[redacted]

COMMITTEES IN THE U.S. CONGRESS 1947-1992

VOLUME 1: COMMITTEE JURISDICTIONS AND MEMBER ROSTERS

COMMITTEES IN THE U.S. CONGRESS 1947-1992

VOLUME 1: COMMITTEE JURISDICTIONS AND MEMBER ROSTERS

GARRISON NELSON
University of Vermont

WITH

CLARK H. BENSEN
POLIDATA

Congressional Quarterly
Washington, D.C.

1414 22nd Street, N.W., Washington, D.C. 20037

Printed in the United States of America

Library of Congress Cataloging-in-Publication Data

Nelson, Garrison, 1942-
Committees in the U.S. Congress, 1947-1992 / Garrison Nelson with Clark H. Bensen.
p. cm.
Contents: v. 1. Committee jurisdictions and member rosters
ISBN 0-87187-729-5
1. United States. Congress--Committees--Directories.
2. Legislators--United States--Directories. I. Bensen, Clark H. (Clark Hamilton), 1952- . II. Title.
JK 1029.N45 1992
328.73'0765'025--dc20 92-40252
CIP

COMMITTEES IN THE U.S. CONGRESS 1947 - 1992

VOLUME I: Committee Jurisdictions and Member Rosters

Garrison Nelson

ABBREVIATED TABLE OF CONTENTS

Detailed Table of Contents

Part I: Senate Standing Committees 1947-1992

(see **Governmental Affairs**)

Part II: Senate Select and Special Committees 1947-1992

(see Senate Standing Committee on **Small Business**)

Part III: House Standing Committees
1947-1992

Part IV: House Select and Special Committees 1947 - 1992

Part V: Joint Committees of Congress 1947-1992

Acknowledgments

This volume is the first of a projected six-volume set documenting all of the assignments to committees in the U.S. Congress from the First Congress in 1789 until the present. The project is an outgrowth of research which I have conducted on leadership recruitment and selection in the U.S. House of Representatives.

In my conversations with House leaders, it became clear to me that the committee assignment process was an important signalling device to members of the House who were assessing their future careers. The decision of members to remain in the House and patiently accrue seniority rather than seek their state's governorship or a seat in the U.S. Senate was clearly related to positive signals which these future leaders received early in their careers from the existing House power structure. The favorable committee assignments given to these talented members of the House was a way of letting them know that they had a future in the House and that the leadership was well aware of their abilities.

I gained an appreciation of this process from three very important members of the House who graciously shared their observations with me about the importance of committee assignments in shaping leadership careers. John W. McCormack (Dem-Mass.) who served as Speaker of the House from 1962 through 1970 first alerted me to this connection. He recounted to me how he was urged by Speaker John Nance Garner (Dem-Tex.) to run for a seat on the Ways and Means Committee in only his third year in the House. McCormack was elected by the Democratic Caucus for this seat in 1931 and it served as his base in advancing his leadership career.

McCormack's career as leader spanned thirty-one years from 1940 through 1970 in which he served as Speaker, floor leader and whip. His was the longest House leadership career in American history. And it was the sponsorship of Representative McCormack by Speaker Garner which established the "Austin-Boston" connection which was to dominate the leadership of the House from 1937 to 1989.

Wilbur Mills (Dem-Ark.) told me of his conversations with Speaker Sam Rayburn (Dem-Tex.) about efforts in Arkansas to get him to run for the U.S. Senate in 1944. According to Mills, Speaker Rayburn told him that, "Wilbur, as long as you are on Ways and Means, there is no point in running for the Senate." Mills heeded Rayburn's advice and remained in the House and by 1956, at the age of 46, he became Chair of Ways and Means and served until 1974 when an unfortunate incident ended his distinguished career as the leader of that powerful committee.

Richard Bolling (Dem-Mo.) shared with me his conversations with Speaker Rayburn about the respective merits of serving on the Ways and Means Committee and the Rules Committee. It was Dick Bolling who clarified for me the linkage between one's committee assignments and ability to shape the legislative agenda. Bolling chaired the House Rules Committee from 1979 to 1983 and also chaired the Select Committee on Committees in 1973. Bolling's extraordinary grasp of congressional history and his enjoyable tolerance of intellectuals played a major role in opening the House to a generation of congressional scholars. He agreed to write a foreword for this work but his death in 1991 prevented this from occurring. I would like to believe that he would have been pleased by it.

I miss these giants of the House.

A project of this scale needs talented personnel and ample funds for it to succeed. I was fortunate to have access to a an eager and extraordinarily capable set of undergraduates at the University of Vermont to assist me in this project. Many students participated in this effort as it stretched through the years. Some of those students are deserving of special mention here. These include Susan Haviland, Marie Race, Jay Shak, Beth Rosenberg, Dan Bryant, Andrew MacGowan, Warren Babb, and Robert Buck.

Clark H. Bensen of Polidata, the former Political Analysis Director of the Republican National Committee, was the person who helped me develop multiple versions of the computerized codebook. It was this detailed codebook and the computer programs developed by Clark which enabled me and my students to retrieve successfully and process fully the twenty-nine variables for the close to 100,000 committee assignments in the total project. For this reason, it is Clark's name which is included on the title page to this volume.

Alan Howard of the University of Vermont's Academic Computing Center updated Clark's listing programs which masterfully converted the densely packed numeric codes to be read easily in text format.

Mary A. Downes, who has been my assistant for the past year, is responsible for the formatting of this volume. I am in awe of her ability to focus clearly on how this information can best be presented in a way to enhance a reader's understanding of congressional committee careers. Her imperturbable determination has often restored my flagging commitment to the project. Her painstaking attentiveness to the more than one million pieces of information in this volume is also greatly appreciated.

Mrs. Ann Gould, the long-time head of the Government Documents section of the University of Vermont's Bailey-Howe Library, is owed my deepest thanks. Her extraordinary willingness to let my students have almost complete and total access to the library's Serial Set of congressional documents defined for me the ideal of the librarian.

Preparing this reference book also required the cooperation of a number of people in the congressional community. I was delighted by the assistance extended to me by the staffs of U.S. Senator Patrick J. Leahy, U.S. Senator Robert Stafford, and that of U.S. Senator and former U.S. Representative James M. Jeffords. These staffs gave me the names of people on Capitol Hill who assisted me in tracking down hard-to-locate pieces of information.

The countless assistants on the Hill who filled in gaps in the book are impossible to identify but I hope that the publication of this book will lighten their research burdens.

The Government Division of the Congressional Research Service in the Library of Congress contains the single greatest collection of talented congressional scholars assembled anywhere. My indebtedness to Carol Hardy-Vincent, Richard Sachs, Judy Schneider, Fred Pauls, Dan Mulhollan, Stanley Bach, Mildred Amer, Sula Richardson, Walter Oleszek and especially Paul Rundquist is boundless. Their encouragement over the years has been immense and their willingness to provide financial support for this project has been greatly appreciated.

Other people who have been readily available for my questions include Richard A. Baker and Donald A. Ritchie of the Senate Historical Office, Roger K. Haley, the Librarian of the Senate; Raymond W. Smock and Bruce A. Ragsdale of the House Historian's Office and E. Raymond Lewis, Chief of the House Library.

The dean of congressional research on the Hill, Floyd M. "Doc" Riddick, the Senate's Parliamentarian Emeritus, was an invaluable source of information and encouragement.

There have been a number of academic supporters of the project who have not wavered over the years in their belief that this was an important use of my time when I often concluded otherwise. Included here would be my fellow toilers in the legislative fields: Dick Fenno, David Brady, Ron Hedlund, Sam Patterson, Sam Kernell, John C. Wahlke and Robert Peabody. It was Raul Hilberg, my colleague at the University of Vermont, who convinced me that big books could be produced at small universities. And it was from the late Jack L. Walker, the quintessential realist, that I learned that the only way to improve a political system was to understand fully how it operated.

Financial support for this project has not been easy to find. The post-1947 portion has been funded primarily by personal loans and by sales of customized databases through my CALLIOPE System. In the university community, financial help was provided by Professors John Cogan of Stanford University, Charles Stewart of the Massachusetts Institute of Technology, Gary Cox and Matt McCubbins of the University of California at San Diego, and Sally Friedman of the State University of New York at Albany. Bruce Brownson and Wayne Walker of Congressional Staff Directory provided assistance during key transitional stages of this project.

Congressional Quarterly's commitment to publish the first two volumes of the set pleases me greatly and for that commitment, I extend my thanks to David Tarr, the Director of CQ Books.

Loan officers Lisa Rutz at the Chittenden Trust, and Dewey Maurice of the Merchants Bank in Burlington, Vermont came to the rescue during the project's final push this year. A timely loan from Dick and Carol Hess of the Political Resources Directory saved last summer's effort.

A project of this magnitude takes its toll on one's good health and good humor. Having others tolerate you when both health and humor are in short supply requires a level of forbearance not always found in academic departments. For this reason, my colleagues in the Political Science Department at the University of Vermont are deserving of special mention. My children Shyla and Ethan were in grammar school when this project was conceived and now that have grown into wonderful adults, they may at last understand what impelled Dad to commit himself to this effort.

-- Garrison Nelson
Burlington, Vermont
November 1992

Preface

The Congressional Committee System

The United States Congress is the most powerful legislative body in the world. Much of its power derives from its highly developed standing committee system. Analysts of legislatures have regularly remarked upon its expertise, its ability to check executive authority, and its stability in the face of changing political conditions.

The standing committees of Congress had their origins in colonial times. Pennsylvania's legislative committee system served as the major model for that of the early Congress. The first Speaker of the U.S. House of Representatives, Frederick A. C. Muhlenberg, had been the speaker of the Pennsylvania Assembly. Furthermore, the names of Pennsylvania's committees were adopted as the names of the earliest congressional committees--Ways and Means, Accounts, Revision of the Laws, Rules, and Unfinished Business.

From the first Congress in 1789 through the end of the 79th Congress in 1947, the standing committee system of the Congress grew dramatically, and on occasion, underwent revisions. However, these revisions were most often confined to one of the two chambers. No coordinated effort to upgrade and streamline the committee system took place before 1946.

The modern congressional committee system dates from the Legislative Reorganization Act of 1946. The massive expenditures required to fund the nation's military effort in World War II and the difficulties involved in legislative oversight of the executive branch during wartime made a revision of the committee system imperative.

Dr. George B. Galloway was the staff director of the Joint Committee on the Organization of Congress in 1946, and in his book Congress at the Crossroads, (New York, 1946, p. 49) he put it this way:

"Congress as an institution is heavily handicapped in many ways in performing its modern functions. Of all its handicaps the rising tide of legislative and other business is undoubtedly the basic obstacle. The business of Congress -- once relatively limited in scope, small in volume, and simple in nature -- has now become almost unlimited in subject matter, enormous in amount, and exceedingly complex in character."

Senator Robert M. LaFollette Jr. (Prog-Wisc.) and Representative A. S. Mike Monroney (Dem-Okla.) were the Co-Chairs on the Joint Committee on the Organization of Congress, which wrote the Legislative Reorganization Act of 1946. It called for a substantial reduction in the number of standing committees, the development of more joint committees to expedite House and Senate business, and the expansion of the Legislative Reference Service of the Library of Congress to assist members in their research efforts. It was the intent of the act to streamline congressional life and to provide adequate support personnel for the membership.

Committees of the House of Representatives

By the time of the act, the number of House committees stood at forty-eight following the addition of the Select Committee on Small Business and the highly controversial Committee on Un-American Activities. The number was shrunk to nineteen. Six committees, four dealing with elections, were abolished outright. The new committee on House Administration took over the elections function as well as the legislative jurisdictions of six other committees. Six committees were also folded into the new committee on Public Lands (now called the Committee on Interior and Insular Affairs).

Fears that many senior members would be upset about the disappearance of their committee chairmanships through consolidation were rendered moot by the stunning victory of the Republicans in the 1946 congressional elections. All of the Democratic chairs lost their posts through the party shift. This fact eased the transition to the new committee structure.

Changes in the committees of the House have been infrequent since 1946. The successful launching of earth-orbiting satellites by the Soviet Union caused anxiety in Congress as well as the nation, and in 1958, the House Committee on Science and Astronautics was created. A payroll scandal in the House concerning Adam Clayton Powell (Dem-NY), the chairman of the Education and Labor Committee led to the creation of the House Committee on Standards of Official Conduct in 1968.

Although the House passed another Legislative Reorganization Act in 1970, the committees were not directly affected. But in 1973, the House Select Committee on Committees, chaired by Representative Richard Bolling (Dem-Mo.) was able to bring about some reform in the committee system. The two major changes were to abolish the House Committee on Internal Security (the successor to Un-American Activities) and to make the Select Committee on Small Business a standing one.

It was in response to President Richard Nixon's expansion of executive power that led the Congress to enact the most important committee system change since 1946. This was the Budget and Impoundment Control Act of 1974, which was intended to limit the president's authority to withhold funds appropriated by Congress for programs and projects which the President opposed. This act created the Budget committees in both the House and Senate. These committees quickly emerged as centers of institutional power.

Another reform movement to alter the House committee system occurred in 1979 with the Select

Committee on Committees chaired by Representative Jerry Patterson (Dem-Cal.). Its major impact was to consolidate overlapping energy jurisdictions within the renamed Committee on Energy and Commerce.

For the most part, the House of Representatives continues to function with the standing committee system which it created in the 1946 Reorganization Act. Apart from the net addition of three committees, what changes have occurred have taken place in the growing number of committee assignments for each of the standing committees and the large number of sub-committees. From 1947 through 1992, the number of assigned places on House standing committees has grown from 486 to 848--a 57% increase. And the number of House subcommittees has grown from 89 in 1947 to 137 in 1992--a 65% increase.

Committees of the Senate

The U.S. Senate functioned without legislative standing committees for the first twenty-eight years of its existence (1789-1817). Its relatively small size and its reliance upon floor speeches had made a standing committee system unnecessary. For the most part, the Senate utilized a series of select and special committees which were appointed to handle each floor vote that came before the chamber.

By 1816, the Senate had grown from 26 members to 36 and on the verge of statehood were the four territories of Indiana, Illinois, Mississippi, and Alabama. As the Senate faced expansion, the need for a standing committee system became more urgent. On December 10, 1816, the Senate created its first eleven legislative standing committees to augment its existing housekeeping ones.

Once in place, Senate committees grew steadily in number with very few abolished. By 1914, the Senate had seventy-four committees. The committee system of the Senate was in danger of outnumbering the membership, which then stood at ninety-six. Many of these committees had ceased to function legislatively and were primarily a source of prestige and staff for their chairs.

Change came to the Senate more emphatically than it did to the House. Forty-one standing committees were abolished in 1921. Virtually all were so-called "sinecure" committees whose impact upon the Senate's legislative business was minimal.

This meant that the Senate was not as heavily encumbered by its committee system as was the House by the convening of the 79th Congress in 1945.

The Legislative Reorganization Act of 1946 reduced the Senate's thirty-three committees to fifteen, with Rules and Administration picking up the jurisdictions of six committees; Public Lands picked up five; while Interstate and Foreign Commerce collected four.

Following the Reorganization Act, the Senate committees remained relatively stable with only two additions--the Committee on Aeronautics and Space Exploration in 1958 as its response to the orbiting of Soviet satellites, and the Budget Committee in 1974 as an outgrowth of the Budgeting and Impoundment Control Act.

By 1975, it became clear that further reform was necessary. Following the recommendations of the Temporary Select Committee to Study the Senate Committee System, the Senate reduced its committees (standing, joint, and special) from 31 to 24; and its sub-committees from 174 to 118. As a result, the average number of assignments per senator dropped from 18 in the 94th Congress to 11 in the 95th.

Senator Adlai E. Stevenson III (Dem-Ill.) chaired the committee which reorganized the Senate's system. Three standing committees were eliminated as the functions of the District of Columbia Committee and Post Office and Civil Service were folded into the newly reconstituted Governmental Affairs Committee. Both of these committees had encountered difficulty in getting senators to serve on them and their departure from the chamber was not greatly lamented. The Aeronautics and Space Exploration Committee, the only standing committee ever chaired by Lyndon Johnson and once filled with the Senate's senior-most members, had fallen on hard times as appropriations for the space program dried up in the 1970's. This committee was absorbed by Commerce under its new designation, the Committee on Commerce, Science and Transportation.

The Senate has shown a greater propensity to revamp its committee system than has the House. One major reason for this is due to the lesser role which committees play in the Senate relative to the House. With unlimited debate and no Rules Committee to restrict amendments, the Senate has been able to conduct more of its legislative business on the floor than has the House. As a result, Senate careers are not as dependent upon committee assignments as House careers are. This lowers the stakes involved in any alteration in committee jurisdictions and makes reform easier to accomplish.

Joint Committees

From 1789 through 1946 joint committees played no major legislative role. Primarily, they dealt with housekeeping items such as printing and the Library of Congress.

As with the standing committees, the joint committees underwent a dramatic change due to the passage of the Legislative Reorganization Act of 1946. It was the hope of the Act's authors that joint committees would enhance communication between the House and the Senate and expedite legislation.

During the 1940's and 1950's a number of joint committees were created. Atomic Energy, the Economic Report, Immigration and Naturalization, and Reduction of Useless Federal Expenditures, were some of the better-known joint committees. In the 81st and 82nd Congresses (1949-1953), there were twelve joint committees in operation.

However, the joint committees lost their appeal as a basis for intercameral cooperation during the 1960's. House members, more plentiful in number, relished the opportunity to serve on committees with equal numbers of Senators. However, the Senate, with its smaller membership, found it increasingly difficult to staff the joint committees and often left vacancies.

The joint committees disappeared gradually. In the Senate's 1977 Reorganization Amendments, the joint committees were reduced to four: Printing, the Library, Taxation, and the Joint Economic Committee. These four are still in existence. Three of these committees are staffed by members from the standing committees: House Administration and Senate Rules and Administration provide members for both the Joint Committees on Printing and the Library, while senior House Ways and Means members join with senior Senate Finance Committee members to staff the Joint Committee on Taxation. Only the Joint Economic Committee chooses its members from the chambers at large.

Select and Special Committees

Select and special committees have been in existence since the first Congress. They are created for the purpose of gathering information in a specific subject area and reporting the information back to the standing committees for legislative action. They have been given "oversight" authority in their investigative roles, but not until recently have special and select committees been given legislative responsibility. For example, the Select Committees on Intelligence in each chamber have the ability to report legislation.

Select committees possess the advantage of being chosen from the membership of more than one standing committee. This enables them to address issues which might fall between the jurisdictional cracks of the standing committees.

Originally, the difference between select and special committees was that select committees were chosen by the chamber's presiding officer while special committees were selected by the parties and the floor leaders. Over the years, this distinction has become blurred. Now the practice seems to be to use the term "select" for committees that are likely to be renewed by the subsequent Congress, while the term "special" appears to be used for committees which are unlikely to survive the close of business of the Congress in which they are appointed. This has given rise to the designations of "permanent select committees" and "temporary select committees."

Historically, the Senate has relied more heavily on select and special committees than has the House. Many select and special committees have been used as launch pads for the ambitions of their chairs. For example, Harry Truman (Dem-Mo.) chaired the Select Committee on the National Defense Program; Estes Kefauver (Dem-Tenn.) chaired the Select Committee on Organized Crime in Interstate Commerce; John Sparkman (Dem-Ala.) chaired the Select Committee on Small Business; John F. Kennedy (Dem-Mass.) chaired the Select Committee on the Senate Reception Room; Lyndon B. Johnson (Dem-Tex.) chaired the Select Committee on Astronautics and Space; Hubert H. Humphrey (DFL-Minn.) chaired the Special Committee on Disarmament; Eugene J. McCarthy (DFL-Minn.) chaired the Select Committee on Unemployment Problems; George McGovern (Dem-S.D.) chaired the Select Committee on Nutrition and Human Needs; Walter Mondale (DFL-Minn.) chaired the Select Committee on Equal Education Opportunity; Frank Church (Dem-Ida.) chaired the Select Committee on Intelligence Activities; and J. Danforth Quayle (Rep-Ind.) chaired the second Select Committee to Study the Senate Committee System. All of the senators listed were serious contenders for their party's presidential and vice presidential nominations. All made use of these committees as platforms to further their careers.

Given the long-term domination of the Senate's standing committees by southern hierarchs, it was unlikely for a junior member with presidential ambitions to gain national attention through his service on the standing committees. Thus, the Senate's select committees provided an excellent vehicle for intensive media exposure for a limited period of time. This satisfied the ambitious junior members while maintaining the hegemony of the senior-most members.

Most of these select and special committees had short lives. In spite of this, many had a great impact on the nation. Senator Estes Kefauver's (Dem-Tenn.) Special Committee to Investigate Organized Crime in Interstate Commerce, 1950-51, held the first nationally televised set of congressional committee hearings; and Senator Sam Ervin's (Dem-N.C.) Select Committee on Presidential Campaign Activities, 1973-74, unravelled the Watergate scandal and led to the resignation of President Nixon.

Committee Assignments and Chairs

House of Representatives

Methods of selection of members for the standing committees has varied over the years. In the House, the original committees were elected by the membership, but almost immediately, it became clear that it was far easier to have the Speaker make the committee assignments. This arrangement of Speaker-appointed committees lasted from 1790 until 1911 when the revolt against Speaker Joseph G. Cannon (Rep-Ill.) stripped that power from the office.

From 1911 through 1974, the Democratic members of the Ways and Means Committee served as the Democratic Committee on Committees and made assignments for their party. This gave the ranking Democratic member on the Ways and Means Committee power comparable to the floor leader. Members of the Ways and Means Committee could not, however, fill their own vacancies. This had to be done by election in the House Democratic Caucus. The major advantage of the system was that it removed arbitrary power from the Speaker, but its major disadvantage was that it created another power base among House Democrats and further blurred the lines between committee power and party power.

After 1974, the power over committee assignments was given to the Democratic Steering and Policy Committee, whose members were elected by the House Democratic Caucus and upon which the party's major leaders served (the Speaker, the Floor Leader, and the Democratic Whip).

Republican House members created their own committee on committees in the wake of the Speaker's loss of power in 1911. Their committee consists of a single member from each state which has at least one Republican House member. Each of these members has votes weighted by the number of Republican members in the state delegation. Thus committee members from large states such as New York, California, Ohio, Illinois, and Pennsylvania have great power. For the most part, the senior-most delegation members of each state (i.e., the "deans") served on the Committee on Committees and endeavored to get their fellow delegation members onto the most prestigious committees.

Other changes which have occurred in recent years include the modification of the "seniority rule" in the House. Prior to the 1970's, the House was committed to the practice of granting the chairmanship of its standing committees to the member of the majority party with the longest continuous period of service on the committee. The seniority rule's major advantage was that it took much of the internal politicking out of the selection process for the committee chairmanship.

The greatest challenge to the seniority rule occurred in 1971-1973 in a series of reforms known as the Subcommittee Bill of Rights, which was adopted by the Democratic Caucus. Under the new rules, committee and subcommittee chairs were to stand for election by the party members of their committees. The most dramatic impact of this change occurred In 1975 when the influx of the newly elected liberal "Watergate class" led to the defeat of three long-time standing committee chairs: W.R. Poage (Dem-Tex.) on Agriculture; F. Edward Hebert (Dem-La.) on Armed Services and Wright Patman (Dem-Tex.) on Banking and Currency. Since then, three other committee chairs have lost their posts: C. Melvin Price (Dem-Ill.) on Armed Services at the beginning of 1985; and Frank Annunzio (Dem-Ill.) on House Administration and Glenn M. Anderson (Dem-Cal.) on Public Works and Transportation, at the end of 1990.

In the wave of post-Watergate reform, Republicans also subjected their senior-most committee and subcommittee members to votes within the House Republican Conference, but the impact has been minimal.

Senate

The assignment of members to Senate committees differs from that of the House because of the continuity principle within that chamber. The Senate is a continuing body and its members hold their assignments for as long as they wish. When vacancies occur, the assignments are referred to each party's committee on committees. In the Democratic Party, the committee making assignments is the Steering Committee and in the Republican Party, it is the Committee on Committees.

Generally speaking, the assignment of members to Senate committees is not as contested as those of the House for the simple reason that the Senate relies less upon its committees than does the House. Due to the importance of floor debate, a Senator need not be a member of the reporting committee to have a material impact upon the legislative outcome of a bill.

The less intense atmosphere of the Senate regarding committee assignments made it possible for Democratic Leader Lyndon Johnson to institute the "Johnson Rule" in 1953. Under this "rule", all Democratic Senators were to have one major committee assignment (i.e., Finance, Appropriations, Foreign Relations, etc.) before any Senator was assigned to a second major committee. This rule strengthened Johnson's influence among junior members.

Conflict within the Senate regarding chairmanships is less intense. No Senate committee chairs have been deposed since the Legislative Reorganization Act was passed.

Overview

The congressional committee system is one of the great contributions of the American system of government. Within the congressional committees, partisanship can be submerged as members come to grips with problems of common interest. The committees often act in united ways when they present their proposals to the full chamber. Thus, they often serve as a counter to the partisan spirit which otherwise pervades the Capitol.

The American congressional committees, with their power to investigate the executive branch through the oversight function and their control of executive spending through the appropriations process, have been successful in providing a further check and balance in the American political constellation which the Founding Fathers did not foresee. However, it is clearly in keeping with their wishes.

Selected Bibliography

Congressional Quarterly, Guide to Congress 4th edition (Washington, D.C.: Congressional Quarterly, Inc., 1991).

Cooper, Joseph, The Origins of Standing Committees and the Development of the Modern House (Houston: Rice University Press, 1970).

Davidson, Roger H., and Walter J. Oleszek, Congress Against Itself (Bloomington: Indiana University Press, 1977).

Fenno, Richard F., Congressmen in Committees (Boston: Little Brown and Co., 1973).

Fenno, Richard F., The Power of the Purse: Appropriations Politics in Congress (Boston: Little Brown and Co., 1966).

Galloway, George E., Congress at the Crossroads (New York: Thomas Y. Crowell, 1946).

Goodwin, George Jr., The Little Legislatures: The Committees of Congress (Amherst: University of Massachusetts Press, 1970).

Hinckley, Barbara The Seniority System in Congress (Bloomington: Indiana University Press, 1971).

Manley, John F., The Politics of Finance: The House Committee on Ways and Means (Boston: Little Brown and Co., 1970).

Morrow, William L., Congressional Committees (New York: Charles Scribner's Sons, 1969).

Nadel, Nark, dir., The Environment Committees: A Study of the House and Senate Interior, Agriculture and Science Committees (New York: Grossman Publishers, for the Ralph Nader Congress Project, 1975).

Ornstein, Norman J., "Changing Congress: The Committee System," The Annals of the American Academy of Political and Social Science Vol. CDXI (January 1974).

Price, David E., dir., The Commerce Committees: A Study of the House and Senate Commerce Committees (New York: Grossman Publishers for the Ralph Nader Congress Project, 1975).

Price, David E., Who Makes the Laws?: Creativity and Power in Senate Committees (Cambridge, Mass.: Schenkman Publishing Co., 1972).

Salamon, Lester M., dir., The Money Committees: A Study of the House and Senate Banking and Currency Committees (New York: Grossman Publishers, for the Ralph Nader Congress Project, 1975).

Schuck, Peter H., dir., The Judiciary Committees: A Study of the House and Senate Judiciary Committees (New York: Grossman Publishers, for the Ralph Nader Congress Project, 1975).

Shepsle, Kenneth A., The Giant Jigsaw Puzzle: Democratic Committee Assignments in the Modern House (Chicago: University of Chicago Press, 1978).

Siff, Ted and Alan Weil, dirs., Ruling Congress: A Study of How the House and Senate Rules Govern the Legislative Process (New York: Grossman Publishers, for the Ralph Nader Congress Project, 1975).

Smith, Stephen S. and Christopher J. Deering, Committees in Congress (Washington, D.C.: Congressional Quarterly, 1984). A revised edition was published in 1990.

Spohn, Richard and McCollum, Charles, dirs., The Revenue Committees: A Study of the House Ways and Means and Senate Finance Committees and the House and Senate Appropriations Committees (New York: Grossman Publishers, for the Ralph Nader Congress Project, 1975).

Strahan, Randall, The New Ways and Means: Reform and Change in a Congressional Committee (Chapel Hill: University of North Carolina Press, 1990).

Stubbs, Walter L., comp., Congressional Committees, 1789-1982: A Checklist (Westport, Conn.: Greenwood Press, 1985).

Introduction to the Volume

This volume, Committee Jurisdictions and Member Rosters, presents Congressional Committee assignment listings from January 3,1947, the opening of the 80th Congress until January 3,1993, the closing of the 102nd Congress.

The 80th Congress was the first Congress convened after the implementation of the 1946 Legislative Reorganization Act (Public Law 79-601), which greatly altered the congressional committee system and which has remained relatively intact for forty-six years.

Membership lists contained in this book were developed from official congressional documents, most notably, the Congressional Directory, which was published by the U.S. Government Printing Office twice each session in the 80th Congress (1947-1949), then once each session from the 81st Congress (1949) through the 95th Congress (1978), and biannually since the 96th Congress (1979-1991). These listings were checked against the daily publication, the Congressional Record and the annual Journals published by each chamber of Congress. Further confirmation of these listings was made by cross-referencing with non-governmental sources such as Congressional Quarterly's biennial listing of "Committee and Subcommittee Assignments" (Washington, D.C.: Congressional Quarterly Inc., 1951-date), the year-end lists of committee and subcommittee assignments prepared by the U.S. Code Congressional and Administrative News (St.Paul, Minn.: West Publishing Co., 1947-date), and with the annual editions of the Congressional Staff Directory (Mount Vernon, Va.: Congressional Staff Directory, 1959-date).

Committee Types

The U.S. Congress functions with a division of legislative labor. In order to make that division work, most committees are given legislative jurisdiction over specific items within the national agenda -- defense, foreign policy, banking, energy, transportation, and housing, etc. Each committee is responsible for a specific area. Other committees cover a broader range of issues, such as the House and Senate Appropriations Committees, which determine federal spending priorities, and the tax-writing House Ways and Means Committee and Senate Finance Committee, which govern revenue policy. A third set of committees deals with the internal functioning of each chamber; these include the Rules, House Administration, and Standards of Official Conduct Committees in the House and the Rules and Administration Committee in the Senate.

Standing Committees:

The standing committees of the Congress are continuing entities, and do not have to be re-created at the beginning of each new Congress. The powers of the standing committees of the Congress have been institutionalized with their legislative responsibilities outlined in the respective Rules of each chamber. For the House of Representatives, the document delineating those responsibilities is the Rules of the House of Representatives, and for the Senate it is the Authority and Rules of Senate Committees.

Below is an example of a jurisdictional statement from the House Standing Committee on Agriculture:

Jurisdiction, 1947

Established by the Legislative Reorganization Act of 1946:

[Section 121.(1)(a)]

Committee on Agriculture.

1. Agriculture generally.
2. Inspection of livestock and meat products.
3. Animal industry and diseases of animals.
4. Adulteration of seeds, insect pests, and protection of birds and animals in forest reserves.
5. Agricultural colleges and experiment stations.
6. Forestry in general, and forest reserves other than those created from the public domain.
7. Agricultural economics and research.
8. Agricultural and industrial chemistry.
9. Dairy industry.
10. Entomology and plant quarantine.
11. Human nutrition and home economics.
12. Plant industry, soils and agricultural engineering.
13. Agricultural extension services.
14. Extension of farm credit and farm security.
15. Rural electrification.
16. Agricultural production and marketing and stabilization of prices of agricultural products.
17. Crop insurance and soil conservation.

Select and Special Committees:

Select and special committees are created for the purpose of investigation and reporting to their respective chambers. Historically, there were distinctions between the select and special committees, but the intent of both terms was to indicate their temporary nature. In the modern Congress, the distinction between selects and specials has disappeared. The "select" designation is the preferred one. These committees are not authorized to introduce legislation. However, the investigative reports which they file with their respective chambers are used as guides for the standing committees to report legislation. The jurisdictional responsibilities of the select and special committees are delineated in the establishing resolutions.

Below is an example of a jurisdictional excerpt from the House Select Committee on Assassinations:

Jurisdiction, 1976

From House Resolution 1540, 94th Congress, Second Session, September 17, 1976:

[Paragraph 2]

The select committee is authorized and directed to conduct a full and complete investigation and study of the circumstances surrounding the death of John F. Kennedy and the death of Martin Luther King, Junior, and of any others the select committee shall determine.

Unlike other select and special committees, the Permanent Select Committees on Intelligence in both the House and the Senate are authorized to report legislation to their respective chambers.

In recent years, the Congress has adopted the concept of designating some select committees as "permanent." Included are those on Aging and Intelligence in the House of Representatives and those on Aging, Intelligence, Ethics and Indian Affairs in the Senate. The jurisdictions of these permanent select committees have become part of the Rules of their respective chambers, and therefore are not re-created at the beginning of each Congress. The post-1946 precedents for permanent select committees were the House Small Business Committee, which was created as a Select Committee but became a Standing Committee in 1973 and the Senate Committee on Small Business, which also began as a Select Committee but became a Standing Committee in 1981. Both select committees had been named at the same time as the standing committees.

Temporary select and special committees are created to deal with an immediate investigative problem which may involve the jurisdictions of a number of committees. These committees are appointed for a specific period of time to conduct investigations and to report back to the full chamber for legislative action. Three of the better-known of these committees were those on Organized Crime in Interstate Commerce, chaired by Senator Estes Kefauver (Dem-Tenn.) in 1950-1951 which catapulted him into a major presidential contender: Improper Activities in the Labor or Management Field (1957-1960), chaired by Senator John McClellan (Dem-Ark.) which gave Senator John F. Kennedy (Dem-Mass.) and his brother, Robert F. Kennedy, the committee's chief counsel, the national exposure which successfully prepared them for the 1960 presidential campaign; and the Select Committee on Presidential Campaign Activities ("Watergate"), chaired by Senator Sam Ervin (Dem-N.C.) in 1973-1974 which led eventually to the resignation of President Richard M. Nixon.

A recent development in the House select committee system involves the reestablishment of three Temporary Select Committees at the beginning of each Congress. These are Narcotics Abuse and Control (since 1976), Children, Youth and Families (since 1983) and Hunger (since 1985). As Temporary Select Committees, their jurisdictions are subject to change between Congresses. However, their temporary status has not prevented these committees from becoming well-established in the committee system.

Joint Committees:

Joint Committees since 1946 have varied in their structures and jurisdictions. Some have acted as standing committees, while others have operated as select committees. It was the original intent of the 1946 Legislative Reorganization Act that joint committees would generate greater cooperation between the House and the Senate. In both the 81st and 82nd Congresses (1949-1953) twelve joint committees were named. The joint committees eventually lost favor with the membership of each chamber and gradually disappeared. In the Senate Committee Reorganization Amendments of 1977, only four joint committees were named. The Joint Committee on the Library and the Joint Committee on Printing, which had existed in some form since the 19th century, were staffed by members of the House Administration Committee and the Senate Rules and Administration Committee. The Joint Committee on Taxation, created in 1926, was to be staffed by the five senior most members of the House Ways and Means Committee and the five senior most members of the Senate Finance Committee. The Joint Economic Committee was the only joint committee with membership independent of the standing committees. These four committees have achieved the continuity of standing committees.

Since 1975 only three temporary joint committees have been appointed: Bicentennial Arrangements (1975-1977), Deficit Reduction (1987-1989) and the last committee included in this volume, the Joint Committee on Congressional Organization which was named in the closing days of 1992.

Jurisdictional Listings

In order to indicate the jurisdictional changes that have occurred over the past 46 years, the book includes "snapshots" of the committees at significant junctures in the committee system.

Senate Standing Committees:

The Senate committee system underwent a major modification with the passage of the Committee System Reorganization Amendments of 1977. This resulted in the renaming of most committees and a redefining of their legislative responsibilities. Senate committees whose titles and jurisdictions were not changed at that time were Appropriations, Armed Services, Finance, Foreign Relations, and Judiciary. These committees have two jurisdictions listed: the 1946 Reorganization Act defining the original jurisdiction in the 80th Congress, and the jurisdiction in effect during the 102nd Congress, as it appears in the Authority and Rules of Senate Committees, revised through March 13, 1991.

The Committee on Banking, Housing, and Urban Affairs changed its name in 1970, but its jurisdiction did not change significantly; thus only two jurisdictions are listed for this committee.

The six Senate standing committees whose names and

jurisdictions were changed in 1977 are Agriculture, Nutrition, and Forestry; Commerce, Science and Transportation; Energy and Natural Resources; Environment and Public Works; Governmental Affairs; and Labor and Human Resources. These committees as well as Rules and Administration contain three jurisdictions: the 1946 Legislative Reorganization Act, the Committee System Reorganization Amendments of 1977 and the jurisdiction from the 102nd Congress.

Committees that were created by the 1946 Act, but which were reorganized out of existence before the 102nd Congress are the District of Columbia and Post Office and Civil Service Committees. There are two jurisdictions listed for these: the 1946 Act and the one in effect during the 94th Congress (1975-1977), which was the last one in which they existed as independent committees. The Senate Committee on Aeronautical and Space Sciences, which was created as a Standing Committee in 1958, was reorganized out of existence in 1977. Two jurisdictions are listed for this committee: the one contained in the establishing resolution, and the one in effect in the 94th Congress.

Three committees created after the 1946 Act and which are in existence today remained relatively unaffected by the Committee Reorganization Amendments of 1977. These committees are the Veterans' Affairs Committee created in 1970, the Budget Committee created in 1974, and the Small Business Committee created in 1981. Two jurisdictions are listed for these committees: the establishing resolutions or Act creating the committees, and the jurisdiction in effect during the 102nd Congress.

Senate Select and Special Committees:

For most of the Senate select and special committees, only the jurisdiction contained in the establishing resolution is included. In addition, for those select committees which no longer exist, the date of termination of the committee is cited, as well as the authority by which the committee was terminated. Wherever possible, the date and number of the committee's final report is also noted.

The Senate select committees which are designated "permanent" include the jurisdiction contained in the establishing resolution and the jurisdiction in effect for the 102nd Congress. In some cases, there will be a note indicating that the jurisdiction has not changed since the select committee's establishment.

House Standing Committees:

Unlike the Senate, the House standing committee system has not undergone major jurisdictional reorganization since 1946. Twelve of the House standing committees which existed at the time of the 1946 Act have had no change in their committee name and only minor modifications in their legislative responsibilities. These committees are Agriculture, Appropriations, Armed Services, District of Columbia, Education and Labor, House Administration, Judiciary, Merchant Marine and Fisheries, Post Office and Civil Service, Rules, Veterans' Affairs, and Ways and Means. The names of five committees changed between the 80th and 102nd Congress with only minor modifications to their jurisdictions. These committees are Banking, Finance and Urban Affairs; Foreign Affairs; Government Operations; Interior and Insular Affairs; and Public Works and Transportation. All of these committees have two jurisdictions listed: that established by the 1946 Reorganization Act and that in effect for the 102nd Congress as it appears in the Rules of the House of Representatives, revised to July 1, 1992.

Four committees were created after 1947 -- Science, Space and Technology (created as Space and Astronautics in 1958); Standards of Official Conduct (created in 1968), Budget (created in 1974); and Small Business (created in 1974). These committees are listed with their establishing jurisdiction and their present jurisdiction, from the Rules of the House of Representatives. Only one House standing committee was terminated between 1947 and 1992 -- the Internal Security Committee, better known as the Committee on Un-American Activities. Its 1947 jurisdiction is listed as well as the jurisdiction in effect during its last Congress, the 93rd (1973-1975).

House Select and Special Committees:

For most of the select committees in the House, only the jurisdiction contained in the establishing resolution is included. The resolution re-creating the committee at the start of each Congress is cited, though not reprinted. For those select committees which no longer exist, the date of termination of the committee is cited, as well as the authority by which the committee was terminated. Wherever possible, the date and number of the committee's final report is also noted.

The two House select committees which have been designated as Permanent -- Aging and Intelligence -- include both the jurisdiction contained in the establishing resolution and that in effect for the 102nd Congress. The three-member House Recording Studio which was first named as a select committee in 1956 continued through 1992 under its original jurisdiction.

Joint Committees:

Four joint committees have existed from the 1946 Legislative Reorganization Act until 1992. These committees -- Library, Printing, Taxation and Economic -- were each created prior to the passage of the 1946 Act. The establishing jurisdiction as well as that in existence for the 102nd Congress, as contained in the Authority and Rules of Senate Committees, are listed for these committees. Two of these committees, the Joint Committees on the Library and Printing did not change their names between the 80th and 102nd Congresses. However, the Joint Committee on Taxation was known as the Joint Committee on Internal Revenue Taxation from its inception in 1926 in the Revenue Act of that year (Public Law 69-20) until 1976, and the Joint Economic Committee, created by the Employment Act of 1946 (Public Law 79-304,) was known as the Joint Committee on the Economic Report until 1956.

The other joint committees listed in this book had lives of varying length but did not survive the Committee System Reorganization Amendments of 1977. For most of these joint committees, only the concurrent resolution or Public Law establishing the committee is listed, as well as information regarding termination.

Membership Rosters

The bulk of this volume is devoted to membership rosters of the committees which have existed during the twenty-three Congresses from January 3,1947 through January 3,1993. The format utilized for each collection of committee assignments is listed in order of their appearance in the book.

Part I: Standing Committees of the U.S. Senate

Senate standing committees are arranged in alphabetical order, according to the current or most recent name of the committee. Within each Senate committee list, Member rosters are arranged chronologically, from the 80th Congress, or date of the committee's creation to the 102nd Congress or the date of its termination. Most of the Senate's standing committees changed their names during the twenty-three Congresses in this compilation. Name changes include Agriculture, Nutrition, and Forestry (originally named Agriculture and Forestry); Banking, Housing, and Urban Affairs (originally named Banking and Currency); Commerce, Science and Transportation (previously named Interstate and Foreign Commerce, 1947-1961 and Commerce 1961-1977); Energy and Natural Resources (previously named Public Lands 1947-1948 and Interior and Insular Affairs 1948-1977); Environment and Public Works (originally named Public Works); Governmental Affairs (previously named Expenditures in the Executive Departments 1947-1952 and Government Operations 1952-1977); and Labor and Human Resources (previously named Labor and Public Welfare 1947-1977 and Human Resources 1977-1979). The Post Office and Civil Service Committee, which did not survive the Senate's 1977 reorganization of its committees, was originally named Civil Service.

Part II: Select and Special Committees of the U.S. Senate

The Senate select and special committees are arranged in chronological order, from the date of their creation (not the date of appointment of their initial membership). In one case in the Senate, two select committees with the same name were appointed--the Temporary Select Committee to Study the Senate Committee System. In the text, these committees are differentiated by including a Roman numeral and the name of the committee chair on the committee title line. The Senate Select Committee to Study the Committee System, which met during the 94th and 95th Congresses (1975-1979) was chaired by Senator Adlai E. Stevenson III (Dem-Ill.) and the more recent Senate Select Committee to Study the Committee System, which met during the 98th Congress (1983-1985) was chaired by Senator J. Danforth Quayle, (Rep-Ind.). These appear in the text as:

SENATE TEMPORARY SELECT COMMITTEE: STUDY THE SENATE COMMITTEE SYSTEM I (Stevenson) / 94th Congress

SENATE TEMPORARY SELECT COMMITTEE: STUDY THE SENATE COMMITTEE SYSTEM II (Quayle) / 98th Congress

Part III. Standing Committees of the U.S. House of Representatives

The House standing committees are arranged in alphabetical order, according to the current or most recent name of the committee. Within each standing committee, Member rosters are arranged chronologically, from the 80th Congress, or the date of the committee's creation to the 102nd Congress or the date of its termination.

The House standing committees whose names have changed since the 80th Congress are: Banking, Finance, and Urban Affairs (previously named Banking and Currency 1947-1975 and Banking, Currency and Housing 1975-1977); Energy and Commerce (originally named Interstate and Foreign Commerce); Foreign Affairs (renamed International Affairs in 1975-1979 and resumed the name Foreign Affairs in 1979); Government Operations (originally known as Expenditures in the Executive Departments); Interior and Insular Affairs (originally known as Public Lands); Public Works and Transportation (originally known as Public Works); and Space, Science and Technology (previously named Science and Astronautics 1958-1975 and Science and Technology 1975-1987). The committee on Un-American Activities, which was so named from 1947-1969 is listed under its final name, Internal Security.

Part IV: Select and Special Committees of the U.S. House of Representatives

House select and special committees are arranged chronologically in order of their creation. As in the Senate, select committees with the same name are differentiated by including a Roman numeral and the name of the committee chair on the committee title line. The first House Select Committee on Committees was chaired by U.S. Representative Richard Bolling (Dem.-Mo.) in the 93rd Congress (1973-1975), and the second House Select Committee on Committees was chaired by U.S. Representative Jerry M. Patterson (Dem-Cal.) in the 96th Congress (1979-1981). These appear in the text as:

HOUSE SELECT COMMITTEE: COMMITTEES I (Bolling)

HOUSE SELECT COMMITTEE: COMMITTEES II (Patterson)

Part V: Joint Committees of the U.S. Congress

Joint committees have members chosen from each of the two congressional chambers. As with the select and special committees, joint committees are listed in chronological order.

Roster Contents

Each Membership Roster contains a complete history of an individual committee for a given Congress. Please refer to the sample membership roster while reading the following guide.

Committee Name and Congress

Each committee section is self-contained. Committee names are included in every individual congressional roster. The committee name appearing on each roster is the one in place at the time of the appointment of members to the committee for that Congress. Changes in the committee's name are noted both in the jurisdiction section at the front of each committee's listing, as well as in the roster of the Congress in which the change occurred.

Service Dates

The first set of the dates listed, "Service Dates of Committee Chair," refers to the original chair of the committee. The first date is the date on which the chair is named and the second date is the ending date of that chair's service. If the original Chair ceases to serve as Chair or leaves that committee before the end of that Congress, the service dates of the succeeding Chair will be listed as well. Congressional documents indicate the date on which a new Chair was selected. The abbreviations **Ch1** and **Ch2** are used to represent the first committee Chair and the second committee Chair.

Senate Standing Committees: The Senate operates on the "seniority rule" which grants the chairmanship of its standing committees to the majority party member with the longest "continuous" (i.e., unbroken) service on the committee. Often, a senior majority party member may be eligible for the chairmanship of two or more standing committees. In such a circumstance, the senior member must choose which standing committee he or she will chair and relinquish the chairmanship of the other committee to another member.

For example, Senator Edward M. Kennedy (Dem-Mass.) was the senior-most majority Democrat on both the Labor and Human Resources and Judiciary Committees in the 100th Congress (1987-1989). Senator Kennedy chose to chair the Labor and Human Resources Committee and relinquished the chair of the Judiciary Committee to Senator Joseph Biden (Dem-Del.).

The Senate is a continuing body and thus does not terminate with the adjournment of a Congress. For Senate standing committees, "Service Dates of Majority Members" indicate the dates of service from the initial appointment of the majority party members to the committee through the appointment of new members to the committee in the subsequent Congress. As above, "Service Dates of Minority Members" indicate the dates of service from the initial appointment of the minority party members to the committee through the appointment of new members to the committee in the subsequent Congress.

Majority parties organize each Congress and the practice has been to select the majority party members earlier than the minority party ones. Party control of the Senate has changed five times over the past twenty-three Congresses from 1947 through 1992. The first Congress in this volume - the 80th - was organized by the Republicans. Democrats replaced the Republicans as the Senate's majority party in the 81st Congress (1949-1951) and the 82nd Congress (1951-1953). With the Eisenhower landslide of 1952, Republicans captured the Senate for the 83rd Congress (1953-1955), but surrendered it to the Democrats in the 84th Congress (1955-1957). Democrats organized the thirteen Senates between 1955 and 1981. Ronald Reagan's triumph over President Jimmy Carter in 1980 gave the Senate Republicans control over the 97th Congress (1981-1983) which they held for two subsequent Congresses. In 1986, the Democrats recaptured the Senate and organized the 100th Congress (1987-1989) and the two which followed.

Third party members have been rare in the Senate. Two U.S. Senators were elected as third party members, but they were assigned to committees by the major parties. They were Senator James Buckley of New York, who was elected as a Conservative in 1970 but who was placed on committees by the Republican Conference and Senator Harry Flood Byrd Jr. of Virginia who was elected as an Independent in 1970, but who was assigned to committees by the Democratic Caucus. Senator Wayne Morse of Oregon left the Republican Party in 1952, sat as an Independent until 1955 when he joined the Democrats. Morse was assigned his committee slots in the 83rd Congress by the majority Republicans whose company he disdained. As a result, he was removed from the Armed Services Committee and placed on the decidedly less-prestigious District of Columbia Committee.

Senate Selects and Specials: Service dates on Senate select and special committees are dated from the time of the appointment of Members to the committee by the President of the Senate or the President pro tempore. The select and special committee members serve through the termination date of the committee either by resolution or by the submission of the committee's final report. For some select and special committees that continue for more than one Congress, there is no listing in the Senate Journal or the Congressional Record of the full complement of committee members after the first Congress in which they are named. This means that the committee members continued their service into the subsequent Congress. In these cases, the ending service date is listed as "Continued." When new members are named to continuing committees, the date on which they are named is used as the starting "service date" for that Congress. This will be indicated in the "Notes" for that roster. If no new members are named to a continuing committee, January 3 will be used as the starting "Service Date."

Because the full listings are seldom published in the Congressional Record or the Senate Journal, the list of members for each Congress has been checked with the Congressional Directory and when possible with committee reports.

Chairs are generally those members chosen first by the majority party. Select and special committees are often comprised of members from different standing committees and therefore, are not bound by strict adherence to the seniority rule in selecting their chairs. In some cases, the chair will be chosen at the committee's first organizational meeting and will not be listed in the Congressional Record or the Senate Journal. The Congressional Directory or the committee's final report was used to determine the chair of these committees during their terms of service.

In recent years, the senior minority member on some of the Senate's select committees, such as Intelligence, has been designated as Vice Chair (VCh) rather than as "Ranking Minority Member" (RM). The Vice Chair is able to preside over the committee in the absence of the chair. This enhances the power of the committee's minority and presumably increases the bipartisanship of the select committee.

House Standings: The House of Representatives is not a continuing body and the service of committee members ends with the termination of each Congress. Since the passage of the 20th Amendment to the Constitution in 1933, the termination of the Congresses is at noon on January 3 of odd numbered years. For House standing committees, "Service Dates of Majority Members" indicate the dates of service from the initial selection of the majority party members to the committee through the termination of the Congress. As above, "Service Dates of Minority Members" indicate the dates of service from the initial selection of the minority party members to the committee through the termination of the Congress.

In some Congresses, the House did not make all of its committee assignments on the same day, nor did all members of each committee get named. Members named at a later date are included in the roster, but their dates of assignment are found under the heading "Vacancies Filled."

As in the Senate, majority parties organize each Congress and the practice has been to select the majority party members earlier than the minority party ones. Party control of the House has changed only three times over the past twenty-three Congresses from 1947 through 1992. The first Congress in this volume - the 80th - was organized by the Republicans. The Democratic Party replaced the Republican Party as the House's majority party in the 81st Congress (1949-1951). The Eisenhower landslide of 1952 gave Republicans a short-lived majority in the House for the 83rd Congress (1953-1955), but the Democrats regained control in 1954 for the 84th Congress (1955-1957). The Democrats have not relinquished their control to this date.

The House followed the "seniority rule" to choose chairs of its standing committees from 1947 through 1974, when three chairs were deposed. An interesting case occurred in 1967, when the House voted not to seat U.S. Representative Adam Clayton Powell (Dem-N.Y.), then the chair of the Education and Labor Committee. Powell, who was only the second black to chair a standing committee, had become embroiled in a number of law suits which limited his ability to manage the committee's business. Although Powell was eventually returned to his seat in the House, the chairmanship of the committee shifted to Carl Perkins (Dem-Ky.)

The House modified its rules in the Legislative Reorganization Act of 1970, resulting in more open committee procedures, but with no direct impact upon committee jurisdictions. Between 1971 to 1973, the Democratic Caucus adopted a series of measures known as the "Subcommittee Bill of Rights," which enabled Democratic members to vote on the continuance of committee chairs. After the 1974 election in which 75 new Democrats entered the House as the "Watergate class," the seniority rule lost its automatic role in selecting committee chairs in the House.

In the post-election Democratic Caucus of 1974, three committee chairs -- W.R. Poage (Dem-Tex.), the Chair of Agriculture; F. Edward Hebert (Dem-La.), the Chair of Armed Services; and Wright Patman (Dem-Tex.), the Chair of Banking and Currency -- were removed from their chairmanships and replaced with more junior members. Since then, three other committee chairs have been deposed. Armed Services Chair Melvin Price (Dem-Ill.) was replaced in 1984 by Les Aspin (Dem-Wisc.), the 7th ranking Democrat on the committee. In the organizational caucus following the 1990 House elections, House Administration Chair Frank Annunzio (Dem-Ill.) and Public Works and Transportation Chair Glenn M. Anderson (Dem-Cal.) were both replaced by younger members of their respective committees.

House Selects and Specials: Service dates on House select and special committees are dated from the time of the appointment of Members to the committee by the Speaker of the House or floor leaders acting in his stead. The select and special committee members serve through the termination date of the committee as determined either by House resolution or by the submission of the committee's final report. For those select and special committees that continue for more than one Congress, the January 3 termination date for each Congress is used. Chairs are generally those members chosen first by the majority party. As in the Senate, select and special committees are often comprised of members from different standing committees and therefore, are not bound by strict adherence to the seniority rule in selecting their chairs. In some cases, the chair will be chosen at the committee's first organizational meeting and will not be listed in the Congressional Record or the House Journal. The Congressional Directory or the committee's final report was used to determine the chair of these committees during their terms of service.

Joint Committees: Because Joint Committees are composed of members of both chambers, the "Service

Dates" are separated by chamber. Only rarely are the majority and minority members of each chamber named on different dates. Service dates of House members are listed first because they have specific termination dates, i.e., the closing date of that Congress.

As with Senate select and special committees, Senate members on joint committees are often not fully listed in the Senate Journal or the Congressional Record after the first Congress in which they are named. No full listing of the committee generally means that the committee members have continued their service into the subsequent Congress. In these cases, the ending "Service Date" is listed as "Continued." When new members are named to continuing committees, the date on which they are named is used as the starting "Service Date" for that Congress. This will be indicated in the "Notes" for that roster. If no new members are named, January 3 is used as the starting "Service Date." The full list of Senate members for each Congress has been checked with the Congressional Directory and when possible with committee reports.

Majority and Minority Listings

Committee members of the Majority Party, or that Party with the most members in the full chamber during that Congress, are listed on the left side of each committee roster. Committee members of the Minority Party are listed on the right side of each committee roster.

Third party members are very rare in the Senate. Wayne Morse of Oregon, who left the Republican Party in 1952, sat as an Independent from 1953 to 1955 and joined the Democratic Party in 1955, was the only third party member to be so seated. In the House only four Representatives have been seated as third party members: Vito Marcantonio (1939-1951) of New York, Leo Isacson (1948-1949) of New York, Henry Frazier Reams (1951-1955) of Ohio and Bernard Sanders (1991-date) of Vermont. Representatives Marcantonio and Isacson were affiliated with the American Labor Party while Representatives Reams and Sanders served as Independents. These four were assigned to committees by the party organizing the House during the Congresses in which they served.

Rank

Each roster lists the committee membership in order of their ranking as indicated by the Congressional Record at the time of appointment. Changes in the ranking after the initial appointments are made are not reflected in the list, but are explained in the "Notes". Exceptions to this rule are rankings on some Select, Special and Joint committees, where discrepancies between the Congressional Record and the committees' own reports are resolved in favor of the committee's reports. In the case of some Joint Committees, no chair or ranking minority member was identified in the Congressional Directory.

The following is a list of abbreviations used in the **Rank** columns:

Chr = First and only Chair of the committee during that Congress.
Ch1 = First Chair of more than one Chair during that Congress.
Ch2 = Second Chair of more than one Chair during that Congress.
Ch3 = Third Chair of more than two Chairs during that Congress.
ChA = Acting Chair for part or all of that Congress
CoCh = Co-Chair during that Congress.
RM = First and only Ranking Minority Member during that Congress.
RM1 = First Ranking Minority Member of more than one Ranking Minority Member during that Congress.
RM2 = Second Ranking Minority Member of more than one Ranking Minority Member during that Congress.
RM3 = Third Ranking Minority Member of more than two Ranking Minority Members during that Congress
VCh = Vice Chair during that Congress.
VCh1 = First Vice Chair of more than one Vice Chair during that Congress.
VCh2 = Second Vice Chair of more than one Vice Chair during that Congress.
CVc = Chair for 1st Session of that Congress, Vice Chair for 2nd Session of that Congress.
VcC = Vice Chair for 1st Session of that Congress, Chair for 2nd Session of that Congress.
Del = Delegate to Congress (from Alaska and Hawaii before their admission to the Union, or from the District of Columbia, Virgin Islands, Guam or American Samoa), not counted in the committee size or party ratio unless otherwise noted.
RsC = Resident Commissioner (from Puerto Rico), not counted in the committee size or party ratio unless otherwise noted.

Name of Member

In most cases, this book uses the formal name of each member in order to correspond with the Biographical Directory of the American Congress 1774-1989, (Washington, D.C.: Government Printing Office, 1989). Informal names such as Bob or Bill are generally not used, even if that is how the member is best known. For those members who are best known by their middle name, e.g., J. William Fulbright (Dem-Ark.) and J. Strom Thurmond (Dem-S.C.), we have generally used an initial to abbreviate the first name. In some cases, nicknames appear in parentheses. Marilyn Lloyd (Dem-Tenn.) was known as Marilyn Lloyd Bouquard between 1978 and 1983 when she resumed her original name.

Party of Member

The party affiliation of each committee member at the time of appointment is listed. The following is a list of abbreviations used in the Party column:

ALP = American Labor Party
Con = Conservative Party
Dem = Democratic Party
DFL = Democratic Farmer Labor Party (Minnesota)
Ind = Independent
NPr = New Progressive (Puerto Rico)
Rep = Republican Party
PpD = Popular Democrat (Puerto Rico)
Ind = Independent

State

The state, territory, or federal district from which each member of the committee is elected is listed. Under the State column the following designations have been used:

Ala. = Alabama
Alas. = Alaska
AmS = American Samoa
Ariz. = Arizona
Ark. = Arkansas
Cal. = California
Colo. = Colorado
Conn. = Connecticut
D.C. = District of Columbia
Del. = Delaware
Fla. = Florida
Ga. = Georgia
Guam = Guam
Hai. = Hawaii
Ida. = Idaho
Ill. = Illinois
Ind. = Indiana
Iowa = Iowa
Kans. = Kansas
Ky. = Kentucky
La. = Louisiana
Mass. = Massachusetts
Md. = Maryland
Me. = Maine
Mich. = Michigan
Minn. = Minnesota
Miss. = Mississippi
Mo. = Missouri
Mont. = Montana
Neb. = Nebraska
Nev. = Nevada
N.C. = North Carolina
N.D. = North Dakota
N.J. = New Jersey
N.H. = New Hampshire
N.M. = New Mexico
N.Y. = New York
Ohio = Ohio
Okla. = Oklahoma
Ore. = Oregon
Penn. = Pennsylvania
P.R. = Puerto Rico
R.I. = Rhode Island
S.C. = South Carolina
S.D. = South Dakota
Tenn. = Tennessee
Tex. = Texas
Utah = Utah
Va. = Virginia
V.I. = Virgin Islands
Vt. = Vermont
W.Va. = West Virginia
Wash. = Washington
Wisc. = Wisconsin
Wyo. = Wyoming

Terms in: House/Comm

As noted above, Representatives are elected to a two-year term, which begins at noon on January 3 of each odd numbered year. Thus, seniority in the House is measured in consecutive terms of service. For example, an "11" under the Terms in: House column indicates that the Representative has served eleven consecutive terms of service in the House. Similarly an "11" under the Terms in: Comm. indicates that the Representative has served eleven consecutive terms of service on the Committee. In other words, the Representative in the example has been on this committee continuously since his first term in the House.

Rank	Name	Party	State	Terms in: House	Terms in: Comm.
RM	Ashbrook, John M.	Rep	Ohio	11	11

In some cases, House members are elected in special elections after the adjournment of Congress. A member so elected is given seniority credit for that Congress, even though he or she was not sworn as a member of that Congress. For example, Robert E. Andrews (Dem-N.J.) was elected on November 6, 1990 both to fill the balance of James J. Florio's term in the 101st Congress and to his own term in the 102nd Congress.

The following example is taken from the House Small Business Committee in the 102nd Congress:

Rank	Name	Party	State	Terms in: House	Terms in: Comm.
24th	Andrews, Robert E.	Dem	N.J.	2	1

Representative Andrews is listed as having served 2 terms in the House. He has been credited for service in both the 101st Congress and the 102nd Congress.

Terms in: Senate/Comm:

Because the Senate is a continuous body, seniority is measured by the number of consecutive years served. Seniority in the Senate begins to accrue when a Senator is sworn in or appointed by a governor to fill a vacancy. Seniority on the committee beings to accrue from the date of initial naming to that committee. In the following example, taken from the Senate Armed Services Committee for the 96th Congress (1979-1981), Carl Levin who began as a Senator on January 3, 1979, is in his first year in the Senate and in his first year on the committee, which was appointed on January 23, 1979.

				Years in:	
Rank	Name	Party	State	Senate	Comm.
10th	Levin, Carl M.	Dem	Mich.	1	1

The next example is taken from the same committee in the 97th Congress (1981-1983), which was appointed on January 5, 1983. Levin's third year of service in the Senate began on January 3, 1983, before his reappointment to this committee; hence, there is a "3" under the column **"Years in: Senate."** Levin's third year of service on the committee began on January 25, 1981, after the appointment of members to this committee for the 97th Congress. As of January 5, 1981, the day members are appointed to the committee for the 97th Congress, Levin is still in his second year of service on the committee; hence, there is a "2" under the column **"Years in: Comm."** Had Levin been reappointed to the committee after January 25, 1981, there would be a "3" under that column.

				Years in:	
Rank	Name	Party	State	Senate	Comm.
8th	Levin, Carl M.	Dem	Mich.	3	2

If a member departs from either chamber and subsequently returns to that same chamber, their previous service is included in the "Terms in: House" or "Terms in: Senate" column. However, if a member returns to the committee, he or she is not credited for prior service.

* Period of Service on the Committee

Upon leaving a committee, a member forfeits whatever seniority he or she had accrued. Therefore, if the member is reassigned to the same committee, former service is not counted, and he or she beings accruing seniority as a new member. When a member serves more than one non-consecutive period of service on the same committee, that fact is marked by the member's name with an asterisk.

The number accompanying the asterisk indicates which period of service the member is serving during that particular Congress. On the sample roster, there is a *1 next to Dennis Eckart's name. This indicates that Eckart is in his first of more than one period of service on this committee. Eckart rejoined the committee in the 99th Congress.

On the sample roster, there is a ***2** next to Peter Peyser's "Terms in: Comm." column, indicating that he served on the committee previously, and then left. He was in his second period of service on the committee in the 97th Congress. Peyser served on the Education and Labor Committee in the 94th Congress.

In extremely rare cases, a member will serve on the same committee for three separate periods. The third period of service is indicated by a ***3**. For example, a series of party changing special elections and appointments led to ratio changes that resulted in A. Willis Robertson (Dem-Va.) serving on the Senate Appropriations Committee three separate times from Jan. 10,1949 until May 12,1951.

Representatives occasionally serve on a committee in a temporary capacity, filling a vacancy until a permanent replacement is named. Temporary members are indicated in the text by a *T. Members do not accrue seniority while serving in a temporary capacity; therefore, temporary service is not reflected under the " Terms in: Comm." column.

Notes

The "Notes" contain information explaining unusual circumstances concerning ranking and committee size.

Chair and Ranking Minority Member: Generally, the Chair of a committee is the majority member with the longest continuous service on that committee. Similarly, the Ranking Minority Member is the minority member with the longest continuous service on that committee. All other members are ranked in order of their seniority. There are however, many exceptions to this rule, and for the Standing committees, these exceptions are explained in the "Notes".

In the following example from the Senate Committee on Banking, Housing and Urban Affairs for the 97th Congress, Jake Garn (Rep-Utah), with 6 years of service on the committee, is Chair, and John Tower (Rep-Tex.), with 20 years of service on the committee, is ranked 2nd. The "Notes" indicate that John Tower was Chair of the powerful Senate Armed Services Committee during the 97th Congress, and chose not to be Chair of Banking, Housing and Urban Affairs.

				Years in:	
Rank	Name	Party	State	Senate	Comm.
Chr	Garn, Jake	Rep	Utah	7	6
2nd	Tower, John G.	Rep	Tex.	20	20

Ratio Changes: Changes in the ratio of majority members to minority members are also explained, wherever possible, in the "Notes". Usually these changes in ratio are due to overall gains by one party or the other in special elections or, in the case of the Senate, by gubernatorial appointments. Before the 95th Congress, a Senate Resolution was necessary in order to change a Senate committee's size. The date of each such Resolution is noted. After the 95th Congress, the date used to indicate size and ratio changes is that of the appointment of additional members (see below under Addition).

Delegates and Resident Commissioners: Territorial Delegates from Alaska (until 1959), and Hawaii (until 1959), the District of Columbia, the Virgin Islands, Guam and American Samoa and the Resident Commissioner from Puerto Rico were not allowed to accrue seniority nor were they included in the committee's party ratio until the 93rd Congress (1973-1975). These changing conditions of their membership are included in the "Notes". If the Delegate or Resident Commissioner is assigned on a different day than the other members of the committee, this is noted as well.

Party Switching and Third Party Members: In addition, the seniority status and affect on the party ratio of a committee member who changes parties in the middle of a Congress, or who does not caucus with either the Democratic or Republican Party is explained in the "Notes" as well. Following is list of members who changed their party affiliation between 1947 and 1992:

Senators:

Wayne Morse of Oregon (Rep to Ind to Dem) switched parties in 1952 and in 1955.

J. Strom Thurmond of South Carolina (Dem to Rep) switched parties in 1964.

Harry F. Byrd, Jr. of Virginia (Dem to Ind) switched parties in 1970.

Representatives:

Vincent J. Dellay of New Jersey (Rep to Dem) switched parties in 1958.

Albert W. Watson of South Carolina (Dem to Rep) switched parties in 1965.

Ogden R. Reid of New York (Rep to Dem) switched parties in 1972.

Donald W. Reigle of Michigan (Rep to Dem) switched parties in 1973.

John Jarman of Oklahoma (Dem to Rep) switched parties in 1975.

Peter A. Peyser of New York (Rep to Dem) switched parties in 1976.

Eugene V. Atkinson of Pennsylvania (Dem to Rep) switched parties in 1981.

Robert Stump of Arizona (Dem to Rep) switched parties in 1983.

W. Phil Gramm of Texas (Dem to Rep) switched parties in 1983.

Andy Ireland of Florida (Dem to Rep) switched parties in 1984.

Bill Grant of Florida (Dem to Rep) switched parties in 1989.

Tommy Robinson of Arkansas (Dem to Rep) switched parties in 1989.

Ranking changes: Occasionally, the original ranking of members as reported in the Congressional Record is changed later in that Congress, and the new ranking is reported in the Congressional Record. These changes are reported in the "Notes". For the Select, Special and Joint committees of both chambers, changes made in ranking after the original appointment are not always reported in the House Journal, Senate Journal or the Congressional Record, but are reflected in the membership listing of the committees' reports. As a rule, standing committee rosters are checked with the Congressional Record; select, special and joint committees are checked with committee reports wherever possible.

Seniority from Abolished Committees: After the Committee System Reorganization Amendments of 1977, several Senate standing committees were consolidated. Many members of committees that were abolished (District of Columbia, Post Office and Civil Service, Aeronautical and Space Sciences) were reassigned to successor committees with their seniority intact. Therefore, their previous service on the abolished committee is included under the "Years in: Comm." column, and explained in the "Notes".

House Budget Committee: Representatives who serve on the House Budget committee are allowed to take a leave of absence from the other committees to which they have been named without forfeiting their seniority. When they return to active service on these committees after having served on the Budget Committee, their absence and seniority status are explained in the Notes.

Vacancies Filled

Committee assignments are made at the beginning of each new Congress. Vacancies on the committees due to the departures of members from the previous Congress, or due to a committee size increase or ratio change are usually filled at this time. Sometimes, vacancies remain after the original assignment of members, and are filled at a later date. Majority vacancies that are filled after the date noted by "Service Dates of Majority Members" and minority vacancies that are filled after the date noted by "Service Dates of Minority Members" are listed in the roster and are noted under the heading Vacancies Filled. The majority or minority status of the member filling the vacancy, the rank of the seat being filled, his or her last name, and the date of assignment are listed under this heading. When more than two vacancies are filled by the same party on the same date, the last names are omitted.

Additions

When the ratio of Democrats to Republicans in the entire chamber changes in the middle of a Congress due to special elections, gubernatorial appointments, unfilled vacancies created by departing members, or a change in the party affiliation of a member, the agreed upon ratio of Democrats to Republicans on a committee may change as well. This results in either the forced departure of a member, or more commonly, to the addition of one or more new committee members. A member added under such circumstances is listed under the heading "Addition". Wherever possible, the reason for his or her addition is explained in the Notes. Unlike members filling existing vacancies, members added to a committee due to a size increase do not appear in the roster of committee members, therefore more information about that member is included. The rank to which they are assigned, their full name, party affiliation, state represented and the date on which they were assigned to the committee are included under the heading Addition.

Changes

All members who leave the committee before the January 3 termination date of the Congress, as well as the members who replace them (if they do so before January 3 of that Congress), are listed under the heading "Changes." The full name of the member, his or her party affiliation, state represented and date of departure or assignment is listed. For departing members, the reason for their departure is noted. Common reasons for departure include death, resignation, and appointment to another office. For replacement members, the member whose seat they are filling is noted.

The House and the Senate have differing procedures regarding notification of departures. In the House, a letter is sent by the resigning member to the Speaker indicating his or her departure from the committee. Generally the date that the letter is published in the House Journal or Congressional Record is the one used for the departure. Occasionally, a member will indicate an effective date of departure different from the date the letter is published, in which case both dates are noted. In the Senate, the departure officially takes place when the replacement member is named to the committee.

Chair changes: When the Chair of a committee changes during a Congress, the name of the original Chair, his or her party affiliation, state represented, the date of departure or cessation of duties as Chair, and reason for departure or cessation is noted under the sub-heading Chair. Also listed are the name of his or her successor and the date of their succession. The date of succession used corresponds to the date of passage of the appropriate Resolution, as reported in the official documents.

Ranking Minority Member changes: No Resolution is required for the succession of Ranking Minority Members. Therefore, when the original Ranking Minority Member of a committee departs a committee or ceases to serve in this capacity during a Congress, it is assumed that the succeeding Ranking Minority Member takes over from his or her predecessor on the date of the predecessor's departure as Ranking Minority Member.

Departures

Under this heading are listed all members who serve on the committee until the end of the Congress, but who do not return to the committee at the beginning of the subsequent Congress. There are two categories of departures: Departures from the House or Senate and Departures from Committee.

Departures from the Chamber: Departures from the respective chamber of Congress can occur for a number of reasons. "Died in office" refers to members who died during their congressional service. "Resigned and retired" refers to those members who leave the Congress to resume private life and retire from politics. In some cases, the resignation was due to illness which impeded the member from carrying out official duties. In other cases, there may have been legal difficulties which made the member's continued service problematical. "Resigned..." for other offices refers to members who leave their congressional chamber to contest for another office or to accept appointment to another office. In these cases, an effort has been made to identify the office sought, if it was an elective post, or the office selected for, if it was an appointive post. House members frequently contest for Senate seats which accounts for a substantial number of departures from the House chamber. Those who are successful are identified as "Elected to U.S. Senate." Those who are not are listed as "Lost Election to U.S. Senate" or "Lost Nomination for U.S. Senate" if they failed to survive their party's primary election.

Some House members from large states will leave the House for state-wide offices such as governor or state attorney general as a way of broadening their constituencies in hopes of obtaining later election to the Senate. A small group of members has returned home for municipal offices, such as mayor. Included here would be Representatives John V. Lindsay (Rep-N.Y.) and Edward I. Koch (Dem-N.Y.), both of whom left the House to be elected Mayor of New York City.

Senators seldom leave the Senate for state or local elective office. Senator Pete Wilson's decision to seek the governorship of California in 1990 was related to Republican efforts to thwart congressional redistricting plans which were likely to emanate from the Democratically-controlled state assembly. At stake was the partisan composition of the largest state delegation ever elected to the House of Representatives -- 52 Members.

Judgeships, both federal and state, often prove alluring to members of Congress who desire to remain in public life but wish to avoid the risks of reelection.

Senators are more likely to leave the chamber to accept appointment to the Cabinet or an ambassadorship.

A few Members have run for President and had to relinquish their congressional seats as a consequence. Senator Barry M. Goldwater (Rep-Ariz.), Representative John B. Anderson (Rep-Ill.), and Representative Jack Kemp (Rep-N.Y.) fall into this category.

Leaving the Congress to accept employment in the private sector is relatively rare. However, it happened most recently when Representative William H. Gray III (Dem-Pa.), the Democratic Whip, left the House in 1991 to become President of the United Negro College Fund.

Electoral factors play a major role in ending congressional committee careers. A number of departures from the chamber are due to a Member's failure to be renominated in the state or district primary of his or her party ("Defeated for Renomination") or the failure to be reelected ("Defeated for Reelection"). In some Senate cases, a Member appointed by a governor to fill a portion of the unexpired term of a departed Senator may fail to win election to fill the balance of the term ("Defeated in Special Election").

Departures from the Committee: Departures from the committee refer to those cases where a Member retains his or her seat in the Congress but leaves the committee assignment. The most common reason for committee departures is assignment to another committee. In these cases, the committee to which the member has been assigned is identified.

Other reasons for committee departures include election to a major party leadership post, such as Speaker, floor leader, or whip. In other cases, the departure may be due to assuming the chairmanship or ranking minority slot on another committee.

In some cases, members leave a committee without a new assignment or leadership role. This generally occurs when election results change the number of seats available to a party on the committee or because a member chooses to focus his or her energy on fewer committee assignments.

The information under the Departures heading is listed in three columns: the first lists the reason for departure, the second lists the full name, state represented and party affiliation of all departing majority members, and the third lists the full name, state represented and party affiliation of all departing minority members.

On the sample roster under the "Departures from the House" heading, Democrat Peter Peyser and Republicans Wendell Bailey, Lawrence DeNardis, Arlen Erdahl, and Eugene Johnston all were defeated for reelection, and thus did not return to the House or the committee in the 98th Congress. Also, Republican Millicent Fenwick lost an election to the U.S. Senate. The "None" in the Majority column indicates that no Democrats from this committee departed for this reason.

Under the "Departures from Committee" heading, Democrat Dennis Eckart left the committee (not the House) in order to take a seat on the Energy and Commerce Committee; no Republicans did the same. Democrat William Ratchford and Republican Kenneth Kramer left the committee (but not the House), and were not assigned to any other committee.

EDUCATION AND LABOR / 97th Congress

Service Dates of Committee Chair: Jan. 28,1981-Jan. 3,1983
Service Dates of Majority Members: Jan. 28,1981-Jan. 3,1983
Service Dates of Minority Members: Jan. 28,1981-Jan. 3,1983

Majority

Rank	Name	Party	State	Terms in: House	Terms in: Comm.
Chr	Perkins, Carl D.	Dem	Ky.	17	17
2nd	Hawkins, Augustus F.	Dem	Cal.	10	10
3rd	Ford, William D.	Dem	Mich.	9	9
4th	Burton, Phillip	Dem	Cal.	10	9
5th	Gaydos, Joseph M.	Dem	Penn.	8	7
6th	Clay, William L.	Dem	Mo.	7	7
7th	Biaggi, Mario	Dem	N.Y.	7	6
8th	Andrews, Ike F.	Dem	N.C.	5	5
9th	Simon, Paul M.	Dem	Ill.	4	4
10th	Miller, George	Dem	Cal.	4	4
11th	Murphy, Austin J.	Dem	Penn.	3	3
12th	Weiss, Theodore S.	Dem	N.Y.	3	3
13th	Corrada-del Rio, Baltasar	NPr	P.R.	3	3
14th	Kildee, Dale E.	Dem	Mich.	3	3
15th	Peyser, Peter A.	Dem	N.Y.	2	*2 2
16th	Williams, Pat	Dem	Mont.	2	2
17th	Ratchford, William R.	Dem	Conn.	2	2
18th	Kogovsek, Raymond P.	Dem	Colo.	2	2
19th	Washington, Harold	Dem	Ill.	1	1
20th	Eckart, Dennis E.	Dem	Ohio	1	*1 1

Minority

Rank	Name	Party	State	Terms in: House	Terms in: Comm.
RM1	Ashbrook, John M.	Rep	Ohio	11	11
RM2	Erlenborn, John N.	Rep	Ill.	9	9
3rd	Jeffords, James M.	Rep	Vt.	4	4
4th	Goodling, William F.	Rep	Penn.	4	4
5th	Coleman, E. Thomas	Rep	Mo.	4	2
6th	Kramer, Kenneth B.	Rep	Colo.	2	2
7th	Erdahl, Arlen I.	Rep	Minn.	2	2
8th	Petri, Thomas E.	Rep	Wisc.	2	2
9th	Fenwick, Millicent H.	Rep	N.J.	4	1
10th	Roukema, Margaret	Rep	N.J.	1	1
11th	Johnston, Eugene	Rep	N.C.	1	1
12th	DeNardis, Lawrence J.	Rep	Conn.	1	1
13th	Craig, Larry E.	Rep	Ida.	1	1
14th	Bailey, Wendell	Rep	Mo.	1	1

*1: Member's 1st period of service on the committee;
*2: Member's 2nd period of service on the committee.

Notes: Baltasar Corrada-del Rio (New Progressive-P.R.), the Resident Commissioner from Puerto Rico was allowed to accrue committee seniority but was not included in the committee's party ratio. The committee was expanded and the party ratio changed to 20 Democrats (excluding Corrada) and 14 Republicans on Aug. 19,1982.

Vacancy Filled:
Majority: 20th seat by Eckart on Feb. 25,1981.

Addition:
Majority: 21st Martinez, Matthew G. Dem Cal. Aug. 19,1982

Changes:

Ranking Member:

	Name	Party	State	Date	Change
RM1	Ashbrook, John M.	Rep	Ohio	Apr. 24,1982	Died in office.
RM2	Erlenborn, John N.	Rep	Ill.	Apr. 24,1982	Succeeded Ashbrook as Ranking Minority Member.

Minority:

Name	Party	State	Date	Change
Ashbrook, John M.	Rep	Ohio	Apr. 24,1982	Died in office.
Gunderson, Steven	Rep	Wisc.	June 9,1982	Replaced Ashbrook.

Departures from the House:	Majority			Minority		
Defeated for Reelection	Peyser, Peter A.	N.Y.	Dem	Bailey, Wendell	Mo.	Rep
				DeNardis, Lawrence J.	Conn.	Rep
				Erdahl, Arlen I.	Minn.	Rep
				Johnston, Eugene	N.C.	Rep
Lost Election to U.S. Senate	None			Fenwick, Millicent H.	N.J.	Rep
Departures from Committee:						
Moved to Energy and Commerce	Eckart, Dennis E.	Ohio	Dem	None		
No new assignment	Ratchford, William R.	Conn.	Dem	Kramer, Kenneth B.	Colo.	Rep

PART I
Standing Committees
U.S. Senate, 1947-1992

AERONAUTICAL AND SPACE SCIENCES

Jurisdiction, 1958

From Senate Resolution 327 as amended, 85th Congress, Second Session, July 24, 1958:

[Paragraph 1]

Committee on Aeronautical and Space Sciences, to consist of fifteen Senators, to which committee shall be referred all proposed legislation, messages, petitions, memorials, and other matters relating primarily to the following subjects:

(A) Aeronautical and space activities, as that term is defined in the National Aeronautics and Space Act of 1958, except those which are peculiar to or primarily associated with the development of weapons systems or military operations.
(B) Matters relating generally to the scientific aspects of such aeronautical and space activities, except those which are peculiar to or primarily associated with the developments of weapons systems or military operations.
(C) National Aeronautics and Space Administration.

(2) Such committee also shall have jurisdiction to survey and review, and to prepare studies and reports upon, aeronautical and space activities of all agencies of the United States, including such activities which are peculiar to or primarily associated with the development of weapons systems or military operations.

Jurisdiction, 1975

Jurisdiction from the Senate Manual for the 94th Congress (1975):

[Rule XXV.(a)]

(1) Committee on Aeronautical and Space Sciences, to which committee shall be referred all proposed legislation, messages, petitions, memorials, and other matters relating primarily to the following subjects:

  (A) Aeronautical and space activities, as that term is defined in the National Aeronautics and Space Act of 1958, except those which are peculiar to or primarily associated with the development of weapons systems or military operations.
  (B) Matters relating generally to the scientific aspects of such aeronautical and space activities, except those which are peculiar to or primarily associated with the development of weapons systems or military operations.
  (C) National Aeronautics and Space Administration.

(2) Such committee also shall have jurisdiction to survey and review, and to prepare studies and reports upon, aeronautical and space activities of all agencies of the United States, including such activities which are peculiar to or primarily associated with the development of weapons systems or military operations.

Reorganization, 1977

The Committee was reorganized into the Standing Committee on Commerce, Science and Transportation following the passage of Senate Resolution 4, the Committee System Reorganization Amendments of 1977, February 4, 1977. Majority members were reassigned on February 11, 1977 and the minority members were reassigned on February 22, 1977.

AERONAUTICAL AND SPACE SCIENCES / 85th Congress

* Created as a standing committee July 24,1958.

Service Dates of Committee Chair: Aug. 24,1958-Jan. 14,1959
Service Dates of Majority Members: Aug. 24,1958-Jan. 14,1959
Service Dates of Minority Members: Aug. 24,1958-Jan. 20,1959

Majority

Rank Name	Party	State	Years in: Senate	Comm.
Chr Johnson, Lyndon B.	Dem	Tex.	10	1
2nd Hayden, Carl	Dem	Ariz.	32	1
3rd Russell, Richard B.	Dem	Ga.	26	1
4th Green, Theodore F.	Dem	R.I.	22	1
5th Magnuson, Warren G.	Dem	Wash.	14	1
6th Anderson, Clinton P.	Dem	N.M.	10	1
7th Kerr, Robert S.	Dem	Okla.	10	1
8th Symington, W. Stuart	Dem	Mo.	6	1

Minority

Rank Name	Party	State	Years in: Senate	Comm.
RM Bridges, H. Styles	Rep	N.H.	22	1
2nd Saltonstall, Leverett	Rep	Mass.	14	1
3rd Wiley, Alexander	Rep	Wisc.	20	1
4th Bricker, John W.	Rep	Ohio	12	1
5th Hickenlooper, Bourke B.	Rep	Iowa	14 *1	1
6th Smith, Margaret Chase	Rep	Me.	10	1
7th Javits, Jacob K.	Rep	N.Y.	2	1

*1: Member's 1st period of service on the committee.

	Majority		Minority	
Departures from the Senate:				
Defeated for Reelection	None		Bricker, John W.	Ohio Rep
Departures from Committee:				
No new assignment	Green, Theodore F.	R.I. Dem	Hickenlooper, Bourke B.	Iowa Rep
	Hayden, Carl	Ariz. Dem	Saltonstall, Leverett	Mass. Rep

AERONAUTICAL AND SPACE SCIENCES / 86th Congress

Service Dates of Committee Chair: Jan. 14,1959-Jan. 3,1961
Service Dates of Majority Members: Jan. 14,1959-Jan. 10,1961
Service Dates of Minority Members: Jan. 20,1959-Jan. 13,1961

Majority

Rank Name	Party	State	Years in: Senate	Comm.
Chr Johnson, Lyndon B.	Dem	Tex.	11	1
2nd Russell, Richard B.	Dem	Ga.	27	1
3rd Magnuson, Warren G.	Dem	Wash.	15	1
4th Anderson, Clinton P.	Dem	N.M.	11	1
5th Kerr, Robert S.	Dem	Okla.	11	1
6th Symington, W. Stuart	Dem	Mo.	7	1
7th Stennis, John C.	Dem	Miss.	12	1
8th Young, Stephen M.	Dem	Ohio	1	1
9th Dodd, Thomas J.	Dem	Conn.	1	1
10th Cannon, Howard W.	Dem	Nev.	1	1

Minority

Rank Name	Party	State	Years in: Senate	Comm.
RM Bridges, H. Styles	Rep	N.H.	23	1
2nd Wiley, Alexander	Rep	Wisc.	21	1
3rd Smith, Margaret Chase	Rep	Me.	11	1
4th Javits, Jacob K.	Rep	N.Y.	3	1
5th Case, Clifford P.	Rep	N.J.	5	1

Changes:
Minority:

Javits, Jacob K.	Rep	N.Y.	Jan. 27,1959	Moved to Banking and Currency.
Martin, Thomas E.	Rep	Iowa	Jan. 27,1959	Replaced Javits; ranked ahead of Case on Jan. 28,1959.

	Majority		Minority	
Departures from the Senate:				
Elected Vice President	Johnson, Lyndon B.	Tex. Dem	None	
Retired	None		Martin, Thomas E.	Iowa Rep

AERONAUTICAL AND SPACE SCIENCES / 87th Congress

Service Dates of Committee Chair: Jan. 10,1961-Jan. 1,1963
Service Dates of Majority Members: Jan. 10,1961-Feb. 25,1963
Service Dates of Minority Members: Jan. 13,1961-Feb. 25,1963

Majority

Rank Name	Party	State	Years in: Senate	Years in: Comm.
Chr Kerr, Robert S.	Dem	Okla.	13	3
2nd Russell, Richard B.	Dem	Ga.	28	3
3rd Magnuson, Warren G.	Dem	Wash.	17	3
4th Anderson, Clinton P.	Dem	N.M.	13	3
5th Symington, W. Stuart	Dem	Mo.	9	3
6th Stennis, John C.	Dem	Miss.	14	2
7th Young, Stephen M.	Dem	Ohio	3	2
8th Dodd, Thomas J.	Dem	Conn.	3	2
9th Cannon, Howard W.	Dem	Nev.	3	2
10th Holland, Spessard L.	Dem	Fla.	15	1

Minority

Rank Name	Party	State	Years in: Senate	Years in: Comm.
RM1 Bridges, H. Styles	Rep	N.H.	25	3
RM2 2nd Wiley, Alexander	Rep	Wisc.	23	3
3rd Smith, Margaret Chase	Rep	Me.	13	3
4th Case, Clifford P.	Rep	N.J.	7	2
5th Hickenlooper, Bourke B.	Rep	Iowa	17 *2	1

*2: Member's 2nd period of service on the committee.

Note: Rankings on this committee for the following members were affected by other chamber service: Richard B. Russell (Dem-Ga.), Chair, Armed Services; Warren G. Magnuson (Dem-Wash.), Chair, Interstate and Foreign Commerce; and Clinton P. Anderson (Dem-N.M.), Chair, Interior and Insular Affairs.

Changes:

Ranking Member:

RM1 Bridges, H. Styles	Rep	N.H.	Nov. 26,1961	Died in office.
RM2 Wiley, Alexander	Rep	Wisc.	Nov. 26,1961	Succeeded Bridges as Ranking Minority Member.

Majority:

Kerr, Robert S.	Dem	Okla.	Jan. 1,1963	Died in office.

Minority:

Bridges, H. Styles	Rep	N.H.	Nov. 26,1961	Died in office.
Capehart, Homer E.	Rep	Ind.	Feb. 2,1962	Replaced Bridges.

Departures from the Senate:

	Majority	Minority		
Defeated for Reelection	None	Wiley, Alexander	Wisc.	Rep
		Capehart, Homer E.	Ind.	Rep

AERONAUTICAL AND SPACE SCIENCES / 88th Congress

Service Dates of Committee Chair: Feb. 25,1963-Jan. 8,1965
Service Dates of Majority Members: Feb. 25,1963-Jan. 8,1965
Service Dates of Minority Members: Feb. 25,1963-Jan. 15,1965

Majority

Rank Name	Party	State	Years in: Senate	Years in: Comm.
Chr Anderson, Clinton P.	Dem	N.M.	15	5
2nd Russell, Richard B.	Dem	Ga.	31	5
3rd Magnuson, Warren G.	Dem	Wash.	19	5
4th Symington, W. Stuart	Dem	Mo.	11	5
5th Stennis, John C.	Dem	Miss.	16	5
6th Young, Stephen M.	Dem	Ohio	5	5
7th Dodd, Thomas J.	Dem	Conn.	5	5
8th Cannon, Howard W.	Dem	Nev.	5	5
9th Holland, Spessard L.	Dem	Fla.	17	3
10th Edmondson, J. Howard	Dem	Okla.	1	1

Minority

Rank Name	Party	State	Years in: Senate	Years in: Comm.
RM Smith, Margaret Chase	Rep	Me.	15	5
2nd Case, Clifford P.	Rep	N.J.	9	5
3rd Hickenlooper, Bourke B.	Rep	Iowa	19 *2	3
4th Curtis, Carl T.	Rep	Neb.	9	1
5th Keating, Kenneth B.	Rep	N.Y.	5	1

*2: Member's 2nd period of service on the committee.

Note: Rankings on this committee for the following members were affected by other chamber service: Richard B. Russell (Dem-Ga.), Chair, Armed Services; and Warren G. Magnuson (Dem-Wash.), Chair, Interstate and Foreign Commerce.

Changes:

Majority:

Edmondson, J. Howard	Dem	Okla.	Nov. 3,1964	Resigned; defeated for nomination.

Departures from the Senate:	Majority			Minority		
Defeated for Reelection	None			Keating, Kenneth B.	N.Y.	Rep
Departures from Committee:						
Moved to Foreign Relations	None			Case, Clifford P.	N.J.	Rep

AERONAUTICAL AND SPACE SCIENCES / 89th Congress

Service Dates of Committee Chair: Jan. 8,1965-Jan. 11,1967
Service Dates of Majority Members: Jan. 8,1965-Jan. 11,1967
Service Dates of Minority Members: Jan. 15,1965-Jan. 16,1967

Majority

Rank	Name	Party	State	Years in: Senate	Years in: Comm.
Chr	Anderson, Clinton P.	Dem	N.M.	17	7
2nd	Russell, Richard B.	Dem	Ga.	32	7
3rd	Magnuson, Warren G.	Dem	Wash.	21	7
4th	Symington, W. Stuart	Dem	Mo.	13	7
5th	Stennis, John C.	Dem	Miss.	18	6
6th	Young, Stephen M.	Dem	Ohio	7	6
7th	Dodd, Thomas J.	Dem	Conn.	7	6
8th	Cannon, Howard W.	Dem	Nev.	7	6
9th	Holland, Spessard L.	Dem	Fla.	19	4
10th	Mondale, Walter F.	DFL	Minn.	1	1
11th	Tydings, Joseph D.	Dem	Md.	1	1

Minority

Rank	Name	Party	State	Years in: Senate	Years in: Comm.
RM	Smith, Margaret Chase	Rep	Me.	17	7
2nd	Hickenlooper, Bourke B.	Rep	Iowa	21	*2 5
3rd	Curtis, Carl T.	Rep	Neb.	11	2
4th	Jordan, Len B.	Rep	Ida.	3	1
5th	Aiken, George D.	Rep	Vt.	25	1

*2: Member's 2nd period of service on the committee.

Note: Rankings on this committee for the following members were affected by other chamber service: Richard B. Russell (Dem-Ga.), Chair, Armed Services; and Warren G. Magnuson (Dem-Wash.), Chair, Interstate and Foreign Commerce.

Changes:
Majority:

Name	Party	State	Date	Change
Tydings, Joseph D.	Dem	Md.	Jan. 14,1966	Moved to Public Works.
Byrd, Harry Flood Jr.	Dem	Va.	Jan. 14,1966	Replaced Tydings.

Departures from Committee:	Majority			Minority		
Moved to Agriculture & Forestry	Byrd, Harry Flood Jr.	Va.	Dem	None		
No new assignment	None			Aiken, George D.	Vt.	Rep

AERONAUTICAL AND SPACE SCIENCES / 90th Congress

Service Dates of Committee Chair: Jan. 11,1967-Jan. 14,1969
Service Dates of Majority Members: Jan. 11,1967-Jan. 14,1969
Service Dates of Minority Members: Jan. 16,1967-Jan. 14,1969

Majority

Rank	Name	Party	State	Years in: Senate	Years in: Comm.
Chr	Anderson, Clinton P.	Dem	N.M.	19	9
2nd	Russell, Richard B.	Dem	Ga.	34	9
3rd	Magnuson, Warren G.	Dem	Wash.	23	9
4th	Symington, W. Stuart	Dem	Mo.	15	9
5th	Stennis, John C.	Dem	Miss.	20	8
6th	Young, Stephen M.	Dem	Ohio	9	8
7th	Dodd, Thomas J.	Dem	Conn.	9	8
8th	Cannon, Howard W.	Dem	Nev.	9	8
9th	Holland, Spessard L.	Dem	Fla.	21	7
10th	Mondale, Walter F.	DFL	Minn.	3	3

Minority

Rank	Name	Party	State	Years in: Senate	Years in: Comm.
RM	Smith, Margaret Chase	Rep	Me.	19	9
2nd	Hickenlooper, Bourke B.	Rep	Iowa	23	*2 7
3rd	Curtis, Carl T.	Rep	Neb.	13	4
4th	Jordan, Len B.	Rep	Ida.	5	3
5th	Brooke, Edward W.	Rep	Mass.	1	1
6th	Percy, Charles H.	Rep	Ill.	1	1

*2: Member's 2nd period of service on the committee.

Note: Rankings on this committee for the following members were affected by other chamber service: Richard B. Russell (Dem-Ga.), Chair, Armed Services; and Warren G. Magnuson (Dem-Wash.), Chair, Interstate and Foreign Commerce.

Changes:

Majority:

Mondale, Walter F.	DFL	Minn.	June 25,1968	Moved to Labor and Public Welfare.

Minority:

Brooke, Edward W.	Rep	Mass.	Sep. 12,1968	Moved to Government Operations.
Percy, Charles H.	Rep	Ill.	Sep. 12,1968	Moved to Government Operations.
Hatfield, Mark O.	Rep	Ore.	Sep. 12,1968	Replaced Brooke.
Goodell, Charles E.	Rep	N.Y.	Sep. 12,1968	Replaced Percy.

	Majority	Minority		
Departures from the Senate:				
Retired	None	Hickenlooper, Bourke B.	Iowa	Rep
Departures from Committee:				
Moved to Finance	None	Jordan, Len B.	Ida.	Rep
Moved to Banking & Currency; Commerce; District of Columbia	None	Goodell, Charles E.	N.Y.	Rep

AERONAUTICAL AND SPACE SCIENCES / 91st Congress

Service Dates of Committee Chair: Jan. 14,1969-Jan. 28,1971
Service Dates of Majority Members: Jan. 14,1969-Jan. 28,1971
Service Dates of Minority Members: Jan. 14,1969-Jan. 29,1971

Majority

Rank	Name	Party	State	Years in: Senate	Years in: Comm.
Chr	Anderson, Clinton P.	Dem	N.M.	21	11
2nd	Russell, Richard B.	Dem	Ga.	37	11
3rd	Magnuson, Warren G.	Dem	Wash.	25	11
4th	Symington, W. Stuart	Dem	Mo.	17	11
5th	Stennis, John C.	Dem	Miss.	22	11
6th	Young, Stephen M.	Dem	Ohio	11	11
7th	Dodd, Thomas J.	Dem	Conn.	11	11
8th	Cannon, Howard W.	Dem	Nev.	11	11
9th	Holland, Spessard L.	Dem	Fla.	23	9

Minority

Rank	Name	Party	State	Years in: Senate	Years in: Comm.
RM	Smith, Margaret Chase	Rep	Me.	21	11
2nd	Curtis, Carl T.	Rep	Neb.	15	6
3rd	Hatfield, Mark O.	Rep	Ore.	3	1
4th	Goldwater, Barry M.	Rep	Ariz.	13	1
5th	Mathias, Charles McC. Jr.	Rep	Md.	1	1
6th	Saxbe, William B.	Rep	Ohio	1	1

Notes: Appointed Senator Ralph Tyler Smith (Rep-Ill.) lost in a special election to Adlai Stevenson (Dem-Ill.), resulting in a change in size and party ratio on this committee to 10 Democrats and 5 Republicans on November 17, 1970. Rankings on this committee for the following members were affected by other chamber service: Richard B. Russell (Dem-Ga.), Chair, Armed Services; and Warren G. Magnuson (Dem-Wash.), Chair, Interstate and Foreign Commerce.

Addition:

Majority: 10th Stevenson, Adlai E. III Dem Ill. Nov. 17,1970

Changes:

Majority:

Russell, Richard B.	Dem	Ga.	Jan. 21,1971	Died in office.

Minority:

Mathias, Charles McC. Jr.	Rep	Md.	Sep. 17,1969	Moved to Government Operations.
Smith, Ralph Tyler	Rep	Ill.	Sep. 18,1969	Replaced Mathias.
Smith, Ralph Tyler	Rep	Ill.	Nov. 16,1970	Resigned; lost special election to Stevenson.

	Majority			Minority		
Departures from the Senate:						
Defeated for Reelection	Dodd, Thomas J.	Conn.	Dem	None		
Retired	Holland, Spessard L.	Fla.	Dem	None		
	Young, Stephen M.	Ohio	Dem			
Departures from Committee:						
Moved to Banking, Housing & Urban Affairs; District of Columbia	Stevenson, Adlai E. III	Ill.	Dem	None		
Moved to Commerce	None			Hatfield, Mark O.	Ore.	Rep
Moved to Armed Services	None			Saxbe, William B.	Ohio	Rep

AERONAUTICAL AND SPACE SCIENCES / 92nd Congress

Service Dates of Committee Chair: Jan. 28,1971-Jan. 3,1973
Service Dates of Majority Members: Jan. 28,1971-Jan. 4,1973
Service Dates of Minority Members: Jan. 29,1971-Jan. 12,1973

Majority

Rank	Name	Party	State	Years in: Senate	Years in: Comm.
Chr	Anderson, Clinton P.	Dem	N.M.	23	13
2nd	Magnuson, Warren G.	Dem	Wash.	27	13
3rd	Symington, W. Stuart	Dem	Mo.	19	13
4th	Stennis, John C.	Dem	Miss.	24	13
5th	Cannon, Howard W.	Dem	Nev.	13	13
6th	Gambrell, David H.	Dem	Ga.	1	1

Minority

Rank	Name	Party	State	Years in: Senate	Years in: Comm.
RM	Curtis, Carl T.	Rep	Neb.	17	8
2nd	Smith, Margaret Chase	Rep	Me.	23	13
3rd	Goldwater, Barry M.	Rep	Ariz.	15	3
4th	Weicker, Lowell P. Jr.	Rep	Conn.	1	1
5th	Buckley, James L.	Con	N.Y.	1	1

Notes: Rankings on this committee for the following members were affected by other chamber service: Richard B. Russell (Dem-Ga.), Chair, Armed Services; Warren G. Magnuson (Dem-Wash.), Chair, Interstate and Foreign Commerce; and Margaret Chase Smith (Rep-Me.), Ranking Minority Member, Armed Services. James L. Buckley of New York was elected as a Conservative, but was assigned by the Republican Conference, serving on the committee with his seniority intact.

Vacancy Filled:
Majority: 6th seat by Gambrell on Feb. 2,1971.

Changes:

	Name	Party	State	Date	Change
Majority:	Gambrell, David H.	Dem	Ga.	Nov. 7,1972	Resigned; defeated for nomination in special election.
Minority:	Buckley, James L.	Con	N.Y.	Feb. 23,1972	Moved to Interior and Insular Affairs.
	Mundt, Karl E.	Rep	S.D.	Feb. 23,1972	Replaced Buckley.

Departures from the Senate:

	Majority			Minority		
Defeated for Reelection	None			Smith, Margaret Chase	Me.	Rep
Retired	Anderson, Clinton P.	N.M.	Dem	Mundt, Karl E.	S.D.	Rep

AERONAUTICAL AND SPACE SCIENCES / 93rd Congress

Service Dates of Committee Chair: Jan. 4,1973-Jan. 17,1975
Service Dates of Majority Members: Jan. 4,1973-Jan. 17,1975
Service Dates of Minority Members: Jan. 12,1973-Jan. 23,1975

Majority

Rank	Name	Party	State	Years in: Senate	Years in: Comm.
Chr	Moss, Frank E.	Dem	Utah	15	1
2nd	Magnuson, Warren G.	Dem	Wash.	29	15
3rd	Symington, W. Stuart	Dem	Mo.	21	15
4th	Stennis, John C.	Dem	Miss.	26	14
5th	Cannon, Howard W.	Dem	Nev.	15	14
6th	Abourezk, James G.	Dem	S.D.	1	1
7th	Haskell, Floyd K.	Dem	Colo.	1	1

Minority

Rank	Name	Party	State	Years in: Senate	Years in: Comm.
RM	Goldwater, Barry M.	Rep	Ariz.	17	4
2nd	Curtis, Carl T.	Rep	Neb.	19	10
3rd	Weicker, Lowell P. Jr.	Rep	Conn.	3	2
4th	Bartlett, Dewey F.	Rep	Okla.	1	1
5th	Helms, Jesse A.	Rep	N.C.	1	1
6th	Domenici, Pete V.	Rep	N.M.	1	1

Notes: The resignation of William Saxbe (Rep-Ohio) upon his appointment as Attorney General, and the appointment of Howard Metzenbaum (Dem-Ohio) to fill his vacancy resulted in a change in size and party ratio on this committee to 8 Democrats and 6 Republicans on Jan. 23,1974. Rankings on this committee for the following members were affected by other chamber service: Warren G. Magnuson (Dem-Wash.), Chair, Commerce; John C. Stennis (Dem-Miss.), Chair, Armed Services; Howard W. Cannon (Dem-Nev.), Chair, Rules and Administration; and Carl T. Curtis (Rep-Neb.), Ranking Minority Member, Agriculture and Forestry. Stuart Symington (Dem-Mo.), was a senior member of the Armed Services committee and the Foreign Relations committee and waived his seniority on this committee.

Addition:
Majority: 8th Metzenbaum, Howard M. Dem Ohio Jan. 23,1974

Changes:

Majority:

Metzenbaum, Howard M.	Dem	Ohio	Dec. 23,1974	Resigned; defeated for nomination.

Departures from Committee:

	Majority		Minority	
Moved to Judiciary	Abourezk, James G.	S.D. Dem	None	
Moved to Finance	Haskell, Floyd K.	Colo. Dem	Curtis, Carl T.	Neb. Rep
Moved to Armed Services	None		Bartlett, Dewey F.	Okla. Rep
Moved to Banking, Housing & Urban Affairs	None		Helms, Jesse A.	N.C. Rep
Moved to Government Operations	None		Weicker, Lowell P. Jr.	Conn. Rep
No new assignment	Magnuson, Warren G.	Wash. Dem	None	

AERONAUTICAL AND SPACE SCIENCES / 94th Congress

Service Dates of Committee Chair: Jan. 17,1975-Jan. 3,1977
Service Dates of Majority Members: Jan. 17,1975-Jan. 10,1977
Service Dates of Minority Members: Jan. 23,1975-Jan. 10,1977

Majority

Rank	Name	Party	State	Years in: Senate	Years in: Comm.
Chr	Moss, Frank E.	Dem	Utah	17	3
2nd	Symington, W. Stuart	Dem	Mo.	23	17
3rd	Stennis, John C.	Dem	Miss.	28	17
4th	Cannon, Howard W.	Dem	Nev.	17	17
5th	Ford, Wendell H.	Dem	Ky.	1	1
6th	Bumpers, Dale	Dem	Ark.	1	1

Minority

Rank	Name	Party	State	Years in: Senate	Years in: Comm.
RM	Goldwater, Barry M.	Rep	Ariz.	19	7
2nd	Domenici, Pete V.	Rep	N.M.	3	3
3rd	Laxalt, Paul	Rep	Nev.	1	1
4th	Garn, Jake	Rep	Utah	1	1

Notes: Norris Cotton (Rep-N.H.), appointed to fill a vacancy caused by the contested election between John Durkin (Dem) and Louis Wyman (Rep), was assigned the 5th minority seat on this committee, changing its size and party ratio to 6 Democrats and 5 Republicans on September 3, 1975. Cotton left the Senate upon the election of Durkin in a special election, resulting in a change to the original committee size and party ratio of 6 Democrats and 4 Republicans on Sep. 19,1975. Rankings on this committee for the following members were affected by other chamber service: John C. Stennis (Dem-Miss.), Chair, Armed Services; and Howard W. Cannon (Dem-Nev.), Chair, Rules and Administration. Stuart Symington (Dem-Mo.), was a senior member of the Armed Services committee and the Foreign Relations committee and waived his seniority on this committee.

Addition:

Minority: 5th Cotton, Norris — Rep N.H. — Sep. 3,1975

Changes:

Majority:

Symington, W. Stuart	Dem	Mo.	Dec. 27,1976	Resigned and retired.

Minority:

Cotton, Norris	Rep	N.H.	Sep. 17,1975	Resigned and retired.

Departures from the Senate:

	Majority		Minority
Defeated for Reelection	Moss, Frank E.	Utah Dem	None

AERONAUTICAL AND SPACE SCIENCES / 95th Congress

* Reorganized into the Committee on COMMERCE, SCIENCE AND TRANSPORTATION.

Service Dates of Committee Chair: Jan. 10,1977-Feb. 11,1977
Service Dates of Majority Members: Jan. 10,1977-Feb. 11,1977
Service Dates of Minority Members: Jan. 10,1977-Feb. 22,1977

Majority

Rank	Name	Party	State	Years in: Senate	Comm.
Chr	Ford, Wendell H.	Dem	Ky.	3	2
2nd	Stennis, John C.	Dem	Miss.	30	18
3rd	Cannon, Howard W.	Dem	Nev.	19	18
4th	Bumpers, Dale	Dem	Ark.	3	2

Minority

Rank	Name	Party	State	Years in: Senate	Comm.
RM	Goldwater, Barry M.	Rep	Ariz.	21	8
2nd	Domenici, Pete V.	Rep	N.M.	5	4
3rd	Laxalt, Paul	Rep	Nev.	3	2
4th	Garn, Jake	Rep	Utah	3	2

Note: Rankings on this committee for the following members were affected by other chamber service: John C. Stennis (Dem-Miss.), Chair of the Armed Services committee; and Howard W. Cannon (Dem-Nev.), Chair of Rules and Administration.

Changes:

Majority:

Name	Party	State	Date	Change
Ford, Wendell H.	Dem	Ky.	Feb. 11,1977	Moved to Energy and Natural Resources.
Stennis, John C.	Dem	Miss.	Feb. 11,1977	Left committee; no new assignment.
Cannon, Howard W.	Dem	Nev.	Feb. 11,1977	Remained on reorganized Commerce, Science and Transportation.
Bumpers, Dale	Dem	Ark.	Feb. 11,1977	Moved to Armed Services.

Minority:

Name	Party	State	Date	Change
Goldwater, Barry M.	Rep	Ariz.	Feb. 22,1977	Remained on reorganized Commerce, Science and Transportation.
Domenici, Pete V.	Rep	N.M.	Feb. 22,1977	Moved to Energy and Natural Resources.
Laxalt, Paul	Rep	Nev.	Feb. 22,1977	Moved to Energy and Natural Resources; Judiciary.
Garn, Jake	Rep	Utah	Feb. 22,1977	Moved to Armed Services.

AGRICULTURE, NUTRITION, AND FORESTRY

AGRICULTURE AND FORESTRY

Jurisdiction, 1947

Established by the Legislative Reorganization Act of 1946:

[Section 102.(1)(a)]

(1) Committee on Agriculture and Forestry, to consist of thirteen Senators, to which committee shall be referred all proposed legislation, messages, petitions, memorials, and other matters relating to the following subjects:

1. Agriculture generally.
2. Inspection of livestock and meat products.
3. Animal industry and diseases of animals.
4. Adulteration of seeds, insect pests, and protection of birds and animals in forest reserves.
5. Agricultural colleges and experiment stations.
6. Forestry in general, and forest reserves other than those created from the public domain.
7. Agricultural economics and research.
8. Agricultural and industrial chemistry.
9. Dairy industry.
10. Entomology and plant quarantine.
11. Human nutrition and home economics.
12. Plant industry, soils, and agricultural engineering.
13. Agricultural educational extension services.
14. Extension of farm credit and farm security.
15. Rural electrification.
16. Agricultural production and marketing and stabilization of prices of agricultural products.
17. Crop insurance and soil conservation.

AGRICULTURE, NUTRITION, AND FORESTRY

Reorganization, 1977

The Committee was reorganized as the Standing Committee on Agriculture, Nutrition and Forestry following the passage of Senate Resolution 4, the Committee System Reorganization Amendments of 1977, February 4, 1977.

Jurisdiction, 1977

[Section 1.(a)(1)]

Committee on Agriculture, Nutrition, and Forestry, to which committee shall be referred all proposed legislation, messages, petitions, memorials, and other matters relating primarily to the following subjects:

1. Agriculture and agricultural commodities.
2. Inspection of livestock, meat, and agricultural products.
3. Animal industry and disease.
4. Pests and pesticides.
5. Agricultural extension services and experiment stations.
6. Forestry, and forest reserves and wilderness areas other than those created from the public domain.
7. Agricultural economics and research.
8. Home economics.
9. Plant industry, soils, and agricultural engineering.
10. Farm credit and farm security.
11. Rural development, rural electrification, and watersheds.

12. Agricultural production, marketing, and stabilization of prices.
13. Crop insurance and soil conservation.
14. Human nutrition.
15. School nutrition programs.
16. Food stamp programs.
17. Food from fresh waters.

(2) Such committee shall also study and review, on a comprehensive basis, matters relating to food, nutrition, and hunger, both in the United States and in foreign countries, and rural affairs, and report thereon from time to time.

Jurisdiction, 1992

Jurisdiction contained in the Standing Rules of the Senate (as revised to March 18, 1992):

[Rule XXV.(1)(a)]

(1) Committee on Agriculture, Nutrition, and Forestry, to which committee shall be referred all proposed legislation, messages, petitions, memorials, and other matters relating primarily to the following subjects:

1. Agricultural economics and research.
2. Agricultural extension services and experiment stations.
3. Agricultural production, marketing, and stabilization of prices.
4. Agriculture and agricultural commodities.
5. Animal industry and diseases.
6. Crop insurance and soil conservation.
7. Farm credit and farm security.
8. Food from fresh waters.
9. Food stamp programs.
10. Forestry, and forest reserves and wilderness areas other than those created from the public domain.
11. Home economics.
12. Human nutrition.
13. Inspection of livestock, meat, and agricultural products.
14. Pests and pesticides.
15. Plant industry, soils, and agricultural engineering.
16. Rural development, rural electrification, and watersheds.
17. School nutrition programs.

(2) Such committee shall also study and review, on a comprehensive basis, matters relating to food, nutrition, and hunger, both in the United States and in foreign countries, and rural affairs, and report thereon from time to time.

AGRICULTURE AND FORESTRY / 80th Congress

Service Dates of Committee Chair: Jan. 6,1947-Jan. 3,1949
Service Dates of Majority Members: Jan. 6,1947-Jan. 10,1949
Service Dates of Minority Members: Jan. 8,1947-Jan. 10,1949

Majority

Rank Name	Party	State	Years in: Senate	Years in: Comm.
Chr Capper, Arthur	Rep	Kans.	28	28
2nd Aiken, George D.	Rep	Vt.	6	6
3rd Bushfield, Harlan J.	Rep	S.D.	5	4
4th Wilson, George A.	Rep	Iowa	4	3
5th Young, Milton R.	Rep	N.D.	2	2
6th Kem, James P.	Rep	Mo.	1	1
7th Thye, Edward J.	Rep	Minn.	1	1

Minority

Rank Name	Party	State	Years in: Senate	Years in: Comm.
RM Thomas, Elmer	Dem	Okla.	20	20
2nd Ellender, Allen J.	Dem	La.	11	11
3rd Lucas, Scott W.	Dem	Ill.	9	8
4th Stewart, A. Tom	Dem	Tenn.	8	8
5th Hoey, Clyde R.	Dem	N.C.	3	2
6th Pepper, Claude D.	Dem	Fla.	11	1

Note: The rankings of majority members Thye and Kem were switched on Dec. 15,1947, with Thye listed ahead of Kem.

Changes:
Majority:

Bushfield, Harlan J.	Rep	S.D.	Sep. 27,1948	Died in office.

	Majority		Minority	
Departures from the Senate:				
Defeated for Reelection	Wilson, George A.	Iowa Rep	None	
Defeated for Renomination	None		Stewart, A. Tom	Tenn. Dem
Retired	Capper, Arthur	Kans. Rep	None	
Departures from Committee:				
Moved to Foreign Relations	None		Pepper, Claude D.	Fla. Dem

AGRICULTURE AND FORESTRY / 81st Congress

Service Dates of Committee Chair: Jan. 10,1949-Jan. 3,1951
Service Dates of Majority Members: Jan. 10,1949-Jan. 15,1951
Service Dates of Minority Members: Jan. 10,1949-Jan. 15,1951

Majority

Rank	Name	Party	State	Years in: Senate	Years in: Comm.
Chr	Thomas, Elmer	Dem	Okla.	22	22
2nd	Ellender, Allen J.	Dem	La.	13	13
3rd	Lucas, Scott W.	Dem	Ill.	11	11
4th	Hoey, Clyde R.	Dem	N.C.	5	5
5th	Johnston, Olin D.	Dem	S.C.	5	1
6th	Holland, Spessard L.	Dem	Fla.	3	1
7th	Gillette, Guy M.	Dem	Iowa	9 *2	1
8th	Anderson, Clinton P.	Dem	N.M.	1	1

Minority

Rank	Name	Party	State	Years in: Senate	Years in: Comm.
RM	Aiken, George D.	Rep	Vt.	9	8
2nd	Young, Milton R.	Rep	N.D.	4	4
3rd	Thye, Edward J.	Rep	Minn.	3	3
4th	Kem, James P.	Rep	Mo.	3	3
5th	Hickenlooper, Bourke B.	Rep	Iowa	5	1

*2: Member's 2nd period of service on the committee.

	Majority		Minority
Departures from the Senate:			
Defeated for Reelection	Lucas, Scott W.	Ill. Dem	None
Defeated for Renomination	Thomas, Elmer	Okla. Dem	None
Departures from Committee:			
Moved to Foreign Relations	Gillette, Guy M.	Iowa Dem	None

AGRICULTURE AND FORESTRY / 82nd Congress

Service Dates of Committee Chair: Jan. 15,1951-Jan. 13,1953
Service Dates of Majority Members: Jan. 15,1951-Jan. 13,1953
Service Dates of Minority Members: Jan. 15,1951-Jan. 13,1953

Majority

Rank	Name	Party	State	Years in: Senate	Years in: Comm.
Chr	Ellender, Allen J.	Dem	La.	15	15
2nd	Hoey, Clyde R.	Dem	N.C.	7	7
3rd	Johnston, Olin D.	Dem	S.C.	7	3
4th	Holland, Spessard L.	Dem	Fla.	5	3
5th	Anderson, Clinton P.	Dem	N.M.	3	3
6th	Eastland, James O.	Dem	Miss.	9	1
7th	Humphrey, Hubert H. Jr.	DFL	Minn.	3 *1	1

Minority

Rank	Name	Party	State	Years in: Senate	Years in: Comm.
RM	Aiken, George D.	Rep	Vt.	11	10
2nd	Young, Milton R.	Rep	N.D.	6	6
3rd	Thye, Edward J.	Rep	Minn.	5	5
4th	Kem, James P.	Rep	Mo.	5	5
5th	Hickenlooper, Bourke B.	Rep	Iowa	7	3
6th	Mundt, Karl E.	Rep	S.D.	3	1

*1: Member's 1st period of service on the committee.

	Majority		Minority	
Departures from the Senate:				
Defeated for Reelection	None		Kem, James P.	Mo. Rep
Departures from Committee:				
Moved to Foreign Relations	Humphrey, Hubert H. Jr.	Minn. DFL	None	

AGRICULTURE AND FORESTRY / 83rd Congress

Service Dates of Committee Chair: Jan. 13,1953-Jan. 11,1955
Service Dates of Majority Members: Jan. 13,1953-Jan. 11,1955
Service Dates of Minority Members: Jan. 13,1953-Jan. 11,1955

Majority

Rank	Name	Party	State	Years in: Senate	Years in: Comm.
Chr	Aiken, George D.	Rep	Vt.	13	12
2nd	Young, Milton R.	Rep	N.D.	8	8
3rd	Thye, Edward J.	Rep	Minn.	7	7
4th	Hickenlooper, Bourke B.	Rep	Iowa	9	5
5th	Mundt, Karl E.	Rep	S.D.	5	2
6th	Williams, John J.	Rep	Del.	7	1
7th	Schoeppel, Andrew F.	Rep	Kans.	5	1
8th	Welker, Herman	Rep	Ida.	3	1

Minority

Rank	Name	Party	State	Years in: Senate	Years in: Comm.
RM	Ellender, Allen J.	Dem	La.	17	17
2nd	Hoey, Clyde R.	Dem	N.C.	9	9
3rd	Johnston, Olin D.	Dem	S.C.	9	5
4th	Holland, Spessard L.	Dem	Fla.	7	5
5th	Anderson, Clinton P.	Dem	N.M.	5	5
6th	Eastland, James O.	Dem	Miss.	11	2
7th	Clements, Earle C.	Dem	Ky.	3	1

Changes:
Minority:

Hoey, Clyde R.	Dem	N.C.	May 12,1954	Died in office.
Humphrey, Hubert H. Jr.	DFL	Minn.	May 18,1954	Replaced Hoey.

Departures from Committee:	Majority			Minority
Moved to Armed Services	Welker, Herman	Ida.	Rep	None

AGRICULTURE AND FORESTRY / 84th Congress

Service Dates of Committee Chair: Jan. 11,1955-Jan. 9,1957
Service Dates of Majority Members: Jan. 11,1955-Jan. 9,1957
Service Dates of Minority Members: Jan. 11,1955-Jan. 9,1957

Majority

Rank	Name	Party	State	Years in: Senate	Years in: Comm.
Chr	Ellender, Allen J.	Dem	La.	19	19
2nd	Johnston, Olin D.	Dem	S.C.	11	7
3rd	Holland, Spessard L.	Dem	Fla.	9	7
4th	Anderson, Clinton P.	Dem	N.M.	7	7
5th	Eastland, James O.	Dem	Miss.	13	4
6th	Clements, Earle C.	Dem	Ky.	5	2
7th	Humphrey, Hubert H. Jr.	DFL	Minn.	7	*2 2
8th	Scott, W. Kerr	Dem	N.C.	1	1

Minority

Rank	Name	Party	State	Years in: Senate	Years in: Comm.
RM	Aiken, George D.	Rep	Vt.	15	14
2nd	Young, Milton R.	Rep	N.D.	10	10
3rd	Thye, Edward J.	Rep	Minn.	9	9
4th	Hickenlooper, Bourke B.	Rep	Iowa	11	7
5th	Mundt, Karl E.	Rep	S.D.	7	4
6th	Williams, John J.	Rep	Del.	9	2
7th	Schoeppel, Andrew F.	Rep	Kans.	7	2

*2: Member's 2nd period of service on the committee.

Changes:
Majority:

Anderson, Clinton P.	Dem	N.M.	Mar. 22,1956	Moved to Finance.
Symington, W. Stuart	Dem	Mo.	Mar. 29,1956	Replaced Anderson.

Departures from the Senate:	Majority			Minority
Defeated for Reelection	Clements, Earle C.	Ky.	Dem	None

AGRICULTURE AND FORESTRY / 85th Congress

Service Dates of Committee Chair: Jan. 9,1957-Jan. 14,1959
Service Dates of Majority Members: Jan. 9,1957-Jan. 14,1959
Service Dates of Minority Members: Jan. 9,1957-Jan. 20,1959

Majority

Rank	Name	Party	State	Years in: Senate	Years in: Comm.
Chr	Ellender, Allen J.	Dem	La.	21	21
2nd	Johnston, Olin D.	Dem	S.C.	13	8
3rd	Holland, Spessard L.	Dem	Fla.	11	8
4th	Eastland, James O.	Dem	Miss.	15	6
5th	Humphrey, Hubert H. Jr.	DFL	Minn.	9	*2 4
6th	Scott, W. Kerr	Dem	N.C.	3	2
7th	Symington, W. Stuart	Dem	Mo.	5	1
8th	Talmadge, Herman E.	Dem	Ga.	1	1

Minority

Rank	Name	Party	State	Years in: Senate	Years in: Comm.
RM	Aiken, George D.	Rep	Vt.	16	16
2nd	Young, Milton R.	Rep	N.D.	12	12
3rd	Thye, Edward J.	Rep	Minn.	11	11
4th	Hickenlooper, Bourke B.	Rep	Iowa	13	8
5th	Mundt, Karl E.	Rep	S.D.	9	6
6th	Williams, John J.	Rep	Del.	11	4
7th	Schoeppel, Andrew F.	Rep	Kans.	9	4

*2: Member's 2nd period of service on the committee.

Changes:

Majority:

Name	Party	State	Date	Note
Scott, W. Kerr	Dem	N.C.	Apr. 16,1958	Died in office.
Proxmire, William	Dem	Wisc.	Apr. 21,1958	Replaced Scott.

Departures from the Senate:

	Majority	Minority
Defeated for Reelection	None	Thye, Edward J. Minn. Rep

AGRICULTURE AND FORESTRY / 86th Congress

Service Dates of Committee Chair: Jan. 14,1959-Jan. 10,1961
Service Dates of Majority Members: Jan. 14,1959-Jan. 10,1961
Service Dates of Minority Members: Jan. 20,1959-Jan. 13,1961

Majority

Rank	Name	Party	State	Years in: Senate	Years in: Comm.
Chr	Ellender, Allen J.	Dem	La.	23	23
2nd	Johnston, Olin D.	Dem	S.C.	15	11
3rd	Holland, Spessard L.	Dem	Fla.	13	11
4th	Eastland, James O.	Dem	Miss.	17	8
5th	Humphrey, Hubert H. Jr.	DFL	Minn.	11	*2 6
6th	Symington, W. Stuart	Dem	Mo.	7	3
7th	Talmadge, Herman E.	Dem	Ga.	3	3
8th	Proxmire, William	Dem	Wisc.	2	1
9th	Jordan, B. Everett	Dem	N.C.	1	1
10th	Young, Stephen M.	Dem	Ohio	1	1
11th	Hart, Philip A.	Dem	Mich.	1	1

Minority

Rank	Name	Party	State	Years in: Senate	Years in: Comm.
RM	Aiken, George D.	Rep	Vt.	19	18
2nd	Young, Milton R.	Rep	N.D.	14	14
3rd	Hickenlooper, Bourke B.	Rep	Iowa	15	11
4th	Mundt, Karl E.	Rep	S.D.	11	9
5th	Williams, John J.	Rep	Del.	13	7
6th	Schoeppel, Andrew F.	Rep	Kans.	11	7

*2: Member's 2nd period of service on the committee.

Changes:

Minority:

Name	Party	State	Date	Note
Williams, John J.	Rep	Del.	Jan. 18,1960	Moved to Foreign Relations.
Cooper, John Sherman	Rep	Ky.	Jan. 18,1960	Replaced Williams.

Departures from Committee:

	Majority	Minority
Became Senate Majority Whip	Humphrey, Hubert H. Jr. Minn. DFL	None
Moved to Appropriations	None	Schoeppel, Andrew F. Kans. Rep
Moved to Foreign Relations	Symington, W. Stuart Mo. Dem	None

AGRICULTURE AND FORESTRY / 87th Congress

Service Dates of Committee Chair: Jan. 10,1961-Feb. 25,1963
Service Dates of Majority Members: Jan. 10,1961-Feb. 25,1963
Service Dates of Minority Members: Jan. 13,1961-Feb. 25,1963

Majority

Rank	Name	Party	State	Years in: Senate	Years in: Comm.
Chr	Ellender, Allen J.	Dem	La.	25	25
2nd	Johnston, Olin D.	Dem	S.C.	17	13
3rd	Holland, Spessard L.	Dem	Fla.	15	13
4th	Eastland, James O.	Dem	Miss.	19	10
5th	Talmadge, Herman E.	Dem	Ga.	5	5
6th	Proxmire, William	Dem	Wisc.	4	3
7th	Jordan, B. Everett	Dem	N.C.	3	2
8th	Young, Stephen M.	Dem	Ohio	3	2
9th	Hart, Philip A.	Dem	Mich.	3	2
10th	McCarthy, Eugene J.	DFL	Minn.	3	1
11th	Neuberger, Maurine B.	Dem	Ore.	1	1

Minority

Rank	Name	Party	State	Years in: Senate	Years in: Comm.
RM	Aiken, George D.	Rep	Vt.	21	20
2nd	Young, Milton R.	Rep	N.D.	16	16
3rd	Hickenlooper, Bourke B.	Rep	Iowa	17	13
4th	Mundt, Karl E.	Rep	S.D.	13	10
5th	Cooper, John Sherman	Rep	Ky.	9	1
6th	Boggs, J. Caleb	Rep	Del.	1	1

Departures from Committee:

	Majority		Minority	
Moved to Commerce	Hart, Philip A.	Mich. Dem	None	
Moved to Foreign Relations	None		Mundt, Karl E.	S.D. Rep
Moved to Armed Services	Young, Stephen M.	Ohio Dem	None	

AGRICULTURE AND FORESTRY / 88th Congress

Service Dates of Committee Chair: Feb. 25,1963-Jan. 8,1965
Service Dates of Majority Members: Feb. 25,1963-Jan. 8,1965
Service Dates of Minority Members: Feb. 25,1963-Jan. 15,1965

Majority

Rank	Name	Party	State	Years in: Senate	Years in: Comm.
Chr	Ellender, Allen J.	Dem	La.	27	27
2nd	Johnston, Olin D.	Dem	S.C.	19	15
3rd	Holland, Spessard L.	Dem	Fla.	17	15
4th	Eastland, James O.	Dem	Miss.	21	13
5th	Talmadge, Herman E.	Dem	Ga.	7	7
6th	Proxmire, William	Dem	Wisc.	6	5
7th	Jordan, B. Everett	Dem	N.C.	5	5
8th	McCarthy, Eugene J.	DFL	Minn.	5	3
9th	Neuberger, Maurine B.	Dem	Ore.	3	3
10th	McGovern, George S.	Dem	S.D.	1	1
11th	Edmondson, J. Howard	Dem	Okla.	1	1

Minority

Rank	Name	Party	State	Years in: Senate	Years in: Comm.
RM	Aiken, George D.	Rep	Vt.	23	23
2nd	Young, Milton R.	Rep	N.D.	18	18
3rd	Hickenlooper, Bourke B.	Rep	Iowa	19	15
4th	Cooper, John Sherman	Rep	Ky.	11	4
5th	Boggs, J. Caleb	Rep	Del.	3	3
6th	Mechem, Edwin L.	Rep	N.M.	1	1

Changes:

Majority:

Name	Party	State	Date	Change
Proxmire, William	Dem	Wisc.	Aug. 23,1963	Moved to Appropriations.
Walters, Herbert S.	Dem	Tenn.	Aug. 27,1963	Replaced Proxmire.
Edmondson, J. Howard	Dem	Okla.	Nov. 3,1964	Resigned; defeated for nomination.
Walters, Herbert S.	Dem	Tenn.	Nov. 3,1964	Resigned and retired.

Minority:

Name	Party	State	Date	Change
Mechem, Edwin L.	Rep	N.M.	Nov. 3,1964	Resigned; defeated for election.

Departures from Committee:

	Majority		Minority	
Moved to Commerce	Neuberger, Maurine B.	Ore. Dem	None	
Moved to Banking & Currency	None		Hickenlooper, Bourke B.	Iowa Rep

AGRICULTURE AND FORESTRY / 89th Congress

Service Dates of Committee Chair: Jan. 8,1965-Jan. 11,1967
Service Dates of Majority Members: Jan. 8,1965-Jan. 11,1967
Service Dates of Minority Members: Jan. 15,1965-Jan. 16,1967

Majority

Rank	Name	Party	State	Years in: Senate	Years in: Comm.
Chr	Ellender, Allen J.	Dem	La.	29	29
2nd	Johnston, Olin D.	Dem	S.C.	21	16
3rd	Holland, Spessard L.	Dem	Fla.	19	16
4th	Eastland, James O.	Dem	Miss.	23	14
5th	Talmadge, Herman E.	Dem	Ga.	9	8
6th	Jordan, B. Everett	Dem	N.C.	7	6
7th	McCarthy, Eugene J.	DFL	Minn.	7	4
8th	McGovern, George S.	Dem	S.D.	3	2
9th	Bass, Ross	Dem	Tenn.	1	1
10th	Montoya, Joseph M.	Dem	N.M.	1	1

Minority

Rank	Name	Party	State	Years in: Senate	Years in: Comm.
RM	Aiken, George D.	Rep	Vt.	25	24
2nd	Young, Milton R.	Rep	N.D.	20	20
3rd	Cooper, John Sherman	Rep	Ky.	13	5
4th	Boggs, J. Caleb	Rep	Del.	5	5
5th	Miller, Jack R.	Rep	Iowa	5	1

Changes:

Majority:

Name	Party	State	Date	Change
Johnston, Olin D.	Dem	S.C.	Apr. 18,1965	Died in office.
McCarthy, Eugene J.	DFL	Minn.	Apr. 26,1965	Moved to Foreign Relations.
Russell, Donald S.	Dem	S.C.	Apr. 26,1965	Replaced Johnston.
Mondale, Walter F.	DFL	Minn.	Apr. 26,1965	Replaced McCarthy.
Russell, Donald S.	Dem	S.C.	Nov. 8,1966	Resigned; defeated for nomination.

	Majority		Minority	
Departures from the Senate:				
Defeated for Renomination	Bass, Ross	Tenn. Dem	None	
Departures from Committee:				
Moved to Foreign Relations	None		Cooper, John Sherman	Ky. Rep

AGRICULTURE AND FORESTRY / 90th Congress

Service Dates of Committee Chair: Jan. 11,1967-Jan. 14,1969
Service Dates of Majority Members: Jan. 11,1967-Jan. 14,1969
Service Dates of Minority Members: Jan. 16,1967-Jan. 14,1969

Majority

Rank	Name	Party	State	Years in: Senate	Years in: Comm.
Chr	Ellender, Allen J.	Dem	La.	31	31
2nd	Holland, Spessard L.	Dem	Fla.	21	19
3rd	Eastland, James O.	Dem	Miss.	25	16
4th	Talmadge, Herman E.	Dem	Ga.	11	11
5th	Jordan, B. Everett	Dem	N.C.	9	8
6th	McGovern, George S.	Dem	S.D.	5	4
7th	Montoya, Joseph M.	Dem	N.M.	3	3
8th	Mondale, Walter F.	DFL	Minn.	3	2
9th	Byrd, Harry Flood Jr.	Dem	Va.	2	1
10th	Hollings, Ernest F.	Dem	S.C.	1	1

Minority

Rank	Name	Party	State	Years in: Senate	Years in: Comm.
RM	Aiken, George D.	Rep	Vt.	27	26
2nd	Young, Milton R.	Rep	N.D.	22	22
3rd	Boggs, J. Caleb	Rep	Del.	7	7
4th	Miller, Jack R.	Rep	Iowa	7	3
5th	Hatfield, Mark O.	Rep	Ore.	1	1

Changes:

Minority:

Name	Party	State	Date	Change
Hatfield, Mark O.	Rep	Ore.	Sep. 12,1968	Moved to Aeronautical and Space Sciences.
Goodell, Charles E.	Rep	N.Y.	Sep. 12,1968	Replaced Hatfield.

Departures from Committee:	Majority		Minority	
Moved to Finance	Byrd, Harry Flood Jr.	Va. Dem	None	
Moved to Banking & Currency	Hollings, Ernest F.	S.C. Dem	None	
Moved to Labor & Public Welfare	Mondale, Walter F.	Minn. DFL	None	
Moved to Appropriations	Montoya, Joseph M.	N.M. Dem	Boggs, J. Caleb	Del. Rep
Moved to Banking & Currency; Commerce; District of Columbia	None		Goodell, Charles E.	N.Y. Rep

AGRICULTURE AND FORESTRY / 91st Congress

Service Dates of Committee Chair: Jan. 14,1969-Jan. 28,1971
Service Dates of Majority Members: Jan. 14,1969-Jan. 28,1971
Service Dates of Minority Members: Jan. 14,1969-Jan. 29,1971

Majority

Rank	Name	Party	State	Years in: Senate	Years in: Comm.
Chr	Ellender, Allen J.	Dem	La.	33	33
2nd	Holland, Spessard L.	Dem	Fla.	23	21
3rd	Eastland, James O.	Dem	Miss.	27	18
4th	Talmadge, Herman E.	Dem	Ga.	13	13
5th	Jordan, B. Everett	Dem	N.C.	11	11
6th	McGovern, George S.	Dem	S.D.	7	6
7th	Allen, James B.	Dem	Ala.	1	1

Minority

Rank	Name	Party	State	Years in: Senate	Years in: Comm.
RM	Aiken, George D.	Rep	Vt.	29	28
2nd	Young, Milton R.	Rep	N.D.	24	24
3rd	Miller, Jack R.	Rep	Iowa	9	4
4th	Curtis, Carl T.	Rep	Neb.	15	1
5th	Cook, Marlow W.	Rep	Ky.	1	1
6th	Dole, Robert J.	Rep	Kans.	1	1

Changes:
Minority:

Cook, Marlow W.	Rep	Ky.	Sep. 17,1969	Moved to Commerce.
Bellmon, Henry	Rep	Okla.	Sep. 17,1969	Replaced Cook.

Departures from the Senate:	Majority			Minority
Retired	Holland, Spessard L.	Fla.	Dem	None

AGRICULTURE AND FORESTRY / 92nd Congress

Service Dates of Committee Chair: Jan. 28,1971-Jan. 4,1973
Service Dates of Majority Members: Jan. 28,1971-Jan. 4,1973
Service Dates of Minority Members: Jan. 29,1971-Jan. 12,1973

Majority

Rank	Name	Party	State	Years in: Senate	Years in: Comm.
Chr	Talmadge, Herman E.	Dem	Ga.	15	15
2nd	Ellender, Allen J.	Dem	La.	35	35
3rd	Eastland, James O.	Dem	Miss.	29	21
4th	Jordan, B. Everett	Dem	N.C.	13	13
5th	McGovern, George S.	Dem	S.D.	9	8
6th	Allen, James B.	Dem	Ala.	3	3
7th	Humphrey, Hubert H. Jr.	DFL	Minn.	17	*3 1
8th	Chiles, Lawton M. Jr.	Dem	Fla.	1	1

Minority

Rank	Name	Party	State	Years in: Senate	Years in: Comm.
RM	Miller, Jack R.	Rep	Iowa	11	7
2nd	Aiken, George D.	Rep	Vt.	31	31
3rd	Young, Milton R.	Rep	N.D.	26	26
4th	Curtis, Carl T.	Rep	Neb.	17	3
5th	Dole, Robert J.	Rep	Kans.	3	3
6th	Bellmon, Henry	Rep	Okla.	3	2

*3: Member's 3rd period of service on the committee.

Note: Rankings on this committee for the following members were affected by other chamber service: Allen J. Ellender (Dem-Ga.), Chair, Appropriations; James O. Eastland (Dem-Miss.), Chair, Judiciary; George D. Aiken (Rep-Vt.), Ranking Minority Member, Foreign Relations; and Milton R. Young (Rep-N.D.), Ranking Minority Member, Appropriations.

Changes:
Majority:

Ellender, Allen J.	Dem	La.	July 27,1972	Died in office.
Edwards, Elaine S.	Dem	La.	Aug. 7,1972	Replaced Ellender.
Edwards, Elaine S.	Dem	La.	Nov. 13,1972	Resigned and retired.

Departures from the Senate:	Majority			Minority		
Defeated for Reelection	None			Miller, Jack R.	Iowa	Rep
Defeated for Renomination	Jordan, B. Everett	N.C.	Dem	None		
Departures from Committee:						
Moved to Appropriations	Chiles, Lawton M. Jr.	Fla.	Dem	None		

AGRICULTURE AND FORESTRY / 93rd Congress

Service Dates of Committee Chair: Jan. 4,1973-Jan. 17,1975
Service Dates of Majority Members: Jan. 4,1973-Jan. 17,1975
Service Dates of Minority Members: Jan. 12,1973-Jan. 23,1975

Majority

Rank	Name	Party	State	Years in: Senate	Years in: Comm.
Chr	Talmadge, Herman E.	Dem	Ga.	17	16
2nd	Eastland, James O.	Dem	Miss.	31	22
3rd	McGovern, George S.	Dem	S.D.	11	10
4th	Allen, James B.	Dem	Ala.	5	4
5th	Humphrey, Hubert H. Jr.	DFL	Minn.	18	*3 2
6th	Hathaway, William D.	Dem	Me.	1	1
7th	Huddleston, Walter D.	Dem	Ky.	1	1
8th	Clark, Richard C.	Dem	Iowa	1	1

Minority

Rank	Name	Party	State	Years in: Senate	Years in: Comm.
RM	Curtis, Carl T.	Rep	Neb.	19	4
2nd	Aiken, George D.	Rep	Vt.	33	32
3rd	Young, Milton R.	Rep	N.D.	28	28
4th	Dole, Robert J.	Rep	Kans.	5	4
5th	Bellmon, Henry	Rep	Okla.	5	4
6th	Helms, Jesse A.	Rep	N.C.	1	1

*3: Member's 3rd period of service on the committee.

Notes: On Jan. 11,1973, the committee was reduced to 13 members, changing the party ratio to 7 Democrats and 6 Republicans. Rankings on this committee for the following members were affected by other chamber service: James O. Eastland (Dem-Miss.), Chair, Judiciary; George D. Aiken (Rep-Vt.), Ranking Minority Member, Foreign Relations; and Milton R. Young (Rep-N.D.), Ranking Minority Member, Appropriations.

Changes:

Majority:

Hathaway, William D. Dem Me. Jan. 11,1973 Ratio change; moved to Labor and Public Welfare.

Departures from the Senate:

	Majority	Minority		
Retired	None	Aiken, George D.	Vt.	Rep

AGRICULTURE AND FORESTRY / 94th Congress

Service Dates of Committee Chair: Jan. 17,1975-Jan. 10,1977
Service Dates of Majority Members: Jan. 17,1975-Jan. 10,1977
Service Dates of Minority Members: Jan. 23,1975-Jan. 10,1977

Majority

Rank	Name	Party	State	Years in: Senate	Years in: Comm.
Chr	Talmadge, Herman E.	Dem	Ga.	19	19
2nd	Eastland, James O.	Dem	Miss.	33	25
3rd	McGovern, George S.	Dem	S.D.	13	12
4th	Allen, James B.	Dem	Ala.	7	7
5th	Humphrey, Hubert H. Jr.	DFL	Minn.	21	*3 4
6th	Huddleston, Walter D.	Dem	Ky.	3	3
7th	Clark, Richard C.	Dem	Iowa	3	3
8th	Stone, Richard B.	Dem	Fla.	1	1
9th	Leahy, Patrick J.	Dem	Vt.	1	1

Minority

Rank	Name	Party	State	Years in: Senate	Years in: Comm.
RM	Dole, Robert J.	Rep	Kans.	7	7
2nd	Young, Milton R.	Rep	N.D.	30	30
3rd	Curtis, Carl T.	Rep	Neb.	21	7
4th	Bellmon, Henry	Rep	Okla.	7	6
5th	Helms, Jesse A.	Rep	N.C.	3	3

*3: Member's 3rd period of service on the committee.

Note: Rankings on this committee for the following members were affected by other chamber service: James O. Eastland (Dem-Miss.), Chair, Judiciary; Milton R. Young (Rep-N.D.), Ranking Minority Member, Appropriations; and Carl T. Curtis (Rep-Neb), Ranking Minority Member, Finance.

AGRICULTURE AND FORESTRY / 95th Congress

* Reorganized as the Committee on AGRICULTURE, NUTRITION, AND FORESTRY on Feb. 4,1977.

Service Dates of Committee Chair: Jan. 10,1977-Feb. 11,1977
Service Dates of Majority Members: Jan. 10,1977-Feb. 11,1977
Service Dates of Minority Members: Jan. 10,1977-Feb. 22,1977

Majority

Rank	Name	Party	State	Years in: Senate	Years in: Comm.
Chr	Talmadge, Herman E.	Dem	Ga.	21	21
2nd	Eastland, James O.	Dem	Miss.	35	26
3rd	McGovern, George S.	Dem	S.D.	15	14
4th	Allen, James B.	Dem	Ala.	9	8
5th	Humphrey, Hubert H. Jr.	DFL	Minn.	23	*3 6
6th	Huddleston, Walter D.	Dem	Ky.	5	5
7th	Clark, Richard C.	Dem	Iowa	5	5
8th	Stone, Richard B.	Dem	Fla.	3	2
9th	Leahy, Patrick J.	Dem	Vt.	3	2
10th	Anderson, Wendell R.	DFL	Minn.	1	*T 1

Minority

Rank	Name	Party	State	Years in: Senate	Years in: Comm.
RM	Dole, Robert J.	Rep	Kans.	9	8
2nd	Young, Milton R.	Rep	N.D.	32	32
3rd	Curtis, Carl T.	Rep	Neb.	23	8
4th	Bellmon, Henry	Rep	Okla.	9	8
5th	Helms, Jesse A.	Rep	N.C.	5	4
6th	Hayakawa, S. I. (Sam)	Rep	Cal.	1	*T 1

*3: Member's 3rd period of service on the committee;
*T: Temporary member of the committee.

Note: Rankings on this committee for the following members were affected by other chamber service: James O. Eastland (Dem-Miss.), Chair, Judiciary; Milton R. Young (Rep-N.D.), Ranking Minority Member, Appropriations; and Carl T. Curtis (Rep-Neb), Ranking Minority Member, Finance.

Changes:
Majority:

Anderson, Wendell R.	DFL	Minn.	Feb. 11,1977	Moved to Environment and Public Works.

AGRICULTURE, NUTRITION, AND FORESTRY / 95th Congress

* Renamed the Committee on AGRICULTURE, NUTRITION, AND FORESTRY on Feb. 4,1977

Service Dates of Committee Chair: Feb. 11,1977-Jan. 23,1979
Service Dates of Majority Members: Feb. 11,1977-Jan. 23,1979
Service Dates of Minority Members: Feb. 22,1977-Jan. 23,1979

Majority

Rank	Name	Party	State	Years in: Senate	Years in: Comm.
Chr	Talmadge, Herman E.	Dem	Ga.	21	21
2nd	Eastland, James O.	Dem	Miss.	35	27
3rd	McGovern, George S.	Dem	S.D.	15	14
4th	Allen, James B.	Dem	Ala.	9	9
5th	Humphrey, Hubert H. Jr.	DFL	Minn.	23	*3 7
6th	Huddleston, Walter D.	Dem	Ky.	5	5
7th	Clark, Richard C.	Dem	Iowa	5	5
8th	Stone, Richard B.	Dem	Fla.	3	3
9th	Leahy, Patrick J.	Dem	Vt.	3	3
10th	Zorinsky, Edward	Dem	Neb.	1	1
11th	Melcher, John	Dem	Mont.	1	1

Minority

Rank	Name	Party	State	Years in: Senate	Years in: Comm.
RM	Dole, Robert J.	Rep	Kans.	9	9
2nd	Young, Milton R.	Rep	N.D.	32	32
3rd	Curtis, Carl T.	Rep	Neb.	23	9
4th	Bellmon, Henry	Rep	Okla.	9	8
5th	Helms, Jesse A.	Rep	N.C.	5	5
6th	Hayakawa, S. I. (Sam)	Rep	Cal.	1	1
7th	Lugar, Richard G.	Rep	Ind.	1	1

*3: Member's 3rd period of service on the committee.

Note: Rankings on this committee for the following members were affected by other chamber service: James O. Eastland (Dem-Miss.), Chair, Judiciary; Milton R. Young (Rep-N.D.), Ranking Minority Member, Appropriations; and Carl T. Curtis (Rep-Neb), Ranking Minority Member, Finance.

Changes:
Majority:

Humphrey, Hubert H. Jr.	DFL	Minn.	Jan. 13,1978	Died in office.
Hodges, Kaneaster Jr.	Dem	Ark.	Jan. 27,1978	Replaced Humphrey.
Allen, James B.	Dem	Ala.	June 1,1978	Died in office.
Allen, Maryon	Dem	Ala.	July 11,1978	Replaced James B. Allen.
Allen, Maryon	Dem	Ala.	Nov. 7,1978	Resigned; defeated for nomination in special election.
Eastland, James O.	Dem	Miss.	Dec. 27,1978	Resigned and retired.

Departures from the Senate:	Majority			Minority		
Defeated for Reelection	Clark, Richard C.	Iowa	Dem	None		
Retired	Hodges, Kaneaster Jr.	Ark.	Dem	Curtis, Carl T.	Neb.	Rep
Departures from Committee:						
Moved to Energy & Natural Resources	None			Bellmon, Henry	Okla.	Rep

AGRICULTURE, NUTRITION, AND FORESTRY / 96th Congress

Service Dates of Committee Chair: Jan. 23,1979-Jan. 3,1981
Service Dates of Majority Members: Jan. 23,1979-Jan. 5,1981
Service Dates of Minority Members: Jan. 23,1979-Jan. 5,1981

Majority

Rank	Name	Party	State	Years in: Senate	Years in: Comm.
Chr	Talmadge, Herman E.	Dem	Ga.	23	23
2nd	McGovern, George S.	Dem	S.D.	17	16
3rd	Huddleston, Walter D.	Dem	Ky.	7	7
4th	Stone, Richard B.	Dem	Fla.	5	5
5th	Leahy, Patrick J.	Dem	Vt.	5	5
6th	Zorinsky, Edward	Dem	Neb.	3	2
7th	Melcher, John	Dem	Mont.	3	2
8th	Stewart, Donald W.	Dem	Ala.	1	1
9th	Pryor, David H.	Dem	Ark.	1	1
10th	Boren, David L.	Dem	Okla.	1	1

Minority

Rank	Name	Party	State	Years in: Senate	Years in: Comm.
RM	Helms, Jesse A.	Rep	N.C.	7	7
2nd	Dole, Robert J.	Rep	Kans.	11	11
3rd	Young, Milton R.	Rep	N.D.	34	34
4th	Hayakawa, S. I. (Sam)	Rep	Cal.	3	3
5th	Lugar, Richard G.	Rep	Ind.	3	2
6th	Cochran, Thad	Rep	Miss.	1	1
7th	Boschwitz, Rudolf E.	Rep	Minn.	1	1
8th	Jepsen, Roger W.	Rep	Iowa	1	1

Note: Rankings on this committee for the following members were affected by other chamber service: Robert J. Dole (Rep-Kans.), Ranking Minority Member, Finance; Milton R. Young (Rep-N.D.), Ranking Minority Member, Appropriations.

Changes:
Majority:

Stone, Richard B.	Dem	Fla.	Jan. 1,1981	Resigned; defeated for renomination.

Departures from the Senate:	Majority			Minority		
Defeated for Reelection	McGovern, George S.	S.D.	Dem	None		
	Stewart, Donald W.	Ala.	Dem			
	Talmadge, Herman E.	Ga.	Dem			
Retired	None			Young, Milton R.	N.D.	Rep

AGRICULTURE, NUTRITION, AND FORESTRY / 97th Congress

Service Dates of Committee Chair: Jan. 5,1981-Jan. 3,1983
Service Dates of Majority Members: Jan. 5,1981-Jan. 3,1983
Service Dates of Minority Members: Jan. 5,1981-Jan. 3,1983

Majority

Rank	Name	Party	State	Years in: Senate	Years in: Comm.
Chr	Helms, Jesse A.	Rep	N.C.	9	8
2nd	Dole, Robert J.	Rep	Kans.	13	12
3rd	Hayakawa, S. I. (Sam)	Rep	Cal.	5	4
4th	Lugar, Richard G.	Rep	Ind.	5	4
5th	Cochran, Thad	Rep	Miss.	3	2
6th	Boschwitz, Rudolf E.	Rep	Minn.	3	2
7th	Jepsen, Roger W.	Rep	Iowa	3	2
8th	Hawkins, Paula	Rep	Fla.	1	1
9th	Andrews, Mark	Rep	N.D.	1	1

Minority

Rank	Name	Party	State	Years in: Senate	Years in: Comm.
RM	Huddleston, Walter D.	Dem	Ky.	9	9
2nd	Leahy, Patrick J.	Dem	Vt.	7	6
3rd	Zorinsky, Edward	Dem	Neb.	5	4
4th	Melcher, John	Dem	Mont.	5	4
5th	Pryor, David H.	Dem	Ark.	3	2
6th	Boren, David L.	Dem	Okla.	3	2
7th	Dixon, Alan J.	Dem	Ill.	1	1
8th	Heflin, Howell T.	Dem	Ala.	3	1

Notes: The resignation of Harrison Williams (Dem-N.J.), and the appointment of Nicholas F. Brady (Rep-N.J.) to fill his vacancy on April 12, 1982, led to a change in size and party ratio on this committee to 10 Republicans and 8 Democrats. Ranking on this committee for the following member was affected by other chamber service: Robert J. Dole (Rep-Kans.), Chair, Finance.

Addition:
Majority: 10th Hatch, Orrin G. Rep Utah Apr. 27,1982

Departures from the Senate:	Majority			Minority		
Retired	Hayakawa, S. I. (Sam)	Cal.	Rep	None		

AGRICULTURE, NUTRITION, AND FORESTRY / 98th Congress

Service Dates of Committee Chair: Jan. 3,1983-Feb. 21,1985
Service Dates of Majority Members: Jan. 3,1983-Feb. 21,1985
Service Dates of Minority Members: Jan. 3,1983-Feb. 21,1985

Majority

Rank	Name	Party	State	Years in: Senate	Years in: Comm.
Chr	Helms, Jesse A.	Rep	N.C.	11	10
2nd	Dole, Robert J.	Rep	Kans.	15	14
3rd	Lugar, Richard G.	Rep	Ind.	7	6
4th	Cochran, Thad	Rep	Miss.	5	4
5th	Boschwitz, Rudolf E.	Rep	Minn.	5	4
6th	Jepsen, Roger W.	Rep	Iowa	5	4
7th	Hawkins, Paula	Rep	Fla.	3	2
8th	Andrews, Mark	Rep	N.D.	3	2
9th	Wilson, Pete	Rep	Cal.	1	1
10th	Hatch, Orrin G.	Rep	Utah	7	1

Minority

Rank	Name	Party	State	Years in: Senate	Years in: Comm.
RM	Huddleston, Walter D.	Dem	Ky.	11	10
2nd	Leahy, Patrick J.	Dem	Vt.	9	8
3rd	Zorinsky, Edward	Dem	Neb.	7	6
4th	Melcher, John	Dem	Mont.	7	6
5th	Pryor, David H.	Dem	Ark.	5	4
6th	Boren, David L.	Dem	Okla.	5	4
7th	Dixon, Alan J.	Dem	Ill.	3	2
8th	Heflin, Howell T.	Dem	Ala.	5	2

Note: Ranking on this committee for the following member was affected by other chamber service: Robert J. Dole (Rep-Kans.), Chair, Finance.

Departures from the Senate:	Majority			Minority		
Defeated for Reelection	Jepsen, Roger W.	Iowa	Rep	Huddleston, Walter D.	Ky.	Dem
Departures from Committee:						
Moved to Select Intelligence	Hatch, Orrin G.	Utah	Rep	None		

AGRICULTURE, NUTRITION, AND FORESTRY / 99th Congress

Service Dates of Committee Chair: Feb. 21,1985-Jan. 6,1987
Service Dates of Majority Members: Feb. 21,1985-Jan. 6,1987
Service Dates of Minority Members: Feb. 21,1985-Jan. 6,1987

Majority

Rank	Name	Party	State	Years in: Senate	Years in: Comm.
Chr	Helms, Jesse A.	Rep	N.C.	13	13
2nd	Dole, Robert J.	Rep	Kans.	17	17
3rd	Lugar, Richard G.	Rep	Ind.	9	8
4th	Cochran, Thad	Rep	Miss.	7	7
5th	Boschwitz, Rudolf E.	Rep	Minn.	7	7
6th	Hawkins, Paula	Rep	Fla.	5	5
7th	Andrews, Mark	Rep	N.D.	5	5
8th	Wilson, Pete	Rep	Cal.	3	3
9th	McConnell, Mitch	Rep	Ky.	1	1

Minority

Rank	Name	Party	State	Years in: Senate	Years in: Comm.
RM	Zorinsky, Edward	Dem	Neb.	9	9
2nd	Leahy, Patrick J.	Dem	Vt.	11	11
3rd	Melcher, John	Dem	Mont.	9	9
4th	Pryor, David H.	Dem	Ark.	7	7
5th	Boren, David L.	Dem	Okla.	7	7
6th	Dixon, Alan J.	Dem	Ill.	5	5
7th	Heflin, Howell T.	Dem	Ala.	7	5
8th	Harkin, Thomas R.	Dem	Iowa	1	1

Note: Ranking on this committee for the following member was affected by other chamber service: Robert J. Dole (Rep-Kans.), Chair, Finance; Patrick J. Leahy (Dem-Vt.), Vice Chair, Select Intelligence.

Departures from the Senate:	Majority			Minority		
Defeated for Reelection	Andrews, Mark	N.D.	Rep	None		
	Hawkins, Paula	Fla.	Rep			
Departures from Committee:						
No new assignment	None			Dixon, Alan J.	Ill.	Dem

AGRICULTURE, NUTRITION, AND FORESTRY / 100th Congress

Service Dates of Committee Chair: Jan. 6,1987-Feb. 2,1989
Service Dates of Majority Members: Jan. 6,1987-Feb. 2,1989
Service Dates of Minority Members: Jan. 6,1987-Feb. 2,1989

Majority

Rank	Name	Party	State	Years in: Senate	Years in: Comm.
Chr	Leahy, Patrick J.	Dem	Vt.	13	12
2nd	Zorinsky, Edward	Dem	Neb.	11	10
3rd	Melcher, John	Dem	Mont.	11	10
4th	Pryor, David H.	Dem	Ark.	9	8
5th	Boren, David L.	Dem	Okla.	9	8
6th	Heflin, Howell T.	Dem	Ala.	9	7
7th	Harkin, Thomas R.	Dem	Iowa	3	2
8th	Conrad, Kent	Dem	N.D.	1	1
9th	Fowler, Wyche Jr.	Dem	Ga.	1	1
10th	Daschle, Thomas A.	Dem	S.D.	1	1

Minority

Rank	Name	Party	State	Years in: Senate	Years in: Comm.
RM1	Helms, Jesse A.	Rep	N.C.	15	14
2nd	Dole, Robert J.	Rep	Kans.	19	18
RM2 3rd	Lugar, Richard G.	Rep	Ind.	11	10
4th	Cochran, Thad	Rep	Miss.	9	8
5th	Boschwitz, Rudolf E.	Rep	Minn.	9	8
6th	McConnell, Mitch	Rep	Ky.	3	2
7th	Bond, Christopher S.	Rep	Mo.	1	1
8th	Wilson, Pete	Rep	Cal.	5	5

Notes: The death of Edward Zorinsky (Dem-Neb.), and the appointment of David K. Karnes (Rep-Neb.) to fill his vacancy on Mar. 10,1987, led to a change in size and party ratio on this committee to 10 Democrats and 9 Republicans. The Republican Conference voted on Jan. 20,1987 to seat Jesse A. Helms (Rep-N.C.) as Ranking Minority Member of Foreign Relations, and to have Richard G. Lugar (Rep-Ind.) succeed Helms as Ranking Minority Member of Agriculture, Nutrition, and Forestry. Ranking on this committee for the following member was affected by other chamber service: Robert J. Dole (Rep-Kans.), Senate Minority Leader and Ranking Minority Member, Finance; Pete Wilson (Rep-Cal.) served on two other important committees in this Congress and was obliged by the Republican Conference rules to waive his seniority.

Addition:

Minority: 9th Karnes, David K. Rep Neb. May 12,1987

Changes:

Ranking Member:

RM1	Helms, Jesse A.	Rep	N.C.	Jan. 20,1987	Republican Conference voted to seat Helms as Ranking Minority Member on Foreign Relations; remained on committee as third ranking member.
RM2	Lugar, Richard G.	Rep	Ind.	Jan. 20,1987	Succeeded Helms as Ranking Minority Member.

Majority:

Zorinsky, Edward	Dem	Neb.	Mar. 6,1987	Died in office.
Breaux, John B.	Dem	La.	May 12,1987	Replaced Zorinsky.

	Majority		Minority	
Departures from the Senate:				
Defeated for Reelection	Melcher, John	Mont. Dem	None	
Defeated for Election	None		Karnes, David K.	Neb. Rep
Departures from Committee:				
No new assignment	Breaux, John B.	La. Dem	None	

AGRICULTURE, NUTRITION, AND FORESTRY / 101st Congress

Service Dates of Committee Chair: Feb. 2,1989-Feb. 5,1991
Service Dates of Majority Members: Feb. 2,1989-Feb. 5,1991
Service Dates of Minority Members: Feb. 2,1989-Feb. 5,1991

Majority

Rank	Name	Party	State	Years in: Senate	Years in: Comm.
Chr	Leahy, Patrick J.	Dem	Vt.	15	15
2nd	Pryor, David H.	Dem	Ark.	11	11
3rd	Boren, David L.	Dem	Okla.	11	11
4th	Heflin, Howell T.	Dem	Ala.	11	9
5th	Harkin, Thomas R.	Dem	Iowa	5	4
6th	Conrad, Kent	Dem	N.D.	3	3
7th	Fowler, Wyche Jr.	Dem	Ga.	3	3
8th	Daschle, Thomas A.	Dem	S.D.	3	3
9th	Baucus, Max S.	Dem	Mont.	11	1
10th	Kerrey, Bob	Dem	Neb.	1	1

Minority

Rank	Name	Party	State	Years in: Senate	Years in: Comm.
RM	Lugar, Richard G.	Rep	Ind.	13	13
2nd	Dole, Robert J.	Rep	Kans.	21	21
3rd	Helms, Jesse A.	Rep	N.C.	17	17
4th	Cochran, Thad	Rep	Miss.	11	11
5th	Boschwitz, Rudolf E.	Rep	Minn.	11	11
6th	McConnell, Mitch	Rep	Ky.	5	4
7th	Bond, Christopher S.	Rep	Mo.	3	3
8th	Wilson, Pete	Rep	Cal.	7	7
9th	Gorton, Slade	Rep	Wash.	7	1

Note: Rankings on this committee for the following members were affected by other chamber service: Robert J. Dole (Rep-Kans.), Senate Minority Whip and Ranking Minority Member, Finance; Jesse A. Helms (Rep-N.C.), Ranking Minority Member, Foreign Relations; Pete Wilson (Rep-Cal.) served on two other important committees in this Congress and was obliged by the Republican Conference rules to waive his seniority.

	Majority	Minority		
Departures from the Senate:				
Elected Governor of California	None	Wilson, Pete	Cal.	Rep
Departures from Committee:				
Moved to Appropriations	None	Gorton, Slade	Wash.	Rep
		Bond, Christopher S.	Mo.	Rep

AGRICULTURE, NUTRITION, AND FORESTRY / 102nd Congress

Service Dates of Committee Chair: Feb. 5,1991-Jan. 2,1993
Service Dates of Majority Members: Feb. 5,1991-Jan. 2,1993
Service Dates of Minority Members: Feb. 5,1991-Jan. 2,1993

Majority

Rank	Name	Party	State	Years in: Senate	Years in: Comm.
Chr	Leahy, Patrick J.	Dem	Vt.	17	17
2nd	Pryor, David H.	Dem	Ark.	13	13
3rd	Boren, David L.	Dem	Okla.	13	13
4th	Heflin, Howell T.	Dem	Ala.	13	11
5th	Harkin, Thomas R.	Dem	Iowa	7	6
6th	Conrad, Kent	Dem	N.D.	5	5
7th	Fowler, Wyche Jr.	Dem	Ga.	5	5
8th	Daschle, Thomas A.	Dem	S.D.	5	5
9th	Baucus, Max S.	Dem	Mont.	13	3
10th	Kerrey, Bob	Dem	Neb.	3	3

Minority

Rank	Name	Party	State	Years in: Senate	Years in: Comm.
RM	Lugar, Richard G.	Rep	Ind.	15	15
2nd	Dole, Robert J.	Rep	Kans.	23	23
3rd	Helms, Jesse A.	Rep	N.C.	19	19
4th	Cochran, Thad	Rep	Miss.	13	13
5th	McConnell, Mitch	Rep	Ky.	7	6
6th	Craig, Larry	Rep	Ida.	1	1
7th	Seymour, John	Rep	Cal.	1	1
8th	Grassley, Charles E.	Rep	Iowa	11	1

Note: Rankings on this committee for the following members were affected by other chamber service: Robert J. Dole (Rep-Kans.), Senate Minority Leader and Ranking Minority Member, Finance; and Jesse A. Helms (Rep-N.C.), Ranking Minority Member, Foreign Relations.

APPROPRIATIONS

Jurisdiction, 1947

Established by the Legislative Reorganization Act of 1946:

[Section 102.(1)(b)]

(1) Committee on Appropriations, to consist of twenty-one Senators, to which committee shall be referred all proposed legislation, messages, petitions, memorials, and other matters relating to the following subjects:

1. Appropriation of the revenue for the support of the Government.

[Section 139.]

(a) No general appropriation bill shall be considered in either House unless, prior to the consideration of such bill, printed committee hearings and reports on such bill have been available for at least three calendar days for the Members of the House in which such bill is to be considered.
(b) The Committees on Appropriations of the two Houses are authorized and directed, acting jointly, to develop a standard appropriation classification schedule which will clearly define in concise and uniform accounts the subtotals of appropriations asked for by agencies in the executive branch of the Government. That part of the printed hearings containing each such agency's request for appropriations shall be preceded by such a schedule.
(c) No general appropriation bill or amendment thereto shall be received or considered in either House if it contains a provision reappropriating unexpended balances of appropriations; except that this provision shall not apply to appropriations in continuation of appropriations for public works on which work has commenced.
(d) The Appropriations Committees of both Houses are authorized and directed to make a study of
  (1) existing permanent appropriations with a view to limiting the number of permanent appropriations and to recommend to their respective Houses what permanent appropriations, if any, should be discontinued; and
  (2) the disposition of funds resulting from the sale of Government property or services by all departments and agencies in the executive branch of the Government with a view to recommending to their respective Houses a uniform system of control with respect to such funds.

Jurisdiction, 1992

Jurisdiction contained in the Standing Rules of the Senate (as revised to March 18, 1992).

[Rule XXV.(1)(b)]

Committee on Appropriations, to which committee shall be referred all proposed legislation, messages, petitions, memorials, and other matters relating to the following subjects:

1. Appropriation of the revenue for the support of the Government, except as provided in subparagraph (e). [Committee on the Budget]
2. Rescission of appropriations contained in appropriation Acts (referred to in section 105 of title 1, United States Code).
3. The amount of new spending authority described in section 401(c)(2) (A) and (B) of the Congressional Budget Act of 1974 which is to be effective for a fiscal year.
4. New spending authority described in section 401(c)(2) (C) of the Congressional Budget Act of 1974 provided in bills and resolutions referred to the committee under section 401(b)(2) of that Act (but subject to the provisions of section 401(b)(3) of the Act).

APPROPRIATIONS / 80th Congress

Service Dates of Committee Chair: Jan. 6,1947-Jan. 10,1949
Service Dates of Majority Members: Jan. 6,1947-Jan. 10,1949
Service Dates of Minority Members: Jan. 8,1947-Jan. 10,1949

Majority

Rank	Name	Party	State	Years in: Senate	Years in: Comm.
Chr	Bridges, H. Styles	Rep	N.H.	11	10
2nd	Gurney, J. Chandler	Rep	S.D.	9	6
3rd	Brooks, C. Wayland	Rep	Ill.	7	6
4th	Reed, Clyde M.	Rep	Kans.	9	4
5th	Ball, Joseph H.	Rep	Minn.	7	4
6th	Ferguson, Homer	Rep	Mich.	5	2
7th	Wherry, Kenneth S.	Rep	Neb.	5	2
8th	Cordon, Guy	Rep	Ore.	3	2
9th	Saltonstall, Leverett	Rep	Mass.	3	1
10th	Young, Milton R.	Rep	N.D.	2	1
11th	Knowland, William F.	Rep	Cal.	2	*1 1
12th	Dworshak, Henry C.	Rep	Ida.	1	*1 1

Minority

Rank	Name	Party	State	Years in: Senate	Years in: Comm.
RM	McKellar, Kenneth D.	Dem	Tenn.	30	24
2nd	Hayden, Carl	Dem	Ariz.	20	20
3rd	Thomas, Elmer	Dem	Okla.	20	16
4th	Tydings, Millard E.	Dem	Md.	20	15
5th	Russell, Richard B.	Dem	Ga.	14	14
6th	McCarran, Patrick A.	Dem	Nev.	14	14
7th	Overton, John H.	Dem	La.	14	14
8th	O'Mahoney, Joseph C.	Dem	Wyo.	14	14
9th	Green, Theodore F.	Dem	R.I.	11	11

*1: Member's 1st period of service on the committee.

Changes:

Minority:

Name	Party	State	Date	Note
Overton, John H.	Dem	La.	May 14,1948	Died in office.
Chavez, Dennis	Dem	N.M.	May 26,1948	Replaced Overton.

Departures from the Senate:

	Majority			Minority		
Defeated for Reelection	Ball, Joseph H.	Minn.	Rep	None		
	Brooks, C. Wayland	Ill.	Rep			
	Dworshak, Henry C.	Ida.	Rep			

Departures from Committee:

	Majority			Minority		
Moved to Armed Services	Knowland, William F.	Cal.	Rep	None		
Moved to Foreign Relations	None			Green, Theodore F.	R.I.	Dem
				Tydings, Millard E.	Md.	Dem

APPROPRIATIONS / 81st Congress

Service Dates of Committee Chair: Jan. 10,1949-Jan. 15,1951
Service Dates of Majority Members: Jan. 10,1949-Jan. 15,1951
Service Dates of Minority Members: Jan. 10,1949-Jan. 15,1951

Majority

Rank	Name	Party	State	Years in: Senate	Years in: Comm.
Chr	McKellar, Kenneth D.	Dem	Tenn.	32	26
2nd	Hayden, Carl	Dem	Ariz.	22	22
3rd	Thomas, Elmer	Dem	Okla.	22	18
4th	Russell, Richard B.	Dem	Ga.	16	16
5th	McCarran, Patrick A.	Dem	Nev.	16	16
6th	O'Mahoney, Joseph C.	Dem	Wyo.	16	16
7th	Chavez, Dennis	Dem	N.M.	14	*2 1
8th	Maybank, Burnet R.	Dem	S.C.	8	*2 1
9th	Ellender, Allen J.	Dem	La.	13	1
10th	Hill, J. Lister	Dem	Ala.	11	1
11th	Kilgore, Harley M.	Dem	W.Va.	9	1
12th	McClellan, John L.	Dem	Ark.	7	1
13th	Robertson, A. Willis	Dem	Va.	3	*1 1

Minority

Rank	Name	Party	State	Years in: Senate	Years in: Comm.
RM	Bridges, H. Styles	Rep	N.H.	13	13
2nd	Gurney, J. Chandler	Rep	S.D.	11	8
3rd	Reed, Clyde M.	Rep	Kans.	11	6
4th	Ferguson, Homer	Rep	Mich.	7	5
5th	Wherry, Kenneth S.	Rep	Neb.	7	4
6th	Cordon, Guy	Rep	Ore.	5	4
7th	Saltonstall, Leverett	Rep	Mass.	5	3
8th	Young, Milton R.	Rep	N.D.	4	3

*1: Member's 1st period of service on the committee;
*2: Member's 2nd period of service on the committee.

Notes: The resignation of Robert Wagner (Dem-N.Y.), and the appointment of John Foster Dulles (Rep-N.Y.) to fill his vacancy on July 8,1949, led to a change in size and party ratio on this committee to 12 Democrats and 9 Republicans on July 26, 1949. The defeat of Dulles by Herbert H. Lehman (Dem-N.Y.) in a special election resulted in a return to the original size and party ratio of 13 Democrats and 8 Republicans on Jan. 12,1950.

Additions:

Majority: 13th Robertson, A. Willis — Dem Va. — Jan. 12,1950
Minority: 9th Knowland, William F. — Rep Cal. — July 26,1949

Changes:

Majority:
Robertson, A. Willis — Dem Va. — July 26,1949 Ratio change; moved to Expenditures in the Executive Departments.
Minority:
Reed, Clyde M. — Rep Kans. — Nov. 8, 1949 Died in office.

	Majority		Minority	
Departures from the Senate:				
Defeated for Renomination	Thomas, Elmer	Okla. Dem	Gurney, J. Chandler	S.D. Rep
Departures from Committee:				
Moved to Expenditures in the Executive Departments	Robertson, A. Willis	Va. Dem	None	

APPROPRIATIONS / 82nd Congress

Service Dates of Committee Chair: Jan. 15,1951-Jan. 3,1953
Service Dates of Majority Members: Jan. 15,1951-Jan. 13,1953
Service Dates of Minority Members: Jan. 15,1951-Jan. 13,1953

Majority

Rank Name	Party	State	Years in: Senate	Years in: Comm.
Chr McKellar, Kenneth D.	Dem	Tenn.	34	28
2nd Hayden, Carl	Dem	Ariz.	24	24
3rd Russell, Richard B.	Dem	Ga.	19	19
4th McCarran, Patrick A.	Dem	Nev.	18	18
5th O'Mahoney, Joseph C.	Dem	Wyo.	18	18
6th Chavez, Dennis	Dem	N.M.	16	*2 3
7th Maybank, Burnet R.	Dem	S.C.	10	*2 3
8th Ellender, Allen J.	Dem	La.	15	3
9th Hill, J. Lister	Dem	Ala.	14	3
10th Kilgore, Harley M.	Dem	W.Va.	11	3
11th McClellan, John L.	Dem	Ark.	9	3

Minority

Rank Name	Party	State	Years in: Senate	Years in: Comm.
RM Bridges, H. Styles	Rep	N.H.	15	15
2nd Ferguson, Homer	Rep	Mich.	9	7
3rd Wherry, Kenneth S.	Rep	Neb.	9	6
4th Cordon, Guy	Rep	Ore.	7	6
5th Saltonstall, Leverett	Rep	Mass.	7	5
6th Young, Milton R.	Rep	N.D.	6	5
7th Knowland, William F.	Rep	Cal.	6	*2 2
8th Thye, Edward J.	Rep	Minn.	5	1
9th Ecton, Zales N.	Rep	Mont.	5	1
10th McCarthy, Joseph R.	Rep	Wisc.	5	*1 1

*1: Member's 1st period of service on the committee; *2: Member's 2nd period of service on the committee.

Note: The death of Arthur Vandenberg (Rep-Mich.), and the appointment of Blair Moody (Dem-Mich.) to fill his vacancy on Apr. 25,1951, led to a change in size and party ratio on this committee to 12 Democrats and 9 Republicans on May 21,1951.

Addition:

Majority: 12th Robertson, A. Willis — Dem Va. — May 21,1951

Changes:

Minority:
McCarthy, Joseph R. — Rep Wisc. — May 21,1951 Ratio change; moved to Rules and Administration.
Wherry, Kenneth S. — Rep Neb. — Nov. 29,1951 Died in office.
McCarthy, Joseph R. — Rep Wisc. — Jan. 14,1952 Replaced Wherry.

Departures from the Senate:	Majority		Minority	
Defeated for Reelection	O'Mahoney, Joseph C.	Wyo. Dem	Ecton, Zales N.	Mont. Rep
Defeated for Renomination	McKellar, Kenneth D.	Tenn. Dem	None	

APPROPRIATIONS / 83rd Congress

Service Dates of Committee Chair: Jan. 13,1953-Jan. 11,1955
Service Dates of Majority Members: Jan. 13,1953-Jan. 11,1955
Service Dates of Minority Members: Jan. 13,1953-Jan. 11,1955

Majority

Rank	Name	Party	State	Years in: Senate	Years in: Comm.
Chr	Bridges, H. Styles	Rep	N.H.	17	17
2nd	Ferguson, Homer	Rep	Mich.	11	9
3rd	Cordon, Guy	Rep	Ore.	9	8
4th	Saltonstall, Leverett	Rep	Mass.	9	7
5th	Young, Milton R.	Rep	N.D.	8	7
6th	Knowland, William F.	Rep	Cal.	8	*2 4
7th	Thye, Edward J.	Rep	Minn.	7	2
8th	McCarthy, Joseph R.	Rep	Wisc.	7	*2 1
9th	Mundt, Karl E.	Rep	S.D.	5	1
10th	Smith, Margaret Chase	Rep	Me.	5	1
11th	Dworshak, Henry C.	Rep	Ida.	6	*2 1
12th	Dirksen, Everett M.	Rep	Ill.	3	1

Minority

Rank	Name	Party	State	Years in: Senate	Years in: Comm.
RM	Hayden, Carl	Dem	Ariz.	26	26
2nd	Russell, Richard B.	Dem	Ga.	21	21
3rd	McCarran, Patrick A.	Dem	Nev.	20	20
4th	Chavez, Dennis	Dem	N.M.	18	*2 5
5th	Maybank, Burnet R.	Dem	S.C.	12	*2 5
6th	Ellender, Allen J.	Dem	La.	17	5
7th	Hill, J. Lister	Dem	Ala.	16	5
8th	Kilgore, Harley M.	Dem	W.Va.	13	5
9th	McClellan, John L.	Dem	Ark.	11	5
10th	Robertson, A. Willis	Dem	Va.	7	*3 2
11th	Magnuson, Warren G.	Dem	Wash.	9	1

*2: Member's 2nd period of service on the committee; *3: Member's 3rd period of service on the committee.

Changes:
Minority:

Name	Party	State	Date	Change
Maybank, Burnet R.	Dem	S.C.	Sep. 1,1954	Died in office.
McCarran, Patrick A.	Dem	Nev.	Sep. 28,1954	Died in office.

Departures from the Senate:
Defeated for Reelection

Majority
Cordon, Guy — Ore. Rep
Ferguson, Homer — Mich. Rep

Minority
None

APPROPRIATIONS / 84th Congress

Service Dates of Committee Chair: Jan. 11,1955-Jan. 9,1957
Service Dates of Majority Members: Jan. 11,1955-Jan. 9,1957
Service Dates of Minority Members: Jan. 11,1955-Jan. 9,1957

Majority

Rank	Name	Party	State	Years in: Senate	Years in: Comm.
Chr	Hayden, Carl	Dem	Ariz.	28	28
2nd	Russell, Richard B.	Dem	Ga.	22	22
3rd	Chavez, Dennis	Dem	N.M.	20	*2 7
4th	Ellender, Allen J.	Dem	La.	19	7
5th	Hill, J. Lister	Dem	Ala.	18	7
6th	Kilgore, Harley M.	Dem	W.Va.	15	7
7th	McClellan, John L.	Dem	Ark.	13	7
8th	Robertson, A. Willis	Dem	Va.	9	*3 4
9th	Magnuson, Warren G.	Dem	Wash.	11	2
10th	Holland, Spessard L.	Dem	Fla.	9	1
11th	Stennis, John C.	Dem	Miss.	8	1
12th	Clements, Earle C.	Dem	Ky.	5	1

Minority

Rank	Name	Party	State	Years in: Senate	Years in: Comm.
RM	Bridges, H. Styles	Rep	N.H.	19	19
2nd	Saltonstall, Leverett	Rep	Mass.	11	9
3rd	Young, Milton R.	Rep	N.D.	10	9
4th	Knowland, William F.	Rep	Cal.	10	*2 6
5th	Thye, Edward J.	Rep	Minn.	9	4
6th	McCarthy, Joseph R.	Rep	Wisc.	9	*2 3
7th	Mundt, Karl E.	Rep	S.D.	7	2
8th	Smith, Margaret Chase	Rep	Me.	7	2
9th	Dworshak, Henry C.	Rep	Ida.	8	*2 2
10th	Dirksen, Everett M.	Rep	Ill.	5	2
11th	Potter, Charles E.	Rep	Mich.	3	1

*2: Member's 2nd period of service on the committee; *3: Member's 3rd period of service on the committee.

Changes:
Majority:

Name	Party	State	Date	Change
Kilgore, Harley M.	Dem	W.Va.	Feb. 28,1956	Died in office.
Johnson, Lyndon B.	Dem	Tex.	Mar. 22,1956	Replaced Kilgore.

Departures from the Senate:
Defeated for Reelection

Majority
Clements, Earle C. — Ky. Dem

Minority
None

APPROPRIATIONS / 85th Congress

Service Dates of Committee Chair: Jan. 9,1957-Jan. 14,1959
Service Dates of Majority Members: Jan. 9,1957-Jan. 14,1959
Service Dates of Minority Members: Jan. 9,1957-Jan. 20,1959

Majority

Rank	Name	Party	State	Years in: Senate	Years in: Comm.
Chr	Hayden, Carl	Dem	Ariz.	30	30
2nd	Russell, Richard B.	Dem	Ga.	24	24
3rd	Chavez, Dennis	Dem	N.M.	22	*2 9
4th	Ellender, Allen J.	Dem	La.	21	8
5th	Hill, J. Lister	Dem	Ala.	19	8
6th	McClellan, John L.	Dem	Ark.	15	8
7th	Robertson, A. Willis	Dem	Va.	11	*3 6
8th	Magnuson, Warren G.	Dem	Wash.	13	4
9th	Holland, Spessard L.	Dem	Fla.	11	2
10th	Stennis, John C.	Dem	Miss.	10	2
11th	Johnson, Lyndon B.	Dem	Tex.	9	1
12th	Pastore, John O.	Dem	R.I.	7	1

Minority

Rank	Name	Party	State	Years in: Senate	Years in: Comm.
RM	Bridges, H. Styles	Rep	N.H.	21	21
2nd	Saltonstall, Leverett	Rep	Mass.	13	11
3rd	Young, Milton R.	Rep	N.D.	12	11
4th	Knowland, William F.	Rep	Cal.	12	*2 8
5th	Thye, Edward J.	Rep	Minn.	11	6
6th	McCarthy, Joseph R.	Rep	Wisc.	11	*2 5
7th	Mundt, Karl E.	Rep	S.D.	9	4
8th	Smith, Margaret Chase	Rep	Me.	9	4
9th	Dworshak, Henry C.	Rep	Ida.	10	*2 4
10th	Dirksen, Everett M.	Rep	Ill.	7	4
11th	Potter, Charles E.	Rep	Mich.	5	2

*2: Member's 2nd period of service on the committee; *3: Member's 3rd period of service on the committee.

Changes:

Minority:

Name	Party	State	Date	Action
McCarthy, Joseph R.	Rep	Wisc.	May 2,1957	Died in office.
Ives, Irving M.	Rep	N.Y.	May 22,1957	Replaced McCarthy.

Departures from the Senate:	Majority	Minority	State	Party
Defeated for Reelection	None	Potter, Charles E.	Mich.	Rep
		Thye, Edward J.	Minn.	Rep
Defeated in Election for Governor	None	Knowland, William F.	Cal.	Rep
Retired	None	Ives, Irving M.	N.Y.	Rep
Departures from Committee:				
Moved to Labor and Public Welfare	None	Dirksen, Everett McK.	Ill.	Rep

APPROPRIATIONS / 86th Congress

Service Dates of Committee Chair: Jan. 14,1959-Jan. 10,1961
Service Dates of Majority Members: Jan. 14,1959-Jan. 10,1961
Service Dates of Minority Members: Jan. 20,1959-Jan. 13,1961

Majority

Rank	Name	Party	State	Years in: Senate	Years in: Comm.
Chr	Hayden, Carl	Dem	Ariz.	32	32
2nd	Russell, Richard B.	Dem	Ga.	27	27
3rd	Chavez, Dennis	Dem	N.M.	24	*2 11
4th	Ellender, Allen J.	Dem	La.	23	11
5th	Hill, J. Lister	Dem	Ala.	22	11
6th	McClellan, John L.	Dem	Ark.	17	11
7th	Robertson, A. Willis	Dem	Va.	13	*3 8
8th	Magnuson, Warren G.	Dem	Wash.	15	7
9th	Holland, Spessard L.	Dem	Fla.	13	5
10th	Stennis, John C.	Dem	Miss.	12	5
11th	Johnson, Lyndon B.	Dem	Tex.	11	3
12th	Pastore, John O.	Dem	R.I.	9	3
13th	Kefauver, C. Estes	Dem	Tenn.	11	1
14th	Monroney, A. S. Mike	Dem	Okla.	9	1
15th	Bible, Alan H.	Dem	Nev.	5	1
16th	Byrd, Robert C.	Dem	W.Va.	1	1
17th	Dodd, Thomas J.	Dem	Conn.	1	1
18th	McGee, Gale W.	Dem	Wyo.	1	1

Minority

Rank	Name	Party	State	Years in: Senate	Years in: Comm.
RM	Bridges, H. Styles	Rep	N.H.	23	23
2nd	Saltonstall, Leverett	Rep	Mass.	15	13
3rd	Young, Milton R.	Rep	N.D.	14	13
4th	Mundt, Karl E.	Rep	S.D.	11	7
5th	Smith, Margaret Chase	Rep	Me.	11	7
6th	Dworshak, Henry C.	Rep	Ida.	12	*2 7
7th	Kuchel, Thomas H.	Rep	Cal.	7	1
8th	Hruska, Roman L.	Rep	Neb.	5	1
9th	Allott, Gordon L.	Rep	Colo.	5	1

*2: Member's 2nd period of service on the committee;
*3: Member's 3rd period of service on the committee.

	Majority		Minority
Departures from the Senate:			
Elected Vice President	Johnson, Lyndon B.	Tex. Dem	None
Departures from Committee:			
Moved to Foreign Relations	Dodd, Thomas J.	Conn. Dem	None

APPROPRIATIONS / 87th Congress

Service Dates of Committee Chair: Jan. 10,1961-Feb. 25,1963
Service Dates of Majority Members: Jan. 10,1961-Feb. 25,1963
Service Dates of Minority Members: Jan. 13,1961-Feb. 25,1963

Majority

Rank	Name	Party	State	Years in: Senate	Years in: Comm.
Chr	Hayden, Carl	Dem	Ariz.	34	34
2nd	Russell, Richard B.	Dem	Ga.	28	28
3rd	Chavez, Dennis	Dem	N.M.	26 *2	13
4th	Ellender, Allen J.	Dem	La.	25	13
5th	Hill, J. Lister	Dem	Ala.	23	13
6th	McClellan, John L.	Dem	Ark.	19	13
7th	Robertson, A. Willis	Dem	Va.	15 *3	10
8th	Magnuson, Warren G.	Dem	Wash.	17	8
9th	Holland, Spessard L.	Dem	Fla.	15	6
10th	Stennis, John C.	Dem	Miss.	14	6
11th	Pastore, John O.	Dem	R.I.	11	5
12th	Kefauver, C. Estes	Dem	Tenn.	13	2
13th	Monroney, A. S. Mike	Dem	Okla.	11	2
14th	Bible, Alan H.	Dem	Nev.	7	2
15th	Byrd, Robert C.	Dem	W.Va.	3	2
16th	McGee, Gale W.	Dem	Wyo.	3	2
17th	Humphrey, Hubert H. Jr.	DFL	Minn.	13	1

Minority

Rank	Name	Party	State	Years in: Senate	Years in: Comm.
RM1	Bridges, H. Styles	Rep	N.H.	25	25
RM2 2nd	Saltonstall, Leverett	Rep	Mass.	17	15
3rd	Young, Milton R.	Rep	N.D.	16	15
4th	Mundt, Karl E.	Rep	S.D.	13	9
5th	Smith, Margaret Chase	Rep	Me.	13	9
6th	Dworshak, Henry C.	Rep	Ida.	14 *2	9
7th	Kuchel, Thomas H.	Rep	Cal.	9	2
8th	Hruska, Roman L.	Rep	Neb.	7	2
9th	Allott, Gordon L.	Rep	Colo.	7	2
10th	Schoeppel, Andrew F.	Rep	Kans.	13	1

*2: Member's 2nd period of service on the committee;
*3: Member's 3rd period of service on the committee.

Changes:

Ranking Member:				
RM1 Bridges, H. Styles	Rep	N.H.	Nov. 26,1961	Died in office.
RM2 Saltonstall, Leverett	Rep	Mass.	Nov. 26,1961	Succeeded Bridges as Ranking Minority Member.
Majority:				
Chavez, Dennis	Dem	N.M.	Nov. 18,1962	Died in office.
Minority:				
Bridges, H. Styles	Rep	N.H.	Nov. 26,1961	Died in office.
Schoeppel, Andrew F.	Rep	Kans.	Jan. 21,1962	Died in office.
Cotton, Norris	Rep	N.H.	Feb. 2,1962	Replaced Bridges.
Case, Clifford P.	Rep	N.J.	Feb. 2,1962	Replaced Schoeppel.
Dworshak, Henry C.	Rep	Ida.	July 23,1962	Died in office.
Javits, Jacob K.	Rep	N.Y.	Aug. 8,1962	Replaced Dworshak.

	Majority	Minority	
Departures from Committee:			
Moved to Banking & Currency	None	Javits, Jacob K.	N.Y. Rep

APPROPRIATIONS / 88th Congress

Service Dates of Committee Chair: Feb. 25,1963-Jan. 8,1965
Service Dates of Majority Members: Feb. 25,1963-Jan. 8,1965
Service Dates of Minority Members: Feb. 25,1963-Jan. 15,1965

Majority

Rank	Name	Party	State	Years in: Senate	Years in: Comm.
Chr	Hayden, Carl	Dem	Ariz.	36	36
2nd	Russell, Richard B.	Dem	Ga.	31	31
3rd	Ellender, Allen J.	Dem	La.	27	15
4th	Hill, J. Lister	Dem	Ala.	26	15
5th	McClellan, John L.	Dem	Ark.	21	15
6th	Robertson, A. Willis	Dem	Va.	17 *3	12
7th	Magnuson, Warren G.	Dem	Wash.	19	11
8th	Holland, Spessard L.	Dem	Fla.	17	9
9th	Stennis, John C.	Dem	Miss.	16	9
10th	Pastore, John O.	Dem	R.I.	13	7
11th	Kefauver, C. Estes	Dem	Tenn.	15	5
12th	Monroney, A. S. Mike	Dem	Okla.	13	5
13th	Bible, Alan H.	Dem	Nev.	9	5
14th	Byrd, Robert C.	Dem	W.Va.	5	5
15th	McGee, Gale W.	Dem	Wyo.	5	5
16th	Humphrey, Hubert H. Jr.	DFL	Minn.	15	3
17th	Mansfield, Michael J.	Dem	Mont.	11	1
18th	Bartlett, E. L. (Bob)	Dem	Alas.	5	1

Minority

Rank	Name	Party	State	Years in: Senate	Years in: Comm.
RM	Saltonstall, Leverett	Rep	Mass.	19	17
2nd	Young, Milton R.	Rep	N.D.	18	17
3rd	Mundt, Karl E.	Rep	S.D.	15	11
4th	Smith, Margaret Chase	Rep	Me.	15	11
5th	Kuchel, Thomas H.	Rep	Cal.	11	5
6th	Hruska, Roman L.	Rep	Neb.	9	5
7th	Allott, Gordon L.	Rep	Colo.	9	5
8th	Cotton, Norris	Rep	N.H.	9	2
9th	Case, Clifford P.	Rep	N.J.	9	2

*3: Member's 3rd period of service on the committee.

Changes:

Majority:

Name	Party	State	Date	Note
Kefauver, C. Estes	Dem	Tenn.	Aug. 10,1963	Died in office.
Proxmire, William	Dem	Wisc.	Aug. 23,1963	Replaced Kefauver.
Humphrey, Hubert H. Jr.	DFL	Minn.	Dec. 29,1964	Resigned; elected Vice President.

APPROPRIATIONS / 89th Congress

Service Dates of Committee Chair: Jan. 8,1965-Jan. 11,1967
Service Dates of Majority Members: Jan. 8,1965-Jan. 11,1967
Service Dates of Minority Members: Jan. 15,1965-Jan. 16,1967

Majority

Rank	Name	Party	State	Years in: Senate	Years in: Comm.
Chr	Hayden, Carl	Dem	Ariz.	38	38
2nd	Russell, Richard B.	Dem	Ga.	32	32
3rd	Ellender, Allen J.	Dem	La.	29	16
4th	Hill, J. Lister	Dem	Ala.	27	16
5th	McClellan, John L.	Dem	Ark.	23	16
6th	Robertson, A. Willis	Dem	Va.	19 *3	14
7th	Magnuson, Warren G.	Dem	Wash.	21	12
8th	Holland, Spessard L.	Dem	Fla.	19	10
9th	Stennis, John C.	Dem	Miss.	18	10
10th	Pastore, John O.	Dem	R.I.	15	8
11th	Monroney, A. S. Mike	Dem	Okla.	15	6
12th	Bible, Alan H.	Dem	Nev.	11	6
13th	Byrd, Robert C.	Dem	W.Va.	7	6
14th	McGee, Gale W.	Dem	Wyo.	7	6
15th	Mansfield, Michael J.	Dem	Mont.	13	2
16th	Bartlett, E. L. (Bob)	Dem	Alas.	7	2
17th	Proxmire, William	Dem	Wisc.	8	2
18th	Yarborough, Ralph W.	Dem	Tex.	8	1

Minority

Rank	Name	Party	State	Years in: Senate	Years in: Comm.
RM	Saltonstall, Leverett	Rep	Mass.	21	19
2nd	Young, Milton R.	Rep	N.D.	20	19
3rd	Mundt, Karl E.	Rep	S.D.	17	13
4th	Smith, Margaret Chase	Rep	Me.	17	13
5th	Kuchel, Thomas H.	Rep	Cal.	13	6
6th	Hruska, Roman L.	Rep	Neb.	11	6
7th	Allott, Gordon L.	Rep	Colo.	11	6
8th	Cotton, Norris	Rep	N.H.	11	3
9th	Case, Clifford P.	Rep	N.J.	11	3

*3: Member's 3rd period of service on the committee.

Changes:
Majority:

Robertson, A. Willis	Dem	Va.	Dec. 30,1966	Resigned; defeated for renomination.

Departures from the Senate:	Majority		Minority	
Retired	None		Saltonstall, Leverett	Mass. Rep

APPROPRIATIONS / 90th Congress

Service Dates of Committee Chair: Jan. 11,1967-Jan. 3,1969
Service Dates of Majority Members: Jan. 11,1967-Jan. 14,1969
Service Dates of Minority Members: Jan. 16,1967-Jan. 14,1969

Majority

Rank	Name	Party	State	Years in: Senate	Years in: Comm.
Chr	Hayden, Carl	Dem	Ariz.	40	40
2nd	Russell, Richard B.	Dem	Ga.	34	34
3rd	Ellender, Allen J.	Dem	La.	31	19
4th	Hill, J. Lister	Dem	Ala.	30	19
5th	McClellan, John L.	Dem	Ark.	25	19
6th	Magnuson, Warren G.	Dem	Wash.	23	14
7th	Holland, Spessard L.	Dem	Fla.	21	13
8th	Stennis, John C.	Dem	Miss.	20	13
9th	Pastore, John O.	Dem	R.I.	17	11
10th	Monroney, A. S. Mike	Dem	Okla.	17	8
11th	Bible, Alan H.	Dem	Nev.	13	8
12th	Byrd, Robert C.	Dem	W.Va.	9	8
13th	McGee, Gale W.	Dem	Wyo.	9	8
14th	Mansfield, Michael J.	Dem	Mont.	15	4
15th	Bartlett, E. L. (Bob)	Dem	Alas.	9	4
16th	Proxmire, William	Dem	Wisc.	10	4
17th	Yarborough, Ralph W.	Dem	Tex.	10	3

Minority

Rank	Name	Party	State	Years in: Senate	Years in: Comm.
RM	Young, Milton R.	Rep	N.D.	22	21
2nd	Mundt, Karl E.	Rep	S.D.	19	15
3rd	Smith, Margaret Chase	Rep	Me.	19	15
4th	Kuchel, Thomas H.	Rep	Cal.	15	8
5th	Hruska, Roman L.	Rep	Neb.	13	8
6th	Allott, Gordon L.	Rep	Colo.	13	8
7th	Cotton, Norris	Rep	N.H.	13	5
8th	Case, Clifford P.	Rep	N.J.	13	5
9th	Javits, Jacob K.	Rep	N.Y.	11	*2 1

*2: Member's 2nd period of service on the committee.

Changes:
Majority:

Bartlett, E. L. (Bob)	Dem	Alas.	Dec. 11,1968	Died in office.

Departures from the Senate:	Majority		Minority	
Defeated for Reelection	Monroney, A. S. Mike	Okla. Dem	None	
Defeated for Renomination	None		Kuchel, Thomas H.	Cal. Rep
Retired	Hill, J. Lister	Ala. Dem	None	
	Hayden, Carl	Ariz. Dem		
Departures from Committee:				
Moved to Foreign Relations	None		Javits, Jacob K.	N.Y. Rep

APPROPRIATIONS / 91st Congress

Service Dates of Committee Chair: Jan. 14,1969-Jan. 21,1971
Service Dates of Majority Members: Jan. 14,1969-Jan. 28,1971
Service Dates of Minority Members: Jan. 14,1969-Jan. 29,1971

Majority

Rank	Name	Party	State	Years in: Senate	Years in: Comm.
Chr	Russell, Richard B.	Dem	Ga.	37	37
2nd	Ellender, Allen J.	Dem	La.	33	21
3rd	McClellan, John L.	Dem	Ark.	27	21
4th	Magnuson, Warren G.	Dem	Wash.	25	17
5th	Holland, Spessard L.	Dem	Fla.	23	15
6th	Stennis, John C.	Dem	Miss.	22	15
7th	Pastore, John O.	Dem	R.I.	19	13
8th	Bible, Alan H.	Dem	Nev.	15	11
9th	Byrd, Robert C.	Dem	W.Va.	11	11
10th	McGee, Gale W.	Dem	Wyo.	11	11

Minority

Rank	Name	Party	State	Years in: Senate	Years in: Comm.
RM	Young, Milton R.	Rep	N.D.	24	23
2nd	Mundt, Karl E.	Rep	S.D.	21	17
3rd	Smith, Margaret Chase	Rep	Me.	21	17
4th	Hruska, Roman L.	Rep	Neb.	15	10
5th	Allott, Gordon L.	Rep	Colo.	15	10
6th	Cotton, Norris	Rep	N.H.	15	7
7th	Case, Clifford P.	Rep	N.J.	15	7
8th	Fong, Hiram L.	Rep	Hai.	10	1
9th	Boggs, J. Caleb	Rep	Del.	9	1
10th	Pearson, James B.	Rep	Kans.	7	1

11th Mansfield, Michael J.	Dem	Mont.	17	6
12th Proxmire, William	Dem	Wisc.	12	6
13th Yarborough, Ralph W.	Dem	Tex.	12	5
14th Montoya, Joseph M.	Dem	N.M.	5	1

Changes:

Majority:

Russell, Richard B.	Dem	Ga.	Jan. 21,1971	Died in office.

	Majority			Minority	
Departures from the Senate:					
Defeated for Renomination	Yarborough, Ralph W.	Tex.	Dem	None	
Retired	Holland, Spessard L.	Fla.	Dem	None	
Departures from Committee:					
Moved to Foreign Relations	None			Pearson, James B.	Kans. Rep

APPROPRIATIONS / 92nd Congress

Service Dates of Committee Chairs: Ch1 Jan. 28,1971-July 27,1972
Ch2 Aug. 2,1972-Jan. 4,1973
Service Dates of Majority Members: Jan. 28,1971-Jan. 4,1973
Service Dates of Minority Members: Jan. 29,1971-Jan. 12,1973

Majority

Rank Name	Party	State	Years in: Senate	Years in: Comm.
Ch1 Ellender, Allen J.	Dem	La.	35	23
Ch2 2nd McClellan, John L.	Dem	Ark.	29	23
3rd Magnuson, Warren G.	Dem	Wash.	27	19
4th Stennis, John C.	Dem	Miss.	24	17
5th Pastore, John O.	Dem	R.I.	21	15
6th Bible, Alan H.	Dem	Nev.	17	13
7th Byrd, Robert C.	Dem	W.Va.	13	13
8th McGee, Gale W.	Dem	Wyo.	13	13
9th Mansfield, Michael J.	Dem	Mont.	19	8
10th Proxmire, William	Dem	Wisc.	14	8
11th Montoya, Joseph M.	Dem	N.M.	7	3
12th Inouye, Daniel K.	Dem	Hai.	9	1
13th Hollings, Ernest F.	Dem	S.C.	5	1

Minority

Rank Name	Party	State	Years in: Senate	Years in: Comm.
RM Young, Milton R.	Rep	N.D.	26	25
2nd Mundt, Karl E.	Rep	S.D.	23	19
3rd Smith, Margaret Chase	Rep	Me.	23	19
4th Hruska, Roman L.	Rep	Neb.	17	13
5th Allott, Gordon L.	Rep	Colo.	17	13
6th Cotton, Norris	Rep	N.H.	17	9
7th Case, Clifford P.	Rep	N.J.	17	9
8th Fong, Hiram L.	Rep	Hai.	12	3
9th Boggs, J. Caleb	Rep	Del.	11	3
10th Percy, Charles H.	Rep	Ill.	5	1
11th Brooke, Edward W.	Rep	Mass.	5	1

Changes:

Chair:				
Ch1 Ellender, Allen J.	Dem	La.	July 27,1972	Died in office.
Ch2 McClellan, John L.	Dem	Ark.	Aug. 2,1972	Succeeded Ellender as Chair.
Majority:				
Ellender, Allen J.	Dem	La.	July 27,1972	Died in office.
Bayh, Birch E.	Dem	Ind.	Aug. 2,1972	Replaced Ellender.
Minority:				
Mundt, Karl E.	Rep	S.D.	Feb. 23,1972	Moved to Public Works.
Percy, Charles H.	Rep	Ill.	Feb. 23,1972	Moved to Foreign Relations.
Hatfield, Mark O.	Rep	Ore.	Feb. 23,1972	Replaced Mundt.
Stevens, Theodore F.	Rep	Alas.	Feb. 23,1972	Replaced Percy.

Departures from the Senate:	Majority	Minority	
Defeated for Reelection	None	Allott, Gordon L.	Colo. Rep
		Boggs, J. Caleb	Del. Rep
		Smith, Margaret Chase	Me. Rep

APPROPRIATIONS / 93rd Congress

Service Dates of Committee Chair: Jan. 4,1973-Jan. 17,1975
Service Dates of Majority Members: Jan. 4,1973-Jan. 17,1975
Service Dates of Minority Members: Jan. 12,1973-Jan. 23,1975

Majority

Rank Name	Party	State	Years in: Senate	Years in: Comm.
Chr McClellan, John L.	Dem	Ark.	31	24
2nd Magnuson, Warren G.	Dem	Wash.	29	20
3rd Stennis, John C.	Dem	Miss.	26	18
4th Pastore, John O.	Dem	R.I.	23	16
5th Bible, Alan H.	Dem	Nev.	19	14
6th Byrd, Robert C.	Dem	W.Va.	15	14
7th McGee, Gale W.	Dem	Wyo.	15	14
8th Mansfield, Michael J.	Dem	Mont.	21	10
9th Proxmire, William	Dem	Wisc.	16	10
10th Montoya, Joseph M.	Dem	N.M.	9	4
11th Inouye, Daniel K.	Dem	Hai.	11	2
12th Hollings, Ernest F.	Dem	S.C.	7	2
13th Bayh, Birch E.	Dem	Ind.	11	1
14th Eagleton, Thomas F.	Dem	Mo.	5	1
15th Chiles, Lawton M. Jr.	Dem	Fla.	3	1

Minority

Rank Name	Party	State	Years in: Senate	Years in: Comm.
RM Young, Milton R.	Rep	N.D.	28	27
2nd Hruska, Roman L.	Rep	Neb.	19	14
3rd Cotton, Norris	Rep	N.H.	19	11
4th Case, Clifford P.	Rep	N.J.	19	11
5th Fong, Hiram L.	Rep	Hai.	14	4
6th Brooke, Edward W.	Rep	Mass.	7	2
7th Hatfield, Mark O.	Rep	Ore.	7	1
8th Stevens, Theodore F.	Rep	Alas.	5	1
9th Mathias, Charles McC. Jr.	Rep	Md.	5	1
10th Schweiker, Richard S.	Rep	Penn.	5	1
11th Bellmon, Henry	Rep	Okla.	5	1

Note: The resignation of Alan Bible (Dem-Nev.), and the appointment of Paul Laxalt (Rep-Nev.) to fill his vacancy on Dec. 18,1974, led to a change in size and party ratio on this committee to 14 Democrats and 12 Republicans.

Addition:
Minority: 12th Laxalt, Paul — Rep Nev. Dec. 18,1974

Changes:
Majority:
Bible, Alan H. — Dem Nev. Dec. 17,1974 Resigned and retired.
Minority:
Cotton, Norris — Rep N.H. Dec. 31,1974 Resigned and retired.

Departures from Committee:	Majority	Minority	
Moved to Aeronautical & Space Sciences; Labor & Public Welfare	None	Laxalt, Paul	Nev. Rep

APPROPRIATIONS / 94th Congress

Service Dates of Committee Chair: Jan. 17,1975-Jan. 10,1977
Service Dates of Majority Members: Jan. 17,1975-Jan. 10,1977
Service Dates of Minority Members: Jan. 23,1975-Jan. 10,1977

Majority

Rank Name	Party	State	Years in: Senate	Years in: Comm.
Chr McClellan, John L.	Dem	Ark.	33	27
2nd Magnuson, Warren G.	Dem	Wash.	31	23
3rd Stennis, John C.	Dem	Miss.	28	21
4th Pastore, John O.	Dem	R.I.	25	19
5th Byrd, Robert C.	Dem	W.Va.	17	17
6th McGee, Gale W.	Dem	Wyo.	17	17
7th Mansfield, Michael J.	Dem	Mont.	23	12
8th Proxmire, William	Dem	Wisc.	18	12
9th Montoya, Joseph M.	Dem	N.M.	11	7
10th Inouye, Daniel K.	Dem	Hai.	13	4
11th Hollings, Ernest F.	Dem	S.C.	9	4
12th Bayh, Birch E.	Dem	Ind.	13	3
13th Eagleton, Thomas F.	Dem	Mo.	7	3
14th Chiles, Lawton M. Jr.	Dem	Fla.	5	3

Minority

Rank Name	Party	State	Years in: Senate	Years in: Comm.
RM Young, Milton R.	Rep	N.D.	30	29
2nd Hruska, Roman L.	Rep	Neb.	21	17
3rd Case, Clifford P.	Rep	N.J.	21	13
4th Fong, Hiram L.	Rep	Hai.	16	7
5th Brooke, Edward W.	Rep	Mass.	9	4
6th Hatfield, Mark O.	Rep	Ore.	9	3
7th Stevens, Theodore F.	Rep	Alas.	7	3
8th Mathias, Charles McC. Jr.	Rep	Md.	7	3
9th Schweiker, Richard S.	Rep	Penn.	7	3
10th Bellmon, Henry	Rep	Okla.	7	3

15th Johnston, J. Bennett Jr.	Dem	La.	3	1
16th Huddleston, Walter D.	Dem	Ky.	3	1

Changes:

Majority:

Pastore, John O.	Dem	R.I.	Dec. 28,1976	Resigned and retired.

Minority:

Hruska, Roman L.	Rep	Neb.	Dec. 27,1976	Resigned and retired.

Departures from the Senate:	Majority		Minority	
Appointed Ambassador to Japan	Mansfield, Michael J.	Mont. Dem	None	
Defeated for Reelection	McGee, Gale W.	Wyo. Dem	None	
	Montoya, Joseph M.	N.M. Dem		
Retired	None		Fong, Hiram L.	Hai. Rep

APPROPRIATIONS / 95th Congress

Service Dates of Committee Chairs: Ch1 Jan. 10,1977-Nov. 28,1977
Ch2 Jan. 27,1978-Jan. 23,1979
Service Dates of Majority Members: Jan. 10,1977-Jan. 23,1979
Service Dates of Minority Members: Jan. 10,1977-Jan. 23,1979

Majority

Rank Name	Party	State	Years in: Senate	Comm.
Ch1 McClellan, John L.	Dem	Ark.	35	29
Ch2 2nd Magnuson, Warren G.	Dem	Wash.	33	24
3rd Stennis, John C.	Dem	Miss.	30	22
4th Byrd, Robert C.	Dem	W.Va.	19	18
5th Proxmire, William	Dem	Wisc.	20	14
6th Inouye, Daniel K.	Dem	Hai.	15	6
7th Hollings, Ernest F.	Dem	S.C.	11	6
8th Bayh, Birch E.	Dem	Ind.	15	5
9th Eagleton, Thomas F.	Dem	Mo.	9	5
10th Chiles, Lawton M. Jr.	Dem	Fla.	7	5
11th Johnston, J. Bennett Jr.	Dem	La.	5	2
12th Huddleston, Walter D.	Dem	Ky.	5	2
13th Riegle, Donald W. Jr.	Dem	Mich.	1	*T 1
14th Melcher, John	Dem	Mont.	1	*T 1
15th Sarbanes, Paul S.	Dem	Md.	1	*T 1
16th DeConcini, Dennis	Dem	Ariz.	1	*T 1

Minority

Rank Name	Party	State	Years in: Senate	Comm.
RM Young, Milton R.	Rep	N.D.	32	31
2nd Case, Clifford P.	Rep	N.J.	23	15
3rd Brooke, Edward W.	Rep	Mass.	11	6
4th Hatfield, Mark O.	Rep	Ore.	11	5
5th Stevens, Theodore F.	Rep	Alas.	9	5
6th Mathias, Charles McC. Jr.	Rep	Md.	9	4
7th Schweiker, Richard S.	Rep	Penn.	9	4
8th Bellmon, Henry	Rep	Okla.	9	4

*T: Temporary member of the committee.

Note: The committee size was expanded and the party ratio changed to 16 Democrats and 9 Republicans on Feb. 11,1977.

Addition:

Minority: 9th Weicker, Lowell P. Jr. Rep Conn. Feb. 22,1977

Changes:

Chair:

Ch1 McClellan, John L.	Dem	Ark.	Nov. 28,1977	Died in office.
Ch2 Magnuson, Warren G.	Dem	Wash.	Jan. 27,1978	Succeeded McClellan as Chair.

Majority:

Riegle, Donald W. Jr.	Dem	Mich.	Feb. 11,1977	Moved to Commerce, Science and Transportation; Human Resources.
Melcher, John	Dem	Mont.	Feb. 11,1977	Moved to Commerce, Science and Transportation.
Sarbanes, Paul S.	Dem	Md.	Feb. 11,1977	Moved to Foreign Relations.
Burdick, Quentin N.	Dem	N.D.	Feb. 11,1977	Replaced Riegle in 13th majority seat.
Leahy, Patrick J.	Dem	Vt.	Feb. 11,1977	Replaced Melcher in 14th majority seat.
Sasser, James R.	Dem	Tenn.	Feb. 11,1977	Replaced Sarbanes in 15th majority seat.
DeConcini, Dennis	Dem	Ariz.	Feb. 11,1977	Became a permanent member, remained in 16th majority seat.
McClellan, John L.	Dem	Ark.	Nov. 28,1977	Died in office.
Bumpers, Dale	Dem	Ark.	Jan. 27,1978	Replaced McClellan.

Departures from the Senate:	Majority	Minority	
Defeated for Reelection	None	Brooke, Edward W.	Mass. Rep
Defeated for Renomination	None	Case, Clifford P.	N.J. Rep

APPROPRIATIONS / 96th Congress

Service Dates of Committee Chair: Jan. 23,1979-Jan. 3,1981
Service Dates of Majority Members: Jan. 23,1979-Jan. 5,1981
Service Dates of Minority Members: Jan. 23,1979-Jan. 5,1981

Majority

Rank	Name	Party	State	Years in: Senate	Years in: Comm.
Chr	Magnuson, Warren G.	Dem	Wash.	35	27
2nd	Stennis, John C.	Dem	Miss.	32	25
3rd	Byrd, Robert C.	Dem	W.Va.	21	21
4th	Proxmire, William	Dem	Wisc.	22	16
5th	Inouye, Daniel K.	Dem	Hai.	17	8
6th	Hollings, Ernest F.	Dem	S.C.	13	8
7th	Bayh, Birch E.	Dem	Ind.	17	7
8th	Eagleton, Thomas F.	Dem	Mo.	11	7
9th	Chiles, Lawton M. Jr.	Dem	Fla.	9	7
10th	Johnston, J. Bennett Jr.	Dem	La.	7	5
11th	Huddleston, Walter D.	Dem	Ky.	7	5
12th	Burdick, Quentin N.	Dem	N.D.	19	2
13th	Leahy, Patrick J.	Dem	Vt.	5	2
14th	Sasser, James R.	Dem	Tenn.	3	2
15th	DeConcini, Dennis	Dem	Ariz.	3	3
16th	Bumpers, Dale	Dem	Ark.	5	1
17th	Durkin, John A.	Dem	N.H.	4	1

Minority

Rank	Name	Party	State	Years in: Senate	Years in: Comm.
RM	Young, Milton R.	Rep	N.D.	34	33
2nd	Hatfield, Mark O.	Rep	Ore.	13	7
3rd	Stevens, Theodore F.	Rep	Alas.	11	7
4th	Mathias, Charles McC. Jr.	Rep	Md.	11	7
5th	Schweiker, Richard S.	Rep	Penn.	11	7
6th	Bellmon, Henry	Rep	Okla.	11	7
7th	Weicker, Lowell P. Jr.	Rep	Conn.	9	2
8th	McClure, James A.	Rep	Ida.	7	1
9th	Laxalt, Paul	Rep	Nev.	5	*2 1
10th	Garn, Jake	Rep	Utah	5	1
11th	Schmitt, Harrison H.	Rep	N.M.	3	1

*2: Member's 2nd period of service on the committee.

Changes:
Majority:

Name	Party	State	Date	Reason
Durkin, John A.	Dem	N.H.	Dec. 29,1980	Resigned; defeated for reelection.

Departures from the Senate:

	Majority		Minority	
Appointed Secretary of Health and Human Services	None		Schweiker, Richard S.	Penn. Rep
Defeated for Reelection	Bayh, Birch E.	Ind. Dem	None	
	Magnuson, Warren G.	Wash. Dem		
Retired	None		Bellmon, Henry	Okla. Rep
			Young, Milton R.	N.D. Rep

Departures from Committee:

	Majority		Minority	
Became Chair of Rules & Administration	None		Mathias, Charles McC. Jr.	Md. Rep

APPROPRIATIONS / 97th Congress

Service Dates of Committee Chair: Jan. 5,1981-Jan. 3,1983
Service Dates of Majority Members: Jan. 5,1981-Jan. 3,1983
Service Dates of Minority Members: Jan. 5,1981-Jan. 3,1983

Majority

Rank	Name	Party	State	Years in: Senate	Years in: Comm.
Chr	Hatfield, Mark O.	Rep	Ore.	14	9
2nd	Stevens, Theodore F.	Rep	Alas.	13	9
3rd	Weicker, Lowell P. Jr.	Rep	Conn.	11	4
4th	McClure, James A.	Rep	Ida.	9	2
5th	Laxalt, Paul	Rep	Nev.	7	*2 2
6th	Garn, Jake	Rep	Utah	7	2
7th	Schmitt, Harrison H.	Rep	N.M.	5	2
8th	Cochran, Thad	Rep	Miss.	3	1
9th	Andrews, Mark	Rep	N.D.	1	1
10th	Abdnor, James	Rep	S.D.	1	1
11th	Kasten, Robert W. Jr.	Rep	Wisc.	1	1
12th	D'Amato, Alfonse M.	Rep	N.Y.	1	1
13th	Mattingly, Mack	Rep	Ga.	1	1
14th	Rudman, Warren B.	Rep	N.H.	1	1
15th	Specter, Arlen	Rep	Penn.	1	1

Minority

Rank	Name	Party	State	Years in: Senate	Years in: Comm.
RM	Proxmire, William	Dem	Wisc.	24	18
2nd	Stennis, John C.	Dem	Miss.	34	26
3rd	Byrd, Robert C.	Dem	W.Va.	23	22
4th	Inouye, Daniel K.	Dem	Hai.	19	10
5th	Hollings, Ernest F.	Dem	S.C.	15	10
6th	Eagleton, Thomas F.	Dem	Mo.	13	9
7th	Chiles, Lawton M. Jr.	Dem	Fla.	11	9
8th	Johnston, J. Bennett Jr.	Dem	La.	9	6
9th	Huddleston, Walter D.	Dem	Ky.	9	6
10th	Burdick, Quentin N.	Dem	N.D.	21	4
11th	Leahy, Patrick J.	Dem	Vt.	7	4
12th	Sasser, James R.	Dem	Tenn.	5	4
13th	DeConcini, Dennis	Dem	Ariz.	5	4
14th	Bumpers, Dale	Dem	Ark.	7	3

*2: Member's 2nd period of service on the committee.

Note: Rankings on this committee for the following members were affected by other chamber service: John C. Stennis (Dem-Miss.), Ranking Minority Member, Armed Services; and Robert C. Byrd (Dem-W.Va.), Senate Minority Leader.

Departures from the Senate:	Majority			Minority
Defeated for Reelection	Schmitt, Harrison H.	N.M.	Rep	None

APPROPRIATIONS / 98th Congress

Service Dates of Committee Chair: Jan. 3,1983-Feb. 21,1985
Service Dates of Majority Members: Jan. 3,1983-Feb. 21,1985
Service Dates of Minority Members: Jan. 3,1983-Feb. 21,1985

Majority

Rank Name	Party	State	Years in: Senate	Years in: Comm.
Chr Hatfield, Mark O.	Rep	Ore.	16	11
2nd Stevens, Theodore F.	Rep	Alas.	15	11
3rd Weicker, Lowell P. Jr.	Rep	Conn.	13	6
4th McClure, James A.	Rep	Ida.	11	4
5th Laxalt, Paul	Rep	Nev.	9	*2 4
6th Garn, Jake	Rep	Utah	9	4
7th Cochran, Thad	Rep	Miss.	5	2
8th Andrews, Mark	Rep	N.D.	3	2
9th Abdnor, James	Rep	S.D.	3	2
10th Kasten, Robert W. Jr.	Rep	Wisc.	3	2
11th D'Amato, Alfonse M.	Rep	N.Y.	3	2
12th Mattingly, Mack	Rep	Ga.	3	2
13th Rudman, Warren B.	Rep	N.H.	3	2
14th Specter, Arlen	Rep	Penn.	3	2
15th Domenici, Pete V.	Rep	N.M.	11	1

Minority

Rank Name	Party	State	Years in: Senate	Years in: Comm.
RM Stennis, John C.	Dem	Miss.	36	28
2nd Byrd, Robert C.	Dem	W.Va.	25	24
3rd Proxmire, William	Dem	Wisc.	26	20
4th Inouye, Daniel K.	Dem	Hai.	21	12
5th Hollings, Ernest F.	Dem	S.C.	17	12
6th Eagleton, Thomas F.	Dem	Mo.	15	10
7th Chiles, Lawton M. Jr.	Dem	Fla.	13	10
8th Johnston, J. Bennett Jr.	Dem	La.	11	8
9th Huddleston, Walter D.	Dem	Ky.	11	8
10th Burdick, Quentin N.	Dem	N.D.	23	6
11th Leahy, Patrick J.	Dem	Vt.	9	6
12th Sasser, James R.	Dem	Tenn.	7	6
13th DeConcini, Dennis	Dem	Ariz.	7	6
14th Bumpers, Dale	Dem	Ark.	9	5

*2: Member's 2nd period of service on the committee.

Departures from the Senate:	Majority	Minority		
Defeated for Reelection	None	Huddleston, Walter D.	Ky.	Dem
Departures from Committee:				
No new assignment	None	Eagleton, Thomas F.	Mo.	Dem

APPROPRIATIONS / 99th Congress

Service Dates of Committee Chair: Feb. 21,1985-Jan. 6,1987
Service Dates of Majority Members: Feb. 21,1985-Jan. 6,1987
Service Dates of Minority Members: Feb. 21,1985-Jan. 6,1987

Majority

Rank Name	Party	State	Years in: Senate	Years in: Comm.
Chr Hatfield, Mark O.	Rep	Ore.	19	13
2nd Stevens, Theodore F.	Rep	Alas.	17	13
3rd Weicker, Lowell P. Jr.	Rep	Conn.	15	9
4th McClure, James A.	Rep	Ida.	13	7
5th Laxalt, Paul	Rep	Nev.	11	*2 7
6th Garn, Jake	Rep	Utah	11	7
7th Cochran, Thad	Rep	Miss.	7	5
8th Andrews, Mark	Rep	N.D.	5	5
9th Abdnor, James	Rep	S.D.	5	5
10th Kasten, Robert W. Jr.	Rep	Wisc.	5	5
11th D'Amato, Alfonse M.	Rep	N.Y.	5	5
12th Mattingly, Mack	Rep	Ga.	5	5
13th Rudman, Warren B.	Rep	N.H.	5	5
14th Specter, Arlen	Rep	Penn.	5	5
15th Domenici, Pete V.	Rep	N.M.	13	3

Minority

Rank Name	Party	State	Years in: Senate	Years in: Comm.
RM Stennis, John C.	Dem	Miss.	38	31
2nd Byrd, Robert C.	Dem	W.Va.	27	27
3rd Proxmire, William	Dem	Wisc.	28	22
4th Inouye, Daniel K.	Dem	Hai.	23	15
5th Hollings, Ernest F.	Dem	S.C.	19	15
6th Chiles, Lawton M. Jr.	Dem	Fla.	15	13
7th Johnston, J. Bennett Jr.	Dem	La.	13	11
8th Burdick, Quentin N.	Dem	N.D.	25	9
9th Leahy, Patrick J.	Dem	Vt.	11	9
10th Sasser, James R.	Dem	Tenn.	9	9
11th DeConcini, Dennis	Dem	Ariz.	9	9
12th Bumpers, Dale	Dem	Ark.	11	8
13th Lautenberg, Frank R.	Dem	N.J.	3	1
14th Harkin, Thomas R.	Dem	Iowa	1	1

*2: Member's 2nd period of service on the committee.

Departures from the Senate:	Majority			Minority
Defeated for Reelection	Abdnor, James	S.D.	Rep	None
	Andrews, Mark	N.D.	Rep	
	Mattingly, Mack	Ga.	Rep	
Retired	Laxalt, Paul	Nev.	Rep	None

APPROPRIATIONS / 100th Congress

Service Dates of Committee Chair: Jan. 6,1987-Jan. 3,1989
Service Dates of Majority Members: Jan. 6,1987-Feb. 2,1989
Service Dates of Minority Members: Jan. 6,1987-Feb. 2,1989

Majority

Rank	Name	Party	State	Years in: Senate	Years in: Comm.
Chr	Stennis, John C.	Dem	Miss.	40	32
2nd	Byrd, Robert C.	Dem	W.Va.	29	28
3rd	Proxmire, William	Dem	Wisc.	30	24
4th	Inouye, Daniel K.	Dem	Hai.	25	16
5th	Hollings, Ernest F.	Dem	S.C.	21	16
6th	Chiles, Lawton M. Jr.	Dem	Fla.	17	15
7th	Johnston, J. Bennett Jr.	Dem	La.	15	12
8th	Burdick, Quentin N.	Dem	N.D.	27	10
9th	Leahy, Patrick J.	Dem	Vt.	13	10
10th	Sasser, James R.	Dem	Tenn.	11	10
11th	DeConcini, Dennis	Dem	Ariz.	11	10
12th	Bumpers, Dale	Dem	Ark.	13	9
13th	Lautenberg, Frank R.	Dem	N.J.	5	2
14th	Harkin, Thomas R.	Dem	Iowa	3	2
15th	Mikulski, Barbara A.	Dem	Md.	1	1
16th	Reid, Harry M.	Dem	Nev.	1	1

Minority

Rank	Name	Party	State	Years in: Senate	Years in: Comm.
RM	Hatfield, Mark O.	Rep	Ore.	20	15
2nd	Stevens, Theodore F.	Rep	Alas.	19	15
3rd	Weicker, Lowell P. Jr.	Rep	Conn.	17	10
4th	McClure, James A.	Rep	Ida.	15	8
5th	Garn, Jake	Rep	Utah	13	8
6th	Cochran, Thad	Rep	Miss.	9	7
7th	Kasten, Robert W. Jr.	Rep	Wisc.	7	7
8th	D'Amato, Alfonse M.	Rep	N.Y.	7	7
9th	Rudman, Warren B.	Rep	N.H.	7	7
10th	Specter, Arlen	Rep	Penn.	7	7
11th	Domenici, Pete V.	Rep	N.M.	15	5
12th	Grassley, Charles E.	Rep	Iowa	7	1
13th	Nickles, Don	Rep	Okla.	7	1

Departures from the Senate:	Majority			Minority		
Defeated for Reelection	None			Weicker, Lowell P. Jr.	Conn.	Rep
Retired	Chiles, Lawton M. Jr.	Fla.	Dem	None		
	Proxmire, William	Wisc.	Dem			
	Stennis, John C.	Miss.	Dem			

APPROPRIATIONS / 101st Congress

Service Dates of Committee Chair: Feb. 2,1989-Feb. 5,1991
Service Dates of Majority Members: Feb. 2,1989-Feb. 5,1991
Service Dates of Minority Members: Feb. 2,1989-Feb. 5,1991

Majority

Rank	Name	Party	State	Years in: Senate	Years in: Comm.
Chr	Byrd, Robert C.	Dem	W.Va.	31	31
2nd	Inouye, Daniel K.	Dem	Hai.	27	19
3rd	Hollings, Ernest F.	Dem	S.C.	23	19
4th	Johnston, J. Bennett Jr.	Dem	La.	17	15
5th	Burdick, Quentin N.	Dem	N.D.	29	12
6th	Leahy, Patrick J.	Dem	Vt.	15	12
7th	Sasser, James R.	Dem	Tenn.	13	12
8th	DeConcini, Dennis	Dem	Ariz.	13	12
9th	Bumpers, Dale	Dem	Ark.	15	11
10th	Lautenberg, Frank R.	Dem	N.J.	7	4
11th	Harkin, Thomas R.	Dem	Iowa	5	4
12th	Mikulski, Barbara A.	Dem	Md.	3	3
13th	Reid, Harry M.	Dem	Nev.	3	3
14th	Adams, Brock	Dem	Wash.	3	1
15th	Fowler, Wyche Jr.	Dem	Ga.	3	1
16th	Kerrey, Bob	Dem	Neb.	1	1

Minority

Rank	Name	Party	State	Years in: Senate	Years in: Comm.
RM	Hatfield, Mark O.	Rep	Ore.	23	17
2nd	Stevens, Theodore F.	Rep	Alas.	21	17
3rd	McClure, James A.	Rep	Ida.	17	11
4th	Garn, Jake	Rep	Utah	15	11
5th	Cochran, Thad	Rep	Miss.	11	9
6th	Kasten, Robert W. Jr.	Rep	Wisc.	9	9
7th	D'Amato, Alfonse M.	Rep	N.Y.	9	9
8th	Rudman, Warren	Rep	N.H.	9	9
9th	Specter, Arlen	Rep	Penn.	9	9
10th	Domenici, Pete V.	Rep	N.M.	17	7
11th	Grassley, Charles E.	Rep	Iowa	9	3
12th	Nickles, Don	Rep	Okla.	9	3
13th	Gramm, W. Phil	Rep	Tex.	5	1

Departures from the Senate:	Majority	Minority		
Retired	None	McClure, James A.	Ida.	Rep
Departures from Committee:				
Moved to Agriculture, Nutrition & Forestry; Finance	None	Grassley, Charles E.	Iowa	Rep

APPROPRIATIONS / 102nd Congress

Service Dates of Committee Chair: Feb. 5,1991-Jan. 3,1993
Service Dates of Majority Members: Feb. 5,1991-Jan. 3,1993
Service Dates of Minority Members: Feb. 5,1991-Jan. 3,1993

Majority

Rank Name	Party	State	Years in: Senate	Years in: Comm.
Chr Byrd, Robert C.	Dem	W.Va.	33	33
2nd Inouye, Daniel K.	Dem	Hai.	29	21
3rd Hollings, Ernest F.	Dem	S.C.	25	21
4th Johnston, J. Bennett Jr.	Dem	La.	19	17
5th Burdick, Quentin N.	Dem	N.D.	31	14
6th Leahy, Patrick J.	Dem	Vt.	17	14
7th Sasser, James R.	Dem	Tenn.	15	14
8th DeConcini, Dennis	Dem	Ariz.	15	14
9th Bumpers, Dale	Dem	Ark.	17	13
10th Lautenberg, Frank R.	Dem	N.J.	9	6
11th Harkin, Thomas R.	Dem	Iowa	7	6
12th Mikulski, Barbara A.	Dem	Md.	5	5
13th Reid, Harry M.	Dem	Nev.	5	5
14th Adams, Brock	Dem	Wash.	5	3
15th Fowler, Wyche Jr.	Dem	Ga.	5	3
16th Kerrey, Bob	Dem	Neb.	3	3

Minority

Rank Name	Party	State	Years in: Senate	Years in: Comm.
RM Hatfield, Mark O.	Rep	Ore.	25	19
2nd Stevens, Theodore F.	Rep	Alas.	23	19
3rd Garn, Jake	Rep	Utah	17	13
4th Cochran, Thad	Rep	Miss.	13	11
5th Kasten, Robert W. Jr.	Rep	Wisc.	11	11
6th D'Amato, Alfonse M.	Rep	N.Y.	11	11
7th Rudman, Warren	Rep	N.H.	11	11
8th Specter, Arlen	Rep	Penn.	11	11
9th Domenici, Pete V.	Rep	N.M.	19	9
11th Nickles, Don	Rep	Okla.	11	5
10th Grassley, Charles E.	Rep	Iowa	11	5
12th Gramm, W. Phil	Rep	Tex.	7	3
13th Bond, Christopher S.	Rep	Mo.	5	1
14th Gorton, Slade	Rep	Wash.	9	1

Changes:

Majority:

Burdick, Quentin N.	Dem	N.D.	Sep. 8,1992	Died in office.
Conrad, Kent	Dem	N.D.	Sep. 18,1992	Replaced Burdick.

ARMED SERVICES

Jurisdiction, 1947

Established by the Legislative Reorganization Act of 1946:

[Section 102.(1)(c)]

Committee on Armed Services, to consist of thirteen Senators, to which committee shall be referred all proposed legislation, messages, petitions, memorials, and other matters relating to the following subjects:

1. Common defense generally.
2. The War Department and the Military Establishment generally.
3. The Navy Department and the Naval Establishment generally.
4. Soldiers' and sailors' homes.
5. Pay, promotion, retirement, and other benefits and privileges of members of the armed forces.
6. Selective service.
7. Size and composition of the Army and Navy.
8. Forts, arsenals, military reservations, and navy yards.
9. Ammunition depots.
10. Maintenance and operation of the Panama Canal, including the administration, sanitation, and government of the Canal Zone.
11. Conservation, development, and use of naval petroleum and oil shale reserves.
12. Strategic and critical materials necessary for the common defense.

Jurisdiction, 1992

Jurisdiction contained in the Standing Rules of the Senate (as revised to March 18, 1992):

[Rule XXV.(1)(c)]

(1) Committee on Armed Services, to which committee shall be referred all proposed legislation, messages, petitions, memorials, and other matters relating to the following subjects:

1. Aeronautical and space activities peculiar to or primarily associated with the development of weapons systems or military operations.
2. Common defense.
3. Department of Defense, the Department of the Army, the Department of the Navy, and the Department of the Air Force, generally.
4. Maintenance and operation of the Panama Canal, including administration, sanitation, and government of the Canal Zone.
5. Military research and development.
6. National security aspects of nuclear energy.
7. Naval petroleum reserves, except those in Alaska.
8. Pay, promotion, retirement, and other benefits and privileges of members of the Armed Forces, including overseas education of civilian and military dependents.
9. Selective service system.
10. Strategic and critical materials necessary for the common defense.

(2) Such committee shall also study and review, on a comprehensive basis, matters relating to the common defense policy of the United States, and report thereon from time to time.

ARMED SERVICES / 80th Congress

Service Dates of Committee Chair: Jan. 6,1947-Jan. 10,1949
Service Dates of Majority Members: Jan. 6,1947-Jan. 10,1949
Service Dates of Minority Members: Jan. 8,1947-Jan. 10,1949

Majority

Rank	Name	Party	State	Years in: Senate	Years in: Comm.
Chr	Gurney, J. Chandler	Rep	S.D.	9	8
2nd	Bridges, H. Styles	Rep	N.H.	11	10
3rd	Robertson, Edward V.	Rep	Wyo.	5	2
4th	Wilson, George A.	Rep	Iowa	4	4
5th	Saltonstall, Leverett	Rep	Mass.	3	2
6th	Morse, Wayne L.	Rep	Ore.	3	2
7th	Baldwin, Raymond E.	Rep	Conn.	1	1

Minority

Rank	Name	Party	State	Years in: Senate	Years in: Comm.
RM	Tydings, Millard E.	Dem	Md.	20	20
2nd	Russell, Richard B.	Dem	Ga.	14	14
3rd	Byrd, Harry Flood	Dem	Va.	14	14
4th	Hill, J. Lister	Dem	Ala.	9	9
5th	Kilgore, Harley M.	Dem	W.Va.	7	6
6th	Maybank, Burnet R.	Dem	S.C.	6	2

Note: Rankings on this committee for the following members were affected by other chamber service: Styles H. Bridges (Rep-N.H.), Chair, Appropriations.

Departures from the Senate:

	Majority			Minority		
Defeated for Reelection	Robertson, Edward V.	Wyo.	Rep	None		
	Wilson, George A.	Iowa	Rep			

Departures from Committee:

	Majority	Minority		
Moved to Appropriations	None	Hill, J. Lister	Ala.	Dem
		Kilgore, Harley M.	W.Va.	Dem
		Maybank, Burnet R.	S.C.	Dem

ARMED SERVICES / 81st Congress

Service Dates of Committee Chair: Jan. 10,1949-Jan. 3,1951
Service Dates of Majority Members: Jan. 10,1949-Jan. 15,1951
Service Dates of Minority Members: Jan. 10,1949-Jan. 15,1951

Majority

Rank	Name	Party	State	Years in: Senate	Years in: Comm.
Chr	Tydings, Millard E.	Dem	Md.	22	22
2nd	Russell, Richard B.	Dem	Ga.	16	16
3rd	Byrd, Harry Flood	Dem	Va.	16	16
4th	Chapman, Virgil M.	Dem	Ky.	1	1
5th	Johnson, Lyndon B.	Dem	Tex.	1	1
6th	Kefauver, C. Estes	Dem	Tenn.	1	1
7th	Hunt, Lester C.	Dem	Wyo.	1	1

Minority

Rank	Name	Party	State	Years in: Senate	Years in: Comm.
RM	Bridges, H. Styles	Rep	N.H.	13	13
2nd	Gurney, J. Chandler	Rep	S.D.	11	11
3rd	Saltonstall, Leverett	Rep	Mass.	5	5
4th	Morse, Wayne L.	Rep	Ore.	5	4
5th	Baldwin, Raymond E.	Rep	Conn.	3	3
6th	Knowland, William F.	Rep	Cal.	4	1

Changes:

Minority:

Name	Party	State	Date	Change
Baldwin, Raymond E.	Rep	Conn.	Dec. 16,1949	Resigned; appointed State Supreme Court Justice.
Cain, Harry P.	Rep	Wash.	Jan. 12,1950	Replaced Baldwin.

Departures from the Senate:

	Majority			Minority		
Defeated for Reelection	Tydings, Millard E.	Md.	Dem	None		
Defeated for Renomination	None			Gurney, J. Chandler	S.D.	Rep

ARMED SERVICES / 82nd Congress

Service Dates of Committee Chair: Jan. 15,1951-Jan. 13,1953
Service Dates of Majority Members: Jan. 15,1951-Jan. 13,1953
Service Dates of Minority Members: Jan. 15,1951-Jan. 13,1953

Majority

Rank	Name	Party	State	Years in: Senate	Years in: Comm.
Chr	Russell, Richard B.	Dem	Ga.	19	18
2nd	Byrd, Harry Flood	Dem	Va.	18	18
3rd	Chapman, Virgil M.	Dem	Ky.	3	3
4th	Johnson, Lyndon B.	Dem	Tex.	3	3
5th	Kefauver, C. Estes	Dem	Tenn.	3	3
6th	Hunt, Lester C.	Dem	Wyo.	3	3
7th	Stennis, John C.	Dem	Miss.	4	1

Minority

Rank	Name	Party	State	Years in: Senate	Years in: Comm.
RM	Bridges, H. Styles	Rep	N.H.	15	15
2nd	Saltonstall, Leverett	Rep	Mass.	7	7
3rd	Morse, Wayne L.	Rep	Ore.	7	6
4th	Knowland, William F.	Rep	Cal.	6	3
5th	Cain, Harry P.	Rep	Wash.	5	2
6th	Flanders, Ralph E.	Rep	Vt.	5	1

Changes:

Majority:

Chapman, Virgil M.	Dem	Ky.	Mar. 8,1951	Died in office.
Long, Russell B.	Dem	La.	Apr. 3,1951	Replaced Chapman.

Minority:

Morse, Wayne L.	Rep	Ore.	Oct. 24,1952	Resigned the Republican Party to become an Independent; lost minority assignment.

	Majority			Minority		
Departures from the Senate:						
Defeated for Reelection	None			Cain, Harry P.	Wash.	Rep
Departures from Committee:						
Moved to Finance	Long, Russell B.	La.	Dem	None		
Moved to Foreign Relations	None			Knowland, William F.	Cal.	Rep
Moved to Public Works	None			Morse, Wayne L.	Ore.	Rep

ARMED SERVICES / 83rd Congress

Service Dates of Committee Chair: Jan. 13,1953-Jan. 11,1955
Service Dates of Majority Members: Jan. 13,1953-Jan. 11,1955
Service Dates of Minority Members: Jan. 13,1953-Jan. 11,1955

Majority

Rank	Name	Party	State	Years in: Senate	Years in: Comm.
Chr	Saltonstall, Leverett	Rep	Mass.	9	9
2nd	Bridges, H. Styles	Rep	N.H.	17	17
3rd	Flanders, Ralph E.	Rep	Vt.	7	2
4th	Smith, Margaret Chase	Rep	Me.	5	1
5th	Hendrickson, Robert C.	Rep	N.J.	5	1
6th	Case, Francis H.	Rep	S.D.	3	1
7th	Duff, James H.	Rep	Penn.	2	1
8th	Cooper, John Sherman	Rep	Ky.	3	1

Minority

Rank	Name	Party	State	Years in: Senate	Years in: Comm.
RM	Russell, Richard B.	Dem	Ga.	21	20
2nd	Byrd, Harry Flood	Dem	Va.	20	20
3rd	Johnson, Lyndon B.	Dem	Tex.	5	5
4th	Kefauver, C. Estes	Dem	Tenn.	5	5
5th	Hunt, Lester C.	Dem	Wyo.	5	5
6th	Stennis, John C.	Dem	Miss.	6	2
7th	Symington, W. Stuart	Dem	Mo.	1	1

Notes: Wayne L. Morse of Oregon resigned the Republican Party at the close of the 82nd Congress. Due to the near parity of Democratic and Republican members, a full vote was taken in the Senate on the membership of the Armed Services committee. On Jan. 13,1953, 88 votes were cast in favor of allowing the membership from the 82nd Congress to continue, except for Morse. As for the two vacancies, Stuart Symington (Rep-Ky.) received 86 votes, John Sherman Cooper (Dem-Mo.) received 83 votes and Morse received seven votes. Ranking on this committee for the following member was affected by other chamber service: Styles H. Bridges (Rep-N.H.), Chair, Appropriations.

Changes:

Minority:

Hunt, Lester C.	Dem	Wyo.	June 19,1954	Died in office.
Jackson, Henry M.	Dem	Wash.	June 25,1954	Replaced Hunt.

Departures from the Senate:	Majority			Minority
Appointed Ambassador to New Zealand	Hendrickson, Robert C.	N.J.	Rep	None
Defeated for Reelection	Cooper, John Sherman	Ky.	Rep	None

ARMED SERVICES / 84th Congress

Service Dates of Committee Chair: Jan. 11,1955-Jan. 9,1957
Service Dates of Majority Members: Jan. 11,1955-Jan. 9,1957
Service Dates of Minority Members: Jan. 11,1955-Jan. 9,1957

Majority

Rank	Name	Party	State	Years in: Senate	Years in: Comm.
Chr	Russell, Richard B.	Dem	Ga.	22	22
2nd	Byrd, Harry Flood	Dem	Va.	22	22
3rd	Johnson, Lyndon B.	Dem	Tex.	7	7
4th	Kefauver, C. Estes	Dem	Tenn.	7	7
5th	Stennis, John C.	Dem	Miss.	8	4
6th	Symington, W. Stuart	Dem	Mo.	3	2
7th	Jackson, Henry M.	Dem	Wash.	3	1
8th	Ervin, Samuel J.	Dem	N.C.	1	1

Minority

Rank	Name	Party	State	Years in: Senate	Years in: Comm.
RM1	Bridges, H. Styles	Rep	N.H.	19	19
RM2 2nd	Saltonstall, Leverett	Rep	Mass.	11	11
3rd	Flanders, Ralph E.	Rep	Vt.	9	4
4th	Smith, Margaret Chase	Rep	Me.	7	2
5th	Case, Francis H.	Rep	S.D.	5	2
6th	Duff, James H.	Rep	Penn.	4	2
7th	Welker, Herman	Rep	Ida.	5	1

Changes:

Ranking Member:

	Name	Party	State	Date	Change
RM1	Bridges, H. Styles	Rep	N.H.	Feb. 23,1955	Switched rank with Saltonstall to be Ranking Minority Member on Appropriations for the duration of the Congress.
RM2	Saltonstall, Leverett	Rep	Mass.	Feb. 23,1955	Succeeded Bridges as Ranking Minority Member.

Departures from the Senate:	Majority	Minority		
Defeated for Reelection	None	Duff, James H.	Penn.	Rep
		Welker, Herman	Ida.	Rep

ARMED SERVICES / 85th Congress

Service Dates of Committee Chair: Jan. 9,1957-Jan. 14,1959
Service Dates of Majority Members: Jan. 9,1957-Jan. 14,1959
Service Dates of Minority Members: Jan. 9,1957-Jan. 20,1959

Majority

Rank	Name	Party	State	Years in: Senate	Years in: Comm.
Chr	Russell, Richard B.	Dem	Ga.	24	24
2nd	Byrd, Harry Flood	Dem	Va.	24	24
3rd	Johnson, Lyndon B.	Dem	Tex.	9	8
4th	Kefauver, C. Estes	Dem	Tenn.	9	8
5th	Stennis, John C.	Dem	Miss.	10	6
6th	Symington, W. Stuart	Dem	Mo.	5	4
7th	Jackson, Henry M.	Dem	Wash.	5	3
8th	Ervin, Samuel J.	Dem	N.C.	3	2

Minority

Rank	Name	Party	State	Years in: Senate	Years in: Comm.
RM1	Bridges, H. Styles	Rep	N.H.	21	21
RM2 2nd	Saltonstall, Leverett	Rep	Mass.	13	12
3rd	Flanders, Ralph E.	Rep	Vt.	11	6
4th	Smith, Margaret Chase	Rep	Me.	9	4
5th	Case, Francis H.	Rep	S.D.	7	4
6th	Bush, Prescott S.	Rep	Conn.	5	1
7th	Barrett, Frank A.	Rep	Wyo.	5	1

Changes:

Ranking Member:

	Name	Party	State	Date	Change
RM1	Bridges, H. Styles	Rep	N.H.	Jan. 22,1957	Switched rank with Saltonstall to be Ranking Minority Member on Appropriations for the duration of the Congress.
RM2	Saltonstall, Leverett	Rep	Mass.	Jan. 22,1957	Succeeded Bridges as Ranking Minority Member.

Departures from the Senate:	Majority	Minority		
Defeated for Reelection	None	Barrett, Frank A.	Wyo.	Rep
Retired	None	Flanders, Ralph E.	Vt.	Rep

Departures from Committee:	Majority			Minority
Moved to Appropriations	Kefauver, C. Estes	Tenn.	Dem	None

ARMED SERVICES / 86th Congress

Service Dates of Committee Chair: Jan. 14,1959-Jan. 10,1961
Service Dates of Majority Members: Jan. 14,1959-Jan. 10,1961
Service Dates of Minority Members: Jan. 20,1959-Jan. 13,1961

Majority

Rank	Name	Party	State	Years in: Senate	Years in: Comm.
Chr	Russell, Richard B.	Dem	Ga.	27	26
2nd	Byrd, Harry Flood	Dem	Va.	26	26
3rd	Johnson, Lyndon B.	Dem	Tex.	11	11
4th	Stennis, John C.	Dem	Miss.	12	8
5th	Symington, W. Stuart	Dem	Mo.	7	7
6th	Jackson, Henry M.	Dem	Wash.	7	5
7th	Ervin, Samuel J.	Dem	N.C.	5	5
8th	Thurmond, J. Strom	Dem	S.C.	4	1
9th	Engle, Clair	Dem	Cal.	1	1
10th	Bartlett, E. L. (Bob)	Dem	Alas.	1	1
11th	Cannon, Howard W.	Dem	Nev.	1	1

Minority

Rank	Name	Party	State	Years in: Senate	Years in: Comm.
RM1	Bridges, H. Styles	Rep	N.H.	23	23
RM2 2nd	Saltonstall, Leverett	Rep	Mass.	15	15
3rd	Smith, Margaret Chase	Rep	Me.	11	7
4th	Case, Francis H.	Rep	S.D.	9	7
5th	Bush, Prescott S.	Rep	Conn.	7	3
6th	Beall, J. Glenn	Rep	Md.	7	1

Changes:

Ranking Member:

RM1	Bridges, H. Styles	Rep	N.H.	Jan. 23,1959	Switched rank with Saltonstall to be Ranking Minority Member on Appropriations for the duration of the Congress.
RM2	Saltonstall, Leverett	Rep	Mass.	Jan. 23,1959	Succeeded Bridges as Ranking Minority Member.

Departures from Senate:

	Majority			Minority
Elected Vice President	Johnson, Lyndon B.	Tex.	Dem	None

ARMED SERVICES / 87th Congress

Service Dates of Committee Chair: Jan. 10,1961-Feb. 25,1963
Service Dates of Majority Members: Jan. 10,1961-Feb. 25,1963
Service Dates of Minority Members: Jan. 13,1961-Feb. 25,1963

Majority

Rank	Name	Party	State	Years in: Senate	Years in: Comm.
Chr	Russell, Richard B.	Dem	Ga.	28	28
2nd	Byrd, Harry Flood	Dem	Va.	28	28
3rd	Stennis, John C.	Dem	Miss.	14	10
4th	Symington, W. Stuart	Dem	Mo.	9	8
5th	Jackson, Henry M.	Dem	Wash.	9	7
6th	Ervin, Samuel J.	Dem	N.C.	7	6
7th	Thurmond, J. Strom	Dem	S.C.	6	2
8th	Engle, Clair	Dem	Cal.	3	2
9th	Bartlett, E. L. (Bob)	Dem	Alas.	3	2
10th	Cannon, Howard W.	Dem	Nev.	3	2
11th	Byrd, Robert C.	Dem	W.Va.	3	1

Minority

Rank	Name	Party	State	Years in: Senate	Years in: Comm.
RM1	Bridges, H. Styles	Rep	N.H.	25	25
RM2 2nd	Saltonstall, Leverett	Rep	Mass.	17	17
3rd	Smith, Margaret Chase	Rep	Me.	13	9
4th	Case, Francis H.	Rep	S.D.	11	9
5th	Bush, Prescott S.	Rep	Conn.	9	5
6th	Beall, J. Glenn	Rep	Md.	9	2

Changes:

Ranking Member:

RM1	Bridges, H. Styles	Rep	N.H.	Jan. 26,1961	Switched rank with Saltonstall to be Ranking Minority Member on Appropriations for duration of Congress.
RM2	Saltonstall, Leverett	Rep	Mass.	Jan. 26,1961	Succeeded Bridges as Ranking Minority Member.

Minority:

Bridges, H. Styles	Rep	N.H.	Nov. 26,1961	Died in office.
Goldwater, Barry M.	Rep	Ariz.	Feb. 2,1962	Replaced Bridges.
Case, Francis H.	Rep	S.D.	June 22,1962	Died in office.
Case, Clifford P.	Rep	N.J.	July 18,1962	Replaced Francis H. Case.

Departures from the Senate:	**Majority**		**Minority**	
Retired	None		Bush, Prescott S.	Conn. Rep
Departures from Committee:				
Moved to Appropriations	Bartlett, E. L. (Bob)	Alas. Dem	None	

ARMED SERVICES / 88th Congress

Service Dates of Committee Chair: Feb. 25,1963-Jan. 8,1965
Service Dates of Majority Members: Feb. 25,1963-Jan. 8,1965
Service Dates of Minority Members: Feb. 25,1963-Jan. 15,1965

Majority

Rank Name	Party	State	Years in: Senate	Years in: Comm.
Chr Russell, Richard B.	Dem	Ga.	31	30
2nd Byrd, Harry Flood	Dem	Va.	30	30
3rd Stennis, John C.	Dem	Miss.	16	13
4th Symington, W. Stuart	Dem	Mo.	11	11
5th Jackson, Henry M.	Dem	Wash.	11	9
6th Ervin, Samuel J.	Dem	N.C.	9	9
7th Thurmond, J. Strom	Dem	S.C.	8	5
8th Engle, Clair	Dem	Cal.	5	5
9th Cannon, Howard W.	Dem	Nev.	5	5
10th Byrd, Robert C.	Dem	W.Va.	5	3
11th Young, Stephen M.	Dem	Ohio	5	1
12th Inouye, Daniel K.	Dem	Hai.	1	1

Minority

Rank Name	Party	State	Years in: Senate	Years in: Comm.
RM Saltonstall, Leverett	Rep	Mass.	19	19
2nd Smith, Margaret Chase	Rep	Me.	15	11
3rd Beall, J. Glenn	Rep	Md.	11	5
4th Goldwater, Barry M.	Rep	Ariz.	11	*1 2
5th Case, Clifford P.	Rep	N.J.	9	1

*1: Member's 1st period of service on the committee.

Notes: On Feb. 28,1963, John C. Stennis (Dem-Miss.) was moved to the 2nd rank on the committee ahead of Harry Flood Byrd (Dem-Va.). J. Strom Thurmond of South Carolina resigned the Democratic Party and joined the Republican Party on Sep. 16,1964. The Republican Party recognized Thurmond's previous service on the committee and awarded him the 3rd minority rank on Sep. 17,1964.

Changes:

Majority:

Engle, Clair	Dem	Cal.	July 30,1964	Died in office.
McIntyre, Thomas J.	Dem	N.H.	Aug. 10,1964	Replaced Engle.
Thurmond, J. Strom	Dem	S.C.	Sep. 16,1964	Resigned Democratic Party; lost majority assignment.

Minority:

Thurmond, J. Strom	Dem	S.C.	Sep. 17,1964	Rejoined committee; ranked 3rd minority.

Departures from the Senate:	**Majority**	**Minority**	
Defeated for Reelection	None	Beall, J. Glenn	Md. Rep
Lost Election for President	None	Goldwater, Barry M.	Ariz. Rep
Departures from Committee:			
Moved to Foreign Relations	None	Case, Clifford P.	N.J. Rep

ARMED SERVICES / 89th Congress

Service Dates of Committee Chair: Jan. 8,1965-Jan. 11,1967
Service Dates of Majority Members: Jan. 8,1965-Jan. 11,1967
Service Dates of Minority Members: Jan. 15,1965-Jan. 16,1967

Majority

Rank	Name	Party	State	Years in: Senate	Years in: Comm.
Chr	Russell, Richard B.	Dem	Ga.	32	32
2nd	Stennis, John C.	Dem	Miss.	18	14
3rd	Byrd, Harry Flood	Dem	Va.	32	32
4th	Symington, W. Stuart	Dem	Mo.	13	12
5th	Jackson, Henry M.	Dem	Wash.	13	11
6th	Ervin, Samuel J.	Dem	N.C.	11	10
7th	Cannon, Howard W.	Dem	Nev.	7	6
8th	Byrd, Robert C.	Dem	W.Va.	7	4
9th	Young, Stephen M.	Dem	Ohio	7	2
10th	Inouye, Daniel K.	Dem	Hai.	3	2
11th	McIntyre, Thomas J.	Dem	N.H.	3	1
12th	Brewster, Daniel B.	Dem	Md.	3	1

Minority

Rank	Name	Party	State	Years in: Senate	Years in: Comm.
RM	Saltonstall, Leverett	Rep	Mass.	21	21
2nd	Smith, Margaret Chase	Rep	Me.	17	13
3rd	Thurmond, J. Strom	Rep	S.C.	10	7
4th	Miller, Jack R.	Rep	Iowa	5	1
5th	Tower, John G.	Rep	Tex.	4	1

Notes: J. Strom Thurmond (Rep-S.C.) served previously on this committee as a Democrat. In the 88th Congress, John C. Stennis (Dem-Miss.) was moved to 2nd rank on the committee ahead of Harry Flood Byrd (Dem-Va.).

Changes:

Majority:

Name	Party	State	Date	Change
Byrd, Harry Flood	Dem	Va.	Nov. 10,1965	Resigned and retired.
Byrd, Harry Flood, Jr.	Dem	Va.	Jan. 14,1966	Replaced Byrd, Sr.

Departures from the Senate:	Majority		Minority	
Retired	None		Saltonstall, Leverett	Mass. Rep

ARMED SERVICES / 90th Congress

Service Dates of Committee Chair: Jan. 11,1967-Jan. 14,1969
Service Dates of Majority Members: Jan. 11,1967-Jan. 14,1969
Service Dates of Minority Members: Jan. 16,1967-Jan. 14,1969

Majority

Rank	Name	Party	State	Years in: Senate	Years in: Comm.
Chr	Russell, Richard B.	Dem	Ga.	34	34
2nd	Stennis, John C.	Dem	Miss.	20	16
3rd	Symington, W. Stuart	Dem	Mo.	15	14
4th	Jackson, Henry M.	Dem	Wash.	15	13
5th	Ervin, Samuel J.	Dem	N.C.	13	13
6th	Cannon, Howard W.	Dem	Nev.	9	8
7th	Byrd, Robert C.	Dem	W.Va.	9	7
8th	Young, Stephen M.	Dem	Ohio	9	4
9th	Inouye, Daniel K.	Dem	Hai.	5	4
10th	McIntyre, Thomas J.	Dem	N.H.	5	3
11th	Brewster, Daniel B.	Dem	Md.	5	3
12th	Byrd, Harry Flood Jr.	Dem	Va.	2	1

Minority

Rank	Name	Party	State	Years in: Senate	Years in: Comm.
RM	Smith, Margaret Chase	Rep	Me.	19	15
2nd	Thurmond, J. Strom	Rep	S.C.	12	9
3rd	Miller, Jack R.	Rep	Iowa	7	3
4th	Tower, John G.	Rep	Tex.	6	3
5th	Pearson, James B.	Rep	Kans.	5	1
6th	Dominick, Peter H.	Rep	Colo.	5	1

Note: J. Strom Thurmond (Rep-S.C.) served previously on this committee as a Democrat.

	Majority		Minority	
Departures from the Senate:				
Defeated for Reelection	Brewster, Daniel B.	Md. Dem	None	
Departures from Committee:				
Moved to Judiciary	Byrd, Robert C.	W.Va. Dem	None	
Moved to Finance	None		Miller, Jack R.	Iowa Rep
Moved to Appropriations	None		Pearson, James B.	Kans. Rep

ARMED SERVICES / 91st Congress

Service Dates of Committee Chair: Jan. 14,1969-Jan. 28,1971
Service Dates of Majority Members: Jan. 14,1969-Jan. 28,1971
Service Dates of Minority Members: Jan. 14,1969-Jan. 29,1971

Majority

Rank	Name	Party	State	Years in: Senate	Years in: Comm.
Chr	Stennis, John C.	Dem	Miss.	22	18
2nd	Russell, Richard B.	Dem	Ga.	37	36
3rd	Symington, W. Stuart	Dem	Mo.	17	17
4th	Jackson, Henry M.	Dem	Wash.	17	15
5th	Ervin, Samuel J.	Dem	N.C.	15	15
6th	Cannon, Howard W.	Dem	Nev.	11	11
7th	Young, Stephen M.	Dem	Ohio	11	6
8th	Inouye, Daniel K.	Dem	Hai.	7	6
9th	McIntyre, Thomas J.	Dem	N.H.	7	5
10th	Byrd, Harry Flood Jr.	Dem	Va.	4	4

Minority

Rank	Name	Party	State	Years in: Senate	Years in: Comm.
RM	Smith, Margaret Chase	Rep	Me.	21	17
2nd	Thurmond, J. Strom	Rep	S.C.	14	11
3rd	Tower, John G.	Rep	Tex.	8	4
4th	Dominick, Peter H.	Rep	Colo.	7	2
5th	Murphy, George L.	Rep	Cal.	5	1
6th	Brooke, Edward W.	Rep	Mass.	3	1
7th	Goldwater, Barry M.	Rep	Ariz.	13 *2	1
8th	Schweiker, Richard S.	Rep	Penn.	1	1

*2: Member's 2nd period of service on the committee.

Notes: Ranking on this committee for the following member was affected by other chamber service: Richard B. Russell (Dem-Ga.), Chair, Appropriations. J. Strom Thurmond (Rep-S.C.) served previously on this committee as a Democrat.

Changes:

Majority:

Russell, Richard B. Dem Ga. Jan. 21,1971 Died in office.

Minority:

Murphy, George L. Rep Cal. Jan. 2,1971 Resigned; defeated for reelection.

	Majority		Minority	
Departures from the Senate:				
Retired	Young, Stephen M.	Ohio Dem	None	
Departures from Committee:				
Moved to Appropriations; District of Columbia	Inouye, Daniel K.	Hai. Dem		
Moved to Appropriations	None		Brooke, Edward W.	Mass. Rep

ARMED SERVICES / 92nd Congress

Service Dates of Committee Chair: Jan. 28,1971-Jan. 4,1973
Service Dates of Majority Members: Jan. 28,1971-Jan. 4,1973
Service Dates of Minority Members: Jan. 29,1971-Jan. 12,1973

Majority

Rank	Name	Party	State	Years in: Senate	Years in: Comm.
Chr	Stennis, John C.	Dem	Miss.	24	21
2nd	Symington, W. Stuart	Dem	Mo.	19	19
3rd	Jackson, Henry M.	Dem	Wash.	19	17
4th	Ervin, Samuel J.	Dem	N.C.	17	17
5th	Cannon, Howard W.	Dem	Nev.	13	13
6th	McIntyre, Thomas J.	Dem	N.H.	9	7
7th	Byrd, Harry Flood Jr.	Ind	Va.	6	6
8th	Hughes, Harold E.	Dem	Iowa	3	1
9th	Bentsen, Lloyd M. Jr.	Dem	Tex.	1	1

Minority

Rank	Name	Party	State	Years in: Senate	Years in: Comm.
RM	Smith, Margaret Chase	Rep	Me.	23	19
2nd	Thurmond, J. Strom	Rep	S.C.	16	13
3rd	Tower, John G.	Rep	Tex.	10	7
4th	Dominick, Peter H.	Rep	Colo.	9	5
5th	Goldwater, Barry M.	Rep	Ariz.	15 *2	3
6th	Schweiker, Richard S.	Rep	Penn.	3	3
7th	Saxbe, William B.	Rep	Ohio	3	1

*2: Member's 2nd period of service on the committee.

Notes: Harry Flood Byrd, Jr. was elected as an Independent, but was appointed to the committee by the Democratic Caucus, serving with his seniority intact. J. Strom Thurmond (Rep-S.C.) served previously on this committee as a Democrat.

	Majority	Minority	
Departures from the Senate:			
Defeated for Reelection	None	Smith, Margaret Chase	Me. Rep

Departures from Committee:

	Majority		Minority	
Moved to Finance	Bentsen, Lloyd M. Jr.	Tex. Dem	None	
Moved to Appropriations	None		Schweiker, Richard S.	Penn. Rep

ARMED SERVICES / 93rd Congress

Service Dates of Committee Chair: Jan. 4,1973-Jan. 17,1975
Service Dates of Majority Members: Jan. 4,1973-Jan. 17,1975
Service Dates of Minority Members: Jan. 12,1973-Jan. 23,1975

Majority

Rank	Name	Party	State	Years in: Senate	Years in: Comm.
Chr	Stennis, John C.	Dem	Miss.	26	22
2nd	Symington, W. Stuart	Dem	Mo.	21	20
3rd	Jackson, Henry M.	Dem	Wash.	21	19
4th	Ervin, Samuel J.	Dem	N.C.	19	18
5th	Cannon, Howard W.	Dem	Nev.	15	14
6th	McIntyre, Thomas J.	Dem	N.H.	11	9
7th	Byrd, Harry Flood Jr.	Ind	Va.	8	7
8th	Hughes, Harold E.	Dem	Iowa	5	2
9th	Nunn, Samuel A.	Dem	Ga.	1	1

Minority

Rank	Name	Party	State	Years in: Senate	Years in: Comm.
RM	Thurmond, J. Strom	Rep	S.C.	18	14
2nd	Tower, John G.	Rep	Tex.	12	8
3rd	Dominick, Peter H.	Rep	Colo.	11	6
4th	Goldwater, Barry M.	Rep	Ariz.	17	*2 4
5th	Saxbe, William B.	Rep	Ohio	5	2
6th	Scott, William L.	Rep	Va.	1	1

*2: Member's 2nd period of service on the committee.

Notes: Harry Flood Byrd, Jr. was elected as an Independent, but was appointed to the committee by the Democratic Caucus, serving with his seniority intact. J. Strom Thurmond (Rep-S.C.) served previously on this committee as a Democrat.

Changes:

Majority:

Ervin, Samuel J.	Dem	N.C.	Dec. 31,1974	Resigned and retired.

Minority:

Saxbe, William B.	Rep	Ohio	Jan. 3,1974	Resigned; appointed Attorney General.
Taft, Robert Jr.	Rep	Ohio	Jan. 23,1974	Replaced Saxbe.

Departures from the Senate:

	Majority		Minority	
Defeated for Reelection	None		Dominick, Peter H.	Colo. Rep
Retired	Hughes, Harold E.	Iowa Dem	None	

ARMED SERVICES / 94th Congress

Service Dates of Committee Chair: Jan. 17,1975-Jan. 10,1977
Service Dates of Majority Members: Jan. 17,1975-Jan. 10,1977
Service Dates of Minority Members: Jan. 23,1975-Jan. 10,1977

Majority

Rank	Name	Party	State	Years in: Senate	Years in: Comm.
Chr	Stennis, John C.	Dem	Miss.	28	25
2nd	Symington, W. Stuart	Dem	Mo.	23	23
3rd	Jackson, Henry M.	Dem	Wash.	23	21
4th	Cannon, Howard W.	Dem	Nev.	17	17
5th	McIntyre, Thomas J.	Dem	N.H.	13	11
6th	Byrd, Harry Flood Jr.	Ind	Va.	10	10
7th	Nunn, Samuel A.	Dem	Ga.	3	3
8th	Culver, John C.	Dem	Iowa	1	1
9th	Hart, Gary W.	Dem	Colo.	1	1
10th	Leahy, Patrick J.	Dem	Vt.	1	1

Minority

Rank	Name	Party	State	Years in: Senate	Years in: Comm.
RM	Thurmond, J. Strom	Rep	S.C.	20	17
2nd	Tower, John G.	Rep	Tex.	14	11
3rd	Goldwater, Barry M.	Rep	Ariz.	19	*2 7
4th	Scott, William L.	Rep	Va.	3	3
5th	Taft, Robert Jr.	Rep	Ohio	5	2
6th	Bartlett, Dewey F.	Rep	Okla.	3	1

*2: Member's 2nd period of service on the committee.

Notes: Harry Flood Byrd, Jr. was elected as an Independent, but was appointed to the committee by the Democratic Caucus, serving with his seniority intact. J. Strom Thurmond (Rep-S.C.) served previously on this committee as a Democrat.

Changes:

Majority:

Symington, W. Stuart	Dem	Mo.	Dec. 27,1976	Resigned and retired.

Minority:

Taft, Robert Jr.	Rep	Ohio	Dec. 28,1976	Resigned; defeated for reelection.

ARMED SERVICES / 95th Congress

Service Dates of Committee Chair: Jan. 10,1977-Jan. 23,1979
Service Dates of Majority Members: Jan. 10,1977-Jan. 23,1979
Service Dates of Minority Members: Jan. 10,1977-Jan. 23,1979

Majority

Rank Name	Party	State	Years in: Senate	Years in: Comm.
Chr Stennis, John C.	Dem	Miss.	30	26
2nd Jackson, Henry M.	Dem	Wash.	25	23
3rd Cannon, Howard W.	Dem	Nev.	19	18
4th McIntyre, Thomas J.	Dem	N.H.	15	13
5th Byrd, Harry Flood Jr.	Ind	Va.	12	11
6th Nunn, Samuel A.	Dem	Ga.	5	5
7th Culver, John C.	Dem	Iowa	3	2
8th Hart, Gary W.	Dem	Colo.	3	2
9th Leahy, Patrick J.	Dem	Vt.	3	2
10th Metzenbaum, Howard M.	Dem	Ohio	2	*T 1

Minority

Rank Name	Party	State	Years in: Senate	Years in: Comm.
RM1 Thurmond, J. Strom	Rep	S.C.	22	18
RM2 2nd Tower, John G.	Rep	Tex.	16	12
3rd Goldwater, Barry M.	Rep	Ariz.	21	*2 8
4th Scott, William L.	Rep	Va.	5	4
5th Bartlett, Dewey F.	Rep	Okla.	5	2
6th Wallop, Malcolm	Rep	Wyo.	1	*T 1

*2: Member's 2nd period of service on the committee;
*T: Temporary member of the committee.

Notes: The committee size was expanded to 18 members, and the party ratio changed to 11 Democrats and 7 Republicans on Feb. 11,1977. Harry Flood Byrd, Jr. of Virginia was elected as an Independent, but was appointed to the committee by the Democratic Caucus, serving with his seniority intact. J. Strom Thurmond (Rep-S.C.) served previously on this committee as a Democrat.

Additions:

Majority:	11th Anderson, Wendell R.	DFL	Minn.	Feb. 11,1977
Minority:	7th Garn, Jake	Rep	Utah	Feb. 22,1977

Changes:

Ranking Member:				
RM1 Thurmond, J. Strom	Rep	S.C.	Jan. 22,1977	Became Ranking Minority Member of Judiciary; remained on committee in 2nd rank.
RM2 Tower, John G.	Rep	Tex.	Jan. 22,1977	Succeeded Thurmond as Ranking Minority Member.
Majority:				
Leahy, Patrick J.	Dem	Vt.	Feb. 11,1977	Moved to Appropriations.
Metzenbaum, Howard M.	Dem	Ohio	Feb. 11,1977	Moved to Judiciary.
Bumpers, Dale	Dem	Ark.	Feb. 11,1977	Replaced Leahy and ranked 9th.
Morgan, Robert B.	Dem	N.C.	Feb. 11,1977	Replaced Metzenbaum and ranked 10th.
Bumpers, Dale	Dem	Ark.	Jan. 27,1978	Moved to Appropriations.
Hatfield, Paul	Dem	Mont.	Jan. 27,1978	Replaced Bumpers.
Hatfield, Paul	Dem	Mont.	Dec. 14,1978	Resigned; defeated for nomination.
Anderson, Wendell R.	DFL	Minn.	Dec. 29,1978	Resigned; lost special election.
Minority:				
Wallop, Malcolm	Rep	Wyo.	Feb. 22,1977	Moved to Environment and Public Works.
Helms, Jesse A.	Rep	N.C.	Feb. 22,1977	Replaced Wallop.
Scott, William L.	Rep	Va.	Jan. 1,1979	Resigned and retired.

	Majority			Minority		
Departures from the Senate:						
Defeated for Reelection	McIntyre, Thomas J.	N.H.	Dem	None		
Retired	None			Bartlett, Dewey F.	Okla.	Rep
Departures from Committee:						
Moved to Appropriations	None			Garn, Jake	Utah	Rep
Moved to Foreign Relations	None			Helms, Jesse A.	N.C.	Rep

ARMED SERVICES / 96th Congress

Service Dates of Committee Chair: Jan. 23,1979-Jan. 5,1981
Service Dates of Majority Members: Jan. 23,1979-Jan. 5,1981
Service Dates of Minority Members: Jan. 23,1979-Jan. 5,1981

Majority

Rank Name	Party	State	Years in: Senate	Years in: Comm.
Chr Stennis, John C.	Dem	Miss.	32	29
2nd Jackson, Henry M.	Dem	Wash.	27	25
3rd Cannon, Howard W.	Dem	Nev.	21	21
4th Byrd, Harry Flood Jr.	Ind	Va.	14	14
5th Nunn, Samuel A.	Dem	Ga.	7	7
6th Culver, John C.	Dem	Iowa	5	5
7th Hart, Gary W.	Dem	Colo.	5	5
8th Morgan, Robert B.	Dem	N.C.	5	2
9th Exon, J. James	Dem	Neb.	1	1
10th Levin, Carl M.	Dem	Mich.	1	1

Minority

Rank Name	Party	State	Years in: Senate	Years in: Comm.
RM Tower, John G.	Rep	Tex.	18	15
2nd Thurmond, J. Strom	Rep	S.C.	24	21
3rd Goldwater, Barry M.	Rep	Ariz.	23	*2 11
4th Warner, John W.	Rep	Va.	1	1
5th Humphrey, Gordon J.	Rep	N.H.	1	1
6th Cohen, William S.	Rep	Me.	1	1
7th Jepsen, Roger W.	Rep	Iowa	1	1

*2: Member's 2nd period of service on the committee.

Notes: Harry Flood Byrd, Jr. was elected as an Independent, but was appointed to the committee by the Democratic Caucus, serving with his seniority intact. Ranking on this committee for the following member was affected by other chamber service: J. Strom Thurmond (Rep-S.C.), Ranking Minority Member, Judiciary. Thurmond served previously on this committee as a Democrat.

Departures from the Senate:

	Majority			Minority
Defeated for Reelection	Culver, John C.	Iowa	Dem	None
	Morgan, Robert B.	N.C.	Dem	

ARMED SERVICES / 97th Congress

Service Dates of Committee Chair: Jan. 5,1981-Jan. 3,1983
Service Dates of Majority Members: Jan. 5,1981-Jan. 3,1983
Service Dates of Minority Members: Jan. 5,1981-Jan. 3,1983

Majority

Rank Name	Party	State	Years in: Senate	Years in: Comm.
Chr Tower, John G.	Rep	Tex.	20	16
2nd Thurmond, J. Strom	Rep	S.C.	26	22
3rd Goldwater, Barry M.	Rep	Ariz.	25	*2 12
4th Warner, John W.	Rep	Va.	3	2
5th Humphrey, Gordon J.	Rep	N.H.	3	2
6th Cohen, William S.	Rep	Me.	3	2
7th Jepsen, Roger W.	Rep	Iowa	3	2
8th Quayle, J. Danforth	Rep	Ind.	1	1
9th Denton, Jeremiah	Rep	Ala.	1	*1 1

Minority

Rank Name	Party	State	Years in: Senate	Years in: Comm.
RM Stennis, John C.	Dem	Miss.	34	30
2nd Jackson, Henry M.	Dem	Wash.	29	27
3rd Cannon, Howard W.	Dem	Nev.	23	22
4th Byrd, Harry Flood Jr.	Ind	Va.	16	15
5th Nunn, Samuel A.	Dem	Ga.	9	9
6th Hart, Gary W.	Dem	Colo.	7	6
7th Exon, J. James	Dem	Neb.	3	2
8th Levin, Carl M.	Dem	Mich.	3	2

*1: Member's 1st period of service on the committee; *2: Member's 2nd period of service on the committee.

Notes: The resignation of Harrison Williams (Dem-N.J.), and the appointment of Nicholas F. Brady (Rep-N.J.) to fill his vacancy on April 12, 1982, led to a change in size and party ratio on this committee to 10 Republicans and 8 Democrats. Harry Flood Byrd, Jr. of Virginia was elected as an Independent, but was appointed to the committee by the Democratic Caucus, serving with his seniority intact. Ranking on this committee for the following member was affected by other chamber service: J. Strom Thurmond (Rep-S.C.), Chair, Judiciary. Thurmond served previously on this committee as a Democrat.

Addition:
Majority: 10th Brady, Nicholas F. Rep N.J. Apr. 20,1982

Changes:
Majority:
Brady, Nicholas F. Rep N.J. Dec. 26,1982 Resigned and retired.

Departures from the Senate:	**Majority**		**Minority**	
Defeated for Reelection	None		Cannon, Howard W.	Nev. Dem
Retired	None		Byrd, Harry Flood Jr.	Va. Ind
Departures from Committee:				
No new assignment	Denton, Jeremiah	Ala. Rep	None	

ARMED SERVICES / 98th Congress

Service Dates of Committee Chair: Jan. 3,1983-Jan. 3,1985
Service Dates of Majority Members: Jan. 3,1983-Feb. 21,1985
Service Dates of Minority Members: Jan. 3,1983-Feb. 21,1985

Majority

Rank	Name	Party	State	Years in: Senate	Years in: Comm.
Chr	Tower, John G.	Rep	Tex.	22	18
2nd	Thurmond, J. Strom	Rep	S.C.	28	24
3rd	Goldwater, Barry M.	Rep	Ariz.	27	*2 14
4th	Warner, John W.	Rep	Va.	5	4
5th	Humphrey, Gordon J.	Rep	N.H.	5	4
6th	Cohen, William S.	Rep	Me.	5	4
7th	Jepsen, Roger W.	Rep	Iowa	5	4
8th	Quayle, J. Danforth	Rep	Ind.	3	2
9th	East, John P.	Rep	N.C.	3	1
10th	Wilson, Pete	Rep	Cal.	1	1

Minority

Rank	Name	Party	State	Years in: Senate	Years in: Comm.
RM1	Jackson, Henry M.	Dem	Wash.	31	29
2nd	Stennis, John C.	Dem	Miss.	36	32
RM2 3rd	Nunn, Samuel A.	Dem	Ga.	11	10
4th	Hart, Gary W.	Dem	Colo.	9	8
5th	Exon, J. James	Dem	Neb.	5	4
6th	Levin, Carl M.	Dem	Mich.	5	4
7th	Kennedy, Edward M.	Dem	Mass.	21	1
8th	Bingaman, Jeff	Dem	N.M.	1	1

*2: Member's 2nd period of service on the committee.

Notes: The death of Henry M. Jackson (Dem-Wash.), and the appointment of Daniel J. Evans (Rep-Wash.) to fill his vacancy on Sep. 8,1983, led to a temporary change in size and party ratio on this committee to 11 Republicans and 8 Democrats. It returned to its original size and party ratio when Evans left the committee on Feb. 9,1984. Rankings on this committee for the following members were affected by other chamber service: J. Strom Thurmond (Rep-S.C.), Chair, Judiciary; and John C. Stennis (Dem-Miss.), Ranking Minority Member, Appropriations. Thurmond served previously on this committee as a Democrat.

Addition:
Majority: 11th Evans, Daniel J. Rep Wash. Sep. 22,1983

Changes:

Ranking Member:					
RM1	Jackson, Henry M.	Dem	Wash.	Sep. 1,1983	Died in office.
RM2	Nunn, Samuel A.	Dem	Ga.	Sep. 1,1983	Succeeded Jackson as Ranking Minority Member.
Majority:					
	Evans, Daniel J.	Rep	Wash.	Feb. 9,1984	Moved to Environment and Public Works.
Minority:					
	Jackson, Henry M.	Dem	Wash.	Sep. 1,1983	Died in office.
	Dixon, Alan J.	Dem	Ill.	Feb. 9,1984	Replaced Jackson.

Departures from the Senate:	**Majority**		**Minority**
Defeated for Reelection	Jepsen, Roger W.	Iowa Rep	None
Retired	Tower, John G.	Tex. Rep	None

ARMED SERVICES / 99th Congress

Service Dates of Committee Chair: Feb. 21,1985-Jan. 3,1987
Service Dates of Majority Members: Feb. 21,1985-Jan. 6,1987
Service Dates of Minority Members: Feb. 21,1985-Jan. 6,1987

Majority

Rank Name	Party	State	Years in: Senate	Years in: Comm.
Chr Goldwater, Barry M.	Rep	Ariz.	29	*2 17
2nd Thurmond, J. Strom	Rep	S.C.	30	27
3rd Warner, John W.	Rep	Va.	7	7
4th Humphrey, Gordon J.	Rep	N.H.	7	7
5th Cohen, William S.	Rep	Me.	7	7
6th Quayle, J. Danforth	Rep	Ind.	5	5
7th East, John P.	Rep	N.C.	5	3
8th Wilson, Pete	Rep	Cal.	3	3
9th Denton, Jeremiah	Rep	Ala.	5	*2 1
10th Gramm, W. Phil	Rep	Tex.	1	1

Minority

Rank Name	Party	State	Years in: Senate	Years in: Comm.
RM Nunn, Samuel A.	Dem	Ga.	13	13
2nd Stennis, John C.	Dem	Miss.	38	35
3rd Hart, Gary W.	Dem	Colo.	11	11
4th Exon, J. James	Dem	Neb.	7	7
5th Levin, Carl M.	Dem	Mich.	7	7
6th Kennedy, Edward M.	Dem	Mass.	23	3
7th Bingaman, Jeff	Dem	N.M.	3	3
8th Dixon, Alan J.	Dem	Ill.	5	2
9th Glenn, John H. Jr.	Dem	Ohio	11	1

*2: Member's 2nd period of service on the committee.

Notes: Rankings on this committee for the following members were affected by other chamber service: J. Strom Thurmond (Rep-S.C.), Chair, Judiciary; and John C. Stennis (Dem-Miss.), Ranking Minority Member, Appropriations. Thurmond served previously on this committee as a Democrat.

Changes:
Majority:

East, John P.	Rep	N.C.	June 29,1986	Died in office.
Broyhill, James T.	Rep	N.C.	July 14,1986	Replaced East.
Broyhill, James T.	Rep	N.C.	Nov. 5,1986	Resigned; defeated for election.

Departures from the Senate:

	Majority		Minority	
Defeated for Reelection	Denton, Jeremiah	Ala. Rep	None	
Retired	Goldwater, Barry M.	Ariz. Rep	Hart, Gary W.	Colo. Dem

ARMED SERVICES / 100th Congress

Service Dates of Committee Chair: Jan. 6,1987-Feb. 2,1989
Service Dates of Majority Members: Jan. 6,1987-Feb. 2,1989
Service Dates of Minority Members: Jan. 6,1987-Feb. 2,1989

Majority

Rank Name	Party	State	Years in: Senate	Years in: Comm.
Chr Nunn, Samuel A.	Dem	Ga.	15	15
2nd Stennis, John C.	Dem	Miss.	40	36
3rd Exon, J. James	Dem	Neb.	9	8
4th Levin, Carl M.	Dem	Mich.	9	8
5th Kennedy, Edward M.	Dem	Mass.	25	5
6th Bingaman, Jeff	Dem	N.M.	5	5
7th Dixon, Alan J.	Dem	Ill.	7	3
8th Glenn, John H. Jr.	Dem	Ohio	13	2
9th Gore, Albert A. Jr.	Dem	Tenn.	3	1
10th Wirth, Timothy E.	Dem	Colo.	1	1
11th Shelby, Richard C.	Dem	Ala.	1	1

Minority

Rank Name	Party	State	Years in: Senate	Years in: Comm.
RM Warner, John W.	Rep	Va.	9	8
2nd Thurmond, J. Strom	Rep	S.C.	32	28
3rd Humphrey, Gordon J.	Rep	N.H.	9	8
4th Cohen, William S.	Rep	Me.	9	8
5th Quayle, J. Danforth	Rep	Ind.	7	7
6th Wilson, Pete	Rep	Cal.	5	5
7th Gramm, W. Phil	Rep	Tex.	3	2
8th Symms, Steven D.	Rep	Ida.	7	1
9th McCain, John	Rep	Ariz.	1	1

Notes: Rankings on this committee for the following members were affected by other chamber service: John C. Stennis (Dem-Miss.), Chair, Appropriations; and J. Strom Thurmond (Rep-S.C.), Ranking Minority Member, Judiciary. Thurmond served previously on this committee as a Democrat.

Changes:
Minority:

Quayle, J. Danforth	Rep	Ind.	Jan. 2,1989	Resigned; elected Vice President.

Departures from the Senate:	Majority		Minority	
Retired	Stennis, John C.	Miss. Dem	None	
Departures from Committee:				
Moved to Appropriations; Budget	None		Gramm, W. Phil	Tex. Rep
Moved to Environment & Public Works; Foreign Relations	None		Humphrey, Gordon J.	N.H. Rep
Moved to Finance	None		Symms, Steven D.	Ida. Rep

ARMED SERVICES / 101st Congress

Service Dates of Committee Chair: Feb. 2,1989-Feb. 5,1991
Service Dates of Majority Members: Feb. 2,1989-Feb. 5,1991
Service Dates of Minority Members: Feb. 2,1989-Feb. 5,1991

Majority

Rank	Name	Party	State	Years in: Senate	Years in: Comm.
Chr	Nunn, Samuel A.	Dem	Ga.	17	17
2nd	Exon, J. James	Dem	Neb.	11	11
3rd	Levin, Carl M.	Dem	Mich.	11	11
4th	Kennedy, Edward M.	Dem	Mass.	27	7
5th	Bingaman, Jeff	Dem	N.M.	7	7
6th	Dixon, Alan J.	Dem	Ill.	9	5
7th	Glenn, John H. Jr.	Dem	Ohio	15	4
8th	Gore, Albert A. Jr.	Dem	Tenn.	5	3
9th	Wirth, Timothy E.	Dem	Colo.	3	3
10th	Shelby, Richard C.	Dem	Ala.	3	3
11th	Byrd, Robert C.	Dem	W.Va.	31	1

Minority

Rank	Name	Party	State	Years in: Senate	Years in: Comm.
RM	Warner, John W.	Rep	Va.	11	11
2nd	Thurmond, J. Strom	Rep	S.C.	34	31
3rd	Cohen, William S.	Rep	Me.	11	11
4th	Wilson, Pete	Rep	Cal.	7	7
5th	McCain, John	Rep	Ariz.	3	3
6th	Wallop, Malcolm	Rep	Wyo.	13	1
7th	Gorton, Slade	Rep	Wash.	7	1
8th	Lott, Trent	Rep	Miss.	1	1
9th	Coats, Daniel R.	Rep	Ind.	1	1

Notes: Ranking on this committee for the following member was affected by other chamber service: J. Strom Thurmond (Rep-S.C.), Ranking Minority Member, Judiciary. Thurmond served previously on this committee as a Democrat.

Departures from the Senate:	Majority	Minority	
Elected Governor	None	Wilson, Pete	Cal. Rep
Departures from Committee:			
Moved to Appropriations	None	Gorton, Slade	Wash. Rep

ARMED SERVICES / 102nd Congress

Service Dates of Committee Chair: Feb. 5,1991-Jan. 3,1993
Service Dates of Majority Members: Feb. 5,1991-Jan. 3,1993
Service Dates of Minority Members: Feb. 5,1991-Jan. 3,1993

Majority

Rank	Name	Party	State	Years in: Senate	Years in: Comm.
Chr	Nunn, Samuel A.	Dem	Ga.	19	19
2nd	Exon, J. James	Dem	Neb.	13	13
3rd	Levin, Carl M.	Dem	Mich.	13	13
4th	Kennedy, Edward M.	Dem	Mass.	29	9
5th	Bingaman, Jeff	Dem	N.M.	9	9
6th	Dixon, Alan J.	Dem	Ill.	11	7
7th	Glenn, John H. Jr.	Dem	Ohio	17	6
8th	Gore, Albert A. Jr.	Dem	Tenn.	7	5
9th	Wirth, Timothy E.	Dem	Colo.	5	5
10th	Shelby, Richard C.	Dem	Ala.	5	5
11th	Byrd, Robert C.	Dem	W.Va.	33	3

Minority

Rank	Name	Party	State	Years in: Senate	Years in: Comm.
RM	Warner, John W.	Rep	Va.	13	13
2nd	Thurmond, J. Strom	Rep	S.C.	36	33
3rd	Cohen, William S.	Rep	Me.	13	13
4th	McCain, John	Rep	Ariz.	5	5
5th	Wallop, Malcolm	Rep	Wyo.	15	3
6th	Lott, Trent	Rep	Miss.	3	3
7th	Coats, Daniel R.	Rep	Ind.	3	3
8th	Mack, Connie III	Rep	Fla.	3	1
9th	Smith, Robert C.	Rep	N.H.	1	1

Notes: Ranking on this committee for the following member was affected by other chamber service: J. Strom Thurmond (Rep-S.C.), Ranking Minority Member, Judiciary. Thurmond served previously on this committee as a Democrat.

BANKING, HOUSING, AND URBAN AFFAIRS

BANKING AND CURRENCY

Jurisdiction, 1947

Established by the Legislative Reorganization Act of 1946:

[Section 102.(1)(d)]

Committee on Banking and Currency, to consist of thirteen Senators, to which committee shall be referred all proposed legislation, messages, petitions, memorials, and other matters relating to the following subjects:

1. Banking and currency generally.
2. Financial aid to commerce and industry, other than matters relating to such aid which are specifically assigned to other committees under this rule.
3. Deposit insurance.
4. Public and private housing.
5. Federal Reserve System.
6. Gold and silver, including the coinage thereof.
7. Issuance of notes and redemption thereof.
8. Valuation and revaluation of the dollar.
9. Control of prices of commodities, rents, or services.

BANKING, HOUSING, AND URBAN AFFAIRS

Renamed the Committee on Banking, Housing, and Urban Affairs on October 26, 1970.

Jurisdiction, 1992

Jurisdiction contained in the Standing Rules of the Senate (as revised to March 18, 1992):

[Rule XXV.(1)(d)]

(1) Committee on Banking, Housing, and Urban Affairs, to which committee shall be referred all proposed legislation, messages, petitions, memorials, and other matters relating to the following subjects:

1. Banks, banking, and financial institutions.
2. Control of prices of commodities, rents, and services.
3. Deposit insurance.
4. Economic stabilization and defense production.
5. Export and foreign trade promotion.
6. Export controls.
7. Federal monetary policy, including Federal Reserve System.
8. Financial aid to commerce and industry.
9. Issuance and redemption of notes.
10. Money and credit, including currency and coinage.
11. Nursing home construction.
12. Public and private housing (including veterans' housing).
13. Renegotiation of Government contracts.
14. Urban development and urban mass transit.

(2) Such committee shall also study and review, on a comprehensive basis, matters relating to international economic policy as it affects United States monetary affairs, credit, and financial institutions; economic growth, urban affairs, and credit, and report thereon from time to time.

BANKING AND CURRENCY / 80th Congress

Service Dates of Committee Chair: Jan. 6,1947-Jan. 10,1949
Service Dates of Majority Members: Jan. 6,1947-Jan. 10,1949
Service Dates of Minority Members: Jan. 8,1947-Jan. 10,1949

Majority

Rank Name	Party	State	Years in: Senate	Years in: Comm.
Chr Tobey, Charles W.	Rep	N.H.	9	8
2nd Buck, C. Douglass	Rep	Del.	5	4
3rd Capehart, Homer E.	Rep	Ind.	3	2
4th Flanders, Ralph E.	Rep	Vt.	1	1
5th Cain, Harry P.	Rep	Wash.	1	1
6th Bricker, John W.	Rep	Ohio	1	1
7th McCarthy, Joseph R.	Rep	Wisc.	1	1

Minority

Rank Name	Party	State	Years in: Senate	Years in: Comm.
RM Wagner, Robert F.	Dem	N.Y.	20	20
2nd Maybank, Burnet R.	Dem	S.C.	6	*2 1
3rd Taylor, Glen H.	Dem	Ida.	3	2
4th Fulbright, J. William	Dem	Ark.	3	2
5th Robertson, A. Willis	Dem	Va.	1	1
6th Sparkman, John J.	Dem	Ala.	1	1

*2: Member's 2nd period of service on the committee.

Note: As a result of the Reorganization Act and the 1946 elections, Burnet R. Maybank (Dem-S.C.) lost his seat on Appropriations, returned to this committee and was credited for his prior service on Banking and Currency (1943-1945) with the second minority rank.

	Majority			Minority
Departures from the Senate:				
Defeated for Reelection	Buck, C. Douglass	Del.	Rep	None
Departures from Committee:				
Moved to District of Columbia	McCarthy, Joseph R.	Wisc.	Rep	None

BANKING AND CURRENCY / 81st Congress

Service Dates of Committee Chair: Jan. 10,1949-Jan. 15,1951
Service Dates of Majority Members: Jan. 10,1949-Jan. 15,1951
Service Dates of Minority Members: Jan. 10,1949-Jan. 15,1951

Majority

Rank Name	Party	State	Years in: Senate	Years in: Comm.
Chr Maybank, Burnet R.	Dem	S.C.	8	*2 3
2nd Wagner, Robert F.	Dem	N.Y.	22	22
3rd Taylor, Glen H.	Dem	Ida.	5	5
4th Fulbright, J. William	Dem	Ark.	5	5
5th Robertson, A. Willis	Dem	Va.	3	3
6th Sparkman, John J.	Dem	Ala.	3	3
7th Frear, J. Allen Jr.	Dem	Del.	1	1
8th Douglas, Paul H.	Dem	Ill.	1	1

Minority

Rank Name	Party	State	Years in: Senate	Years in: Comm.
RM Tobey, Charles W.	Rep	N.H.	11	11
2nd Capehart, Homer E.	Rep	Ind.	5	4
3rd Flanders, Ralph E.	Rep	Vt.	3	3
4th Cain, Harry P.	Rep	Wash.	3	3
5th Bricker, John W.	Rep	Ohio	3	3

*2: Member's 2nd period of service on the committee.

Note: As a result of the Reorganization Act and the 1946 elections, Burnet R. Maybank (Dem-S.C.) lost his seat on Appropriations, returned to this committee and was credited for his prior service on Banking and Currency (1943-1945). Maybank assumed the Chairmanship of the committee due to the ill health and imminent retirement of former Chair Robert F. Wagner (Dem-N.Y.).

Changes:

Majority:

Wagner, Robert F.	Dem	N.Y.	June 28,1949	Resigned and retired.
Long, Russell B.	Dem	La.	July 26,1949	Replaced Wagner.

Minority:

Cain, Harry P.	Rep	Wash.	Jan. 12,1950	Moved to Armed Services.
Ives, Irving M.	Rep	N.Y.	Jan. 12,1950	Replaced Cain.

	Majority			Minority		
Departures from the Senate:						
Defeated for Renomination	Taylor, Glen H.	Ida.	Dem	None		
Departures from Committee:						
Moved to Armed Services; Rules & Administration	None			Flanders, Ralph E.	Vt.	Rep
Moved to Foreign Relations	None			Tobey, Charles W.	N.H.	Rep

BANKING AND CURRENCY / 82nd Congress

Service Dates of Committee Chair: Jan. 15,1951-Jan. 13,1953
Service Dates of Majority Members: Jan. 15,1951-Jan. 13,1953
Service Dates of Minority Members: Jan. 15,1951-Jan. 13,1953

Majority

Rank Name	Party	State	Years in: Senate		Years in: Comm.
Chr Maybank, Burnet R.	Dem	S.C.	10	*2	5
2nd Fulbright, J. William	Dem	Ark.	7		7
3rd Robertson, A. Willis	Dem	Va.	5		5
4th Sparkman, John J.	Dem	Ala.	5		5
5th Frear, J. Allen Jr.	Dem	Del.	3		3
6th Douglas, Paul H.	Dem	Ill.	3		3
7th Long, Russell B.	Dem	La.	3		2

Minority

Rank Name	Party	State	Years in: Senate		Years in: Comm.
RM Capehart, Homer E.	Rep	Ind.	7		6
2nd Bricker, John W.	Rep	Ohio	5		5
3rd Ives, Irving M.	Rep	N.Y.	5		2
4th Schoeppel, Andrew F.	Rep	Kans.	3		1
5th Dirksen, Everett M.	Rep	Ill.	1		1
6th Bennett, Wallace F.	Rep	Utah	1	*1	1

*1: Member's 1st period of service on the committee; *2: Member's 2nd period of service on the committee.

Notes: The death of Arthur Vandenberg (Rep-Mich.), and the appointment of Blair Moody (Dem-Mich.) to fill his vacancy on Apr. 25,1951 led to a change in size and party ratio on this committee to 8 Democrats and 6 Republicans on May 21,1951. As a result of the Reorganization Act and the 1946 elections, Burnet R. Maybank (Dem-S.C.) lost his seat on Appropriations, returned to this committee and was credited for his prior service on Banking and Currency (1943-1945).

Addition:

Majority: 8th Moody, Blair — Dem Mich. — May 21,1951

Changes:

Majority:

Name	Party	State	Date	Change
Long, Russell B.	Dem	La.	Apr. 3,1951	Moved to Armed Services.
Benton, William	Dem	Conn.	Apr. 3,1951	Replaced Long.

Minority:

Name	Party	State	Date	Change
Bennett, Wallace F.	Rep	Utah	May 21,1951	Ratio change; moved to Post Office and Civil Service.

Departures from the Senate:	**Majority**		**Minority**	
Defeated for Reelection	Benton, William	Conn. Dem	None	
Defeated for Election	Moody, Blair	Mich. Dem	None	
Departures from Committee:				
Moved to Government Operations; Judiciary; Appropriations	None		Dirksen, Everett McK.	Ill. Rep
Moved to Agriculture & Forestry; Interstate & Foreign Commerce	None		Schoeppel, Andrew F.	Kans. Rep

BANKING AND CURRENCY / 83rd Congress

Service Dates of Committee Chair: Jan. 13,1953-Jan. 11,1955
Service Dates of Majority Members: Jan. 13,1953-Jan. 11,1955
Service Dates of Minority Members: Jan. 13,1953-Jan. 11,1955

Majority

Rank Name	Party	State	Years in: Senate		Years in: Comm.
Chr Capehart, Homer E.	Rep	Ind.	9		8
2nd Bricker, John W.	Rep	Ohio	7		7
3rd Ives, Irving M.	Rep	N.Y.	7		4
4th Bennett, Wallace F.	Rep	Utah	3	*2	1
5th Bush, Prescott S.	Rep	Conn.	1		1
6th Beall, J. Glenn	Rep	Md.	1		1
7th Payne, Frederick G.	Rep	Me.	1		1
8th Goldwater, Barry M.	Rep	Ariz.	1		1

Minority

Rank Name	Party	State	Years in: Senate		Years in: Comm.
RM1 Maybank, Burnet R.	Dem	S.C.	12	*2	7
RM2 2nd Fulbright, J. William	Dem	Ark.	9		9
3rd Robertson, A. Willis	Dem	Va.	7		7
4th Sparkman, John J.	Dem	Ala.	7		7
5th Frear, J. Allen Jr.	Dem	Del.	5		5
6th Douglas, Paul H.	Dem	Ill.	5		5
7th Lehman, Herbert H.	Dem	N.Y.	4		1

*2: Member's 2nd period of service on the committee.

Note: As a result of the Reorganization Act and the 1946 elections, Burnet R. Maybank (Dem-S.C.) lost his seat on Appropriations, returned to this committee and was credited for his prior service on Banking and Currency (1943-1945).

Changes:

Ranking Member:				
RM1 Maybank, Burnet R.	Dem	S.C.	Sep. 1,1954	Died in office.
RM2 Fulbright, J. William	Dem	Ark.	Sep. 1,1954	Succeeded Maybank as Ranking Minority Member.
Minority:				
Maybank, Burnet R.	Dem	S.C.	Sep. 1,1954	Died in office.

Departures from Committee:	**Majority**	**Minority**	
Moved to Interior & Insular Affairs	None	Goldwater, Barry M.	Ariz. Rep

BANKING AND CURRENCY / 84th Congress

Service Dates of Committee Chair: Jan. 11,1955-Jan. 9,1957
Service Dates of Majority Members: Jan. 11,1955-Jan. 9,1957
Service Dates of Minority Members: Jan. 11,1955-Jan. 9,1957

Majority

Rank	Name	Party	State	Years in: Senate	Years in: Comm.
Chr	Fulbright, J. William	Dem	Ark.	11	11
2nd	Robertson, A. Willis	Dem	Va.	9	9
3rd	Sparkman, John J.	Dem	Ala.	9	9
4th	Frear, J. Allen Jr.	Dem	Del.	7	7
5th	Douglas, Paul H.	Dem	Ill.	7	7
6th	Lehman, Herbert H.	Dem	N.Y.	6	2
7th	Monroney, A. S. Mike	Dem	Okla.	5	1
Third Party					
8th	Morse, Wayne L.	Ind	Ore.	11	1

Minority

Rank	Name	Party	State	Years in: Senate	Years in: Comm.
RM	Capehart, Homer E.	Rep	Ind.	11	10
2nd	Bricker, John W.	Rep	Ohio	9	9
3rd	Ives, Irving M.	Rep	N.Y.	9	5
4th	Bennett, Wallace F.	Rep	Utah	5	*2 2
5th	Bush, Prescott S.	Rep	Conn.	3	2
6th	Beall, J. Glenn	Rep	Md.	3	2
7th	Payne, Frederick G.	Rep	Me.	3	2

*2: Member's 2nd period of service on the committee.

Note: Wayne L. Morse of Oregon was assigned to the committee by the Democratic Caucus as an Independent on Jan. 11,1955. On Feb. 17,1955, he joined the Democratic Party and became the 8th ranking member on the committee, at which time he was allowed to accrue seniority.

	Majority		**Minority**
Departures from the Senate:			
Retired	Lehman, Herbert H.	N.Y. Dem	None
Departures from Committee:			
Moved to Labor and Public Welfare	Morse, Wayne L.	Ore. Dem	None

BANKING AND CURRENCY / 85th Congress

Service Dates of Committee Chair: Jan. 9,1957-Jan. 14,1959
Service Dates of Majority Members: Jan. 9,1957-Jan. 14,1959
Service Dates of Minority Members: Jan. 9,1957-Jan. 20,1959

Majority

Rank	Name	Party	State	Years in: Senate	Years in: Comm.
Chr	Fulbright, J. William	Dem	Ark.	13	12
2nd	Robertson, A. Willis	Dem	Va.	11	11
3rd	Sparkman, John J.	Dem	Ala.	11	11
4th	Frear, J. Allen Jr.	Dem	Del.	9	8
5th	Douglas, Paul H.	Dem	Ill.	9	8
6th	Monroney, A. S. Mike	Dem	Okla.	7	2
7th	Lausche, Frank J.	Dem	Ohio	1	1
8th	Clark, Joseph S.	Dem	Penn.	1	1

Minority

Rank	Name	Party	State	Years in: Senate	Years in: Comm.
RM	Capehart, Homer E.	Rep	Ind.	13	12
2nd	Bricker, John W.	Rep	Ohio	11	11
3rd	Ives, Irving M.	Rep	N.Y.	11	7
4th	Bennett, Wallace F.	Rep	Utah	7	*2 4
5th	Bush, Prescott S.	Rep	Conn.	5	4
6th	Beall, J. Glenn	Rep	Md.	5	4
7th	Payne, Frederick G.	Rep	Me.	5	4

*2: Member's 2nd period of service on the committee.

Changes:

Majority:

Lausche, Frank J.	Dem	Ohio	Aug. 30,1957	Moved later to Government Operations.
Proxmire, William	Dem	Wisc.	Aug. 30,1957	Replaced Lausche.

Minority:

Ives, Irving M.	Rep	N.Y.	May 22,1957	Moved to Appropriations.
Case, Clifford P.	Rep	N.J.	May 22,1957	Replaced Ives.

	Majority			Minority		
Departures from the Senate:						
Defeated for Reelection	None			Bricker, John W.	Ohio	Rep
				Payne, Frederick G.	Me.	Rep
Departures from Committee:						
Moved to Appropriations	Monroney, A. S. Mike	Okla.	Dem	None		
Moved to District of Columbia	None			Case, Clifford P.	N.J.	Rep

BANKING AND CURRENCY / 86th Congress

Service Dates of Committee Chairs: Ch1 Jan. 14,1959-Feb. 6,1959
Ch2 Feb. 6,1959-Jan. 10,1961
Service Dates of Majority Members: Jan. 14,1959-Jan. 10,1961
Service Dates of Minority Members: Jan. 20,1959-Jan. 13,1961

Majority

Rank Name	Party	State	Years in: Senate	Years in: Comm.
Ch1 Fulbright, J. William	Dem	Ark.	15	15
Ch2 2nd Robertson, A. Willis	Dem	Va.	13	13
3rd Sparkman, John J.	Dem	Ala.	13	13
4th Frear, J. Allen Jr.	Dem	Del.	11	11
5th Douglas, Paul H.	Dem	Ill.	11	11
6th Clark, Joseph S.	Dem	Penn.	3	3
7th Proxmire, William	Dem	Wisc.	2	2
8th Byrd, Robert C.	Dem	W.Va.	1	1
9th Williams, Harrison A. Jr.	Dem	N.J.	1	1
10th Muskie, Edmund S.	Dem	Me.	1	1

Minority

Rank Name	Party	State	Years in: Senate	Years in: Comm.
RM Capehart, Homer E.	Rep	Ind.	15	14
2nd Bennett, Wallace F.	Rep	Utah	9	*2 7
3rd Bush, Prescott S.	Rep	Conn.	7	7
4th Beall, J. Glenn	Rep	Md.	7	7
5th Keating, Kenneth B.	Rep	N.Y.	1	1

*2: Member's 2nd period of service on the committee.

Changes:

Chair:

Ch1 Fulbright, J. William	Dem	Ark.	Feb. 6,1959	Became Chair of Foreign Relations; remained on committee.
Ch2 Robertson, A. Willis	Dem	Va.	Feb. 6,1959	Succeeded Fulbright as Chair.

Minority:

Keating, Kenneth B.	Rep	N.Y.	Jan. 27,1959	Moved to Judiciary.
Javits, Jacob K.	Rep	N.Y.	Jan. 27,1959	Replaced Keating.

	Majority			Minority
Departures from the Senate:				
Defeated for Reelection	Frear, J. Allen Jr.	Del.	Dem	None
Departures from Committee:				
Moved to Armed Services	Byrd, Robert C.	W.Va.	Dem	None
Moved to Finance	Fulbright, J. William	Ark.	Dem	None

BANKING AND CURRENCY / 87th Congress

Service Dates of Committee Chair: Jan. 10,1961-Feb. 25,1963
Service Dates of Majority Members: Jan. 10,1961-Feb. 25,1963
Service Dates of Minority Members: Jan. 13,1961-Feb. 25,1963

Majority

Rank	Name	Party	State	Years in: Senate	Years in: Comm.
Chr	Robertson, A. Willis	Dem	Va.	15	15
2nd	Sparkman, John J.	Dem	Ala.	15	15
3rd	Douglas, Paul H.	Dem	Ill.	13	13
4th	Clark, Joseph S.	Dem	Penn.	5	5
5th	Proxmire, William	Dem	Wisc.	4	4
6th	Williams, Harrison A. Jr.	Dem	N.J.	3	2
7th	Muskie, Edmund S.	Dem	Me.	3	2
8th	Long, Edward V.	Dem	Mo.	1	1
9th	Neuberger, Maurine B.	Dem	Ore.	1	1
10th	Blakley, William A.	Dem	Tex.	1	1

Minority

Rank	Name	Party	State	Years in: Senate	Years in: Comm.
RM	Capehart, Homer E.	Rep	Ind.	17	16
2nd	Bennett, Wallace F.	Rep	Utah	11	*2 9
3rd	Bush, Prescott S.	Rep	Conn.	9	9
4th	Beall, J. Glenn	Rep	Md.	9	9
5th	Javits, Jacob K.	Rep	N.Y.	5	*1 2

*1: Member's 1st period of service on the committee;
*2: Member's 2nd period of service on the committee.

Note: Appointed Senator William A. Blakley (Dem-Tex.) lost in a special election to John Tower (Rep-Tex.), whose seating on June 15,1961, led to a change in size and party ratio on this committee to 9 Democrats and 6 Republicans on July 11,1961.

Addition:

Minority: Tower, John G. Rep Tex. July 11,1961

Changes:

Majority:

Name	Party	State	Date	Action
Blakley, William A.	Dem	Tex.	June 14,1961	Resigned; defeated in special election by Tower.

Minority:

Name	Party	State	Date	Action
Javits, Jacob K.	Rep	N.Y.	Aug. 8,1962	Moved to Appropriations.
Murphy, Maurice J. Jr.	Rep	N.H.	Aug. 8,1962	Replaced Javits.
Murphy, Maurice J. Jr.	Rep	N.H.	Nov. 6,1962	Resigned; defeated for nomination in special election.

	Majority	Minority	State	Party
Departures from the Senate:				
Defeated for Reelection	None	Capehart, Homer E.	Ind.	Rep
Retired	None	Bush, Prescott S.	Conn.	Rep
Departures from Committee:				
Moved to Commerce	None	Beall, J. Glenn	Md.	Rep

BANKING AND CURRENCY / 88th Congress

Service Dates of Committee Chair: Feb. 25,1963-Jan. 8,1965
Service Dates of Majority Members: Feb. 25,1963-Jan. 8,1965
Service Dates of Minority Members: Feb. 25,1963-Jan. 15,1965

Majority

Rank	Name	Party	State	Years in: Senate	Years in: Comm.
Chr	Robertson, A. Willis	Dem	Va.	17	17
2nd	Sparkman, John J.	Dem	Ala.	17	17
3rd	Douglas, Paul H.	Dem	Ill.	15	15
4th	Clark, Joseph S.	Dem	Penn.	7	7
5th	Proxmire, William	Dem	Wisc.	6	6
6th	Williams, Harrison A. Jr.	Dem	N.J.	5	5
7th	Muskie, Edmund S.	Dem	Me.	5	5
8th	Long, Edward V.	Dem	Mo.	3	3
9th	Neuberger, Maurine B.	Dem	Ore.	3	3
10th	McIntyre, Thomas J.	Dem	N.H.	1	1

Minority

Rank	Name	Party	State	Years in: Senate	Years in: Comm.
RM	Bennett, Wallace F.	Rep	Utah	13	*2 11
2nd	Tower, John G.	Rep	Tex.	2	2
3rd	Javits, Jacob K.	Rep	N.Y.	7	*2 1
4th	Simpson, Milward L.	Rep	Wyo.	1	1
5th	Dominick, Peter H.	Rep	Colo.	1	1

*2: Member's 2nd period of service on the committee.

Departures from Committee:	Majority		Minority	
Moved to Foreign Relations	Clark, Joseph S.	Penn. Dem	None	
Moved to Commerce; Labor & Public Welfare	None		Dominick, Peter H.	Colo. Rep
Moved to Judiciary	None		Javits, Jacob K.	N.Y. Rep
Moved to Post Office & Civil Service Government Operations	None		Simpson, Milward L.	Wyo. Rep

BANKING AND CURRENCY / 89th Congress

Service Dates of Committee Chair: Jan. 8,1965-Dec. 30,1966
Service Dates of Majority Members: Jan. 8,1965-Jan. 11,1967
Service Dates of Minority Members: Jan. 15,1965-Jan. 16,1967

Majority

Rank	Name	Party	State	Years in: Senate	Years in: Comm.
Chr	Robertson, A. Willis	Dem	Va.	19	19
2nd	Sparkman, John J.	Dem	Ala.	19	19
3rd	Douglas, Paul H.	Dem	Ill.	17	16
4th	Proxmire, William	Dem	Wisc.	8	8
5th	Williams, Harrison A. Jr.	Dem	N.J.	7	6
6th	Muskie, Edmund S.	Dem	Me.	7	6
7th	Long, Edward V.	Dem	Mo.	5	4
8th	Neuberger, Maurine B.	Dem	Ore.	5	4
9th	McIntyre, Thomas J.	Dem	N.H.	3	2
10th	Mondale, Walter F.	DFL	Minn.	1	1

Minority

Rank	Name	Party	State	Years in: Senate	Years in: Comm.
RM	Bennett, Wallace F.	Rep	Utah	15	*2 13
2nd	Tower, John G.	Rep	Tex.	4	4
3rd	Thurmond, J. Strom	Rep	S.C.	10	1
4th	Hickenlooper, Bourke B.	Rep	Iowa	21	*2 1

*2: Member's 2nd period of service on the committee.

Changes:

Majority:

Name	Party	State	Date	Reason
Robertson, A. Willis	Dem	Va.	Dec. 30,1966	Resigned; defeated for renomination.

Departures from the Senate:	Majority		Minority	
Defeated for Reelection	Douglas, Paul H.	Ill. Dem	None	
Retired	Neuberger, Maurine B.	Ore. Dem	None	
Departures from Committee:				
Moved to Judiciary	None		Thurmond, J. Strom	S.C. Rep

BANKING AND CURRENCY / 90th Congress

Service Dates of Committee Chair: Jan. 11,1967-Jan. 14,1969
Service Dates of Majority Members: Jan. 11,1967-Jan. 14,1969
Service Dates of Minority Members: Jan. 16,1967-Jan. 14,1969

Majority

Rank	Name	Party	State	Years in: Senate	Years in: Comm.
Chr	Sparkman, John J.	Dem	Ala.	21	21
2nd	Proxmire, William	Dem	Wisc.	10	10
3rd	Williams, Harrison A. Jr.	Dem	N.J.	9	8
4th	Muskie, Edmund S.	Dem	Me.	9	8
5th	Long, Edward V.	Dem	Mo.	7	7
6th	McIntyre, Thomas J.	Dem	N.H.	5	4
7th	Mondale, Walter F.	DFL	Minn.	3	3
8th	McGee, Gale W.	Dem	Wyo.	9	1
9th	Spong, William B. Jr.	Dem	Va.	1	1

Minority

Rank	Name	Party	State	Years in: Senate	Years in: Comm.
RM	Bennett, Wallace F.	Rep	Utah	17	*2 15
2nd	Tower, John G.	Rep	Tex.	6	6
3rd	Hickenlooper, Bourke B.	Rep	Iowa	23	*2 3
4th	Brooke, Edward W.	Rep	Mass.	1	1
5th	Percy, Charles H.	Rep	Ill.	1	1

*2: Member's 2nd period of service on the committee.

Changes:

Majority:

Name	Party	State	Date	Reason
Long, Edward V.	Dem	Mo.	Dec. 27,1968	Resigned; defeated for renomination.

Departures from the Senate:	Majority	Minority	
Retired	None	Hickenlooper, Bourke B.	Iowa Rep

Departures from Committee:

Moved to Foreign Relations	McGee, Gale W.	Wyo.	Dem	None
Moved to Commerce	Spong, William B. Jr.	Va.	Dem	None

BANKING AND CURRENCY / 91st Congress

* Renamed the Committee on BANKING, HOUSING, AND URBAN AFFAIRS on Oct. 26,1970.

Service Dates of Committee Chair: Jan. 14,1969-Jan. 28,1971
Service Dates of Majority Members: Jan. 14,1969-Jan. 28,1971
Service Dates of Minority Members: Jan. 14,1969-Jan. 29,1971

Majority

Rank	Name	Party	State	Years in: Senate	Years in: Comm.
Chr	Sparkman, John J.	Dem	Ala.	23	23
2nd	Proxmire, William	Dem	Wisc.	12	12
3rd	Williams, Harrison A. Jr.	Dem	N.J.	11	11
4th	Muskie, Edmund S.	Dem	Me.	11	11
5th	McIntyre, Thomas J.	Dem	N.H.	7	6
6th	Mondale, Walter F.	DFL	Minn.	5	5
7th	Hollings, Ernest F.	Dem	S.C.	3	1
8th	Hughes, Harold E.	Dem	Iowa	1	1
9th	Cranston, Alan	Dem	Cal.	1	1

Minority

Rank	Name	Party	State	Years in: Senate	Years in: Comm.
RM	Bennett, Wallace F.	Rep	Utah	19	*2 17
2nd	Tower, John G.	Rep	Tex.	8	8
3rd	Brooke, Edward W.	Rep	Mass.	3	2
4th	Percy, Charles H.	Rep	Ill.	3	2
5th	Goodell, Charles E.	Rep	N.Y.	1	1
6th	Packwood, Robert W.	Rep	Ore.	1	1

*2: Member's 2nd period of service on the committee.

	Majority			Minority		
Departures from the Senate:						
Defeated for Election	None			Goodell, Charles E.	N.Y.	Rep
Departures from Committee:						
Moved to Appropriations	Hollings, Ernest F.	S.C.	Dem	Percy, Charles H.	Ill.	Rep
Moved to Armed Services; Veterans' Affairs	Hughes, Harold E.	Iowa	Dem	None		
Moved to Foreign Relations	Muskie, Edmund S.	Me.	Dem	None		

BANKING, HOUSING, AND URBAN AFFAIRS / 92nd Congress

Service Dates of Committee Chair: Jan. 28,1971-Jan. 4,1973
Service Dates of Majority Members: Jan. 28,1971-Jan. 4,1973
Service Dates of Minority Members: Jan. 29,1971-Jan. 12,1973

Majority

Rank	Name	Party	State	Years in: Senate	Years in: Comm.
Chr	Sparkman, John J.	Dem	Ala.	25	25
2nd	Proxmire, William	Dem	Wisc.	14	14
3rd	Williams, Harrison A. Jr.	Dem	N.J.	13	13
4th	McIntyre, Thomas J.	Dem	N.H.	9	8
5th	Mondale, Walter F.	DFL	Minn.	7	7
6th	Cranston, Alan	Dem	Cal.	3	3
7th	Stevenson, Adlai E. III	Dem	Ill.	1	1
8th	Gambrell, David H.	Dem	Ga.	1	1

Minority

Rank	Name	Party	State	Years in: Senate	Years in: Comm.
RM	Tower, John G.	Rep	Tex.	10	10
2nd	Bennett, Wallace F.	Rep	Utah	21	*2 19
3rd	Brooke, Edward W.	Rep	Mass.	5	5
4th	Packwood, Robert W.	Rep	Ore.	3	3
5th	Roth, William V. Jr.	Rep	Del.	1	1
6th	Brock, William E. III	Rep	Tenn.	1	1
7th	Taft, Robert Jr.	Rep	Ohio	1	1

*2: Member's 2nd period of service on the committee.

Note: Ranking on this committee for the following member was affected by other chamber service: Wallace F. Bennett (Rep-Utah), Ranking Minority Member, Finance.

Vacancy Filled:
Majority: 8th seat by Gambrell on Feb. 2,1971.

Changes:
Majority:

Gambrell, David H.	Dem	Ga.	Nov. 7,1972	Resigned; defeated for nomination in special election.

Departures from Committee:	Majority		Minority	
Moved to Finance; Budget	Mondale, Walter F.	Minn. DFL	None	
Moved to Finance	None		Roth, William V. Jr.	Del. Rep

BANKING, HOUSING, AND URBAN AFFAIRS / 93rd Congress

Service Dates of Committee Chair: Jan. 4,1973-Jan. 17,1975
Service Dates of Majority Members: Jan. 4,1973-Jan. 17,1975
Service Dates of Minority Members: Jan.12,1973-Jan. 23,1975

Majority

Rank Name	Party	State	Years in: Senate	Years in: Comm.
Chr Sparkman, John J.	Dem	Ala.	27	26
2nd Proxmire, William	Dem	Wisc.	16	16
3rd Williams, Harrison A. Jr.	Dem	N.J.	15	14
4th McIntyre, Thomas J.	Dem	N.H.	11	10
5th Cranston, Alan	Dem	Cal.	5	4
6th Stevenson, Adlai E. III	Dem	Ill.	3	2
7th Johnston, J. Bennett Jr.	Dem	La.	1	1
8th Hathaway, William D.	Dem	Me.	1	1
9th Biden, Joseph R. Jr.	Dem	Del.	1	1

Minority

Rank Name	Party	State	Years in: Senate	Years in: Comm.
RM Tower, John G.	Rep	Tex.	12	12
2nd Bennett, Wallace F.	Rep	Utah	23	*2 20
3rd Brooke, Edward W.	Rep	Mass.	7	6
4th Packwood, Robert W.	Rep	Ore.	5	4
5th Brock, William E. III	Rep	Tenn.	3	2
6th Taft, Robert Jr.	Rep	Ohio	3	2
7th Weicker, Lowell P. Jr.	Rep	Conn.	3	1

*2: Member's 2nd period of service on the committee.

Notes: The resignation of William Saxbe (Rep-Ohio), and the appointment of Howard Metzenbaum (Dem-Ohio) to fill his vacancy on Jan. 21,1974, led to a change in size and party ratio on this committee to 9 Democrats and 6 Republicans on Jan. 23,1974. Ranking on this committee for the following member was affected by other chamber service: Wallace F. Bennett (Rep-Utah), Ranking Minority Member, Finance.

Changes:
Minority:

Taft, Robert Jr.	Rep	Ohio	Jan. 23,1974	Ratio change; moved to Armed Services.
Bennett, Wallace F.	Rep	Utah	Dec. 20,1974	Resigned and retired.

Departures from Committee:	Majority		Minority	
Moved to Finance	Hathaway, William D.	Me. Dem	Brock, William E. III	Tenn. Rep
Moved to Appropriations	Johnston, J. Bennett Jr.	La. Dem	None	
Moved to Commerce; Government Operations	None		Weicker, Lowell P. Jr.	Conn. Rep

BANKING, HOUSING, AND URBAN AFFAIRS / 94th Congress

Service Dates of Committee Chair: Jan. 17,1975-Jan. 10,1977
Service Dates of Majority Members: Jan. 17,1975-Jan. 10,1977
Service Dates of Minority Members: Jan. 23,1975-Jan. 10,1977

Majority

Rank Name	Party	State	Years in: Senate	Years in: Comm.
Chr Proxmire, William	Dem	Wisc.	18	18
2nd Sparkman, John J.	Dem	Ala.	29	29
3rd Williams, Harrison A. Jr.	Dem	N.J.	17	17
4th McIntyre, Thomas J.	Dem	N.H.	13	12
5th Cranston, Alan	Dem	Cal.	7	7
6th Stevenson, Adlai E. III	Dem	Ill.	5	4
7th Biden, Joseph R. Jr.	Dem	Del.	3	3
8th Morgan, Robert B.	Dem	N.C.	1	1

Minority

Rank Name	Party	State	Years in: Senate	Years in: Comm.
RM Tower, John G.	Rep	Tex.	14	14
2nd Brooke, Edward W.	Rep	Mass.	9	9
3rd Packwood, Robert W.	Rep	Ore.	7	7
4th Helms, Jesse A.	Rep	N.C.	3	1
5th Garn, Jake	Rep	Utah	1	1

Note: Ranking on this committee for the following member was affected by other chamber service: John J. Sparkman (Dem-Ala.), Chair, Foreign Relations.

BANKING, HOUSING, AND URBAN AFFAIRS / 95th Congress

Service Dates of Committee Chair: Jan. 10,1977-Jan. 23,1979
Service Dates of Majority Members: Jan. 10,1977-Jan. 23,1979
Service Dates of Minority Members: Jan. 10,1977-Jan. 23,1979

Majority

Rank Name	Party	State	Years in: Senate	Years in: Comm.
Chr Proxmire, William	Dem	Wisc.	20	20
2nd Sparkman, John J.	Dem	Ala.	31	31
3rd Williams, Harrison A. Jr.	Dem	N.J.	19	18
4th McIntyre, Thomas J.	Dem	N.H.	15	14
5th Cranston, Alan	Dem	Cal.	9	8
6th Stevenson, Adlai E. III	Dem	Ill.	7	6
7th Biden, Joseph R. Jr.	Dem	Del.	5	5
8th Morgan, Robert B.	Dem	N.C.	3	2
9th Metzenbaum, Howard M.	Dem	Ohio	2	*T 1

Minority

Rank Name	Party	State	Years in: Senate	Years in: Comm.
RM1 Tower, John G.	Rep	Tex.	16	16
RM2 2nd Brooke, Edward W.	Rep	Mass.	11	10
3rd Packwood, Robert W.	Rep	Ore.	9	8
4th Helms, Jesse A.	Rep	N.C.	5	2
5th Garn, Jake	Rep	Utah	3	2
6th Wallop, Malcolm	Rep	Wyo.	1	*T 1

*T: Temporary member of the committee.

Note: Ranking on this committee for the following member was affected by other chamber service: John J. Sparkman (Dem-Ala.), Chair, Foreign Relations.

Changes:

Ranking Member:				
RM1 Tower, John G.	Rep	Tex.	Jan. 22,1977	Became Ranking Minority Member on Armed Services; remained on committee in second rank.
RM2 Brooke, Edward W.	Rep	Mass.	Jan. 22,1977	Succeeded Tower as Ranking Minority Member.
Majority:				
Biden, Joseph R. Jr.	Dem	Del.	Feb. 11,1977	Moved to Judiciary.
Metzenbaum, Howard M.	Dem	Ohio	Feb. 11,1977	Moved to Energy and Natural Resources.
Riegle, Donald W. Jr.	Dem	Mich.	Feb. 11,1977	Replaced Biden.
Sarbanes, Paul S.	Dem	Md.	Feb. 11,1977	Replaced Metzenbaum.
Minority:				
Packwood, Robert W.	Rep	Ore.	Feb. 22,1977	Moved to Commerce, Science and Transportation.
Helms, Jesse A.	Rep	N.C.	Feb. 22,1977	Moved to Armed Services.
Wallop, Malcolm	Rep	Wyo.	Feb. 22,1977	Moved to Judiciary.
Heinz, H. John III	Rep	Penn.	Feb. 22,1977	Replaced Packwood.
Lugar, Richard G.	Rep	Ind.	Feb. 22,1977	Replaced Helms.
Schmitt, Harrison H.	Rep	N.M.	Feb. 22,1977	Replaced Wallop.

	Majority			Minority		
Departures from the Senate:						
Defeated for Reelection	McIntyre, Thomas J.	N.H.	Dem	Brooke, Edward W.	Mass.	Rep
Retired	Sparkman, John J.	Ala.	Dem	None		
Departures from Committee:						
Moved to Appropriations	None			Schmitt, Harrison H.	N.M.	Rep

BANKING, HOUSING, AND URBAN AFFAIRS / 96th Congress

Service Dates of Committee Chair: Jan. 23,1979-Jan. 5,1981
Service Dates of Majority Members: Jan. 23,1979-Jan. 5,1981
Service Dates of Minority Members: Jan. 23,1979-Jan. 5,1981

Majority

Rank Name	Party	State	Years in: Senate	Years in: Comm.
Chr Proxmire, William	Dem	Wisc.	22	22
2nd Williams, Harrison A. Jr.	Dem	N.J.	21	21
3rd Cranston, Alan	Dem	Cal.	11	11
4th Stevenson, Adlai E. III	Dem	Ill.	9	8
5th Morgan, Robert B.	Dem	N.C.	5	5
6th Riegle, Donald W. Jr.	Dem	Mich.	3	2
7th Sarbanes, Paul S.	Dem	Md.	3	2
8th Stewart, Donald W.	Dem	Ala.	1	1
9th Tsongas, Paul E.	Dem	Mass.	1	1

Minority

Rank Name	Party	State	Years in: Senate	Years in: Comm.
RM Garn, Jake	Rep	Utah	5	5
2nd Tower, John G.	Rep	Tex.	18	18
3rd Heinz, H. John III	Rep	Penn.	3	2
4th Armstrong, William L.	Rep	Colo.	1	1
5th Kassebaum, Nancy Landon	Rep	Kans.	1	*1 1
6th Lugar, Richard G.	Rep	Ind.	3	2

*1: Member's 1st period of service on the committee.

Notes: Ranking on this committee for the following member was affected by other chamber service: John G. Tower (Rep-Tex.), Ranking Minority Member, Armed Services. William L. Armstrong (Rep-Colo.) and Nancy Landon Kassebaum (Rep-Kans.) were ranked above Richard G. Lugar (Rep-Ind.) in the original roster.

Changes:

Majority:

Tsongas, Paul E.	Dem	Mass.	May 13,1980	Moved to Foreign Relations
Mitchell, George J.	Dem	Me.	May 19,1980	Replaced Tsongas.

	Majority			Minority		
Departures from the Senate:						
Defeated for Reelection	Morgan, Robert B.	N.C.	Dem	None		
	Stewart, Donald W.	Ala.	Dem			
Retired	Stevenson, Adlai E. III	Ill.	Dem	None		
Departures from Committee:						
Moved to Finance; Veterans' Affairs	Mitchell, George J.	Me.	Dem	None		
Moved to Foreign Relations	None			Kassebaum, Nancy Landon	Kans.	Rep

BANKING, HOUSING, AND URBAN AFFAIRS / 97th Congress

Service Dates of Committee Chair: Jan. 5,1981-Jan. 3,1983
Service Dates of Majority Members: Jan. 5,1981-Jan. 3,1983
Service Dates of Minority Members: Jan. 5,1981-Jan. 3,1983

Majority

Rank	Name	Party	State	Years in: Senate	Years in: Comm.
Chr	Garn, Jake	Rep	Utah	7	6
2nd	Tower, John G.	Rep	Tex.	20	20
3rd	Heinz, H. John III	Rep	Penn.	5	4
4th	Armstrong, William L.	Rep	Colo.	3	2
5th	Lugar, Richard G.	Rep	Ind.	5	4
6th	D'Amato, Alfonse M.	Rep	N.Y.	1	1
7th	Chafee, John H.	Rep	R.I.	5	*1 1
8th	Schmitt, Harrison H.	Rep	N.M.	5	*2 1

Minority

Rank	Name	Party	State	Years in: Senate	Years in: Comm.
RM1	Williams, Harrison A.Jr.	Dem	N.J.	23	22
2nd	Proxmire, William	Dem	Wisc.	24	24
3rd	Cranston, Alan	Dem	Cal.	13	12
RM2 4th	Riegle, Donald W. Jr.	Dem	Mich.	5	4
5th	Sarbanes, Paul S.	Dem	Md.	5	4
6th	Dodd, Christopher J.	Dem	Conn.	1	1
7th	Dixon, Alan J.	Dem	Ill.	1	1

*1: Member's 1st period of service on the committee; *2: Member's 2nd period of service on the committee.

Notes: The resignation of Harrison Williams (Dem-N.J.), and the appointment of Nicholas F. Brady (Rep-N.J.) to fill his vacancy on April 12, 1982, led to a change in size and party ratio on this committee to 9 Republicans and 8 Democrats. Rankings on this committee for the following members were affected by other chamber service: John G. Tower (Rep-Tex.), Chair, Armed Services; William Proxmire (Dem-Wisc.), Ranking Minority Member, Appropriations; and Alan Cranston (Dem-Cal.), Senate Minority Whip. William L. Armstrong (Rep-Colo.) was ranked above Richard G. Lugar (Rep-Ind.) in the 96th Congress.

Addition:

Majority: 9th Brady, Nicholas F. Rep N.J. Apr. 20,1982

Changes:

Ranking Member:					
RM1	Williams, Harrison A. Jr.	Dem	N.J.	Mar. 11,1982	Resigned and retired.
RM2	Riegle, Donald W. Jr.	Dem	Mich.	Apr. 20,1982	Succeeded Williams as Ranking Minority Member.
Majority:					
	Brady, Nicholas F.	Rep	N.J.	Dec. 26,1982	Resigned and retired.
Minority:					
	Williams, Harrison A. Jr.	Dem	N.J.	Mar. 11,1982	Resigned and retired.
	Sasser, James R.	Dem	Tenn.	Apr. 20,1982	Replaced Williams.

	Majority			Minority
Departures from the Senate:				
Defeated for Reelection	Schmitt, Harrison H.	N.M.	Rep	None
Departures from Committee:				
Moved to Energy & Natural Resources	Chafee, John H.	R.I.	Rep	None
No new assignment	Lugar, Richard G.	Ind.	Rep	

BANKING, HOUSING, AND URBAN AFFAIRS / 98th Congress

Service Dates of Committee Chair: Jan. 3,1983-Feb. 21,1985
Service Dates of Majority Members: Jan. 3,1983-Feb. 21,1985
Service Dates of Minority Members: Jan. 3,1983-Feb. 21,1985

Majority

Rank	Name	Party	State	Years in: Senate	Years in: Comm.
Chr	Garn, Jake	Rep	Utah	9	8
2nd	Tower, John G.	Rep	Tex.	22	22
3rd	Heinz, H. John III	Rep	Penn.	7	6
4th	Armstrong, William L.	Rep	Colo.	5	4
5th	D'Amato, Alfonse M.	Rep	N.Y.	3	2
6th	Gorton, Slade	Rep	Wash.	3	1
7th	Hawkins, Paula	Rep	Fla.	3	1
8th	Mattingly, Mack	Rep	Ga.	3	1
9th	Hecht, Chic	Rep	Nev.	1	1
10th	Trible, Paul S. Jr.	Rep	Va.	1	1

Minority

Rank	Name	Party	State	Years in: Senate	Years in: Comm.
RM	Proxmire, William	Dem	Wisc.	26	26
2nd	Cranston, Alan	Dem	Cal.	15	14
3rd	Riegle, Donald W. Jr.	Dem	Mich.	7	6
4th	Sarbanes, Paul S.	Dem	Md.	7	6
5th	Dodd, Christopher J.	Dem	Conn.	3	2
6th	Dixon, Alan J.	Dem	Ill.	3	2
7th	Sasser, James R.	Dem	Tenn.	7	1
8th	Lautenberg, Frank R.	Dem	N.J.	1	1

Note: Ranking on this committee for the following member was affected by other chamber service: John G. Tower (Rep-Tex.), Chair, Armed Services.

Changes:

Majority:

Hawkins, Paula	Rep	Fla.	Feb. 9,1984	Moved to Foreign Relations.
Humphrey, Gordon J.	Rep	N.H.	Feb. 9,1984	Replaced Hawkins.

	Majority			Minority		
Departures from the Senate:						
Retired	Tower, John G.	Tex.	Rep	None		
Departures from Committee:						
Moved to Foreign Relations	Trible, Paul S. Jr.	Va.	Rep	None		
Moved to Budget	None			Lautenberg, Frank R.	N.J.	Dem
No new assignment	Humphrey, Gordon J.	N.H.	Rep	None		

BANKING, HOUSING, AND URBAN AFFAIRS / 99th Congress

Service Dates of Committee Chair: Feb. 21,1985-Jan. 6,1987
Service Dates of Majority Members: Feb. 21,1985-Jan. 6,1987
Service Dates of Minority Members: Feb. 21,1985-Jan. 6,1987

Majority

Rank	Name	Party	State	Years in: Senate	Years in: Comm.
Chr	Garn, Jake	Rep	Utah	11	11
2nd	Heinz, H. John III	Rep	Penn.	9	8
3rd	Armstrong, William L.	Rep	Colo.	7	7
4th	D'Amato, Alfonse M.	Rep	N.Y.	5	5
5th	Gorton, Slade	Rep	Wash.	5	3
6th	Mattingly, Mack	Rep	Ga.	5	3
7th	Hecht, Chic	Rep	Nev.	3	3
8th	Gramm, W. Phil	Rep	Tex.	1	1

Minority

Rank	Name	Party	State	Years in: Senate	Years in: Comm.
RM	Proxmire, William	Dem	Wisc.	28	28
2nd	Cranston, Alan	Dem	Cal.	17	17
3rd	Riegle, Donald W. Jr.	Dem	Mich.	9	9
4th	Sarbanes, Paul S.	Dem	Md.	9	9
5th	Dodd, Christopher J.	Dem	Conn.	5	5
6th	Dixon, Alan J.	Dem	Ill.	5	5
7th	Sasser, James R.	Dem	Tenn.	9	3

	Majority			Minority
Departures from the Senate:				
Defeated for Reelection	Gorton, Slade	Wash.	Rep	None
	Mattingly, Mack	Ga.	Rep	

BANKING, HOUSING, AND URBAN AFFAIRS / 100th Congress

Service Dates of Committee Chair: Jan. 6,1987-Jan. 3,1989
Service Dates of Majority Members: Jan. 6,1987-Feb. 2,1989
Service Dates of Minority Members: Jan. 6,1987-Feb. 2,1989

Majority

Rank Name	Party	State	Years in: Senate	Years in: Comm.
Chr Proxmire, William	Dem	Wisc.	30	30
2nd Cranston, Alan	Dem	Cal.	19	18
3rd Riegle, Donald W. Jr.	Dem	Mich.	11	10
4th Sarbanes, Paul S.	Dem	Md.	11	10
5th Dodd, Christopher J.	Dem	Conn.	7	7
6th Dixon, Alan J.	Dem	Ill.	7	7
7th Sasser, James R.	Dem	Tenn.	11	5
8th Sanford, Terry	Dem	N.C.	1	1
9th Shelby, Richard C.	Dem	Ala.	1	1
10th Graham, Bob	Dem	Fla.	1	1

Minority

Rank Name	Party	State	Years in: Senate	Years in: Comm.
RM Garn, Jake	Rep	Utah	13	12
2nd Heinz, H. John III	Rep	Penn.	11	10
3rd Armstrong, William L.	Rep	Colo.	9	8
4th D'Amato, Alfonse M.	Rep	N.Y.	7	7
5th Hecht, Chic	Rep	Nev.	5	5
6th Gramm, W. Phil	Rep	Tex.	3	2
7th Bond, Christopher S.	Rep	Mo.	1	1
8th Chafee, John H.	Rep	R.I.	11	*2 1

*2: Member's 2nd period of service on the committee.

Note: The death of Edward Zorinsky (Dem-Neb.), and the appointment of David K. Karnes (Rep-Neb.) to fill his vacancy on Mar. 10,1987, led to a change in size and party ratio on this committee to 11 Democrats and 9 Republicans on May 12,1987.

Additions:

Majority:	11th Wirth, Timothy E.	Dem	Colo.	May 12,1987
Minority:	9th Karnes, David K.	Rep	Neb.	May 12,1987

	Majority		Minority	
Departures from the Senate:				
Defeated for Reelection	None		Hecht, Chic	Nev. Rep
Defeated for Election	None		Karnes, David K.	Neb. Rep
Retired	Proxmire, William	Wisc. Dem	None	
Departures from Committee:				
No new assignment	None		Chafee, John H.	R.I. Rep
			Armstrong, William L.	Colo. Rep

BANKING, HOUSING, AND URBAN AFFAIRS / 101st Congress

Service Dates of Committee Chair: Feb. 2,1989-Feb. 5,1991
Service Dates of Majority Members: Feb. 2,1989-Feb. 5,1991
Service Dates of Minority Members: Feb. 2,1989-Feb. 5,1991

Majority

Rank Name	Party	State	Years in: Senate	Years in: Comm.
Chr Riegle, Donald W. Jr.	Dem	Mich.	13	12
2nd Cranston, Alan	Dem	Cal.	21	21
3rd Sarbanes, Paul S.	Dem	Md.	13	12
4th Dodd, Christopher J.	Dem	Conn.	9	9
5th Dixon, Alan J.	Dem	Ill.	9	9
6th Sasser, James R.	Dem	Tenn.	13	7
7th Sanford, Terry	Dem	N.C.	3	3
8th Shelby, Richard C.	Dem	Ala.	3	3
9th Graham, Bob	Dem	Fla.	3	3
10th Wirth, Timothy E.	Dem	Colo.	3	2
11th Kerry, John F.	Dem	Mass.	5	1
12th Bryan, Richard H.	Dem	Nev.	1	1

Minority

Rank Name	Party	State	Years in: Senate	Years in: Comm.
RM Garn, Jake	Rep	Utah	15	15
2nd Heinz, H. John III	Rep	Penn.	13	12
3rd D'Amato, Alfonse M.	Rep	N.Y.	9	9
4th Gramm, W. Phil	Rep	Tex.	5	4
5th Bond, Christopher S.	Rep	Mo.	3	3
6th Mack, Connie III	Rep	Fla.	1	1
7th Roth, William V. Jr.	Rep	Del.	19	1
8th Kassebaum, Nancy Landon	Rep	Kans.	11	*2 1
9th Pressler, Larry L.	Rep	S.D.	11	1

*2: Member's 2nd period of service on the committee.

Note: Ranking on this committee for the following member was affected by other chamber service: Alan Cranston (Dem-Cal.), Senate Majority Whip.

	Majority	Minority	
Departures from Committee:			
No new assignment	None	Pressler, Larry L.	S.D. Rep

BANKING, HOUSING, AND URBAN AFFAIRS / 102nd Congress

Service Dates of Committee Chair: Feb. 5,1991-Jan. 3,1993
Service Dates of Majority Members: Feb. 5,1991-Jan. 3,1993
Service Dates of Minority Members: Feb. 5,1991-Jan. 3,1993

Majority

Rank	Name	Party	State	Years in: Senate	Years in: Comm.
Chr	Riegle, Donald W. Jr.	Dem	Mich.	15	14
2nd	Cranston, Alan	Dem	Cal.	23	23
3rd	Sarbanes, Paul S.	Dem	Md.	15	14
4th	Dodd, Christopher J.	Dem	Conn.	11	11
5th	Dixon, Alan J.	Dem	Ill.	11	11
6th	Sasser, James R.	Dem	Tenn.	15	9
7th	Sanford, Terry	Dem	N.C.	5	5
8th	Shelby, Richard C.	Dem	Ala.	5	5
9th	Graham, Bob	Dem	Fla.	5	5
10th	Wirth, Timothy E.	Dem	Colo.	5	4
11th	Kerry, John F.	Dem	Mass.	7	3
12th	Bryan, Richard H.	Dem	Nev.	3	3

Minority

Rank	Name	Party	State	Years in: Senate	Years in: Comm.
RM	Garn, Jake	Rep	Utah	17	17
2nd	Heinz, H. John III	Rep	Penn.	15	14
3rd	D'Amato, Alfonse M.	Rep	N.Y.	11	11
4th	Gramm, W. Phil	Rep	Tex.	7	6
5th	Bond, Christopher S.	Rep	Mo.	5	5
6th	Mack, Connie III	Rep	Fla.	3	3
7th	Roth, William V. Jr.	Rep	Del.	21	3
8th	Domenici, Pete V.	Rep	N.M.	19	1
9th	Kassebaum, Nancy Landon	Rep	Kans.	13	*2 3

*2: Member's 2nd period of service on the committee.

Notes: Alan Cranston (Dem-Cal.) left his post as Senate Majority Whip on Nov. 13,1990, due to an Ethics committee investigation. He remained on this committee in the second majority rank. Despite less committee seniority, Pete V. Domenici (Rep-N.M.) was ranked before Nancy Landon Kassebaum (Rep-Kans.).

Changes:

Minority:

Heinz, H. John III	Rep	Penn.	May 4,1991	Died in office.
Chafee, John H.	Rep	R.I.	June 4,1991	Replaced Heinz until Nov. 6,1991 (extended on Nov. 20,1991 until the convening of the 2nd Session of the 102nd Congress.)
Chafee, John H.	Rep	R.I.	Jan. 3,1992	Left committee; no new assignment.
Specter, Arlen	Rep	Penn.	Jan. 23,1992	Replaced Chafee.

BUDGET

Jurisdiction, 1974

Jurisdiction established by Public Law 93-344, the Congressional Budget and Impoundment Control Act of 1974, 93rd Congress, Second Session, July 12, 1974 (88 Statutes 297, 301):

[Section 102.(a)(2)]

Such committee shall have the duty--

(A) to report the matters required to be reported by it under titles III and IV of the Congressional Budget Act of 1974;
(B) to make continuing studies of the effect on budget outlays of relevant existing and proposed legislation and to report the results of such studies to the Senate on a recurring basis;
(C) to request and evaluate continuing studies of tax expenditures, to devise methods of coordinating tax expenditures, policies, and programs with direct budget outlays, and to report the results of such studies to the Senate on a recurring basis; and
(D) to review, on a continuing basis, the conduct by the Congressional Budget Office of its functions and duties.

Jurisdiction, 1992

Jurisdiction contained in the Standing Rules of the Senate (as revised to March 18, 1992):

[Rule XXV.(1)(e)]

(1) Committee on the Budget, to which committee shall be referred all concurrent resolutions on the budget (as defined in section 3(a)(4) of the Congressional Budget Act of 1974) and all other matters required to be referred to that committee under titles III and IV of that Act, and messages, petitions, memorials, and other matters relating thereto.

(2) Such committee shall have the duty --

(A) to report the matters required to be reported by it under titles III and IV of the Congressional Budget Act of 1974;
(B) to make continuing studies of the effect on budget outlays of relevant existing and proposed legislation and to report the results of such studies to the Senate on a recurring basis;
(C) to request and evaluate continuing studies of tax expenditures, to devise methods of coordinating tax expenditures, policies, and programs with direct budget outlays, and to report the results of such studies to the Senate on a recurring basis; and
(D) to review, on a continuing basis, the conduct by the Congressional Budget Office of its functions and duties.

BUDGET / 93rd Congress

* Created as a standing committee on July 12,1974.

Service Dates of Committee Chair: July 25,1974-Jan. 17,1975
Service Dates of Majority Members: July 25,1974-Jan. 17,1975
Service Dates of Minority Members: Aug. 7,1974-Jan. 23,1975

Majority

Rank	Name	Party	State	Years in: Senate	Years in: Comm.
Chr	Muskie, Edmund S.	Dem	Me.	16	1
2nd	Magnuson, Warren G.	Dem	Wash.	30	1
3rd	Moss, Frank E.	Dem	Utah	16	1
4th	Mondale, Walter F.	DFL	Minn.	10	1
5th	Hollings, Ernest F.	Dem	S.C.	8	1
6th	Cranston, Alan	Dem	Cal.	6	1
7th	Chiles, Lawton M. Jr.	Dem	Fla.	4	1
8th	Abourezk, James G.	Dem	S.D.	2	1
9th	Biden, Joseph R. Jr.	Dem	Del.	2	1

Minority

Rank	Name	Party	State	Years in: Senate	Years in: Comm.
RM	Dominick, Peter H.	Rep	Colo.	12	1
2nd	Young, Milton R.	Rep	N.D.	30	1
3rd	Hruska, Roman L.	Rep	Neb.	20	1
4th	Javits, Jacob K.	Rep	N.Y.	18	1
5th	Fannin, Paul J.	Rep	Ariz.	10	1
6th	Dole, Robert J.	Rep	Kans.	6	1

	Majority	Minority		
Departures from the Senate:				
Defeated for Reelection	None	Dominick, Peter H.	Colo.	Rep
Departures from Committee:				
No new assignment	None	Fannin, Paul J.	Ariz.	Rep
		Hruska, Roman L.	Neb.	Rep
		Javits, Jacob K.	N.Y.	Rep
		Young, Milton R.	N.D.	Rep

BUDGET / 94th Congress

Service Dates of Committee Chair: Jan. 17,1975-Jan. 10,1977
Service Dates of Majority Members: Jan. 17,1975-Jan. 10,1977
Service Dates of Minority Members: Jan. 23,1975-Jan. 10,1977

Majority

Rank	Name	Party	State	Years in: Senate	Years in: Comm.
Chr	Muskie, Edmund S.	Dem	Me.	17	1
2nd	Magnuson, Warren G.	Dem	Wash.	31	1
3rd	Moss, Frank E.	Dem	Utah	17	1
4th	Mondale, Walter F.	DFL	Minn.	11	1
5th	Hollings, Ernest F.	Dem	S.C.	9	1
6th	Cranston, Alan	Dem	Cal.	7	1
7th	Chiles, Lawton M. Jr.	Dem	Fla.	5	1
8th	Abourezk, James G.	Dem	S.D.	3	1
9th	Biden, Joseph R. Jr.	Dem	Del.	3	1
10th	Nunn, Samuel A.	Dem	Ga.	3	1

Minority

Rank	Name	Party	State	Years in: Senate	Years in: Comm.
RM	Bellmon, Henry	Rep	Okla.	7	1
2nd	Dole, Robert J.	Rep	Kans.	7	1
3rd	Beall, J. Glenn Jr.	Rep	Md.	5	1
4th	Buckley, James L.	Con	N.Y.	5	1
5th	McClure, James A.	Rep	Ida.	3	1
6th	Domenici, Pete V.	Rep	N.M.	3	1

Notes: Ranking on this committee for the following member was affected by other chamber service: Robert J. Dole (Rep-Kans.), Ranking Minority Member, Agriculture, Nutrition, and Forestry. James Buckley of New York was elected as a Conservative but was assigned by the Republican Conference, serving on the committee with his seniority intact.

Changes:

Majority:

Mondale, Walter F.	DFL	Minn.	Dec. 30,1976	Resigned; elected Vice President.

	Majority			Minority		
Departures from the Senate:						
Defeated for Reelection	Moss, Frank E.	Utah	Dem	Beall, J. Glenn Jr.	Md.	Rep
				Buckley, James L.	N.Y.	Con

BUDGET / 95th Congress

Service Dates of Committee Chair: Jan. 10,1977-Jan. 23,1979
Service Dates of Majority Members: Jan. 10,1977-Jan. 23,1979
Service Dates of Minority Members: Jan. 10,1977-Jan. 23,1979

Majority

Rank	Name	Party	State	Years in: Senate	Years in: Comm.
Chr	Muskie, Edmund S.	Dem	Me.	19	3
2nd	Magnuson, Warren G.	Dem	Wash.	33	3
3rd	Hollings, Ernest F.	Dem	S.C.	11	3
4th	Cranston, Alan	Dem	Cal.	9	3
5th	Chiles, Lawton M. Jr.	Dem	Fla.	7	3
6th	Abourezk, James G.	Dem	S.D.	5	3
7th	Biden, Joseph R. Jr.	Dem	Del.	5	3
8th	Nunn, Samuel A.	Dem	Ga.	5	2

Minority

Rank	Name	Party	State	Years in: Senate	Years in: Comm.
RM	Bellmon, Henry	Rep	Okla.	9	2
2nd	Dole, Robert J.	Rep	Kans.	9	3
3rd	McClure, James A.	Rep	Ida.	5	2
4th	Domenici, Pete V.	Rep	N.M.	5	2
5th	Chafee, John H.	Rep	R.I.	1	*T 1
6th	Lugar, Richard G.	Rep	Ind.	1	*T 1

*T: Temporary member of the committee.

Notes: The committee was expanded and the party ratio was changed to 10 Democrats and 6 Republicans on Jan. 11,1977. Ranking on this committee for the following member was affected by other chamber service: Robert J. Dole (Rep-Kans.), Ranking Minority Member, Agriculture, Nutrition, and Forestry.

Additions:

Majority:	9th Anderson, Wendell R.	DFL	Minn.	Jan. 11,1977 (temporary assignment)
	10th Moynihan, Daniel Patrick	Dem	N.Y.	Jan. 11,1977 (temporary assignment)

Changes:

Majority:				
Nunn, Samuel A.	Dem	Ga.	Feb. 11,1977	Left committee; no new assignment.
Johnston, J. Bennett Jr.	Dem	La.	Feb. 11,1977	Replaced Nunn.
Moynihan, Daniel P.	Dem	N.Y.	Feb. 11,1977	Moved to Environment and Public Works.
Sasser, James R.	Dem	Tenn.	Feb. 11,1977	Replaced Moynihan.
Anderson, Wendell R.	DFL	Minn.	Dec. 29,1978	Resigned; lost special election.
Minority:				
Chafee, John H.	Rep	R.I.	Feb. 22,1977	Moved to Environment and Public Works.
Lugar, Richard G.	Rep	Ind.	Feb. 22,1977	Moved to Banking, Housing and Urban Affairs.
Hayakawa, S. I. (Sam)	Rep	Cal.	Feb. 22,1977	Replaced Chafee.
Heinz, H. John III	Rep	Penn.	Feb. 22,1977	Replaced Lugar.

	Majority			Minority		
Departures from the Senate:						
Retired	Abourezk, James G.	S.D.	Dem	None		
Departures from Committee:						
Moved to Judiciary	None			Dole, Robert J.	Kans.	Rep
Moved to Appropriations	None			McClure, James A.	Ida.	Rep
Moved to Foreign Relations	None			Hayakawa, S. I. (Sam)	Cal.	Rep
Moved to Finance	None			Heinz, H. John III	Penn.	Rep
No new assignment	Cranston, Alan	Cal.	Dem	None		

BUDGET / 96th Congress

Service Dates of Committee Chairs: Ch1 Jan. 23,1979-May 7,1980
Ch2 May 13,1980-Jan. 5,1981
Service Dates of Majority Members: Jan. 23,1979-Jan. 5,1981
Service Dates of Minority Members: Jan. 23,1979-Jan. 5,1981

Majority

Rank Name	Party	State	Years in: Senate	Years in: Comm.
Ch1 Muskie, Edmund S.	Dem	Me.	21	5
2nd Magnuson, Warren G.	Dem	Wash.	35	5
Ch2 3rd Hollings, Ernest F.	Dem	S.C.	13	5
4th Chiles, Lawton M. Jr.	Dem	Fla.	9	5
5th Biden, Joseph R. Jr.	Dem	Del.	7	5
6th Johnston, J. Bennett Jr.	Dem	La.	7	2
7th Sasser, James R.	Dem	Tenn.	3	2
8th Hart, Gary W.	Dem	Colo.	5	1
9th Metzenbaum, Howard M.	Dem	Ohio	4	1
10th Riegle, Donald W. Jr.	Dem	Mich.	3	1
11th Moynihan, Daniel Patrick	Dem	N.Y.	3	1
12th Exon, J. James	Dem	Neb.	1	1

Minority

Rank Name	Party	State	Years in: Senate	Years in: Comm.
RM Bellmon, Henry	Rep	Okla.	11	5
2nd Domenici, Pete V.	Rep	N.M.	7	5
3rd Packwood, Robert W.	Rep	Ore.	11	1
4th Armstrong, William L.	Rep	Colo.	1	1
5th Kassebaum, Nancy Landon	Rep	Kans.	1	1
6th Boschwitz, Rudolf E.	Rep	Minn.	1	1
7th Hatch, Orrin G.	Rep	Utah	3	1
8th Pressler, Larry L.	Rep	S.D.	1	1

Note: Ranking on this committee for the following member was affected by other chamber service: Warren G. Magnuson (Dem-Wash.), Chair, Appropriations.

Changes:

Chair:

Ch1	Muskie, Edmund S.	Dem	Me.	May 7,1980	Resigned; appointed Secretary of State.
Ch2	Hollings, Ernest F.	Dem	S.C.	May 13,1980	Succeeded Muskie as Chair.

Majority:

Muskie, Edmund S.	Dem	Me.	May 7,1980	Resigned; appointed Secretary of State.
Mitchell, George J.	Dem	Me.	May 19,1980	Replaced Muskie.

	Majority			Minority		
Departures from the Senate:						
Defeated for Reelection	Magnuson, Warren G.	Wash.	Dem	None		
Retired	None			Bellmon, Henry	Okla.	Rep
Departures from Committee:						
Moved to Finance	Mitchell, George J.	Me.	Dem	None		
Moved to Foreign Relations	None			Pressler, Larry L.	S.D.	Rep
No new assignment	None			Packwood, Robert W.	Ore.	Rep

BUDGET / 97th Congress

Service Dates of Committee Chair: Jan. 5,1981-Jan. 3,1983
Service Dates of Majority Members: Jan. 5,1981-Jan. 3,1983
Service Dates of Minority Members: Jan. 5,1981-Jan. 3,1983

Majority

Rank Name	Party	State	Years in: Senate	Years in: Comm.
Chr Domenici, Pete V.	Rep	N.M.	9	6
2nd Armstrong, William L.	Rep	Colo.	3	2
3rd Kassebaum, Nancy Landon	Rep	Kans.	3	2
4th Boschwitz, Rudolf E.	Rep	Minn.	3	2
5th Hatch, Orrin G.	Rep	Utah	5	2
6th Tower, John G.	Rep	Tex.	20	1
7th Andrews, Mark	Rep	N.D.	1	1
8th Symms, Steven D.	Rep	Ida.	1	1
9th Grassley, Charles E.	Rep	Iowa	1	1
10th Kasten, Robert W. Jr.	Rep	Wisc.	1	1
11th Quayle, J. Danforth	Rep	Ind.	1	1
12th Gorton, Slade	Rep	Wash.	1	1

Minority

Rank Name	Party	State	Years in: Senate	Years in: Comm.
RM Hollings, Ernest F.	Dem	S.C.	15	7
2nd Chiles, Lawton M. Jr.	Dem	Fla.	11	7
3rd Biden, Joseph R. Jr.	Dem	Del.	9	7
4th Johnston, J. Bennett Jr.	Dem	La.	9	4
5th Sasser, James R.	Dem	Tenn.	5	4
6th Hart, Gary W.	Dem	Colo.	7	2
7th Metzenbaum, Howard M.	Dem	Ohio	6	2
8th Riegle, Donald W. Jr.	Dem	Mich.	5	2
9th Moynihan, Daniel Patrick	Dem	N.Y.	5	2
10th Exon, J. James	Dem	Neb.	3	2

BUDGET / 98th Congress

Service Dates of Committee Chair: Jan. 3,1983-Feb. 21,1985
Service Dates of Majority Members: Jan. 3,1983-Feb. 21,1985
Service Dates of Minority Members: Jan. 3,1983-Mar. 5,1985

Majority

Rank Name	Party	State	Years in: Senate	Years in: Comm.
Chr Domenici, Pete V.	Rep	N.M.	11	8
2nd Armstrong, William L.	Rep	Colo.	5	4
3rd Kassebaum, Nancy Landon	Rep	Kans.	5	4
4th Boschwitz, Rudolf E.	Rep	Minn.	5	4
5th Hatch, Orrin G.	Rep	Utah	7	4
6th Tower, John G.	Rep	Tex.	22	2
7th Andrews, Mark	Rep	N.D.	3	2
8th Symms, Steven D.	Rep	Ida.	3	2
9th Grassley, Charles E.	Rep	Iowa	3	2
10th Kasten, Robert W. Jr.	Rep	Wisc.	3	2
11th Quayle, J. Danforth	Rep	Ind.	3	2
12th Gorton, Slade	Rep	Wash.	3	2

Minority

Rank Name	Party	State	Years in: Senate	Years in: Comm.
RM Chiles, Lawton M. Jr.	Dem	Fla.	13	9
2nd Hollings, Ernest F.	Dem	S.C.	17	9
3rd Biden, Joseph R. Jr.	Dem	Del.	11	9
4th Johnston, J. Bennett Jr.	Dem	La.	11	6
5th Sasser, James R.	Dem	Tenn.	7	6
6th Hart, Gary W.	Dem	Colo.	9	4
7th Metzenbaum, Howard M.	Dem	Ohio	8	4
8th Riegle, Donald W. Jr.	Dem	Mich.	7	4
9th Moynihan, Daniel Patrick	Dem	N.Y.	7	4
10th Exon, J. James	Dem	Neb.	5	4

Note: Ranking on this committee for the following member was affected by other chamber service: Ernest F. Hollings (Dem-S.C.), Ranking Minority Member, Commerce, Science, and Transportation.

	Majority			Minority		
Departures from the Senate:						
Retired	Tower, John G.	Tex.	Rep	None		
Departures from Committee:						
No new assignment	None			Biden, Joseph R. Jr.	Del.	Dem

BUDGET / 99th Congress

Service Dates of Committee Chair: Feb. 21,1985-Jan. 6,1987
Service Dates of Majority Members: Feb. 21,1985-Jan. 6,1987
Service Dates of Minority Members: Mar. 5,1985-Jan. 6,1987

Majority

Rank Name	Party	State	Years in: Senate	Years in: Comm.
Chr Domenici, Pete V.	Rep	N.M.	13	11
2nd Armstrong, William L.	Rep	Colo.	7	7
3rd Kassebaum, Nancy Landon	Rep	Kans.	7	7
4th Boschwitz, Rudolf E.	Rep	Minn.	7	7
5th Hatch, Orrin G.	Rep	Utah	9	7
6th Andrews, Mark	Rep	N.D.	5	5
7th Symms, Steven D.	Rep	Ida.	5	5
8th Grassley, Charles E.	Rep	Iowa	5	5
9th Kasten, Robert W. Jr.	Rep	Wisc.	5	5
10th Quayle, J. Danforth	Rep	Ind.	5	5
11th Gorton, Slade	Rep	Wash.	5	5
12th Danforth, John C.	Rep	Mo.	9	1

Minority

Rank Name	Party	State	Years in: Senate	Years in: Comm.
RM Chiles, Lawton M. Jr.	Dem	Fla.	15	11
2nd Hollings, Ernest F.	Dem	S.C.	19	11
3rd Johnston, J. Bennett Jr.	Dem	La.	13	9
4th Sasser, James R.	Dem	Tenn.	9	9
5th Hart, Gary W.	Dem	Colo.	11	7
6th Metzenbaum, Howard M.	Dem	Ohio	10	7
7th Riegle, Donald W. Jr.	Dem	Mich.	9	7
8th Moynihan, Daniel Patrick	Dem	N.Y.	9	7
9th Exon, J. James	Dem	Neb.	7	7
10th Lautenberg, Frank R.	Dem	N.J.	3	1

Note: Ranking on this committee for the following member was affected by other chamber service: Ernest F. Hollings (Dem-S.C.), Ranking Minority Member, Commerce, Science, and Transportation.

	Majority			Minority		
Departures from the Senate:						
Defeated for Reelection	Andrews, Mark	N.D.	Rep	None		
	Gorton, Slade	Wash.	Rep			
Retired	None			Hart, Gary W.	Colo.	Dem
Departures from Committee:						
Moved to Foreign Relations; Rules and Administration	None			Moynihan, Daniel Patrick	N.Y.	Dem
No new assignment	Hatch, Orrin G.	Utah	Rep	Metzenbaum, Howard M.	Ohio	Dem

BUDGET / 100th Congress

Service Dates of Committee Chair: Jan. 6,1987-Jan. 3,1989
Service Dates of Majority Members: Jan. 6,1987-Feb. 2,1989
Service Dates of Minority Members: Jan. 6,1987-Feb. 2,1989

Majority

Rank	Name	Party	State	Years in: Senate	Years in: Comm.
Chr	Chiles, Lawton M. Jr.	Dem	Fla.	17	13
2nd	Hollings, Ernest F.	Dem	S.C.	21	13
3rd	Johnston, J. Bennett Jr.	Dem	La.	15	10
4th	Sasser, James R.	Dem	Tenn.	11	10
5th	Riegle, Donald W. Jr.	Dem	Mich.	11	8
6th	Exon, J. James	Dem	Neb.	9	8
7th	Lautenberg, Frank R.	Dem	N.J.	5	2
8th	Simon, Paul M.	Dem	Ill.	3	1
9th	Sanford, Terry	Dem	N.C.	1	1
10th	Wirth, Timothy E.	Dem	Colo.	1	1
11th	Fowler, Wyche Jr.	Dem	Ga.	1	1
12th	Conrad, Kent	Dem	N.D.	1	1
13th	Dodd, Christopher J.	Dem	Conn.	7	1

Minority

Rank	Name	Party	State	Years in: Senate	Years in: Comm.
RM	Domenici, Pete V.	Rep	N.M.	15	12
2nd	Armstrong, William L.	Rep	Colo.	9	8
3rd	Kassebaum, Nancy Landon	Rep	Kans.	9	8
4th	Boschwitz, Rudolf E.	Rep	Minn.	9	8
5th	Symms, Steven D.	Rep	Ida.	7	7
6th	Grassley, Charles E.	Rep	Iowa	7	7
7th	Kasten, Robert W. Jr.	Rep	Wisc.	7	7
8th	Quayle, J. Danforth	Rep	Ind.	7	7
9th	Danforth, John C.	Rep	Mo.	11	2
10th	Nickles, Don	Rep	Okla.	7	1
11th	Rudman, Warren B.	Rep	N.H.	7	1

Note: Ranking on this committee for the following member was affected by other chamber service: Ernest F. Hollings (Dem-S.C.), Chair, Commerce, Science, and Transportation.

Changes:
Minority:

Quayle, J. Danforth	Rep	Ind.	Jan. 2,1989	Resigned; elected Vice President.

	Majority		Minority	
Departures from the Senate:				
Retired	Chiles, Lawton M. Jr.	Fla. Dem	None	
Departures from Committee:				
Moves to Select Intelligence	None		Danforth, John C.	Mo. Rep
Moves to Banking, Housing & Urban Affairs; Labor & Human Resources	None		Kassebaum, Nancy Landon	Kans. Rep

BUDGET / 101st Congress

Service Dates of Committee Chair: Feb. 2,1989-Mar. 19,1991
Service Dates of Majority Members: Feb. 2,1989-Mar. 19,1991
Service Dates of Minority Members: Feb. 2,1989-Mar. 19,1991

Majority

Rank	Name	Party	State	Years in: Senate	Years in: Comm.
Chr	Sasser, James R.	Dem	Tenn.	13	12
2nd	Hollings, Ernest F.	Dem	S.C.	23	15
3rd	Johnston, J. Bennett Jr.	Dem	La.	17	12
4th	Riegle, Donald W. Jr.	Dem	Mich.	13	11
5th	Exon, J. James	Dem	Neb.	11	11
6th	Lautenberg, Frank R.	Dem	N.J.	7	4
7th	Simon, Paul M.	Dem	Ill.	5	3
8th	Sanford, Terry	Dem	N.C.	3	3
9th	Wirth, Timothy E.	Dem	Colo.	3	3
10th	Fowler, Wyche Jr.	Dem	Ga.	3	3
11th	Conrad, Kent	Dem	N.D.	3	3
12th	Dodd, Christopher J.	Dem	Conn.	9	3
13th	Robb, Charles S.	Dem	Va.	1	1

Minority

Rank	Name	Party	State	Years in: Senate	Years in: Comm.
RM	Domenici, Pete V.	Rep	N.M.	17	14
2nd	Armstrong, William L.	Rep	Colo.	11	11
3rd	Boschwitz, Rudolf E.	Rep	Minn.	11	11
4th	Symms, Steven D.	Rep	Ida.	9	9
5th	Grassley, Charles E.	Rep	Iowa	9	9
6th	Kasten, Robert W. Jr.	Rep	Wisc.	9	9
7th	Nickles, Don	Rep	Okla.	9	3
8th	Rudman, Warren	Rep	N.H.	9	3
9th	Gramm, W. Phil	Rep	Tex.	5	1
10th	Bond, Christopher S.	Rep	Mo.	3	1

Note: Rankings on this committee for the following members were affected by other chamber service: Ernest F. Hollings (Dem-S.C.), Chair, Commerce, Science, and Transportation; and J. Bennett Johnston, Jr. (Dem-La.), Chair, Energy and Natural Resources.

Departures from the Senate:	Majority			Minority		
Defeated for Reelection	None			Boschwitz, Rudolf E.	Minn.	Rep
Retired	None			Armstrong, William L.	Colo.	Rep
Departures from Committee:						
Moved to Select Intelligence	None			Rudman, Warren	N.H.	Rep
No new assignment	Robb, Charles S.	Va.	Dem	None		

BUDGET / 102nd Congress

Service Dates of Committee Chair: Mar. 19,1991-Jan. 3,1993
Service Dates of Majority Members: Mar. 19,1991-Jan. 3,1993
Service Dates of Minority Members: Mar. 19,1991-Jan. 3,1993

Majority

Rank	Name	Party	State	Years in: Senate	Years in: Comm.
Chr	Sasser, James R.	Dem	Tenn.	15	15
2nd	Hollings, Ernest F.	Dem	S.C.	25	17
3rd	Johnston, J. Bennett Jr.	Dem	La.	19	15
4th	Riegle, Donald W. Jr.	Dem	Mich.	15	13
5th	Exon, J. James	Dem	Neb.	13	13
6th	Lautenberg, Frank R.	Dem	N.J.	9	7
7th	Simon, Paul M.	Dem	Ill.	7	5
8th	Sanford, Terry	Dem	N.C.	5	5
9th	Wirth, Timothy E.	Dem	Colo.	5	5
10th	Fowler, Wyche Jr.	Dem	Ga.	5	5
11th	Conrad, Kent	Dem	N.D.	5	5
12th	Dodd, Christopher J.	Dem	Conn.	11	5

Minority

Rank	Name	Party	State	Years in: Senate	Years in: Comm.
RM	Domenici, Pete V.	Rep	N.M.	19	17
2nd	Symms, Steven D.	Rep	Ida.	11	11
3rd	Grassley, Charles E.	Rep	Iowa	11	11
4th	Kasten, Robert W. Jr.	Rep	Wisc.	11	11
5th	Nickles, Don	Rep	Okla.	11	5
6th	Gramm, W. Phil	Rep	Tex.	7	3
7th	Bond, Christopher S.	Rep	Mo.	5	3
8th	Lott, Trent	Rep	Miss.	3	1
9th	Brown, Hank	Rep	Colo.	1	1

Note: Rankings on this committee for the following members were affected by other chamber service: Ernest F. Hollings (Dem-S.C.), Chair, Commerce, Science, and Transportation; and J. Bennett Johnston, Jr. (Dem-La.), Chair, Energy and Natural Resources.

COMMERCE, SCIENCE, AND TRANSPORTATION

INTERSTATE AND FOREIGN COMMERCE

Jurisdiction, 1947

Established by the Legislative Reorganization Act of 1946:

[Section 102.(1)(j)]

Committee on Interstate and Foreign Commerce, to consist of thirteen Senators, to which committee shall be referred all proposed legislation, messages, petitions, memorials, and other matters relating to the following subjects:

1. Interstate and foreign commerce generally.
2. Regulation of interstate railroads, buses, trucks, and pipe lines.
3. Communication by telephone, telegraph, radio, and television.
4. Civil aeronautics.
5. Merchant marine generally.
6. Registering and licensing of vessels and small boats.
7. Navigation and the laws relating thereto, including pilotage.
8. Rules and international arrangements to prevent collisions at sea.
9. Merchant marine officers and seamen.
10. Measures relating to the regulation of common carriers by water and to the inspection of merchant marine vessels, lights and signals, life-saving equipment, and fire protection on such vessels.
11. Coast and Geodetic Survey.
12. The Coast Guard, including lifesaving service, lighthouses, lightships, and ocean derelicts.
13. The United States Coast Guard and Merchant Marine Academies.
14. Weather Bureau.
15. Except as provided in paragraph (c) [Committee on Armed Services], the Panama Canal and interoceanic canals generally.
16. Inland waterways.
17. Fisheries and wildlife, including research, restoration, refuges, and conservation.
18. Bureau of Standards including standardization of weights and measures and the metric system.

COMMERCE

Renamed the Committee on Commerce on April 13, 1961.

COMMERCE, SCIENCE, AND TRANSPORTATION

Reorganization, 1977

The Committee was reorganized as the Standing Committee on Commerce, Science, and Transportation following the passage of Senate Resolution 4, the Committee System Reorganization Amendments of 1977, February 4, 1977.

Jurisdiction, 1977

From Senate Resolution 4, the Committee System Reorganization Amendments of 1977, February 4, 1977:

[Section (f)(1)]

Committee on Commerce, Science, and Transportation, to which committee shall be referred all proposed legislation, messages, petitions, memorials, and other matters relating to the following subjects:

1. Interstate commerce.
2. Transportation.
3. Regulation of interstate common carriers, including railroads, buses, trucks, vessels, pipelines, and civil aviation.
4. Merchant marine and navigation.
5. Marine and ocean navigation, safety, and transportation, including navigational aspects of deepwater ports.
6. Coast Guard.
7. Inland waterways, except construction.
8. Communications.
9. Regulation of consumer products and services, including testing related to toxic substances, other than pesticides, and except for credit, financial services, and housing.
10. Except as provided in paragraph (c), [Committee on Armed Services] the Panama Canal and interoceanic canals generally.
11. Standards and measurement.
12. Highway safety.
13. Science, engineering, and technology research and development and policy.
14. Nonmilitary aeronautical and space sciences.
15. Transportation and commerce aspects of Outer Continental and Shelf lands.
16. Marine fisheries
17. Coastal zone management.
18. Oceans, weather, and atmospheric activities.
19. Sports.

(2) Such committee shall also study and review, on a comprehensive basis, all matters relating to science and technology, oceans policy, transportation, communications, and consumer affairs, and report thereon from time to time.

Jurisdiction, 1992

Jurisdiction as contained in the Standing Rules of the Senate (as revised to March 18, 1992):

[Rule XXV.(1)(f)]

(1) Committee on Commerce, Science, and Transportation, to which committee shall be referred all proposed legislation, messages, petitions, memorials, and other matters relating to the following subjects:

1. Coast Guard.
2. Coastal zone management.
3. Communications.
4. Highway safety.
5. Inland waterways, except construction.
6. Interstate commerce.
7. Marine and ocean navigation, safety, and transportation, including navigational aspects of deepwater ports.
8. Marine fisheries.
9. Merchant marine and navigation.
10. Nonmilitary aeronautical and space sciences.
11. Oceans, weather, and atmospheric activities.
12. Panama Canal and interoceanic canals generally, except as provided in subparagraph (c) [Committee on Armed Services].
13. Regulation of consumer products and services, including testing related to toxic substances, other than pesticides, and except for credit, financial services, and housing.
14. Regulation of interstate common carriers, including railroads, buses, trucks, vessels, pipelines, and civil aviation.
15. Science, engineering, and technology research and development and policy.
16. Sports.
17. Standards and measurement.
18. Transportation.
19. Transportation and commerce aspects of Outer Continental Shelf lands.

(2) Such committee shall also study and review, on a comprehensive basis, all matters relating to science and technology, oceans policy, transportation, communications, and consumer affairs, and report thereon from time to time.

INTERSTATE AND FOREIGN COMMERCE / 80th Congress

Service Dates of Committee Chair: Jan. 6,1947-Jan. 3,1949
Service Dates of Majority Members: Jan. 6,1947-Jan. 10,1949
Service Dates of Minority Members: Jan. 8,1947-Jan. 10,1949

Majority

Rank	Name	Party	State	Years in: Senate	Years in: Comm.
Chr	White, Wallace H. Jr.	Rep	Me.	16	16
2nd	Tobey, Charles W.	Rep	N.H.	9	8
3rd	Reed, Clyde M.	Rep	Kans.	9	8
4th	Brewster, Ralph O.	Rep	Me.	7	6
5th	Hawkes, Albert W.	Rep	N.J.	5	4
6th	Moore, Edward H.	Rep	Okla.	5	4
7th	Capehart, Homer E.	Rep	Ind.	3	2

Minority

Rank	Name	Party	State	Years in: Senate	Years in: Comm.
RM	Johnson, Edwin C.	Dem	Colo.	11	11
2nd	Stewart, A. Tom	Dem	Tenn.	8	6
3rd	McFarland, Ernest W.	Dem	Ariz.	7	6
4th	Magnuson, Warren G.	Dem	Wash.	3	2
5th	Myers, Francis J.	Dem	Penn.	3	2
6th	McMahon, Brien	Dem	Conn.	3	2

Departures from the Senate:

	Majority		Minority	
Defeated for Renomination	None		Stewart, A. Tom	Tenn. Dem
Retired	Hawkes, Albert W.	N.J. Rep	None	
	Moore, Edward H.	Okla. Rep		
	White, Wallace H. Jr.	Me. Rep		

INTERSTATE AND FOREIGN COMMERCE / 81st Congress

Service Dates of Committee Chair: Jan. 10,1949-Jan. 15,1951
Service Dates of Majority Members: Jan. 10,1949-Jan. 15,1951
Service Dates of Minority Members: Jan. 10,1949-Jan. 15,1951

Majority

Rank	Name	Party	State	Years in: Senate	Years in: Comm.
Chr	Johnson, Edwin C.	Dem	Colo.	13	13
2nd	McFarland, Ernest W.	Dem	Ariz.	9	8
3rd	Magnuson, Warren G.	Dem	Wash.	5	5
4th	Myers, Francis J.	Dem	Penn.	5	5
5th	McMahon, Brien	Dem	Conn.	5	5
6th	O'Conor, Herbert R.	Dem	Md.	3	1
7th	Johnson, Lyndon B.	Dem	Tex.	1	1
8th	Kefauver, C. Estes	Dem	Tenn.	1	1

Minority

Rank	Name	Party	State	Years in: Senate	Years in: Comm.
RM	Tobey, Charles W.	Rep	N.H.	11	11
2nd	Reed, Clyde M.	Rep	Kans.	11	11
3rd	Brewster, Ralph O.	Rep	Me.	9	8
4th	Capehart, Homer E.	Rep	Ind.	5	5
5th	Bricker, John W.	Rep	Ohio	3	1

Changes:

Majority:

Name	Party	State	Date	Change
Kefauver, C. Estes	Dem	Tenn.	Aug. 30,1949	Moved to Judiciary.
Hunt, Lester C.	Dem	Wyo.	Aug. 30,1949	Replaced Kefauver.

Minority:

Name	Party	State	Date	Change
Reed, Clyde M.	Rep	Kans.	Nov. 8,1949	Died in office.
Williams, John J.	Rep	Del.	Jan. 12,1950	Replaced Reed.

Departures from the Senate:

	Majority		Minority
Defeated for Reelection	Myers, Francis J.	Penn. Dem	None

INTERSTATE AND FOREIGN COMMERCE / 82nd Congress

Service Dates of Committee Chair: Jan. 15,1951-Jan. 13,1953
Service Dates of Majority Members: Jan. 15,1951-Jan. 13,1953
Service Dates of Minority Members: Jan. 15,1951-Jan. 13,1953

Majority

Rank	Name	Party	State	Years in: Senate	Years in: Comm.
Chr	Johnson, Edwin C.	Dem	Colo.	15	15
2nd	McFarland, Ernest W.	Dem	Ariz.	11	10
3rd	Magnuson, Warren G.	Dem	Wash.	7	7
4th	McMahon, Brien	Dem	Conn.	7	7
5th	O'Conor, Herbert R.	Dem	Md.	5	3
6th	Johnson, Lyndon B.	Dem	Tex.	3	3
7th	Hunt, Lester C.	Dem	Wyo.	3	2

Minority

Rank	Name	Party	State	Years in: Senate	Years in: Comm.
RM	Tobey, Charles W.	Rep	N.H.	13	13
2nd	Brewster, Ralph O.	Rep	Me.	11	10
3rd	Capehart, Homer E.	Rep	Ind.	7	7
4th	Bricker, John W.	Rep	Ohio	5	3
5th	Williams, John J.	Rep	Del.	5	2
6th	Kem, James P.	Rep	Mo.	5	1

Changes:

Majority:

McMahon, Brien	Dem	Conn.	July 28,1952	Died in office.

Minority:

Brewster, Ralph O.	Rep	Me.	Dec. 31,1952	Resigned; defeated for renomination.

	Majority			Minority		
Departures from the Senate:						
Defeated for Reelection	McFarland, Ernest W.	Ariz.	Dem	Kem, James P.	Mo.	Rep
Retired	O'Conor, Herbert R.	Md.	Dem	None		
Departures from Committee:						
Moved to Agriculture & Forestry	None			Williams, John J.	Del.	Rep

INTERSTATE AND FOREIGN COMMERCE / 83rd Congress

Service Dates of Committee Chairs: Ch1 Jan. 13,1953-July 24,1953
Ch2 July 29,1953-Jan. 11,1955
Service Dates of Majority Members: Jan. 13,1953-Jan. 11,1955
Service Dates of Minority Members: Jan. 13,1953-Jan. 11,1955

Majority

Rank	Name	Party	State	Years in: Senate	Years in: Comm.
Ch1	Tobey, Charles W.	Rep	N.H.	15	15
2nd	Capehart, Homer E.	Rep	Ind.	9	9
Ch2 3rd	Bricker, John W.	Rep	Ohio	7	5
4th	Schoeppel, Andrew F.	Rep	Kans.	5	1
5th	Butler, John Marshall	Rep	Md.	3	1
6th	Cooper, John Sherman	Rep	Ky.	3	1
7th	Griswold, Dwight P.	Rep	Neb.	1	1
8th	Potter, Charles E.	Rep	Mich.	1	1

Minority

Rank	Name	Party	State	Years in: Senate	Years in: Comm.
RM	Johnson, Edwin C.	Dem	Colo.	17	17
2nd	Magnuson, Warren G.	Dem	Wash.	9	9
3rd	Johnson, Lyndon B.	Dem	Tex.	5	5
4th	Hunt, Lester C.	Dem	Wyo.	5	4
5th	Pastore, John O.	Dem	R.I.	3	1
6th	Monroney, A. S. Mike	Dem	Okla.	3	1
7th	Smathers, George A.	Dem	Fla.	3	1

Notes: Rankings on this committee were adjusted on Jan. 29,1953, with John Sherman Cooper (Rep-Ky.) and Dwight P. Griswold (Rep-Neb.) switching ranks. The rankings of the original and remaining five majority members were changed on Feb. 13,1954 to the following order: Bricker, Schoeppel, Butler, Potter and Griswold. Ranking on this committee for the following member was affected by other chamber service: Homer E. Capehart (Rep-Ind.), Chair, Banking and Currency.

Changes:

Chair:

Ch1 Tobey, Charles W.	Rep	N.H.	July 24,1953	Died in office.
Ch2 Bricker, John W.	Rep	Ohio	July 29,1953	Succeeded Tobey as Chair.

Majority:

Tobey, Charles W.	Rep	N.H.	July 24,1953	Died in office.
Capehart, Homer E.	Rep	Ind.	Jan. 13,1954	Moved to Foreign Relations.
Cooper, John Sherman	Rep	Ky.	Jan. 13,1954	Moved to Labor and Public Welfare.
Duff, James H.	Rep	Penn.	Jan. 13,1954	Replaced Tobey.
Purtell, William A.	Rep	Conn.	Jan. 13,1954	Replaced Capehart.
Payne, Frederick G.	Rep	Me.	Jan. 13,1954	Replaced Cooper.

Griswold, Dwight P.	Rep	Neb.	Apr. 12,1954	Died in office.
Bowring, Eva K.	Rep	Neb.	May 3,1954	Replaced Griswold.
Bowring, Eva K.	Rep	Neb.	Nov. 7,1954	Resigned and retired.
Abel, Hazel H.	Rep	Neb.	Nov. 30,1954	Replaced Bowring.
Abel, Hazel H.	Rep	Neb.	Dec. 31,1954	Resigned and retired.

Minority:

Hunt, Lester C.	Dem	Wyo.	June 19,1954	Died in office.
Clements, Earle C.	Dem	Ky.	July 1,1954	Replaced Hunt.

	Majority	Minority		
Departures from the Senate:				
Elected Governor	None	Johnson, Edwin C.	Colo.	Dem
Departures from Committee:				
Moved to Finance	None	Johnson, Lyndon B.	Tex.	Dem
Moved to Appropriations	None	Clements, Earle C.	Ky.	Dem

INTERSTATE AND FOREIGN COMMERCE / 84th Congress

Service Dates of Committee Chair: Jan. 11,1955-Jan. 9,1957
Service Dates of Majority Members: Jan. 11,1955-Jan. 9,1957
Service Dates of Minority Members: Jan. 11,1955-Jan. 9,1957

Majority

Rank	Name	Party	State	Years in: Senate	Years in: Comm.
Chr	Magnuson, Warren G.	Dem	Wash.	11	11
2nd	Pastore, John O.	Dem	R.I.	5	2
3rd	Monroney, A. S. Mike	Dem	Okla.	5	2
4th	Smathers, George A.	Dem	Fla.	5	2
5th	Daniel, Price M.	Dem	Tex.	3	1
6th	Ervin, Samuel J.	Dem	N.C.	1	1
7th	Bible, Alan H.	Dem	Nev.	1	1
8th	Thurmond, J. Strom	Dem	S.C.	1	*1 1

Minority

Rank	Name	Party	State	Years in: Senate	Years in: Comm.
RM	Bricker, John W.	Rep	Ohio	9	7
2nd	Schoeppel, Andrew F.	Rep	Kans.	7	2
3rd	Butler, John Marshall	Rep	Md.	5	2
4th	Potter, Charles E.	Rep	Mich.	3	2
5th	Duff, James H.	Rep	Penn.	4	1
6th	Purtell, William A.	Rep	Conn.	3	1
7th	Payne, Frederick G.	Rep	Me.	3	1

*1: Member's 1st period of service on the committee.

Note: J. Strom Thurmond (Dem-S.C.) was appointed to fill a vacancy in the Senate on Dec. 24,1954. Thurmond resigned his seat on Apr. 4,1956 in order to run for the vacancy in a special election, which he won as a write-in candidate on Nov. 7,1956. Thurmond rejoined the committee in the 85th Congress.

Changes:

Majority:

Thurmond, J. Strom	Dem	S.C.	Apr. 4,1956	Resigned; later elected to fill his own vacancy.
Wofford, Thomas A.	Dem	S.C.	Apr. 18,1956	Replaced Thurmond.
Wofford, Thomas A.	Dem	S.C.	Nov. 6,1956	Resigned and retired.

	Majority			Minority		
Departures from the Senate:						
Defeated for Reelection	None			Duff, James H.	Penn.	Rep
Departures from Committee:						
Moved to Judiciary	Ervin, Samuel J.	N.C.	Dem	None		

INTERSTATE AND FOREIGN COMMERCE / 85th Congress

Service Dates of Committee Chair: Jan. 9,1957-Jan. 14,1959
Service Dates of Majority Members: Jan. 9,1957-Jan. 14,1959
Service Dates of Minority Members: Jan. 9,1957-Jan. 20,1959

Majority

Rank	Name	Party	State	Years in: Senate	Years in: Comm.
Chr	Magnuson, Warren G.	Dem	Wash.	13	12
2nd	Pastore, John O.	Dem	R.I.	7	4
3rd	Monroney, A. S. Mike	Dem	Okla.	7	4
4th	Smathers, George A.	Dem	Fla.	7	4
5th	Daniel, Price M.	Dem	Tex.	5	2
6th	Bible, Alan H.	Dem	Nev.	3	2
7th	Thurmond, J. Strom	Dem	S.C.	2 *2	1
8th	Lausche, Frank J.	Dem	Ohio	1	1

Minority

Rank	Name	Party	State	Years in: Senate	Years in: Comm.
RM	Bricker, John W.	Rep	Ohio	11	8
2nd	Schoeppel, Andrew F.	Rep	Kans.	9	4
3rd	Butler, John Marshall	Rep	Md.	7	4
4th	Potter, Charles E.	Rep	Mich.	5	4
5th	Purtell, William A.	Rep	Conn.	5	3
6th	Payne, Frederick G.	Rep	Me.	5	3
7th	Cotton, Norris	Rep	N.H.	3 *1	1

*1: Member's 1st period of service on the committee; *2: Member's 2nd period of service on the committee.

Changes:

Majority:

Name	Party	State	Date	Action
Daniel, Price M.	Dem	Tex.	Jan. 14,1957	Resigned; elected Governor of Texas.
Blakley, William A.	Dem	Tex.	Jan. 17,1957	Replaced Daniel.
Blakley, William A.	Dem	Tex.	Apr. 28,1957	Resigned and retired.
Yarborough, Ralph W.	Dem	Tex.	May 2,1957	Replaced Blakley.

Departures from the Senate:

	Majority	Minority	
Defeated for Reelection	None	Bricker, John W.	Ohio Rep
		Payne, Frederick G.	Me. Rep
		Potter, Charles E.	Mich. Rep
		Purtell, William A.	Conn. Rep

Departures from Committee:

	Majority		Minority
Moved to Appropriations	Bible, Alan H.	Nev. Dem	None

INTERSTATE AND FOREIGN COMMERCE / 86th Congress

Service Dates of Committee Chair: Jan. 14,1959-Jan. 10,1961
Service Dates of Majority Members: Jan. 14,1959-Jan. 10,1961
Service Dates of Minority Members: Jan. 20,1959-Jan. 13,1961

Majority

Rank	Name	Party	State	Years in: Senate	Years in: Comm.
Chr	Magnuson, Warren G.	Dem	Wash.	15	15
2nd	Pastore, John O.	Dem	R.I.	9	7
3rd	Monroney, A. S. Mike	Dem	Okla.	9	7
4th	Smathers, George A.	Dem	Fla.	9	7
5th	Thurmond, J. Strom	Dem	S.C.	4 *2	3
6th	Lausche, Frank J.	Dem	Ohio	3	3
7th	Yarborough, Ralph W.	Dem	Tex.	2	2
8th	Engle, Clair	Dem	Cal.	1	1
9th	Bartlett, E. L. (Bob)	Dem	Alas.	1	1
10th	Hartke, R. Vance	Dem	Ind.	1	1
11th	McGee, Gale W.	Dem	Wyo.	1	1

Minority

Rank	Name	Party	State	Years in: Senate	Years in: Comm.
RM	Schoeppel, Andrew F.	Rep	Kans.	11	7
2nd	Butler, John Marshall	Rep	Md.	9	7
3rd	Cotton, Norris	Rep	N.H.	5 *1	3
4th	Case, Clifford P.	Rep	N.J.	5	1
5th	Morton, Thruston B.	Rep	Ky.	3	1
6th	Scott, Hugh D. Jr.	Rep	Penn.	1	1

*1: Member's 1st period of service on the committee;
*2: Member's 2nd period of service on the committee.

INTERSTATE AND FOREIGN COMMERCE / 87th Congress

* Renamed the Committee on COMMERCE on April 13,1961.

Service Dates of Committee Chair: Jan. 10,1961-Feb. 25,1963
Service Dates of Majority Members: Jan. 10,1961-Feb. 25,1963
Service Dates of Minority Members: Jan. 13,1961-Feb. 25,1963

Majority

Rank	Name	Party	State	Years in: Senate	Years in: Comm.
Chr	Magnuson, Warren G.	Dem	Wash.	17	17
2nd	Pastore, John O.	Dem	R.I.	11	8
3rd	Monroney, A. S. Mike	Dem	Okla.	11	8
4th	Smathers, George A.	Dem	Fla.	11	8
5th	Thurmond, J. Strom	Dem	S.C.	6	*2 5
6th	Lausche, Frank J.	Dem	Ohio	5	5
7th	Yarborough, Ralph W.	Dem	Tex.	4	4
8th	Engle, Clair	Dem	Cal.	3	2
9th	Bartlett, E. L. (Bob)	Dem	Alas.	3	2
10th	Hartke, R. Vance	Dem	Ind.	3	2
11th	McGee, Gale W.	Dem	Wyo.	3	2

Minority

Rank	Name	Party	State	Years in: Senate	Years in: Comm.
RM1	Schoeppel, Andrew F.	Rep	Kans.	13	9
RM2 2nd	Butler, John Marshall	Rep	Md.	11	9
3rd	Cotton, Norris	Rep	N.H.	7	*1 5
4th	Case, Clifford P.	Rep	N.J.	7	2
5th	Morton, Thruston B.	Rep	Ky.	5	2
6th	Scott, Hugh D. Jr.	Rep	Penn.	3	2

*1: Member's 1st period of service on the committee;
*2: Member's 2nd period of service on the committee.

Changes:

Ranking Member:

RM1	Schoeppel, Andrew F.	Rep	Kans.	Jan. 21,1962	Died in office.
RM2	Butler, John Marshall	Rep	Md.	Jan. 21,1962	Succeeded Schoeppel as Ranking Minority Member.

Minority:

Schoeppel, Andrew F.	Rep	Kans.	Jan. 21,1962	Died in office.
Keating, Kenneth B.	Rep	N.Y.	Feb. 2,1962	Replaced Schoeppel.
Case, Clifford P.	Rep	N.J.	July 18,1962	Moved to Armed Services.
Prouty, Winston L.	Rep	Vt.	July 18,1962	Replaced Case.

	Majority			Minority		
Departures from the Senate:						
Retired	None			Butler, John Marshall	Md.	Rep
Departures from Committee:						
Moved to Foreign Relations	Smathers, George A.	Fla.	Dem	None		
Moved to Aeronautical & Space Sciences	None			Keating, Kenneth B.	N.Y.	Rep

COMMERCE / 88th Congress

Service Dates of Committee Chair: Feb. 25,1963-Jan. 8,1965
Service Dates of Majority Members: Feb. 25,1963-Jan. 8,1965
Service Dates of Minority Members: Feb. 25,1963-Jan. 15,1965

Majority

Rank	Name	Party	State	Years in: Senate	Years in: Comm.
Chr	Magnuson, Warren G.	Dem	Wash.	19	19
2nd	Pastore, John O.	Dem	R.I.	13	11
3rd	Monroney, A. S. Mike	Dem	Okla.	13	11
4th	Thurmond, J. Strom	Dem	S.C.	8	*2 7
5th	Lausche, Frank J.	Dem	Ohio	7	7
6th	Yarborough, Ralph W.	Dem	Tex.	6	6
7th	Engle, Clair	Dem	Cal.	5	5
8th	Bartlett, E. L. (Bob)	Dem	Alas.	5	5
9th	Hartke, R. Vance	Dem	Ind.	5	5
10th	McGee, Gale W.	Dem	Wyo.	5	5
11th	Hart, Philip A.	Dem	Mich.	5	1
12th	Cannon, Howard W.	Dem	Nev.	5	1

Minority

Rank	Name	Party	State	Years in: Senate	Years in: Comm.
RM	Cotton, Norris	Rep	N.H.	9	*1 7
2nd	Morton, Thruston B.	Rep	Ky.	7	5
3rd	Scott, Hugh D. Jr.	Rep	Penn.	5	5
4th	Prouty, Winston L.	Rep	Vt.	5	1
5th	Beall, J. Glenn	Rep	Md.	11	1

*1: Member's 1st period of service on the committee;
*2: Member's 2nd period of service on the committee.

Note: J. Strom Thurmond of South Carolina resigned from the Democratic Party and joined the Repubican Party on Sep. 16,1964. The Republican Party recognized Thurmond's previous service on the committee and awarded him the 2nd minority rank on Sep. 17,1964 for the remainder of the 88th Congress.

Changes:
Majority:

Engle, Clair	Dem	Cal.	July 30,1964	Died in office.
Brewster, Daniel B.	Dem	Md.	Aug. 10,1964	Replaced Engle.

Departures from the Senate:	Majority			Minority		
Defeated for Reelection	None			Beall, J. Glenn	Md.	Rep
Departures from Committee:						
Moved to Banking & Currency	Thurmond, J. Strom	S.C.	Dem	None		
Moved to Appropriations	Yarborough, Ralph W.	Tex.	Dem	None		

COMMERCE / 89th Congress

Service Dates of Committee Chair: Jan. 8,1965-Jan. 11,1967
Service Dates of Majority Members: Jan. 8,1965-Jan. 11,1967
Service Dates of Minority Members: Jan. 15,1965-Jan. 16,1967

Majority

Rank	Name	Party	State	Years in: Senate	Years in: Comm.
Chr	Magnuson, Warren G.	Dem	Wash.	21	20
2nd	Pastore, John O.	Dem	R.I.	15	12
3rd	Monroney, A. S. Mike	Dem	Okla.	15	12
4th	Lausche, Frank J.	Dem	Ohio	9	8
5th	Bartlett, E. L. (Bob)	Dem	Alas.	7	6
6th	Hartke, R. Vance	Dem	Ind.	7	6
7th	McGee, Gale W.	Dem	Wyo.	7	6
8th	Hart, Philip A.	Dem	Mich.	7	2
9th	Cannon, Howard W.	Dem	Nev.	7	2
10th	Brewster, Daniel B.	Dem	Md.	3	1
11th	Neuberger, Maurine B.	Dem	Ore.	5	1
12th	Bass, Ross	Dem	Tenn.	1	1

Minority

Rank	Name	Party	State	Years in: Senate	Years in: Comm.
RM	Cotton, Norris	Rep	N.H.	11	*1 9
2nd	Morton, Thruston B.	Rep	Ky.	9	6
3rd	Scott, Hugh D. Jr.	Rep	Penn.	7	6
4th	Prouty, Winston L.	Rep	Vt.	7	3
5th	Pearson, James B.	Rep	Kans.	3	1
6th	Dominick, Peter H.	Rep	Colo.	3	1

*1: Member's 1st period of service on the committee.

Changes:
Majority:

McGee, Gale W.	Dem	Wyo.	Mar. 25,1966	Moved to Foreign Relations.
Long, Russell B.	Dem	La.	Mar. 25,1966	Replaced McGee.

Departures from the Senate:	Majority			Minority		
Defeated for Renomination	Bass, Ross	Tenn.	Dem	None		
Retired	Neuberger, Maurine B.	Ore.	Dem	None		
Departures from Committee:						
Moved to Armed Services	None			Dominick, Peter H.	Colo.	Rep

COMMERCE / 90th Congress

Service Dates of Committee Chair: Jan. 11,1967-Jan. 14,1969
Service Dates of Majority Members: Jan. 11,1967-Jan. 14,1969
Service Dates of Minority Members: Jan. 16,1967-Jan. 14,1969

Majority

Rank	Name	Party	State	Years in: Senate	Years in: Comm.
Chr	Magnuson, Warren G.	Dem	Wash.	23	23
2nd	Pastore, John O.	Dem	R.I.	17	14
3rd	Monroney, A. S. Mike	Dem	Okla.	17	14
4th	Lausche, Frank J.	Dem	Ohio	11	11
5th	Bartlett, E. L. (Bob)	Dem	Alas.	9	8
6th	Hartke, R. Vance	Dem	Ind.	9	8
7th	Hart, Philip A.	Dem	Mich.	9	4
8th	Cannon, Howard W.	Dem	Nev.	9	4
9th	Brewster, Daniel B.	Dem	Md.	5	3
10th	Long, Russell B.	Dem	La.	19	1
11th	Moss, Frank E.	Dem	Utah	9	1
12th	Hollings, Ernest F.	Dem	S.C.	1	1

Minority

Rank	Name	Party	State	Years in: Senate	Years in: Comm.
RM	Cotton, Norris	Rep	N.H.	13	*1 11
2nd	Morton, Thruston B.	Rep	Ky.	11	8
3rd	Scott, Hugh D. Jr.	Rep	Penn.	9	8
4th	Prouty, Winston L.	Rep	Vt.	9	5
5th	Pearson, James B.	Rep	Kans.	5	3
6th	Griffin, Robert P.	Rep	Mich.	1	1

*1: Member's 1st period of service on the committee.

Note: The death of Robert F. Kennedy (Dem-N.Y.) and the appointment of Charles Goodell (Rep-N.Y.) to fill his vacancy on Sep. 12,1968 led to a change in size and party ratio on this committee to 12 Democrats and 7 Republicans.

Addition:
Minority: 7th Hansen, Clifford P. Rep Wyo. Sep. 12,1968

Changes:
Majority:
Bartlett, E. L. (Bob) Dem Alas. Dec. 11,1968 Died in office.
Minority:
Morton, Thruston B. Rep Ky. Dec. 16,1968 Resigned and retired.

Departures from the Senate:	**Majority**			**Minority**
Defeated for Reelection	Brewster, Daniel B.	Md.	Dem	None
	Monroney, A. S. Mike	Okla.	Dem	
Defeated for Renomination	Lausche, Frank J.	Ohio	Dem	None

COMMERCE / 91st Congress

Service Dates of Committee Chair: Jan. 14,1969-Jan. 28,1971
Service Dates of Majority Members: Jan. 14,1969-Jan. 28,1971
Service Dates of Minority Members: Jan. 14,1969-Jan. 29,1971

Majority

Rank	Name	Party	State	Years in: Senate	Years in: Comm.
Chr	Magnuson, Warren G.	Dem	Wash.	25	25
2nd	Pastore, John O.	Dem	R.I.	19	17
3rd	Hartke, R. Vance	Dem	Ind.	11	11
4th	Hart, Philip A.	Dem	Mich.	11	6
5th	Cannon, Howard W.	Dem	Nev.	11	6
6th	Long, Russell B.	Dem	La.	21	3
7th	Moss, Frank E.	Dem	Utah	11	3
8th	Hollings, Ernest F.	Dem	S.C.	3	3
9th	Inouye, Daniel K.	Dem	Hai.	7	1
10th	Tydings, Joseph D.	Dem	Md.	5	1
11th	Spong, William B. Jr.	Dem	Va.	3	1

Minority

Rank	Name	Party	State	Years in: Senate		Years in: Comm.
RM	Cotton, Norris	Rep	N.H.	15	*1	13
2nd	Scott, Hugh D. Jr.	Rep	Penn.	11		10
3rd	Prouty, Winston L.	Rep	Vt.	11		7
4th	Pearson, James B.	Rep	Kans.	7		4
5th	Griffin, Robert P.	Rep	Mich.	3		2
6th	Hansen, Clifford P.	Rep	Wyo.	3		1
7th	Baker, Howard H. Jr.	Rep	Tenn.	3	*1	1
8th	Goodell, Charles E.	Rep	N.Y.	1		1

*1: Member's 1st period of service on the committee.

Changes:
Minority:
Hansen, Clifford P. Rep Wyo. Sep. 17,1969 Moved to Finance.
Cook, Marlow W. Rep Ky. Sep. 17,1969 Replaced Hansen.

Departures from the Senate:	**Majority**			**Minority**		
Defeated for Reelection	Tydings, Joseph D.	Md.	Dem	None		
Defeated for Election	None			Goodell, Charles E.	N.Y.	Rep
Departures from Committee:						
Moved to Foreign Relations	None			Scott, Hugh D. Jr.	Penn.	Rep

COMMERCE / 92nd Congress

Service Dates of Committee Chair: Jan. 28,1971-Jan. 4,1973
Service Dates of Majority Members: Jan. 28,1971-Jan. 4,1973
Service Dates of Minority Members: Jan. 29,1971-Jan. 12,1973

Majority

Rank	Name	Party	State	Years in: Senate	Years in: Comm.
Chr	Magnuson, Warren G.	Dem	Wash.	27	27
2nd	Pastore, John O.	Dem	R.I.	21	19
3rd	Hartke, R. Vance	Dem	Ind.	13	13
4th	Hart, Philip A.	Dem	Mich.	13	8
5th	Cannon, Howard W.	Dem	Nev.	13	8
6th	Long, Russell B.	Dem	La.	23	5
7th	Moss, Frank E.	Dem	Utah	13	5
8th	Hollings, Ernest F.	Dem	S.C.	5	5

Minority

Rank	Name	Party	State	Years in: Senate		Years in: Comm.
RM	Cotton, Norris	Rep	N.H.	17	*1	15
2nd	Prouty, Winston L.	Rep	Vt.	13		9
3rd	Pearson, James B.	Rep	Kans.	9		7
4th	Griffin, Robert P.	Rep	Mich.	5		5
5th	Baker, Howard H. Jr.	Rep	Tenn.	5	*1	3
6th	Cook, Marlow W.	Rep	Ky.	3		2
7th	Hatfield, Mark O.	Rep	Ore.	5		1
8th	Stevens, Theodore F.	Rep	Alas.	3	*1	1

9th Inouye, Daniel K.	Dem	Hai.	9	3	
10th Spong, William B. Jr.	Dem	Va.	5	3	*1: Member's 1st period of service on the committee.

Changes:
Minority:

Prouty, Winston L.	Rep	Vt.	Sep. 10,1971	Died in office.
Beall, J. Glenn Jr.	Rep	Md.	Sep. 21,1971	Replaced Prouty.
Hatfield, Mark O.	Rep	Ore.	Feb. 23,1972	Moved to Appropriations
Weicker, Lowell P. Jr.	Rep	Conn.	Feb. 23,1972	Replaced Hatfield.

	Majority			Minority		
Departures from the Senate:						
Defeated for Reelection	Spong, William B. Jr.	Va.	Dem	None		
Departures from Committee:						
Moved to Banking, Housing & Urban Affairs	None			Weicker, Lowell P. Jr.	Conn.	Rep

COMMERCE / 93rd Congress

Service Dates of Committee Chair: Jan. 4,1973-Jan. 17,1975
Service Dates of Majority Members: Jan. 4,1973-Jan. 17,1975
Service Dates of Minority Members: Jan.12,1973-Jan. 23,1975

Majority

Rank Name	Party	State	Years in: Senate	Years in: Comm.
Chr Magnuson, Warren G.	Dem	Wash.	29	28
2nd Pastore, John O.	Dem	R.I.	23	20
3rd Hartke, R. Vance	Dem	Ind.	15	14
4th Hart, Philip A.	Dem	Mich.	15	10
5th Cannon, Howard W.	Dem	Nev.	15	10
6th Long, Russell B.	Dem	La.	25	7
7th Moss, Frank E.	Dem	Utah	15	6
8th Hollings, Ernest F.	Dem	S.C.	7	6
9th Inouye, Daniel K.	Dem	Hai.	11	4
10th Tunney, John V.	Dem	Cal.	3	1

Minority

Rank Name	Party	State	Years in: Senate	Years in: Comm.
RM Cotton, Norris	Rep	N.H.	19 *1	17
2nd Pearson, James B.	Rep	Kans.	11	8
3rd Griffin, Robert P.	Rep	Mich.	7	6
4th Baker, Howard H. Jr.	Rep	Tenn.	7 *1	4
5th Cook, Marlow W.	Rep	Ky.	5	4
6th Stevens, Theodore F.	Rep	Alas.	5 *1	2
7th Beall, J. Glenn Jr.	Rep	Md.	3	2

*1: Member's 1st period of service on the committee.

Note: The committee size was expanded and the party ratio changed to 11 Democrats and 7 Republicans on Jan, 11,1973.

Addition:
Majority: 11th Stevenson Adlai E. III Dem Ill. Jan. 11,1973

Changes:
Minority:

Cook, Marlow W.	Rep	Ky.	Dec. 27,1974	Resigned; defeated for reelection.
Cotton, Norris	Rep	N.H.	Dec. 31,1974	Resigned and retired; returned to fill a temporary vacancy in the 94th Congress.

	Majority	Minority		
Departures from Committee:				
Moved to Foreign Relations	None	Baker, Howard H. Jr.	Tenn.	Rep

COMMERCE / 94th Congress

Service Dates of Committee Chair: Jan. 17,1975-Jan. 10,1977
Service Dates of Majority Members: Jan. 17,1975-Jan. 10,1977
Service Dates of Minority Members: Jan. 23,1975-Jan. 10,1977

Majority

Rank	Name	Party	State	Years in: Senate	Years in: Comm.
Chr	Magnuson, Warren G.	Dem	Wash.	31	31
2nd	Pastore, John O.	Dem	R.I.	25	23
3rd	Hartke, R. Vance	Dem	Ind.	17	17
4th	Hart, Philip A.	Dem	Mich.	17	12
5th	Cannon, Howard W.	Dem	Nev.	17	12
6th	Long, Russell B.	Dem	La.	27	9
7th	Moss, Frank E.	Dem	Utah	17	9
8th	Hollings, Ernest F.	Dem	S.C.	9	9
9th	Inouye, Daniel K.	Dem	Hai.	13	7
10th	Tunney, John V.	Dem	Cal.	5	3
11th	Stevenson, Adlai E. III	Dem	Ill.	5	3
12th	Ford, Wendell H.	Dem	Ky.	1	1

Minority

Rank	Name	Party	State	Years in: Senate	Years in: Comm.
RM	Pearson, James B.	Rep	Kans.	13	11
2nd	Griffin, Robert P.	Rep	Mich.	9	9
3rd	Stevens, Theodore F.	Rep	Alas.	7	*1 4
4th	Beall, J. Glenn Jr.	Rep	Md.	5	4
5th	Weicker, Lowell P. Jr.	Rep	Conn.	5	*2 1
6th	Buckley, James L.	Con	N.Y.	5	1

*1: Member's 1st period of service on the committee;
*2: Member's 2nd period of service on the committee.

Notes: James Buckley of New York was elected as a Conservative but was assigned by the Republican Conference, serving on the committee with his seniority intact. Norris Cotton (Rep-N.H.), appointed to fill a vacancy caused by the contested election between John Durkin (Dem) and Louis Wyman (Rep), was assigned the 7th minority rank on this committee, changing its size and party ratio to 12 Democrats and 7 Republicans on September 3, 1975. Cotton left the Senate upon the victory of Durkin in a special election, resulting in another change in committee size and party ratio to 13 Democrats and 7 Republicans on Sep. 19,1975.

Additions:

	Rank	Name	Party	State	Date
Majority:	13th	Durkin, John A.	Dem	N.H.	Sep. 19,1975
Minority:	7th	Cotton, Norris	Rep	N.H.	Sep. 3,1975

Changes:

	Name	Party	State	Date	Change
Majority:					
	Hart, Philip A.	Dem	Mich.	Dec. 26,1976	Died in office.
	Pastore, John O.	Dem	R.I.	Dec. 28,1976	Resigned and retired.
	Tunney, John V.	Dem	Cal.	Jan. 1,1977	Resigned; defeated for reelection.
Minority:					
	Cotton, Norris	Rep	N.H.	Sep. 17,1975	Resigned and retired.
	Baker, Howard H. Jr.	Rep	Tenn.	Sep. 19,1975	Replaced Cotton; ranked 3rd minority.

Departures from the Senate:

	Majority			Minority		
Defeated for Reelection	Hartke, R. Vance	Ind.	Dem	Beall, J. Glenn Jr.	Md.	Rep
	Moss, Frank E.	Utah	Dem	Buckley, James L.	N.Y.	Con

COMMERCE / 95th Congress

* Reorganized as the Committee on COMMERCE, SCIENCE AND TRANSPORTATION on Feb. 11,1977.

Service Dates of Committee Chair: Jan. 10,1977-Feb. 11,1977
Service Dates of Majority Members: Jan. 10,1977-Feb. 11,1977
Service Dates of Minority Members: Jan. 10,1977-Feb. 22,1977

Majority

Rank	Name	Party	State	Years in: Senate	Years in: Comm.
Chr	Magnuson, Warren G.	Dem	Wash.	33	33
2nd	Cannon, Howard W.	Dem	Nev.	19	14
3rd	Long, Russell B.	Dem	La.	29	11
4th	Hollings, Ernest F.	Dem	S.C.	11	10
5th	Inouye, Daniel K.	Dem	Hai.	15	8
6th	Stevenson, Adlai E. III	Dem	Ill.	7	4
7th	Ford, Wendell H.	Dem	Ky.	3	2

Minority

Rank	Name	Party	State	Years in: Senate	Years in: Comm.
RM	Pearson, James B.	Rep	Kans.	15	12
2nd	Griffin, Robert P.	Rep	Mich.	11	10
3rd	Baker, Howard H. Jr.	Rep	Tenn.	11	*2 2
4th	Stevens, Theodore F.	Rep	Alas.	9	*1 6
5th	Weicker, Lowell P. Jr.	Rep	Conn.	7	*2 2
6th	Schmitt, Harrison H.	Rep	N.M.	1	*T 1

8th Durkin, John A.	Dem	N.H.	2		2
9th Anderson, Wendell R.	DFL	Minn.	1	*T	1
10th Matsunaga, Spark M.	Dem	Hai.	1	*T	1
11th Moynihan, Daniel Patrick	Dem	N.Y.	1	*T	1

*1: Member's 1st period of service on the committee;
*2: Member's 2nd period of service on the committee;
*T: Temporary member of the committee.

Note: The committee size was temporarily increased to 18 members on Jan. 12,1977, and the party ratio changed to 11 Democrats and 7 Republicans.

Addition:

Minority: 7th Chafee, John H. Rep R.I. Jan. 12,1977

Changes:

Majority:

Anderson, Wendell R.	DFL	Minn.	Feb. 11,1977	Moved to Armed Services; Budget.
Matsunaga, Spark M.	Dem	Hai.	Feb. 11,1977	Moved to Energy and Natural Resources; Veterans' Affairs.
Moynihan, Daniel Patrick	Dem	N.Y.	Feb. 11,1977	Moved to Environment and Public Works.

Minority:

Baker, Howard H. Jr.	Rep	Tenn.	Feb. 22,1977	Moved to Rules and Administration.
Weicker, Lowell P. Jr.	Rep	Conn.	Feb. 22,1977	Moved to Appropriations.
Chafee, John H.	Rep	R.I.	Feb. 22,1977	Moved to Human Resources; Environment and Public Works.

COMMERCE, SCIENCE AND TRANSPORTATION / 95th Congress

Service Dates of Committee Chairs: Ch1 Feb. 11,1977-Jan. 27,1978
Ch2 Jan. 27,1978-Jan. 23,1979
Service Dates of Majority Members: Feb. 11,1977-Jan. 23,1979
Service Dates of Minority Members: Feb. 22,1977-Jan. 23,1979

Majority

Rank Name	Party	State	Years in: Senate	Years in: Comm.
Ch1 Magnuson, Warren G.	Dem	Wash.	33	33
Ch2 2nd Cannon, Howard W.	Dem	Nev.	19	19
3rd Long, Russell B.	Dem	La.	29	11
4th Hollings, Ernest F.	Dem	S.C.	11	11
5th Inouye, Daniel K.	Dem	Hai.	15	9
6th Stevenson, Adlai E. III	Dem	Ill.	7	5
7th Ford, Wendell H.	Dem	Ky.	3	3
8th Durkin, John A.	Dem	N.H.	2	2
9th Zorinsky, Edward	Dem	Neb.	1	1
10th Riegle, Donald W. Jr.	Dem	Mich.	1	1
11th Melcher, John	Dem	Mont.	1	1

Minority

Rank Name	Party	State	Years in: Senate	Years in: Comm.
RM Pearson, James B.	Rep	Kans.	16	13
2nd Griffin, Robert P.	Rep	Mich.	11	11
3rd Stevens, Theodore F.	Rep	Alas.	9	*1 7
4th Goldwater, Barry M.	Rep	Ariz.	21	9
5th Packwood, Robert W.	Rep	Ore.	9	1
6th Schmitt, Harrison H.	Rep	N.M.	1	1
7th Danforth, John C.	Rep	Mo.	1	1

*1: Member's 1st period of service on the committee.

Notes: "Years in committee" for Cannon and Goldwater include their continuous service on the Aeronautical and Space Sciences Committee. The committee size was reduced to 17 members on Jan. 27,1978, and the party ratio changed to 10 Democrats and 7 Republicans. Harrison H. Schmitt's service on the Commerce committee from Jan. 10,1977-Feb. 22,1977 was not counted toward his ranking. Theodore F. Stevens (Rep-Alas.) held his rank from the parent Commerce committee, and was ranked above Barry M. Goldwater (Rep-Ariz.).

Changes:

Chair:

Ch1 Magnuson, Warren G.	Dem	Wash.	Jan. 27,1978	Became Chair of Appropriations; remained on committee.
Ch2 Cannon, Howard W.	Dem	Nev.	Jan. 27,1978	Succeeded Magnuson as Chair.

Majority:

Melcher, John	Dem	Mont.	Jan. 27,1978	Ratio change; moved to Energy and Natural Resources.

Minority:

Pearson, James B.	Rep	Kans.	Dec. 23,1978	Resigned and retired.

	Majority		Minority	
Departures from the Senate:				
Defeated for Reelection	None		Griffin, Robert P.	Mich. Rep
Departures from Committee:				
Moved to Appropriations	Durkin, John A.	N.H. Dem	None	
Moved to Foreign Relations	Zorinsky, Edward	Neb. Dem	None	
Moved to Energy & Natural Resources	None		Stevens, Theodore F.	Alas. Rep

COMMERCE, SCIENCE AND TRANSPORTATION / 96th Congress

Service Dates of Committee Chair: Jan. 23,1979-Jan. 5,1981
Service Dates of Majority Members: Jan. 23,1979-Jan. 5,1981
Service Dates of Minority Members: Jan. 23,1979-Jan. 5,1981

Majority

Rank Name	Party	State	Years in: Senate	Years in: Comm.
Chr Cannon, Howard W.	Dem	Nev.	21	21
2nd Magnuson, Warren G.	Dem	Wash.	35	35
3rd Long, Russell B.	Dem	La.	31	13
4th Hollings, Ernest F.	Dem	S.C.	13	13
5th Inouye, Daniel K.	Dem	Hai.	17	11
6th Stevenson, Adlai E. III	Dem	Ill.	9	7
7th Ford, Wendell H.	Dem	Ky.	5	5
8th Riegle, Donald W. Jr.	Dem	Mich.	3	2
9th Exon, J. James	Dem	Neb.	1	1
10th Heflin, Howell T.	Dem	Ala.	1	1

Minority

Rank Name	Party	State	Years in: Senate	Years in: Comm.
RM Packwood, Robert W.	Rep	Ore.	11	2
2nd Goldwater, Barry M.	Rep	Ariz.	23	11
3rd Schmitt, Harrison H.	Rep	N.M.	3	3
4th Danforth, John C.	Rep	Mo.	3	2
5th Kassebaum, Nancy Landon	Rep	Kans.	1	1
6th Pressler, Larry L.	Rep	S.D.	1	1
7th Warner, John W.	Rep	Va.	1	1

Notes: "Years in committee" for Cannon and Goldwater include their continuous service on the Aeronautical and Space Sciences Committee. Rankings on this committee for the following members were affected by other chamber service: Warren G. Magnuson (Dem-Wash.), Chair, Appropriations; Barry M. Goldwater (Rep-Ariz.), Vice Chair, Select Intelligence. Previous service on the Commerce committee by Harrison H. Schmitt (Rep-N.M) from Jan. 10,1977-Feb. 22,1977 was not counted toward his ranking on this committee.

	Majority		Minority	
Departures from the Senate:				
Retired	Stevenson, Adlai E. III	Ill. Dem	None	
Defeated for Reelection	Magnuson, Warren G.	Wash. Dem	None	
Departures from Committee:				
Moved to Energy & Natural Resources; Rules and Administration	None		Warner, John W.	Va. Rep

COMMERCE, SCIENCE AND TRANSPORTATION / 97th Congress

Service Dates of Committee Chair: Jan. 5,1981-Jan. 3,1983
Service Dates of Majority Members: Jan. 5,1981-Jan. 3,1983
Service Dates of Minority Members: Jan. 5,1981-Jan. 3,1983

Majority

Rank Name	Party	State	Years in: Senate	Years in: Comm.
Chr Packwood, Robert W.	Rep	Ore.	13	4
2nd Goldwater, Barry M.	Rep	Ariz.	25	12
3rd Schmitt, Harrison H.	Rep	N.M.	5	4
4th Danforth, John C.	Rep	Mo.	5	4
5th Kassebaum, Nancy Landon	Rep	Kans.	3	2
6th Pressler, Larry L.	Rep	S.D.	3	2
7th Gorton, Slade	Rep	Wash.	1	*1 1
8th Stevens, Theodore F.	Rep	Alas.	13	*2 1
9th Kasten, Robert W. Jr.	Rep	Wisc.	1	1

Minority

Rank Name	Party	State	Years in: Senate	Years in: Comm.
RM Cannon, Howard W.	Dem	Nev.	23	23
2nd Long, Russell B.	Dem	La.	33	15
3rd Hollings, Ernest F.	Dem	S.C.	15	14
4th Inouye, Daniel K.	Dem	Hai.	19	12
5th Ford, Wendell H.	Dem	Ky.	7	6
6th Riegle, Donald W. Jr.	Dem	Mich.	5	4
7th Exon, J. James	Dem	Neb.	3	2
8th Heflin, Howell T.	Dem	Ala.	3	2

*1: Member's 1st period of service on the committee; *2: Member's 2nd period of service on the committee.

Notes: "Years in committee" for Goldwater and Cannon include their continuous service on the Aeronautical and Space Sciences Committee. Ranking on this committee for the following member was affected by other chamber service: Barry M. Goldwater (Rep-Ariz.), Chair, Select Intelligence. Previous service on the Commerce committee by Harrison H. Schmitt (Rep-N.M.) from Jan. 10,1977-Feb. 22,1977 was not counted toward his ranking.

	Majority		Minority	
Departures from the Senate:				
Defeated for Reelection	Schmitt, Harrison H.	N.M. Rep	Cannon, Howard W.	Nev. Dem

COMMERCE, SCIENCE AND TRANSPORTATION / 98th Congress

Service Dates of Committee Chair: Jan. 3,1983-Feb. 21,1985
Service Dates of Majority Members: Jan. 3,1983-Feb. 21,1985
Service Dates of Minority Members: Jan. 3,1983-Feb. 21,1985

Majority

Rank	Name	Party	State	Years in: Senate	Years in: Comm.
Chr	Packwood, Robert W.	Rep	Ore.	15	6
2nd	Goldwater, Barry M.	Rep	Ariz.	27	14
3rd	Danforth, John C.	Rep	Mo.	7	6
4th	Kassebaum, Nancy Landon	Rep	Kans.	5	4
5th	Pressler, Larry L.	Rep	S.D.	5	4
6th	Gorton, Slade	Rep	Wash.	3	*1 2
7th	Stevens, Theodore F.	Rep	Alas.	15	*2 2
8th	Kasten, Robert W. Jr.	Rep	Wisc.	3	2
9th	Trible, Paul S. Jr.	Rep	Va.	1	1

Minority

Rank	Name	Party	State	Years in: Senate	Years in: Comm.
RM	Hollings, Ernest F.	Dem	S.C.	17	16
2nd	Long, Russell B.	Dem	La.	35	17
3rd	Inouye, Daniel K.	Dem	Hai.	21	14
4th	Ford, Wendell H.	Dem	Ky.	9	8
5th	Riegle, Donald W. Jr.	Dem	Mich.	7	6
6th	Exon, J. James	Dem	Neb.	5	4
7th	Heflin, Howell T.	Dem	Ala.	5	4
8th	Lautenberg, Frank R.	Dem	N.J.	1	1

*1: Member's 1st period of service on the committee; *2: Member's 2nd period of service on the committee.

Notes: "Years in committee" for Goldwater include his continuous service on the Aeronautical and Space Sciences Committee. Rankings on the committee for the following members were affected by other chamber service: Barry M. Goldwater (Rep-Ariz.), Chair, Select Intelligence; and Russell B. Long (Dem-La.), Ranking Minority Member, Finance.

Departures from Committee:	Majority	Minority		
Moved to Appropriations; Budget	None	Lautenberg, Frank R.	N.J.	Dem
No new assignment	None	Heflin, Howell T.	Ala.	Dem

COMMERCE, SCIENCE AND TRANSPORTATION / 99th Congress

Service Dates of Committee Chair: Feb. 21,1985-Jan. 6,1987
Service Dates of Majority Members: Feb. 21,1985-Jan. 6,1987
Service Dates of Minority Members: Feb. 21,1985-Jan. 6,1987

Majority

Rank	Name	Party	State	Years in: Senate	Years in: Comm.
Chr	Danforth, John C.	Rep	Mo.	9	8
2nd	Packwood, Robert W.	Rep	Ore.	17	8
3rd	Goldwater, Barry M.	Rep	Ariz.	29	17
4th	Kassebaum, Nancy Landon	Rep	Kans.	7	7
5th	Pressler, Larry L.	Rep	S.D.	7	7
6th	Gorton, Slade	Rep	Wash.	5	*1 5
7th	Stevens, Theodore F.	Rep	Alas.	17	*2 5
8th	Kasten, Robert W. Jr.	Rep	Wisc.	5	5
9th	Trible, Paul S. Jr.	Rep	Va.	3	3

Minority

Rank	Name	Party	State	Years in: Senate	Years in: Comm.
RM	Hollings, Ernest F.	Dem	S.C.	19	19
2nd	Long, Russell B.	Dem	La.	37	19
3rd	Inouye, Daniel K.	Dem	Hai.	23	17
4th	Ford, Wendell H.	Dem	Ky.	11	11
5th	Riegle, Donald W. Jr.	Dem	Mich.	9	9
6th	Exon, J. James	Dem	Neb.	7	7
7th	Gore, Albert A. Jr.	Dem	Tenn.	1	1
8th	Rockefeller, John D. IV	Dem	W.Va.	1	1

*1: Member's 1st period of service on the committee; *2: Member's 2nd period of service on the committee.

Notes: "Years in committee" for Goldwater include his continuous service on the Aeronautical and Space Sciences Committee. Rankings on the committee for the following members were affected by other chamber service: Robert W. Packwood (Rep-Ore.), Chair, Finance; Barry M. Goldwater (Rep-Ariz.), Chair, Select Intelligence; and Russell B. Long (Dem-La.), Ranking Minority Member, Finance.

Departures from the Senate:	Majority			Minority		
Defeated for Reelection	Gorton, Slade	Wash.	Rep	None		
Retired	Goldwater, Barry M.	Ariz.	Rep	Long, Russell B.	La.	Dem

COMMERCE, SCIENCE AND TRANSPORTATION / 100th Congress

Service Dates of Committee Chair: Jan. 6,1987-Feb. 2,1989
Service Dates of Majority Members: Jan. 6,1987-Feb. 2,1989
Service Dates of Minority Members: Jan. 6,1987-Feb. 2,1989

Majority

Rank	Name	Party	State	Years in: Senate	Years in: Comm.
Chr	Hollings, Ernest F.	Dem	S.C.	21	20
2nd	Inouye, Daniel K.	Dem	Hai.	25	18
3rd	Ford, Wendell H.	Dem	Ky.	13	12
4th	Riegle, Donald W. Jr.	Dem	Mich.	11	10
5th	Exon, J. James	Dem	Neb.	9	8
6th	Gore, Albert A. Jr.	Dem	Tenn.	3	2
7th	Rockefeller, John D. IV	Dem	W.Va.	2	2
8th	Bentsen, Lloyd M. Jr.	Dem	Tex.	17	1
9th	Kerry, John F.	Dem	Mass.	3	1
10th	Breaux, John B.	Dem	La.	1	1
11th	Adams, Brock	Dem	Wash.	1	1

Minority

Rank	Name	Party	State	Years in: Senate	Years in: Comm.
RM	Danforth, John C.	Rep	Mo.	11	10
2nd	Packwood, Robert W.	Rep	Ore.	19	10
3rd	Kassebaum, Nancy Landon	Rep	Kans.	9	8
4th	Pressler, Larry L.	Rep	S.D.	9	8
5th	Stevens, Theodore F.	Rep	Alas.	19	*2 7
6th	Kasten, Robert W. Jr.	Rep	Wisc.	7	7
7th	Trible, Paul S. Jr.	Rep	Va.	5	5
8th	Wilson, Pete	Rep	Cal.	5	1
9th	McCain, John	Rep	Ariz.	1	1

*2: Member's 2nd period of service on the committee.

Note: Ranking on the committee for the following member was affected by other chamber service: Robert W. Packwood (Rep-Ore.), Ranking Minority Member, Finance.

	Majority			Minority		
Departures from the Senate:						
Retired	None			Trible, Paul S. Jr.	Va.	Rep
Departures from Committee:						
Moved to Appropriations	Adams, Brock	Wash.	Dem	None		
Became Chair of Banking, Housing & Urban Affairs	Riegle, Donald W. Jr.	Mich.	Dem	None		
Moved to Governmental Affairs	None			Wilson, Pete	Cal.	Rep
Moved to Banking, Housing & Urban Affairs	None			Kassebaum, Nancy Landon	Kans.	Rep

COMMERCE, SCIENCE AND TRANSPORTATION / 101st Congress

Service Dates of Committee Chair: Feb. 2,1989-Feb. 5,1991
Service Dates of Majority Members: Feb. 2,1989-Feb. 5,1991
Service Dates of Minority Members: Feb. 2,1989-Feb. 5,1991

Majority

Rank	Name	Party	State	Years in: Senate	Years in: Comm.
Chr	Hollings, Ernest F.	Dem	S.C.	23	23
2nd	Inouye, Daniel K.	Dem	Hai.	27	21
3rd	Ford, Wendell H.	Dem	Ky.	15	15
4th	Exon, J. James	Dem	Neb.	11	11
5th	Gore, Albert A. Jr.	Dem	Tenn.	5	4
6th	Rockefeller, John D. IV	Dem	W.Va.	5	4
7th	Bentsen, Lloyd M. Jr.	Dem	Tex.	19	3
8th	Kerry, John F.	Dem	Mass.	5	3
9th	Breaux, John B.	Dem	La.	3	3
10th	Bryan, Richard H.	Dem	Nev.	1	1
11th	Robb, Charles S.	Dem	Va.	1	1

Minority

Rank	Name	Party	State	Years in: Senate	Years in: Comm.
RM	Danforth, John C.	Rep	Mo.	13	12
2nd	Packwood, Robert W.	Rep	Ore.	21	12
3rd	Pressler, Larry L.	Rep	S.D.	11	11
4th	Stevens, Theodore F.	Rep	Alas.	21	*2 9
5th	Kasten, Robert W. Jr.	Rep	Wisc.	9	9
6th	McCain, John	Rep	Ariz.	3	3
7th	Burns, Conrad	Rep	Ida.	1	1
8th	Gorton, Slade	Rep	Wash.	7	*2 1
9th	Lott, Trent	Rep	Miss.	1	1

*2: Member's 2nd period of service on the committee.

Note: Ranking on the committee for the following member was affected by other chamber service: Robert W. Packwood (Rep-Ore.), Ranking Minority Member, Finance.

COMMERCE, SCIENCE AND TRANSPORTATION / 102nd Congress

Service Dates of Committee Chair: Feb. 5,1991-Jan. 3,1993
Service Dates of Majority Members: Feb. 5,1991-Jan. 3,1993
Service Dates of Minority Members: Feb. 5,1991-Jan. 3,1993

Majority

Rank	Name	Party	State	Years in: Senate	Years in: Comm.
Chr	Hollings, Ernest F.	Dem	S.C.	25	25
2nd	Inouye, Daniel K.	Dem	Hai.	29	23
3rd	Ford, Wendell H.	Dem	Ky.	17	17
4th	Exon, J. James	Dem	Neb.	13	13
5th	Gore, Albert A. Jr.	Dem	Tenn.	7	6
6th	Rockefeller, John D. IV	Dem	W.Va.	7	6
7th	Bentsen, Lloyd M. Jr.	Dem	Tex.	21	5
8th	Kerry, John F.	Dem	Mass.	7	5
9th	Breaux, John B.	Dem	La.	5	5
10th	Bryan, Richard H.	Dem	Nev.	3	3
11th	Robb, Charles S.	Dem	Va.	3	3

Minority

Rank	Name	Party	State	Years in: Senate	Years in: Comm.
RM	Danforth, John C.	Rep	Mo.	15	14
2nd	Packwood, Robert W.	Rep	Ore.	23	14
3rd	Pressler, Larry L.	Rep	S.D.	13	13
4th	Stevens, Theodore F.	Rep	Alas.	23	*2 11
5th	Kasten, Robert W. Jr.	Rep	Wisc.	11	11
6th	McCain, John	Rep	Ariz.	5	5
7th	Burns, Conrad	Rep	Ida.	3	3
8th	Gorton, Slade	Rep	Wash.	9	*2 3
9th	Lott, Trent	Rep	Miss.	3	3

*2: Member's 2nd period of service on the committee.

Note: Ranking on the committee for the following member was affected by other chamber service: Robert W. Packwood (Rep-Ore.), Ranking Minority Member, Finance.

DISTRICT OF COLUMBIA

Jurisdiction, 1947

Established by the Legislative Reorganization Act of 1946:

[Section 102.(1)(f)]

(1) Committee on the District of Columbia, to consist of thirteen Senators, to which committee shall be referred all proposed legislation, messages, petitions, memorials, and other matters relating to the following subjects:

1. All measures relating to the municipal affairs of the District of Columbia in general, other than appropriations therefore, including--
2. Public health and safety, sanitation, and quarantine regulations.
3. Regulation of sale of intoxicating liquors.
4. Adulteration of food and drugs.
5. Taxes and tax sales.
6. Insurance, executors, administrators, wills, and divorce.
7. Municipal and juvenile courts.
8. Incorporation and organization of societies.
9. Municipal code and amendments to the criminal and corporation laws.

Jurisdiction, 1975

Jurisdiction contained in the Senate Manual for the 94th Congress (1975):

[Rule XXV.(1)(g)]

(1) Committee on the District of Columbia, to which committee shall be referred all proposed legislation, messages, petitions, memorials, and other matters relating to the following subjects:

1. All measures relating to the municipal affairs of the District of Columbia in general, other than appropriations therefore, including--
2. Public health and safety, sanitation, and quarantine regulations.
3. Regulation of sale of intoxicating liquors.
4. Adulteration of food and drugs.
5. Taxes and tax sales.
6. Insurance, executors, administrators, wills, and divorce.
7. Municipal and juvenile courts.
8. Incorporation and organization of societies.
9. Municipal code and amendments to the criminal and corporation laws.

Reorganization, 1977

The Committee was reorganized into the Standing Committee on Governmental Affairs following the passage of Senate Resolution 4, the Committee System Reorganization Amendments of 1977, February 4, 1977. Majority members were reassigned on February 11, 1977 and minority members were reassigned on February 22, 1977.

DISTRICT OF COLUMBIA / 80th Congress

Service Dates of Committee Chair: Jan. 6,1947-Jan. 3,1949
Service Dates of Majority Members: Jan. 6,1947-Jan. 10,1949
Service Dates of Minority Members: Jan. 8,1947-Jan. 10,1949

Majority

Rank Name	Party	State	Years in: Senate	Years in: Comm.
Chr Buck, C. Douglass	Rep	Del.	5	4
2nd Capper, Arthur	Rep	Kans.	28	28
3rd Ball, Joseph H.	Rep	Minn.	7	1
4th Flanders, Ralph E.	Rep	Vt.	1	1
5th Cooper, John Sherman	Rep	Ky.	1	1
6th Cain, Harry P.	Rep	Wash.	1	1
7th Kem, James P.	Rep	Mo.	1	1

Minority

Rank Name	Party	State	Years in: Senate	Years in: Comm.
RM Johnston, Olin D.	Dem	S.C.	3	2
2nd Holland, Spessard L.	Dem	Fla.	1	1
3rd Sparkman, John J.	Dem	Ala.	1	1
4th Umstead, William B.	Dem	N.C.	1	1
5th McGrath, J. Howard	Dem	R.I.	1	1
6th Stennis, John C.	Dem	Miss.	1	1

Note: Ranking on this committee for the following member was affected by other chamber service: Arthur Capper (Rep-Kans.), Chair, Agriculture and Forestry.

Vacancy Filled:
Minority: 6th seat by Stennis on Nov. 25,1947.

Changes:

Majority:				
Flanders, Ralph E.	Rep	Vt.	Dec. 19,1947	Left committee; no new assignment.
Dworshak, Henry C.	Rep	Ida.	Feb. 5,1948	Replaced Flanders.
Minority:				
Sparkman, John J.	Dem	Ala.	May 26,1948	Moved to Public Works.
Stennis, John C.	Dem	Miss.	May 26,1948	Moved to Post Office and Civil Service.
Feazel, William C.	Dem	La.	May 26,1948	Replaced Sparkman.
Umstead, William B.	Dem	N.C.	Dec. 30,1948	Resigned; defeated for nomination.
Feazel, William C.	Dem	La.	Dec. 30,1948	Resigned and retired.

Departures from the Senate:	**Majority**			**Minority**		
Defeated for Reelection	Ball, Joseph H.	Minn.	Rep	None		
	Buck, C. Douglass	Del.	Rep			
	Cooper, John Sherman	Ky.	Rep			
	Dworshak, Henry C.	Ida.	Rep			
Retired	Capper, Arthur	Kans.	Rep	None		
Departures from Committee:						
Moved to Agriculture & Forestry	None			Holland, Spessard L.	Fla.	Dem
Moved to Public Works	Kem, James P.	Mo.	Rep	None		
Became Ranking Minority Member of Public Works	Cain, Harry P.	Wash.	Rep	None		

DISTRICT OF COLUMBIA / 81st Congress

Service Dates of Committee Chairs: Ch1 Jan. 10,1949-Aug. 23,1949
Ch2 Aug. 30,1949-Jan. 15,1951
Service Dates of Majority Members: Jan. 10,1949-Jan. 15,1951
Service Dates of Minority Members: Jan. 10,1949-Jan. 15,1951

Majority

Rank Name	Party	State	Years in: Senate	Years in: Comm.
Ch1 McGrath, J. Howard	Dem	R.I.	3	3
2nd Johnston, Olin D.	Dem	S.C.	5	5
Ch2 3rd Neely, Matthew M.	Dem	W.Va.	17 *2	1
4th Kefauver, C. Estes	Dem	Tenn.	1	1
5th Hunt, Lester C.	Dem	Wyo.	1	1
6th Frear, J. Allen Jr.	Dem	Del.	1 *1	1
7th Miller, Bert H.	Dem	Ida.	1	1

Minority

Rank Name	Party	State	Years in: Senate	Years in: Comm.
RM Williams, John J.	Rep	Del.	3	1
2nd McCarthy, Joseph R.	Rep	Wisc.	3	1
3rd Mundt, Karl E.	Rep	S.D.	1	1
4th Smith, Margaret Chase	Rep	Me.	1	1
5th Schoeppel, Andrew F.	Rep	Kans.	1	1
6th Hendrickson, Robert C.	Rep	N.J.	1	1

*1: Member's 1st period of service on the committee; *2: Member's 2nd period of service on the committee.

Note: Ranking on this committee for the following member was affected by other chamber service: Olin D.Johnston (Dem-S.C.), Chair, Post Office and Civil Service.

Changes:

Chair:

Ch1	McGrath, J. Howard	Dem	R.I.	Aug. 23,1949	Resigned; appointed Postmaster General.
Ch2	Neely, Matthew M.	Dem	W.Va.	Aug. 30,1949	Succeeded McGrath as Chair.

Majority:

McGrath, J. Howard	Dem	R.I.	Aug. 23,1949	Resigned; appointed Postmaster General.
Leahy, Edward L.	Dem	R.I.	Aug. 30,1949	Replaced McGrath.
Miller, Bert H.	Dem	Ida.	Oct. 8,1949	Died in office.
Pepper, Claude D.	Dem	Fla.	Oct. 13,1949	Replaced Miller.
Leahy, Edward L.	Dem	R.I.	Dec. 18,1950	Resigned; appointed Federal judge.
Pastore, John O.	Dem	R.I.	Dec. 21,1950	Replaced Leahy.

Minority:

Schoeppel, Andrew F.	Rep	Kans.	July 26,1949	Moved to Rules and Administration.
Dulles, John F.	Rep	N.Y.	July 26,1949	Replaced Schoeppel.
Dulles, John F.	Rep	N.Y.	Nov. 8,1949	Resigned; lost special election.
Dworshak, Henry C.	Rep	Ida.	Jan. 12,1950	Replaced Dulles.
Mundt, Karl E.	Rep	S.D.	Jan. 12,1950	Moved to Rules and Administration.
Darby, Harry	Rep	Kans.	Jan. 12,1950	Replaced Mundt.
Darby, Harry	Rep	Kans.	Nov. 28,1950	Resigned and retired.
Nixon, Richard M.	Rep	Cal.	Dec. 4,1950	Replaced Darby.

Departures from the Senate:	**Majority**			**Minority**		
Defeated for Renomination	Pepper, Claude D.	Fla.	Dem	None		
Departures from Committee:						
Moved to Finance	Frear, J. Allen Jr.	Del.	Dem	Williams, John J.	Del.	Rep
Moved to Judiciary	None			Hendrickson, Robert C.	N.J.	Rep
Moved to Appropriations	None			McCarthy, Joseph R.	Wisc.	Rep
Moved to Rules and Administration	None			Smith, Margaret Chase	Me.	Rep
Moved to Expenditures in the Executive Departments; Public Works	None			Dworshak, Henry C.	Ida.	Rep
Moved to Labor & Public Welfare; Expenditures in the Executive Departments	None			Nixon, Richard M.	Cal.	Rep

DISTRICT OF COLUMBIA / 82nd Congress

Service Dates of Committee Chair: Jan. 15,1951-Jan. 13,1953
Service Dates of Majority Members: Jan. 15,1951-Jan. 13,1953
Service Dates of Minority Members: Jan. 15,1951-Jan. 13,1953

Majority

Rank	Name	Party	State	Years in: Senate	Years in: Comm.
Chr	Neely, Matthew M.	Dem	W.Va.	19	*2 3
2nd	Johnston, Olin D.	Dem	S.C.	7	7
3rd	Kefauver, C. Estes	Dem	Tenn.	3	3
4th	Hunt, Lester C.	Dem	Wyo.	3	3
5th	Pastore, John O.	Dem	R.I.	1	1
6th	Clements, Earle C.	Dem	Ky.	1	1
7th	Smith, Willis	Dem	N.C.	1	1

Minority

Rank	Name	Party	State	Years in: Senate	Years in: Comm.
RM	Case, Francis H.	Rep	S.D.	1	*1 1
2nd	Butler, John Marshall	Rep	Md.	1	1
3rd	Welker, Herman	Rep	Ida.	1	1
4th	Bennett, Wallace F.	Rep	Utah	1	1
5th	Vandenberg, Arthur H.	Rep	Mich.	23	*2 1
6th	Duff, James H.	Rep	Penn.	1	1

*1: Member's 1st period of service on the committee; *2: Member's 2nd period of service on the committee.

Note: Ranking on this committee for the following member was affected by other chamber service: Olin D.Johnston (Dem-S.C.), Chair, Post Office and Civil Service.

Vacancy Filled:

Minority: 6th seat by Duff on Jan. 18,1951.

Changes:

Minority:

Vandenberg, Arthur H.	Rep	Mich.	Apr. 18,1951	Died in office.
Dirksen, Everett M.	Rep	Ill.	June 22,1951	Replaced Vandenberg.
Dirksen, Everett M.	Rep	Ill.	Jan. 14,1952	Moved to Rules and Administration.
Seaton, Frederick A.	Rep	Neb.	Jan. 14,1952	Replaced Dirksen.
Seaton, Frederick A.	Rep	Neb.	Nov. 4,1952	Resigned; appointed a presidential adviser.

Departures from Committee:	Majority			Minority		
Moved to Interior & Insular Affairs; Agriculture & Forestry	Clements, Earle C.	Ky.	Dem	None		
Moved to Judiciary	Johnston, Olin D.	S.C.	Dem	None		
Moved to Interstate & Foreign Commerce	Pastore, John O.	R.I.	Dem	None		
Moved to Banking & Currency; Finance	None			Bennett, Wallace F.	Utah	Rep
Moved to Judiciary; Interstate & Foreign Commerce; Government Operations	None			Butler, John Marshall	Md.	Rep
Moved to Armed Services	None			Duff, James H.	Penn.	Rep
Moved to Judiciary; Agriculture & Forestry	None			Welker, Herman	Ida.	Rep
No new assignment	Hunt, Lester C.	Wyo.	Dem	None		
	Kefauver, C. Estes	Tenn.	Dem			

DISTRICT OF COLUMBIA / 83rd Congress

Service Dates of Committee Chair: Jan. 13,1953-Jan. 11,1955
Service Dates of Majority Members: Jan. 13,1953-Jan. 11,1955
Service Dates of Minority Members: Jan. 13,1953-Jan. 11,1955

Majority

Rank	Name	Party	State	Years in: Senate	Years in: Comm.
Chr	Case, Francis H.	Rep	S.D.	3	*1 2
2nd	Barrett, Frank A.	Rep	Wyo.	1	1
3rd	Beall, J. Glenn	Rep	Md.	1	1
4th	Payne, Frederick G.	Rep	Me.	1	1

Minority

Rank	Name	Party	State	Years in: Senate	Years in: Comm.
RM	Neely, Matthew M.	Dem	W.Va.	21	*2 5
2nd	Smith, Willis	Dem	N.C.	3	2
3rd	Gore, Albert A.	Dem	Tenn.	1	1
4th	Mansfield, Michael J.	Dem	Mont.	1	1

Third Party:

Name	Party	State	Years in: Senate	Years in: Comm.
Morse, Wayne L.	Ind	Ore.	9	1

*1: Member's 1st period of service on the committee; *2: Member's 2nd period of service on the committee.

Note: Wayne Morse (Ind-Ore.) was appointed by the majority on May 25,1953. He was not included in the party ratio, nor was he allowed to accrue committee seniority.

Changes:

Majority:

Barrett, Frank A.	Rep	Wyo.	June 29,1954	Left committee; no new assignment.
Crippa, Edward D.	Rep	Wyo.	June 29,1954	Replaced Barrett.
Crippa, Edward D.	Rep	Wyo.	July 9,1954	Moved to Interior and Insular Affairs.
Reynolds, Samuel W.	Rep	Neb.	July 9,1954	Replaced Crippa.
Reynolds, Samuel W.	Rep	Neb.	Nov. 7,1954	Resigned and retired.
Brown, Ernest S.	Rep	Nev.	Nov. 30,1954	Replaced Reynolds.
Brown, Ernest S.	Rep	Nev.	Dec. 1,1954	Resigned; defeated in special election.

Minority:

Smith, Willis	Dem	N.C.	June 26,1953	Died in office.
Lennon, Alton A.	Dem	N.C.	July 15,1953	Replaced Smith.
Lennon, Alton A.	Dem	N.C.	Jan. 13,1954	Moved to Post Office and Civil Service.
Burke, Thomas A.	Dem	Ohio	Jan. 13,1954	Replaced Lennon.
Burke, Thomas A.	Dem	Ohio	May 19,1954	Moved to Government Operations.
Ervin, Samuel J.	Dem	N.C.	June 11,1954	Replaced Burke.

Departures from Committee:

	Majority		Minority	
Moved to Interstate & Foreign Commerce	Payne, Frederick G.	Me. Rep	None	
Moved to Rules & Administration	None		Mansfield, Michael J.	Mont. Dem
Moved to Government Operations; Armed Services; Interstate & Foreign Commerce	None		Ervin, Samuel J.	N.C. Dem
No new assignment	Case, Francis H.	S.D. Rep	None	

DISTRICT OF COLUMBIA / 84th Congress

Service Dates of Committee Chair: Jan. 11,1955-Jan. 9,1957
Service Dates of Majority Members: Jan. 11,1955-Jan. 9,1957
Service Dates of Minority Members: Jan. 11,1955-Jan. 9,1957

Majority

Rank	Name	Party	State	Years in: Senate	Years in: Comm.
Chr	Neely, Matthew M.	Dem	W.Va.	23	*2 7
2nd	Gore, Albert A.	Dem	Tenn.	3	2
3rd	Bible, Alan H.	Dem	Nev.	1	1
4th	McNamara, Patrick V.	Dem	Mich.	1	1

Minority

Rank	Name	Party	State	Years in: Senate	Years in: Comm.
RM	Beall, J. Glenn	Rep	Md.	3	2
2nd	Hruska, Roman L.	Rep	Neb.	1	1
3rd	Case, Clifford P.	Rep	N.J.	1	1
4th	Allott, Gordon L.	Rep	Colo.	1	1

Third Party:

Name	Party	State	Senate	Comm.
Morse, Wayne L.	Ind	Ore.	11	2

*2: Member's 2nd period of service on the committee.

Note: Wayne Morse of Oregon was assigned to the committee as an Independent on Jan. 11,1955 by the Democratic Caucus. On Feb. 17,1955, he joined the Democratic Party and became the 5th ranking member on the committee, at which time he was allowed to accrue seniority.

Changes:

Majority:

Name	Party	State	Date	Change
Gore, Albert A.	Dem	Tenn.	Jan. 12,1956	Moved to Select Committee to Investigate Attempts to Improperly Influence Senators.
Frear, J. Allen Jr.	Dem	Del.	Jan. 12,1956	Replaced Gore.

Departures from Committee:

	Majority		Minority	
Moved to Interior & Insular Affairs	None		Allott, Gordon L.	Colo. Rep
Moved to Judiciary	None		Hruska, Roman L.	Neb. Rep
No new assignment	McNamara, Patrick V.	Mich. Dem	None	

DISTRICT OF COLUMBIA / 85th Congress

Service Dates of Committee Chairs: Ch1 Jan. 9,1957-Jan. 18,1958
Ch2 Feb. 6,1958-Jan. 14,1959
Service Dates of Majority Members: Jan. 9,1957-Jan. 14,1959
Service Dates of Minority Members: Jan. 9,1957-Jan. 20,1959

Majority

Rank	Name	Party	State	Years in: Senate	Years in: Comm.
Ch1	Neely, Matthew M.	Dem	W.Va.	25	*2 8
Ch2 2nd	Bible, Alan H.	Dem	Nev.	3	2
3rd	Morse, Wayne L.	Dem	Ore.	13	4
4th	Frear, J. Allen Jr.	Dem	Del.	9	*2 1
5th	Clark, Joseph S.	Dem	Penn.	1	1

Minority

Rank	Name	Party	State	Years in: Senate	Years in: Comm.
RM	Beall, J. Glenn	Rep	Md.	5	4
2nd	Case, Clifford P.	Rep	N.J.	3	2
3rd	Morton, Thruston B.	Rep	Ky.	1	*1 1
4th	Javits, Jacob K.	Rep	N.Y.	1	1

*1: Member's 1st period of service on the committee; *2: Member's 2nd period of service on the committee.

Note: Wayne Morse (Dem-Ore.) began to accrue seniority on this committee when he joined the Democratic Party on Feb. 17,1955. His previous service was as an Independent.

Changes:

Chair:

Ch1	Neely, Matthew M.	Dem	W.Va.	Jan. 18,1958 Died in office.
Ch2	Bible, Alan H.	Dem	Nev.	Feb. 6,1958 Succeeded Neely as Chair.

Majority:

Neely, Matthew M.	Dem	W.Va.	Jan. 18,1958 Died in office.
Proxmire, William	Dem	Wisc.	Feb. 6,1958 Replaced Neely.

Minority:

Case, Clifford P.	Rep	N.J.	May 22,1957 Moved to Banking and Currency.
Hoblitzell, John D. Jr.	Rep	W.Va.	Jan. 28,1958 Replaced Case.
Hoblitzell, John D. Jr.	Rep	W.Va.	Nov. 4,1958 Resigned; defeated for election.

Departures from Committee:	Majority		Minority	
Moved to Post Office & Civil Service; Labor & Public Welfare	Clark, Joseph S.	Penn. Dem	None	
Moved to Agriculture & Forestry	Proxmire, William	Wisc. Dem	None	
Moved to Aeronautics & Space Sciences; Labor & Public Welfare; Government Operations	None		Javits, Jacob K.	N.Y. Rep
Moved to Rules & Administration; Interstate & Foreign Commerce; Finance	None		Morton, Thruston B.	Ky. Rep

DISTRICT OF COLUMBIA / 86th Congress

Service Dates of Committee Chair: Jan. 14,1959-Jan. 10,1961
Service Dates of Majority Members: Jan. 14,1959-Jan. 10,1961
Service Dates of Minority Members: Jan. 20,1959-Jan. 13,1961

Majority

Rank	Name	Party	State	Years in: Senate	Years in: Comm.
Chr	Bible, Alan H.	Dem	Nev.	5	5
2nd	Morse, Wayne L.	Dem	Ore.	15	6
3rd	Frear, J. Allen Jr.	Dem	Del.	11	*2 4
4th	Hartke, R. Vance	Dem	Ind.	1	1

Minority

Rank	Name	Party	State	Years in: Senate	Years in: Comm.
RM	Beall, J. Glenn	Rep	Md.	7	7
2nd	Case, Francis H.	Rep	S.D.	9	*2 1
3rd	Prouty, Winston L.	Rep	Vt.	1	1

*2: Member's 2nd period of service on the committee.

Note: Wayne Morse (Dem-Ore.) began to accrue seniority on this committee when he joined the Democratic Party on Feb. 17,1955. His previous service was as an Independent.

Departures from the Senate:	Majority		Minority	
Defeated for Reelection	Frear, J. Allen Jr.	Del. Dem	None	
Departures from Committee:				
No new assignment	None		Case, Francis H.	S.D. Rep

DISTRICT OF COLUMBIA / 87th Congress

Service Dates of Committee Chair: Jan. 10,1961-Feb. 25,1963
Service Dates of Majority Members: Jan. 10,1961-Feb. 25,1963
Service Dates of Minority Members: Jan. 13,1961-Feb. 25,1963

Majority

Rank	Name	Party	State	Years in: Senate	Years in: Comm.
Chr	Bible, Alan H.	Dem	Nev.	7	6
2nd	Morse, Wayne L.	Dem	Ore.	17	8
3rd	Hartke, R. Vance	Dem	Ind.	3	2
4th	Smith, Benjamin A. II	Dem	Mass.	1	1

Minority

Rank	Name	Party	State	Years in: Senate	Years in: Comm.
RM	Beall, J. Glenn	Rep	Md.	9	9
2nd	Prouty, Winston L.	Rep	Vt.	3	2
3rd	Miller, Jack R.	Rep	Iowa	1	1

Note: Wayne Morse (Dem-Ore.) began to accrue seniority on this committee when he joined the Democratic Party on Feb. 17,1955. His previous service was as an Independent.

Changes:
Majority:

Smith, Benjamin A. II	Dem	Mass.	Nov. 6,1962	Resigned and retired.

Departures from Committee:	Majority	Minority		
Moved to Government Operations	None	Miller, Jack R.	Iowa	Rep

DISTRICT OF COLUMBIA / 88th Congress

Service Dates of Committee Chair: Feb. 25,1963-Jan. 8,1965
Service Dates of Majority Members: Feb. 25,1963-Jan. 8,1965
Service Dates of Minority Members: Feb. 25,1963-Jan. 15,1965

Majority			Years in:		Minority			Years in:	
Rank Name	Party	State	Senate	Comm.	Rank Name	Party	State	Senate	Comm.
Chr Bible, Alan H.	Dem	Nev.	9	9	RM Beall, J. Glenn	Rep	Md.	11	11
2nd Morse, Wayne L.	Dem	Ore.	19	10	2nd Prouty, Winston L.	Rep	Vt.	5	5
3rd Hartke, R. Vance	Dem	Ind.	5	5	3rd Dominick, Peter H.	Rep	Colo.	1	1
4th McIntyre, Thomas J.	Dem	N.H.	1	1					

Note: Wayne Morse (Dem-Ore.) began to accrue seniority on this committee when he joined the Democratic Party on Feb. 17,1955. His previous service was as an Independent.

	Majority			Minority		
Departures from the Senate:						
Defeated for Reelection	None			Beall, J. Glenn	Md.	Rep
Departures from Committee:						
Moved to Post Office & Civil Service	Hartke, R. Vance	Ind.	Dem	None		

DISTRICT OF COLUMBIA / 89th Congress

Service Dates of Committee Chair: Jan. 8,1965-Jan. 11,1967
Service Dates of Majority Members: Jan. 8,1965-Jan. 11,1967
Service Dates of Minority Members: Jan. 15,1965-Jan. 16,1967

Majority			Years in:		Minority			Years in:	
Rank Name	Party	State	Senate	Comm.	Rank Name	Party	State	Senate	Comm.
Chr Bible, Alan H.	Dem	Nev.	11	10	RM Prouty, Winston L.	Rep	Vt.	7	6
2nd Morse, Wayne L.	Dem	Ore.	21	12	2nd Dominick, Peter H.	Rep	Colo.	3	2
3rd McIntyre, Thomas J.	Dem	N.H.	3	2					
4th Kennedy, Robert F.	Dem	N.Y.	1	1					
5th Tydings, Joseph D.	Dem	Md.	1	1					

Note: Wayne Morse (Dem-Ore.) began to accrue seniority on this committee when he joined the Democratic Party on Feb. 17,1955. His previous service was as an Independent.

Departures from Committee:	Majority			Minority
No new assignment	McIntyre, Thomas J.	N.H.	Dem	None

DISTRICT OF COLUMBIA / 90th Congress

Service Dates of Committee Chair: Jan. 11,1967-Jan. 14,1969
Service Dates of Majority Members: Jan. 11,1967-Jan. 14,1969
Service Dates of Minority Members: Jan. 16,1967-Jan. 14,1969

Majority

Rank	Name	Party	State	Years in: Senate	Years in: Comm.
Chr	Bible, Alan H.	Dem	Nev.	13	13
2nd	Morse, Wayne L.	Dem	Ore.	23	14
3rd	Kennedy, Robert F.	Dem	N.Y.	3	3
4th	Tydings, Joseph D.	Dem	Md.	3	3
5th	Spong, William B. Jr.	Dem	Va.	1	1

Minority

Rank	Name	Party	State	Years in: Senate	Years in: Comm.
RM	Prouty, Winston L.	Rep	Vt.	9	8
2nd	Dominick, Peter H.	Rep	Colo.	5	4
3rd	Morton, Thruston B.	Rep	Ky.	11	*2 1

*2: Member's 2nd period of service on the committee.

Note: Wayne Morse (Dem-Ore.) began to accrue seniority on this committee when he joined the Democratic Party on Feb. 17,1955. His previous service was as an Independent.

Changes:

Majority:

Kennedy, Robert F.	Dem	N.Y.	June 6,1968	Died in office.

Minority:

Morton, Thruston B.	Rep	Ky.	Dec. 16,1968	Resigned and retired.

	Majority			Minority		
Departures from the Senate:						
Defeated for Reelection	Morse, Wayne L.	Ore.	Dem	None		
Departures from Committee:						
No new assignment	None			Dominick, Peter H.	Colo.	Rep

DISTRICT OF COLUMBIA / 91st Congress

Service Dates of Committee Chair: Jan. 14,1969-Jan. 3,1971
Service Dates of Majority Members: Jan. 14,1969-Jan. 28,1971
Service Dates of Minority Members: Jan. 14,1969-Jan. 29,1971

Majority

Rank	Name	Party	State	Years in: Senate	Years in: Comm.
Chr	Tydings, Joseph D.	Dem	Md.	5	5
2nd	Bible, Alan H.	Dem	Nev.	15	15
3rd	Spong, William B. Jr.	Dem	Va.	3	3
4th	Eagleton, Thomas F.	Dem	Mo.	1	1

Minority

Rank	Name	Party	State	Years in: Senate	Years in: Comm.
RM	Prouty, Winston L.	Rep	Vt.	11	10
2nd	Goodell, Charles E.	Rep	N.Y.	1	1
3rd	Mathias, Charles McC. Jr.	Rep	Md.	1	1

Note: Alan H. Bible (Dem-Nev.) waived his seniority to Joseph D. Tydings (Dem-Md.).

	Majority			Minority		
Departures from the Senate:						
Defeated for Reelection	Tydings, Joseph D.	Md.	Dem	None		
Defeated for Election	None			Goodell, Charles E.	N.Y.	Rep
Departures from Committee:						
Moved to Foreign Relations	Spong, William B. Jr.	Va.	Dem	None		
Moved to Rules & Administration	None			Prouty, Winston L.	Vt.	Rep
No new assignment	Bible, Alan H.	Nev.	Dem	None		

DISTRICT OF COLUMBIA / 92nd Congress

Service Dates of Committee Chair: Jan. 28,1971-Jan. 4,1973
Service Dates of Majority Members: Jan. 28,1971-Jan. 4,1973
Service Dates of Minority Members: Jan. 29,1971-Jan. 12,1973

Majority			Years in:		Minority			Years in:	
Rank Name	**Party**	**State**	**Senate**	**Comm.**	**Rank Name**	**Party**	**State**	**Senate**	**Comm.**
Chr Eagleton, Thomas F.	Dem	Mo.	3	3	RM Mathias, Charles McC. Jr.	Rep	Md.	3	3
2nd Inouye, Daniel K.	Dem	Hai.	9	1	2nd Weicker, Lowell P. Jr.	Rep	Conn.	1	1
3rd Stevenson, Adlai E. III	Dem	Ill.	1	1	3rd Buckley, James L.	Con	N.Y.	1	1
4th Tunney, John V.	Dem	Cal.	1	1					

Note: James Buckley of New York was elected as a Conservative but was assigned by the Republican Conference, serving on the committee with his seniority intact.

Changes:
Minority:

Weicker, Lowell P. Jr.	Rep	Conn.	Feb. 23,1972	Moved to Select Committee on Small Business.

Departures from Committee:	**Majority**	**Minority**		
Moved to Interior & Insular Affairs	None	Buckley, James L.	N.Y.	Con

DISTRICT OF COLUMBIA / 93rd Congress

Service Dates of Committee Chair: Jan. 4,1973-Jan. 17,1975
Service Dates of Majority Members: Jan. 4,1973-Jan. 17,1975
Service Dates of Minority Members: Jan. 12,1973-Jan. 23,1975

Majority			Years in:		Minority			Years in:	
Rank Name	**Party**	**State**	**Senate**	**Comm.**	**Rank Name**	**Party**	**State**	**Senate**	**Comm.**
Chr Eagleton, Thomas F.	Dem	Mo.	5	4	RM Mathias, Charles McC. Jr.	Rep	Md.	5	4
2nd Inouye, Daniel K.	Dem	Hai.	11	2	2nd Bartlett, Dewey F.	Rep	Okla.	1	1
3rd Stevenson, Adlai E. III	Dem	Ill.	3	2	3rd Domenici, Pete V.	Rep	N.M.	1	1
4th Tunney, John V.	Dem	Cal.	3	2					

Departures from Committee:	**Majority**			**Minority**		
Moved to Budget	None			Domenici, Pete V.	N.M.	Rep
No new assignment	Tunney, John V.	Cal.	Dem	None		

DISTRICT OF COLUMBIA / 94th Congress

Service Dates of Committee Chair: Jan. 17,1975-Jan. 10,1977
Service Dates of Majority Members: Jan. 17,1975-Jan. 10,1977
Service Dates of Minority Members: Jan. 23,1975-Jan. 10,1977

Majority			Years in:		Minority			Years in:	
Rank Name	**Party**	**State**	**Senate**	**Comm.**	**Rank Name**	**Party**	**State**	**Senate**	**Comm.**
Chr Eagleton, Thomas F.	Dem	Mo.	7	7	RM Mathias, Charles McC. Jr.	Rep	Md.	7	7
2nd Inouye, Daniel K.	Dem	Hai.	13	4	2nd Bartlett, Dewey F.	Rep	Okla.	3	3
3rd Stevenson, Adlai E. III	Dem	Ill.	5	4	3rd Garn, Jake	Rep	Utah	1	1
4th Glenn, John H. Jr.	Dem	Ohio	1	1					

DISTRICT OF COLUMBIA / 95th Congress

* Reorganized into the Committee on GOVERNMENTAL AFFAIRS on Feb. 11,1977.

Service Dates of Committee Chair: Jan. 10,1977-Feb. 11,1977
Service Dates of Majority Members: Jan. 10,1977-Feb. 11,1977
Service Dates of Minority Members: Jan. 10,1977-Feb. 22,1977

Majority

Rank	Name	Party	State	Years in: Senate	Years in: Comm.
Chr	Eagleton, Thomas F.	Dem	Mo.	9	8
2nd	Inouye, Daniel K.	Dem	Hai.	15	6
3rd	Stevenson, Adlai E. III	Dem	Ill.	7	6
4th	Glenn, John H. Jr.	Dem	Ohio	3	2

Minority

Rank	Name	Party	State	Years in: Senate	Years in: Comm.
RM	Mathias, Charles McC. Jr.	Rep	Md.	9	8
2nd	Bartlett, Dewey F.	Rep	Okla.	5	4
3rd	Garn, Jake	Rep	Utah	3	2

Changes:

Majority:

Name	Party	State	Date	Change
Eagleton, Thomas F.	Dem	Mo.	Feb. 11,1977	Moved into reorganized Governmental Affairs.
Inouye, Daniel K.	Dem	Hai.	Feb. 11,1977	Left committee; no new assignment.
Stevenson, Adlai E. III	Dem	Ill.	Feb. 11,1977	Moved to Chair Select Committee to Study the Senate Committee System.
Glenn, John H. Jr.	Dem	Ohio	Feb. 11,1977	Moved into reorganized Governmental Affairs.

Minority:

Name	Party	State	Date	Change
Mathias, Charles McC. Jr.	Rep	Md.	Feb. 22,1977	Moved into reorganized Governmental Affairs.
Bartlett, Dewey F.	Rep	Okla.	Feb. 22,1977	Moved to Permanent Select Committee on Indian Affairs.
Garn, Jake	Rep	Utah	Feb. 22,1977	Moved to Armed Services.

ENERGY AND NATURAL RESOURCES

PUBLIC LANDS

Jurisdiction, 1947

Established by the Legislative Reorganization Act of 1946:

[Section 102.(1)(m)]

Committee on Public Lands, to consist of thirteen Senators, to which committee shall be referred all proposed legislation, messages, petitions, memorials, and other matters relating to the following subjects:

1. Public lands generally, including entry, easements, and grazing thereon.
2. Mineral resources of the public lands.
3. Forfeiture of land grants and alien ownership, including alien ownership of mineral lands.
4. Forest reserves and national parks created from the public domain.
5. Military parks and battlefields, and national cemeteries.
6. Preservation of prehistoric ruins and objects of interest on the public domain.
7. Measures relating generally to Hawaii, Alaska, and the insular possessions of the United States, except those affecting their revenue and appropriations.
8. Irrigation and reclamation, including water supply for reclamation projects, and easements of public lands for irrigation projects.
9. Interstate compacts relating to apportionment of waters for irrigation purposes.
10. Mining interests generally.
11. Mineral land laws and claims and entries thereunder.
12. Geological survey.
13. Mining schools and experimental stations.
14. Petroleum conservation and conservation of the radium supply in the United States.
15. Relations of the United States with the Indians and the Indian tribes.
16. Measures relating to the care, education, and management of Indians, including the care and allotment of Indian lands and general and special measures relating to claims which are paid out of Indian funds.

INTERIOR AND INSULAR AFFAIRS

Renamed the Committee on Interior and Insular Affairs on January 28, 1948.

ENERGY AND NATURAL RESOURCES

Reorganization, 1977

The Committee was reorganized as the Standing Committee on Energy and Natural Resources following the passage of Senate Resolution 4, the Committee System Reorganization Amendments of 1977, February 4, 1977.

Jurisdiction, 1977

From Senate Resolution 4, the Committee System Reorganization Amendments of 1977, February 4, 1977:

[Section (g)(1)]

Committee on Energy and Natural Resources, to which committee shall be referred all proposed legislation, messages, petitions, memorials, and other matters relating to the following subjects:

1. Energy policy.
2. Energy regulation nd conservation.
3. Energy research and development.
4. Solar energy systems.
5. Nonmilitary development of nuclear energy.
6. Naval petroleum reserves in Alaska.
7. Oil and gas production and distribution.
8. Extraction of minerals from oceans and Outer Continental Shelf lands.
9. Energy related aspects of deepwater ports.
10. Hydroelectric power, irrigation, and reclamation.
11. Coal production, distribution, and utilization.
12. Public lands and forests, including farming and grazing thereon, and mineral extraction therefrom.
13. National parks, recreation areas, wilderness areas, wild and scenic rivers, historical sites, military parks and battlefields on the public domain, and preservation of prehistoric ruins and objects of interest.
14. Mining, mineral lands, mining claims, and mineral conservation.
15. Mining education and research.
16. Territorial possessions of the United States, including trusteeships.

(2) Such committee shall also study and review, on a comprehensive basis, matters relating to energy and resources development, and report thereon from time to time.

Jurisdiction, 1992

Jurisdiction contained in the Standing Rules of the Senate (as revised to March 18, 1992):

[Rule XXV.(1)(g)]

(1) Committee on Energy and Natural Resources, to which committee shall be referred all proposed legislation, messages, petitions, memorials, and other matters relating to the following subjects:

1. Coal production, distribution, and utilization.
2. Energy policy.
3. Energy regulation and conservation.
4. Energy related aspects of deepwater ports.
5. Energy research and development.
6. Extraction of minerals from oceans and Outer Continental Shelf lands.
7. Hydroelectric power, irrigation, and reclamation.
8. Mining education and research.
9. Mining, mineral lands, mining claims, and mineral conservation.
10. National parks, recreation areas, wilderness areas, wild and scenic rivers, historical sites, military parks and battlefields, and on the public domain, preservation of prehistoric ruins and objects of interest.
11. Naval petroleum reserves in Alaska.
12. Nonmilitary development of nuclear energy.
13. Oil and gas production and distribution.
14. Public lands and forests, including farming and grazing thereon, and mineral extraction therefrom.
15. Solar energy systems.
16. Territorial possessions of the United States, including trusteeships.

(2) Such committee shall also study and review, on a comprehensive basis, matters relating to energy and resources development, and report thereon from time to time.

PUBLIC LANDS / 80th Congress

* Name changed to INTERIOR AND INSULAR AFFAIRS on Jan. 28,1948.

Service Dates of Committee Chair: Jan. 6,1947-Jan. 10,1949
Service Dates of Majority Members: Jan. 6,1947-Jan. 10,1949
Service Dates of Minority Members: Jan. 8,1947-Jan. 10,1949

Majority

Rank Name	Party	State	Years in: Senate	Years in: Comm.
Chr Butler, Hugh A.	Rep	Neb.	7	6
2nd Millikin, Eugene D.	Rep	Colo.	6	5
3rd Robertson, Edward V.	Rep	Wyo.	5	4
4th Cordon, Guy	Rep	Ore.	3	3
5th Dworshak, Henry C.	Rep	Ida.	1	*1 1
6th Ecton, Zales N.	Rep	Mont.	1	1
7th Malone, George W.	Rep	Nev.	1	1
8th Watkins, Arthur V.	Rep	Utah	1	1

Minority

Rank Name	Party	State	Years in: Senate	Years in: Comm.
RM Hatch, Carl A.	Dem	N.M.	14	14
2nd O'Mahoney, Joseph C.	Dem	Wyo.	14	*1 14
3rd Murray, James E.	Dem	Mont.	13	13
4th Downey, Sheridan	Dem	Cal.	9	6
5th McFarland, Ernest W.	Dem	Ariz.	7	6

*1: Member's 1st period of service on the committee.

Departures from the Senate:

	Majority			Minority		
Appointed Federal Judge	None			Hatch, Carl A.	N.M.	Dem
Defeated for Reelection	Robertson, Edward V.	Wyo.	Rep	None		
	Dworshak, Henry C.	Ida.	Rep			

INTERIOR AND INSULAR AFFAIRS / 81st Congress

Service Dates of Committee Chair: Jan. 10,1949-Jan. 15,1951
Service Dates of Majority Members: Jan. 10,1949-Jan. 15,1951
Service Dates of Minority Members: Jan. 10,1949-Jan. 15,1951

Majority

Rank Name	Party	State	Years in: Senate	Years in: Comm.
Chr O'Mahoney, Joseph C.	Dem	Wyo.	16	*1 16
2nd Murray, James E.	Dem	Mont.	15	15
3rd Downey, Sheridan	Dem	Cal.	11	8
4th McFarland, Ernest W.	Dem	Ariz.	9	8
5th Anderson, Clinton P.	Dem	N.M.	1	1
6th Miller, Bert H.	Dem	Ida.	1	1
7th Kerr, Robert S.	Dem	Okla.	1	1

Minority

Rank Name	Party	State	Years in: Senate	Years in: Comm.
RM Butler, Hugh A.	Rep	Neb.	9	8
2nd Millikin, Eugene D.	Rep	Colo.	8	8
3rd Cordon, Guy	Rep	Ore.	5	5
4th Ecton, Zales N.	Rep	Mont.	3	3
5th Malone, George W.	Rep	Nev.	3	3
6th Watkins, Arthur V.	Rep	Utah	3	3

*1: Member's 1st period of service on the committee.

Changes:

Majority:

Kerr, Robert S.	Dem	Okla.	Aug. 30,1949	Moved to Finance.
Leahy, Edward L.	Dem	R.I.	Aug. 30,1949	Replaced Kerr.
Miller, Bert H.	Dem	Ida.	Oct. 8,1949	Died in office.
Leahy, Edward L.	Dem	R.I.	Jan. 12,1950	Moved to Expenditures in the Executive Departments; Post Office and Civil Service.
Taylor, Glen H.	Dem	Ida.	Jan. 12,1950	Replaced Leahy.
Lehman, Herbert H.	Dem	N.Y.	Jan. 12,1950	Replaced Miller.
Downey, Sheridan	Dem	Cal.	Nov. 30,1950	Resigned and retired.

Departures from the Senate:

	Majority			Minority
Defeated for Renomination	Taylor, Glen H.	Ida.	Dem	None

INTERIOR AND INSULAR AFFAIRS / 82nd Congress

Service Dates of Committee Chair: Jan. 15,1951-Jan. 3,1953
Service Dates of Majority Members: Jan. 15,1951-Jan. 13,1953
Service Dates of Minority Members: Jan. 15,1951-Jan. 13,1953

Majority

Rank Name	Party	State	Years in: Senate	Years in: Comm.
Chr O'Mahoney, Joseph C.	Dem	Wyo.	18	*1 18
2nd Murray, James E.	Dem	Mont.	17	17
3rd McFarland, Ernest W.	Dem	Ariz.	11	10
4th Anderson, Clinton P.	Dem	N.M.	3	3
5th Lehman, Herbert H.	Dem	N.Y.	2	2
6th Long, Russell B.	Dem	La.	3	1
7th Smathers, George A.	Dem	Fla.	1	1

Minority

Rank Name	Party	State	Years in: Senate	Years in: Comm.
RM Butler, Hugh A.	Rep	Neb.	11	10
2nd Millikin, Eugene D.	Rep	Colo.	10	10
3rd Cordon, Guy	Rep	Ore.	7	7
4th Ecton, Zales N.	Rep	Mont.	5	5
5th Malone, George W.	Rep	Nev.	5	5
6th Watkins, Arthur V.	Rep	Utah	5	5

*1: Member's 1st period of service on the committee.

	Majority		Minority	
Departures from the Senate:				
Defeated for Reelection	McFarland, Ernest W.	Ariz. Dem	Ecton, Zales N.	Mont. Rep
	O'Mahoney, Joseph C.	Wyo. Dem		
Departures from Committee:				
Moved to Banking & Currency	Lehman, Herbert H.	N.Y. Dem	None	

INTERIOR AND INSULAR AFFAIRS / 83rd Congress

Service Dates of Committee Chairs: Ch1 Jan. 13,1953-July 1,1954
Ch2 July 9,1954-Jan. 11,1955
Service Dates of Majority Members: Jan. 13,1953-Jan. 11,1955
Service Dates of Minority Members: Jan. 13,1953-Jan. 11,1955

Majority

Rank Name	Party	State	Years in: Senate	Years in: Comm.
Ch1 Butler, Hugh A.	Rep	Neb.	13	12
2nd Millikin, Eugene D.	Rep	Colo.	12	12
Ch2 3rd Cordon, Guy	Rep	Ore.	9	11
4th Malone, George W.	Rep	Nev.	7	7
5th Watkins, Arthur V.	Rep	Utah	7	7
6th Dworshak, Henry C.	Rep	Ida.	6	*2 1
7th Kuchel, Thomas H.	Rep	Cal.	1	1
8th Barrett, Frank A.	Rep	Wyo.	1	1

Minority

Rank Name	Party	State	Years in: Senate	Years in: Comm.
RM Murray, James E.	Dem	Mont.	19	19
2nd Anderson, Clinton P.	Dem	N.M.	5	5
3rd Long, Russell B.	Dem	La.	5	2
4th Smathers, George A.	Dem	Fla.	3	2
5th Clements, Earle C.	Dem	Ky.	3	1
6th Jackson, Henry M.	Dem	Wash.	1	1
7th Daniel, Price M.	Dem	Tex.	1	1

*2: Member's 2nd period of service on the committee.

Note: Ranking on this committee for the following member was affected by other chamber service: Eugene D. Millikin (Rep-Colo.), Chair, Finance.

Changes:

Chair:				
Ch1 Butler, Hugh A.	Rep	Neb.	July 1,1954	Died in office.
Ch2 Cordon, Guy	Rep	Ore.	July 9,1954	Succeeded Butler as Chair.
Majority:				
Butler, Hugh A.	Rep	Neb.	July 1,1954	Died in office.
Crippa, Edward D.	Rep	Wyo.	July 9,1954	Replaced Butler.
Crippa, Edward D.	Rep	Wyo.	Nov. 28,1954	Resigned and retired.
Brown, Ernest S.	Rep	Nev.	Nov. 30,1954	Replaced Crippa.
Brown, Ernest S.	Rep	Nev.	Dec. 1,1954	Resigned; defeated in special election.
Minority:				
Smathers, George A.	Dem	Fla.	May 18,1954	Moved to Finance.
Lennon, Alton A.	Dem	N.C.	May 19,1954	Replaced Smathers.
Clements, Earle C.	Dem	Ky.	July 1,1954	Moved to Interstate and Foreign Commerce.
Burke, Thomas A.	Dem	Ohio	July 1,1954	Replaced Clements.

Lennon, Alton A.	Dem	N.C.	Nov. 28,1954	Resigned; defeated for nomination in special election.
Burke, Thomas A.	Dem	Ohio	Dec. 2,1954	Resigned; defeated in special election.

	Majority		Minority	
Departures from the Senate:				
Defeated for Reelection	Cordon, Guy	Ore. Rep	None	
Departures from Committee:				
Moved to Judiciary; Interstate & Foreign Commerce	None		Daniel, Price M.	Tex. Dem

INTERIOR AND INSULAR AFFAIRS / 84th Congress

Service Dates of Committee Chair: Jan. 11,1955-Jan. 9,1957
Service Dates of Majority Members: Jan. 11,1955-Jan. 9,1957
Service Dates of Minority Members: Jan. 11,1955-Jan. 9,1957

Majority

Rank Name	Party	State	Years in: Senate	Years in: Comm.
Chr Murray, James E.	Dem	Mont.	21	21
2nd Anderson, Clinton P.	Dem	N.M.	7	7
3rd Long, Russell B.	Dem	La.	7	4
4th Jackson, Henry M.	Dem	Wash.	3	2
5th O'Mahoney, Joseph C.	Dem	Wyo.	20	*2 1
6th Scott, W. Kerr	Dem	N.C.	1	*1 1
7th Bible, Alan H.	Dem	Nev.	1	1
8th Neuberger, Richard L.	Dem	Ore.	1	1

Minority

Rank Name	Party	State	Years in: Senate	Years in: Comm.
RM Millikin, Eugene D.	Rep	Colo.	14	14
2nd Malone, George W.	Rep	Nev.	9	9
3rd Watkins, Arthur V.	Rep	Utah	9	9
4th Dworshak, Henry C.	Rep	Ida.	8	*2 2
5th Kuchel, Thomas H.	Rep	Cal.	3	2
6th Barrett, Frank A.	Rep	Wyo.	3	2
7th Goldwater, Barry M.	Rep	Ariz.	3	1

*1: Member's 1st period of service on the committee; *2: Member's 2nd period of service on the committee.

Changes:
Majority:

Scott, W. Kerr	Dem	N.C.	Apr. 12,1956	Moved to Public Works.
Laird, William R. III	Dem	W.Va.	Apr. 12,1956	Replaced Scott.
Long, Russell B.	Dem	La.	May 18,1956	Moved to Foreign Relations.
Scott, W. Kerr	Dem	N.C.	June 18,1956	Reappointed to committee and replaced Long.
Scott, W. Kerr	Dem	N.C.	July 27,1956	Left committee and returned to Public Works.
Humphreys, Robert	Dem	Ky.	July 27,1956	Replaced Scott.
Laird, William R. III	Dem	W.Va.	Nov. 6,1956	Resigned and retired.
Humphreys, Robert	Dem	Ky.	Nov. 6,1956	Resigned and retired.

	Majority	Minority	
Departures from the Senate:			
Retired	None	Millikin, Eugene D.	Colo. Rep

INTERIOR AND INSULAR AFFAIRS / 85th Congress

Service Dates of Committee Chair: Jan. 9,1957-Jan. 14,1959
Service Dates of Majority Members: Jan. 9,1957-Jan. 14,1959
Service Dates of Minority Members: Jan. 9,1957-Jan. 20,1959

Majority

Rank Name	Party	State	Years in: Senate	Years in: Comm.
Chr Murray, James E.	Dem	Mont.	23	23
2nd Anderson, Clinton P.	Dem	N.M.	9	8
3rd Jackson, Henry M.	Dem	Wash.	5	4
4th O'Mahoney, Joseph C.	Dem	Wyo.	22	*2 2
5th Bible, Alan H.	Dem	Nev.	3	2
6th Neuberger, Richard L.	Dem	Ore.	3	2
7th Carroll, John A.	Dem	Colo.	1	1
8th Church, Frank F.	Dem	Ida.	1	1

Minority

Rank Name	Party	State	Years in: Senate	Years in: Comm.
RM Malone, George W.	Rep	Nev.	11	11
2nd Watkins, Arthur V.	Rep	Utah	11	11
3rd Dworshak, Henry C.	Rep	Ida.	10	*2 4
4th Kuchel, Thomas H.	Rep	Cal.	5	4
5th Barrett, Frank A.	Rep	Wyo.	5	4
6th Goldwater, Barry M.	Rep	Ariz.	5	2
7th Allott, Gordon L.	Rep	Colo.	3	1

*2: Member's 2nd period of service on the committee.

Departures from the Senate:
Defeated for Reelection

Majority
None

Minority

Barrett, Frank A.	Wyo.	Rep
Malone, George W.	Nev.	Rep
Watkins, Arthur V.	Utah	Rep

INTERIOR AND INSULAR AFFAIRS / 86th Congress

Service Dates of Committee Chair: Jan. 14,1959-Jan. 3,1961
Service Dates of Majority Members: Jan. 14,1959-Jan. 10,1961
Service Dates of Minority Members: Jan. 20,1959-Jan. 13,1961

Majority

Rank	Name	Party	State	Years in: Senate	Years in: Comm.
Chr	Murray, James E.	Dem	Mont.	25	25
2nd	Anderson, Clinton P.	Dem	N.M.	11	11
3rd	Jackson, Henry M.	Dem	Wash.	7	7
4th	O'Mahoney, Joseph C.	Dem	Wyo.	24	*2 5
5th	Bible, Alan H.	Dem	Nev.	5	5
6th	Neuberger, Richard L.	Dem	Ore.	5	5
7th	Carroll, John A.	Dem	Colo.	3	3
8th	Church, Frank	Dem	Ida.	3	3
9th	Gruening, Ernest	Dem	Alas.	1	1
10th	Moss, Frank E.	Dem	Utah	1	1

Minority

Rank	Name	Party	State	Years in: Senate	Years in: Comm.
RM	Dworshak, Henry C.	Rep	Ida.	12	*2 7
2nd	Kuchel, Thomas H.	Rep	Cal.	7	7
3rd	Goldwater, Barry M.	Rep	Ariz.	7	5
4th	Allott, Gordon L.	Rep	Colo.	5	3
5th	Keating, Kenneth B.	Rep	N.Y.	1	1

*2: Member's 2nd period of service on the committee.

Notes: The admission of Hawaii to the Union on August 21,1959 led to the seating of both of the state's U.S. Senators on this committee. This resulted in a change in size and party ratio to 11 Democrats and 6 Republicans on Sep. 12,1959. Appointed Senator C. Norman Brunsdale (Rep-N.D.) left the Senate upon the seating of Quentin Burdick (Dem-N.D.), who won the special election to fill the vacancy of William Langer. Burdick's seating on Aug. 8,1960 led to another change in size and party ratio on this committee to 12 Democrats and 5 Republicans on Aug. 24,1960.

Additions:

Majority:	11th	Long, Oren E.	Dem	Hai.	Sep. 12,1959
	12th	Burdick, Quentin N.	Dem	N.D.	Aug. 24,1960
Minority:	6th	Fong, Hiram L.	Rep	Hai.	Sep. 12,1959

Changes:

Majority:

Neuberger, Richard L.	Dem	Ore.	Mar. 9,1960	Died in office.
Lusk, Hall S.	Dem	Ore.	Mar. 28,1960	Replaced Neuberger.
Lusk, Hall S.	Dem	Ore.	Nov. 8,1960	Resigned; appointed to State Supreme Court.

Minority:

Keating, Kenneth B.	Rep	N.Y.	Jan. 27,1959	Moved to Rules and Administration.
Martin, Thomas E.	Rep	Iowa	Jan. 27,1959	Replaced Keating.
Martin, Thomas E.	Rep	Iowa	Aug. 24,1960	Ratio change; moved to Rules and Administration.

Departures from the Senate:
Retired

Majority

Murray, James E.	Mont.	Dem
O'Mahoney, Joseph C.	Wyo.	Dem

Minority
None

INTERIOR AND INSULAR AFFAIRS / 87th Congress

Service Dates of Committee Chair: Jan. 10,1961-Feb. 25,1963
Service Dates of Majority Members: Jan. 10,1961-Feb. 25,1963
Service Dates of Minority Members: Jan. 13,1961-Feb. 25,1963

Majority

Rank	Name	Party	State	Years in: Senate	Years in: Comm.
Chr	Anderson, Clinton P.	Dem	N.M.	13	13
2nd	Jackson, Henry M.	Dem	Wash.	9	8
3rd	Bible, Alan H.	Dem	Nev.	7	6
4th	Carroll, John A.	Dem	Colo.	5	5
5th	Church, Frank F.	Dem	Ida.	5	5
6th	Gruening, Ernest	Dem	Alas.	3	2
7th	Moss, Frank E.	Dem	Utah	3	2
8th	Long, Oren E.	Dem	Hai.	2	2
9th	Burdick, Quentin N.	Dem	N.D.	1	1
10th	Metcalf, Lee	Dem	Mont.	1	*1 1
11th	Hickey, John J.	Dem	Wyo.	1	1

Minority

Rank	Name	Party	State	Years in: Senate	Years in: Comm.
RM1	Dworshak, Henry C.	Rep	Ida.	14	*2 9
RM2 2nd	Kuchel, Thomas H.	Rep	Cal.	9	9
3rd	Goldwater, Barry M.	Rep	Ariz.	9	7
4th	Allott, Gordon L.	Rep	Colo.	7	5
5th	Fong, Hiram L.	Rep	Hai.	2	2
6th	Miller, Jack R.	Rep	Iowa	1	1

*1: Member's 1st period of service on the committee;
*2: Member's 2nd period of service on the committee.

Changes:

Ranking Member:

RM1 Dworshak, Henry C.	Rep	Ida.	July 23,1962	Died in office.
RM2 Kuchel, Thomas H.	Rep	Cal.	July 23,1962	Succeeded Dworshak as Ranking Minority Member.

Majority:

Hickey, John J.	Dem	Wyo.	Nov. 6,1962	Resigned; defeated in special election.

Minority:

Fong, Hiram L.	Rep	Hai.	July 11,1961	Moved to Judiciary.
Dirksen, Everett M.	Rep	Ill.	July 11,1961	Replaced Fong.
Goldwater, Barry M.	Rep	Ariz.	Feb. 2,1962	Moved to Armed Services.
Dirksen, Everett M.	Rep	Ill.	Feb. 2,1962	Moved to Rules and Administration.
Murphy, Maurice J. Jr.	Rep	N.H.	Feb. 2,1962	Replaced Goldwater.
Pearson, James B.	Rep	Kans.	Feb. 5,1962	Replaced Dirksen.
Murphy, Maurice J. Jr.	Rep	N.H.	July 18,1962	Moved to Public Works.
Bottum, Joseph H.	Rep	S.D.	July 18,1962	Replaced Murphy.
Dworshak, Henry C.	Rep	Ida.	July 23,1962	Died in office.
Jordan, Len B.	Rep	Ida.	Aug. 8,1962	Replaced Dworshak.

	Majority		Minority	
Departures from the Senate:				
Retired	Long, Oren E.	Hai. Dem	None	
Defeated for Reelection	Carroll, John A.	Colo. Dem	Bottum, Joseph H.	S.D. Rep
Departures from Committee:				
Moved to Government Operations	None		Miller, Jack R.	Iowa Rep
Moved to Commerce	None		Pearson, James B.	Kans. Rep

INTERIOR AND INSULAR AFFAIRS / 88th Congress

Service Dates of Committee Chair: Feb. 25,1963-Jan. 8,1965
Service Dates of Majority Members: Feb. 25,1963-Jan. 8,1965
Service Dates of Minority Members: Feb. 25,1963-Jan. 15,1965

Majority

Rank	Name	Party	State	Years in: Senate		Years in: Comm.
Chr	Jackson, Henry M.	Dem	Wash.	11		11
2nd	Anderson, Clinton P.	Dem	N.M.	15		15
3rd	Bible, Alan H.	Dem	Nev.	9		9
4th	Church, Frank F.	Dem	Ida.	7		7
5th	Gruening, Ernest	Dem	Alas.	5		5
6th	Moss, Frank E.	Dem	Utah	5		5
7th	Burdick, Quentin N.	Dem	N.D.	3		3
8th	Metcalf, Lee	Dem	Mont.	3	*1	3
9th	Hayden, Carl	Dem	Ariz.	36	*2	1
10th	McGovern, George S.	Dem	S.D.	1		1
11th	Nelson, Gaylord A.	Dem	Wisc.	1	*1	1

Minority

Rank	Name	Party	State	Years in: Senate	Years in: Comm.
RM	Kuchel, Thomas H.	Rep	Cal.	11	11
2nd	Allott, Gordon L.	Rep	Colo.	9	7
3rd	Jordan, Len B.	Rep	Ida.	1	1
4th	Simpson, Milward L.	Rep	Wyo.	1	1
5th	Mechem, Edwin L.	Rep	N.M.	1	1
6th	Dominick, Peter H.	Rep	Colo.	1	1

*1: Member's 1st period of service on the committee;
*2: Member's 2nd period of service on the committee.

Note: Ranking on this committee for the following member was affected by other chamber service: Clinton P. Anderson (Dem-N.M.), Chair, Aeronautical and Space Sciences.

Changes:

Majority:

Name	Party	State	Date	Change
Metcalf, Lee	Dem	Mont.	Aug. 23,1963	Moved to Labor and Public Welfare.
Walters, Herbert S.	Dem	Tenn.	Aug. 27,1963	Replaced Metcalf.
Walters, Herbert S.	Dem	Tenn.	Nov. 3,1964	Resigned and retired.

Minority:

Name	Party	State	Date	Change
Mechem, Edwin L.	Rep	N.M.	Nov. 3,1964	Resigned; defeated for election.

Departures from Committee:

	Majority	Minority		
Moved to Commerce; Labor & Public Welfare	None	Dominick, Peter H.	Colo.	Rep

INTERIOR AND INSULAR AFFAIRS / 89th Congress

Service Dates of Committee Chair: Jan. 8,1965-Jan. 11,1967
Service Dates of Majority Members: Jan. 8,1965-Jan. 11,1967
Service Dates of Minority Members: Jan. 15,1965-Jan. 16,1967

Majority

Rank	Name	Party	State	Years in: Senate		Years in: Comm.
Chr	Jackson, Henry M.	Dem	Wash.	13		12
2nd	Anderson, Clinton P.	Dem	N.M.	17		16
3rd	Bible, Alan H.	Dem	Nev.	11		10
4th	Church, Frank F.	Dem	Ida.	9		8
5th	Gruening, Ernest	Dem	Alas.	7		6
6th	Moss, Frank E.	Dem	Utah	7		6
7th	Burdick, Quentin N.	Dem	N.D.	5		5
8th	Hayden, Carl	Dem	Ariz.	38	*2	2
9th	McGovern, George S.	Dem	S.D.	3		2
10th	Nelson, Gaylord A.	Dem	Wisc.	3	*1	2
11th	Metcalf, Lee	Dem	Mont.	5	*2	1

Minority

Rank	Name	Party	State	Years in: Senate	Years in: Comm.
RM	Kuchel, Thomas H.	Rep	Cal.	13	13
2nd	Allott, Gordon L.	Rep	Colo.	11	9
3rd	Jordan, Len B.	Rep	Ida.	3	3
4th	Simpson, Milward L.	Rep	Wyo.	3	2
5th	Fannin, Paul J.	Rep	Ariz.	1	1

*1: Member's 1st period of service on the committee;
*2: Member's 2nd period of service on the committee.

Note: Ranking on this committee for the following member was affected by other chamber service: Clinton P. Anderson (Dem-N.M.), Chair, Aeronautical and Space Sciences.

Departures from the Senate:

	Majority	Minority		
Retired	None	Simpson, Milward L.	Wyo.	Rep

INTERIOR AND INSULAR AFFAIRS / 90th Congress

Service Dates of Committee Chair: Jan. 11,1967-Jan. 14,1969
Service Dates of Majority Members: Jan. 11,1967-Jan. 14,1969
Service Dates of Minority Members: Jan. 16,1967-Jan. 14,1969

Majority

Rank	Name	Party	State	Years in: Senate		Years in: Comm.
Chr	Jackson, Henry M.	Dem	Wash.	15		14
2nd	Anderson, Clinton P.	Dem	N.M.	19		19
3rd	Bible, Alan H.	Dem	Nev.	13		13
4th	Church, Frank F.	Dem	Ida.	11		11
5th	Gruening, Ernest	Dem	Alas.	9		8
6th	Moss, Frank E.	Dem	Utah	9		8
7th	Burdick, Quentin N.	Dem	N.D.	7		7
8th	Hayden, Carl	Dem	Ariz.	40	*2	4
9th	McGovern, George S.	Dem	S.D.	5		4
10th	Nelson, Gaylord A.	Dem	Wisc.	5	*1	4
11th	Metcalf, Lee	Dem	Mont.	7	*2	3

Minority

Rank	Name	Party	State	Years in: Senate	Years in: Comm.
RM	Kuchel, Thomas H.	Rep	Cal.	15	15
2nd	Allott, Gordon L.	Rep	Colo.	13	11
3rd	Jordan, Len B.	Rep	Ida.	5	5
4th	Fannin, Paul J.	Rep	Ariz.	3	3
5th	Hansen, Clifford P.	Rep	Wyo.	1	1
6th	Hatfield, Mark O.	Rep	Ore.	1	1

*1: Member's 1st period of service on the committee;
*2: Member's 2nd period of service on the committee.

Note: Ranking on this committee for the following member was affected by other chamber service: Clinton P. Anderson (Dem-N.M.), Chair, Aeronautical and Space Sciences.

Departures from the Senate:	Majority		Minority	
Defeated for Renomination	Gruening, Ernest	Alas. Dem	Kuchel, Thomas H.	Cal. Rep
Retired	Hayden, Carl	Ariz. Dem	None	

INTERIOR AND INSULAR AFFAIRS / 91st Congress

Service Dates of Committee Chair: Jan. 14,1969-Jan. 28,1971
Service Dates of Majority Members: Jan. 14,1969-Jan. 28,1971
Service Dates of Minority Members: Jan. 14,1969-Jan. 29,1971

Majority

Rank	Name	Party	State	Years in: Senate		Years in: Comm.
Chr	Jackson, Henry M.	Dem	Wash.	17		17
2nd	Anderson, Clinton P.	Dem	N.M.	21		21
3rd	Bible, Alan H.	Dem	Nev.	15		15
4th	Church, Frank F.	Dem	Ida.	13		13
5th	Moss, Frank E.	Dem	Utah	11		11
6th	Burdick, Quentin N.	Dem	N.D.	9		9
7th	McGovern, George S.	Dem	S.D.	7		6
8th	Nelson, Gaylord A.	Dem	Wisc.	7	*1	6
9th	Metcalf, Lee	Dem	Mont.	9	*2	5
10th	Gravel, Mike	Dem	Alas.	1		1

Minority

Rank	Name	Party	State	Years in: Senate	Years in: Comm.
RM	Allott, Gordon L.	Rep	Colo.	15	13
2nd	Jordan, Len B.	Rep	Ida.	7	7
3rd	Fannin, Paul J.	Rep	Ariz.	5	4
4th	Hansen, Clifford P.	Rep	Wyo.	3	2
5th	Hatfield, Mark O.	Rep	Ore.	3	2
6th	Stevens, Theodore F.	Rep	Alas.	1	1
7th	Bellmon, Henry	Rep	Okla.	1	1

*1: Member's 1st period of service on the committee; *2: Member's 2nd period of service on the committee.

Note: Ranking on this committee for the following member was affected by other chamber service: Clinton P. Anderson (Dem-N.M.), Chair, Aeronautical and Space Sciences.

Departures from Committee:	Majority		Minority
Moved to Finance	Nelson, Gaylord A.	Wisc. Dem	None

INTERIOR AND INSULAR AFFAIRS / 92nd Congress

Service Dates of Committee Chair: Jan. 28,1971-Jan. 4,1973
Service Dates of Majority Members: Jan. 28,1971-Jan. 4,1973
Service Dates of Minority Members: Jan. 29,1971-Jan. 12,1973

Majority

Rank	Name	Party	State	Years in: Senate	Years in: Comm.
Chr	Jackson, Henry M.	Dem	Wash.	19	19
2nd	Anderson, Clinton P.	Dem	N.M.	23	23
3rd	Bible, Alan H.	Dem	Nev.	17	17
4th	Church, Frank F.	Dem	Ida.	15	15
5th	Moss, Frank E.	Dem	Utah	13	13
6th	Burdick, Quentin N.	Dem	N.D.	11	11
7th	McGovern, George S.	Dem	S.D.	9	8
8th	Metcalf, Lee	Dem	Mont.	11	*2 7
9th	Gravel, Mike	Dem	Alas.	3	3

Minority

Rank	Name	Party	State	Years in: Senate	Years in: Comm.
RM	Allott, Gordon L.	Rep	Colo.	17	15
2nd	Jordan, Len B.	Rep	Ida.	9	9
3rd	Fannin, Paul J.	Rep	Ariz.	7	7
4th	Hansen, Clifford P.	Rep	Wyo.	5	5
5th	Hatfield, Mark O.	Rep	Ore.	5	5
6th	Stevens, Theodore F.	Rep	Alas.	3	3
7th	Bellmon, Henry	Rep	Okla.	3	3

*2: Member's 2nd period of service on the committee.

Note: Ranking on this committee for the following member was affected by other chamber service: Clinton P. Anderson (Dem-N.M.), Chair, Aeronautical and Space Sciences.

Changes:
Minority:

Stevens, Theodore F.	Rep	Alas.	Feb. 23,1972	Moved to Appropriations
Buckley, James L.	Con	N.Y.	Feb. 23,1972	Replaced Stevens.

	Majority			Minority		
Departures from the Senate:						
Defeated for Reelection	None			Allott, Gordon L.	Colo.	Rep
Retired	Anderson, Clinton P.	N.M.	Dem	Jordan, Len B.	Ida.	Rep
Departures from Committee:						
Moved to Public Works	Burdick, Quentin N.	N.D.	Dem	None		
Moved to Finance	Gravel, Mike	Alas.	Dem	None		
Moved to Foreign Relations	McGovern, George S.	S.D.	Dem	None		
Moved to Aeronautical & Space Sciences	Moss, Frank E.	Utah	Dem	None		
Moved to Appropriations	None			Bellmon, Henry	Okla.	Rep

INTERIOR AND INSULAR AFFAIRS / 93rd Congress

Service Dates of Committee Chair: Jan. 4,1973-Jan. 17,1975
Service Dates of Majority Members: Jan. 4,1973-Jan. 17,1975
Service Dates of Minority Members: Jan. 12,1973-Jan. 23,1975

Majority

Rank	Name	Party	State	Years in: Senate	Years in: Comm.
Chr	Jackson, Henry M.	Dem	Wash.	21	20
2nd	Bible, Alan H.	Dem	Nev.	19	18
3rd	Church, Frank F.	Dem	Ida.	17	16
4th	Metcalf, Lee	Dem	Mont.	13	*2 8
5th	Johnston, J. Bennett Jr.	Dem	La.	1	1
6th	Abourezk, James G.	Dem	S.D.	1	1
7th	Haskell, Floyd K.	Dem	Colo.	1	1
8th	Nelson, Gaylord A.	Dem	Wisc.	11	1

Minority

Rank	Name	Party	State	Years in: Senate	Years in: Comm.
RM	Fannin, Paul J.	Rep	Ariz.	9	8
2nd	Hansen, Clifford P.	Rep	Wyo.	7	6
3rd	Hatfield, Mark O.	Rep	Ore.	7	6
4th	Buckley, James L.	Con	N.Y.	3	1
5th	McClure, James A.	Rep	Ida.	1	1
6th	Bartlett, Dewey F.	Rep	Okla.	1	1

*2: Member's 2nd period of service on the committee.

Notes: James L. Buckley of New York was elected as a Conservative but was assigned by the Republican Conference, serving on the committee with his seniority intact. The resignation of William Saxbe (Rep-Ohio), and the appointment of Howard Metzenbaum (Dem-Ohio) to fill his vacancy on Jan. 21,1974, led to a change in size and party ratio on this committee to 9 Democrats and 6 Republicans on Jan. 23,1974. The resignation of Alan Bible (Dem-Nev.), and the appointment of Paul Laxalt (Rep-Nev.) to fill his vacancy led to another change in size and party ratio on this committee to 8 Democrats and 7 Republicans on Dec. 18,1974.

Vacancy Filled:
Majority: 8th seat by Nelson on May 31,1973.

Additions:

Majority:	9th	Metzenbaum, Howard M.	Dem	Ohio	Jan. 23,1974
Minority:	7th	Laxalt, Paul	Rep	Nev.	Dec. 18,1974

Changes:

Majority:				
Bible, Alan H.	Dem	Nev.	Dec. 17,1974	Resigned and retired.
Metzenbaum, Howard M.	Dem	Ohio	Dec. 23,1974	Resigned; defeated for nomination.
Minority:				
Cotton, Norris	Rep	N.H.	Dec. 31,1974	Resigned and retired.

Departures from Committee:	**Majority**			**Minority**		
Moved to Budget; Commerce	None			Buckley, James L.	N.Y.	Con
Moved to Aeronautical & Space Sciences; Labor & Public Welfare	None			Laxalt, Paul	Nev.	Rep
No new assignment	Nelson, Gaylord A.	Wisc.	Dem	None		

INTERIOR AND INSULAR AFFAIRS / 94th Congress

Service Dates of Committee Chair: Jan. 17,1975-Jan. 10,1977
Service Dates of Majority Members: Jan. 17,1975-Jan. 10,1977
Service Dates of Minority Members: Jan. 23,1975-Jan. 10,1977

Majority

Rank	Name	Party	State	Years in: Senate	Years in: Comm.
Chr	Jackson, Henry M.	Dem	Wash.	23	23
2nd	Church, Frank F.	Dem	Ida.	19	19
3rd	Metcalf, Lee	Dem	Mont.	15*2	11
4th	Johnston, J. Bennett Jr.	Dem	La.	3	3
5th	Abourezk, James G.	Dem	S.D.	3	3
6th	Haskell, Floyd K.	Dem	Colo.	3	3
7th	Glenn, John H. Jr.	Dem	Ohio	1	1
8th	Stone, Richard B.	Dem	Fla.	1	1
9th	Bumpers, Dale	Dem	Ark.	1	1

Minority

Rank	Name	Party	State	Years in: Senate	Years in: Comm.
RM	Fannin, Paul J.	Rep	Ariz.	11	11
2nd	Hansen, Clifford P.	Rep	Wyo.	9	9
3rd	Hatfield, Mark O.	Rep	Ore.	9	9
4th	McClure, James A.	Rep	Ida.	3	3
5th	Bartlett, Dewey F.	Rep	Okla.	3	3

*2: Member's 2nd period of service on the committee.

Departures from the Senate:	**Majority**	**Minority**	
Retired	None	Fannin, Paul J.	Ariz. Rep

INTERIOR AND INSULAR AFFAIRS / 95th Congress

* Reorganized as the Committee on ENERGY AND NATURAL RESOURCES on Feb. 11,1977.

Service Dates of Committee Chair: Jan. 10,1977-Feb. 11,1977
Service Dates of Majority Members: Jan. 10,1977-Feb. 11,1977
Service Dates of Minority Members: Jan. 10,1977-Feb. 22,1977

Majority

Rank	Name	Party	State	Years in: Senate	Years in: Comm.
Chr	Jackson, Henry M.	Dem	Wash.	25	24
2nd	Church, Frank F.	Dem	Ida.	21	21
3rd	Metcalf, Lee	Dem	Mont.	17 *2	13
4th	Johnston, J. Bennett Jr.	Dem	La.	5	5
5th	Abourezk, James G.	Dem	S.D.	5	5
6th	Haskell, Floyd K.	Dem	Colo.	5	5
7th	Glenn, John H. Jr.	Dem	Ohio	3	2
8th	Stone, Richard B.	Dem	Fla.	3	2
9th	Bumpers, Dale	Dem	Ark.	3	2
10th	Sarbanes, Paul S.	Dem	Md.	1 *T	1
11th	Moynihan, Daniel Patrick	Dem	N.Y.	1 *T	1

Minority

Rank	Name	Party	State	Years in: Senate	Years in: Comm.
RM	Hansen, Clifford P.	Rep	Wyo.	11	10
2nd	Hatfield, Mark O.	Rep	Ore.	11	10
3rd	McClure, James A.	Rep	Ida.	5	4
4th	Bartlett, Dewey F.	Rep	Okla.	5	4
5th	Hatch, Orrin G.	Rep	Utah	1 *T	1
6th	Hayakawa, S. I. (Sam)	Rep	Cal.	1 *T	1

*2: Member's 2nd period of service on the committee;
*T: Temporary member of the committee.

Changes:
Majority:

Glenn, John H. Jr.	Dem	Ohio	Feb. 11,1977	Moved to Foreign Relations.
Stone, Richard B.	Dem	Fla.	Feb. 11,1977	Moved to Foreign Relations.
Sarbanes, Paul S.	Dem	Md.	Feb. 11,1977	Moved to Banking, Housing and Urban Affairs; Foreign Relations.
Moynihan, Daniel Patrick	Dem	N.Y.	Feb. 11,1977	Moved to Finance.

Minority:

Hatch, Orrin G.	Rep	Utah	Feb. 22,1977	Moved to Judiciary.
Hayakawa, S. I. (Sam)	Rep	Cal.	Feb. 22,1977	Moved to Budget; Human Resources.

ENERGY AND NATURAL RESOURCES / 95th Congress

Service Dates of Committee Chair: Feb. 11,1977-Jan. 23,1979
Service Dates of Majority Members: Feb. 11,1977-Jan. 23,1979
Service Dates of Minority Members: Feb. 22,1977-Jan. 23,1979

Majority

Rank	Name	Party	State	Years in: Senate	Years in: Comm.
Chr	Jackson, Henry M.	Dem	Wash.	25	25
2nd	Church, Frank F.	Dem	Ida.	21	21
3rd	Metcalf, Lee	Dem	Mont.	17*2	13
4th	Johnston, J. Bennett Jr.	Dem	La.	5	5
5th	Abourezk, James G.	Dem	S.D.	5	5
6th	Haskell, Floyd K.	Dem	Colo.	5	5
7th	Bumpers, Dale	Dem	Ark.	3	3
8th	Ford, Wendell H.	Dem	Ky.	3	1
9th	Durkin, John A.	Dem	N.H.	2	1
10th	Metzenbaum, Howard M.	Dem	Ohio	2 *2	1
11th	Matsunaga, Spark M.	Dem	Hai.	1	1

Minority

Rank	Name	Party	State	Years in: Senate	Years in: Comm.
RM	Hansen, Clifford P.	Rep	Wyo.	11	11
2nd	Hatfield, Mark O.	Rep	Ore.	11	11
3rd	McClure, James A.	Rep	Ida.	5	5
4th	Bartlett, Dewey F.	Rep	Okla.	5	5
5th	Weicker, Lowell P. Jr.	Rep	Conn.	7	1
6th	Domenici, Pete V.	Rep	N.M.	5	1
7th	Laxalt, Paul	Rep	Nev.	3	1

*2: Member's 2nd period of service on the committee.

Note: The seating of Democratic replacements for Lee Metcalf (Dem-Mont.) and Hubert Humphrey (Dem-Minn.) in January 1978 led to a change in committee size and party ratio to 12 Democrats and 7 Republicans on Jan. 27,1978.

Addition:
Majority: 12th Anderson, Wendell R. DFL Minn. Jan. 27,1978

Changes:
Majority:

Metcalf, Lee	Dem	Mont.	Jan. 12,1978	Died in office.
Melcher, John	Dem	Mont.	Jan. 27,1978	Replaced Metcalf.
Anderson, Wendell R.	DFL	Minn.	Dec. 29,1978	Resigned; lost special election.

Minority:

Hansen, Clifford P.	Rep	Wyo.	Dec. 31,1978	Resigned and retired.

	Majority		Minority	
Departures from the Senate:				
Defeated for Reelection	Haskell, Floyd K.	Colo. Dem	None	
Retired	Abourezk, James G.	S.D. Dem	Bartlett, Dewey F.	Okla. Rep
Departures from Committee:				
Moved to Appropriations	None		Laxalt, Paul	Nev. Rep

ENERGY AND NATURAL RESOURCES / 96th Congress

Service Dates of Committee Chair: Jan. 23,1979-Jan. 5,1981
Service Dates of Majority Members: Jan. 23,1979-Jan. 5,1981
Service Dates of Minority Members: Jan. 23,1979-Jan. 5,1981

Majority

Rank	Name	Party	State	Years in: Senate	Years in: Comm.
Chr	Jackson, Henry M.	Dem	Wash.	27	27
2nd	Church, Frank F.	Dem	Ida.	23	23
3rd	Johnston, J. Bennett Jr.	Dem	La.	7	7
4th	Bumpers, Dale	Dem	Ark.	5	5
5th	Ford, Wendell H.	Dem	Ky.	5	2
6th	Durkin, John A.	Dem	N.H.	4	2
7th	Metzenbaum, Howard M.	Dem	Ohio	4	*2 2
8th	Matsunaga, Spark M.	Dem	Hai.	3	2
9th	Melcher, John	Dem	Mont.	3	1
10th	Tsongas, Paul E.	Dem	Mass.	1	1
11th	Bradley, William W.	Dem	N.J.	1	1

Minority

Rank	Name	Party	State	Years in: Senate	Years in: Comm.
RM	Hatfield, Mark O.	Rep	Ore.	13	13
2nd	McClure, James A.	Rep	Ida.	7	7
3rd	Weicker, Lowell P. Jr.	Rep	Conn.	9	2
4th	Domenici, Pete V.	Rep	N.M.	7	2
5th	Stevens, Theodore F.	Rep	Alas.	11	1
6th	Bellmon, Henry	Rep	Okla.	11	1
7th	Wallop, Malcolm	Rep	Wyo.	3	1

*2: Member's 2nd period of service on the committee.

Changes:
Majority:

Durkin, John A.	Dem	N.H.	Dec. 29,1980	Resigned; defeated for reelection.

	Majority		Minority	
Departures from the Senate:				
Defeated for Reelection	Church, Frank F.	Ida. Dem	None	
Retired	None		Bellmon, Henry	Okla. Rep
Departures from Committee:				
Moved to Commerce, Science, & Transportation	None		Stevens, Theodore F.	Alas. Rep

ENERGY AND NATURAL RESOURCES / 97th Congress

Service Dates of Committee Chair: Jan. 5,1981-Jan. 3,1983
Service Dates of Majority Members: Jan. 5,1981-Jan. 3,1983
Service Dates of Minority Members: Jan. 5,1981-Jan. 3,1983

Majority

Rank	Name	Party	State	Years in: Senate	Years in: Comm.
Chr	McClure, James A.	Rep	Ida.	9	8
2nd	Hatfield, Mark O.	Rep	Ore.	14	14
3rd	Weicker, Lowell P. Jr.	Rep	Conn.	11	4
4th	Domenici, Pete V.	Rep	N.M.	9	4
5th	Wallop, Malcolm	Rep	Wyo.	5	2
6th	Warner, John W.	Rep	Va.	3	1
7th	Humphrey, Gordon J.	Rep	N.H.	3	1
8th	Murkowski, Frank H.	Rep	Alas.	1	1
9th	Nickles, Don	Rep	Okla.	1	1
10th	East, John P.	Rep	N.C.	1	1
11th	Heinz, H. John III	Rep	Penn.	5	1

Minority

Rank	Name	Party	State	Years in: Senate	Years in: Comm.
RM	Jackson, Henry M.	Dem	Wash.	29	28
2nd	Johnston, J. Bennett Jr.	Dem	La.	9	9
3rd	Bumpers, Dale	Dem	Ark.	7	6
4th	Ford, Wendell H.	Dem	Ky.	7	4
5th	Metzenbaum, Howard M.	Dem	Ohio	6	*2 4
6th	Matsunaga, Spark M.	Dem	Hai.	5	4
7th	Melcher, John	Dem	Mont.	5	3
8th	Tsongas, Paul E.	Dem	Mass.	3	2
9th	Bradley, William W.	Dem	N.J.	3	2

*2: Member's 2nd period of service on the committee.

Note: Ranking on this committee for the following member was affected by other chamber service: Mark O. Hatfield (Rep-Ore.), Chair, Appropriations.

	Majority		Minority
Departures from Committee:			
Moved to Armed Services	East, John P.	N.C. Rep	None
Moved to Environment & Public Works	Humphrey, Gordon J.	N.H. Rep	None

ENERGY AND NATURAL RESOURCES / 98th Congress

Service Dates of Committee Chair: Jan. 3,1983-Feb. 21,1985
Service Dates of Majority Members: Jan. 3,1983-Feb. 21,1985
Service Dates of Minority Members: Jan. 3,1983-Feb. 21,1985

Majority

Rank Name	Party	State	Years in: Senate	Years in: Comm.
Chr McClure, James A.	Rep	Ida.	11	10
2nd Hatfield, Mark O.	Rep	Ore.	16	16
3rd Weicker, Lowell P. Jr.	Rep	Conn.	13	6
4th Domenici, Pete V.	Rep	N.M.	11	6
5th Wallop, Malcolm	Rep	Wyo.	7	4
6th Warner, John W.	Rep	Va.	5	2
7th Murkowski, Frank H.	Rep	Alas.	3	2
8th Nickles, Don	Rep	Okla.	3	2
9th Hecht, Chic	Rep	Nev.	1	1
10th Chafee, John H.	Rep	R.I.	7	1
11th Heinz, H. John III	Rep	Penn.	7	2

Minority

Rank Name	Party	State	Years in: Senate	Years in: Comm.
RM Johnston, J. Bennett Jr.	Dem	La.	11	10
2nd Jackson, Henry M.	Dem	Wash.	31	30
3rd Bumpers, Dale	Dem	Ark.	9	8
4th Ford, Wendell H.	Dem	Ky.	9	6
5th Metzenbaum, Howard M.	Dem	Ohio	8	*2 6
6th Matsunaga, Spark M.	Dem	Hai.	7	6
7th Melcher, John	Dem	Mont.	7	5
8th Tsongas, Paul E.	Dem	Mass.	5	4
9th Bradley, William W.	Dem	N.J.	5	4

*2: Member's 2nd period of service on the committee.

Notes: The death of Henry M. Jackson (Dem-Wash.) and the appointment of Daniel J. Evans (Rep-Wash.) to fill his vacancy on Sep. 8,1983 led to a temporary change in size and party ratio on this committee to 12 Republicans and 9 Democrats. The increased size was made permanent on Feb. 9,1984. Rankings on this committee for the following members were affected by other chamber service: Mark O. Hatfield (Rep-Ore.), Chair, Appropriations; and Henry M. Jackson (Dem-Wash.), Ranking Minority Member, Armed Services. As Chair of the Special Committee on Aging, John Heinz, III (Rep-Penn) waived his seniority on this committee.

Addition:
Majority: 12th Evans, Daniel J. Rep Wash. Sep. 22,1983

Changes:
Minority:

Name	Party	State	Date	Change
Jackson, Henry M.	Dem	Wash.	Sep. 1,1983	Died in office.
Levin, Carl M.	Dem	Mich.	Feb. 9,1984	Replaced Jackson.

	Majority			Minority		
Departures from the Senate:						
Retired	None			Tsongas, Paul E.	Mass.	Dem
Departures from Committee:						
No new assignment	Chafee, John H.	R.I.	Rep	Matsunaga, Spark M.	Hai.	Dem
	Heinz, H. John III	Penn.	Rep	Levin, Carl M.	Mich.	Dem

ENERGY AND NATURAL RESOURCES / 99th Congress

Service Dates of Committee Chair: Feb. 21,1985-Jan. 6,1987
Service Dates of Majority Members: Feb. 21,1985-Jan. 6,1987
Service Dates of Minority Members: Feb. 21,1985-Jan. 6,1987

Majority

Rank Name	Party	State	Years in: Senate	Years in: Comm.
Chr McClure, James A.	Rep	Ida.	13	13
2nd Hatfield, Mark O.	Rep	Ore.	19	19
3rd Weicker, Lowell P. Jr.	Rep	Conn.	15	8
4th Domenici, Pete V.	Rep	N.M.	13	8
5th Wallop, Malcolm	Rep	Wyo.	9	7
6th Warner, John W.	Rep	Va.	7	5
7th Murkowski, Frank H.	Rep	Alas.	5	5
8th Nickles, Don	Rep	Okla.	5	5
9th Hecht, Chic	Rep	Nev.	3	3
10th Evans, Daniel J.	Rep	Wash.	2	2

Minority

Rank Name	Party	State	Years in: Senate	Years in: Comm.
RM Johnston, J. Bennett Jr.	Dem	La.	13	13
2nd Bumpers, Dale	Dem	Ark.	11	11
3rd Ford, Wendell H.	Dem	Ky.	11	9
4th Metzenbaum, Howard M.	Dem	Ohio	10	*2 9
5th Melcher, John	Dem	Mont.	9	8
6th Bradley, William W.	Dem	N.J.	7	7
7th Bingaman, Jeff	Dem	N.M.	3	1
8th Rockefeller, John D. IV	Dem	W.Va.	1	*1 1

*1: Member's 1st period of service on the committee; *2: Member's 2nd period of service on the committee.

Note: Ranking on this committee for the following member was affected by other chamber service: Mark O. Hatfield (Rep-Ore.), Chair, Appropriations.

Departures from Committee:	Majority			Minority		
Moved to Select Intelligence; Environment & Public Works	Warner, John W.	Va.	Rep	None		
Moved to Finance	None			Rockefeller, John D. IV	W.Va.	Dem

ENERGY AND NATURAL RESOURCES / 100th Congress

Service Dates of Committee Chair: Jan. 6,1987-Feb. 2,1989
Service Dates of Majority Members: Jan. 6,1987-Feb. 2,1989
Service Dates of Minority Members: Jan. 6,1987-Feb. 2,1989

Majority

Rank	Name	Party	State	Years in: Senate	Years in: Comm.
Chr	Johnston, J. Bennett Jr.	Dem	La.	15	15
2nd	Bumpers, Dale	Dem	Ark.	13	12
3rd	Ford, Wendell H.	Dem	Ky.	13	10
4th	Metzenbaum, Howard M.	Dem	Ohio	12 *2	10
5th	Melcher, John	Dem	Mont.	11	9
6th	Bradley, William W.	Dem	N.J.	9	8
7th	Bingaman, Jeff	Dem	N.M.	5	2
8th	Wirth, Timothy E.	Dem	Colo.	1	1
9th	Fowler, Wyche Jr.	Dem	Ga.	1	1
10th	Conrad, Kent	Dem	N.D.	1	1

Minority

Rank	Name	Party	State	Years in: Senate	Years in: Comm.
RM	McClure, James A.	Rep	Ida.	15	14
2nd	Hatfield, Mark O.	Rep	Ore.	20	20
3rd	Weicker, Lowell P. Jr.	Rep	Conn.	17	10
4th	Domenici, Pete V.	Rep	N.M.	15	10
5th	Wallop, Malcolm	Rep	Wyo.	11	8
6th	Murkowski, Frank H.	Rep	Alas.	7	7
7th	Nickles, Don	Rep	Okla.	7	7
8th	Hecht, Chic	Rep	Nev.	5	5
9th	Evans, Daniel J.	Rep	Wash.	4	4

*2: Member's 2nd period of service on the committee.

Note: Ranking on this committee for the following member was affected by other chamber service: Mark O. Hatfield (Rep-Ore.), Ranking Minority Member, Appropriations.

Departures from the Senate:	Majority			Minority		
Defeated for Reelection	Melcher, John	Mont.	Dem	Hecht, Chic	Nev.	Rep
				Weicker, Lowell P. Jr.	Conn.	Rep
Retired	None			Evans, Daniel J.	Wash.	Rep
Departures from Committee:						
Moved to Appropriations	Fowler, Wyche Jr.	Ga.	Dem	None		

ENERGY AND NATURAL RESOURCES / 101st Congress

Service Dates of Committee Chair: Feb. 2,1989-Feb. 5,1991
Service Dates of Majority Members: Feb. 2,1989-Feb. 5,1991
Service Dates of Minority Members: Feb. 2,1989-Feb. 5,1991

Majority

Rank	Name	Party	State	Years in: Senate	Years in: Comm.
Chr	Johnston, J. Bennett Jr.	Dem	La.	17	17
2nd	Bumpers, Dale	Dem	Ark.	15	15
3rd	Ford, Wendell H.	Dem	Ky.	15	12
4th	Metzenbaum, Howard M.	Dem	Ohio	14 *2	12
5th	Bradley, William W.	Dem	N.J.	11	11
6th	Bingaman, Jeff	Dem	N.M.	7	4
7th	Wirth, Timothy E.	Dem	Colo.	3	3
8th	Conrad, Kent	Dem	N.D.	3	3
9th	Heflin, Howell T.	Dem	Ala.	11	1
10th	Rockefeller, John D. IV	Dem	W.Va.	5 *2	1

Minority

Rank	Name	Party	State	Years in: Senate	Years in: Comm.
RM	McClure, James A.	Rep	Ida.	17	17
2nd	Hatfield, Mark O.	Rep	Ore.	23	23
3rd	Domenici, Pete V.	Rep	N.M.	17	12
4th	Wallop, Malcolm	Rep	Wyo.	13	11
5th	Murkowski, Frank H.	Rep	Alas.	9	9
6th	Nickles, Don	Rep	Okla.	9	9
7th	Burns, Conrad	Rep	Ida.	1	1
8th	Garn, Jake	Rep	Utah	15	1
9th	McConnell, Mitch	Rep	Ky.	5	1

*2: Member's 2nd period of service on the committee.

Note: Ranking on this committee for the following member was affected by other chamber service: Mark O. Hatfield (Rep-Ore.), Ranking Minority Member, Appropriations.

Changes:

Majority:

Metzenbaum, Howard M.	Dem	Ohio	May 16,1990	Moved to Environment and Public Works.
Akaka, Daniel K.	Dem	Hai.	May 16,1990	Replaced Metzenbaum.

	Majority			Minority:		
Departures from Senate:						
Retired	None			McClure, James A.	Ida.	Rep
Departures from Committee:						
No new assignment	Heflin, Howell T.	Ala.	Dem	McConnell, Mitch	Ky.	Rep
	Rockefeller, John D. IV	W.Va.	Dem			

ENERGY AND NATURAL RESOURCES / 102nd Congress

Service Dates of Committee Chair: Feb. 5,1991-Jan. 3,1993
Service Dates of Majority Members: Feb. 5,1991-Jan. 3,1993
Service Dates of Minority Members: Feb. 5,1991-Jan. 3,1993

Majority

Rank	Name	Party	State	Years in: Senate	Years in: Comm.
Chr	Johnston, J. Bennett Jr.	Dem	La.	19	19
2nd	Bumpers, Dale	Dem	Ark.	17	17
3rd	Ford, Wendell H.	Dem	Ky.	17	14
4th	Bradley, William W.	Dem	N.J.	13	13
5th	Bingaman, Jeff	Dem	N.M.	9	6
6th	Wirth, Timothy E.	Dem	Colo.	5	5
7th	Conrad, Kent	Dem	N.D.	5	5
8th	Akaka, Daniel K.	Dem	Hai.	1	1
9th	Fowler, Wyche Jr.	Dem	Ga.	5	1
10th	Shelby, Richard C.	Dem	Ala.	5	1
11th	Wellstone, Paul	Dem	Minn.	1	1

Minority

Rank	Name	Party	State	Years in: Senate	Years in: Comm.
RM	Wallop, Malcolm	Rep	Wyo.	15	13
2nd	Hatfield, Mark O.	Rep	Ore.	25	25
3rd	Domenici, Pete V.	Rep	N.M.	19	14
4th	Murkowski, Frank H.	Rep	Alas.	11	11
5th	Nickles, Don	Rep	Okla.	11	11
6th	Burns, Conrad	Rep	Ida.	3	3
7th	Craig, Larry	Rep	Ida.	1	1
8th	Seymour, John	Rep	Cal.	1	1
9th	Garn, Jake	Rep	Utah	17	3

Note: Rankings on this committee for the following members were affected by other chamber service: Mark O. Hatfield (Rep-Ore.), Ranking Minority Member, Appropriations; Pete V. Domenici (Rep-N.M.), Ranking Minority Member, Budget; and Jake Garn (Rep-Utah), Ranking Member, Banking, Housing and Urban Affairs.

ENVIRONMENT AND PUBLIC WORKS

PUBLIC WORKS

Jurisdiction, 1947

Established by the Legislative Reorganization Act of 1946:

[Section 102.(1)(n)]

The Committee on Public Works, to consist of thirteen Senators, to which committee shall be referred all proposed legislation, messages, petitions, memorials and other matters relating to the following subjects:

1. Flood control and improvement of rivers and harbors.
2. Public works for the benefit of navigation, and bridges and dams (other than international bridges and dams).
3. Water power.
4. Oil and other pollution of navigable waters.
5. Public buildings and occupied or improved grounds of the United States generally.
6. Measures relating to the purchase of sites and construction of post offices, customhouses, Federal courthouses, and Government buildings within the District of Columbia.
7. Measures relating to the Capitol building and the Senate and House Office Buildings.
8. Measures relating to the construction or reconstruction, maintenance, and care of the buildings and grounds of the Botanic Gardens, the Library of Congress, and the Smithsonian Institution.
9. Public reservations and parks within the District of Columbia, including Rock Creek Park and the Zoological Park.
10. Measures relating to the construction or maintenance of roads and post roads.

ENVIRONMENT AND PUBLIC WORKS

Reorganization, 1977

The Committee was reorganized as the Standing Committee on Environment and Public Works following the passage of Senate Resolution 4, the Committee System Reorganization Amendments of 1977, February 4, 1977.

Jurisdiction, 1977

Jurisdiction as contained in Senate Resolution 4, the Committee System Reorganization Amendments of 1977, February 4, 1977:

[Rule XXV.(1)(h)]

(1) Committee on Environment and Public Works, to which committee shall be referred all proposed legislation, messages, petitions, memorials, and other matters relating to the following subjects:

1. Environmental Policy.
2. Environmental research and development.
3. Ocean dumping.
4. Fisheries and wildlife.
5. Environmental aspects of Outer Continental Shelf lands.
6. Solid waste disposal and recycling.
7. Environmental effects of toxic substances, other than pesticides.
8. Water resources.
9. Flood control and improvements of rivers and harbors, including environmental aspects of deepwater ports.
10. Public works, bridges, and dams.
11. Water pollution.
12. Air pollution.
13. Noise pollution.

14. Nonmilitary environmental regulation and control of nuclear energy.
15. Regional economic development.
16. Construction and maintenance of highways.
17. Public buildings and improved grounds of the United States generally, including Federal buildings in the District of Columbia.

(2) Such committee shall also study and review, on a comprehensive basis, matters relating to environmental protection and resource utilization and conservation, and report thereon from time to time.

Jurisdiction, 1992

Jurisdiction contained in the Standing Rules of the Senate (as revised to March 18, 1992):

[Rule XXV.(1)(h)]

(1) Committee on Environment and Public Works, to which committee shall be referred all proposed legislation, messages, petitions, memorials, and other matters relating to the following subjects:

1. Air Pollution.
2. Construction and maintenance of highways.
3. Environmental aspects of Outer Continental Shelf lands.
4. Environmental effects of toxic substances, other than pesticides.
5. Environmental policy.
6. Environmental research and development.
7. Fisheries and wildlife.
8. Flood control and improvements of rivers and harbors, including environmental aspects of deepwater ports.
9. Noise pollution.
10. Nonmilitary environmental regulation and control of nuclear energy.
11. Ocean dumping.
12. Public buildings and improved grounds of the United States generally, including Federal buildings in the District of Columbia.
13. Public works, bridges, and dams.
14. Regional economic development.
15. Solid waste disposal and recycling.
16. Water pollution.
17. Water resources.

(2) Such committee shall also study and review, on a comprehensive basis, matters relating to environmental protection and resource utilization and conservation, and report thereon from time to time.

PUBLIC WORKS / 80th Congress

Service Dates of Committee Chair: Jan. 6,1947-Jan. 3,1949
Service Dates of Majority Members: Jan. 6,1947-Jan. 10,1949
Service Dates of Minority Members: Jan. 8,1947-Jan. 10,1949

Majority

Rank Name	Party	State	Years in: Senate	Comm.
Chr Revercomb, W. Chapman	Rep	W.Va.	5 *1	4
2nd Cooper, John Sherman	Rep	Ky.	1 *1	1
3rd Cain, Harry P.	Rep	Wash.	1	1
4th Martin, Edward	Rep	Penn.	1	1
5th Watkins, Arthur V.	Rep	Utah	1	1
6th Williams, John J.	Rep	Del.	1	1
7th Malone, George W.	Rep	Nev.	1	1

Minority

Rank Name	Party	State	Years in: Senate	Comm.
RM1 Overton, John H.	Dem	La.	14	1
RM2 2nd Chavez, Dennis	Dem	N.M.	12 *2	1
3rd Downey, Sheridan	Dem	Cal.	9	1
4th O'Daniel, W. Lee	Dem	Tex.	6	1
5th McClellan, John L.	Dem	Ark.	5	1
6th Holland, Spessard L.	Dem	Fla.	1	1

*1: Member's 1st period of service on the committee; *2: Member's 2nd period of service on the committee.

Vacancy Filled:
Minority: 6th seat by Holland on Nov. 15,1947.

Changes:
Ranking Member:

RM1	Overton, John H.	Dem	La.	May 14,1948	Died in office.
RM2	Chavez, Dennis	Dem	N.M.	May 14,1948	Succeeded Overton as Ranking Minority Member.

Minority:

Overton, John H.	Dem	La.	May 14,1948	Died in office.
Sparkman, John J.	Dem	Ala.	May 26,1948	Replaced Overton.

Departures from the Senate:	Majority			Minority		
Defeated for Reelection	Cooper, John Sherman	Ky.	Rep	None		
	Revercomb, W. Chapman	W.Va.	Rep			
Retired	None			O'Daniel, W. Lee	Tex.	Dem
Departures from Committee:						
Moved to Finance; Interstate & Foreign Commerce; District of Columbia	Williams, John J.	Del.	Rep	None		

PUBLIC WORKS / 81st Congress

Service Dates of Committee Chair: Jan. 10,1949-Jan. 15,1951
Service Dates of Majority Members: Jan. 10,1949-Jan. 15,1951
Service Dates of Minority Members: Jan. 10,1949-Jan. 15,1951

Majority

Rank	Name	Party	State	Years in: Senate	Years in: Comm.
Chr	Chavez, Dennis	Dem	N.M.	14	*2 3
2nd	Downey, Sheridan	Dem	Cal.	11	3
3rd	McClellan, John L.	Dem	Ark.	7	3
4th	Holland, Spessard L.	Dem	Fla.	3	2
5th	Sparkman, John J.	Dem	Ala.	3	1
6th	Stennis, John C.	Dem	Miss.	2	1
7th	Chapman, Virgil M.	Dem	Ky.	1	1
8th	Kerr, Robert S.	Dem	Okla.	1	1

Minority

Rank	Name	Party	State	Years in: Senate	Years in: Comm.
RM	Cain, Harry P.	Rep	Wash.	3	3
2nd	Martin, Edward	Rep	Penn.	3	3
3rd	Watkins, Arthur V.	Rep	Utah	3	3
4th	Malone, George W.	Rep	Nev.	3	3
5th	Kem, James P.	Rep	Mo.	3	1

*2: Member's 2nd period of service on the committee.

Changes:
Majority:

Downey, Sheridan	Dem	Cal.	Nov. 30,1950	Resigned and retired.

Departures from Committee:	Majority			Minority		
Moved to Foreign Relations	Sparkman, John J.	Ala.	Dem	None		
Moved to Interstate & Foreign Commerce	None			Kem, James P.	Mo.	Rep
Moved to Judiciary	None			Watkins, Arthur V.	Utah	Rep

PUBLIC WORKS / 82nd Congress

Service Dates of Committee Chair: Jan. 15,1951-Jan. 13,1953
Service Dates of Majority Members: Jan. 15,1951-Jan. 13,1953
Service Dates of Minority Members: Jan. 15,1951-Jan. 13,1953

Majority

Rank	Name	Party	State	Years in: Senate	Years in: Comm.
Chr	Chavez, Dennis	Dem	N.M.	16	*2 5
2nd	McClellan, John L.	Dem	Ark.	9	5
3rd	Holland, Spessard L.	Dem	Fla.	5	4
4th	Stennis, John C.	Dem	Miss.	4	3
5th	Chapman, Virgil M.	Dem	Ky.	3	3
6th	Kerr, Robert S.	Dem	Okla.	3	3
7th	Hennings, Thomas C. Jr.	Dem	Mo.	1	1

Minority

Rank	Name	Party	State	Years in: Senate	Years in: Comm.
RM	Cain, Harry P.	Rep	Wash.	5	5
2nd	Martin, Edward	Rep	Penn.	5	5
3rd	Malone, George W.	Rep	Nev.	5	5
4th	Dworshak, Henry C.	Rep	Ida.	4	1
5th	Carlson, Frank	Rep	Kans.	1	1
6th	Case, Francis H.	Rep	S.D.	1	1

*2: Member's 2nd period of service on the committee.

Changes:
Majority:

Chapman, Virgil M.	Dem	Ky.	Mar. 8,1951	Died in office.
Clements, Earle C.	Dem	Ky.	Apr. 3,1951	Replaced Chapman.

	Majority			Minority	
Departures from the Senate:					
Defeated for Reelection	None			Cain, Harry P.	Wash. Rep
Departures from Committee:					
Moved to Judiciary	Hennings, Thomas C. Jr.	Mo. Dem		None	
	McClellan, John L.	Ark. Dem			
Moved to Interior & Insular Affairs; Agriculture & Forestry	Clements, Earle C.	Ky. Dem		None	
Moved to Finance; Rules & Administration	None			Carlson, Frank	Kans. Rep
Moved to Appropriations; Interior & Insular Affairs	None			Dworshak, Henry C.	Ida. Rep
Moved to Finance	None			Malone, George W.	Nev. Rep

PUBLIC WORKS / 83rd Congress

Service Dates of Committee Chair: Jan. 13,1953-Jan. 11,1955
Service Dates of Majority Members: Jan. 13,1953-Jan. 11,1955
Service Dates of Minority Members: Jan. 13,1953-Jan. 11,1955

Majority			Years in:		Minority			Years in:	
Rank Name	**Party**	**State**	**Senate**	**Comm.**	**Rank Name**	**Party**	**State**	**Senate**	**Comm.**
Chr Martin, Edward	Rep	Penn.	7	7	RM Chavez, Dennis	Dem	N.M.	18	*2 7
2nd Case, Francis H.	Rep	S.D.	3	2	2nd Holland, Spessard L.	Dem	Fla.	7	6
3rd Bush, Prescott S.	Rep	Conn.	1	1	3rd Stennis, John C.	Dem	Miss.	6	5
4th Kuchel, Thomas H.	Rep	Cal.	1	1	4th Kerr, Robert S.	Dem	Okla.	5	5
5th Beall, J. Glenn	Rep	Md.	1	1	5th Gore, Albert A.	Dem	Tenn.	1	1

Third Party:

Morse, Wayne L.	Ind	Ore.	9	1

*2: Member's 2nd period of service on the committee.

Notes: Wayne L. Morse (Ind-Ore.) was appointed by the majority on May 25,1953. He was not included in the party ratio, nor was he allowed to accrue committee seniority. The committee was expanded and the party ratio changed to 6 Republicans and (excluding Morse) and 6 Democrats on Jan. 13,1954.

Additions:

Majority:	6th Upton, Robert W.	Rep	N.H.	Jan. 13,1954
Minority:	6th Burke, Thomas A.	Dem	Ohio	Jan. 13,1954

Changes:
Majority:

Upton, Robert W.	Rep	N.H.	Nov. 7,1954	Resigned; defeated for nomination in special election.
Brown, Ernest S.	Rep	Nev.	Nov. 30,1954	Replaced Upton.
Brown, Ernest S.	Rep	Nev.	Dec. 1,1954	Moved to Labor and Public Welfare.
Cotton, Norris	Rep	N.H.	Dec. 1,1954	Replaced Brown.

Minority:

Burke, Thomas A.	Dem	Ohio	Dec. 2,1954	Resigned; defeated for election.

Departures from Committee:	Majority		Minority	
Moved to Appropriations	None		Holland, Spessard L.	Fla. Dem
			Stennis, John C.	Miss. Dem
	Third Party			
Moved to Foreign Relations; Banking & Currency	Morse, Wayne L.	Ore. Ind	None	
No new assignment	Beall, J. Glenn	Md. Rep	None	

PUBLIC WORKS / 84th Congress

Service Dates of Committee Chair: Jan. 11,1955-Jan. 9,1957
Service Dates of Majority Members: Jan. 11,1955-Jan. 9,1957
Service Dates of Minority Members: Jan. 11,1955-Jan. 9,1957

Majority

Rank	Name	Party	State	Years in: Senate	Years in: Comm.
Chr	Chavez, Dennis	Dem	N.M.	20	*2 9
2nd	Kerr, Robert S.	Dem	Okla.	7	7
3rd	Gore, Albert A.	Dem	Tenn.	3	2
4th	Symington, W. Stuart	Dem	Mo.	3	1
5th	Thurmond, J. Strom	Dem	S.C.	1	1
6th	McNamara, Patrick V.	Dem	Mich.	1	1
7th	Neuberger, Richard L.	Dem	Ore.	1	1

Minority

Rank	Name	Party	State	Years in: Senate	Years in: Comm.
RM	Martin, Edward	Rep	Penn.	9	9
2nd	Case, Francis H.	Rep	S.D.	5	4
3rd	Bush, Prescott S.	Rep	Conn.	3	2
4th	Kuchel, Thomas H.	Rep	Cal.	3	2
5th	Cotton, Norris	Rep	N.H.	1	1
6th	Hruska, Roman L.	Rep	Neb.	1	1

*2: Member's 2nd period of service on the committee.

Changes:

Majority:

Symington, W. Stuart	Dem	Mo.	Mar. 29,1956	Moved to Agriculture and Forestry.
Thurmond, J. Strom	Dem	S.C.	Apr. 4,1956	Resigned; reelected to fill his own vacancy on November 7,1956.
Scott, W. Kerr	Dem	N.C.	Apr. 12,1956	Replaced Symington.
Wofford, Thomas A.	Dem	S.C.	Apr. 18,1956	Replaced Thurmond.
Scott, W. Kerr	Dem	N.C.	June 18,1956	Moved to Interior and Insular Affairs.
Humphreys, Robert	Dem	Ky.	June 28,1956	Replaced Scott.
Humphreys, Robert	Dem	Ky.	July 27,1956	Moved to Interior and Insular Affairs.
Scott, W. Kerr	Dem	N.C.	July 27,1956	Reappointed to the committee; replaced Humphreys.
Wofford, Thomas A.	Dem	S.C.	Nov. 6,1956	Resigned and retired.

Departures from Committee:	Majority	Minority	
Moved to Armed Services	None	Bush, Prescott S.	Conn. Rep

PUBLIC WORKS / 85th Congress

Service Dates of Committee Chair: Jan. 9,1957-Jan. 14,1959
Service Dates of Majority Members: Jan. 9,1957-Jan. 14,1959
Service Dates of Minority Members: Jan. 9,1957-Jan. 20,1959

Majority

Rank	Name	Party	State	Years in: Senate	Years in: Comm.
Chr	Chavez, Dennis	Dem	N.M.	22	*2 11
2nd	Kerr, Robert S.	Dem	Okla.	9	8
3rd	Gore, Albert A.	Dem	Tenn.	5	4
4th	McNamara, Patrick V.	Dem	Mich.	3	2
5th	Neuberger, Richard L.	Dem	Ore.	3	2
6th	Scott, W. Kerr	Dem	N.C.	3	*2 1
7th	Carroll, John A.	Dem	Colo.	1	1

Minority

Rank	Name	Party	State	Years in: Senate	Years in: Comm.
RM	Martin, Edward	Rep	Penn.	11	11
2nd	Case, Francis H.	Rep	S.D.	7	6
3rd	Kuchel, Thomas H.	Rep	Cal.	5	4
4th	Cotton, Norris	Rep	N.H.	3	3
5th	Hruska, Roman L.	Rep	Neb.	3	2
6th	Revercomb, W. Chapman	Rep	W.Va.	7	*2 1

*2: Member's 2nd period of service on the committee.

Changes:

Majority:

Carroll, John A.	Dem	Colo.	Jan. 30,1958	Moved to Judiciary.
Church, Frank F.	Dem	Ida.	Mar. 11,1958	Replaced Carroll.
Scott, W. Kerr	Dem	N.C.	Apr. 16,1958	Died in office.
Jordan, B. Everett	Dem	N.C.	May 5,1958	Replaced Scott.

Departures from the Senate:	Majority	Minority	
Defeated for Reelection	None	Revercomb, W. Chapman	W.Va. Rep
Retired	None	Martin, Edward	Penn. Rep

Departures from Committee:

	Majority		Minority	
Moved to Foreign Relations	Gore, Albert A.	Tenn. Dem	None	
	Church, Frank F.	Ida. Dem		
Moved to Agriculture & Forestry; Rules & Administration	Jordan, B. Everett	N.C. Dem	None	
Moved to Finance; Judiciary	None		Cotton, Norris	N.H. Rep
Moved to Appropriations	None		Hruska, Roman L.	Neb. Rep
			Kuchel, Thomas H.	Cal. Rep

PUBLIC WORKS / 86th Congress

Service Dates of Committee Chair: Jan. 14,1959-Jan. 10,1961
Service Dates of Majority Members: Jan. 14,1959-Jan. 10,1961
Service Dates of Minority Members: Jan. 20,1959-Jan. 13,1961

Majority

Rank	Name	Party	State	Years in: Senate	Years in: Comm.
Chr	Chavez, Dennis	Dem	N.M.	24	*2 13
2nd	Kerr, Robert S.	Dem	Okla.	11	11
3rd	McNamara, Patrick V.	Dem	Mich.	5	5
4th	Neuberger, Richard L.	Dem	Ore.	5	5
5th	Randolph, Jennings	Dem	W.Va.	1	1
6th	McCarthy, Eugene J.	DFL	Minn.	1	1
7th	Young, Stephen M.	Dem	Ohio	1	1
8th	Muskie, Edmund S.	Dem	Me.	1	1
9th	Gruening, Ernest	Dem	Alas.	1	1
10th	Moss, Frank E.	Dem	Utah	1	1

Minority

Rank	Name	Party	State	Years in: Senate	Years in: Comm.
RM	Case, Francis H.	Rep	S.D.	9	9
2nd	Martin, Thomas E.	Rep	Iowa	5	1
3rd	Cooper, John Sherman	Rep	Ky.	7	*2 1
4th	Scott, Hugh D. Jr.	Rep	Penn.	1	1
5th	Prouty, Winston L.	Rep	Vt.	1	1

*2: Member's 2nd period of service on the committee.

Note: The admission of Hawaii to the Union on August 21,1959 led to the seating of both of the state's U.S. Senators on this committee. This resulted in a change in size and party ratio to 11 Democrats and 6 Republicans on Sep. 12,1959.

Additions:

Majority:	11th	Long, Oren E.	Dem	Hai.	Sep. 12,1959
Minority:	6th	Fong, Hiram L.	Rep	Hai.	Sep. 12,1959

Changes:

Majority:

Neuberger, Richard L.	Dem	Ore.	Mar. 9,1960	Died in office.
Lusk, Hall S.	Dem	Ore.	Mar. 28,1960	Replaced Neuberger.
Lusk, Hall S.	Dem	Ore.	Nov. 8,1960	Resigned; appointed to State Supreme Court.

Departures from the Senate:

	Majority		Minority	
Retired	None		Martin, Thomas E.	Iowa Rep

Departures from Committee:

	Majority		Minority
Moved to Agriculture & Forestry	McCarthy, Eugene J.	Minn. DFL	None

PUBLIC WORKS / 87th Congress

Service Dates of Committee Chair: Jan. 10,1961-Nov. 18,1962
Service Dates of Majority Members: Jan. 10,1961-Feb. 25,1963
Service Dates of Minority Members: Jan. 13,1961-Feb. 25,1963

Majority

Rank	Name	Party	State	Years in: Senate	Years in: Comm.
Chr	Chavez, Dennis	Dem	N.M.	26	*2 15
2nd	Kerr, Robert S.	Dem	Okla.	13	13
3rd	McNamara, Patrick V.	Dem	Mich.	7	6
4th	Randolph, Jennings	Dem	W.Va.	3	2
5th	Young, Stephen M.	Dem	Ohio	3	2
6th	Muskie, Edmund S.	Dem	Me.	3	2
7th	Gruening, Ernest	Dem	Alas.	3	2
8th	Moss, Frank E.	Dem	Utah	3	2

Minority

Rank	Name	Party	State	Years in: Senate	Years in: Comm.
RM1	Case, Francis H.	Rep	S.D.	11	10
RM2 2nd	Cooper, John Sherman	Rep	Ky.	9	*2 2
3rd	Scott, Hugh D. Jr.	Rep	Penn.	3	2
4th	Prouty, Winston L.	Rep	Vt.	3	2
5th	Fong, Hiram L.	Rep	Hai.	2	2
6th	Boggs, J. Caleb	Rep	Del.	1	1

9th Long, Oren E.	Dem	Hai.	2	2	
10th Smith, Benjamin A. II	Dem	Mass.	1	1	
11th Metcalf, Lee	Dem	Mont.	1	1	*2: Member's 2nd period of service on the committee.

Changes:

Ranking Member:

RM1 Case, Francis H.	Rep	S.D.	June 22,1962	Died in office.
RM2 Cooper, John Sherman	Rep	Ky.	June 22,1962	Succeeded Case as Ranking Minority Member.

Majority:

Smith, Benjamin A. II	Dem	Mass.	Nov. 6,1962	Resigned and retired.
Chavez, Dennis	Dem	N.M.	Nov. 18,1962	Died in office.
Kerr, Robert S.	Dem	Okla.	Jan. 1,1963	Died in office.

Minority:

Scott, Hugh D. Jr.	Rep	Penn.	Feb. 2,1962	Moved to Judiciary.
Miller, Jack R.	Rep	Iowa	Feb. 2,1962	Replaced Scott.
Case, Francis H.	Rep	S.D.	June 22,1962	Died in office.
Prouty, Winston L.	Rep	Vt.	July 18,1962	Moved to Commerce.
Murphy, Maurice J. Jr.	Rep	N.H.	July 18,1962	Replaced Case.
Pearson, James B.	Rep	Kans.	July 18,1962	Replaced Prouty.
Murphy, Maurice J. Jr.	Rep	N.H.	Nov. 6,1962	Resigned; defeated for nomination in special election.

Departures from the Senate:	Majority		Minority	
Retired	Long, Oren E.	Hai. Dem	None	

PUBLIC WORKS / 88th Congress

Service Dates of Committee Chair: Feb. 25,1963-Jan. 8,1965
Service Dates of Majority Members: Feb. 25,1963-Jan. 8,1965
Service Dates of Minority Members: Feb. 25,1963-Jan. 15,1965

Majority

Rank Name	Party	State	Years in: Senate	Years in: Comm.
Chr McNamara, Patrick V.	Dem	Mich.	9	9
2nd Randolph, Jennings	Dem	W.Va.	5	5
3rd Young, Stephen M.	Dem	Ohio	5	5
4th Muskie, Edmund S.	Dem	Me.	5	5
5th Gruening, Ernest	Dem	Alas.	5	5
6th Moss, Frank E.	Dem	Utah	5	5
7th Metcalf, Lee	Dem	Mont.	3	3
8th Jordan, B. Everett	Dem	N.C.	5 *2	1
9th Brewster, Daniel B.	Dem	Md.	1	1
10th Inouye, Daniel K.	Dem	Hai.	1	1
11th Bayh, Birch E.	Dem	Ind.	1	1
12th Nelson, Gaylord A.	Dem	Wisc.	1	1

Minority

Rank Name	Party	State	Years in: Senate	Years in: Comm.
RM Cooper, John Sherman	Rep	Ky.	11 *2	5
2nd Fong, Hiram L.	Rep	Hai.	4	4
3rd Boggs, J. Caleb	Rep	Del.	3	3
4th Miller, Jack R.	Rep	Iowa	3	2
5th Pearson, James B.	Rep	Kans.	2	1

*2: Member's 2nd period of service on the committee.

Changes:

Majority:

Brewster, Daniel B.	Dem	Md.	Aug. 10,1964	Moved to Commerce.
Salinger, Pierre E.	Dem	Cal.	Aug. 10,1964	Replaced Brewster.
Salinger, Pierre E.	Dem	Cal.	Dec. 31,1964	Resigned; defeated for election.

Departures from Committee:	Majority		Minority	
Moved to Labor & Public Welfare	Nelson, Gaylord A.	Wisc. Dem	None	
Moved to Agriculture & Forestry; Armed Services	None		Miller, Jack R.	Iowa Rep

PUBLIC WORKS / 89th Congress

Service Dates of Committee Chairs: Ch1 Jan. 8,1965-Apr. 30,1966
Ch2 May 5,1966-Jan. 11,1967
Service Dates of Majority Members: Jan. 8,1965-Jan. 11,1967
Service Dates of Minority Members: Jan. 15,1965-Jan. 16,1967

Majority

Rank	Name	Party	State	Years in: Senate	Years in: Comm.
Ch1	McNamara, Patrick V.	Dem	Mich.	11	10
Ch2	2nd Randolph, Jennings	Dem	W.Va.	7	6
3rd	Young, Stephen M.	Dem	Ohio	7	6
4th	Muskie, Edmund S.	Dem	Me.	7	6
5th	Gruening, Ernest	Dem	Alas.	7	6
6th	Moss, Frank E.	Dem	Utah	7	6
7th	Metcalf, Lee	Dem	Mont.	5	4
8th	Jordan, B. Everett	Dem	N.C.	7	*2 2
9th	Inouye, Daniel K.	Dem	Hai.	3	2
10th	Bayh, Birch E.	Dem	Ind.	3	2
11th	Montoya, Joseph M.	Dem	N.M.	1	1
12th	Harris, Fred R.	Dem	Okla.	1	1

Minority

Rank	Name	Party	State	Years in: Senate	Years in: Comm.
RM	Cooper, John Sherman	Rep	Ky.	13	*2 6
2nd	Fong, Hiram L.	Rep	Hai.	6	6
3rd	Boggs, J. Caleb	Rep	Del.	5	5
4th	Pearson, James B.	Rep	Kans.	3	3
5th	Murphy, George L.	Rep	Cal.	1	1

*2: Member's 2nd period of service on the committee.

Note: The death of Patrick V. McNamara (Dem-Mich.) and his replacement by Robert P. Griffin (Rep-Mich.) on May 11,1966 led to a change in size and party ratio to 11 Democrats and 6 Republicans on May 17,1966.

Addition:

Minority: 6th Griffin, Robert P. Rep Mich. May 17,1966

Changes:

Chair:

Ch1	McNamara, Patrick V.	Dem	Mich.	Apr. 30,1966	Died in office.
Ch2	Randolph, Jennings	Dem	W.Va.	May 5,1966	Succeeded McNamara as chair.

Majority:

Metcalf, Lee	Dem	Mont.	Jan. 14,1966	Moved to Finance.
Tydings, Joseph D.	Dem	Md.	Jan. 14,1966	Replaced Metcalf.
McNamara, Patrick V.	Dem	Mich.	Apr. 30,1966	Died in office.

Departures from Committee:

	Majority		Minority	
Moved to Finance	Harris, Fred R.	Okla. Dem	None	
Moved to Commerce	Moss, Frank E.	Utah Dem	None	
Moved to Armed Services	None		Pearson, James B.	Kans. Rep
Moved to Labor & Public Welfare; Commerce	None		Griffin, Robert P.	Mich. Rep

PUBLIC WORKS / 90th Congress

Service Dates of Committee Chair: Jan. 11,1967-Jan. 14,1969
Service Dates of Majority Members: Jan. 11,1967-Jan. 14,1969
Service Dates of Minority Members: Jan. 16,1967-Jan. 14,1969

Majority

Rank	Name	Party	State	Years in: Senate	Years in: Comm.
Chr	Randolph, Jennings	Dem	W.Va.	9	8
2nd	Young, Stephen M.	Dem	Ohio	9	8
3rd	Muskie, Edmund S.	Dem	Me.	9	8
4th	Gruening, Ernest	Dem	Alas.	9	8
5th	Jordan, B. Everett	Dem	N.C.	9	*2 4
6th	Inouye, Daniel K.	Dem	Hai.	5	4
7th	Bayh, Birch E.	Dem	Ind.	5	4
8th	Montoya, Joseph M.	Dem	N.M.	3	3
9th	Tydings, Joseph D.	Dem	Md.	3	1
10th	Spong, William B. Jr.	Dem	Va.	1	1

Minority

Rank	Name	Party	State	Years in: Senate	Years in: Comm.
RM	Cooper, John Sherman	Rep	Ky.	15	*2 8
2nd	Fong, Hiram L.	Rep	Hai.	8	8
3rd	Boggs, J. Caleb	Rep	Del.	7	7
4th	Murphy, George L.	Rep	Cal.	3	3
5th	Jordan, Len B.	Rep	Ida.	5	1
6th	Baker, Howard H. Jr.	Rep	Tenn.	1	1

*2: Member's 2nd period of service on the committee.

Departures from the Senate:	Majority		Minority	
Defeated for Renomination	Gruening, Ernest	Alas. Dem	None	
Departures from Committee:				
Moved to Commerce	Inouye, Daniel K.	Hai. Dem	None	
	Tydings, Joseph D.	Md. Dem		
Moved to Appropriations	None		Fong, Hiram L.	Hai. Rep
Moved to Finance	None		Jordan, Len B.	Ida. Rep
Moved to Armed Services	None		Murphy, George L.	Cal. Rep

PUBLIC WORKS / 91st Congress

Service Dates of Committee Chair: Jan. 14,1969-Jan. 28,1971
Service Dates of Majority Members: Jan. 14,1969-Jan. 28,1971
Service Dates of Minority Members: Jan. 14,1969-Jan. 29,1971

Majority

Rank	Name	Party	State	Years in: Senate	Comm.
Chr	Randolph, Jennings	Dem	W.Va.	11	11
2nd	Young, Stephen M.	Dem	Ohio	11	11
3rd	Muskie, Edmund S.	Dem	Me.	11	11
4th	Jordan, B. Everett	Dem	N.C.	11	*2 6
5th	Bayh, Birch E.	Dem	Ind.	7	6
6th	Montoya, Joseph M.	Dem	N.M.	5	5
7th	Spong, William B. Jr.	Dem	Va.	3	3
8th	Eagleton, Thomas F.	Dem	Mo.	1	1
9th	Gravel, Mike	Dem	Alas.	1	1

Minority

Rank	Name	Party	State	Years in: Senate	Comm.
RM	Cooper, John Sherman	Rep	Ky.	17	*2 10
2nd	Boggs, J. Caleb	Rep	Del.	9	9
3rd	Baker, Howard H. Jr.	Rep	Tenn.	3	2
4th	Dole, Robert J.	Rep	Kans.	1	1
5th	Gurney, Edward J.	Rep	Fla.	1	1
6th	Packwood, Robert W.	Rep	Ore.	1	1

*2: member's 2nd period of service on the committee.

Departures from the Senate:	Majority		Minority	
Retired	Young, Stephen M.	Ohio Dem	None	
Departures from Committee:				
Moved to Foreign Relations	Spong, William B. Jr.	Va. Dem	None	
Moved to Judiciary	None		Gurney, Edward J.	Fla. Rep
Moved to Labor & Public Welfare	None		Packwood, Robert W.	Ore. Rep

PUBLIC WORKS / 92nd Congress

Service Dates of Committee Chair: Jan. 28,1971-Jan. 4,1973
Service Dates of Majority Members: Jan. 28,1971-Jan. 4,1973
Service Dates of Minority Members: Jan. 29,1971-Jan. 12,1973

Majority

Rank	Name	Party	State	Years in: Senate	Comm.
Chr	Randolph, Jennings	Dem	W.Va.	13	13
2nd	Muskie, Edmund S.	Dem	Me.	13	13
3rd	Jordan, B. Everett	Dem	N.C.	13	*2 8
4th	Bayh, Birch E.	Dem	Ind.	9	8
5th	Montoya, Joseph M.	Dem	N.M.	7	7
6th	Eagleton, Thomas F.	Dem	Mo.	3	3
7th	Gravel, Mike	Dem	Alas.	3	3
8th	Tunney, John V.	Dem	Cal.	1	1
9th	Bentsen, Lloyd M. Jr.	Dem	Tex.	1	1

Minority

Rank	Name	Party	State	Years in: Senate	Comm.
RM	Cooper, John Sherman	Rep	Ky.	19	*2 13
2nd	Boggs, J. Caleb	Rep	Del.	11	11
3rd	Baker, Howard H. Jr.	Rep	Tenn.	5	5
4th	Dole, Robert J.	Rep	Kans.	3	3
5th	Beall, J. Glenn Jr.	Rep	Md.	1	1
6th	Buckley, James L.	Con	N.Y.	1	1
7th	Weicker, Lowell P. Jr.	Rep	Conn.	1	1

*2: Member's 2nd period of service on the committee.

Notes: James L. Buckley of New York was elected as a Conservative but was assigned by the Republican Conference, serving on the committee with his seniority intact.

Changes:

Majority:

Bayh, Birch E.	Dem	Ind.	Aug. 2,1972	Moved to Appropriations.
Edwards, Elaine S.	Dem	La.	Aug. 7,1972	Replaced Bayh.
Edwards, Elaine S.	Dem	La.	Nov. 13,1972	Resigned and retired.

Minority:

Beall, J. Glenn Jr.	Rep	Md.	Sep. 21,1971	Moved to Commerce.
Stafford, Robert T.	Rep	Vt.	Sep. 21,1971	Replaced Beall.
Weicker, Lowell P. Jr.	Rep	Conn.	Feb. 23,1972	Moved to Commerce.
Mundt, Karl E.	Rep	S.D.	Feb. 23,1972	Replaced Weicker.

Departures from the Senate:	Majority			Minority		
Defeated for Reelection	None			Boggs, J. Caleb	Del.	Rep
Defeated for Renomination	Jordan, B. Everett	N.C.	Dem	None		
Retired	None			Cooper, John Sherman	Ky.	Rep
				Mundt, Karl E.	S.D.	Rep
Departures from Committee:						
Moved to Appropriations	Eagleton, Thomas F.	Mo.	Dem	None		
Moved to Commerce	Tunney, John V.	Cal.	Dem	None		
Moved to Finance; Post Office & Civil Service	None			Dole, Robert J.	Kans.	Rep

PUBLIC WORKS / 93rd Congress

Service Dates of Committee Chair: Jan. 4,1973-Jan. 17,1975
Service Dates of Majority Members: Jan. 4,1973-Jan. 17,1975
Service Dates of Minority Members: Jan. 12,1973-Jan. 23,1975

Majority

Rank	Name	Party	State	Years in: Senate	Years in: Comm.
Chr	Randolph, Jennings	Dem	W.Va.	15	14
2nd	Muskie, Edmund S.	Dem	Me.	15	14
3rd	Montoya, Joseph M.	Dem	N.M.	9	8
4th	Gravel, Mike	Dem	Alas.	5	4
5th	Bentsen, Lloyd M. Jr.	Dem	Tex.	3	2
6th	Burdick, Quentin N.	Dem	N.D.	13	1
7th	Clark, Richard C.	Dem	Iowa	1	1
8th	Biden, Joseph R. Jr.	Dem	Del.	1	1

Minority

Rank	Name	Party	State	Years in: Senate	Years in: Comm.
RM	Baker, Howard H. Jr.	Rep	Tenn.	7	6
2nd	Buckley, James L.	Con	N.Y.	3	2
3rd	Stafford, Robert T.	Rep	Vt.	2	2
4th	Scott, William L.	Rep	Va.	1	1
5th	McClure, James A.	Rep	Ida.	1	1
6th	Domenici, Pete V.	Rep	N.M.	1	1

Notes: James L. Buckley of New York was elected as a Conservative but was assigned by the Republican Conference, serving on the committee with his seniority intact.

Departures from Committee:	Majority			Minority		
Moved to Budget; Foreign Relations	Biden, Joseph R. Jr.	Del.	Dem	None		
Moved to Foreign Relations	Clark, Richard C.	Iowa	Dem	None		
Moved to Judiciary; Veterans' Affairs	None			Scott, William L.	Va.	Rep

PUBLIC WORKS / 94th Congress

Service Dates of Committee Chair: Jan. 17,1975-Jan. 10,1977
Service Dates of Majority Members: Jan. 17,1975-Jan. 10,1977
Service Dates of Minority Members: Jan. 23,1975-Jan. 10,1977

Majority

Rank	Name	Party	State	Years in: Senate	Years in: Comm.
Chr	Randolph, Jennings	Dem	W.Va.	17	17
2nd	Muskie, Edmund S.	Dem	Me.	17	17
3rd	Montoya, Joseph M.	Dem	N.M.	11	11
4th	Gravel, Mike	Dem	Alas.	7	7
5th	Bentsen, Lloyd M. Jr.	Dem	Tex.	5	4
6th	Burdick, Quentin N.	Dem	N.D.	15	3
7th	Culver, John C.	Dem	Iowa	1	1
8th	Morgan, Robert B.	Dem	N.C.	1	1
9th	Hart, Gary W.	Dem	Colo.	1	1

Minority

Rank	Name	Party	State	Years in: Senate	Years in: Comm.
RM	Baker, Howard H. Jr.	Rep	Tenn.	9	9
2nd	Buckley, James L.	Con	N.Y.	5	4
3rd	Stafford, Robert T.	Rep	Vt.	4	4
4th	McClure, James A.	Rep	Ida.	3	3
5th	Domenici, Pete V.	Rep	N.M.	3	3

Notes: James L. Buckley of New York was elected as a Conservative but was assigned by the Republican Conference, serving on the committee with his seniority intact.

Departures from the Senate:	Majority			Minority		
Defeated for Reelection	Montoya, Joseph M.	N.M.	Dem	Buckley, James L.	N.Y.	Con

PUBLIC WORKS / 95th Congress

* Renamed the Committee on ENVIRONMENT AND PUBLIC WORKS on Feb. 11,1977.

Service Dates of Committee Chair: Jan. 10,1977-Feb. 11,1977
Service Dates of Majority Members: Jan. 10,1977-Feb. 11,1977
Service Dates of Minority Members: Jan. 10,1977-Feb. 22,1977

Majority

Rank	Name	Party	State	Years in: Senate	Years in: Comm.
Chr	Randolph, Jennings	Dem	W.Va.	19	18
2nd	Muskie, Edmund S.	Dem	Me.	19	18
3rd	Gravel, Mike	Dem	Alas.	9	8
4th	Bentsen, Lloyd M. Jr.	Dem	Tex.	7	6
5th	Burdick, Quentin N.	Dem	N.D.	17	5
6th	Culver, John C.	Dem	Iowa	3	2
7th	Morgan, Robert B.	Dem	N.C.	3	2
8th	Hart, Gary W.	Dem	Colo.	3	2
9th	DeConcini, Dennis	Dem	Ariz.	1	*T 1

Minority

Rank	Name	Party	State	Years in: Senate	Years in: Comm.
RM	Stafford, Robert T.	Rep	Vt.	6	6
2nd	Baker, Howard H. Jr.	Rep	Tenn.	11	10
3rd	McClure, James A.	Rep	Ida.	5	4
4th	Domenici, Pete V.	Rep	N.M.	5	4
5th	Heinz, H. John III	Rep	Penn.	1	*T 1

*T: Temporary member of the committee.

Note: Ranking on this committee for the following member was affected by other chamber service: Howard H. Baker, Jr. (Rep-Tenn.), Senate Minority Leader.

Changes:

Majority:

Name	Party	State	Date	Change
Morgan, Robert B.	Dem	N.C.	Feb. 11,1977	Moved to Armed Services.
DeConcini, Dennis	Dem	Ariz.	Feb. 11,1977	Moved to Judiciary.

Minority:

Name	Party	State	Date	Change
Heinz, H. John III	Rep	Penn.	Feb. 22,1977	Moved to Governmental Affairs; Banking, Housing, & Urban Affairs.

ENVIRONMENT AND PUBLIC WORKS / 95th Congress

Service Dates of Committee Chair: Feb. 11,1977-Jan. 23,1979
Service Dates of Majority Members: Feb. 11,1977-Jan. 23,1979
Service Dates of Minority Members: Feb. 22,1977-Jan. 23,1979

Majority

Rank	Name	Party	State	Years in: Senate	Years in: Comm.
Chr	Randolph, Jennings	Dem	W.Va.	19	19
2nd	Muskie, Edmund S.	Dem	Me.	19	19
3rd	Gravel, Mike	Dem	Alas.	9	9
4th	Bentsen, Lloyd M. Jr.	Dem	Tex.	7	7
5th	Burdick, Quentin N.	Dem	N.D.	17	5
6th	Culver, John C.	Dem	Iowa	3	3
7th	Hart, Gary W.	Dem	Colo.	3	3
8th	Anderson, Wendell R.	DFL	Minn.	1	1
9th	Moynihan, Daniel Patrick	Dem	N.Y.	1	1

Minority

Rank	Name	Party	State	Years in: Senate	Years in: Comm.
RM	Stafford, Robert T.	Rep	Vt.	6	6
2nd	Baker, Howard H. Jr.	Rep	Tenn.	11	11
3rd	McClure, James A.	Rep	Ida.	5	5
4th	Domenici, Pete V.	Rep	N.M.	5	5
5th	Chafee, John H.	Rep	R.I.	1	1
6th	Wallop, Malcolm	Rep	Wyo.	1	1

Note: Ranking on this committee for the following member was affected by other chamber service: Howard H. Baker, Jr. (Rep-Tenn.), Senate Minority Leader.

Changes:

Majority:

Name	Party	State	Date	Change
Anderson, Wendell R.	DFL	Minn.	Jan. 27,1978	Moved to Energy and Natural Resources.
Hodges, Kaneaster Jr.	Dem	Ark.	Jan. 27,1978	Replaced Anderson.

Departures from the Senate:	Majority			Minority
Retired	Hodges, Kaneaster Jr.	Ark.	Dem	None

Departures from Committee:

	Majority			Minority		
Moved to Appropriations	None			McClure, James A.	Ida.	Rep
Moved to Finance; Energy & Natural Resources	None			Wallop, Malcolm	Wyo.	Rep

ENVIRONMENT AND PUBLIC WORKS / 96th Congress

Service Dates of Committee Chair: Jan. 23,1979-Jan. 5,1981
Service Dates of Majority Members: Jan. 23,1979-Jan. 5,1981
Service Dates of Minority Members: Jan. 23,1979-Jan. 5,1981

Majority

Rank	Name	Party	State	Years in: Senate	Years in: Comm.
Chr	Randolph, Jennings	Dem	W.Va.	21	21
2nd	Muskie, Edmund S.	Dem	Me.	21	21
3rd	Gravel, Mike	Dem	Alas.	11	11
4th	Bentsen, Lloyd M. Jr.	Dem	Tex.	9	8
5th	Burdick, Quentin N.	Dem	N.D.	19	7
6th	Culver, John C.	Dem	Iowa	5	5
7th	Hart, Gary W.	Dem	Colo.	5	5
8th	Moynihan, Daniel Patrick	Dem	N.Y.	3	2

Minority

Rank	Name	Party	State	Years in: Senate	Years in: Comm.
RM	Stafford, Robert T.	Rep	Vt.	8	8
2nd	Baker, Howard H. Jr.	Rep	Tenn.	13	13
3rd	Domenici, Pete V.	Rep	N.M.	7	7
4th	Chafee, John H.	Rep	R.I.	3	2
5th	Simpson, Alan K.	Rep	Wyo.	1	1
6th	Pressler, Larry L.	Rep	S.D.	1	1

Note: Ranking on this committee for the following member was affected by other chamber service: Howard H. Baker, Jr. (Rep-Tenn.), Senate Minority Leader.

Changes:

Majority:

Muskie, Edmund S.	Dem	Me.	May 7,1980	Resigned; appointed Secretary of State.
Mitchell, George J.	Dem	Me.	May 19,1980	Replaced Muskie.

Departures from the Senate:

	Majority			Minority		
Defeated for Reelection	Culver, John C.	Iowa	Dem	None		
Defeated for Renomination	Gravel, Mike	Alas.	Dem	None		

Departures from Committee:

	Majority			Minority		
No new assignment	None			Pressler, Larry L.	S.D.	Rep

ENVIRONMENT AND PUBLIC WORKS / 97th Congress

Service Dates of Committee Chair: Jan. 5,1981-Jan. 3,1983
Service Dates of Majority Members: Jan. 5,1981-Jan. 3,1983
Service Dates of Minority Members: Jan. 5,1981-Jan. 3,1983

Majority

Rank	Name	Party	State	Years in: Senate	Years in: Comm.
Chr	Stafford, Robert T.	Rep	Vt.	10	10
2nd	Baker, Howard H. Jr.	Rep	Tenn.	15	14
3rd	Domenici, Pete V.	Rep	N.M.	9	8
4th	Chafee, John H.	Rep	R.I.	5	4
5th	Simpson, Alan K.	Rep	Wyo.	3	2
6th	Abdnor, James	Rep	S.D.	1	1
7th	Symms, Steven D.	Rep	Ida.	1	1
8th	Gorton, Slade	Rep	Wash.	1	1
9th	Murkowski, Frank H.	Rep	Alas.	1	1

Minority

Rank	Name	Party	State	Years in: Senate	Years in: Comm.
RM	Randolph, Jennings	Dem	W.Va.	23	22
2nd	Bentsen, Lloyd M. Jr.	Dem	Tex.	11	10
3rd	Burdick, Quentin N.	Dem	N.D.	21	9
4th	Hart, Gary W.	Dem	Colo.	7	6
5th	Moynihan, Daniel Patrick	Dem	N.Y.	5	4
6th	Mitchell, George J.	Dem	Me.	1	1
7th	Baucus, Max S.	Dem	Mont.	3	1

Note: Ranking on this committee for the following member was affected by other chamber service: Howard H. Baker, Jr. (Rep-Tenn.), Senate Majority Leader.

Departures from Committee:

	Majority			Minority
Moved to Banking, Housing & Urban Affairs	Gorton, Slade	Wash.	Rep	None
Moved to Foreign Relations	Murkowski, Frank H.	Alas.	Rep	None

ENVIRONMENT AND PUBLIC WORKS / 98th Congress

Service Dates of Committee Chair: Jan. 3,1983-Feb. 21,1985
Service Dates of Majority Members: Jan. 3,1983-Feb. 21,1985
Service Dates of Minority Members: Jan. 3,1983-Feb. 21,1985

Majority

Rank	Name	Party	State	Years in: Senate	Years in: Comm.
Chr	Stafford, Robert T.	Rep	Vt.	12	12
2nd	Baker, Howard H. Jr.	Rep	Tenn.	17	16
3rd	Chafee, John H.	Rep	R.I.	7	6
4th	Simpson, Alan K.	Rep	Wyo.	5	4
5th	Abdnor, James	Rep	S.D.	3	2
6th	Symms, Steven D.	Rep	Ida.	3	2
7th	Domenici, Pete V.	Rep	N.M.	11	10
8th	Durenberger, David F.	Rep	Minn.	5	1
9th	Humphrey, Gordon J.	Rep	N.H.	5	1

Minority

Rank	Name	Party	State	Years in: Senate	Years in: Comm.
RM	Randolph, Jennings	Dem	W.Va.	25	24
2nd	Bentsen, Lloyd M. Jr.	Dem	Tex.	13	12
3rd	Burdick, Quentin N.	Dem	N.D.	23	10
4th	Hart, Gary W.	Dem	Colo.	9	8
5th	Moynihan, Daniel Patrick	Dem	N.Y.	7	6
6th	Mitchell, George J.	Dem	Me.	3	3
7th	Baucus, Max S.	Dem	Mont.	5	2

Notes: The committee size was expanded and the party ratio changed to 10 Republicans and 8 Democrats on Feb. 9,1984. Rankings on this committee for the following members were affected by other chamber service: Howard H. Baker, Jr. (Rep-Tenn.), Senate Majority Leader; and Pete V. Domenici (Rep-N.M.), Chair, Budget.

Additions:

Majority:	10th	Evans, Daniel J.	Rep	Wash.	Feb. 9,1984
Minority:	8th	Lautenberg, Frank R.	Dem	N.J.	Feb. 9,1984

	Majority		Minority	
Departures from the Senate:				
Retired	Baker, Howard H. Jr.	Tenn. Rep	Randolph, Jennings	W.Va. Dem
Departures from Committee:				
Moved to Foreign Relations	Evans, Daniel J.	Wash. Rep	None	

ENVIRONMENT AND PUBLIC WORKS / 99th Congress

Service Dates of Committee Chair: Feb. 21,1985-Jan. 6,1987
Service Dates of Majority Members: Feb. 21,1985-Jan. 6,1987
Service Dates of Minority Members: Feb. 21,1985-Jan. 6,1987

Majority

Rank	Name	Party	State	Years in: Senate	Years in: Comm.
Chr	Stafford, Robert T.	Rep	Vt.	14	14
2nd	Chafee, John H.	Rep	R.I.	9	8
3rd	Simpson, Alan K.	Rep	Wyo.	7	7
4th	Abdnor, James	Rep	S.D.	5	5
5th	Symms, Steven D.	Rep	Ida.	5	5
6th	Humphrey, Gordon J.	Rep	N.H.	7	3
7th	Domenici, Pete V.	Rep	N.M.	13	13
8th	Durenberger, David F.	Rep	Minn.	7	3

Minority

Rank	Name	Party	State	Years in: Senate	Years in: Comm.
RM	Bentsen, Lloyd M. Jr.	Dem	Tex.	15	15
2nd	Burdick, Quentin N.	Dem	N.D.	25	13
3rd	Hart, Gary W.	Dem	Colo.	11	11
4th	Moynihan, Daniel Patrick	Dem	N.Y.	9	9
5th	Mitchell, George J.	Dem	Me.	5	5
6th	Baucus, Max S.	Dem	Mont.	7	5
7th	Lautenberg, Frank R.	Dem	N.J.	3	2

Note: Rankings on this committee for the following members were affected by other chamber service: Pete V. Domenici (Rep-N.M.), Chair, Budget; and David F. Durenberger (Rep-Minn.), Chair, Select Committee on Intelligence.

	Majority		Minority	
Departures from the Senate:				
Defeated for Reelection	Abdnor, James	S.D. Rep	None	
Retired	None		Hart, Gary W.	Colo. Dem
Departures from Committee:				
Moved to Special Aging	Domenici, Pete V.	N.M. Rep	None	
Moved to Judiciary; Labor & Human Resources	Humphrey, Gordon J.	N.H. Rep	None	
Moved to Commerce, Science & Transportation	None		Bentsen, Lloyd M. Jr.	Tex. Dem

ENVIRONMENT AND PUBLIC WORKS / 100th Congress

Service Dates of Committee Chair: Jan. 6,1987-Feb. 2,1989
Service Dates of Majority Members: Jan. 6,1987-Feb. 2,1989
Service Dates of Minority Members: Jan. 6,1987-Feb. 2,1989

Majority

Rank	Name	Party	State	Years in: Senate	Years in: Comm.
Chr	Burdick, Quentin N.	Dem	N.D.	27	15
2nd	Moynihan, Daniel Patrick	Dem	N.Y.	11	10
3rd	Mitchell, George J.	Dem	Me.	7	7
4th	Baucus, Max S.	Dem	Mont.	9	7
5th	Lautenberg, Frank R.	Dem	N.J.	5	3
6th	Breaux, John B.	Dem	La.	1	1
7th	Mikulski, Barbara A.	Dem	Md.	1	1
8th	Reid, Harry M.	Dem	Nev.	1	1
9th	Graham, Bob	Dem	Fla.	1	1

Minority

Rank	Name	Party	State	Years in: Senate	Years in: Comm.
RM	Stafford, Robert T.	Rep	Vt.	16	16
2nd	Chafee, John H.	Rep	R.I.	11	10
3rd	Simpson, Alan K.	Rep	Wyo.	9	8
4th	Symms, Steven D.	Rep	Ida.	7	7
5th	Durenberger, David F.	Rep	Minn.	9	5
6th	Warner, John W.	Rep	Va.	9	1
7th	Pressler, Larry L.	Rep	S.D.	9	*2 1

*2: Member's 2nd period of service on the committee.

	Majority			Minority		
Departures from the Senate:						
Retired	None			Stafford, Robert T.	Vt.	Rep
Departures from Committee:						
Moved to Banking, Housing & Urban Affairs	None			Pressler, Larry L.	S.D.	Rep
No new assignment	Mikulski, Barbara A.	Md.	Dem	None		

ENVIRONMENT AND PUBLIC WORKS / 101st Congress

Service Dates of Committee Chair: Feb. 2,1989-Feb. 5,1991
Service Dates of Majority Members: Feb. 2,1989-Feb. 5,1991
Service Dates of Minority Members: Feb. 2,1989-Feb. 5,1991

Majority

Rank	Name	Party	State	Years in: Senate	Years in: Comm.
Chr	Burdick, Quentin N.	Dem	N.D.	29	17
2nd	Moynihan, Daniel Patrick	Dem	N.Y.	13	12
3rd	Mitchell, George J.	Dem	Me.	9	9
4th	Baucus, Max S.	Dem	Mont.	11	9
5th	Lautenberg, Frank R.	Dem	N.J.	7	5
6th	Breaux, John B.	Dem	La.	3	3
7th	Reid, Harry M.	Dem	Nev.	3	3
8th	Graham, Bob	Dem	Fla.	3	3
9th	Lieberman, Joseph I.	Dem	Conn.	1	1

Minority

Rank	Name	Party	State	Years in: Senate	Years in: Comm.
RM	Chafee, John H.	Rep	R.I.	13	12
2nd	Simpson, Alan K.	Rep	Wyo.	11	11
3rd	Symms, Steven D.	Rep	Ida.	9	9
4th	Durenberger, David F.	Rep	Minn.	11	7
5th	Warner, John W.	Rep	Va.	11	3
6th	Jeffords, James M.	Rep	Vt.	1	1
7th	Humphrey, Gordon J.	Rep	N.H.	11	1

Changes:

Majority:

Name	Party	State	Date	Change
Breaux, John B.	Dem	La.	May 16,1990	Moved to Finance.
Metzenbaum, Howard M.	Dem	Ohio	May 16,1990	Replaced Breaux.

	Majority	Minority		
Departures from Senate:				
Elected to State Senate	None	Humphrey, Gordon	N.H.	Rep

ENVIRONMENT AND PUBLIC WORKS / 102nd Congress

Service Dates of Committee Chair: Ch1 Feb. 5,1991-Sep. 8,1992
Ch2 Sep. 15,1992-Jan. 3,1993
Service Dates of Majority Members: Feb. 5,1991-Jan. 3,1993
Service Dates of Minority Members: Feb. 5,1991-Jan. 3,1993

Majority

Rank Name	Party	State	Years in: Senate	Years in: Comm.
Ch1 Burdick, Quentin N.	Dem	N.D.	31	19
Ch2 2nd Moynihan, Daniel P.	Dem	N.Y.	15	14
3rd Mitchell, George J.	Dem	Me.	11	11
4th Baucus, Max S.	Dem	Mont.	13	11
5th Lautenberg, Frank R.	Dem	N.J.	9	7
6th Reid, Harry M.	Dem	Nev.	5	5
7th Graham, Bob	Dem	Fla.	5	5
8th Lieberman, Joseph I.	Dem	Conn.	3	3
9th Metzenbaum, Howard M.	Dem	Ohio	17	1

Minority

Rank Name	Party	State	Years in: Senate	Years in: Comm.
RM Chafee, John H.	Rep	R.I.	15	14
2nd Simpson, Alan K.	Rep	Wyo.	13	13
3rd Symms, Steven D.	Rep	Ida.	11	11
4th Durenberger, David F.	Rep	Minn.	13	9
5th Warner, John W.	Rep	Va.	13	5
6th Jeffords, James M.	Rep	Vt.	3	3
7th Smith, Robert C.	Rep	N.H.	1	1

Note: The death of John Heinz (Rep-Penn.) and the appointment of Harris Wofford (Dem-Penn.) to fill his vacancy on May 9,1991 led to a change in size and party ratio on this committee to 10 Democrats and 7 Republicans on June 4,1991.

Addition:

Majority: 10th Wofford, Harris Dem Penn. June 4,1991

Changes:

Chair:

Ch1 Burdick, Quentin N.	Dem	N.D.	Sep. 8,1992	Died in office.
Ch2 Moynihan, Daniel P.	Dem	N.Y.	Sep. 15,1992	Succeeded Burdick as Chair.

Majority:

Burdick, Quentin N.	Dem	N.D.	Sep. 8,1992	Died in office.
Burdick, Jocelyn	Dem	N.D.	Sep. 18,1992	Replaced Quentin Burdick.

FINANCE

Jurisdiction, 1947

Established by the Legislative Reorganization Act of 1946:

[Section 102.(1)(h)]

Committee on Finance, to consist of thirteen Senators, to which committee shall be referred all proposed legislation, messages, petitions, memorials, and other matters relating to the following subjects:

1. Revenue measures generally.
2. The bonded debt of the United States.
3. The deposit of public moneys.
4. Customs, collection districts, and ports of entry and delivery.
5. Reciprocal trade agreements.
6. Transportation of dutiable goods.
7. Revenue measures relating to the insular possessions.
8. Tariffs and import quotas, and matters related thereto.
9. National social security.
10. Veterans' measures generally.
11. Pensions of all the wars of the United States, general and special.
12. Life insurance issued by the Government on account of service in the armed forces.
13. Compensation of veterans.

Jurisdiction, 1992

Jurisdiction contained in the Standing Rules of the Senate (as revised to March 18,1992):

[Rule XXV (1)(i)]

Committee on Finance, to which committee shall be referred all proposed legislation, messages, petitions, memorials, and other matters relating to the following subjects:

1. Bonded debt of the United States, except as provided in the Congressional Budget Act of 1974.
2. Customs, collection districts, and ports of entry and delivery.
3. Deposit of public moneys.
4. General revenue sharing.
5. Health programs under the Social Security Act and health programs financed by a specific tax or trust fund.
6. National social security.
7. Reciprocal trade agreements.
8. Revenue measures generally, except as provided in the Congressional Budget Act of 1974.
9. Revenue measures relating to the insular possessions.
10. Tariffs and import quotas, and matters related thereto.
11. Transportation of dutiable goods.

FINANCE / 80th Congress

Service Dates of Committee Chair: Jan. 6,1947-Jan. 10,1949
Service Dates of Majority Members: Jan. 6,1947-Jan. 10,1949
Service Dates of Minority Members: Jan. 8,1947-Jan. 10,1949

Majority

Rank	Name	Party	State	Years in: Senate	Years in: Comm.
Chr	Millikin, Eugene D.	Rep	Colo.	6	4
2nd	Taft, Robert A.	Rep	Ohio	9	6
3rd	Butler, Hugh A.	Rep	Neb.	7	4
4th	Brewster, Ralph O.	Rep	Me.	7	3
5th	Bushfield, Harlan J.	Rep	S.D.	5	2
6th	Hawkes, Albert W.	Rep	N.J.	5	2
7th	Martin, Edward	Rep	Penn.	1	1

Minority

Rank	Name	Party	State	Years in: Senate	Years in: Comm.
RM	George, Walter F.	Dem	Ga.	25	22
2nd	Barkley, Alben W.	Dem	Ky.	20 *1	20
3rd	Connally, Thomas T.	Dem	Tex.	18	18
4th	Byrd, Harry Flood	Dem	Va.	14	14
5th	Johnson, Edwin C.	Dem	Colo.	11	10
6th	Lucas, Scott W.	Dem	Ill.	9	4

*1: Member's 1st period of service on the committee.

Note: Ranking on this committee for the following member was affected by other chamber service: Robert A. Taft (Rep-Ohio), Chair, Labor and Public Welfare.

Changes:

Majority:

Bushfield, Harlan J.	Rep	S.D.	Sep. 27,1948	Died in office.

Departures from the Senate:

	Majority			Minority		
Elected Vice President	None			Barkley, Alben W.	Ky.	Dem
Retired	Hawkes, Albert W.	N.J.	Rep	None		

FINANCE / 81st Congress

Service Dates of Committee Chair: Jan. 10,1949-Jan. 15,1951
Service Dates of Majority Members: Jan. 10,1949-Jan. 15,1951
Service Dates of Minority Members: Jan. 10,1949-Jan. 15,1951

Majority

Rank	Name	Party	State	Years in: Senate	Years in: Comm.
Chr	George, Walter F.	Dem	Ga.	27	24
2nd	Connally, Thomas T.	Dem	Tex.	20	20
3rd	Byrd, Harry Flood	Dem	Va.	16	16
4th	Johnson, Edwin C.	Dem	Colo.	13	12
5th	Lucas, Scott W.	Dem	Ill.	11	6
6th	Hoey, Clyde R.	Dem	N.C.	5	1
7th	McGrath, J. Howard	Dem	R.I.	3	1

Minority

Rank	Name	Party	State	Years in: Senate	Years in: Comm.
RM	Millikin, Eugene D.	Rep	Colo.	8	6
2nd	Taft, Robert A.	Rep	Ohio	11	8
3rd	Butler, Hugh A.	Rep	Neb.	9	6
4th	Brewster, Ralph O.	Rep	Me.	9	5
5th	Martin, Edward	Rep	Penn.	3	3
6th	Williams, John J.	Rep	Del.	3 *1	1

*1: Member's 1st period of service on the committee.

Notes: Appointed Senator John Foster Dulles (Rep-N.Y.) lost in a special election to Herbert H. Lehman (Dem-N.Y.), resulting in a change in size and party ratio on this committee to 8 Democrats and 5 Republicans on Jan. 12,1950. Ranking on this committee for the following member was affected by other chamber service: Robert A. Taft (Rep-Ohio), Ranking Minority Member, Labor and Public Welfare.

Addition:

Majority: 8th Myers, Francis J. Dem Penn. Jan. 12,1950

Changes:

Majority:

McGrath, J. Howard	Dem	R.I.	Aug. 23,1949	Resigned; appointed Attorney General.
Kerr, Robert S.	Dem	Okla.	Aug. 30,1949	Replaced McGrath.

Minority:

Williams, John J.	Rep	Del.	Jan. 12,1950	Ratio change; moved to Interstate and Foreign Commerce.

Departures from the Senate:	Majority		Minority	
Defeated for Reelection	Lucas, Scott W.	Ill. Dem	None	
	Myers, Francis J.	Penn. Dem		

FINANCE / 82nd Congress

Service Dates of Committee Chair: Jan. 15,1951-Jan. 13,1953
Service Dates of Majority Members: Jan. 15,1951-Jan. 13,1953
Service Dates of Minority Members: Jan. 15,1951-Jan. 13,1953

Majority						Minority					
				Years in:						Years in:	
Rank	Name	Party	State	Senate	Comm.	Rank	Name	Party	State	Senate	Comm.
Chr	George, Walter F.	Dem	Ga.	29	26	RM	Millikin, Eugene D.	Rep	Colo.	10	9
2nd	Connally, Thomas T.	Dem	Tex.	22	22	2nd	Taft, Robert A.	Rep	Ohio	13	10
3rd	Byrd, Harry Flood	Dem	Va.	18	18	3rd	Butler, Hugh A.	Rep	Neb.	11	9
4th	Johnson, Edwin C.	Dem	Colo.	15	14	4th	Brewster, Ralph O.	Rep	Me.	11	7
5th	Hoey, Clyde R.	Dem	N.C.	7	3	5th	Martin, Edward	Rep	Penn.	5	5
6th	Kerr, Robert S.	Dem	Okla.	3	2	6th	Williams, John J.	Rep	Del.	5	*2 1
7th	Frear, J. Allen Jr.	Dem	Del.	3	1						

*2: Member's 2nd period of service on the committee.

Note: Ranking on this committee for the following member was affected by other chamber service: Robert A. Taft (Rep-Ohio), Ranking Minority Member, Labor and Public Welfare.

Changes:
Minority:

Brewster, Ralph O.	Rep	Me.	May 9,1951	Moved to Foreign Relations.
Flanders, Ralph E.	Rep	Vt.	June 22,1951	Replaced Brewster.

	Majority		Minority	
Departures from the Senate:				
Retired	Connally, Thomas T.	Tex. Dem	None	
Departures from Committee:				
Moved to Foreign Relations	None		Taft, Robert A.	Ohio Rep

FINANCE / 83rd Congress

Service Dates of Committee Chair: Jan. 13,1953-Jan. 11,1955
Service Dates of Majority Members: Jan. 13,1953-Jan. 11,1955
Service Dates of Minority Members: Jan. 13,1953-Jan. 11,1955

Majority						Minority					
				Years in:						Years in:	
Rank	Name	Party	State	Senate	Comm.	Rank	Name	Party	State	Senate	Comm.
Chr	Millikin, Eugene D.	Rep	Colo.	12	10	RM	George, Walter F.	Dem	Ga.	31	28
2nd	Butler, Hugh A.	Rep	Neb.	13	10	2nd	Byrd, Harry Flood	Dem	Va.	20	20
3rd	Martin, Edward	Rep	Penn.	7	7	3rd	Johnson, Edwin C.	Dem	Colo.	17	16
4th	Williams, John J.	Rep	Del.	7	*2 2	4th	Hoey, Clyde R.	Dem	N.C.	9	5
5th	Flanders, Ralph E.	Rep	Vt.	7	2	5th	Kerr, Robert S.	Dem	Okla.	5	4
6th	Malone, George W.	Rep	Nev.	7	1	6th	Frear, J. Allen Jr.	Dem	Del.	5	2
7th	Carlson, Frank	Rep	Kans.	3	1	7th	Long, Russell B.	Dem	La.	5	1
8th	Bennett, Wallace F.	Rep	Utah	3	1						

*2: Member's 2nd period of service on the committee.

Changes:
Majority:

Butler, Hugh A.	Rep	Neb.	July 1,1954	Died in office.
Reynolds, Samuel W.	Rep	Neb.	July 9,1954	Replaced Butler.
Reynolds, Samuel W.	Rep	Neb.	Nov. 7,1954	Resigned and retired.
Abel, Hazel H.	Rep	Neb.	Nov. 30,1954	Replaced Reynolds.
Abel, Hazel H.	Rep	Neb.	Dec. 31,1954	Resigned and retired.

Minority:

Hoey, Clyde R.	Dem	N.C.	May 12,1954	Died in office.
Smathers, George A.	Dem	Fla.	May 18,1954	Replaced Hoey.

Departures from the Senate:	Majority	Minority	
Elected Governor	None	Johnson, Edwin C.	Colo. Dem

FINANCE / 84th Congress

Service Dates of Committee Chair: Jan. 11,1955-Jan. 9,1957
Service Dates of Majority Members: Jan. 11,1955-Jan. 9,1957
Service Dates of Minority Members: Jan. 11,1955-Jan. 9,1957

Majority

Rank	Name	Party	State	Years in: Senate	Years in: Comm.
Chr	Byrd, Harry Flood	Dem	Va.	22	22
2nd	George, Walter F.	Dem	Ga.	33	30
3rd	Kerr, Robert S.	Dem	Okla.	7	6
4th	Frear, J. Allen Jr.	Dem	Del.	7	4
5th	Long, Russell B.	Dem	La.	7	2
6th	Smathers, George A.	Dem	Fla.	5	1
7th	Johnson, Lyndon B.	Dem	Tex.	7	1
8th	Barkley, Alben W.	Dem	Ky.	22	*2 1

Minority

Rank	Name	Party	State	Years in: Senate	Years in: Comm.
RM	Millikin, Eugene D.	Rep	Colo.	14	12
2nd	Martin, Edward	Rep	Penn.	9	9
3rd	Williams, John J.	Rep	Del.	9	*2 4
4th	Flanders, Ralph E.	Rep	Vt.	9	4
5th	Malone, George W.	Rep	Nev.	9	2
6th	Carlson, Frank	Rep	Kans.	5	2
7th	Bennett, Wallace F.	Rep	Utah	5	2

*2: Member's 2nd period of service on the committee.

Note: Ranking on this committee for the following member was affected by other chamber service: Walter F. George (Dem-Ga.), Chair, Foreign Relations.

Changes:

Majority:

Johnson, Lyndon B.	Dem	Tex.	Mar. 22,1956	Moved to Appropriations.
Anderson, Clinton P.	Dem	N.M.	Mar. 22,1956	Replaced Johnson.
Barkley, Alben W.	Dem	Ky.	Apr. 30,1956	Died in Office.
Douglas, Paul H.	Dem	Ill.	May 18,1956	Replaced Barkley.

Departures from the Senate:	Majority		Minority	
Retired	George, Walter F.	Ga. Dem	Millikin, Eugene D.	Colo. Rep

FINANCE / 85th Congress

Service Dates of Committee Chair: Jan. 9,1957-Jan. 14,1959
Service Dates of Majority Members: Jan. 9,1957-Jan. 14,1959
Service Dates of Minority Members: Jan. 9,1957-Jan. 20,1959

Majority

Rank	Name	Party	State	Years in: Senate	Years in: Comm.
Chr	Byrd, Harry Flood	Dem	Va.	24	24
2nd	Kerr, Robert S.	Dem	Okla.	9	8
3rd	Frear, J. Allen Jr.	Dem	Del.	9	6
4th	Long, Russell B.	Dem	La.	9	4
5th	Smathers, George A.	Dem	Fla.	7	3
6th	Anderson, Clinton P.	Dem	N.M.	9	1
7th	Douglas, Paul H.	Dem	Ill.	9	1
8th	Gore, Albert A.	Dem	Tenn.	5	1

Minority

Rank	Name	Party	State	Years in: Senate	Years in: Comm.
RM	Martin, Edward	Rep	Penn.	11	11
2nd	Williams, John J.	Rep	Del.	11	*2 6
3rd	Flanders, Ralph E.	Rep	Vt.	11	6
4th	Malone, George W.	Rep	Nev.	11	4
5th	Carlson, Frank	Rep	Kans.	7	4
6th	Bennett, Wallace F.	Rep	Utah	7	4
7th	Jenner, William E.	Rep	Ind.	11	1

*2: Member's 2nd period of service on the committee.

Departures from the Senate:	Majority	Minority	
Defeated for Reelection	None	Malone, George W.	Nev. Rep
		Flanders, Ralph E.	Vt. Rep
		Jenner, William E.	Ind. Rep
		Martin, Edward	Penn. Rep
Retired	None		

FINANCE / 86th Congress

Service Dates of Committee Chair: Jan. 14,1959-Jan. 10,1961
Service Dates of Majority Members: Jan. 14,1959-Jan. 10,1961
Service Dates of Minority Members: Jan. 20,1959-Jan. 13,1961

Majority

Rank	Name	Party	State	Years in: Senate	Years in: Comm.
Chr	Byrd, Harry Flood	Dem	Va.	26	26
2nd	Kerr, Robert S.	Dem	Okla.	11	10
3rd	Frear, J. Allen Jr.	Dem	Del.	11	8
4th	Long, Russell B.	Dem	La.	11	7
5th	Smathers, George A.	Dem	Fla.	9	5
6th	Anderson, Clinton P.	Dem	N.M.	11	3
7th	Douglas, Paul H.	Dem	Ill.	11	3
8th	Gore, Albert A.	Dem	Tenn.	7	3
9th	Talmadge, Herman E.	Dem	Ga.	3	1
10th	McCarthy, Eugene J.	DFL	Minn.	1	1
11th	Hartke, R. Vance	Dem	Ind.	1	1

Minority

Rank	Name	Party	State	Years in: Senate	Years in: Comm.
RM	Williams, John J.	Rep	Del.	13	*2 9
2nd	Carlson, Frank	Rep	Kans.	9	7
3rd	Bennett, Wallace F.	Rep	Utah	9	7
4th	Butler, John Marshall	Rep	Md.	9	1
5th	Cotton, Norris	Rep	N.H.	5	1
6th	Curtis, Carl T.	Rep	Neb.	5	1

*2: Member's 2nd period of service on the committee.

Changes:
Minority:

Name	Party	State	Date	Change
Cotton, Norris	Rep	N.H.	Jan. 18,1960	Moved to Judiciary.
Morton, Thruston B.	Rep	Ky.	Jan. 18,1960	Replaced Cotton.

Departures from the Senate:

	Majority			Minority
Defeated for Reelection	Frear, J. Allen Jr.	Del.	Dem	None

FINANCE / 87th Congress

Service Dates of Committee Chair: Jan. 10,1961-Feb. 25,1963
Service Dates of Majority Members: Jan. 10,1961-Feb. 25,1963
Service Dates of Minority Members: Jan. 13,1961-Feb. 25,1963

Majority

Rank	Name	Party	State	Years in: Senate	Years in: Comm.
Chr	Byrd, Harry Flood	Dem	Va.	28	28
2nd	Kerr, Robert S.	Dem	Okla.	13	12
3rd	Long, Russell B.	Dem	La.	13	8
4th	Smathers, George A.	Dem	Fla.	11	7
5th	Anderson, Clinton P.	Dem	N.M.	13	5
6th	Douglas, Paul H.	Dem	Ill.	13	5
7th	Gore, Albert A.	Dem	Tenn.	9	5
8th	Talmadge, Herman E.	Dem	Ga.	5	2
9th	McCarthy, Eugene J.	DFL	Minn.	3	2
10th	Hartke, R. Vance	Dem	Ind.	3	2
11th	Fulbright, J. William	Dem	Ark.	17	1

Minority

Rank	Name	Party	State	Years in: Senate	Years in: Comm.
RM	Williams, John J.	Rep	Del.	15	*2 10
2nd	Carlson, Frank	Rep	Kans.	11	9
3rd	Bennett, Wallace F.	Rep	Utah	11	9
4th	Butler, John Marshall	Rep	Md.	11	2
5th	Curtis, Carl T.	Rep	Neb.	7	2
6th	Morton, Thruston B.	Rep	Ky.	5	1

*2: Member's 2nd period of service on the committee.

Changes:
Majority:

Name	Party	State	Date	Change
Kerr, Robert S.	Dem	Okla.	Jan. 1,1963	Died in office.

Departures from the Senate:

	Majority	Minority		
Retired	None	Butler, John Marshall	Md.	Rep

FINANCE / 88th Congress

Service Dates of Committee Chair: Feb. 25,1963-Jan. 8,1965
Service Dates of Majority Members: Feb. 25,1963-Jan. 8,1965
Service Dates of Minority Members: Feb. 25,1963-Jan. 15,1965

Majority						Minority				
			Years in:						Years in:	
Rank Name	Party	State	Senate	Comm.	Rank Name	Party	State	Senate	Comm.
Chr Byrd, Harry Flood	Dem	Va.	30	30	RM Williams, John J.	Rep	Del.	17	*2 13
2nd Long, Russell B.	Dem	La.	15	11	2nd Carlson, Frank	Rep	Kans.	13	11
3rd Smathers, George A.	Dem	Fla.	13	9	3rd Bennett, Wallace F.	Rep	Utah	13	11
4th Anderson, Clinton P.	Dem	N.M.	15	7	4th Curtis, Carl T.	Rep	Neb.	9	5
5th Douglas, Paul H.	Dem	Ill.	15	7	5th Morton, Thruston B.	Rep	Ky.	7	4
6th Gore, Albert A.	Dem	Tenn.	11	7	6th Dirksen, Everett M.	Rep	Ill.	13	1
7th Talmadge, Herman E.	Dem	Ga.	7	5					
8th McCarthy, Eugene J.	DFL	Minn.	5	5					
9th Hartke, R. Vance	Dem	Ind.	5	5					
10th Fulbright, J. William	Dem	Ark.	19	3					
11th Ribicoff, Abraham A.	Dem	Conn.	1	1					

*2: Member's 2nd period of service on the committee.

FINANCE / 89th Congress

Service Dates of Committee Chairs: Ch1 Jan. 8,1965-Nov. 10,1965
Ch2 Jan.14,1966-Jan. 11,1967
Service Dates of Majority Members: Jan. 8,1965-Jan. 11,1967
Service Dates of Minority Members: Jan. 15,1965-Jan. 16,1967

Majority					Minority				
			Years in:					Years in:	
Rank Name	Party	State	Senate	Comm.	Rank Name	Party	State	Senate	Comm.
Ch1 Byrd, Harry Flood	Dem	Va.	32	32	RM Williams, John J.	Rep	Del.	19	*2 15
Ch2 2nd Long, Russell B.	Dem	La.	17	12	2nd Carlson, Frank	Rep	Kans.	15	13
3rd Smathers, George A.	Dem	Fla.	15	11	3rd Bennett, Wallace F.	Rep	Utah	15	13
4th Anderson, Clinton P.	Dem	N.M.	17	9	4th Curtis, Carl T.	Rep	Neb.	11	6
5th Douglas, Paul H.	Dem	Ill.	17	9	5th Morton, Thruston B.	Rep	Ky.	9	5
6th Gore, Albert A.	Dem	Tenn.	13	8	6th Dirksen, Everett M.	Rep	Ill.	15	2
7th Talmadge, Herman E.	Dem	Ga.	9	6					
8th McCarthy, Eugene J.	DFL	Minn.	7	6					
9th Hartke, R. Vance	Dem	Ind.	7	6					
10th Fulbright, J. William	Dem	Ark.	21	4					
11th Ribicoff, Abraham A.	Dem	Conn.	3	2					

*2: Member's 2nd period of service on the committee.

Changes:

Chair:

Ch1 Byrd, Harry Flood	Dem	Va.	Nov. 10,1965	Resigned and retired.
Ch2 Long, Russell B.	Dem	La.	Jan. 14,1966	Succeeded Byrd as Chair.

Majority:

Byrd, Harry Flood	Dem	Va.	Nov. 10,1965	Resigned and retired.
Metcalf, Lee	Dem	Mont.	Jan. 14,1966	Replaced Byrd.

Departures from the Senate:	Majority		Minority
Defeated for Reelection	Douglas, Paul H.	Ill. Dem	None

FINANCE / 90th Congress

Service Dates of Committee Chair: Jan. 11,1967-Jan. 14,1969
Service Dates of Majority Members: Jan. 11,1967-Jan. 14,1969
Service Dates of Minority Members: Jan. 16,1967-Jan. 14,1969

Majority

Rank	Name	Party	State	Years in: Senate	Years in: Comm.
Chr	Long, Russell B.	Dem	La.	19	14
2nd	Smathers, George A.	Dem	Fla.	17	13
3rd	Anderson, Clinton P.	Dem	N.M.	19	11
4th	Gore, Albert A.	Dem	Tenn.	15	11
5th	Talmadge, Herman E.	Dem	Ga.	11	8
6th	McCarthy, Eugene J.	DFL	Minn.	9	8
7th	Hartke, R. Vance	Dem	Ind.	9	8
8th	Fulbright, J. William	Dem	Ark.	23	7
9th	Ribicoff, Abraham A.	Dem	Conn.	5	4
10th	Metcalf, Lee	Dem	Mont.	7	1
11th	Harris, Fred R.	Dem	Okla.	3	1

Minority

Rank	Name	Party	State	Years in: Senate	Years in: Comm.
RM	Williams, John J.	Rep	Del.	21	*2 17
2nd	Carlson, Frank	Rep	Kans.	17	15
3rd	Bennett, Wallace F.	Rep	Utah	17	15
4th	Curtis, Carl T.	Rep	Neb.	13	8
5th	Morton, Thruston B.	Rep	Ky.	11	7
6th	Dirksen, Everett M.	Rep	Ill.	17	4

*2: Member's 2nd period of service on the committee.

Changes:

Majority:

Name	Party	State	Date	Change
Morton, Thruston B.	Rep	Ky.	Dec. 16,1968	Resigned and retired.

	Majority		Minority	
Departures from the Senate:				
Retired	Smathers, George A.	Fla. Dem	Carlson, Frank	Kans. Rep
Departures from Committee:				
No new assignment	Metcalf, Lee	Mont. Dem	None	

FINANCE / 91st Congress

Service Dates of Committee Chair: Jan. 14,1969-Jan. 28,1971
Service Dates of Majority Members: Jan. 14,1969-Jan. 28,1971
Service Dates of Minority Members: Jan. 14,1969-Jan. 29,1971

Majority

Rank	Name	Party	State	Years in: Senate	Years in: Comm.
Chr	Long, Russell B.	Dem	La.	21	17
2nd	Anderson, Clinton P.	Dem	N.M.	21	13
3rd	Gore, Albert A.	Dem	Tenn.	17	13
4th	Talmadge, Herman E.	Dem	Ga.	13	11
5th	McCarthy, Eugene J.	DFL	Minn.	11	11
6th	Hartke, R. Vance	Dem	Ind.	11	11
7th	Fulbright, J. William	Dem	Ark.	25	9
8th	Ribicoff, Abraham A.	Dem	Conn.	7	6
9th	Harris, Fred R.	Dem	Okla.	5	3
10th	Byrd, Harry Flood Jr.	Dem	Va.	4	1

Minority

Rank	Name	Party	State	Years in: Senate	Years in: Comm.
RM1	Williams, John J.	Rep	Del.	23	*2 18
RM2 2nd	Bennett, Wallace F.	Rep	Utah	19	17
3rd	Curtis, Carl T.	Rep	Neb.	15	10
4th	Dirksen, Everett M.	Rep	Ill.	19	6
5th	Miller, Jack R.	Rep	Iowa	9	1
6th	Jordan, Len B.	Rep	Ida.	7	1
7th	Fannin, Paul J.	Rep	Ariz.	5	1

*2: Member's 2nd period of service on the committee.

Changes:

	Name	Party	State	Date	Change
Ranking Member:					
RM1	Williams, John J.	Rep	Del.	Dec. 31,1970	Resigned and retired.
RM2	Bennett, Wallace F.	Rep	Utah	Dec. 31,1970	Succeeded Williams as Ranking Minority Member.
Minority:					
	Dirksen, Everett M.	Rep	Ill.	Sep. 7,1969	Died in office.
	Hansen, Clifford P.	Rep	Wyo.	Sep. 17,1969	Replaced Dirksen.
	Williams, John J.	Rep	Del.	Dec. 31,1970	Resigned and retired.

Departures from the Senate:	Majority		Minority
Defeated for Reelection	Gore, Albert A.	Tenn. Dem	None
Retired	McCarthy, Eugene J.	Minn. DFL	None

FINANCE / 92nd Congress

Service Dates of Committee Chair: Jan. 28,1971-Jan. 4,1973
Service Dates of Majority Members: Jan. 28,1971-Jan. 4,1973
Service Dates of Minority Members: Jan. 29,1971-Jan. 12,1973

Majority

Rank	Name	Party	State	Years in: Senate	Years in: Comm.
Chr	Long, Russell B.	Dem	La.	23	19
2nd	Anderson, Clinton P.	Dem	N.M.	23	15
3rd	Talmadge, Herman E.	Dem	Ga.	15	13
4th	Hartke, R. Vance	Dem	Ind.	13	13
5th	Fulbright, J. William	Dem	Ark.	27	11
6th	Ribicoff, Abraham A.	Dem	Conn.	9	8
7th	Harris, Fred R.	Dem	Okla.	7	5
8th	Byrd, Harry Flood Jr.	Ind	Va.	6	3
9th	Nelson, Gaylord A.	Dem	Wisc.	9	1

Minority

Rank	Name	Party	State	Years in: Senate	Years in: Comm.
RM	Bennett, Wallace F.	Rep	Utah	21	19
2nd	Curtis, Carl T.	Rep	Neb.	17	13
3rd	Miller, Jack R.	Rep	Iowa	11	3
4th	Jordan, Len B.	Rep	Ida.	9	3
5th	Fannin, Paul J.	Rep	Ariz.	7	3
6th	Hansen, Clifford P.	Rep	Wyo.	5	2
7th	Griffin, Robert P.	Rep	Mich.	5	1

Note: Harry Flood Byrd, Jr. of Virginia was elected as an Independent, but continued to be assigned by the Democratic Caucus, serving on the committee with his seniority intact.

	Majority		Minority	
Departures from the Senate:				
Defeated for Reelection	None		Miller, Jack R.	Iowa Rep
Retired	Anderson, Clinton P.	N.M. Dem	Jordan, Len B.	Ida. Rep
	Harris, Fred R.	Okla. Dem		
Departures from Committee:				
Moved to Foreign Relations	None		Griffin, Robert P.	Mich. Rep

FINANCE / 93rd Congress

Service Dates of Committee Chair: Jan. 4,1973-Jan. 17,1975
Service Dates of Majority Members: Jan. 4,1973-Jan. 17,1975
Service Dates of Minority Members: Jan. 12,1973-Jan. 23,1975

Majority

Rank	Name	Party	State	Years in: Senate	Years in: Comm.
Chr	Long, Russell B.	Dem	La.	25	20
2nd	Talmadge, Herman E.	Dem	Ga.	17	14
3rd	Hartke, R. Vance	Dem	Ind.	15	14
4th	Fulbright, J. William	Dem	Ark.	29	12
5th	Ribicoff, Abraham A.	Dem	Conn.	11	10
6th	Byrd, Harry Flood Jr.	Ind	Va.	8	4
7th	Nelson, Gaylord A.	Dem	Wisc.	10	2
8th	Mondale, Walter F.	DFL	Minn.	9	1
9th	Gravel, Mike	Dem	Alas.	5	1
10th	Bentsen, Lloyd M. Jr.	Dem	Tex.	3	1

Minority

Rank	Name	Party	State	Years in: Senate	Years in: Comm.
RM	Bennett, Wallace F.	Rep	Utah	23	20
2nd	Curtis, Carl T.	Rep	Neb.	19	14
3rd	Fannin, Paul J.	Rep	Ariz.	9	4
4th	Hansen, Clifford P.	Rep	Wyo.	7	4
5th	Dole, Robert J.	Rep	Kans.	5	1
6th	Packwood, Robert W.	Rep	Ore.	5	1
7th	Roth, William V. Jr.	Rep	Del.	3	1

Note: Harry Flood Byrd, Jr. of Virginia was elected as an Independent, but continued to be assigned by the Democratic Caucus, serving on the committee with his seniority intact.

Changes:

Majority:

Fulbright, J. William	Dem	Ark.	Dec. 31,1974	Resigned; defeated for renomination.

Minority:

Bennett, Wallace F.	Rep	Utah	Dec. 20,1974	Resigned and retired.

FINANCE / 94th Congress

Service Dates of Committee Chair: Jan. 17,1975-Jan. 10,1977
Service Dates of Majority Members: Jan. 17,1975-Jan. 10,1977
Service Dates of Minority Members: Jan. 23,1975-Jan. 10,1977

Majority

Rank	Name	Party	State	Years in: Senate	Years in: Comm.
Chr	Long, Russell B.	Dem	La.	27	23
2nd	Talmadge, Herman E.	Dem	Ga.	19	17
3rd	Hartke, R. Vance	Dem	Ind.	17	17
4th	Ribicoff, Abraham A.	Dem	Conn.	13	12
5th	Byrd, Harry Flood Jr.	Ind	Va.	10	7
6th	Nelson, Gaylord A.	Dem	Wisc.	13	4
7th	Mondale, Walter F.	DFL	Minn.	11	3
8th	Gravel, Mike	Dem	Alas.	7	3
9th	Bentsen, Lloyd M. Jr.	Dem	Tex.	5	3
10th	Hathaway, William D.	Dem	Me.	3	1
11th	Haskell, Floyd K.	Dem	Colo.	3	1

Minority

Rank	Name	Party	State	Years in: Senate	Years in: Comm.
RM	Curtis, Carl T.	Rep	Neb.	21	17
2nd	Fannin, Paul J.	Rep	Ariz.	11	7
3rd	Hansen, Clifford P.	Rep	Wyo.	9	6
4th	Dole, Robert J.	Rep	Kans.	7	3
5th	Packwood, Robert W.	Rep	Ore.	7	3
6th	Roth, William V. Jr.	Rep	Del.	5	3
7th	Brock, William E. III	Rep	Tenn.	5	1

Note: Harry Flood Byrd, Jr. of Virginia was elected as an Independent, but continued to be assigned by the Democratic Caucus, serving on the committee with his seniority intact.

Changes:

Majority:

Mondale, Walter F.	DFL	Minn.	Dec. 30,1976	Resigned; elected Vice President.

Departures from the Senate:

	Majority			Minority		
Defeated for Reelection	Hartke, R. Vance	Ind.	Dem	Brock, William E. III	Tenn.	Rep
Retired	None			Fannin, Paul J.	Ariz.	Rep

FINANCE / 95th Congress

Service Dates of Committee Chair: Jan. 10,1977-Jan. 23,1979
Service Dates of Majority Members: Jan. 10,1977-Jan. 23,1979
Service Dates of Minority Members: Jan. 10,1977-Jan. 23,1979

Majority

Rank	Name	Party	State	Years in: Senate	Years in: Comm.
Chr	Long, Russell B.	Dem	La.	29	24
2nd	Talmadge, Herman E.	Dem	Ga.	21	18
3rd	Ribicoff, Abraham A.	Dem	Conn.	15	14
4th	Byrd, Harry Flood Jr.	Ind	Va.	12	8
5th	Nelson, Gaylord A.	Dem	Wisc.	15	6
6th	Gravel, Mike	Dem	Alas.	9	5
7th	Bentsen, Lloyd M. Jr.	Dem	Tex.	7	5
8th	Hathaway, William D.	Dem	Me.	5	2
9th	Haskell, Floyd K.	Dem	Colo.	5	2
10th	Zorinsky, Edward	Dem	Neb.	1	*T 1

Minority

Rank	Name	Party	State	Years in: Senate	Years in: Comm.
RM	Curtis, Carl T.	Rep	Neb.	23	18
2nd	Hansen, Clifford P.	Rep	Wyo.	11	8
3rd	Dole, Robert J.	Rep	Kans.	9	4
4th	Packwood, Robert W.	Rep	Ore.	9	4
5th	Roth, William V. Jr.	Rep	Del.	7	4
6th	Schmitt, Harrison H.	Rep	N.M.	1	*T 1

*T: Temporary member of the committee.

Notes: The committee size was expanded and the party ratio changed to 11 Democrats and 7 Republicans on Feb. 11,1977. Harry Flood Byrd, Jr. of Virginia was elected as an Independent, but continued to be assigned by the Democratic Caucus, serving on the committee with his seniority intact.

Additions:

Majority:	11th Moynihan, Daniel Patrick	Dem	N.Y.	Feb. 11,1977
Minority:	7th Danforth, John C.	Rep	Mo.	Feb. 22,1977

Changes:

Majority:

Zorinsky, Edward	Dem	Neb.	Feb. 11,1977	Moved to Agriculture, Nutrition and Forestry.
Matsunaga, Spark M.	Dem	Hai.	Feb. 11,1977	Replaced Zorinsky.

Minority:

Schmitt, Harrison H.	Rep	N.M.	Feb. 22,1977	Moved to Banking, Housing and Urban Affairs.
Laxalt, Paul	Rep	Nev.	Feb. 22,1977	Replaced Schmitt.
Hansen, Clifford P.	Rep	Wyo.	Dec. 31,1978	Resigned and retired.

Departures from the Senate:	Majority		Minority	
Defeated for Reelection	Haskell, Floyd K.	Colo. Dem	None	
	Hathaway, William D.	Me. Dem		
Retired	None		Curtis, Carl T.	Neb. Rep
Departures from Committee:				
Moved to Appropriations	None		Laxalt, Paul	Nev. Rep

FINANCE / 96th Congress

Service Dates of Committee Chair: Jan. 23,1979-Jan. 5,1981
Service Dates of Majority Members: Jan. 23,1979-Jan. 5,1981
Service Dates of Minority Members: Jan. 23,1979-Jan. 5,1981

Majority

Rank	Name	Party	State	Years in: Senate	Years in: Comm.
Chr	Long, Russell B.	Dem	La.	31	27
2nd	Talmadge, Herman E.	Dem	Ga.	23	21
3rd	Ribicoff, Abraham A.	Dem	Conn.	17	16
4th	Byrd, Harry Flood Jr.	Ind	Va.	14	11
5th	Nelson, Gaylord A.	Dem	Wisc.	17	8
6th	Gravel, Mike	Dem	Alas.	11	7
7th	Bentsen, Lloyd M. Jr.	Dem	Tex.	9	7
8th	Matsunaga, Spark M.	Dem	Hai.	3	2
9th	Moynihan, Daniel Patrick	Dem	N.Y.	3	2
10th	Baucus, Max S.	Dem	Mont.	1	1
11th	Boren, David L.	Dem	Okla.	1	1
12th	Bradley, William W.	Dem	N.J.	1	1

Minority:

Rank	Name	Party	State	Years in: Senate	Years in: Comm.
RM	Dole, Robert J.	Rep	Kans.	11	7
2nd	Packwood, Robert W.	Rep	Ore.	11	7
3rd	Roth, William V. Jr.	Rep	Del.	9	7
4th	Danforth, John C.	Rep	Mo.	3	2
5th	Chafee, John H.	Rep	R.I.	3	1
6th	Heinz, H. John III	Rep	Penn.	3	1
7th	Wallop, Malcolm	Rep	Wyo.	3	1
8th	Durenberger, David F.	Rep	Minn.	1	1

Note: Harry Flood Byrd, Jr. of Virginia was elected as an Independent, but continued to be assigned by the Democratic Caucus, serving on the committee with his seniority intact.

Departures from the Senate:	Majority		Minority
Defeated for Reelection	Nelson, Gaylord A.	Wisc. Dem	None
	Talmadge, Herman E.	Ga. Dem	
Defeated for Renomination	Gravel, Mike	Alas. Dem	None
Retired	Ribicoff, Abraham A.	Conn. Dem	None

FINANCE / 97th Congress

Service Dates of Committee Chair: Jan. 5,1981-Jan. 3,1983
Service Dates of Majority Members: Jan. 5,1981-Jan. 3,1983
Service Dates of Minority Members: Jan. 5,1981-Jan. 3,1983

Majority

Rank	Name	Party	State	Years in: Senate	Years in: Comm.
Chr	Dole, Robert J.	Rep	Kans.	13	8
2nd	Packwood, Robert W.	Rep	Ore.	13	8
3rd	Roth, William V. Jr.	Rep	Del.	11	8
4th	Danforth, John C.	Rep	Mo.	5	4
5th	Chafee, John H.	Rep	R.I.	5	2
6th	Heinz, H. John III	Rep	Penn.	5	2
7th	Wallop, Malcolm	Rep	Wyo.	5	2
8th	Durenberger, David F.	Rep	Minn.	3	2
9th	Armstrong, William L.	Rep	Colo.	3	1
10th	Symms, Steven D.	Rep	Ida.	1 *1	1
11th	Grassley, Charles E.	Rep	Iowa	1 *1	1

Minority

Rank	Name	Party	State	Years in: Senate	Years in: Comm.
RM	Long, Russell B.	Dem	La.	33	28
2nd	Byrd, Harry Flood Jr.	Ind	Va.	16	12
3rd	Bentsen, Lloyd M. Jr.	Dem	Tex.	11	9
4th	Matsunaga, Spark M.	Dem	Hai.	5	4
5th	Moynihan, Daniel Patrick	Dem	N.Y.	5	4
6th	Baucus, Max S.	Dem	Mont.	3	2
7th	Boren, David L.	Dem	Okla.	3	2
8th	Bradley, William W.	Dem	N.J.	3	2
9th	Mitchell, George J.	Dem	Me.	1	1

*1: Member's 1st period of service on the committee.

Note: Harry Flood Byrd, Jr. of Virginia was elected as an Independent, but continued to be assigned by the Democratic Caucus, serving on the committee with his seniority intact.

Departures from the Senate:	Majority	Minority		
Retired	None	Byrd, Harry Flood Jr.	Va.	Ind

FINANCE / 98th Congress

Service Dates of Committee Chair: Jan. 3,1983-Feb. 21,1985
Service Dates of Majority Members: Jan. 3,1983-Feb. 21,1985
Service Dates of Minority Members: Jan. 3,1983-Feb. 21,1985

Majority

Rank Name	Party	State	Years in: Senate	Years in: Comm.
Chr Dole, Robert J.	Rep	Kans.	15	10
2nd Packwood, Robert W.	Rep	Ore.	15	10
3rd Roth, William V. Jr.	Rep	Del.	13	10
4th Danforth, John C.	Rep	Mo.	7	6
5th Chafee, John H.	Rep	R.I.	7	4
6th Heinz, H. John III	Rep	Penn.	7	4
7th Wallop, Malcolm	Rep	Wyo.	7	4
8th Durenberger, David F.	Rep	Minn.	5	4
9th Armstrong, William L.	Rep	Colo.	5	2
10th Symms, Steven D.	Rep	Ida.	3	*1 2
11th Grassley, Charles E.	Rep	Iowa	3	*1 2

Minority

Rank Name	Party	State	Years in: Senate	Years in: Comm.
RM Long, Russell B.	Dem	La.	35	30
2nd Bentsen, Lloyd M. Jr.	Dem	Tex.	13	10
3rd Matsunaga, Spark M.	Dem	Hai.	7	6
4th Moynihan, Daniel Patrick	Dem	N.Y.	7	6
5th Baucus, Max S.	Dem	Mont.	5	4
6th Boren, David L.	Dem	Okla.	5	4
7th Bradley, William W.	Dem	N.J.	5	4
8th Mitchell, George J.	Dem	Me.	3	2
9th Pryor, David H.	Dem	Ark.	5	1

*1: Member's 1st period of service on the committee.

FINANCE / 99th Congress

Service Dates of Committee Chair: Feb. 21,1985-Jan. 6,1987
Service Dates of Majority Members: Feb. 21,1985-Jan. 6,1987
Service Dates of Minority Members: Feb. 21,1985-Jan. 6,1987

Majority

Rank Name	Party	State	Years in: Senate	Years in: Comm.
Chr Packwood, Robert W.	Rep	Ore.	17	13
2nd Dole, Robert J.	Rep	Kans.	17	13
3rd Roth, William V. Jr.	Rep	Del.	15	13
4th Danforth, John C.	Rep	Mo.	9	8
5th Chafee, John H.	Rep	R.I.	9	7
6th Heinz, H. John III	Rep	Penn.	9	7
7th Wallop, Malcolm	Rep	Wyo.	9	7
8th Durenberger, David F.	Rep	Minn.	7	7
9th Armstrong, William L.	Rep	Colo.	7	5
10th Symms, Steven D.	Rep	Ida.	5	*1 5
11th Grassley, Charles E.	Rep	Iowa	5	*1 5

Minority

Rank Name	Party	State	Years in: Senate	Years in: Comm.
RM Long, Russell B.	Dem	La.	37	33
2nd Bentsen, Lloyd M. Jr.	Dem	Tex.	15	13
3rd Matsunaga, Spark M.	Dem	Hai.	9	9
4th Moynihan, Daniel Patrick	Dem	N.Y.	9	9
5th Baucus, Max S.	Dem	Mont.	7	7
6th Boren, David L.	Dem	Okla.	7	7
7th Bradley, William W.	Dem	N.J.	7	7
8th Mitchell, George J.	Dem	Me.	5	5
9th Pryor, David H.	Dem	Ark.	7	3

*1: Member's 1st period of service on the committee.

Note: Ranking on this committee for the following member was affected by other chamber service: Robert J. Dole (Rep-Kans.), Senate Majority Leader.

Departures from the Senate:	Majority			Minority		
Retired	None			Long, Russell B.	La.	Dem
Departures from Committee:						
Moved to Appropriations	Grassley, Charles E.	Iowa	Rep	None		
Moved to Armed Services	Symms, Steven D.	Ida.	Rep	None		

FINANCE / 100th Congress

Service Dates of Committee Chair: Jan. 6,1987-Feb. 2,1989
Service Dates of Majority Members: Jan. 6,1987-Feb. 2,1989
Service Dates of Minority Members: Jan. 6,1987-Feb. 2,1989

Majority

Rank Name	Party	State	Years in: Senate	Years in: Comm.
Chr Bentsen, Lloyd M. Jr.	Dem	Tex.	17	15
2nd Matsunaga, Spark M.	Dem	Hai.	11	10
3rd Moynihan, Daniel Patrick	Dem	N.Y.	11	10
4th Baucus, Max S.	Dem	Mont.	9	8
5th Boren, David L.	Dem	Okla.	9	8
6th Bradley, William W.	Dem	N.J.	9	8
7th Mitchell, George J.	Dem	Me.	7	7
8th Pryor, David H.	Dem	Ark.	9	5
9th Riegle, Donald W. Jr.	Dem	Mich.	11	1
10th Rockefeller, John D. IV	Dem	W.Va.	2	1
11th Daschle, Thomas A.	Dem	S.D.	1	1

Minority

Rank Name	Party	State	Years in: Senate	Years in: Comm.
RM Packwood, Robert W.	Rep	Ore.	19	14
2nd Dole, Robert J.	Rep	Kans.	19	14
3rd Roth, William V. Jr.	Rep	Del.	17	14
4th Danforth, John C.	Rep	Mo.	11	10
5th Chafee, John H.	Rep	R.I.	11	8
6th Heinz, H. John III	Rep	Penn.	11	8
7th Wallop, Malcolm	Rep	Wyo.	11	8
8th Durenberger, David F.	Rep	Minn.	9	8
9th Armstrong, William L.	Rep	Colo.	9	7

Note: Ranking on this committee for the following member was affected by other chamber service: Robert J. Dole (Rep-Kans.), Senate Minority Leader.

Departures from Committee:	Majority	Minority	
Moved to Armed Services	None	Wallop, Malcolm	Wyo. Rep

FINANCE / 101st Congress

Service Dates of Committee Chair: Feb. 2,1989-Feb. 5,1991
Service Dates of Majority Members: Feb. 2,1989-Feb. 5,1991
Service Dates of Minority Members: Feb. 2,1989-Feb. 5,1991

Majority

Rank Name	Party	State	Years in: Senate	Years in: Comm.
Chr Bentsen, Lloyd M. Jr.	Dem	Tex.	19	17
2nd Matsunaga, Spark M.	Dem	Hai.	13	12
3rd Moynihan, Daniel Patrick	Dem	N.Y.	13	12
4th Baucus, Max S.	Dem	Mont.	11	11
5th Boren, David L.	Dem	Okla.	11	11
6th Bradley, William W.	Dem	N.J.	11	11
7th Mitchell, George J.	Dem	Me.	9	9
8th Pryor, David H.	Dem	Ark.	11	7
9th Riegle, Donald W. Jr.	Dem	Mich.	13	3
10th Rockefeller, John D. IV	Dem	W.Va.	5	3
11th Daschle, Thomas A.	Dem	S.D.	3	3

Minority

Rank Name	Party	State	Years in: Senate	Years in: Comm.
RM Packwood, Robert W.	Rep	Ore.	21	17
2nd Dole, Robert J.	Rep	Kans.	21	17
3rd Roth, William V. Jr.	Rep	Del.	19	17
4th Danforth, John C.	Rep	Mo.	13	12
5th Chafee, John H.	Rep	R.I.	13	11
6th Heinz, H. John III	Rep	Penn.	13	11
7th Durenberger, David F.	Rep	Minn.	11	11
8th Armstrong, William L.	Rep	Colo.	11	9
9th Symms, Steven D.	Rep	Ida.	9	*2 1

*2: Member's 2nd period of service on the committee.

Note: Ranking on this committee for the following member was affected by other chamber service: Robert J. Dole (Rep-Kans.), Senate Minority Leader.

Changes:

Majority:

Matsunaga, Spark M.	Dem	Hai.	Apr. 15,1990	Died in office.
Breaux, John B.	Dem	La.	May 16,1990	Replaced Matsunaga.

Departures from the Senate:	Majority	Minority	
Retired	None	Armstrong, William L.	Colo. Rep

FINANCE / 102nd Congress

Service Dates of Committee Chair: Feb. 5,1991-Jan. 3,1993
Service Dates of Majority Members: Feb. 5,1991-Jan. 3,1993
Service Dates of Minority Members: Feb. 5,1991-Jan. 3,1993

Majority

Rank	Name	Party	State	Years in: Senate	Years in: Comm.
Chr	Bentsen, Lloyd M. Jr.	Dem	Tex.	21	19
2nd	Moynihan, Daniel Patrick	Dem	N.Y.	15	14
3rd	Baucus, Max S.	Dem	Mont.	13	13
4th	Boren, David L.	Dem	Okla.	13	13
5th	Bradley, William W.	Dem	N.J.	13	13
6th	Mitchell, George J.	Dem	Me.	11	11
7th	Pryor, David H.	Dem	Ark.	13	9
8th	Riegle, Donald W. Jr.	Dem	Mich.	15	5
9th	Rockefeller, John D. IV	Dem	W.Va.	7	5
10th	Daschle, Thomas A.	Dem	S.D.	5	5
11th	Breaux, John B.	Dem	La.	5	1

Minority

Rank	Name	Party	State	Years in: Senate	Years in: Comm.
RM	Packwood, Robert W.	Rep	Ore.	23	19
2nd	Dole, Robert J.	Rep	Kans.	23	19
3rd	Roth, William V. Jr.	Rep	Del.	21	19
4th	Danforth, John C.	Rep	Mo.	15	14
5th	Chafee, John H.	Rep	R.I.	15	13
6th	Heinz, H. John III	Rep	Penn.	15	13
7th	Durenberger, David F.	Rep	Minn.	13	13
8th	Symms, Steven D.	Rep	Ida.	11	*2 3
9th	Grassley, Charles E.	Rep	Iowa	11	*2 1

*2: Member's 2nd period of service on the committee.

Changes:

Minority:

Heinz, H. John III	Rep	Penn.	May 4,1991	Died in office.
Hatch, Orrin G.	Rep	Utah	June 25,1991	Replaced Heinz.

FOREIGN RELATIONS

Jurisdiction, 1947

Established by the Legislative Reorganization Act of 1946:

[Section 102.(1)(i)]

Committee on Foreign Relations, to consist of thirteen Senators, to which committee shall be referred all proposed legislation, messages, petitions, memorials, and other matters relating to the following subjects:

1. Relations of the United States with foreign nations generally.
2. Treaties.
3. Establishment of boundary lines between the United States and foreign nations.
4. Protection of American citizens abroad and expatriation.
5. Neutrality.
6. International conferences and congresses.
7. The American National Red Cross.
8. Intervention abroad and declarations of war.
9. Measures relating to the diplomatic service.
10. Acquisition of land and buildings for embassies and legations in foreign countries.
11. Measures to foster commercial intercourse with foreign nations and to safeguard American business interests abroad.
12. United Nations Organization and international financial and monetary organizations.
13. Foreign loans.

Jurisdiction, 1992

Jurisdiction contained in the Standing Rules of the Senate (as revised to March 18,1992):

[Rule XXV.(1)(j)]

(1) Committee on Foreign Relations, to which committee shall be referred all proposed legislation, messages, petitions, memorials, and other matters relating to the following subjects:

1. Acquisition of land and buildings for embassies and legations in foreign countries.
2. Boundaries of the United States.
3. Diplomatic service.
4. Foreign economic, military, technical, and humanitarian assistance.
5. Foreign loans.
6. International activities of the American National Red Cross and the International Committee of the Red Cross.
7. International aspects of nuclear energy, including nuclear transfer policy.
8. International conferences and congresses.
9. International law as it relates to foreign policy.
10. International Monetary Fund and other international organizations established primarily for international monetary purposes (except that, at the request of the Committee on Banking, Housing, and Urban Affairs, any proposed legislation relating to such subjects reported by the Committee on Foreign Relations shall be referred to the Committee on Banking, Housing, and Urban Affairs).
11. Intervention abroad and declarations of war.
12. Measures to foster commercial intercourse with foreign nations and to safeguard American business interests abroad.
13. National security and international aspects of trusteeships of the United States.
14. Oceans and international environmental and scientific affairs as they relate to foreign policy.
15. Protection of United States citizens abroad and expatriation.
16. Relations of the United States with foreign nations generally.
17. Treaties and executive agreements, except reciprocal trade agreements.
18. United Nations and its affiliated organizations.

19. World Bank group, the regional development banks, and other international organizations established primarily for development assistance purposes.

(2) Such committee shall also study and review, on a comprehensive basis, matters relating to the national security policy, foreign policy, and international economic policy as it relates to foreign policy of the United States, and matters relating to food, hunger, and nutrition in foreign countries, and report thereon from time to time.

FOREIGN RELATIONS / 80th Congress

Service Dates of Committee Chair: Jan. 6,1947-Jan. 10,1949
Service Dates of Majority Members: Jan. 6,1947-Jan. 10,1949
Service Dates of Minority Members: Jan. 8,1947-Jan. 10,1949

Majority

Rank	Name	Party	State	Years in: Senate	Years in: Comm.
Chr	Vandenberg, Arthur H.	Rep	Mich.	19	18
2nd	Capper, Arthur	Rep	Kans.	28	22
3rd	White, Wallace H. Jr.	Rep	Me.	16	12
4th	Wiley, Alexander	Rep	Wisc.	9	2
5th	Smith, H. Alexander	Rep	N.J.	3	1
6th	Hickenlooper, Bourke B.	Rep	Iowa	3	1
7th	Lodge, Henry Cabot Jr.	Rep	Mass.	8	1

Minority

Rank	Name	Party	State	Years in: Senate	Years in: Comm.
RM	Connally, Thomas T.	Dem	Tex.	18	16
2nd	George, Walter F.	Dem	Ga.	25	19
3rd	Wagner, Robert F.	Dem	N.Y.	20	18
4th	Thomas, Elbert D.	Dem	Utah	14	14
5th	Barkley, Alben W.	Dem	Ky.	20	*1 9
6th	Hatch, Carl A.	Dem	N.M.	14	2

*1: Member's 1st period of service on the committee.

Note: Rankings on this committee for the following members were affected by other chamber service: Arthur Capper (Rep-kans.), Chair, Agriculture and Forestry; Walter F. George (Dem-Ga.), Ranking Minority Member, Finance; and Robert F. Wagner (Dem-N.Y.), Ranking Minority Member, Banking and Currency.

	Majority			Minority		
Departures from the Senate:						
Elected Vice President	None			Barkley, Alben W.	Ky.	Dem
Appointed Federal Judge	None			Hatch, Carl A.	N.M.	Dem
Retired	Capper, Arthur	Kans.	Rep	None		
	White, Wallace H. Jr.	Me.	Rep			
Departures from Committee:						
Moved to Judiciary	None			Wagner, Robert F.	N.Y.	Dem

FOREIGN RELATIONS / 81st Congress

Service Dates of Committee Chair: Jan. 10,1949-Jan. 15,1951
Service Dates of Majority Members: Jan. 10,1949-Jan. 15,1951
Service Dates of Minority Members: Jan. 10,1949-Jan. 15,1951

Majority

Rank	Name	Party	State	Years in: Senate	Years in: Comm.
Chr	Connally, Thomas T.	Dem	Tex.	20	18
2nd	George, Walter F.	Dem	Ga.	27	21
3rd	Thomas, Elbert D.	Dem	Utah	16	16
4th	Tydings, Millard E.	Dem	Md.	22	1
5th	Pepper, Claude D.	Dem	Fla.	13	*2 1
6th	Green, Theodore F.	Dem	R.I.	13	*2 1
7th	McMahon, Brien	Dem	Conn.	5	1
8th	Fulbright, J. William	Dem	Ark.	5	1

Minority

Rank	Name	Party	State	Years in: Senate	Years in: Comm.
RM	Vandenberg, Arthur H.	Rep	Mich.	21	20
2nd	Wiley, Alexander	Rep	Wisc.	11	5
3rd	Smith, H. Alexander	Rep	N.J.	5	3
4th	Hickenlooper, Bourke B.	Rep	Iowa	5	3
5th	Lodge, Henry Cabot Jr.	Rep	Mass.	10	3

*2: Member's 2nd period of service on the committee.

Note: Ranking on this committee for the following member was affected by other chamber service: Walter F. George (Dem-Ga.), Chair, Finance.

	Majority			Minority
Departures from the Senate:				
Defeated for Reelection	Thomas, Elbert D.	Utah	Dem	None
	Tydings, Millard E.	Md.	Dem	
Defeated for Renomination	Pepper, Claude D.	Fla.	Dem	None

FOREIGN RELATIONS / 82nd Congress

Service Dates of Committee Chair: Jan. 15,1951-Jan. 3,1953
Service Dates of Majority Members: Jan. 15,1951-Jan. 13,1953
Service Dates of Minority Members: Jan. 15,1951-Jan. 13,1953

Majority

Rank	Name	Party	State	Years in: Senate	Comm.
Chr	Connally, Thomas T.	Dem	Tex.	22	20
2nd	George, Walter F.	Dem	Ga.	29	23
3rd	Green, Theodore F.	Dem	R.I.	15	*2 3
4th	McMahon, Brien	Dem	Conn.	7	3
5th	Fulbright, J. William	Dem	Ark.	7	3
6th	Sparkman, John J.	Dem	Ala.	5	1
7th	Gillette, Guy M.	Dem	Iowa	11	*2 1

Minority

Rank	Name	Party	State	Years in: Senate	Comm.
RM1	Vandenberg, Arthur H.	Rep	Mich.	23	22
RM2 2nd	Wiley, Alexander	Rep	Wisc.	13	7
3rd	Smith, H. Alexander	Rep	N.J.	7	5
4th	Hickenlooper, Bourke B.	Rep	Iowa	7	5
5th	Lodge, Henry Cabot Jr.	Rep	Mass.	12	5
6th	Tobey, Charles W.	Rep	N.H.	13	1

*2: Member's 2nd period of service on the committee.

Note: Ranking on this committee for the following member was affected by other chamber service: Walter F. George (Dem-Ga.), Chair, Finance.

Changes:

Ranking Member:

	Name	Party	State	Date	Change
RM1	Vandenberg, Arthur H.	Rep	Mich.	Apr. 18,1951	Died in office.
RM2	Wiley, Alexander	Rep	Wisc.	Apr. 18,1951	Succeeded Vandenberg as Ranking Minority Member.

Majority:

Name	Party	State	Date	Change
McMahon, Brien	Dem	Conn.	July 28,1952	Died in office.

Minority:

Name	Party	State	Date	Change
Vandenberg, Arthur H.	Rep	Mich.	Apr. 18,1951	Died in office.
Brewster, Ralph O.	Rep	Me.	May 9,1951	Replaced Vandenberg.
Brewster, Ralph O.	Rep	Me.	Dec. 31,1952	Resigned; defeated for renomination.

Departures from the Senate:	Majority			Minority		
Defeated for Reelection	None			Lodge, Henry Cabot Jr.	Mass.	Rep
Retired	Connally, Thomas T.	Tex.	Dem	None		

FOREIGN RELATIONS / 83rd Congress

Service Dates of Committee Chair: Jan. 13,1953-Jan. 11,1955
Service Dates of Majority Members: Jan. 13,1953-Jan. 11,1955
Service Dates of Minority Members: Jan. 13,1953-Jan. 11,1955

Majority

Rank	Name	Party	State	Years in: Senate	Comm.
Chr	Wiley, Alexander	Rep	Wisc.	15	9
2nd	Smith, H. Alexander	Rep	N.J.	9	7
3rd	Hickenlooper, Bourke B.	Rep	Iowa	9	7
4th	Tobey, Charles W.	Rep	N.H.	15	2
5th	Taft, Robert A.	Rep	Ohio	15	1
6th	Langer, William	Rep	N.D.	13	1
7th	Ferguson, Homer	Rep	Mich.	11	1
8th	Knowland, William F.	Rep	Cal.	8	1

Minority

Rank	Name	Party	State	Years in: Senate	Comm.
RM	George, Walter F.	Dem	Ga.	31	25
2nd	Green, Theodore F.	Dem	R.I.	17	*2 5
3rd	Fulbright, J. William	Dem	Ark.	9	5
4th	Sparkman, John J.	Dem	Ala.	7	2
5th	Gillette, Guy M.	Dem	Iowa	13	*2 2
6th	Humphrey, Hubert H. Jr.	DFL	Minn.	5	*1 1
7th	Mansfield, Michael J.	Dem	Mont.	1	1

*1: Member's 1st period of service on the committee; *2: Member's 2nd period of service on the committee.

Changes:

Majority:

Name	Party	State	Date	Change
Tobey, Charles W.	Rep	N.H.	July 24,1953	Died in office.
Taft, Robert A.	Rep	Ohio	July 31,1953	Died in office.
Aiken, George D.	Rep	Vt.	Jan. 13,1954	Replaced Tobey.
Capehart, Homer E.	Rep	Ind.	Jan. 13,1954	Replaced Taft.

Departures from the Senate:

	Majority		Minority	
Defeated for Reelection	Ferguson, Homer	Mich. Rep	Gillette, Guy M.	Iowa Dem

FOREIGN RELATIONS / 84th Congress

Service Dates of Committee Chair: Jan. 11,1955-Jan. 9,1957
Service Dates of Majority Members: Jan. 11,1955-Jan. 9,1957
Service Dates of Minority Members: Jan. 11,1955-Jan. 9,1957

Majority

Rank Name	Party	State	Years in: Senate	Years in: Comm.
Chr George, Walter F.	Dem	Ga.	33	27
2nd Green, Theodore F.	Dem	R.I.	19	*2 7
3rd Fulbright, J. William	Dem	Ark.	11	7
4th Sparkman, John J.	Dem	Ala.	9	4
5th Humphrey, Hubert H. Jr.	DFL	Minn.	7	*1 2
6th Mansfield, Michael J.	Dem	Mont.	3	2
7th Barkley, Alben W.	Dem	Ky.	22	*2 1

Minority

Rank Name	Party	State	Years in: Senate	Years in: Comm.
RM Wiley, Alexander	Rep	Wisc.	17	11
2nd Smith, H. Alexander	Rep	N.J.	11	9
3rd Hickenlooper, Bourke B.	Rep	Iowa	11	9
4th Langer, William	Rep	N.D.	15	2
5th Knowland, William F.	Rep	Cal.	10	2
6th Aiken, George D.	Rep	Vt.	15	1
7th Capehart, Homer E.	Rep	Ind.	11	1

Third Party:

Name	Party	State	Senate	Comm.
Morse, Wayne L.	Ind	Ore.	11	1

*1: Member's 1st period of service on the committee; *2: Member's 2nd period of service on the committee.

Note: Wayne Morse of Oregon was assigned to this committee as an Independent on Jan. 11,1955 by the Democratic Caucus. On Feb. 17,1955, he joined the Democratic Party and became the 8th ranking member on the committee, at which time he was allowed to accrue seniority.

Changes:

Majority:

Barkley, Alben W.	Dem	Ky.	Apr. 30,1956	Died in office.
Long, Russell B.	Dem	La.	May 18,1956	Replaced Barkley.

Departures from the Senate:

	Majority		Minority
Retired	George, Walter F.	Ga. Dem	None

FOREIGN RELATIONS / 85th Congress

Service Dates of Committee Chair: Jan. 9,1957-Jan. 14,1959
Service Dates of Majority Members: Jan. 9,1957-Jan. 14,1959
Service Dates of Minority Members: Jan. 9,1957-Jan. 20,1959

Majority

Rank Name	Party	State	Years in: Senate	Years in: Comm.
Chr Green, Theodore F.	Dem	R.I.	21	*2 8
2nd Fulbright, J. William	Dem	Ark.	13	8
3rd Sparkman, John J.	Dem	Ala.	11	6
4th Humphrey, Hubert H. Jr.	DFL	Minn.	9	*1 4
5th Mansfield, Michael J.	Dem	Mont.	5	4
6th Morse, Wayne L.	Dem	Ore.	13	2
7th Long, Russell B.	Dem	La.	9	1
8th Kennedy, John F.	Dem	Mass.	5	1

Minority

Rank Name	Party	State	Years in: Senate	Years in: Comm.
RM Wiley, Alexander	Rep	Wisc.	19	12
2nd Smith, H. Alexander	Rep	N.J.	13	11
3rd Hickenlooper, Bourke B.	Rep	Iowa	13	11
4th Langer, William	Rep	N.D.	17	4
5th Knowland, William F.	Rep	Cal.	12	4
6th Aiken, George D.	Rep	Vt.	16	3
7th Capehart, Homer E.	Rep	Ind.	13	3

*1: Member's 1st period of service on the committee; *2: Member's 2nd period of service on the committee.

Departures from the Senate:

	Majority	Minority	
Lost Election for Governor	None	Knowland, William F.	Cal. Rep
Retired	None	Smith, H. Alexander	N.J. Rep

FOREIGN RELATIONS / 86th Congress

Service Dates of Committee Chairs: Ch1 Jan. 14,1959-Feb. 6,1959
Ch2 Feb. 6,1959-Jan. 10,1961
Service Dates of Majority Members: Jan. 14,1959-Jan. 10,1961
Service Dates of Minority Members: Jan. 20,1959-Jan. 13,1961

Majority

Rank	Name	Party	State	Years in: Senate	Years in: Comm.
Ch1	Green, Theodore F.	Dem	R.I.	23 *2	11
Ch2 2nd	Fulbright, J. William	Dem	Ark.	15	11
3rd	Sparkman, John J.	Dem	Ala.	13	8
4th	Humphrey, Hubert H. Jr.	DFL	Minn.	11 *1	7
5th	Mansfield, Michael J.	Dem	Mont.	7	7
6th	Morse, Wayne L.	Dem	Ore.	15	5
7th	Long, Russell B.	Dem	La.	11	3
8th	Kennedy, John F.	Dem	Mass.	7	3
9th	Gore, Albert A.	Dem	Tenn.	7	1
10th	Lausche, Frank J.	Dem	Ohio	3	1
11th	Church, Frank F.	Dem	Ida.	3	1

Minority

Rank	Name	Party	State	Years in: Senate	Years in: Comm.
RM	Wiley, Alexander	Rep	Wisc.	21	15
2nd	Hickenlooper, Bourke B.	Rep	Iowa	15	13
3rd	Langer, William	Rep	N.D.	19	7
4th	Aiken, George D.	Rep	Vt.	19	6
5th	Capehart, Homer E.	Rep	Ind.	15	6
6th	Carlson, Frank	Rep	Kans.	9	1

*1: Member's 1st period of service on the committee;
*2: Member's 2nd period of service on the committee.

Changes:

Chair:

Ch1	Green, Theodore F.	Dem	R.I.	Feb. 6,1959	Resigned as Chair; remained on committee.
Ch2	Fulbright, J. William	Dem	Ark.	Feb. 6,1959	Succeeded Green as Chair.

Majority:

Kennedy, John F.	Dem	Mass.	Dec. 22,1960	Resigned; elected President.

Minority:

Langer, William	Rep	N.D.	Nov. 8,1959	Died in office.
Williams, John J.	Rep	Del.	Jan. 18,1960	Replaced Langer.

Departures from the Senate:	Majority			Minority
Retired	Green, Theodore F.	R.I.	Dem	None

FOREIGN RELATIONS / 87th Congress

Service Dates of Committee Chair: Jan. 10,1961-Feb. 25,1963
Service Dates of Majority Members: Jan. 10,1961-Feb. 25,1963
Service Dates of Minority Members: Jan. 13,1961-Feb. 25,1963

Majority

Rank	Name	Party	State	Years in: Senate	Years in: Comm.
Chr	Fulbright, J. William	Dem	Ark.	17	13
2nd	Sparkman, John J.	Dem	Ala.	15	10
3rd	Humphrey, Hubert H. Jr.	DFL	Minn.	13 *1	8
4th	Mansfield, Michael J.	Dem	Mont.	9	8
5th	Morse, Wayne L.	Dem	Ore.	17	6
6th	Long, Russell B.	Dem	La.	13	5
7th	Gore, Albert A.	Dem	Tenn.	9	2
8th	Lausche, Frank J.	Dem	Ohio	5	2
9th	Church, Frank F.	Dem	Ida.	5	2
10th	Symington, W. Stuart	Dem	Mo.	9	1
11th	Dodd, Thomas J.	Dem	Conn.	3	1

Minority

Rank	Name	Party	State	Years in: Senate	Years in: Comm.
RM	Wiley, Alexander	Rep	Wisc.	23	17
2nd	Hickenlooper, Bourke B.	Rep	Iowa	17	15
3rd	Aiken, George D.	Rep	Vt.	21	8
4th	Capehart, Homer E.	Rep	Ind.	17	8
5th	Carlson, Frank	Rep	Kans.	11	2
6th	Williams, John J.	Rep	Del.	15	1

*1: Member's 1st period of service on the committee.

Departures from the Senate:	Majority	Minority		
Defeated for Reelection	None	Capehart, Homer E.	Ind.	Rep
		Wiley, Alexander	Wisc.	Rep

FOREIGN RELATIONS / 88th Congress

Service Dates of Committee Chair: Feb. 25,1963-Jan. 8,1965
Service Dates of Majority Members: Feb. 25,1963-Jan. 8,1965
Service Dates of Minority Members: Feb. 25,1963-Jan. 15,1965

Majority

Rank	Name	Party	State	Years in: Senate	Years in: Comm.
Chr	Fulbright, J. William	Dem	Ark.	19	15
2nd	Sparkman, John J.	Dem	Ala.	17	13
3rd	Humphrey, Hubert H. Jr.	DFL	Minn.	15	*1 11
4th	Mansfield, Michael J.	Dem	Mont.	11	11
5th	Morse, Wayne L.	Dem	Ore.	19	9
6th	Long, Russell B.	Dem	La.	15	7
7th	Gore, Albert A.	Dem	Tenn.	11	5
8th	Lausche, Frank J.	Dem	Ohio	7	5
9th	Church, Frank F.	Dem	Ida.	7	5
10th	Symington, W. Stuart	Dem	Mo.	11	3
11th	Dodd, Thomas J.	Dem	Conn.	5	3
12th	Smathers, George A.	Dem	Fla.	13	1

Minority

Rank	Name	Party	State	Years in: Senate	Years in: Comm.
RM	Hickenlooper, Bourke B.	Rep	Iowa	19	17
2nd	Aiken, George D.	Rep	Vt.	23	10
3rd	Carlson, Frank	Rep	Kans.	13	5
4th	Williams, John J.	Rep	Del.	17	4
5th	Mundt, Karl E.	Rep	S.D.	15	1

*1: Member's 1st period of service on the committee.

Changes:
Majority:

Humphrey, Hubert H. Jr.	DFL	Minn.	Dec. 29,1964	Resigned; elected Vice President.

FOREIGN RELATIONS / 89th Congress

Service Dates of Committee Chair: Jan. 8,1965-Jan. 11,1967
Service Dates of Majority Members: Jan. 8,1965-Jan. 11,1967
Service Dates of Minority Members: Jan. 15,1965-Jan. 16,1967

Majority

Rank	Name	Party	State	Years in: Senate	Years in: Comm.
Chr	Fulbright, J. William	Dem	Ark.	21	16
2nd	Sparkman, John J.	Dem	Ala.	19	14
3rd	Mansfield, Michael J.	Dem	Mont.	13	12
4th	Morse, Wayne L.	Dem	Ore.	21	10
5th	Long, Russell B.	Dem	La.	17	9
6th	Gore, Albert A.	Dem	Tenn.	13	6
7th	Lausche, Frank J.	Dem	Ohio	9	6
8th	Church, Frank F.	Dem	Ida.	9	6
9th	Symington, W. Stuart	Dem	Mo.	13	4
10th	Dodd, Thomas J.	Dem	Conn.	7	4
11th	Smathers, George A.	Dem	Fla.	15	2
12th	Clark, Joseph S.	Dem	Penn.	9	1
13th	Pell, Claiborne D.	Dem	R.I.	5	1

Minority:

Rank	Name	Party	State	Years in: Senate	Years in: Comm.
RM	Hickenlooper, Bourke B.	Rep	Iowa	21	19
2nd	Aiken, George D.	Rep	Vt.	25	12
3rd	Carlson, Frank	Rep	Kans.	15	6
4th	Williams, John J.	Rep	Del.	19	5
5th	Mundt, Karl E.	Rep	S.D.	17	2
6th	Case, Clifford P.	Rep	N.J.	11	1

Changes:
Majority:

Smathers, George A.	Dem	Fla.	Apr. 26,1965	Moved to Judiciary.
McCarthy, Eugene J.	DFL	Minn.	Apr. 26,1965	Replaced Smathers.
Long, Russell B.	Dem	La.	Mar. 25,1966	Moved to Commerce.
McGee, Gale W.	Dem	Wyo.	Mar. 25,1966	Replaced Long.

Departures from Committee:	Majority			Minority
Moved to Banking and Currency	McGee, Gale W.	Wyo.	Dem	None

FOREIGN RELATIONS / 90th Congress

Service Dates of Committee Chair: Jan. 11,1967-Jan. 14,1969
Service Dates of Majority Members: Jan. 11,1967-Jan. 14,1969
Service Dates of Minority Members: Jan. 16,1967-Jan. 14,1969

Majority

Rank	Name	Party	State	Years in: Senate	Years in: Comm.
Chr	Fulbright, J. William	Dem	Ark.	23	19
2nd	Sparkman, John J.	Dem	Ala.	21	16
3rd	Mansfield, Michael J.	Dem	Mont.	15	14
4th	Morse, Wayne L.	Dem	Ore.	23	13
5th	Gore, Albert A.	Dem	Tenn.	15	8
6th	Lausche, Frank J.	Dem	Ohio	11	8
7th	Church, Frank F.	Dem	Ida.	11	8
8th	Symington, W. Stuart	Dem	Mo.	15	7
9th	Dodd, Thomas J.	Dem	Conn.	9	7
10th	Clark, Joseph S.	Dem	Penn.	11	3
11th	Pell, Claiborne D.	Dem	R.I.	7	3
12th	McCarthy, Eugene J.	DFL	Minn.	9	2

Minority

Rank	Name	Party	State	Years in: Senate	Years in: Comm.
RM	Hickenlooper, Bourke B.	Rep	Iowa	23	21
2nd	Aiken, George D.	Rep	Vt.	27	14
3rd	Carlson, Frank	Rep	Kans.	17	8
4th	Williams, John J.	Rep	Del.	21	7
5th	Mundt, Karl E.	Rep	S.D.	19	4
6th	Case, Clifford P.	Rep	N.J.	13	3
7th	Cooper, John Sherman	Rep	Ky.	15	1

Note: Rankings on this committee were adjusted on Sep. 12,1968, with John J. Williams (Rep-Del.) moving from 4th to 7th minority rank and Mundt, Case, and Cooper moving up a rank.

	Majority		Minority	
Departures from the Senate:				
Defeated for Reelection	Clark, Joseph S.	Penn. Dem	None	
	Morse, Wayne L.	Ore. Dem		
Defeated for Renomination	Lausche, Frank J.	Ohio Dem	None	
Retired	None		Carlson, Frank	Kans. Rep
			Hickenlooper, Bourke B.	Iowa Rep
Departures from Committee:				
Moved to Government Operations	McCarthy, Eugene J.	Minn. DFL	None	

FOREIGN RELATIONS / 91st Congress

Service Dates of Committee Chair: Jan. 14,1969-Jan. 28,1971
Service Dates of Majority Members: Jan. 14,1969-Jan. 28,1971
Service Dates of Minority Members: Jan. 14,1969-Jan. 29,1971

Majority

Rank	Name	Party	State	Years in: Senate	Years in: Comm.
Chr	Fulbright, J. William	Dem	Ark.	25	21
2nd	Sparkman, John J.	Dem	Ala.	23	18
3rd	Mansfield, Michael J.	Dem	Mont.	17	17
4th	Gore, Albert A.	Dem	Tenn.	17	11
5th	Church, Frank F.	Dem	Ida.	13	11
6th	Symington, W. Stuart	Dem	Mo.	17	9
7th	Dodd, Thomas J.	Dem	Conn.	11	9
8th	Pell, Claiborne D.	Dem	R.I.	9	5
9th	McGee, Gale W.	Dem	Wyo.	11	*2 1

Minority

Rank	Name	Party	State	Years in: Senate	Years in: Comm.
RM	Aiken, George D.	Rep	Vt.	29	16
2nd	Mundt, Karl E.	Rep	S.D.	21	6
3rd	Case, Clifford P.	Rep	N.J.	15	4
4th	Cooper, John Sherman	Rep	Ky.	17	2
5th	Williams, John J.	Rep	Del.	23	9
6th	Javits, Jacob K.	Rep	N.Y.	13	1

*2: Member's 2nd period of service on the committee.

Note: In the previous Congress, on Sep. 12,1968, John J. Williams (Rep-Del.) was ranked behind minority members Mundt, Case, and Cooper; the members maintained this order until Williams' retirement.

Changes:

Minority:

Williams, John J.	Rep	Del.	Dec. 31,1970	Resigned and retired.

	Majority		Minority
Departures from the Senate:			
Defeated for Reelection	Dodd, Thomas J.	Conn. Dem	None
	Gore, Albert A.	Tenn. Dem	

FOREIGN RELATIONS / 92nd Congress

Service Dates of Committee Chair: Jan. 28,1971-Jan. 4,1973
Service Dates of Majority Members: Jan. 28,1971-Jan. 4,1973
Service Dates of Minority Members: Jan. 29,1971-Jan. 12,1973

Majority

Rank	Name	Party	State	Years in: Senate	Years in: Comm.
Chr	Fulbright, J. William	Dem	Ark.	27	23
2nd	Sparkman, John J.	Dem	Ala.	25	21
3rd	Mansfield, Michael J.	Dem	Mont.	19	19
4th	Church, Frank F.	Dem	Ida.	15	13
5th	Symington, W. Stuart	Dem	Mo.	19	11
6th	Pell, Claiborne D.	Dem	R.I.	11	7
7th	McGee, Gale W.	Dem	Wyo.	13	*2 3
8th	Muskie, Edmund S.	Dem	Me.	13	*1 1
9th	Spong, William B. Jr.	Dem	Va.	5	1

Minority

Rank	Name	Party	State	Years in: Senate	Years in: Comm.
RM	Aiken, George D.	Rep	Vt.	31	18
2nd	Mundt, Karl E.	Rep	S.D.	23	8
3rd	Case, Clifford P.	Rep	N.J.	17	7
4th	Cooper, John Sherman	Rep	Ky.	19	5
5th	Javits, Jacob K.	Rep	N.Y.	15	3
6th	Scott, Hugh D. Jr.	Rep	Penn.	13	1
7th	Pearson, James B.	Rep	Kans.	9	1

*1: Member's 1st period of service on the committee; *2: Member's 2nd period of service on the committee.

Changes:
Minority:

Mundt, Karl E.	Rep	S.D.	Feb. 23,1972	Moved to Aeronautical and Space Sciences, due to terminal illness.
Percy, Charles H.	Rep	Ill.	Feb. 23,1972	Replaced Mundt.

Departures from the Senate:

	Majority			Minority		
Defeated for Reelection	Spong, William B. Jr.	Va.	Dem	None		
Retired	None			Cooper, John Sherman	Ky.	Rep

FOREIGN RELATIONS / 93rd Congress

Service Dates of Committee Chair: Jan. 4,1973-Dec. 31,1974
Service Dates of Majority Members: Jan. 4,1973-Jan. 17,1975
Service Dates of Minority Members: Jan. 12,1973-Jan. 23,1975

Majority

Rank	Name	Party	State	Years in: Senate	Years in: Comm.
Chr	Fulbright, J. William	Dem	Ark.	29	24
2nd	Sparkman, John J.	Dem	Ala.	27	22
3rd	Mansfield, Michael J.	Dem	Mont.	21	20
4th	Church, Frank F.	Dem	Ida.	17	14
5th	Symington, W. Stuart	Dem	Mo.	21	12
6th	Pell, Claiborne D.	Dem	R.I.	13	8
7th	McGee, Gale W.	Dem	Wyo.	15	*2 4
8th	Muskie, Edmund S.	Dem	Me.	15	*1 2
9th	McGovern, George S.	Dem	S.D.	11	1
10th	Humphrey, Hubert H. Jr.	DFL	Minn.	18	*2 1

Minority

Rank	Name	Party	State	Years in: Senate	Years in: Comm.
RM	Aiken, George D.	Rep	Vt.	33	19
2nd	Case, Clifford P.	Rep	N.J.	19	8
3rd	Javits, Jacob K.	Rep	N.Y.	17	4
4th	Scott, Hugh D. Jr.	Rep	Penn.	15	2
5th	Pearson, James B.	Rep	Kans.	11	2
6th	Percy, Charles H.	Rep	Ill.	7	1
7th	Griffin, Robert P.	Rep	Mich.	7	1

*1: Member's 1st period of service on the committee; *2: Member's 2nd period of service on the committee.

Changes:
Majority:

Fulbright, J. William	Dem	Ark.	Dec. 31,1974	Resigned; defeated for renomination.

Departures from the Senate:

	Majority			Minority		
Retired	None			Aiken, George D.	Vt.	Rep

Departures from Committee:

	Majority			Minority
Moved to Budget	Muskie, Edmund S.	Me.	Dem	None

FOREIGN RELATIONS / 94th Congress

Service Dates of Committee Chair: Jan. 17,1975-Jan. 10,1977
Service Dates of Majority Members: Jan. 17,1975-Jan. 10,1977
Service Dates of Minority Members: Jan. 23,1975-Jan. 10,1977

Majority

Rank Name	Party	State	Years in: Senate	Years in: Comm.
Chr Sparkman, John J.	Dem	Ala.	29	25
2nd Mansfield, Michael J.	Dem	Mont.	23	23
3rd Church, Frank F.	Dem	Ida.	19	17
4th Symington, W. Stuart	Dem	Mo.	23	15
5th Pell, Claiborne D.	Dem	R.I.	15	11
6th McGee, Gale W.	Dem	Wyo.	17	*2 7
7th McGovern, George S.	Dem	S.D.	13	3
8th Humphrey, Hubert H. Jr.	DFL	Minn.	21	*2 3
9th Clark, Richard C.	Dem	Iowa	3	1
10th Biden, Joseph R. Jr.	Dem	Del.	3	1

Minority

Rank Name	Party	State	Years in: Senate	Years in: Comm.
RM Case, Clifford P.	Rep	N.J.	21	11
2nd Javits, Jacob K.	Rep	N.Y.	19	7
3rd Scott, Hugh D. Jr.	Rep	Penn.	17	4
4th Pearson, James B.	Rep	Kans.	13	4
5th Percy, Charles H.	Rep	Ill.	9	3
6th Griffin, Robert P.	Rep	Mich.	9	3
7th Baker, Howard H. Jr.	Rep	Tenn.	9	*1 1

*1: Member's 1st period of service on the committee; *2: Member's 2nd period of service on the committee.

Note: The committee was reduced to 16 members on Sep. 19,1975, and the party ratio changed to 10 Democrats and 6 Republicans.

Changes:

Majority:

Symington, W. Stuart	Dem	Mo.	Dec. 27,1976	Resigned and retired.

Minority:

Baker, Howard H. Jr.	Rep	Tenn.	Sep. 19,1975	Ratio change; moved to Commerce.

Departures from the Senate:	Majority		Minority	
Appointed Ambassador to Japan	Mansfield, Michael J.	Mont. Dem	None	
Defeated for Reelection	McGee, Gale W.	Wyo. Dem	None	
Retired	None		Scott, Hugh D. Jr.	Penn. Rep

FOREIGN RELATIONS / 95th Congress

Service Dates of Committee Chair: Jan. 10,1977-Jan. 3,1979
Service Dates of Majority Members: Jan. 10,1977-Jan. 23,1979
Service Dates of Minority Members: Jan. 10,1977-Jan. 23,1979

Majority

Rank Name	Party	State	Years in: Senate	Years in: Comm.
Chr Sparkman, John J.	Dem	Ala.	31	26
2nd Church, Frank F.	Dem	Ida.	21	18
3rd Pell, Claiborne D.	Dem	R.I.	17	13
4th McGovern, George S.	Dem	S.D.	15	5
5th Humphrey, Hubert H. Jr.	DFL	Minn.	23	*2 5
6th Clark, Richard C.	Dem	Iowa	5	2
7th Biden, Joseph R. Jr.	Dem	Del.	5	2
8th Zorinsky, Edward	Dem	Neb.	1	*T 1
9th Matsunaga, Spark M.	Dem	Hai.	1	*T 1

Minority

Rank Name	Party	State	Years in: Senate	Years in: Comm.
RM Case, Clifford P.	Rep	N.J.	23	12
2nd Javits, Jacob K.	Rep	N.Y.	21	8
3rd Pearson, James B.	Rep	Kans.	15	6
4th Percy, Charles H.	Rep	Ill.	11	5
5th Griffin, Robert P.	Rep	Mich.	11	4
6th Danforth, John C.	Rep	Mo.	1	*T 1

*2: Member's 2nd period of service on the committee; *T: Temporary member of the committee.

Note: The committee was expanded and the party ratio changed to 10 Democrats and 6 Republicans on Feb. 11,1977.

Addition:

Majority: 10th Sarbanes, Paul S. Dem Md. Feb. 11,1977

Changes:

Majority:

Zorinsky, Edward	Dem	Neb.	Feb. 11,1977	Moved to Commerce, Science, and Transportation.
Matsunaga, Spark M.	Dem	Hai.	Feb. 11,1977	Moved to Finance.
Glenn, John H. Jr.	Dem	Ohio	Feb. 11,1977	Replaced Zorinsky.
Stone, Richard B.	Dem	Fla.	Feb. 11,1977	Replaced Matsunaga.
Humphrey, Hubert H. Jr.	DFL	Minn.	Jan. 13,1978	Died in office.
Humphrey, Muriel	Dem	Minn.	Feb. 7,1978	Replaced Humphrey.
Humphrey, Muriel	Dem	Minn.	Nov. 7,1978	Resigned and retired.

Minority:

Danforth, John C.	Rep	Mo.	Feb. 22,1977	Moved to Finance.
Baker, Howard H. Jr.	Rep	Tenn.	Feb. 22,1977	Replaced Danforth.
Pearson, James B.	Rep	Kans.	Dec. 23,1978	Resigned and retired.

Departures from the Senate:	Majority			Minority		
Defeated for Reelection	Clark, Richard C.	Iowa	Dem	Griffin, Robert P.	Mich.	Rep
Defeated for Renomination	None			Case, Clifford P.	N.J.	Rep
Retired	Sparkman, John J.	Ala.	Dem	None		

FOREIGN RELATIONS / 96th Congress

Service Dates of Committee Chair: Jan. 23,1979-Jan. 3,1981
Service Dates of Majority Members: Jan. 23,1979-Jan. 5,1981
Service Dates of Minority Members: Jan. 23,1979-Jan. 5,1981

Majority

Rank	Name	Party	State	Years in: Senate	Years in: Comm.
Chr	Church, Frank F.	Dem	Ida.	23	21
2nd	Pell, Claiborne D.	Dem	R.I.	19	15
3rd	McGovern, George S.	Dem	S.D.	17	7
4th	Biden, Joseph R. Jr.	Dem	Del.	7	5
5th	Glenn, John H. Jr.	Dem	Ohio	5	2
6th	Stone, Richard B.	Dem	Fla.	5	2
7th	Sarbanes, Paul S.	Dem	Md.	3	2
8th	Muskie, Edmund S.	Dem	Me.	21	*2 1
9th	Zorinsky, Edward	Dem	Neb.	3	1

Minority

Rank	Name	Party	State	Years in: Senate	Years in: Comm.
RM	Javits, Jacob K.	Rep	N.Y.	23	11
2nd	Percy, Charles H.	Rep	Ill.	13	7
3rd	Baker, Howard H. Jr.	Rep	Tenn.	13	*2 2
4th	Helms, Jesse A.	Rep	N.C.	7	1
5th	Hayakawa, S. I. (Sam)	Rep	Cal.	3	1
6th	Lugar, Richard G.	Rep	Ind.	3	1

*2: Member's 2nd period of service on the committee.

Changes:

Majority:

Muskie, Edmund S.	Dem	Me.	May 7,1980	Resigned; appointed Secretary of State.
Tsongas, Paul E.	Dem	Mass.	May 13,1980	Replaced Muskie.
Stone, Richard B.	Dem	Fla.	Jan. 1,1981	Resigned; defeated for renomination.

Departures from the Senate:	Majority			Minority		
Defeated for Reelection	Church, Frank F.	Ida.	Dem	Javits, Jacob K.	N.Y.	Rep
	McGovern, George S.	S.D.	Dem			

FOREIGN RELATIONS / 97th Congress

Service Dates of Committee Chair: Jan. 5,1981-Jan. 3,1983
Service Dates of Majority Members: Jan. 5,1981-Jan. 3,1983
Service Dates of Minority Members: Jan. 5,1981-Jan. 3,1983

Majority

Rank	Name	Party	State	Years in: Senate	Years in: Comm.
Chr	Percy, Charles H.	Rep	Ill.	15	9
2nd	Baker, Howard H. Jr.	Rep	Tenn.	15	*2 4
3rd	Helms, Jesse A.	Rep	N.C.	9	2
4th	Hayakawa, S. I. (Sam)	Rep	Cal.	5	2
5th	Lugar, Richard G.	Rep	Ind.	5	2
6th	Mathias, Charles McC. Jr.	Rep	Md.	13	1
7th	Kassebaum, Nancy Landon	Rep	Kans.	3	1
8th	Boschwitz, Rudolf E.	Rep	Minn.	3	1
9th	Pressler, Larry L.	Rep	S.D.	3	1

Minority

Rank	Name	Party	State	Years in: Senate	Years in: Comm.
RM	Pell, Claiborne D.	Dem	R.I.	21	16
2nd	Biden, Joseph R. Jr.	Dem	Del.	9	6
3rd	Glenn, John H. Jr.	Dem	Ohio	7	4
4th	Sarbanes, Paul S.	Dem	Md.	5	4
5th	Zorinsky, Edward	Dem	Neb.	5	2
6th	Tsongas, Paul E.	Dem	Mass.	3	1
7th	Cranston, Alan	Dem	Cal.	13	1
8th	Dodd, Christopher J.	Dem	Conn.	1	1

*2: Member's 2nd period of service on the committee.

Departures from the Senate:	Majority			Minority
Retired	Hayakawa, S. I. (Sam)	Cal.	Rep	None

FOREIGN RELATIONS / 98th Congress

Service Dates of Committee Chair: Jan. 3,1983-Jan. 3,1985
Service Dates of Majority Members: Jan. 3,1983-Feb. 21,1985
Service Dates of Minority Members: Jan. 3,1983-Feb. 21,1985

Majority

Rank	Name	Party	State	Years in: Senate	Years in: Comm.
Chr	Percy, Charles H.	Rep	Ill.	17	11
2nd	Baker, Howard H. Jr.	Rep	Tenn.	17	*2 6
3rd	Helms, Jesse A.	Rep	N.C.	11	4
4th	Lugar, Richard G.	Rep	Ind.	7	4
5th	Mathias, Charles McC. Jr.	Rep	Md.	15	2
6th	Kassebaum, Nancy Landon	Rep	Kans.	5	2
7th	Boschwitz, Rudolf E.	Rep	Minn.	5	2
8th	Pressler, Larry L.	Rep	S.D.	5	2
9th	Murkowski, Frank H.	Rep	Alas.	3	1

Minority

Rank	Name	Party	State	Years in: Senate	Years in: Comm.
RM	Pell, Claiborne D.	Dem	R.I.	23	18
2nd	Biden, Joseph R. Jr.	Dem	Del.	11	8
3rd	Glenn, John H. Jr.	Dem	Ohio	9	6
4th	Sarbanes, Paul S.	Dem	Md.	7	6
5th	Zorinsky, Edward	Dem	Neb.	7	4
6th	Tsongas, Paul E.	Dem	Mass.	5	2
7th	Cranston, Alan	Dem	Cal.	15	2
8th	Dodd, Christopher J.	Dem	Conn.	3	2

*2: Member's 2nd period of service on the committee.

Note: The death of Henry M. Jackson (Dem-Wash.) and the appointment of Daniel J. Evans (Rep-Wash.) to fill his vacancy on Sep. 8,1983 led to a change in size and party ratio on this committee to 10 Republicans and 8 Democrats.

Addition:
Majority: 10th Hawkins, Paula   Rep   Fla.   Feb. 9,1984

	Majority			Minority		
Departures from the Senate:						
Defeated for Reelection	Percy, Charles H.	Ill.	Rep	None		
Retired	Baker, Howard H. Jr.	Tenn.	Rep	Tsongas, Paul E.	Mass.	Dem
Departures from Committee:						
Moved to Special Aging	Hawkins, Paula	Fla.	Rep	None		
Moved to Armed Services	None			Glenn, John H. Jr.	Ohio	Dem

FOREIGN RELATIONS / 99th Congress

Service Dates of Committee Chair: Feb. 21,1985-Jan. 6,1987
Service Dates of Majority Members: Feb. 21,1985-Jan. 6,1987
Service Dates of Minority Members: Feb. 21,1985-Jan. 6,1987

Majority

Rank	Name	Party	State	Years in: Senate	Years in: Comm.
Chr	Lugar, Richard G.	Rep	Ind.	9	7
2nd	Helms, Jesse A.	Rep	N.C.	13	7
3rd	Mathias, Charles McC. Jr.	Rep	Md.	17	5
4th	Kassebaum, Nancy Landon	Rep	Kans.	7	5
5th	Boschwitz, Rudolf E.	Rep	Minn.	7	5
6th	Pressler, Larry L.	Rep	S.D.	7	5
7th	Murkowski, Frank H.	Rep	Alas.	5	3
8th	Trible, Paul S. Jr.	Rep	Va.	3	1
9th	Evans, Daniel J.	Rep	Wash.	2	1

Minority

Rank	Name	Party	State	Years in: Senate	Years in: Comm.
RM	Pell, Claiborne D.	Dem	R.I.	25	21
2nd	Biden, Joseph R. Jr.	Dem	Del.	13	11
3rd	Sarbanes, Paul S.	Dem	Md.	9	9
4th	Zorinsky, Edward	Dem	Neb.	9	7
5th	Cranston, Alan	Dem	Cal.	17	5
6th	Dodd, Christopher J.	Dem	Conn.	5	5
7th	Eagleton, Thomas F.	Dem	Mo.	17	1
8th	Kerry, John F.	Dem	Mass.	1	1

*2: Member's 2nd period of service on the committee.

Note: Ranking on this committee for the following member was affected by other chamber service: Jesse A. Helms (Rep-N.C.), Chair, Agriculture, Nutrition, and Forestry.

Departures from the Senate:

	Majority			Minority		
Retired	Mathias, Charles McC. Jr.	Md.	Rep	Eagleton, Thomas F.	Mo.	Dem

FOREIGN RELATIONS / 100th Congress

Service Dates of Committee Chair: Jan. 6,1987-Feb. 2,1989
Service Dates of Majority Members: Jan. 6,1987-Feb. 2,1989
Service Dates of Minority Members: Jan. 6,1987-Feb. 2,1989

Majority

Rank	Name	Party	State	Years in: Senate	Years in: Comm.
Chr	Pell, Claiborne D.	Dem	R.I.	27	22
2nd	Biden, Joseph R. Jr.	Dem	Del.	15	12
3rd	Sarbanes, Paul S.	Dem	Md.	11	10
4th	Zorinsky, Edward	Dem	Neb.	11	8
5th	Cranston, Alan	Dem	Cal.	19	7
6th	Dodd, Christopher J.	Dem	Conn.	7	7
7th	Kerry, John F.	Dem	Mass.	3	2
8th	Simon, Paul M.	Dem	Ill.	3	1
9th	Sanford, Terry	Dem	N.C.	1	1
10th	Adams, Brock	Dem	Wash.	1	1
11th	Moynihan, Daniel Patrick	Dem	N.Y.	11	1

Minority

Rank	Name	Party	State	Years in: Senate	Years in: Comm.
RM1	Lugar, Richard G.	Rep	Ind.	11	8
RM2 2nd	Helms, Jesse A.	Rep	N.C.	15	8
3rd	Kassebaum, Nancy Landon	Rep	Kans.	9	7
4th	Boschwitz, Rudolf E.	Rep	Minn.	9	7
5th	Pressler, Larry L.	Rep	S.D.	9	7
6th	Murkowski, Frank H.	Rep	Alas.	7	5
7th	Trible, Paul S. Jr.	Rep	Va.	5	2
8th	Evans, Daniel J.	Rep	Wash.	4	2
9th	McConnell, Mitch	Rep	Ky.	3	1

Note: On Jan. 20,1987 the Republican Conference voted to make Jesse A. Helms (Rep-N.C.) Ranking Minority Member of Foreign Relations; Richard G. Lugar (Rep-Ind.) succeeded Helms as Ranking Minority Member of Agriculture, Nutrition and Forestry.

Changes:

Ranking Member:

	Name	Party	State	Date	Change
RM1	Lugar, Richard G.	Rep	Ind.	Jan. 20,1987	Lost Republican Conference vote for Ranking Minority Member.
RM2	Helms, Jesse A.	Rep	N.C.	Jan. 20,1987	Won Republican Conference vote for Ranking Minority Member.

Majority:

Name	Party	State	Date	Change
Zorinsky, Edward	Dem	Neb.	Mar. 6,1987	Died in office.

Departures from the Senate:

	Majority			Minority		
Retired	None			Evans, Daniel J.	Wash.	Rep
				Trible, Paul S. Jr.	Va.	Rep

Departures from Committee:

	Majority			Minority
Moved to Appropriations	Adams, Brock	Wash.	Dem	None

FOREIGN RELATIONS / 101st Congress

Service Dates of Committee Chair: Feb. 2,1989-Feb. 5,1991
Service Dates of Majority Members: Feb. 2,1989-Feb. 5,1991
Service Dates of Minority Members: Feb. 2,1989-Feb. 5,1991

Majority

Rank	Name	Party	State	Years in: Senate	Years in: Comm.
Chr	Pell, Claiborne D.	Dem	R.I.	29	25
2nd	Biden, Joseph R. Jr.	Dem	Del.	17	15
3rd	Sarbanes, Paul S.	Dem	Md.	13	12
4th	Cranston, Alan	Dem	Cal.	21	9
5th	Dodd, Christopher J.	Dem	Conn.	9	9
6th	Kerry, John F.	Dem	Mass.	5	4
7th	Simon, Paul M.	Dem	Ill.	5	3
8th	Sanford, Terry	Dem	N.C.	3	3
9th	Moynihan, Daniel Patrick	Dem	N.Y.	13	3
10th	Robb, Charles S.	Dem	Va.	1	1

Minority

Rank	Name	Party	State	Years in: Senate	Years in: Comm.
RM	Helms, Jesse A.	Rep	N.C.	17	11
2nd	Lugar, Richard G.	Rep	Ind.	13	11
3rd	Kassebaum, Nancy Landon	Rep	Kans.	11	9
4th	Boschwitz, Rudolf E.	Rep	Minn.	11	9
5th	Pressler, Larry L.	Rep	S.D.	11	9
6th	Murkowski, Frank H.	Rep	Alas.	9	7
7th	McConnell, Mitch	Rep	Ky.	5	3
8th	Humphrey, Gordon J.	Rep	N.H.	11	1
9th	Mack, Connie III	Rep	Fla.	1	1

	Majority	Minority	
Departures for the Senate:			
Elected to State Senate	None	Humphrey, Gordon J.	N.H. Rep
Defeated for Reelection	None	Boschwitz, Rudolf E.	Minn. Rep
Departures from Committee:			
Moved to Armed Services	None	Mack, Connie III	Fla. Rep

FOREIGN RELATIONS / 102nd Congress

Service Dates of Committee Chair: Feb. 5,1991-Jan. 3,1993
Service Dates of Majority Members: Feb. 5,1991-Jan. 3,1993
Service Dates of Minority Members: Feb. 5,1991-Jan. 3,1993

Majority

Rank	Name	Party	State	Years in: Senate	Years in: Comm.
Chr	Pell, Claiborne D.	Dem	R.I.	31	27
2nd	Biden, Joseph R. Jr.	Dem	Del.	19	17
3rd	Sarbanes, Paul S.	Dem	Md.	15	14
4th	Cranston, Alan	Dem	Cal.	23	11
5th	Dodd, Christopher J.	Dem	Conn.	11	11
6th	Kerry, John F.	Dem	Mass.	7	6
7th	Simon, Paul M.	Dem	Ill.	7	5
8th	Sanford, Terry	Dem	N.C.	5	5
9th	Moynihan, Daniel Patrick	Dem	N.Y.	15	5
10th	Robb, Charles S.	Dem	Va.	3	3

Minority

Rank	Name	Party	State	Years in: Senate	Years in: Comm.
RM	Helms, Jesse A.	Rep	N.C.	19	13
2nd	Lugar, Richard G.	Rep	Ind.	15	13
3rd	Kassebaum, Nancy Landon	Rep	Kans.	13	11
4th	Pressler, Larry L.	Rep	S.D.	13	11
5th	Murkowski, Frank H.	Rep	Alas.	11	9
6th	McConnell, Mitch	Rep	Ky.	7	5
7th	Brown, Hank	Rep	Colo.	1	1
8th	Hatch, Orrin G.	Rep	Utah	15	1

Note: The death of John Heinz (Rep-Penn.) and the appointment of Harris Wofford (Dem-Penn.) to fill his vacancy on May 9,1991 led to a change in size and party ratio to 11 Democrats and 8 Republicans on June 4,1991.

Additions:
Majority: 11th Wofford, Harris Dem Penn. June 4,1991

Changes:

Hatch, Orrin G.	Rep	Utah	June 25,1991	Moved to Finance.
Jeffords, James M.	Rep	Vt.	July 9,1991	Replaced Hatch.

GOVERNMENTAL AFFAIRS

EXPENDITURES IN THE EXECUTIVE DEPARTMENTS

Jurisdiction, 1947

Established by the Legislative Reorganization Act of 1946:

[Section 102.(1)(g)]

(1) Committee on Expenditures in the Executive Departments, to consist of thirteen Senators, to which committee shall be referred all proposed legislation, messages, petitions, memorials, and other matters relating to the following subjects:

(A) Budget and accounting measures, other than appropriations.
(B) Reorganizations in the executive branch of the Government.

(2) Such committee shall have the duty of--

(A) receiving and examining reports of the Comptroller General of the United States and of submitting such recommendations to the Senate as it deems necessary or desirable in connection with the subject matter of such reports;
(B) studying the operation of Government activities at all levels with a view to determining its economy and efficiency;
(C) evaluating the effects of laws enacted to reorganize the legislative and executive branches of the Government;
(D) studying intergovernmental relationships between the United States and the States and municipalities, and between the United States and international organizations of which the United States is a member.

GOVERNMENT OPERATIONS

Renamed the Committee on Government Operations on March 3, 1952.

GOVERNMENTAL AFFAIRS

Reorganization, 1977

The Committee was reorganized as the Standing Committee on Governmental Affairs following the passage of Senate Resolution 4, the Committee System Reorganization Amendments of 1977, February 4, 1977.

Jurisdiction, 1977

From Senate Resolution 4, the Committee System Reorganization Amendments of 1977, February 4, 1977:

[Section (k)(1)]

Committee on Government Affairs, to which committee shall be referred all proposed legislation, messages, petitions, memorials, and other matters relating to the following subjects:

1. Except as provided in the Congressional Budget Act of 1974, budget and accounting measures, other than appropriations.
2. Organization and reorganization of the executive branch of the Government.
3. Intergovernmental relations.
4. Government information.
5. Municipal affairs of the District of Columbia, except appropriations therefor.
6. Federal Civil Service.
7. Status of officers and employees of the United States, including their classification, compensation, and benefits.
8. Postal service.

9. Census and collection of statistics, including economic and social statistics.
10. Archives of the United States.
11. Organization and management of United States nuclear export policy.
12. Congressional organization, except for any part of the matter that amends the rules or orders of the Senate.

(2) Such committee shall have the duty of--

(A) receiving and examining reports of the Comptroller General of the United States, and of submitting such recommendations to the Senate as it deems necessary or desirable in connection with the subject matter of such reports;
(B) studying the efficiency, economy, and effectiveness of all agencies and departments of the government;
(C) evaluating the effects of laws enacted to reorganize the legislative and executive branches of the government;
(D) studying the intergovernmental relationships between the United States and the States and municipalities, and between the United States and international organizations of which the United States is a member.

Jurisdiction, 1992

Jurisdiction contained in Standing Rules of the Senate (as revised to March 18, 1992):

[Rule XXV.(1)(k)]

(1) Committee on Governmental Affairs, to which committee shall be referred all proposed legislation, messages, petitions, memorials, and other matters relating to the following subjects:

1. Archives of the United States.
2. Budget and accounting measures, other than appropriations, except as provided in the Congressional Budget Act of 1974.
3. Census and collection of statistics, including economic and social statistics.
4. Congressional organization, except for any part of the matter that amends the rules or orders of the Senate.
5. Federal Civil Service.
6. Government information.
7. Intergovernmental relations.
8. Municipal affairs of the District of Columbia, except appropriations therefor.
9. Organization and management of United States nuclear export policy.
10. Organization and reorganization of the executive branch of the Government.
11. Postal Service.
12. Status of officers and employees of the United States, including their classification, compensation, and benefits.

(2) Such committee shall have the duty of:

(A) receiving and examining reports of the Comptroller General of the United States and of submitting such recommendations to the Senate as it deems necessary or desirable in connection with the subject matter of such reports;
(B) studying the efficiency, economy, and effectiveness of all agencies and departments of the Government;
(C) evaluating the effects of laws enacted to reorganize the legislative and branches of the Government; and
(D) studying the intergovernmental relationships between the United States and the States and municipalities, and between the United States and international organizations of which the United States is a member.

EXPENDITURES IN THE EXECUTIVE DEPARTMENTS / 80th Congress

Service Dates of Committee Chair: Jan. 6,1947-Jan. 10,1949
Service Dates of Majority Members: Jan. 6,1947-Jan. 10,1949
Service Dates of Minority Members: Jan. 8,1947-Jan. 10,1949

Majority

Rank	Name	Party	State	Years in: Senate	Years in: Comm.
Chr	Aiken, George D.	Rep	Vt.	6	6
2nd	Ferguson, Homer	Rep	Mich.	5	4
3rd	Hickenlooper, Bourke B.	Rep	Iowa	3	2
4th	Bricker, John W.	Rep	Ohio	1	1
5th	Thye, Edward J.	Rep	Minn.	1	1
6th	McCarthy, Joseph R.	Rep	Wisc.	1	1
7th	Ives, Irving M.	Rep	N.Y.	1	1

Minority

Rank	Name	Party	State	Years in: Senate	Years in: Comm.
RM	McClellan, John L.	Dem	Ark.	5	4
2nd	Eastland, James O.	Dem	Miss.	5	1
3rd	Hoey, Clyde R.	Dem	N.C.	3	1
4th	Taylor, Glen H.	Dem	Ida.	3	1
5th	Robertson, A. Willis	Dem	Va.	1	*1 1
6th	O'Conor, Herbert R.	Dem	Md.	1	1

*1: Member's 1st period of service on the committee.

Departures from Committee:	Majority			Minority		
Became Ranking Minority Member of Agriculture and Forestry	Aiken, George D.	Vt.	Rep	None		
Moved to Interstate & Foreign Commerce	Bricker, John W.	Ohio	Rep	None		
Moved to Agriculture & Forestry	Hickenlooper, Bourke B.	Iowa	Rep	None		
Moved to Appropriations	None			Robertson, A. Willis	Va.	Dem
No new assignment	Ferguson, Homer	Mich.	Rep	None		
	Thye, Edward J.	Minn.	Rep			

EXPENDITURES IN THE EXECUTIVE DEPARTMENTS / 81st Congress

Service Dates of Committee Chair: Jan. 10,1949-Jan. 15,1951
Service Dates of Majority Members: Jan. 10,1949-Jan. 15,1951
Service Dates of Minority Members: Jan. 10,1949-Jan. 15,1951

Majority

Rank	Name	Party	State	Years in: Senate	Years in: Comm.
Chr	McClellan, John L.	Dem	Ark.	7	6
2nd	Eastland, James O.	Dem	Miss.	7	3
3rd	Hoey, Clyde R.	Dem	N.C.	5	3
4th	Taylor, Glen H.	Dem	Ida.	5	3
5th	O'Conor, Herbert R.	Dem	Md.	3	3
6th	Long, Russell B.	Dem	La.	1	1
7th	Humphrey, Hubert H. Jr.	DFL	Minn.	1	*1 1

Minority

Rank	Name	Party	State	Years in: Senate	Years in: Comm.
RM	McCarthy, Joseph R.	Rep	Wisc.	3	3
2nd	Ives, Irving M.	Rep	N.Y.	3	3
3rd	Mundt, Karl E.	Rep	S.D.	1	1
4th	Smith, Margaret Chase	Rep	Me.	1	1
5th	Schoeppel, Andrew F.	Rep	Kans.	1	1
6th	Vandenberg, Arthur H.	Rep	Mich.	21	1

*1: Member's 1st period of service on the committee.

Changes:

Majority:

Long, Russell B.	Dem	La.	July 26,1949	Moved to Banking and Currency.
Robertson, A. Willis	Dem	Va.	July 26,1949	Replaced Long.
Robertson, A. Willis	Dem	Va.	Jan. 12,1950	Moved to Appropriations.
Taylor, Glen H.	Dem	Ida.	Jan. 12,1950	Moved to Interior and Insular Affairs.
Leahy, Edward L.	Dem	R.I.	Jan. 12,1950	Replaced Robertson.
Benton, William	Dem	Conn.	Jan. 12,1950	Replaced Taylor.
Leahy, Edward L.	Dem	R.I.	Dec. 18,1950	Resigned; appointed Federal judge.
Pastore, John O.	Dem	R.I.	Dec. 21,1950	Replaced Leahy.

Departures from Committee:	Majority			Minority		
Moved to Labor & Public Welfare	Pastore, John O.	R.I.	Dem	Ives, Irving M.	N.Y.	Rep
Moved to Agriculture & Forestry	Eastland, James O.	Miss.	Dem	None		
Moved to District of Columbia	None			Vandenberg, Arthur H.	Mich.	Rep

EXPENDITURES IN THE EXECUTIVE DEPARTMENTS / 82nd Congress

* Renamed the Committee on GOVERNMENT OPERATIONS on Mar. 3,1952.

Service Dates of Committee Chair: Jan. 15,1951-Jan. 13,1953
Service Dates of Majority Members: Jan. 15,1951-Jan. 13,1953
Service Dates of Minority Members: Jan. 15,1951-Jan. 13,1953

Majority

Rank Name	Party	State	Years in: Senate	Years in: Comm.
Chr McClellan, John L.	Dem	Ark.	9	9
2nd Hoey, Clyde R.	Dem	N.C.	7	5
3rd O'Conor, Herbert R.	Dem	Md.	5	5
4th Humphrey, Hubert H. Jr.	DFL	Minn.	3 *1	3
5th Benton, William	Dem	Conn.	2	2
6th Robertson, A. Willis	Dem	Va.	5 *3	1
7th Monroney, A. S. Mike	Dem	Okla.	1	1

Minority

Rank Name	Party	State	Years in: Senate	Years in: Comm.
RM McCarthy, Joseph R.	Rep	Wisc.	5	5
2nd Mundt, Karl E.	Rep	S.D.	3	3
3rd Smith, Margaret Chase	Rep	Me.	3	3
4th Schoeppel, Andrew F.	Rep	Kans.	3	3
5th Dworshak, Henry C.	Rep	Ida.	4	1
6th Nixon, Richard M.	Rep	Cal.	1	1

*1: Member's 1st period of service on the committee; *3: Member's 3rd period of service on the committee.

Changes:

Majority:

Benton, William	Dem	Conn.	Apr. 3,1951	Moved to Banking and Currency.
Underwood, Thomas R.	Dem	Ky.	Apr. 3,1951	Replaced Benton.
Robertson, A. Willis	Dem	Va.	May 21,1951	Moved to Appropriations.
Moody, Blair	Dem	Mich.	May 21,1951	Replaced Robertson.
Underwood, Thomas R.	Dem	Ky.	Nov. 4,1952	Resigned; defeated in special election.
Moody, Blair	Dem	Mich.	Nov. 4,1952	Resigned; defeated in special election.

Minority:

Nixon, Richard M.	Rep	Cal.	Jan. 1,1953	Resigned; elected Vice President.

Departures from the Senate:	Majority		Minority	
Defeated for Election	Moody, Blair	Mich. Dem	None	
Retired	O'Conor, Herbert R.	Md. Dem	None	
Departures from Committee:				
Moved to Interstate & Foreign Commerce	Monroney, A. S. Mike	Okla. Dem		
Moved to Interstate & Foreign Commerce; Agriculture & Forestry	None		Schoeppel, Andrew F.	Kans. Rep

GOVERNMENT OPERATIONS / 83rd Congress

Service Dates of Committee Chair: Jan. 13,1953-Jan. 11,1955
Service Dates of Majority Members: Jan. 13,1953-Jan. 11,1955
Service Dates of Minority Members: Jan. 13,1953-Jan. 11,1955

Majority

Rank Name	Party	State	Years in: Senate	Years in: Comm.
Chr McCarthy, Joseph R.	Rep	Wisc.	7	7
2nd Mundt, Karl E.	Rep	S.D.	5	5
3rd Smith, Margaret Chase	Rep	Me.	5	5
4th Dworshak, Henry C.	Rep	Ida.	6	2
5th Dirksen, Everett M.	Rep	Ill.	3	1
6th Butler, John Marshall	Rep	Md.	3	1
7th Potter, Charles E.	Rep	Mich.	1	1

Minority

Rank Name	Party	State	Years in: Senate	Years in: Comm.
RM McClellan, John L.	Dem	Ark.	11	10
2nd Hoey, Clyde R.	Dem	N.C.	9	7
3rd Humphrey, Hubert H. Jr.	DFL	Minn.	5 *1	5
4th Jackson, Henry M.	Dem	Wash.	1	1
5th Kennedy, John F.	Dem	Mass.	1	1
6th Symington, W. Stuart	Dem	Mo.	1	1

*1: Member's 1st period of service on the committee.

Changes:
Minority:

Hoey, Clyde R.	Dem	N.C.	July 7,1953	Left committee; no new assignment.
Lennon, Alton A.	Dem	N.C.	July 15,1953	Replaced Hoey.
Humphrey, Hubert H. Jr.	DFL	Minn.	May 18,1954	Moved to Agriculture and Forestry.
Burke, Thomas A.	Dem	Ohio	May 19,1954	Replaced Humphrey.
Lennon, Alton A.	Dem	N.C.	May 19,1954	Moved to Interior and Insular Affairs.
Ervin, Samuel J.	Dem	N.C.	June 11,1954	Replaced Lennon.
Burke, Thomas A.	Dem	Ohio	Dec. 2,1954	Resigned; defeated for election.

Departures from Committee:	Majority			Minority
Moved to Appropriations	Potter, Charles E.	Mich.	Rep	None
No new assignment	Butler, John Marshall	Md.	Rep	None
	Dirksen, Everett McK.	Ill.	Rep	
	Dworshak, Henry C.	Ida.	Rep	

GOVERNMENT OPERATIONS / 84th Congress

Service Dates of Committee Chair: Jan. 11,1955-Jan. 9,1957
Service Dates of Majority Members: Jan. 11,1955-Jan. 9,1957
Service Dates of Minority Members: Jan. 11,1955-Jan. 9,1957

Majority

Rank	Name	Party	State	Years in: Senate	Years in: Comm.
Chr	McClellan, John L.	Dem	Ark.	13	12
2nd	Jackson, Henry M.	Dem	Wash.	3	2
3rd	Kennedy, John F.	Dem	Mass.	3	2
4th	Symington, W. Stuart	Dem	Mo.	3	2
5th	Ervin, Samuel J.	Dem	N.C.	1	1
6th	Humphrey, Hubert H. Jr.	DFL	Minn.	7 *2	1
7th	Thurmond, J. Strom	Dem	S.C.	1 *1	1

Minority

Rank	Name	Party	State	Years in: Senate	Years in: Comm.
RM	McCarthy, Joseph R.	Rep	Wisc.	9	9
2nd	Mundt, Karl E.	Rep	S.D.	7	7
3rd	Smith, Margaret Chase	Rep	Me.	7	7
4th	Cotton, Norris	Rep	N.H.	1	1
5th	Bender, George H.	Rep	Ohio	1	1
6th	Martin, Thomas E.	Rep	Iowa	1	1

*1: Member's 1st period of service on the committee; *2: Member's 2nd period of service on the committee.

Note: J. Strom Thurmond (Dem-S.C.) was appointed to fill a vacancy in the Senate on Dec. 24,1954. Thurmond resigned his seat on Apr. 4,1956 in order to run for the vacancy in a special election, which he won as a write-in candidate on Nov. 7,1956. Thurmond rejoined the committee in the 85th Congress.

Changes:
Majority:

Thurmond, J. Strom	Dem	S.C.	Apr. 4,1956	Resigned; later elected to fill his own vacancy.
Wofford, Thomas A.	Dem	S.C.	Apr. 18,1956	Replaced Thurmond.
Wofford, Thomas A.	Dem	S.C.	Nov. 6,1956	Resigned and retired.

	Majority			Minority		
Departures from the Senate:						
Defeated for Reelection	None			Bender, George H.	Ohio	Rep
Departures from Committee:						
Moved to Foreign Relations	Kennedy, John F.	Mass.	Dem	None		
Moved to Interstate & Foreign Commerce	None			Cotton, Norris	N.H.	Rep

GOVERNMENT OPERATIONS / 85th Congress

Service Dates of Committee Chair: Jan. 9,1957-Jan. 14,1959
Service Dates of Majority Members: Jan. 9,1957-Jan. 14,1959
Service Dates of Minority Members: Jan. 9,1957-Jan. 20,1959

Majority

Rank	Name	Party	State	Years in: Senate	Years in: Comm.
Chr	McClellan, John L.	Dem	Ark.	15	14
2nd	Jackson, Henry M.	Dem	Wash.	5	4
3rd	Symington, W. Stuart	Dem	Mo.	5	4
4th	Ervin, Samuel J.	Dem	N.C.	3	3
5th	Humphrey, Hubert H. Jr.	DFL	Minn.	9	*2 2
6th	Thurmond, J. Strom	Dem	S.C.	2	*2 1
7th	Blakley, William A.	Dem	Tex.	1	1

Minority

Rank	Name	Party	State	Years in: Senate	Years in: Comm.
RM1	McCarthy, Joseph R.	Rep	Wisc.	11	11
RM2 2nd	Mundt, Karl E.	Rep	S.D.	9	8
3rd	Smith, Margaret Chase	Rep	Me.	9	8
4th	Martin, Thomas E.	Rep	Iowa	3	2
5th	Curtis, Carl T.	Rep	Neb.	3	1
6th	Revercomb, W. Chapman	Rep	W.Va.	7	1

*2: Member's 2nd period of service on the committee.

Vacancy Filled:
Majority: 7th seat by Blakley on Jan. 17,1957.

Changes:

	Name	Party	State	Date	Action
Ranking Member:					
RM1	McCarthy, Joseph R.	Rep	Wisc.	May 2,1957	Died in office.
RM2	Mundt, Karl E.	Rep	S.D.	May 2,1957	Succeeded McCarthy as Ranking Minority Member.
Majority:					
	Blakley, William A.	Dem	Tex.	Apr. 28,1957	Resigned and retired.
	Yarborough, Ralph W.	Dem	Tex.	May 2,1957	Replaced Blakley.
	Yarborough, Ralph W.	Dem	Tex.	Jan. 16,1958	Moved to Labor and Public Welfare.
	Lausche, Frank J.	Dem	Ohio	Jan. 16,1958	Replaced Yarborough.
Minority:					
	McCarthy, Joseph R.	Rep	Wisc.	May 2,1957	Died in office.
	Capehart, Homer E.	Rep	Ind.	May 22,1957	Replaced McCarthy.

	Majority			Minority		
Departures from the Senate:						
Defeated for Reelection	None			Revercomb, W. Chapman	W.Va.	Rep
Departures from Committee:						
Moved to Aeronautics & Space Sciences	Symington, W. Stuart	Mo.	Dem	Smith, Margaret Chase	Me.	Rep
Moved to Foreign Relations	Lausche, Frank J.	Ohio	Dem	None		
Moved to Armed Services	Thurmond, J. Strom	S.C.	Dem	None		
Moved to Judiciary; Public Works	None			Martin, Thomas E.	Iowa	Rep

GOVERNMENT OPERATIONS / 86th Congress

Service Dates of Committee Chair: Jan. 14,1959-Jan. 10,1961
Service Dates of Majority Members: Jan. 14,1959-Jan. 10,1961
Service Dates of Minority Members: Jan. 20,1959-Jan. 13,1961

Majority

Rank	Name	Party	State	Years in: Senate	Years in: Comm.
Chr	McClellan, John L.	Dem	Ark.	17	17
2nd	Jackson, Henry M.	Dem	Wash.	7	7
3rd	Ervin, Samuel J.	Dem	N.C.	5	5
4th	Humphrey, Hubert H. Jr.	DFL	Minn.	11	*2 5
5th	Gruening, Ernest	Dem	Alas.	1	1
6th	Muskie, Edmund S.	Dem	Me.	1	1

Minority

Rank	Name	Party	State	Years in: Senate	Years in: Comm.
RM	Mundt, Karl E.	Rep	S.D.	11	11
2nd	Curtis, Carl T.	Rep	Neb.	5	3
3rd	Capehart, Homer E.	Rep	Ind.	15	2

*2: Member's 2nd period of service on the committee.

Changes:

	Name	Party	State	Date	Action
Minority:					
	Capehart, Homer E.	Rep	Ind.	Jan. 18,1960	Left committee; no new assignment.
	Javits, Jacob K.	Rep	N.Y.	Jan. 18,1960	Replaced Capehart.

GOVERNMENT OPERATIONS / 87th Congress

Service Dates of Committee Chair: Jan. 10,1961-Feb. 25,1963
Service Dates of Majority Members: Jan. 10,1961-Feb. 25,1963
Service Dates of Minority Members: Jan. 13,1961-Feb. 25,1963

Majority

Rank	Name	Party	State	Years in: Senate	Years in: Comm.
Chr	McClellan, John L.	Dem	Ark.	19	18
2nd	Jackson, Henry M.	Dem	Wash.	9	8
3rd	Ervin, Samuel J.	Dem	N.C.	7	7
4th	Humphrey, Hubert H. Jr.	DFL	Minn.	13	*2 6
5th	Gruening, Ernest	Dem	Alas.	3	2
6th	Muskie, Edmund S.	Dem	Me.	3	2

Minority

Rank	Name	Party	State	Years in: Senate	Years in: Comm.
RM	Mundt, Karl E.	Rep	S.D.	13	13
2nd	Curtis, Carl T.	Rep	Neb.	7	5
3rd	Javits, Jacob K.	Rep	N.Y.	5	1

*2: Member's 2nd period of service on the committee.

GOVERNMENT OPERATIONS / 88th Congress

Service Dates of Committee Chair: Feb. 25,1963-Jan. 8,1965
Service Dates of Majority Members: Feb. 25,1963-Jan. 8,1965
Service Dates of Minority Members: Feb. 25,1963-Jan. 15,1965

Majority

Rank	Name	Party	State	Years in: Senate	Years in: Comm.
Chr	McClellan, John L.	Dem	Ark.	21	21
2nd	Jackson, Henry M.	Dem	Wash.	11	11
3rd	Ervin, Samuel J.	Dem	N.C.	9	9
4th	Humphrey, Hubert H. Jr.	DFL	Minn.	15	*2 9
5th	Gruening, Ernest	Dem	Alas.	5	5
6th	Muskie, Edmund S.	Dem	Me.	5	5
7th	Pell, Claiborne D.	Dem	R.I.	3	1
8th	McIntyre, Thomas J.	Dem	N.H.	1	1
9th	Ribicoff, Abraham A.	Dem	Conn.	1	1
10th	Brewster, Daniel B.	Dem	Md.	1	1

Minority

Rank	Name	Party	State	Years in: Senate	Years in: Comm.
RM	Mundt, Karl E.	Rep	S.D.	15	15
2nd	Curtis, Carl T.	Rep	Neb.	9	7
3rd	Javits, Jacob K.	Rep	N.Y.	7	4
4th	Miller, Jack R.	Rep	Iowa	3	1
5th	Pearson, James B.	Rep	Kans.	2	1

*2: Member's 2nd period of service on the committee.

Changes:

Majority:

Name	Party	State	Date	Change
McIntyre, Thomas J.	Dem	N.H.	Aug. 10,1964	Moved to Armed Services.
Salinger, Pierre E.	Dem	Cal.	Aug. 10,1964	Replaced McIntyre.
Humphrey, Hubert H. Jr.	DFL	Minn.	Dec. 29,1964	Resigned; elected Vice President.
Salinger, Pierre E.	Dem	Cal.	Dec. 31,1964	Resigned; defeated for election.

Departures from Committee:

	Majority			Minority		
Moved to Armed Services; Commerce	Brewster, Daniel B.	Md.	Dem	None		
Moved to Foreign Relations	Pell, Claiborne D.	R.I.	Dem	None		
Moved to Agriculture & Forestry; Armed Services	None			Miller, Jack R.	Iowa	Rep
Moved to Commerce	None			Pearson, James B.	Kans.	Rep

GOVERNMENT OPERATIONS / 89th Congress

Service Dates of Committee Chair: Jan. 8,1965-Jan. 11,1967
Service Dates of Majority Members: Jan. 8,1965-Jan. 11,1967
Service Dates of Minority Members: Jan. 15,1965-Jan. 16,1967

Majority

Rank	Name	Party	State	Years in: Senate	Years in: Comm.
Chr	McClellan, John L.	Dem	Ark.	23	22
2nd	Jackson, Henry M.	Dem	Wash.	13	12
3rd	Ervin, Samuel J.	Dem	N.C.	11	11
4th	Gruening, Ernest	Dem	Alas.	7	6
5th	Muskie, Edmund S.	Dem	Me.	7	6
6th	Ribicoff, Abraham A.	Dem	Conn.	3	2
7th	Harris, Fred R.	Dem	Okla.	1	1
8th	Kennedy, Robert F.	Dem	N.Y.	1	1
9th	Metcalf, Lee	Dem	Mont.	5	1
10th	Montoya, Joseph M.	Dem	N.M.	1	1

Minority

Rank	Name	Party	State	Years in: Senate	Years in: Comm.
RM	Mundt, Karl E.	Rep	S.D.	17	17
2nd	Curtis, Carl T.	Rep	Neb.	11	9
3rd	Javits, Jacob K.	Rep	N.Y.	9	5
4th	Simpson, Milward L.	Rep	Wyo.	3	1

Vacancies Filled:
Majority: 9th and 10th seats by Metcalf and Montoya respectively on Mar. 8,1965.

Departures from the Senate:	Majority	Minority	
Retired	None	Simpson, Milward L.	Wyo. Rep

GOVERNMENT OPERATIONS / 90th Congress

Service Dates of Committee Chair: Jan. 11,1967-Jan. 14,1969
Service Dates of Majority Members: Jan. 11,1967-Jan. 14,1969
Service Dates of Minority Members: Jan. 16,1967-Jan. 14,1969

Majority

Rank	Name	Party	State	Years in: Senate	Years in: Comm.
Chr	McClellan, John L.	Dem	Ark.	25	24
2nd	Jackson, Henry M.	Dem	Wash.	15	14
3rd	Ervin, Samuel J.	Dem	N.C.	13	13
4th	Gruening, Ernest	Dem	Alas.	9	8
5th	Muskie, Edmund S.	Dem	Me.	9	8
6th	Ribicoff, Abraham A.	Dem	Conn.	5	4
7th	Harris, Fred R.	Dem	Okla.	3	3
8th	Kennedy, Robert F.	Dem	N.Y.	3	3
9th	Metcalf, Lee	Dem	Mont.	7	*T 2
10th	Montoya, Joseph M.	Dem	N.M.	3	*T 2

Minority

Rank	Name	Party	State	Years in: Senate	Years in: Comm.
RM	Mundt, Karl E.	Rep	S.D.	19	19
2nd	Curtis, Carl T.	Rep	Neb.	13	11
3rd	Javits, Jacob K.	Rep	N.Y.	11	7
4th	Hansen, Clifford P.	Rep	Wyo.	1	1
5th	Baker, Howard H. Jr.	Rep	Tenn.	1	1

*T: Temporary member of the committee.

Note: Lee Metcalf (Dem-Mont.) and Joseph M. Montoya (Dem-N.M.) were listed in the Senate Journal of Jan. 11,1967 as temporary members of the committee. Metcalf continued on this committee in the 91st Congress with his seniority intact.

Changes:

Majority:

Kennedy, Robert F.	Dem	N.Y.	June 6,1968	Died in office.

Minority:

Hansen, Clifford P.	Rep	Wyo.	Sep. 12,1968	Moved to Commerce.
Baker, Howard H. Jr.	Rep	Tenn.	Sep. 12,1968	Moved to Judiciary.
Percy, Charles H.	Rep	Ill.	Sep. 12,1968	Replaced Hansen.
Brooke, Edward W.	Rep	Mass.	Sep. 12,1968	Replaced Baker.

Departures from the Senate:	Majority		Minority	
Defeated for Renomination	Gruening, Ernest	Alas. Dem	None	
Departures from Committee:				
Moved to Appropriations	Montoya, Joseph M.	N.M. Dem	None	
Moved to Agriculture & Forestry	None		Curtis, Carl T.	Neb. Rep
Moved to Armed Services	None		Brooke, Edward W.	Mass. Rep

GOVERNMENT OPERATIONS / 91st Congress

Service Dates of Committee Chair: Jan. 14,1969-Jan. 28,1971
Service Dates of Majority Members: Jan. 14,1969-Jan. 28,1971
Service Dates of Minority Members: Jan. 14,1969-Jan. 29,1971

Majority

Rank Name	Party	State	Years in: Senate	Years in: Comm.
Chr McClellan, John L.	Dem	Ark.	27	27
2nd Jackson, Henry M.	Dem	Wash.	17	17
3rd Ervin, Samuel J.	Dem	N.C.	15	15
4th Muskie, Edmund S.	Dem	Me.	11	11
5th Ribicoff, Abraham A.	Dem	Conn.	7	6
6th Harris, Fred R.	Dem	Okla.	5	5
7th Metcalf, Lee	Dem	Mont.	9	4
8th McCarthy, Eugene J.	DFL	Minn.	11	1
9th Allen, James B.	Dem	Ala.	1	1

Minority

Rank Name	Party	State	Years in: Senate	Years in: Comm.
RM Mundt, Karl E.	Rep	S.D.	21	21
2nd Javits, Jacob K.	Rep	N.Y.	13	9
3rd Percy, Charles H.	Rep	Ill.	3	1
4th Griffin, Robert P.	Rep	Mich.	3	1
5th Stevens, Theodore F.	Rep	Alas.	1	1
6th Gurney, Edward J.	Rep	Fla.	1	1

Changes:

Minority:

Griffin, Robert P.	Rep	Mich.	Sep. 17,1969	Moved to Judiciary.
Mathias, Charles McC. Jr.	Rep	Md.	Sep. 17,1969	Replaced Griffin.

	Majority		Minority	
Departures from the Senate:				
Retired	McCarthy, Eugene J.	Minn. DFL	None	
Departures from Committee:				
Moved to Commerce; Veterans' Affairs	None		Stevens, Theodore F.	Alas. Rep

GOVERNMENT OPERATIONS / 92nd Congress

Service Dates of Committee Chairs: Ch1 Jan. 28,1971-Aug. 2,1972
Ch2 Aug. 2,1972-Jan. 4,1973
Service Dates of Majority Members: Jan. 28,1971-Jan. 4,1973
Service Dates of Minority Members: Jan. 29,1971-Jan. 12,1973

Majority

Rank Name	Party	State	Years in: Senate	Years in: Comm.
Ch1 McClellan, John L.	Dem	Ark.	29	29
2nd Jackson, Henry M.	Dem	Wash.	19	19
Ch2 3rd Ervin, Samuel J.	Dem	N.C.	17	17
4th Muskie, Edmund S.	Dem	Me.	13	13
5th Ribicoff, Abraham A.	Dem	Conn.	9	8
6th Harris, Fred R.	Dem	Okla.	7	7
7th Metcalf, Lee	Dem	Mont.	11	6
8th Allen, James B.	Dem	Ala.	3	3
9th Humphrey, Hubert H. Jr.	DFL	Minn.	17	*3 1
10th Chiles, Lawton M. Jr.	Dem	Fla.	1	1

Minority

Rank Name	Party	State	Years in: Senate	Years in: Comm.
RM1 Mundt, Karl E.	Rep	S.D.	23	23
2nd Javits, Jacob K.	Rep	N.Y.	15	12
RM2 3rd Percy, Charles H.	Rep	Ill.	5	3
4th Gurney, Edward J.	Rep	Fla.	3	3
5th Mathias, Charles McC. Jr.	Rep	Md.	3	2
6th Saxbe, William B.	Rep	Ohio	3	1
7th Roth, William V. Jr.	Rep	Del.	1	1
8th Brock, William E. III	Rep	Tenn.	1	1

*3: Member's 3rd period of service on the committee.

Note: Ranking on this committee for the following member was affected by other chamber service: Henry M. Jackson (Dem-Wash.), Chair, Interior and Insular Affairs; Jacob K. Javits (Rep-N.Y.), Ranking Minority Member, Labor and Public Welfare.

Changes:

Chair:

Ch1 McClellan, John L.	Dem	Ark.	Aug. 2,1972	Became Chair of Appropriations; remained on committee.
Ch2 Ervin, Samuel J.	Dem	N.C.	Aug. 2,1972	Succeeded McClellan as Chair.

Ranking Member:

RM1 Mundt, Karl E.	Rep	S.D.	Feb. 23,1972	Moved to 8th minority rank due to illness.
RM2 Percy, Charles H.	Rep	Ill.	Feb. 23,1972	Succeeded Mundt as Ranking Minority Member.

	Majority		Minority	
Departures from the Senate:				
Retired	Harris, Fred R.	Okla. Dem	Mundt, Karl E.	S.D. Rep

Departures from Committee:

Moved to Foreign Relations	Humphrey, Hubert H. Jr.	Minn. DFL	None	
Moved to Appropriations	None		Mathias, Charles McC. Jr.	Md. Rep

GOVERNMFNT OPERATIONS / 93rd Congress

Service Dates of Committee Chair: Jan. 4,1973-Dec. 31,1974
Service Dates of Majority Members: Jan. 4,1973-Jan. 17,1975
Service Dates of Minority Members: Jan. 12,1973-Jan. 23,1975

Majority

Rank Name	Party	State	Years in: Senate	Comm.
Chr Ervin, Samuel J.	Dem	N.C.	19	19
2nd McClellan, John L.	Dem	Ark.	31	30
3rd Jackson, Henry M.	Dem	Wash.	21	20
4th Muskie, Edmund S.	Dem	Me.	15	14
5th Ribicoff, Abraham A.	Dem	Conn.	11	10
6th Metcalf, Lee	Dem	Mont.	13	8
7th Allen, James B.	Dem	Ala.	5	4
8th Chiles, Lawton M. Jr.	Dem	Fla.	3	2
9th Nunn, Samuel A.	Dem	Ga.	1	1
10th Huddleston, Walter D.	Dem	Ky.	1	1

Minority

Rank Name	Party	State	Years in: Senate	Comm.
RM Percy, Charles H.	Rep	Ill.	7	5
2nd Javits, Jacob K.	Rep	N.Y.	17	13
3rd Gurney, Edward J.	Rep	Fla.	5	4
4th Saxbe, William B.	Rep	Ohio	5	2
5th Roth, William V. Jr.	Rep	Del.	3	2
6th Brock, William E. III	Rep	Tenn.	3	2

Notes: In the initial membership list of Jan. 4,1973, Huddleston was erroneously listed in the 9th rank and Nunn in the 10th rank. These rankings were "corrected" on Jan. 9,1973, as listed here. The resignation of William Saxbe (Rep-Ohio), and the appointment of Howard Metzenbaum (Dem-Ohio) to fill his Senate vacancy on Jan. 21,1974, led to a change in size and party ratio on this committee to 10 Democrats and 5 Republicans. Rankings on this committee for the following members were affected by other chamber service: John L. McClellan (Dem-Ark.), Chair, Appropriations; Henry M. Jackson (Dem-Wash.), Chair, Interior and Insular Affairs; and Jacob K. Javits (Rep-N.Y.), Ranking Minority Member, Labor and Public Welfare.

Changes:

Majority:

Ervin, Samuel J.	Dem	N.C.	Dec. 31,1974	Resigned and retired.

Minority:

Saxbe, William B.	Rep	Ohio	Jan. 3,1974	Resigned; appointed Attorney General.
Gurney, Edward J.	Rep	Fla.	Dec. 31,1974	Resigned and retired.

Departures from Committee:	Majority		Minority
Moved to Appropriations	Huddleston, Walter D.	Ky. Dem	None

GOVERNMENT OPERATIONS / 94th Congress

Service Dates of Committee Chair: Jan. 17,1975-Jan. 10,1977
Service Dates of Majority Members: Jan. 17,1975-Jan. 10,1977
Service Dates of Minority Members: Jan. 23,1975-Jan. 10,1977

Majority

Rank Name	Party	State	Years in: Senate	Comm.
Chr Ribicoff, Abraham A.	Dem	Conn.	13	12
2nd McClellan, John L.	Dem	Ark.	33	33
3rd Jackson, Henry M.	Dem	Wash.	23	23
4th Muskie, Edmund S.	Dem	Me.	17	17
5th Metcalf, Lee	Dem	Mont.	15	10
6th Allen, James B.	Dem	Ala.	7	7
7th Chiles, Lawton M. Jr.	Dem	Fla.	5	4
8th Nunn, Samuel A.	Dem	Ga.	3	3
9th Glenn, John H. Jr.	Dem	Ohio	1	1

Minority

Rank Name	Party	State	Years in: Senate	Comm.
RM Percy, Charles H.	Rep	Ill.	9	7
2nd Javits, Jacob K.	Rep	N.Y.	19	16
3rd Roth, William V. Jr.	Rep	Del.	5	4
4th Brock, William E. III	Rep	Tenn.	5	4
5th Weicker, Lowell P. Jr.	Rep	Conn.	5	1

Note: Rankings on this committee for the following members were affected by other chamber service: John L. McClellan (Dem-Ark.), Chair, Appropriations; Henry M. Jackson (Dem-Wash.), Chair, Interior and Insular Affairs; Edmund S. Muskie (Dem-Me.), Chair, Budget; and Jacob K. Javits (Rep-N.Y.), Ranking Minority Member, Labor and Public Welfare.

Departures from Senate:	**Majority**	**Minority**	
Defeated for Reelection	None	Brock, William E. III	Tenn. Rep

GOVERNMENT OPERATIONS / 95th Congress

* Reorganized as the Committee on GOVERNMENTAL AFFAIRS on Feb. 11,1977.

Service Dates of Committee Chair: Jan. 10,1977-Feb. 11,1977
Service Dates of Majority Members: Jan. 10,1977-Feb. 11,1977
Service Dates of Minority Members: Jan. 10,1977-Feb. 22,1977

Majority

Rank	Name	Party	State	Years in: Senate	Years in: Comm.
Chr	Ribicoff, Abraham A.	Dem	Conn.	15	14
2nd	McClellan, John L.	Dem	Ark.	35	34
3rd	Jackson, Henry M.	Dem	Wash.	25	24
4th	Muskie, Edmund S.	Dem	Me.	19	18
5th	Metcalf, Lee	Dem	Mont.	17	12
6th	Allen, James B.	Dem	Ala.	9	8
7th	Chiles, Lawton M. Jr.	Dem	Fla.	7	6
8th	Nunn, Samuel A.	Dem	Ga.	5	5
9th	Glenn, John H. Jr.	Dem	Ohio	3	2
10th	Sasser, James R.	Dem	Tenn.	1	*T 1

Minority

Rank	Name	Party	State	Years in: Senate	Years in: Comm.
RM	Percy, Charles H.	Rep	Ill.	11	9
2nd	Javits, Jacob K.	Rep	N.Y.	21	17
3rd	Roth, William V. Jr.	Rep	Del.	7	6
4th	Weicker, Lowell P. Jr.	Rep	Conn.	7	2
5th	Lugar, Richard G.	Rep	Ind.	1	*T 1
6th	Hatch, Orrin G.	Rep	Utah	1	*T 1

*T: Temporary member of the committee.

Note: Rankings on this committee for the following members were affected by other chamber service: John L. McClellan (Dem-Ark.), Chair, Appropriations; Henry M. Jackson (Dem-Wash.), Chair, Interior and Insular Affairs; Edmund S. Muskie (Dem-Me.), Chair, Budget; and Jacob K. Javits (Rep-N.Y.), Ranking Minority Member, Labor and Public Welfare.

Changes:

Majority:

Name	Party	State	Date	Change
Allen, James B.	Dem	Ala.	Feb. 11,1977	Moved to Judiciary.

Minority:

Name	Party	State	Date	Change
Weicker, Lowell P. Jr.	Rep	Conn.	Feb. 22,1977	Moved to Energy and Natural Resources.
Lugar, Richard G.	Rep	Ind.	Feb. 22,1977	Moved to Agriculture, Nutrition, and Forestry.
Hatch, Orrin G.	Rep	Utah	Feb. 22,1977	Moved to Human Resources.

Departures from Committee:	**Majority**		**Minority**
No new assignment	Sasser, James R.	Tenn. Dem	None

GOVERNMENTAL AFFAIRS / 95th Congress

Service Dates of Committee Chair: Feb. 11,1977-Jan. 23,1979
Service Dates of Majority Members: Feb. 11,1977-Jan. 23,1979
Service Dates of Minority Members: Feb. 22,1977-Jan. 23,1979

Majority

Rank	Name	Party	State	Years in: Senate	Years in: Comm.
Chr	Ribicoff, Abraham A.	Dem	Conn.	15	14
2nd	McClellan, John L.	Dem	Ark.	35	35
3rd	Jackson, Henry M.	Dem	Wash.	25	25
4th	Muskie, Edmund S.	Dem	Me.	19	19
5th	Metcalf, Lee	Dem	Mont.	17	12
6th	Eagleton, Thomas F.	Dem	Mo.	9	9
7th	Chiles, Lawton M. Jr.	Dem	Fla.	7	7
8th	Nunn, Samuel A.	Dem	Ga.	5	5
9th	Glenn, John H. Jr.	Dem	Ohio	3	3
10th	Sasser, James R.	Dem	Tenn.	1	*1 1

Minority

Rank	Name	Party	State	Years in: Senate	Years in: Comm.
RM	Percy, Charles H.	Rep	Ill.	11	9
2nd	Javits, Jacob K.	Rep	N.Y.	21	18
3rd	Roth, William V. Jr.	Rep	Del.	7	7
4th	Stevens, Theodore F.	Rep	Alas.	9	9
5th	Mathias, Charles McC. Jr.	Rep	Md.	9	9
6th	Danforth, John C.	Rep	Mo.	1	1
7th	Heinz, H. John III	Rep	Penn.	1	*1 1

*1: Member's 1st period of service on the committee.

Notes: "Years in committee" for Eagleton and Mathias include their continuous service on the District of Columbia Committee. "Years in committee" for Stevens include his continuous service on the Post Office and Civil Service Committee. William V. Roth, Jr.'s continuous service on the Government Operations committee entitled him to a rank higher than that of Stevens or

Mathias. The committee size was reduced to 16 members on Jan. 27,1978, and the party ratio changed to 9 Democrats and 7 Republicans. Rankings on this committee for the following members were affected by other chamber service: John L. McClellan (Dem-Ark.), Chair, Appropriations; Henry M. Jackson (Dem-Wash.), Chair, Interior and Insular Affairs; Edmund S. Muskie (Dem-Me.), Chair, Budget; and Jacob K. Javits (Rep-N.Y.), Ranking Minority Member, Labor and Public Welfare.

Changes:

Majority:

McClellan, John L.	Dem	Ark.	Nov. 28,1977	Died in office.
Metcalf, Lee	Dem	Mont.	Jan. 12,1978	Died in office.
Humphrey, Muriel	Dem	Minn.	Feb. 7,1978	Replaced McClellan.
Humphrey, Muriel	Dem	Minn.	Nov. 7,1978	Resigned and retired.

Departures from Committee:	Majority			Minority		
Moved to Foreign Relations	Muskie, Edmund S.	Me.	Dem	None		
Moved to Finance	None			Heinz, H. John III	Penn.	Rep

GOVERNMENTAL AFFAIRS / 96th Congress

Service Dates of Committee Chair: Jan. 23,1979-Jan. 3,1981
Service Dates of Majority Members: Jan. 23,1979-Jan. 5,1981
Service Dates of Minority Members: Jan. 23,1979-Jan. 5,1981

Majority

Rank	Name	Party	State	Years in: Senate	Years in: Comm.
Chr	Ribicoff, Abraham A.	Dem	Conn.	17	16
2nd	Jackson, Henry M.	Dem	Wash.	27	27
3rd	Eagleton, Thomas F.	Dem	Mo.	11	11
4th	Chiles, Lawton M. Jr.	Dem	Fla.	9	8
5th	Nunn, Samuel A.	Dem	Ga.	7	7
6th	Glenn, John H. Jr.	Dem	Ohio	5	5
7th	Sasser, James R.	Dem	Tenn.	3	*1 3
8th	Pryor, David H.	Dem	Ark.	1	*1 1
9th	Levin, Carl M.	Dem	Mich.	1	1

Minority

Rank	Name	Party	State	Years in: Senate	Years in: Comm.
RM	Percy, Charles H.	Rep	Ill.	13	11
2nd	Javits, Jacob K.	Rep	N.Y.	23	20
3rd	Roth, William V. Jr.	Rep	Del.	9	8
4th	Stevens, Theodore F.	Rep	Alas.	11	11
5th	Mathias, Charles McC. Jr.	Rep	Md.	11	11
6th	Danforth, John C.	Rep	Mo.	3	2
7th	Cohen, William S.	Rep	Me.	1	1
8th	Durenberger, David F.	Rep	Minn.	1	1

*1: Member's 1st period of service on the committee.

Notes: "Years in committee" for Eagleton, Glenn, and Mathias include their continuous service on the District of Columbia Committee. "Years in committee" for Stevens include his continuous service on the Post Office and Civil Service Committee. William V. Roth, Jr.'s continuous service on the Government Operations committee entitled him to a rank higher than that of Stevens or Mathias. Rankings on this committee for the following members were affected by other chamber service: Henry M. Jackson (Dem-Wash.), Chair, Interior and Insular Affairs; Edmund S. Muskie (Dem-Me.), Chair, Budget; and Jacob K. Javits (Rep-N.Y.), Ranking Minority Member, Labor and Public Welfare.

Departures from the Senate:	Majority			Minority		
Defeated for Reelection	None			Javits, Jacob K.	N.Y.	Rep
Retired	Ribicoff, Abraham A.	Conn.	Dem	None		

GOVERNMENTAL AFFAIRS / 97th Congress

Service Dates of Committee Chair: Jan. 5,1981-Jan. 3,1983
Service Dates of Majority Members: Jan. 5,1981-Jan. 3,1983
Service Dates of Minority Members: Jan. 5,1981-Jan. 3,1983

Majority

Rank Name	Party	State	Years in: Senate	Years in: Comm.
Chr Roth, William V. Jr.	Rep	Del.	11	10
2nd Percy, Charles H.	Rep	Ill.	15	13
3rd Stevens, Theodore F.	Rep	Alas.	13	12
4th Mathias, Charles McC. Jr.	Rep	Md.	13	12
5th Danforth, John C.	Rep	Mo.	5	4
6th Cohen, William S.	Rep	Me.	3	2
7th Durenberger, David F.	Rep	Minn.	3	2
8th Mattingly, Mack	Rep	Ga.	1	1
9th Rudman, Warren B.	Rep	N.H.	1	1

Minority

Rank Name	Party	State	Years in: Senate	Years in: Comm.
RM Eagleton, Thomas F.	Dem	Mo.	13	12
2nd Jackson, Henry M.	Dem	Wash.	29	28
3rd Chiles, Lawton M. Jr.	Dem	Fla.	11	10
4th Nunn, Samuel A.	Dem	Ga.	9	9
5th Glenn, John H. Jr.	Dem	Ohio	7	6
6th Sasser, James R.	Dem	Tenn.	5	*1 4
7th Pryor, David H.	Dem	Ark.	3	*1 2
8th Levin, Carl M.	Dem	Mich.	3	2

*1: Member's 1st period of service on the committee.

Notes: "Years in committee" for Eagleton, Glenn, and Mathias include their continuous service on the District of Columbia Committee. "Years in committee" for Stevens include his continuous service on the Post Office and Civil Service Committee. The resignation of Harrison Williams (Dem-N.J.), and the appointment of Nicholas F. Brady (Rep-N.J.) to fill his vacancy on Apr. 12,1982, led to a change in size and party ratio on this committee to 10 Republicans and 8 Democrats. Rankings on this committee for the following members were affected by other chamber service: Charles H. Percy (Rep-Ill.), Chair, Foreign Relations; Theodore F. Stevens (Rep-Alas.), Senate Majority Whip; and Charles McC. Mathias, Jr. (Rep-Md.), Chair, Rules and Administration.

Addition:
Majority: 10th Schmitt, Harrison H. Rep N.M. Apr. 27,1982

	Majority			Minority		
Departures from the Senate:						
Defeated for Reelection	Schmitt, Harrison H.	N.M.	Rep	None		
Departures from Committee:						
Moved to Banking, Housing & Urban Affairs	Mattingly, Mack	Ga.	Rep	None		
Moved to Finance	None			Pryor, David H.	Ark.	Dem

GOVERNMENTAL AFFAIRS / 98th Congress

Service Dates of Committee Chair: Jan. 3,1983-Feb. 21,1985
Service Dates of Majority Members: Jan. 3,1983-Feb. 21,1985
Service Dates of Minority Members: Jan. 3,1983-Feb. 21,1985

Majority

Rank Name	Party	State	Years in: Senate	Years in: Comm.
Chr Roth, William V. Jr.	Rep	Del.	13	12
2nd Percy, Charles H.	Rep	Ill.	17	15
3rd Stevens, Theodore F.	Rep	Alas.	15	14
4th Mathias, Charles McC. Jr.	Rep	Md.	15	14
5th Cohen, William S.	Rep	Me.	5	4
6th Durenberger, David F.	Rep	Minn.	5	4
7th Rudman, Warren B.	Rep	N.H.	3	2
8th Danforth, John C.	Rep	Mo.	7	6
9th Cochran, Thad	Rep	Miss.	5	1
10th Armstrong, William L.	Rep	Colo.	5	1

Minority

Rank Name	Party	State	Years in: Senate	Years in: Comm.
RM Eagleton, Thomas F.	Dem	Mo.	15	14
2nd Jackson, Henry M.	Dem	Wash.	31	30
3rd Chiles, Lawton M. Jr.	Dem	Fla.	13	12
4th Nunn, Samuel A.	Dem	Ga.	11	10
5th Glenn, John H. Jr.	Dem	Ohio	9	8
6th Sasser, James R.	Dem	Tenn.	7	*1 6
7th Levin, Carl M.	Dem	Mich.	5	4
8th Bingaman, Jeff	Dem	N.M.	1	*1 1

*1: Member's 1st period of service on the committee.

Notes: "Years in committee" for Eagleton, Glenn, and Mathias include their continuous service on the District of Columbia Committee. "Years in committee" for Stevens include his continuous service on the Post Office and Civil Service Committee. The death of Henry M. Jackson (Dem-Wash.), and the appointment of Daniel J. Evans (Rep-Wash.) to fill his vacancy on Sep. 8,1983, led to a temporary change in size and party ratio on this committee to 11 Republicans and 8 Democrats. The committee returned to its original size and ratio upon Evans' departure on Feb. 9,1984. Rankings on this committee for the following members were affected by other chamber service: Charles H. Percy (Rep-Ill.), Chair, Foreign Relations; Theodore F. Stevens (Rep-Alas.), Senate Majority Whip; and Charles McC. Mathias, Jr. (Rep-Md.), Chair, Rules and Administration. John C. Danforth (Rep-Mo.) was ranked below less senior members Warren B. Rudman (Rep-N.H.), David F. Durenberger (Rep-Minn.) and William S. Cohen (Rep-Me.).

Addition:

Majority: 11th Evans, Daniel J. Rep Wash. Sep. 22,1983

Changes:

Majority:

Evans, Daniel J.	Rep	Wash.	Feb. 9,1984	Moved to Select Committee on Aging; Energy and Natural Resources.

Minority:

Jackson, Henry M.	Dem	Wash.	Sep. 1,1983	Died in office.
Pryor, David H.	Dem	Ark.	Feb. 9,1984	Replaced Jackson.

	Majority			Minority		
Departures from the Senate:						
Defeated for Reelection	Percy, Charles H.	Ill.	Rep	None		
Departures from Committee:						
Moved to Budget; became Chair of Commerce, Science & Transportation	Danforth, John C.	Mo.	Rep	None		
Moved to Energy & Natural Resources	None			Bingaman, Jeff	N.M.	Dem
No new assignment	Armstrong, William L.	Colo.	Rep	Pryor, David H.	Ark.	Dem
				Sasser, James R.	Tenn.	Dem

GOVERNMENTAL AFFAIRS / 99th Congress

Service Dates of Committee Chair: Feb. 21,1985-Jan. 6,1987
Service Dates of Majority Members: Feb. 21,1985-Jan. 6,1987
Service Dates of Minority Members: Feb. 21,1985-Jan. 6,1987

Majority

Rank	Name	Party	State	Years in: Senate	Years in: Comm.
Chr	Roth, William V. Jr.	Rep	Del.	15	15
2nd	Stevens, Theodore F.	Rep	Alas.	17	17
3rd	Mathias, Charles McC. Jr.	Rep	Md.	17	16
4th	Cohen, William S.	Rep	Me.	7	7
5th	Durenberger, David F.	Rep	Minn.	7	7
6th	Rudman, Warren B.	Rep	N.H.	5	5
7th	Cochran, Thad	Rep	Miss.	7	3

Minority

Rank	Name	Party	State	Years in: Senate	Years in: Comm.
RM	Eagleton, Thomas F.	Dem	Mo.	17	17
2nd	Chiles, Lawton M. Jr.	Dem	Fla.	15	15
3rd	Nunn, Samuel A.	Dem	Ga.	13	13
4th	Glenn, John H. Jr.	Dem	Ohio	11	11
5th	Levin, Carl M.	Dem	Mich.	7	7
6th	Gore, Albert A. Jr.	Dem	Tenn.	1	1

Notes: "Years in committee" for Mathias, Eagleton, and Glenn include their continuous service on the District of Columbia Committee. "Years in committee" for Stevens include his continuous service on the Post Office and Civil Service Committee. Rankings on this committee for the following members were affected by other chamber service: Theodore F. Stevens (Rep-Alas.), Senate Majority Whip; and Charles McC. Mathias, Jr. (Rep-Md.), Chair, Rules and Administration.

	Majority			Minority		
Departures from the Senate:						
Retired	Mathias, Charles McC. Jr.	Md.	Rep	Eagleton, Thomas F.	Mo.	Dem
Departures from Committee:						
Moved to Labor & Human Resources	Cochran, Thad	Miss.	Rep	None		
Moved to Armed Services	None			Gore, Albert A. Jr.	Tenn.	Dem

GOVERNMENTAL AFFAIRS / 100th Congress

Service Dates of Committee Chair: Jan. 6,1987-Feb. 2,1989
Service Dates of Majority Members: Jan. 6,1987-Feb. 2,1989
Service Dates of Minority Members: Jan. 6,1987-Feb. 2,1989

Majority

Rank	Name	Party	State	Years in: Senate	Years in: Comm.
Chr	Glenn, John H. Jr.	Dem	Ohio	13	12
2nd	Chiles, Lawton M. Jr.	Dem	Fla.	17	16
3rd	Nunn, Samuel A.	Dem	Ga.	15	15
4th	Levin, Carl M.	Dem	Mich.	9	8
5th	Sasser, James R.	Dem	Tenn.	11	*2 1
6th	Pryor, David H.	Dem	Ark.	9	*3 1
7th	Mitchell, George J.	Dem	Me.	7	1
8th	Bingaman, Jeff	Dem	N.M.	5	*2 1

Minority

Rank	Name	Party	State	Years in: Senate	Years in: Comm.
RM	Roth, William V. Jr.	Rep	Del.	17	16
2nd	Stevens, Theodore F.	Rep	Alas.	19	18
3rd	Cohen, William S.	Rep	Me.	9	8
4th	Rudman, Warren B.	Rep	N.H.	7	7
5th	Heinz, H. John III	Rep	Penn.	11	*2 1
6th	Durenberger, David F.	Rep	Minn.	9	8

*2: Member's 2nd period of service on the committee; *3: Member's 3rd period of service on the committee.

Notes: "Years in committee" for Glenn include his continuous service on the District of Columbia Committee. "Years in committee" for Stevens include his continuous service on the Post Office and Civil Service Committee. Rankings on this committee for the following members were affected by other chamber service: Lawton M. Chiles, Jr. (Dem-Fla.), Chair, Budget; Samuel A. Nunn (Dem-Ga.), Chair, Armed Services; and Theodore F. Stevens (Rep-Alas.), Senate Minority Whip.

Changes:
Minority:

Durenberger, David F.	Rep	Minn.	Feb. 19,1987	Left committee; no new assignment.
Trible, Paul S. Jr.	Rep	Va.	Feb. 19,1987	Replaced Durenberger.

	Majority			Minority		
Departures from the Senate:						
Retired	Chiles, Lawton M. Jr.	Fla.	Dem	Trible, Paul S. Jr.	Va.	Rep
Departures from Committee:						
No new assignment	Mitchell, George J.	Me.	Dem	None		

GOVERNMENTAL AFFAIRS / 101st Congress

Service Dates of Committee Chair: Feb. 2,1989-Feb. 5,1991
Service Dates of Majority Members: Feb. 2,1989-Feb. 5,1991
Service Dates of Minority Members: Feb. 2,1989-Feb. 5,1991

Majority

Rank	Name	Party	State	Years in: Senate	Years in: Comm.
Chr	Glenn, John H. Jr.	Dem	Ohio	15	15
2nd	Nunn, Samuel A.	Dem	Ga.	17	17
3rd	Levin, Carl M.	Dem	Mich.	11	11
4th	Sasser, James R.	Dem	Tenn.	13	*2 3
5th	Pryor, David H.	Dem	Ark.	11	*3 3
6th	Bingaman, Jeff	Dem	N.M.	7	*2 1
7th	Kohl, Herbert	Dem	Wisc.	1	1
8th	Lieberman, Joseph I.	Dem	Conn.	1	1

Minority

Rank	Name	Party	State	Years in: Senate	Years in: Comm.
RM	Roth, William V. Jr.	Rep	Del.	19	19
2nd	Stevens, Theodore F.	Rep	Alas.	21	21
3rd	Cohen, William S.	Rep	Me.	11	11
4th	Rudman, Warren	Rep	N.H.	9	9
5th	Heinz, H. John III	Rep	Penn.	13	*2 3
6th	Wilson, Pete	Rep	Cal.	7	1

*2: Member's 2nd period of service on the committee; *3: Member's 3rd period of service on the committee.

Notes: "Years in committee" for Glenn include his continuous service on the District of Columbia Committee. "Years in committee" for Stevens include his continuous service on the Post Office and Civil Service Committee. Rankings on this committee for the following members were affected by other chamber service: Samuel A. Nunn (Dem-Ga.), Chair, Armed Services; and Theodore F. Stevens (Rep-Alas.), Senate Minority Whip.

Changes:
Majority:

Bingaman, Jeff	Dem	N.M.	May 16,1990	Moved to Labor and Human Resources.
Akaka, Daniel K.	Dem	Hai.	May 16,1990	Replaced Bingaman.

Departures from the Senate:	Majority	Minority	
Elected Governor	None	Wilson, Pete	Cal. Rep

GOVERNMENTAL AFFAIRS / 102nd Congress

Service Dates of Committee Chair: Feb. 5,1991-Jan. 3,1993
Service Dates of Majority Members: Feb. 5,1991-Jan. 3,1993
Service Dates of Minority Members: Feb. 5,1991-Jan. 3,1993

Majority

Rank	Name	Party	State	Years in: Senate	Years in: Comm.
Chr	Glenn, John H. Jr.	Dem	Ohio	17	17
2nd	Nunn, Samuel A.	Dem	Ga.	19	19
3rd	Levin, Carl M.	Dem	Mich.	13	13
4th	Sasser, James R.	Dem	Tenn.	15	*2 5
5th	Pryor, David H.	Dem	Ark.	13	*3 5
6th	Kohl, Herbert	Dem	Wisc.	3	3
7th	Lieberman, Joseph I.	Dem	Conn.	3	3
8th	Akaka, Daniel K.	Dem	Hai.	1	1

Minority

Rank	Name	Party	State	Years in: Senate	Years in: Comm.
RM	Roth, William V. Jr.	Rep	Del.	21	21
2nd	Stevens, Theodore F.	Rep	Alas.	23	23
3rd	Cohen, William S.	Rep	Me.	13	13
4th	Rudman, Warren	Rep	N.H.	11	11
5th	Heinz, H. John III	Rep	Penn.	15	*2 5
6th	Seymour, John	Rep	Cal.	1	1

*2: Member's 2nd period of service on the committee; *3: Member's 3rd period of service on the committee.

Notes: "Years in committee" for Glenn include his continuous service on the District of Columbia Committee. "Years in committee" for Stevens include his continuous service on the Post Office and Civil Service Committee. The death of John Heinz (Rep-Penn.), and the appointment of Harris Wofford (Dem-Penn.) to fill his Senate vacancy on May 9,1991 led to a change in size and party ratio on this committee to 8 Democrats and 5 Republicans on June 4,1991. Rankings on this committee for the following members were affected by other chamber service: Samuel A. Nunn (Dem-Ga.), Chair, Armed Services; and Theodore F. Stevens (Rep-Alas.), Senate Minority Whip.

Changes:
Minority:

Heinz, H. John III	Rep	Penn.	May 4,1991	Died in office.

JUDICIARY

Jurisdiction, 1947

Established by the Legislative Reorganization Act of 1946:

[Section 102.(1)(k)]

(k) Committee on the Judiciary, to consist of thirteen Senators, to which committee shall be referred all proposed legislation, messages, petitions, memorials, and other matters relating to the following subjects:

1. Judicial proceedings, civil and criminal, generally.
2. Constitutional amendments.
3. Federal courts and judges.
4. Local courts in the Territories and possessions.
5. Revision and codification of the statutes of the United States.
6. National penitentiaries.
7. Protection of trade and commerce against unlawful restraints and monopolies.
8. Holidays and celebrations.
9. Bankruptcy, mutiny, espionage, and counterfeiting.
10. State and Territorial boundary lines.
11. Meetings of Congress, attendance of Members, and their acceptance of incompatible offices.
12. Civil liberties.
13. Patents, copyrights, and trade-marks.
14. Patent Office.
15. Immigration and naturalization.
16. Apportionment of Representatives.
17. Measures relating to claims against the United States.
18. Interstate compacts generally.

Jurisdiction, 1992

Jurisdiction contained in the <u>Standing Rules of the Senate</u> (as revised to March 18, 1992):

[Rule XXV.(1)(l)]

(1) Committee on the Judiciary, to which committee shall be referred all proposed legislation, messages, petitions, memorials, and other matters relating to the following subjects:

1. Apportionment of Representatives.
2. Bankruptcy, mutiny, espionage, and counterfeiting.
3. Civil liberties.
4. Constitutional amendments.
5. Federal courts and judges.
6. Government information.
7. Holidays and celebrations.
8. Immigration and naturalization.
9. Interstate compacts generally.
10. Judicial proceedings, civil and criminal, generally.
11. Local courts in the territories and possessions.
12. Measures relating to claims against the United States.
13. National penitentiaries.
14. Patent Office.
15. Patents, copyrights, and trademarks.
16. Protection of trade and commerce against unlawful restraints and monopolies.
17. Revision and codification of the statutes of the United States.
18. State and territorial boundary lines.

JUDICIARY / 80th Congress

Service Dates of Committee Chair: Jan. 6,1947-Jan. 10,1949
Service Dates of Majority Members: Jan. 6,1947-Jan. 10,1949
Service Dates of Minority Members: Jan. 8,1947-Jan. 10,1949

Majority

Rank	Name	Party	State	Years in: Senate	Years in: Comm.
Chr	Wiley, Alexander	Rep	Wisc.	9	8
2nd	Langer, William	Rep	N.D.	7	6
3rd	Ferguson, Homer	Rep	Mich.	5	4
4th	Revercomb, W. Chapman	Rep	W.Va.	5	4
5th	Moore, Edward H.	Rep	Okla.	5	2
6th	Donnell, Forrest C.	Rep	Mo.	3	1
7th	Cooper, John Sherman	Rep	Ky.	1	1

Minority

Rank	Name	Party	State	Years in: Senate	Years in: Comm.
RM	McCarran, Patrick A.	Dem	Nev.	14	14
2nd	Kilgore, Harley M.	Dem	W.Va.	7	6
3rd	Eastland, James O.	Dem	Miss.	5	4
4th	Magnuson, Warren G.	Dem	Wash.	3	1
5th	Fulbright, J. William	Dem	Ark.	3	1
6th	McGrath, J. Howard	Dem	R.I.	1	1

	Majority			Minority		
Departures from the Senate:						
Defeated for Reelection	Cooper, John Sherman	Ky.	Rep	None		
	Revercomb, W. Chapman	W.Va.	Rep			
Retired	Moore, Edward H.	Okla.	Rep	None		
Departures from Committee:						
Moved to Foreign Relations	None			Fulbright, J. William	Ark.	Dem

JUDICIARY / 81st Congress

Service Dates of Committee Chair: Jan. 10,1949-Jan. 15,1951
Service Dates of Majority Members: Jan. 10,1949-Jan. 15,1951
Service Dates of Minority Members: Jan. 10,1949-Jan. 15,1951

Majority

Rank	Name	Party	State	Years in: Senate	Years in: Comm.
Chr	McCarran, Patrick A.	Dem	Nev.	16	16
2nd	Kilgore, Harley M.	Dem	W.Va.	9	8
3rd	Eastland, James O.	Dem	Miss.	7	6
4th	Magnuson, Warren G.	Dem	Wash.	5	3
5th	McGrath, J. Howard	Dem	R.I.	3	3
6th	Wagner, Robert F.	Dem	N.Y.	22 *2	1
7th	Broughton, J. Melville	Dem	N.C.	1	1
8th	Miller, Bert H.	Dem	Ida.	1	1

Minority

Rank	Name	Party	State	Years in: Senate	Years in: Comm.
RM	Wiley, Alexander	Rep	Wisc.	11	11
2nd	Langer, William	Rep	N.D.	9	8
3rd	Ferguson, Homer	Rep	Mich.	7	6
4th	Donnell, Forrest C.	Rep	Mo.	5	3
5th	Jenner, William E.	Rep	Ind.	3	1

Changes:

Majority:

Name	Party	State	Date	Change
Broughton, J. Melville	Dem	N.C.	Mar. 6,1949	Died in office.
O'Conor, Herbert R.	Dem	Md.	Mar. 22,1949	Replaced Broughton.
Wagner, Robert F.	Dem	N.Y.	Apr. 4,1949	Left committee; resigned Senate June 28,1949.
Graham, Frank P.	Dem	N.C.	Apr. 4,1949	Replaced Wagner.
McGrath, J. Howard	Dem	R.I.	Aug. 23,1949	Resigned; appointed Postmaster General.
Kefauver, C. Estes	Dem	Tenn.	Aug. 30,1949	Replaced McGrath.
Miller, Bert H.	Dem	Ida.	Oct. 8,1949	Died in office.
Withers, Garrett L.	Dem	Ky.	Jan. 12,1950	Replaced Miller.
Graham, Frank P.	Dem	N.C.	Nov. 26,1950	Resigned; defeated for nomination.
Withers, Garrett L.	Dem	Ky.	Nov. 26,1950	Resigned; elected to State House.
Clements, Earle C.	Dem	Ky.	Dec. 11,1950	Replaced Graham.
Smith, Willis	Dem	N.C.	Dec. 11,1950	Replaced Withers.

	Majority			Minority		
Departures from the Senate:						
Defeated for Reelection	None			Donnell, Forrest C.	Mo.	Rep
Departures from Committee:						
Moved to Rules & Administration; District of Columbia; Post Office & Civil Service	Clements, Earle C.	Ky.	Dem	None		

JUDICIARY / 82nd Congress

Service Dates of Committee Chair: Jan. 15,1951-Jan. 13,1953
Service Dates of Majority Members: Jan. 15,1951-Jan. 13,1953
Service Dates of Minority Members: Jan. 15,1951-Jan. 13,1953

Majority

Rank	Name	Party	State	Years in: Senate	Years in: Comm.
Chr	McCarran, Patrick A.	Dem	Nev.	18	18
2nd	Kilgore, Harley M.	Dem	W.Va.	11	10
3rd	Eastland, James O.	Dem	Miss.	9	9
4th	Magnuson, Warren G.	Dem	Wash.	7	5
5th	O'Conor, Herbert R.	Dem	Md.	5	2
6th	Kefauver, C. Estes	Dem	Tenn.	3	2
7th	Smith, Willis	Dem	N.C.	1	1

Minority

Rank	Name	Party	State	Years in: Senate	Years in: Comm.
RM	Wiley, Alexander	Rep	Wisc.	13	13
2nd	Langer, William	Rep	N.D.	11	10
3rd	Ferguson, Homer	Rep	Mich.	9	9
4th	Jenner, William E.	Rep	Ind.	5	3
5th	Watkins, Arthur V.	Rep	Utah	5	1
6th	Hendrickson, Robert C.	Rep	N.J.	3	1

	Majority			Minority		
Departures from the Senate:						
Retired	O'Conor, Herbert R.	Md.	Dem	None		
Departures from Committee:						
Moved to Appropriations	Magnuson, Warren G.	Wash.	Dem	None		
Moved to Foreign Relations	None			Ferguson, Homer	Mich.	Rep

JUDICIARY / 83rd Congress

Service Dates of Committee Chair: Jan. 13,1953-Jan. 11,1955
Service Dates of Majority Members: Jan. 13,1953-Jan. 11,1955
Service Dates of Minority Members: Jan. 13,1953-Jan. 11,1955

Majority

Rank	Name	Party	State	Years in: Senate	Years in: Comm.
Chr	Langer, William	Rep	N.D.	13	12
2nd	Wiley, Alexander	Rep	Wisc.	15	15
3rd	Jenner, William E.	Rep	Ind.	7	5
4th	Watkins, Arthur V.	Rep	Utah	7	2
5th	Hendrickson, Robert C.	Rep	N.J.	5	2
6th	Dirksen, Everett M.	Rep	Ill.	3	1
7th	Welker, Herman	Rep	Ida.	3	1
8th	Butler, John Marshall	Rep	Md.	3	1

Minority

Rank	Name	Party	State	Years in: Senate	Years in: Comm.
RM1	McCarran, Patrick A.	Dem	Nev.	20	20
RM2 2nd	Kilgore, Harley M.	Dem	W.Va.	13	12
3rd	Eastland, James O.	Dem	Miss.	11	10
4th	Kefauver, C. Estes	Dem	Tenn.	5	4
5th	Smith, Willis	Dem	N.C.	3	3
6th	Johnston, Olin D.	Dem	S.C.	9	1
7th	Hennings, Thomas C. Jr.	Dem	Mo.	3	1

Note: Ranking on this committee for the following member was affected by other chamber service: Alexander Wiley (Rep-Wisc.), Chair, Foreign Relations.

Changes:

Ranking Member:

RM1	McCarran, Patrick A.	Dem	Nev.	Sep. 28,1954	Died in office.
RM2	Kilgore, Harley M.	Dem	W.Va.	Sep. 28,1954	Succeeded McCarran as Ranking Minority Member.

Minority:

Smith, Willis	Dem	N.C.	June 26,1953	Died in office.
McClellan, John L.	Dem	Ark.	July 7,1953	Replaced Smith.
McCarran, Patrick A.	Dem	Nev.	Sep. 28,1954	Died in office.

	Majority			Minority
Departures from the Senate:				
Appointed Ambassador to New Zealand	Hendrickson, Robert C.	N.J.	Rep	None

JUDICIARY / 84th Congress

Service Dates of Committee Chairs: Ch1 Jan. 11,1955-Feb. 28,1956
Ch2 Mar. 2,1956-Jan. 9,1957
Service Dates of Majority Members: Jan. 11,1955-Jan. 9,1957
Service Dates of Minority Members: Jan. 11,1955-Jan. 9,1957

Majority

Rank	Name	Party	State	Years in: Senate	Years in: Comm.
Ch1	Kilgore, Harley M.	Dem	W.Va.	15	14
Ch2 2nd	Eastland, James O.	Dem	Miss.	13	12
3rd	Kefauver, C. Estes	Dem	Tenn.	7	6
4th	Johnston, Olin D.	Dem	S.C.	11	2
5th	Hennings, Thomas C. Jr.	Dem	Mo.	5	2
6th	McClellan, John L.	Dem	Ark.	13	2
7th	Daniel, Price M.	Dem	Tex.	3	1
8th	O'Mahoney, Joseph C.	Dem	Wyo.	20	*2 1

Minority

Rank	Name	Party	State	Years in: Senate	Years in: Comm.
RM	Wiley, Alexander	Rep	Wisc.	17	17
2nd	Langer, William	Rep	N.D.	15	14
3rd	Jenner, William E.	Rep	Ind.	9	7
4th	Watkins, Arthur V.	Rep	Utah	9	4
5th	Dirksen, Everett M.	Rep	Ill.	5	2
6th	Welker, Herman	Rep	Ida.	5	2
7th	Butler, John Marshall	Rep	Md.	5	2

*2: Member's 2nd period of service on the committee.

Changes:

Chair:

Ch1	Kilgore, Harley M.	Dem	W.Va.	Feb. 28,1956	Died in office.
Ch2	Eastland, James O.	Dem	Miss.	Mar. 2,1956	Succeeded Kilgore as Chair.

Majority:

Kilgore, Harley M.	Dem	W.Va.	Feb. 28,1956	Died in office.
Neely, Matthew M.	Dem	W.Va.	Mar. 2,1956	Replaced Kilgore.

	Majority			Minority		
Departures from the Senate:						
Defeated for Reelection	None			Welker, Herman	Ida.	Rep
Departures from Committee:						
No new assignment	Daniel, Price M.	Tex.	Dem	None		

JUDICIARY / 85th Congress

Service Dates of Committee Chair: Jan. 9,1957-Jan. 14,1959
Service Dates of Majority Members: Jan. 9,1957-Jan. 14,1959
Service Dates of Minority Members: Jan. 9,1957-Jan. 20,1959

Majority

Rank	Name	Party	State	Years in: Senate	Years in: Comm.
Chr	Eastland, James O.	Dem	Miss.	15	14
2nd	Kefauver, C. Estes	Dem	Tenn.	9	8
3rd	Johnston, Olin D.	Dem	S.C.	13	4
4th	Hennings, Thomas C. Jr.	Dem	Mo.	7	4
5th	McClellan, John L.	Dem	Ark.	15	4
6th	O'Mahoney, Joseph C.	Dem	Wyo.	22	*2 2
7th	Neely, Matthew M.	Dem	W.Va.	24	*3 1
8th	Ervin, Samuel J.	Dem	N.C.	3	1

Minority

Rank	Name	Party	State	Years in: Senate	Years in: Comm.
RM	Wiley, Alexander	Rep	Wisc.	19	18
2nd	Langer, William	Rep	N.D.	17	16
3rd	Jenner, William E.	Rep	Ind.	11	8
4th	Watkins, Arthur V.	Rep	Utah	11	6
5th	Dirksen, Everett M.	Rep	Ill.	7	4
6th	Butler, John Marshall	Rep	Md.	7	4
7th	Hruska, Roman L.	Rep	Neb.	3	1

*2: Member's 2nd period of service on the committee; *3: Member's 3rd period of service on the committee.

Changes:

Majority:

Neely, Matthew M.	Dem	W.Va.	Jan. 18,1958	Died in office.
Carroll, John A.	Dem	Colo.	Jan. 30,1958	Replaced Neely.

	Majority	Minority		
Departures from the Senate:				
Defeated for Reelection	None	Watkins, Arthur V.	Utah	Rep
Retired	None	Jenner, William E.	Ind.	Rep
Departures from Committee:				
Moved to Finance	None	Butler, John Marshall	Md.	Rep

JUDICIARY / 86th Congress

Service Dates of Committee Chair: Jan. 14,1959-Jan. 10,1961
Service Dates of Majority Members: Jan. 14,1959-Jan. 10,1961
Service Dates of Minority Members: Jan. 20,1959-Jan. 13,1961

Majority

Rank	Name	Party	State	Years in: Senate	Years in: Comm.
Chr	Eastland, James O.	Dem	Miss.	17	17
2nd	Kefauver, C. Estes	Dem	Tenn.	11	10
3rd	Johnston, Olin D.	Dem	S.C.	15	7
4th	Hennings, Thomas C. Jr.	Dem	Mo.	9	7
5th	McClellan, John L.	Dem	Ark.	17	6
6th	O'Mahoney, Joseph C.	Dem	Wyo.	24	*2 5
7th	Ervin, Samuel J.	Dem	N.C.	5	3
8th	Carroll, John A.	Dem	Colo.	3	1
9th	Dodd, Thomas J.	Dem	Conn.	1	1
10th	Hart, Philip A.	Dem	Mich.	1	1

Minority

Rank	Name	Party	State	Years in: Senate	Years in: Comm.
RM	Wiley, Alexander	Rep	Wisc.	21	21
2nd	Langer, William	Rep	N.D.	19	18
3rd	Dirksen, Everett M.	Rep	Ill.	9	7
4th	Hruska, Roman L.	Rep	Neb.	5	3
5th	Martin, Thomas E.	Rep	Iowa	5	1

*2: Member's 2nd period of service on the committee.

Changes:

Majority:

Hennings, Thomas C. Jr.	Dem	Mo.	Sep. 13,1960	Died in office.

Minority:

Martin, Thomas E.	Rep	Iowa	Jan. 27,1959	Moved to Interior and Insular Affairs; Aeronautical and Space Sciences.
Keating, Kenneth B.	Rep	N.Y.	Jan. 27,1959	Replaced Martin.
Langer, William	Rep	N.D.	Nov. 8,1959	Died in office.
Cotton, Norris	Rep	N.H.	Jan. 18,1960	Replaced Langer.

Departures from the Senate:

	Majority			Minority
Retired	O'Mahoney, Joseph C.	Wyo.	Dem	None

JUDICIARY / 87th Congress

Service Dates of Committee Chair: Jan. 10,1961-Feb. 25,1963
Service Dates of Majority Members: Jan. 10,1961-Feb. 25,1963
Service Dates of Minority Members: Jan. 13,1961-Feb. 25,1963

Majority

Rank	Name	Party	State	Years in: Senate	Years in: Comm.
Chr	Eastland, James O.	Dem	Miss.	19	18
2nd	Kefauver, C. Estes	Dem	Tenn.	13	12
3rd	Johnston, Olin D.	Dem	S.C.	17	8
4th	McClellan, John L.	Dem	Ark.	19	8
5th	Ervin, Samuel J.	Dem	N.C.	7	5
6th	Carroll, John A.	Dem	Colo.	5	3
7th	Dodd, Thomas J.	Dem	Conn.	3	2
8th	Hart, Philip A.	Dem	Mich.	3	2
9th	Long, Edward V.	Dem	Mo.	1	1
10th	Blakley, William A.	Dem	Tex.	1	1

Minority

Rank	Name	Party	State	Years in: Senate	Years in: Comm.
RM	Wiley, Alexander	Rep	Wisc.	23	23
2nd	Dirksen, Everett M.	Rep	Ill.	11	9
3rd	Hruska, Roman L.	Rep	Neb.	7	5
4th	Keating, Kenneth B.	Rep	N.Y.	3	2
5th	Cotton, Norris	Rep	N.H.	7	1

Note: Appointed Senator William A. Blakley (Dem-Tex.) lost in a special election to John Tower (Rep-Tex.), whose seating on June 15,1961 led to a change in size and party ratio on this committee to 9 Democrats and 6 Republicans on July 11,1961.

Addition:

Minority: 7th Fong, Hiram L. Rep Hai. July 11,1961

Changes:

Majority:

Blakley, William A.	Dem	Tex.	June 14,1961	Resigned; defeated in special election.

Minority:

Cotton, Norris	Rep	N.H.	Feb. 2,1962	Moved to Appropriations.
Scott, Hugh D. Jr.	Rep	Penn.	Feb. 2,1962	Replaced Cotton.

Departures from the Senate:	Majority		Minority	
Defeated for Reelection	Carroll, John A.	Colo. Dem	Wiley, Alexander	Wisc. Rep

JUDICIARY / 88th Congress

Service Dates of Committee Chair: Feb. 25,1963-Jan. 8,1965
Service Dates of Majority Members: Feb. 25,1963-Jan. 8,1965
Service Dates of Minority Members: Feb. 25,1963-Jan. 15,1965

Majority

Rank Name	Party	State	Years in: Senate	Years in: Comm.
Chr Eastland, James O.	Dem	Miss.	21	21
2nd Kefauver, C. Estes	Dem	Tenn.	15	14
3rd Johnston, Olin D.	Dem	S.C.	19	11
4th McClellan, John L.	Dem	Ark.	21	10
5th Ervin, Samuel J.	Dem	N.C.	9	7
6th Dodd, Thomas J.	Dem	Conn.	5	5
7th Hart, Philip A.	Dem	Mich.	5	5
8th Long, Edward V.	Dem	Mo.	3	3
9th Kennedy, Edward M.	Dem	Mass.	1	1
10th Bayh, Birch E.	Dem	Ind.	1	1

Minority

Rank Name	Party	State	Years in: Senate	Years in: Comm.
RM Dirksen, Everett M.	Rep	Ill.	13	11
2nd Hruska, Roman L.	Rep	Neb.	9	7
3rd Keating, Kenneth B.	Rep	N.Y.	5	5
4th Fong, Hiram L.	Rep	Hai.	4	2
5th Scott, Hugh D. Jr.	Rep	Penn.	5	2

Changes:
Majority:

Kefauver, C. Estes	Dem	Tenn.	Aug. 10,1963	Died in office.
Burdick, Quentin N.	Dem	N.D.	Aug. 23,1963	Replaced Kefauver.

Departures from the Senate:	Majority	Minority	
Defeated for Reelection	None	Keating, Kenneth B.	N.Y. Rep

JUDICIARY / 89th Congress

Service Dates of Committee Chair: Jan. 8,1965-Jan. 11,1967
Service Dates of Majority Members: Jan. 8,1965-Jan. 11,1967
Service Dates of Minority Members: Jan. 15,1965-Jan. 16,1967

Majority

Rank Name	Party	State	Years in: Senate	Years in: Comm.
Chr Eastland, James O.	Dem	Miss.	23	22
2nd Johnston, Olin D.	Dem	S.C.	21	12
3rd McClellan, John L.	Dem	Ark.	23	12
4th Ervin, Samuel J.	Dem	N.C.	11	8
5th Dodd, Thomas J.	Dem	Conn.	7	6
6th Hart, Philip A.	Dem	Mich.	7	6
7th Long, Edward V.	Dem	Mo.	5	4
8th Kennedy, Edward M.	Dem	Mass.	3	2
9th Bayh, Birch E.	Dem	Ind.	3	2
10th Burdick, Quentin N.	Dem	N.D.	5	2
11th Tydings, Joseph D.	Dem	Md.	1	1

Minority

Rank Name	Party	State	Years in: Senate	Years in: Comm.
RM Dirksen, Everett M.	Rep	Ill.	15	13
2nd Hruska, Roman L.	Rep	Neb.	11	9
3rd Fong, Hiram L.	Rep	Hai.	6	4
4th Scott, Hugh D. Jr.	Rep	Penn.	7	3
5th Javits, Jacob K.	Rep	N.Y.	9	1

Changes:
Majority:

Johnston, Olin D.	Dem	S.C.	Apr. 18,1965	Died in office.
Smathers, George A.	Dem	Fla.	Apr. 26,1965	Replaced Johnston.

Departures from Committee:	Majority	Minority	
Moved to Appropriations	None	Javits, Jacob K.	N.Y. Rep

JUDICIARY / 90th Congress

Service Dates of Committee Chair: Jan. 11,1967-Jan. 14,1969
Service Dates of Majority Members: Jan. 11,1967-Jan. 14,1969
Service Dates of Minority Members: Jan. 16,1967-Jan. 14,1969

Majority

Rank Name	Party	State	Years in: Senate	Years in: Comm.
Chr Eastland, James O.	Dem	Miss.	25	24
2nd McClellan, John L.	Dem	Ark.	25	14
3rd Ervin, Samuel J.	Dem	N.C.	13	11
4th Dodd, Thomas J.	Dem	Conn.	9	8
5th Hart, Philip A.	Dem	Mich.	9	8
6th Long, Edward V.	Dem	Mo.	7	7
7th Kennedy, Edward M.	Dem	Mass.	5	4
8th Bayh, Birch E.	Dem	Ind.	5	4
9th Burdick, Quentin N.	Dem	N.D.	7	4
10th Tydings, Joseph D.	Dem	Md.	3	3
11th Smathers, George A.	Dem	Fla.	17	2

Minority

Rank Name	Party	State	Years in: Senate	Years in: Comm.
RM Dirksen, Everett M.	Rep	Ill.	17	15
2nd Hruska, Roman L.	Rep	Neb.	13	11
3rd Fong, Hiram L.	Rep	Hai.	8	6
4th Scott, Hugh D. Jr.	Rep	Penn.	9	5
5th Thurmond, J. Strom	Rep	S.C.	12	1

Note: The death of Robert F. Kennedy (Dem-N.Y.) and the appointment of Charles Goodell (Rep-N.Y.) to fill his Senate vacancy led to a change in size and party ratio on this committee to 11 Democrats and 6 Republicans on Sep. 12,1968.

Addition:

Minority: 6th Baker, Howard H. Jr. Rep Tenn. Sep. 12,1968

Changes:

Majority:

Long, Edward V. Dem Mo. Dec. 27,1968 Resigned; defeated for renomination.

	Majority		Minority	
Departures from the Senate:				
Retired	Smathers, George A.	Fla. Dem	None	
Departures from Committee:				
Moved to Commerce	None		Baker, Howard H. Jr.	Tenn. Rep

JUDICIARY / 91st Congress

Service Dates of Committee Chair: Jan. 14,1969-Jan. 28,1971
Service Dates of Majority Members: Jan. 14,1969-Jan. 28,1971
Service Dates of Minority Members: Jan. 14,1969-Jan. 29,1971

Majority

Rank Name	Party	State	Years in: Senate	Years in: Comm.
Chr Eastland, James O.	Dem	Miss.	27	27
2nd McClellan, John L.	Dem	Ark.	27	16
3rd Ervin, Samuel J.	Dem	N.C.	15	13
4th Dodd, Thomas J.	Dem	Conn.	11	11
5th Hart, Philip A.	Dem	Mich.	11	11
6th Kennedy, Edward M.	Dem	Mass.	7	6
7th Bayh, Birch E.	Dem	Ind.	7	6
8th Burdick, Quentin N.	Dem	N.D.	9	6
9th Tydings, Joseph D.	Dem	Md.	5	5
10th Byrd, Robert C.	Dem	W.Va.	11	1

Minority

Rank Name	Party	State	Years in: Senate	Years in: Comm.
RM1 Dirksen, Everett M.	Rep	Ill.	19	17
RM2 2nd Hruska, Roman L.	Rep	Neb.	15	13
3rd Fong, Hiram L.	Rep	Hai.	10	8
4th Scott, Hugh D. Jr.	Rep	Penn.	11	7
5th Thurmond, J. Strom	Rep	S.C.	14	2
6th Cook, Marlow W.	Rep	Ky.	1	1
7th Mathias, Charles McC. Jr.	Rep	Md.	1	1

Changes:

Ranking Member:

RM1 Dirksen, Everett M. Rep Ill. Sep. 7,1969 Died in office.
RM2 Hruska, Roman L. Rep Neb. Sep. 7,1969 Succeeded Dirksen as Ranking Minority Member.

Minority:

Dirksen, Everett M. Rep Ill. Sep. 7,1969 Died in office.
Griffin, Robert P. Rep Mich. Sep. 17,1969 Replaced Dirksen.

Departures from the Senate:	Majority		Minority	
Defeated for Reelection	Dodd, Thomas J.	Conn. Dem	None	
	Tydings, Joseph D.	Md. Dem		
Departures from Committee:				
Moved to Government Operations	None		Griffin, Robert P.	Mich. Rep

JUDICIARY / 92nd Congress

Service Dates of Committee Chair: Jan. 28,1971-Jan. 4,1973
Service Dates of Majority Members: Jan. 28,1971-Jan. 4,1973
Service Dates of Minority Members: Jan. 29,1971-Jan. 12,1973

Majority

Rank	Name	Party	State	Years in: Senate	Years in: Comm.
Chr	Eastland, James O.	Dem	Miss.	29	29
2nd	McClellan, John L.	Dem	Ark.	29	18
3rd	Ervin, Samuel J.	Dem	N.C.	17	15
4th	Hart, Philip A.	Dem	Mich.	13	13
5th	Kennedy, Edward M.	Dem	Mass.	9	8
6th	Bayh, Birch E.	Dem	Ind.	9	8
7th	Burdick, Quentin N.	Dem	N.D.	11	8
8th	Byrd, Robert C.	Dem	W.Va.	13	3
9th	Tunney, John V.	Dem	Cal.	1	1

Minority

Rank	Name	Party	State	Years in: Senate	Years in: Comm.
RM	Hruska, Roman L.	Rep	Neb.	17	15
2nd	Fong, Hiram L.	Rep	Hai.	12	10
3rd	Scott, Hugh D. Jr.	Rep	Penn.	13	9
4th	Thurmond, J. Strom	Rep	S.C.	16	5
5th	Cook, Marlow W.	Rep	Ky.	3	3
6th	Mathias, Charles McC. Jr.	Rep	Md.	3	3
7th	Gurney, Edward J.	Rep	Fla.	3	1

JUDICIARY / 93rd Congress

Service Dates of Committee Chair: Jan. 4,1973-Jan. 17,1975
Service Dates of Majority Members: Jan. 4,1973-Jan. 17,1975
Service Dates of Minority Members: Jan. 12,1973-Jan. 23,1975

Majority

Rank	Name	Party	State	Years in: Senate	Years in: Comm.
Chr	Eastland, James O.	Dem	Miss.	31	30
2nd	McClellan, John L.	Dem	Ark.	31	20
3rd	Ervin, Samuel J.	Dem	N.C.	19	16
4th	Hart, Philip A.	Dem	Mich.	15	14
5th	Kennedy, Edward M.	Dem	Mass.	11	10
6th	Bayh, Birch E.	Dem	Ind.	11	10
7th	Burdick, Quentin N.	Dem	N.D.	13	10
8th	Byrd, Robert C.	Dem	W.Va.	15	4
9th	Tunney, John V.	Dem	Cal.	3	2

Minority

Rank	Name	Party	State	Years in: Senate	Years in: Comm.
RM	Hruska, Roman L.	Rep	Neb.	19	17
2nd	Fong, Hiram L.	Rep	Hai.	14	12
3rd	Scott, Hugh D. Jr.	Rep	Penn.	15	11
4th	Thurmond, J. Strom	Rep	S.C.	18	6
5th	Cook, Marlow W.	Rep	Ky.	5	4
6th	Mathias, Charles McC. Jr.	Rep	Md.	5	4
7th	Gurney, Edward J.	Rep	Fla.	5	2

Changes:

Majority:

Name	Party	State	Date	Reason
Ervin, Samuel J.	Dem	N.C.	Dec. 31,1974	Resigned and retired.

Minority:

Name	Party	State	Date	Reason
Cook, Marlow W.	Rep	Ky.	Dec. 27,1974	Resigned; defeated for reelection.
Gurney, Edward J.	Rep	Fla.	Dec. 31,1974	Resigned and retired.

JUDICIARY / 94th Congress

Service Dates of Committee Chair: Jan. 17,1975-Jan. 10,1977
Service Dates of Majority Members: Jan. 17,1975-Jan. 10,1977
Service Dates of Minority Members: Jan. 23,1975-Jan. 10,1977

Majority

Rank	Name	Party	State	Years in: Senate	Years in: Comm.
Chr	Eastland, James O.	Dem	Miss.	33	33
2nd	McClellan, John L.	Dem	Ark.	33	22
3rd	Hart, Philip A.	Dem	Mich.	17	17
4th	Kennedy, Edward M.	Dem	Mass.	13	12
5th	Bayh, Birch E.	Dem	Ind.	13	12
6th	Burdick, Quentin N.	Dem	N.D.	15	12
7th	Byrd, Robert C.	Dem	W.Va.	17	7
8th	Tunney, John V.	Dem	Cal.	5	4
9th	Abourezk, James G.	Dem	S.D.	3	1

Minority

Rank	Name	Party	State	Years in: Senate	Years in: Comm.
RM	Hruska, Roman L.	Rep	Neb.	21	19
2nd	Fong, Hiram L.	Rep	Hai.	16	14
3rd	Scott, Hugh D. Jr.	Rep	Penn.	17	13
4th	Thurmond, J. Strom	Rep	S.C.	20	9
5th	Mathias, Charles McC. Jr.	Rep	Md.	7	7
6th	Scott, William L.	Rep	Va.	3	1

Changes:

Majority:

Hart, Philip A.	Dem	Mich.	Dec. 26,1976	Died in office.
Tunney, John V.	Dem	Cal.	Jan. 1,1977	Resigned; defeated for reelection.

Minority:

Hruska, Roman L.	Rep	Neb.	Dec. 27,1976	Resigned and retired.

Departures from the Senate:

	Majority	Minority		
Retired	None	Fong, Hiram L.	Hai.	Rep
		Scott, Hugh D. Jr.	Penn.	Rep

JUDICIARY / 95th Congress

Service Dates of Committee Chair: Jan. 10,1977-Dec. 27,1978
Service Dates of Majority Members: Jan. 10,1977-Jan. 23,1979
Service Dates of Minority Members: Jan. 10,1977-Jan. 23,1979

Majority

Rank	Name	Party	State	Years in: Senate		Years in: Comm.
Chr	Eastland, James O.	Dem	Miss.	35		34
2nd	McClellan, John L.	Dem	Ark.	35		24
3rd	Kennedy, Edward M.	Dem	Mass.	15		14
4th	Bayh, Birch E.	Dem	Ind.	15		14
5th	Burdick, Quentin N.	Dem	N.D.	17		14
6th	Byrd, Robert C.	Dem	W.Va.	19		8
7th	Abourezk, James G.	Dem	S.D.	5		2
8th	Riegle, Donald W. Jr.	Dem	Mich.	1	*T	1
9th	Sasser, James R.	Dem	Tenn.	1	*T	1

Minority

Rank	Name	Party	State	Years in: Senate		Years in: Comm.
RM	Thurmond, J. Strom	Rep	S.C.	22		10
2nd	Mathias, Charles McC. Jr.	Rep	Md.	9		8
3rd	Scott, William L.	Rep	Va.	5		2
4th	Chafee, John H.	Rep	R.I.	1	*T	1
5th	Heinz, H. John III	Rep	Penn.	1	*T	1

*T: Temporary member of the committee.

Note: The committee size and party ratio changed to 11 Democrats and 6 Republicans on Feb. 11,1977.

Additions:

Majority:	10th	Metzenbaum, Howard M.	Dem	Ohio	Feb. 11,1977
	11th	DeConcini, Dennis	Dem	Ariz.	Feb. 11,1977
Minority:	6th	Wallop, Malcolm	Rep	Wyo.	Feb. 22,1977

Changes:

Majority:

Burdick, Quentin N.	Dem	N.D.	Feb. 11,1977	Moved to Appropriations.
Riegle, Donald W. Jr.	Dem	Mich.	Feb. 11,1977	Moved to Banking, Housing and Urban Affairs.
Sasser, James R.	Dem	Tenn.	Feb. 11,1977	Moved to Budget and to Appropriations.
Allen, James B.	Dem	Ala.	Feb. 11,1977	Replaced Burdick.
Biden, Joseph R. Jr.	Dem	Del.	Feb. 11,1977	Replaced Riegle.
Culver, John C.	Dem	Iowa	Feb. 11,1977	Replaced Sasser.

McClellan, John L.	Dem	Ark.	Nov. 28,1977	Died in office.
Hatfield, Paul	Dem	Mont.	Jan. 27,1978	Replaced McClellan.
Allen, James B.	Dem	Ala.	June 1,1978	Died in office.
Allen, Maryon	Dem	Ala.	July 11,1978	Replaced James B. Allen.
Allen, Maryon	Dem	Ala.	Nov. 7,1978	Resigned; defeated for nomination in special election.
Hatfield, Paul	Dem	Mont.	Dec. 14,1978	Resigned; defeated for nomination in special election.
Eastland, James O.	Dem	Miss.	Dec. 27,1978	Resigned and retired.
Minority:				
Chafee, John H.	Rep	R.I.	Feb. 22,1977	Moved to Human Resources.
Heinz, H. John III	Rep	Penn.	Feb. 22,1977	Moved to Budget.
Laxalt, Paul	Rep	Nev.	Feb. 22,1977	Replaced Chafee.
Hatch, Orrin G.	Rep	Utah	Feb. 22,1977	Replaced Heinz.
Scott, William L.	Rep	Va.	Jan. 1,1979	Resigned and retired.

	Majority		Minority	
Departures from the Senate:				
Retired	Abourezk, James G.	S.D. Dem	None	
Departures from Committee:				
Moved to Finance; Energy & Natural Resources	None		Wallop, Malcolm	Wyo. Rep

JUDICIARY / 96th Congress

Service Dates of Committee Chair: Jan. 23,1979-Jan. 5,1981
Service Dates of Majority Members: Jan. 23,1979-Jan. 5,1981
Service Dates of Minority Members: Jan. 23,1979-Jan. 5,1981

Majority

Rank	Name	Party	State	Years in: Senate	Years in: Comm.
Chr	Kennedy, Edward M.	Dem	Mass.	17	16
2nd	Bayh, Birch E.	Dem	Ind.	17	16
3rd	Byrd, Robert C.	Dem	W.Va.	21	11
4th	Biden, Joseph R. Jr.	Dem	Del.	7	2
5th	Culver, John C.	Dem	Iowa	5	2
6th	Metzenbaum, Howard M.	Dem	Ohio	4	2
7th	DeConcini, Dennis	Dem	Ariz.	3	2
8th	Leahy, Patrick J.	Dem	Vt.	5	1
9th	Baucus, Max S.	Dem	Mont.	1	1
10th	Heflin, Howell T.	Dem	Ala.	1	1

Minority

Rank	Name	Party	State	Years in: Senate	Years in: Comm.
RM	Thurmond, J. Strom	Rep	S.C.	24	13
2nd	Mathias, Charles McC. Jr.	Rep	Md.	11	11
3rd	Laxalt, Paul	Rep	Nev.	5	2
4th	Hatch, Orrin G.	Rep	Utah	3	2
5th	Dole, Robert J.	Rep	Kans.	11	1
6th	Cochran, Thad	Rep	Miss.	1	1
7th	Simpson, Alan K.	Rep	Wyo.	1	1

	Majority		Minority	
Departures from the Senate:				
Defeated for Reelection	Bayh, Birch E.	Ind. Dem	None	
	Culver, John C.	Iowa Dem		
Departures from Committee:				
Moved to Appropriations	None		Cochran, Thad	Miss. Rep

JUDICIARY / 97th Congress

Service Dates of Committee Chair: Jan. 5,1981-Jan. 3,1983
Service Dates of Majority Members: Jan. 5,1981-Jan. 3,1983
Service Dates of Minority Members: Jan. 5,1981-Jan. 3,1983

Majority

Rank	Name	Party	State	Years in: Senate	Years in: Comm.
Chr	Thurmond, J. Strom	Rep	S.C.	26	14
2nd	Mathias, Charles McC. Jr.	Rep	Md.	13	12
3rd	Laxalt, Paul	Rep	Nev.	7	4
4th	Hatch, Orrin G.	Rep	Utah	5	4
5th	Dole, Robert J.	Rep	Kans.	13	2
6th	Simpson, Alan K.	Rep	Wyo.	3	2
7th	East, John P.	Rep	N.C.	1	1
8th	Grassley, Charles E.	Rep	Iowa	1	1
9th	Denton, Jeremiah	Rep	Ala.	1	1
10th	Specter, Arlen	Rep	Penn.	1	1

Minority

Rank	Name	Party	State	Years in: Senate	Years in: Comm.
RM	Biden, Joseph R. Jr.	Dem	Del.	9	4
2nd	Kennedy, Edward M.	Dem	Mass.	19	18
3rd	Byrd, Robert C.	Dem	W.Va.	23	12
4th	Metzenbaum, Howard M.	Dem	Ohio	6	4
5th	DeConcini, Dennis	Dem	Ariz.	5	4
6th	Leahy, Patrick J.	Dem	Vt.	7	2
7th	Baucus, Max S.	Dem	Mont.	3	2
8th	Heflin, Howell T.	Dem	Ala.	3	2

Note: Rankings on this committee for the following members were affected by other chamber service: Edward M. Kennedy (Dem-Mass.), Ranking Minority Member, Labor and Human Resources; and Robert C. Byrd (Dem-W.Va.), Senate Minority Leader.

JUDICIARY / 98th Congress

Service Dates of Committee Chair: Jan. 3,1983-Feb. 21,1985
Service Dates of Majority Members: Jan. 3,1983-Feb. 21,1985
Service Dates of Minority Members: Jan. 3,1983-Feb. 21,1985

Majority

Rank	Name	Party	State	Years in: Senate	Years in: Comm.
Chr	Thurmond, J. Strom	Rep	S.C.	28	16
2nd	Mathias, Charles McC. Jr.	Rep	Md.	15	14
3rd	Laxalt, Paul	Rep	Nev.	9	6
4th	Hatch, Orrin G.	Rep	Utah	7	6
5th	Dole, Robert J.	Rep	Kans.	15	4
6th	Simpson, Alan K.	Rep	Wyo.	5	4
7th	East, John P.	Rep	N.C.	3	2
8th	Grassley, Charles E.	Rep	Iowa	3	2
9th	Denton, Jeremiah	Rep	Ala.	3	2
10th	Specter, Arlen	Rep	Penn.	3	2

Minority

Rank	Name	Party	State	Years in: Senate	Years in: Comm.
RM	Biden, Joseph R. Jr.	Dem	Del.	11	6
2nd	Kennedy, Edward M.	Dem	Mass.	21	20
3rd	Byrd, Robert C.	Dem	W.Va.	25	14
4th	Metzenbaum, Howard M.	Dem	Ohio	8	6
5th	DeConcini, Dennis	Dem	Ariz.	7	6
6th	Leahy, Patrick J.	Dem	Vt.	9	4
7th	Baucus, Max S.	Dem	Mont.	5	4
8th	Heflin, Howell T.	Dem	Ala.	5	4

Note: Rankings on this committee for the following members were affected by other chamber service: Edward M. Kennedy (Dem-Mass.), Ranking Minority Member, Labor and Human Resources; and Robert C. Byrd (Dem-W.Va.), Senate Minority Leader.

Departures from Committee:

	Majority		Minority	
Became Senate Majority Leader	Dole, Robert J.	Kans. Rep	None	
No new assignment	None		Baucus, Max S.	Mont. Dem

JUDICIARY / 99th Congress

Service Dates of Committee Chair: Feb. 21,1985-Jan. 6,1987
Service Dates of Majority Members: Feb. 21,1985-Jan. 6,1987
Service Dates of Minority Members: Feb. 21,1985-Jan. 6,1987

Majority

Rank	Name	Party	State	Years in: Senate	Years in: Comm.
Chr	Thurmond, J. Strom	Rep	S.C.	30	19
2nd	Mathias, Charles McC. Jr.	Rep	Md.	17	17
3rd	Laxalt, Paul	Rep	Nev.	11	8
4th	Hatch, Orrin G.	Rep	Utah	9	8
5th	Simpson, Alan K.	Rep	Wyo.	7	7
6th	East, John P.	Rep	N.C.	5	5
7th	Grassley, Charles E.	Rep	Iowa	5	5
8th	Denton, Jeremiah	Rep	Ala.	5	5
9th	Specter, Arlen	Rep	Penn.	5	5
10th	McConnell, Mitch	Rep	Ky.	1	1

Minority

Rank	Name	Party	State	Years in: Senate	Years in: Comm.
RM	Biden, Joseph R. Jr.	Dem	Del.	13	9
2nd	Kennedy, Edward M.	Dem	Mass.	23	22
3rd	Byrd, Robert C.	Dem	W.Va.	27	17
4th	Metzenbaum, Howard M.	Dem	Ohio	10	9
5th	DeConcini, Dennis	Dem	Ariz.	9	9
6th	Leahy, Patrick J.	Dem	Vt.	11	7
7th	Heflin, Howell T.	Dem	Ala.	7	7
8th	Simon, Paul M.	Dem	Ill.	1	1

Note: Rankings on this committee for the following members were affected by other chamber service: Edward M. Kennedy (Dem-Mass.), Ranking Minority Member, Labor and Human Resources; and Robert C. Byrd (Dem-W.Va.), Senate Minority Leader.

Changes:

Majority:

East, John P.	Rep	N.C.	June 29,1986	Died in office.
Broyhill, James T.	Rep	N.C.	July 14,1986	Replaced East.
Broyhill, James T.	Rep	N.C.	Nov. 5,1986	Resigned; defeated for election.

Departures from the Senate:	Majority			Minority
Defeated for Reelection	Denton, Jeremiah	Ala.	Rep	None
Retired	Laxalt, Paul	Nev.	Rep	None
	Mathias, Charles McC. Jr.	Md.	Rep	
Departures from Committee:				
Moved to Foreign Relations	McConnell, Mitch	Ky.	Rep	None

JUDICIARY / 100th Congress

Service Dates of Committee Chair: Jan. 6,1987-Feb. 2,1989
Service Dates of Majority Members: Jan. 6,1987-Feb. 2,1989
Service Dates of Minority Members: Jan. 6,1987-Feb. 2,1989

Majority

Rank	Name	Party	State	Years in: Senate	Years in: Comm.
Chr	Biden, Joseph R. Jr.	Dem	Del.	15	10
2nd	Kennedy, Edward M.	Dem	Mass.	25	24
3rd	Byrd, Robert C.	Dem	W.Va.	29	18
4th	Metzenbaum, Howard M.	Dem	Ohio	12	10
5th	DeConcini, Dennis	Dem	Ariz.	11	10
6th	Leahy, Patrick J.	Dem	Vt.	13	8
7th	Heflin, Howell T.	Dem	Ala.	9	8
8th	Simon, Paul M.	Dem	Ill.	3	2

Minority

Rank	Name	Party	State	Years in: Senate	Years in: Comm.
RM	Thurmond, J. Strom	Rep	S.C.	32	20
2nd	Hatch, Orrin G.	Rep	Utah	11	10
3rd	Simpson, Alan K.	Rep	Wyo.	9	8
4th	Grassley, Charles E.	Rep	Iowa	7	7
5th	Specter, Arlen	Rep	Penn.	7	7
6th	Humphrey, Gordon J.	Rep	N.H.	9	1

Note: Rankings on this committee for the following members were affected by other chamber service: Edward M. Kennedy (Dem-Mass.), Chair, Labor and Human Resources; and Robert C. Byrd (Dem-W.Va.), Senate Majority Leader.

Departures from Committee:	Majority			Minority
Moved to Armed Services	Byrd, Robert C.	W.Va.	Dem	None

JUDICIARY / 101st Congress

Service Dates of Committee Chair: Feb. 2,1989-Feb. 5,1991
Service Dates of Majority Members: Feb. 2,1989-Feb. 5,1991
Service Dates of Minority Members: Feb. 2,1989-Feb. 5,1991

Majority

Rank	Name	Party	State	Years in: Senate	Years in: Comm.
Chr	Biden, Joseph R. Jr.	Dem	Del.	17	12
2nd	Kennedy, Edward M.	Dem	Mass.	27	26
3rd	Metzenbaum, Howard M.	Dem	Ohio	14	12
4th	DeConcini, Dennis	Dem	Ariz.	13	12
5th	Leahy, Patrick J.	Dem	Vt.	15	11
6th	Heflin, Howell T.	Dem	Ala.	11	11
7th	Simon, Paul M.	Dem	Ill.	5	4
8th	Kohl, Herbert	Dem	Wisc.	1	1

Minority:

Rank	Name	Party	State	Years in: Senate	Years in: Comm.
RM	Thurmond, J. Strom	Rep	S.C.	34	23
2nd	Hatch, Orrin G.	Rep	Utah	13	12
3rd	Simpson, Alan K.	Rep	Wyo.	11	11
4th	Grassley, Charles E.	Rep	Iowa	9	9
5th	Specter, Arlen	Rep	Penn.	9	9
6th	Humphrey, Gordon J.	Rep	N.H.	11	3

Note: Ranking on this committee for the following member was affected by other chamber service: Edward M. Kennedy (Dem-Mass.), Chair, Labor and Human Resources.

Departures from Senate	Majority	Minority		
Elected to State Senate	None	Humphrey, Gordon J.	N.H.	Rep

JUDICIARY / 102nd Congress

Service Dates of Committee Chair: Feb. 5,1991-Jan. 3,1993
Service Dates of Majority Members: Feb. 5,1991-Jan. 3,1993
Service Dates of Minority Members: Feb. 5,1991-Jan. 3,1993

Majority

Rank	Name	Party	State	Years in: Senate	Years in: Comm.
Chr	Biden, Joseph R. Jr.	Dem	Del.	19	14
2nd	Kennedy, Edward M.	Dem	Mass.	29	28
3rd	Metzenbaum, Howard M.	Dem	Ohio	16	14
4th	DeConcini, Dennis	Dem	Ariz.	15	14
5th	Leahy, Patrick J.	Dem	Vt.	17	13
6th	Heflin, Howell T.	Dem	Ala.	13	13
7th	Simon, Paul M.	Dem	Ill.	7	6
8th	Kohl, Herbert	Dem	Wisc.	3	3

Minority

Rank	Name	Party	State	Years in: Senate	Years in: Comm.
RM	Thurmond, J. Strom	Rep	S.C.	36	25
2nd	Hatch, Orrin G.	Rep	Utah	15	14
3rd	Simpson, Alan K.	Rep	Wyo.	13	13
4th	Grassley, Charles E.	Rep	Iowa	11	11
5th	Specter, Arlen	Rep	Penn.	11	11
6th	Brown, Hank	Rep	Colo.	1	1

Note: Ranking on this committee for the following member was affected by other chamber service: Edward M. Kennedy (Dem-Mass.), Chair, Labor and Human Resources.

LABOR AND HUMAN RESOURCES

LABOR AND PUBLIC WELFARE

Jurisdiction, 1947

Established by the Legislative Reorganization Act of 1946:

[Section 102.(1)(l)

(1) Committee on Labor and Public Welfare, to consist of thirteen Senators, to which committee shall be referred all proposed legislation, messages, petitions, memorials, and other matters relating to the following subjects:

1. Measures relating to education, labor, or public welfare generally.
2. Mediation and arbitration of labor disputes.
3. Wages and hours of labor.
4. Convict labor and the entry of goods made by convicts into interstate commerce.
5. Regulation or prevention of importation of foreign laborers under contract.
6. Child labor.
7. Labor statistics.
8. Labor standards.
9. School-lunch program.
10. Vocational rehabilitation.
11. Railroad labor and railroad retirement and unemployment, except revenue measures relating thereto.
12. United States Employees' Compensation Commission.
13. Columbia Institution for the Deaf, Dumb, and Blind; Howard University; Freedmen's Hospital; and Saint Elizabeth's Hospital.
14. Public health and quarantine.
15. Welfare of miners.
16. Vocational rehabilitation and education of veterans.
17. Veterans' hospitals, medical care and treatment of veterans.
18. Soldiers' and sailors' civil relief.
19. Readjustment of servicemen to civil life.

HUMAN RESOURCES

Reorganization, 1977

The Committee was reorganized as the Standing Committee on Human Resources following the passage of Senate Resolution 4, the Committee System Reorganization Amendments of 1977, February 4, 1977.

Jurisdiction, 1977

Jurisdiction contained in Senate Resolution 4, the Committee System Reorganization Amendments of 1977, February 4, 1977.

[Rule XXV.(1)(l)]

(1) Committee on Human Resources, to which committee shall be referred all proposed legislation, messages, petitions, memorials, and other matters relating to the following subjects:

1. Measures relating to education, labor, health, and public welfare.
2. Labor standards and labor statistics.
3. Wages and hours of labor.
4. Child labor.
5. Mediation and arbitration of labor disputes

6. Convict labor and the entry of goods made by convicts into interstate commerce.
7. Regulation of foreign laborers.
8. Handicapped individuals.
9. Equal employment opportunity.
10. Occupational safety and health, including the welfare of miners.
11. Private pension plans.
12. Aging.
13. Railway labor and retirement.
14. Public health.
15 Arts and humanities.
16. Gallaudet College, Howard University, and Saint Elizabeth's Hospital.
17. Biomedical research and development.
18. Student loans.
19. Agricultural colleges.
20. Domestic activities of the American National Red Cross.

(2) Such committee shall also study and review, on a comprehensive basis, matters relating to health, education and training, and public welfare, and report thereon from time to time.

LABOR AND HUMAN RESOURCES

The Committee was renamed the Committee on Labor and Human Resources on March 7, 1979.

Jurisdiction, 1992

Jurisdiction as contained in the Standing Rules of the Senate (as revised to March 18, 1992):

[Rule (1)(m)]

(1) Committee on Labor and Human Resources, to which committee shall be referred all proposed legislation, messages, petitions, memorials, and other matters relating to the following subjects:

1. Measures relating to education, labor, health, and public welfare.
2. Aging.
3. Agricultural colleges.
4. Arts and humanities.
5. Biomedical research and development.
6. Child labor.
7. Convict labor and the entry of goods made by convicts into interstate commerce.
8. Domestic activities of the American National Red Cross.
9. Equal employment opportunity.
10. Gallaudet College, Howard University, and Saint Elizabeth's Hospital.
11. Handicapped individuals.
12. Labor standards and labor statistics.
13. Mediation and arbitration of labor disputes.
14. Occupational safety and health, including the welfare of miners.
15. Private pension plans.
16. Public health.
17. Railway labor and retirement.
18. Regulation of foreign laborers.
19. Student loans.
20. Wages and hours of labor.

(2) Such committee shall also study and review, on a comprehensive basis, matters relating to health, education and training, and public welfare, and report thereon from time to time.

LABOR AND PUBLIC WELFARE / 80th Congress

Service Dates of Committee Chair: Jan. 6,1947-Jan. 10,1949
Service Dates of Majority Members: Jan. 6,1947-Jan. 10,1949
Service Dates of Minority Members: Jan. 8,1947-Jan. 10,1949

Majority

Rank	Name	Party	State	Years in: Senate	Years in: Comm.
Chr	Taft, Robert A.	Rep	Ohio	9	8
2nd	Aiken, George D.	Rep	Vt.	6	6
3rd	Ball, Joseph H.	Rep	Minn.	7	*2 4
4th	Smith, H. Alexander	Rep	N.J.	3	2
5th	Morse, Wayne L.	Rep	Ore.	3	*1 2
6th	Donnell, Forrest C.	Rep	Mo.	3	2
7th	Jenner, William E.	Rep	Ind.	1	*2 1
8th	Ives, Irving M.	Rep	N.Y.	1	*1 1

Minority

Rank	Name	Party	State	Years in: Senate	Years in: Comm.
RM	Thomas, Elbert D.	Dem	Utah	14	14
2nd	Murray, James E.	Dem	Mont.	13	13
3rd	Pepper, Claude D.	Dem	Fla.	11	11
4th	Ellender, Allen J.	Dem	La.	11	11
5th	Hill, J. Lister	Dem	Ala.	9	9

*1: Member's 1st period of service on the committee; *2: Member's 2nd period of service on the committee.

	Majority			Minority		
Departures from the Senate:						
Defeated for Reelection	Ball, Joseph H.	Minn.	Rep	None		
Departures from Committee:						
Moved to Banking & Currency	Ives, Irving M.	N.Y.	Rep	None		
Moved to Judiciary	Jenner, William E.	Ind.	Rep	None		
Moved to Appropriations	None			Ellender, Allen J.	La.	Dem

LABOR AND PUBLIC WELFARE / 81st Congress

Service Dates of Committee Chair: Jan. 10,1949-Jan. 3,1951
Service Dates of Majority Members: Jan. 10,1949-Jan. 15,1951
Service Dates of Minority Members: Jan. 10,1949-Jan. 15,1951

Majority

Rank	Name	Party	State	Years in: Senate	Years in: Comm.
Chr	Thomas, Elbert D.	Dem	Utah	16	16
2nd	Murray, James E.	Dem	Mont.	15	15
3rd	Pepper, Claude D.	Dem	Fla.	13	13
4th	Hill, J. Lister	Dem	Ala.	11	11
5th	Neely, Matthew M.	Dem	W.Va.	17	*2 1
6th	Douglas, Paul H.	Dem	Ill.	1	1
7th	Humphrey, Hubert H. Jr.	DFL	Minn.	1	1
8th	Withers, Garrett L.	Dem	Ky.	1	1

Minority

Rank	Name	Party	State	Years in: Senate	Years in: Comm.
RM	Taft, Robert A.	Rep	Ohio	11	11
2nd	Aiken, George D.	Rep	Vt.	9	8
3rd	Smith, H. Alexander	Rep	N.J.	5	5
4th	Morse, Wayne L.	Rep	Ore.	5	*1 5
5th	Donnell, Forrest C.	Rep	Mo.	5	5

*1: Member's 1st period of service on the committee; *2: Member's 2nd period of service on the committee.

Vacancy Filled:
Majority: 8th seat by Withers on January 24,1949.

Changes:
Majority:

Withers, Garrett L.	Dem	Ky.	Jan. 12,1950	Moved to Judiciary.
Lehman, Herbert H.	Dem	N.Y.	Jan. 12,1950	Replaced Withers.

	Majority			Minority		
Departures from the Senate:						
Defeated for Reelection	Thomas, Elbert D.	Utah	Dem	Donnell, Forrest C.	Mo.	Rep
Defeated for Renomination	Pepper, Claude D.	Fla.	Dem	None		

LABOR AND PUBLIC WELFARE / 82nd Congress

Service Dates of Committee Chair: Jan. 15,1951-Jan. 13,1953
Service Dates of Majority Members: Jan. 15,1951-Jan. 13,1953
Service Dates of Minority Members: Jan. 15,1951-Jan. 13,1953

Majority

Rank Name	Party	State	Years in: Senate	Comm.
Chr Murray, James E.	Dem	Mont.	17	17
2nd Hill, J. Lister	Dem	Ala.	14	13
3rd Neely, Matthew M.	Dem	W.Va.	19	*2 3
4th Douglas, Paul H.	Dem	Ill.	3	3
5th Humphrey, Hubert H. Jr.	DFL	Minn.	3	3
6th Lehman, Herbert H.	Dem	N.Y.	2	2
7th Pastore, John O.	Dem	R.I.	1	1

Minority

Rank Name	Party	State	Years in: Senate	Comm.
RM Taft, Robert A.	Rep	Ohio	13	13
2nd Aiken, George D.	Rep	Vt.	11	10
3rd Smith, H. Alexander	Rep	N.J.	7	7
4th Morse, Wayne L.	Rep	Ore.	7	*1 7
5th Ives, Irving M.	Rep	N.Y.	5	*2 1
6th Nixon, Richard M.	Rep	Cal.	1	1

*1: Member's 1st period of service on the committee; *2: Member's 2nd period of service on the committee.

Note: Wayne Morse of Oregon resigned from the Republican Party to become an Independent on Oct. 24,1952, after the adjournment of the 82nd Congress. He was not assigned to any committees in the 83rd Congress until May 25,1953.

Changes:

Minority:

Nixon, Richard M.	Rep	Cal.	Jan. 1,1953	Resigned; elected Vice President.

Departures from Committee:

	Majority		Minority	
Moved to Government Operations; Foreign Relations	Humphrey, Hubert H. Jr.	Minn. DFL	None	
Moved to Interstate & Foreign Commerce	Pastore, John O.	R.I. Dem	None	
Resigned Republican Party; lost minority assignments	None		Morse, Wayne L.	Ore. Rep

LABOR AND PUBLIC WELFARE / 83rd Congress

Service Dates of Committee Chair: Jan. 13,1953-Jan. 11,1955
Service Dates of Majority Members: Jan. 13,1953-Jan. 11,1955
Service Dates of Minority Members: Jan. 13,1953-Jan. 11,1955

Majority

Rank Name	Party	State	Years in: Senate	Comm.
Chr Smith, H. Alexander	Rep	N.J.	9	9
2nd Taft, Robert A.	Rep	Ohio	15	15
3rd Aiken, George D.	Rep	Vt.	13	12
4th Ives, Irving M.	Rep	N.Y.	7	*2 2
5th Purtell, William A.	Rep	Conn.	1	1
6th Barrett, Frank A.	Rep	Wyo.	1	1
7th Goldwater, Barry M.	Rep	Ariz.	1	1

Minority

Rank Name	Party	State	Years in: Senate	Comm.
RM Murray, James E.	Dem	Mont.	19	19
2nd Hill, J. Lister	Dem	Ala.	16	15
3rd Neely, Matthew M.	Dem	W.Va.	21	*2 5
4th Douglas, Paul H.	Dem	Ill.	5	5
5th Lehman, Herbert H.	Dem	N.Y.	4	4
6th Kennedy, John F.	Dem	Mass.	1	1

*2: Member's 2nd period of service on the committee.

Note: Rankings on this committee for the following members were affected by other chamber service: Robert A. Taft (Rep-Ohio), Senate Majority Leader; and George D. Aiken (Rep-Vt.), Chair, Agriculture and Forestry.

Changes:

Majority:

Barrett, Frank A.	Rep	Wyo.	Jan. 21,1953	Moved to Rules and Administration.
Griswold, Dwight P.	Rep	Neb.	Jan. 21,1953	Replaced Barrett; ranked 5th.
Taft, Robert A.	Rep	Ohio	July 31,1953	Died in office.
Aiken, George D.	Rep	Vt.	Jan. 13,1954	Moved to Foreign Relations.
Cooper, John Sherman	Rep	Ky.	Jan. 13,1954	Replaced Taft.
Upton, Robert W.	Rep	N.H.	Jan. 13,1954	Replaced Aiken.

Griswold, Dwight P.	Rep	Neb.	Apr. 12,1954	Died in office.
Bowring, Eva K.	Rep	Neb.	May 3,1954	Replaced Griswold.
Upton, Robert W.	Rep	N.H.	Nov. 7,1954	Resigned; defeated for nomination.
Bowring, Eva K.	Rep	Neb.	Nov. 7,1954	Resigned and retired.
Cotton, Norris	Rep	N.H.	Nov. 30,1954	Replaced Upton.
Hruska, Roman L.	Rep	Neb.	Nov. 30,1954	Replaced Bowring.
Cotton, Norris	Rep	N.H.	Dec. 1,1954	Moved to Public Works.
Brown, Ernest S.	Rep	Nev.	Dec. 1,1954	Replaced Cotton.
Brown, Ernest S.	Rep	Nev.	Dec. 1,1954	Resigned; defeated in special election.

	Majority			Minority:
Departures from the Senate:				
Defeated for Reelection	Cooper, John Sherman	Ky.	Rep	None
Departures from Committee:				
Moved to District of Columbia; Public Works	Hruska, Roman L.	Neb.	Rep	None

LABOR AND PUBLIC WELFARE / 84th Congress

Service Dates of Committee Chair: Jan. 11,1955-Jan. 9,1957
Service Dates of Majority Members: Jan. 11,1955-Jan. 9,1957
Service Dates of Minority Members: Jan. 11,1955-Jan. 9,1957

Majority

Rank	Name	Party	State	Years in: Senate	Years in: Comm.
Chr	Hill, J. Lister	Dem	Ala.	18	17
2nd	Murray, James E.	Dem	Mont.	21	21
3rd	Neely, Matthew M.	Dem	W.Va.	23	*2 7
4th	Douglas, Paul H.	Dem	Ill.	7	7
5th	Lehman, Herbert H.	Dem	N.Y.	6	5
6th	Kennedy, John F.	Dem	Mass.	3	2
7th	McNamara, Patrick V.	Dem	Mich.	1	1

Minority

Rank	Name	Party	State	Years in: Senate	Years in: Comm.
RM	Smith, H. Alexander	Rep	N.J.	11	11
2nd	Ives, Irving M.	Rep	N.Y.	9	*2 4
3rd	Purtell, William A.	Rep	Conn.	3	2
4th	Goldwater, Barry M.	Rep	Ariz.	3	2
5th	Bender, George H.	Rep	Ohio	1	1
6th	Allott, Gordon L.	Rep	Colo.	1	1

*2: Member's 2nd period of service on the committee.

Note: Ranking on this committee for the following member was affected by other chamber service: James E. Murray (Dem-Mont.), Chair, Interior and Insular Affairs.

Changes:
Majority:

Douglas, Paul H.	Dem	Ill.	May 18,1956	Moved to Finance.
Humphreys, Robert	Dem	Ky.	June 28,1956	Replaced Douglas.
Humphreys, Robert	Dem	Ky.	Nov. 6,1956	Resigned and retired.

Departures from the Senate:	Majority			Minority		
Defeated for Reelection	None			Bender, George H.	Ohio	Rep
Retired	Lehman, Herbert H.	N.Y.	Dem	None		

LABOR AND PUBLIC WELFARE / 85th Congress

Service Dates of Committee Chair: Jan. 9,1957-Jan. 14,1959
Service Dates of Majority Members: Jan. 9,1957-Jan. 14,1959
Service Dates of Minority Members: Jan. 9,1957-Jan. 20,1959

Majority

Rank	Name	Party	State	Years in: Senate	Years in: Comm.
Chr	Hill, J. Lister	Dem	Ala.	19	19
2nd	Murray, James E.	Dem	Mont.	23	23
3rd	Neely, Matthew M.	Dem	W.Va.	25	*2 8
4th	Kennedy, John F.	Dem	Mass.	5	4
5th	McNamara, Patrick V.	Dem	Mich.	3	2
6th	Morse, Wayne L.	Dem	Ore.	13	*2 1
7th	Thurmond, J. Strom	Dem	S.C.	2	*1 1

Minority

Rank	Name	Party	State	Years in: Senate	Years in: Comm.
RM	Smith, H. Alexander	Rep	N.J.	13	12
2nd	Ives, Irving M.	Rep	N.Y.	11	*2 6
3rd	Purtell, William A.	Rep	Conn.	5	4
4th	Goldwater, Barry M.	Rep	Ariz.	5	4
5th	Allott, Gordon L.	Rep	Colo.	3	2
6th	Cooper, John Sherman	Rep	Ky.	5	*2 1

*2: Member's 2nd period of service on the committee.

Note: Ranking on this committee for the following member was affected by other chamber service: James E. Murray (Dem-Mont.), Chair, Interior and Insular Affairs.

Changes:

Majority:

Neely, Matthew M.	Dem	W.Va.	Jan. 18,1958	Died in office.
Yarborough, Ralph W.	Dem	Tex.	Jan. 30,1958	Replaced Neely.

	Majority			Minority		
Departures from the Senate:						
Defeated for Reelection	None			Purtell, William A.	Conn.	Rep
Retired	None			Ives, Irving M.	N.Y.	Rep
				Smith, H. Alexander	N.J.	Rep
Departures from Committee:						
Moved to Armed Services	Thurmond, J. Strom	S.C.	Dem	None		
Moved to Appropriations	None			Allott, Gordon L.	Colo.	Rep

LABOR AND PUBLIC WELFARE / 86th Congress

Service Dates of Committee Chair: Jan. 14,1959-Jan. 10,1961
Service Dates of Majority Members: Jan. 14,1959-Jan. 10,1961
Service Dates of Minority Members: Jan. 20,1959-Jan. 13,1961

Majority

Rank	Name	Party	State	Years in: Senate	Years in: Comm.
Chr	Hill, J. Lister	Dem	Ala.	22	21
2nd	Murray, James E.	Dem	Mont.	25	25
3rd	Kennedy, John F.	Dem	Mass.	7	7
4th	McNamara, Patrick V.	Dem	Mich.	5	5
5th	Morse, Wayne L.	Dem	Ore.	15	*2 3
6th	Yarborough, Ralph W.	Dem	Tex.	2	1
7th	Clark, Joseph S.	Dem	Penn.	3	1
8th	Randolph, Jennings	Dem	W.Va.	1	1
9th	Williams, Harrison A. Jr.	Dem	N.J.	1	1

Minority

Rank	Name	Party	State	Years in: Senate	Years in: Comm.
RM	Goldwater, Barry M.	Rep	Ariz.	7	7
2nd	Cooper, John Sherman	Rep	Ky.	7	*2 3
3rd	Dirksen, Everett M.	Rep	Ill.	9	1
4th	Case, Clifford P.	Rep	N.J.	5	1
5th	Javits, Jacob K.	Rep	N.Y.	3	1
6th	Prouty, Winston L.	Rep	Vt.	1	1

*2: Member's 2nd period of service on the committee.

Notes: Appointed Senator C. Norman Brunsdale (Rep-N.D.) left the Senate upon the seating of Quentin Burdick (Dem-N.D.), who won the special election to fill the vacancy caused by the death of William Langer. Burdick's seating on Aug. 8,1960 led to a change in size and party ratio on this committee to 10 Democrats and 5 Republicans on Aug. 24,1960. Ranking on this committee for the following member was affected by other chamber service: James E. Murray (Dem-Mont.), Chair, Interior and Insular Affairs.

Addition:

Majority: 10th Burdick, Quentin N. Dem N.D. Aug. 24,1960

Changes:

Majority:

Kennedy, John F.	Dem	Mass.	Dec. 22,1960	Resigned; elected President.

Minority:

Cooper, John Sherman	Rep	Ky.	Jan. 18,1960	Moved to Agriculture and Forestry.
Brunsdale, C. Norman	Rep	N.D.	Jan. 18,1960	Replaced Cooper.
Brunsdale, C. Norman	Rep	N.D.	Aug. 7,1960	Resigned and retired.

Departures from the Senate:	Majority			Minority
Retired	Murray, James E.	Mont.	Dem	None

LABOR AND PUBLIC WELFARE / 87th Congress

Service Dates of Committee Chair: Jan. 10,1961-Feb. 25,1963
Service Dates of Majority Members: Jan. 10,1961-Feb. 25,1963
Service Dates of Minority Members: Jan. 13,1961-Feb. 25,1963

Majority

Rank	Name	Party	State	Years in: Senate	Years in: Comm.
Chr	Hill, J. Lister	Dem	Ala.	23	23
2nd	McNamara, Patrick V.	Dem	Mich.	7	6
3rd	Morse, Wayne L.	Dem	Ore.	17	*2 5
4th	Yarborough, Ralph W.	Dem	Tex.	4	3
5th	Clark, Joseph S.	Dem	Penn.	5	2
6th	Randolph, Jennings	Dem	W.Va.	3	2
7th	Williams, Harrison A. Jr.	Dem	N.J.	3	2
8th	Burdick, Quentin N.	Dem	N.D.	1	1
9th	Smith, Benjamin A. II	Dem	Mass.	1	1
10th	Pell, Claiborne D.	Dem	R.I.	1	1

Minority

Rank	Name	Party	State	Years in: Senate	Years in: Comm.
RM	Goldwater, Barry M.	Rep	Ariz.	9	9
2nd	Dirksen, Everett M.	Rep	Ill.	11	2
3rd	Case, Clifford P.	Rep	N.J.	7	2
4th	Javits, Jacob K.	Rep	N.Y.	5	2
5th	Prouty, Winston L.	Rep	Vt.	3	2

*2: Member's 2nd period of service on the committee.

Changes:

Majority:

Smith, Benjamin A. II	Dem	Mass.	Nov. 6,1962	Resigned and retired.

Minority:

Dirksen, Everett M.	Rep	Ill.	July 11,1961	Moved to Interior and Insular Affairs.
Tower, John G.	Rep	Tex.	July 11,1961	Replaced Dirksen.
Case, Clifford P.	Rep	N.J.	Feb. 2,1962	Moved to Appropriations.
Murphy, Maurice J. Jr.	Rep	N.H.	Feb. 2,1962	Replaced Case.
Murphy, Maurice J. Jr.	Rep	N.H.	Aug. 8,1962	Moved to Banking and Currency.
Jordan, Len B.	Rep	Ida.	Aug. 8,1962	Replaced Murphy.

LABOR AND PUBLIC WELFARE / 88th Congress

Service Dates of Committee Chair: Feb. 25,1963-Jan. 8,1965
Service Dates of Majority Members: Feb. 25,1963-Jan. 8,1965
Service Dates of Minority Members: Feb. 25,1963-Jan. 15,1965

Majority

Rank	Name	Party	State	Years in: Senate	Years in: Comm.
Chr	Hill, J. Lister	Dem	Ala.	26	26
2nd	McNamara, Patrick V.	Dem	Mich.	9	9
3rd	Morse, Wayne L.	Dem	Ore.	19	*2 7
4th	Yarborough, Ralph W.	Dem	Tex.	6	6
5th	Clark, Joseph S.	Dem	Penn.	7	5
6th	Randolph, Jennings	Dem	W.Va.	5	5
7th	Williams, Harrison A. Jr.	Dem	N.J.	5	5
8th	Burdick, Quentin N.	Dem	N.D.	3	3
9th	Pell, Claiborne D.	Dem	R.I.	3	3
10th	Kennedy, Edward M.	Dem	Mass.	1	1

Minority

Rank	Name	Party	State	Years in: Senate	Years in: Comm.
RM	Goldwater, Barry M.	Rep	Ariz.	11	11
2nd	Javits, Jacob K.	Rep	N.Y.	7	5
3rd	Prouty, Winston L.	Rep	Vt.	5	5
4th	Tower, John G.	Rep	Tex.	2	2
5th	Jordan, Len B.	Rep	Ida.	1	1

*2: Member's 2nd period of service on the committee.

Changes:

Majority:

Burdick, Quentin N.	Dem	N.D.	Aug. 23,1963	Moved to Judiciary.
Metcalf, Lee	Dem	Mont.	Aug. 23,1963	Replaced Burdick.

	Majority		Minority	
Departures from the Senate:				
Lost Election for President	None		Goldwater, Barry M.	Ariz. Rep
Departures from Committee:				
Moved to Interior & Insular Affairs	Metcalf, Lee	Mont. Dem	None	
Moved to Aeronautical & Space Sciences	None		Jordan, Len B.	Ida. Rep
Moved to Armed Services	None		Tower, John G.	Tex. Rep

LABOR AND PUBLIC WELFARE / 89th Congress

Service Dates of Committee Chair: Jan. 8,1965-Jan. 11,1967
Service Dates of Majority Members: Jan. 8,1965-Jan. 11,1967
Service Dates of Minority Members: Jan. 15,1965-Jan. 16,1967

Majority

Rank	Name	Party	State	Years in: Senate	Years in: Comm.
Chr	Hill, J. Lister	Dem	Ala.	27	27
2nd	McNamara, Patrick V.	Dem	Mich.	11	10
3rd	Morse, Wayne L.	Dem	Ore.	21	*2 8
4th	Yarborough, Ralph W.	Dem	Tex.	8	7
5th	Clark, Joseph S.	Dem	Penn.	9	6
6th	Randolph, Jennings	Dem	W.Va.	7	6
7th	Williams, Harrison A. Jr.	Dem	N.J.	7	6
8th	Pell, Claiborne D.	Dem	R.I.	5	4
9th	Kennedy, Edward M.	Dem	Mass.	3	2
10th	Nelson, Gaylord A.	Dem	Wisc.	3	1
11th	Kennedy, Robert F.	Dem	N.Y.	1	1

Minority

Rank	Name	Party	State	Years in: Senate	Years in: Comm.
RM	Javits, Jacob K.	Rep	N.Y.	9	6
2nd	Prouty, Winston L.	Rep	Vt.	7	6
3rd	Dominick, Peter H.	Rep	Colo.	3	1
4th	Murphy, George L.	Rep	Cal.	1	1
5th	Fannin, Paul J.	Rep	Ariz.	1	1

*2: Member's 2nd period of service on the committee.

Note: The death of Patrick V. McNamara (Dem-Mich.) and the appointment of Robert P. Griffin (Rep-Mich.) to fill his vacancy on May 11,1966 led to a change in size and party ratio on this committee to 10 Democrats and 6 Republicans on May 17,1966.

Addition:
Minority: 6th Griffin, Robert P. Rep Mich. May 17,1966

Changes:
Majority:
McNamara, Patrick V. Dem Mich. Apr. 30,1966 Died in office.

LABOR AND PUBLIC WELFARE / 90th Congress

Service Dates of Committee Chair: Jan. 11,1967-Jan. 3,1969
Service Dates of Majority Members: Jan. 11,1967-Jan. 14,1969
Service Dates of Minority Members: Jan. 16,1967-Jan. 14,1969

Majority

Rank	Name	Party	State	Years in: Senate	Years in: Comm.
Chr	Hill, J. Lister	Dem	Ala.	30	29
2nd	Morse, Wayne L.	Dem	Ore.	23	*2 11
3rd	Yarborough, Ralph W.	Dem	Tex.	10	9
4th	Clark, Joseph S.	Dem	Penn.	11	8
5th	Randolph, Jennings	Dem	W.Va.	9	8
6th	Williams, Harrison A. Jr.	Dem	N.J.	9	8
7th	Pell, Claiborne D.	Dem	R.I.	7	7
8th	Kennedy, Edward M.	Dem	Mass.	5	4
9th	Nelson, Gaylord A.	Dem	Wisc.	5	3
10th	Kennedy, Robert F.	Dem	N.Y.	3	3

Minority

Rank	Name	Party	State	Years in: Senate	Years in: Comm.
RM	Javits, Jacob K.	Rep	N.Y.	11	8
2nd	Prouty, Winston L.	Rep	Vt.	9	8
3rd	Dominick, Peter H.	Rep	Colo.	5	3
4th	Murphy, George L.	Rep	Cal.	3	3
5th	Fannin, Paul J.	Rep	Ariz.	3	3
6th	Griffin, Robert P.	Rep	Mich.	1	1

*2: Member's 2nd period of service on the committee.

Changes:
Majority:
Kennedy, Robert F. Dem N.Y. June 6,1968 Died in office.
Mondale, Walter F. DFL Minn. June 25,1968 Replaced Kennedy.

	Majority		Minority	
Departures from the Senate:				
Defeated for Reelection	Clark, Joseph S.	Penn. Dem	None	
	Morse, Wayne L.	Ore. Dem		
Retired	Hill, J. Lister	Ala. Dem	None	
Departures from Committee:				
Moved to Finance	None		Fannin, Paul J.	Ariz. Rep
Moved to Government Operations	None		Griffin, Robert P.	Mich. Rep

LABOR AND PUBLIC WELFARE / 91st Congress

Service Dates of Committee Chair: Jan. 14,1969-Jan. 3,1971
Service Dates of Majority Members: Jan. 14,1969-Jan. 28,1971
Service Dates of Minority Members: Jan. 14,1969-Jan. 29,1971

Majority

Rank	Name	Party	State	Years in: Senate	Years in: Comm.
Chr	Yarborough, Ralph W.	Dem	Tex.	12	11
2nd	Randolph, Jennings	Dem	W.Va.	11	11
3rd	Williams, Harrison A. Jr.	Dem	N.J.	11	11
4th	Pell, Claiborne D.	Dem	R.I.	9	9
5th	Kennedy, Edward M.	Dem	Mass.	7	6
6th	Nelson, Gaylord A.	Dem	Wisc.	7	5
7th	Mondale, Walter F.	DFL	Minn.	5	1
8th	Eagleton, Thomas F.	Dem	Mo.	1	1
9th	Cranston, Alan	Dem	Cal.	1	1
10th	Hughes, Harold E.	Dem	Iowa	1	1

Minority

Rank	Name	Party	State	Years in: Senate	Years in: Comm.
RM	Javits, Jacob K.	Rep	N.Y.	13	10
2nd	Prouty, Winston L.	Rep	Vt.	11	10
3rd	Dominick, Peter H.	Rep	Colo.	7	4
4th	Murphy, George L.	Rep	Cal.	5	4
5th	Schweiker, Richard S.	Rep	Penn.	1	1
6th	Bellmon, Henry	Rep	Okla.	1	1
7th	Saxbe, William B.	Rep	Ohio	1	1

Note: Appointed Senator Ralph Tyler Smith (Rep-Ill.) lost in a special election to Adlai Stevenson (Dem-Ill.) resulting in a change in size and party ratio on this committee to 11 Democrats and 6 Republicans on Nov. 17,1970.

Addition:
Majority: 11th Stevenson, Adlai E. III — Dem — Ill. — Nov. 17,1970

Changes:
Minority:

Name	Party	State	Date	Change
Bellmon, Henry A.	Rep	Okla.	Sep. 17,1969	Moved to Agriculture and Forestry.
Smith, Ralph Tyler	Rep	Ill.	Sep. 18,1969	Replaced Bellmon.
Smith, Ralph Tyler	Rep	Ill.	Nov. 16,1970	Resigned; lost special election.
Murphy, George L.	Rep	Cal.	Jan. 2,1971	Resigned; defeated for reelection.

	Majority	Minority:
Departures from the Senate:		
Defeated for Renomination	Yarborough, Ralph W. Tex. Dem	None
Departures from Committee:		
Moved to Government Operations; Armed Services	None	Saxbe, William B. Ohio Rep

LABOR AND PUBLIC WELFARE / 92nd Congress

Service Dates of Committee Chair: Jan. 28,1971-Jan. 4,1973
Service Dates of Majority Members: Jan. 28,1971-Jan. 4,1973
Service Dates of Minority Members: Jan. 29,1971-Jan. 12,1973

Majority

Rank	Name	Party	State	Years in: Senate	Years in: Comm.
Chr	Williams, Harrison A. Jr.	Dem	N.J.	13	13
2nd	Randolph, Jennings	Dem	W.Va.	13	13
3rd	Pell, Claiborne D.	Dem	R.I.	11	11
4th	Kennedy, Edward M.	Dem	Mass.	9	8
5th	Nelson, Gaylord A.	Dem	Wisc.	9	7
6th	Mondale, Walter F.	DFL	Minn.	7	3
7th	Eagleton, Thomas F.	Dem	Mo.	3	3
8th	Cranston, Alan	Dem	Cal.	3	3
9th	Hughes, Harold E.	Dem	Iowa	3	3
10th	Stevenson, Adlai E. III	Dem	Ill.	1	1

Minority

Rank	Name	Party	State	Years in: Senate	Years in: Comm.
RM	Javits, Jacob K.	Rep	N.Y.	15	13
2nd	Prouty, Winston L.	Rep	Vt.	13	13
3rd	Dominick, Peter H.	Rep	Colo.	9	7
4th	Schweiker, Richard S.	Rep	Penn.	3	3
5th	Packwood, Robert W.	Rep	Ore.	3	1
6th	Taft, Robert Jr.	Rep	Ohio	1	1
7th	Beall, J. Glenn Jr.	Rep	Md.	1	1

Note: Ranking on this committee for the following member was affected by other chamber service: Jennings Randolph (Dem-W.Va.), Chair, Public Works.

Changes:
Minority:

Prouty, Winston L.	Rep	Vt.	Sep. 10,1971	Died in office.
Stafford, Robert T.	Rep	Vt.	Sep. 21,1971	Replaced Prouty.

Departures from Committee:	Majority		Minority		
Moved to Finance	None		Packwood, Robert W.	Ore.	Rep

LABOR AND PUBLIC WELFARE / 93rd Congress

Service Dates of Committee Chair: Jan. 4,1973-Jan. 17,1975
Service Dates of Majority Members: Jan. 4,1973-Jan. 17,1975
Service Dates of Minority Members: Jan. 12,1973-Jan. 23,1975

Majority

Rank	Name	Party	State	Years in: Senate	Years in: Comm.
Chr	Williams, Harrison A. Jr.	Dem	N.J.	15	14
2nd	Randolph, Jennings	Dem	W.Va.	15	14
3rd	Pell, Claiborne D.	Dem	R.I.	13	12
4th	Kennedy, Edward M.	Dem	Mass.	11	10
5th	Nelson, Gaylord A.	Dem	Wisc.	10	8
6th	Mondale, Walter F.	DFL	Minn.	9	5
7th	Eagleton, Thomas F.	Dem	Mo.	5	4
8th	Cranston, Alan	Dem	Cal.	5	4
9th	Hughes, Harold E.	Dem	Iowa	5	4
10th	Stevenson, Adlai E. III	Dem	Ill.	3	3

Minority

Rank	Name	Party	State	Years in: Senate	Years in: Comm.
RM	Javits, Jacob K.	Rep	N.Y.	17	14
2nd	Dominick, Peter H.	Rep	Colo.	11	8
3rd	Schweiker, Richard S.	Rep	Penn.	5	4
4th	Taft, Robert Jr.	Rep	Ohio	3	2
5th	Beall, J. Glenn Jr.	Rep	Md.	3	2
6th	Stafford, Robert T.	Rep	Vt.	2	2

Note: Ranking on this committee for the following member was affected by other chamber service: Jennings Randolph (Dem-W.Va.), Chair, Public Works.

Changes:
Majority:

Stevenson, Adlai E. III	Dem	Ill.	Jan. 11,1973	Moved to Commerce.
Hathaway, William D.	Dem	Me.	Jan. 11,1973	Replaced Stevenson.

Departures from the Senate:	Majority			Minority		
Defeated for Reelection	None			Dominick, Peter H.	Colo.	Rep
Retired	Hughes, Harold E.	Iowa	Dem	None		

LABOR AND PUBLIC WELFARE / 94th Congress

Service Dates of Committee Chair: Jan. 17,1975-Jan. 10,1977
Service Dates of Majority Members: Jan. 17,1975-Jan. 10,1977
Service Dates of Minority Members: Jan. 23,1975-Jan. 10,1977

Majority

Rank	Name	Party	State	Years in: Senate	Years in: Comm.
Chr	Williams, Harrison A. Jr.	Dem	N.J.	17	17
2nd	Randolph, Jennings	Dem	W.Va.	17	17
3rd	Pell, Claiborne D.	Dem	R.I.	15	15
4th	Kennedy, Edward M.	Dem	Mass.	13	12
5th	Nelson, Gaylord A.	Dem	Wisc.	13	11
6th	Mondale, Walter F.	DFL	Minn.	11	7
7th	Eagleton, Thomas F.	Dem	Mo.	7	7
8th	Cranston, Alan	Dem	Cal.	7	7
9th	Hathaway, William D.	Dem	Me.	3	3

Minority

Rank	Name	Party	State	Years in: Senate	Years in: Comm.
RM	Javits, Jacob K.	Rep	N.Y.	19	17
2nd	Schweiker, Richard S.	Rep	Penn.	7	7
3rd	Taft, Robert Jr.	Rep	Ohio	5	4
4th	Beall, J. Glenn Jr.	Rep	Md.	5	4
5th	Stafford, Robert T.	Rep	Vt.	4	4
6th	Laxalt, Paul	Rep	Nev.	1	1

Notes: Norris Cotton (Rep-N.H.), appointed to fill a vacancy caused by the contested election between John Durkin (Dem) and Louis Wyman (Rep), left the Senate upon the victory of Durkin on Sep. 19,1975, resulting in a change in size and party ratio on this committee to 10 Democrats and 6 Republicans. Ranking on this committee for the following member was affected by other chamber service: Jennings Randolph (Dem-W.Va.), Chair, Public Works.

Addition:
Majority: 10th Durkin, John A. Dem N.H. Sep. 19,1975

Changes:
Majority:

Mondale, Walter F.	DFL	Minn.	Dec. 30,1976	Resigned; elected Vice President.

Minority:

Taft, Robert Jr.	Rep	Ohio	Dec. 28,1976	Resigned; defeated for reelection.

Departures from the Senate:	Majority	Minority		
Defeated for Reelection	None	Beall, J. Glenn Jr.	Md.	Rep

LABOR AND PUBLIC WELFARE / 95th Congress

* Reorganized as the Committee on HUMAN RESOURCES on Feb. 11,1977.

Service Dates of Committee Chair: Jan. 10,1977-Feb. 11,1977
Service Dates of Majority Members: Jan. 10,1977-Feb. 11,1977
Service Dates of Minority Members: Jan. 10,1977-Feb. 22,1977

Majority

Rank	Name	Party	State	Years in: Senate	Years in: Comm.
Chr	Williams, Harrison A. Jr.	Dem	N.J.	19	18
2nd	Randolph, Jennings	Dem	W.Va.	19	18
3rd	Pell, Claiborne D.	Dem	R.I.	17	17
4th	Kennedy, Edward M.	Dem	Mass.	15	14
5th	Nelson, Gaylord A.	Dem	Wisc.	15	13
6th	Eagleton, Thomas F.	Dem	Mo.	9	8
7th	Cranston, Alan	Dem	Cal.	9	8
8th	Hathaway, William D.	Dem	Me.	5	4
9th	Durkin, John A.	Dem	N.H.	2	2
10th	Melcher, John	Dem	Mont.	1	*T 1

Minority

Rank	Name	Party	State	Years in: Senate	Years in: Comm.
RM	Javits, Jacob K.	Rep	N.Y.	21	18
2nd	Schweiker, Richard S.	Rep	Penn.	9	8
3rd	Stafford, Robert T.	Rep	Vt.	6	6
4th	Laxalt, Paul	Rep	Nev.	3	2
5th	Danforth, John C.	Rep	Mo.	1	*T 1

*T: Temporary member of the committee.

Notes: The committee size was temporarily increased to 16 members on Jan. 12,1977, and the party ratio changed to 10 Democrats and 6 Republicans. Ranking on this committee for the following member was affected by other chamber service: Jennings Randolph (Dem-W.Va.), Chair, Public Works.

Addition:
Minority: 6th Lugar, Richard G. Rep Ind. Jan. 12,1977

Changes:
Majority:

Durkin, John A.	Dem	N.H.	Feb. 11,1977	Moved to Energy and Natural Resources.
Melcher, John	Dem	Mont.	Feb. 11,1977	Moved to Agriculture, Nutrition, and Forestry.

Minority:

Laxalt, Paul	Rep	Nev.	Feb. 22,1977	Moved to Finance.
Danforth, John C.	Rep	Mo.	Feb. 22,1977	Moved to Governmental Affairs.
Lugar, Richard G.	Rep	Ind.	Feb. 22,1977	Moved to Agriculture, Nutrition, and Forestry.

HUMAN RESOURCES / 95th Congress

Service Dates of Committee Chair: Feb. 11,1977-Jan. 23,1979
Service Dates of Majority Members: Feb. 11,1977-Jan. 23,1979
Service Dates of Minority Members: Feb. 22,1977-Jan. 23,1979

Majority

Rank	Name	Party	State	Years in: Senate	Years in: Comm.
Chr	Williams, Harrison A. Jr.	Dem	N.J.	19	19
2nd	Randolph, Jennings	Dem	W.Va.	19	19
3rd	Pell, Claiborne D.	Dem	R.I.	17	17
4th	Kennedy, Edward M.	Dem	Mass.	15	14
5th	Nelson, Gaylord A.	Dem	Wisc.	15	13
6th	Eagleton, Thomas F.	Dem	Mo.	9	9
7th	Cranston, Alan	Dem	Cal.	9	9
8th	Hathaway, William D.	Dem	Me.	5	5
9th	Riegle, Donald W. Jr.	Dem	Mich.	1	1

Minority

Rank	Name	Party	State	Years in: Senate	Years in: Comm.
RM	Javits, Jacob K.	Rep	N.Y.	21	19
2nd	Schweiker, Richard S.	Rep	Penn.	9	9
3rd	Stafford, Robert T.	Rep	Vt.	6	6
4th	Hatch, Orrin G.	Rep	Utah	1	1
5th	Chafee, John H.	Rep	R.I.	1	1
6th	Hayakawa, S. I. (Sam)	Rep	Cal.	1	1

Note: Ranking on this committee for the following member was affected by other chamber service: Jennings Randolph (Dem-W.Va.), Chair, Environment and Public Works.

	Majority			Minority		
Departures from the Senate:						
Defeated for Reelection	Hathaway, William D.	Me.	Dem	None		
Departures from Committee:						
Moved to Finance	None			Chafee, John H.	R.I.	Rep
Moved to Foreign Relations	None			Hayakawa, S. I. (Sam)	Cal.	Rep

HUMAN RESOURCES / 96th Congress

* Name changed to LABOR AND HUMAN RESOURCES on Mar. 7,1979.

Service Dates of Committee Chair: Jan. 23,1979-Jan. 5,1981
Service Dates of Majority Members: Jan. 23,1979-Jan. 5,1981
Service Dates of Minority Members: Jan. 23,1979-Jan. 5,1981

Majority

Rank	Name	Party	State	Years in: Senate	Years in: Comm.
Chr	Williams, Harrison A. Jr.	Dem	N.J.	21	21
2nd	Randolph, Jennings	Dem	W.Va.	21	21
3rd	Pell, Claiborne D.	Dem	R.I.	19	19
4th	Kennedy, Edward M.	Dem	Mass.	17	16
5th	Nelson, Gaylord A.	Dem	Wisc.	17	15
6th	Eagleton, Thomas F.	Dem	Mo.	11	11
7th	Cranston, Alan	Dem	Cal.	11	11
8th	Riegle, Donald W. Jr.	Dem	Mich.	3	2
9th	Metzenbaum, Howard M.	Dem	Ohio	4	1

Minority

Rank	Name	Party	State	Years in: Senate	Years in: Comm.
RM	Schweiker, Richard S.	Rep	Penn.	11	11
2nd	Javits, Jacob K.	Rep	N.Y.	23	21
3rd	Stafford, Robert T.	Rep	Vt.	8	8
4th	Hatch, Orrin G.	Rep	Utah	3	2
5th	Armstrong, William L.	Rep	Colo.	1	1
6th	Humphrey, Gordon J.	Rep	N.H.	1	1

Note: Rankings on this committee for the following members were affected by other chamber service: Jennings Randolph (Dem-W.Va.), Chair, Environment and Public Works; Jacob K. Javits (Rep-N.Y.), Ranking Minority Member, Foreign Relations.

	Majority			Minority		
Departures from the Senate:						
Appointed Secretary of Health & Human Services	None			Schweiker, Richard S.	Penn.	Rep
Defeated for Reelection	Nelson, Gaylord A.	Wisc.	Dem	Javits, Jacob K.	N.Y.	Rep
Departures from Committee:						
Moved to Foreign Relations	Cranston, Alan	Cal.	Dem	None		
Moved to Finance	None			Armstrong, William L.	Colo.	Rep

LABOR AND HUMAN RESOURCES / 97th Congress

Service Dates of Committee Chair: Jan. 5,1981-Jan. 3,1983
Service Dates of Majority Members: Jan. 5,1981-Jan. 3,1983
Service Dates of Minority Members: Jan. 5,1981-Jan. 3,1983

Majority

Rank	Name	Party	State	Years in: Senate	Years in: Comm.
Chr	Hatch, Orrin G.	Rep	Utah	5	4
2nd	Stafford, Robert T.	Rep	Vt.	10	10
3rd	Quayle, J. Danforth	Rep	Ind.	1	1
4th	Hawkins, Paula	Rep	Fla.	1	*1 1
5th	Nickles, Don	Rep	Okla.	1	1
6th	Weicker, Lowell P. Jr.	Rep	Conn.	11	1
7th	Humphrey, Gordon J.	Rep	N.H.	3	*1 2
8th	Denton, Jeremiah	Rep	Ala.	1	1
9th	East, John P.	Rep	N.C.	1	*1 1

Minority

Rank	Name	Party	State	Years in: Senate	Years in: Comm.
RM	Kennedy, Edward M.	Dem	Mass.	19	18
2nd	Williams, Harrison A. Jr.	Dem	N.J.	23	22
3rd	Randolph, Jennings	Dem	W.Va	23	22
4th	Pell, Claiborne D.	Dem	R.I.	21	20
5th	Eagleton, Thomas F.	Dem	Mo.	13	12
6th	Riegle, Donald W. Jr.	Dem	Mich.	5	4
7th	Metzenbaum, Howard M.	Dem	Ohio	6	2

*1: Member's 1st period of service on the committee.

Notes: Rankings on this committee for the following members were affected by other chamber service: Robert T. Stafford (Rep-Vt.), Chair, Environment and Public Works; Gordon J. Humphrey (Rep-N.H.), Chair of three subcommittees; Harrison A. Williams, Jr. (Dem-N.J.), Ranking Minority Member, Banking, Housing and Urban Affairs; Jennings Randolph (Dem-W.Va.), Ranking Minority Member Environment and Public Works; and Claiborne D. Pell (Dem-R.I.), Ranking Minority Member, Foreign Relations. On Jan. 22,1981, Harrison Williams was moved to the 3rd minority rank.

Changes:
Minority:

Williams, Harrison A. Jr.	Dem	N.J.	Mar. 11,1982	Resigned and retired.
Matsunaga, Spark M.	Dem	Hai.	Apr. 20,1982	Replaced Williams.

Departures from Committee:	Majority			Minority
Moved to Banking, Housing & Urban Affairs	Hawkins, Paula	Fla.	Rep	None
Moved to Armed Services	East, John P.	N.C.	Rep	None

LABOR AND HUMAN RESOURCES / 98th Congress

Service Dates of Committee Chair: Jan. 3,1983-Feb. 21,1985
Service Dates of Majority Members: Jan. 3,1983-Feb. 21,1985
Service Dates of Minority Members: Jan. 3,1983-Feb. 21,1985

Majority

Rank	Name	Party	State	Years in: Senate	Years in: Comm.
Chr	Hatch, Orrin G.	Rep	Utah	7	6
2nd	Stafford, Robert T.	Rep	Vt.	12	12
3rd	Quayle, J. Danforth	Rep	Ind.	3	2
4th	Nickles, Don	Rep	Okla.	3	2
5th	Humphrey, Gordon J.	Rep	N.H.	5	*1 4
6th	Denton, Jeremiah	Rep	Ala.	3	2
7th	Weicker, Lowell P. Jr.	Rep	Conn.	13	2
8th	Grassley, Charles E.	Rep	Iowa	3	1
9th	D'Amato, Alfonse M.	Rep	N.Y.	3	1

Minority:

Rank	Name	Party	State	Years in: Senate	Years in: Comm.
RM	Kennedy, Edward M.	Dem	Mass.	21	20
2nd	Randolph, Jennings	Dem	W.Va.	25	24
3rd	Pell, Claiborne D.	Dem	R.I.	23	22
4th	Eagleton, Thomas F.	Dem	Mo.	15	14
5th	Riegle, Donald W. Jr.	Dem	Mich.	7	6
6th	Metzenbaum, Howard M.	Dem	Ohio	8	4
7th	Matsunaga, Spark M.	Dem	Hai.	7	1

*1: Member's 1st period of service on the committee.

Notes: The committee size was expanded and the party ratio changed to 10 Republicans and 8 Democrats on Feb. 3,1983. Rankings on this committee for the following members were affected by other chamber service: Robert T. Stafford (Rep-Vt.), Chair, Environment and Public Works; Gordon J. Humphrey (Rep-N.H.), Chair of three subcommittees; Jennings Randolph (Dem-W.Va.), Ranking Minority Member, Environment and Public Works; and Claiborne D. Pell (Dem-R.I.), Ranking Minority Member, Foreign Relations.

Additions:

Majority:	10th	Hawkins, Paula	Rep	Fla.	Feb. 3,1983
Minority:	8th	Dodd, Christopher J.	Dem	Conn.	Feb. 3,1983

Changes:

Majority:

D'Amato, Alfonse M.	Rep	N.Y.	Feb. 3,1983	Moved to Joint Economic Committee.
East, John P.	Rep	N.C.	Feb. 3,1983	Replaced D'Amato.
Humphrey, Gordon J.	Rep	N.H.	Feb. 9,1984	Moved to Banking, Housing and Urban Affairs.
Thurmond, J. Strom	Rep	S.C.	Feb. 9,1984	Replaced Humphrey.

	Majority			Minority		
Departures from the Senate:						
Retired	None			Randolph, Jennings	W.Va.	Dem
Departures from Committee:						
Moved to Armed Services	Denton, Jeremiah	Ala.	Rep	None		
Moved to Foreign Relations	None			Eagleton, Thomas F.	Mo.	Dem
No new assignment	East, John P.	N.C.	Rep	Riegle, Donald W. Jr.	Mich.	Dem

LABOR AND HUMAN RESOURCES / 99th Congress

Service Dates of Committee Chair: Feb. 21,1985-Jan. 6,1987
Service Dates of Majority Members: Feb. 21,1985-Jan. 6,1987
Service Dates of Minority Members: Feb. 21,1985-Jan. 6,1987

Majority

Rank	Name	Party	State	Years in: Senate	Years in: Comm.
Chr	Hatch, Orrin G.	Rep	Utah	9	8
2nd	Stafford, Robert T.	Rep	Vt.	14	14
3rd	Quayle, J. Danforth	Rep	Ind.	5	5
4th	Nickles, Don	Rep	Okla.	5	5
5th	Hawkins, Paula	Rep	Fla.	5	*2 3
6th	Thurmond, J. Strom	Rep	S.C.	30	*2 2
7th	Weicker, Lowell P. Jr.	Rep	Conn.	15	5
8th	Wallop, Malcolm	Rep	Wyo.	9	1
9th	Grassley, Charles E.	Rep	Iowa	5	3

Minority

Rank	Name	Party	State	Years in: Senate	Years in: Comm.
RM	Kennedy, Edward M.	Dem	Mass.	23	22
2nd	Pell, Claiborne D.	Dem	R.I.	25	25
3rd	Metzenbaum, Howard M.	Dem	Ohio	10	7
4th	Matsunaga, Spark M.	Dem	Hai.	9	3
5th	Dodd, Christopher J.	Dem	Conn.	5	1
6th	Simon, Paul M.	Dem	Ill.	1	1
7th	Kerry, John F.	Dem	Mass.	1	1

*2: Member's 2nd period of service on the committee.

Note: Rankings on this committee for the following members were affected by other chamber service: Robert T. Stafford (Rep-Vt.), Chair, Environment and Public Works; Lowell P. Weicker (Rep-Conn.), Chair, Small Business; Charles E. Grassley (Rep-Iowa), Chair, two subcommmittees; and Claiborne D. Pell (Dem-R.I.), Ranking Minority Member, Foreign Relations.

	Majority			Minority		
Departures from the Senate:						
Defeated for Reelection	Hawkins, Paula	Fla.	Rep	None		
Departures from Committee:						
Moved to Appropriations	Grassley, Charles E.	Iowa	Rep	None		
Moved to Appropriations; Budget	Nickles, Don	Okla.	Rep	None		
Moved to Small Business	Wallop, Malcolm	Wyo.	Rep	None		
Moved to Commerce, Science & Transportation	None			Kerry, John F.	Mass.	Dem

LABOR AND HUMAN RESOURCES / 100th Congress

Service Dates of Committee Chair: Jan. 6,1987-Feb. 2,1989
Service Dates of Majority Members: Jan. 6,1987-Feb. 2,1989
Service Dates of Minority Members: Jan. 6,1987-Feb. 2,1989

Majority

Rank	Name	Party	State	Years in: Senate	Years in: Comm.
Chr	Kennedy, Edward M.	Dem	Mass.	25	24
2nd	Pell, Claiborne D.	Dem	R.I.	27	26
3rd	Metzenbaum, Howard M.	Dem	Ohio	12	8
4th	Matsunaga, Spark M.	Dem	Hai.	11	5
5th	Dodd, Christopher J.	Dem	Conn.	7	2
6th	Simon, Paul M.	Dem	Ill.	3	2
7th	Harkin, Thomas R.	Dem	Iowa	3	1
8th	Adams, Brock	Dem	Wash.	1	1
9th	Mikulski, Barbara A.	Dem	Md.	1	1

Minority

Rank	Name	Party	State	Years in: Senate	Years in: Comm.
RM	Hatch, Orrin G.	Rep	Utah	11	10
2nd	Stafford, Robert T.	Rep	Vt.	16	16
3rd	Quayle, J. Danforth	Rep	Ind.	7	7
4th	Thurmond, J. Strom	Rep	S.C.	32	*2 3
5th	Weicker, Lowell P. Jr.	Rep	Conn.	17	7
6th	Cochran, Thad	Rep	Miss.	9	1
7th	Humphrey, Gordon J.	Rep	N.H.	9	*2 1

*2: Member's 2nd period of service on the committee.

Note: Rankings on this committee for the following members were affected by other chamber service: Claiborne D. Pell (Dem-R.I.), Chair, Foreign Relations; Robert T. Stafford (Rep-Vt.), Ranking Minority Member, Environment and Public Works; and Lowell P. Weicker (Rep-Conn.), Ranking Minority Member, Small Business.

Changes:
Minority:

Quayle, J. Danforth	Rep	Ind.	Jan. 2,1989	Resigned; elected Vice President.

	Majority	Minority		
Departures from the Senate:				
Defeated for Reelection	None	Weicker, Lowell P. Jr.	Conn.	Rep
Retired	None	Stafford, Robert T.	Vt.	Rep
Departures from Committee:				
Moved to Foreign Relations; Environment & Public Works	None	Humphrey, Gordon J.	N.H.	Rep

LABOR AND HUMAN RESOURCES / 101st Congress

Service Dates of Committee Chair: Feb. 2,1989-Feb. 5,1991
Service Dates of Majority Members: Feb. 2,1989-Feb. 5,1991
Service Dates of Minority Members: Feb. 2,1989-Feb. 5,1991

Majority

Rank	Name	Party	State	Years in: Senate	Years in: Comm.
Chr	Kennedy, Edward M.	Dem	Mass.	27	26
2nd	Pell, Claiborne D.	Dem	R.I.	29	29
3rd	Metzenbaum, Howard M.	Dem	Ohio	14	11
4th	Matsunaga, Spark M.	Dem	Hai.	12	7
5th	Dodd, Christopher J.	Dem	Conn.	9	5
6th	Simon, Paul M.	Dem	Ill.	5	4
7th	Harkin, Thomas R.	Dem	Iowa	5	3
8th	Adams, Brock	Dem	Wash.	3	3
9th	Mikulski, Barbara A.	Dem	Md.	3	3

Minority

Rank	Name	Party	State	Years in: Senate	Years in: Comm.
RM	Hatch, Orrin G.	Rep	Utah	13	12
2nd	Kassebaum, Nancy Landon	Rep	Kans.	11	1
3rd	Jeffords, James M.	Rep	Vt.	1	1
4th	Coats, Daniel R.	Rep	Ind.	1	1
5th	Thurmond, J. Strom	Rep	S.C.	34	*2 5
6th	Durenberger, David F.	Rep	Minn.	11	1
7th	Cochran, Thad	Rep	Miss.	11	3

*2: Member's 2nd period of service on the committee.

Note: Rankings on this committee for the following members were affected by other chamber service: Claiborne D. Pell (Dem-R.I.), Chair, Foreign Relations; J. Strom Thurmond (Rep-S.C.), Ranking Minority Member, Judiciary; and Thad Cochran (Rep-Miss.), Secretary of the Republican Conference.

Changes:
Majority:

Matsunaga, Spark M.	Dem	Hai.	Apr. 15,1990	Died in office.
Bingaman, Jeff	Dem	N.M.	May 16,1990	Replaced Matsunaga.

LABOR AND HUMAN RESOURCES / 102nd Congress

Service Dates of Committee Chair: Feb. 5,1991-Jan. 3,1993
Service Dates of Majority Members: Feb. 5,1991-Jan. 3,1993
Service Dates of Minority Members: Feb. 5,1991-Jan. 3,1993

Majority

Rank	Name	Party	State	Years in: Senate	Years in: Comm.
Chr	Kennedy, Edward M.	Dem	Mass.	29	28
2nd	Pell, Claiborne D.	Dem	R.I.	31	31
3rd	Metzenbaum, Howard M.	Dem	Ohio	16	13
4th	Dodd, Christopher J.	Dem	Conn.	11	7
5th	Simon, Paul M.	Dem	Ill.	7	6
6th	Harkin, Thomas R.	Dem	Iowa	7	5
7th	Adams, Brock	Dem	Wash.	5	5
8th	Mikulski, Barbara A.	Dem	Md.	5	5
9th	Bingaman, Jeff	Dem	N.M.	9	1
10th	Wellstone, Paul	Dem	Minn.	1	1

Minority

Rank	Name	Party	State	Years in: Senate	Years in: Comm.
RM	Hatch, Orrin G.	Rep	Utah	15	14
2nd	Kassebaum, Nancy Landon	Rep	Kans.	13	3
3rd	Jeffords, James M.	Rep	Vt.	3	3
4th	Coats, Daniel R.	Rep	Ind.	3	3
5th	Thurmond, J. Strom	Rep	S.C.	36	*2 7
6th	Durenberger, David F.	Rep	Minn.	13	3
7th	Cochran, Thad	Rep	Miss.	13	5

*2: Member's 2nd period of service on the committee.

Note: Rankings on this committee for the following members were affected by other chamber service: Claiborne D. Pell (Dem-R.I.), Chair, Foreign Relations. J. Strom Thurmond (Rep-S.C.), Ranking Minority Member, Judiciary; and Thad Cochran (Rep-Miss.), Chairman of the Republican Conference.

POST OFFICE AND CIVIL SERVICE

CIVIL SERVICE

Jurisdiction, 1947

Established by the Legislative Reorganization Act of 1946:

[Section 102.(1)(e)]

Committee on Civil Service, to consist of thirteen Senators, to which committee shall be referred all proposed legislation, messages, petitions, memorials, and other matters relating to the following subjects:

1. The Federal civil service generally.
2. The status of officers and employees of the United States, including their compensation, classification, and retirement.
3. The postal service generally, including the railway mail service, and measures relating to ocean mail and pneumatic-tube service; but excluding post roads.
4. Postal-savings banks.
5. Census and the collection of statistics generally.
6. The National Archives.

POST OFFICE AND CIVIL SERVICE

Renamed the Committee on Post Office and Civil Service on April 17, 1947 effective January 1, 1948.

Jurisdiction, 1975

Jurisdiction contained in the Senate Manual for the 94th Congress (1975):

[Section 102.(1)(n)]

Committee on Post Office and Civil Service, to which committee shall be referred all proposed legislation, messages, petitions, memorials, and other matters relating to the following subjects:

1. The Federal civil service generally.
2. The status of officers and employees of the United States, including their compensation, classification, and retirement.
3. The postal service generally, including the railway mail service, and measures relating to ocean mail and pneumatic-tube service; but excluding post roads.
4. Postal-savings banks.
5. Census and the collection of statistics generally.
6. The National Archives.

Reorganization, 1977

The Committee was reorganized into the Standing Committee on Governmental Affairs following the passage of Senate Resolution 4, the Committee System Reorganization Amendments of 1977, February 4, 1977. Majority members were reassigned on February 11, 1977 and minority members were reassigned on February 22, 1977.

CIVIL SERVICE / 80th Congress

* Name changed to POST OFFICE AND CIVIL SERVICE on Apr. 17, 1947.

Service Dates of Committee Chair: Jan. 6,1947-Jan. 10,1949
Service Dates of Majority Members: Jan. 6,1947-Jan. 10,1949
Service Dates of Minority Members: Jan. 8,1947-Jan. 10,1949

Majority

Rank	Name	Party	State	Years in: Senate	Years in: Comm.
Chr	Langer, William	Rep	N.D.	7	*1 6
2nd	Buck, C. Douglass	Rep	Del.	5	4
3rd	Flanders, Ralph E.	Rep	Vt.	1	1
4th	Baldwin, Raymond E.	Rep	Conn.	1	1
5th	Thye, Edward J.	Rep	Minn.	1	1
6th	Williams, John J.	Rep	Del.	1	1
7th	Ecton, Zales N.	Rep	Mont.	1	1

Minority

Rank	Name	Party	State	Years in: Senate	Years in: Comm.
RM1	Chavez, Dennis	Dem	N.M.	12	12
RM2 2nd	McKellar, Kenneth D.	Dem	Tenn.	30	30
3rd	O'Daniel, W. Lee	Dem	Tex.	6	4
4th	Johnston, Olin D.	Dem	S.C.	3	1
5th	Umstead, William B.	Dem	N.C.	1	1
6th	O'Conor, Herbert R.	Dem	Md.	1	1

*1: Member's 1st period of service on the committee.

Note: Ranking on this committee for the following member was affected by other chamber service: Kenneth D. McKellar (Dem-Tenn), Ranking Minority Member, Appropriations. McKellar served as Ranking Minority Member of both committees after succeeding Chavez on May 26,1948.

Changes:

Ranking Member:

RM1	Chavez, Dennis	Dem	N.M.	May 26,1948	Moved to Appropriations.
RM2	McKellar, Kenneth D.	Dem	Tenn.	May 26,1948	Succeeded Chavez as Ranking Minority Member.

Minority:

Chavez, Dennis	Dem	N.M.	May 26,1948	Moved to Appropriations.
Stennis, John C.	Dem	Miss.	May 26,1948	Replaced Chavez.

Departures from the Senate:	**Majority**			**Minority**		
Defeated for Reelection	Buck, C. Douglass	Del.	Rep	None		
Defeated for Nomination	None			Umstead, William B.	N.C.	Dem
Retired	None			O'Daniel, W. Lee	Tex.	Dem
Departures from Committee:						
Moved to District of Columbia; Finance; Interstate & Foreign Commerce	Williams, John J.	Del.	Rep	None		
Moved to Public Works	None			Stennis, John C.	Miss.	Dem

POST OFFICE AND CIVIL SERVICE / 81st Congress

Service Dates of Committee Chair: Jan. 10,1949-Jan. 15,1951
Service Dates of Majority Members: Jan. 10,1949-Jan. 15,1951
Service Dates of Minority Members: Jan. 10,1949-Jan. 15,1951

Majority

Rank	Name	Party	State	Years in: Senate	Years in: Comm.
Chr	Johnston, Olin D.	Dem	S.C.	5	3
2nd	McKellar, Kenneth D.	Dem	Tenn.	32	32
3rd	O'Conor, Herbert R.	Dem	Md.	3	3
4th	Broughton, J. Melville	Dem	N.C.	1	1
5th	Long, Russell B.	Dem	La.	1	1
6th	Neely, Matthew M.	Dem	W.Va.	16	*3 1
7th	Frear, J. Allen Jr.	Dem	Del.	1	1

Minority

Rank	Name	Party	State	Years in: Senate	Years in: Comm.
RM	Langer, William	Rep	N.D.	9	*1 8
2nd	Flanders, Ralph E.	Rep	Vt.	3	3
3rd	Baldwin, Raymond E.	Rep	Conn.	3	3
4th	Thye, Edward J.	Rep	Minn.	3	3
5th	Ecton, Zales N.	Rep	Mont.	3	3
6th	Hendrickson, Robert C.	Rep	N.J.	1	1

*1: Member's 1st period of service on the committee: *3: Member's 3rd period of service on the committee.

Note: Ranking on this committee for the following member was affected by other chamber service: Kenneth D. McKellar (Dem-Tenn), Chair, Appropriations.

Changes:

Majority:

Broughton, J. Melville	Dem	N.C.	Mar. 6,1949	Died in office.
O'Conor, Herbert R.	Dem	Md.	Mar. 22,1949	Moved to Judiciary.
Humphrey, Hubert H. Jr.	DFL	Minn.	Apr. 4,1949	Replaced Broughton.
Graham, Frank P.	Dem	N.C.	Apr. 4,1949	Replaced O'Conor.
Graham, Frank P.	Dem	N.C.	Jan. 12,1950	Moved to Rules and Administration.
Leahy, Edward L.	Dem	R.I.	Jan. 12,1950	Replaced Graham.
Leahy, Edward L.	Dem	R.I.	Dec. 18,1950	Resigned; appointed Federal judge.
Pastore, John O.	Dem	R.I.	Dec. 21,1950	Replaced Leahy.

Minority:

Hendrickson, Robert C.	Rep	N.J.	July 26,1949	Moved to Rules and Administration.
Dulles, John Foster	Rep	N.Y.	July 26,1949	Replaced Hendrickson.
Dulles, John Foster	Rep	N.Y.	Nov. 8,1949	Resigned; lost special election.
Baldwin, Raymond E.	Rep	Conn.	Dec. 16,1949	Resigned; appointed State Supreme Court Justice.
Dworshak, Henry C.	Rep	Ida.	Jan. 12,1950	Replaced Dulles.
Darby, Harry	Rep	Kans.	Jan. 12,1950	Replaced Baldwin.
Darby, Harry	Rep	Kans.	Nov. 28,1950	Resigned and retired.
Carlson, Frank	Rep	Kans.	Dec. 4,1950	Replaced Darby.

Departures from Committee:	Majority		Minority	
Moved to Finance	Frear, J. Allen Jr.	Del. Dem	None	
Moved to Interior & Insular Affairs	Long, Russell B.	La. Dem	None	
Moved to Agriculture & Forestry	Humphrey, Hubert H. Jr.	Minn. DFL	None	
Moved to Appropriations	None		Ecton, Zales N.	Mont. Rep
			Thye, Edward J.	Minn. Rep
Moved to Armed Services; Rules & Administration	None		Flanders, Ralph E.	Vt. Rep
Moved to Expenditures in Executive Departments; Public Works	None		Dworshak, Henry C.	Ida. Rep

POST OFFICE AND CIVIL SERVICE / 82nd Congress

Service Dates of Committee Chair: Jan. 15,1951-Jan. 13,1953
Service Dates of Majority Members: Jan. 15,1951-Jan. 13,1953
Service Dates of Minority Members: Jan. 15,1951-Jan. 13,1953

Majority

Rank	Name	Party	State	Years in: Senate	Years in: Comm.
Chr	Johnston, Olin D.	Dem	S.C.	7	5
2nd	McKellar, Kenneth D.	Dem	Tenn.	34	34
3rd	Neely, Matthew M.	Dem	W.Va.	18 *3	3
4th	Pastore, John O.	Dem	R.I.	1	1
5th	Clements, Earle C.	Dem	Ky.	1	1
6th	Monroney, A. S. Mike	Dem	Okla.	1	1
7th	Smathers, George A.	Dem	Fla.	1	1

Minority

Rank	Name	Party	State	Years in: Senate	Years in: Comm.
RM	Langer, William	Rep	N.D.	11 *1	10
2nd	Carlson, Frank	Rep	Kans.	1	1
3rd	Dirksen, Everett M.	Rep	Ill.	1	1
4th	Welker, Herman	Rep	Ida.	1	1
5th	Butler, John Marshall	Rep	Md.	1	1
6th	Duff, James H.	Rep	Penn.	1	1

*1: Member's 1st period of service on the committee; *3: Member's 3rd period of service on the committee.

Note: Ranking on this committee for the following member was affected by other chamber service: Kenneth D. McKellar (Dem-Tenn), Chair, Appropriations.

Vacancy Filled:

Minority: 6th seat by Duff on Jan. 18,1951.

Changes:

Majority:

Clements, Earle C.	Dem	Ky.	Apr. 3,1951	Moved to Public Works.
Underwood, Thomas R.	Dem	Ky.	Apr. 3,1951	Replaced Clements.
Underwood, Thomas R.	Dem	Ky.	Nov. 4,1952	Resigned; defeated for election.

Minority:

Dirksen, Everett M.	Rep	Ill.	June 22,1951	Moved to District of Columbia.
Bennett, Wallace F.	Rep	Utah	June 22,1951	Replaced Dirksen.
Welker, Herman	Rep	Ida.	Jan. 14,1952	Moved to Rules and Administration.
Seaton, Frederick A.	Rep	Neb.	Jan. 14,1952	Replaced Welker.
Seaton, Frederick A.	Rep	Neb.	Nov. 4,1952	Resigned; appointed presidential adviser.

Departures from the Senate:	Majority		Minority	
Defeated for Renomination	McKellar, Kenneth D.	Tenn. Dem	None	
Departures from Committee:				
Moved to Interstate & Foreign Commerce	Smathers, George A.	Fla. Dem	None	
Moved to Government Operations; Interstate & Foreign Commerce; Judiciary	None		Butler, John Marshall	Md. Rep
Moved to Foreign Relations	None		Langer, William	N.D. Rep
Moved to Banking & Currency; Finance	None		Bennett, Wallace F.	Utah Rep

POST OFFICE AND CIVIL SERVICE / 83rd Congress

Service Dates of Committee Chair: Jan. 13,1953-Jan. 11,1955
Service Dates of Majority Members: Jan. 13,1953-Jan. 11,1955
Service Dates of Minority Members: Jan. 13,1953-Jan. 11,1955

Majority

Rank	Name	Party	State	Years in: Senate	Years in: Comm.
Chr	Carlson, Frank	Rep	Kans.	3	3
2nd	Duff, James H.	Rep	Penn.	2	2
3rd	Jenner, William E.	Rep	Ind.	7	1
4th	Cooper, John Sherman	Rep	Ky.	3	1
5th	Griswold, Dwight P.	Rep	Neb.	1	1
6th	Purtell, William A.	Rep	Conn.	1	1

Minority

Rank	Name	Party	State	Years in: Senate	Years in: Comm.
RM	Johnston, Olin D.	Dem	S.C.	9	7
2nd	Neely, Matthew M.	Dem	W.Va.	20	*3 5
3rd	Pastore, John O.	Dem	R.I.	3	2
4th	Monroney, A. S. Mike	Dem	Okla.	3	2
5th	Daniel, Price M.	Dem	Tex.	1	1

*3: Member's 3rd period of service on the committee.

Note: The committee size and party ratio changed to 7 Republicans and 6 Democrats on Jan. 13,1954.

Additions:

Majority:	7th	Upton, Robert W.	Rep	N.H.	Jan. 13,1954
Minority:	6th	Lennon, Alton A.	Dem	N.C.	Jan. 13,1954

Changes:

Majority:				
Griswold, Dwight P.	Rep	Neb.	Apr. 12,1954	Died in office.
Bowring, Eva K.	Rep	Neb.	May 3,1954	Replaced Griswold.
Bowring, Eva K.	Rep	Neb.	June 29,1954	Left committee; resigned Senate Nov. 7, 1954.
Crippa, Edward D.	Rep	Wyo.	June 29,1954	Replaced Bowring.
Upton, Robert W.	Rep	N.H.	Nov. 7,1954	Resigned; defeated for nomination in special election.
Crippa, Edward D.	Rep	Wyo.	Nov. 28,1954	Resigned and retired.
Cotton, Norris	Rep	N.H.	Nov. 30,1954	Replaced Upton.
Hruska, Roman L.	Rep	Neb.	Nov. 30,1954	Replaced Crippa.
Minority:				
Lennon, Alton A.	Dem	N.C.	Nov. 28,1954	Resigned; defeated for nomination in special election.

Departures from the Senate:	Majority		Minority	
Defeated for Reelection	Cooper, John Sherman	Ky. Rep	None	
Departures from Committee:				
Moved to Interstate & Foreign Commerce	Duff, James H. Purtell, William A.	Penn. Rep Conn. Rep	None	
Moved to Public Works; Government Operations	Cotton, Norris	N.H. Rep	None	
Moved to District of Columbia; Public Works	Hruska, Roman L.	Neb. Rep	None	
Moved to Judiciary; Interstate and Foreign Commerce	None		Daniel, Price M.	Tex. Dem

POST OFFICE AND CIVIL SERVICE / 84th Congress

Service Dates of Committee Chair: Jan. 11,1955-Jan. 9,1957
Service Dates of Majority Members: Jan. 11,1955-Jan. 9,1957
Service Dates of Minority Members: Jan. 11,1955-Jan. 9,1957

Majority

Rank	Name	Party	State	Years in: Senate	Years in: Comm.
Chr	Johnston, Olin D.	Dem	S.C.	11	9
2nd	Neely, Matthew M.	Dem	W.Va.	22 *3	7
3rd	Pastore, John O.	Dem	R.I.	5	4
4th	Monroney, A. S. Mike	Dem	Okla.	5	4
5th	Hennings, Thomas C. Jr.	Dem	Mo.	5	1
6th	Scott, W. Kerr	Dem	N.C.	1	1
7th	Neuberger, Richard L.	Dem	Ore.	1	1

Minority

Rank	Name	Party	State	Years in: Senate	Years in: Comm.
RM	Carlson, Frank	Rep	Kans.	5	5
2nd	Jenner, William E.	Rep	Ind.	9	2
3rd	Langer, William	Rep	N.D.	15 *2	1
4th	Curtis, Carl T.	Rep	Neb.	1	1
5th	Martin, Thomas E.	Rep	Iowa	1	1
6th	Case, Clifford P.	Rep	N.J.	1	1

*2: Member's 2nd period of service on the committee; *3: Member's 3rd period of service on the committee.

Changes:

Majority:

Name	Party	State	Date	Change
Neely, Matthew M.	Dem	W.Va.	Mar. 2,1956	Moved to Judiciary.
Laird, William R. III	Dem	W.Va.	Mar. 22,1956	Replaced Neely.
Laird, William R. III	Dem	W.Va.	Nov. 6,1956	Resigned and retired.

Departures from Committee:

	Majority			Minority		
Moved to Appropriations	Pastore, John O.	R.I.	Dem	None		
Moved to Government Operations	None			Curtis, Carl T.	Neb.	Rep

POST OFFICE AND CIVIL SERVICE / 85th Congress

Service Dates of Committee Chair: Jan. 9,1957-Jan. 14,1959
Service Dates of Majority Members: Jan. 9,1957-Jan. 14,1959
Service Dates of Minority Members: Jan. 9,1957-Jan. 20,1959

Majority

Rank	Name	Party	State	Years in: Senate	Years in: Comm.
Chr	Johnston, Olin D.	Dem	S.C.	13	11
2nd	Monroney, A. S. Mike	Dem	Okla.	7	6
3rd	Hennings, Thomas C. Jr.	Dem	Mo.	7	2
4th	Scott, W. Kerr	Dem	N.C.	3	2
5th	Neuberger, Richard L.	Dem	Ore.	3	2
6th	Church, Frank F.	Dem	Ida.	1	1
7th	Clark, Joseph S.	Dem	Penn.	1 *1	1

Minority

Rank	Name	Party	State	Years in: Senate	Years in: Comm.
RM	Carlson, Frank	Rep	Kans.	7	7
2nd	Jenner, William E.	Rep	Ind.	11	4
3rd	Langer, William	Rep	N.D.	17 *2	2
4th	Martin, Thomas E.	Rep	Iowa	3	2
5th	Case, Clifford P.	Rep	N.J.	3	2
6th	Morton, Thruston B.	Rep	Ky.	1	1

*1: Member's 1st period of service on the committee; *2: Member's 2nd period of service on the committee.

Changes:

Majority:

Name	Party	State	Date	Change
Hennings, Thomas C. Jr.	Dem	Mo.	May 2,1957	Left committee; no new assignment.
Yarborough, Ralph W.	Dem	Tex.	May 2,1957	Replaced Hennings.
Clark, Joseph S.	Dem	Penn.	Aug. 30,1957	Left committee; no new assignment.
Proxmire, William	Dem	Wisc.	Aug. 30,1957	Replaced Clark.
Scott, W. Kerr	Dem	N.C.	Apr. 16,1958	Died in office.
Proxmire, William	Dem	Wisc.	Apr. 21,1958	Moved to Agriculture and Forestry.
Clark, Joseph S.	Dem	Penn.	Apr. 21,1958	Replaced Scott.
Jordan, B. Everett	Dem	N.C.	May 5,1958	Replaced Proxmire.

Minority:

Name	Party	State	Date	Change
Case, Clifford P.	Rep	N.J.	May 22,1957	Moved to Rules and Administration.
Martin, Edward	Rep	Penn.	June 13,1957	Replaced Case.
Martin, Edward	Rep	Penn.	Jan. 28,1958	Left committee; no new assignment.
Hoblitzell, John D. Jr.	Rep	W.Va.	Jan. 28,1958	Replaced Martin.
Hoblitzell, John D. Jr.	Rep	W.Va.	Nov. 4,1958	Resigned; defeated in special election.

Departures from the Senate:	Majority		Minority	
Retired	None		Jenner, William E.	Ind. Rep
Departures from Committee:				
Moved to Foreign Relations	Church, Frank F.	Ida. Dem	None	
Moved to Judiciary; Public Works	None		Martin, Thomas E.	Iowa Rep

POST OFFICE AND CIVIL SERVICE / 86th Congress

Service Dates of Committee Chair: Jan. 14,1959-Jan. 10,1961
Service Dates of Majority Members: Jan. 14,1959-Jan. 10,1961
Service Dates of Minority Members: Jan. 20,1959-Jan. 13,1961

Majority

Rank	Name	Party	State	Years in: Senate	Years in: Comm.
Chr	Johnston, Olin D.	Dem	S.C.	15	13
2nd	Monroney, A. S. Mike	Dem	Okla.	9	8
3rd	Neuberger, Richard L.	Dem	Ore.	5	5
4th	Yarborough, Ralph W.	Dem	Tex.	2	2
5th	Clark, Joseph S.	Dem	Penn.	3	*2 1
6th	Jordan, B. Everett	Dem	N.C.	1	1

Minority

Rank	Name	Party	State	Years in: Senate	Years in: Comm.
RM	Carlson, Frank	Rep	Kans.	9	9
2nd	Langer, William	Rep	N.D.	19	*2 5
3rd	Morton, Thruston B.	Rep	Ky.	3	3

*2: Member's 2nd period of service on the committee.

Changes:

Majority:

Neuberger, Richard L.	Dem	Ore.	Mar. 9,1960	Died in office.
Randolph, Jennings	Dem	W.Va.	Mar. 28,1960	Replaced Neuberger.

Minority:

Langer, William	Rep	N.D.	Nov. 8,1959	Died in office.
Morton, Thruston B.	Rep	Ky.	Jan. 18,1960	Moved to Finance.
Fong, Hiram L.	Rep	Hai.	Jan. 18,1960	Replaced Langer.
Brunsdale, C. Norman	Rep	N.D.	Jan. 18,1960	Replaced Morton.
Brunsdale, C. Norman	Rep	N.D.	Aug. 7,1960	Resigned and retired.
Young, Milton R.	Rep	N.D.	Aug. 24,1960	Replaced Brunsdale.

Departures from Committee for:	Majority	Minority	
No new assignment	None	Young, Milton R.	N.D. Rep

POST OFFICE AND CIVIL SERVICE / 87th Congress

Service Dates of Committee Chair: Jan. 10,1961-Feb. 25,1963
Service Dates of Majority Members: Jan. 10,1961-Feb. 25,1963
Service Dates of Minority Members: Jan. 13,1961-Feb. 25,1963

Majority

Rank	Name	Party	State	Years in: Senate	Years in: Comm.
Chr	Johnston, Olin D.	Dem	S.C.	17	15
2nd	Monroney, A. S. Mike	Dem	Okla.	11	10
3rd	Yarborough, Ralph W.	Dem	Tex.	4	4
4th	Clark, Joseph S.	Dem	Penn.	5	*2 3
5th	Jordan, B. Everett	Dem	N.C.	3	3
6th	Randolph, Jennings	Dem	W.Va.	3	1

Minority

Rank	Name	Party	State	Years in: Senate	Years in: Comm.
RM	Carlson, Frank	Rep	Kans.	11	11
2nd	Fong, Hiram L.	Rep	Hai.	2	1
3rd	Boggs, J. Caleb	Rep	Del.	1	1

*2: Member's 2nd period of service on the committee.

Departures from Committee:	Majority		Minority
Moved to Rules & Administration	Clark, Joseph S.	Penn. Dem	None
Moved to Public Works	Jordan, B. Everett	N.C. Dem	None

POST OFFICE AND CIVIL SERVICE / 88th Congress

Service Dates of Committee Chair: Feb. 25,1963-Jan. 8,1965
Service Dates of Majority Members: Feb. 25,1963-Jan. 8,1965
Service Dates of Minority Members: Feb. 25,1963-Jan. 15,1965

Majority

Rank Name	Party	State	Years in: Senate	Years in: Comm.
Chr Johnston, Olin D.	Dem	S.C.	19	17
2nd Monroney, A. S. Mike	Dem	Okla.	13	13
3rd Yarborough, Ralph W.	Dem	Tex.	6	6
4th Randolph, Jennings	Dem	W.Va.	5	3
5th McGee, Gale W.	Dem	Wyo.	5	1
6th Brewster, Daniel B.	Dem	Md.	1	1

Minority

Rank Name	Party	State	Years in: Senate	Years in: Comm.
RM Carlson, Frank	Rep	Kans.	13	13
2nd Fong, Hiram L.	Rep	Hai.	4	4
3rd Boggs, J. Caleb	Rep	Del.	3	3

POST OFFICE AND CIVIL SERVICE / 89th Congress

Service Dates of Committee Chairs: Ch1 Jan. 8,1965-Apr. 18,1965
Ch2 Apr. 22,1965-Jan. 11,1967
Service Dates of Majority Members: Jan. 8,1965-Jan. 11,1967
Service Dates of Minority Members: Jan. 15,1965-Jan. 16,1967

Majority

Rank Name	Party	State	Years in: Senate	Years in: Comm.
Ch1 Johnston, Olin D.	Dem	S.C.	21	19
Ch2 2nd Monroney, A. S. Mike	Dem	Okla.	15	14
3rd Yarborough, Ralph W.	Dem	Tex.	8	8
4th Randolph, Jennings	Dem	W.Va.	7	5
5th McGee, Gale W.	Dem	Wyo.	7	2
6th Brewster, Daniel B.	Dem	Md.	3	2
7th Hartke, R. Vance	Dem	Ind.	7	1
8th Burdick, Quentin N.	Dem	N.D.	5	1

Minority

Rank Name	Party	State	Years in: Senate	Years in: Comm.
RM Carlson, Frank	Rep	Kans.	15	15
2nd Fong, Hiram L.	Rep	Hai.	6	5
3rd Boggs, J. Caleb	Rep	Del.	5	5
4th Simpson, Milward L.	Rep	Wyo.	3	1

Changes:

Chair:

Ch1 Johnston, Olin D.	Dem	S.C.	Apr. 18,1965	Died in office.
Ch2 Monroney, A. S. Mike	Dem	Okla.	Apr. 22,1965	Succeeded Johnston as Chair.

Majority:

Johnston, Olin D.	Dem	S.C.	Apr. 18,1965	Died in office.
Russell, Donald S.	Dem	S.C.	Apr. 26,1965	Replaced Johnston.
Russell, Donald S.	Dem	S.C.	Nov. 8,1966	Resigned; defeated for nomination.

Departures from the Senate:	Majority	Minority		
Retired	None	Simpson, Milward L.	Wyo.	Rep

POST OFFICE AND CIVIL SERVICE / 90th Congress

Service Dates of Committee Chair: Jan. 11,1967-Jan. 3,1969
Service Dates of Majority Members: Jan. 11,1967-Jan. 14,1969
Service Dates of Minority Members: Jan. 16,1967-Jan. 14,1969

Majority

Rank Name	Party	State	Years in: Senate	Years in: Comm.
Chr Monroney, A. S. Mike	Dem	Okla.	17	16
2nd Yarborough, Ralph W.	Dem	Tex.	10	10
3rd Randolph, Jennings	Dem	W.Va.	9	7
4th McGee, Gale W.	Dem	Wyo.	9	4
5th Brewster, Daniel B.	Dem	Md.	5	4
6th Hartke, R. Vance	Dem	Ind.	9	3
7th Burdick, Quentin N.	Dem	N.D.	7	3
8th Hollings, Ernest F.	Dem	S.C.	1	1

Minority

Rank Name	Party	State	Years in: Senate	Years in: Comm.
RM Carlson, Frank	Rep	Kans.	17	17
2nd Fong, Hiram L.	Rep	Hai.	8	7
3rd Boggs, J. Caleb	Rep	Del.	7	7
4th Fannin, Paul J.	Rep	Ariz.	3	1

Departures from the Senate:	Majority			Minority		
Defeated for Reelection	Brewster, Daniel B.	Md.	Dem	None		
	Monroney, A. S. Mike	Okla.	Dem			
Retired	None			Carlson, Frank	Kans.	Rep

POST OFFICE AND CIVIL SERVICE / 91st Congress

Service Dates of Committee Chair: Jan. 14,1969-Jan. 28,1971
Service Dates of Majority Members: Jan. 14,1969-Jan. 28,1971
Service Dates of Minority Members: Jan. 14,1969-Jan. 29,1971

Majority

Rank	Name	Party	State	Years in: Senate	Years in: Comm.
Chr	McGee, Gale W.	Dem	Wyo.	11	6
2nd	Yarborough, Ralph W.	Dem	Tex.	12	12
3rd	Randolph, Jennings	Dem	W.Va.	11	9
4th	Hartke, R. Vance	Dem	Ind.	11	5
5th	Burdick, Quentin N.	Dem	N.D.	9	5
6th	Hollings, Ernest F.	Dem	S.C.	3	3
7th	Moss, Frank E.	Dem	Utah	11	1

Minority

Rank	Name	Party	State	Years in: Senate	Years in: Comm.
RM	Fong, Hiram L.	Rep	Hai.	10	9
2nd	Boggs, J. Caleb	Rep	Del.	9	9
3rd	Fannin, Paul J.	Rep	Ariz.	5	2
4th	Stevens, Theodore F.	Rep	Alas.	1	1
5th	Bellmon, Henry	Rep	Okla.	1	1

Note: Rankings on this committee for the following members were affected by other chamber service: Ralph W. Yarborough (Dem-Tex.), Chair, Labor and Public Welfare; and Jennings Randolph (Dem-W.Va.), Chair, Public Works.

Departures from the Senate:	Majority			Minority		
Defeated for Renomination	Yarborough, Ralph W.	Tex.	Dem	None		
Departures from Committee for:						
Moved to Veterans' Affairs	Hartke, R. Vance	Ind.	Dem	None		
No new assignment	None			Fannin, Paul J.	Ariz.	Rep

POST OFFICE AND CIVIL SERVICE / 92nd Congress

Service Dates of Committee Chair: Jan. 28,1971-Jan. 4,1973
Service Dates of Majority Members: Jan. 28,1971-Jan. 4,1973
Service Dates of Minority Members: Jan. 29,1971-Jan. 12,1973

Majority

Rank	Name	Party	State	Years in: Senate	Years in: Comm.
Chr	McGee, Gale W.	Dem	Wyo.	13	8
2nd	Randolph, Jennings	Dem	W.Va.	13	11
3rd	Burdick, Quentin N.	Dem	N.D.	11	7
4th	Hollings, Ernest F.	Dem	S.C.	5	5
5th	Moss, Frank E.	Dem	Utah	13	3

Minority

Rank	Name	Party	State	Years in: Senate	Years in: Comm.
RM	Fong, Hiram L.	Rep	Hai.	12	12
2nd	Boggs, J. Caleb	Rep	Del.	11	11
3rd	Stevens, Theodore F.	Rep	Alas.	3	3
4th	Bellmon, Henry	Rep	Okla.	3	3

Note: Ranking on this committee for the following member was affected by other chamber service: Jennings Randolph (Dem-W.Va.), Chair, Public Works.

Departures from the Senate:	Majority	Minority		
Defeated for Reelection	None	Boggs, J. Caleb	Del.	Rep

POST OFFICE AND CIVIL SERVICE / 93rd Congress

Service Dates of Committee Chair: Jan. 4,1973-Jan. 17,1975
Service Dates of Majority Members: Jan. 4,1973-Jan. 17,1975
Service Dates of Minority Members: Jan. 12,1973-Jan. 23,1975

Majority					Minority				
			Years in:					Years in:	
Rank Name	Party	State	Senate	Comm.	Rank Name	Party	State	Senate	Comm.
Chr McGee, Gale W.	Dem	Wyo.	15	10	RM Fong, Hiram L.	Rep	Hai.	14	13
2nd Randolph, Jennings	Dem	W.Va.	15	13	2nd Stevens, Theodore F.	Rep	Alas.	5	4
3rd Burdick, Quentin N.	Dem	N.D.	13	8	3rd Bellmon, Henry	Rep	Okla.	5	4
4th Hollings, Ernest F.	Dem	S.C.	7	6	4th Saxbe, William B.	Rep	Ohio	5	1
5th Moss, Frank E.	Dem	Utah	15	4					

Note: Ranking on this committee for the following member was affected by other chamber service: Jennings Randolph (Dem-W.Va.), Chair, Public Works.

Changes:
Minority:

Saxbe, William B.	Rep	Ohio	Jan. 3,1974	Resigned; appointed Attorney General
Dole, Robert J.	Rep	Kans.	Jan. 24,1974	Replaced Saxbe.

POST OFFICE AND CIVIL SERVICE / 94th Congress

Service Dates of Committee Chair: Jan. 17,1975-Jan. 3,1977
Service Dates of Majority Members: Jan. 17,1975-Jan. 10,1977
Service Dates of Minority Members: Jan. 23,1975-Jan. 10,1977

Majority					Minority				
			Years in:					Years in:	
Rank Name	Party	State	Senate	Comm.	Rank Name	Party	State	Senate	Comm.
Chr McGee, Gale W.	Dem	Wyo.	17	12	RM Fong, Hiram L.	Rep	Hai.	16	16
2nd Randolph, Jennings	Dem	W.Va.	17	15	2nd Stevens, Theodore F.	Rep	Alas.	7	7
3rd Burdick, Quentin N.	Dem	N.D.	15	11	3rd Bellmon, Henry	Rep	Okla.	7	7
4th Hollings, Ernest F.	Dem	S.C.	9	9	4th Dole, Robert J.	Rep	Kans.	7	1
5th Moss, Frank E.	Dem	Utah	17	7					

Notes: Norris Cotton (Rep-N.H.), appointed to fill a vacancy caused by the contested election between John Durkin (Dem) and Louis Wyman (Rep), left the Senate upon the seating of Durkin on Sep. 19,1975, resulting in a change in size and party ratio to 6 Democrats and 3 Republicans. Ranking on this committee for the following member was affected by other chamber service: Jennings Randolph (Dem-W.Va.), Chair, Public Works.

Addition:
Majority: 6th Leahy, Patrick J. Dem Vt. Sep. 19,1975

Changes:
Minority:
Dole, Robert J. Rep Kans. Sep. 19,1975 Ratio change; left committee for no new assignment.

Departures from the Senate:	Majority			Minority		
Defeated for Reelection	McGee, Gale W.	Wyo.	Dem	None		
	Moss, Frank E.	Utah	Dem			
Retired	None			Fong, Hiram L.	Hai.	Rep

POST OFFICE AND CIVIL SERVICE / 95th Congress

* Reorganized into the Committee on GOVERNMENTAL AFFAIRS on Feb. 11,1977.

Service Dates of Committee Chair: Jan. 10,1977-Feb. 11,1977
Service Dates of Majority Members: Jan. 10,1977-Feb. 11,1977
Service Dates of Minority Members: Jan. 10,1977-Feb. 22,1977

Majority

			Years in:	
Rank Name	**Party**	**State**	**Senate**	**Comm.**
Chr Burdick, Quentin N.	Dem	N.D.	17	13
2nd Randolph, Jennings	Dem	W.Va.	19	17
3rd Hollings, Ernest F.	Dem	S.C.	11	10
4th Leahy, Patrick J.	Dem	Vt.	3	2

Minority

			Years in:	
Rank Name	**Party**	**State**	**Senate**	**Comm.**
RM Stevens, Theodore F.	Rep	Alas.	9	8
2nd Bellmon, Henry	Rep	Okla.	9	8

Note: Ranking on this committee for the following member was affected by other chamber service: Jennings Randolph (Dem-W.Va.), Chair, Public Works.

Changes:

Majority:

Burdick, Quentin N.	Dem	N.D.	Feb. 11,1977	Moved to Appropriations.
Randolph, Jennings	Dem	W.Va.	Feb. 11,1977	Left committee; no new assignment.
Hollings, Ernest F.	Dem	S.C.	Feb. 11,1977	Left committee; no new assignment.
Leahy, Patrick J.	Dem	Vt.	Feb. 11,1977	Moved to Appropriations.

Minority:

Stevens, Theodore F.	Rep	Alas.	Feb. 22,1977	Moved to reorganized Governmental Affairs.
Bellmon, Henry	Rep	Okla.	Feb. 22,1977	Left committee; no new assignment.

RULES AND ADMINISTRATION

Jurisdiction, 1947

Established by the Legislative Reorganization Act of 1946:

[Section 102.(1)(o)]

(1) Committee on Rules and Administration, to consist of thirteen Senators, to which committee shall be referred all proposed legislation, messages, petitions, memorials, and other matters relating to the following subjects:

(A) Matters relating to the payment of money out of the contingent fund of the Senate or creating a charge upon the same; except that any resolution relating to substantive matter within the jurisdiction of any other standing committee of the Senate shall be first referred to such committee.
(B) Except as provided in paragraph (n) 8, [Committee on Public Works], matters relating to the Library of Congress and the Senate Library; statuary and pictures; acceptance or purchase of works of art for the Capitol; the Botanic Gardens; management of the Library of Congress; purchase of books and manuscripts; erection of monuments to the memory of individuals.
(C) Except as provided in paragraph (n) 8, matters relating to the Smithsonian Institution and the incorporation of similar institutions.
(D) Matters relating to the election of the President, Vice President, or Members of Congress; corrupt practices; contested elections; credentials and qualifications; Federal elections generally; Presidential succession.
(E) Matters relating to parliamentary rules; floor and gallery rules; Senate Restaurant; administration of the Senate Office Building and of the Senate Wing of the Capitol; assignment of office space; and services to the Senate.
(F) Matters relating to printing and correction of the Congressional Record.

(2) Such committee shall also have the duty of examining all bills, amendments, and joint resolutions after passage by the Senate; and, in cooperation with the Committee on House Administration of the House of Representatives, of examining all bills and joint resolutions which shall have passed both Houses, to see that the same are correctly enrolled; and when signed by the Speaker of the House and the President of the Senate, shall forthwith present the same, when they shall have originated in the Senate, to the President of the United States in person, and report the fact and date of such presentation to the Senate. Such committee shall also have the duty of assigning office space in the Senate Wing of the Capitol and in the Senate Office Building.

Jurisdiction, 1977

Jurisdiction as contained in Senate Resolution 4, the Committee System Reorganization Amendments of 1977, February 4, 1977:

[Rule XXV.(1)(n)]

(1) Committee on Rules and Administration, to which committee shall be referred all proposed legislation, messages, petitions, memorials, and other matters relating to the following subjects:

1. Meetings of the Congress and attendance of Members.
2. Federal elections generally, including the election of the President, Vice President, and Members of the Congress.
3. Credentials and qualifications of Members of the Senate, contested elections, and acceptance of incompatible offices.
4. Presidential succession.
5. Corrupt practices.
6. The United States Capitol and congressional office buildings, the Library of Congress, the Smithsonian Institution (and the incorporation of similar institutions), and the Botanic Gardens.
7. The Government Printing Office, and the printing and correction of the Congressional Record.
8. The Senate Library and statuary, art, and pictures in the Capitol and Senate Office Buildings.
9. Purchase of books and manuscripts and erection of monuments to the memory of individuals.
10. Payment of money out of the contingent fund of the Senate or creating a charge upon the same (except that any resolution relating to substantive matter within the jurisdiction of any other standing committee of the Senate shall

be first referred to such committee).

11. Congressional organization relative to rules and procedures, and Senate rules and regulations, including floor and gallery rules.
12. Administration of the Senate Office Buildings and the Senate wing of the Capitol, including the assignment of office space.
13. Services to the Senate, including the Senate restaurant.

(2) Such committee shall also--

(A) make a continuing study of the organization and operation of the congress of the United States and shall recommend improvements in such organization and operation with a view toward strengthening the Congress, simplifying its operations, improving its relationships with other branches of the United States Government, and enabling it better to meet its responsibilities under the constitution of the United States; and

(B) identify any court proceeding or action which, in the opinion of the Committee, is of vital interest to the Congress as a constitutionally established institution of the Federal Government and call such proceeding or action to the attention of the Senate.

Jurisdiction, 1992

Jurisdiction contained in the Standing Rules of the Senate (as revised to March 18, 1992):

[Rule XXV.(1)(n)]

(1) Committee on Rules and Administration, to which committee shall be referred all proposed legislation, messages, petitions, memorials, and other matters relating to the following subjects:

1. Administration of the Senate Office Buildings and the Senate wing of the Capitol, including the assignment of office space.
2. Congressional organization relative to rules and procedures, and Senate rules and regulations, including floor and gallery rules.
3. Corrupt practices.
4. Credential and qualifications of Members of the Senate, contested elections, and acceptance of incompatible offices.
5. Federal elections generally, including the election of the President, Vice President, and Members of the Congress.
6. Government Printing Office, and the printing and correction of the Congressional Record, as well as those matters provided for under rule XI.
7. Meetings of the Congress and attendance of Members.
8. Payment of money out of the contingent fund of the Senate or creating a charge upon the same (except that any resolution relating to substantive matter within the jurisdiction of any other standing committee of the Senate shall be first referred to such committee).
9. Presidential succession.
10. Purchase of books and manuscripts and erection of monuments to the memory of individuals.
11. Senate Library and statuary, art, and pictures in the Capitol and Senate Office Buildings.
12. Services to the Senate, including the Senate restaurant.
13. United States Capitol and congressional office buildings, the Library of Congress, the Smithsonian Institution (and the incorporation of similar institutions), and the Botanic Gardens.

(2) Such committee shall also:

(A) make a continuing study of the organization and operation of the Congress of the United States and shall recommend improvements in such organization and operation with a view towards strengthening the Congress, simplifying its operations, improving its relationships with other branches of the United States Government, and enabling it better to meet its responsibilities under the Constitution of the United States; and,

(B) identify any court proceeding or action which, in the opinion of the Committee, is of vital interest to the Congress as a constitutionally established institution of the Federal Government and call such proceeding or action to the attention of the Senate.

RULES AND ADMINISTRATION / 80th Congress

Service Dates of Committee Chair: Jan. 6,1947-Jan. 3,1949
Service Dates of Majority Members: Jan. 6,1947-Jan. 10,1949
Service Dates of Minority Members: Jan. 8,1947-Jan. 10,1949

Majority

Rank	Name	Party	State	Years in: Senate	Years in: Comm.
Chr	Brooks, C. Wayland	Rep	Ill.	7	4
2nd	Wherry, Kenneth S.	Rep	Neb.	5	4
3rd	Hickenlooper, Bourke B.	Rep	Iowa	3	1
4th	Knowland, William F.	Rep	Cal.	2	1
5th	Lodge, Henry Cabot Jr.	Rep	Mass.	8 *2	1
6th	Jenner, William E.	Rep	Ind.	1	1
7th	Bricker, John W.	Rep	Ohio	1	1
8th	Ives, Irving M.	Rep	N.Y.	1	1

Minority

Rank	Name	Party	State	Years in: Senate	Years in: Comm.
RM	Hayden, Carl	Dem	Ariz.	20	16
2nd	Green, Theodore F.	Dem	R.I.	11	11
3rd	McMahon, Brien	Dem	Conn.	3	1
4th	Myers, Francis J.	Dem	Penn.	3	1
5th	Holland, Spessard L.	Dem	Fla.	1	1

*2: Member's 2nd period of service on the committee.

Changes:
Minority:

Name	Party	State	Date	Change
Holland, Spessard L.	Dem	Fla.	Nov. 25,1947	Moved to Public Works.
Stennis, John C.	Dem	Miss.	Nov. 25,1947	Replaced Holland.

	Majority			Minority		
Departures from the Senate:						
Defeated for Reelection	Brooks, C. Wayland	Ill.	Rep	None		
Departures from Committee:						
Moved to Interstate & Foreign Commerce	Bricker, John W.	Ohio	Rep	None		
Moved to Agriculture & Forestry	Hickenlooper, Bourke B.	Iowa	Rep	None		
Moved to Foreign Relations	None			McMahon, Brien	Conn.	Dem

RULES AND ADMINISTRATION / 81st Congress

Service Dates of Committee Chair: Jan. 10,1949-Jan. 15,1951
Service Dates of Majority Members: Jan. 10,1949-Jan. 15,1951
Service Dates of Minority Members: Jan. 10,1949-Jan. 15,1951

Majority

Rank	Name	Party	State	Years in: Senate	Years in: Comm.
Chr	Hayden, Carl	Dem	Ariz.	22	18
2nd	Green, Theodore F.	Dem	R.I.	13	13
3rd	Myers, Francis J.	Dem	Penn.	5	3
4th	Stennis, John C.	Dem	Miss.	2	2
5th	Long, Russell B.	Dem	La.	1	1
6th	Gillette, Guy M.	Dem	Iowa	9 *2	1
7th	Hunt, Lester C.	Dem	Wyo.	1	1
8th	Withers, Garrett L.	Dem	Ky.	1	1

Minority

Rank	Name	Party	State	Years in: Senate	Years in: Comm.
RM	Wherry, Kenneth S.	Rep	Neb.	7	6
2nd	Knowland, William F.	Rep	Cal.	4	3
3rd	Lodge, Henry Cabot Jr.	Rep	Mass.	10 *2	3
4th	Jenner, William E.	Rep	Ind.	3	3
5th	Ives, Irving M.	Rep	N.Y.	3	3

*2: Member's 2nd period of service on the committee.

Note: The resignation of Robert Wagner (Dem-N.Y.) and the appointment of John Foster Dulles (Rep-N.Y.) to fill his vacancy on July 8,1949, led to a change in size and party ratio on this committee to 7 Democrats and 6 Republicans on July 26, 1949.

Vacancy Filled:
Majority: 8th seat by Withers on Jan. 24,1949.

Addition:
Minority: 6th Schoeppel, Andrew F. Rep Kans. July 26,1949

Changes:
Majority:

Name	Party	State	Date	Change
Long, Russell B.	Dem	La.	July 26,1949	Ratio change; moved to Banking and Currency.
Hunt, Lester C.	Dem	Wyo.	Aug. 30,1949	Moved to Interstate and Foreign Commerce.
Taylor, Glen H.	Dem	Ida.	Aug. 30,1949	Replaced Hunt.
Myers, Francis J.	Dem	Penn.	Jan. 12,1950	Moved to Finance.

Taylor, Glen H.	Dem	Ida.	Jan. 12,1950	Moved to Interior and Insular Affairs.
Graham, Frank P.	Dem	N.C.	Jan. 12,1950	Replaced Myers.
Benton, William	Dem	Conn.	Jan. 12,1950	Replaced Taylor.
Withers, Garrett L.	Dem	Ky.	Nov. 26,1950	Resigned; elected to State House.
Graham, Frank P.	Dem	N.C.	Nov. 26,1950	Resigned; defeated for nomination in special election.
Clements, Earle C.	Dem	Ky.	Dec. 11,1950	Replaced Withers.
Smith, Willis	Dem	N.C.	Dec. 11,1950	Replaced Graham.
Minority:				
Knowland, William F.	Rep	Cal.	July 26,1949	Moved to Appropriations.
Hendrickson, Robert C.	Rep	N.J.	July 26,1949	Replaced Knowland.
Ives, Irving M.	Rep	N.Y.	Jan. 12,1950	Moved to Banking and Currency.
Mundt, Karl E.	Rep	S.D.	Jan. 12,1950	Replaced Ives.

Departures from Committee:	Majority		Minority	
Moved to Armed Services	Stennis, John C.	Miss. Dem	None	
Moved to Judiciary; District of Columbia	Smith, Willis	N.C. Dem	None	
Moved to Agriculture & Forestry	None		Mundt, Karl E.	S.D. Rep
Moved to Banking & Currency	None		Schoeppel, Andrew F.	Kans. Rep

RULES AND ADMINISTRATION / 82nd Congress

Service Dates of Committee Chair: Jan. 15,1951-Jan. 13,1953
Service Dates of Majority Members: Jan. 15,1951-Jan. 13,1953
Service Dates of Minority Members: Jan. 15,1951-Jan. 13,1953

Majority

Rank	Name	Party	State	Years in: Senate	Years in: Comm.
Chr	Hayden, Carl	Dem	Ariz.	24	20
2nd	Green, Theodore F.	Dem	R.I.	15	15
3rd	Gillette, Guy M.	Dem	Iowa	11	*2 3
4th	Benton, William	Dem	Conn.	2	2
5th	Clements, Earle C.	Dem	Ky.	1	1
6th	Monroney, A. S. Mike	Dem	Okla.	1	1
7th	Hennings, Thomas C. Jr.	Dem	Mo.	1	1

Minority

Rank	Name	Party	State	Years in: Senate	Years in: Comm.
RM1	Wherry, Kenneth S.	Rep	Neb.	9	9
RM2 2nd	Lodge, Henry Cabot Jr.	Rep	Mass.	12	*2 5
3rd	Jenner, William E.	Rep	Ind.	5	5
4th	Hendrickson, Robert C.	Rep	N.J.	3	2
5th	Flanders, Ralph E.	Rep	Vt.	5	1
6th	Smith, Margaret Chase	Rep	Me.	3	1

*2: Member's 2nd period of service on the committee.

Changes:

Ranking Member:				
RM1 Wherry, Kenneth S.	Rep	Neb.	Nov. 29,1951	Died in office.
RM2 Lodge, Henry Cabot Jr.	Rep	Mass.	Nov. 29,1951	Succeeded Wherry as Ranking Minority Member.
Minority:				
Flanders, Ralph E.	Rep	Vt.	June 22,1951	Moved to Finance.
McCarthy, Joseph R.	Rep	Wisc.	June 22,1951	Replaced Flanders.
Wherry, Kenneth S.	Rep	Neb.	Nov. 29,1951	Died in office.
McCarthy, Joseph R.	Rep	Wisc.	Jan. 14,1952	Moved to Appropriations.
Dirksen, Everett M.	Rep	Ill.	Jan. 14,1952	Replaced Wherry.
Welker, Herman	Rep	Ida.	Jan. 14,1952	Replaced McCarthy.

Departures from the Senate:	Majority		Minority	
Defeated for Reelection	Benton, William	Conn. Dem	Lodge, Henry Cabot Jr.	Mass. Rep
Departures from Committee:				
Moved to Interior & Insular Affairs; Agriculture & Forestry	Clements, Earle C.	Ky. Dem	None	
Moved to Interstate & Foreign Commerce	Monroney, A. S. Mike	Okla. Dem	None	
Moved to Armed Services	None		Hendrickson, Robert C.	N.J. Rep
Moved to Appropriations; Armed Services	None		Smith, Margaret Chase	Me. Rep
Moved to Government Operations; Judiciary; Appropriations	None		Dirksen, Everett McK.	Ill. Rep
Moved to Judiciary; Agriculture & Forestry	None		Welker, Herman	Ida. Rep

RULES AND ADMINISTRATION / 83rd Congress

Service Dates of Committee Chair: Jan. 13,1953-Jan. 11,1955
Service Dates of Majority Members: Jan. 13,1953-Jan. 11,1955
Service Dates of Minority Members: Jan. 13,1953-Jan. 11,1955

Majority

Rank	Name	Party	State	Years in: Senate	Years in: Comm.
Chr	Jenner, William E.	Rep	Ind.	7	7
2nd	Carlson, Frank	Rep	Kans.	3	1
3rd	Potter, Charles E.	Rep	Mich.	1	1
4th	Griswold, Dwight P.	Rep	Neb.	1	1
5th	Purtell, William A.	Rep	Conn.	1	1

Minority

Rank	Name	Party	State	Years in: Senate	Years in: Comm.
RM	Hayden, Carl	Dem	Ariz.	26	22
2nd	Green, Theodore F.	Dem	R.I.	17	17
3rd	Gillette, Guy M.	Dem	Iowa	13	*2 5
4th	Hennings, Thomas C. Jr.	Dem	Mo.	3	2

*2: Member's 2nd period of service on the committee.

Changes:

Majority:

Griswold, Dwight P.	Rep	Neb.	Jan. 21,1953	Moved to Labor and Public Welfare.
Barrett, Frank A.	Rep	Wyo.	Jan. 21,1953	Replaced Griswold.
Purtell, William A.	Rep	Conn.	Jan. 13,1954	Moved to Interstate and Foreign Commerce.
McCarthy, Joseph R.	Rep	Wisc.	Jan. 13,1954	Replaced Purtell.

	Majority		Minority	
Departures from the Senate:				
Defeated for Reelection	None		Gillette, Guy M.	Iowa Dem
Departures from Committee:				
Moved to Appropriations	Potter, Charles E.	Mich. Rep	None	
No new assignment	Carlson, Frank	Kans. Rep	None	

RULES AND ADMINISTRATION / 84th Congress

Service Dates of Committee Chair: Jan. 11,1955-Jan. 9,1957
Service Dates of Majority Members: Jan. 11,1955-Jan. 9,1957
Service Dates of Minority Members: Jan. 11,1955-Jan. 9,1957

Majority

Rank	Name	Party	State	Years in: Senate	Years in: Comm.
Chr	Green, Theodore F.	Dem	R.I.	19	19
2nd	Hayden, Carl	Dem	Ariz.	28	24
3rd	Hennings, Thomas C. Jr.	Dem	Mo.	5	4
4th	Gore, Albert A.	Dem	Tenn.	3	1
5th	Mansfield, Michael J.	Dem	Mont.	3	1

Minority

Rank	Name	Party	State	Years in: Senate	Years in: Comm.
RM	Jenner, William E.	Rep	Ind.	9	9
2nd	Barrett, Frank A.	Rep	Wyo.	3	2
3rd	McCarthy, Joseph R.	Rep	Wisc.	9	*2 1
4th	Curtis, Carl T.	Rep	Neb.	1	1

*2: Member's 2nd period of service on the committee.

Note: Ranking on this committee for the following member was affected by other chamber service: Carl Hayden (Dem-Ariz.), Chair, Appropriations.

Departures from Committee:	Majority		Minority	
Moved to Finance	Gore, Albert A.	Tenn. Dem	Jenner, William E.	Ind. Rep
Moved to Armed Services	None		Barrett, Frank A.	Wyo. Rep

RULES AND ADMINISTRATION / 85th Congress

Service Dates of Committee Chair: Jan. 9,1957-Jan. 14,1959
Service Dates of Majority Members: Jan. 9,1957-Jan. 14,1959
Service Dates of Minority Members: Jan. 9,1957-Jan. 20,1959

Majority

Rank	Name	Party	State	Years in: Senate	Years in: Comm.
Chr	Hennings, Thomas C. Jr.	Dem	Mo.	7	6
2nd	Hayden, Carl	Dem	Ariz.	30	26
3rd	Green, Theodore F.	Dem	R.I.	21	21
4th	Mansfield, Michael J.	Dem	Mont.	5	2
5th	Talmadge, Herman E.	Dem	Ga.	1	1

Minority

Rank	Name	Party	State	Years in: Senate	Years in: Comm.
RM	Curtis, Carl T.	Rep	Neb.	3	2
2nd	McCarthy, Joseph R.	Rep	Wisc.	11	*2 3
3rd	Cooper, John Sherman	Rep	Ky.	5	*1 1
4th	Javits, Jacob K.	Rep	N.Y.	1	1

*1: Member's 1st period of service on the committee; *2: Member's 2nd period of service on the committee.

Note: Rankings on this committee for the following members were affected by other chamber service: Carl Hayden (Dem-Ariz.), Chair, Appropriations; Theodore F. Green (Dem-R.I.), Chair, Foreign Relations; and Joseph R. McCarthy (Rep-Wisc.), Ranking Minority Member, Government Operations.

Changes:

Minority:

McCarthy, Joseph R.	Rep	Wisc.	May 2,1957	Died in office.
Case, Clifford P.	Rep	N.J.	May 22,1957	Replaced McCarthy.

Departures from Committee:

	Majority			Minority		
Moved to Finance	Talmadge, Herman E.	Ga.	Dem	None		
Moved to Public Works; Agriculture & Forestry	None			Cooper, John Sherman	Ky.	Rep
Moved to Aeronautical & Space Sciences; Labor & Public Welfare	None			Case, Clifford P.	N.J.	Rep

RULES AND ADMINISTRATION / 86th Congress

Service Dates of Committee Chair: Jan. 14,1959-Sep. 13,1960
Service Dates of Majority Members: Jan. 14,1959-Jan. 10,1961
Service Dates of Minority Members: Jan. 20,1959-Jan. 13,1961

Majority

Rank	Name	Party	State	Years in: Senate	Years in: Comm.
Chr	Hennings, Thomas C. Jr.	Dem	Mo.	9	8
2nd	Hayden, Carl	Dem	Ariz.	32	28
3rd	Green, Theodore F.	Dem	R.I.	23	23
4th	Mansfield, Michael J.	Dem	Mont.	7	5
5th	Jordan, B. Everett	Dem	N.C.	1	1
6th	Cannon, Howard W.	Dem	Nev.	1	1

Minority

Rank	Name	Party	State	Years in: Senate	Years in: Comm.
RM	Curtis, Carl T.	Rep	Neb.	5	5
2nd	Javits, Jacob K.	Rep	N.Y.	3	3
3rd	Morton, Thruston B.	Rep	Ky.	3	1

Note: Rankings on this committee for the following members were affected by other chamber service: Carl Hayden (Dem-Ariz.), Chair, Appropriations; and Theodore F. Green (Dem-R.I.), Chair, Foreign Relations.

Changes:

Majority:

Hennings, Thomas C. Jr.	Dem	Mo.	Sep. 13,1960	Died in office.

Minority:

Javits, Jacob K.	Rep	N.Y.	Jan. 27,1959	Moved to Banking and Currency.
Keating, Kenneth B.	Rep	N.Y.	Jan. 27,1959	Replaced Javits.
Morton, Thruston B.	Rep	Ky.	Jan. 18,1960	Moved to Finance.
Brunsdale, C. Norman	Rep	N.D.	Jan. 18,1960	Replaced Morton.
Brunsdale, C. Norman	Rep	N.D.	Aug. 7,1960	Resigned and retired.
Martin, Thomas E.	Rep	Iowa	Aug. 24,1960	Replaced Brunsdale.

Departures from the Senate:

	Majority			Minority		
Retired	Green, Theodore F.	R.I.	Dem	Martin, Thomas E.	Iowa	Rep

RULES AND ADMINISTRATION / 87th Congress

Service Dates of Committee Chair: Jan. 10,1961-Feb. 25,1963
Service Dates of Majority Members: Jan. 10,1961-Feb. 25,1963
Service Dates of Minority Members: Jan. 13,1961-Feb. 25,1963

Majority

Rank Name	Party	State	Years in: Senate	Years in: Comm.
Chr Mansfield, Michael J.	Dem	Mont.	9	6
2nd Hayden, Carl	Dem	Ariz.	34	30
3rd Jordan, B. Everett	Dem	N.C.	3	2
4th Cannon, Howard W.	Dem	Nev.	3	2
5th Hickey, John J.	Dem	Wyo.	1	1
6th Pell, Claiborne D.	Dem	R.I.	1	1

Minority

Rank Name	Party	State	Years in: Senate	Years in: Comm.
RM Curtis, Carl T.	Rep	Neb.	7	7
2nd Keating, Kenneth B.	Rep	N.Y.	3	2
3rd Miller, Jack R.	Rep	Iowa	1	1

Note: Ranking on this committee for the following member was affected by other chamber service: Carl Hayden (Dem-Ariz.), Chair, Appropriations.

Changes:

Majority:

Hickey, John J.	Dem	Wyo.	Nov. 6,1962	Resigned; defeated in special election.

Minority:

Keating, Kenneth B.	Rep	N.Y.	Feb. 2,1962	Moved to Commerce.
Miller, Jack R.	Rep	Iowa	Feb. 2,1962	Moved to Public Works.
Dirksen, Everett M.	Rep	Ill.	Feb. 2,1962	Replaced Keating.
Pearson, James B.	Rep	Kans.	Feb. 5,1962	Replaced Miller.
Pearson, James B.	Rep	Kans.	July 18,1962	Moved to Public Works.
Bottum, Joseph H.	Rep	S.D.	July 18,1962	Replaced Pearson.

	Majority			Minority		
Departures from the Senate:						
Defeated for Reelection	None			Bottum, Joseph H.	S.D.	Rep
Departures from Committee:						
Moved to Appropriations	Mansfield, Michael J.	Mont.	Dem	None		
Moved to Finance	None			Dirksen, Everett McK.	Ill.	Rep

RULES AND ADMINISTRATION / 88th Congress

Service Dates of Committee Chair: Feb. 25,1963-Jan. 8,1965
Service Dates of Majority Members: Feb. 25,1963-Jan. 8,1965
Service Dates of Minority Members: Feb. 25,1963-Jan. 15,1965

Majority

Rank Name	Party	State	Years in: Senate	Years in: Comm.
Chr Jordan, B. Everett	Dem	N.C.	5	5
2nd Hayden, Carl	Dem	Ariz.	36	32
3rd Cannon, Howard W.	Dem	Nev.	5	5
4th Pell, Claiborne D.	Dem	R.I.	3	3
5th Clark, Joseph S.	Dem	Penn.	7	1
6th Byrd, Robert C.	Dem	W.Va.	5	1

Minority

Rank Name	Party	State	Years in: Senate	Years in: Comm.
RM Curtis, Carl T.	Rep	Neb.	9	9
2nd Cooper, John Sherman	Rep	Ky.	11	*2 1
3rd Scott, Hugh D. Jr.	Rep	Penn.	5	1

*2: Member's 2nd period of service on the committee.

Note: Ranking on this committee for the following member was affected by other chamber service: Carl Hayden (Dem-Ariz.), Chair, Appropriations.

RULES AND ADMINISTRATION / 89th Congress

Service Dates of Committee Chair: Jan. 8,1965-Jan. 11,1967
Service Dates of Majority Members: Jan. 8,1965-Jan. 11,1967
Service Dates of Minority Members: Jan. 15,1965-Jan. 16,1967

Majority

Rank	Name	Party	State	Years in: Senate	Years in: Comm.
Chr	Jordan, B. Everett	Dem	N.C.	7	6
2nd	Hayden, Carl	Dem	Ariz.	38	34
3rd	Cannon, Howard W.	Dem	Nev.	7	6
4th	Pell, Claiborne D.	Dem	R.I.	5	4
5th	Clark, Joseph S.	Dem	Penn.	9	2
6th	Byrd, Robert C.	Dem	W.Va.	7	2

Minority

Rank	Name	Party	State	Years in: Senate	Years in: Comm.
RM	Curtis, Carl T.	Rep	Neb.	11	11
2nd	Cooper, John Sherman	Rep	Ky.	13	*2 2
3rd	Scott, Hugh D. Jr.	Rep	Penn.	7	2

*2: Member's 2nd period of service on the committee.

Note: Ranking on this committee for the following member was affected by other chamber service: Carl Hayden (Dem-Ariz.), Chair, Appropriations.

RULES AND ADMINISTRATION / 90th Congress

Service Dates of Committee Chair: Jan. 11,1967-Jan. 14,1969
Service Dates of Majority Members: Jan. 11,1967-Jan. 14,1969
Service Dates of Minority Members: Jan. 16,1967-Jan. 14,1969

Majority

Rank	Name	Party	State	Years in: Senate	Years in: Comm.
Chr	Jordan, B. Everett	Dem	N.C.	9	8
2nd	Hayden, Carl	Dem	Ariz.	40	36
3rd	Cannon, Howard W.	Dem	Nev.	9	8
4th	Pell, Claiborne D.	Dem	R.I.	7	7
5th	Clark, Joseph S.	Dem	Penn.	11	4
6th	Byrd, Robert C.	Dem	W.Va.	9	4

Minority

Rank	Name	Party	State	Years in: Senate	Years in: Comm.
RM	Curtis, Carl T.	Rep	Neb.	13	13
2nd	Cooper, John Sherman	Rep	Ky.	15	*2 4
3rd	Scott, Hugh D. Jr.	Rep	Penn.	9	4

*2: Member's 2nd period of service on the committee.

Note: Ranking on this committee for the following member was affected by other chamber service: Carl Hayden (Dem-Ariz.), Chair, Appropriations.

Departures from the Senate:	Majority		Minority
Defeated for Reelection	Clark, Joseph S.	Penn. Dem	None
Retired	Hayden, Carl	Ariz. Dem	None

RULES AND ADMINISTRATION / 91st Congress

Service Dates of Committee Chair: Jan. 14,1969-Jan. 28,1971
Service Dates of Majority Members: Jan. 14,1969-Jan. 28,1971
Service Dates of Minority Members: Jan. 14,1969-Jan. 29,1971

Majority

Rank	Name	Party	State	Years in: Senate	Years in: Comm.
Chr	Jordan, B. Everett	Dem	N.C.	11	11
2nd	Cannon, Howard W.	Dem	Nev.	11	11
3rd	Pell, Claiborne D.	Dem	R.I.	9	9
4th	Byrd, Robert C.	Dem	W.Va.	11	6
5th	Allen, James B.	Dem	Ala.	1	1

Minority

Rank	Name	Party	State	Years in: Senate	Years in: Comm.
RM	Curtis, Carl T.	Rep	Neb.	15	15
2nd	Cooper, John Sherman	Rep	Ky.	17	*2 6
3rd	Scott, Hugh D. Jr.	Rep	Penn.	11	6
4th	Thurmond, J. Strom	Rep	S.C.	14	1

*2: Member's 2nd period of service on the committee.

Departures from Committee:	Majority	Minority	
Moved to Veterans' Affairs	None	Thurmond, J. Strom	S.C. Rep
No new assignment	None	Curtis, Carl T.	Neb. Rep

RULES AND ADMINISTRATION / 92nd Congress

Service Dates of Committee Chair: Jan. 28,1971-Jan. 3,1973
Service Dates of Majority Members: Jan. 28,1971-Jan. 4,1973
Service Dates of Minority Members: Jan. 29,1971-Jan. 12,1973

Majority

Rank	Name	Party	State	Years in: Senate	Years in: Comm.
Chr	Jordan, B. Everett	Dem	N.C.	13	13
2nd	Cannon, Howard W.	Dem	Nev.	13	13
3rd	Pell, Claiborne D.	Dem	R.I.	11	11
4th	Byrd, Robert C.	Dem	W.Va.	13	8
5th	Allen, James B.	Dem	Ala.	3	3

Minority

Rank	Name	Party	State	Years in: Senate	Years in: Comm.
RM1	Prouty, Winston L.	Rep	Vt.	13	1
2nd	Cooper, John Sherman	Rep	Ky.	19	*2 8
3rd	Scott, Hugh D. Jr.	Rep	Penn.	13	8
4th	Griffin, Robert P.	Rep	Mich.	5	1

*2: Member's 2nd period of service on the committee.

Note: Rankings on this committee for the following members were affected by other chamber service: John Sherman Cooper (Rep-Ky.), Ranking Minority Member, Public Works; Hugh D. Scott, Jr. (Rep-Penn.), Senate Minority Leader; and Robert P. Griffin (Rep-Mich.), Senate Minority Whip.

Changes:

Ranking Member:

	Name	Party	State	Date	Change
RM1	Prouty, Winston L.	Rep	Vt.	Sep. 10,1971	Died in office.
RM2	Stevens, Theodore F.	Rep	Alas.	Sep. 21,1971	Succeeded Prouty as Ranking Minority Member.
RM2	Stevens, Theodore F.	Rep	Alas.	Feb. 23,1972	Moved to Appropriations.
RM3	Cook, Marlow W.	Rep	Ky.	Feb. 23,1972	Succeeded Stevens as Ranking Minority Member.

Minority:

Name	Party	State	Date	Change
Prouty, Winston L.	Rep	Vt.	Sep. 10,1971	Died in office.
Stevens, Theodore F.	Rep	Alas.	Sep. 21,1971	Replaced Prouty.
Stevens, Theodore F.	Rep	Alas.	Feb. 23,1972	Moved to Appropriations.
Cook, Marlow W.	Rep	Ky.	Feb. 23,1972	Replaced Stevens.

Departures from the Senate:

	Majority			Minority		
Defeated for Renomination	Jordan, B. Everett	N.C.	Dem	None		
Retired	None			Cooper, John Sherman	Ky.	Rep

RULES AND ADMINISTRATION / 93rd Congress

Service Dates of Committee Chair: Jan. 4,1973-Jan. 17,1975
Service Dates of Majority Members: Jan. 4,1973-Jan. 17,1975
Service Dates of Minority Members: Jan. 12,1973-Jan. 23,1975

Majority

Rank	Name	Party	State	Years in: Senate	Years in: Comm.
Chr	Cannon, Howard W.	Dem	Nev.	15	14
2nd	Pell, Claiborne D.	Dem	R.I.	13	12
3rd	Byrd, Robert C.	Dem	W.Va.	15	10
4th	Allen, James B.	Dem	Ala.	5	4
5th	Williams, Harrison A. Jr.	Dem	N.J.	15	1

Minority

Rank	Name	Party	State	Years in: Senate	Years in: Comm.
RM	Cook, Marlow W.	Rep	Ky.	5	1
2nd	Scott, Hugh D. Jr.	Rep	Penn.	15	10
3rd	Griffin, Robert P.	Rep	Mich.	7	2
4th	Hatfield, Mark O.	Rep	Ore.	7	1

Note: Rankings on this committee for the following members were affected by other chamber service: Hugh D. Scott, Jr. (Rep-Penn.), Senate Minority Leader; and Robert P. Griffin (Rep-Mich.), Senate Minority Whip.

Changes:

Minority:

Name	Party	State	Date	Change
Cook, Marlow W.	Rep	Ky.	Dec. 27,1974	Resigned; defeated for reelection.

RULES AND ADMINISTRATION / 94th Congress

Service Dates of Committee Chair: Jan. 17,1975-Jan. 10,1977
Service Dates of Majority Members: Jan. 17,1975-Jan. 10,1977
Service Dates of Minority Members: Jan. 23,1975-Jan. 10,1977

Majority

Rank	Name	Party	State	Years in: Senate	Years in: Comm.
Chr	Cannon, Howard W.	Dem	Nev.	17	17
2nd	Pell, Claiborne D.	Dem	R.I.	15	15
3rd	Byrd, Robert C.	Dem	W.Va.	17	12
4th	Allen, James B.	Dem	Ala.	7	7
5th	Williams, Harrison A. Jr.	Dem	N.J.	17	3

Minority

Rank	Name	Party	State	Years in: Senate	Years in: Comm.
RM	Hatfield, Mark O.	Rep	Ore.	9	3
2nd	Scott, Hugh D. Jr.	Rep	Penn.	17	12
3rd	Griffin, Robert P.	Rep	Mich.	9	4

Notes: Norris Cotton (Rep-N.H.), appointed to fill a vacancy caused by the contested election between John Durkin (Dem) and Louis Wyman (Rep), left the Senate upon the seating of Durkin on Sep. 19,1975. This resulted in an official change in size and party ratio on this committee to 6 Democrats and 3 Republicans on Sep. 22,1975, after Richard Clark (Dem-Iowa) had been seated. Rankings on this committee for the following members were affected by other chamber service: Hugh D. Scott, Jr. (Rep-Penn.), Senate Minority Leader; and Robert P. Griffin (Rep-Mich.), Senate Minority Whip.

Addition:
Majority: 6th Clark, Richard C. Dem Iowa Sep. 19,1975

Departures from the Senate:

	Majority	Minority		
Retired	None	Scott, Hugh D. Jr.	Penn.	Rep

RULES AND ADMINISTRATION / 95th Congress

Service Dates of Committee Chairs: Ch1 Jan. 10,1977-Jan. 27,1978
Ch2 Jan. 27,1978-Jan. 23,1979
Service Dates of Majority Members: Jan. 10,1977-Jan. 23,1979
Service Dates of Minority Members: Jan. 10,1977-Jan. 23,1979

Majority

Rank	Name	Party	State	Years in: Senate	Years in: Comm.
Ch1	Cannon, Howard W.	Dem	Nev.	19	18
Ch2 2nd	Pell, Claiborne D.	Dem	R.I.	17	17
3rd	Byrd, Robert C.	Dem	W.Va.	19	14
4th	Allen, James B.	Dem	Ala.	9	8
5th	Williams, Harrison A. Jr.	Dem	N.J.	19	5
6th	Clark, Richard C.	Dem	Iowa	5	2

Minority

Rank	Name	Party	State	Years in: Senate	Years in: Comm.
RM	Hatfield, Mark O.	Rep	Ore.	11	4
2nd	Griffin, Robert P.	Rep	Mich.	11	6
3rd	Tower, John G.	Rep	Tex.	16	*T 1

*T: Temporary member of the committee.

Note: Ranking on this committee for the following member was affected by other chamber service: Robert P. Griffin (Rep-Mich.), Senate Minority Whip.

Changes:

Chair:

	Name	Party	State	Date	Change
Ch1	Cannon, Howard W.	Dem	Nev.	Jan. 27,1978	Became Chair of Commerce, Science and Transportation; remained on committee.
Ch2	Pell, Claiborne D.	Dem	R.I.	Jan. 27,1978	Succeeded Cannon as Chair.

Majority:

Name	Party	State	Date	Change
Allen, James B.	Dem	Ala.	June 1,1978	Died in office.
Ford, Wendell H.	Dem	Ky.	July 11,1978	Replaced Allen.

Minority:

Name	Party	State	Date	Change
Tower, John G.	Rep	Tex.	Feb. 22,1977	Moved to Select Committee to Study the Senate Committee System.
Baker, Howard H. Jr.	Rep	Tenn.	Feb. 22,1977	Replaced Tower.

Departures from the Senate:

	Majority			Minority		
Defeated for Reelection	Clark, Richard C.	Iowa	Dem	Griffin, Robert P.	Mich.	Rep

RULES AND ADMINISTRATION / 96th Congress

Service Dates of Committee Chair: Jan. 23,1979-Jan. 5,1981
Service Dates of Majority Members: Jan. 23,1979-Jan. 5,1981
Service Dates of Minority Members: Jan. 23,1979-Jan. 5,1981

Majority

Rank	Name	Party	State	Years in: Senate	Comm.
Chr	Pell, Claiborne D.	Dem	R.I.	19	19
2nd	Cannon, Howard W.	Dem	Nev.	21	21
3rd	Byrd, Robert C.	Dem	W.Va.	21	16
4th	Williams, Harrison A. Jr.	Dem	N.J.	21	7
5th	Ford, Wendell H.	Dem	Ky.	5	1
6th	DeConcini, Dennis	Dem	Ariz.	3	1

Minority

Rank	Name	Party	State	Years in: Senate	Comm.
RM	Hatfield, Mark O.	Rep	Ore.	13	7
2nd	Baker, Howard H. Jr.	Rep	Tenn.	13	2
3rd	Tower, John G.	Rep	Tex.	18	1
4th	Schweiker, Richard S.	Rep	Penn.	11	1

Note: Ranking on this committee for the following member was affected by other chamber service: Howard W. Cannon (Dem-Nev.), Chair, Commerce, Science and Transportation.

	Majority		Minority	
Departures from the Senate:				
Appointed Secretary of Health & Human Services	None		Schweiker, Richard S.	Penn. Rep
Departures from Committee:				
No new assignment	DeConcini, Dennis	Ariz. Dem	Tower, John G.	Tex. Rep

RULES AND ADMINISTRATION / 97th Congress

Service Dates of Committee Chair: Jan. 5,1981-Jan. 3,1983
Service Dates of Majority Members: Jan. 5,1981-Jan. 3,1983
Service Dates of Minority Members: Jan. 5,1981-Jan. 3,1983

Majority

Rank	Name	Party	State	Years in: Senate	Comm.
Chr	Mathias, Charles McC. Jr.	Rep	Md.	13	1
2nd	Hatfield, Mark O.	Rep	Ore.	14	8
3rd	Baker, Howard H. Jr.	Rep	Tenn.	15	4
4th	McClure, James A.	Rep	Ida.	9	1
5th	Helms, Jesse A.	Rep	N.C.	9	1
6th	Warner, John W.	Rep	Va.	3 *1	1
7th	Dole, Robert J.	Rep	Kans.	13	1

Minority

Rank	Name	Party	State	Years in: Senate	Comm.
RM	Ford, Wendell H.	Dem	Ky.	7	3
2nd	Cannon, Howard W.	Dem	Nev.	23	22
3rd	Pell, Claiborne D.	Dem	R.I.	21	20
4th	Byrd, Robert C.	Dem	W.Va.	23	18
5th	Williams, Harrison A. Jr.	Dem	N.J.	23	9

*1: Member's 1st period of service.

Note: Rankings on this committee for the following members were affected by other chamber service: Mark O. Hatfield (Rep-Ore.), Chair, Appropriations; Howard H. Baker, Jr. (Rep-Tenn.), Senate Majority Leader; Howard W. Cannon (Dem-Nev.), Ranking Minority Member, Commerce, Science and Transportation; Claiborne D. Pell (Dem-R.I.), Ranking Minority Member, Foreign Relations; Robert C. Byrd (Dem-W.Va.), Senate Minority Leader; and Harrison A. Williams, Jr. (Dem-N.J.), Ranking Minority Member, Banking, Housing and Urban Affairs.

Changes:
Minority:

Name	Party	State	Date	Change
Williams, Harrison A. Jr.	Dem	N.J.	Mar. 11,1982	Resigned and retired.
Inouye, Daniel K.	Dem	Hai.	Apr. 20,1982	Replaced Williams.

	Majority	Minority	
Departures from the Senate:			
Defeated for Reelection	None	Cannon, Howard W.	Nev. Dem

RULES AND ADMINISTRATION / 98th Congress

Service Dates of Committee Chair: Jan. 3,1983-Feb. 21,1985
Service Dates of Majority Members: Jan. 3,1983-Feb. 21,1985
Service Dates of Minority Members: Jan. 3,1983-Mar. 5,1985

Majority

Rank	Name	Party	State	Years in: Senate	Years in: Comm.
Chr	Mathias, Charles McC. Jr.	Rep	Md.	15	2
2nd	Hatfield, Mark O.	Rep	Ore.	16	10
3rd	Baker, Howard H. Jr.	Rep	Tenn.	17	6
4th	McClure, James A.	Rep	Ida .	11	2
5th	Helms, Jesse A.	Rep	N.C	11	2
6th	Warner, John W.	Rep	Va.	5	*1 2
7th	Dole, Robert J.	Rep	Kans.	15	2

Minority

Rank	Name	Party	State	Years in: Senate	Years in: Comm.
RM	Ford, Wendell H.	Dem	Ky.	9	5
2nd	Pell, Claiborne D.	Dem	R.I.	23	22
3rd	Byrd, Robert C.	Dem	W.Va.	25	20
4th	Inouye, Daniel K.	Dem	Hai.	21	1
5th	DeConcini, Dennis	Dem	Ariz.	7	*2 1

*1: Member's 1st period of service; *2: Member's 2nd period of service on the committee.

Note: Rankings on this committee for the following members were affected by other chamber service: Mark O. Hatfield (Rep-Ore.), Chair, Appropriations; Howard H. Baker, Jr. (Rep-Tenn.), Senate Majority Leader; Claiborne D. Pell (Dem-R.I.), Ranking Minority Member, Foreign Relations; and Robert C. Byrd (Dem-W.Va.), Senate Minority Leader.

Departures from the Senate:	Majority		Minority
Retired	Baker, Howard H. Jr.	Tenn. Rep	None

RULES AND ADMINISTRATION / 99th Congress

Service Dates of Committee Chair: Feb. 21,1985-Jan. 3,1987
Service Dates of Majority Members: Feb. 21,1985-Jan. 6,1987
Service Dates of Minority Members: Mar. 5,1985-Jan. 6,1987

Majority

Rank	Name	Party	State	Years in: Senate	Years in: Comm.
Chr	Mathias, Charles McC. Jr.	Rep	Md.	17	5
2nd	Hatfield, Mark O.	Rep	Ore.	19	13
3rd	McClure, James A.	Rep	Ida.	13	5
4th	Helms, Jesse A.	Rep	N.C.	13	5
5th	Warner, John W.	Rep	Va.	7	*1 5
6th	Dole, Robert J.	Rep	Kans.	17	5
7th	Stevens, Theodore F.	Rep	Alas.	17	*2 1

Minority

Rank	Name	Party	State	Years in: Senate	Years in: Comm.
RM	Ford, Wendell H.	Dem	Ky.	11	7
2nd	Pell, Claiborne D.	Dem	R.I.	25	25
3rd	Byrd, Robert C.	Dem	W.Va.	27	23
4th	Inouye, Daniel K.	Dem	Hai.	23	3
5th	DeConcini, Dennis	Dem	Ariz.	9	*2 3

*1: Member's 1st period of service; *2: Member's 2nd period of service on the committee.

Notes: The committee was expanded and the party ratio changed to 8 Republicans and 7 Democrats on Mar. 5,1985. Rankings on this committee for the following members were affected by other chamber service: Mark O. Hatfield (Rep-Ore.), Chair, Appropriations; Claiborne D. Pell (Dem-R.I.), Ranking Minority Member, Foreign Relations; and Robert C. Byrd (Dem-W.Va.), Senate Minority Leader.

Additions:

Majority:	8th Garn, Jake	Rep	Utah	Mar. 5,1985
Minority:	6th Simon, Paul M.	Dem	Ill.	Mar. 5,1985
	7th Gore, Albert A. Jr.	Dem	Tenn.	Mar. 5,1985

	Majority		Minority	
Departures from the Senate:				
Retired	Mathias, Charles McC. Jr.	Md. Rep	None	
Departures from Committee:				
Moved to Budget; Foreign Relations	None		Simon, Paul M.	Ill. Dem

RULES AND ADMINISTRATION / 100th Congress

Service Dates of Committee Chair: Jan. 6,1987-Feb. 2,1989
Service Dates of Majority Members: Jan. 6,1987-Feb. 2,1989
Service Dates of Minority Members: Jan. 6,1987-Feb. 2,1989

Majority

Rank	Name	Party	State	Years in: Senate	Years in: Comm.
Chr	Ford, Wendell H.	Dem	Ky.	13	9
2nd	Pell, Claiborne D.	Dem	R.I.	27	26
3rd	Byrd, Robert C.	Dem	W.Va.	29	24
4th	Inouye, Daniel K.	Dem	Hai.	25	5
5th	DeConcini, Dennis	Dem	Ariz.	11	*2 5
6th	Gore, Albert A. Jr.	Dem	Tenn.	3	2
7th	Moynihan, Daniel Patrick	Dem	N.Y.	11	1
8th	Dodd, Christopher J.	Dem	Conn.	7	1
9th	Adams, Brock	Dem	Wash.	1	1

Minority

Rank	Name	Party	State	Years in: Senate	Years in: Comm.
RM	Stevens, Theodore F.	Rep	Alas.	19	*2 2
2nd	Hatfield, Mark O.	Rep	Ore.	20	14
3rd	McClure, James A.	Rep	Ida.	15	7
4th	Helms, Jesse A.	Rep	N.C.	15	7
5th	Warner, John W.	Rep	Va.	9	*1 7
6th	Dole, Robert J.	Rep	Kans.	19	7
7th	Garn, Jake	Rep	Utah	13	2

*1: Member's 1st period of service; *2: Member's 2nd period of service on the committee.

Note: Rankings on this committee for the following members were affected by other chamber service: Claiborne D. Pell (Dem-R.I.), Chair, Foreign Relations; and Robert C. Byrd (Dem-W.Va.), Senate Majority Leader. Mark O. Hatfield (Rep-Ore.), Ranking Minority Member, Appropriations; James A. McClure (Rep-Ida.), Ranking Minority Member, Energy and Natural Resources; Jesse A. Helms (Rep-N.C.), Ranking Minority Member, Foreign Relations; John W. Warner (Rep-Va.), Ranking Minority Member, Armed Services; and Robert J. Dole, Senate Minority Leader.

Departures from Committee:	Majority	Minority		
Moved to Special Aging	None	Warner, John W.	Va.	Rep

RULES AND ADMINISTRATION / 101st Congress

Service Dates of Committee Chair: Feb. 2,1989-Mar. 19,1991
Service Dates of Majority Members: Feb. 2,1989-Mar. 19,1991
Service Dates of Minority Members: Feb. 2,1989-Mar. 19,1991

Majority

Rank	Name	Party	State	Years in: Senate	Years in: Comm.
Chr	Ford, Wendell H.	Dem	Ky.	15	11
2nd	Pell, Claiborne D.	Dem	R.I.	29	29
3rd	Byrd, Robert C.	Dem	W.Va.	31	26
4th	Inouye, Daniel K.	Dem	Hai.	27	7
5th	DeConcini, Dennis	Dem	Ariz.	13	*2 7
6th	Gore, Albert A. Jr.	Dem	Tenn.	5	4
7th	Moynihan, Daniel Patrick	Dem	N.Y.	13	3
8th	Dodd, Christopher J.	Dem	Conn.	9	3
9th	Adams, Brock	Dem	Wash.	3	3

Minority

Rank	Name	Party	State	Years in: Senate	Years in: Comm.
RM	Stevens, Theodore F.	Rep	Alas.	21	*2 4
2nd	Hatfield, Mark O.	Rep	Ore.	23	16
3rd	McClure, James A.	Rep	Ida.	17	9
4th	Helms, Jesse A.	Rep	N.C.	17	9
5th	Dole, Robert J.	Rep	Kans.	21	9
6th	Garn, Jake	Rep	Utah	15	4
7th	McConnell, Mitch	Rep	Ky.	5	1

*2: Member's 2nd period of service on the committee.

Note: Rankings on this committee for the following members were affected by other chamber service: Claiborne D. Pell (Dem-R.I.), Chair, Foreign Relations; and Robert C. Byrd (Dem-W.Va.), Chair, Appropriations; Mark O. Hatfield (Rep-Ore.), Ranking Minority Member, Appropriations; James A. McClure (Rep-Ida.), Ranking Minority Member, Energy and Natural Resources; Jesse A. Helms (Rep-N.C.), Ranking Minority Member, Foreign Relations; and Robert J. Dole, Senate Minority Leader.

Departures from the Senate:	Majority	Minority		
Retired	None	McClure, James A.	Ida.	Rep

RULES AND ADMINISTRATION / 102nd Congress

Service Dates of Committee Chair: Mar. 19,1991-Jan. 3,1993
Service Dates of Majority Members: Mar. 19,1991-Jan. 3,1993
Service Dates of Minority Members: Mar. 19,1991-Jan. 3,1993

Majority

Rank	Name	Party	State	Years in: Senate	Years in: Comm.
Chr	Ford, Wendell H.	Dem	Ky.	17	13
2nd	Pell, Claiborne D.	Dem	R.I.	31	31
3rd	Byrd, Robert C.	Dem	W.Va.	33	29
4th	Inouye, Daniel K.	Dem	Hai.	29	9
5th	DeConcini, Dennis	Dem	Ariz.	15	*2 9
6th	Gore, Albert A. Jr.	Dem	Tenn.	7	7
7th	Moynihan, Daniel Patrick	Dem	N.Y.	15	5
8th	Dodd, Christopher J.	Dem	Conn.	11	5
9th	Adams, Brock	Dem	Wash.	5	5

Minority

Rank	Name	Party	State	Years in: Senate	Years in: Comm.
RM	Stevens, Theodore F.	Rep	Alas.	23	*2 7
2nd	Hatfield, Mark O.	Rep	Ore.	25	19
3rd	Helms, Jesse A.	Rep	N.C.	19	11
4th	Warner, John W.	Rep	Va.	13	*2 1
5th	Dole, Robert J.	Rep	Kans.	23	11
6th	Garn, Jake	Rep	Utah	17	7
7th	McConnell, Mitch	Rep	Ky.	7	3

*2: Member's 2nd period of service on the committee.

Notes: Rankings on this committee for the following members were affected by other chamber service: Claiborne D. Pell (Dem-R.I.), Chair, Foreign Relations; and Robert C. Byrd (Dem-W.Va.), Chair, Appropriations; Mark O. Hatfield (Rep-Ore.), Ranking Minority Member, Appropriations; Jesse A. Helms (Rep-N.C.), Ranking Minority Member, Foreign Relations; and Robert J. Dole, Senate Minority Leader. John W. Warner (Rep-Va.) returned to the committee after serving on the Select Committee on Aging, and was credited by the Republican Conference with his previous seniority and ranked 4th.

SMALL BUSINESS

Jurisdiction, 1981

From Senate Resolution 101, March 25, 1981:

[Section 3, Rule XXV.(1)(o)]

(1) Committee on Small Business, to which committee shall be referred all proposed legislation, messages, petitions, memorials, and other matters relating to the Small Business Administration.
(2) Any proposed legislation reported by such committee which relates to matters other than the functions of the Small Business Administration shall, at the request of the chairman of any standing committee having jurisdiction over the subject matter extraneous to the functions of the Small Business Administration, be considered and reported by such standing committee prior to its consideration by the Senate; and likewise measures reported by other committees directly relating to the Small Business Administration shall, at the request of the chairman of the Committee on Small Business, be referred to the Committee on Small Business for its consideration of any portions of the measure dealing with the Small Business Administration, and be reported by this committee prior to its consideration by the Senate.
(3) Such committee shall also study and survey by means of research and investigation all problems of American small business enterprises, and report thereon from time to time.

Jurisdiction, 1992

Jurisdiction contained in the Standing Rules of the Senate (as revised to March 18, 1992):

[Rule (1)(o)]

(1) Committee on Small Business, to which committee shall be referred all proposed legislation, messages, petitions, memorials, and other matters relating to the Small Business Administration.
(2) Any proposed legislation reported by such committee which relates to matters other than the functions of the Small Business Administration shall, at the request of the chairman of any standing committee having jurisdiction over the subject matter extraneous to the functions of the Small Business Administration, be considered and reported by such standing committee prior to its consideration by the Senate; and likewise measures reported by other committees directly relating to the Small Business Administration shall, at the request of the chairman of the Committee on Small Business, be referred to the Committee on Small Business for its consideration of any portions of the measure dealing with the Small Business Administration, and be reported by this committee prior to its consideration by the Senate.
(3) Such committee shall also study and survey by means of research and investigation all problems of American small business enterprises, and report thereon from time to time.

SMALL BUSINESS / 97th Congress

* Became the Standing Committee on SMALL BUSINESS on Mar. 25,1981.

Service Dates of Committee Chair: Mar. 25,1981-Jan. 3,1983
Service Dates of Majority Members: Mar. 25,1981-Jan. 3,1983
Service Dates of Minority Members: Mar. 25,1981-Jan. 3,1983

Majority

Rank	Name	Party	State	Years in: Senate	Years in: Comm.
Chr	Weicker, Lowell P. Jr.	Rep	Conn.	11	*2 7
2nd	Packwood, Robert W.	Rep	Ore.	13	6
3rd	Hatch, Orrin G.	Rep	Utah	5	3
4th	Hayakawa, S. I. (Sam)	Rep	Cal.	5	3
5th	Boschwitz, Rudolf E.	Rep	Minn.	3	3
6th	Gorton, Slade	Rep	Wash.	1	1
7th	Nickles, Don	Rep	Okla.	1	1
8th	Rudman, Warren B.	Rep	N.H.	1	1
9th	D'Amato, Alfonse M.	Rep	N.Y.	1	1

Minority

Rank	Name	Party	State	Years in: Senate	Years in: Comm.
RM	Nunn, Samuel A.	Dem	Ga.	9	9
2nd	Huddleston, Walter D.	Dem	Ky.	9	3
3rd	Bumpers, Dale	Dem	Ark.	7	3
4th	Sasser, James R.	Dem	Tenn.	5	3
5th	Baucus, Max S.	Dem	Mont.	3	3
6th	Levin, Carl M.	Dem	Mich.	3	3
7th	Tsongas, Paul E.	Dem	Mass.	3	1
8th	Dixon, Alan J.	Dem	Ill.	1	1

*2: Member's 2nd period of service on the committee.

Notes: "Years in committee" include members' continuous service on the Select Committee on Small Business. Members were appointed to the Select Committee on Jan. 5,1981 and were named to the Standing Committee on Mar. 25,1981.

Departures from the Senate:	Majority			Minority
Retired	Hayakawa, S. I. (Sam)	Cal.	Rep	None

SMALL BUSINESS / 98th Congress

Service Dates of Committee Chair: Jan. 3,1983-Mar. 5,1985
Service Dates of Majority Members: Jan. 3,1983-Mar. 5,1985
Service Dates of Minority Members: Jan. 3,1983-Mar. 5,1985

Majority

Rank	Name	Party	State	Years in: Senate	Years in: Comm.
Chr	Weicker, Lowell P. Jr.	Rep	Conn.	13 *2	8
2nd	Packwood, Robert W.	Rep	Ore.	15	8
3rd	Hatch, Orrin G.	Rep	Utah	7	4
4th	Boschwitz, Rudolf E.	Rep	Minn.	5	4
5th	Gorton, Slade	Rep	Wash.	3	2
6th	Nickles, Don	Rep	Okla.	3	2
7th	Rudman, Warren B.	Rep	N.H.	3	2
8th	D'Amato, Alfonse M.	Rep	N.Y.	3	2
9th	Kasten, Robert W. Jr.	Rep	Wisc.	3	1
10th	Pressler, Larry L.	Rep	S.D.	5 *2	1

Minority

Rank	Name	Party	State	Years in: Senate	Years in: Comm.
RM	Nunn, Samuel A.	Dem	Ga.	11	10
2nd	Huddleston, Walter D.	Dem	Ky.	11	4
3rd	Bumpers, Dale	Dem	Ark.	9	4
4th	Sasser, James R.	Dem	Tenn.	7	4
5th	Baucus, Max S.	Dem	Mont.	5	4
6th	Levin, Carl M.	Dem	Mich.	5	4
7th	Tsongas, Paul E.	Dem	Mass.	5	2
8th	Dixon, Alan J.	Dem	Ill.	3	2
9th	Boren, David L.	Dem	Okla.	5	1

*2: Member's 2nd period of service on the committee.

Note: "Years in committee" include members' continuous service on the Select Committee on Small Business.

	Majority			Minority		
Departures from the Senate:						
Defeated for Reelection	None			Huddleston, Walter D.	Ky.	Dem
Retired	None			Tsongas, Paul E.	Mass.	Dem
Departures from Committee:						
Moved to Select Intelligence	Hatch, Orrin G.	Utah	Rep	None		
No new assignment	Packwood, Robert W.	Ore.	Rep	None		

SMALL BUSINESS / 99th Congress

Service Dates of Committee Chair: Mar. 5,1985-Jan. 6,1987
Service Dates of Majority Members: Mar. 5,1985-Jan. 6,1987
Service Dates of Minority Members: Mar. 5,1985-Jan. 6,1987

Majority

Rank	Name	Party	State	Years in: Senate	Years in: Comm.
Chr	Weicker, Lowell P. Jr.	Rep	Conn.	15 *2	11
2nd	Boschwitz, Rudolf E.	Rep	Minn.	7	7
3rd	Gorton, Slade	Rep	Wash.	5	5
4th	Nickles, Don	Rep	Okla.	5	5
5th	Rudman, Warren B.	Rep	N.H.	5	5
6th	D'Amato, Alfonse M.	Rep	N.Y.	5	5
7th	Kasten, Robert W. Jr.	Rep	Wisc.	5	3
8th	Pressler, Larry L.	Rep	S.D.	7 *2	3
9th	Goldwater, Barry M.	Rep	Ariz.	29 *2	1
10th	Trible, Paul S. Jr.	Rep	Va.	3	1

Minority

Rank	Name	Party	State	Years in: Senate	Years in: Comm.
RM	Bumpers, Dale	Dem	Ark.	11	7
2nd	Nunn, Samuel A.	Dem	Ga.	13	13
3rd	Sasser, James R.	Dem	Tenn.	9	7
4th	Baucus, Max S.	Dem	Mont.	7	7
5th	Levin, Carl M.	Dem	Mich.	7	7
6th	Dixon, Alan J.	Dem	Ill.	5	5
7th	Boren, David L.	Dem	Okla.	7	3
8th	Harkin, Thomas R.	Dem	Iowa	1	1
9th	Kerry, John F.	Dem	Mass.	1	1

*2: Member's 2nd period of service on the committee.

Note: "Years in committee" include members' continuous service on the Select Committee on Small Business. Ranking on this committee for the following member was affected by other chamber service: Samuel A. Nunn (Dem-Ga.), Ranking Minority Member, Armed Services.

Vacancy Filled:
Majority: 10th seat by Trible on Mar. 6,1985.

Departures from the Senate:	**Majority**		**Minority**
Defeated for Reelection	Gorton, Slade	Wash. Rep	None
Retired	Goldwater, Barry M.	Ariz. Rep	None
Departures from Committee:			
Moved to Appropriations; Budget	Nickles, Don	Okla. Rep	None
Moved to Governmental Affairs	Trible, Paul S. Jr.	Va. Rep	None

SMALL BUSINESS / 100th Congress

Service Dates of Committee Chair: Jan. 6,1987-Feb. 2,1989
Service Dates of Majority Members: Jan. 6,1987-Feb. 2,1989
Service Dates of Minority Members: Jan. 6,1987-Feb. 2,1989

Majority

Rank Name	Party	State	Years in: Senate	Years in: Comm.
Chr Bumpers, Dale	Dem	Ark.	13	8
2nd Nunn, Samuel A.	Dem	Ga.	15	15
3rd Sasser, James R.	Dem	Tenn.	11	8
4th Baucus, Max S.	Dem	Mont.	9	8
5th Levin, Carl M.	Dem	Mich.	9	8
6th Dixon, Alan J.	Dem	Ill.	7	7
7th Boren, David L.	Dem	Okla.	9	5
8th Harkin, Thomas R.	Dem	Iowa	3	2
9th Kerry, John F.	Dem	Mass.	3	2
10th Mikulski, Barbara A.	Dem	Md.	1	1

Minority

Rank Name	Party	State	Years in: Senate	Years in: Comm.
RM Weicker, Lowell P. Jr.	Rep	Conn.	17	*2 12
2nd Boschwitz, Rudolf E.	Rep	Minn.	9	8
3rd Rudman, Warren B.	Rep	N.H.	7	7
4th D'Amato, Alfonse M.	Rep	N.Y.	7	7
5th Kasten, Robert W. Jr.	Rep	Wisc.	7	5
6th Pressler, Larry L.	Rep	S.D.	9	*2 5
7th Wallop, Malcolm	Rep	Wyo.	11	1
8th Bond, Christopher S.	Rep	Mo.	1	1

*2: Member's 2nd period of service on the committee.

Notes: "Years in committee" include members' continuous service on the Select Committee on Small Business. The death of Edward Zorinsky (Dem-Neb.) and the appointment of David K. Karnes (Rep-Neb.) to fill his Senate vacancy on Mar. 10,1987, led to a change in size and party ratio to 10 Democrats and 9 Republicans. Ranking on this committee for the following member was affected by other chamber service: Samuel A. Nunn (Dem-Ga.), Ranking Minority Member, Armed Services.

Addition:
Minority: 9th Karnes, David K. Rep Neb. May 12,1987

Departures from the Senate:	**Majority**		**Minority**	
Defeated for Reelection	None		Weicker, Lowell P. Jr.	Conn. Rep
Defeated for Election	None		Karnes, David K.	Neb. Rep
Departures from Committee:				
Becomes Chair of Budget	Sasser, James R.	Tenn. Dem	None	
Moved to Select Intelligence	None		D'Amato, Alfonse M.	N.Y. Rep
No new assignment	None		Rudman, Warren B.	N.H. Rep

SMALL BUSINESS / 101st Congress

Service Dates of Committee Chair: Feb. 2,1989-Mar. 19,1991
Service Dates of Majority Members: Feb. 2,1989-Mar. 19,1991
Service Dates of Minority Members: Feb. 2,1989-Mar. 19,1991

Majority

Rank Name	Party	State	Years in: Senate	Years in: Comm.
Chr Bumpers, Dale	Dem	Ark.	15	11
2nd Nunn, Samuel A.	Dem	Ga.	17	17
3rd Baucus, Max S.	Dem	Mont.	11	11
4th Levin, Carl M.	Dem	Mich.	11	11
5th Dixon, Alan J.	Dem	Ill.	9	9
6th Boren, David L.	Dem	Okla.	11	7
7th Harkin, Thomas R.	Dem	Iowa	5	4
8th Kerry, John F.	Dem	Mass.	5	4
9th Mikulski, Barbara A.	Dem	Md.	3	3
10th Lieberman, Joseph I.	Dem	Conn.	1	1

Minority

Rank Name	Party	State	Years in: Senate	Years in: Comm.
RM Boschwitz, Rudolf E.	Rep	Minn.	11	11
2nd Kasten, Robert W. Jr.	Rep	Wisc.	9	7
3rd Pressler, Larry L.	Rep	S.D.	11	*2 7
4th Wallop, Malcolm	Rep	Wyo.	13	3
5th Bond, Christopher S.	Rep	Mo.	3	3
6th Grassley, Charles E.	Rep	Iowa	9	1
7th Lott, Trent	Rep	Miss.	1	1
8th Burns, Conrad	Rep	Ida.	1	1
9th Stevens, Theodore F.	Rep	Alas.	21	1

*2: Member's 2nd period of service on the committee.

Note: "Years in committee" include members' continuous service on the Select Committee on Small Business. Ranking on this committee for the following member was affected by other chamber service: Samuel A. Nunn (Dem-Ga.), Ranking Minority Member, Armed Services.

	Majority		Minority	
Departures from the Senate:				
Defeated for Reelection	None		Boschwitz, Rudolf E.	Minn. Rep
Departures from Committee:				
Moved to Agriculture, Nutrition & Forestry; Finance	None		Grassley, Charles E.	Iowa Rep
Moved to Budget	None		Lott, Trent	Miss. Rep
No new assignment	Boren, David L.	Okla. Dem	None	

SMALL BUSINESS / 102nd Congress

Service Dates of Committee Chair: Mar. 19,1991-Jan. 3,1993
Service Dates of Majority Members: Mar. 19,1991-Jan. 3,1993
Service Dates of Minority Members: Mar. 19,1991-Jan. 3,1993

Majority

Rank Name	Party	State	Years in: Senate	Years in: Comm.
Chr Bumpers, Dale	Dem	Ark.	17	13
2nd Nunn, Samuel A.	Dem	Ga.	19	19
3rd Baucus, Max S.	Dem	Mont.	13	13
4th Levin, Carl M.	Dem	Mich.	13	13
5th Dixon, Alan J.	Dem	Ill.	11	11
6th Harkin, Thomas R.	Dem	Iowa	7	6
7th Kerry, John F.	Dem	Mass.	7	6
8th Mikulski, Barbara A.	Dem	Md.	5	5
9th Lieberman, Joseph I.	Dem	Conn.	3	3
10th Wellstone, Paul	Dem	Minn.	1	1

Minority

Rank Name	Party	State	Years in: Senate	Years in: Comm.
RM Kasten, Robert W. Jr.	Rep	Wisc.	11	9
2nd Pressler, Larry L.	Rep	S.D.	13	*2 9
3rd Wallop, Malcolm	Rep	Wyo.	15	5
4th Bond, Christopher S.	Rep	Mo.	5	5
5th Burns, Conrad	Rep	Ida.	3	3
6th Stevens, Theodore F.	Rep	Alas.	23	3
7th Mack, Connie III	Rep	Fla.	3	1
8th Seymour, John	Rep	Cal.	1	1

*2: Member's 2nd period of service on the committee.

Notes: "Years in committee" include members' continuous service on the Select Committee on Small Business. Ranking on this committee for the following member was affected by other chamber service: Samuel A. Nunn (Dem-Ga.), Ranking Minority Member, Armed Services. The death of John Heinz (Rep-Penn.) and the appointment of Harris Wofford (Dem-Penn.) to fill his vacancy on May 9,1991 led to a change in size and party ratio on this committee to 11 Democrats and 8 Republicans on June 4,1991.

Addition:
Majority: 11th Wofford, Harris Dem Penn. June 4,1991

VETERANS' AFFAIRS

Jurisdiction, 1970

Jurisdiction established in Public Law 91-510, the Legislative Reorganization Act of 1970, 9lst Congress, Second Session, October 26, 1970 (84 Statutes 1140, 1164):

[Section 131(q)]

Committee on Veterans' Affairs, to which committee shall be referred all proposed legislation, messages, petitions, memorials, and other matters relating to the following subjects:

1. Veterans' measures generally.
2. Pensions of all wars of the United States, general and special.
3. Life insurance issued by the Government on account of service in the armed forces.
4. Compensation of veterans.
5. Vocational rehabilitation and education of veterans.
6. Veterans' hospitals, medical care and treatment of veterans.
7. Soldiers' and sailors' civil relief.
8. Readjustment of servicemen to civil life.
9. National cemeteries; and

(6) by striking out in subparagraph (k) (relating to the Committee on Interior and Insular Affairs) the following item--

5. Military parks and battlefields, and national cemeteries.

and inserting in lieu thereof--

5. Military parks and battlefields.

Jurisdiction, 1992

Jurisdiction contained in the Standing Rules of the Senate (as revised to March 18, 1992):

[Rule XXV.(1)(p)]

Committee on Veterans' Affairs, to which committee shall be referred all proposed legislation, messages, petitions, memorials, and other matters relating to the following subjects:

1. Compensation of veterans.
2. Life insurance issued by the Government on account of service in the Armed Forces.
3. National cemeteries.
4. Pensions of all wars of the United States, general and special.
5. Readjustment of servicemen to civil life.
6. Soldiers' and sailors' civil relief.
7. Veterans' hospitals, medical care and treatment of veterans.
8. Veterans' measures generally.
9. Vocational rehabilitation and education of veterans.

VETERANS' AFFAIRS / 92nd Congress

* Authorized as a Standing Committee on Oct. 20,1970.

Service Dates of Committee Chair: Jan. 28,1971-Jan. 4,1973
Service Dates of Majority Members: Jan. 28,1971-Jan. 4,1973
Service Dates of Minority Members: Jan. 29,1971-Jan. 12,1973

Majority

Rank	Name	Party	State	Years in: Senate	Years in: Comm.
Chr	Hartke, R. Vance	Dem	Ind.	13	1
2nd	Talmadge, Herman E.	Dem	Ga.	15	1
3rd	Randolph, Jennings	Dem	W.Va.	13	1
4th	Hughes, Harold E.	Dem	Iowa	3	1
5th	Cranston, Alan	Dem	Cal.	3	1

Minority

Rank	Name	Party	State	Years in: Senate	Years in: Comm.
RM	Thurmond, J. Strom	Rep	S.C.	16	1
2nd	Hansen, Clifford P.	Rep	Wyo.	5	1
3rd	Cook, Marlow W.	Rep	Ky.	3	1
4th	Stevens, Theodore F.	Rep	Alas.	3	1

Changes:
Minority:

Name	Party	State	Date	Change
Stevens, Theodore F.	Rep	Alas.	Sep. 21,1971	Moved to Rules & Administration to be Ranking Minority Member.
Stafford, Robert T.	Rep	Vt.	Sep. 21,1971	Replaced Stevens.
Cook, Marlow W.	Rep	Ky.	Feb. 23,1972	Moved to Rules & Administration to be Ranking Minority Member.
Saxbe, William B.	Rep	Ohio	Feb. 23,1972	Replaced Cook.

Departures from Committee:	Majority	Minority	
Moved to Post Office & Civil Service	None	Saxbe, William B.	Ohio Rep

VETERANS' AFFAIRS / 93rd Congress

Service Dates of Committee Chair: Jan. 4,1973-Jan. 17,1975
Service Dates of Majority Members: Jan. 4,1973-Jan. 17,1975
Service Dates of Minority Members: Jan. 12,1973-Jan. 23,1975

Majority

Rank	Name	Party	State	Years in: Senate	Years in: Comm.
Chr	Hartke, R. Vance	Dem	Ind.	15	2
2nd	Talmadge, Herman E.	Dem	Ga.	17	2
3rd	Randolph, Jennings	Dem	W.Va.	15	2
4th	Hughes, Harold E.	Dem	Iowa	5	2
5th	Cranston, Alan	Dem	Cal.	5	2

Minority

Rank	Name	Party	State	Years in: Senate	Years in: Comm.
RM	Hansen, Clifford P.	Rep	Wyo.	7	2
2nd	Thurmond, J. Strom	Rep	S.C.	18	2
3rd	Stafford, Robert T.	Rep	Vt.	2	2
4th	McClure, James A.	Rep	Ida.	1	1

Note: Ranking on this committee for the following member was affected by other chamber service: J. Strom Thurmond (Rep-S.C.), Ranking Minority Member, Armed Services.

	Majority		Minority	
Departures from the Senate:				
Retired	Hughes, Harold E.	Iowa Dem	None	
Departures from Committee:				
Moved to Budget	None		McClure, James A.	Ida. Rep

VETERANS' AFFAIRS / 94th Congress

Service Dates of Committee Chair: Jan. 17,1975-Jan. 3,1977
Service Dates of Majority Members: Jan. 17,1975-Jan. 10,1977
Service Dates of Minority Members: Jan. 23,1975-Jan. 10,1977

Majority

Rank	Name	Party	State	Years in: Senate	Years in: Comm.
Chr	Hartke, R. Vance	Dem	Ind.	17	4
2nd	Talmadge, Herman E.	Dem	Ga.	19	4
3rd	Randolph, Jennings	Dem	W.Va.	17	4
4th	Cranston, Alan	Dem	Cal.	7	4
5th	Stone, Richard B.	Dem	Fla.	1	1

Minority

Rank	Name	Party	State	Years in: Senate	Years in: Comm.
RM	Hansen, Clifford P.	Rep	Wyo.	9	4
2nd	Thurmond, J. Strom	Rep	S.C.	20	4
3rd	Stafford, Robert T.	Rep	Vt.	4	4
4th	Scott, William L.	Rep	Va.	3	1

Notes: Norris Cotton (Rep-N.H.), appointed to fill a vacancy caused by the contested election between John Durkin (Dem) and Louis Wyman (Rep), left the Senate upon the victory of Durkin on Sep. 19,1975, resulting in a change in size and party ratio to 6 Democrats and 3 Republicans on Sep. 19,1975. The ranking on this committee for the following member was affected by other chamber service: J. Strom Thurmond (Rep-S.C.), Ranking Minority Member, Armed Services.

Addition:
Majority: 6th Durkin, John A. Dem N.H. Sep. 19,1975

Changes:
Minority:
Scott, William L. Rep Va. Sep. 19,1975 Ratio change; left committee with no new assignment.

Departures from the Senate:	**Majority**		**Minority**
Defeated for Reelection	Hartke, R. Vance	Ind. Dem	None

VETERANS' AFFAIRS / 95th Congress

Service Dates of Committee Chair: Jan. 10,1977-Jan. 23,1979
Service Dates of Majority Members: Jan. 10,1977-Jan. 23,1979
Service Dates of Minority Members: Jan. 10,1977-Jan. 23,1979

Majority

Rank	Name	Party	State	Years in: Senate	Years in: Comm.
Chr	Cranston, Alan	Dem	Cal.	9	6
2nd	Talmadge, Herman E.	Dem	Ga.	21	6
3rd	Randolph, Jennings	Dem	W.Va.	19	6
4th	Stone, Richard B.	Dem	Fla.	3	2
5th	Durkin, John A.	Dem	N.H.	2	2

Minority

Rank	Name	Party	State	Years in: Senate	Years in: Comm.
RM1	Hansen, Clifford P.	Rep	Wyo.	11	6
RM3 2nd	Thurmond, J. Strom	Rep	S.C.	22	6
RM2 3rd	Stafford, Robert T.	Rep	Vt.	6	6

Notes: The committee size and party ratio changed to 6 Democrats and 3 Republicans on Feb. 11,1977. Rankings on this committee for the following members were affected by other chamber service: Herman E. Talmadge (Dem-Ga.), Chair, Agriculture, Nutrition and Forestry; Jennings Randolph (Dem-W.Va.), Chair, Environment and Public Works; and J. Strom Thurmond (Rep-S.C.), Ranking Minority Member, Judiciary. (Thurmond also served as Ranking Minority Member of Armed Services from Jan. 10,1977-Jan. 22,1977). Feb. 3,1978 is the date of the first committee print that lists J. Strom Thurmond Ranking Minority Member of this committee.

Addition:
Majority: 6th Matsunaga, Spark M. Dem Hai. Feb. 11,1977

Changes:
Ranking Member:

RM1	Hansen, Clifford P.	Rep	Wyo.	Feb. 22,1977	Became Ranking Minority Member on Energy and Natural Resources; remained on committee ranked 3rd.
RM2	Stafford, Robert T.	Rep	Vt.	Feb. 22,1977	Succeeded Hansen as Ranking Minority Member.
RM2	Stafford, Robert T.	Rep	Vt.	Feb. 3,1978	Stepped down as Ranking Minority Member; remained on committee ranked 3rd (see Note).
RM3	Thurmond, J. Strom	Rep	S.C.	Feb. 3,1978	Succeeded Stafford as Ranking Minority Member (see Note).

Minority:
Hansen, Clifford P. Rep Wyo. Dec. 31,1978 Resigned and retired.

VETERANS' AFFAIRS / 96th Congress

Service Dates of Committee Chair: Jan. 23,1979-Jan. 5,1981
Service Dates of Majority Members: Jan. 23,1979-Jan. 5,1981
Service Dates of Minority Members: Jan. 23,1979-Jan. 5,1981

Majority

Rank Name	Party	State	Years in: Senate	Years in: Comm.
Chr Cranston, Alan	Dem	Cal.	11	8
2nd Talmadge, Herman E.	Dem	Ga.	23	8
3rd Randolph, Jennings	Dem	W.Va.	21	8
4th Stone, Richard B.	Dem	Fla.	5	5
5th Durkin, John A.	Dem	N.H.	4	4
6th Matsunaga, Spark M.	Dem	Hai.	3	2

Minority

Rank Name	Party	State	Years in: Senate	Years in: Comm.
RM1 Stafford, Robert T.	Rep	Vt.	8	8
2nd Thurmond, J. Strom	Rep	S.C.	24	8
RM2 3rd Simpson, Alan K.	Rep	Wyo.	1	1
4th Humphrey, Gordon J.	Rep	N.H.	1	1

Notes: Rankings on this committee for the following members were affected by other chamber service: Herman E. Talmadge (Dem-Ga.), Chair, Agriculture, Nutrition and Forestry; Jennings Randolph (Dem-W.Va.), Chair, Environment and Public Works; and J. Strom Thurmond (Rep-S.C.), Ranking Minority Member, Judiciary. The Senate Journal of Jan. 23,1979 lists Stafford as the Ranking Minority Member of this committee. The first committee print of the 96th Congress, dated Feb. 22,1979, lists Alan K. Simpson as Ranking Minority Member.

Changes:

Ranking Member:

RM1 Stafford, Robert T.	Rep	Vt.	Feb. 22,1979	Was already Ranking Minority Member on Environment and Public Works; remained on this committee ranked 3rd.
RM2 Simpson, Alan K.	Rep	Wyo.	Feb. 22,1979	Succeeded Stafford as Ranking Minority Member.

Majority:

Durkin, John A.	Dem	N.H.	Dec. 29,1980	Resigned; defeated for reelection.
Stone, Richard B.	Dem	Fla.	Jan. 1,1981	Resigned; defeated for renomination.

	Majority			Minority		
Departures from the Senate:						
Defeated for Reelection	Talmadge, Herman E.	Ga.	Dem	None		
Departures from Committee:						
Moved to Energy & Natural Resources	None			Humphrey, Gordon J.	N.H.	Rep

VETERANS' AFFAIRS / 97th Congress

Service Dates of Committee Chair: Jan. 5,1981-Jan. 3,1983
Service Dates of Majority Members: Jan. 5,1981-Jan. 3,1983
Service Dates of Minority Members: Jan. 5,1981-Jan. 3,1983

Majority

Rank Name	Party	State	Years in: Senate	Years in: Comm.
Chr Simpson, Alan K.	Rep	Wyo.	3	2
2nd Thurmond, J. Strom	Rep	S.C.	26	10
3rd Stafford, Robert T.	Rep	Vt.	10	10
4th Kasten, Robert W. Jr.	Rep	Wisc.	1	1
5th Denton, Jeremiah	Rep	Ala.	1	*1 1
6th Murkowski, Frank H.	Rep	Alas.	1	1
7th Specter, Arlen	Rep	Penn.	1	1

Minority

Rank Name	Party	State	Years in: Senate	Years in: Comm.
RM Cranston, Alan	Dem	Cal.	13	10
2nd Randolph, Jennings	Dem	W.Va.	23	10
3rd Matsunaga, Spark M.	Dem	Hai.	5	4
4th DeConcini, Dennis	Dem	Ariz.	5	1
5th Mitchell, George J.	Dem	Me.	1	1

*1: Member's 1st period of service on the committee.

Note: Rankings on this committee for the following members were affected by other chamber service: J. Strom Thurmond (Rep-S.C.), Chair, Judiciary; and Robert T. Stafford (Rep-Vt.), Chair, Environment and Public Works.

Departures from Committee:	Majority			Minority
Moved to Small Business	Kasten, Robert W. Jr.	Wisc.	Rep	None
No new assignment	Denton, Jeremiah	Ala.	Rep	None

VETERANS' AFFAIRS / 98th Congress

Service Dates of Committee Chair: Jan. 3,1983-Mar. 5,1985
Service Dates of Majority Members: Jan. 3,1983-Mar. 5,1985
Service Dates of Minority Members: Jan. 3,1983-Mar. 5,1985

Majority

Rank	Name	Party	State	Years in: Senate	Years in: Comm.
Chr	Simpson, Alan K.	Rep	Wyo.	5	4
2nd	Thurmond, J. Strom	Rep	S.C.	28	12
3rd	Stafford, Robert T.	Rep	Vt.	12	12
4th	Murkowski, Frank H.	Rep	Alas.	3	2
5th	Specter, Arlen	Rep	Penn.	3	2
6th	Denton, Jeremiah	Rep	Ala.	3	*2 1
7th	Boschwitz, Rudolf E.	Rep	Minn.	5	1

Minority

Rank	Name	Party	State	Years in: Senate	Years in: Comm.
RM	Cranston, Alan	Dem	Cal.	15	12
2nd	Randolph, Jennings	Dem	W.Va.	25	12
3rd	Matsunaga, Spark M.	Dem	Hai.	7	6
4th	DeConcini, Dennis	Dem	Ariz.	7	2
5th	Mitchell, George J.	Dem	Me.	3	2

*2: Member's 2nd period of service on the committee.

Note: Rankings on this committee for the following members were affected by other chamber service: J. Strom Thurmond (Rep-S.C.), Chair, Judiciary; and Robert T. Stafford (Rep-Vt.), Chair, Environment and Public Works.

Vacancies Filled:
Majority: 6th and 7th seats by Denton and Boschwitz respectively on Feb. 15,1983.

Departures from the Senate:	Majority	Minority	
Retired	None	Randolph, Jennings	W.Va. Dem

VETERANS' AFFAIRS / 99th Congress

Service Dates of Committee Chair: Mar. 5,1985-Jan. 6,1987
Service Dates of Majority Members: Mar. 5,1985-Jan. 6,1987
Service Dates of Minority Members: Mar. 5,1985-Jan. 6,1987

Majority

Rank	Name	Party	State	Years in: Senate	Years in: Comm.
Chr	Murkowski, Frank H.	Rep	Alas.	5	5
2nd	Simpson, Alan K.	Rep	Wyo.	7	7
3rd	Thurmond, J. Strom	Rep	S.C.	30	15
4th	Stafford, Robert T.	Rep	Vt.	14	14
5th	Specter, Arlen	Rep	Penn.	5	5
6th	Denton, Jeremiah	Rep	Ala.	5	*2 3
7th	Boschwitz, Rudolf E.	Rep	Minn.	7	3

Minority

Rank	Name	Party	State	Years in: Senate	Years in: Comm.
RM	Cranston, Alan	Dem	Cal.	17	15
2nd	Matsunaga, Spark M.	Dem	Hai.	9	9
3rd	DeConcini, Dennis	Dem	Ariz.	9	5
4th	Mitchell, George J.	Dem	Me.	5	5
5th	Rockefeller, John D. IV	Dem	W.Va.	1	1

*2: Member's 2nd period of service on the committee.

Note: Rankings on this committee for the following members were affected by other chamber service: Alan K. Simpson (Rep-Wyo.), Senate Majority Whip; J. Strom Thurmond (Rep-S.C.), Chair, Judiciary; and Robert T. Stafford (Rep-Vt.), Chair, Environment and Public Works.

Departures from the Senate:	Majority		Minority
Defeated for Reelection	Denton, Jeremiah	Ala. Rep	None
Departures from Committee:			
No new assignment	Boschwitz, Rudolf E.	Minn. Rep	None

VETERANS' AFFAIRS / 100th Congress

Service Dates of Committee Chair: Jan. 6,1987-Feb. 2,1989
Service Dates of Majority Members: Jan. 6,1987-Feb. 2,1989
Service Dates of Minority Members: Jan. 6,1987-Feb. 2,1989

Majority

Rank Name	Party	State	Years in: Senate	Years in: Comm.
Chr Cranston, Alan	Dem	Cal.	19	16
2nd Matsunaga, Spark M.	Dem	Hai.	11	10
3rd DeConcini, Dennis	Dem	Ariz.	11	7
4th Mitchell, George J.	Dem	Me.	7	7
5th Rockefeller, John D. IV	Dem	W.Va.	3	2
6th Graham, Bob	Dem	Fla.	1	1

Minority

Rank Name	Party	State	Years in: Senate	Years in: Comm.
RM Murkowski, Frank H.	Rep	Alas.	7	7
2nd Simpson, Alan K.	Rep	Wyo.	9	8
3rd Thurmond, J. Strom	Rep	S.C.	32	16
4th Stafford, Robert T.	Rep	Vt.	16	16
5th Specter, Arlen	Rep	Penn.	7	7

Note: Rankings on this committee for the following members were affected by other chamber service: Alan K. Simpson (Rep-Wyo.), Senate Minority Whip; J. Strom Thurmond (Rep-S.C.), Ranking Minority Member, Judiciary; and Robert T. Stafford (Rep-Vt.), Ranking Minority Member, Environment and Public Works.

Departures from the Senate:	Majority	Minority		
Retired	None	Stafford, Robert T.	Vt.	Rep

VETERANS' AFFAIRS / 101st Congress

Service Dates of Committee Chair: Feb. 2,1989-Mar. 19,1991
Service Dates of Majority Members: Feb. 2,1989-Mar. 19,1991
Service Dates of Minority Members: Feb. 2,1989-Mar. 19,1991

Majority

Rank Name	Party	State	Years in: Senate	Years in: Comm.
Chr Cranston, Alan	Dem	Cal.	21	19
2nd Matsunaga, Spark M.	Dem	Hai.	13	12
3rd DeConcini, Dennis	Dem	Ariz.	13	9
4th Mitchell, George J.	Dem	Me.	9	9
5th Rockefeller, John D. IV	Dem	W.Va.	5	4
6th Graham, Bob	Dem	Fla.	3	3

Minority

Rank Name	Party	State	Years in: Senate	Years in: Comm.
RM Murkowski, Frank H.	Rep	Alas.	9	9
2nd Simpson, Alan K.	Rep	Wyo.	11	11
3rd Thurmond, J. Strom	Rep	S.C.	34	19
4th Specter, Arlen	Rep	Penn.	9	9
5th Jeffords, James M.	Rep	Vt.	1	1

Note: Rankings on this committee for the following members were affected by other chamber service: Alan K. Simpson (Rep-Wyo.), Senate Minority Whip; and J. Strom Thurmond (Rep-S.C.), Ranking Minority Member, Judiciary.

Changes:

Majority:

Matsunaga, Spark M.	Dem	Hai.	Apr. 15,1990	Died in office.
Akaka, Daniel K.	Dem	Hai.	May 16,1990	Replaced Matsunaga.

VETERANS' AFFAIRS / 102nd Congress

Service Dates of Committee Chair: Mar. 19,1991-Jan. 3,1993
Service Dates of Majority Members: Mar. 19,1991-Jan. 3,1993
Service Dates of Minority Members: Mar. 19,1991-Jan. 3,1993

Majority

Rank	Name	Party	State	Years in: Senate	Years in: Comm.
Chr	Cranston, Alan	Dem	Cal.	23	21
2nd	DeConcini, Dennis	Dem	Ariz.	15	11
3rd	Mitchell, George J.	Dem	Me.	11	11
4th	Rockefeller, John D. IV	Dem	W.Va.	7	7
5th	Graham, Bob	Dem	Fla.	5	5
6th	Akaka, Daniel K.	Dem	Hai.	1	1
7th	Daschle, Thomas A.	Dem	S.D.	5	1

Minority

Rank	Name	Party	State	Years in: Senate	Years in: Comm.
RM	Specter, Arlen	Rep	Penn.	11	11
2nd	Simpson, Alan K.	Rep	Wyo.	13	13
3rd	Thurmond, J. Strom	Rep	S.C.	36	21
4th	Murkowski, Frank H.	Rep	Alas.	11	11
5th	Jeffords, James M.	Rep	Vt.	3	3

Note: Rankings on this committee for the following members were affected by other chamber service: Alan K. Simpson (Rep-Wyo.), Senate Minority Whip; J. Strom Thurmond (Rep-S.C.), Ranking Minority Member, Judiciary; and Frank H. Murkowski (Rep-Alas.), Vice Chair, Select Intelligence.

PART II
Select and Special Committees
U.S. Senate, 1947-1992

SENATE SPECIAL COMMITTEE: TO INVESTIGATE THE NATIONAL DEFENSE PROGRAM

Jurisdiction, 1941

From Senate Resolution 71, 77th Congress, First Session, March 1, 1941:

[Section 1]

Resolved, That a special committee of seven Senators, to be appointed by the President of the Senate, is authorized and directed to make a full and complete study and investigation of the operation of the program for the procurement and construction of supplies, materials, munitions, vehicles, aircraft, vessels, plants, camps, and other articles and facilities in connection with the national defense, including:

(1) the types and terms of contracts awarded on behalf of the United States;
(2) the methods by which such contracts are awarded and contractors selected;
(3) the utilization of the facilities of small business concerns, through subcontracts or otherwise;
(4) the geographic distribution of contracts and location of plants and facilities;
(5) the effect of such program with respect to labor and the migration of labor;
(6) the performance of contracts and the accountings required of contractors;
(7) benefits accruing to contractors with respect to amortization for the purposes of taxation or otherwise;
(8) practices of management or labor, and prices, fees, and charges, which interfere with such program or unduly increase its cost; and
(9) such other matters as the committee deems appropriate.

Termination, 1948

The Special Committee was terminated upon the filing of its Final Report, Senate Report 440 (80-2), on April 28, 1948.

SENATE SPECIAL COMMITTEE: TO INVESTIGATE THE NATIONAL DEFENSE PROGRAM / 80th Congress

Service Dates of Committee Chair: Jan. 6,1947-Apr. 28,1948
Service Dates of Majority Members: Jan. 24,1947-Apr. 28,1948
Service Dates of Minority Members: Jan. 31,1947-Apr. 28,1948

Majority

Rank Name	Party	State	Years in: Senate	Years in: Comm.
Chr Brewster, Ralph O.	Rep	Me.	7	6
2nd Ball, Joseph H.	Rep	Minn.	7	*2 4
3rd Ferguson, Homer	Rep	Mich.	5	4
4th Knowland, William F.	Rep	Cal.	2	2
5th McCarthy, Joseph R.	Rep	Wisc.	1	1
6th Williams, John J.	Rep	Del.	1	1

Minority

Rank Name	Party	State	Years in: Senate	Years in: Comm.
RM Hatch, Carl A.	Dem	N.M.	14	*2 1
2nd Pepper, Claude D.	Dem	Fla.	11	1
3rd McGrath, J. Howard	Dem	R.I.	1	1
4th O'Conor, Herbert R.	Dem	Md.	1	1

*2: Member's 2nd period of service on the committee.

Note: "Service Dates of Majority Members" reflect the appointment date of McCarthy and Williams; all other majority members continued service from the previous Congress without formal reassignment recorded in the Congressional Record.

Changes:

Majority:

Ball, Joseph H.	Rep	Minn.	Mar. 12,1947	Left committee; no new assignment.
Malone, George W.	Rep	Nev.	Mar. 12,1947	Replaced Ball.
Knowland, William F.	Rep	Cal.	Apr. 22,1947	Left committee; no new assignment (effective Apr. 21,1947).
Cain, Harry P.	Rep	Wash.	Apr. 22,1947	Replaced Knowland (effective Apr. 21,1947).

SENATE SPECIAL COMMITTEE: RECONSTRUCTION OF THE SENATE ROOF AND SKYLIGHTS AND REMODELLING OF THE SENATE CHAMBER

Jurisdiction, 1945

Senate Joint Resolution 31 and Public Law 79-155, 59 Statutes 318, July 17, 1945:

[Clause 1]

Resolved by the Senate and House of Representatives of the United States of America in Congress assembled, That the appropriation of $585,000 provided in the Second Deficiency Appropriation Act approved June 27, 1940, as amended and carried forward by the Act of June 8, 1942, for the reconstruction of the roofs and skylights over the Senate and House wings of the United States Capitol, together with such additional amounts as may be provided hereafter for such purpose, shall be available also for the substitution of reinforced concrete roof slab for the skylights over the Senate and House Chambers, reconstruction of ceilings, redecoration, acoustical treatment, improved lighting, and other alterations, changes, and improvements in such Chambers....

Provided further, That the project, insofar as it affects the Senate wing of the Capitol, shall be carried forward by the Architect of the Capitol in accordance with plans to be approved by a committee of five Senators, to be appointed by the President pro tempore of the Senate, upon recommendation of the chairman of the Senate Committee on Public Buildings and Grounds.

Termination, 1951

The Special Committee was terminated by the authority of Senate Resolution 92 (82-1) and with the filing of Senate Document 20 on April 2,1951, at which time all records and files were transferred to the Committee on Rules and Administration.

SENATE SPECIAL COMMITTEE: RECONSTRUCTION OF SENATE ROOF AND SKYLIGHTS AND REMODELLING OF SENATE CHAMBER / 80th Congress

Service Dates of Committee Chair: Feb. 24,1947-Jan. 3,1949
Service Dates of Majority Members: Feb. 24,1947-Continued
Service Dates of Minority Members: Feb. 24,1947-Continued

Majority

Rank	Name	Party	State	Years in: Senate	Years in: Comm.
Chr	Revercomb, W. Chapman	Rep	W.Va.	5	1
2nd	Taft, Robert A.	Rep	Ohio	9	2
3rd	Vandenberg, Arthur H.	Rep	Mich.	19	2

Minority

Rank	Name	Party	State	Years in: Senate	Years in: Comm.
RM	Byrd, Harry Flood	Dem	Va.	14	2
2nd	Green, Theodore F.	Dem	R.I.	11	2

Note: "Service Dates" of majority and minority members reflect the dates of service of Chavez and Kem; all other members continued service from the previous Congress without official reassignment recorded in the Congressional Record.

Changes:

Majority:

Vandenberg, Arthur H.	Rep	Mich.	Feb. 24,1947	Left committee; no new assignment.
Brooks, C. Wayland	Rep	Ill.	Feb. 24,1947	Replaced Vandenberg.

Departures from the Senate:

	Majority		Minority
Defeated for Reelection	Revercomb, W. Chapman	W.Va. Rep	None
	Brooks, C. Wayland	Ill. Rep	

SENATE SPECIAL COMMITTEE: RECONSTRUCTION OF THE SENATE ROOF AND SKYLIGHTS AND REMODELLING OF THE SENATE CHAMBER / 81st Congress

Service Dates of Committee Chair: Mar. 17,1949-Continued
Service Dates of Majority Members: Mar. 17,1949-Continued
Service Dates of Minority Members: Mar. 17,1949-Continued

Majority					Minority				
			Years in:					Years in:	
Rank Name	**Party**	**State**	**Senate**	**Comm.**	**Rank Name**	**Party**	**State**	**Senate**	**Comm.**
Chr Chavez, Dennis	Dem	N.M.	14	1	RM Taft, Robert A.	Rep	Ohio	11	4
2nd Byrd, Harry Flood	Dem	Va.	17	4	2nd Kem, James P.	Rep	Mo.	3	1
3rd Green, Theodore F.	Dem	R.I.	13	4					

Note: "Service Dates" of majority and minority members reflect the dates of service of Chavez and Kem; all other members continued service from the previous Congress without official reassignment recorded in the Congressional Record.

SENATE SELECT COMMITTEE: RECONSTRUCTION OF SENATE ROOF AND SKYLIGHTS AND REMODELLING OF SENATE CHAMBER / 82nd Congress

Service Dates of Committee Chair: Jan. 3,1949-Apr. 2,1951
Service Dates of Majority Members: Jan. 3,1949-Apr. 2,1951
Service Dates of Minority Members: Jan. 3,1949-Apr. 2,1951

Majority					Minority				
			Years in:					Years in:	
Rank Name	**Party**	**State**	**Senate**	**Comm.**	**Rank Name**	**Party**	**State**	**Senate**	**Comm.**
Chr Chavez, Dennis	Dem	N.M.	16	2	RM Taft, Robert A.	Rep	Ohio	13	6
2nd Byrd, Harry Flood	Dem	Va.	18	6	2nd Kem, James P.	Rep	Mo.	5	2
3rd Green, Theodore F.	Dem	R.I.	15	6					

SENATE SPECIAL COMMITTEE: PROBLEMS OF AMERICAN SMALL BUSINESS

Jurisdiction, 1947

From Senate Resolution 20, 80th Congress, First Session, January 24, 1947:

. . . is hereby authorized and directed to study and survey by means of research all the problems of American small business enterprises, obtaining all facts possible in relation thereto which would not only be of public interest, but which would aid the Congress in enacting remedial legislation.

Termination, 1949

The Select Committee was terminated on January 31, 1949 by authority of Senate Resolution 280 (80-2), and upon filing of Senate Document 7 (81-1). Supplemental views, contained in Senate Report 47, were filed on February 10, 1949.

SENATE SPECIAL COMMITTEE: PROBLEMS OF AMERICAN SMALL BUSINESS / 80th Congress

Service Dates of Committee Chair: Jan. 29,1947-Jan. 31,1949
Service Dates of Majority Members: Jan. 29,1947-Jan. 31,1949
Service Dates of Minority Members: Jan. 31,1947-Jan. 31,1949

Majority

Rank Name	Party	State	Years in: Senate	Years in: Comm.
Chr Wherry, Kenneth S.	Rep	Neb.	5	1
2nd Wilson, George A.	Rep	Iowa	5	1
3rd Capehart, Homer E.	Rep	Ind.	3	1
4th Cain, Harry P.	Rep	Wash.	1	1
5th Martin, Edward	Rep	Penn.	1	1
6th Ives, Irving M.	Rep	N.Y.	1	1
7th Ecton, Zales N.	Rep	Mont.	1	1

Minority

Rank Name	Party	State	Years in: Senate	Years in: Comm.
RM Murray, James E.	Dem	Mont.	13	1
2nd Ellender, Allen J.	Dem	La.	11	1
3rd Taylor, Glen H.	Dem	Ida.	3	1
4th Holland, Spessard L.	Dem	Fla.	1	1
5th Umstead, William B.	Dem	N.C.	1	1

Changes:
Minority:

Umstead, William B.	Dem	N.C.	Dec. 30,1948	Resigned; defeated for nomination.

Departures from the Senate:	Majority			Minority
Defeated for Reelection	Wilson, George A.	Iowa	Rep	None

SENATE SELECT COMMITTEE: SMALL BUSINESS

Jurisdiction, 1950

From Senate Resolution 58, as amended, 81st Congress, Second Session, February 20, 1950:

[Paragraph 2]

It shall be the duty of such committee to study and survey by means of research and investigation all problems of American small-business enterprises, and to obtain all facts possible in relation thereto which would not only be of public interest, but which would aid the Congress in enacting remedial legislation, and to report to the Senate from time to time the results of such studies and surveys. No proposed legislation shall be referred to such committee and such committee shall not have power to report by bill or otherwise have legislative jurisdiction.

From the Senate Manual for the 96th Congress (1979):

[Section 70, Paragraphs 2 and 3]

It shall be the duty of such committee to study and survey by means of research and investigation all problems of American small business enterprises, and to obtain all facts possible in relation thereto which would not only be of public interest, but which would aid the Congress in enacting remedial legislation.

Such committee shall from time to time report to the Senate, by bill or otherwise, its recommendations with respect to matters referred to the committee or otherwise within its jurisdiction: Provided, That any proposed legislation reported by such committee which relates to matters other than the functions of the Small Business Administration shall, at the request of the chairman of any standing committee having jurisdiction over the subject matter extraneous to the functions of the Small Business Administration, be considered and reported by such standing committee prior to its consideration by the Senate; and likewise measures reported by other committees directly relating to the Small Business Administration shall, at the request of the chairman of the Committee on Small Business, be referred to the Committee on Small Business for its consideration of any portions of the measure dealing with the Small Business Administration, and be reported by this committee prior to its consideration by the Senate.

Reorganization, 1981

The Select Committee was designated a Standing Committee on March 25, 1981.

SENATE SELECT COMMITTEE: SMALL BUSINESS / 81st Congress

Service Dates of Committee Chair: Apr. 10,1950-Jan. 29,1951
Service Dates of Majority Members: Apr. 10,1950-Jan. 29,1951
Service Dates of Minority Members: Apr. 10,1950-Jan. 29,1951

Majority

Rank	Name	Party	State	Years in: Senate	Years in: Comm.
Chr	Sparkman, John J.	Dem	Ala.	4	1
2nd	McFarland, Ernest W.	Dem	Ariz.	10	1
3rd	O'Conor, Herbert R.	Dem	Md.	4	1
4th	Long, Russell B.	Dem	La.	2	1
5th	Gillette, Guy M.	Dem	Iowa	2	1
6th	Humphrey, Hubert H. Jr.	DFL	Minn.	2	1
7th	Hunt, Lester C.	Dem	Wyo.	2	1
8th	Benton, William	Dem	Conn.	1	1

Minority

Rank	Name	Party	State	Years in: Senate	Years in: Comm.
RM	Tobey, Charles W.	Rep	N.H.	12	1
2nd	Saltonstall, Leverett	Rep	Mass.	6	1
3rd	Thye, Edward J.	Rep	Minn.	4	1
4th	Hendrickson, Robert C.	Rep	N.J.	2	1
5th	Schoeppel, Andrew F.	Rep	Kans.	2	1

SENATE SELECT COMMITTEE: SMALL BUSINESS / 82nd Congress

Service Dates of Committee Chair: Jan. 29,1951-Feb. 6,1953
Service Dates of Majority Members: Jan. 29,1951-Feb. 6,1953
Service Dates of Minority Members: Jan. 29,1951-Feb. 6,1953

Majority

Rank	Name	Party	State	Years in: Senate	Years in: Comm.
Chr	Sparkman, John J.	Dem	Ala.	5	1
2nd	McFarland, Ernest W.	Dem	Ariz.	11	1
3rd	O'Conor, Herbert R.	Dem	Md.	5	1
4th	Long, Russell B.	Dem	La.	3	1
5th	Gillette, Guy M.	Dem	Iowa	3	1
6th	Humphrey, Hubert H. Jr.	DFL	Minn.	3	1
7th	Hunt, Lester C.	Dem	Wyo.	3	1
8th	Benton, William	Dem	Conn.	2	1

Minority

Rank	Name	Party	State	Years in: Senate	Years in: Comm.
RM	Tobey, Charles W.	Rep	N.H.	13	1
2nd	Saltonstall, Leverett	Rep	Mass.	7	1
3rd	Thye, Edward J.	Rep	Minn.	5	1
4th	Hendrickson, Robert C.	Rep	N.J.	3	1
5th	Schoeppel, Andrew F.	Rep	Kans.	3	1

Note: James H. Duff (Rep-Penn.) was sworn into the Senate on Jan. 16, 1951 after completing his term as Governor of Pennsylvania, and after the start of the 82nd Congress. This resulted in a change in size and party ratio on this committee to 7 Democrats and 6 Republicans.

Addition:

Minority: 6th Duff, James H. Rep Penn. Jan. 29,1951

Changes:

Majority:

Name	Party	State	Date	Remarks
McFarland, Ernest W.	Dem	Ariz.	Jan. 29,1951	Ratio change; left committee, no new assignment.
O'Conor, Herbert R.	Dem	Md.	June 12,1951	Left committee; no new assignment.
Moody, Blair	Dem	Mich.	June 12,1951	Replaced O'Conor.

Departures from the Senate:

	Majority		Minority
Defeated for Reelection	Benton, William	Conn. Dem	None
Defeated for Election	Moody, Blair	Mich. Dem	None

SENATE SELECT COMMITTEE: SMALL BUSINESS / 83rd Congress

Service Dates of Committee Chair: Feb. 6,1953-Jan. 14,1955
Service Dates of Majority Members: Feb. 6,1953-Jan. 14,1955
Service Dates of Minority Members: Feb. 6,1953-Jan. 14,1955

Majority

Rank	Name	Party	State	Years in: Senate	Years in: Comm.
Chr	Thye, Edward J.	Rep	Minn.	7	3
2nd	Tobey, Charles W.	Rep	N.H.	15	3
3rd	Ferguson, Homer	Rep	Mich.	11	1
4th	Saltonstall, Leverett	Rep	Mass.	9	3
5th	Hendrickson, Robert C.	Rep	N.J.	5	3
6th	Schoeppel, Andrew F.	Rep	Kans.	5	3
7th	Duff, James H.	Rep	Penn.	3	3

Minority

Rank	Name	Party	State	Years in: Senate	Years in: Comm.
RM	Sparkman, John J.	Dem	Ala.	7	3
2nd	Long, Russell B.	Dem	La.	5	3
3rd	Gillette, Guy M.	Dem	Iowa	13	3
4th	Humphrey, Hubert H. Jr.	DFL	Minn.	5	3
5th	Hunt, Lester C.	Dem	Wyo.	5	3
6th	Smathers, George A.	Dem	Fla.	3	1

Changes:

Majority:

Name	Party	State	Date	Remarks
Tobey, Charles W.	Rep	N.H.	July 24,1953	Died in office.
Goldwater, Barry M.	Rep	Ariz.	Mar. 15,1954	Replaced Tobey.

Minority:

Name	Party	State	Date	Remarks
Hunt, Lester C.	Dem	Wyo.	June 19,1954	Died in office.
Kennedy, John F.	Dem	Mass.	Aug. 9,1954	Replaced Hunt.

Departures from the Senate:

	Majority		Minority	
Defeated for Reelection	Ferguson, Homer	Mich. Rep	None	
Appointed Ambassador to New Zealand	Hendrickson, Robert C.	N.J. Rep	None	
Defeated for Reelection	None		Gillette, Guy M.	Iowa Dem

SENATE SELECT COMMITTEE: SMALL BUSINESS / 84th Congress

Service Dates of Committee Chair: Jan. 14,1955-Feb. 4,1957
Service Dates of Majority Members: Jan. 14,1955-Feb. 4,1957
Service Dates of Minority Members: Jan. 18,1955-May 23,1957

Majority			Years in:		Minority			Years in:	
Rank Name	**Party**	**State**	**Senate**	**Comm.**	**Rank Name**	**Party**	**State**	**Senate**	**Comm.**
Chr Sparkman, John J.	Dem	Ala.	9	5	RM Thye, Edward J.	Rep	Minn.	9	5
2nd Long, Russell B.	Dem	La.	7	5	2nd Saltonstall, Leverett	Rep	Mass.	11	5
3rd Humphrey, Hubert H. Jr.	DFL	Minn.	7	5	3rd Schoeppel, Andrew F.	Rep	Kans.	7	5
4th Smathers, George A.	Dem	Fla.	5	2	4th Duff, James H.	Rep	Penn.	5	4
5th Kennedy, John F.	Dem	Mass.	3	1	5th Goldwater, Barry M.	Rep	Ariz.	3	1
6th Eastland, James O.	Dem	Miss.	13	1	6th Kuchel, Thomas H.	Rep	Cal.	3	1

Third Party:

Morse, Wayne L.	Ind	Ore.	11	1

Note: Wayne L. Morse of Oregon was assigned to the committee as an Independent on Jan. 14,1955. On Feb. 17,1955, he joined the Democratic Party, and was allowed to accrue seniority. "Service Dates of Majority Members" reflects the dates of service of Eastland. It was announced on Jan. 18,1955 that committee members whose service carried over from the 83rd Congress had been reappointed for the 84th Congress.

Vacancy Filled:
Minority: 6th seat by Kuchel on Mar. 30,1955.

	Majority		Minority	
Departures from the Senate:				
Defeated for Reelection	None		Duff, James H.	Penn. Rep
Departures from Committee:				
Moved to Foreign Relations	Kennedy, John F.	Mass. Dem	None	
No new assignment	Eastland, James O.	Miss. Dem	None	

SENATE SELECT COMMITTEE: SMALL BUSINESS / 85th Congress

Service Dates of Committee Chair: Feb. 4,1957-Feb. 4,1959
Service Dates of Majority Members: Feb. 4,1957-Feb. 4,1959
Service Dates of Minority Members: May 23,1957-Feb. 2,1959

Majority			Years in:		Minority			Years in:	
Rank Name	**Party**	**State**	**Senate**	**Comm.**	**Rank Name**	**Party**	**State**	**Senate**	**Comm.**
Chr Sparkman, John J.	Dem	Ala.	11	7	RM Thye, Edward J.	Rep	Minn.	11	8
2nd Long, Russell B.	Dem	La.	9	7	2nd Saltonstall, Leverett	Rep	Mass.	13	8
3rd Humphrey, Hubert H. Jr.	DFL	Minn.	9	7	3rd Schoeppel, Andrew F.	Rep	Kans.	9	8
4th Smathers, George A.	Dem	Fla.	7	4	4th Goldwater, Barry M.	Rep	Ariz.	5	3
5th Morse, Wayne L.	Dem	Ore.	13	3	5th Kuchel, Thomas H.	Rep	Cal.	5	3
6th Monroney, A. S. Mike	Dem	Okla.	7	1	6th Javits, Jacob K.	Rep	N.Y.	1 *1	1
7th Bible, Alan H.	Dem	Nev.	3	1					

*1: Member's 1st period of service on the committee.

Changes:
Majority:

Monroney, A. S. Mike	Dem	Okla.	Aug. 30,1957	Left committee; no new assignment.
Proxmire, William	Dem	Wisc.	Aug. 30,1957	Replaced Monroney.

	Majority		Minority	
Departures from the Senate:				
Defeated for Reelection	None		Thye, Edward J.	Minn. Rep
Departures from Committee:				
Moved to Agriculture & Forestry	Proxmire, William	Wisc. Dem	None	
Moved to Government Operations; Banking & Currency; Aeronautical & Space Sciences; Labor & Public Welfare	None		Javits, Jacob K.	N.Y. Rep
Became Minority Whip	None		Kuchel, Thomas H.	Cal. Rep

SENATE SELECT COMMITTEE: SMALL BUSINESS / 86th Congress

Service Dates of Committee Chair: Feb. 4,1959-Jan. 11,1961
Service Dates of Majority Members: Feb. 4,1959-Jan. 11,1961
Service Dates of Minority Members: Feb. 2,1959-Jan. 13,1961

Majority

Rank	Name	Party	State	Years in: Senate	Years in: Comm.
Chr	Sparkman, John J.	Dem	Ala.	13	9
2nd	Long, Russell B.	Dem	La.	11	9
3rd	Humphrey, Hubert H. Jr.	DFL	Minn.	11	9
4th	Smathers, George A.	Dem	Fla.	9	6
5th	Morse, Wayne L.	Dem	Ore.	15	5
6th	Bible, Alan H.	Dem	Nev.	5	2
7th	Randolph, Jennings	Dem	W.Va.	1	1
8th	Engle, Clair	Dem	Cal.	1	1
9th	Bartlett, E. L. (Bob)	Dem	Alas.	1	1
10th	Williams, Harrison A. Jr.	Dem	N.J.	1	1
11th	Moss, Frank E.	Dem	Utah	1	1

Minority

Rank	Name	Party	State	Years in: Senate	Years in: Comm.
RM	Saltonstall, Leverett	Rep	Mass.	15	9
2nd	Schoeppel, Andrew F.	Rep	Kans.	11	9
3rd	Goldwater, Barry M.	Rep	Ariz.	7	5
4th	Cooper, John Sherman	Rep	Ky.	7	1
5th	Scott, Hugh D. Jr.	Rep	Penn.	1	1
6th	Prouty, Winston L.	Rep	Vt.	1	1

Changes:
Minority:

Name	Party	State	Date	Change
Goldwater, Barry M.	Rep	Ariz.	Feb. 4,1959	Left committee; no new assignment.
Javits, Jacob K.	Rep	N.Y.	Feb. 4,1959	Replaced Goldwater; ranked behind Schoeppel.

SENATE SELECT COMMITTEE: SMALL BUSINESS / 87th Congress

Service Dates of Committee Chair: Jan. 11,1961-Feb. 25,1963
Service Dates of Majority Members: Jan. 11,1961-Feb. 25,1963
Service Dates of Minority Members: Jan. 13,1961-Feb. 25,1963

Majority

Rank	Name	Party	State	Years in: Senate	Years in: Comm.
Chr	Sparkman, John J.	Dem	Ala.	15	11
2nd	Long, Russell B.	Dem	La.	13	11
3rd	Humphrey, Hubert H. Jr.	DFL	Minn.	13	11
4th	Smathers, George A.	Dem	Fla.	11	8
5th	Morse, Wayne L.	Dem	Ore.	17	6
6th	Bible, Alan H.	Dem	Nev.	7	4
7th	Randolph, Jennings	Dem	W.Va.	3	2
8th	Engle, Clair	Dem	Cal.	3	2
9th	Bartlett, E. L. (Bob)	Dem	Alas.	3	2
10th	Williams, Harrison A. Jr.	Dem	N.J.	3	2
11th	Moss, Frank E.	Dem	Utah	3	2

Minority

Rank	Name	Party	State	Years in: Senate	Years in: Comm.
RM	Saltonstall, Leverett	Rep	Mass.	17	11
2nd	Schoeppel, Andrew F.	Rep	Kans.	13	11
3rd	Javits, Jacob K.	Rep	N.Y.	5	*2 2
4th	Cooper, John Sherman	Rep	Ky.	9	2
5th	Scott, Hugh D. Jr.	Rep	Penn.	3	2
6th	Prouty, Winston L.	Rep	Vt.	3	2

*2: Member's 2nd period of service on the committee.

Note: Jacob K. Javits (Rep-N.Y.) was reassigned to the committee in the 86th Congress and credited with his former rank.

Changes:
Minority:

Name	Party	State	Date	Change
Schoeppel, Andrew F.	Rep	Kans.	Jan. 21,1962	Died in office.
Cotton, Norris	Rep	N.H.	Mar. 8,1962	Replaced Schoeppel.

SENATE SELECT COMMITTEE: SMALL BUSINESS / 88th Congress

Service Dates of Committee Chair: Feb. 25,1963-Jan. 8,1965
Service Dates of Majority Members: Feb. 25,1963-Jan. 8,1965
Service Dates of Minority Members: Feb. 25,1963-Jan. 15,1961

Majority

Rank Name	Party	State	Years in: Senate	Years in: Comm.
Chr Sparkman, John J.	Dem	Ala.	17	13
2nd Long, Russell B.	Dem	La.	15	13
3rd Humphrey, Hubert H. Jr.	DFL	Minn.	15	13
4th Smathers, George A.	Dem	Fla.	13	11
5th Morse, Wayne L.	Dem	Ore.	19	9
6th Bible, Alan H.	Dem	Nev.	9	7
7th Randolph, Jennings	Dem	W.Va.	5	5
8th Engle, Clair	Dem	Cal.	5	5
9th Bartlett, E. L. (Bob)	Dem	Alas.	5	5
10th Williams, Harrison A. Jr.	Dem	N.J.	5	5
11th Moss, Frank E.	Dem	Utah	5	5

Minority

Rank Name	Party	State	Years in: Senate	Years in: Comm.
RM Saltonstall, Leverett	Rep	Mass.	19	13
2nd Javits, Jacob K.	Rep	N.Y.	7	*2 5
3rd Cooper, John Sherman	Rep	Ky.	11	5
4th Scott, Hugh D. Jr.	Rep	Penn.	5	5
5th Prouty, Winston L.	Rep	Vt.	5	5
6th Cotton, Norris	Rep	N.H.	9	1

*2: Member's 2nd period of service on the committee.

Note: Jacob K. Javits (Rep-N.Y.) was reassigned to the committee in the 86th Congress and credited with his former rank.

Changes:

Majority:

Engle, Clair	Dem	Cal.	July 30,1964	Died in office.
Humphrey, Hubert H. Jr.	DFL	Minn.	Dec. 29,1964	Resigned; elected Vice President.

SENATE SELECT COMMITTEE: SMALL BUSINESS / 89th Congress

Service Dates of Committee Chair: Jan. 8,1965-Jan. 11,1967
Service Dates of Majority Members: Jan. 8,1965-Jan. 11,1967
Service Dates of Minority Members: Jan. 15,1965-Jan. 18,1967

Majority

Rank Name	Party	State	Years in: Senate	Years in: Comm.
Chr Sparkman, John J.	Dem	Ala.	19	15
2nd Long, Russell B.	Dem	La.	17	15
3rd Smathers, George A.	Dem	Fla.	15	12
4th Morse, Wayne L.	Dem	Ore.	21	10
5th Bible, Alan H.	Dem	Nev.	11	8
6th Randolph, Jennings	Dem	W.Va.	7	6
7th Bartlett, E. L. (Bob)	Dem	Alas.	7	6
8th Williams, Harrison A. Jr.	Dem	N.J.	7	6
9th Moss, Frank E.	Dem	Utah	7	6
10th Nelson, Gaylord A.	Dem	Wisc.	3	1
11th Montoya, Joseph M.	Dem	N.M.	1	1

Minority

Rank Name	Party	State	Years in: Senate	Years in: Comm.
RM Saltonstall, Leverett	Rep	Mass.	21	15
2nd Javits, Jacob K.	Rep	N.Y.	9	*2 6
3rd Cooper, John Sherman	Rep	Ky.	13	6
4th Scott, Hugh D. Jr.	Rep	Penn.	7	6
5th Prouty, Winston L.	Rep	Vt.	7	6
6th Cotton, Norris	Rep	N.H.	11	3

*2: Member's 2nd period of service on the committee.

Note: Jacob K. Javits (Rep-N.Y.) was reassigned to the committee in the 86th Congress and credited with his former rank.

Changes:

Majority:

Moss, Frank E.	Dem	Utah	Mar. 22,1965	Left committee; no new assignment.
Harris, Fred R.	Dem	Okla.	Mar. 22,1965	Replaced Moss.

	Majority	Minority		
Departures from the Senate:				
Retired	None	Saltonstall, Leverett	Mass.	Rep
Departures from Committee:				
Moved to Foreign Relations	None	Cooper, John Sherman	Ky.	Rep
No new assignment	None	Prouty, Winston L.	Vt.	Rep

SENATE SELECT COMMITTEE: SMALL BUSINESS / 90th Congress

Service Dates of Committee Chair: Ch1 Jan. 11,1967-Jan. 16,1967
Ch2 Jan. 16,1967-Jan. 3,1969
Service Dates of Majority Members: Jan. 11,1967-Jan. 14,1969
Service Dates of Minority Members: Jan. 18,1967-Jan. 22,1969

Majority

Rank Name	Party	State	Years in: Senate	Years in: Comm.
Ch1 Sparkman, John J.	Dem	Ala.	21	17
2nd Long, Russell B.	Dem	La.	19	17
Ch2 3rd Smathers, George A.	Dem	Fla.	17	14
4th Morse, Wayne L.	Dem	Ore.	23	12
5th Bible, Alan H.	Dem	Nev.	13	10
6th Randolph, Jennings	Dem	W.Va.	9	8
7th Bartlett, E. L. (Bob)	Dem	Alas.	9	8
8th Williams, Harrison A. Jr.	Dem	N.J.	9	8
9th Nelson, Gaylord A.	Dem	Wisc.	5	3
10th Montoya, Joseph M.	Dem	N.M.	3	3
11th Harris, Fred R.	Dem	Okla.	3	2

Minority

Rank Name	Party	State	Years in: Senate	Years in: Comm.
RM Javits, Jacob K.	Rep	N.Y.	11	*2 8
2nd Scott, Hugh D. Jr.	Rep	Penn.	9	8
3rd Cotton, Norris	Rep	N.H.	13	5
4th Dominick, Peter H.	Rep	Colo.	5	1
5th Baker, Howard H. Jr.	Rep	Tenn.	1	1
6th Hatfield, Mark O.	Rep	Ore.	1	1

*2: Member's 2nd period of service on the committee.

Note: Jacob K. Javits (Rep-N.Y.) was reassigned to the committee in the 86th Congress and credited with his former rank.

Changes:

Chair:

Ch1 Sparkman, John J.	Dem	Ala.	Jan. 16,1967	Stepped down as Chair; remained on committee.
Ch2 Smathers, George A.	Dem	Fla.	Jan. 16,1967	Succeeded Sparkman as Chair.

Majority:

Bartlett, E. L. (Bob)	Dem	Alas.	Dec. 11,1968	Died in office.

	Majority		Minority	
Departures from the Senate:				
Defeated for Reelection	Morse, Wayne L.	Ore. Dem	None	
Retired	Smathers, George A.	Fla. Dem	None	
Departures from Committee:				
Becomes Senate Minority Whip	None		Scott, Hugh D. Jr.	Penn. Rep
No new assignment	None		Cotton, Norris	N.H. Rep

SENATE SELECT COMMITTEE: SMALL BUSINESS / 91st Congress

Service Dates of Committee Chair: Jan. 14,1969-Jan. 28,1971
Service Dates of Majority Members: Jan. 14,1969-Jan. 28,1971
Service Dates of Minority Members: Jan. 22,1969-Feb. 23,1971

Majority

Rank Name	Party	State	Years in: Senate	Years in: Comm.
Chr Bible, Alan H.	Dem	Nev.	15	12
2nd Sparkman, John J.	Dem	Ala.	23	19
3rd Long, Russell B.	Dem	La.	21	19
4th Randolph, Jennings	Dem	W.Va.	11	10
5th Williams, Harrison A. Jr.	Dem	N.J.	11	10
6th Nelson, Gaylord A.	Dem	Wisc.	7	5
7th Montoya, Joseph M.	Dem	N.M.	5	5
8th Harris, Fred R.	Dem	Okla.	5	4
9th McIntyre, Thomas J.	Dem	N.H.	7	1
10th Gravel, Mike	Dem	Alas.	1	1

Minority

Rank Name	Party	State	Years in: Senate	Years in: Comm.
RM Javits, Jacob K.	Rep	N.Y.	13	*2 10
2nd Dominick, Peter H.	Rep	Colo.	7	3
3rd Baker, Howard H. Jr.	Rep	Tenn.	3	3
4th Hatfield, Mark O.	Rep	Ore.	3	3
5th Dole, Robert J.	Rep	Kans.	1	1
6th Cook, Marlow W.	Rep	Ky.	1	1
7th Stevens, Theodore F.	Rep	Alas.	1	1

*2: Member's 2nd period of service on the committee.

Note: Jacob K. Javits (Rep-N.Y.) was reassigned to the committee in the 86th Congress and credited with his former rank.

Departures from Committee:	Majority		Minority	
Moved to Veterans' Affairs	Randolph, Jennings	W.Va. Dem	None	
Moved to Veterans' Affairs; Rules	None		Cook, Marlow W.	Ky. Rep
Moved to Veterans' Affairs; Commerce; Appropriations	None		Stevens, Theodore F.	Alas. Rep
Moved to Joint Atomic Energy	None		Baker, Howard H. Jr.	Tenn. Rep
No new assignment	Gravel, Mike	Alas. Dem	None	

SENATE SELECT COMMITTEE: SMALL BUSINESS / 92nd Congress

Service Dates of Committee Chair: Jan. 28,1971-Jan. 4,1973
Service Dates of Majority Members: Jan. 28,1971-Jan. 4,1973
Service Dates of Minority Members: Feb. 23,1971-Jan. 12,1973

Majority

Rank Name	Party	State	Years in: Senate	Years in: Comm.
Chr Bible, Alan H.	Dem	Nev.	17	14
2nd Sparkman, John J.	Dem	Ala.	25	21
3rd Long, Russell B.	Dem	La.	23	21
4th Williams, Harrison A. Jr.	Dem	N.J.	13	12
5th Nelson, Gaylord A.	Dem	Wisc.	9	7
6th Montoya, Joseph M.	Dem	N.M.	7	7
7th Harris, Fred R.	Dem	Okla.	7	6
8th McIntyre, Thomas J.	Dem	N.H.	9	3
9th Gambrell, David H.	Dem	Ga.	1	1

Minority

Rank Name	Party	State	Years in: Senate	Years in: Comm.
RM Javits, Jacob K.	Rep	N.Y.	15	*2 13
2nd Dominick, Peter H.	Rep	Colo.	9	5
3rd Hatfield, Mark O.	Rep	Ore.	5	5
4th Dole, Robert J.	Rep	Kans.	3	3
5th Gurney, Edward J.	Rep	Fla.	3	1
6th Saxbe, William B.	Rep	Ohio	3	1
7th Beall, J. Glenn Jr.	Rep	Md.	1	1
8th Taft, Robert Jr.	Rep	Ohio	1	1

*2: Member's 2nd period of service on the committee.

Note: Jacob K. Javits (Rep-N.Y.) was reassigned to the committee in the 86th Congress and credited with his former rank.

Vacancy Filled:
Majority: 9th seat by Gambrell on Feb. 3,1971.

Changes:

Majority:

Gambrell, David H.	Dem	Ga.	Nov. 7,1972	Resigned; defeated for nomination.

Minority:

Saxbe, William B.	Rep	Ohio	Feb. 23,1972	Left committee; no new assignment.
Weicker, Lowell P. Jr.	Rep	Conn.	Feb. 23,1972	Replaced Saxbe.

Departures from the Senate:	Majority		Minority	
Retired	Harris, Fred R.	Okla. Dem	None	
Departures from Committee:				
Moved to Banking, Housing & Urban Affairs	Williams, Harrison A. Jr.	N.J. Dem	Weicker, Lowell P. Jr.	Conn. Rep
Moved to Rules	None		Hatfield, Mark O.	Ore. Rep
Moved to Armed Services	None		Taft, Robert Jr.	Ohio Rep
No new assignment	Long, Russell B.	La. Dem	None	
	Montoya, Joseph M.	N.M. Dem		

SENATE SELECT COMMITTEE: SMALL BUSINESS / 93rd Congress

Service Dates of Committee Chair: Ch1 Jan. 4,1973-Dec. 17,1974
Ch2 Dec. 17,1974-Jan. 4,1975
Service Dates of Majority Members: Jan. 4,1973-Jan. 17,1975
Service Dates of Minority Members: Jan. 12,1973-Jan. 23,1975

Majority

Rank Name	Party	State	Years in: Senate	Years in: Comm.
Ch1 Bible, Alan H.	Dem	Nev.	19	16
2nd Sparkman, John J.	Dem	Ala.	27	23
Ch2 3rd Nelson, Gaylord A.	Dem	Wisc.	11	8
4th McIntyre, Thomas J.	Dem	N.H.	11	4
5th Pell, Claiborne D.	Dem	R.I.	13	1
6th Nunn, Samuel A.	Dem	Ga.	1	1
7th Johnston, J. Bennett Jr.	Dem	La.	1	1
8th Hathaway, William D.	Dem	Me.	1	1
9th Abourezk, James G.	Dem	S.D.	1	1
10th Haskell, Floyd K.	Dem	Colo.	1	1

Minority

Rank Name	Party	State	Years in: Senate	Years in: Comm.
RM Javits, Jacob K.	Rep	N.Y.	17	*2 14
2nd Dominick, Peter H.	Rep	Colo.	11	6
3rd Dole, Robert J.	Rep	Kans.	5	4
4th Gurney, Edward J.	Rep	Fla.	5	2
5th Beall, J. Glenn Jr.	Rep	Md.	3	2
6th Buckley, James L.	Con	N.Y.	3	1
7th Scott, William L.	Rep	Va.	1	1

*2: Member's 2nd period of service on the committee.

Notes: Jacob K. Javits (Rep-N.Y.) was reassigned to the committee in the 86th Congress and credited with his former rank.
James Buckley of New York was elected as a Conservative, but was assigned to the committee by the Republican Conference.

Changes:

Chair:				
Ch1 Bible, Alan H.	Dem	Nev.	Dec. 18,1974	Resigned and retired (effective Dec. 17,1974).
Ch2 Nelson, Gaylord A.	Dem	Wisc.	Dec. 18,1974	Succeeded Bible as Chair.
Majority:				
Pell, Claiborne D.	Dem	R.I.	Jan. 18,1973	Left committee; no new assignment.
Clark, Richard C.	Dem	Iowa	Jan. 29,1973	Replaced Pell.
Bible, Alan H.	Dem	Nev.	Dec. 18,1974	Resigned and retired (effective Dec. 17,1974).
Minority:				
Dole, Robert J.	Rep	Kans.	Jan. 24,1974	Moved to Post Office and Civil Service.
Roth, William V. Jr.	Rep	Del.	Feb. 6,1974	Replaced Dole.
Gurney, Edward J.	Rep	Fla.	Dec. 31,1974	Resigned and retired.

	Majority	Minority		
Departures from the Senate:				
Defeated for Reelection	None	Dominick, Peter H.	Colo.	Rep
Departures from Committee:				
Moved to Budget; Commerce	None	Buckley, James L.	N.Y.	Con
Moved to Judiciary; Veterans' Affairs	None	Scott, William L.	Va.	Rep

SENATE SELECT COMMITTEE: SMALL BUSINESS / 94th Congress

Service Dates of Committee Chair: Jan. 17,1975-Jan. 10,1977
Service Dates of Majority Members: Jan. 17,1975-Jan. 10,1977
Service Dates of Minority Members: Jan. 23,1975-Jan. 10,1977

Majority

Rank Name	Party	State	Years in: Senate	Years in: Comm.
Chr Nelson, Gaylord A.	Dem	Wisc.	13	11
2nd Sparkman, John J.	Dem	Ala.	29	25
3rd McIntyre, Thomas J.	Dem	N.H.	13	7
4th Nunn, Samuel A.	Dem	Ga.	3	3
5th Johnston, J. Bennett Jr.	Dem	La.	3	3
6th Hathaway, William D.	Dem	Me.	3	3
7th Abourezk, James G.	Dem	S.D.	3	3
8th Haskell, Floyd K.	Dem	Colo.	3	3
9th Clark, Richard C.	Dem	Iowa	3	2
10th Mondale, Walter F.	DFL	Minn.	11	1

Minority

Rank Name	Party	State	Years in: Senate	Years in: Comm.
RM Javits, Jacob K.	Rep	N.Y.	19	*2 16
2nd Beall, J. Glenn Jr.	Rep	Md.	5	4
3rd Roth, William V. Jr.	Rep	Del.	5	1
4th Brock, William E. III	Rep	Tenn.	5	1
5th Weicker, Lowell P. Jr.	Rep	Conn.	5	*2 1
6th Bartlett, Dewey F.	Rep	Okla.	3	1
7th Laxalt, Paul	Rep	Nev.	1	1

*2: Member's 2nd period of service on the committee.

Note: Jacob K. Javits (Rep-N.Y.) was reassigned to the committee in the 86th Congress and credited with his former rank.

Changes:

Majority:

Clark, Richard C.	Dem	Iowa	Sep. 19,1975	Left committee; no new assignment.
Culver, John C.	Dem	Iowa	Sep. 19,1975	Replaced Clark.
Mondale, Walter F.	DFL	Minn.	Dec. 30,1976	Resigned; elected Vice President.

Minority:

Roth, William V. Jr.	Rep	Del.	Jan. 31,1975	Left committee; no new assignment.
Packwood, Robert W.	Rep	Ore.	June 13,1975	Replaced Roth.

Departures from the Senate:	Majority	Minority	
Defeated for Reelection	None	Beall, J. Glenn Jr.	Md. Rep
		Brock, William E. III	Tenn. Rep

SENATE SELECT COMMITTEE: SMALL BUSINESS / 95th Congress

Service Dates of Committee Chair: Jan. 10,1977-Jan. 23,1979 (Temporary assignment made permanent Feb. 11,1977)
Service Dates of Majority Members: Jan. 10,1977-Jan. 23,1979 (Temporary assignments made permanent Feb. 11,1977)
Service Dates of Minority Members: Jan. 10,1977-Jan. 23,1979 (Temporary assignments made permanent Feb. 22,1977)

Majority

Rank	Name	Party	State	Years in: Senate	Years in: Comm.
Chr	Nelson, Gaylord A.	Dem	Wisc.	15	13
2nd	Sparkman, John J.	Dem	Ala.	31	27
3rd	McIntyre, Thomas J.	Dem	N.H.	15	8
4th	Nunn, Samuel A.	Dem	Ga.	5	5
5th	Johnston, J. Bennett Jr.	Dem	La.	5	5
6th	Hathaway, William D.	Dem	Me.	5	5
7th	Abourezk, James G.	Dem	S.D.	5	5
8th	Haskell, Floyd K.	Dem	Colo.	5	5
9th	Culver, John C.	Dem	Iowa	3	2

Minority

Rank	Name	Party	State	Years in: Senate	Years in: Comm.
RM1	Javits, Jacob K.	Rep	N.Y.	21	*2 18
RM2 2nd	Weicker, Lowell P. Jr.	Rep	Conn.	7	*2 2
3rd	Bartlett, Dewey F.	Rep	Okla.	5	2
4th	Laxalt, Paul	Rep	Nev.	3	2
5th	Packwood, Robert W.	Rep	Ore.	9	2

*2: Member's 2nd period of service on the committee.

Note: Jacob K. Javits (Rep-N.Y.) was reassigned to the committee in the 86th Congress and credited with his former rank.

Changes:

Ranking Member:

RM1 Javits, Jacob K.	Rep	N.Y.	Feb. 22,1977	Left committee; no new assignment.
RM2 Weicker, Lowell P. Jr.	Rep	Conn.	Feb. 22,1977	Succeeded Javits as Ranking Minority Member.

Majority:

Sparkman, John J.	Dem	Ala.	Feb. 11,1977	Left committee; no new assignment.
Johnston, J. Bennett Jr.	Dem	La.	Feb. 11,1977	Moved to Energy; Budget.
Abourezk, James G.	Dem	S.D.	Feb. 11,1977	Moved to Select Indian Affairs as Chair.

Minority:

Javits, Jacob K.	Rep	N.Y.	Feb. 22,1977	Left committee; no new assignment.
Laxalt, Paul	Rep	Nev.	Feb. 22,1977	Moved to Energy & Natural Resources; Judiciary; Finance.

Departures from the Senate:	Majority		Minority	
Defeated for Reelection	Haskell, Floyd K.	Colo. Dem	None	
	Hathaway, William D.	Me. Dem		
	McIntyre, Thomas J.	N.H. Dem		
Retired	None		Bartlett, Dewey F.	Okla. Rep

SENATE SELECT COMMITTEE: SMALL BUSINESS / 96th Congress

Service Dates of Committee Chair: Jan. 23,1979-Jan. 3,1981
Service Dates of Majority Members: Jan. 23,1979-Jan. 5,1981
Service Dates of Minority Members: Jan. 23,1979-Jan. 5,1981

Majority

Rank	Name	Party	State	Years in: Senate	Years in: Comm.
Chr	Nelson, Gaylord A.	Dem	Wisc.	17	15
2nd	Nunn, Samuel A.	Dem	Ga.	7	7
3rd	Culver, John C.	Dem	Iowa	5	4
4th	Huddleston, Walter D.	Dem	Ky.	7	1
5th	Bumpers, Dale	Dem	Ark.	5	1
6th	Morgan, Robert B.	Dem	N.C.	5	1
7th	Sasser, James R.	Dem	Tenn.	3	1
8th	Stewart, Donald W.	Dem	Ala.	1	1
9th	Baucus, Max S.	Dem	Mont.	1	1
10th	Levin, Carl M.	Dem	Mich.	1	1

Minority

Rank	Name	Party	State	Years in: Senate	Years in: Comm.
RM	Weicker, Lowell P. Jr.	Rep	Conn.	9	*2 5
2nd	Packwood, Robert W.	Rep	Ore.	11	4
3rd	Hatch, Orrin G.	Rep	Utah	3	1
4th	Hayakawa, S. I. (Sam)	Rep	Cal.	3	1
5th	Schmitt, Harrison H.	Rep	N.M.	3	1
6th	Boschwitz, Rudolf E.	Rep	Minn.	1	1
7th	Pressler, Larry L.	Rep	S.D.	1	1

*2: Member's 2nd period of service on the committee.

	Majority			Minority		
Departures from the Senate:						
Defeated for Reelection	Culver, John C.	Iowa	Dem	None		
	Morgan, Robert B.	N.C.	Dem			
	Nelson, Gaylord A.	Wisc.	Dem			
	Stewart, Donald W.	Ala.	Dem			
Departures from Committee:						
Moved to Foreign Relations	None			Pressler, Larry L.	S.D.	Rep
Moved to Banking, Housing & Urban Affairs	None			Schmitt, Harrison H.	N.M.	Rep

SENATE SELECT COMMITTEE: SMALL BUSINESS / 97th Congress

* Became the Standing Committee on SMALL BUSINESS on Mar. 25,1981.

Service Dates of Committee Chair: Jan. 5,1981-Mar. 25,1981
Service Dates of Majority Members: Jan. 5,1981-Mar. 25,1981
Service Dates of Minority Members: Jan. 5,1981-Mar. 25,1981

Majority

Rank	Name	Party	State	Years in: Senate	Years in: Comm.
Chr	Weicker, Lowell P. Jr.	Rep	Conn.	11	*2 6
2nd	Packwood, Robert W.	Rep	Ore.	13	6
3rd	Hatch, Orrin G.	Rep	Utah	5	2
4th	Hayakawa, S. I. (Sam)	Rep	Cal.	5	2
5th	Boschwitz, Rudolf E.	Rep	Minn.	3	2
6th	Gorton, Slade	Rep	Wash.	1	1
7th	Nickles, Don	Rep	Okla.	1	1
8th	Rudman, Warren B.	Rep	N.H.	1	1
9th	D'Amato, Alfonse M.	Rep	N.Y.	1	1

Minority

Rank	Name	Party	State	Years in: Senate	Years in: Comm.
RM	Nunn, Samuel A.	Dem	Ga.	9	9
2nd	Huddleston, Walter D.	Dem	Ky.	9	2
3rd	Bumpers, Dale	Dem	Ark.	7	2
4th	Sasser, James R.	Dem	Tenn.	5	2
5th	Baucus, Max S.	Dem	Mont.	3	2
6th	Levin, Carl M.	Dem	Mich.	3	2
7th	Tsongas, Paul E.	Dem	Mass.	3	1
8th	Dixon, Alan J.	Dem	Ill.	1	1

*2: Member's 2nd period of service on the committee.

SENATE SPECIAL COMMITTEE: TO INVESTIGATE ORGANIZED CRIME IN INTERSTATE COMMERCE

Jurisdiction, 1950

From Senate Resolution 202, 81st Congress, Second Session, May 3, 1950:

[Section 1]

To make a full and complete study and investigation of whether organized crime utilizes the facilities of interstate commerce or otherwise operates in interstate commerce in furtherance of any transactions which are in violation of the law of the United States or of the State in which the transactions occur, and, if so, the manner and extent to which, and the identity of the persons, firms, or corporations by which such utilization is being made, what facilities are being used, and whether or not organized crime utilizes such interstate facilities or otherwise operates in interstate commerce for the development of corrupting influences in violation of law of the United States or of the laws of any State.

Termination, 1951

The Special Committee was terminated upon the filing of Senate Report 725 (82-1) on August 31, 1951, at which time all files, papers, documents and other pertinent data were transferred to the Committee on Interstate and Foreign Commerce.

SENATE SPECIAL COMMITTEE: TO INVESTIGATE ORGANIZED CRIME IN INTERSTATE COMMERCE / 81st Congress

Service Dates of Committee Chair: May 10,1950-Continued
Service Dates of Majority Members: May 10,1950-Continued
Service Dates of Minority Members: May 10,1950-Continued

Majority

Rank	Name	Party	State	Years in: Senate	Years in: Comm.
Chr	Kefauver, C. Estes	Dem	Tenn.	2	1
2nd	O'Conor, Herbert R.	Dem	Md.	4	1
3rd	Hunt, Lester C.	Dem	Wyo.	2	1

Minority

Rank	Name	Party	State	Years in: Senate	Years in: Comm.
RM	Tobey, Charles W.	Rep	N.H.	12	1
2nd	Wiley, Alexander	Rep	Wisc.	12	1

SENATE SPECIAL COMMITTEE: TO INVESTIGATE ORGANIZED CRIME IN INTERSTATE COMMERCE / 82nd Congress

Service Dates of Committee Chair: Ch1 Jan. 3,1949-May 1,1951
Ch2 May 1,1951-Aug. 31,1951
Service Dates of Majority Members: Jan. 3,1949-Aug. 31,1951
Service Dates of Minority Members: Jan. 3,1949-Aug. 31,1951

Majority

Rank	Name	Party	State	Years in: Senate	Years in: Comm.
Chr	Kefauver, C. Estes	Dem	Tenn.	3	1
2nd	O'Conor, Herbert R.	Dem	Md.	5	1
3rd	Hunt, Lester C.	Dem	Wyo.	3	1

Minority

Rank	Name	Party	State	Years in: Senate	Years in: Comm.
RM	Tobey, Charles W.	Rep	N.H.	13	1
2nd	Wiley, Alexander	Rep	Wisc.	13	1

Changes:

Chair:

Ch1	Kefauver, C. Estes	Tenn.	Dem	May 1,1951	Resigned as Chair; remained on committee.
Ch2	O'Conor, Herbert R.	Md.	Dem	May 1,1951	Succeeded Kefauver as Chair.

SENATE SPECIAL COMMITTEE: TO STUDY THE RATES OF COMPENSATION OF CERTAIN OFFICERS AND EMPLOYEES OF THE SENATE

Jurisdiction, 1954

From Public Law 83-178, the Legislative-Judiciary Appropriation Act of 1954, 67 Statutes 318, 321, August 1, 1953:

It shall be the duty of said committee to study the rates of compensation now being paid officers and employees of the Senate, including employees of the Senate Office Building under the Architect of the Capitol, but excluding administrative and clerical assistants to Senators and committee employees, to determine whether such rates of compensation bear the proper relationship to each other and whether they are in line with rates now paid by the other branch of Congress.

Termination, 1954

The Special Committee was terminated on January 6,1954.

SENATE SPECIAL COMMITTEE: TO STUDY THE RATES OF COMPENSATION OF CERTAIN OFFICERS AND EMPLOYEES OF THE SENATE / 83rd Congress

Service Dates of Committee Chair: Aug. 3,1953-Jan. 6,1954
Service Dates of Majority Members: Aug. 3,1953-Jan. 6,1954
Service Dates of Minority Members: Aug. 3,1953-Jan. 6,1954

Majority

Rank	Name	Party	State	Years in: Senate	Comm.
Chr	Smith, Margaret Chase	Rep	Me.	5	1
2nd	Potter, Charles E.	Rep	Mich.	1	1
3rd	Carlson, Frank	Rep	Kans.	3	1

Minority

Rank	Name	Party	State	Years in: Senate	Comm.
RM	Johnston, Olin D.	Dem	S.C.	9	1
2nd	Ellender, Allen J.	Dem	La.	17	1
3rd	Hayden, Carl	Dem	Ariz.	27	1

SENATE SELECT COMMITTEE: TO STUDY CENSURE CHARGES (AGAINST SENATOR JOSEPH R. McCARTHY)

Jurisdiction, 1954

From Senate Resolution 301, 83rd Congress, Second Session, June 30, 1954:

Resolved, That the conduct of the Senator from Wisconsin, Mr. McCarthy, is unbecoming a Member of the United States Senate, is contrary to senatorial traditions, and tends to bring the Senate into disrepute, and such conduct is hereby condemned.

Termination, 1954

The Special Committee was terminated upon the filing of Senate Report 2508 (83-2) on November 8,1954.

SENATE SELECT COMMITTEE: TO STUDY CENSURE CHARGES (AGAINST SENATOR JOSEPH R. McCARTHY) / 83rd Congress

Service Dates of Committee Chair: Aug. 5,1954-Nov. 8,1954
Service Dates of Majority Members: Aug. 5,1954-Nov. 8,1954
Service Dates of Minority Members: Aug. 5,1954-Nov. 8,1954

Majority				Years in:		Minority				Years in:	
Rank	Name	Party	State	Senate	Comm.	Rank	Name	Party	State	Senate	Comm.
Chr	Watkins, Arthur V.	Rep	Utah	8	1	VCh	Johnson, Edwin C.	Dem	Colo.	18	1
2nd	Carlson, Frank	Rep	Kans.	4	1	2nd	Stennis, John C.	Dem	Miss.	7	1
3rd	Case, Francis H.	Rep	S.D.	4	1	3rd	Ervin, Samuel J.	Dem	N.C.	1	1

SENATE SPECIAL COMMITTEE: TO INVESTIGATE THE USE OF MAIL COVERS ON SENATOR JOSEPH R. McCARTHY OR ANY OTHER SENATOR

Jurisdiction, 1954

From Senate Resolution, 332, 83rd Congress, Second Session, December 1, 1954:

[Section 1]

A special committee of the Senate to make a full and complete investigation for the purpose of determining all of the facts with respect to:

(1) whether or not during any period of time there has been maintained a cover on mail to or from the junior Senator from Wisconsin, Mr. McCarthy, or any other Senator, or such mail has been otherwise handled in any special manner and without authorization from the junior Senator from Wisconsin, or any other Senator, for the purpose of ascertaining the contents thereof or the identity of persons corresponding with the junior Senator from Wisconsin, or any other Senator, and

(2) in the event the committee determines that any such cover has been maintained or such mail has been so handled, the person or persons responsible therefor, the period during which such cover was maintained or such mail was so handled, and all other matters connected with the maintenance of such cover or so handling such mail.

Termination, 1954

The Special Committee was terminated upon filing Senate Report 251 (83-2) on December 3, 1954.

SENATE SPECIAL COMMITTEE: TO INVESTIGATE THE USE OF MAIL COVERS ON SENATOR JOSEPH R. McCARTHY OR ANY OTHER SENATOR / 83rd Congress

Service Dates of Committee Chair: Dec. 1,1954-Dec. 3,1954
Service Dates of Minority Member: Dec. 1,1954-Dec. 3,1954

Majority						Minority					
				Years in:						Years in:	
Rank	Name	Party	State	Senate	Comm.	Rank	Name	Party	State	Senate	Comm.
Chr	Ferguson, Homer	Rep	Mich.	12	1	RM	George, Walter F.	Dem	Ga.	33	1

SENATE SPECIAL SUB-COMMITTEE: DISARMAMENT

Jurisdiction, 1955

From Senate Resolution 93, as amended, 84th Congress, First Session, July 25, 1955:

[Section 2]

The said Committee shall, without limiting the scope of the study hereby authorized, direct its attention to the following matters:

1. Efforts made by the United Nations in seeking the control and reduction of military forces and armaments of all types;
2. Disarmament proposals developed by the United States and other governments as well as by private groups and individuals;
3. Methods by which the attitudes of the American people and their Government on the subject of disarmament and world peace may be communicated abroad;
4. The relationship of armaments to the state of the world economy;
5. The relationship of underlying international tension to the problems of disarmament;
6. The dangers implicit in unilateral reduction of armaments; and
7. Methods of assuring that plans for reduction of armaments shall not endanger the security of the United States.

Termination, 1958

The Special Subcommittee was terminated upon the filing of Senate Report 2501 (85-2) on October 13, 1958. A permanent subcommittee of the Senate Foreign Relations Committee was established on July 15, 1958.

Senate Special Sub-Committee: DISARMAMENT / 84th Congress

Service Dates of Committee Chair: Aug. 2,1955-Jan. 9,1957
Service Dates of Majority Members: Aug. 2,1955-Jan. 9,1957
Service Dates of Minority Members: Aug. 2,1955-Jan. 9,1957

Majority

Rank Name	Party	State	Years in: Senate	Years in: Comm.
Chr Humphrey, Hubert H. Jr.	DFL	Minn.	7	1
2nd Byrd, Harry Flood	Dem	Va.	23	1
3rd Sparkman, John J.	Dem	Ala.	9	1
4th Barkley, Alben W.	Dem	Ky.	23	1
5th Pastore, John O.	Dem	R.I.	5	1
6th Symington, W. Stuart	Dem	Mo.	3	1

Minority

Rank Name	Party	State	Years in: Senate	Years in: Comm.
RM Bridges, H. Styles	Rep	N.H.	19	1
2nd Wiley, Alexander	Rep	Wisc.	17	1
3rd Hickenlooper, Bourke B.	Rep	Iowa	11	1
4th Saltonstall, Leverett	Rep	Mass.	11	1
5th Knowland, William F.	Rep	Cal.	10	1
6th Bricker, John W.	Rep	Ohio	9	1

Changes:
Majority:

Barkley, Alben W.	Dem	Ky.	Apr. 30,1956 Died in office.
Long, Russell B.	Dem	La.	May 18,1956 Replaced Barkley; ranked 4th.

SENATE SPECIAL SUB-COMMITTEE: DISARMAMENT / 85th Congress

Service Dates of Committee Chair: Jan. 9,1957-Jan. 31,1959
Service Dates of Majority Members: Jan. 9,1957-Jan. 31,1959
Service Dates of Minority Members: Jan. 9,1957-Jan. 31,1959

Majority

Rank Name	Party	State	Years in: Senate	Years in: Comm.
Chr Humphrey, Hubert H. Jr.	DFL	Minn.	9	2
2nd Byrd, Harry Flood	Dem	Va.	24	2
3rd Sparkman, John J.	Dem	Ala.	11	2
4th Long, Russell B.	Dem	La.	9	1
5th Pastore, John O.	Dem	R.I.	7	2
6th Symington, W. Stuart	Dem	Mo.	5	2

Minority

Rank Name	Party	State	Years in: Senate	Years in: Comm.
RM Bridges, H. Styles	Rep	N.H.	21	2
2nd Wiley, Alexander	Rep	Wisc.	19	2
3rd Hickenlooper, Bourke B.	Rep	Iowa	13	2
4th Saltonstall, Leverett	Rep	Mass.	13	2
5th Knowland, William F.	Rep	Cal.	12	2
6th Bricker, John W.	Rep	Ohio	11	2

Note: "Service Dates" of committee members reflect service on the parent Foreign Relations Committee.

SENATE SPECIAL COMMITTEE: SENATE RECEPTION ROOM

Jurisdiction, 1955

From Senate Resolution 145, 84th Congress, First Session, August 2, 1955:

[Section 2]

It shall be the duty of the committee to select five outstanding persons from all persons, but not a living person, who have served as Members of the Senate since the formation of the Government of the United States, whose paintings shall be placed in the five unfilled spaces in the Senate reception room. The committee is authorized to seek advice and recommendations from such historians and other sources, including the general public, as it deems advisable.

Termination, 1957

The Special Committee was terminated upon filing of Senate Report 279 (85-1) on May 1, 1957.

SENATE SPECIAL COMMITTEE: SENATE RECEPTION ROOM / 84th Congress

Service Dates of Committee Chair: Ch1 Aug. 2,1955-Apr. 11,1956
Ch2 Apr. 11,1956-Continued
Service Dates of Majority Members: Aug. 2,1955-Continued
Service Dates of Minority Members: Aug. 2,1955-Continued

Majority

Rank Name	Party	State	Years in: Senate	Years in: Comm.
Ch1 Johnson, Lyndon B.	Dem	Tex.	7	1
2nd Russell, Richard B.	Dem	Ga.	23	1
3rd Mansfield, Michael J.	Dem	Mont.	3	1

Minority

Rank Name	Party	State	Years in: Senate	Years in: Comm.
RM Bridges, H. Styles	Rep	N.H.	19	1
2nd Millikin, Eugene D.	Rep	Colo.	14	1

Changes:

	Name	Party	State	Date	Change
Chair:					
Ch1	Johnson, Lyndon B.	Dem	Tex.	Apr. 11,1956	Left committee; no new assignment.
Ch2	Kennedy, John F.	Dem	Mass.	Apr. 11,1956	Replaced Johnson as Chair.
Majority:					
	Johnson, Lyndon B.	Dem	Tex.	Apr. 11,1956	Left committee; no new assignment.
	Kennedy, John F.	Dem	Mass.	Apr. 11,1956	Replaced Johnson.
Minority:					
	Millikin, Eugene D.	Rep	Colo.	June 13,1956	Left committee; no new assignment.
	Bricker, John W.	Rep	Ohio	June 13,1956	Replaced Millikin.

SENATE SPECIAL COMMITTEE: SENATE RECEPTION ROOM / 85th Congress

Service Dates of Committee Chair: Jan. 3,1957-May 1,1957
Service Dates of Majority Members: Jan. 3,1957-May 1,1957
Service Dates of Minority Members: Jan. 3,1957-May 1,1957

Majority

Rank Name	Party	State	Years in: Senate	Years in: Comm.
Chr Kennedy, John F.	Dem	Mass.	5	1
2nd Russell, Richard B.	Dem	Ga.	24	2
3rd Mansfield, Michael J.	Dem	Mont.	5	2

Minority

Rank Name	Party	State	Years in: Senate	Years in: Comm.
RM Bricker, John W.	Rep	Ohio	11	1
2nd Bridges, H. Styles	Rep	N.H.	21	2

SENATE SELECT COMMITTEE: CONTRIBUTION INVESTIGATION

Jurisdiction, 1956

From Senate Resolution 205, 84th Congress, Second Session, February 6, 1956:

[Section 1]

Resolved, That there is hereby established a select committee to investigate the circumstances involving an alleged improper attempt through political contributions to influence the vote of the junior Senator from South Dakota, Mr. [Francis] Case, in connection with the Senate's consideration of the bill S. 1853, the natural-gas bill.

Termination, 1956

The Select Committee was extended by Senate Resolution 218 and Senate Resolution 227 and was terminated upon the filing of Senate Report 1724 on April 7, 1956.

SENATE SELECT COMMITTEE: CONTRIBUTION INVESTIGATION / 84th Congress

Service Dates of Committee Chair: Feb. 7,1956-Apr. 7,1956
Service Dates of Majority Members: Feb. 7,1956-Apr. 7,1956
Service Dates of Minority Members: Feb. 7,1956-Apr. 7,1956

Majority

			Years in:	
Rank Name	**Party**	**State**	**Senate**	**Comm.**
Chr George, Walter F.	Dem	Ga.	34	1
2nd Hayden, Carl	Dem	Ariz.	29	1

Minority

			Years in:	
Rank Name	**Party**	**State**	**Senate**	**Comm.**
RM Bridges, H. Styles	Rep	N.H.	20	1
2nd Thye, Edward J.	Rep	Minn.	10	1

SENATE SPECIAL COMMITTEE: TO INVESTIGATE POLITICAL ACTIVITIES, LOBBYING AND CAMPAIGN CONTRIBUTIONS

Jurisdiction, 1956

From Senate Resolution 219, 84th Congress, Second Session, February 22, 1956:

[Section 1]

Resolved, That there is hereby established a special committee which is authorized and directed to investigate the subject of attempts to influence improperly or illegally the Senate or any Member thereof, or any candidate therefor, or any officer or employee of the executive branch of the Government, through campaign contributions, political activities, lobbying, or any and all other activities or practices.

[Section 3.(a)]

The special committee shall report to the Senate by January 31, 1957, and shall include in its report specific recommendations:

(1) to improve and modernize the Federal election laws;

(2) to improve and strengthen the Federal Corrupt Practices Act, the Hatch Act, and the Federal Regulation of Lobbying Act, and related laws; and

(3) to insure appropriate administrative action in connection with all persons, organizations, associations, or corporations believed to be guilty of wrongdoing punishable by law.

Termination, 1957

The Special Committee was extended by Senate Resolutions 47 and 128 (85-1) and terminated upon the filing of its final report Senate Report 395 (85-1) on May 31, 1957.

SENATE SELECT COMMITTEE: TO INVESTIGATE POLITICAL ACTIVITIES, LOBBYING AND CAMPAIGN CONTRIBUTIONS / 84th Congress

Service Dates of Committee Chair: Feb. 23,1956-Continued
Service Dates of Majority Members: Feb. 23,1956-Continued
Service Dates of Minority Members: Feb. 23,1956-Continued

Majority						Minority				
			Years in:						Years in:	
Rank Name	Party	State	Senate	Comm.		Rank Name	Party	State	Senate	Comm.
Chr McClellan, John L.	Dem	Ark.	14	1		VCh Bridges, H. Styles	Rep	N.H.	20	1
2nd Gore, Albert A.	Dem	Tenn.	4	1		2nd Thye, Edward J.	Rep	Minn.	10	1
3rd Anderson, Clinton P.	Dem	N.M.	8	1		3rd Purtell, William A.	Rep	Conn.	4	1
4th Kennedy, John F.	Dem	Mass.	4	1		4th Goldwater, Barry M.	Rep	Ariz.	4	1

SENATE SELECT COMMITTEE: TO INVESTIGATE POLITICAL ACTIVITIES, LOBBYING AND CAMPAIGN CONTRIBUTIONS / 85th Congress

Service Dates of Committee Chair: Jan. 3,1957-May 31,1957
Service Dates of Majority Members: Jan. 3,1957-May 31,1957
Service Dates of Minority Members: Jan. 3,1957-May 31,1957

Majority						Minority				
			Years in:						Years in:	
Rank Name	Party	State	Senate	Comm.		Rank Name	Party	State	Senate	Comm.
Chr McClellan, John L.	Dem	Ark.	15	1		VCh Bridges, H. Styles	Rep	N.H.	21	1
2nd Gore, Albert A.	Dem	Tenn.	5	1		2nd Thye, Edward J.	Rep	Minn.	11	1
3rd Anderson, Clinton P.	Dem	N.M.	9	1		3rd Purtell, William A.	Rep	Conn.	5	1
4th Kennedy, John F.	Dem	Mass.	5	1		4th Goldwater, Barry M.	Rep	Ariz.	5	1

SENATE SPECIAL COMMITTEE: STUDY THE FOREIGN AID PROGRAM

Jurisdiction, 1956

From Senate Resolution 285, 84th Congress, Second Session, July 11, 1956:

[Section 1]

Resolved, That there shall be established a committee which shall make exhaustive studies of the extent to which foreign assistance by the United States Government serves, can be made to serve, or does not serve, the national interest, to the end that such studies and recommendations based thereon may be available to the Senate in considering foreign aid policies for the future.

[Section 3]

The committee shall, without limiting the scope of the study hereby authorized, direct its attention to the following matters:

(a) The proper objectives of foreign aid programs and the criteria which can be used to measure accomplishment.
(b) The capability of the United States to extend aid, in terms of the Nation's economic, technical, personnel, and other resources.
(c) The need and willingness of foreign countries to receive aid, and their capacity to make effective use thereof.
(d) The various kinds of foreign aid and alternatives thereto as well as the methods by which and conditions on which aid might be furnished.
(e) The related actions which should be taken to make foreign aid effective in achieving national objectives.

Termination, 1957

The committee was terminated by authority of Senate Resolution 35 (85-1) on June 20, 1957. The committee submitted its final report, Senate Report 300 (85-1), on May 13, 1957.

SENATE SPECIAL COMMITTEE: STUDY THE FOREIGN AID PROGRAM / 84th Congress

Service Dates of Committee Chair: July 11,1956-Jan. 3,1957
Service Dates of Majority Members: July 11,1956-Jan. 9,1957
Service Dates of Minority Members: July 11,1956-Jan. 9,1957

Majority

Rank	Name	Party	State	Years in: Senate	Years in: Comm.
Chr	George, Walter F.	Dem	Ga.	34	1
2nd	Green, Theodore F.	Dem	R.I.	20	1
3rd	Fulbright, J. William	Dem	Ark.	12	1
4th	Sparkman, John J.	Dem	Ala.	10	1
5th	Humphrey, Hubert H. Jr.	DFL	Minn.	8	1
6th	Mansfield, Michael J.	Dem	Mont.	4	1
7th	Morse, Wayne L.	Dem	Ore.	12	1
8th	Long, Russell B.	Dem	La.	8	1
9th	Hayden, Carl	Dem	Ariz.	30	1
10th	Russell, Richard B.	Dem	Ga.	24	1

Minority

Rank	Name	Party	State	Years in: Senate	Years in: Comm.
RM	Wiley, Alexander	Rep	Wisc.	18	1
2nd	Smith, H. Alexander	Rep	N.J.	12	1
3rd	Hickenlooper, Bourke B.	Rep	Iowa	12	1
4th	Langer, William	Rep	N.D.	16	1
5th	Knowland, William F.	Rep	Cal.	11	1
6th	Aiken, George D.	Rep	Vt.	16	1
7th	Capehart, Homer E.	Rep	Ind.	12	1
8th	Bridges, H. Styles	Rep	N.H.	20	1
9th	Saltonstall, Leverett	Rep	Mass.	12	1

Departures from the Senate:

	Majority		Minority
Retired	George, Walter F.	Ga. Dem	None

SENATE SELECT COMMITTEE: STUDY THE FOREIGN AID PROGRAM / 85th Congress

Service Dates of Committee Chair: Jan. 9,1957-May 13,1957
Service Dates of Majority Members: Jan. 9,1957-May 13,1957
Service Dates of Minority Members: Jan. 9,1957-May 13,1957

Majority

Rank	Name	Party	State	Years in: Senate	Years in: Comm.
Chr	Green, Theodore F.	Dem	R.I.	21	1
2nd	Fulbright, J. William	Dem	Ark.	13	1
3rd	Sparkman, John J.	Dem	Ala.	11	1
4th	Humphrey, Hubert H. Jr.	DFL	Minn.	9	1
5th	Mansfield, Michael J.	Dem	Mont.	5	1
6th	Morse, Wayne L.	Dem	Ore.	13	1
7th	Long, Russell B.	Dem	La.	9	1
8th	Kennedy, John F.	Dem	Mass.	5	1
9th	Hayden, Carl	Dem	Ariz.	30	1
10th	Russell, Richard B.	Dem	Ga.	24	1

Minority

Rank	Name	Party	State	Years in: Senate	Years in: Comm.
RM	Wiley, Alexander	Rep	Wisc.	19	1
2nd	Smith, H. Alexander	Rep	N.J.	13	1
3rd	Hickenlooper, Bourke B.	Rep	Iowa	13	1
4th	Langer, William	Rep	N.D.	17	1
5th	Knowland, William F.	Rep	Cal.	12	1
6th	Aiken, George D.	Rep	Vt.	16	1
7th	Capehart, Homer E.	Rep	Ind.	13	1
8th	Bridges, H. Styles	Rep	N.H.	21	1
9th	Saltonstall, Leverett	Rep	Mass.	13	1

Note: "Service Dates" of committee members reflect service on the Senate Foreign Relations Committee, from which most of the membership was drawn.

SENATE SELECT COMMITTEE: IMPROPER ACTIVITIES IN THE LABOR OR MANAGEMENT FIELD

Jurisdiction, 1957

From Senate Resolution 74, 85th Congress, First Session, January 30, 1957:

[Section 1]

Resolved, That there is hereby established a select committee which is authorized and directed to conduct an investigation and study of the extent to which criminal or other improper practices or activities are, or have been, engaged in the field of labor-management relations or in groups or organizations of employees or employers to the detriment of the interests of the public, employers or employees, and to determine whether any changes are required in the laws of the United States in order to protect such interests against the occurrence of such practices or activities.

Termination, 1960

The Select Committee was extended by Senate Resolutions 44 (86-1) and 249 (86-2) and was terminated upon the filing of Senate Report 1139 (86-2) on March 31, 1960.

SENATE SELECT COMMITTEE: IMPROPER ACTIVITIES IN THE LABOR OR MANAGEMENT FIELD / 85th Congress

Service Dates of Committee Chair: Jan. 30,1957-Continued
Service Dates of Majority Members: Jan. 30,1957-Continued
Service Dates of Minority Members: Jan. 30,1957-Continued

Majority

Rank Name	Party	State	Years in: Senate	Years in: Comm.
Chr McClellan, John L.	Dem	Ark.	15	1
2nd Kennedy, John F.	Dem	Mass.	5	1
3rd Ervin, Samuel J.	Dem	N.C.	3	1
4th McNamara, Patrick V.	Dem	Mich.	3	1

Minority

Rank Name	Party	State	Years in: Senate	Years in: Comm.
VCh Ives, Irving M.	Rep	N.Y.	11	1
2nd Goldwater, Barry M.	Rep	Ariz.	5	1
3rd McCarthy, Joseph R.	Rep	Wisc.	11	1
4th Mundt, Karl E.	Rep	S.D.	9	1

Changes:

Majority:				
McNamara, Patrick V.	Dem	Mich.	Apr. 22,1958	Left committee; no new assignment.
Church, Frank F.	Dem	Ida.	Apr. 22,1958	Replaced McNamara.
Minority:				
McCarthy, Joseph R.	Rep	Wisc.	May 2,1957	Died in office.
Curtis, Carl T.	Rep	Neb.	May 8,1957	Replaced McCarthy.

Departures from the Senate:

	Majority	Minority		
Retired	None	Ives, Irving M.	N.Y.	Rep

SENATE SELECT COMMITTEE: IMPROPER ACTIVITIES IN THE LABOR OR MANAGEMENT FIELD / 86th Congress

Service Dates of Committee Chair: Jan. 3,1959-Mar. 31,1960
Service Dates of Majority Members: Jan. 3,1959-Mar. 31,1960
Service Dates of Minority Members: Feb. 4,1959-Mar. 31,1960

Majority

Rank	Name	Party	State	Years in: Senate	Years in: Comm.
Chr	McClellan, John L.	Dem	Ark.	17	3
2nd	Kennedy, John F.	Dem	Mass.	7	3
3rd	Ervin, Samuel J.	Dem	N.C.	5	3
4th	Church, Frank F.	Dem	Ida.	3	1

Minority

Rank	Name	Party	State	Years in: Senate	Years in: Comm.
VCh	Mundt, Karl E.	Rep	S.D.	11	3
2nd	Goldwater, Barry M.	Rep	Ariz.	7	3
3rd	Curtis, Carl T.	Rep	Neb.	5	2
4th	Capehart, Homer E.	Rep	Ind.	15	1

Note: "Service Dates of Minority Members" reflect the dates of service of Capehart; all other members continued service from the previous Congress without official reassignment recorded in the Congressional Record.

SENATE SPECIAL COMMITTEE: SPACE AND ASTRONAUTICS

Jurisdiction, 1958

From Senate Resolution 256, 85th Congress, Second Session, February 6, 1958:

[Section 1]

Resolved, That there is hereby established a special committee which is authorized and directed to conduct a thorough and complete study and investigation with respect to all aspects and problems relating to the exploration of outer space and the control, development, and use of astronautical resources, personnel, equipment, and facilities.

Termination, 1959

The Special Committee was terminated upon the filing of Senate Report 100 (86-1) on March 11, 1959. The Senate Standing Committee on Aeronautical and Space Sciences was created pursuant to Senate Resolution 327 (85-2), agreed to on July 24, 1958, with members appointed on August 24, 1958.

SENATE SPECIAL COMMITTEE: SPACE AND ASTRONAUTICS / 85th Congress

Service Dates of Committee Chair: Feb. 10,1958-Continued
Service Dates of Majority Members: Feb. 10,1958-Continued
Service Dates of Minority Members: Feb. 10,1958-Continued

Majority

Rank	Name	Party	State	Years in: Senate	Years in: Comm.
Chr	Johnson, Lyndon B.	Dem	Tex.	10	1
2nd	Russell, Richard B.	Dem	Ga.	26	1
3rd	Green, Theodore F.	Dem	R.I.	22	1
4th	McClellan, John L.	Dem	Ark.	16	1
5th	Magnuson, Warren G.	Dem	Wash.	14	1
6th	Anderson, Clinton P.	Dem	N.M.	10	1
7th	Symington, W. Stuart	Dem	Mo.	6	1

Minority

Rank	Name	Party	State	Years in: Senate	Years in: Comm.
RM	Bridges, H. Styles	Rep	N.H.	22	1
2nd	Wiley, Alexander	Rep	Wisc.	20	1
3rd	Hickenlooper, Bourke B.	Rep	Iowa	14	1
4th	Saltonstall, Leverett	Rep	Mass.	14	1
5th	Bricker, John W.	Rep	Ohio	12	1
6th	Mundt, Karl E.	Rep	S.D.	10	1

Departures from the Senate:

	Majority	Minority		
Defeated for Reelection	None	Bricker, John W.	Ohio	Rep

SENATE SPECIAL COMMITTEE: SPACE AND ASTRONAUTICS / 86th Congress

Service Dates of Committee Chair: Jan. 3,1959-Mar. 11,1959
Service Dates of Majority Members: Jan. 3,1959-Mar. 11,1959
Service Dates of Minority Members: Jan. 3,1959-Mar. 11,1959

Majority

Rank	Name	Party	State	Years in: Senate	Years in: Comm.
Chr	Johnson, Lyndon B.	Dem	Tex.	11	1
2nd	Russell, Richard B.	Dem	Ga.	27	1
3rd	Green, Theodore F.	Dem	R.I.	23	1
4th	McClellan, John L.	Dem	Ark.	17	1
5th	Magnuson, Warren G.	Dem	Wash.	15	1
6th	Anderson, Clinton P.	Dem	N.M.	11	1
7th	Symington, W. Stuart	Dem	Mo.	7	1

Minority

Rank	Name	Party	State	Years in: Senate	Years in: Comm.
RM	Bridges, H. Styles	Rep	N.H.	23	1
2nd	Wiley, Alexander	Rep	Wisc.	21	1
3rd	Hickenlooper, Bourke B.	Rep	Iowa	15	1
4th	Saltonstall, Leverett	Rep	Mass.	15	1
5th	Mundt, Karl E.	Rep	S.D.	11	1

SENATE SPECIAL COMMITTEE: SENATE MEMORABILIA

Jurisdiction, 1958

from Senate Resolution 318, 85th Congress, Second Session, June 26, 1958:

[Section 2]

It shall be the function of the committee to conduct a full and complete study for the purpose of determining the desirability and feasibility of providing an appropriate means of preserving selected documents, records, and memorabilia of the United States Senate having historical significance or value. In the event the committee finds that it is desirable and feasible to preserve such documents, records, and memorabilia, the committee shall consider in its study practical means for determining what records, documents, and memorabilia should be preserved, and where such documents, records, and memorabilia might be made available for public inspection.

Termination, 1959

The Special Committee was extended by Senate Resolution 72 (86-1) and Senate Resolution 100 (86-1). A draft report was filed on October 13,1958 and the committee was terminated on April 2, 1959.

SENATE SPECIAL COMMITTEE: SENATE MEMORABILIA / 85th Congress

Service Dates of Committee Chair: Aug. 22,1958-Continued
Service Dates of Majority Members: Aug. 22,1958-Continued
Service Dates of Minority Members: Aug. 22,1958-Continued

Majority

Rank	Name	Party	State	Years in: Senate	Years in: Comm.
Chr	Anderson, Clinton P.	Dem	N.M.	10	1
2nd	Mansfield, Michael J.	Dem	Mont.	6	1
3rd	Talmadge, Herman E.	Dem	Ga.	2	1

Minority

Rank	Name	Party	State	Years in: Senate	Years in: Comm.
RM	Bennett, Wallace F.	Rep	Utah	8	1
2nd	Case, Francis H.	Rep	S.D.	8	1

SENATE SPECIAL COMMITTEE: SENATE MEMORABILIA / 86th Congress

Service Dates of Committee Chair: Jan. 3,1959-Apr. 2,1959
Service Dates of Majority Members: Jan. 3,1959-Apr. 2,1959
Service Dates of Minority Members: Jan. 3,1959-Apr. 2,1959

Majority

Rank	Name	Party	State	Years in: Senate	Years in: Comm.
Chr	Anderson, Clinton P.	Dem	N.M.	11	1
2nd	Mansfield, Michael J.	Dem	Mont.	7	1
3rd	Talmadge, Herman E.	Dem	Ga.	3	1

Minority

Rank	Name	Party	State	Years in: Senate	Years in: Comm.
RM	Bennett, Wallace F.	Rep	Utah	9	1
2nd	Case, Francis H.	Rep	S.D.	9	1

SENATE SELECT COMMITTEE: NATIONAL WATER RESOURCES

Jurisdiction, 1959

From Senate Resolution 48, 86th Congress, First Session, April 20, 1959:

[Section 1]

Resolved, That there shall be established a select committee which shall make exhaustive studies of the extent to which water resources activities in the United States are related to the national interest, and the extent and character of water resource activities, both governmental and nongovernmental, that can be expected to be required to provide the quantity and quality of water for use by the population, agriculture, and industry between the present time and 1980, along with suitable provision for related recreational and fish and wildlife values, to the end that such studies and the recommendations based thereon may be available to the Senate in considering water resources policies for the future.

Termination, 1961

The Select Committee was terminated upon the filing of Senate Report 29 (87-1) on January 30, 1961.

SENATE SELECT COMMITTEE: NATIONAL WATER RESOURCES / 86th Congress

Service Dates of Committee Chair: Apr. 24,1959-Jan. 30,1961
Service Dates of Majority Members: Apr. 24,1959-Jan. 30,1961
Service Dates of Minority Members: Apr. 24,1959-Jan. 30,1961

Majority

Rank	Name	Party	State	Years in: Senate	Years in: Comm.
Chr	Kerr, Robert S.	Dem	Okla.	11	1
2nd	Chavez, Dennis	Dem	N.M.	24	1
3rd	Ellender, Allen J.	Dem	La.	23	1
4th	Magnuson, Warren G.	Dem	Wash.	15	1
5th	Anderson, Clinton P.	Dem	N.M.	11	1
6th	Jackson, Henry M.	Dem	Wash.	7	1
7th	Engle, Clair	Dem	Cal.	1	1
8th	Hart, Philip A.	Dem	Mich.	1	1

Minority

Rank	Name	Party	State	Years in: Senate	Years in: Comm.
VCh	Kuchel, Thomas H.	Rep	Cal.	7	1
2nd	Young, Milton R.	Rep	N.D.	15	1
3rd	Schoeppel, Andrew F.	Rep	Kans.	11	1
4th	Case, Francis H.	Rep	S.D.	9	1

Note: Senate Resolution 111, agreed to on Apr. 28,1959, changed the size and party ratio on this committee to 10 Democrats and 6 Republicans. Senate Resolution 121, agreed to on June 1,9159, added James E. Murray (Dem-Mont.) to the committee as an *ex officio* member.

Additions:

	Rank Name	Party	State	Date
Majority:	9th McGee, Gale W.	Dem	Wyo.	May 12,1959
	10th Moss, Frank E.	Dem	Utah	May 12,1959
	ex officio Murray, James E.	Dem	Mont.	June 1,1959
Minority:	5th Martin, Thomas E.	Rep	Iowa	May 12,1959
	6th Scott, Hugh D. Jr.	Rep	Penn.	May 12,1959

SENATE SPECIAL COMMITTEE: UNEMPLOYMENT PROBLEMS

Jurisdiction, 1959

From Senate Resolution 196, 86th Congress, First Session, September 12, 1959:

[Section 2]

It shall be the duty of such committee to make a full and complete investigation and study of unemployment conditions in the United States, giving particular consideration to areas of critical unemployment for the purpose of determining what can be done to alleviate such conditions and to report its findings and recommendations to the Senate . . . No proposed legislation shall be referred to such committee, and such committee shall not have power to report by bill or otherwise have legislative jurisdiction.

Termination, 1960

The Special Committee was extended by Senate Resolution 252 (86-2) until June 30, 1960; however, its major work was completed with the filing of Senate Report 1206 (86-2) on March 30, 1960.

SENATE SPECIAL COMMITTEE: UNEMPLOYMENT PROBLEMS / 86th Congress

Service Dates of Committee Chair: Sep. 15,1959-June 30,1960
Service Dates of Majority Members: Sep. 15,1959-June 30,1960
Service Dates of Minority Members: Sep. 15,1959-June 30,1960

Majority

Rank	Name	Party	State	Years in: Senate	Years in: Comm.
Chr	McCarthy, Eugene J.	DFL	Minn.	1	1
2nd	McNamara, Patrick V.	Dem	Mich.	5	1
3rd	Clark, Joseph S.	Dem	Penn.	3	1
4th	Randolph, Jennings	Dem	W.Va.	1	1
5th	Hartke, R. Vance	Dem	Ind.	1	1
6th	McGee, Gale W.	Dem	Wyo.	1	1

Minority

Rank	Name	Party	State	Years in: Senate	Years in: Comm.
RM	Cooper, John Sherman	Rep	Ky.	8	1
2nd	Prouty, Winston L.	Rep	Vt.	1	1
3rd	Scott, Hugh D. Jr.	Rep	Penn.	1	1

SENATE SPECIAL COMMITTEE: AGING

AGING

Jurisdiction, 1961

From Senate Resolution 73, 87th Congress, First Session, February 13, 1961:

[Section 2]

It shall be the duty of such committee to make a full and complete study and investigation of any and all matters pertaining to problems of older people, including but not limited to, problems of maintaining health, of assuring adequate income, of finding employment, of engaging in productive and rewarding activity, of securing proper housing, and when necessary, care or assistance. No proposed legislation shall be referred to such committee, and such committee shall not have power to report by bill or otherwise have legislative jurisdiction.

AGING (Permanent)

Reorganization, 1977

By authority of Senate Resolution 4, the Committee Systems Reorganization Amendments of 1977, 95th Congress, First Session, the committee became the Permanent Select Committee on Aging.

Jurisdiction, 1977

From Senate Resolution 4, the Committee System Reorganization Amendments of 1977, 95th Congress, First Session, February 4, 1977:

[Section 104]

(b.1) It shall be the duty of the special committee to conduct a continuing study of any and all matters pertaining to problems and opportunities of older people, including, but not limited to, problems and opportunities of maintaining health, of assuring adequate income, of finding employment, of engaging in productive and rewarding activity, of securing proper housing, and, when necessary, of obtaining care or assistance. No proposed legislation shall be referred to such committee, and such committee shall not have power to report by bill, or otherwise have legislative jurisdiction.

(d) All records and papers of the temporary special committee on Aging, established by Senate Resolution 33, 87th Congress, are transferred to the Special Committee.

Jurisdiction, 1992

From Authority and Rules of Senate Committees, Senate Document 102-6, printed under the authority of Senate Resolution 58 (102-1), agreed to March 13, 1991:

[Section 104]

(b.1) It shall be the duty of the special committee to conduct a continuing study of any and all matters pertaining to problems and opportunities of older people, including, but not limited to, problems and opportunities of maintaining health, of assuring adequate income, of finding employment, of engaging in productive and rewarding activity, of securing proper housing, and, when necessary, of obtaining care or assistance. No proposed legislation shall be referred to such committee, and such committee shall not have power to report by bill, or otherwise have legislative jurisdiction.

SENATE SPECIAL COMMITTEE: AGING / 87th Congress

Service Dates of Committee Chair: Feb. 20,1961-Continued
Service Dates of Majority Members: Feb. 20,1961-Continued
Service Dates of Minority Members: Feb. 20,1961-Continued

Majority

Rank	Name	Party	State	Years in: Senate	Years in: Comm.
Chr	McNamara, Patrick V.	Dem	Mich.	7	1
2nd	Smathers, George A.	Dem	Fla.	11	1
3rd	Engle, Clair	Dem	Cal.	3	1
4th	Williams, Harrison A. Jr.	Dem	N.J.	3	1
5th	Long, Oren E.	Dem	Hai.	2	1
6th	Neuberger, Maurine B.	Dem	Ore.	1	1
7th	Morse, Wayne L.	Dem	Ore.	17	1
8th	Bible, Alan H.	Dem	Nev.	7	1
9th	Clark, Joseph S.	Dem	Penn.	5	1
10th	Church, Frank F.	Dem	Ida.	5	1
11th	Randolph, Jennings	Dem	W.Va.	3	1
12th	Muskie, Edmund S.	Dem	Me.	3	1
13th	Long, Edward V.	Dem	Mo.	1	1
14th	Smith, Benjamin A. II	Dem	Mass.	1	1

Minority

Rank	Name	Party	State	Years in: Senate	Years in: Comm.
RM	Dirksen, Everett M.	Rep	Ill.	11	1
2nd	Goldwater, Barry M.	Rep	Ariz.	9	1
3rd	Cotton, Norris	Rep	N.H.	7	1
4th	Carlson, Frank	Rep	Kans.	11	1
5th	Bennett, Wallace F.	Rep	Utah	11	1
6th	Bush, Prescott S.	Rep	Conn.	9	1
7th	Keating, Kenneth B.	Rep	N.Y.	3 *1	1

*1: Member's 1st period of service on the committee.

Note: Senate Resolution 111 (87-1), agreed to on Mar. 22,1961, changed the size and party ratio on the committee. On the majority side, the 7th through 14th seats were added, and on the minority side the 4th through 7th seats were added, with the additional members being appointed on Mar. 27,1961.

Changes:

Majority:

Name	Party	State	Date	Change
Smith, Benjamin A. II	Dem	Mass.	Nov. 6,1962	Resigned and retired.

Minority:

Name	Party	State	Date	Change
Keating, Kenneth B.	Rep	N.Y.	Mar. 28,1961	Left committee; no new assignment.
Javits, Jacob K.	Rep	N.Y.	Mar. 28,1961	Replaced Keating.
Cotton, Norris	Rep	N.H.	Mar. 15,1962	Had already moved to Appropriations.
Prouty, Winston L.	Rep	Vt.	Mar. 15,1962	Replaced Cotton.

	Majority			Minority		
Departures from the Senate:						
Retired	Long, Oren E.	Hai.	Dem	Bush, Prescott S.	Conn.	Rep
Departures from Committee:						
Moved to Banking and Currency	None			Javits, Jacob K.	N.Y.	Rep
No new assignment	None			Bennett, Wallace F.	Utah	Rep

SENATE SPECIAL COMMITTEE: AGING / 88th Congress

Service Dates of Committee Chair: Mar. 1,1963-Continued
Service Dates of Majority Members: Mar. 1,1963-Continued
Service Dates of Minority Members: Feb. 19,1963-Continued

Majority

Rank	Name	Party	State	Years in: Senate	Years in: Comm.
Chr	Smathers, George A.	Dem	Fla.	13	3
2nd	McNamara, Patrick V.	Dem	Mich.	9	3
3rd	Engle, Clair	Dem	Cal.	5	3
4th	Williams, Harrison A. Jr.	Dem	N.J.	5	3
5th	Neuberger, Maurine B.	Dem	Ore.	3	3
6th	Morse, Wayne L.	Dem	Ore.	19	3
7th	Bible, Alan H.	Dem	Nev.	9	3
8th	Clark, Joseph S.	Dem	Penn.	7	3
9th	Church, Frank F.	Dem	Ida.	7	3
10th	Randolph, Jennings	Dem	W.Va.	5	3
11th	Muskie, Edmund S.	Dem	Me.	5	3
12th	Long, Edward V.	Dem	Mo.	3	3

Minority

Rank	Name	Party	State	Years in: Senate	Years in: Comm.
RM	Dirksen, Everett M.	Rep	Ill.	13	2
2nd	Goldwater, Barry M.	Rep	Ariz.	11	2
3rd	Carlson, Frank	Rep	Kans.	13	2
4th	Prouty, Winston L.	Rep	Vt.	5	1
5th	Keating, Kenneth B.	Rep	N.Y.	5 *2	1
6th	Fong, Hiram L.	Rep	Hai.	4	1
7th	Mechem, Edwin L.	Rep	N.M.	1	1

13th Moss, Frank E.	Dem	Utah	5	1	
14th Kennedy, Edward M.	Dem	Mass.	1	1	*2: Member's 2nd period of service on the committee.

Note: "Service Dates of Majority Members" reflect the dates of service of Moss and Kennedy; "Service Dates of Minority Members" reflect the dates of service of Keating, Fong and Mechem. All other members continued service from the previous Congress without official reassignment recorded in the Congressional Record.

Changes:

Majority:

Clark, Joseph S.	Dem	Penn.	Dec. 19,1963	Left committee; no new assignment.
Yarborough, Ralph W.	Dem	Tex.	Dec. 19,1963	Replaced Clark.
Engle, Clair	Dem	Cal.	July 30,1964	Died in office.
Young, Stephen M.	Dem	Ohio	Aug. 10,1964	Replaced Engle.

Minority:

Mechem, Edwin L.	Rep	N.M.	Nov. 3,1964	Resigned; defeated for election.

Departures from the Senate:	**Majority**	**Minority**	
Defeated for Reelection	None	Keating, Kenneth B.	N.Y. Rep
Lost Election for President	None	Goldwater, Barry M.	Ariz. Rep

SENATE SPECIAL COMMITTEE: AGING / 89th Congress

Service Dates of Committee Chair: Jan. 3,1965-Jan. 17,1967
Service Dates of Majority Members: Jan. 3,1965-Continued
Service Dates of Minority Members: Feb. 1,1965-Continued

Majority

Rank Name	Party	State	Years in: Senate	Years in: Comm.
Chr Smathers, George A.	Dem	Fla.	15	4
2nd McNamara, Patrick V.	Dem	Mich.	11	4
3rd Williams, Harrison A. Jr.	Dem	N.J.	7	4
4th Neuberger, Maurine B.	Dem	Ore.	5	4
5th Morse, Wayne L.	Dem	Ore.	21	4
6th Bible, Alan H.	Dem	Nev.	11	4
7th Church, Frank F.	Dem	Ida.	9	4
8th Randolph, Jennings	Dem	W.Va.	7	4
9th Muskie, Edmund S.	Dem	Me.	7	4
10th Long, Edward V.	Dem	Mo.	5	4
11th Moss, Frank E.	Dem	Utah	7	2
12th Kennedy, Edward M.	Dem	Mass.	3	2
13th Yarborough, Ralph W.	Dem	Tex.	8	2
14th Young, Stephen M.	Dem	Ohio	7	1

Minority

Rank Name	Party	State	Years in: Senate	Years in: Comm.
RM Dirksen, Everett M.	Rep	Ill.	15	4
2nd Carlson, Frank	Rep	Kans.	15	4
3rd Prouty, Winston L.	Rep	Vt.	7	3
4th Fong, Hiram L.	Rep	Hai.	6	2
5th Allott, Gordon L.	Rep	Colo.	11	1
6th Miller, Jack R.	Rep	Iowa	5	1
7th Pearson, James B.	Rep	Kans.	4	1

Note: "Service Dates of Minority Members" reflect the dates of service of Allott, Miller and Pearson; all other minority members continued service from the previous Congress without official reassignment recorded in the Congressional Record.

Changes:

Majority:

McNamara, Patrick V.	Dem	Mich.	Apr. 30,1966	Died in office.

Departures from the Senate:	**Majority**		**Minority**	
Retired	Neuberger, Maurine B.	Ore. Dem	None	
Departures from Committee:				
Moved to Armed Services	None		Pearson, James B.	Kans. Rep
No new assignment	None		Allott, Gordon L.	Colo. Rep

SENATE SPECIAL COMMITTEE: AGING / 90th Congress

Service Dates of Committee Chair: Jan. 17,1967-Continued
Service Dates of Majority Members: Jan. 18,1967-Continued
Service Dates of Minority Members: Jan. 25,1967-Continued

Majority

Rank Name	Party	State	Years in: Senate	Years in: Comm.
Chr Williams, Harrison A. Jr.	Dem	N.J.	9	6
2nd Smathers, George A.	Dem	Fla.	17	6
3rd Morse, Wayne L.	Dem	Ore.	23	6
4th Bible, Alan H.	Dem	Nev.	13	6
5th Church, Frank F.	Dem	Ida.	11	6
6th Randolph, Jennings	Dem	W.Va.	9	6
7th Long, Edward V.	Dem	Mo.	7	6
8th Muskie, Edmund S.	Dem	Me.	9	6
9th Moss, Frank E.	Dem	Utah	9	4
10th Kennedy, Edward M.	Dem	Mass.	5	4
11th Yarborough, Ralph W.	Dem	Tex.	10	4
12th Young, Stephen M.	Dem	Ohio	9	3
13th Mondale, Walter F.	DFL	Minn.	3	1

Minority

Rank Name	Party	State	Years in: Senate	Years in: Comm.
RM Dirksen, Everett M.	Rep	Ill.	17	6
2nd Carlson, Frank	Rep	Kans.	17	6
3rd Prouty, Winston L.	Rep	Vt.	9	5
4th Fong, Hiram L.	Rep	Hai.	8	4
5th Miller, Jack R.	Rep	Iowa	7	2
6th Morton, Thruston B.	Rep	Ky.	11	1
7th Hansen, Clifford P.	Rep	Wyo.	1	1

Note: "Service Dates" of majority and minority members reflect the dates of service of Mondale, Morton and Hansen; all other members continued service from the previous Congress without official reassignment recorded in the Congressional Record.

Changes:

Majority:

Long, Edward V.	Dem	Mo.	Dec. 27,1968	Resigned; defeated for renomination.

Minority:

Morton, Thruston B.	Rep	Ky.	Dec. 16,1968	Resigned and retired.

Departures from the Senate:

	Majority			Minority		
Defeated for Reelection	Morse, Wayne L.	Ore.	Dem	None		
Retired	Smathers, George A.	Fla.	Dem	Carlson, Frank	Kans.	Rep

SENATE SPECIAL COMMITTEE: AGING / 91st Congress

Service Dates of Committee Chair: Jan. 3,1969-Continued
Service Dates of Majority Members: Jan. 14,1969-Continued
Service Dates of Minority Members: Jan. 22,1969-Continued

Majority

Rank Name	Party	State	Years in: Senate	Years in: Comm.
Chr Williams, Harrison A. Jr.	Dem	N.J.	11	8
2nd Bible, Alan H.	Dem	Nev.	15	8
3rd Church, Frank F.	Dem	Ida.	13	8
4th Randolph, Jennings	Dem	W.Va.	11	8
5th Muskie, Edmund S.	Dem	Me.	11	8
6th Moss, Frank E.	Dem	Utah	11	6
7th Kennedy, Edward M.	Dem	Mass.	7	6
8th Yarborough, Ralph W.	Dem	Tex.	12	6
9th Young, Stephen M.	Dem	Ohio	11	5
10th Mondale, Walter F.	DFL	Minn.	5	2
11th Hartke, R. Vance	Dem	Ind.	11	1

Minority

Rank Name	Party	State	Years in: Senate	Years in: Comm.
RM1 Dirksen, Everett M.	Rep	Ill.	19	8
RM2 2nd Prouty, Winston L.	Rep	Vt.	11	7
3rd Fong, Hiram L.	Rep	Hai.	10	6
4th Miller, Jack R.	Rep	Iowa	9	4
5th Hansen, Clifford P.	Rep	Wyo.	3	2
6th Murphy, George L.	Rep	Cal.	5	1
7th Fannin, Paul J.	Rep	Ariz.	5	1
8th Gurney, Edward J.	Rep	Fla.	1	1
9th Saxbe, William B.	Rep	Ohio	1	1

Note: "Service Dates" of majority and minority members reflect the dates of service of Hansen, Murphy, Fannin, Gurney and Saxbe; all other members continued service from the previous Congress without official reassignment recorded in the Congressional Record.

Changes:

Ranking Member:

RM1 Dirksen, Everett M.	Rep	Ill.	Sep. 7,1969	Died in office.
RM2 Prouty, Winston L.	Rep	Vt.	Sep. 7,1969	Succeeded Dirksen as Ranking Minority Member.

Minority:

Dirksen, Everett M.	Rep	Ill.	Sep. 7,1969	Died in office.
Smith, Ralph Tyler	Rep	Ill.	Oct. 9,1969	Replaced Dirksen.
Smith, Ralph Tyler	Rep	Ill.	Nov. 16,1970	Resigned; defeated for election.
Murphy, George L.	Rep	Cal.	Jan. 2,1971	Resigned, defeated for reelection.

Departures from the Senate:	Majority			Minority
Defeated for Renomination	Yarborough, Ralph W.	Tex.	Dem	None
Retired	Young, Stephen M.	Ohio	Dem	None

SENATE SPECIAL COMMITTEE: AGING / 92nd Congress

Service Dates of Committee Chair: Jan. 29,1971-Continued
Service Dates of Majority Members: Jan. 28,1971-Continued
Service Dates of Minority Members: Feb. 17,1971-Continued

Majority

Rank	Name	Party	State	Years in: Senate	Years in: Comm.
Chr	Church, Frank F.	Dem	Ida.	15	10
2nd	Williams, Harrison A. Jr.	Dem	N.J.	13	10
3rd	Bible, Alan H.	Dem	Nev.	17	10
4th	Randolph, Jennings	Dem	W.Va.	13	10
5th	Muskie, Edmund S.	Dem	Me.	13	10
6th	Moss, Frank E.	Dem	Utah	13	8
7th	Kennedy, Edward M.	Dem	Mass.	9	8
8th	Mondale, Walter F.	DFL	Minn.	7	5
9th	Hartke, R. Vance	Dem	Ind.	13	3
10th	Pell, Claiborne D.	Dem	R.I.	11	*1 1
11th	Eagleton, Thomas F.	Dem	Mo.	3	1

Minority

Rank	Name	Party	State	Years in: Senate	Years in: Comm.
RM1	Prouty, Winston L.	Rep	Vt.	13	9
RM2 2nd	Fong, Hiram L.	Rep	Hai.	12	8
3rd	Miller, Jack R.	Rep	Iowa	11	7
4th	Hansen, Clifford P.	Rep	Wyo.	5	5
5th	Fannin, Paul J.	Rep	Ariz.	7	3
6th	Gurney, Edward J.	Rep	Fla.	3	3
7th	Saxbe, William B.	Rep	Ohio	3	3
8th	Brooke, Edward W.	Rep	Mass.	5	1
9th	Percy, Charles H.	Rep	Ill.	5	1

*1: Member's 1st period of service on the committee.

Note: "Service Dates" of majority and minority members reflect the dates of service of Pell, Eagleton, Brooke and Percy; all other members continued service from the previous Congress without official reassignment recorded in the Congressional Record.

Changes:

Ranking Member:

RM1	Prouty, Winston L.	Rep	Vt.	Sep. 10,1971	Died in office.
RM2	Fong, Hiram L.	Rep	Hai.	Sep. 10,1971	Succeeded Prouty as Ranking Minority Member.

Minority:

Prouty, Winston L.	Rep	Vt.	Sep. 10,1971	Died in office.
Stafford, Robert T.	Rep	Vt.	Sep. 17,1971	Replaced Prouty.

	Majority		Minority	
Departures from the Senate:				
Defeated for Reelection	None		Miller, Jack R.	Iowa Rep
Departures from Committee:				
No new assignment	Pell, Claiborne D.	R.I. Dem	Fannin, Paul J.	Ariz. Rep

SENATE SPECIAL COMMITTEE: AGING / 93rd Congress

Service Dates of Committee Chair: Jan. 4,1973-Continued
Service Dates of Majority Members: Jan. 4,1973-Continued
Service Dates of Minority Members: Jan. 12,1973-Continued

Majority

Rank	Name	Party	State	Years in: Senate	Years in: Comm.
Chr	Church, Frank F.	Dem	Ida.	17	12
2nd	Williams, Harrison A. Jr.	Dem	N.J.	15	12
3rd	Bible, Alan H.	Dem	Nev.	19	12
4th	Randolph, Jennings	Dem	W.Va.	15	12
5th	Muskie, Edmund S.	Dem	Me.	15	12
6th	Moss, Frank E.	Dem	Utah	15	10
7th	Kennedy, Edward M.	Dem	Mass.	11	10

Minority

Rank	Name	Party	State	Years in: Senate	Years in: Comm.
RM	Fong, Hiram L.	Rep	Hai.	14	10
2nd	Hansen, Clifford P.	Rep	Wyo.	7	6
3rd	Gurney, Edward J.	Rep	Fla.	5	4
4th	Saxbe, William B.	Rep	Ohio	5	4
5th	Brooke, Edward W.	Rep	Mass.	7	2
6th	Percy, Charles H.	Rep	Ill.	7	2
7th	Stafford, Robert T.	Rep	Vt.	2	2

8th Mondale, Walter F.	DFL	Minn.	9	6	8th Beall, J. Glenn Jr.	Rep	Md.	3		1
9th Hartke, R. Vance	Dem	Ind.	15	4	9th Domenici, Pete V.	Rep	N.M.	1	*1	1
10th Eagleton, Thomas F.	Dem	Mo.	5	2						
11th Tunney, John V.	Dem	Cal.	3	1						
12th Chiles, Lawton M. Jr.	Dem	Fla.	3	1	*1: Member's 1st period of service on the committee.					

Note: Senate Resolution 20 (93-1), agreed to on Jan. 18,1973, changed the size and party ratio to 13 Democrats and 9 Republicans. "Service Dates" of majority and minority members reflect the dates of service of Tunney, Chiles, Beall and Domenici; all other members continued service from the previous Congress without official reassignment recorded in the Congressional Record.

Addition:

Majority: 13th Pell, Claiborne D. Dem R.I. Jan. 18,1973 Ranked below Hartke.

Changes:

Majority:

Bible, Alan H.	Dem	Nev.	Dec. 17,1974	Resigned and retired.

Minority:

Saxbe, William B.	Rep	Ohio	Jan. 3,1974	Resigned; appointed Attorney General.
Brock, William E. III	Rep	Tenn.	Jan. 24,1974	Replaced Saxbe.
Gurney, Edward J.	Rep	Fla.	Dec. 31,1974	Resigned and retired.

SENATE SPECIAL COMMITTEE: AGING / 94th Congress

Service Dates of Committee Chair: Jan. 17,1975-Feb. 11,1977
Service Dates of Majority Members: Jan. 17,1975-Feb. 11,1977
Service Dates of Minority Members: Jan. 27,1975-Feb. 22,1977

Majority						**Minority**					
			Years in:						**Years in:**		
Rank Name	**Party**	**State**	**Senate**		**Comm.**	**Rank Name**	**Party**	**State**	**Senate**		**Comm.**
Chr Church, Frank F.	Dem	Ida.	19		14	RM Fong, Hiram L.	Rep	Hai.	16		12
2nd Williams, Harrison A. Jr.	Dem	N.J.	17		14	2nd Hansen, Clifford P.	Rep	Wyo.	9		9
3rd Randolph, Jennings	Dem	W.Va.	17		14	3rd Brooke, Edward W.	Rep	Mass.	9		4
4th Muskie, Edmund S.	Dem	Me.	17		14	4th Percy, Charles H.	Rep	Ill.	9		4
5th Moss, Frank E.	Dem	Utah	17		12	5th Stafford, Robert T.	Rep	Vt.	4		4
6th Kennedy, Edward M.	Dem	Mass.	13		12	6th Beall, J. Glenn Jr.	Rep	Md.	5		3
7th Mondale, Walter F.	DFL	Minn.	11		8	7th Domenici, Pete V.	Rep	N.M.	3	*1	3
8th Hartke, R. Vance	Dem	Ind.	17		6	8th Brock, William E. III	Rep	Tenn.	5		2
9th Pell, Claiborne D.	Dem	R.I.	15	*2	2	9th Bartlett, Dewey F.	Rep	Okla.	3		1
10th Eagleton, Thomas F.	Dem	Mo.	7		4						
11th Tunney, John V.	Dem	Cal.	5		3						
12th Chiles, Lawton M. Jr.	Dem	Fla.	5		3	*1: Member's 1st period of service on the committee.					
13th Clark, Richard C.	Dem	Iowa	3		1	*2: Member's 2nd period of service on the committee.					

Notes: Claiborne D. Pell (Dem-R.I.) was reappointed to this committee in the 93rd Congress and ranked below R. Vance Hartke (Dem-Ind.). Senate Resolution 258 (94-1), agreed to on Sep. 19,1975, changed the size and party ratio on this committee to 14 Democrats and 9 Republicans. "Service Dates" of majority and minority members reflect the dates of service of Clark and Bartlett; all other members continued service from the previous Congress without official reassignment recorded in the Congressional Record.

Additions:

Majority: 14th Durkin, John A. Dem N.H. Sep. 19,1975

Changes:

Majority:

Mondale, Walter F.	DFL	Minn.	Dec. 30,1976	Resigned; elected Vice President.
Tunney, John V.	Dem	Cal.	Jan. 1,1977	Resigned; defeated for reelection.

Departures from the Senate:	**Majority**			**Minority**		
Defeated for Reelection	Hartke, R. Vance	Ind.	Dem	Brock, William E. III	Tenn.	Rep
	Moss, Frank E.	Utah	Dem	Beall, J. Glenn Jr.	Md.	Rep
Retired	None			Fong, Hiram L.	Hai.	Rep

Departures from Committee:

	Majority		Minority	
Moved to Special Committee on Official Conduct	Clark, Richard C.	Iowa Dem	Stafford, Robert T.	Vt. Rep
	Eagleton, Thomas F.	Mo. Dem		
Moved to Energy	Durkin, John A.	N.H. Dem	None	
Moved to Select Indian Affairs	None		Hansen, Clifford P.	Wyo. Rep
Became Ranking Minority Member of Interior & Insular Affairs	None		Bartlett, Dewey F.	Okla. Rep
No new assignment	Kennedy, Edward M.	Mass. Dem	None	
	Pell, Claiborne D.	R.I. Dem		
	Randolph, Jennings	W.Va. Dem		
	Williams, Harrison A. Jr.	N.J. Dem		

SENATE SPECIAL COMMITTEE: AGING (Permanent) / 95th Congress

* Became the Permanent Special Committee on AGING on Feb. 4,1977.

Service Dates of Committee Chair: Feb. 11,1977-Jan. 23,1979
Service Dates of Majority Members: Feb. 11,1977-Jan. 23,1979
Service Dates of Minority Members: Feb. 22,1977-Continued

Majority

Rank	Name	Party	State	Years in: Senate	Years in: Comm.
Chr	Church, Frank F.	Dem	Ida.	21	16
2nd	Muskie, Edmund S.	Dem	Me.	19	16
3rd	Chiles, Lawton M. Jr.	Dem	Fla.	7	5
4th	Glenn, John H. Jr.	Dem	Ohio	3	1
5th	Melcher, John	Dem	Mont.	1	1
6th	DeConcini, Dennis	Dem	Ariz.	1	1

Minority

Rank	Name	Party	State	Years in: Senate	Years in: Comm.
RM	Domenici, Pete V.	Rep	N.M.	5	*1 5
2nd	Brooke, Edward W.	Rep	Mass.	11	7
3rd	Percy, Charles H.	Rep	Ill.	11	7

*1: Member's 1st period of service on the committee.

	Majority		Minority	
Departures from the Senate:				
Defeated for Reelection	None		Brooke, Edward W.	Mass. Rep
Departures from Committee:				
Moved to Rules and Administration	DeConcini, Dennis	Ariz. Dem	None	
Moved to Foreign Relations	Muskie, Edmund S.	Me. Dem	None	

SENATE SPECIAL COMMITTEE: AGING (Permanent) / 96th Congress

Service Dates of Committee Chair: Jan. 23,1979-Jan. 5,1981
Service Dates of Majority Members: Jan. 23,1979-Jan. 5,1981
Service Dates of Minority Members: Jan. 23,1979-Jan. 5,1981

Majority

Rank	Name	Party	State	Years in: Senate	Years in: Comm.
Chr	Chiles, Lawton M. Jr.	Dem	Fla.	9	7
2nd	Church, Frank F.	Dem	Ida.	23	18
3rd	Glenn, John H. Jr.	Dem	Ohio	5	2
4th	Melcher, John	Dem	Mont.	3	2
5th	Pryor, David H.	Dem	Ark.	1	1
6th	Bradley, William W.	Dem	N.J.	1	1

Minority

Rank	Name	Party	State	Years in: Senate	Years in: Comm.
RM	Domenici, Pete V.	Rep	N.M.	7	*1 7
2nd	Percy, Charles H.	Rep	Ill.	13	8
3rd	Kassebaum, Nancy Landon	Rep	Kans.	1	1
4th	Cohen, William S.	Rep	Me.	1	1

*1: Member's 1st period of service on the committee.

Notes: "Service Dates of Minority Members" reflect the dates of service of Kassebaum and Cohen; all other minority members continued service from the previous Congress. Senate Resolution 101 (96-1), agreed to on March 13, 1979, changed the size and party ratio on this committee to 7 Democrats and 5 Republicans. Minority membership was officially renamed at this time, with H. John Heinz III (Rep-Penn.) ranked third.

Additions:

Majority:	7th	Burdick, Quentin N.	Dem	N.D.	Mar. 13,1979
Minority:	5th	Heinz, H. John III	Rep	Penn.	Mar. 13,1979 (ranked 3rd)

Departures from the Senate:	Majority		Minority
Defeated for Reelection	Church, Frank F.	Ida. Dem	None

SENATE SPECIAL COMMITTEE: AGING (Permanent) / 97th Congress

Service Dates of Committee Chair: Jan. 5,1981-Jan. 3,1983
Service Dates of Majority Members: Jan. 5,1981-Jan. 3,1983
Service Dates of Minority Members: Jan. 5,1981-Jan. 3,1983

Majority

Rank Name	Party	State	Years in: Senate	Years in: Comm.
Chr Heinz, H. John III	Rep	Penn.	5	2
2nd Domenici, Pete V.	Rep	N.M.	9	*1 9
3rd Percy, Charles H.	Rep	Ill.	15	10
4th Kassebaum, Nancy Landon	Rep	Kans.	3	2
5th Cohen, William S.	Rep	Me.	3	2
6th Pressler, Larry L.	Rep	S.D.	3	1
7th Grassley, Charles E.	Rep	Iowa	1	1

Minority

Rank Name	Party	State	Years in: Senate	Years in: Comm.
RM Chiles, Lawton M. Jr.	Dem	Ark.	11	9
2nd Glenn, John H. Jr.	Dem	Ohio	7	4
3rd Melcher, John	Dem	Mont.	5	4
4th Pryor, David H.	Dem	Ark.	3	2
5th Bradley, William W.	Dem	N.J.	3	2
6th Burdick, Quentin N.	Dem	N.D.	21	2

*1: Member's 1st period of service on the committee.

Note: Senate Resolution 24 (97-1), agreed to on Jan. 19,1981, changed the size and party ratio on the committee to 8 Republicans and 7 Democrats.

Additions:

Majority:	8th Durenberger, David F.	Rep	Minn.	Jan. 22,1981 (for 97th Congress only).
Minority:	7th Dodd, Christopher J.	Dem	Conn.	Jan. 21,1981

Departures from Committee:	Majority		Minority
Moved to Environment & Public Works	Durenberger, David F.	Minn. Rep	None

SENATE SPECIAL COMMITTEE: AGING (Permanent) / 98th Congress

Service Dates of Committee Chair: Jan. 3,1983-Mar. 5,1985
Service Dates of Majority Members: Jan. 3,1983-Mar. 5,1985
Service Dates of Minority Members: Jan. 3,1983-Mar. 5,1985

Majority

Rank Name	Party	State	Years in: Senate	Years in: Comm.
Chr Heinz, H. John III	Rep	Penn.	7	4
2nd Domenici, Pete V.	Rep	N.M.	11	*1 10
3rd Percy, Charles H.	Rep	Ill.	17	12
4th Kassebaum, Nancy Landon	Rep	Kans.	5	4
5th Cohen, William S.	Rep	Me.	5	4
6th Pressler, Larry L.	Rep	S.D.	5	2
7th Grassley, Charles E.	Rep	Iowa	3	2
8th Wilson, Pete	Rep	Cal.	1	1

Minority

Rank Name	Party	State	Years in: Senate	Years in: Comm.
RM Glenn, John H. Jr.	Dem	Ohio	9	6
2nd Chiles, Lawton M. Jr.	Dem	Fla.	13	10
3rd Melcher, John	Dem	Mont.	7	6
4th Pryor, David H.	Dem	Ark.	5	4
5th Bradley, William W.	Dem	N.J.	5	4
6th Burdick, Quentin N.	Dem	N.D.	23	4
7th Dodd, Christopher J.	Dem	Conn.	3	2

*1: Member's 1st pericd of service on the committee.

Note: Senate Resolution 338, agreed to on Feb. 9,1984, changed the size and party ratio on this committee to 10 Republicans and 9 Democrats.

Additions:

Majority:	9th	Warner, John W.	Rep	Va.	Feb. 9,1984
	10th	Evans, Daniel J.	Rep	Wash.	Feb. 9,1984
Minority:	8th	Johnston, J. Bennett Jr.	Dem	La.	Feb. 9,1984
	9th	Bingaman, Jeff	Dem	N.M.	Feb. 9,1984

Departures from the Senate:	Majority		Minority
Defeated for Reelection	Percy, Charles H.	Ill. Rep	None
Departures from Committee:			
Moved to Select Ethics	Kassebaum, Nancy Landon	Kans. Rep	None
No new assignment	Domenici, Pete V.	N.M. Rep	None

SENATE SPECIAL COMMITTEE: AGING (Permanent) / 99th Congress

Service Dates of Committee Chair: Mar. 5,1985-Jan. 6,1987
Service Dates of Majority Members: Mar. 5,1985-Jan. 6,1987
Service Dates of Minority Members: Mar. 5,1985-Jan. 6,1987

Majority

Rank	Name	Party	State	Years in: Senate	Years in: Comm.
Chr	Heinz, H. John III	Rep	Penn.	9	7
2nd	Cohen, William S.	Rep	Me.	7	7
3rd	Pressler, Larry L.	Rep	S.D.	7	5
4th	Grassley, Charles E.	Rep	Iowa	5	5
5th	Wilson, Pete	Rep	Cal.	3	3
6th	Warner, John W.	Rep	Va.	7	2
7th	Evans, Daniel J.	Rep	Wash.	2	2
8th	Denton, Jeremiah	Rep	Ala.	5 *2	1
9th	Nickles, Don	Rep	Okla.	5	1
10th	Hawkins, Paula	Rep	Fla.	5	1

Minority

Rank	Name	Party	State	Years in: Senate	Years in: Comm.
RM	Glenn, John H. Jr.	Dem	Ohio	11	9
2nd	Chiles, Lawton M. Jr.	Dem	Fla.	15	13
3rd	Melcher, John	Dem	Mont.	9	9
4th	Pryor, David H.	Dem	Ark.	7	7
5th	Bradley, William W.	Dem	N.J.	7	7
6th	Burdick, Quentin N.	Dem	N.D.	25	6
7th	Dodd, Christopher J.	Dem	Conn.	5	5
8th	Johnston, J. Bennett Jr.	Dem	La.	13	2
9th	Bingaman, Jeff	Dem	N.M.	3	2

*2: Member's 2nd period of service on the committee.

	Majority		Minority	
Departures from the Senate:				
Defeated for Reelection	Denton, Jeremiah	Ala. Rep	None	
	Hawkins, Paula	Fla. Rep		
Departures from Committee:				
Moved to Select Indian Affairs	Evans, Daniel J.	Wash. Rep	None	
Moved to Appropriations; Budget	Nickles, Don	Okla. Rep	None	
Moved to Environment & Public Works	Warner, John W.	Va. Rep		
Moved to Governmental Affairs	None		Bingaman, Jeff	N.M. Dem
Moved to Budget; Rules & Administration	None		Dodd, Christopher J.	Conn. Dem

SENATE SPECIAL COMMITTEE: AGING (Permanent) / 100th Congress

Service Dates of Committee Chair: Jan. 6,1987-Jan. 3,1989
Service Dates of Majority Members: Jan. 6,1987-Feb. 2,1989
Service Dates of Minority Members: Jan. 6,1987-Feb. 2,1989

Majority

Rank	Name	Party	State	Years in: Senate	Years in: Comm.
Chr	Melcher, John	Dem	Mont.	11	10
2nd	Glenn, John H. Jr.	Dem	Ohio	13	10
3rd	Chiles, Lawton M. Jr.	Dem	Fla.	17	15
4th	Pryor, David H.	Dem	Ark.	9	8
5th	Bradley, William W.	Dem	N.J.	9	8
6th	Burdick, Quentin N.	Dem	N.D.	27	8
7th	Johnston, J. Bennett Jr.	Dem	La.	15	3
8th	Breaux, John B.	Dem	La.	1	1
9th	Shelby, Richard C.	Dem	Ala.	1	1
10th	Reid, Harry M.	Dem	Nev.	1	1

Minority

Rank	Name	Party	State	Years in: Senate	Years in: Comm.
RM	Heinz, H. John III	Rep	Penn.	11	8
2nd	Cohen, William S.	Rep	Me.	9	8
3rd	Pressler, Larry L.	Rep	S.D.	9	6
4th	Grassley, Charles E.	Rep	Iowa	7	6
5th	Wilson, Pete	Rep	Cal.	5	5
6th	Domenici, Pete V.	Rep	N.M.	15 *2	1
7th	Chafee, John H.	Rep	R.I.	11	1
8th	Durenberger, David F.	Rep	Minn.	9 *2	1
9th	Simpson, Alan K.	Rep	Wyo.	9	1

*2: Member's 2nd period of service on the committee.

	Majority		Minority	
Departures from the Senate:				
Defeated for Reelection	Melcher, John	Mont. Dem	None	
Retired	Chiles, Lawton M. Jr.	Fla. Dem	None	
Departures from Committee:				
Moved to Labor & Human Resources	None		Durenberger, David F.	Minn. Rep
No new assignment	None		Chafee, John H.	R.I. Rep

SENATE SPECIAL COMMITTEE: AGING (Permanent) / 101st Congress

Service Dates of Committee Chair: Feb. 2,1989-Mar. 19,1991
Service Dates of Majority Members: Feb. 2,1989-Mar. 19,1991
Service Dates of Minority Members: Feb. 2,1989-Mar. 19,1991

Majority

Rank	Name	Party	State	Years in: Senate	Years in: Comm.
Chr	Pryor, David H.	Dem	Ark.	11	11
2nd	Glenn, John H. Jr.	Dem	Ohio	15	12
3rd	Bradley, William W.	Dem	N.J.	11	11
4th	Burdick, Quentin N.	Dem	N.D.	29	10
5th	Johnston, J. Bennett Jr.	Dem	La.	17	5
6th	Breaux, John B.	Dem	La.	3	3
7th	Shelby, Richard C.	Dem	Ala.	3	3
8th	Reid, Harry M.	Dem	Nev.	3	3
9th	Graham, Bob	Dem	Fla.	3	1
10th	Kohl, Herb	Dem	Wisc.	1	1

Minority

Rank	Name	Party	State	Years in: Senate	Years in: Comm.
RM	Heinz, H. John III	Rep	Penn.	13	11
2nd	Cohen, William S.	Rep	Me.	11	11
3rd	Pressler, Larry L.	Rep	S.D.	11	9
4th	Grassley, Charles E.	Rep	Iowa	9	9
5th	Wilson, Pete	Rep	Cal.	7	7
6th	Domenici, Pete V.	Rep	N.M.	17	*2 3
7th	Simpson, Alan K.	Rep	Wyo.	11	3
8th	Warner, John W.	Rep	Va.	11	1
9th	Kassebaum, Nancy Landon	Rep	Kans.	11	1

*2: Member's 2nd period of service on the committee.

	Majority	Minority		
Departures from the Senate:				
Elected Governor	None	Wilson, Pete	Cal.	Rep
Departures from Committee:				
Moved to Banking, Housing & Urban Affairs	None	Domenici, Pete V.	N.M.	Rep
Moved to Select Indian Affairs	None	Kassebaum, Nancy Landon	Kans.	Rep
Moved to Rules & Administration;	None	Warner, John W.	Va.	Rep

SENATE SPECIAL COMMITTEE: AGING (Permanent) / 102nd Congress

Service Dates of Committee Chair: Mar. 19,1991-Jan. 3,1993
Service Dates of Majority Members: Mar. 19,1991-Jan. 3,1993
Service Dates of Minority Members: Mar. 19,1991-Jan. 3,1993

Majority

Rank	Name	Party	State	Years in: Senate	Years in: Comm.
Chr	Pryor, David H.	Dem	Ark.	13	13
2nd	Glenn, John H. Jr.	Dem	Ohio	17	14
3rd	Bradley, William W.	Dem	N.J.	13	13
4th	Burdick, Quentin N.	Dem	N.D.	31	12
5th	Johnston, J. Bennett Jr.	Dem	La.	19	7
6th	Breaux, John B.	Dem	La.	5	5
7th	Shelby, Richard C.	Dem	Ala.	5	5
8th	Reid, Harry M.	Dem	Nev.	5	5
9th	Graham, Bob	Dem	Fla.	5	3
10th	Kohl, Herb	Dem	Wisc.	3	3
11th	Sanford, Terry	Dem	N.C.	5	1

Minority

Rank	Name	Party	State	Years in: Senate	Years in: Comm.
RM1	Heinz, H. John III	Rep	Penn.	15	13
RM2 2nd	Cohen, William S.	Rep	Me.	13	13
3rd	Pressler, Larry L.	Rep	S.D.	13	11
4th	Grassley, Charles E.	Rep	Iowa	11	11
5th	Simpson, Alan K.	Rep	Wyo.	13	5
6th	Jeffords, James	Rep	Vt.	3	1
7th	McCain, John	Rep	Ariz.	5	1
8th	Durenberger, David F.	Rep	Minn.	13	*3 1
9th	Craig, Larry E.	Rep	Ida.	1	1
10th	Burns, Conrad	Rep	Mont.	3	1

*3: Member's 3rd period of service on the committee.

Changes:

Ranking Member:				
RM1 Heinz, John	Rep	Penn.	Apr. 4,1991	Died in office.
RM2 Cohen, William S.	Rep	Me.	Apr. 4,1991	Succeeded Heinz as Ranking Minority Member.
Majority:				
Burdick, Quentin N.	Dem	N.D.	Sep. 8,1992	Died in office.
Burdick, Jocelyn	Dem	N.D.	Sep. 18,1992	Replaced Quentin Burdick.
Minority:				
Heinz, John	Rep	Penn.	Apr. 4,1991	Died in office.
Specter, Arlen	Rep	Penn.	June 6,1991	Replaced Heinz.

SENATE SPECIAL COMMITTEE: NATIONAL FUELS AND ENERGY STUDY GROUP

Jurisdiction, 1961

From Senate Resolution 105, 87th Congress, First Session, September 11, 1961:

[Section 1]

(a) make a full and complete investigation and study (including the holding of public hearings in appropriate parts of the Nation) of the current and prospective fuel and energy resources of the United States and the present and probable future rates of consumption thereof; and

(b) make a full and complete investigation and study of the existing and prospective governmental policies and laws effecting the fuels and energy industries with the view of determining what, if any, changes and implementation of these policies and laws may be advisable in order to coordinate and provide an effective national fuels policy to assure the availability of fuels and energy adequate for an expanding economy and for the security of the United States, taking into account the investment by private enterprise for the maintenance of efficient and adequate fuels and necessary related industries and the necessity for the maintenance of an adequate force of skilled workers.

Termination, 1962

The Special Committee was terminated upon the filing of Senate Report 159 (87-2) on October 2, 1962.

SENATE SPECIAL COMMITTEE: NATIONAL FUELS AND ENERGY STUDY GROUP / 87th Congress

Service Dates of Committee Chair: Sep. 11,1961-Oct. 2,1962
Service Dates of Majority Members: Sep. 11,1961-Oct. 2,1962
Service Dates of Minority Members: Sep. 11,1961-Oct. 2,1962

Majority

Rank	Name	Party	State	Years in: Senate	Years in: Comm.
Chr	Anderson, Clinton P.	Dem	N.M.	13	1
2nd	Jackson, Henry M.	Dem	Wash.	9	1
3rd	Bible, Alan H.	Dem	Nev.	7	1
4th	Carroll, John A.	Dem	Colo.	5	1
5th	Church, Frank F.	Dem	Ida.	5	1
6th	Gruening, Ernest	Dem	Alas.	3	1
7th	Moss, Frank E.	Dem	Utah	3	1
8th	Long, Oren E.	Dem	Hai.	3	1
9th	Burdick, Quentin N.	Dem	N.D.	2	1
10th	Metcalf, Lee	Dem	Mont.	1	1
11th	Hickey, John J.	Dem	Wyo.	1	1
12th	Randolph, Jennings	Dem	W.Va.	3	1
13th	Engle, Clair	Dem	Cal.	3	1

Minority

Rank	Name	Party	State	Years in: Senate	Years in: Comm.
RM1	Dworshak, Henry C.	Rep	Ida.	14	1
RM2 2nd	Kuchel, Thomas H.	Rep	Cal.	9	1
3rd	Goldwater, Barry M.	Rep	Ariz.	9	1
4th	Allott, Gordon L.	Rep	Colo.	7	1
5th	Miller, Jack R.	Rep	Iowa	1	1
6th	Dirksen, Everett M.	Rep	Ill.	11	1
7th	Cotton, Norris	Rep	N.H.	7	1

Note: Jennings Randolph (Dem-W.Va.), Clair Engle (Dem-Cal.) and Norris Cotton (Rep-N.H.) were appointed to the Special Committee on Sep. 21, 1961 to serve in an *"officio* capacity" with the membership of the Senate Standing Committee on Interior and Insular Affairs.

Changes:

Ranking Member:

	Name	Party	State	Date	Change
RM1	Dworshak, Henry C.	Rep	Ida.	July 23,1962	Died in office.
RM2	Kuchel, Thomas H.	Rep	Cal.	July 23,1962	Succeeded Dworshak as Ranking Minority Member.

Minority:

Name	Party	State	Date	Change
Dworshak, Henry C.	Rep	Ida.	July 23,1962	Died in office.

SENATE SELECT COMMITTEE: ETHICS

STANDARDS AND CONDUCT

Jurisdiction, 1964

From Senate Resolution 338, as amended, 88th Congress, Second Session, July 24, 1964

[Section 2]

(a) It shall be the duty of the select committee to:
(1) receive complaints and investigate allegations of improper conduct which may reflect upon the Senate, violations of law, and violations of rules and regulations of the Senate, relating to the conduct of individuals in the performance of their duties as Members of the Senate, or as officers or employees of the Senate, and to make appropriate findings of fact and conclusions with respect thereto;
(2) recommend to the Senate by report or resolution by a majority vote of the full committee disciplinary action to be taken with respect to such violations which the select committee shall determine, after according to the individuals concerned due notice and opportunity for hearing, to have occurred;
(3) recommend to the Senate, by report or resolution, such additional rules or regulations as the select committee shall determine to be necessary or desirable to insure proper standards of conduct by Members of the Senate, and by officers or employees of the Senate, in the performance of their duties and the discharge of their responsibilities; and
(4) report violations by a majority vote of the full committee of any law to the proper Federal and State authorities.

(b) The Select Committee from time to time shall transmit to the Senate its recommendation as to any legislative measures which it may consider to be necessary for the effective discharge of its duties.

ETHICS (Permanent)

By authority of Senate Resolution 4, the Committee Systems Reorganization Amendments of 1977, 95th Congress, First Session, the committee became the Permanent Select Committee on Ethics on February 4, 1977.

Jurisdiction, 1992

From Authority and Rules of Senate Committees, Senate Document 102-6, printed under the authority of Senate Resolution 58 (102-1), agreed to March 13, 1991:

[Section 2 (a)]

It shall be the duty of the Select Committee to--
(1) receive complaints and investigate allegations of improper conduct which may reflect upon the Senate, violations of law, violations of the Senate Code of official Conduct and violations of rules and regulations of the Senate, relating to the conduct of individuals in the performance of their duties as Members of the Senate, or as officers or employees of the Senate, and to make appropriate findings of fact and conclusions with respect thereto;
(2) recommend to the Senate by report or resolution by a majority vote of the full committee disciplinary action (including, but not limited to, in the case of a Member: censure, expulsion, or recommendation to the appropriate party conference regarding such Member's seniority or positions of responsibility; and in the case of an officer or employee: suspension or dismissal) to be taken with respect to such violations which the Select Committee shall determine, after according to the individuals concerned due notice and opportunity for hearing to have occurred.
(3) recommend to the Senate, by report or resolution, such additional rules or regulations as the Select Committee shall determine to be necessary or desirable to insure proper standards of conduct by Members of the Senate, and by officers or employees of the Senate, in the performance of their duties and the discharge of their responsibilities; and
(4) report violations by a majority vote of the full committee of any law to the proper Federal and State authorities.

SENATE SELECT COMMITTEE: STANDARDS AND CONDUCT / 89th Congress

Service Dates of Committee Chair: July 9,1965-Continued
Service Dates of Majority Members: July 9,1965-Continued
Service Dates of Minority Members: July 9,1965-Continued

Majority

Rank Name	Party	State	Years in: Senate	Years in: Comm.
Chr Stennis, John C.	Dem	Miss.	18	1
2nd Monroney, A. S. Mike	Dem	Okla.	15	1
3rd McCarthy, Eugene J.	DFL	Minn.	7	1

Minority

Rank Name	Party	State	Years in: Senate	Years in: Comm.
VCh Bennett, Wallace F.	Rep	Utah	15	1
2nd Cooper, John Sherman	Rep	Ky.	13	1
3rd Pearson, James B.	Rep	Kans.	4	1

SENATE SELECT COMMITTEE: STANDARDS AND CONDUCT / 90th Congress

Service Dates of Committee Chair: Jan. 3,1967-Continued
Service Dates of Majority Members: Jan. 3,1967-Continued
Service Dates of Minority Members: Jan. 3,1967-Continued

Majority

Rank Name	Party	State	Years in: Senate	Years in: Comm.
Chr Stennis, John C.	Dem	Miss.	20	2
2nd Monroney, A. S. Mike	Dem	Okla.	17	2
3rd McCarthy, Eugene J.	DFL	Minn.	9	2

Minority

Rank Name	Party	State	Years in: Senate	Years in: Comm.
VCh Bennett, Wallace F.	Rep	Utah	17	2
2nd Cooper, John Sherman	Rep	Ky.	15	2
3rd Pearson, James B.	Rep	Kans.	5	2

Departures from the Senate:

	Majority		Minority
Defeated for Reelection	Monroney, A. S. Mike	Okla. Dem	None

SENATE SELECT COMMITTEE: STANDARDS AND CONDUCT / 91st Congress

Service Dates of Committee Chair: Jan. 3,1969-Continued
Service Dates of Majority Members: Jan. 3,1969-Continued
Service Dates of Minority Members: Jan. 3,1969-Continued

Majority

Rank Name	Party	State	Years in: Senate	Years in: Comm.
Chr Stennis, John C.	Dem	Miss.	22	4
2nd McCarthy, Eugene J.	DFL	Minn.	11	4
3rd Talmadge, Herman E.	Dem	Ga.	14	1

Minority

Rank Name	Party	State	Years in: Senate	Years in: Comm.
VCh Bennett, Wallace F.	Rep	Utah	19	4
2nd Cooper, John Sherman	Rep	Ky.	17	4
3rd Pearson, James B.	Rep	Kans.	7	4

Vacancy Filled:

Majority: 3rd seat by Talmadge on Feb. 23,1970.

Changes:

Minority:

Pearson, James B.	Rep	Kans.	Oct. 29,1969	Left committee; no new assignment.
Jordan, Len B.	Rep	Ida.	Oct. 29,1969	Replaced Pearson.

Departures from the Senate:

	Majority		Minority
Retired	McCarthy, Eugene J.	Minn. DFL	None

SENATE SELECT COMMITTEE: STANDARDS AND CONDUCT / 92nd Congress

Service Dates of Committee Chair: Jan. 3,1971-Continued
Service Dates of Majority Members: Jan. 3,1971-Continued
Service Dates of Minority Members: Jan. 3,1971-Continued

Majority

Rank Name	Party	State	Years in: Senate	Years in: Comm.
Chr Stennis, John C.	Dem	Miss.	24	6
2nd Talmadge, Herman E.	Dem	Ga.	15	1
3rd Spong, William B. Jr.	Dem	Va.	5	1

Minority

Rank Name	Party	State	Years in: Senate	Years in: Comm.
VCh Bennett, Wallace F.	Rep	Utah	21	6
2nd Cooper, John Sherman	Rep	Ky.	19	6
3rd Jordan, Len B.	Rep	Ida.	9	2

Vacancy Filled:
Majority: 3rd by Spong on July 14,1971.

Departures from the Senate:

	Majority			Minority		
Defeated for Reelection	Spong, William B. Jr.	Va.	Dem	None		
Retired	None			Cooper, John Sherman	Ky.	Rep
				Jordan, Len B.	Ida.	Rep

SENATE SELECT COMMITTEE: STANDARDS AND CONDUCT / 93rd Congress

Service Dates of Committee Chair: Ch1 Jan. 3,1973-Apr. 4,1974
Ch2 Apr. 4,1974-Continued
Service Dates of Majority Members: Apr. 18,1973-Continued
Service Dates of Minority Members: Jan. 11,1973-Continued

Majority

Rank Name	Party	State	Years in: Senate	Years in: Comm.
Ch1 Stennis, John C.	Dem	Miss.	26	8
2nd Talmadge, Herman E.	Dem	Ga.	17	3
Ch2 3rd Cannon, Howard W.	Dem	Nev.	15	1

Minority

Rank Name	Party	State	Years in: Senate	Years in: Comm.
VCh Bennett, Wallace F.	Rep	Utah	23	8
2nd Curtis, Carl T.	Rep	Neb.	19	1
3rd Brooke, Edward W.	Rep	Mass.	7	1

Note: "Service Dates" of majority and minority members reflect the dates of service of Cannon, Curtis and Brooke; all other members continued service from the previous Congress without official reassignment recorded in the Congressional Record.

Changes:

Chair:

Ch1 Stennis, John C.	Dem	Miss.	Apr. 4,1974	Resigned as Chair (effective Mar. 21,1974); remained on committee.
Ch2 Cannon, Howard W.	Dem	Nev.	Apr. 4,1974	Succeeded Stennis as Chair (effective Mar. 21,1974).

Minority:

Bennett, Wallace F.	Rep	Utah	Dec. 20,1974	Resigned and retired.

SENATE SELECT COMMITTEE: STANDARDS AND CONDUCT / 94th Congress

Service Dates of Committee Chair: Continued-Feb. 11,1977
Service Dates of Majority Members: Continued-Feb. 11,1977
Service Dates of Minority Members: Feb. 7,1975-Feb. 22,1977

Majority

Rank Name	Party	State	Years in: Senate	Years in: Comm.
Chr Cannon, Howard W.	Dem	Nev.	17	2
2nd Stennis, John C.	Dem	Miss.	28	10
3rd Talmadge, Herman E.	Dem	Ga.	19	5

Minority

Rank Name	Party	State	Years in: Senate	Years in: Comm.
VCh Curtis, Carl T.	Rep	Neb.	21	3
2nd Brooke, Edward W.	Rep	Mass.	9	3
3rd Young, Milton R.	Rep	N.D.	30	1

Notes: "Service Dates of Minority Members" reflect the dates of service of Young; all other minority members continued service from the previous Congress without official reassignment recorded in the Congressional Record. Carl T. Curtis (Rep-Neb) was selected as Vice Chair of the Committee on Jan. 27,1976 (reported Feb. 3,1976).

Members not assigned to Permanent Select Committee on Ethics:

Majority			Minority		
Cannon, Howard W.	Nev.	Dem	Curtis, Carl T.	Neb.	Rep
Stennis, John C.	Miss.	Dem	Brooke, Edward W.	Mass.	Rep
Talmadge, Herman E.	Ga.	Dem	Young, Milton R.	N.D.	Rep

SENATE SELECT COMMITTEE: ETHICS (Permanent) / 95th Congress

* Renamed Select Committee on ETHICS and made Permanent on Feb. 4,1977.

Service Dates of Committee Chair: Feb. 11,1977-Continued
Service Dates of Majority Members: Feb. 11,1977-Apr. 10,1979
Service Dates of Minority Members: Feb. 22,1977-Apr. 10,1979

Majority

Rank	Name	Party	State	Years in: Senate	Years in: Comm.
Chr	Stevenson, Adlai E. III	Dem	Ill.	7	1
2nd	Ribicoff, Abraham A.	Dem	Conn.	15	1
3rd	Morgan, Robert B.	Dem	N.C.	3	1

Minority

Rank	Name	Party	State	Years in: Senate	Years in: Comm.
VCh	Schmitt, Harrison H.	Rep	N.M.	1	1
2nd	Tower, John G.	Rep	Tex.	16	1
3rd	Weicker, Lowell P. Jr.	Rep	Conn.	7	1

Note: The appointment of James B. Pearson (Rep-Kans.) to replace John G. Tower (Rep-Tex.) on Feb. 28,1978 was vitiated on Mar. 2,1978. Pearson's role on the committee was declared to be "solely for the purpose of such initial review or investigations as to which Mr. Tower has disqualified himself," namely, investigations into Korean plans to improperly influence the U.S. Senate, contained in Senate Report 1314 (95-2), printed Oct. 10,1978.

Changes:

Minority:

Name	Party	State	Date	Change
Tower, John G.	Rep	Tex.	Feb. 28,1978	Left committee temporarily due to inquiry.
Pearson, James B.	Rep	Kans.	Feb. 28,1978	Replaced Tower.
Pearson, James B.	Rep	Kans.	Mar. 2,1978	Order of Feb. 28,1978 vitiated upon dismissal of complaint against Tower.
Tower, John G.	Rep	Tex.	Mar. 2,1978	Order of Feb. 28,1978 vitiated upon dismissal of complaint against Tower.
Weicker, Lowell P. Jr.	Rep	Conn.	Apr. 13,1978	Left committee; no new assignment.
Mathias, Charles McC. Jr.	Rep	Md.	Apr. 13,1978	Replaced Weicker.

Departures from Committee:

	Majority			Minority		
Moved to Rules	None			Tower, John G.	Tex.	Rep
No new assignment	Ribicoff, Abraham A.	Conn.	Dem	Mathias, Charles McC. Jr.	Md.	Rep

SENATE SELECT COMMITTEE: ETHICS (Permanent) / 96th Congress

Service Dates of Committee Chair: Ch1 Apr. 10,1979-Oct. 31,1979
Ch2 Oct. 31,1979-Jan. 6,1981
Service Dates of Majority Members: Apr. 10,1979-Jan. 6,1981
Service Dates of Minority Members: Apr. 10,1979-Jan. 6,1981

Majority

Rank	Name	Party	State	Years in: Senate	Years in: Comm.
Ch1	Stevenson, Adlai E. III	Dem	Ill.	9	3
2nd	Morgan, Robert B.	Dem	N.C.	5	3
3rd	Burdick, Quentin N.	Dem	N.D.	19	1

Minority

Rank	Name	Party	State	Years in: Senate	Years in: Comm.
VCh1	Schmitt, Harrison H.	Rep	N.M.	3	3
2nd	Hatfield, Mark O.	Rep	Ore.	13	1
3rd	Helms, Jesse A.	Rep	N.C.	7	*1 1

*1: Member's 1st period of service on the committee.

Changes:

Chair:

Rank	Name	Party	State	Date	Change
Ch1	Stevenson, Adlai E. III	Dem	Ill.	Oct. 31,1979	Left committee; no new assignment.
Ch2	Heflin, Howell T.	Dem	Ala.	Oct. 31,1979	Replaced Stevenson as Chair.

Vice Chair:

Rank	Name	Party	State	Date	Change
VCh1	Schmitt, Harrison H.	Rep	N.M.	Oct. 31,1979	Left committee; no new assignment.
VCh2	Wallop, Malcolm	Rep	Wyo.	Oct. 31,1979	Replaced Schmitt as Vice Chair.

Majority:

Stevenson, Adlai E. III	Dem	Ill.	Oct. 31,1979	Left committee; no new assignment.
Heflin, Howell T.	Dem	Ala.	Oct. 31,1979	Replaced Stevenson.
Burdick, Quentin N.	Dem	N.D.	Jan. 25,1980	Left committee; no new assignment.
Pryor, David H.	Dem	Ark.	Jan. 25,1980	Replaced Burdick.

Minority:

Schmitt, Harrison H.	Rep	N.M.	Oct. 31,1979	Left committee; no new assignment.
Wallop, Malcolm	Rep	Wyo.	Oct. 31,1979	Replaced Schmitt.
Hatfield, Mark O.	Rep	Ore.	Jan. 28,1980	Left committee; no new assignment.
Cochran, Thad	Rep	Miss.	Jan. 28,1980	Replaced Hatfield.

Departures from the Senate:	**Majority**			**Minority**		
Defeated for Reelection	Morgan, Robert B.	N.C.	Dem	None		
Departures from Committee:						
Moved to Rules & Administration	None			Helms, Jesse A.	N.C.	Rep

SENATE SELECT COMMITTEE: ETHICS (Permanent) / 97th Congress

Service Dates of Committee Chair: Jan. 6,1981-Jan. 3,1983
Service Dates of Majority Members: Jan. 6,1981-Jan. 3,1983
Service Dates of Minority Members: Jan. 6,1981-Jan. 3,1983

Majority

Rank	Name	Party	State	Years in: Senate	Years in: Comm.
Chr	Wallop, Malcolm	Rep	Wyo.	5	2
2nd	Cochran, Thad	Rep	Miss.	3	1
3rd	Mattingly, Mack	Rep	Ga.	1	1

Minority

Rank	Name	Party	State	Years in: Senate	Years in: Comm.
VCh	Heflin, Howell T.	Dem	Ala.	3	2
2nd	Pryor, David H.	Dem	Ark.	3	1
3rd	Eagleton, Thomas F.	Dem	Mo.	13	1

Changes:

Majority:

Cochran, Thad	Rep	Miss.	Jan. 21,1981	Left committee; no new assignment.
Helms, Jesse A.	Rep	N.C.	Jan. 21,1981	Replaced Cochran.

Departures from Committee:	**Majority**			**Minority**
Moved to Banking, Housing & Urban Affairs	Mattingly, Mack	Ga.	Rep	None
No new assignment	Wallop, Malcolm	Wyo.	Rep	None

SENATE SELECT COMMITTEE: ETHICS (Permanent) / 98th Congress

Service Dates of Committee Chair: Jan. 3,1983-Jan. 3,1985
Service Dates of Majority Members: Jan. 3,1983-Mar. 5,1985
Service Dates of Minority Members: Jan. 3,1983-Mar. 5,1985

Majority

Rank	Name	Party	State	Years in: Senate	Years in: Comm.
Chr	Stevens, Theodore F.	Rep	Alas.	15	1
2nd	Helms, Jesse A.	Rep	N.C.	11	*2 2
3rd	Durenberger, David F.	Rep	Minn.	5	1

Minority

Rank	Name	Party	State	Years in: Senate	Years in: Comm.
VCh	Heflin, Howell T.	Dem	Ala.	5	4
2nd	Pryor, David H.	Dem	Ark.	5	3
3rd	Eagleton, Thomas F.	Dem	Mo.	15	2

*2: Member's 2nd period of service on the committee.

Departures from Committee:	**Majority**			**Minority**		
Became Chair of Select Intelligence	Durenberger, David F.	Minn.	Rep	None		
Moved to Rules & Administration	Stevens, Theodore F.	Alas.	Rep	None		
Moved to Foreign Relations	None			Eagleton, Thomas F.	Mo.	Dem

SENATE SELECT COMMITTEE: ETHICS (Permanent) / 99th Congress

Service Dates of Committee Chair: Mar. 5,1985-Jan. 6,1987
Service Dates of Majority Members: Mar. 5,1985-Jan. 6,1987
Service Dates of Minority Members: Mar. 5,1985-Jan. 6,1987

Majority

Rank	Name	Party	State	Years in: Senate	Years in: Comm.
Chr	Rudman, Warren B.	Rep	N.H.	5	1
2nd	Helms, Jesse A.	Rep	N.C.	13	*2 5
3rd	Kassebaum, Nancy Landon	Rep	Kans.	7	1

Minority

Rank	Name	Party	State	Years in: Senate	Years in: Comm.
VCh	Heflin, Howell T.	Dem	Ala.	7	6
2nd	Pryor, David H.	Dem	Ark.	7	6
3rd	Long, Russell B.	Dem	La.	37	1

*2: Member's 2nd period of service on the committee.

Departures from the Senate:	Majority	Minority		
Retired	None	Long, Russell B.	La.	Dem

SENATE SELECT COMMITTEE: ETHICS (Permanent) / 100th Congress

Service Dates of Committee Chair: Jan. 6,1987-Feb. 2,1989
Service Dates of Majority Members: Jan. 6,1987-Feb. 2,1989
Service Dates of Minority Members: Jan. 6,1987-Feb. 2,1989

Majority

Rank	Name	Party	State	Years in: Senate	Years in: Comm.
Chr	Heflin, Howell T.	Dem	Ala.	9	8
2nd	Pryor, David H.	Dem	Ark.	9	7
3rd	Sanford, Terry	Dem	N.C.	1	1

Minority

Rank	Name	Party	State	Years in: Senate	Years in: Comm.
VCh	Rudman, Warren B.	Rep	N.H.	7	2
2nd	Helms, Jesse A.	Rep	N.C.	15	*2 6
3rd	Kassebaum, Nancy Landon	Rep	Kans.	9	2

*2: Member's 2nd period of service on the committee.

Departures from Committee:	Majority	Minority		
Moved to Banking Housing & Urban Affairs; Labor & Human Resources	None	Kassebaum, Nancy Landon	Kans.	Rep

SENATE SELECT COMMITTEE: ETHICS (Permanent) / 101st Congress

Service Dates of Committee Chair: Feb. 2,1989-Continued
Service Dates of Majority Members: Feb. 2,1989-Continued
Service Dates of Minority Members: Feb. 2,1989-Continued

Majority

Rank	Name	Party	State	Years in: Senate	Years in: Comm.
Chr	Heflin, Howell T.	Dem	Ala.	11	10
2nd	Pryor, David H.	Dem	Ark.	11	10
3rd	Sanford, Terry	Dem	N.C.	3	3

Minority

Rank	Name	Party	State	Years in: Senate	Years in: Comm.
VCh	Rudman, Warren B.	Rep	N.H.	9	4
2nd	Helms, Jesse A.	Rep	N.C.	17	*2 9
3rd	Lott, Trent	Rep	Miss.	1	1

*2: Member's 2nd period of service on the committee.

SENATE SELECT COMMITTEE: ETHICS The Keating Five Investigation / Continued into 102nd Congress

Majority					Minority				
			Years in:					Years in:	
Rank Name	Party	State	Senate	Comm.	Rank Name	Party	State	Senate	Comm.
Chr Heflin, Howell T.	Dem	Ala.	13	12	VCh Rudman, Warren B.	Rep	N.H.	11	6
2nd Pryor, David H.	Dem	Ark.	13	11	2nd Helms, Jesse A.	Rep	N.C.	19	*2 10
3rd Sanford, Terry	Dem	N.C.	5	5	3rd Lott, Trent	Rep	Miss.	3	2

*2: Member's 2nd period of service on the committee.

Notes: Senate Resolution 169, agreed to on Aug. 2,1991, provided that the members of the committee for the 101st Congress (except for David Pryor) would continue the committee's inquiry and investigation of "the Keating Five," while the membership of the committee for all other business would be as listed for the 102nd Congress. Senate Resolution 169 also stipulated that Jeff Bingaman (Dem-N.M.) was a member of the committee only for matters not relating to the Keating Five Investigation. Pryor rejoined the committee on Sep. 10,1991 only for matters relating to the Keating Five Investigation. Senate Report 223 (102-1), entitled "Investigation of Senator Alan Cranston," was filed on Nov. 20,1991, at which time the specially constituted committee ceased to function.

Changes:

Majority:

Pryor, David H.	Dem	Ark.	May 22,1991	Left committee; no new assignment.
Bingaman, Jeff	Dem	N.M.	May 22,1991	Replaced Pryor.
Bingaman, Jeff	Dem	N.M.	Aug. 2,1991	Removed from committee matters involving the Keating Five.
Pryor, David H.	Dem	Ark.	Sep. 10,1991	Rejoined committee (see Notes).

Departures from Committee:	Majority			Minority		
No new assignment	Heflin, Howell T.	Ala.	Dem	Helms, Jesse A.	N.C.	Rep

SENATE SELECT COMMITTEE: ETHICS (Permanent) / 102nd Congress

Service Dates of Committee Chair: Aug. 2,1991-Jan. 3,1993
Service Dates of Majority Members: Aug. 2,1991-Jan. 3,1993
Service Dates of Minority Members: Aug. 2,1991-Jan. 3,1993

Majority					Minority				
			Years in:					Years in:	
Rank Name	Party	State	Senate	Comm.	Rank Name	Party	State	Senate	Comm.
Chr Sanford, Terry	Dem	N.C.	5	5	VCh Rudman, Warren B.	Rep	N.H.	11	7
2nd Bingaman, Jeff	Dem	N.M.	9	1	2nd Lott, Trent	Rep	Miss.	3	3
3rd Bryan, Richard	Dem	Nev.	3	1	3rd Gorton, Slade	Rep	Wash.	9	1

Note: Senate Resolution 169, agreed to on Aug. 2,1991, provided that the members of the committee for the 101st Congress (except for David Pryor) would continue the committee's inquiries and investigation of "the Keating Five," while the membership of the committee for all other business would be as listed here.

SENATE SPECIAL COMMITTEE: ORGANIZATION OF THE CONGRESS

Jurisdiction, 1966

From Senate Resolution 293, 89th Congress, Second Session, August 26, 1966:

[Section 1]

Resolved, That a special committee . . . is hereby established . . . for the purpose of receiving and considering a bill, when introduced, and germane amendments relating thereto, having for its purpose the carrying out of the recommendations contained in the report of the Joint Committee on the Organization of the Congress, Report No. 1414, July 28, 1966.

Termination, 1968

The Special Committee was extended and terminated by authority of Senate Resolution 247 (90-2), agreed to on March 15, 1968. The Special Committee concluded its business on June 30, 1968.

SENATE SPECIAL COMMITTEE: ORGANIZATION OF THE CONGRESS / 89th Congress

Service Dates of Committee Chair: Aug. 26,1966-Continued
Service Dates of Majority Members: Aug. 26,1966-Continued
Service Dates of Minority Members: Aug. 26,1966-Continued

Majority

Rank	Name	Party	State	Years in: Senate	Years in: Comm.
Chr	Monroney, A. S. Mike	Dem	Okla.	16	1
2nd	Sparkman, John J.	Dem	Ala.	20	1
3rd	Metcalf, Lee	Dem	Mont.	6	1

Minority

Rank	Name	Party	State	Years in: Senate	Years in: Comm.
RM	Mundt, Karl E.	Rep	S.D.	18	1
2nd	Case, Clifford P.	Rep	N.J.	12	1
3rd	Boggs, J. Caleb	Rep	Del.	6	1

SENATE SPECIAL COMMITTEE: ORGANIZATION OF THE CONGRESS / 90th Congress

Service Dates of Committee Chair: Jan. 3,1967-June 30,1968
Service Dates of Majority Members: Jan. 3,1967-June 30,1968
Service Dates of Minority Members: Jan. 3,1967-June 30,1968

Majority

Rank	Name	Party	State	Years in: Senate	Years in: Comm.
Chr	Monroney, A. S. Mike	Dem	Okla.	17	1
2nd	Sparkman, John J.	Dem	Ala.	21	1
3rd	Metcalf, Lee	Dem	Mont.	7	1

Minority

Rank	Name	Party	State	Years in: Senate	Years in: Comm.
RM	Mundt, Karl E.	Rep	S.D.	19	1
2nd	Case, Clifford P.	Rep	N.J.	13	1
3rd	Boggs, J. Caleb	Rep	Del.	7	1

SENATE SELECT COMMITTEE: NUTRITION AND HUMAN NEEDS

Jurisdiction, 1968

From Senate Resolution 281, 90th Congress, Second Session, July 30, 1968:

[Section 2]

Resolved, That there is established a select committee of the Senate . . . to study the [unmet] food, medical, and other related basic needs among the people of the United States and to report back to the appropriate committees of the Senate and terminate its activities not later than June 30, 1969. Such report may contain such recommendations as the committee finds necessary to establish a coordinated program or programs which will assure every United States resident adequate food, medical assistance, and other related basic necessities of life and health and shall in addition contain appropriate procedures for congressional consideration and oversight of such coordinated programs.

From Senate Resolution 68, 91st Congress, First Session, January 28, 1969:

[Section 1]

Resolved, That the Select Committee on Nutrition and Human Needs as established under S. Res. 281 is authorized to examine, investigate, and make a complete study of any and all matters pertaining to the lack of food, medical assistance, and other related necessities of life and health including, but not limited to, such matters as:

(a) the extent and cause of hunger and malnutrition in the United States, including educational, health, welfare, and other matters related to malnutrition,
(b) the failure of food programs to reach many citizens who lack adequate quantity or quality of food,
(c) the means by which this Nation can bring an adequate supply of nutritious food and other related necessities to every American,
(d) the divisions of responsibility and authority within Congress and the executive branch, including appropriate procedures for congressional consideration and oversight of coordinated programs to assure that every resident of the United States has adequate food, medical assistance, and other basic related necessities of life and health; and
(e) the degree of additional Federal action desirable in these areas.

Termination, 1977

The Select Committee was terminated on December 31, 1977, by authority of Senate Resolution 4 (95-1), agreed to February 4, 1977, at which time its authority was transferred to the Senate Standing Committee on Agriculture, Nutrition and Forestry.

SENATE SELECT COMMITTEE: NUTRITION AND HUMAN NEEDS / 90th Congress

Service Dates of Committee Chair: Aug. 2,1968-Continued
Service Dates of Majority Members: Aug. 2,1968-Continued
Service Dates of Minority Members: Aug. 2,1968-Continued

Majority

Rank	Name	Party	State	Years in: Senate	Years in: Comm.
Chr	McGovern, George S.	Dem	S.D.	6	1
2nd	Ellender, Allen J.	Dem	La.	32	1
3rd	Talmadge, Herman E.	Dem	Ga.	12	1
4th	Yarborough, Ralph W.	Dem	Tex.	12	1
5th	Clark, Joseph S.	Dem	Penn.	12	1
6th	Nelson, Gaylord A.	Dem	Wisc.	6 *1	1
7th	Hart, Philip A.	Dem	Mich.	10	1
8th	Mondale, Walter F.	DFL	Minn.	4	1

Minority

Rank	Name	Party	State	Years in: Senate	Years in: Comm.
RM	Javits, Jacob K.	Rep	N.Y.	12	1
2nd	Prouty, Winston L.	Rep	Vt.	10	1
3rd	Boggs, J. Caleb	Rep	Del.	8	1
4th	Hatfield, Mark O.	Rep	Ore.	2 *1	1
5th	Percy, Charles H.	Rep	Ill.	2	1

*1: Member's 1st period of service on the committee.

Vacancy Filled:
Minority: 5th seat by Percy on Sep. 6,1968.

Additions:
Minority: 6th Goodell, Charles E. Rep N.Y. Oct. 10,1968

	Majority		**Minority**	
Departures from the Senate:				
Defeated for Reelection	Clark, Joseph S.	Penn. Dem	None	
Departures from Committee:				
Moved to Appropriations	None		Boggs, J. Caleb	Del. Rep
Moved to Banking & Currency; Commerce; District of Columbia	None		Goodell, Charles E.	N.Y. Rep
No new assignment	Nelson, Gaylord A.	Wisc. Dem	Hatfield, Mark O.	Ore. Rep
			Prouty, Winston L.	Vt. Rep

SENATE SELECT COMMITTEE: NUTRITION AND HUMAN NEEDS / 91st Congress

Service Dates of Committee Chair: Jan. 3,1969-Continued
Service Dates of Majority Members: Jan. 14,1969-Continued
Service Dates of Minority Members: Jan. 22,1969-Continued

Majority

Rank	Name	Party	State	Years in: Senate	Years in: Comm.
Chr	McGovern, George S.	Dem	S.D.	7	1
2nd	Ellender, Allen J.	Dem	La.	33	1
3rd	Talmadge, Herman E.	Dem	Ga.	13	1
4th	Yarborough, Ralph W.	Dem	Tex.	12	1
5th	Hart, Philip A.	Dem	Mich.	11	1
6th	Mondale, Walter F.	DFL	Minn.	5	1
7th	Kennedy, Edward M.	Dem	Mass.	7	1
8th	Pell, Claiborne D.	Dem	R.I.	9	1

Minority

Rank	Name	Party	State	Years in: Senate	Years in: Comm.
RM	Javits, Jacob K.	Rep	N.Y.	13	1
2nd	Percy, Charles H.	Rep	Ill.	3	1
3rd	Cook, Marlow W.	Rep	Ky.	1 *1	1
4th	Dole, Robert J.	Rep	Kans.	1	1
5th	Dominick, Peter H.	Rep	Colo.	7	1

*1: Member's 1st period of service on the committee.

Note: "Service Dates" of majority and minority members reflect the dates of service of Kennedy, Cook, Dole and Dominick; all other members continued service from the previous Congress without official reassignment recorded in the Congressional Record.

Vacancy Filled:
Majority: 8th seat by Pell on Jan. 23,1969.

Additions:
Minority: 6th Cook, Marlow W. Rep Ky. Feb. 4,1970

Changes:
Minority:

Cook, Marlow W.	Rep	Ky.	Sep. 17,1969	Moved to Commerce.
Bellmon, Henry	Rep	Okla.	June 25,1970	Replaced Cook.

	Majority		**Minority**	
Departures from the Senate:				
Defeated for Renomination	Yarborough, Ralph W.	Tex. Dem	None	
Departures from Committee:				
Moved to Special Aging	Pell, Claiborne D.	R.I. Dem	None	
No new assignment	None		Dominick, Peter H.	Colo. Rep
			Javits, Jacob K.	N.Y. Rep

SENATE SELECT COMMITTEE: NUTRITION AND HUMAN NEEDS / 92nd Congress

Service Dates of Committee Chair: Jan. 3,1971-Continued
Service Dates of Majority Members: Jan. 28,1971-Continued
Service Dates of Minority Members: Feb. 18,1971-Continued

Majority

Rank	Name	Party	State	Years in: Senate	Years in: Comm.
Chr	McGovern, George S.	Dem	S.D.	9	3
2nd	Ellender, Allen J.	Dem	La.	35	3
3rd	Talmadge, Herman E.	Dem	Ga.	15	3
4th	Hart, Philip A.	Dem	Mich.	13	3
5th	Mondale, Walter F.	DFL	Minn.	7	3
6th	Kennedy, Edward M.	Dem	Mass.	9	3
7th	Nelson, Gaylord A.	Dem	Wisc.	9	*2 1
8th	Cranston, Alan	Dem	Cal.	3	1

Minority

Rank	Name	Party	State	Years in: Senate	Years in: Comm.
RM	Percy, Charles H.	Rep	Ill.	5	3
2nd	Dole, Robert J.	Rep	Kans.	3	3
3rd	Cook, Marlow W.	Rep	Ky.	3	*2 1
4th	Bellmon, Henry	Rep	Okla.	3	1
5th	Schweiker, Richard S.	Rep	Penn.	3	1
6th	Taft, Robert Jr.	Rep	Ohio	1	1

*2: Member's 2nd period of service on the committee.

Note: "Service Dates" of majority and minority members reflect the dates of service of Nelson, Cranston, Schweiker and Taft; all other members continued service from the previous Congress without official reassignment recorded in the Congressional Record.

Changes:

Majority:

Ellender, Allen J.	Dem	La.	July 27,1972	Died in office.
Humphrey, Hubert H. Jr.	DFL	Minn.	Aug. 2,1972	Replaced Ellender.

SENATE SELECT COMMITTEE: NUTRITION AND HUMAN NEEDS / 93rd Congress

Service Dates of Committee Chair: Jan. 3,1973-Continued
Service Dates of Majority Members: Jan. 3,1973-Continued
Service Dates of Minority Members: Jan. 3,1973-Continued

Majority

Rank	Name	Party	State	Years in: Senate	Years in: Comm.
Chr	McGovern, George S.	Dem	S.D.	11	5
2nd	Talmadge, Herman E.	Dem	Ga.	17	5
3rd	Hart, Philip A.	Dem	Mich.	15	5
4th	Mondale, Walter F.	DFL	Minn.	9	5
5th	Kennedy, Edward M.	Dem	Mass.	11	5
6th	Nelson, Gaylord A.	Dem	Wisc.	11	*2 2
7th	Cranston, Alan	Dem	Cal.	5	2
8th	Humphrey, Hubert H. Jr.	DFL	Minn.	18	1

Minority

Rank	Name	Party	State	Years in: Senate	Years in: Comm.
RM	Percy, Charles H.	Rep	Ill.	7	5
2nd	Dole, Robert J.	Rep	Kans.	5	5
3rd	Cook, Marlow W.	Rep	Ky.	5	*2 2
4th	Bellmon, Henry	Rep	Okla.	5	3
5th	Schweiker, Richard S.	Rep	Penn.	5	2
6th	Taft, Robert Jr.	Rep	Ohio	3	2

*2: Member's 2nd period of service on the committee.

Changes:

Minority:

Cook, Marlow W.	Rep	Ky.	Dec. 27,1974	Resigned; defeated for reelection.

SENATE SELECT COMMITTEE: NUTRITION AND HUMAN NEEDS / 94th Congress

Service Dates of Committee Chair: Jan. 3,1975-Continued
Service Dates of Majority Members: Jan. 3,1975-Continued
Service Dates of Minority Members: Feb. 3,1975-Continued

Majority

Rank	Name	Party	State	Years in: Senate	Years in: Comm.
Chr	McGovern, George S.	Dem	S.D.	13	7
2nd	Talmadge, Herman E.	Dem	Ga.	19	7
3rd	Hart, Philip A.	Dem	Mich.	17	7
4th	Mondale, Walter F.	DFL	Minn.	11	7
5th	Kennedy, Edward M.	Dem	Mass.	13	7
6th	Nelson, Gaylord A.	Dem	Wisc.	13	*2 4
7th	Cranston, Alan	Dem	Cal.	7	4
8th	Humphrey, Hubert H. Jr.	DFL	Minn.	20	3

Minority

Rank	Name	Party	State	Years in: Senate	Years in: Comm.
RM	Percy, Charles H.	Rep	Ill.	9	7
2nd	Dole, Robert J.	Rep	Kans.	7	7
3rd	Bellmon, Henry	Rep	Okla.	7	5
4th	Schweiker, Richard S.	Rep	Penn.	7	4
5th	Taft, Robert Jr.	Rep	Ohio	5	4
6th	Hatfield, Mark O.	Rep	Ore.	9	*2 1

*2: Member's 2nd period of service on the committee.

Note: "Service Dates of Minority Members" reflect the dates of service of Hatfield; all other minority members continued service from the previous Congress without official reassignment recorded in the Congressional Record.

Changes:

Majority:

Name	Party	State	Date	Reason
Hart, Philip A.	Dem	Mich.	Dec. 26,1976	Died in office.
Mondale, Walter F.	DFL	Minn.	Dec. 30,1976	Resigned; elected Vice President.

Minority:

Name	Party	State	Date	Reason
Taft, Robert Jr.	Rep	Ohio	Dec. 28,1976	Resigned; defeated for reelection.

Departures from Committee:

	Majority		Minority	
Became Senate Majority Whip	Cranston, Alan	Cal. Dem	None	
Moved to Special Committee on Official Conduct as Chair	Nelson, Gaylord A.	Wisc. Dem	None	
Moved to Select Committee on Indian Affairs	None		Hatfield, Mark O.	Ore. Rep
No new assignment	Talmadge, Herman E.	Ga. Dem	Bellmon, Henry	Okla. Rep

SENATE SELECT COMMITTEE: NUTRITION AND HUMAN NEEDS / 95th Congress

Service Dates of Committee Chair: Jan. 3,1975-Dec. 31,1977
Service Dates of Majority Members: Feb. 11,1977-Dec. 31,1977
Service Dates of Minority Members: Feb. 24,1977-Dec. 31,1977

Majority

Rank	Name	Party	State	Years in: Senate	Years in: Comm.
Chr	McGovern, George S.	Dem	S.D.	15	9
2nd	Kennedy, Edward M.	Dem	Mass.	15	9
3rd	Humphrey, Hubert H. Jr.	DFL	Minn.	22	5
4th	Leahy, Patrick J.	Dem	Vt.	3	1
5th	Zorinsky, Edward	Dem	Neb.	1	1

Minority

Rank	Name	Party	State	Years in: Senate	Years in: Comm.
RM	Percy, Charles H.	Rep	Ill.	11	9
2nd	Dole, Robert J.	Rep	Kans.	9	9
3rd	Schweiker, Richard S.	Rep	Penn.	9	7

Note: "Service Dates of Majority Members" reflect the dates of service of Leahy and Zorinsky; all other majority members continued service from the previous Congress without official reassignment recorded in the Congressional Record.

SENATE SELECT COMMITTEE: EQUAL EDUCATIONAL OPPORTUNITY

Jurisdiction, 1970

From Senate Resolution 359, 91st Congress, Second Session, February 19, 1970:

[Section 1]

Resolved, That (a) there is hereby established a select committee of the Senate . . . to study the effectiveness of existing laws and policies in assuring equality of educational opportunity, including policies of the United States with regard to segregation on the ground of race, color, or national origin, whatever the form of such segregation and whatever the origin or cause of such segregation, and to examine the extent to which policies are applied uniformly in all regions of the United States.

Termination, 1972

The Select Committee was extended by Senate Resolution 326 (92-2), agreed to June 20,1972, and terminated by its authority on December 31, 1972. The findings of the Select Committee are contained in Committee Print Y4.Eq2:Eq2/2.

SENATE SELECT COMMITTEE: EQUAL EDUCATIONAL OPPORTUNITY / 91st Congress

Service Dates of Committee Chair: Feb. 25,1970-Jan. 28,1971
Service Dates of Majority Members: Feb. 25,1970-Jan. 28,1971
Service Dates of Minority Members: Mar. 4,1970-Mar. 2,1971

Majority

Rank	Name	Party	State	Years in: Senate	Years in: Comm.
Chr	Mondale, Walter F.	DFL	Minn.	6	1
2nd	McClellan, John L.	Dem	Ark.	28	1
3rd	Magnuson, Warren G.	Dem	Wash.	26	1
4th	Randolph, Jennings	Dem	W.Va.	12	1
5th	Dodd, Thomas J.	Dem	Conn.	12	1
6th	Inouye, Daniel K.	Dem	Hai.	8	1
7th	Bayh, Birch E.	Dem	Ind.	8	1
8th	Spong, William B. Jr.	Dem	Va.	4	1
9th	Hughes, Harold E.	Dem	Iowa	2	1

Minority

Rank	Name	Party	State	Years in: Senate	Years in: Comm.
RM	Hruska, Roman L.	Rep	Neb.	16	1
2nd	Javits, Jacob K.	Rep	N.Y.	14	1
3rd	Dominick, Peter H.	Rep	Colo.	8	1
4th	Brooke, Edward W.	Rep	Mass.	4	1
5th	Hatfield, Mark O.	Rep	Ore.	4	1
6th	Cook, Marlow W.	Rep	Ky.	2	1

Departures from the Senate:	Majority		Minority
Defeated for Reelection	Dodd, Thomas J.	Conn. Dem	None

SENATE SELECT COMMITTEE: EQUAL EDUCATIONAL OPPORTUNITY / 92nd Congress

Service Dates of Committee Chair: Jan. 28,1971-Dec. 31,1972
Service Dates of Majority Members: Jan. 28,1971-Dec. 31,1972
Service Dates of Minority Members: Mar. 2,1971-Dec. 31,1972

Majority

Rank	Name	Party	State	Years in: Senate	Years in: Comm.
Chr	Mondale, Walter F.	DFL	Minn.	7	1
2nd	McClellan, John L.	Dem	Ark.	29	1
3rd	Magnuson, Warren G.	Dem	Wash.	27	1
4th	Ervin, Samuel J.	Dem	N.C.	17	1
5th	Randolph, Jennings	Dem	W.Va.	13	1
6th	Inouye, Daniel K.	Dem	Hai.	9	1
7th	Bayh, Birch E.	Dem	Ind.	9	1
8th	Hughes, Harold E.	Dem	Iowa	3	1
9th	Spong, William B. Jr.	Dem	Va.	5	1

Minority

Rank	Name	Party	State	Years in: Senate	Years in: Comm.
RM	Hruska, Roman L.	Rep	Neb.	17	1
2nd	Javits, Jacob K.	Rep	N.Y.	15	1
3rd	Dominick, Peter H.	Rep	Colo.	9	1
4th	Brooke, Edward W.	Rep	Mass.	5	1
5th	Hatfield, Mark O.	Rep	Ore.	5	1
6th	Cook, Marlow W.	Rep	Ky.	3	1

Changes:

Majority:

Hughes, Harold E.	Dem	Iowa	Feb. 24,1971	Left committee; no new assignment.
Stevenson, Adlai E. III	Dem	Ill.	Feb. 24,1971	Replaced Hughes.

SENATE SPECIAL COMMITTEE: NATIONAL EMERGENCIES AND DELEGATED EMERGENCY POWERS (Ad Hoc)

TERMINATION OF THE NATIONAL EMERGENCY

Jurisdiction, 1972

From Senate Resolution 304, 92nd Congress, Second Session, June 23, 1972.

[Section 2]

It shall be the function of the special committee to conduct a study and investigation with respect to the matter of terminating the national emergency proclaimed by the President of the United States on December 16, 1950, and announced in Presidential Proclamation Numbered 2914, dated the same date. In carrying out such study and investigation the special committee shall:

(1) consult and confer with the President and his advisers;
(2) consider the problems which may arise as the result of terminating such national emergency; and
(3) consider what administrative or legislative actions might be necessary or desirable as the result of terminating special legislative powers that were conferred on the President and other officers, boards and commissions as the result of the President proclaiming a national emergency.

NATIONAL EMERGENCIES AND DELEGATED EMERGENCY POWERS

Jurisdiction, 1974

From Senate Resolution 242, Ninety-Third Congress, Second Session, March 1, 1974.

[Section 2]

It shall be the function of such special committee, in accordance with the provisions of that Senate Resolution 9 not inconsistent with this resolution, to conduct a study and investigation with respect to the termination of existing states of national emergencies proclaimed by President of the United States in 1933, 1950, 1970, and 1971, and with respect to delegated emergency powers.

Termination, 1976

The Special Committee was terminated upon the filing of its final report, Senate Report 922 (94-2), on May 28, 1976.

SENATE SPECIAL COMMITTEE: TERMINATION OF THE NATIONAL EMERGENCY / 92nd Congress

Service Dates of Committee Chair: Sep. 18,1972-Jan. 6,1973
Service Dates of Majority Members: Sep. 18,1972-Jan. 6,1973
Service Dates of Minority Members: Sep. 18,1972-Jan. 6,1973

Majority

Rank	Name	Party	State	Years in: Senate	Years in: Comm.
CoCh	Church, Frank F.	Dem	Ida.	16	1
2nd	Hart, Philip A.	Dem	Mich.	14	1
3rd	Pell, Claiborne D.	Dem	R.I.	12	1
4th	Stevenson, Adlai E. III	Dem	Ill.	2	1

Minority

Rank	Name	Party	State	Years in: Senate	Years in: Comm.
CoCh	Mathias, Charles McC. Jr.	Rep	Md.	4	1
2nd	Hansen, Clifford P.	Rep	Wyo.	6	1
3rd	Pearson, James B.	Rep	Kans.	11	1
4th	Case, Clifford P.	Rep	N.J.	18	1

SENATE SPECIAL COMMITTEE: TERMINATION OF THE NATIONAL EMERGENCY / 93rd Congress

* Name changed to NATIONAL EMERGENCIES AND DELEGATED EMERGENCY POWERS on March 1, 1974.

Service Dates of Committee Chair: Jan. 6,1973-Continued
Service Dates of Majority Members: Jan. 6,1973-Continued
Service Dates of Minority Members: Jan. 6,1973-Continued

Majority

Rank	Name	Party	State	Years in: Senate	Years in: Comm.
CoCh	Church, Frank F.	Dem	Ida.	17	1
2nd	Hart, Philip A.	Dem	Mich.	15	1
3rd	Pell, Claiborne D.	Dem	R.I.	13	1
4th	Stevenson, Adlai E. III	Dem	Ill.	3	1

Minority

Rank	Name	Party	State	Years in: Senate	Years in: Comm.
CoCh	Mathias, Charles McC. Jr.	Rep	Md.	5	1
2nd	Case, Clifford P.	Rep	N.J.	19	1
3rd	Pearson, James B.	Rep	Kans.	11	1
4th	Hansen, Clifford P.	Rep	Wyo.	7	1

Note: Minority rankings on the committee were corrected on Feb. 20,1973 as listed here. The original order reported Jan. 6,1973 was as follows: Mathias, Hansen, Pearson, and Case.

SENATE SPECIAL COMMITTEE: NATIONAL EMERGENCIES AND DELEGATED EMERGENCY POWERS / 94th Congress

Service Dates of Committee Chair: Jan. 3,1975-Apr. 23,1976
Service Dates of Majority Members: Jan. 3,1975-Apr. 23,1976
Service Dates of Minority Members: Jan. 3,1975-Apr. 23,1976

Majority

Rank	Name	Party	State	Years in: Senate	Years in: Comm.
CoCh	Church, Frank F.	Dem	Ida.	19	3
2nd	Hart, Philip A.	Dem	Mich.	17	3
3rd	Pell, Claiborne D.	Dem	R.I.	15	3
4th	Stevenson, Adlai E. III	Dem	Ill.	5	3

Minority

Rank	Name	Party	State	Years in: Senate	Years in: Comm.
CoCh	Mathias, Charles McC. Jr.	Rep	Md.	7	3
2nd	Case, Clifford P.	Rep	N.J.	21	3
3rd	Pearson, James B.	Rep	Kans.	13	3
4th	Hansen, Clifford P.	Rep	Wyo.	9	3

SENATE SPECIAL COMMITTEE: STUDY QUESTIONS RELATED TO SECRET AND CONFIDENTIAL DOCUMENTS (Ad Hoc)

STUDY QUESTIONS RELATED TO SECRET AND CONFIDENTIAL GOVERNMENT DOCUMENTS (Ad Hoc)

Jurisdiction, 1972

From Senate Resolution 299, 92nd Congress, Second Session, September 11, 1972:

[Paragraph 2]

The committee shall conduct a study and report its findings and recommendations to the Senate . . . on all questions relating to the secrecy, confidentiality, and classification of Government documents committed to the Senate, or any Member thereof, and propose guidelines with respect thereto; and, the laws and rules relating to secrecy, confidentiality, and classification of Government documents, and the authority therefor.

The first Special Committee was terminated by authority of Senate Resolution 299 on January 2, 1977.

STUDY QUESTIONS RELATED TO SECRET AND CONFIDENTIAL DOCUMENTS (Ad Hoc)

The Special Ad Hoc Committee was renamed and reauthorized with identical jurisdiction by Senate Resolution 13 (93-1), agreed to January 9, 1973.

Termination, 1973

The second Special Ad Hoc Committee was terminated upon the filing of Senate Report 466 (93-1) on October 12, 1973.

SENATE SPECIAL COMMITTEE: STUDY QUESTIONS RELATED TO SECRET AND CONFIDENTIAL GOVERNMENT DOCUMENTS (Ad Hoc) / 92nd Congress

Service Dates of Committee Chair: Sep. 22,1972-Jan. 2,1973
Service Dates of Majority Members: Sep. 22,1972-Jan. 2,1973
Service Dates of Minority Members: Sep. 22,1972-Jan. 2,1973

Majority					Minority				
			Years in:					Years in:	
Rank Name	Party	State	Senate	Comm.	Rank Name	Party	State	Senate	Comm.
Chr Mansfield, Michael J.	Dem	Mont.	20	1	CoCh Scott, Hugh D. Jr.	Rep	Penn.	14	1
2nd Pastore, John O.	Dem	R.I.	22	1	2nd Javits, Jacob K.	Rep	N.Y.	16	1
3rd Hughes, Harold E.	Dem	Iowa	4	1	3rd Hatfield, Mark O.	Rep	Ore.	6	1
4th Cranston, Alan	Dem	Cal.	4	1	4th Gurney, Edward J.	Rep	Fla.	4	1
5th Gravel, Mike	Dem	Alas.	4	1	5th Cook, Marlow W.	Rep	Ky.	4	1

SENATE SPECIAL COMMITTEE: STUDY QUESTIONS RELATED TO SECRET AND CONFIDENTIAL DOCUMENTS (Ad Hoc) / 93rd Congress

Service Dates of Committee Chair: Jan. 11,1973-Oct. 12,1973
Service Dates of Majority Members: Jan. 11,1973-Oct. 12,1973
Service Dates of Minority Members: Jan. 11,1973-Oct. 12,1973

Majority					Minority				
			Years in:					Years in:	
Rank Name	Party	State	Senate	Comm.	Rank Name	Party	State	Senate	Comm.
Chr Mansfield, Michael J.	Dem	Mont.	21	1	CoCh Scott, Hugh D. Jr.	Rep	Penn.	15	1
2nd Pastore, John O.	Dem	R.I.	23	1	2nd Javits, Jacob K.	Rep	N.Y.	17	1
3rd Hughes, Harold E.	Dem	Iowa	5	1	3rd Hatfield, Mark O.	Rep	Ore.	7	1
4th Cranston, Alan	Dem	Cal.	5	1	4th Gurney, Edward J.	Rep	Fla.	5	1
5th Gravel, Mike	Dem	Alas.	5	1	5th Cook, Marlow W.	Rep	Ky.	5	1

SENATE SELECT COMMITTEE: PRESIDENTIAL CAMPAIGN ACTIVITIES ("WATERGATE")

Jurisdiction, 1973

From Senate Resolution 60, as amended, 93rd Congress, First Session, February 7, 1973:

[Section 1]

(a) That there is hereby established a select committee of the Senate, which may be called, for convenience of expression, the Select Committee on Presidential Campaign Activities, to conduct an investigation and study of the extent, if any, to which illegal, improper, or unethical activities were engaged in by any persons, acting either individually or in combination with others, in the presidential election of 1972, or in any related campaign or canvass conducted by or in behalf of any person seeking nomination or election as the candidate of any political party for the office of President of the United States in such election, and to determine whether in its judgment any occurrences which may be revealed by the investigation and study indicate the necessity or desirability of the enactment of new congressional legislation to safeguard the electoral process by which the President of the United States is chosen.

Termination, 1974

The Select Committee expired 90 days after the filing of Senate Report 981 (93-2) on June 28, 1974. Senate Resolution 369 (93-2), agreed to on July 29, 1974, authorized and directed that all records of the Select Committee be transferred to the Library of Congress, and that the Senate Committee on Rules and Administration "exercise exclusive control of access to and the use of such records."

SENATE SELECT COMMITTEE: PRESIDENTIAL CAMPAIGN ACTIVITIES (WATERGATE) / 93rd Congress

Service Dates of Committee Chair: Feb. 8,1973-June 28,1974
Service Dates of Majority Members: Feb. 8,1973-June 28,1974
Service Dates of Minority Members: Feb. 8,1973-June 28,1974

Majority

Rank	Name	Party	State	Years in: Senate	Years in: Comm.
Chr	Ervin, Samuel J.	Dem	N.C.	19	1
2nd	Talmadge, Herman E.	Dem	Ga.	17	1
3rd	Inouye, Daniel K.	Dem	Hai.	11	1
4th	Montoya, Joseph M.	Dem	N.M.	9	1

Minority

Rank	Name	Party	State	Years in: Senate	Years in: Comm.
VCh	Baker, Howard H. Jr.	Rep	Tenn.	7	1
2nd	Gurney, Edward J.	Rep	Fla.	5	1
3rd	Weicker, Lowell P. Jr.	Rep	Conn.	3	1

SENATE SELECT COMMITTEE: STUDY GOVERNMENTAL OPERATIONS WITH RESPECT TO INTELLIGENCE ACTIVITIES

Jurisdiction, 1975

From Senate Resolution 21, 94th Congress, First Session, January 27, 1975:

[Section 1]

Resolved, That (a) there is hereby established a select committee of the Senate which may be called, for convenience of expression, the Select Committee To Study Governmental Operations With Respect to Intelligence Activities to conduct an investigation and study of the extent, if any, to which illegal, improper, or unethical activities were engaged in by any agency or by any persons, acting either individually or in combination with others, in carrying out any intelligence or surveillance activities by or on behalf of any agency of the Federal Government.

Termination, 1976

The Select Committee was extended by Senate Resolution 377 (94-2) and terminated by its authority on May 31, 1976. The Select Committee's final report, Senate Report 755 (94-2), was filed on April 28, 1976.

SENATE SELECT COMMITTEE: STUDY GOVERNMENTAL OPERATIONS WITH RESPECT TO INTELLIGENCE ACTIVITIES / 94th Congress

Service Dates of Committee Chair: Jan. 27,1975-May 31,1976
Service Dates of Majority Members: Jan. 27,1975-May 31,1976
Service Dates of Minority Members: Jan. 27,1975-May 31,1976

Majority					Minority				
			Years in:					Years in:	
Rank Name	Party	State	Senate	Comm.	Rank Name	Party	State	Senate	Comm.
Chr Church, Frank F.	Dem	Ida.	19	1	RM Tower, John G.	Rep	Tex.	14	1
2nd Hart, Philip A.	Dem	Mich.	17	1	2nd Baker, Howard H. Jr.	Rep	Tenn.	9	1
3rd Mondale, Walter F.	DFL	Minn.	11	1	3rd Goldwater, Barry M.	Rep	Ariz.	19	1
4th Huddleston, Walter D.	Dem	Ky.	3	1	4th Mathias, Charles McC. Jr.	Rep	Md.	7	1
5th Morgan, Robert B.	Dem	N.C.	1	1	5th Schweiker, Richard S.	Rep	Penn.	7	1
6th Hart, Gary W.	Dem	Colo.	1	1					

Departures from Committee:	Majority		Minority	
Members not assigned to Permanent Select Committee on Intelligence	Church, Frank F.	Ida. Dem	Tower, John G.	Tex. Rep
	Hart, Philip A.	Mich. Dem	Mathias, Charles McC. Jr.	Md. Rep
	Mondale, Walter F.	Minn. DFL	Schweiker, Richard S.	Penn. Rep

SENATE SELECT COMMITTEE: INTELLIGENCE (Permanent)

Jurisdiction, 1976

From Senate Resolution 400, 94th Congress, Second Session, May 19, 1976:

[Section 1]

Resolved, That it is the purpose of this resolution to establish a new select committee of the Senate, to be known as the Select Committee on Intelligence, to oversee and make continuing studies of the intelligence activities and programs of the United States Government, and to submit to the Senate appropriate proposals for legislation and report to the Senate concerning such intelligence activities and programs. In carrying out this purpose, the Select Committee on Intelligence shall make every effort to assure that the appropriate departments and agencies of the United States provide informed and timely intelligence necessary for the executive and legislative branches to make sound decisions affecting the security and vital interests of the Nation. It is further the purpose of this resolution to provide vigilant legislative oversight over the intelligence activities of the United States to assure that such activities are in conformity with the Constitution and laws of the United States.

[Section 13a]

The select committee shall make a study with respect to the following matters, taking into consideration with respect to each such matter, all relevant aspects of the effectiveness of planning, gathering, use, security, and dissemination of intelligence:

(1) the quality of the analytical capabilities of United States foreign intelligence agencies and means for integrating more closely analytical intelligence and policy formulation;
(2) the extent and nature of the authority of the departments and agencies of the executive branch to engage in intelligence activities and the desirability of developing charters for each intelligence agency or department;
(3) the organization of intelligence activities in the executive branch to maximize the effectiveness of the conduct, oversight, and accountability of intelligence activities; to reduce duplication or overlap; and to improve the morale of the personnel of the foreign intelligence agencies;
(4) the conduct of covert and clandestine activities and the procedures by which Congress is informed of such activities;
(5) the desirability of changing any law, Senate rule or procedure, or any Executive order, rule, or regulation to improve the protection of intelligence secrets and provide for disclosure of information for which there is no compelling reason for secrecy;
(6) the desirability of establishing a standing committee of the Senate on intelligence activities;
(7) the desirability of establishing a joint committee of the Senate and the House of Representatives on intelligence activities in lieu of having separate committees in each House of Congress, or of establishing procedures under which separate committees on intelligence activities of the two Houses of Congress would receive joint briefings from the intelligence agencies and coordinate their policies with respect to the safeguarding of sensitive intelligence information;
(8) the authorization of funds for the intelligence activities of the Government and whether disclosure of any of the amounts of such funds is in the public interest; and
(9) the development of a uniform set of definitions for terms to be used in policies or guidelines which may be adopted by the executive or legislative branches to govern, clarify, and strengthen the operation of intelligence activities.

Jurisdiction, 1992

From Authority and Rules of Senate Committees, Senate Document 102-6, printed under the authority of Senate Resolution 58 (102-1), agreed to March 13, 1991:

[Section 3.(a)]

There shall be referred to the select committee all proposed legislation, messages, petitions, memorials, and other matters relating to the following:

(1) the Central Intelligence Agency and the Director of Central Intelligence.
(2) Intelligence activities of all other departments and agencies of the government, including, but not limited to, the intelligence activities of the Defense Intelligence Agency, the National Security Agency, and other agencies of the Department of Defense; the Department of State; the Department of Justice; and the Department of the Treasury.
(3) The organization or reorganization of any department or agency of the Government to the extent that the organization or reorganization relates to a function or activity involving intelligence activities.
(4) Authorizations for appropriations, both direct and indirect, for the following:
  (A) The Central Intelligence Agency and Director of Central Intelligence.
  (B) The Defense Intelligence Agency.
  (C) The National Security Agency.
  (D) The intelligence activities of other agencies and subdivisions of the Department of Defense.
  (E) The intelligence activities of the Department of State.
  (F) The intelligence activities of the Federal Bureau of Investigation, including all activities of the Intelligence Division.
  (G) Any department, agency, or subdivision which is the successor to any agency named in clause (A).(B), or (C); and the activities of any department, agency, or subdivision which is the successor to any department, agency, bureau, or subdivision named in clause (D), (E), or (F) to the extent that the activities of such successor department, agency, or subdivision are activities described in clause (D), (E), or (F).

SENATE SELECT COMMITTEE: INTELLIGENCE (Permanent) / 94th Congress

Service Dates of Committee Chair: May 20,1976-Continued
Service Dates of Majority Members: May 20,1976-Continued
Service Dates of Minority Members: May 20,1976-Continued

Majority

Rank Name	Party	State	Years in: Senate	Years in: Comm.
Chr Inouye, Daniel K.	Dem	Hai.	14	1
2nd Bayh, Birch E.	Dem	Ind.	14	1
3rd Stevenson, Adlai E. III	Dem	Ill.	6	1
4th Hathaway, William D.	Dem	Me.	4	1
5th Huddleston, Walter D.	Dem	Ky.	4	1
6th Biden, Joseph R. Jr.	Dem	Del.	4	1
7th Morgan, Robert B.	Dem	N.C.	2	1
8th Hart, Gary W.	Dem	Colo.	2	1

Minority

Rank Name	Party	State	Years in: Senate	Years in: Comm.
VCh Case, Clifford P.	Rep	N.J.	22	1
2nd Thurmond, J. Strom	Rep	S.C.	20	1
3rd Baker, Howard H. Jr.	Rep	Tenn.	10	1
4th Hatfield, Mark O.	Rep	Ore.	10	1
5th Goldwater, Barry M.	Rep	Ariz.	20	1
6th Stafford, Robert T.	Rep	Vt.	5	1
7th Garn, Jake	Rep	Utah	2	1

Note: The Majority and Minority Leaders of the Senate are *ex officio* members of the committee, but do no vote and are not counted for purposes of determining a quorum.

Departures from Committee:	Majority	Minority	State	Party
Became Senate Minority Leader; Moved to Foreign Relations; Rules	None	Baker, Howard H. Jr.	Tenn.	Rep
Became Ranking Minority Member of Judiciary	None	Thurmond, J. Strom	S.C.	Rep
No new assignment	None	Hatfield, Mark O.	Ore.	Rep
		Stafford, Robert T.	Vt.	Rep

SENATE SELECT COMMITTEE: INTELLIGENCE (Permanent) / 95th Congress

Service Dates of Committee Chair: Ch1 Jan. 3,1977-Jan. 27,1978
Ch2 Jan. 27,1978-Continued
Service Dates of Majority Members: Jan. 3,1977-Continued
Service Dates of Minority Members: Jan. 3,1977-Continued

Majority

Rank	Name	Party	State	Years in: Senate	Years in: Comm.
Ch1	Inouye, Daniel K.	Dem	Hai.	15	1
Ch2	Bayh, Birch E.	Dem	Ind.	15	1
3rd	Stevenson, Adlai E. III	Dem	Ill.	7	1
4th	Hathaway, William D.	Dem	Me.	5	1
5th	Huddleston, Walter D.	Dem	Ky.	5	1
6th	Biden, Joseph R. Jr.	Dem	Del.	5	1
7th	Morgan, Robert B.	Dem	N.C.	3	1
8th	Hart, Gary W.	Dem	Colo.	3	1
9th	Moynihan, Daniel Patrick	Dem	N.Y.	1	1

Minority

Rank	Name	Party	State	Years in: Senate	Years in: Comm.
VCh	Goldwater, Barry M.	Rep	Ariz.	21	1
2nd	Case, Clifford P.	Rep	N.J.	23	1
3rd	Garn, Jake	Rep	Utah	3	1
4th	Mathias, Charles McC. Jr.	Rep	Md.	9	*1 1
5th	Pearson, James B.	Rep	Kans.	15	1
6th	Chafee, John H.	Rep	R.I.	1	1
7th	Lugar, Richard G.	Rep	Ind.	1	1
8th	Wallop, Malcolm	Rep	Wyo.	1	1

*1: Member's 1st period of service on the committee.

Notes: Daniel Patrick Moynihan (Dem-N.Y.) was appointed to the committee on Feb. 11,1977 "as an at-large member...for a term expiring at the end of the 97th Congress." The Majority and Minority Leaders of the Senate are *ex officio* members of the committee, but do no vote and are not counted for purposes of determining a quorum.

Vacancies Filled:
Majority: 9th seat by Moynihan on Feb. 11,1977.
Minority: 4th seat by Mathias on Jan. 14,1977; 5th through 7th seats on Feb. 21,1977, 8th seat by Wallop on Feb. 24,1977.

Changes:
Chair:

Ch1 Inouye, Daniel K.	Dem	Hai.	Jan. 27,1978	Resigned as Chair, remained on committee in ranked 9th.
Ch2 Bayh, Birch E.	Dem	Ind.	Jan. 27,1978	Won caucus election; succeeded Inouye as Chair.

Minority:

Pearson, James B.	Rep	Kans.	Dec. 23,1978	Resigned and retired.

	Majority			Minority		
Departures from the Senate:						
Defeated for Reelection	Hathaway, William D.	Me.	Dem	None		
Defeated for Renomination	None			Case, Clifford P.	N.J.	Rep
Departures from Committee:						
Moved to Budget	Hart, Gary W.	Colo.	Dem	None		
No new assignment	Morgan, Robert B.	N.C.	Dem	Mathias, Charles McC. Jr.	Md.	Rep

SENATE SELECT COMMITTEE: INTELLIGENCE (Permanent) / 96th Congress

Service Dates of Committee Chair: Jan. 23,1979-Jan. 3,1981
Service Dates of Majority Members: Jan. 23,1979-Jan. 6,1981
Service Dates of Minority Members: Jan. 23,1979-Continued

Majority

Rank	Name	Party	State	Years in: Senate	Years in: Comm.
Chr	Bayh, Birch E.	Dem	Ind.	17	3
2nd	Stevenson, Adlai E. III	Dem	Ill.	9	3
3rd	Huddleston, Walter D.	Dem	Ky.	7	3
4th	Biden, Joseph R. Jr.	Dem	Del.	7	3
5th	Moynihan, Daniel Patrick	Dem	N.Y.	3	3
6th	Inouye, Daniel K.	Dem	Hai.	17	3
7th	Jackson, Henry M.	Dem	Wash.	27	1

Minority

Rank	Name	Party	State	Years in: Senate	Years in: Comm.
VCh	Goldwater, Barry M.	Rep	Ariz.	23	3
2nd	Garn, Jake	Rep	Utah	5	3
3rd	Chafee, John H.	Rep	R.I.	3	3
4th	Lugar, Richard G.	Rep	Ind.	3	3
5th	Wallop, Malcolm	Rep	Wyo.	3	3
6th	Durenberger, David F.	Rep	Minn.	1	1

*2: Member's 2nd period of service on the committee.

Notes: "Service Dates" of majority and minority members reflect the dates of service of Jackson and Durenberger; all other members continued service from the previous Congress without official reassignment recorded in the Congressional Record. Senate Resolution 176 (96-1), agreed to on June 6,1979, changed the size and party ratio on this committee to 8 Democrats and 7 Republicans. The Majority and Minority Leaders of the Senate are *ex officio* members of the committee, but do no vote and are not counted for purposes of determining a quorum.

Additions:

Majority:	8th Leahy, Patrick J.	Dem	Vt.	June 6,1979	
Minority:	7th Mathias, Charles McC. Jr.	Rep	Md.	June 6,1979	(ranked 3rd minority)

Departures from the Senate:	**Majority**			**Minority**		
Defeated for Reelection	Bayh, Birch E.	Ind.	Dem	None		
Retired	Stevenson, Adlai E. III	Ill.	Dem	None		
Departures from Committee:						
Moved to Foreign Relations; Rules	None			Mathias, Charles McC. Jr.	Md.	Rep

SENATE SELECT COMMITTEE: INTELLIGENCE (Permanent) / 97th Congress

Service Dates of Committee Chair: Jan. 6,1981-Continued
Service Dates of Majority Members: Jan. 6,1981-Continued
Service Dates of Minority Members: Jan. 3,1981-Continued

Majority

Rank Name	Party	State	Years in: Senate	Years in: Comm.
Chr Goldwater, Barry M.	Rep	Ariz.	25	5
2nd Garn, Jake	Rep	Utah	7	5
3rd Chafee, John H.	Rep	R.I.	5	4
4th Lugar, Richard G.	Rep	Ind.	5	4
5th Wallop, Malcolm	Rep	Wyo.	5	4
6th Durenberger, David F.	Rep	Minn.	3	2
7th Roth, William V. Jr.	Rep	Del.	11	1
8th Schmitt, Harrison H.	Rep	N.M.	5	1

Minority

Rank Name	Party	State	Years in: Senate	Years in: Comm.
VCh Moynihan, Daniel Patrick	Dem	N.Y.	5	4
2nd Huddleston, Walter D.	Dem	Ky.	9	5
3rd Biden, Joseph R. Jr.	Dem	Del.	9	5
4th Inouye, Daniel K.	Dem	Hai.	19	5
5th Jackson, Henry M.	Dem	Wash.	29	2
6th Leahy, Patrick J.	Dem	Vt.	7	2
7th Bentsen, Lloyd M. Jr.	Dem	Tex.	11	1

Notes: On Jan. 22,1981 it was announced that the President pro tempore had appointed Lloyd M. Bentsen Jr. (Dem-Tex) to the committee for a term expiring at the end of the 97th Congress; Walter D. Huddleston (Dem-Ky.) and Joseph Biden (Dem-Del.) were appointed to the committee for terms expiring at the end of the 1st session of the 98th Congress. The Majority and Minority Leaders of the Senate are *ex officio* members of the committee, but do no vote and are not counted for purposes of determining a quorum.

Vacancy Filled:
Minority: 7th seat by Bentsen on Jan. 22,1981 for term expiring at end of the 97th Congress.

Departures from the Senate:	**Majority**			**Minority**
Defeated for Reelection	Schmitt, Harrison H.	N.M.	Rep	None

SENATE SELECT COMMITTEE: INTELLIGENCE (Permanent) / 98th Congress

Service Dates of Committee Chair: Jan. 3,1983-Jan. 3,1985
Service Dates of Majority Members: Jan. 3,1983-Jan. 3,1985
Service Dates of Minority Members: Jan. 3,1983-Jan. 3,1985

Majority

Rank	Name	Party	State	Years in: Senate	Years in: Comm.
Chr	Goldwater, Barry M.	Rep	Ariz.	27	7
2nd	Garn, Jake	Rep	Utah	9	7
3rd	Chafee, John H.	Rep	R.I.	7	6
4th	Lugar, Richard G.	Rep	Ind.	7	6
5th	Wallop, Malcolm	Rep	Wyo.	7	6
6th	Durenberger, David F.	Rep	Minn.	5	4
7th	Roth, William V. Jr.	Rep	Del.	13	2
8th	Cohen, William S.	Rep	Me.	5	1

Minority

Rank	Name	Party	State	Years in: Senate	Years in: Comm.
VCh	Moynihan, Daniel Patrick	Dem	N.Y.	7	6
2nd	Huddleston, Walter D.	Dem	Ky.	11	7
3rd	Biden, Joseph R. Jr.	Dem	Del.	11	*2 7
4th	Inouye, Daniel K.	Dem	Hai.	21	7
5th	Jackson, Henry M.	Dem	Wash.	31	4
6th	Leahy, Patrick J.	Dem	Vt.	9	4
7th	Bentsen, Lloyd M. Jr.	Dem	Tex.	13	2

*2: Member's 2nd period of service on the committee.

Notes: On Jan. 3,1993 it was announced that the President pro tempore had appointed Daniel Patrick Moynihan (Dem-N.Y.), Daniel K. Inouye (Dem-Hai.), and Lloyd M. Bentsen Jr. (Dem-Tex.) to the committee for terms expiring at the end of the 98th Congress; Henry M. Jackson (Dem-Wash.) and Patrick J. Leahy (Dem-Vt.) were appointed to the committee for terms expiring at the end of the 99th Congress. On Jan. 23,1984, Walter D. Huddleston (Dem-Ky.) and Joseph R. Biden (Dem-Del.), whose terms were to expire at the end of the 1st session of the 98th Congress, were reappointed to the committee for the remainder of the Congress. The Majority and Minority Leaders of the Senate are *ex officio* members of the committee, but do no vote and are not counted for purposes of determining a quorum.

Changes:

Minority:

Name	Party	State	Date	Change
Jackson, Henry M.	Dem	Wash.	Sep. 1,1983	Died in office.
Nunn, Samuel A.	Dem	Ga.	Sep. 12,1983	Replaced Jackson.

	Majority			Minority		
Departures from the Senate:						
Defeated for Reelection	None			Huddleston, Walter D.	Ky.	Dem
Departures from Committee:						
Moved to Rules	Garn, Jake	Utah	Rep	None		
Moved to Labor & Human Resources	Wallop, Malcolm	Wyo.	Rep	None		
No new assignment	Chafee, John H.	R.I.	Rep	Biden, Joseph R. Jr.	Del.	Dem
	Goldwater, Barry M.	Ariz.	Rep	Moynihan, Daniel Patrick	N.Y.	Dem
	Lugar, Richard G.	Ind.	Rep	Inouye, Daniel K.	Hai.	Dem

SENATE SELECT COMMITTEE: INTELLIGENCE (Permanent) / 99th Congress

Service Dates of Committee Chair: Jan. 3,1985-Jan. 3,1987
Service Dates of Majority Members: Jan. 3,1985-Jan. 12,1987
Service Dates of Minority Members: Jan. 3,1985-Jan. 12,1987

Majority

Rank	Name	Party	State	Years in: Senate	Years in: Comm.
Chr	Durenberger, David F.	Rep	Minn.	7	6
2nd	Roth, William V. Jr.	Rep	Del.	15	4
3rd	Cohen, William S.	Rep	Me.	7	3
4th	Hatch, Orrin G.	Rep	Utah	9	1
5th	Murkowski, Frank H.	Rep	Alas.	5	1
6th	Specter, Arlen	Rep	Penn.	5	1
7th	Hecht, Chic	Rep	Nev.	3	1
8th	McConnell, Mitch	Rep	Ky.	1	1

Minority

Rank	Name	Party	State	Years in: Senate	Years in: Comm.
VCh	Leahy, Patrick J.	Dem	Vt.	11	6
2nd	Bentsen, Lloyd M. Jr.	Dem	Tex.	15	4
3rd	Nunn, Samuel A.	Dem	Ga.	13	2
4th	Eagleton, Thomas F.	Dem	Mo.	17	1
5th	Hollings, Ernest F.	Dem	S.C.	19	1
6th	Bradley, William W.	Dem	N.J.	7	1
7th	Boren, David L.	Dem	Okla.	7	1

Notes: The Majority and Minority Leaders of the Senate are *ex officio* members of the committee, but do no vote and are not counted for purposes of determining a quorum. On Jan. 3,1985, it was announced that the President pro tempore had appointed Thomas F. Eagleton (Dem-Mo.) for 2 years; Ernest F. Hollings (Dem-S.C.) for 4 years; William W. Bradley (Dem-N.J.) for 6 years and David L. Boren (Dem-Okla.) for 8 years.

	Majority			Minority		
Departures from the Senate:						
Retired	None			Eagleton, Thomas F.	Mo.	Dem
Departures from Committee:						
Moved to Special Aging	Durenberger, David F.	Minn.	Rep	None		
Moved to Foreign Relations	McConnell, Mitch	Ky.	Rep	None		

SENATE SELECT COMMITTEE: INTELLIGENCE (Permanent) / 100th Congress

Service Dates of Committee Chair: Jan. 12,1987-Feb. 2,1989
Service Dates of Majority Members: Jan. 12,1987-Feb. 2,1989
Service Dates of Minority Members: Jan. 12,1987-Feb. 2,1989

Majority

Rank	Name	Party	State	Years in: Senate	Years in: Comm.
Chr	Boren, David L.	Dem	Okla.	9	3
2nd	Leahy, Patrick J.	Dem	Vt.	13	8
3rd	Bentsen, Lloyd M. Jr.	Dem	Tex.	17	6
4th	Nunn, Samuel A.	Dem	Ga.	15	4
5th	Hollings, Ernest F.	Dem	S.C.	21	3
6th	Bradley, William W.	Dem	N.J.	9	3
7th	DeConcini, Dennis	Dem	Ariz.	11	1
8th	Cranston, Alan	Dem	Cal.	19	1

Minority

Rank	Name	Party	State	Years in: Senate	Years in: Comm.
VCh	Cohen, William S.	Rep	Me.	9	5
2nd	Roth, William V. Jr.	Rep	Del.	17	7
3rd	Hatch, Orrin G.	Rep	Utah	11	3
4th	Murkowski, Frank H.	Rep	Alas.	7	3
5th	Specter, Arlen	Rep	Penn.	7	3
6th	Hecht, Chic	Rep	Nev.	5	3
7th	Warner, John W.	Rep	Va.	9	*2 1

*2: Member's 2nd period of service on the committee.

Note: The Majority and Minority Leaders of the Senate are *ex officio* members of the committee, but do no vote and are not counted for purposes of determining a quorum.

Changes:

Majority:

Leahy, Patrick J.	Dem	Vt.	Feb. 17,1987	Left committee; no new assignment.
Metzenbaum, Howard M.	Dem	Ohio	Feb. 17,1987	Replaced Leahy.

	Majority			Minority		
Departures from the Senate:						
Defeated for Reelection	None			Hecht, Chic	Nev.	Rep
Departures from Committee:						
Moved to Banking, Housing & Urban Affairs	None			Roth, William V. Jr.	Del.	Rep
No new assignment	Bentsen, Lloyd M. Jr.	Tex.	Dem	None		

SENATE SELECT COMMITTEE: INTELLIGENCE (Permanent) / 101st Congress

Service Dates of Committee Chair: Feb. 2,1989-Feb. 5,1991
Service Dates of Majority Members: Feb. 2,1989-Feb. 5,1991
Service Dates of Minority Members: Feb. 2,1989-Feb. 5,1991

Majority

Rank	Name	Party	State	Years in: Senate	Years in: Comm.
Chr	Boren, David L.	Dem	Okla.	11	5
2nd	Nunn, Samuel A.	Dem	Ga.	17	6
3rd	Hollings, Ernest F.	Dem	S.C.	23	5
4th	Bradley, William W.	Dem	N.J.	11	5
5th	DeConcini, Dennis	Dem	Ariz.	13	3
6th	Cranston, Alan	Dem	Cal.	21	3
7th	Metzenbaum, Howard M.	Dem	Ohio	13	2
8th	Glenn, John H. Jr.	Dem	Ohio	15	1

Minority

Rank	Name	Party	State	Years in: Senate	Years in: Comm.
VCh	Cohen, William S.	Rep	Me.	11	7
2nd	Hatch, Orrin G.	Rep	Utah	13	5
3rd	Murkowski, Frank H.	Rep	Alas.	9	5
4th	Specter, Arlen	Rep	Penn.	9	5
5th	Warner, John W.	Rep	Va.	11	*2 3
6th	D'Amato, Alfonse M.	Rep	N.Y.	9	1
7th	Danforth, John C.	Rep	Mo.	13	1

*2: Member's 2nd period of service on the committee.

Note: The Majority and Minority Leaders of the Senate are *ex officio* members of the committee, but do no vote and are not counted for purposes of determining a quorum.

Departures from Committee:	Majority	Minority		
Moved to Foreign Relations	None	Hatch, Orrin G.	Utah	Rep
Became Ranking Minority Member, Veterans' Affairs	None	Specter, Arlen	Penn.	Rep
No new assignment	None	Cohen, William S.	Me.	Rep

SENATE SELECT COMMITTEE: INTELLIGENCE (Permanent) / 102nd Congress

Service Dates of Committee Chair: Feb. 5,1991-Jan. 3,1993
Service Dates of Majority Members: Feb. 5,1991-Jan. 3,1993
Service Dates of Minority Members: Feb. 5,1991-Jan. 3,1993

Majority

Rank	Name	Party	State	Years in: Senate	Years in: Comm.
Chr	Boren, David L.	Dem	Okla.	13	7
2nd	Nunn, Samuel A.	Dem	Ga.	19	8
3rd	Hollings, Ernest F.	Dem	S.C.	25	7
4th	Bradley, William W.	Dem	N.J.	13	7
5th	DeConcini, Dennis	Dem	Ariz.	15	5
6th	Cranston, Alan	Dem	Cal.	23	5
7th	Metzenbaum, Howard M.	Dem	Ohio	15	4
8th	Glenn, John H. Jr.	Dem	Ohio	17	3

Minority

Rank	Name	Party	State	Years in: Senate	Years in: Comm.
VCh	Murkowski, Frank H.	Rep	Alas.	11	7
2nd	Warner, John W.	Rep	Va.	13	*2 5
3rd	D'Amato, Alfonse M.	Rep	N.Y.	11	3
4th	Danforth, John C.	Rep	Mo.	15	3
5th	Rudman, Warren B.	Rep	N.H.	11	1
6th	Gorton, Slade	Rep	Wash.	3	1
7th	Chafee, John H.	Rep	R.I.	15	1

*2: Member's 2nd period of service on the committee.

Note: The Majority and Minority Leaders of the Senate are *ex officio* members of the committee, but do no vote and are not counted for purposes of determining a quorum.

Changes:
Majority:

Nunn, Samuel A.	Dem	Ga.	Jan. 23,1992	Left committee; no new assignment.
Kerrey, Bob	Dem	Neb.	Jan. 23,1992	Replaced Nunn.

SENATE TEMPORARY SELECT COMMITTEE: STUDY THE SENATE COMMITTEE SYSTEM I (Stevenson)

Jurisdiction, 1976

From Senate Resolution 109, 94th Congress, Second Session, March 31, 1976:

[Section 2]

It shall be the function of the select committee to conduct a thorough study of the Senate committee system, the structure, jurisdiction, number, and optimum size of Senate committees, the number of subcommittees, committee rules and procedures, media coverage of meetings, staffing, and other committee facilities, and to make recommendations which promote optimum utilization of Senators' time, optimum effectiveness of committees in the creation and oversight of Federal programs, clear and consistent procedures for the referral of legislation falling within the jurisdiction of two or more committees, and workable methods for the regular review and revision of committee jurisdictions.

Termination, 1977

The Select Committee filed its final report, Senate Report 1395 (94-2) on November 15, 1976 and submitted its recommendations to the full Senate on March 1, 1977, at which time the Select Committee was terminated.

SENATE TEMPORARY SELECT COMMITTEE: STUDY THE SENATE COMMITTEE SYSTEM I (Stevenson) / 94th Congress

Service Dates of Committee Chair: Apr. 1,1976-Mar. 1,1977
Service Dates of Majority Members: Apr. 1,1976-Mar. 1,1977
Service Dates of Minority Members: Apr. 6,1976-Mar. 1,1977

Majority

Rank	Name	Party	State	Years in: Senate	Years in: Comm.
Chr	Stevenson, Adlai E. III	Dem	Ill.	6	1
2nd	Nelson, Gaylord A.	Dem	Wisc.	14	1
3rd	Metcalf, Lee	Dem	Mont.	16	1
4th	Bentsen, Lloyd M. Jr.	Dem	Tex.	6	1
5th	Chiles, Lawton M. Jr.	Dem	Fla.	6	1
6th	Nunn, Samuel A.	Dem	Ga.	4	1

Minority

Rank	Name	Party	State	Years in: Senate	Years in: Comm.
CoCh	Brock, William E. III	Rep	Tenn.	6	1
2nd	Hansen, Clifford P.	Rep	Wyo.	10	1
3rd	Goldwater, Barry M.	Rep	Ariz.	20	1
4th	Packwood, Robert W.	Rep	Ore.	8	1
5th	Domenici, Pete V.	Rep	N.M.	4	1
6th	Helms, Jesse A.	Rep	N.C.	4	1

Changes:

Majority:

Nunn, Samuel A.	Dem	Ga.	Apr. 12,1976	Left committee; no new assignment.
Moss, Frank E.	Dem	Utah	Apr. 12,1976	Replaced Nunn.

SENATE SPECIAL COMMITTEE: OFFICIAL CONDUCT

Jurisdiction, 1977

From Senate Resolution 36, 95th Congress, First Session, January 18, 1977:

[Section 2.(a)]

It shall be the function and duty of the special committee to conduct a complete study of all matters relating to standards of conduct of Members, officers, and employees of the Senate in the performance of their official duties, and to recommend to the Senate a Code of Official Conduct for Members, officers, and employees of the Senate. Such study and recommended Code of Official Conduct shall include, but not be limited to, standards for:

(1) annual public disclosure of income, assets, debts, gifts, and other financial items.
(2) restrictions on, or the elimination of outside income from honoraria, legal fees, gifts, and other sources of financial or in-kind remuneration,
(3) conflicts of interest arising out of investments in securities, commodities, real estate, or other sources,
(4) office accounts, and excess campaign contributions,
(5) Senate travel,
(6) engaging in business or professional activities or employment, or other remunerative activities, so as to avoid any conflict with the conscientious performance of official duties.

Termination, 1977

The Special Committee was terminated upon filing its final report, Senate Report 49 (95-1) and reporting Senate Resolution 110 on March 10, 1977.

SENATE SPECIAL COMMITTEE: OFFICIAL CONDUCT / 95th Congress

Service Dates of Committee Chair: Jan. 19,1977-Mar. 10,1977
Service Dates of Majority Members: Jan. 19,1977-Mar. 10,1977
Service Dates of Minority Members: Jan. 19,1977-Mar. 10,1977

Majority

Rank	Name	Party	State	Years in: Senate	Years in: Comm.
Chr	Nelson, Gaylord A.	Dem	Wisc.	15	1
2nd	Ribicoff, Abraham A.	Dem	Conn.	15	1
3rd	Inouye, Daniel K.	Dem	Hai.	15	1
4th	Eagleton, Thomas F.	Dem	Mo.	9	1
5th	Nunn, Samuel A.	Dem	Ga.	5	1
6th	Clark, Richard C.	Dem	Iowa	5	1
7th	Glenn, John H. Jr.	Dem	Ohio	3	1
8th	Melcher, John	Dem	Mont.	1	1

Minority

Rank	Name	Party	State	Years in: Senate	Years in: Comm.
CoCh	Thurmond, J. Strom	Rep	S.C.	22	1
2nd	Javits, Jacob K.	Rep	N.Y.	21	1
3rd	Griffin, Robert P.	Rep	Mich.	11	1
4th	Packwood, Robert W.	Rep	Ore.	9	1
5th	Stafford, Robert T.	Rep	Vt.	6	1
6th	Laxalt, Paul	Rep	Nev.	3	1
7th	Chafee, John H.	Rep	R.I.	1	1

SENATE SELECT COMMITTEE: INDIAN AFFAIRS

INDIAN AFFAIRS

Jurisdiction, 1977

From Senate Resolution 4, 95th Congress, First Session, February 4, 1977:

[Section 105.(b)(2)]

It shall be the duty of the select committee to conduct a study of any and all matters pertaining to problems and opportunities of Indians, including but not limited to, Indian land management and trust responsibilities, Indian education, health, special services, and loan programs, and Indian claims against the United States.

INDIAN AFFAIRS (Permanent)

Reorganization, 1984

The Select Committee was made a Permanent Select Committee by authority of Senate Resolution 127 (98-2) agreed to June 6, 1984.

Jurisdiction, 1992

From Authority and Rules of Senate Committees, Senate Document 102-6, printed under the authority of Senate Resolution 58 (102-1), agreed to March 13, 1991:

[Section 2]

It shall be the duty of the select committee to conduct a study of any and all matters pertaining to problems and opportunities of Indians, including but not limited to, Indian land management and trust responsibilities, Indian education, health, special services, and loan programs, and Indian claims against the United States.

SENATE SELECT COMMITTEE: INDIAN AFFAIRS / 95th Congress

Service Dates of Committee Chair: Feb. 11,1977-Jan. 3,1979
Service Dates of Majority Members: Feb. 11,1977-Jan. 23,1979
Service Dates of Minority Members: Feb. 24,1977-Jan. 23,1979

Majority

Rank Name	Party	State	Years in: Senate	Years in: Comm.
Chr Abourezk, James G.	Dem	S.D.	5	1
2nd Metzenbaum, Howard M.	Dem	Ohio	2	1
3rd Melcher, John	Dem	Mont.	1	1

Minority

Rank Name	Party	State	Years in: Senate	Years in: Comm.
RM Bartlett, Dewey F.	Rep	Okla.	5	1
2nd Hatfield, Mark O.	Rep	Ore.	11	1

	Majority			Minority		
Departures from the Senate:						
Retired	Abourezk, James G.	S.D.	Dem	Bartlett, Dewey F.	Okla.	Rep
Departures from Committee:						
Moved to Labor & Human Resources; Budget	Metzenbaum, Howard M.	Ohio	Dem	None		

SENATE SELECT COMMITTEE: INDIAN AFFAIRS / 96th Congress

Service Dates of Committee Chair: Jan. 23,1979-Jan. 19,1981
Service Dates of Majority Members: Jan. 23,1979-Jan. 19,1981
Service Dates of Minority Members: Jan. 23,1979-Jan. 21,1981

Majority

Rank	Name	Party	State	Years in: Senate	Years in: Comm.
Chr	Melcher, John	Dem	Mont.	3	2
2nd	Inouye, Daniel K.	Dem	Hai.	17	1
3rd	DeConcini, Dennis	Dem	Ariz.	3	1

Minority

Rank	Name	Party	State	Years in: Senate	Years in: Comm.
RM1	Armstrong, William L.	Rep	Colo.	1	1
RM2 2nd	Hatfield, Mark O.	Rep	Ore.	13	2

Changes:

Ranking Member:

RM1	Armstrong, William L.	Rep	Colo.	Feb. 6,1979	Left committee; no new assignment.
RM2	Hatfield, Mark O.	Rep	Ore.	Feb. 6,1979	Succeeded Armstrong as Ranking Minority Member.

Minority:

Armstrong, William L.	Rep	Colo.	Feb. 6,1979	Left committee; no new assignment.
Cohen, William S.	Rep	Me.	Feb. 6,1979	Replaced Armstrong.

Departures from Committee:

	Majority	Minority
No new assignment	None	Hatfield, Mark O. Ore. Rep

SENATE SELECT COMMITTEE: INDIAN AFFAIRS / 97th Congress

Service Dates of Committee Chair: Jan. 19,1981-Jan. 3,1983
Service Dates of Majority Members: Jan. 19,1981-Jan. 3,1983
Service Dates of Minority Members: Jan. 21,1981-Jan. 3,1983

Majority

Rank	Name	Party	State	Years in: Senate	Years in: Comm.
Chr	Cohen, William S.	Rep	Me.	3	2
2nd	Goldwater, Barry M.	Rep	Ariz.	25	1
3rd	Andrews, Mark	Rep	N.D.	1	1
4th	Gorton, Slade	Rep	Wash.	1	1

Minority

Rank	Name	Party	State	Years in: Senate	Years in: Comm.
RM	Melcher, John	Dem	Mont.	5	4
2nd	Inouye, Daniel K.	Dem	Hai.	19	2
3rd	DeConcini, Dennis	Dem	Ariz.	5	2

Departures from Committee:

	Majority	Minority
Moved to Select Intelligence	Cohen, William S. Me. Rep	None

SENATE SELECT COMMITTEE: INDIAN AFFAIRS / 98th Congress

* Became the Permanent Select Committee on INDIAN AFFAIRS on June 6, 1984.

Service Dates of Committee Chair: Jan. 3,1983-Mar. 5,1985
Service Dates of Majority Members: Jan. 3,1983-Mar. 5,1985
Service Dates of Minority Members: Jan. 3,1983-Mar. 5,1985

Majority

Rank	Name	Party	State	Years in: Senate	Years in: Comm.
Chr	Andrews, Mark	Rep	N.D.	3	2
2nd	Goldwater, Barry M.	Rep	Ariz.	27	2
3rd	Gorton, Slade	Rep	Wash.	3	2
4th	Murkowski, Frank H.	Rep	Alas.	3	1

Minority

Rank	Name	Party	State	Years in: Senate	Years in: Comm.
RM	Melcher, John	Dem	Mont.	7	6
2nd	Inouye, Daniel K.	Dem	Hai.	21	4
3rd	DeConcini, Dennis	Dem	Ariz.	7	4

SENATE SELECT COMMITTEE: INDIAN AFFAIRS (Permanent) / 99th Congress

Service Dates of Committee Chair: Mar. 5,1985-Jan. 3,1987
Service Dates of Majority Members: Mar. 5,1985-Jan. 6,1987
Service Dates of Minority Members: Mar. 5,1985-Jan. 6,1987

Majority

Rank	Name	Party	State	Years in: Senate	Years in: Comm.
Chr	Andrews, Mark	Rep	N.D.	5	5
2nd	Goldwater, Barry M.	Rep	Ariz.	29	5
3rd	Gorton, Slade	Rep	Wash.	5	5
4th	Murkowski, Frank H.	Rep	Alas.	5	3
5th	Abdnor, James	Rep	S.D.	5	1

Minority

Rank	Name	Party	State	Years in: Senate	Years in: Comm.
RM	Melcher, John	Dem	Mont.	9	9
2nd	Inouye, Daniel K.	Dem	Hai.	23	7
3rd	DeConcini, Dennis	Dem	Ariz.	9	7
4th	Burdick, Quentin N.	Dem	N.D.	25	1

Departures from the Senate:

	Majority		Minority
Defeated for Reelection	Abdnor, James	S.D. Rep	None
	Andrews, Mark	N.D. Rep	
	Gorton, Slade	Wash. Rep	
Retired	Goldwater, Barry M.	Ariz. Rep	None

SENATE SELECT COMMITTEE: INDIAN AFFAIRS (Permanent) / 100th Congress

Service Dates of Committee Chair: Jan. 6,1987-Feb. 2,1989
Service Dates of Majority Members: Jan. 6,1987-Feb. 2,1989
Service Dates of Minority Members: Jan. 6,1987-Feb. 2,1989

Majority

Rank	Name	Party	State	Years in: Senate	Years in: Comm.
Chr	Inouye, Daniel K.	Dem	Hai.	25	8
2nd	Melcher, John	Dem	Mont.	11	10
3rd	DeConcini, Dennis	Dem	Ariz.	11	8
4th	Burdick, Quentin N.	Dem	N.D.	27	2
5th	Daschle, Thomas A.	Dem	S.D.	1	1

Minority

Rank	Name	Party	State	Years in: Senate	Years in: Comm.
RM	Evans, Daniel J.	Rep	Wash.	4	1
2nd	Murkowski, Frank H.	Rep	Alas.	7	5
3rd	McCain, John	Rep	Ariz.	1	1

Departures from the Senate:

	Majority		Minority	
Defeated for Reelection	Melcher, John	Mont. Dem	None	
Retired	None		Evans, Daniel J.	Wash. Rep

SENATE SELECT COMMITTEE: INDIAN AFFAIRS (Permanent) / 101st Congress

Service Dates of Committee Chair: Feb. 2,1989-Feb. 5,1991
Service Dates of Majority Members: Feb. 2,1989-Feb. 5,1991
Service Dates of Minority Members: Feb. 2,1989-Feb. 5,1991

Majority

Rank	Name	Party	State	Years in: Senate	Years in: Comm.
Chr	Inouye, Daniel K.	Dem	Hai.	27	11
2nd	DeConcini, Dennis	Dem	Ariz.	13	11
3rd	Burdick, Quentin N.	Dem	N.D.	29	4
4th	Daschle, Thomas A.	Dem	S.D.	3	3
5th	Conrad, Kent	Dem	N.D.	3	1

Minority

Rank	Name	Party	State	Years in: Senate	Years in: Comm.
RM	McCain, John	Rep	Ariz.	3	3
2nd	Murkowski, Frank H.	Rep	Alas.	9	7
3rd	Cochran, Thad	Rep	Miss.	11	1

Note: The committee size and party ratio was changed to 6 Democrats and 4 Republicans on Apr. 11,1989.

Additions:

Majority:	6th	Reid, Harry M.	Dem	Nev.	Apr. 11,1989
Minority:	4th	Gorton, Slade	Rep	Wash.	Apr. 11,1989

SENATE SELECT COMMITTEE: INDIAN AFFAIRS (Permanent) / 102nd Congress

Service Dates of Committee Chair: Feb. 5,1991-Jan. 3,1993
Service Dates of Majority Members: Feb. 5,1991-Jan. 3,1993
Service Dates of Minority Members: Feb. 5,1991-Jan. 3,1993

Majority

Rank	Name	Party	State	Years in: Senate	Years in: Comm.
Chr	Inouye, Daniel K.	Dem	Hai.	29	13
2nd	DeConcini, Dennis	Dem	Ariz.	15	13
3rd	Burdick, Quentin N.	Dem	N.D.	31	6
4th	Daschle, Thomas A.	Dem	S.D.	5	5
5th	Conrad, Kent	Dem	N.D.	5	3
6th	Reid, Harry M.	Dem	Nev.	5	2
7th	Simon, Paul	Dem	Ill.	7	1
8th	Akaka, Daniel K.	Dem	Hai.	1	1
9th	Wellstone, Paul	DFL	Minn.	1	1

Minority

Rank	Name	Party	State	Years in: Senate	Years in: Comm.
RM	McCain, John	Rep	Ariz.	5	5
2nd	Murkowski, Frank H.	Rep	Alas.	11	9
3rd	Cochran, Thad	Rep	Miss.	13	3
4th	Gorton, Slade	Rep	Wash.	3	2
5th	Domenici, Pete V.	Rep	N.M.	19	1
6th	Kassebaum, Nancy Landon	Rep	Kans.	13	1
7th	Nickles, Don	Rep	Okla.	11	1

Changes:

Majority:

Burdick, Quentin N.	Dem	N.D.	Sep. 8,1992	Died in office.
Burdick, Jocelyn	Dem	N.D.	Sep. 18,1992	Replaced Quentin Burdick.

SENATE SPECIAL SUB-COMMITTEE: INVESTIGATION OF ACTIVITIES RELATING TO INDIVIDUALS REPRESENTING INTERESTS OF FOREIGN GOVERNMENTS

Jurisdiction, 1980

From a "unanimous consent agreement," 96th Congress, Second Session, July 24, 1980:

[Paragraph 1]

. . . for the purpose of conducting an investigation of activities relating to individuals representing the interests of foreign governments

Termination, 1980

The Special Sub-Committee was terminated upon the filing of its final report, Senate Report 1015 (96-2), on October 2, 1980.

Senate Special Sub-Committee: INVESTIGATION OF ACTIVITIES RELATING TO INDIVIDUALS REPRESENTING INTERESTS OF FOREIGN GOVERNMENTS / 96th Congress

Service Dates of Committee Chair: July 24,1980-Oct. 2,1980
Service Dates of Majority Members: July 25,1980-Oct. 2,1980
Service Dates of Minority Members: July 25,1980-Oct. 2,1980

Majority

Rank	Name	Party	State	Years in: Senate	Years in: Comm.
Chr	Bayh, Birch E.	Dem	Ind.	18	1
2nd	Pell, Claiborne D.	Dem	R.I.	20	1
3rd	DeConcini, Dennis	Dem	Ariz.	4	1
4th	Leahy, Patrick J.	Dem	Vt.	6	1
5th	Baucus, Max S.	Dem	Mont.	2	1

Minority

Rank	Name	Party	State	Years in: Senate	Years in: Comm.
VCh	Thurmond, J. Strom	Rep	S.C.	25	1
2nd	Mathias, Charles McC. Jr.	Rep	Md.	12	1
3rd	Dole, Robert J.	Rep	Kans.	12	1
4th	Lugar, Richard G.	Rep	Ind.	4	1

SENATE SELECT COMMITTEE: TO STUDY LAW ENFORCEMENT UNDERCOVER ACTIVITIES OF COMPONENTS OF THE DEPARTMENT OF JUSTICE

Jurisdiction, 1982

From Senate Resolution 350, 97th Congress, Second Session, March 14,1982:

[Section 2 a]

There is hereby established a select committee of the Senate...to conduct an investigation and study of activities of components of the Department of Justice in connection with their law enforcement undercover operations or of any persons acting individually or in combination with others, in connection with such operations, and to recommend such legislation as the select committee deems necessary or desirable.

Termination, 1983

The Select Committee was extended by Senate Resolution 517, 97th Congress, Second Session, agreed to December 15,1982, and terminated by its authority on January 15, 1983. The Select Committee filed its final report, Senate Report 682 (97-2), on December 15, 1982.

SENATE SELECT COMMITTEE: TO STUDY LAW ENFORCEMENT UNDERCOVER ACTIVITIES OF COMPONENTS OF THE DEPARTMENT OF JUSTICE / 97th Congress

Service Dates of Committee Chair: Mar. 29,1982-Jan. 15,1983
Service Dates of Majority Members: Mar. 29,1982-Jan. 15,1983
Service Dates of Minority Members: Mar. 29,1982-Jan. 15,1983

Majority

Rank Name	Party	State	Years in: Senate	Years in: Comm.
Chr Mathias, Charles McC. Jr.	Rep	Md.	14	1
2nd McClure, James A.	Rep	Ida.	10	1
3rd Simpson, Alan K.	Rep	Wyo.	4	1
4th Rudman, Warren B.	Rep	N.H.	2	1

Minority

Rank Name	Party	State	Years in: Senate	Years in: Comm.
VCh Huddleston, Walter D.	Dem	Ky.	10	1
2nd Inouye, Daniel K.	Dem	Hai.	20	1
3rd DeConcini, Dennis	Dem	Ariz.	6	1
4th Leahy, Patrick J.	Dem	Vt.	8	1

SENATE SPECIAL COMMITTEE: SECURITY AND COOPERATION IN EUROPE

Jurisdiction, 1983

From Senate Resolution 286, 98th Congress, First Session, November 18, 1983:

[Section 2c]

The Special Committee is authorized and directed to monitor the acts of the signatories which reflect compliance with or violation of the articles of the Final Act of the Conference on Security and Cooperation in Europe, with particular regard to the provisions relating to Cooperations in Humanitarian Fields. The Special Committee is further authorized and directed to monitor and encourage the development of programs and activities of the United States Government and private organizations with a view toward taking advantage of the provisions of the Final Act to expand East-West economic cooperation and a greater interchange of people and ideas between East and West.

Termination, 1985

The Special Committee was terminated by authority of Public Law 99-7, signed March 27, 1985.

SENATE SPECIAL COMMITTEE: SECURITY AND COOPERATION IN EUROPE / 98th Congress

Service Dates of Committee Chair: Nov. 18,1983-Mar. 27,1985
Service Dates of Majority Members: Nov. 18,1983-Mar. 27,1985
Service Dates of Minority Members: Jan. 31,1984-Mar. 27,1985

Majority

Rank Name	Party	State	Years in: Senate	Years in: Comm.
Chr Dole, Robert J.	Rep	Kans.	15	1
2nd Hatch, Orrin G.	Rep	Utah	7	1
3rd Heinz, H. John III	Rep	Penn.	7	1
4th D'Amato, Alfonse M.	Rep	N.Y.	3	1

Minority

Rank Name	Party	State	Years in: Senate	Years in: Comm.
CoCh DeConcini, Dennis	Dem	Ariz.	8	1
2nd Leahy, Patrick J.	Dem	Vt.	10	1
3rd Pell, Claiborne D.	Dem	R.I.	24	1

SENATE TEMPORARY SELECT COMMITTEE: STUDY THE SENATE COMMITTEE SYSTEM II (Quayle)

Jurisdiction, 1985

From Senate Resolution 127, 98th Congress, Second Session, June 6,1984:

[Section 3]

It shall be the function of the select committee to conduct a thorough study of the Senate committee system, the structure, jurisdiction, number, and optimum size of Senate committees, the number of subcommittees, committee rules and procedures, media coverage of meetings, staffing, and other committee facilities, and to make recommendations which promote optimum utilization of Senators' time, optimum effectiveness of committees in the creation and oversight of Federal programs, clear and consistent procedures for the referral of legislation falling within the jurisdiction of two or more committees, and workable methods of the regular review and revision of committee jurisdictions.

Termination, 1984

The Select Committee was terminated upon the filing of its final report, Senate Print 98-254 on December 14, 1984.

SENATE TEMPORARY SELECT COMMITTEE: STUDY THE SENATE COMMITTEE SYSTEM II (Quayle) / 98th Congress

Service Dates of Committee Chair: June 13,1984-Dec. 14,1984
Service Dates of Majority Members: June 13,1984-Dec. 14,1984
Service Dates of Minority Members: June 13,1984-Dec. 14,1984

Majority

Rank Name	Party	State	Years in: Senate	Years in: Comm.
Chr Quayle, J. Danforth	Rep	Ind.	4	1
2nd Mathias, Charles McC. Jr.	Rep	Md.	16	1
3rd Garn, Jake	Rep	Utah	10	1
4th Wallop, Malcolm	Rep	Wyo.	8	1
5th Kasten, Robert W. Jr.	Rep	Wisc.	4	1
6th Rudman, Warren B.	Rep	N.H.	4	1

Minority

Rank Name	Party	State	Years in: Senate	Years in: Comm.
RM Long, Russell B.	Dem	La.	36	1
2nd Melcher, John	Dem	Mont.	8	1
3rd Johnston, J. Bennett Jr.	Dem	La.	12	1
4th Ford, Wendell H.	Dem	Ky.	10	1
5th Matsunaga, Spark M.	Dem	Hai.	8	1
6th Dixon, Alan J.	Dem	Ill.	4	1

SENATE SPECIAL COMMITTEE: IMPEACHMENT TRIAL

Jurisdiction, 1986

From Rule XI of the Rules of Procedure and Practice in the Senate When Sitting on Impeachment Trials:

"That in the trial of any impeachment the Presiding Officer of the Senate, upon the order of the Senate, shall appoint a committee of twelve Senators to receive evidence and take testimony... the committee so appointed shall report to the Senate in writing a certified copy of the transcript of the proceedings and testimony had and given before such committee..."

Each of the authorizing resolutions cited below follow Rule XI as quoted above. Impeachment proceedings against Judge Harry E. Claiborne authorized by Senate Resolution 481 (99-2), August 14, 1986. Impeachment proceedings against Judge Alcee L. Hastings authorized by Senate Resolution 38 (101-1) March 16, 1989 (for membership roster, see page 321 of this Volume). Impeachment proceedings against Judge Walter L. Nixon, Jr. authorized by Senate Resolution 128, (101-1) May 11, 1989 (for membership roster, see page 321 of this Volume).

Termination, Claiborne

The Special Committee on the Impeachment Trial of Judge Harry E. Claiborne concluded its hearings on September 23, 1986. Transcripts are contained in Senate Hearing 99-812, Parts I-IV. A summary report is contained in Senate Report 99-511, filed October 1, 1986.

Termination, Hastings

The Special Committee on the Impeachment Trial of Judge Alcee L. Hastings concluded its hearings on August 3, 1989. Transcripts are contained in Senate Hearing 101-194, Parts 1-2A.

Termination, Nixon

The Special Committee on the Impeachment Trial of Judge Walter L. Nixon, Jr. concluded its hearings on September 13, 1989. Transcripts are contained in Senate Hearing 101-247, Parts 1-3.

SENATE SELECT COMMITTEE: IMPEACHMENT TRIAL OF JUDGE HARRY E. CLAIBORNE / 99th Congress

Service Dates of Committee Chair: Aug. 14,1986-Oct. 1,1986
Service Dates of Majority Members: Aug. 14,1986-Oct. 1,1986
Service Dates of Minority Members: Aug. 14,1986-Oct. 1,1986

Majority

Rank	Name	Party	State	Years in: Senate	Years in: Comm.
Chr	Mathias, Charles McC. Jr.	Rep	Md.	18	1
2nd	Hatch, Orrin G.	Rep	Utah	10	1
3rd	Warner, John W.	Rep	Va.	8	1
4th	Rudman, Warren B.	Rep	N.H.	6	1
5th	Pressler, Larry L.	Rep	S.D.	8	1
6th	McConnell, Mitch	Rep	Ky.	2	1

Minority

Rank	Name	Party	State	Years in: Senate	Years in: Comm.
VCh	Sarbanes, Paul S.	Dem	Md.	10	1
2nd	Heflin, Howell T.	Dem	Ala.	8	1
3rd	DeConcini, Dennis	Dem	Ariz.	10	1
4th	Pryor, David H.	Dem	Ark.	8	1
5th	Gore, Albert A. Jr.	Dem	Tenn.	2	1
6th	Bingaman, Jeff	Dem	N.M.	4	1

SENATE SELECT COMMITTEE: SECRET MILITARY ASSISTANCE TO IRAN AND THE NICARAGUAN OPPOSITION

Jurisdiction, 1987

From Senate Resolution 23, 100th Congress, First Session, January 6, 1987:

[Section 1.(b)]

The purpose of the select committee is--

(1) to conduct an investigation into, and study of, all matters which have any tendency to reveal the full facts about--

(A) any activity of--
- (i) the National Security Council or of any member or staff thereof.
- (ii) any other department, agency, or entity of the United States Government or of any officer or employee thereof.
- (iii) any foreign government, or of any agency or instrumentality thereof, or of any officer or employee thereof, or
- (iv) any other individual, group, corporation, entity, or organization, which relates to--
  - (I) the direct or indirect sale, shipment, or other provision of arms, or the direct or indirect provision of material, funds, or other assistance, to Iran,
  - (II) the use of the proceeds from any transaction described in subclause (I) to provide assistance to any faction or insurgency in Nicaragua or in any other foreign country, or to further any political purpose or activity within the United States, or to further any purpose of any nature whatsoever.
  - (III) the generation and use of any other money, item of value, or service to provide assistance to the Nicaraguan democratic resistance, or
  - (IV) the provision or coordination of support for persons or entities engaged as insurgents in armed conflict with Government of Nicaragua, in order to determine whether any such activity was illegal, improper, unauthorized or unethical;

(B) any other activity, circumstance, material, or transaction having a tendency to prove or disprove that any official of the United States Government, or any other person, acting either individually or in combination with others, engaged in any activity which was illegal, improper, unauthorized, or unethical, in connection with any activity described in subclause (I), (II), (III), or (IV) of clause (A) or in connection with the operations described in clause (C); and

(C) the suitability of the structure and operations of the National Security Council, and persons serving as staff, consultants, or agents thereto, for any function related to the formulation, implementation, or conduct of American national security policy; and

(2) (A) to make such findings of fact as are warranted and appropriate;
(B) to make such recommendations, including recommendations for new legislation and amendments to existing laws and any administrative or other actions, as the select committee may determine to be necessary and desirable; and
(C) to fulfil the Constitutional oversight and informing function of the Congress with respect to the matters described in this section.

Termination, 1987

The Select Committee was terminated upon the filing of its final report, Senate Report 216 (100-1), jointly with the House Select Committee to Investigate Covert Arms Transactions with Iran, on November 17, 1987.

SENATE SELECT COMMITTEE: SECRET MILITARY ASSISTANCE TO IRAN AND THE NICARAGUAN OPPOSITION / 100th Congress

Service Dates of Committee Chair: Jan. 12,1987-Nov. 17,1987
Service Dates of Majority Members: Jan. 12,1987-Nov. 17,1987
Service Dates of Minority Members: Jan. 12,1987-Nov. 17,1987

Majority

Rank Name	Party	State	Years in: Senate	Years in: Comm.
Chr Inouye, Daniel K.	Dem	Hai.	25	1
2nd Mitchell, George J.	Dem	Me.	7	1
3rd Nunn, Samuel A.	Dem	Ga.	15	1
4th Sarbanes, Paul S.	Dem	Md.	11	1
5th Heflin, Howell T.	Dem	Ala.	9	1
6th Boren, David L.	Dem	Okla.	9	1

Minority

Rank Name	Party	State	Years in: Senate	Years in: Comm.
VCh Rudman, Warren B.	Rep	N.H.	7	1
2nd McClure, James A.	Rep	Ida.	15	1
3rd Hatch, Orrin G.	Rep	Utah	11	1
4th Cohen, William S.	Rep	Me.	9	1
5th Trible, Paul S. Jr.	Rep	Va.	5	1

SENATE SPECIAL COMMITTEE: IMPEACHMENT TRIALS (Hastings and Nixon)

* **Jurisdictions** and **terminations** for these two Special Committees contained on page 319 of this Volume.

SENATE SPECIAL COMMITTEE: IMPEACHMENT TRIAL OF JUDGE ALCEE L. HASTINGS / 101st Congress

Service Dates of Committee Chair: Mar. 16,1989-Aug. 3,1989
Service Dates of Majority Members: Mar. 16,1989-Aug. 3,1989
Service Dates of Minority Members: Mar. 16,1989-Aug. 3,1989

Majority

Rank Name	Party	State	Years in: Senate	Years in: Comm.
Chr Bingaman, Jeff	Dem	N.M.	7	1
2nd Leahy, Patrick J.	Dem	Vt.	15	1
3rd Pryor, David H.	Dem	Ark.	11	1
4th Bryan, Richard H.	Dem	Nev.	1	1
5th Kerrey, Bob	Dem	Neb.	1	1
6th Lieberman, Joseph I.	Dem	Conn.	1	1

Minority

Rank Name	Party	State	Years in: Senate	Years in: Comm.
VCh Specter, Arlen	Rep	Penn.	9	1
2nd Durenberger, David F.	Rep	Minn.	11	1
3rd Rudman, Warren	Rep	N.H.	9	1
4th Bond, Christopher S.	Rep	Mo.	3	1
5th Gorton, Slade	Rep	Wash.	7	1
6th Burns, Conrad	Rep	Mont.	1	1

SENATE SPECIAL COMMITTEE: IMPEACHMENT TRIAL OF JUDGE WALTER L. NIXON, Jr. / 101st Congress

Service Dates of Committee Chair: May 11,1989-Sep. 13,1989
Service Dates of Majority Members: May 11,1989-Sep. 13,1989
Service Dates of Minority Members: May 11,1989-Sep. 13,1989

Majority

Rank Name	Party	State	Years in: Senate	Years in: Comm.
Chr Fowler, Wyche Jr.	Dem	Ga.	3	1
2nd Heflin, Howell T.	Dem	Ala.	11	1
3rd Wirth, Timothy E.	Dem	Colo.	3	1
4th Reid, Harry M.	Dem	Nev.	3	1
5th Robb, Charles S.	Dem	Va.	1	1
6th Kohl, Herbert	Dem	Wisc.	1	1

Minority

Rank Name	Party	State	Years in: Senate	Years in: Comm.
VCh Hatch, Orrin G.	Rep	Utah	13	1
2nd Danforth, John C.	Rep	Mo.	13	1
3rd Chafee, John H.	Rep	R.I.	13	1
4th Murkowski, Frank H.	Rep	Alas.	9	1
5th Jeffords, James M.	Rep	Vt.	1	1
6th Mack, Connie III	Rep	Fla.	1	1

SENATE SELECT COMMITTEE: POW/MIA AFFAIRS

Jurisdiction, 1991

Jurisdiction from Senate Resolution 82, 102nd Congress, First Session, August 2, 1991:

[Section 2]

All messages, petitions, memorials and other matters relating to United States personnel unaccounted for from military conflicts shall be referred to the select committee concurrently with referral to any other committee of the Senate with jurisdiction.

Termination, 1992

The Select Committee is to be terminated at the end of the 102nd Congress.

TEMPORARY SENATE SELECT COMMITTEE: POW/MIA AFFAIRS / 102nd Congress

Service Dates of Committee Chair: Aug. 2,1991-Jan. 3,1993
Service Dates of Majority Members: Aug. 2,1991-Jan. 3,1993
Service Dates of Minority Members: Aug. 2,1991-Jan. 3,1993

Majority

Rank	Name	Party	State	Years in: Senate	Years in: Comm.
Chr	Kerry, John F.	Dem	Mass.	7	1
2nd	Daschle, Thomas A.	Dem	S.D.	5	1
3rd	DeConcini, Dennis	Dem	Ariz.	15	1
4th	Kerrey, Bob	Dem	Neb.	3	1
5th	Reid, Harry M.	Dem	Nev.	5	1
6th	Robb, Charles S.	Dem	Va.	3	1

Minority

Rank	Name	Party	State	Years in: Senate	Years in: Comm.
VCh	Smith, Robert C.	Rep	N.H.	1	1
2nd	McCain, John	Rep	Ariz.	5	1
3rd	Brown, Hank	Rep	Colo.	1	1
4th	Grassley, Charles E.	Rep	Iowa	11	1
5th	Kassebaum, Nancy Landon	Rep	Kans.	13	1
6th	Helms, Jesse A.	Rep	N.C.	19	1

Notes: Robert Smith (Rep-N.H.) was designated Vice Chair of the committee on Sep. 17,1991. Other than the Chair of the committee, majority members were listed alphabetically.

Vacancy Filled:
Minority: 2nd seat by McCain on Sep. 17,1991.

Changes:
Majority:

DeConcini, Dennis	Dem	Ariz.	Oct. 30,1991	Left committee; no new assignment.
Kohl, Herbert	Dem	Wisc.	Oct. 30,1991	Replaced DeConcini.

PART III
Standing Committees
U.S. House of Representatives, 1947-1992

AGRICULTURE

Jurisdiction, 1947

Established by the Legislative Reorganization Act of 1946:

[Section 121.(1)(a)]

Committee on Agriculture.

1. Agriculture generally.
2. Inspection of livestock and meat products.
3. Animal industry and diseases of animals.
4. Adulteration of seeds, insect pests, and protection of birds and animals in forest reserves.
5. Agricultural colleges and experiment stations.
6. Forestry in general, and forest reserves other than those created from the public domain.
7. Agricultural economics and research.
8. Agricultural and industrial chemistry.
9. Dairy industry.
10. Entomology and plant quarantine.
11. Human nutrition and home economics.
12. Plant industry, soils, and agricultural engineering.
13. Agricultural educational extension services.
14. Extension of farm credit and farm security.
15. Rural electrification.
16. Agricultural production and marketing and stabilization of prices of agricultural products.
17. Crop insurance and soil conservation.

Jurisdiction, 1992

Jurisdiction contained in <u>Rules of the House of Representatives</u> (as revised to July 1, 1992):

[Rule X. 1. (a)]

Committee on Agriculture.

(1) Adulteration of seeds, insect pests, and protection of birds and animals in forest reserves.
(2) Agriculture generally.
(3) Agricultural and industrial chemistry.
(4) Agricultural colleges and experiment stations.
(5) Agricultural economics and research.
(6) Agricultural education extension services.
(7) Agricultural production and marketing and stabilization of prices of agricultural products, and commodities (not including distribution outside of the United States).
(8) Animal industry and diseases of animals.
(9) Crop insurance and soil conservation.
(10) Dairy industry.
(11) Entomology and plant quarantine.
(12) Extension of farm credit and farm security.
(13) Forestry in general, and forest reserves other than those created from the public domain.
(14) Human nutrition and home economics.
(15) Inspection of livestock and meat products.
(16) Plant industry, soils, and agricultural engineering.
(17) Rural electrification.
(18) Commodities exchanges.
(19) Rural development.

AGRICULTURE / 80th Congress

Service Dates of Committee Chair: Jan. 14,1947-Jan. 3,1949
Service Dates of Majority Members: Jan. 14,1947-Jan. 3,1949
Service Dates of Minority Members: Jan. 16,1947-Jan. 3,1949

Majority

Rank	Name	Party	State	Terms in: House	Terms in: Comm.
Chr	Hope, Clifford R.	Rep	Kans.	11	11
2nd	Andresen, August H.	Rep	Minn.	11	*2 7
3rd	Johnson, Anton J.	Rep	Ill.	5	5
4th	Murray, Reid F.	Rep	Wisc.	5	5
5th	Clevenger, Cliff	Rep	Ohio	5	5
6th	Gillie, George W.	Rep	Ind.	5	4
7th	Hall, Edwin Arthur	Rep	N.Y.	5	4
8th	Hill, William S.	Rep	Colo.	4	3
9th	Hoeven, Charles B.	Rep	Iowa	3	2
10th	Simpson, Sidney E.	Rep	Ill.	3	1
11th	Gross, Chester H.	Rep	Penn.	4	1
12th	Fuller, Hadwen C.	Rep	N.Y.	3	1
13th	Bramblett, Ernest K.	Rep	Cal.	1	1
14th	Dague, Paul B.	Rep	Penn.	1	1
15th	Goff, Abe McGregor	Rep	Ida.	1	1
16th	Cotton, Norris	Rep	N.H.	1	1
Del.	Farrington, Joseph R.	Rep.	Hai.	3	3

Minority

Rank	Name	Party	State	Terms in: House	Terms in: Comm.
RM	Flannagan, John W. Jr.	Dem	Va.	9	9
2nd	Cooley, Harold D.	Dem	N.C.	8	7
3rd	Zimmerman, Orville	Dem	Mo.	7	5
4th	Pace, Stephen	Dem	Ga.	6	5
5th	Poage, William R.	Dem	Tex.	6	4
6th	Grant, George M.	Dem	Ala.	6	4
7th	Granger, Walter K.	Dem	Utah	4	3
8th	Gathings, Ezekiel C.	Dem	Ark.	5	3
9th	McMillan, John L.	Dem	S.C.	5	3
10th	Worley, Eugene	Dem	Tex.	4	2
11th	Abernethy, Thomas G.	Dem	Miss.	3	2
Del.	Bartlett, E. L. (Bob)	Dem	Alas.	2	1
RsC.	Fernos-Isern, Antonio	PpD	P.R.	2	1

*2: Member's 2nd period of service on the committee.

Note: Territorial Delegates Joseph Farrington (Rep-Hai.) and E.L. (Bob) Bartlett (Dem-Alas.) and Antonio Fernos-Isern (Popular Democrat-P.R.), the Resident Commissioner for Puerto-Rico were not allowed to accrue seniority nor were they included in the committee's party ratio.

Changes:

Majority:

Name	Party	State	Date	Change
Clevenger, Cliff	Rep	Ohio	July 23,1947	Moved to Appropriations.
Arnold, Samuel W.	Rep	Mo.	July 23,1947	Replaced Clevenger.

Minority:

Name	Party	State	Date	Change
Zimmerman, Orville	Dem	Mo.	Apr. 7,1948	Died in office.
Peden, Preston E.	Dem	Okla.	May 12,1948	Replaced Zimmerman.
Peden, Preston E.	Dem	Okla.	Aug. 7,1948	Left committee; defeated for renomination.
Albert, Carl	Dem	Okla.	Aug. 7,1948	Replaced Peden.

Departures from the House:

	Majority			Minority		
Elected Mayor of Macomb	Johnson, Anton J.	Ill.	Rep	None		
Defeated for Reelection	Fuller, Hadwen C.	N.Y.	Rep	None		
	Gillie, George W.	Ind.	Rep			
	Goff, Abe McGregor	Ida.	Rep			
	Gross, Chester H.	Penn.	Rep			
	Arnold, Samuel W.	Mo.	Rep	None		
Retired	None			Flannagan, John W. Jr.	Va.	Dem

AGRICULTURE / 81st Congress

Service Dates of Committee Chair: Jan. 18,1949-Jan. 3,1951
Service Dates of Majority Members: Jan. 18,1949-Jan. 3,1951
Service Dates of Minority Members: Jan. 18,1949-Jan. 3,1951

Majority

Rank	Name	Party	State	Terms in: House	Terms in: Comm.
Chr	Cooley, Harold D.	Dem	N.C.	9	8
2nd	Pace, Stephen	Dem	Ga.	7	6
3rd	Poage, William R.	Dem	Tex.	7	5
4th	Grant, George M.	Dem	Ala.	7	5
5th	Granger, Walter K.	Dem	Utah	5	4
6th	Gathings, Ezekiel C.	Dem	Ark.	6	4
7th	McMillan, John L.	Dem	S.C.	6	4
8th	Worley, Eugene	Dem	Tex.	5	3
9th	Abernethy, Thomas G.	Dem	Miss.	4	3
10th	Albert, Carl	Dem	Okla.	2	2
11th	Abbitt, Watkins M.	Dem	Va.	2	1
12th	Polk, James G.	Dem	Ohio	6	*2 1
13th	Sutton, James P.	Dem	Tenn.	1	1
14th	O'Sullivan, Eugene D.	Dem	Neb.	1	1
15th	Davies, John C.	Dem	N.Y.	1	1
16th	White, Cecil F.	Dem	Cal.	1	1
17th	Lind, James F.	Dem	Penn.	1	1
Del.	Bartlett, E. L. (Bob)	Dem	Alas.	3	2
RsC.	Fernos-Isern, Antonio	PpD	P.R.	3	2

Minority

Rank	Name	Party	State	Terms in: House	Terms in: Comm.
RM	Hope, Clifford R.	Rep	Kans.	12	12
2nd	Andresen, August H.	Rep	Minn.	12	*2 8
3rd	Murray, Reid F.	Rep	Wisc.	6	6
4th	Hall, Edwin Arthur	Rep	N.Y.	6	5
5th	Hill, William S.	Rep	Colo.	5	4
6th	Hoeven, Charles B.	Rep	Iowa	4	3
7th	Simpson, Sidney E.	Rep	Ill.	4	2
8th	Bramblett, Ernest K.	Rep	Cal.	2	2
9th	Dague, Paul B.	Rep	Penn.	2	2
10th	Cotton, Norris	Rep	N.H.	2	2
Del.	Farrington, Joseph R.	Rep.	Hai.	4	4

*2: Member's 2nd period of service on the committee.

Note: Territorial Delegates Joseph Farrington (Rep-Hai.) and E.L. (Bob) Bartlett (Dem-Alas.) and Antonio Fernos-Isern (Popular Democrat-P.R.), the Resident Commissioner for Puerto-Rico were not allowed to accrue seniority nor were they included in the committee's party ratio.

Changes:

Majority:

Name	Party	State	Date	Change
Worley, Eugene	Dem	Tex.	Mar. 28,1950	Left committee; later resigned House for federal judgeship Apr. 3,1950.
Christopher, George H.	Dem	Mo.	Mar. 30,1950	Replaced Worley.

Minority:

Name	Party	State	Date	Change
Cotton, Norris	Rep	N.H.	June 21,1950	Left committee; moved to Appropriations on Aug. 29,1950.
Guill, Ben H.	Rep	Tex.	June 21,1950	Replaced Cotton.

Departures from the House:	**Majority**			**Minority**		
Defeated for Reelection	Davies, John C.	N.Y.	Dem	Guill, Ben H.	Tex.	Rep
	O'Sullivan, Eugene D.	Neb.	Dem			
	White, Cecil F.	Cal.	Dem			
	Christopher, George H.	Mo.	Dem			
Retired	Pace, Stephen	Ga.	Dem	None		
Departures from Committee:						
Moved to Ways & Means	Granger, Walter K.	Utah	Dem	None		

AGRICULTURE / 82nd Congress

Service Dates of Committee Chair: Jan. 12,1951-Jan. 3,1953
Service Dates of Majority Members: Jan. 12,1951-Jan. 3,1953
Service Dates of Minority Members: Jan. 15,1951-Jan. 3,1953

Majority

Rank Name	Party	State	Terms in: House	Comm.
Chr Cooley, Harold D.	Dem	N.C.	10	9
2nd Poage, William R.	Dem	Tex.	8	6
3rd Grant, George M.	Dem	Ala.	8	6
4th Gathings, Ezekiel C.	Dem	Ark.	7	5
5th McMillan, John L.	Dem	S.C.	7	5
6th Abernethy, Thomas G.	Dem	Miss.	5	4
7th Albert, Carl	Dem	Okla.	3	3
8th Abbitt, Watkins M.	Dem	Va.	3	2
9th Polk, James G.	Dem	Ohio	7	*2 2
10th Sutton, James P.	Dem	Tenn.	2	2
11th Lind, James F.	Dem	Penn.	2	2
12th Wheeler, William M.	Dem	Ga.	3	1
13th Thompson, Clark W.	Dem	Tex.	4	1
14th Jones, Paul C.	Dem	Mo.	3	1
15th Herlong, Albert S. Jr.	Dem	Fla.	2	1
16th McCarthy, Eugene J.	DFL	Minn.	2	1
17th Patten, Harold A.	Dem	Ariz.	2	1
Del. Bartlett, E. L. (Bob)	Dem	Alas.	4	3
RsC. Fernos-Isern, Antonio	PpD	P.R.	4	3

Minority

Rank Name	Party	State	Terms in: House	Comm.
RM Hope, Clifford R.	Rep	Kans.	13	13
2nd Andresen, August H.	Rep	Minn.	13	*2 9
3rd Murray, Reid F.	Rep	Wisc.	7	7
4th Hall, Edwin Arthur	Rep	N.Y.	7	6
5th Hill, William S.	Rep	Colo.	6	5
6th Hoeven, Charles B.	Rep	Iowa	5	4
7th Simpson, Sidney E.	Rep	Ill.	5	3
8th Bramblett, Ernest K.	Rep	Cal.	3	3
9th Dague, Paul B.	Rep	Penn.	3	3
10th Harvey, Ralph	Rep	Ind.	3	*1 1
11th Lovre, Harold O.	Rep	S.D.	2	1
12th Belcher, Page H.	Rep	Okla.	1	1
13th Ostertag, Harold C.	Rep	N.Y.	1	1
Del. Farrington, Joseph R.	Rep.	Hai.	5	5

*1: Member's 1st period of service on the committee;
*2: Member's 2nd period of service on the committee.

Note: Territorial Delegates Joseph Farrington (Rep-Hai.) and E.L. (Bob) Bartlett (Dem-Alas.) and Antonio Fernos-Isern (Popular Democrat-P.R.), the Resident Commissioner for Puerto-Rico were not allowed to accrue seniority nor were they included in the committee's party ratio.

Changes:
Minority:

Murray, Reid F.	Rep	Wisc.	Apr. 29,1952	Died in office.
McIntire, Clifford G.	Rep	Me.	June 16,1952	Replaced Murray.

	Majority		Minority	
Departures from the House:				
Defeated for Reelection	Lind, James F.	Penn. Dem	None	
Defeated for Renomination	None		Hall, Edwin Arthur	N.Y. Rep
Departures from Committee:				
Moved to Interior & Insular Affairs; Banking & Currency	McCarthy, Eugene J.	Minn. DFL	None	
Moved to Armed Services	Patten, Harold A.	Ariz. Dem	None	
Moved to Appropriations	None		Ostertag, Harold C.	N.Y. Rep

AGRICULTURE / 83rd Congress

Service Dates of Committee Chair: Jan. 19,1953-Jan. 3,1955
Service Dates of Majority Members: Jan. 19,1953-Jan. 3,1955
Service Dates of Minority Members: Jan. 19,1953-Jan. 3,1955

Majority

Rank Name	Party	State	Terms in: House	Terms in: Comm.
Chr Hope, Clifford R.	Rep	Kans.	14	14
2nd Andresen, August H.	Rep	Minn.	14*2	10
3rd Hill, William S.	Rep	Colo.	7	6
4th Hoeven, Charles B.	Rep	Iowa	6	5
5th Simpson, Sidney E.	Rep	Ill.	6	4
6th Bramblett, Ernest K.	Rep	Cal.	4	4
7th Dague, Paul B.	Rep	Penn.	4	4
8th Harvey, Ralph	Rep	Ind.	4 *1	2
9th Lovre, Harold O.	Rep	S.D.	3	2
10th Belcher, Page H.	Rep	Okla.	2	2
11th McIntire, Clifford G.	Rep	Me.	2	2
12th Golden, James S.	Rep	Ky.	3	1
13th Williams, William R.	Rep	N.Y.	2	1
14th King, Karl C.	Rep	Penn.	2	1
15th Harrison, Robert D.	Rep	Neb.	2	1
16th Wampler, William C.	Rep	Va.	1 *1	1
Del. Farrington, Joseph R.	Rep.	Hai.	6	6

Minority

Rank Name	Party	State	Terms in: House	Terms in: Comm.
RM Cooley, Harold D.	Dem	N.C.	11	10
2nd Poage, William R.	Dem	Tex.	9	7
3rd Grant, George M.	Dem	Ala.	9	7
4th Gathings, Ezekiel C.	Dem	Ark.	8	6
5th McMillan, John L.	Dem	S.C.	8	6
6th Abernethy, Thomas G.	Dem	Miss.	6	5
7th Albert, Carl	Dem	Okla.	4	4
8th Abbitt, Watkins M.	Dem	Va.	4	3
9th Polk, James G.	Dem	Ohio	8 *2	3
10th Sutton, James P.	Dem	Tenn.	3	3
11th Wheeler, William M.	Dem	Ga.	4	2
12th Thompson, Clark W.	Dem	Tex.	5	2
13th Jones, Paul C.	Dem	Mo.	4	2
14th Herlong, Albert S. Jr.	Dem	Fla.	3	2
Del. Bartlett, E. L. (Bob)	Dem	Alas.	5	4
RsC. Fernos-Isern, Antonio	PpD	P.R.	5	4

*1: Member's 1st period of service on the committee; *2: Member's 2nd period of service on the committee.

Notes: Territorial Delegates Joseph Farrington (Rep-Hai.) and E.L. (Bob) Bartlett (Dem-Alas.) and Antonio Fernos-Isern (Popular Democrat-P.R.), the Resident Commissioner for Puerto-Rico were not allowed to accrue seniority nor were they included in the committee's party ratio. Farrington was appointed on Jan. 22,1953 and Bartlett and Fernos-Isern were appointed on Jan. 26,1953.

Changes:

Majority:

Farrington, Joseph R.	Rep.	Hai.	June 19,1954	Died in office.
Farrington, Mary E. Pruett	Rep.	Hai.	Aug. 5,1954	Replaced Joseph Farrington.

	Majority			Minority		
Departures from the House:						
Defeated for Reelection	Wampler, William C.	Va.	Rep	None		
Defeated for Renomination	None			Wheeler, William M.	Ga.	Dem
Lost Nomination to U.S. Senate	None			Sutton, James P.	Tenn.	Dem
Retired	Bramblett, Ernest K.	Cal.	Rep	None		
	Golden, James S.	Ky.	Rep			
Departures from Committee:						
Moved to Ways & Means	None			Herlong, Albert S. Jr.	Fla.	Dem

AGRICULTURE / 84th Congress

Service Dates of Committee Chair: Jan. 13,1955-Jan. 3,1957
Service Dates of Majority Members: Jan. 13,1955-Jan. 3,1957
Service Dates of Minority Members: Jan. 20,1955-Jan. 3,1957

Majority

Rank Name	Party	State	Terms in: House	Terms in: Comm.
Chr Cooley, Harold D.	Dem	N.C.	12	11
2nd Poage, William R.	Dem	Tex.	10	8
3rd Grant, George M.	Dem	Ala.	10	8
4th Gathings, Ezekiel C.	Dem	Ark.	9	7
5th McMillan, John L.	Dem	S.C.	9	7
6th Abernethy, Thomas G.	Dem	Miss.	7	6
7th Albert, Carl	Dem	Okla.	5	5
8th Abbitt, Watkins M.	Dem	Va.	5	4
9th Polk, James G.	Dem	Ohio	9	*2 4
10th Thompson, Clark W.	Dem	Tex.	6	3
11th Jones, Paul C.	Dem	Mo.	5	3
12th Watts, John C.	Dem	Ky.	3	1
13th Hagen, Harlan F.	Dem	Cal.	2	1
14th Johnson, Lester R.	Dem	Wisc.	2	1
15th Anfuso, Victor L.	Dem	N.Y.	2	1
16th Bass, Ross	Dem	Tenn.	1	1
17th Knutson, Coya G.	DFL	Minn.	1	1
18th Jennings, William Pat	Dem	Va.	1	1
19th Matthews, Donald R.	Dem	Fla.	2	1
Del. Bartlett, E. L. (Bob)	Dem	Alas.	6	5
RsC. Fernos-Isern, Antonio	PpD	P.R.	6	5

Minority

Rank Name	Party	State	Terms in: House	Terms in: Comm.
RM Hope, Clifford R.	Rep	Kans.	15	15
2nd Andresen, August H.	Rep	Minn.	15*2	11
3rd Hill, William S.	Rep	Colo.	8	7
4th Hoeven, Charles B.	Rep	Iowa	7	6
5th Simpson, Sidney E.	Rep	Ill.	7	5
6th Dague, Paul B.	Rep	Penn.	5	5
7th Harvey, Ralph	Rep	Ind.	5	*1 3
8th Lovre, Harold O.	Rep	S.D.	4	3
9th Belcher, Page H.	Rep	Okla.	3	3
10th McIntire, Clifford G.	Rep	Me.	3	3
11th Williams, William R.	Rep	N.Y.	3	2
12th King, Karl C.	Rep	Penn.	3	2
13th Harrison, Robert D.	Rep	Neb.	3	2
14th Laird, Melvin R.	Rep	Wisc.	2	1
15th Dixon, Henry Aldous	Rep	Utah	1	1
Del. Farrington, Mary E. Pruett	Rep.	Hai.	2	2

*1: Member's 1st period of service on the committee;
*2: Member's 2nd period of service on the committee.

Notes: Territorial Delegates E.L. (Bob) Bartlett (Dem-Alas.) and Mary E. Pruett Farrington (Rep-Hai.) and Antonio Fernos-Isern (Popular Democrat-P.R.), the Resident Commissioner for Puerto Rico were not allowed to accrue seniority nor were they included in the committee's party ratio, which was set at 19 Democrats and 15 Republicans on Jan. 20,1955. Bartlett, Fernos-Isern, and Farrington were appointed on Jan. 20,1955.

Vacancy Filled:
Majority: 19th seat by Matthews on Jan. 31,1955.

	Majority	Minority	
Departures from the House:			
Defeated for Reelection	None	Lovre, Harold O.	S.D. Rep
		Farrington, Mary E. Pruett	Hai. Rep
Retired	None	Hope, Clifford R.	Kans. Rep
		King, Karl C.	Penn. Rep
Departures from Committee:			
Moved to Appropriations	None	Laird, Melvin R.	Wisc. Rep

AGRICULTURE / 85th Congress

Service Dates of Committee Chair: Jan. 10,1957-Jan. 3,1959
Service Dates of Majority Members: Jan. 10,1957-Jan. 3,1959
Service Dates of Minority Members: Jan. 16,1957-Jan. 3,1959

Majority

Rank Name	Party	State	Terms in: House	Terms in: Comm.
Chr Cooley, Harold D.	Dem	N.C.	13	12
2nd Poage, William R.	Dem	Tex.	11	9
3rd Grant, George M.	Dem	Ala.	11	9
4th Gathings, Ezekiel C.	Dem	Ark.	10	8
5th McMillan, John L.	Dem	S.C.	10	8
6th Abernethy, Thomas G.	Dem	Miss.	8	7
7th Albert, Carl	Dem	Okla.	6	6
8th Abbitt, Watkins M.	Dem	Va.	6	5
9th Polk, James G.	Dem	Ohio	10 *2	5
10th Thompson, Clark W.	Dem	Tex.	7	4
11th Jones, Paul C.	Dem	Mo.	6	4
12th Watts, John C.	Dem	Ky.	4	2
13th Hagen, Harlan F.	Dem	Cal.	3	2
14th Johnson, Lester R.	Dem	Wisc.	3	2
15th Anfuso, Victor L.	Dem	N.Y.	3	2
16th Bass, Ross	Dem	Tenn.	2	2
17th Knutson, Coya G.	DFL	Minn.	2	2
18th Jennings, William Pat	Dem	Va.	2	2
19th Matthews, Donald R.	Dem	Fla.	3	2
Del. Bartlett, E. L. (Bob)	Dem	Alas.	7	6
RsC. Fernos-Isern, Antonio	PpD	P.R.	7	6
Del. Burns, John A.	Dem.	Hai.	1	1

Minority

Rank Name	Party	State	Terms in: House	Terms in: Comm.
RM1 Andresen, August H.	Rep	Minn.	16*2	12
RM2 2nd Hill, William S.	Rep	Colo.	9	8
3rd Hoeven, Charles B.	Rep	Iowa	8	7
4th Simpson, Sidney E.	Rep	Ill.	8	6
5th Dague, Paul B.	Rep	Penn.	6	6
6th Harvey, Ralph	Rep	Ind.	6 *1	4
7th Belcher, Page H.	Rep	Okla.	4	4
8th McIntire, Clifford G.	Rep	Me.	4	4
9th Williams, William R.	Rep	N.Y.	4	3
10th Harrison, Robert D.	Rep	Neb.	4	3
11th Dixon, Henry Aldous	Rep	Utah	2	2
12th Smith, Wint	Rep	Kans.	6	1
13th Krueger, Otto	Rep	N.D.	3	1
14th Teague, Charles M.	Rep	Cal.	2	1
15th Tewes, Donald E.	Rep	Wisc.	1	1

*1: Member's 1st period of service on the committee;
*2: Member's 2nd period of service on the committee.

Notes: Territorial Delegates E.L.(Bob) Bartlett (Dem-Alas.) and John A. Burns (Dem-Hai.) and Antonio Fernos-Isern (Popular Democrat-P.R.), the Resident Commissioner for Puerto Rico were not allowed to accrue seniority nor were they included in the committee's party ratio.

Changes:

Ranking Member:

RM1 Andresen, August H.	Rep	Minn.	Jan. 14,1958	Died in office.
RM2 Hill, William S.	Rep	Colo.	Jan. 14,1958	Succeeded Andresen as Ranking Minority Member.

Minority:

Andresen, August H.	Rep	Minn.	Jan. 14,1958	Died in office.
Quie, Albert H.	Rep	Minn.	Mar. 6,1958	Replaced Andresen.
Simpson, Sidney E.	Rep	Ill.	Oct. 26,1958	Died in office.

Departures from the House:	Majority		Minority	
Elected to U.S. Senate	Bartlett, E. L. (Bob)	Alas. Dem	None	
Defeated for Reelection	Knutson, Coya G.	Minn. DFL	Harrison, Robert D.	Neb. Rep
			Harvey, Ralph	Ind. Rep
			Tewes, Donald E.	Wisc. Rep
Retired	None		Hill, William S.	Colo. Rep
			Krueger, Otto	N.D. Rep
			Williams, William R.	N.Y. Rep

Departures from Committee:			
Moved to Merchant Marine & Fisheries; Science & Astronautics	Anfuso, Victor L.	N.Y. Dem	None
Moved to Ways & Means	Watts, John C.	Ky. Dem	None

AGRICULTURE / 86th Congress

Service Dates of Committee Chair: Jan. 19,1959-Jan. 3,1961
Service Dates of Majority Members: Jan. 19,1959-Jan. 3,1961
Service Dates of Minority Members: Jan. 19,1959-Jan. 3,1961

Majority

Rank	Name	Party	State	Terms in: House	Terms in: Comm.
Chr	Cooley, Harold D.	Dem	N.C.	14	13
2nd	Poage, William R.	Dem	Tex.	12	10
3rd	Grant, George M.	Dem	Ala.	12	10
4th	Gathings, Ezekiel C.	Dem	Ark.	11	9
5th	McMillan, John L.	Dem	S.C.	11	9
6th	Abernethy, Thomas G.	Dem	Miss.	9	8
7th	Albert, Carl	Dem	Okla.	7	7
8th	Abbitt, Watkins M.	Dem	Va.	7	6
9th	Polk, James G.	Dem	Ohio	11	*2 6
10th	Thompson, Clark W.	Dem	Tex.	8	5
11th	Jones, Paul C.	Dem	Mo.	7	5
12th	Hagen, Harlan F.	Dem	Cal.	4	3
13th	Johnson, Lester R.	Dem	Wisc.	4	3
14th	Bass, Ross	Dem	Tenn.	3	3
15th	Jennings, William Pat	Dem	Va.	3	3
16th	Matthews, Donald R.	Dem	Fla.	4	3
17th	McGovern, George S.	Dem	S.D.	2	1
18th	Coad, Merwin	Dem	Iowa	2	1
19th	Breeding, J. Floyd	Dem	Kans.	2	1
20th	Stubblefield, Frank A.	Dem	Ky.	1	1
21st	McSween, Harold B.	Dem	La.	1	1
22nd	Hogan, Earl	Dem	Ind.	1	1
RsC.	Fernos-Isern, Antonio	PpD	P.R.	8	7
Del.	Burns, John A.	Dem	Hai.	2	2

Minority

Rank	Name	Party	State	Terms in: House	Terms in: Comm.
RM	Hoeven, Charles B.	Rep	Iowa	9	8
2nd	Dague, Paul B.	Rep	Penn.	7	7
3rd	Belcher, Page H.	Rep	Okla.	5	5
4th	McIntire, Clifford G.	Rep	Me.	5	5
5th	Dixon, Henry Aldous	Rep	Utah	3	3
6th	Smith, Wint	Rep	Kans.	7	2
7th	Teague, Charles M.	Rep	Cal.	3	2
8th	Quie, Albert H.	Rep	Minn.	2	2
9th	Short, Don L.	Rep	N.D.	1	1
10th	May, Catherine D.	Rep	Wash.	1	1
11th	Pirnie, Alexander	Rep	N.Y.	1	1
12th	Latta, Delbert L.	Rep	Ohio	1	1

*2: Member's 2nd period of service on the committee.

Notes: Territorial Delegate John A. Burns (Dem-Hai.) and Antonio Fernos-Isern (Popular Democrat-P.R.), the Resident Commissioner for Puerto Rico were not allowed to accrue seniority nor were they included in the committee's party ratio.

Changes:

Majority:

Polk, James G.	Dem	Ohio	Apr. 28,1959	Died in office.
Levering, Robert W.	Dem	Ohio	May 25,1959	Replaced Polk.
Burns, John a.	Dem	Hai.	Aug. 21,1953	Resigned; lost election for Governor.

Departures from the House:

	Majority			Minority		
Defeated for Reelection	Hogan, Earl	Ind.	Dem	None		
	Levering, Robert W.	Ohio	Dem			
Lost Election to U.S. Senate:	McGovern, George S.	S.D.	Dem	None		
Retired	None			Dixon, Henry Aldous	Utah	Rep
				Smith, Wint	Kans.	Rep

Departures from Committee:

	Majority	Minority		
Moved to Armed Services	None	Pirnie, Alexander	N.Y.	Rep

AGRICULTURE / 87th Congress

Service Dates of Committee Chair: Feb. 6,1961-Jan. 3,1963
Service Dates of Majority Members: Feb. 6,1961-Jan. 3,1963
Service Dates of Minority Members: Feb. 13,1961-Jan. 3,1963

Majority

Rank Name	Party	State	Terms in: House	Comm.
Chr Cooley, Harold D.	Dem	N.C.	15	14
2nd Poage, William R.	Dem	Tex.	13	11
3rd Grant, George M.	Dem	Ala.	13	11
4th Gathings, Ezekiel C.	Dem	Ark.	12	10
5th McMillan, John L.	Dem	S.C.	12	10
6th Abernethy, Thomas G.	Dem	Miss.	10	9
7th Albert, Carl	Dem	Okla.	8	8
8th Abbitt, Watkins M.	Dem	Va.	8	7
9th Thompson, Clark W.	Dem	Tex.	9	6
10th Jones, Paul C.	Dem	Mo.	8	6
11th Hagen, Harlan F.	Dem	Cal.	5	4
12th Johnson, Lester R.	Dem	Wisc.	5	4
13th Bass, Ross	Dem	Tenn.	4	4
14th Jennings, William Pat	Dem	Va.	4	4
15th Matthews, Donald R.	Dem	Fla.	5	4
16th Coad, Merwin	Dem	Iowa	3	2
17th Breeding, J. Floyd	Dem	Kans.	3	2
18th Stubblefield, Frank A.	Dem	Ky.	2	2
19th McSween, Harold B.	Dem	La.	2	2
20th Inouye, Daniel K.	Dem	Hai.	2	1
21st Harding, Ralph R.	Dem	Ida.	1	1
RsC. Fernos-Isern, Antonio	PpD	P.R.	9	8

Minority

Rank Name	Party	State	Terms in: House	Comm.
RM Hoeven, Charles B.	Rep	Iowa	10	9
2nd Dague, Paul B.	Rep	Penn.	8	8
3rd Belcher, Page H.	Rep	Okla.	6	6
4th McIntire, Clifford G.	Rep	Me.	6	6
5th Teague, Charles M.	Rep	Cal.	4	3
6th Quie, Albert H.	Rep	Minn.	3	3
7th Short, Don L.	Rep	N.D.	2	2
8th May, Catherine D.	Rep	Wash.	2	2
9th Latta, Delbert L.	Rep	Ohio	2	2
10th Harvey, Ralph	Rep	Ind.	7 *2	1
11th Findley, Paul	Rep	Ill.	1 *1	1
12th Dole, Robert J.	Rep	Kans.	1	1
13th Beermann, Ralph F.	Rep	Neb.	1	1
14th Reifel, Benjamin	Rep	S.D.	1	1

*1: Member's 1st period of service on the committee;
*2: Member's 2nd period of service on the committee.

Note: Antonio Fernos-Isern (Popular Democrat-P.R.), the Resident Commissioner for Puerto Rico, was not allowed to accrue seniority nor was he included in the committee's party ratio.

Changes:

Majority:

Thompson, Clark W.	Dem	Tex.	Jan. 16,1962	Moved to Ways and Means.
Albert, Carl	Dem	Okla.	Jan. 18,1962	Left committee; elected House Majority Leader.
Hagan, G. Elliott	Dem	Ga.	Jan. 18,1962	Replaced Thompson.
Purcell, Graham B.	Dem	Tex.	Feb. 6,1962	Replaced Albert.

Departures from the House:	Majority			Minority		
Elected to U.S. Senate	Inouye, Daniel K.	Hai.	Dem	None		
Defeated for Reelection	Breeding, J. Floyd	Kans.	Dem	None		
Defeated for Renomination	McSween, Harold B.	La.	Dem	None		
Retired	Coad, Merwin	Iowa	Dem	None		
Departures from Committee:						
Moved to Ways & Means	Jennings, William Pat	Va.	Dem	None		
	Bass, Ross	Tenn.	Dem			
Moved to Appropriations	None			Reifel, Benjamin	S.D.	Rep

AGRICULTURE / 88th Congress

Service Dates of Committee Chair: Jan. 17,1963-Jan. 3,1965
Service Dates of Majority Members: Jan. 17,1963-Jan. 3,1965
Service Dates of Minority Members: Jan. 24,1963-Jan. 3,1965

Majority

Rank	Name	Party	State	Terms in: House	Terms in: Comm.
Chr	Cooley, Harold D.	Dem	N.C.	16	15
2nd	Poage, William R.	Dem	Tex.	14	12
3rd	Grant, George M.	Dem	Ala.	14	12
4th	Gathings, Ezekiel C.	Dem	Ark.	13	11
5th	McMillan, John L.	Dem	S.C.	13	11
6th	Abernethy, Thomas G.	Dem	Miss.	11	10
7th	Abbitt, Watkins M.	Dem	Va.	9	8
8th	Jones, Paul C.	Dem	Mo.	9	7
9th	Hagen, Harlan F.	Dem	Cal.	6	5
10th	Johnson, Lester R.	Dem	Wisc.	6	5
11th	Matthews, Donald R.	Dem	Fla.	6	5
12th	Stubblefield, Frank A.	Dem	Ky.	3	3
13th	Harding, Ralph R.	Dem	Ida.	2	2
14th	Hagan, G. Elliott	Dem	Ga.	2	2
15th	Purcell, Graham B.	Dem	Tex.	2	2
16th	Morrison, James H.	Dem	La.	11	1
17th	Rosenthal, Benjamin S.	Dem	N.Y.	2	1
18th	Duncan, Robert B.	Dem	Ore.	1	1
19th	Olson, Alec G.	DFL	Minn.	1	1
20th	Leggett, Robert L.	Dem	Cal.	1	1
21st	Matsunaga, Spark M.	Dem	Hai.	1	*1 1
RsC.	Fernos-Isern, Antonio	PpD	P.R.	10	9

Minority

Rank	Name	Party	State	Terms in: House	Terms in: Comm.
RM	Hoeven, Charles B.	Rep	Iowa	11	10
2nd	Dague, Paul B.	Rep	Penn.	9	9
3rd	Belcher, Page H.	Rep	Okla.	7	7
4th	McIntire, Clifford G.	Rep	Me.	7	7
5th	Teague, Charles M.	Rep	Cal.	5	4
6th	Quie, Albert H.	Rep	Minn.	4	4
7th	Short, Don L.	Rep	N.D.	3	3
8th	May, Catherine D.	Rep	Wash.	3	3
9th	Latta, Delbert L.	Rep	Ohio	3	3
10th	Harvey, Ralph	Rep	Ind.	8	*2 2
11th	Findley, Paul	Rep	Ill.	2	*1 2
12th	Dole, Robert J.	Rep	Kans.	2	2
13th	Beermann, Ralph F.	Rep	Neb.	2	2
14th	Hutchinson, J. Edward	Rep	Mich.	1	1

*1: Member's 1st period of service on the committee;
*2: Member's 2nd period of service on the committee.

Note: Antonio Fernos-Isern (Popular Democrat-P.R.), the Resident Commissioner for Puerto Rico, was not allowed to accrue seniority nor was he included in the committee's party ratio. Fernos-Isern was appointed on Jan. 18,1963.

	Majority			Minority		
Departures from the House:						
Defeated for Reelection	Grant, George M.	Ala.	Dem	Beermann, Ralph F.	Neb.	Rep
	Harding, Ralph R.	Ida.	Dem	Short, Don L.	N.D.	Rep
Lost Election to U.S. Senate	None			McIntire, Clifford G.	Me.	Rep
Retired	Johnson, Lester R.	Wisc.	Dem	Hoeven, Charles B.	Iowa	Rep
	Fernos-Isern, Antonio	P.R.	PpD			
Departures from Committee:						
Moved to Appropriations	Duncan, Robert B.	Ore.	Dem	None		
	Matthews, Donald R.	Fla.	Dem			
Moved to Armed Services	Hagan, G. Elliott	Ga.	Dem	None		
	Leggett, Robert L.	Cal.	Dem			
Moved to Foreign Affairs	Rosenthal, Benjamin S.	N.Y.	Dem	None		
Moved to Judiciary	None			Hutchinson, J. Edward	Mich.	Rep

AGRICULTURE / 89th Congress

Service Dates of Committee Chair: Jan. 18,1965-Dec. 30,1966
Service Dates of Majority Members: Jan. 18,1965-Jan. 3,1967
Service Dates of Minority Members: Jan. 21,1965-Jan. 3,1967

Majority

Rank	Name	Party	State	Terms in: House	Terms in: Comm.
Chr	Cooley, Harold D.	Dem	N.C.	17	16
2nd	Poage, William R.	Dem	Tex.	15	13
3rd	Gathings, Ezekiel C.	Dem	Ark.	14	12
4th	McMillan, John L.	Dem	S.C.	14	12
5th	Abernethy, Thomas G.	Dem	Miss.	12	11
6th	Abbitt, Watkins M.	Dem	Va.	10	9
7th	Jones, Paul C.	Dem	Mo.	10	8
8th	Hagen, Harlan F.	Dem	Cal.	7	6
9th	Stubblefield, Frank A.	Dem	Ky.	4	4
10th	Purcell, Graham B.	Dem	Tex.	3	3
11th	Morrison, James H.	Dem	La.	12	2
12th	Olson, Alec G.	DFL	Minn.	2	2
13th	Matsunaga, Spark M.	Dem	Hai.	2	*1 2
14th	O'Neal, Maston E. Jr.	Dem	Ga.	1	1
15th	Foley, Thomas S.	Dem	Wash.	1	1
16th	Resnick, Joseph Y.	Dem	N.Y.	1	1
17th	Stalbaum, Lynn E.	Dem	Wisc.	1	1
18th	de la Garza, E. (Kika)	Dem	Tex.	1	1
19th	Vigorito, Joseph P.	Dem	Penn.	1	1
20th	Mackie, John C.	Dem	Mich.	1	1
21st	Redlin, Rolland	Dem	N.D.	1	1
22nd	Bandstra, Bert	Dem	Iowa	1	1
23rd	Greigg, Stanley L.	Dem	Iowa	1	1
24th	Callan, Clair A.	Dem	Neb.	1	1
RsC.	Polanco-Abreu, Santiago	PpD	P.R.	1	1

Minority

Rank	Name	Party	State	Terms in: House	Terms in: Comm.
RM	Dague, Paul B.	Rep	Penn.	10	10
2nd	Belcher, Page H.	Rep	Okla.	8	8
3rd	Teague, Charles M.	Rep	Cal.	6	5
4th	Quie, Albert H.	Rep	Minn.	5	5
5th	May, Catherine D.	Rep	Wash.	4	4
6th	Latta, Delbert L.	Rep	Ohio	4	4
7th	Harvey, Ralph	Rep	Ind.	9	*2 3
8th	Findley, Paul	Rep	Ill.	3	*1 3
9th	Dole, Robert J.	Rep	Kans.	3	3
10th	Burton, Laurence J.	Rep	Utah	2	1
11th	Walker, Prentiss L.	Rep	Miss.	1	1

*1: Member's 1st period of service on the committee;
*2: Member's 2nd period of service on the committee.

Note: Santiago Polanco-Abreu (Popular Democrat-P.R.), the Resident Commissioner for Puerto Rico, was not allowed to accrue seniority nor was he included in the committee's party ratio.

Changes:

Majority:

Name	Party	State	Date	Change
Mackie, John C.	Dem	Mich.	Oct. 18,1966	Moved to Public Works.
Jones, Walter B.	Dem	N.C.	Oct. 21,1966	Replaced Mackie.
Cooley, Harold D.	Dem	N.C.	Dec. 30,1966	Defeated for reelection.

Minority:

Name	Party	State	Date	Change
Latta, Delbert L.	Rep	Ohio	Feb. 7,1966	Left committee to comply with the Republican Conference rule that members of Rules Committee not have dual committee assignments.
Hansen, George V.	Rep	Ida.	Feb. 7,1966	Replaced Latta.
Dague, Paul B.	Rep	Penn.	Dec. 30,1966	Resigned and retired.
Harvey, Ralph	Rep	Ind.	Dec. 30,1966	Resigned; defeated for renomination.

	Majority			Minority		
Departures from the House:						
Defeated for Reelection	Bandstra, Bert	Iowa	Dem	None		
	Callan, Clair A.	Neb.	Dem			
	Greigg, Stanley L.	Iowa	Dem			
	Hagen, Harlan F.	Cal.	Dem			
	Olson, Alec G.	Minn.	DFL			
	Redlin, Rolland	N.D.	Dem			
	Stalbaum, Lynn E.	Wisc.	Dem			
Defeated for Renomination	Morrison, James H.	La.	Dem			
Lost Election to U.S. Senate	None			Walker, Prentiss L.	Miss.	Rep
Departures from Committee:						
Moved to Rules	Matsunaga, Spark M.	Hai.	Dem	None		
Moved to Select Small Business	None			Burton, Laurence J.	Utah	Rep
Moved to Foreign Affairs	None			Findley, Paul	Ill.	Rep
Moved to House Administration	None			Quie, Albert H.	Minn.	Rep

AGRICULTURE / 90th Congress

Service Dates of Committee Chair: Jan. 23,1967-Jan. 3,1969
Service Dates of Majority Members: Jan. 23,1967-Jan. 3,1969
Service Dates of Minority Members: Jan. 26,1967-Jan. 3,1969

Majority

Rank Name	Party	State	Terms in: House	Terms in: Comm.
Chr Poage, William R.	Dem	Tex.	16	14
2nd Gathings, Ezekiel C.	Dem	Ark.	15	13
3rd McMillan, John L.	Dem	S.C.	15	13
4th Abernethy, Thomas G.	Dem	Miss.	13	12
5th Abbitt, Watkins M.	Dem	Va.	11	10
6th Jones, Paul C.	Dem	Mo.	11	9
7th Stubblefield, Frank A.	Dem	Ky.	5	5
8th Purcell, Graham B.	Dem	Tex.	4	4
9th O'Neal, Maston E. Jr.	Dem	Ga.	2	2
10th Foley, Thomas S.	Dem	Wash.	2	2
11th Resnick, Joseph Y.	Dem	N.Y.	2	2
12th de la Garza, E. (Kika)	Dem	Tex.	2	2
13th Vigorito, Joseph P.	Dem	Penn.	2	2
14th Jones, Walter B.	Dem	N.C.	2	2
15th Dow, John G.	Dem	N.Y.	2 *1	1
16th Nichols, William F.	Dem	Ala.	1	1
17th Montgomery, G.V. (Sonny)	Dem	Miss.	1	1
18th Brasco, Frank J.	Dem	N.Y.	1	1
19th Stuckey, Williamson S.Jr.	Dem	Ga.	1	1
20th Rarick, John R.	Dem	La.	1	1
RsC. Polanco-Abreu, Santiago	PpD	P.R.	2	2

Minority

Rank Name	Party	State	Terms in: House	Terms in: Comm.
RM Belcher, Page H.	Rep	Okla.	9	9
2nd Teague, Charles M.	Rep	Cal.	7	6
3rd May, Catherine D.	Rep	Wash.	5	5
4th Dole, Robert J.	Rep	Kans.	4	4
5th Hansen, George V.	Rep	Ida.	2 *1	2
6th Wampler, William C.	Rep	Va.	2 *2	1
7th Goodling, George A.	Rep	Penn.	3	1
8th Miller, Clarence E.	Rep	Ohio	1	1
9th Burke, J. Herbert	Rep	Fla.	1	1
10th Mathias, Robert B.	Rep	Cal.	1	1
11th Mayne, Wiley	Rep	Iowa	1	1
12th Zwach, John M.	Rep	Minn.	1	1
13th Kleppe, Thomas S.	Rep	N.D.	1	1
14th Price, Robert D.	Rep	Tex.	1	1
15th Myers, John T.	Rep	Ind.	1	1

*1: Member's 1st period of service on the committee;
*2: Member's 2nd period of service on the committee.

Note: Santiago Polanco-Abreu (Popular Democrat-P.R.), the Resident Commissioner for Puerto Rico, was not allowed to accrue seniority nor was he included in the committee's party ratio. Polanco-Abreu was included on the committee listing in the Congressional Directory but not in the House Journal or Congressional Record for Jan. 23,1967. However, as a Resident Commissioner, he was elected to a four-year term in 1966 and his appointment date of Jan. 18,1965 may have been holding in this case.

Changes:

Majority:

Stuckey, Williamson S.Jr. Dem Ga. May 25,1967 Moved to Interstate and Foreign Commerce.

	Majority			Minority		
Departures from the House:						
Elected to the U.S. Senate	None			Dole, Robert J.	Kans.	Rep
Defeated for Reelection	Dow, John G.	N.Y.	Dem	None		
	Polanco-Abreu, Santiago	P.R.	PpD			
Lost Election to U.S. Senate	None			Hansen, George V.	Ida.	Rep
Lost Nomination to U.S. Senate	Resnick, Joseph Y.	N.Y.	Dem	None		
Retired	Gathings, Ezekiel C.	Ark.	Dem	None		
	Jones, Paul C.	Mo.	Dem			
Departures from Committee:						
Moved to Banking & Currency	Brasco, Frank J.	N.Y.	Dem	None		
Moved to Armed Services	Nichols, William F.	Ala.	Dem	None		
Moved to Foreign Affairs	None			Burke, J. Herbert	Fla.	Rep

AGRICULTURE / 91st Congress

Service Dates of Committee Chair: Jan. 29,1969-Jan. 3,1971
Service Dates of Majority Members: Jan. 29,1969-Jan. 3,1971
Service Dates of Minority Members: Jan. 29,1969-Jan. 3,1971

Majority

Rank Name	Party	State	Terms in: House	Terms in: Comm.
Chr Poage, William R.	Dem	Tex.	17	15
2nd McMillan, John L.	Dem	S.C.	16	14
3rd Abernethy, Thomas G.	Dem	Miss.	14	13
4th Abbitt, Watkins M.	Dem	Va.	12	11
5th Stubblefield, Frank A.	Dem	Ky.	6	6
6th Purcell, Graham B.	Dem	Tex.	5	5
7th O'Neal, Maston E. Jr.	Dem	Ga.	3	3
8th Foley, Thomas S.	Dem	Wash.	3	3
9th de la Garza, E. (Kika)	Dem	Tex.	3	3
10th Vigorito, Joseph P.	Dem	Penn.	3	3
11th Jones, Walter B.	Dem	N.C.	3	3
12th Montgomery, G.V. (Sonny)	Dem	Miss.	2	2
13th Sisk, B. F.	Dem	Cal.	8	1
14th Alexander, William V. Jr.	Dem	Ark.	1	1
15th Burlison, Bill D.	Dem	Mo.	1	1
16th Lowenstein, Allard K.	Dem	N.Y.	1	1
17th Rarick, John R.	Dem	La.	2	2
18th Jones, Ed	Dem	Tenn.	1	1
RsC. Cordova-Diaz, Jorge L.	NPr	P.R.	1	1

Minority

Rank Name	Party	State	Terms in: House	Terms in: Comm.
RM Belcher, Page H.	Rep	Okla.	10	10
2nd Teague, Charles M.	Rep	Cal.	8	7
3rd May, Catherine D.	Rep	Wash.	6	6
4th Wampler, William C.	Rep	Va.	3	*2 2
5th Goodling, George A.	Rep	Penn.	4	2
6th Miller, Clarence E.	Rep	Ohio	2	2
7th Mathias, Robert B.	Rep	Cal.	2	2
8th Mayne, Wiley	Rep	Iowa	2	2
9th Zwach, John M.	Rep	Minn.	2	2
10th Kleppe, Thomas S.	Rep	N.D.	2	2
11th Price, Robert D.	Rep	Tex.	2	2
12th Myers, John T.	Rep	Ind.	2	2
13th Sebelius, Keith G.	Rep	Kans.	1	1
14th McKneally, Martin B.	Rep	N.Y.	1	1
15th Mizell, Wilmer D.	Rep	N.C.	1	1

*2: Member's 2nd period of service on the committee.

Notes: Jorge L. Cordova-Diaz (New Progressive-P.R.), the Resident Commissioner for Puerto Rico, was appointed by the majority in this Congress. He was not allowed to accrue seniority nor was he included in the committee's party ratio. Democratic Party gains in the 1969 special elections in Wisconsin and Montana led to the passage of House Resolution 470, agreed to on July 8,1969, changing the size and party ratio on this committee to 19 Democrats and 15 Republicans. John R. Rarick (Dem-La.) was stripped of his seniority by the Democratic Caucus on Jan. 29,1969 by a vote of 101 to 73 for backing American Independent presidential candidate George C. Wallace.

Vacancy Filled:
Majority: 18th seat by Ed Jones on Apr. 2,1969.

Addition:
Majority: 19th Melcher, John Dem Mont. July 8,1969

Departures from the House:	**Majority**		**Minority**	
Defeated for Reelection	Lowenstein, Allard K.	N.Y. Dem	May, Catherine D.	Wash. Rep
			McKneally, Martin B.	N.Y. Rep
Lost Election to U.S. Senate	None		Kleppe, Thomas S.	N.D. Rep
Retired	O'Neal, Maston E. Jr.	Ga. Dem	None	
Departures from Committee:				
Moved to Armed Services	Montgomery, G.V. (Sonny)	Miss. Dem		
Moved to Appropriations	None		Myers, John T.	Ind. Rep
No new assignment	Cordova-Diaz, Jorge L.	P.R. NPr		

AGRICULTURE / 92nd Congress

Service Dates of Committee Chair: Feb. 4,1971-Jan. 3,1973
Service Dates of Majority Members: Feb. 4,1971-Jan. 3,1973
Service Dates of Minority Members: Feb. 4,1971-Jan. 3,1973

Majority

Rank	Name	Party	State	Terms in: House	Terms in: Comm.
Chr	Poage, William R.	Dem	Tex.	18	16
2nd	McMillan, John L.	Dem	S.C.	17	15
3rd	Abernethy, Thomas G.	Dem	Miss.	15	14
4th	Abbitt, Watkins M.	Dem	Va.	13	12
5th	Stubblefield, Frank A.	Dem	Ky.	7	7
6th	Purcell, Graham B.	Dem	Tex.	6	6
7th	Foley, Thomas S.	Dem	Wash.	4	4
8th	de la Garza, E. (Kika)	Dem	Tex.	4	4
9th	Vigorito, Joseph P.	Dem	Penn.	4	4
10th	Jones, Walter B.	Dem	N.C.	4	4
11th	Sisk, B. F.	Dem	Cal.	9	2
12th	Alexander, William V. Jr.	Dem	Ark.	2	2
13th	Burlison, Bill D.	Dem	Mo.	2	2
14th	Rarick, John R.	Dem	La.	3	3
15th	Jones, Ed	Dem	Tenn.	2	2
16th	Melcher, John	Dem	Mont.	2	2
17th	Dow, John G.	Dem	N.Y.	3	*2 1
18th	Mathis, M. Dawson	Dem	Ga.	1	1
19th	Bergland, Bob	DFL	Minn.	1	1
20th	Link, Arthur A.	Dem	N.D.	1	1
21st	Denholm, Frank E.	Dem	S.D.	1	1
22nd	Matsunaga, Spark M.	Dem	Hai.	5	*2 1

Minority

Rank	Name	Party	State	Terms in: House	Terms in: Comm.
RM	Belcher, Page H.	Rep	Okla.	11	11
2nd	Teague, Charles M.	Rep	Cal.	9	8
3rd	Wampler, William C.	Rep	Va.	4	*2 3
4th	Goodling, George A.	Rep	Penn.	5	3
5th	Miller, Clarence E.	Rep	Ohio	3	3
6th	Mathias, Robert B.	Rep	Cal.	3	3
7th	Mayne, Wiley	Rep	Iowa	3	3
8th	Zwach, John M.	Rep	Minn.	3	3
9th	Price, Robert D.	Rep	Tex.	3	3
10th	Sebelius, Keith G.	Rep	Kans.	2	2
11th	Mizell, Wilmer D.	Rep	N.C.	2	2
12th	Findley, Paul	Rep	Ill.	6	*2 1
13th	Kyl, John H.	Rep	Iowa	6	1
14th	Robinson, J. Kenneth	Rep	Va.	1	1

*2: Member's 2nd period of service on the committee.

Vacancy Filled:
Majority: 22nd seat by Matsunaga on Mar. 11,1971.

Changes:
Minority:

Name	Party	State	Date	Action
Robinson, J. Kenneth	Rep	Va.	Oct. 27,1971	Moved to Appropriations.
Baker, LaMar	Rep	Tenn.	Feb. 7,1972	Replaced Robinson.

	Majority			Minority		
Departures from the House:						
Retired	Abbitt, Watkins M.	Va.	Dem	Belcher, Page H.	Okla.	Rep
	Abernethy, Thomas G.	Miss.	Dem			
Elected Governor	Link, Arthur A.	N.D.	Dem	None		
Defeated for Reelection	Dow, John G.	N.Y.	Dem	Kyl, John H.	Iowa	Rep
	Purcell, Graham B.	Tex.	Dem	Cordova, Jorge L.	P.R.	NPr
Defeated for Renomination	McMillan, John L.	S.C.	Dem	None		
Departures from Committee:						
Moved to Appropriations	Burlison, Bill D.	Mo.	Dem	Miller, Clarence E.	Ohio	Rep

AGRICULTURE / 93rd Congress

Service Dates of Committee Chair: Jan. 24,1973-Jan. 3,1975
Service Dates of Majority Members: Jan. 24,1973-Jan. 3,1975
Service Dates of Minority Members: Jan. 24,1973-Jan. 3,1975

Majority

Rank	Name	Party	State	Terms in: House	Terms in: Comm.
Chr	Poage, William R.	Dem	Tex.	19	17
2nd	Stubblefield, Frank A.	Dem	Ky.	8	8
3rd	Foley, Thomas S.	Dem	Wash.	5	5
4th	de la Garza, E. (Kika)	Dem	Tex.	5	5
5th	Vigorito, Joseph P.	Dem	Penn.	5	5
6th	Jones, Walter B.	Dem	N.C.	5	5
7th	Sisk, B. F.	Dem	Cal.	10	3
8th	Alexander, William V. Jr.	Dem	Ark.	3	3
9th	Rarick, John R.	Dem	La.	4	4
10th	Jones, Ed	Dem	Tenn.	3	3
11th	Melcher, John	Dem	Mont.	3	3
12th	Mathis, M. Dawson	Dem	Ga.	2	2
13th	Bergland, Bob	DFL	Minn.	2	2
14th	Denholm, Frank E.	Dem	S.D.	2	2
15th	Matsunaga, Spark M.	Dem	Hai.	6	*2 2
16th	Brown, George E. Jr.	Dem	Cal.	5	1
17th	Bowen, David R.	Dem	Miss.	1	1
18th	Rose, Charles G. III	Dem	N.C.	1	1
19th	Litton, Jerry	Dem	Mo.	1	1
20th	Gunter, William D. Jr.	Dem	Fla.	1	1

Minority

Rank	Name	Party	State	Terms in: House	Terms in: Comm.
RM1	Teague, Charles M.	Rep	Cal.	10	9
RM2 2nd	Wampler, William C.	Rep	Va.	5	*2 4
3rd	Goodling, George A.	Rep	Penn.	6	4
4th	Mathias, Robert B.	Rep	Cal.	4	4
5th	Mayne, Wiley	Rep	Iowa	4	4
6th	Zwach, John M.	Rep	Minn.	4	4
7th	Price, Robert D.	Rep	Tex.	4	4
8th	Sebelius, Keith G.	Rep	Kans.	3	3
9th	Mizell, Wilmer D.	Rep	N.C.	3	3
10th	Findley, Paul	Rep	Ill.	7	*2 2
11th	Baker, LaMar	Rep	Tenn.	2	2
12th	Thone, Charles	Rep	Neb.	2	1
13th	Symms, Steven D.	Rep	Ida.	1	1
14th	Young, Edward L.	Rep	S.C.	1	1
15th	Johnson, James P.	Rep	Colo.	1	1
16th	Madigan, Edward R.	Rep	Ill.	1	1

*2: Member's 2nd period of service on the committee.

Changes:

Ranking Member:

RM1	Teague, Charles M.	Rep	Cal.	Jan. 1,1974	Died in office.
RM2	Wampler, William C.	Rep	Va.	Jan. 1,1974	Succeeded Teague.

Majority:

Stubblefield, Frank A.	Dem	Ky.	Dec. 31,1974	Resigned; defeated for renomination.

Minority:

Teague, Charles M.	Rep	Cal.	Jan. 1,1974	Died in office.
Peyser, Peter A.	Rep	N.Y.	May 1,1974	Replaced Teague.

Departures from the House:

	Majority			Minority		
Retired	None			Goodling, George A.	Penn.	Rep
				Zwach, John M.	Minn.	Rep
Defeated for Reelection	Denholm, Frank E.	S.D.	Dem	Baker, LaMar	Tenn.	Rep
				Mathias, Robert B.	Cal.	Rep
				Mayne, Wiley	Iowa	Rep
				Mizell, Wilmer D.	N.C.	Rep
				Price, Robert D.	Tex.	Rep
				Young, Edward L.	S.C.	Rep
Defeated for Renomination	Rarick, John R.	La.	Dem	None		
Lost Nomination for U.S. Senate	Gunter, William D. Jr.	Fla.	Dem	None		

Departures from Committee:

Moved to Appropriations	Alexander, William V. Jr	Ark.	Dem	None
No new assignment	Matsunaga, Spark M.	Hai.	Dem	None
	Sisk, B. F.	Cal.	Dem	

AGRICULTURE / 94th Congress

Service Dates of Committee Chair: Jan. 23,1975-Jan. 3,1977
Service Dates of Majority Members: Jan. 23,1975-Jan. 3,1977
Service Dates of Minority Members: Jan. 28,1975-Jan. 3,1977

Majority

Rank	Name	Party	State	Terms in: House	Terms in: Comm.
Chr	Foley, Thomas S.	Dem	Wash.	6	6
2nd	Poage, William R.	Dem	Tex.	20	18
3rd	de la Garza, E. (Kika)	Dem	Tex.	6	6
4th	Vigorito, Joseph P.	Dem	Penn.	6	6
5th	Jones, Walter B.	Dem	N.C.	6	6
6th	Jones, Ed	Dem	Tenn.	4	4
7th	Melcher, John	Dem	Mont.	4	4
8th	Mathis, M. Dawson	Dem	Ga.	3	3
9th	Bergland, Bob	DFL	Minn.	3	3
10th	Brown, George E. Jr.	Dem	Cal.	6	2
11th	Bowen, David R.	Dem	Miss.	2	2
12th	Rose, Charles G. III	Dem	N.C.	2	2
13th	Litton, Jerry	Dem	Mo.	2	2
14th	Breckinridge, John B.	Dem	Ky.	2	1
15th	Richmond, Frederick W.	Dem	N.Y.	1	1
16th	Nolan, Richard M.	DFL	Minn.	1	1
17th	Weaver, James H.	Dem	Ore.	1	1
18th	Baldus, Alvin J.	Dem	Wisc.	1	1
19th	Krebs, John H.	Dem	Cal.	1	1
20th	Harkin, Thomas R.	Dem	Iowa	1	1
21st	Hightower, Jack E.	Dem	Tex.	1	1
22nd	Bedell, Berkley W.	Dem	Iowa	1	1
23rd	McHugh, Matthew F.	Dem	N.Y.	1	1
24th	English, Glenn L. Jr.	Dem	Okla.	1	1
25th	Fithian, Floyd J.	Dem	Ind.	1	1
26th	Jenrette, John W. Jr.	Dem	S.C.	1	1
27th	D'Amours, Norman E.	Dem	N.H.	1	1
28th	Thornton, Raymond H. Jr.	Dem	Ark.	2	1

Minority

Rank	Name	Party	State	Terms in: House	Terms in: Comm.
RM	Wampler, William C.	Rep	Va.	6	*2 5
2nd	Sebelius, Keith G.	Rep	Kans.	4	4
3rd	Findley, Paul	Rep	Ill.	8	*2 3
4th	Thone, Charles	Rep	Neb.	3	2
5th	Symms, Steven D.	Rep	Ida.	2	2
6th	Johnson, James P.	Rep	Colo.	2	2
7th	Madigan, Edward R.	Rep	Ill.	2	2
8th	Peyser, Peter A.	Rep	N.Y.	3	2
9th	Heckler, Margaret M.	Rep	Mass.	5	1
10th	Jeffords, James M.	Rep	Vt.	1	1
11th	Kelly, Richard	Rep	Fla.	1	1
12th	Grassley, Charles E.	Rep	Iowa	1	1
13th	Hagedorn, Thomas M.	Rep	Minn.	1	1
14th	Moore, W. Henson	Rep	La.	1	1

*2: Member's 2nd period of service on the committee.

Note: William R. Poage (Dem-Tex.) was unseated as Chair of this committee on Jan. 16,1975 by the Democratic Caucus by a vote of 146-114.

Vacancy Filled:
Majority: 28th seat by Thornton on Dec. 17,1975.

Changes:
Majority:

Name	Party	State	Date	Change
D'Amours, Norman E.	Dem	N.H.	Apr. 8,1976	Moved to Banking, Currency and Housing.
Litton, Jerry	Dem	Mo.	Aug. 3,1976	Died in office.

Departures from the House:

	Majority		Minority	
Elected to U.S. Senate	Melcher, John	Mont. Dem	None	
Defeated for Reelection	Vigorito, Joseph P.	Penn. Dem	None	
Lost Nomination to U.S. Senate	None		Peyser, Peter A.	N.Y. Rep

AGRICULTURE / 95th Congress

Service Dates of Committee Chair: Jan. 19,1977-Jan. 3,1979
Service Dates of Majority Members: Jan. 19,1977-Jan. 3,1979
Service Dates of Minority Members: Jan. 19,1977-Jan. 3,1979

Majority

Rank	Name	Party	State	Terms in: House	Terms in: Comm.
Chr	Foley, Thomas S.	Dem	Wash.	7	7
2nd	Poage, William R.	Dem	Tex.	21	19
3rd	de la Garza, E. (Kika)	Dem	Tex.	7	7
4th	Jones, Walter B.	Dem	N.C.	7	7
5th	Jones, Ed	Dem	Tenn.	5	5
6th	Mathis, M. Dawson	Dem	Ga.	4	4
7th	Bergland, Bob	Dem	Minn.	4	4
8th	Brown, George E. Jr.	Dem	Cal.	7	3
9th	Bowen, David R.	Dem	Miss.	3	3
10th	Rose, Charles G. III	Dem	N.C.	3	3
11th	Breckinridge, John B.	Dem	Ky.	3	2
12th	Richmond, Frederick W.	Dem	N.Y.	2	2
13th	Nolan, Richard M.	DFL	Minn.	2	2
14th	Weaver, James H.	Dem	Ore.	2	2
15th	Baldus, Alvin J.	Dem	Wisc.	2	2
16th	Krebs, John H.	Dem	Cal.	2	2
17th	Harkin, Thomas R.	Dem	Iowa	2	2
18th	Hightower, Jack E.	Dem	Tex.	2	2
19th	Bedell, Berkley W.	Dem	Iowa	2	2
20th	McHugh, Matthew F.	Dem	N.Y.	2	2
21st	English, Glenn L. Jr.	Dem	Okla.	2	2
22nd	Fithian, Floyd J.	Dem	Ind.	2	2
23rd	Jenrette, John W. Jr.	Dem	S.C.	2	2
24th	Thornton, Raymond H. Jr.	Dem	Ark.	3	2
25th	Panetta, Leon E.	Dem	Cal.	1	1
26th	Skelton, Ike	Dem	Mo.	1	1
27th	Ammerman, Joseph S.	Dem	Penn.	1	1
28th	Huckaby, T. Jerry	Dem	La.	1	1
29th	Glickman, Daniel R.	Dem	Kans.	1	1
30th	Akaka, Daniel K.	Dem	Hai.	1	1
31st	Volkmer, Harold L.	Dem	Mo.	1	*T 1

Minority

Rank	Name	Party	State	Terms in: House	Terms in: Comm.
RM	Wampler, William C.	Rep	Va.	7	*2 6
2nd	Sebelius, Keith G.	Rep	Kans.	5	5
3rd	Findley, Paul	Rep	Ill.	9	*2 4
4th	Thone, Charles	Rep	Neb.	4	3
5th	Symms, Steven D.	Rep	Ida.	3	3
6th	Johnson, James P.	Rep	Colo.	3	3
7th	Madigan, Edward R.	Rep	Ill.	3	3
8th	Heckler, Margaret M.	Rep	Mass.	6	2
9th	Jeffords, James M.	Rep	Vt.	2	2
10th	Kelly, Richard	Rep	Fla.	2	2
11th	Grassley, Charles E.	Rep	Iowa	2	2
12th	Hagedorn, Thomas M.	Rep	Minn.	2	2
13th	Moore, W. Henson	Rep	La.	2	2
14th	Coleman, E. Thomas	Rep	Mo.	2	1
15th	Marlenee, Ron	Rep	Mont.	1	1

*2: Member's 2nd period of service on the committee;
*T: Temporary member of the committee.

Note: William R. Poage (Dem-Tex.) was unseated as Chair of this committee by the Democratic Caucus at the beginning of the 94th Congress.

Vacancy Filled:
Majority: 31st seat by Volkmer on Jan. 27,1977.

Changes:
Majority:

Bergland, Bob	Dem	Minn.	Jan. 22,1977	Resigned; appointed Secretary of Agriculture.
Whitley, Charles O. Sr.	Dem	N.C.	Mar. 16,1977	Replaced Bergland.
McHugh, Matthew F.	Dem	N.Y.	Jan. 25,1978	Moved to Appropriations.
Risenhoover, Theodore M.	Dem	Okla.	Feb. 22,1978	Replaced McHugh
Poage, William R.	Dem	Tex.	Dec. 31,1978	Resigned and retired.

Departures from the House:	Majority			Minority		
Elected Governor	None			Thone, Charles	Neb.	Rep
Defeated for Reelection	Ammerman, Joseph S.	Penn.	Dem	None		
	Krebs, John H.	Cal.	Dem			
Defeated for Renomination	Breckinridge, John B.	Ky.	Dem	None		
	Risenhoover, Theodore M.	Okla.	Dem			
Lost Nomination to U.S. Senate	Thornton, Raymond H. Jr.	Ark.	Dem	None		

Departures from Committee:

Moved to Appropriations	Hightower, Jack E.	Tex.	Dem	None		
	Jenrette, John W. Jr.	S.C.	Dem			
Moved to Science & Technology	Volkmer, Harold L.	Mo.	Dem	None		
Moved to Ways & Means	None			Moore, W. Henson	La.	Rep

AGRICULTURE / 96th Congress

Service Dates of Committee Chair: Jan. 24,1979-Jan. 3,1981
Service Dates of Majority Members: Jan. 24,1979-Jan. 3,1981
Service Dates of Minority Members: Jan. 24,1979-Jan. 3,1981

Majority

Rank	Name	Party	State	Terms in: House	Terms in: Comm.
Chr	Foley, Thomas S.	Dem	Wash.	8	8
2nd	de la Garza, E. (Kika)	Dem	Tex.	8	8
3rd	Jones, Walter B.	Dem	N.C.	8	8
4th	Jones, Ed	Dem	Tenn.	6	6
5th	Mathis, M. Dawson	Dem	Ga.	5	5
6th	Brown, George E. Jr.	Dem	Cal.	8	4
7th	Bowen, David R.	Dem	Miss.	4	4
8th	Rose, Charles G. III	Dem	N.C.	4	4
9th	Richmond, Frederick W.	Dem	N.Y.	3	3
10th	Nolan, Richard M.	DFL	Minn.	3	3
11th	Weaver, James H.	Dem	Ore.	3	3
12th	Baldus, Alvin J.	Dem	Wisc.	3	3
13th	Harkin, Thomas R.	Dem	Iowa	3	3
14th	Bedell, Berkley W.	Dem	Iowa	3	3
15th	English, Glenn L. Jr.	Dem	Okla.	3	3
16th	Fithian, Floyd J.	Dem	Ind.	3	3
17th	Panetta, Leon E.	Dem	Cal.	2	2
18th	Skelton, Ike	Dem	Mo.	2	2
19th	Huckaby, T. Jerry	Dem	La.	2	2
20th	Glickman, Daniel R.	Dem	Kans.	2	2
21st	Akaka, Daniel K.	Dem	Hai.	2	2
22nd	Whitley, Charles O. Sr.	Dem	N.C.	2	2
23rd	Coelho, Anthony L.	Dem	Cal.	1	1
24th	Daschle, Thomas A.	Dem	S.D.	1	1
25th	Hance, Kent	Dem	Tex.	1	1
26th	Anthony, Beryl F. Jr.	Dem	Ark.	1	1
27th	Stenholm, Charles W.	Dem	Tex.	1	1

Minority

Rank	Name	Party	State	Terms in: House	Terms in: Comm.
RM	Wampler, William C.	Rep	Va.	8	*2 7
2nd	Sebelius, Keith G.	Rep	Kans.	6	6
3rd	Findley, Paul	Rep	Ill.	10	*2 5
4th	Symms, Steven D.	Rep	Ida.	4	4
5th	Johnson, James P.	Rep	Colo.	4	4
6th	Madigan, Edward R.	Rep	Ill.	4	4
7th	Heckler, Margaret M.	Rep	Mass.	7	3
8th	Jeffords, James M.	Rep	Vt.	3	3
9th	Kelly, Richard	Rep	Fla.	3	3
10th	Grassley, Charles E.	Rep	Iowa	3	3
11th	Hagedorn, Thomas M.	Rep	Minn.	3	3
12th	Coleman, E. Thomas	Rep	Mo.	3	2
13th	Marlenee, Ron	Rep	Mont.	2	2
14th	Hopkins, Larry J.	Rep	Ky.	1	1
15th	Thomas, William M.	Rep	Cal.	1	1

*2: Member's 2nd period of service on the committee.

Changes:

Minority:

Symms, Steven D.	Rep	Ida.	Oct. 1,1980	Left committee; later elected to U.S. Senate.
Hansen, George V.	Rep	Ida.	Oct. 1,1980	Replaced Symms.

Departures from the House:

	Majority			Minority		
Elected to U.S. Senate	None			Grassley, Charles E.	Iowa	Rep
Defeated for Reelection	Baldus, Alvin J.	Wisc.	Dem	None		
Defeated for Renomination	None			Kelly, Richard	Fla.	Rep
Lost Nomination to U.S. Senate	Mathis, M. Dawson	Ga.	Dem	None		
Retired	Nolan, Richard M.	Minn.	DFL	Johnson, James P.	Colo.	Rep
				Sebelius, Keith G.	Kans.	Rep

Departures from Committee:

Moved to Appropriations	Akaka, Daniel K.	Hai.	Dem	None		
Moved to Ways and Means	Hance, Kent	Tex.	Dem	None		
Moved to Science & Technology	None			Heckler, Margaret M.	Mass.	Rep
No new assignment	Skelton, Ike	Mo.	Dem	Madigan, Edward R.	Ill.	Rep

AGRICULTURE / 97th Congress

Service Dates of Committee Chair: Jan. 28,1981-Jan. 3,1983
Service Dates of Majority Members: Jan. 28,1981-Jan. 3,1983
Service Dates of Minority Members: Jan. 28,1981-Jan. 3,1983

Majority

Rank	Name	Party	State	Terms in: House	Terms in: Comm.
Chr	de la Garza, E. (Kika)	Dem	Tex.	9	9
2nd	Foley, Thomas S.	Dem	Wash.	9	9
3rd	Jones, Walter B.	Dem	N.C.	9	9
4th	Jones, Ed	Dem	Tenn.	7	7
5th	Brown, George E. Jr.	Dem	Cal.	9	5
6th	Bowen, David R.	Dem	Miss.	5	5
7th	Rose, Charles G. III	Dem	N.C.	5	5
8th	Richmond, Frederick W.	Dem	N.Y.	4	4
9th	Weaver, James H.	Dem	Ore.	4	4
10th	Harkin, Thomas R.	Dem	Iowa	4	4
11th	Bedell, Berkley W.	Dem	Iowa	4	4
12th	English, Glenn L. Jr.	Dem	Okla.	4	4
13th	Fithian, Floyd J.	Dem	Ind.	4	4
14th	Panetta, Leon E.	Dem	Cal.	3	3
15th	Huckaby, T. Jerry	Dem	La.	3	3
16th	Glickman, Daniel R.	Dem	Kans.	3	3
17th	Whitley, Charles O. Sr.	Dem	N.C.	3	3
18th	Coelho, Anthony L.	Dem	Cal.	2	2
19th	Daschle, Thomas A.	Dem	S.D.	2	2
20th	Anthony, Beryl F. Jr.	Dem	Ark.	2	2
21st	Stenholm, Charles W.	Dem	Tex.	2	2
22nd	Volkmer, Harold L.	Dem	Mo.	3	1
23rd	Hatcher, Charles F.	Dem	Ga.	1	1
24th	Dorgan, Byron L.	Dem	N.D.	1	1

Minority

Rank	Name	Party	State	Terms in: House	Terms in: Comm.
RM	Wampler, William C.	Rep	Va.	9	*2 8
2nd	Findley, Paul	Rep	Ill.	11	*2 6
3rd	Jeffords, James M.	Rep	Vt.	4	4
4th	Hagedorn, Thomas M.	Rep	Minn.	4	4
5th	Coleman, E. Thomas	Rep	Mo.	4	3
6th	Marlenee, Ron	Rep	Mont.	3	3
7th	Hopkins, Larry J.	Rep	Ky.	2	2
8th	Thomas, William M.	Rep	Cal.	2	2
9th	Hansen, George V.	Rep	Ida.	5	*2 2
10th	Stangeland, Arlan	Rep	Minn.	3	1
11th	Roberts, Pat	Rep	Kans.	1	1
12th	Emerson, Bill	Rep	Mo.	1	1
13th	Napier, John L.	Rep	S.C.	1	1
14th	Skeen, Joe	Rep	N.M.	1	1
15th	Morrison, Sid	Rep	Wash.	1	1
16th	Roberts, Clint	Rep	S.D.	1	1
17th	Gunderson, Steven	Rep	Wisc.	1	1
18th	Evans, Cooper	Rep	Iowa	1	1
19th	Chappie, Eugene A.	Rep	Cal.	1	1

*2: Member's 2nd period of service on the committee.

Note: Ranking on this committee for the following member was affected by other chamber service: Thomas S. Foley (Dem-Wash.), House Majority Whip.

Changes:

Majority:

Anthony, Beryl F. Jr.	Dem	Ark.	Oct. 7,1981	Moved to Ways and Means.
Albosta, Donald J.	Dem	Mich.	Dec. 16,1981	Replaced Anthony.
Richmond, Frederick W.	Dem	N.Y.	Aug. 25,1982	Resigned and retired.

Departures from the House:	**Majority**			**Minority**		
Defeated for Reelection	None			Findley, Paul	Ill.	Rep
				Hagedorn, Thomas M.	Minn.	Rep
				Napier, John L.	S.C.	Rep
				Roberts, Clint	S.D.	Rep
				Wampler, William C.	Va.	Rep
Lost Election to U.S. Senate	Fithian, Floyd J.	Ind.	Dem	None		
Retired	Bowen, David R.	Miss.	Dem	None		
Departures from Committee:						
No new assignment	Albosta, Donald J.	Mich.	Dem	None		
Moved to Ways and Means	Dorgan, Byron L.	N.D.	Dem	Thomas, William M.	Cal.	Rep

AGRICULTURE / 98th Congress

Service Dates of Committee Chair: Jan. 6,1983-Jan. 3,1985
Service Dates of Majority Members: Jan. 6,1983-Jan. 3,1985
Service Dates of Minority Members: Jan. 6,1983-Jan. 3,1985

Majority

Rank	Name	Party	State	Terms in: House	Terms in: Comm.
Chr	de la Garza, E. (Kika)	Dem	Tex.	10	10
2nd	Foley, Thomas S.	Dem	Wash.	10	10
3rd	Jones, Walter B.	Dem	N.C.	10	10
4th	Jones, Ed	Dem	Tenn.	8	8
5th	Brown, George E. Jr.	Dem	Cal.	10	6
6th	Rose, Charles G. III	Dem	N.C.	6	6
7th	Weaver, James H.	Dem	Ore.	5	5
8th	Harkin, Thomas R.	Dem	Iowa	5	5
9th	Bedell, Berkley W.	Dem	Iowa	5	5
10th	English, Glenn L. Jr.	Dem	Okla.	5	5
11th	Panetta, Leon E.	Dem	Cal.	4	4
12th	Huckaby, T. Jerry	Dem	La.	4	4
13th	Glickman, Daniel R.	Dem	Kans.	4	4
14th	Whitley, Charles O. Sr.	Dem	N.C.	4	4
15th	Coelho, Anthony L.	Dem	Cal.	3	3
16th	Daschle, Thomas A.	Dem	S.D.	3	3
17th	Stenholm, Charles W.	Dem	Tex.	3	3
18th	Volkmer, Harold L.	Dem	Mo.	4	2
19th	Hatcher, Charles F.	Dem	Ga.	2	2
20th	Tallon, Robin	Dem	S.C.	1	1
21st	Staggers, Harley O. Jr.	Dem	W.Va.	1	1
22nd	Durbin, Richard J.	Dem	Ill.	1	1
23rd	Evans, Lane	Dem	Ill.	1	1
24th	Thomas, Robert Lindsay	Dem	Ga.	1	1
25th	Olin, James R.	Dem	Va.	1	1
26th	Penny, Timothy J.	Dem	Minn.	1	1

Minority

Rank	Name	Party	State	Terms in: House	Terms in: Comm.
RM	Madigan, Edward R.	Rep	Ill.	6	6
2nd	Jeffords, James M.	Rep	Vt.	5	5
3rd	Coleman, E. Thomas	Rep	Mo.	5	4
4th	Marlenee, Ron	Rep	Mont.	4	4
5th	Hopkins, Larry J.	Rep	Ky.	3	3
6th	Hansen, George V.	Rep	Ida.	6	*2 3
7th	Stangeland, Arlan	Rep	Minn.	4	2
8th	Roberts, Pat	Rep	Kans.	2	2
9th	Emerson, Bill	Rep	Mo.	2	2
10th	Skeen, Joe	Rep	N.M.	2	2
11th	Morrison, Sid	Rep	Wash.	2	2
12th	Gunderson, Steven	Rep	Wisc.	2	2
13th	Evans, Cooper	Rep	Iowa	2	2
14th	Chappie, Eugene A.	Rep	Cal.	2	2
15th	Franklin, Webb	Rep	Miss.	1	1

*2: Member's 2nd period of service on the committee.

Note: Ranking on this committee for the following member was affected by other chamber service: Thomas S. Foley (Dem-Wash.), House Majority Whip.

	Majority			Minority		
Departures from the House:						
Elected to U.S. Senate	Harkin, Thomas R.	Iowa	Dem	None		
Defeated for Reelection	None			Hansen, George V.	Ida.	Rep
Departures from Committee:						
Moved to Appropriations	Durbin, Richard J.	Ill.	Dem	Skeen, Joe	N.M.	Rep

AGRICULTURE / 99th Congress

Service Dates of Committee Chair: Jan. 7,1985-Jan. 3,1987
Service Dates of Majority Members: Jan. 30,1985-Jan. 3,1987
Service Dates of Minority Members: Jan. 30,1985-Jan. 3,1987

Majority

Rank	Name	Party	State	Terms in: House	Terms in: Comm.
Chr	de la Garza, E. (Kika)	Dem	Tex.	11	11
2nd	Foley, Thomas S.	Dem	Wash.	11	11
3rd	Jones, Walter B.	Dem	N.C.	11	11
4th	Jones, Ed	Dem	Tenn.	9	9
5th	Brown, George E. Jr.	Dem	Cal.	11	7
6th	Rose, Charles G. III	Dem	N.C.	7	7
7th	Weaver, James H.	Dem	Ore.	6	6
8th	Bedell, Berkley W.	Dem	Iowa	6	6
9th	English, Glenn L. Jr.	Dem	Okla.	6	6
10th	Panetta, Leon E.	Dem	Cal.	5	5
11th	Huckaby, T. Jerry	Dem	La.	5	5
12th	Glickman, Daniel R.	Dem	Kans.	5	5
13th	Whitley, Charles O. Sr.	Dem	N.C.	5	5
14th	Coelho, Anthony L.	Dem	Cal.	4	4
15th	Daschle, Thomas A.	Dem	S.D.	4	4
16th	Stenholm, Charles W.	Dem	Tex.	4	4
17th	Volkmer, Harold L.	Dem	Mo.	5	3
18th	Hatcher, Charles F.	Dem	Ga.	3	3
19th	Tallon, Robin	Dem	S.C.	2	2
20th	Staggers, Harley O. Jr.	Dem	W.Va.	2	2
21st	Evans, Lane	Dem	Ill.	2	2
22nd	Thomas, Robert Lindsay	Dem	Ga.	2	2
23rd	Olin, James R.	Dem	Va.	2	2
24th	Penny, Timothy J.	Dem	Minn.	2	2
25th	Stallings, Richard H.	Dem	Ida.	1	1
26th	Bruce, Terry L.	Dem	Ill.	1	*T 1

Minority

Rank	Name	Party	State	Terms in: House	Terms in: Comm.
RM	Madigan, Edward R.	Rep	Ill.	7	7
2nd	Jeffords, James M.	Rep	Vt.	6	6
3rd	Coleman, E. Thomas	Rep	Mo.	6	5
4th	Marlenee, Ron	Rep	Mont.	5	5
5th	Hopkins, Larry J.	Rep	Ky.	4	4
6th	Stangeland, Arlan	Rep	Minn.	5	3
7th	Roberts, Pat	Rep	Kans.	3	3
8th	Emerson, Bill	Rep	Mo.	3	3
9th	Morrison, Sid	Rep	Wash.	3	3
10th	Gunderson, Steven	Rep	Wisc.	3	3
11th	Evans, Cooper	Rep	Iowa	3	3
12th	Chappie, Eugene A.	Rep	Cal.	3	3
13th	Franklin, Webb	Rep	Miss.	2	2
14th	Lewis, Tom	Rep	Fla.	2	1
15th	Smith, Robert F.	Rep	Ore.	2	1
16th	Combest, Larry	Rep	Tex.	1	1
17th	Schuette, Bill	Rep	Mich.	1	1

*T: Temporary member of the committee.

Note: Ranking on this committee for the following member was affected by other chamber service: Thomas S. Foley (Dem-Wash.), House Majority Whip.

Vacancy Filled: Majority: 26th seat filled by Bruce on Feb. 6,1985.

Changes:

Majority:

Bruce, Terry L.	Dem	Ill.	Dec. 30,1985	Temporary term expired.
Bruce, Terry L.	Dem	Ill.	Jan. 29,1986	Replaced himself.

	Majority			Minority		
Departures from the House:						
Elected to U.S. Senate	Daschle, Thomas A.	S.D.	Dem	None		
Defeated for Reelection	None			Franklin, Webb	Miss.	Rep
Retired	Bedell, Berkley W.	Iowa	Dem	Chappie, Eugene A.	Cal.	Rep
	Whitley, Charles O. Sr.	N.C.	Dem	Evans, T. Cooper	Iowa	Rep
	Weaver, James H.	Ore.	Dem			
Departures from Committee:						
Elected Majority Leader	Foley, Thomas S.	Wash.	Dem	None		
Moved to Energy & Commerce	Bruce, Terry L.	Ill.	Dem	None		

AGRICULTURE / 100th Congress

Service Dates of Committee Chair: Jan. 8,1987-Jan. 3,1989
Service Dates of Majority Members: Jan. 22,1987-Jan. 3,1989
Service Dates of Minority Members: Jan. 21,1987-Jan. 3,1989

Majority

Rank	Name	Party	State	Terms in: House	Terms in: Comm.
Chr	de la Garza, E. (Kika)	Dem	Tex.	12	12
2nd	Jones, Walter B.	Dem	N.C.	12	12
3rd	Jones, Ed	Dem	Tenn.	10	10
4th	Brown, George E. Jr.	Dem	Cal.	12	8
5th	Rose, Charles G. III	Dem	N.C.	8	8
6th	English, Glenn L. Jr.	Dem	Okla.	7	7
7th	Panetta, Leon E.	Dem	Cal.	6	6
8th	Huckaby, T. Jerry	Dem	La.	6	6
9th	Glickman, Daniel R.	Dem	Kans.	6	6
10th	Coelho, Anthony L.	Dem	Cal.	5	5
11th	Stenholm, Charles W.	Dem	Tex.	5	5
12th	Volkmer, Harold L.	Dem	Mo.	6	4
13th	Hatcher, Charles F.	Dem	Ga.	4	4
14th	Tallon, Robin	Dem	S.C.	3	3
15th	Staggers, Harley O. Jr.	Dem	W.Va.	3	3
16th	Evans, Lane	Dem	Ill.	3	3
17th	Thomas, Robert Lindsay	Dem	Ga.	3	3
18th	Olin, James R.	Dem	Va.	3	3
19th	Penny, Timothy J.	DFL	Minn.	3	3
20th	Stallings, Richard H.	Dem	Ida.	2	2
21st	Nagle, David R.	Dem	Iowa	1	1
22nd	Jontz, James	Dem	Ind.	1	1
23rd	Johnson, Tim	Dem	S.D.	1	1
24th	Harris, Claude	Dem	Ala.	1	1
25th	Campbell, Ben Nighthorse	Dem	Colo.	1	1
26th	Espy, Mike	Dem	Miss.	1	1

Minority

Rank	Name	Party	State	Terms in: House	Terms in: Comm.
RM	Madigan, Edward R.	Rep	Ill.	8	8
2nd	Jeffords, James M.	Rep	Vt.	7	7
3rd	Coleman, E. Thomas	Rep	Mo.	7	6
4th	Marlenee, Ron	Rep	Mont.	6	6
5th	Hopkins, Larry J.	Rep	Ky.	5	5
6th	Stangeland, Arlan	Rep	Minn.	6	4
7th	Roberts, Pat	Rep	Kans.	4	4
8th	Emerson, Bill	Rep	Mo.	4	4
9th	Morrison, Sid	Rep	Wash.	4	4
10th	Gunderson, Steven	Rep	Wisc.	4	4
11th	Lewis, Tom	Rep	Fla.	3	2
12th	Smith, Robert F.	Rep	Ore.	3	2
13th	Combest, Larry	Rep	Tex.	2	2
14th	Schuette, Bill	Rep	Mich.	2	2
15th	Grandy, Fred	Rep	Iowa	1	1
16th	Herger, Wally	Rep	Cal.	1	1
17th	Holloway, Clyde C.	Rep	La.	1	1

Changes:

Majority:

Name	Party	State	Date	Change
Thomas, Robert Lindsay	Dem	Ga.	Oct. 21,1987	Moved to Appropriations.
Lancaster, H. Martin	Dem	N.C.	Dec. 15,1987	Replaced Thomas.
Evans, Lane	Dem	Ill.	June 8,1988	Had already moved to Armed Services on May 18,1988.

Departures from the House:

	Majority	Minority
Elected to U.S. Senate	None	Jeffords, James M. Vt. Rep
Retired	Jones, Ed Tenn. Dem	None

AGRICULTURE / 101st Congress

Service Dates of Committee Chair: Jan. 3,1989-Jan. 3,1991
Service Dates of Majority Members: Jan. 19,1989-Jan. 3,1991
Service Dates of Minority Members: Jan. 20,1989-Jan. 3,1991

Majority

Rank	Name	Party	State	Terms in: House	Terms in: Comm.
Chr	de la Garza, E. (Kika)	Dem	Tex.	13	13
2nd	Jones, Walter B.	Dem	N.C.	13	13
3rd	Brown, George E. Jr.	Dem	Cal.	13	9
4th	Rose, Charles G. III	Dem	N.C.	9	9
5th	English, Glenn L. Jr.	Dem	Okla.	8	8
6th	Panetta, Leon E.	Dem	Cal.	7	7
7th	Huckaby, T. Jerry	Dem	La.	7	7
8th	Glickman, Daniel R.	Dem	Kans.	7	7
9th	Coelho, Anthony L.	Dem	Cal.	6	6
10th	Stenholm, Charles W.	Dem	Tex.	6	6
11th	Volkmer, Harold L.	Dem	Mo.	7	5
12th	Hatcher, Charles F.	Dem	Ga.	5	5
13th	Tallon, Robin	Dem	S.C.	4	4
14th	Staggers, Harley O. Jr.	Dem	W.Va.	4	4
15th	Olin, James R.	Dem	Va.	4	4
16th	Penny, Timothy J.	Dem	Minn.	4	4
17th	Stallings, Richard H.	Dem	Ida.	3	3
18th	Nagle, David R.	Dem	Iowa	2	2
19th	Jontz, James	Dem	Ind.	2	2
20th	Johnson, Tim	Dem	S.D.	2	2
21st	Harris, Claude	Dem	Ala.	2	2
22nd	Campbell, Ben Nighthorse	Dem	Colo.	2	2
23rd	Espy, Mike	Dem	Miss.	2	2
24th	Sarpalius, Bill	Dem	Tex.	1	1
25th	Long, Jill	Dem	Ill.	1	1
26th	Dyson, Royden	Dem	Md.	5	*T 1
27th	Lancaster, H. Martin	Dem	N.C.	2	*T 2

Minority

Rank	Name	Party	State	Terms in: House	Terms in: Comm.
RM	Madigan, Edward R.	Rep	Ill.	9	9
2nd	Coleman, E. Thomas	Rep	Mo.	8	7
3rd	Marlenee, Ron	Rep	Mont.	7	7
4th	Hopkins, Larry J.	Rep	Ky.	6	6
5th	Stangeland, Arlan	Rep	Minn.	7	5
6th	Roberts, Pat	Rep	Kans.	5	5
7th	Emerson, Bill	Rep	Mo.	5	5
8th	Morrison, Sid	Rep	Wash.	5	5
9th	Gunderson, Steven	Rep	Wisc.	5	5
10th	Lewis, Tom	Rep	Fla.	4	3
11th	Smith, Robert F.	Rep	Ore.	4	3
12th	Combest, Larry	Rep	Tex.	3	3
13th	Schuette, Bill	Rep	Mich.	3	3
14th	Grandy, Fred	Rep	Iowa	2	2
15th	Herger, Wally	Rep	Cal.	2	2
16th	Holloway, Clyde C.	Rep	La.	2	2
17th	Walsh, James T.	Rep	N.Y.	1	1
18th	Grant, Bill	Rep	Fla.	3	1

*T: Temporary member of the committee.

Note: Bill Grant of Florida resigned from the Democratic Party and joined the Republican Party on Feb. 22,1989, thereby losing his majority committee assignments. Jill Long (Dem-Ill.) was ranked above temporary members Dyson and Lancaster upon her assignment to the committee.

Vacancy Filled:
Majority: 26th and 27th seats by Dyson and Lancaster respectively on Jan. 27,1989; 25th seat by Long on Apr. 27,1989.
Minority: 18th seat by Grant as a Republican, on May 4,1989.

Changes:
Majority:

Coelho, Anthony L.	Dem	Cal.	June 15,1989	Resigned and retired.
Condit, Gary	Dem	Cal.	Oct. 16,1989	Replaced Coelho; ranked before Dyson Nov. 8,1989.

Departures from the House:	**Majority**			**Minority**		
Defeated for Reelection	Dyson, Royden	Md.	Dem	Stangeland, Arlan	Minn.	Rep
				Grant, Bill	Fla.	Rep
Lost Election to U.S. Senate	None			Schuette, Bill	Mich.	Rep
Departures from Committee:						
Moved to Energy and Commerce	Harris, Claude	Ala.	Dem	Holloway, Clyde C.	La.	Rep
Moved to Ways and Means	None			Grandy, Fred	Iowa	Rep
No new assignment	Lancaster, H. Martin	N.C.	Dem	None		

AGRICULTURE / 102nd Congress

Service Dates of Committee Chair: Jan. 24,1991-Jan. 3,1993
Service Dates of Majority Members: Jan. 24,1991-Jan. 3,1993
Service Dates of Minority Members: Jan. 24,1991-Jan. 3,1993

Majority

Rank Name	Party	State	Terms in: House	Terms in: Comm.
Chr de la Garza, E. (Kika)	Dem	Tex.	14	14
2nd Jones, Walter B.	Dem	N.C.	14	14
3rd Brown, George E. Jr.	Dem	Cal.	14	10
4th Rose, Charles G. III	Dem	N.C.	10	10
5th English, Glenn L. Jr.	Dem	Okla.	9	9
6th Panetta, Leon E.	Dem	Cal.	8	8
7th Huckaby, T. Jerry	Dem	La.	8	8
8th Glickman, Daniel R.	Dem	Kans.	8	8
9th Stenholm, Charles W.	Dem	Tex.	7	7
10th Volkmer, Harold L.	Dem	Mo.	8	6
11th Hatcher, Charles F.	Dem	Ga.	6	6
12th Tallon, Robin	Dem	S.C.	5	5
13th Staggers, Harley O. Jr.	Dem	W.Va.	5	5
14th Olin, James R.	Dem	Va.	5	5
15th Penny, Timothy J.	Dem	Minn.	5	5
16th Stallings, Richard H.	Dem	Ida.	4	4
17th Nagle, David R.	Dem	Iowa	3	3
18th Jontz, James	Dem	Ind.	3	3
19th Johnson, Tim	Dem	S.D.	3	3
20th Campbell, Ben Nighthorse	Dem	Colo.	3	3
21st Espy, Mike	Dem	Miss.	3	3
22nd Sarpalius, Bill	Dem	Tex.	2	2
23rd Long, Jill L.	Dem	Ill.	2	2
24th Condit, Gary	Dem	Cal.	2	2
25th Peterson, Collin C.	Dem	Minn.	1	1
26th Dooley, Calvin	Dem	Cal.	1	1
27th Kopetski, Mike	Dem	Ore.	1	1

Minority

Rank Name	Party	State	Terms in: House	Terms in: Comm.
RM1 Madigan, Edward R.	Rep	Ill.	10	10
RM2 2nd Coleman, E. Thomas	Rep	Mo.	9	8
3rd Marlenee, Ron	Rep	Mont.	8	8
4th Hopkins, Larry J.	Rep	Ky.	7	7
5th Roberts, Pat	Rep	Kans.	6	6
6th Emerson, Bill	Rep	Mo.	6	6
7th Morrison, Sid	Rep	Wash.	6	6
8th Gunderson, Steven	Rep	Wisc.	6	6
9th Lewis, Tom	Rep	Fla.	5	4
10th Smith, Robert F.	Rep	Ore.	5	4
11th Combest, Larry	Rep	Tex.	4	4
12th Herger, Wally	Rep	Cal.	3	3
13th Walsh, James T.	Rep	N.Y.	3	2
14th Camp, Dave	Rep	Mich.	1	1
15th Allard, Wayne	Rep	Colo.	1	1
16th Barrett, Bill	Rep	Neb.	1	1
17th Nussle, Jim	Rep	Iowa	1	1
18th Boehner, John A.	Rep	Ohio	1	1

Changes:

Ranking Member:

RM1 Madigan, Edward R.	Rep	Ill.	Mar. 8,1991	Resigned House; appointed Secretary of Agriculture.
RM2 Coleman, E. Thomas	Rep	Mo.	Mar. 8,1991	Succeeded Madigan as Ranking Minority Member.

Majority:

Jones, Walter B.	Dem	N.C.	Sep. 15,1992	Died in office.

Minority:

Madigan, Edward R.	Rep	Ill.	Mar. 8,1991	Resigned House; appointed Secretary of Agriculture.
Ewing, Thomas W.	Rep	Ill.	July 11,1991	Replaced Madigan.

APPROPRIATIONS

Jurisdiction, 1947

Established by the Legislative Reorganization Act of 1946:

[Section 121.(1)(b)]

Committee on Appropriations.

1. Appropriation of the revenue for the support of the Government.

[Sec. 139]

(a) No general appropriation bill shall be considered in either House unless, prior to the consideration of such bill, printed committee hearings and reports on such bill have been available for at least three calendar days for the Members of the House in which such bill is to be considered.
(b) The Committees on Appropriations of the two Houses are authorized and directed, acting jointly, to develop a standard appropriation classification schedule which will clearly define in concise and uniform accounts the subtotals of appropriations asked for by agencies in the executive branch of the Government. That part of the printed hearings containing each such agency's request for appropriations shall be preceded by such a schedule.
(c) No general appropriation bill or amendment thereto shall be received or considered in either House if it contains a provision reappropriating unexpended balances of appropriations; except that this provision shall not apply to appropriations in continuation of appropriations for public works on which work has commenced.
(d) The Appropriations Committees of both Houses are authorized and directed to make a study of (1) existing permanent appropriations with a view to limiting the number of permanent appropriations and to recommend to their respective Houses what permanent appropriations, if any, should be discontinued; and (2) the disposition of funds resulting from the sale of Government property or services by all departments and agencies in the executive branch of the Government with a view to recommending to their respective Houses a uniform system of control with respect to such funds.

Jurisdiction, 1992

Jurisdiction contained in Rules of the House of Representatives (as revised to July 1, 1992):

[Rule X. 1. (b)]

Committee on Appropriations.

(1) Appropriation of the revenue for the support of the Government.
(2) Rescissions of appropriations contained in appropriation Acts.
(3) Transfers of unexpended balances.
(4) The amount of new spending authority (as described in the Congressional Budget Act of 1974) which is to be effective for a fiscal year, including bills and resolutions (reported by other committees) which provide new spending authority and are referred to the committee under clause 4(a).

The committee shall include separate headings for "Rescissions" and "Transfers of Unexpended Balances" in any bill or resolution as reported from the committee under its jurisdiction specified in subparagraph (2) or (3), with all proposed rescissions and proposed transfers listed therein; and shall include a separate section with respect to such rescissions or transfers in the accompanying committee report. In addition to its jurisdiction under the preceding provisions of this paragraph, the committee shall have the fiscal oversight function provided for in clause 2(b) (3) and the budget hearing function provided for in clause 4(a).

Additional functions of the Committee on Appropriations:

[Rule X. 4.(a)(1)]

(A) The Committee on Appropriations shall, within thirty days after the transmittal of the Budget to the Congress each year, hold hearings on the Budget as a whole with particular reference to--

(i) the basic recommendations and budgetary policies of the President in the presentation of the Budget; and
(ii) the fiscal, financial, and economic assumptions used as bases in arriving at total estimated expenditures and receipts.

(B) In holding hearings pursuant to subdivision (A), the committee shall receive testimony from the Secretary of the Treasury, the Director of the Office of Management and Budget, the Chairman of the Council of Economic Advisers, and such other persons as the committee may desire.

[Rule X. 4.(a)(2)]

Whenever any bill or resolution which provides new spending authority described in section 401(c) (2) (C) of the Congressional Budget Act of 1974 is reported by a committee of the House and the amount of new budget authority which will be required for the fiscal year involved if such bill or resolution is enacted as so reported exceeds the appropriate allocation of new budget authority reported as described in clause 4(h) in connection with the most recently agreed to concurrent resolution on the budget for such fiscal year, such bill or resolution shall then be referred to the Committee on Appropriations with instructions to report it, with the committee's recommendations and (if the committee deems it desirable) with an amendment limiting the total amount of new spending authority provided in the bill or resolution, within 15 calendar days (not counting any day on which the House is not in session) beginning with the day following the day on which it is so referred. If the Committee on Appropriations fails to report the bill or resolution within such 15-day period, the committee shall be automatically discharged from further consideration of the bill or resolution and the bill or resolution shall be placed on the appropriate calendar.

[Rule 4.(a)(3)]

In addition, the Committee on Appropriations shall study on a continuing basis those provisions of law which (on the first day of the first fiscal year for which the congressional budget process is effective) provide spending authority or permanent budget authority, and shall report to the House from time to time its recommendations for terminating or modifying such provisions.

APPROPRIATIONS / 80th Congress

Service Dates of Committee Chair: Jan. 7,1947-Jan. 3,1949
Service Dates of Majority Members: Jan. 7,1947-Jan. 3,1949
Service Dates of Minority Members: Jan. 8,1947-Jan. 3,1949

Majority

Rank	Name	Party	State	Terms in: House	Terms in: Comm.
Chr	Taber, John	Rep	N.Y.	13	13
2nd	Wigglesworth, Richard B.	Rep	Mass.	11	10
3rd	Plumley, Charles A.	Rep	Vt.	8	6
4th	Dirksen, Everett M.	Rep	Ill.	8	6
5th	Engel, Albert J.	Rep	Mich.	7	6
6th	Stefan, Karl	Rep	Neb.	7	5
7th	Case, Francis H.	Rep	S.D.	6	5
8th	Keefe, Frank B.	Rep	Wisc.	5	5
9th	Johnson, Noble J.	Rep	Ind.	8	4
10th	Jones, Robert F.	Rep	Ohio	5	4
11th	Jensen, Ben F.	Rep	Iowa	5	3
12th	Andersen, H. Carl	Rep	Minn.	5	3
13th	Ploeser, Walter C.	Rep	Mo.	4	3
14th	Tibbott, Harve	Rep	Penn.	5	3
15th	Horan, Walter F.	Rep	Wash.	3	2
16th	Canfield, Gordon	Rep	N.J.	4	2
17th	Schwabe, George B.	Rep	Okla.	2	*1 2
18th	Fenton, Ivor D.	Rep	Penn.	5	1
19th	Church, Ralph E.	Rep	Ill.	6	1
20th	Griffiths, Percy W.	Rep	Ohio	3	1
21st	Stockman, Lowell	Rep	Ore.	3	1
22nd	Phillips, John	Rep	Cal.	3	1
23rd	Scrivner, Errett P.	Rep	Kans.	3	1
24th	Robertson, Charles R.	Rep	N.D.	3	1
25th	Coudert, Frederic R. Jr.	Rep	N.Y.	1	1

Minority

Rank	Name	Party	State	Terms in: House	Terms in: Comm.
RM	Cannon, Clarence	Dem	Mo.	13	10
2nd	Ludlow, Louis	Dem	Ind.	10	9
3rd	Kerr, John H.	Dem	N.C.	13	5
4th	Mahon, George H.	Dem	Tex.	7	5
5th	Sheppard, Harry R.	Dem	Cal.	6	5
6th	Thomas, Albert	Dem	Tex.	6	4
7th	Hendricks, Joseph E.	Dem	Fla.	6	4
8th	Kirwan, Michael J.	Dem	Ohio	6	3
9th	Norrell, William F.	Dem	Ark.	5	3
10th	Gore, Albert A.	Dem	Tenn.	5	3
11th	Whitten, Jamie L.	Dem	Miss.	4	3
12th	D'Alesandro, Thomas Jr.	Dem	Md.	5	2
13th	Andrews, George W.	Dem	Ala.	3	2
14th	Rooney, John J.	Dem	N.Y.	3	2
15th	Gary, J. Vaughn	Dem	Va.	2	2
16th	Bates, Joe B.	Dem	Ky.	6	6
17th	O'Brien, Thomas J.	Dem	Ill.	6	3
18th	Fogarty, John E.	Dem	R.I.	4	1

*1: Member's 1st period of service on the committee.

Vacancies Filled:
Majority: 18th through 25th seats were filled on Jan. 14,1947.
Minority: 16th through 18th seats were filled on Jan. 16,1947.

Changes:
Majority:

Name	Party	State	Date	Change
Jones, Robert F.	Rep	Ohio	July 23,1947	Left committee; resigned House Sep. 2,1947 appointed to Federal Communications Commission.
Clevenger, Cliff	Rep	Ohio	July 23,1947	Replaced Jones.
Johnson, Noble J.	Rep	Ind.	June 19,1948	Left committee; later resigned House for federal judgeship on July 1,1948.
Wilson, Earl	Rep	Ind.	June 19,1948	Replaced Johnson.

Minority:

Name	Party	State	Date	Change
D'Alesandro, Thomas Jr.	Dem	Md.	May 16,1947	Resigned House; elected Mayor of Baltimore
Jackson, Henry M.	Dem	Wash.	July 24,1947	Replaced D'Alesandro.

Departures from the House:

	Majority			Minority		
Defeated for Reelection	Griffiths, Percy W.	Ohio	Rep	None		
	Ploeser, Walter C.	Mo.	Rep			
	Schwabe, George B.	Okla.	Rep			
	Tibbott, Harve	Penn.	Rep			
Defeated for Renomination	Robertson, Charles R.	N.D.	Rep	None		
Retired	Dirksen, Everett McK.	Ill.	Rep	Hendricks, Joseph E.	Fla.	Dem
				Ludlow, Louis	Ind.	Dem

Departures from Committee:

	Majority			Minority		
Moved to House Administration	Wilson, Earl	Ind.	Rep	None		
Moved to Ways & Means	None			O'Brien, Thomas J.	Ill.	Dem

APPROPRIATIONS / 81st Congress

Service Dates of Committee Chair: Jan. 18,1949-Jan. 3,1951
Service Dates of Majority Members: Jan. 18,1949-Jan. 3,1951
Service Dates of Minority Members: Jan. 18,1949-Jan. 3,1951

Majority

Rank	Name	Party	State	Terms in: House	Terms in: Comm.
Chr	Cannon, Clarence	Dem	Mo.	14	11
2nd	Kerr, John H.	Dem	N.C.	14	6
3rd	Mahon, George H.	Dem	Tex.	8	6
4th	Sheppard, Harry R.	Dem	Cal.	7	6
5th	Thomas, Albert	Dem	Tex.	7	5
6th	Kirwan, Michael J.	Dem	Ohio	7	4
7th	Norrell, William F.	Dem	Ark.	6	4
8th	Gore, Albert A.	Dem	Tenn.	6	4
9th	Whitten, Jamie L.	Dem	Miss.	5	4
10th	Andrews, George W.	Dem	Ala.	4	3
11th	Rooney, John J.	Dem	N.Y.	4	3
12th	Gary, J. Vaughn	Dem	Va.	3	3
13th	Bates, Joe B.	Dem	Ky.	7	7
14th	Fogarty, John E.	Dem	R.I.	5	2
15th	Jackson, Henry M.	Dem	Wash.	5	2
16th	Sikes, Robert L. F.	Dem	Fla.	5	1
17th	Fernandez, Antonio M.	Dem	N.M.	4	1
18th	Stigler, William G.	Dem	Okla.	4	1
19th	Hedrick, Erland H.	Dem	W.Va.	3	1
20th	Preston, Prince H. Jr.	Dem	Ga.	2	1
21st	Passman, Otto E.	Dem	La.	2	1
22nd	Rabaut, Louis C.	Dem	Mich.	7	*2 1
23rd	Flood, Daniel J.	Dem	Penn.	2	*2 1
24th	McGrath, Christopher C.	Dem	N.Y.	1	1
25th	Yates, Sidney R.	Dem	Ill.	1	*1 1
26th	Furcolo, Foster	Dem	Mass.	1	1
27th	Kruse, Edward H. Jr.	Dem	Ind.	1	1

Minority

Rank	Name	Party	State	Terms in: House	Terms in: Comm.
RM	Taber, John	Rep	N.Y.	14	14
2nd	Wigglesworth, Richard B.	Rep	Mass.	12	11
3rd	Plumley, Charles A.	Rep	Vt.	9	7
4th	Engel, Albert J.	Rep	Mich.	8	7
5th	Stefan, Karl	Rep	Neb.	8	6
6th	Case, Francis H.	Rep	S.D.	7	6
7th	Keefe, Frank B.	Rep	Wisc.	6	6
8th	Jensen, Ben F.	Rep	Iowa	6	4
9th	Andersen, H. Carl	Rep	Minn.	6	4
10th	Horan, Walter F.	Rep	Wash.	4	3
11th	Canfield, Gordon	Rep	N.J.	5	3
12th	Fenton, Ivor D.	Rep	Penn.	6	2
13th	Church, Ralph E.	Rep	Ill.	7	2
14th	Stockman, Lowell	Rep	Ore.	4	2
15th	Phillips, John	Rep	Cal.	4	2
16th	Scrivner, Errett P.	Rep	Kans.	4	2
17th	Coudert, Frederic R. Jr.	Rep	N.Y.	2	2
18th	Clevenger, Cliff	Rep	Ohio	6	2

*1: Member's 1st period of service on the committee;
*2: Member's 2nd period of service on the committee.

Changes:

Minority:

Name	Party	State	Date	Change
Church, Ralph E.	Rep	Ill.	Mar. 21,1950	Died in office.
Wilson, Earl	Rep	Ind.	Mar. 30,1950	Replaced Church.
Plumley, Charles A.	Rep	Vt.	Aug. 29,1950	Left committee; no new assignment.
Cotton, Norris	Rep	N.H.	Aug. 29,1950	Replaced Plumley.

Departures from the House:

	Majority		Minority	
Elected to U.S. Senate	None		Case, Francis H.	S.D. Rep
Defeated for Reelection	Kruse, Edward H. Jr.	Ind. Dem	None	
Lost Nomination for Governor	None		Engel, Albert J.	Mich. Rep
Retired	None		Keefe, Frank B.	Wisc. Rep

APPROPRIATIONS / 82nd Congress

Service Dates of Committee Chair: Jan. 3,1951-Jan. 3,1953
Service Dates of Majority Members: Jan. 3,1951-Jan. 3,1953
Service Dates of Minority Members: Jan. 4,1951-Jan. 3,1953

Majority

Rank	Name	Party	State	Terms in: House	Terms in: Comm.
Chr	Cannon, Clarence	Dem	Mo.	15	12
2nd	Kerr, John H.	Dem	N.C.	15	7
3rd	Mahon, George H.	Dem	Tex.	9	7
4th	Sheppard, Harry R.	Dem	Cal.	8	7
5th	Thomas, Albert	Dem	Tex.	8	6
6th	Kirwan, Michael J.	Dem	Ohio	8	5
7th	Norrell, William F.	Dem	Ark.	7	5
8th	Gore, Albert A.	Dem	Tenn.	7	5
9th	Whitten, Jamie L.	Dem	Miss.	6	5
10th	Andrews, George W.	Dem	Ala.	5	4
11th	Rooney, John J.	Dem	N.Y.	5	4
12th	Gary, J. Vaughn	Dem	Va.	4	4
13th	Bates, Joe B.	Dem	Ky.	8	8
14th	Fogarty, John E.	Dem	R.I.	6	3
15th	Jackson, Henry M.	Dem	Wash.	6	3
16th	Sikes, Robert L. F.	Dem	Fla.	6	2
17th	Fernandez, Antonio M.	Dem	N.M.	5	2
18th	Stigler, William G.	Dem	Okla.	5	2
19th	Hedrick, Erland H.	Dem	W.Va.	4	2
20th	Preston, Prince H. Jr.	Dem	Ga.	3	2
21st	Passman, Otto E.	Dem	La.	3	2
22nd	Rabaut, Louis C.	Dem	Mich.	8 *2	2
23rd	Flood, Daniel J.	Dem	Penn.	3 *2	2
24th	McGrath, Christopher C.	Dem	N.Y.	2	2
25th	Yates, Sidney R.	Dem	Ill.	2 *1	2
26th	Furcolo, Foster	Dem	Mass.	2	2
27th	Marshall, Fred	DFL	Minn.	2	1
28th	Denton, Winfield K.	Dem	Ind.	2 *1	1
29th	Riley, John J.	Dem	S.C.	3	1
30th	Sieminski, Alfred D.	Dem	N.J.	1	1

Minority

Rank	Name	Party	State	Terms in: House	Terms in: Comm.
RM	Taber, John	Rep	N.Y.	15	15
2nd	Wigglesworth, Richard B.	Rep	Mass.	13	12
3rd	Stefan, Karl	Rep	Neb.	9	7
4th	Jensen, Ben F.	Rep	Iowa	7	5
5th	Andersen, H. Carl	Rep	Minn.	7	5
6th	Horan, Walter F.	Rep	Wash.	5	4
7th	Canfield, Gordon	Rep	N.J.	6	4
8th	Fenton, Ivor D.	Rep	Penn.	7	3
9th	Stockman, Lowell	Rep	Ore.	5	3
10th	Phillips, John	Rep	Cal.	5	3
11th	Scrivner, Errett P.	Rep	Kans.	5	3
12th	Coudert, Frederic R. Jr.	Rep	N.Y.	3	3
13th	Clevenger, Cliff	Rep	Ohio	7	3
14th	Wilson, Earl	Rep	Ind.	6 *2	2
15th	Cotton, Norris	Rep	N.H.	3	2
16th	Davis, Glenn R.	Rep	Wisc.	3 *1	1
17th	James, Benjamin F.	Rep	Penn.	2	1
18th	Ford, Gerald R. Jr.	Rep	Mich.	2	1
19th	Busbey, Fred E.	Rep	Ill.	3	1
20th	Schwabe, George B.	Rep	Okla.	3 *2	1

*1: Member's 1st period of service on the committee;
*2: Member's 2nd period of service on the committee.

Vacancies Filled:
Majority: 27th through the 30th seats on Jan. 12,1951.
Minority: 16th through the 20th seats on Jan. 15,1951.

Changes:

Majority:

Name	Party	State	Date	Change
Stigler, William G.	Dem	Okla.	Aug. 21,1952	Died in office.
Furcolo, Foster	Dem	Mass.	Sep. 30,1952	Resigned House; elected State Treasurer.

Minority:

Name	Party	State	Date	Change
Stefan, Karl	Rep	Neb.	Oct. 2,1951	Died in office.
Aandahl, Fred G.	Rep	N.D.	Oct. 17,1951	Replaced Stefan.
Schwabe, George B.	Rep	Okla.	Apr. 2,1952	Died in office.
Miller, Edward T.	Rep	Md.	Apr. 30,1952	Replaced Schwabe.

Departures from the House:

	Majority			Minority		
Elected to U.S. Senate	Gore, Albert A.	Tenn.	Dem	None		
	Jackson, Henry M.	Wash.	Dem			
Elected County Judge	McGrath, Christopher C.	N.Y.	Dem	None		
Defeated for Reelection	Denton, Winfield K.	Ind.	Dem	None		
	Flood, Daniel J.	Penn.	Dem			
Defeated for Renomination	Bates, Joe B.	Ky.	Dem	None		
	Kerr, John H.	N.C.	Dem			
Lost Nomination to U.S. Senate	None			Aandahl, Fred G.	N.D.	Rep
Lost Nomination for Governor	Hedrick, Erland H.	W.Va.	Dem	None		
Retired	None			Stockman, Lowell	Ore.	Rep

APPROPRIATIONS / 83rd Congress

Service Dates of Committee Chair: Jan. 14,1953-Jan. 3,1955
Service Dates of Majority Members: Jan. 14,1953-Jan. 3,1955
Service Dates of Minority Members: Jan. 14,1953-Jan. 3,1955

Majority

Rank	Name	Party	State	Terms in: House		Terms in: Comm.
Chr	Taber, John	Rep	N.Y.	16		16
2nd	Wigglesworth, Richard B.	Rep	Mass.	14		13
3rd	Jensen, Ben F.	Rep	Iowa	8		6
4th	Andersen, H. Carl	Rep	Minn.	8		6
5th	Horan, Walter F.	Rep	Wash.	6		5
6th	Canfield, Gordon	Rep	N.J.	7		5
7th	Fenton, Ivor D.	Rep	Penn.	8		4
8th	Phillips, John	Rep	Cal.	6		4
9th	Scrivner, Errett P.	Rep	Kans.	6		4
10th	Coudert, Frederic R. Jr.	Rep	N.Y.	4		4
11th	Clevenger, Cliff	Rep	Ohio	8		4
12th	Wilson, Earl	Rep	Ind.	7	*2	3
13th	Cotton, Norris	Rep	N.H.	4		3
14th	Davis, Glenn R.	Rep	Wisc.	4	*1	2
15th	James, Benjamin F.	Rep	Penn.	3		2
16th	Ford, Gerald R. Jr.	Rep	Mich.	3		2
17th	Busbey, Fred E.	Rep	Ill.	4		2
18th	Miller, Edward T.	Rep	Md.	4		2
19th	Vursell, Charles W.	Rep	Ill.	6		1
20th	Hand, T. Millet II	Rep	N.J.	5		1
21st	Ostertag, Harold C.	Rep	N.Y.	2		1
22nd	Hunter, Allan O.	Rep	Cal.	2		1
23rd	Bow, Frank T.	Rep	Ohio	2		1
24th	Budge, Hamer H.	Rep	Ida.	2	*1	1
25th	Jonas, Charles Raper	Rep	N.C.	1	*1	1
26th	Krueger, Otto	Rep	N.D.	1		1
27th	Hruska, Roman L	Rep	Neb.	1		1
28th	Coon, Samuel H	Rep	Ore.	1		1
29th	Laird, Melvin R	Rep	Wisc.	1	*1	1
30th	Cederberg, Elford A	Rep	Mich.	1	*1	1

Minority

Rank	Name	Party	State	Terms in: House		Terms in: Comm.
RM	Cannon, Clarence	Dem	Mo.	16		13
2nd	Mahon, George H.	Dem	Tex.	10		8
3rd	Sheppard, Harry R.	Dem	Cal.	9		8
4th	Thomas, Albert	Dem	Tex.	9		7
5th	Kirwan, Michael J.	Dem	Ohio	9		6
6th	Norrell, William F.	Dem	Ark.	8		6
7th	Whitten, Jamie L.	Dem	Miss.	7		6
8th	Andrews, George W.	Dem	Ala.	6		5
9th	Rooney, John J.	Dem	N.Y.	6		5
10th	Gary, J. Vaughn	Dem	Va.	5		5
11th	Fogarty, John E.	Dem	R.I.	7		4
12th	Sikes, Robert L. F.	Dem	Fla.	7		3
13th	Fernandez, Antonio M.	Dem	N.M.	6		3
14th	Preston, Prince H. Jr.	Dem	Ga.	4		3
15th	Passman, Otto E.	Dem	La.	4		3
16th	Rabaut, Louis C.	Dem	Mich.	9	*2	3
17th	Yates, Sidney R.	Dem	Ill.	3	*1	3
18th	Marshall, Fred	DFL	Minn.	3		2
19th	Riley, John J.	Dem	S.C.	4		2
20th	Sieminski, Alfred D.	Dem	N.J.	2		2

*1: Member's 1st period of service on the committee;
*2: Member's 2nd period of service on the committee.

Changes:

Majority:

Name	Party	State	Date	Reason
Cotton, Norris	Rep	N.H.	Nov. 7,1954	Resigned; elected to U.S. Senate.
Hruska, Roman L.	Rep	Neb.	Nov. 8,1954	Resigned; elected to U.S. Senate.

	Majority	State	Party	Minority
Departures from the House:				
Defeated for Reelection	Busbey, Fred E.	Ill.	Rep	None
	Hunter, Allan O.	Cal.	Rep	
Departures from Committee:				
Moved to Merchant Marine & Fisheries; Post Office & Civil Service	Cederberg, Elford A.	Mich.	Rep	None
Moved to Education & Labor	Coon, Samuel H.	Ore.	Rep	None
Moved to Government Operations	Jonas, Charles Raper	N.C.	Rep	None
	Krueger, Otto	N.D.	Rep	
Moved to Agriculture	Laird, Melvin R.	Wisc.	Rep	None
No new assignment	Budge, Hamer H.	Ida.	Rep	None

APPROPRIATIONS / 84th Congress

Service Dates of Committee Chair: Jan. 5,1955-Jan. 3,1957
Service Dates of Majority Members: Jan. 5,1955-Jan. 3,1957
Service Dates of Minority Members: Jan. 10,1955-Jan. 3,1957

Majority

Rank	Name	Party	State	Terms in: House	Terms in: Comm.
Chr	Cannon, Clarence	Dem	Mo.	17	14
2nd	Mahon, George H.	Dem	Tex.	11	9
3rd	Sheppard, Harry R.	Dem	Cal.	10	9
4th	Thomas, Albert	Dem	Tex.	10	8
5th	Kirwan, Michael J.	Dem	Ohio	10	7
6th	Norrell, William F.	Dem	Ark.	9	7
7th	Whitten, Jamie L.	Dem	Miss.	8	7
8th	Andrews, George W.	Dem	Ala.	7	6
9th	Rooney, John J.	Dem	N.Y.	7	6
10th	Gary, J. Vaughn	Dem	Va.	6	6
11th	Fogarty, John E.	Dem	R.I.	8	5
12th	Sikes, Robert L. F.	Dem	Fla.	8	4
13th	Fernandez, Antonio M.	Dem	N.M.	7	4
14th	Preston, Prince H. Jr.	Dem	Ga.	5	4
15th	Passman, Otto E.	Dem	La.	5	4
16th	Rabaut, Louis C.	Dem	Mich.	10 *2	4
17th	Yates, Sidney R.	Dem	Ill.	4 *1	4
18th	Marshall, Fred	DFL	Minn.	4	3
19th	Riley, John J.	Dem	S.C.	5	3
20th	Sieminski, Alfred D.	Dem	N.J.	3	3
21st	Evins, Joseph L.	Dem	Tenn.	5	1
22nd	Lanham, Henderson L.	Dem	Ga.	5	1
23rd	Deane, Charles B.	Dem	N.C.	5	1
24th	Shelley, John F.	Dem	Cal.	4	1
25th	Boland, Edward P.	Dem	Mass.	2	1
26th	Magnuson, Donald H.	Dem	Wash.	2	1
27th	Natcher, William H.	Dem	Ky.	2	1
28th	Flood, Daniel J.	Dem	Penn.	4 *3	1
29th	Denton, Winfield K.	Dem	Ind.	3 *2	1
30th	Murray, James C.	Dem	Ill.	1	1

Minority

Rank	Name	Party	State	Terms in: House	Terms in: Comm.
RM	Taber, John	Rep	N.Y.	17	17
2nd	Wigglesworth, Richard B.	Rep	Mass.	15	14
3rd	Jensen, Ben F.	Rep	Iowa	9	7
4th	Andersen, H. Carl	Rep	Minn.	9	7
5th	Horan, Walter F.	Rep	Wash.	7	6
6th	Canfield, Gordon	Rep	N.J.	8	6
7th	Fenton, Ivor D.	Rep	Penn.	9	5
8th	Phillips, John	Rep	Cal.	7	5
9th	Scrivner, Errett P.	Rep	Kans.	7	5
10th	Coudert, Frederic R. Jr.	Rep	N.Y.	5	5
11th	Clevenger, Cliff	Rep	Ohio	9	5
12th	Wilson, Earl	Rep	Ind.	8 *2	4
13th	Davis, Glenn R.	Rep	Wisc.	5 *1	3
14th	James, Benjamin F.	Rep	Penn.	4	3
15th	Ford, Gerald R. Jr.	Rep	Mich.	4	3
16th	Miller, Edward T.	Rep	Md.	5	3
17th	Vursell, Charles W.	Rep	Ill.	7	2
18th	Hand, T. Millet II	Rep	N.J.	6	2
19th	Ostertag, Harold C.	Rep	N.Y.	3	2
20th	Bow, Frank T.	Rep	Ohio	3	2

*1: Member's 1st period of service on the committee;
*2: Member's 2nd period of service on the committee;
*3: Member's 3rd period of service on the committee.

Vacancies Filled:
Majority: 21st through the 30th seats on Jan. 13,1955.

Changes:

Majority:

Fernandez, Antonio M.	Dem	N.M.	Nov. 7,1956	Died in office.

Minority:

Hand, T. Millet II	Rep	N.J.	Dec. 26,1956	Died in office.

Departures from the House:	Majority			Minority		
Defeated for Reelection	Murray, James C.	Ill.	Dem	None		
Defeated for Renomination	Deane, Charles B.	N.C.	Dem	None		
Lost Nomination to U.S. Senate	None			Davis, Glenn R.	Wisc.	Rep
Retired	None			Phillips, John	Cal.	Rep

APPROPRIATIONS / 85th Congress

Service Dates of Committee Chair: Jan. 3,1957-Jan. 3,1959
Service Dates of Majority Members: Jan. 3,1957-Jan. 3,1959
Service Dates of Minority Members: Jan. 7,1957-Jan. 3,1959

Majority

Rank	Name	Party	State	Terms in: House	Terms in: Comm.
Chr	Cannon, Clarence	Dem	Mo.	18	15
2nd	Mahon, George H.	Dem	Tex.	12	10
3rd	Sheppard, Harry R.	Dem	Cal.	11	10
4th	Thomas, Albert	Dem	Tex.	11	9
5th	Kirwan, Michael J.	Dem	Ohio	11	8
6th	Norrell, William F.	Dem	Ark.	10	8
7th	Whitten, Jamie L.	Dem	Miss.	9	8
8th	Andrews, George W.	Dem	Ala.	8	7
9th	Rooney, John J.	Dem	N.Y.	8	7
10th	Gary, J. Vaughn	Dem	Va.	7	7
11th	Fogarty, John E.	Dem	R.I.	9	6
12th	Sikes, Robert L. F.	Dem	Fla.	9	5
13th	Preston, Prince H. Jr.	Dem	Ga.	6	5
14th	Passman, Otto E.	Dem	La.	6	5
15th	Rabaut, Louis C.	Dem	Mich.	11	*2 5
16th	Yates, Sidney R.	Dem	Ill.	5	*1 5
17th	Marshall, Fred	DFL	Minn.	5	4
18th	Riley, John J.	Dem	S.C.	6	4
19th	Sieminski, Alfred D.	Dem	N.J.	4	4
20th	Evins, Joseph L.	Dem	Tenn.	6	2
21st	Lanham, Henderson L.	Dem	Ga.	6	2
22nd	Shelley, John F.	Dem	Cal.	5	2
23rd	Boland, Edward P.	Dem	Mass.	3	2
24th	Magnuson, Donald H.	Dem	Wash.	3	2
25th	Natcher, William H.	Dem	Ky.	3	2
26th	Flood, Daniel J.	Dem	Penn.	5	*3 2
27th	Denton, Winfield K.	Dem	Ind.	4	*2 2
28th	Steed, Thomas J.	Dem	Okla.	5	1
29th	Alexander, Hugh Q.	Dem	N.C.	3	1
30th	Bowler, James B.	Dem	Ill.	3	1

Minority

Rank	Name	Party	State	Terms in: House	Terms in: Comm.
RM	Taber, John	Rep	N.Y.	18	18
2nd	Wigglesworth, Richard B.	Rep	Mass.	16	15
3rd	Jensen, Ben F.	Rep	Iowa	10	8
4th	Andersen, H. Carl	Rep	Minn.	10	8
5th	Horan, Walter F.	Rep	Wash.	8	7
6th	Canfield, Gordon	Rep	N.J.	9	7
7th	Fenton, Ivor D.	Rep	Penn.	10	6
8th	Scrivner, Errett P.	Rep	Kans.	8	6
9th	Coudert, Frederic R. Jr.	Rep	N.Y.	6	6
10th	Clevenger, Cliff	Rep	Ohio	10	6
11th	Wilson, Earl	Rep	Ind.	9	*2 5
12th	James, Benjamin F.	Rep	Penn.	5	4
13th	Ford, Gerald R. Jr.	Rep	Mich.	5	4
14th	Miller, Edward T.	Rep	Md.	6	4
15th	Vursell, Charles W.	Rep	Ill.	8	3
16th	Ostertag, Harold C.	Rep	N.Y.	4	3
17th	Bow, Frank T.	Rep	Ohio	4	3
18th	Budge, Hamer H.	Rep	Ida.	4	*2 1
19th	Jonas, Charles Raper	Rep	N.C.	3	*2 1
20th	Laird, Melvin R.	Rep	Wisc.	3	*2 1

*1: Member's 1st period of service on the committee;
*2: Member's 2nd period of service on the committee;
*3: Member's 3rd period of service on the committee.

Vacancies Filled:
Majority: 28th through the 30th seats on Jan. 10,1957.
Minority: 13th through the 20th seats on Jan. 16,1957.

Changes:

Majority:

Name	Party	State	Date	Change
Bowler, James B.	Dem	Ill.	July 18,1957	Died in office.
Boyle, Charles A.	Dem	Ill.	July 23,1957	Replaced Bowler.
Lanham, Henderson L.	Dem	Ga.	Nov. 10,1957	Died in office.
Santangelo, Alfred E.	Dem	N.Y.	Jan. 16,1958	Replaced Lanham.

Minority:

Name	Party	State	Date	Change
James, Benjamin F.	Rep	Penn.	June 11,1958	Left committee due to "worsening physical condition"; no new assignment.
Cederberg, Elford A.	Rep	Mich.	June 11,1958	Replaced James.
Coudert, Frederic R. Jr.	Rep	N.Y.	July 31,1958	Left committee; no new assignment.
Lipscomb, Glenard P.	Rep	Cal.	July 31,1958	Replaced Coudert.
Wigglesworth, Richard B.	Rep	Mass.	Aug. 23,1958	Left committee; resigned Nov. 13,1958 to become Ambassador to Canada.
May, Edwin H. Jr.	Rep	Conn.	Aug. 23,1958	Replaced Wigglesworth.

Departures from the House:

	Majority		Minority	
Defeated for Reelection	None		Miller, Edward T.	Md. Rep
			Scrivner, Errett P.	Kans. Rep
			Vursell, Charles W.	Ill. Rep
			Wilson, Earl	Ind. Rep
			May, Edwin H. Jr.	Conn. Rep
Defeated for Renomination	Sieminski, Alfred D.	N.J. Dem	None	
Retired	None		Clevenger, Cliff	Ohio Rep

APPROPRIATIONS / 86th Congress

Service Dates of Committee Chair: Jan. 7,1959-Jan. 3,1961
Service Dates of Majority Members: Jan. 7,1959-Jan. 3,1961
Service Dates of Minority Members: Jan. 15,1959-Jan. 3,1961

Majority

Rank	Name	Party	State	Terms in: House		Terms in: Comm.
Chr	Cannon, Clarence	Dem	Mo.	19		16
2nd	Mahon, George H.	Dem	Tex.	13		11
3rd	Sheppard, Harry R.	Dem	Cal.	12		11
4th	Thomas, Albert	Dem	Tex.	12		10
5th	Kirwan, Michael J.	Dem	Ohio	12		9
6th	Norrell, William F.	Dem	Ark.	11		9
7th	Whitten, Jamie L.	Dem	Miss.	10		9
8th	Andrews, George W.	Dem	Ala.	9		8
9th	Rooney, John J.	Dem	N.Y.	9		8
10th	Gary, J. Vaughn	Dem	Va.	8		8
11th	Fogarty, John E.	Dem	R.I.	10		7
12th	Sikes, Robert L. F.	Dem	Fla.	10		6
13th	Preston, Prince H. Jr.	Dem	Ga.	7		6
14th	Passman, Otto E.	Dem	La.	7		6
15th	Rabaut, Louis C.	Dem	Mich.	12	*2	6
16th	Yates, Sidney R.	Dem	Ill.	6	*1	6
17th	Marshall, Fred	DFL	Minn.	6		5
18th	Riley, John J.	Dem	S.C.	7		5
19th	Evins, Joseph L.	Dem	Tenn.	7		3
20th	Shelley, John F.	Dem	Cal.	6		3
21st	Boland, Edward P.	Dem	Mass.	4		3
22nd	Magnuson, Donald H.	Dem	Wash.	4		3
23rd	Natcher, William H.	Dem	Ky.	4		3
24th	Flood, Daniel J.	Dem	Penn.	6	*3	3
25th	Denton, Winfield K.	Dem	Ind.	5	*2	3
26th	Steed, Thomas J.	Dem	Okla.	6		2
27th	Alexander, Hugh Q.	Dem	N.C.	4		2
28th	Boyle, Charles A.	Dem	Ill.	3		2
29th	Santangelo, Alfred E.	Dem	N.Y.	2		2
30th	Montoya, Joseph M.	Dem	N.M.	2		1

Minority

Rank	Name	Party	State	Terms in: House		Terms in: Comm.
RM	Taber, John	Rep	N.Y.	19		19
2nd	Jensen, Ben F.	Rep	Iowa	11		9
3rd	Andersen, H. Carl	Rep	Minn.	11		9
4th	Horan, Walter F.	Rep	Wash.	9		8
5th	Canfield, Gordon	Rep	N.J.	10		8
6th	Fenton, Ivor D.	Rep	Penn.	11		7
7th	Ford, Gerald R. Jr.	Rep	Mich.	6		5
8th	Ostertag, Harold C.	Rep	N.Y.	5		4
9th	Bow, Frank T.	Rep	Ohio	5		4
10th	Budge, Hamer H.	Rep	Ida.	5	*2	2
11th	Jonas, Charles Raper	Rep	N.C.	4	*2	2
12th	Laird, Melvin R.	Rep	Wisc.	4	*2	2
13th	Cederberg, Elford A.	Rep	Mich.	4	*2	2
14th	Lipscomb, Glenard P.	Rep	Cal.	4		2
15th	Rhodes, John J.	Rep	Ariz.	4		1
16th	Pillion, John R.	Rep	N.Y.	4		1
17th	Weaver, Phillip H.	Rep	Neb.	3		1
18th	Minshall, William E. Jr.	Rep	Ohio	3		1
19th	Thomson, E. Keith	Rep	Wyo.	3		1
20th	Michel, Robert H.	Rep	Ill.	2	*1	1

*1: Member's 1st period of service on the committee;
*2: Member's 2nd period of service on the committee;
*3: Member's 3rd period of service on the committee.

Vacancies Filled:
Majority: 30th seat by Montoya on Jan. 19,1959.
Minority: 15th through 20th seats on Jan. 19,1959.

Changes:

Majority:

Name	Party	State	Date	Change
Boyle, Charles A.	Dem	Ill.	Nov. 4,1959	Died in office.
Shipley, George E.	Dem	Ill.	Jan. 12,1960	Replaced Boyle.

Minority:

Name	Party	State	Date	Change
Budge, Hamer H.	Rep	Ida.	Jan. 19,1959	Moved to Rules.
Conte, Silvio O.	Rep	Mass.	Jan. 19,1959	Replaced Budge.
Thomson, E. Keith	Rep	Wyo.	Dec. 9,1960	Died in office.

Departures from the House:

	Majority			Minority		
Defeated for Renomination	Preston, Prince H. Jr.	Ga.	Dem	None		
Retired	None			Canfield, Gordon	N.J.	Rep

APPROPRIATIONS / 87th Congress

Service Dates of Committee Chair: Jan. 23,1961-Jan. 3,1963
Service Dates of Majority Members: Jan. 23,1961-Jan. 3,1963
Service Dates of Minority Members: Jan. 23,1961-Jan. 3,1963

Majority

Rank	Name	Party	State	Terms in: House		Terms in: Comm.
Chr	Cannon, Clarence	Dem	Mo.	20		17
2nd	Mahon, George H.	Dem	Tex.	14		12
3rd	Sheppard, Harry R.	Dem	Cal.	13		12
4th	Thomas, Albert	Dem	Tex.	13		11
5th	Kirwan, Michael J.	Dem	Ohio	13		10
6th	Norrell, William F.	Dem	Ark.	12		10
7th	Whitten, Jamie L.	Dem	Miss.	11		10
8th	Andrews, George W.	Dem	Ala.	10		9
9th	Rooney, John J.	Dem	N.Y.	10		9
10th	Gary, J. Vaughn	Dem	Va.	9		9
11th	Fogarty, John E.	Dem	R.I.	11		8
12th	Sikes, Robert L. F.	Dem	Fla.	11		7
13th	Passman, Otto E.	Dem	La.	8		7
14th	Rabaut, Louis C.	Dem	Mich.	13	*2	7
15th	Yates, Sidney R.	Dem	Ill.	7	*1	7
16th	Marshall, Fred	DFL	Minn.	7		6
17th	Riley, John J.	Dem	S.C.	8		6
18th	Evins, Joseph L.	Dem	Tenn.	8		4
19th	Shelley, John F.	Dem	Cal.	7		4
20th	Boland, Edward P.	Dem	Mass.	5		4
21st	Magnuson, Donald H.	Dem	Wash.	5		4
22nd	Natcher, William H.	Dem	Ky.	5		4
23rd	Flood, Daniel J.	Dem	Penn.	7	*3	4
24th	Denton, Winfield K.	Dem	Ind.	6	*2	4
25th	Steed, Thomas J.	Dem	Okla.	7		3
26th	Alexander, Hugh Q.	Dem	N.C.	5		3
27th	Santangelo, Alfred E.	Dem	N.Y.	3		3
28th	Montoya, Joseph M.	Dem	N.M.	3		2
29th	Shipley, George E.	Dem	Ill.	2		2
30th	Slack, John M. Jr.	Dem	W.Va.	2		1

Minority

Rank	Name	Party	State	Terms in: House		Terms in: Comm.
RM	Taber, John	Rep	N.Y.	20		20
2nd	Jensen, Ben F.	Rep	Iowa	12		10
3rd	Andersen, H. Carl	Rep	Minn.	12		10
4th	Horan, Walter F.	Rep	Wash.	10		9
5th	Fenton, Ivor D.	Rep	Penn.	12		8
6th	Ford, Gerald R. Jr.	Rep	Mich.	7		6
7th	Ostertag, Harold C.	Rep	N.Y.	6		5
8th	Bow, Frank T.	Rep	Ohio	6		5
9th	Jonas, Charles Raper	Rep	N.C.	5	*2	3
10th	Laird, Melvin R.	Rep	Wisc.	5	*2	3
11th	Cederberg, Elford A.	Rep	Mich.	5	*2	3
12th	Lipscomb, Glenard P.	Rep	Cal.	5		3
13th	Rhodes, John J.	Rep	Ariz.	5		2
14th	Pillion, John R.	Rep	N.Y.	5		2
15th	Weaver, Phillip H.	Rep	Neb.	4		2
16th	Minshall, William E. Jr.	Rep	Ohio	4		2
17th	Michel, Robert H.	Rep	Ill.	3	*1	2
18th	Conte, Silvio O.	Rep	Mass.	2		2
19th	Milliken, William H. Jr.	Rep	Penn.	2		1
20th	Wilson, Earl	Rep	Ind.	10	*3	1

*1: Member's 1st period of service on the committee;
*2: Member's 2nd period of service on the committee;
*3: Member's 3rd period of service on the committee.

Vacancies Filled:
Majority: 30th seat by Slack on Feb. 6,1961.
Minority: 19th and 20th seats by Milliken and Wilson respectively on Feb. 13,1961.

Changes:

Majority:

Norrell, William F.	Dem	Ark.	Feb. 15,1961	Died in office.
Alford, T. Dale	Dem	Ark.	Mar. 6,1961	Replaced Norrell.
Rabaut, Louis C.	Dem	Mich.	Nov. 12,1961	Died in office.
Lesinski, John Jr.	Dem	Mich.	Jan. 18,1962	Replaced Rabaut.
Riley, John J.	Dem	S.C.	Jan. 1,1962	Died in office.
Flynt, John James Jr.	Dem	Ga.	Jan. 18,1962	Replaced Riley.
Marshall, Fred	DFL	Minn.	Aug. 28,1962	Left committee; no new assignment.
Smith, Neal	Dem	Iowa	Aug. 28,1962	Replaced Marshall.

Minority:

Andersen, H. Carl	Rep	Minn.	Oct. 11,1962	Left committee; defeated for reelection.
Langen, Odin	Rep	Minn.	Oct. 11,1962	Replaced Anderson.

Departures from the House:

	Majority			Minority		
Defeated for Reelection	Alexander, Hugh Q.	N.C.	Dem	Fenton, Ivor D.	Penn.	Rep
	Magnuson, Donald H.	Wash.	Dem			
	Santangelo, Alfred E.	N.Y.	Dem			
Defeated for Renomination	None			Weaver, Phillip H.	Neb.	Rep
Lost Election to U.S. Senate	Yates, Sidney R.	Ill.	Dem	None		
Lost Nomination for Governor	Alford, T. Dale	Ark.	Dem			
Retired	None			Taber, John	N.Y.	Rep

APPROPRIATIONS / 88th Congress

Service Dates of Committee Chairs: Ch1 Jan. 17,1963-May 12,1964
Ch2 May 18,1964-Jan. 3,1965
Service Dates of Majority Members: Jan. 17,1963-Jan. 3,1965
Service Dates of Minority Members: Jan. 17,1963-Jan. 3,1965

Majority

Rank	Name	Party	State	Terms in: House	Terms in: Comm.
Ch1	Cannon, Clarence	Dem	Mo.	21	18
Ch2 2nd	Mahon, George H.	Dem	Tex.	15	13
3rd	Sheppard, Harry R.	Dem	Cal.	14	13
4th	Thomas, Albert	Dem	Tex.	14	12
5th	Kirwan, Michael J.	Dem	Ohio	14	11
6th	Whitten, Jamie L.	Dem	Miss.	12	11
7th	Andrews, George W.	Dem	Ala.	11	10
8th	Rooney, John J.	Dem	N.Y.	11	10
9th	Gary, J. Vaughn	Dem	Va.	10	10
10th	Fogarty, John E.	Dem	R.I.	12	9
11th	Sikes, Robert L. F.	Dem	Fla.	12	8
12th	Passman, Otto E.	Dem	La.	9	8
13th	Evins, Joseph L.	Dem	Tenn.	9	5
14th	Shelley, John F.	Dem	Cal.	8	5
15th	Boland, Edward P.	Dem	Mass.	6	5
16th	Natcher, William H.	Dem	Ky.	6	5
17th	Flood, Daniel J.	Dem	Penn.	8 *3	5
18th	Denton, Winfield K.	Dem	Ind.	7 *2	5
19th	Steed, Thomas J.	Dem	Okla.	8	4
20th	Montoya, Joseph M.	Dem	N.M.	4	3
21st	Shipley, George E.	Dem	Ill.	3	3
22nd	Slack, John M. Jr.	Dem	W.Va.	3	2
23rd	Lesinski, John Jr.	Dem	Mich.	7	2
24th	Flynt, John James Jr.	Dem	Ga.	6	2
25th	Smith, Neal	Dem	Iowa	3	2
26th	Giaimo, Robert N.	Dem	Conn.	3	1
27th	Hansen, Julia Butler	Dem	Wash.	3	1
28th	Finnegan, Edward R.	Dem	Ill.	2	1
29th	Joelson, Charles S.	Dem	N.J.	2	1
30th	Addabbo, Joseph P.	Dem	N.Y.	2	1

Minority

Rank	Name	Party	State	Terms in: House	Terms in: Comm.
RM	Jensen, Ben F.	Rep	Iowa	13	11
2nd	Horan, Walter F.	Rep	Wash.	11	10
3rd	Ford, Gerald R. Jr.	Rep	Mich.	8	7
4th	Ostertag, Harold C.	Rep	N.Y.	7	6
5th	Bow, Frank T.	Rep	Ohio	7	6
6th	Jonas, Charles Raper	Rep	N.C.	6 *2	4
7th	Laird, Melvin R.	Rep	Wisc.	6 *2	4
8th	Cederberg, Elford A.	Rep	Mich.	6 *2	4
9th	Lipscomb, Glenard P.	Rep	Cal.	6	4
10th	Rhodes, John J.	Rep	Ariz.	6	3
11th	Pillion, John R.	Rep	N.Y.	6	3
12th	Minshall, William E. Jr.	Rep	Ohio	5	3
13th	Michel, Robert H.	Rep	Ill.	4 *1	3
14th	Conte, Silvio O.	Rep	Mass.	3	3
15th	Milliken, William H. Jr.	Rep	Penn.	3	2
16th	Wilson, Earl	Rep	Ind.	11 *3	2
17th	Langen, Odin	Rep	Minn.	3	2
18th	Harrison, William Henry	Rep	Wyo.	4 *1	1
19th	Reifel, Benjamin	Rep	S.D.	2	1
20th	Wyman, Louis C.	Rep	N.H.	1 *1	1

*1: Member's 1st period of service on the committee;
*2: Member's 2nd period of service on the committee;
*3: Member's 3rd period of service on the committee.

Vacancies Filled:
Minority: 18th through the 20th seats on Jan. 24,1963.

Changes:

Chair:

Ch1	Cannon, Clarence	Dem	Mo.	May 12,1964	Died in office.
Ch2	Mahon, George H.	Dem	Tex.	May 18,1964	Succeeded Cannon as chair.

Majority:

Shelley, John F.	Dem	Cal.	Dec. 10,1963	Left committee; resigned Jan. 7,1964 to become Mayor of San Francisco.
McFall, John J.	Dem	Cal.	Dec. 10,1963	Replaced Shelley.
Cannon, Clarence	Dem	Mo.	May 12,1964	Died in office.
Hull, William R. Jr.	Dem	Mo.	June 2,1964	Replaced Cannon.
Montoya, Joseph M.	Dem	N.M.	Nov. 3,1964	Resigned; elected to U.S. Senate.
Finnegan, Edward R.	Dem	Ill.	Dec. 6,1964	Resigned; appointed to state circuit court.

Minority:

Milliken, William H. Jr.	Rep	Penn.	Oct. 2,1964	Left committee; no new assignment.
Weaver, James D.	Rep	Penn.	Oct. 2,1964	Replaced Milliken.

Departures from the House:

Defeated for Reelection

Majority
None

Minority

Harrison, William Henry	Wyo.	Rep
Horan, Walter F.	Wash.	Rep
Jensen, Ben F.	Iowa	Rep
Pillion, John R.	N.Y.	Rep
Wilson, Earl	Ind.	Rep
Wyman, Louis C.	N.H.	Rep
Weaver, James D.	Penn.	Rep

Defeated for Renomination	Lesinski, John Jr.	Mich. Dem	None	
Retired	Gary, J. Vaughn	Va. Dem	Ostertag, Harold C.	N.Y. Rep
	Sheppard, Harry R.	Cal. Dem		
Departures from Committee:				
Became House Minority Leader	None		Ford, Gerald R. Jr.	Mich. Rep

APPROPRIATIONS / 89th Congress

Service Dates of Committee Chair: Jan. 18,1965-Jan. 3,1967
Service Dates of Majority Members: Jan. 18,1965-Jan. 3,1967
Service Dates of Minority Members: Jan. 21,1965-Jan. 3,1967

Majority

Rank	Name	Party	State	Terms in: House	Terms in: Comm.
Chr	Mahon, George H.	Dem	Tex.	16	14
2nd	Thomas, Albert	Dem	Tex.	15	13
3rd	Kirwan, Michael J.	Dem	Ohio	15	12
4th	Whitten, Jamie L.	Dem	Miss.	13	12
5th	Andrews, George W.	Dem	Ala.	12	11
6th	Rooney, John J.	Dem	N.Y.	12	11
7th	Fogarty, John E.	Dem	R.I.	13	10
8th	Sikes, Robert L. F.	Dem	Fla.	13	9
9th	Passman, Otto E.	Dem	La.	10	9
10th	Evins, Joseph L.	Dem	Tenn.	10	6
11th	Boland, Edward P.	Dem	Mass.	7	6
12th	Natcher, William H.	Dem	Ky.	7	6
13th	Flood, Daniel J.	Dem	Penn.	9	*3 6
14th	Denton, Winfield K.	Dem	Ind.	8	*2 6
15th	Steed, Thomas J.	Dem	Okla.	9	5
16th	Shipley, George E.	Dem	Ill.	4	4
17th	Slack, John M. Jr.	Dem	W.Va.	4	3
18th	Flynt, John James Jr.	Dem	Ga.	7	3
19th	Smith, Neal	Dem	Iowa	4	3
20th	Giaimo, Robert N.	Dem	Conn.	4	2
21st	Hansen, Julia Butler	Dem	Wash.	4	2
22nd	Joelson, Charles S.	Dem	N.J.	3	2
23rd	Addabbo, Joseph P.	Dem	N.Y.	3	2
24th	McFall, John J.	Dem	Cal.	5	2
25th	Hull, William R. Jr.	Dem	Mo.	6	2
26th	Matthews, Donald R.	Dem	Fla.	7	1
27th	Cohelan, Jeffrey	Dem	Cal.	4	1
28th	Morris, Thomas G.	Dem	N.M.	4	1
29th	Patten, Edward J.	Dem	N.J.	2	1
30th	Long, Clarence D.	Dem	Md.	2	1
31st	Marsh, John O. Jr.	Dem	Va.	2	1
32nd	Duncan, Robert B.	Dem	Ore.	2	*1 1
33rd	Yates, Sidney R.	Dem	Ill.	8	*2 1
34th	Farnum, Billie S.	Dem	Mich.	1	1

Minority

Rank	Name	Party	State	Terms in: House	Terms in: Comm.
RM	Bow, Frank T.	Rep	Ohio	8	7
2nd	Jonas, Charles Raper	Rep	N.C.	7	*2 5
3rd	Laird, Melvin R.	Rep	Wisc.	7	*2 5
4th	Cederberg, Elford A.	Rep	Mich.	7	*2 5
5th	Lipscomb, Glenard P.	Rep	Cal.	7	5
6th	Rhodes, John J.	Rep	Ariz.	7	4
7th	Minshall, William E. Jr.	Rep	Ohio	6	4
8th	Michel, Robert H.	Rep	Ill.	5	*1 4
9th	Conte, Silvio O.	Rep	Mass.	4	4
10th	Langen, Odin	Rep	Minn.	4	3
11th	Reifel, Benjamin	Rep	S.D.	3	2
12th	Davis, Glenn R.	Rep	Wisc.	6	*2 1
13th	Robison, Howard W.	Rep	N.Y.	5	1
14th	Shriver, Garner E.	Rep	Kans.	3	1
15th	McDade, Joseph M.	Rep	Penn.	2	1
16th	Andrews, Mark	Rep	N.D.	2	1

*1: Member's 1st period of service on the committee;
*2: Member's 2nd period of service on the committee;
*3: Member's 3rd period of service on the committee.

Changes:

Majority:

Thomas, Albert	Dem	Tex.	Feb. 15,1966	Died in office.
Casey, Robert R.	Dem	Tex.	Mar. 8,1966	Replaced Thomas.
Denton, Winfield K.	Dem	Ind.	Dec. 30,1966	Resigned House; defeated for reelection.

Departures from the House:

	Majority		Minority
Defeated for Reelection	Farnum, Billie S.	Mich. Dem	None
Defeated for Renomination	Matthews, Donald R.	Fla. Dem	None
Lost Election to U.S. Senate	Duncan, Robert B.	Ore. Dem	None
Died in office Jan. 10,1967	Fogarty, John E.	R.I. Dem	None

APPROPRIATIONS / 90th Congress

Service Dates of Committee Chair: Jan. 18,1967-Jan. 3,1969
Service Dates of Majority Members: Jan. 18,1967-Jan. 3,1969
Service Dates of Minority Members: Jan. 18,1967-Jan. 3,1969

Majority

Rank	Name	Party	State	Terms in: House		Terms in: Comm.
Chr	Mahon, George H.	Dem	Tex.	17		15
2nd	Kirwan, Michael J.	Dem	Ohio	16		13
3rd	Whitten, Jamie L.	Dem	Miss.	14		13
4th	Andrews, George W.	Dem	Ala.	13		12
5th	Rooney, John J.	Dem	N.Y.	13		12
6th	Sikes, Robert L. F.	Dem	Fla.	14		10
7th	Passman, Otto E.	Dem	La.	11		10
8th	Evins, Joseph L.	Dem	Tenn.	11		7
9th	Boland, Edward P.	Dem	Mass.	8		7
10th	Natcher, William H.	Dem	Ky.	8		7
11th	Flood, Daniel J.	Dem	Penn.	10	*3	7
12th	Steed, Thomas J.	Dem	Okla.	10		6
13th	Shipley, George E.	Dem	Ill.	5		5
14th	Slack, John M. Jr.	Dem	W.Va.	5		4
15th	Flynt, John James Jr.	Dem	Ga.	8		4
16th	Smith, Neal	Dem	Iowa	5		4
17th	Giaimo, Robert N.	Dem	Conn.	5		3
18th	Hansen, Julia Butler	Dem	Wash.	5		3
19th	Joelson, Charles S.	Dem	N.J.	4		3
20th	Addabbo, Joseph P	Dem	N.Y.	4		3
21st	McFall, John J.	Dem	Cal.	6		3
22nd	Hull, William R. Jr.	Dem	Mo.	7		3
23rd	Cohelan, Jeffrey	Dem	Cal.	5		2
24th	Morris, Thomas G.	Dem	N.M.	5		2
25th	Patten, Edward J.	Dem	N.J.	3		2
26th	Long, Clarence D.	Dem	Md.	3		2
27th	Marsh, John O. Jr.	Dem	Va.	3		2
28th	Yates, Sidney R.	Dem	Ill.	9	*2	2
29th	Casey, Robert R.	Dem	Tex.	5		2
30th	Pryor, David H.	Dem	Ark.	2		1

Minority

Rank	Name	Party	State	Terms in: House		Terms in: Comm.
RM	Bow, Frank T.	Rep	Ohio	9		8
2nd	Jonas, Charles Raper	Rep	N.C.	8	*2	6
3rd	Laird, Melvin R.	Rep	Wisc.	8	*2	6
4th	Cederberg, Elford A.	Rep	Mich.	8	*2	6
5th	Lipscomb, Glenard P.	Rep	Cal.	8		6
6th	Rhodes, John J.	Rep	Ariz.	8		5
7th	Minshall, William E. Jr.	Rep	Ohio	7		5
8th	Michel, Robert H.	Rep	Ill.	6	*1	5
9th	Conte, Silvio O.	Rep	Mass.	5		5
10th	Langen, Odin	Rep	Minn.	5		4
11th	Reifel, Benjamin	Rep	S.D.	4		3
12th	Davis, Glenn R.	Rep	Wisc.	7	*2	2
13th	Robison, Howard W.	Rep	N.Y.	6		2
14th	Shriver, Garner E.	Rep	Kans.	4		2
15th	McDade, Joseph M.	Rep	Penn.	3		2
16th	Andrews, Mark	Rep	N.D.	3		2
17th	Harrison, William Henry	Rep	Wyo.	5	*2	1
18th	Wyman, Louis C.	Rep	N.H.	2	*2	1
19th	Talcott, Burt L.	Rep	Cal.	3		1
20th	Reid, Charlotte T.	Rep	Ill.	3		1
21st	Riegle, Donald W. Jr.	Rep	Mich.	1		1

*1: Member's 1st period of service on the committee;
*2: Member's 2nd period of service on the committee;
*3: Member's 3rd period of service on the committee.

Vacancies Filled:
Minority: 17th through the 21st seats on Jan. 26,1967.

Changes:
Minority:

Harrison, William Henry	Rep	Wyo.	Oct. 3,1968	Left committee; defeated for renomination.
Wyatt, Wendell	Rep	Ore.	Oct. 3,1968	Replaced Harrison.

Departures from the House:

	Majority		Minority
Defeated for Reelection	Morris, Thomas G.	N.M. Dem	None

APPROPRIATIONS / 91st Congress

Service Dates of Committee Chair: Jan. 3,1969-Jan. 3,1971
Service Dates of Majority Members: Jan. 3,1969-Jan. 3,1971
Service Dates of Minority Members: Jan. 3,1969-Jan. 3,1971

Majority

Rank Name	Party	State	Terms in: House	Terms in: Comm.
Chr Mahon, George H.	Dem	Tex.	18	16
2nd Kirwan, Michael J.	Dem	Ohio	17	14
3rd Whitten, Jamie L.	Dem	Miss.	15	14
4th Andrews, George W.	Dem	Ala.	14	13
5th Rooney, John J.	Dem	N.Y.	14	13
6th Sikes, Robert L. F.	Dem	Fla.	15	11
7th Passman, Otto E.	Dem	La.	12	11
8th Evins, Joseph L.	Dem	Tenn.	12	8
9th Boland, Edward P.	Dem	Mass.	9	8
10th Natcher, William H.	Dem	Ky.	9	8
11th Flood, Daniel J.	Dem	Penn.	11	*3 8
12th Steed, Thomas J.	Dem	Okla.	11	7
13th Shipley, George E.	Dem	Ill.	6	6
14th Slack, John M. Jr.	Dem	W.Va.	6	5
15th Flynt, John James Jr.	Dem	Ga.	9	5
16th Smith, Neal	Dem	Iowa	6	5
17th Giaimo, Robert N.	Dem	Conn.	6	4
18th Hansen, Julia Butler	Dem	Wash.	6	4
19th Joelson, Charles S.	Dem	N.J.	5	4
20th Addabbo, Joseph P.	Dem	N.Y.	5	4
21st McFall, John J.	Dem	Cal.	7	4
22nd Hull, William R. Jr.	Dem	Mo.	8	4
23rd Cohelan, Jeffrey	Dem	Cal.	6	3
24th Patten, Edward J.	Dem	N.J.	4	3
25th Long, Clarence D.	Dem	Md.	4	3
26th Marsh, John O. Jr.	Dem	Va.	4	3
27th Yates, Sidney R.	Dem	Ill.	10	*2 3
28th Casey, Robert R.	Dem	Tex.	6	3
29th Pryor, David H.	Dem	Ark.	3	2
30th Evans, Frank E.	Dem	Colo.	3	1

Minority

Rank Name	Party	State	Terms in: House	Terms in: Comm.
RM Bow, Frank T.	Rep	Ohio	10	9
2nd Jonas, Charles Raper	Rep	N.C.	9	*2 7
3rd Laird, Melvin R.	Rep	Wisc.	9	*2 7
4th Cederberg, Elford A.	Rep	Mich.	9	*2 7
5th Lipscomb, Glenard P.	Rep	Cal.	9	7
6th Rhodes, John J.	Rep	Ariz.	9	6
7th Minshall, William E. Jr.	Rep	Ohio	8	6
8th Michel, Robert H.	Rep	Ill.	7	*1 6
9th Conte, Silvio O.	Rep	Mass.	6	6
10th Langen, Odin	Rep	Minn.	6	5
11th Reifel, Benjamin	Rep	S.D.	5	4
12th Davis, Glenn R.	Rep	Wisc.	8	*2 3
13th Robison, Howard W.	Rep	N.Y.	7	3
14th Shriver, Garner E.	Rep	Kans.	5	3
15th McDade, Joseph M.	Rep	Penn.	4	3
16th Andrews, Mark	Rep	N.D.	4	3
17th Wyman, Louis C.	Rep	N.H.	3	*2 2
18th Talcott, Burt L.	Rep	Cal.	4	2
19th Reid, Charlotte T.	Rep	Ill.	4	2
20th Riegle, Donald W. Jr.	Rep	Mich.	2	2
21st Wyatt, Wendell	Rep	Ore.	4	2

*1: Member's 1st period of service on the committee;
*2: Member's 2nd period of service on the committee;
*3: Member's 3rd period of service on the committee.

Vacancy Filled:
Majority: 30th seat by Evans on Jan. 29,1969.

Changes:
Majority:

Joelson, Charles S.	Dem	N.J.	Sep. 4,1969	Resigned; appointed state Superior Court Judge.
Obey, David R.	Dem	Wisc.	Nov. 12,1969	Replaced Joelson.
Kirwan, Michael J.	Dem	Ohio	July 27,1970	Died in office.

Minority:

Laird, Melvin R.	Rep	Wisc.	Jan. 21,1969	Resigned; appointed Secretary of Defense.
Edwards, W. J. (Jack)	Rep	Ala.	Jan. 29,1969	Replaced Laird.
Lipscomb, Glenard P.	Rep	Cal.	Feb. 1,1970	Died in office.
Clawson, Del M.	Rep	Cal.	Feb. 17,1970	Replaced Lipscomb.
Reifel, Benjamin	Rep	S.D.	Oct. 14,1970	Left committee; no new assignment.
Scherle, William J.	Rep	Iowa	Nov. 25,1970	Replaced Reifel.

Departures from the House:

	Majority		Minority	
Defeated for Reelection	None		Langen, Odin	Minn. Rep
Defeated for Renomination	Cohelan, Jeffrey	Cal. Dem	None	
Retired	Marsh, John O. Jr.	Va. Dem	None	

APPROPRIATIONS / 92nd Congress

Service Dates of Committee Chair: Feb. 4,1971-Jan. 3,1973
Service Dates of Majority Members: Feb. 4,1971-Jan. 3,1973
Service Dates of Minority Members: Feb. 4,1971-Jan. 3,1973

Majority

Rank	Name	Party	State	Terms in: House		Terms in: Comm.
Chr	Mahon, George H.	Dem	Tex.	19		17
2nd	Whitten, Jamie L.	Dem	Miss.	16		15
3rd	Andrews, George W.	Dem	Ala.	15		14
4th	Rooney, John J.	Dem	N.Y.	15		14
5th	Sikes, Robert L. F.	Dem	Fla.	16		12
6th	Passman, Otto E.	Dem	La.	13		12
7th	Evins, Joseph L.	Dem	Tenn.	13		9
8th	Boland, Edward P.	Dem	Mass.	10		9
9th	Natcher, William H.	Dem	Ky.	10		9
10th	Flood, Daniel J.	Dem	Penn.	12	*3	9
11th	Steed, Thomas J.	Dem	Okla.	12		8
12th	Shipley, George E.	Dem	Ill.	7		7
13th	Slack, John M. Jr.	Dem	W.Va.	7		6
14th	Flynt, John James Jr.	Dem	Ga.	10		6
15th	Smith, Neal	Dem	Iowa	7		6
16th	Giaimo, Robert N.	Dem	Conn.	7		5
17th	Hansen, Julia Butler	Dem	Wash.	7		5
18th	Addabbo, Joseph P.	Dem	N.Y.	6		5
19th	McFall, John J.	Dem	Cal.	8		5
20th	Hull, William R. Jr.	Dem	Mo.	9		5
21st	Patten, Edward J.	Dem	N.J.	5		4
22nd	Long, Clarence D.	Dem	Md.	5		4
23rd	Yates, Sidney R.	Dem	Ill.	11	*2	4
24th	Casey, Robert R.	Dem	Tex.	7		4
25th	Pryor, David H.	Dem	Ark.	4		3
26th	Evans, Frank E.	Dem	Colo.	4		2
27th	Obey, David R.	Dem	Wisc.	2		2
28th	Roybal, Edward R.	Dem	Cal.	5		1
29th	Hathaway, William D.	Dem	Me.	4		1
30th	Galifianakis, Nick	Dem	N.C.	3		1
31st	Stokes, Louis	Dem	Ohio	2		1
32nd	Roush, J. Edward	Dem	Ind.	6		1
33rd	McKay, K. Gunn	Dem	Utah	1		1

Minority

Rank	Name	Party	State	Terms in: House		Terms in: Comm.
RM	Bow, Frank T.	Rep	Ohio	11		10
2nd	Jonas, Charles Raper	Rep	N.C.	10	*2	8
3rd	Cederberg, Elford A.	Rep	Mich.	10	*2	8
4th	Rhodes, John J.	Rep	Ariz.	10		7
5th	Minshall, William E. Jr.	Rep	Ohio	9		7
6th	Michel, Robert H.	Rep	Ill.	8	*1	7
7th	Conte, Silvio O.	Rep	Mass.	7		7
8th	Davis, Glenn R.	Rep	Wisc.	9	*2	4
9th	Robison, Howard W.	Rep	N.Y.	8		4
10th	Shriver, Garner E.	Rep	Kans.	6		4
11th	McDade, Joseph M.	Rep	Penn.	5		4
12th	Andrews, Mark	Rep	N.D.	5		4
13th	Wyman, Louis C.	Rep	N.H.	4	*2	3
14th	Talcott, Burt L.	Rep	Cal.	5		3
15th	Reid, Charlotte T.	Rep	Ill.	5		3
16th	Riegle, Donald W. Jr.	Rep	Mich.	3		3
17th	Wyatt, Wendell	Rep	Ore.	5		3
18th	Edwards, W. J. (Jack)	Rep	Ala.	4		2
19th	Clawson, Del M.	Rep	Cal.	5		2
20th	Scherle, William J.	Rep	Iowa	3		2
21st	McEwen, Robert C.	Rep	N.Y.	4		1
22nd	Myers, John T.	Rep	Ind.	3		1

*1: Member's 1st period of service on the committee;
*2: Member's 2nd period of service on the committee;
*3: Member's 3rd period of service on the committee.

Changes:

Majority:

Name	Party	State	Date	Change
Andrews, George W.	Dem	Ala.	Dec. 25,1971	Died in office.
Bevill, Tom	Dem	Ala.	Jan. 27,1972	Replaced Andrews.

Minority:

Name	Party	State	Date	Change
Reid, Charlotte T.	Rep	Ill.	Oct. 7,1971	Resigned; appointed to Federal Communications Commission.
Robinson, J. Kenneth	Rep	Va.	Oct. 27,1971	Replaced Reid.
Bow, Frank T.	Rep	Ohio	Nov. 13,1972	Died in office.

Departures from the House:

	Majority			Minority		
Elected to U.S. Senate	Hathaway, William D.	Me.	Dem	None		
Lost Election to U.S. Senate	Galifianakis, Nick	N.C.	Dem	None		
Lost Nomination to U.S. Senate	Pryor, David H.	Ark.	Dem	None		
Retired	Hull, William R. Jr.	Mo.	Dem	Jonas, Charles Raper	N.C.	Rep

APPROPRIATIONS / 93rd Congress

Service Dates of Committee Chair: Jan. 6,1973-Jan. 3,1975
Service Dates of Majority Members: Jan. 6,1973-Jan. 3,1975
Service Dates of Minority Members: Jan. 6,1973-Jan. 3,1975

Majority

Rank	Name	Party	State	Terms in: House	Terms in: Comm.
Chr	Mahon, George H.	Dem	Tex.	20	18
2nd	Whitten, Jamie L.	Dem	Miss.	17	16
3rd	Rooney, John J.	Dem	N.Y.	16	15
4th	Sikes, Robert L. F.	Dem	Fla.	17	13
5th	Passman, Otto E.	Dem	La.	14	13
6th	Evins, Joseph L.	Dem	Tenn.	14	10
7th	Boland, Edward P.	Dem	Mass.	11	10
8th	Natcher, William H.	Dem	Ky.	11	10
9th	Flood, Daniel J.	Dem	Penn.	13	*3 10
10th	Steed, Thomas J.	Dem	Okla.	13	9
11th	Shipley, George E.	Dem	Ill.	8	8
12th	Slack, John M. Jr.	Dem	W.Va.	8	7
13th	Flynt, John James Jr.	Dem	Ga.	11	7
14th	Smith, Neal	Dem	Iowa	8	7
15th	Giaimo, Robert N.	Dem	Conn.	8	6
16th	Hansen, Julia Butler	Dem	Wash.	8	6
17th	Addabbo, Joseph P.	Dem	N.Y.	7	6
18th	McFall, John J.	Dem	Cal.	9	6
19th	Patten, Edward J.	Dem	N.J.	6	5
20th	Long, Clarence D.	Dem	Md.	6	5
21st	Yates, Sidney R.	Dem	Ill.	12	*2 5
22nd	Casey, Robert R.	Dem	Tex.	8	5
23rd	Evans, Frank E.	Dem	Colo.	5	3
24th	Obey, David R.	Dem	Wisc.	3	3
25th	Roybal, Edward R.	Dem	Cal.	6	2
26th	Stokes, Louis	Dem	Ohio	3	2
27th	Roush, J. Edward	Dem	Ind.	7	2
28th	McKay, K. Gunn	Dem	Utah	2	2
29th	Bevill, Tom	Dem	Ala.	4	2
30th	Green, Edith S.	Dem	Ore.	10	1
31st	Tiernan, Robert O.	Dem	R.I.	4	1
32nd	Chappell, William V. Jr.	Dem	Fla.	3	1
33rd	Burlison, Bill D.	Dem	Mo.	3	1

Minority

Rank	Name	Party	State	Terms in: House	Terms in: Comm.
RM	Cederberg, Elford A.	Rep	Mich.	11	*2 9
2nd	Rhodes, John J.	Rep	Ariz.	11	8
3rd	Minshall, William E. Jr.	Rep	Ohio	10	8
4th	Michel, Robert H.	Rep	Ill.	9	*1 8
5th	Conte, Silvio O.	Rep	Mass.	8	8
6th	Davis, Glenn R.	Rep	Wisc.	10	*2 5
7th	Robison, Howard W.	Rep	N.Y.	9	5
8th	Shriver, Garner E.	Rep	Kans.	7	5
9th	McDade, Joseph M.	Rep	Penn.	6	5
10th	Andrews, Mark	Rep	N.D.	6	5
11th	Wyman, Louis C.	Rep	N.H.	5	*2 4
12th	Talcott, Burt L.	Rep	Cal.	6	4
13th	Riegle, Donald W. Jr.	Rep	Mich.	4	4
14th	Wyatt, Wendell	Rep	Ore.	6	4
15th	Edwards, W. J. (Jack)	Rep	Ala.	5	3
16th	Clawson, Del M.	Rep	Cal.	6	3
17th	Scherle, William J.	Rep	Iowa	4	3
18th	McEwen, Robert C.	Rep	N.Y.	5	2
19th	Myers, John T.	Rep	Ind.	4	2
20th	Robinson, J. Kenneth	Rep	Va.	2	2
21st	Miller, Clarence E.	Rep	Ohio	4	1
22nd	Ruth, Earl B.	Rep	N.C.	3	1

*1: Member's 1st period of service on the committee;
*2: Member's 2nd period of service on the committee;
*3: Member's 3rd period of service on the committee.

Vacancies Filled:
Majority: 30th through the 33rd seats on Jan. 24,1973.
Minority: 21st and 22nd seats by Miller and Ruth respectively on Jan. 24,1973.

Changes:

Majority:

Rooney, John J.	Dem	N.Y.	Dec. 31,1974	Resigned and retired.
Hansen, Julia Butler	Dem	Wash.	Dec. 31,1974	Resigned and retired.
Green, Edith S.	Dem	Ore.	Dec. 31,1974	Resigned and retired.

Minority:

Clawson, Del M.	Rep	Cal.	Jan. 24,1973	Moved to Rules.
Veysey, Victor V.	Rep	Cal.	Jan. 24,1973	Replaced Clawson.
Riegle, Donald W. Jr.	Rep	Mich.	Mar. 5,1973	Resigned Republican Party, Feb. 27,1973; moved to Foreign Affairs.
Coughlin, R. Lawrence	Rep	Penn.	Mar. 7,1973	Replaced Riegle.
Rhodes, John J.	Rep	Ariz.	Dec. 7,1973	Left committee; elected House Minority Leader.
Young, C. W. Bill	Rep	Fla.	Dec. 20,1973	Replaced Rhodes.
Minshall, William E. Jr.	Rep	Ohio	Dec. 31,1974	Resigned and retired.
Davis, Glenn R.	Rep	Wisc.	Dec. 31,1974	Resigned; defeated for renomination.
Wyman, Louis C.	Rep	N.H.	Dec. 31,1974	Resigned; appointed to U.S. Senate.

Departures from the House:

	Majority			Minority		
Defeated for Reelection	None			Ruth, Earl B.	N.C.	Rep
				Scherle, William J.	Iowa	Rep
				Veysey, Victor V.	Cal.	Rep
Defeated for Renomination	Tiernan, Robert O.	R.I.	Dem	None		
Retired	None			Robison, Howard W.	N.Y.	Rep
				Wyatt, Wendell	Ore.	Rep

APPROPRIATIONS / 94th Congress

Service Dates of Committee Chair: Jan. 20,1975-Jan. 3,1977
Service Dates of Majority Members: Jan. 20,1975-Jan. 3,1977
Service Dates of Minority Members: Jan. 28,1975-Jan. 3,1977

Majority

Rank Name	Party	State	Terms in: House	Terms in: Comm.
Chr Mahon, George H.	Dem	Tex.	21	19
2nd Whitten, Jamie L.	Dem	Miss.	18	17
3rd Sikes, Robert L. F.	Dem	Fla.	18	14
4th Passman, Otto E.	Dem	La.	15	14
5th Evins, Joseph L.	Dem	Tenn.	15	11
6th Boland, Edward P.	Dem	Mass.	12	11
7th Natcher, William H.	Dem	Ky.	12	11
8th Flood, Daniel J.	Dem	Penn.	14 *3	11
9th Steed, Thomas J.	Dem	Okla.	14	10
10th Shipley, George E.	Dem	Ill.	9	9
11th Slack, John M. Jr.	Dem	W.Va.	9	8
12th Flynt, John James Jr.	Dem	Ga.	12	8
13th Smith, Neal	Dem	Iowa	9	8
14th Giaimo, Robert N.	Dem	Conn.	9	7
15th Addabbo, Joseph P.	Dem	N.Y.	8	7
16th McFall, John J.	Dem	Cal.	10	7
17th Patten, Edward J.	Dem	N.J.	7	6
18th Long, Clarence D.	Dem	Md.	7	6
19th Yates, Sidney R.	Dem	Ill.	13 *2	6
20th Casey, Robert R.	Dem	Tex.	9	6
21st Evans, Frank E.	Dem	Colo.	6	4
22nd Obey, David R.	Dem	Wisc.	4	4
23rd Roybal, Edward R.	Dem	Cal.	7	3
24th Stokes, Louis	Dem	Ohio	4	3
25th Roush, J. Edward	Dem	Ind.	8	3
26th McKay, K. Gunn	Dem	Utah	3	3
27th Bevill, Tom	Dem	Ala.	5	3
28th Chappell, William V. Jr.	Dem	Fla.	4	2
29th Burlison, Bill D.	Dem	Mo.	4	2
30th Alexander, William V. Jr.	Dem	Ark.	4	1
31st Koch, Edward I.	Dem	N.Y.	4	1
32nd Burke, Yvonne Brathwaite	Dem	Cal.	2	1
33rd Murtha, John P. Jr.	Dem	Penn.	2	1
34th Traxler, J. Bob	Dem	Mich.	2	1
35th Duncan, Robert B.	Dem	Ore.	3 *2	1
36th Early, Joseph D.	Dem	Mass.	1	1
37th Baucus, Max S.	Dem	Mont.	1	1

Minority

Rank Name	Party	State	Terms in: House	Terms in: Comm.
RM Cederberg, Elford A.	Rep	Mich.	12 *2	10
2nd Michel, Robert H.	Rep	Ill.	10 *1	9
3rd Conte, Silvio O.	Rep	Mass.	9	9
4th Shriver, Garner E.	Rep	Kans.	8	6
5th McDade, Joseph M.	Rep	Penn.	7	6
6th Andrews, Mark	Rep	N.D.	7	6
7th Talcott, Burt L.	Rep	Cal.	7	5
8th Edwards, W. J. (Jack)	Rep	Ala.	6	4
9th McEwen, Robert C.	Rep	N.Y.	6	3
10th Myers, John T.	Rep	Ind.	5	3
11th Robinson, J. Kenneth	Rep	Va.	3	3
12th Miller, Clarence E.	Rep	Ohio	5	2
13th Coughlin, R. Lawrence	Rep	Penn.	4	2
14th Young, C. W. Bill	Rep	Fla.	3	2
15th Kemp, Jack F.	Rep	N.Y.	3	1
16th Armstrong, William L.	Rep	Colo.	2	1
17th Regula, Ralph S.	Rep	Ohio	2	1
18th Burgener, Clair W.	Rep	Cal.	2	1

*1: Member`s 1st period of service on the committee;
*2: Member's 2nd period of service on the committee;
*3: Member's 3rd period of service on the committee.

Changes:

Majority:

Casey, Robert R.	Dem	Tex.	Jan. 22,1976	Resigned; appointed to Federal Maritime Commission.
Wilson, Charles	Dem	Tex.	Feb. 3,1976	Replaced Casey.

Departures from the House:

	Majority			Minority		
Defeated for Reelection	Roush, J. Edward	Ind.	Dem	Shriver, Garner E.	Kans.	Rep
				Talcott, Burt L.	Cal.	Rep
Defeated for Renomination	Passman, Otto E.	La.	Dem	None		
Retired	Evins, Joseph L.	Tenn.	Dem	None		

APPROPRIATIONS / 95th Congress

Service Dates of Committee Chair: Jan. 19,1977-Jan. 3,1979
Service Dates of Majority Members: Jan. 19,1977-Jan. 3,1979
Service Dates of Minority Members: Jan. 19,1977-Jan. 3,1979

Majority

Rank	Name	Party	State	Terms in: House	Terms in: Comm.
Chr	Mahon, George H.	Dem	Tex.	22	20
2nd	Whitten, Jamie L.	Dem	Miss.	19	18
3rd	Sikes, Robert L. F.	Dem	Fla.	19	15
4th	Boland, Edward P.	Dem	Mass.	13	12
5th	Natcher, William H.	Dem	Ky.	13	12
6th	Flood, Daniel J.	Dem	Penn.	15	*3 12
7th	Steed, Thomas J.	Dem	Okla.	15	11
8th	Shipley, George E.	Dem	Ill.	10	10
9th	Slack, John M. Jr.	Dem	W.Va.	10	9
10th	Flynt, John James Jr.	Dem	Ga.	13	9
11th	Smith, Neal	Dem	Iowa	10	9
12th	Giaimo, Robert N.	Dem	Conn.	10	8
13th	Addabbo, Joseph P.	Dem	N.Y.	9	8
14th	McFall, John J.	Dem	Cal.	11	8
15th	Patten, Edward J.	Dem	N.J.	8	7
16th	Long, Clarence D.	Dem	Md.	8	7
17th	Yates, Sidney R.	Dem	Ill.	14	*2 7
18th	Evans, Frank E.	Dem	Colo.	7	5
19th	Obey, David R.	Dem	Wisc.	5	5
20th	Roybal, Edward R.	Dem	Cal.	8	4
21st	Stokes, Louis	Dem	Ohio	5	4
22nd	McKay, K. Gunn	Dem	Utah	4	4
23rd	Bevill, Tom	Dem	Ala.	6	4
24th	Chappell, William V. Jr.	Dem	Fla.	5	3
25th	Burlison, Bill D.	Dem	Mo.	5	3
26th	Alexander, William V. Jr.	Dem	Ark.	5	2
27th	Koch, Edward I.	Dem	N.Y.	5	2
28th	Burke, Yvonne Brathwaite	Dem	Cal.	3	2
29th	Murtha, John P. Jr.	Dem	Penn.	3	2
30th	Traxler, J. Bob	Dem	Mich.	3	2
31st	Duncan, Robert B.	Dem	Ore.	4	*2 2
32nd	Early, Joseph D.	Dem	Mass.	2	2
33rd	Baucus, Max S.	Dem	Mont.	2	2
34th	Wilson, Charles	Dem	Tex.	2	2
35th	Boggs, Corinne C. (Lindy)	Dem	La.	3	1
36th	Benjamin, Adam Jr.	Dem	Ind.	1	1
37th	Dicks, Norman D.	Dem	Wash.	1	1

Minority

Rank	Name	Party	State	Terms in: House	Terms in: Comm.
RM	Cederberg, Elford A.	Rep	Mich.	13	*2 11
2nd	Michel, Robert H.	Rep	Ill.	11	*1 10
3rd	Conte, Silvio O.	Rep	Mass.	10	10
4th	McDade, Joseph M.	Rep	Penn.	8	7
5th	Andrews, Mark	Rep	N.D.	8	7
6th	Edwards, W. J. (Jack)	Rep	Ala.	7	5
7th	McEwen, Robert C.	Rep	N.Y.	7	4
8th	Myers, John T.	Rep	Ind.	6	4
9th	Robinson, J. Kenneth	Rep	Va.	4	4
10th	Miller, Clarence E.	Rep	Ohio	6	3
11th	Coughlin, R. Lawrence	Rep	Penn.	5	3
12th	Young, C. W. Bill	Rep	Fla.	4	3
13th	Kemp, Jack F.	Rep	N.Y.	4	2
14th	Armstrong, William L.	Rep	Colo.	3	2
15th	Regula, Ralph S.	Rep	Ohio	3	2
16th	Burgener, Clair W.	Rep	Cal.	3	2
17th	O'Brien, George M.	Rep	Ill.	3	1
18th	Smith, Virginia D.	Rep	Neb.	2	1

*1: Member's 1st period of service on the committee;
*2: Member's 2nd period of service on the committee;
*3: Member's 3rd period of service on the committee.

Changes:

Majority:

Koch, Edward I.	Dem	N.Y.	Dec. 31,1977	Resigned House; elected Mayor of New York City.
McHugh, Matthew F.	Dem	N.Y.	Jan. 25,1978	Replaced Koch.
Baucus, Max S.	Dem	Mont.	Dec. 14,1978	Resigned House; elected to the U.S. Senate.
McFall, John J.	Dem	Cal.	Dec. 31,1978	Resigned House; defeated for reelection.

Minority:

Cederberg, Elford A.	Rep	Mich.	Dec. 31,1978	Resigned House; defeated for reelection.

Departures from the House:

	Majority			Minority		
Elected to U.S. Senate	None			Armstrong, William L.	Colo.	Rep
Lost Election for State Attorney General	Burke, Yvonne Brathwaite	Cal.	Dem	None		
Retired	Evans, Frank E.	Colo.	Dem	None		
	Flynt, John James Jr.	Ga.	Dem			
	Mahon, George H.	Tex.	Dem			
	Shipley, George E.	Ill.	Dem			
	Sikes, Robert L. F.	Fla.	Dem			

APPROPRIATIONS / 96th Congress

Service Dates of Committee Chair: Jan. 24,1979-Jan. 3,1981
Service Dates of Majority Members: Jan. 24,1979-Jan. 3,1981
Service Dates of Minority Members: Jan. 24,1979-Jan. 3,1981

Majority

Rank	Name	Party	State	Terms in: House	Terms in: Comm.
Chr	Whitten, Jamie L.	Dem	Miss.	20	19
2nd	Boland, Edward P.	Dem	Mass.	14	13
3rd	Natcher, William H.	Dem	Ky.	14	13
4th	Flood, Daniel J.	Dem	Penn.	16	*3 13
5th	Steed, Thomas J.	Dem	Okla.	16	12
6th	Slack, John M. Jr.	Dem	W.Va.	11	10
7th	Smith, Neal	Dem	Iowa	11	10
8th	Giaimo, Robert N.	Dem	Conn.	11	9
9th	Addabbo, Joseph P.	Dem	N.Y.	10	9
10th	Patten, Edward J.	Dem	N.J.	9	8
11th	Long, Clarence D.	Dem	Md.	9	8
12th	Yates, Sidney R.	Dem	Ill.	15	*2 8
13th	Obey, David R.	Dem	Wisc.	6	6
14th	Roybal, Edward R.	Dem	Cal.	9	5
15th	Stokes, Louis	Dem	Ohio	6	5
16th	McKay, K. Gunn	Dem	Utah	5	5
17th	Bevill, Tom	Dem	Ala.	7	5
18th	Chappell, William V. Jr.	Dem	Fla.	6	4
19th	Burlison, Bill D.	Dem	Mo.	6	4
20th	Alexander, William V. Jr.	Dem	Ark.	6	3
21st	Murtha, John P. Jr.	Dem	Penn.	4	3
22nd	Traxler, J. Bob	Dem	Mich.	4	3
23rd	Duncan, Robert B.	Dem	Ore.	5	*2 3
24th	Early, Joseph D.	Dem	Mass.	3	3
25th	Wilson, Charles	Dem	Tex.	4	3
26th	Boggs, Corinne C. (Lindy)	Dem	La.	4	2
27th	Benjamin, Adam Jr.	Dem	Ind.	2	2
28th	Dicks, Norman D.	Dem	Wash.	2	2
29th	McHugh, Matthew F.	Dem	N.Y.	3	2
30th	Ginn, Ronald B. (Bo)	Dem	Ga.	4	1
31st	Lehman, William	Dem	Fla.	4	1
32nd	Hightower, Jack E.	Dem	Tex.	3	1
33rd	Jenrette, John W. Jr.	Dem	S.C.	3	1
34th	Sabo, Martin Olav	DFL	Minn.	1	1
35th	Dixon, Julian C.	Dem	Cal.	1	1
36th	Stewart, Bennett M.	Dem	Ill.	1	1

Minority

Rank	Name	Party	State	Terms in: House	Terms in: Comm.
RM	Conte, Silvio O.	Rep	Mass.	11	11
2nd	Michel, Robert H.	Rep	Ill.	12	*1 11
3rd	McDade, Joseph M.	Rep	Penn.	9	8
4th	Andrews, Mark	Rep	N.D.	9	8
5th	Edwards, Jack	Rep	Ala.	8	6
6th	McEwen, Robert C.	Rep	N.Y.	8	5
7th	Myers, John T.	Rep	Ind.	7	5
8th	Robinson, J. Kenneth	Rep	Va.	5	5
9th	Miller, Clarence E.	Rep	Ohio	7	4
10th	Coughlin, R. Lawrence	Rep	Penn.	6	4
11th	Young, C. W. Bill	Rep	Fla.	5	4
12th	Kemp, Jack F.	Rep	N.Y.	5	3
13th	Regula, Ralph S.	Rep	Ohio	4	3
14th	Burgener, Clair W.	Rep	Cal.	4	3
15th	O'Brien, George M.	Rep	Ill.	4	2
16th	Smith, Virginia D.	Rep	Neb.	3	2
17th	Rudd, Eldon D.	Rep	Ariz.	2	1
18th	Pursell, Carl D.	Rep	Mich.	2	1

*1: Member`s 1st period of service on the committee;
*2: Member's 2nd period of service on the committee;
*3: Member's 3rd period of service on the committee.

Note: Ranking on this committee for the following member was affected by other chamber service: Robert H. Michel (Rep-Ill.), House Minority Whip.

Changes:

Majority:

Flood, Daniel J.	Dem	Penn.	Jan. 31,1980	Resigned and retired.
Fazio, Victor H.	Dem	Cal.	Feb. 26,1980	Replaced Flood.
Slack, John M. Jr.	Dem	W.Va	Mar. 17,1980	Died in office.
Hefner, W. G. (Bill)	Dem	N.C.	July 2,1980	Replaced Slack.
Jenrette, John W. Jr.	Dem	S.C.	Dec. 10,1980	Resigned; defeated for reelection.

Departures from the House:

	Majority			Minority		
Elected to U.S. Senate	None			Andrews, Mark	N.D.	Rep
Defeated for Reelection	Burlison, Bill D.	Mo.	Dem	None		
	McKay, K. Gunn	Utah	Dem			
Defeated for Renomination	Duncan, Robert B.	Ore.	Dem	None		
	Stewart, Bennett M.	Ill.	Dem			
Retired	Giaimo, Robert N.	Conn.	Dem	McEwen, Robert C.	N.Y.	Rep
	Patten, Edward J.	N.J.	Dem			
	Steed, Thomas J.	Okla.	Dem			

Departures from Committee:

Became House Minority Leader	None	Michel, Robert H.	Ill. Rep

APPROPRIATIONS / 97th Congress

Service Dates of Committee Chair: Jan. 28,1981-Jan. 3,1983
Service Dates of Majority Members: Jan. 28,1981-Jan. 3,1983
Service Dates of Minority Members: Jan. 28,1981-Jan. 3,1983

Majority

Rank Name	Party	State	Terms in: House	Terms in: Comm.
Chr Whitten, Jamie L.	Dem	Miss.	21	20
2nd Boland, Edward P.	Dem	Mass.	15	14
3rd Natcher, William H.	Dem	Ky.	15	14
4th Smith, Neal	Dem	Iowa	12	11
5th Addabbo, Joseph P.	Dem	N.Y.	11	10
6th Long, Clarence D.	Dem	Md.	10	9
7th Yates, Sidney R.	Dem	Ill.	16	*2 9
8th Obey, David R.	Dem	Wisc.	7	7
9th Roybal, Edward R.	Dem	Cal.	10	6
10th Stokes, Louis	Dem	Ohio	7	6
11th Bevill, Tom	Dem	Ala.	8	6
12th Chappell, William V. Jr.	Dem	Fla.	7	5
13th Alexander, William V. Jr.	Dem	Ark.	7	4
14th Murtha, John P. Jr.	Dem	Penn.	5	4
15th Traxler, J. Bob	Dem	Mich.	5	4
16th Early, Joseph D.	Dem	Mass.	4	4
17th Wilson, Charles	Dem	Tex.	5	4
18th Boggs, Corinne C. (Lindy)	Dem	La.	5	3
19th Benjamin, Adam Jr.	Dem	Ind.	3	3
20th Dicks, Norman D.	Dem	Wash.	3	3
21st McHugh, Matthew F.	Dem	N.Y.	4	3
22nd Ginn, Ronald B. (Bo)	Dem	Ga.	5	2
23rd Lehman, William	Dem	Fla.	5	2
24th Hightower, Jack E.	Dem	Tex.	4	2
25th Sabo, Martin Olav	Dem	Minn.	2	2
26th Dixon, Julian C.	Dem	Cal.	2	2
27th Fazio, Victor H.	Dem	Cal.	2	2
28th Hefner, W. G. (Bill)	Dem	N.C.	4	2
29th AuCoin, Les	Dem	Ore.	4	1
30th Akaka, Daniel K.	Dem	Hai.	3	1
31st Watkins, Wesley W.	Dem	Okla.	3	1
32nd Gray, William H. III	Dem	Penn.	2	1
33rd Dwyer, Bernard J.	Dem	N.J.	1	1

Minority

Rank Name	Party	State	Terms in: House	Terms in: Comm.
RM Conte, Silvio O.	Rep	Mass.	12	12
2nd McDade, Joseph M.	Rep	Penn.	10	9
3rd Edwards, Jack	Rep	Ala.	9	7
4th Myers, John T.	Rep	Ind.	8	6
5th Robinson, J. Kenneth	Rep	Va.	6	6
6th Miller, Clarence E.	Rep	Ohio	8	5
7th Coughlin, R. Lawrence	Rep	Penn.	7	5
8th Young, C. W. Bill	Rep	Fla.	6	5
9th Kemp, Jack F.	Rep	N.Y.	6	4
10th Regula, Ralph S.	Rep	Ohio	5	4
11th Burgener, Clair W.	Rep	Cal.	5	4
12th O'Brien, George M.	Rep	Ill.	5	3
13th Smith, Virginia D.	Rep	Neb.	4	3
14th Rudd, Eldon D.	Rep	Ariz.	3	2
15th Pursell, Carl D.	Rep	Mich.	3	2
16th Edwards, M. H. (Mickey)	Rep	Okla.	3	1
17th Livingston, Robert L.	Rep	La.	3	1
18th Green, S. William	Rep	N.Y.	3	1
19th Loeffler, Thomas G.	Rep	Tex.	2	1
20th Lewis, Jerry	Rep	Cal.	2	1
21st Campbell, Carroll A. Jr.	Rep	S.C.	2	1
22nd Porter, John Edward	Rep	Ill.	2	1

*2: Member's 2nd period of service on the committee.

Changes:

Majority:

Benjamin, Adam Jr.	Dem	Ind.	Sep. 7,1982	Died in office.
Ratchford, William R.	Dem	Conn.	Sep. 22,1982	Replaced Benjamin.

Departures from the House:	**Majority**		**Minority**	
Lost Nomination for Governor	Ginn, Ronald B. (Bo)	Ga. Dem	None	
Retired	None		Burgener, Clair W.	Cal. Rep
Departures from Committee:				
Moved to Ways & Means	None		Campbell, Carroll A. Jr.	S.C. Rep

APPROPRIATIONS / 98th Congress

Service Dates of Committee Chair: Jan. 6,1983-Jan. 3,1985
Service Dates of Majority Members: Jan. 6,1983-Jan. 3,1985
Service Dates of Minority Members: Jan. 6,1983-Jan. 3,1985

Majority

Rank	Name	Party	State	Terms in: House	Terms in: Comm.
Chr	Whitten, Jamie L.	Dem	Miss.	22	21
2nd	Boland, Edward P.	Dem	Mass.	16	15
3rd	Natcher, William H.	Dem	Ky.	16	15
4th	Smith, Neal	Dem	Iowa	13	12
5th	Addabbo, Joseph P.	Dem	N.Y.	12	11
6th	Long, Clarence D.	Dem	Md.	11	10
7th	Yates, Sidney R.	Dem	Ill.	17	*2 10
8th	Obey, David R.	Dem	Wisc.	8	8
9th	Roybal, Edward R.	Dem	Cal.	11	7
10th	Stokes, Louis	Dem	Ohio	8	7
11th	Bevill, Tom	Dem	Ala.	9	7
12th	Chappell, William V. Jr.	Dem	Fla.	8	6
13th	Alexander, William V. Jr.	Dem	Ark.	8	5
14th	Murtha, John P. Jr.	Dem	Penn.	6	5
15th	Traxler, J. Bob	Dem	Mich.	6	5
16th	Early, Joseph D.	Dem	Mass.	5	5
17th	Wilson, Charles	Dem	Tex.	6	5
18th	Boggs, Corinne C. (Lindy)	Dem	La.	6	4
19th	Dicks, Norman D.	Dem	Wash.	4	4
20th	McHugh, Matthew F.	Dem	N.Y.	5	4
21st	Lehman, William	Dem	Fla.	6	3
22nd	Hightower, Jack E.	Dem	Tex.	5	3
23rd	Sabo, Martin Olav	Dem	Minn.	3	3
24th	Dixon, Julian C.	Dem	Cal.	3	3
25th	Fazio, Victor H.	Dem	Cal.	3	3
26th	Hefner, W. G. (Bill)	Dem	N.C.	5	3
27th	AuCoin, Les	Dem	Ore.	5	2
28th	Akaka, Daniel K.	Dem	Hai.	4	2
29th	Watkins, Wesley W.	Dem	Okla.	4	2
30th	Gray, William H. III	Dem	Penn.	3	2
31st	Dwyer, Bernard J.	Dem	N.J.	2	2
32nd	Ratchford, William R.	Dem	Conn.	3	2
33rd	Boner, William H.	Dem	Tenn.	3	1
34th	Hoyer, Steny H.	Dem	Md.	2	1
35th	Carr, M. Robert	Dem	Mich.	4	1
36th	Mrazek, Robert J.	Dem	N.Y.	1	1

Minority

Rank	Name	Party	State	Terms in: House	Terms in: Comm.
RM	Conte, Silvio O.	Rep	Mass.	13	13
2nd	McDade, Joseph M.	Rep	Penn.	11	10
3rd	Edwards, Jack	Rep	Ala.	10	8
4th	Myers, John T.	Rep	Ind.	9	7
5th	Robinson, J. Kenneth	Rep	Va.	7	7
6th	Miller, Clarence E.	Rep	Ohio	9	6
7th	Coughlin, R. Lawrence	Rep	Penn.	8	6
8th	Young, C. W. Bill	Rep	Fla.	7	6
9th	Kemp, Jack F.	Rep	N.Y.	7	5
10th	Regula, Ralph S.	Rep	Ohio	6	5
11th	O'Brien, George M.	Rep	Ill.	6	4
12th	Smith, Virginia D.	Rep	Neb.	5	4
13th	Rudd, Eldon D.	Rep	Ariz.	4	3
14th	Pursell, Carl D.	Rep	Mich.	4	3
15th	Edwards, M.H. (Mickey)	Rep	Okla.	4	2
16th	Livingston, Robert L.	Rep	La.	4	2
17th	Green, S. William	Rep	N.Y.	4	2
18th	Loeffler, Thomas G.	Rep	Tex.	3	2
19th	Lewis, Jerry	Rep	Cal.	3	2
20th	Porter, John Edward	Rep	Ill.	3	2
21st	Rogers, Harold	Rep	Ky.	2	1

*2: Member's 2nd period of service on the committee.

Departures from the House:

	Majority			Minority		
Defeated for Reelection	Hightower, Jack E.	Tex.	Dem	None		
	Long, Clarence D.	Md.	Dem			
	Ratchford, William R.	Conn.	Dem			
Retired	None			Edwards, W.J. (Jack)	Ala.	Rep
				Robinson, J. Kenneth	Va.	Rep

APPROPRIATIONS / 99th Congress

Service Dates of Committee Chair: Jan. 7,1985-Jan. 3,1987
Service Dates of Majority Members: Jan. 30,1985-Jan. 3,1987
Service Dates of Minority Members: Jan. 30,1985-Jan. 3,1987

Majority

Rank	Name	Party	State	Terms in: House	Terms in: Comm.
Chr	Whitten, Jamie L.	Dem	Miss.	23	22
2nd	Boland, Edward P.	Dem	Mass.	17	16
3rd	Natcher, William H.	Dem	Ky.	17	16
4th	Smith, Neal	Dem	Iowa	14	13
5th	Addabbo, Joseph P.	Dem	N.Y.	13	12
6th	Yates, Sidney R.	Dem	Ill.	18	*2 11
7th	Obey, David R.	Dem	Wisc.	9	9
8th	Roybal, Edward R.	Dem	Cal.	12	8
9th	Stokes, Louis	Dem	Ohio	9	8
10th	Bevill, Tom	Dem	Ala.	10	8
11th	Chappell, William V. Jr.	Dem	Fla.	9	7
12th	Alexander, William V. Jr.	Dem	Ark.	9	6
13th	Murtha, John P. Jr.	Dem	Penn.	7	6
14th	Traxler, J. Bob	Dem	Mich.	7	6
15th	Early, Joseph D.	Dem	Mass.	6	6
16th	Wilson, Charles	Dem	Tex.	7	6
17th	Boggs, Corinne C. (Lindy)	Dem	La.	7	5
18th	Dicks, Norman D.	Dem	Wash.	5	5
19th	McHugh, Matthew F.	Dem	N.Y.	6	5
20th	Lehman, William	Dem	Fla.	7	4
21st	Sabo, Martin Olav	Dem	Minn.	4	4
22nd	Dixon, Julian C.	Dem	Cal.	4	4
23rd	Fazio, Victor H.	Dem	Cal.	4	4
24th	Hefner, W. G. (Bill)	Dem	N.C.	6	4
25th	AuCoin, Les	Dem	Ore.	6	3
26th	Akaka, Daniel K.	Dem	Hai.	5	3
27th	Watkins, Wesley W.	Dem	Okla.	5	3
28th	Gray, William H. III	Dem	Penn.	4	3
29th	Dwyer, Bernard J.	Dem	N.J.	3	3
30th	Boner, William H.	Dem	Tenn.	4	2
31st	Hoyer, Steny H.	Dem	Md.	3	2
32nd	Carr, M. Robert	Dem	Mich.	5	2
33rd	Mrazek, Robert J.	Dem	N.Y.	2	2
34th	Durbin, Richard J.	Dem	Ill.	2	1
35th	Coleman, Ronald D.	Dem	Tex.	2	1

Minority

Rank	Name	Party	State	Terms in: House	Terms in: Comm.
RM	Conte, Silvio O.	Rep	Mass.	14	14
2nd	McDade, Joseph M.	Rep	Penn.	12	11
3rd	Myers, John T.	Rep	Ind.	10	8
4th	Miller, Clarence E.	Rep	Ohio	10	7
5th	Coughlin, R. Lawrence	Rep	Penn.	9	7
6th	Young, C. W. Bill	Rep	Fla.	8	7
7th	Kemp, Jack F.	Rep	N.Y.	8	6
8th	Regula, Ralph S.	Rep	Ohio	7	6
9th	O'Brien, George M.	Rep	Ill.	7	5
10th	Smith, Virginia D.	Rep	Neb.	6	5
11th	Rudd, Eldon D.	Rep	Ariz.	5	4
12th	Pursell, Carl D.	Rep	Mich.	5	4
13th	Edwards, M.H. (Mickey)	Rep	Okla.	5	3
14th	Livingston, Robert L.	Rep	La.	5	3
15th	Green, S. William	Rep	N.Y.	5	3
16th	Loeffler, Thomas G.	Rep	Tex.	4	3
17th	Lewis, Jerry	Rep	Cal.	4	3
18th	Porter, John Edward	Rep	Ill.	4	3
19th	Rogers, Harold	Rep	Ky.	3	2
20th	Skeen, Joe	Rep	N.M.	3	1
21st	Wolf, Frank R.	Rep	Va.	3	1
22nd	Lowery, William	Rep	Cal.	3	1

*2: Member's 2nd period of service on the committee.

Changes:

Majority:

Name	Party	State	Date	Change
Addabbo, Joseph P.	Dem	N.Y.	Apr. 10,1986	Died in office.
Mollohan, Alan B.	Dem	W.Va.	May 1,1986	Replaced Addabbo.

Minority:

Name	Party	State	Date	Change
O'Brien, George M.	Rep	Ill.	July 17,1986	Died in office.
Michel, Robert H.	Rep	Ill.	July 23,1986	Replaced O'Brien; returned to committee.

Departures from the House:	**Majority**	**Minority**		
Lost Nomination for Governor	None	Loeffler, Thomas G.	Tex.	Rep
Retired	None	Rudd, Eldon D.	Ariz.	Rep
Departures from Committee:				
No new assignment	None	Michel, Robert H.	Ill.	Rep

APPROPRIATIONS / 100th Congress

Service Dates of Committee Chair: Jan. 6,1987-Jan. 3,1989
Service Dates of Majority Members: Jan. 6,1987-Jan. 3,1989
Service Dates of Minority Members: Jan. 21,1987-Jan. 3,1989

Majority

Rank Name	Party	State	Terms in: House	Terms in: Comm.
Chr Whitten, Jamie L.	Dem	Miss.	24	23
2nd Boland, Edward P.	Dem	Mass.	18	17
3rd Natcher, William H.	Dem	Ky.	18	17
4th Smith, Neal	Dem	Iowa	15	14
5th Yates, Sidney R.	Dem	Ill.	19	*2 12
6th Obey, David R.	Dem	Wisc.	10	10
7th Roybal, Edward R.	Dem	Cal.	13	9
8th Stokes, Louis	Dem	Ohio	10	9
9th Bevill, Tom	Dem	Ala.	11	9
10th Chappell, William V. Jr.	Dem	Fla.	10	8
11th Alexander, William V. Jr.	Dem	Ark.	10	7
12th Murtha, John P. Jr.	Dem	Penn.	8	7
13th Traxler, J. Bob	Dem	Mich.	8	7
14th Early, Joseph D.	Dem	Mass.	7	7
15th Wilson, Charles	Dem	Tex.	8	7
16th Boggs, Corinne C. (Lindy)	Dem	La.	8	6
17th Dicks, Norman D.	Dem	Wash.	6	6
18th McHugh, Matthew F.	Dem	N.Y.	7	6
19th Lehman, William	Dem	Fla.	8	5
20th Sabo, Martin Olav	DFL	Minn.	5	5
21st Dixon, Julian C.	Dem	Cal.	5	5
22nd Fazio, Victor H.	Dem	Cal.	5	5
23rd Hefner, W. G. (Bill)	Dem	N.C.	7	5
24th AuCoin, Les	Dem	Ore.	7	4
25th Akaka, Daniel K.	Dem	Hai.	6	4
26th Watkins, Wesley W.	Dem	Okla.	6	4
27th Gray, William H. III	Dem	Penn.	5	4
28th Dwyer, Bernard J.	Dem	N.J.	4	4
29th Boner, William H.	Dem	Tenn.	5	3
30th Hoyer, Steny H.	Dem	Md.	4	3
31st Carr, M. Robert	Dem	Mich.	6	3
32nd Mrazek, Robert J.	Dem	N.Y.	3	3
33rd Durbin, Richard J.	Dem	Ill.	3	2
34th Coleman, Ronald D.	Dem	Tex.	3	2
35th Mollohan, Alan B.	Dem	W.Va.	3	2

Minority

Rank Name	Party	State	Terms in: House	Terms in: Comm.
RM Conte, Silvio O.	Rep	Mass.	15	15
2nd McDade, Joseph M.	Rep	Penn.	13	12
3rd Myers, John T.	Rep	Ind.	11	9
4th Miller, Clarence E.	Rep	Ohio	11	8
5th Coughlin, R. Lawrence	Rep	Penn.	10	8
6th Young, C. W. Bill	Rep	Fla.	9	8
7th Kemp, Jack F.	Rep	N.Y.	9	7
8th Regula, Ralph S.	Rep	Ohio	8	7
9th Smith, Virginia D.	Rep	Neb.	7	6
10th Pursell, Carl D.	Rep	Mich.	6	5
11th Edwards, M.H. (Mickey)	Rep	Okla.	6	4
12th Livingston, Robert L.	Rep	La.	6	4
13th Green, S. William	Rep	N.Y.	6	4
14th Lewis, Jerry	Rep	Cal.	5	4
15th Porter, John Edward	Rep	Ill.	5	4
16th Rogers, Harold	Rep	Ky.	4	3
17th Skeen, Joe	Rep	N.M.	4	2
18th Wolf, Frank R.	Rep	Va.	4	2
19th Lowery, William	Rep	Cal.	4	2
20th Weber, Vin	Rep	Minn.	4	1
21st DeLay, Thomas D.	Rep	Tex.	2	1
22nd Kolbe, Jim	Rep	Ariz.	2	1

*2: Member's 2nd period of service on the committee.

Changes:

Majority:

Boner, William H.	Dem	Tenn.	Oct. 5,1987	Resigned House; elected Mayor of Nashville.
Thomas, Robert Lindsay	Dem	Ga.	Oct. 21,1987	Replaced Boner.

Departures from the House:

	Majority		Minority	
Defeated for Reelection	Chappell, William V. Jr.	Fla. Dem	None	
Retired	Boland, Edward P.	Mass. Dem	None	
Lost Nomination for President	None		Kemp, Jack F.	N.Y. Rep

APPROPRIATIONS / 101st Congress

Service Dates of Committee Chair: Jan. 3,1989-Jan. 3,1991
Service Dates of Majority Members: Jan. 3,1989-Jan. 3,1991
Service Dates of Minority Members: Jan. 20,1989-Jan. 3,1991

Majority

Rank	Name	Party	State	Terms in: House	Terms in: Comm.
Chr	Whitten, Jamie L.	Dem	Miss.	25	24
2nd	Natcher, William H.	Dem	Ky.	19	18
3rd	Smith, Neal	Dem	Iowa	16	15
4th	Yates, Sidney R.	Dem	Ill.	20	*2 13
5th	Obey, David R.	Dem	Wisc.	11	11
6th	Roybal, Edward R.	Dem	Cal.	14	10
7th	Stokes, Louis	Dem	Ohio	11	10
8th	Bevill, Tom	Dem	Ala.	12	10
9th	Alexander, William V. Jr.	Dem	Ark.	11	8
10th	Murtha, John P. Jr.	Dem	Penn.	9	8
11th	Traxler, J. Bob	Dem	Mich.	9	8
12th	Early, Joseph D.	Dem	Mass.	8	8
13th	Wilson, Charles	Dem	Tex.	9	8
14th	Boggs, Corinne C. (Lindy)	Dem	La.	9	7
15th	Dicks, Norman D.	Dem	Wash.	7	7
16th	McHugh, Matthew F.	Dem	N.Y.	8	7
17th	Lehman, William	Dem	Fla.	9	6
18th	Sabo, Martin Olav	Dem	Minn.	6	6
19th	Dixon, Julian C.	Dem	Cal.	6	6
20th	Fazio, Victor H.	Dem	Cal.	6	6
21st	Hefner, W. G. (Bill)	Dem	N.C.	8	6
22nd	AuCoin, Les	Dem	Ore.	8	5
23rd	Akaka, Daniel K.	Dem	Hai.	7	5
24th	Watkins, Wesley W.	Dem	Okla.	7	5
25th	Gray, William H. III	Dem	Penn.	6	5
26th	Dwyer, Bernard J.	Dem	N.J.	5	5
27th	Hoyer, Steny H.	Dem	Md.	5	4
28th	Carr, M. Robert	Dem	Mich.	7	4
29th	Mrazek, Robert J.	Dem	N.Y.	4	4
30th	Durbin, Richard J.	Dem	Ill.	4	3
31st	Coleman, Ronald D.	Dem	Tex.	4	3
32nd	Mollohan, Alan B.	Dem	W.Va.	4	3
33rd	Thomas, Robert Lindsay	Dem	Ga.	4	2
34th	Atkins, Chester G.	Dem	Mass.	3	1
35th	Chapman, Jim	Dem	Tex.	3	1

Minority

Rank	Name	Party	State	Terms in: House	Terms in: Comm.
RM	Conte, Silvio O.	Rep	Mass.	16	16
2nd	McDade, Joseph M.	Rep	Penn.	14	13
3rd	Myers, John T.	Rep	Ind.	12	10
4th	Miller, Clarence E.	Rep	Ohio	12	9
5th	Coughlin, R. Lawrence	Rep	Penn.	11	9
6th	Young, C. W. Bill	Rep	Fla.	10	9
7th	Regula, Ralph S.	Rep	Ohio	9	8
8th	Smith, Virginia D.	Rep	Neb.	8	7
9th	Pursell, Carl D.	Rep	Mich.	7	6
10th	Edwards, M.H. (Mickey)	Rep	Okla.	7	5
11th	Livingston, Robert L.	Rep	La.	7	5
12th	Green, S. William	Rep	N.Y.	7	5
13th	Lewis, Jerry	Rep	Cal.	6	5
14th	Porter, John Edward	Rep	Ill.	6	5
15th	Rogers, Harold	Rep	Ky.	5	4
16th	Skeen, Joe	Rep	N.M.	5	3
17th	Wolf, Frank R.	Rep	Va.	5	3
18th	Lowery, William	Rep	Cal.	5	3
19th	Weber, Vin	Rep	Minn.	5	2
20th	DeLay, Thomas D.	Rep	Tex.	3	2
21st	Kolbe, Jim	Rep	Ariz.	3	2
22nd	Gallo, Dean A.	Rep	N.J.	3	1

*2: Member's 2nd period of service on the committee.

Changes:

Majority:

Akaka, Daniel K.	Dem	Hai.	May 16,1990	Resigned; appointed to U.S. Senate.
Kaptur, Marcy	Dem	Ohio	May 24,1990	Replaced Akaka.

Departures from the House:

	Majority			Minority		
Lost Nomination for Governor	Watkins, Wesley W.	Okla.	Dem	None		
Retired	Boggs, Corinne C. (Lindy)	La.	Dem	Smith, Virginia D.	Neb.	Rep

APPROPRIATIONS / 102nd Congress

Service Dates of Committee Chair: Jan. 3,1991-Jan. 3,1993
Service Dates of Majority Members: Jan. 3,1991-Jan. 3,1993
Service Dates of Minority Members: Jan. 3,1991-Jan. 3,1993

Majority

Rank	Name	Party	State	Terms in: House	Terms in: Comm.
Chr	Whitten, Jamie L.	Dem	Miss.	26	25
2nd	Natcher, William H.	Dem	Ky.	20	19
3rd	Smith, Neal	Dem	Iowa	17	16
4th	Yates, Sidney R.	Dem	Ill.	21	*2 14
5th	Obey, David R.	Dem	Wisc.	12	12
6th	Roybal, Edward R.	Dem	Cal.	15	11
7th	Stokes, Louis	Dem	Ohio	12	11
8th	Bevill, Tom	Dem	Ala.	13	11
9th	Alexander, William V. Jr.	Dem	Ark.	12	9
10th	Murtha, John P. Jr.	Dem	Penn.	10	9
11th	Traxler, J. Bob	Dem	Mich.	10	9
12th	Early, Joseph D.	Dem	Mass.	9	9
13th	Wilson, Charles	Dem	Tex.	10	9
14th	Dicks, Norman D.	Dem	Wash.	8	8
15th	McHugh, Matthew F.	Dem	N.Y.	9	8
16th	Lehman, William	Dem	Fla.	10	7
17th	Sabo, Martin Olav	Dem	Minn.	7	7
18th	Dixon, Julian C.	Dem	Cal.	7	7
19th	Fazio, Victor H.	Dem	Cal.	7	7
20th	Hefner, W. G. (Bill)	Dem	N.C.	9	7
21st	AuCoin, Les	Dem	Ore.	9	6
22nd	Gray, William H. III	Dem	Penn.	7	6
23rd	Dwyer, Bernard J.	Dem	N.J.	6	6
24th	Hoyer, Steny H.	Dem	Md.	6	6
25th	Carr, M. Robert	Dem	Mich.	8	5
26th	Mrazek, Robert J.	Dem	N.Y.	5	5
27th	Durbin, Richard J.	Dem	Ill.	5	4
28th	Coleman, Ronald D.	Dem	Tex.	5	4
29th	Mollohan, Alan B.	Dem	W.Va.	5	4
30th	Thomas, Robert Lindsay	Dem	Ga.	5	3
31st	Atkins, Chester G.	Dem	Mass.	4	2
32nd	Chapman, Jim	Dem	Tex.	4	2
33rd	Kaptur, Marcy	Dem	Ohio	5	2
34th	Smith, Lawrence J.	Dem	Fla.	3	1
35th	Skaggs, David E.	Dem	Colo.	3	1
36th	Price, David E.	Dem	N.C.	3	1
37th	Pelosi, Nancy	Dem	Cal.	3	1

Minority

Rank	Name	Party	State	Terms in: House	Terms in: Comm.
RM1	Conte, Silvio O.	Rep	Mass.	17	17
RM2 2nd	McDade, Joseph M.	Rep	Penn.	15	14
3rd	Myers, John T.	Rep	Ind.	13	11
4th	Miller, Clarence E.	Rep	Ohio	13	10
5th	Coughlin, R. Lawrence	Rep	Penn.	12	10
6th	Young, C. W. Bill	Rep	Fla.	11	10
7th	Regula, Ralph S.	Rep	Ohio	10	9
8th	Pursell, Carl D.	Rep	Mich.	8	7
9th	Edwards, M. H. (Mickey)	Rep	Okla.	8	6
10th	Livingston, Robert L.	Rep	La.	8	6
11th	Green, S. William	Rep	N.Y.	8	6
12th	Lewis, Jerry	Rep	Cal.	7	6
13th	Porter, John Edward	Rep	Ill.	7	6
14th	Rogers, Harold	Rep	Ky.	6	5
15th	Skeen, Joe	Rep	N.M.	6	4
16th	Wolf, Frank R.	Rep	Va.	6	4
17th	Lowery, William	Rep	Cal.	6	4
18th	Weber, Vin	Rep	Minn.	6	3
19th	DeLay, Thomas D.	Rep	Tex.	4	3
20th	Kolbe, Jim	Rep	Ariz.	4	3
21st	Gallo, Dean A.	Rep	N.J.	4	2
22nd	Vucanovich, Barbara F.	Rep	Nev.	5	1

*2: Member's 2nd period of service on the committee.

Note: Due to ill health, Chair Jaime L. Whitten (Dem-Miss.) turned over many of his duties as Chair to William H. Natcher (Dem-Ky.) in a letter dated June 9,1992. Whitten retained the title of Chair throughout the remainder of the 102nd Congress.

Changes:

Ranking Member:

RM1	Conte, Silvio O.	Rep	Mass.	Feb. 8,1991	Died in office.
RM2	McDade, Joseph M.	Rep	Penn.	Feb. 8,1991	Succeeded Conte as Ranking Minority Member.

Majority:

Gray, William H. III	Dem	Penn.	Sep. 11,1991	Resigns to become President of United Negro College Fund.
Visclosky, Peter J.	Dem	Ind.	Oct. 9,1991	Replaced Gray.

Minority:

Conte, Silvio O.	Rep	Mass.	Feb. 8,1991	Died in office.
Lightfoot, Jim Ross	Rep	Iowa	Feb. 28,1991	Replaced Conte.

ARMED SERVICES

Jurisdiction, 1947

Established by the Legislative Reorganization Act of 1946:

[Section 121.(1)(c)]

Committee on Armed Services.

1. Common defense generally.
2. The War Department and the Military Establishment generally.
3. The Navy Department and the Naval Establishment generally.
4. Soldiers' and sailors' homes.
5. Pay, promotion, retirement, and other benefits and privileges of members of the armed forces.
6. Selective service.
7. Size and composition of the Arm# and Navy.
8. Forts, arsenals, military reservations, and navy yards.
9. Ammunition depots.
10. Conservation, development, and use of naval petroleum and oil shale reserves.
11. Strategic and critical materials necessary for the common defense.
12. Scientific research and development in support of the armed services.

Jurisdiction, 1992

Jurisdiction contained in Rules of the House of Representatives, (as revised to July 1, 1992):

[Rule X. 1. (c)]

Committee on Armed Services.

(1) Common defense generally.
(2) The Department of Defense generally, including the Departments of the Army, Navy and Air Force generally.
(3) Ammunition depots; forts; arsenals; Army, Navy, and Air Force reservations and establishments.
(4) Conservation, development, and use of naval petroleum and oil shale reserves.
(5) Pay, promotion, retirement, and other benefits and privileges of members of the armed forces.
(6) Scientific research and development in support of the armed services.
(7) Selective service.
(8) Size and composition of the Army, Navy, and Air Force.
(9) Soldiers' and sailors' homes.
(10) Strategic and critical materials necessary for the common defense.
(11) Military applications of nuclear energy.

In addition to its legislative jurisdiction under the preceding provisions of this paragraph (and its general oversight function under clause 2(b)(1)), the committee shall have the special oversight function provided for in clause 3(a) with respect to international arms control and disarmament, and military dependents education.

[Rule X. 3.(a)]

The Committee on Armed Services shall have the function of reviewing and studying, on a continuing basis, all laws, programs, and Government activities dealing with or involving international arms control and disarmament and the education of military dependents in schools.

ARMED SERVICES / 80th Congress

Service Dates of Committee Chair: Jan. 14,1947-Jan. 3,1949
Service Dates of Majority Members: Jan. 14,1947-Jan. 3,1949
Service Dates of Minority Members: Jan. 16,1947-Jan. 3,1949

Majority

Rank	Name	Party	State	Terms in: House	Terms in: Comm.
Chr	Andrews, Walter G.	Rep	N.Y.	9	8
2nd	Short, Dewey	Rep	Mo.	8	7
3rd	Arends, Leslie C.	Rep	Ill.	7	7
4th	Cole, W. Sterling	Rep	N.Y.	7	6
5th	Clason, Charles R.	Rep	Mass.	6	6
6th	Thomas, J. Parnell	Rep	N.J.	6	6
7th	Bates, George J.	Rep	Mass.	6	6
8th	Shafer, Paul W.	Rep	Mich.	6	5
9th	Hess, William E.	Rep	Ohio	9	*2 5
10th	Elston, Charles H.	Rep	Ohio	5	5
11th	Anderson, John Z.	Rep	Cal.	5	5
12th	Blackney, William W.	Rep	Mich.	6	4
13th	Smith, Margaret Chase	Rep	Me.	5	3
14th	Johnson, J. Leroy	Rep	Cal.	3	3
15th	Towe, Harry L.	Rep	N.J.	3	2
16th	Bishop, Cecil W. (Runt)	Rep	Ill.	4	*1 2
17th	Gavin, Leon H.	Rep	Penn.	3	1
18th	Norblad, A. Walter Jr.	Rep	Ore.	2	1
19th	Van Zandt, James E.	Rep	Penn.	4	1
Del.	Farrington, Joseph R.	Rep.	Hai.	3	3

Minority

Rank	Name	Party	State	Terms in: House	Terms in: Comm.
RM	Vinson, Carl	Dem	Ga.	18	17
2nd	Drewry, Patrick Henry	Dem	Va.	15	14
3rd	Thomason, R. Ewing	Dem	Tex.	9	9
4th	Brooks, Overton	Dem	La.	6	6
5th	Johnson, Lyndon B.	Dem	Tex.	6	6
6th	Kilday, Paul J.	Dem	Tex.	5	5
7th	Durham, Carl T.	Dem	N.C.	5	4
8th	Sasscer, Lansdale G.	Dem	Md.	5	4
9th	Heffernan, James J.	Dem	N.Y.	4	4
10th	Rivers, L. Mendel	Dem	S.C.	4	4
11th	Sikes, Robert L. F.	Dem	Fla.	4	*2 2
12th	Philbin, Philip J.	Dem	Mass.	3	3
13th	Hebert, F. Edward	Dem	La.	4	3
14th	Winstead, W. Arthur	Dem	Miss.	3	3
Del.	Bartlett, E. L. (Bob)	Dem	Alas.	2	2
RsC.	Fernos-Isern, Antonio	PpD	P.R.	2	1

*1: Member's 1st period of service on the committee;
*2: Member's 2nd period of service on the committee.

Note: Territorial Delegates Joseph Farrington (Rep-Hai.) and E.L. (Bob) Bartlett (Dem-Alas.) and Antonio Fernos-Isern (Popular Democrat-P.R.), the Resident Commissioner for Puerto-Rico were not allowed to accrue seniority nor were they included in the committee's party ratio.

Changes:

Minority:

Thomason, R. Ewing	Dem	Tex.	July 26,1947	Left committee; resigned House for federal judgeship on July 31,1947.
Havenner, Franck R.	Dem	Cal.	July 26,1947	Replaced Thomason.
Drewry, Patrick Henry	Dem	Va.	Dec. 21,1947	Died in office.
Price, C. Melvin	Dem	Ill.	Jan. 20,1948	Replaced Drewry.

Departures from the House:	Majority			Minority		
Elected to U.S. Senate	Smith, Margaret Chase	Me.	Rep	Johnson, Lyndon B.	Tex.	Dem
Defeated for Reelection	Clason, Charles R.	Mass.	Rep	None		
	Hess, William E.	Ohio	Rep			
Retired	Andrews, Walter G.	N.Y.	Rep	None		
Departures from Committee:						
Moved to Appropriations	None			Sikes, Robert L. F.	Fla.	Dem
No new assignment	Bishop, Cecil W. (Runt)	Ill.	Rep	None		

ARMED SERVICES / 81st Congress

Service Dates of Committee Chair: Jan. 18,1949-Jan. 3,1951
Service Dates of Majority Members: Jan. 18,1949-Jan. 3,1951
Service Dates of Minority Members: Jan. 18,1949-Jan. 3,1951

Majority

Rank Name	Party	State	Terms in: House	Terms in: Comm.
Chr Vinson, Carl	Dem	Ga.	19	18
2nd Brooks, Overton	Dem	La.	7	7
3rd Kilday, Paul J.	Dem	Tex.	6	6
4th Durham, Carl T.	Dem	N.C.	6	5
5th Sasscer, Lansdale G.	Dem	Md.	6	5
6th Heffernan, James J.	Dem	N.Y.	5	5
7th Rivers, L. Mendel	Dem	S.C.	5	5
8th Philbin, Philip J.	Dem	Mass.	4	4
9th Hebert, F. Edward	Dem	La.	5	4
10th Winstead, W. Arthur	Dem	Miss.	4	4
11th Havenner, Franck R.	Dem	Cal.	5	*3 2
12th Price, C. Melvin	Dem	Ill.	3	*2 2
13th Fisher, O. Clark	Dem	Tex.	4	1
14th Hardy, Porter Jr.	Dem	Va.	2	1
15th Green, William J. Jr.	Dem	Penn.	2	1
16th Doyle, Clyde G.	Dem	Cal.	2	1
17th deGraffenreid, Edward	Dem	Ala.	1	1
18th Walsh, John R.	Dem	Ind.	1	1
19th Clemente, L. Gary	Dem	N.Y.	1	1
Del. Bartlett, E. L. (Bob)	Dem	Alas.	3	3
RsC. Fernos-Isern, Antonio	PpD	P.R.	3	2

Minority

Rank Name	Party	State	Terms in: House	Terms in: Comm.
RM Short, Dewey	Rep	Mo.	9	8
2nd Arends, Leslie C.	Rep	Ill.	8	8
3rd Cole, W. Sterling	Rep	N.Y.	8	7
4th Thomas, J. Parnell	Rep	N.J.	7	7
5th Bates, George J.	Rep	Mass.	7	7
6th Shafer, Paul W.	Rep	Mich.	7	6
7th Elston, Charles H.	Rep	Ohio	6	6
8th Anderson, John Z.	Rep	Cal.	6	6
9th Blackney, William W.	Rep	Mich.	7	5
10th Johnson, J. Leroy	Rep	Cal.	4	4
11th Towe, Harry L.	Rep	N.J.	4	3
12th Gavin, Leon H.	Rep	Penn.	4	2
13th Norblad, A. Walter Jr.	Rep	Ore.	3	2
14th Van Zandt, James E.	Rep	Penn.	5	2
Del. Farrington, Joseph R.	Rep.	Hai.	4	4

*2: Member's 2nd period of service on the committee;
*3: Member's 3rd period of service on the committee.

Note: Territorial Delegates Joseph Farrington (Rep-Hai.) and E.L. (Bob) Bartlett (Dem-Alas.) and Antonio Fernos-Isern (Popular Democrat-P.R.), the Resident Commissioner for Puerto-Rico were not allowed to accrue seniority nor were they included in the committee's party ratio.

Changes:
Minority:

Bates, George J.	Rep	Mass.	Nov. 1,1949	Died in office.
Thomas, J. Parnell	Rep	N.J.	Jan. 2,1950	Resigned and retired.
Patterson, James T.	Rep	Conn.	Jan. 9,1950	Replaced Bates.
Meyer, Herbert A.	Rep	Kans.	Mar. 1,1950	Replaced Thomas.
Meyer, Herbert A.	Rep	Kans.	Oct. 2,1950	Died in office.

Departures from the House:

	Majority		Minority
Defeated for Reelection	Walsh, John R.	Ind. Dem	None

ARMED SERVICES / 82nd Congress

Service Dates of Committee Chair: Jan. 3,1951-Jan. 3,1953
Service Dates of Majority Members: Jan. 3,1951-Jan. 3,1953
Service Dates of Minority Members: Jan. 4,1951-Jan. 3,1953

Majority

Rank	Name	Party	State	Terms in: House		Terms in: Comm.
Chr	Vinson, Carl	Dem	Ga.	20		19
2nd	Brooks, Overton	Dem	La.	8		8
3rd	Kilday, Paul J.	Dem	Tex.	7		7
4th	Durham, Carl T.	Dem	N.C.	7		6
5th	Sasscer, Lansdale G.	Dem	Md.	7		6
6th	Heffernan, James J.	Dem	N.Y.	6		6
7th	Rivers, L. Mendel	Dem	S.C.	6		6
8th	Philbin, Philip J.	Dem	Mass.	5		5
9th	Hebert, F. Edward	Dem	La.	6		5
10th	Winstead, W. Arthur	Dem	Miss.	5		5
11th	Havenner, Franck R.	Dem	Cal.	6	*3	3
12th	Price, C. Melvin	Dem	Ill.	4	*2	3
13th	Fisher, O. Clark	Dem	Tex.	5		2
14th	Hardy, Porter Jr.	Dem	Va.	3		2
15th	Green, William J. Jr.	Dem	Penn.	3		2
16th	Doyle, Clyde G.	Dem	Cal.	3		2
17th	deGraffenreid, Edward	Dem	Ala.	2		2
18th	Clemente, L. Gary	Dem	N.Y.	2		2
19th	Wickersham, Victor E.	Dem	Okla.	5	*1	1
Del.	Bartlett, E. L. (Bob)	Dem	Alas.	4		4
RsC.	Fernos-Isern, Antonio	PpD	P.R.	4		3

Minority

Rank	Name	Party	State	Terms in: House		Terms in: Comm.
RM	Short, Dewey	Rep	Mo.	10		9
2nd	Arends, Leslie C.	Rep	Ill.	9		9
3rd	Cole, W. Sterling	Rep	N.Y.	9		8
4th	Shafer, Paul W.	Rep	Mich.	8		7
5th	Elston, Charles H.	Rep	Ohio	7		7
6th	Anderson, John Z.	Rep	Cal.	7		7
7th	Blackney, William W.	Rep	Mich.	8		6
8th	Johnson, J. Leroy	Rep	Cal.	5		5
9th	Towe, Harry L.	Rep	N.J.	5		4
10th	Gavin, Leon H.	Rep	Penn.	5		3
11th	Norblad, A. Walter Jr.	Rep	Ore.	4		3
12th	Van Zandt, James E.	Rep	Penn.	6		3
13th	Patterson, James T.	Rep	Conn.	3		2
14th	Cunningham, Paul	Rep	Iowa	6		1
15th	Bates, William H.	Rep	Mass.	2		1
16th	Hess, William E.	Rep	Ohio	10	*3	1
Del.	Farrington, Joseph R.	Rep.	Hai.	5		5

*1: Member's 1st period of service on the committee; *2: Member's 2nd period of service on the committee;
*3: Member's 3rd period of service on the committee.

Note: Territorial Delegates Joseph Farrington (Rep-Hai.) and E.L. (Bob) Bartlett (Dem-Alas.) and Antonio Fernos-Isern (Popular Democrat-P.R.), the Resident Commissioner for Puerto-Rico were not allowed to accrue seniority nor were they included in the committee's party ratio.

Vacancy Filled:
Majority: 19th seat by Wickersham on Jan. 12,1951.
Minority: 14th through 16th seats on Jan. 15,1951.

Changes:
Minority:

Name	Party	State	Date	Change
Towe, Harry L.	Rep	N.J.	Sep. 7,1951	Resigned; appointed state Assistant Attorney General.
Nelson, Charles P.	Rep	Me.	Oct. 17,1951	Replaced Towe.
Anderson, John Z.	Rep	Cal.	July 3,1952	Left committee; no new assignment.
Devereux, James P. S.	Rep	Md.	July 3,1952	Replaced Anderson.

Departures from the House:

	Majority			Minority		
Defeated for Reelection	Clemente, L. Gary	N.Y.	Dem	None		
	Havenner, Franck R.	Cal.	Dem			
Defeated for Renomination	deGraffenreid, Edward	Ala.	Dem	None		
Lost Nomination to U.S. Senate	Sasscer, Lansdale G.	Md.	Dem	None		
Retired	Heffernan, James J.	N.Y.	Dem	Blackney, William W.	Mich.	Rep
				Elston, Charles H.	Ohio	Rep

ARMED SERVICES / 83rd Congress

Service Dates of Committee Chair: Jan. 19,1953-Jan. 3,1955
Service Dates of Majority Members: Jan. 19,1953-Jan. 3,1955
Service Dates of Minority Members: Jan. 19,1953-Jan. 3,1955

Majority

Rank	Name	Party	State	Terms in: House	Terms in: Comm.
Chr	Short, Dewey	Rep	Mo.	11	10
2nd	Arends, Leslie C.	Rep	Ill.	10	10
3rd	Cole, W. Sterling	Rep	N.Y.	10	9
4th	Shafer, Paul W.	Rep	Mich.	9	8
5th	Johnson, J. Leroy	Rep	Cal.	6	6
6th	Gavin, Leon H.	Rep	Penn.	6	4
7th	Norblad, A. Walter Jr.	Rep	Ore.	5	4
8th	Van Zandt, James E.	Rep	Penn.	7	4
9th	Patterson, James T.	Rep	Conn.	4	3
10th	Cunningham, Paul	Rep	Iowa	7	2
11th	Bates, William H.	Rep	Mass.	3	2
12th	Hess, William E.	Rep	Ohio	11	*3 2
13th	Nelson, Charles P.	Rep	Me.	3	2
14th	Devereux, James P. S.	Rep	Md.	2	2
15th	Bishop, Cecil W. (Runt)	Rep	Ill.	7	*2 1
16th	O'Konski, Alvin E.	Rep	Wisc.	6	1
17th	Smith, Wint	Rep	Kans.	4	1
18th	Bray, William G.	Rep	Ind.	2	1
19th	Wilson, Robert C.	Rep	Cal.	1	1
Del.	Farrington, Joseph R.	Rep.	Hai.	6	6

Minority

Rank	Name	Party	State	Terms in: House	Terms in: Comm.
RM	Vinson, Carl	Dem	Ga.	21	20
2nd	Brooks, Overton	Dem	La.	9	9
3rd	Kilday, Paul J.	Dem	Tex.	8	8
4th	Durham, Carl T.	Dem	N.C.	8	7
5th	Rivers, L. Mendel	Dem	S.C.	7	7
6th	Philbin, Philip J.	Dem	Mass.	6	6
7th	Hebert, F. Edward	Dem	La.	7	6
8th	Winstead, W. Arthur	Dem	Miss.	6	6
9th	Price, C. Melvin	Dem	Ill.	5	*2 4
10th	Fisher, O. Clark	Dem	Tex.	6	3
11th	Hardy, Porter Jr.	Dem	Va.	4	3
12th	Green, William J. Jr.	Dem	Penn.	4	3
13th	Doyle, Clyde G.	Dem	Cal.	4	3
14th	Wickersham, Victor E.	Dem	Okla.	6	*1 2
15th	Miller, George P.	Dem	Cal.	5	1
16th	Patten, Harold A.	Dem	Ariz.	3	1
17th	Bennett, Charles E.	Dem	Fla.	3	1
Del.	Bartlett, E. L. (Bob)	Dem	Alas.	5	5
RsC.	Fernos-Isern, Antonio	PpD	P.R.	5	4

*1: Member's 1st period of service on the committee; *2: Member's 2nd period of service on the committee;
*3: Member's 3rd period of service on the committee.

Notes: Territorial Delegates Joseph Farrington (Rep-Hai.) and E.L. (Bob) Bartlett (Dem-Alas.) and Antonio Fernos-Isern (Popular Democrat-P.R.), the Resident Commissioner for Puerto-Rico were not allowed to accrue seniority nor were they included in the committee's party ratio. Farrington was appointed on Jan. 22,1953 and Bartlett and Fernos-Isern were appointed on Jan. 26,1953.

Changes:

Majority:

Name	Party	State	Date	Change
Farrington, Joseph R.	Rep.	Hai.	June 19,1954	Died in office.
Farrington, Mary E. Pruett	Rep.	Hai.	Aug. 5,1954	Replaced Joseph Farrington.
Shafer, Paul W.	Rep	Mich.	Aug. 17,1954	Died in office.

	Majority		Minority	
Departures from the House:				
Defeated for Reelection	Bishop, Cecil W. (Runt)	Ill. Rep	None	
Retired	None		Patten, Harold A.	Ariz. Dem
Departures from Committee:				
No new assignment	Smith, Wint	Kans. Rep	None	

ARMED SERVICES / 84th Congress

Service Dates of Committee Chair: Jan. 13,1955-Jan. 3,1957
Service Dates of Majority Members: Jan. 13,1955-Jan. 3,1957
Service Dates of Minority Members: Jan. 20,1955-Jan. 3,1957

Majority

Rank Name	Party	State	Terms in: House	Terms in: Comm.
Chr Vinson, Carl	Dem	Ga.	22	21
2nd Brooks, Overton	Dem	La.	10	10
3rd Kilday, Paul J.	Dem	Tex.	9	9
4th Durham, Carl T.	Dem	N.C.	9	8
5th Rivers, L. Mendel	Dem	S.C.	8	8
6th Philbin, Philip J.	Dem	Mass.	7	7
7th Hebert, F. Edward	Dem	La.	8	7
8th Winstead, W. Arthur	Dem	Miss.	7	7
9th Price, C. Melvin	Dem	Ill.	6 *2	5
10th Fisher, O. Clark	Dem	Tex.	7	4
11th Hardy, Porter Jr.	Dem	Va.	5	4
12th Green, William J. Jr.	Dem	Penn.	5	4
13th Doyle, Clyde G.	Dem	Cal.	5	4
14th Wickersham, Victor E.	Dem	Okla.	7 *1	3
15th Miller, George P.	Dem	Cal.	6	2
16th Bennett, Charles E.	Dem	Fla.	4	2
17th Holtzman, Lester	Dem	N.Y.	2	1
18th Mollohan, Robert H.	Dem	W.Va.	2 *1	1
19th Lankford, Richard E.	Dem	Md.	1	1
20th Huddleston, George Jr.	Dem	Ala.	1	1
Del. Bartlett, E. L. (Bob)	Dem	Alas.	6	5
RsC. Fernos-Isern, Antonio	PpD	P.R.	6	5

Minority

Rank Name	Party	State	Terms in: House	Terms in: Comm.
RM Short, Dewey	Rep	Mo.	12	11
2nd Arends, Leslie C.	Rep	Ill.	11	11
3rd Cole, W. Sterling	Rep	N.Y.	11	10
4th Johnson, J. Leroy	Rep	Cal.	7	7
5th Gavin, Leon H.	Rep	Penn.	7	5
6th Norblad, A. Walter Jr.	Rep	Ore.	6	5
7th Van Zandt, James E.	Rep	Penn.	8	5
8th Patterson, James T.	Rep	Conn.	5	4
9th Cunningham, Paul	Rep	Iowa	8	3
10th Bates, William H.	Rep	Mass.	4	3
11th Hess, William E.	Rep	Ohio	12 *3	3
12th Nelson, Charles P.	Rep	Me.	4	3
13th Devereux, James P. S.	Rep	Md.	3	3
14th O'Konski, Alvin E.	Rep	Wisc.	7	2
15th Bray, William G.	Rep	Ind.	3	2
16th Wilson, Robert C.	Rep	Cal.	2	2
17th Osmers, Frank C. Jr.	Rep	N.J.	5	1
Del. Farrington, Mary E. Pruett	Rep.	Hai.	2	2

*1: Member's 1st period of service on the committee; *2: Member's 2nd period of service on the committee;
*3: Member's 3rd period of service on the committee.

Notes: Territorial Delegates E.L. Bartlett (Dem-Alas.) and Mary E. Pruett Farrington (Rep-Hai.) and Antonio Fernos-Isern (Popular Democrat-P.R.), the Resident Commissioner for Puerto-Rico were not allowed to accrue seniority nor were they included in the committee's party ratio. Bartlett, Fernos-Isern, and Mrs. Farrington were appointed on Jan. 20,1955.

Departures from the House:	Majority		Minority	
Defeated for Reelection	None		Johnson, J. Leroy	Cal. Rep
			Short, Dewey	Mo. Rep
			Farrington, Mary E. Pruett	Hai. Rep
Defeated for Renomination	Wickersham, Victor E.	Okla. Dem	None	
Lost Election for Governor	Mollohan, Robert H.	W.Va. Dem	None	
Retired	None		Nelson, Charles P.	Me. Rep

ARMED SERVICES / 85th Congress

Service Dates of Committee Chair: Jan. 3,1957-Jan. 3,1959
Service Dates of Majority Members: Jan. 3,1957-Jan. 3,1959
Service Dates of Minority Members: Jan. 7,1957-Jan. 3,1959

Majority

Rank	Name	Party	State	Terms in: House	Terms in: Comm.
Chr	Vinson, Carl	Dem	Ga.	23	22
2nd	Brooks, Overton	Dem	La.	11	11
3rd	Kilday, Paul J.	Dem	Tex.	10	10
4th	Durham, Carl T.	Dem	N.C.	10	9
5th	Rivers, L. Mendel	Dem	S.C.	9	9
6th	Philbin, Philip J.	Dem	Mass.	8	8
7th	Hebert, F. Edward	Dem	La.	9	8
8th	Winstead, W. Arthur	Dem	Miss.	8	8
9th	Price, C. Melvin	Dem	Ill.	7 *2	6
10th	Fisher, O. Clark	Dem	Tex.	8	5
11th	Hardy, Porter Jr.	Dem	Va.	6	5
12th	Green, William J. Jr.	Dem	Penn.	6	5
13th	Doyle, Clyde G.	Dem	Cal.	6	5
14th	Miller, George P.	Dem	Cal.	7	3
15th	Bennett, Charles E.	Dem	Fla.	5	3
16th	Holtzman, Lester	Dem	N.Y.	3	2
17th	Lankford, Richard E.	Dem	Md.	2	2
18th	Huddleston, George Jr.	Dem	Ala.	2	2
19th	Byrne, James A.	Dem	Penn.	3	1
20th	Morris, Toby	Dem	Okla.	4	1
Del.	Bartlett, E. L. (Bob)	Dem	Alas.	7	6
RsC.	Fernos-Isern, Antonio	PpD	P.R.	7	6
Del.	Burns, John A.	Dem.	Hai.	1	1

Minority

Rank	Name	Party	State	Terms in: House	Terms in: Comm.
RM	Arends, Leslie C.	Rep	Ill.	12	12
2nd	Cole, W. Sterling	Rep	N.Y.	12	11
3rd	Gavin, Leon H.	Rep	Penn.	8	6
4th	Norblad, A. Walter Jr.	Rep	Ore.	7	6
5th	Van Zandt, James E.	Rep	Penn.	9	6
6th	Patterson, James T.	Rep	Conn.	6	5
7th	Cunningham, Paul	Rep	Iowa	9	4
8th	Bates, William H.	Rep	Mass.	5	4
9th	Hess, William E.	Rep	Ohio	13 *3	4
10th	Devereux, James P. S.	Rep	Md.	4	4
11th	O'Konski, Alvin E.	Rep	Wisc.	8	3
12th	Bray, William G.	Rep	Ind.	4	3
13th	Wilson, Robert C.	Rep	Cal.	3	3
14th	Osmers, Frank C. Jr.	Rep	N.J.	6	2
15th	St. George, Katharine	Rep	N.Y.	6	1
16th	Reece, B. Carroll	Rep	Tenn.	16 *2	1
17th	Gubser, Charles S.	Rep	Cal.	3	1

*2: Member's 2nd period of service on the committee;
*3: Member's 3rd period of service on the committee.

Notes: Territorial Delegates E.L. (Bob) Bartlett (Dem-Alas.) and John A. Burns (Dem-Hai.) and Antonio Fernos-Isern (Popular Democrat-P.R.), the Resident Commissioner for Puerto Rico were not allowed to accrue seniority nor were they included in the committee's party ratio. Bartlett, Fernos-Isern and Burns were appointed on Jan 10,1957.

Vacancies Filled:
Majority: 19th and 20th seats by Byrne and Morris respectively on Jan. 10,1957.
Minority: 15th through the 17th seats on Jan. 16,1957.

Changes:

Majority:

Name	Party	State	Date	Change
Holtzman, Lester	Dem	N.Y.	Jan. 10,1957	Moved to Judiciary.
Kitchin, A. Paul	Dem	N.C.	Jan. 10,1957	Replaced Holtzman.

Minority:

Name	Party	State	Date	Change
Cole, W. Sterling	Rep	N.Y.	Dec. 1,1957	Resigned; appointed Director General of the International Atomic Energy Agency.
Becker, Frank J.	Rep	N.Y.	Feb. 3,1958	Replaced Cole.

Departures from the House:

	Majority		Minority	
Elected to U.S. Senate	Bartlett, E. L. (Bob)	Alas. Dem	None	
Defeated for Reelection	None		Cunningham, Paul	Iowa Rep
			Patterson, James T.	Conn. Rep
			Devereux, James P. S.	Md. Rep
Lost Election for Governor	None			

Departures from Committee:

	Majority		Minority	
Moved to Science & Astronautics	Brooks, Overton	La. Dem	None	
	Miller, George P.	Cal. Dem		
Moved to Ways & Means	Green, William J. Jr.	Penn. Dem	None	
Moved to Rules	None		Reece, B. Carroll	Tenn. Rep

ARMED SERVICES / 86th Congress

Service Dates of Committee Chair: Jan. 19,1959-Jan. 3,1961
Service Dates of Majority Members: Jan. 19,1959-Jan. 3,1961
Service Dates of Minority Members: Jan. 19,1959-Jan. 3,1961

Majority

Rank	Name	Party	State	Terms in: House	Comm.
Chr	Vinson, Carl	Dem	Ga.	24	23
2nd	Kilday, Paul J.	Dem	Tex.	11	11
3rd	Durham, Carl T.	Dem	N.C.	11	10
4th	Rivers, L. Mendel	Dem	S.C.	10	10
5th	Philbin, Philip J.	Dem	Mass.	9	9
6th	Hebert, F. Edward	Dem	La.	10	9
7th	Winstead, W. Arthur	Dem	Miss.	9	9
8th	Price, C. Melvin	Dem	Ill.	8 *2	7
9th	Fisher, O. Clark	Dem	Tex.	9	6
10th	Hardy, Porter Jr.	Dem	Va.	7	6
11th	Doyle, Clyde G.	Dem	Cal.	7	6
12th	Bennett, Charles E.	Dem	Fla.	6	4
13th	Lankford, Richard E.	Dem	Md.	3	3
14th	Huddleston, George Jr.	Dem	Ala.	3	3
15th	Byrne, James A.	Dem	Penn.	4	2
16th	Morris, Toby	Dem	Okla.	5	2
17th	Kitchin, A. Paul	Dem	N.C.	2	2
18th	Anderson, LeRoy H.	Dem	Mont.	2	1
19th	Brewster, Daniel B.	Dem	Md.	1	1
20th	Kowalski, Frank	Dem	Conn.	1	1
21st	Wampler, Fred	Dem	Ind.	1	1
22nd	Stratton, Samuel S.	Dem	N.Y.	1	1
23rd	Cohelan, Jeffrey	Dem	Cal.	1	1
RsC.	Fernos-Isern, Antonio	PpD	P.R.	8	7
Del.	Burns, John A.	Dem	Hai.	2	2

Minority

Rank	Name	Party	State	Terms in: House	Comm.
RM	Arends, Leslie C.	Rep	Ill.	13	13
2nd	Gavin, Leon H.	Rep	Penn.	9	7
3rd	Norblad, A. Walter Jr.	Rep	Ore.	8	7
4th	Van Zandt, James E.	Rep	Penn.	10	7
5th	Bates, William H.	Rep	Mass.	6	5
6th	Hess, William E.	Rep	Ohio	14 *3	5
7th	O'Konski, Alvin E.	Rep	Wisc.	9	4
8th	Bray, William G.	Rep	Ind.	5	4
9th	Wilson, Robert C.	Rep	Cal.	4	4
10th	Osmers, Frank C. Jr.	Rep	N.J.	7	3
11th	St. George, Katharine	Rep	N.Y.	7	2
12th	Gubser, Charles S.	Rep	Cal.	4	2
13th	Becker, Frank J.	Rep	N.Y.	4	2
14th	Chamberlain, Charles E.	Rep	Mich.	2	1

*2: Member's 2nd period of service on the committee;
*3: Member's 3rd period of service on the committee.

Notes: Antonio Fernos-Isern (Popular Democrat-P.R.), the Resident Commissioner for Puerto Rico and Territorial Delegate John A. Burns (Dem-Hai.) were not allowed to accrue seniority nor were they included in the committee's party ratio.

Changes:

Majority:

Burns, John A.	Dem	Hai.	Aug. 21,1953	Resigned; lost election for Governor.

	Majority			Minority		
Departures from the House:						
Defeated for Reelection	Wampler, Fred	Ind.	Dem	None		
Defeated for Renomination	Morris, Toby	Okla.	Dem	None		
Lost Nomination to U.S. Senate	Anderson, LeRoy H.	Mont.	Dem	None		
Retired	Durham, Carl T.	N.C.	Dem	Hess, William E.	Ohio	Rep
Departures from Committee:						
Moved to Rules	None			St. George, Katharine	N.Y.	Rep

ARMED SERVICES / 87th Congress

Service Dates of Committee Chair: Feb. 6,1961-Jan. 3,1963
Service Dates of Majority Members: Feb. 6,1961-Jan. 3,1963
Service Dates of Minority Members: Feb. 13,1961-Jan. 3,1963

Majority

Rank Name	Party	State	Terms in: House	Terms in: Comm.
Chr Vinson, Carl	Dem	Ga.	25	24
2nd Kilday, Paul J.	Dem	Tex.	12	12
3rd Rivers, L. Mendel	Dem	S.C.	11	11
4th Philbin, Philip J.	Dem	Mass.	10	10
5th Hebert, F. Edward	Dem	La.	11	10
6th Winstead, W. Arthur	Dem	Miss.	10	10
7th Price, C. Melvin	Dem	Ill.	9	*2 8
8th Fisher, O. Clark	Dem	Tex.	10	7
9th Hardy, Porter Jr.	Dem	Va.	8	7
10th Doyle, Clyde G.	Dem	Cal.	8	7
11th Bennett, Charles E.	Dem	Fla.	7	5
12th Lankford, Richard E.	Dem	Md.	4	4
13th Huddleston, George Jr.	Dem	Ala.	4	4
14th Byrne, James A.	Dem	Penn.	5	3
15th Kitchin, A. Paul	Dem	N.C.	3	3
16th Brewster, Daniel B.	Dem	Md.	2	2
17th Kowalski, Frank	Dem	Conn.	2	2
18th Stratton, Samuel S.	Dem	N.Y.	2	2
19th Cohelan, Jeffrey	Dem	Cal.	2	2
20th Wickersham, Victor E.	Dem	Okla.	8	*2 1
21st Pike, Otis G.	Dem	N.Y.	1	1
RsC. Fernos-Isern, Antonio	PpD	P.R.	9	8

Minority

Rank Name	Party	State	Terms in: House	Terms in: Comm.
RM Arends, Leslie C.	Rep	Ill.	14	14
2nd Gavin, Leon H.	Rep	Penn.	10	8
3rd Norblad, A. Walter Jr.	Rep	Ore.	9	8
4th Van Zandt, James E.	Rep	Penn.	11	8
5th Bates, William H.	Rep	Mass.	7	6
6th O'Konski, Alvin E.	Rep	Wisc.	10	5
7th Bray, William G.	Rep	Ind.	6	5
8th Wilson, Robert C.	Rep	Cal.	5	5
9th Osmers, Frank C. Jr.	Rep	N.J.	8	4
10th Gubser, Charles S.	Rep	Cal.	5	3
11th Becker, Frank J.	Rep	N.Y.	5	3
12th Chamberlain, Charles E.	Rep	Mich.	3	2
13th Pirnie, Alexander	Rep	N.Y.	2	1
14th Hall, Durward G.	Rep	Mo.	1	1
15th Clancy, Donald D.	Rep	Ohio	1	1
16th Stafford, Robert T.	Rep	Vt.	1	1

*2: Member's 2nd period of service on the committee.

Note: Antonio Fernos-Isern (Popular Democrat-P.R.), the Resident Commissioner for Puerto Rico, was not allowed to accrue seniority nor was he included in the committee's party ratio.

Changes:

Majority:

Kilday, Paul J.	Dem	Tex.	Sep. 24,1961	Resigned; appointed federal judge.
Rutherford, J. T.	Dem	Tex.	Sep. 25,1961	Replaced Kilday.

Departures from the House:

	Majority			Minority	
Elected to U.S. Senate	Brewster, Daniel B.	Md.	Dem	None	
Defeated for Reelection	Kitchin, A. Paul	N.C.	Dem	None	
	Rutherford, J. T.	Tex.	Dem		
Lost Nomination to U.S. Senate	Kowalski, Frank	Conn.	Dem	Van Zandt, James E.	Penn. Rep

ARMED SERVICES / 88th Congress

Service Dates of Committee Chair: Jan. 17,1963-Jan. 3,1965
Service Dates of Majority Members: Jan. 17,1963-Jan. 3,1965
Service Dates of Minority Members: Jan. 24,1963-Jan. 3,1965

Majority

Rank	Name	Party	State	Terms in: House	Terms in: Comm.
Chr	Vinson, Carl	Dem	Ga.	26	25
2nd	Rivers, L. Mendel	Dem	S.C.	12	12
3rd	Philbin, Philip J.	Dem	Mass.	11	11
4th	Hebert, F. Edward	Dem	La.	12	11
5th	Winstead, W. Arthur	Dem	Miss.	11	11
6th	Price, C. Melvin	Dem	Ill.	10	*2 9
7th	Fisher, O. Clark	Dem	Tex.	11	8
8th	Hardy, Porter Jr.	Dem	Va.	9	8
9th	Doyle, Clyde G.	Dem	Cal.	9	8
10th	Bennett, Charles E.	Dem	Fla.	8	6
11th	Lankford, Richard E.	Dem	Md.	5	5
12th	Huddleston, George Jr.	Dem	Ala.	5	5
13th	Byrne, James A.	Dem	Penn.	6	4
14th	Stratton, Samuel S.	Dem	N.Y.	3	3
15th	Cohelan, Jeffrey	Dem	Cal.	3	3
16th	Wickersham, Victor E.	Dem	Okla.	9	*2 2
17th	Pike, Otis G.	Dem	N.Y.	2	2
18th	Kilgore, Joe M.	Dem	Tex.	5	1
19th	Ichord, Richard H.	Dem	Mo.	2	1
20th	Nedzi, Lucien N.	Dem	Mich.	2	1
21st	Long, Clarence D.	Dem	Md.	1	1
RsC.	Fernos-Isern, Antonio	PpD	P.R.	10	9

Minority

Rank	Name	Party	State	Terms in: House	Terms in: Comm.
RM	Arends, Leslie C.	Rep	Ill.	15	15
2nd	Gavin, Leon H.	Rep	Penn.	11	9
3rd	Norblad, A. Walter Jr.	Rep	Ore.	10	9
4th	Bates, William H.	Rep	Mass.	8	7
5th	O'Konski, Alvin E.	Rep	Wisc.	11	6
6th	Bray, William G.	Rep	Ind.	7	6
7th	Wilson, Robert C.	Rep	Cal.	6	6
8th	Osmers, Frank C. Jr.	Rep	N.J.	9	5
9th	Gubser, Charles S.	Rep	Cal.	6	4
10th	Becker, Frank J.	Rep	N.Y.	6	4
11th	Chamberlain, Charles E.	Rep	Mich.	4	3
12th	Pirnie, Alexander	Rep	N.Y.	3	2
13th	Hall, Durward G.	Rep	Mo.	2	2
14th	Clancy, Donald D.	Rep	Ohio	2	2
15th	Stafford, Robert T.	Rep	Vt.	2	2
16th	Foreman, Edgar F.	Rep	Tex.	1	*1 1

*1: Member's 1st period of service on the committee;
*2: Member's 2nd period of service on the committee.

Note: Antonio Fernos-Isern (Popular Democrat-P.R.), the Resident Commissioner for Puerto Rico, was not allowed to accrue seniority nor was he included in the committee's party ratio. Fernos-Isern was appointed on Jan. 18,1963.

Changes:

Majority:

Doyle, Clyde G.	Dem	Cal.	Mar. 14,1963	Died in office.
Burkhalter, Everett G.	Dem	Cal.	May 2,1963	Replaced Doyle.

Minority:

Gavin, Leon H.	Rep	Penn.	Sep. 15,1963	Died in office.
Schweiker, Richard S.	Rep	Penn.	Sep. 25,1963	Replaced Gavin.
Norblad, A. Walter Jr.	Rep	Ore.	Sep. 20,1964	Died in office.
Stinson, K. William	Rep	Wash.	Oct. 1,1964	Replaced Norblad.

Departures from the House:

	Majority			Minority		
Defeated for Reelection	Huddleston, George Jr.	Ala.	Dem	Foreman, Edgar F.	Tex.	Rep
	Winstead, W. Arthur	Miss.	Dem	Osmers, Frank C. Jr.	N.J.	Rep
				Stinson, K. William	Wash.	Rep
Defeated for Renomination	Wickersham, Victor E.	Okla.	Dem	None		
Retired	Burkhalter, Everett G.	Cal.	Dem	Becker, Frank J.	N.Y.	Rep
	Kilgore, Joe M.	Tex.	Dem			
	Lankford, Richard E.	Md.	Dem			
	Vinson, Carl	Ga.	Dem			
	Fernos-Isern, Antonio	P.R.	PpD			

Departures from Committee:

	Majority			Minority
Moved to Appropriations	Cohelan, Jeffrey	Cal.	Dem	None
	Long, Clarence D.	Md.	Dem	

ARMED SERVICES / 89th Congress

Service Dates of Committee Chair: Jan. 18,1965-Jan. 3,1967
Service Dates of Majority Members: Jan. 18,1965-Jan. 3,1967
Service Dates of Minority Members: Jan. 21,1965-Jan. 3,1967

Majority

Rank	Name	Party	State	Terms in: House	Terms in: Comm.
Chr	Rivers, L. Mendel	Dem	S.C.	13	13
2nd	Philbin, Philip J.	Dem	Mass.	12	12
3rd	Hebert, F. Edward	Dem	La.	13	12
4th	Price, C. Melvin	Dem	Ill.	11	*2 10
5th	Fisher, O. Clark	Dem	Tex.	12	9
6th	Hardy, Porter Jr.	Dem	Va.	10	9
7th	Bennett, Charles E.	Dem	Fla.	9	7
8th	Byrne, James A.	Dem	Penn.	7	5
9th	Stratton, Samuel S.	Dem	N.Y.	4	4
10th	Pike, Otis G.	Dem	N.Y.	3	3
11th	Ichord, Richard H.	Dem	Mo.	3	2
12th	Nedzi, Lucien N.	Dem	Mich.	3	2
13th	Lennon, Alton A.	Dem	N.C.	5	1
14th	Randall, William J.	Dem	Mo.	4	1
15th	Hagan, G. Elliott	Dem	Ga.	3	1
16th	Wilson, Charles H.	Dem	Cal.	2	1
17th	Leggett, Robert L.	Dem	Cal.	2	1
18th	Irwin, Donald J.	Dem	Conn.	2	1
19th	Johnson, Jed Jr.	Dem	Okla.	1	1
20th	Evans, Frank E.	Dem	Colo.	1	1
21st	Love, Rodney M.	Dem	Ohio	1	1
22nd	Hicks, Floyd V.	Dem	Wash.	1	1
23rd	Machen, Hervey G.	Dem	Md.	1	1
24th	Long, Speedy O.	Dem	La.	1	1
25th	Walker, E. S. Johnny	Dem	N.M.	1	1
RsC.	Polanco-Abreu, Santiago	PpD	P.R.	1	1

Minority

Rank	Name	Party	State	Terms in: House	Terms in: Comm.
RM	Bates, William H.	Rep	Mass.	9	8
2nd	Arends, Leslie C.	Rep	Ill.	16	16
3rd	O'Konski, Alvin E.	Rep	Wisc.	12	7
4th	Bray, William G.	Rep	Ind.	8	7
5th	Wilson, Robert C.	Rep	Cal.	7	7
6th	Gubser, Charles S.	Rep	Cal.	7	5
7th	Chamberlain, Charles E.	Rep	Mich.	5	4
8th	Pirnie, Alexander	Rep	N.Y.	4	3
9th	Hall, Durward G.	Rep	Mo.	3	3
10th	Clancy, Donald D.	Rep	Ohio	3	3
11th	Stafford, Robert T.	Rep	Vt.	3	3
12th	Schweiker, Richard S.	Rep	Penn.	3	2

*2: Member's 2nd period of service on the committee.

Notes: Santiago Polanco-Abreu (Popular Democrat-P.R.), the Resident Commissioner for Puerto Rico, was not allowed to accrue seniority nor was he included in the committee's party ratio. A change in the rules of the Republican Conference prevented House Minority Whip Leslie C. Arends (Rep-Ill.) from serving as Ranking Minority Member on this committee.

Departures from the House:

	Majority		Minority
Defeated for Reelection	Johnson, Jed Jr.	Okla. Dem	None
	Love, Rodney M.	Ohio Dem	

ARMED SERVICES / 90th Congress

Service Dates of Committee Chair: Jan. 18,1967-Jan. 3,1969
Service Dates of Majority Members: Jan. 18,1967-Jan. 3,1969
Service Dates of Minority Members: Jan. 26,1967-Jan. 3,1969

Majority

Rank	Name	Party	State	Terms in: House	Terms in: Comm.
Chr	Rivers, L. Mendel	Dem	S.C.	14	14
2nd	Philbin, Philip J.	Dem	Mass.	13	13
3rd	Hebert, F. Edward	Dem	La.	14	13
4th	Price, C. Melvin	Dem	Ill.	12	*2 11
5th	Fisher, O. Clark	Dem	Tex.	13	10
6th	Hardy, Porter Jr.	Dem	Va.	11	10
7th	Bennett, Charles E.	Dem	Fla.	10	8
8th	Byrne, James A.	Dem	Penn.	8	6
9th	Stratton, Samuel S.	Dem	N.Y.	5	5
10th	Pike, Otis G.	Dem	N.Y.	4	4
11th	Ichord, Richard H.	Dem	Mo.	4	3
12th	Nedzi, Lucien N.	Dem	Mich.	4	3
13th	Lennon, Alton A.	Dem	N.C.	6	2
14th	Randall, William J.	Dem	Mo.	5	2
15th	Hagan, G. Elliott	Dem	Ga.	4	2
16th	Wilson, Charles H.	Dem	Cal.	3	2
17th	Leggett, Robert L.	Dem	Cal.	3	2
18th	Irwin, Donald J.	Dem	Conn.	3	2
19th	Evans, Frank E.	Dem	Colo.	2	2
20th	Hicks, Floyd V.	Dem	Wash.	2	2
21st	Machen, Hervey G.	Dem	Md.	2	2
22nd	Long, Speedy O.	Dem	La.	2	2
23rd	Walker, E. S. Johnny	Dem	N.M.	2	2
RsC.	Polanco-Abreu, Santiago	PpD	P.R.	2	2

Minority

Rank	Name	Party	State	Terms in: House	Terms in: Comm.
RM	Bates, William H.	Rep	Mass.	10	9
2nd	Arends, Leslie C.	Rep	Ill.	17	17
3rd	O'Konski, Alvin E.	Rep	Wisc.	13	8
4th	Bray, William G.	Rep	Ind.	9	8
5th	Wilson, Robert C.	Rep	Cal.	8	8
6th	Gubser, Charles S.	Rep	Cal.	8	6
7th	Chamberlain, Charles E.	Rep	Mich.	6	5
8th	Pirnie, Alexander	Rep	N.Y.	5	4
9th	Hall, Durward G.	Rep	Mo.	4	4
10th	Clancy, Donald D.	Rep	Ohio	4	4
11th	Stafford, Robert T.	Rep	Vt.	4	4
12th	Schweiker, Richard S.	Rep	Penn.	4	3
13th	Halleck, Charles A.	Rep	Ind.	17	1
14th	King, Carleton J.	Rep	N.Y.	4	1
15th	Dickinson, William L.	Rep	Ala.	2	1
16th	Whalen, Charles W. Jr.	Rep	Ohio	1	1
17th	Smith, James V.	Rep	Okla.	1	1

*2: Member's 2nd period of service on the committee.

Notes: Santiago Polanco-Abreu (Popular Democrat-P.R.), the Resident Commissioner for Puerto Rico, was not allowed to accrue seniority nor was he included in the committee's party ratio. Polanco-Abreu was included on the committee listing in the Congressional Directory but not in the House Journal or Congressional Record for Jan. 23,1967. However, as a Resident Commissioner, he was elected to a four-year term in 1966 and his appointment date of Jan. 18,1965 may have been holding in this case. Republican Convention rules prevented House Minority Whip Leslie C. Arends (Rep-Ill.) from serving as Ranking Minority Member on this committee.

Departures from the House:	Majority			Minority		
Elected to U.S. Senate	None			Schweiker, Richard S.	Penn.	Rep
Defeated for Reelection	Irwin, Donald J.	Conn.	Dem	Smith, James V.	Okla.	Rep
	Machen, Hervey G.	Md.	Dem			
	Walker, E. S. Johnny	N.M.	Dem			
	Polanco-Abreu, Santiago	P.R.	PpD			
Retired	Hardy, Porter Jr.	Va.	Dem	Halleck, Charles A.	Ind.	Rep

ARMED SERVICES / 91st Congress

Service Dates of Committee Chairs: Ch1 Jan. 3,1969-Dec. 28,1970
Ch2 Dec. 30,1970-Jan. 3,1971
Service Dates of Majority Members: Jan. 3,1969-Jan. 3,1971
Service Dates of Minority Members: Jan. 29,1969-Jan. 3,1971

Majority

Rank	Name	Party	State	Terms in: House	Terms in: Comm.
Ch1	Rivers, L. Mendel	Dem	S.C.	15	15
Ch2 2nd	Philbin, Philip J.	Dem	Mass.	14	14
3rd	Hebert, F. Edward	Dem	La.	15	14
4th	Price, C. Melvin	Dem	Ill.	13 *2	12
5th	Fisher, O. Clark	Dem	Tex.	14	11
6th	Bennett, Charles E.	Dem	Fla.	11	9
7th	Byrne, James A.	Dem	Penn.	9	7
8th	Stratton, Samuel S.	Dem	N.Y.	6	6
9th	Pike, Otis G.	Dem	N.Y.	5	5
10th	Ichord, Richard H.	Dem	Mo.	5	4
11th	Nedzi, Lucien N.	Dem	Mich.	5	4
12th	Lennon, Alton A.	Dem	N.C.	7	3
13th	Randall, William J.	Dem	Mo.	6	3
14th	Hagan, G. Elliott	Dem	Ga.	5	3
15th	Wilson, Charles H.	Dem	Cal.	4	3
16th	Leggett, Robert L.	Dem	Cal.	4	3
17th	Evans, Frank E.	Dem	Colo.	3	3
18th	Hicks, Floyd V.	Dem	Wash.	3	3
19th	Long, Speedy O.	Dem	La.	3	3
20th	White, Richard C.	Dem	Tex.	3	1
21st	Nichols, William F.	Dem	Ala.	2	1
22nd	Brinkley, Jack T.	Dem	Ga.	2	1
23rd	Mollohan, Robert H.	Dem	W.Va.	3 *2	1
RsC.	Cordova-Diaz, Jorge L.	NPr	P.R.	1	1

Minority

Rank	Name	Party	State	Terms in: House	Terms in: Comm.
RM1	Bates, William H.	Rep	Mass.	11	10
RM2 2nd	Arends, Leslie C.	Rep	Ill.	18	18
3rd	O'Konski, Alvin E.	Rep	Wisc.	14	9
4th	Bray, William G.	Rep	Ind.	10	9
5th	Wilson, Robert C.	Rep	Cal.	9	9
6th	Gubser, Charles S.	Rep	Cal.	9	7
7th	Chamberlain, Charles E.	Rep	Mich.	7	6
8th	Pirnie, Alexander	Rep	N.Y.	6	5
9th	Hall, Durward G.	Rep	Mo.	5	5
10th	Clancy, Donald D.	Rep	Ohio	5	5
11th	Stafford, Robert T.	Rep	Vt.	5	5
12th	King, Carleton J.	Rep	N.Y.	5	2
13th	Dickinson, William L.	Rep	Ala.	3	2
14th	Whalen, Charles W. Jr.	Rep	Ohio	2	2
15th	Foreman, Edgar F.	Rep	N.M.	2 *2	1
16th	Hunt, John E.	Rep	N.J.	2	1
17th	Whitehurst, G. William	Rep	Va.	1	1

*2: Member's 2nd period of service on the committee.

Notes: Jorge L. Cordova-Diaz (New Progressive-P.R.), the Resident Commissioner for Puerto Rico, was assigned to the committee by the majority in this Congress. He was not allowed to accrue seniority nor was he included in the committee's party ratio. Cordova-Diaz was appointed on Jan. 29,1969.

Vacancies Filled:
Majority: 20th through the 23rd seats on Jan. 29,1969.

Changes:

	Name	Party	State	Date	Change
Chair:					
Ch1	Rivers, L. Mendel	Dem	S.C.	Dec. 28,1970	Died in office.
Ch2	Philbin, Philip J.	Dem	Mass.	Dec. 30,1970	Succeeded Rivers as Chair for remainder of Congress.
Ranking Member:					
RM1	Bates, William H.	Rep	Mass.	June 22,1969	Died in office.
RM2	Arends, Leslie C.	Rep	Ill.	June 22,1969	Succeeded Bates as Ranking Minority Member.
Majority:					
	Evans, Frank E.	Dem	Colo.	Jan. 29,1969	Moved to Appropriations.
	Daniel, W. C. (Dan)	Dem	Va.	Jan. 29,1969	Replaced Evans.
	Rivers, L. Mendel	Dem	S.C.	Dec. 28,1970	Died in office.
Minority:					
	Chamberlain, Charles E.	Rep	Mich.	Mar. 5,1969	Moved to Ways and Means.
	Corbett, Robert J.	Rep	Penn.	Mar. 20,1969	Replaced Chamberlain.
	Bates, William H.	Rep	Mass.	June 22,1969	Died in office.
	Beall, J. Glenn Jr.	Rep	Md.	Oct. 7,1969	Replaced Bates.

Departures from the House:	**Majority**		**Minority**	
Elected to U.S. Senate	None		Beall, J. Glenn Jr.	Md. Rep
Defeated for Reelection	None		Foreman, Edgar F.	N.M. Rep
Defeated for Renomination	Philbin, Philip J.	Mass. Dem	None	
Departures from Committee:				
No new assignment	Cordova-Diaz, Jorge L.	P.R. NPr	Corbett, Robert J.	Penn. Rep

ARMED SERVICES / 92nd Congress

Service Dates of Committee Chair: Feb. 4,1971-Jan. 3,1973
Service Dates of Majority Members: Feb. 4,1971-Jan. 3,1973
Service Dates of Minority Members: Feb. 4,1971-Jan. 3,1973

Majority

Rank	Name	Party	State	Terms in: House	Terms in: Comm.
Chr	Hebert, F. Edward	Dem	La.	16	15
2nd	Price, C. Melvin	Dem	Ill.	14	*2 13
3rd	Fisher, O. Clark	Dem	Tex.	15	12
4th	Bennett, Charles E.	Dem	Fla.	12	10
5th	Byrne, James A.	Dem	Penn.	10	8
6th	Stratton, Samuel S.	Dem	N.Y.	7	7
7th	Pike, Otis G.	Dem	N.Y.	6	6
8th	Ichord, Richard H.	Dem	Mo.	6	5
9th	Nedzi, Lucien N.	Dem	Mich.	6	5
10th	Lennon, Alton A.	Dem	N.C.	8	4
11th	Randall, William J.	Dem	Mo.	7	4
12th	Hagan, G. Elliott	Dem	Ga.	6	4
13th	Wilson, Charles H.	Dem	Cal.	5	4
14th	Leggett, Robert L.	Dem	Cal.	5	4
15th	Hicks, Floyd V.	Dem	Wash.	4	4
16th	Long, Speedy O.	Dem	La.	4	4
17th	White, Richard C.	Dem	Tex.	4	2
18th	Nichols, William F.	Dem	Ala.	3	2
19th	Brinkley, Jack T.	Dem	Ga.	3	2
20th	Mollohan, Robert H.	Dem	W.Va.	4	*2 2
21st	Daniel, W. C. (Dan)	Dem	Va.	2	2
22nd	Montgomery, G.V. (Sonny)	Dem	Miss.	3	1
23rd	Harrington, Michael J.	Dem	Mass.	2	1
24th	Runnels, Harold L.	Dem	N.M.	1	1
25th	Aspin, Les	Dem	Wisc.	1	1

Minority

Rank	Name	Party	State	Terms in: House	Terms in: Comm.
RM	Arends, Leslie C.	Rep	Ill.	19	19
2nd	O'Konski, Alvin E.	Rep	Wisc.	15	10
3rd	Bray, William G.	Rep	Ind.	11	10
4th	Wilson, Robert C.	Rep	Cal.	10	10
5th	Gubser, Charles S.	Rep	Cal.	10	8
6th	Pirnie, Alexander	Rep	N.Y.	7	6
7th	Hall, Durward G.	Rep	Mo.	6	6
8th	Clancy, Donald D.	Rep	Ohio	6	6
9th	Stafford, Robert T.	Rep	Vt.	6	6
10th	King, Carleton J.	Rep	N.Y.	6	3
11th	Dickinson, William L.	Rep	Ala.	4	3
12th	Whalen, Charles W. Jr.	Rep	Ohio	3	3
13th	Hunt, John E.	Rep	N.J.	3	2
14th	Whitehurst, G. William	Rep	Va.	2	2
15th	Young, C. W. Bill	Rep	Fla.	1	1
16th	Spence, Floyd D.	Rep	S.C.	1	1

*2: Member's 2nd period of service on the committee.

Changes:

Minority:

Name	Party	State	Date	Change
Stafford, Robert T.	Rep	Vt.	Sep. 16,1971	Resigned; appointed to U.S. Senate.
Whalen, Charles W. Jr.	Rep	Ohio	Oct. 27,1971	Moved to Foreign Affairs.
Powell, Walter E.	Rep	Ohio	Feb. 7,1972	Replaced Stafford.
Conover, William S. II	Rep	Penn.	May 31,1972	Replaced Whalen.

	Majority			Minority		
Departures from the House:						
Elected State District Attorney	Long, Speedy O.	La.	Dem	None		
Defeated for Reelection	None			O'Konski, Alvin E.	Wisc.	Rep
				Cordova-Diaz, Jorge L.	P.R.	NPr
Defeated for Renomination	Byrne, James A.	Penn.	Dem	Conover, William S. II	Penn.	Rep
	Hagan, G. Elliott	Ga.	Dem			
Retired	Lennon, Alton A.	N.C.	Dem	Hall, Durward G.	Mo.	Rep
				Pirnie, Alexander	N.Y.	Rep
Departures from Committee:						
Moved to Foreign Affairs	Harrington, Michael J.	Mass.	Dem	None		
Moved to Ways & Means	None			Clancy, Donald D.	Ohio	Rep

ARMED SERVICES / 93rd Congress

Service Dates of Committee Chair: Jan. 24,1973-Jan. 3,1975
Service Dates of Majority Members: Jan. 24,1973-Jan. 3,1975
Service Dates of Minority Members: Jan. 24,1973-Jan. 3,1975

Majority

Rank	Name	Party	State	Terms in: House	Terms in: Comm.
Chr	Hebert, F. Edward	Dem	La.	17	16
2nd	Price, C. Melvin	Dem	Ill.	15	*2 14
3rd	Fisher, O. Clark	Dem	Tex.	16	13
4th	Bennett, Charles E.	Dem	Fla.	13	11
5th	Stratton, Samuel S.	Dem	N.Y.	8	8
6th	Pike, Otis G.	Dem	N.Y.	7	7
7th	Ichord, Richard H.	Dem	Mo.	7	6
8th	Nedzi, Lucien N.	Dem	Mich.	7	6
9th	Randall, William J.	Dem	Mo.	8	5
10th	Wilson, Charles H.	Dem	Cal.	6	5
11th	Leggett, Robert L.	Dem	Cal.	6	5
12th	Hicks, Floyd V.	Dem	Wash.	5	5
13th	White, Richard C.	Dem	Tex.	5	3
14th	Nichols, William F.	Dem	Ala.	4	3
15th	Brinkley, Jack T.	Dem	Ga.	4	3
16th	Mollohan, Robert H.	Dem	W.Va.	5	*2 3
17th	Daniel, W. C. (Dan)	Dem	Va.	3	3
18th	Montgomery, G.V. (Sonny)	Dem	Miss.	4	2
19th	Runnels, Harold L.	Dem	N.M.	2	2
20th	Aspin, Les	Dem	Wisc.	2	2
21st	Dellums, Ronald V.	Dem	Cal.	2	1
22nd	Davis, Mendel J.	Dem	S.C.	2	1
23rd	Jones, James R.	Dem	Okla.	1	1
24th	Schroeder, Patricia S.	Dem	Colo.	1	1

Minority

Rank	Name	Party	State	Terms in: House	Terms in: Comm.
RM	Bray, William G.	Rep	Ind.	12	11
2nd	Arends, Leslie C.	Rep	Ill.	20	20
3rd	Wilson, Robert C.	Rep	Cal.	11	11
4th	Gubser, Charles S.	Rep	Cal.	11	9
5th	King, Carleton J.	Rep	N.Y.	7	4
6th	Dickinson, William L.	Rep	Ala.	5	4
7th	Hunt, John E.	Rep	N.J.	4	3
8th	Whitehurst, G. William	Rep	Va.	3	3
9th	Young, C. W. Bill	Rep	Fla.	2	2
10th	Spence, Floyd D.	Rep	S.C.	2	2
11th	Powell, Walter E.	Rep	Ohio	2	2
12th	Price, Robert D.	Rep	Tex.	4	1
13th	Treen, David C.	Rep	La.	1	1
14th	Armstrong, William L.	Rep	Colo.	1	1
15th	O'Brien, George M.	Rep	Ill.	1	1
16th	Beard, Robin L. Jr.	Rep	Tenn.	1	1
17th	Mitchell, Donald J.	Rep	N.Y.	1	1
18th	Holt, Marjorie S.	Rep	Md.	1	1
19th	Daniel, Robert W. Jr.	Rep	Va.	1	1

*2: Member's 2nd period of service on the committee.

Notes: Democratic Party gains in the 1974 special elections in Pennsylvania, Michigan, and Ohio, led to the passage of House Resolution 979 agreed to on Mar. 13,1979, which changed the size and party ratio on this committee to 25 Democrats and 19 Republicans. Ranking on this committee for the following member was affected by other chamber service: Leslie C. Arends (Rep-Ill.), House Minority Whip, stepped aside as Ranking Minority Member during his last term in Congress.

Addition:

Majority:	25th	Murtha, John P. Jr.	Dem	Penn.	Mar. 13,1974

Changes:

Majority:				
Pike, Otis G.	Dem	N.Y.	Dec. 18,1974	Moved to Ways and Means.
Fisher, O. Clark	Dem	Tex.	Dec. 31,1974	Resigned and retired.
Minority:				
Young, C. W. Bill	Rep	Fla.	Dec. 20,1973	Moved to Appropriations.
Hillis, Elwood H.	Rep	Ind.	Feb. 13,1974	Replaced Young.
Arends, Leslie C.	Rep	Ill.	Dec. 31,1974	Resigned and retired.
Gubser, Charles S.	Rep	Cal.	Dec. 31,1974	Resigned and retired.
King, Carleton J.	Rep	N.Y.	Dec. 31,1974	Resigned; defeated for reelection.

Departures from the House:

	Majority		Minority	
Defeated for Reelection	None		Bray, William G.	Ind. Rep
			Hunt, John E.	N.J. Rep
			Price, Robert D.	Tex. Rep
			Powell, Walter E.	Ohio Rep
Retired	None			

Departures from Committee:

Moved to Ways & Means	Jones, James R.	Okla. Dem	None	
Moved to Appropriations	Murtha, John P. Jr.	Penn. Dem	Armstrong, William L.	Colo. Rep

ARMED SERVICES / 94th Congress

Service Dates of Committee Chair: Jan. 23,1975-Jan. 3,1977
Service Dates of Majority Members: Jan. 23,1975-Jan. 3,1977
Service Dates of Minority Members: Jan. 28,1975-Jan. 3,1977

Majority

Rank	Name	Party	State	Terms in: House	Terms in: Comm.
Chr	Price, C. Melvin	Dem	Ill.	16 *2	15
2nd	Hebert, F. Edward	Dem	La.	18	17
3rd	Bennett, Charles E.	Dem	Fla.	14	12
4th	Stratton, Samuel S.	Dem	N.Y.	9	9
5th	Ichord, Richard H.	Dem	Mo.	8	7
6th	Nedzi, Lucien N.	Dem	Mich.	8	7
7th	Randall, William J.	Dem	Mo.	9	6
8th	Wilson, Charles H.	Dem	Cal.	7	6
9th	Leggett, Robert L.	Dem	Cal.	7	6
10th	Hicks, Floyd V.	Dem	Wash.	6	6
11th	White, Richard C.	Dem	Tex.	6	4
12th	Nichols, William F.	Dem	Ala.	5	4
13th	Brinkley, Jack T.	Dem	Ga.	5	4
14th	Mollohan, Robert H.	Dem	W.Va.	6 *2	4
15th	Daniel, W. C. (Dan)	Dem	Va.	4	4
16th	Montgomery, G.V. (Sonny)	Dem	Miss.	5	3
17th	Runnels, Harold L.	Dem	N.M.	3	3
18th	Aspin, Les	Dem	Wisc.	3	3
19th	Dellums, Ronald V.	Dem	Cal.	3	2
20th	Davis, Mendel J.	Dem	S.C.	3	2
21st	Schroeder, Patricia S.	Dem	Colo.	2	2
22nd	Kazen, Abraham Jr.	Dem	Tex.	5	1
23rd	Won Pat, Antonio Borja	Dem	Guam	2	1
24th	Carr, M. Robert	Dem	Mich.	1	1
25th	Lloyd, James F.	Dem	Cal.	1	1
26th	McDonald, Lawrence P.	Dem	Ga.	1	1
27th	Downey, Thomas J.	Dem	N.Y.	1	1

Minority

Rank	Name	Party	State	Terms in: House	Terms in: Comm.
RM	Wilson, Robert C.	Rep	Cal.	12	12
2nd	Dickinson, William L.	Rep	Ala.	6	5
3rd	Whitehurst, G. William	Rep	Va.	4	4
4th	Spence, Floyd D.	Rep	S.C.	3	3
5th	Treen, David C.	Rep	La.	2	2
6th	O'Brien, George M.	Rep	Ill.	2	2
7th	Beard, Robin L. Jr.	Rep	Tenn.	2	2
8th	Mitchell, Donald J.	Rep	N.Y.	2	2
9th	Holt, Marjorie S.	Rep	Md.	2	2
10th	Daniel, Robert W. Jr.	Rep	Va.	2	2
11th	Hillis, Elwood H.	Rep	Ind.	3	2
12th	Hinshaw, Andrew J.	Rep	Cal.	2	1
13th	Schulze, Richard T.	Rep	Penn.	1	1

*2: Member's 2nd period of service on the committee.

Notes: Edward F. Hebert (Dem-La.) was unseated as Chair of this committee by the Democratic Caucus on Jan. 16,1975 by a vote of 152-133. Territorial Delegate Antonio Borja Won Pat (Dem-Guam) was allowed to accrue committee seniority, but was not included in the committee's party ratio of 26 Democrats and 13 Republicans.

	Majority		Minority	
Departures from the House:				
Defeated for Renomination	None		Hinshaw, Andrew J.	Cal. Rep
Retired	Hebert, F. Edward	La. Dem	None	
	Hicks, Floyd V.	Wash. Dem		
	Randall, William J.	Mo. Dem		
Departures from Committee:				
Moved to Appropriations	None		O'Brien, George M.	Ill. Rep
Moved to Ways & Means	None		Schulze, Richard T.	Penn. Rep

ARMED SERVICES / 95th Congress

Service Dates of Committee Chair: Jan. 19,1977-Jan. 3,1979
Service Dates of Majority Members: Jan. 19,1977-Jan. 3,1979
Service Dates of Minority Members: Jan. 19,1977-Jan. 3,1979

Majority

Rank	Name	Party	State	Terms in: House		Terms in: Comm.
Chr	Price, C. Melvin	Dem	Ill.	17	*2	16
2nd	Bennett, Charles E.	Dem	Fla.	15		13
3rd	Stratton, Samuel S.	Dem	N.Y.	10		10
4th	Ichord, Richard H.	Dem	Mo.	9		8
5th	Nedzi, Lucien N.	Dem	Mich.	9		8
6th	Wilson, Charles H.	Dem	Cal.	8		7
7th	Leggett, Robert L.	Dem	Cal.	8		7
8th	White, Richard C.	Dem	Tex.	7		5
9th	Nichols, William F.	Dem	Ala.	6		5
10th	Brinkley, Jack T.	Dem	Ga.	6		5
11th	Mollohan, Robert H.	Dem	W.Va.	7	*2	5
12th	Daniel, W. C. (Dan)	Dem	Va.	5		5
13th	Montgomery, G.V. (Sonny)	Dem	Miss.	6		4
14th	Runnels, Harold L.	Dem	N.M.	4		4
15th	Aspin, Les	Dem	Wisc.	4		4
16th	Dellums, Ronald V.	Dem	Cal.	4		3
17th	Davis, Mendel J.	Dem	S.C.	4		3
18th	Schroeder, Patricia S.	Dem	Colo.	3		3
19th	Kazen, Abraham Jr.	Dem	Tex.	6		2
20th	Won Pat, Antonio Borja	Dem	Guam	3		2
21st	Carr, M. Robert	Dem	Mich.	2		2
22nd	Lloyd, James F.	Dem	Cal.	2		2
23rd	McDonald, Lawrence P.	Dem	Ga.	2		2
24th	Downey, Thomas J.	Dem	N.Y.	2		2
25th	Byron, Goodloe E.	Dem	Md.	4		1
26th	Whitley, Charles O. Sr.	Dem	N.C.	1		1
27th	Tonry, Richard A.	Dem	La.	1		1
28th	Breckinridge, John B.	Dem	Ky.	3	*T	1

Minority

Rank	Name	Party	State	Terms in: House	Terms in: Comm.
RM	Wilson, Robert C.	Rep	Cal.	13	13
2nd	Dickinson, William L.	Rep	Ala.	7	6
3rd	Whitehurst, G. William	Rep	Va.	5	5
4th	Spence, Floyd D.	Rep	S.C.	4	4
5th	Treen, David C.	Rep	La.	3	3
6th	Beard, Robin L. Jr.	Rep	Tenn.	3	3
7th	Mitchell, Donald J.	Rep	N.Y.	3	3
8th	Holt, Marjorie S.	Rep	Md.	3	3
9th	Daniel, Robert W. Jr.	Rep	Va.	3	3
10th	Hillis, Elwood H.	Rep	Ind.	4	3
11th	Emery, David F.	Rep	Me.	2	1
12th	Trible, Paul S. Jr.	Rep	Va.	1	1
13th	Badham, Robert E.	Rep	Cal.	1	1

*2: Member's 2nd period of service on the committee;
*T: Temporary member of the committee.

Note: Territorial Delegate Antonio Borja Won Pat (Dem-Guam) was allowed to accrue committee seniority, but was not included in the committee's party ratio of 27 Democrats and 13 Republicans.

Vacancy Filled:
Majority: 28th seat by Breckinridge on Feb. 22,1978.

Changes:
Majority:

Tonry, Richard A.	Dem	La.	May 4,1977	Resigned and retired.
Stump, Robert	Dem	Ariz.	Feb. 22,1978	Replaced Tonry.
Byron, Goodloe E.	Dem	Md.	Oct. 11,1978	Died in office.

	Majority			Minority
Departures from the House:				
Defeated for Renomination	Breckinridge, John B.	Ky.	Dem	None
Retired	Leggett, Robert L.	Cal.	Dem	None
Departures from Committee:				
Moved to Ways & Means	Downey, Thomas J.	N.Y.	Dem	None
No new assignment	Whitley, Charles O. Sr.	N.C.	Dem	None

ARMED SERVICES / 96th Congress

Service Dates of Committee Chair: Jan. 24,1979-Jan. 3,1981
Service Dates of Majority Members: Jan. 24,1979-Jan. 3,1981
Service Dates of Minority Members: Jan. 24,1979-Jan. 3,1981

Majority

Rank Name	Party	State	Terms in: House	Terms in: Comm.
Chr Price, C. Melvin	Dem	Ill.	18	*2 17
2nd Bennett, Charles E.	Dem	Fla.	16	14
3rd Stratton, Samuel S.	Dem	N.Y.	11	11
4th Ichord, Richard H.	Dem	Mo.	10	9
5th Nedzi, Lucien N.	Dem	Mich.	10	9
6th Wilson, Charles H.	Dem	Cal.	9	8
7th White, Richard C.	Dem	Tex.	8	6
8th Nichols, William	Dem	Ala.	7	6
9th Brinkley, Jack T.	Dem	Ga.	7	6
10th Mollohan, Robert H.	Dem	W.Va.	8	*2 6
11th Daniel, W. C. (Dan)	Dem	Va.	6	6
12th Montgomery, G.V. (Sonny)	Dem	Miss.	7	5
13th Runnels, Harold L.	Dem	N.M.	5	5
14th Aspin, Les	Dem	Wisc.	5	5
15th Dellums, Ronald V.	Dem	Cal.	5	4
16th Davis, Mendel J.	Dem	S.C.	5	4
17th Schroeder, Patricia S.	Dem	Colo.	4	4
18th Kazen, Abraham Jr.	Dem	Tex.	7	3
19th Won Pat, Antonio Borja	Dem	Guam	4	3
20th Carr, M. Robert	Dem	Mich.	3	3
21st Lloyd, James F.	Dem	Cal.	3	3
22nd McDonald, Lawrence P.	Dem	Ga.	3	3
23rd Stump, Robert	Dem	Ariz.	2	2
24th Fazio, Victor H.	Dem	Cal.	1	1
25th Leach, A. Claude Jr.	Dem	La.	1	1
26th Byron, Beverly B.	Dem	Md.	1	1
27th Mavroules, Nicholas	Dem	Mass.	1	1
28th Wyatt, Joseph P. Jr.	Dem	Tex.	1	1
29th Bailey, Donald A.	Dem	Penn.	1	1

Minority

Rank Name	Party	State	Terms in: House	Terms in: Comm.
RM Wilson, Robert C.	Rep	Cal.	14	14
2nd Dickinson, William L.	Rep	Ala.	8	7
3rd Whitehurst, G. William	Rep	Va.	6	6
4th Spence, Floyd D.	Rep	S.C.	5	5
5th Treen, David C.	Rep	La.	4	4
6th Beard, Robin L. Jr.	Rep	Tenn.	4	4
7th Mitchell, Donald J.	Rep	N.Y.	4	4
8th Holt, Marjorie S.	Rep	Md.	4	4
9th Daniel, Robert W. Jr.	Rep	Va.	4	4
10th Hillis, Elwood H.	Rep	Ind.	5	4
11th Emery, David F.	Rep	Me.	3	2
12th Trible, Paul S. Jr.	Rep	Va.	2	2
13th Badham, Robert E.	Rep	Cal.	2	2
14th Dougherty, Charles F.	Rep	Penn.	1	1
15th Courter, James A.	Rep	N.J.	1	1
16th Evans, Melvin H.	Rep	V.I.	1	1

*2: Member's 2nd period of service on the committee.

Note: Territorial Delegates Antonio Borja Won Pat (Dem-Guam) and Melvin H. Evans (Rep-Virgin Islands), were allowed to accrue committee seniority, but were not included in the committee's party ratio of 28 Democrats and 15 Republicans.

Changes:

Majority:

Fazio, Victor H.	Dem	Cal.	Feb. 26,1980	Moved to Appropriations.
Hutto, Earl D.	Dem	Fla.	Mar. 19,1980	Replaced Fazio.
Runnels, Harold L.	Dem	N.M.	Aug. 5,1980	Died in office.
Skelton, Ike	Dem	Mo.	Sep. 16,1980	Replaced Runnels.

Minority:

Treen, David C.	Rep	La.	Mar. 10,1980	Resigned; elected Governor of Louisiana.
Hopkins, Larry J.	Rep	Ky.	Mar. 10,1980	Replaced Treen.

Departures from the House:

	Majority			Minority		
Defeated for Reelection	Carr, M. Robert	Mich.	Dem	Evans, Melvin H.	V.I.	Rep
	Leach, A. Claude Jr.	La.	Dem			
	Lloyd, James F.	Cal.	Dem			
Defeated for Renomination	Wilson, Charles H.	Cal.	Dem	None		
Retired	Davis, Mendel J.	S.C.	Dem	Wilson, Robert C.	Cal.	Rep
	Ichord, Richard H.	Mo.	Dem			
	Nedzi, Lucien N.	Mich.	Dem			
	Wyatt, Joseph P. Jr.	Tex.	Dem			

ARMED SERVICES / 97th Congress

Service Dates of Committee Chair: Jan. 28,1981-Jan. 3,1983
Service Dates of Majority Members: Jan. 28,1981-Jan. 3,1983
Service Dates of Minority Members: Jan. 28,1981-Jan. 3,1983

Majority

Rank	Name	Party	State	Terms in: House		Terms in: Comm.
Chr	Price, C. Melvin	Dem	Ill.	19	*2	18
2nd	Bennett, Charles E.	Dem	Fla.	17		15
3rd	Stratton, Samuel S.	Dem	N.Y.	12		12
4th	White, Richard C.	Dem	Tex.	9		7
5th	Nichols, William	Dem	Ala.	8		7
6th	Brinkley, Jack T.	Dem	Ga.	8		7
7th	Mollohan, Robert H.	Dem	W.Va.	9	*2	7
8th	Daniel, W. C. (Dan)	Dem	Va.	7		7
9th	Montgomery, G.V. (Sonny)	Dem	Miss.	8		6
10th	Aspin, Les	Dem	Wisc.	6		6
11th	Dellums, Ronald V.	Dem	Cal.	6		5
12th	Schroeder, Patricia S.	Dem	Colo.	5		5
13th	Kazen, Abraham Jr.	Dem	Tex.	8		4
14th	Won Pat, Antonio Borja	Dem	Guam	5		4
15th	McDonald, Lawrence P.	Dem	Ga.	4		4
16th	Stump, Robert	Dem	Ariz.	3		3
17th	Byron, Beverly B.	Dem	Md.	2		2
18th	Mavroules, Nicholas	Dem	Mass.	2		2
19th	Bailey, Donald A.	Dem	Penn.	2		2
20th	Hutto, Earl D.	Dem	Fla.	2		2
21st	Skelton, Ike	Dem	Mo.	3		1
22nd	Leath, J. Marvin	Dem	Tex.	2		1
23rd	McCurdy, Dave	Dem	Okla.	1		1
24th	Foglietta, Thomas M.	Dem	Penn.	1		1
25th	Dyson, Royden	Dem	Md.	1		1
26th	Hertel, Dennis M.	Dem	Mich.	1		1

Minority

Rank	Name	Party	State	Terms in: House		Terms in: Comm.
RM	Dickinson, William L.	Rep	Ala.	9		8
2nd	Whitehurst, G. William	Rep	Va.	7		7
3rd	Spence, Floyd D.	Rep	S.C.	6		6
4th	Beard, Robin L. Jr.	Rep	Tenn.	5		5
5th	Mitchell, Donald J.	Rep	N.Y.	5		5
6th	Holt, Marjorie S.	Rep	Md.	5		5
7th	Daniel, Robert W. Jr.	Rep	Va.	5		5
8th	Hillis, Elwood H.	Rep	Ind.	6	*1	5
9th	Emery, David F.	Rep	Me.	4		3
10th	Trible, Paul S. Jr.	Rep	Va.	3		3
11th	Badham, Robert E.	Rep	Cal.	3		3
12th	Dougherty, Charles F.	Rep	Penn.	2		2
13th	Courter, James A.	Rep	N.J.	2		2
14th	Hopkins, Larry J.	Rep	Ky.	2		2
15th	Davis, Robert W.	Rep	Mich.	2		1
16th	Kramer, Kenneth B.	Rep	Colo.	2		1
17th	Hunter, Duncan L.	Rep	Cal.	1		1
18th	Nelligan, James L.	Rep	Penn.	1		1
19th	Hartnett, Thomas F.	Rep	S.C.	1		1

*1: Member's 1st period of service on the committee;
*2: Member's 2nd period of service on the committee.

Notes: Territorial Delegate Antonio Borja Won Pat (Dem-Guam) was allowed to accrue committee seniority, but was not included in the original party ratio of 25 Democrats and 19 Republicans. The committee was expanded and the party ratio changed to 26 Democrats (excluding Won Pat) and 19 Republicans on Sep. 22,1982.

Addition:

Majority: 27th Bouquard, Marilyn Lloyd Dem Tenn. Sep. 22,1982

Changes:

Majority:

Name	Party	State	Date	Change
Bailey, Donald A.	Dem	Penn.	Feb. 25,1981	Moved to Ways and Means.
Smith, Joseph F.	Dem	Penn.	Oct. 7,1981	Replaced Bailey.

Departures from the House:

	Majority		Minority	
Elected to U.S. Senate	None			
Defeated for Reelection	None		Trible, Paul S. Jr.	Va. Rep
			Daniel, Robert W. Jr.	Va. Rep
			Dougherty, Charles F.	Penn. Rep
			Nelligan, James L.	Penn. Rep
Defeated for Renomination	Smith, Joseph F.	Penn. Dem	None	
Lost Election to U.S. Senate	None		Beard, Robin L. Jr.	Tenn. Rep
Retired	Brinkley, Jack T.	Ga. Dem	Emery, David F.	Me. Rep
	Mollohan, Robert H.	W.Va. Dem	Mitchell, Donald J.	N.Y. Rep
	White, Richard C.	Tex. Dem		

ARMED SERVICES / 98th Congress

Service Dates of Committee Chair: Jan. 6,1983-Jan. 3,1985
Service Dates of Majority Members: Jan. 6,1983-Jan. 3,1985
Service Dates of Minority Members: Jan. 6,1983-Jan. 3,1985

Majority

Rank	Name	Party	State	Terms in: House	Terms in: Comm.
Chr	Price, C. Melvin	Dem	Ill.	20 *2	19
2nd	Bennett, Charles E.	Dem	Fla.	18	16
3rd	Stratton, Samuel S.	Dem	N.Y.	13	13
4th	Nichols, William	Dem	Ala.	9	8
5th	Daniel, W. C. (Dan)	Dem	Va.	8	8
6th	Montgomery, G.V. (Sonny)	Dem	Miss.	9	7
7th	Aspin, Les	Dem	Wisc.	7	7
8th	Dellums, Ronald V.	Dem	Cal.	7	6
9th	Schroeder, Patricia S.	Dem	Colo.	6	6
10th	Kazen, Abraham Jr.	Dem	Tex.	9	5
11th	Won Pat, Antonio Borja	Dem	Guam	6	5
12th	McDonald, Lawrence P.	Dem	Ga.	5	5
13th	Byron, Beverly B.	Dem	Md.	3	3
14th	Mavroules, Nicholas	Dem	Mass.	3	3
15th	Hutto, Earl D.	Dem	Fla.	3	3
16th	Skelton, Ike	Dem	Mo.	4	2
17th	Leath, J. Marvin	Dem	Tex.	3	2
18th	McCurdy, Dave	Dem	Okla.	2	2
19th	Foglietta, Thomas M.	Dem	Penn.	2	2
20th	Dyson, Royden	Dem	Md.	2	2
21st	Hertel, Dennis M.	Dem	Mich.	2	2
22nd	Bouquard, Marilyn Lloyd	Dem	Tenn.	5	2
23rd	Sisisky, Norman	Dem	Va.	1	1
24th	Ray, Richard	Dem	Ga.	1	1
25th	Spratt, John M. Jr.	Dem	S.C.	1	1
26th	McCloskey, Francis X.	Dem	Ind.	1	1
27th	Britt, Charles Robin	Dem	N.C.	1	1
28th	Ortiz, Solomon P.	Dem	Tex.	1	1
29th	Coleman, Ronald D.	Dem	Tex.	1	1

Minority

Rank	Name	Party	State	Terms in: House	Terms in: Comm.
RM	Dickinson, William L.	Rep	Ala.	10	9
2nd	Whitehurst, G. William	Rep	Va.	8	8
3rd	Spence, Floyd D.	Rep	S.C.	7	7
4th	Holt, Marjorie S.	Rep	Md.	6	6
5th	Hillis, Elwood H.	Rep	Ind.	7 *1	6
6th	Badham, Robert E.	Rep	Cal.	4	4
7th	Stump, Robert	Rep	Ariz.	4	4
8th	Courter, James A.	Rep	N.J.	3	3
9th	Hopkins, Larry J.	Rep	Ky.	3	3
10th	Davis, Robert W.	Rep	Mich.	3	2
11th	Kramer, Kenneth B.	Rep	Colo.	3	2
12th	Hunter, Duncan L.	Rep	Cal.	2	2
13th	Hartnett, Thomas F.	Rep	S.C.	2	2
14th	Crane, Daniel B.	Rep	Ill.	3	1
15th	Martin, David O'B.	Rep	N.Y.	2	1
16th	Kasich, John R.	Rep	Ohio	1	1

*1: Member's 1st period of service on the committee;
*2: Member's 2nd period of service on the committee.

Notes: Robert Stump of Arizona resigned from the Democratic Party and joined the Republican Party on Jan. 3,1983. Recognizing Stump's previous service on this committee, the Republican Conference assigned him the 7th minority rank. Territorial Delegate Antonio Borja Won Pat (Dem-Guam) was allowed to accrue committee seniority, but was not included in the party ratio of 28 Democrats and 16 Republicans. Marilyn Lloyd Bouquard (Dem-Tenn.) first voted in this Congress under the resumed name Marilyn Lloyd on Apr. 12,1983

Changes:

Majority:

McDonald, Lawrence P.	Dem	Ga.	Sep. 1,1983	Died in office.
Darden, George W. (Buddy)	Dem	Ga.	Nov. 17,1983	Replaced McDonald.

	Majority			Minority		
Departures from the House:						
Defeated for Reelection	Britt, Charles Robin	N.C.	Dem	Crane, Daniel B.	Ill.	Rep
	Won Pat, Antonio Borja	Guam	Dem			
Defeated for Renomination	Kazen, Abraham Jr.	Tex.	Dem	None		
Departures from Committee:						
Moved to Appropriations	Coleman, Ronald D.	Tex.	Dem	None		

ARMED SERVICES / 99th Congress

Service Dates of Committee Chair: Jan. 7,1985-Jan. 3,1987
Service Dates of Majority Members: Jan. 30,1985-Jan. 3,1987
Service Dates of Minority Members: Jan. 30,1985-Jan. 3,1987

Majority

Rank Name	Party	State	Terms in: House	Terms in: Comm.
Chr Aspin, Les	Dem	Wisc.	8	8
2nd Price, C. Melvin	Dem	Ill.	21 *2	20
3rd Bennett, Charles E.	Dem	Fla.	19	17
4th Stratton, Samuel S.	Dem	N.Y.	14	14
5th Nichols, William	Dem	Ala.	10	9
6th Daniel, W. C. (Dan)	Dem	Va.	9	9
7th Montgomery, G.V. (Sonny)	Dem	Miss.	10	8
8th Dellums, Ronald V.	Dem	Cal.	8	7
9th Schroeder, Patricia S.	Dem	Colo.	7	7
10th Byron, Beverly B.	Dem	Md.	4	4
11th Mavroules, Nicholas	Dem	Mass.	4	4
12th Hutto, Earl D.	Dem	Fla.	4	4
13th Skelton, Ike	Dem	Mo.	5	3
14th Leath, J. Marvin	Dem	Tex.	4	3
15th McCurdy, Dave	Dem	Okla.	3	3
16th Foglietta, Thomas M.	Dem	Penn.	3	3
17th Dyson, Royden	Dem	Md.	3	3
18th Hertel, Dennis M.	Dem	Mich.	3	3
19th Lloyd, Marilyn	Dem	Tenn.	6	3
20th Sisisky, Norman	Dem	Va.	2	2
21st Ray, Richard	Dem	Ga.	2	2
22nd Spratt, John M. Jr.	Dem	S.C.	2	2
23rd McCloskey, Francis X.	Dem	Ind.	2	2
24th Ortiz, Solomon P.	Dem	Tex.	2	2
25th Darden, George W. (Buddy)	Dem	Ga.	2	2
26th Robinson, Tommy F.	Dem	Ark.	1	1
27th Bustamante, Albert G.	Dem	Tex.	1	1

Minority

Rank Name	Party	State	Terms in: House	Terms in: Comm.
RM Dickinson, William L.	Rep	Ala.	11	10
2nd Whitehurst, G. William	Rep	Va.	9	9
3rd Spence, Floyd D.	Rep	S.C.	8	8
4th Holt, Marjorie S.	Rep	Md.	7	7
5th Hillis, Elwood H.	Rep	Ind.	8 *1	7
6th Badham, Robert E.	Rep	Cal.	5	5
7th Stump, Robert	Rep	Ariz.	5	5
8th Courter, James A.	Rep	N.J.	4	4
9th Hopkins, Larry J.	Rep	Ky.	4	4
10th Davis, Robert W.	Rep	Mich.	4	3
11th Kramer, Kenneth B.	Rep	Colo.	4	3
12th Hunter, Duncan L.	Rep	Cal.	3	3
13th Hartnett, Thomas F.	Rep	S.C.	3	3
14th Martin, David O'B.	Rep	N.Y.	3	2
15th Kasich, John R.	Rep	Ohio	2	2
16th Carney, William	Rep	N.Y.	4	1
17th Martin, Lynn M.	Rep	Ill.	3	1
18th Bateman, Herbert H.	Rep	Va.	2	1
19th Sweeney, Mac	Rep	Tex.	1	1
20th Blaz, Ben Garrido	Rep	Guam	1	1

*1: Member's 1st period of service on the committee;
*2: Member's 2nd period of service on the committee.

Notes: Territorial Delegate Ben Blaz (Rep-Guam) was allowed to accrue committee seniority but was not included in the original party ratio of 27 Democrats and 19 Republicans. In a secret ballot vote of the Democratic Caucus on Jan. 4,1985, C. Melvin Price (Dem-Ill.) was removed as Chair by a vote of 118 to 121. He was replaced by Les Aspin (Dem-Wisc.), who was chosen over Charles Bennett (Dem-Fla.) by a vote of 125 to 103. The contested election in Indiana between Francis McCloskey (Dem) and Richard McIntire (Rep) was decided on a floor vote of the House on May 1,1985 in favor of McCloskey, 236 to 190. The committee was expanded to 49 members and the party ratio changed to 28 Democrats and 20 Republicans (excluding Blaz) on Oct. 10,1986.

Vacancy Filled:
Majority: 23rd seat was filled by McCloskey on May 8,1985.

Additions:

Majority:	28th	Abercrombie, Neil	Dem	Hai.	Oct. 10,1986	
Minority:	21st	Hillis, Elwood H.	Rep	Ind.	Oct. 10,1986	Ranked 5th on minority.

Changes:
Minority:

Hillis, Elwood H.	Rep	Ind.	Sep. 26,1986	Left committee; no new assignment (re-added on Oct. 10,1986).
Hansen, James V.	Rep	Utah	Sep. 26,1986	Replaced Hillis.

Departures from the House:

	Majority			Minority		
Defeated for Renomination	Abercrombie, Neil	Hai.	Dem	None		
Lost Election to U.S. Senate	None			Kramer, Kenneth B.	Colo.	Rep
Lost Election for Lt. Governor	None			Hartnett, Thomas F.	S.C.	Rep
Retired	None			Carney, William	N.Y.	Rep
				Holt, Marjorie S.	Md.	Rep
				Whitehurst, G. William	Va.	Rep
				Hillis, Elwood H.	Ind.	Rep

ARMED SERVICES / 100th Congress

Service Dates of Committee Chair: Jan. 22,1987-Jan. 3,1989
Service Dates of Majority Members: Jan. 22,1987-Jan. 3,1989
Service Dates of Minority Members: Jan. 21,1987-Jan. 3,1989

Majority

Rank	Name	Party	State	Terms in: House	Terms in: Comm.
Chr	Aspin, Les	Dem	Wisc.	9	9
2nd	Price, C. Melvin	Dem	Ill.	22	*2 21
3rd	Bennett, Charles E.	Dem	Fla.	20	18
4th	Stratton, Samuel S.	Dem	N.Y.	15	15
5th	Nichols, William	Dem	Ala.	11	10
6th	Daniel, W. C. (Dan)	Dem	Va.	10	10
7th	Montgomery, G.V. (Sonny)	Dem	Miss.	11	9
8th	Dellums, Ronald V.	Dem	Cal.	9	8
9th	Schroeder, Patricia S.	Dem	Colo.	8	8
10th	Byron, Beverly B.	Dem	Md.	5	5
11th	Mavroules, Nicholas	Dem	Mass.	5	5
12th	Hutto, Earl D.	Dem	Fla.	5	5
13th	Skelton, Ike	Dem	Mo.	6	4
14th	Leath, J. Marvin	Dem	Tex.	5	4
15th	McCurdy, Dave	Dem	Okla.	4	4
16th	Foglietta, Thomas M.	Dem	Penn.	4	4
17th	Dyson, Royden	Dem	Md.	4	4
18th	Hertel, Dennis M.	Dem	Mich.	4	4
19th	Lloyd, Marilyn	Dem	Tenn.	7	4
20th	Sisisky, Norman	Dem	Va.	3	3
21st	Ray, Richard	Dem	Ga.	3	3
22nd	Spratt, John M. Jr.	Dem	S.C.	3	3
23rd	McCloskey, Francis X.	Dem	Ind.	3	3
24th	Ortiz, Solomon P.	Dem	Tex.	3	3
25th	Darden, George W. (Buddy)	Dem	Ga.	3	3
26th	Robinson, Tommy F.	Dem	Ark.	2	2
27th	Bustamante, Albert G.	Dem	Tex.	2	2
28th	Boxer, Barbara	Dem	Cal.	3	1
29th	Hochbrueckner, George J.	Dem	N.Y.	1	1
30th	Brennan, Joseph E.	Dem	Me.	1	1
31st	Pickett, Owen B.	Dem	Va.	1	1

Minority

Rank	Name	Party	State	Terms in: House	Terms in: Comm.
RM	Dickinson, William L.	Rep	Ala.	12	11
2nd	Spence, Floyd D.	Rep	S.C.	9	9
3rd	Badham, Robert E.	Rep	Cal.	6	6
4th	Stump, Robert	Rep	Ariz.	6	6
5th	Courter, James A.	Rep	N.J.	5	5
6th	Hopkins, Larry J.	Rep	Ky.	5	5
7th	Davis, Robert W.	Rep	Mich.	5	4
8th	Hunter, Duncan L.	Rep	Cal.	4	4
9th	Martin, David O'B.	Rep	N.Y.	4	3
10th	Kasich, John R.	Rep	Ohio	3	3
11th	Martin, Lynn M.	Rep	Ill.	4	2
12th	Bateman, Herbert H.	Rep	Va.	3	2
13th	Sweeney, Mac	Rep	Tex.	2	2
14th	Blaz, Ben Garrido	Rep	Guam	2	2
15th	Ireland, Andrew P.	Rep	Fla.	6	1
16th	Hansen, James V.	Rep	Utah	4	2
17th	Rowland, John G.	Rep	Conn.	2	1
18th	Weldon, Curt	Rep	Penn.	1	1
19th	Kyl, Jon	Rep	Ariz.	1	1
20th	Ravenel, Arthur Jr.	Rep	S.C.	1	1
21st	Davis, Jack	Rep	Ill.	1	1

*2: Member's 2nd period of service on the committee.

Notes: Territorial Delegate Ben Blaz (Rep-Guam) was allowed to accrue committee seniority but was not included in the party ratio of 31 Democrats and 20 Republicans. James V. Hansen (Rep-Utah) was ranked behind Andrew P. Ireland (Rep-Fla.) despite two weeks more committee seniority. In the 99th Congress, the Democratic Caucus elected Les Aspin (Dem-Wisc.) Chair of this committee over more senior members.

Changes:

Majority:

Name	Party	State	Date	Change
Daniel, W. C. (Dan)	Dem	Va.	Jan. 23,1988	Died in office.
Lancaster, H. Martin	Dem	N.C.	Mar. 2,1988	Replaced Daniel.
Price, C. Melvin	Dem	Ill.	Apr. 2,1988	Died in office.
Evans, Lane	Dem	Ill.	May 18,1988	Replaced Price.
Nichols, William	Dem	Ala.	Dec. 13,1988	Died in office.

	Majority			Minority		
Departures from the House:						
Defeated for Reelection	None			Davis, Jack	Ill.	Rep
				Sweeney, Mac	Tex.	Rep
Retired	Stratton, Samuel S.	N.Y.	Dem	Badham, Robert E.	Cal.	Rep
Departures from Committee:						
Ceased active membership while serving on Budget	Boxer, Barbara	Cal.	Dem	None		
Moved to Rules	None			Martin, Lynn M.	Ill.	Rep

ARMED SERVICES / 101st Congress

Service Dates of Committee Chair: Jan. 3,1989-Jan. 3,1991
Service Dates of Majority Members: Jan. 19,1989-Jan. 3,1991
Service Dates of Minority Members: Jan. 20,1989-Jan. 3,1991

Majority

Rank	Name	Party	State	Terms in: House	Terms in: Comm.
Chr	Aspin, Les	Dem	Wisc.	10	10
2nd	Bennett, Charles E.	Dem	Fla.	21	19
3rd	Montgomery, G.V. (Sonny)	Dem	Miss.	12	10
4th	Dellums, Ronald V.	Dem	Cal.	10	9
5th	Schroeder, Patricia S.	Dem	Colo.	9	9
6th	Byron, Beverly B.	Dem	Md.	6	6
7th	Mavroules, Nicholas	Dem	Mass.	6	6
8th	Hutto, Earl D.	Dem	Fla.	6	6
9th	Skelton, Ike	Dem	Mo.	7	5
10th	Leath, J. Marvin	Dem	Tex.	6	5
11th	McCurdy, Dave	Dem	Okla.	5	5
12th	Foglietta, Thomas M.	Dem	Penn.	5	5
13th	Dyson, Royden	Dem	Md.	5	5
14th	Hertel, Dennis M.	Dem	Mich.	5	5
15th	Lloyd, Marilyn	Dem	Tenn.	8	5
16th	Sisisky, Norman	Dem	Va.	4	4
17th	Ray, Richard	Dem	Ga.	4	4
18th	Spratt, John M. Jr.	Dem	S.C.	4	4
19th	McCloskey, Francis X.	Dem	Ind.	4	4
20th	Ortiz, Solomon P.	Dem	Tex.	4	4
21st	Darden, George W. (Buddy)	Dem	Ga.	4	4
22nd	Robinson, Tommy F.	Dem	Ark.	3	3
23rd	Bustamante, Albert G.	Dem	Tex.	3	3
24th	Hochbrueckner, George J.	Dem	N.Y.	2	2
25th	Brennan, Joseph E.	Dem	Me.	2	2
26th	Pickett, Owen B.	Dem	Va.	2	2
27th	Lancaster, H. Martin	Dem	N.C.	2	2
28th	Evans, Lane	Dem	Ill.	4	2
29th	Bilbray, James H.	Dem	Nev.	2	1
30th	Tanner, John S.	Dem	Tenn.	1	1
31st	McNulty, Michael R.	Dem	N.Y.	1	1

Minority

Rank	Name	Party	State	Terms in: House	Terms in: Comm.
RM	Dickinson, William L.	Rep	Ala.	13	12
2nd	Spence, Floyd D.	Rep	S.C.	10	10
3rd	Stump, Robert	Rep	Ariz.	7	7
4th	Courter, James A.	Rep	N.J.	6	6
5th	Hopkins, Larry J.	Rep	Ky.	6	6
6th	Davis, Robert W.	Rep	Mich.	6	5
7th	Hunter, Duncan L.	Rep	Cal.	5	5
8th	Martin, David O'B.	Rep	N.Y.	5	4
9th	Kasich, John R.	Rep	Ohio	4	4
10th	Bateman, Herbert H.	Rep	Va.	4	3
11th	Blaz, Ben Garrido	Rep	Guam	3	3
12th	Ireland, Andrew P.	Rep	Fla.	7	2
13th	Hansen, James V.	Rep	Utah	5	3
14th	Rowland, John G.	Rep	Conn.	3	2
15th	Weldon, Curt	Rep	Penn.	2	2
16th	Kyl, Jon	Rep	Ariz.	2	2
17th	Ravenel, Arthur Jr.	Rep	S.C.	2	2
18th	Dornan, Robert K.	Rep	Cal.	6	1
19th	Hefley, Joel	Rep	Colo.	2	1
20th	McCrery, Jim	Rep	La.	2	1
21st	Machtley, Ronald K.	Rep	R.I.	1	1

Notes: Territorial Delegate Ben Blaz (Rep-Guam) was allowed to accrue committee seniority but was not included in the party ratio of 31 Democrats and 20 Republicans. In the 99th Congress, the Democratic Caucus elected Les Aspin (Dem-Wisc.) Chair of this committee over more senior members. Tommy F. Robinson of Arkansas resigned from the Democratic Party on July 28,1989 and lost his majority assignment. This change and the replacement of Larkin Smith (Rep-Miss.) by Gene Taylor (Dem-Miss.) on Oct. 24,1989, led to a change in size and party ratio on this committee to 32 Democrats and 21 Republicans (excluding Blaz) on November 3,1989.

Additions:

Majority:	32nd Taylor, Gene	Dem	Miss.	Nov. 8,1989
Minority:	22nd Smith, Robert C.	Rep	N.H.	Nov. 3,1989

Changes:

Majority:

Robinson, Tommy F.	Dem	Ark.	July 31,1989	Resigned from the Democratic Party on July 28,1989; lost majority assignments.
Browder, Glen	Dem	Ala.	Nov. 8,1989	Replaced Robinson.

Departures from the House:

	Majority			Minority		
Elected to U.S. Senate	None			Smith, Robert C.	N.H.	Rep
Defeated for Reelection	Dyson, Royden	Md.	Dem	None		
Lost Election For Governor	Brennan, Joseph E.	Me.	Dem	Rowland, John G.	Conn.	Rep
Retired	Leath, J. Marvin	Tex.	Dem	Courter, James A.	N.J.	Rep

ARMED SERVICES / 102nd Congress

Service Dates of Committee Chair: Jan. 24,1991-Jan. 3,1993
Service Dates of Majority Members: Jan. 24,1991-Jan. 3,1993
Service Dates of Minority Members: Jan. 24,1991-Jan. 3,1993

Majority

Rank	Name	Party	State	Terms in: House	Terms in: Comm.
Chr	Aspin, Les	Dem	Wisc.	11	11
2nd	Bennett, Charles E.	Dem	Fla.	22	20
3rd	Montgomery, G.V. (Sonny)	Dem	Miss.	13	11
4th	Dellums, Ronald V.	Dem	Cal.	11	10
5th	Schroeder, Patricia S.	Dem	Colo.	10	10
6th	Byron, Beverly B.	Dem	Md.	7	7
7th	Mavroules, Nicholas	Dem	Mass.	7	7
8th	Hutto, Earl D.	Dem	Fla.	7	7
9th	Skelton, Ike	Dem	Mo.	8	6
10th	McCurdy, Dave	Dem	Okla.	6	6
11th	Foglietta, Thomas M.	Dem	Penn.	6	6
12th	Hertel, Dennis M.	Dem	Mich.	6	6
13th	Lloyd, Marilyn	Dem	Tenn.	9	6
14th	Sisisky, Norman	Dem	Va.	5	5
15th	Ray, Richard	Dem	Ga.	5	5
16th	Spratt, John M. Jr.	Dem	S.C.	5	5
17th	McCloskey, Francis X.	Dem	Ind.	5	5
18th	Ortiz, Solomon P.	Dem	Tex.	5	5
19th	Darden, George W. (Buddy)	Dem	Ga.	5	5
20th	Bustamante, Albert G.	Dem	Tex.	4	4
21st	Boxer, Barbara	Dem	Cal.	5	4
22nd	Hochbrueckner, George J.	Dem	N.Y.	3	3
23rd	Pickett, Owen B.	Dem	Va.	3	3
24th	Lancaster, H. Martin	Dem	N.C.	3	3
25th	Evans, Lane	Dem	Ill.	5	3
26th	Bilbray, James H.	Dem	Nev.	3	2
27th	Tanner, John S.	Dem	Tenn.	2	2
28th	McNulty, Michael R.	Dem	N.Y.	2	2
29th	Browder, Glen	Dem	Ala.	2	2
30th	Taylor, Gene	Dem	Miss.	2	2
31st	Abercrombie, Neil	Dem	Hai.	2	*2 1
32nd	Andrews, Thomas H.	Dem	Me.	1	1
33rd	Edwards, Chet	Dem	Tex.	1	1

Minority

Rank	Name	Party	State	Terms in: House	Terms in: Comm.
RM	Dickinson, William L.	Rep	Ala.	14	13
2nd	Spence, Floyd D.	Rep	S.C.	11	11
3rd	Stump, Robert	Rep	Ariz.	8	8
4th	Hopkins, Larry J.	Rep	Ky.	7	7
5th	Davis, Robert W.	Rep	Mich.	7	6
6th	Hunter, Duncan L.	Rep	Cal.	6	6
7th	Martin, David O'B.	Rep	N.Y.	6	5
8th	Kasich, John R.	Rep	Ohio	5	5
9th	Bateman, Herbert H.	Rep	Va.	5	4
10th	Blaz, Ben Garrido	Rep	Guam	4	4
11th	Ireland, Andrew P.	Rep	Fla.	8	3
12th	Hansen, James V.	Rep	Utah	6	4
13th	Weldon, Curt	Rep	Penn.	3	3
14th	Kyl, Jon	Rep	Ariz.	3	3
15th	Ravenel, Arthur Jr.	Rep	S.C.	3	3
16th	Dornan, Robert K.	Rep	Cal.	7	2
17th	Hefley, Joel	Rep	Colo.	3	2
18th	McCrery, Jim	Rep	La.	3	2
19th	Machtley, Ronald K.	Rep	R.I.	2	2
20th	Saxton, H. James	Rep	N.J.	4	1
21st	Cunningham, Randy	Rep	Cal.	1	1
22nd	Franks, Gary	Rep	Conn.	1	1

*2: Member's 2nd period of service on the committee.

Notes: Territorial Delegate Ben Blaz (Rep-Guam) was allowed to accrue committee seniority but was not included in the party ratio of 33 Democrats and 21 Republicans. Barbara Boxer (Dem-Cal.), having served on the Budget Committee during the previous three Congresses, returned to active service on this committee with her seniority intact. In the 99th Congress, the Democratic Caucus elected Les Aspin (Dem-Wisc.) Chair of this committee over more senior members.

BANKING, FINANCE AND URBAN AFFAIRS

BANKING AND CURRENCY

Jurisdiction, 1947

Established by the Legislative Reorganization Act of 1946:

[Section 121.(1)(d)]

Committee on Banking and Currency.

1. Banking and currency generally.
2. Financial aid to commerce and industry, other than matters relating to such aid which are specifically assigned to other committees under this rule.
3. Deposit insurance.
4. Public and private housing.
5. Federal Reserve System.
6. Gold and silver, including the coinage thereof.
7. Issuance of notes and redemption thereof.
8. Valuation and revaluation of the dollar.
9. Control of prices of commodities, rents, or services.

BANKING, CURRENCY AND HOUSING

Renamed the Committee on Banking, Currency and Housing on January 3, 1975.

BANKING, FINANCE AND URBAN AFFAIRS

Renamed the Committee on Banking, Finance and Urban Affairs on January 4, 1977.

Jurisdiction, 1992

Jurisdiction contained in Rules of the House of Representatives, (as revised to July 1, 1992):

[Rule X. 1. (d)]

Committee on Banking, Finance and Urban Affairs.

(1) Banks and banking, including deposit insurance and Federal monetary policy.
(2) Money and credit, including currency and the issuance of notes and redemption thereof; gold and silver, including the coinage thereof; valuation and revaluation of the dollar.
(3) Urban development.
(4) Public and private housing.
(5) Economic stabilization, defense production, renegotiation, and control of the price of commodities, rents, and services.
(6) International finance.
(7) Financial aid to commerce and industry (other than transportation).
(8) International Financial and Monetary organizations.

BANKING AND CURRENCY / 80th Congress

Service Dates of Committee Chair: Jan. 14,1947-Jan. 3,1949
Service Dates of Majority Members: Jan. 14,1947-Jan. 3,1949
Service Dates of Minority Members: Jan. 16,1947-Jan. 3,1949

Majority

Rank	Name	Party	State	Terms in: House	Terms in: Comm.
Chr	Wolcott, Jesse P.	Rep	Mich.	9	8
2nd	Gamble, Ralph A.	Rep	N.Y.	6	6
3rd	Smith, Frederick C.	Rep	Ohio	5	4
4th	Kunkel, John C.	Rep	Penn.	5	4
5th	Talle, Henry O.	Rep	Iowa	5	3
6th	Sundstrom, Frank L.	Rep	N.J.	3	3
7th	McMillen, Rolla C.	Rep	Ill.	3	3
8th	Kilburn, Clarence E.	Rep	N.Y.	5	2
9th	Buffett, Howard H.	Rep	Neb.	3	*1 2
10th	Cole, Albert M.	Rep	Kans.	2	1
11th	Hull, Merlin	Rep	Wisc.	8	5
12th	Stratton, William G.	Rep	Ill.	2	1
13th	Scott, Hardie	Rep	Penn.	1	1
14th	Banta, Parke M.	Rep	Mo.	1	1
15th	Fletcher, Charles K.	Rep	Cal.	1	1
16th	Foote, Ellsworth B.	Rep	Conn.	1	1

Minority

Rank	Name	Party	State	Terms in: House	Terms in: Comm.
RM	Spence, Brent	Dem	Ky.	9	8
2nd	Brown, Paul	Dem	Ga.	8	7
3rd	Patman, J.W. Wright	Dem	Tex.	10	6
4th	Monroney, A. S. Mike	Dem	Okla.	5	5
5th	Folger, John H.	Dem	N.C.	4	4
6th	Hays, L. Brooks	Dem	Ark.	3	3
7th	Riley, John J.	Dem	S.C.	2	2
8th	Rains, Albert	Dem	Ala.	2	2
9th	O'Toole, Donald L.	Dem	N.Y.	6	1
10th	Buchanan, Frank	Dem	Penn.	2	1
11th	Boggs, T. Hale	Dem	La.	2	*2 1

*1: Member's 1st period of service on the committee;
*2: Member's 2nd period of service on the committee.

Note: Ranking on this committee for the following member was affected by other chamber service: Merlin Hull (Rep-Wisc.) served previously on this committee as a Progressive. Elected as a Republican to the 80th Congress, Hull was allowed to accrue seniority only after joining the Republican Conference.

Changes:

Majority:

Foote, Ellsworth B.	Rep	Conn.	Dec. 18,1947	Moved to Judiciary.
Nicholson, Donald W.	Rep	Mass.	Dec. 18,1947	Replaced Foote.

Minority:

O'Toole, Donald L.	Dem	N.Y.	Dec. 4,1947	Moved to Merchant Marine and Fisheries.
Multer, Abraham J.	Dem	N.Y.	Dec. 4,1947	Replaced O'Toole.

Departures from the House:	**Majority**			**Minority**		
Defeated for Reelection	Banta, Parke M.	Mo.	Rep	None		
	Buffett, Howard H.	Neb.	Rep			
	Fletcher, Charles K.	Cal.	Rep			
	Sundstrom, Frank L.	N.J.	Rep			
Defeated for Renomination	None			Riley, John J.	S.C.	Dem
Retired	Stratton, William G.	Ill.	Rep	Folger, John H.	N.C.	Dem
Departures from Committee:						
Moved to Ways & Means	None			Boggs, T. Hale	La.	Dem

BANKING AND CURRENCY / 81st Congress

Service Dates of Committee Chair: Jan. 18,1949-Jan. 3,1951
Service Dates of Majority Members: Jan. 18,1949-Jan. 3,1951
Service Dates of Minority Members: Jan. 18,1949-Jan. 3,1951

Majority

Rank	Name	Party	State	Terms in: House		Terms in: Comm.
Chr	Spence, Brent	Dem	Ky.	10		9
2nd	Brown, Paul	Dem	Ga.	9		8
3rd	Patman, J.W. Wright	Dem	Tex.	11		7
4th	Monroney, A. S. Mike	Dem	Okla.	6		6
5th	Hays, L. Brooks	Dem	Ark.	4		4
6th	Rains, Albert	Dem	Ala.	3		3
7th	Buchanan, Frank	Dem	Penn.	3		2
8th	Multer, Abraham J.	Dem	N.Y.	2		2
9th	Deane, Charles B.	Dem	N.C.	2		1
10th	O'Brien, George D.	Dem	Mich.	5		1
11th	Woodhouse, Chase Going	Dem	Conn.	2	*2	1
12th	McKinnon, Clinton D.	Dem	Cal.	1		1
13th	Addonizio, Hugh J.	Dem	N.J.	1		1
14th	Dollinger, Isidore	Dem	N.Y.	1		1
15th	Mitchell, Hugh B.	Dem	Wash.	1		1
16th	O'Hara, Barratt	Dem	Ill.	1	*1	1

Minority

Rank	Name	Party	State	Terms in: House		Terms in: Comm.
RM	Wolcott, Jesse P.	Rep	Mich.	10		9
2nd	Gamble, Ralph A.	Rep	N.Y.	7		7
3rd	Smith, Frederick C.	Rep	Ohio	6		5
4th	Kunkel, John C.	Rep	Penn.	6		5
5th	Talle, Henry O.	Rep	Iowa	6		4
6th	McMillen, Rolla C.	Rep	Ill.	4		4
7th	Kilburn, Clarence E.	Rep	N.Y.	6		3
8th	Cole, Albert M.	Rep	Kans.	3		2
9th	Hull, Merlin	Rep	Wisc.	9		6
10th	Scott, Hardie	Rep	Penn.	2		2
11th	Nicholson, Donald W.	Rep	Mass.	2	*1	2

*1: Member's 1st period of service on the committee;
*2: Member's 2nd period of service on the committee.

Note: Ranking on this committee for the following member was affected by other chamber service: Merlin Hull (Rep-Wisc.) served previously on this committee as a Progressive. Elected as a Republican to the 80th Congress, Hull was allowed to accrue seniority only after joining the Republican Conference.

Changes:

Majority:

Mitchell, Hugh B.	Dem	Wash.	June 20,1950	Moved to Education and Labor.
Bolling, Richard W.	Dem	Mo.	June 20,1950	Replaced Mitchell.

	Majority			Minority		
Departures from the House:						
Elected to the U.S. Senate	Monroney, A. S. Mike	Okla.	Dem	None		
Defeated for Reelection	O'Hara, Barratt	Ill.	Dem	None		
	Woodhouse, Chase Going	Conn.	Dem			
Lost Nomination to U.S. Senate	None			Kunkel, John C.	Penn.	Rep
Retired	None			McMillen, Rolla C.	Ill.	Rep
				Smith, Frederick C.	Ohio	Rep
Departures from Committee:						
Moved to Foreign Affairs	Hays, L. Brooks	Ark.	Dem	None		

BANKING AND CURRENCY / 82nd Congress

Service Dates of Committee Chair: Jan. 12,1951-Jan. 3,1953
Service Dates of Majority Members: Jan. 12,1951-Jan. 3,1953
Service Dates of Minority Members: Jan. 15,1951-Jan. 3,1953

Majority

Rank Name	Party	State	Terms in: House	Terms in: Comm.
Chr Spence, Brent	Dem	Ky.	11	10
2nd Brown, Paul	Dem	Ga.	10	9
3rd Patman, J.W. Wright	Dem	Tex.	12	8
4th Rains, Albert	Dem	Ala.	4	4
5th Buchanan, Frank	Dem	Penn.	4	3
6th Multer, Abraham J.	Dem	N.Y.	3	3
7th Deane, Charles B.	Dem	N.C.	3	2
8th O'Brien, George D.	Dem	Mich.	6	2
9th McKinnon, Clinton D.	Dem	Cal.	2	2
10th Addonizio, Hugh J.	Dem	N.J.	2	2
11th Dollinger, Isidore	Dem	N.Y.	2	2
12th Bolling, Richard W.	Dem	Mo.	2	2
13th Burton, Clarence G.	Dem	Va.	3	1
14th Fugate, Thomas B.	Dem	Va.	2	1
15th Kluczynski, John C.	Dem	Ill.	1	1

Minority

Rank Name	Party	State	Terms in: House	Terms in: Comm.
RM Wolcott, Jesse P.	Rep	Mich.	11	10
2nd Gamble, Ralph A.	Rep	N.Y.	8	8
3rd Talle, Henry O.	Rep	Iowa	7	5
4th Kilburn, Clarence E.	Rep	N.Y.	7	4
5th Cole, Albert M.	Rep	Kans.	4	3
6th Hull, Merlin	Rep	Wisc.	10	7
7th Scott, Hardie	Rep	Penn.	3	3
8th Nicholson, Donald W.	Rep	Mass.	3 *1	3
9th McDonough, Gordon L.	Rep	Cal.	4	1
10th Widnall, William B.	Rep	N.J.	2	1
11th Buffett, Howard H.	Rep	Neb.	4 *2	1
12th Betts, Jackson E.	Rep	Ohio	1	1

*1: Member's 1st period of service on the committee; *2: Member's 2nd period of service on the committee.

Note: Ranking on this committee for the following member was affected by other chamber service: Merlin Hull (Rep-Wisc.) served previously on this committee as a Progressive. Elected as a Republican to the 80th Congress, Hull was allowed to accrue seniority only after joining the Republican Conference.

Changes:

Majority:

Buchanan, Frank	Dem	Penn.	Apr. 27,1951	Died in office.
Barrett, William A.	Dem	Penn.	June 13,1951	Replaced Buchanan.
Kluczynski, John C.	Dem	Ill.	July 25,1951	Moved to Public Works.
Hays, Wayne L.	Dem	Ohio	Aug. 9,1951	Replaced Kluczynski.

Departures from the House:	Majority			Minority		
Defeated for Reelection	Burton, Clarence G.	Va.	Dem	Cole, Albert M.	Kans.	Rep
Lost Nomination to U.S. Senate	McKinnon, Clinton D.	Cal.	Dem	None		
Retired	Fugate, Thomas B.	Va.	Dem	Buffett, Howard H.	Neb.	Rep
				Scott, Hardie	Penn.	Rep
Departures from Committee:						
Moved to Rules	None			Nicholson, Donald W.	Mass.	Rep

BANKING AND CURRENCY / 83rd Congress

Service Dates of Committee Chair: Jan. 19,1953-Jan. 3,1955
Service Dates of Majority Members: Jan. 19,1953-Jan. 3,1955
Service Dates of Minority Members: Jan. 19,1953-Jan. 3,1955

Majority

Rank	Name	Party	State	Terms in: House	Terms in: Comm.
Chr	Wolcott, Jesse P.	Rep	Mich.	12	11
2nd	Gamble, Ralph A.	Rep	N.Y.	9	9
3rd	Talle, Henry O.	Rep	Iowa	8	6
4th	Kilburn, Clarence E.	Rep	N.Y.	8	5
5th	Hull, Merlin	Rep	Wisc.	11	8
6th	McDonough, Gordon L.	Rep	Cal.	5	2
7th	Widnall, William B.	Rep	N.J.	3	2
8th	Betts, Jackson E.	Rep	Ohio	2	2
9th	D'Ewart, Wesley A.	Rep	Mont.	5	1
10th	George, Myron V.	Rep	Kans.	3	1
11th	Mumma, Walter M.	Rep	Penn.	2	1
12th	McVey, William E.	Rep	Ill.	2	1
13th	Merrill, D. Bailey	Rep	Ind.	1	1
14th	Oakman, Charles G.	Rep	Mich.	1	1
15th	Hiestand, Edgar W.	Rep	Cal.	1	1
16th	Stringfellow, Douglas R.	Rep	Utah	1	1

Minority

Rank	Name	Party	State	Terms in: House	Terms in: Comm.
RM	Spence, Brent	Dem	Ky.	12	11
2nd	Brown, Paul	Dem	Ga.	11	10
3rd	Patman, J.W. Wright	Dem	Tex.	13	9
4th	Rains, Albert	Dem	Ala.	5	5
5th	Multer, Abraham J.	Dem	N.Y.	4	4
6th	Deane, Charles B.	Dem	N.C.	4	3
7th	O'Brien, George D.	Dem	Mich.	7	3
8th	Addonizio, Hugh J.	Dem	N.J.	3	3
9th	Dollinger, Isidore	Dem	N.Y.	3	3
10th	Bolling, Richard W.	Dem	Mo.	3	3
11th	Barrett, William A.	Dem	Penn.	4	*2 2
12th	Hays, Wayne L.	Dem	Ohio	3	2
13th	O'Hara, Barratt	Dem	Ill.	2	*2 1

*2: Member's 2nd period of service on the committee.

Notes: Democratic Party gains in the 1953 special elections in New Jersey and Wisconsin led to a change in the size and party ratio on this committee to 16 Republicans and 14 Democrats on Jan. 25,1954. Ranking on this committee for the following member was affected by other chamber service: Merlin Hull (Rep-Wisc.) served previously on this committee as a Progressive. Elected as a Republican to the 80th Congress, Hull was allowed to accrue seniority only after joining the Republican Conference.

Addition:

Minority:	14th	McCarthy, Eugene J.	DFL	Minn.	Jan. 25,1954

Changes:

Majority:

Hull, Merlin	Rep	Wisc.	May 17,1953	Died in office.
Van Pelt, William K.	Rep	Wisc.	Jan. 21,1954	Replaced Hull.

Departures from the House:	**Majority**		**Minority**	
Defeated for Reelection	Merrill, D. Bailey	Ind. Rep	None	
	Oakman, Charles G.	Mich. Rep		
Defeated for Renomination	None		O'Brien, George D.	Mich. Dem
Lost Election to U.S. Senate	D'Ewart, Wesley A.	Mont. Rep	None	
Retired	Stringfellow, Douglas R.	Utah Rep	None	
Departures from Committee:				
Moved to Rules	None		Bolling, Richard W.	Mo. Dem
Moved to Appropriations	None		Deane, Charles B.	N.C. Dem
Moved to Interstate & Foreign Commerce	None		Dollinger, Isidore	N.Y. Dem
Moved to Foreign Affairs	None		Hays, Wayne L.	Ohio Dem
Moved to Ways & Means	None		McCarthy, Eugene J.	Minn. DFL
No new assignment	George, Myron V.	Kans. Rep	None	
	Van Pelt, William K.	Wisc. Rep		

BANKING AND CURRENCY / 84th Congress

Service Dates of Committee Chair: Jan. 13,1955-Jan. 3,1957
Service Dates of Majority Members: Jan. 13,1955-Jan. 3,1957
Service Dates of Minority Members: Jan. 20,1955-Jan. 3,1957

Majority

Rank	Name	Party	State	Terms in: House	Terms in: Comm.
Chr	Spence, Brent	Dem	Ky.	13	12
2nd	Brown, Paul	Dem	Ga.	12	11
3rd	Patman, J.W. Wright	Dem	Tex.	14	10
4th	Rains, Albert	Dem	Ala.	6	6
5th	Multer, Abraham J.	Dem	N.Y.	5	5
6th	Addonizio, Hugh J.	Dem	N.J.	4	4
7th	Barrett, William A.	Dem	Penn.	5	*2 3
8th	O'Hara, Barratt	Dem	Ill.	3	*2 2
9th	Buchanan, Vera D.	Dem	Penn.	3	1
10th	Sullivan, Leonor Kretzer	Dem	Mo.	2	1
11th	Fountain, Lawrence H.	Dem	N.C.	2	1
12th	Reuss, Henry S.	Dem	Wisc.	1	1
13th	Griffiths, Martha W.	Dem	Mich.	1	1
14th	Ashley, Thomas L.	Dem	Ohio	1	1
15th	Vanik, Charles A.	Dem	Ohio	1	1
16th	Davidson, Irwin D.	Dem	N.Y.	1	1
17th	Bell, John J.	Dem	Tex.	1	1

Minority

Rank	Name	Party	State	Terms in: House	Terms in: Comm.
RM	Wolcott, Jesse P.	Rep	Mich.	13	12
2nd	Gamble, Ralph A.	Rep	N.Y.	10	10
3rd	Talle, Henry O.	Rep	Iowa	9	7
4th	Kilburn, Clarence E.	Rep	N.Y.	9	6
5th	McDonough, Gordon L.	Rep	Cal.	6	3
6th	Widnall, William B.	Rep	N.J.	4	3
7th	Betts, Jackson E.	Rep	Ohio	3	3
8th	Mumma, Walter M.	Rep	Penn.	3	2
9th	McVey, William E.	Rep	Ill.	3	2
10th	Hiestand, Edgar W.	Rep	Cal.	2	2
11th	Nicholson, Donald W.	Rep	Mass.	5	*2 1
12th	Bolton, Oliver P.	Rep	Ohio	2	*1 1
13th	Bass, Perkins	Rep	N.H.	1	1

*1: Member's 1st period of service on the committee;
*2: Member's 2nd period of service on the committee.

Note: The committee size was expanded and the party ratio changed to 17 Democrats an 13 Republicans on Jan. 20,1955.

Changes:

Majority:

Buchanan, Vera D.	Dem	Penn.	Nov. 26,1955	Died in office.
Davidson, Irwin D.	Dem	N.Y.	Jan. 19,1956	Moved to Judiciary.
Holland, Elmer J.	Dem	Penn.	Feb. 23,1956	Replaced Buchanan.
Healey, James C.	Dem	N.Y.	Feb. 23,1956	Replaced Holland.

Departures from the House:	Majority		Minority	
Appointed Ohio Director of Commerce	None		Bolton, Oliver P.	Ohio Rep
Defeated for Renomination	Bell, John J.	Tex. Dem	None	
Retired	None		Gamble, Ralph A.	N.Y. Rep
			Wolcott, Jesse P.	Mich. Rep
Departures from Committee:				
Moved to Foreign Affairs	Fountain, Lawrence H.	N.C. Dem	None	
	O'Hara, Barratt	Ill. Dem		
Moved to Education & Labor	Holland, Elmer J.	Penn. Dem	Nicholson, Donald W.	Mass. Rep

BANKING AND CURRENCY / 85th Congress

Service Dates of Committee Chair: Jan. 10,1957-Jan. 3,1959
Service Dates of Majority Members: Jan. 10,1957-Jan. 3,1959
Service Dates of Minority Members: Jan. 16,1957-Jan. 3,1959

Majority

Rank Name	Party	State	Terms in: House	Terms in: Comm.
Chr Spence, Brent	Dem	Ky.	14	13
2nd Brown, Paul	Dem	Ga.	13	12
3rd Patman, J.W. Wright	Dem	Tex.	15	11
4th Rains, Albert	Dem	Ala.	7	7
5th Multer, Abraham J.	Dem	N.Y.	6	6
6th Addonizio, Hugh J.	Dem	N.J.	5	5
7th Barrett, William A.	Dem	Penn.	6	*2 4
8th Sullivan, Leonor Kretzer	Dem	Mo.	3	2
9th Reuss, Henry S.	Dem	Wisc.	2	2
10th Griffiths, Martha W.	Dem	Mich.	2	2
11th Ashley, Thomas L.	Dem	Ohio	2	2
12th Vanik, Charles A.	Dem	Ohio	2	2
13th Healey, James C.	Dem	N.Y.	2	2
14th Rutherford, J. T.	Dem	Tex.	2	1
15th Coad, Merwin	Dem	Iowa	1	1
16th Anderson, LeRoy H.	Dem	Mont.	1	1
17th Breeding, J. Floyd	Dem	Kans.	1	1

Minority

Rank Name	Party	State	Terms in: House	Terms in: Comm.
RM Talle, Henry O.	Rep	Iowa	10	8
2nd Kilburn, Clarence E.	Rep	N.Y.	10	7
3rd McDonough, Gordon L.	Rep	Cal.	7	4
4th Widnall, William B.	Rep	N.J.	5	4
5th Betts, Jackson E.	Rep	Ohio	4	4
6th Mumma, Walter M.	Rep	Penn.	4	3
7th McVey, William E.	Rep	Ill.	4	3
8th Hiestand, Edgar W.	Rep	Cal.	3	3
9th Bass, Perkins	Rep	N.H.	2	2
10th Seely-Brown, Horace Jr.	Rep	Conn.	5	1
11th Siler, Eugene	Rep	Ky.	2	1
12th Henderson, John E.	Rep	Ohio	2	1
13th Chamberlain, Charles E.	Rep	Mich.	1	1

*2: Member's 2nd period of service on the committee.

Changes:
Minority:
McVey, William E. Rep Ill. Aug. 10,1958 Died in office.

	Majority		Minority	
Departures from the House:				
Defeated for Reelection	None		Seely-Brown, Horace Jr.	Conn. Rep
			Talle, Henry O.	Iowa Rep
Departures from Committee:				
Moved to Armed Services	Anderson, LeRoy H.	Mont. Dem	Chamberlain, Charles E.	Mich. Rep
Moved to Agriculture	Breeding, J. Floyd	Kans. Dem	None	
	Coad, Merwin	Iowa Dem		
Moved to Ways & Means	None		Betts, Jackson E.	Ohio Rep
			Mumma, Walter M.	Penn. Rep
Moved to Judiciary	None		Henderson, John E.	Ohio Rep

BANKING AND CURRENCY / 86th Congress

Service Dates of Committee Chair: Jan. 19,1959-Jan. 3,1961
Service Dates of Majority Members: Jan. 19,1959-Jan. 3,1961
Service Dates of Minority Members: Jan. 19,1959-Jan. 3,1961

Majority

Rank Name	Party	State	Terms in: House	Terms in: Comm.
Chr Spence, Brent	Dem	Ky.	15	14
2nd Brown, Paul	Dem	Ga.	14	13
3rd Patman, J.W. Wright	Dem	Tex.	16	12
4th Rains, Albert	Dem	Ala.	8	8
5th Multer, Abraham J.	Dem	N.Y.	7	7
6th Addonizio, Hugh J.	Dem	N.J.	6	6
7th Barrett, William A.	Dem	Penn.	7	*2 5
8th Sullivan, Leonor Kretzer	Dem	Mo.	4	3
9th Reuss, Henry S.	Dem	Wisc.	3	3
10th Griffiths, Martha W.	Dem	Mich.	3	3
11th Ashley, Thomas L.	Dem	Ohio	3	3
12th Vanik, Charles A.	Dem	Ohio	3	3
13th Healey, James C.	Dem	N.Y.	3	3

Minority

Rank Name	Party	State	Terms in: House	Terms in: Comm.
RM Kilburn, Clarence E.	Rep	N.Y.	11	8
2nd McDonough, Gordon L.	Rep	Cal.	8	5
3rd Widnall, William B.	Rep	N.J.	6	5
4th Hiestand, Edgar W.	Rep	Cal.	4	4
5th Bass, Perkins	Rep	N.H.	3	3
6th Siler, Eugene	Rep	Ky.	3	2
7th Fino, Paul A.	Rep	N.Y.	4	1
8th Dwyer, Florence P.	Rep	N.J.	2	1
9th Derwinski, Edward J.	Rep	Ill.	1	1
10th Halpern, Seymour	Rep	N.Y.	1	1
11th Milliken, William H. Jr.	Rep	Penn.	1	1

14th Rutherford, J. T.	Dem	Tex.	3	2	
15th Barr, Joseph W.	Dem	Ind.	1	1	
16th Burke, James A.	Dem	Mass.	1	1	
17th Moorhead, William S.	Dem	Penn.	1	1	
18th Miller, Clement W.	Dem	Cal.	1	1	
19th Johnson, Byron L.	Dem	Colo.	1	1	*2: Member's 2nd period of service on the committee.

Changes:

Majority:

Healey, James C.	Dem	N.Y.	Aug. 27,1959	Moved to Interstate and Foreign Commerce.
Inouye, Daniel K.	Dem	Hai.	Aug. 27,1959	Replaced Healey.

Minority:

Hiestand, Edgar W.	Rep	Cal.	June 30,1960	Left committee; no new assignment.
Schneebeli, Herman T.	Rep	Penn.	June 30,1960	Replaced Hiestand.

	Majority			Minority		
Departures from the House:						
Defeated for Reelection	Barr, Joseph W.	Ind.	Dem	None		
	Johnson, Byron L.	Colo.	Dem			
Retired	Brown, Paul	Ga.	Dem	None		
Departures from Committee:						
Moved to Ways & Means	Burke, James A.	Mass.	Dem	Schneebeli, Herman T.	Penn.	Rep
Moved to Agriculture	Inouye, Daniel K.	Hai.	Dem	None		
Moved to Public Works	None			Bass, Perkins	N.H.	Rep
Moved to Appropriations	None			Milliken, William H. Jr.	Penn.	Rep

BANKING AND CURRENCY / 87th Congress

Service Dates of Committee Chair: Feb. 6,1961-Jan. 3,1963
Service Dates of Majority Members: Feb. 6,1961-Jan. 3,1963
Service Dates of Minority Members: Feb. 13,1961-Jan. 3,1963

Majority

Rank Name	Party	State	Terms in: House	Terms in: Comm.
Chr Spence, Brent	Dem	Ky.	16	15
2nd Patman, J.W. Wright	Dem	Tex.	17	13
3rd Rains, Albert	Dem	Ala.	9	9
4th Multer, Abraham J.	Dem	N.Y.	8	8
5th Addonizio, Hugh J.	Dem	N.J.	7	7
6th Barrett, William A.	Dem	Penn.	8 *2	6
7th Sullivan, Leonor Kretzer	Dem	Mo.	5	4
8th Reuss, Henry S.	Dem	Wisc.	4	4
9th Griffiths, Martha W.	Dem	Mich.	4	4
10th Ashley, Thomas L.	Dem	Ohio	4	4
11th Vanik, Charles A.	Dem	Ohio	4	4
12th Rutherford, J. T.	Dem	Tex.	4	3
13th Moorhead, William S.	Dem	Penn.	2	2
14th Miller, Clement W.	Dem	Cal.	2	2
15th Gilbert, Jacob H.	Dem	N.Y.	2	1
16th Finnegan, Edward R.	Dem	Ill.	1	1
17th Stephens, Robert G. Jr.	Dem	Ga.	1	1
18th St Germain, Fernand J.	Dem	R.I.	1	1

Minority

Rank Name	Party	State	Terms in: House	Terms in: Comm.
RM Kilburn, Clarence E.	Rep	N.Y.	12	9
2nd McDonough, Gordon L.	Rep	Cal.	9	6
3rd Widnall, William B.	Rep	N.J.	7	6
4th Siler, Eugene	Rep	Ky.	4	3
5th Fino, Paul A.	Rep	N.Y.	5	2
6th Dwyer, Florence P.	Rep	N.J.	3	2
7th Derwinski, Edward J.	Rep	Ill.	2	2
8th Halpern, Seymour	Rep	N.Y.	2	2
9th Harvey, James	Rep	Mich.	1	1
10th Moorehead, Tom V.	Rep	Ohio	1	1
11th Rousselot, John H.	Rep	Cal.	1 *1	1
12th Scranton, William W.	Rep	Penn.	1	1

*1: Member's 1st period of service on the committee;
*2: Member's 2nd period of service on the committee.

Changes:

Majority:

Rutherford, J. T.	Dem	Tex.	Sep. 25,1961	Moved to Armed Services.
Griffiths, Martha W.	Dem	Mich.	Jan. 18,1962	Moved to Ways and Means.
Gilbert, Jacob H.	Dem	N.Y.	Jan. 18,1962	Moved to Judiciary.
Carey, Hugh L.	Dem	N.Y.	Jan. 18,1962	Replaced Rutherford.
Gonzalez, Henry B.	Dem	Tex.	Jan. 18,1962	Replaced Griffiths.
Ryan, Harold M.	Dem	Mich.	Feb. 28,1962	Replaced Gilbert.
Addonizio, Hugh J.	Dem	N.J.	June 30,1962	Resigned; elected mayor of Newark.
Miller, Clement W.	Dem	Cal.	Oct. 7,1962	Died in office.

Departures from the House:	Majority			Minority		
Elected Governor	None			Scranton, William W.	Penn.	Rep
Defeated for Reelection	None			McDonough, Gordon L.	Cal.	Rep
	None			Moorehead, Tom V.	Ohio	Rep
Retired	Spence, Brent	Ky.	Dem	None		
Departures from Committee:						
Moved to Appropriations	Finnegan, Edward R.	Ill.	Dem	None		
Moved to Education & Labor	Carey, Hugh L.	N.Y.	Dem	None		
Moved to Public Works	Ryan, Harold M.	Mich.	Dem	None		
Moved to Foreign Affairs	None			Derwinski, Edward J.	Ill.	Rep
				Rousselot, John H.	Cal.	Rep

BANKING AND CURRENCY / 88th Congress

Service Dates of Committee Chair: Jan. 17,1963-Jan. 3,1965
Service Dates of Majority Members: Jan. 17,1963-Jan. 3,1965
Service Dates of Minority Members: Jan. 24,1963-Jan. 3,1965

Majority

Rank Name	Party	State	Terms in: House	Terms in: Comm.
Chr Patman, J.W. Wright	Dem	Tex.	18	14
2nd Rains, Albert	Dem	Ala.	10	10
3rd Multer, Abraham J.	Dem	N.Y.	9	9
4th Barrett, William A.	Dem	Penn.	9	*2 7
5th Sullivan, Leonor Kretzer	Dem	Mo.	6	5
6th Reuss, Henry S.	Dem	Wisc.	5	5
7th Ashley, Thomas L.	Dem	Ohio	5	5
8th Vanik, Charles A.	Dem	Ohio	5	5
9th Moorhead, William S.	Dem	Penn.	3	3
10th Stephens, Robert G. Jr.	Dem	Ga.	2	2
11th St Germain, Fernand J.	Dem	R.I.	2	2
12th Gonzalez, Henry B.	Dem	Tex.	2	2
13th Pepper, Claude D.	Dem	Fla.	1	1
14th Minish, Joseph G.	Dem	N.J.	1	1
15th Weltner, Charles L.	Dem	Ga.	1	1
16th Hanna, Richard T.	Dem	Cal.	1	1
17th Grabowski, Bernard F.	Dem	Conn.	1	1
18th Wilson, Charles H.	Dem	Cal.	1	1

Minority

Rank Name	Party	State	Terms in: House	Terms in: Comm.
RM Kilburn, Clarence E.	Rep	N.Y.	13	10
2nd Widnall, William B.	Rep	N.J.	8	7
3rd Siler, Eugene	Rep	Ky.	5	4
4th Fino, Paul A.	Rep	N.Y.	6	3
5th Dwyer, Florence P.	Rep	N.J.	4	3
6th Halpern, Seymour	Rep	N.Y.	3	3
7th Harvey, James	Rep	Mich.	2	2
8th Bolton, Oliver P.	Rep	Ohio	3	*2 1
9th Brock, William E. III	Rep	Tenn.	1	1
10th Taft, Robert Jr.	Rep	Ohio	1	1
11th McDade, Joseph M.	Rep	Penn.	1	1
12th Lloyd, Sherman P.	Rep	Utah	1	*1 1
13th Talcott, Burt L.	Rep	Cal.	1	1

*1: Member's 1st period of service on the committee;
*2: Member's 2nd period of service on the committee.

Note: House Resolution 429, agreed to on July 8,1963, led to a change in size and party ratio to 19 Democrats and 14 Republicans.

Additions:

Majority:	19th	White, Compton I. Jr.	Dem	Ida.	July 25,1963
Minority:	14th	Clawson, Del M.	Rep	Cal.	July 9,1963

Departures from the House:	Majority			Minority		
Defeated for Reelection	None			Bolton, Oliver P.	Ohio	Rep
Lost Election to U.S. Senate	None			Taft, Robert Jr.	Ohio	Rep
Lost Nomination to U.S. Senate	None			Lloyd, Sherman P.	Utah	Rep
Retired	Rains, Albert	Ala.	Dem	Kilburn, Clarence E.	N.Y.	Rep
				Siler, Eugene	Ky.	Rep
Departures from Committee:						
Moved to Rules	Pepper, Claude D.	Fla.	Dem	None		
Moved to Ways & Means	Vanik, Charles A.	Ohio	Dem	None		
Moved to Post Office & Civil Service; Armed Services; Veterans' Affairs	Wilson, Charles H.	Cal.	Dem	None		
Moved to Appropriations	None			McDade, Joseph M.	Penn.	Rep

BANKING AND CURRENCY / 89th Congress

Service Dates of Committee Chair: Jan. 18,1965-Jan. 3,1967
Service Dates of Majority Members: Jan. 18,1965-Jan. 3,1967
Service Dates of Minority Members: Jan. 21,1965-Jan. 3,1967

Majority

Rank	Name	Party	State	Terms in: House	Terms in: Comm.
Chr	Patman, J.W. Wright	Dem	Tex.	19	15
2nd	Multer, Abraham J.	Dem	N.Y.	10	10
3rd	Barrett, William A.	Dem	Penn.	10	*2 8
4th	Sullivan, Leonor Kretzer	Dem	Mo.	7	6
5th	Reuss, Henry S.	Dem	Wisc.	6	6
6th	Ashley, Thomas L.	Dem	Ohio	6	6
7th	Moorhead, William S.	Dem	Penn.	4	4
8th	Stephens, Robert G. Jr.	Dem	Ga.	3	3
9th	St Germain, Fernand J.	Dem	R.I.	3	3
10th	Gonzalez, Henry B.	Dem	Tex.	3	3
11th	Minish, Joseph G.	Dem	N.J.	2	2
12th	Weltner, Charles L.	Dem	Ga.	2	2
13th	Hanna, Richard T.	Dem	Cal.	2	2
14th	Grabowski, Bernard F.	Dem	Conn.	2	2
15th	White, Compton I. Jr.	Dem	Ida.	2	2
16th	Gettys, Thomas S.	Dem	S.C.	2	1
17th	Todd, Paul H. Jr.	Dem	Mich.	1	1
18th	Ottinger, Richard L.	Dem	N.Y.	1	1
19th	Cabell, Earle	Dem	Tex.	1	1
20th	McGrath, Thomas C. Jr.	Dem	N.J.	1	1
21st	Hansen, John R.	Dem	Iowa	1	1
22nd	Annunzio, Frank	Dem	Ill.	1	1

Minority

Rank	Name	Party	State	Terms in: House	Terms in: Comm.
RM	Widnall, William B.	Rep	N.J.	9	8
2nd	Fino, Paul A.	Rep	N.Y.	7	4
3rd	Dwyer, Florence P.	Rep	N.J.	5	4
4th	Halpern, Seymour	Rep	N.Y.	4	4
5th	Harvey, James	Rep	Mich.	3	3
6th	Brock, William E. III	Rep	Tenn.	2	2
7th	Talcott, Burt L.	Rep	Cal.	2	2
8th	Clawson, Del M.	Rep	Cal.	2	2
9th	Johnson, Albert W.	Rep	Penn.	2	1
10th	Stanton, J. William	Rep	Ohio	1	1
11th	Mize, Chester L.	Rep	Kans.	1	1

*2: Member's 2nd period of service on the committee.

Changes:

Majority:

Cabell, Earle	Dem	Tex.	Mar. 8,1966	Moved to Science and Astronautics.
Rees, Thomas M.	Dem	Cal.	Mar. 8,1966	Replaced Cabell.
Ottinger, Richard L.	Dem	N.Y.	Oct. 18,1966	Moved to Interstate and Foreign Commerce.

Departures from the House:

	Majority			Minority		
Defeated for Reelection	Grabowski, Bernard F.	Conn.	Dem	None		
	Hansen, John R.	Iowa	Dem			
	McGrath, Thomas C. Jr.	N.J.	Dem			
	Todd, Paul H. Jr.	Mich.	Dem			
	White, Compton I. Jr.	Ida.	Dem			
Retired	Weltner, Charles L.	Ga.	Dem	None		
Departures from Committee:						
Moved to Appropriations	None			Talcott, Burt L.	Cal.	Rep
No new assignment	None			Harvey, James	Mich.	Rep

BANKING AND CURRENCY / 90th Congress

Service Dates of Committee Chair: Jan. 23,1967-Jan. 3,1969
Service Dates of Majority Members: Jan. 23,1967-Jan. 3,1969
Service Dates of Minority Members: Jan. 26,1967-Jan. 3,1969

Majority

Rank Name	Party	State	Terms in: House	Terms in: Comm.
Chr Patman, J.W. Wright	Dem	Tex.	20	16
2nd Multer, Abraham J.	Dem	N.Y.	11	11
3rd Barrett, William A.	Dem	Penn.	11	*2 9
4th Sullivan, Leonor Kretzer	Dem	Mo.	8	7
5th Reuss, Henry S.	Dem	Wisc.	7	7
6th Ashley, Thomas L.	Dem	Ohio	7	7
7th Moorhead, William S.	Dem	Penn.	5	5
8th Stephens, Robert G. Jr.	Dem	Ga.	4	4
9th St Germain, Fernand J.	Dem	R.I.	4	4
10th Gonzalez, Henry B.	Dem	Tex.	4	4
11th Minish, Joseph G.	Dem	N.J.	3	3
12th Hanna, Richard T.	Dem	Cal.	3	3
13th Gettys, Thomas S.	Dem	S.C.	3	2
14th Annunzio, Frank	Dem	Ill.	2	2
15th Rees, Thomas M.	Dem	Cal.	2	2
16th Bingham, Jonathan B.	Dem	N.Y.	2	1
17th Galifianakis, Nick	Dem	N.C.	1	1
18th Bevill, Tom	Dem	Ala.	1	1
19th Kyros, Peter N.	Dem	Me.	1	1

Minority

Rank Name	Party	State	Terms in: House	Terms in: Comm.
RM Widnall, William B.	Rep	N.J.	10	9
2nd Fino, Paul A.	Rep	N.Y.	8	5
3rd Dwyer, Florence P.	Rep	N.J.	6	5
4th Halpern, Seymour	Rep	N.Y.	5	5
5th Brock, William E. III	Rep	Tenn.	3	3
6th Clawson, Del M.	Rep	Cal.	3	3
7th Johnson, Albert W.	Rep	Penn.	3	2
8th Stanton, J. William	Rep	Ohio	2	2
9th Mize, Chester L.	Rep	Kans.	2	2
10th Lloyd, Sherman P.	Rep	Utah	2	*2 1
11th Blackburn, Benjamin B.	Rep	Ga.	1	1
12th Brown, Garry E.	Rep	Mich.	1	1
13th Williams, Lawrence G.	Rep	Penn.	1	1
14th Wylie, Chalmers P.	Rep	Ohio	1	1

*2: Member's 2nd period of service on the committee.

Changes:

Majority:

Kyros, Peter N.	Dem	Me.	May 25,1967	Moved to Interstate and Foreign Commerce.
Multer, Abraham J.	Dem	N.Y.	Dec. 31,1967	Resigned; elected to State Supreme Court.
Griffin, Charles H.	Dem	Miss.	Apr. 3,1968	Replaced Kyros.
Wolff, Lester L.	Dem	N.Y.	Apr. 3,1968	Replaced Multer.

Minority:

Fino, Paul A.	Rep	N.Y.	Dec. 31,1968	Resigned; elected to State Supreme Court.

Departures from Committee:

Moved to House Administration; Foreign Affairs	Bingham, Jonathan B.	N.Y.	Dem	None		
Moved to Foreign Affairs	Wolff, Lester L.	N.Y.	Dem	Lloyd, Sherman P.	Utah	Rep

BANKING AND CURRENCY / 91st Congress

Service Dates of Committee Chair: Jan. 29,1969-Jan. 3,1971
Service Dates of Majority Members: Jan. 29,1969-Jan. 3,1971
Service Dates of Minority Members: Jan. 29,1969-Jan. 3,1971

Majority

Rank	Name	Party	State	Terms in: House	Terms in: Comm.
Chr	Patman, J.W. Wright	Dem	Tex.	21	17
2nd	Barrett, William A.	Dem	Penn.	12	*2 10
3rd	Sullivan, Leonor Kretzer	Dem	Mo.	9	8
4th	Reuss, Henry S.	Dem	Wisc.	8	8
5th	Ashley, Thomas L.	Dem	Ohio	8	8
6th	Moorhead, William S.	Dem	Penn.	6	6
7th	Stephens, Robert G. Jr.	Dem	Ga.	5	5
8th	St Germain, Fernand J.	Dem	R.I.	5	5
9th	Gonzalez, Henry B.	Dem	Tex.	5	5
10th	Minish, Joseph G.	Dem	N.J.	4	4
11th	Hanna, Richard T.	Dem	Cal.	4	4
12th	Gettys, Thomas S.	Dem	S.C.	4	3
13th	Annunzio, Frank	Dem	Ill.	3	3
14th	Rees, Thomas M.	Dem	Cal.	3	3
15th	Galifianakis, Nick	Dem	N.C.	2	2
16th	Bevill, Tom	Dem	Ala.	2	2
17th	Griffin, Charles H.	Dem	Miss.	2	2
18th	Hanley, James M.	Dem	N.Y.	3	1
19th	Brasco, Frank J.	Dem	N.Y.	2	1
20th	Chappell, William V. Jr.	Dem	Fla.	1	1

Minority

Rank	Name	Party	State	Terms in: House	Terms in: Comm.
RM	Widnall, William B.	Rep	N.J.	11	10
2nd	Dwyer, Florence P.	Rep	N.J.	7	6
3rd	Halpern, Seymour	Rep	N.Y.	6	6
4th	Brock, William E. III	Rep	Tenn.	4	4
5th	Clawson, Del M.	Rep	Cal.	4	4
6th	Johnson, Albert W.	Rep	Penn.	4	3
7th	Stanton, J. William	Rep	Ohio	3	3
8th	Mize, Chester L.	Rep	Kans.	3	3
9th	Blackburn, Benjamin B.	Rep	Ga.	2	2
10th	Brown, Garry E.	Rep	Mich.	2	2
11th	Williams, Lawrence G.	Rep	Penn.	2	2
12th	Wylie, Chalmers P.	Rep	Ohio	2	2
13th	Heckler, Margaret M.	Rep	Mass.	2	1
14th	Cowger, William O.	Rep	Ky.	2	1
15th	Beall, J. Glenn Jr.	Rep	Md.	1	1

*2: Member's 2nd period of service on the committee.

Note: The death of William H. Bates (Rep-Mass.), and his replacement by Michael J. Harrington (Dem-Mass.) on Oct. 3,1969, led to the passage of House Resolution 673, agreed to Nov. 12,1969, changing the size and party ratio on this committee to 21 Democrats and 15 Republicans.

Addition:

Majority: 21st Harrington, Michael J. Dem Mass. Nov. 12,1969

Changes:

Minority:

Name	Party	State	Date	Change
Beall, J. Glenn Jr.	Rep	Md.	Oct. 7,1969	Moved to Armed Services.
Crane, Philip M.	Rep	Ill.	Dec. 23,1969	Replaced Beall.
Clawson, Del M.	Rep	Cal.	Feb. 17,1970	Moved to Appropriations.
MacGregor, Clark	Rep	Minn.	Mar. 5,1970	Replaced Clawson.
MacGregor, Clark	Rep	Minn.	Sep. 16,1970	Left committee; no new assignment.
Rousselot, John H.	Rep	Cal.	Sep. 23,1970	Replaced MacGregor.

Departures from the House:

	Majority		Minority	
Elected to U.S. Senate	None		Brock, William E. III	Tenn. Rep
Defeated for Reelection	None		Cowger, William O.	Ky. Rep
			Mize, Chester L.	Kans. Rep

Departures from Committee:

	Majority		Minority	
Moved to Appropriations	Galifianakis, Nick	N.C. Dem	None	
Moved to Armed Services	Harrington, Michael J.	Mass. Dem	None	
Moved to Foreign Affairs	None		Halpern, Seymour	N.Y. Rep

BANKING AND CURRENCY / 92nd Congress

Service Dates of Committee Chair: Feb. 4,1971-Jan. 3,1973
Service Dates of Majority Members: Feb. 4,1971-Jan. 3,1973
Service Dates of Minority Members: Feb. 4,1971-Jan. 3,1973

Majority

Rank	Name	Party	State	Terms in: House	Terms in: Comm.
Chr	Patman, J.W. Wright	Dem	Tex.	22	18
2nd	Barrett, William A.	Dem	Penn.	13	*2 11
3rd	Sullivan, Leonor Kretzer	Dem	Mo.	10	9
4th	Reuss, Henry S.	Dem	Wisc.	9	9
5th	Ashley, Thomas L.	Dem	Ohio	9	9
6th	Moorhead, William S.	Dem	Penn.	7	7
7th	Stephens, Robert G. Jr.	Dem	Ga.	6	6
8th	St Germain, Fernand J.	Dem	R.I.	6	6
9th	Gonzalez, Henry B.	Dem	Tex.	6	6
10th	Minish, Joseph G.	Dem	N.J.	5	5
11th	Hanna, Richard T.	Dem	Cal.	5	5
12th	Gettys, Thomas S.	Dem	S.C.	5	4
13th	Annunzio, Frank	Dem	Ill.	4	4
14th	Rees, Thomas M.	Dem	Cal.	4	4
15th	Bevill, Tom	Dem	Ala.	3	3
16th	Griffin, Charles H.	Dem	Miss.	3	3
17th	Hanley, James M.	Dem	N.Y.	4	2
18th	Brasco, Frank J.	Dem	N.Y.	3	2
19th	Chappell, William V. Jr.	Dem	Fla.	2	2
20th	Koch, Edward I.	Dem	N.Y.	2	1
21st	Cotter, William R.	Dem	Conn.	1	1
22nd	Mitchell, Parren J.	Dem	Md.	1	1

Minority

Rank	Name	Party	State	Terms in: House	Terms in: Comm.
RM	Widnall, William B.	Rep	N.J.	12	11
2nd	Dwyer, Florence P.	Rep	N.J.	8	7
3rd	Johnson, Albert W.	Rep	Penn.	5	4
4th	Stanton, J. William	Rep	Ohio	4	4
5th	Blackburn, Benjamin B.	Rep	Ga.	3	3
6th	Brown, Garry E.	Rep	Mich.	3	3
7th	Williams, Lawrence G.	Rep	Penn.	3	3
8th	Wylie, Chalmers P.	Rep	Ohio	3	3
9th	Heckler, Margaret M.	Rep	Mass.	3	2
10th	Crane, Philip M.	Rep	Ill.	2	2
11th	Rousselot, John H.	Rep	Cal.	3	*2 2
12th	McKinney, Stewart B.	Rep	Conn.	1	1
13th	Lent, Norman F.	Rep	N.Y.	1	1
14th	Archer, William R.	Rep	Tex.	1	1
15th	Frenzel, William E.	Rep	Minn.	1	1

*2: Member's 2nd period of service on the committee.

Changes:

Majority:

Name	Party	State	Date	Change
Bevill, Tom	Dem	Ala.	Jan. 27,1972	Moved to Appropriations.
Curlin, William P. Jr.	Dem	Ky.	Jan. 27,1972	Replaced Bevill.

	Majority			Minority		
Departures from the House:						
Retired	Griffin, Charles H.	Miss.	Dem	Dwyer, Florence P.	N.J.	Rep
	Curlin, William P. Jr.	Ky.	Dem			
Departures from Committee:						
Moved to Appropriations	Chappell, William V. Jr.	Fla.	Dem	None		
Moved to Ways & Means	None			Archer, William R.	Tex.	Rep
Moved to Interstate & Foreign Commerce	None			Lent, Norman F.	N.Y.	Rep

BANKING AND CURRENCY / 93rd Congress

Service Dates of Committee Chair: Jan. 24,1973-Jan. 3,1975
Service Dates of Majority Members: Jan. 24,1973-Jan. 3,1975
Service Dates of Minority Members: Jan. 24,1973-Jan. 3,1975

Majority

Rank	Name	Party	State	Terms in: House	Terms in: Comm.
Chr	Patman, J.W. Wright	Dem	Tex.	23	19
2nd	Barrett, William A.	Dem	Penn.	14 *2	12
3rd	Sullivan, Leonor Kretzer	Dem	Mo.	11	10
4th	Reuss, Henry S.	Dem	Wisc.	10	10
5th	Ashley, Thomas L.	Dem	Ohio	10	10
6th	Moorhead, William S.	Dem	Penn.	8	8
7th	Stephens, Robert G. Jr.	Dem	Ga.	7	7
8th	St Germain, Fernand J.	Dem	R.I.	7	7
9th	Gonzalez, Henry B.	Dem	Tex.	7	7
10th	Minish, Joseph G.	Dem	N.J.	6	6
11th	Hanna, Richard T.	Dem	Cal.	6	6
12th	Gettys, Thomas S.	Dem	S.C.	6	5
13th	Annunzio, Frank	Dem	Ill.	5	5
14th	Rees, Thomas M.	Dem	Cal.	5	5
15th	Hanley, James M.	Dem	N.Y.	5	3
16th	Brasco, Frank J.	Dem	N.Y.	4	3
17th	Koch, Edward I.	Dem	N.Y.	3	2
18th	Cotter, William R.	Dem	Conn.	2	2
19th	Mitchell, Parren J.	Dem	Md.	2	2
20th	Fauntroy, Walter E.	Dem	D.C.	2	1
21st	Young, Andrew J.	Dem	Ga.	1	1
22nd	Moakley, John Joseph	Dem	Mass.	1	1
23rd	Stark, Fortney H. (Pete)	Dem	Cal.	1	1

Minority

Rank	Name	Party	State	Terms in: House	Terms in: Comm.
RM	Widnall, William B.	Rep	N.J.	13	12
2nd	Johnson, Albert W.	Rep	Penn.	6	5
3rd	Stanton, J. William	Rep	Ohio	5	5
4th	Blackburn, Benjamin B.	Rep	Ga.	4	4
5th	Brown, Garry E.	Rep	Mich.	4	4
6th	Williams, Lawrence G.	Rep	Penn.	4	4
7th	Wylie, Chalmers P.	Rep	Ohio	4	4
8th	Heckler, Margaret M.	Rep	Mass.	4	3
9th	Crane, Philip M.	Rep	Ill.	3	3
10th	Rousselot, John H.	Rep	Cal.	4 *2	3
11th	McKinney, Stewart B.	Rep	Conn.	2	2
12th	Frenzel, William E.	Rep	Minn.	2	2
13th	Roncallo, Angelo D.	Rep	N.Y.	1	1
14th	Conlan, John B.	Rep	Ariz.	1	1
15th	Burgener, Clair W.	Rep	Cal.	1	1
16th	Rinaldo, Matthew J.	Rep	N.J.	1	1

*2: Member's 2nd period of service on the committee.

Notes: Delegate Walter E. Fauntroy (Dem-D.C.) was allowed to accrue committee seniority, but was not included in the original party ratio of 22 Democrats and 16 Republicans. Donald W. Riegle, Jr. of Michigan resigned the Republican Party and joined the Democratic Party on Feb. 27,1973, leading to the passage of House Resolution 324, agreed to Mar. 26,1973, changing the party ratio on this committee to 23 Democrats (excluding Fauntroy) and 16 Republicans.

Addition:

Majority: 24th Boggs, Corinne C. (Lindy) Dem La. Mar. 27,1973

Changes:

Majority:

Hanna, Richard T.	Dem	Cal.	Dec. 31,1974	Resigned and retired.
Gettys, Thomas S.	Dem	S.C.	Dec. 31,1974	Resigned and retired.

Minority:

Widnall, William B.	Rep	N.J.	Dec. 31,1974	Resigned; defeated for reelection.

Departures from the House:	Majority			Minority		
Defeated for Reelection	None			Blackburn, Benjamin B.	Ga.	Rep
				Roncallo, Angelo D.	N.Y.	Rep
Defeated for Renomination	None			Williams, Lawrence G.	Penn.	Rep
Retired	Brasco, Frank J.	N.Y.	Dem	None		
Departures from Committee:						
Moved to Ways & Means	Cotter, William R.	Conn.	Dem	Crane, Philip M.	Ill.	Rep
	Stark, Fortney H. (Pete)	Cal.	Dem	Frenzel, William E.	Minn.	Rep
Moved to Appropriations	Koch, Edward I.	N.Y.	Dem	Burgener, Clair W.	Cal.	Rep
Moved to Rules	Moakley, John Joseph	Mass.	Dem	None		
	Young, Andrew J.	Ga.	Dem			
Moved to Agriculture	None			Heckler, Margaret M.	Mass.	Rep
Moved to Interstate & Foreign Commerce; Merchant Marine & Fisheries	None			Rinaldo, Matthew J.	N.J.	Rep

BANKING, CURRENCY AND HOUSING / 94th Congress

* Name changed from BANKING AND CURRENCY on Jan. 3,1975.

Service Dates of Committee Chair: Jan. 23,1975-Jan. 3,1977
Service Dates of Majority Members: Jan. 23,1975-Jan. 3,1977
Service Dates of Minority Members: Jan. 28,1975-Jan. 3,1977

Majority

Rank	Name	Party	State	Terms in: House	Terms in: Comm.
Chr	Reuss, Henry S.	Dem	Wisc.	11	11
2nd	Patman, J.W. Wright	Dem	Tex.	24	20
3rd	Barrett, William A.	Dem	Penn.	15*2	13
4th	Sullivan, Leonor Kretzer	Dem	Mo.	12	11
5th	Ashley, Thomas L.	Dem	Ohio	11	11
6th	Moorhead, William S.	Dem	Penn.	9	9
7th	Stephens, Robert G. Jr.	Dem	Ga.	8	8
8th	St Germain, Fernand J.	Dem	R.I.	8	8
9th	Gonzalez, Henry B.	Dem	Tex.	8	8
10th	Minish, Joseph G.	Dem	N.J.	7	7
11th	Annunzio, Frank	Dem	Ill.	6	6
12th	Rees, Thomas M.	Dem	Cal.	6	6
13th	Hanley, James M.	Dem	N.Y.	6	4
14th	Mitchell, Parren J.	Dem	Md.	3	3
15th	Fauntroy, Walter E.	Dem	D.C.	3	2
16th	Boggs, Corinne C. (Lindy)	Dem	La.	2	2
17th	Neal, Stephen L.	Dem	N.C.	1	1
18th	Patterson, Jerry M.	Dem	Cal.	1	1
19th	Blanchard, James J.	Dem	Mich.	1	1
20th	Maguire, G. Andrew	Dem	N.J.	1	1
21st	Ford, Harold E.	Dem	Tenn.	1	1
22nd	Hubbard, Carroll Jr.	Dem	Ky.	1	1
23rd	LaFalce, John J.	Dem	N.Y.	1	1
24th	Spellman, Gladys Noon	Dem	Md.	1	1
25th	AuCoin, Les	Dem	Ore.	1	1
26th	Tsongas, Paul E.	Dem	Mass.	1	1
27th	Derrick, Butler C. Jr.	Dem	S.C.	1	1
28th	Hayes, Philip H.	Dem	Ind.	1	1
29th	Hannaford, Mark W.	Dem	Cal.	1	1

Minority

Rank	Name	Party	State	Terms in: House	Terms in: Comm.
RM	Johnson, Albert W.	Rep	Penn.	7	6
2nd	Stanton, J. William	Rep	Ohio	6	6
3rd	Brown, Garry E.	Rep	Mich.	5	5
4th	Wylie, Chalmers P.	Rep	Ohio	5	5
5th	Rousselot, John H.	Rep	Cal.	5 *2	4
6th	McKinney, Stewart B.	Rep	Conn.	3	3
7th	Conlan, John B.	Rep	Ariz.	2	2
8th	Hansen, George V.	Rep	Ida.	3	1
9th	Schulze, Richard T.	Rep	Penn.	1	1
10th	Gradison, Willis D. Jr.	Rep	Ohio	1	1
11th	Hyde, Henry J.	Rep	Ill.	1	1
12th	Kelly, Richard	Rep	Fla.	1	1
13th	Grassley, Charles E.	Rep	Iowa	1	1
14th	Fenwick, Millicent H.	Rep	N.J.	1	1

*2: Member's 2nd period of service on the committee.

Notes: Delegate Walter E. Fauntroy (Dem-D.C.) was allowed to accrue seniority, but was not included in the committee's original party ratio of 28 Democrats and 14 Republicans. J.W. Wright Patman (Dem-Tex.) was succeeded as Chair of this committee by Henry S. Reuss (Dem-Wisc.), who, in a vote of the Democratic Caucus on Jan. 22,1975, received 152 votes to Patman's 117. Neither William A. Barrett (Dem-Penn.) nor Leonor Kretzer Sullivan (Dem-Mo.) contested the race. The resignation of Robert R. Casey (Dem-Tex.) and his replacement by Ronald E. Paul (Rep-Tex.) on Apr. 7,1976 led to a change in size and party ratio on this committee to 28 Democrats (excluding Fauntroy) and 15 Republicans.

Addition:

Minority:	15th	Paul, Ronald E.	Rep	Tex.	Apr. 14,1976

Changes:

Majority:

Maguire, G. Andrew	Dem	N.J.	Mar. 18,1975	Moved to Interstate and Foreign Commerce.
Evans, David W.	Dem	Ind.	Mar. 18,1975	Replaced Maguire.
Ford, Harold E.	Dem	Tenn.	Sep. 30,1975	Moved to Ways and Means.
Allen, Clifford R.	Dem	Tenn.	Dec. 17,1975	Replaced Ford.
Patman, J.W. Wright	Dem	Tex.	Mar. 7,1976	Died in office.
Barrett, William A.	Dem	Penn.	Apr. 12,1976	Died in office.
D'Amours, Norman E.	Dem	N.H.	Apr. 8,1976	Replaced Patman.
Lundine, Stanley N.	Dem	N.Y.	Apr. 8,1976	Replaced terminally ill Barrett.

Departures from the House:	**Majority**			**Minority**		
Defeated for Reelection	None			Johnson, Albert W.	Penn.	Rep
				Paul, Ronald E.	Tex.	Rep
Lost Nomination to U.S. Senate	Hayes, Philip H.	Ind.	Dem	Conlan, John B.	Ariz.	Rep
Retired	Rees, Thomas M.	Cal.	Dem	None		
	Stephens, Robert G. Jr.	Ga.	Dem			
	Sullivan, Leonor Kretzer	Mo.	Dem			
Departures from Committee:						
Moved to Appropriations	Boggs, Corinne C. (Lindy)	La.	Dem	None		
Moved to Ways & Means	None			Gradison, Willis D. Jr.	Ohio	Rep
				Schulze, Richard T.	Penn.	Rep

BANKING, FINANCE AND URBAN AFFAIRS / 95th Congress

* Name changed from BANKING, CURRENCY AND HOUSING on Jan. 4,1977.

Service Dates of Committee Chair: Jan. 19,1977-Jan. 3,1979
Service Dates of Majority Members: Jan. 19,1977-Jan. 3,1979
Service Dates of Minority Members: Jan. 19,1977-Jan. 3,1979

Majority

Rank	Name	Party	State	Terms in: House	Terms in: Comm.
Chr	Reuss, Henry S.	Dem	Wisc.	12	12
2nd	Ashley, Thomas L.	Dem	Ohio	12	12
3rd	Moorhead, William S.	Dem	Penn.	10	10
4th	St Germain, Fernand J.	Dem	R.I.	9	9
5th	Gonzalez, Henry B.	Dem	Tex.	9	9
6th	Minish, Joseph G.	Dem	N.J.	8	8
7th	Annunzio, Frank	Dem	Ill.	7	7
8th	Hanley, James M.	Dem	N.Y.	7	5
9th	Mitchell, Parren J.	Dem	Md.	4	4
10th	Fauntroy, Walter E.	Dem	D.C.	4	3
11th	Neal, Stephen L.	Dem	N.C.	2	2
12th	Patterson, Jerry M.	Dem	Cal.	2	2
13th	Blanchard, James J.	Dem	Mich.	2	2
14th	Hubbard, Carroll Jr.	Dem	Ky.	2	2
15th	LaFalce, John J.	Dem	N.Y.	2	2
16th	Spellman, Gladys Noon	Dem	Md.	2	2
17th	AuCoin, Les	Dem	Ore.	2	2
18th	Tsongas, Paul E.	Dem	Mass.	2	2
19th	Derrick, Butler C. Jr.	Dem	S.C.	2	2
20th	Hannaford, Mark W.	Dem	Cal.	2	2
21st	Evans, David W.	Dem	Ind.	2	2
22nd	Allen, Clifford R.	Dem	Tenn.	2	2
23rd	D'Amours, Norman E.	Dem	N.H.	2	2
24th	Lundine, Stanley N.	Dem	N.Y.	2	2
25th	Badillo, Herman	Dem	N.Y.	4	1
26th	Pattison, Edward W.	Dem	N.Y.	2	1
27th	Cavanaugh, John J.	Dem	Neb.	1	1
28th	Oakar, Mary Rose	Dem	Ohio	1	1
29th	Mattox, James A.	Dem	Tex.	1	1
30th	Vento, Bruce F.	DFL	Minn.	1	1
31st	Barnard, D. Douglas Jr.	Dem	Ga.	1	1
32nd	Watkins, Wesley W.	Dem	Okla.	1	1

Minority

Rank	Name	Party	State	Terms in: House	Terms in: Comm.
RM	Stanton, J. William	Rep	Ohio	7	7
2nd	Brown, Garry E.	Rep	Mich.	6	6
3rd	Wylie, Chalmers P.	Rep	Ohio	6	6
4th	Rousselot, John H.	Rep	Cal.	6	*2 5
5th	McKinney, Stewart B.	Rep	Conn.	4	4
6th	Hansen, George V.	Rep	Ida.	4	2
7th	Hyde, Henry J.	Rep	Ill.	2	2
8th	Kelly, Richard	Rep	Fla.	2	2
9th	Grassley, Charles E.	Rep	Iowa	2	2
10th	Fenwick, Millicent H.	Rep	N.J.	2	2
11th	Leach, James A. S.	Rep	Iowa	1	1
12th	Steers, Newton I. Jr.	Rep	Md.	1	1
13th	Evans, Thomas B. Jr.	Rep	Del.	1	1
14th	Caputo, Bruce F.	Rep	N.Y.	1	1
15th	Hollenbeck, Harold C.	Rep	N.J.	1	1

*2: Member's 2nd period of service on the committee.

Notes: Delegate Walter E. Fauntroy (Dem-D.C.) was allowed to accrue seniority, but was not included in the committee's original party ratio of 31 Democrats and 15 Republicans. The resignation of Edward I. Koch (Dem-N.Y.), and his replacement by S. William Green (Rep-N.Y.) on Feb. 21,1978 led to a change in size and party ratio on this committee to 31 Democrats (excluding Fauntroy) and 16 Republicans.

Addition:

Minority: 16th Green, S. William Rep N.Y. Feb. 22,1978

Changes:

Majority:

Badillo, Herman	Dem	N.Y.	Dec. 31,1977	Resigned; appointed Deputy Mayor of New York City.
Garcia, Robert	Dem	N.Y.	Feb. 22,1978	Replaced Badillo.
Allen, Clifford R.	Dem	Tenn.	June 18,1978	Died in office.

Departures from the House:	**Majority**			**Minority**		
Defeated for Reelection	Hannaford, Mark W.	Cal.	Dem	Brown, Garry E.	Mich.	Rep
	Pattison, Edward W.	N.Y.	Dem	Steers, Newton I. Jr.	Md.	Rep
Elected to U.S. Senate	Tsongas, Paul E.	Mass.	Dem	None		
Lost Nomination for Lt. Governor	None			Caputo, Bruce F.	N.Y.	Rep
Departures from Committee:						
Moved to Rules	Derrick, Butler C. Jr.	S.C.	Dem	None		
Moved to District of Columbia; Foreign Affairs	None			Fenwick, Millicent H.	N.J.	Rep
Moved to Standards of Official Conduct	None			Hollenbeck, Harold C.	N.J.	Rep
No new assignment	None			Grassley, Charles E.	Iowa	Rep
				Rousselot, John H.	Cal.	Rep

BANKING, FINANCE AND URBAN AFFAIRS / 96th Congress

Service Dates of Committee Chair: Jan. 24,1979-Jan. 3,1981
Service Dates of Majority Members: Jan. 24,1979-Jan. 3,1981
Service Dates of Minority Members: Jan. 24,1979-Jan. 3,1981

Majority

Rank	Name	Party	State	Terms in: House	Terms in: Comm.
Chr	Reuss, Henry S.	Dem	Wisc.	13	13
2nd	Ashley, Thomas L.	Dem	Ohio	13	13
3rd	Moorhead, William S.	Dem	Penn.	11	11
4th	St Germain, Fernand J.	Dem	R.I.	10	10
5th	Gonzalez, Henry B.	Dem	Tex.	10	10
6th	Minish, Joseph G.	Dem	N.J.	9	9
7th	Annunzio, Frank	Dem	Ill.	8	8
8th	Hanley, James M.	Dem	N.Y.	8	6
9th	Mitchell, Parren J.	Dem	Md.	5	5
10th	Fauntroy, Walter E.	Dem	D.C.	5	4
11th	Neal, Stephen L.	Dem	N.C.	3	3
12th	Patterson, Jerry M.	Dem	Cal.	3	3
13th	Blanchard, James J.	Dem	Mich.	3	3
14th	Hubbard, Carroll Jr.	Dem	Ky.	3	3
15th	LaFalce, John J.	Dem	N.Y.	3	3
16th	Spellman, Gladys Noon	Dem	Md.	3	3
17th	AuCoin, Les	Dem	Ore.	3	3
18th	Evans, David W.	Dem	Ind.	3	3
19th	D'Amours, Norman E.	Dem	N.H.	3	3
20th	Lundine, Stanley N.	Dem	N.Y.	3	3
21st	Cavanaugh, John J.	Dem	Neb.	2	2
22nd	Oakar, Mary Rose	Dem	Ohio	2	2
23rd	Mattox, James A.	Dem	Tex.	2	2
24th	Vento, Bruce F.	DFL	Minn.	2	2
25th	Barnard, D. Douglas Jr.	Dem	Ga.	2	2
26th	Watkins, Wesley W.	Dem	Okla.	2	2
27th	Garcia, Robert	Dem	N.Y.	2	2
28th	Lowry, Michael E.	Dem	Wash.	1	1

Minority

Rank	Name	Party	State	Terms in: House	Terms in: Comm.
RM	Stanton, J. William	Rep	Ohio	8	8
2nd	Wylie, Chalmers P.	Rep	Ohio	7	7
3rd	McKinney, Stewart B.	Rep	Conn.	5	5
4th	Hansen, George V.	Rep	Ida.	5	3
5th	Hyde, Henry J.	Rep	Ill.	3	3
6th	Kelly, Richard	Rep	Fla.	3	3
7th	Leach, James A. S.	Rep	Iowa	2	2
8th	Evans, Thomas B. Jr.	Rep	Del.	2	2
9th	Green, S. William	Rep	N.Y.	2	2
10th	Paul, Ronald E.	Rep	Tex.	2	*2 1
11th	Bethune, Edwin R.	Rep	Ark.	1	1
12th	Shumway, Norman D.	Rep	Cal.	1	1
13th	Campbell, Carroll A. Jr.	Rep	S.C.	1	1
14th	Ritter, Donald L.	Rep	Penn.	1	1
15th	Hinson, Jon C.	Rep	Miss.	1	1
16th	Porter, John Edward	Rep	Ill.	1	1

*2: Member's 2nd period of service on the committee.

Note: Delegate Walter E. Fauntroy (Dem-D.C.) was allowed to accrue seniority, but was not included in the committee's original party ratio of 27 Democrats and 16 Republicans.

Vacancy Filled:

Minority: 16th seat by Porter on Feb. 7,1980.

Departures from the House:	**Majority**			**Minority**		
Defeated for Reelection	Ashley, Thomas L.	Ohio	Dem	None		
Defeated for Renomination	None			Kelly, Richard	Fla.	Rep
Retired	Cavanaugh, John J.	Neb.	Dem	None		
	Hanley, James M.	N.Y.	Dem			
	Moorhead, William S.	Penn.	Dem			
Departures from Committee:						
Moved to Appropriations	AuCoin, Les	Ore.	Dem	Campbell, Carroll A. Jr.	S.C.	Rep
	Watkins, Wesley W.	Okla.	Dem	Green, S. William	N.Y.	Rep
				Porter, John Edward	Ill.	Rep
Moved to Energy & Commerce	None			Ritter, Donald L.	Penn.	Rep

BANKING, FINANCE AND URBAN AFFAIRS / 97th Congress

Service Dates of Committee Chair: Jan. 28,1981-Jan. 3,1983
Service Dates of Majority Members: Jan. 28,1981-Jan. 3,1983
Service Dates of Minority Members: Jan. 28,1981-Jan. 3,1983

Majority

Rank	Name	Party	State	Terms in: House	Terms in: Comm.
Chr	St Germain, Fernand J.	Dem	R.I.	11	11
2nd	Reuss, Henry S.	Dem	Wisc.	14	14
3rd	Gonzalez, Henry B.	Dem	Tex.	11	11
4th	Minish, Joseph G.	Dem	N.J.	10	10
5th	Annunzio, Frank	Dem	Ill.	9	9
6th	Mitchell, Parren J.	Dem	Md.	6	6
7th	Fauntroy, Walter E.	Dem	D.C.	6	5
8th	Neal, Stephen L.	Dem	N.C.	4	4
9th	Patterson, Jerry M.	Dem	Cal.	4	4
10th	Blanchard, James J.	Dem	Mich.	4	4
11th	Hubbard, Carroll Jr.	Dem	Ky.	4	4
12th	LaFalce, John J.	Dem	N.Y.	4	4
13th	Spellman, Gladys Noon	Dem	Md.	4	4
14th	Evans, David W.	Dem	Ind.	4	4
15th	D'Amours, Norman E.	Dem	N.H.	4	4
16th	Lundine, Stanley N.	Dem	N.Y.	4	4
17th	Oakar, Mary Rose	Dem	Ohio	3	3
18th	Mattox, James A.	Dem	Tex.	3	3
19th	Vento, Bruce F.	Dem	Minn.	3	3
20th	Barnard, D. Douglas Jr.	Dem	Ga.	3	3
21st	Garcia, Robert	Dem	N.Y.	3	3
22nd	Lowry, Michael E.	Dem	Wash.	2	2
23rd	Schumer, Charles E.	Dem	N.Y.	1	1
24th	Frank, Barney	Dem	Mass.	1	1
25th	Patman, William N.	Dem	Tex.	1	1
26th	Coyne, William J.	Dem	Penn.	1	1

Minority

Rank	Name	Party	State	Terms in: House	Terms in: Comm.
RM	Stanton, J. William	Rep	Ohio	9	9
2nd	Wylie, Chalmers P.	Rep	Ohio	8	8
3rd	McKinney, Stewart B.	Rep	Conn.	6	6
4th	Hansen, George V.	Rep	Ida.	6	4
5th	Hyde, Henry J.	Rep	Ill.	4	4
6th	Leach, James A. S.	Rep	Iowa	3	3
7th	Evans, Thomas B. Jr.	Rep	Del.	3	3
8th	Paul, Ronald E.	Rep	Tex.	3	*2 2
9th	Bethune, Edwin R.	Rep	Ark.	2	2
10th	Shumway, Norman D.	Rep	Cal.	2	2
11th	Hinson, Jon C.	Rep	Miss.	2	2
12th	Parris, Stanford E.	Rep	Va.	2	1
13th	Weber, Ed	Rep	Ohio	1	1
14th	McCollum, Bill	Rep	Fla.	1	1
15th	Carman, Gregory W.	Rep	N.Y.	1	1
16th	Wortley, George	Rep	N.Y.	1	1
17th	Roukema, Margaret	Rep	N.J.	1	1
18th	Lowery, William	Rep	Cal.	1	1
19th	Coyne, James K.	Rep	Penn.	1	1

*2: Member's 2nd period of service on the committee.

Notes: Delegate Walter E. Fauntroy (Dem-D.C.) was allowed to accrue seniority, but was not included in the committee's party ratio of 25 Democrats and 19 Republicans. Ranking on this committee for the following member was affected by other chamber service: Henry S. Reuss (Dem-Wisc.), Chair, Joint Economic Committee.

Changes:

Majority:				
Spellman, Gladys Noon	Dem	Md.	Feb. 24,1981	Seat declared vacant; Spellman unable to resign due to a paralyzing stroke.
Hoyer, Steny H.	Dem	Md.	June 8,1981	Replaced Spellman.
Minority:				
Hinson, Jon C.	Rep	Miss.	Apr. 13,1981	Resigned and retired.
Bereuter, Douglas K.	Rep	Neb.	Apr. 29,1981	Replaced Hinson.
Hyde, Henry J.	Rep	Ill.	June 24,1981	Moved to Foreign Affairs.
Dreier, David	Rep	Cal.	July 24,1981	Replaced Hyde.

Departures from the House:	Majority			Minority		
Appointed Federal Judge	None			Carman, Gregory W.	N.Y.	Rep
Elected Governor	Blanchard, James J.	Mich.	Dem	None		
Elected State Attorney General	Mattox, James A.	Tex.	Dem	None		
Defeated for Reelection	None			Coyne, James K.	Penn.	Rep
				Evans, Thomas B. Jr.	Del.	Rep
				Weber, Ed	Ohio	Rep
Defeated for Renomination	Evans, David W.	Ind.	Dem	None		
Retired	Reuss, Henry S.	Wisc.	Dem	Stanton, J. William	Ohio	Rep
Departures from Committee:						
Moved to Appropriations	Hoyer, Steny H.	Md.	Dem	None		

BANKING, FINANCE AND URBAN AFFAIRS / 98th Congress

Service Dates of Committee Chair: Jan. 6,1983-Jan. 3,1985
Service Dates of Majority Members: Jan. 6,1983-Jan. 3,1985
Service Dates of Minority Members: Jan. 6,1983-Jan. 3,1985

Majority

Rank Name	Party	State	Terms in: House	Terms in: Comm.
Chr St Germain, Fernand J.	Dem	R.I.	12	12
2nd Gonzalez, Henry B.	Dem	Tex.	12	12
3rd Minish, Joseph G.	Dem	N.J.	11	11
4th Annunzio, Frank	Dem	Ill.	10	10
5th Mitchell, Parren J.	Dem	Md.	7	7
6th Fauntroy, Walter E.	Dem	D.C.	7	6
7th Neal, Stephen L.	Dem	N.C.	5	5
8th Patterson, Jerry M.	Dem	Cal.	5	5
9th Hubbard, Carroll Jr.	Dem	Ky.	5	5
10th LaFalce, John J.	Dem	N.Y.	5	5
11th D'Amours, Norman E.	Dem	N.H.	5	5
12th Lundine, Stanley N.	Dem	N.Y.	5	5
13th Oakar, Mary Rose	Dem	Ohio	4	4
14th Vento, Bruce F.	Dem	Minn.	4	4
15th Barnard, D. Douglas Jr.	Dem	Ga.	4	4
16th Garcia, Robert	Dem	N.Y.	4	4
17th Lowry, Michael E.	Dem	Wash.	3	3
18th Schumer, Charles E.	Dem	N.Y.	2	2
19th Frank, Barney	Dem	Mass.	2	2
20th Patman, William N.	Dem	Tex.	2	2
21st Coyne, William J.	Dem	Penn.	2	2
22nd Roemer, Charles (Buddy)	Dem	La.	2	1
23rd Lehman, Richard H.	Dem	Cal.	1	1
24th Morrison, Bruce A.	Dem	Conn.	1	1
25th Cooper, Jim	Dem	Tenn.	1	1
26th Kaptur, Marcy	Dem	Ohio	1	1
27th Erdreich, Ben	Dem	Ala.	1	1
28th Levin, Sander M.	Dem	Mich.	1	1
29th Carper, Thomas R.	Dem	Del.	1	1
30th Torres, Esteban Edward	Dem	Cal.	1	1

Minority

Rank Name	Party	State	Terms in: House	Terms in: Comm.
RM Wylie, Chalmers P.	Rep	Ohio	9	9
2nd McKinney, Stewart B.	Rep	Conn.	7	7
3rd Hansen, George V.	Rep	Ida.	7	5
4th Leach, James A. S.	Rep	Iowa	4	4
5th Paul, Ronald E.	Rep	Tex.	4	*2 3
6th Bethune, Edwin R.	Rep	Ark.	3	3
7th Shumway, Norman D.	Rep	Cal.	3	3
8th Parris, Stanford E.	Rep	Va.	3	2
9th McCollum, Bill	Rep	Fla.	2	2
10th Wortley, George	Rep	N.Y.	2	2
11th Roukema, Margaret	Rep	N.J.	2	2
12th Lowery, William	Rep	Cal.	2	2
13th Bereuter, Douglas K.	Rep	Neb.	3	2
14th Dreier, David	Rep	Cal.	2	2
15th Hiler, John P.	Rep	Ind.	2	1
16th Ridge, Thomas J.	Rep	Penn.	1	1
17th Bartlett, Steve	Rep	Tex.	1	1

*2: Member's 2nd period of service on the committee.

Notes: Delegate Walter E. Fauntroy (Dem-D.C.) was allowed to accrue seniority, but was not included in the committee's original party ratio of 29 Democrats and 17 Republicans. The committee was expanded and the party ratio changed to 30 Democrats (excluding Fauntroy) and 18 Republicans on May 16,1984.

Additions:

Majority:	31st	Kleczka, Gerald D.	Dem	Wisc.	May 16,1984
Minority:	18th	Edwards, W.J. (Jack)	Rep	Ala.	May 17,1984

Departures from the House:	Majority			Minority		
Defeated for Reelection	Minish, Joseph G.	N.J.	Dem	Hansen, George V.	Ida.	Rep
	Patman, William N.	Tex.	Dem			
	Patterson, Jerry M.	Cal.	Dem			
Lost Election to U.S. Senate	D'Amours, Norman E.	N.H.	Dem	Bethune, Edwin R.	Ark.	Rep
Lost Nomination to U.S. Senate	None			Paul, Ronald E.	Tex.	Rep
Retired	None			Edwards, W.J. (Jack)	Ala.	Rep

Departures from Committee:

Moved to Ways & Means	Coyne, William J.	Penn. Dem		
Moved to Appropriations	None		Lowery, William	Cal. Rep
Moved to Merchant Marine & Fisheries	Lowry, Michael E.	Wash. Dem		

BANKING, FINANCE AND URBAN AFFAIRS / 99th Congress

Service Dates of Committee Chair: Jan. 7,1985-Jan. 3,1987
Service Dates of Majority Members: Jan. 30,1985-Jan. 3,1987
Service Dates of Minority Members: Jan. 30,1985-Jan. 3,1987

Majority

Rank	Name	Party	State	Terms in: House	Terms in: Comm.
Chr	St Germain, Fernand J.	Dem	R.I.	13	13
2nd	Gonzalez, Henry B.	Dem	Tex.	13	13
3rd	Annunzio, Frank	Dem	Ill.	11	11
4th	Mitchell, Parren J.	Dem	Md.	8	8
5th	Fauntroy, Walter E.	Dem	D.C.	8	7
6th	Neal, Stephen L.	Dem	N.C.	6	6
7th	Hubbard, Carroll Jr.	Dem	Ky.	6	6
8th	LaFalce, John J.	Dem	N.Y.	6	6
9th	Lundine, Stanley N.	Dem	N.Y.	6	6
10th	Oakar, Mary Rose	Dem	Ohio	5	5
11th	Vento, Bruce F.	Dem	Minn.	5	5
12th	Barnard, D. Douglas Jr.	Dem	Ga.	5	5
13th	Garcia, Robert	Dem	N.Y.	5	5
14th	Schumer, Charles E.	Dem	N.Y.	3	3
15th	Frank, Barney	Dem	Mass.	3	3
16th	Roemer, Charles (Buddy)	Dem	La.	3	2
17th	Lehman, Richard H.	Dem	Cal.	2	2
18th	Morrison, Bruce A.	Dem	Conn.	2	2
19th	Cooper, Jim	Dem	Tenn.	2	2
20th	Kaptur, Marcy	Dem	Ohio	2	2
21st	Erdreich, Ben	Dem	Ala.	2	2
22nd	Levin, Sander M.	Dem	Mich.	2	2
23rd	Carper, Thomas R.	Dem	Del.	2	2
24th	Torres, Esteban Edward	Dem	Cal.	2	2
25th	Kleczka, Gerald D.	Dem	Wisc.	2	2
26th	Nelson, Bill	Dem	Fla.	4	1
27th	Kanjorski, Paul E.	Dem	Penn.	1	1
28th	Gordon, Bart	Dem	Tenn.	1	1
29th	Manton, Thomas J.	Dem	N.Y.	1	1
30th	Fuster, Jaime B.	Dem	P.R.	1	1

Minority

Rank	Name	Party	State	Terms in: House	Terms in: Comm.
RM	Wylie, Chalmers P.	Rep	Ohio	10	10
2nd	McKinney, Stewart B.	Rep	Conn.	8	8
3rd	Leach, James A. S.	Rep	Iowa	5	5
4th	Shumway, Norman D.	Rep	Cal.	4	4
5th	Parris, Stanford E.	Rep	Va.	4	3
6th	McCollum, Bill	Rep	Fla.	3	3
7th	Wortley, George	Rep	N.Y.	3	3
8th	Roukema, Margaret	Rep	N.J.	3	3
9th	Bereuter, Douglas K.	Rep	Neb.	4	3
10th	Dreier, David	Rep	Cal.	3	3
11th	Hiler, John P.	Rep	Ind.	3	2
12th	Ridge, Thomas J.	Rep	Penn.	2	2
13th	Bartlett, Steve	Rep	Tex.	2	2
14th	Roth, Tobias A.	Rep	Wisc.	4	1
15th	Chandler, Rodney	Rep	Wash.	2	1
16th	McCandless, Alfred A.	Rep	Cal.	2	1
17th	Grotberg, John E.	Rep	Ill.	1	1
18th	Kolbe, Jim	Rep	Ariz.	1	1
19th	McMillan, J. Alex	Rep	N.C.	1	1

Note: Delegate Walter E. Fauntroy (Dem-D.C.) and Jaime B. Fuster (Dem-P.R.), the Resident Commissioner of Puerto Rico, were allowed to accrue seniority, but were not included in the committee's original party ratio of 28 Democrats and 19 Republicans.

Changes:

Minority:

Grotberg, John E.	Rep	Ill.	Nov. 15,1986	Died in office.

	Majority		Minority	
Departures from the House:				
Elected Lt. Governor	Lundine, Stanley N.	N.Y. Dem	None	
Lost Nomination for Lt. Governor	Mitchell, Parren J.	Md. Dem	None	
Departures from Committee:				
Moved to Ways & Means	Levin, Sander M.	Mich. Dem	Chandler, Rodney	Wash. Rep
Moved to Foreign Affairs	Fuster, Jaime B.	P.R. Dem	None	
Moved to Energy & Commerce	Cooper, Jim	Tenn. Dem	None	
Moved to Appropriations	Kolbe, Jim	Ariz. Dem	None	

BANKING, FINANCE AND URBAN AFFAIRS / 100th Congress

Service Dates of Committee Chair: Jan. 8,1987-Jan. 3,1989
Service Dates of Majority Members: Jan. 22,1987-Jan. 3,1989
Service Dates of Minority Members: Jan. 21,1987-Jan. 3,1989

Majority

Rank	Name	Party	State	Terms in: House	Terms in: Comm.
Chr	St Germain, Fernand J.	Dem	R.I.	14	14
2nd	Gonzalez, Henry B.	Dem	Tex.	14	14
3rd	Annunzio, Frank	Dem	Ill.	12	12
4th	Fauntroy, Walter E.	Dem	D.C.	9	8
5th	Neal, Stephen L.	Dem	N.C.	7	7
6th	Hubbard, Carroll Jr.	Dem	Ky.	7	7
7th	LaFalce, John J.	Dem	N.Y.	7	7
8th	Oakar, Mary Rose	Dem	Ohio	6	6
9th	Vento, Bruce F.	DFL	Minn.	6	6
10th	Barnard, D. Douglas Jr.	Dem	Ga.	6	6
11th	Garcia, Robert	Dem	N.Y.	6	6
12th	Schumer, Charles E.	Dem	N.Y.	4	4
13th	Frank, Barney	Dem	Mass.	4	4
14th	Roemer, Charles (Buddy)	Dem	La.	4	3
15th	Lehman, Richard H.	Dem	Cal.	3	3
16th	Morrison, Bruce A.	Dem	Conn.	3	3
17th	Kaptur, Marcy	Dem	Ohio	3	3
18th	Erdreich, Ben	Dem	Ala.	3	3
19th	Carper, Thomas R.	Dem	Del.	3	3
20th	Torres, Esteban Edward	Dem	Cal.	3	3
21st	Kleczka, Gerald D.	Dem	Wisc.	3	3
22nd	Nelson, Bill	Dem	Fla.	5	2
23rd	Kanjorski, Paul E.	Dem	Penn.	2	2
24th	Gordon, Bart	Dem	Tenn.	2	2
25th	Manton, Thomas J.	Dem	N.Y.	2	2
26th	Patterson, Elizabeth J.	Dem	S.C.	1	1
27th	McMillen, C. Thomas	Dem	Md.	1	1
28th	Kennedy, Joseph P. II	Dem	Mass.	1	1
29th	Flake, Floyd H.	Dem	N.Y.	1	1
30th	Mfume, Kweisi	Dem	Md.	1	1
31st	Price, David E.	Dem	N.C.	1	1

Minority

Rank	Name	Party	State	Terms in: House	Terms in: Comm.
RM	Wylie, Chalmers P.	Rep	Ohio	11	11
2nd	McKinney, Stewart B.	Rep	Conn.	9	9
3rd	Leach, James A. S.	Rep	Iowa	6	6
4th	Shumway, Norman D.	Rep	Cal.	5	5
5th	Parris, Stanford E.	Rep	Va.	5	4
6th	McCollum, Bill	Rep	Fla.	4	4
7th	Wortley, George	Rep	N.Y.	4	4
8th	Roukema, Margaret	Rep	N.J.	4	4
9th	Bereuter, Douglas K.	Rep	Neb.	5	4
10th	Dreier, David	Rep	Cal.	4	4
11th	Hiler, John P.	Rep	Ind.	4	3
12th	Ridge, Thomas J.	Rep	Penn.	3	3
13th	Bartlett, Steve	Rep	Tex.	3	3
14th	Roth, Tobias A.	Rep	Wisc.	5	2
15th	McCandless, Alfred A.	Rep	Cal.	3	2
16th	McMillan, J. Alex	Rep	N.C.	2	2
17th	Saxton, H. James	Rep	N.J.	2	1
18th	Swindall, Patrick Lynn	Rep	Ga.	2	1
19th	Saiki, Patricia F.	Rep	Hai.	1	1
20th	Bunning, Jim	Rep	Ky.	1	1

Note: Delegate Walter E. Fauntroy (Dem-D.C.) was allowed to accrue seniority, but was not included in the committee's party ratio of 30 Democrats and 20 Republicans.

Changes:

Majority:

Gordon, Bart	Dem	Tenn.	Feb. 19,1987	Moved to Rules.
Pelosi, Nancy	Dem	Cal.	June 18,1987	Replaced Gordon.
Roemer, Charles (Buddy)	Dem	La.	Mar. 14,1988	Resigned; elected Governor of Louisiana.
Ackerman, Gary L.	Dem	N.Y.	May 18,1988	Replaced Roemer.

Minority:

McKinney, Stewart B.	Rep	Conn.	May 7,1987	Died in office.
DioGuardi, Joseph J.	Rep	N.Y.	June 18,1987	Replaced McKinney.

	Majority			Minority		
Departures from the House:						
Defeated for Reelection	St Germain, Fernand J.	R.I.	Dem	Swindall, Patrick Lynn	Ga.	Rep
				DioGuardi, Joseph J.	N.Y.	Rep
Retired	None			Wortley, George	N.Y.	Rep
Departures from Committee:						
Moved to Energy and Commerce	Manton, Thomas J.	N.Y.	Dem	McMillan, J. Alex	N.C.	Rep
No new assignment	Ackerman, Gary L.	N.Y.	Dem	None		

BANKING, FINANCE AND URBAN AFFAIRS / 101st Congress

Service Dates of Committee Chair: Jan. 3,1989-Jan. 3,1991
Service Dates of Majority Members: Jan. 19,1989-Jan. 3,1991
Service Dates of Minority Members: Jan. 20,1989-Jan. 3,1991

Majority

Rank Name	Party	State	Terms in: House	Terms in: Comm.
Chr Gonzalez, Henry B.	Dem	Tex.	15	15
2nd Annunzio, Frank	Dem	Ill.	13	13
3rd Fauntroy, Walter E.	Dem	D.C.	10	9
4th Neal, Stephen L.	Dem	N.C.	8	8
5th Hubbard, Carroll Jr.	Dem	Ky.	8	8
6th LaFalce, John J.	Dem	N.Y.	8	8
7th Oakar, Mary Rose	Dem	Ohio	7	7
8th Vento, Bruce F.	Dem	Minn.	7	7
9th Barnard, D. Douglas Jr.	Dem	Ga.	7	7
10th Garcia, Robert	Dem	N.Y.	7	7
11th Schumer, Charles E.	Dem	N.Y.	5	5
12th Frank, Barney	Dem	Mass.	5	5
13th Lehman, Richard H.	Dem	Cal.	4	4
14th Morrison, Bruce A.	Dem	Conn.	4	4
15th Kaptur, Marcy	Dem	Ohio	4	4
16th Erdreich, Ben	Dem	Ala.	4	4
17th Carper, Thomas R.	Dem	Del.	4	4
18th Torres, Esteban Edward	Dem	Cal.	4	4
19th Kleczka, Gerald D.	Dem	Wisc.	4	4
20th Nelson, Bill	Dem	Fla.	6	3
21st Kanjorski, Paul E.	Dem	Penn.	3	3
22nd Patterson, Elizabeth J.	Dem	S.C.	2	2
23rd McMillen, C. Thomas	Dem	Md.	2	2
24th Kennedy, Joseph P. II	Dem	Mass.	2	2
25th Flake, Floyd H.	Dem	N.Y.	2	2
26th Mfume, Kweisi	Dem	Md.	2	2
27th Price, David E.	Dem	N.C.	2	2
28th Pelosi, Nancy	Dem	Cal.	2	2
29th McDermott, James A.	Dem	Wash.	1	1
30th Hoagland, Peter	Dem	Neb.	1	1
31st Neal, Richard E.	Dem	Mass.	1	1

Minority

Rank Name	Party	State	Terms in: House	Terms in: Comm.
RM Wylie, Chalmers P.	Rep	Ohio	12	12
2nd Leach, James A. S.	Rep	Iowa	7	7
3rd Shumway, Norman D.	Rep	Cal.	6	6
4th Parris, Stanford E.	Rep	Va.	6	5
5th McCollum, Bill	Rep	Fla.	5	5
6th Roukema, Margaret	Rep	N.J.	5	5
7th Bereuter, Douglas K.	Rep	Neb.	6	5
8th Dreier, David	Rep	Cal.	5	5
9th Hiler, John P.	Rep	Ind.	5	4
10th Ridge, Thomas J.	Rep	Penn.	4	4
11th Bartlett, Steve	Rep	Tex.	4	4
12th Roth, Tobias A.	Rep	Wisc.	6	3
13th McCandless, Alfred A.	Rep	Cal.	4	3
14th Saxton, H. James	Rep	N.J.	3	2
15th Saiki, Patricia F.	Rep	Hai.	2	2
16th Bunning, Jim	Rep	Ky.	2	2
17th Baker, Richard H.	Rep	La.	2	1
18th Stearns, Cliff	Rep	Fla.	1	1
19th Gillmor, Paul E.	Rep	Ohio	1	1
20th Paxon, L. William	Rep	N.Y.	1	1

Note: Delegate Walter E. Fauntroy (Dem-D.C.) was allowed to accrue seniority, but was not included in the committee's party ratio of 30 Democrats and 20 Republicans.

Changes:

Majority:

Garcia, Robert	Dem	N.Y.	Jan. 7,1990	Resigned and retired.
McMillen, C. Thomas	Dem	Md.	Feb. 27,1990	Moved to Energy and Commerce.
Engel, Eliot L.	Dem	N.Y.	Apr. 4,1990	Replaced Garcia.
Kaptur, Marcy	Dem	Ohio	May 24,1990	Moved to Appropriations.
Weiss, Theodore S.	Dem	N.Y.	July 12,1990	Replaced McMillen.
Lantos, Tom	Dem	Cal.	July 12,1990	Replaced Kaptur.

Departures from the House:	Majority			Minority		
Defeated for Reelection	None			Hiler, John P.	Ind.	Rep
				Parris, Stanford E.	Va.	Rep
Lost Election to U.S. Senate	None			Saiki, Patricia F.	Hai.	Rep
Lost Election for Governor	Morrison, Bruce A.	Conn.	Dem	None		
Lost Nomination for Governor	Nelson, Bill	Fla.	Dem	None		
Lost Mayoral Election	Fauntroy, Walter E.	D.C.	Dem	None		
Retired	None			Shumway, Norman D.	Cal.	Rep

Departures from Committee:

Moved to Energy & Commerce	Lehman, Richard H.	Cal.	Dem	None		
Moved to Appropriations	Price, David E.	N.C.	Dem	None		
Moved to Appropriations; Standards of Official Conduct	Pelosi, Nancy	Cal.	Dem	None		
Moved to Standards of Official Conduct; Ways & Means	McDermott, James A.	Wash.	Dem	Bunning, Jim	Ky.	Rep
Moved to Rules	None			Dreier, David	Cal.	Rep
Moved to Armed Services	None			Saxton, H. James	N.J.	Rep
No new assignment	Engel, Eliot L.	N.Y.	Dem	None		
	Lantos, Tom	Cal.	Dem			

BANKING, FINANCE AND URBAN AFFAIRS / 102nd Congress

Service Dates of Committee Chair: Jan. 24,1991-Jan. 3,1993
Service Dates of Majority Members: Jan. 24,1991-Jan. 3,1993
Service Dates of Minority Members: Jan. 24,1991-Jan. 3,1993

Majority

Rank	Name	Party	State	Terms in: House	Terms in: Comm.
Chr	Gonzalez, Henry B.	Dem	Tex.	16	16
2nd	Annunzio, Frank	Dem	Ill.	14	14
3rd	Neal, Stephen L.	Dem	N.C.	9	9
4th	Hubbard, Carroll Jr.	Dem	Ky.	9	9
5th	LaFalce, John J.	Dem	N.Y.	9	9
6th	Oakar, Mary Rose	Dem	Ohio	8	8
7th	Vento, Bruce F.	Dem	Minn.	8	8
8th	Barnard, D. Douglas Jr.	Dem	Ga.	8	8
9th	Schumer, Charles E.	Dem	N.Y.	6	6
10th	Frank, Barney	Dem	Mass.	6	6
11th	Erdreich, Ben	Dem	Ala.	5	5
12th	Carper, Thomas R.	Dem	Del.	5	5
13th	Torres, Esteban Edward	Dem	Cal.	5	5
14th	Kleczka, Gerald D.	Dem	Wisc.	5	5
15th	Kanjorski, Paul E.	Dem	Penn.	4	4
16th	Patterson, Elizabeth J.	Dem	S.C.	3	3
17th	Kennedy, Joseph P. II	Dem	Mass.	3	3
18th	Flake, Floyd H.	Dem	N.Y.	3	3
19th	Mfume, Kweisi	Dem	Md.	3	3
20th	Hoagland, Peter	Dem	Neb.	2	2
21st	Neal, Richard E.	Dem	Mass.	2	2
22nd	Luken, Charles	Dem	Ohio	1	1
23rd	Waters, Maxine	Dem	Cal.	1	1
24th	LaRocco, Larry	Dem	Ida.	1	1
25th	Orton, Bill	Dem	Utah	1	1
26th	Bacchus, Jim	Dem	Fla.	1	1
27th	Moran, James P. Jr.	Dem	Va.	1	1
28th	Cox, John W. Jr.	Dem	Ill.	1	1
29th	Weiss, Theodore S.	Dem	N.Y.	8	*T 2
30th	Slattery, Jim	Dem	Kans.	5	*T 1
31st	Ackerman, Gary L.	Dem	N.Y.	5	*T 1

Minority

Rank	Name	Party	State	Terms in: House	Terms in: Comm.
RM	Wylie, Chalmers P.	Rep	Ohio	13	13
2nd	Leach, James A. S.	Rep	Iowa	8	8
3rd	McCollum, Bill	Rep	Fla.	6	6
4th	Roukema, Margaret	Rep	N.J.	6	6
5th	Bereuter, Douglas K.	Rep	Neb.	7	6
6th	Ridge, Thomas J.	Rep	Penn.	5	5
7th	Bartlett, Steve	Rep	Tex.	5	5
8th	Roth, Tobias A.	Rep	Wisc.	7	4
9th	McCandless, Alfred A.	Rep	Cal.	5	4
10th	Baker, Richard H.	Rep	La.	3	2
11th	Stearns, Cliff	Rep	Fla.	2	2
12th	Gillmor, Paul E.	Rep	Ohio	2	2
13th	Paxon, L. William	Rep	N.Y.	2	2
14th	Duncan, John J. Jr.	Rep	Tenn.	2	1
15th	Campbell, Tom	Rep	Cal.	2	1
16th	Hancock, Melton D.	Rep	Mo.	2	1
17th	Riggs, Frank	Rep	Cal.	1	1
18th	Nussle, Jim	Rep	Iowa	1	1
19th	Armey, Richard	Rep	Tex.	4	1
20th	Thomas, Craig	Rep	Wyo.	2	1

Third Party:

Name	Party	State	Terms in: House	Terms in: Comm.
Sanders, Bernard	Ind	Vt.	1	1

*T: Temporary member of the committee.

Vacancies Filled:

Minority: 19th and 20th seats by Armey and Thomas respectively on Feb. 6,1991.

Note: Bernard Sanders (Ind-Vt.) was elected to the 102nd Congress as an Independent. Assigned to the committee by the Democratic Caucus on Jan. 24,1991, he was not allowed to accrue seniority, nor was he included in the committee's party ratio.

Changes:

Majority:

Weiss, Theodore S.	Dem	N.Y.	Sep. 14,1992	Died in office.

Minority:

Bartlett, Steve	Rep	Tex.	Mar. 11,1991	Resigned House; ran for Mayor of Dallas.
Johnson, Sam	Rep	Tex.	June 7,1991	Replaced Bartlett.

BUDGET

Jurisdiction, 1974

Established by Public Law 93-344, the Congressional Budget and Impoundment Control Act of 1974, 93rd Congress, Second Session, July 12, 1974 (88 Statutes 297, 300):

[Section 101.(c)]

(c) Rule XI of the Rules of the House of Representatives is amended by redesignating clauses 5 through 33 as clauses 6 through 34, respectively, and by inserting after clause 4 the following new clause:

Committee on the Budget.

(a) All concurrent resolutions on the budget (as defined in section 3(a) (4) of the Congressional Budget Act of 1974) and other matters required to be referred to the committee under titles III and IV of that Act.
(b) The committee shall have the duty--

   (1) to report the matters required to be reported by it under titles III and IV of the Congressional Budget Act of 1974;
   (2) to make continuing studies of the effect on budget outlays of relevant existing and proposed legislation and to report the results of such studies to the House on a recurring basis;
   (3) to request and evaluate continuing studies of tax expenditures, to devise methods of coordinating tax expenditures, policies, and programs with direct budget outlays, and to report the results of such studies to the House on a recurring basis; and
   (4) to review, on a continuing basis, the conduct by the Congressional Budget Office of its functions and duties.

Jurisdiction, 1992

Jurisdiction contained in Rules of the House of Representatives, (as revised to July 1, 1992):

[Rule X. 1. (e) (2)]

All concurrent resolutions on the budget (as defined in section 3(a) (4) of the Congressional Budget Act of 1974) and other matters required to be referred to the committee under titles III and IV of that Act.

[Rule X. 1. (e) (3)]

The committee shall have the duty--

(A) to report the matters required to be reported by it under titles III and IV of the Congressional Budget Act of 1974;
(B) to make continuing studies of the effect on budget outlays of relevant existing and proposed legislation and to report the results of such studies to the House on a recurring basis;
(C) to request and evaluate continuing studies of tax expenditures, to devise methods of coordinating tax expenditures, policies, and programs with direct budget outlays, and to report the results of such studies to the House on a recurring basis; and
(D) to review, on a continuing basis, the conduct by the Congressional Budget Office of its functions and duties.

[Rule X. 3. (b)]

The Committee on the Budget shall have the function of--

(1) making continuing studies of the effect on budget outlays of relevant existing and proposed legislation, and reporting the results of such studies to the House on a recurring basis; and
(2) requesting and evaluating continuing studies of tax expenditures, devising methods of coordinating tax expenditures, policies, and programs with direct budget outlays, and reporting the results of such studies to the House on a recurring basis.

[Rule X. 4. (b)]

The Committee on the Budget shall have the duty--

(1) to review on a continuing basis the conduct by the Congressional Budget Office of its functions and duties;
(2) to hold hearings, and receive testimony from Members of Congress and such appropriate representatives of Federal departments and agencies, the general public, and national organizations as it deems desirable, in developing the first concurrent resolution on the budget for each fiscal year;
(3) to make all reports required of it by the Congressional Budget Act of 1974, including the reporting of reconciliation bills and resolutions when so required;
(4) to study on a continuing basis those provisions of law which exempt Federal agencies or any of their activities or outlays from inclusion in the Budget of the United States Government, and to report to the House from time to time its recommendations for terminating or modifying such provisions; and
(5) to study on a continuing basis proposals designed to improve and facilitate methods of congressional budget-making, and to report to the House from time to time the results of such study together with its recommendations.

Relevant provisions of the Congressional Budget and Impoundment Control Act of 1974:

[Section 3.(a)]

The term "concurrent resolution on the budget" means--

(A) a concurrent resolution setting forth the congressional budget for the United States Government for a fiscal year as provided in section 301;
(B) a concurrent resolution reaffirming or revising the congressional budget for the United States Government for a fiscal year as provided in section 310; and
(C) any other concurrent resolution revising the congressional budget for the United States Government for a fiscal year as described in section 304.

BUDGET / 93rd Congress

* Created as a standing committee on July 12,1974.

Service Dates of Committee Chair: Aug. 14,1974-Jan. 3,1975
Service Dates of Majority Members: Aug. 14,1974-Jan. 3,1975
Service Dates of Minority Members: Aug. 14,1974-Jan. 3,1975

Majority

Rank	Name	Party	State	Terms in: House	Terms in: Comm.
Chr	Ullman, Albert C.	Dem	Ore.	9	1
2nd	Whitten, Jamie L.	Dem	Miss.	17	1
3rd	Bolling, Richard W.	Dem	Mo.	13	1
4th	O'Neill, Thomas P. Jr.	Dem	Mass.	11	1
5th	Griffiths, Martha W.	Dem	Mich.	10	1
6th	Wright, James C. Jr.	Dem	Tex.	10	1
7th	Ashley, Thomas L.	Dem	Ohio	10	1
8th	Giaimo, Robert N.	Dem	Conn.	8	1
9th	Smith, Neal	Dem	Iowa	8	1
10th	Burke, James A.	Dem	Mass.	8	1
11th	O'Hara, James G.	Dem	Mich.	8	1
12th	Leggett, Robert L.	Dem	Cal.	6	1
13th	Adams, Brock	Dem	Wash.	5	1
14th	Mitchell, Parren J.	Dem	Md.	2	1

Minority

Rank	Name	Party	State	Terms in: House	Terms in: Comm.
RM	Rhodes, John J.	Rep	Ariz.	11	1
2nd	Cederberg, Elford A.	Rep	Mich.	11	1
3rd	Broyhill, Joel T.	Rep	Va.	11	1
4th	Michel, Robert H.	Rep	Ill.	9	1
5th	Latta, Delbert L.	Rep	Ohio	8	1
6th	Schneebeli, Herman T.	Rep	Penn.	8	1
7th	Broyhill, James T.	Rep	N.C.	6	1
8th	Clawson, Del M.	Rep	Cal.	6	1
9th	Hastings, James F.	Rep	N.Y.	3	1

Note: Due to the nature of rotating membership on the Budget committee, the Democratic Caucus does not necessarily use committee seniority to determine rank. When in the majority, the Democratic Caucus reserves the second rank for the House Majority Leader.

Changes:

Majority:

Griffiths, Martha W.	Dem	Mich.	Dec. 31,1974	Resigned and retired.

Minority:

Broyhill, Joel T.	Rep	Va.	Dec. 31,1974	Resigned; defeated for reelection.

Departures from Committee:	Majority			Minority		
Becomes Minority Whip	None			Michel, Robert H.	Ill.	Rep
No new assignment	Bolling, Richard W.	Mo.	Dem	Rhodes, John J.	Ariz.	Rep
	Burke, James A.	Mass.	Dem			
	Ullman, Albert C.	Ore.	Dem			
	Whitten, Jamie L.	Miss.	Dem			

BUDGET / 94th Congress

Service Dates of Committee Chair: Feb. 5,1975-Jan. 3,1977
Service Dates of Majority Members: Feb. 5,1975-Jan. 3,1977
Service Dates of Minority Members: Jan. 28,1975-Jan. 3,1977

Majority

Rank	Name	Party	State	Terms in: House	Terms in: Comm.
Chr	Adams, Brock	Dem	Wash.	6	2
2nd	O'Neill, Thomas P. Jr.	Dem	Mass.	12	2
3rd	Wright, James C. Jr.	Dem	Tex.	11	2
4th	Ashley, Thomas L.	Dem	Ohio	11	2
5th	Giaimo, Robert N.	Dem	Conn.	9	2
6th	Smith, Neal	Dem	Iowa	9	2
7th	O'Hara, James G.	Dem	Mich.	9	2
8th	Leggett, Robert L.	Dem	Cal.	7	2
9th	Mitchell, Parren J.	Dem	Md.	3	2
10th	Burleson, Omar T.	Dem	Tex.	15	1
11th	Landrum, Phillip M.	Dem	Ga.	12	1
12th	Gibbons, Sam M.	Dem	Fla.	7	1
13th	Mink, Patsy T.	Dem	Hai.	6	1
14th	Stokes, Louis	Dem	Ohio	4	1
15th	Runnels, Harold L.	Dem	N.M.	3	1
16th	Holtzman, Elizabeth	Dem	N.Y.	2	1
17th	Derrick, Butler C. Jr.	Dem	S.C.	1 *1	1

Minority

Rank	Name	Party	State	Terms in: House	Terms in: Comm.
RM	Latta, Delbert L.	Rep	Ohio	9	2
2nd	Cederberg, Elford A.	Rep	Mich.	12	2
3rd	Schneebeli, Herman T.	Rep	Penn.	9	2
4th	Broyhill, James T.	Rep	N.C.	7	2
5th	Clawson, Del M.	Rep	Cal.	7	2
6th	Hastings, James F.	Rep	N.Y.	4	2
7th	Shriver, Garner E.	Rep	Kans.	8	1
8th	Conable, Barber B. Jr.	Rep	N.Y.	6	1

*1: Member's 1st period of service on the committee.

Note: Due to the nature of rotating membership on the Budget committee, the Democratic Caucus does not necessarily use committee seniority to determine rank. When in the majority, the Democratic Caucus reserves the second rank for the House Majority Leader.

Changes:

Minority:

Hastings, James F.	Rep	N.Y.	Jan. 20,1976	Resigned; became President of Associated Industries of New York State.
Holt, Marjorie S.	Rep	Md.	Jan. 27,1976	Replaced Hastings.
Clawson, Del M.	Rep	Cal.	Sep. 14,1976	Left committee; no new assignment.
Rousselot, John H.	Rep	Cal.	Sep. 22,1976	Replaced Clawson.

Departures from the House:	Majority			Minority		
Appointed Secretary of Transportation	Adams, Brock	Wash.	Dem	None		
Defeated for Reelection	None			Shriver, Garner E.	Kans.	Rep
Lost Nomination to U.S. Senate	O'Hara, James G.	Mich.	Dem	None		
Retired	Landrum, Phillip M.	Ga.	Dem	Schneebeli, Herman T.	Penn.	Rep
	Mink, Patsy T.	Hai.	Dem			
Departures from Committee:						
Became Speaker of the House	O'Neill, Thomas P. Jr.	Mass.	Dem			
Became Chair of Small Business	Smith, Neal	Iowa	Dem			
No new assignment	Gibbons, Sam M.	Fla.	Dem	Cederberg, Elford A.	Mich.	Rep
	Runnels, Harold L.	N.M.	Dem			

BUDGET / 95th Congress

Service Dates of Committee Chair: Jan. 11,1977-Jan. 3,1979
Service Dates of Majority Members: Jan. 11,1977-Jan. 3,1979
Service Dates of Minority Members: Jan. 11,1977-Jan. 3,1979

Majority

Rank Name	Party	State	Terms in: House	Terms in: Comm.
Chr Giaimo, Robert N.	Dem	Conn.	10	3
2nd Wright, James C. Jr.	Dem	Tex.	12	3
3rd Ashley, Thomas L.	Dem	Ohio	12	3
4th Leggett, Robert L.	Dem	Cal.	8	3
5th Mitchell, Parren J.	Dem	Md.	4	3
6th Burleson, Omar T.	Dem	Tex.	16	2
7th Stokes, Louis	Dem	Ohio	5	2
8th Holtzman, Elizabeth	Dem	N.Y.	3	2
9th Derrick, Butler C. Jr.	Dem	S.C.	2	*1 2
10th Pike, Otis G.	Dem	N.Y.	9	1
11th Fraser, Donald M.	DFL	Minn.	8	1
12th Obey, David R.	Dem	Wisc.	5	1
13th Lehman, William	Dem	Fla.	3	1
14th Simon, Paul M.	Dem	Ill.	2	1
15th Mineta, Norman Y.	Dem	Cal.	2	1
16th Fisher, Joseph L.	Dem	Va.	2	1
17th Mattox, James A.	Dem	Tex.	1	1

Minority

Rank Name	Party	State	Terms in: House	Terms in: Comm.
RM Latta, Delbert L.	Rep	Ohio	10	3
2nd Broyhill, James T.	Rep	N.C.	8	3
3rd Conable, Barber B. Jr.	Rep	N.Y.	7	2
4th Holt, Marjorie S.	Rep	Md.	3	2
5th Rousselot, John H.	Rep	Cal.	6	2
6th Duncan, John J.	Rep	Tenn.	7	1
7th Burgener, Clair W.	Rep	Cal.	3	1
8th Regula, Ralph S.	Rep	Ohio	3	1

*1: Member's 1st period of service on the committee.

Note: Due to the nature of rotating membership on the Budget committee, the Democratic Caucus does not necessarily use committee seniority to determine rank. When in the majority, the Democratic Caucus reserves the second rank for the House Majority Leader.

Changes:

Majority:

Burleson, Omar T.	Dem	Tex.	Dec. 31,1978	Resigned and retired.

	Majority		Minority	
Departures from the House:				
Lost Nomination to U.S. Senate	Fraser, Donald M.	Minn. DFL	None	
Retired	Leggett, Robert L.	Cal. Dem	None	
	Pike, Otis G.	N.Y. Dem		
Departures from Committee:				
Moved to Rules	Derrick, Butler C. Jr.	S.C. Dem	None	
Moved to Appropriations	Lehman, William	Fla. Dem	None	
Returned to Small Business	Mitchell, Parren J.	Md. Dem	None	
No new assignment	Fisher, Joseph L.	Va. Dem	Rousselot, John H.	Cal. Rep

BUDGET / 96th Congress

Service Dates of Committee Chair: Jan. 24,1979-Jan. 3,1981
Service Dates of Majority Members: Jan. 24,1979-Jan. 3,1981
Service Dates of Minority Members: Jan. 24,1979-Jan. 3,1981

Majority

Rank Name	Party	State	Terms in: House	Terms in: Comm.
Chr Giaimo, Robert N.	Dem	Conn.	11	4
2nd Wright, James C. Jr.	Dem	Tex.	13	4
3rd Ashley, Thomas L.	Dem	Ohio	13	4
4th Stokes, Louis	Dem	Ohio	6	3
5th Holtzman, Elizabeth	Dem	N.Y.	4	3
6th Obey, David R.	Dem	Wisc.	6	2
7th Simon, Paul M.	Dem	Ill.	3	2
8th Mineta, Norman Y.	Dem	Cal.	3	2
9th Mattox, James A.	Dem	Tex.	2	2
10th Jones, James R.	Dem	Okla.	4	1
11th Solarz, Stephen J.	Dem	N.Y.	3	1
12th Brodhead, William M.	Dem	Mich.	3	1
13th Wirth, Timothy E.	Dem	Colo.	3	1
14th Panetta, Leon E.	Dem	Cal.	2	1
15th Gephardt, Richard A.	Dem	Mo.	2	1
16th Nelson, Bill	Dem	Fla.	1	1
17th Gray, William H. III	Dem	Penn.	1	*1 1

Minority

Rank Name	Party	State	Terms in: House	Terms in: Comm.
RM Latta, Delbert L.	Rep	Ohio	11	4
2nd Broyhill, James T.	Rep	N.C.	9	4
3rd Conable, Barber B. Jr.	Rep	N.Y.	8	3
4th Holt, Marjorie S.	Rep	Md.	4	3
5th Duncan, John J.	Rep	Tenn.	8	2
6th Burgener, Clair W.	Rep	Cal.	4	2
7th Regula, Ralph S.	Rep	Ohio	4	2
8th Shuster, E. G. (Bud)	Rep	Penn.	4	1

*1: Member's 1st period of service on the committee.

Note: Due to the nature of rotating membership on the Budget committee, the Democratic Caucus does not necessarily use committee seniority to determine rank. When in the majority, the Democratic Caucus reserves the second rank for the House Majority Leader.

Changes:

Minority:

Duncan, John J.	Rep	Tenn.	Jan. 31,1979	Left committee; no new assignment.
Frenzel, William E.	Rep	Minn.	Jan. 31,1979	Replaced Duncan.
Burgener, Clair W.	Rep	Cal.	Feb. 8,1979	Left committee; no new assignment.
Rudd, Eldon D.	Rep	Ariz.	Feb. 8,1979	Replaced Burgener.

	Majority		Minority	
Departures from the House:				
Defeated for Reelection	Ashley, Thomas L.	Ohio Dem	None	
Lost Election to U.S. Senate	Holtzman, Elizabeth	N.Y. Dem	None	
Retired	Giaimo, Robert N.	Conn. Dem	None	
Departures from Committee:				
Moved to Appropriations	Gray, William H. III	Penn. Dem		
Moved to Energy & Commerce	None		Broyhill, James T.	N.C. Rep
Became Chair of Standards of Official Conduct	Stokes, Louis	Ohio Dem	None	
No new assignment	Brodhead, William M.	Mich. Dem	Holt, Marjorie S.	Md. Rep
			Conable, Barber B. Jr.	N.Y. Rep

BUDGET / 97th Congress

Service Dates of Committee Chair: Jan. 28,1981-Jan. 3,1983
Service Dates of Majority Members: Jan. 28,1981-Jan. 3,1983
Service Dates of Minority Members: Jan. 28,1981-Jan. 3,1983

Majority

Rank	Name	Party	State	Terms in: House	Terms in: Comm.
Chr	Jones, James R.	Dem	Okla.	5	2
2nd	Wright, James C. Jr.	Dem	Tex.	14	5
3rd	Obey, David R.	Dem	Wisc.	7	3
4th	Simon, Paul M.	Dem	Ill.	4	3
5th	Mineta, Norman Y.	Dem	Cal.	4	3
6th	Mattox, James A.	Dem	Tex.	3	3
7th	Solarz, Stephen J.	Dem	N.Y.	4	2
8th	Wirth, Timothy E.	Dem	Colo.	4	2
9th	Panetta, Leon E.	Dem	Cal.	3	2
10th	Gephardt, Richard A.	Dem	Mo.	3	2
11th	Nelson, Bill	Dem	Fla.	2	2
12th	Aspin, Les	Dem	Wisc.	6	1
13th	Hefner, W. G. (Bill)	Dem	N.C.	4	1
14th	Downey, Thomas J.	Dem	N.Y.	4	1
15th	Benjamin, Adam Jr.	Dem	Ind.	3	1
16th	Donnelly, Brian J.	Dem	Mass.	2	1
17th	Anthony, Beryl F. Jr.	Dem	Ark.	2	1
18th	Gramm, W. Phil	Dem	Tex.	2	1

Minority

Rank	Name	Party	State	Terms in: House	Terms in: Comm.
RM	Latta, Delbert L.	Rep	Ohio	12	5
2nd	Regula, Ralph S.	Rep	Ohio	5	3
3rd	Shuster, E. G. (Bud)	Rep	Penn.	5	2
4th	Frenzel, William E.	Rep	Minn.	6	2
5th	Rudd, Eldon D.	Rep	Ariz.	3	2
6th	Trible, Paul S. Jr.	Rep	Va.	3	1
7th	Bethune, Edwin R.	Rep	Ark.	2	1
8th	Martin, Lynn M.	Rep	Ill.	1	1
9th	Smith, Albert Lee Jr.	Rep	Ala.	1	1
10th	Johnston, Eugene	Rep	N.C.	1	1
11th	Fiedler, Bobbi	Rep	Cal.	1	1
12th	Kemp, Jack F.	Rep	N.Y.	6	1

Note: Due to the nature of rotating membership on the Budget committee, the Democratic Caucus does not necessarily use committee seniority to determine rank. When in the majority, the Democratic Caucus reserves the second rank for the House Majority Leader.

Vacancy Filled:
Minority: 12th seat by Kemp on Feb. 5,1981.

Changes:

Majority:

Anthony, Beryl F. Jr.	Dem	Ark.	Oct. 7,1981	Moved to Ways and Means.
Lowry, Michael E.	Dem	Wash.	Oct. 28,1981	Replaced Anthony.
Benjamin, Adam Jr.	Dem	Ind.	Sep. 7,1982	Died in office.

Minority:

Rudd, Eldon D.	Rep	Ariz.	Feb. 5,1981	Left committee; no new assignment.
Martin, James G.	Rep	N.C.	Feb. 5,1981	Replaced Rudd.

Departures from the House:

	Majority			Minority		
Elected to U.S. Senate	None			Trible, Paul S. Jr.	Va.	Rep
Elected State Attorney General	Mattox, James A.	Tex.	Dem	None		
Defeated for Reelection	None			Johnston, Eugene	N.C.	Rep
				Smith, Albert Lee Jr.	Ala.	Rep

Departures from Committee:

	Majority			Minority		
Moved to Science & Technology	Mineta, Norman Y.	Cal.	Dem	None		
	Simon, Paul M.	Ill.	Dem			
Moved to Joint Economic Committee	Obey, David R.	Wisc.	Dem	None		
No new assignment	None			Martin, James G.	N.C.	Rep
				Regula, Ralph S.	Ohio	Rep

BUDGET / 98th Congress

Service Dates of Committee Chair: Jan. 6,1983-Jan. 3,1985
Service Dates of Majority Members: Jan. 6,1983-Jan. 3,1985
Service Dates of Minority Members: Jan. 6,1983-Jan. 3,1985

Majority

Rank	Name	Party	State	Terms in: House	Terms in: Comm.
Chr	Jones, James R.	Dem	Okla.	6	3
2nd	Wright, James C. Jr.	Dem	Tex.	15	6
3rd	Solarz, Stephen J.	Dem	N.Y.	5	3
4th	Wirth, Timothy E.	Dem	Colo.	5	3
5th	Panetta, Leon E.	Dem	Cal.	4	3
6th	Gephardt, Richard A.	Dem	Mo.	4	3
7th	Nelson, Bill	Dem	Fla.	3	3
8th	Aspin, Les	Dem	Wisc.	7	2
9th	Hefner, W. G. (Bill)	Dem	N.C.	5	2
10th	Downey, Thomas J.	Dem	N.Y.	5	2
11th	Donnelly, Brian J.	Dem	Mass.	3	2
12th	Lowry, Michael E.	Dem	Wash.	3	2
13th	Derrick, Butler C. Jr.	Dem	S.C.	5	*2 1
14th	Miller, George	Dem	Cal.	5	1
15th	Gray, William H. III	Dem	Penn.	3	*2 1
16th	Williams, Pat	Dem	Mont.	3	1
17th	Ferraro, Geraldine A.	Dem	N.Y.	3	1
18th	Wolpe, Howard E.	Dem	Mich.	3	1
19th	Frost, J. Martin III	Dem	Tex.	3	1
20th	Fazio, Victor H.	Dem	Cal.	3	1

Minority

Rank	Name	Party	State	Terms in: House	Terms in: Comm.
RM	Latta, Delbert L.	Rep	Ohio	13	6
2nd	Shuster, E. G. (Bud)	Rep	Penn.	6	3
3rd	Frenzel, William E.	Rep	Minn.	7	3
4th	Kemp, Jack F.	Rep	N.Y.	7	2
5th	Bethune, Edwin R.	Rep	Ark.	3	2
6th	Gramm, W. Phil	Rep	Tex.	3	2
7th	Martin, Lynn M.	Rep	Ill.	2	2
8th	Fiedler, Bobbi	Rep	Cal.	2	2
9th	Loeffler, Thomas G.	Rep	Tex.	3	1
10th	Gradison, Willis D. Jr.	Rep	Ohio	5	1
11th	Mack, Connie III	Rep	Fla.	1	1

*2: Member's 2nd period of service on the committee.

Notes: Due to the nature of rotating membership on the Budget committee, the Democratic Caucus does not necessarily use committee seniority to determine rank. When in the majority, the Democratic Caucus reserves the second rank for the House Majority Leader. W. Phil Gramm of Texas switched from the Democratic Party to the Republican Party on Jan. 5,1983. Upon Gramm's victory in a special election to fill his own vacancy, the Republican Conference recognized his previous service on the committee and assigned him the 6th rank on Mar. 1,1983.

Addition:

	Name	Party	State	Date	Note
Minority:	Gramm, W. Phil	Rep	Tex.	Mar. 1,1983	Ranked 6th on committee.

	Majority			Minority		
Departures from the House:						
Elected to U.S. Senate	None			Gramm, W. Phil	Tex.	Rep
Lost Election for Vice President	Ferraro, Geraldine A.	N.Y.	Dem	None		
Lost Election to U.S. Senate	None			Bethune, Edwin R.	Ark.	Rep
Departures from Committee:						
Becomes Chair of Armed Services	Aspin, Les	Wisc.	Dem	None		
Moves to Ways and Means	Donnelly, Brian J.	Mass.	Dem	None		
Moves to Banking, Housing & Urban Affairs	Nelson, Bill	Fla.	Dem	None		
Returns to House Administration	Panetta, Leon E.	Cal.	Dem	None		
Moves to Education & Labor; returns to Post Office & Civil Service	Solarz, Stephen J.	N.Y.	Dem	None		
Returns to Science & Technology	Wirth, Timothy E.	Colo.	Dem			
No new assignment	Gephardt, Richard A.	Mo.	Dem	Frenzel, William E.	Minn.	Rep
	Jones, James R.	Okla.	Dem	Shuster, E. G. (Bud)	Penn.	Rep

BUDGET / 99th Congress

Service Dates of Committee Chair: Jan. 7,1985-Jan. 3,1987
Service Dates of Majority Members: Jan. 30,1985-Jan. 3,1987
Service Dates of Minority Members: Jan. 30,1985-Jan. 3,1987

Majority

Rank Name	Party	State	Terms in: House	Terms in: Comm.
Chr Gray, William H. III	Dem	Penn.	4	*2 2
2nd Wright, James C. Jr.	Dem	Tex.	16	7
3rd Hefner, W. G. (Bill)	Dem	N.C.	6	3
4th Downey, Thomas J.	Dem	N.Y.	6	3
5th Lowry, Michael E.	Dem	Wash.	4	3
6th Derrick, Butler C. Jr.	Dem	S.C.	6	*2 2
7th Miller, George	Dem	Cal.	6	2
8th Williams, Pat	Dem	Mont.	4	2
9th Wolpe, Howard E.	Dem	Mich.	4	2
10th Frost, J. Martin III	Dem	Tex.	4	2
11th Fazio, Victor H.	Dem	Cal.	4	2
12th Russo, Martin A.	Dem	Ill.	6	1
13th Jenkins, Edgar L.	Dem	Ga.	5	1
14th Barnes, Michael D.	Dem	Md.	4	1
15th Leath, J. Marvin	Dem	Tex.	4	1
16th Schumer, Charles E.	Dem	N.Y.	3	1
17th Boxer, Barbara	Dem	Cal.	2	1
18th MacKay, Kenneth H.	Dem	Fla.	2	1
19th Slattery, Jim	Dem	Kans.	2	1
20th Atkins, Chester G.	Dem	Mass.	1	1

Minority

Rank Name	Party	State	Terms in: House	Terms in: Comm.
RM Latta, Delbert L.	Rep	Ohio	14	6
2nd Kemp, Jack F.	Rep	N.Y.	8	3
3rd Martin, Lynn M.	Rep	Ill.	3	3
4th Fiedler, Bobbi	Rep	Cal.	3	3
5th Gradison, Willis D. Jr.	Rep	Ohio	6	2
6th Loeffler, Thomas G.	Rep	Tex.	4	2
7th Mack, Connie III	Rep	Fla.	2	2
8th Goodling, William F.	Rep	Penn.	6	1
9th Moore, W. Henson	Rep	La.	6	1
10th Smith, Denny	Rep	Ore.	3	1
11th Weber, Vin	Rep	Minn.	3	1
12th Brown, Hank	Rep	Colo.	3	1
13th Boulter, Beau	Rep	Tex.	1	1

*2: Member's 2nd period of service on the committee.

Note: Due to the nature of rotating membership on the Budget committee, the Democratic Caucus does not necessarily use committee seniority to determine rank. When in the majority, the Democratic Caucus reserves the second rank for the House Majority Leader.

Vacancies Filled:
Minority: Gradison was ranked 5th and Moore was ranked 9th on Feb. 7,1985.

	Majority			Minority		
Departures from the House:						
Lost Election to U.S. Senate	None			Moore, W. Henson	La.	Rep
Lost Nomination to U.S. Senate	Barnes, Michael D.	Md.	Dem	Fiedler, Bobbi	Cal.	Rep
Lost Nomination for Governor	None			Loeffler, Thomas G.	Tex.	Rep
Departures from Committee:						
Becomes Speaker of the House	Wright, James C. Jr.	Tex.	Dem	None		
No new assignment	Downey, Thomas J.	N.Y.	Dem	Martin, Lynn M.	Ill.	Rep
	Hefner, W. G. (Bill)	N.C.	Dem			
Moved to Ways and Means	None			Brown, Hank	Colo.	Rep
Moved to Select Committee on Children, Youth & Families	None			Kemp, Jack F.	N.Y.	Rep
Moved to Appropriations	None			Weber, Vin	Minn.	Rep

BUDGET / 100th Congress

Service Dates of Committee Chair: Jan. 6,1987-Jan. 3,1989
Service Dates of Majority Members: Jan. 6,1987-Jan. 3,1989
Service Dates of Minority Members: Jan. 21,1987-Jan. 3,1989

Majority

Rank	Name	Party	State	Terms in: House	Terms in: Comm.
Chr	Gray, William H. III	Dem	Penn.	5	*2 3
2nd	Foley, Thomas S.	Dem	Wash.	12	1
3rd	Lowry, Michael E.	Dem	Wash.	5	4
4th	Derrick, Butler C. Jr.	Dem	S.C.	7	*2 3
5th	Miller, George	Dem	Cal.	7	3
6th	Williams, Pat	Dem	Mont.	5	3
7th	Wolpe, Howard E.	Dem	Mich.	5	3
8th	Frost, J. Martin III	Dem	Tex.	5	3
9th	Fazio, Victor H.	Dem	Cal.	5	3
10th	Russo, Martin A.	Dem	Ill.	7	2
11th	Jenkins, Edgar L.	Dem	Ga.	6	2
12th	Leath, J. Marvin	Dem	Tex.	5	2
13th	Schumer, Charles E.	Dem	N.Y.	4	2
14th	Boxer, Barbara	Dem	Cal.	3	2
15th	MacKay, Kenneth H.	Dem	Fla.	3	2
16th	Slattery, Jim	Dem	Kans.	3	2
17th	Atkins, Chester G.	Dem	Mass.	2	2
18th	Oberstar, James L.	DFL	Minn.	7	1
19th	Guarini, Frank J.	Dem	N.J.	5	1
20th	Durbin, Richard J.	Dem	Ill.	3	1
21st	Espy, Mike	Dem	Miss.	1	1

Minority

Rank	Name	Party	State	Terms in: House	Terms in: Comm.
RM	Latta, Delbert L.	Rep	Ohio	15	7
2nd	Gradison, Willis D. Jr.	Rep	Ohio	7	3
3rd	Mack, Connie III	Rep	Fla.	3	3
4th	Goodling, William F.	Rep	Penn.	7	2
5th	Smith, Denny	Rep	Ore.	4	2
6th	Boulter, Beau	Rep	Tex.	2	2
7th	Edwards, M. H. (Mickey)	Rep	Okla.	6	1
8th	Thomas, William M.	Rep	Cal.	5	1
9th	Rogers, Harold	Rep	Ky.	4	1
10th	Sundquist, Don	Rep	Tenn.	3	1
11th	Johnson, Nancy L.	Rep	Conn.	3	1
12th	Armey, Richard	Rep	Tex.	2	1
13th	Buechner, Jack	Rep	Mo.	1	1
14th	Houghton, Amory Jr.	Rep	N.Y.	1	1

*2: Member's 2nd period of service on the committee.

Notes: The resignation of Charles (Buddy) Roemer (Dem-La.) and his replacement by Jim McCrery (Rep-La.) on Apr. 26,1988, led to a change in size and party ratio on this committee to 21 Democrats and 15 Republicans on May 18,1988. Due to the nature of rotating membership on the Budget committee, the Democratic Caucus does not necessarily use committee seniority to determine rank. When in the majority, the Democratic Caucus reserves the second rank for the House Majority Leader.

Addition:

Minority: 15th McCrery, Jim Rep La. May 18,1988

	Majority		Minority	
Departures from the House:				
Elected to U.S. Senate	None		Mack, Connie III	Fla. Rep
Lost Election to U.S. Senate	Lowry, Michael E.	Wash. Dem	Boulter, Beau	Tex. Rep
	MacKay, Kenneth H.	Fla. Dem		
Retired	None		Latta, Delbert L.	Ohio Rep
Departures from Committee:				
Moved to Appropriations	Atkins, Chester G.	Mass. Dem	None	
Moved to House Administration	Frost, J. Martin III	Tex. Dem	None	
Moved to Ways and Means	None		Johnson, Nancy L.	Conn. Rep
			Sundquist, Don	Tenn. Rep
Returned to Education & Labor	Miller, George	Cal. Dem	None	
Returned to Interior & Insular Affairs	Williams, Pat	Mont. Dem	None	
Returned to Science, Space & Technology	Wolpe, Howard E.	Mich. Dem	None	
No new assignment	Derrick, Butler C. Jr.	S.C. Dem	Edwards, M.H. (Mickey)	Okla. Rep
	Fazio, Victor H.	Cal. Dem		
	Gray, William H. III	Penn. Dem		

BUDGET / 101st Congress

Service Dates of Committee Chair: Jan. 3,1989-Jan. 3,1991
Service Dates of Majority Members: Jan. 19,1989-Jan. 3,1991
Service Dates of Minority Members: Jan. 20,1989-Jan. 3,1991

Majority

Rank Name	Party	State	Terms in: House	Terms in: Comm.
Chr Panetta, Leon E.	Dem	Cal.	7	1
2nd Foley, Thomas S.	Dem	Wash.	13	2
3rd Russo, Martin A.	Dem	Ill.	8	3
4th Jenkins, Edgar L.	Dem	Ga.	7	3
5th Leath, J. Marvin	Dem	Tex.	6	3
6th Schumer, Charles E.	Dem	N.Y.	5	3
7th Boxer, Barbara	Dem	Cal.	4	3
8th Slattery, Jim	Dem	Kans.	4	3
9th Oberstar, James L.	Dem	Minn.	8	2
10th Guarini, Frank J.	Dem	N.J.	6	2
11th Durbin, Richard J.	Dem	Ill.	4	2
12th Espy, Mike	Dem	Miss.	2	2
13th Kildee, Dale E.	Dem	Mich.	7	1
14th Beilenson, Anthony C.	Dem	Cal.	7	1
15th Huckaby, T. Jerry	Dem	La.	7	1
16th Sabo, Martin Olav	Dem	Minn.	6	1
17th Dwyer, Bernard J.	Dem	N.J.	5	1
18th Berman, Howard L.	Dem	Cal.	4	1
19th Wise, Robert E. Jr.	Dem	W.Va.	4	1
20th Kaptur, Marcy	Dem	Ohio	4	1
21st Bryant, John	Dem	Tex.	4	1

Minority

Rank Name	Party	State	Terms in: House	Terms in: Comm.
RM Frenzel, William E.	Rep	Minn.	10	1
2nd Gradison, Willis D. Jr.	Rep	Ohio	8	4
3rd Goodling, William F.	Rep	Penn.	8	3
4th Smith, Denny	Rep	Ore.	5	3
5th Thomas, William M.	Rep	Cal.	6	2
6th Rogers, Harold	Rep	Ky.	5	2
7th Armey, Richard	Rep	Tex.	3	2
8th Buechner, Jack	Rep	Mo.	2	2
9th Houghton, Amory Jr.	Rep	N.Y.	2	2
10th McCrery, Jim	Rep	La.	2	2
11th Kasich, John R.	Rep	Ohio	4	1
12th Gallo, Dean A.	Rep	N.J.	3	1
13th Schuette, Bill	Rep	Mich.	3	1
14th Bentley, Helen Delich	Rep	Md.	3	1

Notes: Due to the nature of rotating membership on the Budget committee, the Democratic Caucus does not necessarily use committee seniority to determine rank. When in the majority, the Democratic Caucus reserves the second rank for the House Majority Leader. As the senior most House minority member on this committee, William E. Frenzel (Rep-Minn.) was chosen Ranking Minority Member.

Changes:

Majority:

Foley, Thomas S.	Dem	Wash.	June 6,1989	Left committee; elected Speaker of the House.
Gephardt, Richard A.	Dem	Mo.	Oct. 16,1989	Replaced Foley in 2nd seat as new House Majority Leader.
Kaptur, Marcy	Dem	Ohio	May 24,1990	Moved to Appropriations.
Spratt, John M. Jr.	Dem	S.C.	June 14,1990	Replaced Kaptur.

Departures from the House:	**Majority**			**Minority**		
Defeated for Reelection	None			Buechner, Jack	Mo.	Rep
				Smith, Denny	Ore.	Rep
Lost Election to U.S. Senate	None			Schuette, Bill	Mich.	Rep
Retired	Leath, J. Marvin	Tex.	Dem	Frenzel, William E.	Minn.	Rep
Departures from Committee:						
Moved to House Administration	Russo, Martin A.	Ill.	Dem	None		
Moved to Interior & Insular Affairs	Schumer, Charles E.	N.Y.	Dem	None		
Moved to Banking, Finance & Urban Affairs; returned to Veterans' Affairs	Slattery, Jim	Kans.	Dem	None		
Returned to Armed Services	Boxer, Barbara	Cal.	Dem	None		
Returned to Foreign Affairs	None			Goodling, William F.	Penn.	Rep
No new assignment	Jenkins, Edgar L.	Ga.	Dem	None		

BUDGET / 102nd Congress

Service Dates of Committee Chair: Jan. 24,1991-Jan. 3,1993
Service Dates of Majority Members: Jan. 24,1991-Jan. 3,1993
Service Dates of Minority Members: Jan. 24,1991-Jan. 3,1993

Majority

Rank	Name	Party	State	Terms in: House	Terms in: Comm.
Chr	Panetta, Leon E.	Dem	Cal.	8	2
2nd	Gephardt, Richard A.	Dem	Mo.	8	2
3rd	Oberstar, James L.	Dem	Minn.	9	3
4th	Guarini, Frank J.	Dem	N.J.	7	3
5th	Durbin, Richard J.	Dem	Ill.	5	3
6th	Espy, Mike	Dem	Miss.	3	3
7th	Kildee, Dale E.	Dem	Mich.	8	2
8th	Beilenson, Anthony C.	Dem	Cal.	8	2
9th	Huckaby, T. Jerry	Dem	La.	8	2
10th	Sabo, Martin Olav	Dem	Minn.	7	2
11th	Dwyer, Bernard J.	Dem	N.J.	6	2
12th	Berman, Howard L.	Dem	Cal.	5	2
13th	Wise, Robert E. Jr.	Dem	W.Va.	5	2
14th	Bryant, John	Dem	Tex.	5	2
15th	Spratt, John M. Jr.	Dem	S.C.	5	2
16th	Pease, Donald J.	Dem	Ohio	8	1
17th	Stenholm, Charles W.	Dem	Tex.	7	1
18th	Matsui, Robert T.	Dem	Cal.	7	1
19th	Frank, Barney	Dem	Mass.	6	1
20th	Cooper, Jim	Dem	Tenn.	5	1
21st	Slaughter, Louise M.	Dem	N.Y.	3	*2 1
22nd	Payne, Lewis F. Jr.	Dem	Va.	3	1
23rd	Parker, Mike	Dem	Miss.	2	1

Minority

Rank	Name	Party	State	Terms in: House	Terms in: Comm.
RM	Gradison, Willis D. Jr.	Rep	Ohio	9	5
2nd	McMillan, J. Alex	Rep	N.C.	4	1
3rd	Thomas, William M.	Rep	Cal.	7	3
4th	Rogers, Harold	Rep	Ky.	6	3
5th	Armey, Richard	Rep	Tex.	4	3
6th	Houghton, Amory Jr.	Rep	N.Y.	3	3
7th	McCrery, Jim	Rep	La.	3	3
8th	Kasich, John R.	Rep	Ohio	5	2
9th	Gallo, Dean A.	Rep	N.J.	4	2
10th	Bentley, Helen Delich	Rep	Md.	4	2
11th	Dannemeyer, William E.	Rep	Cal.	7	1
12th	Miller, John R.	Rep	Wash.	4	1
13th	Shays, Christopher	Rep	Conn.	3	1
14th	Santorum, Rick	Rep	Penn.	1	1

*2: Member's second period of service on committee.

Note: Due to the nature of rotating membership on the Budget committee, the Democratic Caucus does not necessarily use committee seniority to determine rank. When in the majority, the Democratic Caucus reserves the second rank for the House Majority Leader.

Changes:

Minority:

Gallo, Dean A.	Rep	N.J.	Jan. 30,1991	Left committee; no new assignment.
Kolbe, Jim	Rep	Ariz.	Jan. 30,1991	Replaced Gallo; ranked ahead of Shays.
Armey, Richard	Rep	Tex.	July 9,1991	Left committee (effective June 30,1991); no new assignment.
Paxon, L. William	Rep	N.Y.	July 9,1991	Replaced Armey.

DISTRICT OF COLUMBIA

Jurisdiction, 1947

Established by the Legislative Reorganization Act of 1946:

[Section 121.(1)(f)]

Committee on the District of Columbia.

1. All measures relating to the municipal affairs of the District of Columbia in general, other than appropriations therefor, including--
2. Public health and safety, sanitation, and quarantine regulations.
3. Regulation of sale of intoxicating liquors.
4. Adulteration of food and drugs.
5. Taxes and tax sales.
6. Insurance, executors, administrators, wills, and divorce.
7. Municipal and juvenile courts.
8. Incorporation and organization of societies.
9. Municipal code and amendments to the criminal and corporation laws.

Jurisdiction, 1992

Jurisdiction contained in Rules of the House of Representatives (as revised to July 1, 1992):

[Rule X. 1. (f)]

Committee on the District of Columbia.

(1) All measures relating to the municipal affairs of the District of Columbia in general, other than appropriations therefor, including--
(2) Adulteration of foods and drugs.
(3) Incorporation and organization of societies.
(4) Insurance, executors, administrators, wills, and divorce.
(5) Municipal code and amendments to the criminal and corporation laws.
(6) Municipal and juvenile courts.
(7) Public health and safety, sanitation, and quarantine regulations.
(8) Regulation of sale of intoxicating liquors.
(9) Taxes and tax sales.
(10) Saint Elizabeth's Hospital.

DISTRICT OF COLUMBIA / 80th Congress

Service Dates of Committee Chair: Jan. 14,1947-Jan. 3,1949
Service Dates of Majority Members: Jan. 14,1947-Jan. 3,1949
Service Dates of Minority Members: Jan. 16,1947-Jan. 3,1949

Majority

Rank Name	Party	State	Terms in: House	Terms in: Comm.
Chr Dirksen, Everett M.	Rep	Ill.	8	8
2nd Bates, George J.	Rep	Mass.	6	6
3rd Simpson, Sidney E.	Rep	Ill.	3	3
4th Beall, J. Glenn	Rep	Md.	3	3
5th O'Hara, Joseph P.	Rep	Minn.	4	2
6th Talle, Henry O.	Rep	Iowa	5	1
7th Miller, Arthur L.	Rep	Neb.	3	1
8th Auchincloss, James C.	Rep	N.J.	3	*2 1
9th McDowell, John R.	Rep	Penn.	2	1
10th Allen, John J. Jr.	Rep	Cal.	1	1
11th McMahon, Gregory	Rep	N.Y.	1	1
12th Youngblood, Harold F.	Rep	Mich.	1	1
13th McGarvey, Robert N.	Rep	Penn.	1	1
14th Jones, Homer R.	Rep	Wash.	1	1

Minority

Rank Name	Party	State	Terms in: House	Terms in: Comm.
RM McMillan, John L.	Dem	S.C.	5	5
2nd Harris, Oren	Dem	Ark.	4	4
3rd Hebert, F. Edward	Dem	La.	4	4
4th Abernethy, Thomas G.	Dem	Miss.	3	3
5th Smith, Howard W.	Dem	Va.	9	*2 3
6th Klein, Arthur G.	Dem	N.Y.	4	1
7th Teague, Olin E.	Dem	Tex.	2	1
8th Deane, Charles B.	Dem	N.C.	1	1
9th Kennedy, John F.	Dem	Mass.	1	1
10th Jones, Robert E. Jr.	Dem	Ala.	1	1
11th Davis, James C.	Dem	Ga.	1	1

*2: Member's 2nd period of service on the committee.

Vacancies Filled:
Majority: 14th seat by Homer Jones on Jan. 23,1947.
Minority: 10th seat by Robert Jones on Feb. 26,1947; 11th seat by Davis on Mar. 18,1947.

Changes:
Minority:

Name	Party	State	Date	Change
Hebert, F. Edward	Dem	La.	Dec. 8,1947	Moved to Un-American Activities.
Price, Emory H.	Dem	Fla.	Apr. 14,1948	Replaced Hebert.

	Majority			Minority		
Departures from the House:						
Defeated for Reelection	Jones, Homer R.	Wash.	Rep	None		
	McDowell, John R.	Penn.	Rep			
	McGarvey, Robert N.	Penn.	Rep			
	McMahon, Gregory	N.Y.	Rep			
	Youngblood, Harold F.	Mich.	Rep			
Defeated for Renomination	None			Price, Emory H.	Fla.	Dem
Retired	Dirksen, Everett McK.	Ill.	Rep	None		
Departures from Committee:						
Moved to Banking & Currency	None			Deane, Charles B.	N.C.	Dem

DISTRICT OF COLUMBIA / 81st Congress

Service Dates of Committee Chair: Jan. 18,1949-Jan. 3,1951
Service Dates of Majority Members: Jan. 18,1949-Jan. 3,1951
Service Dates of Minority Members: Jan. 18,1949-Jan. 3,1951

Majority

Rank Name	Party	State	Terms in: House	Terms in: Comm.
Chr McMillan, John L.	Dem	S.C.	6	6
2nd Harris, Oren	Dem	Ark.	5	5
3rd Abernethy, Thomas G.	Dem	Miss.	4	4
4th Smith, Howard W.	Dem	Va.	10	*2 4
5th Klein, Arthur G.	Dem	N.Y.	5	2
6th Teague, Olin E.	Dem	Tex.	3	2
7th Kennedy, John F.	Dem	Mass.	2	2
8th Jones, Robert E. Jr.	Dem	Ala.	2	2
9th Davis, James C.	Dem	Ga.	2	2
10th Granger, Walter K.	Dem	Utah	5	1
11th Morrison, James H.	Dem	La.	4	1

Minority

Rank Name	Party	State	Terms in: House	Terms in: Comm.
RM1 Bates, George J.	Rep	Mass.	7	7
RM2 2nd Simpson, Sidney E.	Rep	Ill.	4	4
3rd Beall, J. Glenn	Rep	Md.	4	4
4th O'Hara, Joseph P.	Rep	Minn.	5	3
5th Talle, Henry O.	Rep	Iowa	6	2
6th Miller, Arthur L.	Rep	Neb.	4	2
7th Auchincloss, James C.	Rep	N.J.	4	*2 2
8th Allen, John J. Jr.	Rep	Cal.	2	2
9th James, Benjamin F.	Rep	Penn.	1	1
10th Wadsworth, James W. Jr.	Rep	N.Y.	9	1

12th Miller, George P.	Dem	Cal.	3	1	
13th Buchanan, Frank	Dem	Penn.	3	1	
14th Redden, Monroe M.	Dem	N.C.	2	1	
15th Jones, Paul C.	Dem	Mo.	2	1	*2: Member's 2nd period of service on the committee.

Vacancy Filled:
Minority: 10th seat by Wadsworth on Jan. 31,1949.

Changes:
Ranking Member:

RM1 Bates, George J.	Rep	Mass.	Nov. 1,1949	Died in office.
RM2 Simpson, Sidney E.	Rep	Ill.	Nov. 1,1949	Succeeded Bates as Ranking Minority Member.

Minority:

Bates, George J.	Rep	Mass.	Nov. 1,1949	Died in office.
Kearns, Carroll D.	Rep	Penn.	Apr. 4,1950	Replaced Bates.

Departures from the House:	Majority			Minority		
Appointed Chair of National Security Training Commission	None			Wadsworth, James W. Jr.	N.Y.	Rep
Departures from Committee:						
Moved to Ways & Means	Granger, Walter K.	Utah	Dem	None		
Moved to Appropriations	None			James, Benjamin F.	Penn.	Rep

DISTRICT OF COLUMBIA / 82nd Congress

Service Dates of Committee Chair: Jan. 12,1951-Jan. 3,1953
Service Dates of Majority Members: Jan. 12,1951-Jan. 3,1953
Service Dates of Minority Members: Jan. 15,1951-Jan. 3,1953

Majority

Rank Name	Party	State	Terms in: House	Terms in: Comm.
Chr McMillan, John L.	Dem	S.C.	7	7
2nd Harris, Oren	Dem	Ark.	6	6
3rd Abernethy, Thomas G.	Dem	Miss.	5	5
4th Smith, Howard W.	Dem	Va.	11	*2 5
5th Klein, Arthur G.	Dem	N.Y.	6	3
6th Teague, Olin E.	Dem	Tex.	4	3
7th Kennedy, John F.	Dem	Mass.	3	3
8th Jones, Robert E. Jr.	Dem	Ala.	3	3
9th Davis, James C.	Dem	Ga.	3	3
10th Morrison, James H.	Dem	La.	5	2
11th Miller, George P.	Dem	Cal.	4	2
12th Buchanan, Frank	Dem	Penn.	4	2
13th Redden, Monroe M.	Dem	N.C.	3	2
14th Jones, Paul C.	Dem	Mo.	3	2

Minority

Rank Name	Party	State	Terms in: House	Terms in: Comm.
RM Simpson, Sidney E.	Rep	Ill.	5	5
2nd Beall, J. Glenn	Rep	Md.	5	5
3rd O'Hara, Joseph P.	Rep	Minn.	6	4
4th Talle, Henry O.	Rep	Iowa	7	3
5th Miller, Arthur L.	Rep	Neb.	5	3
6th Auchincloss, James C.	Rep	N.J.	5	*2 3
7th Allen, John J. Jr.	Rep	Cal.	3	3
8th Kearns, Carroll D.	Rep	Penn.	3	2
9th Sittler, Edward L. Jr.	Rep	Penn.	1	1
10th Hagen, Harold C.	Rep	Minn.	5	1
11th Patterson, James T.	Rep	Conn.	3	1

*2: Member's 2nd period of service on the committee.

Vacancies Filled:
Minority: 10th seat by Hagen and the 11th seat by Patterson on Jan. 25,1951.

Changes:
Majority:

Buchanan, Frank	Dem	Penn.	Apr. 27,1951	Died in office.
Sutton, James P. (Pat)	Dem	Tenn.	May 17,1951	Replaced Buchanan.

Departures from the House:	Majority			Minority		
Elected to U.S. Senate	Kennedy, John F.	Mass.	Dem	Beall, J. Glenn	Md.	Rep
Defeated for Reelection				Sittler, Edward L. Jr.	Penn.	Rep
Retired	Redden, Monroe M.	N.C.	Dem	None		
Departures from Committee:						
Moved to Armed Services	Miller, George P.	Cal.	Dem	None		

DISTRICT OF COLUMBIA / 83rd Congress

Service Dates of Committee Chair: Jan. 19,1953-Jan. 3,1955
Service Dates of Majority Members: Jan. 19,1953-Jan. 3,1955
Service Dates of Minority Members: Jan. 19,1953-Jan. 3,1955

Majority

Rank Name	Party	State	Terms in: House		Terms in: Comm.
Chr Simpson, Sidney E.	Rep	Ill.	6		6
2nd O'Hara, Joseph P.	Rep	Minn.	7		5
3rd Talle, Henry O.	Rep	Iowa	8		4
4th Miller, Arthur L.	Rep	Neb.	6		4
5th Auchincloss, James C.	Rep	N.J.	6	*2	4
6th Allen, John J. Jr.	Rep	Cal.	4		4
7th Kearns, Carroll D.	Rep	Penn.	4		3
8th Hagen, Harold C.	Rep	Minn.	6		2
9th Patterson, James T.	Rep	Conn.	4		2
10th Gubser, Charles S.	Rep	Cal.	1		1
11th Broyhill, Joel T.	Rep	Va.	1	*1	1
12th Hyde, DeWitt S.	Rep	Md.	1		1
13th Hillelson, Jeffrey P.	Rep	Mo.	1		1

Minority

Rank Name	Party	State	Terms in: House		Terms in: Comm.
RM McMillan, John L.	Dem	S.C.	8		8
2nd Harris, Oren	Dem	Ark.	7		7
3rd Abernethy, Thomas G.	Dem	Miss.	6		6
4th Smith, Howard W.	Dem	Va.	12	*2	6
5th Klein, Arthur G.	Dem	N.Y.	7		4
6th Teague, Olin E.	Dem	Tex.	5		4
7th Jones, Robert E. Jr.	Dem	Ala.	4		4
8th Davis, James C.	Dem	Ga.	4		4
9th Morrison, James H.	Dem	La.	6		3
10th Jones, Paul C.	Dem	Mo.	4		3
11th Sutton, James P. (Pat)	Dem	Tenn.	3		2
12th Moss, John E. Jr.	Dem	Cal.	1		1

*1: Member's 1st period of service on the committee; *2: Member's 2nd period of service on the committee.

Changes:
Minority:

Moss, John E. Jr.	Dem	Cal.	Feb. 12,1953	Moved to Post Office and Civil Service.
Friedel, Samuel N.	Dem	Md.	Feb. 12,1953	Replaced Moss.

	Majority		Minority	
Departures from the House:				
Defeated for Reelection	Hagen, Harold C.	Minn. Rep	None	
	Hillelson, Jeffrey P.	Mo. Rep		
Lost Nomination to U.S. Senate	None		Sutton, James P.	Tenn. Dem
Departures from Committee:				
Moved to House Administration	None		Jones, Paul C.	Mo. Dem
Moved to Government Operations	None		Jones, Robert E. Jr.	Ala. Dem
Moved to Interstate & Foreign Commerce	None		Friedel, Samuel N.	Md. Dem

DISTRICT OF COLUMBIA / 84th Congress

Service Dates of Committee Chair: Jan. 13,1955-Jan. 3,1957
Service Dates of Majority Members: Jan. 13,1955-Jan. 3,1957
Service Dates of Minority Members: Jan. 20,1955-Jan. 3,1957

Majority

Rank Name	Party	State	Terms in: House		Terms in: Comm.
Chr McMillan, John L.	Dem	S.C.	9		9
2nd Harris, Oren	Dem	Ark.	8		8
3rd Abernethy, Thomas G.	Dem	Miss.	7		7
4th Smith, Howard W.	Dem	Va.	13	*2	7
5th Klein, Arthur G.	Dem	N.Y.	8		5
6th Teague, Olin E.	Dem	Tex.	6		5
7th Davis, James C.	Dem	Ga.	5		5
8th Morrison, James H.	Dem	La.	7		4
9th Dawson, William L.	Dem	Ill.	7		1
10th Williams, John Bell	Dem	Miss.	5		1
11th Steed, Thomas J.	Dem	Okla.	4		1
12th Wier, Roy W.	DFL	Minn.	4		1
13th Jones, Woodrow W.	Dem	N.C.	4		1
14th Rutherford, J. T.	Dem	Tex.	1		1

Minority

Rank Name	Party	State	Terms in: House		Terms in: Comm.
RM Simpson, Sidney E.	Rep	Ill.	7		7
2nd O'Hara, Joseph P.	Rep	Minn.	8		6
3rd Talle, Henry O.	Rep	Iowa	9		5
4th Miller, Arthur L.	Rep	Neb.	7		5
5th Auchincloss, James C.	Rep	N.J.	7	*2	5
6th Allen, John J. Jr.	Rep	Cal.	5		5
7th Kearns, Carroll D.	Rep	Penn.	5		4
8th Patterson, James T.	Rep	Conn.	5		3
9th Gubser, Charles S.	Rep	Cal.	2		2
10th Broyhill, Joel T.	Rep	Va.	2	*1	2
11th Hyde, DeWitt S.	Rep	Md.	2		2

*1: Member's 1st period of service on the committee;
*2: Member's 2nd period of service on the committee.

Changes:

Majority:

Klein, Arthur G.	Dem	N.Y.	Dec. 31,1956	Resigned; elected state supreme court justice.

	Majority			Minority		
Departures from the House:						
Retired	Jones, Woodrow W.	N.C.	Dem	None		
Departures from Committee:						
Moved to Banking & Currency	Rutherford, J. T.	Tex.	Dem	None		
Moved to Appropriations	Steed, Thomas J.	Okla.	Dem	None		
Moved to Armed Services	None			Gubser, Charles S.	Cal.	Rep

DISTRICT OF COLUMBIA / 85th Congress

Service Dates of Committee Chair: Jan. 10,1957-Jan. 3,1959
Service Dates of Majority Members: Jan. 10,1957-Jan. 3,1959
Service Dates of Minority Members: Jan. 16,1957-Jan. 3,1959

Majority

Rank	Name	Party	State	Terms in: House	Terms in: Comm.
Chr	McMillan, John L.	Dem	S.C.	10	10
2nd	Harris, Oren	Dem	Ark.	9	9
3rd	Abernethy, Thomas G.	Dem	Miss.	8	8
4th	Smith, Howard W.	Dem	Va.	14	*2 8
5th	Teague, Olin E.	Dem	Tex.	7	6
6th	Davis, James C.	Dem	Ga.	6	6
7th	Morrison, James H.	Dem	La.	8	5
8th	Dawson, William L.	Dem	Ill.	8	2
9th	Williams, John Bell	Dem	Miss.	6	2
10th	Wier, Roy W.	DFL	Minn.	5	2
11th	Multer, Abraham J.	Dem	N.Y.	6	1
12th	Dowdy, John V.	Dem	Tex.	4	1
13th	Matthews, Donald R.	Dem	Fla.	3	1
14th	Granahan, Kathryn E.	Dem	Penn.	2	1

Minority

Rank	Name	Party	State	Terms in: House	Terms in: Comm.
RM	Simpson, Sidney E.	Rep	Ill.	8	8
2nd	O'Hara, Joseph P.	Rep	Minn.	9	7
3rd	Talle, Henry O.	Rep	Iowa	10	6
4th	Miller, Arthur L.	Rep	Neb.	8	6
5th	Auchincloss, James C.	Rep	N.J.	8	*2 6
6th	Allen, John J. Jr.	Rep	Cal.	6	6
7th	Kearns, Carroll D.	Rep	Penn.	6	5
8th	Patterson, James T.	Rep	Conn.	6	4
9th	Broyhill, Joel T.	Rep	Va.	3	*1 3
10th	Hyde, DeWitt S.	Rep	Md.	3	3
11th	Holt, Joseph F.	Rep	Cal.	3	1

*1: Member's 1st period of service on the committee; *2: Member's 2nd period of service on the committee.

Changes:

Majority:				
Granahan, Kathryn E.	Dem	Penn.	Jan. 16,1958	Moved to Government Operations.
Mitchell, Harlan Erwin	Dem	Ga.	Jan. 27,1958	Replaced Granahan.
Minority:				
Simpson, Sidney E.	Rep	Ill.	Oct. 26,1958	Died in office.

	Majority			Minority		
Departures from the House:						
Defeated for Reelection	None			Allen, John J. Jr.	Cal.	Rep
				Hyde, DeWitt S.	Md.	Rep
				Miller, Arthur L.	Neb.	Rep
				Patterson, James T.	Conn.	Rep
				Talle, Henry O.	Iowa	Rep
Retired	None			O'Hara, Joseph P.	Minn.	Rep
Departures from Committee:						
Moved to Science & Astronautics	Teague, Olin E.	Tex.	Dem	None		
	Mitchell, Harlan Erwin	Ga.	Dem			
Moved to Government Operations	None			Holt, Joseph F.	Cal.	Rep
No new assignment	Harris, Oren	Ark.	Dem	None		

DISTRICT OF COLUMBIA / 86th Congress

Service Dates of Committee Chair: Jan. 19,1959-Jan. 3,1961
Service Dates of Majority Members: Jan. 19,1959-Jan. 3,1961
Service Dates of Minority Members: Jan. 19,1959-Jan. 3,1961

Majority

Rank	Name	Party	State	Terms in: House	Terms in: Comm.
Chr	McMillan, John L.	Dem	S.C.	11	11
2nd	Abernethy, Thomas G.	Dem	Miss.	9	9
3rd	Smith, Howard W.	Dem	Va.	15	*2 9
4th	Davis, James C.	Dem	Ga.	7	7
5th	Morrison, James H.	Dem	La.	9	6
6th	Dawson, William L.	Dem	Ill.	9	3
7th	Williams, John Bell	Dem	Miss.	7	3
8th	Wier, Roy W.	DFL	Minn.	6	3
9th	Multer, Abraham J.	Dem	N.Y.	7	2
10th	Dowdy, John V.	Dem	Tex.	5	2
11th	Matthews, Donald R.	Dem	Fla.	4	2
12th	Loser, J. Carlton	Dem	Tenn.	2	1
13th	Harmon, Randall S.	Dem	Ind.	1	1
14th	Foley, John R.	Dem	Md.	1	1
15th	Irwin, Donald J.	Dem	Conn.	1	1
16th	Morris, Thomas G.	Dem	N.M.	1	1

Minority

Rank	Name	Party	State	Terms in: House	Terms in: Comm.
RM	Auchincloss, James C.	Rep	N.J.	9	*2 7
2nd	Kearns, Carroll D.	Rep	Penn.	7	6
3rd	Broyhill, Joel T.	Rep	Va.	4	*1 4
4th	Springer, William L.	Rep	Ill.	5	1
5th	Nelsen, Ancher	Rep	Minn.	1	1
6th	O'Konski, Alvin E.	Rep	Wisc.	9	1
7th	Smith, Wint	Rep	Kans.	7	1
8th	Derounian, Steven B.	Rep	N.Y.	4	1
9th	Weis, Jessica McC.	Rep	N.Y.	1	1

*1: Member's 1st period of service on the committee;
*2: Member's 2nd period of service on the committee.

Vacancies Filled:
Minority: 6th through the 9th seats on Jan. 29,1959.

Changes:
Majority:

Morris, Thomas G.	Dem	N.M.	Feb. 10,1960	Moved to Science and Astronautics.
Vanik, Charles A.	Dem	Ohio	Mar. 24,1960	Replaced Morris.

	Majority			Minority		
Departures from the House:						
Defeated for Reelection	Foley, John R.	Md.	Dem	None		
	Harmon, Randall S.	Ind.	Dem			
	Irwin, Donald J.	Conn.	Dem			
	Wier, Roy W.	Minn.	DFL			
Retired	None			Smith, Wint	Kans.	Rep
Departures from Committee:						
Moved to Merchant Marine & Fisheries	Vanik, Charles A.	Ohio	Dem	None		
Moved to Ways & Means	None			Derounian, Steven B.	N.Y.	Rep
No new assignment	Matthews, Donald R.	Fla.	Dem	None		

DISTRICT OF COLUMBIA / 87th Congress

Service Dates of Committee Chair: Feb. 6,1961-Jan. 3,1963
Service Dates of Majority Members: Feb. 6,1961-Jan. 3,1963
Service Dates of Minority Members: Feb. 13,1961-Jan. 3,1963

Majority

Rank	Name	Party	State	Terms in: House	Terms in: Comm.
Chr	McMillan, John L.	Dem	S.C.	12	12
2nd	Abernethy, Thomas G.	Dem	Miss.	10	10
3rd	Smith, Howard W.	Dem	Va.	16	*2 10
4th	Davis, James C.	Dem	Ga.	8	8
5th	Morrison, James H.	Dem	La.	10	7
6th	Dawson, William L.	Dem	Ill.	10	4
7th	Williams, John Bell	Dem	Miss.	8	4
8th	Multer, Abraham J.	Dem	N.Y.	8	3
9th	Dowdy, John V.	Dem	Tex.	6	3
10th	Loser, J. Carlton	Dem	Tenn.	3	2

Minority

Rank	Name	Party	State	Terms in: House	Terms in: Comm.
RM	Auchincloss, James C.	Rep	N.J.	10	*2 8
2nd	Kearns, Carroll D.	Rep	Penn.	8	7
3rd	Broyhill, Joel T.	Rep	Va.	5	*1 5
4th	Springer, William L.	Rep	Ill.	6	2
5th	Nelsen, Ancher	Rep	Minn.	2	2
6th	O'Konski, Alvin E.	Rep	Wisc.	10	2
7th	Weis, Jessica McC.	Rep	N.Y.	2	2
8th	Harsha, William H. Jr.	Rep	Ohio	1	1
9th	Mathias, Charles McC. Jr.	Rep	Md.	1	1
10th	Tupper, Stanley R.	Rep	Me.	1	1

11th Huddleston, George Jr.	Dem	Ala.	4	1
12th Whitener, Basil L.	Dem	N.C.	3	1
13th Burke, Frank W.	Dem	Ky.	2	1
14th Cohelan, Jeffrey	Dem	Cal.	2	1
15th St Germain, Fernand J.	Dem	R.I.	1	1

*1: Member's 1st period of service on the committee;
*2: Member's 2nd period of service on the committee.

Vacancy Filled:
Minority: 10th seat by Tupper on July 24,1961.

Departures from the House:	Majority			Minority		
Defeated for Reelection	Burke, Frank W.	Ky.	Dem	None		
	Loser, J. Carlton	Tenn.	Dem			
Defeated for Renomination	Davis, James C.	Ga.	Dem	Kearns, Carroll D.	Penn.	Rep
Retired	None			Weis, Jessica McC.	N.Y.	Rep
Departures from Committee:						
Moved to Agriculture	Morrison, James H.	La.	Dem	None		
No new assignment	None			Tupper, Stanley R.	Me.	Rep

DISTRICT OF COLUMBIA / 88th Congress

Service Dates of Committee Chair: Jan. 17,1963-Jan. 3,1965
Service Dates of Majority Members: Jan. 17,1963-Jan. 3,1965
Service Dates of Minority Members: Jan. 24,1963-Jan. 3,1965

Majority

Rank Name	Party	State	Terms in: House	Terms in: Comm.
Chr McMillan, John L.	Dem	S.C.	13	13
2nd Abernethy, Thomas G.	Dem	Miss.	11	11
3rd Smith, Howard W.	Dem	Va.	17	*2 11
4th Dawson, William L.	Dem	Ill.	11	5
5th Williams, John Bell	Dem	Miss.	9	5
6th Multer, Abraham J.	Dem	N.Y.	9	4
7th Dowdy, John V.	Dem	Tex.	7	4
8th Huddleston, George Jr.	Dem	Ala.	5	2
9th Whitener, Basil L.	Dem	N.C.	4	2
10th Cohelan, Jeffrey	Dem	Cal.	3	2
11th St Germain, Fernand J.	Dem	R.I.	2	2
12th Trimble, James W.	Dem	Ark.	10	1
13th Sisk, B. F.	Dem	Cal.	5	1
14th Diggs, Charles C. Jr.	Dem	Mich.	5	1
15th Hagan, G. Elliott	Dem	Ga.	2	1

Minority

Rank Name	Party	State	Terms in: House	Terms in: Comm.
RM1 Broyhill, Joel T.	Rep	Va.	6	*1 6
RM2 2nd Auchincloss, James C.	Rep	N.J.	11	*2 9
3rd Springer, William L.	Rep	Ill.	7	3
4th Nelsen, Ancher	Rep	Minn.	3	3
5th O'Konski, Alvin E.	Rep	Wisc.	11	3
6th Harsha, William H. Jr.	Rep	Ohio	2	2
7th Mathias, Charles McC. Jr.	Rep	Md.	2	2
8th Schwengel, Frederick D.	Rep	Iowa	5	1
9th Horton, Frank J.	Rep	N.Y.	1	1
10th Roudebush, Richard L.	Rep	Ind.	2	1

*1: Member's 1st period of service on the committee;
*2: Member's 2nd period of service on the committee.

Note: Ranking on this committee for the following member was affected by other chamber service: James C. Auchincloss (Rep-N.J.), Ranking Minority Member, Public Works.

Vacancies Filled:
Minority: 9th seat by Horton on Jan. 29,1963 and the 10th seat by Roudebush on May 15,1963.

Changes:
Ranking Member:

RM1 Broyhill, Joel T.	Rep	Va.	Jan. 22,1964	Moved to Ways and Means.
RM2 Auchincloss, James C.	Rep	N.J.	Jan. 22,1964	Succeeded Broyhill as Ranking Minority Member.

Minority:

Broyhill, Joel T.	Rep	Va.	Jan. 22,1964	Moved to Ways and Means.

Departures from the House:	Majority			Minority		
Defeated for Reelection	Huddleston, George Jr.	Ala.	Dem	Schwengel, Frederick D.	Iowa	Rep
Retired	None			Auchincloss, James C.	N.J.	Rep
Departures from Committee:						
Moved to Appropriations	Cohelan, Jeffrey	Cal.	Dem	None		
Moved to Government Operations	St Germain, Fernand J.	R.I.	Dem	None		

DISTRICT OF COLUMBIA / 89th Congress

Service Dates of Committee Chair: Jan. 18,1965-Jan. 3,1967
Service Dates of Majority Members: Jan. 18,1965-Jan. 3,1967
Service Dates of Minority Members: Jan. 21,1965-Jan. 3,1967

Majority

Rank	Name	Party	State	Terms in: House	Terms in: Comm.
Chr	McMillan, John L.	Dem	S.C.	14	14
2nd	Abernethy, Thomas G.	Dem	Miss.	12	12
3rd	Smith, Howard W.	Dem	Va.	18 *2	12
4th	Dawson, William L.	Dem	Ill.	12	6
5th	Multer, Abraham J.	Dem	N.Y.	10	5
6th	Dowdy, John V.	Dem	Tex.	8	5
7th	Whitener, Basil L.	Dem	N.C.	5	3
8th	Trimble, James W.	Dem	Ark.	11	2
9th	Sisk, B. F.	Dem	Cal.	6	2
10th	Diggs, Charles C. Jr.	Dem	Mich.	6	2
11th	Hagan, G. Elliott	Dem	Ga.	3	2
12th	Fuqua, Don	Dem	Fla.	2	1
13th	Fraser, Donald M.	DFL	Minn.	2	1
14th	Sickles, Carlton R.	Dem	Md.	2	1
15th	Huot, J. Oliva	Dem	N.H.	1	1
16th	Grider, George W.	Dem	Tenn.	1	1
17th	Williams, John Bell	Dem	Miss.	10	6

Minority

Rank	Name	Party	State	Terms in: House	Terms in: Comm.
RM	Nelsen, Ancher	Rep	Minn.	4	4
2nd	Springer, William L.	Rep	Ill.	8	4
3rd	O'Konski, Alvin E.	Rep	Wisc.	12	4
4th	Harsha, William H. Jr.	Rep	Ohio	3	3
5th	Mathias, Charles McC. Jr.	Rep	Md.	3	3
6th	Horton, Frank J.	Rep	N.Y.	2	2
7th	Roudebush, Richard L.	Rep	Ind.	3	2
8th	Broyhill, Joel T.	Rep	Va.	7 *2	1

*2: Member's 2nd period of service on the committee.

Notes: John Bell Williams (Dem-Miss.) lost his seniority in the Democratic Caucus for backing Republican presidential candidate Barry Goldwater. Ranking on this committee for the following member was affected by other chamber service: William L. Springer (Rep-Ill.), Ranking Minority Member, Interstate and Foreign Commerce.

	Majority			Minority		
Departures from the House:						
Defeated for Reelection	Grider, George W.	Tenn.	Dem	None		
	Huot, J. Oliva	N.H.	Dem			
	Trimble, James W.	Ark.	Dem			
Defeated for Renomination	Smith, Howard W.	Va.	Dem	None		
Lost Nomination for Governor	Sickles, Carlton R.	Md.	Dem	None		
Departures from Committee:						
Moved to Un-American Activities	None			Roudebush, Richard L.	Ind.	Rep
Unassigned in 90th Congress	Williams, John Bell	Miss.	Dem	None		

DISTRICT OF COLUMBIA / 90th Congress

Service Dates of Committee Chair: Jan. 23,1967-Jan. 3,1969
Service Dates of Majority Members: Jan. 23,1967-Jan. 3,1969
Service Dates of Minority Members: Jan. 26,1967-Jan. 3,1969

Majority

Rank	Name	Party	State	Terms in: House	Terms in: Comm.
Chr	McMillan, John L.	Dem	S.C.	15	15
2nd	Abernethy, Thomas G.	Dem	Miss.	13	13
3rd	Dawson, William L.	Dem	Ill.	13	7
4th	Multer, Abraham J.	Dem	N.Y.	11	6
5th	Dowdy, John V.	Dem	Tex.	9	6
6th	Whitener, Basil L.	Dem	N.C.	6	4
7th	Sisk, B. F.	Dem	Cal.	7	3
8th	Diggs, Charles C. Jr.	Dem	Mich.	7	3
9th	Hagan, G. Elliott	Dem	Ga.	4	3
10th	Fuqua, Don	Dem	Fla.	3	2
11th	Fraser, Donald M.	DFL	Minn.	3	2
12th	Adams, Brock	Dem	Wash.	2 *1	1
13th	Jacobs, Andrew Jr.	Dem	Ind.	2	1
14th	Walker, E. S. Johnny	Dem	N.M.	2	1

Minority

Rank	Name	Party	State	Terms in: House	Terms in: Comm.
RM	Nelsen, Ancher	Rep	Minn.	5	5
2nd	Springer, William L.	Rep	Ill.	9	5
3rd	O'Konski, Alvin E.	Rep	Wisc.	13	5
4th	Harsha, William H. Jr.	Rep	Ohio	4	4
5th	Mathias, Charles McC. Jr.	Rep	Md.	4	4
6th	Horton, Frank J.	Rep	N.Y.	3	3
7th	Broyhill, Joel T.	Rep	Va.	8 *2	2
8th	Winn, Larry Jr.	Rep	Kans.	1	1
9th	Gude, Gilbert	Rep	Md.	1	1
10th	Zwach, John M.	Rep	Minn.	1	1
11th	Steiger, Sam	Rep	Ariz.	1	1

*1: Member's 1st period of service on the committee;
*2: Member's 2nd period of service on the committee.

Note: Ranking on this committee for the following member was affected by other chamber service: William L. Springer (Rep-Ill.), Ranking Minority Member, Interstate and Foreign Commerce.

Vacancy Filled:
Majority: 14th seat by Walker on May 25,1967.

Changes:
Majority:

Multer, Abraham J.	Dem	N.Y.	Dec. 31,1967	Resigned; elected to State Supreme Court.
Kyros, Peter N.	Dem	Me.	Apr. 3,1968	Replaced Multer.

Departures from the House:	Majority			Minority		
Elected to U.S. Senate	None			Mathias, Charles McC. Jr.	Md.	Rep
Defeated for Reelection	Walker, E. S. Johnny	N.M.	Dem	None		
	Whitener, Basil L.	N.C.	Dem			
Departures from Committee:						
Moved to Agriculture	Sisk, B. F.	Cal.	Dem	None		
Moved to Veterans' Affairs	None			Zwach, John M.	Minn.	Rep

DISTRICT OF COLUMBIA / 91st Congress

Service Dates of Committee Chair: Jan. 29,1969-Jan. 3,1971
Service Dates of Majority Members: Jan. 29,1969-Jan. 3,1971
Service Dates of Minority Members: Jan. 29,1969-Jan. 3,1971

Majority

Rank	Name	Party	State	Terms in: House	Terms in: Comm.
Chr	McMillan, John L.	Dem	S.C.	16	16
2nd	Abernethy, Thomas G.	Dem	Miss.	14	14
3rd	Dawson, William L.	Dem	Ill.	14	8
4th	Dowdy, John V	Dem	Tex.	10	7
5th	Diggs, Charles C. Jr.	Dem	Mich.	8	4
6th	Hagan, G. Elliott	Dem	Ga.	5	4
7th	Fuqua, Don	Dem	Fla.	4	3
8th	Fraser, Donald M.	DFL	Minn.	4	3
9th	Adams, Brock	Dem	Wash.	3	*1 2
10th	Jacobs, Andrew Jr.	Dem	Ind.	3	2
11th	Kyros, Peter N.	Dem	Me.	2	2
12th	Hungate, William L.	Dem	Mo.	4	1
13th	Cabell, Earle	Dem	Tex.	3	1
14th	Blanton, Leonard Ray	Dem	Tenn.	2	1

Minority

Rank	Name	Party	State	Terms in: House	Terms in: Comm.
RM	Nelsen, Ancher	Rep	Minn.	6	6
2nd	Springer, William L.	Rep	Ill.	10	6
3rd	O'Konski, Alvin E.	Rep	Wisc.	14	6
4th	Harsha, William H. Jr.	Rep	Ohio	5	5
5th	Horton, Frank J.	Rep	N.Y.	4	4
6th	Broyhill, Joel T.	Rep	Va.	9	*2 3
7th	Winn, Larry Jr.	Rep	Kans.	2	2
8th	Gude, Gilbert	Rep	Md.	2	2
9th	Steiger, Sam	Rep	Ariz.	2	2
10th	May, Catherine D.	Rep	Wash.	6	1
11th	Hogan, Lawrence J.	Rep	Md.	1	1

*1: Member's 1st period of service on the committee;
*2: Member's 2nd period of service on the committee.

Note: Ranking on this committee for the following member was affected by other chamber service: William L. Springer (Rep-Ill.), Ranking Minority Member, Interstate and Foreign Commerce.

Changes:
Majority:

Dawson, William L.	Dem	Ill.	Nov. 9,1970	Died in office.

Minority:

May, Catherine D.	Rep	Wash.	July 24,1969	Moved to Joint Committee on Atomic Energy.
Steiger, Sam	Rep	Ariz.	Oct. 7,1969	Moved to Government Operations.
Thomson, Vernon W.	Rep	Wisc.	Oct. 7,1969	Replaced May.
Smith, Henry P. III	Rep	N.Y.	Oct. 31,1969	Replaced Steiger.
Horton, Frank J.	Rep	N.Y.	Dec. 17,1969	Left committee; no new assignment.
Landgrebe, Earl F.	Rep	Ind.	Dec. 17,1969	Replaced Horton.

Departures from Committee:	Majority			Minority		
Moved to Government Operations	Fuqua, Don	Fla.	Dem	None		
Moved to Merchant Marine & Fisheries	Kyros, Peter N.	Me.	Dem	None		
Moved to Judiciary	None			Hogan, Lawrence J.	Md.	Rep
Moved to Veterans' Affairs	None			Winn, Larry Jr.	Kans.	Rep
No new assignment	Adams, Brock	Wash.	Dem	None		

DISTRICT OF COLUMBIA / 92nd Congress

Service Dates of Committee Chair: Feb. 4,1971-Jan. 3,1973
Service Dates of Majority Members: Feb. 4,1971-Jan. 3,1973
Service Dates of Minority Members: Feb. 4,1971-Jan. 3,1973

Majority

Rank	Name	Party	State	Terms in: House	Terms in: Comm.
Chr	McMillan, John L.	Dem	S.C.	17	17
2nd	Abernethy, Thomas G.	Dem	Miss.	15	15
3rd	Dowdy, John V.	Dem	Tex.	11	8
4th	Diggs, Charles C. Jr.	Dem	Mich.	9	5
5th	Hagan, G. Elliott	Dem	Ga.	6	5
6th	Fraser, Donald M.	DFL	Minn.	5	4
7th	Jacobs, Andrew Jr.	Dem	Ind.	4	3
8th	Hungate, William L.	Dem	Mo.	5	2
9th	Cabell, Earle	Dem	Tex.	4	2
10th	Blanton, Leonard Ray	Dem	Tenn.	3	2
11th	Stuckey, Williamson S.Jr.	Dem	Ga.	3	1
12th	Mikva, Abner J.	Dem	Ill.	2	1
13th	Link, Arthur A.	Dem	N.D.	1	1
14th	Dellums, Ronald V.	Dem	Cal.	1	1
15th	Green, Edith S.	Dem	Ore.	9	1
Del.	Fauntroy, Walter E.	Dem	D.C.	1	1

Minority

Rank	Name	Party	State	Terms in: House	Terms in: Comm.
RM	Nelsen, Ancher	Rep	Minn.	7	7
2nd	Springer, William L.	Rep	Ill.	11	7
3rd	O'Konski, Alvin E.	Rep	Wisc.	15	7
4th	Harsha, William H. Jr.	Rep	Ohio	6	6
5th	Broyhill, Joel T.	Rep	Va.	10 *2	4
6th	Gude, Gilbert	Rep	Md.	3	3
7th	Thomson, Vernon W.	Rep	Wisc.	6	2
8th	Smith, Henry P. III	Rep	N.Y.	4	2
9th	Landgrebe, Earl F.	Rep	Ind.	2	2
10th	McKinney, Stewart B.	Rep	Conn.	1	1

*2: Member's 2nd period of service on the committee.

Notes: Delegate Walter E. Fauntroy (Dem-D.C.) was not allowed to accrue seniority, nor was he included in the committee's party ratio of 15 Democrats and 10 Republicans. Fauntroy was added to the committee on Apr. 21,1971. Ranking on this committee for the following member was affected by other chamber service: William L. Springer (Rep-Ill.), Ranking Minority Member, Interstate and Foreign Commerce.

Vacancy Filled:
Majority: 15th seat by Green on June 17,1971.

Changes:
Majority:

Name	Party	State	Date	Change
Hungate, William L.	Dem	Mo.	Dec. 10,1971	Left committee; no new assignment.
Rees, Thomas M.	Dem	Cal.	Apr. 27,1972	Replaced Hungate.
Blanton, Leonard Ray	Dem	Tenn.	May 8,1972	Left committee; no new assignment.
Adams, Brock	Dem	Wash.	Aug. 2,1972	Replaced Blanton.

Departures from the House:	Majority			Minority		
Appointed to Federal Power Comm.	None			Springer, William L.	Ill.	Rep
Elected Governor	Link, Arthur A.	N.D.	Dem	None		
Defeated for Reelection	Cabell, Earle	Tex.	Dem	O'Konski, Alvin E.	Wisc.	Rep
	Jacobs, Andrew Jr.	Ind.	Dem			
	Mikva, Abner J.	Ill.	Dem			
Defeated for Renomination	Hagan, G. Elliott	Ga.	Dem	None		
	McMillan, John L.	S.C.	Dem			
Retired	Abernethy, Thomas G.	Miss.	Dem	None		
	Dowdy, John V.	Tex.	Dem			
Departures from Committee:						
Moved to Appropriations	Green, Edith S.	Ore.	Dem	None		

DISTRICT OF COLUMBIA / 93rd Congress

Service Dates of Committee Chair: Jan. 24,1973-Jan. 3,1975
Service Dates of Majority Members: Jan. 24,1973-Jan. 3,1975
Service Dates of Minority Members: Jan. 24,1973-Jan. 3,1975

Majority

Rank	Name	Party	State	Terms in: House	Terms in: Comm.
Chr	Diggs, Charles C. Jr.	Dem	Mich.	10	6
2nd	Fraser, Donald M.	DFL	Minn.	6	5
3rd	Stuckey, Williamson S. Jr.	Dem	Ga.	4	2
4th	Dellums, Ronald V.	Dem	Cal.	2	2
5th	Rees, Thomas M.	Dem	Cal.	5	2
6th	Adams, Brock	Dem	Wash.	5	*2 2
7th	Fauntroy, Walter E.	Dem	D.C.	2	2
8th	Howard, James J.	Dem	N.J.	5	1
9th	Mann, James R.	Dem	S.C.	3	1
10th	Mazzoli, Romano L.	Dem	Ky.	2	1
11th	Aspin, Les	Dem	Wisc.	2	1
12th	Rangel, Charles B.	Dem	N.Y.	2	1
13th	Breckinridge, John B.	Dem	Ky.	1	1
14th	Stark, Fortney H. (Pete)	Dem	Cal.	1	*1 1

Minority

Rank	Name	Party	State	Terms in: House	Terms in: Comm.
RM	Nelsen, Ancher	Rep	Minn.	8	8
2nd	Harsha, William H. Jr.	Rep	Ohio	7	7
3rd	Broyhill, Joel T.	Rep	Va.	11	*2 5
4th	Gude, Gilbert	Rep	Md.	4	4
5th	Thomson, Vernon W.	Rep	Wisc.	7	3
6th	Smith, Henry P. III	Rep	N.Y.	5	3
7th	Landgrebe, Earl F.	Rep	Ind.	3	3
8th	McKinney, Stewart B.	Rep	Conn.	2	2
9th	Symms, Steven D.	Rep	Ida.	1	1
10th	Ketchum, William M.	Rep	Cal.	1	1
11th	Taylor, Gene	Rep	Mo.	1	1

*1: Member's 1st period of service on the committee; *2: Member's 2nd period of service on the committee.

Note: Delegate Walter E. Fauntroy (Dem-D.C.) was allowed to accrue seniority, but was not included in the committee's party ratio of 13 Democrats and 11 Republicans.

Changes:

Minority:

Name	Party	State	Date	Change
Thomson, Vernon W.	Rep	Wisc.	Feb. 20,1973	Moved to Select Committee on Small Business.
Shuster, E. G. (Bud)	Rep	Penn.	Feb. 20,1973	Replaced Thomson.
Symms, Steven D.	Rep	Ida.	Nov. 15,1973	Moved to Interior and Insular Affairs.
Ketchum, William M.	Rep	Cal.	Nov. 15,1973	Moved to Science and Astronautics.
Beard, Robin L. Jr.	Rep	Tenn.	Nov. 15,1973	Replaced Symms.
Taylor, Gene	Rep	Mo.	Feb. 21,1974	Moved to Post Office and Civil Service.
Burgener, Clair W.	Rep	Cal.	May 1,1974	Replaced Ketchum.
Nelsen, Ancher	Rep	Minn.	Dec. 31,1974	Resigned and retired.
Broyhill, Joel T.	Rep	Va.	Dec. 31,1974	Resigned; defeated for reelection.

	Majority			Minority		
Departures from the House:						
Defeated for Reelection	None			Landgrebe, Earl F.	Ind.	Rep
Retired	None			Smith, Henry P. III	N.Y.	Rep
Departures from Committee:						
Moved to Small Business	Breckinridge, John B.	Ky.	Dem	None		
Moved to Ways & Means	Rangel, Charles B.	N.Y.	Dem	None		
	Stark, Fortney H. (Pete)	Cal.	Dem			
Moved to Post Office & Civil Service	None			Beard, Robin L. Jr.	Tenn.	Rep
Moved to Appropriations	None			Burgener, Clair W.	Cal.	Rep
Became Chair of Budget	Adams, Brock	Wash.	Dem	Shuster, E. G. (Bud)	Penn.	Rep

DISTRICT OF COLUMBIA / 94th Congress

Service Dates of Committee Chair: Jan. 20,1975-Jan. 3,1977
Service Dates of Majority Members: Jan. 20,1975-Jan. 3,1977
Service Dates of Minority Members: Jan. 28,1975-Jan. 3,1977

Majority

Rank	Name	Party	State	Terms in: House	Terms in: Comm.
Chr	Diggs, Charles C. Jr.	Dem	Mich.	11	7
2nd	Fraser, Donald M.	DFL	Minn.	7	6
3rd	Stuckey, Williamson S.Jr.	Dem	Ga.	5	3
4th	Dellums, Ronald V.	Dem	Cal.	3	3
5th	Rees, Thomas M.	Dem	Cal.	6	3
6th	Fauntroy, Walter E.	Dem	D.C.	3	3
7th	Howard, James J.	Dem	N.J.	6	2
8th	Mann, James R.	Dem	S.C.	4	2
9th	Mazzoli, Romano L.	Dem	Ky.	3	2
10th	Aspin, Les	Dem	Wisc.	3	2
11th	Harris, Herbert E. II	Dem	Va.	1	1
12th	Daniel, W. C. (Dan)	Dem	Va.	4	1
13th	Litton, Jerry	Dem	Mo.	2	1
14th	Meyner, Helen S.	Dem	N.J.	1	1
15th	Nowak, Henry J.	Dem	N.Y.	1	1
16th	Sharp, Philip R.	Dem	Ind.	1	1
17th	Florio, James J.	Dem	N.J.	1	1

Minority

Rank	Name	Party	State	Terms in: House	Terms in: Comm.
RM	Gude, Gilbert	Rep	Md.	5	5
2nd	Harsha, William H. Jr.	Rep	Ohio	8	8
3rd	McKinney, Stewart B.	Rep	Conn.	3	3
4th	Biester, Edward G. Jr.	Rep	Penn.	5	1
5th	Railsback, Thomas F.	Rep	Ill.	5	1
6th	Daniel, Robert W. Jr.	Rep	Va.	2	1
7th	Whalen, Charles W. Jr.	Rep	Ohio	5	1

Notes: Delegate Walter E. Fauntroy (Dem-D.C.) was allowed to accrue seniority, but was not included in the committee's party ratio of 16 Democrats and 7 Republicans. Ranking on this committee for the following member was affected by other chamber service: William H. Harsha, Jr. (Rep-Ohio), Ranking Minority Member, Public Works and Transportation.

Vacancy Filled:
Minority: 7th seat by Whalen on Feb. 20,1975.

Changes:
Majority:

Name	Party	State	Date	Change
Aspin, Les	Dem	Wisc.	Mar. 5,1975	Moved to Government Operations.
Howard, James J.	Dem	N.J.	Mar. 10,1975	Left committee; no new assignment.
Florio, James J.	Dem	N.J.	Apr. 8,1976	Moved to Interior and Insular Affairs.
Litton, Jerry	Dem	Mo.	Aug. 3,1976	Died in office.

Departures from the House:	Majority			Minority		
Retired	Rees, Thomas M.	Cal.	Dem	Biester, Edward G. Jr.	Penn.	Rep
	Stuckey, Williamson S. Jr.	Ga.	Dem	Gude, Gilbert	Md.	Rep
Departures from Committee:						
Moved to Budget	Fraser, Donald M.	Minn.	DFL	None		
Moved to Small Business	Nowak, Henry J.	N.Y.	Dem	None		
Moved to Interior & Insular Affairs	Sharp, Philip R.	Ind.	Dem	None		
No new assignment	None			Harsha, William H. Jr.	Ohio	Rep

DISTRICT OF COLUMBIA / 95th Congress

Service Dates of Committee Chair: Jan. 19,1977-Jan. 3,1979
Service Dates of Majority Members: Jan. 19,1977-Jan. 3,1979
Service Dates of Minority Members: Jan. 19,1977-Jan. 3,1979

Majority

Rank	Name	Party	State	Terms in: House	Terms in: Comm.
Chr	Diggs, Charles C. Jr.	Dem	Mich.	12	8
2nd	Dellums, Ronald V.	Dem	Cal.	4	4
3rd	Fauntroy, Walter E.	Dem	D.C.	4	4
4th	Mann, James R.	Dem	S.C.	5	3
5th	Mazzoli, Romano L.	Dem	Ky.	4	3
6th	Harris, Herbert E. II	Dem	Va.	2	2
7th	Daniel, W. C. (Dan)	Dem	Va.	5	2
8th	Meyner, Helen S.	Dem	N.J.	2	2
9th	Stark, Fortney H. (Pete)	Dem	Cal.	3	*T 1
10th	Rose, Charles G. III	Dem	N.C.	3	*T 1
11th	D'Amours, Norman E.	Dem	N.H.	2	*T 1
12th	Risenhoover, Theodore M	Dem	Okla.	2	*T 1
13th	Applegate, Douglas	Dem	Ohio	1	*T 1
14th	Collins, Cardiss	Dem	Ill.	3	*T 1

Minority

Rank	Name	Party	State	Terms in: House	Terms in: Comm.
RM	McKinney, Stewart B.	Rep	Conn.	4	4
2nd	Railsback, Thomas F.	Rep	Ill.	6	2
3rd	Daniel, Robert W. Jr.	Rep	Va.	3	2
4th	Whalen, Charles W. Jr.	Rep	Ohio	6	2
5th	Coleman, E. Thomas	Rep	Mo.	2	1
6th	Marks, Marc L.	Rep	Penn.	1	1
7th	Steers, Newton I. Jr.	Rep	Md.	1	1

*T: Temporary member of the committee.

Note: Delegate Walter E. Fauntroy (Dem-D.C.) was allowed to accrue seniority, but was not included in the committee's party ratio of 13 Democrats and 7 Republicans.

Vacancies Filled:
Majority: 9th through the 13th seats on Jan. 27,1977 and the 14th seat by Collins on Feb. 9,1977.

Changes:
Minority:

Name	Party	State	Date	Change
Railsback, Thomas F.	Rep	Ill.	Jan. 26,1977	Left committee; no new assignment.

	Majority			Minority		
Departures from the House:						
Defeated for Reelection	Meyner, Helen S.	N.J.	Dem	Steers, Newton I. Jr.	Md.	Rep
Defeated for Renomination	Risenhoover, Theodore M.	Okla.	Dem	None		
Retired	Mann, James R.	S.C.	Dem	Whalen, Charles W. Jr.	Ohio	Rep
Departures from Committee:						
Moved to Education & Labor	None			Coleman, E. Thomas	Mo.	Rep
Temporary term expired; no new assignment	Applegate, Douglas	Ohio	Dem	None		
	Collins, Cardiss	Ill.	Dem			
	D'Amours, Norman E.	N.H.	Dem			
	Rose, Charles G. III	N.C.	Dem			
	Stark, Fortney H. (Pete)	Cal.	Dem			

DISTRICT OF COLUMBIA / 96th Congress

Service Dates of Committee Chair: Jan. 24,1979-Jan. 3,1981
Service Dates of Majority Members: Jan. 24,1979-Jan. 3,1981
Service Dates of Minority Members: Jan. 24,1979-Jan. 3,1981

Majority

Rank	Name	Party	State	Terms in: House	Terms in: Comm.
Chr	Dellums, Ronald V.	Dem	Cal.	5	5
2nd	Diggs, Charles C. Jr.	Dem	Mich.	13	9
3rd	Fauntroy, Walter E.	Dem	D.C.	5	5
4th	Mazzoli, Romano L.	Dem	Ky.	5	4
5th	Harris, Herbert E. II	Dem	Va.	3	*T 3
6th	Daniel, W. C. (Dan)	Dem	Va.	6	3
7th	Leland, G. T. (Mickey)	Dem	Tex.	1	*T 1
8th	Moffett, Anthony J.(Toby)	Dem	Conn.	3	*T 1
9th	Gray, William H. III	Dem	Penn.	1	*T 1
10th	Barnes, Michael D.	Dem	Md.	1	1

Minority

Rank	Name	Party	State	Terms in: House	Terms in: Comm.
RM	McKinney, Stewart B.	Rep	Conn.	5	5
2nd	Daniel, Robert W. Jr.	Rep	Va.	4	3
3rd	Marks, Marc L.	Rep	Penn.	2	2
4th	Fenwick, Millicent H.	Rep	N.J.	3	1
5th	Jeffries, James E.	Rep	Kans.	1	1

*T: Temporary member of the committee.

Notes: Delegate Walter E. Fauntroy (Dem-D.C.) was allowed to accrue seniority, but was not included in the committee's party ratio of 9 Democrats and 5 Republicans. Charles C. Diggs, Jr. (Dem-Mich.) was convicted of mail fraud in October 1978, after the adjournment of the 95th Congress and obliged by the Democratic Caucus to relinquish the chairmanship of this committee.

Vacancies Filled:
Majority: 7th seat by Leland on Jan. 31,1979; 8th and 9th seats by Moffett and Gray respectively on Feb. 21,1979; and 10th seat by Barnes on June 26,1979.

Changes:
Majority:

Daniel, W. C. (Dan)	Dem	Va.	Jan. 31,1979	Left committee; no new assignment.
Stark, Fortney H. (Pete)	Dem	Cal.	Feb. 8,1979	Replaced Daniel; ranked 6th.
Diggs, Charles C. Jr.	Dem	Mich.	June 3,1980	Resigned and retired.

	Majority			Minority		
Departures from the House:						
Defeated for Reelection	Harris, Herbert E. II	Va.	Dem	None		
Departures from Committee:						
Moved to Education & Labor	None			Fenwick, Millicent H.	N.J.	Rep
Moved to Veterans' Affairs; Public Works & Transportation	None			Jeffries, James E.	Kans.	Rep
No new assignment	Moffett, Anthony J.(Toby)	Conn.	Dem	Marks, Marc L.	Penn.	Rep
				Daniel, Robert W. Jr.	Va.	Rep

DISTRICT OF COLUMBIA / 97th Congress

Service Dates of Committee Chair: Jan. 28,1981-Jan. 3,1983
Service Dates of Majority Members: Jan. 28,1981-Jan. 3,1983
Service Dates of Minority Members: Jan. 28,1981-Jan. 3,1983

Majority

Rank	Name	Party	State	Terms in: House	Terms in: Comm.
Chr	Dellums, Ronald V.	Dem	Cal.	6	6
2nd	Fauntroy, Walter E.	Dem	D.C.	6	6
3rd	Mazzoli, Romano L.	Dem	Ky.	6	5
4th	Stark, Fortney H. (Pete)	Dem	Cal.	5	*2 2
5th	Leland, G. T. (Mickey)	Dem	Tex.	2	2
6th	Gray, William H. III	Dem	Penn.	2	2
7th	Barnes, Michael D.	Dem	Md.	2	2
8th	Dymally, Mervyn M.	Dem	Cal.	1	1

Minority

Rank	Name	Party	State	Terms in: House	Terms in: Comm.
RM	McKinney, Stewart B.	Rep	Conn.	6	6
2nd	Parris, Stanford E.	Rep	Va.	2	1
3rd	Bliley, Thomas J. Jr.	Rep	Va.	1	1
4th	Holt, Marjorie S.	Rep	Md.	5	1

*2: Member's 2nd period of service on the committee.

Note: Delegate Walter E. Fauntroy (Dem-D.C.) was allowed to accrue seniority, but was not included in the committee's party ratio of 7 Democrats and 4 Republicans.

Vacancies Filled:
Majority: 8th seat by Dymally on Apr. 30,1981.
Minority: 4th seat by Holt on Apr. 29,1981.

DISTRICT OF COLUMBIA / 98th Congress

Service Dates of Committee Chair: Jan. 6,1983-Jan. 3,1985
Service Dates of Majority Members: Jan. 6,1983-Jan. 3,1985
Service Dates of Minority Members: Jan. 6,1983-Jan. 3,1985

Majority

Rank	Name	Party	State	Terms in: House	Terms in: Comm.
Chr	Dellums, Ronald V.	Dem	Cal.	7	7
2nd	Fauntroy, Walter E.	Dem	D.C.	7	7
3rd	Mazzoli, Romano L.	Dem	Ky.	7	6
4th	Stark, Fortney H. (Pete)	Dem	Cal.	6	*2 3
5th	Leland, G. T. (Mickey)	Dem	Tex.	3	3
6th	Gray, William H. III	Dem	Penn.	3	3
7th	Barnes, Michael D.	Dem	Md.	3	3
8th	Dymally, Mervyn M.	Dem	Cal.	2	2

Minority

Rank	Name	Party	State	Terms in: House	Terms in: Comm.
RM	McKinney, Stewart B.	Rep	Conn.	7	7
2nd	Parris, Stanford E.	Rep	Va.	3	2
3rd	Bliley, Thomas J. Jr.	Rep	Va.	2	2
4th	Holt, Marjorie S.	Rep	Md.	6	2

*2: Member's 2nd period of service on the committee.

Note: Delegate Walter E. Fauntroy (Dem-D.C.) was allowed to accrue seniority, but was not included in the committee's party ratio of 7 Democrats and 4 Republicans.

Departures from Committee:	**Majority**	**Minority**		
No new assignment	None	Holt, Marjorie S.	Md.	Rep

DISTRICT OF COLUMBIA / 99th Congress

Service Dates of Committee Chair: Jan. 7,1985-Jan. 3,1987
Service Dates of Majority Members: Jan. 30,1985-Jan. 3,1987
Service Dates of Minority Members: Jan. 30,1985-Jan. 3,1987

Majority

Rank	Name	Party	State	Terms in: House	Terms in: Comm.
Chr	Dellums, Ronald V.	Dem	Cal.	8	8
2nd	Fauntroy, Walter E.	Dem	D.C.	8	8
3rd	Mazzoli, Romano L.	Dem	Ky.	8	7
4th	Stark, Fortney H. (Pete)	Dem	Cal.	7	*2 4
5th	Leland, G. T. (Mickey)	Dem	Tex.	4	4
6th	Gray, William H. III	Dem	Penn.	4	4
7th	Barnes, Michael D.	Dem	Md.	4	4
8th	Dymally, Mervyn M.	Dem	Cal.	3	3

Minority

Rank	Name	Party	State	Terms in: House	Terms in: Comm.
RM	McKinney, Stewart B.	Rep	Conn.	8	8
2nd	Parris, Stanford E.	Rep	Va.	4	3
3rd	Bliley, Thomas J. Jr.	Rep	Va.	3	3
4th	Combest, Larry	Rep	Tex.	1	1

*2: Member's 2nd period of service on the committee.

Note: Delegate Walter E. Fauntroy (Dem-D.C.) was allowed to accrue seniority, but was not included in the committee's party ratio of 7 Democrats and 4 Republicans.

Vacancy Filled:
Minority: 4th seat by Combest on Oct. 1,1985.

Changes:
Majority:

Leland, G. T. (Mickey)	Dem	Tex.	Feb. 21,1985	Left committee; no new assignment.
Wheat, Alan	Dem	Mo.	Feb. 27,1985	Replaced Leland.

Departures from the House:	**Majority**			**Minority**
Lost Nomination to U.S. Senate	Barnes, Michael D.	Md.	Dem	None

DISTRICT OF COLUMBIA / 100th Congress

Service Dates of Committee Chair: Jan. 8,1987-Jan. 3,1989
Service Dates of Majority Members: Jan. 22,1987-Jan. 3,1989
Service Dates of Minority Members: Jan. 21,1987-Jan. 3,1989

Majority

Rank	Name	Party	State	Terms in: House	Terms in: Comm.
Chr	Dellums, Ronald V.	Dem	Cal.	9	9
2nd	Fauntroy, Walter E.	Dem	D.C.	9	9
3rd	Mazzoli, Romano L.	Dem	Ky.	9	8
4th	Stark, Fortney H. (Pete)	Dem	Cal.	8	*2 5
5th	Gray, William H. III	Dem	Penn.	5	5
6th	Dymally, Mervyn M.	Dem	Cal.	4	4
7th	Wheat, Alan	Dem	Mo.	3	2
8th	Morrison, Bruce A.	Dem	Conn.	3	1

Minority

Rank	Name	Party	State	Terms in: House	Terms in: Comm.
RM1	McKinney, Stewart B.	Rep	Conn.	9	9
RM2	2nd Parris, Stanford E.	Rep	Va.	5	4
3rd	Bliley, Thomas J. Jr.	Rep	Va.	4	4
4th	Combest, Larry	Rep	Tex.	2	2

*2: Member's 2nd period of service on the committee.

Note: Delegate Walter E. Fauntroy (Dem-D.C.) was allowed to accrue seniority, but was not included in the committee's party ratio of 7 Democrats and 4 Republicans.

Vacancy Filled:
Majority: 8th seat by Morrison on Sep. 10,1987.

Changes:

Ranking Member:

RM1 McKinney, Stewart B.	Rep	Conn.	May 7,1987	Died in office.
RM2 Parris, Stanford E.	Rep	Va.	May 7,1987	Succeeded McKinney as Ranking Minority Member.

Minority:

McKinney, Stewart B.	Rep	Conn.	May 7,1987	Died in office.
Martin, Lynn M.	Rep	Ill.	May 18,1987	Replaced McKinney.

Departures from Committee:	Majority			Minority		
Moved to Rules	None			Martin, Lynn M.	Ill.	Rep
No new assignment	Mazzoli, Romano L.	Ky.	Dem	None		

DISTRICT OF COLUMBIA / 101st Congress

Service Dates of Committee Chair: Jan. 3,1989-Jan. 3,1991
Service Dates of Majority Members: Jan. 19,1989-Jan. 3,1991
Service Dates of Minority Members: Jan. 20,1989-Jan. 3,1991

Majority

Rank Name	Party	State	Terms in: House	Terms in: Comm.
Chr Dellums, Ronald V.	Dem	Cal.	10	10
2nd Fauntroy, Walter E.	Dem	D.C.	10	10
3rd Stark, Fortney H. (Pete)	Dem	Cal.	9	*2 6
4th Gray, William H. III	Dem	Penn.	6	6
5th Dymally, Mervyn M.	Dem	Cal.	5	5
6th Wheat, Alan	Dem	Mo.	4	3
7th Morrison, Bruce A.	Dem	Conn.	4	2
8th McDermott, James A.	Dem	Wash.	1	1

Minority

Rank Name	Party	State	Terms in: House	Terms in: Comm.
RM Parris, Stanford E.	Rep	Va.	6	5
2nd Bliley, Thomas J. Jr.	Rep	Va.	5	5
3rd Combest, Larry	Rep	Tex.	3	3
4th Rohrabacher, Dana	Rep	Cal.	1	1

*2: Member's 2nd period of service on the committee.

Note: Delegate Walter E. Fauntroy (Dem-D.C.) was allowed to accrue seniority, but was not included in the committee's party ratio of 7 Democrats and 4 Republicans.

Vacancy Filled:
Majority: 8th seat by McDermott on Nov. 8,1989.

Departures from the House:	Majority			Minority		
Defeated for Reelection	None			Parris, Stanford E.	Va.	Rep
Lost Election for Governor	Morrison, Bruce A.	Conn.	Dem	None		
Lost Election for Mayor	Fauntroy, Walter E.	D.C.	Dem	None		

DISTRICT OF COLUMBIA / 102nd Congress

Service Dates of Committee Chair: Jan. 24,1991-Jan. 3,1993
Service Dates of Majority Members: Jan. 24,1991-Jan. 3,1993
Service Dates of Minority Members: Jan. 24,1991-Jan. 3,1993

Majority

Rank	Name	Party	State	Terms in: House	Terms in: Comm.
Chr	Dellums, Ronald V.	Dem	Cal.	11	11
2nd	Stark, Fortney H. (Pete)	Dem	Cal.	10	*2 7
3rd	Gray, William H. III	Dem	Penn.	7	7
4th	Dymally, Mervyn M.	Dem	Cal.	6	6
5th	Wheat, Alan	Dem	Mo.	5	4
6th	McDermott, James A.	Dem	Wash.	2	3
7th	Norton, Eleanor Holmes	Dem	D.C.	1	1
8th	Levin, Sander M.	Dem	Mich.	5	1

Minority

Rank	Name	Party	State	Terms in: House	Terms in: Comm.
RM	Bliley, Thomas J. Jr.	Rep	Va.	6	6
2nd	Combest, Larry	Rep	Tex.	4	4
3rd	Rohrabacher, Dana	Rep	Cal.	2	3
4th	Lowery, William	Rep	Cal.	6	1

*2: Member's 2nd period of service on the committee.

Note: Delegate Eleanor Holmes Norton (Dem-D.C.) was allowed to accrue seniority, but was not included in the committee's party ratio of 7 Democrats and 4 Republicans.

Vacancies Filled:
Majority: 8th seat by Levin on Apr. 24,1991.
Minority: 4th seat by Lowery on Feb. 6,1991.

Changes:
Majority:

Name	Party	State	Date	Reason
Gray, William H. III	Dem	Penn.	Sep. 11,1991	Resigned to become President of United Negro College Fund.

EDUCATION AND LABOR

Jurisdiction, 1947

Established by the Legislative Reorganization Act of 1946:

[Section 121.(1)(g)]

Committee on Education and Labor.

1. Measures relating to education or labor generally.
2. Mediation and arbitration of labor disputes.
3. Wages and hours of labor.
4. Convict labor and the entry of goods made by convicts into interstate commerce.
5. Regulation or prevention of importation of foreign laborers under contract.
6. Child labor.
7. Labor statistics.
8. Labor standards.
9. School-lunch program.
10. Vocational rehabilitation.
11. United States Employees' Compensation Commission.
12. Columbia Institution for the Deaf, Dumb, and Blind; Howard University; Freedmen's Hospital; and Saint Elizabeth's Hospital.
13. Welfare of miners.

Jurisdiction, 1992

Jurisdiction contained in Rules of the House of Representatives, (as revised to July 1, 1992):

[Rule X. 1. (g)]

Committee on Education and Labor.

(1) Measures relating to education or labor generally.
(2) Child labor.
(3) Columbia Institution for the Deaf, Dumb, and Blind; Howard University; Freedmen's Hospital.
(4) Convict labor and the entry of goods made by convicts into interstate commerce.
(5) Labor standards.
(6) Labor statistics.
(7) Mediation and arbitration of labor disputes.
(8) Regulation or prevention of importation of foreign laborers under contract.
(9) Food programs for children in schools.
(10) United States Employees' Compensation Commission.
(11) Vocational rehabilitation.
(12) Wages and hours of labor.
(13) Welfare of miners.
(14) Work incentive programs.

In addition to its legislative jurisdiction under the preceding provisions of this paragraph (and its general oversight function under clause 2(b)(1)), the committee shall have the special oversight function provided for in clause 3(c) with respect to domestic educational programs and institutions, and programs of student assistance, which are within the jurisdiction of other committees.

[Rule X. 3.(c)]

The Committee on Education and Labor shall have the function of reviewing, studying, and coordinating, on a continuing basis, all laws, programs, and Government activities dealing with or involving domestic educational programs and institutions, and programs of student assistance, which are within the jurisdiction of other committees.

EDUCATION AND LABOR / 80th Congress

Service Dates of Committee Chair: Jan. 14,1947-Jan. 3,1949
Service Dates of Majority Members: Jan. 14,1947-Jan. 3,1949
Service Dates of Minority Members: Jan. 16,1947-Jan. 3,1949

Majority

Rank	Name	Party	State	Terms in: House	Terms in: Comm.
Chr	Hartley, Fred A. Jr.	Rep	N.J.	10	10
2nd	Landis, Gerald W.	Rep	Ind.	5	5
3rd	Hoffman, Clare E.	Rep	Mich.	7	*1 5
4th	McCowen, Edward O.	Rep	Ohio	3	3
5th	Schwabe, Max	Rep	Mo.	3	3
6th	McConnell, Samuel K. Jr.	Rep	Penn.	3	2
7th	Gwinn, Ralph W.	Rep	N.Y.	2	2
8th	Buck, Ellsworth B.	Rep	N.Y.	3	2
9th	Brehm, Walter E.	Rep	Ohio	3	1
10th	Smith, Wint	Rep	Kans.	1	1
11th	Kersten, Charles J.	Rep	Wisc.	1	*1 1
12th	MacKinnon, George E.	Rep	Minn.	1	1
13th	Owens, Thomas L.	Rep	Ill.	1	1
14th	Kearns, Carroll D.	Rep	Penn.	1	1
15th	Nixon, Richard M.	Rep	Cal.	1	1

Minority

Rank	Name	Party	State	Terms in: House	Terms in: Comm.
RM	Lesinski, John	Dem	Mich.	8	8
2nd	Barden, Graham A.	Dem	N.C.	7	7
3rd	Kelley, Augustine B.	Dem	Penn.	4	4
4th	Fisher, O. Clark	Dem	Tex.	3	3
5th	Powell, Adam Clayton Jr.	Dem	N.Y.	2	*1 2
6th	Wood, John S.	Dem	Ga.	4	2
7th	Madden, Ray J.	Dem	Ind.	3	1
8th	Klein, Arthur G.	Dem	N.Y.	4	1
9th	Kennedy, John F.	Dem	Mass.	1	1
10th	Lucas, Wingate H.	Dem	Tex.	1	1

*1: Member's 1st period of service on the committee.

Changes:

Majority:

Name	Party	State	Date	Change
Owens, Thomas L.	Rep	Ill.	June 7,1948	Died in office.

Departures from the House:

	Majority	State	Party	Minority	State	Party
Defeated for Reelection	Kersten, Charles J.	Wisc.	Rep	None		
	Landis, Gerald W.	Ind.	Rep			
	MacKinnon, George E.	Minn.	Rep			
	McCowen, Edward O.	Ohio	Rep			
	Schwabe, Max	Mo.	Rep			
Retired	Buck, Ellsworth B.	N.Y.	Rep	None		
	Hartley, Fred A. Jr.	N.J.	Rep			

Departures from Committee:

	Majority	State	Party	Minority	State	Party
Moved to Rules	None			Madden, Ray J.	Ind.	Dem
Moved to Armed Services	None			Fisher, O. Clark	Tex.	Dem
Moved to Interstate & Foreign Commerce	None			Klein, Arthur G.	N.Y.	Dem
No new assignment	Hoffman, Clare E.	Mich.	Rep			

EDUCATION AND LABOR / 81st Congress

Service Dates of Committee Chairs: Ch1 Jan. 18,1949-May 27,1950
Ch2 June 6,1950-Jan. 3,1951
Service Dates of Majority Members: Jan. 18,1949-Jan. 3,1951
Service Dates of Minority Members: Jan. 18,1949-Jan. 3,1951

Majority

Rank Name	Party	State	Terms in: House	Terms in: Comm.
Ch1 Lesinski, John	Dem	Mich.	9	9
Ch2 2nd Barden, Graham A.	Dem	N.C.	8	8
3rd Kelley, Augustine B.	Dem	Penn.	5	5
4th Powell, Adam Clayton Jr.	Dem	N.Y.	3 *1	3
5th Wood, John S.	Dem	Ga.	5	3
6th Kennedy, John F.	Dem	Mass.	2	2
7th Lucas, Wingate H.	Dem	Tex.	2	2
8th Bailey, Cleveland M.	Dem	W.Va.	2	1
9th Irving, Theodore Leonard	Dem	Mo.	1	1
10th Perkins, Carl D.	Dem	Ky.	1	1
11th Howell, Charles R.	Dem	N.J.	1	1
12th Sims, Hugo S. Jr.	Dem	S.C.	1	1
13th Jacobs, Andrew Sr.	Dem	Ind.	1	1
14th Burke, Thomas H.	Dem	Ohio	1	1
15th Steed, Thomas J.	Dem	Okla.	1	1
16th Wier, Roy W.	DFL	Minn.	1	1

Minority

Rank Name	Party	State	Terms in: House	Terms in: Comm.
RM McConnell, Samuel K. Jr.	Rep	Penn.	4	3
2nd Gwinn, Ralph W.	Rep	N.Y.	3	3
3rd Brehm, Walter E.	Rep	Ohio	4	2
4th Smith, Wint	Rep	Kans.	2	2
5th Kearns, Carroll D.	Rep	Penn.	2	2
6th Nixon, Richard M.	Rep	Cal.	2	2
7th Morton, Thruston B.	Rep	Ky.	2	1
8th Werdel, Thomas H.	Rep	Cal.	1	1
9th Velde, Harold H.	Rep	Ill.	1	1

*1: Member's 1st period of service on the committee.

Changes:

Chair:

Ch1 Lesinski, John	Dem	Mich.	May 27,1950	Died in office.
Ch2 Barden, Graham A.	Dem	N.C.	June 6,1958	Succeeded Lesinski as Chair.

Majority:

Lesinski, John	Dem	Mich.	May 27,1950	Died in office.
Mitchell, Hugh B.	Dem	Wash.	June 20,1950	Replaced Lesinski.

Minority:

Nixon, Richard M.	Rep	Cal.	Nov. 30,1950	Resigned; elected to U.S. Senate.

	Majority			Minority
Departures from the House:				
Defeated for Reelection	Burke, Thomas H.	Ohio	Dem	None
	Jacobs, Andrew Sr.	Ind.	Dem	None
Defeated for Renomination	Sims, Hugo S. Jr.	S.C.	Dem	
Departures from Committee:				
Moved to Rules	Mitchell, Hugh B.	Wash.	Dem	None

EDUCATION AND LABOR / 82nd Congress

Service Dates of Committee Chair: Jan. 12,1951-Jan. 3,1953
Service Dates of Majority Members: Jan. 12,1951-Jan. 3,1953
Service Dates of Minority Members: Jan. 15,1951-Jan. 3,1953

Majority

Rank Name	Party	State	Terms in: House	Terms in: Comm.
Chr Barden, Graham A.	Dem	N.C.	9	9
2nd Kelley, Augustine B.	Dem	Penn.	6	6
3rd Powell, Adam Clayton Jr.	Dem	N.Y.	4 *1	4
4th Wood, John S.	Dem	Ga.	6	4
5th Kennedy, John F.	Dem	Mass.	3	3
6th Lucas, Wingate H.	Dem	Tex.	3	3
7th Bailey, Cleveland M.	Dem	W.Va.	3	2
8th Irving, Theodore Leonard	Dem	Mo.	2	2
9th Perkins, Carl D.	Dem	Ky.	2	2
10th Howell, Charles R.	Dem	N.J.	2	2
11th Steed, Thomas J.	Dem	Okla.	2	2

Minority

Rank Name	Party	State	Terms in: House	Terms in: Comm.
RM McConnell, Samuel K. Jr.	Rep	Penn.	5	4
2nd Gwinn, Ralph W.	Rep	N.Y.	4	4
3rd Brehm, Walter E.	Rep	Ohio	5	3
4th Smith, Wint	Rep	Kans.	3	3
5th Kearns, Carroll D.	Rep	Penn.	3	3
6th Morton, Thruston B.	Rep	Ky.	3	2
7th Werdel, Thomas H.	Rep	Cal.	2	2
8th Velde, Harold H.	Rep	Ill.	2	2
9th Potter, Charles E.	Rep	Mich.	3	1
10th Vail, Richard B.	Rep	Ill.	2	1
11th Berry, Ellis Y.	Rep	S.D.	1 *1	1

12th Wier, Roy W.	DFL	Minn.	2	2	
13th Tackett, Boyd	Dem	Ark.	2	1	
14th Greenwood, Ernest	Dem	N.Y.	1	1	*1: Member's 1st period of service on the committee.

Changes:

Majority:

Steed, Thomas J.	Dem	Okla.	Aug. 10,1951	Moved to Public Works.
Elliott, Carl A.	Dem	Ala.	Oct. 20,1951	Replaced Steed.

Minority:

Berry, Ellis Y.	Rep	S.D.	Oct. 19,1951	Moved to Interior and Insular Affairs.
Potter, Charles E.	Rep	Mich.	Nov. 4,1952	Resigned; elected to U.S. Senate.

Departures from the House:	Majority			Minority		
Appointed Assistant Secretary of State	None			Morton, Thruston B.	Ky.	Rep
Elected to U.S. Senate	Kennedy, John F.	Mass.	Dem	None		
Defeated for Reelection	Greenwood, Ernest	N.Y.	Dem	Vail, Richard B.	Ill.	Rep
	Irving, Theodore Leonard	Mo.	Dem	Werdel, Thomas H.	Cal.	Rep
Lost Nomination for Governor	Tackett, Boyd	Ark.	Dem	None		
Retired	Wood, John S.	Ga.	Dem	Brehm, Walter E.	Ohio	Rep

EDUCATION AND LABOR / 83rd Congress

Service Dates of Committee Chair: Jan. 19,1953-Jan. 3,1955
Service Dates of Majority Members: Jan. 19,1953-Jan. 3,1955
Service Dates of Minority Members: Jan. 19,1953-Jan. 3,1955

Majority

Rank Name	Party	State	Terms in: House	Comm.
Chr McConnell, Samuel K. Jr	Rep	Penn.	6	5
2nd Gwinn, Ralph W.	Rep	N.Y.	5	5
3rd Smith, Wint	Rep	Kans.	4	4
4th Kearns, Carroll D.	Rep	Penn.	4	4
5th Velde, Harold H.	Rep	Ill.	3	3
6th Hoffman, Clare E.	Rep	Mich.	10	*2 1
7th Kersten, Charles J.	Rep	Wisc.	3	*2 1
8th Berry, Ellis Y.	Rep	S.D.	2	*2 1
9th Harrison, William Henry	Rep	Wyo.	2	1
10th Bosch, Albert H.	Rep	N.Y.	1	1
11th Holt, Joseph F.	Rep	Cal.	1	1
12th Rhodes, John J.	Rep	Ariz.	1	1
13th Wainwright, Stuyvesant II	Rep	N.Y.	1	1
14th Frelinghuysen, Peter H.B.	Rep	N.J.	1	1
15th Young, Clifton	Rep	Nev.	1	1

Minority

Rank Name	Party	State	Terms in: House	Comm.
RM Barden, Graham A.	Dem	N.C.	10	10
2nd Kelley, Augustine B.	Dem	Penn.	7	7
3rd Powell, Adam Clayton Jr.	Dem	N.Y.	5	*1 5
4th Lucas, Wingate H.	Dem	Tex.	4	4
5th Bailey, Cleveland M.	Dem	W.Va.	4	3
6th Perkins, Carl D.	Dem	Ky.	3	3
7th Howell, Charles R.	Dem	N.J.	3	3
8th Wier, Roy W.	DFL	Minn.	3	3
9th Elliott, Carl A.	Dem	Ala.	3	2
10th Landrum, Phillip M.	Dem	Ga.	1	1
11th Metcalf, Lee	Dem	Mont.	1	1
12th Miller, Howard S.	Dem	Kans.	1	1

*1: Member's 1st period of service on the committee; *2: Member's 2nd period of service on the committee.

Note: House seats left vacant in the 82nd Congress in Georgia and Illinois were filled by Democrats in 1953, which led to a change in the size and party ratio of this committee to 15 Republicans and 13 Democrats on Apr. 22,1953.

Vacancy Filled:

Majority: 15th seat by Young on Feb. 9,1954.

Addition:

Minority: 13th Bowler, James B. Dem Ill. July 14,1953

Departures from the House:	Majority			Minority		
Defeated for Reelection	Kersten, Charles J.	Wisc.	Rep	Miller, Howard S.	Kans.	Dem
Defeated for Renomination	None			Lucas, Wingate H.	Tex.	Dem
Lost Election to U.S. Senate	Harrison, William Henry	Wyo.	Rep	Howell, Charles R.	N.J.	Dem
Departures from Committee:						
No new assignment	Berry, Ellis Y.	S.D.	Rep	None		
	Young, Clifton	Nev.	Rep			

EDUCATION AND LABOR / 84th Congress

Service Dates of Committee Chair: Jan. 13,1955-Jan. 3,1957
Service Dates of Majority Members: Jan. 13,1955-Jan. 3,1957
Service Dates of Minority Members: Jan. 20,1955-Jan. 3,1957

Majority

Rank Name	Party	State	Terms in: House	Comm.
Chr Barden, Graham A.	Dem	N.C.	11	11
2nd Kelley, Augustine B.	Dem	Penn.	8	8
3rd Powell, Adam Clayton Jr.	Dem	N.Y.	6	*1 6
4th Bailey, Cleveland M.	Dem	W.Va.	5	4
5th Perkins, Carl D.	Dem	Ky.	4	4
6th Wier, Roy W.	DFL	Minn.	4	4
7th Elliott, Carl A.	Dem	Ala.	4	3
8th Landrum, Phillip M.	Dem	Ga.	2	2
9th Metcalf, Lee	Dem	Mont.	2	2
10th Bowler, James B.	Dem	Ill.	2	2
11th Chudoff, Earl	Dem	Penn.	4	1
12th Green, Edith S.	Dem	Ore.	1	1
13th Roosevelt, James	Dem	Cal.	1	1
14th Zelenko, Herbert	Dem	N.Y.	1	1
15th McDowell, Harris B. Jr.	Dem	Del.	1	1
16th Thompson, Frank Jr.	Dem	N.J.	1	1
17th Udall, Stewart L.	Dem	Ariz.	1	1

Minority

Rank Name	Party	State	Terms in: House	Comm.
RM McConnell, Samuel K. Jr.	Rep	Penn.	7	6
2nd Gwinn, Ralph W.	Rep	N.Y.	6	6
3rd Smith, Wint	Rep	Kans.	5	5
4th Kearns, Carroll D.	Rep	Penn.	5	5
5th Velde, Harold H.	Rep	Ill.	4	4
6th Hoffman, Clare E.	Rep	Mich.	11	*2 2
7th Bosch, Albert H.	Rep	N.Y.	2	2
8th Holt, Joseph F.	Rep	Cal.	2	2
9th Rhodes, John J.	Rep	Ariz.	2	2
10th Wainwright, Stuyvesant II	Rep	N.Y.	2	2
11th Frelinghuysen, Peter H.B	Rep	N.J.	2	2
12th Coon, Samuel H.	Rep	Ore.	2	1
13th Fjare, Orvin B.	Rep	Mont.	1	1

*1: Member's 1st period of service on the committee;
*2: Member's 2nd period of service on the committee.

Note: The committee's size was set at 30 members on Jan. 20,1955.

Vacancy Filled:
Majority: 17th seat by Udall on Jan. 31,1955.

	Majority		Minority	
Departures from the House:				
Defeated for Reelection	McDowell, Harris B. Jr.	Del. Dem	Coon, Samuel H.	Ore. Rep
			Fjare, Orvin B.	Mont. Rep
Retired	None		Velde, Harold H.	Ill. Rep
Departures from Committee:				
Moved to Appropriations	Bowler, James B.	Ill. Dem	None	
Moved to Judiciary	Chudoff, Earl	Penn. Dem	None	
Moved to Agriculture	None		Smith, Wint	Kans. Rep

EDUCATION AND LABOR / 85th Congress

Service Dates of Committee Chair: Jan. 10,1957-Jan. 3,1959
Service Dates of Majority Members: Jan. 10,1957-Jan. 3,1959
Service Dates of Minority Members: Jan. 16,1957-Jan. 3,1959

Majority

Rank Name	Party	State	Terms in: House	Comm.
Chr Barden, Graham A.	Dem	N.C.	12	12
2nd Kelley, Augustine B.	Dem	Penn.	9	9
3rd Powell, Adam Clayton Jr.	Dem	N.Y.	7	*1 7
4th Bailey, Cleveland M.	Dem	W.Va.	6	5
5th Perkins, Carl D.	Dem	Ky.	5	5
6th Wier, Roy W.	DFL	Minn.	5	5
7th Elliott, Carl A.	Dem	Ala.	5	4
8th Landrum, Phillip M.	Dem	Ga.	3	3
9th Metcalf, Lee	Dem	Mont.	3	3
10th Green, Edith S.	Dem	Ore.	2	2
11th Roosevelt, James	Dem	Cal.	2	2
12th Zelenko, Herbert	Dem	N.Y.	2	2
13th Thompson, Frank Jr.	Dem	N.J.	2	2
14th Udall, Stewart L.	Dem	Ariz.	2	2

Minority

Rank Name	Party	State	Terms in: House	Comm.
RM1 McConnell, Samuel K. Jr. Rep	Penn.		8	7
RM2 2nd Gwinn, Ralph W.	Rep	N.Y.	7	7
3rd Kearns, Carroll D.	Rep	Penn.	6	6
4th Hoffman, Clare E.	Rep	Mich.	12	*2 3
5th Bosch, Albert H.	Rep	N.Y.	3	3
6th Holt, Joseph F.	Rep	Cal.	3	3
7th Rhodes, John J.	Rep	Ariz.	3	3
8th Wainwright, Stuyvesant II	Rep	N.Y.	3	3
9th Frelinghuysen, Peter H.B	Rep	N.J.	3	3
10th Nicholson, Donald W.	Rep	Mass.	6	1
11th Ayres, William H.	Rep	Ohio	4	1
12th Griffin, Robert P.	Rep	Mich.	1	1
13th Haskell, Harry G. Jr.	Rep	Del.	1	1

15th Holland, Elmer J.	Dem	Penn.	3	*2 1	
16th Teller, Ludwig	Dem	N.Y.	1	1	*1: Member's 1st period of service on the committee;
17th McGovern, George S.	Dem	S.D.	1	1	*2: Member's 2nd period of service on the committee.

Changes:

Ranking Member:

RM1 McConnell, Samuel K. Jr.	Rep	Penn.	Sep. 1,1957	Resigned and retired.
RM2 Gwinn, Ralph W.	Rep	N.Y.	Sep. 1,1957	Succeeded McConnell as Ranking Minority Member.

Majority:

Kelley, Augustine B.	Dem	Penn.	Nov. 20,1957	Died in office.
Dent, John H.	Dem	Penn.	Jan. 27,1958	Replaced Kelley.

Minority:

McConnell, Samuel K. Jr.	Rep	Penn.	Sep. 1,1957	Resigned and retired.
Lafore, John A. Jr.	Rep	Penn.	Jan. 16,1958	Replaced McConnell.

Departures from the House:	Majority		Minority	
Defeated for Reelection	None		Haskell, Harry G. Jr.	Del. Rep
Retired	None		Gwinn, Ralph W.	N.Y. Rep
			Nicholson, Donald W.	Mass. Rep

Departures from Committee:				
Moved to Agriculture	McGovern, George S.	S.D. Dem	None	
Moved to Ways and Means	Metcalf, Lee	Mont. Dem	None	
Moved to Appropriations	None		Rhodes, John J.	Ariz. Rep

EDUCATION AND LABOR / 86th Congress

Service Dates of Committee Chair: Jan. 19,1959-Jan. 3,1961
Service Dates of Majority Members: Jan. 19,1959-Jan. 3,1961
Service Dates of Minority Members: Jan. 19,1959-Jan. 3,1961

Majority

Rank Name	Party	State	Terms in: House	Terms in: Comm.
Chr Barden, Graham A.	Dem	N.C.	13	13
2nd Powell, Adam Clayton Jr.	Dem	N.Y.	8	*1 8
3rd Bailey, Cleveland M.	Dem	W.Va.	7	6
4th Perkins, Carl D.	Dem	Ky.	6	6
5th Wier, Roy W.	DFL	Minn.	6	6
6th Elliott, Carl A.	Dem	Ala.	6	5
7th Landrum, Phillip M.	Dem	Ga.	4	4
8th Green, Edith S.	Dem	Ore.	3	3
9th Roosevelt, James	Dem	Cal.	3	3
10th Zelenko, Herbert	Dem	N.Y.	3	3
11th Thompson, Frank Jr.	Dem	N.J.	3	3
12th Udall, Stewart L.	Dem	Ariz.	3	3
13th Holland, Elmer J.	Dem	Penn.	4	*2 2
14th Teller, Ludwig	Dem	N.Y.	2	2
15th Dent, John H.	Dem	Penn.	2	2
16th Pucinski, Roman C.	Dem	Ill.	1	1
17th Daniels, Dominick V.	Dem	N.J.	1	1
18th Brademas, John	Dem	Ind.	1	1
19th Giaimo, Robert N.	Dem	Conn.	1	1
20th O'Hara, James G.	Dem	Mich.	1	1

Minority

Rank Name	Party	State	Terms in: House	Terms in: Comm.
RM Kearns, Carroll D.	Rep	Penn.	7	7
2nd Hoffman, Clare E.	Rep	Mich.	13	*2 4
3rd Bosch, Albert H.	Rep	N.Y.	4	4
4th Holt, Joseph F.	Rep	Cal.	4	4
5th Wainwright, Stuyvesant II	Rep	N.Y.	4	4
6th Frelinghuysen, Peter H.B.	Rep	N.J.	4	4
7th Ayres, William H.	Rep	Ohio	5	2
8th Griffin, Robert P.	Rep	Mich.	2	2
9th Lafore, John A. Jr.	Rep	Penn.	2	2
10th Hiestand, Edgar W.	Rep	Cal.	4	1

*1: Member's 1st period of service on the committee;
*2: Member's 2nd period of service on the committee.

Changes:

Minority:

Bosch, Albert H.	Rep	N.Y.	Feb. 25,1959	Moved to Ways and Means.
Quie, Albert H.	Rep	Minn.	May 14,1959	Replaced Bosch.
Lafore, John A. Jr.	Rep	Penn.	Jan. 18,1960	Moved to Ways and Means.
Goodell, Charles E.	Rep	N.Y.	Jan. 18,1960	Replaced Lafore.

Departures from the House:	Majority		Minority	
Defeated for Reelection	Wier, Roy W.	Minn. DFL	Wainwright, Stuyvesant II	N.Y. Rep
Defeated for Renomination	Teller, Ludwig	N.Y. Dem	None	
Retired	Barden, Graham A.	N.C. Dem	Holt, Joseph F.	Cal. Rep

Departures from Committee:

Moved to Rules	Elliott, Carl A.	Ala. Dem	None
Unassigned in 87th Congress: appointed Secretary of Interior	Udall, Stewart L.	Ariz. Dem	None

EDUCATION AND LABOR / 87th Congress

Service Dates of Committee Chair: Feb. 6,1961-Jan. 3,1963
Service Dates of Majority Members: Feb. 6,1961-Jan. 3,1963
Service Dates of Minority Members: Feb. 13,1961-Jan. 3,1963

Majority

Rank	Name	Party	State	Terms in: House		Comm.
Chr	Powell, Adam Clayton Jr.	Dem	N.Y.	9	*1	9
2nd	Bailey, Cleveland M.	Dem	W.Va.	8		7
3rd	Perkins, Carl D.	Dem	Ky.	7		7
4th	Landrum, Phillip M.	Dem	Ga.	5		5
5th	Green, Edith S.	Dem	Ore.	4		4
6th	Roosevelt, James	Dem	Cal.	4		4
7th	Zelenko, Herbert	Dem	N.Y.	4		4
8th	Thompson, Frank Jr.	Dem	N.J.	4		4
9th	Holland, Elmer J.	Dem	Penn.	5	*2	3
10th	Dent, John H.	Dem	Penn.	3		3
11th	Pucinski, Roman C.	Dem	Ill.	2		2
12th	Daniels, Dominick V.	Dem	N.J.	2		2
13th	Brademas, John	Dem	Ind.	2		2
14th	Giaimo, Robert N.	Dem	Conn.	2		2
15th	O'Hara, James G.	Dem	Mich.	2		2
16th	Scott, Ralph J.	Dem	N.C.	3		1
17th	Smith, Neal	Dem	Iowa	2		1
18th	Joelson, Charles S.	Dem	N.J.	1		1
19th	Hansen, Julia Butler	Dem	Wash.	2		1

Minority

Rank	Name	Party	State	Terms in: House		Comm.
RM	Kearns, Carroll D.	Rep	Penn.	8		8
2nd	Hoffman, Clare E.	Rep	Mich.	14	*2	5
3rd	Frelinghuysen, Peter H.B.	Rep	N.J.	5		5
4th	Ayres, William H.	Rep	Ohio	6		3
5th	Griffin, Robert P.	Rep	Mich.	3		3
6th	Hiestand, Edgar W.	Rep	Cal.	5		2
7th	Quie, Albert H.	Rep	Minn.	3		2
8th	Goodell, Charles E.	Rep	N.Y.	2		2
9th	Garland, Peter A.	Rep	Me.	1		1
10th	Bruce, Donald C.	Rep	Ind.	1		1
11th	Ashbrook, John M.	Rep	Ohio	1		1
12th	Martin, David T.	Rep	Neb.	1		1

*1: Member's 1st period of service on the committee;
*2: Member's 2nd period of service on the committee.

Vacancy Filled:
Majority: 19th seat by Hansen on Mar. 6,1961.

Changes:
Majority:

Smith, Neal	Dem	Iowa	Aug. 28,1962	Moved to Appropriations.

Departures from the House:

	Majority		Minority	
Defeated for Reelection	Bailey, Cleveland M.	W.Va. Dem	Hiestand, Edgar W.	Cal. Rep
Defeated for Renomination	Zelenko, Herbert	N.Y. Dem	Garland, Peter A.	Me. Rep
			Kearns, Carroll D.	Penn. Rep
Retired	None		Hoffman, Clare E.	Mich. Rep

Departures from Committee:

Moved to Appropriations	Giaimo, Robert N.	Conn. Dem	None
	Hansen, Julia Butler	Wash. Dem	
	Joelson, Charles S.	N.J. Dem	

EDUCATION AND LABOR / 88th Congress

Service Dates of Committee Chair: Jan. 17,1963-Jan. 3,1965
Service Dates of Majority Members: Jan. 17,1963-Jan. 3,1965
Service Dates of Minority Members: Jan. 24,1963-Jan. 3,1965

Majority

Rank	Name	Party	State	Terms in: House	Terms in: Comm.
Chr	Powell, Adam Clayton Jr.	Dem	N.Y.	10	*1 10
2nd	Perkins, Carl D.	Dem	Ky.	8	8
3rd	Landrum, Phillip M.	Dem	Ga.	6	6
4th	Green, Edith S.	Dem	Ore.	5	5
5th	Roosevelt, James	Dem	Cal.	5	5
6th	Thompson, Frank Jr.	Dem	N.J.	5	5
7th	Holland, Elmer J.	Dem	Penn.	6	*2 4
8th	Dent, John H.	Dem	Penn.	4	4
9th	Pucinski, Roman C.	Dem	Ill.	3	3
10th	Daniels, Dominick V.	Dem	N.J.	3	3
11th	Brademas, John	Dem	Ind.	3	3
12th	O'Hara, James G.	Dem	Mich.	3	3
13th	Scott, Ralph J.	Dem	N.C.	4	2
14th	Carey, Hugh L.	Dem	N.Y.	2	1
15th	Hawkins, Augustus F.	Dem	Cal.	1	1
16th	Sickles, Carlton R.	Dem	Md.	1	1
17th	Gibbons, Sam M.	Dem	Fla.	1	1
18th	Gill, Thomas P.	Dem	Hai.	1	1
19th	Brown, George E. Jr.	Dem	Cal.	1	1

Minority

Rank	Name	Party	State	Terms in: House	Terms in: Comm.
RM	Frelinghuysen, Peter H.B.	Rep	N.J.	6	6
2nd	Ayres, William H.	Rep	Ohio	7	4
3rd	Griffin, Robert P.	Rep	Mich.	4	4
4th	Quie, Albert H.	Rep	Minn.	4	3
5th	Goodell, Charles E.	Rep	N.Y.	3	3
6th	Bruce, Donald C.	Rep	Ind.	2	2
7th	Ashbrook, John M.	Rep	Ohio	2	2
8th	Martin, David T.	Rep	Neb.	2	2
9th	Bell, Alphonzo	Rep	Cal.	2	1
10th	Snyder, M. G. (Gene)	Rep	Ky.	1	1
11th	Findley, Paul	Rep	Ill.	2	1
12th	Taft, Robert Jr.	Rep	Ohio	1	1

*1: Member's 1st period of service on the committee;
*2: Member's 2nd period of service on the committee.

Vacancies Filled:
Majority: 19th seat by Brown on Jan. 31,1963.
Minority: 11th and 12th seats by Findley and Taft respectively on Feb. 7,1963.

Departures from the House:	Majority			Minority		
Defeated for Reelection	None			Snyder, M. G. (Gene)	Ky.	Rep
Lost Election to U.S. Senate	Gill, Thomas P.	Hai.	Dem	None		
Lost Nomination to U.S. Senate	None			Bruce, Donald C.	Ind.	Rep
				Taft, Robert Jr.	Ohio	Rep
Departures from Committee:						
Moved to Science & Astronautics	Brown, George E. Jr.	Cal.	Dem	None		
Moved to Ways and Means	Landrum, Phillip M.	Ga.	Dem	None		
No new assignment	None			Frelinghuysen, Peter H.B.	N.J.	Rep

EDUCATION AND LABOR / 89th Congress

Service Dates of Committee Chair: Jan. 18,1965-Jan. 3,1967
Service Dates of Majority Members: Jan. 18,1965-Jan. 3,1967
Service Dates of Minority Members: Jan. 21,1965-Jan. 3,1967

Majority

Rank	Name	Party	State	Terms in: House	Terms in: Comm.
Chr	Powell, Adam Clayton Jr.	Dem	N.Y.	11	*1 11
2nd	Perkins, Carl D.	Dem	Ky.	9	9
3rd	Green, Edith S.	Dem	Ore.	6	6
4th	Roosevelt, James	Dem	Cal.	6	6
5th	Thompson, Frank Jr.	Dem	N.J.	6	6
6th	Holland, Elmer J.	Dem	Penn.	7	*2 5
7th	Dent, John H.	Dem	Penn.	5	5
8th	Pucinski, Roman C.	Dem	Ill.	4	4
9th	Daniels, Dominick V.	Dem	N.J.	4	4
10th	Brademas, John	Dem	Ind.	4	4
11th	O'Hara, James G.	Dem	Mich.	4	4
12th	Scott, Ralph J.	Dem	N.C.	5	3
13th	Carey, Hugh L.	Dem	N.Y.	3	2
14th	Hawkins, Augustus F.	Dem	Cal.	2	2
15th	Sickles, Carlton R.	Dem	Md.	2	2
16th	Gibbons, Sam M.	Dem	Fla.	2	2
17th	Ford, William D.	Dem	Mich.	1	1
18th	Hathaway, William D.	Dem	Me.	1	1
19th	Mink, Patsy T.	Dem	Hai.	1	*1 1
20th	Scheuer, James H.	Dem	N.Y.	1	1
21st	Meeds, Lloyd	Dem	Wash.	1	1

Minority

Rank	Name	Party	State	Terms in: House	Terms in: Comm.
RM	Ayres, William H.	Rep	Ohio	8	5
2nd	Griffin, Robert P.	Rep	Mich.	5	5
3rd	Quie, Albert H.	Rep	Minn.	5	4
4th	Goodell, Charles E.	Rep	N.Y.	4	4
5th	Ashbrook, John M.	Rep	Ohio	3	3
6th	Martin, David T.	Rep	Neb.	3	3
7th	Bell, Alphonzo	Rep	Cal.	3	2
8th	Findley, Paul	Rep	Ill.	3	2
9th	Reid, Ogden R.	Rep	N.Y.	2	1
10th	Andrews, A. Glenn	Rep	Ala.	1	1

*1: Member's 1st period of service on the committee;
*2: Member's 2nd period of service on the committee.

Changes:

Majority:

Name	Party	State	Date	Note
Roosevelt, James	Dem	Cal.	Sep. 30,1965	Resigned; appointed U.S. representative to UNESCO.
Burton, Phillip	Dem	Cal.	Oct. 20,1965	Replaced Roosevelt.

Minority:

Name	Party	State	Date	Note
Griffin, Robert P.	Rep	Mich.	May 10,1966	Resigned; appointed to U.S. Senate.
Findley, Paul	Rep	Ill.	May 12,1965	Left committee; no new assignment.
Gurney, Edward J.	Rep	Fla.	May 12,1965	Replaced Griffin.
Erlenborn, John N.	Rep	Ill.	May 24,1966	Replaced Findley.

	Majority			Minority		
Departures from the House:						
Defeated for Reelection	None			Andrews, A. Glenn	Ala.	Rep
Lost Nomination for Governor	Sickles, Carlton R.	Md.	Dem	None		
Retired	Scott, Ralph J.	N.C.	Dem	None		
Departures from Committee:						
Unassigned in 90th Congress; seat declared vacant	Powell, Adam Clayton Jr.	N.Y.	Dem	None		
No new assignment	None			Martin, David T.	Neb.	Rep

EDUCATION AND LABOR / 90th Congress

Service Dates of Committee Chair: Jan. 23,1967-Jan. 3,1969
Service Dates of Majority Members: Jan. 23,1967-Jan. 3,1969
Service Dates of Minority Members: Jan. 26,1967-Jan. 3,1969

Majority

Rank Name	Party	State	Terms in: House	Terms in: Comm.
Chr Perkins, Carl D.	Dem	Ky.	10	10
2nd Green, Edith S.	Dem	Ore.	7	7
3rd Thompson, Frank Jr.	Dem	N.J.	7	7
4th Holland, Elmer J.	Dem	Penn.	8	*2 6
5th Dent, John H.	Dem	Penn.	6	6
6th Pucinski, Roman C.	Dem	Ill.	5	5
7th Daniels, Dominick V.	Dem	N.J.	5	5
8th Brademas, John	Dem	Ind.	5	5
9th O'Hara, James G.	Dem	Mich.	5	5
10th Carey, Hugh L.	Dem	N.Y.	4	3
11th Hawkins, Augustus F.	Dem	Cal.	3	3
12th Gibbons, Sam M.	Dem	Fla.	3	3
13th Ford, William D.	Dem	Mich.	2	2
14th Hathaway, William D.	Dem	Me.	2	2
15th Mink, Patsy T.	Dem	Hai.	2	*1 2
16th Scheuer, James H.	Dem	N.Y.	2	2
17th Meeds, Lloyd	Dem	Wash.	2	2
18th Burton, Phillip	Dem	Cal.	3	2
19th Albert, Carl	Dem	Okla.	11	1

Minority

Rank Name	Party	State	Terms in: House	Terms in: Comm.
RM Ayres, William H.	Rep	Ohio	9	6
2nd Quie, Albert H.	Rep	Minn.	6	5
3rd Goodell, Charles E.	Rep	N.Y.	5	5
4th Ashbrook, John M.	Rep	Ohio	4	4
5th Bell, Alphonzo	Rep	Cal.	4	3
6th Reid, Ogden R.	Rep	N.Y.	3	2
7th Gurney, Edward J.	Rep	Fla.	3	2
8th Erlenborn, John N.	Rep	Ill.	2	2
9th Scherle, William J.	Rep	Iowa	1	1
10th Dellenback, John R.	Rep	Ore.	1	1
11th Esch, Marvin L.	Rep	Mich.	1	1
12th Eshleman, Edwin D.	Rep	Penn.	1	1
13th Gardner, James C.	Rep	N.C.	1	1
14th Steiger, William A.	Rep	Wisc.	1	1

*1: Member's 1st period of service on the committee;
*2: Member's 2nd period of service on the committee.

Vacancy Filled:
Majority: 19th seat by Albert on Mar. 16,1967.

Changes:
Majority:

Holland, Elmer J.	Dem	Penn.	Aug. 9,1968	Died in office.

Minority:

Goodell, Charles E.	Rep	N.Y.	Sep. 9,1968	Resigned; appointed to U.S. Senate.
Collins, James M.	Rep	Tex.	Sep. 19,1968	Replaced Goodell.

	Majority		Minority	
Departures from the House:				
Elected to U.S. Senate	None		Gurney, Edward J.	Fla. Rep
Lost Election for Governor	None		Gardner, James C.	N.C. Rep
Departures from Committee:				
Moved to Ways and Means	Gibbons, Sam M.	Fla. Dem	None	
No new assignment	Albert, Carl	Okla. Dem	None	

EDUCATION AND LABOR / 91st Congress

Service Dates of Committee Chair: Jan. 29,1969-Jan. 3,1971
Service Dates of Majority Members: Jan. 29,1969-Jan. 3,1971
Service Dates of Minority Members: Jan. 29,1969-Jan. 3,1971

Majority

Rank	Name	Party	State	Terms in: House		Terms in: Comm.
Chr	Perkins, Carl D.	Dem	Ky.	11		11
2nd	Green, Edith S.	Dem	Ore.	8		8
3rd	Thompson, Frank Jr.	Dem	N.J.	8		8
4th	Dent, John H.	Dem	Penn.	7		7
5th	Pucinski, Roman C.	Dem	Ill.	6		6
6th	Daniels, Dominick V.	Dem	N.J.	6		6
7th	Brademas, John	Dem	Ind.	6		6
8th	O'Hara, James G.	Dem	Mich.	6		6
9th	Carey, Hugh L.	Dem	N.Y.	5		4
10th	Hawkins, Augustus F.	Dem	Cal.	4		4
11th	Ford, William D.	Dem	Mich.	3		3
12th	Hathaway, William D.	Dem	Me.	3		3
13th	Mink, Patsy T.	Dem	Hai.	3	*1	3
14th	Scheuer, James H.	Dem	N.Y.	3		3
15th	Meeds, Lloyd	Dem	Wash.	3		3
16th	Burton, Phillip	Dem	Cal.	4		3
17th	Gaydos, Joseph M.	Dem	Penn.	2		1
18th	Stokes, Louis	Dem	Ohio	1		1
19th	Clay, William L.	Dem	Mo.	1		1
20th	Powell, Adam Clayton Jr.	Dem	N.Y.	13	*2	1

Minority

Rank	Name	Party	State	Terms in: House	Terms in: Comm.
RM	Ayres, William H.	Rep	Ohio	10	7
2nd	Quie, Albert H.	Rep	Minn.	7	6
3rd	Ashbrook, John M.	Rep	Ohio	5	5
4th	Bell, Alphonzo	Rep	Cal.	5	4
5th	Reid, Ogden R.	Rep	N.Y.	4	3
6th	Erlenborn, John N.	Rep	Ill.	3	3
7th	Scherle, William J.	Rep	Iowa	2	2
8th	Dellenback, John R.	Rep	Ore.	2	2
9th	Esch, Marvin L.	Rep	Mich.	2	2
10th	Eshleman, Edwin D.	Rep	Penn.	2	2
11th	Steiger, William A.	Rep	Wisc.	2	2
12th	Collins, James M.	Rep	Tex.	2	2
13th	Landgrebe, Earl F.	Rep	Ind.	1	1
14th	Hansen, Orval H.	Rep	Ida.	1	1
15th	Ruth, Earl B.	Rep	N.C.	1	1

*1: Member's 1st period of service on the committee;
*2: Member's 2nd period of service on the committee.

Note: Adam Clayton Powell (Dem-N.Y.), was stripped of his seniority by a censure ruling of the House on Feb. 14,1967.

Changes:

Majority:

Carey, Hugh L.	Dem	N.Y.	Dec. 17,1970	Moved to Ways and Means.

Minority:

Scherle, William J.	Rep	Iowa	Nov. 25,1970	Moved to Appropriations.

	Majority			Minority		
Departures from the House:						
Defeated for Reelection	None			Ayres, William H.	Ohio	Rep
Defeated for Renomination	Powell, Adam Clayton Jr.	N.Y.	Dem	None		
Departures from Committee:						
Moved to Appropriations	Hathaway, William D.	Me.	Dem	None		
	Stokes, Louis	Ohio	Dem			
Moved to Interstate & Foreign Commerce	None			Collins, James M.	Tex.	Rep

EDUCATION AND LABOR / 92nd Congress

Service Dates of Committee Chair: Feb. 4,1971-Jan. 3,1973
Service Dates of Majority Members: Feb. 4,1971-Jan. 3,1973
Service Dates of Minority Members: Feb. 4,1971-Jan. 3,1973

Majority

Rank	Name	Party	State	Terms in: House		Terms in: Comm.
Chr	Perkins, Carl D.	Dem	Ky.	12		12
2nd	Green, Edith S.	Dem	Ore.	9		9
3rd	Thompson, Frank Jr.	Dem	N.J.	9		9
4th	Dent, John H.	Dem	Penn.	8		8
5th	Pucinski, Roman C.	Dem	Ill.	7		7
6th	Daniels, Dominick V.	Dem	N.J.	7		7
7th	Brademas, John	Dem	Ind.	7		7
8th	O'Hara, James G.	Dem	Mich.	7		7
9th	Hawkins, Augustus F.	Dem	Cal.	5		5
10th	Ford, William D.	Dem	Mich.	4		4
11th	Mink, Patsy T.	Dem	Hai.	4	*1	4
12th	Scheuer, James H.	Dem	N.Y.	4		4
13th	Meeds, Lloyd	Dem	Wash.	4		4
14th	Burton, Phillip	Dem	Cal.	5		4
15th	Gaydos, Joseph M.	Dem	Penn.	3		2
16th	Clay, William L.	Dem	Mo.	2		2
17th	Chisholm, Shirley A.	Dem	N.Y.	2		1
18th	Biaggi, Mario	Dem	N.Y.	2		1
19th	Grasso, Ella T.	Dem	Conn.	1		1
20th	Hicks, Louise Day	Dem	Mass.	1		1
21st	Mazzoli, Romano L.	Dem	Ky.	1		1
22nd	Badillo, Herman	Dem	N.Y.	1		1

Minority

Rank	Name	Party	State	Terms in: House		Terms in: Comm.
RM	Quie, Albert H.	Rep	Minn.	8		7
2nd	Ashbrook, John M.	Rep	Ohio	6		6
3rd	Bell, Alphonzo	Rep	Cal.	6		5
4th	Reid, Ogden R.	Rep	N.Y.	5		4
5th	Erlenborn, John N.	Rep	Ill.	4		4
6th	Dellenback, John R.	Rep	Ore.	3		3
7th	Esch, Marvin L.	Rep	Mich.	3		3
8th	Eshleman, Edwin D.	Rep	Penn.	3		3
9th	Steiger, William A.	Rep	Wisc.	3		3
10th	Landgrebe, Earl F.	Rep	Ind.	2		2
11th	Hansen, Orval H.	Rep	Ida.	2		2
12th	Ruth, Earl B.	Rep	N.C.	2		2
13th	Forsythe, Edwin B.	Rep	N.J.	2		1
14th	Veysey, Victor V.	Rep	Cal.	1		1
15th	Kemp, Jack F.	Rep	N.Y.	1		1
16th	Peyser, Peter A.	Rep	N.Y.	1	*1	1

*1: Member's 1st period of service on the committee.

Changes:

Minority:

Reid, Ogden R.	Rep	N.Y.	Mar. 27,1972	Left the Republican Party; moved to Foreign Affairs as a Democrat.
Carlson, Clifford D.	Rep	Ill.	May 3,1972	Replaced Reid.

Departures from the House:	**Majority**			**Minority**		
Defeated for Reelection	Hicks, Louise Day	Mass.	Dem	None		
Defeated for Renomination	Scheuer, James H.	N.Y.	Dem	None		
Lost Election to U.S. Senate	Pucinski, Roman C.	Ill.	Dem	None		
Retired	None			Carlson, Clifford D.	Ill.	Rep
Departures from Committee:						
Moved to Appropriations	Green, Edith S.	Ore.	Dem	Ruth, Earl B.	N.C.	Rep
				Veysey, Victor V.	Cal.	Rep

EDUCATION AND LABOR / 93rd Congress

Service Dates of Committee Chair: Jan. 24,1973-Jan. 3,1975
Service Dates of Majority Members: Jan. 24,1973-Jan. 3,1975
Service Dates of Minority Members: Jan. 24,1973-Jan. 3,1975

Majority

Rank	Name	Party	State	Terms in: House	Terms in: Comm.
Chr	Perkins, Carl D.	Dem	Ky.	13	13
2nd	Thompson, Frank Jr.	Dem	N.J.	10	10
3rd	Dent, John H.	Dem	Penn.	9	9
4th	Daniels, Dominick V.	Dem	N.J.	8	8
5th	Brademas, John	Dem	Ind.	8	8
6th	O'Hara, James G.	Dem	Mich.	8	8
7th	Hawkins, Augustus F.	Dem	Cal.	6	6
8th	Ford, William D.	Dem	Mich.	5	5
9th	Mink, Patsy T.	Dem	Hai.	5	*1 5
10th	Meeds, Lloyd	Dem	Wash.	5	5
11th	Burton, Phillip	Dem	Cal.	6	5
12th	Gaydos, Joseph M.	Dem	Penn.	4	3
13th	Clay, William L.	Dem	Mo.	3	3
14th	Chisholm, Shirley A.	Dem	N.Y.	3	2
15th	Biaggi, Mario	Dem	N.Y.	3	2
16th	Grasso, Ella T.	Dem	Conn.	2	2
17th	Mazzoli, Romano L.	Dem	Ky.	2	2
18th	Badillo, Herman	Dem	N.Y.	2	2
19th	Andrews, Ike F.	Dem	N.C.	1	1
20th	Lehman, William	Dem	Fla.	1	1
21st	Benitez, Jaime	PpD	P.R.	1	1

Minority

Rank	Name	Party	State	Terms in: House	Terms in: Comm.
RM	Quie, Albert H.	Rep	Minn.	9	8
2nd	Ashbrook, John M.	Rep	Ohio	7	7
3rd	Bell, Alphonzo	Rep	Cal.	7	6
4th	Erlenborn, John N.	Rep	Ill.	5	5
5th	Dellenback, John R.	Rep	Ore.	4	4
6th	Esch, Marvin L.	Rep	Mich.	4	4
7th	Eshleman, Edwin D.	Rep	Penn.	4	4
8th	Steiger, William A.	Rep	Wisc.	4	4
9th	Landgrebe, Earl F.	Rep	Ind.	3	3
10th	Hansen, Orval H.	Rep	Ida.	3	3
11th	Forsythe, Edwin B.	Rep	N.J.	3	2
12th	Kemp, Jack F.	Rep	N.Y.	2	2
13th	Peyser, Peter A.	Rep	N.Y.	2	*1 2
14th	Towell, David G.	Rep	Nev.	1	1
15th	Sarasin, Ronald A.	Rep	Conn.	1	1
16th	Huber, Robert J.	Rep	Mich.	1	1

*1: Member's 1st period of service on the committee.

Note: Jamie Benitez (Popular Democrat-P.R.), the Resident Commissioner from Puerto Rico, was allowed to accrue seniority but was not included in the committee's size or party ratio of 20 Democrats and 16 Republicans.

Departures from the House:	Majority		Minority	
Elected Governor	Grasso, Ella T.	Conn. Dem	None	
Defeated for Reelection	None		Dellenback, John R.	Ore. Rep
			Huber, Robert J.	Mich. Rep
			Landgrebe, Earl F.	Ind. Rep
			Towell, David G.	Nev. Rep
Defeated for Renomination	None		Hansen, Orval H.	Ida. Rep
Departures from Committee:				
Moved to Judiciary	Badillo, Herman	N.Y. Dem	None	
	Mazzoli, Romano L.	Ky. Dem		
Moved to Government Operations	None		Forsythe, Edwin B.	N.J. Rep
Moved to Appropriations	None		Kemp, Jack F.	N.Y. Rep
Moved to Ways and Means	None		Steiger, William A.	Wisc. Rep

EDUCATION AND LABOR / 94th Congress

Service Dates of Committee Chair: Jan. 20,1975-Jan. 3,1977
Service Dates of Majority Members: Jan. 20,1975-Jan. 3,1977
Service Dates of Minority Members: Jan. 28,1975-Jan. 3,1977

Majority

Rank	Name	Party	State	Terms in: House	Terms in: Comm.
Chr	Perkins, Carl D.	Dem	Ky.	14	14
2nd	Thompson, Frank Jr.	Dem	N.J.	11	11
3rd	Dent, John H.	Dem	Penn.	10	10
4th	Daniels, Dominick V.	Dem	N.J.	9	9
5th	Brademas, John	Dem	Ind.	9	9
6th	O'Hara, James G.	Dem	Mich.	9	9
7th	Hawkins, Augustus F.	Dem	Cal.	7	7
8th	Ford, William D.	Dem	Mich.	6	6
9th	Mink, Patsy T.	Dem	Hai.	6	*1 6
10th	Meeds, Lloyd	Dem	Wash.	6	6
11th	Burton, Phillip	Dem	Cal.	7	6
12th	Gaydos, Joseph M.	Dem	Penn.	5	4
13th	Clay, William L.	Dem	Mo.	4	4
14th	Chisholm, Shirley A.	Dem	N.Y.	4	3
15th	Biaggi, Mario	Dem	N.Y.	4	3
16th	Andrews, Ike F.	Dem	N.C.	2	2
17th	Lehman, William	Dem	Fla.	2	2
18th	Benitez, Jaime	PpD	P.R.	2	2
19th	Blouin, Michael T.	Dem	Iowa	1	1
20th	Cornell, Robert J.	Dem	Wisc.	1	1
21st	Risenhoover, Theodore M.	Dem	Okla.	1	1
22nd	Simon, Paul M.	Dem	Ill.	1	1
23rd	Beard, Edward P.	Dem	R.I.	1	1
24th	Zeferetti, Leo C.	Dem	N.Y.	1	1
25th	Miller, George	Dem	Cal.	1	1
26th	Mottl, Ronald M.	Dem	Ohio	1	1
27th	Hall, Tim L.	Dem	Ill.	1	1

Minority

Rank	Name	Party	State	Terms in: House	Terms in: Comm.
RM	Quie, Albert H.	Rep	Minn.	10	9
2nd	Ashbrook, John M.	Rep	Ohio	8	8
3rd	Bell, Alphonzo	Rep	Cal.	8	7
4th	Erlenborn, John N.	Rep	Ill.	6	6
5th	Esch, Marvin L.	Rep	Mich.	5	5
6th	Eshleman, Edwin D.	Rep	Penn.	5	5
7th	Peyser, Peter A.	Rep	N.Y.	3	*1 3
8th	Sarasin, Ronald A.	Rep	Conn.	2	2
9th	Buchanan, John H. Jr.	Rep	Ala.	6	1
10th	Jeffords, James M.	Rep	Vt.	1	1
11th	Pressler, Larry L.	Rep	S.D.	1	1
12th	Goodling, William F.	Rep	Penn.	1	1
13th	Smith, Virginia D.	Rep	Neb.	1	1

*1: Member's 1st period of service on the committee.

Note: Jamie Benitez (Popular Democrat-P.R.), the Resident Commissioner from Puerto Rico, was allowed to accrue seniority but was not included in the committee's size or party ratio of 26 Democrats and 13 Republicans.

Changes:

Majority:

Risenhoover, Theodore M.	Dem	Okla.	Dec. 17,1975	Moved to Public Works and Transportation.

Departures from the House:	Majority			Minority		
Defeated for Reelection	Benitez, Jaime	P.R.	Dem	None		
	Hall, Tim L.	Ill.	Dem			
Lost Election to U.S. Senate	None			Esch, Marvin L.	Mich.	Rep
Lost Nomination to U.S. Senate	Mink, Patsy T.	Hai.	Dem	Bell, Alphonzo	Cal.	Rep
	O'Hara, James G.	Mich.	Dem	Peyser, Peter A.	N.Y.	Rep
Retired	Daniels, Dominick V.	N.J.	Dem	Eshleman, Edwin D.	Penn.	Rep
Departures from Committee:						
Moved to Rules	Chisholm, Shirley A.	N.Y.	Dem	None		
	Meeds, Lloyd	Wash.	Dem			
Moved to Budget	Lehman, William	Fla.	Dem			
Moved to Appropriations	None			Smith, Virginia D.	Neb.	Rep

EDUCATION AND LABOR / 95th Congress

Service Dates of Committee Chair: Jan. 19,1977-Jan. 3,1979
Service Dates of Majority Members: Jan. 19,1977-Jan. 3,1979
Service Dates of Minority Members: Jan. 19,1977-Jan. 3,1979

Majority

Rank	Name	Party	State	Terms in: House	Terms in: Comm.
Chr	Perkins, Carl D.	Dem	Ky.	15	15
2nd	Thompson, Frank Jr.	Dem	N.J.	12	12
3rd	Dent, John H.	Dem	Penn.	11	11
4th	Brademas, John	Dem	Ind.	10	10
5th	Hawkins, Augustus F.	Dem	Cal.	8	8
6th	Ford, William D.	Dem	Mich.	7	7
7th	Burton, Phillip	Dem	Cal.	8	7
8th	Gaydos, Joseph M.	Dem	Penn.	6	5
9th	Clay, William L.	Dem	Mo.	5	5
10th	Biaggi, Mario	Dem	N.Y.	5	4
11th	Andrews, Ike F.	Dem	N.C.	3	3
12th	Blouin, Michael T.	Dem	Iowa	2	2
13th	Cornell, Robert J.	Dem	Wisc.	2	2
14th	Simon, Paul M.	Dem	Ill.	2	2
15th	Beard, Edward P.	Dem	R.I.	2	2
16th	Zeferetti, Leo C.	Dem	N.Y.	2	2
17th	Miller, George	Dem	Cal.	2	2
18th	Mottl, Ronald M.	Dem	Ohio	2	2
19th	Myers, Michael O. (Ozzie)	Dem	Penn.	2	1
20th	Murphy, Austin J.	Dem	Penn.	1	1
21st	LeFante, Joseph A.	Dem	N.J.	1	1
22nd	Weiss, Theodore S.	Dem	N.Y.	1	1
23rd	Heftel, Cecil	Dem	Hai.	1	1
24th	Corrada-del Rio, Baltasar	NPr	P.R.	1	1
25th	Kildee, Dale E.	Dem	Mich.	1	1

Minority

Rank	Name	Party	State	Terms in: House	Terms in: Comm.
RM	Quie, Albert H.	Rep	Minn.	11	10
2nd	Ashbrook, John M.	Rep	Ohio	9	9
3rd	Erlenborn, John N.	Rep	Ill.	7	7
4th	Sarasin, Ronald A.	Rep	Conn.	3	3
5th	Buchanan, John H. Jr.	Rep	Ala.	7	2
6th	Jeffords, James M.	Rep	Vt.	2	2
7th	Pressler, Larry L.	Rep	S.D.	2	2
8th	Goodling, William F.	Rep	Penn.	2	2
9th	Shuster, E. G. (Bud)	Rep	Penn.	3	1
10th	Pettis, Shirley N.	Rep	Cal.	2	1
11th	Pursell, Carl D.	Rep	Mich.	1	1
12th	Edwards, M. H. (Mickey)	Rep	Okla.	1	1

Note: Baltasar Corrada-del Rio (New Progressive-P.R.), the Resident Commissioner from Puerto Rico, was allowed to accrue seniority but was not included in the committee's party ratio of 24 Democrats and 12 Republicans.

Changes:

Majority:

LeFante, Joseph A.	Dem	N.J.	Dec. 14,1978	Resigned and retired.

	Majority		Minority	
Departures from the House:				
Elected to U.S. Senate	None		Pressler, Larry L.	S.D. Rep
Elected Governor	None		Quie, Albert H.	Minn. Rep
Defeated for Reelection	Blouin, Michael T.	Iowa Dem	None	
	Cornell, Robert J.	Wisc. Dem		
Lost Election for Governor	None		Sarasin, Ronald A.	Conn. Rep
Retired	Dent, John H.	Penn. Dem	Pettis, Shirley N.	Cal. Rep
Departures from Committee:				
Moved to Ways and Means	Heftel, Cecil	Hai. Dem	None	
Moved to Interstate & Foreign Commerce	Mottl, Ronald M.	Ohio Dem	None	
Moved to Rules	Zeferetti, Leo C.	N.Y. Dem	None	
Moved to Appropriations	None		Pursell, Carl D.	Mich. Rep
Moved to Budget	None		Shuster, E. G. (Bud)	Penn. Rep

EDUCATION AND LABOR / 96th Congress

Service Dates of Committee Chair: Jan. 24,1979-Jan. 3,1981
Service Dates of Majority Members: Jan. 24,1979-Jan. 3,1981
Service Dates of Minority Members: Jan. 24,1979-Jan. 3,1981

Majority

Rank	Name	Party	State	Terms in: House	Terms in: Comm.
Chr	Perkins, Carl D.	Dem	Ky.	16	16
2nd	Thompson, Frank Jr.	Dem	N.J.	13	13
3rd	Brademas, John	Dem	Ind.	11	11
4th	Hawkins, Augustus F.	Dem	Cal.	9	9
5th	Ford, William D.	Dem	Mich.	8	8
6th	Burton, Phillip	Dem	Cal.	9	8
7th	Gaydos, Joseph M.	Dem	Penn.	7	6
8th	Clay, William L.	Dem	Mo.	6	6
9th	Biaggi, Mario	Dem	N.Y.	6	5
10th	Andrews, Ike F.	Dem	N.C.	4	4
11th	Simon, Paul M.	Dem	Ill.	3	3
12th	Beard, Edward P.	Dem	R.I.	3	3
13th	Miller, George	Dem	Cal.	3	3
14th	Myers, Michael O.(Ozzie)	Dem	Penn.	3	2
15th	Murphy, Austin J.	Dem	Penn.	2	2
16th	Weiss, Theodore S.	Dem	N.Y.	2	2
17th	Corrada-del Rio, Baltasar	NPr	P.R.	2	2
18th	Kildee, Dale E.	Dem	Mich.	2	2
19th	Peyser, Peter A.	Dem	N.Y.	1 *2	1
20th	Stack, Edward J.	Dem	Fla.	1	1
21st	Williams, Pat	Dem	Mont.	1	1
22nd	Ratchford, William R.	Dem	Conn.	1	1
23rd	Kogovsek, Raymond P.	Dem	Colo.	1	1
24th	Bailey, Donald A.	Dem	Penn.	1 *T	1

Minority

Rank	Name	Party	State	Terms in: House	Terms in: Comm.
RM	Ashbrook, John M.	Rep	Ohio	10	10
2nd	Erlenborn, John N.	Rep	Ill.	8	8
3rd	Buchanan, John H. Jr.	Rep	Ala.	8	3
4th	Jeffords, James M.	Rep	Vt.	3	3
5th	Goodling, William F.	Rep	Penn.	3	3
6th	Edwards, M. H. (Mickey)	Rep	Okla.	2	2
7th	Coleman, E. Thomas	Rep	Mo.	3	1
8th	Kramer, Kenneth B.	Rep	Colo.	1	1
9th	Erdahl, Arlen I.	Rep	Minn.	1	1
10th	Tauke, Thomas J.	Rep	Iowa	1	1
11th	Crane, Daniel B.	Rep	Ill.	1	1
12th	Hinson, Jon C.	Rep	Miss.	1	1
13th	Petri, Thomas E.	Rep	Wisc.	1	1

*2: Member's 2nd period of service on the committee;
*T: Temporary member of the committee.

Note: Baltasar Corrada-del Rio (New Progressive-P.R.), the Resident Commissioner from Puerto Rico, was allowed to accrue seniority but was not included in the committee's party ratio of 23 Democrats and 13 Republicans.

Vacancies Filled:
Majority: 24th seat by Bailey on Jan. 31,1979.
Minority: 13th seat by Petri on Apr. 9,1979.

Changes:
Majority:

Name	Party	State	Date	Change
Bailey, Donald A.	Dem	Penn.	May 15,1980	Left committee; no new assignment.
Musto, Raphael	Dem	Penn.	May 15,1980	Replaced Bailey.
Myers, Michael O. (Ozzie)	Dem	Penn.	Oct. 2,1980	Expelled from the House.

	Majority			Minority		
Departures from the House:						
Defeated for Reelection	Beard, Edward P.	R.I.	Dem	None		
	Brademas, John	Ind.	Dem			
	Thompson, Frank Jr.	N.J.	Dem			
	Musto, Raphael	Penn.	Dem			
Defeated for Renomination	Stack, Edward J.	Fla.	Dem	Buchanan, John H. Jr.	Ala.	Rep
Departures from Committee:						
Moved to Small Business	None			Crane, Daniel B.	Ill.	Rep
Moved to Appropriations	None			Edwards, M.H. (Mickey)	Okla.	Rep
Moved to Interior & Insular Affairs	None			Hinson, Jon C.	Miss.	Rep
Moved to Energy & Commerce	None			Tauke, Thomas J.	Iowa	Rep

EDUCATION AND LABOR / 97th Congress

Service Dates of Committee Chair: Jan. 28,1981-Jan. 3,1983
Service Dates of Majority Members: Jan. 28,1981-Jan. 3,1983
Service Dates of Minority Members: Jan. 28,1981-Jan. 3,1983

Majority

Rank	Name	Party	State	Terms in: House	Terms in: Comm.
Chr	Perkins, Carl D.	Dem	Ky.	17	17
2nd	Hawkins, Augustus F.	Dem	Cal.	10	10
3rd	Ford, William D.	Dem	Mich.	9	9
4th	Burton, Phillip	Dem	Cal.	10	9
5th	Gaydos, Joseph M.	Dem	Penn.	8	7
6th	Clay, William L.	Dem	Mo.	7	7
7th	Biaggi, Mario	Dem	N.Y.	7	6
8th	Andrews, Ike F.	Dem	N.C.	5	5
9th	Simon, Paul M.	Dem	Ill.	4	4
10th	Miller, George	Dem	Cal.	4	4
11th	Murphy, Austin J.	Dem	Penn.	3	3
12th	Weiss, Theodore S.	Dem	N.Y.	3	3
13th	Corrada-del Rio, Baltasar	NPr	P.R.	3	3
14th	Kildee, Dale E.	Dem	Mich.	3	3
15th	Peyser, Peter A.	Dem	N.Y.	2	*2 2
16th	Williams, Pat	Dem	Mont.	2	2
17th	Ratchford, William R.	Dem	Conn.	2	2
18th	Kogovsek, Raymond P.	Dem	Colo.	2	2
19th	Washington, Harold	Dem	Ill.	1	1
20th	Eckart, Dennis E.	Dem	Ohio	1	*1 1

Minority

Rank	Name	Party	State	Terms in: House	Terms in: Comm.
RM1	Ashbrook, John M.	Rep	Ohio	11	11
RM2	Erlenborn, John N.	Rep	Ill.	9	9
3rd	Jeffords, James M.	Rep	Vt.	4	4
4th	Goodling, William F.	Rep	Penn.	4	4
5th	Coleman, E. Thomas	Rep	Mo.	4	2
6th	Kramer, Kenneth B.	Rep	Colo.	2	2
7th	Erdahl, Arlen I.	Rep	Minn.	2	2
8th	Petri, Thomas E.	Rep	Wisc.	2	2
9th	Fenwick, Millicent H.	Rep	N.J.	4	1
10th	Roukema, Margaret	Rep	N.J.	1	1
11th	Johnston, Eugene	Rep	N.C.	1	1
12th	DeNardis, Lawrence J.	Rep	Conn.	1	1
13th	Craig, Larry E.	Rep	Ida.	1	1
14th	Bailey, Wendell	Rep	Mo.	1	1

*1: Member's 1st period of service on the committee;
*2: Member's 2nd period of service on the committee.

Notes: Baltasar Corrada-del Rio (New Progressive-P.R.), the Resident Commissioner from Puerto Rico was allowed to accrue committee seniority but was not included in the committee's party ratio. The committee was expanded and the party ratio changed to 20 Democrats (excluding Corrada) and 14 Republicans on Aug. 19,1982.

Vacancy Filled:
Majority: 20th seat by Eckart on Feb. 25,1981.

Addition:
Majority: 21st Martinez, Matthew G. Dem Cal. Aug. 19,1982

Changes:
Ranking Member:

RM1	Ashbrook, John M.	Rep	Ohio	Apr. 24,1982	Died in office.
RM2	Erlenborn, John N.	Rep	Ill.	Apr. 24,1982	Succeeded Ashbrook as Ranking Minority Member.

Minority:

Ashbrook, John M.	Rep	Ohio	Apr. 24,1982	Died in office.
Gunderson, Steven	Rep	Wisc.	June 9,1982	Replaced Ashbrook.

	Majority			Minority		
Departures from the House:						
Defeated for Reelection	Peyser, Peter A.	N.Y.	Dem	Bailey, Wendell	Mo.	Rep
				DeNardis, Lawrence J.	Conn.	Rep
				Erdahl, Arlen I.	Minn.	Rep
				Johnston, Eugene	N.C.	Rep
Lost Election to U.S. Senate	None			Fenwick, Millicent H.	N.J.	Rep
Departures from Committee:						
Moved to Energy and Commerce	Eckart, Dennis E.	Ohio	Dem	None		
No new assignment	Ratchford, William R.	Conn.	Dem	Kramer, Kenneth B.	Colo.	Rep

EDUCATION AND LABOR / 98th Congress

Service Dates of Committee Chairs: Ch1 Jan. 6,1983-Aug. 3,1984
Ch2 Sep. 6,1984-Jan. 3,1985
Service Dates of Majority Members: Jan. 6,1983-Jan. 3,1985
Service Dates of Minority Members: Jan. 6,1983-Jan. 3,1985

Majority

Rank Name	Party	State	Terms in: House	Terms in: Comm.
Ch1 Perkins, Carl D.	Dem	Ky.	18	18
Ch2 2nd Hawkins, Augustus F.	Dem	Cal.	11	11
3rd Ford, William D.	Dem	Mich.	10	10
4th Burton, Phillip	Dem	Cal.	11	10
5th Gaydos, Joseph M.	Dem	Penn.	9	8
6th Clay, William L.	Dem	Mo.	8	8
7th Biaggi, Mario	Dem	N.Y.	8	7
8th Andrews, Ike F.	Dem	N.C.	6	6
9th Simon, Paul M.	Dem	Ill.	5	5
10th Miller, George	Dem	Cal.	5	5
11th Murphy, Austin J.	Dem	Penn.	4	4
12th Weiss, Theodore S.	Dem	N.Y.	4	4
13th Corrada-del Rio, Baltasar	NPr	P.R.	4	4
14th Kildee, Dale E.	Dem	Mich.	4	4
15th Williams, Pat	Dem	Mont.	3	3
16th Kogovsek, Raymond P.	Dem	Colo.	3	3
17th Washington, Harold	Dem	Ill.	2	2
18th Martinez, Matthew G.	Dem	Cal.	2	2
19th Owens, Major R.	Dem	N.Y.	1	1
20th Harrison, Frank	Dem	Penn.	1	1
21st Boucher, Frederick C.	Dem	Va.	1	1

Minority

Rank Name	Party	State	Terms in: House	Terms in: Comm.
RM Erlenborn, John N.	Rep	Ill.	10	10
2nd Jeffords, James M.	Rep	Vt.	5	5
3rd Goodling, William F.	Rep	Penn.	5	5
4th Coleman, E. Thomas	Rep	Mo.	5	3
5th Petri, Thomas E.	Rep	Wisc.	3	3
6th Roukema, Margaret	Rep	N.J.	2	2
7th Craig, Larry E.	Rep	Ida.	2	2
8th Gunderson, Steven	Rep	Wisc.	2	2
9th Bartlett, Steve	Rep	Tex.	1	1
10th Packard, Ron	Rep	Cal.	1	1
11th Nielson, Howard C.	Rep	Utah	1	1

Notes: Baltasar Corrada-del Rio (New Progressive-P.R.), the Resident Commissioner from Puerto Rico, was allowed to accrue seniority, but was not included in the committee's party ratio of 20 Democrats and 11 Republicans. The committee was expanded and the party ratio changed to 22 Democrats (excluding Corrada) and 13 Republicans on July 19,1983.

Vacancy Filled:
Minority: 11th seat by Nielson on Apr. 21,1983.

Additions:

	Rank	Name	Party	State	Date
Majority:	22nd	Burton, Sala	Dem	Cal.	July 19,1983 (to rank ahead of temporary members Eckart and Penny.)
	23rd	Hayes, Charles A.	Dem	Ill.	Nov. 3,1983
Minority:	12th	Tauke, Thomas J.	Rep	Iowa	Jan. 26,1984
	13th	McCain, John	Rep	Ariz.	Jan. 26,1984

Changes:

Name	Party	State	Date	Change
Chair:				
Ch1 Perkins, Carl D.	Dem	Ky.	Aug. 3,1984	Died in office.
Ch2 Hawkins, Augustus F.	Dem	Cal.	Sep. 6,1984	Succeeded Perkins as Chair.
Majority:				
Weiss, Theodore S.	Dem	N.Y.	Feb. 2,1983	Moved to Foreign Affairs.
Ackerman, Gary L.	Dem	N.Y.	Mar. 24,1983	Replaced Weiss.
Burton, Phillip	Dem	Cal.	Apr. 10,1983	Died in office.
Washington, Harold	Dem	Ill.	Apr. 30,1983	Resigned; elected Mayor of Chicago.
Eckart, Dennis E.	Dem	Ohio	May 24,1983	Replaced Burton; temporary term.
Penny, Timothy J.	Dem	Minn.	May 24,1983	Replaced Washington; temporary term.
Eckart, Dennis E.	Dem	Ohio	Nov. 18,1983	Temporary term expired on last day of 1st Session.
Penny, Timothy J.	Dem	Minn.	Nov. 18,1983	Temporary term expired on last day of 1st Session.
Eckart, Dennis E.	Dem	Ohio	Feb. 9,1984	Replaced himself.
Penny, Timothy J.	Dem	Minn.	Feb. 9,1984	Replaced himself.
Perkins, Carl D.	Dem	Ky.	Aug. 3,1984	Died in office.
Minority:				
Craig, Larry E.	Rep	Ida.	Mar. 2,1983	Moved to Government Operations.
Chandler, Rodney	Rep	Wash.	June 8,1983	Replaced Craig.

Departures from the House:	**Majority**		**Minority**	
Elected to U.S. Senate	Simon, Paul M.	Ill. Dem	None	
Elected Mayor of San Juan	Corrada-del Rio, Baltasar	P.R. Dem	None	
Defeated for Reelection	Andrews, Ike F.	N.C. Dem	None	
Defeated for Renomination	Harrison, Frank	Penn. Dem	None	
Retired	Kogovsek, Raymond P.	Colo. Dem	Erlenborn, John N.	Ill. Rep
Departures from Committee:				
Moved to Rules	Burton, Sala	Cal. Dem	None	
Ceases active membership to serve on Budget	Miller, George	Cal. Dem	None	
Moved to Science & Technology	None		Packard, Ron	Cal. Rep
Moved to Foreign Affairs	None		McCain, John	Ariz. Rep
No new assignment	Ackerman, Gary L.	N.Y. Dem	None	

EDUCATION AND LABOR / 99th Congress

Service Dates of Committee Chair: Jan. 7,1985-Jan. 3,1987
Service Dates of Majority Members: Jan. 30,1985-Jan. 3,1987
Service Dates of Minority Members: Jan. 30,1985-Jan. 3,1987

Majority

Rank	Name	Party	State	Terms in: House	Terms in: Comm.
Chr	Hawkins, Augustus F.	Dem	Cal.	12	12
2nd	Ford, William D.	Dem	Mich.	11	11
3rd	Gaydos, Joseph M.	Dem	Penn.	10	9
4th	Clay, William L.	Dem	Mo.	9	9
5th	Biaggi, Mario	Dem	N.Y.	9	8
6th	Murphy, Austin J.	Dem	Penn.	5	5
7th	Kildee, Dale E.	Dem	Mich.	5	5
8th	Williams, Pat	Dem	Mont.	4	4
9th	Martinez, Matthew G.	Dem	Cal.	3	3
10th	Owens, Major R.	Dem	N.Y.	2	2
11th	Boucher, Frederick C.	Dem	Va.	2	2
12th	Hayes, Charles A.	Dem	Ill.	2	2
13th	Perkins, Carl C. (Chris)	Dem	Ky.	2	1
14th	Bruce, Terry L.	Dem	Ill.	1	1
15th	Solarz, Stephen J.	Dem	N.Y.	6	*T 1
16th	Dymally, Mervyn M.	Dem	Cal.	3	*T 1
17th	Eckart, Dennis E.	Dem	Ohio	3	*T 1
18th	Penny, Timothy J.	Dem	Minn.	2	*T 1
19th	Atkins, Chester G.	Dem	Mass.	1	*T 1

Minority

Rank	Name	Party	State	Terms in: House	Terms in: Comm.
RM	Jeffords, James M.	Rep	Vt.	6	6
2nd	Goodling, William F.	Rep	Penn.	6	6
3rd	Coleman, E. Thomas	Rep	Mo.	6	4
4th	Petri, Thomas E.	Rep	Wisc.	4	4
5th	Roukema, Margaret	Rep	N.J.	3	3
6th	Gunderson, Steven	Rep	Wisc.	3	3
7th	Bartlett, Steve	Rep	Tex.	2	2
8th	Nielson, Howard C.	Rep	Utah	2	2
9th	Chandler, Rodney	Rep	Wash.	2	2
10th	Tauke, Thomas J.	Rep	Iowa	4	2
11th	Armey, Richard	Rep	Tex.	1	1
12th	Fawell, Harris W.	Rep	Ill.	1	1
13th	Henry, Paul B.	Rep	Mich.	1	1

*T: Temporary member of the committee.

Note: The committee was expanded and the party ratio changed to 20 Democrats and 14 Republicans on Aug. 7,1986.

Vacancies Filled:
Majority: 15th through 19th seats on Feb. 6,1985.

Additions:

Majority:	20th	Waldon, Alton R.	Dem	N.Y.	Aug. 7,1986 Ranked behind Bruce.
Minority:	14th	Dornan, Robert K.	Rep	Cal.	Oct. 10,1986

Changes:
Majority:

Solarz, Stephen J.	Dem	N.Y.	Dec. 30,1985	Temporary term expired on last day of 1st Session.
Dymally, Mervyn M.	Dem	Cal.	Dec. 30,1985	Temporary term expired on last day of 1st Session.
Eckart, Dennis E.	Dem	Ohio	Dec. 30,1985	Temporary term expired on last day of 1st Session.
Penny, Timothy J.	Dem	Minn.	Dec. 30,1985	Temporary term expired on last day of 1st Session.
Atkins, Chester G.	Dem	Mass.	Dec. 30,1985	Temporary term expired on last day of 1st Session.
Solarz, Stephen J.	Dem	N.Y.	Jan. 29,1986	Replaced himself.
Dymally, Mervyn M.	Dem	Cal.	Jan. 29,1986	Replaced himself.
Eckart, Dennis E.	Dem	Ohio	Jan. 29,1986	Replaced himself.
Penny, Timothy J.	Dem	Minn.	Jan. 29,1986	Replaced himself.
Atkins, Chester G.	Dem	Mass.	Jan. 29,1986	Replaced himself.

Minority:

Nielson, Howard C.	Rep	Utah	Feb. 27,1985	Moved to Government Operations.
McKernan, John R. Jr.	Rep	Me.	Feb. 27,1985	Replaced Nielson and ranked below Tauke.

	Majority			Minority		
Departures from the House:						
Elected Governor	None			McKernan, John R. Jr.	Me.	Rep
Defeated for Renomination	Waldon, Alton R.	N.Y.	Dem	None		
Departures from Committee:						
Moved to Energy and Commerce	Boucher, Frederick C.	Va.	Dem	None		
	Bruce, Terry L.	Ill.	Dem			
No new assignment	Dymally, Mervyn M.	Cal.	Dem	Chandler, Rodney	Wash.	Rep
	Eckart, Dennis E.	Ohio	Dem	Dornan, Robert K.	Cal.	Rep

EDUCATION AND LABOR / 100th Congress

Service Dates of Committee Chair: Jan. 8,1987-Jan. 3,1989
Service Dates of Majority Members: Jan. 22,1987-Jan. 3,1989
Service Dates of Minority Members: Jan. 21,1987-Jan. 3,1989

Majority

Rank	Name	Party	State	Terms in: House	Terms in: Comm.
Chr	Hawkins, Augustus F.	Dem	Cal.	13	13
2nd	Ford, William D.	Dem	Mich.	12	12
3rd	Gaydos, Joseph M.	Dem	Penn.	11	10
4th	Clay, William L.	Dem	Mo.	10	10
5th	Biaggi, Mario	Dem	N.Y.	10	9
6th	Murphy, Austin J.	Dem	Penn.	6	6
7th	Kildee, Dale E.	Dem	Mich.	6	6
8th	Williams, Pat	Dem	Mont.	5	5
9th	Martinez, Matthew G.	Dem	Cal.	4	4
10th	Owens, Major R.	Dem	N.Y.	3	3
11th	Hayes, Charles A.	Dem	Ill.	3	3
12th	Perkins, Carl C. (Chris)	Dem	Ky.	3	2
13th	Sawyer, Thomas C.	Dem	Ohio	1	1
14th	Solarz, Stephen J.	Dem	N.Y.	7	1
15th	Wise, Robert E. Jr.	Dem	W.Va.	3	1
16th	Penny, Timothy J.	DFL	Minn.	3	*2 1
17th	Richardson, Bill	Dem	N.M.	3	1
18th	Robinson, Tommy F.	Dem	Ark.	2	*T 1
19th	Visclosky, Peter J.	Dem	Ind.	2	1
20th	Atkins, Chester G.	Dem	Mass.	2	1
21st	Jontz, James	Dem	Ind.	1	1

Minority

Rank	Name	Party	State	Terms in: House	Terms in: Comm.
RM	Jeffords, James M.	Rep	Vt.	7	7
2nd	Goodling, William F.	Rep	Penn.	7	7
3rd	Coleman, E. Thomas	Rep	Mo.	7	5
4th	Petri, Thomas E.	Rep	Wisc.	5	5
5th	Roukema, Margaret	Rep	N.J.	4	4
6th	Gunderson, Steven	Rep	Wisc.	4	4
7th	Bartlett, Steve	Rep	Tex.	3	3
8th	Tauke, Thomas J.	Rep	Iowa	5	3
9th	Armey, Richard	Rep	Tex.	2	2
10th	Fawell, Harris W.	Rep	Ill.	2	2
11th	Henry, Paul B.	Rep	Mich.	2	2
12th	Grandy, Fred	Rep	Iowa	1	1
13th	Ballenger, Cass	Rep	N.C.	1	1

*2: Member's 2nd period of service on the committee;
*T: Temporary member of the committee.

Note: Stephen J. Solarz (Dem-N.Y.), Timothy J. Penny (DFL-Minn), and Chester G. Atkins (Dem-Mass.) served as temporary members in the previous Congress.

Changes:
Majority:

Biaggi, Mario	Dem	N.Y.	Aug. 5,1988	Resigned and retired.

	Majority			Minority		
Departures from the House:						
Elected to U.S. Senate	None			Jeffords, James M.	Vt.	Rep
Departures from Committee:						
Moved to Appropriations	Atkins, Chester G.	Mass.	Dem	None		
Moved to Select Intelligence	Solarz, Stephen J.	N.Y.	Dem	None		
Moved to Budget	Wise, Robert E. Jr.	W.Va.	Dem	None		
No new assignment	Penny, Timothy J.	Minn.	DFL	None		
	Richardson, Bill	N.M.	Dem			
	Robinson, Tommy F.	Ark.	Dem			

EDUCATION AND LABOR / 101st Congress

Service Dates of Committee Chair: Jan. 3,1989-Jan. 3,1991
Service Dates of Majority Members: Jan. 19,1989-Jan. 3,1991
Service Dates of Minority Members: Jan. 20,1989-Jan. 3,1991

Majority

Rank	Name	Party	State	Terms in: House	Terms in: Comm.
Chr	Hawkins, Augustus F.	Dem	Cal.	14	14
2nd	Ford, William D.	Dem	Mich.	13	13
3rd	Gaydos, Joseph M.	Dem	Penn.	12	11
4th	Clay, William L.	Dem	Mo.	11	11
5th	Miller, George	Dem	Cal.	8	7
6th	Murphy, Austin J.	Dem	Penn.	7	7
7th	Kildee, Dale E.	Dem	Mich.	7	7
8th	Williams, Pat	Dem	Mont.	6	6
9th	Martinez, Matthew G.	Dem	Cal.	5	5
10th	Owens, Major R.	Dem	N.Y.	4	4
11th	Hayes, Charles A.	Dem	Ill.	4	4
12th	Perkins, Carl C. (Chris)	Dem	Ky.	4	3
13th	Sawyer, Thomas C.	Dem	Ohio	2	2
14th	Payne, Donald M.	Dem	N.J.	2	1
15th	Lowey, Nita M.	Dem	N.Y.	1	1
16th	Poshard, Glenn	Dem	Ill.	1	1
17th	Unsoeld, Jolene	Dem	Wash.	1	1
18th	Rahall, Nick Joe II	Dem	W.Va.	7	*T 1
19th	Fuster, Jaime B.	Dem	P.R.	3	*T 1
20th	Visclosky, Peter J.	Dem	Ind.	3	*T 2
21st	Jontz, James	Dem	Ind.	2	*T 2
22nd	Mfume, Kweisi	Dem	Md.	2	*T 1

Minority

Rank	Name	Party	State	Terms in: House	Terms in: Comm.
RM	Goodling, William F.	Rep	Penn.	8	8
2nd	Coleman, E. Thomas	Rep	Mo.	8	6
3rd	Petri, Thomas E.	Rep	Wisc.	6	6
4th	Roukema, Margaret	Rep	N.J.	5	5
5th	Gunderson, Steven	Rep	Wisc.	5	5
6th	Bartlett, Steve	Rep	Tex.	4	4
7th	Tauke, Thomas J.	Rep	Iowa	6	4
8th	Armey, Richard	Rep	Tex.	3	3
9th	Fawell, Harris W.	Rep	Ill.	3	3
10th	Henry, Paul B.	Rep	Mich.	3	3
11th	Grandy, Fred	Rep	Iowa	2	2
12th	Ballenger, Cass	Rep	N.C.	2	2
13th	Smith, Peter P.	Rep	Vt.	1	1

*T: Temporary member of the committee.

Notes: Jaime Fuster (Dem-P.R.) the Resident Commissioner from Puerto Rico, was temporarily assigned to the committee, but was not included in the original party ratio of 21 Democrats and 13 Republicans. The committee was expanded and the party ratio changed to 22 Democrats (excluding Fuster) and 13 Republicans on Oct. 10,1990. George Miller (Dem-Cal.), having served on the Budget Committee during the previous three Congresses, returned to active service on this committee with his seniority intact. Tommy F. Robinson of Arkansas resigned from the Democratic Party on July 28,1989 and joined the Republican Party. He was assigned to the committee by the minority, having served previously as a Democrat.

Vacancies Filled:

Majority: 18th through 22nd seats on Jan. 27,1989.

Addition:

Majority:	23rd Mink, Patsy T.	Dem	Hai.	Oct. 10,1990	Ranked behind Serrano.

Changes:

Majority:				
Mfume, Kweisi	Dem	Md.	Feb. 27,1990	Temporary term expired.
Washington, Craig	Dem	Tex.	Feb. 27,1990	Replaced Mfume, ranked behind Unsoeld.
Visclosky, Peter J.	Dem	Ind.	Apr. 4,1990	Temporary term expired.
Serrano, Jose E.	Dem	N.Y.	Apr. 4,1990	Replaced Visclosky, ranked behind Washington.
Rahall, Nick Joe II	Dem	W.Va.	June 14,1990	Temporary term terminated.
Mfume, Kweisi	Dem	Md.	June 14,1990	Replaced Rahall.
Minority:				
Armey, Richard	Rep	Tex.	Aug. 3,1989	Moved to Government Operations.
Robinson, Tommy F.	Rep	Ark.	Aug. 3,1989	Replaced Armey.

Departures from the House:	Majority			Minority		
Defeated for Reelection	None			Smith, Peter P.	Vt.	Rep
Lost Election to U.S. Senate	None			Tauke, Thomas J.	Iowa	Rep
Lost Election for Governor	None			Robinson, Tommy F.	Ark.	Rep
Retired	Hawkins, Augustus F.	Cal.	Dem	None		

Departures from Committee:

Moved to Interior & Insular Affairs	Jontz, James	Ind.	Dem	None		
Moved to Public Works & Transportation	Poshard, Glenn	Ill.	Dem	None		
Moved to Joint Economic	Mfume, Kweisi	Md.	Dem	None		
Moved to Ways and Means	None			Grandy, Fred	Iowa	Rep

EDUCATION AND LABOR / 102nd Congress

Service Dates of Committee Chair: Jan. 24,1991-Jan. 3,1993
Service Dates of Majority Members: Jan. 24,1991-Jan. 3,1993
Service Dates of Minority Members: Jan. 24,1991-Jan. 3,1993

Majority

Rank	Name	Party	State	Terms in: House	Terms in: Comm.
Chr	Ford, William D.	Dem	Mich.	14	14
2nd	Gaydos, Joseph M.	Dem	Penn.	13	12
3rd	Clay, William L.	Dem	Mo.	12	12
4th	Miller, George	Dem	Cal.	9	8
5th	Murphy, Austin J.	Dem	Penn.	8	8
6th	Kildee, Dale E.	Dem	Mich.	8	8
7th	Williams, Pat	Dem	Mont.	7	7
8th	Martinez, Matthew G.	Dem	Cal.	6	6
9th	Owens, Major R.	Dem	N.Y.	5	5
10th	Hayes, Charles A.	Dem	Ill.	5	5
11th	Perkins, Carl C. (Chris)	Dem	Ky.	5	4
12th	Sawyer, Thomas C.	Dem	Ohio	3	3
13th	Payne, Donald M.	Dem	N.J.	3	2
14th	Lowey, Nita M.	Dem	N.Y.	2	2
15th	Unsoeld, Jolene	Dem	Wash.	2	2
16th	Washington, Craig	Dem	Tex.	2	2
17th	Serrano, Jose E.	Dem	N.Y.	2	2
18th	Mink, Patsy T.	Dem	Hai.	8	*2 2
19th	Andrews, Robert E.	Dem	N.J.	1	1
20th	Jefferson, William J.	Dem	La.	1	1
21st	Reed, John F.	Dem	R.I.	1	1
22nd	Roemer, Timothy J.	Dem	Ind.	1	1
23rd	Visclosky, Peter J.	Dem	Ind.	4	*T 1
24th	de Lugo, Ron	Dem	V.I.	9	*T 1
25th	Fuster, Jaime B.	Dem	P.R.	4	*T 1

Minority

Rank	Name	Party	State	Terms in: House	Terms in: Comm.
RM	Goodling, William F.	Rep	Penn.	9	9
2nd	Coleman, E. Thomas	Rep	Mo.	9	7
3rd	Petri, Thomas E.	Rep	Wisc.	7	7
4th	Roukema, Margaret	Rep	N.J.	6	6
5th	Gunderson, Steven	Rep	Wisc.	6	6
6th	Bartlett, Steve	Rep	Tex.	5	5
7th	Armey, Richard	Rep	Tex.	4	4
8th	Fawell, Harris W.	Rep	Ill.	4	4
9th	Henry, Paul B.	Rep	Mich.	4	4
10th	Ballenger, Cass	Rep	N.C.	3	3
11th	Molinari, Susan	Rep	N.Y.	2	1
12th	Barrett, Bill	Rep	Neb.	1	1
13th	Boehner, John A.	Rep	Ohio	1	1
14th	Klug, Scott L.	Rep	Wisc.	1	1

*2: Member's 2nd period of service on the committee;
*T: Temporary member of the committee.

Notes: Territorial Delegate Ron de Lugo (Dem-V.I.) and Resident Commissioner Jaime Fuster (Dem-P.R.) were allowed to accrue committee seniority but were not included in the original party ratio of 23 Democrats and 14 Republicans. Peter J. Visclosky (Dem-Ind.) and Jaime B. Fuster (Dem-P.R) served as temporary members in the previous Congress. The committee was expanded and the party ratio changed to 24 Democrats (excluding De Lugo and Fuster) and 15 Republicans on Oct. 9,1991.

Additions:

Majority:	26th Pastor, Ed	Dem	Ariz.	Oct. 9,1991
Minority:	15th Cunningham, Randy	Rep	Cal.	Oct. 23,1991

Changes:

Majority:

Visclosky, Peter J.	Dem	Ind.	June 27,1991	Resigned committee; no new assignment.
Olver, John W.	Dem	Mass.	June 27,1991	Replaced Visclosky.
Fuster, Jaime B.	Dem	P.R.	Mar. 4,1992	Resigned and retired.

Minority:

Bartlett, Steve	Rep	Tex.	Mar. 11,1991	Resigned House; ran for Mayor of Dallas.
Edwards, M. H. (Mickey)	Rep	Okla.	Apr. 16,1991	Replaced Bartlett.

ENERGY AND COMMERCE

INTERSTATE AND FOREIGN COMMERCE

Jurisdiction, 1947

Established by the Legislative Reorganization Act of 1946:

[Section 121.(1)(k)]

Committee on Interstate and Foreign Commerce.

1. Interstate and foreign commerce generally.
2. Regulation of interstate and foreign transportation, except transportation by water not subject to the jurisdiction of the Interstate Commerce Commission.
3. Regulation of interstate and foreign communications.
4. Civil aeronautics.
5. Weather bureau.
6. Interstate oil compacts; and petroleum and natural gas, except on the public lands.
7. Securities and exchanges.
8. Regulation of interstate transmission of power, except the installation of connections between Government water power projects.
9. Railroad labor and railroad retirement and unemployment, except revenue measures relating thereto.
10. Public health and quarantine.
11. Inland waterways.
12. Bureau of Standards, standardization of weights and measures, and the metric system.

ENERGY AND COMMERCE

Renamed the Committee on Energy and Commerce on March 25, 1980, effective January 3, 1981.

Jurisdiction, 1992

Jurisdiction contained in Rules of the House of Representatives, (as revised to July 1, 1992):

[Rule X. 1. (h)]

Committee on Energy and Commerce.

(1) Interstate and foreign commerce, generally.
(2) National energy policy generally.
(3) Measures relating to the exploration, production, storage, supply, marketing, pricing, and regulation of energy resources, including all fossils, fuels, solar energy, and other unconventional or renewable energy resources.
(4) Measures relating to the conservation of energy resources.
(5) Measures relating to the commercial application of energy technology.
(6) Measures relating to energy information generally.
(7) Measures relating to
    (A) the generation and marketing of power (except by federally chartered or Federal regional power marketing authorities,
    (B) the reliability and interstate transmission of, and ratemaking for, all power, and
    (C) the siting of generation facilities; except the installation of interconnections between Government waterpower projects.
(8) Interstate energy compacts.
(9) Measures relating to general management of the Department of Energy, and the management and all functions of the Federal Energy Regulatory Commission.
(10) Inland waterways.
(11) Railroads, including railroad labor, railroad retirement and unemployment, except revenue measures related thereto.

(12) Regulations of interstate and foreign communications.
(13) Securities and exchanges.
(14) Consumer affairs and consumer protection.
(15) Travel and tourism.
(16) Public health and quarantine.
(17) Health and health facilities, except health care supported by payroll deductions.
(18) Biomedical research and development.

Such committee shall have the same jurisdiction with respect to regulation of nuclear facilities and of use of nuclear energy as it has with respect to regulation of nonnuclear facilities and of use of nonnuclear energy.

In addition to its legislative jurisdiction under the preceding provisions of this paragraph (and its general oversight functions under clause 2(b)(1)), such committee shall have the special oversight functions provided for in clause (3)(h) with respect to all laws, programs, and Government activities affecting nuclear and other energy.

[Rule X. 3. (h)]

The Committee on Energy and Commerce shall have the function of reviewing and studying on a continuing basis, all laws, programs and government activities relating to nuclear and other energy.

INTERSTATE AND FOREIGN COMMERCE / 80th Congress

Service Dates of Committee Chair: Jan. 14,1947-Jan. 3,1949
Service Dates of Majority Members: Jan. 14,1947-Jan. 3,1949
Service Dates of Minority Members: Jan. 16,1947-Jan. 3,1949

Majority

Rank	Name	Party	State	Terms in: House	Terms in: Comm.
Chr	Wolverton, Charles A.	Rep	N.J.	11	*2 8
2nd	Hinshaw, Carl	Rep	Cal.	5	5
3rd	Howell, G. Evan	Rep	Ill.	4	4
4th	Hall, Leonard W.	Rep	N.Y.	5	3
5th	O'Hara, Joseph P.	Rep	Minn.	4	3
6th	Gillette, Wilson D.	Rep	Penn.	4	2
7th	Hale, Robert	Rep	Me.	3	1
8th	Ellsworth, M. Harris	Rep	Ore.	3	1
9th	Bennett, Marion T.	Rep	Mo.	3	1
10th	Dolliver, James I.	Rep	Iowa	2	1
11th	Elsaesser, Edward J.	Rep	N.Y.	2	1
12th	Heselton, John W.	Rep	Mass.	2	1
13th	Scott, Hugh D. Jr.	Rep	Penn.	3	*2 1
14th	Miller, William J.	Rep	Conn.	3	1
15th	Carson, Henderson H.	Rep	Ohio	2	1
16th	Bennett, John B.	Rep	Mich.	2	1

Minority

Rank	Name	Party	State	Terms in: House	Terms in: Comm.
RM	Lea, Clarence F.	Dem	Cal.	16	14
2nd	Crosser, Robert	Dem	Ohio	16	13
3rd	Bulwinkle, Alfred L.	Dem	N.C.	13	9
4th	Chapman, Virgil M.	Dem	Ky.	11	9
5th	Beckworth, Lindley G.	Dem	Tex.	5	3
6th	Priest, J. Percy	Dem	Tenn.	4	3
7th	Harris, Oren	Dem	Ark.	4	3
8th	Sadowski, George G.	Dem	Mich.	6	*2 3
9th	Harless, Richard F.	Dem	Ariz.	3	3
10th	Rogers, Dwight L.	Dem	Fla.	2	2
11th	Rabin, Benjamin J.	Dem	N.Y.	2	2

*2: Member's 2nd period of service on the committee.

Changes:

Majority:

Name	Party	State	Date	Change
Howell, G. Evan	Rep	Ill.	Oct. 5,1947	Resigned; appointed federal judge.
Busbey, Fred E.	Rep	Ill.	Dec. 18,1947	Replaced Howell.

Minority:

Name	Party	State	Date	Change
Rabin, Benjamin J.	Dem	N.Y.	Dec. 31,1947	Resigned; elected to state supreme court.
Keogh, Eugene J.	Dem	N.Y.	Jan. 20,1948	Replaced Rabin.

Departures from the House:

	Majority			Minority		
Elected to U.S. Senate	None			Chapman, Virgil M.	Ky.	Dem
Defeated for Reelection	Bennett, Marion T.	Mo.	Rep	None		
	Carson, Henderson H.	Ohio	Rep			
	Elsaesser, Edward J.	N.Y.	Rep			
	Miller, William J.	Conn.	Rep			
	Busbey, Fred E.	Ill.	Rep			
Lost Nomination for Governor	None			Harless, Richard F.	Ariz.	Dem
Retired	None			Lea, Clarence F.	Cal.	Dem

INTERSTATE AND FOREIGN COMMERCE / 81st Congress

Service Dates of Committee Chair: Jan. 18,1949-Jan. 3,1951
Service Dates of Majority Members: Jan. 18,1949-Jan. 3,1951
Service Dates of Minority Members: Jan. 18,1949-Jan. 3,1951

Majority

Rank	Name	Party	State	Terms in: House	Terms in: Comm.
Chr	Crosser, Robert	Dem	Ohio	17	14
2nd	Bulwinkle, Alfred L.	Dem	N.C.	14	10
3rd	Beckworth, Lindley G.	Dem	Tex.	6	4
4th	Priest, J. Percy	Dem	Tenn.	5	4
5th	Harris, Oren	Dem	Ark.	5	4
6th	Sadowski, George G.	Dem	Mich.	7	*2 4
7th	Rogers, Dwight L.	Dem	Fla.	3	3
8th	Keogh, Eugene J.	Dem	N.Y.	7	2
9th	Klein, Arthur G.	Dem	N.Y.	5	1
10th	Stanley, Thomas B.	Dem	Va.	3	1
11th	Sullivan, John B.	Dem	Mo.	3	*2 1
12th	Granahan, William T.	Dem	Penn.	2	1
13th	Biemiller, Andrew J.	Dem	Wisc.	2	1
14th	McGuire, John A.	Dem	Conn.	1	1
15th	Wilson, George H.	Dem	Okla.	1	1
16th	Linehan, Neil J.	Dem	Ill.	1	1
17th	Underwood, Thomas R.	Dem	Ky.	1	1

Minority

Rank	Name	Party	State	Terms in: House	Terms in: Comm.
RM	Wolverton, Charles A.	Rep	N.J.	12	*2 9
2nd	Hinshaw, Carl	Rep	Cal.	6	6
3rd	Hall, Leonard W.	Rep	N.Y.	6	4
4th	O'Hara, Joseph P.	Rep	Minn.	5	4
5th	Gillette, Wilson D.	Rep	Penn.	5	3
6th	Hale, Robert	Rep	Me.	4	2
7th	Ellsworth, M. Harris	Rep	Ore.	4	2
8th	Dolliver, James I.	Rep	Iowa	3	2
9th	Heselton, John W.	Rep	Mass.	3	2
10th	Scott, Hugh D. Jr.	Rep	Penn.	4	*2 2
11th	Bennett, John B.	Rep	Mich.	3	2

*2: Member's 2nd period of service on the committee.

Changes:

Majority:

Name	Party	State	Date	Change
Bulwinkle, Alfred L.	Dem	N.C.	Aug. 31,1950	Died in office.
Carlyle, F. Ertel	Dem	N.C.	Dec. 11,1950	Replaced Bulwinkle.

Departures from the House:	Majority			Minority		
Defeated for Reelection	Biemiller, Andrew J.	Wisc.	Dem	None		
	Linehan, Neil J.	Ill.	Dem			
	Wilson, George H.	Okla.	Dem			
Defeated for Renomination	Sadowski, George G.	Mich.	Dem	None		
Departures from Committee:						
Moved to Ways and Means	Keogh, Eugene J.	N.Y.	Dem	None		
Moved to Rules	None			Ellsworth, M. Harris	Ore.	Rep

INTERSTATE AND FOREIGN COMMERCE / 82nd Congress

Service Dates of Committee Chair: Jan. 12,1951-Jan. 3,1953
Service Dates of Majority Members: Jan. 12,1951-Jan. 3,1953
Service Dates of Minority Members: Jan. 15,1951-Jan. 3,1953

Majority

Rank	Name	Party	State	Terms in: House	Terms in: Comm.
Chr	Crosser, Robert	Dem	Ohio	18	15
2nd	Beckworth, Lindley G.	Dem	Tex.	7	5
3rd	Priest, J. Percy	Dem	Tenn.	6	5
4th	Harris, Oren	Dem	Ark.	6	5
5th	Rogers, Dwight L.	Dem	Fla.	4	4
6th	Klein, Arthur G.	Dem	N.Y.	6	2
7th	Stanley, Thomas B.	Dem	Va.	4	2
8th	Sullivan, John B.	Dem	Mo.	4	*2 2
9th	Granahan, William T.	Dem	Penn.	3	2
10th	McGuire, John A.	Dem	Conn.	2	2
11th	Underwood, Thomas R.	Dem	Ky.	2	2
12th	Carlyle, F. Ertel	Dem	N.C.	2	2
13th	Williams, John Bell	Dem	Miss.	3	1
14th	Mack, Peter F. Jr.	Dem	Ill.	2	1

Minority

Rank	Name	Party	State	Terms in: House	Terms in: Comm.
RM	Wolverton, Charles A.	Rep	N.J.	13	*2 10
2nd	Hinshaw, Carl	Rep	Cal.	7	7
3rd	Hall, Leonard W.	Rep	N.Y.	7	5
4th	O'Hara, Joseph P.	Rep	Minn.	6	5
5th	Gillette, Wilson D.	Rep	Penn.	6	4
6th	Hale, Robert	Rep	Me.	5	3
7th	Dolliver, James I.	Rep	Iowa	4	3
8th	Heselton, John W.	Rep	Mass.	4	3
9th	Scott, Hugh D. Jr.	Rep	Penn.	5	*2 3
10th	Bennett, John B.	Rep	Mich.	4	3
11th	Hoffman, Richard W.	Rep	Ill.	2	1
12th	Chenoweth, J. Edgar	Rep	Colo.	5	1
13th	Beamer, John V.	Rep	Ind.	1	1

15th Thornberry, W. Homer	Dem	Tex.	2	1	
16th Heller, Louis B.	Dem	N.Y.	2	1	
17th Roberts, Kenneth A.	Dem	Ala.	1	1	*2: Member's 2nd period of service on the committee.

Changes:

Majority:

Sullivan, John B.	Dem	Mo.	Jan. 29,1951	Died in office.
Underwood, Thomas R.	Dem	Ky.	Mar. 17,1951	Resigned; appointed to U.S. Senate.
Moulder, Morgan M.	Dem	Mo.	Apr. 3,1951	Replaced Sullivan.
Staggers, Harley O.	Dem	W.Va.	Apr. 6,1951	Replaced Underwood.

Minority:

Gillette, Wilson D.	Rep	Penn.	July 30,1951	Resigned committee; died in office on Aug. 1,1951.
Denny, Harmar D. Jr.	Rep	Penn.	Aug. 1,1951	Replaced Gillette.
Hall, Leonard W.	Rep	N.Y.	Dec. 31,1952	Resigned; became County Surrogate and Chair of Republican National Committee.

Departures from the House:	**Majority**		**Minority**	
Defeated for Reelection	McGuire, John A.	Conn. Dem	Denny, Harmar D. Jr.	Penn. Rep
Lost Nomination to U.S. Senate	Beckworth, Lindley G.	Tex. Dem	None	
Departures from Committee:				
Moved to Post Office & Civil Service	Staggers, Harley O.	W.Va. Dem	None	
Moved to Rules	None		Chenoweth, J. Edgar	Colo. Rep
			Scott, Hugh D. Jr.	Penn. Rep

INTERSTATE AND FOREIGN COMMERCE / 83rd Congress

Service Dates of Committee Chair: Jan. 19,1953-Jan. 3,1955
Service Dates of Majority Members: Jan. 19,1953-Jan. 3,1955
Service Dates of Minority Members: Jan. 19,1953-Jan. 3,1955

Majority

Rank Name	Party	State	Terms in: House	Terms in: Comm.
Chr Wolverton, Charles A.	Rep	N.J.	14	*2 11
2nd Hinshaw, Carl	Rep	Cal.	8	8
3rd O'Hara, Joseph P.	Rep	Minn.	7	6
4th Hale, Robert	Rep	Me.	6	4
5th Dolliver, James I.	Rep	Iowa	5	4
6th Heselton, John W.	Rep	Mass.	5	4
7th Bennett, John B.	Rep	Mich.	5	4
8th Hoffman, Richard W.	Rep	Ill.	3	2
9th Beamer, John V.	Rep	Ind.	2	2
10th Springer, William L.	Rep	Ill.	2	1
11th Bush, Alvin R.	Rep	Penn.	2	1
12th Schenck, Paul F.	Rep	Ohio	2	1
13th Carrigg, Joseph L.	Rep	Penn.	2	1
14th Warburton, Herbert B.	Rep	Del.	1	1
15th Derounian, Steven B.	Rep	N.Y.	1	1
16th Pelly, Thomas M.	Rep	Wash.	1	1
17th Younger, J. Arthur	Rep	Cal.	1	*1 1

Minority

Rank Name	Party	State	Terms in: House	Terms in: Comm.
RM Crosser, Robert	Dem	Ohio	19	16
2nd Priest, J. Percy	Dem	Tenn.	7	6
3rd Harris, Oren	Dem	Ark.	7	6
4th Rogers, Dwight L.	Dem	Fla.	5	5
5th Klein, Arthur G.	Dem	N.Y.	7	3
6th Stanley, Thomas B.	Dem	Va.	5	3
7th Granahan, William T.	Dem	Penn.	4	3
8th Carlyle, F. Ertel	Dem	N.C.	3	3
9th Williams, John Bell	Dem	Miss.	4	2
10th Mack, Peter F. Jr.	Dem	Ill.	3	2
11th Thornberry, W. Homer	Dem	Tex.	3	2
12th Heller, Louis B.	Dem	N.Y.	3	2
13th Roberts, Kenneth A.	Dem	Ala.	2	2
14th Moulder, Morgan M.	Dem	Mo.	3	2

*1: Member's 1st period of service on the committee;
*2: Member's 2nd period of service on the committee.

Changes:

Minority:

Stanley, Thomas B.	Dem	Va.	Feb. 3,1953	Resigned; elected Governor of Virginia.
Staggers, Harley O.	Dem	W.Va.	Feb. 6,1953	Replaced Stanley.
Heller, Louis B.	Dem	N.Y.	July 21,1954	Resigned; elected New York City judge.
Rogers, Dwight L.	Dem	Fla.	Dec. 1,1954	Died in office.

Departures from the House:	**Majority**		**Minority**	
Defeated for Renomination	None		Crosser, Robert	Ohio Dem
Lost Election to U.S. Senate	Warburton, Herbert B.	Del. Rep	None	
Departures from Committee:				
Moved to Merchant Marine & Fisheries	Pelly, Thomas M.	Wash. Rep	None	
Moved to Government Operations	Younger, J. Arthur	Cal. Rep	None	
Moved to Rules	None		Thornberry, W. Homer	Tex. Dem

INTERSTATE AND FOREIGN COMMERCE / 84th Congress

Service Dates of Committee Chair: Jan. 13,1955-Oct. 12,1956
Service Dates of Majority Members: Jan. 13,1955-Jan. 3,1957
Service Dates of Minority Members: Jan. 20,1955-Jan. 3,1957

Majority

Rank	Name	Party	State	Terms in: House	Terms in: Comm.
Chr	Priest, J. Percy	Dem	Tenn.	8	7
2nd	Harris, Oren	Dem	Ark.	8	7
3rd	Klein, Arthur G.	Dem	N.Y.	8	4
4th	Granahan, William T.	Dem	Penn.	5	4
5th	Carlyle, F. Ertel	Dem	N.C.	4	4
6th	Williams, John Bell	Dem	Miss.	5	3
7th	Mack, Peter F. Jr.	Dem	Ill.	4	3
8th	Roberts, Kenneth A.	Dem	Ala.	3	3
9th	Moulder, Morgan M.	Dem	Mo.	4	3
10th	Staggers, Harley O.	Dem	W.Va.	4	3
11th	Dollinger, Isidore	Dem	N.Y.	4	1
12th	Rogers, Walter E.	Dem	Tex.	3	1
13th	Dies, Martin Jr.	Dem	Tex.	9	1
14th	Friedel, Samuel N.	Dem	Md.	2	1
15th	Flynt, John James Jr.	Dem	Ga.	2	1
16th	Macdonald, Torbert H.	Dem	Mass.	1	1
17th	Hayworth, Don	Dem	Mich.	1	1

Minority

Rank	Name	Party	State	Terms in: House	Terms in: Comm.
RM	Wolverton, Charles A.	Rep	N.J.	15 *2	12
2nd	Hinshaw, Carl	Rep	Cal.	9	9
3rd	O'Hara, Joseph P.	Rep	Minn.	8	7
4th	Hale, Robert	Rep	Me.	7	5
5th	Dolliver, James I.	Rep	Iowa	6	5
6th	Heselton, John W.	Rep	Mass.	6	5
7th	Bennett, John B.	Rep	Mich.	6	5
8th	Hoffman, Richard W.	Rep	Ill.	4	3
9th	Beamer, John V.	Rep	Ind.	3	3
10th	Springer, William L.	Rep	Ill.	3	2
11th	Bush, Alvin R.	Rep	Penn.	3	2
12th	Schenck, Paul F.	Rep	Ohio	3	2
13th	Carrigg, Joseph L.	Rep	Penn.	3	2
14th	Derounian, Steven B.	Rep	N.Y.	2	2

*2: Member's 2nd period of service on the committee.

Note: J. Percy Priest (Dem-Tenn) died in office after the adjournment of the 84th Congress. The Chairmanship of the committee was left vacant until the start of the 85th Congress.

Changes:

Majority:

Name	Party	State	Date	Change
Granahan, William T.	Dem	Penn.	May 25,1956	Died in office.
Rhodes, George M.	Dem	Penn.	July 24,1956	Replaced Granahan.
Priest, J. Percy	Dem	Tenn.	Oct. 12,1956	Died in office.
Klein, Arthur G.	Dem	N.Y.	Dec. 31,1956	Resigned; elected to State Supreme Court.

Minority:

Name	Party	State	Date	Change
Hinshaw, Carl	Rep	Cal.	Aug. 5,1956	Died in office.

Departures from the House:

	Majority		Minority	
Defeated for Reelection	Hayworth, Don	Mich. Dem	Dolliver, James I.	Iowa Rep
Defeated for Renomination	Carlyle, F. Ertel	N.C. Dem	None	
Retired	None		Hoffman, Richard W.	Ill. Rep

INTERSTATE AND FOREIGN COMMERCE / 85th Congress

Service Dates of Committee Chair: Jan. 10,1957-Jan. 3,1959
Service Dates of Majority Members: Jan. 10,1957-Jan. 3,1959
Service Dates of Minority Members: Jan. 16,1957-Jan. 3,1959

Majority

Rank	Name	Party	State	Terms in: House	Terms in: Comm.
Chr	Harris, Oren	Dem	Ark.	9	8
2nd	Williams, John Bell	Dem	Miss.	6	4
3rd	Mack, Peter F. Jr.	Dem	Ill.	5	4
4th	Roberts, Kenneth A.	Dem	Ala.	4	4
5th	Moulder, Morgan M.	Dem	Mo.	5	4
6th	Staggers, Harley O.	Dem	W.Va.	5	4
7th	Dollinger, Isidore	Dem	N.Y.	5	2
8th	Rogers, Walter E.	Dem	Tex.	4	2
9th	Dies, Martin Jr.	Dem	Tex.	10	2
10th	Friedel, Samuel N.	Dem	Md.	3	2
11th	Flynt, John James Jr.	Dem	Ga.	3	2
12th	Macdonald, Torbert H.	Dem	Mass.	2	2

Minority

Rank	Name	Party	State	Terms in: House	Terms in: Comm.
RM	Wolverton, Charles A.	Rep	N.J.	16 *2	13
2nd	O'Hara, Joseph P.	Rep	Minn.	9	8
3rd	Hale, Robert	Rep	Me.	8	6
4th	Heselton, John W.	Rep	Mass.	7	6
5th	Bennett, John B.	Rep	Mich.	7	6
6th	Beamer, John V.	Rep	Ind.	4	4
7th	Springer, William L.	Rep	Ill.	4	3
8th	Bush, Alvin R.	Rep	Penn.	4	3
9th	Schenck, Paul F.	Rep	Ohio	4	3
10th	Carrigg, Joseph L.	Rep	Penn.	4	3
11th	Derounian, Steven B.	Rep	N.Y.	3	3
12th	Younger, J. Arthur	Rep	Cal.	3 *2	1

13th Rhodes, George M.	Dem	Penn.	5	2	13th Avery, William H.	Rep	Kans.	2	1
14th Jarman, John	Dem	Okla.	4	1	14th Alger, Bruce R.	Rep	Tex.	2	1
15th O'Brien, Leo W.	Dem	N.Y.	4	1	15th Neal, William E.	Rep	W.Va.	2	1
16th Moss, John E. Jr.	Dem	Cal.	3	1					
17th Dingell, John D. Jr.	Dem	Mich.	2	1					
18th Loser, J. Carlton	Dem	Tenn.	1	1					

*2: Member's 2nd period of service on the committee.

Changes:
Majority:

Dies, Martin Jr.	Dem	Tex.	July 21,1958	Left committee; lost nomination to U.S. Senate.
Kilgore, Joe M.	Dem	Tex.	July 21,1958	Replaced Dies.

Departures from the House:	**Majority**		**Minority**	
Defeated for Reelection	None		Beamer, John V.	Ind. Rep
			Carrigg, Joseph L.	Penn. Rep
			Hale, Robert	Me. Rep
			Neal, William E.	W.Va. Rep
Retired	None		Heselton, John W.	Mass. Rep
			O'Hara, Joseph P.	Minn. Rep
			Wolverton, Charles A.	N.J. Rep
Departures from Committee:				
Moved to District of Columbia; Judiciary	Loser, J. Carlton	Tenn. Dem	None	
Moved to Ways and Means	None		Alger, Bruce R.	Tex. Rep

INTERSTATE AND FOREIGN COMMERCE / 86th Congress

Service Dates of Committee Chair: Jan. 19,1959-Jan. 3,1961
Service Dates of Majority Members: Jan. 19,1959-Jan. 3,1961
Service Dates of Minority Members: Jan. 19,1959-Jan. 3,1961

Majority

Rank Name	Party	State	Terms in: House	Terms in: Comm.
Chr Harris, Oren	Dem	Ark.	10	9
2nd Williams, John Bell	Dem	Miss.	7	5
3rd Mack, Peter F. Jr.	Dem	Ill.	6	5
4th Roberts, Kenneth A.	Dem	Ala.	5	5
5th Moulder, Morgan M.	Dem	Mo.	6	5
6th Staggers, Harley O.	Dem	W.Va.	6	5
7th Dollinger, Isidore	Dem	N.Y.	6	3
8th Rogers, Walter E.	Dem	Tex.	5	3
9th Friedel, Samuel N.	Dem	Md.	4	3
10th Flynt, John James Jr.	Dem	Ga.	4	3
11th Macdonald, Torbert H.	Dem	Mass.	3	3
12th Rhodes, George M.	Dem	Penn.	6	3
13th Jarman, John	Dem	Okla.	5	2
14th O'Brien, Leo W.	Dem	N.Y.	5	2
15th Moss, John E. Jr.	Dem	Cal.	4	2
16th Dingell, John D. Jr.	Dem	Mich.	3	2
17th Kilgore, Joe M.	Dem	Tex.	3	2
18th Rogers, Paul G.	Dem	Fla.	3	1
19th Hemphill, Robert W.	Dem	S.C.	2	1
20th Rostenkowski, Daniel D.	Dem	Ill.	1	1
21st Brock, Lawrence	Dem	Neb.	1	1

Minority

Rank Name	Party	State	Terms in: House	Terms in: Comm.
RM Bennett, John B.	Rep	Mich.	8	7
2nd Springer, William L.	Rep	Ill.	5	4
3rd Bush, Alvin R.	Rep	Penn.	5	4
4th Schenck, Paul F.	Rep	Ohio	5	4
5th Derounian, Steven B.	Rep	N.Y.	4	4
6th Younger, J. Arthur	Rep	Cal.	4	*2 2
7th Avery, William H.	Rep	Kans.	3	2
8th Collier, Harold R.	Rep	Ill.	2	1
9th Glenn, Milton W.	Rep	N.J.	2	1
10th Devine, Samuel L.	Rep	Ohio	1	1
11th Nelsen, Ancher	Rep	Minn.	1	1
12th Keith, Hastings	Rep	Mass.	1	1

*2: Member's 2nd period of service on the committee.

Changes:
Majority:

Dollinger, Isidore	Dem	N.Y.	Aug. 27,1959	Left committee; resigned to become District Attorney Dec. 31, 1959.
Healey, James C.	Dem	N.Y.	Aug. 27,1959	Replaced Dollinger.

Minority:

Bush, Alvin R.	Rep	Penn.	Nov. 5,1959	Died in office.
Curtin, Willard S.	Rep	Penn.	Jan. 18,1960	Replaced Bush.

Departures from the House:	Majority		Minority	
Defeated for Reelection	Brock, Lawrence	Neb. Dem	None	
Departures from Committee:				
Moved to Ways and Means	None		Derounian, Steven B.	N.Y. Rep

INTERSTATE AND FOREIGN COMMERCE / 87th Congress

Service Dates of Committee Chair: Feb. 6,1961-Jan. 3,1963
Service Dates of Majority Members: Feb. 6,1961-Jan. 3,1963
Service Dates of Minority Members: Feb. 13,1961-Jan. 3,1963

Majority

Rank	Name	Party	State	Terms in: House	Terms in: Comm.
Chr	Harris, Oren	Dem	Ark.	11	10
2nd	Williams, John Bell	Dem	Miss.	8	6
3rd	Mack, Peter F. Jr.	Dem	Ill.	7	6
4th	Roberts, Kenneth A.	Dem	Ala.	6	6
5th	Moulder, Morgan M.	Dem	Mo.	7	6
6th	Staggers, Harley O.	Dem	W.Va.	7	6
7th	Rogers, Walter E.	Dem	Tex.	6	4
8th	Friedel, Samuel N.	Dem	Md.	5	4
9th	Flynt, John James Jr.	Dem	Ga.	5	4
10th	Macdonald, Torbert H.	Dem	Mass.	4	4
11th	Rhodes, George M.	Dem	Penn.	7	4
12th	Jarman, John	Dem	Okla.	6	3
13th	O'Brien, Leo W.	Dem	N.Y.	6	3
14th	Moss, John E. Jr.	Dem	Cal.	5	3
15th	Dingell, John D. Jr.	Dem	Mich.	4	3
16th	Kilgore, Joe M.	Dem	Tex.	4	3
17th	Rogers, Paul G.	Dem	Fla.	4	2
18th	Hemphill, Robert W.	Dem	S.C.	3	2
19th	Rostenkowski, Daniel D.	Dem	Ill.	2	2
20th	Healey, James C.	Dem	N.Y.	4	2

Minority

Rank	Name	Party	State	Terms in: House	Terms in: Comm.
RM	Bennett, John B.	Rep	Mich.	9	8
2nd	Springer, William L.	Rep	Ill.	6	5
3rd	Schenck, Paul F.	Rep	Ohio	6	5
4th	Younger, J. Arthur	Rep	Cal.	5	*2 3
5th	Avery, William H.	Rep	Kans.	4	3
6th	Collier, Harold R.	Rep	Ill.	3	2
7th	Glenn, Milton W.	Rep	N.J.	3	2
8th	Devine, Samuel L.	Rep	Ohio	2	2
9th	Nelsen, Ancher	Rep	Minn.	2	2
10th	Keith, Hastings	Rep	Mass.	2	2
11th	Curtin, Willard S.	Rep	Penn.	3	2
12th	Sibal, Abner W.	Rep	Conn.	1	1
13th	Thomson, Vernon W.	Rep	Wisc.	1	1

*2: Member's 2nd period of service on the committee.

Changes:

Majority:

Name	Party	State	Date	Change
Flynt, John James Jr.	Dem	Ga.	Jan. 18,1962	Moved to Appropriations.
Kornegay, Horace R.	Dem	N.C.	Jan. 18,1962	Replaced Flynt.

Minority:

Name	Party	State	Date	Change
Avery, William H.	Rep	Kans.	Mar. 28,1961	Moved to Rules.
Dominick, Peter H.	Rep	Colo.	Mar. 28,1961	Replaced Avery.

Departures from the House:	Majority		Minority	
Elected to U.S. Senate	None		Dominick, Peter H.	Colo. Rep
Defeated for Reelection	Mack, Peter F. Jr.	Ill. Dem	None	
Retired	Moulder, Morgan M.	Mo. Dem	None	
Departures from Committee:				
Moved to Armed Services	Kilgore, Joe M.	Tex. Dem	None	
Moved to Ways and Means	None		Collier, Harold R.	Ill. Rep
Moved to Foreign Affairs	None		Thomson, Vernon W.	Wisc. Rep

INTERSTATE AND FOREIGN COMMERCE / 88th Congress

Service Dates of Committee Chair: Jan. 17,1963-Jan. 3,1965
Service Dates of Majority Members: Jan. 17,1963-Jan. 3,1965
Service Dates of Minority Members: Jan. 24,1963-Jan. 3,1965

Majority

Rank	Name	Party	State	Terms in: House	Terms in: Comm.
Chr	Harris, Oren	Dem	Ark.	12	11
2nd	Williams, John Bell	Dem	Miss.	9	7
3rd	Roberts, Kenneth A.	Dem	Ala.	7	7
4th	Staggers, Harley O.	Dem	W.Va.	8	7
5th	Rogers, Walter E.	Dem	Tex.	7	5
6th	Friedel, Samuel N.	Dem	Md.	6	5
7th	Macdonald, Torbert H.	Dem	Mass.	5	5
8th	Rhodes, George M.	Dem	Penn.	8	5
9th	Jarman, John	Dem	Okla.	7	4
10th	O'Brien, Leo W.	Dem	N.Y.	7	4
11th	Moss, John E. Jr.	Dem	Cal.	6	4
12th	Dingell, John D. Jr.	Dem	Mich.	5	4
13th	Rogers, Paul G.	Dem	Fla.	5	3
14th	Hemphill, Robert W.	Dem	S.C.	4	3
15th	Rostenkowski, Daniel D.	Dem	Ill.	3	3
16th	Healey, James C.	Dem	N.Y.	5	3
17th	Kornegay, Horace R.	Dem	N.C.	2	2
18th	Hull, William R. Jr.	Dem	Mo.	5	1
19th	Long, Gillis W.	Dem	La.	1	1
20th	Van Deerlin, Lionel	Dem	Cal.	1	1

Minority

Rank	Name	Party	State	Terms in: House	Terms in: Comm.
RM1	Bennett, John B.	Rep	Mich.	10	9
RM2 2nd	Springer, William L.	Rep	Ill.	7	6
3rd	Schenck, Paul F.	Rep	Ohio	7	6
4th	Younger, J. Arthur	Rep	Cal.	6	*2 4
5th	Glenn, Milton W.	Rep	N.J.	4	3
6th	Devine, Samuel L.	Rep	Ohio	3	3
7th	Nelsen, Ancher	Rep	Minn.	3	3
8th	Keith, Hastings	Rep	Mass.	3	3
9th	Curtin, Willard S.	Rep	Penn.	4	3
10th	Sibal, Abner W.	Rep	Conn.	2	2
11th	Cunningham, Glenn C.	Rep	Neb.	4	1
12th	Broyhill, James T.	Rep	N.C.	1	1
13th	Brotzman, Donald G.	Rep	Colo.	1	*1 1

*1: Member's 1st period of service on the committee;
*2: Member's 2nd period of service on the committee.

Changes:

Ranking Member:

RM1	Bennett, John B.	Rep	Mich.	Aug. 9,1964	Died in office.
RM2	Springer, William L.	Rep	Ill.	Aug. 9,1964	Succeeded Bennett as Ranking Minority Member.

Majority:

Rhodes, George M.	Dem	Penn.	Jan. 21,1964	Moved to Ways and Means.
Pickle, J. J. (Jake)	Dem	Tex.	Feb. 25,1964	Replaced Rhodes.
Hemphill, Robert W.	Dem	S.C.	May 1,1964	Resigned; appointed federal judge.
Rostenkowski, Daniel D.	Dem	Ill.	May 5,1964	Moved to Ways and Means.
Watson, Albert W.	Dem	S.C.	May 20,1964	Replaced Hemphill.
Rooney, Fred B.	Dem	Penn.	May 20,1964	Replaced Rostenkowski.
Hull, William R. Jr.	Dem	Mo.	June 2,1964	Moved to Appropriations.

Minority:

Bennett, John B.	Rep	Mich.	Aug. 9,1964	Died in office.
Harvey, James	Rep	Mich.	Oct. 1,1964	Replaced Bennett.

Departures from the House:

	Majority			Minority		
Defeated for Reelection	Healey, James C.	N.Y.	Dem	Brotzman, Donald G.	Colo.	Rep
	Roberts, Kenneth A.	Ala.	Dem	Glenn, Milton W.	N.J.	Rep
				Schenck, Paul F.	Ohio	Rep
				Sibal, Abner W.	Conn.	Rep
Defeated for Renomination	Long, Gillis W.	La.	Dem	None		

INTERSTATE AND FOREIGN COMMERCE / 89th Congress

Service Dates of Committee Chairs: Ch1 Jan. 18,1965-Jan. 13,1966
Ch2 Jan. 13,1966-Jan. 3,1967
Service Dates of Majority Members: Jan. 18,1965-Jan. 3,1967
Service Dates of Minority Members: Jan. 21,1965-Jan. 3,1967

Majority

Rank Name	Party	State	Terms in: House	Terms in: Comm.
Ch1 Harris, Oren	Dem	Ark.	13	12
Ch2 2nd Staggers, Harley O.	Dem	W.Va.	9	8
3rd Rogers, Walter E.	Dem	Tex.	8	6
4th Friedel, Samuel N.	Dem	Md.	7	6
5th Macdonald, Torbert H.	Dem	Mass.	6	6
6th Jarman, John	Dem	Okla.	8	5
7th O'Brien, Leo W.	Dem	N.Y.	8	5
8th Moss, John E. Jr.	Dem	Cal.	7	5
9th Dingell, John D. Jr.	Dem	Mich.	6	5
10th Rogers, Paul G.	Dem	Fla.	6	4
11th Kornegay, Horace R.	Dem	N.C.	3	3
12th Van Deerlin, Lionel	Dem	Cal.	2	2
13th Pickle, J. J. (Jake)	Dem	Tex.	2	2
14th Rooney, Fred B.	Dem	Penn.	2	2
15th Murphy, John M.	Dem	N.Y.	2	1
16th Satterfield, David E. III	Dem	Va.	1	1
17th Ronan, Daniel J.	Dem	Ill.	1	1
18th Huot, J. Oliva	Dem	N.H.	1	1
19th MacKay, James A.	Dem	Ga.	1	1
20th Gilligan, John J.	Dem	Ohio	1	1
21st Farnsley, Charles R. P.	Dem	Ky.	1	1
22nd Williams, John Bell	Dem	Miss.	10	8

Minority

Rank Name	Party	State	Terms in: House	Terms in: Comm.
RM Springer, William L.	Rep	Ill.	8	7
2nd Younger, J. Arthur	Rep	Cal.	7	*2 5
3rd Devine, Samuel L.	Rep	Ohio	4	4
4th Nelsen, Ancher	Rep	Minn.	4	4
5th Keith, Hastings	Rep	Mass.	4	4
6th Curtin, Willard S.	Rep	Penn.	5	4
7th Cunningham, Glenn C.	Rep	Neb.	5	2
8th Broyhill, James T.	Rep	N.C.	2	2
9th Harvey, James	Rep	Mich.	3	2
10th Watson, Albert W.	Dem	S.C.	2	*1 2
11th Carter, Tim Lee	Rep	Ky.	1	1

*1: Member's 1st period of service on the committee;
*2: Member's 2nd period of service on the committee.

Notes: John Bell Williams of Mississippi and Albert W. Watson of South Carolina were stripped of their seniority by the Democratic Caucus on Jan. 9,1965 for backing Republican presidential candidate Barry Goldwater. Williams chose to remain seated as a Democrat. While still a Democrat, Watson was assigned to this committee by the Republican Conference. He resigned from the House and from the Democratic Party on Feb. 1,1965 and was reelected to fill his own vacancy as a Republican on June 15,1965.

Changes:

Chair:				
Ch1 Harris, Oren	Dem	Ark.	Jan. 13,1966	Resigned; appointed federal judge.
Ch2 Staggers, Harley O.	Dem	W.Va.	Jan. 13,1966	Succeeded Harris as Chair.
Majority:				
Harris, Oren	Dem	Ark.	Jan. 13,1966	Resigned; appointed federal judge.
Adams, Brock	Dem	Wash.	Mar. 8,1966	Replaced Harris.
O'Brien, Leo W.	Dem	N.Y.	Oct. 18,1966	Left committee; no new assignment.
Ottinger, Richard L.	Dem	N.Y.	Oct. 18,1966	Replaced O'Brien.
Farnsley, Charles R. P.	Dem	Ky.	Oct. 21,1966	Left committee; no new assignment.
Anderson, William R.	Dem	Tenn.	Oct. 21,1966	Replaced Farnsley.
Minority:				
Watson, Albert W.	Dem	S.C.	Feb. 1,1965	Resigned House; later filled own vacancy as a Republican.
Callaway, Howard H.	Rep	Ga.	Mar. 3,1965	Replaced Watson.
Callaway, Howard H.	Rep	Ga.	June 23,1965	Left committee; no new assignment.
Watson, Albert W.	Rep	S.C.	June 23,1965	Replaced Callaway.
Curtin, Willard S.	Rep	Penn.	Oct. 19,1966	Left committee; no new assignment.
Watkins, G. Robert	Rep	Penn.	Oct. 19,1966	Replaced Curtin.

	Majority			Minority
Departures from the House:				
Defeated for Reelection	Gilligan, John J.	Ohio	Dem	None
	Huot, J. Oliva	N.H.	Dem	
	MacKay, James A.	Ga.	Dem	
Retired	Rogers, Walter E.	Tex.	Dem	None
Departures from Committee:				
Moved to Rules	Anderson, William R.	Tenn.	Dem	None
No new assignment	Williams, John Bell	Miss.	Dem	None

INTERSTATE AND FOREIGN COMMERCE / 90th Congress

Service Dates of Committee Chair: Jan. 23,1967-Jan. 3,1969
Service Dates of Majority Members: Jan. 23,1967-Jan. 3,1969
Service Dates of Minority Members: Jan. 26,1967-Jan. 3,1969

Majority

Rank	Name	Party	State	Terms in: House		Comm.
Chr	Staggers, Harley O.	Dem	W.Va.	10		9
2nd	Friedel, Samuel N.	Dem	Md.	8		7
3rd	Macdonald, Torbert H.	Dem	Mass.	7		7
4th	Jarman, John	Dem	Okla.	9		6
5th	Moss, John E. Jr.	Dem	Cal.	8		6
6th	Dingell, John D. Jr.	Dem	Mich.	7		6
7th	Rogers, Paul G.	Dem	Fla.	7		5
8th	Kornegay, Horace R.	Dem	N.C.	4		4
9th	Van Deerlin, Lionel	Dem	Cal.	3		3
10th	Pickle, J. J. (Jake)	Dem	Tex.	3		3
11th	Rooney, Fred B.	Dem	Penn.	3		3
12th	Murphy, John M.	Dem	N.Y.	3		2
13th	Satterfield, David E. III	Dem	Va.	2		2
14th	Ronan, Daniel J.	Dem	Ill.	2		2
15th	Adams, Brock	Dem	Wash.	2		2
16th	Ottinger, Richard L.	Dem	N.Y.	2	*1	2
17th	Blanton, Leonard Ray	Dem	Tenn.	1		1
18th	Stuckey, Williamson S.Jr.	Dem	Ga.	1		1
19th	Kyros, Peter N.	Dem	Me.	1		1

Minority

Rank	Name	Party	State	Terms in: House		Comm.
RM	Springer, William L.	Rep	Ill.	9		8
2nd	Younger, J. Arthur	Rep	Cal.	8	*2	6
3rd	Devine, Samuel L.	Rep	Ohio	5		5
4th	Nelsen, Ancher	Rep	Minn.	5		5
5th	Keith, Hastings	Rep	Mass.	5		5
6th	Cunningham, Glenn C.	Rep	Neb.	6		3
7th	Broyhill, James T.	Rep	N.C.	3		3
8th	Harvey, James	Rep	Mich.	4		3
9th	Watson, Albert W.	Rep	S.C.	3	*2	2
10th	Carter, Tim Lee	Rep	Ky.	2		2
11th	Watkins, G. Robert	Rep	Penn.	2		2
12th	Brotzman, Donald G.	Rep	Colo.	2	*2	1
13th	Brown, Clarence J. Jr.	Rep	Ohio	2		1
14th	Kuykendall, Dan H.	Rep	Tenn.	1		1

*1: Member's 1st period of service on the committee;
*2: Member's 2nd period of service on the committee.

Vacancies Filled:
Majority: 18th and 19th seats by Stuckey and Kyros respectively on May 25,1967.

Changes:
Minority:

Name	Party	State	Date	Change
Younger, J. Arthur	Rep	Cal.	June 20,1967	Died in office.
Skubitz, Joe	Rep	Kans.	Aug. 1,1967	Replaced Younger.

Departures from the House:

	Majority			Minority
Retired	Kornegay, Horace R.	N.C.	Dem	None

INTERSTATE AND FOREIGN COMMERCE / 91st Congress

Service Dates of Committee Chair: Jan. 29,1969-Jan. 3,1971
Service Dates of Majority Members: Jan. 29,1969-Jan. 3,1971
Service Dates of Minority Members: Jan. 29,1969-Jan. 3,1971

Majority

Rank	Name	Party	State	Terms in: House		Comm.
Chr	Staggers, Harley O.	Dem	W.Va.	11		10
2nd	Friedel, Samuel N.	Dem	Md.	9		8
3rd	Macdonald, Torbert H.	Dem	Mass.	8		8
4th	Jarman, John	Dem	Okla.	10		7
5th	Moss, John E. Jr.	Dem	Cal.	9		7
6th	Dingell, John D. Jr.	Dem	Mich.	8		7
7th	Rogers, Paul G.	Dem	Fla.	8		6
8th	Van Deerlin, Lionel	Dem	Cal.	4		4
9th	Pickle, J. J. (Jake)	Dem	Tex.	4		4
10th	Rooney, Fred B.	Dem	Penn.	4		4
11th	Murphy, John M.	Dem	N.Y.	4		3
12th	Satterfield, David E. III	Dem	Va.	3		3
13th	Ronan, Daniel J.	Dem	Ill.	3		3
14th	Adams, Brock	Dem	Wash.	3		3
15th	Ottinger, Richard L.	Dem	N.Y.	3	*1	3

Minority

Rank	Name	Party	State	Terms in: House		Comm.
RM	Springer, William L.	Rep	Ill.	10		9
2nd	Devine, Samuel L.	Rep	Ohio	6		6
3rd	Nelsen, Ancher	Rep	Minn.	6		6
4th	Keith, Hastings	Rep	Mass.	6		6
5th	Cunningham, Glenn C.	Rep	Neb.	7		4
6th	Broyhill, James T.	Rep	N.C.	4		4
7th	Harvey, James	Rep	Mich.	5		4
8th	Watson, Albert W.	Rep	S.C.	4	*2	3
9th	Carter, Tim Lee	Rep	Ky.	3		3
10th	Watkins, G. Robert	Rep	Penn.	3		3
11th	Brotzman, Donald G.	Rep	Colo.	3	*2	2
12th	Brown, Clarence J. Jr.	Rep	Ohio	3		2
13th	Kuykendall, Dan H.	Rep	Tenn.	2		2
14th	Skubitz, Joe	Rep	Kans.	4		2
15th	Thompson, S. Fletcher	Rep	Ga.	2		1

16th Blanton, Leonard Ray	Dem	Tenn.	2	2	16th Hastings, James F.	Rep	N.Y.	1	1
17th Stuckey, Williamson S.Jr.	Dem	Ga.	2	2					
18th Kyros, Peter N.	Dem	Me.	2	2					
19th Eckhardt, Robert C.	Dem	Tex.	2	1					
20th Tiernan, Robert O.	Dem	R.I.	2	1					
21st Preyer, L. Richardson	Dem	N.C.	1	1					

*1: Member's 1st period of service on the committee;
*2: Member's 2nd period of service on the committee.

Changes:

Majority:

Ronan, Daniel J.	Dem	Ill.	Aug. 13,1969	Died in office.
Ottinger, Richard L.	Dem	N.Y.	Dec. 8,1970	Resigned; lost election to U.S. Senate.
Podell, Bertram L.	Dem	N.Y.	Dec. 8,1970	Replaced Ottinger.

Minority:

Watkins, G. Robert	Rep	Penn.	Aug. 7,1970	Died in office.
Schmitz, John G.	Rep	Cal.	Sep. 23,1970	Replaced Watkins.

	Majority			Minority		
Departures from the House:						
Defeated for Renomination	Friedel, Samuel N.	Md.	Dem	Cunningham, Glenn C.	Neb.	Rep
Lost Election for Governor	None			Watson, Albert W.	S.C.	Rep
Departures from Committee:						
Moved to Ways and Means	None			Brotzman, Donald G.	Colo.	Rep

INTERSTATE AND FOREIGN COMMERCE / 92nd Congress

Service Dates of Committee Chair: Feb. 4,1971-Jan. 3,1973
Service Dates of Majority Members: Feb. 4,1971-Jan. 3,1973
Service Dates of Minority Members: Feb. 4,1971-Jan. 3,1973

Majority

Rank Name	Party	State	Terms in: House	Terms in: Comm.
Chr Staggers, Harley O.	Dem	W.Va.	12	11
2nd Macdonald, Torbert H.	Dem	Mass.	9	9
3rd Jarman, John	Dem	Okla.	11	8
4th Moss, John E. Jr.	Dem	Cal.	10	8
5th Dingell, John D. Jr.	Dem	Mich.	9	8
6th Rogers, Paul G.	Dem	Fla.	9	7
7th Van Deerlin, Lionel	Dem	Cal.	5	5
8th Pickle, J. J. (Jake)	Dem	Tex.	5	5
9th Rooney, Fred B.	Dem	Penn.	5	5
10th Murphy, John M.	Dem	N.Y.	5	4
11th Satterfield, David E. III	Dem	Va.	4	4
12th Adams, Brock	Dem	Wash.	4	4
13th Blanton, Leonard Ray	Dem	Tenn.	3	3
14th Stuckey, Williamson S.Jr.	Dem	Ga.	3	3
15th Kyros, Peter N.	Dem	Me.	3	3
16th Eckhardt, Robert C.	Dem	Tex.	3	2
17th Tiernan, Robert O.	Dem	R.I.	3	2
18th Preyer, L. Richardson	Dem	N.C.	2	2
19th Podell, Bertram L.	Dem	N.Y.	3	2
20th Helstoski, Henry	Dem	N.J.	4	1
21st Symington, James W.	Dem	Mo.	2	1
22nd Carney, Charles J.	Dem	Ohio	2	1
23rd Metcalfe, Ralph H.	Dem	Ill.	1	1
24th Byron, Goodloe E.	Dem	Md.	1	1
25th Roy, William R.	Dem	Kans.	1	1

Minority

Rank Name	Party	State	Terms in: House	Terms in: Comm.
RM Springer, William L.	Rep	Ill.	11	10
2nd Devine, Samuel L.	Rep	Ohio	7	7
3rd Nelsen, Ancher	Rep	Minn.	7	7
4th Keith, Hastings	Rep	Mass.	7	7
5th Broyhill, James T.	Rep	N.C.	5	5
6th Harvey, James	Rep	Mich.	6	5
7th Carter, Tim Lee	Rep	Ky.	4	4
8th Brown, Clarence J. Jr.	Rep	Ohio	4	3
9th Kuykendall, Dan H.	Rep	Tenn.	3	3
10th Skubitz, Joe	Rep	Kans.	5	3
11th Thompson, S. Fletcher	Rep	Ga.	3	2
12th Hastings, James F.	Rep	N.Y.	2	2
13th Schmitz, John G.	Rep	Cal.	2	2
14th Collins, James M.	Rep	Tex.	3	1
15th Frey, Louis Jr.	Rep	Fla.	2	1
16th Ware, John H. III	Rep	Penn.	2	1
17th McCollister, John Y.	Rep	Neb.	1	1
18th Shoup, Richard G.	Rep	Mont.	1	1

	Majority			Minority		
Departures from the House:						
Appointed to Federal Power Commission	None			Springer, William L.	Ill.	Rep
Defeated for Renomination	None			Schmitz, John G.	Cal.	Rep
Lost Election to U.S. Senate	Blanton, Leonard Ray	Tenn.	Dem	Thompson, S. Fletcher	Ga.	Rep
Retired	None			Keith, Hastings	Mass.	Rep
Departures from Committee:						
Moved to Appropriations	Tiernan, Robert O.	R.I.	Dem	None		

INTERSTATE AND FOREIGN COMMERCE / 93rd Congress

Service Dates of Committee Chair: Jan. 24,1973-Jan. 3,1975
Service Dates of Majority Members: Jan. 24,1973-Jan. 3,1975
Service Dates of Minority Members: Jan. 24,1973-Jan. 3,1975

Majority

Rank	Name	Party	State	Terms in: House	Terms in: Comm.
Chr	Staggers, Harley O.	Dem	W.Va.	13	12
2nd	Macdonald, Torbert H.	Dem	Mass.	10	10
3rd	Jarman, John	Dem	Okla.	12	9
4th	Moss, John E. Jr.	Dem	Cal.	11	9
5th	Dingell, John D. Jr.	Dem	Mich.	10	9
6th	Rogers, Paul G.	Dem	Fla.	10	8
7th	Van Deerlin, Lionel	Dem	Cal.	6	6
8th	Pickle, J. J. (Jake)	Dem	Tex.	6	6
9th	Rooney, Fred B.	Dem	Penn.	6	6
10th	Murphy, John M.	Dem	N.Y.	6	5
11th	Satterfield, David E. III	Dem	Va.	5	5
12th	Adams, Brock	Dem	Wash.	5	5
13th	Stuckey, Williamson S.Jr.	Dem	Ga.	4	4
14th	Kyros, Peter N.	Dem	Me.	4	4
15th	Eckhardt, Robert C.	Dem	Tex.	4	3
16th	Preyer, L. Richardson	Dem	N.C.	3	3
17th	Podell, Bertram L.	Dem	N.Y.	4	3
18th	Helstoski, Henry	Dem	N.J.	5	2
19th	Symington, James W.	Dem	Mo.	3	2
20th	Carney, Charles J.	Dem	Ohio	3	2
21st	Metcalfe, Ralph H.	Dem	Ill.	2	2
22nd	Byron, Goodloe E.	Dem	Md.	2	2
23rd	Roy, William R.	Dem	Kans.	2	2
24th	Breckinridge, John B.	Dem	Ky.	1	1

Minority

Rank	Name	Party	State	Terms in: House	Terms in: Comm.
RM	Devine, Samuel L.	Rep	Ohio	8	8
2nd	Nelsen, Ancher	Rep	Minn.	8	8
3rd	Broyhill, James T.	Rep	N.C.	6	6
4th	Harvey, James	Rep	Mich.	7	6
5th	Carter, Tim Lee	Rep	Ky.	5	5
6th	Brown, Clarence J. Jr.	Rep	Ohio	5	4
7th	Kuykendall, Dan H.	Rep	Tenn.	4	4
8th	Skubitz, Joe	Rep	Kans.	6	4
9th	Hastings, James F.	Rep	N.Y.	3	3
10th	Collins, James M.	Rep	Tex.	4	2
11th	Frey, Louis Jr.	Rep	Fla.	3	2
12th	Ware, John H. III	Rep	Penn.	3	2
13th	McCollister, John Y.	Rep	Neb.	2	2
14th	Shoup, Richard G.	Rep	Mont.	2	2
15th	Goldwater, Barry M. Jr.	Rep	Cal.	3	1
16th	Lent, Norman F.	Rep	N.Y.	2	1
17th	Heinz, H. John III	Rep	Penn.	2	1
18th	Hudnut, William H. III	Rep	Ind.	1	1
19th	Young, Samuel H.	Rep	Ill.	1	1

Note: Democratic Party gains in the 1974 special elections in Pennsylvania, Michigan, and Ohio, led to the passage of House Resolution 979 agreed to on Mar. 13,1974, changing the size and party ratio on this committee to 25 Democrats and 19 Republicans on Mar. 13,1974.

Addition:

Majority:	25th	Luken, Thomas A.	Dem	Ohio	Mar. 13,1974

Changes:

Minority:

Harvey, James	Rep	Mich.	Jan. 31,1974	Resigned; appointed Federal judge.
Madigan, Edward R.	Rep	Ill.	May 1,1974	Replaced Harvey.
Nelsen, Ancher	Rep	Minn.	Dec. 31,1974	Resigned and retired.

	Majority			Minority		
Departures from the House:						
Defeated for Reelection	Luken, Thomas A.	Ohio	Dem	Hudnut, William H. III	Ind.	Rep
	Kyros, Peter N.	Me.	Dem	Kuykendall, Dan H.	Tenn.	Rep
				Shoup, Richard G.	Mont.	Rep
				Young, Samuel H.	Ill.	Rep
Defeated for Renomination	Podell, Bertram L.	N.Y.	Dem	None		
Lost Election to U.S. Senate	Roy, William R.	Kans.	Dem	None		
Retired	None			Ware, John H. III	Penn.	Rep
Departures from Committee:						
Moved to Small Business; Agriculture	Breckinridge, John B.	Ky.	Dem	None		
Moved to Ways and Means	Helstoski, Henry	N.J.	Dem	None		
	Pickle, J. J. (Jake)	Tex.	Dem			
Moved to Public Works & Transportation	None			Goldwater, Barry M. Jr.	Cal.	Rep

INTERSTATE AND FOREIGN COMMERCE / 94th Congress

Service Dates of Committee Chair: Jan. 20,1975-Jan. 3,1977
Service Dates of Majority Members: Jan. 20,1975-Jan. 3,1977
Service Dates of Minority Members: Jan. 28,1975-Jan. 3,1977

Majority

Rank	Name	Party	State	Terms in: House	Terms in: Comm.
Chr	Staggers, Harley O.	Dem	W.Va.	14	13
2nd	Macdonald, Torbert H.	Dem	Mass.	11	11
3rd	Jarman, John	Dem	Okla.	13	10
4th	Moss, John E. Jr.	Dem	Cal.	12	10
5th	Dingell, John D. Jr.	Dem	Mich.	11	10
6th	Rogers, Paul G.	Dem	Fla.	11	9
7th	Van Deerlin, Lionel	Dem	Cal.	7	7
8th	Rooney, Fred B.	Dem	Penn.	7	7
9th	Murphy, John M.	Dem	N.Y.	7	6
10th	Satterfield, David E. III	Dem	Va.	6	6
11th	Adams, Brock	Dem	Wash.	6	6
12th	Stuckey, Williamson S.Jr.	Dem	Ga.	5	5
13th	Eckhardt, Robert C.	Dem	Tex.	5	4
14th	Preyer, L. Richardson	Dem	N.C.	4	4
15th	Symington, James W.	Dem	Mo.	4	3
16th	Carney, Charles J.	Dem	Ohio	4	3
17th	Metcalfe, Ralph H.	Dem	Ill.	3	3
18th	Byron, Goodloe E.	Dem	Md.	3	3
19th	Scheuer, James H.	Dem	N.Y.	5	1
20th	Ottinger, Richard L.	Dem	N.Y.	4	*2 1
21st	Waxman, Henry A.	Dem	Cal.	1	1
22nd	Krueger, Robert C.	Dem	Tex.	1	1
23rd	Wirth, Timothy E.	Dem	Colo.	1	1
24th	Sharp, Philip R.	Dem	Ind.	1	1
25th	Brodhead, William M.	Dem	Mich.	1	1
26th	Hefner, W. G. (Bill)	Dem	N.C.	1	1
27th	Florio, James J.	Dem	N.J.	1	1
28th	Moffett, Anthony J.(Toby)	Dem	Conn.	1	1
29th	Santini, James D.	Dem	Nev.	1	1

Minority

Rank	Name	Party	State	Terms in: House	Terms in: Comm.
RM	Devine, Samuel L.	Rep	Ohio	9	9
2nd	Broyhill, James T.	Rep	N.C.	7	7
3rd	Carter, Tim Lee	Rep	Ky.	6	6
4th	Brown, Clarence J. Jr.	Rep	Ohio	6	5
5th	Skubitz, Joe	Rep	Kans.	7	5
6th	Hastings, James F.	Rep	N.Y.	4	4
7th	Collins, James M.	Rep	Tex.	5	3
8th	Frey, Louis Jr.	Rep	Fla.	4	3
9th	McCollister, John Y.	Rep	Neb.	3	3
10th	Lent, Norman F.	Rep	N.Y.	3	2
11th	Heinz, H. John III	Rep	Penn.	3	2
12th	Madigan, Edward R.	Rep	Ill.	2	2
13th	Moorhead, Carlos J.	Rep	Cal.	2	1
14th	Rinaldo, Matthew J.	Rep	N.J.	2	1

*2: Member's 2nd period of service on the committee.

Note: John Jarman of Oklahoma resigned from the Democratic Party on Jan. 24,1975 and lost his majority assignments.

Changes:

Majority:

Name	Party	State	Date	Change
Jarman, John	Dem	Okla.	Jan. 30,1975	Moved to Science and Technology as a Republican.
Maguire, G. Andrew	Dem	N.J.	Mar. 18,1975	Replaced Jarman.
Hefner, W. G. (Bill)	Dem	N.C.	Apr. 8,1976	Moved to Public Works and Transportation.
Russo, Martin A.	Dem	Ill.	Apr. 13,1976	Replaced Hefner.
Macdonald, Torbert H.	Dem	Mass.	May 21,1976	Died in office.

Minority:

Name	Party	State	Date	Change
Hastings, James F.	Rep	N.Y.	Jan. 20,1976	Resigned and retired.
Moore, W. Henson	Rep	La.	Jan. 27,1976	Replaced Hastings.

	Majority			Minority		
Departures from the House:						
Elected to U.S. Senate	None			Heinz, H. John III	Penn.	Rep
Lost Election to U.S. Senate	None			McCollister, John Y.	Neb.	Rep
Lost Nomination to U.S. Senate	Symington, James W.	Mo.	Dem	None		
Retired	Stuckey, Williamson S.Jr.	Ga.	Dem	None		
Departures from Committee:						
Unassigned in 95th; appointed Secretary of Transportation	Adams, Brock	Wash.	Dem	None		
Moved to Ways and Means	Brodhead, William M.	Mich.	Dem	None		
Moved to Armed Services	Byron, Goodloe E.	Md.	Dem	None		

INTERSTATE AND FOREIGN COMMERCE / 95th Congress

Service Dates of Committee Chair: Jan. 19,1977-Jan. 3,1979
Service Dates of Majority Members: Jan. 19,1977-Jan. 3,1979
Service Dates of Minority Members: Jan. 19,1977-Jan. 3,1979

Majority

Rank	Name	Party	State	Terms in: House	Terms in: Comm.
Chr	Staggers, Harley O.	Dem	W.Va.	15	14
2nd	Moss, John E. Jr.	Dem	Cal.	13	11
3rd	Dingell, John D. Jr.	Dem	Mich.	12	11
4th	Rogers, Paul G.	Dem	Fla.	12	10
5th	Van Deerlin, Lionel	Dem	Cal.	8	8
6th	Rooney, Fred B.	Dem	Penn.	8	8
7th	Murphy, John M.	Dem	N.Y.	8	7
8th	Satterfield, David E. III	Dem	Va.	7	7
9th	Eckhardt, Robert C.	Dem	Tex.	6	5
10th	Preyer, L. Richardson	Dem	N.C.	5	5
11th	Carney, Charles J.	Dem	Ohio	5	4
12th	Metcalfe, Ralph H.	Dem	Ill.	4	4
13th	Scheuer, James H.	Dem	N.Y.	6	2
14th	Ottinger, Richard L.	Dem	N.Y.	5	*2 2
15th	Waxman, Henry A.	Dem	Cal.	2	2
16th	Krueger, Robert C.	Dem	Tex.	2	2
17th	Wirth, Timothy E.	Dem	Colo.	2	2
18th	Sharp, Philip R.	Dem	Ind.	2	2
19th	Florio, James J.	Dem	N.J.	2	2
20th	Moffett, Anthony J.(Toby)	Dem	Conn.	2	2
21st	Santini, James D.	Dem	Nev.	2	2
22nd	Maguire, G. Andrew	Dem	N.J.	2	2
23rd	Russo, Martin A.	Dem	Ill.	2	2
24th	Markey, Edward J.	Dem	Mass.	2	1
25th	Luken, Thomas A.	Dem	Ohio	2	*2 1
26th	Walgren, Douglas	Dem	Penn.	1	1
27th	Gammage, Robert A.	Dem	Tex.	1	1
28th	Gore, Albert A. Jr.	Dem	Tenn.	1	1
29th	Mikulski, Barbara A.	Dem	Md.	1	1

Minority

Rank	Name	Party	State	Terms in: House	Terms in: Comm.
RM	Devine, Samuel L.	Rep	Ohio	10	10
2nd	Broyhill, James T.	Rep	N.C.	8	8
3rd	Carter, Tim Lee	Rep	Ky.	7	7
4th	Brown, Clarence J. Jr.	Rep	Ohio	7	6
5th	Skubitz, Joe	Rep	Kans.	8	6
6th	Collins, James M.	Rep	Tex.	6	4
7th	Frey, Louis Jr.	Rep	Fla.	5	4
8th	Lent, Norman F.	Rep	N.Y.	4	3
9th	Madigan, Edward R.	Rep	Ill.	3	3
10th	Moorhead, Carlos J.	Rep	Cal.	3	2
11th	Rinaldo, Matthew J.	Rep	N.J.	3	2
12th	Moore, W. Henson	Rep	La.	2	2
13th	Stockman, David A.	Rep	Mich.	1	1
14th	Marks, Marc L.	Rep	Penn.	1	1

*2: Member's 2nd period of service on the committee.

Changes:

Majority:

Metcalfe, Ralph H.	Dem	Ill.	Oct. 10,1978	Died in office.
Moss, John E. Jr.	Dem	Cal.	Dec. 31,1978	Resigned and retired.

Minority:

Skubitz, Joe	Rep	Kans.	Dec. 31,1978	Resigned and retired.

Departures from the House:

	Majority			Minority		
Defeated for Reelection	Carney, Charles J.	Ohio	Dem	None		
	Gammage, Robert A.	Tex.	Dem			
	Rooney, Fred B.	Penn.	Dem			
Lost Election to U.S. Senate	Krueger, Robert C.	Tex.	Dem	None		
Lost Nomination for Governor	None			Frey, Louis Jr.	Fla.	Rep
Retired	Rogers, Paul G.	Fla.	Dem	None		

Departures from Committee:

	Majority			Minority		
Moved to Ways and Means	None			Moore, W. Henson	La.	Rep

INTERSTATE AND FOREIGN COMMERCE / 96th Congress

Service Dates of Committee Chair: Jan. 24,1979-Jan. 3,1981
Service Dates of Majority Members: Jan. 24,1979-Jan. 3,1981
Service Dates of Minority Members: Jan. 24,1979-Jan. 3,1981

Majority

Rank	Name	Party	State	Terms in: House	Terms in: Comm.
Chr	Staggers, Harley O.	Dem	W.Va.	16	15
2nd	Dingell, John D. Jr.	Dem	Mich.	13	12
3rd	Van Deerlin, Lionel	Dem	Cal.	9	9
4th	Murphy, John M.	Dem	N.Y.	9	8
5th	Satterfield, David E. III	Dem	Va.	8	8
6th	Eckhardt, Robert C.	Dem	Tex.	7	6
7th	Preyer, L. Richardson	Dem	N.C.	6	6
8th	Scheuer, James H.	Dem	N.Y.	7	3
9th	Ottinger, Richard L.	Dem	N.Y.	6	*2 3
10th	Waxman, Henry A.	Dem	Cal.	3	3
11th	Wirth, Timothy E.	Dem	Colo.	3	3
12th	Sharp, Philip R.	Dem	Ind.	3	3
13th	Florio, James J.	Dem	N.J.	3	3
14th	Moffett, Anthony J.(Toby)	Dem	Conn.	3	3
15th	Santini, James D.	Dem	Nev.	3	3
16th	Maguire, G. Andrew	Dem	N.J.	3	3
17th	Russo, Martin A.	Dem	Ill.	3	3
18th	Markey, Edward J.	Dem	Mass.	3	2
19th	Luken, Thomas A.	Dem	Ohio	3	*2 2
20th	Walgren, Douglas	Dem	Penn.	2	2
21st	Gore, Albert A. Jr.	Dem	Tenn.	2	2
22nd	Mikulski, Barbara A.	Dem	Md.	2	2
23rd	Mottl, Ronald M.	Dem	Ohio	3	1
24th	Gramm, W. Phil	Dem	Tex.	1	1
25th	Swift, Allan B.	Dem	Wash.	1	1
26th	Leland, G. T. (Mickey)	Dem	Tex.	1	1
27th	Shelby, Richard C.	Dem	Ala.	1	1

Minority

Rank	Name	Party	State	Terms in: House	Terms in: Comm.
RM1	Devine, Samuel L.	Rep	Ohio	11	11
RM2 2nd	Broyhill, James T.	Rep	N.C.	9	9
3rd	Carter, Tim Lee	Rep	Ky.	8	8
4th	Brown, Clarence J. Jr.	Rep	Ohio	8	7
5th	Collins, James M.	Rep	Tex.	7	5
6th	Lent, Norman F.	Rep	N.Y.	5	4
7th	Madigan, Edward R.	Rep	Ill.	4	4
8th	Moorhead, Carlos J.	Rep	Cal.	4	3
9th	Rinaldo, Matthew J.	Rep	N.J.	4	3
10th	Stockman, David A.	Rep	Mich.	2	2
11th	Marks, Marc L.	Rep	Penn.	2	2
12th	Corcoran, Thomas J.	Rep	Ill.	2	1
13th	Lee, Gary A.	Rep	N.Y.	1	1
14th	Loeffler, Thomas G.	Rep	Tex.	1	1
15th	Dannemeyer, William E.	Rep	Cal.	1	1

*2: Member's 2nd period of service on the committee.

Changes:

Ranking Member:

RM1	Devine, Samuel L.	Rep Ohio	June 27,1979	Elected Chairman of the Republican Conference; remained on committee.
RM2	Broyhill, James T.	Rep N.C.	June 27,1979	Succeeded Devine as Ranking Minority Member.

Majority:

Russo, Martin A.	Dem Ill.	Oct. 23,1979	Moved to Ways and Means.
Matsui, Robert T.	Dem Cal.	Nov. 7,1979	Replaced Russo.

	Majority			Minority		
Departures from the House:						
Defeated for Reelection	Eckhardt, Robert C.	Tex.	Dem	Devine, Samuel L.	Ohio	Rep
	Maguire, G. Andrew	N.J.	Dem			
	Murphy, John M.	N.Y.	Dem			
	Preyer, L. Richardson	N.C.	Dem			
	Van Deerlin, Lionel	Cal.	Dem			
Retired	Satterfield, David E. III	Va.	Dem	Carter, Tim Lee	Ky.	Rep
	Staggers, Harley O.	W.Va.	Dem			
Departures from Committee:						
Moved to Ways and Means	Matsui, Robert T.	Cal.	Dem	None		
Moved to Appropriations	None			Loeffler, Thomas G.	Tex.	Rep
Unassigned in 97th; appointed Director Office of Management and Budget	None			Stockman, David A.	Mich.	Rep

ENERGY AND COMMERCE / 97th Congress

* Name changed from the Committee on INTERSTATE AND FOREIGN COMMERCE on Mar. 25,1980 to go into effect Jan. 3,1981

Service Dates of Committee Chair: Jan. 28,1981-Jan. 3,1983
Service Dates of Majority Members: Jan. 28,1981-Jan. 3,1983
Service Dates of Minority Members: Jan. 28,1981-Jan. 3,1983

Majority

Rank	Name	Party	State	Terms in: House	Terms in: Comm.
Chr	Dingell, John D. Jr.	Dem	Mich.	14	13
2nd	Scheuer, James H.	Dem	N.Y.	8	4
3rd	Ottinger, Richard L.	Dem	N.Y.	7	*2 4
4th	Waxman, Henry A.	Dem	Cal.	4	4
5th	Wirth, Timothy E.	Dem	Colo.	4	4
6th	Sharp, Philip R.	Dem	Ind.	4	4
7th	Florio, James J.	Dem	N.J.	4	4
8th	Moffett, Anthony J.(Toby)	Dem	Conn.	4	4
9th	Santini, James D.	Dem	Nev.	4	4
10th	Markey, Edward J.	Dem	Mass.	4	3
11th	Luken, Thomas A.	Dem	Ohio	4	*2 3
12th	Walgren, Douglas	Dem	Penn.	3	3
13th	Gore, Albert A. Jr.	Dem	Tenn.	3	3
14th	Mikulski, Barbara A.	Dem	Md.	3	3
15th	Mottl, Ronald M.	Dem	Ohio	4	2
16th	Gramm, W. Phil	Dem	Tex.	2	2
17th	Swift, Allan B.	Dem	Wash.	2	2
18th	Leland, G. T. (Mickey)	Dem	Tex.	2	2
19th	Shelby, Richard C.	Dem	Ala.	2	2
20th	Collins, Cardiss	Dem	Ill.	5	1
21st	Synar, Michael L.	Dem	Okla.	2	1
22nd	Tauzin, W. J. (Billy)	Dem	La.	2	1
23rd	Wyden, Ron	Dem	Ore.	1	1
24th	Hall, Ralph M.	Dem	Tex.	1	1

Minority

Rank	Name	Party	State	Terms in: House	Terms in: Comm.
RM	Broyhill, James T.	Rep	N.C.	10	10
2nd	Brown, Clarence J. Jr.	Rep	Ohio	9	8
3rd	Collins, James M.	Rep	Tex.	8	6
4th	Lent, Norman F.	Rep	N.Y.	6	5
5th	Madigan, Edward R.	Rep	Ill.	5	5
6th	Moorhead, Carlos J.	Rep	Cal.	5	4
7th	Rinaldo, Matthew J.	Rep	N.J.	5	4
8th	Marks, Marc L.	Rep	Penn.	3	3
9th	Corcoran, Thomas J.	Rep	Ill.	3	2
10th	Lee, Gary A.	Rep	N.Y.	2	2
11th	Dannemeyer, William E.	Rep	Cal.	2	2
12th	Whittaker, Robert	Rep	Kans.	2	1
13th	Tauke, Thomas J.	Rep	Iowa	2	1
14th	Ritter, Donald L.	Rep	Penn.	2	1
15th	Rogers, Harold	Rep	Ky.	1	1
16th	Benedict, Cleve	Rep	W.Va.	1	1
17th	Coats, Daniel R.	Rep	Ind.	1	1
18th	Bliley, Thomas J. Jr.	Rep	Va.	1	1

*2: Member's 2nd period of service on the committee.

	Majority			Minority		
Departures from the House:						
Defeated for Renomination	Mottl, Ronald M.	Ohio	Dem	Lee, Gary A.	N.Y.	Rep
Lost Election to U.S. Senate	Moffett, Anthony J.(Toby)	Conn.	Dem	Benedict, Cleve	W.Va.	Rep
				Collins, James M.	Tex.	Rep
Lost Nomination to U.S. Senate	Santini, James D.	Nev.	Dem	None		
Lost Election for Governor	None			Brown, Clarence J. Jr.	Ohio	Rep
Retired	None			Marks, Marc L.	Penn.	Rep
Departures from Committee:						
Moved to Appropriations	None			Rogers, Harold	Ky.	Rep
No new assignment	Gramm, W. Phil	Tex.	Dem	None		

ENERGY AND COMMERCE / 98th Congress

Service Dates of Committee Chair: Jan. 6,1983-Jan. 3,1985
Service Dates of Majority Members: Jan. 6,1983-Jan. 3,1985
Service Dates of Minority Members: Jan. 6,1983-Jan. 3,1985

Majority

Rank	Name	Party	State	Terms in: House	Terms in: Comm.
Chr	Dingell, John D. Jr.	Dem	Mich.	15	14
2nd	Scheuer, James H.	Dem	N.Y.	9	5
3rd	Ottinger, Richard L.	Dem	N.Y.	8	*2 5
4th	Waxman, Henry A.	Dem	Cal.	5	5
5th	Wirth, Timothy E.	Dem	Colo.	5	5
6th	Sharp, Philip R.	Dem	Ind.	5	5
7th	Florio, James J.	Dem	N.J.	5	5
8th	Markey, Edward J.	Dem	Mass.	5	4
9th	Luken, Thomas A.	Dem	Ohio	5	*2 4
10th	Walgren, Douglas	Dem	Penn.	4	4
11th	Gore, Albert A. Jr.	Dem	Tenn.	4	4
12th	Mikulski, Barbara A.	Dem	Md.	4	4
13th	Swift, Allan B.	Dem	Wash.	3	3
14th	Leland, G. T. (Mickey)	Dem	Tex.	3	3
15th	Shelby, Richard C.	Dem	Ala.	3	3
16th	Collins, Cardiss	Dem	Ill.	6	2
17th	Synar, Michael L.	Dem	Okla.	3	2
18th	Tauzin, W. J. (Billy)	Dem	La.	3	2
19th	Wyden, Ron	Dem	Ore.	2	2
20th	Hall, Ralph M.	Dem	Tex.	2	2
21st	Eckart, Dennis E.	Dem	Ohio	2	1
22nd	Dowdy, Wayne	Dem	Miss.	2	1
23rd	Richardson, Bill	Dem	N.M.	1	1
24th	Slattery, Jim	Dem	Kans.	1	1
25th	Sikorski, Gerry	Dem	Minn.	1	1
26th	Bryant, John	Dem	Tex.	1	1
27th	Bates, Jim	Dem	Cal.	1	1

Minority

Rank	Name	Party	State	Terms in: House	Terms in: Comm.
RM	Broyhill, James T.	Rep	N.C.	11	11
2nd	Lent, Norman F.	Rep	N.Y.	7	6
3rd	Madigan, Edward R.	Rep	Ill.	6	6
4th	Moorhead, Carlos J.	Rep	Cal.	6	5
5th	Rinaldo, Matthew J.	Rep	N.J.	6	5
6th	Corcoran, Thomas J.	Rep	Ill.	4	3
7th	Dannemeyer, William E.	Rep	Cal.	3	3
8th	Whittaker, Robert	Rep	Kans.	3	2
9th	Tauke, Thomas J.	Rep	Iowa	3	2
10th	Ritter, Donald L.	Rep	Penn.	3	2
11th	Coats, Daniel R.	Rep	Ind.	2	2
12th	Bliley, Thomas J. Jr.	Rep	Va.	2	2
13th	Fields, Jack	Rep	Tex.	2	1
14th	Oxley, Michael G.	Rep	Ohio	2	1
15th	Nielson, Howard C.	Rep	Utah	1	1

*2: Member's 2nd period of service on the committee.

Departures from the House:	Majority		Minority	
Elected to U.S. Senate	Gore, Albert A. Jr.	Tenn. Dem	None	
Lost Nomination to U.S. Senate	None		Corcoran, Thomas J.	Ill. Rep
Retired	Ottinger, Richard L.	N.Y. Dem	None	

ENERGY AND COMMERCE / 99th Congress

Service Dates of Committee Chair: Jan. 7,1985-Jan. 3,1987
Service Dates of Majority Members: Jan. 30,1985-Jan. 3,1987
Service Dates of Minority Members: Jan. 30,1985-Jan. 3,1987

Majority

Rank	Name	Party	State	Terms in: House	Terms in: Comm.
Chr	Dingell, John D. Jr.	Dem	Mich.	16	15
2nd	Scheuer, James H.	Dem	N.Y.	10	6
3rd	Waxman, Henry A.	Dem	Cal.	6	6
4th	Wirth, Timothy E.	Dem	Colo.	6	6
5th	Sharp, Philip R.	Dem	Ind.	6	6
6th	Florio, James J.	Dem	N.J.	6	6
7th	Markey, Edward J.	Dem	Mass.	6	5
8th	Luken, Thomas A.	Dem	Ohio	6	*2 5
9th	Walgren, Douglas	Dem	Penn.	5	5
10th	Mikulski, Barbara A.	Dem	Md.	5	5
11th	Swift, Allan B.	Dem	Wash.	4	4
12th	Leland, G. T. (Mickey)	Dem	Tex.	4	4
13th	Shelby, Richard C.	Dem	Ala.	4	4

Minority

Rank	Name	Party	State	Terms in: House	Terms in: Comm.
RM1	Broyhill, James T.	Rep	N.C.	12	12
RM2 2nd	Lent, Norman F.	Rep	N.Y.	8	7
3rd	Madigan, Edward R.	Rep	Ill.	7	7
4th	Moorhead, Carlos J.	Rep	Cal.	7	6
5th	Rinaldo, Matthew J.	Rep	N.J.	7	6
6th	Dannemeyer, William E.	Rep	Cal.	4	4
7th	Whittaker, Robert	Rep	Kans.	4	3
8th	Tauke, Thomas J.	Rep	Iowa	4	3
9th	Ritter, Donald L.	Rep	Penn.	4	3
10th	Coats, Daniel R.	Rep	Ind.	3	3
11th	Bliley, Thomas J. Jr.	Rep	Va.	3	3
12th	Fields, Jack	Rep	Tex.	3	2
13th	Oxley, Michael G.	Rep	Ohio	3	2

Rank Name	Party	State	House	Comm.	Rank Name	Party	State	House	Comm.
14th Collins, Cardiss	Dem	Ill.	7	3	14th Nielson, Howard C.	Rep	Utah	2	2
15th Synar, Michael L.	Dem	Okla.	4	3	15th Bilirakis, Michael	Rep	Fla.	2	1
16th Tauzin, W. J. (Billy)	Dem	La.	4	3	16th Schaefer, Daniel L.	Rep	Colo.	2	1
17th Wyden, Ron	Dem	Ore.	3	3	17th Eckert, Fred J.	Rep	N.Y.	1	1
18th Hall, Ralph M.	Dem	Tex.	3	3					
19th Eckart, Dennis E.	Dem	Ohio	3	2					
20th Dowdy, Wayne	Dem	Miss.	3	2					
21st Richardson, Bill	Dem	N.M.	2	2					
22nd Slattery, Jim	Dem	Kans.	2	2					
23rd Sikorski, Gerry	Dem	Minn.	2	2					
24th Bryant, John	Dem	Tex.	2	2					
25th Bates, Jim	Dem	Cal.	2	2					

*2: Member's 2nd period of service on the committee.

Changes:

Ranking Member:

RM1 Broyhill, James T.	Rep	N.C.	July 13,1986	Resigned; appointed to U.S. Senate.
RM2 Lent, Norman F.	Rep	N.Y.	July 13,1986	Succeeded Broyhill as Ranking Minority Member.

Minority:

Broyhill, James T.	Rep	N.C.	July 13,1986	Resigned; appointed to U.S. Senate.
Lott, Trent	Rep	Miss.	July 23,1986	Replaced Broyhill.

Departures from the House:	**Majority**		**Minority**	
Elected to U.S. Senate	Mikulski, Barbara A.	Md. Dem	None	
	Shelby, Richard C.	Ala. Dem		
	Wirth, Timothy E.	Colo. Dem		
Defeated for Reelection	None		Eckert, Fred J.	N.Y. Rep
Departures from Committee:				
No new assignment	None		Lott, Trent	Cal. Rep

ENERGY AND COMMERCE / 100th Congress

Service Dates of Committee Chair: Jan. 8,1987-Jan. 3,1989
Service Dates of Majority Members: Jan. 22,1987-Jan. 3,1989
Service Dates of Minority Members: Jan. 21,1987-Jan. 3,1989

Majority			Terms in:		**Minority**			Terms in:	
Rank Name	**Party**	**State**	**House**	**Comm.**	**Rank Name**	**Party**	**State**	**House**	**Comm.**
Chr Dingell, John D. Jr.	Dem	Mich.	17	16	RM Lent, Norman F.	Rep	N.Y.	9	8
2nd Scheuer, James H.	Dem	N.Y.	11	7	2nd Madigan, Edward R.	Rep	Ill.	8	8
3rd Waxman, Henry A.	Dem	Cal.	7	7	3rd Moorhead, Carlos J.	Rep	Cal.	8	7
4th Sharp, Philip R.	Dem	Ind.	7	7	4th Rinaldo, Matthew J.	Rep	N.J.	8	7
5th Florio, James J.	Dem	N.J.	7	7	5th Dannemeyer, William E.	Rep	Cal.	5	5
6th Markey, Edward J.	Dem	Mass.	7	6	6th Whittaker, Robert	Rep	Kans.	5	4
7th Luken, Thomas A.	Dem	Ohio	7 *2	6	7th Tauke, Thomas J.	Rep	Iowa	5	4
8th Walgren, Douglas	Dem	Penn.	6	6	8th Ritter, Donald L.	Rep	Penn.	5	4
9th Swift, Allan B.	Dem	Wash.	5	5	9th Coats, Daniel R.	Rep	Ind.	4	4
10th Leland, G. T. (Mickey)	Dem	Tex.	5	5	10th Bliley, Thomas J. Jr.	Rep	Va.	4	4
11th Collins, Cardiss	Dem	Ill.	8	4	11th Fields, Jack	Rep	Tex.	4	3
12th Synar, Michael L.	Dem	Okla.	5	4	12th Oxley, Michael G.	Rep	Ohio	4	3
13th Tauzin, W. J. (Billy)	Dem	La.	5	4	13th Nielson, Howard C.	Rep	Utah	3	3
14th Wyden, Ron	Dem	Ore.	4	4	14th Bilirakis, Michael	Rep	Fla.	3	2
15th Hall, Ralph M.	Dem	Tex.	4	4	15th Schaefer, Daniel L.	Rep	Colo.	3	2
16th Eckart, Dennis E.	Dem	Ohio	4	3	16th Barton, Joe L.	Rep	Tex.	2	1
17th Dowdy, Wayne	Dem	Miss.	4	3	17th Callahan, H. L. (Sonny)	Rep	Ala.	2	1
18th Richardson, Bill	Dem	N.M.	3	3					
19th Slattery, Jim	Dem	Kans.	3	3					
20th Sikorski, Gerry	DFL	Minn.	3	3					
21st Bryant, John	Dem	Tex.	3	3					
22nd Bates, Jim	Dem	Cal.	3	3					
23rd Boucher, Frederick C.	Dem	Va.	3	1					
24th Cooper, Jim	Dem	Tenn.	3	1					
25th Bruce, Terry L.	Dem	Ill.	2	1					

*2: Member's 2nd period of service on the committee.

Departures from the House:	**Majority**		**Minority**	
Appointed to U.S. Senate	None		Coats, Daniel R.	Ind. Rep
Lost Election to U.S. Senate	Dowdy, Wayne	Miss. Dem	None	

ENERGY AND COMMERCE / 101st Congress

Service Dates of Committee Chair: Jan. 3,1989-Jan. 3,1991
Service Dates of Majority Members: Jan. 19,1989-Jan. 3,1991
Service Dates of Minority Members: Jan. 20,1989-Jan. 3,1991

Majority

Rank	Name	Party	State	Terms in: House	Terms in: Comm.
Chr	Dingell, John D. Jr.	Dem	Mich.	18	17
2nd	Scheuer, James H.	Dem	N.Y.	12	8
3rd	Waxman, Henry A.	Dem	Cal.	8	8
4th	Sharp, Philip R.	Dem	Ind.	8	8
5th	Florio, James J.	Dem	N.J.	8	8
6th	Markey, Edward J.	Dem	Mass.	8	7
7th	Luken, Thomas A.	Dem	Ohio	8	*2 7
8th	Walgren, Douglas	Dem	Penn.	7	7
9th	Swift, Allan B.	Dem	Wash.	6	6
10th	Leland, G. T. (Mickey)	Dem	Tex.	6	6
11th	Collins, Cardiss	Dem	Ill.	9	5
12th	Synar, Michael L.	Dem	Okla.	6	5
13th	Tauzin, W. J. (Billy)	Dem	La.	6	5
14th	Wyden, Ron	Dem	Ore.	5	5
15th	Hall, Ralph M.	Dem	Tex.	5	5
16th	Eckart, Dennis E.	Dem	Ohio	5	4
17th	Richardson, Bill	Dem	N.M.	4	4
18th	Slattery, Jim	Dem	Kans.	4	4
19th	Sikorski, Gerry	Dem	Minn.	4	4
20th	Bryant, John	Dem	Tex.	4	4
21st	Bates, Jim	Dem	Cal.	4	4
22nd	Boucher, Frederick C.	Dem	Va.	4	2
23rd	Cooper, Jim	Dem	Tenn.	4	2
24th	Bruce, Terry L.	Dem	Ill.	3	2
25th	Rowland, J. Roy	Dem	Ga.	4	1
26th	Manton, Thomas J.	Dem	N.Y.	3	1

Minority

Rank	Name	Party	State	Terms in: House	Terms in: Comm.
RM	Lent, Norman F.	Rep	N.Y.	10	9
2nd	Madigan, Edward R.	Rep	Ill.	9	9
3rd	Moorhead, Carlos J.	Rep	Cal.	9	8
4th	Rinaldo, Matthew J.	Rep	N.J.	9	8
5th	Dannemeyer, William E.	Rep	Cal.	6	6
6th	Whittaker, Robert	Rep	Kans.	6	5
7th	Tauke, Thomas J.	Rep	Iowa	6	5
8th	Ritter, Donald L.	Rep	Penn.	6	5
9th	Bliley, Thomas J. Jr.	Rep	Va.	5	5
10th	Fields, Jack	Rep	Tex.	5	4
11th	Oxley, Michael G.	Rep	Ohio	5	4
12th	Nielson, Howard C.	Rep	Utah	4	4
13th	Bilirakis, Michael	Rep	Fla.	4	3
14th	Schaefer, Daniel L.	Rep	Colo.	4	3
15th	Barton, Joe L.	Rep	Tex.	3	2
16th	Callahan, H. L. (Sonny)	Rep	Ala.	3	2
17th	McMillan, J. Alex	Rep	N.C.	3	1

*2: Member's 2nd period of service on the committee.

Changes:

Majority:

Leland, G. T. (Mickey)	Dem	Tex.	Aug. 7,1989	Died in office.
Towns, Edolphus	Dem	N.Y.	Nov. 8,1989	Replaced Leland.
Florio, James J.	Dem	N.J.	Jan. 16,1990	Resigned; elected Governor of New Jersey.
McMillen, C. Thomas	Dem	Md.	Feb. 27,1990	Replaced Florio.

Departures from the House:

	Majority			Minority		
Defeated for Reelection	Bates, Jim	Cal.	Dem	None		
	Walgren, Douglas	Penn.	Dem			
Lost Election to U.S. Senate	None			Tauke, Thomas J.	Iowa	Rep
Retired	Luken, Thomas A.	Ohio	Dem	Nielson, Howard C.	Utah	Rep
				Whittaker, Robert	Kans.	Rep

ENERGY AND COMMERCE / 102nd Congress

Service Dates of Committee Chair: Jan. 24,1991-Jan. 3,1993
Service Dates of Majority Members: Jan. 24,1991-Jan. 3,1993
Service Dates of Minority Members: Jan. 24,1991-Jan. 3,1993

Majority

Rank	Name	Party	State	Terms in: House	Terms in: Comm.
Chr	Dingell, John D. Jr.	Dem	Mich.	19	18
2nd	Scheuer, James H.	Dem	N.Y.	13	9
3rd	Waxman, Henry A.	Dem	Cal.	9	9
4th	Sharp, Philip R.	Dem	Ind.	9	9
5th	Markey, Edward J.	Dem	Mass.	9	8
6th	Swift, Allan B.	Dem	Wash.	7	7
7th	Collins, Cardiss	Dem	Ill.	10	6
8th	Synar, Michael L.	Dem	Okla.	7	6
9th	Tauzin, W. J. (Billy)	Dem	La.	7	6
10th	Wyden, Ron	Dem	Ore.	6	6
11th	Hall, Ralph M.	Dem	Tex.	6	6
12th	Eckart, Dennis E.	Dem	Ohio	6	5
13th	Richardson, Bill	Dem	N.M.	5	5
14th	Slattery, Jim	Dem	Kans.	5	5
15th	Sikorski, Gerry	Dem	Minn.	5	5
16th	Bryant, John	Dem	Tex.	5	5
17th	Boucher, Frederick C.	Dem	Va.	5	3
18th	Cooper, Jim	Dem	Tenn.	5	3
19th	Bruce, Terry L.	Dem	Ill.	4	3
20th	Rowland, J. Roy	Dem	Ga.	5	2
21st	Manton, Thomas J.	Dem	N.Y.	4	2
22nd	Towns, Edolphus	Dem	N.Y.	5	*T 2
23rd	McMillen, C. Thomas	Dem	Md.	3	*T 2
24th	Studds, Gerry E.	Dem	Mass.	10	1
25th	Kostmayer, Peter H.	Dem	Penn.	7	1
26th	Lehman, Richard H.	Dem	Cal.	5	1
27th	Harris, Claude	Dem	Ala.	3	1

Minority

Rank	Name	Party	State	Terms in: House	Terms in: Comm.
RM	Lent, Norman F.	Rep	N.Y.	11	10
2nd	Madigan, Edward R.	Rep	Ill.	10	10
3rd	Moorhead, Carlos J.	Rep	Cal.	10	9
4th	Rinaldo, Matthew J.	Rep	N.J.	10	9
5th	Dannemeyer, William E.	Rep	Cal.	7	7
6th	Ritter, Donald L.	Rep	Penn.	7	6
7th	Bliley, Thomas J. Jr.	Rep	Va.	6	6
8th	Fields, Jack	Rep	Tex.	6	5
9th	Oxley, Michael G.	Rep	Ohio	6	5
10th	Bilirakis, Michael	Rep	Fla.	5	4
11th	Schaefer, Daniel L.	Rep	Colo.	5	4
12th	Barton, Joe L.	Rep	Tex.	4	3
13th	Callahan, H. L. (Sonny)	Rep	Ala.	4	3
14th	McMillan, J. Alex	Rep	N.C.	4	2
15th	Hastert, J. Dennis	Rep	Ill.	3	1
16th	Holloway, Clyde C.	Rep	La.	3	1

*T: Temporary member of the committee.

Changes:

Minority:

Madigan, Edward R.	Rep	Ill.	Mar. 8,1991	Resigned House; appointed Secretary of Agriculture.
Upton, Frederick S.	Rep	Mich.	Mar. 11,1991	Replaced Madigan.

FOREIGN AFFAIRS

Jurisdiction, 1947

Established by the Legislative Reorganization Act of 1946:

[Section 121.(1)(i)]

Committee on Foreign Affairs.

1. Relations of the United States with foreign nations generally.
2. Establishment of boundary lines between the United States and foreign nations.
3. Protection of American citizens abroad and expatriation.
4. Neutrality.
5. International conferences and congresses.
6. The American National Red Cross.
7. Intervention abroad and declarations of war.
8. Measures relating to the diplomatic service.
9. Acquisition of land and buildings for embassies and legations in foreign countries.
10. Measures to foster commercial intercourse with foreign nations and to safeguard American business interests abroad.
11. United Nations Organization and international financial and monetary organizations.
12. Foreign loans.

INTERNATIONAL RELATIONS

Renamed the Committee on International Relations on March 19, 1975.

FOREIGN AFFAIRS

Resumed name of Committee on Foreign Affairs on February 5, 1979.

Jurisdiction, 1992

Jurisdiction contained in Rules of the House of Representatives (as revised to July 1, 1992):

[Rule X. 1. (i)]

Committee on Foreign Affairs.

(1) Relations of the United States with foreign nations generally.
(2) Acquisition of land and buildings for embassies and legations in foreign countries.
(3) Establishment of boundary lines between the United States and foreign nations.
(4) Foreign loans.
(5) International conferences and congresses.
(6) Intervention abroad and declarations of war.
(7) Measures relating to the diplomatic service.
(8) Measures to foster commercial intercourse with foreign nations and to safeguard American business interests abroad.
(9) Neutrality.
(10) Protection of American citizens abroad and expatriation.
(11) The American National Red Cross.
(12) United Nations Organizations.
(13) Measures relating to international economic policy.

(14) Export controls, including nonproliferation of nuclear technology and nuclear hardware.
(15) International commodity agreements (other than those involving sugar), including all agreements for cooperation in the export of nuclear technology and nuclear hardware.
(16) Trading with the enemy.
(17) International education.

In addition to its legislative jurisdiction under the preceding provisions of this paragraph (and its general oversight function under clause 2(b)(1)), the committee shall have the special oversight functions provided for in clause 3(d) with respect to customs administration, intelligence activities relating to foreign policy, international financial and monetary organizations, and international fishing agreements.

[Rule X. 3.(d)]

The Committee on Foreign Affairs shall have the function of reviewing and studying, on a continuing basis, all laws, programs, and Government activities dealing with or involving customs administration, intelligence activities relating to foreign policy, international financial and monetary organizations, and international fishing agreements.

FOREIGN AFFAIRS / 80th Congress

Service Dates of Committee Chair: Jan. 14,1947-Jan. 3,1949
Service Dates of Majority Members: Jan. 14,1947-Jan. 3,1949
Service Dates of Minority Members: Jan. 16,1947-Jan. 3,1949

Majority

Rank	Name	Party	State	Terms in: House	Terms in: Comm.
Chr	Eaton, Charles A.	Rep	N.J.	12	12
2nd	Chiperfield, Robert B.	Rep	Ill.	5	5
3rd	Vorys, John M.	Rep	Ohio	5	5
4th	Mundt, Karl E.	Rep	S.D.	5	4
5th	Jonkman, Bartel J.	Rep	Mich.	5	4
6th	Bolton, Frances P.	Rep	Ohio	5	4
7th	Gerlach, Charles L.	Rep	Penn.	5	3
8th	Smith, Lawrence H.	Rep	Wisc.	4	2
9th	Merrow, Chester E.	Rep	N.H.	3	2
10th	Judd, Walter H.	Rep	Minn.	3	1
11th	Fulton, James G.	Rep	Penn.	2	*1 1
12th	Javits, Jacob K.	Rep	N.Y.	1	1
13th	Lodge, John Davis	Rep	Conn.	1	1
14th	Jackson, Donald L.	Rep	Cal.	1	1

Minority

Rank	Name	Party	State	Terms in: House	Terms in: Comm.
RM	Bloom, Sol	Dem	N.Y.	13	11
2nd	Kee, John	Dem	W.Va.	8	8
3rd	Richards, James P.	Dem	S.C.	8	7
4th	Pfeifer, Joseph L.	Dem	N.Y.	7	7
5th	Jarman, Pete	Dem	Ala.	6	5
6th	Courtney, Wirt	Dem	Tenn.	5	5
7th	Gordon, Thomas S.	Dem	Ill.	3	3
8th	Douglas, Helen Gahagan	Dem	Cal.	2	2
9th	Mansfield, Michael J.	Dem	Mont.	3	*2 2
10th	Morgan, Thomas E.	Dem	Penn.	2	2
11th	Colmer, William M.	Dem	Miss.	8	1

*1: Member's 1st period of service on the committee; *2: Member's 2nd period of service on the committee.

Changes:

Majority:

Name	Party	State	Date	Change
Gerlach, Charles L.	Rep	Penn.	May 5,1947	Died in office.
Maloney, Franklin J.	Rep	Penn.	July 15,1947	Replaced Gerlach.
Mundt, Karl E.	Rep	S.D.	Dec. 30,1948	Resigned; elected to U.S. Senate.

	Majority		Minority	
Departures from the House:				
Defeated for Reelection	Maloney, Franklin J.	Penn. Rep	None	
Defeated for Renomination	Jonkman, Bartel J.	Mich. Rep	Courtney, Wirt	Tenn. Dem
			Jarman, Pete	Ala. Dem
Departures from Committee:				
Moved to Rules	None		Colmer, William M.	Miss. Dem

FOREIGN AFFAIRS / 81st Congress

Service Dates of Committee Chairs: Ch1 Jan. 18,1949-Mar. 7,1949
Ch2 Mar. 11,1949-Jan. 3,1951
Service Dates of Majority Members: Jan. 18,1949-Jan. 3,1951
Service Dates of Minority Members: Jan. 18,1949-Jan. 3,1951

Majority

Rank Name	Party	State	Terms in: House		Terms in: Comm.
Ch1 Bloom, Sol	Dem	N.Y.	14		12
Ch2 2nd Kee, John	Dem	W.Va.	9		9
3rd Richards, James P.	Dem	S.C.	9		8
4th Pfeifer, Joseph L.	Dem	N.Y.	8		8
5th Gordon, Thomas S.	Dem	Ill.	4		4
6th Douglas, Helen Gahagan	Dem	Cal.	3		3
7th Mansfield, Michael J.	Dem	Mont.	4	*2	2
8th Morgan, Thomas E.	Dem	Penn.	3		3
9th Battle, Laurie C.	Dem	Ala.	2		1
10th Smathers, George A.	Dem	Fla.	2		1
11th Carnahan, Albert S. J.	Dem	Mo.	2	*2	1
12th Chatham, Richard Thurmond	Dem	N.C.	1		1
13th Zablocki, Clement J.	Dem	Wisc.	1		1
14th Ribicoff, Abraham A.	Dem	Conn.	1		1

Minority

Rank Name	Party	State	Terms in: House		Terms in: Comm.
RM Eaton, Charles A.	Rep	N.J.	13		13
2nd Chiperfield, Robert B.	Rep	Ill.	6		6
3rd Vorys, John M.	Rep	Ohio	6		6
4th Bolton, Frances P.	Rep	Ohio	6		5
5th Smith, Lawrence H.	Rep	Wisc.	5		3
6th Merrow, Chester E.	Rep	N.H.	4		3
7th Judd, Walter H.	Rep	Minn.	4		2
8th Fulton, James G.	Rep	Penn.	3	*1	2
9th Javits, Jacob K.	Rep	N.Y.	2		2
10th Lodge, John Davis	Rep	Conn.	2		2
11th Jackson, Donald L.	Rep	Cal.	2		2

*1: Member's 1st period of service on the committee;
*2: Member's 2nd period of service on the committee.

Changes:

Chair:

Ch1 Bloom, Sol	Dem	N.Y.	Mar. 7,1949	Died in office.
Ch2 Kee, John	Dem	W.Va.	Mar.11,1949	Succeeded Bloom as chair.

Majority:

Bloom, Sol	Dem	N.Y.	Mar. 7,1949	Died in office.
Burleson, Omar T.	Dem	Tex.	Mar. 16,1949	Replaced Bloom.

Departures from the House:	Majority			Minority		
Elected to U.S. Senate	Smathers, George A.	Fla.	Dem	None		
Elected Governor	None			Lodge, John Davis	Conn.	Rep
Defeated for Renomination	Pfeifer, Joseph L.	N.Y.	Dem	None		
Lost Election to U.S. Senate	Douglas, Helen Gahagan	Cal.	Dem	None		

FOREIGN AFFAIRS / 82nd Congress

Service Dates of Committee Chairs: Ch1 Jan. 12,1951-May 8,1951
Ch2 May 15,1951-Jan. 3,1953
Service Dates of Majority Members: Jan. 12,1951-Jan. 3,1953
Service Dates of Minority Members: Jan. 15,1951-Jan. 3,1953

Majority

Rank Name	Party	State	Terms in: House		Terms in: Comm.
Ch1 Kee, John	Dem	W.Va.	10		10
Ch2 2nd Richards, James P.	Dem	S.C.	10		9
3rd Gordon, Thomas S.	Dem	Ill.	5		5
4th Mansfield, Michael J.	Dem	Mont.	5	*2	3
5th Morgan, Thomas E.	Dem	Penn.	4		4
6th Battle, Laurie C.	Dem	Ala.	3		2
7th Carnahan, Albert S. J.	Dem	Mo.	3	*2	2
8th Chatham, Richard Thurmond	Dem	N.C.	2		2
9th Zablocki, Clement J.	Dem	Wisc.	2		2
10th Ribicoff, Abraham A.	Dem	Conn.	2		2
11th Burleson, Omar T.	Dem	Tex.	3		2
12th Hays, L. Brooks	Dem	Ark.	5		1
13th Holifield, Chet	Dem	Cal.	5		1
14th Roosevelt, Franklin D. Jr.	Dem	N.Y.	2		1
15th Kelly, Edna F.	Dem	N.Y.	2		1

Minority

Rank Name	Party	State	Terms in: House		Terms in: Comm.
RM Eaton, Charles A.	Rep	N.J.	14		14
2nd Chiperfield, Robert B.	Rep	Ill.	7		7
3rd Vorys, John M.	Rep	Ohio	7		7
4th Bolton, Frances P.	Rep	Ohio	7		6
5th Smith, Lawrence H.	Rep	Wisc.	6		4
6th Merrow, Chester E.	Rep	N.H.	5		4
7th Judd, Walter H.	Rep	Minn.	5		3
8th Fulton, James G.	Rep	Penn.	4	*1	3
9th Javits, Jacob K.	Rep	N.Y.	3		3
10th Jackson, Donald L.	Rep	Cal.	3		3
11th Herter, Christian A.	Rep	Mass.	5		1
12th Reece, B. Carroll	Rep	Tenn.	13		1

*1: Member's 1st period of service on the committee; *2: Member's 2nd period of service on the committee.

Changes:
Chair:

Ch1 Kee, John	Dem	W.Va.	May 8,1951	Died in office.
Ch2 Richards, James P.	Dem	S.C.	May 15,1951	Succeeded Kee as Chair.

Majority:

Kee, John	Dem	W.Va.	May 8,1951	Died in office.
Lanham, Henderson L.	Dem	Ga.	July 18,1951	Replaced Kee.

	Majority			Minority		
Departures from the House:						
Elected to U.S. Senate	Mansfield, Michael J.	Mont.	Dem	None		
Elected Governor	None			Herter, Christian A.	Mass.	Rep
Lost Election to U.S. Senate	Ribicoff, Abraham A.	Conn.	Dem	None		
Retired	None			Eaton, Charles A.	N.J.	Rep
Departures from Committee:						
Moved to Government Operations	Holifield, Chet	Cal.	Dem	None		
Moved to Rules	None			Reece, B. Carroll	Tenn.	Rep

FOREIGN AFFAIRS / 83rd Congress

Service Dates of Committee Chair: Jan. 19,1953-Jan. 3,1955
Service Dates of Majority Members: Jan. 19,1953-Jan. 3,1955
Service Dates of Minority Members: Jan. 19,1953-Jan. 3,1955

Majority

Rank	Name	Party	State	Terms in: House		Terms in: Comm.
Chr	Chiperfield, Robert B.	Rep	Ill.	8		8
2nd	Vorys, John M.	Rep	Ohio	8		8
3rd	Bolton, Frances P.	Rep	Ohio	8		7
4th	Smith, Lawrence H.	Rep	Wisc.	7		5
5th	Merrow, Chester E.	Rep	N.H.	6		5
6th	Judd, Walter H.	Rep	Minn.	6		4
7th	Fulton, James G.	Rep	Penn.	5	*1	4
8th	Javits, Jacob K.	Rep	N.Y.	4		4
9th	Jackson, Donald L.	Rep	Cal.	4		4
10th	LeCompte, Karl M.	Rep	Iowa	8		1
11th	Radwan, Edmund P.	Rep	N.Y.	2		1
12th	Morano, Albert P.	Rep	Conn.	2		1
13th	Church, Marguerite Stitt	Rep	Ill.	2		1
14th	Adair, E. Ross	Rep	Ind.	2		1
15th	Prouty, Winston L.	Rep	Vt.	2		1
16th	Bentley, Alvin M.	Rep	Mich.	1		1

Minority

Rank	Name	Party	State	Terms in: House		Terms in: Comm.
RM	Richards, James P.	Dem	S.C.	11		10
2nd	Gordon, Thomas S.	Dem	Ill.	6		6
3rd	Morgan, Thomas E.	Dem	Penn.	5		5
4th	Battle, Laurie C.	Dem	Ala.	4		3
5th	Carnahan, Albert S. J.	Dem	Mo.	4	*2	3
6th	Chatham, Richard Thurmond	Dem	N.C.	3		3
7th	Zablocki, Clement J.	Dem	Wisc.	3		3
8th	Burleson, Omar T.	Dem	Tex.	4		3
9th	Hays, L. Brooks	Dem	Ark.	6		2
10th	Roosevelt, Franklin D. Jr.	Dem	N.Y.	3		2
11th	Kelly, Edna F.	Dem	N.Y.	3		2
12th	Lanham, Henderson L.	Dem	Ga.	4		2
13th	Harrison, Burr P.	Dem	Va.	5		1

*1: Member's 1st period of service on the committee; *2: Member's 2nd period of service on the committee.

Note: Democratic Party gains in the 1953 special elections in New Jersey and Wisconsin led to an increase in the size of this committee to 16 Republicans and 14 Democrats on Jan. 25,1954.

Addition:
Minority: 14th Dodd, Thomas J. Dem Conn. Jan. 25,1954

Changes:
Majority:

Javits, Jacob K.	Rep	N.Y.	Dec. 31,1954	Resigned; elected State Attorney General.

	Majority	Minority		
Departures from the House:				
Lost Nomination to U.S. Senate	None	Battle, Laurie C.	Ala.	Dem
Lost Nomination for Governor	None	Roosevelt, Franklin D.Jr.	N.Y.	Dem
Departures from Committee:				
Moved to Appropriations	None	Lanham, Henderson L.	Ga.	Dem
No new assignment	None	Harrison, Burr P.	Va.	Dem

FOREIGN AFFAIRS / 84th Congress

Service Dates of Committee Chair: Jan. 13,1955-Jan. 3,1957
Service Dates of Majority Members: Jan. 13,1955-Jan. 3,1957
Service Dates of Minority Members: Jan. 20,1955-Jan. 3,1957

Majority

Rank Name	Party	State	Terms in: House	Terms in: Comm.
Chr Richards, James P.	Dem	S.C.	12	11
2nd Gordon, Thomas S.	Dem	Ill.	7	7
3rd Morgan, Thomas E.	Dem	Penn.	6	6
4th Carnahan, Albert S. J.	Dem	Mo.	5	*2 4
5th Chatham, Richard Thurmond	Dem	N.C.	4	4
6th Zablocki, Clement J.	Dem	Wisc.	4	4
7th Burleson, Omar T.	Dem	Tex.	5	4
8th Hays, L. Brooks	Dem	Ark.	7	3
9th Kelly, Edna F.	Dem	N.Y.	4	3
10th Dodd, Thomas J.	Dem	Conn.	2	2
11th Hays, Wayne L.	Dem	Ohio	4	1
12th Donovan, James G.	Dem	N.Y.	3	1
13th Jarman, John	Dem	Okla.	3	1
14th Byrd, Robert C.	Dem	W.Va.	2	1
15th Selden, Armistead I. Jr.	Dem	Ala.	2	1
16th Pilcher, John L.	Dem	Ga.	2	1
17th Williams, Harrison A. Jr.	Dem	N.J.	2	1

Minority

Rank Name	Party	State	Terms in: House	Terms in: Comm.
RM Chiperfield, Robert B.	Rep	Ill.	9	9
2nd Vorys, John M.	Rep	Ohio	9	9
3rd Bolton, Frances P.	Rep	Ohio	9	8
4th Smith, Lawrence H.	Rep	Wisc.	8	6
5th Merrow, Chester E.	Rep	N.H.	7	6
6th Judd, Walter H.	Rep	Minn.	7	5
7th Fulton, James G.	Rep	Penn.	6	*1 5
8th Jackson, Donald L.	Rep	Cal.	5	5
9th LeCompte, Karl M.	Rep	Iowa	9	2
10th Radwan, Edmund P.	Rep	N.Y.	3	2
11th Morano, Albert P.	Rep	Conn.	3	2
12th Church, Marguerite Stitt	Rep	Ill.	3	2
13th Adair, E. Ross	Rep	Ind.	3	2
14th Prouty, Winston L.	Rep	Vt.	3	2
15th Bentley, Alvin M.	Rep	Mich.	2	2

*1: Member's 1st period of service on the committee; *2: Member's 2nd period of service on the committee.

Departures from the House:	Majority			Minority
Appointed Presidential Assistant	Richards, James P.	S.C.	Dem	None
Defeated for Reelection	Donovan, James G.	N.Y.	Dem	None
	Williams, Harrison A. Jr.	N.J.	Dem	
Defeated for Renomination	Chatham, Richard Thurmond	N.C.	Dem	None
Lost Election to U.S. Senate	Dodd, Thomas J.	Conn.	Dem	None

FOREIGN AFFAIRS / 85th Congress

Service Dates of Committee Chair: Jan. 3,1957-Jan. 3,1959
Service Dates of Majority Members: Jan. 3,1957-Jan. 3,1959
Service Dates of Minority Members: Jan. 7,1957-Jan. 3,1959

Majority

Rank Name	Party	State	Terms in: House	Terms in: Comm.
Chr Gordon, Thomas S.	Dem	Ill.	8	8
2nd Morgan, Thomas E.	Dem	Penn.	7	7
3rd Carnahan, Albert S. J.	Dem	Mo.	6	*2 5
4th Zablocki, Clement J.	Dem	Wisc.	5	5
5th Burleson, Omar T.	Dem	Tex.	6	5
6th Hays, L. Brooks	Dem	Ark.	8	4
7th Kelly, Edna F.	Dem	N.Y.	5	4
8th Hays, Wayne L.	Dem	Ohio	5	2
9th Jarman, John	Dem	Okla.	4	2
10th Byrd, Robert C.	Dem	W.Va.	3	2
11th Selden, Armistead I. Jr.	Dem	Ala.	3	2
12th Pilcher, John L.	Dem	Ga.	3	2
13th O'Hara, Barratt	Dem	Ill.	4	1
14th Fountain, Lawrence H.	Dem	N.C.	3	1
15th Fascell, Dante B.	Dem	Fla.	2	1
16th Coffin, Frank M.	Dem	Me.	1	1
17th Farbstein, Leonard	Dem	N.Y.	1	1

Minority

Rank Name	Party	State	Terms in: House	Terms in: Comm.
RM Chiperfield, Robert B.	Rep	Ill.	10	10
2nd Vorys, John M.	Rep	Ohio	10	10
3rd Bolton, Frances P.	Rep	Ohio	10	9
4th Smith, Lawrence H.	Rep	Wisc.	9	7
5th Merrow, Chester E.	Rep	N.H.	8	7
6th Judd, Walter H.	Rep	Minn.	8	6
7th Fulton, James G.	Rep	Penn.	7	*1 6
8th Jackson, Donald L.	Rep	Cal.	6	6
9th LeCompte, Karl M.	Rep	Iowa	10	3
10th Radwan, Edmund P.	Rep	N.Y.	4	3
11th Morano, Albert P.	Rep	Conn.	4	3
12th Church, Marguerite Stitt	Rep	Ill.	4	3
13th Adair, E. Ross	Rep	Ind.	4	3
14th Prouty, Winston L.	Rep	Vt.	4	3
15th Bentley, Alvin M.	Rep	Mich.	3	3

*1: Member's 1st period of service on the committee; *2: Member's 2nd period of service on the committee.

Vacancies Filled:
Majority: 13th through the 17th seats on Jan. 7,1957.

Changes:

Majority:

Jarman, John	Dem	Okla.	Jan. 10,1957	Moved to Interstate and Foreign Commerce.
Saund, Dalip S.	Dem	Cal.	Jan. 10,1957	Replaced Jarman.

Minority:

Smith, Lawrence H.	Rep	Wisc.	Jan. 22,1958	Died in office.
Curtis, Laurence	Rep	Mass.	Feb. 3,1958	Replaced Smith.

Departures from the House:	Majority			Minority		
Elected to U.S. Senate	Byrd, Robert C.	W.Va.	Dem	Prouty, Winston L.	Vt.	Rep
Defeated for Reelection	Hays, L. Brooks	Ark.	Dem	Morano, Albert P.	Conn.	Rep
Retired	Gordon, Thomas S.	Ill.	Dem	LeCompte, Karl M.	Iowa	Rep
				Radwan, Edmund P.	N.Y.	Rep
				Vorys, John M.	Ohio	Rep

FOREIGN AFFAIRS / 86th Congress

Service Dates of Committee Chair: Jan. 19,1959-Jan. 3,1961
Service Dates of Majority Members: Jan. 19,1959-Jan. 3,1961
Service Dates of Minority Members: Jan. 19,1959-Jan. 3,1961

Majority

Rank	Name	Party	State	Terms in: House	Terms in: Comm.
Chr	Morgan, Thomas E.	Dem	Penn.	8	8
2nd	Carnahan, Albert S. J.	Dem	Mo.	7	*2 6
3rd	Zablocki, Clement J.	Dem	Wisc.	6	6
4th	Burleson, Omar T.	Dem	Tex.	7	6
5th	Kelly, Edna F.	Dem	N.Y.	6	5
6th	Hays, Wayne L.	Dem	Ohio	6	3
7th	Selden, Armistead I. Jr.	Dem	Ala.	4	3
8th	Pilcher, John L.	Dem	Ga.	4	3
9th	O'Hara, Barratt	Dem	Ill.	5	2
10th	Fountain, Lawrence H.	Dem	N.C.	4	2
11th	Fascell, Dante B.	Dem	Fla.	3	2
12th	Coffin, Frank M.	Dem	Me.	2	2
13th	Farbstein, Leonard	Dem	N.Y.	2	2
14th	Saund, Dalip S.	Dem	Cal.	2	2
15th	Diggs, Charles C. Jr.	Dem	Mich.	3	1
16th	Beckworth, Lindley G.	Dem	Tex.	9	1
17th	McDowell, Harris B. Jr.	Dem	Del.	2	1
18th	Murphy, William T.	Dem	Ill.	1	1
19th	Meyer, William H.	Dem	Vt.	1	1
20th	Gallagher, Cornelius E.	Dem	N.J.	1	1
21st	Bowles, Chester B.	Dem	Conn.	1	1

Minority

Rank	Name	Party	State	Terms in: House	Terms in: Comm.
RM	Chiperfield, Robert B.	Rep	Ill.	11	11
2nd	Bolton, Frances P.	Rep	Ohio	11	10
3rd	Merrow, Chester E.	Rep	N.H.	9	8
4th	Judd, Walter H.	Rep	Minn.	9	7
5th	Fulton, James G.	Rep	Penn.	8	*1 7
6th	Jackson, Donald L.	Rep	Cal.	7	7
7th	Church, Marguerite Stitt	Rep	Ill.	5	4
8th	Adair, E. Ross	Rep	Ind.	5	4
9th	Bentley, Alvin M.	Rep	Mich.	4	4
10th	Curtis, Laurence	Rep	Mass.	4	2
11th	Wainwright, Stuyvesant II	Rep	N.Y.	4	1

*1: Member's 1st period of service on the committee;
*2: Member's 2nd period of service on the committee.

Departures from the House:	Majority			Minority		
Appointed Presidential Advisor	Bowles, Chester B.	Conn.	Dem	None		
Defeated for Reelection	Meyer, William H.	Vt.	Dem	Wainwright, Stuyvesant II	N.Y.	Rep
Defeated for Renomination	Carnahan, Albert S. J.	Mo.	Dem	None		
Lost Election to U.S. Senate	None			Bentley, Alvin M.	Mich.	Rep
Lost Election for Governor	Coffin, Frank M.	Me.	Dem			
Retired	None			Jackson, Donald L.	Cal.	Rep
Departures from Committee:						
Moved to Veterans' Affairs	None			Fulton, James G.	Penn.	Rep

FOREIGN AFFAIRS / 87th Congress

Service Dates of Committee Chair: Feb. 6,1961-Jan. 3,1963
Service Dates of Majority Members: Feb. 6,1961-Jan. 3,1963
Service Dates of Minority Members: Feb. 13,1961-Jan. 3,1963

Majority

Rank	Name	Party	State	Terms in: House	Terms in: Comm.
Chr	Morgan, Thomas E.	Dem	Penn.	9	9
2nd	Zablocki, Clement J.	Dem	Wisc.	7	7
3rd	Burleson, Omar T.	Dem	Tex.	8	7
4th	Kelly, Edna F.	Dem	N.Y.	7	6
5th	Hays, Wayne L.	Dem	Ohio	7	4
6th	Selden, Armistead I. Jr.	Dem	Ala.	5	4
7th	Pilcher, John L.	Dem	Ga.	5	4
8th	O'Hara, Barratt	Dem	Ill.	6	3
9th	Fountain, Lawrence H.	Dem	N.C.	5	3
10th	Fascell, Dante B.	Dem	Fla.	4	3
11th	Farbstein, Leonard	Dem	N.Y.	3	3
12th	Saund, Dalip S.	Dem	Cal.	3	3
13th	Diggs, Charles C. Jr.	Dem	Mich.	4	2
14th	Beckworth, Lindley G.	Dem	Tex.	10	2
15th	McDowell, Harris B. Jr.	Dem	Del.	3	2
16th	Murphy, William T.	Dem	Ill.	2	2
17th	Gallagher, Cornelius E.	Dem	N.J.	2	2
18th	Nix, Robert N. C.	Dem	Penn.	3	1
19th	Johnson, Thomas F.	Dem	Md.	2	1
20th	Monagan, John S.	Dem	Conn.	2	1

Minority

Rank	Name	Party	State	Terms in: House	Terms in: Comm.
RM	Chiperfield, Robert B.	Rep	Ill.	12	12
2nd	Bolton, Frances P.	Rep	Ohio	12	11
3rd	Merrow, Chester E.	Rep	N.H.	10	9
4th	Judd, Walter H.	Rep	Minn.	10	8
5th	Church, Marguerite Stitt	Rep	Ill.	6	5
6th	Adair, E. Ross	Rep	Ind.	6	5
7th	Curtis, Laurence	Rep	Mass.	5	3
8th	Mailliard, William S.	Rep	Cal.	5	1
9th	Frelinghuysen, Peter H.B.	Rep	N.J.	5	1
10th	Broomfield, William S.	Rep	Mich.	3	1
11th	Barry, Robert R.	Rep	N.Y.	2	1
12th	Whalley, J. Irving	Rep	Penn.	2	1
13th	Seely-Brown, Horace Jr.	Rep	Conn.	6	1

Departures from the House:

	Majority			Minority		
Defeated for Reelection	Johnson, Thomas F.	Md.	Dem	Judd, Walter H.	Minn.	Rep
	Saund, Dalip S.	Cal.	Dem			
Lost Election to U.S. Senate	None			Seely-Brown, Horace Jr.	Conn.	Rep
Lost Nomination to U.S. Senate	None			Curtis, Laurence	Mass.	Rep
				Merrow, Chester E.	N.H.	Rep
Retired	None			Chiperfield, Robert B.	Ill.	Rep
				Church, Marguerite Stitt	Ill.	Rep

FOREIGN AFFAIRS / 88th Congress

Service Dates of Committee Chair: Jan. 17,1963-Jan. 3,1965
Service Dates of Majority Members: Jan. 17,1963-Jan. 3,1965
Service Dates of Minority Members: Jan. 24,1963-Jan. 3,1965

Majority

Rank	Name	Party	State	Terms in: House	Terms in: Comm.
Chr	Morgan, Thomas E.	Dem	Penn.	10	10
2nd	Zablocki, Clement J.	Dem	Wisc.	8	8
3rd	Burleson, Omar T.	Dem	Tex.	9	8
4th	Kelly, Edna F.	Dem	N.Y.	8	7
5th	Hays, Wayne L.	Dem	Ohio	8	5
6th	Selden, Armistead I. Jr.	Dem	Ala.	6	5
7th	Pilcher, John L.	Dem	Ga.	6	5
8th	O'Hara, Barratt	Dem	Ill.	7	4
9th	Fountain, Lawrence H.	Dem	N.C.	6	4
10th	Fascell, Dante B.	Dem	Fla.	5	4
11th	Farbstein, Leonard	Dem	N.Y.	4	4
12th	Diggs, Charles C. Jr.	Dem	Mich.	5	3
13th	Beckworth, Lindley G.	Dem	Tex.	11	3
14th	McDowell, Harris B. Jr.	Dem	Del.	4	3
15th	Murphy, William T.	Dem	Ill.	3	3
16th	Gallagher, Cornelius E.	Dem	N.J.	3	3

Minority

Rank	Name	Party	State	Terms in: House	Terms in: Comm.
RM	Bolton, Frances P.	Rep	Ohio	13	12
2nd	Adair, E. Ross	Rep	Ind.	7	6
3rd	Mailliard, William S.	Rep	Cal.	6	2
4th	Frelinghuysen, Peter H.B.	Rep	N.J.	6	2
5th	Broomfield, William S.	Rep	Mich.	4	2
6th	Barry, Robert R.	Rep	N.Y.	3	2
7th	Whalley, J. Irving	Rep	Penn.	3	2
8th	Gross, Harold R.	Rep	Iowa	8	1
9th	Berry, Ellis Y.	Rep	S.D.	7	1
10th	Derwinski, Edward J.	Rep	Ill.	3	1
11th	Morse, F. Bradford	Rep	Mass.	2	1
12th	Battin, James F.	Rep	Mont.	2	1
13th	Thomson, Vernon W.	Rep	Wisc.	2	1

17th Nix, Robert N. C.	Dem	Penn.	4	2
18th Monagan, John S.	Dem	Conn.	3	2
19th Fraser, Donald M.	DFL	Minn.	1	1
20th Cameron, Ronald Brooks	Dem	Cal.	1	1

Departures from the House:	**Majority**			**Minority**		
Defeated for Reelection	None			Barry, Robert R.	N.Y.	Rep
Retired	Pilcher, John L.	Ga.	Dem	None		
Departures from Committee:						
Moved to Ways and Means	None			Battin, James F.	Mont.	Rep

FOREIGN AFFAIRS / 89th Congress

Service Dates of Committee Chair: Jan. 18,1965-Jan. 3,1967
Service Dates of Majority Members: Jan. 18,1965-Jan. 3,1967
Service Dates of Minority Members: Jan. 21,1965-Jan. 3,1967

Majority

Rank Name	Party	State	Terms in: House	Terms in: Comm.
Chr Morgan, Thomas E.	Dem	Penn.	11	11
2nd Zablocki, Clement J.	Dem	Wisc.	9	9
3rd Burleson, Omar T.	Dem	Tex.	10	9
4th Kelly, Edna F.	Dem	N.Y.	9	8
5th Hays, Wayne L.	Dem	Ohio	9	6
6th Selden, Armistead I. Jr.	Dem	Ala.	7	6
7th O'Hara, Barratt	Dem	Ill.	8	5
8th Fountain, Lawrence H.	Dem	N.C.	7	5
9th Fascell, Dante B.	Dem	Fla.	6	5
10th Farbstein, Leonard	Dem	N.Y.	5	5
11th Diggs, Charles C. Jr.	Dem	Mich.	6	4
12th Beckworth, Lindley G.	Dem	Tex.	12	4
13th McDowell, Harris B. Jr.	Dem	Del.	5	4
14th Murphy, William T.	Dem	Ill.	4	4
15th Gallagher, Cornelius E.	Dem	N.J.	4	4
16th Nix, Robert N. C.	Dem	Penn.	5	3
17th Monagan, John S.	Dem	Conn.	4	3
18th Fraser, Donald M.	DFL	Minn.	2	2
19th Cameron, Ronald Brooks	Dem	Cal.	2	2
20th Rosenthal, Benjamin S.	Dem	N.Y.	3	1
21st Roybal, Edward R.	Dem	Cal.	2	1
22nd Culver, John C.	Dem	Iowa	1	1
23rd Hamilton, Lee H.	Dem	Ind.	1	1
24th McVicker, Roy H.	Dem	Colo.	1	1

Minority

Rank Name	Party	State	Terms in: House	Terms in: Comm.
RM Bolton, Frances P.	Rep	Ohio	14	13
2nd Adair, E. Ross	Rep	Ind.	8	7
3rd Mailliard, William S.	Rep	Cal.	7	3
4th Frelinghuysen, Peter H.B.	Rep	N.J.	7	3
5th Broomfield, William S.	Rep	Mich.	5	3
6th Whalley, J. Irving	Rep	Penn.	4	3
7th Gross, Harold R.	Rep	Iowa	9	2
8th Berry, Ellis Y.	Rep	S.D.	8	2
9th Derwinski, Edward J.	Rep	Ill.	4	2
10th Morse, F. Bradford	Rep	Mass.	3	2
11th Thomson, Vernon W.	Rep	Wisc.	3	2
12th Fulton, James G.	Rep	Penn.	11	*2 1

*2: Member's 2nd period of service on the committee.

Departures from the House:	**Majority**			**Minority**
Defeated for Reelection	Cameron, Ronald Brooks	Cal.	Dem	None
	McDowell, Harris B. Jr.	Del.	Dem	
	McVicker, Roy H.	Colo.	Dem	
Defeated for Renomination	Beckworth, Lindley G.	Tex.	Dem	None

FOREIGN AFFAIRS / 90th Congress

Service Dates of Committee Chair: Jan. 23,1967-Jan. 3,1969
Service Dates of Majority Members: Jan. 23,1967-Jan. 3,1969
Service Dates of Minority Members: Jan. 26,1967-Jan. 3,1969

Majority

Rank Name	Party	State	Terms in: House	Terms in: Comm.
Chr Morgan, Thomas E.	Dem	Penn.	12	12
2nd Zablocki, Clement J.	Dem	Wisc.	10	10
3rd Burleson, Omar T.	Dem	Tex.	11	10
4th Kelly, Edna F.	Dem	N.Y.	10	9
5th Hays, Wayne L.	Dem	Ohio	10	7
6th Selden, Armistead I. Jr.	Dem	Ala.	8	7
7th O'Hara, Barratt	Dem	Ill.	9	6
8th Fountain, Lawrence H.	Dem	N.C.	8	6
9th Fascell, Dante B.	Dem	Fla.	7	6
10th Farbstein, Leonard	Dem	N.Y.	6	6
11th Diggs, Charles C. Jr.	Dem	Mich.	7	5
12th Murphy, William T.	Dem	Ill.	5	5
13th Gallagher, Cornelius E.	Dem	N.J.	5	5
14th Nix, Robert N. C.	Dem	Penn.	6	4
15th Monagan, John S.	Dem	Conn.	5	4
16th Fraser, Donald M.	DFL	Minn.	3	3
17th Rosenthal, Benjamin S.	Dem	N.Y.	4	2
18th Roybal, Edward R.	Dem	Cal.	3	2
19th Culver, John C.	Dem	Iowa	2	2
20th Hamilton, Lee H.	Dem	Ind.	2	2
21st Tunney, John V.	Dem	Cal.	2	1

Minority

Rank Name	Party	State	Terms in: House	Terms in: Comm.
RM Bolton, Frances P.	Rep	Ohio	15	14
2nd Adair, E. Ross	Rep	Ind.	9	8
3rd Mailliard, William S.	Rep	Cal.	8	4
4th Frelinghuysen, Peter H.B.	Rep	N.J.	8	4
5th Broomfield, William S.	Rep	Mich.	6	4
6th Whalley, J. Irving	Rep	Penn.	5	4
7th Gross, Harold R.	Rep	Iowa	10	3
8th Berry, Ellis Y.	Rep	S.D.	9	3
9th Derwinski, Edward J.	Rep	Ill.	5	3
10th Morse, F. Bradford	Rep	Mass.	4	3
11th Thomson, Vernon W.	Rep	Wisc.	4	3
12th Fulton, James G.	Rep	Penn.	12	*2 2
13th Findley, Paul	Rep	Ill.	4	1
14th Buchanan, John H. Jr.	Rep	Ala.	2	1
15th Taft, Robert Jr.	Rep	Ohio	2	1

*2: Member's 2nd period of service on the committee.

Changes:

Majority:

Burleson, Omar T.	Dem	Tex.	July 30,1968	Moved to Ways and Means.
Kazen, Abraham Jr.	Dem	Tex.	Oct. 10,1968	Replaced Burleson.

Departures from the House:	Majority			Minority		
Defeated for Reelection	None			Bolton, Frances P.	Ohio	Rep
Defeated for Renomination	Kelly, Edna F.	N.Y.	Dem	None		
	O'Hara, Barratt	Ill.	Dem			
Lost Nomination to U.S. Senate	Selden, Armistead I. Jr.	Ala.	Dem	None		

FOREIGN AFFAIRS / 91st Congress

Service Dates of Committee Chair: Jan. 29,1969-Jan. 3,1971
Service Dates of Majority Members: Jan. 29,1969-Jan. 3,1971
Service Dates of Minority Members: Jan. 29,1969-Jan. 3,1971

Majority

Rank Name	Party	State	Terms in: House	Terms in: Comm.
Chr Morgan, Thomas E.	Dem	Penn.	13	13
2nd Zablocki, Clement J.	Dem	Wisc.	11	11
3rd Hays, Wayne L.	Dem	Ohio	11	8
4th Fountain, Lawrence H.	Dem	N.C.	9	7
5th Fascell, Dante B.	Dem	Fla.	8	7
6th Farbstein, Leonard	Dem	N.Y.	7	7
7th Diggs, Charles C. Jr.	Dem	Mich.	8	6
8th Murphy, William T.	Dem	Ill.	6	6
9th Gallagher, Cornelius E.	Dem	N.J.	6	6
10th Nix, Robert N. C.	Dem	Penn.	7	5
11th Monagan, John S.	Dem	Conn.	6	5
12th Fraser, Donald M.	DFL	Minn.	4	4
13th Rosenthal, Benjamin S.	Dem	N.Y.	5	3

Minority

Rank Name	Party	State	Terms in: House	Terms in: Comm.
RM Adair, E. Ross	Rep	Ind.	10	9
2nd Mailliard, William S.	Rep	Cal.	9	5
3rd Frelinghuysen, Peter H.B.	Rep	N.J.	9	5
4th Broomfield, William S.	Rep	Mich.	7	5
5th Whalley, J. Irving	Rep	Penn.	6	5
6th Gross, Harold R.	Rep	Iowa	11	4
7th Berry, Ellis Y.	Rep	S.D.	10	4
8th Derwinski, Edward J.	Rep	Ill.	6	4
9th Morse, F. Bradford	Rep	Mass.	5	4
10th Thomson, Vernon W.	Rep	Wisc.	5	4
11th Fulton, James G.	Rep	Penn.	13	*2 3
12th Findley, Paul	Rep	Ill.	5	2
13th Buchanan, John H. Jr.	Rep	Ala.	3	2

14th Roybal, Edward R.	Dem	Cal.	4	3	14th Taft, Robert Jr.	Rep	Ohio	3	2
15th Culver, John C.	Dem	Iowa	3	3	15th Lloyd, Sherman P.	Rep	Utah	3	1
16th Hamilton, Lee H.	Dem	Ind.	3	3	16th Burke, J. Herbert	Rep	Fla.	2	1
17th Tunney, John V.	Dem	Cal.	3	2	17th Roth, William V. Jr.	Rep	Del.	2	1
18th Kazen, Abraham Jr.	Dem	Tex.	2	2					
19th Wolff, Lester L.	Dem	N.Y.	3	1					
20th Bingham, Jonathan B.	Dem	N.Y.	3	1					
21st Yatron, Gus	Dem	Penn.	1	1					

*2: Member's 2nd period of service on the committee.

	Majority			Minority		
Departures from the House:						
Elected to U.S Senate	Tunney, John V.	Cal.	Dem	Roth, William V. Jr.	Del.	Rep
				Taft, Robert Jr.	Ohio	Rep
Defeated for Reelection	None			Adair, E. Ross	Ind.	Rep
Defeated for Renomination	Farbstein, Leonard	N.Y.	Dem	None		
Retired	Murphy, William T.	Ill.	Dem	Berry, Ellis Y.	S.D.	Rep
Departures from Committee:						
Moved to Appropriations	Roybal, Edward R.	Cal.	Dem	None		

FOREIGN AFFAIRS / 92nd Congress

Service Dates of Committee Chair: Feb. 4,1971-Jan. 3,1973
Service Dates of Majority Members: Feb. 4,1971-Jan. 3,1973
Service Dates of Minority Members: Feb. 4,1971-Jan. 3,1973

Majority			Terms in:		Minority			Terms in:	
Rank Name	**Party**	**State**	**House**	**Comm.**	**Rank Name**	**Party**	**State**	**House**	**Comm.**
Chr Morgan, Thomas E.	Dem	Penn.	14	14	RM Mailliard, William S.	Rep	Cal.	10	6
2nd Zablocki, Clement J.	Dem	Wisc.	12	12	2nd Frelinghuysen, Peter H.B.	Rep	N.J.	10	6
3rd Hays, Wayne L.	Dem	Ohio	12	9	3rd Broomfield, William S.	Rep	Mich.	8	6
4th Fountain, Lawrence H.	Dem	N.C.	10	8	4th Whalley, J. Irving	Rep	Penn.	7	6
5th Fascell, Dante B.	Dem	Fla.	9	8	5th Gross, Harold R.	Rep	Iowa	12	5
6th Diggs, Charles C. Jr.	Dem	Mich.	9	7	6th Derwinski, Edward J.	Rep	Ill.	7	5
7th Gallagher, Cornelius E.	Dem	N.J.	7	7	7th Morse, F. Bradford	Rep	Mass.	6	5
8th Nix, Robert N. C.	Dem	Penn.	8	6	8th Thomson, Vernon W.	Rep	Wisc.	6	5
9th Monagan, John S.	Dem	Conn.	7	6	9th Fulton, James G.	Rep	Penn.	14	*2 4
10th Fraser, Donald M.	DFL	Minn.	5	5	10th Findley, Paul	Rep	Ill.	6	3
11th Rosenthal, Benjamin S.	Dem	N.Y.	6	4	11th Buchanan, John H. Jr.	Rep	Ala.	4	3
12th Culver, John C.	Dem	Iowa	4	4	12th Lloyd, Sherman P.	Rep	Utah	4	2
13th Hamilton, Lee H.	Dem	Ind.	4	4	13th Burke, J. Herbert	Rep	Fla.	3	2
14th Kazen, Abraham Jr.	Dem	Tex.	3	3	14th Halpern, Seymour	Rep	N.Y.	7	1
15th Wolff, Lester L.	Dem	N.Y.	4	2	15th Vander Jagt, Guy A.	Rep	Mich.	4	1
16th Bingham, Jonathan B.	Dem	N.Y.	4	2	16th Steele, Robert H.	Rep	Conn.	2	1
17th Yatron, Gus	Dem	Penn.	2	2	17th du Pont, Pierre S. IV	Rep	Del.	1	1
18th Taylor, Roy A.	Dem	N.C.	7	1					
19th Davis, John W.	Dem	Ga.	6	1					
20th Murphy, Morgan F.	Dem	Ill.	1	1					
21st Dellums, Ronald V.	Dem	Cal.	1	1					

*2: Member's 2nd period of service on the committee.

Note: Ogden Reid of New York resigned from the Republican Party and joined the Democratic Party on Mar. 22,1972. House Resolution 922, agreed to Apr. 12,1972, led to a change in size and party ratio on this committee to 22 Democrats and 17 Republicans; Reid was added the following day.

Addition:
Majority: 22nd Reid, Ogden R. Dem N.Y. Apr. 13,1972

Changes:
Minority:

Fulton, James G.	Rep	Penn.	Oct. 6,1971	Died in office.
Whalen, Charles W. Jr.	Rep	Ohio	Oct. 27,1971	Replaced Fulton.
Morse, F. Bradford	Rep	Mass.	May 1,1972	Resigned; appointed Undersecretary of State.
Mathias, Robert B.	Rep	Cal.	May 31,1972	Replaced Morse.

Departures from the House:	Majority		Minority	
Defeated for Reelection	Monagan, John S.	Conn. Dem	Lloyd, Sherman P.	Utah Rep
Defeated for Renomination	Gallagher, Cornelius E.	N.J. Dem	None	
Retired	None		Halpern, Seymour	N.Y. Rep
			Whalley, J. Irving	Penn. Rep
Departures from Committee:				
Moved to Armed Services	Dellums, Ronald V.	Cal. Dem	None	
Moved to Rules	Murphy, Morgan F.	Ill. Dem	None	

FOREIGN AFFAIRS / 93rd Congress

Service Dates of Committee Chair: Jan. 24,1973-Jan. 3,1975
Service Dates of Majority Members: Jan. 24,1973-Jan. 3,1975
Service Dates of Minority Members: Jan. 24,1973-Jan. 3,1975

Majority

Rank	Name	Party	State	Terms in: House	Terms in: Comm.
Chr	Morgan, Thomas E.	Dem	Penn.	15	15
2nd	Zablocki, Clement J.	Dem	Wisc.	13	13
3rd	Hays, Wayne L.	Dem	Ohio	13	10
4th	Fountain, Lawrence H.	Dem	N.C.	11	9
5th	Fascell, Dante B.	Dem	Fla.	10	9
6th	Diggs, Charles C. Jr.	Dem	Mich.	10	8
7th	Nix, Robert N. C.	Dem	Penn.	9	7
8th	Fraser, Donald M.	DFL	Minn.	6	6
9th	Rosenthal, Benjamin S.	Dem	N.Y.	7	5
10th	Culver, John C.	Dem	Iowa	5	5
11th	Hamilton, Lee H.	Dem	Ind.	5	5
12th	Kazen, Abraham Jr.	Dem	Tex.	4	4
13th	Wolff, Lester L.	Dem	N.Y.	5	3
14th	Bingham, Jonathan B.	Dem	N.Y.	5	3
15th	Yatron, Gus	Dem	Penn.	3	3
16th	Taylor, Roy A.	Dem	N.C.	8	2
17th	Davis, John W.	Dem	Ga.	7	2
18th	Reid, Ogden R.	Dem	N.Y.	6	2
19th	Harrington, Michael J.	Dem	Mass.	3	1
20th	Ryan, Leo J.	Dem	Cal.	1	1
21st	Wilson, Charles	Dem	Tex.	1	1
22nd	Riegle, Donald W. Jr.	Dem	Mich.	4	1

Minority

Rank	Name	Party	State	Terms in: House	Terms in: Comm.
RM1	Mailliard, William S.	Rep	Cal.	11	7
RM2 2nd	Frelinghuysen, Peter H.B.	Rep	N.J.	11	7
3rd	Broomfield, William S.	Rep	Mich.	9	7
4th	Gross, Harold R.	Rep	Iowa	13	6
5th	Derwinski, Edward J.	Rep	Ill.	8	6
6th	Thomson, Vernon W.	Rep	Wisc.	7	6
7th	Findley, Paul	Rep	Ill.	7	4
8th	Buchanan, John H. Jr.	Rep	Ala.	5	4
9th	Burke, J. Herbert	Rep	Fla.	4	3
10th	Vander Jagt, Guy A.	Rep	Mich.	5	2
11th	Steele, Robert H.	Rep	Conn.	3	2
12th	du Pont, Pierre S. IV	Rep	Del.	2	2
13th	Whalen, Charles W. Jr.	Rep	Ohio	4	2
14th	Mathias, Robert B.	Rep	Cal.	4	2
15th	Biester, Edward G. Jr.	Rep	Penn.	4	1
16th	Winn, Larry Jr.	Rep	Kans.	4	1
17th	Gilman, Benjamin A.	Rep	N.Y.	1	1
18th	Guyer, Tennyson	Rep	Ohio	1	1

Note: Donald Riegle resigned from the Republican Party and joined the Democratic Party on Feb. 27,1973.

Vacancy Filled:
Majority: 22nd seat by Riegle on Mar. 27,1973.

Changes:

Ranking Member:

RM1 Mailliard, William S.	Rep	Cal.	Mar. 5,1974	Resigned; appointed Ambassador to Organization of American States.
RM2 Frelinghuysen, Peter H.B.	Rep	N.J.	Mar. 5,1974	Succeeded Mailliard as Ranking Minority Member.

Minority:

Mailliard, William S.	Rep	Cal.	Mar. 5,1974	Resigned; appointed Ambassador to Organization of American States.
Lagomarsino, Robert J.	Rep	Cal.	Mar. 21,1974	Replaced Mailliard.
Thomson, Vernon W.	Rep	Wisc.	Dec. 31,1974	Resigned; defeated for reelection.

Departures from the House:	Majority		Minority	
Elected to U.S. Senate	Culver, John C.	Iowa Dem	None	
Defeated for Reelection	None		Mathias, Robert B.	Cal. Rep
Defeated for Renomination	Davis, John W.	Ga. Dem	None	
Lost Election for Governor	None		Steele, Robert H.	Conn. Rep
Lost Nomination for Governor	Reid, Ogden R.	N.Y. Dem	None	
Retired	None		Frelinghuysen, Peter H.B.	N.J. Rep
			Gross, Harold R.	Iowa Rep
Departures from Committee:				
Moved to Armed Services	Kazen, Abraham Jr.	Tex. Dem	None	
Moved to Ways and Means	None		Vander Jagt, Guy A.	Mich. Rep

FOREIGN AFFAIRS / 94th Congress

* Renamed the Committee on INTERNATIONAL RELATIONS on Mar. 19,1975.

Service Dates of Committee Chair: Jan. 20,1975-Jan. 3,1977
Service Dates of Majority Members: Jan. 20,1975-Jan. 3,1977
Service Dates of Minority Members: Jan. 28,1975-Jan. 3,1977

Majority

Rank Name	Party	State	Terms in: House	Terms in: Comm.
Chr Morgan, Thomas E.	Dem	Penn.	16	16
2nd Zablocki, Clement J.	Dem	Wisc.	14	14
3rd Hays, Wayne L.	Dem	Ohio	14	11
4th Fountain, Lawrence H.	Dem	N.C.	12	10
5th Fascell, Dante B.	Dem	Fla.	11	10
6th Diggs, Charles C. Jr.	Dem	Mich.	11	9
7th Nix, Robert N. C.	Dem	Penn.	10	8
8th Fraser, Donald M.	DFL	Minn.	7	7
9th Rosenthal, Benjamin S.	Dem	N.Y.	8	6
10th Hamilton, Lee H.	Dem	Ind.	6	6
11th Wolff, Lester L.	Dem	N.Y.	6	4
12th Bingham, Jonathan B.	Dem	N.Y.	6	4
13th Yatron, Gus	Dem	Penn.	4	4
14th Taylor, Roy A.	Dem	N.C.	9	3
15th Harrington, Michael J.	Dem	Mass.	4	2
16th Ryan, Leo J.	Dem	Cal.	2	2
17th Wilson, Charles	Dem	Tex.	2	2
18th Riegle, Donald W. Jr.	Dem	Mich.	5	2
19th Collins, Cardiss	Dem	Ill.	2	1
20th Solarz, Stephen J.	Dem	N.Y.	1	1
21st Meyner, Helen S.	Dem	N.J.	1	1
22nd Bonker, Don L.	Dem	Wash.	1	1
23rd Studds, Gerry E.	Dem	Mass.	2	1

Minority

Rank Name	Party	State	Terms in: House	Terms in: Comm.
RM Broomfield, William S.	Rep	Mich.	10	8
2nd Derwinski, Edward J.	Rep	Ill.	9	7
3rd Findley, Paul	Rep	Ill.	8	5
4th Buchanan, John H. Jr.	Rep	Ala.	6	5
5th Burke, J. Herbert	Rep	Fla.	5	4
6th du Pont, Pierre S. IV	Rep	Del.	3	3
7th Whalen, Charles W. Jr.	Rep	Ohio	5	3
8th Biester, Edward G. Jr.	Rep	Penn.	5	2
9th Winn, Larry Jr.	Rep	Kans.	5	2
10th Gilman, Benjamin A.	Rep	N.Y.	2	2
11th Guyer, Tennyson	Rep	Ohio	2	2
12th Lagomarsino, Robert J.	Rep	Cal.	2	2

Vacancy Filled:
Majority: 23rd seat by Studds on Feb. 18,1976.

Changes:
Majority:

Wilson, Charles	Dem	Tex.	Feb. 3,1976	Moved to Appropriations.
Hays, Wayne L.	Dem	Ohio	Sep. 1,1976	Resigned and retired.
Riegle, Donald W. Jr.	Dem	Mich.	Dec. 30,1976	Resigned; elected to U.S. Senate.

Departures from the House:

	Majority		Minority	
Elected Governor	None		du Pont, Pierre S. IV	Del. Rep
Retired	Morgan, Thomas E.	Penn. Dem	Biester, Edward G. Jr.	Penn. Rep
	Taylor, Roy A.	N.C. Dem		

INTERNATIONAL RELATIONS / 95th Congress

Service Dates of Committee Chair: Jan. 19,1977-Jan. 3,1979
Service Dates of Majority Members: Jan. 19,1977-Jan. 3,1979
Service Dates of Minority Members: Jan. 19,1977-Jan. 3,1979

Majority

Rank Name	Party	State	Terms in: House	Terms in: Comm.
Chr Zablocki, Clement J.	Dem	Wisc.	15	15
2nd Fountain, Lawrence H.	Dem	N.C.	13	11
3rd Fascell, Dante B.	Dem	Fla.	12	11
4th Diggs, Charles C. Jr.	Dem	Mich.	12	10
5th Nix, Robert N. C.	Dem	Penn.	11	9
6th Fraser, Donald M.	DFL	Minn.	8	8
7th Rosenthal, Benjamin S.	Dem	N.Y.	9	7
8th Hamilton, Lee H.	Dem	Ind.	7	7
9th Wolff, Lester L.	Dem	N.Y.	7	5
10th Bingham, Jonathan B.	Dem	N.Y.	7	5
11th Yatron, Gus	Dem	Penn.	5	5
12th Harrington, Michael J.	Dem	Mass.	5	3
13th Ryan, Leo J.	Dem	Cal.	3	3
14th Collins, Cardiss	Dem	Ill.	3	2
15th Solarz, Stephen J.	Dem	N.Y.	2	2
16th Meyner, Helen S.	Dem	N.J.	2	2
17th Bonker, Don L.	Dem	Wash.	2	2
18th Studds, Gerry E.	Dem	Mass.	3	2
19th Ireland, Andrew P.	Dem	Fla.	1	1
20th Pease, Donald J.	Dem	Ohio	1	1
21st Beilenson, Anthony C.	Dem	Cal.	1	1
22nd de la Garza, E. (Kika)	Dem	Tex.	7	*T 1
23rd Danielson, George E.	Dem	Cal.	4	*T 1
24th Bedell, Berkley W.	Dem	Iowa	2	*T 1
25th Cavanaugh, John J.	Dem	Neb.	1	*T 1

Minority

Rank Name	Party	State	Terms in: House	Terms in: Comm.
RM Broomfield, William S.	Rep	Mich.	11	9
2nd Derwinski, Edward J.	Rep	Ill.	10	8
3rd Findley, Paul	Rep	Ill.	9	6
4th Buchanan, John H. Jr.	Rep	Ala.	7	6
5th Burke, J. Herbert	Rep	Fla.	6	5
6th Whalen, Charles W. Jr.	Rep	Ohio	6	4
7th Winn, Larry Jr.	Rep	Kans.	6	3
8th Gilman, Benjamin A.	Rep	N.Y.	3	3
9th Guyer, Tennyson	Rep	Ohio	3	3
10th Lagomarsino, Robert J.	Rep	Cal.	3	3
11th Goodling, William F.	Rep	Penn.	2 *1	1
12th Pettis, Shirley N.	Rep	Cal.	2	1

*T: Temporary member of the committee.

Vacancies Filled:
Majority: 22nd through the 25th seats on Jan. 27,1977.

Changes:

Majority:

Bedell, Berkley W.	Dem	Iowa	Apr. 20,1977	Left committee; no new assignment.
Fowler, Wyche Jr.	Dem	Ga.	Apr. 20,1977	Replaced Bedell and ranked 22nd.
Ryan, Leo J.	Dem	Cal.	Nov. 18,1978	Died in office.

Minority:

Pettis, Shirley N.	Rep	Cal.	Sep. 20,1978	Left committee; no new assignment.
Pritchard, Joel M.	Rep	Wash.	Sep. 20,1978	Replaced Pettis.

	Majority			Minority		
Departures from the House:						
Defeated for Reelection	Meyner, Helen S.	N.J.	Dem	Burke, J. Herbert	Fla.	Rep
Defeated for Renomination	Nix, Robert N. C.	Penn.	Dem	None		
Lost Nomination to U.S. Senate	Fraser, Donald M.	Minn.	DFL	None		
Retired	Harrington, Michael J.	Mass.	Dem	Whalen, Charles W. Jr.	Ohio	Rep
Departures from Committee:						
Moved to Ways and Means	Fowler, Wyche Jr.	Ga.	Dem	None		
Moved to Rules	Beilenson, Anthony C.	Cal.	Dem	None		
Moved to Post Office & Civil Service	Cavanaugh, John J.	Neb.	Dem	None		
No new assignment	Danielson, George E.	Cal.	Dem	None		
	de la Garza, E. (Kika)	Tex.	Dem			

INTERNATIONAL RELATIONS / 96th Congress

* Resumed the name Committee on FOREIGN AFFAIRS on Feb. 5,1979.

Service Dates of Committee Chair: Jan. 24,1979-Jan. 3,1981
Service Dates of Majority Members: Jan. 24,1979-Jan. 3,1981
Service Dates of Minority Members: Jan. 24,1979-Jan. 3,1981

Majority

Rank	Name	Party	State	Terms in: House	Terms in: Comm.
Chr	Zablocki, Clement J.	Dem	Wisc.	16	16
2nd	Fountain, Lawrence H.	Dem	N.C.	14	12
3rd	Fascell, Dante B.	Dem	Fla.	13	12
4th	Diggs, Charles C. Jr.	Dem	Mich.	13	11
5th	Rosenthal, Benjamin S.	Dem	N.Y.	10	8
6th	Hamilton, Lee H.	Dem	Ind.	8	8
7th	Wolff, Lester L.	Dem	N.Y.	8	6
8th	Bingham, Jonathan B.	Dem	N.Y.	8	6
9th	Yatron, Gus	Dem	Penn.	6	6
10th	Collins, Cardiss	Dem	Ill.	4	3
11th	Solarz, Stephen J.	Dem	N.Y.	3	3
12th	Bonker, Don L.	Dem	Wash.	3	3
13th	Studds, Gerry E.	Dem	Mass.	4	3
14th	Ireland, Andrew P.	Dem	Fla.	2	2
15th	Pease, Donald J.	Dem	Ohio	2	2
16th	Mica, Daniel A.	Dem	Fla.	1	1
17th	Barnes, Michael D.	Dem	Md.	1	1
18th	Gray, William H. III	Dem	Penn.	1	1
19th	Hall, Tony P.	Dem	Ohio	1	1
20th	Wolpe, Howard E.	Dem	Mich.	1	1
21st	Bowen, David R.	Dem	Miss.	4	*T 1
22nd	Fithian, Floyd J.	Dem	Ind.	3	*T 1

Minority

Rank	Name	Party	State	Terms in: House	Terms in: Comm.
RM	Broomfield, William S.	Rep	Mich.	12	10
2nd	Derwinski, Edward J.	Rep	Ill.	11	9
3rd	Findley, Paul	Rep	Ill.	10	7
4th	Buchanan, John H. Jr.	Rep	Ala.	8	7
5th	Winn, Larry Jr.	Rep	Kans.	7	4
6th	Gilman, Benjamin A.	Rep	N.Y.	4	4
7th	Guyer, Tennyson	Rep	Ohio	4	4
8th	Lagomarsino, Robert J.	Rep	Cal.	4	4
9th	Goodling, William F.	Rep	Penn.	3	*1 2
10th	Pritchard, Joel M.	Rep	Wash.	4	2
11th	Fenwick, Millicent H.	Rep	N.J.	3	1
12th	Quayle, J. Danforth	Rep	Ind.	2	1

*T: Temporary member of the committee.

Vacancies Filled:
Majority: 21st and 22nd seats by Bowen and Fithian respectively on Jan. 31,1979.

Changes:
Majority:

Name	Party	State	Date	Change
Diggs, Charles C. Jr.	Dem	Mich.	June 3,1980	Resigned and retired.
Bedell, Berkley W.	Dem	Iowa	July 2,1980	Replaced Diggs.
Fithian, Floyd J.	Dem	Ind.	Nov. 19,1980	Left committee; no new assignment.
Crockett, George W. Jr.	Dem	Mich.	Nov. 19,1980	Replaced Fithian and ranked 21st.

	Majority			Minority		
Departures from the House:						
Elected to U.S. Senate	None			Quayle, J. Danforth	Ind.	Rep
Defeated for Reelection	Wolff, Lester L.	N.Y.	Dem	None		
Defeated for Renomination	None			Buchanan, John H. Jr.	Ala.	Rep
Departures from Committee:						
Moved to Energy and Commerce	Collins, Cardiss	Ill.	Dem	None		
Moved to Appropriations	Gray, William H. III	Penn.	Dem	None		
Moved to Rules	Hall, Tony P.	Ohio	Dem	None		
Moved to Ways and Means	Pease, Donald J.	Ohio	Dem	None		
No new assignment	Bedell, Berkley W.	Iowa	Dem	None		

FOREIGN AFFAIRS / 97th Congress

Service Dates of Committee Chair: Jan. 28,1981-Jan. 3,1983
Service Dates of Majority Members: Jan. 28,1981-Jan. 3,1983
Service Dates of Minority Members: Jan. 28,1981-Jan. 3,1983

Majority

Rank Name	Party	State	Terms in: House	Terms in: Comm.
Chr Zablocki, Clement J.	Dem	Wisc.	17	17
2nd Fountain, Lawrence H.	Dem	N.C.	15	13
3rd Fascell, Dante B.	Dem	Fla.	14	13
4th Rosenthal, Benjamin S.	Dem	N.Y.	11	9
5th Hamilton, Lee H.	Dem	Ind.	9	9
6th Bingham, Jonathan B.	Dem	N.Y.	9	7
7th Yatron, Gus	Dem	Penn.	7	7
8th Solarz, Stephen J.	Dem	N.Y.	4	4
9th Bonker, Don L.	Dem	Wash.	4	4
10th Studds, Gerry E.	Dem	Mass.	5	4
11th Ireland, Andrew P.	Dem	Fla.	3	3
12th Mica, Daniel A.	Dem	Fla.	2	2
13th Barnes, Michael D.	Dem	Md.	2	2
14th Wolpe, Howard E.	Dem	Mich.	2	2
15th Crockett, George W. Jr.	Dem	Mich.	2	2
16th Shamansky, Robert N.	Dem	Ohio	1	1
17th Gejdenson, Samuel	Dem	Conn.	1	1
18th Dymally, Mervyn M.	Dem	Cal.	1	1
19th Eckart, Dennis E.	Dem	Ohio	1	1
20th Lantos, Tom	Dem	Cal.	1	1
21st Bowen, David R.	Dem	Miss.	5	1

Minority

Rank Name	Party	State	Terms in: House	Terms in: Comm.
RM Broomfield, William S.	Rep	Mich.	13	11
2nd Derwinski, Edward J.	Rep	Ill.	12	10
3rd Findley, Paul	Rep	Ill.	11	8
4th Winn, Larry Jr.	Rep	Kans.	8	5
5th Gilman, Benjamin A.	Rep	N.Y.	5	5
6th Guyer, Tennyson	Rep	Ohio	5	5
7th Lagomarsino, Robert J.	Rep	Cal.	5	5
8th Goodling, William F.	Rep	Penn.	4 *1	3
9th Pritchard, Joel M.	Rep	Wash.	5	3
10th Fenwick, Millicent H.	Rep	N.J.	4	2
11th Dornan, Robert K.	Rep	Cal.	3 *1	1
12th Leach, James A. S.	Rep	Iowa	3	1
13th Erdahl, Arlen I.	Rep	Minn.	2	1
14th Roth, Tobias A.	Rep	Wisc.	2	1
15th Snowe, Olympia J. B.	Rep	Me.	2	1
16th LeBoutillier, John	Rep	N.Y.	1	1

*1: Member's 1st period of service on the committee.

Note: David R. Bowen (Dem-Miss.) served as a temporary member of this committee in the previous Congress.

Vacancy Filled:
Majority: 21st seat by Bowen on Feb. 25,1981.

Changes:
Minority:

Guyer, Tennyson	Rep	Ohio	Apr. 12,1981	Died in office.
Hyde, Henry J.	Rep	Ill.	June 24,1981	Replaced Guyer.

	Majority			Minority		
Departures from the House:						
Defeated for Reelection	Shamansky, Robert N.	Ohio	Dem	Erdahl, Arlen I.	Minn.	Rep
				Findley, Paul	Ill.	Rep
				LeBoutillier, John	N.Y.	Rep
Defeated for Renomination	None			Derwinski, Edward J.	Ill.	Rep
Lost Nomination to U.S. Senate	None			Dornan, Robert K.	Cal.	Rep
Lost Election to U.S. Senate	None			Fenwick, Millicent H.	N.J.	Rep
Retired	Bingham, Jonathan B.	N.Y.	Dem	None		
	Bowen, David R.	Miss.	Dem			
	Fountain, Lawrence H.	N.C.	Dem			
Died in office, Jan. 4,1983	Rosenthal, Benjamin S.	N.Y.	Dem	None		
Departures from Committee:						
Moved to Energy and Commerce	Eckart, Dennis E.	Ohio	Dem	None		
No new assignment	None			Goodling, William F.	Penn.	Rep

FOREIGN AFFAIRS / 98th Congress

Service Dates of Committee Chairs: Ch1 Jan. 6,1983-Dec. 3,1983
Ch2 Jan. 25,1984-Jan. 3,1985
Service Dates of Majority Members: Jan. 6,1983-Jan. 3,1985
Service Dates of Minority Members: Jan. 6,1983-Jan. 3,1985

Majority

Rank Name	Party	State	Terms in: House	Terms in: Comm.
Ch1 Zablocki, Clement J.	Dem	Wisc.	18	18
Ch2 2nd Fascell, Dante B.	Dem	Fla.	15	14
3rd Hamilton, Lee H.	Dem	Ind.	10	10
4th Yatron, Gus	Dem	Penn.	8	8
5th Solarz, Stephen J.	Dem	N.Y.	5	5
6th Bonker, Don L.	Dem	Wash.	5	5
7th Studds, Gerry E.	Dem	Mass.	6	5
8th Ireland, Andrew P.	Dem	Fla.	4	4
9th Mica, Daniel A.	Dem	Fla.	3	3
10th Barnes, Michael D.	Dem	Md.	3	3
11th Wolpe, Howard E.	Dem	Mich.	3	3
12th Crockett, George W. Jr.	Dem	Mich.	3	3
13th Gejdenson, Samuel	Dem	Conn.	2	2
14th Dymally, Mervyn M.	Dem	Cal.	2	2
15th Lantos, Tom	Dem	Cal.	2	2
16th Kostmayer, Peter H.	Dem	Penn.	3	1
17th Torricelli, Robert G.	Dem	N.J.	1	1
18th Smith, Lawrence J.	Dem	Fla.	1	1
19th Berman, Howard L.	Dem	Cal.	1	1
20th Reid, Harry M.	Dem	Nev.	1	1
21st Levine, Mel	Dem	Cal.	1	1
22nd Feighan, Edward F.	Dem	Ohio	1	1
23rd Weiss, Theodore S.	Dem	N.Y.	4	1
24th Garcia, Robert	Dem	N.Y.	4	*T 1

Minority

Rank Name	Party	State	Terms in: House	Terms in: Comm.
RM Broomfield, William S.	Rep	Mich.	14	12
2nd Winn, Larry Jr.	Rep	Kans.	9	6
3rd Gilman, Benjamin A.	Rep	N.Y.	6	6
4th Lagomarsino, Robert J.	Rep	Cal.	6	6
5th Pritchard, Joel M.	Rep	Wash.	6	4
6th Leach, James A. S.	Rep	Iowa	4	2
7th Roth, Tobias A.	Rep	Wisc.	3	2
8th Snowe, Olympia J. B.	Rep	Me.	3	2
9th Hyde, Henry J.	Rep	Ill.	5	2
10th Solomon, Gerald B. H.	Rep	N.Y.	3	1
11th Bereuter, Douglas K.	Rep	Neb.	3	1
12th Siljander, Mark D.	Rep	Mich.	2	1
13th Zschau, Ed	Rep	Cal.	1	1

*T: Temporary member of the committee.

Note: Andrew Ireland of Florida resigned from the Democratic Party and joined the Republican Party on July 5,1984, but it was not until Sep. 11, 1984 that the Democratic Caucus terminated his majority assignments.

Vacancy Filled: 23rd seat by Weiss on Feb. 2,1983.

Changes:

Chair:

Ch1 Zablocki, Clement J.	Dem	Wisc.	Dec. 3,1983	Died in office.
Ch2 Fascell, Dante B.	Dem	Fla.	Jan. 25,1984	Succeeded Zablocki as Chair.

Majority:

Garcia, Robert	Dem	N.Y.	Nov. 18,1983	Temporary term expired on last day of 1st Session.
Zablocki, Clement J.	Dem	Wisc.	Dec. 3,1983	Died in office.
Garcia, Robert	Dem	N.Y.	Feb. 9,1984	Replaced himself.
Ackerman, Gary L.	Dem	N.Y.	Feb. 29,1984	Replaced Zablocki to rank behind Weiss.
Ireland, Andrew P.	Dem	Fla.	Sep. 11,1984	Resigned Democratic Party; lost majority assignment.
MacKay, Kenneth H.	Dem	Fla.	Sep. 13,1984	Replaced Ireland.

Minority:

Pritchard, Joel M.	Rep	Wash.	Sep. 18,1984	Left committee; no new assignment.
Goodling, William F.	Rep	Penn.	Sep. 19,1984	Replaced Pritchard and ranked behind Lagomarsino.

	Majority	Minority	
Departures from the House:			
Retired	None	Winn, Larry Jr.	Kans. Rep
Departures from Committee:			
Ceases active membership to serve on Budget	None	Goodling, William F.	Penn. Rep

FOREIGN AFFAIRS / 99th Congress

Service Dates of Committee Chair: Jan. 7,1985-Jan. 3,1987
Service Dates of Majority Members: Jan. 30,1985-Jan. 3,1987
Service Dates of Minority Members: Jan. 30,1985-Jan. 3,1987

Majority

Rank	Name	Party	State	Terms in: House	Terms in: Comm.
Chr	Fascell, Dante B.	Dem	Fla.	16	15
2nd	Hamilton, Lee H.	Dem	Ind.	11	11
3rd	Yatron, Gus	Dem	Penn.	9	9
4th	Solarz, Stephen J.	Dem	N.Y.	6	6
5th	Bonker, Don L.	Dem	Wash.	6	6
6th	Studds, Gerry E.	Dem	Mass.	7	6
7th	Mica, Daniel A.	Dem	Fla.	4	4
8th	Barnes, Michael D.	Dem	Md.	4	4
9th	Wolpe, Howard E.	Dem	Mich.	4	4
10th	Crockett, George W. Jr.	Dem	Mich.	4	4
11th	Gejdenson, Samuel	Dem	Conn.	3	3
12th	Dymally, Mervyn M.	Dem	Cal.	3	3
13th	Lantos, Tom	Dem	Cal.	3	3
14th	Kostmayer, Peter H.	Dem	Penn.	4	2
15th	Torricelli, Robert G.	Dem	N.J.	2	2
16th	Smith, Lawrence J.	Dem	Fla.	2	2
17th	Berman, Howard L.	Dem	Cal.	2	2
18th	Reid, Harry M.	Dem	Nev.	2	2
19th	Levine, Mel	Dem	Cal.	2	2
20th	Feighan, Edward F.	Dem	Ohio	2	2
21st	Weiss, Theodore S.	Dem	N.Y.	5	2
22nd	Ackerman, Gary L.	Dem	N.Y.	2	2
23rd	MacKay, Kenneth H.	Dem	Fla.	2	2
24th	Udall, Morris K.	Dem	Ariz.	13	1
25th	Garcia, Robert	Dem	N.Y.	5	*T 2

Minority

Rank	Name	Party	State	Terms in: House	Terms in: Comm.
RM	Broomfield, William S.	Rep	Mich.	15	13
2nd	Gilman, Benjamin A.	Rep	N.Y.	7	7
3rd	Lagomarsino, Robert J.	Rep	Cal.	7	7
4th	Leach, James A. S.	Rep	Iowa	5	3
5th	Roth, Tobias A.	Rep	Wisc.	4	3
6th	Snowe, Olympia J. B.	Rep	Me.	4	3
7th	Hyde, Henry J.	Rep	Ill.	6	3
8th	Solomon, Gerald B. H.	Rep	N.Y.	4	2
9th	Bereuter, Douglas K.	Rep	Neb.	4	2
10th	Siljander, Mark D.	Rep	Mich.	3	2
11th	Zschau, Ed	Rep	Cal.	2	2
12th	Dornan, Robert K.	Rep	Cal.	4 *2	1
13th	Smith, Christopher H.	Rep	N.J.	3	1
14th	Mack, Connie III	Rep	Fla.	2	1
15th	DeWine, Michael	Rep	Ohio	2	1
16th	Burton, Dan	Rep	Ind.	2	1
17th	McCain, John	Rep	Ariz.	2	1

*T: Temporary member of the committee.

Vacancy Filled:
Majority: 25th seat by Garcia on Feb. 6,1985 for the 1st Session only.

Changes:
Majority:

Garcia, Robert	Dem	N.Y.	Dec. 30,1985	Temporary term expired on last day of 1st Session.
Garcia, Robert	Dem	N.Y.	Jan. 29,1986	Replaced himself.

Departures from the House:	Majority			Minority		
Elected to U.S. Senate	Reid, Harry M.	Nev.	Dem	McCain, John	Ariz.	Rep
Defeated for Renomination	None			Siljander, Mark D.	Mich.	Rep
Lost Election to U.S. Senate	None			Zschau, Ed	Cal.	Rep
Lost Nomination to U.S. Senate	Barnes, Michael D.	Md.	Dem	None		
Departures from Committee:						
No new assignment	Garcia, Robert	N.Y.	Dem	None		

FOREIGN AFFAIRS / 100th Congress

Service Dates of Committee Chair: Jan. 6,1987-Jan. 3,1989
Service Dates of Majority Members: Jan. 6,1987-Jan. 3,1989
Service Dates of Minority Members: Jan. 6,1987-Jan. 3,1989

Majority

Rank	Name	Party	State	Terms in: House	Terms in: Comm.
Chr	Fascell, Dante B.	Dem	Fla.	17	16
2nd	Hamilton, Lee H.	Dem	Ind.	12	12
3rd	Yatron, Gus	Dem	Penn.	10	10
4th	Solarz, Stephen J.	Dem	N.Y.	7	7
5th	Bonker, Don L.	Dem	Wash.	7	7
6th	Studds, Gerry E.	Dem	Mass.	8	7
7th	Mica, Daniel A.	Dem	Fla.	5	5
8th	Wolpe, Howard E.	Dem	Mich.	5	5
9th	Crockett, George W. Jr.	Dem	Mich.	5	5
10th	Gejdenson, Samuel	Dem	Conn.	4	4
11th	Dymally, Mervyn M.	Dem	Cal.	4	4
12th	Lantos, Tom	Dem	Cal.	4	4
13th	Kostmayer, Peter H.	Dem	Penn.	5	3
14th	Torricelli, Robert G.	Dem	N.J.	3	3
15th	Smith, Lawrence J.	Dem	Fla.	3	3
16th	Berman, Howard L.	Dem	Cal.	3	3
17th	Levine, Mel	Dem	Cal.	3	3
18th	Feighan, Edward F.	Dem	Ohio	3	3
19th	Weiss, Theodore S.	Dem	N.Y.	6	3
20th	Ackerman, Gary L.	Dem	N.Y.	3	3
21st	MacKay, Kenneth H.	Dem	Fla.	3	3
22nd	Udall, Morris K.	Dem	Ariz.	14	2
23rd	Atkins, Chester G.	Dem	Mass.	2	1
24th	Clarke, James McClure	Dem	N.C.	2	1
25th	Fuster, Jaime B.	Dem	P.R.	2	1
26th	Bilbray, James H.	Dem	Nev.	1	1
27th	Owens, Wayne	Dem	Utah	2	1

Minority

Rank	Name	Party	State	Terms in: House	Terms in: Comm.
RM	Broomfield, William S.	Rep	Mich.	16	14
2nd	Gilman, Benjamin A.	Rep	N.Y.	8	8
3rd	Lagomarsino, Robert J.	Rep	Cal.	8	8
4th	Leach, James A. S.	Rep	Iowa	6	4
5th	Roth, Tobias A.	Rep	Wisc.	5	4
6th	Snowe, Olympia J. B.	Rep	Me.	5	4
7th	Hyde, Henry J.	Rep	Ill.	7	4
8th	Solomon, Gerald B. H.	Rep	N.Y.	5	3
9th	Bereuter, Douglas K.	Rep	Neb.	5	3
10th	Dornan, Robert K.	Rep	Cal.	5	*2 2
11th	Smith, Christopher H.	Rep	N.J.	4	2
12th	Mack, Connie III	Rep	Fla.	3	2
13th	DeWine, Michael	Rep	Ohio	3	2
14th	Burton, Dan	Rep	Ind.	3	2
15th	Meyers, Jan	Rep	Kans.	2	1
16th	Miller, John R.	Rep	Wash.	2	1
17th	Lukens, Donald E. (Buz)	Rep	Ohio	3	1
18th	Blaz, Ben Garrido	Rep	Guam	2	1

*2: Member's 2nd period of service on the committee.

Notes: Territorial Delegates Jaime Fuster (Dem-Puerto Rico) and Ben Blaz (Rep-Guam) were allowed to accrue seniority but were not included in the committee size or party ratio. The replacement of Kenneth H. MacKay (Dem-Fla.) by Fofo Sunia (Dem-A.Sm.), the Territorial Delegate for American Samoa, changed the official party ratio to 25 Democrats (excluding Fuster and Sunia) and 17 Republicans (excluding Blaz).

Vacancies Filled:
Majority: 27th seat by Owens on Jan. 22,1987.
Minority: 15th through the 18th seats on Jan. 21,1987.

Changes:
Majority:

Name	Party	State	Date	Change
MacKay, Kenneth H.	Dem	Fla.	Jan. 22,1987	Returned to Science, Space and Technology.
Sunia, Fofo I. F.	Dem	A.Sm.	Jan. 22,1987	Replaced MacKay.
Sunia, Fofo I. F.	Dem	A.Sm.	Sep. 6,1988	Resigned and retired.

	Majority		Minority	
Departures from the House:				
Elected to U.S. Senate	None		Mack, Connie III	Fla. Rep
Lost Nomination to U.S. Senate	Bonker, Don L.	Wash. Dem	None	
	Mica, Daniel A.	Fla. Dem		
Departures from Committee:				
Moved to Armed Services	Bilbray, James H.	Nev. Dem	Dornan, Robert K.	Cal. Rep
Moved to Appropriations	Atkins, Chester G.	Mass. Dem	None	
Moved to Rules	None		Solomon, Gerald B.H.	N.Y. Rep

FOREIGN AFFAIRS / 101st Congress

Service Dates of Committee Chair: Jan. 3,1989-Jan. 3,1991
Service Dates of Majority Members: Jan. 19,1989-Jan. 3,1991
Service Dates of Minority Members: Jan. 20,1989-Jan. 3,1991

Majority

Rank	Name	Party	State	Terms in: House	Terms in: Comm.
Chr	Fascell, Dante B.	Dem	Fla.	18	17
2nd	Hamilton, Lee H.	Dem	Ind.	13	13
3rd	Yatron, Gus	Dem	Penn.	11	11
4th	Solarz, Stephen J.	Dem	N.Y.	8	8
5th	Studds, Gerry E.	Dem	Mass.	9	8
6th	Wolpe, Howard E.	Dem	Mich.	6	6
7th	Crockett, George W. Jr.	Dem	Mich.	6	6
8th	Gejdenson, Samuel	Dem	Conn.	5	5
9th	Dymally, Mervyn M.	Dem	Cal.	5	5
10th	Lantos, Tom	Dem	Cal.	5	5
11th	Kostmayer, Peter H.	Dem	Penn.	6	4
12th	Torricelli, Robert G.	Dem	N.J.	4	4
13th	Smith, Lawrence J.	Dem	Fla.	4	4
14th	Berman, Howard L.	Dem	Cal.	4	4
15th	Levine, Mel	Dem	Cal.	4	4
16th	Feighan, Edward F.	Dem	Ohio	4	4
17th	Weiss, Theodore S.	Dem	N.Y.	7	4
18th	Ackerman, Gary L.	Dem	N.Y.	4	4
19th	Udall, Morris K.	Dem	Ariz.	15	3
20th	Clarke, James McClure	Dem	N.C.	3	2
21st	Fuster, Jaime B.	Dem	P.R.	3	2
22nd	Owens, Wayne	Dem	Utah	3	2
23rd	Johnston, Harry A.	Dem	Fla.	1	1
24th	Engel, Eliot L.	Dem	N.Y.	1	1
25th	Faleomavaega, Eni F. H.	Dem	A.Sm.	1	1
26th	Bosco, Douglas H.	Dem	Cal.	4	*T 1
27th	McCloskey, Francis X.	Dem	Ind.	4	*T 1
28th	Payne, Donald M.	Dem	N.J.	2	*T 1

Minority

Rank	Name	Party	State	Terms in: House	Terms in: Comm.
RM	Broomfield, William S.	Rep	Mich.	17	15
2nd	Gilman, Benjamin A.	Rep	N.Y.	9	9
3rd	Lagomarsino, Robert J.	Rep	Cal.	9	9
4th	Leach, James A. S.	Rep	Iowa	7	5
5th	Roth, Tobias A.	Rep	Wisc.	6	5
6th	Snowe, Olympia J. B.	Rep	Me.	6	5
7th	Hyde, Henry J.	Rep	Ill.	8	5
8th	Bereuter, Douglas K.	Rep	Neb.	6	4
9th	Smith, Christopher H.	Rep	N.J.	5	3
10th	DeWine, Michael	Rep	Ohio	4	3
11th	Burton, Dan	Rep	Ind.	4	3
12th	Meyers, Jan	Rep	Kans.	3	2
13th	Miller, John R.	Rep	Wash.	3	2
14th	Lukens, Donald E. (Buz)	Rep	Ohio	4	2
15th	Blaz, Ben Garrido	Rep	Guam	3	2
16th	Gallegly, Elton	Rep	Cal.	2	1
17th	Houghton, Amory Jr.	Rep	N.Y.	2	1
18th	Goss, Porter J.	Rep	Fla.	1	1

*T: Temporary member of the committee.

Notes: Territorial Delegates Eni Faleomavaega (Dem-American Samoa) and Ben Blaz (Rep-Guam) and Resident Commissioner Jaime Fuster (Dem-Puerto Rico) were allowed to accrue committee seniority but were not included in the original party ratio of 26 Democrats and 17 Republicans. The death of Claude Pepper (Dem-Fla.) and his replacement by Ileana Ros-Lehtinen (Rep-Fla.) on Sep. 6,1989 led to a change in size and party ratio to 26 Democrats (excluding Fuster and Faleomavaega) and 18 Republicans (excluding Blaz) on Oct. 5,1989.

Vacancies Filled:
Majority: 26th through 28th seats on Jan. 27,1989.

Addition:
Minority: 19th Ros-Lehtinen, Ileana Rep Fla. Oct. 5,1989

Changes:
Minority:
Lukens, Donald E. (Buz) Rep Ohio Oct. 24,1990 Resigned; defeated for renomination.

Departures from the House:	Majority			Minority		
Elected Lt. Governor	None			DeWine, Michael	Ohio	Rep
Defeated for Reelection	Bosco, Douglas H.	Cal.	Dem	None		
	Clarke, James McClure	N.C.	Dem			
Retired	Crockett, George W. Jr.	Mich.	Dem	None		
Departures from Committee:						
Moved to Appropriations	Smith, Lawrence J.	Fla.	Dem	None		

FOREIGN AFFAIRS / 102nd Congress

Service Dates of Committee Chair: Jan. 3,1991-Jan. 3,1993
Service Dates of Majority Members: Jan. 3,1991-Jan. 3,1993
Service Dates of Minority Members: Jan. 3,1991-Jan. 3,1993

Majority

Rank	Name	Party	State	Terms in: House	Terms in: Comm.
Chr	Fascell, Dante B.	Dem	Fla.	19	18
2nd	Hamilton, Lee H.	Dem	Ind.	14	14
3rd	Yatron, Gus	Dem	Penn.	12	12
4th	Solarz, Stephen J.	Dem	N.Y.	9	9
5th	Wolpe, Howard E.	Dem	Mich.	7	7
6th	Gejdenson, Samuel	Dem	Conn.	6	6
7th	Dymally, Mervyn M.	Dem	Cal.	6	6
8th	Lantos, Tom	Dem	Cal.	6	6
9th	Torricelli, Robert G.	Dem	N.J.	5	5
10th	Berman, Howard L.	Dem	Cal.	5	5
11th	Levine, Mel	Dem	Cal.	5	5
12th	Feighan, Edward F.	Dem	Ohio	5	5
13th	Weiss, Theodore S.	Dem	N.Y.	8	5
14th	Ackerman, Gary L.	Dem	N.Y.	5	5
15th	Udall, Morris K.	Dem	Ariz.	16	4
16th	Fuster, Jaime B.	Dem	P.R.	4	3
17th	Owens, Wayne	Dem	Utah	4	3
18th	Johnston, Harry A.	Dem	Fla.	2	2
19th	Engel, Eliot L.	Dem	N.Y.	2	2
20th	Faleomavaega, Eni F. H.	Dem	A.Sm.	2	2
21st	Studds, Gerry E.	Dem	Mass.	10	*T 9
22nd	Murphy, Austin J.	Dem	Penn.	8	*T 1
23rd	Kostmayer, Peter H.	Dem	Penn.	7	*T 5
24th	Foglietta, Thomas M.	Dem	Penn.	6	*T 1
25th	McCloskey, Francis X.	Dem	Ind.	5	*T 2
26th	Sawyer, Thomas C.	Dem	Ohio	3	*T 1
27th	Payne, Donald M.	Dem	N.J.	3	*T 2
28th	Orton, Bill	Dem	Utah	1	*T 1

Minority

Rank	Name	Party	State	Terms in: House	Terms in: Comm.
RM	Broomfield, William S.	Rep	Mich.	18	16
2nd	Gilman, Benjamin A.	Rep	N.Y.	10	10
3rd	Lagomarsino, Robert J.	Rep	Cal.	10	10
4th	Goodling, William F.	Rep	Penn.	9	*2 8
5th	Leach, James A. S.	Rep	Iowa	8	6
6th	Roth, Tobias A.	Rep	Wisc.	7	6
7th	Snowe, Olympia J. B.	Rep	Me.	7	6
8th	Hyde, Henry J.	Rep	Ill.	9	6
9th	Bereuter, Douglas K.	Rep	Neb.	7	5
10th	Smith, Christopher H.	Rep	N.J.	6	4
11th	Burton, Dan	Rep	Ind.	5	4
12th	Meyers, Jan	Rep	Kans.	4	3
13th	Miller, John R.	Rep	Wash.	4	3
14th	Blaz, Ben Garrido	Rep	Guam	4	3
15th	Gallegly, Elton	Rep	Cal.	3	2
16th	Houghton, Amory Jr.	Rep	N.Y.	3	2
17th	Goss, Porter J.	Rep	Fla.	2	2
18th	Ros-Lehtinen, Ileana	Rep	Fla.	2	2

*2: Member's 2nd period of service on the committee;
*T: Temporary member of the committee.

Notes: Territorial Delegates Eni Faleomavaega (Dem-American Samoa) and Ben Blaz (Rep-Guam) and Resident Commissioner Jaime Fuster (Dem-Puerto Rico) were allowed to accrue committee seniority but were not included in the party ratio. William F. Goodling (Rep-Penn.), having served on the Budget Committee during the previous three Congresses, returned to active service on this committee with his seniority intact.

Changes:

Majority:

Udall, Morris K.	Dem	Ariz.	May 4,1991	Resigned and retired.
Fuster, Jaime B.	Dem	P.R.	Mar. 4,1992	Resigned and retired.
Colorado, Antonio J.	Dem	P.R.	Mar. 17,1992	Replaced Udall (ranked after Faleomavaega on Aug. 11,1992).
Weiss, Theodore S.	Dem	N.Y.	Sep. 14,1992	Died in office.

GOVERNMENT OPERATIONS

EXPENDITURES IN THE EXECUTIVE DEPARTMENTS

Jurisdiction, 1947

Established by the Legislative Reorganization Act of 1946:

[Section 121.(1)(h)]

Committee on Expenditures in the Executive Departments.

(A) Budget and accounting measures, other than appropriations.
(B) Reorganizations in the executive branch of the Government.

[Section 121.(2)]

Such committee shall have the duty of--

(A) receiving and examining reports of the Comptroller General of the United States and of submitting such recommendations to the House as it deems necessary or desirable in connection with the subject matter of such reports;
(B) studying the operation of Government activities at all levels with a view to determining its economy and efficiency;
(C) evaluating the effects of laws enacted to reorganize the legislative and executive branches of the Government;
(D) Studying intergovernmental relationships between the United States and the States and municipalities, and between the United States and international organizations of which the United States is a member.

GOVERNMENT OPERATIONS

Renamed Committee on Government Operations on July 3, 1952.

Jurisdiction, 1992

Jurisdiction contained in Rules of the House of Representatives, (as revised to July 1, 1992):

[Rule X. 1. (j)]

Committee on Government Operations.

(1) Budget and accounting measures, other than appropriations.
(2) The overall economy and efficiency of Government operations and activities, including Federal procurement.
(3) Reorganizations in the executive branch of the Government.
(4) Intergovernmental relationships between the United States and the States and municipalities, and general revenue sharing.
(5) National archives.
(6) Measures providing for off-budget treatment of Federal agencies or programs.
(7) Measures providing exemption from reduction under any order issued under part C of the Balanced Budget and Emergency Deficit Control Act of 1985.

In addition to its legislative jurisdiction under the preceding provisions of this paragraph (and its oversight functions under clause 2(b) (1) and (2)), the committee shall have the function of performing the activities and conducting the studies which are provided for in clause 4(c).

[Rule X. 4. (c)(1)]

The Committee on Government Operations shall have the general function of--

(A) receiving and examining reports of the Comptroller General of the United States and of submitting such recommendations to the House as it deems necessary or desirable in connection with the subject matter of such reports;
(B) evaluating the effects of laws enacted to reorganize the legislative and executive branches of the Government; and
(C) studying intergovernmental relationships between the United States and the States and municipalities, and between the United States and international organizations of which the United States is a member.

[Rule X. 4. (c)(2)]

In addition to its duties under subparagraph (1), the Committee on Government Operations may at any time conduct investigations of any matter without regard to the provisions of clause 1, 2, or 3 (or this clause) conferring jurisdiction over such matter upon another standing committee. The committee's findings and recommendations in any such investigation shall be made available to the other standing committee or committees having jurisdiction over the matter involved (and included in the report of any such other committee when required by clause 2(1)(3) of Rule XI).

EXPENDITURES IN THE EXECUTIVE DEPARTMENTS / 80th Congress

Service Dates of Committee Chair: Jan. 14,1947-Jan. 3,1949
Service Dates of Majority Members: Jan. 14,1947-Jan. 3,1949
Service Dates of Minority Members: Jan. 16,1947-Jan. 3,1949

Majority

Rank	Name	Party	State	Terms in: House	Terms in: Comm.
Chr	Hoffman, Clare E.	Rep	Mich.	7	7
2nd	Bender, George H.	Rep	Ohio	5	*1 4
3rd	Rich, Robert F.	Rep	Penn.	9	*2 2
4th	Latham, Henry J.	Rep	N.Y.	2	2
5th	Wadsworth, James W. Jr.	Rep	N.Y.	8	1
6th	Harness, Forest A.	Rep	Ind.	5	1
7th	Brown, Clarence J.	Rep	Ohio	5	*1 1
8th	Rizley, Ross	Rep	Okla.	4	1
9th	Chenoweth, J. Edgar	Rep	Colo.	4	1
10th	Busbey, Fred E.	Rep	Ill.	2	1
11th	Snyder, Melvin C.	Rep	W.Va.	1	1
12th	Boggs, J. Caleb	Rep	Del.	1	1
13th	Riehlman, R. Walter	Rep	N.Y.	1	1
14th	Jenkins, Mitchell	Rep	Penn.	1	1
15th	Coffin, Howard A.	Rep	Mich.	1	1

Minority

Rank	Name	Party	State	Terms in: House	Terms in: Comm.
RM	Manasco, Carter	Dem	Ala.	4	4
2nd	Dawson, William L.	Dem	Ill.	3	3
3rd	Delaney, John J.	Dem	N.Y.	10	1
4th	Holifield, Chet	Dem	Cal.	3	1
5th	Lanham, Henderson L.	Dem	Ga.	1	1
6th	Dorn, W. J. Bryan	Dem	S.C.	1	*1 1
7th	Hardy, Porter Jr.	Dem	Va.	1	*1 1
8th	Karsten, Frank M.	Dem	Mo.	1	1
9th	Deane, Charles B.	Dem	N.C.	1	1
10th	Wilson, J. Frank	Dem	Tex.	1	1

*1: Member's 1st period of service on the committee;
*2: Member's 2nd period of service on the committee.

Changes:

Majority:

Name	Party	State	Date	Change
Coffin, Howard A.	Rep	Mich.	Jan. 23,1947	Moved to Public Works.
Judd, Walter H.	Rep	Minn.	Jan. 23,1947	Replaced Coffin; ranked 3rd.
Jenkins, Mitchell	Rep	Penn.	Dec. 18,1947	Left committee; moved to Select Committee to Investigate Transactions on Commodity Exchanges.
Harvey, Ralph	Rep	Ind.	Dec. 18,1947	Replaced Jenkins.
Boggs, J. Caleb	Rep	Del.	Mar. 25,1948	Moved to Judiciary.

Minority:

Name	Party	State	Date	Change
Deane, Charles B.	Dem	N.C.	Feb. 26,1947	Moved to House Administration.
McCormack, John W.	Dem	Mass.	Feb. 26,1947	Replaced Deane; ranked 2nd on minority.
Delaney, John J.	Dem	N.Y.	Nov. 18,1948	Died in office.

Third Party:

Name	Party	State	Date	Change
Isacson, Leo	ALP	N.Y.	Mar. 25,1948	Replaced Boggs.

Departures from the House:	Majority			Minority		
Defeated for Reelection	Bender, George H.	Ohio	Rep	None		
	Busbey, Fred E.	Ill.	Rep			
	Chenoweth, J. Edgar	Colo.	Rep			
	Harness, Forest A.	Ind.	Rep			
	Snyder, Melvin C.	W.Va.	Rep			
	Third Party					
	Isacson, Leo	N.Y.	ALP			
Defeated for Renomination	None			Manasco, Carter	Ala.	Dem
Lost Election to U.S. Senate	Rizley, Ross	Okla.	Rep	None		
Lost Nomination to U.S. Senate	None			Dorn, W. J. Bryan	S.C.	Dem
Departures from Committee:						
Moved to District of Columbia	Wadsworth, James W. Jr.	N.Y.	Rep	None		
Moved to Judiciary	None			Wilson, J. Frank	Tex.	Dem
No new assignment	Brown, Clarence J.	Ohio	Rep	None		
	Judd, Walter H.	Minn.	Rep			
	Latham, Henry J.	N.Y.	Rep			

EXPENDITURES IN THE EXECUTIVE DEPARTMENTS / 81st Congress

Service Dates of Committee Chair: Jan. 18,1949-Jan. 3,1951
Service Dates of Majority Members: Jan. 18,1949-Jan. 3,1951
Service Dates of Minority Members: Jan. 18,1949-Jan. 3,1951

Majority

Rank	Name	Party	State	Terms in: House	Terms in: Comm.
Chr	Dawson, William L.	Dem	Ill.	4	4
2nd	Holifield, Chet	Dem	Cal.	4	2
3rd	Lanham, Henderson L.	Dem	Ga.	2	2
4th	Hardy, Porter Jr.	Dem	Va.	2	*1 2
5th	Karsten, Frank M.	Dem	Mo.	2	2
6th	McCormack, John W.	Dem	Mass.	12	2
7th	Bonner, Herbert C.	Dem	N.C.	6	1
8th	Sadowski, George G.	Dem	Mich.	7	1
9th	Huber, Walter B.	Dem	Ohio	3	1
10th	Blatnik, John A.	DFL	Minn.	2	*1 1
11th	Donohue, Harold D.	Dem	Mass.	2	*1 1
12th	Wagner, Earl T.	Dem	Ohio	1	1
13th	Coffey, Robert L. Jr.	Dem	Penn.	1	1
14th	Bolton, William P.	Dem	Md.	1	1
15th	Burnside, Maurice G.	Dem	W.Va.	1	1
16th	Bolling, Richard W.	Dem	Mo.	1	1
17th	Tauriello, Anthony F.	Dem	N.Y.	1	1
18th	Heller, Louis B.	Dem	N.Y.	1	1

Minority

Rank	Name	Party	State	Terms in: House	Terms in: Comm.
RM	Hoffman, Clare E.	Rep	Mich.	8	8
2nd	Rich, Robert F.	Rep	Penn.	10	*2 3
3rd	Riehlman, R. Walter	Rep	N.Y.	2	2
4th	Harvey, Ralph	Rep	Ind.	2	2
5th	Halleck, Charles A.	Rep	Ind.	8	1
6th	Lovre, Harold O.	Rep	S.D.	1	1
7th	Pfeiffer, William L.	Rep	N.Y.	1	1

*1: Member's 1st period of service on the committee;
*2: Member's 2nd period of service on the committee.

Vacancy Filled:
Majority: 18th seat by Heller on Mar. 16,1949.

Changes:
Majority:

Coffey, Robert L. Jr.	Dem	Penn.	Apr. 20,1949	Died in office.
Heller, Louis B.	Dem	N.Y.	June 24,1949	Moved to Public Lands.
Roosevelt, Franklin D. Jr.	Dem	N.Y.	June 24,1949	Replaced Coffey.
Shelley, John F.	Dem	Cal.	Jan. 26,1950	Replaced Heller.

Departures from the House:	Majority			Minority		
Defeated for Reelection	Bolton, William P.	Md.	Dem	None		
	Huber, Walter B.	Ohio	Dem			
	Tauriello, Anthony F.	N.Y.	Dem			
	Wagner, Earl T.	Ohio	Dem			
Defeated for Renomination	Sadowski, George G.	Mich.	Dem	None		
Retired	None			Pfeiffer, William L.	N.Y.	Rep
				Rich, Robert F.	Penn.	Rep

Departures from Committee:

Moved to Foreign Affairs	Roosevelt, Franklin D. Jr.	N.Y. Dem	None	
Moved to House Administration	None		Halleck, Charles A.	Ind. Rep
Moved to Agriculture	None		Harvey, Ralph	Ind. Rep
			Lovre, Harold O.	S.D. Rep

EXPENDITURES IN THE EXECUTIVE DEPARTMENTS / 82nd Congress

* Renamed the Committee on GOVERNMENT OPERATIONS on July 3,1952.

Service Dates of Committee Chair: Jan. 12,1951-Jan. 3,1953
Service Dates of Majority Members: Jan. 12,1951-Jan. 3,1953
Service Dates of Minority Members: Jan. 15,1951-Jan. 3,1953

Majority

Rank	Name	Party	State	Terms in: House		Terms in: Comm.
Chr	Dawson, William L.	Dem	Ill.	5		5
2nd	Holifield, Chet	Dem	Cal.	5		3
3rd	Lanham, Henderson L.	Dem	Ga.	3		3
4th	Hardy, Porter Jr.	Dem	Va.	3	*1	3
5th	Karsten, Frank M.	Dem	Mo.	3		3
6th	McCormack, John W.	Dem	Mass.	13		3
7th	Bonner, Herbert C.	Dem	N.C.	7		2
8th	Blatnik, John A.	DFL	Minn.	3	*1	2
9th	Donohue, Harold D.	Dem	Mass.	3	*1	2
10th	Burnside, Maurice G.	Dem	W.Va.	2		2
11th	Bolling, Richard W.	Dem	Mo.	2		2
12th	Shelley, John F.	Dem	Cal.	2		2
13th	Dorn, W. J. Bryan	Dem	S.C.	2	*2	1
14th	Fine, Sidney A.	Dem	N.Y.	1		1
15th	Lantaff, William C.	Dem	Fla.	1		1
16th	Baring, Walter S.	Dem	Nev.	2		1

Minority

Rank	Name	Party	State	Terms in: House		Terms in: Comm.
RM	Hoffman, Clare E.	Rep	Mich.	9		9
2nd	Riehlman, R. Walter	Rep	N.Y.	3		3
3rd	Harden, Cecil M.	Rep	Ind.	2		1
4th	Bender, George H.	Rep	Ohio	6	*2	1
5th	Brownson, Charles B.	Rep	Ind.	1		1
6th	Curtis, Thomas B.	Rep	Mo.	1		1
7th	Miller, William E.	Rep	N.Y.	1	*1	1
8th	Church, Marguerite Stitt	Rep	Ill.	1		1
9th	Meader, George	Rep	Mich.	1		1
10th	McVey, William E.	Rep	Ill.	1		1
11th	Bush, Alvin R.	Rep	Penn.	1		1

*1: Member's 1st period of service on the committee;
*2: Member's 2nd period of service on the committee.

Vacancy Filled:
Majority: 16th seat by Baring on Feb. 14,1951.

Changes:
Minority:

Miller, William E.	Rep	N.Y.	Oct. 17,1951	Moved to Judiciary.
Osmers, Frank C. Jr.	Rep	N.J.	Feb. 4,1952	Replaced Miller.

Departures from the House:

	Majority		Minority	
Defeated for Reelection	Baring, Walter S.	Nev. Dem	None	
	Burnside, Maurice G.	W.Va. Dem		

Departures from Committee:

Moved to Interstate & Foreign Commerce	None		Bush, Alvin R.	Penn. Rep
Moved to Ways and Means	None		Curtis, Thomas B.	Mo. Rep
Moved to Banking & Currency	None		McVey, William E.	Ill. Rep
No new assignment	Blatnik, John A.	Minn. DFL	None	
	Bolling, Richard W.	Mo. Dem		
	Bonner, Herbert C.	N.C. Dem		
	Donohue, Harold D.	Mass. Dem		
	Dorn, W. J. Bryan	S.C. Dem		
	Hardy, Porter Jr.	Va. Dem		
	Lanham, Henderson L.	Ga. Dem		
	Shelley, John F.	Cal. Dem		

GOVERNMENT OPERATIONS / 83rd Congress

Service Dates of Committee Chair: Jan. 19,1953-Jan. 3,1955
Service Dates of Majority Members: Jan. 19,1953-Jan. 3,1955
Service Dates of Minority Members: Jan. 19,1953-Jan. 3,1955

Majority

Rank	Name	Party	State	Terms in: House		Terms in: Comm.
Chr	Hoffman, Clare E.	Rep	Mich.	10		10
2nd	Riehlman, R. Walter	Rep	N.Y.	4		4
3rd	Harden, Cecil M.	Rep	Ind.	3		2
4th	Bender, George H.	Rep	Ohio	7	*2	2
5th	Brownson, Charles B.	Rep	Ind.	2		2
6th	Church, Marguerite Stitt	Rep	Ill.	2		2
7th	Meader, George	Rep	Mich.	2		2
8th	Osmers, Frank C. Jr.	Rep	N.J.	4		2
9th	Brown, Clarence J.	Rep	Ohio	8	*2	1
10th	Graham, Louis E.	Rep	Penn.	8		1
11th	Judd, Walter H.	Rep	Minn.	6	*2	1
12th	McDonough, Gordon L.	Rep	Cal.	5		1
13th	St. George, Katharine	Rep	N.Y.	4		1
14th	Miller, William E.	Rep	N.Y.	2	*2	1
15th	Hillelson, Jeffrey P.	Rep	Mo.	1		1
16th	Poff, Richard H.	Rep	Va.	1		1

Minority

Rank	Name	Party	State	Terms in: House	Terms in: Comm.
RM	Dawson, William L.	Dem	Ill.	6	6
2nd	Holifield, Chet	Dem	Cal.	6	4
3rd	Karsten, Frank M.	Dem	Mo.	4	4
4th	McCormack, John W.	Dem	Mass.	14	4
5th	Fine, Sidney A.	Dem	N.Y.	2	2
6th	Lantaff, William C.	Dem	Fla.	2	2
7th	Chudoff, Earl	Dem	Penn.	3	1
8th	Ikard, Frank N.	Dem	Tex.	2	1
9th	Brooks, Jack B.	Dem	Tex.	1	1
10th	Holtzman, Lester	Dem	N.Y.	1	1
11th	Condon, Robert L.	Dem	Cal.	1	1
12th	Dodd, Thomas J.	Dem	Conn.	1	1
13th	Mollohan, Robert H.	Dem	W.Va.	1	1
14th	Fountain, Lawrence H.	Dem	N.C.	1	1

*2: Member's 2nd period of service on the committee.

Changes:

Majority:

Name	Party	State	Date	Change
Poff, Richard H.	Rep	Va.	Jan. 21,1954	Moved to Judiciary.
Lipscomb, Glenard P.	Rep	Cal.	Jan. 21,1954	Replaced Poff.
Bender, George H.	Rep	Ohio	Dec. 15,1954	Resigned; elected to U.S. Senate.

Minority:

Name	Party	State	Date	Change
Fine, Sidney A.	Dem	N.Y.	Mar. 30,1953	Moved to Judiciary.
Pilcher, John L.	Dem	Ga.	Mar. 30,1953	Replaced Fine.
Dodd, Thomas J.	Dem	Conn.	Jan. 25,1954	Moved to Foreign Affairs.
Williams, Harrison A. Jr.	Dem	N.J.	Jan. 25,1954	Replaced Dodd.

	Majority			Minority		
Departures from the House:						
Defeated for Reelection	Graham, Louis E.	Penn.	Rep	Condon, Robert L.	Cal.	Dem
	Hillelson, Jeffrey P.	Mo.	Rep			
Retired	None			Lantaff, William C.	Fla.	Dem
Departures from Committee:						
Moved to Armed Services	Osmers, Frank C. Jr.	N.J.	Rep	None		
Moved to Ways and Means	None			Karsten, Frank M.	Mo.	Dem
				Ikard, Frank N.	Tex.	Dem
Moved to Foreign Affairs	None			Pilcher, John L.	Ga.	Dem
				Williams, Harrison A. Jr.	N.J.	Dem
No new assignment	Judd, Walter H.	Minn.	Rep	None		
	McDonough, Gordon L.	Cal.	Rep			
	Miller, William E.	N.Y.	Rep			
	St. George, Katharine	N.Y.	Rep			
	Church, Marguerite Stitt	Ill.	Rep			

GOVERNMENT OPERATIONS / 84th Congress

Service Dates of Committee Chair: Jan. 13,1955-Jan. 3,1957
Service Dates of Majority Members: Jan. 13,1955-Jan. 3,1957
Service Dates of Minority Members: Jan. 20,1955-Jan. 3,1957

Majority

Rank	Name	Party	State	Terms in: House	Terms in: Comm.
Chr	Dawson, William L.	Dem	Ill.	7	7
2nd	Holifield, Chet	Dem	Cal.	7	5
3rd	McCormack, John W.	Dem	Mass.	15	5
4th	Chudoff, Earl	Dem	Penn.	4	2
5th	Brooks, Jack B.	Dem	Tex.	2	2
6th	Holtzman, Lester	Dem	N.Y.	2	2
7th	Mollohan, Robert H.	Dem	W.Va.	2	2
8th	Fountain, Lawrence H.	Dem	N.C.	2	2
9th	Hardy, Porter Jr.	Dem	Va.	5	*2 1
10th	Blatnik, John A.	DFL	Minn.	5	*2 1
11th	Jones, Robert E. Jr.	Dem	Ala.	5	1
12th	Garmatz, Edward A.	Dem	Md.	5	1
13th	Moss, John E. Jr.	Dem	Cal.	2	1
14th	Kilgore, Joe M.	Dem	Tex.	1	1
15th	Fascell, Dante B.	Dem	Fla.	1	1
16th	Griffiths, Martha W.	Dem	Mich.	1	1
17th	Reuss, Henry S.	Dem	Wisc.	1	1

Minority

Rank	Name	Party	State	Terms in: House	Terms in: Comm.
RM	Hoffman, Clare E.	Rep	Mich.	11	11
2nd	Riehlman, R. Walter	Rep	N.Y.	5	5
3rd	Harden, Cecil M.	Rep	Ind.	4	3
4th	Brownson, Charles B.	Rep	Ind.	3	3
5th	Meader, George	Rep	Mich.	3	3
6th	Brown, Clarence J.	Rep	Ohio	9	*2 2
7th	Lipscomb, Glenard P.	Rep	Cal.	2	2
8th	Reece, B. Carroll	Rep	Tenn.	15	*2 1
9th	Younger, J. Arthur	Rep	Cal.	2	1
10th	Knox, Victor A.	Rep	Mich.	2	1
11th	Krueger, Otto	Rep	N.D.	2	1
12th	Jonas, Charles Raper	Rep	N.C.	2	1
13th	Minshall, William E. Jr.	Rep	Ohio	1	1

*2: Member's 2nd period of service on the committee.

Note: The committee's size was set at 30 members on Jan. 20,1955.

	Majority		Minority	
Departures from the House:				
Lost Election for Governor	Mollohan, Robert H.	W.Va. Dem	None	
Departures from Committee:				
Moved to Judiciary	Holtzman, Lester	N.Y. Dem	None	
Moved to Appropriations	None		Jonas, Charles Raper	N.C. Rep
Moved to Agriculture	None		Krueger, Otto	N.D. Rep
Moved to Armed Services	None		Reece, B. Carroll	Tenn. Rep
Moved to Interstate & Foreign Commerce	None		Younger, J. Arthur	Cal. Rep

GOVERNMENT OPERATIONS / 85th Congress

Service Dates of Committee Chair: Jan. 10,1957-Jan. 3,1959
Service Dates of Majority Members: Jan. 10,1957-Jan. 3,1959
Service Dates of Minority Members: Jan. 16,1957-Jan. 3,1959

Majority

Rank	Name	Party	State	Terms in: House	Terms in: Comm.
Chr	Dawson, William L.	Dem	Ill.	8	8
2nd	Holifield, Chet	Dem	Cal.	8	6
3rd	McCormack, John W.	Dem	Mass.	16	6
4th	Chudoff, Earl	Dem	Penn.	5	3
5th	Brooks, Jack B.	Dem	Tex.	3	3
6th	Fountain, Lawrence H.	Dem	N.C.	3	3
7th	Hardy, Porter Jr.	Dem	Va.	6	*2 2
8th	Blatnik, John A.	DFL	Minn.	6	*2 2
9th	Jones, Robert E. Jr.	Dem	Ala.	6	2
10th	Garmatz, Edward A.	Dem	Md.	6	2
11th	Moss, John E. Jr.	Dem	Cal.	3	2
12th	Kilgore, Joe M.	Dem	Tex.	2	2
13th	Fascell, Dante B.	Dem	Fla.	2	2
14th	Griffiths, Martha W.	Dem	Mich.	2	2
15th	Reuss, Henry S.	Dem	Wisc.	2	2
16th	Brooks, Overton	Dem	La.	11	1
17th	Kee, Maude Elizabeth	Dem	W.Va.	4	1

Minority

Order	Name	Party	State	Terms in: Chamber	Terms in: Committee
RM	Hoffman, Clare E.	Rep	Mich.	12	12
2nd	Riehlman, R. Walter	Rep	N.Y.	6	6
3rd	Harden, Cecil M.	Rep	Ind.	5	4
4th	Brownson, Charles B.	Rep	Ind.	4	4
5th	Meader, George	Rep	Mich.	4	4
6th	Brown, Clarence J.	Rep	Ohio	10	*2 3
7th	Lipscomb, Glenard P.	Rep	Cal.	3	3
8th	Knox, Victor A.	Rep	Mich.	3	2
9th	Minshall, William E. Jr.	Rep	Ohio	2	2
10th	May, Edwin H. Jr.	Rep	Conn.	1	1
11th	Michel, Robert H.	Rep	Ill.	1	1
12th	Smith, H. Allen	Rep	Cal.	1	1
13th	Dwyer, Florence P.	Rep	N.J.	1	1

*2: Member's 2nd period of service on the committee.

Changes:

Majority:

Chudoff, Earl	Dem	Penn.	Jan. 5,1958	Resigned; elected Philadelphia judge.
Granahan, Kathryn E.	Dem	Penn.	Jan. 16,1958	Replaced Chudoff.

Minority:

Smith, H. Allen	Rep	Cal.	Jan. 16,1958	Moved to Judiciary.
Westland, Alfred John	Rep	Wash.	Mar. 28,1958	Replaced Smith.

Departures from the House:	Majority	Minority		
Defeated for Reelection	None	Brownson, Charles B.	Ind.	Rep
		Harden, Cecil M.	Ind.	Rep
		May, Edwin H. Jr.	Conn.	Rep
Departures from Committee:				
Moved to Ways and Means	None	Knox, Victor A.	Mich.	Rep
Moved to Appropriations	None	Michel, Robert H.	Ill.	Rep
		Minshall, William E. Jr.	Ohio	Rep
No new assignment	None	Lipscomb, Glenard P.	Cal.	Rep

GOVERNMENT OPERATIONS / 86th Congress

Service Dates of Committee Chair: Jan. 19,1959-Jan. 3,1961
Service Dates of Majority Members: Jan. 19,1959-Jan. 3,1961
Service Dates of Minority Members: Jan. 19,1959-Jan. 3,1961

Majority

Rank	Name	Party	State	Terms in: House	Terms in: Comm.
Chr	Dawson, William L.	Dem	Ill.	9	9
2nd	Holifield, Chet	Dem	Cal.	9	7
3rd	McCormack, John W.	Dem	Mass.	17	7
4th	Brooks, Jack B.	Dem	Tex.	4	4
5th	Fountain, Lawrence H.	Dem	N.C.	4	4
6th	Hardy, Porter Jr.	Dem	Va.	7	*2 3
7th	Blatnik, John A.	DFL	Minn.	7	*2 3
8th	Jones, Robert E. Jr.	Dem	Ala.	7	3
9th	Garmatz, Edward A.	Dem	Md.	7	3
10th	Moss, John E. Jr.	Dem	Cal.	4	3
11th	Kilgore, Joe M.	Dem	Tex.	3	3
12th	Fascell, Dante B.	Dem	Fla.	3	3
13th	Griffiths, Martha W.	Dem	Mich.	3	3
14th	Reuss, Henry S.	Dem	Wisc.	3	3
15th	Brooks, Overton	Dem	La.	12	2
16th	Kee, Maude Elizabeth	Dem	W.Va.	5	2
17th	Granahan, Kathryn E.	Dem	Penn.	3	2
18th	Monagan, John S.	Dem	Conn.	1	1
19th	Smith, Neal	Dem	Iowa	1	1

Minority

Rank	Name	Party	State	Terms in: House	Terms in: Comm.
RM	Hoffman, Clare E.	Rep	Mich.	13	13
2nd	Riehlman, R. Walter	Rep	N.Y.	7	7
3rd	Meader, George	Rep	Mich.	5	5
4th	Brown, Clarence J.	Rep	Ohio	11	*2 4
5th	Dwyer, Florence P.	Rep	N.J.	2	2
6th	Westland, Alfred John	Rep	Wash.	4	2
7th	Holt, Joseph F.	Rep	Cal.	4	1
8th	Griffin, Robert P.	Rep	Mich.	2	1
9th	Wallhauser, George M.	Rep	N.J.	1	1
10th	Weis, Jessica McC.	Rep	N.Y.	1	1
11th	Langen, Odin	Rep	Minn.	1	1

*2: Member's 2nd period of service on the committee.

Changes:

Minority:

Westland, Alfred John	Rep	Wash.	Jan. 21,1959	Moved to Joint Committee on Atomic Energy.
Barry, Robert R.	Rep	N.Y.	Jan. 29,1959	Replaced Westland.

Departures from the House:	Majority	Minority		
Retired	None	Holt, Joseph F.	Cal.	Rep
Departures from Committee:				
Moved to Science & Astronautics	None	Weis, Jessica McC.	N.Y.	Rep
Moved to Foreign Affairs	None	Barry, Robert R.	N.Y.	Rep

GOVERNMENT OPERATIONS / 87th Congress

Service Dates of Committee Chair: Feb. 6,1961-Jan. 3,1963
Service Dates of Majority Members: Feb. 6,1961-Jan. 3,1963
Service Dates of Minority Members: Feb. 13,1961-Jan. 3,1963

Majority

Rank Name	Party	State	Terms in: House	Terms in: Comm.
Chr Dawson, William L.	Dem	Ill.	10	10
2nd Holifield, Chet	Dem	Cal.	10	8
3rd McCormack, John W.	Dem	Mass.	18	8
4th Brooks, Jack B.	Dem	Tex.	5	5
5th Fountain, Lawrence H.	Dem	N.C.	5	5
6th Hardy, Porter Jr.	Dem	Va.	8	*2 4
7th Blatnik, John A.	DFL	Minn.	8	*2 4
8th Jones, Robert E. Jr.	Dem	Ala.	8	4
9th Garmatz, Edward A.	Dem	Md.	8	4
10th Moss, John E. Jr.	Dem	Cal.	5	4
11th Kilgore, Joe M.	Dem	Tex.	4	4
12th Fascell, Dante B.	Dem	Fla.	4	4
13th Griffiths, Martha W.	Dem	Mich.	4	4
14th Reuss, Henry S.	Dem	Wisc.	4	4
15th Brooks, Overton	Dem	La.	13	3
16th Kee, Maude Elizabeth	Dem	W.Va.	6	3
17th Granahan, Kathryn E.	Dem	Penn.	4	3
18th Monagan, John S.	Dem	Conn.	2	2
19th Smith, Neal	Dem	Iowa	2	2

Minority

Rank Name	Party	State	Terms in: House	Terms in: Comm.
RM Hoffman, Clare E.	Rep	Mich.	14	14
2nd Riehlman, R. Walter	Rep	N.Y.	8	8
3rd Meader, George	Rep	Mich.	6	6
4th Brown, Clarence J.	Rep	Ohio	12	*2 5
5th Dwyer, Florence P.	Rep	N.J.	3	3
6th Griffin, Robert P.	Rep	Mich.	3	2
7th Wallhauser, George M.	Rep	N.J.	2	2
8th Langen, Odin	Rep	Minn.	2	2
9th Anderson, John B.	Rep	Ill.	1	1
10th Schweiker, Richard S.	Rep	Penn.	1	1
11th Morse, F. Bradford	Rep	Mass.	1	1

*2: Member's 2nd period of service on the committee.

Changes:

Majority:

Brooks, Overton	Dem	La.	Sep. 16,1961	Died in office.
McCormack, John W.	Dem	Mass.	Jan. 10,1962	Left committee; elected Speaker of the House.
Griffiths, Martha W.	Dem	Mich.	Jan. 18,1962	Moved to Ways and Means.
Lankford, Richard E.	Dem	Md.	Jan. 18,1962	Replaced Brooks.
Bass, Ross	Dem	Tenn.	Jan. 18,1962	Replaced McCormack.
Nedzi, Lucien N.	Dem	Mich.	Jan. 18,1962	Replaced Griffiths.

	Majority		Minority	
Departures from the House:				
Appointed Treasurer of U.S.	Granahan, Kathryn E.	Penn. Dem	None	
Retired	None		Hoffman, Clare E.	Mich. Rep
Departures from Committee:				
Moved to Interior & Insular Affairs	Kee, Maude Elizabeth	W.Va. Dem	None	
Moved to Armed Services	Kilgore, Joe M.	Tex. Dem	None	
	Nedzi, Lucien N.	Mich. Dem		
Moved to Ways and Means	Bass, Ross	Tenn. Dem	None	
Moved to Foreign Affairs	None		Morse, F. Bradford	Mass. Rep
No new assignment	Smith, Neal	Iowa Dem	Langen, Odin	Minn. Rep

GOVERNMENT OPERATIONS / 88th Congress

Service Dates of Committee Chair: Jan. 17,1963-Jan. 3,1965
Service Dates of Majority Members: Jan. 17,1963-Jan. 3,1965
Service Dates of Minority Members: Jan. 24,1963-Jan. 3,1965

Majority

Rank Name	Party	State	Terms in: House	Terms in: Comm.
Chr Dawson, William L.	Dem	Ill.	11	11
2nd Holifield, Chet	Dem	Cal.	11	9
3rd Brooks, Jack B.	Dem	Tex.	6	6
4th Fountain, Lawrence H.	Dem	N.C.	6	6
5th Hardy, Porter Jr.	Dem	Va.	9	*2 5
6th Blatnik, John A.	DFL	Minn.	9	*2 5
7th Jones, Robert E. Jr.	Dem	Ala.	9	5
8th Garmatz, Edward A.	Dem	Md.	9	5
9th Moss, John E. Jr.	Dem	Cal.	6	5
10th Fascell, Dante B.	Dem	Fla.	5	5
11th Reuss, Henry S.	Dem	Wisc.	5	5
12th Monagan, John S.	Dem	Conn.	3	3
13th Lankford, Richard E.	Dem	Md.	5	2
14th Macdonald, Torbert H.	Dem	Mass.	5	1
15th Roush, J. Edward	Dem	Ind.	3	1
16th Moorhead, William S.	Dem	Penn.	3	1
17th Gallagher, Cornelius E.	Dem	N.J.	3	1
18th Randall, William J.	Dem	Mo.	3	1
19th Rosenthal, Benjamin S.	Dem	N.Y.	2	1

Minority

Rank Name	Party	State	Terms in: House	Terms in: Comm.
RM Riehlman, R. Walter	Rep	N.Y.	9	9
2nd Meader, George	Rep	Mich.	7	7
3rd Brown, Clarence J.	Rep	Ohio	13	*2 6
4th Dwyer, Florence P.	Rep	N.J.	4	4
5th Griffin, Robert P.	Rep	Mich.	4	3
6th Wallhauser, George M.	Rep	N.J.	3	3
7th Anderson, John B.	Rep	Ill.	2	2
8th Schweiker, Richard S.	Rep	Penn.	2	2
9th Reid, Ogden R.	Rep	N.Y.	1	1
10th Horton, Frank J.	Rep	N.Y.	1	1
11th Stinson, K. William	Rep	Wash.	1	1
12th McClory, Robert	Rep	Ill.	1	1

*2: Member's 2nd period of service on the committee.

Changes:
Minority:

Schweiker, Richard S.	Rep	Penn.	Dec. 2,1963	Already had moved to Armed Services.
Johnson, Albert W.	Rep	Penn.	Dec. 2,1963	Replaced Schweiker.
Johnson, Albert W.	Rep	Penn.	May 14,1964	Left committee; no new assignment.
Baker, Irene Bailey	Rep	Tenn.	May 14,1964	Replaced Johnson.

	Majority			Minority		
Departures from the House:						
Defeated for Reelection	None			Meader, George	Mich.	Rep
				Riehlman, R. Walter	N.Y.	Rep
				Stinson, K. William	Wash.	Rep
Retired	Lankford, Richard E.	Md.	Dem	Wallhauser, George M.	N.J.	Rep
				Baker, Irene Bailey	Tenn.	Rep
Departures from Committee:						
Moved to Judiciary	None			McClory, Robert	Ill.	Rep
No new assignment	None			Anderson, John B.	Ill.	Rep

GOVERNMENT OPERATIONS / 89th Congress

Service Dates of Committee Chair: Jan. 18,1965-Jan. 3,1967
Service Dates of Majority Members: Jan. 18,1965-Jan. 3,1967
Service Dates of Minority Members: Jan. 21,1965-Jan. 3,1967

Majority

Rank Name	Party	State	Terms in: House	Terms in: Comm.
Chr Dawson, William L.	Dem	Ill.	12	12
2nd Holifield, Chet	Dem	Cal.	12	10
3rd Brooks, Jack B.	Dem	Tex.	7	7
4th Fountain, Lawrence H.	Dem	N.C.	7	7
5th Hardy, Porter Jr.	Dem	Va.	10	*2 6
6th Blatnik, John A.	DFL	Minn.	10	*2 6
7th Jones, Robert E. Jr.	Dem	Ala.	10	6
8th Garmatz, Edward A.	Dem	Md.	10	6
9th Moss, John E. Jr.	Dem	Cal.	7	6
10th Fascell, Dante B.	Dem	Fla.	6	6
11th Reuss, Henry S.	Dem	Wisc.	6	6
12th Monagan, John S.	Dem	Conn.	4	4
13th Macdonald, Torbert H.	Dem	Mass.	6	2
14th Roush, J. Edward	Dem	Ind.	4	2
15th Moorhead, William S.	Dem	Penn.	4	2
16th Gallagher, Cornelius E.	Dem	N.J.	4	2
17th Randall, William J.	Dem	Mo.	4	2
18th Rosenthal, Benjamin S.	Dem	N.Y.	3	2
19th Wright, James C. Jr.	Dem	Tex.	6	1
20th St Germain, Fernand J.	Dem	R.I.	3	1
21st King, David S.	Dem	Utah	3	1
22nd Dow, John G.	Dem	N.Y.	1	1
23rd Helstoski, Henry	Dem	N.J.	1	1

Minority

Rank Name	Party	State	Terms in: House	Terms in: Comm.
RM1 Brown, Clarence J.	Rep	Ohio	14	*2 7
RM2 2nd Dwyer, Florence P.	Rep	N.J.	5	5
3rd Griffin, Robert P.	Rep	Mich.	5	4
4th Reid, Ogden R.	Rep	N.Y.	2	2
5th Horton, Frank J.	Rep	N.Y.	2	2
6th Latta, Delbert L.	Rep	Ohio	4	1
7th Rumsfeld, Donald	Rep	Ill.	2	1
8th Dickinson, William L.	Rep	Ala.	1	1
9th Erlenborn, John N.	Rep	Ill.	1	1
10th Callaway, Howard H.	Rep	Ga.	1	1
11th Gurney, Edward J.	Rep	Fla.	2	1

*2: Member's 2nd period of service on the committee.

Vacancy Filled:
Minority: 11th seat by Gurney on Feb. 3,1965.

Changes:

Ranking Member:

RM1 Brown, Clarence J.	Rep	Ohio	Aug. 23,1965	Died in office.
RM2 Dwyer, Florence P.	Rep	N.J.	Aug. 23,1965	Succeeded Brown as Ranking Minority Member.

Minority:

Gurney, Edward J.	Rep	Fla.	May 12,1965	Moved to Education and Labor.
Wydler, John W.	Rep	N.Y.	May 12,1965	Replaced Gurney.
Brown, Clarence J.	Rep	Ohio	Aug. 23,1965	Died in office.
Dole, Robert J.	Rep	Kans.	Aug. 31,1965	Replaced Brown.
Latta, Delbert L.	Rep	Ohio	Sep. 1,1965	Moved to Rules on Aug. 31,1965.
Brown, Clarence J. Jr.	Rep	Ohio	Jan. 12,1966	Replaced Latta.
Griffin, Robert P.	Rep	Mich.	May 10,1966	Resigned; appointed to U.S. Senate.
Edwards, W. J. (Jack)	Rep	Ala.	May 24,1966	Replaced Griffin.

	Majority			Minority		
Departures from the House:						
Defeated for Reelection	King, David S.	Utah	Dem			
Lost Election for Governor	None			Callaway, Howard H.	Ga.	Rep
Departures from Committee:						
Moved to Agriculture	Dow, John G.	N.Y.	Dem	None		
Moved to Armed Services	None			Dickinson, William L.	Ala.	Rep
Moved to Merchant Marine & Fisheries	Helstoski, Henry	N.J.	Dem	None		

GOVERNMENT OPERATIONS / 90th Congress

Service Dates of Committee Chair: Jan. 23,1967-Jan. 3,1969
Service Dates of Majority Members: Jan. 23,1967-Jan. 3,1969
Service Dates of Minority Members: Jan. 26,1967-Jan. 3,1969

Majority

Rank	Name	Party	State	Terms in: House	Terms in: Comm.
Chr	Dawson, William L.	Dem	Ill.	13	13
2nd	Holifield, Chet	Dem	Cal.	13	11
3rd	Brooks, Jack B.	Dem	Tex.	8	8
4th	Fountain, Lawrence H.	Dem	N.C.	8	8
5th	Hardy, Porter Jr.	Dem	Va.	11	*2 7
6th	Blatnik, John A.	DFL	Minn.	11	*2 7
7th	Jones, Robert E. Jr.	Dem	Ala.	11	7
8th	Garmatz, Edward A.	Dem	Md.	11	7
9th	Moss, John E. Jr.	Dem	Cal.	8	7
10th	Fascell, Dante B.	Dem	Fla.	7	7
11th	Reuss, Henry S.	Dem	Wisc.	7	7
12th	Monagan, John S.	Dem	Conn.	5	5
13th	Macdonald, Torbert H.	Dem	Mass.	7	3
14th	Roush, J. Edward	Dem	Ind.	5	3
15th	Moorhead, William S.	Dem	Penn.	5	3
16th	Gallagher, Cornelius E.	Dem	N.J.	5	3
17th	Randall, William J.	Dem	Mo.	5	3
18th	Rosenthal, Benjamin S.	Dem	N.Y.	4	3
19th	Wright, James C. Jr.	Dem	Tex.	7	2
20th	St Germain, Fernand J.	Dem	R.I.	4	2

Minority

Rank	Name	Party	State	Terms in: House	Terms in: Comm.
RM	Dwyer, Florence P.	Rep	N.J.	6	6
2nd	Reid, Ogden R.	Rep	N.Y.	3	3
3rd	Horton, Frank J.	Rep	N.Y.	3	3
4th	Rumsfeld, Donald	Rep	Ill.	3	2
5th	Erlenborn, John N.	Rep	Ill.	2	2
6th	Wydler, John W.	Rep	N.Y.	3	2
7th	Dole, Robert J.	Rep	Kans.	4	2
8th	Brown, Clarence J. Jr.	Rep	Ohio	2	2
9th	Edwards, W. J. (Jack)	Rep	Ala.	2	2
10th	Vander Jagt, Guy A.	Rep	Mich.	2	1
11th	Myers, John T.	Rep	Ind.	1	1
12th	Thompson, S. Fletcher	Rep	Ga.	1	1
13th	Cowger, William O.	Rep	Ky.	1	1
14th	Heckler, Margaret M.	Rep	Mass.	1	1
15th	Gude, Gilbert	Rep	Md.	1	1

*2: Member's 2nd period of service on the committee.

Changes:

Minority:

Dole, Robert J.	Rep	Kans.	Jan. 30,1968	Left committee; no new assignment.
McCloskey, Paul N. Jr.	Rep	Cal.	Jan. 30,1968	Replaced Dole.

Departures from the House:	**Majority**			**Minority**		
Defeated for Reelection	Roush, J. Edward	Ind.	Dem	None		
Retired	Hardy, Porter Jr.	Va.	Dem	None		
Departures from Committee:						
Moved to Appropriations	None			Edwards, W.J. (Jack)	Ala.	Rep
Moved to Banking & Currency	None			Heckler, Margaret M.	Mass.	Rep
Moved to Interstate & Foreign Commerce	None			Thompson, S. Fletcher	Ga.	Rep

GOVERNMENT OPERATIONS / 91st Congress

Service Dates of Committee Chairs: Ch1 Jan. 29,1969-Nov. 9,1970
Ch2 Nov. 18,1970-Jan. 3,1971
Service Dates of Majority Members: Jan. 29,1969-Jan. 3,1971
Service Dates of Minority Members: Jan. 29,1969-Jan. 3,1971

Majority

Rank	Name	Party	State	Terms in: House	Terms in: Comm.
Ch1	Dawson, William L.	Dem	Ill.	14	14
Ch2 2nd	Holifield, Chet	Dem	Cal.	14	12
3rd	Brooks, Jack B.	Dem	Tex.	9	9
4th	Fountain, Lawrence H.	Dem	N.C.	9	9
5th	Blatnik, John A.	DFL	Minn.	12	*2 8
6th	Jones, Robert E. Jr.	Dem	Ala.	12	8
7th	Garmatz, Edward A.	Dem	Md.	12	8
8th	Moss, John E. Jr.	Dem	Cal.	9	8
9th	Fascell, Dante B.	Dem	Fla.	8	8
10th	Reuss, Henry S.	Dem	Wisc.	8	8
11th	Monagan, John S.	Dem	Conn.	6	6
12th	Macdonald, Torbert H.	Dem	Mass.	8	4
13th	Moorhead, William S.	Dem	Penn.	6	4
14th	Gallagher, Cornelius E.	Dem	N.J.	6	4
15th	Randall, William J.	Dem	Mo.	6	4
16th	Rosenthal, Benjamin S.	Dem	N.Y.	5	4
17th	Wright, James C. Jr.	Dem	Tex.	8	3
18th	St Germain, Fernand J.	Dem	R.I.	5	3
19th	Culver, John C.	Dem	Iowa	3	1
20th	Hicks, Floyd V.	Dem	Wash.	3	1

Minority

Rank	Name	Party	State	Terms in: House	Terms in: Comm.
RM	Dwyer, Florence P.	Rep	N.J.	7	7
2nd	Reid, Ogden R.	Rep	N.Y.	4	4
3rd	Horton, Frank J.	Rep	N.Y.	4	4
4th	Rumsfeld, Donald	Rep	Ill.	4	3
5th	Erlenborn, John N.	Rep	Ill.	3	3
6th	Wydler, John W.	Rep	N.Y.	4	3
7th	Brown, Clarence J. Jr.	Rep	Ohio	3	3
8th	Vander Jagt, Guy A.	Rep	Mich.	3	2
9th	Myers, John T.	Rep	Ind.	2	2
10th	Cowger, William O.	Rep	Ky.	2	2
11th	Gude, Gilbert	Rep	Md.	2	2
12th	McCloskey, Paul N. Jr.	Rep	Cal.	2	2
13th	Findley, Paul	Rep	Ill.	5	1
14th	Buchanan, John H. Jr.	Rep	Ala.	3	1
15th	Weicker, Lowell P. Jr.	Rep	Conn.	1	1

*2: Member's 2nd period of service on the committee.

Changes:

Chair:

Ch1	Dawson, William L.	Dem	Ill.	Nov. 9,1970	Died in office.
Ch2	Holifield, Chet	Dem	Cal.	Nov. 18,1970	Succeeded Dawson as Chair.

Majority:

Name	Party	State	Date	Note
Dawson, William L.	Dem	Ill.	Nov. 9,1970	Died in office.
Collins, George W.	Dem	Ill.	Dec. 8,1970	Replaced Dawson.

Minority:

Name	Party	State	Date	Note
Rumsfeld, Donald	Rep	Ill.	May 25,1969	Resigned; appointed Assistant Director of the Office of Economic Opportunity.
Steiger, Sam	Rep	Ariz.	Oct. 7,1969	Replaced Rumsfeld.

	Majority		Minority	
Departures from the House:				
Elected to U.S. Senate	None		Weicker, Lowell P. Jr.	Conn. Rep
Defeated for Reelection	None		Cowger, William O.	Ky. Rep
Departures from Committee:				
Moved to Agriculture	None		Findley, Paul	Ill. Rep
Moved to Appropriations	None		Myers, John T.	Ind. Rep
No new assignment	Blatnik, John A.	Minn. DFL	None	

GOVERNMENT OPERATIONS / 92nd Congress

Service Dates of Committee Chair: Feb. 4,1971-Jan. 3,1973
Service Dates of Majority Members: Feb. 4,1971-Jan. 3,1973
Service Dates of Minority Members: Feb. 4,1971-Jan. 3,1973

Majority

Rank	Name	Party	State	Terms in: House	Terms in: Comm.
Chr	Holifield, Chet	Dem	Cal.	15	13
2nd	Brooks, Jack B.	Dem	Tex.	10	10
3rd	Fountain, Lawrence H.	Dem	N.C.	10	10
4th	Jones, Robert E. Jr.	Dem	Ala.	13	9
5th	Garmatz, Edward A.	Dem	Md.	13	9
6th	Moss, John E. Jr.	Dem	Cal.	10	9
7th	Fascell, Dante B.	Dem	Fla.	9	9
8th	Reuss, Henry S.	Dem	Wisc.	9	9
9th	Monagan, John S.	Dem	Conn.	7	7
10th	Macdonald, Torbert H.	Dem	Mass.	9	5
11th	Moorhead, William S.	Dem	Penn.	7	5
12th	Gallagher, Cornelius E.	Dem	N.J.	7	5
13th	Randall, William J.	Dem	Mo.	7	5
14th	Rosenthal, Benjamin S.	Dem	N.Y.	6	5
15th	Wright, James C. Jr.	Dem	Tex.	9	4
16th	St Germain, Fernand J.	Dem	R.I.	6	4
17th	Culver, John C.	Dem	Iowa	4	2
18th	Hicks, Floyd V.	Dem	Wash.	4	2
19th	Collins, George W.	Dem	Ill.	2	2
20th	Fuqua, Don	Dem	Fla.	5	1
21st	Conyers, John Jr.	Dem	Mich.	4	1
22nd	Alexander, William V. Jr.	Dem	Ark.	2	1
23rd	Abzug, Bella S.	Dem	N.Y.	1	1

Minority

Rank	Name	Party	State	Terms in: House	Terms in: Comm.
RM	Dwyer, Florence P.	Rep	N.J.	8	8
2nd	Reid, Ogden R.	Rep	N.Y.	5	5
3rd	Horton, Frank J.	Rep	N.Y.	5	5
4th	Erlenborn, John N.	Rep	Ill.	4	4
5th	Wydler, John W.	Rep	N.Y.	5	4
6th	Brown, Clarence J. Jr.	Rep	Ohio	4	4
7th	Vander Jagt, Guy A.	Rep	Mich.	4	3
8th	Gude, Gilbert	Rep	Md.	3	3
9th	McCloskey, Paul N. Jr.	Rep	Cal.	3	3
10th	Buchanan, John H. Jr.	Rep	Ala.	4	2
11th	Steiger, Sam	Rep	Ariz.	3	2
12th	Brown, Garry E.	Rep	Mich.	3	1
13th	Goldwater, Barry M. Jr.	Rep	Cal.	2	1
14th	Robinson, J. Kenneth	Rep	Va.	1	1
15th	Powell, Walter E.	Rep	Ohio	1	1
16th	Thone, Charles	Rep	Neb.	1	1

Changes:

Majority:

Collins, George W.	Dem	Ill.	Dec. 8,1972	Died in office.

Minority:

Robinson, J. Kenneth	Rep	Va.	Oct. 27,1971	Moved to Appropriations.
Heinz, H. John III	Rep	Penn.	Dec. 9,1971	Replaced Robinson.
Powell, Walter E.	Rep	Ohio	Feb. 7,1972	Moved to Armed Services.
Mallary, Richard W.	Rep	Vt.	Feb. 7,1972	Replaced Powell.
Reid, Ogden R.	Rep	N.Y.	Mar. 27,1972	Moved to Foreign Affairs as a Democrat.

Departures from the House:	**Majority**			**Minority**		
Defeated for Reelection	Monagan, John S.	Conn.	Dem	None		
Defeated for Renomination	Gallagher, Cornelius E.	N.J.	Dem	None		
Retired	Garmatz, Edward A.	Md.	Dem	Dwyer, Florence P.	N.J.	Rep
Departures from Committee:						
Became Ranking Minority Member of Aeronautical & Space Sciences	None			Goldwater, Barry M. Jr.	Cal.	Rep
Moved to Interstate & Foreign Commerce	None			Heinz, H. John III	Penn.	Rep

GOVERNMENT OPERATIONS / 93rd Congress

Service Dates of Committee Chair: Jan. 24,1973-Dec. 31,1974
Service Dates of Majority Members: Jan. 24,1973-Jan. 3,1975
Service Dates of Minority Members: Jan. 24,1973-Jan. 3,1975

Majority

Rank	Name	Party	State	Terms in: House	Terms in: Comm.
Chr	Holifield, Chet	Dem	Cal.	16	14
2nd	Brooks, Jack B.	Dem	Tex.	11	11
3rd	Fountain, Lawrence H.	Dem	N.C.	11	11
4th	Jones, Robert E. Jr.	Dem	Ala.	14	10
5th	Moss, John E. Jr.	Dem	Cal.	11	10
6th	Fascell, Dante B.	Dem	Fla.	10	10
7th	Reuss, Henry S.	Dem	Wisc.	10	10
8th	Macdonald, Torbert H.	Dem	Mass.	10	6
9th	Moorhead, William S.	Dem	Penn.	8	6
10th	Randall, William J.	Dem	Mo.	8	6
11th	Rosenthal, Benjamin S.	Dem	N.Y.	7	6
12th	Wright, James C. Jr.	Dem	Tex.	10	5
13th	St Germain, Fernand J.	Dem	R.I.	7	5
14th	Culver, John C.	Dem	Iowa	5	3
15th	Hicks, Floyd V.	Dem	Wash.	5	3
16th	Fuqua, Don	Dem	Fla.	6	2
17th	Conyers, John Jr.	Dem	Mich.	5	2
18th	Alexander, William V. Jr.	Dem	Ark.	3	2
19th	Abzug, Bella S.	Dem	N.Y.	2	2
20th	Donohue, Harold D.	Dem	Mass.	14	*2 1
21st	Stanton, James V.	Dem	Ohio	2	1
22nd	Ryan, Leo J.	Dem	Cal.	1	1
23rd	Collins, Cardiss	Dem	Ill.	1	1

Minority

Rank	Name	Party	State	Terms in: House	Terms in: Comm.
RM	Horton, Frank J.	Rep	N.Y.	6	6
2nd	Erlenborn, John N.	Rep	Ill.	5	5
3rd	Wydler, John W.	Rep	N.Y.	6	5
4th	Brown, Clarence J. Jr.	Rep	Ohio	5	5
5th	Vander Jagt, Guy A.	Rep	Mich.	5	4
6th	Gude, Gilbert	Rep	Md.	4	4
7th	McCloskey, Paul N. Jr.	Rep	Cal.	4	4
8th	Buchanan, John H. Jr.	Rep	Ala.	5	3
9th	Steiger, Sam	Rep	Ariz.	4	3
10th	Brown, Garry E.	Rep	Mich.	4	2
11th	Thone, Charles	Rep	Neb.	2	2
12th	Mallary, Richard W.	Rep	Vt.	2	2
13th	Parris, Stanford E.	Rep	Va.	1	1
14th	Regula, Ralph S.	Rep	Ohio	1	1
15th	Hinshaw, Andrew J.	Rep	Cal.	1	1
16th	Steelman, Alan W.	Rep	Tex.	1	1
17th	Pritchard, Joel M.	Rep	Wash.	1	1
18th	Hanrahan, Robert P.	Rep	Ill.	1	1

*2: Member's 2nd period of service on the committee.

Note: Democratic Party gains in the 1974 special elections in Ohio and California, led to the passage of House Resolution 1238, agreed to on July 17,1974, changing the size and party ratio on this committee to 24 Democrats and 18 Republicans.

Vacancy Filled:
Majority: 23rd seat by Collins on June 19,1973.

Addition:
Majority: 24th Burton, John L. Dem Cal. July 29,1974

Changes:
Majority:

Holifield, Chet	Dem	Cal.	Dec. 31,1974	Resigned and retired.
Donohue, Harold D.	Dem	Mass.	Dec. 31,1974	Resigned and retired.

Departures from the House:	Majority			Minority		
Elected to U.S. Senate	Culver, John C.	Iowa	Dem	None		
Defeated for Reelection	None			Hanrahan, Robert P.	Ill.	Rep
				Parris, Stanford E.	Va.	Rep
Lost Election to U.S. Senate	None			Mallary, Richard W.	Vt.	Rep
Departures from Committee:						
Moved to Appropriations	Alexander, William V. Jr.	Ark.	Dem	Regula, Ralph S.	Ohio	Rep
Moved to Education and Labor	None			Buchanan, John H. Jr.	Ala	Rep
Became Chair of Public Works & Transportation	Jones, Robert E. Jr.	Ala.	Dem	None		
Moved to Armed Services	None			Hinshaw, Andrew J.	Cal.	Rep
Moved to Ways and Means	None			Vander Jagt, Guy A.	Mich.	Rep

GOVERNMENT OPERATIONS / 94th Congress

Service Dates of Committee Chair: Jan. 20,1975-Jan. 3,1977
Service Dates of Majority Members: Jan. 20,1975-Jan. 3,1977
Service Dates of Minority Members: Jan. 28,1975-Jan. 3,1977

Majority

Rank	Name	Party	State	Terms in: House	Terms in: Comm.
Chr	Brooks, Jack B.	Dem	Tex.	12	12
2nd	Fountain, Lawrence H.	Dem	N.C.	12	12
3rd	Moss, John E. Jr.	Dem	Cal.	12	11
4th	Fascell, Dante B.	Dem	Fla.	11	11
5th	Reuss, Henry S.	Dem	Wisc.	11	11
6th	Macdonald, Torbert H.	Dem	Mass.	11	7
7th	Moorhead, William S.	Dem	Penn.	9	7
8th	Randall, William J.	Dem	Mo.	9	7
9th	Rosenthal, Benjamin S.	Dem	N.Y.	8	7
10th	Wright, James C. Jr.	Dem	Tex.	11	6
11th	St Germain, Fernand J.	Dem	R.I.	8	6
12th	Hicks, Floyd V.	Dem	Wash.	6	4
13th	Fuqua, Don	Dem	Fla.	7	3
14th	Conyers, John Jr.	Dem	Mich.	6	3
15th	Abzug, Bella S.	Dem	N.Y.	3	3
16th	Stanton, James V.	Dem	Ohio	3	2
17th	Ryan, Leo J.	Dem	Cal.	2	2
18th	Collins, Cardiss	Dem	Ill.	2	2
19th	Burton, John L.	Dem	Cal.	2	2
20th	Preyer, L. Richardson	Dem	N.C.	4	1
21st	Harrington, Michael J.	Dem	Mass.	4	1
22nd	Drinan, Robert F.	Dem	Mass.	3	1
23rd	Mezvinsky, Edward M.	Dem	Iowa	2	1
24th	Jordan, Barbara C.	Dem	Tex.	2	1
25th	English, Glenn L. Jr.	Dem	Okla.	1	1
26th	Levitas, Elliott H.	Dem	Ga.	1	1
27th	Evans, David W.	Dem	Ind.	1	1
28th	Moffett, Anthony J.(Toby)	Dem	Conn.	1	1
29th	Maguire, G. Andrew	Dem	N.J.	1	1

Minority

Rank	Name	Party	State	Terms in: House	Terms in: Comm.
RM	Horton, Frank J.	Rep	N.Y.	7	7
2nd	Erlenborn, John N.	Rep	Ill.	6	6
3rd	Wydler, John W.	Rep	N.Y.	7	6
4th	Brown, Clarence J. Jr.	Rep	Ohio	6	6
5th	Gude, Gilbert	Rep	Md.	5	5
6th	McCloskey, Paul N. Jr.	Rep	Cal.	5	5
7th	Steiger, Sam	Rep	Ariz.	5	4
8th	Brown, Garry E.	Rep	Mich.	5	3
9th	Thone, Charles	Rep	Neb.	3	3
10th	Steelman, Alan W.	Rep	Tex.	2	2
11th	Pritchard, Joel M.	Rep	Wash.	2	2
12th	Forsythe, Edwin B.	Rep	N.J.	4	1
13th	Kasten, Robert W. Jr.	Rep	Wisc.	1	1
14th	Gradison, Willis D. Jr.	Rep	Ohio	1	1

Changes:

Majority:

Name	Party	State	Date	Change
Reuss, Henry S.	Dem	Wisc.	Feb. 20,1975	Left committee to Chair Banking, Currency and Housing.
Aspin, Les	Dem	Wisc.	Feb. 19,1975	Replaced Reuss.
Macdonald, Torbert H.	Dem	Mass.	May 21,1976	Died in office.

	Majority			Minority		
Departures from the House:						
Defeated for Reelection	Mezvinsky, Edward M.	Iowa	Dem	None		
Lost Election to U.S. Senate	None			Steelman, Alan W.	Tex.	Rep
				Steiger, Sam	Ariz.	Rep
Lost Nomination to U.S. Senate	Abzug, Bella S.	N.Y.	Dem	None		
	Stanton, James V.	Ohio	Dem			
Retired	Hicks, Floyd V.	Wash.	Dem	Gude, Gilbert	Md.	Rep
	Randall, William J.	Mo.	Dem			
Departures from Committee:						
Became House Majority Leader	Wright, James C. Jr.	Tex.	Dem	None		
Moved to Ways and Means	None			Gradison, Willis D. Jr.	Ohio	Rep

GOVERNMENT OPERATIONS / 95th Congress

Service Dates of Committee Chair: Jan. 19,1977-Jan. 3,1979
Service Dates of Majority Members: Jan. 19,1977-Jan. 3,1979
Service Dates of Minority Members: Jan. 19,1977-Jan. 3,1979

Majority

Rank	Name	Party	State	Terms in: House	Terms in: Comm.
Chr	Brooks, Jack B.	Dem	Tex.	13	13
2nd	Fountain, Lawrence H.	Dem	N.C.	13	13
3rd	Moss, John E. Jr.	Dem	Cal.	13	12
4th	Fascell, Dante B.	Dem	Fla.	12	12
5th	Moorhead, William S.	Dem	Penn.	10	8
6th	Rosenthal, Benjamin S.	Dem	N.Y.	9	8
7th	St Germain, Fernand J.	Dem	R.I.	9	7
8th	Fuqua, Don	Dem	Fla.	8	4
9th	Conyers, John Jr.	Dem	Mich.	7	4
10th	Ryan, Leo J.	Dem	Cal.	3	3
11th	Collins, Cardiss	Dem	Ill.	3	3
12th	Burton, John L.	Dem	Cal.	3	3
13th	Preyer, L. Richardson	Dem	N.C.	5	2
14th	Harrington, Michael J.	Dem	Mass.	5	2
15th	Drinan, Robert F.	Dem	Mass.	4	2
16th	Jordan, Barbara C.	Dem	Tex.	3	2
17th	English, Glenn L. Jr.	Dem	Okla.	2	2
18th	Levitas, Elliott H.	Dem	Ga.	2	2
19th	Evans, David W.	Dem	Ind.	2	2
20th	Moffett, Anthony J.(Toby)	Dem	Conn.	2	2
21st	Maguire, G. Andrew	Dem	N.J.	2	2
22nd	Aspin, Les	Dem	Wisc.	4	2
23rd	Waxman, Henry A.	Dem	Cal.	2	1
24th	Hightower, Jack E.	Dem	Tex.	2	1
25th	Jenrette, John W. Jr.	Dem	S.C.	2	1
26th	Fithian, Floyd J.	Dem	Ind.	2	1
27th	Blouin, Michael T.	Dem	Iowa	2	1
28th	Kostmayer, Peter H.	Dem	Penn.	1	1
29th	Weiss, Theodore S.	Dem	N.Y.	1	1

Minority

Rank	Name	Party	State	Terms in: House	Terms in: Comm.
RM	Horton, Frank J.	Rep	N.Y.	8	8
2nd	Erlenborn, John N.	Rep	Ill.	7	7
3rd	Wydler, John W.	Rep	N.Y.	8	7
4th	Brown, Clarence J. Jr.	Rep	Ohio	7	7
5th	McCloskey, Paul N. Jr.	Rep	Cal.	6	6
6th	Brown, Garry E.	Rep	Mich.	6	4
7th	Thone, Charles	Rep	Neb.	4	4
8th	Pritchard, Joel M.	Rep	Wash.	3	3
9th	Forsythe, Edwin B.	Rep	N.J.	5	2
10th	Kasten, Robert W. Jr.	Rep	Wisc.	2	2
11th	Kindness, Thomas N.	Rep	Ohio	2	1
12th	Corcoran, Thomas J.	Rep	Ill.	1	1
13th	Quayle, J. Danforth	Rep	Ind.	1	1
14th	Walker, Robert S.	Rep	Penn.	1	1

Changes:

Majority:

Name	Party	State	Date	Change
Ryan, Leo J.	Dem	Cal.	Nov. 18,1978	Died in office.
Moss, John E. Jr.	Dem	Cal.	Dec. 31,1978	Resigned and retired.

Minority:

Name	Party	State	Date	Change
Forsythe, Edwin B.	Rep	N.J.	Mar. 3,1977	Moved to Science and Technology.
Stangeland, Arlan	Rep	Minn.	Mar. 3,1977	Replaced Forsythe.
Pritchard, Joel M.	Rep	Wash.	June 14,1977	Moved to International Affairs.
Cunningham, John E.	Rep	Wash.	June 14,1977	Replaced Pritchard.

Departures from the House:	Majority			Minority		
Elected Governor	None			Thone, Charles	Neb.	Rep
Defeated for Reelection	Blouin, Michael T.	Iowa	Dem	Brown, Garry E.	Mich.	Rep
				Cunningham, John E.	Wash.	Rep
Lost Election for Governor	None			Kasten, Robert W. Jr.	Wisc.	Rep
Retired	Harrington, Michael J.	Mass.	Dem	None		
	Jordan, Barbara C.	Tex.	Dem			

Departures from Committee:	Majority			Minority		
Moved to Appropriations	Hightower, Jack E.	Tex.	Dem	None		
	Jenrette, John W. Jr.	S.C.	Dem			
Moved to Interstate & Foreign Commerce	None			Corcoran, Thomas J.	Ill.	Rep
Moved to Foreign Affairs	None			Quayle, J. Danforth	Ind.	Rep

GOVERNMENT OPERATIONS / 96th Congress

Service Dates of Committee Chair: Jan. 24,1979-Jan. 3,1981
Service Dates of Majority Members: Jan. 24,1979-Jan. 3,1981
Service Dates of Minority Members: Jan. 24,1979-Jan. 3,1981

Majority

Rank	Name	Party	State	Terms in: House	Terms in: Comm.
Chr	Brooks, Jack B.	Dem	Tex.	14	14
2nd	Fountain, Lawrence H.	Dem	N.C.	14	14
3rd	Fascell, Dante B.	Dem	Fla.	13	13
4th	Moorhead, William S.	Dem	Penn.	11	9
5th	Rosenthal, Benjamin S.	Dem	N.Y.	10	9
6th	St Germain, Fernand J.	Dem	R.I.	10	8
7th	Fuqua, Don	Dem	Fla.	9	5
8th	Conyers, John Jr.	Dem	Mich.	8	5
9th	Collins, Cardiss	Dem	Ill.	4	4
10th	Burton, John L.	Dem	Cal.	4	4
11th	Preyer, L. Richardson	Dem	N.C.	6	3
12th	Drinan, Robert F.	Dem	Mass.	5	3
13th	English, Glenn L. Jr.	Dem	Okla.	3	3
14th	Levitas, Elliott H.	Dem	Ga.	3	3
15th	Evans, David W.	Dem	Ind.	3	3
16th	Moffett, Anthony J.(Toby)	Dem	Conn.	3	3
17th	Maguire, G. Andrew	Dem	N.J.	3	3
18th	Aspin, Les	Dem	Wisc.	5	3
19th	Waxman, Henry A.	Dem	Cal.	3	2
20th	Fithian, Floyd J.	Dem	Ind.	3	2
21st	Kostmayer, Peter H.	Dem	Penn.	2	2
22nd	Weiss, Theodore S.	Dem	N.Y.	2	2
23rd	Synar, Michael L.	Dem	Okla.	1	1
24th	Matsui, Robert T.	Dem	Cal.	1	1
25th	Atkinson, Eugene V.	Dem	Penn.	1	1

Minority

Rank	Name	Party	State	Terms in: House	Terms in: Comm.
RM	Horton, Frank J.	Rep	N.Y.	9	9
2nd	Erlenborn, John N.	Rep	Ill.	8	8
3rd	Wydler, John W.	Rep	N.Y.	9	8
4th	Brown, Clarence J. Jr.	Rep	Ohio	8	8
5th	McCloskey, Paul N. Jr.	Rep	Cal.	7	7
6th	Kindness, Thomas N.	Rep	Ohio	3	2
7th	Walker, Robert S.	Rep	Penn.	2	2
8th	Stangeland, Arlan	Rep	Minn.	2	2
9th	Butler, M. Caldwell	Rep	Va.	5	1
10th	Williams, Lyle	Rep	Ohio	1	1
11th	Jeffries, James E.	Rep	Kans.	1	1
12th	Snowe, Olympia J. B.	Rep	Me.	1	1
13th	Grisham, Wayne R.	Rep	Cal.	1	1
14th	Deckard, H. Joel	Rep	Ind.	1	1

	Majority		Minority	
Departures from the House:				
Defeated for Reelection	Kostmayer, Peter H.	Penn. Dem	None	
	Maguire, G. Andrew	N.J. Dem		
	Preyer, L. Richardson	N.C. Dem		
Retired	Drinan, Robert F.	Mass. Dem	Wydler, John W.	N.Y. Rep
	Moorhead, William S.	Penn. Dem		
Departures from Committee:				
Moved to Budget	Aspin, Les	Wisc. Dem	None	
Moved to Ways and Means	Matsui, Robert T.	Cal. Dem	None	
Became Chair of Banking, Finance & Urban Affairs	St Germain, Fernand J.	R.I. Dem	None	
Moved to Post Office & Civil Service; Public Works & Transportation	None		Grisham, Wayne R.	Cal. Rep
Moved to Veterans' Affairs; Public Works & Transportation	None		Jeffries, James E.	Kans. Rep
Moved to Foreign Affairs	None		Snowe, Olympia J. B.	Me. Rep
Moved to Agriculture	None		Stangeland, Arlan	Minn. Rep

GOVERNMENT OPERATIONS / 97th Congress

Service Dates of Committee Chair: Jan. 28,1981-Jan. 3,1983
Service Dates of Majority Members: Jan. 28,1981-Jan. 3,1983
Service Dates of Minority Members: Jan. 28,1981-Jan. 3,1983

Majority

Rank	Name	Party	State	Terms in: House	Terms in: Comm.
Chr	Brooks, Jack B.	Dem	Tex.	15	15
2nd	Fountain, Lawrence H.	Dem	N.C.	15	15
3rd	Fascell, Dante B.	Dem	Fla.	14	14
4th	Rosenthal, Benjamin S.	Dem	N.Y.	11	10
5th	Fuqua, Don	Dem	Fla.	10	6
6th	Conyers, John Jr.	Dem	Mich.	9	6
7th	Collins, Cardiss	Dem	Ill.	5	5
8th	Burton, John L.	Dem	Cal.	5	5
9th	English, Glenn L. Jr.	Dem	Okla.	4	4
10th	Levitas, Elliott H.	Dem	Ga.	4	4
11th	Evans, David W.	Dem	Ind.	4	4
12th	Moffett, Anthony J.(Toby)	Dem	Conn.	4	4
13th	Waxman, Henry A.	Dem	Cal.	4	3
14th	Fithian, Floyd J.	Dem	Ind.	4	3
15th	Weiss, Theodore S.	Dem	N.Y.	3	3
16th	Synar, Michael L.	Dem	Okla.	2	2
17th	Atkinson, Eugene V.	Dem	Penn.	2	2
18th	Neal, Stephen L.	Dem	N.C.	4	1
19th	Barnard, D. Douglas Jr.	Dem	Ga.	3	1
20th	Peyser, Peter A.	Dem	N.Y.	5	1
21st	Frank, Barney	Dem	Mass.	1	1
22nd	Washington, Harold	Dem	Ill.	1	1
23rd	Lantos, Tom	Dem	Cal.	1	1

Minority

Rank	Name	Party	State	Terms in: House	Terms in: Comm.
RM	Horton, Frank J.	Rep	N.Y.	10	10
2nd	Erlenborn, John N.	Rep	Ill.	9	9
3rd	Brown, Clarence J. Jr.	Rep	Ohio	9	9
4th	McCloskey, Paul N. Jr.	Rep	Cal.	8	8
5th	Kindness, Thomas N.	Rep	Ohio	4	3
6th	Walker, Robert S.	Rep	Penn.	3	3
7th	Butler, M. Caldwell	Rep	Va.	6	2
8th	Williams, Lyle	Rep	Ohio	2	2
9th	Deckard, H. Joel	Rep	Ind.	2	2
10th	Clinger, William F. Jr.	Rep	Penn.	2	1
11th	McGrath, Raymond J.	Rep	N.Y.	1	1
12th	Daub, Hal	Rep	Neb.	1	1
13th	Hiler, John P.	Rep	Ind.	1	1
14th	Dreier, David	Rep	Cal.	1	1
15th	Bailey, Wendell	Rep	Mo.	1	1
16th	DeNardis, Lawrence J.	Rep	Conn.	1	1
17th	Gregg, Judd	Rep	N.H.	1	1

Note: Eugene Atkinson of Pennsylvania resigned from the Democratic Party and joined the Republican Party on Oct. 14,1981, resulting in a change in the party ratio to 22 Democrats and 18 Republicans.

Changes:

Majority:

Name	Party	State	Date	Change
Atkinson, Eugene V.	Dem	Penn.	Oct. 14,1981	Resigned Democractic Party; lost majority assignment.
Kennelly, Barbara B.	Dem	Conn.	Feb. 24,1982	Replaced Atkinson.

Minority:

Name	Party	State	Date	Change
Dreier, David	Rep	Cal.	July 24,1981	Moved to Banking, Finance, and Urban Affairs.
Oxley, Michael G.	Rep	Ohio	Sep. 16,1981	Replaced Dreier.
Atkinson, Eugene V.	Rep	Penn.	Oct. 14,1981	Rejoined committee as a Republican.

Departures from the House:

	Majority	State	Party	Minority	State	Party
Defeated for Reelection	Peyser, Peter A.	N.Y.	Dem	Atkinson, Eugene V.	Penn.	Rep
				Bailey, Wendell	Mo.	Rep
				Deckard, H. Joel	Ind.	Rep
				DeNardis, Lawrence J.	Conn.	Rep
Defeated for Renomination	Evans, David W.	Ind.	Dem	None		
Lost Election to U.S. Senate	Fithian, Floyd J.	Ind.	Dem	None		
	Moffett, Anthony J.(Toby)	Conn.	Dem			
Lost Nomination to U.S. Senate	None			McCloskey, Paul N. Jr.	Cal.	Rep
Lost Election for Governor	None			Brown, Clarence J. Jr.	Ohio	Rep
Retired	Burton, John L.	Cal.	Dem	Butler, M. Caldwell	Va.	Rep
	Fountain, Lawrence H.	N.C.	Dem			
Died in office, Jan. 4,1983	Rosenthal, Benjamin S.	N.Y.	Dem	None		

Departures from Committee:

	Majority	State	Party	Minority	State	Party
Moved to Ways and Means	Kennelly, Barbara B.	Conn.	Dem	None		
Moved to Banking, Finance & Urban Affairs	None			Hiler, John P.	Ind.	Rep
Moved to Post Office & Civil Service	None			Daub, Hal	Neb.	Rep
No new assignment	Washington, Harold	Ill.	Dem	None		

GOVERNMENT OPERATIONS / 98th Congress

Service Dates of Committee Chair: Jan. 6,1983-Jan. 3,1985
Service Dates of Majority Members: Jan. 6,1983-Jan. 3,1985
Service Dates of Minority Members: Jan. 6,1983-Jan. 3,1985

Majority

Rank Name	Party	State	Terms in: House	Terms in: Comm.
Chr Brooks, Jack B.	Dem	Tex.	16	16
2nd Fascell, Dante B.	Dem	Fla.	15	15
3rd Fuqua, Don	Dem	Fla.	11	7
4th Conyers, John Jr.	Dem	Mich.	10	7
5th Collins, Cardiss	Dem	Ill.	6	6
6th English, Glenn L. Jr.	Dem	Okla.	5	5
7th Levitas, Elliott H.	Dem	Ga.	5	5
8th Waxman, Henry A.	Dem	Cal.	5	4
9th Weiss, Theodore S.	Dem	N.Y.	4	4
10th Synar, Michael L.	Dem	Okla.	3	3
11th Neal, Stephen L.	Dem	N.C.	5	2
12th Barnard, D. Douglas Jr.	Dem	Ga.	4	2
13th Frank, Barney	Dem	Mass.	2	2
14th Lantos, Tom	Dem	Cal.	2	2
15th Coleman, Ronald D.	Dem	Tex.	1	1
16th Wise, Robert E. Jr.	Dem	W.Va.	1	1
17th Boxer, Barbara	Dem	Cal.	1	1
18th Levin, Sander M.	Dem	Mich.	1	1
19th MacKay, Kenneth H.	Dem	Fla.	1	1
20th Levine, Mel	Dem	Cal.	1	1
21st Owens, Major R.	Dem	N.Y.	1	1
22nd Towns, Edolphus	Dem	N.Y.	1	1
23rd Spratt, John M. Jr.	Dem	S.C.	1	1
24th Kolter, Joseph P.	Dem	Penn.	1	1
25th Erdreich, Ben	Dem	Ala.	1	1

Minority

Rank Name	Party	State	Terms in: House	Terms in: Comm.
RM Horton, Frank J.	Rep	N.Y.	11	11
2nd Erlenborn, John N.	Rep	Ill.	10	10
3rd Kindness, Thomas N.	Rep	Ohio	5	4
4th Walker, Robert S.	Rep	Penn.	4	4
5th Williams, Lyle	Rep	Ohio	3	3
6th Clinger, William F. Jr.	Rep	Penn.	3	2
7th McGrath, Raymond J.	Rep	N.Y.	2	2
8th Gregg, Judd	Rep	N.H.	2	2
9th Burton, Dan	Rep	Ind.	1	1
10th McKernan, John R. Jr.	Rep	Me.	1	1
11th Lewis, Tom	Rep	Fla.	1	1
12th McCandless, Alfred A.	Rep	Cal.	1	1
13th Craig, Larry E.	Rep	Ida.	2	1
14th Schaefer, Daniel L.	Rep	Colo.	1	1

Vacancies Filled:
Minority: 13th seat by Craig on Mar. 1,1983 and the 14th seat by Schaefer on Apr. 21,1983.

Changes:
Majority:

Fascell, Dante B.	Dem	Fla.	Jan. 25,1984	Left committee to chair Foreign Affairs.
Kleczka, Gerald D.	Dem	Wisc.	May 16,1984	Replaced Fascell.
MacKay, Kenneth H.	Dem	Fla.	Sep. 13,1984	Moved to Foreign Affairs.
Darden, George W. (Buddy)	Dem	Ga.	Sep. 13,1984	Replaced MacKay.

	Majority			Minority		
Departures from the House:						
Defeated for Reelection	Levitas, Elliott H.	Ga.	Dem	Williams, Lyle	Ohio	Rep
Retired	None			Erlenborn, John N.	Ill.	Rep
Departures from Committee:						
Moved to Appropriations	Coleman, Ronald D.	Tex.	Dem	None		
Moved to Interior & Insular Affairs	Darden, George W. (Buddy)	Ga.	Dem	None		
Moved to Foreign Affairs; Post Office & Civil Service	None			Burton, Dan	Ind.	Rep
Moved to Ways and Means	None			Gregg, Judd	N.H.	Rep
				McGrath, Raymond J.	N.Y.	Rep
Moved to Agriculture				Lewis, Tom	Fla.	Rep
Moved to Energy and Commerce	None			Schaefer, Daniel L.	Colo.	Rep

GOVERNMENT OPERATIONS / 99th Congress

Service Dates of Committee Chair: Jan. 7,1985-Jan. 3,1987
Service Dates of Majority Members: Jan. 30,1985-Jan. 3,1987
Service Dates of Minority Members: Jan. 30,1985-Jan. 3,1987

Majority

Rank Name	Party	State	Terms in: House	Terms in: Comm.
Chr Brooks, Jack B.	Dem	Tex.	17	17
2nd Fuqua, Don	Dem	Fla.	12	8
3rd Conyers, John Jr.	Dem	Mich.	11	8
4th Collins, Cardiss	Dem	Ill.	7	7
5th English, Glenn L. Jr.	Dem	Okla.	6	6
6th Waxman, Henry A.	Dem	Cal.	6	5
7th Weiss, Theodore S.	Dem	N.Y.	5	5
8th Synar, Michael L.	Dem	Okla.	4	4
9th Neal, Stephen L.	Dem	N.C.	6	3
10th Barnard, D. Douglas Jr.	Dem	Ga.	5	3
11th Frank, Barney	Dem	Mass.	3	3
12th Lantos, Tom	Dem	Cal.	3	3
13th Wise, Robert E. Jr.	Dem	W.Va.	2	2
14th Boxer, Barbara	Dem	Cal.	2	2
15th Levin, Sander M.	Dem	Mich.	2	2
16th Levine, Mel	Dem	Cal.	2	2
17th Owens, Major R.	Dem	N.Y.	2	2
18th Towns, Edolphus	Dem	N.Y.	2	2
19th Spratt, John M. Jr.	Dem	S.C.	2	2
20th Kolter, Joseph P.	Dem	Penn.	2	2
21st Erdreich, Ben	Dem	Ala.	2	2
22nd Kleczka, Gerald D.	Dem	Wisc.	2	2
23rd Bustamante, Albert G.	Dem	Tex.	1	1

Minority

Rank Name	Party	State	Terms in: House	Terms in: Comm.
RM Horton, Frank J.	Rep	N.Y.	12	12
2nd Kindness, Thomas N.	Rep	Ohio	6	5
3rd Walker, Robert S.	Rep	Penn.	5	5
4th Clinger, William F. Jr.	Rep	Penn.	4	3
5th McKernan, John R. Jr.	Rep	Me.	2	2
6th McCandless, Alfred A.	Rep	Cal.	2	2
7th Craig, Larry E.	Rep	Ida.	3	2
8th Saxton, H. James	Rep	N.J.	1	1
9th Swindall, Patrick Lynn	Rep	Ga.	1	1
10th DeLay, Thomas D.	Rep	Tex.	1	1
11th Monson, David S.	Rep	Utah	1	1
12th DioGuardi, Joseph J.	Rep	N.Y.	1	1
13th Rowland, John G.	Rep	Conn.	1	1
14th Armey, Richard	Rep	Tex.	1	1
15th Lightfoot, Jim Ross	Rep	Iowa	1	1
16th Miller, John R.	Rep	Wash.	1	1

Changes:

Majority:				
Levine, Mel	Dem	Cal.	Feb. 19,1985	Moved to Interior and Insular Affairs on Feb. 6,1985.
Martinez, Matthew G.	Dem	Cal.	Feb. 27,1985	Replaced Levine.
Minority:				
McKernan, John R. Jr.	Rep	Me.	Feb. 27,1985	Moved to Education and Labor.
Nielson, Howard C.	Rep	Utah	Feb. 27,1985	Replaced McKernan, ranked below Craig.
Monson, David S.	Rep	Utah	June 19,1985	Moved to Public Works and Transportation.
Rowland, John G.	Rep	Conn.	Oct. 10,1985	Moved to Public Works and Transportation.
Boulter, Beau	Rep	Tex.	Oct. 10,1985	Replaced Monson.
Grotberg, John E.	Rep	Ill.	Oct. 10,1985	Replaced Rowland.
Grotberg, John E.	Rep	Ill.	Nov. 15,1986	Died in office.

	Majority			Minority		
Departures from the House:						
Lost Election to U.S. Senate	None			Kindness, Thomas N.	Ohio	Rep
Retired	Fuqua, Don	Fla.	Dem	None		
Departures from Committee:						
Ceases active membership while serving on Budget	Boxer, Barbara	Cal.	Dem	None		
Moved to Ways and Means	Levin, Sander M.	Mich.	Dem			
Moved to Budget	None			Armey, Richard	Tex.	Rep
Moved to Appropriations	None			DeLay, Thomas D.	Tex.	Rep
Moved to Foreign Affairs	None			Miller, John R.	Wash.	Rep
Moved to Banking, Finance & Urban Affairs	None			Saxton, H. James	N.J.	Rep
				Swindall, Patrick Lynn	Ga.	Rep

GOVERNMENT OPERATIONS / 100th Congress

Service Dates of Committee Chair: Jan. 8,1987-Jan. 3,1989
Service Dates of Majority Members: Jan. 22,1987-Jan. 3,1989
Service Dates of Minority Members: Jan. 21,1987-Jan. 3,1989

Majority

Rank	Name	Party	State	Terms in: House	Terms in: Comm.
Chr	Brooks, Jack B.	Dem	Tex.	18	18
2nd	Conyers, John Jr.	Dem	Mich.	12	9
3rd	Collins, Cardiss	Dem	Ill.	8	8
4th	English, Glenn L. Jr.	Dem	Okla.	7	7
5th	Waxman, Henry A.	Dem	Cal.	7	6
6th	Weiss, Theodore S.	Dem	N.Y.	6	6
7th	Synar, Michael L.	Dem	Okla.	5	5
8th	Neal, Stephen L.	Dem	N.C.	7	4
9th	Barnard, D. Douglas Jr.	Dem	Ga.	6	4
10th	Frank, Barney	Dem	Mass.	4	4
11th	Lantos, Tom	Dem	Cal.	4	4
12th	Wise, Robert E. Jr.	Dem	W.Va.	3	3
13th	Owens, Major R.	Dem	N.Y.	3	3
14th	Towns, Edolphus	Dem	N.Y.	3	3
15th	Spratt, John M. Jr.	Dem	S.C.	3	3
16th	Kolter, Joseph P.	Dem	Penn.	3	3
17th	Erdreich, Ben	Dem	Ala.	3	3
18th	Kleczka, Gerald D.	Dem	Wisc.	3	3
19th	Bustamante, Albert G.	Dem	Tex.	2	2
20th	Martinez, Matthew G.	Dem	Cal.	4	2
21st	Sawyer, Thomas C.	Dem	Ohio	1	1
22nd	Skaggs, David E.	Dem	Colo.	1	1
23rd	Slaughter, Louise M.	Dem	N.Y.	1	1
24th	Grant, Bill	Dem	Fla.	1	1

Minority

Rank	Name	Party	State	Terms in: House	Terms in: Comm.
RM	Horton, Frank J.	Rep	N.Y.	13	13
2nd	Walker, Robert S.	Rep	Penn.	6	6
3rd	Clinger, William F. Jr.	Rep	Penn.	5	4
4th	McCandless, Alfred A.	Rep	Cal.	3	3
5th	Craig, Larry E.	Rep	Ida.	4	3
6th	Nielson, Howard C.	Rep	Utah	3	2
7th	DioGuardi, Joseph J.	Rep	N.Y.	2	2
8th	Lightfoot, Jim Ross	Rep	Iowa	2	2
9th	Boulter, Beau	Rep	Tex.	2	2
10th	Lukens, Donald E. (Buz)	Rep	Ohio	3	1
11th	Houghton, Amory Jr.	Rep	N.Y.	1	1
12th	Hastert, J. Dennis	Rep	Ill.	1	1
13th	Kyl, Jon	Rep	Ariz.	1	1
14th	Konnyu, Ernest L.	Rep	Cal.	1	1
15th	Inhofe, James M.	Rep	Okla.	1	1

Changes:

Majority:

Skaggs, David E.	Dem	Colo.	Apr. 7,1987	Moved to Science, Space and Technology.
Pelosi, Nancy	Dem	Cal.	June 18,1987	Replaced Skaggs.

Minority:

Konnyu, Ernest L.	Rep	Cal.	Nov. 4,1987	Moved to Merchant Marine and Fisheries.
Shays, Christopher	Rep	Conn.	Nov. 4,1987	Replaced Konnyu.

	Majority			Minority		
Departures from the House:						
Defeated for Reelection	None			DioGuardi, Joseph J.	N.Y.	Rep
Lost Election to U.S. Senate	None			Boulter, Beau	Tex.	Rep
Departures from Committee:						
Became Chair of Judiciary	Brooks, Jack B.	Tex.	Dem	None		
Moved to Post Office & Civil Service	Sawyer, Thomas C.	Ohio	Dem	None		
Moved to Foreign Affairs	None			Houghton, Amory Jr.	N.Y.	Rep
Moved to Public Works & Transportation	None			Craig, Larry E.	Ida.	Rep
Moved to Merchant Marine & Fisheries	None			Inhofe, James M.	Okla.	Rep
Moved to Interior & Insular Affairs	None			Lightfoot, Jim Ross	Iowa	Rep

GOVERNMENT OPERATIONS / 101st Congress

Service Dates of Committee Chair: Jan. 3,1989-Jan. 3,1991
Service Dates of Majority Members: Jan. 19,1989-Jan. 3,1991
Service Dates of Minority Members: Jan. 20,1989-Jan. 3,1991

Majority

Rank Name	Party	State	Terms in: House	Terms in: Comm.
Chr Conyers, John Jr.	Dem	Mich.	13	10
2nd Collins, Cardiss	Dem	Ill.	9	9
3rd English, Glenn L. Jr.	Dem	Okla.	8	8
4th Waxman, Henry A.	Dem	Cal.	8	7
5th Weiss, Theodore S.	Dem	N.Y.	7	7
6th Synar, Michael L.	Dem	Okla.	6	6
7th Neal, Stephen L.	Dem	N.C.	8	5
8th Barnard, D. Douglas Jr.	Dem	Ga.	7	5
9th Frank, Barney	Dem	Mass.	5	5
10th Lantos, Tom	Dem	Cal.	5	5
11th Wise, Robert E. Jr.	Dem	W.Va.	4	4
12th Boxer, Barbara	Dem	Cal.	4	4
13th Owens, Major R.	Dem	N.Y.	4	4
14th Towns, Edolphus	Dem	N.Y.	4	4
15th Spratt, John M. Jr.	Dem	S.C.	4	4
16th Kolter, Joseph P.	Dem	Penn.	4	4
17th Erdreich, Ben	Dem	Ala.	4	4
18th Kleczka, Gerald D.	Dem	Wisc.	4	4
19th Bustamante, Albert G.	Dem	Tex.	3	3
20th Martinez, Matthew G.	Dem	Cal.	5	3
21st Slaughter, Louise M.	Dem	N.Y.	2	2
22nd Grant, Bill	Dem	Fla.	2	2
23rd Pelosi, Nancy	Dem	Cal.	2	2
24th Payne, Donald M.	Dem	N.J.	2	1

Minority

Rank Name	Party	State	Terms in: House	Terms in: Comm.
RM Horton, Frank J.	Rep	N.Y.	14	14
2nd Walker, Robert S.	Rep	Penn.	7	7
3rd Clinger, William F. Jr.	Rep	Penn.	6	5
4th McCandless, Alfred A.	Rep	Cal.	4	4
5th Nielson, Howard C.	Rep	Utah	4	3
6th Lukens, Donald E. (Buz)	Rep	Ohio	4	2
7th Hastert, J. Dennis	Rep	Ill.	2	2
8th Kyl, Jon	Rep	Ariz.	2	2
9th Shays, Christopher	Rep	Conn.	2	2
10th Smith, Peter P.	Rep	Vt.	1	1
11th Schiff, Steven H.	Rep	N.M.	1	1
12th Douglas, Charles	Rep	N.H.	1	1
13th Smith, Larkin	Rep	Miss.	1	1
14th Cox, C. Christopher	Rep	Cal.	1	1
15th Thomas, Craig	Rep	Wyo.	1	1

Note: Barbara Boxer (Dem-Cal.), having served on the Budget Committee during the previous two Congresses, returned to active service on this committee with her seniority intact.

Vacancy Filled:
Minority: 15th seat by Thomas on May 4,1989.

Changes:

Majority:

Grant, Bill	Dem	Fla.	Feb. 22,1989	Resigned Democratic Party; lost majority assignment.
Bates, Jim	Dem	Cal.	Mar. 1,1989	Replaced Grant.
Slaughter, Louise M.	Dem	N.Y.	July 25,1989	Moved to Rules.
Condit, Gary	Dem	Cal.	Oct. 16,1989	Replaced Slaughter.
Kolter, Joseph P.	Dem	Penn.	Feb. 5,1990	Left committee; no new assignment.
Eckart, Dennis E.	Dem	Ohio	Apr. 4,1990	Replaced Kolter.
Spratt, John M. Jr.	Dem	S.C.	June 14,1990	Moved to Budget.
Mink, Patsy T.	Dem	Hai.	Oct. 10,1990	Replaced Spratt.

Minority:

Walker, Robert S.	Rep	Penn.	May 10,1989	Left committee; no new assignment.
Armey, Richard	Rep	Tex.	Aug. 3,1989	Replaced Walker; ranked below Nielson.
Smith, Larkin	Rep	Miss.	Aug. 13,1989	Died in office.
Ros-Lehtinen, Ileana	Rep	Fla.	Nov. 3,1989	Replaced Smith.
Lukens, Donald E. (Buz)	Rep	Ohio	Oct. 24,1990	Resigned; defeated for renomination.

Departures from the House:

	Majority			Minority		
Defeated for Reelection	Bates, Jim	Cal.	Dem	Douglas, Charles	N.H.	Rep
				Smith, Peter P.	Vt.	Rep
Retired	None			Nielson, Howard C.	Utah	Rep

Departures from Committee:

Moved to Budget	Frank, Barney	Mass. Dem	None	
Moved to Appropriations; Standards of Official Conduct	Pelosi, Nancy	Cal. Dem	None	
Moved to Banking, Finance & Urban Affairs	None		Armey, Richard	Tex. Rep
No new assignment	Eckart, Dennis E.	Ohio Dem	None	

GOVERNMENT OPERATIONS / 102nd Congress

Service Dates of Committee Chair: Jan. 24,1991-Jan. 3,1993
Service Dates of Majority Members: Jan. 24,1991-Jan. 3,1993
Service Dates of Minority Members: Jan. 24,1991-Jan. 3,1993

Majority

Rank	Name	Party	State	Terms in: House	Terms in: Comm.
Chr	Conyers, John Jr.	Dem	Mich.	14	11
2nd	Collins, Cardiss	Dem	Ill.	10	10
3rd	English, Glenn L. Jr.	Dem	Okla.	9	9
4th	Waxman, Henry A.	Dem	Cal.	9	8
5th	Weiss, Theodore S.	Dem	N.Y.	8	8
6th	Synar, Michael L.	Dem	Okla.	7	7
7th	Neal, Stephen L.	Dem	N.C.	9	6
8th	Barnard, D. Douglas Jr.	Dem	Ga.	8	6
9th	Lantos, Tom	Dem	Cal.	6	6
10th	Wise, Robert E. Jr.	Dem	W.Va.	5	5
11th	Boxer, Barbara	Dem	Cal.	5	5
12th	Owens, Major R.	Dem	N.Y.	5	5
13th	Towns, Edolphus	Dem	N.Y.	5	5
14th	Erdreich, Ben	Dem	Ala.	5	5
15th	Kleczka, Gerald D.	Dem	Wisc.	5	5
16th	Bustamante, Albert G.	Dem	Tex.	4	4
17th	Martinez, Matthew G.	Dem	Cal.	6	4
18th	Payne, Donald M.	Dem	N.J.	3	2
19th	Condit, Gary	Dem	Cal.	2	2
20th	Mink, Patsy T.	Dem	Hai.	8	2
21st	Thornton, Ray	Dem	Ark.	1	1
22nd	Peterson, Collin C.	Dem	Minn.	1	1
23rd	DeLauro, Rosa	Dem	Conn.	1	1
24th	Luken, Charles	Dem	Ohio	1	1
25th	Cox, John W. Jr.	Dem	Ill.	1	1

Minority

Rank	Name	Party	State	Terms in: House	Terms in: Comm.
RM	Horton, Frank J.	Rep	N.Y.	15	15
2nd	Clinger, William F. Jr.	Rep	Penn.	7	6
3rd	McCandless, Alfred A.	Rep	Cal.	5	5
4th	Hastert, J. Dennis	Rep	Ill.	3	3
5th	Kyl, Jon	Rep	Ariz.	3	3
6th	Shays, Christopher	Rep	Conn.	3	3
7th	Schiff, Steven H.	Rep	N.M.	2	2
8th	Cox, C. Christopher	Rep	Cal.	2	2
9th	Thomas, Craig	Rep	Wyo.	2	2
10th	Ros-Lehtinen, Ileana	Rep	Fla.	2	2
11th	Machtley, Ronald K.	Rep	R.I.	2	1
12th	Zimmer, Richard	Rep	N.J.	1	1
13th	Zeliff, William	Rep	N.H.	1	1
14th	Hobson, David L.	Rep	Ohio	1	1
15th	Klug, Scott L.	Rep	Wisc.	1	1

Third Party:

Name	Party	State	House	Comm.
Sanders, Bernard	Ind	Vt.	1	1

Note: Bernard Sanders (Ind-Vt.) was elected to the 102nd Congress as an Independent. Assigned to the committee by the Democratic Caucus on Jan. 24,1991, he was not allowed to accrue seniority, nor was he included in the party ratio.

Changes:

Majority:

Weiss, Theodore S.	Dem	N.Y.	Sep. 14,1992	Died in office.

HOUSE ADMINISTRATION

Jurisdiction, 1947

Established by the Legislative Reorganization Act of 1946:

[Section 121.(1)(j)]

(1) Committee on House Administration.

(A) Employment of persons by the House, including clerks for Members and committees, and reporters of debates.
(B) Expenditure of the contingent fund of the House.
(C) The auditing and settling of all accounts which may be charged to the contingent fund.
(D) Measures relating to accounts of the House generally.
(E) Appropriations from the contingent fund.
(F) Measures relating to services to the House, including the House Restaurant and administration of the House Office Buildings and of the House wing of the Capitol.
(G) Measures relating to the travel of Members of the House.
(H) Measures relating to the assignment of office space for Members and committees.
(I) Measures relating to the disposition of useless executive papers.
(J) Except as provided in paragraph (o) 8, matters relating to the Library of Congress and the House Library; statuary and pictures; acceptance or purchase of works of art for the Capitol; the Botanic Gardens; management of the Library of Congress; purchase of books and manuscripts; erection of monuments to the memory of individuals.
(K) Except as provided in paragraph (o) 8, matters relating to the Smithsonian Institution and the incorporation of similar institutions.
(L) Matters relating to printing and correction of the Congressional Record.
(M) Measures relating to the election of the President, Vice President, or Members of Congress; corrupt practices; contested.elections; credentials and qualifications; and Federal elections generally.

(2) Such committee shall also have the duty of--

(A) Examining all bills, amendments, and joint resolution after passage by the House; and in cooperation with the Senate Committee on Rules and Administration, of examining all bills and joint resolutions which shall have passed both Houses, to see that they are correctly enrolled; and when signed by the Speaker of the House and the President of the Senate, shall forthwith present the same, when they shall have originated in the House, to the President of the United States in person, and report the fact and date of such presentation to the House;
(B) reporting to the Sergeant at Arms of the House the travel of Members of the House;
(C) arranging a suitable program for each day observed by the House of Representatives as a memorial day in memory of Members of the Senate and House of Representatives who have died during the preceding period, and to arrange for the publication of the proceedings thereof.

Jurisdiction, 1992

Jurisdiction contained in Rules of the House of Representatives, (as revised to July 1, 1992):

[Rule X. 1. (k)]

Committee on House Administration.

(1) Appropriations from the contingent fund.
(2) Auditing and settling of all accounts which may be charged to the contingent fund.
(3) Employment of persons by the House, including clerks for Members and committees, and reporters of debates.
(4) Except as provided in clause l(p) (4) [Committee on Public Works and Transportation], matters relating to the Library of Congress and the House Library; statuary and pictures; acceptance or purchase of works of art for the Capitol; the Botanic Gardens; management of the Library of Congress; purchase of books and manuscripts; erection of monuments to the memory of individuals.
(5) Except as provided in clause l(p)(4), matters relating to the Smithsonian Institution and the incorporation of similar

institutions.

(6) Expenditure of contingent fund of the House.

(7) Matters relating to printing and correction of the Congressional Record.

(8) Measures relating to accounts of the House generally.

(9) Measures relating to assignment of office space for Members and committees.

(10) Measures relating to the disposition of useless executive papers.

(11) Measures relating to the election of the President, Vice President, or Members of Congress; corrupt practices; contested elections; credentials and qualifications; and Federal elections generally.

(12) Measures relating to services to the House, including the House Restaurant, parking facilities and administration of the House Office Buildings and of the House wing of the Capitol.

(13) Measures relating to the travel of Members of the House.

(14) Measures relating to the raising, reporting and use of campaign contributions for candidates for office of Representative in the House of Representatives and of Resident Commissioner to the United States from Puerto Rico.

(15) Measures relating to the compensation, retirement and other benefits of the Members, officers, and employees of the Congress.

In addition to its legislative jurisdiction under the preceding provisions of this paragraph (and its general oversight function under clause 2(b)(1)), the committee shall have the function of performing the duties which are provided for in clause 4(d).

[Rule X. 4. (d)]

The Committee on House Administration shall have the function of--

(1) examining all bills, amendments, and joint resolutions after passage by the House and, in cooperation with the Senate, examining all bills and joint resolutions which shall have passed both Houses to see that they are correctly enrolled, forthwith presenting those which originated in the House to the President of the United States in person after their signature by the Speaker of the House and the President of the Senate and reporting the fact and date of such presentation to the House;

(2) reporting to the Sergeant-at-Arms of the House concerning the travel of Members of the House; and

(3) providing, through the House Information Systems a scheduling service which may be used by all the committees and subcommittees of the House to eliminate, insofar as possible, any meeting and scheduling conflicts.

HOUSE ADMINISTRATION / 80th Congress

Service Dates of Committee Chair: Jan. 14,1947-Jan. 3,1949
Service Dates of Majority Members: Jan. 14,1947-Jan. 3,1949
Service Dates of Minority Members: Jan. 16,1947-Jan. 3,1949

Majority

Rank	Name	Party	State	Terms in: House	Terms in: Comm.
Chr	LeCompte, Karl M.	Rep	Iowa	5	4
2nd	Gamble, Ralph A.	Rep	N.Y.	6	6
3rd	Bishop, Cecil W. (Runt)	Rep	Ill.	4	4
4th	Sundstrom, Frank L.	Rep	N.J.	3	3
5th	Vursell, Charles W.	Rep	Ill.	3	3
6th	Landis, Gerald W.	Rep	Ind.	5	3
7th	Cole, William C.	Rep	Mo.	3 *1	1
8th	Corbett, Robert J.	Rep	Penn.	3 *1	1
9th	Busbey, Fred E.	Rep	Ill.	2	1
10th	Gallagher, James	Rep	Penn.	2	1
11th	McMahon, Gregory	Rep	N.Y.	1	1
12th	Riehlman, R. Walter	Rep	N.Y.	1	1
13th	Boggs, J. Caleb	Rep	Del.	1	1
14th	Coffin, Howard A.	Rep	Mich.	1	1

Minority

Rank	Name	Party	State	Terms in: House	Terms in: Comm.
RM	Norton, Mary T.	Dem	N.J.	12	10
2nd	McCormack, John W.	Dem	Mass.	11 *2	1
3rd	Pickett, Tom	Dem	Tex.	2	2
4th	Stanley, Thomas B.	Dem	Va.	2	1
5th	Harrison, Burr P.	Dem	Va.	2	1
6th	Passman, Otto E.	Dem	La.	1	1
7th	Burleson, Omar T.	Dem	Tex.	1	1
8th	Meade, Hugh A.	Dem	Md.	1	1
9th	Morris, Toby	Dem	Okla.	1	1
10th	Smathers, George A.	Dem	Fla.	1	1
11th	Williams, John Bell	Dem	Miss.	1	1

*1: Member's 1st period of service on the committee; *2: Member's 2nd period of service on the committee.

Notes: Vito Marcantonio (American Labor Party-N.Y.) was assigned by the majority to replace Boggs on Mar. 25,1948 but was not allowed to accrue committee seniority, nor was he included in the committee's party ratio. As House Minority Whip, John W. McCormack (Dem-Mass.) was assigned the second rank on this committee, the only committee on which he served.

Changes:

Majority:

Name	Party	State	Date	Change
Busbey, Fred E.	Rep	Ill.	Dec. 18,1947	Moved to Interstate and Foreign Commerce.
Harvey, Ralph	Rep	Ind.	Dec. 18,1947	Replaced Busbey.
Boggs, J. Caleb	Rep	Del.	Mar. 25,1948	Moved to Judiciary.
Marcantonio, Vito	ALP	N.Y.	Mar. 25,1948	Replaced Boggs; not included in party ratio.

Minority:

Name	Party	State	Date	Change
McCormack, John W.	Dem	Mass.	Feb. 26,1947	Moved to Expenditures in the Executive Departments.
Deane, Charles B.	Dem	N.C.	Feb. 26,1947	Replaced McCormack.
Pickett, Tom	Dem	Tex.	July 23,1947	Moved to Public Works.
Meade, Hugh A.	Dem	Md.	Dec. 4,1947	Moved to Merchant Marine and Fisheries.
Garmatz, Edward A.	Dem	Md.	Dec. 4,1947	Replaced Pickett.
Regan, Kenneth M.	Dem	Tex.	Dec. 4,1947	Replaced Meade.
Morris, Toby	Dem	Okla.	June 4,1948	Left committee; no new assignment.
Williams, John Bell	Dem	Miss.	June 4,1948	Moved to Post Office and Civil Service.

	Majority	State	Party	Minority	State	Party
Departures from the House:						
Defeated for Reelection	Coffin, Howard A.	Mich.	Rep	None		
	Cole, William C.	Mo.	Rep			
	Landis, Gerald W.	Ind.	Rep			
	McMahon, Gregory	N.Y.	Rep			
	Sundstrom, Frank L.	N.J.	Rep			
Defeated for Renomination	Gallagher, James	Penn.	Rep	None		
Departures from Committee:						
Moved to Public Works	Vursell, Charles W.	Ill.	Rep	None		
Moved to Appropriations	None			Passman, Otto E.	La.	Dem
No new assignment	Corbett, Robert J.	Penn.	Rep	None		
	Gamble, Ralph A.	N.Y.	Rep			
	Riehlman, R. Walter	N.Y.	Rep			
	Harvey, Ralph	Ind.	Rep			

HOUSE ADMINISTRATION / 81st Congress

Service Dates of Committee Chair: Jan. 18,1949-Jan. 3,1951
Service Dates of Majority Members: Jan. 18,1949-Jan. 3,1951
Service Dates of Minority Members: Jan. 18,1949-Jan. 3,1951

Majority

Rank	Name	Party	State	Terms in: House	Terms in: Comm.
Chr	Norton, Mary T.	Dem	N.J.	13	11
2nd	Stanley, Thomas B.	Dem	Va.	3	2
3rd	Harrison, Burr P.	Dem	Va.	3	2
4th	Burleson, Omar T.	Dem	Tex.	2	2
5th	Smathers, George A.	Dem	Fla.	2	2
6th	Deane, Charles B.	Dem	N.C.	2	2
7th	Garmatz, Edward A.	Dem	Md.	2	2
8th	Regan, Kenneth M.	Dem	Tex.	2	2
9th	Trimble, James W.	Dem	Ark.	3	1
10th	Albert, Carl	Dem	Okla.	2	1
11th	Wheeler, William M.	Dem	Ga.	2	1
12th	Jones, Paul C.	Dem	Mo.	2 *1	1
13th	Hays, Wayne L.	Dem	Ohio	1 *1	1
14th	Cavalcante, Anthony	Dem	Penn.	1	1
15th	Christopher, George H.	Dem	Mo.	1	1
16th	Woodhouse, Chase Going	Dem	Conn.	2	1
17th	Kelly, Edna F.	Dem	N.Y.	1	1

Minority

Rank	Name	Party	State	Terms in: House	Terms in: Comm.
RM	LeCompte, Karl M.	Rep	Iowa	6	5
2nd	Bishop, Cecil W. (Runt)	Rep	Ill.	5	5
3rd	Wilson, Earl	Rep	Ind.	5 *2	1
4th	James, Benjamin F.	Rep	Penn.	1	1
5th	Widnall, William B.	Rep	N.J.	1	1

Third Party:

Name	Party	State	Terms in: House	Terms in: Comm.
Marcantonio, Vito	ALP	N.Y.	7	2

*1: Member's 1st period of service on the committee;
*2: Member's 2nd period of service on the committee.

Note: Vito Marcantonio (American Labor Party-N.Y.) was assigned by the Republican Conference on Jan. 18,1949, but was not allowed to accrue seniority, nor was he included in the committee's party ratio.

Vacancies Filled:
Majority: 16th seat by Woodhouse on Mar. 31,1949 and the 17th seat by Kelly on Jan. 26,1950.
Minority: 5th seat by Widnall on Mar. 1,1950.

Changes:
Minority:

Name	Party	State	Date	Change
Wilson, Earl	Rep	Ind.	Mar. 30,1950	Moved to Appropriations.

Departures from the House:	**Majority**			**Minority**		
Elected to U.S. Senate	Smathers, George A.	Fla.	Dem	None		
Defeated for Reelection	Cavalcante, Anthony	Penn.	Dem	None		
	Christopher, George H.	Mo.	Dem			
	Woodhouse, Chase Going	Conn.	Dem			
	Marcantonio, Vito	N.Y.	ALP			
Retired	Norton, Mary T.	N.J.	Dem	None		
Departures from Committee:						
Moved to Ways and Means	Harrison, Burr P.	Va.	Dem			
Moved to Appropriations	None			James, Benjamin F.	Penn.	Rep
Moved to Banking & Currency	None			Widnall, William B.	N.J.	Rep

HOUSE ADMINISTRATION / 82nd Congress

Service Dates of Committee Chair: Jan. 3,1951-Jan. 3,1953
Service Dates of Majority Members: Jan. 3,1951-Jan. 3,1953
Service Dates of Minority Members: Jan. 15,1951-Jan. 3,1953

Majority

Rank	Name	Party	State	Terms in: House		Terms in: Comm.
Chr	Stanley, Thomas B.	Dem	Va.	4		3
2nd	Burleson, Omar T.	Dem	Tex.	3		3
3rd	Deane, Charles B.	Dem	N.C.	3		3
4th	Garmatz, Edward A.	Dem	Md.	3		3
5th	Regan, Kenneth M.	Dem	Tex.	3		3
6th	Trimble, James W.	Dem	Ark.	4		2
7th	Albert, Carl	Dem	Okla.	3		2
8th	Wheeler, William M.	Dem	Ga.	3		2
9th	Jones, Paul C.	Dem	Mo.	3	*1	2
10th	Hays, Wayne L.	Dem	Ohio	2	*1	2
11th	Kelly, Edna F.	Dem	N.Y.	2		2
12th	O'Neill, Harry P.	Dem	Penn.	2		1
13th	McKinnon, Clinton D.	Dem	Cal.	2		1
14th	Bosone, Reva Z. B.	Dem	Utah	2		1
15th	Howell, Charles R.	Dem	N.J.	2		1

Minority

Rank	Name	Party	State	Terms in: House		Terms in: Comm.
RM	LeCompte, Karl M.	Rep	Iowa	7		6
2nd	Bishop, Cecil W. (Runt)	Rep	Ill.	6		6
3rd	Halleck, Charles A.	Rep	Ind.	9	*1	1
4th	Morano, Albert P.	Rep	Conn.	1		1
5th	Radwan, Edmund P.	Rep	N.Y.	1		1
6th	Van Pelt, William K.	Rep	Wisc.	1	*1	1
7th	Sittler, Edward L. Jr.	Rep	Penn.	1		1
8th	Schenck, Paul F.	Rep	Ohio	1		1

*1: Member's 1st period of service on the committee.

Vacancies Filled:
Majority: 12th seat through the 15th seat on Jan. 12,1951.
Minority: 8th seat by Schenck on Feb. 4,1952.

Changes:

Majority:				
Jones, Paul C.	Dem	Mo.	Jan. 12,1951	Moved to Agriculture.
Kelly, Edna F.	Dem	N.Y.	Jan. 12,1951	Moved to Foreign Affairs.
Aspinall, Wayne N.	Dem	Colo.	Jan. 12,1951	Replaced Jones.
Anfuso, Victor L.	Dem	N.Y.	Jan. 12,1951	Replaced Kelly.
Minority:				
Sittler, Edward L. Jr.	Rep	Penn.	Oct. 4,1951	Moved to Veterans Affairs.
Carrigg, Joseph L.	Rep	Penn.	Feb. 4,1952	Replaced Sittler.
Radwan, Edmund P.	Rep	N.Y.	Feb. 20,1952	Moved to Veterans Affairs.
Van Pelt, William K.	Rep	Wisc.	Feb. 20,1952	Moved to Merchant Marine and Fisheries.
Harrison, Robert D.	Rep	Neb.	Feb. 20,1952	Replaced Radwan.
Ross, Robert Tripp	Rep	N.Y.	Mar. 5,1952	Replaced Van Pelt.

	Majority			Minority		
Departures from the House:						
Appointed N.Y. City Magistrate	Anfuso, Victor L.	N.Y.	Dem	None		
Defeated for Reelection	Bosone, Reva Z. B.	Utah	Dem	Ross, Robert Tripp	N.Y.	Rep
	O'Neill, Harry P.	Penn.	Dem			
Lost Nomination to U.S. Senate	McKinnon, Clinton D.	Cal.	Dem	None		
Departures from Committee:						
No new assignment	Albert, Carl	Okla.	Dem	None		
	Aspinall, Wayne N.	Colo.	Dem			
	Hays, Wayne L.	Ohio	Dem			
	Howell, Charles R.	N.J.	Dem			
	Wheeler, William M.	Ga.	Dem			

HOUSE ADMINISTRATION / 83rd Congress

Service Dates of Committee Chair: Jan. 14,1953-Jan. 3,1955
Service Dates of Majority Members: Jan. 14,1953-Jan. 3,1955
Service Dates of Minority Members: Jan. 14,1953-Jan. 3,1955

Majority

Rank Name	Party	State	Terms in: House	Terms in: Comm.
Chr LeCompte, Karl M.	Rep	Iowa	8	7
2nd Bishop, Cecil W. (Runt)	Rep	Ill.	7	7
3rd Halleck, Charles A.	Rep	Ind.	10	*1 2
4th Morano, Albert P.	Rep	Conn.	2	2
5th Schenck, Paul F.	Rep	Ohio	2	2
6th Carrigg, Joseph L.	Rep	Penn.	2	2
7th Harrison, Robert D.	Rep	Neb.	2	2
8th Corbett, Robert J.	Rep	Penn.	6	*2 1
9th Bennett, John B.	Rep	Mich.	5	1
10th Van Pelt, William K.	Rep	Wisc.	2	*2 1
11th Hillings, Patrick J.	Rep	Cal.	2	1
12th Cole, William C.	Rep	Mo.	4	*2 1
13th Scherer, Gordon H.	Rep	Ohio	1	1
14th Bolton, Oliver P.	Rep	Ohio	1	1

Minority

Rank Name	Party	State	Terms in: House	Terms in: Comm.
RM1 Stanley, Thomas B.	Dem	Va.	5	4
RM2 2nd Burleson, Omar T.	Dem	Tex.	4	4
3rd Deane, Charles B.	Dem	N.C.	4	4
4th Garmatz, Edward A.	Dem	Md.	4	4
5th Regan, Kenneth M.	Dem	Tex.	4	4
6th Trimble, James W.	Dem	Ark.	5	3
7th Byrd, Robert C.	Dem	W.Va.	1	1
8th Campbell, Courtney W.	Dem	Fla.	1	1
9th Moss, John E. Jr.	Dem	Cal.	1	1
10th Friedel, Samuel N.	Dem	Md.	1	1
11th Pilcher, John L.	Dem	Ga.	1	1

*1: Member's 1st period of service on the committee; *2: Member's 2nd period of service on the committee.

Vacancies Filled:
Majority: 14th seat by Bolton on Jan. 19,1953.
Minority: 7th through the 10th seats on Jan. 19,1953 and the 11th seat by Pilcher on Feb. 12,1953.

Changes:

Ranking Minority Member:

Name	Party	State	Date	Change
RM1 Stanley, Thomas B.	Dem	Va.	Feb. 3,1953	Resigned; elected Governor of Virginia.
RM2 Burleson, Omar T.	Dem	Tex.	Feb. 3,1953	Succeeded Stanley as Ranking Minority Member.

Majority:

Name	Party	State	Date	Change
Scherer, Gordon H.	Rep	Ohio	Jan. 16,1953	Moved to Public Works.
Van Pelt, William K.	Rep	Wisc.	Jan. 21,1954	Moved to Banking and Currency.
Halleck, Charles A.	Rep	Ind.	Apr. 29,1954	Left committee; no new assignment.
Neal, William E.	Rep	W.Va.	Apr. 29,1954	Replaced Scherer.
Merrill, D. Bailey	Rep	Ind.	Apr. 29,1954	Replaced Van Pelt.
Lipscomb, Glenard P.	Rep	Cal.	Apr. 29,1954	Replaced Halleck.

Minority:

Name	Party	State	Date	Change
Stanley, Thomas B.	Dem	Va.	Feb. 3,1953	Resigned; elected Governor of Virginia.
Pilcher, John L.	Dem	Ga.	Mar. 30,1953	Moved to Government Operations.
Ashmore, Robert T.	Dem	S.C.	July 8,1953	Replaced Stanley.
Hays, Wayne L.	Dem	Ohio	Mar. 11,1954	Replaced Pilcher.

Departures from the House:

	Majority		Minority	
Defeated for Reelection	Bishop, Cecil W. (Runt)	Ill. Rep	Campbell, Courtney W.	Fla. Dem
	Cole, William C.	Mo. Rep		
	Merrill, D. Bailey	Ind. Rep		
	Neal, William E.	W.Va. Rep		
Defeated for Renomination	None		Regan, Kenneth M.	Tex. Dem

HOUSE ADMINISTRATION / 84th Congress

Service Dates of Committee Chair: Jan. 5,1955-Jan. 3,1957
Service Dates of Majority Members: Jan. 5,1955-Jan. 3,1957
Service Dates of Minority Members: Jan. 10,1955-Jan. 3,1957

Majority

Rank	Name	Party	State	Terms in: House	Terms in: Comm.
Chr	Burleson, Omar T.	Dem	Tex.	5	5
2nd	Deane, Charles B.	Dem	N.C.	5	5
3rd	Garmatz, Edward A.	Dem	Md.	5	5
4th	Trimble, James W.	Dem	Ark.	6	4
5th	Byrd, Robert C.	Dem	W.Va.	2	2
6th	Moss, John E. Jr.	Dem	Cal.	2	2
7th	Friedel, Samuel N.	Dem	Md.	2	2
8th	Ashmore, Robert T.	Dem	S.C.	2	2
9th	Hays, Wayne L.	Dem	Ohio	4	*2 2
10th	Dowdy, John V.	Dem	Tex.	3	1
11th	Long, George S.	Dem	La.	2	1
12th	Haley, James A.	Dem	Fla.	2	1
13th	Alexander, Hugh Q.	Dem	N.C.	2	1
14th	Thompson, Frank Jr.	Dem	N.J.	1	1

Minority

Rank	Name	Party	State	Terms in: House	Terms in: Comm.
RM	LeCompte, Karl M.	Rep	Iowa	9	8
2nd	Morano, Albert P.	Rep	Conn.	3	3
3rd	Schenck, Paul F.	Rep	Ohio	3	3
4th	Carrigg, Joseph L.	Rep	Penn.	3	3
5th	Harrison, Robert D.	Rep	Neb.	3	3
6th	Corbett, Robert J.	Rep	Penn.	7	*2 2
7th	Bennett, John B.	Rep	Mich.	6	2
8th	Hillings, Patrick J.	Rep	Cal.	3	2
9th	Bolton, Oliver P.	Rep	Ohio	2	2
10th	Lipscomb, Glenard P.	Rep	Cal.	2	2
11th	Halleck, Charles A.	Rep	Ind.	11	*2 1

*2: Member's 2nd period of service on the committee.

Vacancies Filled:
Majority: 10th through 14th seats on Jan. 13,1955.
Minority: 11th seat by Halleck on Jan. 13,1955.

Changes:
Majority:

Name	Party	State	Date	Change
Garmatz, Edward A.	Dem	Md.	Jan. 13,1955	Moved to Merchant Marine and Fisheries.
Deane, Charles B.	Dem	N.C.	Jan. 13,1955	Moved to Banking and Currency.
Moss, John E. Jr.	Dem	Cal.	Jan. 13,1955	Moved to Government Operations.
Trimble, James W.	Dem	Ark.	Jan. 13,1955	Moved to Rules.
Jones, Paul C.	Dem	Mo.	Jan. 13,1955	Replaced Garmatz; ranked 6th.
Rhodes, George M.	Dem	Penn.	Jan. 13,1955	Replaced Deane; ranked 7th.
Lesinski, John Jr.	Dem	Mich.	Jan. 13,1955	Replaced Moss; ranked 8th.
Smith, Frank E.	Dem	Miss.	Jan. 13,1955	Replaced Trimble; ranked 9th.
Haley, James A.	Dem	Fla.	Mar. 16,1955	Moved to Veterans Affairs.
Abbitt, Watkins M.	Dem	Va.	Jan. 19,1956	Replaced Haley.

	Majority		Minority	
Departures from the House:				
Appointed Ohio Director of Commerce	None		Bolton, Oliver P.	Ohio Rep
Departures from Committee:				
Moved to District of Columbia; Judiciary	Dowdy, John V.	Tex. Dem	None	
Moved to Appropriations	Alexander, Hugh Q.	N.C. Dem	None	

HOUSE ADMINISTRATION / 85th Congress

Service Dates of Committee Chair: Jan. 10,1957-Jan. 3,1959
Service Dates of Majority Members: Jan. 10,1957-Jan. 3,1959
Service Dates of Minority Members: Jan. 16,1957-Jan. 3,1959

Majority

Rank Name	Party	State	Terms in: House		Terms in: Comm.
Chr Burleson, Omar T.	Dem	Tex.	6		6
2nd Byrd, Robert C.	Dem	W.Va.	3		3
3rd Friedel, Samuel N.	Dem	Md.	3		3
4th Ashmore, Robert T.	Dem	S.C.	3		3
5th Hays, Wayne L.	Dem	Ohio	5	*2	3
6th Jones, Paul C.	Dem	Mo.	6	*2	2
7th Rhodes, George M.	Dem	Penn.	5		2
8th Lesinski, John Jr.	Dem	Mich.	4		2
9th Smith, Frank E.	Dem	Miss.	4		2
10th Long, George S.	Dem	La.	3		2
11th Thompson, Frank Jr.	Dem	N.J.	2		2
12th Abbitt, Watkins M.	Dem	Va.	6		2
13th Elliott, Carl A.	Dem	Ala.	5		1
14th Green, Edith S.	Dem	Ore.	2		1

Minority

Rank Name	Party	State	Terms in: House		Terms in: Comm.
RM LeCompte, Karl M.	Rep	Iowa	10		9
2nd Morano, Albert P.	Rep	Conn.	4		4
3rd Schenck, Paul F.	Rep	Ohio	4		4
4th Carrigg, Joseph L.	Rep	Penn.	4		4
5th Harrison, Robert D.	Rep	Neb.	4		4
6th Corbett, Robert J.	Rep	Penn.	8	*2	3
7th Bennett, John B.	Rep	Mich.	7		3
8th Hillings, Patrick J.	Rep	Cal.	4		3
9th Lipscomb, Glenard P.	Rep	Cal.	3		3
10th Halleck, Charles A.	Rep	Ind.	12	*2	2
11th Ray, John H.	Rep	N.Y.	3		1

*2: Member's 2nd period of service on the committee.

Note: George M. Rhodes, John Lesinski (Dem-Mich), and Frank E. Smith (Dem-Miss.), were added to the committee in the 84th Congress and ranked ahead of George S. Long (Dem-La.), Frank Thompson (Dem-N.J.) and Watkins M. Abbitt (Dem-Va.).

Changes:

Majority:

Long, George S.	Dem	La.	Mar. 22,1958	Died in office.
Everett, Robert A.	Dem	Tenn.	Apr. 3,1958	Replaced Long.

Departures from the House:	Majority		Minority	
Elected to U.S. Senate	Byrd, Robert C.	W.Va. Dem	None	
Defeated for Reelection	None		Carrigg, Joseph L.	Penn. Rep
			Harrison, Robert D.	Neb. Rep
			Morano, Albert P.	Conn. Rep
Lost Election for State Attorney General	None		Hillings, Patrick J.	Cal. Rep
Retired	None		LeCompte, Karl M.	Iowa Rep

HOUSE ADMINISTRATION / 86th Congress

Service Dates of Committee Chair: Jan. 7,1959-Jan. 3,1961
Service Dates of Majority Members: Jan. 7,1959-Jan. 3,1961
Service Dates of Minority Members: Jan. 19,1959-Jan. 3,1961

Majority

Rank Name	Party	State	Terms in: House	Terms in: Comm.
Chr Burleson, Omar T.	Dem	Tex.	7	7
2nd Friedel, Samuel N.	Dem	Md.	4	4
3rd Ashmore, Robert T.	Dem	S.C.	4	4
4th Hays, Wayne L.	Dem	Ohio	6 *2	4
5th Jones, Paul C.	Dem	Mo.	7 *2	3
6th Rhodes, George M.	Dem	Penn.	6	3
7th Lesinski, John Jr.	Dem	Mich.	5	3
8th Smith, Frank E.	Dem	Miss.	5	3
9th Thompson, Frank Jr.	Dem	N.J.	3	3
10th Abbitt, Watkins M.	Dem	Va.	7	3
11th Elliott, Carl A.	Dem	Ala.	6	2
12th Green, Edith S.	Dem	Ore.	3	2
13th Everett, Robert A.	Dem	Tenn.	2	2
14th Slack, John M. Jr.	Dem	W.Va.	1	1
15th Casey, Robert R.	Dem	Tex.	1	1
16th Carter, Steven V.	Dem	Iowa	1	1

Minority

Rank Name	Party	State	Terms in: House	Terms in: Comm.
RM Schenck, Paul F.	Rep	Ohio	5	5
2nd Corbett, Robert J.	Rep	Penn.	9 *2	4
3rd Bennett, John B.	Rep	Mich.	8	4
4th Lipscomb, Glenard P.	Rep	Cal.	4	4
5th Halleck, Charles A.	Rep	Ind.	13 *2	3
6th Ray, John H.	Rep	N.Y.	4	2
7th Mailliard, William S.	Rep	Cal.	4	1
8th Curtin, Willard S.	Rep	Penn.	2 *1	1
9th Simpson, Edna Oakes	Rep	Ill.	1	1

*1: Member's 1st period of service on the committee;
*2: Member's 2nd period of service on the committee.

Vacancies Filled:
Majority: 14th through the 16th seats on Jan. 19,1959.

Changes:

Majority:				
Carter, Steven V.	Dem	Iowa	Nov. 4,1959	Died in office.
George, Newell A.	Dem	Kans.	Feb. 10,1960	Replaced Carter.
Minority:				
Ray, John H.	Rep	N.Y.	Feb. 25,1959	Moved to Judiciary.
Chamberlain, Charles E.	Rep	Mich.	Mar. 5,1959	Replaced Ray.
Halleck, Charles A.	Rep	Ind.	May 14,1959	Left committee; elected House Minority Leader.
Goodell, Charles E.	Rep	N.Y.	June 23,1959	Replaced Halleck.
Curtin, Willard S.	Rep	Penn.	Jan. 18,1960	Moved to Interstate and Foreign Commerce.
Kyl, John H.	Rep	Iowa	Jan. 18,1960	Replaced Curtin.

	Majority		Minority	
Departures from the House:				
Defeated for Reelection	George, Newell A.	Kans. Dem	None	
Retired	None		Simpson, Edna Oakes	Ill. Rep
Departures from Committee:				
Moved to Science & Astronautics	Casey, Robert R.	Tex. Dem	None	
Moved to Rules	Elliott, Carl A.	Ala. Dem	None	
Moved to Appropriations	Slack, John M. Jr.	W.Va. Dem	None	
Moved to Foreign Affairs	None		Mailliard, William S.	Cal. Rep

HOUSE ADMINISTRATION / 87th Congress

Service Dates of Committee Chair: Feb. 6,1961-Jan. 3,1963
Service Dates of Majority Members: Feb. 6,1961-Jan. 3,1963
Service Dates of Minority Members: Feb. 13,1961-Jan. 3,1963

Majority

Rank	Name	Party	State	Terms in: House	Terms in: Comm.
Chr	Burleson, Omar T.	Dem	Tex.	8	8
2nd	Friedel, Samuel N.	Dem	Md.	5	5
3rd	Ashmore, Robert T.	Dem	S.C.	5	5
4th	Hays, Wayne L.	Dem	Ohio	7	*2 5
5th	Jones, Paul C.	Dem	Mo.	8	*2 4
6th	Rhodes, George M.	Dem	Penn.	7	4
7th	Lesinski, John Jr.	Dem	Mich.	6	4
8th	Smith, Frank E.	Dem	Miss.	6	4
9th	Thompson, Frank Jr.	Dem	N.J.	4	4
10th	Abbitt, Watkins M.	Dem	Va.	8	4
11th	Green, Edith S.	Dem	Ore.	4	3
12th	Everett, Robert A.	Dem	Tenn.	3	3
13th	McFall, John J.	Dem	Cal.	3	1
14th	Giaimo, Robert N.	Dem	Conn.	2	1
15th	Carey, Hugh L.	Dem	N.Y.	1	1

Minority

Rank	Name	Party	State	Terms in: House	Terms in: Comm.
RM	Schenck, Paul F.	Rep	Ohio	6	6
2nd	Corbett, Robert J.	Rep	Penn.	10	*2 5
3rd	Bennett, John B.	Rep	Mich.	9	5
4th	Lipscomb, Glenard P.	Rep	Cal.	5	5
5th	Chamberlain, Charles E.	Rep	Mich.	3	2
6th	Goodell, Charles E.	Rep	N.Y.	2	2
7th	Kyl, John H.	Rep	Iowa	2	*1 2
8th	Hiestand, Edgar W.	Rep	Cal.	5	1
9th	Anderson, John B.	Rep	Ill.	1	1
10th	McVey, Walter L.	Rep	Kans.	1	1

*1: Member's 1st period of service on the committee;
*2: Member's 2nd period of service on the committee.

Changes:

Majority:

Lesinski, John Jr.	Dem	Mich.	Jan. 18,1962	Moved to Appropriations.
Carey, Hugh L.	Dem	N.Y.	Jan. 18,1962	Moved to Banking and Currency.
Nedzi, Lucien N.	Dem	Mich.	Jan. 18,1962	Replaced Lesinski.
Waggonner, Joe D. Jr.	Dem	La.	Jan. 18,1962	Replaced Carey.
Smith, Frank E.	Dem	Miss.	Nov. 14,1962	Resigned after renomination defeat; appointed to Board of Directors, Tennessee Valley Authority.

Departures from the House:	Majority			Minority		
Defeated for Reelection	None			Hiestand, Edgar W.	Cal.	Rep
Defeated for Renomination	None			McVey, Walter L.	Kans.	Rep
Departures from Committee:						
Moved to Appropriations	Giaimo, Robert N.	Conn.	Dem	None		
Moved to Merchant Marine & Fisheries	Green, Edith S.	Ore.	Dem	None		
Moved to Armed Services	Nedzi, Lucien N.	Mich.	Dem	None		

HOUSE ADMINISTRATION / 88th Congress

Service Dates of Committee Chair: Jan. 17,1963-Jan. 3,1965
Service Dates of Majority Members: Jan. 17,1963-Jan. 3,1965
Service Dates of Minority Members: Jan. 17,1963-Jan. 3,1965

Majority

Rank	Name	Party	State	Terms in: House	Terms in: Comm.
Chr	Burleson, Omar T.	Dem	Tex.	9	9
2nd	Friedel, Samuel N.	Dem	Md.	6	6
3rd	Ashmore, Robert T.	Dem	S.C.	6	6
4th	Hays, Wayne L.	Dem	Ohio	8	*2 6
5th	Jones, Paul C.	Dem	Mo.	9	*2 5
6th	Rhodes, George M.	Dem	Penn.	8	5
7th	Thompson, Frank Jr.	Dem	N.J.	5	5
8th	Abbitt, Watkins M.	Dem	Va.	9	5
9th	Everett, Robert A.	Dem	Tenn.	4	4
10th	McFall, John J.	Dem	Cal.	4	2
11th	Waggonner, Joe D. Jr.	Dem	La.	2	2
12th	Perkins, Carl D.	Dem	Ky.	8	1
13th	Dent, John H.	Dem	Penn.	4	1

Minority

Rank	Name	Party	State	Terms in: House	Terms in: Comm.
RM	Schenck, Paul F.	Rep	Ohio	7	7
2nd	Corbett, Robert J.	Rep	Penn.	11	*2 6
3rd	Bennett, John B.	Rep	Mich.	10	6
4th	Lipscomb, Glenard P.	Rep	Cal.	6	6
5th	Chamberlain, Charles E.	Rep	Mich.	4	3
6th	Goodell, Charles E.	Rep	N.Y.	3	3
7th	Kyl, John H.	Rep	Iowa	3	*1 3
8th	Anderson, John B.	Rep	Ill.	2	2
9th	Curtin, Willard S.	Rep	Penn.	4	*2 1
10th	Skubitz, Joe	Rep	Kans.	1	1

14th Gibbons, Sam M.	Dem	Fla.	1		1	*1: Member's 1st period of service on the committee;
15th Nedzi, Lucien N.	Dem	Mich.	2	*2	1	*2: Member's 2nd period of service on the committee.

Vacancies Filled:
Majority: 15th seat by Nedzi on July 25,1963.
Minority: 9th and 10th seats by Curtin and Skubitz respectively on Jan. 24,1963.

Changes:
Majority:

McFall, John J.	Dem	Cal.	Dec. 10,1963	Moved to Appropriations.
Rhodes, George M.	Dem	Penn.	Jan. 21,1964	Moved to Ways and Means.
Brademas, John	Dem	Ind.	Feb. 25,1964	Replaced McFall.
Davis, John W.	Dem	Ga.	Feb. 25,1964	Replaced Rhodes.

Minority:

Anderson, John B.	Rep	Ill.	Feb. 4,1963	Moved to Joint Committee on Atomic Energy.
Devine, Samuel L.	Rep	Ohio	Feb. 4,1963	Replaced Anderson.
Bennett, John B.	Rep	Mich.	Aug. 9,1964	Died in office.

Departures from the House:	**Majority:**		**Minority**	
Defeated for Reelection	None		Kyl, John H.	Iowa Rep
			Schenck, Paul F.	Ohio Rep
Departures from Committee:				
Moved to Public Works	Everett, Robert A.	Tenn. Dem	Skubitz, Joe	Kans. Rep

HOUSE ADMINISTRATION / 89th Congress

Service Dates of Committee Chair: Jan. 18,1965-Jan. 3,1967
Service Dates of Majority Members: Jan. 18,1965-Jan. 3,1967
Service Dates of Minority Members: Jan. 21,1965-Jan. 3,1967

Majority

Rank Name	Party	State	House (Terms in)		Comm. (Terms in)
Chr Burleson, Omar T.	Dem	Tex.	10		10
2nd Friedel, Samuel N.	Dem	Md.	7		7
3rd Ashmore, Robert T.	Dem	S.C.	7		7
4th Hays, Wayne L.	Dem	Ohio	9	*2	7
5th Jones, Paul C.	Dem	Mo.	10	*2	6
6th Thompson, Frank Jr.	Dem	N.J.	6		6
7th Abbitt, Watkins M.	Dem	Va.	10		6
8th Waggonner, Joe D. Jr.	Dem	La.	3		3
9th Perkins, Carl D.	Dem	Ky.	9		2
10th Dent, John H.	Dem	Penn.	5		2
11th Gibbons, Sam M.	Dem	Fla.	2		2
12th Nedzi, Lucien N.	Dem	Mich.	3	*2	2
13th Brademas, John	Dem	Ind.	4		2
14th Davis, John W.	Dem	Ga.	3		2
15th Gray, Kenneth J.	Dem	Ill.	6		1
16th Hawkins, Augustus F.	Dem	Cal.	2	*1	1
17th Bingham, Jonathan B.	Dem	N.Y.	1	*1	1

Minority

Rank Name	Party	State	House (Terms in)		Comm. (Terms in)
RM Lipscomb, Glenard P.	Rep	Cal.	7		7
2nd Corbett, Robert J.	Rep	Penn.	12	*2	7
3rd Chamberlain, Charles E.	Rep	Mich.	5		4
4th Goodell, Charles E.	Rep	N.Y.	4		4
5th Curtin, Willard S.	Rep	Penn.	5	*2	2
6th Devine, Samuel L.	Rep	Ohio	4		2
7th Erlenborn, John N.	Rep	Ill.	1		1
8th Dickinson, William L.	Rep	Ala.	1		1

*1: Member's 1st period of service on the committee;
*2: Member's 2nd period of service on the committee.

Note: Ranking on this committee for the following member was affected by other chamber service: Robert J. Corbett (Rep-Penn), Ranking Minority Member, Post Office and Civil Service.

Changes:
Minority:

Erlenborn, John N.	Rep	Ill.	May 24,1966	Moved to Education and Labor.
Conable, Barber B. Jr.	Rep	N.Y.	May 24,1966	Replaced Erlenborn.
Curtin, Willard S.	Rep	Penn.	Oct. 20,1966	Left committee; no new assignment.
Cleveland, James C.	Rep	N.H.	Oct. 20,1966	Replaced Curtin.

Departures from Committee:	**Majority**		**Minority**
Moved to Banking and Currency	Bingham, Jonathan B.	N.Y. Dem	None
Became Chair of Education & Labor	Perkins, Carl D.	Ky. Dem	None
No new assignment	Hawkins, Augustus F.	Cal. Dem	None

HOUSE ADMINISTRATION / 90th Congress

Service Dates of Committee Chairs: Ch1 Jan. 18,1967-July 30,1968
Ch2 July 30,1968-Jan. 3,1969
Service Dates of Majority Members: Jan. 18,1967-Jan. 3,1969
Service Dates of Minority Members: Jan. 18,1967-Jan. 3,1969

Majority

Rank Name	Party	State	Terms in: House	Terms in: Comm.
Ch1 Burleson, Omar T.	Dem	Tex.	11	11
Ch2 2nd Friedel, Samuel N.	Dem	Md.	8	8
3rd Ashmore, Robert T.	Dem	S.C.	8	8
4th Hays, Wayne L.	Dem	Ohio	10 *2	8
5th Jones, Paul C.	Dem	Mo.	11 *2	7
6th Thompson, Frank Jr.	Dem	N.J.	7	7
7th Abbitt, Watkins M.	Dem	Va.	11	7
8th Waggonner, Joe D. Jr.	Dem	La.	4	4
9th Dent, John H.	Dem	Penn.	6	3
10th Gibbons, Sam M.	Dem	Fla.	3	3
11th Nedzi, Lucien N.	Dem	Mich.	4 *2	3
12th Brademas, John	Dem	Ind.	5	3
13th Davis, John W.	Dem	Ga.	4	3
14th Gray, Kenneth J.	Dem	Ill.	7	2

Minority

Rank Name	Party	State	Terms in: House	Terms in: Comm.
RM Lipscomb, Glenard P.	Rep	Cal.	8	8
2nd Corbett, Robert J.	Rep	Penn.	13 *2	8
3rd Chamberlain, Charles E.	Rep	Mich.	6	5
4th Goodell, Charles E.	Rep	N.Y.	5	5
5th Devine, Samuel L.	Rep	Ohio	5	3
6th Dickinson, William L.	Rep	Ala.	2	2
7th Conable, Barber B. Jr.	Rep	N.Y.	2	2
8th Cleveland, James C.	Rep	N.H.	3	2
9th Kyl, John H.	Rep	Iowa	4 *2	1
10th Quie, Albert H.	Rep	Minn.	6	1
11th Schwengel, Frederick D.	Rep	Iowa	6	1

*2: Member's 2nd period of service on the committee.

Note: Ranking on this committee for the following member was affected by other chamber service: Robert J. Corbett (Rep-Penn), Ranking Minority Member, Post Office and Civil Service.

Vacancies Filled:
Minority: 9th through 11th seats on Jan. 26,1967.

Changes:

Chair:

Ch1 Burleson, Omar T.	Dem	Tex.	July 30,1968	Moved to Ways and Means.
Ch2 Friedel, Samuel N.	Dem	Md.	July 30,1968	Succeeded Burleson as Chair.

Majority:

Burleson, Omar T.	Dem	Tex.	July 30,1968	Moved to Ways and Means.

Minority:

Conable, Barber B. Jr.	Rep	N.Y.	Jan. 26,1967	Moved to Ways and Means.
Cowger, William O.	Rep	Ky.	Jan. 26,1967	Replaced Conable.
Goodell, Charles E.	Rep	N.Y.	Sep. 9,1968	Resigned; appointed to U.S. Senate.
McEwen, Robert C.	Rep	N.Y.	Sep. 18,1968	Replaced Goodell.

Departures from the House:

	Majority			Minority
Retired	Ashmore, Robert T.	S.C.	Dem	None
	Jones, Paul C.	Mo.	Dem	

HOUSE ADMINISTRATION / 91st Congress

Service Dates of Committee Chair: Jan. 3,1969-Jan. 3,1971
Service Dates of Majority Members: Jan. 3,1969-Jan. 3,1971
Service Dates of Minority Members: Jan. 3,1969-Jan. 3,1971

Majority

Rank	Name	Party	State	Terms in: House		Comm.
Chr	Friedel, Samuel N.	Dem	Md.	9		9
2nd	Hays, Wayne L.	Dem	Ohio	11	*2	9
3rd	Thompson, Frank Jr.	Dem	N.J.	8		8
4th	Abbitt, Watkins M.	Dem	Va.	12		8
5th	Waggonner, Joe D. Jr.	Dem	La.	5		5
6th	Dent, John H.	Dem	Penn.	7		4
7th	Gibbons, Sam M.	Dem	Fla.	4		4
8th	Nedzi, Lucien N.	Dem	Mich.	5	*2	4
9th	Brademas, John	Dem	Ind.	6		4
10th	Davis, John W.	Dem	Ga.	5		4
11th	Gray, Kenneth J.	Dem	Ill.	8		3
12th	Hawkins, Augustus F.	Dem	Cal.	4	*2	1
13th	Gettys, Thomas S.	Dem	S.C.	4		1
14th	Bingham, Jonathan B.	Dem	N.Y.	3	*2	1

Minority

Rank	Name	Party	State	Terms in: House		Comm.
RM1	Lipscomb, Glenard P.	Rep	Cal.	9		9
2nd	Corbett, Robert J.	Rep	Penn.	14	*2	9
3rd	Chamberlain, Charles E.	Rep	Mich.	7		6
RM2 4th	Devine, Samuel L.	Rep	Ohio	6		4
5th	Dickinson, William L.	Rep	Ala.	3		3
6th	Cleveland, James C.	Rep	N.H.	4		3
7th	Kyl, John H.	Rep	Iowa	5	*2	2
8th	Quie, Albert H.	Rep	Minn.	7		2
9th	Schwengel, Frederick D.	Rep	Iowa	7		2
10th	Cowger, William O.	Rep	Ky.	2		2
11th	McEwen, Robert C.	Rep	N.Y.	3		2

*2: Member's 2nd period of service on the committee.

Vacancies Filled:

Majority: The 12th through the 14th seats on Jan. 29,1969.

Changes:

Ranking Member:

RM1	Lipscomb, Glenard P.	Rep	Cal.	Feb. 1,1970	Died in office.
RM2	Devine, Samuel L.	Rep	Ohio	Feb. 1,1970	Succeeded Lipscomb as Ranking Minority Member.

Majority:

Gibbons, Sam M.	Dem	Fla.	Jan. 14,1969	Moved to Ways and Means.
Podell, Bertram L.	Dem	N.Y.	Jan. 29,1969	Replaced Gibbons.

Minority:

Cowger, William O.	Rep	Ky.	Jan. 29,1969	Moved to Banking and Currency.
Harvey, James	Rep	Mich.	Jan. 29,1969	Replaced Cowger.
Quie, Albert H.	Rep	Minn.	Feb. 7,1969	Left committee; no new assignment.
Pettis, Jerry L.	Rep	Cal.	Feb. 7,1969	Replaced Quie.
Chamberlain, Charles E.	Rep	Mich.	Mar. 5,1969	Moved to Ways and Means.
Corbett, Robert J.	Rep	Penn.	Mar. 20,1969	Moved to Armed Services.
Hansen, Orval H.	Rep	Ida.	Mar. 20,1969	Replaced Chamberlain.
Crane, Philip M.	Rep	Ill.	Dec. 23,1969	Replaced Corbett.
Lipscomb, Glenard P.	Rep	Cal.	Feb. 1,1970	Died in office.
Wold, John S.	Rep	Wyo.	Mar. 5,1970	Replaced Lipscomb.
Pettis, Jerry L.	Rep	Cal.	Apr. 30,1970	Moved to Ways and Means.
Schmitz, John G.	Rep	Cal.	July 23,1970	Replaced Pettis.

Departures from the House:

	Majority			Minority		
Defeated for Renomination	Friedel, Samuel N.	Md.	Dem	None		
Lost Election to U.S. Senate	None			Wold, John S.	Wyo.	Rep

HOUSE ADMINISTRATION / 92nd Congress

Service Dates of Committee Chair: Jan. 22,1971-Jan. 3,1973
Service Dates of Majority Members: Jan. 22,1971-Jan. 3,1973
Service Dates of Minority Members: Jan. 22,1971-Jan. 3,1973

Majority

Rank	Name	Party	State	Terms in: House		Comm.
Chr	Hays, Wayne L.	Dem	Ohio	12	*2	10
2nd	Thompson, Frank Jr.	Dem	N.J.	9		9
3rd	Abbitt, Watkins M.	Dem	Va.	13		9
4th	Waggonner, Joe D. Jr.	Dem	La.	6		6
5th	Dent, John H.	Dem	Penn.	8		5
6th	Nedzi, Lucien N.	Dem	Mich.	6	*2	5
7th	Brademas, John	Dem	Ind.	7		5
8th	Davis, John W.	Dem	Ga.	6		5
9th	Gray, Kenneth J.	Dem	Ill.	9		4
10th	Hawkins, Augustus F.	Dem	Cal.	5	*2	2
11th	Gettys, Thomas S.	Dem	S.C.	5		2
12th	Bingham, Jonathan B.	Dem	N.Y.	4	*2	2
13th	Podell, Bertram L.	Dem	N.Y.	3		2
14th	Annunzio, Frank	Dem	Ill.	4		1
15th	Gaydos, Joseph M.	Dem	Penn.	3		1

Minority

Rank	Name	Party	State	Terms in: House		Comm.
RM	Devine, Samuel L.	Rep	Ohio	7		5
2nd	Dickinson, William L.	Rep	Ala.	4		4
3rd	Cleveland, James C.	Rep	N.H.	5		4
4th	Kyl, John H.	Rep	Iowa	6	*2	3
5th	Schwengel, Frederick D.	Rep	Iowa	8		3
6th	McEwen, Robert C.	Rep	N.Y.	4		3
7th	Harvey, James	Rep	Mich.	6		2
8th	Hansen, Orval H.	Rep	Ida.	2		2
9th	Crane, Philip M.	Rep	Ill.	2		2
10th	Schmitz, John G.	Rep	Cal.	2		2

*2: Member's 2nd period of service on the committee.

Vacancies Filled:

Majority: 14th and 15th seats by Annunzio and Gaydos respectively on Feb. 4,1971.

Changes:

Majority:				
Waggonner, Joe D. Jr.	Dem	La.	Feb. 3,1971	Moved to Ways and Means.
Davis, John W.	Dem	Ga.	Feb. 4,1971	Moved to Foreign Affairs.
Jones, Ed	Dem	Tenn.	Feb. 4,1971	Replaced Waggonner.
Mollohan, Robert H.	Dem	W.Va.	Mar. 1,1971	Replaced Davis.
Minority:				
Kyl, John H.	Rep	Iowa	Feb. 4,1971	Moved to Agriculture.
McEwen, Robert C.	Rep	N.Y.	Feb. 4,1971	Moved to Appropriations.
Schmitz, John G.	Rep	Cal.	Feb. 4,1971	Moved to Internal Security.
Ware, John H. III	Rep	Penn.	Feb. 4,1971	Replaced Kyl.
Veysey, Victor V.	Rep	Cal.	Feb. 4,1971	Replaced McEwen.
Frenzel, William E.	Rep	Minn.	Feb. 4,1971	Replaced Schmitz.

Departures from the House:	**Majority**			**Minority**		
Defeated for Reelection	None			Schwengel, Frederick D.	Iowa	Rep
Retired	Abbitt, Watkins M.	Va.	Dem	None		

HOUSE ADMINISTRATION / 93rd Congress

Service Dates of Committee Chair: Jan. 6,1973-Jan. 3,1975
Service Dates of Majority Members: Jan. 6,1973-Jan. 3,1975
Service Dates of Minority Members: Jan. 6,1973-Jan. 3,1975

Majority

Rank	Name	Party	State	Terms in: House	Terms in: Comm.
Chr	Hays, Wayne L.	Dem	Ohio	13	*2 11
2nd	Thompson, Frank Jr.	Dem	N.J.	10	10
3rd	Dent, John H.	Dem	Penn.	9	6
4th	Nedzi, Lucien N.	Dem	Mich.	7	*2 6
5th	Brademas, John	Dem	Ind.	8	6
6th	Gray, Kenneth J.	Dem	Ill.	10	5
7th	Hawkins, Augustus F.	Dem	Cal.	6	*2 3
8th	Gettys, Thomas S.	Dem	S.C.	6	3
9th	Bingham, Jonathan B.	Dem	N.Y.	5	*2 3
10th	Podell, Bertram L.	Dem	N.Y.	4	3
11th	Annunzio, Frank	Dem	Ill.	5	2
12th	Gaydos, Joseph M.	Dem	Penn.	4	2
13th	Jones, Ed	Dem	Tenn.	3	2
14th	Mollohan, Robert H.	Dem	W.Va.	5	2
15th	Koch, Edward I.	Dem	N.Y.	3	1

Minority

Rank	Name	Party	State	Terms in: House	Terms in: Comm.
RM1	Devine, Samuel L.	Rep	Ohio	8	6
RM2 2nd	Dickinson, William L.	Rep	Ala.	5	5
3rd	Cleveland, James C.	Rep	N.H.	6	5
4th	Harvey, James	Rep	Mich.	7	3
5th	Hansen, Orval H.	Rep	Ida.	3	3
6th	Crane, Philip M.	Rep	Ill.	3	2
7th	Ware, John H. III	Rep	Penn.	3	2
8th	Veysey, Victor V.	Rep	Cal.	2	2
9th	Frenzel, William E.	Rep	Minn.	2	*1 2
10th	Wiggins, Charles E.	Rep	Cal.	4	1
11th	Hastings, James F.	Rep	N.Y.	3	1

*1: Member's 1st period of service on the committee;
*2: Member's 2nd period of service on the committee.

Notes: House Resolution 158, agreed to on Jan. 24,1973, set the committee's size set at 26 with a party ratio of 15 Democrats and 11 Republicans. Democratic Party gains in the 1974 special elections in Ohio and California, led to the passage of House Resolution 1238, agreed to on July 17,1974, changing the size and party ratio on this committee to 16 Democrats and 11 Republicans.

Vacancies Filled:
Majority: 15th seat by Koch on Jan. 24,1973.
Minority: 10th and 11th seats by Wiggins and Hastings respectively on Jan. 24,1973.

Addition:
Majority: 16th Van Deerlin, Lionel Dem Cal. July 29,1974

Changes:
Ranking Member:

RM1 Devine, Samuel L.	Rep	Ohio	Jan. 24,1973	Became Ranking Minority Member of Interstate and Foreign Commerce; remained on committee.
RM2 Dickinson, William L.	Rep	Ala.	Jan. 24,1973	Succeeded Devine as Ranking Minority Member.
Majority:				
Bingham, Jonathan B.	Dem	N.Y.	Jan. 24,1973	Moved to Interior and Insular Affairs.
Mathis, M. Dawson	Dem	Ga.	Jan. 24,1973	Replaced Bingham.
Gray, Kenneth J.	Dem	Ill.	Dec. 31,1974	Resigned and retired.
Gettys, Thomas S.	Dem	S.C.	Dec. 31,1974	Resigned and retired.
Minority:				
Veysey, Victor V.	Rep	Cal.	Jan. 24,1973	Moved to Appropriations.
Froehlich, Harold V.	Rep	Wisc.	Jan. 24,1973	Replaced Veysey.
Harvey, James	Rep	Mich.	Jan. 31,1974	Resigned; appointed federal judge.
Butler, M. Caldwell	Rep	Va.	Feb. 21,1974	Replaced Harvey.

	Majority			Minority		
Departures from the House:						
Defeated for Reelection	None			Froehlich, Harold V.	Wisc.	Rep
Defeated for Renomination	Podell, Bertram L.	N.Y.	Dem	Hansen, Orval H.	Ida.	Rep
Retired	None			Ware, John H. III	Penn.	Rep
Departures from Committee:						
Moved to Appropriations	Koch, Edward I.	N.Y.	Dem	None		
Moved to Ways and Means	None			Crane, Philip M.	Ill.	Rep
No new assignment	None			Hastings, James F.	N.Y.	Rep

HOUSE ADMINISTRATION / 94th Congress

Service Dates of Committee Chairs: Ch1 Jan. 23,1975-June 21,1976
Ch2 June 23,1976-Jan. 3,1977
Service Dates of Majority Members: Jan. 23,1975-Jan. 3,1977
Service Dates of Minority Members: Jan. 28,1975-Jan. 3,1977

Majority

Rank	Name	Party	State	Terms in: House	Terms in: Comm.
Ch1	Hays, Wayne L.	Dem	Ohio	14	*2 12
Ch2 2nd	Thompson, Frank Jr.	Dem	N.J.	11	11
3rd	Dent, John H.	Dem	Penn.	10	7
4th	Nedzi, Lucien N.	Dem	Mich.	8	*2 7
5th	Brademas, John	Dem	Ind.	9	7
6th	Hawkins, Augustus F.	Dem	Cal.	7	*2 4
7th	Annunzio, Frank	Dem	Ill.	6	3
8th	Gaydos, Joseph M.	Dem	Penn.	5	3
9th	Jones, Ed	Dem	Tenn.	4	3
10th	Mollohan, Robert H.	Dem	W.Va.	6	3
11th	Mathis, M. Dawson	Dem	Ga.	3	2
12th	Van Deerlin, Lionel	Dem	Cal.	7	2
13th	Minish, Joseph G.	Dem	N.J.	7	1
14th	Davis, Mendel J.	Dem	S.C.	3	1
15th	Rose, Charles G. III	Dem	N.C.	2	1
16th	Boggs, Corinne C. (Lindy)	Dem	La.	2	1
17th	Burton, John L.	Dem	Cal.	2	1

Minority

Rank	Name	Party	State	Terms in: House	Terms in: Comm.
RM	Dickinson, William L.	Rep	Ala.	6	6
2nd	Devine, Samuel L.	Rep	Ohio	9	7
3rd	Cleveland, James C.	Rep	N.H.	7	6
4th	Wiggins, Charles E.	Rep	Cal.	5	2
5th	Butler, M. Caldwell	Rep	Va.	3	2
6th	Burke, J. Herbert	Rep	Fla.	5	1
7th	Holt, Marjorie S.	Rep	Md.	2	1
8th	Moore, W. Henson	Rep	La.	1	1

*2: Member's 2nd period of service on the committee.

Note: Ranking on this committee for the following member was affected by other chamber service: Samuel L. Devine (Rep-Ohio), Ranking Minority Member, Interstate and Foreign Commerce.

Changes:

Chair:

Ch1	Hays, Wayne L.	Dem	Ohio	June 21,1976	Resigned as Chair; remained on committee until retirement.
Ch2	Thompson, Frank Jr.	Dem	N.J.	June 23,1976	Succeeded Hays as Chair.

Majority:

Hays, Wayne L.	Dem	Ohio	Sep. 1,1976	Resigned and retired.
Pattison, Edward W.	Dem	N.Y.	Sep. 15,1976	Replaced Hays.

Minority:

Butler, M. Caldwell	Rep	Va.	Mar. 21,1975	Left committee; no new assignment.
Frenzel, William E.	Rep	Minn.	Mar. 21,1975	Replaced Butler.
Holt, Marjorie S.	Rep	Md.	Apr. 14,1976	Had moved to Budget Jan. 27,1976.
Paul, Ronald E.	Rep	Tex.	Apr. 14,1976	Replaced Holt.

	Majority			Minority		
Departures from the House:						
Defeated for Reelection	None			Paul, Ronald E.	Tex.	Rep
Departures from Committee:						
Moved to Appropriations	Boggs, Corinne C. (Lindy)	La.	Dem	None		
Moved to Interior & Insular Affairs	Mathis, M. Dawson	Ga.	Dem	None		
No new assignment	None			Moore, W. Henson	La.	Rep

HOUSE ADMINISTRATION / 95th Congress

Service Dates of Committee Chair: Jan. 19,1977-Jan. 3,1979
Service Dates of Majority Members: Jan. 19,1977-Jan. 3,1979
Service Dates of Minority Members: Jan. 19,1977-Jan. 3,1979

Majority

Rank	Name	Party	State	Terms in: House	Terms in: Comm.
Chr	Thompson, Frank Jr.	Dem	N.J.	12	12
2nd	Dent, John H.	Dem	Penn.	11	8
3rd	Nedzi, Lucien N.	Dem	Mich.	9	*2 8
4th	Brademas, John	Dem	Ind.	10	8
5th	Hawkins, Augustus F.	Dem	Cal.	8	*2 5
6th	Annunzio, Frank	Dem	Ill.	7	4
7th	Gaydos, Joseph M.	Dem	Penn.	6	4
8th	Jones, Ed	Dem	Tenn.	5	4
9th	Mollohan, Robert H.	Dem	W.Va.	7	4
10th	Van Deerlin, Lionel	Dem	Cal.	8	3
11th	Minish, Joseph G.	Dem	N.J.	8	2
12th	Davis, Mendel J.	Dem	S.C.	4	2
13th	Rose, Charles G. III	Dem	N.C.	3	2
14th	Burton, John L.	Dem	Cal.	3	2
15th	Pattison, Edward W.	Dem	N.Y.	2	2
16th	Panetta, Leon E.	Dem	Cal.	1	1
17th	Ammerman, Joseph S.	Dem	Penn.	1	1

Minority

Rank	Name	Party	State	Terms in: House	Terms in: Comm.
RM	Dickinson, William L.	Rep	Ala.	7	7
2nd	Devine, Samuel L.	Rep	Ohio	10	8
3rd	Cleveland, James C.	Rep	N.H.	8	7
4th	Wiggins, Charles E.	Rep	Cal.	6	3
5th	Burke, J. Herbert	Rep	Fla.	6	2
6th	Frenzel, William E.	Rep	Minn.	4	*2 2
7th	Stockman, David A.	Rep	Mich.	1	1
8th	Badham, Robert E.	Rep	Cal.	1	1

*1: Member's 1st period of service on the committee;
*2: Member's 2nd period of service on the committee.

Note: Ranking on this committee for the following member was affected by other chamber service: Samuel L. Devine (Rep-Ohio), Ranking Minority Member, Interstate and Foreign Commerce.

	Majority			Minority		
Departures from the House:						
Defeated for Reelection	Ammerman, Joseph S.	Penn.	Dem	Burke, J. Herbert	Fla.	Rep
	Pattison, Edward W.	N.Y.	Dem			
Retired	Dent, John H.	Penn.	Dem	Wiggins, Charles E.	Cal.	Rep
Departures from Committee:						
Ceases active membership to serve on Budget	Panetta, Leon E.	Cal.	Dem	None		

HOUSE ADMINISTRATION / 96th Congress

Service Dates of Committee Chair: Jan. 24,1979-Jan. 3,1981
Service Dates of Majority Members: Jan. 24,1979-Jan. 3,1981
Service Dates of Minority Members: Jan. 24,1979-Jan. 3,1981

Majority

Rank	Name	Party	State	Terms in: House	Terms in: Comm.
Chr	Thompson, Frank Jr.	Dem	N.J.	13	13
ChA 2nd	Nedzi, Lucien N.	Dem	Mich.	10	*2 9
3rd	Brademas, John	Dem	Ind.	11	9
4th	Hawkins, Augustus F.	Dem	Cal.	9	*2 6
5th	Annunzio, Frank	Dem	Ill.	8	5
6th	Gaydos, Joseph M.	Dem	Penn.	7	5
7th	Jones, Ed	Dem	Tenn.	6	5
8th	Mollohan, Robert H.	Dem	W.Va.	8	5
9th	Van Deerlin, Lionel	Dem	Cal.	9	4
10th	Minish, Joseph G.	Dem	N.J.	9	3
11th	Davis, Mendel J.	Dem	S.C.	5	3
12th	Rose, Charles G. III	Dem	N.C.	4	3
13th	Burton, John L.	Dem	Cal.	4	3
14th	Peyser, Peter A.	Dem	N.Y.	4	1
15th	Ratchford, William R.	Dem	Conn.	1	1
16th	Fazio, Victor H.	Dem	Cal.	1	1

Minority

Rank	Name	Party	State	Terms in: House	Terms in: Comm.
RM	Dickinson, William L.	Rep	Ala.	8	8
2nd	Devine, Samuel L.	Rep	Ohio	11	9
3rd	Cleveland, James C.	Rep	N.H.	9	8
4th	Frenzel, William E.	Rep	Minn.	5	*2 3
5th	Stockman, David A.	Rep	Mich.	2	2
6th	Badham, Robert E.	Rep	Cal.	2	2
7th	Gingrich, Newton L.	Rep	Ga.	1	1
8th	Lewis, Jerry	Rep	Cal.	1	1
9th	Campbell, Carroll A. Jr.	Rep	S.C.	1	1

*2: Member's 2nd period of service on the committee.

Note: Ranking on this committee for the following member was affected by other chamber service: Samuel L. Devine (Rep-Ohio), Ranking Minority Member, Interstate and Foreign Commerce.

Changes:

Chair:				
Chr Thompson, Frank Jr.	Dem	N.J.	June 18,1980	Due to Democratic Party Caucus rules, interrupts service as Chair.
ChA Nedzi, Lucien N.	Dem	Mich.	June 18,1980	Acting Chair during interruption of service by Thompson.
Majority:				
Fazio, Victor H.	Dem	Cal.	Feb. 26,1980	Moved to Appropriations.
Swift, Allan B.	Dem	Wash.	Mar. 19,1980	Replaced Fazio.
Minority:				
Devine, Samuel L.	Rep	Ohio	June 27,1979	Left committee; elected Chairman of the Republican Conference.
Loeffler, Thomas G.	Rep	Tex.	June 27,1979	Replaced Devine.

	Majority		Minority	
Departures from the House:				
Defeated for Reelection	Brademas, John	Ind. Dem	None	
	Thompson, Frank Jr.	N.J. Dem		
	Van Deerlin, Lionel	Cal. Dem		
Retired	Davis, Mendel J.	S.C. Dem	Cleveland, James C.	N.H. Rep
	Nedzi, Lucien N.	Mich. Dem		
Departures from Committee:				
Unassigned in 97th; appointed Director Office of Management and Budget	None		Stockman, David A.	Mich. Rep
Moved to Post Office & Civil Service; Government Operations	Peyser, Peter A.	N.Y. Dem	None	
Moved to Appropriations	None		Campbell, Carroll A. Jr.	S.C. Rep
			Lewis, Jerry	Cal. Rep
			Loeffler, Thomas G.	Tex. Rep

HOUSE ADMINISTRATION / 97th Congress

Service Dates of Committee Chair: Jan. 28,1981-Jan. 3,1983
Service Dates of Majority Members: Jan. 28,1981-Jan. 3,1983
Service Dates of Minority Members: Jan. 28,1981-Jan. 3,1983

Majority

Rank	Name	Party	State	Terms in: House	Terms in: Comm.
Chr	Hawkins, Augustus F.	Dem	Cal.	10	*2 7
2nd	Annunzio, Frank	Dem	Ill.	9	6
3rd	Gaydos, Joseph M.	Dem	Penn.	8	6
4th	Jones, Ed	Dem	Tenn.	7	6
5th	Mollohan, Robert H.	Dem	W.Va.	9	6
6th	Minish, Joseph G.	Dem	N.J.	10	4
7th	Rose, Charles G. III	Dem	N.C.	5	4
8th	Burton, John L.	Dem	Cal.	5	4
9th	Ratchford, William R.	Dem	Conn.	2	2
10th	Swift, Allan B.	Dem	Wash.	2	2
11th	Coyne, William J.	Dem	Penn.	1	1

Minority

Rank	Name	Party	State	Terms in: House	Terms in: Comm.
RM	Frenzel, William E.	Rep	Minn.	6	*2 4
2nd	Dickinson, William L.	Rep	Ala.	9	9
3rd	Badham, Robert E.	Rep	Cal.	3	3
4th	Gingrich, Newton L.	Rep	Ga.	2	2
5th	Thomas, William M.	Rep	Cal.	2	1
6th	Lee, Gary A.	Rep	N.Y.	2	1
7th	Coyne, James K.	Rep	Penn.	1	1
8th	Martin, Lynn M.	Rep	Ill.	1	1

*2: Member's 2nd period of service on the committee.

Note: Ranking on this committee for the following member was affected by other chamber service: William L. Dickinson (Rep-Ala.), Ranking Minority Member, Armed Services.

	Majority		Minority	
Departures from the House:				
Defeated for Reelection	None		Coyne, James K.	Penn. Rep
Defeated for Renomination	None		Lee, Gary A.	N.Y. Rep
Retired	Burton, John L.	Cal. Dem	None	
	Mollohan, Robert H.	W.Va. Dem		
Departures from Committee:				
No new assignment	Ratchford, William R.	Conn. Dem	None	

HOUSE ADMINISTRATION / 98th Congress

Service Dates of Committee Chairs: Ch1 Jan. 6,1983-Sep. 6,1984
Ch2 Sep. 6,1984-Jan. 3,1985
Service Dates of Majority Members: Jan. 6,1983-Jan. 3,1985
Service Dates of Minority Members: Jan. 6,1983-Jan. 3,1985

Majority

Rank	Name	Party	State	Terms in: House	Terms in: Comm.
Ch1	Hawkins, Augustus F.	Dem	Cal.	11	*2 8
Ch2	2nd Annunzio, Frank	Dem	Ill.	10	7
3rd	Gaydos, Joseph M.	Dem	Penn.	9	7
4th	Jones, Ed	Dem	Tenn.	8	7
5th	Minish, Joseph G.	Dem	N.J.	11	5
6th	Rose, Charles G. III	Dem	N.C.	6	5
7th	Swift, Allan B.	Dem	Wash.	3	3
8th	Coyne, William J.	Dem	Penn.	2	2
9th	Foley, Thomas S.	Dem	Wash.	10	1
10th	Oakar, Mary Rose	Dem	Ohio	4	1
11th	Coelho, Anthony L.	Dem	Cal.	3	1
12th	Bates, Jim	Dem	Cal.	1	1

Minority

Rank	Name	Party	State	Terms in: House	Terms in: Comm.
RM	Frenzel, William E.	Rep	Minn.	7	*2 5
2nd	Dickinson, William L.	Rep	Ala.	10	10
3rd	Badham, Robert E.	Rep	Cal.	4	4
4th	Gingrich, Newton L.	Rep	Ga.	3	3
5th	Thomas, William M.	Rep	Cal.	3	2
6th	Martin, Lynn M.	Rep	Ill.	2	2
7th	Chandler, Rodney	Rep	Wash.	1	1

*2: Member's 2nd period of service on the committee.

Note: Ranking on this committee for the following member was affected by other chamber service: William L. Dickinson (Rep-Ala.), Ranking Minority Member, Armed Services.

Changes:

Chair:

Ch1 Hawkins, Augustus F.	Dem	Cal.	Sep. 6,1984	Left committee to Chair Education and Labor.
Ch2 Annunzio, Frank	Dem	Ill.	Sep. 6,1984	Succeeded Hawkins as Chair.

Majority:

Hawkins, Augustus F.	Dem	Cal.	Sep. 6,1984	Left committee to Chair Education and Labor.

Minority:

Martin, Lynn M.	Rep	Ill.	June 8,1983	Moved earlier to Public Works and Transportation.
Vucanovich, Barbara	Rep	Nev.	June 8,1983	Replaced Martin.
Chandler, Rodney	Rep	Wash.	July 20,1983	Moved to Education and Labor.
Roberts, Pat	Rep	Kans.	July 20,1983	Replaced Chandler.

	Majority		Minority
Departures from the House:			
Defeated for Reelection	Minish, Joseph G.	N.J. Dem	None
Departures from Committee:			
Moved to Ways and Means	Coyne, William J.	Penn. Dem	None

HOUSE ADMINISTRATION / 99th Congress

Service Dates of Committee Chair: Jan. 7,1985-Jan. 3,1987
Service Dates of Majority Members: Jan. 30,1985-Jan. 3,1987
Service Dates of Minority Members: Jan. 30,1985-Jan. 3,1987

Majority

Rank	Name	Party	State	Terms in: House	Terms in: Comm.
Chr	Annunzio, Frank	Dem	Ill.	11	8
2nd	Gaydos, Joseph M.	Dem	Penn.	10	8
3rd	Jones, Ed	Dem	Tenn.	9	8
4th	Rose, Charles G. III	Dem	N.C.	7	6
5th	Panetta, Leon E.	Dem	Cal.	5	5
6th	Swift, Allan B.	Dem	Wash.	4	4
7th	Foley, Thomas S.	Dem	Wash.	11	2
8th	Oakar, Mary Rose	Dem	Ohio	5	2
9th	Coelho, Anthony L.	Dem	Cal.	4	2
10th	Bates, Jim	Dem	Cal.	2	2
11th	Clay, William L.	Dem	Mo.	9	1
12th	Gejdenson, Samuel	Dem	Conn.	3	1

Minority

Rank	Name	Party	State	Terms in: House	Terms in: Comm.
RM	Frenzel, William E.	Rep	Minn.	8	*2 6
2nd	Dickinson, William L.	Rep	Ala.	11	11
3rd	Badham, Robert E.	Rep	Cal.	5	5
4th	Gingrich, Newton L.	Rep	Ga.	4	4
5th	Thomas, William M.	Rep	Cal.	4	3
6th	Vucanovich, Barbara	Rep	Nev.	2	2
7th	Roberts, Pat	Rep	Kans.	3	2

*2: Member's 2nd period of service on the committee.

Notes: Ranking on this committee for the following member was affected by other chamber service: William L. Dickinson (Rep-Ala.), Ranking Minority Member, Armed Services. Leon Panetta (Dem-Cal.) having served on the Budget Committee during the previous three Congresses, returned to active service on this committee with his seniority intact.

Departures from Committee:	**Majority**		**Minority**
Becomes House Majority Leader	Foley, Thomas S.	Wash. Dem	None

HOUSE ADMINISTRATION / 100th Congress

Service Dates of Committee Chair: Jan. 8,1987-Jan. 3,1989
Service Dates of Majority Members: Jan. 22,1987-Jan. 3,1989
Service Dates of Minority Members: Jan. 6,1987-Jan. 3,1989

Majority

Rank Name	Party	State	Terms in: House	Terms in: Comm.
Chr Annunzio, Frank	Dem	Ill.	12	9
2nd Gaydos, Joseph M.	Dem	Penn.	11	9
3rd Jones, Ed	Dem	Tenn.	10	9
4th Rose, Charles G. III	Dem	N.C.	8	7
5th Panetta, Leon E.	Dem	Cal.	6	6
6th Swift, Allan B.	Dem	Wash.	5	5
7th Oakar, Mary Rose	Dem	Ohio	6	3
8th Coelho, Anthony L.	Dem	Cal.	5	3
9th Bates, Jim	Dem	Cal.	3	3
10th Clay, William L.	Dem	Mo.	10	2
11th Gejdenson, Samuel	Dem	Conn.	4	2
12th Kolter, Joseph P.	Dem	Penn.	3	1

Minority

Rank Name	Party	State	Terms in: House	Terms in: Comm.
RM Frenzel, William E.	Rep	Minn.	9	*2 7
2nd Dickinson, William L.	Rep	Ala.	12	12
3rd Badham, Robert E.	Rep	Cal.	6	6
4th Gingrich, Newton L.	Rep	Ga.	5	5
5th Thomas, William M.	Rep	Cal.	5	4
6th Vucanovich, Barbara	Rep	Nev.	3	3
7th Roberts, Pat	Rep	Kans.	4	3

*2: Member's 2nd period of service on the committee.

Note: Ranking on this committee for the following member was affected by other chamber service: William L. Dickinson (Rep-Ala.), Ranking Minority Member, Armed Services.

Vacancy Filled:
Majority: 12th seat by Kolter on Sep. 10,1987.

	Majority		**Minority**	
Departures from the House:				
Retired	Jones, Ed	Tenn. Dem	Badham, Robert E.	Cal. Rep
Departures from Committee:				
Moved to Budget	None		Frenzel, William E.	Minn. Rep

HOUSE ADMINISTRATION / 101st Congress

Service Dates of Committee Chair: Jan. 3,1989-Jan. 3,1991
Service Dates of Majority Members: Jan. 19,1989-Jan. 3,1991
Service Dates of Minority Members: Jan. 20,1989-Jan. 3,1991

Majority

Rank Name	Party	State	Terms in: House	Terms in: Comm.
Chr Annunzio, Frank	Dem	Ill.	13	10
2nd Gaydos, Joseph M.	Dem	Penn.	12	10
3rd Rose, Charles G. III	Dem	N.C.	9	8
4th Panetta, Leon E.	Dem	Cal.	7	7
5th Swift, Allan B.	Dem	Wash.	6	6
6th Oakar, Mary Rose	Dem	Ohio	7	4
7th Coelho, Anthony L.	Dem	Cal.	6	4
8th Bates, Jim	Dem	Cal.	4	4
9th Clay, William L.	Dem	Mo.	11	3
10th Gejdenson, Samuel	Dem	Conn.	5	3
11th Kolter, Joseph P.	Dem	Penn.	4	2
12th Flippo, Ronnie G.	Dem	Ala.	7	1
13th Frost, J. Martin III	Dem	Tex.	6	1

Minority

Rank Name	Party	State	Terms in: House	Terms in: Comm.
RM1 Gingrich, Newton L.	Rep	Ga.	6	6
2nd Dickinson, William L.	Rep	Ala.	13	13
RM2 3rd Thomas, William M.	Rep	Cal.	6	5
4th Vucanovich, Barbara F.	Rep	Nev.	4	4
5th Roberts, Pat	Rep	Kans.	5	4
6th Gillmor, Paul E.	Rep	Ohio	1	1
7th Hiler, John P.	Rep	Ind.	5	1
8th Walsh, James T.	Rep	N.Y.	1	1

Note: Ranking on this committee for the following member was affected by other chamber service: William L. Dickinson (Rep-Ala.), Ranking Minority Member, Armed Services.

Vacancies Filled:
Minority: 7th seat by Hiler on Feb. 22,1989; 8th seat by Walsh in Mar. 2,1989.

Changes:
Ranking Member:

RM1 Gingrich, Newton L.	Rep	Ga.	Apr. 10,1989	Had been elected House Minority Whip; remained on committee in third rank.
RM2 Thomas, William M.	Rep	Cal.	Apr. 10,1989	Succeeded Gingrich as Ranking Minority Member.

Majority:

Coelho, Anthony L.	Dem	Cal.	June 15,1989	Resigned and retired.
Manton, Thomas J.	Dem	N.Y.	Oct. 16,1989	Replaced Coelho.

	Majority			Minority		
Departures from the House:						
Defeated for Reelection	Bates, Jim	Cal.	Dem	Hiler, John P.	Ind.	Rep
Lost Nomination for Governor	Flippo, Ronnie G.	Ala.	Dem	None		
Departures from Committee:						
Moved to Appropriations	None			Vucanovich, Barbara F.	Nev.	Rep

HOUSE ADMINISTRATION / 102nd Congress

Service Dates of Committee Chair: Jan. 3,1991-Jan. 3,1993
Service Dates of Majority Members: Jan. 3,1991-Jan. 3,1993
Service Dates of Minority Members: Jan. 3,1991-Jan. 3,1993

Majority

Rank Name	Party	State	Terms in: House	Terms in: Comm.
Chr Rose, Charles G. III	Dem	N.C.	10	9
2nd Annunzio, Frank	Dem	Ill.	14	11
3rd Gaydos, Joseph M.	Dem	Penn.	13	11
4th Panetta, Leon E.	Dem	Cal.	8	4
5th Swift, Allan B.	Dem	Wash.	7	7
6th Oakar, Mary Rose	Dem	Ohio	8	5
7th Clay, William L.	Dem	Mo.	12	4
8th Gejdenson, Samuel	Dem	Conn.	6	4
9th Kolter, Joseph P.	Dem	Penn.	5	3
10th Frost, J. Martin III	Dem	Tex.	7	2
11th Manton, Thomas J.	Dem	N.Y.	4	2
12th Russo, Martin A.	Dem	Ill.	9	1
13th Gray, William H. III	Dem	Penn.	7	1
14th Hoyer, Steny H.	Dem	Md.	6	1
15th Kleczka, Gerald D.	Dem	Wisc.	5	1

Minority

Rank Name	Party	State	Terms in: House	Terms in: Comm.
RM Thomas, William M.	Rep	Cal.	7	6
2nd Dickinson, William L.	Rep	Ala.	14	14
3rd Gingrich, Newton L.	Rep	Ga.	7	7
4th Roberts, Pat	Rep	Kans.	6	5
5th Gillmor, Paul E.	Rep	Ohio	2	2
6th Walsh, James T.	Rep	N.Y.	2	2
7th Edwards, M. H. (Mickey)	Rep	Okla.	8	1
8th Livingston, Robert L.	Rep	La.	8	1
9th Barrett, Bill	Rep	Neb.	1	1

Notes: Frank Annunzio (Dem-Ill.) was unseated as Chair of this committee by the Democratic Caucus on Dec. 5,1990 by a vote of 127-125. A second vote seated Charles G. Rose III (Dem-N.C.) as Chair over Joseph M. Gaydos (Dem-Penn.) by a vote of 158-64. Rankings on this committee for the following members were affected by other chamber service: William L. Dickinson (Rep-Ala.), Ranking Minority Member, Armed Services; and Newton L. Gingrich (Rep-Ga.), House Minority Whip.

Changes:
Majority:

Gray, William H. III	Dem	Penn.	Sep. 11,1991	Resigns to become President of United Negro College Fund.
Kildee, Dale	Dem	Mich.	Oct. 30,1991	Replaced Gray.

INTERIOR AND INSULAR AFFAIRS

PUBLIC LANDS

Jurisdiction, 1947

Established by the Legislative Reorganization Act of 1946:

[Section 121.(1)(n)]

Committee on Public Lands.

1. Public lands generally, including entry, easements, and grazing thereon.
2. Mineral resources of the public lands.
3. Forfeiture of land grants and alien ownership, including alien ownership of mineral lands.
4. Forest reserves and national parks created from the public domain.
5. Military parks and battlefields, and national cemeteries.
6. Preservation of prehistoric ruins and objects of interest on the public domain.
7. Measures relating generally to Hawaii, Alaska, and the insular possessions of the United States, except those affecting the revenue and appropriations.
8. Irrigation and reclamation, including water supply for reclamation projects, and easements of public lands for irrigation projects, and acquisition of private lands when necessary to complete irrigation projects.
9. Interstate compacts relating to apportionment of waters for irrigation purposes.
10. Mining interests generally.
11. Mineral land laws and claims and entries thereunder.
12. Geological survey.
13. Mining schools and experimental stations.
14. Petroleum conservation on the public lands and conservation of the radium supply in the United States.
15. Relations of the United States with the Indians and the Indian tribes.
16. Measures relating to the care, education, and management of Indians, including the care and allotment of Indian lands and general and special measures relating to claims which are paid out of Indian funds.

INTERIOR AND INSULAR AFFAIRS

Renamed the Committee on Interior and Insular Affairs on February 2, 1951.

Jurisdiction, 1992

Jurisdiction contained in <u>Rules of the House of Representatives</u> (as revised to July 1, 1992):

[Rule X. 1. (l)]

Committee on Interior and Insular Affairs.

(1) Forest reserves and national parks created from the public domain.
(2) Forfeiture of land grants and alien ownership, including alien ownership of mineral lands.
(3) Geological Survey.
(4) Interstate compacts relating to apportionment of waters for irrigation purposes.
(5) Irrigation and reclamation, including water supply for reclamation projects, and easements of public lands for irrigation projects, and acquisition of private lands when necessary to complete irrigation projects.
(6) Measures relating to the care and management of Indians, including the care and allotment of Indian lands and general and special measures relating to claims which are paid out of Indian funds.
(7) Measures relating generally to the insular possessions of the United States, except those affecting the revenue and appropriations.
(8) Military parks and battlefields; national cemeteries administered by the Secretary of the Interior, and parks within the District of Columbia.

(9) Mineral land laws and claims and entries thereunder.
(10) Mineral resources of the public lands.
(11) Mining interests generally.
(12) Mining schools and experimental stations.
(13) Petroleum conservation on the public lands and conservation of the radium supply in the United States.
(14) Preservation of prehistoric ruins and objects of interest on the public domain.
(15) Public lands, generally, including entry, easements, and grazing thereon.
(16) Relations of the United States with the Indians and the Indian tribes.
(17) Regulation of the domestic nuclear energy industry, including regulation of research and development reactors and nuclear regulatory research.

In addition to its legislative jurisdiction under the preceding provisions of this paragraph (and its general oversight function under clause 2(b)(1)), the committee shall have the special oversight functions provided for in clause 3(e) with respect to all programs affecting Indians and nonmilitary nuclear energy and research and development including the disposal of nuclear waste.

[Rule X. 3.(e)]

The Committee on Interior and Insular Affairs shall have the function of reviewing and studying, on a continuing basis, all laws, programs, and Government activities dealing with Indians and nonmilitary nuclear energy and research and development including the disposal of nuclear waste.

PUBLIC LANDS / 80th Congress

Service Dates of Committee Chair: Jan. 14,1947-Jan. 3,1949
Service Dates of Majority Members: Jan. 14,1947-Jan. 3,1949
Service Dates of Minority Members: Jan. 16,1947-Jan. 3,1949

Majority

Rank Name	Party	State	Terms in: House	Terms in: Comm.
Chr Welch, Richard J.	Rep	Cal.	12	12
2nd Crawford, Fred L.	Rep	Mich.	7	7
3rd LeCompte, Karl M.	Rep	Iowa	5	5
4th Rockwell, Robert F.	Rep	Colo.	4	4
5th Lemke, William	Rep	N.D.	7	*2 3
6th Barrett, Frank A.	Rep	Wyo.	3	3
7th Taylor, Dean P.	Rep	N.Y.	3	3
8th LeFevre, Jay	Rep	N.Y.	3	3
9th Miller, Arthur L.	Rep	Neb.	3	3
10th D'Ewart, Wesley A.	Rep	Mont.	2	2
11th Poulson, Norris	Rep	Cal.	2	1
12th Russell, Charles H.	Rep	Nev.	1	1
13th Sanborn, John C.	Rep	Ida.	1	1
14th Jenison, Edward H.	Rep	Ill.	1	*1 1
15th Dawson, William A.	Rep	Utah	1	1
Del. Farrington, Joseph R.	Rep.	Hai.	3	3

Minority

Rank Name	Party	State	Terms in: House	Terms in: Comm.
RM Somers, Andrew L.	Dem	N.Y.	12	12
2nd Peterson, J. Hardin	Dem	Fla.	8	8
3rd Bell, C. Jasper	Dem	Mo.	7	7
4th Murdock, John R.	Dem	Ariz.	6	6
5th Fernandez, Antonio M.	Dem	N.M.	3	3
6th Engle, Clair	Dem	Cal.	3	3
7th Hedrick, Erland H.	Dem	W.Va.	2	2
8th Peden, Preston E.	Dem	Okla.	1	1
9th Redden, Monroe M.	Dem	N.C.	1	1
10th Carroll, John A.	Dem	Colo.	1	1
Del. Bartlett, E. L. (Bob)	Dem	Alas.	2	2
RsC. Fernos-Isern, Antonio	PpD	P.R.	2	1

*1: Member's 1st period of service on the committee;
*2: Member's 2nd period of service on the committee.

Notes: Territorial Delegates Joseph Farrington (Rep-Hai.) and E.L. (Bob) Bartlett (Dem-Alas.) and Antonio Fernos-Isern (Popular Democrat-P.R.) the Resident Commissioner for Puerto-Rico were not allowed to accrue seniority nor were they included in the committee's party ratio. Rockwell was confirmed as the 4th majority seat and Lemke the 5th on Jan. 20,1947.

Changes:
Minority:

Peden, Preston E.	Dem	Okla.	May 12,1948	Moved to Agriculture.
Morris, Toby	Dem	Okla.	May 25,1948	Replaced Peden.

Departures from the House:

	Majority		Minority	
Defeated for Reelection	Dawson, William A.	Utah Rep	None	
	Rockwell, Robert F.	Colo. Rep		
	Russell, Charles H.	Nev. Rep		
Retired	None		Bell, C. Jasper	Mo. Dem

Departures from Committee:

	Majority		Minority	
Moved to Ways and Means	None		Carroll, John A.	Colo. Dem
Moved to Appropriations	None		Fernandez, Antonio M.	N.M. Dem
			Hedrick, Erland H.	W.Va. Dem
Moved to Post Office & Civil Service	Jenison, Edward H.	Ill. Rep	None	
No new assignment	LeCompte, Karl M.	Iowa Rep	None	

PUBLIC LANDS / 81st Congress

Service Dates of Committee Chairs: Ch1 Jan. 18,1949-Apr. 6,1949
Ch2 Apr. 13,1949-Jan. 3,1951
Service Dates of Majority Members: Jan. 18,1949-Jan. 3,1951
Service Dates of Minority Members: Jan. 18,1949-Jan. 3,1951

Majority

Rank Name	Party	State	Terms in: House	Terms in: Comm.
Ch1 Somers, Andrew L.	Dem	N.Y.	13	13
Ch2 2nd Peterson, J. Hardin	Dem	Fla.	9	9
3rd Murdock, John R.	Dem	Ariz.	7	7
4th Engle, Clair	Dem	Cal.	4	4
5th Redden, Monroe M.	Dem	N.C.	2	2
6th Morris, Toby	Dem	Okla.	2	2
7th Regan, Kenneth M.	Dem	Tex.	2	1
8th Bentsen, Lloyd M. Jr.	Dem	Tex.	2	1
9th White, Compton I.	Dem	Ida.	8	*2 1
10th Baring, Walter S.	Dem	Nev.	1	*1 1
11th Bosone, Reva Z. B.	Dem	Utah	1	1
12th Marshall, Fred	DFL	Minn.	1	1
13th O'Neill, Harry P.	Dem	Penn.	1	1
14th Aspinall, Wayne N.	Dem	Colo.	1	1
15th Miles, John E.	Dem	N.M.	1	1
Del. Bartlett, E. L. (Bob)	Dem	Alas.	3	3
RsC. Fernos-Isern, Antonio	PpD	P.R.	3	2

Minority

Rank Name	Party	State	Terms in: House	Terms in: Comm.
RM1 Welch, Richard J.	Rep	Cal.	13	13
RM2 2nd Crawford, Fred L.	Rep	Mich.	8	8
3rd Lemke, William	Rep	N.D.	8	*2 4
4th Barrett, Frank A.	Rep	Wyo.	4	4
5th Taylor, Dean P.	Rep	N.Y.	4	4
6th LeFevre, Jay	Rep	N.Y.	4	4
7th Miller, Arthur L.	Rep	Neb.	4	4
8th D'Ewart, Wesley A.	Rep	Mont.	3	3
9th Poulson, Norris	Rep	Cal.	3	2
10th Sanborn, John C.	Rep	Ida.	2	2
Del. Farrington, Joseph R.	Rep.	Hai.	4	4

*1: Member's 1st period of service on the committee;
*2: Member's 2nd period of service on the committee.

Note: Territorial Delegates Joseph Farrington (Rep-Hai.) and E.L. Bartlett (Dem-Alas.) and Antonio Fernos-Isern (Popular Democrat-P.R.) the Resident Commissioner for Puerto-Rico were not allowed to accrue seniority nor were they included in the committee's party ratio.

Changes:

Chair:				
Ch1 Somers, Andrew L.	Dem	N.Y.	Apr. 6,1949	Died in office.
Ch2 Peterson, J. Hardin	Dem	Fla.	Apr. 13,1949	Succeeded Somers as Chair.
Ranking Member:				
RM1 Welch, Richard J.	Rep	Cal.	Sep. 10,1949	Died in office.
RM2 Crawford, Fred L.	Rep	Mich.	Sep. 10,1949	Succeeded Welch as Ranking Minority Member.
Majority:				
Somers, Andrew L.	Dem	N.Y.	Apr. 6,1949	Died in office.
Heller, Louis B.	Dem	N.Y.	June 24,1949	Replaced Somers.
Minority:				
Welch, Richard J.	Rep	Cal.	Sep. 10,1949	Died in office.
Saylor, John P.	Rep	Penn.	Oct. 17,1949	Replaced Welch.
Lemke, William	Rep	N.D.	May 30,1950	Died in office.
Jenison, Edward H.	Rep	Ill.	June 20,1950	Replaced Lemke.
Barrett, Frank A.	Rep	Wyo.	Dec. 31,1950	Resigned; elected Governor of Wyoming.

Departures from the House:	Majority		Minority	
Lost Nomination to U.S. Senate	White, Compton I.	Ida. Dem	Sanborn, John C.	Ida. Rep
Lost Election for Governor	Miles, John E.	N.M. Dem	None	
Retired	Peterson, J. Hardin	Fla. Dem	LeFevre, Jay	N.Y. Rep

Departures from Committee:

	Majority		Minority
Moved to Appropriations	Marshall, Fred	Minn. DFL	None
Moved to Interstate & Foreign Commerce	Heller, Louis B.	N.Y. Dem	None

PUBLIC LANDS / 82nd Congress

* Name changed to the Committee on INTERIOR AND INSULAR AFFAIRS on Feb. 2,1951.

Service Dates of Committee Chair: Jan. 12,1951-Jan. 3,1953
Service Dates of Majority Members: Jan. 12,1951-Jan. 3,1953
Service Dates of Minority Members: Jan. 15,1951-Jan. 3,1953

Majority

Rank	Name	Party	State	Terms in: House		Terms in: Comm.
Chr	Murdock, John R.	Dem	Ariz.	8		8
2nd	Engle, Clair	Dem	Cal.	5		5
3rd	Redden, Monroe M.	Dem	N.C.	3		3
4th	Morris, Toby	Dem	Okla.	3		3
5th	Regan, Kenneth M.	Dem	Tex.	3		2
6th	Bentsen, Lloyd M. Jr.	Dem	Tex.	3		2
7th	Baring, Walter S.	Dem	Nev.	2	*1	2
8th	Bosone, Reva Z. B.	Dem	Utah	2		2
9th	O'Neill, Harry P.	Dem	Penn.	2		2
10th	Aspinall, Wayne N.	Dem	Colo.	2		2
11th	Dawson, William L.	Dem	Ill.	5		1
12th	Fine, Sidney A.	Dem	N.Y.	1		1
13th	Yorty, Samuel W.	Dem	Cal.	1		1
14th	McMullen, Chester B.	Dem	Fla.	1		1
15th	Donovan, James G.	Dem	N.Y.	1		1
Del.	Bartlett, E. L. (Bob)	Dem	Alas.	4		4
RsC.	Fernos-Isern, Antonio	PpD	P.R.	4		3

Minority

Rank	Name	Party	State	Terms in: House		Terms in: Comm.
RM	Crawford, Fred L.	Rep	Mich.	9		9
2nd	Taylor, Dean P.	Rep	N.Y.	5		5
3rd	Miller, Arthur L.	Rep	Neb.	5		5
4th	D'Ewart, Wesley A.	Rep	Mont.	4		4
5th	Poulson, Norris	Rep	Cal.	4		3
6th	Saylor, John P.	Rep	Penn.	2		2
7th	Jenison, Edward H.	Rep	Ill.	3	*2	2
8th	Aandahl, Fred G.	Rep	N.D.	1		1
9th	Harrison, William Henry	Rep	Wyo.	1	*1	1
10th	Wharton, J. Ernest	Rep	N.Y.	1		1
11th	Budge, Hamer H.	Rep	Ida.	1	*1	1
12th	Bow, Frank T.	Rep	Ohio	1		1
Del.	Farrington, Joseph R.	Rep.	Hai.	5		5

*1: Member's 1st period of service on the committee;
*2: Member's 2nd period of service on the committee.

Notes: Territorial Delegates Joseph Farrington (Rep-Hai.) and E.L. Bartlett (Dem-Alas.) and Antonio Fernos-Isern (Popular Democrat-P.R.) the Resident Commissioner for Puerto-Rico were not allowed to accrue seniority nor were they included in the committee's party ratio.

Changes:

Majority:

Fine, Sidney A.	Dem	N.Y.	Feb. 26,1952	Moved to Judiciary.
O'Brien, Leo W.	Dem	N.Y.	Apr. 24,1952	Replaced Fine.

Minority:

Aandahl, Fred G.	Rep	N.D.	Oct. 17,1951	Moved to Appropriations.
Berry, Ellis Y.	Rep	S.D.	Oct. 19,1951	Replaced Aandahl.

Departures from the House:	Majority			Minority		
Defeated for Reelection	Baring, Walter S.	Nev.	Dem	Jenison, Edward H.	Ill.	Rep
	Bosone, Reva Z. B.	Utah	Dem			
	Murdock, John R.	Ariz.	Dem			
	O'Neill, Harry P.	Penn.	Dem			
Defeated for Renomination	Morris, Toby	Okla.	Dem	Crawford, Fred L.	Mich.	Rep
Retired	McMullen, Chester B.	Fla.	Dem	None		
	Redden, Monroe M.	N.C.	Dem			
Departures from Committee:						
Moved to Appropriations	None			Bow, Frank T.	Ohio	Rep
				Budge, Hamer H.	Ida.	Rep
Moved to Judiciary	None			Taylor, Dean P.	N.Y.	Rep
No new assignment	Dawson, William L.	Ill.	Dem	None		

INTERIOR AND INSULAR AFFAIRS / 83rd Congress

Service Dates of Committee Chair: Jan. 19,1953-Jan. 3,1955
Service Dates of Majority Members: Jan. 19,1953-Jan. 3,1955
Service Dates of Minority Members: Jan. 19,1953-Jan. 3,1955

Majority

Rank Name	Party	State	Terms in: House	Terms in: Comm.
Chr Miller, Arthur L.	Rep	Neb.	6	6
2nd D'Ewart, Wesley A.	Rep	Mont.	5	5
3rd Poulson, Norris	Rep	Cal.	5	4
4th Saylor, John P.	Rep	Penn.	3	3
5th Harrison, William Henry	Rep	Wyo.	2	*1 2
6th Wharton, J. Ernest	Rep	N.Y.	2	2
7th Berry, Ellis Y.	Rep	S.D.	2	2
8th Gross, Harold R.	Rep	Iowa	3	1
9th Bender, George H.	Rep	Ohio	7	1
10th Dawson, William A.	Rep	Utah	2	1
11th Westland, Alfred John	Rep	Wash.	1	1
12th Pillion, John R.	Rep	N.Y.	1	1
13th Young, Clifton	Rep	Nev.	1	1
14th Hosmer, Craig	Rep	Cal.	1	1
15th Rhodes, John J.	Rep	Ariz.	1	1
Del. Farrington, Joseph R.	Rep.	Hai.	6	6

Minority

Rank Name	Party	State	Terms in: House	Terms in: Comm.
RM Engle, Clair	Dem	Cal.	6	6
2nd Regan, Kenneth M.	Dem	Tex.	4	3
3rd Bentsen, Lloyd M. Jr.	Dem	Tex.	4	3
4th Aspinall, Wayne N.	Dem	Colo.	3	3
5th Yorty, Samuel W.	Dem	Cal.	2	2
6th Donovan, James G.	Dem	N.Y.	2	2
7th O'Brien, Leo W.	Dem	N.Y.	2	2
8th McCarthy, Eugene J.	DFL	Minn.	3	1
9th Rogers, Walter E.	Dem	Tex.	2	1
10th Pfost, Gracie B.	Dem	Ida.	1	1
11th Haley, James A.	Dem	Fla.	1	1
12th Shuford, George A.	Dem	N.C.	1	1
Del. Bartlett, E. L. (Bob)	Dem	Alas.	5	5
Res. Fernos-Isern, Antonio	PpD	P.R.	5	4

*1: Member's 1st period of service on the committee.

Notes: Territorial Delegates Joseph Farrington (Rep-Hai.) and E.L Bartlett (Dem-Alas.) and Antonio Fernos-Isern (Popular Democrat-P.R.), the Resident Commissioner for Puerto-Rico were not allowed to accrue seniority nor were they included in the committee's party ratio. Farrington was appointed on Jan. 22,1953 and Bartlett and Fernos-Isern were appointed on Jan. 26,1953.

Changes:

Majority:

Poulson, Norris	Rep	Cal.	June 11,1953	Resigned; elected Mayor of Los Angeles.
Budge, Hamer H.	Rep	Ida.	Aug. 1,1953	Replaced Poulson.
Farrington, Joseph R.	Rep.	Hai.	June 19,1954	Died in office.
Farrington, Mary E. Pruett	Rep.	Hai.	Aug. 5,1954	Replaced Joseph Farrington.
Bender, George H.	Rep	Ohio	Dec. 15,1954	Resigned; elected to U.S. Senate.

Minority:

McCarthy, Eugene J.	DFL	Minn.	Jan. 25,1954	Moved to Banking and Currency.

	Majority			Minority		
Departures from the House:						
Defeated for Renomination	None			Regan, Kenneth M.	Tex.	Dem
Lost Election to U.S. Senate	D'Ewart, Wesley A.	Mont.	Rep	None		
	Harrison, William Henry	Wyo.	Rep			
Lost Nomination to U.S. Senate	None			Yorty, Samuel W.	Cal.	Dem
Retired	None			Bentsen, Lloyd M. Jr.	Tex.	Dem
Departures from Committee:						
Moved to Foreign Affairs	None			Donovan, James G.	N.Y.	Dem
No new assignment	Gross, Harold R.	Iowa	Rep	None		

INTERIOR AND INSULAR AFFAIRS / 84th Congress

Service Dates of Committee Chair: Jan. 13,1955-Jan. 3,1957
Service Dates of Majority Members: Jan. 13,1955-Jan. 3,1957
Service Dates of Minority Members: Jan. 20,1955-Jan. 3,1957

Majority

Rank Name	Party	State	Terms in: House	Terms in: Comm.
Chr Engle, Clair	Dem	Cal.	7	7
2nd Aspinall, Wayne N.	Dem	Colo.	4	4
3rd O'Brien, Leo W.	Dem	N.Y.	3	3
4th Rogers, Walter E.	Dem	Tex.	3	2
5th Pfost, Gracie B.	Dem	Ida.	2	2
6th Haley, James A.	Dem	Fla.	2	2
7th Shuford, George A.	Dem	N.C.	2	2
8th Powell, Adam Clayton Jr.	Dem	N.Y.	6	*2 1
9th Edmondson, Edmond A.	Dem	Okla.	2	1
10th Metcalf, Lee	Dem	Mont.	2	1
11th Christopher, George H.	Dem	Mo.	2	1
12th Sisk, B. F.	Dem	Cal.	1	1
13th Udall, Stewart L.	Dem	Ariz.	1	1
14th Diggs, Charles C. Jr.	Dem	Mich.	1	1
15th Rutherford, J. T.	Dem	Tex.	1	1
16th Green, Edith S.	Dem	Ore.	1	1
Del. Bartlett, E. L. (Bob)	Dem	Alas.	6	6
RsC. Fernos-Isern, Antonio	PpD	P.R.	6	5

Minority

Rank Name	Party	State	Terms in: House	Terms in: Comm.
RM Miller, Arthur L.	Rep	Neb.	7	7
2nd Saylor, John P.	Rep	Penn.	4	4
3rd Wharton, J. Ernest	Rep	N.Y.	3	3
4th Berry, Ellis Y.	Rep	S.D.	3	3
5th Dawson, William A.	Rep	Utah	3	2
6th Westland, Alfred John	Rep	Wash.	2	2
7th Pillion, John R.	Rep	N.Y.	2	2
8th Young, Clifton	Rep	Nev.	2	2
9th Hosmer, Craig	Rep	Cal.	2	2
10th Rhodes, John J.	Rep	Ariz.	2	2
11th Budge, Hamer H.	Rep	Ida.	3	*2 2
12th Chenoweth, J. Edgar	Rep	Colo.	7	*2 1
13th Utt, James B.	Rep	Cal.	2	1
Del. Farrington, Mary E. Pruett	Rep.	Hai.	2	2

*2: Member's 2nd period of service on the committee.

Notes: The committee's size was set at 29 members on Jan. 20,1955. Territorial Delegates E.L. Bartlett (Dem-Alas.) Mary E. Pruett Farrington (Rep-Hai.) and Antonio Fernos-Isern (Popular Democrat-P.R.), the Resident Commissioner for Puerto-Rico were not allowed to accrue seniority nor were they included in the committee's party ratio. Bartlett, Fernos-Isern, and Farrington were appointed on Jan. 20,1955.

Vacancy Filled:
Majority: 16th seat by Green on Jan. 31,1955.

	Majority		Minority	
Departures from the House:				
Defeated for Reelection	None		Farrington, Mary E. Pruett	Hai. Rep
Lost Election to U.S. Senate	None		Young, Clifton	Nev. Rep
Departures from Committee:				
Moved to House Administration	Green, Edith S.	Ore. Dem	None	
No new assignment	None		Budge, Hamer H.	Ida. Rep

INTERIOR AND INSULAR AFFAIRS / 85th Congress

Service Dates of Committee Chair: Jan. 10,1957-Jan. 3,1959
Service Dates of Majority Members: Jan. 10,1957-Jan. 3,1959
Service Dates of Minority Members: Jan. 16,1957-Jan. 3,1959

Majority

Rank	Name	Party	State	Terms in: House		Terms in: Comm.
Chr	Engle, Clair	Dem	Cal.	8		8
2nd	Aspinall, Wayne N.	Dem	Colo.	5		5
3rd	O'Brien, Leo W.	Dem	N.Y.	4		4
4th	Rogers, Walter E.	Dem	Tex.	4		3
5th	Pfost, Gracie B.	Dem	Ida.	3		3
6th	Haley, James A.	Dem	Fla.	3		3
7th	Shuford, George A.	Dem	N.C.	3		3
8th	Powell, Adam Clayton Jr.	Dem	N.Y.	7	*2	2
9th	Edmondson, Edmond A.	Dem	Okla.	3		2
10th	Metcalf, Lee	Dem	Mont.	3		2
11th	Christopher, George H.	Dem	Mo.	3		2
12th	Sisk, B. F.	Dem	Cal.	2		2
13th	Udall, Stewart L.	Dem	Ariz.	2		2
14th	Diggs, Charles C. Jr.	Dem	Mich.	2		2
15th	Rutherford, J. T.	Dem	Tex.	2		2
16th	Baring, Walter S.	Dem	Nev.	3	*2	1
17th	Ullman, Albert C.	Dem	Ore.	1		1
Del.	Bartlett, E. L. (Bob)	Dem	Alas.	7		7
RsC.	Fernos-Isern, Antonio	PpD	P.R.	7		6
Del.	Burns, John A.	Dem.	Hai.	1		1

Minority

Rank	Name	Party	State	Terms in: House		Terms in: Comm.
RM	Miller, Arthur L.	Rep	Neb.	8		8
2nd	Saylor, John P.	Rep	Penn.	5		5
3rd	Wharton, J. Ernest	Rep	N.Y.	4		4
4th	Berry, Ellis Y.	Rep	S.D.	4		4
5th	Dawson, William A.	Rep	Utah	4		3
6th	Westland, Alfred John	Rep	Wash.	3		3
7th	Pillion, John R.	Rep	N.Y.	3		3
8th	Hosmer, Craig	Rep	Cal.	3		3
9th	Rhodes, John J.	Rep	Ariz.	3		3
10th	Chenoweth, J. Edgar	Rep	Colo.	8	*2	2
11th	Utt, James B.	Rep	Cal.	3		2
12th	Thomson, E. Keith	Rep	Wyo.	2		1
13th	Weaver, Phillip H.	Rep	Neb.	2		1
14th	Collier, Harold R.	Rep	Ill.	1		1

*2: Member's 2nd period of service on the committee.

Notes: Territorial Delegates E.L. Bartlett (Dem-Alas.) and John A. Burns (Dem-Hai.) and Antonio Fernos-Isern (Popular Democrat-P.R.), the Resident Commissioner for Puerto Rico were not allowed to accrue seniority nor were they included in the committee's party ratio.

Changes:

Majority:

Name	Party	State	Date	Change
Metcalf, Lee	Dem	Mont.	Feb. 26,1958	Moved to Select Committee on Astronautics and Space Exploration.
Anderson, LeRoy H.	Dem	Mont.	Feb. 26,1958	Replaced Metcalf.

Departures from the House:	Majority		Minority	
Elected to U.S. Senate	Engle, Clair	Cal. Dem	None	
	Bartlett, E.L. (Bob)	Alas. Dem		
Defeated for Reelection	None		Dawson, William A.	Utah Rep
			Miller, Arthur L.	Neb. Rep
Retired	Shuford, George A.	N.C. Dem	None	
Departures from Committee:				
Moved to Foreign Affairs	Diggs, Charles C. Jr.	Mich. Dem	None	
Moved to Appropriations	None		Pillion, John R.	N.Y. Rep
			Rhodes, John J.	Ariz. Rep
			Thomson, E. Keith	Wyo. Rep
			Weaver, Phillip H.	Neb. Rep
Moved to Ways and Means	None		Utt, James B.	Cal. Rep

INTERIOR AND INSULAR AFFAIRS / 86th Congress

Service Dates of Committee Chair: Jan. 19,1959-Jan. 3,1961
Service Dates of Majority Members: Jan. 19,1959-Jan. 3,1961
Service Dates of Minority Members: Jan. 19,1959-Jan. 3,1961

Majority

Rank	Name	Party	State	Terms in: House		Terms in: Comm.
Chr	Aspinall, Wayne N.	Dem	Colo.	6		6
2nd	O'Brien, Leo W.	Dem	N.Y.	5		5
3rd	Rogers, Walter E.	Dem	Tex.	5		4
4th	Pfost, Gracie B.	Dem	Ida.	4		4
5th	Haley, James A.	Dem	Fla.	4		4
6th	Powell, Adam Clayton Jr.	Dem	N.Y.	8	*2	3
7th	Edmondson, Edmond A.	Dem	Okla.	4		3
8th	Christopher, George H.	Dem	Mo.	4		3
9th	Sisk, B. F.	Dem	Cal.	3		3
10th	Udall, Stewart L.	Dem	Ariz.	3		3
11th	Rutherford, J. T.	Dem	Tex.	3		3
12th	Baring, Walter S.	Dem	Nev.	4	*2	2
13th	Ullman, Albert C.	Dem	Ore.	2		2
14th	Anderson, LeRoy H.	Dem	Mont.	2		2
15th	Saund, Dalip S.	Dem	Cal.	2		1
16th	McGinley, Donald F.	Dem	Neb.	1		1
17th	Morris, Thomas G.	Dem	N.M.	1		1
18th	Rivers, Ralph J.	Dem	Alas.	1		1
19th	Burdick, Quentin N.	Dem	N.D.	1		1
RsC.	Fernos-Isern, Antonio	Dem	P.R.	8		7
Del.	Burns, John A.	Dem.	Hai.	2		2

Minority

Rank	Name	Party	State	Terms in: House		Terms in: Comm.
RM	Saylor, John P.	Rep	Penn.	6		6
2nd	Wharton, J. Ernest	Rep	N.Y.	5		5
3rd	Berry, Ellis Y.	Rep	S.D.	5		5
4th	Westland, Alfred John	Rep	Wash.	4		4
5th	Hosmer, Craig	Rep	Cal.	4		4
6th	Chenoweth, J. Edgar	Rep	Colo.	9	*2	3
7th	Collier, Harold R.	Rep	Ill.	2		2
8th	Withrow, Gardner R.	Rep	Wisc.	10		1
9th	Wilson, Robert C.	Rep	Cal.	4		1
10th	Cunningham, Glenn C.	Rep	Neb.	2		1
11th	Langen, Odin	Rep	Minn.	1		1
12th	Simpson, Edna Oakes	Rep	Ill.	1		1

*2: Member's 2nd period of service on the committee.

Notes: Antonio Fernos-Isern (Popular Democrat-P.R.), the Resident Commissioner for Puerto Rico and territorial Delegate John A. Burns (Dem-Hai.) were not allowed to accrue seniority nor were they included in the committee's party ratio.

Changes:

Majority:

Christopher, George H.	Dem	Mo.	Jan. 23,1959	Died in office.
Randall, William J.	Dem	Mo.	Mar. 11,1959	Replaced Christopher.
Burns, John A.	Dem	Hai.	Aug. 21,1959	Resigned; lost election for Governor.
Burdick, Quentin N.	Dem	N.D.	Aug. 8,1960	Resigned; elected to U.S. Senate.
Taylor, Roy A.	Dem	N.C.	Aug. 23,1960	Replaced Burdick.

Minority:

Collier, Harold R.	Rep	Ill.	Jan. 18,1960	Left committee; no new assignment.
Kyl, John H.	Rep	Iowa	Jan. 18,1960	Replaced Collier.

Departures from the House:	Majority			Minority		
Defeated for Reelection	McGinley, Donald F.	Neb.	Dem	None		
Lost Nomination to U.S. Senate	Anderson, LeRoy H.	Mont.	Dem	None		
Retired	None			Simpson, Edna Oakes	Ill.	Rep
				Withrow, Gardner R.	Wisc.	Rep

Departures from Committee:	Majority			Minority		
Became Chair of Education & Labor	Powell, Adam Clayton Jr.	N.Y.	Dem	None		
Moved to Rules	Sisk, B. F.	Cal.	Dem	None		
Unassigned in 87th; appointed Secretary of Interior	Udall, Stewart L.	Ariz.	Dem	None		
Moved to Ways and Means	Ullman, Albert C.	Ore.	Dem	None		
Moved to Science & Astronautics	Randall, William J.	Mo.	Dem	None		
No new assignment	None			Wilson, Robert C.	Cal.	Rep

INTERIOR AND INSULAR AFFAIRS / 87th Congress

Service Dates of Committee Chair: Feb. 6,1961-Jan. 3,1963
Service Dates of Majority Members: Feb. 6,1961-Jan. 3,1963
Service Dates of Minority Members: Feb. 13,1961-Jan. 3,1963

Majority

Rank	Name	Party	State	Terms in: House		Terms in: Comm.
Chr	Aspinall, Wayne N.	Dem	Colo.	7		7
2nd	O'Brien, Leo W.	Dem	N.Y.	6		6
3rd	Rogers, Walter E.	Dem	Tex.	6		5
4th	Pfost, Gracie B.	Dem	Ida.	5		5
5th	Haley, James A.	Dem	Fla.	5		5
6th	Edmondson, Edmond A.	Dem	Okla.	5		4
7th	Rutherford, J. T.	Dem	Tex.	4		4
8th	Baring, Walter S.	Dem	Nev.	5	*2	3
9th	Saund, Dalip S.	Dem	Cal.	3		2
10th	Morris, Thomas G.	Dem	N.M.	2		2
11th	Rivers, Ralph J.	Dem	Alas.	2		2
12th	Taylor, Roy A.	Dem	N.C.	2		2
13th	King, David S.	Dem	Utah	2	*1	1
14th	Johnson, Harold T.	Dem	Cal.	2		1
15th	Hansen, Julia Butler	Dem	Wash.	2		1
16th	Olsen, Arnold	Dem	Mont.	1		1
17th	Carey, Hugh L.	Dem	N.Y.	1		1
18th	Ichord, Richard H.	Dem	Mo.	1		1
RsC.	Fernos-Isern, Antonio	PpD	P.R.	9		8

Minority

Rank	Name	Party	State	Terms in: House		Terms in: Comm.
RM	Saylor, John P.	Rep	Penn.	7		7
2nd	Wharton, J. Ernest	Rep	N.Y.	6		6
3rd	Berry, Ellis Y.	Rep	S.D.	6		6
4th	Westland, Alfred John	Rep	Wash.	5		5
5th	Hosmer, Craig	Rep	Cal.	5		5
6th	Chenoweth, J. Edgar	Rep	Colo.	10	*2	4
7th	Cunningham, Glenn C.	Rep	Neb.	3		2
8th	Langen, Odin	Rep	Minn.	2		2
9th	Kyl, John H.	Rep	Iowa	2	*1	2
10th	Harrison, William Henry	Rep	Wyo.	3	*2	1
11th	Durno, Edwin R.	Rep	Ore.	1		1
12th	Dominick, Peter H.	Rep	Colo.	1		1
13th	Nygaard, Hjalmar C.	Rep	N.D.	1		1

*1: Member's 1st period of service on the committee;
*2: Member's 2nd period of service on the committee.

Notes: Antonio Fernos-Isern (Popular Democrat-P.R.), the Resident Commissioner for Puerto Rico, was not allowed to accrue seniority nor was he included in the committee's party ratio. House Resolution 355, agreed to on June 21,1961, led to a change in size and party ratio to 19 Democrats and 14 Republicans.

Additions:

Majority:	19th	Udall, Morris K.	Dem	Ariz.	Jan. 18,1962
Minority:	14th	Ashbrook, John M.	Rep	Ohio	Jan. 30,1962

Departures from the House:	**Majority**			**Minority**		
Elected to U.S. Senate	None			Dominick, Peter H.	Colo.	Rep
Defeated for Reelection	Rutherford, J. T.	Tex.	Dem	None		
	Saund, Dalip S.	Cal.	Dem			
Lost Election to U.S. Senate	King, David S.	Utah	Dem	None		
	Pfost, Gracie B.	Ida.	Dem			
Lost Nomination to U.S. Senate	None			Durno, Edwin R.	Ore.	Rep
Departures from Committee:						
Moved to Appropriations	Hansen, Julia Butler	Wash.	Dem	Harrison, William Henry	Wyo.	Rep
Moved to Armed Services	Ichord, Richard H.	Mo.	Dem	None		
Moved to Public Works	Olsen, Arnold	Mont.	Dem	None		
Moved to Interstate & Foreign Commerce	None			Cunningham, Glenn C.	Neb.	Rep
Moved to Un-American Activities	None			Ashbrook, John M.	Ohio	Rep
No new assignment	None			Langen, Odin	Minn.	Rep

INTERIOR AND INSULAR AFFAIRS / 88th Congress

Service Dates of Committee Chair: Jan. 17,1963-Jan. 3,1965
Service Dates of Majority Members: Jan. 17,1963-Jan. 3,1965
Service Dates of Minority Members: Jan. 24,1963-Jan. 3,1965

Majority

Rank	Name	Party	State	Terms in: House	Terms in: Comm.
Chr	Aspinall, Wayne N.	Dem	Colo.	8	8
2nd	O'Brien, Leo W.	Dem	N.Y.	7	7
3rd	Rogers, Walter E.	Dem	Tex.	7	6
4th	Haley, James A.	Dem	Fla.	6	6
5th	Edmondson, Edmond A.	Dem	Okla.	6	5
6th	Baring, Walter S.	Dem	Nev.	6	*2 4
7th	Morris, Thomas G.	Dem	N.M.	3	3
8th	Rivers, Ralph J.	Dem	Alas.	3	3
9th	Taylor, Roy A.	Dem	N.C.	3	3
10th	Johnson, Harold T.	Dem	Cal.	3	2
11th	Carey, Hugh L.	Dem	N.Y.	2	2
12th	Udall, Morris K.	Dem	Ariz.	2	2
13th	Kee, Maude Elizabeth	Dem	W.Va.	7	1
14th	Roberts, Herbert Ray	Dem	Tex.	2	1
15th	Duncan, Robert B.	Dem	Ore.	1	1
16th	White, Compton I. Jr.	Dem	Ida.	1	1
17th	Marsh, John O. Jr.	Dem	Va.	1	1
18th	Roybal, Edward R.	Dem	Cal.	1	1
19th	Gill, Thomas P.	Dem	Hai.	1	1
RsC.	Fernos-Isern, Antonio	PpD	P.R.	10	9

Minority

Rank	Name	Party	State	Terms in: House	Terms in: Comm.
RM	Saylor, John P.	Rep	Penn.	8	8
2nd	Wharton, J. Ernest	Rep	N.Y.	7	7
3rd	Berry, Ellis Y.	Rep	S.D.	7	7
4th	Westland, Alfred John	Rep	Wash.	6	6
5th	Hosmer, Craig	Rep	Cal.	6	6
6th	Chenoweth, J. Edgar	Rep	Colo.	11	*2 5
7th	Kyl, John H.	Rep	Iowa	3	*1 3
8th	Nygaard, Hjalmar C.	Rep	N.D.	2	2
9th	Abele, Homer E.	Rep	Ohio	1	1
10th	Skubitz, Joe	Rep	Kans.	1	1
11th	Reid, Charlotte T.	Rep	Ill.	1	1
12th	Burton, Laurence J.	Rep	Utah	1	1
13th	Morton, Rogers C. B.	Rep	Md.	1	1
14th	Martin, Pat Minor	Rep	Cal.	1	1

*1: Member's 1st period of service on the committee;
*2: Member's 2nd period of service on the committee.

Note: Antonio Fernos-Isern (Popular Democrat-P.R.), the Resident Commissioner for Puerto Rico, was not allowed to accrue seniority nor was he included in the committee's party ratio. He was appointed on Jan. 18,1963.

Vacancy Filled:
Minority: 14th seat by Martin on Feb. 7,1962.

Changes:

Majority:

Name	Party	State	Date	Change
Roberts, Herbert Ray	Dem	Tex.	Feb. 25,1964	Moved to Public Works.
Burton, Phillip	Dem	Cal.	Feb. 25,1964	Replaced Roberts.

Minority:

Name	Party	State	Date	Change
Nygaard, Hjalmar C.	Rep	N.D.	July 18,1963	Died in office.
Andrews, Mark	Rep	N.D.	Oct. 30,1963	Replaced Nygaard.

	Majority			Minority		
Departures from the House:						
Defeated for Reelection	None			Abele, Homer E.	Ohio	Rep
				Chenoweth, J. Edgar	Colo.	Rep
				Kyl, John H.	Iowa	Rep
				Martin, Pat Minor	Cal.	Rep
				Westland, Alfred John	Wash.	Rep
				Wharton, J. Ernest	N.Y.	Rep
Lost Election to U.S. Senate	Gill, Thomas P.	Hai.	Dem	None		
Retired	Kee, Maude Elizabeth	W.Va.	Dem	None		
	Fernos-Isern, Antonio	P.R.	PpD			
Departures from Committee:						
Moved to Appropriations	Duncan, Robert B.	Ore.	Dem	Andrews, Mark	N.D.	Rep
	Marsh, John O. Jr.	Va.	Dem			
	Morris, Thomas G.	N.M.	Dem			
Moved to Foreign Affairs	Roybal, Edward R.	Cal.	Dem	None		

INTERIOR AND INSULAR AFFAIRS / 89th Congress

Service Dates of Committee Chair: Jan. 18,1965-Jan. 3,1967
Service Dates of Majority Members: Jan. 18,1965-Jan. 3,1967
Service Dates of Minority Members: Jan. 21,1965-Jan. 3,1967

Majority

Rank	Name	Party	State	Terms in: House		Terms in: Comm.
Chr	Aspinall, Wayne N.	Dem	Colo.	9		9
2nd	O'Brien, Leo W.	Dem	N.Y.	8		8
3rd	Rogers, Walter E.	Dem	Tex.	8		7
4th	Haley, James A.	Dem	Fla.	7		7
5th	Edmondson, Edmond A.	Dem	Okla.	7		6
6th	Baring, Walter S.	Dem	Nev.	7	*2	5
7th	Rivers, Ralph J.	Dem	Alas.	4		4
8th	Taylor, Roy A.	Dem	N.C.	4		4
9th	Johnson, Harold T.	Dem	Cal.	4		3
10th	Carey, Hugh L.	Dem	N.Y.	3		3
11th	Udall, Morris K.	Dem	Ariz.	3		3
12th	White, Compton I. Jr.	Dem	Ida.	2		2
13th	Burton, Phillip	Dem	Cal.	2		2
14th	King, David S.	Dem	Utah	3	*2	1
15th	Moeller, Walter H.	Dem	Ohio	3		1
16th	Tunney, John V.	Dem	Cal.	1		1
17th	Bingham, Jonathan B.	Dem	N.Y.	1	*1	1
18th	Foley, Thomas S.	Dem	Wash.	1		1
19th	Craley, N. Neiman Jr.	Dem	Penn.	1		1
20th	Race, John A.	Dem	Wisc.	1		1
21st	White, Richard C.	Dem	Tex.	1		1
22nd	Roncalio, Teno	Dem	Wyo.	1	*1	1
RsC.	Polanco-Abreu, Santiago	PpD	P.R.	1		1

Minority

Rank	Name	Party	State	Terms in: House	Terms in: Comm.
RM	Saylor, John P.	Rep	Penn.	9	9
2nd	Berry, Ellis Y.	Rep	S.D.	8	8
3rd	Hosmer, Craig	Rep	Cal.	7	7
4th	Skubitz, Joe	Rep	Kans.	2	2
5th	Reid, Charlotte T.	Rep	Ill.	2	2
6th	Burton, Laurence J.	Rep	Utah	2	2
7th	Morton, Rogers C. B.	Rep	Md.	2	2
8th	Wyatt, Wendell	Rep	Ore.	2	1
9th	Hansen, George V.	Rep	Ida.	1	1
10th	Smith, Henry P. III	Rep	N.Y.	1	1
11th	Reinecke, Ed	Rep	Cal.	1	1

*1: Member's 1st period of service on the committee;
*2: Member's 2nd period of service on the committee.

Note: Santiago Polanco-Abreu (Popular Democrat-P.R.), the Resident Commissioner for Puerto Rico, was not allowed to accrue seniority nor was he included in the committee's party ratio.

Changes:

Majority:

O'Brien, Leo W.	Dem	N.Y.	Dec. 30,1966	Resigned; appointed chair county planning board.
Rivers, Ralph J.	Dem	Alas.	Dec. 30,1966	Resigned; defeated for reelection.

Minority:

Smith, Henry P. III	Rep	N.Y.	Feb. 16,1966	Moved to Judiciary.
Kupferman, Theodore R.	Rep	N.Y.	Feb. 23,1966	Replaced Smith.

	Majority			Minority		
Departures from the House:						
Defeated for Reelection	Craley, N. Neiman Jr.	Penn.	Dem	None		
	King, David S.	Utah	Dem			
	Moeller, Walter H.	Ohio	Dem			
	Race, John A.	Wisc.	Dem			
	White, Compton I. Jr.	Ida.	Dem			
Lost Election to U.S. Senate	Roncalio, Teno	Wyo.	Dem	None		
Retired	Rogers, Walter E.	Tex.	Dem	None		
Departures from Committee:						
Moved to Banking & Currency	Bingham, Jonathan B.	N.Y.	Dem	None		
Moved to Appropriations	None			Reid, Charlotte T.	Ill.	Rep

INTERIOR AND INSULAR AFFAIRS / 90th Congress

Service Dates of Committee Chair: Jan. 23,1967-Jan. 3,1969
Service Dates of Majority Members: Jan. 23,1967-Jan. 3,1969
Service Dates of Minority Members: Jan. 26,1967-Jan. 3,1969

Majority

Rank	Name	Party	State	Terms in: House	Terms in: Comm.
Chr	Aspinall, Wayne N.	Dem	Colo.	10	10
2nd	Haley, James A.	Dem	Fla.	8	8
3rd	Edmondson, Edmond A.	Dem	Okla.	8	7
4th	Baring, Walter S.	Dem	Nev.	8	*2 6
5th	Taylor, Roy A.	Dem	N.C.	5	5
6th	Johnson, Harold T.	Dem	Cal.	5	4
7th	Carey, Hugh L.	Dem	N.Y.	4	4
8th	Udall, Morris K.	Dem	Ariz.	4	4
9th	Burton, Phillip	Dem	Cal.	3	3
10th	Tunney, John V.	Dem	Cal.	2	2
11th	Foley, Thomas S.	Dem	Wash.	2	2
12th	White, Richard C.	Dem	Tex.	2	2
13th	Kastenmeier, Robert W.	Dem	Wisc.	5	1
14th	O'Hara, James G.	Dem	Mich.	5	1
15th	Ryan, William Fitts	Dem	N.Y.	4	1
16th	Mink, Patsy T.	Dem	Hai.	2	1
17th	Kee, James	Dem	W.Va.	2	1
18th	Meeds, Lloyd	Dem	Wash.	2	1
19th	Kazen, Abraham Jr.	Dem	Tex.	1	1
RsC.	Polanco-Abreu, Santiago	Dem	P.R.	2	2

Minority

Rank	Name	Party	State	Terms in: House	Terms in: Comm.
RM	Saylor, John P.	Rep	Penn.	10	10
2nd	Berry, Ellis Y.	Rep	S.D.	9	9
3rd	Hosmer, Craig	Rep	Cal.	8	8
4th	Skubitz, Joe	Rep	Kans.	3	3
5th	Burton, Laurence J.	Rep	Utah	3	3
6th	Morton, Rogers C. B.	Rep	Md.	3	3
7th	Wyatt, Wendell	Rep	Ore.	3	2
8th	Hansen, George V.	Rep	Ida.	2	2
9th	Reinecke, Ed	Rep	Cal.	2	2
10th	Kupferman, Theodore R.	Rep	N.Y.	2	2
11th	Kyl, John H.	Rep	Iowa	4	*2 1
12th	Steiger, Sam	Rep	Ariz.	1	1
13th	Pollock, Howard W.	Rep	Alas.	1	1
14th	McClure, James A.	Rep	Ida.	1	1

*2: Member's 2nd period of service on the committee.

Note: Santiago Polanco-Abreu (Popular Democrat-P.R.), the Resident Commissioner for Puerto Rico, was not allowed to accrue seniority nor was he included in the committee's party ratio. Polanco-Abreu was included on the committee listing in the Congressional Directory but not in the House Journal or Congressional Record for Jan. 23,1967. However, as a Resident Commissioner, he was elected to a four-year term in 1966 and his appointment date of Jan. 18,1965 may have been holding in this case.

Changes:

Minority:

Name	Party	State	Date	Change
Wyatt, Wendell	Rep	Ore.	Oct. 3,1968	Moved to Appropriations.

	Majority			Minority		
Departures from the House:						
Elected State Supreme Court Justice	None			Kupferman, Theodore R.	N.Y.	Rep
Defeated for Reelection	Polanco-Abreu, Sanitago	P.R.	Dem	None		
Lost Election to U.S. Senate	None			Hansen, George V.	Ida.	Rep
Departures from Committee:						
Moved to Armed Services	White, Richard C.	Tex.	Dem	None		
Moved to Ways and Means	None			Morton, Rogers C. B.	Md.	Rep
Unassigned in 91st; elected Lieutenant Governor	None			Reinecke, Ed	Cal.	Rep

INTERIOR AND INSULAR AFFAIRS / 91st Congress

Service Dates of Committee Chair: Jan. 29,1969-Jan. 3,1971
Service Dates of Majority Members: Jan. 29,1969-Jan. 3,1971
Service Dates of Minority Members: Jan. 29,1969-Jan. 3,1971

Majority

Rank	Name	Party	State	Terms in: House	Terms in: Comm.
Chr	Aspinall, Wayne N.	Dem	Colo.	11	11
2nd	Haley, James A.	Dem	Fla.	9	9
3rd	Edmondson, Edmond A.	Dem	Okla.	9	8
4th	Baring, Walter S.	Dem	Nev.	9	*2 7
5th	Taylor, Roy A.	Dem	N.C.	6	6
6th	Johnson, Harold T.	Dem	Cal.	6	5
7th	Carey, Hugh L.	Dem	N.Y.	5	5
8th	Udall, Morris K.	Dem	Ariz.	5	5
9th	Burton, Phillip	Dem	Cal.	4	4
10th	Tunney, John V.	Dem	Cal.	3	3
11th	Foley, Thomas S.	Dem	Wash.	3	3
12th	Kastenmeier, Robert W.	Dem	Wisc.	6	2
13th	O'Hara, James G.	Dem	Mich.	6	2
14th	Ryan, William Fitts	Dem	N.Y.	5	2
15th	Mink, Patsy T.	Dem	Hai.	3	2
16th	Kee, James	Dem	W.Va.	3	2
17th	Meeds, Lloyd	Dem	Wash.	3	2
18th	Kazen, Abraham Jr.	Dem	Tex.	2	2
19th	Burlison, Bill D.	Dem	Mo.	1	1
RsC.	Cordova-Diaz, Jorge L.	NPr	P.R.	1	1

Minority

Rank	Name	Party	State	Terms in: House	Terms in: Comm.
RM	Saylor, John P.	Rep	Penn.	11	11
2nd	Berry, Ellis Y.	Rep	S.D.	10	10
3rd	Hosmer, Craig	Rep	Cal.	9	9
4th	Skubitz, Joe	Rep	Kans.	4	4
5th	Burton, Laurence J.	Rep	Utah	4	4
6th	Kyl, John H.	Rep	Iowa	5	*2 2
7th	Steiger, Sam	Rep	Ariz.	2	2
8th	Pollock, Howard W.	Rep	Alas.	2	2
9th	McClure, James A.	Rep	Ida.	2	2
10th	Clausen, Don H.	Rep	Cal.	4	1
11th	Ruppe, Philip E.	Rep	Mich.	2	1
12th	Wold, John S.	Rep	Wyo.	1	1
13th	Camp, John N. Happy	Rep	Okla.	1	1
14th	Lujan, Manuel Jr.	Rep	N.M.	1	1

*2: Member's 2nd period of service on the committee.

Note: Jorge L. Cordova-Diaz (New Progressive-P.R.), the Resident Commissioner for Puerto Rico, was appointed by the majority in the 91st Congress. He was not allowed to accrue seniority nor was he included in the committee's party ratio.

Changes:

Majority:

Carey, Hugh L.	Dem	N.Y.	Dec. 17,1970	Moved to Ways and Means.

Departures from the House:

	Majority			Minority		
Elected to U.S. Senate	Tunney, John V.	Cal.	Dem	None		
Lost Election to U.S. Senate	None			Burton, Laurence J.	Utah	Rep
				Wold, John S.	Wyo.	Rep
Lost Nomination for Governor	None			Pollock, Howard W.	Alas.	Rep
Retired	None			Berry, Ellis Y.	S.D.	Rep

INTERIOR AND INSULAR AFFAIRS / 92nd Congress

Service Dates of Committee Chair: Feb. 4,1971-Jan. 3,1973
Service Dates of Majority Members: Feb. 4,1971-Jan. 3,1973
Service Dates of Minority Members: Feb. 4,1971-Jan. 3,1973

Majority

Rank	Name	Party	State	Terms in: House	Terms in: Comm.
Chr	Aspinall, Wayne N.	Dem	Colo.	12	12
2nd	Haley, James A.	Dem	Fla.	10	10
3rd	Edmondson, Edmond A.	Dem	Okla.	10	9
4th	Baring, Walter S.	Dem	Nev.	10	*2 8
5th	Taylor, Roy A.	Dem	N.C.	7	7
6th	Johnson, Harold T.	Dem	Cal.	7	6
7th	Udall, Morris K.	Dem	Ariz.	6	6
8th	Burton, Phillip	Dem	Cal.	5	5
9th	Foley, Thomas S.	Dem	Wash.	4	4
10th	Kastenmeier, Robert W.	Dem	Wisc.	7	3
11th	O'Hara, James G.	Dem	Mich.	7	3
12th	Ryan, William Fitts	Dem	N.Y.	6	3
13th	Mink, Patsy T.	Dem	Hai.	4	3
14th	Kee, James	Dem	W.Va.	4	3
15th	Meeds, Lloyd	Dem	Wash.	4	3
16th	Kazen, Abraham Jr.	Dem	Tex.	3	3
17th	Burlison, Bill D.	Dem	Mo.	2	2
18th	Stephens, Robert G. Jr.	Dem	Ga.	6	1
19th	Vigorito, Joseph P.	Dem	Penn.	4	1
20th	Melcher, John	Dem	Mont.	2	1
21st	Roncalio, Teno	Dem	Wyo.	2	*2 1
22nd	Begich, Nicholas J.	Dem	Alas.	1	1
23rd	Abourezk, James G.	Dem	S.D.	1	1

Minority

Rank	Name	Party	State	Terms in: House	Terms in: Comm.
RM	Saylor, John P.	Rep	Penn.	12	12
2nd	Hosmer, Craig	Rep	Cal.	10	10
3rd	Skubitz, Joe	Rep	Kans.	5	5
4th	Kyl, John H.	Rep	Iowa	6	*2 3
5th	Steiger, Sam	Rep	Ariz.	3	3
6th	McClure, James A.	Rep	Ida.	3	3
7th	Clausen, Don H.	Rep	Cal.	5	2
8th	Ruppe, Philip E.	Rep	Mich.	3	2
9th	Camp, John N. Happy	Rep	Okla.	2	2
10th	Lujan, Manuel Jr.	Rep	N.M.	2	2
11th	Lloyd, Sherman P.	Rep	Utah	4	1
12th	Dellenback, John R.	Rep	Ore.	3	1
13th	Sebelius, Keith G.	Rep	Kans.	2	1
14th	McKevitt, James D.	Rep	Colo.	1	1
15th	Terry, John H.	Rep	N.Y.	1	1
RsC.	Cordova-Diaz, Jorge L.	NPr	P.R.	2	2

*2: Member's 2nd period of service on the committee.

Note: Jorge L. Cordova-Diaz (New Progressive-P.R.), the Resident Commissioner for Puerto Rico, was appointed by the minority in the 92nd Congress. He was not allowed to accrue seniority nor was he included in the committee's party ratio.

Changes:

Majority:

Ryan, William Fitts	Dem	N.Y.	Sep. 17,1972	Died in office.
Begich, Nicholas J.	Dem	Alas.	Dec. 29,1972	Died in office.

Departures from the House:	**Majority**			**Minority**		
Elected to U.S. Senate	Abourezk, James G.	S.D.	Dem	McClure, James A.	Ida.	Rep
Defeated for Reelection	None			Kyl, John H.	Iowa	Rep
				Lloyd, Sherman P.	Utah	Rep
				McKevitt, James D.	Colo.	Rep
				Cordova-Diaz, Jorge L.	P.R.	NPr
Defeated for Renomination	Aspinall, Wayne N.	Colo.	Dem	None		
	Baring, Walter S.	Nev.	Dem			
	Kee, James	W.Va.	Dem			
Lost Election to U.S. Senate	Edmondson, Edmond A.	Okla.	Dem	None		
Retired	None			Terry, John H.	N.Y.	Rep
Departures from Committee:						
Moved to Appropriations	Burlison, Bill D.	Mo.	Dem	None		

INTERIOR AND INSULAR AFFAIRS / 93rd Congress

Service Dates of Committee Chair: Jan. 24,1973-Jan. 3,1975
Service Dates of Majority Members: Jan. 24,1973-Jan. 3,1975
Service Dates of Minority Members: Jan. 24,1973-Jan. 3,1975

Majority

Rank Name	Party	State	Terms in: House	Terms in: Comm.
Chr Haley, James A.	Dem	Fla.	11	11
2nd Taylor, Roy A.	Dem	N.C.	8	8
3rd Johnson, Harold T.	Dem	Cal.	8	7
4th Udall, Morris K.	Dem	Ariz.	7	7
5th Burton, Phillip	Dem	Cal.	6	6
6th Foley, Thomas S.	Dem	Wash.	5	5
7th Kastenmeier, Robert W.	Dem	Wisc.	8	4
8th O'Hara, James G.	Dem	Mich.	8	4
9th Mink, Patsy T.	Dem	Hai.	5	4
10th Meeds, Lloyd	Dem	Wash.	5	4
11th Kazen, Abraham Jr.	Dem	Tex.	4	4
12th Stephens, Robert G. Jr.	Dem	Ga.	7	2
13th Vigorito, Joseph P.	Dem	Penn.	5	2
14th Melcher, John	Dem	Mont.	3	2
15th Roncalio, Teno	Dem	Wyo.	3	*2 2
16th Bingham, Jonathan B.	Dem	N.Y.	5	*2 1
17th Seiberling, John F.	Dem	Ohio	2	1
18th Runnels, Harold L.	Dem	N.M.	2	1
19th Burke, Yvonne Brathwaite	Dem	Cal.	1	1
20th Won Pat, Antonio Borja	Dem	Guam	1	1
21st Owens, D. Wayne	Dem	Utah	1	1
22nd de Lugo, Ron	Dem	V.I.	1	*1 1
23rd Jones, James R.	Dem	Okla.	1	1

Minority

Rank Name	Party	State	Terms in: House	Terms in: Comm.
RM1 Saylor, John P.	Rep	Penn.	13	13
RM2 2nd Hosmer, Craig	Rep	Cal.	11	11
3rd Skubitz, Joe	Rep	Kans.	6	6
4th Steiger, Sam	Rep	Ariz.	4	4
5th Clausen, Don H.	Rep	Cal.	6	3
6th Ruppe, Philip E.	Rep	Mich.	4	3
7th Camp, John N. Happy	Rep	Okla.	3	3
8th Lujan, Manuel Jr.	Rep	N.M.	3	3
9th Dellenback, John R.	Rep	Ore.	4	2
10th Sebelius, Keith G.	Rep	Kans.	3	2
11th Regula, Ralph S.	Rep	Ohio	1	1
12th Steelman, Alan W.	Rep	Tex.	1	1
13th Maraziti, Joseph J.	Rep	N.J.	1	1
14th Towell, David G.	Rep	Nev.	1	1
15th Martin, James G.	Rep	N.C.	1	1
16th Ketchum, William M.	Rep	Cal.	1	1
17th Cronin, Paul W.	Rep	Mass.	1	1
18th Young, Donald E.	Rep	Alas.	1	1

*1: Member's 1st period of service on the committee;
*2: Member's 2nd period of service on the committee.

Note: Territorial Delegates Antonio Borja Won Pat (Dem-Guam) and Ron de Lugo (Dem-Virgin Islands), were allowed to accrue committee seniority, but were not included in the party ratio of 21 Democrats and 18 Republicans.

Vacancy Filled:
Minority: 18th seat by Young on Mar. 14,1973.

Changes:
Ranking Member:

RM1 Saylor, John P.	Rep	Penn.	Oct. 28,1973	Died in office.
RM2 Hosmer, Craig	Rep	Cal.	Oct. 28,1973	Succeeded Saylor as Ranking Minority Member.

Changes:
Minority:

Maraziti, Joseph J.	Rep	N.J.	May 29,1973	Moved to Judiciary.
Bauman, Robert E.	Rep	Md.	Sep. 6,1973	Replaced Maraziti.
Saylor, John P.	Rep	Penn.	Oct. 28,1973	Died in office.
Symms, Steven D.	Rep	Ida.	Nov. 15,1973	Replaced Saylor.
Hosmer, Craig	Rep	Cal.	Dec. 31,1974	Resigned and retired.

Departures from the House:

	Majority			Minority		
Defeated for Reelection	None			Camp, John N. Happy	Okla.	Rep
				Cronin, Paul W.	Mass.	Rep
				Dellenback, John R.	Ore.	Rep
				Towell, David G.	Nev.	Rep
Lost Election to U.S. Senate	Owens, D. Wayne	Utah	Dem	None		

Departures from Committee:

Moved to Appropriations	Burke, Yvonne Brathwaite	Cal.	Dem	Regula, Ralph S.	Ohio	Rep
Moved to Ways and Means	Jones, James R.	Okla.	Dem	Martin, James O.	N.C.	Rep
No new assignment	O'Hara, James G.	Mich.	Dem	None		

INTERIOR AND INSULAR AFFAIRS / 94th Congress

Service Dates of Committee Chair: Jan. 20,1975-Jan. 3,1977
Service Dates of Majority Members: Jan. 20,1975-Jan. 3,1977
Service Dates of Minority Members: Jan. 28,1975-Jan. 3,1977

Majority

Rank	Name	Party	State	Terms in: House	Terms in: Comm.
Chr	Haley, James A.	Dem	Fla.	12	12
2nd	Taylor, Roy A.	Dem	N.C.	9	9
3rd	Johnson, Harold T.	Dem	Cal.	9	8
4th	Udall, Morris K.	Dem	Ariz.	8	8
5th	Burton, Phillip	Dem	Cal.	7	7
6th	Foley, Thomas S.	Dem	Wash.	6	6
7th	Kastenmeier, Robert W.	Dem	Wisc.	9	5
8th	Mink, Patsy T.	Dem	Hai.	6	5
9th	Meeds, Lloyd	Dem	Wash.	6	5
10th	Kazen, Abraham Jr.	Dem	Tex.	5	5
11th	Stephens, Robert G. Jr.	Dem	Ga.	8	3
12th	Vigorito, Joseph P.	Dem	Penn.	6	3
13th	Melcher, John	Dem	Mont.	4	3
14th	Roncalio, Teno	Dem	Wyo.	4 *2	3
15th	Bingham, Jonathan B.	Dem	N.Y.	6 *2	2
16th	Seiberling, John F.	Dem	Ohio	3	2
17th	Runnels, Harold L.	Dem	N.M.	3	2
18th	Won Pat, Antonio Borja	Dem	Guam	2	2
19th	de Lugo, Ron	Dem	V.I.	2 *1	2
20th	Eckhardt, Robert C.	Dem	Tex.	5	1
21st	Byron, Goodloe E.	Dem	Md.	3	1
22nd	Benitez, Jaime	PpD	P.R.	2 *1	1
23rd	Santini, James D.	Dem	Nev.	1	1
24th	Tsongas, Paul E.	Dem	Mass.	1	1
25th	Howe, Allan T.	Dem	Utah	1	1
26th	Weaver, James H.	Dem	Ore.	1	1
27th	Carr, M. Robert	Dem	Mich.	1	1
28th	Miller, George	Dem	Cal.	1	1
29th	Risenhoover, Theodore M.	Dem	Okla.	1	1

Minority

Rank	Name	Party	State	Terms in: House	Terms in: Comm.
RM	Skubitz, Joe	Rep	Kans.	7	7
2nd	Steiger, Sam	Rep	Ariz.	5	5
3rd	Clausen, Don H.	Rep	Cal.	7	4
4th	Ruppe, Philip E.	Rep	Mich.	5	4
5th	Lujan, Manuel Jr.	Rep	N.M.	4	4
6th	Sebelius, Keith G.	Rep	Kans.	4	3
7th	Steelman, Alan W.	Rep	Tex.	2	2
8th	Ketchum, William M.	Rep	Cal.	2	2
9th	Young, Donald E.	Rep	Alas.	2	2
10th	Bauman, Robert E.	Rep	Md.	2	2
11th	Symms, Steven D.	Rep	Ida.	2	2
12th	Johnson, James P.	Rep	Colo.	2	1
13th	Lagomarsino, Robert J.	Rep	Cal.	2	1
14th	Smith, Virginia D.	Rep	Neb.	1	1

*1: Member's 1st period of service on the committee;
*2: Member's 2nd period of service on the committee.

Note: Territorial Delegates Antonio Borja Won Pat (Dem-Guam) and Ron de Lugo (Dem-Virgin Islands), and Resident Commissioner Jaime Benitez (Popular Democrat-P.R.) were allowed to accrue seniority, but were not included in the committee's party ratio of 26 Democrats and 14 Republicans.

Changes:

Majority:

Name	Party	State	Date	Change
Foley, Thomas S.	Dem	Wash.	Feb. 4,1975	Left committee to become Chair of Agriculture.
Patman, J.W. Wright	Dem	Tex.	Feb. 5,1975	Replaced Foley.
Patman, J.W. Wright	Dem	Tex.	Mar. 7,1976	Died in office.
Florio, James J.	Dem	N.J.	Apr. 8,1976	Replaced Patman.

Minority:

Name	Party	State	Date	Change
Ketchum, William M.	Rep	Cal.	May 15,1975	Moved to Ways and Means.
Pettis, Shirley N.	Rep	Cal.	May 15,1975	Replaced Ketchum.

Departures from the House:

	Majority		Minority	
Elected to U.S. Senate	Melcher, John	Mont. Dem	None	
Defeated for Reelection	Benitez, Jaime	P.R. Dem	None	
	Howe, Allan T.	Utah Dem		
	Vigorito, Joseph P.	Penn. Dem		
Lost Election to U.S. Senate	None		Steelman, Alan W.	Tex. Rep
			Steiger, Sam	Ariz. Rep
Lost Nomination to U.S. Senate	Mink, Patsy T.	Hai. Dem	None	
Retired	Haley, James A.	Fla. Dem	None	
	Stephens, Robert G. Jr.	Ga. Dem		
	Taylor, Roy A.	N.C. Dem		

Departures from Committee:

Became Chair of Public Works & Transportation	Johnson, Harold T.	Cal. Dem	None	
Moved to Appropriations	None		Smith, Virginia D.	Neb. Rep
Moved to Education & Labor; International Relations	None		Pettis, Shirley N.	Cal. Rep

INTERIOR AND INSULAR AFFAIRS / 95th Congress

Service Dates of Committee Chair: Jan. 19,1977-Jan. 3,1979
Service Dates of Majority Members: Jan. 19,1977-Jan. 3,1979
Service Dates of Minority Members: Jan. 19,1977-Jan. 3,1979

Majority

Rank Name	Party	State	Terms in: House	Terms in: Comm.
Chr Udall, Morris K.	Dem	Ariz.	9	9
2nd Burton, Phillip	Dem	Cal.	8	8
3rd Kastenmeier, Robert W.	Dem	Wisc.	10	6
4th Meeds, Lloyd	Dem	Wash.	7	6
5th Kazen, Abraham Jr.	Dem	Tex.	6	6
6th Roncalio, Teno	Dem	Wyo.	5	*2 4
7th Bingham, Jonathan B.	Dem	N.Y.	7	*2 3
8th Seiberling, John F.	Dem	Ohio	4	3
9th Runnels, Harold L.	Dem	N.M.	4	3
10th Won Pat, Antonio Borja	Dem	Guam	3	3
11th de Lugo, Ron	Dem	V.I.	3	*1 3
12th Eckhardt, Robert C.	Dem	Tex.	6	2
13th Byron, Goodloe E.	Dem	Md.	4	2
14th Santini, James D.	Dem	Nev.	2	2
15th Tsongas, Paul E.	Dem	Mass.	2	2
16th Weaver, James H.	Dem	Ore.	2	2
17th Carr, M. Robert	Dem	Mich.	2	2
18th Miller, George	Dem	Cal.	2	2
19th Risenhoover, Theodore M.	Dem	Okla.	2	2
20th Florio, James J.	Dem	N.J.	2	2
21st Mathis, M. Dawson	Dem	Ga.	4	1
22nd Sharp, Philip R.	Dem	Ind.	2	1
23rd McHugh, Matthew F.	Dem	N.Y.	2	1
24th Krebs, John H.	Dem	Cal.	2	1
25th Markey, Edward J.	Dem	Mass.	2	1
26th Kostmayer, Peter H.	Dem	Penn.	1	1
27th Corrada, Baltasar	NPr	P.R.	1	1
28th Murphy, Austin J.	Dem	Penn.	1	1
29th Rahall, Nick J. II	Dem	W.Va.	1	1
30th Vento, Bruce F.	DFL	Minn.	1	1
31st Huckaby, T. Jerry	Dem	La.	1	1
32nd Gudger, V. Lamar	Dem	N.C.	1	1

Minority

Rank Name	Party	State	Terms in: House	Terms in: Comm.
RM Skubitz, Joe	Rep	Kans.	8	8
2nd Clausen, Don H.	Rep	Cal.	8	5
3rd Ruppe, Philip E.	Rep	Mich.	6	5
4th Lujan, Manuel Jr.	Rep	N.M.	5	5
5th Sebelius, Keith G.	Rep	Kans.	5	4
6th Young, Donald E.	Rep	Alas.	3	3
7th Bauman, Robert E.	Rep	Md.	3	3
8th Symms, Steven D.	Rep	Ida.	3	3
9th Johnson, James P.	Rep	Colo.	3	2
10th Lagomarsino, Robert J.	Rep	Cal.	3	2
11th Marriott, D. Daniel	Rep	Utah	1	1
12th Marlenee, Ron	Rep	Mont.	1	1
13th Rudd, Eldon D.	Rep	Ariz.	1	1
14th Edwards, M. H. (Mickey)	Rep	Okla.	1	1

*1: Member's 1st period of service on the committee;
*2: Member's 2nd period of service on the committee.

Note: Territorial Delegates Antonio Borja Won Pat (Dem-Guam) and Ron de Lugo (Dem-Virgin Islands), and Resident Commissioner Baltasar Corrada (New Progressive-P.R.) were allowed to accrue seniority, but were not included in the committee's party ratio of 29 Democrats and 14 Republicans.

Changes:

Majority:

McHugh, Matthew F.	Dem	N.Y.	Jan. 25,1978	Moved to Appropriations.
Howard, James J.	Dem	N.J.	Feb. 22,1978	Replaced McHugh.
Byron, Goodloe E.	Dem	Md.	Oct. 11,1978	Died in office.
Roncalio, Teno	Dem	Wyo.	Dec. 30,1978	Resigned and retired.

Minority:

Skubitz, Joe	Rep	Kans.	Dec. 31,1978	Resigned and retired.

	Majority		Minority	
Departures from the House:				
Elected to U.S. Senate	Tsongas, Paul E.	Mass. Dem	None	
Defeated for Reelection	de Lugo, Ron	V.I. Dem	None	
	Krebs, John H.	Cal. Dem		
Defeated for Renomination	Risenhoover, Theodore M.	Okla. Dem	None	
Retired	Meeds, Lloyd	Wash. Dem	Ruppe, Philip E.	Mich. Rep
Departures from Committee:				
Moved to Appropriations	None		Rudd, Eldon D.	Ariz. Rep
No new assignment	None		Bauman, Robert E.	Md. Rep

INTERIOR AND INSULAR AFFAIRS / 96th Congress

Service Dates of Committee Chair: Jan. 24,1979-Jan. 3,1981
Service Dates of Majority Members: Jan. 24,1979-Jan. 3,1981
Service Dates of Minority Members: Jan. 24,1979-Jan. 3,1981

Majority

Rank	Name	Party	State	Terms in: House	Terms in: Comm.
Chr	Udall, Morris K.	Dem	Ariz.	10	10
2nd	Burton, Phillip	Dem	Cal.	9	9
3rd	Kastenmeier, Robert W.	Dem	Wisc.	11	7
4th	Kazen, Abraham Jr.	Dem	Tex.	7	7
5th	Bingham, Jonathan B.	Dem	N.Y.	8	*2 4
6th	Seiberling, John F.	Dem	Ohio	5	4
7th	Runnels, Harold L.	Dem	N.M.	5	4
8th	Won Pat, Antonio Borja	Dem	Guam	4	4
9th	Eckhardt, Robert C.	Dem	Tex.	7	3
10th	Santini, James D.	Dem	Nev.	3	3
11th	Weaver, James H.	Dem	Ore.	3	3
12th	Carr, M. Robert	Dem	Mich.	3	3
13th	Miller, George	Dem	Cal.	3	3
14th	Florio, James J.	Dem	N.J.	3	3
15th	Mathis, M. Dawson	Dem	Ga.	5	2
16th	Sharp, Philip R.	Dem	Ind.	3	2
17th	Markey, Edward J.	Dem	Mass.	3	2
18th	Kostmayer, Peter H.	Dem	Penn.	2	2
19th	Corrada, Baltasar	NPr	P.R.	2	2
20th	Murphy, Austin J.	Dem	Penn.	2	2
21st	Rahall, Nick J. II	Dem	W.Va.	2	2
22nd	Vento, Bruce F.	DFL	Minn.	2	2
23rd	Huckaby, T. Jerry	Dem	La.	2	2
24th	Gudger, V. Lamar	Dem	N.C.	2	2
25th	Howard, James J.	Dem	N.J.	8	2
26th	Patterson, Jerry M.	Dem	Cal.	3	1
27th	Kogovsek, Raymond P.	Dem	Colo.	1	1
28th	Williams, Pat	Dem	Mont.	1	1

Minority

Rank	Name	Party	State	Terms in: House	Terms in: Comm.
RM	Clausen, Don H.	Rep	Cal.	9	6
2nd	Lujan, Manuel Jr.	Rep	N.M.	6	6
3rd	Sebelius, Keith G.	Rep	Kans.	6	5
4th	Young, Donald E.	Rep	Alas.	4	4
5th	Symms, Steven D.	Rep	Ida.	4	4
6th	Johnson, James P.	Rep	Colo.	4	3
7th	Lagomarsino, Robert J.	Rep	Cal.	4	3
8th	Marriott, D. Daniel	Rep	Utah	2	2
9th	Marlenee, Ron	Rep	Mont.	2	2
10th	Edwards, M. H. (Mickey)	Rep	Okla.	2	2
11th	Cheney, Richard B.	Rep	Wyo.	1	1
12th	Pashayan, Charles S. Jr.	Rep	Cal.	1	1
13th	Whittaker, Robert	Rep	Kans.	1	1
14th	Bereuter, Douglas K.	Rep	Neb.	1	1
15th	Evans, Melvin H.	Rep	V.I.	1	1

*2: Member's 2nd period of service on the committee.

Note: Territorial Delegates Antonio Borja Won Pat (Dem-Guam) and Melvin H. Evans (Rep-Virgin Islands), and Resident Commissioner Baltasar Corrada (New Progressive-P.R.), were allowed to accrue seniority, but were not included in the committee's party ratio of 26 Democrats and 14 Republicans.

Changes:

Majority:

Runnels, Harold L.	Dem	N.M.	Aug. 5,1980	Died in office.

	Majority		Minority	
Departures from the House:				
Elected to U.S. Senate	None		Symms, Steven D.	Ida. Rep
Defeated for Reelection	Carr, M. Robert	Mich. Dem	Evans, Melvin H.	V.I. Rep
	Eckhardt, Robert C.	Tex. Dem		
	Gudger, V. Lamar	N.C. Dem		
	Kostmayer, Peter H.	Penn. Dem		
Lost Nomination to U.S. Senate	Mathis, M. Dawson	Ga. Dem	None	
Retired	None		Johnson, James P.	Colo. Rep
			Sebelius, Keith G.	Kans. Rep

Departures from Committee:

	Majority		Minority	
Became Chair of Public Works & Transportation	Howard, James J.	N.J. Dem	None	
Moved to Appropriations	None		Edwards, M.H. (Mickey)	Okla. Rep
Moved to Energy & Commerce	None		Whittaker, Robert	Kans. Rep

INTERIOR AND INSULAR AFFAIRS / 97th Congress

Service Dates of Committee Chair: Jan. 28,1981-Jan. 3,1983
Service Dates of Majority Members: Jan. 28,1981-Jan. 3,1983
Service Dates of Minority Members: Jan. 28,1981-Jan. 3,1983

Majority

Rank	Name	Party	State	Terms in: House	Terms in: Comm.
Chr	Udall, Morris K.	Dem	Ariz.	11	11
2nd	Burton, Phillip	Dem	Cal.	10	10
3rd	Kastenmeier, Robert W.	Dem	Wisc.	12	8
4th	Kazen, Abraham Jr.	Dem	Tex.	8	8
5th	Bingham, Jonathan B.	Dem	N.Y.	9	*2 5
6th	Seiberling, John F.	Dem	Ohio	6	5
7th	Won Pat, Antonio Borja	Dem	Guam	5	5
8th	Santini, James D.	Dem	Nev.	4	4
9th	Weaver, James H.	Dem	Ore.	4	4
10th	Miller, George	Dem	Cal.	4	4
11th	Florio, James J.	Dem	N.J.	4	4
12th	Sharp, Philip R.	Dem	Ind.	4	3
13th	Markey, Edward J.	Dem	Mass.	4	3
14th	Corrada, Baltasar	NPr	P.R.	3	3
15th	Murphy, Austin J.	Dem	Penn.	3	3
16th	Rahall, Nick Joe II	Dem	W.Va.	3	3
17th	Vento, Bruce F.	Dem	Minn.	3	3
18th	Huckaby, T. Jerry	Dem	La.	3	3
19th	Patterson, Jerry M.	Dem	Cal.	4	2
20th	Kogovsek, Raymond P.	Dem	Colo.	2	2
21st	Williams, Pat	Dem	Mont.	2	2
22nd	Kildee, Dale E.	Dem	Mich.	3	1
23rd	Coelho, Anthony L.	Dem	Cal.	2	1
24th	Byron, Beverly B.	Dem	Md.	2	1
25th	de Lugo, Ron	Dem	V.I.	4	*2 1
26th	Gejdenson, Samuel	Dem	Conn.	1	1

Minority

Rank	Name	Party	State	Terms in: House	Terms in: Comm.
RM	Lujan, Manuel Jr.	Rep	N.M.	7	7
2nd	Clausen, Don H.	Rep	Cal.	10	7
3rd	Young, Donald E.	Rep	Alas.	5	5
4th	Lagomarsino, Robert J.	Rep	Cal.	5	4
5th	Marriott, D. Daniel	Rep	Utah	3	3
6th	Marlenee, Ron	Rep	Mont.	3	3
7th	Cheney, Richard B.	Rep	Wyo.	2	2
8th	Pashayan, Charles S. Jr.	Rep	Cal.	2	2
9th	Bereuter, Douglas K.	Rep	Neb.	2	2
10th	Hinson, Jon C.	Rep	Miss.	2	1
11th	Martin, David O'B.	Rep	N.Y.	1	1
12th	Craig, Larry E.	Rep	Ida.	1	1
13th	Hendon, William M.	Rep	N.C.	1	*1 1
14th	Brown, Hank	Rep	Colo.	1	1
15th	Staton, David (Mick)	Rep	W.Va.	1	1
16th	Smith, Denny	Rep	Ore.	1	1
17th	Hansen, James V.	Rep	Utah	1	1

*1: Member's 1st period of service on the committee;
*2: Member's 2nd period of service on the committee.

Notes: Territorial Delegates Antonio Borja Won Pat (Dem-Guam) and Ron de Lugo (Dem-Virgin Islands), and Resident Commissioner Baltasar Corrada (New Progressive-P.R.) were allowed to accrue seniority, but were not included in the committee's party ratio of 23 Democrats and 17 Republicans. Ranking on this committee for the following member was affected by other chamber service: Don H. Clausen (Rep-Cal.), Ranking Minority Member, Public Works and Transportation.

Changes:

Minority:

Hinson, Jon C.	Rep	Miss.	Apr. 13,1981	Resigned and retired.
Emerson, Bill	Rep	Mo.	Dec. 10,1981	Replaced Hinson.

Departures from the House:

	Majority		Minority	
Defeated for Reelection	None		Clausen, Don H.	Cal. Rep
			Hendon, William M.	N.C. Rep
			Staton, David (Mick)	W.Va. Rep
Lost Nomination to U.S. Senate	Santini, James D.	Nev. Dem	None	
Retired	Bingham, Jonathan B.	N.Y. Dem	None	

Departures from Committee:

	Majority		Minority	
Moved to Budget	Miller, George	Cal. Dem	None	
Moved to Foreign Affairs	None		Bereuter, Douglas K.	Neb. Rep
Moved to Armed Services	None		Martin, David O'B.	N.Y. Rep
Ceased active membership to serve on Budget	Williams, Pat	Mont. Dem	None	
No new assignment	Kastenmeier, Robert W.	Wisc. Dem	None	

INTERIOR AND INSULAR AFFAIRS / 98th Congress

Service Dates of Committee Chair: Jan. 6,1983-Jan. 3,1985
Service Dates of Majority Members: Jan. 6,1983-Jan. 3,1985
Service Dates of Minority Members: Jan. 6,1983-Jan. 3,1985

Majority

Rank	Name	Party	State	Terms in: House	Terms in: Comm.
Chr	Udall, Morris K.	Dem	Ariz.	12	12
2nd	Burton, Phillip	Dem	Cal.	11	11
3rd	Kazen, Abraham Jr.	Dem	Tex.	9	9
4th	Seiberling, John F.	Dem	Ohio	7	6
5th	Won Pat, Antonio Borja	Dem	Guam	6	6
6th	Weaver, James H.	Dem	Ore.	5	5
7th	Miller, George	Dem	Cal.	5	5
8th	Florio, James J.	Dem	N.J.	5	5
9th	Sharp, Philip R.	Dem	Ind.	5	4
10th	Markey, Edward J.	Dem	Mass.	5	4
11th	Corrada, Baltasar	NPr	P.R.	4	4
12th	Murphy, Austin J.	Dem	Penn.	4	4
13th	Rahall, Nick Joe II	Dem	W.Va.	4	4
14th	Vento, Bruce F.	Dem	Minn.	4	4
15th	Huckaby, T. Jerry	Dem	La.	4	4
16th	Patterson, Jerry M.	Dem	Cal.	5	3
17th	Kogovsek, Raymond P.	Dem	Colo.	3	3
18th	Kildee, Dale E.	Dem	Mich.	4	2
19th	Coelho, Anthony L.	Dem	Cal.	3	2
20th	Byron, Beverly B.	Dem	Md.	3	2
21st	de Lugo, Ron	Dem	V.I.	5	*2 2
22nd	Gejdenson, Samuel	Dem	Conn.	2	2
23rd	Patman, William N.	Dem	Tex.	2	1
24th	Kostmayer, Peter H.	Dem	Penn.	3	*2 1
25th	Moody, Jim	Dem	Wisc.	1	1
26th	Mollohan, Alan B.	Dem	W.Va.	1	1
27th	Clarke, James McClure	Dem	N.C.	1	1
28th	McNulty, James F. Jr.	Dem	Ariz.	1	1
29th	Lehman, Richard H.	Dem	Cal.	1	1

Minority

Rank	Name	Party	State	Terms in: House	Terms in: Comm.
RM	Lujan, Manuel Jr.	Rep	N.M.	8	8
2nd	Young, Donald E.	Rep	Alas.	6	6
3rd	Lagomarsino, Robert J.	Rep	Cal.	6	5
4th	Marriott, D. Daniel	Rep	Utah	4	4
5th	Marlenee, Ron	Rep	Mont.	4	4
6th	Cheney, Richard B.	Rep	Wyo.	3	3
7th	Pashayan, Charles S. Jr.	Rep	Cal.	3	3
8th	Craig, Larry E.	Rep	Ida.	2	2
9th	Brown, Hank	Rep	Colo.	2	2
10th	Smith, Denny	Rep	Ore.	2	2
11th	Hansen, James V.	Rep	Utah	2	2
12th	Emerson, Bill	Rep	Mo.	2	2
13th	McCain, John	Rep	Ariz.	1	1
14th	Vucanovich, Barbara	Rep	Nev.	1	1

*2: Member's 2nd period of service on the committee.

Note: Territorial Delegates Antonio Borja Won Pat (Dem-Guam) and Ron de Lugo (Dem-Virgin Islands), and Resident Commissioner Baltasar Corrada (New Progressive-P.R.) were allowed to accrue seniority, but were not included in the committee's party ratio of 26 Democrats and 14 Republicans.

Changes:

Majority:

Name	Party	State	Date	Change
Burton, Phillip	Dem	Cal.	Apr. 10,1983	Died in office.
Boxer, Barbara	Dem	Cal.	May 24,1983	Replaced Burton.
Boxer, Barbara	Dem	Cal.	July 12,1983	Moved to Interior and Insular Affairs on May 24,1983.
Burton, Sala	Dem	Cal.	July 19,1983	Replaced Boxer.
Florio, James J.	Dem	N.J.	Feb. 29,1984	Moved to Veterans' Affairs.
Richardson, Bill	Dem	N.M.	Feb. 29,1984	Replaced Florio.

Departures from the House:	Majority			Minority		
Elected Mayor of San Juan	Corrada, Baltasar	P.R.	Dem	None		
Defeated for Reelection	Clarke, James McClure	N.C.	Dem	None		
	McNulty, James F. Jr.	Ariz.	Dem			
	Patman, William N.	Tex.	Dem			
	Patterson, Jerry M.	Cal.	Dem			
	Won Pat, Antonio Borja	Guam	Dem			
Defeated for Renomination	Kazen, Abraham Jr.	Tex.	Dem	None		
Lost Nomination for Governor	None			Marriott, D. Daniel	Utah	Rep
Retired	Kogovsek, Raymond P.	Colo.	Dem	None		
Departures from Committee:						
Moved to Rules	Burton, Sala	Cal.	Dem	None		
Moved to Budget; Judiciary	None			Brown, Hank	Colo.	Rep

INTERIOR AND INSULAR AFFAIRS / 99th Congress

Service Dates of Committee Chair: Jan. 7,1985-Jan. 3,1987
Service Dates of Majority Members: Jan. 30,1985-Jan. 3,1987
Service Dates of Minority Members: Jan. 30,1985-Jan. 3,1987

Majority

Rank Name	Party	State	Terms in: House	Terms in: Comm.
Chr Udall, Morris K.	Dem	Ariz.	13	13
2nd Seiberling, John F.	Dem	Ohio	8	7
3rd Weaver, James H.	Dem	Ore.	6	6
4th Miller, George	Dem	Cal.	6	6
5th Sharp, Philip R.	Dem	Ind.	6	5
6th Markey, Edward J.	Dem	Mass.	6	5
7th Murphy, Austin J.	Dem	Penn.	5	5
8th Rahall, Nick Joe II	Dem	W.Va.	5	5
9th Vento, Bruce F.	Dem	Minn.	5	5
10th Huckaby, T. Jerry	Dem	La.	5	5
11th Kildee, Dale E.	Dem	Mich.	5	3
12th Coelho, Anthony L.	Dem	Cal.	4	3
13th Byron, Beverly B.	Dem	Md.	4	3
14th de Lugo, Ron	Dem	V.I.	6 *2	3
15th Gejdenson, Samuel	Dem	Conn.	3	3
16th Kostmayer, Peter H.	Dem	Penn.	4 *2	2
17th Moody, Jim	Dem	Wisc.	2	2
18th Mollohan, Alan B.	Dem	W.Va.	2	2
19th Lehman, Richard H.	Dem	Cal.	2	2
20th Richardson, Bill	Dem	N.M.	2	2
21st Sunia, Fofo I. F.	Dem	A.Sm.	3	1
22nd Darden, George W. (Buddy)	Dem	Ga.	2	1
23rd Visclosky, Peter J.	Dem	Ind.	1	1
24th Fuster, Jaime B.	Dem	P.R.	1	1
25th Levine, Mel	Dem	Cal.	2 *T	1

Minority

Rank Name	Party	State	Terms in: House	Terms in: Comm.
RM Young, Donald E.	Rep	Alas.	7	7
2nd Lujan, Manuel Jr.	Rep	N.M.	9	9
3rd Lagomarsino, Robert J.	Rep	Cal.	7	6
4th Marlenee, Ron	Rep	Mont.	5	5
5th Cheney, Richard B.	Rep	Wyo.	4	4
6th Pashayan, Charles S. Jr.	Rep	Cal.	4	4
7th Craig, Larry E.	Rep	Ida.	3	3
8th Smith, Denny	Rep	Ore.	3	3
9th Hansen, James V.	Rep	Utah	3	3
10th Emerson, Bill	Rep	Mo.	3	3
11th McCain, John	Rep	Ariz.	2	2
12th Vucanovich, Barbara	Rep	Nev.	2	2
13th Hendon, William M.	Rep	N.C.	2 *2	1
14th Strang, Michael L.	Rep	Colo.	1	1
15th Blaz, Ben Garrido	Rep	Guam	1	1
16th Barton, Joe L.	Rep	Tex.	1	1

*2: Member's 2nd period of service on the committee;
*T: Temporary member of the committee.

Notes: Territorial Delegates Ron de Lugo (Dem-Virgin Islands), Fofo I.F. Sunia (Dem-American Samoa), and Ben Garrido Blaz (Rep-Guam), and Resident Commissioner Jamie B. Fuster (Dem-P.R.), were allowed to accrue seniority, but were not included in the committee's party ratio of 22 Democrats and 15 Republicans. Ranking on this committee for the following member was affected by other chamber service: Manuel Lujan, Jr. (Rep-N.M.), Ranking Minority Member, Science and Technology.

Vacancy Filled:
Majority: 25th seat by Levine on Feb. 6,1985.

Changes:
Majority:

Mollohan, Alan B.	Dem	W.Va.	May 1,1986	Moved to Appropriations.
Atkins, Chester G.	Dem	Mass.	July 29,1986	Replaced Mollohan.

	Majority		Minority	
Departures from the House:				
Elected to U.S. Senate	None		McCain, John	Ariz. Rep
Defeated for Reelection	None		Hendon, William M.	N.C. Rep
			Strang, Michael L.	Colo. Rep
Retired	Seiberling, John F.	Ohio Dem	None	
	Weaver, James H.	Ore. Dem		
Departures from Committee:				
Moved to Ways and Means	Moody, Jim	Wisc. Dem	None	
Moved to Foreign Affairs; Standards of Official Conduct	Atkins, Chester G.	Mass. Dem	None	
Moved to Energy and Commerce	None		Barton, Joe L.	Tex. Rep

INTERIOR AND INSULAR AFFAIRS / 100th Congress

Service Dates of Committee Chair: Jan. 8,1987-Jan. 3,1989
Service Dates of Majority Members: Jan. 22,1987-Jan. 3,1989
Service Dates of Minority Members: Jan. 21,1987-Jan. 3,1989

Majority

Rank	Name	Party	State	Terms in: House	Terms in: Comm.
Chr	Udall, Morris K.	Dem	Ariz.	14	14
2nd	Miller, George	Dem	Cal.	7	7
3rd	Sharp, Philip R.	Dem	Ind.	7	6
4th	Markey, Edward J.	Dem	Mass.	6	6
5th	Murphy, Austin J.	Dem	Penn.	6	6
6th	Rahall, Nick Joe II	Dem	W.Va.	6	6
7th	Vento, Bruce F.	DFL	Minn.	6	6
8th	Huckaby, T. Jerry	Dem	La.	6	6
9th	Kildee, Dale E.	Dem	Mich.	6	4
10th	Coelho, Anthony L.	Dem	Cal.	5	4
11th	Byron, Beverly B.	Dem	Md.	5	4
12th	de Lugo, Ron	Dem	V.I.	7	*2 4
13th	Gejdenson, Samuel	Dem	Conn.	4	4
14th	Kostmayer, Peter H.	Dem	Penn.	5	*2 3
15th	Lehman, Richard H.	Dem	Cal.	3	3
16th	Richardson, Bill	Dem	N.M.	3	3
17th	Sunia, Fofo I. F.	Dem	A.Sm.	4	2
18th	Darden, George W. (Buddy)	Dem	Ga.	3	2
19th	Visclosky, Peter J.	Dem	Ind.	2	2
20th	Fuster, Jaime B.	Dem	P.R.	2	2
21st	Levine, Mel	Dem	Cal.	3	2
22nd	Clarke, James McClure	Dem	N.C.	2	*2 1
23rd	Owens, Wayne	Dem	Utah	2	*2 1
24th	Lewis, John	Dem	Ga.	1	1
25th	Campbell, Ben Nighthorse	Dem	Colo.	1	1
26th	DeFazio, Peter A.	Dem	Ore.	1	1

Minority

Rank	Name	Party	State	Terms in: House	Terms in: Comm.
RM	Young, Donald E.	Rep	Alas.	8	8
2nd	Lujan, Manuel Jr.	Rep	N.M.	10	10
3rd	Lagomarsino, Robert J.	Rep	Cal.	8	7
4th	Marlenee, Ron	Rep	Mont.	6	6
5th	Cheney, Richard B.	Rep	Wyo.	5	5
6th	Pashayan, Charles S. Jr.	Rep	Cal.	5	5
7th	Craig, Larry E.	Rep	Ida.	4	4
8th	Smith, Denny	Rep	Ore.	4	4
9th	Hansen, James V.	Rep	Utah	4	4
10th	Emerson, Bill	Rep	Mo.	4	4
11th	Vucanovich, Barbara	Rep	Nev.	3	3
12th	Blaz, Ben Garrido	Rep	Guam	2	2
13th	Rhodes, John J. III	Rep	Ariz.	1	1
14th	Gallegly, Elton	Rep	Cal.	1	1
15th	Baker, Richard H.	Rep	La.	1	1

*2: Member's 2nd period of service on the committee.

Notes: Territorial Delegates Ron de Lugo (Dem-Virgin Islands), Fofo I.F. Sunia (Dem-American Samoa), and Ben Garrido Blaz (Rep-Guam), and Resident Commissioner Jamie B. Fuster (Dem-P.R.), were allowed to accrue seniority, but were not included in the committee's party ratio of 23 Democrats and 14 Republicans. Ranking on this committee for the following member was affected by other chamber service: Manuel Lujan, Jr. (Rep-N.M.), Ranking Minority Member, Science and Technology.

Changes:

Majority:

Name	Party	State	Date	Change
Sunia, Fofo I. F.	Dem	A.Sm.	Sep. 6,1988	Resigned and retired.

Minority:

Name	Party	State	Date	Change
Emerson, Bill	Rep	Mo.	Sep. 23,1988	Moved to Public Works and Transportation.

	Majority			Minority		
Departures from the House:						
Appointed Secretary of Interior	None			Lujan, Manuel Jr.	N.M.	Rep
Departures from Committee:						
Moved to Budget	Huckaby, T. Jerry	La.	Dem	None		
	Kildee, Dale E.	Mich.	Dem			
Moved to Banking, Finance & Urban Affairs	None			Baker, Richard H.	La.	Rep
Moved to Rules	None			Pashayan, Charles S. Jr.	Cal.	Rep

INTERIOR AND INSULAR AFFAIRS / 101st Congress

Service Dates of Committee Chair: Jan. 3,1989-Jan. 3,1991
Service Dates of Majority Members: Jan. 19,1989-Jan. 3,1991
Service Dates of Minority Members: Jan. 20,1989-Jan. 3,1991

Majority

Rank	Name	Party	State	Terms in: House	Terms in: Comm.
Chr	Udall, Morris K.	Dem	Ariz.	15	15
2nd	Miller, George	Dem	Cal.	8	8
3rd	Sharp, Philip R.	Dem	Ind.	8	7
4th	Markey, Edward J.	Dem	Mass.	7	7
5th	Murphy, Austin J.	Dem	Penn.	7	7
6th	Rahall, Nick Joe II	Dem	W.Va.	7	7
7th	Vento, Bruce F.	Dem	Minn.	7	7
8th	Williams, Pat	Dem	Mont.	6	6
9th	Coelho, Anthony L.	Dem	Cal.	6	5
10th	Byron, Beverly B.	Dem	Md.	6	5
11th	de Lugo, Ron	Dem	V.I.	8	*2 5
12th	Gejdenson, Samuel	Dem	Conn.	5	5
13th	Kostmayer, Peter H.	Dem	Penn.	6	*2 4
14th	Lehman, Richard H.	Dem	Cal.	4	4
15th	Richardson, Bill	Dem	N.M.	4	4
16th	Darden, George W. (Buddy)	Dem	Ga.	4	3
17th	Visclosky, Peter J.	Dem	Ind.	3	3
18th	Fuster, Jaime B.	Dem	P.R.	3	3
19th	Levine, Mel	Dem	Cal.	4	3
20th	Clarke, James McClure	Dem	N.C.	3	*2 2
21st	Owens, Wayne	Dem	Utah	3	*2 2
22nd	Lewis, John	Dem	Ga.	2	2
23rd	Campbell, Ben Nighthorse	Dem	Colo.	2	2
24th	DeFazio, Peter A.	Dem	Ore.	2	2
25th	Faleomavaega, Eni F. H.	Dem	A.Sm.	1	1
26th	McDermott, James A.	Dem	Wash.	1	1

Minority

Rank	Name	Party	State	Terms in: House	Terms in: Comm.
RM	Young, Donald E.	Rep	Alas.	9	9
2nd	Lagomarsino, Robert J.	Rep	Cal.	9	8
3rd	Marlenee, Ron	Rep	Mont.	7	7
4th	Cheney, Richard B.	Rep	Wyo.	6	6
5th	Craig, Larry E.	Rep	Ida.	5	5
6th	Smith, Denny	Rep	Ore.	5	5
7th	Hansen, James V.	Rep	Utah	5	5
8th	Vucanovich, Barbara F.	Rep	Nev.	4	4
9th	Blaz, Ben Garrido	Rep	Guam	3	3
10th	Rhodes, John J. III	Rep	Ariz.	2	2
11th	Gallegly, Elton	Rep	Cal.	2	2
12th	Parris, Stanford E.	Rep	Va.	6	1
13th	Smith, Robert F.	Rep	Ore.	4	1
14th	Lightfoot, Jim Ross	Rep	Iowa	3	1
15th	Thomas, Craig	Rep	Wyo.	1	1

*2: Member's 2nd period of service on the committee.

Notes: Territorial Delegates Ron de Lugo (Dem-Virgin Islands), Eni F.H. Faleomavaega (Dem-American Samoa), Ben Garrido Blaz (Rep-Guam), and Resident Commissioner Jaime Fuster (Dem-Puerto Rico) were allowed to accrue seniority but were not included in the committee's party ratio of 23 Democrats and 14 Republicans.

Vacancies Filled:
Minority: 15th seat by Thomas on May 4,1989.

Changes:

Majority:

Coelho, Anthony L.	Dem	Cal.	June 15,1989	Resigned and retired.
Johnson, Tim	Dem	S.D.	Oct. 16,1989	Replaced Coelho.

Minority:

Cheney, Richard B.	Rep	Wyo.	Mar. 17,1989	Resigned; appointed Secretary of Defense.
Duncan, James Jr.	Rep	Tenn.	May 4,1989	Replaced Cheney.

Departures from the House:

	Majority			Minority		
Elected to U.S. Senate	None			Craig, Larry E.	Ida.	Rep
Defeated for Reelection	Clarke, James McClure	N.C.	Dem	Parris, Stanford E.	Va.	Rep
				Smith, Denny	Ore.	Rep

Departures from Committee:

	Majority			Minority
Moved to Standards of Official Conduct; Ways and Means	McDermott, James A.	Wash.	Dem	None

INTERIOR AND INSULAR AFFAIRS / 102nd Congress

Service Dates of Committee Chair: Ch1 Jan. 24,1991-May 4,1991
Ch2 May 4,1991-Jan. 3,1993
Service Dates of Majority Members: Jan. 24,1991-Jan. 3,1993
Service Dates of Minority Members: Jan. 24,1991-Jan. 3,1993

Majority

Rank	Name	Party	State	Terms in: House	Terms in: Comm.
Ch1	Udall, Morris K.	Dem	Ariz.	16	16
Ch2 2nd	Miller, George	Dem	Cal.	9	9
3rd	Sharp, Philip R.	Dem	Ind.	9	8
4th	Markey, Edward J.	Dem	Mass.	8	8
5th	Murphy, Austin J.	Dem	Penn.	8	8
6th	Rahall, Nick Joe II	Dem	W.Va.	8	8
7th	Vento, Bruce F.	Dem	Minn.	8	8
8th	Williams, Pat	Dem	Mont.	7	7
9th	Byron, Beverly B.	Dem	Md.	7	6
10th	de Lugo, Ron	Dem	V.I.	9	*2 6
11th	Gejdenson, Samuel	Dem	Conn.	6	6
12th	Kostmayer, Peter H.	Dem	Penn.	7	*2 5
13th	Lehman, Richard H.	Dem	Cal.	5	5
14th	Richardson, Bill	Dem	N.M.	5	5
15th	Darden, George W. (Buddy)	Dem	Ga.	5	4
16th	Visclosky, Peter J.	Dem	Ind.	4	4
17th	Fuster, Jaime B.	Dem	P.R.	4	4
18th	Levine, Mel	Dem	Cal.	5	4
19th	Owens, Wayne	Dem	Utah	4	*2 3
20th	Lewis, John	Dem	Ga.	3	3
21st	Campbell, Ben Nighthorse	Dem	Colo.	3	3
22nd	DeFazio, Peter A.	Dem	Ore.	3	3
23rd	Faleomavaega, Eni F. H.	Dem	A.Sm.	2	2
24th	Johnson, Tim	Dem	S.D.	3	2
25th	Schumer, Charles E.	Dem	N.Y.	6	1
26th	Jontz, James	Dem	Ind.	3	1
27th	Hoagland, Peter	Dem	Neb.	2	1
28th	Johnston, Harry A.	Dem	Fla.	2	1
29th	LaRocco, Larry	Dem	Ida.	1	1

Minority

Rank	Name	Party	State	Terms in: House	Terms in: Comm.
RM	Young, Donald E.	Rep	Alas.	10	10
2nd	Lagomarsino, Robert J.	Rep	Cal.	10	9
3rd	Marlenee, Ron	Rep	Mont.	8	8
4th	Hansen, James V.	Rep	Utah	6	6
5th	Vucanovich, Barbara F.	Rep	Nev.	5	5
6th	Blaz, Ben Garrido	Rep	Guam	4	4
7th	Rhodes, John J. III	Rep	Ariz.	3	3
8th	Gallegly, Elton	Rep	Cal.	3	3
9th	Smith, Robert F.	Rep	Ore.	5	2
10th	Lightfoot, Jim Ross	Rep	Iowa	4	2
11th	Thomas, Craig	Rep	Wyo.	2	2
12th	Duncan, John J. Jr.	Rep	Tenn.	3	1
13th	Schulze, Richard T.	Rep	Penn.	9	1
14th	Hefley, Joel	Rep	Colo.	3	1
15th	Taylor, Charles H.	Rep	N.C.	1	1
16th	Doolittle, John T.	Rep	Cal.	1	1
17th	Allard, Wayne	Rep	Colo.	1	1

*2: Member's 2nd period of service on the committee.

Notes: Territorial Delegates Ron de Lugo (Dem-Virgin Islands), Eni F.H. Faleomavaega (Dem-American Samoa), Ben Garrido Blaz (Rep-Guam), and Resident Commissioner Jaime Fuster (Dem-Puerto Rico) were allowed to accrue seniority but were not included in the committee's party ratio of 26 Democrats and 16 Republicans.

Changes:

Chair:

Ch1 Udall, Morris K.	Dem	Ariz.	May 4,1991	Resigned and retired.
Ch2 Miller, George	Dem	Cal.	May 9,1991	Succeeded Udall as Chair.

Majority:

Udall, Morris K.	Dem	Ariz.	May 4,1991	Resigned and retired.
Abercrombie, Neil	Dem	Hai.	Oct. 9,1991	Replaced Udall.
Visclosky, Peter J.	Dem	Ind.	Oct. 9,1991	Moved to Appropriations.
Dooley, Calvin	Dem	Cal.	Oct. 9,1991	Replaced Visclosky.
Fuster, Jaime B.	Dem	P.R.	Mar. 4,1992	Resigned and retired.
Colorado, Antonio J.	Dem	P.R.	Mar. 17,1992	Replaced Fuster.

Minority:

Lightfoot, Jim Ross	Rep	Iowa	Feb. 28,1991	Moved to Appropriations.
Baker, Richard H.	Rep	La.	July 11,1991	Replaced Lightfoot.

INTERNAL SECURITY

UN-AMERICAN ACTIVITIES

Jurisdiction, 1947

Established by the Legislative Reorganization Act of 1946:

[Section 121.(1)(q)]

(1) Committee on Un-American Activities.

(A) Un-American activities.

(2) The Committee on Un-American Activities, as a whole or by subcommittee, is authorized to make from time to time investigations of

(i) the extent, character, and objects of un-American propaganda activities in the United States,
(ii) the diffusion within the United States of subversive and un-American propaganda that is instigated from foreign countries or of a domestic origin and attacks the principle of the form of government as guaranteed by our Constitution, and
(iii) all other questions in relation thereto that would aid Congress in any necessary remedial legislation. The Committee on Un-American Activities shall report to the House (or to the Clerk of the House if the House is not in session) the results of any such investigation, together with such recommendations as it deems advisable.

For the purpose of any such investigation, the Committee on Un-American Activities, or any subcommittee thereof, is authorized to sit and act at such times and places within the United States, whether or not the House is sitting, has recessed, or has adjourned, to hold such hearings, to require the attendance of such witnesses and the production of such books, papers, and documents, and to take such testimony, as it deems necessary. Subpoenas may be issued under the signature of the chairman of the committee or any subcommittee, or by any member designated by any such chairman, and may be served by any person designated by any such chairman or member.

INTERNAL SECURITY

Renamed the Committee on Internal Security on February 18, 1969.

Jurisdiction, 1973

Jurisdiction contained in Jefferson's Manual and Rules of the House of Representatives for the 93rd Congress (1973):

[Rule X. 11.]

(1) Committee on Internal Security.

(a) Communist and other subversive activities affecting the internal security of the United States.
(b) The Committee on Internal Security, acting as a whole or by subcommittee, is authorized to make investigations from time to time of

(1) the extent, character, objectives, and activities within the United States of organizations or groups, whether of foreign or domestic origin, their members, agents, and affiliates, which seek to establish, or assist in the establishment of, a totalitarian dictatorship within the United States, or to overthrow or alter, or assist in the overthrow or alteration of, the form of government of the United States or of any State thereof, by force, violence, treachery, espionage, sabotage, insurrection, or any unlawful means,

(2) the extent, character, objectives, and activities within the United States of organizations or groups, their members, agents, and affiliates, which incite or employ acts of force, violence, terrorism, or any unlawful means, to obstruct or oppose the lawful authority of the Government of the United States in the execution of any law or policy affecting the internal security of the United States, and

(3) all other questions, including the administration and execution of any law of the United States, or any portion of law, relating to the foregoing that would aid the Congress or any committee of the House in any necessary remedial legislation. The Committee on Internal Security shall report to the House (or to the Clerk of the House if the House is not in session) the results of any such investigation, together with such recommendations as it deems advisable. For the purpose of any such investigation, the Committee on Internal Security, or any subcommittee thereof, is authorized to sit and act at such times and places within the United States, whether the House is in session, has recessed, or has adjourned, to hold such hearings, and to require, by subpoena or otherwise, the attendance and testimony of such witnesses and the production of such books, records, correspondence, memorandums, papers, and documents, as it deems necessary. Subpoenas may be issued under the signature of the chairman of the committee or any subcommittee, or by any member designated by any such chairman, and may be served by any person designated by any such chairman or member.

Termination, 1975

The Committee was terminated by authority of House Resolution 5 (93-1), agreed to on January 14, 1975. All property and records were transferred at that time to the House Judiciary Committee.

UN-AMERICAN ACTIVITIES / 80th Congress

Service Dates of Committee Chair: Jan. 14,1947-Jan. 3,1949
Service Dates of Majority Members: Jan. 14,1947-Jan. 3,1949
Service Dates of Minority Members: Jan. 16,1947-Jan. 3,1949

Majority

Rank	Name	Party	State	Terms in: House	Terms in: Comm.
Chr	Thomas, J. Parnell	Rep	N.J.	6	2
2nd	Mundt, Karl E.	Rep	S.D.	5	2
3rd	McDowell, John R.	Rep	Penn.	2	2
4th	Nixon, Richard M.	Rep	Cal.	1	1
5th	Vail, Richard B.	Rep	Ill.	1	1

Minority

Rank	Name	Party	State	Terms in: House	Terms in: Comm.
RM	Wood, John S.	Dem	Ga.	4	2
2nd	Rankin, John E.	Dem	Miss.	14	2
3rd	Peterson, J. Hardin	Dem	Fla.	8	2
4th	Bonner, Herbert C.	Dem	N.C.	5	2

Changes:

Majority:

Name	Party	State	Date	Change
Mundt, Karl E.	Rep	S.D.	Dec. 30,1948	Resigned; elected to U.S. Senate

Minority:

Name	Party	State	Date	Change
Bonner, Herbert C.	Dem	N.C.	Nov. 17,1947	Left committee; no new assignment.
Hebert, F. Edward	Dem	La.	Dec. 9,1947	Replaced Bonner.

Departures from the House:

Defeated for Reelection

Majority		Minority
McDowell, John R.	Penn. Rep	None
Vail, Richard B.	Ill. Rep	

Departures from Committee:

No new assignment

Majority	Minority	
None	Peterson, J. Hardin	Fla. Dem
	Rankin, John E.	Miss. Dem
	Hebert, F. Edward	La. Dem

UN-AMERICAN ACTIVITIES / 81st Congress

Service Dates of Committee Chair: Jan. 18,1949-Jan. 3,1951
Service Dates of Majority Members: Jan. 18,1949-Jan. 3,1951
Service Dates of Minority Members: Jan. 31,1949-Jan. 3,1951

Majority

Rank Name	Party	State	Terms in: House	Terms in: Comm.
Chr Wood, John S.	Dem	Ga.	5	3
2nd Walter, Francis E.	Dem	Penn.	9	1
3rd Harrison, Burr P.	Dem	Va.	3	1
4th McSweeney, John	Dem	Ohio	5	1
5th Moulder, Morgan M.	Dem	Mo.	1	1

Minority

Rank Name	Party	State	Terms in: House	Terms in: Comm.
RM1 Thomas, J. Parnell	Rep	N.J.	7	3
RM2 2nd Nixon, Richard M.	Rep	Cal.	2	2
RM3 3rd Case, Francis H.	Rep	S.D.	7	1
4th Velde, Harold H.	Rep	Ill.	1	1

Changes:

Ranking Member:

RM1 Thomas, J. Parnell	Rep	N.J.	Jan. 2,1950	Resigned and retired.
RM2 Nixon, Richard M.	Rep	Cal.	Jan. 2,1950	Succeeded Thomas as Ranking Minority Member.
RM2 Nixon, Richard M.	Rep	Cal.	Nov. 30,1950	Resigned; elected to U.S. Senate.
RM3 Case, Francis H.	Rep	S.D.	Nov. 30,1950	Succeeded Nixon as Ranking Minority Member.

Minority:

Thomas, J. Parnell	Rep	N.J.	Jan. 2,1950	Resigned and retired.
Kearney, Bernard W.	Rep	N.Y.	Jan. 9,1950	Replaced Thomas.
Nixon, Richard M.	Rep	Cal.	Nov. 30,1950	Resigned; elected to U.S. Senate.
Jackson, Donald L.	Rep	Cal.	Dec. 14,1950	Replaced Nixon.

	Majority			Minority		
Departures from the House:						
Elected to U.S. Senate	None			Case, Francis H.	S.D.	Rep
Defeated for Reelection	McSweeney, John	Ohio	Dem	None		
Departures from Committee:						
Moved to Ways and Means	Harrison, Burr P.	Va.	Dem	None		

UN-AMERICAN ACTIVITIES / 82nd Congress

Service Dates of Committee Chair: Jan. 12,1951-Jan. 3,1953
Service Dates of Majority Members: Jan. 12,1951-Jan. 3,1953
Service Dates of Minority Members: Jan. 15,1951-Jan. 3,1953

Majority

Rank Name	Party	State	Terms in: House	Terms in: Comm.
Chr Wood, John S.	Dem	Ga.	6	4
2nd Walter, Francis E.	Dem	Penn.	10	2
3rd Moulder, Morgan M.	Dem	Mo.	2	2
4th Doyle, Clyde G.	Dem	Cal.	3	1
5th Frazier, James B. Jr.	Dem	Tenn.	2	1

Minority

Rank Name	Party	State	Terms in: House	Terms in: Comm.
RM Velde, Harold H.	Rep	Ill.	2	2
2nd Kearney, Bernard W.	Rep	N.Y.	5	2
3rd Jackson, Donald L.	Rep	Cal.	3	2
4th Potter, Charles E.	Rep	Mich.	3	1

Changes:

Minority:

Potter, Charles E.	Rep	Mich.	Nov. 4,1952	Resigned; elected to U.S. Senate.

	Majority			Minority
Departures from the House:				
Retired	Wood, John S.	Ga.	Dem	None

UN-AMERICAN ACTIVITIES / 83rd Congress

Service Dates of Committee Chair: Jan. 19,1953-Jan. 3,1955
Service Dates of Majority Members: Jan. 19,1953-Jan. 3,1955
Service Dates of Minority Members: Jan. 19,1953-Jan. 3,1955

Majority

Rank	Name	Party	State	Terms in: House	Terms in: Comm.
Chr	Velde, Harold H.	Rep	Ill.	3	3
2nd	Kearney, Bernard W.	Rep	N.Y.	6	3
3rd	Jackson, Donald L.	Rep	Cal.	4	3
4th	Clardy, Kit	Rep	Mich.	1	1
5th	Scherer, Gordon H.	Rep	Ohio	1	1

Minority

Rank	Name	Party	State	Terms in: House	Terms in: Comm.
RM	Walter, Francis E.	Dem	Penn.	11	3
2nd	Moulder, Morgan M.	Dem	Mo.	3	3
3rd	Doyle, Clyde G.	Dem	Cal.	4	2
4th	Frazier, James B. Jr.	Dem	Tenn.	3	2

Departures from the House:

	Majority		Minority	
Defeated for Reelection	Clardy, Kit	Mich. Rep	None	

UN-AMERICAN ACTIVITIES / 84th Congress

Service Dates of Committee Chair: Jan. 13,1955-Jan. 3,1957
Service Dates of Majority Members: Jan. 13,1955-Jan. 3,1957
Service Dates of Minority Members: Jan. 20,1955-Jan. 3,1957

Majority

Rank	Name	Party	State	Terms in: House	Terms in: Comm.
Chr	Walter, Francis E.	Dem	Penn.	12	4
2nd	Moulder, Morgan M.	Dem	Mo.	4	4
3rd	Doyle, Clyde G.	Dem	Cal.	5	3
4th	Frazier, James B. Jr.	Dem	Tenn.	4	3
5th	Willis, Edwin E.	Dem	La.	4	1

Minority

Rank	Name	Party	State	Terms in: House	Terms in: Comm.
RM	Velde, Harold H.	Rep	Ill.	4	4
2nd	Kearney, Bernard W.	Rep	N.Y.	7	4
3rd	Jackson, Donald L.	Rep	Cal.	5	4
4th	Scherer, Gordon H.	Rep	Ohio	2	2

Departures from the House:

	Majority		Minority	
Retired	None		Velde, Harold H.	Ill. Rep

UN-AMERICAN ACTIVITIES / 85th Congress

Service Dates of Committee Chair: Jan. 10,1957-Jan. 3,1959
Service Dates of Majority Members: Jan. 10,1957-Jan. 3,1959
Service Dates of Minority Members: Jan. 16,1957-Jan. 3,1959

Majority

Rank	Name	Party	State	Terms in: House	Terms in: Comm.
Chr	Walter, Francis E.	Dem	Penn.	13	5
2nd	Moulder, Morgan M.	Dem	Mo.	5	5
3rd	Doyle, Clyde G.	Dem	Cal.	6	4
4th	Frazier, James B. Jr.	Dem	Tenn.	5	4
5th	Willis, Edwin E.	Dem	La.	5	2

Minority

Rank	Name	Party	State	Terms in: House	Terms in: Comm.
RM	Kearney, Bernard W.	Rep	N.Y.	8	5
2nd	Jackson, Donald L.	Rep	Cal.	6	5
3rd	Scherer, Gordon H.	Rep	Ohio	3	3
4th	McIntosh, Robert J.	Rep	Mich.	1	1

Changes:

Majority:

Name	Party	State	Date	Change
Frazier, James B. Jr.	Dem	Tenn.	Jan. 15,1958	Moved to Ways and Means.
Tuck, William M.	Dem	Va.	Jan. 16,1958	Replaced Frazier.

Departures from the House:

	Majority	Minority	
Defeated for Reelection	None	McIntosh, Robert J.	Mich. Rep
Retired	None	Kearney, Bernard W.	N.Y. Rep

UN-AMERICAN ACTIVITIES / 86th Congress

Service Dates of Committee Chair: Jan. 19,1959-Jan. 3,1961
Service Dates of Majority Members: Jan. 19,1959-Jan. 3,1961
Service Dates of Minority Members: Jan. 19,1959-Jan. 3,1961

Majority

Rank Name	Party	State	Terms in: House	Terms in: Comm.
Chr Walter, Francis E.	Dem	Penn.	14	6
2nd Moulder, Morgan M.	Dem	Mo.	6	6
3rd Doyle, Clyde G.	Dem	Cal.	7	5
4th Willis, Edwin E.	Dem	La.	6	3
5th Tuck, William M.	Dem	Va.	4	2

Minority

Rank Name	Party	State	Terms in: House	Terms in: Comm.
RM Jackson, Donald L.	Rep	Cal.	7	6
2nd Scherer, Gordon H.	Rep	Ohio	4	4
3rd Miller, William E.	Rep	N.Y.	5	1
4th Johansen, August E.	Rep	Mich.	3	1

	Majority	Minority		
Departures from the House:				
Retired	None	Jackson, Donald L.	Cal.	Rep
Departures from Committee:				
No new assignment	None	Miller, William E.	N.Y.	Rep

UN-AMERICAN ACTIVITIES / 87th Congress

Service Dates of Committee Chair: Feb. 6,1961-Jan. 3,1963
Service Dates of Majority Members: Feb. 6,1961-Jan. 3,1963
Service Dates of Minority Members: Feb. 13,1961-Jan. 3,1963

Majority

Rank Name	Party	State	Terms in: House	Terms in: Comm.
Chr Walter, Francis E.	Dem	Penn.	15	7
2nd Moulder, Morgan M.	Dem	Mo.	7	7
3rd Doyle, Clyde G.	Dem	Cal.	8	6
4th Willis, Edwin E.	Dem	La.	7	4
5th Tuck, William M.	Dem	Va.	5	3

Minority

Rank Name	Party	State	Terms in: House	Terms in: Comm.
RM Scherer, Gordon H.	Rep	Ohio	5	5
2nd Johansen, August E.	Rep	Mich.	4	2
3rd Bruce, Donald C.	Rep	Ind.	1	1
4th Schadeberg, Henry C.	Rep	Wisc.	1	1

	Majority			Minority		
Departures from the House:						
Retired	Moulder, Morgan M.	Mo.	Dem	Scherer, Gordon H.	Ohio	Rep

UN-AMERICAN ACTIVITIES / 88th Congress

Service Dates of Committee Chairs: Ch1 Jan. 17,1963-May 31,1963
Ch2 June 5,1963-Jan. 3,1965
Service Dates of Majority Members: Jan. 17,1963-Jan. 3,1965
Service Dates of Minority Members: Jan. 24,1963-Jan. 3,1965

Majority

Rank Name	Party	State	Terms in: House	Terms in: Comm.
Ch1 Walter, Francis E.	Dem	Penn.	16	8
2nd Doyle, Clyde G.	Dem	Cal.	9	7
Ch2 3rd Willis, Edwin E.	Dem	La.	8	5
4th Tuck, William M.	Dem	Va.	6	4
5th Pool, Joe Richard	Dem	Tex.	1	1

Minority

Rank Name	Party	State	Terms in: House	Terms in: Comm.
RM Johansen, August E.	Rep	Mich.	5	3
2nd Bruce, Donald C.	Rep	Ind.	2	2
3rd Schadeberg, Henry C.	Rep	Wisc.	2	2
4th Ashbrook, John M.	Rep	Ohio	2	1

Changes:

Chair:				
Ch1 Walter, Francis E.	Dem	Penn.	May 31,1963	Died in office.
Ch2 Willis, Edwin E.	Dem	La.	June 5,1963	Succeeded Walter as Chair.
Majority:				
Doyle, Clyde G.	Dem	Cal.	Mar. 14,1963	Died in office.
Ichord, Richard H.	Dem	Mo.	May 29,1963	Replaced Doyle.
Walter, Francis E.	Dem	Penn.	May 31,1963	Died in office.
Senner, George F. Jr.	Dem	Ariz.	July 25,1963	Replaced Walter.

Departures from the House:	Majority	Minority	
Defeated for Reelection	None	Johansen, August E.	Mich. Rep
		Schadeberg, Henry C.	Wisc. Rep
Lost Nomination to U.S. Senate	None	Bruce, Donald C.	Ind. Rep

UN-AMERICAN ACTIVITIES / 89th Congress

Service Dates of Committee Chair: Jan. 18,1965-Jan. 3,1967
Service Dates of Majority Members: Jan. 18,1965-Jan. 3,1967
Service Dates of Minority Members: Jan. 21,1965-Jan. 3,1967

Majority

Rank Name	Party	State	Terms in: House	Terms in: Comm.
Chr Willis, Edwin E.	Dem	La.	9	6
2nd Tuck, William M.	Dem	Va.	7	5
3rd Pool, Joe Richard	Dem	Tex.	2	2
4th Ichord, Richard H.	Dem	Mo.	3	2
5th Senner, George F. Jr.	Dem	Ariz.	2	2
6th Weltner, Charles L.	Dem	Ga.	2	1

Minority

Rank Name	Party	State	Terms in: House	Terms in: Comm.
RM Ashbrook, John M.	Rep	Ohio	3	2
2nd Clawson, Del M.	Rep	Cal.	2	1
3rd Buchanan, John H. Jr.	Rep	Ala.	1	1

Departures from the House:	Majority		Minority	
Defeated for Reelection	Senner, George F. Jr.	Ariz. Dem	None	
Retired	Weltner, Charles L.	Ga. Dem	None	
Departures from Committee:				
Moved to Foreign Affairs	None		Buchanan, John H. Jr.	Ala. Rep

UN-AMERICAN ACTIVITIES / 90th Congress

Service Dates of Committee Chair: Jan. 23,1967-Jan. 3,1969
Service Dates of Majority Members: Jan. 23,1967-Jan. 3,1969
Service Dates of Minority Members: Jan. 26,1967-Jan. 3,1969

Majority

Rank Name	Party	State	Terms in: House	Terms in: Comm.
Chr Willis, Edwin E.	Dem	La.	10	7
2nd Tuck, William M.	Dem	Va.	8	6
3rd Pool, Joe Richard	Dem	Tex.	3	3
4th Ichord, Richard H.	Dem	Mo.	4	3
5th Culver, John C.	Dem	Iowa	2	1

Minority

Rank Name	Party	State	Terms in: House	Terms in: Comm.
RM Ashbrook, John M.	Rep	Ohio	4	3
2nd Clawson, Del M.	Rep	Cal.	3	2
3rd Roudebush, Richard L.	Rep	Ind.	4	1
4th Watson, Albert W.	Rep	S.C.	3	1

Changes:

Majority:

Pool, Joe Richard — Dem Tex. — July 14,1968 Died in office.

Departures from the House:	Majority		Minority
Defeated for Renomination	Willis, Edwin E.	La. Dem	None
Retired	Tuck, William M.	Va. Dem	None
Departures from Committee:			
Moved to Government Operations	Culver, John C.	Iowa Dem	None

UN-AMERICAN ACTIVITIES / 91st Congress

* Renamed the Committee on INTERNAL SECURITY on Feb. 18,1969.

Service Dates of Committee Chair: Jan. 29,1969-Jan. 3,1971
Service Dates of Majority Members: Jan. 29,1969-Jan. 3,1971
Service Dates of Minority Members: Jan. 29,1969-Jan. 3,1971

Majority

Rank	Name	Party	State	Terms in: House	Terms in: Comm.
Chr	Ichord, Richard H.	Dem	Mo.	5	4
2nd	Pepper, Claude D.	Dem	Fla.	4	1
3rd	Edwards, Edwin W.	Dem	La.	3	1
4th	Preyer, L. Richardson	Dem	N.C.	1	1
5th	Stokes, Louis	Dem	Ohio	1	1

Minority

Rank	Name	Party	State	Terms in: House	Terms in: Comm.
RM	Ashbrook, John M.	Rep	Ohio	5	4
2nd	Clawson, Del M.	Rep	Cal.	4	3
3rd	Roudebush, Richard L.	Rep	Ind.	5	2
4th	Watson, Albert W.	Rep	S.C.	4	2

Changes:

Minority:

Clawson, Del M.	Rep	Cal.	Feb. 5,1969	Left committee; no new assignment.
Scherle, William J.	Rep	Iowa	Feb. 7,1969	Replaced Clawson.
Scherle, William J.	Rep	Iowa	Nov. 25,1970	Moved to Appropriations.

Departures from the House:

	Majority	Minority		
Lost Election to U.S. Senate	None	Roudebush, Richard L.	Ind.	Rep
Lost Election for Governor	None	Watson, Albert W.	S.C.	Rep

Departures from Committee:

	Majority			Minority
Moved to Appropriations	Stokes, Louis	Ohio	Dem	None

INTERNAL SECURITY / 92nd Congress

Service Dates of Committee Chair: Feb. 4,1971-Jan. 3,1973
Service Dates of Majority Members: Feb. 4,1971-Jan. 3,1973
Service Dates of Minority Members: Feb. 4,1971-Jan. 3,1973

Majority

Rank	Name	Party	State	Terms in: House	Terms in: Comm.
Chr	Ichord, Richard H.	Dem	Mo.	6	5
2nd	Pepper, Claude D.	Dem	Fla.	5	2
3rd	Edwards, Edwin W.	Dem	La.	4	2
4th	Preyer, L. Richardson	Dem	N.C.	2	2
5th	Drinan, Robert F.	Dem	Mass.	1	1

Minority

Rank	Name	Party	State	Terms in: House	Terms in: Comm.
RM	Ashbrook, John M.	Rep	Ohio	6	5
2nd	Zion, Roger H.	Rep	Ind.	3	1
3rd	Thompson, S. Fletcher	Rep	Ga.	3	1
4th	Schmitz, John G.	Rep	Cal.	2	1

Changes:

Majority:

Edwards, Edwin W.	Dem	La.	Feb. 16,1972	Left committee; resigned May 9, 1972 to become Governor of Louisiana.
Davis, Mendel J.	Dem	S.C.	Apr. 27,1972	Replaced Edwards.

Departures from the House:

	Majority	Minority		
Defeated for Renomination	None	Schmitz, John G.	Cal.	Rep
Lost Election to U.S. Senate	None	Thompson, S. Fletcher	Ga.	Rep

INTERNAL SECURITY / 93rd Congress

* The committee was terminated on Jan. 14,1975.

Service Dates of Committee Chair: Jan. 24,1973-Jan. 3,1975
Service Dates of Majority Members: Jan. 24,1973-Jan. 3,1975
Service Dates of Minority Members: Jan. 24,1973-Jan. 3,1975

Majority

Rank	Name	Party	State	Terms in: House	Terms in: Comm.
Chr	Ichord, Richard H.	Dem	Mo.	7	6
2nd	Pepper, Claude D.	Dem	Fla.	6	3
3rd	Preyer, L. Richardson	Dem	N.C.	3	3
4th	Drinan, Robert F.	Dem	Mass.	2	2
5th	Davis, Mendel J.	Dem	S.C.	2	2

Minority

Rank	Name	Party	State	Terms in: House	Terms in: Comm.
RM	Ashbrook, John M.	Rep	Ohio	7	6
2nd	Zion, Roger H.	Rep	Ind.	4	2
3rd	Burke, J. Herbert	Rep	Fla.	4	1
4th	Guyer, Tennyson	Rep	Ohio	1	1

	Majority			Minority		
Departures from the House:						
Defeated for Reelection	None			Zion, Roger H.	Ind.	Rep
Departures from Committee (Abolished):						
Moved to House Administration	Davis, Mendel J.	S.C.	Dem	Burke, J. Herbert	Fla.	Rep
Moved to Government Operations	Drinan, Robert F.	Mass.	Dem	None		
Moved to Judiciary	None			Ashbrook, John M.	Ohio	Rep
No new assignment	Ichord, Richard H.	Mo.	Dem	Guyer, Tennyson	Ohio	Rep
	Pepper, Claude D.	Fla.	Dem			
	Preyer, L. Richardson	N.C.	Dem			

JUDICIARY

Jurisdiction, 1947

Established by the Legislative Reorganization Act of 1946:

[Section 121.(1)(l)]

Committee on the Judiciary.

1. Judicial proceedings, civil and criminal, generally.
2. Constitutional amendments.
3. Federal courts and judges.
4. Local courts in the Territories and possessions.
5. Revision and codification of the statutes of the United States.
6. National penitentiaries.
7. Protection of trade and commerce against unlawful restraints and monopolies.
8. Holidays and celebrations.
9. Bankruptcy, mutiny, espionage, and counterfeiting.
10. State and Territorial boundary lines.
11. Meetings of Congress, attendance of Members, and their acceptance of incompatible offices.
12. Civil liberties.
13. Patents, copyrights, and trade-marks.
14. Patent Office.
15. Immigration and naturalization.
16. Apportionment of Representatives.
17. Measures relating to claims against the United States.
18. Interstate compacts generally.
19. Presidential succession.

Jurisdiction, 1992

Jurisdiction contained in <u>Rules of the House of Representatives</u>, (as revised to July 1, 1992):

[Rule X. 1. (m)]

Committee on the Judiciary.

(1) Judicial proceedings, civil and criminal generally.
(2) Apportionment of Representatives.
(3) Bankruptcy, mutiny, espionage, and counterfeiting.
(4) Civil liberties.
(5) Constitutional amendments.
(6) Federal courts and judges.
(7) Immigration and naturalization.
(8) Interstate compacts generally.
(9) Local courts in the Territories and possessions.
(10) Measures relating to claims against the United States.
(11) Meetings of Congress, attendance of Members and their acceptance of incompatible offices.
(12) National penitentiaries.
(13) Patent Office.
(14) Patents, copyrights, and trademarks.
(15) Presidential succession.
(16) Protection of trade and commerce against unlawful restraints and monopolies.
(17) Revision and codification of the Statutes of the United States.
(18) State and territorial boundary lines.
(19) Communist and other subversive activities affecting the internal security of the United States.

JUDICIARY / 80th Congress

Service Dates of Committee Chair: Jan. 14,1947-Jan. 3,1949
Service Dates of Majority Members: Jan. 14,1947-Jan. 3,1949
Service Dates of Minority Members: Jan. 16,1947-Jan. 3,1949

Majority

Rank Name	Party	State	Terms in: House	Terms in: Comm.
Chr Michener, Earl C.	Rep	Mich.	14	*2 7
2nd Robsion, John M.	Rep	Ky.	13	7
3rd Reed, Chauncey W.	Rep	Ill.	7	6
4th Gwynne, John W.	Rep	Iowa	7	6
5th Graham, Louis E.	Rep	Penn.	5	5
6th Springer, Raymond S.	Rep	Ind.	5	5
7th Fellows, Frank	Rep	Me.	4	3
8th Lewis, Earl R.	Rep	Ohio	4	3
9th Jennings, John Jr.	Rep	Tenn.	5	3
10th Goodwin, Angier L.	Rep	Mass.	3	*1 2
11th Case, Clifford P.	Rep	N.J.	2	1
12th Chadwick, E. Wallace	Rep	Penn.	1	1
13th Reeves, Albert L. Jr.	Rep	Mo.	1	1
14th Keating, Kenneth B.	Rep	N.Y.	1	1
15th Devitt, Edward J.	Rep	Minn.	1	1

Minority

Rank Name	Party	State	Terms in: House	Terms in: Comm.
RM Celler, Emanuel	Dem	N.Y.	13	10
2nd Walter, Francis E.	Dem	Penn.	8	7
3rd Hobbs, Sam	Dem	Ala.	7	7
4th Byrne, William T.	Dem	N.Y.	6	6
5th Kefauver, C. Estes	Dem	Tenn.	5	5
6th Bryson, Joseph R.	Dem	S.C.	5	4
7th Cravens, Fadjo	Dem	Ark.	5	4
8th Lane, Thomas J.	Dem	Mass.	4	3
9th Gorski, Martin	Dem	Ill.	3	3
10th Feighan, Michael A.	Dem	Ohio	3	3
11th Chelf, Frank L.	Dem	Ky.	2	2
12th Gossett, Ed	Dem	Tex.	5	5

*1: Member's 1st period of service on the committee; *2: Member's 2nd period of service on the committee.

Note: "Terms in Committee" for Ed Gossett (Dem-Tex.) include his previous service on the Immigration and Naturalization Committee, as well as the Revision of the Laws Committee, both of which were absorbed by the Judiciary Committee. Gossett's previous committee service, however, was not counted toward his ranking on the Judiciary committee.

Changes:

Majority:

Springer, Raymond S.	Rep	Ind.	Aug. 28,1947	Died in office.
Goodwin, Angier L.	Rep	Mass.	Dec. 18,1947	Moved to Ways and Means.
Foote, Ellsworth B.	Rep	Conn.	Dec. 18,1947	Replaced Springer.
McCulloch, William M.	Rep	Ohio	Dec. 18,1947	Replaced Goodwin.
Robsion, John M.	Rep	Ky.	Feb. 17,1948	Died in office.
Boggs, J. Caleb	Rep	Del.	Mar. 25,1948	Replaced Robsion.

Departures from the House:

	Majority		Minority	
Elected to U.S. Senate	None		Kefauver, C. Estes	Tenn. Dem
Defeated for Reelection	Foote, Ellsworth B.	Conn. Rep	None	
	Devitt, Edward J.	Minn. Rep		
	Lewis, Earl R.	Ohio Rep		
	Reeves, Albert L. Jr.	Mo. Rep		
Defeated for Renomination	Chadwick, E. Wallace	Penn. Rep	None	
	Gwynne, John W.	Iowa Rep		
Retired	None		Cravens, Fadjo	Ark. Dem

JUDICIARY / 81st Congress

Service Dates of Committee Chair: Jan. 18,1949-Jan. 3,1951
Service Dates of Majority Members: Jan. 18,1949-Jan. 3,1951
Service Dates of Minority Members: Jan. 18,1949-Jan. 3,1951

Majority

Rank	Name	Party	State	Terms in: House		Terms in: Comm.
Chr	Celler, Emanuel	Dem	N.Y.	14		11
2nd	Walter, Francis E.	Dem	Penn.	9		8
3rd	Hobbs, Sam	Dem	Ala.	8		8
4th	Byrne, William T.	Dem	N.Y.	7		7
5th	Bryson, Joseph R.	Dem	S.C.	6		5
6th	Lane, Thomas J.	Dem	Mass.	5		4
7th	Gorski, Martin	Dem	Ill.	4		4
8th	Feighan, Michael A.	Dem	Ohio	4		4
9th	Chelf, Frank L.	Dem	Ky.	3		3
10th	Gossett, Ed	Dem	Tex.	6		6
11th	Wilson, J. Frank	Dem	Tex.	2		1
12th	Ramsay, Robert L.	Dem	W.Va.	5	*2	1
13th	Gilmer, William F.(Dixie)	Dem	Okla.	1		1
14th	Tackett, Boyd	Dem	Ark.	1		1
15th	Willis, Edwin E.	Dem	La.	1		1
16th	Denton, Winfield K.	Dem	Ind.	1		1
17th	Frazier, James B. Jr.	Dem	Tenn.	1		1

Minority

Rank	Name	Party	State	Terms in: House		Terms in: Comm.
RM	Michener, Earl C.	Rep	Mich.	15	*2	8
2nd	Reed, Chauncey W.	Rep	Ill.	8		7
3rd	Graham, Louis E.	Rep	Penn.	6		6
4th	Fellows, Frank	Rep	Me.	5		4
5th	Jennings, John Jr.	Rep	Tenn.	6		4
6th	Case, Clifford P.	Rep	N.J.	3		2
7th	Keating, Kenneth B.	Rep	N.Y.	2		2
8th	McCulloch, William M.	Rep	Ohio	2		2
9th	Boggs, J. Caleb	Rep	Del.	2		2
10th	Goodwin, Angier L.	Rep	Mass.	4	*2	1

*2: Member's 2nd period of service on the committee.

Note: "Terms in Committee" for Ed Gossett (Dem-Tex.) include his previous service on the Immigration and Naturalization Committee, as well as the Revision of the Laws Committee, both of which were absorbed by the Judiciary Committee. Gossett's previous committee service, however, was not counted toward his ranking on the Judiciary committee.

Changes:

Majority:

Gorski, Martin	Dem	Ill.	Dec. 4,1949	Died in office.
Rodino, Peter W. Jr.	Dem	N.J.	Jan. 26,1950	Replaced Gorski.

	Majority			Minority		
Departures from the House:						
Defeated for Reelection	Gilmer, William F.(Dixie)	Okla.	Dem	None		
Defeated for Renomination	None			Jennings, John Jr.	Tenn.	Rep
Retired	Hobbs, Sam	Ala.	Dem	Michener, Earl C.	Mich.	Rep
Departures from Committee:						
Moved to Appropriations	Denton, Winfield K.	Ind.	Dem	None		
Moved to Education and Labor	Tackett, Boyd	Ark.	Dem	None		

JUDICIARY / 82nd Congress

Service Dates of Committee Chair: Jan. 12,1951-Jan. 3,1953
Service Dates of Majority Members: Jan. 12,1951-Jan. 3,1953
Service Dates of Minority Members: Jan. 15,1951-Jan. 3,1953

Majority

Rank	Name	Party	State	Terms in: House	Terms in: Comm.
Chr	Celler, Emanuel	Dem	N.Y.	15	12
2nd	Walter, Francis E.	Dem	Penn.	10	9
3rd	Byrne, William T.	Dem	N.Y.	8	8
4th	Bryson, Joseph R.	Dem	S.C.	7	6
5th	Lane, Thomas J.	Dem	Mass.	6	5
6th	Feighan, Michael A.	Dem	Ohio	5	5
7th	Chelf, Frank L.	Dem	Ky.	4	4
8th	Gossett, Ed	Dem	Tex.	7	7
9th	Wilson, J. Frank	Dem	Tex.	3	2
10th	Ramsay, Robert L.	Dem	W.Va.	6	*2 2
11th	Willis, Edwin E.	Dem	La.	2	2
12th	Frazier, James B. Jr.	Dem	Tenn.	2	2
13th	Rodino, Peter W. Jr.	Dem	N.J.	2	2
14th	Jones, Woodrow W.	Dem	N.C.	2	1
15th	Forrester, Elijah L.	Dem	Ga.	1	1
16th	Rogers, Byron G.	Dem	Colo.	1	1
17th	Machrowicz, Thaddeus M.	Dem	Mich.	1	1

Minority

Rank	Name	Party	State	Terms in: House	Terms in: Comm.
RM	Reed, Chauncey W.	Rep	Ill.	9	8
2nd	Graham, Louis E.	Rep	Penn.	7	7
3rd	Fellows, Frank	Rep	Me.	6	5
4th	Case, Clifford P.	Rep	N.J.	4	3
5th	Keating, Kenneth B.	Rep	N.Y.	3	3
6th	McCulloch, William M.	Rep	Ohio	3	3
7th	Boggs, J. Caleb	Rep	Del.	3	3
8th	Goodwin, Angier L.	Rep	Mass.	5	*2 2
9th	Jonas, Edgar A.	Rep	Ill.	2	1
10th	Thompson, Ruth	Rep	Mich.	1	1
11th	Hillings, Patrick J.	Rep	Cal.	1	1
12th	Crumpacker, Shepard J.Jr.	Rep	Ind.	1	1

*2: Member's 2nd period of service on the committee.

Notes: The death of John B. Sullivan (Dem-Mo.), and the election of Claude I. Bakewell (Rep-Mo.) to fill his vacancy on Mar. 19,1951 led to a change in size and party ratio on this committee to 17 Democrats and 13 Republicans on May 10,1951 (reported May 14,1951). "Terms in Committee" for Ed Gossett (Dem-Tex.) include his previous service on the Immigration and Naturalization Committee, as well as the Revision of the Laws Committee, both of which were absorbed by the Judiciary Committee. Gossett's previous committee service, however, was not counted toward his ranking on the Judiciary committee.

Addition:

Minority: 13th Bakewell, Claude I. Rep Mo. May 10,1951

Changes:

Majority:

Name	Party	State	Date	Action
Machrowicz, Thaddeus M.	Dem	Mich.	July 16,1951	Moved to Public Works.
Gossett, Ed	Dem	Tex.	July 31,1951	Resigned and retired.
Pickett, Tom	Dem	Tex.	Aug. 9,1951	Replaced Machrowicz.
Donohue, Harold D.	Dem	Mass.	Aug. 9,1951	Replaced Gossett.
Byrne, William T.	Dem	N.Y.	Jan. 27,1952	Died in office.
Fine, Sidney A.	Dem	N.Y.	Feb. 26,1952	Replaced Byrne.
Pickett, Tom	Dem	Tex.	June 25,1952	Left committee; resigned House on June 30,1952.

Minority:

Name	Party	State	Date	Action
Fellows, Frank	Rep	Me.	Aug. 27,1951	Died in office.
Miller, William E.	Rep	N.Y.	Oct. 17,1951	Replaced Fellows.
Goodwin, Angier L.	Rep	Mass.	July 2,1952	Moved to Ways and Means.

	Majority			Minority		
Departures from the House:						
Elected Governor	None			Boggs, J. Caleb	Del.	Rep
Defeated for Renomination	Ramsay, Robert L.	W.Va.	Dem	None		
Defeated for Reelection	None			Bakewell, Claude I.	Mo.	Rep
Departures from Committee:						
No new assignment	Fine, Sidney A.	N.Y.	Dem	None		

JUDICIARY / 83rd Congress

Service Dates of Committee Chair: Jan. 19,1953-Jan. 3,1955
Service Dates of Majority Members: Jan. 19,1953-Jan. 3,1955
Service Dates of Minority Members: Jan. 19,1953-Jan. 3,1955

Majority

Rank	Name	Party	State	Terms in: House	Terms in: Comm.
Chr	Reed, Chauncey W.	Rep	Ill.	10	9
2nd	Graham, Louis E.	Rep	Penn.	8	8
3rd	Case, Clifford P.	Rep	N.J.	5	4
4th	Keating, Kenneth B.	Rep	N.Y.	4	4
5th	McCulloch, William M.	Rep	Ohio	4	4
6th	Jonas, Edgar A.	Rep	Ill.	3	2
7th	Thompson, Ruth	Rep	Mich.	2	2
8th	Hillings, Patrick J.	Rep	Cal.	2	2
9th	Crumpacker, Shepard J.Jr.	Rep	Ind.	2	2
10th	Miller, William E.	Rep	N.Y.	2	2
11th	Taylor, Dean P.	Rep	N.Y.	6	1
12th	Burdick, Usher L.	Rep	N.D.	8	1
13th	Meader, George	Rep	Mich.	2	*1 1
14th	Curtis, Laurence	Rep	Mass.	1	1
15th	Robsion, John M. Jr.	Rep	Ky.	1	1
16th	Hyde, DeWitt S.	Rep	Md.	1	1

Minority

Rank	Name	Party	State	Terms in: House	Terms in: Comm.
RM	Celler, Emanuel	Dem	N.Y.	16	13
2nd	Walter, Francis E.	Dem	Penn.	11	10
3rd	Bryson, Joseph R.	Dem	S.C.	8	7
4th	Lane, Thomas J.	Dem	Mass.	7	6
5th	Feighan, Michael A.	Dem	Ohio	6	6
6th	Chelf, Frank L.	Dem	Ky.	5	5
7th	Wilson, J. Frank	Dem	Tex.	4	3
8th	Willis, Edwin E.	Dem	La.	3	3
9th	Frazier, James B. Jr.	Dem	Tenn.	3	3
10th	Rodino, Peter W. Jr.	Dem	N.J.	3	3
11th	Jones, Woodrow W.	Dem	N.C.	3	2
12th	Forrester, Elijah L.	Dem	Ga.	2	2
13th	Rogers, Byron G.	Dem	Colo.	2	2
14th	Donohue, Harold D.	Dem	Mass.	4	2

*1: Member's 1st period of service on the committee.

Changes:

Majority:

Name	Party	State	Date	Note
Case, Clifford P.	Rep	N.J.	Aug. 16,1953	Resigned; elected to U.S. Senate in 1954.
Poff, Richard H.	Rep	Va.	Jan. 21,1954	Replaced Case.

Minority:

Name	Party	State	Date	Note
Bryson, Joseph R.	Dem	S.C.	Mar. 10,1953	Died in office.
Fine, Sidney A.	Dem	N.Y.	Mar. 30,1953	Replaced Bryson.

Departures from the House:	Majority		Minority	
Appointed State Judge	None		Wilson, J. Frank	Tex. Dem
Defeated for Reelection	Graham, Louis E.	Penn. Rep	None	
	Jonas, Edgar A.	Ill. Rep		
Departures from Committee:				
No new assignment	Meader, George	Mich. Rep	None	

JUDICIARY / 84th Congress

Service Dates of Committee Chair: Jan. 13,1955-Jan. 3,1957
Service Dates of Majority Members: Jan. 13,1955-Jan. 3,1957
Service Dates of Minority Members: Jan. 20,1955-Jan. 3,1957

Majority

Rank Name	Party	State	Terms in: House	Terms in: Comm.
Chr Celler, Emanuel	Dem	N.Y.	17	14
2nd Walter, Francis E.	Dem	Penn.	12	11
3rd Lane, Thomas J.	Dem	Mass.	8	7
4th Feighan, Michael A.	Dem	Ohio	7	7
5th Chelf, Frank L.	Dem	Ky.	6	6
6th Willis, Edwin E.	Dem	La.	4	4
7th Frazier, James B. Jr.	Dem	Tenn.	4	4
8th Rodino, Peter W. Jr.	Dem	N.J.	4	4
9th Jones, Woodrow W.	Dem	N.C.	4	3
10th Forrester, Elijah L.	Dem	Ga.	3	3
11th Rogers, Byron G.	Dem	Colo.	3	3
12th Donohue, Harold D.	Dem	Mass.	5	3
13th Fine, Sidney A.	Dem	N.Y.	3	*2 2
14th Brooks, Jack B.	Dem	Tex.	2	1
15th Tuck, William M.	Dem	Va.	2	1
16th Ashmore, Robert T.	Dem	S.C.	2	1
17th Quigley, James M.	Dem	Penn.	1	1
18th Boyle, Charles A.	Dem	Ill.	1	1

Minority

Rank Name	Party	State	Terms in: House	Terms in: Comm.
RM1 Reed, Chauncey W.	Rep	Ill.	11	10
RM2 2nd Keating, Kenneth B.	Rep	N.Y.	5	5
3rd McCulloch, William M.	Rep	Ohio	5	5
4th Thompson, Ruth	Rep	Mich.	3	3
5th Hillings, Patrick J.	Rep	Cal.	3	3
6th Crumpacker, Shepard J.Jr.	Rep	Ind.	3	3
7th Miller, William E.	Rep	N.Y.	3	3
8th Taylor, Dean P.	Rep	N.Y.	7	2
9th Burdick, Usher L.	Rep	N.D.	9	2
10th Curtis, Laurence	Rep	Mass.	2	2
11th Robsion, John M. Jr.	Rep	Ky.	2	2
12th Hyde, DeWitt S.	Rep	Md.	2	2
13th Poff, Richard H.	Rep	Va.	2	2
14th Scott, Hugh D. Jr.	Rep	Penn.	7	*2 1

*2: Member's 2nd period of service on the committee.

Changes:

Ranking Member:				
RM1 Reed, Chauncey W.	Rep	Ill.	Feb. 9,1956	Died in office.
RM2 Keating, Kenneth B.	Rep	N.Y.	Feb. 9,1956	Succeeded Reed as Ranking Minority Member.
Majority:				
Fine, Sidney A.	Dem	N.Y.	Jan. 2,1956	Resigned; elected to State Supreme Court.
Davidson, Irwin D.	Dem	N.Y.	Jan. 19,1956	Replaced Fine.
Davidson, Irwin D.	Dem	N.Y.	Dec. 31,1956	Resigned; elected state judge.
Minority:				
Reed, Chauncey W.	Rep	Ill.	Feb. 9,1956	Died in office.
Cramer, William C.	Rep	Fla.	May 23,1956	Replaced Reed.

Departures from the House:	**Majority**		**Minority**	
Defeated for Reelection	Quigley, James M.	Penn. Dem	None	
Defeated for Renomination	None		Thompson, Ruth	Mich. Rep
Retired	Jones, Woodrow W.	N.C. Dem	Crumpacker, Shepard J.Jr.	Ind. Rep
Departures from Committee:				
Moved to Rules	None		Scott, Hugh D. Jr.	Penn. Rep

JUDICIARY / 85th Congress

Service Dates of Committee Chair: Jan. 10,1957-Jan. 3,1959
Service Dates of Majority Members: Jan. 10,1957-Jan. 3,1959
Service Dates of Minority Members: Jan. 16,1957-Jan. 3,1959

Majority

Rank	Name	Party	State	Terms in: House	Terms in: Comm.
Chr	Celler, Emanuel	Dem	N.Y.	18	15
2nd	Walter, Francis E.	Dem	Penn.	13	12
3rd	Lane, Thomas J.	Dem	Mass.	9	8
4th	Feighan, Michael A.	Dem	Ohio	8	8
5th	Chelf, Frank L.	Dem	Ky.	7	7
6th	Willis, Edwin E.	Dem	La.	5	5
7th	Frazier, James B. Jr.	Dem	Tenn.	5	5
8th	Rodino, Peter W. Jr.	Dem	N.J.	5	5
9th	Forrester, Elijah L.	Dem	Ga.	4	4
10th	Rogers, Byron G.	Dem	Colo.	4	4
11th	Donohue, Harold D.	Dem	Mass.	6	4
12th	Brooks, Jack B.	Dem	Tex.	3	2
13th	Tuck, William M.	Dem	Va.	3	2
14th	Ashmore, Robert T.	Dem	S.C.	3	2
15th	Boyle, Charles A.	Dem	Ill.	2	2
16th	Chudoff, Earl	Dem	Penn.	5	1
17th	Dowdy, John V.	Dem	Tex.	4	1
18th	Holtzman, Lester	Dem	N.Y.	3	1

Minority

Rank	Name	Party	State	Terms in: House	Terms in: Comm.
RM	Keating, Kenneth B.	Rep	N.Y.	6	6
2nd	McCulloch, William M.	Rep	Ohio	6	6
3rd	Hillings, Patrick J.	Rep	Cal.	4	4
4th	Miller, William E.	Rep	N.Y.	4	4
5th	Taylor, Dean P.	Rep	N.Y.	8	3
6th	Burdick, Usher L.	Rep	N.D.	10	3
7th	Curtis, Laurence	Rep	Mass.	3	3
8th	Robsion, John M. Jr.	Rep	Ky.	3	3
9th	Hyde, DeWitt S.	Rep	Md.	3	3
10th	Poff, Richard H.	Rep	Va.	3	3
11th	Cramer, William C.	Rep	Fla.	2	2
12th	Moore, Arch A. Jr.	Rep	W.Va.	1	1
13th	Keeney, Russell W.	Rep	Ill.	1	1
14th	Nimtz, F. Jay	Rep	Ind.	1	1

Changes:

Majority:

Name	Party	State	Date	Change
Boyle, Charles A.	Dem	Ill.	July 23,1957	Moved to Appropriations.
Montoya, Joseph M.	Dem	N.M.	July 23,1957	Replaced Boyle.
Chudoff, Earl	Dem	Penn.	Jan. 5,1958	Resigned; elected Philadelphia judge.
Frazier, James B. Jr.	Dem	Tenn.	Jan. 15,1958	Moved to Ways and Means.
Whitener, Basil L.	Dem	N.C.	Jan. 16,1958	Replaced Chudoff.
Libonati, Roland V.	Dem	Ill.	Jan. 16,1958	Replaced Frazier.

Minority:

Name	Party	State	Date	Change
Keeney, Russell W.	Rep	Ill.	Jan. 11,1958	Died in office.
Smith, H. Allen	Rep	Cal.	Jan. 16,1958	Replaced Keeney.
Curtis, Laurence	Rep	Mass.	Feb. 3,1958	Moved to Foreign Affairs.
Cretella, Albert W.	Rep	Conn.	Mar. 4,1958	Replaced Curtis.

Departures from the House:	**Majority**	**Minority**		
Elected to U.S. Senate	None	Keating, Kenneth B.	N.Y.	Rep
Defeated for Reelection	None	Hyde, DeWitt S.	Md.	Rep
		Nimtz, F. Jay	Ind.	Rep
		Robsion, John M. Jr.	Ky.	Rep
		Cretella, Albert W.	Conn.	Rep
Lost Election for Attorney General	None	Hillings, Patrick J.	Cal.	Rep
Retired	None	Burdick, Usher L.	N.D.	Rep
Departures from Committee:				
Moved to Appropriations	Montoya, Joseph M. N.M. Dem	None		
Moved to Public Works	None	Taylor, Dean P.	N.Y.	Rep

JUDICIARY / 86th Congress

Service Dates of Committee Chair: Jan. 19,1959-Jan. 3,1961
Service Dates of Majority Members: Jan. 19,1959-Jan. 3,1961
Service Dates of Minority Members: Jan. 19,1959-Jan. 3,1961

Majority

Rank	Name	Party	State	Terms in: House	Terms in: Comm.
Chr	Celler, Emanuel	Dem	N.Y.	19	16
2nd	Walter, Francis E.	Dem	Penn.	14	13
3rd	Lane, Thomas J.	Dem	Mass.	10	9
4th	Feighan, Michael A.	Dem	Ohio	9	9
5th	Chelf, Frank L.	Dem	Ky.	8	8
6th	Willis, Edwin E.	Dem	La.	6	6
7th	Rodino, Peter W. Jr.	Dem	N.J.	6	6
8th	Forrester, Elijah L.	Dem	Ga.	5	5
9th	Rogers, Byron G.	Dem	Colo.	5	5
10th	Donohue, Harold D.	Dem	Mass.	7	5
11th	Brooks, Jack B.	Dem	Tex.	4	3
12th	Tuck, William M.	Dem	Va.	4	3
13th	Ashmore, Robert T.	Dem	S.C.	4	3
14th	Dowdy, John V.	Dem	Tex.	5	2
15th	Holtzman, Lester	Dem	N.Y.	4	2
16th	Whitener, Basil L.	Dem	N.C.	2	2
17th	Libonati, Roland V.	Dem	Ill.	2	2
18th	Loser, J. Carlton	Dem	Tenn.	2	1
19th	Toll, Herman	Dem	Penn.	1	1
20th	Kastenmeier, Robert W.	Dem	Wisc.	1	1
21st	Kasem, George A.	Dem	Cal.	1	1

Minority

Rank	Name	Party	State	Terms in: House	Terms in: Comm.
RM	McCulloch, William M.	Rep	Ohio	7	7
2nd	Miller, William E.	Rep	N.Y.	5	5
3rd	Poff, Richard H.	Rep	Va.	4	4
4th	Cramer, William C.	Rep	Fla.	3	3
5th	Moore, Arch A. Jr.	Rep	W.Va.	2	2
6th	Smith, H. Allen	Rep	Cal.	2	2
7th	Meader, George	Rep	Mich.	5	*2 1
8th	Bosch, Albert H.	Rep	N.Y.	4	1
9th	Henderson, John E.	Rep	Ohio	3	1
10th	Lindsay, John V.	Rep	N.Y.	1	1
11th	Cahill, William T.	Rep	N.J.	1	1

*2: Member's 2nd period of service on the committee.

Changes:

Minority:

Name	Party	State	Date	Change
Bosch, Albert H.	Rep	N.Y.	Feb. 25,1959	Moved to Ways and Means.
Ray, John H.	Rep	N.Y.	Feb. 25,1959	Replaced Bosch.

	Majority			Minority		
Departures from the House:						
Defeated for Reelection	Kasem, George A.	Cal.	Dem	None		
Retired	None			Henderson, John E.	Ohio	Rep
Departures from Committee:						
No new assignment	None			Smith, H. Allen	Cal.	Rep

JUDICIARY / 87th Congress

Service Dates of Committee Chair: Feb. 6,1961-Jan. 3,1963
Service Dates of Majority Members: Feb. 6,1961-Jan. 3,1963
Service Dates of Minority Members: Feb. 13,1961-Jan. 3,1963

Majority

Rank	Name	Party	State	Terms in: House	Terms in: Comm.
Chr	Celler, Emanuel	Dem	N.Y.	20	17
2nd	Walter, Francis E.	Dem	Penn.	15	14
3rd	Lane, Thomas J.	Dem	Mass.	11	10
4th	Feighan, Michael A.	Dem	Ohio	10	10
5th	Chelf, Frank L.	Dem	Ky.	9	9
6th	Willis, Edwin E.	Dem	La.	7	7
7th	Rodino, Peter W. Jr.	Dem	N.J.	7	7
8th	Forrester, Elijah L.	Dem	Ga.	6	6
9th	Rogers, Byron G.	Dem	Colo.	6	6
10th	Donohue, Harold D.	Dem	Mass.	8	6
11th	Brooks, Jack B.	Dem	Tex.	5	4
12th	Tuck, William M.	Dem	Va.	5	4
13th	Ashmore, Robert T.	Dem	S.C.	5	4

Minority

Rank	Name	Party	State	Terms in: House	Terms in: Comm.
RM	McCulloch, William M.	Rep	Ohio	8	8
2nd	Miller, William E.	Rep	N.Y.	6	6
3rd	Poff, Richard H.	Rep	Va.	5	5
4th	Cramer, William C.	Rep	Fla.	4	4
5th	Moore, Arch A. Jr.	Rep	W.Va.	3	3
6th	Meader, George	Rep	Mich.	6	*2 2
7th	Lindsay, John V.	Rep	N.Y.	2	2
8th	Cahill, William T.	Rep	N.J.	2	2
9th	Ray, John H.	Rep	N.Y.	5	2
10th	Shriver, Garner E.	Rep	Kans.	1	1
11th	MacGregor, Clark	Rep	Minn.	1	1
12th	Mathias, Charles McC. Jr.	Rep	Md.	1	1
13th	Battin, James F.	Rep	Mont.	1	1

Rank Name	Party	State	House	Comm.	Rank Name	Party	State	House	Comm.
14th Dowdy, John V.	Dem	Tex.	6	3	14th Bromwell, James E.	Rep	Iowa	1	1
15th Holtzman, Lester	Dem	N.Y.	5	3					
16th Whitener, Basil L.	Dem	N.C.	3	3					
17th Libonati, Roland V.	Dem	Ill.	3	3					
18th Loser, J. Carlton	Dem	Tenn.	3	2					
19th Toll, Herman	Dem	Penn.	2	2					
20th Kastenmeier, Robert W.	Dem	Wisc.	2	2					

*2: Member's 2nd period of service on the committee.

Note: House Resolution 157, agreed to Feb. 9,1961, led to a change in size and party ratio on this committee to 21 Democrats and 14 Republicans.

Addition:

Majority: 21st Peterson, M. Blaine — Dem — Utah — Mar. 6,1961

Changes:

Majority:

Holtzman, Lester	Dem	N.Y.	Dec. 31,1961	Resigned; elected to State Supreme Court.
Gilbert, Jacob H.	Dem	N.Y.	Jan. 18,1962	Replaced Holtzman.

Minority:

Ray, John H.	Rep	N.Y.	Aug. 15,1962	Left committee; no new assignment.
King, Carleton J.	Rep	N.Y.	Aug. 16,1962	Replaced Ray.

	Majority		Minority	
Departures from the House:				
Defeated for Reelection	Lane, Thomas J.	Mass. Dem	None	
	Loser, J. Carlton	Tenn. Dem		
	Peterson, M. Blaine	Utah Dem		
Departures from Committee:				
Moved to Foreign Affairs	None		Battin, James F.	Mont. Rep

JUDICIARY / 88th Congress

Service Dates of Committee Chair: Jan. 17,1963-Jan. 3,1965
Service Dates of Majority Members: Jan. 17,1963-Jan. 3,1965
Service Dates of Minority Members: Jan. 24,1963-Jan. 3,1965

Majority			Terms in:		Minority			Terms in:	
Rank Name	**Party**	**State**	**House**	**Comm.**	**Rank Name**	**Party**	**State**	**House**	**Comm.**
Chr Celler, Emanuel	Dem	N.Y.	21	18	RM McCulloch, William M.	Rep	Ohio	9	9
2nd Walter, Francis E.	Dem	Penn.	16	15	2nd Miller, William E.	Rep	N.Y.	7	7
3rd Feighan, Michael A.	Dem	Ohio	11	11	3rd Poff, Richard H.	Rep	Va.	6	6
4th Chelf, Frank L.	Dem	Ky.	10	10	4th Cramer, William C.	Rep	Fla.	5	5
5th Willis, Edwin E.	Dem	La.	8	8	5th Moore, Arch A. Jr.	Rep	W.Va.	4	4
6th Rodino, Peter W. Jr.	Dem	N.J.	8	8	6th Meader, George	Rep	Mich.	7	*2 3
7th Forrester, Elijah L.	Dem	Ga.	7	7	7th Lindsay, John V.	Rep	N.Y.	3	3
8th Rogers, Byron G.	Dem	Colo.	7	7	8th Cahill, William T.	Rep	N.J.	3	3
9th Donohue, Harold D.	Dem	Mass.	9	7	9th Shriver, Garner E.	Rep	Kans.	2	2
10th Brooks, Jack B.	Dem	Tex.	6	5	10th MacGregor, Clark	Rep	Minn.	2	2
11th Tuck, William M.	Dem	Va.	6	5	11th Mathias, Charles McC. Jr.	Rep	Md.	2	2
12th Ashmore, Robert T.	Dem	S.C.	6	5	12th Bromwell, James E.	Rep	Iowa	2	2
13th Dowdy, John V.	Dem	Tex.	7	4	13th King, Carleton J.	Rep	N.Y.	2	2
14th Whitener, Basil L.	Dem	N.C.	4	4	14th Martin, Pat Minor	Rep	Cal.	1	1
15th Libonati, Roland V.	Dem	Ill.	4	4					
16th Toll, Herman	Dem	Penn.	3	3					
17th Kastenmeier, Robert W.	Dem	Wisc.	3	3					
18th Gilbert, Jacob H.	Dem	N.Y.	3	2					
19th Corman, James C.	Dem	Cal.	2	1					
20th St. Onge, William L.	Dem	Conn.	1	1					
21st Senner, George F. Jr.	Dem	Ariz.	1	1					

*2: Member's 2nd period of service on the committee.

Changes:

Majority:

Walter, Francis E.	Dem	Penn.	May 31,1963	Died in office.
Edwards, Don	Dem	Cal.	July 25,1963	Replaced Walter.

Departures from the House:	Majority			Minority		
Defeated for Reelection	None			Bromwell, James E.	Iowa	Rep
				Martin, Pat Minor	Cal.	Rep
				Meader, George	Mich.	Rep
Lost Election for Vice President	None			Miller, William E.	N.Y.	Rep
Retired	Forrester, Elijah L.	Ga.	Dem	None		
	Libonati, Roland V.	Ill.	Dem			
Departures from Committee:						
Moved to Appropriations	None			Shriver, Garner E.	Kans.	Rep

JUDICIARY / 89th Congress

Service Dates of Committee Chair: Jan. 18,1965-Jan. 3,1967
Service Dates of Majority Members: Jan. 18,1965-Jan. 3,1967
Service Dates of Minority Members: Jan. 21,1965-Jan. 3,1967

Majority

Rank	Name	Party	State	Terms in: House	Terms in: Comm.
Chr	Celler, Emanuel	Dem	N.Y.	22	19
2nd	Feighan, Michael A.	Dem	Ohio	12	12
3rd	Chelf, Frank L.	Dem	Ky.	11	11
4th	Willis, Edwin E.	Dem	La.	9	9
5th	Rodino, Peter W. Jr.	Dem	N.J.	9	9
6th	Rogers, Byron G.	Dem	Colo.	8	8
7th	Donohue, Harold D.	Dem	Mass.	10	8
8th	Brooks, Jack B.	Dem	Tex.	7	6
9th	Tuck, William M.	Dem	Va.	7	6
10th	Ashmore, Robert T.	Dem	S.C.	7	6
11th	Dowdy, John V.	Dem	Tex.	8	5
12th	Whitener, Basil L.	Dem	N.C.	5	5
13th	Toll, Herman	Dem	Penn.	4	4
14th	Kastenmeier, Robert W.	Dem	Wisc.	4	4
15th	Gilbert, Jacob H.	Dem	N.Y.	4	3
16th	Corman, James C.	Dem	Cal.	3	2
17th	St. Onge, William L.	Dem	Conn.	2	2
18th	Senner, George F. Jr.	Dem	Ariz.	2	2
19th	Edwards, Don	Dem	Cal.	2	2
20th	Hungate, William L.	Dem	Mo.	2	1
21st	Tenzer, Herbert	Dem	N.Y.	1	1
22nd	Conyers, John Jr.	Dem	Mich.	1	1
23rd	Grider, George W.	Dem	Tenn.	1	1
24th	Jacobs, Andrew Jr.	Dem	Ind.	1	1

Minority

Rank	Name	Party	State	Terms in: House	Terms in: Comm.
RM	McCulloch, William M.	Rep	Ohio	10	10
2nd	Poff, Richard H.	Rep	Va.	7	7
3rd	Cramer, William C.	Rep	Fla.	6	6
4th	Moore, Arch A. Jr.	Rep	W.Va.	5	5
5th	Lindsay, John V.	Rep	N.Y.	4	4
6th	Cahill, William T.	Rep	N.J.	4	4
7th	MacGregor, Clark	Rep	Minn.	3	3
8th	Mathias, Charles McC. Jr.	Rep	Md.	3	3
9th	King, Carleton J.	Rep	N.Y.	3	3
10th	Hutchinson, J. Edward	Rep	Mich.	2	1
11th	McClory, Robert	Rep	Ill.	2	1

Changes:
Minority:

Lindsay, John V.	Rep	N.Y.	Dec. 31,1965	Resigned; elected Mayor of New York City.
Smith, Henry P. III	Rep	N.Y.	Feb. 16,1966	Replaced Lindsay.

Departures from the House:	Majority			Minority		
Defeated for Reelection	Chelf, Frank L.	Ky.	Dem	None		
	Grider, George W.	Tenn.	Dem			
	Senner, George F. Jr.	Ariz.	Dem			
Retired	Toll, Herman	Penn.	Dem	None		
Departures from Committee:						
Moved to Ways and Means	Gilbert, Jacob H.	N.Y.	Dem	None		
Moved to Armed Services	None			King, Carleton J.	N.Y.	Rep
No new assignment	None			Cramer, William C.	Fla.	Rep

JUDICIARY / 90th Congress

Service Dates of Committee Chair: Jan. 23,1967-Jan. 3,1969
Service Dates of Majority Members: Jan. 23,1967-Jan. 3,1969
Service Dates of Minority Members: Jan. 26,1967-Jan. 3,1969

Majority

Rank	Name	Party	State	Terms in: House	Terms in: Comm.
Chr	Celler, Emanuel	Dem	N.Y.	23	20
2nd	Feighan, Michael A.	Dem	Ohio	13	13
3rd	Willis, Edwin E.	Dem	La.	10	10
4th	Rodino, Peter W. Jr.	Dem	N.J.	10	10
5th	Rogers, Byron G.	Dem	Colo.	9	9
6th	Donohue, Harold D.	Dem	Mass.	11	9
7th	Brooks, Jack B.	Dem	Tex.	8	7
8th	Tuck, William M.	Dem	Va.	8	7
9th	Ashmore, Robert T.	Dem	S.C.	8	7
10th	Dowdy, John V.	Dem	Tex.	9	6
11th	Whitener, Basil L.	Dem	N.C.	6	6
12th	Kastenmeier, Robert W.	Dem	Wisc.	5	5
13th	Corman, James C.	Dem	Cal.	4	3
14th	St. Onge, William L.	Dem	Conn.	3	3
15th	Edwards, Don	Dem	Cal.	3	3
16th	Hungate, William L.	Dem	Mo.	3	2
17th	Tenzer, Herbert	Dem	N.Y.	2	2
18th	Conyers, John Jr.	Dem	Mich.	2	2
19th	Jacobs, Andrew Jr.	Dem	Ind.	2	2
20th	Eilberg, Joshua	Dem	Penn.	1	1

Minority

Rank	Name	Party	State	Terms in: House	Terms in: Comm.
RM	McCulloch, William M.	Rep	Ohio	11	11
2nd	Poff, Richard H.	Rep	Va.	8	8
3rd	Moore, Arch A. Jr.	Rep	W.Va.	6	6
4th	Cahill, William T.	Rep	N.J.	5	5
5th	MacGregor, Clark	Rep	Minn.	4	4
6th	Mathias, Charles McC. Jr.	Rep	Md.	4	4
7th	Hutchinson, J. Edward	Rep	Mich.	3	2
8th	McClory, Robert	Rep	Ill.	3	2
9th	Smith, Henry P. III	Rep	N.Y.	2	2
10th	Roth, William V. Jr.	Rep	Del.	1	1
11th	Meskill, Thomas J.	Rep	Conn.	1	1
12th	Sandman, Charles W. Jr.	Rep	N.J.	1	1
13th	Railsback, Thomas F.	Rep	Ill.	1	1
14th	Biester, Edward G. Jr.	Rep	Penn.	1	1
15th	Wiggins, Charles E.	Rep	Cal.	1	1

Changes:

Majority:

Corman, James C.	Dem	Cal.	Aug. 1,1968	Moved to Ways and Means.
Tenzer, Herbert	Dem	N.Y.	Oct. 10,1968	Left committee; no new assignment.
Ryan, William Fitts	Dem	N.Y.	Oct. 10,1968	Replaced Corman.
Waldie, Jerome R.	Dem	Cal.	Oct. 10,1968	Replaced Tenzer.

Departures from the House:	Majority			Minority		
Elected to U.S. Senate	None			Mathias, Charles McC. Jr.	Md.	Rep
Elected Governor	None			Moore, Arch A. Jr.	W.Va.	Rep
Defeated for Reelection	Whitener, Basil L.	N.C.	Dem	None		
Defeated for Renomination	Willis, Edwin E.	La.	Dem	None		
Retired	Ashmore, Robert T.	S.C.	Dem	None		
	Tuck, William M.	Va.	Dem			
Departures from Committee:						
Moved to Foreign Affairs	None			Roth, William V. Jr.	Del.	Rep

JUDICIARY / 91st Congress

Service Dates of Committee Chair: Jan. 29,1969-Jan. 3,1971
Service Dates of Majority Members: Jan. 29,1969-Jan. 3,1971
Service Dates of Minority Members: Jan. 29,1969-Jan. 3,1971

Majority

Rank	Name	Party	State	Terms in: House	Terms in: Comm.
Chr	Celler, Emanuel	Dem	N.Y.	24	21
2nd	Feighan, Michael A.	Dem	Ohio	14	14
3rd	Rodino, Peter W. Jr.	Dem	N.J.	11	11
4th	Rogers, Byron G.	Dem	Colo.	10	10
5th	Donohue, Harold D.	Dem	Mass.	12	10
6th	Brooks, Jack B.	Dem	Tex.	9	8
7th	Dowdy, John V.	Dem	Tex.	10	7
8th	Kastenmeier, Robert W.	Dem	Wisc.	6	6
9th	St. Onge, William L.	Dem	Conn.	4	4
10th	Edwards, Don	Dem	Cal.	4	4
11th	Hungate, William L.	Dem	Mo.	4	3
12th	Conyers, John Jr.	Dem	Mich.	3	3
13th	Jacobs, Andrew Jr.	Dem	Ind.	3	3
14th	Eilberg, Joshua	Dem	Penn.	2	2
15th	Ryan, William Fitts	Dem	N.Y.	5	2
16th	Waldie, Jerome R.	Dem	Cal.	3	2
17th	Edwards, Edwin W.	Dem	La.	3	1
18th	Flowers, Walter	Dem	Ala.	1	1
19th	Mann, James R.	Dem	S.C.	1	1
20th	Mikva, Abner J.	Dem	Ill.	1	*1 1

Minority

Rank	Name	Party	State	Terms in: House	Terms in: Comm.
RM	McCulloch, William M.	Rep	Ohio	12	12
2nd	Poff, Richard H.	Rep	Va.	9	9
3rd	Cahill, William T.	Rep	N.J.	6	6
4th	MacGregor, Clark	Rep	Minn.	5	5
5th	Hutchinson, J. Edward	Rep	Mich.	4	3
6th	McClory, Robert	Rep	Ill.	4	3
7th	Smith, Henry P. III	Rep	N.Y.	3	3
8th	Meskill, Thomas J.	Rep	Conn.	2	2
9th	Sandman, Charles W. Jr.	Rep	N.J.	2	2
10th	Railsback, Thomas F.	Rep	Ill.	2	2
11th	Biester, Edward G. Jr.	Rep	Penn.	2	2
12th	Wiggins, Charles E.	Rep	Cal.	2	2
13th	Dennis, David W.	Rep	Ind.	1	1
14th	Fish, Hamilton Jr.	Rep	N.Y.	1	1
15th	Coughlin, R. Lawrence	Rep	Penn.	1	1

*1: Member's 1st period of service on the committee.

Changes:

Majority:

Name	Party	State	Date	Change
St. Onge, William L.	Dem	Conn.	May 1,1970	Died in office.

Minority:

Name	Party	State	Date	Change
Cahill, William T.	Rep	N.J.	Jan. 19,1970	Resigned; elected Governor of New Jersey.
Mayne, Wiley	Rep	Iowa	Feb. 16,1970	Replaced Cahill.

Departures from the House:

	Majority		Minority	
Elected Governor	None		Meskill, Thomas J.	Conn. Rep
Defeated for Renomination	Feighan, Michael A.	Ohio Dem	None	
	Rogers, Byron G.	Colo. Dem		
Lost Election to U.S. Senate	None		MacGregor, Clark	Minn. Rep

JUDICIARY / 92nd Congress

Service Dates of Committee Chair: Feb. 4,1971-Jan. 3,1973
Service Dates of Majority Members: Feb. 4,1971-Jan. 3,1973
Service Dates of Minority Members: Feb. 4,1971-Jan. 3,1973

Majority

Rank	Name	Party	State	Terms in: House	Terms in: Comm.
Chr	Celler, Emanuel	Dem	N.Y.	25	22
2nd	Rodino, Peter W. Jr.	Dem	N.J.	12	12
3rd	Donohue, Harold D.	Dem	Mass.	13	11
4th	Brooks, Jack B.	Dem	Tex.	10	9
5th	Dowdy, John V.	Dem	Tex.	11	8
6th	Kastenmeier, Robert W.	Dem	Wisc.	7	7
7th	Edwards, Don	Dem	Cal.	5	5
8th	Hungate, William L.	Dem	Mo.	5	4
9th	Conyers, John Jr.	Dem	Mich.	4	4
10th	Jacobs, Andrew Jr.	Dem	Ind.	4	4
11th	Eilberg, Joshua	Dem	Penn.	3	3
12th	Ryan, William Fitts	Dem	N.Y.	6	3
13th	Waldie, Jerome R.	Dem	Cal.	4	3
14th	Edwards, Edwin W.	Dem	La.	4	2
15th	Flowers, Walter	Dem	Ala.	2	2
16th	Mann, James R.	Dem	S.C.	2	2
17th	Mikva, Abner J.	Dem	Ill.	2	*1 2
18th	Sarbanes, Paul S.	Dem	Md.	1	1
19th	Seiberling, John F.	Dem	Ohio	1	1
20th	Abourezk, James G.	Dem	S.D.	1	1
21st	Danielson, George E.	Dem	Cal.	1	1
22nd	Drinan, Robert F.	Dem	Mass.	1	1

Minority

Rank	Name	Party	State	Terms in: House	Terms in: Comm.
RM	McCulloch, William M.	Rep	Ohio	13	13
2nd	Poff, Richard H.	Rep	Va.	10	10
3rd	Hutchinson, J. Edward	Rep	Mich.	5	4
4th	McClory, Robert	Rep	Ill.	5	4
5th	Smith, Henry P. III	Rep	N.Y.	4	4
6th	Sandman, Charles W. Jr.	Rep	N.J.	3	3
7th	Railsback, Thomas F.	Rep	Ill.	3	3
8th	Biester, Edward G. Jr.	Rep	Penn.	3	3
9th	Wiggins, Charles E.	Rep	Cal.	3	3
10th	Dennis, David W.	Rep	Ind.	2	2
11th	Fish, Hamilton Jr.	Rep	N.Y.	2	2
12th	Coughlin, R. Lawrence	Rep	Penn.	2	2
13th	Mayne, Wiley	Rep	Iowa	3	2
14th	Hogan, Lawrence J.	Rep	Md.	2	1
15th	Keating, William J.	Rep	Ohio	1	1
16th	McKevitt, James D.	Rep	Colo.	1	1

*1: Member's 1st period of service on the committee.

Changes:

Majority:				
Edwards, Edwin W.	Dem	La.	May 9,1972	Resigned; elected Governor of Louisiana.
Ryan, William Fitts	Dem	N.Y.	Sep. 17,1972	Died in office.
Rangel, Charles B.	Dem	N.Y.	Oct. 12,1972	Replaced Edwards.
Minority:				
Poff, Richard H.	Rep	Va.	Aug. 29,1972	Resigned; appointed to State Supreme Court.

Departures from the House:	**Majority**			**Minority**		
Elected to U.S. Senate	Abourezk, James G.	S.D.	Dem	None		
Defeated for Reelection	Jacobs, Andrew Jr.	Ind.	Dem	McKevitt, James D.	Colo.	Rep
	Mikva, Abner J.	Ill.	Dem			
Defeated for Renomination	Celler, Emanuel	N.Y.	Dem	None		
Retired	Dowdy, John V.	Tex.	Dem	McCulloch, William M.	Ohio	Rep
Departures from Committee:						
Moved to Foreign Affairs	None			Biester, Edward G. Jr.	Penn.	Rep

JUDICIARY / 93rd Congress

Service Dates of Committee Chair: Jan. 24,1973-Jan. 3,1975
Service Dates of Majority Members: Jan. 24,1973-Jan. 3,1975
Service Dates of Minority Members: Jan. 24,1973-Jan. 3,1975

Majority

Rank Name	Party	State	Terms in: House	Terms in: Comm.
Chr Rodino, Peter W. Jr.	Dem	N.J.	13	13
2nd Donohue, Harold D.	Dem	Mass.	14	12
3rd Brooks, Jack B.	Dem	Tex.	11	10
4th Kastenmeier, Robert W.	Dem	Wisc.	8	8
5th Edwards, Don	Dem	Cal.	6	6
6th Hungate, William L.	Dem	Mo.	6	5
7th Conyers, John Jr.	Dem	Mich.	5	5
8th Eilberg, Joshua	Dem	Penn.	4	4
9th Waldie, Jerome R.	Dem	Cal.	5	4
10th Flowers, Walter	Dem	Ala.	3	3
11th Mann, James R.	Dem	S.C.	3	3
12th Sarbanes, Paul S.	Dem	Md.	2	2
13th Seiberling, John F.	Dem	Ohio	2	2
14th Danielson, George E.	Dem	Cal.	2	2
15th Drinan, Robert F.	Dem	Mass.	2	2
16th Rangel, Charles B.	Dem	N.Y.	2	2
17th Jordan, Barbara C.	Dem	Tex.	1	1
18th Thornton, Raymond H. Jr.	Dem	Ark.	1	1
19th Holtzman, Elizabeth	Dem	N.Y.	1	1
20th Owens, D. Wayne	Dem	Utah	1	1
21st Mezvinsky, Edward M.	Dem	Iowa	1	1

Minority

Rank Name	Party	State	Terms in: House	Terms in: Comm.
RM Hutchinson, J. Edward	Rep	Mich.	6	5
2nd McClory, Robert	Rep	Ill.	6	5
3rd Smith, Henry P. III	Rep	N.Y.	5	5
4th Sandman, Charles W. Jr.	Rep	N.J.	4	4
5th Railsback, Thomas F.	Rep	Ill.	4	4
6th Wiggins, Charles E.	Rep	Cal.	4	4
7th Dennis, David W.	Rep	Ind.	3	3
8th Fish, Hamilton Jr.	Rep	N.Y.	3	3
9th Coughlin, R. Lawrence	Rep	Penn.	3	3
10th Mayne, Wiley	Rep	Iowa	4	3
11th Hogan, Lawrence J.	Rep	Md.	3	2
12th Keating, William J.	Rep	Ohio	2	2
13th Butler, M. Caldwell	Rep	Va.	2	1
14th Cohen, William S.	Rep	Me.	1	1
15th Lott, Trent	Rep	Miss.	1	1
16th Froehlich, Harold V.	Rep	Wisc.	1	1
17th Moorhead, Carlos J.	Rep	Cal.	1	1

Changes:

Majority:

Donohue, Harold D.	Dem	Mass.	Dec. 31,1974	Resigned and retired.

Minority:

Coughlin, R. Lawrence	Rep	Penn.	Mar. 7,1973	Moved to Appropriations.
Maraziti, Joseph J.	Rep	N.J.	May 29,1973	Replaced Coughlin.
Keating, William J.	Rep	Ohio	Jan. 3,1974	Resigned; became President and CEO of Cincinnati Inquirer.
Latta, Delbert L.	Rep	Ohio	Feb. 13,1974	Replaced Keating.
Latta, Delbert L.	Rep	Ohio	Nov. 21,1974	Moved earlier to Budget.
McCloskey, Paul N. Jr.	Rep	Cal.	Nov. 21,1974	Replaced Latta.

	Majority			Minority		
Departures from the House:						
Defeated for Reelection	None			Dennis, David W.	Ind.	Rep
				Froehlich, Harold V.	Wisc.	Rep
				Mayne, Wiley	Iowa	Rep
				Sandman, Charles W. Jr.	N.J.	Rep
				Maraziti, Joseph J.	N.J.	Rep
Lost Election to U.S. Senate	Owens, D. Wayne	Utah	Dem	None		
Lost Nomination for Governor	Waldie, Jerome R.	Cal.	Dem	Hogan, Lawrence J.	Md.	Rep
Retired	None			Smith, Henry P. III	N.Y.	Rep
Departures from Committee:						
Moved to Ways and Means	Rangel, Charles B.	N.Y.	Dem	None		
Moved to Post Office & Civil Service; Rules	None			Lott, Trent	Miss.	Rep
No new assignment	None			McCloskey, Paul N. Jr.	Cal.	Rep

JUDICIARY / 94th Congress

Service Dates of Committee Chair: Jan. 20,1975-Jan. 3,1977
Service Dates of Majority Members: Jan. 20,1975-Jan. 3,1977
Service Dates of Minority Members: Jan. 28,1975-Jan. 3,1977

Majority

Rank Name	Party	State	Terms in: House	Terms in: Comm.
Chr Rodino, Peter W. Jr.	Dem	N.J.	14	14
2nd Brooks, Jack B.	Dem	Tex.	12	11
3rd Kastenmeier, Robert W.	Dem	Wisc.	9	9
4th Edwards, Don	Dem	Cal.	7	7
5th Hungate, William L.	Dem	Mo.	7	6
6th Conyers, John Jr.	Dem	Mich.	6	6
7th Eilberg, Joshua	Dem	Penn.	5	5
8th Flowers, Walter	Dem	Ala.	4	4
9th Mann, James R.	Dem	S.C.	4	4
10th Sarbanes, Paul S.	Dem	Md.	3	3
11th Seiberling, John F.	Dem	Ohio	3	3
12th Danielson, George E.	Dem	Cal.	3	3
13th Drinan, Robert F.	Dem	Mass.	3	3
14th Jordan, Barbara C.	Dem	Tex.	2	2
15th Thornton, Raymond H. Jr.	Dem	Ark.	2	2
16th Holtzman, Elizabeth	Dem	N.Y.	2	2
17th Mezvinsky, Edward M.	Dem	Iowa	2	2
18th Badillo, Herman	Dem	N.Y.	3	1
19th Mazzoli, Romano L.	Dem	Ky.	3	1
20th Pattison, Edward W.	Dem	N.Y.	1	1
21st Dodd, Christopher J.	Dem	Conn.	1	1
22nd Hughes, William J.	Dem	N.J.	1	1
23rd Russo, Martin A.	Dem	Ill.	1	1

Minority

Rank Name	Party	State	Terms in: House	Terms in: Comm.
RM Hutchinson, J. Edward	Rep	Mich.	7	6
2nd McClory, Robert	Rep	Ill.	7	6
3rd Railsback, Thomas F.	Rep	Ill.	5	5
4th Wiggins, Charles E.	Rep	Cal.	5	5
5th Fish, Hamilton Jr.	Rep	N.Y.	4	4
6th Butler, M. Caldwell	Rep	Va.	3	2
7th Cohen, William S.	Rep	Me.	2	2
8th Moorhead, Carlos J.	Rep	Cal.	2	2
9th Ashbrook, John M.	Rep	Ohio	8	1
10th Hyde, Henry J.	Rep	Ill.	1	1
11th Kindness, Thomas N.	Rep	Ohio	1	1

Changes:

Majority:

Thornton, Raymond H. Jr.	Dem	Ark.	Dec. 17,1975	Moved to Agriculture.
Russo, Martin A.	Dem	Ill.	Apr. 13,1976	Moved to Interstate and Foreign Commerce.
Hall, Sam B. Jr.	Dem	Tex.	July 21,1976	Replaced Thornton.

	Majority			Minority	
Departures from the House:					
Elected to U.S. Senate	Sarbanes, Paul S.	Md.	Dem	None	
Defeated for Reelection	Mezvinsky, Edward M.	Iowa	Dem	None	
Retired	Hungate, William L.	Mo.	Dem	Hutchinson, J. Edward	Mich. Rep
Departures from Committee:					
Moved to Banking, Finance & Urban Affairs	Badillo, Herman	N.Y.	Dem	None	
	Pattison, Edward W.	N.Y.	Dem		
Moved to Rules	Dodd, Christopher J.	Conn.	Dem	None	

JUDICIARY / 95th Congress

Service Dates of Committee Chair: Jan. 19,1977-Jan. 3,1979
Service Dates of Majority Members: Jan. 19,1977-Jan. 3,1979
Service Dates of Minority Members: Jan. 19,1977-Jan. 3,1979

Majority

Rank	Name	Party	State	Terms in: House	Terms in: Comm.
Chr	Rodino, Peter W. Jr.	Dem	N.J.	15	15
2nd	Brooks, Jack B.	Dem	Tex.	13	12
3rd	Kastenmeier, Robert W.	Dem	Wisc.	10	10
4th	Edwards, Don	Dem	Cal.	8	8
5th	Conyers, John Jr.	Dem	Mich.	7	7
6th	Eilberg, Joshua	Dem	Penn.	6	6
7th	Flowers, Walter	Dem	Ala.	5	5
8th	Mann, James R.	Dem	S.C.	5	5
9th	Seiberling, John F.	Dem	Ohio	4	4
10th	Danielson, George E.	Dem	Cal.	4	4
11th	Drinan, Robert F.	Dem	Mass.	4	4
12th	Jordan, Barbara C.	Dem	Tex.	3	3
13th	Holtzman, Elizabeth	Dem	N.Y.	3	3
14th	Mazzoli, Romano L.	Dem	Ky.	4	2
15th	Hughes, William J.	Dem	N.J.	2	2
16th	Hall, Sam B. Jr.	Dem	Tex.	2	2
17th	Gudger, V. Lamar	Dem	N.C.	1	1
18th	Volkmer, Harold L.	Dem	Mo.	1	1
19th	Harris, Herbert E. II	Dem	Va.	2	1
20th	Santini, James D.	Dem	Nev.	2	*T 1
21st	Ertel, Allen E.	Dem	Penn.	1	*T 1
22nd	Evans, Billy Lee	Dem	Ga.	1	*T 1
23rd	Beilenson, Anthony C.	Dem	Cal.	1	*T 1

Minority

Rank	Name	Party	State	Terms in: House	Terms in: Comm.
RM	McClory, Robert	Rep	Ill.	8	7
2nd	Railsback, Thomas F.	Rep	Ill.	6	6
3rd	Wiggins, Charles E.	Rep	Cal.	6	6
4th	Fish, Hamilton Jr.	Rep	N.Y.	5	5
5th	Butler, M. Caldwell	Rep	Va.	4	3
6th	Cohen, William S.	Rep	Me.	3	3
7th	Moorhead, Carlos J.	Rep	Cal.	3	3
8th	Ashbrook, John M.	Rep	Ohio	9	2
9th	Hyde, Henry J.	Rep	Ill.	2	2
10th	Kindness, Thomas N.	Rep	Ohio	2	2
11th	Sawyer, Harold S.	Rep	Mich.	1	1

*T: Temporary member of the committee.

Vacancies Filled:
Majority: 19th through the 23rd seats on Jan. 27,1977.

Departures from the House:	**Majority**			**Minority**		
Elected to U.S. Senate	None			Cohen, William S.	Me.	Rep
Defeated for Reelection	Eilberg, Joshua	Penn.	Dem	None		
Lost Nomination to U.S. Senate	Flowers, Walter	Ala.	Dem	None		
Retired	Jordan, Barbara C.	Tex.	Dem	Wiggins, Charles E.	Cal.	Rep
	Mann, James R.	S.C.	Dem			
Departures from Committee:						
Moved to Rules	Beilenson, Anthony C.	Cal.	Dem	None		
Moved to Science & Technology	Ertel, Allen E.	Penn.	Dem	None		
No new assignment	Evans, Billy Lee	Ga.	Dem	None		
	Santini, James D.	Nev.	Dem			

JUDICIARY / 96th Congress

Service Dates of Committee Chair: Jan. 24,1979-Jan. 3,1981
Service Dates of Majority Members: Jan. 24,1979-Jan. 3,1981
Service Dates of Minority Members: Jan. 24,1979-Jan. 3,1981

Majority

Rank	Name	Party	State	Terms in: House	Terms in: Comm.
Chr	Rodino, Peter W. Jr.	Dem	N.J.	16	16
2nd	Brooks, Jack B.	Dem	Tex.	14	13
3rd	Kastenmeier, Robert W.	Dem	Wisc.	11	11
4th	Edwards, Don	Dem	Cal.	9	9
5th	Conyers, John Jr.	Dem	Mich.	8	8
6th	Seiberling, John F.	Dem	Ohio	5	5
7th	Danielson, George E.	Dem	Cal.	5	5
8th	Drinan, Robert F.	Dem	Mass.	5	5
9th	Holtzman, Elizabeth	Dem	N.Y.	4	4
10th	Mazzoli, Romano L.	Dem	Ky.	5	3
11th	Hughes, William J.	Dem	N.J.	3	3
12th	Hall, Sam B. Jr.	Dem	Tex.	3	3
13th	Gudger, V. Lamar	Dem	N.C.	2	2
14th	Volkmer, Harold L.	Dem	Mo.	2	2
15th	Harris, Herbert E. II	Dem	Va.	3	2
16th	Synar, Michael L.	Dem	Okla.	1	1
17th	Matsui, Robert T.	Dem	Cal.	1	1
18th	Mikva, Abner J.	Dem	Ill.	5	*2 1
19th	Barnes, Michael D.	Dem	Md.	1	*T 1
20th	Shelby, Richard C.	Dem	Ala.	1	*T 1

Minority

Rank	Name	Party	State	Terms in: House	Terms in: Comm.
RM	McClory, Robert	Rep	Ill.	9	8
2nd	Railsback, Thomas F.	Rep	Ill.	7	7
3rd	Fish, Hamilton Jr.	Rep	N.Y.	6	6
4th	Butler, M. Caldwell	Rep	Va.	5	4
5th	Moorhead, Carlos J.	Rep	Cal.	4	4
6th	Ashbrook, John M.	Rep	Ohio	10	3
7th	Hyde, Henry J.	Rep	Ill.	3	3
8th	Kindness, Thomas N.	Rep	Ohio	3	3
9th	Sawyer, Harold S.	Rep	Mich.	2	2
10th	Lungren, Daniel E.	Rep	Cal.	1	1
11th	Sensenbrenner, F. Jas. Jr.	Rep	Wisc.	1	1

*2: Member's 2nd period of service on the committee;
*T: Temporary member of the committee.

Vacancies Filled:
Majority: 18th through the 20th seats on Jan. 31,1979.

Changes:
Majority:

Mikva, Abner J.	Dem	Ill.	Sep. 26,1979	Resigned; appointed federal judge.
Matsui, Robert T.	Dem	Cal.	Nov. 7,1979	Moved to Interstate and Foreign Commerce.
Glickman, Daniel R.	Dem	Kans.	Jan. 23,1980	Replaced Mikva.
Carr, M. Robert	Dem	Mich.	Feb. 6,1980	Replaced Matsui.
Shelby, Richard C.	Dem	Ala.	Mar. 3,1980	Left committee; letter dated Feb. 28,1980; no new assignment.
Evans, Billy Lee	Dem	Ga.	Mar. 19,1980	Replaced Shelby; temporary assignment.

Departures from the House:	**Majority**			**Minority**
Defeated for Reelection	Gudger, V. Lamar	N.C.	Dem	None
	Harris, Herbert E. II	Va.	Dem	
	Carr, M. Robert	Mich.	Dem	
Lost Election to U.S. Senate	Holtzman, Elizabeth	N.Y.	Dem	None
Retired	Drinan, Robert F.	Mass.	Dem	None
Departures from Committee:				
Moved to Agriculture	Volkmer, Harold L.	Mo.	Dem	None
No new assignment	Barnes, Michael D.	Md.	Dem	None

JUDICIARY / 97th Congress

Service Dates of Committee Chair: Jan. 28,1981-Jan. 3,1983
Service Dates of Majority Members: Jan. 28,1981-Jan. 3,1983
Service Dates of Minority Members: Jan. 28,1981-Jan. 3,1983

Majority

Rank	Name	Party	State	Terms in: House	Terms in: Comm.
Chr	Rodino, Peter W. Jr.	Dem	N.J.	17	17
2nd	Brooks, Jack B.	Dem	Tex.	15	14
3rd	Kastenmeier, Robert W.	Dem	Wisc.	12	12
4th	Edwards, Don	Dem	Cal.	10	10
5th	Conyers, John Jr.	Dem	Mich.	9	9
6th	Seiberling, John F.	Dem	Ohio	6	6
7th	Danielson, George E.	Dem	Cal.	6	6
8th	Mazzoli, Romano L.	Dem	Ky.	6	4
9th	Hughes, William J.	Dem	N.J.	4	4
10th	Hall, Sam B. Jr.	Dem	Tex.	4	4
11th	Synar, Michael L.	Dem	Okla.	2	2
12th	Schroeder, Patricia S.	Dem	Colo.	5	1
13th	Evans, Billy Lee	Dem	Ga.	3	*1 1
14th	Glickman, Daniel R.	Dem	Kans.	3	1
15th	Washington, Harold	Dem	Ill.	1	1
16th	Frank, Barney	Dem	Mass.	1	1

Minority

Rank	Name	Party	State	Terms in: House	Terms in: Comm.
RM	McClory, Robert	Rep	Ill.	10	9
2nd	Railsback, Thomas F.	Rep	Ill.	8	8
3rd	Fish, Hamilton Jr.	Rep	N.Y.	7	7
4th	Butler, M. Caldwell	Rep	Va.	6	5
5th	Moorhead, Carlos J.	Rep	Cal.	5	5
6th	Ashbrook, John M.	Rep	Ohio	11	4
7th	Hyde, Henry J.	Rep	Ill.	4	4
8th	Kindness, Thomas N.	Rep	Ohio	4	4
9th	Sawyer, Harold S.	Rep	Mich.	3	3
10th	Lungren, Daniel E.	Rep	Cal.	2	2
11th	Sensenbrenner, F. Jas. Jr.	Rep	Wisc.	2	2
12th	McCollum, Bill	Rep	Fla.	1	1

*1: Member's 1st period of service on the committee.

Changes:

Majority:

Name	Party	State	Date	Change
Danielson, George E.	Dem	Cal.	Mar. 9,1982	Resigned; appointed state judge.
Crockett, George W. Jr.	Dem	Mich.	Mar. 31,1982	Replaced Danielson.

Minority:

Name	Party	State	Date	Change
Ashbrook, John M.	Rep	Ohio	Apr. 24,1982	Died in office.
Shaw, E. Clay Jr.	Rep	Fla.	June 9,1982	Replaced Ashbrook.

Departures from the House:

	Majority	State	Party	Minority	State	Party
Defeated for Renomination	Evans, Billy Lee	Ga.	Dem	Railsback, Thomas F.	Ill.	Rep
Retired	None			Butler, M. Caldwell	Va.	Rep
				McClory, Robert	Ill.	Rep

JUDICIARY / 98th Congress

Service Dates of Committee Chair: Jan. 6,1983-Jan. 3,1985
Service Dates of Majority Members: Jan. 6,1983-Jan. 3,1985
Service Dates of Minority Members: Jan. 6,1983-Jan. 3,1985

Majority

Rank	Name	Party	State	Terms in: House	Terms in: Comm.
Chr	Rodino, Peter W. Jr.	Dem	N.J.	18	18
2nd	Brooks, Jack B.	Dem	Tex.	16	15
3rd	Kastenmeier, Robert W.	Dem	Wisc.	13	13
4th	Edwards, Don	Dem	Cal.	11	11
5th	Conyers, John Jr.	Dem	Mich.	10	10
6th	Seiberling, John F.	Dem	Ohio	7	7
7th	Mazzoli, Romano L.	Dem	Ky.	7	5
8th	Hughes, William J.	Dem	N.J.	5	5
9th	Hall, Sam B. Jr.	Dem	Tex.	5	5
10th	Synar, Michael L.	Dem	Okla.	3	3
11th	Schroeder, Patricia S.	Dem	Colo.	6	2
12th	Glickman, Daniel R.	Dem	Kans.	4	2
13th	Washington, Harold	Dem	Ill.	2	2
14th	Frank, Barney	Dem	Mass.	2	2
15th	Crockett, George W. Jr.	Dem	Mich.	3	2
16th	Schumer, Charles E.	Dem	N.Y.	2	1

Minority

Rank	Name	Party	State	Terms in: House	Terms in: Comm.
RM	Fish, Hamilton Jr.	Rep	N.Y.	8	8
2nd	Moorhead, Carlos J.	Rep	Cal.	6	6
3rd	Hyde, Henry J.	Rep	Ill.	5	5
4th	Kindness, Thomas N.	Rep	Ohio	5	5
5th	Sawyer, Harold S.	Rep	Mich.	4	4
6th	Lungren, Daniel E.	Rep	Cal.	3	3
7th	Sensenbrenner, F. Jas. Jr.	Rep	Wisc.	3	3
8th	McCollum, Bill	Rep	Fla.	2	2
9th	Shaw, E. Clay Jr.	Rep	Fla.	2	2
10th	Gekas, George W.	Rep	Penn.	1	1
11th	DeWine, Michael	Rep	Ohio	1	1

17th Morrison, Bruce A.	Dem	Conn.	1	1
18th Feighan, Edward F.	Dem	Ohio	1	1
19th Smith, Lawrence J.	Dem	Fla.	1	1
20th Berman, Howard L.	Dem	Cal.	1	1

Changes:

Majority:

Washington, Harold	Dem	Ill.	Apr. 30,1983	Resigned; elected Mayor of Chicago.
Boucher, Frederick C.	Dem	Va.	May 24,1983	Replaced Washington; temporary term.
Boucher, Frederick C.	Dem	Va.	Nov. 18,1983	Temporary term expired on last day of 1st Session.
Boucher, Frederick C.	Dem	Va.	Feb. 29,1984	Replaced himself.

Departures from the House:	Majority		Minority	
Retired	None		Sawyer, Harold S.	Mich. Rep

JUDICIARY / 99th Congress

Service Dates of Committee Chair: Jan. 7,1985-Jan. 3,1987
Service Dates of Majority Members: Jan. 30,1985-Jan. 3,1987
Service Dates of Minority Members: Jan. 30,1985-Jan. 3,1987

Majority

Rank Name	Party	State	Terms in: House	Terms in: Comm.
Chr Rodino, Peter W. Jr.	Dem	N.J.	19	19
2nd Brooks, Jack B.	Dem	Tex.	17	16
3rd Kastenmeier, Robert W.	Dem	Wisc.	14	14
4th Edwards, Don	Dem	Cal.	12	12
5th Conyers, John Jr.	Dem	Mich.	11	11
6th Seiberling, John F.	Dem	Ohio	8	8
7th Mazzoli, Romano L.	Dem	Ky.	8	6
8th Hughes, William J.	Dem	N.J.	6	6
9th Hall, Sam B. Jr.	Dem	Tex.	6	6
10th Synar, Michael L.	Dem	Okla.	4	4
11th Schroeder, Patricia S.	Dem	Colo.	7	3
12th Glickman, Daniel R.	Dem	Kans.	5	3
13th Frank, Barney	Dem	Mass.	3	3
14th Crockett, George W. Jr.	Dem	Mich.	4	3
15th Schumer, Charles E.	Dem	N.Y.	3	2
16th Morrison, Bruce A.	Dem	Conn.	2	2
17th Feighan, Edward F.	Dem	Ohio	2	2
18th Smith, Lawrence J.	Dem	Fla.	2	2
19th Berman, Howard L.	Dem	Cal.	2	2
20th Boucher, Frederick C.	Dem	Va.	2	2
21st Staggers, Harley O. Jr.	Dem	W.Va.	2	1

Minority

Rank Name	Party	State	Terms in: House	Terms in: Comm.
RM Fish, Hamilton Jr.	Rep	N.Y.	9	9
2nd Moorhead, Carlos J.	Rep	Cal.	7	7
3rd Hyde, Henry J.	Rep	Ill.	6	6
4th Kindness, Thomas N.	Rep	Ohio	6	6
5th Lungren, Daniel E.	Rep	Cal.	4	4
6th Sensenbrenner, F. Jas. Jr.	Rep	Wisc.	4	4
7th McCollum, Bill	Rep	Fla.	3	3
8th Shaw, E. Clay Jr.	Rep	Fla.	3	3
9th Gekas, George W.	Rep	Penn.	2	2
10th DeWine, Michael	Rep	Ohio	2	2
11th Dannemeyer, William E.	Rep	Cal.	4	1
12th Brown, Hank	Rep	Colo.	3	1
13th Swindall, Patrick Lynn	Rep	Ga.	1	1
14th Coble, Howard	Rep	N.C.	1	1

Changes:

Majority:

Hall, Sam B. Jr.	Dem	Tex.	May 27,1985	Resigned; appointed federal judge.
Bryant, John	Dem	Tex.	June 5,1985	Replaced Hall.

Departures from the House:	Majority		Minority	
Lost Election to U.S. Senate	None		Kindness, Thomas N.	Ohio Rep
Retired	Seiberling, John F.	Ohio Dem	None	
Departures from Committee:				
Moved to Ways and Means	None		Brown, Hank	Colo. Rep

JUDICIARY / 100th Congress

Service Dates of Committee Chair: Jan. 8,1987-Jan. 3,1989
Service Dates of Majority Members: Jan. 22,1987-Jan. 3,1989
Service Dates of Minority Members: Jan. 21,1987-Jan. 3,1989

Majority

Rank	Name	Party	State	Terms in: House	Terms in: Comm.
Chr	Rodino, Peter W. Jr.	Dem	N.J.	20	20
2nd	Brooks, Jack B.	Dem	Tex.	18	17
3rd	Kastenmeier, Robert W.	Dem	Wisc.	15	15
4th	Edwards, Don	Dem	Cal.	13	13
5th	Conyers, John Jr.	Dem	Mich.	12	12
6th	Mazzoli, Romano L.	Dem	Ky.	9	7
7th	Hughes, William J.	Dem	N.J.	7	7
8th	Synar, Michael L.	Dem	Okla.	5	5
9th	Schroeder, Patricia S.	Dem	Colo.	8	4
10th	Glickman, Daniel R.	Dem	Kans.	6	4
11th	Frank, Barney	Dem	Mass.	4	4
12th	Crockett, George W. Jr.	Dem	Mich.	5	4
13th	Schumer, Charles E.	Dem	N.Y.	4	3
14th	Morrison, Bruce A.	Dem	Conn.	3	3
15th	Feighan, Edward F.	Dem	Ohio	3	3
16th	Smith, Lawrence J.	Dem	Fla.	3	3
17th	Berman, Howard L.	Dem	Cal.	3	3
18th	Boucher, Frederick C.	Dem	Va.	3	3
19th	Staggers, Harley O. Jr.	Dem	W.Va.	3	2
20th	Bryant, John	Dem	Tex.	3	2
21st	Cardin, Benjamin L.	Dem	Md.	1	1

Minority

Rank	Name	Party	State	Terms in: House	Terms in: Comm.
RM	Fish, Hamilton Jr.	Rep	N.Y.	10	10
2nd	Moorhead, Carlos J.	Rep	Cal.	8	8
3rd	Hyde, Henry J.	Rep	Ill.	7	7
4th	Lungren, Daniel E.	Rep	Cal.	5	5
5th	Sensenbrenner, F. Jas. Jr.	Rep	Wisc.	5	5
6th	McCollum, Bill	Rep	Fla.	4	4
7th	Shaw, E. Clay Jr.	Rep	Fla.	4	4
8th	Gekas, George W.	Rep	Penn.	3	3
9th	DeWine, Michael	Rep	Ohio	3	3
10th	Dannemeyer, William E.	Rep	Cal.	5	2
11th	Swindall, Patrick Lynn	Rep	Ga.	2	2
12th	Coble, Howard	Rep	N.C.	2	2
13th	Slaughter, D. French Jr.	Rep	Va.	2	1
14th	Smith, Lamar S.	Rep	Tex.	1	1

Changes:
Minority:

Name	Party	State	Date	Change
Shaw, E. Clay Jr.	Rep	Fla.	July 7,1988	Moved to Ways and Means.

Departures from the House:

	Majority			Minority		
Defeated for Reelection	None			Swindall, Patrick Lynn	Ga.	Rep
Retired	Rodino, Peter W. Jr.	N.J.	Dem	Lungren, Daniel E.	Cal.	Rep

JUDICIARY / 101st Congress

Service Dates of Committee Chair: Jan. 3,1989-Jan. 3,1991
Service Dates of Majority Members: Jan. 19,1989-Jan. 3,1991
Service Dates of Minority Members: Jan. 20,1989-Jan. 3,1991

Majority

Rank	Name	Party	State	Terms in: House	Terms in: Comm.
Chr	Brooks, Jack B.	Dem	Tex.	19	18
2nd	Kastenmeier, Robert W.	Dem	Wisc.	16	16
3rd	Edwards, Don	Dem	Cal.	14	14
4th	Conyers, John Jr.	Dem	Mich.	13	13
5th	Mazzoli, Romano L.	Dem	Ky.	10	8
6th	Hughes, William J.	Dem	N.J.	8	8
7th	Synar, Michael L.	Dem	Okla.	6	6
8th	Schroeder, Patricia S.	Dem	Colo.	9	5
9th	Glickman, Daniel R.	Dem	Kans.	7	5
10th	Frank, Barney	Dem	Mass.	5	5
11th	Crockett, George W. Jr.	Dem	Mich.	6	5
12th	Schumer, Charles E.	Dem	N.Y.	5	4
13th	Morrison, Bruce A.	Dem	Conn.	4	4
14th	Feighan, Edward F.	Dem	Ohio	4	4
15th	Smith, Lawrence J.	Dem	Fla.	4	4
16th	Berman, Howard L.	Dem	Cal.	4	4

Minority

Rank	Name	Party	State	Terms in: House	Terms in: Comm.
RM	Fish, Hamilton Jr.	Rep	N.Y.	11	11
2nd	Moorhead, Carlos J.	Rep	Cal.	9	9
3rd	Hyde, Henry J.	Rep	Ill.	8	8
4th	Sensenbrenner, F. Jas. Jr.	Rep	Wisc.	6	6
5th	McCollum, Bill	Rep	Fla.	5	5
6th	Gekas, George W.	Rep	Penn.	4	4
7th	DeWine, Michael	Rep	Ohio	4	4
8th	Dannemeyer, William E.	Rep	Cal.	6	3
9th	Coble, Howard	Rep	N.C.	3	3
10th	Slaughter, D. French Jr.	Rep	Va.	3	2
11th	Smith, Lamar S.	Rep	Tex.	2	2
12th	Smith, Larkin	Rep	Miss.	1	1
13th	Douglas, Charles	Rep	N.H.	1	1
14th	James, Craig T.	Rep	Fla.	1	1

17th Boucher, Frederick C.	Dem	Va.	4	4
18th Staggers, Harley O. Jr.	Dem	W.Va.	4	3
19th Bryant, John	Dem	Tex.	4	3
20th Cardin, Benjamin L.	Dem	Md.	2	2
21st Sangmeister, George E.	Dem	Ill.	1	1

Note: The committee was expanded and the party ratio changed to 22 Democrats and 14 Republicans on Feb. 27,1990.

Addition:

Majority: 22nd Washington, Craig Dem Tex. Feb. 27,1990

Changes:

Majority:

Cardin, Benjamin L.	Dem	Md.	Oct. 16,1989	Moved to Ways and Means.
Levine, Mel	Dem	Cal.	Nov. 8,1989	Replaced Cardin; ranked above Sangmeister.

Minority:

Smith, Larkin	Rep	Miss.	Aug. 13,1989	Died in office.
Campbell, Tom	Rep	Cal.	Nov. 21,1989	Replaced Smith.

Departures from the House:	**Majority**		**Minority**	
Elected Lt. Governor	None		DeWine, Michael	Ohio Rep
Defeated for Reelection	Kastenmeier, Robert W.	Wisc. Dem	Douglas, Charles	N.H. Rep
Lost Election for Governor	Morrison, Bruce A.	Conn. Dem	None	
Retired	Crockett, George W. Jr.	Mich. Dem	None	
Departures from Committee:				
Moved to Appropriations	Smith, Lawrence J.	Fla. Dem	None	
Moved to Budget	None		Dannemeyer, William E.	Cal. Rep

JUDICIARY / 102nd Congress

Service Dates of Committee Chair: Jan. 24,1991-Jan. 3,1993
Service Dates of Majority Members: Jan. 24,1991-Jan. 3,1993
Service Dates of Minority Members: Jan. 24,1991-Jan. 3,1993

Majority

Rank Name	Party	State	Terms in: House	Terms in: Comm.
Chr Brooks, Jack B.	Dem	Tex.	20	19
2nd Edwards, Don	Dem	Cal.	15	15
3rd Conyers, John Jr.	Dem	Mich.	14	14
4th Mazzoli, Romano L.	Dem	Ky.	11	9
5th Hughes, William J.	Dem	N.J.	9	9
6th Synar, Michael L.	Dem	Okla.	7	7
7th Schroeder, Patricia S.	Dem	Colo.	10	6
8th Glickman, Daniel R.	Dem	Kans.	8	6
9th Frank, Barney	Dem	Mass.	6	6
10th Schumer, Charles E.	Dem	N.Y.	6	5
11th Feighan, Edward F.	Dem	Ohio	5	5
12th Berman, Howard L.	Dem	Cal.	5	5
13th Boucher, Frederick C.	Dem	Va.	5	5
14th Staggers, Harley O. Jr.	Dem	W.Va.	5	4
15th Bryant, John	Dem	Tex.	5	4
16th Levine, Mel	Dem	Cal.	5	2
17th Sangmeister, George E.	Dem	Ill.	2	2
18th Washington, Craig	Dem	Tex.	2	2
19th Hoagland, Peter	Dem	Neb.	2	1
20th Kopetski, Mike	Dem	Ore.	1	1
21st Reed, John F.	Dem	R.I.	1	1

Minority

Rank Name	Party	State	Terms in: House	Terms in: Comm.
RM Fish, Hamilton Jr.	Rep	N.Y.	12	12
2nd Moorhead, Carlos J.	Rep	Cal.	10	10
3rd Hyde, Henry J.	Rep	Ill.	9	9
4th Sensenbrenner, F. Jas. Jr.	Rep	Wisc.	7	7
5th McCollum, Bill	Rep	Fla.	6	5
6th Gekas, George W.	Rep	Penn.	5	5
7th Coble, Howard	Rep	N.C.	4	4
8th Slaughter, D. French Jr.	Rep	Va.	4	3
9th Smith, Lamar S.	Rep	Tex.	3	3
10th James, Craig T.	Rep	Fla.	2	2
11th Campbell, Tom	Rep	Cal.	2	2
12th Schiff, Steven H.	Rep	N.M.	2	1
13th Ramstad, Jim	Rep	Minn.	1	1

Note: Mel Levine (Dem-Cal.) was appointed to the committee in the 101st Congress and ranked above George E. Sangmeister (Dem-Ill.).

Changes:

Minority:

Slaughter, D. French Jr.	Rep	Va.	Nov. 5,1991	Resigned and retired.
Allen, George F.	Rep	Va.	Nov. 12,1991	Replaced Slaughter.

MERCHANT MARINE AND FISHERIES

Jurisdiction, 1947

Established by the Legislative Reorganization Act of 1946:

[Section 121.(1)(m)]

Committee on Merchant Marine and Fisheries.

1. Merchant marine generally.
2. Registering and licensing of vessels and small boats.
3. Navigation and the laws relating thereto, including pilotage.
4. Rules and international arrangements to prevent collisions at sea.
5. Merchant marine officers and seamen.
6. Measures relating to the regulation of common carriers by water (except matters subject to the jurisdiction of the Interstate Commerce Commission) and to the inspection of merchant marine vessels, lights and signals, lifesaving equipment, and fire protection on such vessels.
7. The Coast Guard, including lifesaving service, lighthouses, lightships, and ocean derelicts.
8. United States Coast Guard and Merchant Marine Academies.
9. Coast and Geodetic Survey.
10. The Panama Canal and the maintenance and operation of the Panama Canal, including the administration, sanitation, and government of the Canal Zone; and interoceanic canals generally.
11. Fisheries and wildlife, including research, restoration, refuges, and conservation.

Jurisdiction, 1992

Jurisdiction contained in <u>Rules of the House of Representatives</u>, (as revised to July 1, 1992):

[Rule X. 1. (n)]

Committee on Merchant Marine and Fisheries.

(1) Merchant marine generally.
(2) Oceanography and Marine Affairs, including coastal zone management.
(3) Coast Guard, including lifesaving service, lighthouses, lightships, and ocean derelicts.
(4) Fisheries and wildlife, including research, restoration, refuges, and conservation.
(5) Measures relating to the regulation of common carriers by water (except matters subject to the jurisdiction of the Interstate Commerce Commission) and to the inspection of merchant marine vessels, lights and signals, lifesaving equipment, and fire protection on such vessels.
(6) Merchant marine officers and seamen.
(7) Navigation and the laws relating thereto, including pilotage.
(8) Panama Canal and the maintenance and operation of the Panama Canal, including the administration, sanitation, and government of the Canal Zone; and interoceanic canals generally.
(9) Registering and licensing of vessels and small boats.
(10) Rules and international arrangements to prevent collisions at sea.
(11) United States Coast Guard and Merchant Marine Academies, and State Maritime Academies.
(12) International fishing agreements.

MERCHANT MARINE AND FISHERIES / 80th Congress

Service Dates of Committee Chairs: Ch1 Jan. 14,1947-May 24,1947
Ch2 June 4,1947-Jan. 3,1949
Service Dates of Majority Members: Jan. 14,1947-Jan. 3,1949
Service Dates of Minority Members: Jan. 16,1947-Jan. 3,1949

Majority

Rank Name	Party	State	Terms in: House	Terms in: Comm.
Ch1 Bradley, Frederick V.	Rep	Mich.	5	5
Ch2 2nd Weichel, Alvin F.	Rep	Ohio	3	3
3rd Hand, T. Millet II	Rep	N.J.	2	2
4th Latham, Henry J.	Rep	N.Y.	2	1
5th Potts, David M.	Rep	N.Y.	1	1
6th Bradley, Willis W.	Rep	Cal.	1	1
7th Maloney, Franklin J.	Rep	Penn.	1	1
8th Tollefson, Thor C.	Rep	Wash.	1	1
9th Burke, Raymond H.	Rep	Ohio	1	1
10th Allen, John J. Jr.	Rep	Cal.	1	1
11th Seely-Brown, Horace Jr.	Rep	Conn.	1 *1	1
12th Brophy, John C.	Rep	Wisc.	1	1
13th Nodar, Robert J. Jr.	Rep	N.Y.	1	1
14th Miller, Edward T.	Rep	Md.	1	1

Minority

Rank Name	Party	State	Terms in: House	Terms in: Comm.
RM Bland, Schuyler Otis	Dem	Va.	16	14
2nd Hart, Edward J.	Dem	N.J.	7	7
3rd Bonner, Herbert C.	Dem	N.C.	5	5
4th Domengeaux, James	Dem	La.	4 *2	2
5th Jackson, Henry M.	Dem	Wash.	4	4
6th Keogh, Eugene J.	Dem	N.Y.	6 *1	3
7th King, Cecil R.	Dem	Cal.	4 *2	1
8th Price, Emory H.	Dem	Fla.	3	1
9th Havenner, Franck R.	Dem	Cal.	4	1
10th Rayfiel, Leo F.	Dem	N.Y.	2	1
11th Preston, Prince H. Jr.	Dem	Ga.	1	1

*1: Member's 1st period of service on the committee; *2: Member's 2nd period of service on the committee.

Note: James Domengeaux (Dem-La.) temporarily left the Congress to serve in the Armed Forces in April, 1944. Reelected to fill his own vacancy, Domengeaux returned to the House and to this committee in November 1944 with his ranking intact.

Changes:

Chair:				
Ch1 Bradley, Frederick V.	Rep	Mich.	May 24,1947	Died in office.
Ch2 Weichel, Alvin F.	Rep	Ohio	June 4,1947	Succeeded Bradley as Chair.
Majority:				
Bradley, Frederick V.	Rep	Mich.	May 24,1947	Died in office.
Maloney, Franklin J.	Rep	Penn.	July 15,1947	Moved to Foreign Affairs.
Jenkins, Mitchell	Rep	Penn.	July 15,1947	Replaced Bradley.
Potter, Charles E.	Rep	Mich.	Dec. 18,1947	Replaced Maloney.
Minority:				
Jackson, Henry M.	Dem	Wash.	July 24,1947	Moved to Appropriations.
Havenner, Franck R.	Dem	Cal.	July 26,1947	Moved to Armed Services.
Rayfiel, Leo F.	Dem	N.Y.	Sep. 13,1947	Resigned; appointed federal judge.
O'Toole, Donald L.	Dem	N.Y.	Dec. 4,1947	Replaced Jackson.
Meade, Hugh A.	Dem	Md.	Dec. 4,1947	Replaced Havenner.
Thompson, Clark W.	Dem	Tex.	Dec. 4,1947	Replaced Rayfiel.
Keogh, Eugene J.	Dem	N.Y.	Jan. 20,1948	Moved to Interstate and Foreign Commerce.
Boykin, Frank W.	Dem	Ala.	June 10,1948	Replaced Keogh.

	Majority		Minority	
Departures from the House:				
Appointed Asst. County Attorney	Jenkins, Mitchell	Penn. Rep	None	
Defeated for Reelection	Bradley, Willis W.	Cal. Rep	None	
	Brophy, John C.	Wisc. Rep		
	Burke, Raymond H.	Ohio Rep		
	Nodar, Robert J. Jr.	N.Y. Rep		
	Potts, David M.	N.Y. Rep		
	Seely-Brown, Horace Jr.	Conn. Rep		
Defeated for Renomination	None		Price, Emory H.	Fla. Dem
			Meade, Hugh A.	Md. Dem
Lost Nomination to U.S. Senate	None		Domengeaux, James	La. Dem
Departures from Committee:				
Moved to Ways and Means	None		King, Cecil R.	Cal. Dem
Moved to Appropriations	None		Preston, Prince H. Jr.	Ga. Dem

MERCHANT MARINE AND FISHERIES / 81st Congress

Service Dates of Committee Chairs: Ch1 Jan. 18,1949-Feb. 16,1950
Ch2 Feb. 23,1950-Jan. 3,1951
Service Dates of Majority Members: Jan. 18,1949-Jan. 3,1951
Service Dates of Minority Members: Jan. 18,1949-Jan. 3,1951

Majority

Rank Name	Party	State	Terms in: House	Terms in: Comm.
Ch1 Bland, Schuyler Otis	Dem	Va.	17	15
Ch2 2nd Hart, Edward J.	Dem	N.J.	8	8
3rd Bonner, Herbert C.	Dem	N.C.	6	6
4th O'Toole, Donald L.	Dem	N.Y.	7	2
5th Thompson, Clark W.	Dem	Tex.	3	2
6th Boykin, Frank W.	Dem	Ala.	8	2
7th Garmatz, Edward A.	Dem	Md.	2	1
8th Wickersham, Victor E.	Dem	Okla.	4	1
9th Barrett, William A.	Dem	Penn.	2	1
10th Hare, James B.	Dem	S.C.	1	1
11th Bennett, Charles E.	Dem	Fla.	1 *1	1
12th Welch, Philip J.	Dem	Mo.	1	1
13th Breen, Edward G.	Dem	Ohio	1	1
14th Murphy, James J.	Dem	N.Y.	1	1
15th Fugate, Thomas B.	Dem	Va.	1	1
Del. Bartlett, E.L. (Bob)	Dem	Alas.	3	1

Minority

Rank Name	Party	State	Terms in: House	Terms in: Comm.
RM Weichel, Alvin F.	Rep	Ohio	4	4
2nd Hand, T. Millet II	Rep	N.J.	3	3
3rd Latham, Henry J.	Rep	N.Y.	3	2
4th Tollefson, Thor C.	Rep	Wash.	2	2
5th Allen, John J. Jr.	Rep	Cal.	2	2
6th Miller, Edward T.	Rep	Md.	2	2
7th Potter, Charles E.	Rep	Mich.	2	2
8th Lichtenwalter, Franklin H.	Rep	Penn.	2	1
9th Jonas, Edgar A.	Rep	Ill.	1	1
10th Nelson, Charles P.	Rep	Me.	1	1

Note: Territorial Delegate E.L. (Bob) Bartlett (Dem-Alas.) was assigned to the committee on Aug. 2,1949, but was not allowed to accrue seniority nor was he included in the committee's party ratio.

Changes:

Chair:

Ch1 Bland, Schuyler Otis	Dem	Va.	Feb. 16,1950	Died in office.
Ch2 Hart, Edward J.	Dem	N.J.	Feb. 23,1950	Succeeded Bland as Chair.

Majority:

Bland, Schuyler Otis	Dem	Va.	Feb. 16,1950	Died in office.
Shelley, John F.	Dem	Cal.	Mar. 13,1950	Replaced Bland.
Hare, James B.	Dem	S.C.	Sep. 21,1950	Left committee; defeated for renomination.
Robeson, Edward J. Jr.	Dem	Va.	Sep. 21,1950	Replaced Hare.

	Majority	Minority
Departures from the House:		
Retired	None	Lichtenwalter, Franklin H. Penn. Rep
Departures from Committee:		
Moved to Banking and Currency	Fugate, Thomas B. Va. Dem	None
Moved to Agriculture	Thompson, Clark W. Tex. Dem	None
Moved to Armed Services	Wickersham, Victor E. Okla. Dem	None
Moved to Judiciary	None	Jonas, Edgar A. Ill. Rep
Moved to Rules	None	Latham, Henry J. N.Y. Rep
Moved to Education and Labor; Un-American Activities	None	Potter, Charles E. Mich. Rep

MERCHANT MARINE AND FISHERIES / 82nd Congress

Service Dates of Committee Chair: Jan. 12,1951-Jan. 3,1953
Service Dates of Majority Members: Jan. 12,1951-Jan. 3,1953
Service Dates of Minority Members: Jan. 15,1951-Jan. 3,1953

Majority

Rank	Name	Party	State	Terms in: House	Terms in: Comm.
Chr	Hart, Edward J.	Dem	N.J.	9	9
2nd	Bonner, Herbert C.	Dem	N.C.	7	7
3rd	O'Toole, Donald L.	Dem	N.Y.	8	3
4th	Boykin, Frank W.	Dem	Ala.	9	3
5th	Garmatz, Edward A.	Dem	Md.	3	2
6th	Barrett, William A.	Dem	Penn.	3	2
7th	Bennett, Charles E.	Dem	Fla.	2 *1	2
8th	Welch, Philip J.	Dem	Mo.	2	2
9th	Breen, Edward G.	Dem	Ohio	2	2
10th	Murphy, James J.	Dem	N.Y.	2	2
11th	Shelley, John F.	Dem	Cal.	2	2
12th	Robeson, Edward J. Jr.	Dem	Va.	2	2
13th	McCormack, John W.	Dem	Mass.	13	1
14th	Buchanan, Vera D.	Dem	Penn.	1	1
15th	Ikard, Frank N.	Dem	Tex.	1	1
Del.	Bartlett, E.L. (Bob)	Dem	Alas.	4	2

Minority

Rank	Name	Party	State	Terms in: House	Terms in: Comm.
RM	Weichel, Alvin F.	Rep	Ohio	5	5
2nd	Hand, T. Millet II	Rep	N.J.	4	4
3rd	Tollefson, Thor C.	Rep	Wash.	3	3
4th	Allen, John J. Jr.	Rep	Cal.	3	3
5th	Miller, Edward T.	Rep	Md.	3	3
6th	Nelson, Charles P.	Rep	Me.	2	2
7th	Butler, John C.	Rep	N.Y.	5	1
8th	Seely-Brown, Horace Jr.	Rep	Conn.	2 *2	1
9th	Kersten, Charles J.	Rep	Wisc.	2	1
10th	Vaughn, Albert C.	Rep	Penn.	1	1
11th	Sheehan, Timothy P.	Rep	Ill.	1	1
12th	Mumma, Walter M.	Rep	Penn.	1 *1	1

*1: Member's 1st period of service on the committee;
*2: Member's 2nd period of service on the committee.

Note: Territorial Delegate E.L. (Bob) Bartlett (Dem-Alas.) was not allowed to accrue seniority, nor was he included in the committee's party ratio.

Vacancies Filled:
Majority: 14th seat by Mrs. Buchanan on Aug. 16,1951 and the 15th seat by Ikard on Sep. 25,1951.

Changes:

Majority:				
Barrett, William A.	Dem	Penn.	June 13,1951	Moved to Banking and Currency.
Breen, Edward G.	Dem	Ohio	Oct. 1,1951	Resigned and retired.
Buchanan, Vera D.	Dem	Penn.	Jan. 29,1952	Moved to Public Works.
Chudoff, Earl	Dem	Penn.	Mar. 11,1952	Replaced Barrett.
Minority:				
Vaughn, Albert C.	Rep	Penn.	Sep. 1,1951	Died in office.
Nelson, Charles P.	Rep	Me.	Oct. 17,1951	Moved to Armed Services.
Van Pelt, William K.	Rep	Wisc.	Feb. 20,1952	Replaced Vaughn.
McIntire, Clifford G.	Rep	Me.	Feb. 20,1952	Replaced Nelson.
King, Karl C.	Rep	Penn.	Feb. 20,1952	Assigned to committee before subsequent vacancies were officially announced.
Miller, Edward T.	Rep	Md.	Apr. 30,1952	Moved to Appropriations.
McIntire, Clifford G.	Rep	Me.	June 16,1952	Moved to Agriculture.

	Majority		Minority	
Departures from the House:				
Defeated for Reelection	Murphy, James J.	N.Y. Dem	None	
	O'Toole, Donald L.	N.Y. Dem		
Defeated for Renomination	None		Butler, John C.	N.Y. Rep
Lost Nomination for Governor	Welch, Philip J.	Mo. Dem	None	
Departures from Committee:				
Moved to Armed Services	Bennett, Charles E.	Fla. Dem	None	
Moved to Government Operations	Ikard, Frank N.	Tex. Dem	None	
	Chudoff, Earl	Penn. Dem		
Moved to Appropriations	None		Hand, T. Millet II	N.J. Rep
Moved to Education and Labor	None		Kersten, Charles J.	Wisc. Rep
Moved to Agriculture	None		King, Karl C.	Penn. Rep
No new assignment	McCormack, John W.	Mass. Dem	None	

MERCHANT MARINE AND FISHERIES / 83rd Congress

Service Dates of Committee Chair: Jan. 19,1953-Jan. 3,1955
Service Dates of Majority Members: Jan. 19,1953-Jan. 3,1955
Service Dates of Minority Members: Jan. 19,1953-Jan. 3,1955

Majority

Rank	Name	Party	State	Terms in: House	Terms in: Comm.
Chr	Weichel, Alvin F.	Rep	Ohio	6	6
2nd	Tollefson, Thor C.	Rep	Wash.	4	4
3rd	Allen, John J. Jr.	Rep	Cal.	4	4
4th	Seely-Brown, Horace Jr.	Rep	Conn.	3	*2 2
5th	Sheehan, Timothy P.	Rep	Ill.	2	2
6th	Mumma, Walter M.	Rep	Penn.	2	*1 2
7th	Van Pelt, William K.	Rep	Wisc.	2	2
8th	Norblad, A. Walter Jr.	Rep	Ore.	5	*1 1
9th	Osmers, Frank C. Jr.	Rep	N.J.	4	1
10th	Wainwright, Stuyvesant II	Rep	N.Y.	1	1
11th	Clardy, Kit	Rep	Mich.	1	1
12th	Ray, John H.	Rep	N.Y.	1	1
13th	Mailliard, William S.	Rep	Cal.	1	1
14th	Dorn, Francis E.	Rep	N.Y.	1	1

Minority

Rank	Name	Party	State	Terms in: House	Terms in: Comm.
RM	Hart, Edward J.	Dem	N.J.	10	10
2nd	Bonner, Herbert C.	Dem	N.C.	8	8
3rd	Boykin, Frank W.	Dem	Ala.	10	4
4th	Garmatz, Edward A.	Dem	Md.	4	3
5th	Shelley, John F.	Dem	Cal.	3	3
6th	Robeson, Edward J. Jr.	Dem	Va.	3	3
7th	Keogh, Eugene J.	Dem	N.Y.	9	*2 1
8th	Delaney, James J.	Dem	N.Y.	4	1
9th	Dies, Martin Jr.	Dem	Tex.	8	1
10th	Sullivan, Leonor Kretzer	Dem	Mo.	1	1
11th	Thompson, T. Ashton	Dem	La.	1	1
12th	Magnuson, Donald H.	Dem	Wash.	1	1
13th	O'Neill, Thomas P. Jr.	Dem	Mass.	1	1
14th	Campbell, Courtney W.	Dem	Fla.	1	1
Del.	Bartlett, E.L. (Bob)	Dem	Alas.	5	3

*1: Member's 1st period of service on the committee; *2: Member's 2nd period of service on the committee.

Note: Territorial Delegate E.L. (Bob) Bartlett (Dem-Alas.) was not allowed to accrue seniority, nor was he included in the committee's party ratio. He was assigned to the committee on Jan. 26,1953.

Vacancy Filled:
Minority: 14th seat by Campbell on Feb. 12,1953.

Changes:
Minority:

Keogh, Eugene J.	Dem	N.Y.	July 27,1954	Moved to Ways and Means.

	Majority		Minority	
Departures from the House:				
Defeated for Reelection	Clardy, Kit	Mich. Rep	Campbell, Courtney W.	Fla. Dem
Retired	Weichel, Alvin F.	Ohio Rep	Hart, Edward J.	N.J. Dem
Departures from Committee:				
Moved to Armed Services	Osmers, Frank C. Jr.	N.J. Rep	None	
Moved to Rules	None		Delaney, James J.	N.Y. Dem
			O'Neill, Thomas P. Jr.	Mass. Dem
Moved to Appropriations	None		Shelley, John F.	Cal. Dem
Moved to Interstate & Foreign Commerce	None		Dies, Martin Jr.	Tex. Dem
Became Chair of Interstate & Foreign Commerce	None		Donald H.	Wash. Dem
No new assignment	Wainwright, Stuyvesant II	N.Y. Rep		
	Mumma, Walter M.	Penn. Rep		
	Norblad, A. Walter Jr.	Ore. Rep		

MERCHANT MARINE AND FISHERIES / 84th Congress

Service Dates of Committee Chair: Jan. 13,1955-Jan. 3,1957
Service Dates of Majority Members: Jan. 13,1955-Jan. 3,1957
Service Dates of Minority Members: Jan. 20,1955-Jan. 3,1957

Majority

Rank	Name	Party	State	Terms in: House	Terms in: Comm.
Chr	Bonner, Herbert C.	Dem	N.C.	9	9
2nd	Boykin, Frank W.	Dem	Ala.	11	5
3rd	Garmatz, Edward A.	Dem	Md.	5	4
4th	Robeson, Edward J. Jr.	Dem	Va.	4	4
5th	Sullivan, Leonor Kretzer	Dem	Mo.	2	2
6th	Thompson, T. Ashton	Dem	La.	2	2
7th	Miller, George P.	Dem	Cal.	6	1
8th	Kluczynski, John C.	Dem	Ill.	3	1
9th	Byrne, James A.	Dem	Penn.	2 *1	1
10th	Bell, John J.	Dem	Tex.	1	1
11th	Tumulty, T. James	Dem	N.J.	1	1
12th	Davidson, Irwin D.	Dem	N.Y.	1	1
13th	Zelenko, Herbert	Dem	N.Y.	1	1
14th	Clark, Frank M.	Dem	Penn.	1	1
15th	Ashley, Thomas L.	Dem	Ohio	1	1
16th	Machrowicz, Thaddeus M.	Dem	Mich.	3	1
Del.	Bartlett, E.L. (Bob)	Dem	Alas.	6	4

Minority

Rank	Name	Party	State	Terms in: House	Terms in: Comm.
RM	Tollefson, Thor C.	Rep	Wash.	5	5
2nd	Allen, John J. Jr.	Rep	Cal.	5	5
3rd	Seely-Brown, Horace Jr.	Rep	Conn.	4 *2	3
4th	Sheehan, Timothy P.	Rep	Ill.	3	3
5th	Van Pelt, William K.	Rep	Wisc.	3	3
6th	Ray, John H.	Rep	N.Y.	2	2
7th	Mailliard, William S.	Rep	Cal.	2	2
8th	Dorn, Francis E.	Rep	N.Y.	2	2
9th	Bush, Alvin R.	Rep	Penn.	3	1
10th	Pelly, Thomas M.	Rep	Wash.	2	1
11th	Cederberg, Elford A.	Rep	Mich.	2	1
12th	Baumhart, Albert D. Jr.	Rep	Ohio	2	1
13th	Chase, Jackson B.	Rep	Neb.	1	1

*1: Member's 1st period of service on the committee;
*2: Member's 2nd period of service on the committee.

Note: Territorial Delegate E.L. (Bob) Bartlett (Dem-Alas.) was not allowed to accrue seniority, nor was he included in the committee's party ratio. He was assigned to the committee on Jan. 20,1955.

Vacancy Filled:
Majority: 16th seat by Machrowitz on Jan. 31,1955.

Changes:

Majority:

Machrowicz, Thaddeus M.	Dem	Mich.	Jan. 12,1956	Moved to Ways and Means.
Dingell, John D. Jr.	Dem	Mich.	Jan. 19,1956	Replaced Machrowitz.
Davidson, Irwin D.	Dem	N.Y.	Dec. 31,1956	Resigned; elected state judge.

Minority:

Bush, Alvin R.	Rep	Penn.	Jan. 27,1955	Moved to Public Works.
Mumma, Walter M.	Rep	Penn.	Feb. 2,1955	Replaced Bush.
Mumma, Walter M.	Rep	Penn.	Feb. 10,1955	Left committee; no new assignment.
Norblad, A. Walter Jr.	Rep	Ore.	Apr. 11,1956	Replaced Mumma.

	Majority		Minority	
Departures from the House:				
Elected State Judge	None		Chase, Jackson B.	Neb. Rep
Defeated for Reelection	Tumulty, T. James	N.J. Dem	None	
Defeated for Renomination	Bell, John J.	Tex. Dem	None	
Departures from Committee:				
Moved to Armed Services	Byrne, James A.	Penn. Dem	None	
Moved to Banking & Currency	None		Seely-Brown, Horace Jr.	Conn. Rep
No new assignment	None		Norblad, A. Walter Jr.	Ore. Rep

MERCHANT MARINE AND FISHERIES / 85th Congress

Service Dates of Committee Chair: Jan. 10,1957-Jan. 3,1959
Service Dates of Majority Members: Jan. 10,1957-Jan. 3,1959
Service Dates of Minority Members: Jan. 16,1957-Jan. 3,1959

Majority

Rank	Name	Party	State	Terms in: House	Terms in: Comm.
Chr	Bonner, Herbert C.	Dem	N.C.	10	10
2nd	Boykin, Frank W.	Dem	Ala.	12	6
3rd	Garmatz, Edward A.	Dem	Md.	6	5
4th	Robeson, Edward J. Jr.	Dem	Va.	5	5
5th	Sullivan, Leonor Kretzer	Dem	Mo.	3	3
6th	Thompson, T. Ashton	Dem	La.	3	3
7th	Miller, George P.	Dem	Cal.	7	2
8th	Kluczynski, John C.	Dem	Ill.	4	2
9th	Zelenko, Herbert	Dem	N.Y.	2	2
10th	Clark, Frank M.	Dem	Penn.	2	2
11th	Ashley, Thomas L.	Dem	Ohio	2	2
12th	Dingell, John D. Jr.	Dem	Mich.	2	2
13th	Rivers, L. Mendel	Dem	S.C.	9	1
14th	Macdonald, Torbert H.	Dem	Mass.	2	1
15th	Lennon, Alton A.	Dem	N.C.	1	1
16th	Santangelo, Alfred E.	Dem	N.Y.	1	1
17th	Young, John A.	Dem	Tex.	1	1
Del.	Bartlett, E.L. (Bob)	Dem	Alas.	7	5

Minority

Rank	Name	Party	State	Terms in: House	Terms in: Comm.
RM	Tollefson, Thor C.	Rep	Wash.	6	6
2nd	Allen, John J. Jr.	Rep	Cal.	6	6
3rd	Sheehan, Timothy P.	Rep	Ill.	4	4
4th	Van Pelt, William K.	Rep	Wisc.	4	4
5th	Ray, John H.	Rep	N.Y.	3	3
6th	Mailliard, William S.	Rep	Cal.	3	3
7th	Dorn, Francis E.	Rep	N.Y.	3	3
8th	Pelly, Thomas M.	Rep	Wash.	3	2
9th	Cederberg, Elford A.	Rep	Mich.	3	2
10th	Baumhart, Albert D. Jr.	Rep	Ohio	3	2
11th	Gross, Harold R.	Rep	Iowa	5	1
12th	Dellay, Vincent J.	Rep	N.J.	1	1
13th	Curtin, Willard S.	Rep	Penn.	1	1
14th	McIntosh, Robert J.	Rep	Mich.	1	1

Notes: Territorial Delegate E.L. (Bob) Bartlett (Dem-Alas.) was not allowed to accrue seniority, nor was he included in the committee's party ratio. Vincent J. Dellay of New Jersey resigned from the Republican Party on Jan. 14,1958. He left the committee on Jan. 20,1958 and was reassigned by the Democratic Caucus on Jan. 27.1958. The committee size and party ratio remained constant.

Changes:

Majority:

Name	Party	State	Date	Change
Santangelo, Alfred E.	Dem	N.Y.	Jan. 16,1958	Moved to Appropriations.
Dellay, Vincent J.	Dem	N.J.	Jan. 27,1958	Replaced Santangelo.
Young, John A.	Dem	Tex.	July 21,1958	Moved to Public Works.
Nix, Robert N. C.	Dem	Penn.	July 21,1958	Replaced Young.

Minority:

Name	Party	State	Date	Change
Dellay, Vincent J.	Rep	N.J.	Jan. 20,1958	Resigned Republican Party; lost minority assignment.
Glenn, Milton W.	Rep	N.J.	Jan. 20,1958	Replaced Dellay.

Departures from the House:	**Majority**		**Minority**	
Elected to U.S. Senate	Bartlett, E.L. (Bob)	Alas. Dem	None	
Defeated for Reelection	None		Allen, John J. Jr.	Cal. Rep
			McIntosh, Robert J.	Mich. Rep
			Sheehan, Timothy P.	Ill. Rep
Defeated for Renomination	Dellay, Vincent J.	N.J. Dem	None	
	Robeson, Edward J. Jr.	Va. Dem		
Departures from Committee:				
No new assignment	Kluczynski, John C.	Ill. Dem	Cederberg, Elford A.	Mich. Rep

MERCHANT MARINE AND FISHERIES / 86th Congress

Service Dates of Committee Chair: Jan. 19,1959-Jan. 3,1961
Service Dates of Majority Members: Jan. 19,1959-Jan. 3,1961
Service Dates of Minority Members: Jan. 19,1959-Jan. 3,1961

Majority

Rank	Name	Party	State	Terms in: House	Terms in: Comm.
Chr	Bonner, Herbert C.	Dem	N.C.	11	11
2nd	Boykin, Frank W.	Dem	Ala.	13	7
3rd	Garmatz, Edward A.	Dem	Md.	7	6
4th	Sullivan, Leonor Kretzer	Dem	Mo.	4	4
5th	Thompson, T. Ashton	Dem	La.	4	4
6th	Miller, George P.	Dem	Cal.	8	3
7th	Zelenko, Herbert	Dem	N.Y.	3	3
8th	Clark, Frank M.	Dem	Penn.	3	3
9th	Ashley, Thomas L.	Dem	Ohio	3	3
10th	Dingell, John D. Jr.	Dem	Mich.	3	3
11th	Rivers, L. Mendel	Dem	S.C.	10	2
12th	Macdonald, Torbert H.	Dem	Mass.	3	2
13th	Lennon, Alton A.	Dem	N.C.	2	2
14th	Nix, Robert N. C.	Dem	Penn.	2	2
15th	Anfuso, Victor L.	Dem	N.Y.	4	1
16th	Oliver, James C.	Dem	Me.	4	*2 1
17th	Downing, Thomas N.	Dem	Va.	1	1
18th	Flynn, Gerald T.	Dem	Wisc.	1	1
19th	Casey, Robert R.	Dem	Tex.	1	1
20th	Johnson, Thomas F.	Dem	Md.	1	1

Minority

Rank	Name	Party	State	Terms in: House	Terms in: Comm.
RM	Tollefson, Thor C.	Rep	Wash.	7	7
2nd	Van Pelt, William K.	Rep	Wisc.	5	5
3rd	Ray, John H.	Rep	N.Y.	4	4
4th	Mailliard, William S.	Rep	Cal.	4	4
5th	Dorn, Francis E.	Rep	N.Y.	4	4
6th	Pelly, Thomas M.	Rep	Wash.	4	3
7th	Baumhart, Albert D. Jr.	Rep	Ohio	4	3
8th	Gross, Harold R.	Rep	Iowa	6	2
9th	Curtin, Willard S.	Rep	Penn.	2	2
10th	Glenn, Milton W.	Rep	N.J.	2	2
11th	Hoffman, Elmer J.	Rep	Ill.	1	1

*2: Member's 2nd period of service on the committee.

	Majority			Minority		
Departures from the House:						
Defeated for Reelection	Flynn, Gerald T.	Wisc.	Dem	Dorn, Francis E.	N.Y.	Rep
	Oliver, James C.	Me.	Dem			
Retired	None			Baumhart, Albert D. Jr.	Ohio	Rep
Departures from Committee:						
Moved to Foreign Affairs	Nix, Robert N. C.	Penn.	Dem	None		
Moved to Rules	None			Hoffman, Elmer J.	Ill.	Rep
No new assignment	None			Curtin, Willard S.	Penn.	Rep

MERCHANT MARINE AND FISHERIES / 87th Congress

Service Dates of Committee Chair: Feb. 6,1961-Jan. 3,1963
Service Dates of Majority Members: Feb. 6,1961-Jan. 3,1963
Service Dates of Minority Members: Feb. 13,1961-Jan. 3,1963

Majority

Rank	Name	Party	State	Terms in: House	Terms in: Comm.
Chr	Bonner, Herbert C.	Dem	N.C.	12	12
2nd	Boykin, Frank W.	Dem	Ala.	14	8
3rd	Garmatz, Edward A.	Dem	Md.	8	7
4th	Sullivan, Leonor Kretzer	Dem	Mo.	5	5
5th	Thompson, T. Ashton	Dem	La.	5	5
6th	Miller, George P.	Dem	Cal.	9	4
7th	Zelenko, Herbert	Dem	N.Y.	4	4
8th	Clark, Frank M.	Dem	Penn.	4	4
9th	Ashley, Thomas L.	Dem	Ohio	4	4
10th	Dingell, John D. Jr.	Dem	Mich.	4	4
11th	Rivers, L. Mendel	Dem	S.C.	11	3
12th	Macdonald, Torbert H.	Dem	Mass.	4	3
13th	Lennon, Alton A.	Dem	N.C.	3	3
14th	Anfuso, Victor L.	Dem	N.Y.	5	2
15th	Downing, Thomas N.	Dem	Va.	2	2
16th	Casey, Robert R.	Dem	Tex.	2	2

Minority

Rank	Name	Party	State	Terms in: House	Terms in: Comm.
RM	Tollefson, Thor C.	Rep	Wash.	8	8
2nd	Van Pelt, William K.	Rep	Wisc.	6	6
3rd	Ray, John H.	Rep	N.Y.	5	5
4th	Mailliard, William S.	Rep	Cal.	5	5
5th	Pelly, Thomas M.	Rep	Wash.	5	4
6th	Gross, Harold R.	Rep	Iowa	7	3
7th	Glenn, Milton W.	Rep	N.J.	3	3
8th	McDonough, Gordon L.	Rep	Cal.	9	1
9th	Ellsworth, Robert F.	Rep	Kans.	1	1
10th	Morse, F. Bradford	Rep	Mass.	1	*1 1
11th	Goodling, George A.	Rep	Penn.	1	*1 1
12th	Tupper, Stanley R.	Rep	Me.	1	1

17th Johnson, Thomas F.	Dem	Md.	2		2	
18th Byrne, James A.	Dem	Penn.	5	*2	1	*1: Member's 1st period of service on the committee;
19th Vanik, Charles A.	Dem	Ohio	4		1	*2: Member's 2nd period of service on the committee.

Changes:

Majority:

Miller, George P.	Dem	Cal.	Sep. 21,1961	Left committee; had been elected Chair of Science and Astronautics.
Hagen, Harlan F.	Dem	Cal.	Sep. 25,1961	Replaced Miller.

Departures from the House:	**Majority**			**Minority**		
Elected State Judge	Anfuso, Victor L.	N.Y.	Dem	None		
Defeated for Reelection	Johnson, Thomas F.	Md.	Dem	McDonough, Gordon L.	Cal.	Rep
Defeated for Renomination	Boykin, Frank W.	Ala.	Dem	None		
	Zelenko, Herbert	N.Y.	Dem			
Retired	None			Ray, John H.	N.Y.	Rep
Departures from Committee:						
Moved to Government Operations	Macdonald, Torbert H.	Mass.	Dem			
Moved to Foreign Affairs	None			Gross, Harold R.	Iowa	Rep
				Morse, F. Bradford	Mass.	Rep

MERCHANT MARINE AND FISHERIES / 88th Congress

Service Dates of Committee Chair: Jan. 17,1963-Jan. 3,1965
Service Dates of Majority Members: Jan. 17,1963-Jan. 3,1965
Service Dates of Minority Members: Jan. 24,1963-Jan. 3,1965

Majority

Rank Name	Party	State	Terms in: House		Comm.
Chr Bonner, Herbert C.	Dem	N.C.	13		13
2nd Garmatz, Edward A.	Dem	Md.	9		8
3rd Sullivan, Leonor Kretzer	Dem	Mo.	6		6
4th Thompson, T. Ashton	Dem	La.	6		6
5th Clark, Frank M.	Dem	Penn.	5		5
6th Ashley, Thomas L.	Dem	Ohio	5		5
7th Dingell, John D. Jr.	Dem	Mich.	5		5
8th Rivers, L. Mendel	Dem	S.C.	12		4
9th Lennon, Alton A.	Dem	N.C.	4		4
10th Downing, Thomas N.	Dem	Va.	3		3
11th Casey, Robert R.	Dem	Tex.	3		3
12th Byrne, James A.	Dem	Penn.	6	*2	2
13th Vanik, Charles A.	Dem	Ohio	5		2
14th Hagen, Harlan F.	Dem	Cal.	6		2
15th Green, Edith S.	Dem	Ore.	5		1
16th Rogers, Paul G.	Dem	Fla.	5		1
17th Stubblefield, Frank A.	Dem	Ky.	3		1
18th Murphy, John M.	Dem	N.Y.	1		1
19th Gilbert, Jacob H.	Dem	N.Y.	3		1

Minority

Rank Name	Party	State	Terms in: House		Comm.
RM Tollefson, Thor C.	Rep	Wash.	9		9
2nd Van Pelt, William K.	Rep	Wisc.	7		7
3rd Mailliard, William S.	Rep	Cal.	6		6
4th Pelly, Thomas M.	Rep	Wash.	6		5
5th Glenn, Milton W.	Rep	N.J.	4		4
6th Ellsworth, Robert F.	Rep	Kans.	2		2
7th Goodling, George A.	Rep	Penn.	2	*1	2
8th Tupper, Stanley R.	Rep	Me.	2		2
9th Mosher, Charles A.	Rep	Ohio	2		1
10th Grover, James R. Jr.	Rep	N.Y.	1		1
11th Morton, Rogers C. B.	Rep	Md.	1		1
12th Keith, Hastings	Rep	Mass.	3		1

*1: Member's 1st period of service on the committee;
*2: Member's 2nd period of service on the committee.

Vacancies Filled:

Majority: 19th seat by Gilbert on Jan. 31,1963.
Minority: 12th seat by Keith on Feb. 7,1963.

Departures from the House:	**Majority**			**Minority**		
Defeated for Reelection	None			Glenn, Milton W.	N.J.	Rep
				Goodling, George A.	Penn.	Rep
				Tollefson, Thor C.	Wash.	Rep
				Van Pelt, William K.	Wisc.	Rep
Departures from Committee:						
Moved to Ways and Means	Vanik, Charles A.	Ohio	Dem	None		
No new assignment	Rivers, L. Mendel	S.C.	Dem	None		

MERCHANT MARINE AND FISHERIES / 89th Congress

Service Dates of Committee Chairs: Ch1 Jan. 18,1965-Nov. 7,1965
Ch2 Jan. 10,1966-Jan. 3,1967
Service Dates of Majority Members: Jan. 18,1965-Jan. 3,1967
Service Dates of Minority Members: Jan. 21,1965-Jan. 3,1967

Majority

Rank	Name	Party	State	Terms in: House	Terms in: Comm.
Ch1	Bonner, Herbert C.	Dem	N.C.	14	14
Ch2 2nd	Garmatz, Edward A.	Dem	Md.	10	9
3rd	Sullivan, Leonor Kretzer	Dem	Mo.	7	7
4th	Thompson, T. Ashton	Dem	La.	7	7
5th	Clark, Frank M.	Dem	Penn.	6	6
6th	Ashley, Thomas L.	Dem	Ohio	6	6
7th	Dingell, John D. Jr.	Dem	Mich.	6	6
8th	Lennon, Alton A.	Dem	N.C.	5	5
9th	Downing, Thomas N.	Dem	Va.	4	4
10th	Casey, Robert R.	Dem	Tex.	4	4
11th	Byrne, James A.	Dem	Penn.	7	*2 3
12th	Hagen, Harlan F.	Dem	Cal.	7	3
13th	Green, Edith S.	Dem	Ore.	6	2
14th	Rogers, Paul G.	Dem	Fla.	6	2
15th	Stubblefield, Frank A.	Dem	Ky.	4	2
16th	Murphy, John M.	Dem	N.Y.	2	2
17th	Gilbert, Jacob H.	Dem	N.Y.	4	2
18th	Tuten, J. Russell	Dem	Ga.	2	1
19th	St. Onge, William L.	Dem	Conn.	2	1
20th	Dow, John G.	Dem	N.Y.	1	1
21st	Clevenger, Raymond F.	Dem	Mich.	1	1

Minority

Rank	Name	Party	State	Terms in: House	Terms in: Comm.
RM	Mailliard, William S.	Rep	Cal.	7	7
2nd	Pelly, Thomas M.	Rep	Wash.	7	6
3rd	Ellsworth, Robert F.	Rep	Kans.	3	3
4th	Tupper, Stanley R.	Rep	Me.	3	3
5th	Mosher, Charles A.	Rep	Ohio	3	2
6th	Grover, James R. Jr.	Rep	N.Y.	2	2
7th	Morton, Rogers C. B.	Rep	Md.	2	2
8th	Keith, Hastings	Rep	Mass.	4	2
9th	Edwards, W. J. (Jack)	Rep	Ala.	1	1
10th	Watkins, G. Robert	Rep	Penn.	1	1

*2: Member's 2nd period of service on the committee.

Note: House Resolution 806, agreed to on Mar. 29,1966, led to a change in size and party ratio on this committee to 22 Democrats and 10 Republicans.

Addition:

Majority:	22nd	Thomas, Lera	Dem	Tex.	Mar. 30,1966

Changes:

Chair:

Ch1	Bonner, Herbert C.	Dem	N.C.	Nov. 7,1965	Died in office.
Ch2	Garmatz, Edward A.	Dem	Md.	Jan. 10,1966	Succeeded Bonner as chair.

Majority:

Thompson, T. Ashton	Dem	La.	July 1,1965	Died in office.
Karth, Joseph E.	DFL	Minn.	Aug. 5,1965	Replaced Thompson.
Bonner, Herbert C.	Dem	N.C.	Nov. 7,1965	Died in office.
Casey, Robert R.	Dem	Tex.	Mar. 8,1966	Moved to Appropriations.
Hathaway, William D.	Dem	Me.	Mar. 8,1966	Replaced Bonner.
Jones, Walter B.	Dem	N.C.	Mar. 8,1966	Replaced Casey.

Minority:

Ellsworth, Robert F.	Rep	Kans.	Mar. 18,1965	Had already moved to Joint Economic Committee.
Reinecke, Ed	Rep	Cal.	Mar. 18,1965	Replaced Ellsworth.

	Majority			Minority		
Departures from the House:						
Defeated for Reelection	Clevenger, Raymond F.	Mich.	Dem	None		
	Hagen, Harlan F.	Cal.	Dem			
Defeated for Renomination	Tuten, J. Russell	Ga.	Dem	None		
Retired	Thomas, Lera	Tex.	Dem	Tupper, Stanley R.	Me.	Rep
Departures from Committee:						
Moved to Ways and Means	Gilbert, Jacob H.	N.Y.	Dem	None		

MERCHANT MARINE AND FISHERIES / 90th Congress

Service Dates of Committee Chair: Jan. 23,1967-Jan. 3,1969
Service Dates of Majority Members: Jan. 23,1967-Jan. 3,1969
Service Dates of Minority Members: Jan. 26,1967-Jan. 3,1969

Majority

Rank	Name	Party	State	Terms in: House	Terms in: Comm.
Chr	Garmatz, Edward A.	Dem	Md.	11	10
2nd	Sullivan, Leonor Kretzer	Dem	Mo.	8	8
3rd	Clark, Frank M.	Dem	Penn.	7	7
4th	Ashley, Thomas L.	Dem	Ohio	7	7
5th	Dingell, John D. Jr.	Dem	Mich.	7	7
6th	Lennon, Alton A.	Dem	N.C.	6	6
7th	Downing, Thomas N.	Dem	Va.	5	5
8th	Byrne, James A.	Dem	Penn.	8	*2 4
9th	Green, Edith S.	Dem	Ore.	7	3
10th	Rogers, Paul G.	Dem	Fla.	7	3
11th	Stubblefield, Frank A.	Dem	Ky.	5	3
12th	Murphy, John M.	Dem	N.Y.	3	3
13th	St. Onge, William L.	Dem	Conn.	3	2
14th	Dow, John G.	Dem	N.Y.	2	2
15th	Karth, Joseph E.	DFL	Minn.	5	2
16th	Hathaway, William D.	Dem	Me.	2	2
17th	Jones, Walter B.	Dem	N.C.	2	2
18th	Hanna, Richard T.	Dem	Cal.	3	1
19th	Helstoski, Henry	Dem	N.J.	2	1

Minority

Rank	Name	Party	State	Terms in: House	Terms in: Comm.
RM	Mailliard, William S.	Rep	Cal.	8	8
2nd	Pelly, Thomas M.	Rep	Wash.	8	7
3rd	Mosher, Charles A.	Rep	Ohio	4	3
4th	Grover, James R. Jr.	Rep	N.Y.	3	3
5th	Morton, Rogers C. B.	Rep	Md.	3	3
6th	Keith, Hastings	Rep	Mass.	5	3
7th	Edwards, W. J. (Jack)	Rep	Ala.	2	2
8th	Watkins, G. Robert	Rep	Penn.	2	2
9th	Reinecke, Ed	Rep	Cal.	2	2
10th	Schadeberg, Henry C.	Rep	Wisc.	3	1
11th	Roth, William V. Jr.	Rep	Del.	1	1
12th	Dellenback, John R.	Rep	Ore.	1	1
13th	Pollock, Howard W.	Rep	Alas.	1	1
14th	Ruppe, Philip E.	Rep	Mich.	1	1
15th	Button, Daniel E.	Rep	N.Y.	1	1

*2: Member's 2nd period of service on the committee.

Changes:

Majority:

Green, Edith S.	Dem	Ore.	Oct. 17,1967	Left committee; no new assignment.
Leggett, Robert L.	Dem	Cal.	Apr. 3,1968	Replaced Green.

	Majority			Minority		
Departures from the House:						
Defeated for Reelection	Dow, John G.	N.Y.	Dem	None		
Departures from Committee:						
Moved to Science & Astronautics	Helstoski, Henry	N.J.	Dem	None		
Moved to Appropriations	None			Edwards, W.J. (Jack)	Ala.	Rep
Moved to Ways and Means	None			Morton, Rogers C. B.	Md.	Rep
				Roth, William V. Jr.	Del.	Rep
Unassigned in 91st; elected Lieutenant Governor	None			Reinecke, Ed	Cal.	Rep

MERCHANT MARINE AND FISHERIES / 91st Congress

Service Dates of Committee Chair: Jan. 29,1969-Jan. 3,1971
Service Dates of Majority Members: Jan. 29,1969-Jan. 3,1971
Service Dates of Minority Members: Jan. 29,1969-Jan. 3,1971

Majority

Rank	Name	Party	State	Terms in: House	Terms in: Comm.
Chr	Garmatz, Edward A.	Dem	Md.	12	11
2nd	Sullivan, Leonor Kretzer	Dem	Mo.	9	9
3rd	Clark, Frank M.	Dem	Penn.	8	8
4th	Ashley, Thomas L.	Dem	Ohio	8	8
5th	Dingell, John D. Jr.	Dem	Mich.	8	8
6th	Lennon, Alton A.	Dem	N.C.	7	7
7th	Downing, Thomas N.	Dem	Va.	6	6
8th	Byrne, James A.	Dem	Penn.	9	*2 5
9th	Rogers, Paul G.	Dem	Fla.	8	4
10th	Stubblefield, Frank A.	Dem	Ky.	6	4
11th	Murphy, John M.	Dem	N.Y.	4	4
12th	St. Onge, William L.	Dem	Conn.	4	3
13th	Karth, Joseph E.	DFL	Minn.	6	3
14th	Hathaway, William D.	Dem	Me.	3	3
15th	Jones, Walter B.	Dem	N.C.	3	3
16th	Hanna, Richard T.	Dem	Cal.	4	2
17th	Leggett, Robert L.	Dem	Cal.	4	2
18th	Feighan, Michael A.	Dem	Ohio	14	1
19th	Annunzio, Frank	Dem	Ill.	3	1
20th	Long, Speedy O.	Dem	La.	3	1
21st	Biaggi, Mario	Dem	N.Y.	1	1

Minority

Rank	Name	Party	State	Terms in: House	Terms in: Comm.
RM	Mailliard, William S.	Rep	Cal.	9	9
2nd	Pelly, Thomas M.	Rep	Wash.	9	8
3rd	Mosher, Charles A.	Rep	Ohio	5	4
4th	Grover, James R. Jr.	Rep	N.Y.	4	4
5th	Keith, Hastings	Rep	Mass.	6	4
6th	Watkins, G. Robert	Rep	Penn.	3	3
7th	Schadeberg, Henry C.	Rep	Wisc.	4	2
8th	Dellenback, John R.	Rep	Ore.	2	2
9th	Pollock, Howard W.	Rep	Alas.	2	2
10th	Ruppe, Philip E.	Rep	Mich.	2	2
11th	Button, Daniel E.	Rep	N.Y.	2	2
12th	Goodling, George A.	Rep	Penn.	4	*2 1
13th	Bray, William G.	Rep	Ind.	10	1
14th	McCloskey, Paul N. Jr.	Rep	Cal.	2	1
15th	Frey, Louis Jr.	Rep	Fla.	1	1
16th	McDonald, Jack H.	Rep	Mich.	2	1

*2: Member's 2nd period of service on the committee.

Vacancy Filled:
Minority: 16th seat by McDonald on July 24,1969.

Changes:

Majority:

Name	Party	State	Date	Change
St. Onge, William L.	Dem	Conn.	May 1,1970	Died in office.
Griffin, Charles H.	Dem	Miss.	May 14,1970	Replaced St. Onge.
Hanna, Richard T.	Dem	Cal.	Dec. 10,1970	Left committee; no new assignment.
Anderson, Glenn M.	Dem	Cal.	Dec. 10,1970	Replaced Hanna.

Minority:

Name	Party	State	Date	Change
Watkins, G. Robert	Rep	Penn.	Aug. 7,1970	Died in office.
Snyder, M. G. (Gene)	Rep	Ky.	Sep. 23,1970	Replaced Watkins.

	Majority			Minority		
Departures from the House:						
Defeated for Reelection	None			Button, Daniel E.	N.Y.	Rep
				Schadeberg, Henry C.	Wisc.	Rep
Defeated for Renomination	Feighan, Michael A.	Ohio	Dem	None		
Lost Nomination for Governor	None			Pollock, Howard W.	Alas.	Rep
Departures from Committee:						
Moved to House Administration	Annunzio, Frank	Ill.	Dem	None		
Moved to Appropriations	Hathaway, William D.	Me.	Dem	None		
Moved to Interior & Insular Affairs	None			Dellenback, John R.	Ore.	Rep
Moved to Interstate & Foreign Commerce	None			Frey, Louis Jr.	Fla.	Rep

MERCHANT MARINE AND FISHERIES / 92nd Congress

Service Dates of Committee Chair: Feb. 4,1971-Jan. 3,1973
Service Dates of Majority Members: Feb. 4,1971-Jan. 3,1973
Service Dates of Minority Members: Feb. 4,1971-Jan. 3,1973

Majority

Rank	Name	Party	State	Terms in: House	Terms in: Comm.
Chr	Garmatz, Edward A.	Dem	Md.	13	12
2nd	Sullivan, Leonor Kretzer	Dem	Mo.	10	10
3rd	Clark, Frank M.	Dem	Penn.	9	9
4th	Ashley, Thomas L.	Dem	Ohio	9	9
5th	Dingell, John D. Jr.	Dem	Mich.	9	9
6th	Lennon, Alton A.	Dem	N.C.	8	8
7th	Downing, Thomas N.	Dem	Va.	7	7
8th	Byrne, James A.	Dem	Penn.	10	*2 6
9th	Rogers, Paul G.	Dem	Fla.	9	5
10th	Stubblefield, Frank A.	Dem	Ky.	7	5
11th	Murphy, John M.	Dem	N.Y.	5	5
12th	Karth, Joseph E.	DFL	Minn.	7	4
13th	Jones, Walter B.	Dem	N.C.	4	4
14th	Leggett, Robert L.	Dem	Cal.	5	3
15th	Long, Speedy O.	Dem	La.	4	2
16th	Biaggi, Mario	Dem	N.Y.	2	2
17th	Griffin, Charles H.	Dem	Miss.	3	2
18th	Anderson, Glenn M.	Dem	Cal.	2	2
19th	de la Garza, E. (Kika)	Dem	Tex.	4	1
20th	Kyros, Peter N.	Dem	Me.	3	1
21st	Tiernan, Robert O.	Dem	R.I.	3	1
22nd	Stanton, James V.	Dem	Ohio	1	1

Minority

Rank	Name	Party	State	Terms in: House	Terms in: Comm.
RM	Pelly, Thomas M.	Rep	Wash.	10	9
2nd	Mailliard, William S.	Rep	Cal.	10	10
3rd	Mosher, Charles A.	Rep	Ohio	6	5
4th	Grover, James R. Jr.	Rep	N.Y.	5	5
5th	Keith, Hastings	Rep	Mass.	7	5
6th	Ruppe, Philip E.	Rep	Mich.	3	3
7th	Goodling, George A.	Rep	Penn.	5	*2 2
8th	Bray, William G.	Rep	Ind.	11	2
9th	McCloskey, Paul N. Jr.	Rep	Cal.	3	2
10th	McDonald, Jack H.	Rep	Mich.	3	2
11th	Snyder, M. G. (Gene)	Rep	Ky.	4	2
12th	Steele, Robert H.	Rep	Conn.	2	1
13th	Forsythe, Edwin B.	Rep	N.J.	2	1
14th	du Pont, Pierre S. IV	Rep	Del.	1	1
15th	Mills, William O.	Rep	Md.	1	1

*2: Member's 2nd period of service on the committee.

Note: Ranking on this committee for the following member was affected by other chamber service: William S. Mailliard (Rep-Cal.), Ranking Minority Member, Foreign Affairs.

Vacancy Filled:
Minority: 15th seat by Mills on June 3,1971.

Changes:
Majority:

Karth, Joseph E.	DFL	Minn.	Oct. 6,1971	Moved to Ways and Means.
Metcalfe, Ralph H.	Dem	Ill.	Jan. 27,1972	Replaced Karth.
Long, Speedy O.	Dem	La.	Oct. 12,1972	Left committee; no new assignment.
Breaux, John B.	Dem	La.	Oct. 12,1972	Replaced Long.

	Majority		Minority	
Departures from the House:				
Defeated for Renomination	Byrne, James A.	Penn. Dem	McDonald, Jack H.	Mich. Rep
Retired	Garmatz, Edward A.	Md. Dem	Keith, Hastings	Mass. Rep
	Griffin, Charles H.	Miss. Dem	Pelly, Thomas M.	Wash. Rep
	Lennon, Alton A.	N.C. Dem		
Departures from Committee:				
Moved to Government Operations	Stanton, James V.	Ohio Dem	None	
Moved to Appropriations	Tiernan, Robert O.	R.I. Dem	None	

MERCHANT MARINE AND FISHERIES / 93rd Congress

Service Dates of Committee Chair: Jan. 24,1973-Jan. 3,1975
Service Dates of Majority Members: Jan. 24,1973-Jan. 3,1975
Service Dates of Minority Members: Jan. 24,1973-Jan. 3,1975

Majority

Rank	Name	Party	State	Terms in: House	Terms in: Comm.
Chr	Sullivan, Leonor Kretzer	Dem	Mo.	11	11
2nd	Clark, Frank M.	Dem	Penn.	10	10
3rd	Ashley, Thomas L.	Dem	Ohio	10	10
4th	Dingell, John D. Jr.	Dem	Mich.	10	10
5th	Downing, Thomas N.	Dem	Va.	8	8
6th	Rogers, Paul G.	Dem	Fla.	10	6
7th	Stubblefield, Frank A.	Dem	Ky.	8	6
8th	Murphy, John M.	Dem	N.Y.	6	6
9th	Jones, Walter B.	Dem	N.C.	5	5
10th	Leggett, Robert L.	Dem	Cal.	6	4
11th	Biaggi, Mario	Dem	N.Y.	3	3
12th	Anderson, Glenn M.	Dem	Cal.	3	3
13th	de la Garza, E. (Kika)	Dem	Tex.	5	2
14th	Kyros, Peter N.	Dem	Me.	4	2
15th	Metcalfe, Ralph H.	Dem	Ill.	2	2
16th	Breaux, John B.	Dem	La.	2	2
17th	Rooney, Fred B.	Dem	Penn.	6	1
18th	Eckhardt, Robert C.	Dem	Tex.	4	1
19th	Sarbanes, Paul S.	Dem	Md.	2	1
20th	Ginn, Ronald B. (Bo)	Dem	Ga.	1	1
21st	Studds, Gerry E.	Dem	Mass.	1	1
22nd	Bowen, David R.	Dem	Miss.	1	1

Minority

Rank	Name	Party	State	Terms in: House	Terms in: Comm.
RM	Grover, James R. Jr.	Rep	N.Y.	6	6
2nd	Mailliard, William S.	Rep	Cal.	11	11
3rd	Mosher, Charles A.	Rep	Ohio	7	6
4th	Ruppe, Philip E.	Rep	Mich.	4	4
5th	Goodling, George A.	Rep	Penn.	6	*2 3
6th	Bray, William G.	Rep	Ind.	12	3
7th	McCloskey, Paul N. Jr.	Rep	Cal.	4	3
8th	Snyder, M. G. (Gene)	Rep	Ky.	5	3
9th	Steele, Robert H.	Rep	Conn.	3	2
10th	Forsythe, Edwin B.	Rep	N.J.	3	2
11th	du Pont, Pierre S. IV	Rep	Del.	2	2
12th	Mills, William O.	Rep	Md.	2	2
13th	Cohen, William S.	Rep	Me.	1	1
14th	Lott, Trent	Rep	Miss.	1	1
15th	Treen, David C.	Rep	La.	1	1
16th	Pritchard, Joel M.	Rep	Wash.	1	1
17th	Young, Edward L.	Rep	S.C.	1	1

*2: Member's 2nd period of service on the committee.

Note: Rankings on this committee for the following members were affected by other chamber service: William S. Mailliard (Rep-Cal.), Ranking Minority Member, Foreign Affairs; and Charles A. Mosher (Rep-Ohio), Ranking Minority Member, Science and Astronautics.

Vacancy Filled:
Minority: 17th seat by Young on Feb. 20,1973.

Changes:

Majority:

Clark, Frank M.	Dem	Penn.	Dec. 31,1974	Resigned; defeated for reelection.
Stubblefield, Frank A.	Dem	Ky.	Dec. 31,1974	Resigned; defeated for renomination.

Minority:

Bray, William G.	Rep	Ind.	Feb. 5,1973	Left committee; no new assignment.
Young, Donald E.	Rep	Alas.	Mar. 14,1973	Replaced Bray.
Mills, William O.	Rep	Md.	May 24,1973	Died in office.
Bauman, Robert E.	Rep	Md.	Sep. 6,1973	Replaced Mills.
Mailliard, William S.	Rep	Cal.	Mar. 5,1974	Resigned; appointed Ambassador to Organization of American States
Lagomarsino, Robert J.	Rep	Cal.	May 1,1974	Replaced Mailliard.

	Majority			Minority		
Departures from the House:						
Defeated for Reelection	Kyros, Peter N.	Me.	Dem	Grover, James R. Jr.	N.Y.	Rep
				Young, Edward L.	S.C.	Rep
Lost Election for Governor	None			Steele, Robert H.	Conn.	Rep
Retired	None			Goodling, George A.	Penn.	Rep
Departures from Committee:						
Moved to Interior & Insular Affairs	Eckhardt, Robert C.	Tex.	Dem	Lagomarsino, Robert J.	Cal.	Rep
Moved to Small Business	None			Cohen, William S.	Me.	Rep
Moved to Post Office & Civil Service; Rules	None			Lott, Trent	Miss.	Rep

MERCHANT MARINE AND FISHERIES / 94th Congress

Service Dates of Committee Chair: Jan. 20,1975-Jan. 3,1977
Service Dates of Majority Members: Jan. 20,1975-Jan. 3,1977
Service Dates of Minority Members: Jan. 28,1975-Jan. 3,1977

Majority

Rank	Name	Party	State	Terms in: House	Terms in: Comm.
Chr	Sullivan, Leonor Kretzer	Dem	Mo.	12	12
2nd	Ashley, Thomas L.	Dem	Ohio	11	11
3rd	Dingell, John D. Jr.	Dem	Mich.	11	11
4th	Downing, Thomas N.	Dem	Va.	9	9
5th	Rogers, Paul G.	Dem	Fla.	11	7
6th	Murphy, John M.	Dem	N.Y.	7	7
7th	Jones, Walter B.	Dem	N.C.	6	6
8th	Leggett, Robert L.	Dem	Cal.	7	5
9th	Biaggi, Mario	Dem	N.Y.	4	4
10th	Anderson, Glenn M.	Dem	Cal.	4	4
11th	de la Garza, E. (Kika)	Dem	Tex.	6	3
12th	Metcalfe, Ralph H.	Dem	Ill.	3	3
13th	Breaux, John B.	Dem	La.	3	3
14th	Rooney, Fred B.	Dem	Penn.	7	2
15th	Sarbanes, Paul S.	Dem	Md.	3	2
16th	Ginn, Ronald B. (Bo)	Dem	Ga.	2	2
17th	Studds, Gerry E.	Dem	Mass.	2	2
18th	Bowen, David R.	Dem	Miss.	2	2
19th	Eilberg, Joshua	Dem	Penn.	5	1
20th	de Lugo, Ron	Dem	V.I.	2	1
21st	Hubbard, Carroll Jr.	Dem	Ky.	1	1
22nd	Bonker, Don L.	Dem	Wash.	1	1
23rd	AuCoin, Les	Dem	Ore.	1	1
24th	D'Amours, Norman E.	Dem	N.H.	1	1
25th	Patterson, Jerry M.	Dem	Cal.	1	1
26th	Zeferetti, Leo C.	Dem	N.Y.	1	1
27th	Oberstar, James L.	DFL	Minn.	1	1

Minority

Rank	Name	Party	State	Terms in: House	Terms in: Comm.
RM	Ruppe, Philip E.	Rep	Mich.	5	5
2nd	Mosher, Charles A.	Rep	Ohio	8	7
3rd	McCloskey, Paul N. Jr.	Rep	Cal.	5	4
4th	Snyder, M. G. (Gene)	Rep	Ky.	6	4
5th	Forsythe, Edwin B.	Rep	N.J.	4	3
6th	du Pont, Pierre S. IV	Rep	Del.	3	3
7th	Treen, David C.	Rep	La.	2	2
8th	Pritchard, Joel M.	Rep	Wash.	2	2
9th	Young, Donald E.	Rep	Alas.	2	2
10th	Bauman, Robert E.	Rep	Md.	2	2
11th	Lent, Norman F.	Rep	N.Y.	3	1
12th	Rinaldo, Matthew J.	Rep	N.J.	2	1
13th	Emery, David F.	Rep	Me.	1	1

Note: Ranking on this committee for the following member was affected by other chamber service: Charles A. Mosher (Rep-Ohio), Ranking Minority Member, Science and Astronautics.

	Majority			Minority		
Departures from the House:						
Elected to U.S. Senate	Sarbanes, Paul S.	Md.	Dem	None		
Elected Governor	None			du Pont, Pierre S. IV	Del.	Rep
Retired	Downing, Thomas N.	Va.	Dem	Mosher, Charles A.	Ohio	Rep
	Sullivan, Leonor Kretzer	Mo.	Dem			
Departures from Committee:						
No new assignment	None			Rinaldo, Matthew J.	N.J.	Rep

MERCHANT MARINE AND FISHERIES / 95th Congress

Service Dates of Committee Chair: Jan. 19,1977-Jan. 3,1979
Service Dates of Majority Members: Jan. 19,1977-Jan. 3,1979
Service Dates of Minority Members: Jan. 19,1977-Jan. 3,1979

Majority

Rank Name	Party	State	Terms in: House	Terms in: Comm.
Chr Murphy, John M.	Dem	N.Y.	8	8
2nd Ashley, Thomas L.	Dem	Ohio	12	12
3rd Dingell, John D. Jr.	Dem	Mich.	12	12
4th Rogers, Paul G.	Dem	Fla.	12	8
5th Jones, Walter B.	Dem	N.C.	7	7
6th Leggett, Robert L.	Dem	Cal.	8	6
7th Biaggi, Mario	Dem	N.Y.	5	5
8th Anderson, Glenn M.	Dem	Cal.	5	5
9th de la Garza, E. (Kika)	Dem	Tex.	7	4
10th Metcalfe, Ralph H.	Dem	Ill.	4	4
11th Breaux, John B.	Dem	La.	4	4
12th Rooney, Fred B.	Dem	Penn.	8	3
13th Ginn, Ronald B. (Bo)	Dem	Ga.	3	3
14th Studds, Gerry E.	Dem	Mass.	3	3
15th Bowen, David R.	Dem	Miss.	3	3
16th Eilberg, Joshua	Dem	Penn.	6	2
17th de Lugo, Ron	Dem	V.I.	3	2
18th Hubbard, Carroll Jr.	Dem	Ky.	2	2
19th Bonker, Don L.	Dem	Wash.	2	2
20th AuCoin, Les	Dem	Ore.	2	2
21st D'Amours, Norman E.	Dem	N.H.	2	2
22nd Patterson, Jerry M.	Dem	Cal.	2	2
23rd Zeferetti, Leo C.	Dem	N.Y.	2	2
24th Oberstar, James L.	DFL	Minn.	2	2
25th Hughes, William J.	Dem	N.J.	2	1
26th Mikulski, Barbara A.	Dem	Md.	1	1
27th Bonior, David E.	Dem	Mich.	1	1
28th Akaka, Daniel K.	Dem	Hai.	1	1

Minority

Rank Name	Party	State	Terms in: House	Terms in: Comm.
RM Ruppe, Philip E.	Rep	Mich.	6	6
2nd McCloskey, Paul N. Jr.	Rep	Cal.	6	5
3rd Snyder, M. G. (Gene)	Rep	Ky.	7	5
4th Forsythe, Edwin B.	Rep	N.J.	5	4
5th Treen, David C.	Rep	La.	3	3
6th Pritchard, Joel M.	Rep	Wash.	3	3
7th Young, Donald E.	Rep	Alas.	3	3
8th Bauman, Robert E.	Rep	Md.	3	3
9th Lent, Norman F.	Rep	N.Y.	4	2
10th Emery, David F.	Rep	Me.	2	2
11th Dornan, Robert K.	Rep	Cal.	1	1
12th Evans, Thomas B. Jr.	Rep	Del.	1	1
13th Trible, Paul S. Jr.	Rep	Va.	1	1

Note: Rankings on this committee for the following members were affected by other chamber service: Thomas L. Ashley (Dem-Ohio), Chair, Select Committee on Energy (ad hoc); John D. Dingell, Jr. (Dem-Mich.), Chair, Energy and Power Subcommittee of Interstate and Foreign Commerce; and Paul G. Rogers (Dem-Fla.), Chair, Health and Environment Subcommittee of Interstate and Foreign Commerce.

Changes:

Majority:

Metcalfe, Ralph H.	Dem	Ill.	Oct. 10,1978	Died in office.

Departures from the House:	Majority		Minority	
Defeated for Reelection	de Lugo, Ron	V.I. Dem	None	
	Eilberg, Joshua	Penn. Dem		
	Rooney, Fred B.	Penn. Dem		
Retired	Leggett, Robert L.	Cal. Dem	Ruppe, Philip E.	Mich. Rep
	Rogers, Paul G.	Fla. Dem		
Departures from Committee:				
Moved to Appropriations	Ginn, Ronald B. (Bo)	Ga. Dem	None	
Moved to Interior & Insular Affairs	Patterson, Jerry M.	Cal. Dem	None	
Moved to Rules	Zeferetti, Leo C.	N.Y. Dem	None	

MERCHANT MARINE AND FISHERIES / 96th Congress

Service Dates of Committee Chair: Jan. 24,1979-Jan. 3,1981
Service Dates of Majority Members: Jan. 24,1979-Jan. 3,1981
Service Dates of Minority Members: Jan. 24,1979-Jan. 3,1981

Majority

Rank Name	Party	State	Terms in: House	Terms in: Comm.
Chr Murphy, John M.	Dem	N.Y.	9	9
ChA 2nd Ashley, Thomas L.	Dem	Ohio	13	13
3rd Dingell, John D. Jr.	Dem	Mich.	13	13
4th Jones, Walter B.	Dem	N.C.	8	8
5th Biaggi, Mario	Dem	N.Y.	6	6
6th Anderson, Glenn M.	Dem	Cal.	6	6
7th de la Garza, E. (Kika)	Dem	Tex.	8	5
8th Breaux, John B.	Dem	La.	5	5
9th Studds, Gerry E.	Dem	Mass.	4	4
10th Bowen, David R.	Dem	Miss.	4	4
11th Hubbard, Carroll Jr.	Dem	Ky.	3	3
12th Bonker, Don L.	Dem	Wash.	3	3
13th AuCoin, Les	Dem	Ore.	3	3
14th D'Amours, Norman E.	Dem	N.H.	3	3
15th Oberstar, James L.	DFL	Minn.	3	3
16th Hughes, William J.	Dem	N.J.	3	2
17th Mikulski, Barbara A.	Dem	Md.	2	2
18th Bonior, David E.	Dem	Mich.	2	2
19th Akaka, Daniel K.	Dem	Hai.	2	2
20th Myers, Michael O. (Ozzie)	Dem	Penn.	3	1
21st Wyatt, Joseph P. Jr.	Dem	Tex.	1	1
22nd Lowry, Michael E.	Dem	Wash.	1	1
23rd Hutto, Earl D.	Dem	Fla.	1	1
24th Stack, Edward J.	Dem	Fla.	1	1
25th Donnelly, Brian J.	Dem	Mass.	1	1

Minority

Rank Name	Party	State	Terms in: House	Terms in: Comm.
RM McCloskey, Paul N. Jr.	Rep	Cal.	7	6
2nd Snyder, M. G. (Gene)	Rep	Ky.	8	6
3rd Forsythe, Edwin B.	Rep	N.J.	6	5
4th Treen, David C.	Rep	La.	4	4
5th Pritchard, Joel M.	Rep	Wash.	4	4
6th Young, Donald E.	Rep	Alas.	4	4
7th Bauman, Robert E.	Rep	Md.	4	4
8th Lent, Norman F.	Rep	N.Y.	5	3
9th Emery, David F.	Rep	Me.	3	3
10th Dornan, Robert K.	Rep	Cal.	2	2
11th Evans, Thomas B. Jr.	Rep	Del.	2	2
12th Trible, Paul S. Jr.	Rep	Va.	2	2
13th Davis, Robert W.	Rep	Mich.	1	1
14th Carney, William	Rep	N.Y.	1	1
15th Evans, Melvin H.	Rep	V.I.	1	1

*1: Member's 1st period of service on the committee.

Note: Rankings on this committee for the following members were affected by other chamber service: Thomas L. Ashley (Dem-Ohio), Chair, Select Committee on Energy (ad hoc); and John D. Dingell, Jr. (Dem-Mich.), Chair, Energy and Power Subcommittee of Interstate and Foreign Commerce.

Changes:

Chair:				
Chr Murphy, John M.	Dem	N.Y.	June 18,1980	Due to Democratic Party Caucus rules, interrupts service as Chair.
ChA Ashley, Thomas L.	Dem	Ohio	June 18,1980	Acting Chair during ethics investigation of Murphy.
Majority:				
Myers, Michael O. (Ozzie)	Dem	Penn.	Oct. 2,1980	Expelled from the House due to involvement in Abscam.
Minority:				
Treen, David C.	Rep	La.	Mar. 10,1980	Resigned; elected Governor of Louisiana.
Livingston, Robert L.	Rep	La.	Mar. 10,1980	Replaced Treen.

	Majority			Minority		
Departures from the House:						
Defeated for Reelection	Ashley, Thomas L.	Ohio	Dem	Bauman, Robert E.	Md.	Rep
	Murphy, John M.	N.Y.	Dem	Evans, Melvin H.	V.I.	Rep
Defeated for Renomination	Stack, Edward J.	Fla.	Dem	None		
Retired	Wyatt, Joseph P. Jr.	Tex.	Dem	None		
Departures from Committee:						
Moved to Appropriations	Akaka, Daniel K.	Hai.	Dem	Livingston, Robert L.	La.	Rep
	AuCoin, Les	Ore.	Dem			
Moved to Rules	Bonior, David E.	Mich.	Dem			
Moved to Foreign Affairs	None			Dornan, Robert K.	Cal.	Rep
Moved to Budget	None			Trible, Paul S. Jr.	Va.	Rep
Became Chair of Agriculture	de la Garza, E. (Kika)	Tex.	Dem	None		
Became Chair of Energy & Commerce	Dingell, John D. Jr.	Mich.	Dem	None		

MERCHANT MARINE AND FISHERIES / 97th Congress

Service Dates of Committee Chair: Jan. 28,1981-Jan. 3,1983
Service Dates of Majority Members: Jan. 28,1981-Jan. 3,1983
Service Dates of Minority Members: Jan. 28,1981-Jan. 3,1983

Majority			Terms in:		Minority			Terms in:	
Rank Name	Party	State	House	Comm.	Rank Name	Party	State	House	Comm.
Chr Jones, Walter B.	Dem	N.C.	9	9	RM Snyder, M. G. (Gene)	Rep	Ky.	9	7
2nd Biaggi, Mario	Dem	N.Y.	7	7	2nd McCloskey, Paul N. Jr.	Rep	Cal.	8	7
3rd Anderson, Glenn M.	Dem	Cal.	7	7	3rd Forsythe, Edwin B.	Rep	N.J.	7	6
4th Breaux, John B.	Dem	La.	6	6	4th Pritchard, Joel M.	Rep	Wash.	5	5
5th Studds, Gerry E.	Dem	Mass.	5	5	5th Young, Donald E.	Rep	Alas.	5	5
6th Bowen, David R.	Dem	Miss.	5	5	6th Lent, Norman F.	Rep	N.Y.	6	4
7th Hubbard, Carroll Jr.	Dem	Ky.	4	4	7th Emery, David F.	Rep	Me.	4	4
8th Bonker, Don L.	Dem	Wash.	4	4	8th Evans, Thomas B. Jr.	Rep	Del.	3	3
9th D'Amours, Norman E.	Dem	N.H.	4	4	9th Davis, Robert W.	Rep	Mich.	2	2
10th Oberstar, James L.	Dem	Minn.	4	4	10th Carney, William	Rep	N.Y.	2	2
11th Hughes, William J.	Dem	N.J.	4	3	11th Dougherty, Charles F.	Rep	Penn.	2	1
12th Mikulski, Barbara A.	Dem	Md.	3	3	12th Shumway, Norman D.	Rep	Cal.	2	1
13th Lowry, Michael E.	Dem	Wash.	2	2	13th Fields, Jack	Rep	Tex.	1	1
14th Hutto, Earl D.	Dem	Fla.	2	2	14th Schneider, Claudine	Rep	R.I.	1	1
15th Donnelly, Brian J.	Dem	Mass.	2	2	15th Shaw, E. Clay Jr.	Rep	Fla.	1	1
16th Tauzin, W. J. (Billy)	Dem	La.	2	1					
17th Foglietta, Thomas M.	Dem	Penn.	1	1					
18th Patman, William N.	Dem	Tex.	1	1					
19th Sunia, Fofo I. F.	Dem	A.Sm.	1	1					
20th Hertel, Dennis M.	Dem	Mich.	1	1					
21st Dyson, Royden	Dem	Md.	1	1					

*1: Member's 1st period of service on the committee.

Note: Ranking on this committee for the following member was affected by other chamber service: Paul N McCloskey, Jr. (Rep-Cal.), Ranking Minority Member, Manpower and Housing Subcommittee of Government Operations. McCloskey also announced his candidacy for the Senate during this Congress.

Changes:

Majority:

Lowry, Michael E.	Dem	Wash.	Dec. 10,1981	Ceased active membership on committee; had moved to Budget on Oct. 28,1981.
Smith, Joseph F.	Dem	Penn.	Dec. 16,1981	Replaced Lowry.

Minority:

Shaw, E. Clay Jr.	Rep	Fla.	Aug. 3,1982	Moved to Judiciary; letter dated July 29,1981.
Ashbrook, Jean	Rep	Ohio	July 29,1982	Replaced Shaw.

Departures from the House:	Majority		Minority	
Defeated for Reelection	None		Dougherty, Charles F.	Penn. Rep
			Evans, Thomas B. Jr.	Del. Rep
Defeated for Renomination	Smith, Joseph F.	Penn. Dem	None	
Lost Election to U.S. Senate	None		Emery, David F.	Me. Rep
Lost Nomination to U.S. Senate	None		McCloskey, Paul N. Jr.	Cal. Rep
Retired	Bowen, David R.	Miss. Dem	Ashbrook, Jean	Ohio Rep
Departures from Committee:				
Moved to Interior & Insular Affairs	Patman, William N.	Tex. Dem	None	

MERCHANT MARINE AND FISHERIES / 98th Congress

Service Dates of Committee Chair: Jan. 6,1983-Jan. 3,1985
Service Dates of Majority Members: Jan. 6,1983-Jan. 3,1985
Service Dates of Minority Members: Jan. 6,1983-Jan. 3,1985

Majority

Rank Name	Party	State	Terms in: House	Terms in: Comm.
Chr Jones, Walter B.	Dem	N.C.	10	10
2nd Biaggi, Mario	Dem	N.Y.	8	8
3rd Anderson, Glenn M.	Dem	Cal.	8	8
4th Breaux, John B.	Dem	La.	7	7
5th Studds, Gerry E.	Dem	Mass.	6	6
6th Hubbard, Carroll Jr.	Dem	Ky.	5	5
7th Bonker, Don L.	Dem	Wash.	5	5
8th D'Amours, Norman E.	Dem	N.H.	5	5
9th Oberstar, James L.	Dem	Minn.	5	5
10th Hughes, William J.	Dem	N.J.	5	4
11th Mikulski, Barbara A.	Dem	Md.	4	4
12th Hutto, Earl D.	Dem	Fla.	3	3
13th Donnelly, Brian J.	Dem	Mass.	3	3
14th Tauzin, W. J. (Billy)	Dem	La.	3	2
15th Foglietta, Thomas M.	Dem	Penn.	2	2
16th Sunia, Fofo I. F.	Dem	A.Sm.	2	2
17th Hertel, Dennis M.	Dem	Mich.	2	2
18th Dyson, Royden	Dem	Md.	2	2
19th Lipinski, William O.	Dem	Ill.	1	1
20th Borski, Robert A.	Dem	Penn.	1	1
21st Carper, Thomas R.	Dem	Del.	1	1
22nd Bosco, Douglas H.	Dem	Cal.	1	1
23rd Tallon, Robin	Dem	S.C.	1	1
24th Thomas, Robert Lindsay	Dem	Ga.	1	1
25th Boxer, Barbara	Dem	Cal.	1	1
26th Ortiz, Solomon P.	Dem	Tex.	1	1

Minority

Rank Name	Party	State	Terms in: House	Terms in: Comm.
RM1 Forsythe, Edwin B.	Rep	N.J.	8	7
RM2 2nd Snyder, M. G. (Gene)	Rep	Ky.	10	8
3rd Pritchard, Joel M.	Rep	Wash.	6	6
4th Young, Donald E.	Rep	Alas.	6	6
5th Lent, Norman F.	Rep	N.Y.	7	5
6th Davis, Robert W.	Rep	Mich.	3	3
7th Carney, William	Rep	N.Y.	3	3
8th Shumway, Norman D.	Rep	Cal.	3	2
9th Fields, Jack	Rep	Tex.	2	2
10th Schneider, Claudine	Rep	R.I.	2	2
11th Sawyer, Harold S.	Rep	Mich.	4	1
12th Bateman, Herbert H.	Rep	Va.	1	1
13th McKernan, John R. Jr.	Rep	Me.	1	1
14th Franklin, Webb	Rep	Miss.	1	1

*1: Member's 1st period of service on the committee.

Note: Ranking on this committee for the following member was affected by other chamber service: M.G. (Gene) Snyder (Rep-Ky.), Ranking Minority Member, Public Works and Transportation.

Changes:

Ranking Member:

RM1 Forsythe, Edwin B.	Rep	N.J.	Mar. 29,1984	Died in office.
RM2 Snyder, M. G. (Gene)	Rep	Ky.	Mar. 29,1984	Succeeded Forsythe as Ranking Minority Member.

Majority:

Donnelly, Brian J.	Dem	Mass.	Feb. 2,1983	Moved to Public Works and Transportation.
Donnelly, Brian J.	Dem	Mass.	Feb. 2,1983	Temporarily filled his own vacancy (1st Session only).
Donnelly, Brian J.	Dem	Mass.	Nov. 18,1983	Temporary term expired on last day of 1st Session.
Bennett, Charles E.	Dem	Fla.	Feb. 29,1984	Replaced Donnelly.

Minority:

Forsythe, Edwin B.	Rep	N.J.	Mar. 29,1984	Died in office.
Hartnett, Thomas F.	Rep	S.C.	June 14,1984	Replaced Forsythe.

Departures from the House:	Majority		Minority	
Lost Election to U.S. Senate	D'Amours, Norman E.	N.H. Dem	None	
Retired	None		Pritchard, Joel M.	Wash. Rep
			Sawyer, Harold S.	Mich. Rep

Departures from Committee:	Majority		Minority
Moved to Budget	Boxer, Barbara	Cal. Dem	None
Moved to Interior & Insular Affairs	Sunia, Fofo I. F.	A.Sm. Dem	None

MERCHANT MARINE AND FISHERIES / 99th Congress

Service Dates of Committee Chair: Jan. 7,1985-Jan. 3,1987
Service Dates of Majority Members: Jan. 30,1985-Jan. 3,1987
Service Dates of Minority Members: Jan. 30,1985-Jan. 3,1987

Majority

Rank Name	Party	State	Terms in: House	Terms in: Comm.
Chr Jones, Walter B.	Dem	N.C.	11	11
2nd Biaggi, Mario	Dem	N.Y.	9	9
3rd Anderson, Glenn M.	Dem	Cal.	9	9
4th Breaux, John B.	Dem	La.	8	8
5th Studds, Gerry E.	Dem	Mass.	7	7
6th Hubbard, Carroll Jr.	Dem	Ky.	6	6
7th Bonker, Don L.	Dem	Wash.	6	6
8th Oberstar, James L.	Dem	Minn.	6	6
9th Hughes, William J.	Dem	N.J.	6	5
10th Mikulski, Barbara A.	Dem	Md.	5	5
11th Lowry, Michael E.	Dem	Wash.	4	4
12th Hutto, Earl D.	Dem	Fla.	4	4
13th Tauzin, W. J. (Billy)	Dem	La.	4	3
14th Foglietta, Thomas M.	Dem	Penn.	3	3
15th Hertel, Dennis M.	Dem	Mich.	3	3
16th Dyson, Royden	Dem	Md.	3	3
17th Lipinski, William O.	Dem	Ill.	2	2
18th Borski, Robert A.	Dem	Penn.	2	2
19th Carper, Thomas R.	Dem	Del.	2	2
20th Bosco, Douglas H.	Dem	Cal.	2	2
21st Tallon, Robin	Dem	S.C.	2	2
22nd Thomas, Robert Lindsay	Dem	Ga.	2	2
23rd Ortiz, Solomon P.	Dem	Tex.	2	2
24th Bennett, Charles E.	Dem	Fla.	19	*2 2
25th Manton, Thomas J.	Dem	N.Y.	1	1

Minority

Rank Name	Party	State	Terms in: House	Terms in: Comm.
RM Lent, Norman F.	Rep	N.Y.	8	6
2nd Snyder, M. G. (Gene)	Rep	Ky.	11	9
3rd Young, Donald E.	Rep	Alas.	7	7
4th Davis, Robert W.	Rep	Mich.	4	4
5th Carney, William	Rep	N.Y.	4	4
6th Shumway, Norman D.	Rep	Cal.	4	3
7th Fields, Jack	Rep	Tex.	3	3
8th Schneider, Claudine	Rep	R.I.	3	3
9th Bateman, Herbert H.	Rep	Va.	2	2
10th McKernan, John R. Jr.	Rep	Me.	2	2
11th Franklin, Webb	Rep	Miss.	2	2
12th Hartnett, Thomas F.	Rep	S.C.	3	2
13th Chappie, Eugene A.	Rep	Cal.	3	1
14th Saxton, H. James	Rep	N.J.	1	1
15th Callahan, H. L. (Sonny)	Rep	Ala.	1	1
16th Miller, John R.	Rep	Wash.	1	1
17th Bentley, Helen Delich	Rep	Md.	1	1

*2: Member's 2nd period of service on the committee.

Notes Rankings on this committee for the following members were affected by other chamber service: M.G. (Gene) Snyder (Rep-Ky.), Ranking Minority Member, Public Works and Transportation; Donald E. Young (Rep-Alas.), Ranking Minority Member, Interior and Insular Affairs; Michael E. Lowry (Dem-Wash.), while continuing to serve on the Budget Committee, returned to active service on this committee with his seniority intact.

Departures from the House:	Majority			Minority		
Elected to U.S. Senate	Breaux, John B.	La.	Dem	None		
	Mikulski, Barbara A.	Md.	Dem			
Elected Governor	None			McKernan, John R. Jr.	Me.	Rep
Defeated for Reelection	None			Franklin, Webb	Miss.	Rep
Lost Election for Lt. Governor	None			Hartnett, Thomas F.	S.C.	Rep
Retired	None			Carney, William	N.Y.	Rep
				Chappie, Eugene A.	Cal.	Rep
				Snyder, M. G. (Gene)	Ky.	Rep
Departures from Committee:						
Moved to Budget	Oberstar, James L.	Minn.	Dem	None		
Moved to Energy & Commerce	None			Callahan, H. L. (Sonny)	Ala.	Rep

MERCHANT MARINE AND FISHERIES / 100th Congress

Service Dates of Committee Chair: Jan. 8,1987-Jan. 3,1989
Service Dates of Majority Members: Jan. 22,1987-Jan. 3,1989
Service Dates of Minority Members: Jan. 21,1987-Jan. 3,1989

Majority

Rank	Name	Party	State	Terms in: House	Terms in: Comm.
Chr	Jones, Walter B.	Dem	N.C.	12	12
2nd	Biaggi, Mario	Dem	N.Y.	10	10
3rd	Anderson, Glenn M.	Dem	Cal.	10	10
4th	Studds, Gerry E.	Dem	Mass.	8	8
5th	Hubbard, Carroll Jr.	Dem	Ky.	7	7
6th	Bonker, Don L.	Dem	Wash.	7	7
7th	Hughes, William J.	Dem	N.J.	7	6
8th	Lowry, Michael E.	Dem	Wash.	5	5
9th	Hutto, Earl D.	Dem	Fla.	5	5
10th	Tauzin, W. J. (Billy)	Dem	La.	5	4
11th	Foglietta, Thomas M.	Dem	Penn.	4	4
12th	Hertel, Dennis M.	Dem	Mich.	4	4
13th	Dyson, Royden	Dem	Md.	4	4
14th	Lipinski, William O.	Dem	Ill.	3	3
15th	Borski, Robert A.	Dem	Penn.	3	3
16th	Carper, Thomas R.	Dem	Del.	3	3
17th	Bosco, Douglas H.	Dem	Cal.	3	3
18th	Tallon, Robin	Dem	S.C.	3	3
19th	Thomas, Robert Lindsay	Dem	Ga.	3	3
20th	Ortiz, Solomon P.	Dem	Tex.	3	3
21st	Bennett, Charles E.	Dem	Fla.	20	*2 3
22nd	Manton, Thomas J.	Dem	N.Y.	2	2
23rd	Pickett, Owen B.	Dem	Va.	1	1
24th	Brennan, Joseph E.	Dem	Me.	1	1
25th	Hochbrueckner, George J.	Dem	N.Y.	1	1

Minority

Rank	Name	Party	State	Terms in: House	Terms in: Comm.
RM	Davis, Robert W.	Rep	Mich.	5	5
2nd	Young, Donald E.	Rep	Alas.	8	8
3rd	Lent, Norman F.	Rep	N.Y.	9	7
4th	Shumway, Norman D.	Rep	Cal.	5	4
5th	Fields, Jack	Rep	Tex.	4	4
6th	Schneider, Claudine	Rep	R.I.	4	4
7th	Bateman, Herbert H.	Rep	Va.	3	3
8th	Saxton, H. James	Rep	N.J.	2	2
9th	Miller, John R.	Rep	Wash.	2	2
10th	Bentley, Helen Delich	Rep	Md.	2	2
11th	Coble, Howard	Rep	N.C.	2	1
12th	Sweeney, Mac	Rep	Tex.	2	1
13th	DioGuardi, Joseph J.	Rep	N.Y.	2	1
14th	Weldon, Curt	Rep	Penn.	1	1
15th	Saiki, Patricia F.	Rep	Hai.	1	1
16th	Herger, Wally	Rep	Cal.	1	1
17th	Bunning, Jim	Rep	Ky.	1	1

*2: Member's 2nd period of service on the committee.

Note: Rankings on this committee for the following members were affected by other chamber service: Donald E. Young (Rep-Alas.), Ranking Minority Member, Interior and Insular Affairs; and Norman F. Lent (Rep-N.Y.), Ranking Minority Member, Energy and Commerce.

Changes:

Majority:

Thomas, Robert Lindsay	Dem	Ga.	Oct. 21,1987	Moved to Appropriations.
Clement, Bob	Dem	Tenn.	Mar. 2,1988	Replaced Thomas.
Biaggi, Mario	Dem	N.Y.	Aug. 5,1988	Resigned and retired.
Solarz, Stephen J.	Dem	N.Y.	Oct. 6,1988	Replaced Biaggi.

Minority:

DioGuardi, Joseph J.	Rep	N.Y.	Nov. 4,1987	Had already moved to Banking, Finance and Urban Affairs on June 18,1987.
Konnyu, Ernest L.	Rep	Cal.	Nov. 4,1987	Replaced DioGuardi.

Departures from the House:	Majority			Minority		
Defeated for Reelection	None			Sweeney, Mac	Tex.	Rep
Defeated for Renomination	None			Konnyu, Ernest L.	Cal.	Rep
Lost Election to U.S. Senate	Lowry, Michael E.	Wash.	Dem	None		
Lost Nomination to U.S. Senate	Bonker, Don L.	Wash.	Dem	None		
Departures from Committee:						
No new assignment	Anderson, Glenn M.	Cal.	Dem	None		

MERCHANT MARINE AND FISHERIES / 101st Congress

Service Dates of Committee Chair: Jan. 3,1989-Jan. 3,1991
Service Dates of Majority Members: Jan. 19,1989-Jan. 3,1991
Service Dates of Minority Members: Jan. 20,1989-Jan. 3,1991

Majority

Rank	Name	Party	State	Terms in: House	Terms in: Comm.
Chr	Jones, Walter B.	Dem	N.C.	13	13
2nd	Studds, Gerry E.	Dem	Mass.	9	9
3rd	Hubbard, Carroll Jr.	Dem	Ky.	8	8
4th	Hughes, William J.	Dem	N.J.	8	7
5th	Hutto, Earl D.	Dem	Fla.	6	6
6th	Tauzin, W. J. (Billy)	Dem	La.	6	5
7th	Foglietta, Thomas M.	Dem	Penn.	5	5
8th	Hertel, Dennis M.	Dem	Mich.	5	5
9th	Dyson, Royden	Dem	Md.	5	5
10th	Lipinski, William O.	Dem	Ill.	4	4
11th	Borski, Robert A.	Dem	Penn.	4	4
12th	Carper, Thomas R.	Dem	Del.	4	4
13th	Bosco, Douglas H.	Dem	Cal.	4	4
14th	Tallon, Robin	Dem	S.C.	4	4
15th	Ortiz, Solomon P.	Dem	Tex.	4	4
16th	Bennett, Charles E.	Dem	Fla.	21	*2 4
17th	Manton, Thomas J.	Dem	N.Y.	3	3
18th	Pickett, Owen B.	Dem	Va.	2	2
19th	Brennan, Joseph E.	Dem	Me.	2	2
20th	Hochbrueckner, George J.	Dem	N.Y.	2	2
21st	Clement, Bob	Dem	Tenn.	2	2
22nd	Solarz, Stephen J.	Dem	N.Y.	8	2
23rd	Pallone, Frank Jr.	Dem	N.J.	2	1
24th	Laughlin, Greg H.	Dem	Tex.	1	1
25th	Lowey, Nita M.	Dem	N.Y.	1	1
26th	Unsoeld, Jolene	Dem	Wash.	1	1

Minority

Rank	Name	Party	State	Terms in: House	Terms in: Comm.
RM	Davis, Robert W.	Rep	Mich.	6	6
2nd	Young, Donald E.	Rep	Alas.	9	9
3rd	Lent, Norman F.	Rep	N.Y.	10	8
4th	Shumway, Norman D.	Rep	Cal.	6	5
5th	Fields, Jack	Rep	Tex.	5	5
6th	Schneider, Claudine	Rep	R.I.	5	5
7th	Bateman, Herbert H.	Rep	Va.	4	4
8th	Saxton, H. James	Rep	N.J.	3	3
9th	Miller, John R.	Rep	Wash.	3	3
10th	Bentley, Helen Delich	Rep	Md.	3	3
11th	Coble, Howard	Rep	N.C.	3	2
12th	Weldon, Curt	Rep	Penn.	2	2
13th	Saiki, Patricia F.	Rep	Hai.	2	2
14th	Herger, Wally	Rep	Cal.	2	2
15th	Bunning, Jim	Rep	Ky.	2	2
16th	Inhofe, James M.	Rep	Okla.	2	1
17th	Goss, Porter J.	Rep	Fla.	1	1

*2: Member's 2nd period of service on the committee.

Notes: The death of Larkin Smith (Rep-Miss.) and his replacement by Gene Taylor (Dem-Miss.) on Oct. 24,1989, led to a change in size and party ratio on this committee to 27 Democrats and 18 Republicans on Nov. 8,1989. Rankings on this committee for the following members were affected by other chamber service: Donald E. Young (Rep-Alas.), Ranking Minority Member, Interior and Insular Affairs; and Norman F. Lent (Rep-N.Y.), Ranking Minority Member, Energy and Commerce.

Additions:

Majority:	27th	Taylor, Gene	Dem	Miss.	Nov. 8,1989
Minority:	18th	Ravenel, Arthur Jr.	Rep	S.C.	Nov. 9,1989

Departures from the House:	**Majority**			**Minority**		
Defeated for Reelection	Bosco, Douglas H.	Cal.	Dem	None		
	Dyson, Royden	Md.	Dem			
Lost Election to U.S. Senate	None			Saiki, Patricia F.	Hai.	Rep
				Schneider, Claudine	R.I.	Rep
Lost Election for Governor	Brennan, Joseph E.	Me.	Dem	None		
Retired	None			Shumway, Norman D.	Cal.	Rep
Departures from Committee:						
Moved to Ways and Means; Standards of Official Conduct	None			Bunning, Jim	Ky.	Rep
Moved to Budget	None			Miller, John R.	Wash.	Rep

MERCHANT MARINE AND FISHERIES / 102nd Congress

Service Dates of Committee Chair: Ch1 Jan. 24,1991-Sep. 15,1992
ChA Sep. 15,1992-Jan. 3,1993
Service Dates of Majority Members: Jan. 24,1991-Jan. 3,1993
Service Dates of Minority Members: Jan. 24,1991-Jan. 3,1993

Majority

Rank Name	Party	State	Terms in: House	Terms in: Comm.
Chr Jones, Walter B.	Dem	N.C.	14	14
ChA 2nd Studds, Gerry E.	Dem	Mass.	10	10
3rd Hubbard, Carroll Jr.	Dem	Ky.	9	9
4th Hughes, William J.	Dem	N.J.	9	8
5th Hutto, Earl D.	Dem	Fla.	7	7
6th Tauzin, W. J. (Billy)	Dem	La.	7	6
7th Foglietta, Thomas M.	Dem	Penn.	6	6
8th Hertel, Dennis M.	Dem	Mich.	6	6
9th Lipinski, William O.	Dem	Ill.	5	5
10th Borski, Robert A.	Dem	Penn.	5	5
11th Carper, Thomas R.	Dem	Del.	5	5
12th Tallon, Robin	Dem	S.C.	5	5
13th Ortiz, Solomon P.	Dem	Tex.	5	5
14th Bennett, Charles E.	Dem	Fla.	22	*2 5
15th Manton, Thomas J.	Dem	N.Y.	4	4
16th Pickett, Owen B.	Dem	Va.	3	3
17th Hochbrueckner, George J.	Dem	N.Y.	3	3
18th Clement, Bob	Dem	Tenn.	3	3
19th Solarz, Stephen J.	Dem	N.Y.	9	3
20th Pallone, Frank Jr.	Dem	N.J.	3	2
21st Laughlin, Greg H.	Dem	Tex.	2	2
22nd Lowey, Nita M.	Dem	N.Y.	2	2
23rd Unsoeld, Jolene	Dem	Wash.	2	2
24th Taylor, Gene	Dem	Miss.	2	2
25th Anderson, Glenn M.	Dem	Cal.	12	1
26th Reed, John F.	Dem	R.I.	1	1
27th Jefferson, William J.	Dem	La.	1	1
28th Abercrombie, Neil	Dem	Hai.	2	1
29th Faleomavaega, Eni F. H.	Dem	A.Sm.	2	1

Minority

Rank Name	Party	State	Terms in: House	Terms in: Comm.
RM Davis, Robert W.	Rep	Mich.	7	7
2nd Young, Donald E.	Rep	Alas.	10	10
3rd Lent, Norman F.	Rep	N.Y.	11	9
4th Fields, Jack	Rep	Tex.	6	6
5th Bateman, Herbert H.	Rep	Va.	5	5
6th Saxton, H. James	Rep	N.J.	4	4
7th Bentley, Helen Delich	Rep	Md.	4	4
8th Coble, Howard	Rep	N.C.	4	3
9th Weldon, Curt	Rep	Penn.	3	3
10th Herger, Wally	Rep	Cal.	3	3
11th Inhofe, James M.	Rep	Okla.	3	2
12th Goss, Porter J.	Rep	Fla.	2	2
13th Ravenel, Arthur Jr.	Rep	S.C.	3	2
14th Callahan, H. L. (Sonny)	Rep	Ala.	4	1
15th Gilchrest, Wayne T.	Rep	Md.	1	1
16th Doolittle, John T.	Rep	Cal.	1	1
17th Cunningham, Randy	Rep	Cal.	1	1

*2: Member's 2nd period of service on the committee.

Note: Rankings on this committee for the following members were affected by other chamber service: Donald E. Young (Rep-Alas.), Ranking Minority Member, Interior and Insular Affairs; and Norman F. Lent (Rep-N.Y.), Ranking Minority Member, Energy and Commerce.

Changes:

Chair:

Ch1 Jones, Walter B.	Dem	N.C.	Sep. 15,1992	Died in office.
ChA Studds, Gerry E.	Dem	Mass.	Sep. 15,1992	Succeeded Jones as Acting Chair.

Majority:

Abercrombie, Neil	Dem	Hai.	Oct. 9,1991	Moved to Interior and Insular Affairs.
Lancaster, H. Martin	Dem	N.C.	Oct. 30,1991	Replaced Abercrombie.
Clement, Bob	Dem	Tenn.	Feb. 5,1992	Moved to Veterans' Affairs.
Blackwell, Lucien E.	Dem	Penn.	Feb. 5,1992	Replaced Clement.
Jones, Walter B.	Dem	N.C.	Sep. 15,1992	Died in office.

POST OFFICE AND CIVIL SERVICE

Jurisdiction, 1947

Established by the Legislative Reorganization Act of 1946:

[Section 121. (1) (e)]

Committee on Post Office and Civil Service.

1. The Federal civil service generally.
2. The status of officers and employees of the United States, including their compensation, classification, and retirement.
3. The postal service generally, including the railway mail service, and measures relating to ocean mail and pneumatic-tube service; but excluding post roads.
4. Postal-savings banks.
5. Census and the collection of statistics generally.
6. The National Archives.

Jurisdiction, 1992

Jurisdiction contained in Rules of the House of Representatives, (as revised to July 1, 1992):

[Rule X. 1. (o)]

Committee on Post Office and Civil Service.

(1) Census and the collection of statistics generally.
(2) All Federal Civil Service, including intergovernmental personnel.
(3) Postal-savings banks.
(4) Postal service generally, including the railway mail service, and measures relating to ocean mail and pneumatic tube service; but excluding post roads.
(5) Status of officers and employees of the United States, including their compensation, classification, and retirement.
(6) Hatch Act.
(7) Holidays and celebrations.
(8) Population and demography.

POST OFFICE AND CIVIL SERVICE / 80th Congress

Service Dates of Committee Chair: Jan. 14,1947-Jan. 3,1949
Service Dates of Majority Members: Jan. 14,1947-Jan. 3,1949
Service Dates of Minority Members: Jan. 16,1947-Jan. 3,1949

Majority

Rank	Name	Party	State	Terms in: House		Terms in: Comm.
Chr	Rees, Edward H.	Rep	Kans.	6		6
2nd	Stevenson, William H.	Rep	Wisc.	4		4
3rd	Butler, John C.	Rep	N.Y.	4		3
4th	Cole, William C.	Rep	Mo.	3	*1	3
5th	Vursell, Charles W.	Rep	Ill.	3		3
6th	Hagen, Harold C.	Rep	Minn.	3		3
7th	Corbett, Robert J.	Rep	Penn.	3		2
8th	Scoblick, James P.	Rep	Penn.	2		1
9th	Twyman, Robert J.	Rep	Ill.	1		1
10th	St. George, Katharine	Rep	N.Y.	1	*1	1
11th	Morton, Thruston B.	Rep	Ky.	1		1
12th	Sadlak, Antoni N.	Rep	Conn.	1		1
13th	Youngblood, Harold F.	Rep	Mich.	1		1
14th	Jones, Homer R.	Rep	Wash.	1		1
15th	Love, Francis J.	Rep	W.Va.	1		1

Minority

Rank	Name	Party	State	Terms in: House	Terms in: Comm.
RM	Murray, Thomas J.	Dem	Tenn.	3	3
2nd	Lyle, John E. Jr.	Dem	Tex.	2	2
3rd	Morrison, James H.	Dem	La.	3	2
4th	Miller, George P.	Dem	Cal.	2	2
5th	Combs, Jesse M.	Dem	Tex.	2	2
6th	Clements, Earle C.	Dem	Ky.	2	1
7th	Almond, J. Lindsay Jr.	Dem	Va.	2	1
8th	Albert, Carl	Dem	Okla.	1	1
9th	Battle, Laurie C.	Dem	Ala.	1	1
10th	Davis, James C.	Dem	Ga.	1	1

*1: Member's 1st period of service on the committee.

Changes:

Minority:

Clements, Earle C.	Dem	Ky.	Jan. 6,1948	Resigned; elected Governor of Kentucky.
Almond, J. Lindsay Jr.	Dem	Va.	Apr. 17,1948	Resigned; elected Governor of Virginia.
Williams, John Bell	Dem	Miss.	May 12,1948	Replaced Clements.
Whitaker, John A.	Dem	Ky.	May 12,1948	Replaced Almond.
Albert, Carl	Dem	Okla.	Aug. 7,1948	Moved to Agriculture.

	Majority			Minority		
Departures from the House:						
Defeated for Reelection	Butler, John C.	N.Y.	Rep	None		
	Cole, William C.	Mo.	Rep			
	Jones, Homer R.	Wash.	Rep			
	Love, Francis J.	W.Va.	Rep			
	Twyman, Robert J.	Ill.	Rep			
	Youngblood, Harold F.	Mich.	Rep			
Defeated for Renomination	Scoblick, James P.	Penn.	Rep	None		
	Stevenson, William H.	Wisc.	Rep			
Departures from Committee:						
Moved to Education & Labor	Morton, Thruston B.	Ky.	Rep	None		
Moved to Public Works	Vursell, Charles W.	Ill.	Rep	None		
Moved to Foreign Affairs	None			Battle, Laurie C.	Ala.	Dem
Moved to Ways and Means	None			Combs, Jesse M.	Tex.	Dem
Moved to Rules	None			Lyle, John E. Jr.	Tex.	Dem

POST OFFICE AND CIVIL SERVICE / 81st Congress

Service Dates of Committee Chair: Jan. 18,1949-Jan. 3,1951
Service Dates of Majority Members: Jan. 18,1949-Jan. 3,1951
Service Dates of Minority Members: Jan. 18,1949-Jan. 3,1951

Majority

Rank	Name	Party	State	Terms in: House	Terms in: Comm.
Chr	Murray, Thomas J.	Dem	Tenn.	4	4
2nd	Morrison, James H.	Dem	La.	4	3
3rd	Miller, George P.	Dem	Cal.	3	3
4th	Davis, James C.	Dem	Ga.	2	2
5th	Williams, John Bell	Dem	Miss.	2	2
6th	Whitaker, John A.	Dem	Ky.	2	2
7th	Crook, Thurman C.	Dem	Ind.	1	1
8th	Karst, Raymond W.	Dem	Mo.	1	1
9th	Thornberry, W. Homer	Dem	Tex.	1	1
10th	Buckley, James V.	Dem	Ill.	1	1
11th	Carlyle, F. Ertel	Dem	N.C.	1	1
12th	McCarthy, Eugene J.	DFL	Minn.	1	1
13th	Herlong, Albert S. Jr.	Dem	Fla.	1	1
14th	Gorski, Chester C.	Dem	N.Y.	1	1
15th	Rhodes, George M.	Dem	Penn.	1	1

Minority

Rank	Name	Party	State	Terms in: House	Terms in: Comm.
RM	Rees, Edward H.	Rep	Kans.	7	7
2nd	Hagen, Harold C.	Rep	Minn.	4	4
3rd	Corbett, Robert J.	Rep	Penn.	4	3
4th	St. George, Katharine	Rep	N.Y.	2 *1	2
5th	Sadlak, Antoni N.	Rep	Conn.	2	2
6th	Jenison, Edward H.	Rep	Ill.	2	1
7th	Burdick, Usher L.	Rep	N.D.	6	1
8th	Withrow, Gardner R.	Rep	Wisc.	5 *2	1
9th	Gross, Harold R.	Rep	Iowa	1	1
10th	Golden, James S.	Rep	Ky.	1	1

*1: Member's 1st period of service on the committee;
*2: Member's 2nd period of service on the committee.

Changes:

Majority:

Carlyle, F. Ertel	Dem	N.C.	Dec. 11,1950	Moved to Interstate and Foreign Commerce.

Minority:

Jenison, Edward H.	Rep	Ill.	June 20,1950	Moved to Public Lands.

	Majority			Minority
Departures from the House:				
Defeated for Reelection	Buckley, James V.	Ill.	Dem	None
	Crook, Thurman C.	Ind.	Dem	
	Gorski, Chester C.	N.Y.	Dem	
	Karst, Raymond W.	Mo.	Dem	
Departures from Committee:				
Moved to Agriculture	Herlong, Albert S. Jr.	Fla.	Dem	None
	McCarthy, Eugene J.	Minn.	DFL	
Moved to Interstate & Foreign Commerce	Thornberry, W. Homer	Tex.	Dem	None
	Williams, John Bell	Miss.	Dem	

POST OFFICE AND CIVIL SERVICE / 82nd Congress

Service Dates of Committee Chair: Jan. 12,1951-Jan. 3,1953
Service Dates of Majority Members: Jan. 12,1951-Jan. 3,1953
Service Dates of Minority Members: Jan. 15,1951-Jan. 3,1953

Majority

Rank	Name	Party	State	Terms in: House	Terms in: Comm.
Chr	Murray, Thomas J.	Dem	Tenn.	5	5
2nd	Morrison, James H.	Dem	La.	5	4
3rd	Miller, George P.	Dem	Cal.	4	4
4th	Davis, James C.	Dem	Ga.	3	3
5th	Whitaker, John A.	Dem	Ky.	3	3
6th	Rhodes, George M.	Dem	Penn.	2	2
7th	Karsten, Frank M.	Dem	Mo.	3	1
8th	Burnside, Maurice G.	Dem	W.Va.	2	1
9th	Lesinski, John Jr.	Dem	Mich.	1	1
10th	Jarman, John	Dem	Okla.	1	1
11th	Anfuso, Victor L.	Dem	N.Y.	1	1
12th	Lantaff, William C.	Dem	Fla.	1	1

Minority

Rank	Name	Party	State	Terms in: House	Terms in: Comm.
RM	Rees, Edward H.	Rep	Kans.	8	8
2nd	Hagen, Harold C.	Rep	Minn.	5	5
3rd	Corbett, Robert J.	Rep	Penn.	5	4
4th	St. George, Katharine	Rep	N.Y.	3 *1	3
5th	Sadlak, Antoni N.	Rep	Conn.	3	3
6th	Burdick, Usher L.	Rep	N.D.	7	2
7th	Withrow, Gardner R.	Rep	Wisc.	6 *2	2
8th	Gross, Harold R.	Rep	Iowa	2	2
9th	Golden, James S.	Rep	Ky.	2	2
10th	Williams, William R.	Rep	N.Y.	1	1
11th	Armstrong, Orland K.	Rep	Mo.	1	1

Third Party:

13th Reams, Henry Frazier	Ind	Ohio	1	1

*1: Member's 1st period of service on the committee; *2: Member's 2nd period of service on the committee.

Note: Henry Frazier Reams (Independent-Ohio) was assigned by the Democratic Caucus to the 13th majority rank on Jan. 12,1951, but was not allowed to accrue seniority.

Changes:

Majority:

Whitaker, John A.	Dem	Ky.	Dec. 15,1951	Died in office.

Departures from the House:	Majority			Minority		
Appointed N.Y. City Magistrate	Anfuso, Victor L.	N.Y.	Dem	None		
Defeated for Reelection	Burnside, Maurice G.	W.Va.	Dem	None		
Retired	None			Armstrong, Orland K.	Mo.	Rep

Departures from Committee:						
Moved to Armed Services	Miller, George P.	Cal.	Dem	None		
Moved to Agriculture	None			Golden, James S.	Ky.	Rep
				Williams, William R.	N.Y.	Rep
Moved to Judiciary	None			Burdick, Usher L.	N.D.	Rep
Moved to Ways and Means	None			Sadlak, Antoni N.	Conn.	Rep
No new assignment	Karsten, Frank M.	Mo.	Dem	None		
	Lantaff, William C.	Fla.	Dem			

POST OFFICE AND CIVIL SERVICE / 83rd Congress

Service Dates of Committee Chair: Jan. 19,1953-Jan. 3,1955
Service Dates of Majority Members: Jan. 19,1953-Jan. 3,1955
Service Dates of Minority Members: Jan. 19,1953-Jan. 3,1955

Majority

Rank Name	Party	State	Terms in: House		Terms in: Comm.
Chr Rees, Edward H.	Rep	Kans.	9		9
2nd Hagen, Harold C.	Rep	Minn.	6		6
3rd Corbett, Robert J.	Rep	Penn.	6		5
4th St. George, Katharine	Rep	N.Y.	4	*1	4
5th Withrow, Gardner R.	Rep	Wisc.	7	*2	3
6th Gross, Harold R.	Rep	Iowa	3		3
7th Harden, Cecil M.	Rep	Ind.	3		1
8th Cole, William C.	Rep	Mo.	4	*2	1
9th Cretella, Albert W.	Rep	Conn.	1		1
10th Gubser, Charles S.	Rep	Cal.	1		1
11th Bonin, Edward J.	Rep	Penn.	1		1
12th Broyhill, Joel T.	Rep	Va.	1		1
13th Bolton, Oliver P.	Rep	Ohio	1		1

Minority

Rank Name	Party	State	Terms in: House		Terms in: Comm.
RM Murray, Thomas J.	Dem	Tenn.	6		6
2nd Morrison, James H.	Dem	La.	6		5
3rd Davis, James C.	Dem	Ga.	4		4
4th Rhodes, George M.	Dem	Penn.	3		3
5th Lesinski, John Jr.	Dem	Mich.	2		2
6th Jarman, John	Dem	Okla.	2		2
7th Staggers, Harley O.	Dem	W.Va.	3	*1	1
8th Withers, Garrett L.	Dem	Ky.	2		1
9th Dowdy, John V.	Dem	Tex.	2		1
10th Boland, Edward P.	Dem	Mass.	1		1
11th Alexander, Hugh Q.	Dem	N.C.	1		1

Third Party:

12th Reams, Henry Frazier	Ind	Ohio	2	2

*1: Member's 1st period of service on the committee; *2: Member's 2nd period of service on the committee.

Note: Henry Frazier Reams (Independent-Ohio) was assigned by the Republican Conference to the 12th minority rank on Jan. 19,1953, but was not allowed to accrue seniority.

Changes:

Minority:

Staggers, Harley O.	Dem	W.Va.	Feb. 6,1953	Moved to Interstate and Foreign Commerce.
Moss, John E. Jr.	Dem	Cal.	Feb. 12,1953	Replaced Staggers.
Withers, Garrett L.	Dem	Ky.	Apr. 30,1953	Died in office.
Tuck, William M.	Dem	Va.	May 19,1953	Replaced Withers.

Departures from the House:	Majority			Minority		
Defeated for Reelection	Bonin, Edward J.	Penn.	Rep	Reams, Henry Frazier	Ohio	Ind
	Cole, William C.	Mo.	Rep			
	Hagen, Harold C.	Minn.	Rep			

Departures from Committee:

	Majority		Minority	
Moved to Banking & Currency	Bolton, Oliver P.	Ohio Rep	None	
Moved to Public Works	Withrow, Gardner R.	Wisc. Rep	None	
Moved to Appropriations	None		Boland, Edward P.	Mass. Dem
Moved to Foreign Affairs	None		Jarman, John	Okla. Dem
Moved to Judiciary	None		Tuck, William M.	Va. Dem

POST OFFICE AND CIVIL SERVICE / 84th Congress

Service Dates of Committee Chair: Jan. 13,1955-Jan. 3,1957
Service Dates of Majority Members: Jan. 13,1955-Jan. 3,1957
Service Dates of Minority Members: Jan. 20,1955-Jan. 3,1957

Majority

Rank Name	Party	State	Terms in: House	Terms in: Comm.
Chr Murray, Thomas J.	Dem	Tenn.	7	7
2nd Morrison, James H.	Dem	La.	7	6
3rd Davis, James C.	Dem	Ga.	5	5
4th Rhodes, George M.	Dem	Penn.	4	4
5th Lesinski, John Jr.	Dem	Mich.	3	3
6th Dowdy, John V.	Dem	Tex.	3	2
7th Alexander, Hugh Q.	Dem	N.C.	2	2
8th Moss, John E. Jr.	Dem	Cal.	2	2
9th Robeson, Edward J. Jr.	Dem	Va.	4	1
10th Pfost, Gracie B.	Dem	Ida.	2	1
11th Fascell, Dante B.	Dem	Fla.	1	1
12th Clark, Frank M.	Dem	Penn.	1	1
13th Tumulty, T. James	Dem	N.J.	1	1
14th Kilgore, Joe M.	Dem	Tex.	1	1

Minority

Rank Name	Party	State	Terms in: House	Terms in: Comm.
RM Rees, Edward H.	Rep	Kans.	10	10
2nd Corbett, Robert J.	Rep	Penn.	7	6
3rd St. George, Katharine	Rep	N.Y.	5	*1 5
4th Gross, Harold R.	Rep	Iowa	4	4
5th Harden, Cecil M.	Rep	Ind.	4	2
6th Cretella, Albert W.	Rep	Conn.	2	2
7th Gubser, Charles S.	Rep	Cal.	2	2
8th Broyhill, Joel T.	Rep	Va.	2	2
9th Cederberg, Elford A.	Rep	Mich.	2	1
10th Henderson, John E.	Rep	Ohio	1	1
11th Johansen, August E.	Rep	Mich.	1	1

*1: Member's 1st period of service on the committee.

Changes:

Majority:

Clark, Frank M.	Dem	Penn.	Jan. 28,1955	Moved to Public Works.
Holifield, Chet	Dem	Cal.	Feb. 28,1955	Replaced Clark.
Rhodes, George M.	Dem	Penn.	July 24,1956	Moved to Interstate and Foreign Commerce.

	Majority		Minority	
Departures from the House:				
Defeated for Reelection	Tumulty, T. James	N.J. Dem	None	
Departures from Committee:				
Moved to Appropriations	Alexander, Hugh Q.	N.C. Dem	None	
Moved to District of Columbia; Judiciary	Dowdy, John V.	Tex. Dem	None	
Moved to Foreign Affairs	Fascell, Dante B.	Fla. Dem	None	
Moved to Public Works	Kilgore, Joe M.	Tex. Dem	None	
Moved to Interstate & Foreign Commerce	Moss, John E. Jr.	Cal. Dem	None	
Moved to Armed Services	None		Gubser, Charles S.	Cal. Rep
			St. George, Katharine	N.Y. Rep
Moved to Banking & Currency	None		Henderson, John E.	Ohio Rep

POST OFFICE AND CIVIL SERVICE / 85th Congress

Service Dates of Committee Chair: Jan. 10,1957-Jan. 3,1959
Service Dates of Majority Members: Jan. 10,1957-Jan. 3,1959
Service Dates of Minority Members: Jan. 16,1957-Jan. 3,1959

Majority

Rank Name	Party	State	Terms in: House	Terms in: Comm.
Chr Murray, Thomas J.	Dem	Tenn.	8	8
2nd Morrison, James H.	Dem	La.	8	7
3rd Davis, James C.	Dem	Ga.	6	6
4th Lesinski, John Jr.	Dem	Mich.	4	4
5th Robeson, Edward J. Jr.	Dem	Va.	5	2
6th Pfost, Gracie B.	Dem	Ida.	3	2
7th Holifield, Chet	Dem	Cal.	8 *2	2
8th Granahan, Kathryn E.	Dem	Penn.	2	1
9th Beckworth, Lindley G.	Dem	Tex.	8 *2	1
10th Porter, Charles O.	Dem	Ore.	1	1
11th Santangelo, Alfred E.	Dem	N.Y.	1	1
12th Young, John A.	Dem	Tex.	1	1
13th Hemphill, Robert W.	Dem	S.C.	1	1
14th Scott, Ralph J.	Dem	N.C.	1	1

Minority

Rank Name	Party	State	Terms in: House	Terms in: Comm.
RM Rees, Edward H.	Rep	Kans.	11	11
2nd Corbett, Robert J.	Rep	Penn.	8	7
3rd Gross, Harold R.	Rep	Iowa	5	5
4th Harden, Cecil M.	Rep	Ind.	5	3
5th Cretella, Albert W.	Rep	Conn.	3	3
6th Broyhill, Joel T.	Rep	Va.	3	3
7th Cederberg, Elford A.	Rep	Mich.	3	2
8th Johansen, August E.	Rep	Mich.	2	2
9th Wainwright, Stuyvesant II	Rep	N.Y.	3	1
10th Cunningham, Glenn C.	Rep	Neb.	1	1
11th Dennison, David S.	Rep	Ohio	1	1

*2: Member's 2nd period of service on the committee.

Changes:

Majority:

Santangelo, Alfred E.	Dem	N.Y.	Jan. 16,1958	Moved to Appropriations.
Dellay, Vincent J.	Dem	N.J.	Jan. 27,1958	Replaced Santangelo.
Pfost, Gracie B.	Dem	Ida.	July 18,1958	Moved to Public Works.
Young, John A.	Dem	Tex.	July 21,1958	Moved to Public Works.

Departures from the House:

	Majority			Minority		
Defeated for Reelection	None			Cretella, Albert W.	Conn.	Rep
				Dennison, David S.	Ohio	Rep
				Harden, Cecil M.	Ind.	Rep
Defeated for Renomination	Robeson, Edward J. Jr.	Va.	Dem	None		
	Dellay, Vincent J.	N.J.	Dem			

Departures from Committee:

	Majority			Minority		
Moved to Foreign Affairs	Beckworth, Lindley G.	Tex.	Dem	Wainwright, Stuyvesant II	N.Y.	Rep
Moved to Interstate & Foreign Commerce	Hemphill, Robert W.	S.C.	Dem	None		
No new assignment	None			Cederberg, Elford A.	Mich.	Rep

POST OFFICE AND CIVIL SERVICE / 86th Congress

Service Dates of Committee Chair: Jan. 19,1959-Jan. 3,1961
Service Dates of Majority Members: Jan. 19,1959-Jan. 3,1961
Service Dates of Minority Members: Jan. 19,1959-Jan. 3,1961

Majority

Rank Name	Party	State	Terms in: House	Terms in: Comm.
Chr Murray, Thomas J.	Dem	Tenn.	9	9
2nd Morrison, James H.	Dem	La.	9	8
3rd Davis, James C.	Dem	Ga.	7	7
4th Lesinski, John Jr.	Dem	Mich.	5	5
5th Holifield, Chet	Dem	Cal.	9 *2	3
6th Granahan, Kathryn E.	Dem	Penn.	3	2
7th Porter, Charles O.	Dem	Ore.	2	2
8th Scott, Ralph J.	Dem	N.C.	2	2
9th Shipley, George E.	Dem	Ill.	1	1
10th Levering, Robert W.	Dem	Ohio	1	1
11th Dulski, Thaddeus J.	Dem	N.Y.	1	1
12th Prokop, Stanley A.	Dem	Penn.	1	1

Minority

Rank Name	Party	State	Terms in: House	Terms in: Comm.
RM Rees, Edward H.	Rep	Kans.	12	12
2nd Corbett, Robert J.	Rep	Penn.	9	8
3rd Gross, Harold R.	Rep	Iowa	6	6
4th Broyhill, Joel T.	Rep	Va.	4	4
5th Johansen, August E.	Rep	Mich.	3	3
6th Cunningham, Glenn C.	Rep	Neb.	2	2
7th Wallhauser, George M.	Rep	N.J.	1	1
8th Barry, Robert R.	Rep	N.Y.	1	1
9th St. George, Katharine	Rep	N.Y.	7 *2	1

13th Foley, John R.	Dem	Md.	1	1	
14th Irwin, Donald J.	Dem	Conn.	1	1	
15th Harmon, Randall S.	Dem	Ind.	1	1	
16th Alford, T. Dale	Dem	Ark.	1	1	*2: Member's 2nd period of service on the committee.

Vacancy Filled:
Minority: 9th seat by St. George on Jan. 29,1959.

Changes:
Majority:

Levering, Robert W.	Dem	Ohio	May 21,1959	Moved to Agriculture.
Oliver, James C.	Dem	Me.	May 25,1959	Replaced Levering.
Shipley, George E.	Dem	Ill.	Jan. 12,1960	Moved to Appropriations.
Gilbert, Jacob H.	Dem	N.Y.	Mar. 17,1960	Replaced Shipley.

	Majority			Minority		
Departures from the House:						
Defeated for Reelection	Foley, John R.	Md.	Dem	None		
	Harmon, Randall S.	Ind.	Dem			
	Irwin, Donald J.	Conn.	Dem			
	Porter, Charles O.	Ore.	Dem			
	Prokop, Stanley A.	Penn.	Dem			
	Oliver, James C.	Me.	Dem			
Retired	None			Rees, Edward H.	Kans.	Rep
Departures from Committee:						
Moved to Banking & Currency	Gilbert, Jacob H.	N.Y.	Dem	None		
Moved to Education and Labor	Scott, Ralph J.	N.C.	Dem	None		
No new assignment	Holifield, Chet	Cal.	Dem	None		

POST OFFICE AND CIVIL SERVICE / 87th Congress

Service Dates of Committee Chair: Feb. 6,1961-Jan. 3,1963
Service Dates of Majority Members: Feb. 6,1961-Jan. 3,1963
Service Dates of Minority Members: Feb. 13,1961-Jan. 3,1963

Majority			Terms in:		Minority			Terms in:	
Rank Name	**Party**	**State**	**House**	**Comm.**	**Rank Name**	**Party**	**State**	**House**	**Comm.**
Chr Murray, Thomas J.	Dem	Tenn.	10	10	RM Corbett, Robert J.	Rep	Penn.	10	9
2nd Morrison, James H.	Dem	La.	10	9	2nd Gross, Harold R.	Rep	Iowa	7	7
3rd Davis, James C.	Dem	Ga.	8	8	3rd Broyhill, Joel T.	Rep	Va.	5	5
4th Lesinski, John Jr.	Dem	Mich.	6	6	4th Johansen, August E.	Rep	Mich.	4	4
5th Granahan, Kathryn E.	Dem	Penn.	4	3	5th Cunningham, Glenn C.	Rep	Neb.	3	3
6th Dulski, Thaddeus J.	Dem	N.Y.	2	2	6th Wallhauser, George M.	Rep	N.J.	2	2
7th Alford, T. Dale	Dem	Ark.	2	2	7th Barry, Robert R.	Rep	N.Y.	2	2
8th Henderson, David N.	Dem	N.C.	1	1	8th St. George, Katharine	Rep	N.Y.	8	*2 2
9th Olsen, Arnold	Dem	Mont.	1	1	9th Rousselot, John H.	Rep	Cal.	1	*1 1
10th Addabbo, Joseph P.	Dem	N.Y.	1	1	10th Derwinski, Edward J.	Rep	Ill.	2	1
11th Ichord, Richard H.	Dem	Mo.	1	1	11th Ellsworth, Robert F.	Rep	Kans.	1	1
12th Peterson, M. Blaine	Dem	Utah	1	1					
13th Hagan, G. Elliott	Dem	Ga.	1	1					
14th Norrell, Catherine D.	Dem	Ark.	1	1					

*1: Member's 1st period of service on the committee;
*2: Member's 2nd period of service on the committee.

Vacancies Filled:
Majority: 13th seat by Hagan on Mar. 6,1961 and the 14th seat by Norrell on May 15,1961.
Minority: 10th seat by Derwinski on Feb. 20,1961 and the 11th seat by Ellsworth on Sep. 7,1961.

Changes:
Majority:

Alford, T. Dale	Dem	Ark.	Mar. 6,1961	Moved to Appropriations.
Peterson, M. Blaine	Dem	Utah	Mar. 6,1961	Moved to Judiciary.
Udall, Morris K.	Dem	Ariz.	June 29,1961	Replaced Alford.
Daniels, Dominick V.	Dem	N.J.	Aug. 14,1961	Replaced Peterson.
Hagan, G. Elliott	Dem	Ga.	Jan. 18,1962	Moved to Agriculture.
Lesinski, John Jr.	Dem	Mich.	Jan. 18,1962	Moved to Appropriations.
Beckworth, Lindley G.	Dem	Tex.	Jan. 18,1962	Replaced Hagan.
Moeller, Walter H.	Dem	Ohio	Jan. 18,1962	Replaced Lesinski.

Departures from the House:	Majority		Minority	
Appointed U.S. Treasurer	Granahan, Kathryn E.	Penn. Dem	None	
Appt. Deputy Assistant Secretary of State	Norrell, Catherine D.	Ark. Dem	None	
Defeated for Reelection	Moeller, Walter H.	Ohio Dem	Rousselot, John H.	Cal. Rep
Defeated for Renomination	Davis, James C.	Ga. Dem	None	
Departures from Committee:				
Moved to Appropriations	Addabbo, Joseph P.	N.Y. Dem	None	
Moved to Armed Services	Ichord, Richard H.	Mo. Dem	None	

POST OFFICE AND CIVIL SERVICE / 88th Congress

Service Dates of Committee Chair: Jan. 17,1963-Jan. 3,1965
Service Dates of Majority Members: Jan. 17,1963-Jan. 3,1965
Service Dates of Minority Members: Jan. 24,1963-Jan. 3,1965

Majority

Rank	Name	Party	State	Terms in: House	Terms in: Comm.
Chr	Murray, Thomas J.	Dem	Tenn.	11	11
2nd	Morrison, James H.	Dem	La.	11	10
3rd	Dulski, Thaddeus J.	Dem	N.Y.	3	3
4th	Henderson, David N.	Dem	N.C.	2	2
5th	Olsen, Arnold	Dem	Mont.	2	2
6th	Udall, Morris K.	Dem	Ariz.	2	*1 2
7th	Daniels, Dominick V.	Dem	N.J.	3	2
8th	Beckworth, Lindley G.	Dem	Tex.	11	*3 2
9th	Staggers, Harley O.	Dem	W.Va.	8	*2 1
10th	Nix, Robert N. C.	Dem	Penn.	4	1
11th	Burkhalter, Everett G.	Dem	Cal.	1	1
12th	Edwards, Don	Dem	Cal.	1	1
13th	Pool, Joe Richard	Dem	Tex.	1	1
14th	Watson, Albert W.	Dem	S.C.	1	1

Minority

Rank	Name	Party	State	Terms in: House	Terms in: Comm.
RM	Corbett, Robert J.	Rep	Penn.	11	10
2nd	Gross, Harold R.	Rep	Iowa	8	8
3rd	Broyhill, Joel T.	Rep	Va.	6	6
4th	Johansen, August E.	Rep	Mich.	5	5
5th	Cunningham, Glenn C.	Rep	Neb.	4	4
6th	Wallhauser, George M.	Rep	N.J.	3	3
7th	Barry, Robert R.	Rep	N.Y.	3	3
8th	St. George, Katharine	Rep	N.Y.	9	*2 3
9th	Derwinski, Edward J.	Rep	Ill.	3	2
10th	Ellsworth, Robert F.	Rep	Kans.	2	2
11th	Abele, Homer E.	Rep	Ohio	1	1

*1: Member's 1st period of service on the committee; *2: Member's 2nd period of service on the committee;
*3: Member's 3rd period of service on the committee.

Changes:

Majority:				
Burkhalter, Everett G.	Dem	Cal.	May 2,1963	Moved to Armed Services.
Roybal, Edward R.	Dem	Cal.	May 2,1963	Replaced Burkhalter.
Edwards, Don	Dem	Cal.	July 25,1963	Moved to Judiciary.
Wilson, Charles H.	Dem	Cal.	July 25,1963	Replaced Edwards.
Watson, Albert W.	Dem	S.C.	May 20,1964	Moved to Interstate and Foreign Commerce.
Green, William J. III	Dem	Penn.	Aug. 7,1964	Replaced Watson.
Minority:				
Broyhill, Joel T.	Rep	Va.	Jan. 22,1964	Moved to Ways and Means.
Johnson, Albert W.	Rep	Penn.	Feb. 7,1964	Replaced Broyhill.

Departures from the House:	Majority		Minority	
Defeated for Reelection	None		Abele, Homer E.	Ohio Rep
			Barry, Robert R.	N.Y. Rep
			Johansen, August E.	Mich. Rep
			St. George, Katharine	N.Y. Rep
			Wallhauser, George M.	N.J. Rep
Retired	None			
Departures from Committee:				
Moved to Foreign Affairs	Roybal, Edward R.	Cal. Dem	None	
Moved to Armed Services; Veterans' Affairs	Wilson, Charles H.	Cal. Dem	None	

POST OFFICE AND CIVIL SERVICE / 89th Congress

Service Dates of Committee Chair: Jan. 18,1965-Dec. 30,1966
Service Dates of Majority Members: Jan. 18,1965-Jan. 3,1967
Service Dates of Minority Members: Jan. 21,1965-Jan. 3,1967

Majority

Rank	Name	Party	State	Terms in: House	Terms in: Comm.
Chr	Murray, Thomas J.	Dem	Tenn.	12	12
2nd	Morrison, James H.	Dem	La.	12	11
3rd	Dulski, Thaddeus J.	Dem	N.Y.	4	4
4th	Henderson, David N.	Dem	N.C.	3	3
5th	Olsen, Arnold	Dem	Mont.	3	3
6th	Udall, Morris K.	Dem	Ariz.	3	*1 3
7th	Daniels, Dominick V.	Dem	N.J.	4	3
8th	Beckworth, Lindley G.	Dem	Tex.	12	*3 3
9th	Staggers, Harley O.	Dem	W.Va.	9	*2 2
10th	Nix, Robert N. C.	Dem	Penn.	5	2
11th	Pool, Joe Richard	Dem	Tex.	2	2
12th	Green, William J. III	Dem	Penn.	2	2
13th	Matsunaga, Spark M.	Dem	Hai.	2	1
14th	Krebs, Paul J.	Dem	N.J.	1	1
15th	Clevenger, Raymond F.	Dem	Mich.	1	1
16th	Hanley, James M.	Dem	N.Y.	1	1
17th	Tunney, John V.	Dem	Cal.	1	1

Minority

Rank	Name	Party	State	Terms in: House	Terms in: Comm.
RM	Corbett, Robert J.	Rep	Penn.	12	11
2nd	Gross, Harold R.	Rep	Iowa	9	9
3rd	Cunningham, Glenn C.	Rep	Neb.	5	5
4th	Derwinski, Edward J.	Rep	Ill.	4	3
5th	Ellsworth, Robert F.	Rep	Kans.	3	3
6th	Johnson, Albert W.	Rep	Penn.	2	2
7th	Buchanan, John H. Jr.	Rep	Ala.	1	1
8th	Broyhill, James T.	Rep	N.C.	2	1

*1: Member's 1st period of service on the committee;
*2: Member's 2nd period of service on the committee;
*3: Member's 3rd period of service on the committee.

Note: The death of John F. Baldwin (Rep-Cal.) and his replacement by Jerome R. Waldie (Dem-Cal.), on June 20,1966 led to the passage of House Resolution 916, agreed to on July 18,1966, changing the size and party ratio on this committee to 18 Democrats and 8 Republicans.

Vacancy Filled:
Minority: 8th seat by Broyhill on Feb. 3,1965.

Addition:
Majority: 18th Waldie, Jerome R. Dem Cal. July 18,1966

Changes:
Majority:

Name	Party	State	Date	Change
Staggers, Harley O.	Dem	W.Va.	Oct. 14,1965	Left committee to take chairmanship responsibilities for Interstate and Foreign Commerce; formally elected Chair on Jan. 13,1966.
Wilson, Charles H.	Dem	Cal.	Oct. 21,1965	Replaced Staggers.
Murray, Thomas J.	Dem	Tenn.	Dec. 30,1966	Resigned House; defeated for renomination.

	Majority			Minority		
Departures from the House:						
Appointed to State Office of Consumer Protection	Krebs, Paul J.	N.J.	Dem	None		
Defeated for Reelection	Clevenger, Raymond F.	Mich.	Dem	None		
Defeated for Renomination	Beckworth, Lindley G.	Tex.	Dem	None		
	Morrison, James H.	La.	Dem			
Lost Nomination to U.S. Senate	None			Ellsworth, Robert F.	Kans.	Rep
Departures from Committee:						
Moved to Foreign Affairs	Tunney, John V.	Cal.	Dem	Buchanan, John H. Jr.	Ala.	Rep
Moved to Rules	Matsunaga, Spark M.	Hai.	Dem	None		

POST OFFICE AND CIVIL SERVICE / 90th Congress

Service Dates of Committee Chair: Jan. 23,1967-Jan. 3,1969
Service Dates of Majority Members: Jan. 23,1967-Jan. 3,1969
Service Dates of Minority Members: Jan. 26,1967-Jan. 3,1969

Majority

Rank	Name	Party	State	Terms in: House	Terms in: Comm.
Chr	Dulski, Thaddeus J.	Dem	N.Y.	5	5
2nd	Henderson, David N.	Dem	N.C.	4	4
3rd	Olsen, Arnold	Dem	Mont.	4	4
4th	Udall, Morris K.	Dem	Ariz.	4	*1 4
5th	Daniels, Dominick V.	Dem	N.J.	5	4
6th	Nix, Robert N. C.	Dem	Penn.	6	3
7th	Pool, Joe Richard	Dem	Tex.	3	3
8th	Green, William J. III	Dem	Penn.	3	3
9th	Hanley, James M.	Dem	N.Y.	2	2
10th	Wilson, Charles H.	Dem	Cal.	3	*2 2
11th	Waldie, Jerome R.	Dem	Cal.	2	2
12th	White, Richard C.	Dem	Tex.	2	1
13th	Ford, William D.	Dem	Mich.	2	1
14th	Hamilton, Lee H.	Dem	Ind.	2	1
15th	Brasco, Frank J.	Dem	N.Y.	1	1

Minority

Rank	Name	Party	State	Terms in: House	Terms in: Comm.
RM	Corbett, Robert J.	Rep	Penn.	13	12
2nd	Gross, Harold R.	Rep	Iowa	10	10
3rd	Cunningham, Glenn C.	Rep	Neb.	6	6
4th	Derwinski, Edward J.	Rep	Ill.	5	4
5th	Johnson, Albert W.	Rep	Penn.	3	3
6th	Broyhill, James T.	Rep	N.C.	3	2
7th	Button, Daniel E.	Rep	N.Y.	1	1
8th	Scott, William L.	Rep	Va.	1	1
9th	Ruppe, Philip E.	Rep	Mich.	1	1
10th	McClure, James A.	Rep	Ida.	1	1
11th	Thompson, S. Fletcher	Rep	Ga.	1	1

*1: Member's 1st period of service on the committee;
*2: Member's 2nd period of service on the committee.

Changes:

Majority:

Pool, Joe Richard	Dem	Tex.	July 14,1968	Died in office.
Green, William J. III	Dem	Penn.	Aug. 1,1968	Moved to Ways and Means.
Tiernan, Robert O.	Dem	R.I.	Aug. 2,1968	Replaced Pool.
Purcell, Graham B.	Dem	Tex.	Oct. 10,1968	Replaced Green.

Departures from Committee:

	Majority	Minority		
Moved to Interstate & Foreign Commerce	None	Ruppe, Philip E.	Mich.	Rep
		Thompson, S. Fletcher	Ga.	Rep
No new assignment	None	Broyhill, James T.	N.C.	Rep

POST OFFICE AND CIVIL SERVICE / 91st Congress

Service Dates of Committee Chair: Jan. 29,1969-Jan. 3,1971
Service Dates of Majority Members: Jan. 29,1969-Jan. 3,1971
Service Dates of Minority Members: Jan. 29,1969-Jan. 3,1971

Majority

Rank	Name	Party	State	Terms in: House	Terms in: Comm.
Chr	Dulski, Thaddeus J.	Dem	N.Y.	6	6
2nd	Henderson, David N.	Dem	N.C.	5	5
3rd	Olsen, Arnold	Dem	Mont.	5	5
4th	Udall, Morris K.	Dem	Ariz.	5	*1 5
5th	Daniels, Dominick V.	Dem	N.J.	6	5
6th	Nix, Robert N. C.	Dem	Penn.	7	4
7th	Hanley, James M.	Dem	N.Y.	3	3
8th	Wilson, Charles H.	Dem	Cal.	4	*2 3
9th	Waldie, Jerome R.	Dem	Cal.	3	3
10th	White, Richard C.	Dem	Tex.	3	2
11th	Ford, William D.	Dem	Mich.	3	2
12th	Hamilton, Lee H.	Dem	Ind.	3	2
13th	Brasco, Frank J.	Dem	N.Y.	2	2
14th	Tiernan, Robert O.	Dem	R.I.	2	2
15th	Purcell, Graham B.	Dem	Tex.	5	2

Minority

Rank	Name	Party	State	Terms in: House	Terms in: Comm.
RM	Corbett, Robert J.	Rep	Penn.	14	13
2nd	Gross, Harold R.	Rep	Iowa	11	11
3rd	Cunningham, Glenn C.	Rep	Neb.	7	7
4th	Derwinski, Edward J.	Rep	Ill.	6	5
5th	Johnson, Albert W.	Rep	Penn.	4	4
6th	Button, Daniel E.	Rep	N.Y.	2	2
7th	Scott, William L.	Rep	Va.	2	2
8th	McClure, James A.	Rep	Ida.	2	2
9th	Meskill, Thomas J.	Rep	Conn.	2	1
10th	Lukens, Donald E. (Buz)	Rep	Ohio	2	1
11th	Hogan, Lawrence J.	Rep	Md.	1	1

*1: Member's 1st period of service on the committee;
*2: Member's 2nd period of service on the committee.

Departures from the House:	Majority		Minority	
Elected Governor	None		Meskill, Thomas J.	Conn. Rep
Defeated for Reelection	Olsen, Arnold	Mont. Dem	Button, Daniel E.	N.Y. Rep
Defeated for Renomination	None		Cunningham, Glenn C.	Neb. Rep
Lost Nomination for Governor	None		Lukens, Donald E. (Buz)	Ohio Rep
Departures from Committee:				
Moved to Merchant Marine & Fisheries	Tiernan, Robert O.	R.I. Dem	None	

POST OFFICE AND CIVIL SERVICE / 92nd Congress

Service Dates of Committee Chair: Feb. 4,1971-Jan. 3,1973
Service Dates of Majority Members: Feb. 4,1971-Jan. 3,1973
Service Dates of Minority Members: Feb. 4,1971-Jan. 3,1973

Majority

Rank Name	Party	State	Terms in: House	Terms in: Comm.
Chr Dulski, Thaddeus J.	Dem	N.Y.	7	7
2nd Henderson, David N.	Dem	N.C.	6	6
3rd Udall, Morris K.	Dem	Ariz.	6 *1	6
4th Daniels, Dominick V.	Dem	N.J.	7	6
5th Nix, Robert N. C.	Dem	Penn.	8	5
6th Hanley, James M.	Dem	N.Y.	4	4
7th Wilson, Charles H.	Dem	Cal.	5 *2	4
8th Waldie, Jerome R.	Dem	Cal.	4	4
9th White, Richard C.	Dem	Tex.	4	3
10th Ford, William D.	Dem	Mich.	4	3
11th Hamilton, Lee H.	Dem	Ind.	4	3
12th Brasco, Frank J.	Dem	N.Y.	3	3
13th Purcell, Graham B.	Dem	Tex.	6	3
14th Bevill, Tom	Dem	Ala.	3	1
15th Chappell, William V. Jr.	Dem	Fla.	2	1

Minority

Rank Name	Party	State	Terms in: House	Terms in: Comm.
RM1 Corbett, Robert J.	Rep	Penn.	15	14
RM2 2nd Gross, Harold R.	Rep	Iowa	12	12
3rd Derwinski, Edward J.	Rep	Ill.	7	6
4th Johnson, Albert W.	Rep	Penn.	5	5
5th Scott, William L.	Rep	Va.	3	3
6th McClure, James A.	Rep	Ida.	3	3
7th Hogan, Lawrence J.	Rep	Md.	2	2
8th Rousselot, John H.	Rep	Cal.	3 *2	1
9th Hillis, Elwood H.	Rep	Ind.	1	1
10th Powell, Walter E.	Rep	Ohio	1	1
11th Young, C. W. Bill	Rep	Fla.	1	1

*1: Member's 1st period of service on the committee;
*2: Member's 2nd period of service on the committee.

Vacancy Filled:
Minority: 11th seat by Young on Mar. 3,1971.

Changes:

Ranking Member:				
RM1 Corbett, Robert J.	Rep	Penn.	Apr. 25,1971	Died in office.
RM2 Gross, Harold R.	Rep	Iowa	Apr. 25,1971	Succeeded Corbett as Ranking Minority Member.
Majority:				
Bevill, Tom	Dem	Ala.	Jan. 27,1972	Moved to Appropriations.
Andrews, Elizabeth B.	Dem	Ala.	Apr. 27,1972	Replaced Bevill.
Minority:				
Corbett, Robert J.	Rep	Penn.	Apr. 25,1971	Died in office.
Mills, William O.	Rep	Md.	June 3,1971	Replaced Corbett.
Young, C. W. Bill	Rep	Fla.	Feb. 3,1972	Left committee; no new assignment.
Mallary, Richard W.	Rep	Vt.	Feb. 7,1972	Replaced Young.

Departures from the House:	Majority		Minority	
Elected to U.S. Senate	None		McClure, James A.	Ida. Rep
			Scott, William L.	Va. Rep
Defeated for Reelection	Purcell, Graham B.	Tex. Dem	None	
Retired	Andrews, Elizabeth B.	Ala. Dem	None	
Departures from Committee:				
Moved to Appropriations	Chappell, William V. Jr.	Fla. Dem	None	
No new assignment	Hamilton, Lee H.	Ind. Dem	None	

POST OFFICE AND CIVIL SERVICE / 93rd Congress

Service Dates of Committee Chair: Jan. 24,1973-Dec. 31,1974
Service Dates of Majority Members: Jan. 24,1973-Jan. 3,1975
Service Dates of Minority Members: Jan. 24,1973-Jan. 3,1975

Majority

Rank	Name	Party	State	Terms in: House	Terms in: Comm.
Chr	Dulski, Thaddeus J.	Dem	N.Y.	8	8
2nd	Henderson, David N.	Dem	N.C.	7	7
3rd	Udall, Morris K.	Dem	Ariz.	7 *1	7
4th	Daniels, Dominick V.	Dem	N.J.	8	7
5th	Nix, Robert N. C.	Dem	Penn.	9	6
6th	Hanley, James M.	Dem	N.Y.	5	5
7th	Wilson, Charles H.	Dem	Cal.	6 *2	5
8th	Waldie, Jerome R.	Dem	Cal.	5	5
9th	White, Richard C.	Dem	Tex.	5	4
10th	Ford, William D.	Dem	Mich.	5	4
11th	Brasco, Frank J.	Dem	N.Y.	4	4
12th	Clay, William L.	Dem	Mo.	3	1
13th	Schroeder, Patricia S.	Dem	Colo.	1	1
14th	Moakley, John Joseph	Dem	Mass.	1	1
15th	Lehman, William	Dem	Fla.	1	1

Minority

Rank	Name	Party	State	Terms in: House	Terms in: Comm.
RM	Gross, Harold R.	Rep	Iowa	13	13
2nd	Derwinski, Edward J.	Rep	Ill.	8	7
3rd	Johnson, Albert W.	Rep	Penn.	6	6
4th	Hogan, Lawrence J.	Rep	Md.	3	3
5th	Rousselot, John H.	Rep	Cal.	4 *2	2
6th	Hillis, Elwood H.	Rep	Ind.	2	2
7th	Powell, Walter E.	Rep	Ohio	2	2
8th	Mills, William O.	Rep	Md.	2	2
9th	Mallary, Richard W.	Rep	Vt.	2	2
10th	Hinshaw, Andrew J.	Rep	Cal.	1	1
11th	Bafalis, Louis A. (Skip)	Rep	Fla.	1	1

*1: Member's 1st period of service on the committee;
*2: Member's 2nd period of service on the committee.

Note: The resignation of James Harvey (Rep-Mich.) and his replacement by J. Bob Traxler (Dem-Mich.) on Apr. 23,1974 led to the passage of House Resolution 1102, agreed to May 15,1974, changing the size and party ratio on this committee to 16 Democrats and 11 Republicans.

Addition:

Majority:	16th	Traxler, J. Bob	Dem	Mich.	May 29,1974

Changes:

Majority:				
Dulski, Thaddeus J.	Dem	N.Y.	Dec. 31,1974	Resigned and retired.
Minority:				
Mills, William O.	Rep	Md.	May 24,1973	Died in office.
Hillis, Elwood H.	Rep	Ind.	Feb. 13,1974	Moved to Armed Services.
Taylor, Gene	Rep	Mo.	Feb. 21,1974	Replaced Mills.
Collins, James M.	Rep	Tex.	Feb. 21,1974	Replaced Hillis.

	Majority			Minority		
Departures from the House:						
Lost Nomination for Governor	Waldie, Jerome R.	Cal.	Dem	Hogan, Lawrence J.	Md.	Rep
Lost Election to U.S. Senate	None			Mallary, Richard W.	Vt.	Rep
Retired	Brasco, Frank J.	N.Y.	Dem	Gross, Harold R.	Iowa	Rep
				Powell, Walter E.	Ohio	Rep
Departures from Committee:						
Moved to Rules	Moakley, John Joseph	Mass.	Dem	None		
Moved to Appropriations	Traxler, J. Bob	Mich.	Dem	None		
Moved to Ways and Means	None			Bafalis, Louis A. (Skip)	Fla.	Rep

POST OFFICE AND CIVIL SERVICE / 94th Congress

Service Dates of Committee Chair: Jan. 20,1975-Jan. 3,1977
Service Dates of Majority Members: Jan. 20,1975-Jan. 3,1977
Service Dates of Minority Members: Jan. 28,1975-Jan. 3,1977

Majority

Rank	Name	Party	State	Terms in: House		Terms in: Comm.
Chr	Henderson, David N.	Dem	N.C.	8		8
2nd	Udall, Morris K.	Dem	Ariz.	8	*1	8
3rd	Daniels, Dominick V.	Dem	N.J.	9		8
4th	Nix, Robert N. C.	Dem	Penn.	10		7
5th	Hanley, James M.	Dem	N.Y.	6		6
6th	Wilson, Charles H.	Dem	Cal.	7	*2	6
7th	White, Richard C.	Dem	Tex.	6		5
8th	Ford, William D.	Dem	Mich.	6		5
9th	Clay, William L.	Dem	Mo.	4		2
10th	Schroeder, Patricia S.	Dem	Colo.	2		2
11th	Lehman, William	Dem	Fla.	2		2
12th	Spellman, Gladys Noon	Dem	Md.	1		1
13th	Neal, Stephen L.	Dem	N.C.	1		1
14th	Harris, Herbert E. II	Dem	Va.	1		1
15th	Brodhead, William M.	Dem	Mich.	1		1
16th	Simon, Paul M.	Dem	Ill.	1		1
17th	Mineta, Norman Y.	Dem	Cal.	1		1
18th	Jenrette, John W. Jr.	Dem	S.C.	1		1
19th	Solarz, Stephen J.	Dem	N.Y.	1		1

Minority

Rank	Name	Party	State	Terms in: House		Terms in: Comm.
RM	Derwinski, Edward J.	Rep	Ill.	9		8
2nd	Johnson, Albert W.	Rep	Penn.	7		7
3rd	Rousselot, John H.	Rep	Cal.	5	*2	3
4th	Hinshaw, Andrew J.	Rep	Cal.	2		2
5th	Collins, James M.	Rep	Tex.	5		2
6th	Taylor, Gene	Rep	Mo.	2		2
7th	Gilman, Benjamin A.	Rep	N.Y.	2		1
8th	Beard, Robin L. Jr.	Rep	Tenn.	2		1
9th	Lott, Trent	Rep	Miss.	2		1

*1: Member's 1st period of service on the committee;
*2: Member's 2nd period of service on the committee.

Departures from the House:	Majority			Minority		
Defeated for Reelection	None			Johnson, Albert W.	Penn.	Rep
Defeated for Renomination	None			Hinshaw, Andrew J.	Cal.	Rep
Retired	Daniels, Dominick V.	N.J.	Dem	None		
	Henderson, David N.	N.C.	Dem			
Departures from Committee:						
Moved to Ways and Means	Brodhead, William M.	Mich.	Dem	None		
Moved to Government Operations	Jenrette, John W. Jr.	S.C.	Dem	None		
Moved to Budget	Mineta, Norman Y.	Cal.	Dem	None		
	Simon, Paul M.	Ill.	Dem			
Moved to Science & Technology	Neal, Stephen L.	N.C.	Dem	None		
No new assignment	None			Beard, Robin L. Jr.	Tenn.	Rep

POST OFFICE AND CIVIL SERVICE / 95th Congress

Service Dates of Committee Chair: Jan. 19,1977-Jan. 3,1979
Service Dates of Majority Members: Jan. 19,1977-Jan. 3,1979
Service Dates of Minority Members: Jan. 19,1977-Jan. 3,1979

Majority

Rank	Name	Party	State	Terms in: House		Terms in: Comm.
Chr	Nix, Robert N. C.	Dem	Penn.	11		8
2nd	Udall, Morris K.	Dem	Ariz.	9	*1	9
3rd	Hanley, James M.	Dem	N.Y.	7		7
4th	Wilson, Charles H.	Dem	Cal.	8	*2	7
5th	White, Richard C.	Dem	Tex.	7		6
6th	Ford, William D.	Dem	Mich.	7		6
7th	Clay, William L.	Dem	Mo.	5		3
8th	Schroeder, Patricia S.	Dem	Colo.	3		3
9th	Lehman, William	Dem	Fla.	3		3
10th	Spellman, Gladys Noon	Dem	Md.	2		2
11th	Harris, Herbert E. II	Dem	Va.	2		2
12th	Solarz, Stephen J.	Dem	N.Y.	2		2
13th	Myers, Michael O. (Ozzie)	Dem	Penn.	2		1

Minority

Rank	Name	Party	State	Terms in: House		Terms in: Comm.
RM	Derwinski, Edward J.	Rep	Ill.	10		9
2nd	Rousselot, John H.	Rep	Cal.	6	*2	4
3rd	Collins, James M.	Rep	Tex.	6		3
4th	Taylor, Gene	Rep	Mo.	3		3
5th	Gilman, Benjamin A.	Rep	N.Y.	3		2
6th	Lott, Trent	Rep	Miss.	3		2
7th	Leach, James A. S.	Rep	Iowa	1		1
8th	Corcoran, Thomas J.	Rep	Ill.	1		1

14th Heftel, Cecil	Dem	Hai.	1	1	
15th Howard, James J.	Dem	N.J.	7	1	*1: Member's 1st period of service on the committee;
16th Metcalfe, Ralph H.	Dem	Ill.	4 *T	1	*2: Member's 2nd period of service on the committee;
17th Ryan, Leo J.	Dem	Cal.	3 *T	1	*T Temporary committee member.

Note: Ranking on this committee for the following member was affected by other chamber service: Morris K. Udall (Dem-Ariz.), Chair, Interior and Insular Affairs.

Vacancies Filled:

Majority: 15th and 16th seats by Howard and Metcalfe respectively on Jan. 27,1977; the 17th seat by Ryan on Feb. 9,1977.

Changes:

Majority:

Howard, James J.	Dem	N.J.	Feb. 22,1978	Moved to Interior and Insular Affairs.
Garcia, Robert	Dem	N.Y.	Feb. 22,1978	Replaced Howard.
Metcalfe, Ralph H.	Dem	Ill.	Oct. 10,1978	Died in office.
Ryan, Leo J.	Dem	Cal.	Nov. 18,1978	Died in office.

	Majority		Minority	
Departures from the House:				
Defeated for Renomination	Nix, Robert N. C.	Penn. Dem	None	
Departures from Committee:				
Ceases active membership to serve on Budget	Solarz, Stephen J.	N.Y. Dem	None	
Moved to Ways and Means	Heftel, Cecil	Hai. Dem	None	
Moved to Appropriations	Lehman, William	Fla. Dem	None	
Moved to Merchant Marine & Fisheries	Myers, Michael O. (Ozzie)	Penn. Dem	None	
Moved to Science & Technology	White, Richard C.	Tex. Dem	None	
No new assignment	None		Collins, James M.	Tex. Rep
			Lott, Trent	Miss. Rep
			Rousselot, John H.	Cal. Rep

POST OFFICE AND CIVIL SERVICE / 96th Congress

Service Dates of Committee Chair: Jan. 24,1979-Jan. 3,1981
Service Dates of Majority Members: Jan. 24,1979-Jan. 3,1981
Service Dates of Minority Members: Jan. 24,1979-Jan. 3,1981

Majority

Rank Name	Party	State	Terms in: House	Terms in: Comm.
Chr Hanley, James M.	Dem	N.Y.	8	8
2nd Udall, Morris K.	Dem	Ariz.	10 *1	10
3rd Wilson, Charles H.	Dem	Cal.	9 *2	8
4th Ford, William D.	Dem	Mich.	8	7
5th Clay, William L.	Dem	Mo.	6	4
6th Schroeder, Patricia S.	Dem	Colo.	4	4
7th Spellman, Gladys Noon	Dem	Md.	3	3
8th Harris, Herbert E. II	Dem	Va.	3	3
9th Garcia, Robert	Dem	N.Y.	2	2
10th Leland, G. T. (Mickey)	Dem	Tex.	1	1
11th Ferraro, Geraldine A.	Dem	N.Y.	1	1
12th Stenholm, Charles W.	Dem	Tex.	1	1
13th Albosta, Donald J.	Dem	Mich.	1	1
14th Cavanaugh, John J.	Dem	Neb.	2	1
15th Oakar, Mary Rose	Dem	Ohio	2	1
16th Yatron, Gus	Dem	Penn.	6	1

Minority

Rank Name	Party	State	Terms in: House	Terms in: Comm.
RM Derwinski, Edward J.	Rep	Ill.	11	10
2nd Taylor, Gene	Rep	Mo.	4	4
3rd Gilman, Benjamin A.	Rep	N.Y.	4	3
4th Leach, James A. S.	Rep	Iowa	2	2
5th Corcoran, Thomas J.	Rep	Ill.	2	2
6th Courter, James A.	Rep	N.J.	1	1
7th Pashayan, Charles S. Jr.	Rep	Cal.	1	1
8th Dannemeyer, William E.	Rep	Cal.	1	1
9th Crane, Daniel B.	Rep	Ill.	1	1

*1: Member's 1st period of service on the committee;
*2: Member's 2nd period of service on the committee.

Note: Ranking on this committee for the following member was affected by other chamber service: Morris K. Udall (Dem-Ariz.), Chair, Interior and Insular Affairs.

Vacancies Filled:

Majority: 13th seat by Albosta on Jan. 31,1979; the 14th seat by Cavanaugh on June 26,1979; and the 15th and 16th seats by Oakar and Yatron respectively on July 18,1979.

Changes:

Majority:

Stenholm, Charles W.	Dem	Tex.	Dec. 19,1979	Moved to Small Business.

Departures from the House:	Majority			Minority		
Defeated for Reelection	Harris, Herbert E. II	Va.	Dem	None		
Defeated for Renomination	Wilson, Charles H.	Cal.	Dem	None		
Retired	Cavanaugh, John J.	Neb.	Dem	None		
	Hanley, James M.	N.Y.	Dem			
Departures from Committee:						
Moved to Foreign Affairs	None			Leach, James A. S.	Iowa	Rep

POST OFFICE AND CIVIL SERVICE / 97th Congress

Service Dates of Committee Chair: Jan. 28,1981-Jan. 3,1983
Service Dates of Majority Members: Jan. 28,1981-Jan. 3,1983
Service Dates of Minority Members: Jan. 28,1981-Jan. 3,1983

Majority

Rank	Name	Party	State	Terms in: House	Terms in: Comm.
Chr	Ford, William D.	Dem	Mich.	9	8
2nd	Udall, Morris K.	Dem	Ariz.	11	*1 11
3rd	Clay, William L.	Dem	Mo.	7	5
4th	Schroeder, Patricia S.	Dem	Colo.	5	5
5th	Spellman, Gladys Noon	Dem	Md.	4	4
6th	Garcia, Robert	Dem	N.Y.	3	3
7th	Leland, G. T. (Mickey)	Dem	Tex.	2	2
8th	Ferraro, Geraldine A.	Dem	N.Y.	2	2
9th	Albosta, Donald J.	Dem	Mich.	2	2
10th	Yatron, Gus	Dem	Penn.	7	2
11th	Oakar, Mary Rose	Dem	Ohio	3	2
12th	Danielson, George E.	Dem	Cal.	6	1
13th	Dellums, Ronald V.	Dem	Cal.	6	1
14th	Solarz, Stephen J.	Dem	N.Y.	4	4
15th	Peyser, Peter A.	Dem	N.Y.	5	1
16th	de Lugo, Ron	Dem	V.I.	4	*1 1
17th	Savage, Gus	Dem	Ill.	1	1

Minority

Rank	Name	Party	State	Terms in: House	Terms in: Comm.
RM	Derwinski, Edward J.	Rep	Ill.	12	11
2nd	Taylor, Gene	Rep	Mo.	5	5
3rd	Gilman, Benjamin A.	Rep	N.Y.	5	4
4th	Corcoran, Thomas J.	Rep	Ill.	3	3
5th	Courter, James A.	Rep	N.J.	2	2
6th	Pashayan, Charles S. Jr.	Rep	Cal.	2	2
7th	Dannemeyer, William E.	Rep	Cal.	2	2
8th	Crane, Daniel B.	Rep	Ill.	2	2
9th	Grisham, Wayne R.	Rep	Cal.	2	1
10th	Wolf, Frank R.	Rep	Va.	1	1
11th	Bailey, Wendell	Rep	Mo.	1	1

*1: Member's 1st period of service on the committee;
*2: Member's 2nd period of service on the committee.

Notes: Territorial Delegate Ron de Lugo (Dem-V.I.) was allowed to accrue seniority but was not included in the party ratio of 16 Democrats and 11 Republicans. Rankings on this committee for the following members were affected by other chamber service: Morris K. Udall (Dem-Ariz.), Chair, Interior and Insular Affairs; and Stephen J. Solarz (Dem-N.Y.), active member of Budget Committee.

Vacancy Filled:

Majority: 17th seat by Savage on Apr. 30,1981.
Minority: 11th seat by Bailey on Dec. 10,1981.

Changes:

Majority:

Spellman, Gladys Noon	Dem	Md.	Feb. 24,1981	Seat declared vacant.
Solarz, Stephen J.	Dem	N.Y.	Mar. 9,1981	Ceases active membership on committee.
Schumer, Charles E.	Dem	N.Y.	Apr. 30,1981	Replaced Spellman and ranked 11th.
Peyser, Peter A.	Dem	N.Y.	June 8,1981	Left committee; no new assignment.
Hoyer, Steny H.	Dem	Md.	June 8,1981	Replaced Solarz and ranked 12th.
Danielson, George E.	Dem	Cal.	Mar. 9,1982	Resigned; appointed state judge.
Daschle, Thomas A.	Dem	S.D.	Mar. 31,1982	Replaced Peyser.

Departures from the House:	Majority			Minority		
Defeated for Reelection	None			Bailey, Wendell	Mo.	Rep
Defeated for Renomination	None			Derwinski, Edward J.	Ill.	Rep
				Grisham, Wayne R.	Cal.	Rep
Departures from Committee:						
Moved to Budget	Ferraro, Geraldine A.	N.Y.	Dem	None		
Moved to Appropriations	Hoyer, Steny H.	Md.	Dem	None		
No new assignment	Savage, Gus	Ill.	Dem	None		

POST OFFICE AND CIVIL SERVICE / 98th Congress

Service Dates of Committee Chair: Jan. 6,1983-Jan. 3,1985
Service Dates of Majority Members: Jan. 6,1983-Jan. 3,1985
Service Dates of Minority Members: Jan. 6,1983-Jan. 3,1985

Majority

Rank Name	Party	State	Terms in: House	Terms in: Comm.
Chr Ford, William D.	Dem	Mich.	10	9
2nd Udall, Morris K.	Dem	Ariz.	12	*1 12
3rd Clay, William L.	Dem	Mo.	8	6
4th Schroeder, Patricia S.	Dem	Colo.	6	6
5th Garcia, Robert	Dem	N.Y.	4	4
6th Leland, G. T. (Mickey)	Dem	Tex.	3	3
7th Albosta, Donald J.	Dem	Mich.	3	3
8th Yatron, Gus	Dem	Penn.	8	3
9th Oakar, Mary Rose	Dem	Ohio	4	3
10th Hall, Katie	Dem	Ind.	2	1
11th Sikorski, Gerry	Dem	Minn.	1	1
12th Dellums, Ronald V.	Dem	Cal.	7	*T 2
13th Daschle, Thomas A.	Dem	S.D.	3	*T 2
14th de Lugo, Ron	Dem	V.I.	5	*T 2
15th Schumer, Charles E.	Dem	N.Y.	2	*T 2
16th Bosco, Douglas H.	Dem	Cal.	1	*T 1

Minority

Rank Name	Party	State	Terms in: House	Terms in: Comm.
RM Taylor, Gene	Rep	Mo.	6	6
2nd Gilman, Benjamin A.	Rep	N.Y.	6	5
3rd Corcoran, Thomas J.	Rep	Ill.	4	4
4th Courter, James A.	Rep	N.J.	3	3
5th Pashayan, Charles S. Jr.	Rep	Cal.	3	3
6th Dannemeyer, William E.	Rep	Cal.	3	3
7th Crane, Daniel B.	Rep	Ill.	3	3
8th Wolf, Frank R.	Rep	Va.	2	2
9th Mack, Connie III	Rep	Fla.	1	1

*1: Member's 1st period of service on the committee;
*2: Member's 2nd period of service on the committee;
*T: Temporary member of the committee.

Notes: The 12th through the 16th seats on the majority were to be filled by the named members only for the 1st Session of the 98th Congress. Territorial Delegate Ron de Lugo (Dem-V.I.) was allowed to accrue committee seniority, but was not included in the committee's party ratio of 15 Democrats and 9 Republicans. Ranking on this committee for the following member was affected by other chamber service: Morris K. Udall (Dem-Ariz.), Chair, Interior and Insular Affairs.

Changes:

Majority:

Name	Party	State	Date	Change
Dellums, Ronald V.	Dem	Cal.	Feb. 3,1983	Left committee; no new assignment.
McCloskey, Francis X.	Dem	Ind.	Nov. 17,1983	Replaced Dellums.
Daschle, Thomas A.	Dem	S.D.	Nov. 18,1983	Temporary term expired on last day of 1st Session.
Schumer, Charles E.	Dem	N.Y.	Nov. 18,1983	Temporary term expired on last day of 1st Session.
Bosco, Douglas H.	Dem	Cal.	Nov. 18,1983	Temporary term expired on last day of 1st Session.
de Lugo, Ron	Dem	V.I.	Nov. 18,1983	Temporary term expired on last day of 1st Session.
Ackerman, Gary L.	Dem	N.Y.	Feb. 29,1984	Replaced Daschle.
de Lugo, Ron	Dem	V.I.	Feb. 29,1984	Replaced himself.
Bosco, Douglas H.	Dem	Cal.	Feb. 29,1984	Replaced himself.
Dymally, Mervyn M.	Dem	Cal.	Feb. 29,1984	Replaced Schumer.

	Majority		Minority	
Departures from the House:				
Defeated for Reelection	Albosta, Donald J.	Mich. Dem	Crane, Daniel B.	Ill. Rep
Defeated for Renomination	Hall, Katie	Ind. Dem	None	
Lost Nomination to U.S. Senate	None		Corcoran, Thomas J.	Ill. Rep
Departures from Committee:				
Moved to Foreign Affairs	Udall, Morris K.	Ariz. Dem	Mack, Connie III	Fla. Rep
Moved to Appropriations	None		Wolf, Frank R.	Va. Rep
No new assignment	Bosco, Douglas H.	Cal. Dem	None	

POST OFFICE AND CIVIL SERVICE / 99th Congress

Service Dates of Committee Chair: Jan. 7,1985-Jan. 3,1987
Service Dates of Majority Members: Jan. 30,1985-Jan. 3,1987
Service Dates of Minority Members: Jan. 30,1985-Jan. 3,1987

Majority

Rank	Name	Party	State	Terms in: House	Terms in: Comm.
Chr	Ford, William D.	Dem	Mich.	11	10
2nd	Clay, William L.	Dem	Mo.	9	7
3rd	Schroeder, Patricia S.	Dem	Colo.	7	7
4th	Solarz, Stephen J.	Dem	N.Y.	6	6
5th	Garcia, Robert	Dem	N.Y.	5	5
6th	Leland, G. T. (Mickey)	Dem	Tex.	4	4
7th	Yatron, Gus	Dem	Penn.	9	4
8th	Oakar, Mary Rose	Dem	Ohio	5	4
9th	Sikorski, Gerry	Dem	Minn.	2	2
10th	McCloskey, Francis X.	Dem	Ind.	2	2
11th	Ackerman, Gary L.	Dem	N.Y.	2	2
12th	Foley, Thomas S.	Dem	Wash.	11	1
13th	Dymally, Mervyn M.	Dem	Cal.	3	*T 2
14th	de Lugo, Ron	Dem	V.I.	6	*T 3

Minority

Rank	Name	Party	State	Terms in: House	Terms in: Comm.
RM	Taylor, Gene	Rep	Mo.	7	7
2nd	Gilman, Benjamin A.	Rep	N.Y.	7	6
3rd	Pashayan, Charles S. Jr.	Rep	Cal.	4	4
4th	Horton, Frank J.	Rep	N.Y.	12	1
5th	Myers, John T.	Rep	Ind.	10	1
6th	Young, Donald E.	Rep	Alas.	7	1
7th	Hansen, James V.	Rep	Utah	3	1
8th	Burton, Dan	Rep	Ind.	2	1

*T: Temporary member of the committee.

Notes: The contested election between Francis X. McCloskey (Dem-Ind.) and Richard McIntire (Rep-Ind.) was decided on a floor vote on May 1,1985 in favor of McCloskey. McCloskey rejoined the committee with his seniority and ranking intact. Territorial Delegate Ron de Lugo (Dem-V.I.) was allowed to accrue seniority, but was not included in committee's party ratio of 13 Democrats and 8 Republicans. Stephen J. Solarz (Dem-N.Y.), having served on the Budget Committee during the previous three Congresses, returned to active service on this committee with his seniority intact.

Vacancy Filled:
Majority: 14th seat by de Lugo on Feb. 6,1985 for the first session only.

Changes:
Majority:

Name	Party	State	Date	Change
Foley, Thomas S.	Dem	Wash.	Feb. 27,1985	Left committee; no new assignment.
Udall, Morris K.	Dem	Ariz.	Feb. 27,1985	Temporary term; replaced Foley for the 1st Session only.
de Lugo, Ron	Dem	V.I.	Dec. 30,1985	Temporary term expired on last day of 1st Session.
Udall, Morris K.	Dem	Ariz.	Dec. 30,1985	Temporary term expired on last day of 1st Session.
de Lugo, Ron	Dem	V.I.	Jan. 29,1986	Replaced himself.
Udall, Morris K.	Dem	Ariz.	Jan. 29,1986	Replaced himself.

Departures from Committee:	Majority	Minority		
No new assignment	None	Hansen, James V.	Utah	Rep

POST OFFICE AND CIVIL SERVICE / 100th Congress

Service Dates of Committee Chair: Jan. 8,1987-Jan. 3,1989
Service Dates of Majority Members: Jan. 22,1987-Jan. 3,1989
Service Dates of Minority Members: Jan. 21,1987-Jan. 3,1989

Majority

Rank	Name	Party	State	Terms in: House		Terms in: Comm.
Chr	Ford, William D.	Dem	Mich.	12		11
2nd	Clay, William L.	Dem	Mo.	10		8
3rd	Schroeder, Patricia S.	Dem	Colo.	8		8
4th	Solarz, Stephen J.	Dem	N.Y.	7		7
5th	Garcia, Robert	Dem	N.Y.	6		6
6th	Leland, G. T. (Mickey)	Dem	Tex.	5		5
7th	Yatron, Gus	Dem	Penn.	10		5
8th	Oakar, Mary Rose	Dem	Ohio	6		5
9th	Sikorski, Gerry	DFL	Minn.	3		3
10th	McCloskey, Francis X.	Dem	Ind.	3		3
11th	Ackerman, Gary L.	Dem	N.Y.	3		3
12th	Dymally, Mervyn M.	Dem	Cal.	4		3
13th	Udall, Morris K.	Dem	Ariz.	14	*2	2
14th	de Lugo, Ron	Dem	V.I.	7	*2	1

Minority

Rank	Name	Party	State	Terms in: House	Terms in: Comm.
RM	Taylor, Gene	Rep	Mo.	8	8
2nd	Gilman, Benjamin A.	Rep	N.Y.	8	7
3rd	Pashayan, Charles S. Jr.	Rep	Cal.	5	5
4th	Horton, Frank J.	Rep	N.Y.	13	2
5th	Myers, John T.	Rep	Ind.	11	2
6th	Young, Donald E.	Rep	Alas.	8	2
7th	Burton, Dan	Rep	Ind.	3	2
8th	Morella, Constance A.	Rep	Md.	1	1

*2: Member's 2nd period of service on the committee.

Note: Territorial Delegate Ron de Lugo (Dem-V.I.) was allowed to accrue seniority, but was not included in the committee's party ratio of 13 Democrats and 8 Republicans.

Changes:
Majority:

Name	Party	State	Date	Change
Solarz, Stephen J.	Dem	N.Y.	Oct. 11,1988	Moved to Merchant Marine and Fisheries (letter effective Oct. 6,1988).

	Majority	Minority	State	Party
Departures from the House:				
Retired	None	Taylor, Gene	Mo.	Rep
Departures from Committee:				
Moved to Rules	None	Pashayan, Charles S. Jr.	Cal.	Rep

POST OFFICE AND CIVIL SERVICE / 101st Congress

Service Dates of Committee Chair: Jan. 3,1989-Jan. 3,1991
Service Dates of Majority Members: Jan. 19,1989-Jan. 3,1991
Service Dates of Minority Members: Jan. 20,1989-Jan. 3,1991

Majority

Rank	Name	Party	State	Terms in: House		Terms in: Comm.
Chr	Ford, William D.	Dem	Mich.	13		12
2nd	Clay, William L.	Dem	Mo.	11		9
3rd	Schroeder, Patricia S.	Dem	Colo.	9		9
4th	Garcia, Robert	Dem	N.Y.	7		7
5th	Leland, G. T. (Mickey)	Dem	Tex.	6		6
6th	Yatron, Gus	Dem	Penn.	11		6
7th	Oakar, Mary Rose	Dem	Ohio	7		6
8th	Sikorski, Gerry	Dem	Minn.	4		4
9th	McCloskey, Francis X.	Dem	Ind.	4		4
10th	Ackerman, Gary L.	Dem	N.Y.	4		4
11th	Dymally, Mervyn M.	Dem	Cal.	5		4
12th	Sawyer, Thomas C.	Dem	Ohio	2		1
13th	Kanjorski, Paul E.	Dem	Penn.	3		1
14th	Udall, Morris K.	Dem	Ariz.	15	*2	3
15th	de Lugo, Ron	Dem	V.I.	8	*2	2

Minority

Rank	Name	Party	State	Terms in: House	Terms in: Comm.
RM	Gilman, Benjamin A.	Rep	N.Y.	9	8
2nd	Horton, Frank J.	Rep	N.Y.	14	3
3rd	Myers, John T.	Rep	Ind.	12	3
4th	Young, Donald E.	Rep	Alas.	9	3
5th	Burton, Dan	Rep	Ind.	4	3
6th	Morella, Constance A.	Rep	Md.	2	2
7th	Ridge, Thomas J.	Rep	Penn.	4	1
8th	Chandler, Rodney	Rep	Wash.	4	1

*2: Member's 2nd period of service on the committee.

Notes: Territorial Delegate Ron de Lugo (Dem-V.I.) was allowed to accrue seniority, but was not included in the committee's party ratio of 14 Democrats and 8 Republicans. Morris K. Udall (Dem-Ariz.) waived his committee seniority. Tommy Robinson of Arkansas resigned from the Democratic Party and joined the Republican Party on July 28,1989. Due to this and other Republican Party gains in the 101st Congress, the committee size and party ratio changed to 14 Democrats and 9 Republicans on Aug. 3,1989.

Vacancies Filled:
Majority: 14th and 15th seats by Kanjorski and de Lugo respectively on Mar. 1,1989.
Minority: 7th and 8th seats by Ridge and Chandler respectively on Feb. 22,1989.

Addition:
Minority: 9th Robinson, Tommy F. Rep Ark. Aug. 3,1989

Changes:
Majority:

Leland, G. T. (Mickey)	Dem	Tex.	Aug. 7,1989	Died in office.
Hayes, Charles A.	Dem	Ill.	Oct. 16,1989	Replaced Leland; ranked above Udall, Nov. 8,1989.
Garcia, Robert	Dem	N.Y.	Jan. 7,1990	Resigned and retired.
McNulty, Michael R.	Dem	N.Y.	Feb. 27,1990	Replaced Garcia; ranked after Hayes, May 24,1990.

Departures from the House:	**Majority**		**Minority**	
Lost Election for Governor	None		Robinson, Tommy F.	Ark. Rep
Departures from Committee:				
Moved to Education & Labor	de Lugo, Ron	V.I. Dem	None	
Became Chair of Education & Labor	Ford, William D.	Mich. Dem	None	

POST OFFICE AND CIVIL SERVICE / 102nd Congress

Service Dates of Committee Chair: Jan. 24,1991-Jan. 3,1993
Service Dates of Majority Members: Jan. 24,1991-Jan. 3,1993
Service Dates of Minority Members: Jan. 24,1991-Jan. 3,1993

Majority

Rank	Name	Party	State	Terms in: House	Terms in: Comm.
Chr	Clay, William L.	Dem	Mo.	12	10
2nd	Schroeder, Patricia S.	Dem	Colo.	10	10
3rd	Yatron, Gus	Dem	Penn.	12	7
4th	Oakar, Mary Rose	Dem	Ohio	8	7
5th	Sikorski, Gerry	Dem	Minn.	5	5
6th	McCloskey, Francis X.	Dem	Ind.	5	5
7th	Ackerman, Gary L.	Dem	N.Y.	5	5
8th	Dymally, Mervyn M.	Dem	Cal.	6	5
9th	Sawyer, Thomas C.	Dem	Ohio	3	2
10th	Kanjorski, Paul E.	Dem	Penn.	4	2
11th	Hayes, Charles A.	Dem	Ill.	5	2
12th	McNulty, Michael R.	Dem	N.Y.	2	2
13th	Moran, James P. Jr.	Dem	Va.	1	1
14th	Udall, Morris K.	Dem	Ariz.	16	*2 4
15th	Norton, Eleanor Holmes	Dem	D.C.	1	1

Minority

Rank	Name	Party	State	Terms in: House	Terms in: Comm.
RM	Gilman, Benjamin A.	Rep	N.Y.	10	9
2nd	Horton, Frank J.	Rep	N.Y.	15	4
3rd	Myers, John T.	Rep	Ind.	13	4
4th	Young, Donald E.	Rep	Alas.	10	4
5th	Burton, Dan	Rep	Ind.	5	4
6th	Morella, Constance A.	Rep	Md.	3	3
7th	Ridge, Thomas J.	Rep	Penn.	5	2
8th	Chandler, Rodney	Rep	Wash.	5	2

*2: Member's 2nd period of service on the committee.

Notes: Eleanor Holmes Norton (Dem-D.C.) was allowed to accrue committee seniority, but was not included in the committee's party ratio. Appointed on Feb. 6,1991, Norton was ranked ahead of Morris K. Udall (Dem-Ariz.), who waived his committee seniority.

Vacancy Filled:
Majority: 15th seat by Norton on Feb. 6,1991.

Changes:
Majority:

Udall, Morris K.	Dem	Ariz.	May 4,1991	Resigned and retired.
Collins, Barbara-Rose	Dem	Mich.	May 9,1991	Replaced Udall.

PUBLIC WORKS AND TRANSPORTATION

PUBLIC WORKS

Jurisdiction, 1947

Established by the Legislative Reorganization Act of 1946:

[Section 121.(1)(o)]

Committee on Public Works.

1. Flood control and improvement of rivers and harbors.
2. Public works for the benefit of navigation, including bridges and dams (other than international bridges and dams).
3. Water power.
4. Oil and other pollution of navigable waters.
5. Public buildings and occupied or improved grounds of the United States generally.
6. Measures relating to the purchase of sites and construction of post offices, customhouses, Federal courthouses, and Government buildings within the District of Columbia.
7. Measures relating to the Capitol Building and the Senate and House Office Buildings.
8. Measures relating to the construction or reconstruction, maintenance, and care of the buildings and grounds of the Botanic Gardens, the Library of Congress, and the Smithsonian Institution.
9. Public reservations and parks within the District of Columbia, including Rock Creek Park and the Zoological Park.
10. Measures relating to the construction or maintenance of roads and post roads, other than appropriations therefore; but it shall not be in order for any bill providing general legislation in relation to roads to contain any provision for any specific road, nor for any bill in relation to a specific road to embrace a provision in relation to any other specific road.

PUBLIC WORKS AND TRANSPORTATION

Renamed the Committee on Public Works and Transportation on January 5, 1975.

Jurisdiction, 1992

Jurisdiction contained in <u>Rules of the House of Representatives</u>, (as revised to July 1, 1992):

[Rule X. 1. (p)]

Committee on Public Works and Transportation.

(1) Flood control and improvement of rivers and harbors.
(2) Measures relating to the Capitol Building and the Senate and House Office Buildings.
(3) Measures relating to the construction or maintenance of roads and post roads, other than appropriations therefor; but it shall not be in order for any bill providing general legislation in relation to roads to contain any provision for any specific road, nor for any bill in relation to a specific road to embrace a provision in relation to any other specific road.
(4) Measures relating to the construction or reconstruction, maintenance, and care of the buildings and grounds of the Botanic Gardens, the Library of Congress, and the Smithsonian Institute.
(5) Measures relating to the purchase of sites and construction of post offices, customhouses, Federal courthouses, and Government buildings within the District of Columbia.
(6) Oil and other pollution of navigable waters.
(7) Public buildings and occupied or improved grounds of the United States generally.
(8) Public works for the benefit of navigation, including bridges and dams (other than international bridges and dams).
(9) Water power.
(10) Transportation, including civil aviation except railroads, railroad labor and pensions.

(11) Roads and the safety thereof.
(12) Water transportation subject to the jurisdiction of the Interstate Commerce Commission.
(13) Related transportation regulatory agencies, except
(A) the Interstate Commerce Commission as it relates to railroads;
(B) Federal Railroad Administration; and
(C) Amtrak.

PUBLIC WORKS / 80th Congress

Service Dates of Committee Chair: Jan. 14,1947-Jan. 3,1949
Service Dates of Majority Members: Jan. 14,1947-Jan. 3,1949
Service Dates of Minority Members: Jan. 16,1947-Jan. 3,1949

Majority

Rank	Name	Party	State	Terms in: House	Terms in: Comm.
Chr	Dondero, George A.	Rep	Mich.	8	8
2nd	Angell, Homer D.	Rep	Ore.	5	5
3rd	Bender, George H.	Rep	Ohio	5	5
4th	McGregor, J. Harry	Rep	Ohio	5	5
5th	Cunningham, Paul	Rep	Iowa	4	4
6th	Wilson, Earl	Rep	Ind.	4	4
7th	Auchincloss, James C.	Rep	N.J.	3	3
8th	Beall, J. Glenn	Rep	Md.	3	3
9th	Arnold, Samuel W.	Rep	Mo.	3	3
10th	McDonough, Gordon L.	Rep	Cal.	2	2
11th	Clippinger, Roy	Rep	Ill.	2	1
12th	Rohrbough, Edward G.	Rep	W.Va.	2	1
13th	Norman, Fred	Rep	Wash.	2 *2	1
14th	Macy, W. Kingsland	Rep	N.Y.	1	1
15th	Muhlenberg, Frederick A.	Rep	Penn.	1	1
16th	Coffin, Howard A.	Rep	Mich.	1	1

Minority

Rank	Name	Party	State	Terms in: House	Terms in: Comm.
RM1	Mansfield, Joseph J.	Dem	Tex.	16	16
RM2 2nd	Whittington, William M.	Dem	Miss.	12	12
3rd	Buckley, Charles A.	Dem	N.Y.	7	7
4th	Boykin, Frank W.	Dem	Ala.	7	7
5th	Elliott, Alfred J.	Dem	Cal.	6	6
6th	Larcade, Henry D. Jr.	Dem	La.	3	3
7th	Stigler, William G.	Dem	Okla.	3	3
8th	Fallon, George H.	Dem	Md.	2	2
9th	Davis, Clifford	Dem	Tenn.	5	2
10th	Trimble, James W.	Dem	Ark.	2	1
11th	Blatnik, John A.	DFL	Minn.	1	1

*2: Member's 2nd period of service on the committee.

Vacancy Filled:
Majority: 16th seat by Coffin on Jan. 23,1947.

Changes:
Ranking Member:

RM1 Mansfield, Joseph J.	Dem	Tex.	July 12,1947	Died in office.
RM2 Whittington, William M.	Dem	Miss.	July 12,1947	Succeeded Mansfield as Ranking Minority Member.

Majority:

Norman, Fred	Rep	Wash.	Apr. 18,1947	Died in office.
McGarvey, Robert N.	Rep	Penn.	May 1,1947	Replaced Norman.
Arnold, Samuel W.	Rep	Mo.	July 23,1947	Moved to Agriculture.
Mack, Russell V.	Rep	Wash.	July 23,1947	Replaced Arnold.
Wilson, Earl	Rep	Ind.	June 19,1948	Moved to Appropriations.

Minority:

Mansfield, Joseph J.	Dem	Tex.	July 12,1947	Died in office.
Pickett, Tom	Dem	Tex.	July 23,1947	Replaced Mansfield.
Boykin, Frank W.	Dem	Ala.	June 10,1948	Moved to Merchant Marine and Fisheries.
Jones, Robert E. Jr.	Dem	Ala.	June 10,1948	Replaced Boykin.

Departures from the House:

	Majority			Minority		
Defeated for Reelection	Bender, George H.	Ohio	Rep	None		
	McGarvey, Robert N.	Penn.	Rep			
	Coffin, Howard A.	Mich.	Rep			
	Muhlenberg, Frederick A.	Penn.	Rep			
	Rohrbough, Edward G.	W.Va.	Rep			
Retired	Clippinger, Roy	Ill.	Rep	Elliott, Alfred J.	Cal.	Dem

Departures from Committee:

	Majority			Minority		
Moved to Appropriations	None			Stigler, William G.	Okla.	Dem

PUBLIC WORKS / 81st Congress

Service Dates of Committee Chair: Jan. 18,1949-Jan. 3,1951
Service Dates of Majority Members: Jan. 18,1949-Jan. 3,1951
Service Dates of Minority Members: Jan. 18,1949-Jan. 3,1951

Majority

Rank	Name	Party	State	Terms in: House	Terms in: Comm.
Chr	Whittington, William M.	Dem	Miss.	13	13
2nd	Buckley, Charles A.	Dem	N.Y.	8	8
3rd	Larcade, Henry D. Jr.	Dem	La.	4	4
4th	Fallon, George H.	Dem	Md.	3	3
5th	Davis, Clifford	Dem	Tenn.	6	3
6th	Trimble, James W.	Dem	Ark.	3	2
7th	Blatnik, John A.	DFL	Minn.	2	2
8th	Pickett, Tom	Dem	Tex.	3	2
9th	Jones, Robert E. Jr.	Dem	Ala.	2	2
10th	Lanham, Henderson L.	Dem	Ga.	2	1
11th	Secrest, Robert T.	Dem	Ohio	6	*2 1
12th	Davenport, Harry J.	Dem	Penn.	1	1
13th	Quinn, T. Vincent	Dem	N.Y.	1	1
14th	Moulder, Morgan M.	Dem	Mo.	1	1
15th	Marsalis, John H.	Dem	Colo.	1	1
16th	Chesney, Chester A.	Dem	Ill.	1	1

Minority

Rank	Name	Party	State	Terms in: House	Terms in: Comm.
RM	Dondero, George A.	Rep	Mich.	9	9
2nd	Angell, Homer D.	Rep	Ore.	6	6
3rd	McGregor, J. Harry	Rep	Ohio	6	6
4th	Cunningham, Paul	Rep	Iowa	5	5
5th	Auchincloss, James C.	Rep	N.J.	4	4
6th	Beall, J. Glenn	Rep	Md.	4	4
7th	McDonough, Gordon L.	Rep	Cal.	3	3
8th	Macy, W. Kingsland	Rep	N.Y.	2	2
9th	Mack, Russell V.	Rep	Wash.	2	2
10th	Vursell, Charles W.	Rep	Ill.	4	1
11th	Ford, Gerald R. Jr.	Rep	Mich.	1	1

*2: Member's 2nd period of service on the committee.

	Majority		Minority	
Departures from the House:				
Defeated for Reelection	Chesney, Chester A.	Ill. Dem	Macy, W. Kingsland	N.Y. Rep
	Davenport, Harry J.	Penn. Dem		
	Marsalis, John H.	Colo. Dem		
Retired	Whittington, William M.	Miss. Dem	None	
Departures from Committee:				
Moved to Armed Services	None		Cunningham, Paul	Iowa Rep
Moved to Appropriations	None		Ford, Gerald R. Jr.	Mich. Rep
Moved to Banking & Currency	None		McDonough, Gordon L.	Cal. Rep

PUBLIC WORKS / 82nd Congress

Service Dates of Committee Chair: Jan. 12,1951-Jan. 3,1953
Service Dates of Majority Members: Jan. 12,1951-Jan. 3,1953
Service Dates of Minority Members: Jan. 15,1951-Jan. 3,1953

Majority

Rank	Name	Party	State	Terms in: House	Terms in: Comm.
Chr	Buckley, Charles A.	Dem	N.Y.	9	9
2nd	Larcade, Henry D. Jr.	Dem	La.	5	5
3rd	Fallon, George H.	Dem	Md.	4	4
4th	Davis, Clifford	Dem	Tenn.	7	4
5th	Trimble, James W.	Dem	Ark.	4	3
6th	Blatnik, John A.	DFL	Minn.	3	3
7th	Pickett, Tom	Dem	Tex.	4	3
8th	Jones, Robert E. Jr.	Dem	Ala.	3	3
9th	Lanham, Henderson L.	Dem	Ga.	3	2
10th	Secrest, Robert T.	Dem	Ohio	7	*2 2
11th	Quinn, T. Vincent	Dem	N.Y.	2	2
12th	Moulder, Morgan M.	Dem	Mo.	2	2
13th	Chudoff, Earl	Dem	Penn.	2	1
14th	Dempsey, John J.	Dem	N.M.	4	1
15th	Smith, Frank E.	Dem	Miss.	1	1

Minority

Rank	Name	Party	State	Terms in: House	Terms in: Comm.
RM	Dondero, George A.	Rep	Mich.	10	10
2nd	Angell, Homer D.	Rep	Ore.	7	7
3rd	McGregor, J. Harry	Rep	Ohio	7	7
4th	Auchincloss, James C.	Rep	N.J.	5	5
5th	Beall, J. Glenn	Rep	Md.	5	5
6th	Mack, Russell V.	Rep	Wash.	3	3
7th	Vursell, Charles W.	Rep	Ill.	5	2
8th	Scudder, Hubert B.	Rep	Cal.	2	1
9th	George, Myron V.	Rep	Kans.	2	1
10th	Bray, William G.	Rep	Ind.	1	1
11th	Baker, Howard H.	Rep	Tenn.	1	1
12th	Wood, John T.	Rep	Ida.	1	1

*2: Member's 2nd period of service on the committee.

Changes:

Majority:

Chudoff, Earl	Dem	Penn.	Jan. 17,1951	Moved to Select Committee to Investigate Abuses in Education, Training and Loan Guaranty Programs of World War II Veterans.
Moulder, Morgan M.	Dem	Mo.	Apr. 2,1951	Moved to Interstate and Foreign Commerce.
Watts, John C.	Dem	Ky.	May 2,1951	Replaced Chudoff.
Magee, Clare	Dem	Mo.	June 13,1951	Replaced Moulder.
Secrest, Robert T.	Dem	Ohio	July 2,1951	Moved to Veterans Affairs.
Lanham, Henderson L.	Dem	Ga.	July 18,1951	Moved to Foreign Affairs.
Machrowicz, Thaddeus M.	Dem	Mich.	July 18,1951	Replaced Secrest.
Kluczynski, John C.	Dem	Ill.	July 25,1951	Replaced Lanham.
Pickett, Tom	Dem	Tex.	Aug. 9,1951	Moved to Judiciary.
Steed, Thomas J.	Dem	Okla.	Aug. 10,1951	Replaced Pickett.
Quinn, T. Vincent	Dem	N.Y.	Dec. 30,1951	Resigned; elected District Attorney of New York City.
Buchanan, Vera D.	Dem	Penn.	Jan. 29,1952	Replaced Quinn.

	Majority			Minority		
Departures from the House:						
Elected to U.S. Senate	None			Beall, J. Glenn	Md.	Rep
Defeated for Reelection	None			Wood, John T.	Ida.	Rep
Retired	Larcade, Henry D. Jr.	La.	Dem	None		
	Magee, Clare	Mo.	Dem			
Departures from Committee:						
Moved to Ways and Means	None			Baker, Howard H.	Tenn.	Rep
Moved to Armed Services	None			Bray, William G.	Ind.	Rep
Moved to Appropriations	None			Vursell, Charles W.	Ill.	Rep

PUBLIC WORKS / 83rd Congress

Service Dates of Committee Chair: Jan. 19,1953-Jan. 3,1955
Service Dates of Majority Members: Jan. 19,1953-Jan. 3,1955
Service Dates of Minority Members: Jan. 19,1953-Jan. 3,1955

Majority

Rank	Name	Party	State	Terms in: House	Terms in: Comm.
Chr	Dondero, George A.	Rep	Mich.	11	11
2nd	Angell, Homer D.	Rep	Ore.	8	8
3rd	McGregor, J. Harry	Rep	Ohio	8	8
4th	Auchincloss, James C.	Rep	N.J.	6	6
5th	Mack, Russell V.	Rep	Wash.	4	4
6th	Scudder, Hubert B.	Rep	Cal.	3	2
7th	George, Myron V.	Rep	Kans.	3	2
8th	Brownson, Charles B.	Rep	Ind.	2	1
9th	Bush, Alvin R.	Rep	Penn.	2	1
10th	Oakman, Charles G.	Rep	Mich.	1	1
11th	Small, Frank Jr.	Rep	Md.	1	1
12th	Warburton, Herbert B.	Rep	Del.	1	1
13th	Neal, William E.	Rep	W.Va.	1	1
14th	Becker, Frank J.	Rep	N.Y.	1	1
15th	Stauffer, S. Walter	Rep	Penn.	1 *1	1
16th	Scherer, Gordon H.	Rep	Ohio	1	1

Minority

Rank	Name	Party	State	Terms in: House	Terms in: Comm.
RM	Buckley, Charles A.	Dem	N.Y.	10	10
2nd	Fallon, George H.	Dem	Md.	5	5
3rd	Davis, Clifford	Dem	Tenn.	8	5
4th	Trimble, James W.	Dem	Ark.	5	4
5th	Blatnik, John A.	DFL	Minn.	4	4
6th	Jones, Robert E. Jr.	Dem	Ala.	4	4
7th	Dempsey, John J.	Dem	N.M.	5	2
8th	Smith, Frank E.	Dem	Miss.	2	2
9th	Watts, John C.	Dem	Ky.	2	2
10th	Machrowicz, Thaddeus M.	Dem	Mich.	2	2
11th	Kluczynski, John C.	Dem	Ill.	2	2
12th	Steed, Thomas J.	Dem	Okla.	3	2
13th	Buchanan, Vera D.	Dem	Penn.	2	2

*1: Member's 1st period of service on the committee.

	Majority			Minority		
Departures from the House:						
Defeated for Reelection	Neal, William E.	W.Va.	Rep	None		
	Oakman, Charles G.	Mich.	Rep			
	Small, Frank Jr.	Md.	Rep			
	Stauffer, S. Walter	Penn.	Rep			
Defeated for Renomination	Angell, Homer D.	Ore.	Rep	None		
Lost Election to U.S. Senate	Warburton, Herbert B.	Del.	Rep	None		
Departures from Committee:						
Moved to Merchant Marine & Fisheries	Bush, Alvin R.	Penn.	Rep	None		
Moved to Banking & Currency	None			Buchanan, Vera D.	Penn.	Dem
Moved to Rules	None			Trimble, James W.	Ark.	Dem
Moved to Agriculture	None			Watts, John C.	Ky.	Dem
No new assignment	Brownson, Charles B.	Ind.	Rep	None		

PUBLIC WORKS / 84th Congress

Service Dates of Committee Chair: Jan. 13,1955-Jan. 3,1957
Service Dates of Majority Members: Jan. 13,1955-Jan. 3,1957
Service Dates of Minority Members: Jan. 20,1955-Jan. 3,1957

Majority

Rank	Name	Party	State	Terms in: House	Terms in: Comm.
Chr	Buckley, Charles A.	Dem	N.Y.	11	11
2nd	Fallon, George H.	Dem	Md.	6	6
3rd	Davis, Clifford	Dem	Tenn.	9	6
4th	Blatnik, John A.	DFL	Minn.	5	5
5th	Jones, Robert E. Jr.	Dem	Ala.	5	5
6th	Dempsey, John J.	Dem	N.M.	6	3
7th	Smith, Frank E.	Dem	Miss.	3	3
8th	Machrowicz, Thaddeus M.	Dem	Mich.	3	3
9th	Kluczynski, John C.	Dem	Ill.	3	3
10th	Steed, Thomas J.	Dem	Okla.	4	3
11th	Thompson, T. Ashton	Dem	La.	2	1
12th	Gentry, Brady P.	Dem	Tex.	2	1
13th	Burnside, Maurice G.	Dem	W.Va.	3	1
14th	Blitch, Iris F.	Dem	Ga.	1	1
15th	Wright, James C. Jr.	Dem	Tex.	1	1
16th	Hull, William R. Jr.	Dem	Mo.	1	1
17th	Gray, Kenneth J.	Dem	Ill.	1	1

Minority

Rank	Name	Party	State	Terms in: House	Terms in: Comm.
RM	Dondero, George A.	Rep	Mich.	12	12
2nd	McGregor, J. Harry	Rep	Ohio	9	9
3rd	Auchincloss, James C.	Rep	N.J.	7	7
4th	Mack, Russell V.	Rep	Wash.	5	5
5th	Scudder, Hubert B.	Rep	Cal.	4	3
6th	George, Myron V.	Rep	Kans.	4	3
7th	Becker, Frank J.	Rep	N.Y.	2	2
8th	Scherer, Gordon H.	Rep	Ohio	2	2
9th	Withrow, Gardner R.	Rep	Wisc.	8	*2 1
10th	Cramer, William C.	Rep	Fla.	1	1
11th	Baldwin, John F. Jr.	Rep	Cal.	1	1
12th	Schwengel, Frederick D.	Rep	Iowa	1	*1 1
13th	Alger, Bruce R.	Rep	Tex.	1	1

*1: Member's 1st period of service on the committee;
*2: Member's 2nd period of service on the committee.

Notes: House Resolution 119, agreed to Jan. 31,1955, increased the size and the party ratio on this committee to 19 Democrats and 15 Republicans.

Additions:

	Rank	Name	Party	State	Date
Majority:	18th	Clark, Frank M.	Dem	Penn.	Jan. 31,1955
	19th	Rogers, Paul G.	Dem	Fla.	Jan. 31,1955
Minority:	14th	Bush, Alvin R.	Rep	Penn.	Feb. 16,1955
	15th	Nicholson, Donald W.	Rep	Mass.	Feb. 16,1955

Changes:

Majority:

Name	Party	State	Date	Change
Machrowicz, Thaddeus M.	Dem	Mich.	Jan. 12,1956	Moved to Ways and Means.
Dingell, John D. Jr.	Dem	Mich.	Jan. 19,1956	Replaced Machrowicz.

	Majority		Minority	
Departures from the House:				
Defeated for Reelection	Burnside, Maurice G.	W.Va. Dem	None	
Retired	Gentry, Brady P.	Tex. Dem	Dondero, George A.	Mich. Rep
Departures from Committee:				
Moved to Appropriations	Steed, Thomas J.	Okla. Dem		
Moved to Interstate & Foreign Commerce	Dingell, John D. Jr.	Mich. Dem	Alger, Bruce R.	Tex. Rep
Moved to Education and Labor	None		Nicholson, Donald W.	Mass. Rep
No new assignment	None		Bush, Alvin R.	Penn. Rep

PUBLIC WORKS / 85th Congress

Service Dates of Committee Chair: Jan. 10,1957-Jan. 3,1959
Service Dates of Majority Members: Jan. 10,1957-Jan. 3,1959
Service Dates of Minority Members: Jan. 16,1957-Jan. 3,1959

Majority

Rank Name	Party	State	Terms in: House	Terms in: Comm.
Chr Buckley, Charles A.	Dem	N.Y.	12	12
2nd Fallon, George H.	Dem	Md.	7	7
3rd Davis, Clifford	Dem	Tenn.	10	7
4th Blatnik, John A.	DFL	Minn.	6	6
5th Jones, Robert E. Jr.	Dem	Ala.	6	6
6th Dempsey, John J.	Dem	N.M.	7	4
7th Smith, Frank E.	Dem	Miss.	4	4
8th Kluczynski, John C.	Dem	Ill.	4	4
9th Thompson, T. Ashton	Dem	La.	3	2
10th Blitch, Iris F.	Dem	Ga.	2	2
11th Wright, James C. Jr.	Dem	Tex.	2	2
12th Hull, William R. Jr.	Dem	Mo.	2	2
13th Gray, Kenneth J.	Dem	Ill.	2	2
14th Clark, Frank M.	Dem	Penn.	2	2
15th Rogers, Paul G.	Dem	Fla.	2	2
16th Edmondson, Edmond A.	Dem	Okla.	3	1
17th Kilgore, Joe M.	Dem	Tex.	2	1
18th McFall, John J.	Dem	Cal.	1	1
19th Brown, Charles H.	Dem	Mo.	1	1

Minority

Rank Name	Party	State	Terms in: House	Terms in: Comm.
RM McGregor, J. Harry	Rep	Ohio	10	10
2nd Auchincloss, James C.	Rep	N.J.	8	8
3rd Mack, Russell V.	Rep	Wash.	6	6
4th Scudder, Hubert B.	Rep	Cal.	5	4
5th George, Myron V.	Rep	Kans.	5	4
6th Becker, Frank J.	Rep	N.Y.	3	3
7th Scherer, Gordon H.	Rep	Ohio	3	3
8th Withrow, Gardner R.	Rep	Wisc.	9	*2 2
9th Cramer, William C.	Rep	Fla.	2	2
10th Baldwin, John F. Jr.	Rep	Cal.	2	2
11th Schwengel, Frederick D.	Rep	Iowa	2	*1 2
12th Stauffer, S. Walter	Rep	Penn.	2	*2 1
13th Byrne, Emmet F.	Rep	Ill.	1	1
14th Dooley, Edwin B.	Rep	N.Y.	1	1
15th Broomfield, William S.	Rep	Mich.	1	1

*1: Member's 1st period of service on the committee;
*2: Member's 2nd period of service on the committee.

Changes:

Majority:

Dempsey, John J.	Dem	N.M.	Mar. 11,1958	Died in office.
Pfost, Gracie B.	Dem	Ida.	July 18,1958	Replaced Pfost.
Kilgore, Joe M.	Dem	Tex.	July 21,1958	Moved to Interstate and Foreign Commerce.
Young, John A.	Dem	Tex.	July 21,1958	Replaced Kilgore.

Minority:

Becker, Frank J.	Rep	N.Y.	Feb. 3,1958	Moved to Armed Services.
Robison, Howard W.	Rep	N.Y.	Feb. 3,1958	Replaced Becker.
McGregor, J. Harry	Rep	Ohio	Oct. 7,1958	Died in office.

Departures from the House:	**Majority**		**Minority**	
Defeated for Reelection	None		Byrne, Emmet F.	Ill. Rep
			George, Myron V.	Kans. Rep
			Stauffer, S. Walter	Penn. Rep
Retired	None		Scudder, Hubert B.	Cal. Rep
Departures from Committee:				
Moved to Interstate & Foreign Commerce	Rogers, Paul G.	Fla. Dem	None	

PUBLIC WORKS / 86th Congress

Service Dates of Committee Chair: Jan. 19,1959-Jan. 3,1961
Service Dates of Majority Members: Jan. 19,1959-Jan. 3,1961
Service Dates of Minority Members: Jan. 19,1959-Jan. 3,1961

Majority

Rank Name	Party	State	Terms in: House	Terms in: Comm.
Chr Buckley, Charles A.	Dem	N.Y.	13	13
2nd Fallon, George H.	Dem	Md.	8	8
3rd Davis, Clifford	Dem	Tenn.	11	8
4th Blatnik, John A.	DFL	Minn.	7	7
5th Jones, Robert E. Jr.	Dem	Ala.	7	7
6th Smith, Frank E.	Dem	Miss.	5	5
7th Kluczynski, John C.	Dem	Ill.	5	5
8th Thompson, T. Ashton	Dem	La.	4	3
9th Blitch, Iris F.	Dem	Ga.	3	3
10th Wright, James C. Jr.	Dem	Tex.	3	3
11th Hull, William R. Jr.	Dem	Mo.	3	3
12th Gray, Kenneth J.	Dem	Ill.	3	3
13th Clark, Frank M.	Dem	Penn.	3	3
14th Edmondson, Edmond A.	Dem	Okla.	4	2
15th McFall, John J.	Dem	Cal.	2	2
16th Brown, Charles H.	Dem	Mo.	2	2
17th Pfost, Gracie B.	Dem	Ida.	4	2
18th Young, John A.	Dem	Tex.	2	2
19th Hargis, Denver D.	Dem	Kans.	1	1
20th Burke, Frank W.	Dem	Ky.	1	1
21st Johnson, Harold T.	Dem	Cal.	1	1
22nd Cook, Robert E.	Dem	Ohio	1	1

Minority

Rank Name	Party	State	Terms in: House	Terms in: Comm.
RM Auchincloss, James C.	Rep	N.J.	9	9
2nd Mack, Russell V.	Rep	Wash.	7	7
3rd Scherer, Gordon H.	Rep	Ohio	4	4
4th Withrow, Gardner R.	Rep	Wisc.	10	*2 3
5th Cramer, William C.	Rep	Fla.	3	3
6th Baldwin, John F. Jr.	Rep	Cal.	3	3
7th Schwengel, Frederick D.	Rep	Iowa	3	*1 3
8th Dooley, Edwin B.	Rep	N.Y.	2	2
9th Broomfield, William S.	Rep	Mich.	2	2
10th Robison, Howard W.	Rep	N.Y.	2	2
11th Taylor, Dean P.	Rep	N.Y.	9	*2 1
12th Mumma, Walter M.	Rep	Penn.	5	1

*1: Member's 1st period of service on the committee;
*2: Member's 2nd period of service on the committee.

Changes:

Minority:

Mack, Russell V.	Rep	Wash.	Mar. 28,1960	Died in office.
Schneebeli, Herman T.	Rep	Penn.	June 30,1960	Replaced Mack.

Departures from the House:

	Majority		Minority	
Defeated for Reelection	Brown, Charles H.	Mo. Dem	None	
	Hargis, Denver D.	Kans. Dem		
Retired	None		Taylor, Dean P.	N.Y. Rep
			Withrow, Gardner R.	Wisc. Rep

Departures from Committee:

	Majority		Minority	
Moved to Foreign Affairs	None		Broomfield, William S.	Mich. Rep
No new assignment			Mumma, Walter M.	Penn. Rep

PUBLIC WORKS / 87th Congress

Service Dates of Committee Chair: Feb. 6,1961-Jan. 3,1963
Service Dates of Majority Members: Feb. 6,1961-Jan. 3,1963
Service Dates of Minority Members: Feb. 13,1961-Jan. 3,1963

Majority

Rank	Name	Party	State	Terms in: House	Terms in: Comm.
Chr	Buckley, Charles A.	Dem	N.Y.	14	14
2nd	Fallon, George H.	Dem	Md.	9	9
3rd	Davis, Clifford	Dem	Tenn.	12	9
4th	Blatnik, John A.	DFL	Minn.	8	8
5th	Jones, Robert E. Jr.	Dem	Ala.	8	8
6th	Smith, Frank E.	Dem	Miss.	6	6
7th	Kluczynski, John C.	Dem	Ill.	6	6
8th	Thompson, T. Ashton	Dem	La.	5	4
9th	Blitch, Iris F.	Dem	Ga.	4	4
10th	Wright, James C. Jr.	Dem	Tex.	4	4
11th	Hull, William R. Jr.	Dem	Mo.	4	4
12th	Gray, Kenneth J.	Dem	Ill.	4	4
13th	Clark, Frank M.	Dem	Penn.	4	4
14th	Edmondson, Edmond A.	Dem	Okla.	5	3
15th	McFall, John J.	Dem	Cal.	3	3
16th	Pfost, Gracie B.	Dem	Ida.	5	3
17th	Young, John A.	Dem	Tex.	3	3
18th	Burke, Frank W.	Dem	Ky.	2	2
19th	Johnson, Harold T.	Dem	Cal.	2	2
20th	Cook, Robert E.	Dem	Ohio	2	2

Minority

Rank	Name	Party	State	Terms in: House	Terms in: Comm.
RM	Auchincloss, James C.	Rep	N.J.	10	10
2nd	Scherer, Gordon H.	Rep	Ohio	5	5
3rd	Cramer, William C.	Rep	Fla.	4	4
4th	Baldwin, John F. Jr.	Rep	Cal.	4	4
5th	Schwengel, Frederick D.	Rep	Iowa	4	*1 4
6th	Dooley, Edwin B.	Rep	N.Y.	3	3
7th	Robison, Howard W.	Rep	N.Y.	3	3
8th	Schneebeli, Herman T.	Rep	Penn.	2	2
9th	Bass, Perkins	Rep	N.H.	4	1
10th	McVey, Walter L.	Rep	Kans.	1	1
11th	King, Carleton J.	Rep	N.Y.	1	1
12th	Harsha, William H. Jr.	Rep	Ohio	1	1
13th	Harvey, James	Rep	Mich.	1	1
14th	Kunkel, John C.	Rep	Penn.	7	1

*1: Member's 1st period of service on the committee.

Vacancy Filled:
Minority: 14th seat by Kunkel on May 23,1961.

Changes:

Majority:

Name	Party	State	Date	Note
Smith, Frank E.	Dem	Miss.	Nov. 14,1962	Resigned; defeated for renomination and appointed to board of the Tennessee Valley Authority.
Cook, Robert E.	Dem	Ohio	Dec. 13,1962	Resigned; defeated for reelection.

Minority:

Name	Party	State	Date	Note
Schneebeli, Herman T.	Rep	Penn.	May 23,1961	Moved to Ways and Means.
Reece, Louise G.	Rep	Tenn.	May 23,1961	Replaced Schneebeli.

Departures from the House:

	Majority			Minority		
Defeated for Reelection	Burke, Frank W.	Ky.	Dem	None		
Defeated for Renomination	None			Dooley, Edwin B.	N.Y.	Rep
				McVey, Walter L.	Kans.	Rep
Lost Election to U.S. Senate	Pfost, Gracie B.	Ida.	Dem	Bass, Perkins	N.H.	Rep
Retired	Blitch, Iris F.	Ga.	Dem	Scherer, Gordon H.	Ohio	Rep
				Reece, Louise G.	Tenn.	Rep

Departures from Committee:

	Majority			Minority		
Moved to Interstate & Foreign Commerce	Hull, William R. Jr.	Mo.	Dem	None		
No new assignment	None			King, Carleton J.	N.Y.	Rep

PUBLIC WORKS / 88th Congress

Service Dates of Committee Chair: Jan. 17,1963-Jan. 3,1965
Service Dates of Majority Members: Jan. 17,1963-Jan. 3,1965
Service Dates of Minority Members: Jan. 24,1963-Jan. 3,1965

Majority

Rank	Name	Party	State	Terms in: House	Terms in: Comm.
Chr	Buckley, Charles A.	Dem	N.Y.	15	15
2nd	Fallon, George H.	Dem	Md.	10	10
3rd	Davis, Clifford	Dem	Tenn.	13	10
4th	Blatnik, John A.	DFL	Minn.	9	9
5th	Jones, Robert E. Jr.	Dem	Ala.	9	9
6th	Kluczynski, John C.	Dem	Ill.	7	7
7th	Thompson, T. Ashton	Dem	La.	6	5
8th	Wright, James C. Jr.	Dem	Tex.	5	5
9th	Gray, Kenneth J.	Dem	Ill.	5	5
10th	Clark, Frank M.	Dem	Penn.	5	5
11th	Edmondson, Edmond A.	Dem	Okla.	6	4
12th	McFall, John J.	Dem	Cal.	4	4
13th	Young, John A.	Dem	Tex.	4	4
14th	Johnson, Harold T.	Dem	Cal.	3	3
15th	Dorn, W. J. Bryan	Dem	S.C.	8	1
16th	Henderson, David N.	Dem	N.C.	2	1
17th	Olsen, Arnold	Dem	Mont.	2	1
18th	Ryan, Harold M.	Dem	Mich.	2	1
19th	Tuten, J. Russell	Dem	Ga.	1	1
20th	Murphy, John M.	Dem	N.Y.	1	1

Minority

Rank	Name	Party	State	Terms in: House	Terms in: Comm.
RM	Auchincloss, James C.	Rep	N.J.	11	11
2nd	Cramer, William C.	Rep	Fla.	5	5
3rd	Baldwin, John F. Jr.	Rep	Cal.	5	5
4th	Schwengel, Frederick D.	Rep	Iowa	5	*1 5
5th	Robison, Howard W.	Rep	N.Y.	4	4
6th	Harsha, William H. Jr.	Rep	Ohio	2	2
7th	Harvey, James	Rep	Mich.	2	2
8th	Kunkel, John C.	Rep	Penn.	8	2
9th	McLoskey, Robert T.	Rep	Ill.	1	1
10th	Grover, James R. Jr.	Rep	N.Y.	1	1
11th	Quillen, James H.	Rep	Tenn.	1	1
12th	Rich, Carl W.	Rep	Ohio	1	1
13th	Cleveland, James C.	Rep	N.H.	1	1
14th	Clausen, Don H.	Rep	Cal.	1	1

*1: Member's 1st period of service on the committee.

Vacancy Filled:
Minority: 14th seat by Clausen on Jan. 29,1963.

Changes:
Majority:

McFall, John J.	Dem	Cal.	Dec. 10,1963	Moved to Appropriations.
Young, John A.	Dem	Tex.	Dec. 10,1963	Moved to Rules.
Rivers, Ralph J.	Dem	Alas.	Feb. 25,1964	Replaced McFall.
Roberts, Herbert Ray	Dem	Tex.	Feb. 25,1964	Replaced Young.

Departures from the House:	Majority			Minority		
Defeated for Reelection	None			McLoskey, Robert T.	Ill.	Rep
				Rich, Carl W.	Ohio	Rep
				Schwengel, Frederick D.	Iowa	Rep
Defeated for Renomination	Buckley, Charles A.	N.Y.	Dem	None		
	Davis, Clifford	Tenn.	Dem			
	Ryan, Harold M.	Mich.	Dem			
Retired	None			Auchincloss, James C.	N.J.	Rep
Departures from Committee:						
Moved to Interstate & Foreign Commerce	Murphy, John M.	N.Y.	Dem	None		
Moved to Rules	None			Quillen, James H.	Tenn.	Rep
Moved to Appropriations	None			Robison, Howard W.	N.Y.	Rep
No new assignment	None			Harvey, James	Mich.	Rep

PUBLIC WORKS / 89th Congress

Service Dates of Committee Chair: Jan. 18,1965-Jan. 3,1967
Service Dates of Majority Members: Jan. 18,1965-Jan. 3,1967
Service Dates of Minority Members: Jan. 21,1965-Jan. 3,1967

Majority

Rank	Name	Party	State	Terms in: House	Terms in: Comm.
Chr	Fallon, George H.	Dem	Md.	11	11
2nd	Blatnik, John A.	DFL	Minn.	10	10
3rd	Jones, Robert E. Jr.	Dem	Ala.	10	10
4th	Kluczynski, John C.	Dem	Ill.	8	8
5th	Thompson, T. Ashton	Dem	La.	7	6
6th	Wright, James C. Jr.	Dem	Tex.	6	6
7th	Gray, Kenneth J.	Dem	Ill.	6	6
8th	Clark, Frank M.	Dem	Penn.	6	6
9th	Edmondson, Edmond A.	Dem	Okla.	7	5
10th	Johnson, Harold T.	Dem	Cal.	4	4
11th	Dorn, W. J. Bryan	Dem	S.C.	9	2
12th	Henderson, David N.	Dem	N.C.	3	2
13th	Olsen, Arnold	Dem	Mont.	3	2
14th	Tuten, J. Russell	Dem	Ga.	2	2
15th	Rivers, Ralph J.	Dem	Alas.	4	2
16th	Roberts, Herbert Ray	Dem	Tex.	3	2
17th	Everett, Robert A.	Dem	Tenn.	5	1
18th	McCarthy, Richard D.	Dem	N.Y.	1	1
19th	Kee, James	Dem	W.Va.	1	1
20th	Schmidhauser, John R.	Dem	Iowa	1	1
21st	Sweeney, Robert E.	Dem	Ohio	1	1
22nd	Howard, James J.	Dem	N.J.	1	1
23rd	Dyal, Kenneth W.	Dem	Cal.	1	1

Minority

Rank	Name	Party	State	Terms in: House	Terms in: Comm.
RM	Cramer, William C.	Rep	Fla.	6	6
2nd	Baldwin, John F. Jr.	Rep	Cal.	6	6
3rd	Harsha, William H. Jr.	Rep	Ohio	3	3
4th	Kunkel, John C.	Rep	Penn.	9	3
5th	Grover, James R. Jr.	Rep	N.Y.	2	2
6th	Cleveland, James C.	Rep	N.H.	2	2
7th	Clausen, Don H.	Rep	Cal.	2	2
8th	Halleck, Charles A.	Rep	Ind.	16	1
9th	Reid, Charlotte T.	Rep	Ill.	2	1
10th	McEwen, Robert C.	Rep	N.Y.	1	1
11th	Martin, James D.	Rep	Ala.	1	1

Changes:

Majority:

Thompson, T. Ashton	Dem	La.	July 1,1965	Died in office.
Edwards, Edwin W.	Dem	La.	Oct. 21,1965	Replaced Thompson.
Tuten, J. Russell	Dem	Ga.	Oct. 18,1966	Left committee; defeated for renomination.
Sweeney, Robert E.	Dem	Ohio	Oct. 18,1966	Left committee; retired at end of Congress.
Mackie, John C.	Dem	Mich.	Oct. 18,1966	Replaced Tuten.
Secrest, Robert T.	Dem	Ohio	Oct. 18,1966	Replaced Sweeney.
Rivers, Ralph J.	Dem	Alas.	Dec. 30,1966	Resigned House; defeated for reelection.
Secrest, Robert T.	Dem	Ohio	Dec. 30,1966	Resigned House; defeated for reelection.

Minority:

Baldwin, John F. Jr.	Rep	Cal.	Mar. 9,1966	Died in office.
Skubitz, Joe	Rep	Kans.	May 24,1966	Replaced Baldwin.
Martin, James D.	Rep	Ala.	Oct. 21,1966	Left committee; defeated in election for Governor.
Duncan, John J.	Rep	Tenn.	Oct. 21,1966	Replaced Martin.
Kunkel, John C.	Rep	Penn.	Dec. 30,1966	Resigned and retired.

Departures from the House:

	Majority			Minority
Defeated for Reelection	Dyal, Kenneth W.	Cal.	Dem	None
	Schmidhauser, John R.	Iowa	Dem	
	Mackie, John C.	Mich.	Dem	

Departures from Committee:

	Majority	Minority		
Moved to Armed Services	None	Halleck, Charles A.	Ind.	Rep
Moved to Appropriations	None	Reid, Charlotte T.	Ill.	Rep

PUBLIC WORKS / 90th Congress

Service Dates of Committee Chair: Jan. 23,1967-Jan. 3,1969
Service Dates of Majority Members: Jan. 23,1967-Jan. 3,1969
Service Dates of Minority Members: Jan. 26,1967-Jan. 3,1969

Majority

Rank	Name	Party	State	Terms in: House	Terms in: Comm.
Chr	Fallon, George H.	Dem	Md.	12	12
2nd	Blatnik, John A.	DFL	Minn.	11	11
3rd	Jones, Robert E. Jr.	Dem	Ala.	11	11
4th	Kluczynski, John C.	Dem	Ill.	9	9
5th	Wright, James C. Jr.	Dem	Tex.	7	7
6th	Gray, Kenneth J.	Dem	Ill.	7	7
7th	Clark, Frank M.	Dem	Penn.	7	7
8th	Edmondson, Edmond A.	Dem	Okla.	8	6
9th	Johnson, Harold T.	Dem	Cal.	5	5
10th	Dorn, W. J. Bryan	Dem	S.C.	10	3
11th	Henderson, David N.	Dem	N.C.	4	3
12th	Olsen, Arnold	Dem	Mont.	4	3
13th	Roberts, Herbert Ray	Dem	Tex.	4	3
14th	Everett, Robert A.	Dem	Tenn.	6	2
15th	McCarthy, Richard D.	Dem	N.Y.	2	2
16th	Kee, James	Dem	W.Va.	2	2
17th	Howard, James J.	Dem	N.J.	2	2
18th	Edwards, Edwin W.	Dem	La.	2	2
19th	Waldie, Jerome R.	Dem	Cal.	2	1

Minority

Rank	Name	Party	State	Terms in: House	Terms in: Comm.
RM	Cramer, William C.	Rep	Fla.	7	7
2nd	Harsha, William H. Jr.	Rep	Ohio	4	4
3rd	Grover, James R. Jr.	Rep	N.Y.	3	3
4th	Cleveland, James C.	Rep	N.H.	3	3
5th	Clausen, Don H.	Rep	Cal.	3	3
6th	McEwen, Robert C.	Rep	N.Y.	2	2
7th	Skubitz, Joe	Rep	Kans.	3	2
8th	Duncan, John J.	Rep	Tenn.	2	2
9th	Schwengel, Frederick D.	Rep	Iowa	6	*2 1
10th	Schadeberg, Henry C.	Rep	Wisc.	3	1
11th	Snyder, M. G. (Gene)	Rep	Ky.	2	1
12th	Denney, Robert V.	Rep	Neb.	1	1
13th	Zion, Roger H.	Rep	Ind.	1	1
14th	McDonald, Jack H.	Rep	Mich.	1	1
15th	Hammerschmidt, John Paul	Rep	Ark.	1	1

*2: Member's 2nd period of service on the committee.

Changes:

Majority:

Name	Party	State	Date	Change
Waldie, Jerome R.	Dem	Cal.	Oct. 10,1968	Moved to Judiciary.

Minority:

Name	Party	State	Date	Change
Skubitz, Joe	Rep	Kans.	Aug. 1,1967	Moved to Interstate and Foreign Commerce.
Miller, Clarence E.	Rep	Ohio	Nov. 15,1967	Replaced Skubitz.

Departures from Committee:	Majority		Minority
Moved to Internal Security	Edwards, Edwin W.	La. Dem	None
Unassigned in 91st; died in office Jan. 26,1969	Everett, Robert A.	Tenn. Dem	None

PUBLIC WORKS / 91st Congress

Service Dates of Committee Chair: Jan. 29,1969-Jan. 3,1971
Service Dates of Majority Members: Jan. 29,1969-Jan. 3,1971
Service Dates of Minority Members: Jan. 29,1969-Jan. 3,1971

Majority

Rank	Name	Party	State	Terms in: House	Terms in: Comm.
Chr	Fallon, George H.	Dem	Md.	13	13
2nd	Blatnik, John A.	DFL	Minn.	12	12
3rd	Jones, Robert E. Jr.	Dem	Ala.	12	12
4th	Kluczynski, John C.	Dem	Ill.	10	10
5th	Wright, James C. Jr.	Dem	Tex.	8	8
6th	Gray, Kenneth J.	Dem	Ill.	8	8
7th	Clark, Frank M.	Dem	Penn.	8	8
8th	Edmondson, Edmond A.	Dem	Okla.	9	7
9th	Johnson, Harold T.	Dem	Cal.	6	6
10th	Dorn, W. J. Bryan	Dem	S.C.	11	4
11th	Henderson, David N.	Dem	N.C.	5	4
12th	Olsen, Arnold	Dem	Mont.	5	4
13th	Roberts, Herbert Ray	Dem	Tex.	5	4
14th	McCarthy, Richard D.	Dem	N.Y.	3	3
15th	Kee, James	Dem	W.Va.	3	3
16th	Howard, James J.	Dem	N.J.	3	3
17th	Anderson, Glenn M.	Dem	Cal.	1	1
18th	Caffery, Patrick T.	Dem	La.	1	1
19th	Obey, David R.	Dem	Wisc.	1	1

Minority

Rank	Name	Party	State	Terms in: House	Terms in: Comm.
RM	Cramer, William C.	Rep	Fla.	8	8
2nd	Harsha, William H. Jr.	Rep	Ohio	5	5
3rd	Grover, James R. Jr.	Rep	N.Y.	4	4
4th	Cleveland, James C.	Rep	N.H.	4	4
5th	Clausen, Don H.	Rep	Cal.	4	4
6th	McEwen, Robert C.	Rep	N.Y.	3	3
7th	Duncan, John J.	Rep	Tenn.	3	3
8th	Schwengel, Frederick D.	Rep	Iowa	7	*2 2
9th	Schadeberg, Henry C.	Rep	Wisc.	4	2
10th	Snyder, M. G. (Gene)	Rep	Ky.	3	2
11th	Denney, Robert V.	Rep	Neb.	2	2
12th	Zion, Roger H.	Rep	Ind.	2	2
13th	McDonald, Jack H.	Rep	Mich.	2	2
14th	Hammerschmidt, John Paul	Rep	Ark.	2	2
15th	Miller, Clarence E.	Rep	Ohio	2	2

*2: Member's 2nd period of service on the committee.

Vacancy Filled:
Majority: 19th seat by Obey on Apr. 15,1969.

Changes:
Majority:

Obey, David R.	Dem	Wisc.	Nov. 12,1969	Moved to Appropriations.
Roe, Robert A.	Dem	N.J.	Feb. 16,1970	Replaced Obey.

Departures from the House:	**Majority**			**Minority**		
Appointed Federal Judge	None			Denney, Robert V.	Neb.	Rep
Defeated for Reelection	Olsen, Arnold	Mont.	Dem	Schadeberg, Henry C.	Wisc.	Rep
Defeated for Renomination	Fallon, George H.	Md.	Dem	None		
Lost Election to U.S. Senate	None			Cramer, William C.	Fla.	Rep
Lost Nomination to U.S. Senate	McCarthy, Richard D.	N.Y.	Dem	None		
Departures from Committee:						
Moved to Ways and Means	None			Duncan, John J.	Tenn.	Rep
Moved to Appropriations	None			McEwen, Robert C.	N.Y.	Rep

PUBLIC WORKS / 92nd Congress

Service Dates of Committee Chair: Feb. 4,1971-Jan. 3,1973
Service Dates of Majority Members: Feb. 4,1971-Jan. 3,1973
Service Dates of Minority Members: Feb. 4,1971-Jan. 3,1973

Majority

Rank	Name	Party	State	Terms in: House	Terms in: Comm.
Chr	Blatnik, John A.	DFL	Minn.	13	13
2nd	Jones, Robert E. Jr.	Dem	Ala.	13	13
3rd	Kluczynski, John C.	Dem	Ill.	11	11
4th	Wright, James C. Jr.	Dem	Tex.	9	9
5th	Gray, Kenneth J.	Dem	Ill.	9	9
6th	Clark, Frank M.	Dem	Penn.	9	9
7th	Edmondson, Edmond A.	Dem	Okla.	10	8
8th	Johnson, Harold T.	Dem	Cal.	7	7
9th	Dorn, W. J. Bryan	Dem	S.C.	12	5
10th	Henderson, David N.	Dem	N.C.	6	5
11th	Roberts, Herbert Ray	Dem	Tex.	6	5
12th	Kee, James	Dem	W.Va.	4	4
13th	Howard, James J.	Dem	N.J.	4	4
14th	Anderson, Glenn M.	Dem	Cal.	2	2
15th	Caffery, Patrick T.	Dem	La.	2	2
16th	Roe, Robert A.	Dem	N.J.	2	2
17th	Collins, George W.	Dem	Ill.	2	1
18th	Roncalio, Teno	Dem	Wyo.	2	1
19th	Begich, Nicholas J.	Dem	Alas.	1	1
20th	McCormack, Mike	Dem	Wash.	1	1
21st	Rangel, Charles B.	Dem	N.Y.	1	1
22nd	Stanton, James V.	Dem	Ohio	1	1
23rd	Abzug, Bella S.	Dem	N.Y.	1	1

Minority

Rank	Name	Party	State	Terms in: House	Terms in: Comm.
RM	Harsha, William H. Jr.	Rep	Ohio	6	6
2nd	Grover, James R. Jr.	Rep	N.Y.	5	5
3rd	Cleveland, James C.	Rep	N.H.	5	5
4th	Clausen, Don H.	Rep	Cal.	5	5
5th	Schwengel, Frederick D.	Rep	Iowa	8	*2 3
6th	Snyder, M. G. (Gene)	Rep	Ky.	4	3
7th	Zion, Roger H.	Rep	Ind.	3	3
8th	McDonald, Jack H.	Rep	Mich.	3	3
9th	Hammerschmidt, John Paul	Rep	Ark.	3	3
10th	Miller, Clarence E.	Rep	Ohio	3	3
11th	Mizell, Wilmer D.	Rep	N.C.	2	1
12th	Terry, John H.	Rep	N.Y.	1	1
13th	Thone, Charles	Rep	Neb.	1	1
14th	Baker, LaMar	Rep	Tenn.	1	1

*2: Member's 2nd period of service on the committee.

Changes:

Majority:

Rangel, Charles B.	Dem	N.Y.	Oct. 12,1972	Moved to Judiciary.
Breaux, John B.	Dem	La.	Oct. 12,1972	Replaced Rangel.
Collins, George W.	Dem	Ill.	Dec. 8,1972	Died in office.
Begich, Nicholas J.	Dem	Alas.	Dec. 29,1972	Died in office.

Departures from the House:	Majority		Minority	
Defeated for Reelection	None		Schwengel, Frederick D.	Iowa Rep
Defeated for Renomination	Kee, James	W.Va. Dem	McDonald, Jack H.	Mich. Rep
Lost Election to U.S. Senate	Edmondson, Edmond A.	Okla. Dem	None	
Retired	Caffery, Patrick T.	La. Dem	Terry, John H.	N.Y. Rep
Departures from Committee:				
Moved to Appropriations	None		Miller, Clarence E.	Ohio Rep
Moved to Agriculture	None		Thone, Charles	Neb. Rep

PUBLIC WORKS / 93rd Congress

Service Dates of Committee Chair: Jan. 24,1973-Dec. 31,1974
Service Dates of Majority Members: Jan. 24,1973-Jan. 3,1975
Service Dates of Minority Members: Jan. 24,1973-Jan. 3,1975

Majority

Rank Name	Party	State	Terms in: House	Terms in: Comm.
Chr Blatnik, John A.	DFL	Minn.	14	14
2nd Jones, Robert E. Jr.	Dem	Ala.	14	14
3rd Kluczynski, John C.	Dem	Ill.	12	12
4th Wright, James C. Jr.	Dem	Tex.	10	10
5th Gray, Kenneth J.	Dem	Ill.	10	10
6th Clark, Frank M.	Dem	Penn.	10	10
7th Johnson, Harold T.	Dem	Cal.	8	8
8th Dorn, W. J. Bryan	Dem	S.C.	13	6
9th Henderson, David N.	Dem	N.C.	7	6
10th Roberts, Herbert Ray	Dem	Tex.	7	6
11th Howard, James J.	Dem	N.J.	5	5
12th Anderson, Glenn M.	Dem	Cal.	3	3
13th Roe, Robert A.	Dem	N.J.	3	3
14th Roncalio, Teno	Dem	Wyo.	3	2
15th McCormack, Mike	Dem	Wash.	2	2
16th Stanton, James V.	Dem	Ohio	2	2
17th Abzug, Bella S.	Dem	N.Y.	2	2
18th Breaux, John B.	Dem	La.	2	2
19th Studds, Gerry E.	Dem	Mass.	1	1
20th Burke, Yvonne Brathwaite	Dem	Cal.	1 *1	1
21st Ginn, Ronald B. (Bo)	Dem	Ga.	1	1
22nd Milford, Dale	Dem	Tex.	1	1
23rd Vander Veen, Richard F.	Dem	Mich.	1	1

Minority

Rank Name	Party	State	Terms in: House	Terms in: Comm.
RM Harsha, William H. Jr.	Rep	Ohio	7	7
2nd Grover, James R. Jr.	Rep	N.Y.	6	6
3rd Cleveland, James C.	Rep	N.H.	6	6
4th Clausen, Don H.	Rep	Cal.	6	6
5th Snyder, M. G. (Gene)	Rep	Ky.	5	4
6th Zion, Roger H.	Rep	Ind.	4	4
7th Hammerschmidt, John Paul	Rep	Ark.	4	4
8th Mizell, Wilmer D.	Rep	N.C.	3	2
9th Baker, LaMar	Rep	Tenn.	2	2
10th Shuster, E. G. (Bud)	Rep	Penn.	1	1
11th Walsh, William F.	Rep	N.Y.	1	1
12th Cochran, Thad	Rep	Miss.	1	1
13th Bafalis, Louis A. (Skip)	Rep	Fla.	1	1
14th Abdnor, James	Rep	S.D.	1	1
15th Hanrahan, Robert P.	Rep	Ill.	1	1
16th Taylor, Gene	Rep	Mo.	1	1

*1: Member's 1st period of service on the committee.

Note: The resignation of James Harvey (Rep-Mich.) and his replacement by J. Bob Traxler (Dem-Mich.) on Apr. 23,1974 led to the passage of House Resolution 1103, agreed to May 15,1974, changing the size and party ratio on this committee to 24 Democrats and 16 Republicans on May 15,1974. House Resolution 1243, agreed to July 18,1974, led to another change in size and party ratio to 26 Democrats and 16 Republicans; however, the 26th majority rank was left vacant for the remainder of the Congress.

Vacancy Filled:
Majority: 23rd seat by Vander Veen on Mar. 13,1974.

Additions:

Majority:	24th Traxler, J. Bob	Dem	Mich.	May 29,1974
	25th Collins, Cardiss	Dem	Ill.	July 29,1974

Changes:
Majority:

Vander Veen, Richard F.	Dem	Mich.	Dec. 18,1974	Moved to Ways and Means.
Blatnik, John A.	DFL	Minn.	Dec. 31,1974	Resigned and retired
Gray, Kenneth J.	Dem	Ill.	Dec. 31,1974	Resigned and retired.
Clark, Frank M.	Dem	Penn.	Dec. 31,1974	Resigned; defeated for reelection.
Dorn, W. J. Bryan	Dem	S.C.	Dec. 31,1974	Resigned; lost election for governor.

Departures from the House:

	Majority		Minority	
Defeated for Reelection	None		Baker, LaMar	Tenn. Rep
			Grover, James R. Jr.	N.Y. Rep
			Hanrahan, Robert P.	Ill. Rep
			Mizell, Wilmer D.	N.C. Rep
			Zion, Roger H.	Ind. Rep

Departures from Committee:

	Majority		Minority	
Moved to Appropriations	Burke, Yvonne Brathwaite	Cal. Dem	None	
	Traxler, J. Bob	Mich. Dem		
Moved to International Relations	Collins, Cardiss	Ill. Dem	None	
Moved to Ways and Means	None		Bafalis, Louis A. (Skip)	Fla. Rep

PUBLIC WORKS AND TRANSPORTATION / 94th Congress

* Renamed the Committee on PUBLIC WORKS AND TRANSPORTATION on Jan. 5,1975.

Service Dates of Committee Chair: Jan. 20,1975-Jan. 3,1977
Service Dates of Majority Members: Jan. 20,1975-Jan. 3,1977
Service Dates of Minority Members: Jan. 28,1975-Jan. 3,1977

Majority

Rank	Name	Party	State	Terms in: House	Terms in: Comm.
Chr	Jones, Robert E. Jr.	Dem	Ala.	15	15
2nd	Kluczynski, John C.	Dem	Ill.	13	13
3rd	Wright, James C. Jr.	Dem	Tex.	11	11
4th	Johnson, Harold T.	Dem	Cal.	9	9
5th	Henderson, David N.	Dem	N.C.	8	7
6th	Roberts, Herbert Ray	Dem	Tex.	8	7
7th	Howard, James J.	Dem	N.J.	6	6
8th	Anderson, Glenn M.	Dem	Cal.	4	4
9th	Roe, Robert A.	Dem	N.J.	4	4
10th	Roncalio, Teno	Dem	Wyo.	4	3
11th	McCormack, Mike	Dem	Wash.	3	3
12th	Stanton, James V.	Dem	Ohio	3	3
13th	Abzug, Bella S.	Dem	N.Y.	3	3
14th	Breaux, John B.	Dem	La.	3	3
15th	Studds, Gerry E.	Dem	Mass.	2	2
16th	Ginn, Ronald B. (Bo)	Dem	Ga.	2	2
17th	Milford, Dale	Dem	Tex.	2	2
18th	Mineta, Norman Y.	Dem	Cal.	1	1
19th	Holland, Kenneth L.	Dem	S.C.	1	1
20th	Howe, Allan T.	Dem	Utah	1	1
21st	Levitas, Elliott H.	Dem	Ga.	1	1
22nd	Oberstar, James L.	DFL	Minn.	1	1
23rd	Ambro, Jerome A. Jr.	Dem	N.Y.	1	1
24th	Nowak, Henry J.	Dem	N.Y.	1	1
25th	Edgar, Robert W.	Dem	Penn.	1	1
26th	Lloyd, Marilyn	Dem	Tenn.	1	1
27th	Fary, John G.	Dem	Ill.	1	1

Minority

Rank	Name	Party	State	Terms in: House	Terms in: Comm.
RM	Harsha, William H. Jr.	Rep	Ohio	8	8
2nd	Cleveland, James C.	Rep	N.H.	7	7
3rd	Clausen, Don H.	Rep	Cal.	7	7
4th	Snyder, M. G. (Gene)	Rep	Ky.	6	5
5th	Hammerschmidt, John Paul	Rep	Ark.	5	5
6th	Shuster, E. G. (Bud)	Rep	Penn.	2	2
7th	Walsh, William F.	Rep	N.Y.	2	2
8th	Cochran, Thad	Rep	Miss.	2	2
9th	Abdnor, James	Rep	S.D.	2	2
10th	Taylor, Gene	Rep	Mo.	2	2
11th	Goldwater, Barry M. Jr.	Rep	Cal.	4	1
12th	Hagedorn, Thomas M.	Rep	Minn.	1	1
13th	Myers, Gary A.	Rep	Penn.	1	1

Vacancy Filled:
Majority: 27th seat by Fary on Sep. 9,1975.

Changes:
Majority:

Kluczynski, John C.	Dem	Ill.	Jan. 26,1975	Died in office.
Risenhoover, Theodore M.	Dem	Okla.	Dec. 17,1975	Replaced Kluczynski.
Studds, Gerry E.	Dem	Mass.	Feb. 18,1976	Moved to International Relations.
Hefner, W. G. (Bill)	Dem	N.C.	Apr. 8,1976	Replaced Studds.

Departures from the House:

	Majority			Minority
Defeated for Reelection	Howe, Allan T.	Utah	Dem	None
Lost Nomination to U.S. Senate	Abzug, Bella S.	N.Y.	Dem	None
	Stanton, James V.	Ohio	Dem	
Retired	Henderson, David N.	N.C.	Dem	None
	Jones, Robert E. Jr.	Ala.	Dem	

Departures from Committee:

Moved to Ways and Means	Holland, Kenneth L.	S.C.	Dem	None
Became House Majority Leader	Wright, James C. Jr.	Tex.	Dem	None

PUBLIC WORKS AND TRANSPORTATION / 95th Congress

Service Dates of Committee Chair: Jan. 19,1977-Jan. 3,1979
Service Dates of Majority Members: Jan. 19,1977-Jan. 3,1979
Service Dates of Minority Members: Jan. 19,1977-Jan. 3,1979

Majority

Rank	Name	Party	State	Terms in: House	Terms in: Comm.
Chr	Johnson, Harold T.	Dem	Cal.	10	10
2nd	Roberts, Herbert Ray	Dem	Tex.	9	8
3rd	Howard, James J.	Dem	N.J.	7	7
4th	Anderson, Glenn M.	Dem	Cal.	5	5
5th	Roe, Robert A.	Dem	N.J.	5	5
6th	Roncalio, Teno	Dem	Wyo.	5	4
7th	McCormack, Mike	Dem	Wash.	4	4
8th	Breaux, John B.	Dem	La.	4	4
9th	Ginn, Ronald B. (Bo)	Dem	Ga.	3	3
10th	Milford, Dale	Dem	Tex.	3	3
11th	Mineta, Norman Y.	Dem	Cal.	2	2
12th	Levitas, Elliott H.	Dem	Ga.	2	2
13th	Oberstar, James L.	DFL	Minn.	2	2
14th	Ambro, Jerome A. Jr.	Dem	N.Y.	2	2
15th	Nowak, Henry J.	Dem	N.Y.	2	2
16th	Edgar, Robert W.	Dem	Penn.	2	2
17th	Lloyd, Marilyn	Dem	Tenn.	2	2
18th	Fary, John G.	Dem	Ill.	2	2
19th	Risenhoover, Theodore M.	Dem	Okla.	2	2
20th	Hefner, W. G. (Bill)	Dem	N.C.	2	2
21st	Cornwell, David L.	Dem	Ind.	1	1
22nd	Young, Robert A.	Dem	Mo.	1	1
23rd	Bonior, David E.	Dem	Mich.	1	1
24th	Ertel, Allen E.	Dem	Penn.	1	1
25th	Evans, Billy Lee	Dem	Ga.	1	1
26th	Flippo, Ronnie G.	Dem	Ala.	1	1
27th	Rahall, Nick J. II	Dem	W.Va.	1	1
28th	Stump, Robert	Dem	Ariz.	1	1
29th	Applegate, Douglas	Dem	Ohio	1	1

Minority

Rank	Name	Party	State	Terms in: House	Terms in: Comm.
RM	Harsha, William H. Jr.	Rep	Ohio	9	9
2nd	Cleveland, James C.	Rep	N.H.	8	8
3rd	Clausen, Don H.	Rep	Cal.	8	8
4th	Snyder, M. G. (Gene)	Rep	Ky.	7	6
5th	Hammerschmidt, John Paul	Rep	Ark.	6	6
6th	Shuster, E. G. (Bud)	Rep	Penn.	3	3
7th	Walsh, William F.	Rep	N.Y.	3	3
8th	Cochran, Thad	Rep	Miss.	3	3
9th	Abdnor, James	Rep	S.D.	3	3
10th	Taylor, Gene	Rep	Mo.	3	3
11th	Goldwater, Barry M. Jr.	Rep	Cal.	5	2
12th	Hagedorn, Thomas M.	Rep	Minn.	2	2
13th	Myers, Gary A.	Rep	Penn.	2	2
14th	Stangeland, Arlan	Rep	Minn.	1	1

Notes: The resignation of Richard A. Tonry (Dem-La.) and his replacement by Robert L. Livingston, Jr. (Rep-La.) on Sep. 7,1977 led to a change in size and party ratio on this committee to 29 Democrats and 15 Republicans. Marilyn Lloyd (Dem-Tenn.) changed her name to Marilyn Lloyd Bouquard during the adjournment of the 95th Congress.

Vacancy Filled:
Minority: 14th seat by Stangeland on Mar. 3,1977.

Addition:

Minority:	15th	Livingston, Robert L.	Rep	La.	Sep. 28,1977

Changes:

Majority:				
Roncalio, Teno	Dem	Wyo.	Dec. 30,1978	Resigned and retired.
Minority:				
Walsh, William F.	Rep	N.Y.	Oct. 14,1978	Left committee; no new assignment.
Cunningham, John E.	Rep	Wash.	Oct. 14,1978	Replaced Walsh.
Cochran, Thad	Rep	Miss.	Dec. 26,1978	Resigned; elected to U.S. Senate.

	Majority			Minority		
Departures from the House:						
Defeated for Reelection	Cornwell, David L.	Ind.	Dem	Cunningham, John E.	Wash.	Rep
Defeated for Renomination	Milford, Dale	Tex.	Dem	None		
	Risenhoover, Theodore M.	Okla.	Dem			
Retired	None			Myers, Gary A.	Penn.	Rep
Departures from Committee:						
Moved to Appropriations	Ginn, Ronald B. (Bo)	Ga.	Dem	None		
No new assignment	Stump, Robert	Ariz.	Dem	None		

PUBLIC WORKS AND TRANSPORTATION / 96th Congress

Service Dates of Committee Chair: Jan. 24,1979-Jan. 3,1981
Service Dates of Majority Members: Jan. 24,1979-Jan. 3,1981
Service Dates of Minority Members: Jan. 24,1979-Jan. 3,1981

Majority

Rank	Name	Party	State	Terms in: House	Terms in: Comm.
Chr	Johnson, Harold T.	Dem	Cal.	11	11
2nd	Roberts, Herbert Ray	Dem	Tex.	10	9
3rd	Howard, James J.	Dem	N.J.	8	8
4th	Anderson, Glenn M.	Dem	Cal.	6	6
5th	Roe, Robert A.	Dem	N.J.	6	6
6th	McCormack, Mike	Dem	Wash.	5	5
7th	Breaux, John B.	Dem	La.	5	5
8th	Mineta, Norman Y.	Dem	Cal.	3	3
9th	Levitas, Elliott H.	Dem	Ga.	3	3
10th	Oberstar, James L.	DFL	Minn.	3	3
11th	Ambro, Jerome A. Jr.	Dem	N.Y.	3	3
12th	Nowak, Henry J.	Dem	N.Y.	3	3
13th	Edgar, Robert W.	Dem	Penn.	3	3
14th	Bouquard, Marilyn Lloyd	Dem	Tenn.	3	3
15th	Fary, John G.	Dem	Ill.	3	3
16th	Hefner, W. G. (Bill)	Dem	N.C.	3	3
17th	Young, Robert A.	Dem	Mo.	2	2
18th	Bonior, David E.	Dem	Mich.	2	2
19th	Ertel, Allen E.	Dem	Penn.	2	2
20th	Evans, Billy Lee	Dem	Ga.	2	2
21st	Flippo, Ronnie G.	Dem	Ala.	2	2
22nd	Rahall, Nick J. II	Dem	W.Va.	2	2
23rd	Applegate, Douglas	Dem	Ohio	2	2
24th	Ferraro, Geraldine A.	Dem	N.Y.	1	1
25th	Donnelly, Brian J.	Dem	Mass.	1	1
26th	Hutto, Earl D.	Dem	Fla.	1	1
27th	Atkinson, Eugene V.	Dem	Penn.	1	1
28th	Albosta, Donald J.	Dem	Mich.	1	1
29th	Leath, J. Marvin	Dem	Tex.	1	1
30th	Boner, William H.	Dem	Tenn.	1	1
31st	Tauzin, W. J. (Billy)	Dem	La.	4	1

Minority

Rank	Name	Party	State	Terms in: House	Terms in: Comm.
RM	Harsha, William H. Jr.	Rep	Ohio	10	10
2nd	Cleveland, James C.	Rep	N.H.	9	9
3rd	Clausen, Don H.	Rep	Cal.	9	9
4th	Snyder, M. G. (Gene)	Rep	Ky.	8	7
5th	Hammerschmidt, John Paul	Rep	Ark.	7	7
6th	Shuster, E. G. (Bud)	Rep	Penn.	4	4
7th	Abdnor, James	Rep	S.D.	4	4
8th	Taylor, Gene	Rep	Mo.	4	4
9th	Goldwater, Barry M. Jr.	Rep	Cal.	6	3
10th	Hagedorn, Thomas M.	Rep	Minn.	3	3
11th	Stangeland, Arlan	Rep	Minn.	2	2
12th	Livingston, Robert L.	Rep	La.	2	2
13th	Gingrich, Newton L.	Rep	Ga.	1	1
14th	Clinger, William F. Jr.	Rep	Penn.	1	1
15th	Solomon, Gerald B. H.	Rep	N.Y.	1	1
16th	Lewis, Jerry	Rep	Cal.	1	1
17th	Royer, William	Rep	Cal.	1	1

Note: Marilyn Lloyd Bouquard (Dem-Tenn.) changed her name from Marilyn Lloyd during the adjournment of the 95th Congress.

Vacancies Filled:

Majority: 31st seat by Tauzin on June 18,1980.
Minority: 17th seat by Royer on Apr. 9,1979.

Changes:

Majority:

Name	Party	State	Date	Change
Hutto, Earl D.	Dem	Fla.	Mar. 19,1980	Moved to Armed Services.
Hutchinson, John G.	Dem	W.Va.	June 18,1980	Replaced Hutto.
Hefner, W. G. (Bill)	Dem	N.C.	July 2,1980	Moved to Appropriations.

Departures from the House:

	Majority			Minority		
Elected to U.S. Senate	None			Abdnor, James	S.D.	Rep
Defeated for Reelection	Hutchinson, John G.	W.Va.	Dem	Royer, William	Cal.	Rep
	Ambro, Jerome A. Jr.	N.Y.	Dem			
	Johnson, Harold T.	Cal.	Dem			
	McCormack, Mike	Wash.	Dem			
Retired	Roberts, Herbert Ray	Tex.	Dem	Cleveland, James C.	N.H.	Rep
				Harsha, William H. Jr.	Ohio	Rep

Departures from Committee:

Moved to Rules	Bonior, David E.	Mich. Dem	None		
Moved to Armed Services	Leath, J. Marvin	Tex. Dem	None		
	Tauzin, W. J. (Billy)	La. Dem	None		
Moved to Appropriations	None		Lewis, Jerry	Cal.	Rep
			Livingston, Robert L.	La.	Rep
No new assignment	None		Taylor, Gene	Mo.	Rep

PUBLIC WORKS AND TRANSPORTATION / 97th Congress

Service Dates of Committee Chair: Jan. 28,1981-Jan. 3,1983
Service Dates of Majority Members: Jan. 28,1981-Jan. 3,1983
Service Dates of Minority Members: Jan. 28,1981-Jan. 3,1983

Majority

Rank Name	Party	State	Terms in: House	Terms in: Comm.
Chr Howard, James J.	Dem	N.J.	9	9
2nd Anderson, Glenn M.	Dem	Cal.	7	7
3rd Roe, Robert A.	Dem	N.J.	7	7
4th Breaux, John B.	Dem	La.	6	6
5th Mineta, Norman Y.	Dem	Cal.	4	4
6th Levitas, Elliott H.	Dem	Ga.	4	4
7th Oberstar, James L.	Dem	Minn.	4	4
8th Nowak, Henry J.	Dem	N.Y.	4	4
9th Edgar, Robert W.	Dem	Penn.	4	4
10th Bouquard, Marilyn Lloyd	Dem	Tenn.	4	4
11th Fary, John G.	Dem	Ill.	4	4
12th Young, Robert A.	Dem	Mo.	3	3
13th Ertel, Allen E.	Dem	Penn.	3	3
14th Evans, Billy Lee	Dem	Ga.	3	3
15th Flippo, Ronnie G.	Dem	Ala.	3	3
16th Rahall, Nick Joe II	Dem	W.Va.	3	3
17th Applegate, Douglas	Dem	Ohio	3	3
18th Ferraro, Geraldine A.	Dem	N.Y.	2	2
19th Atkinson, Eugene V.	Dem	Penn.	2	2
20th Albosta, Donald J.	Dem	Mich.	2	2
21st Boner, William H.	Dem	Tenn.	2	2
22nd de Lugo, Ron	Dem	V.I.	4	1
23rd Savage, Gus	Dem	Ill.	1	1
24th Sunia, Fofo I. F.	Dem	A.Sm.	1	1
25th Roemer, Charles (Buddy)	Dem	La.	1	1
26th Donnelly, Brian J.	Dem	Mass.	2	2
27th Kogovsek, Raymond P.	Dem	Colo.	2	1

Minority

Rank Name	Party	State	Terms in: House	Terms in: Comm.
RM Clausen, Don H.	Rep	Cal.	10	10
2nd Snyder, M. G. (Gene)	Rep	Ky.	9	8
3rd Hammerschmidt, John Paul	Rep	Ark.	8	8
4th Shuster, E. G. (Bud)	Rep	Penn.	5	5
5th Goldwater, Barry M. Jr.	Rep	Cal.	7	4
6th Hagedorn, Thomas M.	Rep	Minn.	4	4
7th Stangeland, Arlan	Rep	Minn.	3	3
8th Gingrich, Newton L.	Rep	Ga.	2	2
9th Clinger, William F. Jr.	Rep	Penn.	2	2
10th Solomon, Gerald B. H.	Rep	N.Y.	2	2
11th Hollenbeck, Harold C.	Rep	N.J.	3	1
12th Deckard, H. Joel	Rep	Ind.	2	1
13th Grisham, Wayne R.	Rep	Cal.	2	1
14th Jeffries, James E.	Rep	Kans.	2	1
15th Fields, Jack	Rep	Tex.	1	1
16th Molinari, Guy V.	Rep	N.Y.	1	1
17th Shaw, E. Clay Jr.	Rep	Fla.	1	1
18th McEwen, Bob	Rep	Ohio	1	1
19th Wolf, Frank R.	Rep	Va.	1	1

Notes: Territorial Delegates Ron de Lugo (Dem-Virgin Islands) and Fofo I. F. Sunia (Dem-American Samoa) were allowed to accrue seniority but were not included in the committee's party ratio. Eugene Atkinson of Pennsylvania resigned from the Democratic Party on Oct. 14,1981, and was reappointed to the committee as a Republican. To accommodate Atkinson's switch, the party ratio was changed to 25 Democrats (excluding de Lugo and Sunia) and 20 Republicans on Feb. 24,1982. Brian J. Donnelly (Dem-Mass.) was ranked 26th according to both the House Journal and The Congressional Record.

Vacancy Filled:
Majority: 27th seat by Kogovsek on Feb. 25,1981.

Addition:
Majority: 28th Kennelly, Barbara B. Dem Conn. Feb. 24,1982 to rank above Dowdy

Changes:
Majority:

Atkinson, Eugene V.	Dem	Penn.	Oct. 14,1981	Resigned Democratic Party; lost majority assignment.
Dowdy, Wayne	Dem	Miss.	Dec. 16,1981	Replaced Atkinson.

Minority:

Atkinson, Eugene V.	Rep	Penn.	Oct. 14,1981	Rejoined committee as a Republican.

Departures from the House:	Majority			Minority		
Defeated for Reelection	None			Clausen, Don H.	Cal.	Rep
				Deckard, H. Joel	Ind.	Rep
				Hagedorn, Thomas M.	Minn.	Rep
				Hollenbeck, Harold C.	N.J.	Rep
				Atkinson, Eugene V.	Penn.	Rep
Defeated for Renomination	Evans, Billy Lee	Ga.	Dem	Grisham, Wayne R.	Cal.	Rep
	Fary, John G.	Ill.	Dem			
Lost Nomination to U.S. Senate	None			Goldwater, Barry M. Jr.	Cal.	Rep
Lost Nomination for Governor	Ertel, Allen E.	Penn.	Dem	None		
Retired	None			Jeffries, James E.	Kans.	Rep
Departures from Committee:						
Moved to Appropriations	Boner, William H.	Tenn.	Dem	None		
Moved to Banking, Finance & Urban Affairs	Roemer, Charles (Buddy)	La.	Dem	None		
Moved to Ways and Means	Kennelly, Barbara B.	Conn.	Dem	Flippo, Ronnie G.	Ala.	Dem
Moved to Energy and Commerce	Dowdy, Wayne	Miss.	Dem	Fields, Jack	Tex.	Rep
Moved to Foreign Affairs	None			Solomon, Gerald B.H.	N.Y.	Rep
No new assignment	Kogovsek, Raymond P.	Colo.	Dem	None		
	Bouquard, Marilyn Lloyd	Tenn.	Dem			

PUBLIC WORKS AND TRANSPORTATION / 98th Congress

Service Dates of Committee Chair: Jan. 6,1983-Jan. 3,1985
Service Dates of Majority Members: Jan. 6,1983-Jan. 3,1985
Service Dates of Minority Members: Jan. 6,1983-Jan. 3,1985

Majority

Rank	Name	Party	State	Terms in: House	Terms in: Comm.
Chr	Howard, James J.	Dem	N.J.	10	10
2nd	Anderson, Glenn M.	Dem	Cal.	8	8
3rd	Roe, Robert A.	Dem	N.J.	8	8
4th	Breaux, John B.	Dem	La.	7	7
5th	Mineta, Norman Y.	Dem	Cal.	5	5
6th	Levitas, Elliott H.	Dem	Ga.	5	5
7th	Oberstar, James L.	Dem	Minn.	5	5
8th	Nowak, Henry J.	Dem	N.Y.	5	5
9th	Edgar, Robert W.	Dem	Penn.	5	5
10th	Young, Robert A.	Dem	Mo.	4	4
11th	Rahall, Nick Joe II	Dem	W.Va.	4	4
12th	Applegate, Douglas	Dem	Ohio	4	4
13th	Ferraro, Geraldine A.	Dem	N.Y.	3	3
14th	Donnelly, Brian J.	Dem	Mass.	3	3
15th	Albosta, Donald J.	Dem	Mich.	3	3
16th	de Lugo, Ron	Dem	V.I.	5	2
17th	Savage, Gus	Dem	Ill.	2	2
18th	Sunia, Fofo I. F.	Dem	A.Sm.	2	2
19th	Hall, Katie	Dem	Ind.	2	1
20th	Bosco, Douglas H.	Dem	Cal.	1	1
21st	McNulty, James F. Jr.	Dem	Ariz.	1	1
22nd	Moody, Jim	Dem	Wisc.	1	1
23rd	Borski, Robert A.	Dem	Penn.	1	1
24th	Kolter, Joseph P.	Dem	Penn.	1	1
25th	Valentine, I.T. Jr. (Tim)	Dem	N.C.	1	1
26th	Towns, Edolphus	Dem	N.Y.	1	1
27th	Lipinski, William O.	Dem	Ill.	1	1
28th	Andrews, Michael A.	Dem	Tex.	1	1
29th	Vandergriff, Tom	Dem	Tex.	1	1
30th	Rowland, J. Roy	Dem	Ga.	1	1
31st	Clarke, James McClure	Dem	N.C.	1	1
32nd	Wise, Robert E. Jr.	Dem	W.Va.	1	1

Minority

Rank	Name	Party	State	Terms in: House	Terms in: Comm.
RM	Snyder, M. G. (Gene)	Rep	Ky.	10	9
2nd	Hammerschmidt, John Paul	Rep	Ark.	9	9
3rd	Shuster, E. G. (Bud)	Rep	Penn.	6	6
4th	Stangeland, Arlan	Rep	Minn.	4	4
5th	Gingrich, Newton L.	Rep	Ga.	3	3
6th	Clinger, William F. Jr.	Rep	Penn.	3	3
7th	Molinari, Guy V.	Rep	N.Y.	2	2
8th	Shaw, E. Clay Jr.	Rep	Fla.	2	2
9th	McEwen, Bob	Rep	Ohio	2	2
10th	Wolf, Frank R.	Rep	Va.	2	2
11th	Petri, Thomas E.	Rep	Wisc.	3	1
12th	Daub, Hal	Rep	Neb.	2	1
13th	Martin, Lynn M.	Rep	Ill.	2	1
14th	Weber, Vin	Rep	Minn.	2	1
15th	Smith, Robert F.	Rep	Ore.	1	1
16th	Sundquist, Don	Rep	Tenn.	1	1
17th	Johnson, Nancy L.	Rep	Conn.	1	1
18th	Packard, Ron	Rep	Cal.	1	1

Note: Territorial Delegates Ron de Lugo (Dem-Virgin Islands) and Fofo I. F. Sunia (Dem-American Samoa) were allowed to accrue seniority but were not included in the committee's party ratio.

Vacancies Filled:
Majority: 14th seat by Donnelly on Feb. 2,1983.
Minority: 13th seat by Martin on Mar. 1,1983.

Departures from the House:	**Majority**		**Minority**	
Defeated for Reelection	Albosta, Donald J.	Mich. Dem	None	
	Clarke, James McClure	N.C. Dem		
	Levitas, Elliott H.	Ga. Dem		
	McNulty, James F. Jr.	Ariz. Dem		
	Vandergriff, Tom	Tex. Dem		
Defeated for Renomination	Hall, Katie	Ind. Dem	None	
Lost Election for Vice President	Ferraro, Geraldine A.	N.Y. Dem	None	
Departures from Committee:				
Moved to Ways and Means	Donnelly, Brian J.	Mass. Dem	Daub, Hal	Neb. Rep
Moved to Armed Services	None		Martin, Lynn M.	Ill. Rep
Moved to Agriculture	None		Smith, Robert F.	Ore. Rep
Moved to Budget	None		Weber, Vin	Minn. Rep
Moved to Appropriations	None		Wolf, Frank R.	Va. Rep

PUBLIC WORKS AND TRANSPORTATION / 99th Congress

Service Dates of Committee Chair: Jan. 7,1985-Jan. 3,1987
Service Dates of Majority Members: Jan. 30,1985-Jan. 3,1987
Service Dates of Minority Members: Jan. 30,1985-Jan. 3,1987

Majority

Rank Name	Party	State	Terms in: House	Terms in: Comm.
Chr Howard, James J.	Dem	N.J.	11	11
2nd Anderson, Glenn M.	Dem	Cal.	9	9
3rd Roe, Robert A.	Dem	N.J.	9	9
4th Breaux, John B.	Dem	La.	8	8
5th Mineta, Norman Y.	Dem	Cal.	6	6
6th Oberstar, James L.	Dem	Minn.	6	6
7th Nowak, Henry J.	Dem	N.Y.	6	6
8th Edgar, Robert W.	Dem	Penn.	6	6
9th Young, Robert A.	Dem	Mo.	5	5
10th Rahall, Nick Joe II	Dem	W.Va.	5	5
11th Applegate, Douglas	Dem	Ohio	5	5
12th de Lugo, Ron	Dem	V.I.	6	3
13th Savage, Gus	Dem	Ill.	3	3
14th Sunia, Fofo I. F.	Dem	A.Sm.	3	3
15th Bosco, Douglas H.	Dem	Cal.	2	2
16th Moody, Jim	Dem	Wisc.	2	2
17th Borski, Robert A.	Dem	Penn.	2	2
18th Kolter, Joseph P.	Dem	Penn.	2	2
19th Valentine, I.T. Jr. (Tim)	Dem	N.C.	2	2
20th Towns, Edolphus	Dem	N.Y.	2	2
21st Lipinski, William O.	Dem	Ill.	2	2
22nd Andrews, Michael A.	Dem	Tex.	2	2
23rd Rowland, J. Roy	Dem	Ga.	2	2
24th Wise, Robert E. Jr.	Dem	W.Va.	2	2
25th Gray, Kenneth J.	Dem	Ill.	11	*2 1
26th Atkins, Chester G.	Dem	Mass.	1	1
27th Visclosky, Peter J.	Dem	Ind.	1	1
28th Traficant, James A. Jr.	Dem	Ohio	1	1
29th Perkins, Carl C. (Chris)	Dem	Ky.	2	*T 1

Minority

Rank Name	Party	State	Terms in: House	Terms in: Comm.
RM Snyder, M. G. (Gene)	Rep	Ky.	11	10
2nd Hammerschmidt, John Paul	Rep	Ark.	10	10
3rd Shuster, E. G. (Bud)	Rep	Penn.	7	7
4th Stangeland, Arlan	Rep	Minn.	5	5
5th Gingrich, Newton L.	Rep	Ga.	4	4
6th Clinger, William F. Jr.	Rep	Penn.	4	4
7th Molinari, Guy V.	Rep	N.Y.	3	3
8th Shaw, E. Clay Jr.	Rep	Fla.	3	3
9th McEwen, Bob	Rep	Ohio	3	3
10th Petri, Thomas E.	Rep	Wisc.	4	2
11th Sundquist, Don	Rep	Tenn.	2	2
12th Johnson, Nancy L.	Rep	Conn.	2	2
13th Packard, Ron	Rep	Cal.	2	2
14th Boehlert, Sherwood L.	Rep	N.Y.	2	1
15th DeLay, Thomas D.	Rep	Tex.	1	1
16th Callahan, H. L. (Sonny)	Rep	Ala.	1	1
17th Gallo, Dean A.	Rep	N.J.	1	1
18th Bentley, Helen Delich	Rep	Md.	1	1
19th Lightfoot, Jim Ross	Rep	Iowa	1	1

*2: Member's 2nd period of service on the committee;
*T: Temporary member of the committee.

Note: Territorial Delegates Ron de Lugo (Dem-Virgin Islands) and Fofo Sunia (Dem-American Samoa) were allowed to accrue seniority but were not included in the committee's party ratio. The committee was expanded and the party ratio changed to 28 Democrats (excluding de Lugo and Sunia) and 20 Republicans on May 2,1985. The committee was expanded again and the party ratio changed to 29 Democrats (excluding de Lugo and Sunia) and 21 Republicans on Sep. 12,1985.

Vacancy Filled:
Majority: 29th seat by Perkins for the 1st Session only on Feb. 6,1985.

Additions:

Majority:	30th	Long, Cathy	Dem	La.	May 2,1985	Ranked below Traficant.
	31st	Chapman, Jim	Dem	Tex.	Sep. 12,1985	Ranked below Long.
Minority:	20th	Monson, David S.	Rep	Utah	June 19,1985	
	21st	Rowland, John G.	Rep	Conn.	Oct. 8,1985	

Changes:

Majority:

Perkins, Carl C. (Chris)	Dem	Ky.	Dec. 30,1985	Temporary term expired on last day of 1st Session.
Perkins, Carl C. (Chris)	Dem	Ky.	Jan. 29,1986	Replaced himself.
Andrews, Michael A.	Dem	Tex.	July 29,1986	Moved to Ways and Means.
Atkins, Chester G.	Dem	Mass.	July 29,1986	Moved to Interior and Insular Affairs.
Biaggi, Mario	Dem	N.Y.	Oct. 10,1986	Replaced Andrews.

Departures from the House:	**Majority**			**Minority**		
Elected to U.S. Senate	Breaux, John B.	La.	Dem	None		
Defeated for Reelection	Young, Robert A.	Mo.	Dem	None		
Lost Election to U.S. Senate	Edgar, Robert W.	Penn.	Dem	None		
Retired	Long, Cathy	La.	Dem	Snyder, M. G. (Gene)	Ky.	Rep
				Monson, David S.	Utah	Rep
Departures from Committee:						
Moved to Ways and Means	Moody, Jim	Wisc.	Dem	None		
Moved to Science, Space & Technology	Perkins, Carl C. (Chris)	Ky.	Dem	None		
No new assignment	Biaggi, Mario	N.Y.	Dem	None		

PUBLIC WORKS AND TRANSPORTATION / 100th Congress

Service Dates of Committee Chairs: Ch1 Jan. 6,1987-Mar. 25,1988
Ch2 Apr. 20,1988-Jan. 3,1989
Service Dates of Majority Members: Jan. 6,1987-Jan. 3,1989
Service Dates of Minority Members: Jan. 6,1987-Jan. 3,1989

Majority

Rank	Name	Party	State	Terms in: House	Terms in: Comm.
Ch1	Howard, James J.	Dem	N.J.	12	12
Ch2 2nd	Anderson, Glenn M.	Dem	Cal.	10	10
3rd	Roe, Robert A.	Dem	N.J.	10	10
4th	Mineta, Norman Y.	Dem	Cal.	7	7
5th	Oberstar, James L.	DFL	Minn.	7	7
6th	Nowak, Henry J.	Dem	N.Y.	7	7
7th	Rahall, Nick Joe II	Dem	W.Va.	6	6
8th	Applegate, Douglas	Dem	Ohio	6	6
9th	de Lugo, Ron	Dem	V.I.	7	4
10th	Savage, Gus	Dem	Ill.	4	4
11th	Sunia, Fofo I. F.	Dem	A.Sm.	4	4
12th	Bosco, Douglas H.	Dem	Cal.	3	3
13th	Borski, Robert A.	Dem	Penn.	3	3
14th	Kolter, Joseph P.	Dem	Penn.	3	3
15th	Valentine, I.T. Jr. (Tim)	Dem	N.C.	3	3
16th	Towns, Edolphus	Dem	N.Y.	3	3
17th	Lipinski, William O.	Dem	Ill.	3	3
18th	Rowland, J. Roy	Dem	Ga.	3	3
19th	Wise, Robert E. Jr.	Dem	W.Va.	3	3
20th	Gray, Kenneth J.	Dem	Ill.	12	*2 2
21st	Visclosky, Peter J.	Dem	Ind.	2	2
22nd	Traficant, James A. Jr.	Dem	Ohio	2	2
23rd	Chapman, Jim	Dem	Tex.	2	2
24th	Lancaster, H. Martin	Dem	N.C.	1	1
25th	Slaughter, Louise M.	Dem	N.Y.	1	1
26th	Lewis, John	Dem	Ga.	1	1
27th	DeFazio, Peter A.	Dem	Ore.	1	1
28th	Cardin, Benjamin L.	Dem	Md.	1	1
29th	Grant, Bill	Dem	Fla.	1	1
30th	Skaggs, David E.	Dem	Colo.	1	1
31st	Hayes, James A.	Dem	La.	1	1
32nd	Perkins, Carl C. (Chris)	Dem	Ky.	3	*2 1

Minority

Rank	Name	Party	State	Terms in: House	Terms in: Comm.
RM	Hammerschmidt, John Paul	Rep	Ark.	11	11
2nd	Shuster, E. G. (Bud)	Rep	Penn.	8	8
3rd	Stangeland, Arlan	Rep	Minn.	6	6
4th	Gingrich, Newton L.	Rep	Ga.	5	5
5th	Clinger, William F. Jr.	Rep	Penn.	5	5
6th	Molinari, Guy V.	Rep	N.Y.	4	4
7th	Shaw, E. Clay Jr.	Rep	Fla.	4	4
8th	McEwen, Bob	Rep	Ohio	4	4
9th	Petri, Thomas E.	Rep	Wisc.	5	3
10th	Sundquist, Don	Rep	Tenn.	3	3
11th	Johnson, Nancy L.	Rep	Conn.	3	3
12th	Packard, Ron	Rep	Cal.	3	3
13th	Boehlert, Sherwood L.	Rep	N.Y.	3	2
14th	DeLay, Thomas D.	Rep	Tex.	2	2
15th	Callahan, H. L. (Sonny)	Rep	Ala.	2	2
16th	Gallo, Dean A.	Rep	N.J.	2	2
17th	Bentley, Helen Delich	Rep	Md.	2	2
18th	Lightfoot, Jim Ross	Rep	Iowa	2	2
19th	Rowland, John G.	Rep	Conn.	2	2
20th	Hastert, J. Dennis	Rep	Ill.	1	1

*2: Member's 2nd period of service on the committee.

Note: Territorial Delegates Ron de Lugo (Dem-Virgin Islands) and Fofo I. F. Sunia (Dem-American Samoa) were allowed to accrue seniority but were not included in the committee's party ratio.

Vacancies Filled:
Majority: 32nd seat by Perkins on Jan. 22,1987.
Minority: 20th seat by Hastert on Jan. 21,1987.

Changes:

Chair:				
Ch1 Howard, James J.	Dem	N.J.	Mar, 25,1988	Died in office.
Ch2 Anderson, Glenn M.	Dem	Cal.	Apr. 20,1988	Succeeded Howard as Chair.
Majority:				
Lancaster, H. Martin	Dem	N.C.	Mar. 2,1988	Moved to Armed Services (reported Mar. 9,1987).
Clement, Bob	Dem	Tenn.	Mar. 2,1988	Replaced Lancaster (reported Mar. 9,1987).
Howard, James J.	Dem	N.J.	Mar. 25,1988	Died in office.
Payne, Lewis F. Jr.	Dem	Va.	July 13,1988	Replaced Howard.
Sunia, Fofo I. F.	Dem	A.Sm.	Sep. 6,1988	Resigned and retired.
Gray, Kenneth J.	Dem	Ill.	Oct. 3,1988	Left committee; no new assignment.
Costello, Jerry F.	Dem	Ill.	Oct. 6,1988	Replaced Gray.
Minority:				
Rowland, John G.	Rep	Conn.	Jan. 21,1987	Moved to Armed Services.
Callahan, H. L. (Sonny)	Rep	Ala.	Jan. 21,1987	Moved to Energy and Commerce.
DeLay, Thomas D.	Rep	Tex.	Jan. 21,1987	Moved to Appropriations.
Inhofe, James M.	Rep	Okla.	Jan. 21,1987	Replaced John Rowland.
Ballenger, Cass	Rep	N.C.	Jan. 21,1987	Replaced Callahan.
Upton, Frederick S.	Rep	Mich.	Jan. 21,1987	Replaced DeLay.
Shaw, E. Clay Jr.	Rep	Fla.	July 7,1988	Moved to Ways and Means.
Emerson, Bill	Rep	Mo.	Sep. 23,1988	Replaced Shaw.

Departures from Committee:	**Majority**			**Minority**		
Moved to Appropriations	Chapman, Jim	Tex.	Dem	None		
Moved to Energy & Commerce	Rowland, J. Roy	Ga.	Dem	None		
Moved to Appropriations; Budget	None			Gallo, Dean A.	N.J.	Rep
Moved to Ways and Means	None			Johnson, Nancy L.	Conn.	Rep
				Sundquist, Don	Tenn.	Rep
Ceased active membership to serve on Budget	Wise, Robert E. Jr.	W.Va.	Dem	Bentley, Helen Delich	Md.	Rep
No new assignment	Perkins, Carl C. (Chris)	Ky.	Dem			

PUBLIC WORKS AND TRANSPORTATION / 101st Congress

Service Dates of Committee Chair: Jan. 3,1989-Jan. 3,1991
Service Dates of Majority Members: Jan. 19,1989-Jan. 3,1991
Service Dates of Minority Members: Jan. 20,1989-Jan. 3,1991

Majority

Rank Name	Party	State	Terms in: House	Terms in: Comm.
Chr Anderson, Glenn M.	Dem	Cal.	11	11
2nd Roe, Robert A.	Dem	N.J.	11	11
3rd Mineta, Norman Y.	Dem	Cal.	8	8
4th Oberstar, James L.	Dem	Minn.	8	8
5th Nowak, Henry J.	Dem	N.Y.	8	8
6th Rahall, Nick Joe II	Dem	W.Va.	7	7
7th Applegate, Douglas	Dem	Ohio	7	7
8th de Lugo, Ron	Dem	V.I.	8	5
9th Savage, Gus	Dem	Ill.	5	5
10th Bosco, Douglas H.	Dem	Cal.	4	4
11th Borski, Robert A.	Dem	Penn.	4	4
12th Kolter, Joseph P.	Dem	Penn.	4	4
13th Valentine, I.T. Jr. (Tim)	Dem	N.C.	4	4
14th Towns, Edolphus	Dem	N.Y.	4	4
15th Lipinski, William O.	Dem	Ill.	4	4
16th Visclosky, Peter J.	Dem	Ind.	3	3
17th Traficant, James A. Jr.	Dem	Ohio	3	3
18th Slaughter, Louise M.	Dem	N.Y.	2	2
19th Lewis, John	Dem	Ga.	2	2

Minority

Rank Name	Party	State	Terms in: House	Terms in: Comm.
RM Hammerschmidt, John Paul	Rep	Ark.	12	12
2nd Shuster, E. G. (Bud)	Rep	Penn.	9	9
3rd Stangeland, Arlan	Rep	Minn.	7	7
4th Gingrich, Newton L.	Rep	Ga.	6	6
5th Clinger, William F. Jr.	Rep	Penn.	6	6
6th Molinari, Guy V.	Rep	N.Y.	5	5
7th McEwen, Bob	Rep	Ohio	5	5
8th Petri, Thomas E.	Rep	Wisc.	6	4
9th Packard, Ron	Rep	Cal.	4	4
10th Boehlert, Sherwood L.	Rep	N.Y.	4	3
11th Lightfoot, Jim Ross	Rep	Iowa	3	3
12th Hastert, J. Dennis	Rep	Ill.	2	2
13th Inhofe, James M.	Rep	Okla.	2	2
14th Ballenger, Cass	Rep	N.C.	2	2
15th Upton, Frederick S.	Rep	Mich.	2	2
16th Emerson, Bill	Rep	Mo.	5	2
17th Craig, Larry E.	Rep	Ida.	5	1
18th Duncan, James Jr.	Rep	Tenn.	2	1
19th Hancock, Melton D.	Rep	Mo.	1	1

20th DeFazio, Peter A.	Dem	Ore.	2	2	20th Cox, C. Christopher	Rep	Cal.	1	1
21st Cardin, Benjamin L.	Dem	Md.	2	2					
22nd Grant, Bill	Dem	Fla.	2	2					
23rd Skaggs, David E.	Dem	Coio.	2	2					
24th Hayes, James A.	Dem	La.	2	2					
25th Clement, Bob	Dem	Tenn.	2	2					
26th Payne, Lewis F. Jr.	Dem	Tex.	2	2					
27th Costello, Jerry F.	Dem	Ill.	2	2					
28th Pallone, Frank Jr.	Dem	N.J.	2	1					
29th Jones, Ben	Dem	Ga.	1	1					
30th Parker, Mike	Dem	Miss.	1	1					
31st Laughlin, Greg H.	Dem	Tex.	1	1					

Notes: Territorial Delegate Ron de Lugo (Dem-Virgin Islands) was allowed to accrue seniority but was not included in the committee's party ratio. House Resolution 353, agreed to on Mar. 7,1990, listed the order of Republican membership on the committee, with Bill Grant (Rep-Fla.) ranked directly behind Bill Emerson (Rep-Mo.).

Changes:

Majority:

Grant, Bill	Dem	Fla.	Feb. 22,1989	Resigned Democratic Party; lost Majority assignment.
Perkins, Carl C. (Chris)	Dem	Ky.	Mar. 1,1989	Replaced Grant on temporary assignment.
Perkins, Carl C. (Chris)	Dem	Ky.	Apr. 27,1989	Left committee; temporary assignment terminated.
Browder, Glen	Dem	Ala.	Apr. 27,1989	Replaced Perkins.
Slaughter, Louise M.	Dem	N.Y.	July 25,1989	Moved to Rules.
Cardin, Benjamin L.	Dem	Md.	Oct. 16,1989	Moved to Ways and Means.
Geren, Pete	Dem	Tex.	Oct. 16,1989	Replaced Slaughter.
Towns, Edolphus	Dem	N.Y.	Nov. 8,1989	Moved to Energy and Commerce.
Browder, Glen	Dem	Ala.	Nov. 8,1989	Moved to Armed Services.
Sangmeister, George E.	Dem	Ill.	Nov. 8,1989	Replaced Cardin.
Ackerman, Gary L.	Dem	N.Y.	Feb. 27,1990	Replaced Towns.
Perkins, Carl C. (Chris)	Dem	Ky.	Feb. 27,1990	Replaced Browder.

Minority:

Gingrich, Newton L.	Rep	Ga.	Apr. 18,1989	Left committee; elected Minority Whip.
Grant, Bill	Rep	Fla.	Apr. 18,1989	Replaced Gingrich.
Molinari, Guy V.	Rep	N.Y.	Jan. 1,1990	Resigned; elected county official.
Molinari, Susan	Rep	N.Y.	Mar. 28,1990	Replaced Guy Molinari.

Departures from the House:	**Majority**			**Minority**		
Elected to U.S. Senate	None			Craig, Larry E.	Ida.	Rep
Defeated for Reelection	Bosco, Douglas H.	Cal.	Dem	Stangeland, Arlan	Minn.	Rep
				Grant, Bill	Fla.	Rep
Departures from Committee:						
Moved to Banking, Finance & Urban Affairs; Standards of Official Conduct	Ackerman, Gary L.	N.Y.	Dem	None		
Moved to Appropriations	Skaggs, David E.	Colo.	Dem	None		
Moved to Energy and Commerce	None			Hastert, J. Dennis	Ill.	Rep
Moved to Rules	None			McEwen, Bob	Ohio	Rep
No new assignment	Perkins, Carl C. (Chris)	Ky.	Dem	None		

PUBLIC WORKS AND TRANSPORTATION / 102nd Congress

Service Dates of Committee Chair: Jan. 24,1991-Jan. 3,1993
Service Dates of Majority Members: Jan. 24,1991-Jan. 3,1993
Service Dates of Minority Members: Jan. 24,1991-Jan. 3,1993

Majority

Rank	Name	Party	State	Terms in: House	Terms in: Comm.
Chr	Roe, Robert A.	Dem	N.J.	12	12
2nd	Anderson, Glenn M.	Dem	Cal.	12	12
3rd	Mineta, Norman Y.	Dem	Cal.	9	9
4th	Oberstar, James L.	Dem	Minn.	9	9
5th	Nowak, Henry J.	Dem	N.Y.	9	9
6th	Rahall, Nick Joe II	Dem	W.Va.	8	8
7th	Applegate, Douglas	Dem	Ohio	8	8
8th	de Lugo, Ron	Dem	V.I.	8	6
9th	Savage, Gus	Dem	Ill.	9	6
10th	Borski, Robert A.	Dem	Penn.	5	5
11th	Kolter, Joseph P.	Dem	Penn.	5	5
12th	Valentine, I.T. Jr. (Tim)	Dem	N.C.	5	5
13th	Lipinski, William O.	Dem	Ill.	5	5
14th	Visclosky, Peter J.	Dem	Ind.	4	4
15th	Traficant, James A. Jr.	Dem	Ohio	4	4
16th	Lewis, John	Dem	Ga.	3	3
17th	DeFazio, Peter A.	Dem	Ore.	3	3
18th	Hayes, James A.	Dem	La.	3	3
19th	Clement, Bob	Dem	Tenn.	3	3
20th	Payne, Lewis F. Jr.	Dem	Va.	3	3
21st	Costello, Jerry F.	Dem	Ill.	3	3
22nd	Pallone, Frank Jr.	Dem	N.J.	3	2
23rd	Jones, Ben	Dem	Ga.	2	2
24th	Parker, Mike	Dem	Miss.	2	2
25th	Laughlin, Greg H.	Dem	Tex.	2	2
26th	Geren, Pete	Dem	Tex.	2	2
27th	Sangmeister, George E.	Dem	Ill.	2	2
28th	Poshard, Glenn	Dem	Ill.	2	1
29th	Swett, Dick	Dem	N.H.	1	1
30th	Brewster, Bill	Dem	Okla.	1	1
31st	Cramer, Bud	Dem	Ala.	1	1
32nd	DeLauro, Rosa	Dem	Conn.	1	1
33rd	Horn, Joan Kelly	Dem	Mo.	1	1
34th	Collins, Barbara-Rose	Dem	Mich.	1	1
35th	Peterson, Pete	Dem	Fla.	1	1
36th	Norton, Eleanor Holmes	Dem	D.C.	1	1

Minority

Rank	Name	Party	State	Terms in: House	Terms in: Comm.
RM	Hammerschmidt, John Paul	Rep	Ark.	13	13
2nd	Shuster, E. G. (Bud)	Rep	Penn.	10	10
3rd	Clinger, William F. Jr.	Rep	Penn.	7	7
4th	Petri, Thomas E.	Rep	Wisc.	7	5
5th	Packard, Ron	Rep	Cal.	5	5
6th	Boehlert, Sherwood L.	Rep	N.Y.	5	4
7th	Bentley, Helen Delich	Rep	Md.	4	4
8th	Lightfoot, Jim Ross	Rep	Iowa	4	4
8th	Inhofe, James M.	Rep	Okla.	3	3
9th	Ballenger, Cass	Rep	N.C.	3	3
10th	Upton, Frederick S.	Rep	Mich.	3	3
11th	Emerson, Bill	Rep	Mo.	6	3
12th	Duncan, John J. Jr.	Rep	Tenn.	3	2
13th	Hancock, Melton D.	Rep	Mo.	2	2
14th	Cox, C. Christopher	Rep	Cal.	2	2
15th	Molinari, Susan	Rep	N.Y.	2	2
16th	Hobson, David L.	Rep	Ohio	1	1
17th	Riggs, Frank	Rep	Cal.	1	1
18th	Taylor, Charles H.	Rep	N.C.	1	1
19th	Nichols, Dick	Rep	Kans.	1	1
20th	Zeliff, William	Rep	N.H.	1	1

Notes: Territorial Delegates Ron de Lugo (Dem-Virgin Islands) and Eleanor Holmes Norton (Dem-D.C.) were allowed to accrue seniority but were not included in the committee's party ratio. Glenn M. Anderson (Dem-Cal.) was unseated as Chair of this committee by the Democratic Caucus on Dec. 5,1990 by a vote of 152-100. A second vote seated Robert A. Roe (Dem-N.J.) as Chair over Norman Y. Mineta (Dem-Cal.) by a vote of 121-107. Helen Delich Bentley (Rep-Md.), having served on the Budget Committee during the previous Congress, returned to active service on this committee with her seniority intact.

Changes:

Majority:

Name	Party	State	Date	Change
Visclosky, Peter J.	Dem	Ind.	Oct. 9,1991	Moved to Appropriations.
Blackwell, Lucien E.	Dem	Penn.	Nov. 26,1991	Replaced Visclosky.

Minority:

Name	Party	State	Date	Change
Lightfoot, Jim Ross	Rep	Iowa	Feb. 28,1991	Moved to Appropriations.
Ewing, Thomas W.	Rep	Ill.	July 11,1991	Replaced Lightfoot.
Upton, Frederick S.	Rep	Mich.	Oct. 17,1991	Left committee; no new assignment.
Gillmor, Paul E.	Rep	Ohio	Oct. 17.1991	Replaced Upton.

RULES

Jurisdiction, 1947

Established by the Legislative Reorganization Act of 1946:

[Section 121.(1)(p)]

Committee on Rules.

1. The rules, joint rules, and order of business of the House.
2. Recesses and final adjournments of Congress.

Jurisdiction, 1992

Jurisdiction contained in Rules of the House of Representatives, (as revised to July 1, 1992):

[Rule X. 1. (q)]

Committee on Rules.

(1) The rules and joint rules (other than rules or joint rules relating to the Code of Official Conduct), and order of business of the House.
(2) Recesses and final adjournments of Congress.
(3) The Committee on Rules is authorized to sit and act whether or not the House is in session.

RULES / 80th Congress

Service Dates of Committee Chair: Jan. 14,1947-Jan. 3,1949
Service Dates of Majority Members: Jan. 14,1947-Jan. 3,1949
Service Dates of Minority Members: Jan. 9,1947-Jan. 3,1949

Majority

Rank	Name	Party	State	Terms in: House	Terms in: Comm.
Chr	Allen, Leo E.	Rep	Ill.	8	5
2nd	Brown, Clarence J.	Rep	Ohio	5	3
3rd	Wadsworth, James W. Jr.	Rep	N.Y.	8	1
4th	Harness, Forest A.	Rep	Ind.	5	1
5th	Chenoweth, J. Edgar	Rep	Colo.	4	*1 1
6th	Rizley, Ross	Rep	Okla.	4	1
7th	Herter, Christian A.	Rep	Mass.	3	1
8th	Rich, Robert F.	Rep	Penn.	9	1

Minority

Rank	Name	Party	State	Terms in: House	Terms in: Comm.
RM	Sabath, Adolph J.	Dem	Ill.	21	10
2nd	Cox, Edward E.	Dem	Ga.	12	9
3rd	Smith, Howard W.	Dem	Va.	9	8
4th	Clark, J. Bayard	Dem	N.C.	10	8

*1: Member's 1st period of service on the committee.

	Majority		Minority	
Departures from the House:				
Defeated for Reelection	Chenoweth, J. Edgar	Colo. Rep	None	
	Harness, Forest A.	Ind. Rep		
Lost Election to U.S. Senate	Rizley, Ross	Okla. Rep	None	
Retired	None		Clark, J. Bayard	N.C. Dem
Departures from Committee:				
No new assignment	Rich, Robert F.	Penn. Rep	None	

RULES / 81st Congress

Service Dates of Committee Chair: Jan. 18,1949-Jan. 3,1951
Service Dates of Majority Members: Jan. 18,1949-Jan. 3,1951
Service Dates of Minority Members: Jan. 18,1949-Jan. 3,1951

Majority

Rank	Name	Party	State	Terms in: House		Terms in: Comm.
Chr	Sabath, Adolph J.	Dem	Ill.	22		11
2nd	Cox, Edward E.	Dem	Ga.	13		10
3rd	Smith, Howard W.	Dem	Va.	10		9
4th	Colmer, William M.	Dem	Miss.	9	*2	1
5th	Madden, Ray J.	Dem	Ind.	4		1
6th	Lyle, John E. Jr.	Dem	Tex.	3		1
7th	McSweeney, John	Dem	Ohio	5		1
8th	Delaney, James J.	Dem	N.Y.	2	*1	1

Minority

Rank	Name	Party	State	Terms in: House	Terms in: Comm.
RM	Allen, Leo E.	Rep	Ill.	9	6
2nd	Brown, Clarence J.	Rep	Ohio	6	4
3rd	Wadsworth, James W. Jr.	Rep	N.Y.	9	2
4th	Herter, Christian A.	Rep	Mass.	4	2

*1: Member's 1st period of service on the committee;
*2: Member's 2nd period of service on the committee.

Departures from the House:	Majority		Minority	
Appointed Chair of National Security Training Commission	None		Wadsworth, James W. Jr.	N.Y. Rep
Defeated for Reelection	McSweeney, John	Ohio Dem	None	
Departures from Committee:				
Moved to Foreign Affairs	None		Herter, Christian A.	Mass. Rep

RULES / 82nd Congress

Service Dates of Committee Chair: Jan. 3,1951-Nov. 6,1952
Service Dates of Majority Members: Jan. 3,1951-Jan. 3,1953
Service Dates of Minority Members: Jan. 4,1951-Jan. 3,1953

Majority

Rank	Name	Party	State	Terms in: House		Terms in: Comm.
Chr	Sabath, Adolph J.	Dem	Ill.	23		12
2nd	Cox, Edward E.	Dem	Ga.	14		11
3rd	Smith, Howard W.	Dem	Va.	11		10
4th	Colmer, William M.	Dem	Miss.	10	*2	2
5th	Madden, Ray J.	Dem	Ind.	5		2
6th	Lyle, John E. Jr.	Dem	Tex.	4		2
7th	Delaney, James J.	Dem	N.Y.	3	*1	2
8th	Mitchell, Hugh B.	Dem	Wash.	2		1

Minority

Rank	Name	Party	State	Terms in: House	Terms in: Comm.
RM	Allen, Leo E.	Rep	Ill.	10	7
2nd	Brown, Clarence J.	Rep	Ohio	7	5
3rd	Ellsworth, M. Harris	Rep	Ore.	5	1
4th	Latham, Henry J.	Rep	N.Y.	4	1

*1: Member's 1st period of service on the committee;
*2: Member's 2nd period of service on the committee.

Vacancy Filled:
Majority: 8th seat by Mitchell on Jan. 12,1951.

Changes:
Majority:

Sabath, Adolph J.	Dem	Ill.	Nov. 6,1952	Died in office.
Cox, Edward E.	Dem	Ga.	Dec. 24,1952	Died in office.

Departures from the House:	Majority		Minority
Lost Election for Governor	Mitchell, Hugh B.	Wash. Dem	None
Departures from Committee:			
Moved to Merchant Marine & Fisheries	Delaney, James J.	N.Y. Dem	None

RULES / 83rd Congress

Service Dates of Committee Chair: Jan. 14,1953-Jan. 3,1955
Service Dates of Majority Members: Jan. 14,1953-Jan. 3,1955
Service Dates of Minority Members: Jan. 14,1953-Jan. 3,1955

Majority

Rank	Name	Party	State	Terms in: House	Terms in: Comm.
Chr	Allen, Leo E.	Rep	Ill.	11	8
2nd	Brown, Clarence J.	Rep	Ohio	8	6
3rd	Ellsworth, M. Harris	Rep	Ore.	6	2
4th	Latham, Henry J.	Rep	N.Y.	5	2
5th	Scott, Hugh D. Jr.	Rep	Penn.	6	*1 1
6th	Nicholson, Donald W.	Rep	Mass.	4	1
7th	Chenoweth, J. Edgar	Rep	Colo.	6	*2 1
8th	Reece, B. Carroll	Rep	Tenn.	14	*1 1

Minority

Rank	Name	Party	State	Terms in: House	Terms in: Comm.
RM	Smith, Howard W.	Dem	Va.	12	11
2nd	Colmer, William M.	Dem	Miss.	11	*2 3
3rd	Madden, Ray J.	Dem	Ind.	6	3
4th	Lyle, John E. Jr.	Dem	Tex.	5	3

*1: Member's 1st period of service on the committee;
*2: Member's 2nd period of service on the committee.

	Majority		Minority	
Departures from the House:				
Retired	None		Lyle, John E. Jr.	Tex. Dem
Departures from Committee:				
Moved to Interior & Insular Affairs	Chenoweth, J. Edgar	Colo. Rep	None	
Moved to Banking and Currency	Nicholson, Donald W.	Mass. Rep	None	
Moved to Government Operations	Reece, B. Carroll	Tenn. Rep	None	
Moved to Judiciary	Scott, Hugh D. Jr.	Penn. Rep	None	

RULES / 84th Congress

Service Dates of Committee Chair: Jan. 13,1955-Jan. 3,1957
Service Dates of Majority Members: Jan. 13,1955-Jan. 3,1957
Service Dates of Minority Members: Jan. 20,1955-Jan. 3,1957

Majority

Rank	Name	Party	State	Terms in: House	Terms in: Comm.
Chr	Smith, Howard W.	Dem	Va.	13	12
2nd	Colmer, William M.	Dem	Miss.	12	*2 4
3rd	Madden, Ray J.	Dem	Ind.	7	4
4th	Delaney, James J.	Dem	N.Y.	5	*2 1
5th	Trimble, James W.	Dem	Ark.	6	1
6th	Thornberry, W. Homer	Dem	Tex.	4	1
7th	Bolling, Richard W.	Dem	Mo.	4	1
8th	O'Neill, Thomas P. Jr.	Dem	Mass.	2	1

Minority

Rank	Name	Party	State	Terms in: House	Terms in: Comm.
RM	Allen, Leo E.	Rep	Ill.	12	9
2nd	Brown, Clarence J.	Rep	Ohio	9	7
3rd	Ellsworth, M. Harris	Rep	Ore.	7	3
4th	Latham, Henry J.	Rep	N.Y.	6	3

*2: Member's 2nd period of service on the committee.

	Majority	Minority	
Departures from the House:			
Defeated for Reelection	None	Ellsworth, M. Harris	Ore. Rep

RULES / 85th Congress

Service Dates of Committee Chair: Jan. 3,1957-Jan. 3,1959
Service Dates of Majority Members: Jan. 3,1957-Jan. 3,1959
Service Dates of Minority Members: Jan. 7,1957-Jan. 3,1959

Majority

Rank	**Name**	**Party**	**State**	**Terms in: House**	**Comm.**
Chr	Smith, Howard W.	Dem	Va.	14	13
2nd	Colmer, William M.	Dem	Miss.	13	*2 5
3rd	Madden, Ray J.	Dem	Ind.	8	5
4th	Delaney, James J.	Dem	N.Y.	6	*2 2
5th	Trimble, James W.	Dem	Ark.	7	2
6th	Thornberry, W. Homer	Dem	Tex.	5	2
7th	Bolling, Richard W.	Dem	Mo.	5	2
8th	O'Neill, Thomas P. Jr.	Dem	Mass.	3	2

Minority

Rank	**Name**	**Party**	**State**	**Terms in: House**	**Comm.**
RM	Allen, Leo E.	Rep	Ill.	13	10
2nd	Brown, Clarence J.	Rep	Ohio	10	8
3rd	Latham, Henry J.	Rep	N.Y.	7	4
4th	Scott, Hugh D. Jr.	Rep	Penn.	8	*2 1

*2: Member's 2nd period of service on the committee.

Vacancy Filled:
Minority: 4th seat by Scott on Jan. 16,1957.

Changes:
Minority:

Latham, Henry J.	Rep	N.Y.	Dec. 31,1958	Resigned; elected to the State Supreme Court.

Departures from the House:	**Majority**	**Minority**		
Elected to U.S. Senate	None	Scott, Hugh D. Jr.	Penn.	Rep

RULES / 86th Congress

Service Dates of Committee Chair: Jan. 7,1959-Jan. 3,1961
Service Dates of Majority Members: Jan. 7,1959-Jan. 3,1961
Service Dates of Minority Members: Jan. 15,1959-Jan. 3,1961

Majority

Rank	**Name**	**Party**	**State**	**Terms in: House**	**Comm.**
Chr	Smith, Howard W.	Dem	Va.	15	14
2nd	Colmer, William M.	Dem	Miss.	14	*2 6
3rd	Madden, Ray J.	Dem	Ind.	9	6
4th	Delaney, James J.	Dem	N.Y.	7	*2 3
5th	Trimble, James W.	Dem	Ark.	8	3
6th	Thornberry, W. Homer	Dem	Tex.	6	3
7th	Bolling, Richard W.	Dem	Mo.	6	3
8th	O'Neill, Thomas P. Jr.	Dem	Mass.	4	3

Minority

Rank	**Name**	**Party**	**State**	**Terms in: House**	**Comm.**
RM	Allen, Leo E.	Rep	Ill.	14	11
2nd	Brown, Clarence J.	Rep	Ohio	11	9
3rd	Reece, B. Carroll	Rep	Tenn.	17	*2 1
4th	Budge, Hamer H.	Rep	Ida.	5	1

*2: Member's 2nd period of service on the committee.

Vacancies Filled:
Minority: 3rd and 4th seats by Reece and Budge respectively on Jan. 19,1959.

Departures from the House:	**Majority**	**Minority**		
Defeated for Reelection	None	Budge, Hamer H.	Ida.	Rep
Retired	None	Allen, Leo E.	Ill.	Rep

RULES / 87th Congress

Service Dates of Committee Chair: Jan. 23,1961-Jan. 3,1963
Service Dates of Majority Members: Jan. 23,1961-Jan. 3,1963
Service Dates of Minority Members: Jan. 23,1961-Jan. 3,1963

Majority

Rank	Name	Party	State	Terms in: House	Terms in: Comm.
Chr	Smith, Howard W.	Dem	Va.	16	15
2nd	Colmer, William M.	Dem	Miss.	15	*2 7
3rd	Madden, Ray J.	Dem	Ind.	10	7
4th	Delaney, James J.	Dem	N.Y.	8	*2 4
5th	Trimble, James W.	Dem	Ark.	9	4
6th	Thornberry, W. Homer	Dem	Tex.	7	4
7th	Bolling, Richard W.	Dem	Mo.	7	4
8th	O'Neill, Thomas P. Jr.	Dem	Mass.	5	4

Minority

Rank	Name	Party	State	Terms in: House	Terms in: Comm.
RM	Brown, Clarence J.	Rep	Ohio	12	10
2nd	Reece, B. Carroll	Rep	Tenn.	18	*2 2
3rd	St. George, Katharine	Rep	N.Y.	8	1
4th	Smith, H. Allen	Rep	Cal.	3	1

*2: Member's 2nd period of service on the committee.

Note: House Resolution 127, agreed to by the full House on a vote of 217-212 on Jan. 31,1961, led to a temporary change in size and party ratio on this committee to 10 Democrats and 5 Republicans.

Vacancies Filled:
Minority: 3rd and 4th seats by St. George and Smith respectively on Feb. 13,1961.

Additions:

Majority:	9th Elliott, Carl A.	Dem	Ala.	Feb. 6,1961
	10th Sisk, B. F.	Dem	Cal.	Feb. 6,1961
Minority:	5th Hoffman, Elmer J.	Rep	Ill.	Feb. 13,1961

Changes:
Minority:

Reece, B. Carroll	Rep	Tenn.	Mar. 19,1961	Died in office.
Avery, William H.	Rep	Kans.	Mar. 28,1961	Replaced Reece.

RULES / 88th Congress

Service Dates of Committee Chair: Jan. 17,1963-Jan. 3,1965
Service Dates of Majority Members: Jan. 17,1963-Jan. 3,1965
Service Dates of Minority Members: Jan. 17,1963-Jan. 3,1965

Majority

Rank	Name	Party	State	Terms in: House	Terms in: Comm.
Chr	Smith, Howard W.	Dem	Va.	17	16
2nd	Colmer, William M.	Dem	Miss.	16	*2 8
3rd	Madden, Ray J.	Dem	Ind.	11	8
4th	Delaney, James J.	Dem	N.Y.	9	*2 5
5th	Trimble, James W.	Dem	Ark.	10	5
6th	Thornberry, W. Homer	Dem	Tex.	8	5
7th	Bolling, Richard W.	Dem	Mo.	8	5
8th	O'Neill, Thomas P. Jr.	Dem	Mass.	6	5
9th	Elliott, Carl A.	Dem	Ala.	8	2
10th	Sisk, B. F.	Dem	Cal.	5	2

Minority

Rank	Name	Party	State	Terms in: House	Terms in: Comm.
RM	Brown, Clarence J.	Rep	Ohio	13	11
2nd	St. George, Katharine	Rep	N.Y.	9	2
3rd	Smith, H. Allen	Rep	Cal.	4	2
4th	Hoffman, Elmer J.	Rep	Ill.	3	2
5th	Avery, William H.	Rep	Kans.	5	2

*2: Member's 2nd period of service on the committee.

Changes:
Majority:

Thornberry, W. Homer	Dem	Tex.	Dec. 10,1963	Left committee; appointed federal judge on Dec. 20,1963.
Young, John A.	Dem	Tex.	Dec. 10,1963	Replaced Thornberry.

Minority:

Hoffman, Elmer J.	Rep	Ill.	June 16,1964	Left committee; no new assignment.
Anderson, John B.	Rep	Ill.	June 16,1964	Replaced Hoffman.
Avery, William H.	Rep	Kans.	June 24,1964	Left committee; no new assignment, elected Governor of Kansas in 1964.
Martin, David T.	Rep	Neb.	June 24,1964	Replaced Avery.

Departures from the House:

	Majority		Minority	
Defeated for Reelection	None		St. George, Katharine	N.Y. Rep
Defeated for Renomination	Elliott, Carl A.	Ala. Dem	None	

RULES / 89th Congress

Service Dates of Committee Chair: Jan. 18,1965-Jan. 3,1967
Service Dates of Majority Members: Jan. 18,1965-Jan. 3,1967
Service Dates of Minority Members: Jan. 21,1965-Jan. 3,1967

Majority

Rank	Name	Party	State	Terms in: House	Terms in: Comm.
Chr	Smith, Howard W.	Dem	Va.	18	17
2nd	Colmer, William M.	Dem	Miss.	17	*2 9
3rd	Madden, Ray J.	Dem	Ind.	12	9
4th	Delaney, James J.	Dem	N.Y.	10	*2 6
5th	Trimble, James W.	Dem	Ark.	11	6
6th	Bolling, Richard W.	Dem	Mo.	9	6
7th	O'Neill, Thomas P. Jr.	Dem	Mass.	7	6
8th	Sisk, B. F.	Dem	Cal.	6	3
9th	Young, John A.	Dem	Tex.	5	2
10th	Pepper, Claude D.	Dem	Fla.	2	1

Minority

Rank	Name	Party	State	Terms in: House	Terms in: Comm.
RM1	Brown, Clarence J.	Rep	Ohio	14	12
RM2 2nd	Smith, H. Allen	Rep	Cal.	5	3
3rd	Anderson, John B.	Rep	Ill.	3	2
4th	Martin, David T.	Rep	Neb.	3	2
5th	Quillen, James H.	Rep	Tenn.	2	1

*2: Member's 2nd period of service on the committee.

Changes:

Ranking Member:

RM1	Brown, Clarence J.	Rep	Ohio	Aug. 23,1965	Died in office.
RM2	Smith, H. Allen	Rep	Cal.	Aug. 23,1965	Succeeded Brown as Ranking Minority Member.

Minority:

Brown, Clarence J.	Rep	Ohio	Aug. 23,1965	Died in office.
Latta, Delbert L.	Rep	Ohio	Aug. 31,1965	Replaced Brown.

Departures from the House:

	Majority		Minority
Defeated for Reelection	Trimble, James W.	Ark. Dem	None
Defeated for Renomination	Smith, Howard W.	Va. Dem	None

RULES / 90th Congress

Service Dates of Committee Chair: Jan. 18,1967-Jan. 3,1969
Service Dates of Majority Members: Jan. 18,1967-Jan. 3,1969
Service Dates of Minority Members: Jan. 18,1967-Jan. 3,1969

Majority

Rank	Name	Party	State	Terms in: House	Terms in: Comm.
Chr	Colmer, William M.	Dem	Miss.	18	*2 10
2nd	Madden, Ray J.	Dem	Ind.	13	10
3rd	Delaney, James J.	Dem	N.Y.	11	*2 7
4th	Bolling, Richard W.	Dem	Mo.	10	7
5th	O'Neill, Thomas P. Jr.	Dem	Mass.	8	7
6th	Sisk, B. F.	Dem	Cal.	7	4
7th	Young, John A.	Dem	Tex.	6	3
8th	Pepper, Claude D.	Dem	Fla.	3	2
9th	Matsunaga, Spark M.	Dem	Hai.	3	1
10th	Anderson, William R.	Dem	Tenn.	2	1

Minority

Rank	Name	Party	State	Terms in: House	Terms in: Comm.
RM	Smith, H. Allen	Rep	Cal.	6	4
2nd	Anderson, John B.	Rep	Ill.	4	3
3rd	Martin, David T.	Rep	Neb.	4	3
4th	Quillen, James H.	Rep	Tenn.	3	2
5th	Latta, Delbert L.	Rep	Ohio	5	2

*2: Member's 2nd period of service on the committee.

RULES / 91st Congress

Service Dates of Committee Chair: Jan. 3,1969-Jan. 3,1971
Service Dates of Majority Members: Jan. 3,1969-Jan. 3,1971
Service Dates of Minority Members: Jan. 3,1969-Jan. 3,1971

Majority

Rank	Name	Party	State	Terms in: House	Terms in: Comm.
Chr	Colmer, William M.	Dem	Miss.	19	*2 11
2nd	Madden, Ray J.	Dem	Ind.	14	11
3rd	Delaney, James J.	Dem	N.Y.	12	*2 8
4th	Bolling, Richard W.	Dem	Mo.	11	8
5th	O'Neill, Thomas P. Jr.	Dem	Mass.	9	8
6th	Sisk, B. F.	Dem	Cal.	8	5
7th	Young, John A.	Dem	Tex.	7	4
8th	Pepper, Claude D.	Dem	Fla.	4	3
9th	Matsunaga, Spark M.	Dem	Hai.	4	2
10th	Anderson, William R.	Dem	Tenn.	3	2

Minority

Rank	Name	Party	State	Terms in: House	Terms in: Comm.
RM	Smith, H. Allen	Rep	Cal.	7	5
2nd	Anderson, John B.	Rep	Ill.	5	4
3rd	Martin, David T.	Rep	Neb.	5	4
4th	Quillen, James H.	Rep	Tenn.	4	3
5th	Latta, Delbert L.	Rep	Ohio	6	3

*2: Member's 2nd period of service on the committee.

RULES / 92nd Congress

Service Dates of Committee Chair: Feb. 4,1971-Jan. 3,1973
Service Dates of Majority Members: Feb. 4,1971-Jan. 3,1973
Service Dates of Minority Members: Feb. 4,1971-Jan. 3,1973

Majority

Rank	Name	Party	State	Terms in: House	Terms in: Comm.
Chr	Colmer, William M.	Dem	Miss.	20	*2 12
2nd	Madden, Ray J.	Dem	Ind.	15	12
3rd	Delaney, James J.	Dem	N.Y.	13	*2 9
4th	Bolling, Richard W.	Dem	Mo.	12	9
5th	O'Neill, Thomas P. Jr.	Dem	Mass.	10	9
6th	Sisk, B. F.	Dem	Cal.	9	6
7th	Young, John A.	Dem	Tex.	8	5
8th	Pepper, Claude D.	Dem	Fla.	5	4
9th	Matsunaga, Spark M.	Dem	Hai.	5	3
10th	Anderson, William R.	Dem	Tenn.	4	3

Minority

Rank	Name	Party	State	Terms in: House	Terms in: Comm.
RM	Smith, H. Allen	Rep	Cal.	8	6
2nd	Anderson, John B.	Rep	Ill.	6	5
3rd	Martin, David T.	Rep	Neb.	6	5
4th	Quillen, James H.	Rep	Tenn.	5	4
5th	Latta, Delbert L.	Rep	Ohio	7	4

*2: Member's 2nd period of service on the committee.

Departures from the House:

	Majority		Minority	
Defeated for Reelection	Anderson, William R.	Tenn. Dem	None	
Retired	Colmer, William M.	Miss. Dem	Smith, H. Allen	Cal. Rep

RULES / 93rd Congress

Service Dates of Committee Chair: Jan. 6,1973-Jan. 3,1975
Service Dates of Majority Members: Jan. 6,1973-Jan. 3,1975
Service Dates of Minority Members: Jan. 6,1973-Jan. 3,1975

Majority

Rank	Name	Party	State	Terms in: House	Terms in: Comm.
Chr	Madden, Ray J.	Dem	Ind.	16	13
2nd	Delaney, James J.	Dem	N.Y.	14	*2 10
3rd	Bolling, Richard W.	Dem	Mo.	13	10
4th	O'Neill, Thomas P. Jr.	Dem	Mass.	11	10
5th	Sisk, B. F.	Dem	Cal.	10	7
6th	Young, John A.	Dem	Tex.	9	6
7th	Pepper, Claude D.	Dem	Fla.	6	5
8th	Matsunaga, Spark M.	Dem	Hai.	6	4
9th	Murphy, Morgan F.	Dem	Ill.	2	1
10th	Long, Gillis W.	Dem	La.	2	1

Minority

Rank	Name	Party	State	Terms in: House	Terms in: Comm.
RM	Martin, David T.	Rep	Neb.	7	6
2nd	Anderson, John B.	Rep	Ill.	7	6
3rd	Quillen, James H.	Rep	Tenn.	6	5
4th	Latta, Delbert L.	Rep	Ohio	8	5
5th	Clawson, Del M.	Rep	Cal.	6	1

*2: Member's 2nd period of service on the committee.

Note: John B. Anderson (Rep-Ill.) was listed as the Ranking Minority Member of this committee on Jan. 6,1973. However, as Chairman of the Republican Caucus, Anderson was not allowed to serve in this capacity, and the order was amended as listed.

Vacancies Filled:
Majority: 9th and 10th seats by Murphy and Long respectively Jan. 24,1973.
Minority: 5th seat by Clawson on Jan. 24,1973.

Changes:

Majority:				
O'Neill, Thomas P. Jr.	Dem	Mass.	Jan. 24,1973	Left committee; elected House Majority Leader.
McSpadden, Clem Rogers	Dem	Okla.	Jan. 24,1973	Replaced O'Neill.
Minority:				
Martin, David T.	Rep	Neb.	Dec. 31,1974	Resigned and retired.

Departures from the House:	**Majority**		**Minority**
Lost Nomination for Governor	McSpadden, Clem Rogers	Okla. Dem	None

RULES / 94th Congress

Service Dates of Committee Chair: Jan. 20,1975-Jan. 3,1977
Service Dates of Majority Members: Jan. 20,1975-Jan. 3,1977
Service Dates of Minority Members: Jan. 28,1975-Jan. 3,1977

Majority

Rank	Name	Party	State	Terms in: House	Terms in: Comm.
Chr	Madden, Ray J.	Dem	Ind.	17	14
2nd	Delaney, James J.	Dem	N.Y.	15 *2	11
3rd	Bolling, Richard W.	Dem	Mo.	14	11
4th	Sisk, B. F.	Dem	Cal.	11	8
5th	Young, John A.	Dem	Tex.	10	7
6th	Pepper, Claude D.	Dem	Fla.	7	6
7th	Matsunaga, Spark M.	Dem	Hai.	7	5
8th	Murphy, Morgan F.	Dem	Ill.	3	2
9th	Long, Gillis W.	Dem	La.	3	2
10th	Moakley, John Joseph	Dem	Mass.	2	1
11th	Young, Andrew J.	Dem	Ga.	2	1

Minority

Rank	Name	Party	State	Terms in: House	Terms in: Comm.
RM	Quillen, James H.	Rep	Tenn.	7	6
2nd	Anderson, John B.	Rep	Ill.	8	7
3rd	Latta, Delbert L.	Rep	Ohio	9	6
4th	Clawson, Del M.	Rep	Cal.	7	2
5th	Lott, Trent	Rep	Miss.	2	1

*2: Member's 2nd period of service on the committee.

Note: Ranking on the committee for the following member was affected by other chamber service: John B. Anderson (Rep-Ill.), Chairman of the Republican Caucus.

Departures from the House:	**Majority**		**Minority**
Elected to U.S. Senate	Matsunaga, Spark M.	Hai. Dem	None
Defeated for Renomination	Madden, Ray J.	Ind. Dem	None
Departures from Committee:			
Unassigned in 95th; appointed Ambassador to United Nations	Young, Andrew J.	Ga. Dem	None

RULES / 95th Congress

Service Dates of Committee Chair: Jan. 19,1977-Dec. 31,1978
Service Dates of Majority Members: Jan. 19,1977-Jan. 3,1979
Service Dates of Minority Members: Jan. 19,1977-Jan. 3,1979

Majority

Rank	Name	Party	State	Terms in: House	Terms in: Comm.
Chr	Delaney, James J.	Dem	N.Y.	16	*2 12
2nd	Bolling, Richard W.	Dem	Mo.	15	12
3rd	Sisk, B. F.	Dem	Cal.	12	9
4th	Young, John A.	Dem	Tex.	11	8
5th	Pepper, Claude D.	Dem	Fla.	8	7
6th	Murphy, Morgan F.	Dem	Ill.	4	3
7th	Long, Gillis W.	Dem	La.	4	3
8th	Moakley, John Joseph	Dem	Mass.	3	2
9th	Meeds, Lloyd	Dem	Wash.	7	1
10th	Chisholm, Shirley A.	Dem	N.Y.	5	1
11th	Dodd, Christopher J.	Dem	Conn.	2	1

Minority

Rank	Name	Party	State	Terms in: House	Terms in: Comm.
RM	Quillen, James H.	Rep	Tenn.	8	7
2nd	Anderson, John B.	Rep	Ill.	9	8
3rd	Latta, Delbert L.	Rep	Ohio	10	7
4th	Clawson, Del M.	Rep	Cal.	8	3
5th	Lott, Trent	Rep	Miss.	3	2

*2: Member's 2nd period of service on the committee.

Note: Ranking on the committee for the following member was affected by other chamber service: John B. Anderson (Rep-Ill.), Chairman of the Republican Caucus.

Changes:

Majority:

Delaney, James J.	Dem	N.Y.	Dec. 31,1978	Resigned and retired.

Minority:

Clawson, Del M.	Rep	Cal.	Sep. 26,1978	Left committee; resigned Dec. 31,1978.
Bauman, Robert E.	Rep	Md.	Sep. 26,1978	Replaced Clawson.

Departures from the House:

	Majority			Minority
Defeated for Renomination	Young, John A.	Tex.	Dem	None
Retired	Meeds, Lloyd	Wash.	Dem	None
	Sisk, B. F.	Cal.	Dem	

RULES / 96th Congress

Service Dates of Committee Chair: Jan. 24,1979-Jan. 3,1981
Service Dates of Majority Members: Jan. 24,1979-Jan. 3,1981
Service Dates of Minority Members: Jan. 24,1979-Jan. 3,1981

Majority

Rank	Name	Party	State	Terms in: House	Terms in: Comm.
Chr	Bolling, Richard W.	Dem	Mo.	16	13
2nd	Pepper, Claude D.	Dem	Fla.	9	8
3rd	Murphy, Morgan F.	Dem	Ill.	5	4
4th	Long, Gillis W.	Dem	La.	5	4
5th	Moakley, John Joseph	Dem	Mass.	4	3
6th	Chisholm, Shirley A.	Dem	N.Y.	6	2
7th	Dodd, Christopher J.	Dem	Conn.	3	2
8th	Zeferetti, Leo C.	Dem	N.Y.	3	1
9th	Derrick, Butler C. Jr.	Dem	S.C.	3	1
10th	Beilenson, Anthony C.	Dem	Cal.	2	1
11th	Frost, J. Martin III	Dem	Tex.	1	1

Minority

Rank	Name	Party	State	Terms in: House	Terms in: Comm.
RM	Quillen, James H.	Rep	Tenn.	9	8
2nd	Anderson, John B.	Rep	Ill.	10	9
3rd	Latta, Delbert L.	Rep	Ohio	11	8
4th	Lott, Trent	Rep	Miss.	4	3
5th	Bauman, Robert E.	Rep	Md.	4	2

Note: Ranking on the committee for the following member was affected by other chamber service: John B. Anderson (Rep-Ill.), Chairman of the Republican Caucus.

Changes:

Minority:

Anderson, John B.	Rep	Ill.	May 8,1980	Left committee; lost election for President.
Taylor, Gene	Rep	Mo.	May 14,1980	Replaced Anderson.

Departures from the House:	Majority		Minority	
Elected to U.S. Senate	Dodd, Christopher J.	Conn. Dem	None	
Defeated for Reelection	None		Baumann, Robert E.	Md. Rep
Retired	Murphy, Morgan F.	Ill. Dem	None	

RULES / 97th Congress

Service Dates of Committee Chair: Jan. 28,1981-Jan. 3,1983
Service Dates of Majority Members: Jan. 28,1981-Jan. 3,1983
Service Dates of Minority Members: Jan. 28,1981-Jan. 3,1983

Majority

Rank Name	Party	State	Terms in: House	Terms in: Comm.
Chr Bolling, Richard W.	Dem	Mo.	17	14
2nd Pepper, Claude D.	Dem	Fla.	10	9
3rd Long, Gillis W.	Dem	La.	6	5
4th Moakley, John Joseph	Dem	Mass.	5	4
5th Chisholm, Shirley A.	Dem	N.Y.	7	3
6th Zeferetti, Leo C.	Dem	N.Y.	4	2
7th Derrick, Butler C. Jr.	Dem	S.C.	4	2
8th Beilenson, Anthony C.	Dem	Cal.	3	2
9th Frost, J. Martin III	Dem	Tex.	2	2
10th Bonior, David E.	Dem	Mich.	3	1
11th Hall, Tony P.	Dem	Ohio	2	1

Minority

Rank Name	Party	State	Terms in: House	Terms in: Comm.
RM Quillen, James H.	Rep	Tenn.	10	9
2nd Latta, Delbert L.	Rep	Ohio	12	9
3rd Lott, Trent	Rep	Miss.	5	4
4th Taylor, Gene	Rep	Mo.	5	2
5th Rhodes, John J.	Rep	Ariz.	13	1

Departures from the House:	Majority		Minority	
Defeated for Reelection	Zeferetti, Leo C.	N.Y. Dem	None	
Retired	Bolling, Richard W.	Mo. Dem	Rhodes, John J.	Ariz. Rep
	Chisholm, Shirley A.	N.Y. Dem		

RULES / 98th Congress

Service Dates of Committee Chair: Jan. 6,1983-Jan. 3,1985
Service Dates of Majority Members: Jan. 6,1983-Jan. 3,1985
Service Dates of Minority Members: Jan. 6,1983-Jan. 3,1985

Majority

Rank Name	Party	State	Terms in: House	Terms in: Comm.
Chr Pepper, Claude D.	Dem	Fla.	11	10
2nd Long, Gillis W.	Dem	La.	7	6
3rd Moakley, John Joseph	Dem	Mass.	6	5
4th Derrick, Butler C. Jr.	Dem	S.C.	5	3
5th Beilenson, Anthony C.	Dem	Cal.	4	3
6th Frost, J. Martin III	Dem	Tex.	3	3
7th Bonior, David E.	Dem	Mich.	4	2
8th Hall, Tony P.	Dem	Ohio	3	2
9th Wheat, Alan	Dem	Mo.	1	1

Minority

Rank Name	Party	State	Terms in: House	Terms in: Comm.
RM Quillen, James H.	Rep	Tenn.	11	10
2nd Latta, Delbert L.	Rep	Ohio	13	10
3rd Lott, Trent	Rep	Miss.	6	5
4th Taylor, Gene	Rep	Mo.	6	3

Departures from Committee:	Majority		Minority
Unassigned in 99th; died in office Jan. 20,1985	Long, Gillis W.	La. Dem	None

RULES / 99th Congress

Service Dates of Committee Chair: Jan. 7,1985-Jan. 3,1987
Service Dates of Majority Members: Jan. 30,1985-Jan. 3,1987
Service Dates of Minority Members: Jan. 30,1985-Jan. 3,1987

Majority

Rank	Name	Party	State	Terms in: House	Terms in: Comm.
Chr	Pepper, Claude D.	Dem	Fla.	12	11
2nd	Moakley, John Joseph	Dem	Mass.	7	6
3rd	Derrick, Butler C. Jr.	Dem	S.C.	6	4
4th	Beilenson, Anthony C.	Dem	Cal.	5	4
5th	Frost, J. Martin III	Dem	Tex.	4	4
6th	Bonior, David E.	Dem	Mich.	5	3
7th	Hall, Tony P.	Dem	Ohio	4	3
8th	Wheat, Alan	Dem	Mo.	2	2
9th	Burton, Sala	Dem	Cal.	2	1

Minority

Rank	Name	Party	State	Terms in: House	Terms in: Comm.
RM	Quillen, James H.	Rep	Tenn.	12	11
2nd	Latta, Delbert L.	Rep	Ohio	14	11
3rd	Lott, Trent	Rep	Miss.	7	6
4th	Taylor, Gene	Rep	Mo.	7	4

RULES / 100th Congress

Service Dates of Committee Chair: Jan. 6,1987-Jan. 3,1989
Service Dates of Majority Members: Jan. 6,1987-Jan. 3,1989
Service Dates of Minority Members: Jan. 6,1987-Jan. 3,1989

Majority

Rank	Name	Party	State	Terms in: House	Terms in: Comm.
Chr	Pepper, Claude D.	Dem	Fla.	13	12
2nd	Moakley, John Joseph	Dem	Mass.	8	7
3rd	Derrick, Butler C. Jr.	Dem	S.C.	7	5
4th	Beilenson, Anthony C.	Dem	Cal.	6	5
5th	Frost, J. Martin III	Dem	Tex.	5	5
6th	Bonior, David E.	Dem	Mich.	6	4
7th	Hall, Tony P.	Dem	Ohio	5	4
8th	Wheat, Alan	Dem	Mo.	3	3
9th	Burton, Sala	Dem	Cal.	3	2

Minority

Rank	Name	Party	State	Terms in: House	Terms in: Comm.
RM	Quillen, James H.	Rep	Tenn.	13	12
2nd	Latta, Delbert L.	Rep	Ohio	15	12
3rd	Lott, Trent	Rep	Miss.	8	7
4th	Taylor, Gene	Rep	Mo.	8	5

Changes:

Majority:

Name	Party	State	Date	Note
Burton, Sala	Dem	Cal.	Feb. 1,1987	Died in office.
Gordon, Bart	Dem	Tenn.	Feb. 19,1987	Replaced Burton.

Departures from the House:

	Majority	Minority	State	Party
Elected to U.S. Senate	None	Lott, Trent	Miss.	Rep
Retired	None	Latta, Delbert L.	Ohio	Rep
		Taylor, Gene	Mo.	Rep

RULES / 101st Congress

Service Dates of Committee Chairs: Ch1 Jan. 3,1989-May 30,1989
Ch2 June 7,1989-Jan. 3,1991
Service Dates of Majority Members: Jan. 3,1989-Jan. 3,1991
Service Dates of Minority Members: Jan. 20,1989-Jan. 3,1991

Majority

Rank Name	Party	State	Terms in: House	Terms in: Comm.
Ch1 Pepper, Claude D.	Dem	Fla.	14	13
Ch2 2nd Moakley, John Joseph	Dem	Mass.	9	8
3rd Derrick, Butler C. Jr.	Dem	S.C.	8	6
4th Beilenson, Anthony C.	Dem	Cal.	7	6
5th Frost, J. Martin III	Dem	Tex.	6	6
6th Bonior, David E.	Dem	Mich.	7	5
7th Hall, Tony P.	Dem	Ohio	6	5
8th Wheat, Alan	Dem	Mo.	4	4
9th Gordon, Bart	Dem	Tenn.	3	2

Minority

Rank Name	Party	State	Terms in: House	Terms in: Comm.
RM Quillen, James H.	Rep	Tenn.	14	13
2nd Solomon, Gerald B. H.	Rep	N.Y.	6	1
3rd Martin, Lynn M.	Rep	Ill.	5	1
4th Pashayan, Charles S. Jr.	Rep	Cal.	6	1

Changes:

Chair:

Ch1 Pepper, Claude D.	Dem	Fla.	May 30,1989	Died in office.
Ch2 Moakley, John Joseph	Dem	Mass.	June 7,1989	Succeeded Pepper as Chair.

Majority:

Pepper, Claude D.	Dem	Fla.	May 30,1989	Died in office.
Slaughter, Louise M.	Dem	N.Y.	June 14,1989	Replaced Pepper.

Departures from the House:

	Majority	Minority	State	Party
Defeated for Reelection	None	Pashayan, Charles S. Jr.	Cal.	Rep
Lost Election to U.S. Senate	None	Martin, Lynn M.	Ill.	Rep

RULES / 102nd Congress

Service Dates of Committee Chair: Jan. 3,1991-Jan. 3,1993
Service Dates of Majority Members: Jan. 3,1991-Jan. 3,1993
Service Dates of Minority Members: Jan. 3,1991-Jan. 3,1993

Majority

Rank Name	Party	State	Terms in: House	Terms in: Comm.
Chr Moakley, John Joseph	Dem	Mass.	10	9
2nd Derrick, Butler C. Jr.	Dem	S.C.	9	7
3rd Beilenson, Anthony C.	Dem	Cal.	8	7
4th Frost, J. Martin III	Dem	Tex.	7	7
5th Bonior, David E.	Dem	Mich.	8	6
6th Hall, Tony P.	Dem	Ohio	7	6
7th Wheat, Alan	Dem	Mo.	5	5
8th Gordon, Bart	Dem	Tenn.	4	3
9th Slaughter, Louise M.	Dem	N.Y.	3	2

Minority

Rank Name	Party	State	Terms in: House	Terms in: Comm.
RM Solomon, Gerald B. H.	Rep	N.Y.	7	2
2nd Quillen, James H.	Rep	Tenn.	15	14
3rd Dreier, David	Rep	Cal.	6	1
4th McEwen, Bob	Rep	Ohio	6	1

Note: James H. Quillen (Rep-Tenn.) waived his seniority on this committee at the December 1990 Republican Conference and was designated Republican Chair Emeritus.

SCIENCE, SPACE, AND TECHNOLOGY

SCIENCE AND ASTRONAUTICS

Jurisdiction, 1958

Established by House Resolution 580 as amended, 85th Congress, Second Session, July 21, 1958 for the House Committee on Science and Astronautics:

[Paragraph 3.17]

Committee on Science and Astronautics.

(a) Astronautical research and development, including resources, personnel, equipment, and facilities.
(b) Bureau of Standards, standardization of weights and measures, and the metric system.
(c) National Aeronautics and Space Administration.
(d) National Aeronautics and Space Council.
(e) National Science Foundation.
(f) Outer space, including exploration and control thereof.
(g) Science Scholarships.
(h) Scientific research and development.

SCIENCE AND TECHNOLOGY

Renamed the Committee on Science and Technology on January 3, 1975.

SCIENCE, SPACE, AND TECHNOLOGY

Renamed the Committee on Science, Space, and Technology on January 6, 1987.

Jurisdiction, 1992

Jurisdiction contained in Rules of the House of Representatives, (as revised to July 1, 1992):

[Rule X. 1. (r)]

Committee on Science, Space, and Technology.

(1) Astronautical research and development, including resources, personnel, equipment, and facilities.
(2) Bureau of Standards, standardization of weights and measures and the metric system.
(3) National Aeronautics and Space Administration.
(4) National Aeronautics and Space Council.
(5) National Science Foundation.
(6) Outer space, including exploration and control thereof.
(7) Science Scholarships.
(8) Scientific research and development, and demonstration, and projects therefor, and all federally owned or operated nonmilitary energy laboratories.
(9) Civil aviation research and development.
(10) Environmental research and development.
(11) All energy research, development, and demonstration, and projects, therefor, and all federally-owned or operated nonmilitary energy laboratories.
(12) National Weather Service.

In addition to its legislative jurisdiction under the preceding provisions of this paragraph (and its general oversight function under clause 2(b)(1)), the committee shall have the special oversight function provided for in clause 3(f) with respect to all nonmilitary research and development.

[Rule X. 3. (f)]

(f) The Committee on Science, Space, and Technology shall have the function of reviewing and studying, on a continuing basis, all laws, programs, and Government activities dealing with or involving nonmilitary research and development.

SCIENCE AND ASTRONAUTICS / 86th Congress

* Approved as a standing committee on July 21,1958; began service as a standing committee on Jan. 3,1959.

Service Dates of Committee Chair: Jan. 19,1959-Jan. 3,1961
Service Dates of Majority Members: Jan. 19,1959-Jan. 3,1961
Service Dates of Minority Members: Jan. 19,1959-Jan. 3,1961

Majority

Rank Name	Party	State	Terms in: House	Terms in: Comm.
Chr Brooks, Overton	Dem	La.	12	2
2nd McCormack, John W.	Dem	Mass.	17	*1 2
3rd Miller, George P.	Dem	Cal.	8	1
4th Teague, Olin E.	Dem	Tex.	8	1
5th Anfuso, Victor L.	Dem	N.Y.	4	1
6th Sisk, B. F.	Dem	Cal.	3	2
7th Mitchell, Harlan Erwin	Dem	Ga.	2	1
8th Quigley, James M.	Dem	Penn.	2	1
9th Hall, David M.	Dem	N.C.	1	1
10th Wolf, Leonard G.	Dem	Iowa	1	1
11th Karth, Joseph E.	DFL	Minn.	1	1
12th Hechler, Kenneth	Dem	W.Va.	1	1
13th Daddario, Emilio Q.	Dem	Conn.	1	1
14th Moeller, Walter H.	Dem	Ohio	1	*1 1
15th King, David S.	Dem	Utah	1	1
16th Roush, J. Edward	Dem	Ind.	1	1

Minority

Rank Name	Party	State	Terms in: House	Terms in: Comm.
RM Martin, Joseph W. Jr.	Rep	Mass.	18	2
2nd Fulton, James G.	Rep	Penn.	8	2
3rd McDonough, Gordon L.	Rep	Cal.	8	2
4th Chenoweth, J. Edgar	Rep	Colo.	9	1
5th Osmers, Frank C. Jr.	Rep	N.J.	7	1
6th Van Pelt, William K.	Rep	Wisc.	5	1
7th Baumhart, Albert D. Jr.	Rep	Ohio	4	1
8th Bass, Perkins	Rep	N.H.	3	1
9th Riehlman, R. Walter	Rep	N.Y.	7	1

*1: Member's 1st period of service on the committee.

Note: "Terms in committee" for Overton Brooks (Dem-La.), John W. McCormack (Dem-Mass.), B. F. Sisk (Dem-Cal.), Joseph W. Martin, Jr. (Rep-Mass.), James G. Fulton (Rep-Penn.) and Gordon L. McDonough (Rep-Cal.) include their previous service on the House Select Committee on Astronautics and Space Exploration.

Vacancy Filled:
Minority: 9th seat by Riehlman on Jan. 29,1959.

Changes:
Majority:

Hall, David M.	Dem	N.C.	Jan. 29,1960	Died in office.
Morris, Thomas G.	Dem	N.M.	Feb. 10,1960	Replaced Hall.

Departures from the House:	Majority			Minority		
Elected State Senator	Mitchell, Harlan Erwin	Ga.	Dem	None		
Defeated for Reelection	Quigley, James M.	Penn.	Dem	None		
	Wolf, Leonard G.	Iowa	Dem			
Retired	None			Baumhart, Albert D. Jr.	Ohio	Rep
Departures from Committee:						
Moved to Rules	Sisk, B. F.	Cal.	Dem			
Moved to Merchant Marine & Fisheries	None			McDonough, Gordon L.	Cal.	Rep
No new assignment	McCormack, John W.	Mass.	Dem	Osmers, Frank C. Jr.	N.J.	Rep

SCIENCE AND ASTRONAUTICS / 87th Congress

Service Dates of Committee Chairs: Ch1 Feb. 6,1961-Sep. 16,1961
Ch2 Sep. 21,1961-Jan. 3,1963
Service Dates of Majority Members: Feb. 6,1961-Jan. 3,1963
Service Dates of Minority Members: Feb. 13,1961-Jan. 3,1963

Majority

Rank Name	Party	State	Terms in: House	Terms in: Comm.
Ch1 Brooks, Overton	Dem	La.	13	3
Ch2 2nd Miller, George P.	Dem	Cal.	9	2
3rd Teague, Olin E.	Dem	Tex.	9	2
4th Anfuso, Victor L.	Dem	N.Y.	5	2
5th Karth, Joseph E.	DFL	Minn.	2	2
6th Hechler, Kenneth	Dem	W.Va.	2	2
7th Daddario, Emilio Q.	Dem	Conn.	2	2
8th Moeller, Walter H.	Dem	Ohio	2 *1	2
9th King, David S.	Dem	Utah	2	2
10th Roush, J. Edward	Dem	Ind.	2	2
11th Morris, Thomas G.	Dem	N.M.	2	2
12th Casey, Robert R.	Dem	Tex.	2	1
13th Randall, William J.	Dem	Mo.	2	1
14th Davis, John W.	Dem	Ga.	1	1
15th Ryan, William Fitts	Dem	N.Y.	1	1
16th Corman, James C.	Dem	Cal.	1	1

Minority

Rank Name	Party	State	Terms in: House	Terms in: Comm.
RM Martin, Joseph W. Jr.	Rep	Mass.	19	3
2nd Fulton, James G.	Rep	Penn.	9	3
3rd Chenoweth, J. Edgar	Rep	Colo.	10	2
4th Van Pelt, William K.	Rep	Wisc.	6	2
5th Bass, Perkins	Rep	N.H.	4	2
6th Riehlman, R. Walter	Rep	N.Y.	8	2
7th Weis, Jessica McC.	Rep	N.Y.	2	1
8th Mosher, Charles A.	Rep	Ohio	1	1
9th Roudebush, Richard L.	Rep	Ind.	1	1
10th Bell, Alphonzo Jr.	Rep	Cal.	1	1

*1: Member's 1st period of service on the committee.

Notes: "Terms in committee" for Overton Brooks (Dem-La.), Joseph W. Martin, Jr. (Rep-Mass.), and James G. Fulton (Rep-Penn.) include their previous service on the House Select Committee on Astronautics and Space Exploration. House Resolution 355, agreed to on June 21,1961, led to a change in size and party ratio on this committee to 17 Democrats and 10 Republicans. J. Edward Roush (Dem-Ind.) took his seat in the 10th rank on June 29,1961 after an election challenge to him was rejected. House Resolution 643, agreed to on May 17,1962, led to another change in size and party ratio to 18 Democrats and 11 Republicans.

Additions:

	Rank	Name	Party	State	Date
Majority:	17th	McCormack, John W.	Dem	Mass.	May 15,1961
	18th	Riley, Corinne B.	Dem	S.C.	May 17,1962
Minority:	11th	Pelly, Thomas M.	Rep	Wash.	Sep. 7,1961

Changes:

	Name	Party	State	Date	Change
Chair:					
Ch1	Brooks, Overton	Dem	La.	Sep. 16,1961	Died in office.
Ch2	Miller, George P.	Dem	Cal.	Sep. 21,1961	Succeeded Brooks as Chair.
Majority:					
	Brooks, Overton	Dem	La.	Sep. 16,1961	Died in office.
	McCormack, John W.	Dem	Mass.	Jan. 10,1962	Left committee; elected Speaker of the House.
	Downing, Thomas N.	Dem	Va.	Jan. 18,1962	Replaced Brooks.
	Waggonner, Joe D. Jr.	Dem	La.	Jan. 18,1962	Replaced McCormack.

	Majority			Minority		
Departures from the House:						
Elected State Supreme Court Judge	Anfuso, Victor L.	N.Y.	Dem	None		
Defeated for Reelection	Moeller, Walter H.	Ohio	Dem	None		
Lost Election to U.S. Senate	King, David S.	Utah	Dem	Bass, Perkins	N.H.	Rep
Retired	Riley, Corinne B.	S.C.	Dem	Weis, Jessica McC.	N.Y.	Rep
Departures from Committee:						
Moved to Judiciary	Corman, James C.	Cal.	Dem	None		

SCIENCE AND ASTRONAUTICS / 88th Congress

Service Dates of Committee Chair: Jan. 17,1963-Jan. 3,1965
Service Dates of Majority Members: Jan. 17,1963-Jan. 3,1965
Service Dates of Minority Members: Jan. 24,1963-Jan. 3,1965

Majority

Rank	Name	Party	State	Terms in: House	Terms in: Comm.
Chr	Miller, George P.	Dem	Cal.	10	3
2nd	Teague, Olin E.	Dem	Tex.	10	3
3rd	Karth, Joseph E.	DFL	Minn.	3	3
4th	Hechler, Kenneth	Dem	W.Va.	3	3
5th	Daddario, Emilio Q.	Dem	Conn.	3	3
6th	Roush, J. Edward	Dem	Ind.	3	3
7th	Morris, Thomas G.	Dem	N.M.	3	3
8th	Casey, Robert R.	Dem	Tex.	3	2
9th	Randall, William J.	Dem	Mo.	3	2
10th	Davis, John W.	Dem	Ga.	2	2
11th	Ryan, William Fitts	Dem	N.Y.	2	2
12th	Downing, Thomas N.	Dem	Va.	3	2
13th	Waggonner, Joe D. Jr.	Dem	La.	2	2
14th	Patten, Edward J.	Dem	N.J.	1	1
15th	Fulton, Richard H.	Dem	Tenn.	1	1
16th	Fuqua, Don	Dem	Fla.	1	1
17th	Staebler, Neil	Dem	Mich.	1	1
18th	Albert, Carl	Dem	Okla.	9	1

Minority

Rank	Name	Party	State	Terms in: House	Terms in: Comm.
RM	Martin, Joseph W. Jr.	Rep	Mass.	20	4
2nd	Fulton, James G.	Rep	Penn.	10	4
3rd	Chenoweth, J. Edgar	Rep	Colo.	11	3
4th	Van Pelt, William K.	Rep	Wisc.	7	3
5th	Riehlman, R. Walter	Rep	N.Y.	9	3
6th	Mosher, Charles A.	Rep	Ohio	2	2
7th	Roudebush, Richard L.	Rep	Ind.	2	2
8th	Bell, Alphonzo	Rep	Cal.	2	2
9th	Pelly, Thomas M.	Rep	Wash.	6	2
10th	Rumsfeld, Donald	Rep	Ill.	1	1
11th	Weaver, James D.	Rep	Penn.	1	1
12th	Gurney, Edward J.	Rep	Fla.	1	1
13th	Wydler, John W.	Rep	N.Y.	1	1

Note: "Terms in committee" for Joseph W. Martin, Jr. (Rep-Mass.), and James G. Fulton (Rep-Penn.) include their previous service on the House Select Committee on Astronautics and Space Exploration.

	Majority			Minority		
Departures from the House:						
Defeated for Reelection	None			Chenoweth, J. Edgar	Colo.	Rep
				Riehlman, R. Walter	N.Y.	Rep
				Van Pelt, William K.	Wisc.	Rep
				Weaver, James D.	Penn.	Rep
Lost Election for Governor	Staebler, Neil	Mich.	Dem	None		
Departures from Committee:						
Moved to Ways and Means	Fulton, Richard H.	Tenn.	Dem	None		
Moved to Appropriations	Morris, Thomas G.	N.M.	Dem	None		
	Patten, Edward J.	N.J.	Dem	None		
Moved to Armed Services	Randall, William J.	Mo.	Dem	None		

SCIENCE AND ASTRONAUTICS / 89th Congress

Service Dates of Committee Chair: Jan. 18,1965-Jan. 3,1967
Service Dates of Majority Members: Jan. 18,1965-Jan. 3,1967
Service Dates of Minority Members: Jan. 21,1965-Jan. 3,1967

Majority

Rank	Name	Party	State	Terms in: House	Terms in: Comm.
Chr	Miller, George P.	Dem	Cal.	11	4
2nd	Teague, Olin E.	Dem	Tex.	11	4
3rd	Karth, Joseph E.	DFL	Minn.	4	4
4th	Hechler, Kenneth	Dem	W.Va.	4	4
5th	Daddario, Emilio Q.	Dem	Conn.	4	4
6th	Roush, J. Edward	Dem	Ind.	4	4
7th	Casey, Robert R.	Dem	Tex.	4	3
8th	Davis, John W.	Dem	Ga.	3	3
9th	Ryan, William Fitts	Dem	N.Y.	3	3
10th	Downing, Thomas N.	Dem	Va.	4	3
11th	Waggonner, Joe D. Jr.	Dem	La.	3	3
12th	Fuqua, Don	Dem	Fla.	2	2

Minority

Rank	Name	Party	State	Terms in: House	Terms in: Comm.
RM	Martin, Joseph W. Jr.	Rep	Mass.	21	5
2nd	Fulton, James G.	Rep	Penn.	11	5
3rd	Mosher, Charles A.	Rep	Ohio	3	3
4th	Roudebush, Richard L.	Rep	Ind.	3	3
5th	Bell, Alphonzo	Rep	Cal.	3	3
6th	Pelly, Thomas M.	Rep	Wash.	7	3
7th	Rumsfeld, Donald	Rep	Ill.	2	2
8th	Gurney, Edward J.	Rep	Fla.	2	2
9th	Wydler, John W.	Rep	N.Y.	2	2
10th	Conable, Barber B. Jr.	Rep	N.Y.	1	1

13th Albert, Carl	Dem	Okla.	10	2	
14th Taylor, Roy A.	Dem	N.C.	4	*1 1	
15th Brown, George E. Jr.	Dem	Cal.	2	*1 1	
16th Moeller, Walter H.	Dem	Ohio	3	*2 1	
17th Anderson, William R.	Dem	Tenn.	1	1	
18th Adams, Brock	Dem	Wash.	1	1	
19th Wolff, Lester L.	Dem	N.Y.	1	1	
20th Vivian, Weston E.	Dem	Mich.	1	1	*1: Member's 1st period of service on the committee;
21st Schisler, D. Gale	Dem	Ill.	1	1	*2: Member`s 2nd period of service on the committee.

Note: "Terms in committee" for Joseph W. Martin, Jr. (Rep-Mass.), and James G. Fulton (Rep-Penn.) include their previous service on the House Select Committee on Astronautics and Space Exploration.

Changes:

Majority:

Casey, Robert R.	Dem	Tex.	Mar. 8,1966	Moved to Appropriations.
Adams, Brock	Dem	Wash.	Mar. 8,1966	Moved to Interstate and Foreign Commerce.
Green, William J. III	Dem	Penn.	Mar. 8,1966	Replaced Casey.
Cabell, Earle	Dem	Tex.	Mar. 8,1966	Replaced Adams.
Anderson, William R.	Dem	Tenn.	Oct. 21,1966	Moved to Interstate and Foreign Commerce.

Departures from the House:	**Majority**			**Minority**		
Defeated for Reelection	Moeller, Walter H.	Ohio	Dem	None		
	Schisler, D. Gale	Ill.	Dem			
	Vivian, Weston E.	Mich.	Dem			
Defeated for Renomination	None			Martin, Joseph W. Jr.	Mass.	Rep
Departures from Committee:						
Moved to Ways and Means	None			Conable, Barber B. Jr.	N.Y.	Rep
No new assignment	Taylor, Roy A.	N.C.	Dem	None		

SCIENCE AND ASTRONAUTICS / 90th Congress

Service Dates of Committee Chair: Jan. 23,1967-Jan. 3,1969
Service Dates of Majority Members: Jan. 23,1967-Jan. 3,1969
Service Dates of Minority Members: Jan. 26,1967-Jan. 3,1969

Majority

Rank Name	Party	State	Terms in: House	Terms in: Comm.
Chr Miller, George P.	Dem	Cal.	12	5
2nd Teague, Olin E.	Dem	Tex.	12	5
3rd Karth, Joseph E.	DFL	Minn.	5	5
4th Hechler, Kenneth	Dem	W.Va.	5	5
5th Daddario, Emilio Q.	Dem	Conn.	5	5
6th Roush, J. Edward	Dem	Ind.	5	5
7th Davis, John W.	Dem	Ga.	4	4
8th Ryan, William Fitts	Dem	N.Y.	4	4
9th Downing, Thomas N.	Dem	Va.	5	4
10th Waggonner, Joe D. Jr.	Dem	La.	4	4
11th Fuqua, Don	Dem	Fla.	3	3
12th Albert, Carl	Dem	Okla.	11	3
13th Brown, George E. Jr.	Dem	Cal.	3	*1 2
14th Wolff, Lester L.	Dem	N.Y.	2	2
15th Green, William J. III	Dem	Penn.	3	2
16th Cabell, Earle	Dem	Tex.	2	2
17th Brinkley, Jack T.	Dem	Ga.	1	1
18th Eckhardt, Robert C.	Dem	Tex.	1	1

Minority

Rank Name	Party	State	Terms in: House	Terms in: Comm.
RM Fulton, James G.	Rep	Penn.	12	6
2nd Mosher, Charles A.	Rep	Ohio	4	4
3rd Roudebush, Richard L.	Rep	Ind.	4	4
4th Bell, Alphonzo	Rep	Cal.	4	4
5th Pelly, Thomas M.	Rep	Wash.	8	4
6th Rumsfeld, Donald	Rep	Ill.	3	3
7th Gurney, Edward J.	Rep	Fla.	3	3
8th Wydler, John W.	Rep	N.Y.	3	3
9th Vander Jagt, Guy A.	Rep	Mich.	2	1
10th Winn, Larry Jr.	Rep	Kans.	1	1
11th Pettis, Jerry L.	Rep	Cal.	1	1
12th Lukens, Donald E. (Buz)	Rep	Ohio	1	1
13th Hunt, John E.	Rep	N.J.	1	1

*1: Member's 1st period of service on the committee;
*2: Member`s 2nd period of service on the committee.

Note: "Terms in committee" for James G. Fulton (Rep-Penn.) include his previous service on the House Select Committee on Astronautics and Space Exploration.

Changes:

Majority:

Albert, Carl	Dem	Okla.	Mar. 16,1967	Moved to Education and Labor.
Tiernan, Robert O.	Dem	R.I.	May 25,1967	Replaced Albert.
Wolff, Lester L.	Dem	N.Y.	Apr. 3,1968	Moved to Banking and Currency.
Podell, Bertram L.	Dem	N.Y.	Apr. 3,1968	Replaced Wolff.
Green, William J. III	Dem	Penn.	Aug. 1,1968	Moved to Ways and Means.
Ryan, William Fitts	Dem	N.Y.	Oct. 10,1968	Moved to Judiciary.

Departures from the House:	Majority			Minority		
Elected to U.S. Senate	None			Gurney, Edward J.	Fla.	Rep
Defeated for Reelection	Roush, J. Edward	Ind.	Dem	None		
Departures from Committee:						
Moved to Armed Services	Brinkley, Jack T.	Ga.	Dem	Hunt, John E.	N.J.	Rep
Moved to Interstate & Foreign Commerce	Eckhardt, Robert C.	Tex.	Dem	None		
	Tiernan, Robert O.	R.I.	Dem			

SCIENCE AND ASTRONAUTICS / 91st Congress

Service Dates of Committee Chair: Jan. 29,1969-Jan. 3,1971
Service Dates of Majority Members: Jan. 29,1969-Jan. 3,1971
Service Dates of Minority Members: Jan. 29,1969-Jan. 3,1971

Majority

Rank	Name	Party	State	Terms in: House	Terms in: Comm.
Chr	Miller, George P.	Dem	Cal.	13	6
2nd	Teague, Olin E.	Dem	Tex.	13	6
3rd	Karth, Joseph E.	DFL	Minn.	6	6
4th	Hechler, Kenneth	Dem	W.Va.	6	6
5th	Daddario, Emilio Q.	Dem	Conn.	6	6
6th	Davis, John W.	Dem	Ga.	5	5
7th	Downing, Thomas N.	Dem	Va.	6	5
8th	Waggonner, Joe D. Jr.	Dem	La.	5	5
9th	Fuqua, Don	Dem	Fla.	4	4
10th	Brown, George E. Jr.	Dem	Cal.	4	*1 3
11th	Cabell, Earle	Dem	Tex.	3	3
12th	Podell, Bertram L.	Dem	N.Y.	2	2
13th	Aspinall, Wayne N.	Dem	Colo.	11	1
14th	Taylor, Roy A.	Dem	N.C.	6	*2 1
15th	Helstoski, Henry	Dem	N.J.	3	1
16th	Biaggi, Mario	Dem	N.Y.	1	1
17th	Symington, James W.	Dem	Mo.	1	1
18th	Koch, Edward I.	Dem	N.Y.	1	1

Minority

Rank	Name	Party	State	Terms in: House	Terms in: Comm.
RM	Fulton, James G.	Rep	Penn.	13	7
2nd	Mosher, Charles A.	Rep	Ohio	5	5
3rd	Roudebush, Richard L.	Rep	Ind.	5	5
4th	Bell, Alphonzo	Rep	Cal.	5	5
5th	Pelly, Thomas M.	Rep	Wash.	9	5
6th	Rumsfeld, Donald	Rep	Ill.	4	4
7th	Wydler, John W.	Rep	N.Y.	4	4
8th	Vander Jagt, Guy A.	Rep	Mich.	3	2
9th	Winn, Larry Jr.	Rep	Kans.	2	2
10th	Pettis, Jerry L.	Rep	Cal.	2	2
11th	Lukens, Donald E. (Buz)	Rep	Ohio	2	2
12th	Price, Robert D.	Rep	Tex.	2	1
13th	Weicker, Lowell P. Jr.	Rep	Conn.	1	1
14th	Frey, Louis Jr.	Rep	Fla.	1	1

*1: Member's 1st period of service on the committee;
*2: Member`s 2nd period of service on the committee.

Note: "Terms in committee" for James G. Fulton (Rep-Penn.) include his previous service on the House Select Committee on Astronautics and Space Exploration.

Changes:

Majority:

Podell, Bertram L.	Dem	N.Y.	Dec. 8,1970	Moved to Interstate and Foreign Commerce.

Minority:

Rumsfeld, Donald	Rep	Ill.	May 25,1969	Resigned; appointed Assistant Director of the Office of Economic Opportunity.
Goldwater, Barry M. Jr.	Rep	Cal.	June 3,1969	Replaced Rumsfeld.
Pettis, Jerry L.	Rep	Cal.	Apr. 30,1970	Moved to Ways and Means.

Departures from the House:	Majority			Minority		
Elected to U.S. Senate	None			Weicker, Lowell P. Jr.	Conn.	Rep
Lost Election to U.S. Senate	None			Roudebush, Richard L.	Ind.	Rep
Lost Nomination to U.S. Senate	Brown, George E. Jr.	Cal.	Dem	None		
Lost Election for Governor	Daddario, Emilio Q.	Conn.	Dem	None		
Lost Nomination for Governor	None			Lukens, Donald E. (Buz)	Ohio	Rep

Departures from Committee:

Moved to Foreign Affairs	Taylor, Roy A.	N.C. Dem	Vander Jagt, Guy A.	Mich. Rep
Moved to Education & Labor	Biaggi, Mario	N.Y. Dem	None	
Moved to Interstate & Foreign Commerce	Helstoski, Henry	N.J. Dem	None	
Moved to Banking & Currency	Koch, Edward I.	N.Y. Dem	None	
Moved to Ways and Means	Waggonner, Joe D. Jr.	La. Dem	None	
No new assignment	Aspinall, Wayne N.	Colo. Dem	None	

SCIENCE AND ASTRONAUTICS / 92nd Congress

Service Dates of Committee Chair: Feb. 4,1971-Jan. 3,1973
Service Dates of Majority Members: Feb. 4,1971-Jan. 3,1973
Service Dates of Minority Members: Feb. 4,1971-Jan. 3,1973

Majority

Rank	Name	Party	State	Terms in: House	Terms in: Comm.
Chr	Miller, George P.	Dem	Cal.	14	7
2nd	Teague, Olin E.	Dem	Tex.	14	7
3rd	Karth, Joseph E.	DFL	Minn.	7	7
4th	Hechler, Kenneth	Dem	W.Va.	7	7
5th	Davis, John W.	Dem	Ga.	6	6
6th	Downing, Thomas N.	Dem	Va.	7	6
7th	Fuqua, Don	Dem	Fla.	5	5
8th	Cabell, Earle	Dem	Tex.	4	4
9th	Symington, James W.	Dem	Mo.	2	2
10th	Hanna, Richard T.	Dem	Cal.	5	1
11th	Flowers, Walter	Dem	Ala.	2	1
12th	Roe, Robert A.	Dem	N.J.	2	1
13th	Seiberling, John F.	Dem	Ohio	1	1
14th	Cotter, William R.	Dem	Conn.	1	1
15th	Rangel, Charles B.	Dem	N.Y.	1	1
16th	Murphy, Morgan F.	Dem	Ill.	1	1
17th	McCormack, Mike	Dem	Wash.	1	1
18th	Davis, Mendel J.	Dem	S.C.	1	1

Minority

Rank	Name	Party	State	Terms in: House	Terms in: Comm.
RM1	Fulton, James G.	Rep	Penn.	14	8
RM2 2nd	Mosher, Charles A.	Rep	Ohio	6	6
3rd	Bell, Alphonzo	Rep	Cal.	6	6
4th	Pelly, Thomas M.	Rep	Wash.	10	6
5th	Wydler, John W.	Rep	N.Y.	5	5
6th	Winn, Larry Jr.	Rep	Kans.	3	3
7th	Price, Robert D.	Rep	Tex.	3	2
8th	Frey, Louis Jr.	Rep	Fla.	2	2
9th	Goldwater, Barry M. Jr.	Rep	Cal.	2	2
10th	Esch, Marvin L.	Rep	Mich.	3	1
11th	Coughlin, R. Lawrence	Rep	Penn.	2	1
12th	Camp, John N. Happy	Rep	Okla.	2	1

Note: "Terms in committee" for James G. Fulton (Rep-Penn.) include his previous service on the House Select Committee on Astronautics and Space Exploration.

Vacancy Filled:
Majority: 18th seat by Davis on June 3,1971.

Changes:

Ranking Member:

RM1	Fulton, James G.	Rep	Penn.	Oct. 6,1971	Died in office.
RM2	Mosher, Charles A.	Rep	Ohio	Oct. 6,1971	Succeeded Fulton as Ranking Minority Member.

Majority:

Karth, Joseph E.	DFL	Minn.	Oct. 6,1971	Moved to Ways and Means.
Bergland, Bob	DFL	Minn.	Jan. 27,1972	Replaced Karth.

Minority:

Fulton, James G.	Rep	Penn.	Oct. 6,1971	Died in office.

Departures from the House:	**Majority**		**Minority**	
Defeated for Reelection	Cabell, Earle	Tex. Dem	None	
Defeated for Renomination	Miller, George P.	Cal. Dem	None	
Retired	None		Pelly, Thomas M.	Wash. Rep
Departures from Committee:				
Moved to Armed Services	Davis, Mendel J.	S.C. Dem	Price, Robert D.	Tex. Rep
Moved to Rules	Murphy, Morgan F.	Ill. Dem	None	
Moved to District of Columbia	Rangel, Charles B.	N.Y. Dem	None	
Moved to Interior & Insular Affairs	Seiberling, John F.	Ohio Dem	None	

SCIENCE AND ASTRONAUTICS / 93rd Congress

Service Dates of Committee Chair: Jan. 24,1973-Jan. 3,1975
Service Dates of Majority Members: Jan. 24,1973-Jan. 3,1975
Service Dates of Minority Members: Jan. 24,1973-Jan. 3,1975

Majority

Rank Name	Party	State	Terms in: House	Terms in: Comm.
Chr Teague, Olin E.	Dem	Tex.	15	8
2nd Hechler, Kenneth	Dem	W.Va.	8	8
3rd Davis, John W.	Dem	Ga.	7	7
4th Downing, Thomas N.	Dem	Va.	8	7
5th Fuqua, Don	Dem	Fla.	6	6
6th Symington, James W.	Dem	Mo.	3	3
7th Hanna, Richard T.	Dem	Cal.	6	2
8th Flowers, Walter	Dem	Ala.	3	2
9th Roe, Robert A.	Dem	N.J.	3	2
10th Cotter, William R.	Dem	Conn.	2	2
11th McCormack, Mike	Dem	Wash.	2	2
12th Bergland, Bob	DFL	Minn.	2	2
13th Pickle, J. J. (Jake)	Dem	Tex.	6	1
14th Brown, George E. Jr.	Dem	Cal.	5	*2 1
15th Milford, Dale	Dem	Tex.	1	1
16th Thornton, Raymond H. Jr.	Dem	Ark.	1	1
17th Gunter, William D. Jr.	Dem	Fla.	1	1

Minority

Rank Name	Party	State	Terms in: House	Terms in: Comm.
RM Mosher, Charles A.	Rep	Ohio	7	7
2nd Bell, Alphonzo	Rep	Cal.	7	7
3rd Wydler, John W.	Rep	N.Y.	6	6
4th Winn, Larry Jr.	Rep	Kans.	4	4
5th Frey, Louis Jr.	Rep	Fla.	3	3
6th Goldwater, Barry M. Jr.	Rep	Cal.	3	3
7th Esch, Marvin L.	Rep	Mich.	4	2
8th Coughlin, R. Lawrence	Rep	Penn.	3	2
9th Camp, John N. Happy	Rep	Okla.	3	2
10th Conlan, John B.	Rep	Ariz.	1	1
11th Parris, Stanford E.	Rep	Va.	1	1
12th Cronin, Paul W.	Rep	Mass.	1	1
13th Martin, James G.	Rep	N.C.	1	1

*2: Member's 2nd period of service on the committee.

Changes:

Majority:

Hanna, Richard T.	Dem	Cal.	Dec. 31,1974	Resigned and retired.

Minority:

Coughlin, R. Lawrence	Rep	Penn.	Mar. 7,1973	Moved to Appropriations.
Ketchum, William M.	Rep	Cal.	Nov. 15,1973	Replaced Coughlin.

	Majority			Minority		
Departures from the House:						
Defeated for Reelection	None			Camp, John N. Happy	Okla.	Rep
				Cronin, Paul W.	Mass.	Rep
				Parris, Stanford E.	Va.	Rep
Defeated for Renomination	Davis, John W.	Ga.	Dem	None		
Lost Nomination to U.S. Senate	Gunter, William D. Jr.	Fla.	Dem	None		
Departures from Committee:						
Moved to Ways and Means	Cotter, William R.	Conn.	Dem	Martin, James G.	N.C.	Rep
	Pickle, J. J. (Jake)	Tex.	Dem			

SCIENCE AND TECHNOLOGY / 94th Congress

* Name changed from the Committee on SCIENCE AND ASTRONAUTICS on Jan. 3,1975.

Service Dates of Committee Chair: Jan. 20,1975-Jan. 3,1977
Service Dates of Majority Members: Jan. 20,1975-Jan. 3,1977
Service Dates of Minority Members: Jan. 28,1975-Jan. 3,1977

Majority

Rank	Name	Party	State	Terms in: House	Terms in: Comm.
Chr	Teague, Olin E.	Dem	Tex.	16	9
2nd	Hechler, Kenneth	Dem	W.Va.	9	9
3rd	Downing, Thomas N.	Dem	Va.	9	8
4th	Fuqua, Don	Dem	Fla.	7	7
5th	Symington, James W.	Dem	Mo.	4	4
6th	Flowers, Walter	Dem	Ala.	4	3
7th	Roe, Robert A.	Dem	N.J.	4	3
8th	McCormack, Mike	Dem	Wash.	3	3
9th	Bergland, Bob	DFL	Minn.	3	3
10th	Brown, George E. Jr.	Dem	Cal.	6	*2 2
11th	Milford, Dale	Dem	Tex.	2	2
12th	Thornton, Raymond H. Jr.	Dem	Ark.	2	2
13th	Scheuer, James H.	Dem	N.Y.	5	1
14th	Ottinger, Richard L.	Dem	N.Y.	4	1
15th	Waxman, Henry A.	Dem	Cal.	1	1
16th	Hayes, Philip H.	Dem	Ind.	1	1
17th	Harkin, Thomas R.	Dem	Iowa	1	1
18th	Lloyd, James F.	Dem	Cal.	1	1
19th	Ambro, Jerome A. Jr.	Dem	N.Y.	1	1
20th	Dodd, Christopher J.	Dem	Conn.	1	1
21st	Blouin, Michael T.	Dem	Iowa	1	1
22nd	Hall, Tim L.	Dem	Ill.	1	1
23rd	Krueger, Robert C.	Dem	Tex.	1	1
24th	Lloyd, Marilyn	Dem	Tenn.	1	1
25th	Blanchard, James J.	Dem	Mich.	1	1

Minority

Rank	Name	Party	State	Terms in: House	Terms in: Comm.
RM	Mosher, Charles A.	Rep	Ohio	8	8
2nd	Bell, Alphonzo	Rep	Cal.	8	8
3rd	Jarman, John	Rep	Okla.	13	1
4th	Wydler, John W.	Rep	N.Y.	7	7
5th	Winn, Larry Jr.	Rep	Kans.	5	5
6th	Frey, Louis Jr.	Rep	Fla.	4	4
7th	Goldwater, Barry M. Jr.	Rep	Cal.	4	4
8th	Esch, Marvin L.	Rep	Mich.	5	3
9th	Conlan, John B.	Rep	Ariz.	2	2
10th	Ketchum, William M.	Rep	Cal.	2	2
11th	Myers, Gary A.	Rep	Penn.	1	1
12th	Emery, David F.	Rep	Me.	1	1

*2: Member's 2nd period of service on the committee.

Note: John Jarman of Oklahoma resigned the Democratic Party on Jan. 24, 1975, joined the Republican Party, and was awarded the 3rd minority rank on this committee.

Changes:

Majority:

Bergland, Bob	DFL	Minn.	Feb. 19,1975	Left committee; no new assignment.
Wirth, Timothy E.	Dem	Colo.	Feb. 19,1975	Replaced Bergland.

Minority:

Ketchum, William M.	Rep	Cal.	Mar. 24,1975	Moved to Ways and Means.
Pressler, Larry L.	Rep	S.D.	May 15,1975	Replaced Ketchum.

Departures from the House:

	Majority			Minority		
Defeated for Reelection	Hall, Tim L.	Ill.	Dem	None		
Lost Election to U.S. Senate	None			Esch, Marvin L.	Mich.	Rep
Lost Nomination to U.S. Senate	Hayes, Philip H.	Ind.	Dem	Bell, Alphonzo	Cal.	Rep
	Symington, James W.	Mo.	Dem	Conlan, John B.	Ariz.	Rep
Lost Nomination for Governor	Hechler, Kenneth	W.Va.	Dem	None		
Retired	Downing, Thomas N.	Va.	Dem	Jarman, John	Okla.	Rep
				Mosher, Charles A.	Ohio	Rep

Departures from Committee:

	Majority			Minority		
Moved to Government Operations	Blouin, Michael T.	Iowa	Dem	None		
	Waxman, Henry A.	Cal.	Dem			
Moved to Rules	Dodd, Christopher J.	Conn.	Dem			
Moved to Small Business	None			Pressler, Larry L.	S.D.	Rep
Moved to Armed Services	None			Emery, David F.	Me.	Rep

SCIENCE AND TECHNOLOGY / 95th Congress

Service Dates of Committee Chair: Jan. 19,1977-Dec. 31,1978
Service Dates of Majority Members: Jan. 19,1977-Jan. 3,1979
Service Dates of Minority Members: Jan. 19,1977-Jan. 3,1979

Majority

Rank Name	Party	State	Terms in: House	Terms in: Comm.
Chr Teague, Olin E.	Dem	Tex.	17	10
2nd Fuqua, Don	Dem	Fla.	8	8
3rd Flowers, Walter	Dem	Ala.	5	4
4th Roe, Robert A.	Dem	N.J.	5	4
5th McCormack, Mike	Dem	Wash.	4	4
6th Brown, George E. Jr.	Dem	Cal.	7	*2 3
7th Milford, Dale	Dem	Tex.	3	3
8th Thornton, Raymond H. Jr.	Dem	Ark.	3	3
9th Scheuer, James H.	Dem	N.Y.	6	2
10th Ottinger, Richard L.	Dem	N.Y.	5	2
11th Harkin, Thomas R.	Dem	Iowa	2	2
12th Lloyd, James F.	Dem	Cal.	2	2
13th Ambro, Jerome A. Jr.	Dem	N.Y.	2	2
14th Krueger, Robert C.	Dem	Tex.	2	2
15th Lloyd, Marilyn	Dem	Tenn.	2	2
16th Blanchard, James J.	Dem	Mich.	2	2
17th Wirth, Timothy E.	Dem	Colo.	2	2
18th Neal, Stephen L.	Dem	N.C.	2	1
19th Downey, Thomas J.	Dem	N.Y.	2	1
20th Walgren, Douglas	Dem	Penn.	1	1
21st Flippo, Ronnie G.	Dem	Ala.	1	1
22nd Glickman, Daniel R.	Dem	Kans.	1	1
23rd Gammage, Robert A.	Dem	Tex.	1	1
24th Beilenson, Anthony C.	Dem	Cal.	1	1
25th Gore, Albert A. Jr.	Dem	Tenn.	1	1
26th Watkins, Wesley W.	Dem	Okla.	1	1
27th Tonry, Richard A.	Dem	La.	1	1

Minority

Rank Name	Party	State	Terms in: House	Terms in: Comm.
RM Wydler, John W.	Rep	N.Y.	8	8
2nd Winn, Larry Jr.	Rep	Kans.	6	6
3rd Frey, Louis Jr.	Rep	Fla.	5	5
4th Goldwater, Barry M. Jr.	Rep	Cal.	5	5
5th Myers, Gary A.	Rep	Penn.	2	2
6th Fish, Hamilton Jr.	Rep	N.Y.	5	1
7th Lujan, Manuel Jr.	Rep	N.M.	5	1
8th Pursell, Carl D.	Rep	Mich.	1	1
9th Hollenbeck, Harold C.	Rep	N.J.	1	1
10th Rudd, Eldon D.	Rep	Ariz.	1	1
11th Dornan, Robert K.	Rep	Cal.	1	1
12th Walker, Robert S.	Rep	Penn.	1	1
13th Forsythe, Edwin B.	Rep	N.J.	5	1

*2: Member's 2nd period of service on the committee.

Note: Marilyn Lloyd (Dem-Tenn.) changed her name to Marilyn Lloyd Bouquard during the adjournment of the 95th Congress.

Vacancy Filled:
Minority: 13th seat by Forsythe on Mar. 3,1977.

Changes:
Majority:

Tonry, Richard A.	Dem	La.	May 4,1977	Resigned and retired.
Young, Robert A.	Dem	Mo.	July 20,1977	Replaced Tonry.
Teague, Olin E.	Dem	Tex.	Dec. 31,1978	Resigned and retired.

Departures from the House:	**Majority**			**Minority**		
Defeated for Reelection	Gammage, Robert A.	Tex.	Dem	None		
Defeated for Renomination	Milford, Dale	Tex.	Dem	None		
Lost Election to U.S. Senate	Krueger, Robert C.	Tex.	Dem	None		
Lost Nomination to U.S. Senate	Flowers, Walter	Ala.	Dem	None		
	Thornton, Raymond H. Jr.	Ark.	Dem			
Lost Nomination for Governor	None			Frey, Louis Jr.	Fla.	Rep
Retired	None			Myers, Gary A.	Penn.	Rep
Departures from Committee:						
Ceases active membership to serve on Budget	Wirth, Timothy E.	Colo.	Dem	None		
Moved to Rules	Beilenson, Anthony C.	Cal.	Dem			
Moved to Ways and Means	Downey, Thomas J.	N.Y.	Dem	None		
Moved to Appropriations	None			Pursell, Carl D.	Mich.	Rep
				Rudd, Eldon D.	Ariz.	Rep

SCIENCE AND TECHNOLOGY / 96th Congress

Service Dates of Committee Chair: Jan. 24,1979-Jan. 3,1981
Service Dates of Majority Members: Jan. 24,1979-Jan. 3,1981
Service Dates of Minority Members: Jan. 24,1979-Jan. 3,1981

Majority

Rank	Name	Party	State	Terms in: House	Terms in: Comm.
Chr	Fuqua, Don	Dem	Fla.	9	9
2nd	Roe, Robert A.	Dem	N.J.	6	5
3rd	McCormack, Mike	Dem	Wash.	5	5
4th	Brown, George E. Jr.	Dem	Cal.	8	*2 4
5th	Scheuer, James H.	Dem	N.Y.	7	3
6th	Ottinger, Richard L.	Dem	N.Y.	6	3
7th	Harkin, Thomas R.	Dem	Iowa	3	3
8th	Lloyd, James F.	Dem	Cal.	3	3
9th	Ambro, Jerome A. Jr.	Dem	N.Y.	3	3
10th	Bouquard, Marilyn Lloyd	Dem	Tenn.	3	3
11th	Blanchard, James J.	Dem	Mich.	3	3
12th	Neal, Stephen L.	Dem	N.C.	3	2
13th	Walgren, Douglas	Dem	Penn.	2	2
14th	Flippo, Ronnie G.	Dem	Ala.	2	2
15th	Glickman, Daniel R.	Dem	Kans.	2	2
16th	Gore, Albert A. Jr.	Dem	Tenn.	2	2
17th	Watkins, Wesley W.	Dem	Okla.	2	2
18th	Young, Robert A.	Dem	Mo.	2	2
19th	White, Richard C.	Dem	Tex.	8	1
20th	Volkmer, Harold L.	Dem	Mo.	2	1
21st	Pease, Donald J.	Dem	Ohio	2	1
22nd	Wolpe, Howard E.	Dem	Mich.	1	1
23rd	Mavroules, Nicholas	Dem	Mass.	1	1
24th	Nelson, Bill	Dem	Fla.	1	1
25th	Anthony, Beryl F. Jr.	Dem	Ark.	1	1
26th	Lundine, Stanley N.	Dem	N.Y.	3	1
27th	Ertel, Allen E.	Dem	Penn.	2	1

Minority

Rank	Name	Party	State	Terms in: House	Terms in: Comm.
RM	Wydler, John W.	Rep	N.Y.	9	9
2nd	Winn, Larry Jr.	Rep	Kans.	7	7
3rd	Goldwater, Barry M. Jr.	Rep	Cal.	6	6
4th	Fish, Hamilton Jr.	Rep	N.Y.	6	2
5th	Lujan, Manuel Jr.	Rep	N.M.	6	2
6th	Hollenbeck, Harold C.	Rep	N.J.	2	2
7th	Dornan, Robert K.	Rep	Cal.	2	2
8th	Walker, Robert S.	Rep	Penn.	2	2
9th	Forsythe, Edwin B.	Rep	N.J.	6	2
10th	Kramer, Kenneth B.	Rep	Colo.	1	1
11th	Carney, William	Rep	N.Y.	1	1
12th	Davis, Robert W.	Rep	Mich.	1	1
13th	Roth, Tobias A.	Rep	Wisc.	1	1
14th	Ritter, Donald L.	Rep	Penn.	1	1
15th	Royer, William	Rep	Cal.	1	1

*2: Member's 2nd period of service on the committee.

Note: Marilyn Lloyd Bouquard (Dem-Tenn.), changed her name from Marilyn Lloyd during the adjournment of the 95th Congress.

Vacancies Filled:
Majority: 26th and 27th seats by Lundine and Ertel respectively on Jan. 31,1979.
Minority: 15th seat by Royer on June 27,1979.

Changes:
Majority:

Neal, Stephen L.	Dem	N.C.	Jan. 31,1979	Left committee; no new assignment.
Hance, Kent	Dem	Tex.	Jan. 31,1979	Replaced Neal.

	Majority			Minority		
Departures from the House:						
Defeated for Reelection	Ambro, Jerome A. Jr.	N.Y.	Dem	Royer, William	Cal.	Rep
	Lloyd, James F.	Cal.	Dem			
	McCormack, Mike	Wash.	Dem			
Retired	None			Wydler, John W.	N.Y.	Rep
Departures from Committee:						
Moved to Budget	Anthony, Beryl F. Jr.	Ark.	Dem	None		
Moved to Small Business	Mavroules, Nicholas	Mass.	Dem	None		
Moved to Ways and Means	Pease, Donald J.	Ohio	Dem	None		
	Hance, Kent	Tex.	Dem			
Moved to Appropriations	Watkins, Wesley W.	Okla.	Dem	None		
Moved to Armed Services	None			Davis, Robert W.	Mich.	Rep
				Kramer, Kenneth B.	Colo.	Rep
Moved to Foreign Affairs	None			Dornan, Robert K.	Cal.	Rep
				Roth, Tobias A.	Wisc.	Rep
Moved to Energy and Commerce	None			Ritter, Donald L.	Penn.	Rep

SCIENCE AND TECHNOLOGY / 97th Congress

Service Dates of Committee Chair: Jan. 28,1981-Jan. 3,1983
Service Dates of Majority Members: Jan. 28,1981-Jan. 3,1983
Service Dates of Minority Members: Jan. 28,1981-Jan. 3,1983

Majority

Rank Name	Party	State	Terms in: House	Terms in: Comm.
Chr Fuqua, Don	Dem	Fla.	10	10
2nd Roe, Robert A.	Dem	N.J.	7	6
3rd Brown, George E. Jr.	Dem	Cal.	9	*2 5
4th Scheuer, James H.	Dem	N.Y.	8	4
5th Ottinger, Richard L.	Dem	N.Y.	7	4
6th Harkin, Thomas R.	Dem	Iowa	4	4
7th Bouquard, Marilyn Lloyd	Dem	Tenn.	4	4
8th Blanchard, James J.	Dem	Mich.	4	4
9th Walgren, Douglas	Dem	Penn.	3	3
10th Flippo, Ronnie G.	Dem	Ala.	3	3
11th Glickman, Daniel R.	Dem	Kans.	3	3
12th Gore, Albert A. Jr.	Dem	Tenn.	3	3
13th Young, Robert A.	Dem	Mo.	3	3
14th White, Richard C.	Dem	Tex.	9	2
15th Volkmer, Harold L.	Dem	Mo.	3	2
16th Wolpe, Howard E.	Dem	Mich.	2	2
17th Nelson, Bill	Dem	Fla.	2	2
18th Lundine, Stanley N.	Dem	N.Y.	4	2
19th Ertel, Allen E.	Dem	Penn.	3	2
20th Shamansky, Robert N.	Dem	Ohio	1	1
21st Hall, Ralph M.	Dem	Tex.	1	1
22nd McCurdy, Dave	Dem	Okla.	1	1
23rd Dymally, Mervyn M.	Dem	Cal.	1	1

Minority

Rank Name	Party	State	Terms in: House	Terms in: Comm.
RM Winn, Larry Jr.	Rep	Kans.	8	8
2nd Goldwater, Barry M. Jr.	Rep	Cal.	7	7
3rd Fish, Hamilton Jr.	Rep	N.Y.	7	3
4th Lujan, Manuel Jr.	Rep	N.M.	7	3
5th Hollenbeck, Harold C.	Rep	N.J.	3	3
6th Walker, Robert S.	Rep	Penn.	3	3
7th Forsythe, Edwin B.	Rep	N.J.	7	3
8th Carney, William	Rep	N.Y.	2	2
9th Heckler, Margaret M.	Rep	Mass.	8	1
10th Sensenbrenner, F. Jas. Jr.	Rep	Wisc.	2	1
11th Weber, Vin	Rep	Minn.	1	1
12th Gregg, Judd	Rep	N.H.	1	1
13th McGrath, Raymond J.	Rep	N.Y.	1	1
14th Skeen, Joe	Rep	N.M.	1	1
15th Schneider, Claudine	Rep	R.I.	1	1
16th Dunn, Jim	Rep	Mich.	1	1
17th Lowery, William	Rep	Cal.	1	1

*2: Member's 2nd period of service on the committee.

	Majority		Minority	
Departures from the House:				
Elected Governor	Blanchard, James J.	Mich. Dem	None	
Defeated for Reelection	Shamansky, Robert N.	Ohio Dem	Dunn, Jim	Mich. Rep
			Heckler, Margaret M.	Mass. Rep
			Hollenbeck, Harold C.	N.J. Rep
Lost Nomination to U.S. Senate	None		Goldwater, Barry M. Jr.	Cal. Rep
Lost Nomination for Governor	Ertel, Allen E.	Penn. Dem	None	
Retired	White, Richard C.	Tex. Dem	None	
Departures from Committee:				
Moved to Ways and Means	Flippo, Ronnie G.	Ala. Dem		
	Wolpe, Howard E.	Mich. Dem		
Moved to Select Committee on Children, Youth & Families	None		Fish, Hamilton Jr.	N.Y. Rep
Moved to Public Works & Transportation	None		Weber, Vin	Minn. Rep
No new assignment	None		Forsythe, Edwin B.	N.J. Rep

SCIENCE AND TECHNOLOGY / 98th Congress

Service Dates of Committee Chair: Jan. 6,1983-Jan. 3,1985
Service Dates of Majority Members: Jan. 6,1983-Jan. 3,1985
Service Dates of Minority Members: Jan. 6,1983-Jan. 3,1985

Majority

Rank	Name	Party	State	Terms in: House	Terms in: Comm.
Chr	Fuqua, Don	Dem	Fla.	11	11
2nd	Roe, Robert A.	Dem	N.J.	8	7
3rd	Brown, George E. Jr.	Dem	Cal.	10	*2 6
4th	Scheuer, James H.	Dem	N.Y.	9	5
5th	Ottinger, Richard L.	Dem	N.Y.	8	5
6th	Harkin, Thomas R.	Dem	Iowa	5	5
7th	Bouquard, Marilyn Lloyd	Dem	Tenn.	5	5
8th	Walgren, Douglas	Dem	Penn.	4	4
9th	Glickman, Daniel R.	Dem	Kans.	4	4
10th	Gore, Albert A. Jr.	Dem	Tenn.	4	4
11th	Young, Robert A.	Dem	Mo.	4	4
12th	Volkmer, Harold L.	Dem	Mo.	4	3
13th	Nelson, Bill	Dem	Fla.	3	3
14th	Lundine, Stanley N.	Dem	N.Y.	5	3
15th	Hall, Ralph M.	Dem	Tex.	2	2
16th	McCurdy, Dave	Dem	Okla.	2	2
17th	Dymally, Mervyn M.	Dem	Cal.	2	2
18th	Simon, Paul M.	Dem	Ill.	5	1
19th	Mineta, Norman Y.	Dem	Cal.	5	1
20th	Durbin, Richard J.	Dem	Ill.	1	1
21st	Andrews, Michael A.	Dem	Tex.	1	1
22nd	MacKay, Kenneth H.	Dem	Fla.	1	1
23rd	Valentine, I.T. Jr. (Tim)	Dem	N.C.	1	1
24th	Reid, Harry M.	Dem	Nev.	1	1
25th	Torricelli, Robert G.	Dem	N.J.	1	1
26th	Boucher, Frederick C.	Dem	Va.	1	1

Minority

Rank	Name	Party	State	Terms in: House	Terms in: Comm.
RM	Winn, Larry Jr.	Rep	Kans.	9	9
2nd	Lujan, Manuel Jr.	Rep	N.M.	8	4
3rd	Walker, Robert S.	Rep	Penn.	4	4
4th	Carney, William	Rep	N.Y.	3	3
5th	Sensenbrenner, F. Jas. Jr.	Rep	Wisc.	3	2
6th	Gregg, Judd	Rep	N.H.	2	2
7th	McGrath, Raymond J.	Rep	N.Y.	2	2
8th	Skeen, Joe	Rep	N.M.	2	2
9th	Schneider, Claudine	Rep	R.I.	2	2
10th	Lowery, William	Rep	Cal.	2	2
11th	Chandler, Rodney	Rep	Wash.	1	1
12th	Bateman, Herbert H.	Rep	Va.	1	1
13th	Boehlert, Sherwood L.	Rep	N.Y.	1	1
14th	McCandless, Alfred A.	Rep	Cal.	1	1
15th	Lewis, Tom	Rep	Fla.	1	1

*1: Member's 1st period of service on the committee;
*2: Member's 2nd period of service on the committee.

Note: Marilyn Lloyd Bouquard (Dem-Tenn.) first voted in this Congress under the resumed name Marilyn Lloyd on Apr. 12,1983.

	Majority			Minority		
Departures from the House:						
Elected to U.S. Senate	Gore, Albert A. Jr.	Tenn.	Dem	None		
	Harkin, Thomas R.	Iowa	Dem			
	Simon, Paul M.	Ill.	Dem			
Retired	Ottinger, Richard L.	N.Y.	Dem	Winn, Larry Jr.	Kans.	Rep
Departures from Committee:						
Ceased active membership to serve on Budget	MacKay, Kenneth H.	Fla.	Dem	None		
Moved to Appropriations	Durbin, Richard J.	Ill.	Dem	Lowery, William	Cal.	Rep
				Skeen, Joe	N.M.	Rep
Moved to Education and Labor	Dymally, Mervyn M.	Cal.	Dem	None		
Moved to Armed Services	None			Bateman, Herbert H.	Va.	Rep
				Carney, William	N.Y.	Rep
Moved to Banking, Finance & Urban Affairs	None			Chandler, Rodney	Wash.	Rep
				McCandless, Alfred A.	Cal.	Rep
Moved to Ways and Means	None			Gregg, Judd	N.H.	Rep
				McGrath, Raymond J.	N.Y.	Rep

SCIENCE AND TECHNOLOGY / 99th Congress

Service Dates of Committee Chair: Jan. 7,1985-Jan. 3,1987
Service Dates of Majority Members: Jan. 30,1985-Jan. 3,1987
Service Dates of Minority Members: Jan. 30,1985-Jan. 3,1987

Majority

Rank	Name	Party	State	Terms in: House		Terms in: Comm.
Chr	Fuqua, Don	Dem	Fla.	12		12
2nd	Roe, Robert A.	Dem	N.J.	9		8
3rd	Brown, George E. Jr.	Dem	Cal.	11	*2	7
4th	Scheuer, James H.	Dem	N.Y.	10		6
5th	Lloyd, Marilyn	Dem	Tenn.	6		6
6th	Wirth, Timothy E.	Dem	Colo.	6		5
7th	Walgren, Douglas	Dem	Penn.	5		5
8th	Glickman, Daniel R.	Dem	Kans.	5		5
9th	Young, Robert A.	Dem	Mo.	5		5
10th	Volkmer, Harold L.	Dem	Mo.	5		4
11th	Nelson, Bill	Dem	Fla.	4		4
12th	Lundine, Stanley N.	Dem	N.Y.	6		4
13th	Hall, Ralph M.	Dem	Tex.	3		3
14th	McCurdy, Dave	Dem	Okla.	3		3
15th	Mineta, Norman Y.	Dem	Cal.	6		2
16th	Andrews, Michael A.	Dem	Tex.	2		2
17th	Valentine, I.T. Jr. (Tim)	Dem	N.C.	2		2
18th	Reid, Harry M.	Dem	Nev.	2		2
19th	Torricelli, Robert G.	Dem	N.J.	2		2
20th	Boucher, Frederick C.	Dem	Va.	2		2
21st	Bruce, Terry L.	Dem	Ill.	1		1
22nd	Stallings, Richard H.	Dem	Ida.	1		1
23rd	Gordon, Bart	Dem	Tenn.	1		1
24th	Traficant, James A. Jr.	Dem	Ohio	1		1

Minority

Rank	Name	Party	State	Terms in: House		Terms in: Comm.
RM	Lujan, Manuel Jr.	Rep	N.M.	9		5
2nd	Walker, Robert S.	Rep	Penn.	5		5
3rd	Sensenbrenner, F. Jas. Jr.	Rep	Wisc.	4		3
4th	Schneider, Claudine	Rep	R.I.	3		3
5th	Boehlert, Sherwood L.	Rep	N.Y.	2		2
6th	Lewis, Tom	Rep	Fla.	2		2
7th	Ritter, Donald L.	Rep	Penn.	4	*2	1
8th	Morrison, Sid	Rep	Wash.	3		1
9th	Packard, Ron	Rep	Cal.	2		1
10th	Meyers, Jan	Rep	Kans.	1		1
11th	Smith, Robert C.	Rep	N.H.	1		1
12th	Henry, Paul B.	Rep	Mich.	1		1
13th	Fawell, Harris W.	Rep	Ill.	1		1
14th	Cobey, William W. Jr.	Rep	N.C.	1		1
15th	Barton, Joe L.	Rep	Tex.	1		1
16th	Slaughter, D. French Jr.	Rep	Va.	1		1
17th	Monson, David S.	Rep	Utah	1		1

*2: Member's 2nd period of service on the committee.

Note: Timothy E. Wirth (Dem-Colo.), having served on the Budget Committee during the previous three Congresses, returned to active service on this committee with his seniority intact.

Changes:

Majority:

Andrews, Michael A.	Dem	Tex.	July 29,1986	Moved to Ways and Means.
Chapman, Jim	Dem	Tex.	July 29,1986	Replaced Andrews.

Departures from the House:	Majority			Minority		
Elected to U.S. Senate	Reid, Harry M.	Nev.	Dem	None		
	Wirth, Timothy E.	Colo.	Dem			
Elected Lieutenant Governor	Lundine, Stanley N.	N.Y.	Dem	None		
Defeated for Reelection	Young, Robert A.	Mo.	Dem	Cobey, William W. Jr.	N.C.	Rep
Retired	Fuqua, Don	Fla.	Dem	Monson, David S.	Utah	Rep
Departures from Committee:						
Moved to Energy and Commerce	None			Barton, Joe L.	Tex.	Rep
Moved to Foreign Affairs	None			Meyers, Jan	Kans.	Rep

SCIENCE, SPACE, AND TECHNOLOGY / 100th Congress

* Renamed the Committee on SCIENCE, SPACE, AND TECHNOLOGY on Jan. 6,1987.

Service Dates of Committee Chair: Jan. 8,1987-Jan. 3,1989
Service Dates of Majority Members: Jan. 22,1987-Jan. 3,1989
Service Dates of Minority Members: Jan. 21,1987-Jan. 3,1989

Majority

Rank	Name	Party	State	Terms in: House	Terms in: Comm.
Chr	Roe, Robert A.	Dem	N.J.	10	9
2nd	Brown, George E. Jr.	Dem	Cal.	12	*2 8
3rd	Scheuer, James H.	Dem	N.Y.	11	7
4th	Lloyd, Marilyn	Dem	Tenn.	7	7
5th	Walgren, Douglas	Dem	Penn.	6	6
6th	Glickman, Daniel R.	Dem	Kans.	6	6
7th	Volkmer, Harold L.	Dem	Mo.	6	5
8th	Nelson, Bill	Dem	Fla.	5	5
9th	Hall, Ralph M.	Dem	Tex.	4	4
10th	McCurdy, Dave	Dem	Okla.	4	4
11th	Mineta, Norman Y.	Dem	Cal.	7	3
12th	MacKay, Kenneth H.	Dem	Fla.	3	3
13th	Valentine, I.T. Jr. (Tim)	Dem	N.C.	3	3
14th	Torricelli, Robert G.	Dem	N.J.	3	3
15th	Boucher, Frederick C.	Dem	Va.	3	3
16th	Bruce, Terry L.	Dem	Ill.	2	2
17th	Stallings, Richard H.	Dem	Ida.	2	2
18th	Gordon, Bart	Dem	Tenn.	2	2
19th	Traficant, James A. Jr.	Dem	Ohio	2	2
20th	Chapman, Jim	Dem	Tex.	2	2
21st	Hamilton, Lee H.	Dem	Ind.	12	1
22nd	Nowak, Henry J.	Dem	N.Y.	7	1
23rd	Perkins, Carl C. (Chris)	Dem	Ky.	3	1
24th	McMillen, C. Thomas	Dem	Md.	1	1
25th	Price, David E.	Dem	N.C.	1	1
26th	Nagle, David R.	Dem	Iowa	1	1
27th	Hayes, James A.	Dem	La.	1	1

Minority

Rank	Name	Party	State	Terms in: House	Terms in: Comm.
RM	Lujan, Manuel Jr.	Rep	N.M.	10	6
2nd	Walker, Robert S.	Rep	Penn.	6	6
3rd	Sensenbrenner, F. Jas. Jr.	Rep	Wisc.	5	4
4th	Schneider, Claudine	Rep	R.I.	4	4
5th	Boehlert, Sherwood L.	Rep	N.Y.	3	3
6th	Lewis, Tom	Rep	Fla.	3	3
7th	Ritter, Donald L.	Rep	Penn.	5	*2 2
8th	Morrison, Sid	Rep	Wash.	4	2
9th	Packard, Ron	Rep	Cal.	3	2
10th	Smith, Robert C.	Rep	N.H.	2	2
11th	Henry, Paul B.	Rep	Mich.	2	2
12th	Fawell, Harris W.	Rep	Ill.	2	2
13th	Slaughter, D. French Jr.	Rep	Va.	2	2
14th	Smith, Lamar S.	Rep	Tex.	1	1
15th	Konnyu, Ernest L.	Rep	Cal.	1	1
16th	Buechner, Jack	Rep	Mo.	1	1
17th	Hefley, Joel	Rep	Colo.	1	1
18th	Morella, Constance A.	Rep	Md.	1	1

*2: Member's 2nd period of service on the committee.

Notes: The committee was expanded and the party ratio changed to 29 Democrats and 19 Republicans on Nov. 4,1987. Kenneth H. MacKay (Dem-Fla.), while continuing to serve on the Budget Committee, returned to active service on this committee with his seniority intact.

Additions:

Majority:	28th	Hochbrueckner, George J.	Dem	N.Y.	Dec. 15,1987
	29th	Kanjorski, Paul E.	Dem	Penn.	Dec. 15,1987
Minority:	19th	Shays, Christopher	Rep	Conn.	Nov. 4,1987

Changes:

Majority:

Gordon, Bart	Dem	Tenn.	Feb. 19,1987	Moved to Rules.
Skaggs, David E.	Dem	Colo.	Mar. 30,1987	Replaced Gordon.

	Majority			Minority		
Departures from the House:						
Appointed Secretary of Interior	None			Lujan, Manuel Jr.	N.M.	Rep
Defeated for Renomination	None			Konnyu, Ernest L.	Cal.	Rep
Lost Election to U.S. Senate	MacKay, Kenneth H.	Fla.	Dem	None		
Departures from Committee:						
Moved to Appropriations	Chapman, Jim	Tex.	Dem			
Moved to Post Office & Civil Service	Kanjorski, Paul E.	Penn.	Dem	None		
Moved to Armed Services	None			Hefley, Joel	Colo.	Rep
No new assignment	Hochbrueckner, George J.	N.Y.	Dem	None		

SCIENCE, SPACE, AND TECHNOLOGY / 101st Congress

Service Dates of Committee Chair: Jan. 3,1989-Jan. 3,1991
Service Dates of Majority Members: Jan. 19,1989-Jan. 3,1991
Service Dates of Minority Members: Jan. 20,1989-Jan. 3,1991

Majority

Rank	Name	Party	State	Terms in: House	Terms in: Comm.
Chr	Roe, Robert A.	Dem	N.J.	11	10
2nd	Brown, George E. Jr.	Dem	Cal.	13	*2 9
3rd	Scheuer, James H.	Dem	N.Y.	12	8
4th	Lloyd, Marilyn	Dem	Tenn.	8	8
5th	Walgren, Douglas	Dem	Penn.	7	7
6th	Glickman, Daniel R.	Dem	Kans.	7	7
7th	Volkmer, Harold L.	Dem	Mo.	7	6
8th	Wolpe, Howard E.	Dem	Mich.	6	6
9th	Nelson, Bill	Dem	Fla.	6	6
10th	Hall, Ralph M.	Dem	Tex.	5	5
11th	McCurdy, Dave	Dem	Okla.	5	5
12th	Mineta, Norman Y.	Dem	Cal.	8	4
13th	Valentine, I.T. Jr. (Tim)	Dem	N.C.	4	4
14th	Torricelli, Robert G.	Dem	N.J.	4	4
15th	Boucher, Frederick C.	Dem	Va.	4	4
16th	Bruce, Terry L.	Dem	Ill.	3	3
17th	Stallings, Richard H.	Dem	Ida.	3	3
18th	Traficant, James A. Jr.	Dem	Ohio	3	3
19th	Hamilton, Lee H.	Dem	Ind.	13	2
20th	Nowak, Henry J.	Dem	N.Y.	8	2
21st	Perkins, Carl C. (Chris)	Dem	Ky.	4	2
22nd	McMillen, C. Thomas	Dem	Md.	2	2
23rd	Price, David E.	Dem	N.C.	2	2
24th	Nagle, David R.	Dem	Iowa	2	2
25th	Hayes, James A.	Dem	La.	2	2
26th	Skaggs, David E.	Dem	Colo.	2	2
27th	Costello, Jerry F.	Dem	Ill.	2	2
28th	Johnston, Harry A.	Dem	Fla.	1	1
29th	Tanner, John	Dem	Tenn.	1	1
30th	Browder, Glen	Dem	Ala.	1	1

Minority

Rank	Name	Party	State	Terms in: House	Terms in: Comm.
RM	Walker, Robert S.	Rep	Penn.	7	7
2nd	Sensenbrenner, F. Jas. Jr.	Rep	Wisc.	6	5
3rd	Schneider, Claudine	Rep	R.I.	5	5
4th	Boehlert, Sherwood L.	Rep	N.Y.	4	4
5th	Lewis, Tom	Rep	Fla.	4	4
6th	Ritter, Donald L.	Rep	Penn.	6	*2 3
7th	Morrison, Sid	Rep	Wash.	5	3
8th	Packard, Ron	Rep	Cal.	4	3
9th	Smith, Robert C.	Rep	N.H.	3	3
10th	Henry, Paul B.	Rep	Mich.	3	3
11th	Fawell, Harris W.	Rep	Ill.	3	3
12th	Slaughter, D. French Jr.	Rep	Va.	3	3
13th	Smith, Lamar S.	Rep	Tex.	2	2
14th	Buechner, Jack	Rep	Mo.	2	2
15th	Morella, Constance A.	Rep	Md.	2	2
16th	Shays, Christopher	Rep	Conn.	2	2
17th	Rohrabacher, Dana	Rep	Cal.	1	1
18th	Schiff, Steven H.	Rep	N.M.	1	1
19th	Campbell, Tom	Rep	Cal.	1	1

*2: Member's 2nd period of service on the committee.

Note: Howard E. Wolpe (Dem-Mich.), having served on the Budget Committee during the previous three Congresses, returned to active service on this committee with his seniority intact.

Vacancy Filled:
Majority: 30th seat by Browder on Apr. 27,1989.

Changes:
Minority:

Smith, Robert C.	Rep	N.H.	Mar. 7,1990	Moved to Armed Services.
Rhodes, John J. III	Rep	Ariz.	Mar. 7,1990	Replaced Smith.

Departures from the House:	**Majority**		**Minority**	
Defeated for Reelection	Walgren, Douglas	Penn. Dem	Buechner, Jack	Mo. Rep
Lost Nomination for Governor	Nelson, Bill	Fla. Dem	None	
Lost Election to U.S. Senate	None		Schneider, Claudine	R.I. Rep
Departure from Committee:				
Became Chair of Joint Economic	Hamilton, Lee H.	Ind. Dem	None	
Moved to Appropriations	Skaggs, David E.	Colo. Dem	None	
	Price, David E.	N.C. Dem		
Moved to Interior & Insular Affairs	Johnston, Harry A.	Fla. Dem	None	
Moved to Select Aging	Roe, Robert A.	N.J. Dem	None	
Moved to Budget	None		Shays, Christopher	Conn. Rep

SCIENCE, SPACE, AND TECHNOLOGY / 102nd Congress

Service Dates of Committee Chair: Jan. 24,1991-Jan. 3,1993
Service Dates of Majority Members: Jan. 24,1991-Jan. 3,1993
Service Dates of Minority Members: Jan. 24,1991-Jan. 3,1993

Majority

Rank Name	Party	State	Terms in: House	Terms in: Comm.
Chr Brown, George E. Jr.	Dem	Cal.	14	*2 10
2nd Scheuer, James H.	Dem	N.Y.	13	9
3rd Lloyd, Marilyn	Dem	Tenn.	9	9
4th Glickman, Daniel R.	Dem	Kans.	8	8
5th Volkmer, Harold L.	Dem	Mo.	8	7
6th Wolpe, Howard E.	Dem	Mich.	7	7
7th Hall, Ralph M.	Dem	Tex.	6	6
8th McCurdy, Dave	Dem	Okla.	6	6
9th Mineta, Norman Y.	Dem	Cal.	9	5
10th Valentine, I.T. Jr. (Tim)	Dem	N.C.	5	5
11th Torricelli, Robert G.	Dem	N.J.	5	5
12th Boucher, Frederick C.	Dem	Va.	5	5
13th Bruce, Terry L.	Dem	Ill.	4	4
14th Stallings, Richard H.	Dem	Ida.	4	4
15th Traficant, James A. Jr.	Dem	Ohio	4	4
16th Nowak, Henry J.	Dem	N.Y.	9	3
17th Perkins, Carl C. (Chris)	Dem	Ky.	5	3
18th McMillen, C. Thomas	Dem	Md.	3	3
19th Nagle, David R.	Dem	Iowa	3	3
20th Hayes, James A.	Dem	La.	3	3
21st Costello, Jerry F.	Dem	Ill.	3	3
22nd Tanner, John S.	Dem	Tenn.	2	2
23rd Browder, Glen	Dem	Ala.	2	2
24th Geren, Pete	Dem	Tex.	2	1
25th Thornton, Ray	Dem	Ark.	1	1
26th Bacchus, Jim	Dem	Fla.	1	1
27th Roemer, Timothy J.	Dem	Ind.	1	1
28th Cramer, Bud	Dem	Ala.	1	1
29th Swett, Dick	Dem	N.H.	1	1
30th Kopetski, Mike	Dem	Ore.	1	1
31st Horn, Joan Kelly	Dem	Mo.	1	1
32nd Collins, Barbara-Rose	Dem	Mich.	1	1

Minority

Rank Name	Party	State	Terms in: House	Terms in: Comm.
RM Walker, Robert S.	Rep	Penn.	8	8
2nd Sensenbrenner, F. Jas. Jr.	Rep	Wisc.	7	6
3rd Boehlert, Sherwood L.	Rep	N.Y.	5	5
4th Lewis, Tom	Rep	Fla.	5	5
5th Ritter, Donald L.	Rep	Penn.	7	*2 4
6th Morrison, Sid	Rep	Wash.	6	4
7th Packard, Ron	Rep	Cal.	5	4
8th Henry, Paul B.	Rep	Mich.	4	4
9th Fawell, Harris W.	Rep	Ill.	4	4
10th Slaughter, D. French Jr.	Rep	Va.	4	4
11th Smith, Lamar S.	Rep	Tex.	3	3
12th Morella, Constance A.	Rep	Md.	3	3
13th Rohrabacher, Dana	Rep	Cal.	2	2
14th Schiff, Steven H.	Rep	N.M.	2	2
15th Campbell, Tom	Rep	Cal.	2	2
16th Rhodes, John J. III	Rep	Ariz.	3	2
17th Barton, Joe L.	Rep	Tex.	4	1
18th Zimmer, Richard	Rep	N.J.	1	1
19th Gilchrest, Wayne T.	Rep	Md.	1	1

*2: Member's 2nd period of service on the committee.

Note: The death of Silvio O. Conte (Rep-Mass.) and his replacement by John W. Olver (Dem-Mass.) led to a change in size and party ratio on this committee to 33 Democrats and 20 Republicans on June 27,1991.

Additions:

Majority:	33rd Engel, Eliot L.	Dem	N.Y.	June 27,1991
Minority:	20th Johnson, Sam	Rep	Tex.	Sep. 19,1991

Changes:

Majority:

Collins, Barbara-Rose	Dem	Mich.	May 20,1991	Moved to Post Office and Civil Service.
Olver, John W.	Dem	Mass.	June 27,1991	Replaced Collins.

Minority:

Slaughter, D. French Jr.	Rep	Va.	Nov. 5,1991	Resigned and retired.
Allen, George F.	Rep	Va.	Nov. 12,1991	Replaced Slaughter.

SMALL BUSINESS

Jurisdiction, 1974

Established by House Resolution 988, as amended, 93rd Congress, Second Session, October 8, 1974:

[Section 321]

Rule X of the Rules of the House of Representatives, as amended by the previous sections, is further amended by adding at the end thereof the following:

(t) Committee on Small Business.

(1) Assistance to and protection of small business, including financial aid.
(2) Participation of small-business enterprises in Federal procurement and Government contracts. In addition to its legislative jurisdiction under the preceding provisions of this paragraph (and its general oversight function under clause 2(b) (1), the committee shall have the special oversight function provided for in clause 3(f) with respect to the problems of small business.

Jurisdiction, 1992

Jurisdiction contained in Rules of the House of Representatives, (as revised to July 1, 1992):

[Rule X. 1. (s)]

Committee on Small Business.

(1) Assistance to and protection of small business, including financial aid.
(2) Participation of small-business enterprises in Federal procurement and Government contracts.

In addition to its legislative jurisdiction under the preceding provisions of this paragraph (and its general oversight function under clause 2(b)(1)), the committee shall have the special oversight function provided for in clause 3. (g) with respect to the problems of small business.

[Rule X. 3.(g)]

The Committee on Small Business shall have the function of studying and investigating, on a continuing basis, the problems of all types of small business.

SMALL BUSINESS / 94th Congress

Service Dates of Committee Chairs: Ch1 Jan. 20,1975-Aug. 30,1976
Ch2 Aug. 31,1976-Jan. 3,1977
Service Dates of Majority Members: Jan. 20,1975-Jan. 3,1977
Service Dates of Minority Members: Jan. 28,1975-Jan. 3,1977

Majority

Rank Name	Party	State	Terms in: House	Terms in: Comm.
Ch1 Evins, Joseph L.	Dem	Tenn.	15	14
Ch2 2nd Steed, Thomas J.	Dem	Okla.	14	12
3rd Kluczynski, John C.	Dem	Ill.	13	7
4th Dingell, John D. Jr.	Dem	Mich.	11	7
5th Smith, Neal	Dem	Iowa	9	6
6th Corman, James C.	Dem	Cal.	8	6
7th Addabbo, Joseph P.	Dem	N.Y.	8	5
8th Hungate, William L.	Dem	Mo.	7	4
9th St Germain, Fernand J.	Dem	R.I.	8	3
10th Carney, Charles J.	Dem	Ohio	4	3
11th Mitchell, Parren J.	Dem	Md.	3	3
12th Bergland, Bob	DFL	Minn.	3	3
13th Gonzalez, Henry B.	Dem	Tex.	8	1
14th Hanley, James M.	Dem	N.Y.	6	1
15th Yatron, Gus	Dem	Penn.	4	1
16th Breckinridge, John B.	Dem	Ky.	2	1
17th LaFalce, John J.	Dem	N.Y.	1	1
18th Krebs, John H.	Dem	Cal.	1	1
19th Bedell, Berkley W.	Dem	Iowa	1	1
20th Richmond, Frederick W.	Dem	N.Y.	1	1
21st Evans, David W.	Dem	Ind.	1	1
22nd Russo, Martin A.	Dem	Ill.	1	1
23rd Baldus, Alvin J.	Dem	Wisc.	1	1
24th Nolan, Richard M.	DFL	Minn.	1	1
25th Derrick, Butler C. Jr.	Dem	S.C.	1	1

Minority

Rank Name	Party	State	Terms in: House	Terms in: Comm.
RM Conte, Silvio O.	Rep	Mass.	9	6
2nd Stanton, J. William	Rep	Ohio	6	4
3rd McDade, Joseph M.	Rep	Penn.	7	3
4th McCollister, John Y.	Rep	Neb.	3	2
5th Broomfield, William S.	Rep	Mich.	10	1
6th Carter, Tim Lee	Rep	Ky.	6	1
7th Fish, Hamilton Jr.	Rep	N.Y.	4	1
8th Butler, M. Caldwell	Rep	Va.	3	1
9th Cohen, William S.	Rep	Me.	2	1
10th Fenwick, Millicent H.	Rep	N.J.	1	1
11th Kindness, Thomas N.	Rep	Ohio	1	1
12th Goodling, William F.	Rep	Penn.	1	1

*1: Member's 1st period of service on the committee.

Note: "Terms in committee" reflect members' previous service on the House Select Committee on Small Business.

Changes:

Chair:

Name	Party	State	Date	Change
Ch1 Evins, Joseph L.	Dem	Tenn.	Aug. 23,1976	Left committee effective Aug. 30,1976; no new assignment.
Ch2 Steed, Thomas J.	Dem	Okla.	Aug. 31,1976	Succeeded Evins as Chair.

Majority:

Name	Party	State	Date	Change
Kluczynski, John C.	Dem	Ill.	Jan. 26,1975	Died in office.
Derrick, Butler C. Jr.	Dem	S.C.	Feb. 6,1975	Ceased active membership on committee, serving on Budget.
Badillo, Herman	Dem	N.Y.	Feb. 19,1975	Replaced Kluczynski.
Hightower, Jack E.	Dem	Tex.	Feb. 19,1975	Replaced Derrick.
Evans, David W.	Dem	Ind.	Mar. 18,1975	Moved to Banking, Currency and Housing.
Mitchell, Parren J.	Dem	Md.	May 15,1975	Ceased active membership on committee; serving on Budget.
Downey, Thomas J.	Dem	N.Y.	June 4,1975	Replaced Evans.
Fithian, Floyd J.	Dem	Ind.	June 4,1975	Replaced Mitchell.
Evins, Joseph L.	Dem	Tenn.	Aug. 23,1976	Left committee effective Aug. 30,1976; no new assignment.
Hungate, William L.	Dem	Mo.	Aug. 23,1976	Left committee effective Sep. 7,1976; no new assignment.
Ichord, Richard H.	Dem	Mo.	Aug. 31,1976	Replaced Evins.

	Majority			Minority		
Departures from the House:						
Lost Election to U.S. Senate	None			McCollister, John Y.	Neb.	Rep
Departures from Committee:						
Moved to Interior & Insular Affairs	Krebs, John H.	Cal.	Dem	None		
Moved to Science & Technology	Downey, Thomas J.	N.Y.	Dem	Fish, Hamilton Jr.	N.Y.	Rep
Moved to Government Operations	Fithian, Floyd J.	Ind.	Dem	Kindness, Thomas N.	Ohio	Rep
	Hightower, Jack E.	Tex.	Dem			
Moved to International Relations	None			Goodling, William F.	Penn.	Rep

SMALL BUSINESS / 95th Congress

Service Dates of Committee Chair: Jan. 19,1977-Jan. 3,1979
Service Dates of Majority Members: Jan. 19,1977-Jan. 3,1979
Service Dates of Minority Members: Jan. 19,1977-Jan. 3,1979

Majority

Rank	Name	Party	State	Terms in: House	Terms in: Comm.
Chr	Smith, Neal	Dem	Iowa	10	7
2nd	Steed, Thomas J.	Dem	Okla.	15	13
3rd	Dingell, John D. Jr.	Dem	Mich.	12	8
4th	Corman, James C.	Dem	Cal.	9	7
5th	Addabbo, Joseph P.	Dem	N.Y.	9	6
6th	St Germain, Fernand J.	Dem	R.I.	9	4
7th	Carney, Charles J.	Dem	Ohio	5	4
8th	Bergland, Bob	Dem	Minn.	4	4
9th	Gonzalez, Henry B.	Dem	Tex.	9	2
10th	Hanley, James M.	Dem	N.Y.	7	2
11th	Yatron, Gus	Dem	Penn.	5	2
12th	Breckinridge, John B.	Dem	Ky.	3	2
13th	LaFalce, John J.	Dem	N.Y.	2	2
14th	Bedell, Berkley W.	Dem	Iowa	2	2
15th	Richmond, Frederick W.	Dem	N.Y.	2	2
16th	Russo, Martin A.	Dem	Ill.	2	2
17th	Baldus, Alvin J.	Dem	Wisc.	2	2
18th	Nolan, Richard M.	DFL	Minn.	2	2
19th	Badillo, Herman	Dem	N.Y.	4	2
20th	Ichord, Richard H.	Dem	Mo.	9	2
21st	Nowak, Henry J.	Dem	N.Y.	2	1
22nd	Luken, Thomas A.	Dem	Ohio	2	1
23rd	LeFante, Joseph A.	Dem	N.J.	1	1
24th	Ireland, Andrew P.	Dem	Fla.	1	1
25th	Kildee, Dale E.	Dem	Mich.	1	1

Minority

Rank	Name	Party	State	Terms in: House	Terms in: Comm.
RM	Conte, Silvio O.	Rep	Mass.	10	7
2nd	Stanton, J. William	Rep	Ohio	7	5
3rd	McDade, Joseph M.	Rep	Penn.	8	4
4th	Broomfield, William S.	Rep	Mich.	11	2
5th	Carter, Tim Lee	Rep	Ky.	7	2
6th	Butler, M. Caldwell	Rep	Va.	4	2
7th	Cohen, William S.	Rep	Me.	3	2
8th	Fenwick, Millicent H.	Rep	N.J.	2	2
9th	Kasten, Robert W. Jr.	Rep	Wisc.	2	1
10th	Pressler, Larry L.	Rep	S.D.	2	1
11th	Quayle, J. Danforth	Rep	Ind.	1	1
12th	Marriott, D. Daniel	Rep	Utah	1	1

Notes: "Terms in committee" reflect members' previous service on the House Select Committee on Small Business. Rankings on this committee for the following members were affected by other chamber service: Thomas J. Steed (Dem-Okla.), Chair, Treasury, Postal Service, General Government Subcommittee of Appropriations; and John D. Dingell Jr. (Dem-Mich.), Chair, Energy and Power subcommittee of Interstate and Foreign Commerce.

Changes:

Majority:

Name	Party	State	Date	Change
Bergland, Bob	Dem	Minn.	Jan. 22,1977	Resigned; appointed Secretary of Agriculture.
Skelton, Ike	Dem	Mo.	Jan. 27,1977	Replaced Bergland.
Yatron, Gus	Dem	Penn.	Feb. 7,1977	Left committee; no new assignment.
Fowler, Wyche Jr.	Dem	Ga.	Apr. 20,1977	Replaced Yatron.
Badillo, Herman	Dem	N.Y.	Dec. 31,1977	Resigned; appointed Deputy Mayor of New York City.
Evans, Billy Lee	Dem	Ga.	Feb. 22,1978	Replaced Badillo.
LeFante, Joseph A.	Dem	N.J.	Dec. 14,1978	Resigned and retired.

	Majority			Minority		
Departures from the House:						
Elected to U.S. Senate	None			Cohen, William S.	Me.	Rep
				Pressler, Larry L.	S.D.	Rep
Defeated for Reelection	Carney, Charles J.	Ohio	Dem	None		
Defeated for Renomination	Breckinridge, John B.	Ky.	Dem	None		
Lost Election for Governor	None			Kasten, Robert W. Jr.	Wisc.	Rep
Departures from Committee:						
Moved to Ways and Means	Fowler, Wyche Jr.	Ga.	Dem	None		
Moved to Government Operations	None			Butler, M. Caldwell	Va.	Rep
Moved to District of Columbia; Foreign Affairs	None			Fenwick, Millicent H.	N.J.	Rep

SMALL BUSINESS / 96th Congress

Service Dates of Committee Chair: Jan. 24,1979-Jan. 3,1981
Service Dates of Majority Members: Jan. 24,1979-Jan. 3,1981
Service Dates of Minority Members: Jan. 24,1979-Jan. 3,1981

Majority

Rank	Name	Party	State	Terms in: House	Terms in: Comm.
Chr	Smith, Neal	Dem	Iowa	11	8
2nd	Steed, Thomas J.	Dem	Okla.	16	14
3rd	Dingell, John D. Jr.	Dem	Mich.	13	9
4th	Corman, James C.	Dem	Cal.	10	8
5th	Addabbo, Joseph P.	Dem	N.Y.	10	7
6th	St Germain, Fernand J.	Dem	R.I.	10	5
7th	Mitchell, Parren J.	Dem	Md.	5	5
8th	Gonzalez, Henry B.	Dem	Tex.	10	3
9th	Hanley, James M.	Dem	N.Y.	8	3
10th	LaFalce, John J.	Dem	N.Y.	3	3
11th	Bedell, Berkley W.	Dem	Iowa	3	3
12th	Richmond, Frederick W.	Dem	N.Y.	3	3
13th	Russo, Martin A.	Dem	Ill.	3	3
14th	Baldus, Alvin J.	Dem	Wisc.	3	3
15th	Nolan, Richard M.	DFL	Minn.	3	3
16th	Ichord, Richard H.	Dem	Mo.	10	3
17th	Nowak, Henry J.	Dem	N.Y.	3	2
18th	Luken, Thomas A.	Dem	Ohio	3	2
19th	Ireland, Andrew P.	Dem	Fla.	2	2
20th	Kildee, Dale E.	Dem	Mich.	2	2
21st	Skelton, Ike	Dem	Mo.	2	2
22nd	Evans, Billy Lee	Dem	Ga.	2	2
23rd	Barnard, D. Douglas Jr.	Dem	Ga.	2	1
24th	Leach, A. Claude Jr.	Dem	La.	1	1
25th	Hall, Tony P.	Dem	Ohio	1	1
26th	Spellman, Gladys Noon	Dem	Md.	3	*T 1

Minority

Rank	Name	Party	State	Terms in: House	Terms in: Comm.
RM	McDade, Joseph M.	Rep	Penn.	9	5
2nd	Conte, Silvio O.	Rep	Mass.	11	8
3rd	Stanton, J. William	Rep	Ohio	8	6
4th	Broomfield, William S.	Rep	Mich.	12	3
5th	Carter, Tim Lee	Rep	Ky.	8	3
6th	Quayle, J. Danforth	Rep	Ind.	2	2
7th	Marriott, D. Daniel	Rep	Utah	2	2
8th	Roth, Tobias A.	Rep	Wisc.	1	1
9th	Williams, Lyle	Rep	Ohio	1	1
10th	Snowe, Olympia J. B.	Rep	Me.	1	1
11th	Bereuter, Douglas K.	Rep	Neb.	1	1
12th	Bethune, Edwin R.	Rep	Ark.	1	1
13th	Erdahl, Arlen I.	Rep	Minn.	1	1
14th	Tauke, Thomas J.	Rep	Iowa	1	1
15th	Porter, John Edward	Rep	Ill.	1	1

*2: Member's 2nd period of service on the committee;
*T: Temporary member of the committee.

Notes: "Terms in committee" reflect members' previous service on the House Select Committee on Small Business. Rankings on this committee for the following members were affected by other chamber service: Thomas J. Steed (Dem-Okla.), Chair, Treasury, Postal Service, and General Government Subcommittee of Appropriations; John D. Dingell Jr. (Dem-Mich.), Chair, Energy and Power Subcommittee of Interstate and Foreign Commerce; Silvio O. Conte (Rep-Mass.), Ranking Minority Member, Appropriations; and J. William Stanton (Rep-Ohio), Ranking Minority Member, Banking, Finance and Urban Affairs. Parren J. Mitchell (Dem-Md.), having served on the Budget Committee during the previous three Congresses, returned to active service on this committee with his seniority intact.

Vacancies Filled:
Majority: 25th seat by Hall on Jan. 31,1979 and the 26th seat by Spellman on Feb. 6,1980.
Minority: 15th seat by Porter on Feb. 7,1980.

Changes:
Majority:

Russo, Martin A.	Dem	Ill.	Oct. 23,1979	Moved to Ways and Means.
Stenholm, Charles W.	Dem	Tex.	Dec. 19,1979	Replace Russo.

Departures from the House:

	Majority			Minority		
Elected to U.S. Senate	None			Quayle, J. Danforth	Ind.	Rep
Defeated for Reelection	Baldus, Alvin J.	Wisc.	Dem	None		
	Corman, James C.	Cal.	Dem			
	Leach, A. Claude Jr.	La.	Dem			
Retired	Hanley, James M.	N.Y.	Dem	Carter, Tim Lee	Ky.	Rep
	Ichord, Richard H.	Mo.	Dem			
	Nolan, Richard M.	Minn.	DFL			
	Steed, Thomas J.	Okla.	Dem			

Departures from Committee:

Moved to Government Operations	Barnard, D. Douglas Jr.	Ga.	Dem	None			
Became Chair of Energy & Commerce	Dingell, John D. Jr.	Mich.	Dem	None			
Moved to Rules	Hall, Tony P.	Ohio	Dem	None			
Moved to Interior & Insular Affairs	Kildee, Dale E.	Mich.	Dem				
Became Chair of Banking, Finance & Urban Affairs	St Germain, Fernand J.	R.I.	Dem	None			
Unassigned in 97th; resigned and retired Feb. 24,1981	Spellman, Gladys Noon	Md.	Dem	None			
Moved to Budget	None				Bethune, Edwin R.	Ark.	Rep
Moved to Foreign Affairs	None				Erdahl, Arlen I.	Minn.	Rep
					Roth, Tobias A.	Wisc.	Rep
Moved to Appropriations	None				Porter, John Edward	Ill.	Rep
Moved to Energy and Commerce	None				Tauke, Thomas J.	Iowa	Rep

SMALL BUSINESS / 97th Congress

Service Dates of Committee Chair: Jan. 28,1981-Jan. 3,1983
Service Dates of Majority Members: Jan. 28,1981-Jan. 3,1983
Service Dates of Minority Members: Jan. 28,1981-Jan. 3,1983

Majority

Rank	Name	Party	State	Terms in: House	Terms in: Comm.
Chr	Mitchell, Parren J.	Dem	Md.	6	6
2nd	Smith, Neal	Dem	Iowa	12	9
3rd	Addabbo, Joseph P.	Dem	N.Y.	11	8
4th	Gonzalez, Henry B.	Dem	Tex.	11	4
5th	LaFalce, John J.	Dem	N.Y.	4	4
6th	Bedell, Berkley W.	Dem	Iowa	4	4
7th	Richmond, Frederick W.	Dem	N.Y.	4	4
8th	Nowak, Henry J.	Dem	N.Y.	4	3
9th	Luken, Thomas A.	Dem	Ohio	4	3
10th	Ireland, Andrew P.	Dem	Fla.	3	3
11th	Skelton, Ike	Dem	Mo.	3	3
12th	Evans, Billy Lee	Dem	Ga.	3	3
13th	Stenholm, Charles W.	Dem	Tex.	2	2
14th	Mazzoli, Romano L.	Dem	Ky.	6	1
15th	Mavroules, Nicholas	Dem	Mass.	2	1
16th	Crockett, George W. Jr.	Dem	Mich.	2	1
17th	Hatcher, Charles F.	Dem	Ga.	1	1
18th	Wyden, Ron	Dem	Ore.	1	1
19th	Eckart, Dennis E.	Dem	Ohio	1	1
20th	Dorgan, Byron L.	Dem	N.D.	1	1
21st	Savage, Gus	Dem	Ill.	1	1
22nd	Roemer, Charles (Buddy)	Dem	La.	1	1
23rd	Fary, John G.	Dem	Ill.	4	1

Minority

Rank	Name	Party	State	Terms in: House	Terms in: Comm.
RM	McDade, Joseph M.	Rep	Penn.	10	6
2nd	Conte, Silvio O.	Rep	Mass.	12	9
3rd	Stanton, J. William	Rep	Ohio	9	7
4th	Broomfield, William S.	Rep	Mich.	13	4
5th	Marriott, D. Daniel	Rep	Utah	3	3
6th	Williams, Lyle	Rep	Ohio	2	2
7th	Snowe, Olympia J. B.	Rep	Me.	2	2
8th	Bereuter, Douglas K.	Rep	Neb.	2	2
9th	Crane, Daniel B.	Rep	Ill.	2	1
10th	Hiler, John P.	Rep	Ind.	1	1
11th	Staton, David (Mick)	Rep	W.Va.	1	1
12th	Weber, Vin	Rep	Minn.	1	1
13th	Daub, Hal	Rep	Neb.	1	1
14th	Smith, Christopher H.	Rep	N.J.	1	1
15th	Weber, Ed	Rep	Ohio	1	1
16th	Dreier, David	Rep	Cal.	1	1
17th	Molinari, Guy V.	Rep	N.Y.	1	1

Note: "Terms in committee" reflect members' previous service on the House Select Committee on Small Business. Rankings on this committee for the following members were affected by other chamber service: Neal Smith (Dem-Iowa), Chair, Commerce, Justice, State and the Judiciary Subcommittee of Appropriations; Joseph P. Addabbo (Dem-N.Y.), Chair, Defense Subcommittee of Appropriations; Silvio O. Conte (Rep-Mass.), Ranking Minority Member, Appropriations; and J. William Stanton (Rep-Ohio), Ranking Minority Member, Banking, Finance and Urban Affairs.

Vacancy Filled:
Minority: 17th seat by Molinari on Apr. 29,1981.

Changes:

Majority:

Richmond, Frederick W.	Dem	N.Y.	Aug. 25,1982	Resigned and retired.
Crockett, George W. Jr.	Dem	Mich.	May 18,1982	Moved to Judiciary.

Minority:

Bereuter, Douglas K.	Rep	Neb.	Apr. 29,1981	Moved to Banking, Finance, and Urban Affairs.
Siljander, Mark D.	Rep	Mich.	Apr. 29,1981	Replaced Bereuter.

Departures from the House:	Majority			Minority		
Defeated for Reelection	None			Staton, David (Mick)	W.Va.	Rep
				Weber, Ed	Ohio	Rep
Defeated for Renomination	Evans, Billy Lee	Ga.	Dem	None		
	Fary, John G.	Ill.	Dem			
Retired	None			Stanton, J. William	Ohio	Rep
Departures from Committee:						
Moved to Ways and Means	Dorgan, Byron L.	N.D.	Dem	None		
Moved to Armed Services	None			Crane, Daniel B.	Ill.	Rep
Moved to Joint Economic Committee	None			Snowe, Olympia J. B.	Me.	Rep
Moved to Foreign Affairs	None			Siljander, Mark D.	Mich.	Rep

SMALL BUSINESS / 98th Congress

Service Dates of Committee Chair: Jan. 6,1983-Jan. 3,1985
Service Dates of Majority Members: Jan. 6,1983-Jan. 3,1985
Service Dates of Minority Members: Jan. 6,1983-Jan. 3,1985

Majority

Rank Name	Party	State	Terms in: House	Terms in: Comm.
Chr Mitchell, Parren J.	Dem	Md.	7	7
2nd Smith, Neal	Dem	Iowa	13	10
3rd Addabbo, Joseph P.	Dem	N.Y.	12	9
4th Gonzalez, Henry B.	Dem	Tex.	12	5
5th LaFalce, John J.	Dem	N.Y.	5	5
6th Bedell, Berkley W.	Dem	Iowa	5	5
7th Nowak, Henry J.	Dem	N.Y.	5	4
8th Luken, Thomas A.	Dem	Ohio	5	4
9th Ireland, Andrew P.	Dem	Fla.	4	4
10th Skelton, Ike	Dem	Mo.	4	4
11th Stenholm, Charles W.	Dem	Tex.	3	3
12th Mazzoli, Romano L.	Dem	Ky.	7	2
13th Mavroules, Nicholas	Dem	Mass.	3	2
14th Hatcher, Charles F.	Dem	Ga.	2	2
15th Wyden, Ron	Dem	Ore.	2	2
16th Eckart, Dennis E.	Dem	Ohio	2	2
17th Savage, Gus	Dem	Ill.	2	2
18th Roemer, Charles (Buddy)	Dem	La.	2	2
19th Sisisky, Norman	Dem	Va.	1	1
20th McCloskey, Francis X.	Dem	Ind.	1	1
21st Torres, Esteban Edward	Dem	Cal.	1	1
22nd Vandergriff, Tom	Dem	Tex.	1	1
23rd Cooper, Jim	Dem	Tenn.	1	1
24th Olin, James R.	Dem	Va.	1	1
25th Britt, Charles Robin	Dem	N.C.	1	1
26th Ray, Richard	Dem	Ga.	1	1

Minority

Rank Name	Party	State	Terms in: House	Terms in: Comm.
RM McDade, Joseph M.	Rep	Penn.	11	7
2nd Conte, Silvio O.	Rep	Mass.	13	10
3rd Broomfield, William S.	Rep	Mich.	14	5
4th Marriott, D. Daniel	Rep	Utah	4	4
5th Williams, Lyle	Rep	Ohio	3	3
6th Hiler, John P.	Rep	Ind.	2	2
7th Weber, Vin	Rep	Minn.	2	2
8th Daub, Hal	Rep	Neb.	2	2
9th Smith, Christopher H.	Rep	N.J.	2	2
10th Dreier, David	Rep	Cal.	2	2
11th Molinari, Guy V.	Rep	N.Y.	2	2
12th Roth, Tobias A.	Rep	Wisc.	3	1
13th Chappie, Eugene A.	Rep	Cal.	2	1
14th Boehlert, Sherwood L.	Rep	N.Y.	1	1
15th Bilirakis, Michael	Rep	Fla.	1	1

Notes: "Terms in committee" reflect members' previous service on the House Select Committee on Small Business. Andrew Ireland of Florida resigned the Democratic Party and joined the Republican Party on July 5,1984. The Democratic Caucus terminated his majority assignments on Sep. 11, 1984. On Sep. 19,1984, the Republican Conference assigned Ireland the 5th minority rank on this committee. This resulted in a change in committee size and party ratio to 26 Democrats and 16 Republicans. Rankings on this committee for the following members were affected by other chamber service: Neal Smith (Dem-Iowa), Chair, Commerce, Justice, State and the Judiciary Subcommittee of Appropriations; Joseph P. Addabbo (Dem-N.Y.), Chair, Defense Subcommittee of Appropriations and Silvio O. Conte (Rep-Mass.), Ranking Minority Member, Appropriations.

Addition:

Minority: 16th Ireland, Andrew P. Rep Fla. Sep. 19,1984 Ranked below Williams.

Changes:

Majority:

McCloskey, Francis X.	Dem	Ind.	Nov. 17,1983	Moved to Post Office and Civil Service.
Hayes, Charles A.	Dem	Ill.	Nov. 3,1983	Replaced McCloskey before formal letter of resignation.
Ireland, Andrew P.	Dem	Fla.	Sep. 11,1984	Resigned Democratic Party; lost majority assignment.

Minority:

Marriott, D. Daniel	Rep	Utah	Feb. 3,1983	Left committee to be Ranking Minority Member on Select Committee on Children, Youth and Families.
Schaefer, Daniel L.	Rep	Colo.	Apr. 21,1983	Replaced Marriott.

	Majority			Minority		
Departures from the House:						
Defeated for Reelection	Britt, Charles Robin	N.C.	Dem	Williams, Lyle	Ohio	Rep
	Vandergriff, Tom	Tex.	Dem			
Departures from Committee:						
Moved to Energy and Commerce	None			Bilirakis, Michael	Fla.	Rep
				Schaefer, Daniel L.	Colo.	Rep
Moved to Public Works & Transportation	None			Boehlert, Sherwood L.	N.Y.	Rep
Moved to Merchant Marine & Fisheries	None			Chappie, Eugene A.	Cal.	Rep
Moved to Ways and Means	None			Daub, Hal	Neb.	Rep
Moved to Veterans' Affairs	None			Molinari, Guy V.	N.Y.	Rep
Moved to Banking, Finance & Urban Affairs	None			Roth, Tobias A.	Wisc.	Rep
Moved to Foreign Affairs				Smith, Christopher H.	N.J.	Rep

SMALL BUSINESS / 99th Congress

Service Dates of Committee Chair: Jan. 7,1985-Jan. 3,1987
Service Dates of Majority Members: Jan. 30,1985-Jan. 3,1987
Service Dates of Minority Members: Jan. 30,1985-Jan. 3,1987

Majority

Rank Name	Party	State	Terms in: House	Terms in: Comm.
Chr Mitchell, Parren J.	Dem	Md.	8	8
2nd Smith, Neal	Dem	Iowa	14	11
3rd Addabbo, Joseph P.	Dem	N.Y.	13	10
4th Gonzalez, Henry B.	Dem	Tex.	13	6
5th LaFalce, John J.	Dem	N.Y.	6	6
6th Bedell, Berkley W.	Dem	Iowa	6	6
7th Nowak, Henry J.	Dem	N.Y.	6	5
8th Luken, Thomas A.	Dem	Ohio	6	5
9th Skelton, Ike	Dem	Mo.	5	5
10th Stenholm, Charles W.	Dem	Tex.	4	4
11th Mazzoli, Romano L.	Dem	Ky.	8	3
12th Mavroules, Nicholas	Dem	Mass.	4	3
13th Hatcher, Charles F.	Dem	Ga.	3	3
14th Wyden, Ron	Dem	Ore.	3	3
15th Eckart, Dennis E.	Dem	Ohio	3	3
16th Savage, Gus	Dem	Ill.	3	3
17th Roemer, Charles (Buddy)	Dem	La.	3	3
18th Sisisky, Norman	Dem	Va.	2	2
19th Torres, Esteban Edward	Dem	Cal.	2	2
20th Cooper, Jim	Dem	Tenn.	2	2
21st Olin, James R.	Dem	Va.	2	2
22nd Ray, Richard	Dem	Ga.	2	2
23rd Hayes, Charles A.	Dem	Ill.	2	2
24th Martinez, Matthew G.	Dem	Cal.	3	1
25th Robinson, Tommy F.	Dem	Ark.	1	*T 1

Minority

Rank Name	Party	State	Terms in: House	Terms in: Comm.
RM McDade, Joseph M.	Rep	Penn.	12	7
2nd Conte, Silvio O.	Rep	Mass.	14	11
3rd Broomfield, William S.	Rep	Mich.	15	6
4th Ireland, Andrew P.	Rep	Fla.	5	5
5th Hiler, John P.	Rep	Ind.	3	3
6th Weber, Vin	Rep	Minn.	3	3
7th Dreier, David	Rep	Cal.	3	3
8th Slaughter, D. French Jr.	Rep	Va.	1	1
9th Kolbe, Jim	Rep	Ariz.	1	1
10th Cobey, William W. Jr.	Rep	N.C.	1	1
11th Smith, Robert C.	Rep	N.H.	1	1
12th Coble, Howard	Rep	N.C.	1	1
13th DioGuardi, Joseph J.	Rep	N.Y.	1	1
14th Meyers, Jan	Rep	Kans.	1	1
15th Gallo, Dean A.	Rep	N.J.	1	1
16th McMillan, J. Alex	Rep	N.C.	1	1
17th Grotberg, John E.	Rep	Ill.	1	1

*T: Temporary member of the committee.

Notes: "Terms in committee" reflect members' previous service on the House Select Committee on Small Business. The committee size was expanded and the party ratio changed to 26 Democrats and 18 Republicans on Sep. 12,1985. Rankings on this committee for the following members were affected by other chamber service: Neal Smith (Dem-Iowa), Chair, Commerce, Justice, State and the Judiciary Subcommittee of Appropriations; Joseph P. Addabbo (Dem-N.Y.), Chair, Defense Subcommittee of Appropriations; and Silvio O. Conte (Rep-Mass.), Ranking Minority Member, Appropriations. Andrew P. Ireland (Rep-Fla.) served previously on this committee as a Democrat.

Vacancy Filled:
Majority: 25th seat by Robinson on Feb. 6,1985 for the First Session only.

Additions:

Majority:	26th	Chapman, Jim	Dem	Tex.	Sep. 12,1985	Ranked below Long.
Minority:	18th	McKinney, Stewart B.	Rep	Conn.	Oct. 10,1985	

Changes:

Majority:

Martinez, Matthew G.	Dem	Cal.	Feb. 27,1985	Moved to Government Operations.
Long, Cathy	Dem	La.	May 2,1985	Replaced Martinez; ranked below Hayes.
Robinson, Tommy F.	Dem	Ark.	Dec. 30,1985	Temporary term expired on last day of First Session.
Robinson, Tommy F.	Dem	Ark.	Jan. 29,1986	Replaced himself.
Addabbo, Joseph P.	Dem	N.Y.	Apr. 10,1986	Died in office.
Waldon, Alton R.	Dem	N.Y.	Aug. 7,1986	Replaced Addabbo.
Chapman, Jim	Dem	Tex.	July 29,1986	Moved to Science and Technology.

Minority:

Grotberg, John E.	Rep	Ill.	Oct. 10,1985	Moved to Government Operations.
Combest, Larry	Rep	Tex.	Oct. 10,1985	Replaced Grotberg.

	Majority			**Minority**		
Departures from the House:						
Defeated for Reelection	None			Cobey, William W. Jr.	N.C.	Rep
Defeated for Renomination	Waldon, Alton R.	N.Y.	Dem	None		
Lost Nomination for Lt. Governor	Mitchell, Parren J.	Md.	Dem	None		
Retired	Bedell, Berkley W.	Iowa	Dem	None		
	Long, Cathy	La.	Dem			
Departures from Committee:						
Moved to Science, Space & Technology	Nowak, Henry J.	N.Y.	Dem	None		
Moved to Veterans' Affairs	None			Smith, Robert C.	N.H.	Rep
Moved to Education and Labor	Robinson, Tommy F.	Ark.	Dem	None		
Moved to Merchant Marine & Fisheries	None			Coble, Howard	N.C.	Rep
				DioGuardi, Joseph J.	N.Y.	Rep
Moved to Appropriations	None			Kolbe, Jim	Ariz.	Rep
				Weber, Vin	Minn.	Rep
No new assignment	Stenholm, Charles W.	Tex.	Dem	None		

SMALL BUSINESS / 100th Congress

Service Dates of Committee Chair: Jan. 8,1987-Jan. 3,1989
Service Dates of Majority Members: Jan. 22,1987-Jan. 3,1989
Service Dates of Minority Members: Jan. 21,1987-Jan. 3,1989

Majority

Rank	Name	Party	State	Terms in: House	Terms in: Comm.
Chr	LaFalce, John J.	Dem	N.Y.	7	7
2nd	Smith, Neal	Dem	Iowa	15	12
3rd	Gonzalez, Henry B.	Dem	Tex.	14	7
4th	Luken, Thomas A.	Dem	Ohio	7	6
5th	Skelton, Ike	Dem	Mo.	6	6
6th	Mazzoli, Romano L.	Dem	Ky.	9	4
7th	Mavroules, Nicholas	Dem	Mass.	5	4
8th	Hatcher, Charles F.	Dem	Ga.	4	4
9th	Wyden, Ron	Dem	Ore.	4	4
10th	Eckart, Dennis E.	Dem	Ohio	4	4
11th	Savage, Gus	Dem	Ill.	4	4
12th	Roemer, Charles (Buddy)	Dem	La.	4	4
13th	Sisisky, Norman	Dem	Va.	3	3
14th	Torres, Esteban Edward	Dem	Cal.	3	3
15th	Cooper, Jim	Dem	Tenn.	3	3
16th	Olin, James R.	Dem	Va.	3	3
17th	Ray, Richard	Dem	Ga.	3	3
18th	Hayes, Charles A.	Dem	Ill.	3	3
19th	Conyers, John Jr.	Dem	Mich.	12	1
20th	Bilbray, James H.	Dem	Nev.	1	1
21st	Mfume, Kweisi	Dem	Md.	1	1
22nd	Flake, Floyd H.	Dem	N.Y.	1	1
23rd	Lancaster, H. Martin	Dem	N.C.	1	1
24th	Campbell, Ben Nighthorse	Dem	Colo.	1	1
25th	DeFazio, Peter A.	Dem	Ore.	1	1
26th	Price, David E.	Dem	N.C.	1	1
27th	Martinez, Matthew G.	Dem	Cal.	4	*2 1

Minority

Rank	Name	Party	State	Terms in: House	Terms in: Comm.
RM	McDade, Joseph M.	Rep	Penn.	13	9
2nd	Conte, Silvio O.	Rep	Mass.	15	12
3rd	Broomfield, William S.	Rep	Mich.	16	7
4th	Ireland, Andrew P.	Rep	Fla.	6	6
5th	Hiler, John P.	Rep	Ind.	4	4
6th	Dreier, David	Rep	Cal.	4	4
7th	Slaughter, D. French Jr.	Rep	Va.	2	2
8th	Meyers, Jan	Rep	Kans.	2	2
9th	Gallo, Dean A.	Rep	N.J.	2	2
10th	McMillan, J. Alex	Rep	N.C.	2	2
11th	McKinney, Stewart B.	Rep	Conn.	9	2
12th	Combest, Larry	Rep	Tex.	2	2
13th	Baker, Richard H.	Rep	La.	1	1
14th	Rhodes, John J. III	Rep	Ariz.	1	1
15th	Hefley, Joel	Rep	Colo.	1	1
16th	Upton, Frederick S.	Rep	Mich.	1	1
17th	Gallegly, Elton	Rep	Cal.	1	1

*2: Member's 2nd period of service on the committee.

Notes: "Terms in committee" reflect members' previous service on the House Select Committee on Small Business. Rankings on this committee for the following members were affected by other chamber service: Neal Smith (Dem-Iowa), Chair, Commerce, Justice, State and the Judiciary Subcommittee of Appropriations; Silvio O. Conte (Rep-Mass.), Ranking Minority Member, Appropriations. Henry B. Gonzalez (Dem-Tex.), did not seek the Chairmanship of the committee.

Vacancies Filled:
Majority: 26th and 27th seats by Price and Martinez respectively on Mar. 30,1987.

Changes:
Majority:

Roemer, Charles (Buddy)	Dem	La.	Mar. 14,1988	Resigned; elected Governor of Louisiana.

Minority:

McKinney, Stewart B.	Rep	Conn.	May 7,1987	Died in office.
Holloway, Clyde C.	Rep	La.	June 18,1987	Replaced McKinney.

Departures from Committee:	Majority			Minority		
Became Chair of Banking, Finance & Urban Affairs	Gonzalez, Henry B.	Tex.	Dem	None		
Moved to Foreign Affairs	None			Gallegly, Elton	Cal.	Rep
Moved to Appropriations; Budget	None			Gallo, Dean A.	N.J.	Rep
Moved to Energy and Commerce	None			McMillan, J. Alex	N.C.	Rep
No new assignment	Campbell, Ben Nighthorse	Colo.	Dem	None		
	DeFazio, Peter A.	Ore.	Dem	None		
	Martinez, Matthew G.	Cal.	Dem	None		
	Price, David E.	N.C.	Dem	None		

SMALL BUSINESS / 101st Congress

Service Dates of Committee Chair: Jan. 3,1989-Jan. 3,1991
Service Dates of Majority Members: Jan. 19,1989-Jan. 3,1991
Service Dates of Minority Members: Jan. 20,1989-Jan. 3,1991

Majority

Rank Name	Party	State	Terms in: House	Terms in: Comm.
Chr LaFalce, John J.	Dem	N.Y.	8	8
2nd Smith, Neal	Dem	Iowa	16	13
3rd Luken, Thomas A.	Dem	Ohio	8	7
4th Skelton, Ike	Dem	Mo.	7	7
5th Mazzoli, Romano L.	Dem	Ky.	10	5
6th Mavroules, Nicholas	Dem	Mass.	6	5
7th Hatcher, Charles F.	Dem	Ga.	5	5
8th Wyden, Ron	Dem	Ore.	5	5
9th Eckart, Dennis E.	Dem	Ohio	5	5
10th Savage, Gus	Dem	Ill.	5	5
11th Sisisky, Norman	Dem	Va.	4	4
12th Torres, Esteban Edward	Dem	Cal.	4	4
13th Cooper, Jim	Dem	Tenn.	4	4
14th Olin, James R.	Dem	Va.	4	4
15th Ray, Richard	Dem	Ga.	4	4
16th Hayes, Charles A.	Dem	Ill.	4	4
17th Conyers, John Jr.	Dem	Mich.	13	2
18th Bilbray, James H.	Dem	Nev.	2	2
19th Mfume, Kweisi	Dem	Md.	2	2
20th Flake, Floyd H.	Dem	N.Y.	2	2
21st Lancaster, H. Martin	Dem	N.C.	2	2
22nd McNulty, Michael R.	Dem	N.Y.	1	1
23rd Sarpalius, Bill	Dem	Tex.	1	1
24th Hoagland, Peter	Dem	Neb.	1	1
25th Neal, Richard E.	Dem	Mass.	1	1
26th Poshard, Glenn	Dem	Ill.	1	1
27th Engel, Eliot L.	Dem	N.Y.	1	1

Minority

Rank Name	Party	State	Terms in: House	Terms in: Comm.
RM McDade, Joseph M.	Rep	Penn.	14	10
2nd Conte, Silvio O.	Rep	Mass.	16	13
3rd Broomfield, William S.	Rep	Mich.	17	8
4th Ireland, Andrew P.	Rep	Fla.	7	7
5th Hiler, John P.	Rep	Ind.	5	5
6th Dreier, David	Rep	Cal.	5	5
7th Slaughter, D. French Jr.	Rep	Va.	3	3
8th Meyers, Jan	Rep	Kans.	3	3
9th Combest, Larry	Rep	Tex.	3	3
10th Baker, Richard H.	Rep	La.	2	2
11th Rhodes, John J. III	Rep	Ariz.	2	2
12th Hefley, Joel	Rep	Colo.	2	2
13th Upton, Frederick S.	Rep	Mich.	2	2
14th Holloway, Clyde C.	Rep	La.	2	2
15th Hancock, Melton D.	Rep	Mo.	1	1
16th Campbell, Tom	Rep	Cal.	1	1
17th Machtley, Ronald K.	Rep	R.I.	1	1

Notes: "Terms in committee" reflect members' previous service on the House Select Committee on Small Business. Rankings on this committee for the following members were affected by other chamber service: Neal Smith (Dem-Iowa), Chair, Commerce, Justice, State and the Judiciary Subcommittee of Appropriations; and Silvio O. Conte (Rep-Mass.), Ranking Minority Member, Appropriations.

Vacancies Filled:
Majority: 27th seat by Engel on Jan. 27,1989.
Minority: 17th seat by Machtley on May 4,1989.

Changes:

Majority:				
Hayes, Charles A.	Dem	Ill.	Oct. 26,1989	Moved to Post Office and Civil Service.
McNulty, Michael R.	Dem	N.Y.	Feb. 27,1990	Moved to Post Office and Civil Service.
Serrano, Jose E.	Dem	N.Y.	Apr. 4,1990	Replaced Hayes.
Minority:				
Campbell, Tom	Rep	Cal.	Mar. 28,1990	Moved to Judiciary.
Molinari, Susan	Rep	N.Y.	Mar. 28,1990	Replaced Campbell.

	Majority			Minority		
Departures from the House:						
Defeated for Reelection	None			Hiler, John P.	Ind.	Rep
Retired	Luken, Thomas A.	Ohio	Dem	None		
Departures from Committee:						
Moved to Budget	Cooper, Jim	Tenn.	Dem	None		
Moved to Interior & Insular Affairs; Judiciary	Hoagland, Peter	Neb.	Dem	None		
Moved to Rules	None			Dreier, David	Cal.	Rep
Moved to Energy and Commerce	None			Holloway, Clyde C.	La.	Rep
Moved to Education and Labor	None			Molinari, Susan	N.Y.	Rep
No new assignment	None			Rhodes, John J. III	Ariz.	Rep

SMALL BUSINESS / 102nd Congress

Service Dates of Committee Chair: Jan. 24,1991-Jan. 3,1993
Service Dates of Majority Members: Jan. 24,1991-Jan. 3,1993
Service Dates of Minority Members: Jan. 24,1991-Jan. 3,1993

Majority

Rank	Name	Party	State	Terms in: House	Terms in: Comm.
Chr	LaFalce, John J.	Dem	N.Y.	9	9
2nd	Smith, Neal	Dem	Iowa	17	14
3rd	Skelton, Ike	Dem	Mo.	8	8
4th	Mazzoli, Romano L.	Dem	Ky.	11	6
5th	Mavroules, Nicholas	Dem	Mass.	7	6
6th	Hatcher, Charles F.	Dem	Ga.	6	6
7th	Wyden, Ron	Dem	Ore.	6	6
8th	Eckart, Dennis E.	Dem	Ohio	6	6
9th	Savage, Gus	Dem	Ill.	6	6
10th	Sisisky, Norman	Dem	Va.	5	5
11th	Torres, Esteban Edward	Dem	Cal.	5	5
12th	Olin, James R.	Dem	Va.	5	5
13th	Ray, Richard	Dem	Ga.	5	5
14th	Conyers, John Jr.	Dem	Mich.	14	3
15th	Bilbray, James H.	Dem	Nev.	3	3
16th	Mfume, Kweisi	Dem	Md.	3	3
17th	Flake, Floyd H.	Dem	N.Y.	3	3
18th	Lancaster, H. Martin	Dem	N.C.	3	3
19th	Sarpalius, Bill	Dem	Tex.	2	2
20th	Neal, Richard E.	Dem	Mass.	2	2
21st	Poshard, Glenn	Dem	Ill.	2	2
22nd	Engel, Eliot L.	Dem	N.Y.	2	2
23rd	Serrano, Jose E.	Dem	N.Y.	2	2
24th	Andrews, Robert E.	Dem	N.J.	2	1
25th	Andrews, Thomas H.	Dem	Me.	1	1
26th	Dooley, Calvin	Dem	Cal.	1	1
27th	Orton, Bill	Dem	Utah	1	1

Minority

Rank	Name	Party	State	Terms in: House	Terms in: Comm.
RM1	McDade, Joseph M.	Rep	Penn.	15	11
2nd	Conte, Silvio O.	Rep	Mass.	17	14
3rd	Broomfield, William S.	Rep	Mich.	18	9
RM2 4th	Ireland, Andrew P.	Rep	Fla.	7	8
5th	Slaughter, D. French Jr.	Rep	Va.	4	4
6th	Meyers, Jan	Rep	Kans.	4	4
7th	Combest, Larry	Rep	Tex.	4	4
8th	Baker, Richard H.	Rep	La.	3	3
9th	Hefley, Joel	Rep	Colo.	3	3
10th	Upton, Frederick S.	Rep	Mich.	3	3
11th	Hancock, Melton D.	Rep	Mo.	2	1
12th	Machtley, Ronald K.	Rep	R.I.	2	1
13th	Ramstad, Jim	Rep	Minn.	1	1
14th	Camp, Dave	Rep	Mich.	1	1
15th	Franks, Gary	Rep	Conn.	1	1
16th	Allard, Wayne	Rep	Colo.	1	1
17th	Boehner, John A.	Rep	Ohio	1	1

Notes: "Terms in committee" reflect members' previous service on the House Select Committee on Small Business. Rankings on this committee for the following members were affected by other chamber service: Neal Smith (Dem-Iowa), Chair, Commerce, Justice, State and the Judiciary Subcommittee of Appropriations; Silvio O. Conte (Rep-Mass.), Ranking Minority Member, Appropriations; and William S. Broomfield (Rep-Mich.), Ranking Minority Member, Foreign Affairs.

Changes:

Ranking Member:

	Name	Party	State	Date	Change
RM1	McDade, Joseph M.	Rep	Penn.	Feb. 8,1991	Became Ranking Minority Member of Appropriations; remained on committee.
RM2	Ireland, Andrew P.	Rep	Fla.	Feb. 8,1991	Succeeded McDade as Ranking Minority Member.

Majority:

Name	Party	State	Date	Change
Engel, Eliot L.	Dem	N.Y.	July 9,1991	Moved to Science, Space and Technology (letter dated June 28,1991).
Dooley, Calvin	Dem	Cal.	Oct. 9,1991	Moved to Interior and Insular Affairs.
Pastor, Ed	Dem	Penn.	Oct. 9,1991	Replaced Engel.

Minority:

Name	Party	State	Date	Change
Conte, Silvio O.	Rep	Mass.	Feb. 8,1991	Died in office.
Johnson, Sam	Rep	Tex.	June 7,1991	Replaced Conte.
Upton, Frederick S.	Rep	Mich.	July 11,1991	Left committee, no new assignment.
Zeliff, William	Rep	N.H.	July 11,1991	Replaced Upton.
Slaughter, D. French Jr.	Rep	Va.	Nov. 5,1991	Resigned and retired.
Allen, George F.	Rep	Va.	Nov. 12,1991	Replaced Slaughter.

STANDARDS OF OFFICIAL CONDUCT

Jurisdiction, 1967

Established by House Resolution 418, 90th Congress, First Session, April 3, 1967:

[Paragraph 2, Sections (a) through (c)]

(a) Measures relating to the Code of Official Conduct.
(b) Measures relating to financial disclosure by Members, officers, and employees of the House of Representatives.
(c) The committee is authorized--

(1) to recommend to the House of Representatives, from time to time, such legislative or administrative actions as the committee may deem appropriate to establish or enforce standards of official conduct for Members, officers, and employees of the House of Representatives;
(2) to investigate, subject to paragraph (d) of this clause, any alleged violation, by a Member, officer, or employee of the House of Representatives, of the Code of Official Conduct or of any law, rule, regulation, or other standard of conduct applicable to the conduct of such Member, officer, or employee in the performance of his duties or the discharge of his responsibilities and, after notice and a hearing, shall recommend to the House of Representatives, by resolution or otherwise, such action as the committee may deem appropriate in the circumstances;
(3) to report to the appropriate Federal or State authorities, with approval of the House of Representatives, any substantial evidence of a violation, by a Member, officer, or employee of the House of Representatives, of any law applicable to the performance of his duties or the discharge of his responsibilities, which may have been disclosed in a committee investigation; and
(4) to give consideration to the request of a Member, officer, or employee of the House of Representatives, for an advisory opinion with respect to the general propriety of any current or proposed conduct of such Member, officer, or employee and, with appropriate deletions to assure the privacy of the individual concerned, to publish such opinion for the guidance of other Members, officers, and employees of the House of Representatives.

Jurisdiction, 1992

Jurisdiction contained in Rules of the House of Representatives, (as revised to July 1, 1992):

[Rule X. 1. (t)]

Committee on Standards of Official Conduct.

(1) Measures relating to the Code of Official Conduct.

In addition to its legislative jurisdiction under the preceding provision of this paragraph (and its general oversight function under clause 2(b)(1)), the committee shall have the functions with respect to recommendations, studies, investigations, and reports which are provided for in clause 4(e), and the functions designated in titles I and V of the Ethics in Government Act of 1978 and sections 7342, 7351 and 7353 of title 5, United States Code.

[Rule X. 4. (e)(1)]

The Committee on Standards of Official Conduct is authorized;

(A) to recommend to the House from time to time such administrative actions as it may deem appropriate to establish or enforce standards of official conduct for Members, officers, and employees of the House, and any letter or reproval or other administrative action of the committee pursuant to an investigation under subdivision (B) shall only be issued or implemented as a part of a report required by such subdivision;
(B) to investigate, subject to subparagraph (2) of this paragraph, any alleged violation, by a Member, officer, or employee of the House, of the Code of Official Conduct or of any law, rule, regulation, or other standard of conduct applicable to the conduct of such Member, officer, or employee in the performance of his duties or the discharge of his responsibilities, and after notice and hearing (unless the right to a hearing is waived by the Member, officer,

or employee), shall report to the House its findings of fact and recommendations, if any, upon the final disposition of any such investigation, and such action as the committee may deem appropriate in the circumstances;

(C) to report to the appropriate Federal or State authorities, with the approval of the House, any substantial evidence of a violation, by a Member, officer, or employee of the House, of any law applicable to the performance of his duties or the discharge of his responsibilities, which may have been disclosed in a committee investigation;

(D) to give consideration to the request of any Member, officer, or employee of the House for an advisory opinion with respect to the general propriety of any current or proposed conduct of such Member, officer, or employee and, with appropriate deletions to assure the privacy of the individual concerned, to publish such opinion for the guidance of other Members, officers, and employees of the House; and

(E) to give consideration to the request of any Member, officer, or employee of the House for a written waiver in exceptional circumstances with respect to clause 4 of rule XLIII.

STANDARDS OF OFFICIAL CONDUCT / 90th Congress

Service Dates of Committee Chair: May 1,1967-Jan. 3,1969
Service Dates of Majority Members: May 1,1967-Jan. 3,1969
Service Dates of Minority Members: May 1,1967-Jan. 3,1969

Majority

Rank	Name	Party	State	Terms in: House	Terms in: Comm.
Chr	Price, C. Melvin	Dem	Ill.	12	1
2nd	Teague, Olin E.	Dem	Tex.	12	1
3rd	Evins, Joseph L.	Dem	Tenn.	11	1
4th	Abbitt, Watkins M.	Dem	Va.	11	1
5th	Aspinall, Wayne N.	Dem	Colo.	10	1
6th	Kelly, Edna F.	Dem	N.Y.	10	1

Minority

Rank	Name	Party	State	Terms in: House	Terms in: Comm.
RM	Halleck, Charles A.	Rep	Ind.	17	1
2nd	Arends, Leslie C.	Rep	Ill.	17	1
3rd	Betts, Jackson E.	Rep	Ohio	9	1
4th	Stafford, Robert T.	Rep	Vt.	4	1
5th	Quillen, James H.	Rep	Tenn.	3	1
6th	Williams, Lawrence G.	Rep	Penn.	1	1

	Majority			Minority		
Departures from the House:						
Defeated for Renomination	Kelly, Edna F.	N.Y.	Dem	None		
Retired	None			Halleck, Charles A.	Ind.	Rep
Departures from Committee:						
No new assignment	Evins, Joseph L.	Tenn.	Dem	None		

STANDARDS OF OFFICIAL CONDUCT / 91st Congress

Service Dates of Committee Chair: Jan. 29,1969-Jan. 3,1971
Service Dates of Majority Members: Jan. 29,1969-Jan. 3,1971
Service Dates of Minority Members: Jan. 29,1969-Jan. 3,1971

Majority

Rank	Name	Party	State	Terms in: House	Terms in: Comm.
Chr	Price, C. Melvin	Dem	Ill.	13	2
2nd	Teague, Olin E.	Dem	Tex.	13	2
3rd	Abbitt, Watkins M.	Dem	Va.	12	2
4th	Aspinall, Wayne N.	Dem	Colo.	11	2
5th	Hebert, F. Edward	Dem	La.	15	1
6th	Holifield, Chet	Dem	Cal.	14	1

Minority

Rank	Name	Party	State	Terms in: House	Terms in: Comm.
RM1	Arends, Leslie C.	Rep	Ill.	18	2
RM2 2nd	Betts, Jackson E.	Rep	Ohio	10	2
3rd	Stafford, Robert T.	Rep	Vt.	5	2
4th	Quillen, James H.	Rep	Tenn.	4	2
5th	Williams, Lawrence G.	Rep	Penn.	2	2
6th	Hutchinson, J. Edward	Rep	Mich.	4	1

Changes:

Ranking Member:				
RM1 Arends, Leslie C.	Rep	Ill.	July 24,1969	Left committee; became Ranking Minority Member of Armed Services June 22,1969.
RM2 Betts, Jackson E.	Rep	Ohio	July 24,1969	Succeeded Arends as Ranking Minority Member.
Minority:				
Arends, Leslie C.	Rep	Ill.	July 24,1969	Left committee; no new assignment.
Reid, Charlotte T.	Rep	Ill.	Oct. 7,1969	Replaced Arends.

STANDARDS OF OFFICIAL CONDUCT / 92nd Congress

Service Dates of Committee Chair: Feb. 4,1971-Jan. 3,1973
Service Dates of Majority Members: Feb. 4,1971-Jan. 3,1973
Service Dates of Minority Members: Feb. 4,1971-Jan. 3,1973

Majority			Terms in:		Minority			Terms in:	
Rank Name	Party	State	House	Comm.	Rank Name	Party	State	House	Comm.
Chr Price, C. Melvin	Dem	Ill.	14	3	RM Betts, Jackson E.	Rep	Ohio	11	3
2nd Teague, Olin E.	Dem	Tex.	14	3	2nd Stafford, Robert T.	Rep	Vt.	6	3
3rd Abbitt, Watkins M.	Dem	Va.	13	3	3rd Quillen, James H.	Rep	Tenn.	5	3
4th Aspinall, Wayne N.	Dem	Colo.	12	3	4th Williams, Lawrence G.	Rep	Penn.	3	3
5th Hebert, F. Edward	Dem	La.	16	2	5th Hutchinson, J. Edward	Rep	Mich.	5	2
6th Holifield, Chet	Dem	Cal.	15	2	6th Reid, Charlotte T.	Rep	Ill.	5	2

Changes:

Minority:

Stafford, Robert T.	Rep	Vt.	Sep. 16,1971	Resigned; appointed to U.S. Senate.
Reid, Charlotte T.	Rep	Ill.	Oct. 7,1971	Resigned; appointed to Federal Communications Commission.
King, Carleton J.	Rep	N.Y.	Oct. 27,1971	Replaced Stafford.
Spence, Floyd D.	Rep	S.C.	Oct. 27,1971	Replaced Reid.

Departures from the House:	Majority			Minority		
Defeated for Renomination	Aspinall, Wayne N.	Colo.	Dem	None		
Retired	Abbitt, Watkins M.	Va.	Dem	Betts, Jackson E.	Ohio	Rep

STANDARDS OF OFFICIAL CONDUCT / 93rd Congress

Service Dates of Committee Chair: Jan. 24,1973-Jan. 3,1975
Service Dates of Majority Members: Jan. 24,1973-Jan. 3,1975
Service Dates of Minority Members: Jan. 24,1973-Jan. 3,1975

Majority			Terms in:		Minority			Terms in:	
Rank Name	Party	State	House	Comm.	Rank Name	Party	State	House	Comm.
Chr Price, C. Melvin	Dem	Ill.	15	4	RM Quillen, James H.	Rep	Tenn.	6	4
2nd Teague, Olin E.	Dem	Tex.	15	4	2nd Williams, Lawrence G.	Rep	Penn.	4	4
3rd Hebert, F. Edward	Dem	La.	17	3	3rd Hutchinson, J. Edward	Rep	Mich.	6	3
4th Holifield, Chet	Dem	Cal.	16	3	4th King, Carleton J.	Rep	N.Y.	7	2
5th Flynt, John James Jr.	Dem	Ga.	11	1	5th Spence, Floyd D.	Rep	S.C.	2	2
6th Foley, Thomas S.	Dem	Wash.	5	1	6th Hunt, John E.	Rep	N.J.	4	1

Changes:

Majority:

Holifield, Chet	Dem	Cal.	Dec. 31,1974	Resigned and retired.

Minority:

King, Carleton J.	Rep	N.Y.	Dec. 31,1974	Resigned; defeated for reelection.

Departures from the House:	Majority	Minority		
Defeated for Reelection	None	Hunt, John E.	N.J.	Rep
Defeated for Renomination	None	Williams, Lawrence G.	Penn.	Rep

STANDARDS OF OFFICIAL CONDUCT / 94th Congress

Service Dates of Committee Chairs: Ch1 Jan. 20,1975-Feb. 5,1975
Ch2 Feb. 5,1975-Jan. 3,1977
Service Dates of Majority Members: Jan. 20,1975-Jan. 3,1977
Service Dates of Minority Members: Jan. 28,1975-Jan. 3,1977

Majority

Rank Name	Party	State	Terms in: House	Terms in: Comm.
Ch1 Price, C. Melvin	Dem	Ill.	16	5
2nd Teague, Olin E.	Dem	Tex.	16	5
3rd Hebert, F. Edward	Dem	La.	18	4
Ch2 4th Flynt, John James Jr.	Dem	Ga.	12	2
5th Foley, Thomas S.	Dem	Wash.	6	2
6th Bennett, Charles E.	Dem	Fla.	14	1

Minority

Rank Name	Party	State	Terms in: House	Terms in: Comm.
RM Spence, Floyd D.	Rep	S.C.	3	3
2nd Quillen, James H.	Rep	Tenn.	7	5
3rd Hutchinson, J. Edward	Rep	Mich.	7	4
4th Quie, Albert H.	Rep	Minn.	10	1
5th Mitchell, Donald J.	Rep	N.Y.	2	1
6th Cochran, Thad	Rep	Miss.	2	1

Note: Rankings on this committee for the following members were affected by other chamber service: Olin E. Teague (Dem-Tex.), Chair, Science and Technology; James H. Quillen (Rep-Tenn.), Ranking Minority Member, Rules; and J. Edward Hutchinson (Rep-Mich.), Ranking Minority Member, Judiciary. Edward F. Hebert (Dem-La.), was unseated as Chair of the Armed Services committee by Price and did not seek the Chairmanship of this committee.

Changes:

Chair:

Ch1 Price, C. Melvin	Dem	Ill.	Feb. 5,1975	Elected Chair of Armed Services; remained on committee.
Ch2 Flynt, John James Jr.	Dem	Ga.	Feb. 5,1975	Succeeded Price as Chair.

	Majority			Minority		
Departures from the House:						
Retired	Hebert, F. Edward	La.	Dem	Hutchinson, J. Edward	Mich.	Rep
Departures from Committee:						
No new assignment	Foley, Thomas S.	Wash.	Dem	Mitchell, Donald J.	N.Y.	Rep
	Price, C. Melvin	Ill.	Dem			

STANDARDS OF OFFICIAL CONDUCT / 95th Congress

Service Dates of Committee Chair: Jan. 19,1977-Jan. 3,1979
Service Dates of Majority Members: Jan. 19,1977-Jan. 3,1979
Service Dates of Minority Members: Jan. 19,1977-Jan. 3,1979

Majority

Rank Name	Party	State	Terms in: House	Terms in: Comm.
Chr Flynt, John James Jr.	Dem	Ga.	13	3
2nd Teague, Olin E.	Dem	Tex.	17	6
3rd Bennett, Charles E.	Dem	Fla.	15	2
4th Hamilton, Lee H.	Dem	Ind.	7	1
5th Preyer, L. Richardson	Dem	N.C.	5	1
6th Flowers, Walter	Dem	Ala.	5	1

Minority

Rank Name	Party	State	Terms in: House	Terms in: Comm.
RM Spence, Floyd D.	Rep	S.C.	4	4
2nd Quillen, James H.	Rep	Tenn.	8	6
3rd Quie, Albert H.	Rep	Minn.	11	2
4th Cochran, Thad	Rep	Miss.	3	2
5th Fenwick, Millicent H.	Rep	N.J.	2	1
6th Caputo, Bruce F.	Rep	N.Y.	1	1

Note: Rankings on this committee for the following members were affected by other chamber service: Olin E. Teague (Dem-Tex.), Chair, Science and Technology; James H. Quillen (Rep-Tenn.), Ranking Minority Member, Rules.

Vacancy Filled:
Minority: 6th seat by Caputo on Jan. 26,1977

Changes:

Majority:

Teague, Olin E.	Dem	Tex.	Dec. 31,1978	Resigned and retired.

Minority:

Cochran, Thad	Rep	Miss.	Dec. 26,1978	Resigned; elected to U.S. Senate.

Departures from the House:	Majority			Minority		
Elected Governor	None			Quie, Albert H.	Minn.	Rep
Lost Nomination to U.S. Senate	Flowers, Walter	Ala.	Dem	None		
Lost Nomination for Lt. Governor	None			Caputo, Bruce F.	N.Y.	Rep
Retired	Flynt, John James Jr.	Ga.	Dem	None		
Departures from Committee:						
Moved to District of Columbia; Foreign Affairs	None			Fenwick, Millicent H.	N.J.	Rep
No new assignment	None			Quillen, James H.	Tenn.	Rep

STANDARDS OF OFFICIAL CONDUCT / 96th Congress

Service Dates of Committee Chair: Jan. 31,1979-Jan. 3,1981
Service Dates of Majority Members: Jan. 31,1979-Jan. 3,1981
Service Dates of Minority Members: Jan. 24,1979-Jan. 3,1981

Majority			Terms in:		Minority			Terms in:	
Rank Name	Party	State	House	Comm.	Rank Name	Party	State	House	Comm.
Chr Bennett, Charles E.	Dem	Fla.	16	3	RM Spence, Floyd D.	Rep	S.C.	5	5
2nd Hamilton, Lee H.	Dem	Ind.	8	2	2nd Hollenbeck, Harold C.	Rep	N.J.	2	1
3rd Preyer, L. Richardson	Dem	N.C.	6	2	3rd Livingston, Robert L.	Rep	La.	2	1
4th Slack, John M. Jr.	Dem	W.Va.	11	1	4th Thomas, William M.	Rep	Cal.	1	1
5th Murphy, Morgan F.	Dem	Ill.	5	1	5th Sensenbrenner, F. Jas. Jr.	Rep	Wisc.	1	1
6th Murtha, John P. Jr.	Dem	Penn.	4	1	6th Cheney, Richard B.	Rep	Wyo.	1	1

Note: On Feb. 5,1980 and Mar. 18,1980, during the "Abscam" investigation, John P. Murtha, Jr. (Dem-Penn.) was replaced temporarily by Wyche Fowler (Dem-Ga.).

Vacancy Filled:
Minority: 6th seat by Cheney on Jan. 31,1979.

Changes:
Majority:

Murphy, Morgan F.	Dem	Ill.	Dec. 20,1979	Left committee; no new assignment.
Stokes, Louis	Dem	Ohio	Feb. 6,1980	Replaced Murphy.
Slack, John M. Jr.	Dem	W.Va.	Mar. 17,1980	Died in office.
Rahall, Nick J. II	Dem	W.Va.	Mar. 26,1980	Replaced Slack.

Departures from the House:	Majority			Minority		
Defeated for Reelection	Preyer, L. Richardson	N.C.	Dem	None		
Departures from Committee:						
Moved to Select Intelligence	Hamilton, Lee H.	Ind.	Dem	None		
Moved to Public Works & Transportation	None			Hollenbeck, Harold C.	N.J.	Rep
Moved to Appropriations	None			Livingston, Robert L.	La.	Rep
Moved to Science & Technology	None			Sensenbrenner, F. Jas. Jr.	Wisc.	Rep
Moved to House Administration	None			Thomas, William M.	Cal.	Rep
No new assignment	Bennett, Charles E.	Fla.	Dem	Cheney, Richard B.	Wyo.	Rep
	Murtha, John P. Jr.	Penn.	Dem			

STANDARDS OF OFFICIAL CONDUCT / 97th Congress

Service Dates of Committee Chair: Jan. 28,1981-Jan. 3,1983
Service Dates of Majority Members: Jan. 28,1981-Jan. 3,1983
Service Dates of Minority Members: Jan. 28,1981-Jan. 3,1983

Majority

Rank Name	Party	State	Terms in: House	Terms in: Comm.
Chr Stokes, Louis	Dem	Ohio	7	*1 2
2nd Rahall, Nick Joe II	Dem	W.Va.	3	2
3rd Alexander, William V. Jr.	Dem	Ark.	7	1
4th Wilson, Charles	Dem	Tex.	5	1
5th Holland, Kenneth L.	Dem	S.C.	4	1
6th Bailey, Donald A.	Dem	Penn.	2	1

Minority

Rank Name	Party	State	Terms in: House	Terms in: Comm.
RM Spence, Floyd D.	Rep	S.C.	6	6
2nd Conable, Barber B. Jr.	Rep	N.Y.	9	1
3rd Myers, John T.	Rep	Ind.	8	1
4th Forsythe, Edwin B.	Rep	N.J.	7	1
5th Brown, Hank	Rep	Colo.	1	1
6th Hansen, James V.	Rep	Utah	1	1

*1: Member's 1st period of service on the committee.

	Majority		Minority
Departures from the House:			
Defeated for Reelection	Holland, Kenneth L.	S.C. Dem	None
Defeated for Renomination	Bailey, Donald A.	Penn. Dem	None
Departures from Committee:			
No new assignment	Alexander, William V. Jr.	Ark. Dem	None
	Wilson, Charles	Tex. Dem	

STANDARDS OF OFFICIAL CONDUCT / 98th Congress

Service Dates of Committee Chair: Jan. 6,1983-Jan. 3,1985
Service Dates of Majority Members: Jan. 6,1983-Jan. 3,1985
Service Dates of Minority Members: Jan. 6,1983-Jan. 3,1985

Majority

Rank Name	Party	State	Terms in: House	Terms in: Comm.
Chr Stokes, Louis	Dem	Ohio	8	*1 3
2nd Rahall, Nick Joe II	Dem	W.Va.	4	3
3rd Jenkins, Edgar L.	Dem	Ga.	4	1
4th Dixon, Julian C.	Dem	Cal.	3	1
5th Fazio, Victor H.	Dem	Cal.	3	1
6th Coyne, William J.	Dem	Penn.	2	1

Minority

Rank Name	Party	State	Terms in: House	Terms in: Comm.
RM Spence, Floyd D.	Rep	S.C.	7	7
2nd Conable, Barber B. Jr.	Rep	N.Y.	10	2
3rd Myers, John T.	Rep	Ind.	9	2
4th Forsythe, Edwin B.	Rep	N.J.	8	2
5th Brown, Hank	Rep	Colo.	2	2
6th Hansen, James V.	Rep	Utah	2	2

*1: Member's 1st period of service on the committee.

Changes:
Minority:

Forsythe, Edwin B.	Rep	N.J.	Mar. 29,1984	Died in office.
Bliley, Thomas J. Jr.	Rep	Va.	May 9,1984	Replaced Forsythe.

	Majority		Minority	
Departures from the House:				
Retired	None		Conable, Barber B. Jr.	N.Y. Rep
Departures from Committee:				
Moved to Budget; Judiciary	None		Brown, Hank	Colo. Rep
No new assignment	Rahall, Nick Joe II	W.Va. Dem	Bliley, Thomas J. Jr.	Va. Rep
	Stokes, Louis	Ohio Dem		

STANDARDS OF OFFICIAL CONDUCT / 99th Congress

Service Dates of Committee Chair: Jan. 7,1985-Jan. 3,1987
Service Dates of Majority Members: Jan. 30,1985-Jan. 3,1987
Service Dates of Minority Members: Jan. 30,1985-Jan. 3,1987

Majority			Terms in:		Minority			Terms in:	
Rank Name	**Party**	**State**	**House**	**Comm.**	**Rank Name**	**Party**	**State**	**House**	**Comm.**
Chr Dixon, Julian C.	Dem	Cal.	4	2	RM Spence, Floyd D.	Rep	S.C.	8	8
2nd Jenkins, Edgar L.	Dem	Ga.	5	2	2nd Myers, John T.	Rep	Ind.	10	3
3rd Fazio, Victor H.	Dem	Cal.	4	2	3rd Hansen, James V.	Rep	Utah	3	3
4th Coyne, William J.	Dem	Penn.	3	2	4th Whitehurst, G. William	Rep	Va.	9	1
5th Dwyer, Bernard J.	Dem	N.J.	3	1	5th Pursell, Carl D.	Rep	Mich.	5	1
6th Mollohan, Alan B.	Dem	W.Va.	2	1	6th Wortley, George	Rep	N.Y.	3	1

Note: Ranking on this committee for the following member was affected by other chamber service: Edgar L. Jenkins (Dem-Ga.) served on both the Budget Committee and the Ways and Means Committee.

	Majority			Minority		
Departures from the House:						
Retired	None			Whitehurst, G. William	Va.	Rep
Departures from Committee:						
Moved to Budget	Jenkins, Edgar L.	Ga.	Dem	None		
Moved to Select Children, Youth & Families	None			Wortley, George	N.Y.	Rep
No new assignment	Coyne, William J.	Penn.	Dem	Pursell, Carl D.	Mich.	Rep

STANDARDS OF OFFICIAL CONDUCT / 100th Congress

Service Dates of Committee Chair: Feb. 19,1987-Jan. 3,1989
Service Dates of Majority Members: Feb. 19,1987-Jan. 3,1989
Service Dates of Minority Members: Jan. 21,1987-Jan. 3,1989

Majority			Terms in:		Minority			Terms in:	
Rank Name	**Party**	**State**	**House**	**Comm.**	**Rank Name**	**Party**	**State**	**House**	**Comm.**
Chr Dixon, Julian C.	Dem	Cal.	5	3	RM1 Spence, Floyd D.	Rep	S.C.	9	9
2nd Fazio, Victor H.	Dem	Cal.	5	3	RM2 2nd Myers, John T.	Rep	Ind.	11	4
3rd Dwyer, Bernard J.	Dem	N.J.	4	2	3rd Hansen, James V.	Rep	Utah	4	4
4th Mollohan, Alan B.	Dem	W.Va.	3	2	4th Pashayan, Charles S. Jr.	Rep	Cal.	5	1
5th Gaydos, Joseph M.	Dem	Penn.	11	1	5th Petri, Thomas E.	Rep	Wisc.	5	1
6th Atkins, Chester G.	Dem	Mass.	2	1	6th Craig, Larry E.	Rep	Ida.	4	1

Changes:

Ranking Member:				
RM1 Spence, Floyd D.	Rep	S.C.	June 1,1988	Left committee; no new assignment.
RM2 Myers, John T.	Rep	Ind.	June 1,1988	Succeeded Spence as Ranking Minority Member.
Minority:				
Spence, Floyd D.	Rep	S.C.	June 1,1988	Left committee; no new assignment.
Brown, Hank	Rep	Colo.	June 2,1988	Replaced Spence.

STANDARDS OF OFFICIAL CONDUCT / 101st Congress

Service Dates of Committee Chair: Jan. 3,1989-Jan. 3,1991
Service Dates of Majority Members: Jan. 3,1989-Jan. 3,1991
Service Dates of Minority Members: Jan. 3,1989-Jan. 3,1991

Majority			Terms in:		Minority			Terms in:	
Rank Name	Party	State	House	Comm.	Rank Name	Party	State	House	Comm.
Chr Dixon, Julian C.	Dem	Cal.	6	4	RM Myers, John T.	Rep	Ind.	12	5
2nd Fazio, Victor H.	Dem	Cal.	6	4	2nd Hansen, James V.	Rep	Utah	5	5
3rd Dwyer, Bernard J.	Dem	N.J.	5	3	3rd Pashayan, Charles S. Jr.	Rep	Cal.	6	2
4th Mollohan, Alan B.	Dem	W.Va.	4	3	4th Petri, Thomas E.	Rep	Wisc.	6	2
5th Gaydos, Joseph M.	Dem	Penn.	12	2	5th Craig, Larry E.	Rep	Ida.	5	2
6th Atkins, Chester G.	Dem	Mass.	3	2	6th Brown, Hank	Rep	Colo.	5 *T	2

*T: Temporary member of the committee.

Changes:
Minority:

Brown, Hank	Rep	Colo.	July 18,1989	Left committee; no new assignment.
Grandy, Fred	Rep	Iowa	July 18,1989	Replaced Brown.

	Majority			Minority		
Departures from the House:						
Elected to U.S. Senate	None			Craig, Larry E.	Ida.	Rep
Defeated for Reelection	None			Pashayan, Charles S. Jr.	Cal.	Rep
Departures from Committee:						
No new assignment	Dixon, Julian C.	Cal.	Dem	Myers, John T.	Ind.	Rep
	Fazio, Victor H.	Cal.	Dem	Petri, Thomas E.	Wisc.	Rep
	Dwyer, Bernard J.	N.J.	Dem			
	Mollohan, Alan B.	W.Va.	Dem			
	Gaydos, Joseph M.	Penn.	Dem			
	Atkins, Chester G.	Mass.	Dem			

STANDARDS OF OFFICIAL CONDUCT / 102nd Congress

Service Dates of Committee Chair: Feb. 6,1991-Jan. 3,1993
Service Dates of Majority Members: Feb. 6,1991-Jan. 3,1993
Service Dates of Minority Members: Feb. 6,1991-Jan. 3,1993

Majority			Terms in:		Minority			Terms in:	
Rank Name	Party	State	House	Comm.	Rank Name	Party	State	House	Comm.
Chr Stokes, Louis	Dem	Ohio	12 *2	1	RM Hansen, James V.	Rep	Utah	6	6
2nd McHugh, Matthew F.	Dem	N.Y.	9	1	2nd Grandy, Fred	Rep	Iowa	3	2
3rd Ackerman, Gary L.	Dem	N.Y.	5	1	3rd Johnson, Nancy L.	Rep	Conn.	5	1
4th Darden, George W. (Buddy)	Dem	Ga.	5	1	4th Bunning, Jim	Rep	Ky.	3	1
5th Cardin, Benjamin L.	Dem	Md.	3	1	5th Kyl, Jon	Rep	Ariz.	3	1
6th Pelosi, Nancy	Dem	Cal.	3	1	6th Goss, Porter J.	Rep	Fla.	2	1
7th McDermott, James A.	Dem	Wash.	2	1	7th Hobson, David L.	Rep	Ohio	1	1

*2: Member's 2nd period of service on the committee.

Note: On Oct. 9,1991, Louis Stokes (Dem-Ohio), Chair of this committee, excused himself from the committee's investigation of the House Bank run by the Sergeant-at-Arms. Kweisi Mfume (Dem-Md.) acted as a member of the committee during this investigation according to Congressional Record Oct. 9,1991 (H7675). Mfume later filled a vacancy on the committee.

Changes:
Majority:

Ackerman, Gary L.	Dem	N.Y.	July 28,1992	Left committee; no new assignment.
Mfume, Kweisi	Dem	Md.	Aug. 11,1992	Replaced Ackerman.

VETERANS' AFFAIRS

Jurisdiction, 1947

Established by the Legislative Reorganization Act of 1946:

[Section 121.(1)(r)]

Committee on Veterans' Affairs.

1. Veterans' measures generally.
2. Pensions of all the wars of the United States, general and special.
3. Life insurance issued by the Government on account of service in the armed forces.
4. Compensation, vocational rehabilitation, and education of veterans.
5. Veterans' hospitals, medical care, and treatment of veterans.
6. Soldiers' and sailors' civil relief.
7. Readjustment of servicemen to civil life.

Jurisdiction, 1992

Jurisdiction contained in Rules of the House of Representatives, (as revised to July 1, 1992):

[Rule X. 1. (u)]

Committee on Veterans' Affairs.

(1) Veterans' measures generally.
(2) Cemeteries of the United States in which veterans of any war or conflict are or may be buried, whether in the United States or abroad, except cemeteries administered by the Secretary of the Interior.
(3) Compensation, vocational rehabilitation, and education of veterans.
(4) Life insurance issued by the Government on account of service in the Armed Forces.
(5) Pensions of all the wars of the United States, general and special.
(6) Readjustment of servicemen to civil life.
(7) Soldiers' and sailors' civil relief.
(8) Veterans' hospitals, medical care, and treatment of veterans.

VETERANS' AFFAIRS / 80th Congress

Service Dates of Committee Chair: Jan. 14,1947-Jan. 3,1949
Service Dates of Majority Members: Jan. 14,1947-Jan. 3,1949
Service Dates of Minority Members: Jan. 16,1947-Jan. 3,1949

Majority

Rank	Name	Party	State	Terms in: House	Terms in: Comm.
Chr	Rogers, Edith Nourse	Rep	Mass.	12	12
2nd	Kearney, Bernard W.	Rep	N.Y.	3	3
3rd	O'Konski, Alvin E.	Rep	Wisc.	3	3
4th	Ramey, Homer A.	Rep	Ohio	3	2
5th	Mathews, Frank A. Jr.	Rep	N.J.	2	2
6th	Crow, William J.	Rep	Penn.	1	1
7th	Meade, W. Howes	Rep	Ky.	1	1
8th	Vail, Richard B.	Rep	Ill.	1	1
9th	Meyer, Herbert A.	Rep	Kans.	1	1
10th	Mitchell, Edward A.	Rep	Ind.	1	1
11th	Patterson, James T.	Rep	Conn.	1	1
12th	Phillips, Dayton E.	Rep	Tenn.	1	1
13th	Ross, Robert Tripp	Rep	N.Y.	1	1
14th	Sarbacher, George W. Jr.	Rep	Penn.	1	1
15th	Bakewell, Claude I.	Rep	Mo.	1	1
16th	Davis, Glenn R.	Rep	Wisc.	1	1

Minority

Rank	Name	Party	State	Terms in: House	Terms in: Comm.
RM	Rankin, John E.	Dem	Miss.	14	14
2nd	Allen, A. Leonard	Dem	La.	6	4
3rd	Huber, Walter B.	Dem	Ohio	2	2
4th	Price, C. Melvin	Dem	Ill.	2	1
5th	Teague, Olin E.	Dem	Tex.	2	1
6th	Johnson, Glen D.	Dem	Okla.	1	1
7th	Evins, Joseph L.	Dem	Tenn.	1	1
8th	Lusk, Georgia L.	Dem	N.M.	1	1
9th	Wheeler, William M.	Dem	Ga.	1	1
10th	Jones, Hamilton C.	Dem	N.C.	1	1
11th	Donohue, Harold D.	Dem	Mass.	1	1

Vacancy Filled:
Majority: 16th seat by Davis on May 23,1947.

Changes:
Minority:

Price, C. Melvin	Dem	Ill.	Jan. 20,1948	Moved to Armed Services.

Departures from the House:

	Majority			Minority		
Appointed Deputy Assistant Attorney General	Mathews, Frank A. Jr.	N.J.	Rep	None		
Defeated for Reelection	Bakewell, Claude I.	Mo.	Rep	None		
	Crow, William J.	Penn.	Rep			
	Meade, W. Howes	Ky.	Rep			
	Mitchell, Edward A.	Ind.	Rep			
	Ramey, Homer A.	Ohio	Rep			
	Ross, Robert Tripp	N.Y.	Rep			
	Sarbacher, George W. Jr.	Penn.	Rep			
	Vail, Richard B.	Ill.	Rep			
Defeated for Renomination	None			Lusk, Georgia L.	N.M.	Dem
Lost Nomination to U.S. Senate	None			Johnson, Glen D.	Okla.	Dem

VETERANS' AFFAIRS / 81st Congress

Service Dates of Committee Chair: Jan. 18,1949-Jan. 3,1951
Service Dates of Majority Members: Jan. 18,1949-Jan. 3,1951
Service Dates of Minority Members: Jan. 18,1949-Jan. 3,1951

Majority

Rank	Name	Party	State	Terms in: House	Terms in: Comm.
Chr	Rankin, John E.	Dem	Miss.	15	15
2nd	Allen, A. Leonard	Dem	La.	7	5
3rd	Huber, Walter B.	Dem	Ohio	3	3
4th	Teague, Olin E.	Dem	Tex.	3	2
5th	Evins, Joseph L.	Dem	Tenn.	2	2
6th	Wheeler, William M.	Dem	Ga.	2	2
7th	Jones, Hamilton C.	Dem	N.C.	2	2
8th	Donohue, Harold D.	Dem	Mass.	2	2
9th	Burton, Clarence G.	Dem	Va.	2	1
10th	Mack, Peter F. Jr.	Dem	Ill.	1	1
11th	Magee, Clare	Dem	Mo.	1	1
12th	Chudoff, Earl	Dem	Penn.	1	1
13th	Staggers, Harley O.	Dem	W.Va.	1	1
14th	Rodino, Peter W. Jr.	Dem	N.J.	1	1
15th	Noland, James E.	Dem	Ind.	1	1
16th	Elliott, Carl A.	Dem	Ala.	1	1
17th	Patten, Harold A.	Dem	Ariz.	1	1

Minority

Rank	Name	Party	State	Terms in: House	Terms in: Comm.
RM	Rogers, Edith Nourse	Rep	Mass.	13	13
2nd	Kearney, Bernard W.	Rep	N.Y.	4	4
3rd	O'Konski, Alvin E.	Rep	Wisc.	4	4
4th	Meyer, Herbert A.	Rep	Kans.	2	2
5th	Patterson, James T.	Rep	Conn.	2	2
6th	Phillips, Dayton E.	Rep	Tenn.	2	2
7th	Davis, Glenn R.	Rep	Wisc.	2	2
8th	Scudder, Hubert B.	Rep	Cal.	1	1
9th	Harden, Cecil M.	Rep	Ind.	1	1
10th	Hoffman, Richard W.	Rep	Ill.	1	1

Changes:
Majority:

Rodino, Peter W. Jr.	Dem	N.J.	Jan. 26,1950	Moved to Judiciary.
Hays, Wayne L.	Dem	Ohio	Mar. 30,1950	Replaced Rodino.

Minority:

Patterson, James T.	Rep	Conn.	Jan. 9,1950	Moved to Armed Services.
Meyer, Herbert A.	Rep	Kans.	Mar. 1,1950	Moved to Armed Services.
Bates, William H.	Rep	Mass.	Mar. 1,1950	Replaced Patterson.

Departures from the House:

	Majority			Minority		
Defeated for Reelection	Huber, Walter B.	Ohio	Dem	None		
	Noland, James E.	Ind.	Dem			
Defeated for Renomination	None			Phillips, Dayton E.	Tenn.	Rep

Departures from Committee:

Moved to Banking and Currency	Burton, Clarence G.	Va. Dem	None	
Moved to Public Works	Chudoff, Earl	Penn. Dem	Scudder, Hubert B.	Cal. Rep
Moved to Interstate & Foreign Commerce	Mack, Peter F. Jr.	Ill. Dem	Hoffman, Richard W.	Ill. Rep
Moved to Agriculture	Patten, Harold A.	Ariz. Dem	None	
	Wheeler, William M.	Ga. Dem		
Moved to Armed Services	None		Bates, William H.	Mass. Rep
Moved to Appropriations	None		Davis, Glenn R.	Wisc. Rep
Moved to Expenditures in the Executive Departments	None		Harden, Cecil M.	Ind. Rep

VETERANS' AFFAIRS / 82nd Congress

Service Dates of Committee Chair: Jan. 12,1951-Jan. 3,1953
Service Dates of Majority Members: Jan. 12,1951-Jan. 3,1953
Service Dates of Minority Members: Jan. 15,1951-Jan. 3,1953

Majority

Rank	Name	Party	State	Terms in: House	Terms in: Comm.
Chr	Rankin, John E.	Dem	Miss.	16	16
2nd	Allen, A. Leonard	Dem	La.	8	6
3rd	Teague, Olin E.	Dem	Tex.	4	3
4th	Evins, Joseph L.	Dem	Tenn.	3	3
5th	Jones, Hamilton C.	Dem	N.C.	3	3
6th	Donohue, Harold D.	Dem	Mass.	3	3
7th	Magee, Clare	Dem	Mo.	2	2
8th	Staggers, Harley O.	Dem	W.Va.	2	2
9th	Elliott, Carl A.	Dem	Ala.	2	2
10th	Hays, Wayne L.	Dem	Ohio	2	2
11th	Dorn, W. J. Bryan	Dem	S.C.	2	1
12th	Rogers, Walter E.	Dem	Tex.	1	1
13th	Secrest, Robert T.	Dem	Ohio	7 *2	1

Minority

Rank	Name	Party	State	Terms in: House	Terms in: Comm.
RM	Rogers, Edith Nourse	Rep	Mass.	14	14
2nd	Kearney, Bernard W.	Rep	N.Y.	5	5
3rd	O'Konski, Alvin E.	Rep	Wisc.	5	5
4th	Devereux, James P. S.	Rep	Md.	1	1
5th	Ayres, William H.	Rep	Ohio	1	1
6th	Adair, E. Ross	Rep	Ind.	1	1
7th	Hunter, Allan O.	Rep	Cal.	1	1
8th	Springer, William L.	Rep	Ill.	1	1
9th	Prouty, Winston L.	Rep	Vt.	1	1
10th	Denny, Harmar D. Jr.	Rep	Penn.	1	1

*2: Member's 2nd period of service on the committee.

Vacancy Filled:
Majority: 13th seat by Secrest on July 18,1951.

Changes:

Majority:

Staggers, Harley O.	Dem	W.Va.	Apr. 6,1951	Moved to Interstate and Foreign Commerce.
Magee, Clare	Dem	Mo.	June 13,1951	Moved to Public Works.
Donohue, Harold D.	Dem	Mass.	Aug. 9,1951	Moved to Judiciary.
Hays, Wayne L.	Dem	Ohio	Aug. 9,1951	Moved to Banking and Currency.
Kee, Maude Elizabeth	Dem	W.Va.	Aug. 9,1951	Replaced Staggers.
Buchanan, Vera D.	Dem	Penn.	Aug. 9,1951	Replaced Magee.
Buchanan, Vera D.	Dem	Penn.	Aug. 16,1951	Moved to Merchant Marine and Fisheries.
Elliott, Carl A.	Dem	Ala.	Oct. 20,1951	Moved to Education and Labor.

Minority:

Denny, Harmar D. Jr.	Rep	Penn.	Aug. 1,1951	Moved to Interstate and Foreign Commerce.
Sittler, Edward L. Jr.	Rep	Penn.	Oct. 4,1951	Replaced Denny.
Devereux, James P. S.	Rep	Md.	July 3,1952	Moved to Armed Services.
Radwan, Edmund P.	Rep	N.Y.	Feb. 20,1952	Replaced Devereux.

Departures from the House:	Majority		Minority	
Defeated for Reelection	Jones, Hamilton C.	N.C. Dem	Sittler, Edward L. Jr.	Penn. Rep
Defeated for Renomination	Rankin, John E.	Miss. Dem	None	
Retired	Allen, A. Leonard	La. Dem	None	
Departures from Committee:				
Moved to Interior & Insular Affairs	Rogers, Walter E.	Tex. Dem	None	
Moved to Appropriations	None		Hunter, Allan O.	Cal. Rep
Moved to Armed Services	None		O'Konski, Alvin E.	Wisc. Rep

VETERANS' AFFAIRS / 83rd Congress

Service Dates of Committee Chair: Jan. 19,1953-Jan. 3,1955
Service Dates of Majority Members: Jan. 19,1953-Jan. 3,1955
Service Dates of Minority Members: Jan. 19,1953-Jan. 3,1955

Majority

Rank	Name	Party	State	Terms in: House		Comm.
Chr	Rogers, Edith Nourse	Rep	Mass.	15		15
2nd	Kearney, Bernard W.	Rep	N.Y.	6		6
3rd	Ayres, William H.	Rep	Ohio	2		2
4th	Adair, E. Ross	Rep	Ind.	2		2
5th	Springer, William L.	Rep	Ill.	2		2
6th	Prouty, Winston L.	Rep	Vt.	2		2
7th	Radwan, Edmund P.	Rep	N.Y.	2		2
8th	Mack, Russell V.	Rep	Wash.	4		1
9th	Saylor, John P.	Rep	Penn.	3	*1	1
10th	Bonin, Edward J.	Rep	Penn.	1		1
11th	Frelinghuysen, Peter H.B.	Rep	N.J.	1		1
12th	Mailliard, William S.	Rep	Cal.	1		1
13th	Fino, Paul A.	Rep	N.Y.	1		1
14th	Cretella, Albert W.	Rep	Conn.	1		1

Minority

Rank	Name	Party	State	Terms in: House		Comm.
RM	Teague, Olin E.	Dem	Tex.	5		4
2nd	Evins, Joseph L.	Dem	Tenn.	4		4
3rd	Dorn, W. J. Bryan	Dem	S.C.	3		2
4th	Secrest, Robert T.	Dem	Ohio	8	*2	2
5th	Kee, Maude Elizabeth	Dem	W.Va.	2		2
6th	Long, George S.	Dem	La.	1		1
7th	Hagen, Harlan F.	Dem	Cal.	1		1
8th	Byrne, James A.	Dem	Penn.	1		1
9th	Gentry, Brady P.	Dem	Tex.	1		1
10th	Matthews, Donald R.	Dem	Fla.	1		1
11th	Edmondson, Edmond A.	Dem	Okla.	1		1
12th	Selden, Armistead I. Jr.	Dem	Ala.	1		1

*1: Member's 1st period of service on the committee; *2: Member's 2nd period of service on the committee.

Note: Democratic party gains in the 1953 special elections in New Jersey and Wisconsin led to a change in size and party ratio on this committee to 14 Republicans and 14 Democrats on Jan. 25,1954.

Additions:

Minority:

13th	Natcher, William H.	Dem	Ky.	Jan. 25,1954
14th	Johnson, Lester R.	Dem	Wisc.	Jan. 25,1954

Changes:

Minority:

Secrest, Robert T. — Dem — Ohio — Sep. 26,1954 — Resigned; appointed to Federal Trade Commission.

	Majority			Minority		
Departures from the House:						
Defeated for Reelection	Bonin, Edward J.	Penn.	Rep	None		
Departures from Committee:						
Moved to Appropriations	None			Evins, Joseph L.	Tenn.	Dem
				Natcher, William H.	Ky.	Dem
Moved to Public Works	None			Gentry, Brady P.	Tex.	Dem
Moved to Agriculture	None			Hagen, Harlan F.	Cal.	Dem
				Johnson, Lester R.	Wisc.	Dem
Moved to Foreign Affairs	None			Selden, Armistead I. Jr.	Ala.	Dem
No new assignment	Cretella, Albert W.	Conn.	Rep	None		
	Frelinghuysen, Peter H.B.	N.J.	Rep			
	Mack, Russell V.	Wash.	Rep			
	Mailliard, William S.	Cal.	Rep			
	Prouty, Winston L.	Vt.	Rep			
	Radwan, Edmund P.	N.Y.	Rep			
	Saylor, John P.	Penn.	Rep			
	Springer, William L.	Ill.	Rep			

VETERANS' AFFAIRS / 84th Congress

Service Dates of Committee Chair: Jan. 13,1955-Jan. 3,1957
Service Dates of Majority Members: Jan. 13,1955-Jan. 3,1957
Service Dates of Minority Members: Jan. 20,1955-Jan. 3,1957

Majority

Rank	Name	Party	State	Terms in: House		Terms in: Comm.
Chr	Teague, Olin E.	Dem	Tex.	6		5
2nd	Dorn, W. J. Bryan	Dem	S.C.	4		3
3rd	Kee, Maude Elizabeth	Dem	W.Va.	3		3
4th	Long, George S.	Dem	La.	2		2
5th	Byrne, James A.	Dem	Penn.	2		2
6th	Matthews, Donald R.(Billy)	Dem	Fla.	2		2
7th	Edmondson, Edmond A.	Dem	Okla.	2		2
8th	Boykin, Frank W.	Dem	Ala.	11	*2	1
9th	Aspinall, Wayne N.	Dem	Colo.	4		1
10th	O'Brien, Leo W.	Dem	N.Y.	3		1
11th	Shuford, George A.	Dem	N.C.	2		1
12th	Christopher, George H.	Dem	Mo.	2		1
13th	Diggs, Charles C. Jr.	Dem	Mich.	1		1
14th	Sisk, B. F.	Dem	Cal.	1		1

Minority

Rank	Name	Party	State	Terms in: House		Terms in: Comm.
RM	Rogers, Edith Nourse	Rep	Mass.	16		16
2nd	Kearney, Bernard W.	Rep	N.Y.	7		7
3rd	Ayres, William H.	Rep	Ohio	3		3
4th	Adair, E. Ross	Rep	Ind.	3		3
5th	Fino, Paul A.	Rep	N.Y.	2		2
6th	Weaver, Phillip H.	Rep	Neb.	1		1
7th	Avery, William H.	Rep	Kans.	1		1
8th	Thomson, E. Keith	Rep	Wyo.	1		1
9th	Siler, Eugene	Rep	Ky.	1		1
10th	Teague, Charles M.	Rep	Cal.	1	*1	1

*1: Member's 1st period of service on the committee;
*2: Member's 2nd period of service on the committee.

Changes:

Majority:

Matthews, Donald R.(Billy)	Dem	Fla.	Jan. 31,1955	Moved to Agriculture.
Haley, James A.	Dem	Fla.	Mar. 16,1955	Replaced Matthews.

Departures from Committee:	Majority			Minority		
Moved to Armed Services	Byrne, James A.	Penn.	Dem	None		
Moved to Public Works	Edmondson, Edmond A.	Okla.	Dem	None		
Moved to Interstate & Foreign Commerce	O'Brien, Leo W.	N.Y.	Dem	Avery, William H.	Kans.	Rep
Moved to Banking and Currency	None			Siler, Eugene	Ky.	Rep
Moved to Agriculture	None			Teague, Charles M.	Cal.	Rep
Moved to Interior & Insular Affairs	None			Thomson, E. Keith	Wyo.	Rep

VETERANS' AFFAIRS / 85th Congress

Service Dates of Committee Chair: Jan. 10,1957-Jan. 3,1959
Service Dates of Majority Members: Jan. 10,1957-Jan. 3,1959
Service Dates of Minority Members: Jan. 16,1957-Jan. 3,1959

Majority

Rank	Name	Party	State	Terms in: House		Terms in: Comm.
Chr	Teague, Olin E.	Dem	Tex.	7		6
2nd	Dorn, W. J. Bryan	Dem	S.C.	5		4
3rd	Kee, Maude Elizabeth	Dem	W.Va.	4		4
4th	Long, George S.	Dem	La.	3		3
5th	Boykin, Frank W.	Dem	Ala.	12	*2	2
6th	Aspinall, Wayne N.	Dem	Colo.	5		2
7th	Shuford, George A.	Dem	N.C.	3		2
8th	Christopher, George H.	Dem	Mo.	3		2
9th	Diggs, Charles C. Jr.	Dem	Mich.	2		2
10th	Sisk, B. F.	Dem	Cal.	2		2
11th	Haley, James A.	Dem	Fla.	3		2
12th	Baring, Walter S.	Dem	Nev.	3		1
13th	Whitener, Basil L.	Dem	N.C.	1		1

Minority

Rank	Name	Party	State	Terms in: House		Terms in: Comm.
RM	Rogers, Edith Nourse	Rep	Mass.	17		17
2nd	Kearney, Bernard W.	Rep	N.Y.	8		8
3rd	Ayres, William H.	Rep	Ohio	4		4
4th	Adair, E. Ross	Rep	Ind.	4		4
5th	Fino, Paul A.	Rep	N.Y.	3		3
6th	Weaver, Phillip H.	Rep	Neb.	2		2
7th	Saylor, John P.	Rep	Penn.	5	*2	1
8th	Dwyer, Florence P.	Rep	N.J.	1		1
9th	Smith, H. Allen	Rep	Cal.	1		1
10th	Teague, Charles M.	Rep	Cal.	2	*2	1

*2: Member's 2nd period of service on the committee.

Note: The committee was expanded and the party ratio changed to 14 Democrats and 10 Republicans on Feb. 26,1958.

Vacancy Filled:
Minority: 10th seat by Charles Teague on Mar. 18,1957.

Addition:
Majority: 14th Everett, Robert A. Dem Tenn. Feb. 26,1958.

Changes:
Majority:

Whitener, Basil L.	Dem	N.C.	Jan. 16,1958	Moved to Judiciary.
Mitchell, Harlan Erwin	Dem	Ga.	Jan. 27,1958	Replaced Whitener.
Long, George S.	Dem	La.	Mar. 22,1958	Died in office.
Nix, Robert N. C.	Dem	Penn.	July 21,1958	Replaced Long.

Departures from the House:	**Majority**			**Minority**		
Retired	Shuford, George A.	N.C.	Dem	Kearney, Bernard W.	N.Y.	Rep
Departures from Committee:						
Became Chair of Interior & Insular Affairs	Aspinall, Wayne N.	Colo.	Dem	None		
Moved to Foreign Affairs	Diggs, Charles C. Jr.	Mich.	Dem	None		
Moved to Science & Astronautics	Sisk, B. F.	Cal.	Dem	None		
Moved to Banking and Currency	None			Dwyer, Florence P.	N.J.	Rep
Moved to Appropriations	None			Weaver, Phillip H.	Neb.	Rep

VETERANS' AFFAIRS / 86th Congress

Service Dates of Committee Chair: Jan. 19,1959-Jan. 3,1961
Service Dates of Majority Members: Jan. 19,1959-Jan. 3,1961
Service Dates of Minority Members: Jan. 19,1959-Jan. 3,1961

Majority

Rank Name	Party	State	Terms in: House	Terms in: Comm.
Chr Teague, Olin E.	Dem	Tex.	8	7
2nd Dorn, W. J. Bryan	Dem	S.C.	6	5
3rd Kee, Maude Elizabeth	Dem	W.Va.	5	5
4th Boykin, Frank W.	Dem	Ala.	13 *2	3
5th Christopher, George H.	Dem	Mo.	4	3
6th Haley, James A.	Dem	Fla.	4	3
7th Baring, Walter S.	Dem	Nev.	4	2
8th Mitchell, Harlan Erwin	Dem	Ga.	2	2
9th Everett, Robert A.	Dem	Tenn.	2	2
10th Nix, Robert N. C.	Dem	Penn.	2	2
11th Quigley, James M.	Dem	Penn.	2	1
12th Slack, John M. Jr.	Dem	W.Va.	1	1
13th Flynn, Gerald T.	Dem	Wisc.	1	1
14th Dulski, Thaddeus J.	Dem	N.Y.	1	1
15th Carter, Steven V.	Dem	Iowa	1	1
16th George, Newell A.	Dem	Kans.	1	1

Minority

Rank Name	Party	State	Terms in: House	Terms in: Comm.
RM Rogers, Edith Nourse	Rep	Mass.	18	18
2nd Ayres, William H.	Rep	Ohio	5	5
3rd Adair, E. Ross	Rep	Ind.	5	5
4th Fino, Paul A.	Rep	N.Y.	4	4
5th Saylor, John P.	Rep	Penn.	6 *2	2
6th Smith, H. Allen	Rep	Cal.	2	2
7th Teague, Charles M.	Rep	Cal.	3 *2	2
8th Halpern, Seymour	Rep	N.Y.	1	1

*2: Member's 2nd period of service on the committee.

Vacancy Filled:
Minority: 8th seat by Halpern on Jan. 29,1959.

Changes:
Majority:

Christopher, George H.	Dem	Mo.	Jan. 23,1959	Died in office.
Randall, William J.	Dem	Mo.	Mar. 11,1959	Replaced Christopher.
Carter, Steven V.	Dem	Iowa	Nov. 4,1959	Died in office.

Minority:

Rogers, Edith Nourse	Rep	Mass.	Sep. 10,1960	Died in office.

Departures from the House:	**Majority**			**Minority**		
Elected State Senator	Mitchell, Harlan Erwin	Ga.	Dem	None		
Defeated for Reelection	Flynn, Gerald T.	Wisc.	Dem	None		
	George, Newell A.	Kans.	Dem			
	Quigley, James M.	Penn.	Dem			
Departures from Committee:						
Moved to Foreign Affairs	Nix, Robert N. C.	Penn.	Dem	None		
Moved to Appropriations	Slack, John M. Jr.	W.Va.	Dem	None		
Moved to Rules	None			Smith, H. Allen	Cal.	Rep

VETERANS' AFFAIRS / 87th Congress

Service Dates of Committee Chair: Feb. 6,1961-Jan. 3,1963
Service Dates of Majority Members: Feb. 6,1961-Jan. 3,1963
Service Dates of Minority Members: Feb. 13,1961-Jan. 3,1963

Majority

Rank	Name	Party	State	Terms in: House	Terms in: Comm.
Chr	Teague, Olin E.	Dem	Tex.	9	8
2nd	Dorn, W. J. Bryan	Dem	S.C.	7	6
3rd	Kee, Maude Elizabeth	Dem	W.Va.	6	6
4th	Boykin, Frank W.	Dem	Ala.	14	*2 4
5th	Haley, James A.	Dem	Fla.	5	4
6th	Baring, Walter S.	Dem	Nev.	5	3
7th	Everett, Robert A.	Dem	Tenn.	3	3
8th	Dulski, Thaddeus J.	Dem	N.Y.	2	2
9th	Randall, William J.	Dem	Mo.	2	2
10th	Libonati, Roland V.	Dem	Ill.	3	1
11th	McDowell, Harris B. Jr.	Dem	Del.	3	1
12th	Hansen, Julia Butler	Dem	Wash.	2	1
13th	Hagan, G. Elliott	Dem	Ga.	1	1
14th	Kornegay, Horace R.	Dem	N.C.	1	1
15th	Addabbo, Joseph P.	Dem	N.Y.	1	1

Minority

Rank	Name	Party	State	Terms in: House	Terms in: Comm.
RM	Ayres, William H.	Rep	Ohio	6	6
2nd	Adair, E. Ross	Rep	Ind.	6	6
3rd	Fino, Paul A.	Rep	N.Y.	5	5
4th	Saylor, John P.	Rep	Penn.	7	*2 3
5th	Teague, Charles M.	Rep	Cal.	4	*2 3
6th	Halpern, Seymour	Rep	N.Y.	2	2
7th	Fulton, James G.	Rep	Penn.	9	1
8th	Harrison, William Henry	Rep	Wyo.	3	1
9th	Schadeberg, Henry C.	Rep	Wisc.	1	1
10th	Ellsworth, Robert F.	Rep	Kans.	1	1

*2: Member's 2nd period of service on the committee.

Changes:

Majority:

Name	Party	State	Date	Change
Hansen, Julia Butler	Dem	Wash.	Mar. 6,1961	Moved to Education and Labor.
Hagan, G. Elliott	Dem	Ga.	Jan. 18,1962	Moved to Agriculture.
Roberts, Herbert Ray	Dem	Tex.	Feb. 6,1962	Replaced Hansen.
Rosenthal, Benjamin S.	Dem	N.Y.	Mar. 7,1962	Replaced Hagan.

	Majority			Minority		
Departures from the House:						
Defeated for Renomination	Boykin, Frank W.	Ala.	Dem	None		
Departures from Committee:						
Moved to Appropriations	Addabbo, Joseph P.	N.Y.	Dem	Harrison, William Henry	Wyo.	Rep
Moved to Government Operations	Randall, William J.	Mo.	Dem	None		
Moved to Agriculture; Government Operations	Rosenthal, Benjamin S.	N.Y.	Dem	None		
No new assignment	None			Fulton, James G.	Penn.	Rep

VETERANS' AFFAIRS / 88th Congress

Service Dates of Committee Chair: Jan. 17,1963-Jan. 3,1965
Service Dates of Majority Members: Jan. 17,1963-Jan. 3,1965
Service Dates of Minority Members: Jan. 24,1963-Jan. 3,1965

Majority

Rank	Name	Party	State	Terms in: House		Comm.
Chr	Teague, Olin E.	Dem	Tex.	10		9
2nd	Dorn, W. J. Bryan	Dem	S.C.	8		7
3rd	Kee, Maude Elizabeth	Dem	W.Va.	7		7
4th	Haley, James A.	Dem	Fla.	6		5
5th	Baring, Walter S.	Dem	Nev.	6		4
6th	Everett, Robert A.	Dem	Tenn.	4		4
7th	Dulski, Thaddeus J.	Dem	N.Y.	3		3
8th	Libonati, Roland V.	Dem	Ill.	4		2
9th	McDowell, Harris B. Jr.	Dem	Del.	4		2
10th	Kornegay, Horace R.	Dem	N.C.	2		2
11th	Roberts, Herbert Ray	Dem	Tex.	2		2
12th	Secrest, Robert T.	Dem	Ohio	9	*3	1
13th	Edwards, Don	Dem	Cal.	1	*1	1
14th	Marsh, John O. Jr.	Dem	Va.	1		1
15th	Brown, George E. Jr.	Dem	Cal.	1		1

Minority

Rank	Name	Party	State	Terms in: House		Comm.
RM	Ayres, William H.	Rep	Ohio	7		7
2nd	Adair, E. Ross	Rep	Ind.	7		7
3rd	Fino, Paul A.	Rep	N.Y.	6		6
4th	Saylor, John P.	Rep	Penn.	8	*2	4
5th	Teague, Charles M.	Rep	Cal.	5	*2	4
6th	Halpern, Seymour	Rep	N.Y.	3		3
7th	Schadeberg, Henry C.	Rep	Wisc.	2		2
8th	Ellsworth, Robert F.	Rep	Kans.	2		2
9th	Bromwell, James E.	Rep	Iowa	2		1

*1: Member's 1st period of service on the committee;
*2: Member's 2nd period of service on the committee;
*3: Member's 3rd period of service on the committee.

Vacancy Filled:
Minority: 9th seat by Bromwell on Feb. 27,1963.

Changes:
Majority:

Edwards, Don	Dem	Cal.	July 25,1963	Moved to Judiciary.
Rooney, Fred B.	Dem	Penn.	Aug. 12,1963	Replaced Edwards.
Rooney, Fred B.	Dem	Penn.	May 20,1964	Moved to Interstate and Foreign Commerce.

Departures from the House:

	Majority			Minority		
Defeated for Reelection	None			Bromwell, James E.	Iowa	Rep
				Schadeberg, Henry C.	Wisc.	Rep
Retired	Kee, Maude Elizabeth	W.Va.	Dem	None		
	Libonati, Roland V.	Ill.	Dem			

Departures from Committee:

Moved to Appropriations	Marsh, John O. Jr.	Va.	Dem	None

VETERANS' AFFAIRS / 89th Congress

Service Dates of Committee Chair: Jan. 18,1965-Jan. 3,1967
Service Dates of Majority Members: Jan. 18,1965-Jan. 3,1967
Service Dates of Minority Members: Jan. 21,1965-Jan. 3,1967

Majority

Rank	Name	Party	State	Terms in: House		Comm.
Chr	Teague, Olin E.	Dem	Tex.	11		10
2nd	Dorn, W. J. Bryan	Dem	S.C.	9		8
3rd	Haley, James A.	Dem	Fla.	7		6
4th	Baring, Walter S.	Dem	Nev.	7		5
5th	Everett, Robert A.	Dem	Tenn.	5		5
6th	Dulski, Thaddeus J.	Dem	N.Y.	4		4
7th	McDowell, Harris B. Jr.	Dem	Del.	5		3
8th	Kornegay, Horace R.	Dem	N.C.	3		3
9th	Roberts, Herbert Ray	Dem	Tex.	3		3
10th	Secrest, Robert T.	Dem	Ohio	10	*3	2
11th	Brown, George E. Jr.	Dem	Cal.	2		2
12th	Wilson, Charles H.	Dem	Cal.	2		1
13th	Satterfield, David E. III	Dem	Va.	1		1
14th	Roncalio, Teno	Dem	Wyo.	1		1

Minority

Rank	Name	Party	State	Terms in: House		Comm.
RM	Adair, E. Ross	Rep	Ind.	8		8
2nd	Ayres, William H.	Rep	Ohio	8		8
3rd	Fino, Paul A.	Rep	N.Y.	7		7
4th	Saylor, John P.	Rep	Penn.	9	*2	5
5th	Teague, Charles M.	Rep	Cal.	6	*2	5
6th	Halpern, Seymour	Rep	N.Y.	4		4
7th	Ellsworth, Robert F.	Rep	Kans.	3		3
8th	Duncan, John J.	Rep	Tenn.	1		1

15th Helstoski, Henry	Dem	N.J.	1	1
16th Resnick, Joseph Y.	Dem	N.Y.	1	1
17th Hanley, James M.	Dem	N.Y.	1	1

*2: Member's 2nd period of service on the committee;
*3: Member's 3rd period of service on the committee.

Note: Ranking on this committee for the following member was affected by other chamber service: William H. Ayres (Rep-Ohio), Ranking Minority Member, Education and Labor.

Changes:
Majority:

Wilson, Charles H.	Dem	Cal.	Oct. 21,1965	Moved to Post Office and Civil Service.
Pucinski, Roman C.	Dem	Ill.	Mar. 8,1966	Replaced Wilson.
Secrest, Robert T.	Dem	Ohio	Dec. 30,1966	Resigned; defeated for reelection.

Departures from the House:	Majority			Minority		
Defeated for Reelection	McDowell, Harris B. Jr.	Del.	Dem	None		
Lost Election to U.S. Senate	Roncalio, Teno	Wyo.	Dem	None		
Lost Nomination to U.S. Senate	None			Ellsworth, Robert F.	Kans.	Rep

VETERANS' AFFAIRS / 90th Congress

Service Dates of Committee Chair: Jan. 23,1967-Jan. 3,1969
Service Dates of Majority Members: Jan. 23,1967-Jan. 3,1969
Service Dates of Minority Members: Jan. 26,1967-Jan. 3,1969

Majority

Rank Name	Party	State	Terms in: House	Terms in: Comm.
Chr Teague, Olin E.	Dem	Tex.	12	11
2nd Dorn, W. J. Bryan	Dem	S.C.	10	9
3rd Haley, James A.	Dem	Fla.	8	7
4th Baring, Walter S.	Dem	Nev.	8	6
5th Everett, Robert A.	Dem	Tenn.	6	6
6th Dulski, Thaddeus J.	Dem	N.Y.	5	5
7th Kornegay, Horace R.	Dem	N.C.	4	4
8th Roberts, Herbert Ray	Dem	Tex.	4	4
9th Brown, George E. Jr.	Dem	Cal.	3	3
10th Satterfield, David E. III	Dem	Va.	2	2
11th Helstoski, Henry	Dem	N.J.	2	2
12th Resnick, Joseph Y.	Dem	N.Y.	2	2
13th Hanley, James M.	Dem	N.Y.	2	2
14th Pucinski, Roman C.	Dem	Ill.	5	2

Minority

Rank Name	Party	State	Terms in: House	Terms in: Comm.
RM Adair, E. Ross	Rep	Ind.	9	9
2nd Ayres, William H.	Rep	Ohio	9	9
3rd Fino, Paul A.	Rep	N.Y.	8	8
4th Saylor, John P.	Rep	Penn.	10	*2 6
5th Teague, Charles M.	Rep	Cal.	7	*2 6
6th Halpern, Seymour	Rep	N.Y.	5	5
7th Duncan, John J.	Rep	Tenn.	2	2
8th Kupferman, Theodore R.	Rep	N.Y.	2	1
9th Hammerschmidt, John Paul	Rep	Ark.	1	1
10th Scott, William L.	Rep	Va.	1	1
11th Heckler, Margaret M.	Rep	Mass.	1	1

*2: Member's 2nd period of service on the committee.

Note: Ranking on this committee for the following member was affected by other chamber service: William H. Ayres (Rep-Ohio), Ranking Minority Member, Education and Labor.

Changes:
Minority:

Fino, Paul A.	Rep	N.Y.	Dec. 31,1968	Resigned; elected to State Supreme Court.

Departures from the House:	Majority			Minority		
Elected State Supreme Court Judge	None			Kupferman, Theodore R.	N.Y.	Rep
Lost Nomination to U.S. Senate	Resnick, Joseph Y.	N.Y.	Dem	None		
Retired	Kornegay, Horace R.	N.C.	Dem	None		
Departures from Committee:						
Unassigned in 91st; died in office Jan. 26,1969	Everett, Robert A.	Tenn.	Dem	None		
Moved to Banking and Currency	Hanley, James M.	N.Y.	Dem	None		

VETERANS' AFFAIRS / 91st Congress

Service Dates of Committee Chair: Jan. 29,1969-Jan. 3,1971
Service Dates of Majority Members: Jan. 29,1969-Jan. 3,1971
Service Dates of Minority Members: Jan. 29,1969-Jan. 3,1971

Majority

Rank	Name	Party	State	Terms in: House	Terms in: Comm.
Chr	Teague, Olin E.	Dem	Tex.	13	12
2nd	Dorn, W. J. Bryan	Dem	S.C.	11	10
3rd	Haley, James A.	Dem	Fla.	9	8
4th	Baring, Walter S.	Dem	Nev.	9	7
5th	Dulski, Thaddeus J.	Dem	N.Y.	6	6
6th	Roberts, Herbert Ray	Dem	Tex.	5	5
7th	Brown, George E. Jr.	Dem	Cal.	4	4
8th	Satterfield, David E. III	Dem	Va.	3	3
9th	Helstoski, Henry	Dem	N.J.	3	3
10th	Pucinski, Roman C.	Dem	Ill.	6	3
11th	Edwards, Don	Dem	Cal.	4	*2 1
12th	Roybal, Edward R.	Dem	Cal.	4	1
13th	Montgomery, G.V. (Sonny)	Dem	Miss.	2	1
14th	Chisholm, Shirley A.	Dem	N.Y.	1	1

Minority

Rank	Name	Party	State	Terms in: House	Terms in: Comm.
RM	Teague, Charles M.	Rep	Cal.	8	*2 7
2nd	Adair, E. Ross	Rep	Ind.	10	10
3rd	Ayres, William H.	Rep	Ohio	10	10
4th	Saylor, John P.	Rep	Penn.	11	*2 7
5th	Halpern, Seymour	Rep	N.Y.	6	6
6th	Duncan, John J.	Rep	Tenn.	3	3
7th	Hammerschmidt, John Paul	Rep	Ark.	2	2
8th	Scott, William L.	Rep	Va.	2	2
9th	Heckler, Margaret M.	Rep	Mass.	2	2
10th	Zwach, John M.	Rep	Minn.	2	1
11th	Denney, Robert V.	Rep	Neb.	2	1

*2: Member's 2nd period of service on the committee.

Note: Rankings on this committee for the following members were affected by other chamber service: E. Ross Adair (Rep-Ind.), Ranking Minority Member, Foreign Affairs; William H. Ayres (Rep-Ohio), Ranking Minority Member, Education and Labor; John P. Saylor (Rep-Penn.), Interior and Insular Affairs.

Vacancy Filled:
Majority: 14th seat by Chisholm on Feb. 18,1969.

	Majority			Minority		
Departures from the House:						
Appointed Federal Judge	None			Denney, Robert V.	Neb.	Rep
Defeated for Reelection	None			Adair, E. Ross	Ind.	Rep
				Ayres, William H.	Ohio	Rep
Lost Nomination to U.S. Senate	Brown, George E. Jr.	Cal.	Dem	None		
Departures from Committee:						
Moved to Appropriations	Roybal, Edward R.	Cal.	Dem	None		
Moved to Ways and Means	None			Duncan, John J.	Tenn.	Rep
Moved to Foreign Affairs	None			Halpern, Seymour	N.Y.	Rep

VETERANS' AFFAIRS / 92nd Congress

Service Dates of Committee Chair: Feb. 4,1971-Jan. 3,1973
Service Dates of Majority Members: Feb. 4,1971-Jan. 3,1973
Service Dates of Minority Members: Feb. 4,1971-Jan. 3,1973

Majority

Rank	Name	Party	State	Terms in: House	Terms in: Comm.
Chr	Teague, Olin E.	Dem	Tex.	14	13
2nd	Dorn, W. J. Bryan	Dem	S.C.	12	11
3rd	Haley, James A.	Dem	Fla.	10	9
4th	Baring, Walter S.	Dem	Nev.	10	8
5th	Dulski, Thaddeus J.	Dem	N.Y.	7	7
6th	Roberts, Herbert Ray	Dem	Tex.	6	6
7th	Satterfield, David E. III	Dem	Va.	4	4
8th	Helstoski, Henry	Dem	N.J.	4	4
9th	Pucinski, Roman C.	Dem	Ill.	7	4
10th	Edwards, Don	Dem	Cal.	5	*2 2
11th	Montgomery, G.V. (Sonny)	Dem	Miss.	3	2
12th	Chisholm, Shirley A.	Dem	N.Y.	2	2
13th	Carney, Charles J.	Dem	Ohio	2	1
14th	Hicks, Louise Day	Dem	Mass.	1	1
15th	Danielson, George E.	Dem	Cal.	1	1
16th	Grasso, Ella T.	Dem	Conn.	1	1

Minority

Rank	Name	Party	State	Terms in: House	Terms in: Comm.
RM	Teague, Charles M.	Rep	Cal.	9	*2 8
2nd	Saylor, John P.	Rep	Penn.	12	*2 8
3rd	Hammerschmidt, John Paul	Rep	Ark.	3	3
4th	Scott, William L.	Rep	Va.	3	3
5th	Heckler, Margaret M.	Rep	Mass.	3	3
6th	Zwach, John M.	Rep	Minn.	3	2
7th	Wylie, Chalmers P.	Rep	Ohio	3	1
8th	Winn, Larry Jr.	Rep	Kans.	3	1
9th	Ruth, Earl B.	Rep	N.C.	2	1
10th	Hillis, Elwood H.	Rep	Ind.	1	1

*2: Member's 2nd period of service on the committee.

Note: Ranking on this committee for the following member was affected by other chamber service: John P. Saylor (Rep-Penn.), Interior and Insular Affairs.

Changes:
Majority:

Chisholm, Shirley A.	Dem	N.Y.	Mar. 30,1971	Left committee; no new assignment.
Wolff, Lester L.	Dem	N.Y.	Apr. 6,1971	Replaced Chisholm.

Departures from the House:	Majority			Minority		
Elected to U.S. Senate	None			Scott, William L.	Va.	Rep
Defeated for Reelection	Hicks, Louise Day	Mass.	Dem	None		
Defeated for Renomination	Baring, Walter S.	Nev.	Dem	None		
Lost Election to U.S. Senate	Pucinski, Roman C.	Ill.	Dem	None		
Departures from Committee:						
Moved to Appropriations	None			Ruth, Earl B.	N.C.	Rep
Moved to Foreign Affairs	None			Winn, Larry Jr.	Kans.	Rep

VETERANS' AFFAIRS / 93rd Congress

Service Dates of Committee Chair: Jan. 24,1973-Dec. 31,1974
Service Dates of Majority Members: Jan. 24,1973-Jan. 3,1975
Service Dates of Minority Members: Jan. 24,1973-Jan. 3,1975

Majority

Rank	Name	Party	State	Terms in: House	Terms in: Comm.
Chr	Dorn, W. J. Bryan	Dem	S.C.	13	12
2nd	Teague, Olin E.	Dem	Tex.	15	14
3rd	Haley, James A.	Dem	Fla.	11	10
4th	Dulski, Thaddeus J.	Dem	N.Y.	8	8
5th	Roberts, Herbert Ray	Dem	Tex.	7	7
6th	Satterfield, David E. III	Dem	Va.	5	5
7th	Helstoski, Henry	Dem	N.J.	5	5
8th	Edwards, Don	Dem	Cal.	6	*2 3
9th	Montgomery, G.V. (Sonny)	Dem	Miss.	4	3
10th	Carney, Charles J.	Dem	Ohio	3	2
11th	Danielson, George E.	Dem	Cal.	2	2
12th	Grasso, Ella T.	Dem	Conn.	2	2
13th	Wolff, Lester L.	Dem	N.Y.	5	2
14th	Brinkley, Jack T.	Dem	Ga.	4	1
15th	Wilson, Charles	Dem	Tex.	1	1

Minority

Rank	Name	Party	State	Terms in: House	Terms in: Comm.
RM	Hammerschmidt, John Paul	Rep	Ark.	4	4
2nd	Saylor, John P.	Rep	Penn.	13	*2 9
3rd	Teague, Charles M.	Rep	Cal.	10	*2 9
4th	Heckler, Margaret M.	Rep	Mass.	4	4
5th	Zwach, John M.	Rep	Minn.	4	3
6th	Wylie, Chalmers P.	Rep	Ohio	4	2
7th	Hillis, Elwood H.	Rep	Ind.	2	2
8th	Maraziti, Joseph J.	Rep	N.J.	1	1
9th	Abdnor, James	Rep	S.D.	1	1
10th	Huber, Robert J.	Rep	Mich.	1	1
11th	Walsh, William F.	Rep	N.Y.	1	1

*2: Member's 2nd period of service on the committee.

Note: Rankings on this committee for the following members were affected by other chamber service: Olin E. Teague (Dem-Tex.), Chair, Science and Astronautics; John P. Saylor (Rep-Penn.), Ranking Minority Member, Interior and Insular Affairs; and Charles M. Teague (Rep-Cal.), Ranking Minority Member, Agriculture.

Changes:
Majority:

Dorn, W. J. Bryan	Dem	S.C.	Dec. 31,1974	Resigned; lost election for Governor.
Dulski, Thaddeus J.	Dem	N.Y.	Dec. 31,1974	Resigned and retired.

Minority:

Saylor, John P.	Rep	Penn.	Oct. 28,1973	Died in office.
Teague, Charles M.	Rep	Cal.	Jan. 1,1974	Died in office.
Moorhead, Carlos J.	Rep	Cal.	Mar. 21,1974	Replaced Saylor.
Guyer, Tennyson	Rep	Ohio	Mar. 21,1974	Replaced Charles Teague.

Departures from the House:	Majority			Minority		
Elected Governor	Grasso, Ella T.	Conn.	Dem	None		
Defeated for Reelection	None			Huber, Robert J.	Mich.	Rep
				Maraziti, Joseph J.	N.J.	Rep
Retired	None			Zwach, John M.	Minn.	Rep

Departures from Committee:

Moved to Interstate & Foreign Commerce	None			Moorhead, Carlos J.	Cal. Rep
Moved to Ways and Means	Helstoski, Henry	N.J.	Dem	None	
No new assignment	Haley, James A.	Fla.	Dem	None	

VETERANS' AFFAIRS / 94th Congress

Service Dates of Committee Chair: Jan. 20,1975-Jan. 3,1977
Service Dates of Majority Members: Jan. 20,1975-Jan. 3,1977
Service Dates of Minority Members: Jan. 28,1975-Jan. 3,1977

Majority

Rank Name	Party	State	Terms in: House	Terms in: Comm.
Chr Roberts, Herbert Ray	Dem	Tex.	8	8
2nd Teague, Olin E.	Dem	Tex.	16	15
3rd Satterfield, David E. III	Dem	Va.	6	6
4th Edwards, Don	Dem	Cal.	7	*2 4
5th Montgomery, G.V. (Sonny)	Dem	Miss.	5	4
6th Carney, Charles J.	Dem	Ohio	4	3
7th Danielson, George E.	Dem	Cal.	3	3
8th Wolff, Lester L.	Dem	N.Y.	6	3
9th Brinkley, Jack T.	Dem	Ga.	5	2
10th Wilson, Charles	Dem	Tex.	2	2
11th Mottl, Ronald M.	Dem	Ohio	1	1
12th Cornell, Robert J.	Dem	Wisc.	1	1
13th Hefner, W. G. (Bill)	Dem	N.C.	1	1
14th Hannaford, Mark W.	Dem	Cal.	1	1
15th Ford, Harold E.	Dem	Tenn.	1	1
16th Beard, Edward P.	Dem	R.I.	1	1
17th Edgar, Robert W.	Dem	Penn.	1	1
18th Wirth, Timothy E.	Dem	Colo.	1	1
19th Holland, Kenneth L.	Dem	S.C.	1	1

Minority

Rank Name	Party	State	Terms in: House	Terms in: Comm.
RM Hammerschmidt, John Paul	Rep	Ark.	5	5
2nd Heckler, Margaret M.	Rep	Mass.	5	5
3rd Wylie, Chalmers P.	Rep	Ohio	5	3
4th Hillis, Elwood H.	Rep	Ind.	3	3
5th Abdnor, James	Rep	S.D.	2	2
6th Walsh, William F.	Rep	N.Y.	2	2
7th Guyer, Tennyson	Rep	Ohio	2	2
8th Hansen, George V.	Rep	Ida.	3	1
9th O'Brien, George M.	Rep	Ill.	2	1

*2: Member's 2nd period of service on the committee.

Note: Ranking on this committee for the following member was affected by other chamber service: Olin E. Teague (Dem-Tex.), Chair, Science and Astronautics.

Changes:

Majority:

Wirth, Timothy E.	Dem	Colo.	Feb. 19,1975	Moved to Science and Technology.
McHugh, Matthew F.	Dem	N.Y.	Mar. 12,1975	Replaced Wirth.
Ford, Harold E.	Dem	Tenn.	Sep. 30,1975	Moved to Ways and Means.
Allen, Clifford R.	Dem	Tenn.	Dec. 17,1975	Replaced Ford.
Wilson, Charles	Dem	Tex.	Feb. 3,1976	Moved to Appropriations.
Hall, Sam B. Jr.	Dem	Tex.	July 21,1976	Replaced Wilson.

Departures from Committee:

	Majority			Minority	
Moved to Ways and Means	Holland, Kenneth L.	S.C.	Dem	None	
Moved to Interior & Insular Affairs	McHugh, Matthew F.	N.Y.	Dem		
Moved to Appropriations	None			O'Brien, George M.	Ill. Rep

VETERANS' AFFAIRS / 95th Congress

Service Dates of Committee Chair: Jan. 19,1977-Jan. 3,1979
Service Dates of Majority Members: Jan. 19,1977-Jan. 3,1979
Service Dates of Minority Members: Jan. 19,1977-Jan. 3,1979

Majority

Rank	Name	Party	State	Terms in: House	Terms in: Comm.
Chr	Roberts, Herbert Ray	Dem	Tex.	9	9
2nd	Teague, Olin E.	Dem	Tex.	17	16
3rd	Satterfield, David E. III	Dem	Va.	7	7
4th	Edwards, Don	Dem	Cal.	8	*2 5
5th	Montgomery, G.V. (Sonny)	Dem	Miss.	6	5
6th	Carney, Charles J.	Dem	Ohio	5	4
7th	Danielson, George E.	Dem	Cal.	4	4
8th	Wolff, Lester L.	Dem	N.Y.	7	4
9th	Brinkley, Jack T.	Dem	Ga.	6	3
10th	Mottl, Ronald M.	Dem	Ohio	2	2
11th	Cornell, Robert J.	Dem	Wisc.	2	2
12th	Hefner, W. G. (Bill)	Dem	N.C.	2	2
13th	Hannaford, Mark W.	Dem	Cal.	2	2
14th	Beard, Edward P.	Dem	R.I.	2	2
15th	Edgar, Robert W.	Dem	Penn.	2	2
16th	Allen, Clifford R.	Dem	Tenn.	2	2
17th	Hall, Sam B. Jr.	Dem	Tex.	2	2
18th	Applegate, Douglas	Dem	Ohio	1	1
19th	Barnard, D. Douglas Jr.	Dem	Ga.	1	1

Minority

Rank	Name	Party	State	Terms in: House	Terms in: Comm.
RM	Hammerschmidt, John Paul	Rep	Ark.	6	6
2nd	Heckler, Margaret M.	Rep	Mass.	6	6
3rd	Wylie, Chalmers P.	Rep	Ohio	6	4
4th	Hillis, Elwood H.	Rep	Ind.	4	4
5th	Abdnor, James	Rep	S.D.	3	3
6th	Walsh, William F.	Rep	N.Y.	3	3
7th	Guyer, Tennyson	Rep	Ohio	3	3
8th	Hansen, George V.	Rep	Ida.	4	2
9th	Sawyer, Harold S.	Rep	Mich.	1	1

*2: Member's 2nd period of service on the committee.

Note: Ranking on this committee for the following member was affected by other chamber service: Olin E. Teague (Dem-Tex.), Chair, Science and Astronautics.

Changes:

Majority:

Allen, Clifford R.	Dem	Tenn.	June 18,1978	Died in office.
Cornwell, David L.	Dem	Ind.	Sep. 20,1978	Replaced Allen.
Teague, Olin E.	Dem	Tex.	Dec. 31,1978	Resigned and retired.

	Majority			Minority		
Departures from the House:						
Defeated for Reelection	Carney, Charles J.	Ohio	Dem	None		
	Cornell, Robert J.	Wisc.	Dem			
	Hannaford, Mark W.	Cal.	Dem			
	Cornwell, David L.	Ind.	Dem			
Retired	None			Walsh, William F.	N.Y.	Rep
Departures from Committee:						
Moved to Small Business	Barnard, D. Douglas Jr.	Ga.	Dem	None		

VETERANS' AFFAIRS / 96th Congress

Service Dates of Committee Chair: Jan. 24,1979-Jan. 3,1981
Service Dates of Majority Members: Jan. 24,1979-Jan. 3,1981
Service Dates of Minority Members: Jan. 24,1979-Jan. 3,1981

Majority

Rank	Name	Party	State	Terms in: House	Terms in: Comm.
Chr	Roberts, Herbert Ray	Dem	Tex.	10	10
2nd	Satterfield, David E. III	Dem	Va.	8	8
3rd	Edwards, Don	Dem	Cal.	9	*2 6
4th	Montgomery, G.V. (Sonny)	Dem	Miss.	7	6
5th	Danielson, George E.	Dem	Cal.	5	5
6th	Wolff, Lester L.	Dem	N.Y.	8	5
7th	Brinkley, Jack T.	Dem	Ga.	7	4
8th	Mottl, Ronald M.	Dem	Ohio	3	3
9th	Hefner, W. G. (Bill)	Dem	N.C.	3	3
10th	Beard, Edward P.	Dem	R.I.	3	3
11th	Edgar, Robert W.	Dem	Penn.	3	3
12th	Hall, Sam B. Jr.	Dem	Tex.	3	3
13th	Applegate, Douglas	Dem	Ohio	2	2
14th	Leath, J. Marvin	Dem	Tex.	1	1
15th	Boner, William H.	Dem	Tenn.	1	1
16th	Gramm, W. Phil	Dem	Tex.	1	1
17th	Shelby, Richard C.	Dem	Ala.	1	1
18th	Hall, Tony P.	Dem	Ohio	1	1
19th	Mica, Daniel A.	Dem	Fla.	1	1
20th	Daschle, Thomas A.	Dem	S.D.	1	1
21st	Coelho, Anthony L.	Dem	Cal.	1	1

Minority

Rank	Name	Party	State	Terms in: House	Terms in: Comm.
RM	Hammerschmidt, John Paul	Rep	Ark.	7	7
2nd	Heckler, Margaret M.	Rep	Mass.	7	7
3rd	Wylie, Chalmers P.	Rep	Ohio	7	5
4th	Hillis, Elwood H.	Rep	Ind.	5	5
5th	Abdnor, James	Rep	S.D.	4	4
6th	Guyer, Tennyson	Rep	Ohio	4	4
7th	Hansen, George V.	Rep	Ida.	5	3
8th	Sawyer, Harold S.	Rep	Mich.	2	2
9th	Grisham, Wayne R.	Rep	Cal.	1	1
10th	Deckard, H. Joel	Rep	Ind.	1	1
11th	Lee, Gary A.	Rep	N.Y.	1	1

*2: Member's 2nd period of service on the committee.

Changes:

Majority:

Hall, Tony P.	Dem	Ohio	Jan. 31,1979	Moved to Small Business.
Beard, Edward P.	Dem	R.I.	Feb. 8,1979	Left committee; no new assignment.
Leach, A. Claude Jr.	Dem	La.	Feb. 6,1980	Replaced Hall.
Downey, Thomas J.	Dem	N.Y.	Mar. 19,1980	Replaced Beard.
Downey, Thomas J.	Dem	N.Y.	June 18,1980	Left committee; no new assignment.
Hutchinson, John G.	Dem	W.Va.	June 18,1980	Replaced Downey.

Minority:

Hansen, George V.	Rep	Ida.	Oct. 1,1980	Moved to Agriculture.
Solomon, Gerald B. H.	Rep	N.Y.	Oct. 1,1980	Replaced Hansen.

Departures from the House:	**Majority**			**Minority**		
Elected to U.S. Senate	None			Abdnor, James	S.D.	Rep
Defeated for Reelection	Wolff, Lester L.	N.Y.	Dem	None		
	Hutchinson, John G.	W.Va.	Dem			
	Leach, A. Claude Jr.	La.	Dem			
Retired	Roberts, Herbert Ray	Tex.	Dem	None		
	Satterfield, David E. III	Va.	Dem			
Departures from Committee:						
Moved to Interior & Insular Affairs	Coelho, Anthony L.	Cal.	Dem	None		
Moved to Budget	Hefner, W. G. (Bill)	N.C.	Dem	None		
Moved to Public Works & Transportation	None			Deckard, H. Joel	Ind.	Rep
Moved to Post Office & Civil Service; Public Works & Transportation	None			Grisham, Wayne R.	Cal.	Rep
Moved to House Administration	None			Lee, Gary A.	N.Y.	Rep

VETERANS' AFFAIRS / 97th Congress

Service Dates of Committee Chair: Jan. 28,1981-Jan. 3,1983
Service Dates of Majority Members: Jan. 28,1981-Jan. 3,1983
Service Dates of Minority Members: Jan. 28,1981-Jan. 3,1983

Majority

Rank	Name	Party	State	Terms in: House	Terms in: Comm.
Chr	Montgomery, G.V. (Sonny)	Dem	Miss.	8	7
2nd	Edwards, Don	Dem	Cal.	10	*2 7
3rd	Danielson, George E.	Dem	Cal.	6	6
4th	Brinkley, Jack T.	Dem	Ga.	8	5
5th	Mottl, Ronald M.	Dem	Ohio	4	4
6th	Edgar, Robert W.	Dem	Penn.	4	4
7th	Hall, Sam B. Jr.	Dem	Tex.	4	4
8th	Applegate, Douglas	Dem	Ohio	3	3
9th	Leath, J. Marvin	Dem	Tex.	2	2
10th	Boner, William H.	Dem	Tenn.	2	2
11th	Shelby, Richard C.	Dem	Ala.	2	2
12th	Mica, Daniel A.	Dem	Fla.	2	2
13th	Daschle, Thomas A.	Dem	S.D.	2	2
14th	Stump, Robert	Dem	Ariz.	3	*1 1
15th	Gramm, W. Phil	Dem	Tex.	2	*T 2
16th	Murphy, Austin J.	Dem	Penn.	3	1
17th	Dorgan, Byron L.	Dem	N.D.	1	1
18th	Won Pat, Antonio Borja	Dem	Guam	5	1

Minority

Rank	Name	Party	State	Terms in: House	Terms in: Comm.
RM	Hammerschmidt, John Paul	Rep	Ark.	8	8
2nd	Heckler, Margaret M.	Rep	Mass.	8	8
3rd	Wylie, Chalmers P.	Rep	Ohio	8	6
4th	Hillis, Elwood H.	Rep	Ind.	6	6
5th	Guyer, Tennyson	Rep	Ohio	5	5
6th	Sawyer, Harold S.	Rep	Mich.	3	3
7th	Solomon, Gerald B. H.	Rep	N.Y.	2	1
8th	Jeffries, James E.	Rep	Kans.	2	1
9th	McEwen, Bob	Rep	Ohio	1	1
10th	Dunn, Jim	Rep	Mich.	1	1
11th	Smith, Christopher H.	Rep	N.J.	1	1
12th	Smith, Albert Lee Jr.	Rep	Ala.	1	1
13th	Smith, Denny	Rep	Ore.	1	1
14th	Siljander, Mark D.	Rep	Mich.	1	1

*1: Member's 1st period of service on the committee;
*2: Member's 2nd period of service on the committee;
*T: Temporary member of the committee.

Notes: Territorial Delegate Antonio Won Pat (Dem-Guam) was allowed to accrue seniority but was not included in the committee's party ratio. Eugene V. Atkinson of Pennsylvania resigned the Democratic Party and joined the Republican Party on Oct. 14,1981. This change and the resignation of John C. Hinson (Rep-Miss.) and his replacement by Wayne Dowdy (Dem-Miss.) on July 9,1981 led to a change in size and party ratio to 18 Democrats (excluding Won Pat) and 15 Republicans on Dec. 16,1981. Ranking on this committee for the following member was affected by other chamber service: Don Edwards (Dem-Cal.), Chair, Civil and Constitutional Rights Subcommittee of Judiciary. Phil Gramm (Dem-Tex.) was assigned as a temporary member of this committee while he served on the Budget Committee, and was therefore ranked behind Robert Stump (Dem-Ariz.)

Vacancies Filled:

Majority: 16th and 17th seats by Murphy and Dorgan respectively (to rank above Gramm) on Feb. 25,1981, and the 18th seat by Won Pat on Apr. 30,1981.
Minority: 14th seat by Siljander on Apr. 29,1981.

Additions:

Majority:	19th	Dowdy, Wayne	Dem	Miss.	Dec. 16,1981
Minority:	15th	Nelligan, James L.	Rep	Penn.	Mar. 18,1982

Changes:

Majority:

Danielson, George E.	Dem	Cal.	Mar. 9,1982	Resigned; appointed state judge.
Martinez, Matthew G.	Dem	Cal.	Aug. 19,1982	Replaced Danielson.

Minority:

Guyer, Tennyson	Rep	Ohio	Apr. 12,1981	Died in office.
Napier, John L.	Rep	S.C.	Dec. 10,1981	Replaced Guyer.

Departures from the House:

	Majority			Minority		
Defeated for Reelection	None			Dunn, Jim	Mich.	Rep
				Heckler, Margaret M.	Mass.	Rep
				Smith, Albert Lee Jr.	Ala.	Rep
				Napier, John L.	S.C.	Rep
				Nelligan, James L.	Penn.	Rep
Defeated for Renomination	Mottl, Ronald M.	Ohio	Dem	None		
Retired	Brinkley, Jack T.	Ga.	Dem	Jeffries, James E.	Kans.	Rep

Departures from Committee:

Moved to Appropriations	Boner, William H.	Tenn. Dem	None	
Moved to Ways and Means	Dorgan, Byron L.	N.D. Dem	None	
Resigned Democratic Party; lost majority assignment	Stump Robert	Ariz. Dem	None	
	Gramm, Phil	Tex. Dem		
Moved to Merchant Marine & Fisheries	None		Sawyer, Harold S.	Mich. Rep
Moved to Foreign Affairs	None		Siljander, Mark D.	Mich. Rep
No new assignment	Murphy, Austin J.	Penn. Dem	None	
	Won Pat, Antonio Borja	Guam Dem		

VETERANS' AFFAIRS / 98th Congress

Service Dates of Committee Chair: Jan. 6,1983-Jan. 3,1985
Service Dates of Majority Members: Jan. 6,1983-Jan. 3,1985
Service Dates of Minority Members: Jan. 6,1983-Jan. 3,1985

Majority

Rank	Name	Party	State	Terms in: House	Terms in: Comm.
Chr	Montgomery, G.V. (Sonny)	Dem	Miss.	9	8
2nd	Edwards, Don	Dem	Cal.	11	*2 8
3rd	Edgar, Robert W.	Dem	Penn.	5	5
4th	Hall, Sam B. Jr.	Dem	Tex.	5	5
5th	Applegate, Douglas	Dem	Ohio	4	4
6th	Leath, J. Marvin	Dem	Tex.	3	3
7th	Shelby, Richard C.	Dem	Ala.	3	3
8th	Mica, Daniel A.	Dem	Fla.	3	3
9th	Daschle, Thomas A.	Dem	S.D.	3	3
10th	Dowdy, Wayne	Dem	Miss.	2	2
11th	Martinez, Matthew G.	Dem	Cal.	2	2
12th	Evans, Lane	Dem	Ill.	1	1
13th	Kaptur, Marcy	Dem	Ohio	1	1
14th	Harrison, Frank	Dem	Penn.	1	1
15th	Mollohan, Alan B.	Dem	W.Va.	1	1
16th	Penny, Timothy J.	Dem	Minn.	1	1
17th	Staggers, Harley O. Jr.	Dem	W.Va.	1	1
18th	Rowland, J. Roy	Dem	Ga.	1	1
19th	Slattery, Jim	Dem	Kans.	1	1
20th	Bryant, John	Dem	Tex.	1	1
21st	Richardson, Bill	Dem	N.M.	1	1

Minority

Rank	Name	Party	State	Terms in: House	Terms in: Comm.
RM	Hammerschmidt, John Paul	Rep	Ark.	9	9
2nd	Wylie, Chalmers P.	Rep	Ohio	9	7
3rd	Hillis, Elwood H.	Rep	Ind.	7	7
4th	Solomon, Gerald B. H.	Rep	N.Y.	3	2
5th	McEwen, Bob	Rep	Ohio	2	2
6th	Smith, Christopher H.	Rep	N.J.	2	2
7th	Smith, Denny	Rep	Ore.	2	2
8th	Gramm, W. Phil	Rep	Tex.	3	3
9th	Burton, Dan	Rep	Ind.	1	1
10th	Sundquist, Don	Rep	Tenn.	1	1
11th	Bilirakis, Michael	Rep	Fla.	1	1
12th	Johnson, Nancy L.	Rep	Conn.	1	1

*2: Member's 2nd period of service on the committee.

Notes: Phil Gramm of Texas resigned the Democratic Party on Jan. 5,1983. After winning the special election to fill his own vacancy, Gramm returned to the House on Feb. 22,1983 as a Republican. The Republican Conference awarded Gramm the 8th minority rank on this committee on Mar. 1,1983. Ranking on this committee for the following member was affected by other chamber service: Don Edwards (Dem-Cal.), Chair, Civil and Constitutional Rights Subcommittee of Judiciary.

Vacancy Filled:
Minority: 8th seat by Gramm on Mar. 1,1983.

Changes:
Majority:

Richardson, Bill	Dem	N.M.	Feb. 29,1984	Moved to Interior and Insular Affairs.
Florio, James J.	Dem	N.J.	Feb. 29,1984	Replaced Richardson.

	Majority		Minority	
Departures from the House:				
Elected to U.S. Senate	None		Gramm, W. Phil	Tex. Rep
Defeated for Renomination	Harrison, Frank	Penn. Dem	None	
Departures from Committee:				
Moved to Budget	Leath, J. Marvin	Tex. Dem	Smith, Denny	Ore. Rep
Moved to Government Operations	Martinez, Matthew G.	Cal. Dem	None	
Ceased active membership to serve on Budget	Slattery, Jim	Kans. Dem	None	

VETERANS' AFFAIRS / 99th Congress

Service Dates of Committee Chair: Jan. 7,1985-Jan. 3,1987
Service Dates of Majority Members: Jan. 30,1985-Jan. 3,1987
Service Dates of Minority Members: Jan. 30,1985-Jan. 3,1987

Majority

Rank Name	Party	State	Terms in: House	Terms in: Comm.
Chr Montgomery, G.V. (Sonny)	Dem	Miss.	10	9
2nd Edwards, Don	Dem	Cal.	12	*2 9
3rd Edgar, Robert W.	Dem	Penn.	6	6
4th Hall, Sam B. Jr.	Dem	Tex.	6	6
5th Applegate, Douglas	Dem	Ohio	5	5
6th Shelby, Richard C.	Dem	Ala.	4	4
7th Mica, Daniel A.	Dem	Fla.	4	4
8th Daschle, Thomas A.	Dem	S.D.	4	4
9th Dowdy, Wayne	Dem	Miss.	3	3
10th Evans, Lane	Dem	Ill.	2	2
11th Kaptur, Marcy	Dem	Ohio	2	2
12th Mollohan, Alan B.	Dem	W.Va.	2	2
13th Penny, Timothy J.	Dem	Minn.	2	2
14th Staggers, Harley O. Jr.	Dem	W.Va.	2	2
15th Rowland, J. Roy	Dem	Ga.	2	2
16th Bryant, John	Dem	Tex.	2	2
17th Florio, James J.	Dem	N.J.	6	2
18th Gray, Kenneth J.	Dem	Ill.	11	1
19th Kanjorski, Paul E.	Dem	Penn.	1	1
20th Robinson, Tommy F.	Dem	Ark.	1	1

Minority

Rank Name	Party	State	Terms in: House	Terms in: Comm.
RM Hammerschmidt, John Paul	Rep	Ark.	10	10
2nd Wylie, Chalmers P.	Rep	Ohio	10	8
3rd Hillis, Elwood H.	Rep	Ind.	8	8
4th Solomon, Gerald B. H.	Rep	N.Y.	4	3
5th McEwen, Bob	Rep	Ohio	3	3
6th Smith, Christopher H.	Rep	N.J.	3	3
7th Burton, Dan	Rep	Ind.	2	2
8th Sundquist, Don	Rep	Tenn.	2	2
9th Bilirakis, Michael	Rep	Fla.	2	2
10th Johnson, Nancy L.	Rep	Conn.	2	2
11th Molinari, Guy V.	Rep	N.Y.	3	1
12th Ridge, Thomas J.	Rep	Penn.	2	1
13th Hendon, William M.	Rep	N.C.	2	1
14th Rowland, John G.	Rep	Conn.	1	1

*2: Member's 2nd period of service on the committee.

Note: Ranking on this committee for the following member was affected by other chamber service: Don Edwards (Dem-Cal.), Chair, Civil and Constitutional Rights Subcommittee of Judiciary.

Changes:

Majority:

Hall, Sam B. Jr.	Dem	Tex.	May 27,1985	Resigned; appointed federal judge.
McCloskey, Francis X.	Dem	Ind.	May 1,1986	Replaced Hall.
Mollohan, Alan B.	Dem	W.Va.	May 1,1986	Moved to Appropriations.
Stenholm, Charles W.	Dem	Tex.	Oct. 10,1986	Replaced Mollohan.

	Majority		Minority	
Departures from the House:				
Elected to U.S. Senate	Daschle, Thomas A.	S.D. Dem	None	
	Shelby, Richard C.	Ala. Dem		
Defeated for Reelection	None		Hendon, William M.	N.C. Rep
Lost Election to U.S. Senate	Edgar, Robert W.	Penn. Dem	None	
Retired	None		Hillis, Elwood H.	Ind. Rep
Departures from Committee:				
Moved to Budget	None		Johnson, Nancy L.	Conn. Rep
			Sundquist, Don	Tenn. Rep
Moved to Select Hunger	None		Molinari, Guy V.	N.Y. Rep
No new assignment	McCloskey, Francis X.	Ind. Dem	None	

VETERANS' AFFAIRS / 100th Congress

Service Dates of Committee Chair: Jan. 8,1987-Jan. 3,1989
Service Dates of Majority Members: Jan. 22,1987-Jan. 3,1989
Service Dates of Minority Members: Jan. 21,1987-Jan. 3,1989

Majority

Rank	Name	Party	State	Terms in: House	Terms in: Comm.
Chr	Montgomery, G.V. (Sonny)	Dem	Miss.	11	10
2nd	Edwards, Don	Dem	Cal.	13	*2 10
3rd	Applegate, Douglas	Dem	Ohio	6	6
4th	Mica, Daniel A.	Dem	Fla.	5	5
5th	Dowdy, Wayne	Dem	Miss.	4	4
6th	Evans, Lane	Dem	Ill.	3	3
7th	Kaptur, Marcy	Dem	Ohio	3	3
8th	Penny, Timothy J.	DFL	Minn.	3	3
9th	Staggers, Harley O. Jr.	Dem	W.Va.	3	3
10th	Rowland, J. Roy	Dem	Ga.	3	3
11th	Bryant, John	Dem	Tex.	3	3
12th	Florio, James J.	Dem	N.J.	7	3
13th	Gray, Kenneth J.	Dem	Ill.	12	2
14th	Kanjorski, Paul E.	Dem	Penn.	2	2
15th	Robinson, Tommy F.	Dem	Ark.	2	2
16th	Stenholm, Charles W.	Dem	Tex.	5	2
17th	Harris, Claude	Dem	Ala.	1	1
18th	Kennedy, Joseph P. II	Dem	Mass.	1	1
19th	Patterson, Elizabeth J.	Dem	S.C.	1	1
20th	Johnson, Tim	Dem	S.D.	1	1
21st	Jontz, James	Dem	Ind.	1	1

Minority

Rank	Name	Party	State	Terms in: House	Terms in: Comm.
RM	Solomon, Gerald B. H.	Rep	N.Y.	5	4
2nd	Hammerschmidt, John Paul	Rep	Ark.	11	11
3rd	Wylie, Chalmers P.	Rep	Ohio	11	9
4th	Stump, Robert	Rep	Ariz.	6	*2 1
5th	McEwen, Bob	Rep	Ohio	4	4
6th	Smith, Christopher H.	Rep	N.J.	4	4
7th	Burton, Dan	Rep	Ind.	3	3
8th	Bilirakis, Michael	Rep	Fla.	3	3
9th	Ridge, Thomas J.	Rep	Penn.	3	2
10th	Rowland, John G.	Rep	Conn.	2	2
11th	Dornan, Robert K.	Rep	Cal.	5	1
12th	Smith, Robert C.	Rep	N.H.	2	1
13th	Davis, Jack	Rep	Ill.	1	1

*2: Member's 2nd period of service on the committee.

Notes: Rankings on this committee for the following members were affected by other chamber service: Don Edwards (Dem-Cal.), Chair, Civil and Constitutional Rights Subcommittee of Judiciary; John Paul Hammerschmidt (Rep-Ark.), Ranking Minority Member, Public Works and Transportation; and Chalmers P. Wylie (Rep-Ohio), Ranking Minority Member, Banking, Finance and Urban Affairs. Robert Stump (Rep-Ariz.) served previously on this committee as a Democrat. Stump joined the Republican Party on Jan. 3,1983, and was awarded the 4th minority rank on this committee in the 100th Congress.

Changes:

Majority:

Gray, Kenneth J.	Dem	Ill.	Oct. 3,1988	Left committee; no new assignment.
Payne, Lewis F. Jr.	Dem	Va.	Oct. 6,1988	Replaced Gray.

	Majority			Minority		
Departures from the House:						
Defeated for Reelection	None			Davis, Jack	Ill.	Rep
Lost Election to U.S. Senate	Dowdy, Wayne	Miss.	Dem	None		
Lost Nomination to U.S. Senate	Mica, Daniel A.	Fla.	Dem	None		
Departures from Committee:						
Moved to Budget	Bryant, John	Tex.	Dem	None		
	Kaptur, Marcy	Ohio	Dem			
Moved to Armed Services	None			Dornan, Robert K.	Cal.	Rep
Moved to Rules	None			Solomon, Gerald B.H.	N.Y.	Rep

VETERANS' AFFAIRS / 101st Congress

Service Dates of Committee Chair: Jan. 3,1989-Jan. 3,1991
Service Dates of Majority Members: Jan. 19,1989-Jan. 3,1991
Service Dates of Minority Members: Jan. 20,1989-Jan. 3,1991

Majority

Rank	Name	Party	State	Terms in: House	Terms in: Comm.
Chr	Montgomery, G.V. (Sonny)	Dem	Miss.	12	11
2nd	Edwards, Don	Dem	Cal.	14	*2 11
3rd	Applegate, Douglas	Dem	Ohio	7	7
4th	Evans, Lane	Dem	Ill.	4	4
5th	Penny, Timothy J.	Dem	Minn.	4	4
6th	Staggers, Harley O. Jr.	Dem	W.Va.	4	4
7th	Rowland, J. Roy	Dem	Ga.	4	4
8th	Florio, James J.	Dem	N.J.	8	4
9th	Kanjorski, Paul E.	Dem	Penn.	3	3
10th	Robinson, Tommy F.	Dem	Ark.	3	3
11th	Stenholm, Charles W.	Dem	Tex.	6	3
12th	Harris, Claude	Dem	Ala.	2	2
13th	Kennedy, Joseph P. II	Dem	Mass.	2	2
14th	Patterson, Elizabeth J.	Dem	S.C.	2	2
15th	Johnson, Tim	Dem	S.D.	2	2
16th	Jontz, James	Dem	Ind.	2	2
17th	Payne, Lewis F. Jr.	Dem	Va.	2	2
18th	Morrison, Bruce A.	Dem	Conn.	4	1
19th	Sangmeister, George E.	Dem	Ill.	1	1
20th	Parker, Mike	Dem	Miss.	1	1
21st	Jones, Ben	Dem	Ga.	1	1

Minority

Rank	Name	Party	State	Terms in: House	Terms in: Comm.
RM	Stump, Robert	Rep	Ariz.	7	*2 2
2nd	Hammerschmidt, John Paul	Rep	Ark.	12	12
3rd	Wylie, Chalmers P.	Rep	Ohio	12	10
4th	McEwen, Bob	Rep	Ohio	5	5
5th	Smith, Christopher H.	Rep	N.J.	5	5
6th	Burton, Dan	Rep	Ind.	4	4
7th	Bilirakis, Michael	Rep	Fla.	4	4
8th	Ridge, Thomas J.	Rep	Penn.	4	3
9th	Rowland, John G.	Rep	Conn.	3	3
10th	Smith, Robert C.	Rep	N.H.	3	2
11th	James, Craig T.	Rep	Fla.	1	1
12th	Stearns, Cliff	Rep	Fla.	1	1
13th	Paxon, L. William	Rep	N.Y.	1	1

*2: Member's 2nd period of service on the committee.

Note: Rankings on this committee for the following members were affected by other chamber service: Don Edwards (Dem-Cal.), Chair, Civil and Constitutional Rights Subcommittee of Judiciary; John Paul Hammerschmidt (Rep-Ark.), Ranking Minority Member, Public Works and Transportation; and Chalmers P. Wylie (Rep-Ohio), Ranking Minority Member, Banking, Finance and Urban Affairs. Robert Stump (Rep-Ariz.) served previously on this committee as a Democrat. Stump joined the Republican Party on Jan. 3,1983, and was awarded the 4th minority rank on this committee in the 100th Congress.

Vacancy Filled:
Minority: 13th seat by Paxon on May 4,1989.

Changes:
Majority:

Name	Party	State	Date	Change
Kanjorski, Paul E.	Dem	Penn.	Mar. 1,1989	Moved to Post Office and Civil Service.
Long, Jill	Dem	Ill.	Apr. 27,1989	Replaced Kanjorski.
Robinson, Tommy F.	Dem	Ark.	July 28,1989	Resigned Democratic Party; lost Majority assignment.
Johnson, Tim	Dem	S.D.	Oct. 17,1989	Moved to Interior and Insular Affairs (letter dated Oct. 12,1989).
Geren, Pete	Dem	Tex.	Nov. 8,1989	Replaced Robinson.
Florio, James J.	Dem	N.J.	Jan. 16,1990	Resigned; elected Governor of New Jersey.
Hochbrueckner, George J.	Dem	N.Y.	Feb. 27,1990	Replaced Johnson.

	Majority			Minority		
Departures from the House:						
Elected to U.S. Senate	None			Smith, Robert C.	N.H.	Rep
Lost Election for Governor	Morrison, Bruce A.	Conn.	Dem	Rowland, John G.	Conn.	Rep
Departures from Committee:						
Moved to Select Narcotic Abuse & Control	Hochbruechner, George J.	N.Y.	Dem	None		
Moved to Interior & Insular Affairs	Jontz, James	Ind.	Dem	None		
Moved to Budget	Parker, Mike	Miss.	Dem	None		
	Payne, Lewis F. Jr.	Va.	Dem			
	Stenholm, Charles W.	Tex.	Dem			
Moved to Rules	None			McEwen, Bob	Ohio	Rep

VETERANS' AFFAIRS / 102nd Congress

Service Dates of Committee Chair: Jan. 24,1991-Jan. 3,1993
Service Dates of Majority Members: Jan. 24,1991-Jan. 3,1993
Service Dates of Minority Members: Jan. 24,1991-Jan. 3,1993

Majority

Rank	Name	Party	State	Terms in: House	Terms in: Comm.
Chr	Montgomery, G.V. (Sonny)	Dem	Miss.	13	12
2nd	Edwards, Don	Dem	Cal.	15*2	12
3rd	Applegate, Douglas	Dem	Ohio	8	8
4th	Evans, Lane	Dem	Ill.	5	5
5th	Penny, Timothy J.	Dem	Minn.	5	5
6th	Staggers, Harley O. Jr.	Dem	W.Va.	5	5
7th	Rowland, J. Roy	Dem	Ga.	5	5
8th	Slattery, Jim	Dem	Kans.	5	1
9th	Harris, Claude	Dem	Ala.	3	3
10th	Kennedy, Joseph P. II	Dem	Mass.	3	3
11th	Patterson, Elizabeth J.	Dem	S.C.	3	3
12th	Sangmeister, George E.	Dem	Ill.	2	2
13th	Jones, Ben	Dem	Ga.	2	2
14th	Long, Jill L.	Dem	Ill.	2	2
15th	Peterson, Pete	Dem	Fla.	1	1
16th	Edwards, Chet	Dem	Tex.	1	1
17th	Waters, Maxine	Dem	Cal.	1	1
18th	Brewster, Bill	Dem	Okla.	1	1
19th	Pickett, Owen B.	Dem	Va.	3	1
20th	Geren, Pete	Dem	Tex.	2	2
21st	Clement, Bob	Dem	Tenn.	3	1

Minority

Rank	Name	Party	State	Terms in: House	Terms in: Comm.
RM	Stump, Robert	Rep	Ariz.	8	*2 3
2nd	Hammerschmidt, John Paul	Rep	Ark.	13	13
3rd	Wylie, Chalmers P.	Rep	Ohio	13	11
4th	Smith, Christopher H.	Rep	N.J.	6	6
5th	Burton, Dan	Rep	Ind.	5	5
6th	Bilirakis, Michael	Rep	Fla.	5	5
7th	Ridge, Thomas J.	Rep	Penn.	5	4
8th	James, Craig T.	Rep	Fla.	2	2
9th	Stearns, Cliff	Rep	Fla.	2	2
10th	Paxon, L. William	Rep	N.Y.	2	2
11th	Spence, Floyd D.	Rep	S.C.	11	1
12th	Nichols, Dick	Rep	Kans.	1	1
13th	Santorum, Rick	Rep	Penn.	1	1

*2: Member's 2nd period of service on the committee.

Vacancy Filled:
Majority: 21st seat by Clement on Feb. 5,1992.

Notes: Rankings on this committee for the following members were affected by other chamber service: Don Edwards (Dem-Cal.), Chair, Civil and Constitutional Rights Subcommittee of Judiciary; John Paul Hammerschmidt (Rep-Ark.), Ranking Minority Member, Public Works and Transportation; and Chalmers P. Wylie (Rep-Ohio), Ranking Minority Member, Banking, Finance and Urban Affairs. Robert Stump (Rep-Ariz.) served previously on this committee as a Democrat. Stump joined the Republican Party on Jan. 3,1983, and was awarded the 4th minority rank on this committee in the 100th Congress. Jim Slattery (Dem-Kans.), having served on the Budget Committee during the previous three Congresses, returned to active service on this committee with his seniority intact. Having served on this committee for only one month during the previous Congress, Pete Geren (Dem-Tex.) was ranked below Owen B. Pickett (Dem-Va.).

WAYS AND MEANS

Jurisdiction, 1947

Established by the Legislative Reorganization Act of 1946:

[Section 121.(1)(s)]

Committee on Ways and Means.

1. Revenue measures generally.
2. The bonded debt of the United States.
3. The deposit of public moneys.
4. Customs, collection districts, and ports of entry and delivery.
5. Reciprocal trade agreements.
6. Transportation of dutiable goods.
7. Revenue measures relating to the insular possessions.
8. National social security.

Jurisdiction, 1992

Jurisdiction contained in Rules of the House of Representatives, (as revised to July 1, 1992):

[Rule X. 1. (v)]

Committee on Ways and Means.

(1) Customs, collection districts, and ports of entry and delivery.
(2) Reciprocal trade agreements.
(3) Revenue measures generally.
(4) Revenue measures relating to the insular possessions.
(5) The bonded debt of the United States (subject to the last sentence of clause 4(g) of this rule).
(6) The deposit of public moneys.
(7) Transportation of dutiable goods.
(8) Tax exempt foundations and charitable trusts.
(9) National social security, except
 (A) health care and facilities programs that are supported from general revenues as opposed to payroll deductions and
 (B) work incentive programs.

[Rule X, Clause 4. (g) last sentence]

The views and estimates submitted by the Committee on Ways and Means under the preceding sentence shall include a specific recommendation, made after holding public hearings, as to the appropriate level of the public debt which should be set forth in the concurrent resolution on the budget referred to in such sentence and serve as the basis for an increase or decrease in the statutory limit on such debt under the procedures provided by Rule XLIX.

WAYS AND MEANS / 80th Congress

Service Dates of Committee Chair: Jan. 7,1947-Jan. 3,1949
Service Dates of Majority Members: Jan. 7,1947-Jan. 3,1949
Service Dates of Minority Members: Jan. 9,1947-Jan. 3,1949

Majority

Rank	Name	Party	State	Terms in: House	Terms in: Comm.
Chr	Knutson, Harold	Rep	Minn.	16	8
2nd	Reed, Daniel A.	Rep	N.Y.	15	8
3rd	Woodruff, Roy O.	Rep	Mich.	15	8
4th	Jenkins, Thomas A.	Rep	Ohio	12	8
5th	Gearhart, Bertrand W.	Rep	Cal.	7	5
6th	Simpson, Richard M.	Rep	Penn.	6	3
7th	Kean, Robert W.	Rep	N.J.	5	3
8th	Gifford, Charles L.	Rep	Mass.	14	2
9th	Curtis, Carl T.	Rep	Neb.	5	2
10th	Mason, Noah M.	Rep	Ill.	6	1
11th	Martin, Thomas E.	Rep	Iowa	5	1
12th	Grant, Robert A.	Rep	Ind.	5	1
13th	Holmes, O. H. (Hal)	Rep	Wash.	3	1
14th	Ellis, Hubert S.	Rep	W.Va.	3	1
15th	Byrnes, John W.	Rep	Wisc.	2	1

Minority

Rank	Name	Party	State	Terms in: House	Terms in: Comm.
RM	Doughton, Robert L.	Dem	N.C.	19	12
2nd	Cooper, Jere	Dem	Tenn.	10	9
3rd	Dingell, John D.	Dem	Mich.	8	7
4th	West, Milton H.	Dem	Tex.	8	5
5th	Mills, Wilbur D.	Dem	Ark.	5	4
6th	Gregory, Noble J.	Dem	Ky.	6	3
7th	Camp, A. Sidney	Dem	Ga.	5	3
8th	Lynch, Walter A.	Dem	N.Y.	5	3
9th	Forand, Aime J.	Dem	R.I.	5	3
10th	Eberharter, Herman P.	Dem	Penn.	6	3

Vacancies Filled:
Majority: 10th through 15th seats on Jan. 14,1947.

Changes:
Majority:

Gifford, Charles L.	Rep	Mass.	Aug. 23,1947	Died in office.
Goodwin, Angier L.	Rep	Mass.	Dec. 18,1947	Replaced Gifford.

Minority:

West, Milton H.	Dem	Tex.	Oct. 28,1948	Died in office.

Departures from the House:	**Majority**		**Minority**
Defeated for Reelection	Ellis, Hubert S.	W.Va. Rep	None
	Gearhart, Bertrand W.	Cal. Rep	
	Grant, Robert A.	Ind. Rep	
	Knutson, Harold	Minn. Rep	
Departures from Committee:			
No new assignment	Goodwin, Angier L.	Mass. Rep	None

WAYS AND MEANS / 81st Congress

Service Dates of Committee Chair: Jan. 5,1949-Jan. 3,1951
Service Dates of Majority Members: Jan. 5,1949-Jan. 3,1951
Service Dates of Minority Members: Jan. 5,1949-Jan. 3,1951

Majority

Rank	Name	Party	State	Terms in: House	Terms in: Comm.
Chr	Doughton, Robert L.	Dem	N.C.	20	13
2nd	Cooper, Jere	Dem	Tenn.	11	10
3rd	Dingell, John D.	Dem	Mich.	9	8
4th	Mills, Wilbur D.	Dem	Ark.	6	5
5th	Gregory, Noble J.	Dem	Ky.	7	4
6th	Camp, A. Sidney	Dem	Ga.	6	4
7th	Lynch, Walter A.	Dem	N.Y.	6	4
8th	Forand, Aime J.	Dem	R.I.	6	4
9th	Eberharter, Herman P.	Dem	Penn.	7	4
10th	King, Cecil R.	Dem	Cal.	5 *2	1
11th	O'Brien, Thomas J.	Dem	Ill.	7	1
12th	Combs, Jesse M.	Dem	Tex.	3	1

Minority

Rank	Name	Party	State	Terms in: House	Terms in: Comm.
RM	Reed, Daniel A.	Rep	N.Y.	16	9
2nd	Woodruff, Roy O.	Rep	Mich.	16	9
3rd	Jenkins, Thomas A.	Rep	Ohio	13	9
4th	Simpson, Richard M.	Rep	Penn.	7	4
5th	Kean, Robert W.	Rep	N.J.	6	4
6th	Curtis, Carl T.	Rep	Neb.	6	3
7th	Mason, Noah M.	Rep	Ill.	7	2
8th	Martin, Thomas E.	Rep	Iowa	6	2
9th	Holmes, O. H. (Hal)	Rep	Wash.	4	2
10th	Byrnes, John W.	Rep	Wisc.	3	2

13th Boggs, T. Hale	Dem	La.	3	1
14th Carroll, John A.	Dem	Colo.	2	1
15th Young, Stephen M.	Dem	Ohio	4	1

*2: Member's 2nd period of service on the committee.

Departures from the House:	Majority			Minority
Defeated for Reelection	Young, Stephen M.	Ohio	Dem	None
Lost Election to U.S. Senate	Carroll, John A.	Colo.	Dem	None
Lost Election for Governor	Lynch, Walter A.	N.Y.	Dem	None

WAYS AND MEANS / 82nd Congress

Service Dates of Committee Chair: Jan. 3,1951-Jan. 3,1953
Service Dates of Majority Members: Jan. 3,1951-Jan. 3,1953
Service Dates of Minority Members: Jan. 4,1951-Jan. 3,1953

Majority

Rank Name	Party	State	Terms in: House	Terms in: Comm.
Chr Doughton, Robert L.	Dem	N.C.	21	14
2nd Cooper, Jere	Dem	Tenn.	12	11
3rd Dingell, John D.	Dem	Mich.	10	9
4th Mills, Wilbur D.	Dem	Ark.	7	6
5th Gregory, Noble J.	Dem	Ky.	8	5
6th Camp, A. Sidney	Dem	Ga.	7	5
7th Forand, Aime J.	Dem	R.I.	7	5
8th Eberharter, Herman P.	Dem	Penn.	8	5
9th King, Cecil R.	Dem	Cal.	6	*2 2
10th O'Brien, Thomas J.	Dem	Ill.	8	2
11th Combs, Jesse M.	Dem	Tex.	4	2
12th Boggs, T. Hale	Dem	La.	4	2
13th Keogh, Eugene J.	Dem	N.Y.	8	*1 1
14th Granger, Walter K.	Dem	Utah	6	1
15th Harrison, Burr P.	Dem	Va.	4	*1 1

Minority

Rank Name	Party	State	Terms in: House	Terms in: Comm.
RM Reed, Daniel A.	Rep	N.Y.	17	10
2nd Woodruff, Roy O.	Rep	Mich.	17	10
3rd Jenkins, Thomas A.	Rep	Ohio	14	10
4th Simpson, Richard M.	Rep	Penn.	8	5
5th Kean, Robert W.	Rep	N.J.	7	5
6th Curtis, Carl T.	Rep	Neb.	7	4
7th Mason, Noah M.	Rep	Ill.	8	3
8th Martin, Thomas E.	Rep	Iowa	7	3
9th Holmes, O. H. (Hal)	Rep	Wash.	5	3
10th Byrnes, John W.	Rep	Wisc.	4	3

*1: Member's 1st period of service on the committee;
*2: Member's 2nd period of service on the committee.

Changes:
Minority:

Woodruff, Roy O.	Rep	Mich.	July 2,1952	Left committee; no new assignment.
Goodwin, Angier L.	Rep	Mass.	July 2,1952	Replaced Woodruff.

Departures from the House:	Majority			Minority
Lost Election to U.S. Senate	Granger, Walter K.	Utah	Dem	None
Retired	Combs, Jesse M.	Tex.	Dem	None
	Doughton, Robert L.	N.C.	Dem	
Departures from Committee:				
Moved to Foreign Affairs	Harrison, Burr P.	Va.	Dem	None
Moved to Merchant Marine & Fisheries	Keogh, Eugene J.	N.Y.	Dem	None

WAYS AND MEANS / 83rd Congress

Service Dates of Committee Chair: Jan. 14,1953-Jan. 3,1955
Service Dates of Majority Members: Jan. 14,1953-Jan. 3,1955
Service Dates of Minority Members: Jan. 14,1953-Jan. 3,1955

Majority

Rank	Name	Party	State	Terms in: House		Comm.
Chr	Reed, Daniel A.	Rep	N.Y.	18		11
2nd	Jenkins, Thomas A.	Rep	Ohio	15		11
3rd	Simpson, Richard M.	Rep	Penn.	9		6
4th	Kean, Robert W.	Rep	N.J.	8		6
5th	Curtis, Carl T.	Rep	Neb.	8		5
6th	Mason, Noah M.	Rep	Ill.	9		4
7th	Martin, Thomas E.	Rep	Iowa	8		4
8th	Holmes, O. H. (Hal)	Rep	Wash.	6		4
9th	Byrnes, John W.	Rep	Wisc.	5		4
10th	Goodwin, Angier L.	Rep	Mass.	6	*2	2
11th	Sadlak, Antoni N.	Rep	Conn.	4		1
12th	Baker, Howard H.	Rep	Tenn.	2		1
13th	Curtis, Thomas B.	Rep	Mo.	2		1
14th	Knox, Victor A.	Rep	Mich.	1	*1	1
15th	Utt, James B.	Rep	Cal.	1	*1	1

Minority

Rank	Name	Party	State	Terms in: House		Comm.
RM	Cooper, Jere	Dem	Tenn.	13		12
2nd	Dingell, John D.	Dem	Mich.	11		10
3rd	Mills, Wilbur D.	Dem	Ark.	8		7
4th	Gregory, Noble J.	Dem	Ky.	9		6
5th	Camp, A. Sidney	Dem	Ga.	8		6
6th	Forand, Aime J.	Dem	R.I.	8		6
7th	Eberharter, Herman P.	Dem	Penn.	9		6
8th	King, Cecil R.	Dem	Cal.	7	*2	3
9th	O'Brien, Thomas J.	Dem	Ill.	9		3
10th	Boggs, T. Hale	Dem	La.	5		3

*1: Member's 1st period of service on the committee;
*2: Member's 2nd period of service on the committee.

Changes:

Majority:

Name	Party	State	Date	Change
Curtis, Carl T.	Rep	Neb.	Dec. 31,1954	Resigned; elected to U.S. Senate.

Minority:

Name	Party	State	Date	Change
Camp, A. Sidney	Dem	Ga.	July 24,1954	Died in office.
Keogh, Eugene J.	Dem	N.Y.	July 27,1954	Replaced Camp.

	Majority			Minority
Departures from the House:				
Elected to U.S. Senate	Martin, Thomas E.	Iowa	Rep	None
Defeated for Reelection	Goodwin, Angier L.	Mass.	Rep	None
Departures from Committee:				
Moved to Government Operations	Knox, Victor A.	Mich.	Rep	None
Moved to Interior & Insular Affairs	Utt, James B.	Cal.	Rep	None

WAYS AND MEANS / 84th Congress

Service Dates of Committee Chair: Jan. 5,1955-Jan. 3,1957
Service Dates of Majority Members: Jan. 5,1955-Jan. 3,1957
Service Dates of Minority Members: Jan. 10,1955-Jan. 3,1957

Majority

Rank	Name	Party	State	Terms in: House		Comm.
Chr	Cooper, Jere	Dem	Tenn.	14		13
2nd	Dingell, John D.	Dem	Mich.	12		11
3rd	Mills, Wilbur D.	Dem	Ark.	9		8
4th	Gregory, Noble J.	Dem	Ky.	10		7
5th	Forand, Aime J.	Dem	R.I.	9		7
6th	Eberharter, Herman P.	Dem	Penn.	10		7
7th	King, Cecil R.	Dem	Cal.	8	*2	4
8th	O'Brien, Thomas J.	Dem	Ill.	10		4
9th	Boggs, T. Hale	Dem	La.	6		4
10th	Keogh, Eugene J.	Dem	N.Y.	10	*2	2
11th	Harrison, Burr P.	Dem	Va.	6	*2	1
12th	Karsten, Frank M.	Dem	Mo.	5		1
13th	Herlong, Albert S. Jr.	Dem	Fla.	4		1
14th	McCarthy, Eugene J.	DFL	Minn.	4		1
15th	Ikard, Frank N.	Dem	Tex.	3		1

Minority

Rank	Name	Party	State	Terms in: House		Comm.
RM	Reed, Daniel A.	Rep	N.Y.	19		12
2nd	Jenkins, Thomas A.	Rep	Ohio	16		12
3rd	Simpson, Richard M.	Rep	Penn.	10		7
4th	Kean, Robert W.	Rep	N.J.	9		7
5th	Mason, Noah M.	Rep	Ill.	10		5
6th	Holmes, O. H. (Hal)	Rep	Wash.	7		5
7th	Byrnes, John W.	Rep	Wisc.	6		5
8th	Sadlak, Antoni N.	Rep	Conn.	5		2
9th	Baker, Howard H.	Rep	Tenn.	3		2
10th	Curtis, Thomas B.	Rep	Mo.	3		2

*2: Member's 2nd period of service on the committee.

Changes:

Majority:

Dingell, John D.	Dem	Mich.	Sep. 19,1955	Died in office.
Machrowicz, Thaddeus M.	Dem	Mich.	Jan. 12,1956	Replaced Dingell.

WAYS AND MEANS / 85th Congress

Service Dates of Committee Chairs: Ch1 Jan. 3,1957-Dec. 18,1957
Ch2 Jan. 7,1958-Jan. 3,1959
Service Dates of Majority Members: Jan. 3,1957-Jan. 3,1959
Service Dates of Minority Members: Jan. 7,1957-Jan. 3,1959

Majority

Rank Name	Party	State	Terms in: House	Terms in: Comm.
Ch1 Cooper, Jere	Dem	Tenn.	15	14
Ch2 2nd Mills, Wilbur D.	Dem	Ark.	10	9
3rd Gregory, Noble J.	Dem	Ky.	11	8
4th Forand, Aime J.	Dem	R.I.	10	8
5th Eberharter, Herman P.	Dem	Penn.	11	8
6th King, Cecil R.	Dem	Cal.	9	*2 5
7th O'Brien, Thomas J.	Dem	Ill.	11	5
8th Boggs, T. Hale	Dem	La.	7	5
9th Keogh, Eugene J.	Dem	N.Y.	11	*2 3
10th Harrison, Burr P.	Dem	Va.	7	*2 2
11th Karsten, Frank M.	Dem	Mo.	6	2
12th Herlong, Albert S. Jr.	Dem	Fla.	5	2
13th McCarthy, Eugene J.	DFL	Minn.	5	2
14th Ikard, Frank N.	Dem	Tex.	4	2
15th Machrowicz, Thaddeus M.	Dem	Mich.	4	2

Minority

Rank Name	Party	State	Terms in: House	Terms in: Comm.
RM Reed, Daniel A.	Rep	N.Y.	20	13
2nd Jenkins, Thomas A.	Rep	Ohio	17	13
3rd Simpson, Richard M.	Rep	Penn.	11	8
4th Kean, Robert W.	Rep	N.J.	10	8
5th Mason, Noah M.	Rep	Ill.	11	6
6th Holmes, O. H. (Hal)	Rep	Wash.	8	6
7th Byrnes, John W.	Rep	Wisc.	7	6
8th Sadlak, Antoni N.	Rep	Conn.	6	3
9th Baker, Howard H.	Rep	Tenn.	4	3
10th Curtis, Thomas B.	Rep	Mo.	4	3

*2: Member's 2nd period of service on the committee.

Changes:

Chair:

Ch1 Cooper, Jere	Dem	Tenn.	Dec. 18,1957	Died in office.
Ch2 Mills, Wilbur D.	Dem	Ark.	Jan. 7,1958	Succeeded Cooper as Chair.

Majority:

Cooper, Jere	Dem	Tenn.	Dec. 18,1957	Died in office.
Frazier, James B. Jr.	Dem	Tenn.	Jan. 15,1958	Replaced Cooper.
Eberharter, Herman P.	Dem	Penn.	Sep. 9,1958	Died in office.

Departures from the House:

	Majority		Minority	
Elected to U.S. Senate	McCarthy, Eugene J.	Minn. DFL	Sadlak, Antoni N.	Conn. Rep
Defeated for Reelection	None		None	
Defeated for Renomination	Gregory, Noble J.	Ky. Dem		
Lost Election to U.S. Senate	None		Kean, Robert W.	N.J. Rep
Retired	None		Holmes, O. H. (Hal)	Wash. Rep
			Jenkins, Thomas A.	Ohio Rep

WAYS AND MEANS / 86th Congress

Service Dates of Committee Chair: Jan. 7,1959-Jan. 3,1961
Service Dates of Majority Members: Jan. 7,1959-Jan. 3,1961
Service Dates of Minority Members: Jan. 15,1959-Jan. 3,1961

Majority

Rank	Name	Party	State	Terms in: House	Terms in: Comm.
Chr	Mills, Wilbur D.	Dem	Ark.	11	10
2nd	Forand, Aime J.	Dem	R.I.	11	9
3rd	King, Cecil R.	Dem	Cal.	10	*2 6
4th	O'Brien, Thomas J.	Dem	Ill.	12	6
5th	Boggs, T. Hale	Dem	La.	8	6
6th	Keogh, Eugene J.	Dem	N.Y.	12	*2 4
7th	Harrison, Burr P.	Dem	Va.	8	*2 3
8th	Karsten, Frank M.	Dem	Mo.	7	3
9th	Herlong, Albert S. Jr.	Dem	Fla.	6	3
10th	Ikard, Frank N.	Dem	Tex.	5	3
11th	Machrowicz, Thaddeus M.	Dem	Mich.	5	3
12th	Frazier, James B. Jr.	Dem	Tenn.	6	2
13th	Green, William J. Jr.	Dem	Penn.	7	1
14th	Watts, John C.	Dem	Ky.	5	1
15th	Metcalf, Lee	Dem	Mont.	4	1

Minority

Rank	Name	Party	State	Terms in: House	Terms in: Comm.
RM1	Reed, Daniel A.	Rep	N.Y.	21	14
RM2 2nd	Simpson, Richard M.	Rep	Penn.	12	9
RM3 3rd	Mason, Noah M.	Rep	Ill.	12	7
4th	Byrnes, John W.	Rep	Wisc.	8	7
5th	Baker, Howard H.	Rep	Tenn.	5	4
6th	Curtis, Thomas B.	Rep	Mo.	5	4
7th	Knox, Victor A.	Rep	Mich.	4	*2 1
8th	Utt, James B.	Rep	Cal.	4	*2 1
9th	Betts, Jackson E.	Rep	Ohio	5	1
10th	Alger, Bruce R.	Rep	Tex.	3	1

*2: Member's 2nd period of service on the committee.

Vacancies Filled:
Minority: 7th through the 10th seats on Jan. 19,1959.

Changes:
Ranking Member:

RM1	Reed, Daniel A.	Rep	N.Y.	Feb. 19,1959	Died in office.
RM2	Simpson, Richard M.	Rep	Penn.	Feb. 19,1959	Succeeded Reed as Ranking Minority Member.
RM2	Simpson, Richard M.	Rep	Penn.	Jan. 7,1960	Died in office.
RM3	Mason, Noah M.	Rep	Ill.	Jan. 7,1960	Succeeded Simpson as Ranking Minority Member.

Minority:

Reed, Daniel A.	Rep	N.Y.	Feb. 19,1959	Died in office.
Bosch, Albert H.	Rep	N.Y.	Feb. 25,1959	Replaced Reed.
Simpson, Richard M.	Rep	Penn.	Jan. 7,1960	Died in office.
Lafore, John A. Jr.	Rep	Penn.	Jan. 18,1960	Replaced Simpson.
Lafore, John A. Jr.	Rep	Penn.	Aug. 30,1960	Left committee; defeated for renomination.
Mumma, Walter M.	Rep	Penn.	Aug. 30,1960	Replaced Lafore.
Bosch, Albert H.	Rep	N.Y.	Dec. 31,1960	Resigned; elected state judge.

Departures from the House:	Majority		Minority
Elected to U.S. Senate	Metcalf, Lee	Mont. Dem	None
Retired	Forand, Aime J.	R.I. Dem	None

WAYS AND MEANS / 87th Congress

Service Dates of Committee Chair: Jan. 3,1961-Jan. 3,1963
Service Dates of Majority Members: Jan. 3,1961-Jan. 3,1963
Service Dates of Minority Members: Jan. 23,1961-Jan. 3,1963

Majority

Rank	Name	Party	State	Terms in: House		Terms in: Comm.
Chr	Mills, Wilbur D.	Dem	Ark.	12		11
2nd	King, Cecil R.	Dem	Cal.	11	*2	7
3rd	O'Brien, Thomas J.	Dem	Ill.	13		7
4th	Boggs, T. Hale	Dem	La.	9		7
5th	Keogh, Eugene J.	Dem	N.Y.	13	*2	5
6th	Harrison, Burr P.	Dem	Va.	9	*2	4
7th	Karsten, Frank M.	Dem	Mo.	8		4
8th	Herlong, Albert S. Jr.	Dem	Fla.	7		4
9th	Ikard, Frank N.	Dem	Tex.	6		4
10th	Machrowicz, Thaddeus M.	Dem	Mich.	6		4
11th	Frazier, James B. Jr.	Dem	Tenn.	7		3
12th	Green, William J. Jr.	Dem	Penn.	8		2
13th	Watts, John C.	Dem	Ky.	6		2
14th	Ullman, Albert C.	Dem	Ore.	3		1
15th	Burke, James A.	Dem	Mass.	2		1

Minority

Rank	Name	Party	State	Terms in: House		Terms in: Comm.
RM	Mason, Noah M.	Rep	Ill.	13		8
2nd	Byrnes, John W.	Rep	Wisc.	9		8
3rd	Baker, Howard H.	Rep	Tenn.	6		5
4th	Curtis, Thomas B.	Rep	Mo.	6		5
5th	Knox, Victor A.	Rep	Mich.	5	*2	2
6th	Utt, James B.	Rep	Cal.	5	*2	2
7th	Betts, Jackson E.	Rep	Ohio	6		2
8th	Alger, Bruce R.	Rep	Tex.	4		2
9th	Mumma, Walter M.	Rep	Penn.	6		2
10th	Derounian, Steven B.	Rep	N.Y.	5		1

*2: Member's 2nd period of service on the committee.

Vacancy Filled:
Minority: 10th seat by Derounian on Feb. 13,1961.

Changes:

Majority:

Name	Party	State	Date	Change
Machrowicz, Thaddeus M.	Dem	Mich.	Sep. 18,1961	Resigned; appointed federal judge.
Ikard, Frank N.	Dem	Tex.	Dec. 15,1961	Resigned; became Executive Vice President of American Petroleum Institute.
Thompson, Clark W.	Dem	Tex.	Jan. 16,1962	Replaced Ikard.
Griffiths, Martha W.	Dem	Mich.	Jan. 16,1962	Replaced Machrowicz.

Minority:

Name	Party	State	Date	Change
Mumma, Walter M.	Rep	Penn.	Feb. 25,1961	Died in office.
Schneebeli, Herman T.	Rep	Penn.	Mar. 8,1961	Replaced Mumma.

Departures from the House:

	Majority			Minority		
Defeated for Renomination	Frazier, James B. Jr.	Tenn.	Dem	None		
Retired	Harrison, Burr P.	Va.	Dem	Mason, Noah M.	Ill.	Rep

WAYS AND MEANS / 88th Congress

Service Dates of Committee Chair: Jan. 9,1963-Jan. 3,1965
Service Dates of Majority Members: Jan. 9,1963-Jan. 3,1965
Service Dates of Minority Members: Jan. 17,1963-Jan. 3,1965

Majority

Rank	Name	Party	State	Terms in: House		Terms in: Comm.
Chr	Mills, Wilbur D.	Dem	Ark.	13		12
2nd	King, Cecil R.	Dem	Cal.	12	*2	8
3rd	O'Brien, Thomas J.	Dem	Ill.	14		8
4th	Boggs, T. Hale	Dem	La.	10		8
5th	Keogh, Eugene J.	Dem	N.Y.	14	*2	6
6th	Karsten, Frank M.	Dem	Mo.	9		5
7th	Herlong, Albert S. Jr.	Dem	Fla.	8		5
8th	Green, William J. Jr.	Dem	Penn.	9		3
9th	Watts, John C.	Dem	Ky.	7		3
10th	Ullman, Albert C.	Dem	Ore.	4		2
11th	Burke, James A.	Dem	Mass.	3		2
12th	Thompson, Clark W.	Dem	Tex.	10		2

Minority

Rank	Name	Party	State	Terms in: House		Terms in: Comm.
RM	Byrnes, John W.	Rep	Wisc.	10		9
2nd	Baker, Howard H.	Rep	Tenn.	7		6
3rd	Curtis, Thomas B.	Rep	Mo.	7		6
4th	Knox, Victor A.	Rep	Mich.	6	*2	3
5th	Utt, James B.	Rep	Cal.	6	*2	3
6th	Betts, Jackson E.	Rep	Ohio	7		3
7th	Alger, Bruce R.	Rep	Tex.	5		3
8th	Derounian, Steven B.	Rep	N.Y.	6		2
9th	Schneebeli, Herman T.	Rep	Penn.	3		2
10th	Collier, Harold R.	Rep	Ill.	4		1

13th Griffiths, Martha W.	Dem	Mich.	5	2	
14th Bass, Ross	Dem	Tenn.	5	1	
15th Jennings, William Pat	Dem	Va.	5	1	

*2: Member's 2nd period of service on the committee.

Vacancies Filled:
Majority: 14th and 15th seats by Bass and Jennings respectively on Jan. 17,1963.
Minority: 10th seat by Collier on Jan. 24,1963.

Changes:
Majority:

Green, William J. Jr.	Dem	Penn.	Dec. 21,1963	Died in office.
Rhodes, George M.	Dem	Penn.	Jan. 21,1964	Replaced Green.
O'Brien, Thomas J.	Dem	Ill.	Apr. 14,1964	Died in office.
Rostenkowski, Daniel D.	Dem	Ill.	May 5,1964	Replaced O'Brien.
Bass, Ross	Dem	Tenn.	Nov. 3,1964	Resigned; appointed to U.S. Senate.

Minority:

Baker, Howard H.	Rep	Tenn.	Jan. 7,1964	Died in office.
Broyhill, Joel T.	Rep	Va.	Jan. 22,1964	Replaced Baker.

Departures from the House:

	Majority	Minority		
Defeated for Reelection	None	Alger, Bruce R.	Tex.	Rep
		Derounian, Steven B.	N.Y.	Rep
		Knox, Victor A.	Mich.	Rep

WAYS AND MEANS / 89th Congress

Service Dates of Committee Chair: Jan. 7,1965-Jan. 3,1967
Service Dates of Majority Members: Jan. 7,1965-Jan. 3,1967
Service Dates of Minority Members: Jan. 21,1965-Jan. 3,1967

Majority

Rank Name	Party	State	Terms in: House	Terms in: Comm.
Chr Mills, Wilbur D.	Dem	Ark.	14	13
2nd King, Cecil R.	Dem	Cal.	13	*2 9
3rd Boggs, T. Hale	Dem	La.	11	9
4th Keogh, Eugene J.	Dem	N.Y.	15	*2 7
5th Karsten, Frank M.	Dem	Mo.	10	6
6th Herlong, Albert S. Jr.	Dem	Fla.	9	6
7th Watts, John C.	Dem	Ky.	8	4
8th Ullman, Albert C.	Dem	Ore.	5	3
9th Burke, James A.	Dem	Mass.	4	3
10th Thompson, Clark W.	Dem	Tex.	11	3
11th Griffiths, Martha W.	Dem	Mich.	6	3
12th Jennings, William Pat	Dem	Va.	6	2
13th Rhodes, George M.	Dem	Penn.	9	2
14th Rostenkowski, Daniel D.	Dem	Ill.	4	2
15th Landrum, Phillip M.	Dem	Ga.	7	1
16th Vanik, Charles A.	Dem	Ohio	6	1
17th Fulton, Richard H.	Dem	Tenn.	2	1

Minority

Rank Name	Party	State	Terms in: House	Terms in: Comm.
RM Byrnes, John W.	Rep	Wisc.	11	10
2nd Curtis, Thomas B.	Rep	Mo.	8	7
3rd Utt, James B.	Rep	Cal.	7	*2 4
4th Betts, Jackson E.	Rep	Ohio	8	4
5th Schneebeli, Herman T.	Rep	Penn.	4	3
6th Collier, Harold R.	Rep	Ill.	5	2
7th Broyhill, Joel T.	Rep	Va.	7	2
8th Battin, James F.	Rep	Mont.	3	1

*2: Member's 2nd period of service on the committee.

Changes:
Majority:

Thompson, Clark W.	Dem	Tex.	Dec. 30,1966	Resigned and retired.

Departures from the House:

	Majority			Minority
Defeated for Reelection	Jennings, William Pat	Va.	Dem	None
Retired	Keogh, Eugene J.	N.Y.	Dem	None

WAYS AND MEANS / 90th Congress

Service Dates of Committee Chair: Jan. 10,1967-Jan. 3,1969
Service Dates of Majority Members: Jan. 10,1967-Jan. 3,1969
Service Dates of Minority Members: Jan. 16,1967-Jan. 3,1969

Majority

Rank Name	Party	State	Terms in: House	Terms in: Comm.
Chr Mills, Wilbur D.	Dem	Ark.	15	14
2nd King, Cecil R.	Dem	Cal.	14 *2	10
3rd Boggs, T. Hale	Dem	La.	12	10
4th Karsten, Frank M.	Dem	Mo.	11	7
5th Herlong, Albert S. Jr.	Dem	Fla.	10	7
6th Watts, John C.	Dem	Ky.	9	5
7th Ullman, Albert C.	Dem	Ore.	6	4
8th Burke, James A.	Dem	Mass.	5	4
9th Griffiths, Martha W.	Dem	Mich.	7	4
10th Rhodes, George M.	Dem	Penn.	10	3
11th Rostenkowski, Daniel D.	Dem	Ill.	5	3
12th Landrum, Phillip M.	Dem	Ga.	8	2
13th Vanik, Charles A.	Dem	Ohio	7	2
14th Fulton, Richard H.	Dem	Tenn.	3	2
15th Gilbert, Jacob H.	Dem	N.Y.	5	1

Minority

Rank Name	Party	State	Terms in: House	Terms in: Comm.
RM Byrnes, John W.	Rep	Wisc.	12	11
2nd Curtis, Thomas B.	Rep	Mo.	9	8
3rd Utt, James B.	Rep	Cal.	8 *2	5
4th Betts, Jackson E.	Rep	Ohio	9	5
5th Schneebeli, Herman T.	Rep	Penn.	5	4
6th Collier, Harold R.	Rep	Ill.	6	3
7th Broyhill, Joel T.	Rep	Va.	8	3
8th Battin, James F.	Rep	Mont.	4	2
9th Conable, Barber B. Jr.	Rep	N.Y.	2	1
10th Bush, George H. W.	Rep	Tex.	1	1

*2: Member's 2nd period of service on the committee.

Vacancies Filled:
Majority: The 15th seat by Gilbert on Jan. 17,1967.
Minority: The 9th and 10th seats by Conable and Bush respectively on Jan. 26,1967.

Changes:
Majority:

Name	Party	State	Date	Change
Herlong, Albert S. Jr.	Dem	Fla.	July 23,1968	Left committee; later appointed to Securities and Exchanges Commission.
Burleson, Omar T.	Dem	Tex.	July 30,1968	Replaced Herlong.
King, Cecil R.	Dem	Cal.	July 31,1968	Left committee; no new assignment.
Rhodes, George M.	Dem	Penn.	July 31,1968	Left committee; no new assignment.
Corman, James C.	Dem	Cal.	Aug. 1,1968	Replaced King.
Green, William J. III	Dem	Penn.	Aug. 1,1968	Replaced Rhodes.

Departures from the House:	Majority			Minority		
Lost Election to U.S. Senate	None			Curtis, Thomas B.	Mo.	Rep
Retired	Karsten, Frank M.	Mo.	Dem	None		

WAYS AND MEANS / 91st Congress

Service Dates of Committee Chair: Jan. 3,1969-Jan. 3,1971
Service Dates of Majority Members: Jan. 3,1969-Jan. 3,1971
Service Dates of Minority Members: Jan. 3,1969-Jan. 3,1971

Majority

Rank Name	Party	State	Terms in: House	Terms in: Comm.
Chr Mills, Wilbur D.	Dem	Ark.	16	15
2nd Boggs, T. Hale	Dem	La.	13	11
3rd Watts, John C.	Dem	Ky.	10	6
4th Ullman, Albert C.	Dem	Ore.	7	5
5th Burke, James A.	Dem	Mass.	6	5
6th Griffiths, Martha W.	Dem	Mich.	8	5
7th Rostenkowski, Daniel D.	Dem	Ill.	6	4
8th Landrum, Phillip M.	Dem	Ga.	9	3
9th Vanik, Charles A.	Dem	Ohio	8	3
10th Fulton, Richard H.	Dem	Tenn.	4	3
11th Gilbert, Jacob H.	Dem	N.Y.	6	2
12th Burleson, Omar T.	Dem	Tex.	12	2

Minority

Rank Name	Party	State	Terms in: House	Terms in: Comm.
RM Byrnes, John W.	Rep	Wisc.	13	12
2nd Utt, James B.	Rep	Cal.	9 *2	6
3rd Betts, Jackson E.	Rep	Ohio	10	6
4th Schneebeli, Herman T.	Rep	Penn.	6	5
5th Collier, Harold R.	Rep	Ill.	7	4
6th Broyhill, Joel T.	Rep	Va.	9	4
7th Battin, James F.	Rep	Mont.	5	3
8th Conable, Barber B. Jr.	Rep	N.Y.	3	2
9th Bush, George H. W.	Rep	Tex.	2	2
10th Morton, Rogers C. B.	Rep	Md.	4	1

13th Corman, James C.	Dem	Cal.	5	2	
14th Green, William J. III	Dem	Penn.	4	2	
15th Gibbons, Sam M.	Dem	Fla.	4	1	*2: Member's 2nd period of service on the committee.

Vacancy Filled:
Majority: 15th seat by Gibbons on Jan. 14,1969.
Minority: 10th seat by Morton on Jan. 29,1969.

Changes:
Majority:

Gilbert, Jacob H.	Dem	N.Y.	Dec. 15,1970	Left committee following defeat for renomination.
Carey, Hugh L.	Dem	N.Y.	Dec. 16,1970	Replaced Gilbert.

Minority:

Battin, James F.	Rep	Mont.	Feb. 27,1969	Resigned; appointed federal judge.
Chamberlain, Charles E.	Rep	Mich.	Mar. 5,1969	Replaced Battin.
Utt, James B.	Rep	Cal.	Mar. 1,1970	Died in office.
Pettis, Jerry L.	Rep	Cal.	Apr. 30,1970	Replaced Utt.

Departures from the House:	Majority	Minority		
Lost Election to U.S. Senate	None	Bush, George H. W.	Tex.	Rep

WAYS AND MEANS / 92nd Congress

Service Dates of Committee Chair: Jan. 22,1971-Jan. 3,1973
Service Dates of Majority Members: Jan. 22,1971-Jan. 3,1973
Service Dates of Minority Members: Jan. 22,1971-Jan. 3,1973

Majority

Rank Name	Party	State	Terms in: House	Terms in: Comm.
Chr Mills, Wilbur D.	Dem	Ark.	17	16
2nd Boggs, T. Hale	Dem	La.	14	12
3rd Watts, John C.	Dem	Ky.	11	7
4th Ullman, Albert C.	Dem	Ore.	8	6
5th Burke, James A.	Dem	Mass.	7	6
6th Griffiths, Martha W.	Dem	Mich.	9	6
7th Rostenkowski, Daniel D.	Dem	Ill.	7	5
8th Landrum, Phillip M.	Dem	Ga.	10	4
9th Vanik, Charles A.	Dem	Ohio	9	4
10th Fulton, Richard H.	Dem	Tenn.	5	4
11th Burleson, Omar T.	Dem	Tex.	13	3
12th Corman, James C.	Dem	Cal.	6	3
13th Green, William J. III	Dem	Penn.	5	3
14th Gibbons, Sam M.	Dem	Fla.	5	2
15th Carey, Hugh L.	Dem	N.Y.	6	2

Minority

Rank Name	Party	State	Terms in: House	Terms in: Comm.
RM Byrnes, John W.	Rep	Wisc.	14	13
2nd Betts, Jackson E.	Rep	Ohio	11	7
3rd Schneebeli, Herman T.	Rep	Penn.	7	6
4th Collier, Harold R.	Rep	Ill.	8	5
5th Broyhill, Joel T.	Rep	Va.	10	5
6th Conable, Barber B. Jr.	Rep	N.Y.	4	3
7th Morton, Rogers C. B.	Rep	Md.	5	2
8th Chamberlain, Charles E.	Rep	Mich.	8	2
9th Pettis, Jerry L.	Rep	Cal.	3	2
10th Duncan, John J.	Rep	Tenn.	4	1

Vacancy Filled:
Minority: 10th seat by Duncan on Feb. 4,1971.

Changes:
Majority:

Boggs, T. Hale	Dem	La.	Feb. 2,1971	Left committee; elected House Majority Leader.
Waggonner, Joe D. Jr.	Dem	La.	Feb. 4,1971	Replaced Boggs.
Watts, John C.	Dem	Ky.	Sep. 24,1971	Died in office.
Karth, Joseph E.	DFL	Minn.	Oct. 6,1971	Replaced Watts.

Minority:

Morton, Rogers C. B.	Rep	Md.	Jan. 29,1971	Resigned; appointed Secretary of the Interior.
Brotzman, Donald G.	Rep	Colo.	Feb. 4,1971	Replaced Morton.

Departures from the House:	Majority	Minority		
Retired	None	Betts, Jackson E.	Ohio	Rep
		Byrnes, John W.	Wisc.	Rep

WAYS AND MEANS / 93rd Congress

Service Dates of Committee Chair: Jan. 24,1973-Jan. 3,1975
Service Dates of Majority Members: Jan. 24,1973-Jan. 3,1975
Service Dates of Minority Members: Jan. 24,1973-Jan. 3,1975

Majority

Rank Name	Party	State	Terms in: House	Terms in: Comm.
Chr Mills, Wilbur D.	Dem	Ark.	18	17
2nd Ullman, Albert C.	Dem	Ore.	9	7
3rd Burke, James A.	Dem	Mass.	8	7
4th Griffiths, Martha W.	Dem	Mich.	10	7
5th Rostenkowski, Daniel D.	Dem	Ill.	8	6
6th Landrum, Phillip M.	Dem	Ga.	11	5
7th Vanik, Charles A.	Dem	Ohio	10	5
8th Fulton, Richard H.	Dem	Tenn.	6	5
9th Burleson, Omar T.	Dem	Tex.	14	4
10th Corman, James C.	Dem	Cal.	7	4
11th Green, William J. III	Dem	Penn.	6	4
12th Gibbons, Sam M.	Dem	Fla.	6	3
13th Carey, Hugh L.	Dem	N.Y.	7	3
14th Waggonner, Joe D. Jr.	Dem	La.	7	2
15th Karth, Joseph E.	DFL	Minn.	8	2

Minority

Rank Name	Party	State	Terms in: House	Terms in: Comm.
RM Schneebeli, Herman T.	Rep	Penn.	8	7
2nd Collier, Harold R.	Rep	Ill.	9	6
3rd Broyhill, Joel T.	Rep	Va.	11	6
4th Conable, Barber B. Jr.	Rep	N.Y.	5	4
5th Chamberlain, Charles E.	Rep	Mich.	9	3
6th Pettis, Jerry L.	Rep	Cal.	4	3
7th Duncan, John J.	Rep	Tenn.	5	2
8th Brotzman, Donald G.	Rep	Colo.	5	2
9th Clancy, Donald D.	Rep	Ohio	7	1
10th Archer, William R.	Rep	Tex.	2	1

Changes:

Majority:

Name	Party	State	Date	Change
Carey, Hugh L.	Dem	N.Y.	Dec. 17,1974	Left committee; resigned Dec. 31,1974 to become Governor of New York.
Griffiths, Martha W.	Dem	Mich.	Dec. 17,1974	Left committee; resigned Dec. 31,1974.
Pike, Otis G.	Dem	N.Y.	Dec. 18,1974	Replaced Carey.
Vander Veen, Richard F.	Dem	Mich.	Dec. 18,1974	Replaced Griffiths.

Minority:

Name	Party	State	Date	Change
Broyhill, Joel T.	Rep	Va.	Dec. 31,1974	Resigned; defeated for reelection.
Chamberlain, Charles E.	Rep	Mich.	Dec. 31,1974	Resigned and retired.

Departures from the House:	Majority	Minority	
Defeated for Reelection	None	Brotzman, Donald G.	Colo. Rep
Retired	None	Collier, Harold R.	Ill. Rep

WAYS AND MEANS / 94th Congress

Service Dates of Committee Chair: Jan. 20,1975-Jan. 3,1977
Service Dates of Majority Members: Jan. 20,1975-Jan. 3,1977
Service Dates of Minority Members: Jan. 23,1975-Jan. 3,1977

Majority

Rank Name	Party	State	Terms in: House	Terms in: Comm.
Chr Ullman, Albert C.	Dem	Ore.	10	8
2nd Mills, Wilbur D.	Dem	Ark.	19	18
3rd Burke, James A.	Dem	Mass.	9	8
4th Rostenkowski, Daniel D.	Dem	Ill.	9	7
5th Landrum, Phillip M.	Dem	Ga.	12	6
6th Vanik, Charles A.	Dem	Ohio	11	6
7th Fulton, Richard H.	Dem	Tenn.	7	6
8th Burleson, Omar T.	Dem	Tex.	15	5
9th Corman, James C.	Dem	Cal.	8	5
10th Green, William J. III	Dem	Penn.	7	5
11th Gibbons, Sam M.	Dem	Fla.	7	4
12th Waggonner, Joe D. Jr.	Dem	La.	8	3
13th Karth, Joseph E.	DFL	Minn.	9	3
14th Pike, Otis G.	Dem	N.Y.	8	2
15th Vander Veen, Richard F.	Dem	Mich.	2	2
16th Pickle, J. J. (Jake)	Dem	Tex.	7	1

Minority

Rank Name	Party	State	Terms in: House	Terms in: Comm.
RM Schneebeli, Herman T.	Rep	Penn.	9	8
2nd Conable, Barber B. Jr.	Rep	N.Y.	6	5
3rd Pettis, Jerry L.	Rep	Cal.	5	4
4th Duncan, John J.	Rep	Tenn.	6	3
5th Clancy, Donald D.	Rep	Ohio	8	2
6th Archer, William R.	Rep	Tex.	3	2
7th Vander Jagt, Guy A.	Rep	Mich.	6	1
8th Steiger, William A.	Rep	Wisc.	5	1
9th Crane, Philip M.	Rep	Ill.	4	1
10th Frenzel, William E.	Rep	Minn.	3	1
11th Martin, James G.	Rep	N.C.	2	1
12th Bafalis, Louis A. (Skip)	Rep	Fla.	2	1

17th Helstoski, Henry	Dem	N.J.	6	1
18th Rangel, Charles B.	Dem	N.Y.	3	1
19th Cotter, William R.	Dem	Conn.	3	1
20th Stark, Fortney H. (Pete)	Dem	Cal.	2	1
21st Jones, James R.	Dem	Okla.	2	1
22nd Jacobs, Andrew Jr.	Dem	Ind.	5	1
23rd Mikva, Abner J.	Dem	Ill.	3	1
24th Keys, Martha E.	Dem	Kans.	1	1
25th Fisher, Joseph L.	Dem	Va.	1	1

Note: Wilbur D. Mills (Dem-Ark.) announced at the end of the previous Congress on Dec. 11,1974, that he would not resume chairmanship of this committee in the 94th Congress due to ill health.

Changes:

Majority:

Fulton, Richard H.	Dem	Tenn.	Aug. 14,1975	Resigned; elected Mayor of Nashville.
Ford, Harold E.	Dem	Tenn.	Sep. 30,1975	Replaced Fulton.

Minority:

Pettis, Jerry L.	Rep	Cal.	Feb. 14,1975	Died in office.
Ketchum, William M.	Rep	Cal.	Mar. 21,1975	Replaced Pettis.

Departures from the House:	Majority			Minority		
Defeated for Reelection	Helstoski, Henry	N.J.	Dem	Clancy, Donald D.	Ohio	Rep
	Vander Veen, Richard F.	Mich.	Dem			
Lost Election to U.S. Senate	Green, William J. III	Penn.	Dem	None		
Retired	Karth, Joseph E.	Minn.	DFL	Schneebeli, Herman T.	Penn.	Rep
	Landrum, Phillip M.	Ga.	Dem			
	Mills, Wilbur D.	Ark.	Dem			

WAYS AND MEANS / 95th Congress

Service Dates of Committee Chair: Jan. 19,1977-Jan. 3,1979
Service Dates of Majority Members: Jan. 19,1977-Jan. 3,1979
Service Dates of Minority Members: Jan. 19,1977-Jan. 3,1979

Majority

Rank Name	Party	State	Terms in: House	Terms in: Comm.
Chr Ullman, Albert C.	Dem	Ore.	11	9
2nd Burke, James A.	Dem	Mass.	10	9
3rd Rostenkowski, Daniel D.	Dem	Ill.	10	8
4th Vanik, Charles A.	Dem	Ohio	12	7
5th Burleson, Omar T.	Dem	Tex.	16	6
6th Corman, James C.	Dem	Cal.	9	6
7th Gibbons, Sam M.	Dem	Fla.	8	5
8th Waggonner, Joe D. Jr.	Dem	La.	9	4
9th Pike, Otis G.	Dem	N.Y.	9	3
10th Pickle, J. J. (Jake)	Dem	Tex.	8	2
11th Rangel, Charles B.	Dem	N.Y.	4	2
12th Cotter, William R.	Dem	Conn.	4	2
13th Stark, Fortney H. (Pete)	Dem	Cal.	3	2
14th Jones, James R.	Dem	Okla.	3	2
15th Jacobs, Andrew Jr.	Dem	Ind.	6	2
16th Mikva, Abner J.	Dem	Ill.	4	2
17th Keys, Martha E.	Dem	Kans.	2	2
18th Fisher, Joseph L.	Dem	Va.	2	2
19th Ford, Harold E.	Dem	Tenn.	2	2
20th Holland, Kenneth L.	Dem	S.C.	2	1
21st Brodhead, William M.	Dem	Mich.	2	1
22nd Jenkins, Edgar L.	Dem	Ga.	1	1
23rd Gephardt, Richard A.	Dem	Mo.	1	1
24th Tucker, James G. Jr.	Dem	Ark.	1	1
25th Lederer, Raymond F.	Dem	Penn.	1	1

Minority

Rank Name	Party	State	Terms in: House	Terms in: Comm.
RM Conable, Barber B. Jr.	Rep	N.Y.	7	6
2nd Duncan, John J.	Rep	Tenn.	7	4
3rd Archer, William R.	Rep	Tex.	4	3
4th Vander Jagt, Guy A.	Rep	Mich.	7	2
5th Steiger, William A.	Rep	Wisc.	6	2
6th Crane, Philip M.	Rep	Ill.	5	2
7th Frenzel, William E.	Rep	Minn.	4	2
8th Martin, James G.	Rep	N.C.	3	2
9th Bafalis, Louis A. (Skip)	Rep	Fla.	3	2
10th Ketchum, William M.	Rep	Cal.	3	2
11th Schulze, Richard T.	Rep	Penn.	2	1
12th Gradison, Willis D. Jr.	Rep	Ohio	2	1

Changes:

Majority:

Burleson, Omar T.	Dem	Tex.	Dec. 31,1978	Resigned and retired.

Minority:

Ketchum, William M.	Rep	Cal.	June 24,1978	Died in office.
Rousselot, John H.	Rep	Cal.	June 29,1978	Replaced Ketchum.
Steiger, William A.	Rep	Wisc.	Dec. 4,1978	Died in office.

Departures from the House:	Majority			Minority
Defeated for Reelection	Keys, Martha E.	Kans.	Dem	None
Lost Nomination to U.S. Senate	Tucker, James G. Jr.	Ark.	Dem	None
Retired	Burke, James A.	Mass.	Dem	None
	Pike, Otis G.	N.Y.	Dem	
	Waggonner, Joe D. Jr.	La.	Dem	

WAYS AND MEANS / 96th Congress

Service Dates of Committee Chair: Jan. 24,1979-Jan. 3,1981
Service Dates of Majority Members: Jan. 24,1979-Jan. 3,1981
Service Dates of Minority Members: Jan. 24,1979-Jan. 3,1981

Majority

Rank Name	Party	State	Terms in: House	Terms in: Comm.
Chr Ullman, Albert C.	Dem	Ore.	12	10
2nd Rostenkowski, Daniel D.	Dem	Ill.	11	9
3rd Vanik, Charles A.	Dem	Ohio	13	8
4th Corman, James C.	Dem	Cal.	10	7
5th Gibbons, Sam M.	Dem	Fla.	9	6
6th Pickle, J. J. (Jake)	Dem	Tex.	9	3
7th Rangel, Charles B.	Dem	N.Y.	5	3
8th Cotter, William R.	Dem	Conn.	5	3
9th Stark, Fortney H. (Pete)	Dem	Cal.	4	3
10th Jones, James R.	Dem	Okla.	4	3
11th Jacobs, Andrew Jr.	Dem	Ind.	7	3
12th Mikva, Abner J.	Dem	Ill.	5	3
13th Fisher, Joseph L.	Dem	Va.	3	3
14th Ford, Harold E.	Dem	Tenn.	3	3
15th Holland, Kenneth L.	Dem	S.C.	3	2
16th Brodhead, William M.	Dem	Mich.	3	2
17th Jenkins, Edgar L.	Dem	Ga.	2	2
18th Gephardt, Richard A.	Dem	Mo.	2	2
19th Lederer, Raymond F.	Dem	Penn.	2	2
20th Downey, Thomas J.	Dem	N.Y.	3	1
21st Heftel, Cecil	Dem	Hai.	2	1
22nd Fowler, Wyche Jr.	Dem	Ga.	2	1
23rd Guarini, Frank J.	Dem	N.J.	1	1
24th Shannon, James M.	Dem	Mass.	1	1

Minority

Rank Name	Party	State	Terms in: House	Terms in: Comm.
RM Conable, Barber B. Jr.	Rep	N.Y.	8	7
2nd Duncan, John J.	Rep	Tenn.	8	5
3rd Archer, William R.	Rep	Tex.	5	4
4th Vander Jagt, Guy A.	Rep	Mich.	8	3
5th Crane, Philip M.	Rep	Ill.	6	3
6th Frenzel, William E.	Rep	Minn.	5	3
7th Martin, James G.	Rep	N.C.	4	3
8th Bafalis, Louis A. (Skip)	Rep	Fla.	4	3
9th Schulze, Richard T.	Rep	Penn.	3	2
10th Gradison, Willis D. Jr.	Rep	Ohio	3	2
11th Rousselot, John H.	Rep	Cal.	7	2
12th Moore, W. Henson	Rep	La.	3	1

Changes:

Majority:

Mikva, Abner J.	Dem	Ill.	Sep. 26,1979	Resigned; appointed federal judge.
Russo, Martin A.	Dem	Ill.	Oct. 23,1979	Replaced Mikva.

Departures from the House:	Majority			Minority
Defeated for Reelection	Corman, James C.	Cal.	Dem	None
	Fisher, Joseph L.	Va.	Dem	
	Ullman, Albert C.	Ore.	Dem	
Retired	Vanik, Charles A.	Ohio	Dem	None
Departures from Committee:				
Unassigned in 97th Congress pending indictment	Lederer, Raymond F.	Penn.	Dem	None

WAYS AND MEANS / 97th Congress

Service Dates of Committee Chair: Jan. 28,1981-Jan. 3,1983
Service Dates of Majority Members: Jan. 28,1981-Jan. 3,1983
Service Dates of Minority Members: Jan. 28,1981-Jan. 3,1983

Majority

Rank Name	Party	State	Terms in: House	Terms in: Comm.
Chr Rostenkowski, Daniel D.	Dem	Ill.	12	10
2nd Gibbons, Sam M.	Dem	Fla.	10	7
3rd Pickle, J. J. (Jake)	Dem	Tex.	10	4
4th Rangel, Charles B.	Dem	N.Y.	6	4
5th Cotter, William R.	Dem	Conn.	6	4
6th Stark, Fortney H. (Pete)	Dem	Cal.	5	4
7th Jones, James R.	Dem	Okla.	5	4
8th Jacobs, Andrew Jr.	Dem	Ind.	8	4
9th Ford, Harold E.	Dem	Tenn.	4	4
10th Holland, Kenneth L.	Dem	S.C.	4	3
11th Brodhead, William M.	Dem	Mich.	4	3
12th Jenkins, Edgar L.	Dem	Ga.	3	3
13th Gephardt, Richard A.	Dem	Mo.	3	3
14th Downey, Thomas J.	Dem	N.Y.	4	2
15th Heftel, Cecil	Dem	Hai.	3	2
16th Fowler, Wyche Jr.	Dem	Ga.	3	2
17th Guarini, Frank J.	Dem	N.J.	2	2
18th Shannon, James M.	Dem	Mass.	2	2
19th Russo, Martin A.	Dem	Ill.	4	2
20th Pease, Donald J.	Dem	Ohio	3	1
21st Hance, Kent	Dem	Tex.	2	1
22nd Matsui, Robert T.	Dem	Cal.	2	1
23rd Bailey, Donald A.	Dem	Penn.	2	1

Minority

Rank Name	Party	State	Terms in: House	Terms in: Comm.
RM Conable, Barber B. Jr.	Rep	N.Y.	9	8
2nd Duncan, John J.	Rep	Tenn.	9	6
3rd Archer, William R.	Rep	Tex.	6	5
4th Vander Jagt, Guy A.	Rep	Mich.	9	4
5th Crane, Philip M.	Rep	Ill.	7	4
6th Frenzel, William E.	Rep	Minn.	6	4
7th Martin, James G.	Rep	N.C.	5	4
8th Bafalis, Louis A. (Skip)	Rep	Fla.	5	4
9th Schulze, Richard T.	Rep	Penn.	4	3
10th Gradison, Willis D. Jr.	Rep	Ohio	4	3
11th Rousselot, John H.	Rep	Cal.	8	3
12th Moore, W. Henson	Rep	La.	4	2

Vacancy Filled:
Majority: 23rd seat by Bailey on Feb. 25,1981.

Changes:
Majority:

Cotter, William R.	Dem	Conn.	Sep. 8,1981	Died in office.
Anthony, Beryl F. Jr.	Dem	Ark.	Oct. 7,1981	Replaced Cotter.

Departures from the House:

	Majority		Minority	
Defeated for Reelection	None		Rousselot, John H.	Cal. Rep
Defeated for Renomination	Bailey, Donald A.	Penn. Dem	None	
Lost Nomination for Governor	None		Bafalis, Louis A. (Skip)	Fla. Rep
Retired	Brodhead, William M.	Mich. Dem	None	
	Holland, Kenneth L.	S.C. Dem		

WAYS AND MEANS / 98th Congress

Service Dates of Committee Chair: Jan. 6,1983-Jan. 3,1985
Service Dates of Majority Members: Jan. 6,1983-Jan. 3,1985
Service Dates of Minority Members: Jan. 6,1983-Jan. 3,1985

Majority

Rank	Name	Party	State	Terms in: House	Terms in: Comm.
Chr	Rostenkowski, Daniel D.	Dem	Ill.	13	11
2nd	Gibbons, Sam M.	Dem	Fla.	11	8
3rd	Pickle, J. J. (Jake)	Dem	Tex.	11	5
4th	Rangel, Charles B.	Dem	N.Y.	7	5
5th	Stark, Fortney H. (Pete)	Dem	Cal.	6	5
6th	Jones, James R.	Dem	Okla.	6	5
7th	Jacobs, Andrew Jr.	Dem	Ind.	9	5
8th	Ford, Harold E.	Dem	Tenn.	5	5
9th	Jenkins, Edgar L.	Dem	Ga.	4	4
10th	Gephardt, Richard A.	Dem	Mo.	4	4
11th	Downey, Thomas J.	Dem	N.Y.	5	3
12th	Heftel, Cecil	Dem	Hai.	4	3
13th	Fowler, Wyche Jr.	Dem	Ga.	4	3
14th	Guarini, Frank J.	Dem	N.J.	3	3
15th	Shannon, James M.	Dem	Mass.	3	3
16th	Russo, Martin A.	Dem	Ill.	5	3
17th	Pease, Donald J.	Dem	Ohio	4	2
18th	Hance, Kent	Dem	Tex.	3	2
19th	Matsui, Robert T.	Dem	Cal.	3	2
20th	Anthony, Beryl F. Jr.	Dem	Ark.	3	2
21st	Flippo, Ronnie G.	Dem	Ala.	4	1
22nd	Dorgan, Byron L.	Dem	N.D.	2	1
23rd	Kennelly, Barbara B.	Dem	Conn.	2	1

Minority

Rank	Name	Party	State	Terms in: House	Terms in: Comm.
RM	Conable, Barber B. Jr.	Rep	N.Y.	10	9
2nd	Duncan, John J.	Rep	Tenn.	10	7
3rd	Archer, William R.	Rep	Tex.	7	6
4th	Vander Jagt, Guy A.	Rep	Mich.	10	5
5th	Crane, Philip M.	Rep	Ill.	8	5
6th	Frenzel, William E.	Rep	Mich.	7	5
7th	Martin, James G.	Rep	N.C.	6	5
8th	Schulze, Richard T.	Rep	Penn.	5	4
9th	Gradison, Willis D. Jr.	Rep	Ohio	5	4
10th	Moore, W. Henson	Rep	La.	5	3
11th	Campbell, Carroll A. Jr.	Rep	S.C.	3	1
12th	Thomas, William M.	Rep	Cal.	3	1

Departures from the House:	Majority		Minority	
Elected Governor	None		Martin, James G.	N.C. Rep
Lost Nomination to U.S. Senate	Hance, Kent	Tex. Dem	None	
	Shannon, James M.	Mass. Dem		
Retired	None		Conable, Barber B. Jr.	N.Y. Rep

WAYS AND MEANS / 99th Congress

Service Dates of Committee Chair: Jan. 7,1985-Jan. 3,1987
Service Dates of Majority Members: Jan. 30,1985-Jan. 3,1987
Service Dates of Minority Members: Jan. 30,1985-Jan. 3,1987

Majority

Rank	Name	Party	State	Terms in: House	Terms in: Comm.
Chr	Rostenkowski, Daniel D.	Dem	Ill.	14	12
2nd	Gibbons, Sam M.	Dem	Fla.	12	9
3rd	Pickle, J. J. (Jake)	Dem	Tex.	12	6
4th	Rangel, Charles B.	Dem	N.Y.	8	6
5th	Stark, Fortney H. (Pete)	Dem	Cal.	7	6
6th	Jones, James R.	Dem	Okla.	7	6
7th	Jacobs, Andrew Jr.	Dem	Ind.	10	6
8th	Ford, Harold E.	Dem	Tenn.	6	6
9th	Jenkins, Edgar L.	Dem	Ga.	5	5
10th	Gephardt, Richard A.	Dem	Mo.	5	5
11th	Downey, Thomas J.	Dem	N.Y.	6	4
12th	Heftel, Cecil	Dem	Hai.	5	4
13th	Fowler, Wyche Jr.	Dem	Ga.	5	4
14th	Guarini, Frank J.	Dem	N.J.	4	4
15th	Russo, Martin A.	Dem	Ill.	6	4
16th	Pease, Donald J.	Dem	Ohio	5	3

Minority

Rank	Name	Party	State	Terms in: House	Terms in: Comm.
RM	Duncan, John J.	Rep	Tenn.	11	8
2nd	Archer, William R.	Rep	Tex.	8	7
3rd	Vander Jagt, Guy A.	Rep	Mich.	11	6
4th	Crane, Philip M.	Rep	Ill.	9	6
5th	Frenzel, William E.	Rep	Minn.	8	6
6th	Schulze, Richard T.	Rep	Penn.	6	5
7th	Gradison, Willis D. Jr.	Rep	Ohio	6	5
8th	Moore, W. Henson	Rep	La.	6	4
9th	Campbell, Carroll A. Jr.	Rep	S.C.	4	2
10th	Thomas, William M.	Rep	Cal.	4	2
11th	McGrath, Raymond J.	Rep	N.Y.	3	1
12th	Daub, Hal	Rep	Neb.	3	1
13th	Gregg, Judd	Rep	N.H.	3	1

17th Matsui, Robert T.	Dem	Cal.	4	3
18th Anthony, Beryl F. Jr.	Dem	Ark.	4	3
19th Flippo, Ronnie G.	Dem	Ala.	5	2
20th Dorgan, Byron L.	Dem	N.D.	3	2
21st Kennelly, Barbara B.	Dem	Conn.	3	2
22nd Donnelly, Brian J.	Dem	Mass.	4	1
23rd Coyne, William J.	Dem	Penn.	3	1

Changes:

Majority:

Heftel, Cecil	Dem	Hai.	July 11,1986	Resigned; lost election for Governor.
Andrews, Michael A.	Dem	Tex.	July 29,1986	Replaced Heftel.

Departures from the House:	Majority			Minority		
Elected to U.S. Senate	Fowler, Wyche Jr.	Ga.	Dem	None		
Elected Governor	None			Campbell, Carroll A. Jr.	S.C.	Rep
Lost Election to U.S. Senate	Jones, James R.	Okla.	Dem	Moore, W. Henson	La.	Rep

WAYS AND MEANS / 100th Congress

Service Dates of Committee Chair: Jan. 6,1987-Jan. 3,1989
Service Dates of Majority Members: Jan. 6,1987-Jan. 3,1989
Service Dates of Minority Members: Jan. 21,1987-Jan. 3,1989

Majority

Rank Name	Party	State	Terms in: House	Terms in: Comm.
Chr Rostenkowski, Daniel D.	Dem	Ill.	15	13
2nd Gibbons, Sam M.	Dem	Fla.	13	10
3rd Pickle, J. J. (Jake)	Dem	Tex.	13	7
4th Rangel, Charles B.	Dem	N.Y.	9	7
5th Stark, Fortney H. (Pete)	Dem	Cal.	8	7
6th Jacobs, Andrew Jr.	Dem	Ind.	11	7
7th Ford, Harold E.	Dem	Tenn.	7	7
8th Jenkins, Edgar L.	Dem	Ga.	6	6
9th Gephardt, Richard A.	Dem	Mo.	6	6
10th Downey, Thomas J.	Dem	N.Y.	7	5
11th Guarini, Frank J.	Dem	N.J.	5	5
12th Russo, Martin A.	Dem	Ill.	7	5
13th Pease, Donald J.	Dem	Ohio	6	4
14th Matsui, Robert T.	Dem	Cal.	5	4
15th Anthony, Beryl F. Jr.	Dem	Ark.	5	4
16th Flippo, Ronnie G.	Dem	Ala.	6	3
17th Dorgan, Byron L.	Dem	N.D.	4	3
18th Kennelly, Barbara B.	Dem	Conn.	4	3
19th Donnelly, Brian J.	Dem	Mass.	5	2
20th Coyne, William J.	Dem	Penn.	4	2
21st Andrews, Michael A.	Dem	Tex.	3	2
22nd Levin, Sander M.	Dem	Mich.	3	1
23rd Moody, Jim	Dem	Wisc.	3	1

Minority

Rank Name	Party	State	Terms in: House	Terms in: Comm.
RM1 Duncan, John J.	Rep	Tenn.	12	9
RM2 2nd Archer, William R.	Rep	Tex.	9	8
3rd Vander Jagt, Guy A.	Rep	Mich.	12	7
4th Crane, Philip M.	Rep	Ill.	10	7
5th Frenzel, William E.	Rep	Minn.	9	7
6th Schulze, Richard T.	Rep	Penn.	7	6
7th Gradison, Willis D. Jr.	Rep	Ohio	7	6
8th Thomas, William M.	Rep	Cal.	5	3
9th McGrath, Raymond J.	Rep	N.Y.	4	2
10th Daub, Hal	Rep	Neb.	4	2
11th Gregg, Judd	Rep	N.H.	4	2
12th Brown, Hank	Rep	Colo.	4	1
13th Chandler, Rodney	Rep	Wash.	3	1

Changes:

Ranking Member:

RM1 Duncan, John J.	Rep	Tenn.	June 2,1988	Died in office.
RM2 Archer, William R.	Rep	Tex.	June 2,1988	Succeeded Duncan as Ranking Minority Member.

Minority:

Duncan, John J.	Rep	Tenn.	June 2,1988	Died in office.
Shaw, E. Clay Jr.	Rep	Fla.	July 7,1988	Replaced Duncan.

Departures from the House:	Majority	Minority		
Elected Governor	None	Gregg, Judd	N.H.	Rep
Lost Nomination to U.S. Senate	None	Daub, Hal	Neb.	Rep

WAYS AND MEANS / 101st Congress

Service Dates of Committee Chair: Jan. 3,1989-Jan. 3,1991
Service Dates of Majority Members: Jan. 3,1989-Jan. 3,1991
Service Dates of Minority Members: Jan. 20,1989-Jan. 3,1991

Majority

Rank	Name	Party	State	Terms in: House	Terms in: Comm.
Chr	Rostenkowski, Daniel D.	Dem	Ill.	16	14
2nd	Gibbons, Sam M.	Dem	Fla.	14	11
3rd	Pickle, J. J. (Jake)	Dem	Tex.	14	8
4th	Rangel, Charles B.	Dem	N.Y.	10	8
5th	Stark, Fortney H. (Pete)	Dem	Cal.	9	8
6th	Jacobs, Andrew Jr.	Dem	Ind.	12	8
7th	Ford, Harold E.	Dem	Tenn.	8	8
8th	Jenkins, Edgar L.	Dem	Ga.	7	7
9th	Gephardt, Richard A.	Dem	Mo.	7	7
10th	Downey, Thomas J.	Dem	N.Y.	8	6
11th	Guarini, Frank J.	Dem	N.J.	6	6
12th	Russo, Martin A.	Dem	Ill.	8	6
13th	Pease, Donald J.	Dem	Ohio	7	5
14th	Matsui, Robert T.	Dem	Cal.	6	5
15th	Anthony, Beryl F. Jr.	Dem	Ark.	6	5
16th	Flippo, Ronnie G.	Dem	Ala.	7	4
17th	Dorgan, Byron L.	Dem	N.D.	5	4
18th	Kennelly, Barbara B.	Dem	Conn.	5	4
19th	Donnelly, Brian J.	Dem	Mass.	6	3
20th	Coyne, William J.	Dem	Penn.	5	3
21st	Andrews, Michael A.	Dem	Tex.	4	3
22nd	Levin, Sander M.	Dem	Mich.	4	2
23rd	Moody, Jim	Dem	Wisc.	4	2

Minority

Rank	Name	Party	State	Terms in: House	Terms in: Comm.
RM	Archer, William R.	Rep	Tex.	10	9
2nd	Vander Jagt, Guy A.	Rep	Mich.	13	8
3rd	Crane, Philip M.	Rep	Ill.	11	8
4th	Frenzel, William E.	Rep	Minn.	10	8
5th	Schulze, Richard T.	Rep	Penn.	8	7
6th	Gradison, Willis D. Jr.	Rep	Ohio	8	7
7th	Thomas, William M.	Rep	Cal.	6	4
8th	McGrath, Raymond J.	Rep	N.Y.	5	3
9th	Brown, Hank	Rep	Colo.	5	2
10th	Chandler, Rodney	Rep	Wash.	4	2
11th	Shaw, E. Clay Jr.	Rep	Fla.	5	2
12th	Sundquist, Don	Rep	Tenn.	4	1
13th	Johnson, Nancy L.	Rep	Conn.	4	1

Changes:

Majority:

Name	Party	State	Date	Note
Gephardt, Richard A.	Dem	Mo.	Oct. 16,1989	Left committee; earlier elected House Majority Leader.
Cardin, Benjamin L.	Dem	Md.	Oct. 16,1989	Replaced Gephardt.

Departures from the House:

	Majority			Minority		
Elected to U.S. Senate	None			Brown, Hank	Colo.	Rep
Lost Nomination for Governor	Flippo, Ronnie G.	Ala.	Dem	None		
Retired	None			Frenzel, William E.	Minn.	Rep

WAYS AND MEANS / 102nd Congress

Service Dates of Committee Chair: Jan. 3,1991-Jan. 3,1993
Service Dates of Majority Members: Jan. 3,1991-Jan. 3,1993
Service Dates of Minority Members: Jan. 3,1991-Jan. 3,1993

Majority

Rank Name	Party	State	Terms in: House	Terms in: Comm.
Chr Rostenkowski, Daniel D.	Dem	Ill.	17	15
2nd Gibbons, Sam M.	Dem	Fla.	15	12
3rd Pickle, J. J. (Jake)	Dem	Tex.	15	9
4th Rangel, Charles B.	Dem	N.Y.	11	9
5th Stark, Fortney H. (Pete)	Dem	Cal.	10	9
6th Jacobs, Andrew Jr.	Dem	Ind.	13	9
7th Ford, Harold E.	Dem	Tenn.	9	9
8th Jenkins, Edgar L.	Dem	Ga.	8	8
9th Downey, Thomas J.	Dem	N.Y.	9	7
10th Guarini, Frank J.	Dem	N.J.	7	7
11th Russo, Martin A.	Dem	Ill.	9	7
12th Pease, Donald J.	Dem	Ohio	8	6
13th Matsui, Robert T.	Dem	Cal.	7	6
14th Anthony, Beryl F. Jr.	Dem	Ark.	7	6
15th Dorgan, Byron L.	Dem	N.D.	6	5
16th Kennelly, Barbara B.	Dem	Conn.	6	5
17th Donnelly, Brian J.	Dem	Mass.	7	4
18th Coyne, William J.	Dem	Penn.	6	4
19th Andrews, Michael A.	Dem	Tex.	5	4
20th Levin, Sander M.	Dem	Mich.	5	3
21st Moody, Jim	Dem	Wisc.	5	3
22nd Cardin, Benjamin L.	Dem	Md.	3	2
23rd McDermott, James A.	Dem	Wash.	2	1

Minority

Rank Name	Party	State	Terms in: House	Terms in: Comm.
RM Archer, William R.	Rep	Tex.	11	10
2nd Vander Jagt, Guy A.	Rep	Mich.	14	9
3rd Crane, Philip M.	Rep	Ill.	12	9
4th Schulze, Richard T.	Rep	Penn.	9	8
5th Gradison, Willis D. Jr.	Rep	Ohio	9	8
6th Thomas, William M.	Rep	Cal.	7	5
7th McGrath, Raymond J.	Rep	N.Y.	6	4
8th Chandler, Rodney	Rep	Wash.	5	3
9th Shaw, E. Clay Jr.	Rep	Fla.	6	3
10th Sundquist, Don	Rep	Tenn.	5	2
11th Johnson, Nancy L.	Rep	Conn.	5	2
12th Bunning, Jim	Rep	Ky.	3	1
13th Grandy, Fred	Rep	Iowa	3	1

PART IV

Select and Special Committees

U.S. House of Representatives, 1947-1992

HOUSE SPECIAL COMMITTEE: RECONSTRUCTION OF ROOF AND SKYLIGHTS OVER THE HOUSE WING OF THE CAPITOL AND REMODELING OF THE HOUSE CHAMBER

Jurisdiction, 1945

From Public Law 79-155, 59 Statutes 318, July 17, 1945:

[Clause 1]

That the appropriation of $585,000 provided in the Second Deficiency Appropriation Act, approved June 27, 1940, as amended and carried forward by the Act of June 8, 1942, for the reconstruction of the roofs and skylights over the Senate and House wings of the United States Capitol, together with such additional amounts as may be provided hereafter for such purpose, shall be available also for the substitution of reinforced concrete roof slab for the skylights over the Senate and House Chambers, reconstruction of ceilings, redecoration, acoustical treatment, improved lighting, and other alterations, changes, and improvements in such Chambers.

Termination, 1952

The Special Committee was terminated upon filing its final report, House Document 531 (82-2), on February 19, 1952.

HOUSE SPECIAL COMMITTEE: RECONSTRUCTION OF ROOF AND SKYLIGHTS OVER THE HOUSE WING OF THE CAPITOL AND REMODELING OF THE HOUSE CHAMBER / 80th Congress

Service Dates of Committee Chair: Jan. 20,1947-Feb. 2,1949
Service Dates of Majority Members: Jan. 20,1947-Feb. 2,1949
Service Dates of Minority Members: Jan. 20,1947-Feb. 2,1949

Majority			Terms in:		Minority			Terms in:	
Rank Name	**Party**	**State**	**House**	**Comm.**	**Rank Name**	**Party**	**State**	**House**	**Comm.**
Chr McGregor, J. Harry	Rep	Ohio	5	2	RM Bloom, Sol	Dem	N.Y.	13	2
2nd Sundstrom, Frank L.	Rep	N.J.	3	1	2nd Bell, C. Jasper	Dem	Mo.	7	2
3rd Goodwin, Angier L.	Rep	Mass.	3	1					

Departures from the House:	Majority			Minority		
Defeated for Reelection	Sundstrom, Frank L.	N.J.	Rep	None		
Retired	None			Bell, C. Jasper	Mo.	Dem

HOUSE SPECIAL COMMITTEE: RECONSTRUCTION OF ROOF AND SKYLIGHTS OVER THE HOUSE WING OF THE CAPITOL AND REMODELING OF THE HOUSE CHAMBER / 81st Congress

Service Dates of Committee Chair: Ch1 Feb. 2,1949-Mar. 7,1949
Ch2 Mar. 7,1949-Jan. 3,1951
Service Dates of Majority Members: Feb. 2,1949-Jan. 3,1951
Service Dates of Minority Members: Feb. 2,1949-Jan. 3,1951

Majority			Terms in:		Minority			Terms in:	
Rank Name	**Party**	**State**	**House**	**Comm.**	**Rank Name**	**Party**	**State**	**House**	**Comm.**
Ch1 Bloom, Sol	Dem	N.Y.	14	3	RM McGregor, J. Harry	Rep	Ohio	6	3
Ch2 2nd Trimble, James W.	Dem	Ark.	3	1	2nd Goodwin, Angier L.	Rep	Mass.	4	2
3rd Smathers, George A.	Dem	Fla.	2	1					

Changes:
Chair:

Ch1	Bloom, Sol	Dem	N.Y.	Mar. 7,1949	Died in office.
Ch2	Trimble, James W.	Dem	Ark.	Mar. 7,1949	Succeeded Bloom.

Majority:

Bloom, Sol	Dem	N.Y.	Mar. 7,1949	Died in office.
Heffernan, James J.	Dem	N.Y.	Mar. 15,1949	Replaced Bloom.

Departures from the House:	Majority		Minority
Elected to U.S. Senate	Smathers, George A.	Fla. Dem	None

HOUSE SPECIAL COMMITTEE: RECONSTRUCTION OF ROOF AND SKYLIGHTS OVER THE HOUSE WING OF THE CAPITOL AND REMODELING OF THE HOUSE CHAMBER / 82nd Congress

Service Dates of Committee Chair: Jan. 29,1951-Jan. 26,1953
Service Dates of Majority Members: Jan. 29,1951-Jan. 26,1953
Service Dates of Minority Members: Jan. 29,1951-Jan. 26,1953

Majority

Rank	Name	Party	State	Terms in: House	Terms in: Comm.
Chr	Trimble, James W.	Dem	Ark.	4	2
2nd	Heffernan, James J.	Dem	N.Y.	6	2
3rd	Jones, Robert E. Jr.	Dem	Ala.	3	1

Minority

Rank	Name	Party	State	Terms in: House	Terms in: Comm.
RM	McGregor, J. Harry	Rep	Ohio	7	4
2nd	Goodwin, Angier L.	Rep	Mass.	5	3

Departures from the House:	Majority		Minority
Retired	Heffernan, James J.	N.Y. Dem	None

HOUSE SPECIAL COMMITTEE: RECONSTRUCTION OF ROOF AND SKYLIGHTS OVER THE HOUSE WING OF THE CAPITOL AND REMODELING OF THE HOUSE CHAMBER / 83rd Congress

Service Dates of Committee Chair: Jan. 26,1953-Jan. 3,1955
Service Dates of Majority Members: Jan. 26,1953-Jan. 3,1955
Service Dates of Minority Members: Jan. 26,1953-Jan. 3,1955

Majority

Rank	Name	Party	State	Terms in: House	Terms in: Comm.
Chr	McGregor, J. Harry	Rep	Ohio	8	5
2nd	Goodwin, Angier L.	Rep	Mass.	6	4
3rd	Broyhill, Joel T.	Rep	Va.	1	1

Minority

Rank	Name	Party	State	Terms in: House	Terms in: Comm.
RM	Trimble, James W.	Dem	Ark.	5	3
2nd	Jones, Robert E. Jr.	Dem	Ala.	4	2

HOUSE SELECT COMMITTEE: SMALL BUSINESS

Jurisdiction, 1947

From House Resolution 18, 80th Congress, First Session, February 26, 1947:

[Paragraph 3]

The committee is authorized and directed to conduct a study and investigation of the problems of small business, existing, arising, or that may arise with particular reference to

(1) whether the potentialities of small business are being adequately developed and, if not, what factors have hindered and are hindering the normal operation of established small business and/or its development and enterprise;

(2) whether agencies, departments of the Government or Government owned or controlled corporations are properly, adequately, or equitably serving the needs of small business;

(3) whether small business is being treated fairly and the public welfare properly and justly served through the allotments of valuable materials in which there are shortages, in the granting of priorities or preferences in the use, sales, or purchase of said materials; and

(4) the need for a sound program for the solution of the postwar problems of small business.

From House Resolution 114, 84th Congress, First Session, January 27, 1955:

[Paragraphs 2-3]

The committee is authorized and directed to conduct a study and investigation of the problems of all types of small business, existing, arising, or that may arise, with particular reference to

(1) the factors which have impeded or may impede the normal operations, growth, and development of the potentialities of small business;

(2) the administration of Federal laws relating specifically to small business to determine whether such laws adequately serve the needs of small business;

(3) whether Government agencies adequately serve and give due consideration to the problems of small business;

(4) whether priorities and preferences established and allocations made by the Federal Government with respect to scarce materials adequately serve the needs of small business; and

(5) methods of solving the special problems of small business arising by reason of the existing national emergency: Provided, That the committee shall not invade any subject matter under active investigation by any standing committee of the House.

Reorganization, 1975

The Select Committee was reorganized on Jan. 3,1975 as the House Standing Committee on Small Business.

HOUSE SELECT COMMITTEE: SMALL BUSINESS / 80th Congress

Service Dates of Committee Chair: Apr. 1,1947-Jan. 3,1949
Service Dates of Majority Members: Apr. 1,1947-Jan. 3,1949
Service Dates of Minority Members: Apr. 1,1947-Jan. 3,1949

Majority

Rank Name	Party	State	Terms in: House	Terms in: Comm.
Chr Ploeser, Walter C.	Rep	Mo.	4	4
2nd Stevenson, William H.	Rep	Wisc.	4	3
3rd Howell, G. Evan	Rep	Ill.	4	3
4th Hill, William S.	Rep	Colo.	4	1
5th Riehlman, R. Walter	Rep	N.Y.	1	1

Minority

Rank Name	Party	State	Terms in: House	Terms in: Comm.
RM Patman, J.W. Wright	Dem	Tex.	10	4
2nd Keogh, Eugene J.	Dem	N.Y.	6	3
3rd Jackson, Henry M.	Dem	Wash.	4	3
4th Kefauver, C. Estes	Dem	Tenn.	5	3

Changes:

Majority:

Name	Party	State	Date	Change
Howell, G. Evan	Rep	Ill.	Oct. 5,1947	Resigned; appointed Federal Judge.
Lichtenwalter, Franklin H.	Rep	Penn.	Dec. 15,1947	Replaced Howell.

Minority:

Name	Party	State	Date	Change
Kefauver, C. Estes	Dem	Tenn.	Aug. 14,1948	Left committee; no new assignment (subsequent to adjournment).
Hardy, Porter Jr.	Dem	Va.	Aug. 14,1948	Replaced Kefauver (subsequent to adjournment).

	Majority		Minority	
Departures from the House:				
Defeated for Reelection	Ploeser, Walter C.	Mo. Rep	None	
Defeated for Renomination	Stevenson, William H.	Wisc. Rep	None	
Departures from Committee:				
No new assignment	None		Jackson, Henry M.	Wash. Dem

HOUSE SELECT COMMITTEE: SMALL BUSINESS / 81st Congress

Service Dates of Committee Chair: Feb. 2,1949-Jan. 3,1951
Service Dates of Majority Members: Feb. 2,1949-Jan. 3,1951
Service Dates of Minority Members: Feb. 2,1949-Jan. 3,1951

Majority

Rank Name	Party	State	Terms in: House	Terms in: Comm.
Chr Patman, J.W. Wright	Dem	Tex.	11	5
2nd Keogh, Eugene J.	Dem	N.Y.	7	4
3rd Hardy, Porter Jr.	Dem	Va.	2	2
4th Mansfield, Michael J.	Dem	Mont.	4	1
5th Evins, Joseph L.	Dem	Tenn.	2	1

Minority

Rank Name	Party	State	Terms in: House	Terms in: Comm.
RM Halleck, Charles A.	Rep	Ind.	8	*2 1
2nd Hill, William S.	Rep	Colo.	5	2
3rd Riehlman, R. Walter	Rep	N.Y.	2	2
4th Lichtenwalter, Franklin H.	Rep	Penn.	2	2

*2: Member's 2nd period of service on the committee.

Changes:

Majority:

Name	Party	State	Date	Change
Hardy, Porter Jr.	Dem	Va.	Apr. 8,1949	Left committee; no new assignment.
Burton, Clarence G.	Dem	Va.	Apr. 8,1949	Replaced Hardy.

	Majority		Minority	
Departures from the House:				
Retired	None		Lichtenwalter, Franklin H.	Penn. Rep
Departures from Committee:				
Moved to Ways and Means	Keogh, Eugene J.	N.Y. Dem	None	

HOUSE SELECT COMMITTEE: SMALL BUSINESS / 82nd Congress

Service Dates of Committee Chair: Feb. 12,1951-Jan. 3,1953
Service Dates of Majority Members: Feb. 12,1951-Jan. 3,1953
Service Dates of Minority Members: Feb. 12,1951-Jan. 3,1953

Majority

Rank	Name	Party	State	Terms in: House	Terms in: Comm.
Chr	Patman, J.W. Wright	Dem	Tex.	12	6
2nd	Mansfield, Michael J.	Dem	Mont.	5	2
3rd	Evins, Joseph L.	Dem	Tenn.	3	2
4th	Burton, Clarence G.	Dem	Va.	3	2
5th	Multer, Abraham J.	Dem	N.Y.	3	1
6th	McKinnon, Clinton D.	Dem	Cal.	2	1

Minority

Rank	Name	Party	State	Terms in: House	Terms in: Comm.
RM	Halleck, Charles A.	Rep	Ind.	9 *2	2
2nd	Hill, William S.	Rep	Colo.	6	3
3rd	Riehlman, R. Walter	Rep	N.Y.	3	3
4th	Seely-Brown, Horace Jr.	Rep	Conn.	2	1
5th	Curtis, Thomas B.	Rep	Mo.	1	1

*2: Member's 2nd period of service on the committee.

	Majority		Minority	
Departures from the House:				
Elected to U.S. Senate	Mansfield, Michael J.	Mont. Dem	None	
Defeated for Reelection	Burton, Clarence G.	Va. Dem	None	
Lost Nomination for U.S. Senate	McKinnon, Clinton D.	Cal. Dem	None	
Departure from Committee:				
Moved to Ways and Means	None		Curtis, Thomas B.	Mo. Rep
Became House Majority Leader			Halleck, Charles A.	Ind. Rep

HOUSE SELECT COMMITTEE: SMALL BUSINESS / 83rd Congress

Service Dates of Committee Chair: Feb. 3,1953-Jan. 3,1955
Service Dates of Majority Members: Feb. 3,1953-Jan. 3,1955
Service Dates of Minority Members: Feb. 3,1953-Jan. 3,1955

Majority

Rank	Name	Party	State	Terms in: House	Terms in: Comm.
Chr	Hill, William S.	Rep	Colo.	7	4
2nd	Riehlman, R. Walter	Rep	N.Y.	4	4
3rd	Seely-Brown, Horace Jr.	Rep	Conn.	3	2
4th	McCulloch, William M.	Rep	Ohio	4	1
5th	Sheehan, Timothy P.	Rep	Ill.	2	1
6th	Hosmer, Craig	Rep	Cal.	1 *1	1

Minority

Rank	Name	Party	State	Terms in: House	Terms in: Comm.
RM	Patman, J.W. Wright	Dem	Tex.	13	7
2nd	Evins, Joseph L.	Dem	Tenn.	4	3
3rd	Multer, Abraham J.	Dem	N.Y.	4	2
4th	Yates, Sidney R.	Dem	Ill.	3	1
5th	Steed, Thomas J.	Dem	Okla.	3	1

*1: Member's first period of service on the committee.

Departures from Committee:	Majority		Minority
No new assignment	Hosmer, Craig	Cal. Rep	None

HOUSE SELECT COMMITTEE: SMALL BUSINESS / 84th Congress

Service Dates of Committee Chair: Jan. 27,1955-Jan. 3,1957
Service Dates of Majority Members: Jan. 27,1955-Jan. 3,1957
Service Dates of Minority Members: Jan. 27,1955-Jan. 3,1957

Majority

Rank	Name	Party	State	Terms in: House	Terms in: Comm.
Chr	Patman, J.W. Wright	Dem	Tex.	14	8
2nd	Evins, Joseph L.	Dem	Tenn.	5	4
3rd	Multer, Abraham J.	Dem	N.Y.	5	3
4th	Yates, Sidney R.	Dem	Ill.	4	2
5th	Steed, Thomas J.	Dem	Okla.	4	2
6th	Roosevelt, James	Dem	Cal.	1	1

Minority

Rank	Name	Party	State	Terms in: House	Terms in: Comm.
RM	Hill, William S.	Rep	Colo.	8	5
2nd	Riehlman, R. Walter	Rep	N.Y.	5	5
3rd	Seely-Brown, Horace Jr.	Rep	Conn.	4	3
4th	McCulloch, William M.	Rep	Ohio	5	2
5th	Sheehan, Timothy P.	Rep	Ill.	3	2

HOUSE SELECT COMMITTEE: SMALL BUSINESS / 85th Congress

Service Dates of Committee Chair: Feb. 4,1957-Jan. 3,1959
Service Dates of Majority Members: Feb. 4,1957-Jan. 3,1959
Service Dates of Minority Members: Feb. 4,1957-Jan. 3,1959

Majority

Rank	Name	Party	State	Terms in: House	Terms in: Comm.
Chr	Patman, J.W. Wright	Dem	Tex.	15	9
2nd	Evins, Joseph L.	Dem	Tenn.	6	5
3rd	Multer, Abraham J.	Dem	N.Y.	6	4
4th	Yates, Sidney R.	Dem	Ill.	5	3
5th	Steed, Thomas J.	Dem	Okla.	5	3
6th	Roosevelt, James	Dem	Cal.	2	2
7th	Brown, Charles H.	Dem	Mo.	1	1

Minority

Rank	Name	Party	State	Terms in: House	Terms in: Comm.
RM	Hill, William S.	Rep	Colo.	9	6
2nd	Riehlman, R. Walter	Rep	N.Y.	6	6
3rd	Seely-Brown, Horace Jr.	Rep	Conn.	5	4
4th	McCulloch, William M.	Rep	Ohio	6	3
5th	Sheehan, Timothy P.	Rep	Ill.	4	3
6th	Hosmer, Craig	Rep	Cal.	3 *2	1

*2: Member's 2nd period of service on the committee.

Changes:

Minority:

Name	Party	State	Date	Change
Hosmer, Craig	Rep	Cal.	Feb. 20,1958	Left committee; no new assignment.
Moore, Arch A. Jr.	Rep	W.Va.	Feb. 20,1958	Replaced Hosmer.

	Majority	Minority	
Departures from the House:			
Defeated for Reelection	None	Seely-Brown, Horace Jr.	Conn. Rep
		Sheehan, Timothy P.	Ill. Rep
Retired	None	Hill, William S.	Colo. Rep
Departures from Committee:			
Moved to Science and Astronautics	None	Riehlman, R. Walter	N.Y. Rep

HOUSE SELECT COMMITTEE: SMALL BUSINESS / 86th Congress

Service Dates of Committee Chair: Feb. 11,1959-Jan. 3,1961
Service Dates of Majority Members: Feb. 11,1959-Jan. 3,1961
Service Dates of Minority Members: Feb. 11,1959-Jan. 3,1961

Majority

Rank	Name	Party	State	Terms in: House	Terms in: Comm.
Chr	Patman, J.W. Wright	Dem	Tex.	16	10
2nd	Evins, Joseph L.	Dem	Tenn.	7	6
3rd	Multer, Abraham J.	Dem	N.Y.	7	5
4th	Yates, Sidney R.	Dem	Ill.	6	4
5th	Steed, Thomas J.	Dem	Okla.	6	4
6th	Roosevelt, James	Dem	Cal.	3	3
7th	Brown, Charles H.	Dem	Mo.	2	2

Minority

Rank	Name	Party	State	Terms in: House	Terms in: Comm.
RM	McCulloch, William M.	Rep	Ohio	7	4
2nd	Moore, Arch A. Jr.	Rep	W.Va.	2	2
3rd	Avery, William H.	Rep	Kans.	3	1
4th	Smith, H. Allen	Rep	Cal.	2	1
5th	Robison, Howard W.	Rep	N.Y.	2	1
6th	Quie, Albert H.	Rep	Minn.	2	1

Changes:
Minority:

Name	Party	State	Date	Change
Quie, Albert H.	Rep	Minn.	May 14,1959	Left committee; no new assignment.
Derwinski, Edward J.	Rep	Ill.	July 28,1959	Replaced Quie.

Departures from the House:

	Majority	State	Party	Minority
Defeated for Reelection	Brown, Charles H.	Mo.	Dem	None

HOUSE SELECT COMMITTEE: SMALL BUSINESS / 87th Congress

Service Dates of Committee Chair: Feb. 7,1961-Jan. 3,1963
Service Dates of Majority Members: Feb. 7,1961-Jan. 3,1963
Service Dates of Minority Members: Feb. 17,1961-Jan. 3,1963

Majority

Rank	Name	Party	State	Terms in: House	Terms in: Comm.
Chr	Patman, J.W. Wright	Dem	Tex.	17	11
2nd	Evins, Joseph L.	Dem	Tenn.	8	7
3rd	Multer, Abraham J.	Dem	N.Y.	8	6
4th	Yates, Sidney R.	Dem	Ill.	7	5
5th	Steed, Thomas J.	Dem	Okla.	7	5
6th	Roosevelt, James	Dem	Cal.	4	4
7th	Alford, T. Dale	Dem	Ark.	2	1

Minority

Rank	Name	Party	State	Terms in: House	Terms in: Comm.
RM	McCulloch, William M.	Rep	Ohio	8	5
2nd	Moore, Arch A. Jr.	Rep	W.Va.	3	3
3rd	Avery, William H.	Rep	Kans.	4	2
4th	Smith, H. Allen	Rep	Cal.	3	2
5th	Robison, Howard W.	Rep	N.Y.	3	2
6th	Derwinski, Edward J.	Rep	Ill.	2	2

Changes:
Minority:

Name	Party	State	Date	Change
Derwinski, Edward J.	Rep	Ill.	Mar. 7,1961	Left committee; no new assignment.
Harvey, Ralph	Rep	Ind.	Mar. 7,1961	Replaced Derwinski.

Departures from the House:

	Majority	State	Party	Minority
Lost Election to U.S. Senate	Yates, Sidney R.	Ill.	Dem	None
Lost Nomination for Governor	Alford, T. Dale	Ark.	Dem	None

HOUSE SELECT COMMITTEE: SMALL BUSINESS / 88th Congress

Service Dates of Committee Chair: Jan. 31,1963-Jan. 3,1965
Service Dates of Majority Members: Jan. 31,1963-Jan. 3,1965
Service Dates of Minority Members: Jan. 31,1963-Jan. 3,1965

Majority

Rank	Name	Party	State	Terms in: House	Terms in: Comm.
Chr	Evins, Joseph L.	Dem	Tenn.	9	8
2nd	Patman, J.W. Wright	Dem	Tex.	18	12
3rd	Multer, Abraham J.	Dem	N.Y.	9	7
4th	Steed, Thomas J.	Dem	Okla.	8	6
5th	Roosevelt, James	Dem	Cal.	5	5
6th	Kluczynski, John C.	Dem	Ill.	7	1
7th	Dingell, John D. Jr.	Dem	Mich.	5	1

Minority

Rank	Name	Party	State	Terms in: House	Terms in: Comm.
RM	McCulloch, William M.	Rep	Ohio	9	6
2nd	Moore, Arch A. Jr.	Rep	W.Va.	4	4
3rd	Avery, William H.	Rep	Kans.	5	3
4th	Smith, H. Allen	Rep	Cal.	4	3
5th	Robison, Howard W.	Rep	N.Y.	4	3
6th	Harvey, Ralph	Rep	Ind.	8	2

	Majority	Minority		
Departures from the House:				
Elected Governor	None	Avery, William H.	Kans.	Rep
Departures from Committee:				
Moved to Appropriations	None	Robison, Howard W.	N.Y.	Rep
No new assignment	None	McCulloch, William M.	Ohio	Rep

HOUSE SELECT COMMITTEE: SMALL BUSINESS / 89th Congress

Service Dates of Committee Chair: Feb. 16,1965-Jan. 3,1967
Service Dates of Majority Members: Feb. 16,1965-Jan. 3,1967
Service Dates of Minority Members: Feb. 16,1965-Jan. 3,1967

Majority

Rank	Name	Party	State	Terms in: House	Terms in: Comm.
Chr	Evins, Joseph L.	Dem	Tenn.	10	9
2nd	Patman, J.W. Wright	Dem	Tex.	19	13
3rd	Multer, Abraham J.	Dem	N.Y.	10	8
4th	Steed, Thomas J.	Dem	Okla.	9	7
5th	Roosevelt, James	Dem	Cal.	6	6
6th	Kluczynski, John C.	Dem	Ill.	8	2
7th	Dingell, John D. Jr.	Dem	Mich.	6	2
8th	Smith, Neal	Dem	Iowa	4	1
9th	Weltner, Charles L.	Dem	Ga.	2	1

Minority

Rank	Name	Party	State	Terms in: House	Terms in: Comm.
RM	Moore, Arch A. Jr.	Rep	W.Va.	5	5
2nd	Smith, H. Allen	Rep	Cal.	5	4
3rd	Harvey, Ralph	Rep	Ind.	9	3
4th	Conte, Silvio O.	Rep	Mass.	4	1
5th	Broyhill, James T.	Rep	N.C.	2	1
6th	Horton, Frank J.	Rep	N.Y.	2	1

Changes:

Majority:				
Roosevelt, James	Dem	Cal.	Sep. 17,1965	Resigned House Sep. 30,1965; appointed UNESCO Representative.
Corman, James C.	Dem	Cal.	Sep. 20,1965	Replaced Roosevelt.
Weltner, Charles L.	Dem	Ga.	Oct. 10,1966	Left committee due to imminent retirement.
Irwin, Donald J.	Dem	Conn.	Oct. 10,1966	Replaced Weltner.
Minority:				
Harvey, Ralph	Rep	Ind.	Dec. 30,1966	Defeated for Renomination.

	Majority	Minority		
Departures from the House:				
No new assignment	None	Smith, H. Allen	Cal.	Rep

HOUSE SELECT COMMITTEE: SMALL BUSINESS / 90th Congress

Service Dates of Committee Chair: Feb. 1,1967-Jan. 3,1969
Service Dates of Majority Members: Feb. 1,1967-Jan. 3,1969
Service Dates of Minority Members: Feb. 1,1967-Jan. 3,1969

Majority

Rank Name	Party	State	Terms in: House	Terms in: Comm.
Chr Evins, Joseph L.	Dem	Tenn.	11	10
2nd Patman, J.W. Wright	Dem	Tex.	20	14
3rd Multer, Abraham J.	Dem	N.Y.	11	9
4th Steed, Thomas J.	Dem	Okla.	10	8
5th Kluczynski, John C.	Dem	Ill.	9	3
6th Dingell, John D. Jr.	Dem	Mich.	7	3
7th Smith, Neal	Dem	Iowa	5	2
8th Corman, James C.	Dem	Cal.	4	2
9th Irwin, Donald J.	Dem	Conn.	3	2

Minority

Rank Name	Party	State	Terms in: House	Terms in: Comm.
RM Moore, Arch A. Jr.	Rep	W.Va.	6	6
2nd Conte, Silvio O.	Rep	Mass.	5	2
3rd Broyhill, James T.	Rep	N.C.	3	2
4th Horton, Frank J.	Rep	N.Y.	3	2
5th Morton, Rogers C. B.	Rep	Md.	3	1
6th Burton, Laurence J.	Rep	Utah	3	1

Changes:

Majority:

Name	Party	State	Date	Note
Multer, Abraham J.	Dem	N.Y.	Dec. 6,1967	Left committee; elected to State Supreme Court Dec. 31,1967.
Addabbo, Joseph P.	Dem	N.Y.	Dec. 6,1967	Replaced Multer.

	Majority		Minority	
Departures from the House:				
Elected Governor	None		Moore, Arch A. Jr.	W.Va. Rep
Defeated for Reelection	Irwin, Donald J.	Conn. Dem	None	
Departures from Committee:				
Moved to Ways and Means	None		Morton, Rogers C. B.	Md. Rep

HOUSE SELECT COMMITTEE: SMALL BUSINESS / 91st Congress

Service Dates of Committee Chair: Feb. 5,1969-Jan. 3,1971
Service Dates of Majority Members: Feb. 5,1969-Jan. 3,1971
Service Dates of Minority Members: Feb. 5,1969-Jan. 3,1971

Majority

Rank Name	Party	State	Terms in: House	Terms in: Comm.
Chr Evins, Joseph L.	Dem	Tenn.	12	11
2nd Patman, J.W. Wright	Dem	Tex.	21	15
3rd Steed, Thomas J.	Dem	Okla.	11	9
4th Kluczynski, John C.	Dem	Ill.	10	4
5th Dingell, John D. Jr.	Dem	Mich.	8	4
6th Smith, Neal	Dem	Iowa	6	3
7th Corman, James C.	Dem	Cal.	5	3
8th Addabbo, Joseph P.	Dem	N.Y.	5	2
9th Hungate, William L.	Dem	Mo.	4	1

Minority

Rank Name	Party	State	Terms in: House	Terms in: Comm.
RM Conte, Silvio O.	Rep	Mass.	6	3
2nd Broyhill, James T.	Rep	N.C.	4	3
3rd Horton, Frank J.	Rep	N.Y.	4	3
4th Burton, Laurence J.	Rep	Utah	4	2
5th Stanton, J. William	Rep	Ohio	3	1
6th Button, Daniel E.	Rep	N.Y.	2	1

	Majority	Minority	
Departures from the House:			
Defeated for Reelection	None	Button, Daniel E.	N.Y. Rep
Lost Election to U.S. Senate	None	Burton, Laurence J.	Utah Rep

HOUSE SELECT COMMITTEE: SMALL BUSINESS / 92nd Congress

Service Dates of Committee Chair: Mar. 3,1971-Jan. 3,1973
Service Dates of Majority Members: Mar. 3,1971-Jan. 3.1973
Service Dates of Minority Members: Mar. 3,1971-Jan. 3,1973

Majority

Rank Name	Party	State	Terms in: House	Terms in: Comm.
Chr Evins, Joseph L.	Dem	Tenn.	13	12
2nd Patman, J.W. Wright	Dem	Tex.	22	16
3rd Steed, Thomas J.	Dem	Okla.	12	10
4th Kluczynski, John C.	Dem	Ill.	11	5
5th Dingell, John D. Jr.	Dem	Mich.	9	5
6th Smith, Neal	Dem	Iowa	7	4
7th Corman, James C.	Dem	Cal.	6	4
8th Addabbo, Joseph P.	Dem	N.Y.	6	3
9th Hungate, William L.	Dem	Mo.	5	2
10th St Germain, Fernand J.	Dem	R.I.	6	1
11th Carney, Charles J.	Dem	Ohio	2	1
12th Mitchell, Parren J.	Dem	Md.	1	1

Minority

Rank Name	Party	State	Terms in: House	Terms in: Comm.
RM Conte, Silvio O.	Rep	Mass.	7	4
2nd Broyhill, James T.	Rep	N.C.	5	4
3rd Horton, Frank J.	Rep	N.Y.	5	4
4th Stanton, J. William	Rep	Ohio	4	2
5th McDade, Joseph M.	Rep	Penn.	5	1
6th Lujan, Manuel Jr.	Rep	N.M.	2	1
7th McKevitt, James D.	Rep	Colo.	1	1

Changes:

Majority:

Patman, J.W. Wright	Dem	Tex.	May 4,1971	Left committee; no new assignment.
Bergland, Bob	DFL	Minn.	May 4,1971	Replaced Patman.

	Majority	Minority	
Departures from the House:			
Defeated for Reelection	None	McKevitt, James D.	Colo. Rep
Departures from Committee:			
No new assignment	None	Horton, Frank J.	N.Y. Rep
		Lujan, Manuel Jr.	N.M. Rep

HOUSE SELECT COMMITTEE: SMALL BUSINESS / 93rd Congress

Service Dates of Committee Chair: Feb. 7,1973-Jan. 3,1975
Service Dates of Majority Members: Feb. 7,1973-Jan. 3,1975
Service Dates of Minority Members: Feb. 7,1973-Jan. 3,1975

Majority

Rank Name	Party	State	Terms in: House	Terms in: Comm.
Chr Evins, Joseph L.	Dem	Tenn.	14	13
2nd Steed, Thomas J.	Dem	Okla.	13	11
3rd Kluczynski, John C.	Dem	Ill.	12	6
4th Dingell, John D. Jr.	Dem	Mich.	10	6
5th Smith, Neal	Dem	Iowa	8	5
6th Corman, James C.	Dem	Cal.	7	5
7th Addabbo, Joseph P.	Dem	N.Y.	7	4
8th Hungate, William L.	Dem	Mo.	6	3
9th St Germain, Fernand J.	Dem	R.I.	7	2
10th Carney, Charles J.	Dem	Ohio	3	2
11th Mitchell, Parren J.	Dem	Md.	2	2
12th Bergland, Bob	DFL	Minn.	2	2

Minority

Rank Name	Party	State	Terms in: House	Terms in: Comm.
RM Conte, Silvio O.	Rep	Mass.	8	5
2nd Broyhill, James T.	Rep	N.C.	6	5
3rd Stanton, J. William	Rep	Ohio	5	3
4th McDade, Joseph M.	Rep	Penn.	6	2
5th Thomson, Vernon W.	Rep	Wisc.	7	1
6th Kemp, Jack F.	Rep	N.Y.	2	1
7th McCollister, John Y.	Rep	Neb.	2	1

	Majority	Minority	
Departures from House:			
Defeated for Reelection	None	Thomson, Vernon W.	Wisc. Rep
Departures from Committee:			
Moved to Appropriations		Kemp, Jack F.	N.Y. Rep
No new assignment	None	Broyhill, James T.	N.C. Rep

HOUSE SELECT COMMITTEE: NEWSPRINT AND PAPER SUPPLY

Jurisdiction, 1947

From House Resolution 58, 80th Congress, First Session, February 26, 1947:

[Paragraph 2]

The committee is authorized to conduct a study and investigation of all matters related to the need for adequate supplies, for use in the United States (including use in time of war), of newsprint, printing and wrapping paper, paper products, paper pulp and pulpwood, and of all matters related to means by which adequate supplies thereof may be produced or secured, with particular reference to--

(1) the short-range and long-range possibilities of increased production thereof in the continental United States (including Alaska);
(2) the short-range and long-range prospects of securing increased supplies thereof from Canada and other sources outside the United States; and
(3) the extent to which agencies or officers of the United States may be able to assist in furthering the objectives of securing increased production and supplies thereof.

Termination, 1948

The Select Committee was terminated upon the filing of its final report, House Report 2471 (80-2) on December 31, 1948.

HOUSE SELECT COMMITTEE: NEWSPRINT AND PAPER SUPPLY / 80th Congress

Service Dates of Committee Chair: Mar. 3,1947-Dec. 31,1948
Service Dates of Majority Members: Mar. 3,1947-Dec. 31,1948
Service Dates of Minority Members: Mar. 3,1947-Dec. 31,1948

Majority

Rank	Name	Party	State	Terms in: House	Terms in: Comm.
Chr	Brown, Clarence J.	Rep	Ohio	5	1
2nd	Wolverton, Charles A.	Rep	N.J.	11	1
3rd	Shafer, Paul W.	Rep	Mich.	6	1
4th	Vursell, Charles W.	Rep	Ill.	3	1

Minority

Rank	Name	Party	State	Terms in: House	Terms in: Comm.
RM	Beckworth, Lindley G.	Dem	Tex.	5	1
2nd	Harless, Richard F.	Dem	Ariz.	3	1
3rd	Sikes, Robert L. F.	Dem	Fla.	4	1

HOUSE SELECT COMMITTEE: FOREIGN AID

Jurisdiction, 1947

From House Resolution 296, 80th Congress, First Session, July 22, 1947:

[Paragraph 2]

The committee is authorized and directed to make a study of

(1) actual and prospective needs of foreign nations and people, including those within the United States military zones, both for relief in terms of food, clothing, and so forth, and of economic rehabilitation;
(2) resources and facilities available to meet such needs within and without the continental United States;
(3) existing or contemplated agencies, whether private, public, domestic, or international qualified to deal with such needs;
(4) any or all measures which might assist in assessing relative needs and in correlating such assistance as the United States can properly make without weakening its domestic economy.

Termination, 1948

The Select Committee was extended by House Resolution 476 (80-2) and terminated upon the filing of its final report, House Report 1845 (80-2), on May 1, 1948.

HOUSE SELECT COMMITTEE: FOREIGN AID / 80th Congress

Service Dates of Committee Chair: July 29,1947-May 1,1948
Service Dates of Majority Members: July 29,1947-May 1,1948
Service Dates of Minority Members: July 29,1947-May 1,1948

Majority

Rank	Name	Party	State	Terms in: House	Terms in: Comm.
Chr	Eaton, Charles A.	Rep	N.J.	12	1
VCh	Herter, Christian A.	Rep	Mass.	3	1
3rd	Jenkins, Mitchell	Rep	Penn.	1	1
4th	Wolverton, Charles A.	Rep	N.J.	11	1
5th	Andresen, August H.	Rep	Minn.	11	1
6th	Case, Francis H.	Rep	S.D.	6	1
7th	Kunkel, John C.	Rep	Penn.	5	1
8th	Vorys, John M.	Rep	Ohio	5	1
9th	Vursell, Charles W.	Rep	Ill.	3	1
10th	Macy, W. Kingsland	Rep	N.Y.	1	1
11th	Nixon, Richard M.	Rep	Cal.	1	1

Minority

Rank	Name	Party	State	Terms in: House	Terms in: Comm.
RM1	Colmer, William M.	Dem	Miss.	8	1
2nd	Richards, James P.	Dem	S.C.	8	1
3rd	Walter, Francis E.	Dem	Penn.	8	1
4th	Cooley, Harold D.	Dem	N.C.	8	1
5th	Mahon, George H.	Dem	Tex.	7	1
6th	Brooks, Overton	Dem	La.	6	1
7th	Keogh, Eugene J.	Dem	N.Y.	6	1
8th	Monroney, A. S. Mike	Dem	Okla.	5	1

Changes:

Ranking Member:

RM1	Colmer, William M.	Dem	Miss.	Aug. 19,1947	Left committee; no new assignment.
RM2	Cox, Edward E.	Dem	Ga.	Aug. 19,1947	Replaced Colmer as Ranking Minority Member

HOUSE SELECT COMMITTEE: TO INVESTIGATE COMMODITY TRANSACTIONS

Jurisdiction, 1947

From House Resolution 404, 80th Congress, First Session, December 18, 1947:

[Paragraph 2]

The committee is authorized to conduct a full and complete investigation of purchases and sales of commodities, including transactions in the purchase and sale of commodities for future delivery, and including (a) the activities of any department or agency of the United States Government in connection with the purchase and sale of commodities, and into any other activities of any such agency or department that may have heretofore affected, or may hereafter affect, the price of food and other commodities; and (b) the private acts, and official activities of any individual in the United States Government in connection with the purchase or sale of commodities.

Termination, 1948

The Select Committee was terminated upon filing its final report, House Report 2472 (80-2) on December 31,1948.

HOUSE SELECT COMMITTEE: TO INVESTIGATE COMMODITY TRANSACTIONS / 80th Congress

Service Dates of Committee Chair: Dec. 19,1947-Dec. 31,1948
Service Dates of Majority Members: Dec. 19,1947-Dec. 31,1948
Service Dates of Minority Members: Dec. 19,1947-Dec. 31,1948

Majority

Rank	Name	Party	State	Terms in: House	Terms in: Comm.
Chr	Andresen, August H.	Rep	Minn.	11	1
2nd	Crawford, Fred L.	Rep	Mich.	7	1
3rd	Buffett, Howard H.	Rep	Neb.	3	1
4th	Jenkins, Mitchell	Rep	Penn.	1	1

Minority

Rank	Name	Party	State	Terms in: House	Terms in: Comm.
RM	McCormack, John W.	Dem	Mass.	11	1
2nd	Carroll, John A.	Dem	Colo.	1	1
3rd	Rains, Albert	Dem	Ala.	2	1

HOUSE SPECIAL COMMITTEE: INVESTIGATE CAMPAIGN EXPENDITURES

Jurisdiction, 1948

From House Resolution 461, 80th Congress, Second Session, March 1, 1948:

[Section 1 through 6]

Resolved, That a special committee of five members be appointed by the Speaker of the House of Representatives to investigate and report to the House not later than January 3, 1949, with respect to the following matters:

1. The extent and nature of expenditures made by all candidates for the House of Representatives in connection with their campaign for nomination and election to such office.
2. The amounts subscribed, contributed, or expended, and the value of services rendered, and facilities made available (including personal services, use of advertising space, radio time, office space, moving-picture films, and automobile and other transportation facilities) by any individual, individuals, or group of individuals, committee, partnership, corporation, or labor union, to or on behalf of each such candidate in connection with any such campaign or for the purpose of influencing the votes cast or to be cast at any convention or election held in 1948 to which a candidate for the House of Representatives is to be nominated or elected.
3. The use of any other means or influence (including the promise or use of patronage) for the purpose of aiding or influencing the nomination or election of any such candidates.
4. The amounts, if any, raised contributed, and expended by any individual, individuals, or group of individuals, committee, partnership, corporation, or labor union, including any political committee thereof, in connection with any such election, and the amounts received by any political committee from any corporation, labor union, individual, individuals, or group of individuals, committee, or partnership.
5. The violations, if any, of the following statutes of the United States:
   (a) The Federal Corrupt Practices Act.
   (b) Title 18, sections 61 to 62b, inclusive, United States Code, 1940 edition, relating to pernicious political activities, commonly referred to as the "Hatch Act."
   (c) The provisions of section 304, Public Law 101, Eightieth Congress, chapter 120, first session, referred to as the "Labor Management Relations Act, 1947."
   (d) Any statute or legislative act of the United States, or of the State within which a candidate is seeking nomination or reelection to the House of Representatives, the violation of which Federal or State statute, or statutes, would affect the qualification of a Member of the House of Representatives within the meaning of article I, section 5, of the Constitution of the United States.
6. Such other matters relating to the election of Members of the House of Representatives in 1948, and the campaigns of candidates in connection therewith, as the committee deems to be of public interest, and which in its opinion will aid the House of Representatives in enacting remedial legislation, or in deciding any contests that may be instituted involving the right to a seat in the House of Representatives.

The last two Special Committees to Investigate Campaign Expenditures dealt with the congressional elections of 1972. Their mandates were similar to their predecessors with the addition of the enforcement of the provisions concerning congressional elections in the Federal Election Campaign Act of 1971.

HOUSE SPECIAL COMMITTEE: INVESTIGATE CAMPAIGN EXPENDITURES / 80th Congress

Service Dates of Committee Chair: Mar. 17,1948-Jan. 3,1949
Service Dates of Majority Members: Mar. 17,1948-Jan. 3,1949
Service Dates of Minority Members: Mar. 17,1948-Jan. 3,1949

Majority

Rank	Name	Party	State	Terms in: House	Terms in: Comm.
Chr	Rizley, Ross	Rep	Okla.	4	1
2nd	Fellows, Frank	Rep	Me.	4	1
3rd	Harness, Forest A.	Rep	Ind.	5	1

Minority

Rank	Name	Party	State	Terms in: House	Terms in: Comm.
RM	Harris, Oren	Dem	Ark.	4	1
2nd	Fogarty, John E.	Dem	R.I.	4	1

Departures from the House:	Majority		Minority	
Defeated for Reelection	Harness, Forest A.	Ind. Rep	None	
Lost Election to U.S. Senate	Rizley, Ross	Okla. Rep	None	
Departures from Committee:				
No new assignment	None		Harris, Oren	Ark. Dem
			Fogarty, John E.	R.I. Dem

HOUSE SPECIAL COMMITTEE: INVESTIGATE CAMPAIGN EXPENDITURES / 81st Congress

Service Dates of Committee Chair: June 30,1950-Jan. 3,1951
Service Dates of Majority Members: June 30,1950-Jan. 3,1951
Service Dates of Minority Members: June 30,1950-Jan. 3,1951

Majority

Rank	Name	Party	State	Terms in: House	Terms in: Comm.
Chr	Mansfield, Michael J.	Dem	Mont.	4	1
2nd	Chelf, Frank L.	Dem	Ky.	3	1
3rd	Deane, Charles B.	Dem	N.C.	2	1

Minority

Rank	Name	Party	State	Terms in: House	Terms in: Comm.
RM	Fellows, Frank	Rep	Me.	5	2
2nd	Jennings, John Jr.	Rep	Tenn.	6	1

Departures from the House:	Majority		Minority	
Defeated for Renomination	None		Jennings, John Jr.	Tenn. Rep
Departures from Committee:				
No new assignment	Mansfield, Michael J.	Mont. Dem	Fellows, Frank	Me. Rep
	Chelf, Frank L.	Ky. Dem		
	Deane, Charles B.	N.C. Dem		

HOUSE SPECIAL COMMITTEE: INVESTIGATE CAMPAIGN EXPENDITURES / 82nd Congress

Service Dates of Committee Chair: June 16,1952-Jan. 3,1953
Service Dates of Majority Members: June 16,1952-Jan. 3,1953
Service Dates of Minority Members: June 16,1952-Jan. 3,1953

Majority

Rank	Name	Party	State	Terms in: House	Terms in: Comm.
Chr	Boggs, T. Hale	Dem	La.	4	1
2nd	Karsten, Frank M.	Dem	Mo.	3	1
3rd	Rooney, John J.	Dem	N.Y.	5	1

Minority

Rank	Name	Party	State	Terms in: House	Terms in: Comm.
RM	Keating, Kenneth B.	Rep	N.Y.	3	1
2nd	McCulloch, William M.	Rep	Ohio	3	1

Departures from Committee:	Majority		Minority	
No new assignment	Rooney, John J.	N.Y. Dem	McCulloch, William M.	Ohio Rep

HOUSE SPECIAL COMMITTEE: INVESTIGATE CAMPAIGN EXPENDITURES / 83rd Congress

Service Dates of Committee Chair: Aug. 9,1954-Jan. 3,1955
Service Dates of Majority Members: Aug. 9,1954-Jan. 3,1955
Service Dates of Minority Members: Aug. 9,1954-Jan. 3,1955

Majority

Rank	Name	Party	State	Terms in: House	Terms in: Comm.
Chr	Bishop, Cecil W. (Runt)	Rep	Ill.	7	1
2nd	Keating, Kenneth B.	Rep	N.Y.	4	2
3rd	Baker, Howard H.	Rep	Tenn.	2	1

Minority

Rank	Name	Party	State	Terms in: House	Terms in: Comm.
RM	Boggs, T. Hale	Dem	La.	5	2
2nd	Karsten, Frank M.	Dem	Mo.	4	2

	Majority		Minority	
Departures from the House:				
Defeated for Reelection	Bishop, Cecil W. (Runt)	Ill. Rep	None	
Departures from Committee:				
Moved to Ways and Means	Baker, Howard H.	Tenn. Rep	Karsten, Frank M.	Mo. Dem
No new assignment	None		Boggs, T. Hale	La. Dem

HOUSE SPECIAL COMMITTEE: INVESTIGATE CAMPAIGN EXPENDITURES / 84th Congress

Service Dates of Committee Chair: July 25,1956-Jan. 3,1957
Service Dates of Majority Members: July 25,1956-Jan. 3,1957
Service Dates of Minority Members: July 25,1956-Jan. 3,1957

Majority

Rank	Name	Party	State	Terms in: House	Terms in: Comm.
Chr	Davis, Clifford	Dem	Tenn.	9	1
2nd	Jones, Robert E. Jr.	Dem	Ala.	5	1
3rd	Bolling, Richard W.	Dem	Mo.	4	1

Minority

Rank	Name	Party	State	Terms in: House	Terms in: Comm.
RM	Keating, Kenneth B.	Rep	N.Y.	5	3
2nd	Hillings, Patrick J.	Rep	Cal.	3	1

	Majority		Minority	
Departures from Committee:				
No new assignment	Bolling, Richard W.	Mo. Dem	Hillings, Patrick J.	Cal. Rep

HOUSE SPECIAL COMMITTEE: INVESTIGATE CAMPAIGN EXPENDITURES / 85th Congress

Service Dates of Committee Chair: Aug. 19,1958-Jan. 3,1959
Service Dates of Majority Members: Aug. 19,1958-Jan. 3,1959
Service Dates of Minority Members: Aug. 19,1958-Jan. 3,1959

Majority

Rank	Name	Party	State	Terms in: House	Terms in: Comm.
Chr	Davis, Clifford	Dem	Tenn.	10	2
2nd	Jones, Robert E. Jr.	Dem	Ala.	6	2
3rd	O'Neill, Thomas P. Jr.	Dem	Mass.	3 *1	1

Minority

Rank	Name	Party	State	Terms in: House	Terms in: Comm.
RM	Keating, Kenneth B.	Rep	N.Y.	6	4
2nd	Dennison, David S.	Rep	Ohio	1	1

*1: Member's first period of service on the committee.

	Majority		Minority	
Departures from the House:				
Elected to U.S. Senate	None		Keating, Kenneth B.	N.Y. Rep
Defeated for Reelection	None		Dennison, David S.	Ohio Rep
Departures from Committee:				
No new assignment	O'Neill, Thomas P. Jr.	Mass. Dem	None	

HOUSE SPECIAL COMMITTEE: INVESTIGATE CAMPAIGN EXPENDITURES / 86th Congress

Service Dates of Committee Chair: July 1,1960-Jan. 3,1961
Service Dates of Majority Members: July 1,1960-Jan. 3,1961
Service Dates of Minority Members: July 1,1960-Jan. 3,1961

Majority

Rank	Name	Party	State	Terms in: House	Terms in: Comm.
Chr	Davis, Clifford	Dem	Tenn.	11	3
2nd	Jones, Robert E. Jr.	Dem	Ala.	7	3
3rd	O'Brien, Leo W.	Dem	N.Y.	5	1

Minority

Rank	Name	Party	State	Terms in: House	Terms in: Comm.
RM	Cramer, William C.	Rep	Fla.	3	1
2nd	Devine, Samuel L.	Rep	Ohio	1	1

Departures from Committee:	Majority		Minority		
No new assignment	None		Cramer, William C.	Fla.	Rep

HOUSE SPECIAL COMMITTEE: INVESTIGATE CAMPAIGN EXPENDITURES / 87th Congress

Service Dates of Committee Chair: Aug. 14,1962-Jan. 3,1963
Service Dates of Majority Members: Aug. 14,1962-Jan. 3,1963
Service Dates of Minority Members: Aug. 14,1962-Jan. 3,1963

Majority

Rank	Name	Party	State	Terms in: House	Terms in: Comm.
Chr	Davis, Clifford	Dem	Tenn.	12	4
2nd	Jones, Robert E. Jr.	Dem	Ala.	8	4
3rd	O'Brien, Leo W.	Dem	N.Y.	6	2

Minority

Rank	Name	Party	State	Terms in: House	Terms in: Comm.
RM	Cramer, William C.	Rep	Fla.	4	2
2nd	Devine, Samuel L.	Rep	Ohio	2	2

HOUSE SPECIAL COMMITTEE: INVESTIGATE CAMPAIGN EXPENDITURES / 88th Congress

Service Dates of Committee Chair: July 23,1964-Jan. 3,1965
Service Dates of Majority Members: July 23,1964-Jan. 3,1965
Service Dates of Minority Members: July 23,1964-Jan. 3,1965

Majority

Rank	Name	Party	State	Terms in: House	Terms in: Comm.
Chr	Davis, Clifford	Dem	Tenn.	13	5
2nd	Jones, Paul C.	Dem	Mo.	9	5
3rd	O'Brien, Leo W.	Dem	N.Y.	7	3

Minority

Rank	Name	Party	State	Terms in: House	Terms in: Comm.
RM	Devine, Samuel L.	Rep	Ohio	3	3
2nd	Bromwell, James E.	Rep	Iowa	2	1

	Majority			Minority		
Departures from the House:						
Defeated for Reelection	None			Bromwell, James E.	Iowa	Rep
Defeated for Renomination	Davis, Clifford	Tenn.	Dem	None		
Departures from Committee:						
No new assignment	Jones, Paul C.	Mo.	Dem	None		
	O'Brien, Leo W.	N.Y.	Dem			

HOUSE SPECIAL COMMITTEE: INVESTIGATE CAMPAIGN EXPENDITURES / 89th Congress

Service Dates of Committee Chair: Aug. 11,1966-Jan. 3,1967
Service Dates of Majority Members: Aug. 11,1966-Jan. 3,1967
Service Dates of Minority Members: Aug. 11,1966-Jan. 3,1967

Majority

Rank	Name	Party	State	Terms in: House	Terms in: Comm.
Chr	O'Neill, Thomas P. Jr.	Dem	Mass.	7	*2 1
2nd	Smith, Neal	Dem	Iowa	4	1
3rd	Davis, John W.	Dem	Ga.	3	1

Minority

Rank	Name	Party	State	Terms in: House	Terms in: Comm.
RM	Devine, Samuel L.	Rep	Ohio	4	4
2nd	Goodell, Charles E.	Rep	N.Y.	4	1

*2: Member's 2nd period of service on the committee.

Departures from Committee:	Majority		Minority	
No new assignment	None		Goodell, Charles E.	N.Y. Rep

HOUSE SPECIAL COMMITTEE: INVESTIGATE CAMPAIGN EXPENDITURES / 90th Congress

Service Dates of Committee Chair: Aug. 2,1968-Jan. 3,1969
Service Dates of Majority Members: Aug. 2,1968-Jan. 3,1969
Service Dates of Minority Members: Aug. 2,1968-Jan. 3,1969

Majority

Rank	Name	Party	State	Terms in: House	Terms in: Comm.
Chr	O'Neill, Thomas P. Jr.	Dem	Mass.	8	*2 2
2nd	Smith, Neal	Dem	Iowa	5	2
3rd	Davis, John W.	Dem	Ga.	4	2

Minority

Rank	Name	Party	State	Terms in: House	Terms in: Comm.
RM	Devine, Samuel L.	Rep	Ohio	5	5
2nd	Kyl, John H.	Rep	Iowa	4	1

*2: Member's 2nd period of service on the committee.

Changes:

Majority:

Davis, John W.	Dem	Ga.	Sep. 12,1968	Left committee; no new assignment.
Anderson, William R.	Dem	Tenn.	Sep. 12,1968	Replaced Davis.

HOUSE SPECIAL COMMITTEE: INVESTIGATE CAMPAIGN EXPENDITURES / 91st Congress

Service Dates of Committee Chair: Aug. 4,1970-Jan. 3,1971
Service Dates of Majority Members: Aug. 4,1970-Jan. 3,1971
Service Dates of Minority Members: Aug. 4,1970-Jan. 3,1971

Majority

Rank	Name	Party	State	Terms in: House	Terms in: Comm.
Chr	O'Neill, Thomas P. Jr.	Dem	Mass.	9	*2 3
2nd	Smith, Neal	Dem	Iowa	6	3
3rd	Anderson, William R.	Dem	Tenn.	3	2

Minority

Rank	Name	Party	State	Terms in: House	Terms in: Comm.
RM	Devine, Samuel L.	Rep	Ohio	6	6
2nd	Kyl, John H.	Rep	Iowa	5	2

*2: Member's 2nd period of service on the committee.

Departures from Committee:	Majority		Minority	
No new assignment	Anderson, William R.	Tenn. Dem	Kyl, John H.	Iowa Rep

HOUSE SPECIAL COMMITTEE: INVESTIGATE CAMPAIGN EXPENDITURES / 92nd Congress

Service Dates of Committee Chair: Feb. 29,1972-Jan. 3,1973
Service Dates of Majority Members: Feb. 29,1972-Jan. 3,1973
Service Dates of Minority Members: Feb. 29,1972-Jan. 3,1973

Majority

Rank	Name	Party	State	Terms in: House	Terms in: Comm.
Chr	O'Neill, Thomas P. Jr.	Dem	Mass.	10	*2 4
2nd	Smith, Neal	Dem	Iowa	7	4
3rd	Leggett, Robert L.	Dem	Cal.	5	1

Minority

Rank	Name	Party	State	Terms in: House	Terms in: Comm.
RM	Devine, Samuel L.	Rep	Ohio	7	7
2nd	Harvey, James	Rep	Mich.	6	1

*2: Member's 2nd period of service on the committee.

Departures from Committee:	Majority		Minority	
Became House Majority Leader	O'Neill, Thomas P. Jr.	Mass. Dem	None	
No new assignment	None		Harvey, James	Mich. Rep

HOUSE SPECIAL COMMITTEE: INVESTIGATE CAMPAIGN EXPENDITURES / 93rd Congress

Service Dates of Committee Chair: Mar. 15,1973-Jan. 3,1975
Service Dates of Majority Members: Mar. 15,1973-Jan. 3,1975
Service Dates of Minority Members: Mar. 15,1973-Jan. 3,1975

Majority

Rank	Name	Party	State	Terms in: House	Terms in: Comm.
Chr	Smith, Neal	Dem	Iowa	8	5
2nd	Leggett, Robert L.	Dem	Cal.	6	2
3rd	Long, Gillis W.	Dem	La.	2	1

Minority

Rank	Name	Party	State	Terms in: House	Terms in: Comm.
RM	Dickinson, William L.	Rep	Ala.	5	1
2nd	Devine, Samuel L.	Rep	Ohio	8	8

HOUSE SELECT COMMITTEE: INVESTIGATE THE FEDERAL COMMUNICATIONS COMMISSION

Jurisdiction, 1948

From House Resolution 691, 80th Congress, Second Session, June 19, 1948:

[Paragraph 2]

The committee is authorized, empowered, and directed to conduct a study and investigation of the organization, personnel, and activities of the Federal Communications Commission with a view to determining whether or not such Commission in its organization, in the selection and appointment of personnel, and in the conduct of its functions and activities, has been, and is, acting in accordance with law and the public interest; including (but not limiting the foregoing authority) a study and investigation of the Commission's licensing and license renewal activities; the Commission's power and authority, if any, to promulgate and issue its so-called "Blue Book", and the extent to which, if any, the same has been, or is being, used as the basis or excuse for regulation by the Commission, directly or indirectly, of radio-program content at licensed radio stations; whether the Commission has licensed, or proposes to license, any radio station or stations owned or controlled by persons who are members of or affiliated with subversive or Communist front organizations or who might permit the facilities of such radio stations to be used contrary to the public interest; and whether there has been, or is, any concerted movement or effort to procure the concentration of radio station licenses, including frequency modulation, amplitude modulation, and television, in the hands of a limited class of persons or concerns rather than a distribution of such licenses on a geographical and equitable basis, as provided by the Communications Act of 1934, as amended.

Termination, 1949

The Select Committee was terminated upon the filing of its final report, House Report 2479, on January 3, 1949.

HOUSE SELECT COMMITTEE: INVESTIGATE THE FEDERAL COMMUNICATIONS COMMISSION / 80th Congress

Service Dates of Committee Chair: June 29,1948-Jan. 3,1949
Service Dates of Majority Members: June 29,1948-Jan. 3,1949
Service Dates of Minority Members: June 29,1948-Jan. 3,1949

Majority

Rank	Name	Party	State	Terms in: House	Terms in: Comm.
Chr	Harness, Forest A.	Rep	Ind.	5	1
2nd	Hall, Leonard W.	Rep	N.Y.	5	1
3rd	Elston, Charles H.	Rep	Ohio	5	1

Minority

Rank	Name	Party	State	Terms in: House	Terms in: Comm.
RM	Priest, J. Percy	Dem	Tenn.	4	1
2nd	Harris, Oren	Dem	Ark.	4	1

HOUSE SELECT COMMITTEE: LOBBYING ACTIVITIES

Jurisdiction, 1949

From House Resolution 298, 81st Congress, First Session, August 12, 1949:

The committee is authorized and directed to conduct a study and investigation of --

(1) all lobbying activities intended to influence, encourage, promote, or retard legislation; and
(2) all activities of agencies of the Federal Government intended to influence, encourage, promote, or retard legislation.

Termination, 1951

The Select Committee was terminated by authority of House Resolution 298 (81-1) at the end of the 81st Congress, and upon filing of House Report 3239 (Part II) on January 3, 1951.

HOUSE SELECT COMMITTEE: LOBBYING ACTIVITIES / 81st Congress

Service Dates of Committee Chair: Oct. 6,1949-Jan. 2,1951
Service Dates of Majority Members: Oct. 6,1949-Jan. 2,1951
Service Dates of Minority Members: Oct. 6,1949-Jan. 2,1951

Majority

Rank	Name	Party	State	Terms in: House	Terms in: Comm.
Chr	Buchanan, Frank	Dem	Penn.	3	1
2nd	Lanham, Henderson L.	Dem	Ga.	2	1
3rd	Albert, Carl	Dem	Okla.	2	1
4th	Doyle, Clyde G.	Dem	Cal.	2	1

Minority

Rank	Name	Party	State	Terms in: House	Terms in: Comm.
RM	Halleck, Charles A.	Rep	Ind.	8	1
2nd	Brown, Clarence J.	Rep	Ohio	6	1
3rd	O'Hara, Joseph P.	Rep	Minn.	5	1

HOUSE SELECT COMMITTEE: TO INVESTIGATE AND STUDY THE USE OF CHEMICALS, PESTICIDES, AND INSECTICIDES IN AND WITH RESPECT TO FOOD PRODUCTS

Jurisdiction, 1950

From House Resolution 323, 81st Congress, Second Session, June 20, 1950:

[Paragraph 2]

The committee is authorized and directed to conduct a full and complete investigation and study of--

(1) the nature, extent, and effect of the use of chemicals, compounds, and synthetics in the production, processing, preparation, and packaging of food products to determine the effect of the use of such chemicals, compounds, and synthetics
 (A) upon the health and welfare of the Nation and
 (B) upon the stability and well-being of our agricultural economy;
(2) the nature, extent, and effect of the use of pesticides and insecticides with respect to food and food products, particularly the effect of such use of pesticides and insecticides upon the health and welfare of the consumer by reason of toxic residues remaining on such food and food products as a result of such use; and
(3) the nature, effect, and extent of the use of chemicals, compounds, and synthetics in the manufacture of fertilizer, particularly the effect of such use of chemicals, compounds, and synthetics upon
 (A) the condition of the soil as a result of the use of such fertilizer,
 (B) the quantity and quality of the vegetation growing from such soil,
 (C) the health of animals consuming such vegetation, and
 (D) the quantity and quality of food produced from such soil, and
 (E) the public health and welfare generally.

From House Resolution 447, 82nd Congress, First Session, October 15, 1951:

[Amendment to extending resolution, H. Res. 74, February 2, 1951]

Resolved, That H. Res. 74, Eighty-second Congress, is amended by adding, after the words "H. Res. 323," in the fourth line, a comma and the following language: "and an investigation and study of the nature, extent, and effect of the use of chemicals, compounds, and synthetics in the production, processing, preparation, and packaging of cosmetics to determine the effect of the use of such chemicals, compounds, and synthetics upon the health and welfare of the Nation".

Termination, 1952

The Select Committee was terminated upon the filing of its final report, House Report 2500 (82-2), on July 10, 1952.

HOUSE SELECT COMMITTEE: TO INVESTIGATE AND STUDY THE USE OF CHEMICALS, PESTICIDES, AND INSECTICIDES IN AND WITH RESPECT TO FOOD PRODUCTS / 81st Congress

Service Dates of Committee Chair: July 20,1950-Jan. 3,1951
Service Dates of Majority Members: July 20,1950-Jan. 3,1951
Service Dates of Minority Members: July 20,1950-Jan. 3,1951

Majority

Rank	Name	Party	State	Terms in: House	Terms in: Comm.
Chr	Delaney, James J.	Dem	N.Y.	2	1
2nd	Abernethy, Thomas G.	Dem	Miss.	4	1
3rd	Hedrick, Erland H.	Dem	W.Va.	3	1
4th	Jones, Paul C.	Dem	Mo.	2	1

Minority

Rank	Name	Party	State	Terms in: House	Terms in: Comm.
RM	Keefe, Frank B.	Rep	Wisc.	6	1
2nd	Miller, Arthur L.	Rep	Neb.	4	1
3rd	McDonough, Gordon L.	Rep	Cal.	3	1

Departures from the House:

	Majority		Minority
Retired	Keefe, Frank B.	Wisc. Rep	None

HOUSE SELECT COMMITTEE: TO INVESTIGATE AND STUDY THE USE OF CHEMICALS, PESTICIDES, AND INSECTICIDES IN AND WITH RESPECT TO FOOD PRODUCTS / 82nd Congress

Service Dates of Committee Chair: Feb. 12,1951-July 10,1952
Service Dates of Majority Members: Feb. 12,1951-July 10,1952
Service Dates of Minority Members: Feb. 12,1951-July 10,1952

Majority

Rank	Name	Party	State	Terms in: House	Terms in: Comm.
Chr	Delaney, James J.	Dem	N.Y.	3	2
2nd	Abernethy, Thomas G.	Dem	Miss.	5	2
3rd	Hedrick, Erland H.	Dem	W.Va.	4	2
4th	Jones, Paul C.	Dem	Mo.	3	2

Minority

Rank	Name	Party	State	Terms in: House	Terms in: Comm.
RM	Miller, Arthur L.	Rep	Neb.	5	2
2nd	McDonough, Gordon L.	Rep	Cal.	4	2
3rd	Horan, Walter F.	Rep	Wash.	5	1

HOUSE SELECT COMMITTEE: INVESTIGATE EDUCATIONAL AND TRAINING AND LOAN GUARANTY PROGRAMS UNDER GI BILL

INVESTIGATE EDUCATIONAL AND TRAINING PROGRAMS UNDER GI BILL

Jurisdiction, 1950

From House Resolution 474, 81st Congress, Second Session, August 28, 1950:

[Paragraph 2]

The committee is authorized and directed to conduct a full and complete investigation and study of the alleged abuses in the education and training program of World War II veterans, and of action taken or the lack of action taken by the responsible officers and employees of the Veterans' Administration and State approving authorities to prevent abuses under the Servicemen's Re-adjustment Act, as amended.

INVESTIGATE EDUCATIONAL AND TRAINING AND LOAN GUARANTY PROGRAMS UNDER GI BILL

Jurisdiction, 1951

From House Resolution 93, 82nd Congress, First Session, February 2, 1951:

[Paragraph 2]

The committee is authorized and directed, effective January 3, 1951, to conduct a full and complete investigation, evaluation, and study of the alleged abuses in the education and training and loan guaranty programs of World War II veterans, and of action taken, or the lack of action taken by the responsible officers and employees of the Veterans' Administration and State approving agencies to prevent abuses under Public Laws 16 and 346 (Seventy-eighth Congress), as amended.

Termination, 1952

The Select Committee was terminated upon the filing of its final report, House Report 2501 (82-2) on September 11, 1952.

HOUSE SELECT COMMITTEE: INVESTIGATE EDUCATIONAL AND TRAINING PROGRAMS UNDER GI BILL / 81st Congress

Service Dates of Committee Chair: Sep. 20,1950-Jan. 3,1951
Service Dates of Majority Members: Sep. 20,1950-Jan. 3,1951
Service Dates of Minority Members: Sep. 20,1950-Jan. 3,1951

Majority

Rank	Name	Party	State	Terms in: House	Terms in: Comm.
Chr	Teague, Olin E.	Dem	Tex.	3	1
2nd	Engle, Clair	Dem	Cal.	4	1
3rd	Evins, Joseph L.	Dem	Tenn.	2	1
4th	Bolling, Richard W.	Dem	Mo.	1	1
5th	Chudoff, Earl	Dem	Penn.	1	1

Minority

Rank	Name	Party	State	Terms in: House	Terms in: Comm.
RM	Kearney, Bernard W.	Rep	N.Y.	4	1
2nd	Weichel, Alvin F.	Rep	Ohio	4	1
3rd	Beall, J. Glenn	Rep	Md.	4	1
4th	Scudder, Hubert B.	Rep	Cal.	1	1

Departures from the House:

	Majority			Minority		
No new assignment	Bolling, Richard W.	Mo.	Dem	Kearney, Bernard W.	N.Y.	Rep

HOUSE SELECT COMMITTEE: INVESTIGATE EDUCATIONAL, TRAINING AND LOAN GUARANTY PROGRAMS UNDER GI BILL / 82nd Congress

Service Dates of Committee Chair: Feb. 12,1951-Sep. 11,1952
Service Dates of Majority Members: Feb. 12,1951-Sep. 11,1952
Service Dates of Minority Members: Feb. 12,1951-Sep. 11,1952

Majority

Rank Name	Party	State	Terms in: House	Comm.
Chr Teague, Olin E.	Dem	Tex.	4	2
2nd Engle, Clair	Dem	Cal.	5	2
3rd Evins, Joseph L.	Dem	Tenn.	3	2
4th Chudoff, Earl	Dem	Penn.	2	2
5th Patten, Harold A.	Dem	Ariz.	2	1

Minority

Rank Name	Party	State	Terms in: House	Comm.
RM Weichel, Alvin F.	Rep	Ohio	5	2
2nd Beall, J. Glenn	Rep	Md.	5	2
3rd Scudder, Hubert B.	Rep	Cal.	2	2
4th Morton, Thruston B.	Rep	Ky.	3	1

HOUSE SELECT COMMITTEE: TO INVESTIGATE AND STUDY THE KATYN FOREST MASSACRE

Jurisdiction, 1952

From House Resolution 390, 82nd Congress, First Session, September 18, 1951, as amended by House Resolution 539, 82nd Congress, Second Session, March 11, 1952:

[Paragraph 2]

The Committee is authorized and directed to conduct a full and complete investigation and study of the facts, evidence, and extenuating circumstances both before and after the massacre of thousands of Polish officers buried in mass graves in the Katyn Forest on the banks of the Dnieper River in the vicinity of Smolensk, Union of Soviet Socialist Republics, which was then a Nazi-occupied territory formerly having been occupied and under the control of the Union of Soviet Socialist Republics.

Termination, 1952

The Select Committee was terminated upon the filing of its final report, House Report 2505 (82-2), on December 22, 1952.

HOUSE SELECT COMMITTEE: TO INVESTIGATE AND STUDY THE KATYN FOREST MASSACRE / 82nd Congress

Service Dates of Committee Chair: Sep. 24,1951-Dec. 22,1952
Service Dates of Majority Members: Sep. 24,1951-Dec. 22,1952
Service Dates of Minority Members: Sep. 24,1951-Dec. 22,1952

Majority

Rank Name	Party	State	Terms in: House	Terms in: Comm.
Chr Madden, Ray J.	Dem	Ind.	5	1
2nd Flood, Daniel J.	Dem	Penn.	3	1
3rd Furcolo, Foster	Dem	Mass.	2	1
4th Machrowicz, Thaddeus M.	Dem	Mich.	1	1

Minority

Rank Name	Party	State	Terms in: House	Terms in: Comm.
RM Dondero, George A.	Rep	Mich.	10	1
2nd O'Konski, Alvin E.	Rep	Wisc.	5	1
3rd Sheehan, Timothy P.	Rep	Ill.	1	1

HOUSE SPECIAL COMMITTEE: TO INVESTIGATE AND STUDY EDUCATIONAL AND PHILANTHROPIC FOUNDATIONS AND OTHER COMPARABLE ORGANIZATIONS WHICH ARE EXEMPT FROM FEDERAL INCOME TAXATION

HOUSE SELECT COMMITTEE: TO INVESTIGATE AND STUDY EDUCATIONAL AND PHILANTHROPIC FOUNDATIONS AND OTHER COMPARABLE ORGANIZATIONS WHICH ARE EXEMPT FROM FEDERAL INCOME TAXATION

Jurisdiction, 1952

From House Resolution 561, 82nd Congress, Second Session, April 4, 1952:

[Paragraph 2]

The committee is authorized and directed to conduct a full and complete investigation and study of educational and philanthropic foundations and other comparable organizations which are exempt from Federal income taxation to determine which such foundations and organizations are using their resources for purposes other than the purposes for which they were established, and especially to determine which such foundations and organizations are using their resources for un-American and subversive activities or for purposes not in the interest or tradition of the United States.

The final report of this Select Committee, House Report 2514 (82-2), was filed on January 1, 1953. The Committee was reorganized as a Special Committee by House Resolution 217 (83-1) on July 27, 1953.

HOUSE SPECIAL COMMITTEE: TO INVESTIGATE AND STUDY EDUCATIONAL AND PHILANTHROPIC FOUNDATIONS AND OTHER COMPARABLE ORGANIZATIONS WHICH ARE EXEMPT FROM FEDERAL INCOME TAXATION

Reorganization, 1953

The Select Committee was reorganized as a Special Committee by House Resolution 217 (83-1) on July 27, 1953:

The committee is authorized and directed to conduct a full and complete investigation and study of educational and philanthropic foundations and other comparable organizations which are exempt from Federal income taxation to determine if any foundations and organizations are using their resources for purposes other than the purposes for which they were established, and especially to determine which such foundations and organizations are using their resources for un-American and subversive activities; for political purposes; propaganda, or attempts to influence legislation.

Termination, 1954

The Special Committee was terminated upon the filing of its final report, House Report 2681 (83-2) on December 16, 1954.

HOUSE SELECT COMMITTEE: TO INVESTIGATE AND STUDY EDUCATIONAL AND PHILANTHROPIC FOUNDATIONS AND OTHER COMPARABLE ORGANIZATIONS WHICH ARE EXEMPT FROM FEDERAL INCOME TAXATION / 82nd Congress

Service Dates of Committee Chair: Ch1 Apr. 30,1952-Dec. 24,1952
ChA Dec. 24,1952-Jan. 3,1953
Service Dates of Majority Members: Apr. 30,1952-Jan. 3,1953
Service Dates of Minority Members: Apr. 30,1952-Jan. 3,1953

Majority

Rank	Name	Party	State	Terms in: House	Terms in: Comm.
Ch1	Cox, Edward E.	Dem	Ga.	14	1
ChA	Hays, L. Brooks	Dem	Ark.	5	1
3rd	O'Toole, Donald L.	Dem	N.Y.	8	1
4th	Forand, Aime J.	Dem	R.I.	7	1

Minority

Rank	Name	Party	State	Terms in: House	Terms in: Comm.
RM	Simpson, Richard M.	Rep	Penn.	8	1
2nd	Goodwin, Angier L.	Rep	Mass.	5	1
3rd	Reece, B. Carroll	Rep	Tenn.	13	1

Changes:

Chair:

	Name	Party	State	Date	Remarks
Ch1	Cox, Edward E.	Dem	Ga.	Dec. 24,1952	Died in office.
ChA	Hays, L. Brooks	Dem	Ark.	Dec. 24,1952	Succeeded Cox as Acting Chair for remainder of the Congress.

Majority:

Name	Party	State	Date	Remarks
Cox, Edward E.	Dem	Ga.	Dec. 24,1952	Died in office.

	Majority			Minority		
Departures from the House:						
Defeated for Reelection	O'Toole, Donald L.	N.Y.	Dem	None		
Members not appointed to the Reorganized Committee:						
	Forand, Aime J.	R.I.	Dem	Simpson, Richard M.	Penn.	Rep
	Hays, L. Brooks	Ark.	Dem			

HOUSE SPECIAL COMMITTEE: TO INVESTIGATE AND STUDY EDUCATIONAL AND PHILANTHROPIC FOUNDATIONS AND OTHER COMPARABLE ORGANIZATIONS WHICH ARE EXEMPT FROM FEDERAL INCOME TAXATION / 83rd Congress

Service Dates of Committee Chair: Aug. 4,1953-Dec. 16,1954
Service Dates of Majority Members: Aug. 4,1953-Dec. 16,1954
Service Dates of Minority Members: Aug. 4,1953-Dec. 16,1954

Majority

Rank	Name	Party	State	Terms in: House	Terms in: Comm.
Chr	Reece, B. Carroll	Rep	Tenn.	14	2
2nd	Wolcott, Jesse P.	Rep	Mich.	12	1
3rd	Goodwin, Angier L.	Rep	Mass.	6	2

Minority

Rank	Name	Party	State	Terms in: House	Terms in: Comm.
RM	Hays, Wayne L.	Dem	Ohio	3	1
2nd	Pfost, Gracie B.	Dem	Ida.	1	1

HOUSE SELECT COMMITTEE: CURRENT PORNOGRAPHIC MATERIALS

Jurisdiction, 1952

From House Resolution 596, 82nd Congress, Second Session, May 12, 1952:

[Paragraph 2]

The select committee is authorized and directed to conduct a full and complete investigation and study

(1) to determine the extent to which current literature--books, magazines, and comic books--containing immoral, obscene, or otherwise offense matter, or placing improper emphasis on crime, violence, and corruption, are being made available to the people of the United States through the United States mails and otherwise; and

(2) to determine the adequacy of existing law to prevent the publication and distribution of books containing immoral, offensive, and other undesirable matter.

Termination, 1952

The Select Committee was terminated upon the filing of its final report, House Report 2510 (82-2) on December 31, 1952.

HOUSE SELECT COMMITTEE: CURRENT PORNOGRAPHIC MATERIALS / 82nd Congress

Service Dates of Committee Chair: June 16,1952-Jan. 3,1953
Service Dates of Majority Members: June 16,1952-Jan. 3,1953
Service Dates of Minority Members: June 16,1952-Jan. 3,1953

Majority

Rank	Name	Party	State	Terms in: House	Terms in: Comm.
Chr	Gathings, Ezekiel C.	Dem	Ark.	7	1
2nd	Celler, Emanuel	Dem	N.Y.	15	1
3rd	Walter, Francis E.	Dem	Penn.	10	1
4th	Miller, George P.	Dem	Cal.	4	1
5th	Bosone, Reva Z. B.	Dem	Utah	2	1

Minority

Rank	Name	Party	State	Terms in: House	Terms in: Comm.
RM	Rees, Edward H.	Rep	Kans.	8	1
2nd	Graham, Louis E.	Rep	Penn.	7	1
3rd	St. George, Katharine	Rep	N.Y.	3	1
4th	Kearns, Carroll D.	Rep	Penn.	3	1

HOUSE SELECT COMMITTEE: COMMUNIST AGGRESSION

Jurisdiction, 1953

From House Resolution 346, 83rd Congress, First Session, July 27, 1953:

[Paragraph 2]

The committee is authorized and directed to conduct a full and complete investigation and study of said seizure and forced "incorporation" of Lithuania, Latvia, and Estonia by the Union of Soviet Socialist Republics and the treatment of the said Baltic peoples during and following said seizure and "incorporation".

From House Resolution 438, 83rd Congress, Second Session, March 4, 1954:

[Paragraph 2]

The committee is authorized and directed to conduct a full and complete investigation and study of

(1) said seizure and forced "incorporation" of Lithuania, Latvia, and Estonia by the Union of Soviet Socialist Republics and the treatment of the said Baltic peoples during and following said seizure and "incorporation"; and

(2) the subversion and destruction of free institutions and human liberties in all other areas controlled, directly or indirectly, by world communism, including the treatment of the peoples in such areas.

Termination, 1954

The Select Committee was terminated upon the filing of its final report, House Report 2684 (83-2), on December 31, 1954.

HOUSE SELECT COMMITTEE: COMMUNIST AGGRESSION / 83rd Congress

Service Dates of Committee Chair: Aug. 4,1953-Dec. 31,1954
Service Dates of Majority Members: Aug. 4,1953-Dec. 31,1954
Service Dates of Minority Members: Aug. 4,1953-Dec. 31,1954

Majority

Rank	Name	Party	State	Terms in: House	Terms in: Comm.
Chr	Kersten, Charles J.	Rep	Wisc.	3	1
2nd	Busbey, Fred E.	Rep	Ill.	4	1
3rd	Bentley, Alvin M.	Rep	Mich.	1	1
4th	Bonin, Edward J.	Rep	Penn.	1	1

Minority

Rank	Name	Party	State	Terms in: House	Terms in: Comm.
RM	Madden, Ray J.	Dem	Ind.	6	1
2nd	Machrowicz, Thaddeus M.	Dem	Mich.	2	1
3rd	Dodd, Thomas J.	Dem	Conn.	1	1

Note: House Resolution 438 (83-2) changed the size and party ratio of the committee to 5 Republicans and 4 Democrats on Mar. 4,1954.

Additions:

Majority:	5th	Hillings, Patrick J.	Rep	Cal.	Mar. 10,1954
Minority:	4th	Feighan, Michael A.	Dem	Ohio	Mar. 10,1954

HOUSE SELECT COMMITTEE: SURVIVOR BENEFITS

Jurisdiction, 1954

From House Resolution 549, 83rd Congress, Second Session, August 4, 1954:

[Paragraph 2]

The committee is authorized and directed
(1) to conduct a full and complete investigation and study of the benefits provided under Federal law for the surviving dependents of deceased members and former members of the Armed Forces, and
(2) on the basis of such investigation, and study, to make such recommendations as it may deem advisable and to prepare such legislation as it may consider appropriate to carry out such recommendations.

Termination, 1956

The Select Committee was extended by House Resolution 35 (84-1) and terminated by its authority on January 15, 1956.

HOUSE SELECT COMMITTEE: SURVIVOR BENEFITS / 83rd Congress

Service Dates of Committee Chair: Aug. 20,1954-Jan. 3,1955
Service Dates of Majority Members: Aug. 20,1954-Jan. 3,1955
Service Dates of Minority Members: Aug. 20,1954-Jan. 3,1955

Majority

Rank	Name	Party	State	Terms in: House	Terms in: Comm.
Chr	Bates, William H.	Rep	Mass.	3	1
2nd	Kean, Robert W.	Rep	N.J.	8	1
3rd	Kearney, Bernard W.	Rep	N.Y.	6	1

Minority

Rank	Name	Party	State	Terms in: House	Terms in: Comm.
RM	Teague, Olin E.	Dem	Tex.	5	1
2nd	Hardy, Porter Jr.	Dem	Va.	4	1

Departures from Committee:

	Majority		Minority
No new assignment	Kearney, Bernard W.	N.Y. Rep	None

HOUSE SELECT COMMITTEE: SURVIVOR BENEFITS / 84th Congress

Service Dates of Committee Chair: Feb. 8,1955-Jan. 15,1956
Service Dates of Majority Members: Feb. 8,1955-Jan. 15,1956
Service Dates of Minority Members: Feb. 8,1955-Jan. 15,1956

Majority

Rank	Name	Party	State	Terms in: House	Terms in: Comm.
Chr	Hardy, Porter Jr.	Dem	Va.	5	2
2nd	Kilday, Paul J.	Dem	Tex.	9	1
3rd	Teague, Olin E.	Dem	Tex.	6	2

Minority

Rank	Name	Party	State	Terms in: House	Terms in: Comm.
RM	Bates, William H.	Rep	Mass.	4	2
2nd	Kean, Robert W.	Rep	N.J.	9	2

HOUSE SELECT COMMITTEE: CONDUCT AN INVESTIGATION AND STUDY OF THE FINANCIAL POSITION OF THE WHITE COUNTY BRIDGE COMMISSION

Jurisdiction, 1955

From House Resolution 244, 84th Congress, First Session, May 25, 1955:

[Paragraph 2]

The committee is authorized and directed to conduct a full and complete investigation and study of the financial position of the White County Bridge Commission established by Public Law 37, Seventy-Seventh Congress, with a view to ascertaining when it may be expected that the bridge and approaches thereto operated by such Commission near New Harmony, Indiana, will become free of tolls, and what money has been received, and what expenditures have been made, by such Commission since its establishment in 1941.

Termination, 1956

The Select Committee was terminated upon the filing of its final report, House Report 2052 (84-2), on April 25, 1956.

HOUSE SELECT COMMITTEE: CONDUCT AN INVESTIGATION AND STUDY OF THE FINANCIAL POSITION OF THE WHITE COUNTY BRIDGE COMMISSION / 84th Congress

Service Dates of Committee Chair: June 7,1955-Apr. 25,1956
Service Dates of Majority Members: June 7,1955-Apr. 25,1956
Service Dates of Minority Members: June 7,1955-Apr. 25,1956

Majority

Rank	Name	Party	State	Terms in: House	Terms in: Comm.
Chr	Denton, Winfield K.	Dem	Ind.	3	1
2nd	Price, C. Melvin	Dem	Ill.	6	1

Minority

Rank	Name	Party	State	Terms in: House	Terms in: Comm.
RM	Simpson, Sidney E.	Rep	Ill.	7	1

HOUSE SELECT COMMITTEE: HOUSE RECORDING STUDIO

Jurisdiction, 1956

From Public Law 84-624, 84th Congress, Second Session, Legislative Branch Appropriations Act for 1957 (70 Statutes 356), June 27, 1956:

[Section 105.(b)]

The House Recording Studio shall assist Members of the House of Representatives in making disk, film, and tape recordings, and in performing such other functions and duties in connection with the making of such recordings as may be necessary.... The House Recording Studio shall be for the exclusive use of Members of the House of Representatives (including the Delegates and the Resident Commissioner from Puerto Rico)....

HOUSE SELECT COMMITTEE: HOUSE RECORDING STUDIO / 84th Congress

Service Dates of Committee Chair: July 25,1956-Jan. 3,1957
Service Dates of Majority Members: July 25,1956-Jan. 3,1957
Service Dates of Minority Members: July 25,1956-Jan. 3,1957

Majority			Terms in:		Minority			Terms in:	
Rank Name	**Party**	**State**	**House**	**Comm.**	**Rank Name**	**Party**	**State**	**House**	**Comm.**
Chr Gary, J. Vaughn	Dem	Va.	6	1	RM Bow, Frank T.	Rep	Ohio	3	1
2nd Evins, Joseph L.	Dem	Tenn.	5	1					

HOUSE SELECT COMMITTEE: HOUSE RECORDING STUDIO / 85th Congress

Service Dates of Committee Chair: Jan. 28,1957-Jan. 3,1959
Service Dates of Majority Members: Jan. 28,1957-Jan. 3,1959
Service Dates of Minority Members: Jan. 28,1957-Jan. 3,1959

Majority			Terms in:		Minority			Terms in:	
Rank Name	**Party**	**State**	**House**	**Comm.**	**Rank Name**	**Party**	**State**	**House**	**Comm.**
Chr Gary, J. Vaughn	Dem	Va.	7	2	RM Bow, Frank T.	Rep	Ohio	4	2
2nd Evins, Joseph L.	Dem	Tenn.	6	2					

Departures from Committee:	**Majority**		**Minority**
No new assignment	Evins, Joseph L.	Tenn. Dem	None

HOUSE SELECT COMMITTEE: HOUSE RECORDING STUDIO / 86th Congress

Service Dates of Committee Chair: Feb. 11,1959-Jan. 3,1961
Service Dates of Majority Members: Feb. 11,1959-Jan. 3,1961
Service Dates of Minority Members: Feb. 11,1959-Jan. 3,1961

Majority			Terms in:		Minority			Terms in:	
Rank Name	**Party**	**State**	**House**	**Comm.**	**Rank Name**	**Party**	**State**	**House**	**Comm.**
Chr Gary, J. Vaughn	Dem	Va.	8	3	RM Bow, Frank T.	Rep	Ohio	5	3
2nd O'Brien, Leo W.	Dem	N.Y.	5	1					

HOUSE SELECT COMMITTEE: HOUSE RECORDING STUDIO / 87th Congress

Service Dates of Committee Chair: Apr. 20,1961-Jan. 3,1963
Service Dates of Majority Members: Apr. 20,1961-Jan. 3,1963
Service Dates of Minority Members: Apr. 20,1961-Jan. 3,1963

Majority

Rank Name	Party	State	Terms in: House	Comm.
Chr Gary, J. Vaughn	Dem	Va.	9	4
2nd O'Brien, Leo W.	Dem	N.Y.	6	2

Minority

Rank Name	Party	State	Terms in: House	Comm.
RM Bow, Frank T.	Rep	Ohio	6	4

HOUSE SELECT COMMITTEE: HOUSE RECORDING STUDIO / 88th Congress

Service Dates of Committee Chair: Jan. 31,1963-Jan. 3,1965
Service Dates of Majority Members: Jan. 31,1963-Jan. 3,1965
Service Dates of Minority Members: Jan. 31,1963-Jan. 3,1965

Majority

Rank Name	Party	State	Terms in: House	Comm.
Chr Gary, J. Vaughn	Dem	Va.	10	5
2nd O'Brien, Leo W.	Dem	N.Y.	7	3

Minority

Rank Name	Party	State	Terms in: House	Comm.
RM Bow, Frank T.	Rep	Ohio	7	5

	Majority		Minority	
Departures from the House:				
Retired	Gary, J. Vaughn	Va. Dem	None	
Departures from Committee:				
No new assignment	None		Bow, Frank T.	Ohio Rep

HOUSE SELECT COMMITTEE: HOUSE RECORDING STUDIO / 89th Congress

Service Dates of Committee Chair: Feb. 3,1965-Dec. 30,1966
Service Dates of Majority Members: Feb. 3,1965-Jan. 3,1967
Service Dates of Minority Members: Feb. 3,1965-Jan. 3,1967

Majority

Rank Name	Party	State	Terms in: House	Comm.
Chr O'Brien, Leo W.	Dem	N.Y.	8	4
2nd Steed, Thomas J.	Dem	Okla.	9	1

Minority

Rank Name	Party	State	Terms in: House	Comm.
RM Devine, Samuel L.	Rep	Ohio	4	1

Changes:

Majority:

O'Brien, Leo W.	Dem	N.Y.	Dec. 30,1966	Resigned; appointed Chair of County Planning Board.

HOUSE SELECT COMMITTEE: HOUSE RECORDING STUDIO / 90th Congress

Service Dates of Committee Chair: Jan. 26,1967-Jan. 3,1969
Service Dates of Majority Members: Jan. 26,1967-Jan. 3,1969
Service Dates of Minority Members: Jan. 26,1967-Jan. 3,1969

Majority

Rank Name	Party	State	Terms in: House	Comm.
Chr Steed, Thomas J.	Dem	Okla.	10	2
2nd Irwin, Donald J.	Dem	Conn.	3	1

Minority

Rank Name	Party	State	Terms in: House	Comm.
RM Devine, Samuel L.	Rep	Ohio	5	2

	Majority		Minority	
Departures from the House:				
Defeated for Reelection	Irwin, Donald J.	Conn. Dem	None	
Departures from Committee:				
No new assignment	None		Devine, Samuel L.	Ohio Rep

HOUSE SELECT COMMITTEE: HOUSE RECORDING STUDIO / 91st Congress

Service Dates of Committee Chair: Feb. 6,1969-Jan. 3,1971
Service Dates of Majority Members: Feb. 6,1969-Jan. 3,1971
Service Dates of Minority Members: Feb. 6,1969-Jan. 3,1971

Majority

Rank Name	Party	State	Terms in: House	Terms in: Comm.
Chr Steed, Thomas J.	Dem	Okla.	11	3
2nd Cohelan, Jeffrey	Dem	Cal.	6	1

Minority

Rank Name	Party	State	Terms in: House	Terms in: Comm.
RM Kyl, John H.	Rep	Iowa	5	1

	Majority			Minority		
Departures from the House:						
Defeated for Renomination	Cohelan, Jeffrey	Cal.	Dem	None		
Departure from Committee:						
Moved to Agriculture	None			Kyl, John H.	Iowa	Rep

HOUSE SELECT COMMITTEE: HOUSE RECORDING STUDIO / 92nd Congress

Service Dates of Committee Chair: Feb. 1,1971-Jan. 3,1973
Service Dates of Majority Members: Feb. 1,1971-Dec. 8,1971
Service Dates of Minority Members: Feb. 1,1971-Jan. 3,1973

Majority

Rank Name	Party	State	Terms in: House	Terms in: Comm.
Chr Steed, Thomas J.	Dem	Okla.	12	4
2nd Bolling, Richard W.	Dem	Mo.	12	1

Minority

Rank Name	Party	State	Terms in: House	Terms in: Comm.
RM Crane, Philip M.	Rep	Ill.	2	1

Changes:

Majority:

Bolling, Richard W.	Dem	Mo.	Dec. 8,1971	Left committee; no new assignment.
Rees, Thomas M.	Dem	Cal.	Dec. 8,1971	Replaced Bolling.

	Majority			Minority
Departures from Committee:				
No new assignment	Steed, Thomas J.	Okla.	Dem	None

HOUSE SELECT COMMITTEE: HOUSE RECORDING STUDIO / 93rd Congress

Service Dates of Committee Chair: Feb. 8,1973-Jan. 3,1975
Service Dates of Majority Members: Feb. 8,1973-Jan. 3,1975
Service Dates of Minority Members: Feb. 8,1973-Jan. 3,1975

Majority

Rank Name	Party	State	Terms in: House	Terms in: Comm.
Chr Rees, Thomas M.	Dem	Cal.	5	2
2nd Rose, Charles G. III	Dem	N.C.	1	1

Minority

Rank Name	Party	State	Terms in: House	Terms in: Comm.
RM Crane, Philip M.	Rep	Ill.	3	2

HOUSE SELECT COMMITTEE: HOUSE RECORDING STUDIO / 94th Congress

Service Dates of Committee Chair: Feb. 18,1975-Jan. 3,1977
Service Dates of Majority Members: Feb. 18,1975-Jan. 3,1977
Service Dates of Minority Members: Feb. 18,1975-Jan. 3,1977

Majority

Rank	Name	Party	State	Terms in: House	Terms in: Comm.
Chr	Rees, Thomas M.	Dem	Cal.	6	3
2nd	Rose, Charles G. III	Dem	N.C.	2	2

Minority

Rank	Name	Party	State	Terms in: House	Terms in: Comm.
RM	Crane, Philip M.	Rep	Ill.	4	3

Departures from the House:

	Majority			Minority
Retired	Rees, Thomas M.	Cal.	Dem	None

HOUSE SELECT COMMITTEE: HOUSE RECORDING STUDIO / 95th Congress

Service Dates of Committee Chair: Jan. 31,1977-Jan. 3,1979
Service Dates of Majority Members: Jan. 31,1977-Jan. 3,1979
Service Dates of Minority Members: Jan. 31,1977-Jan. 3,1979

Majority

Rank	Name	Party	State	Terms in: House	Terms in: Comm.
Chr	Rose, Charles G. III	Dem	N.C.	3	3
2nd	Boggs, Corinne C. (Lindy)	Dem	La.	3	1

Minority

Rank	Name	Party	State	Terms in: House	Terms in: Comm.
RM	Crane, Philip M.	Rep	Ill.	5	4

Departures from Committee:

	Majority	Minority		
No new assignment	None	Crane, Philip M.	Ill.	Rep

HOUSE SELECT COMMITTEE: HOUSE RECORDING STUDIO / 96th Congress

Service Dates of Committee Chair: May 2,1979-Jan. 3,1981
Service Dates of Majority Members: May 2,1979-Jan. 3,1981
Service Dates of Minority Members: May 2,1979-Jan. 3,1981

Majority

Rank	Name	Party	State	Terms in: House	Terms in: Comm.
Chr	Rose, Charles G. III	Dem	N.C.	4	4
2nd	Boggs, Corinne C. (Lindy)	Dem	La.	4	2

Minority

Rank	Name	Party	State	Terms in: House	Terms in: Comm.
RM	Dornan, Robert K.	Rep	Cal.	2	1

HOUSE SELECT COMMITTEE: HOUSE RECORDING STUDIO / 97th Congress

Service Dates of Committee Chair: Apr. 9,1981-Jan. 3,1983
Service Dates of Majority Members: Apr. 9,1981-Jan. 3,1983
Service Dates of Minority Members: Apr. 9,1981-Jan. 3,1983

Majority

Rank	Name	Party	State	Terms in: House	Terms in: Comm.
Chr	Rose, Charles G. III	Dem	N.C.	5	5
2nd	Boggs, Corinne C. (Lindy)	Dem	La.	5	3

Minority

Rank	Name	Party	State	Terms in: House	Terms in: Comm.
RM	Dornan, Robert K.	Rep	Cal.	3	2

Departures from the House:

	Majority	Minority		
Lost Nomination for U.S. Senate	None	Dornan, Robert K.	Cal.	Rep

HOUSE SELECT COMMITTEE: HOUSE RECORDING STUDIO / 98th Congress

Service Dates of Committee Chair: Mar. 2,1983-Jan. 3,1985
Service Dates of Majority Members: Mar. 2,1983-Jan. 3,1985
Service Dates of Minority Members: Mar. 2,1983-Jan. 3,1985

Majority						Minority					
				Terms in:						Terms in:	
Rank	Name	Party	State	House	Comm.	Rank	Name	Party	State	House	Comm.
Chr	Rose, Charles G. III	Dem	N.C.	6	6	RM	Badham, Robert E.	Rep	Cal.	4	1
2nd	Boggs, Corinne C. (Lindy)	Dem	La.	6	4						

HOUSE SELECT COMMITTEE: HOUSE RECORDING STUDIO / 99th Congress

Service Dates of Committee Chair: May 22,1985-Jan. 3,1987
Service Dates of Majority Members: May 22,1985-Jan. 3,1987
Service Dates of Minority Members: May 22,1985-Jan. 3,1987

Majority						Minority					
				Terms in:						Terms in:	
Rank	Name	Party	State	House	Comm.	Rank	Name	Party	State	House	Comm.
Chr	Rose, Charles G. III	Dem	N.C.	7	7	RM	Badham, Robert E.	Rep	Cal.	5	2
2nd	Boggs, Corinne C. (Lindy)	Dem	La.	7	5						

Departures from Committee:	Majority			Minority
No new assignment	Boggs, Corinne C. (Lindy)	La.	Dem	None

HOUSE SELECT COMMITTEE: HOUSE RECORDING STUDIO / 100th Congress

Service Dates of Committee Chair: Mar. 2,1987-Jan. 3,1989
Service Dates of Majority Members: Mar. 2,1987-Jan. 3,1989
Service Dates of Minority Members: Mar. 2,1987-Jan. 3,1989

Majority						Minority					
				Terms in:						Terms in:	
Rank	Name	Party	State	House	Comm.	Rank	Name	Party	State	House	Comm.
Chr	Rose, Charles G. III	Dem	N.C.	8	8	RM	Badham, Robert E.	Rep	Cal.	6	3
2nd	Swift, Allan B.	Dem	Wash	5	1						

Departures from the House:	Majority	Minority		
Retired	None	Badham, Robert E.	Rep	Cal.

HOUSE SELECT COMMITTEE: HOUSE RECORDING STUDIO / 101st Congress

Service Dates of Committee Chair: Feb. 23,1989-Jan. 3,1991
Service Dates of Majority Members: Feb. 23,1989-Jan. 3,1991
Service Dates of Minority Members: Feb. 23,1989-Jan. 3,1991

Majority						Minority					
				Terms in:						Terms in:	
Rank	Name	Party	State	House	Comm.	Rank	Name	Party	State	House	Comm.
Chr	Rose, Charles G. III	Dem	N.C.	9	9	RM	Boehlert, Sherwood L.	Rep	N.Y.	4	1
2nd	Swift, Allan B.	Dem	Wash	6	2						

HOUSE SELECT COMMITTEE: HOUSE RECORDING STUDIO / 102nd Congress

Service Dates of Committee Chair: Feb. 18,1992-Jan. 3,1993
Service Dates of Majority Members: Feb. 18,1992-Jan. 3,1993
Service Dates of Minority Members: Feb. 18,1992-Jan. 3,1993

Majority

Rank	Name	Party	State	Terms in: House	Terms in: Comm.
Chr	Rose, Charles G. III	Dem	N.C.	10	10
2nd	Swift, Allan B.	Dem	Wash	7	3

Minority

Rank	Name	Party	State	Terms in: House	Terms in: Comm.
RM	Boehlert, Sherwood L.	Rep	N.Y.	5	2

HOUSE SELECT COMMITTEE: ASTRONAUTICS AND SPACE EXPLORATION

Jurisdiction, 1958

From House Resolution 496, 85th Congress, Second Session, March 5, 1958:

[Paragraph 2]

The select committee is authorized and directed to conduct a thorough and complete study and investigation with respect to all aspects and problems relating to the exploration of outer space and the control, development, and use of astronautical resources, personnel, equipment, and facilities. All bills and resolutions introduced in the House, and all bills and resolutions from the Senate, proposing legislation in the field of astronautics and space exploration shall be referred to the select committee.

The Select Committee was reorganized by House Resolution 580 into the House Standing Committee on Science and Astronautics on July 21, 1958. Membership of the reorganized committee was appointed on January 7, 1959.

HOUSE SELECT COMMITTEE: ASTRONAUTICS AND SPACE EXPLORATION / 85th Congress

Service Dates of Committee Chair: Mar. 5,1958-Jan. 7,1959
Service Dates of Majority Members: Mar. 5,1958-Jan. 7,1959
Service Dates of Minority Members: Mar. 5,1958-Jan. 7,1959

Majority

Rank Name	Party	State	Terms in: House	Terms in: Comm.
Chr McCormack, John W.	Dem	Mass.	16	1
2nd Brooks, Overton	Dem	La.	11	1
3rd Hays, L. Brooks	Dem	Ark.	8	1
4th O'Brien, Leo W.	Dem	N.Y.	4	1
5th Metcalf, Lee	Dem	Mont.	3	1
6th Natcher, William H.	Dem	Ky.	3	1
7th Sisk, B. F.	Dem	Cal.	2	1

Minority

Rank Name	Party	State	Terms in: House	Terms in: Comm.
RM Martin, Joseph W. Jr.	Rep	Mass.	17	1
2nd Arends, Leslie C.	Rep	Ill.	12	1
3rd McDonough, Gordon L.	Rep	Cal.	7	1
4th Fulton, James G.	Rep	Penn.	7	1
5th Keating, Kenneth B.	Rep	N.Y.	6	1
6th Ford, Gerald R. Jr.	Rep	Mich.	5	1

Departures from the House:	Majority		Minority	
Elected to U.S. Senate	None		Keating, Kenneth B.	N.Y. Rep
Defeated for Reelection	Hays, L. Brooks	Ark. Dem	None	
Members not assigned to reorganized Committee on Science and Astronautics:				
Moved to Ways and Means	Metcalf, Lee	Mont. Dem	None	
No new assignment	Natcher, William H.	Ky. Dem	Ford, Gerald R. Jr.	Mich. Rep
	O'Brien, Leo W.	N.Y. Dem	Arends, Leslie C.	Ill. Rep

HOUSE SELECT COMMITTEE: EXPORT CONTROL

Jurisdiction, 1961

From House Resolution 403, 87th Congress, First Session, September 7, 1961:

[Paragraph 2]

The committee is authorized and directed to conduct a full and complete investigation and study of the administration, operation, and enforcement of the Export Control Act of 1949 (63 Stat. 7), as amended, with a view to assessing the accomplishments under that Act, determining whether improvements can be made in the administration, operation, or enforcement thereof, and improving congressional oversight and guidance over the formation of United States policies involved in such Act. In carrying out such investigation and study, the committee shall give particular attention to the following matters:

(1) The problems involved in the control of trade between the United States and foreign countries, particularly the foreign countries comprising the Sino-Soviet bloc.
(2) Present methods and procedures in the formulation of policy with respect to the determination of which articles, materials, supplies, and technical data shall be controlled under such Act, and the extent of such control.
(3) Procedures followed under such Act in obtaining information, advice, and opinions with respect to determinations of which articles, materials, supplies, and technical data shall be controlled under such Act, from departments and agencies of the United States which are concerned with aspects of our domestic or foreign policies and operations which have a bearing on exports.
(4) The extent to which decisions heretofore made under such Act concerning the control of exports have adversely affected the security of the United States.
(5) Whether or not such Act is being administered by the appropriate department of the Federal Government.
(6) The interrelationship between such Act and related Acts (such as the Mutual Defense Assistance Control Act of 1951, and the Trading With the Enemy Act) and other discussions or agreements entered into by the United States (such as the coordinating committee (COCOM) discussions and agreements) which affect or relate to the control of trade between the United States and foreign countries.

Termination, 1962

The Select Committee was terminated upon the filing of its final report, House Report 1753 (87-2), on May 31, 1962.

HOUSE SELECT COMMITTEE: EXPORT CONTROL / 87th Congress

Service Dates of Committee Chair: Sep. 15,1961-May 31,1962
Service Dates of Majority Members: Sep. 15,1961-May 31,1962
Service Dates of Minority Members: Sep. 15,1961-May 31,1962

Majority

Rank	Name	Party	State	Terms in: House	Terms in: Comm.
Chr	Kitchin, A. Paul	Dem	N.C.	3	1
2nd	Boland, Edward P.	Dem	Mass.	5	1
3rd	Sisk, B. F.	Dem	Cal.	4	1

Minority

Rank	Name	Party	State	Terms in: House	Terms in: Comm.
RM	Lipscomb, Glenard P.	Rep	Cal.	5	1
2nd	Latta, Delbert L.	Rep	Ohio	2	1

HOUSE SELECT COMMITTEE: GOVERNMENT RESEARCH

Jurisdiction, 1963

From House Resolution 504, 88th Congress, First Session, September 11, 1963:

[Paragraph 2]

The said committee is directed to make a complete, full, and thorough investigation of the numerous research programs being conducted by sundry departments and agencies of the Federal Government and, without limiting the generality of the foregoing, the committee shall give special attention to the following:
(1) the overall total amount of annual expenditures on research programs;
(2) what departments and agencies of the Government are conducting research and at what costs;
(3) the amounts being expended by the various agencies and departments in grants and contracts for research to colleges, private industry, and every form of student scholarships;
(4) what facilities, if any, exist for coordinating the various and sundry research programs, including grants to colleges and universities as well as scholarship grants.

Termination, 1965

The Select Committee was extended by House Resolution 810 (88-2) and terminated on January 3, 1965. Its final report, House Report 1941 (Part 2), was filed on February 18, 1965.

HOUSE SELECT COMMITTEE: GOVERNMENT RESEARCH / 88th Congress

Service Dates of Committee Chair: Sep. 11,1963-Jan. 3,1965
Service Dates of Majority Members: Sep. 11,1963-Jan. 3,1965
Service Dates of Minority Members: Sep. 11,1963-Jan. 3,1965

Majority

Rank Name	Party	State	Terms in: House	Terms in: Comm.
Chr Elliott, Carl A.	Dem	Ala.	8	1
2nd Fogarty, John E.	Dem	R.I.	12	1
3rd Miller, George P.	Dem	Cal.	10	1
4th Price, C. Melvin	Dem	Ill.	10	1
5th Landrum, Phillip M.	Dem	Ga.	6	1

Minority

Rank Name	Party	State	Terms in: House	Terms in: Comm.
RM Brown, Clarence J.	Rep	Ohio	13	1
2nd Anderson, John B.	Rep	Ill.	2	1
3rd Cleveland, James C.	Rep	N.H.	1	1
4th Martin, Pat Minor	Rep	Cal.	1	1

HOUSE SELECT COMMITTEE: WELFARE AND EDUCATION OF CONGRESSIONAL PAGES

Jurisdiction, 1964

From House Resolution 847, 88th Congress, Second Session, September 30, 1964:

[Paragraph 2]

The Committee is authorized and directed to conduct a full and complete investigation and study of all of the factors relating to the general welfare and education of congressional pages, including, but not limited to, a study and investigation of the residential, dining, recreational, educational, and physical training facilities and opportunities for such pages, and rates of pay, hours of work, and other conditions governing the employment of such pages.

[Paragraph 4]

The committee shall report to the House as soon as practicable during the present Congress the results of its investigation and study, together with recommendations regarding the feasibility and desirability of raising the minimum age for Capitol pages to eighteen years, of requiring secondary school graduation as a prerequisite for appointment as a Capitol page, and of providing for the establishment and construction of a Capitol page school and residence, and such other recommendations as it deems advisable.

Termination, 1965

The Select Committee was terminated upon the filing of its final report, House Report 1945 (88-2), on January 2, 1965.

HOUSE SELECT COMMITTEE: WELFARE AND EDUCATION OF CONGRESSIONAL PAGES / 88th Congress

Service Dates of Committee Chair: Oct. 2,1964-Jan. 2,1965
Service Dates of Majority Members: Oct. 2,1964-Jan. 2,1965
Service Dates of Minority Members: Oct. 2,1964-Jan. 2,1965

Majority

Rank	Name	Party	State	Terms in: House	Terms in: Comm.
Chr	Green, Edith S.	Dem	Ore.	5	1
2nd	Gibbons, Sam M.	Dem	Fla.	1	1
3rd	Wilson, Charles H.	Dem	Cal.	1	1

Minority

Rank	Name	Party	State	Terms in: House	Terms in: Comm.
RM	Broomfield, William S.	Rep	Mich.	4	1
2nd	Curtin, Willard S.	Rep	Penn.	4	1

HOUSE SELECT COMMITTEE: STANDARDS AND CONDUCT

Jurisdiction, 1966

From House Resolution 1013, 89th Congress, Second Session, October 19, 1966:

[Section 2 (a)]

It shall be the duty of the Select Committee in its discretion to--

(1) investigate allegations of improper conduct which may reflect upon the House, violations of law, and violations of rules and regulations of the House, relating to the conduct of individuals in the performance of their duties as Members of the House, or as officers or employees of the House, and to make appropriate findings of fact and conclusions with respect thereto;

(2) recommend to the House, by report or resolution by a two-thirds vote (eight members) of the Select Committee, disciplinary action to be taken with respect to such violations which the Select Committee shall determine, after according to the individuals concerned due notice and opportunity for hearing, to have occurred.

Termination, 1966

The Select Committee was terminated upon the filing of its final report, House Report 2338 (89-2) on December 27, 1966. The Standing Committee on Standards of Official Conduct was created by House Resolution 418 (90-1) on April 3, 1967 with membership appointed on May 1,1967.

HOUSE SELECT COMMITTEE: STANDARDS AND CONDUCT / 89th Congress

Service Dates of Committee Chair: Oct. 20,1966-Dec. 27,1966
Service Dates of Majority Members: Oct. 20,1966-Dec. 27,1966
Service Dates of Minority Members: Oct. 20,1966-Dec. 27,1966

Majority

Rank Name	Party	State	Terms in: House	Terms in: Comm.
Chr Bennett, Charles E.	Dem	Fla.	9	1
2nd Brooks, Jack B.	Dem	Tex.	7	1
3rd Nix, Robert N. C.	Dem	Penn.	5	1
4th Carey, Hugh L.	Dem	N.Y.	3	1
5th Cameron, Ronald Brooks	Dem	Cal.	2	1
6th Ronan, Daniel J.	Dem	Ill.	1	1

Minority

Rank Name	Party	State	Terms in: House	Terms in: Comm.
RM Gross, Harold R.	Rep	Iowa	9	1
2nd Broyhill, Joel T.	Rep	Va.	7	1
3rd Michel, Robert H.	Rep	Ill.	5	1
4th May, Catherine D.	Rep	Wash.	4	1
5th Latta, Delbert L.	Rep	Ohio	4	1
6th Stafford, Robert T.	Rep	Vt.	3	1

HOUSE SELECT COMMITTEE: IN RE ADAM CLAYTON POWELL

Jurisdiction, 1967

From House Resolution 1, as amended, 90th Congress, First Session, January 10, 1967:

[Paragraph 1]

That the question of the right of Adam Clayton Powell to be sworn in as a Representative from the State of New York in the Ninetieth Congress, as well as his final right to a seat therein as such Representative, be referred to a special committee.... Until such committee shall report upon and the House staff decide such question and right, the said Adam Clayton Powell shall not be sworn in or permitted to occupy a seat in this House.

[Paragraph 3]

Until such question and right have been decided, the said Adam Clayton Powell shall be entitled to all the pay, allowances, and emoluments authorized for Members of the House.

Termination, 1967

The Select Committee was terminated upon the filing of its final report, House Report 27 (90-1), on February 23, 1967.

HOUSE SELECT COMMITTEE: IN RE ADAM CLAYTON POWELL / 90th Congress

Service Dates of Committee Chair: Jan. 19,1967-Feb. 23,1967
Service Dates of Majority Members: Jan. 19,1967-Feb. 23,1967
Service Dates of Minority Members: Jan. 19,1967-Feb. 23,1967

Majority

Rank	Name	Party	State	Terms in: House	Terms in: Comm.
Chr	Celler, Emanuel	Dem	N.Y.	23	1
2nd	Corman, James C.	Dem	Cal.	4	1
3rd	Pepper, Claude D.	Dem	Fla.	3	1
4th	Conyers, John Jr.	Dem	Mich.	2	1
5th	Jacobs, Andrew Jr.	Dem	Ind.	2	1

Minority

Rank	Name	Party	State	Terms in: House	Terms in: Comm.
RM	Moore, Arch A. Jr.	Rep	W.Va.	6	1
2nd	Teague, Charles M.	Rep	Cal.	7	1
3rd	MacGregor, Clark	Rep	Minn.	4	1
4th	Thomson, Vernon W.	Rep	Wisc.	4	1

HOUSE SELECT COMMITTEE: HOUSE BEAUTY SHOP

Jurisdiction, 1967

From House Resolution 1000, 90th Congress, First Session, December 6, 1967:

[Section 1 (b)]

Effective upon the date of approval of this resolution, until otherwise ordered by the House, the management of the House Beauty Shop and all matters connected therewith shall be under the direction of the Select Committee herein created and shall be operated under such rules and regulations as such Committee may prescribe for the operation and the employment of necessary assistance for the conduct of said Beauty Shop by such business methods as may produce the best results consistent with economical and modern management.

Termination, 1969

The Select Committee was extended by House Resolution 258 (91-1), agreed to February 19, 1969, and reauthorized by Public Law 91-145 on December 12, 1969. The Select Committee was terminated at the end of the 91st Congress, Second Session, after which time its functions were transferred to the House Administration Subcommittee on Services.

HOUSE SELECT COMMITTEE: HOUSE BEAUTY SHOP / 90th Congress

Service Dates of Committee Chair: Dec. 6,1967-Jan. 3,1969
Service Dates of Majority Members: Dec. 6,1967-Jan. 3,1969
Service Dates of Minority Members: Dec. 6,1967-Jan. 3,1969

Majority					Minority				
			Terms in:					Terms in:	
Rank Name	Party	State	House	Comm.	Rank Name	Party	State	House	Comm.
Chr Griffiths, Martha W.	Dem	Mich.	7	1	RM May, Catherine D.	Rep	Wash.	5	1
2nd Green, Edith S.	Dem	Ore.	7	1					

HOUSE BEAUTY SHOP / 91st Congress

Service Dates of Committee Chair: Feb. 19,1969-Jan. 3,1971
Service Dates of Majority Members: Feb. 19,1969-Jan. 3,1971
Service Dates of Minority Members: Feb. 19,1969-Jan. 3,1971

Majority					Minority				
			Terms in:					Terms in:	
Rank Name	Party	State	House	Comm.	Rank Name	Party	State	House	Comm.
Chr Griffiths, Martha W.	Dem	Mich.	8	2	RM May, Catherine D.	Rep	Wash.	6	2
2nd Green, Edith S.	Dem	Ore.	8	2					

Departures from the House:	Majority	Minority	
Defeated for Reelection	None	May, Catherine D.	Wash. Rep

HOUSE BEAUTY SHOP / 92nd Congress

Service Dates of Committee Chair: Feb. 22,1971-Jan. 3,1973
Service Dates of Majority Members: Feb. 22,1971-Jan. 3,1973
Service Dates of Minority Members: Feb. 22,1971-Jan. 3,1973

Majority

Rank	Name	Party	State	Terms in: House	Terms in: Comm.
Chr	Griffiths, Martha W.	Dem	Mich.	9	3
2nd	Green, Edith S.	Dem	Ore.	9	3

Minority

Rank	Name	Party	State	Terms in: House	Terms in: Comm.
RM	Heckler, Margaret M.	Rep	Mass.	3	1

HOUSE BEAUTY SHOP / 93rd Congress

Service Dates of Committee Chair: Feb. 5,1973-Dec. 31,1974
Service Dates of Majority Members: Feb. 5,1973-Dec. 31,1974
Service Dates of Minority Members: Feb. 5,1973-Jan. 3,1975

Majority

Rank	Name	Party	State	Terms in: House	Terms in: Comm.
Chr	Griffiths, Martha W.	Dem	Mich.	10	4
2nd	Green, Edith S.	Dem	Ore.	10	4

Minority

Rank	Name	Party	State	Terms in: House	Terms in: Comm.
RM	Heckler, Margaret M.	Rep	Mass.	4	2

Changes:

Majority:

Griffiths, Martha W.	Dem	Mich.	Dec. 31,1974	Resigned and retired.
Green, Edith S.	Dem	Ore.	Dec. 31,1974	Resigned and retired.

Departures from Committee:
No new assignment

Majority
None

Minority
Heckler, Margaret M. Mass. Rep

HOUSE BEAUTY SHOP / 94th Congress

Service Dates of Committee Chair: Mar. 24,1975-Jan. 3,1977
Service Dates of Majority Members: Mar. 24,1975-Jan. 3,1977
Service Dates of Minority Members: Mar. 24,1975-Jan. 3,1977

Majority

Rank	Name	Party	State	Terms in: House	Terms in: Comm.
Chr	Burke, Yvonne Brathwaite	Dem	Cal.	2	1
2nd	Meyner, Helen S.	Dem	N.J.	1	1

Minority

Rank	Name	Party	State	Terms in: House	Terms in: Comm.
RM	Smith, Virginia D.	Rep	Neb.	1	1

HOUSE SELECT COMMITTEE: PARKING ON HOUSE SIDE OF THE CAPITOL

Jurisdiction, 1969

From House Resolution 282, 91st Congress, First Session, March 13, 1969:

[Section 1 (b)]

The said committee is hereby authorized to exercise direction over the Sergeant at Arms of the House of Representatives in the assignment of space for outdoor parking of automobiles in squares 639, south of 635, and 692, located adjacent to the House Office Buildings, and for all other outdoor parking of automobiles on the House side of the United States Capitol Grounds.

[Section 2]

The House Office Building Commission...is hereby authorized to delegate so much of such duties as pertain to the direction and supervision of the Architect of the Capitol in the assignment of space for parking of automobiles in the garages in the Rayburn House Office Building, the Cannon House Office Building, and the two underground garages in squares 637 and 691, located adjacent to the House Office Buildings, and the issuance of regulations governing such assignments, to the select committee herein created.

Termination, 1975

The Select Committee was extended by House Resolutions 24 (92-1) and 145 (93-1) and terminated at the end of the 93rd Congress. A Subcommittee on Parking was created by the Committee on House Administration.

HOUSE SELECT COMMITTEE: PARKING ON HOUSE SIDE OF THE CAPITOL / 91st Congress

Service Dates of Committee Chair: Mar. 13,1969-Jan. 3,1971
Service Dates of Majority Members: Mar. 13,1969-Jan. 3,1971
Service Dates of Minority Members: Mar. 13,1969-Jan. 3,1971

Majority

Rank	Name	Party	State	Terms in: House	Terms in: Comm.
Chr	Sisk, B. F.	Dem	Cal.	8	1
2nd	Hays, Wayne L.	Dem	Ohio	11	1

Minority

Rank	Name	Party	State	Terms in: House	Terms in: Comm.
RM	Gross, Harold R.	Rep	Iowa	11	1

HOUSE SELECT COMMITTEE: PARKING ON HOUSE SIDE OF THE CAPITOL / 92nd Congress

Service Dates of Committee Chair: Feb. 10,1971-Jan. 3,1973
Service Dates of Majority Members: Feb. 10,1971-Jan. 3,1973
Service Dates of Minority Members: Feb. 10,1971-Jan. 3,1973

Majority

Rank	Name	Party	State	Terms in: House	Terms in: Comm.
Chr	Sisk, B. F.	Dem	Cal.	9	2
2nd	Hays, Wayne L.	Dem	Ohio	12	2

Minority

Rank	Name	Party	State	Terms in: House	Terms in: Comm.
RM	Gross, Harold R.	Rep	Iowa	12	2

HOUSE SELECT COMMITTEE: PARKING ON HOUSE SIDE OF THE CAPITOL / 93rd Congress

Service Dates of Committee Chair: Feb. 7,1973-Jan. 3,1975
Service Dates of Majority Members: Feb. 7,1973-Jan. 3,1975
Service Dates of Minority Members: Feb. 7,1973-Jan. 3,1975

Majority

Rank	Name	Party	State	Terms in: House	Comm.
Chr	Sisk, B. F.	Dem	Cal.	10	3
2nd	Hays, Wayne L.	Dem	Ohio	13	3

Minority

Rank	Name	Party	State	Terms in: House	Comm.
RM	Gross, Harold R.	Rep	Iowa	13	3

HOUSE SELECT COMMITTEE: CRIME

Jurisdiction, 1969

From House Resolution 17, 91st Congress, First Session, May 1, 1969:

[Section 2]

The committee is authorized and directed to conduct a full and complete investigation and study of all aspects of crime in the United States, including:

(1) its elements, causes, and extent;
(2) the preparation, collection, and dissemination of statistics thereon, and the availability of reciprocity of information among law enforcement agencies, Federal, State, and local, including exchange of information with foreign nations;
(3) the adequacy of law enforcement and the administration of justice, including constitutional issues pertaining thereto;
(4) the effect of crime and disturbances in the metropolitan urban areas;
(5) the effect, directly or indirectly, of crime on the commerce of the Nation;
(6) the treatment and rehabilitation of persons convicted of crimes;
(7) measures for the reduction, control, or prevention of crime;
(8) measures for the improvement of
 (a) detection of crime,
 (b) law enforcement, including increased cooperation among the agencies thereof,
 (c) the administration of justice; and
(9) measures and programs for increased respect for the law.

Termination, 1973

The Select Committee was extended by House Resolution 115 (92-1), and House Resolution 256 (93-1). It was terminated upon the filing of its final report, House Report 358 (93-1) on June 29, 1973.

HOUSE SELECT COMMITTEE: CRIME / 91st Congress

Service Dates of Committee Chair: May 1,1969-Jan. 3,1971
Service Dates of Majority Members: May 1,1969-Jan. 3,1971
Service Dates of Minority Members: May 1,1969-Jan. 3,1970

Majority

Rank Name	Party	State	Terms in: House	Terms in: Comm.
Chr Pepper, Claude D.	Dem	Fla.	4	1
2nd Griffiths, Martha W.	Dem	Mich.	8	1
3rd Nix, Robert N. C.	Dem	Penn.	7	1
4th Waldie, Jerome R.	Dem	Cal.	3	1

Minority

Rank Name	Party	State	Terms in: House	Terms in: Comm.
RM1 Watson, Albert W.	Rep	S.C.	4	1
RM2 2nd Wiggins, Charles E.	Rep	Cal.	2	1
3rd Denney, Robert V.	Rep	Neb.	2	1

Changes:

Ranking Member:				
Watson, Albert W.	Rep	S.C.	Nov. 16,1970	Left committee (effective Nov. 4,1970); no new assignment.
Wiggins, Charles E.	Rep	Cal.	Nov. 16,1970	Succeeded Watson as Ranking Minority Member (effective Nov. 4,1970).
Minority:				
Denney, Robert V.	Rep	Neb.	July 30,1970	Left committee; no new assignment.
Steiger, Sam	Rep	Ariz.	July 30,1970	Replaced Denney.
Watson, Albert W.	Rep	S.C.	Nov. 16,1970	Left committee (effective Nov. 4,1970); no new assignment.
Winn, Larry Jr.	Rep	Kans.	Nov. 16,1970	Replaced Watson.

Departures from Committee:

	Majority		Minority
No new assignment	Griffiths, Martha W.	Mich. Dem	None
	Nix, Robert N. C.	Penn. Dem	

HOUSE SELECT COMMITTEE: CRIME / 92nd Congress

Service Dates of Committee Chair: Mar. 15,1971-Jan. 3,1973
Service Dates of Majority Members: Mar. 15,1971-Jan. 3,1973
Service Dates of Minority Members: Mar. 15,1971-Jan. 3,1973

Majority

Rank	Name	Party	State	Terms in: House	Terms in: Comm.
Chr	Pepper, Claude D.	Dem	Fla.	5	2
2nd	Waldie, Jerome R.	Dem	Cal.	4	2
3rd	Brasco, Frank J.	Dem	N.Y.	3	1
4th	Mann, James R.	Dem	S.C.	2	1
5th	Murphy, Morgan F.	Dem	Ill.	1	1
6th	Rangel, Charles B.	Dem	N.Y.	1	1

Minority

Rank	Name	Party	State	Terms in: House	Terms in: Comm.
RM	Wiggins, Charles E.	Rep	Cal.	3	2
2nd	Steiger, Sam	Rep	Ariz.	3	2
3rd	Winn, Larry Jr.	Rep	Kans.	3	2
4th	Sandman, Charles W. Jr.	Rep	N.J.	3	1
5th	Keating, William J.	Rep	Ohio	1	1

HOUSE SELECT COMMITTEE: CRIME / 93rd Congress

Service Dates of Committee Chair: Feb. 28,1973-June 29,1973
Service Dates of Majority Members: Feb. 28,1973-June 29,1973
Service Dates of Minority Members: Feb. 28,1973-June 29,1973

Majority

Rank	Name	Party	State	Terms in: House	Terms in: Comm.
Chr	Pepper, Claude D.	Dem	Fla.	6	3
2nd	Waldie, Jerome R.	Dem	Cal.	5	3
3rd	Brasco, Frank J.	Dem	N.Y.	4	2
4th	Mann, James R.	Dem	S.C.	3	2
5th	Murphy, Morgan F.	Dem	Ill.	2	2
6th	Rangel, Charles B.	Dem	N.Y.	2	2

Minority

Rank	Name	Party	State	Terms in: House	Terms in: Comm.
RM	Wiggins, Charles E.	Rep	Cal.	4	3
2nd	Steiger, Sam	Rep	Ariz.	4	3
3rd	Winn, Larry Jr.	Rep	Kans.	4	3
4th	Sandman, Charles W. Jr.	Rep	N.J.	4	2
5th	Keating, William J.	Rep	Ohio	2	2

HOUSE SELECT COMMITTEE: HOUSE RESTAURANT

Jurisdiction, 1969

From House Resolution 472, 91st Congress, First Session, July 10, 1969:

[Section 1 (b)]

On and after July 15, 1969, until otherwise ordered by the House, the Architect of the Capitol shall perform the duties vested in him by section 208 of Public Law 812, 76th Congress (40 U.S.C. 174k) under the direction of the select committee herein created.

From House Resolution 317, 92nd Congress, First Session, March 25, 1971:

[Section 2 (a)]

Notwithstanding any other authority with respect to the jurisdiction and control over the management of the House Restaurant and the cafeteria and other food service facilities of the House of Representatives, the jurisdiction over such restaurant and facilities and authority over the direction and supervision of the immediate management and operation thereof shall be vested in the Committee on House Administration; and the immediate management and operation of such restaurant and facilities may be vested in such official or other authority, acting as the agent of the committee, as the committee may designate.

Termination, 1975

The Select Committee was extended by House Resolution 111 (93-2) and terminated at the end of the 93rd Congress. An Ad Hoc Subcommittee on the Restaurant was created by the Committee on House Administration.

HOUSE SELECT COMMITTEE: HOUSE RESTAURANT / 91st Congress

Service Dates of Committee Chair: July 10,1969-Jan. 3,1971
Service Dates of Majority Members: July 10,1969-Jan. 3,1971
Service Dates of Minority Members: July 10,1969-Jan. 3,1971

Majority

Rank	Name	Party	State	Terms in: House	Terms in: Comm.
Chr	Kluczynski, John C.	Dem	Ill.	10	1
2nd	Steed, Thomas J.	Dem	Okla.	11	1
3rd	Cabell, Earle	Dem	Tex.	3	1

Minority

Rank	Name	Party	State	Terms in: House	Terms in: Comm.
RM	Collier, Harold R.	Rep	Ill.	7	1
2nd	Thomson, Vernon W.	Rep	Wisc.	5	1

HOUSE RESTAURANT / 92nd Congress

Service Dates of Committee Chair: Mar. 29,1971-Jan. 3,1973
Service Dates of Majority Members: Mar. 29,1971-Jan. 3,1973
Service Dates of Minority Members: Mar. 29,1971-June 30,1972

Majority

Rank	Name	Party	State	Terms in: House	Terms in: Comm.
Chr	Kluczynski, John C.	Dem	Ill.	11	2
2nd	Steed, Thomas J.	Dem	Okla.	12	2
3rd	Cabell, Earle	Dem	Tex.	4	2

Minority

Rank	Name	Party	State	Terms in: House	Terms in: Comm.
RM1	Collier, Harold R.	Rep	Ill.	8	2
RM2	2nd Thomson, Vernon W.	Rep	Wisc.	6	2

Changes:

Ranking Member:

Collier, Harold R.	Rep	Ill.	June 30,1972	Left committee; no new assignment.
Thomson, Vernon W.	Rep	Wisc.	June 30,1972	Succeeded Collier as Ranking Minority Member.

Minority:

Collier, Harold R.	Rep	Ill.	June 30,1972	Left committee; no new assignment.
Johnson, Albert W.	Rep	Penn.	July 18,1972	Replaced Collier.

Departures from the House:	Majority			Minority
Defeated for Reelection	Cabell, Earle	Tex.	Dem	None

HOUSE RESTAURANT / 93rd Congress

Service Dates of Committee Chair: Feb. 7,1973-Jan. 3,1975
Service Dates of Majority Members: Feb. 7,1973-Jan. 3,1975
Service Dates of Minority Members: Feb. 7,1973-Jan. 3,1975

Majority

Rank Name	Party	State	Terms in: House	Terms in: Comm.
Chr Kluczynski, John C.	Dem	Ill.	12	3
2nd Steed, Thomas J.	Dem	Okla.	13	3
3rd Burke, James A.	Dem	Mass.	8	1

Minority

Rank Name	Party	State	Terms in: House	Terms in: Comm.
RM Thomson, Vernon W.	Rep	Wisc.	7	3
2nd Johnson, Albert W.	Rep	Penn.	6	2

HOUSE SELECT COMMITTEE: UNITED STATES INVOLVEMENT IN SOUTHEAST ASIA

Jurisdiction, 1970

Title of House Resolution 976, as amended, 91st Congress, Second Session, June 8, 1970:

Resolution to authorize a select committee of the House to study firsthand the recent developments in Southeast Asia and then report its findings to the House of Representatives within forty-five days of its adoption.

Termination, 1970

The Select Committee was terminated upon the filing of its final report, House Report 1276 (91-2) on July 6, 1970.

HOUSE SELECT COMMITTEE: UNITED STATES INVOLVEMENT IN SOUTHEAST ASIA / 91st Congress

Service Dates of Committee Chair: June 15,1970-July 6,1970
Service Dates of Majority Members: June 15,1970-July 6,1970
Service Dates of Minority Members: June 15,1970-July 6,1970

Majority					Minority				
			Terms in:					Terms in:	
Rank Name	Party	State	House	Comm.	Rank Name	Party	State	House	Comm.
Chr Montgomery, G.V. (Sonny)	Dem	Miss.	2	1	RM Adair, E. Ross	Rep	Ind.	10	1
2nd Smith, Neal	Dem	Iowa	6	1	2nd Robison, Howard W.	Rep	N.Y.	7	1
3rd Hawkins, Augustus F.	Dem	Cal.	4	1	3rd Keith, Hastings	Rep	Mass.	6	1
4th Anderson, William R.	Dem	Tenn.	3	1	4th Clancy, Donald D.	Rep	Ohio	5	1
5th Hamilton, Lee H.	Dem	Ind.	3	1	5th Watson, Albert W.	Rep	S.C.	4	1
6th Mollohan, Robert H.	Dem	W.Va.	3	1	6th Hansen, Orval H.	Rep	Ida.	1	1

HOUSE SELECT COMMITTEE: COMMITTEES I (Bolling)

Jurisdiction, 1973

From House Resolution 132, 93rd Congress, First Session, January 31, 1973:

[Paragraph 2]

The select committee is authorized and directed to conduct a thorough and complete study with respect to the operation and implementation of rules X and XI of the Rules of the House of Representatives, including committee structure of the House, the number and optimum size of committees, their jurisdiction, the number of subcommittees, committee rules and procedures, media coverage of meetings, staffing, space, equipment, and other committee facilities.

Termination, 1974

The Select Committee was terminated by authority of House Resolution 132 (93-1) at the end of the 93rd Congress on December 20,1974.

HOUSE SELECT COMMITTEE: COMMITTEES I (Bolling) / 93rd Congress

Service Dates of Committee Chair: Jan. 31,1973-Dec. 20,1974
Service Dates of Majority Members: Jan. 31,1973-Dec. 20,1974
Service Dates of Minority Members: Jan. 31,1973-Dec. 20,1974

Majority

Rank Name	Party	State	Terms in: House	Terms in: Comm.
Chr Bolling, Richard W.	Dem	Mo.	13	1
2nd Stephens, Robert G. Jr.	Dem	Ga.	7	1
3rd Culver, John C.	Dem	Iowa	5	1
4th Meeds, Lloyd	Dem	Wash.	5	1
5th Sarbanes, Paul S.	Dem	Md.	2	1

Minority

Rank Name	Party	State	Terms in: House	Terms in: Comm.
VCh Martin, David T.	Rep	Neb.	7	1
2nd Frelinghuysen, Peter H.B.	Rep	N.J.	11	1
3rd Wiggins, Charles E.	Rep	Cal.	4	1
4th Steiger, William A.	Rep	Wisc.	4	1
5th Young, C. W. Bill	Rep	Fla.	2	1

HOUSE SELECT COMMITTEE: AGING (Permanent)

Jurisdiction, 1974

From House Resolution 988, as amended, 93rd Congress, Second Session, October 2, 1974:

[Section 6 (h)]

There shall be in the House the permanent Select Committee on Aging, which shall not have legislative jurisdiction but which shall have jurisdiction--

(1) to conduct a continuing comprehensive study and review of the problems of the older American, including but not limited to income maintenance, housing, health (including medical research), welfare, employment, education, recreation, and participation in family and community life [as] self-respecting citizens;
(2) to study the use of all practicable means and methods of encouraging the development of public and private programs and policies which will assist the older American in taking a full part in national life and which will encourage the utilization of the knowledge, skills, special aptitudes, and abilities of older Americans to contribute to a better quality of life for all Americans;
(3) to develop policies that would encourage the coordination of both governmental and private programs designed to deal with problems of aging; and
(4) to review any recommendations made by the President or by the White House Conference on Aging relating to programs or policies affecting older Americans.

Jurisdiction, 1992

The jurisdiction of the Permanent Select Committee has not changed since its inception in 1974.

HOUSE SELECT COMMITTEE: AGING (Permanent) / 94th Congress

Service Dates of Committee Chair: Feb. 6,1975-Jan. 3,1977
Service Dates of Majority Members: Feb. 6,1975-Jan. 3,1977
Service Dates of Minority Members: Feb. 6,1975-Jan. 3,1977

Majority

Rank	Name	Party	State	Terms in: House	Terms in: Comm.
Chr	Randall, William J.	Dem	Mo.	9	1
2nd	Pepper, Claude D.	Dem	Fla.	7	1
3rd	Matsunaga, Spark M.	Dem	Hai.	7	1
4th	Roybal, Edward R.	Dem	Cal.	7	1
5th	Rooney, Fred B.	Dem	Penn.	7	1
6th	Biaggi, Mario	Dem	N.Y.	4	1
7th	Flowers, Walter	Dem	Ala.	4	1
8th	Andrews, Ike F.	Dem	N.C.	2	1
9th	Burton, John L.	Dem	Cal.	2	1
10th	Beard, Edward P.	Dem	R.I.	1	1
11th	Blouin, Michael T.	Dem	Iowa	1	1
12th	Bonker, Don L.	Dem	Wash.	1	1
13th	Downey, Thomas J.	Dem	N.Y.	1	1
14th	Florio, James J.	Dem	N.J.	1	1
15th	Ford, Harold E.	Dem	Tenn.	1	1
16th	Hughes, William J.	Dem	N.J.	1	1
17th	Lloyd, Marilyn	Dem	Tenn.	1	1
18th	Santini, James D.	Dem	Nev.	1	1

Minority

Rank	Name	Party	State	Terms in: House	Terms in: Comm.
RM	Wilson, Robert C.	Rep	Cal.	12	1
2nd	Wampler, William C.	Rep	Va.	6	1
3rd	Hammerschmidt, John Paul	Rep	Ark.	5	1
4th	Heinz, H. John III	Rep	Penn.	3	1
5th	Cohen, William S.	Rep	Me.	2	1
6th	Sarasin, Ronald A.	Rep	Conn.	2	1
7th	Walsh, William F.	Rep	N.Y.	2	1
8th	Grassley, Charles E.	Rep	Iowa	1	1

Vacancy Filled:
Majority: 3rd seat by Matsunaga on Feb. 10,1975

Additions:

Majority:	19th Risenhoover, Theodore M.	Dem	Okla.	Feb. 27,1975
Minority:	9th Gude, Gilbert	Rep	Md.	Feb. 27,1975

Departures from the House:	**Majority**			**Minority**		
Elected to U.S. Senate	Matsunaga, Spark M.	Hai.	Dem	Heinz, H. John III	Penn.	Rep
Retired	Randall, William J.	Mo.	Dem	Gude, Gilbert	Md.	Rep

HOUSE SELECT COMMITTEE: AGING (Permanent) / 95th Congress

Service Dates of Committee Chair: Jan. 19,1977-Jan. 3,1979
Service Dates of Majority Members: Jan. 19,1977-Jan. 3,1979
Service Dates of Minority Members: Jan. 31,1977-Jan. 3,1979

Majority

Rank Name	Party	State	Terms in: House	Terms in: Comm.
Chr Pepper, Claude D.	Dem	Fla.	8	2
2nd Roybal, Edward R.	Dem	Cal.	8	2
3rd Rooney, Fred B.	Dem	Penn.	8	2
4th Biaggi, Mario	Dem	N.Y.	5	2
5th Flowers, Walter	Dem	Ala.	5	2
6th Andrews, Ike F.	Dem	N.C.	3	2
7th Burton, John L.	Dem	Cal.	3	2
8th Beard, Edward P.	Dem	R.I.	2	2
9th Blouin, Michael T.	Dem	Iowa	2	2
10th Bonker, Don L.	Dem	Wash.	2	2
11th Downey, Thomas J.	Dem	N.Y.	2	2
12th Florio, James J.	Dem	N.J.	2	2
13th Ford, Harold E.	Dem	Tenn.	2	2
14th Hughes, William J.	Dem	N.J.	2	2
15th Lloyd, Marilyn	Dem	Tenn.	2	2
16th Santini, James D.	Dem	Nev.	2	2
17th Risenhoover, Theodore M.	Dem	Okla.	2	2
18th Drinan, Robert F.	Dem	Mass.	4	1
19th Evans, David W.	Dem	Ind.	2	1
20th Meyner, Helen S.	Dem	N.J.	2	1
21st Russo, Martin A.	Dem	Ill.	2	1
22nd Lundine, Stanley N.	Dem	N.Y.	2	1
23rd Oakar, Mary Rose	Dem	Ohio	1	1

Minority

Rank Name	Party	State	Terms in: House	Terms in: Comm.
RM1 Wilson, Robert C.	Rep	Cal.	13	2
RM2 2nd Wampler, William C.	Rep	Va.	7	2
3rd Hammerschmidt, John Paul	Rep	Ark.	6	2
4th Cohen, William S.	Rep	Me.	3	2
5th Sarasin, Ronald A.	Rep	Conn.	3	2
6th Walsh, William F.	Rep	N.Y.	3	2
7th Grassley, Charles E.	Rep	Iowa	2	2
8th Abdnor, James	Rep	S.D.	3	1
9th Cochran, Thad	Rep	Miss.	3	1
10th Rinaldo, Matthew J.	Rep	N.J.	3	1
11th Marks, Marc L.	Rep	Penn.	1	1

Note: Marilyn Lloyd (Dem-Tenn.) changed her name to Marilyn Lloyd Bouquard during the adjournment of the 95th Congress.

Changes:

Ranking Member:				
RM1 Wilson, Robert C.	Rep	Cal.	Aug. 1,1977	Moved to Select Intelligence as Ranking Minority Member.
RM2 Wampler, William C.	Rep	Va.	Aug. 1,1977	Succeeded Wilson as Ranking Minority Member.
Minority:				
Wilson, Robert C.	Rep	Cal.	Aug. 1,1977	Moved to Select Intelligence as Ranking Minority Member.
Regula, Ralph S.	Rep	Ohio	Aug. 1,1977	Replaced Wilson.
Walsh, William F.	Rep	N.Y.	July 25,1978	Left committee; no new assignment.
Cunningham, John E.	Rep	Wash.	July 25,1978	Replaced Walsh.
Cochran, Thad	Rep	Miss.	Dec. 26,1978	Resigned; elected to U.S. Senate.

Departures from the House:	**Majority**			**Minority**		
Elected to U.S. Senate	None			Cohen, William S.	Me.	Rep
Defeated for Reelection	Blouin, Michael T.	Iowa	Dem	Cunningham, John E.	Wash.	Rep
	Meyner, Helen S.	N.J.	Dem			
	Rooney, Fred B.	Penn.	Dem			
Defeated for Renomination	Risenhoover, Theodore M.	Okla.	Dem	None		
Lost Nomination for U.S. Senate	Flowers, Walter	Ala.	Dem	None		
Lost Election for Governor	None			Sarasin, Ronald A.	Conn.	Rep

HOUSE SELECT COMMITTEE: AGING (Permanent) / 96th Congress

Service Dates of Committee Chair: Jan. 25,1979-Jan. 3,1981
Service Dates of Majority Members: Jan. 25,1979-Jan. 3,1981
Service Dates of Minority Members: Jan. 25,1979-Jan. 3,1981

Majority

Rank	Name	Party	State	Terms in: House	Terms in: Comm.
Chr	Pepper, Claude D.	Dem	Fla.	9	3
2nd	Roybal, Edward R.	Dem	Cal.	9	3
3rd	Biaggi, Mario	Dem	N.Y.	6	3
4th	Andrews, Ike F.	Dem	N.C.	4	3
5th	Burton, John L.	Dem	Cal.	4	3
6th	Beard, Edward P.	Dem	R.I.	3	3
7th	Bonker, Don L.	Dem	Wash.	3	3
8th	Downey, Thomas J.	Dem	N.Y.	3	3
9th	Florio, James J.	Dem	N.J.	3	3
10th	Ford, Harold E.	Dem	Tenn.	3	3
11th	Hughes, William J.	Dem	N.J.	3	3
12th	Bouquard, Marilyn Lloyd	Dem	Tenn.	3	3
13th	Santini, James D.	Dem	Nev.	3	3
14th	Drinan, Robert F.	Dem	Mass.	5	2
15th	Evans, David W.	Dem	Ind.	3	2
16th	Russo, Martin A.	Dem	Ill.	3	2
17th	Lundine, Stanley N.	Dem	N.Y.	3	2
18th	Oakar, Mary Rose	Dem	Ohio	2	2
19th	Holtzman, Elizabeth	Dem	N.Y.	4	1
20th	Lloyd, James F.	Dem	Cal.	3	1
21st	Luken, Thomas A.	Dem	Ohio	3	1
22nd	Watkins, Wesley W.	Dem	Okla.	2	1
23rd	Gudger, V. Lamar	Dem	N.C.	2	1
24th	Ferraro, Geraldine A.	Dem	N.Y.	1	1
25th	Byron, Beverly B.	Dem	Md.	1	1
26th	Ratchford, William R.	Dem	Conn.	1	1
27th	Mica, Daniel A.	Dem	Fla.	1	1
28th	Stack, Edward J.	Dem	Fla.	1	1
29th	Waxman, Henry A.	Dem	Cal.	3	1
30th	Synar, Michael L.	Dem	Okla.	1	1

Minority

Rank	Name	Party	State	Terms in: House	Terms in: Comm.
RM	Grassley, Charles E.	Rep	Iowa	3	3
2nd	Wampler, William C.	Rep	Va.	8	3
3rd	Hammerschmidt, John Paul	Rep	Ark.	7	3
4th	Abdnor, James	Rep	S.D.	4	2
5th	Rinaldo, Matthew J.	Rep	N.J.	4	2
6th	Marks, Marc L.	Rep	Penn.	2	2
7th	Regula, Ralph S.	Rep	Ohio	4	2
8th	Dornan, Robert K.	Rep	Cal.	2	1
10th	Hollenbeck, Harold C.	Rep	N.J.	2	1
11th	Green, S. William	Rep	N.Y.	2	1
12th	Whittaker, Robert	Rep	Kans.	1	1
13th	Shumway, Norman D.	Rep	Cal.	1	1
14th	Hopkins, Larry J.	Rep	Ky.	1	1
15th	Snowe, Olympia J. B.	Rep	Me.	1	1
16th	Lungren, Daniel E.	Rep	Cal.	1	1

Notes: The minority membership following William Green as originally appointed on Jan. 25,1979 was listed as follows: Hopkins, Lungren, Shumway, Snowe and Whittaker. These members were reappointed on Feb. 21,1979 in the order shown above. Marilyn Lloyd Bouquard (Dem-Tenn.) changed her name from Marilyn Lloyd during the adjournment of the 95th Congress.

Vacancies Filled:
Majority: 29th and 30th seats by Waxman and Synar respectively on Feb. 21,1979.
Minority: 6th seat by Marks on Feb. 21,1979.

Changes:
Majority:

Beard, Edward P.	Dem	R.I.	Feb. 8,1979	Left committee; no new assignment.
Atkinson, Eugene V.	Dem	Penn.	Feb. 21,1979	Replaced Beard.

	Majority			Minority		
Departures from the House:						
Elected to U.S. Senate	None			Abdnor, James	S.D.	Rep
				Grassley, Charles E.	Iowa	Rep
Defeated for Reelection	Gudger, V. Lamar	N.C.	Dem	None		
	Lloyd, James F.	Cal.	Dem			
Defeated for Renomination	Stack, Edward J.	Fla.	Dem	None		
Lost Election to U.S. Senate	Holtzman, Elizabeth	N.Y.	Dem	None		
Retired	Drinan, Robert F.	Mass.	Dem	None		
Departures from Committee:						
Moved to Appropriations	Watkins, Wesley W.	Okla.	Dem	Green, S. William	N.Y.	Rep
Moved to Energy & Commerce	None			Whittaker, Robert	Kans.	Rep
No new assignment	Russo, Martin A.	Ill.	Dem	Hopkins, Larry J.	Ky.	Rep

HOUSE SELECT COMMITTEE: AGING (Permanent) / 97th Congress

Service Dates of Committee Chair: Feb. 5,1981-Jan. 3,1983
Service Dates of Majority Members: Feb. 5,1981-Jan. 3,1983
Service Dates of Minority Members: Feb. 5,1981-Jan. 3,1983

Majority

Rank	Name	Party	State	Terms in: House	Terms in: Comm.
Chr	Pepper, Claude D.	Dem	Fla.	10	4
2nd	Roybal, Edward R.	Dem	Cal.	10	4
3rd	Biaggi, Mario	Dem	N.Y.	7	4
4th	Andrews, Ike F.	Dem	N.C.	5	4
5th	Burton, John L.	Dem	Cal.	5	4
6th	Bonker, Don L.	Dem	Wash.	4	4
7th	Downey, Thomas J.	Dem	N.Y.	4	4
8th	Florio, James J.	Dem	N.J.	4	4
9th	Ford, Harold E.	Dem	Tenn.	4	4
10th	Hughes, William J.	Dem	N.J.	4	4
11th	Bouquard, Marilyn Lloyd	Dem	Tenn.	4	4
12th	Santini, James D.	Dem	Nev.	4	4
13th	Evans, David W.	Dem	Ind.	4	3
14th	Lundine, Stanley N.	Dem	N.Y.	4	3
15th	Oakar, Mary Rose	Dem	Ohio	3	3
16th	Luken, Thomas A.	Dem	Ohio	4	2
17th	Ferraro, Geraldine A.	Dem	N.Y.	2	2
18th	Byron, Beverly B.	Dem	Md.	2	2
19th	Ratchford, William R.	Dem	Conn.	2	2
20th	Mica, Daniel A.	Dem	Fla.	2	2
21st	Waxman, Henry A.	Dem	Cal.	4	2
22nd	Synar, Michael L.	Dem	Okla.	2	2
23rd	Atkinson, Eugene V.	Dem	Penn.	2	2
24th	Derrick, Butler C. Jr.	Dem	S.C.	4	1
25th	Vento, Bruce F.	Dem	Minn.	3	1
26th	Frank, Barney	Dem	Mass.	1	1
27th	Lantos, Tom	Dem	Cal.	1	1
28th	Shamansky, Robert N.	Dem	Ohio	1	1
29th	Wyden, Ron	Dem	Ore.	1	1
30th	Albosta, Donald J.	Dem	Mich.	2	1
31st	Crockett, George W. Jr.	Dem	Mich.	2	1

Minority

Rank	Name	Party	State	Terms in: House	Terms in: Comm.
RM	Rinaldo, Matthew J.	Rep	N.J.	5	3
2nd	Wampler, William C.	Rep	Va.	9	4
3rd	Hammerschmidt, John Paul	Rep	Ark.	8	4
4th	Marks, Marc L.	Rep	Penn.	3	3
5th	Regula, Ralph S.	Rep	Ohio	5	3
6th	Dornan, Robert K.	Rep	Cal.	3	2
7th	Hollenbeck, Harold C.	Rep	N.J.	3	2
8th	Shumway, Norman D.	Rep	Cal.	2	2
9th	Snowe, Olympia J. B.	Rep	Me.	2	2
10th	Lungren, Daniel E.	Rep	Cal.	2	2
11th	Fenwick, Millicent H.	Rep	N.J.	4	1
12th	Jeffords, James M.	Rep	Vt.	4	1
13th	Bereuter, Douglas K.	Rep	Neb.	2	1
14th	Tauke, Thomas J.	Rep	Iowa	2	1
15th	Petri, Thomas E.	Rep	Wisc.	2	1
16th	Gregg, Judd	Rep	N.H.	1	1
17th	Coats, Daniel R.	Rep	Ind.	1	1
18th	Wortley, George	Rep	N.Y.	1	1
19th	Daub, Hal	Rep	Neb.	1	1
20th	Craig, Larry E.	Rep	Ida.	1	1
21st	Roberts, Pat	Rep	Kans.	1	1
22nd	Hendon, William M.	Rep	N.C.	1	1
23rd	Carman, Gregory W.	Rep	N.Y.	1	1

Notes: The committee size and party ratio changed to 32 Democrats and 23 Republicans on May 13,1981. Eugene V. Atkinson of Pennsylvania resigned the Democratic Party and joined the Republican Party on Oct. 14,1981, leading to another change in size and party ratio to 31 Democrats and 24 Republicans on Oct. 14,1982.

Vacancies Filled:
Majority: 30th and 31st seats by Albosta and Crockett respectively on Mar. 3,1981.
Minority: 7th seat by Hollenbeck on Mar. 3,1981.

Addition:

Majority:	32nd	Boner, William H.	Dem	Tenn.	May 13,1981	
Minority:	24th	Atkinson, Eugene V.	Rep	Penn.	Oct. 14,1982	(Rejoined the committee as a Republican.)

Changes:

	Name	Party	State	Date	Change
Majority:					
	Atkinson, Eugene V.	Dem	Penn.	Oct. 14,1982	Resigned Democratic Party; lost majority assignments.
Minority:					
	Bereuter, Douglas K.	Rep	Neb.	Apr. 29,1981	Moved to Banking, Finance & Urban Affairs.
	Evans, T. Cooper	Rep	Iowa	Sep. 21,1981	Replaced Bereuter.
	Dornan, Robert K.	Rep	Cal.	Aug. 12,1982	Left committee; no new assignment.
	Heckler, Margaret M.	Rep	Mass.	Aug. 12,1982	Replaced Dornan.

Departures from the House:	Majority			Minority		
Defeated for Reelection	Shamansky, Robert N.	Ohio	Dem	Hollenbeck, Harold C.	N.J.	Rep
				Wampler, William C.	Va.	Rep
				Hendon, William M.	N.C.	Rep
				Atkinson, Eugene V.	Penn.	Rep
				Heckler, Margaret M.	Mass.	Rep
Defeated for Renomination	Evans, David W.	Ind.	Dem	None		
Lost Election to U.S. Senate	None			Fenwick, Millicent H.	N.J.	Rep
Lost Nomination to U.S. Senate	Santini, James D.	Nev.	Dem	None		
Retired	Burton, John L.	Cal.	Dem	Carman, Gregory W.	N.Y.	Rep
				Marks, Marc L.	Penn.	Rep
Departures from Committee:						
Moved to Select Children, Youth & Families	None			Coats, Daniel R.	Ind.	Rep
Moved to Public Works & Transportation	None			Petri, Thomas E.	Wisc.	Rep

HOUSE SELECT COMMITTEE: AGING (Permanent) / 98th Congress

Service Dates of Committee Chair: Feb. 8,1983-Jan. 3,1985
Service Dates of Majority Members: Feb. 8,1983-Jan. 3,1985
Service Dates of Minority Members: Feb. 8,1983-Jan. 3,1985

Majority

Rank	Name	Party	State	Terms in: House	Terms in: Comm.
Chr	Roybal, Edward R.	Dem	Cal.	11	5
2nd	Pepper, Claude D.	Dem	Fla.	11	5
3rd	Biaggi, Mario	Dem	N.Y.	8	5
4th	Andrews, Ike F.	Dem	N.C.	6	5
5th	Bonker, Don L.	Dem	Wash.	5	5
6th	Downey, Thomas J.	Dem	N.Y.	5	5
7th	Florio, James J.	Dem	N.J.	5	5
8th	Ford, Harold E.	Dem	Tenn.	5	5
9th	Hughes, William J.	Dem	N.J.	5	5
10th	Bouquard, Marilyn Lloyd	Dem	Tenn.	5	5
11th	Lundine, Stanley N.	Dem	N.Y.	5	4
12th	Oakar, Mary Rose	Dem	Ohio	4	4
13th	Luken, Thomas A.	Dem	Ohio	5	3
14th	Ferraro, Geraldine A.	Dem	N.Y.	3	3
15th	Byron, Beverly B.	Dem	Md.	3	3
16th	Ratchford, William R.	Dem	Conn.	3	3
17th	Mica, Daniel A.	Dem	Fla.	3	3
18th	Waxman, Henry A.	Dem	Cal.	5	3
19th	Synar, Michael L.	Dem	Okla.	3	3
20th	Derrick, Butler C. Jr.	Dem	S.C.	5	2
21st	Vento, Bruce F.	Dem	Minn.	4	2
22nd	Frank, Barney	Dem	Mass.	2	2
23rd	Lantos, Tom	Dem	Cal.	2	2
24th	Wyden, Ron	Dem	Ore.	2	2
25th	Albosta, Donald J.	Dem	Mich.	3	2
26th	Crockett, George W. Jr.	Dem	Mich.	3	2
27th	Boner, William H.	Dem	Tenn.	3	2
28th	Skelton, Ike	Dem	Mo.	4	1
29th	Hertel, Dennis M.	Dem	Mich.	2	1
30th	Borski, Robert A.	Dem	Penn.	1	1
31st	Boucher, Frederick C.	Dem	Va.	1	1
32nd	Erdreich, Ben	Dem	Ala.	1	1
33rd	MacKay, Kenneth H.	Dem	Fla.	1	1
34th	Reid, Harry M.	Dem	Nev.	1	1
35th	Sisisky, Norman	Dem	Va.	1	1
36th	Vandergriff, Tom	Dem	Tex.	1	1
37th	Wise, Robert E. Jr.	Dem	W.Va.	1	1

Minority

Rank	Name	Party	State	Terms in: House	Terms in: Comm.
RM	Rinaldo, Matthew J.	Rep	N.J.	6	4
2nd	Hammerschmidt, John Paul	Rep	Ark.	9	5
3rd	Regula, Ralph S.	Rep	Ohio	6	4
4th	Shumway, Norman D.	Rep	Cal.	3	3
5th	Snowe, Olympia J. B.	Rep	Me.	3	3
6th	Lungren, Daniel E.	Rep	Cal.	3	3
7th	Jeffords, James M.	Rep	Vt.	5	2
8th	Tauke, Thomas J.	Rep	Iowa	3	2
9th	Gregg, Judd	Rep	N.H.	2	2
10th	Wortley, George	Rep	N.Y.	2	2
11th	Daub, Hal	Rep	Neb.	2	2
12th	Craig, Larry E.	Rep	Ida.	2	2
13th	Roberts, Pat	Rep	Kans.	2	2
14th	Evans, T. Cooper	Rep	Iowa	2	2
15th	Courter, James A.	Rep	N.J.	3	1
16th	Williams, Lyle	Rep	Ohio	3	1
17th	Schneider, Claudine	Rep	R.I.	2	1
18th	Ridge, Thomas J.	Rep	Penn.	1	1
19th	McCain, John	Rep	Ariz.	1	1
20th	Bilirakis, Michael	Rep	Fla.	1	1

Notes: Due to Republican Party gains at the beginning of the 98th Congress, the size and party ratio on this committee was changed to 38 Democrats and 22 Republicans on Mar. 3,1983. Marilyn Lloyd Bouquard (Dem-Tenn.) first voted in this Congress under the resumed name Marilyn Lloyd on Apr. 12,1983.

Additions:

Majority:	38th Richardson, Bill	Dem	N.M.	Mar. 3,1983
Minority:	21st Gekas, George W.	Rep	Penn	Mar. 3,1983
	22nd Siljander, Mark D.	Rep	Mich.	Mar. 3,1983

Changes:

Minority:

Lungren, Daniel E.	Rep	Cal.	Feb. 22,1983	Moved to Joint Economic (reported Mar. 3,1983).
Smith, Christopher H.	Rep	N.J.	Mar. 3,1983	Replaced Lungren.
Roberts, Pat	Rep	Kans.	July 11,1983	Moved to House Administration (reported July 14,1983).
DeWine, Michael	Rep	Ohio	July 14,1983	Replaced Roberts.

Departures from the House:	**Majority**			**Minority**		
Defeated for Reelection	Albosta, Donald J.	Mich.	Dem	Williams, Lyle	Ohio	Rep
	Andrews, Ike F.	N.C.	Dem			
	Ratchford, William R.	Conn.	Dem			
	Vandergriff, Tom	Tex.	Dem			
Lost Election for Vice President	Ferraro, Geraldine A.	N.Y.	Dem	None		
Departures from Committee:						
Moved to Energy & Commerce	None			Bilirakis, Michael	Fla.	Rep
Moved to Ways and Means	None			Daub, Hal	Neb.	Rep
				Gregg, Judd	N.H.	Rep
Moved to Foreign Affairs	None			DeWine, Michael	Ohio	Rep
No new assignment	None			Craig, Larry E.	Ida.	Rep

HOUSE SELECT COMMITTEE: AGING (Permanent) / 99th Congress

Service Dates of Committee Chair: Feb. 6,1985-Jan. 3,1987
Service Dates of Majority Members: Feb. 6,1985-Jan. 3,1987
Service Dates of Minority Members: Feb. 21,1985-Jan. 3,1987

Majority

Rank Name	Party	State	Terms in: House	Terms in: Comm.
Chr Roybal, Edward R.	Dem	Cal.	12	6
2nd Pepper, Claude D.	Dem	Fla.	12	6
3rd Biaggi, Mario	Dem	N.Y.	9	6
4th Bonker, Don L.	Dem	Wash.	6	6
5th Downey, Thomas J.	Dem	N.Y.	6	6
6th Florio, James J.	Dem	N.J.	6	6
7th Ford, Harold E.	Dem	Tenn.	6	6
8th Hughes, William J.	Dem	N.J.	6	6
9th Lloyd, Marilyn	Dem	Tenn.	6	6
10th Lundine, Stanley N.	Dem	N.Y.	6	5
11th Oakar, Mary Rose	Dem	Ohio	5	5
12th Luken, Thomas A.	Dem	Ohio	6	4
13th Byron, Beverly B.	Dem	Md.	4	4
14th Mica, Daniel A.	Dem	Fla.	4	4
15th Waxman, Henry A.	Dem	Cal.	6	4
16th Synar, Michael L.	Dem	Okla.	4	4
17th Derrick, Butler C. Jr.	Dem	S.C.	6	3
18th Vento, Bruce F.	Dem	Minn.	5	3
19th Frank, Barney	Dem	Mass.	3	3
20th Lantos, Tom	Dem	Cal.	3	3
21st Wyden, Ron	Dem	Ore.	3	3
22nd Crockett, George W. Jr.	Dem	Mich.	4	3
23rd Boner, William H.	Dem	Tenn.	4	3
24th Skelton, Ike	Dem	Mo.	5	2
25th Hertel, Dennis M.	Dem	Mich.	3	2
26th Borski, Robert A.	Dem	Penn.	2	2
27th Boucher, Frederick C.	Dem	Va.	2	2
28th Erdreich, Ben	Dem	Ala.	2	2
29th MacKay, Kenneth H.	Dem	Fla.	2	2
30th Reid, Harry M.	Dem	Nev.	2	2
31st Sisisky, Norman	Dem	Va.	2	2
32nd Wise, Robert E. Jr.	Dem	W.Va.	2	2

Minority

Rank Name	Party	State	Terms in: House	Terms in: Comm.
RM Rinaldo, Matthew J.	Rep	N.J.	7	5
2nd Hammerschmidt, John Paul	Rep	Ark.	10	6
3rd Regula, Ralph S.	Rep	Ohio	7	5
4th Shumway, Norman D.	Rep	Cal.	4	4
5th Snowe, Olympia J. B.	Rep	Me.	4	4
6th Jeffords, James M.	Rep	Vt.	6	3
7th Tauke, Thomas J.	Rep	Iowa	4	3
8th Wortley, George	Rep	N.Y.	3	3
9th Courter, James A.	Rep	N.J.	4	2
10th Schneider, Claudine	Rep	R.I.	3	2
11th Ridge, Thomas J.	Rep	Penn.	2	2
12th McCain, John	Rep	Ariz.	2	2
13th Gekas, George W.	Rep	Penn.	2	2
14th Siljander, Mark D.	Rep	Mich.	3	2
15th Smith, Christopher H.	Rep	N.J.	3	2
16th Boehlert, Sherwood L.	Rep	N.Y.	2	1
17th Saxton, H. James	Rep	N.J.	1	1
18th Bentley, Helen Delich	Rep	Md.	1	1
19th Lightfoot, Jim Ross	Rep	Iowa	1	1
20th Fawell, Harris W.	Rep	Ill.	1	1
21st Meyers, Jan	Rep	Kans.	1	1
22nd Blaz, Ben Garrido	Rep	Guam	1	1
23rd Swindall, Patrick Lynn	Rep	Ga.	1	1
24th Henry, Paul B.	Rep	Mich.	1	1
25th Kolbe, Jim	Rep	Ariz.	1	1
26th Schuette, Bill	Rep	Mich.	1	1

33rd Richardson, Bill	Dem	N.M.	2	2
34th Volkmer, Harold L.	Dem	Mo.	5	1
35th Gordon, Bart	Dem	Tenn.	1	1
36th Manton, Thomas J.	Dem	N.Y.	1	1
37th Robinson, Tommy F.	Dem	Ark.	1	1
38th Stallings, Richard H.	Dem	Ida.	1	1

	Majority			Minority		
Departures from the House:						
Elected to U.S. Senate	Reid, Harry M.	Nev.	Dem	McCain, John	Ariz.	Rep
Elected Lieutenant Governor	Lundine, Stanley N.	N.Y.	Dem	None		
Defeated for Renomination	None			Siljander, Mark D.	Mich.	Rep
Departures from Committee:						
Moved to Appropriations	None			Kolbe, Jim	Ariz.	Rep
No new assignment	None			Gekas, George W.	Penn.	Rep

HOUSE SELECT COMMITTEE: AGING (Permanent) / 100th Congress

Service Dates of Committee Chair: Jan. 21,1987-Jan. 3,1989
Service Dates of Majority Members: Jan. 21,1987-Jan. 3,1989
Service Dates of Minority Members: Feb. 2,1987-Jan. 3,1989

Majority

Rank Name	Party	State	Terms in: House	Terms in: Comm.
Chr Roybal, Edward R.	Dem	Cal.	13	7
2nd Pepper, Claude D.	Dem	Fla.	13	7
3rd Biaggi, Mario	Dem	N.Y.	10	7
4th Bonker, Don L.	Dem	Wash.	7	7
5th Downey, Thomas J.	Dem	N.Y.	7	7
6th Florio, James J.	Dem	N.J.	7	7
7th Ford, Harold E.	Dem	Tenn.	7	7
8th Hughes, William J.	Dem	N.J.	7	7
9th Lloyd, Marilyn	Dem	Tenn.	7	7
10th Oakar, Mary Rose	Dem	Ohio	6	6
11th Luken, Thomas A.	Dem	Ohio	7	5
12th Byron, Beverly B.	Dem	Md.	5	5
13th Mica, Daniel A.	Dem	Fla.	5	5
14th Waxman, Henry A.	Dem	Cal.	7	5
15th Synar, Michael L.	Dem	Okla.	5	5
16th Derrick, Butler C. Jr.	Dem	S.C.	7	4
17th Vento, Bruce F.	Dem	Minn.	6	4
18th Frank, Barney	Dem	Mass.	4	4
19th Lantos, Tom	Dem	Cal.	4	4
20th Wyden, Ron	Dem	Ore.	4	4
21st Crockett, George W. Jr.	Dem	Mich.	5	4
22nd Boner, William H.	Dem	Tenn.	5	4
23rd Skelton, Ike	Dem	Mo.	6	3
24th Hertel, Dennis M.	Dem	Mich.	4	3
25th Borski, Robert A	Dem	Penn.	3	3
26th Boucher, Frederick C.	Dem	Va.	3	3
27th Erdreich, Ben	Dem	Ala.	3	3
28th MacKay, Kenneth H.	Dem	Fla.	3	3
29th Sisisky, Norman	Dem	Va.	3	3
30th Wise, Robert E. Jr.	Dem	W.Va.	3	3
31st Richardson, Bill	Dem	N.M.	3	3
32nd Volkmer, Harold L.	Dem	Mo.	6	2
33rd Gordon, Bart	Dem	Tenn.	2	2
34th Manton, Thomas J.	Dem	N.Y.	2	2
35th Robinson, Tommy F.	Dem	Ark.	2	2
36th Stallings, Richard H.	Dem	Ida.	2	2
37th Clarke, James McClure	Dem	N.C.	2	1
38th Kennedy, Joseph P. II	Dem	Mass.	1	1
39th Slaughter, Louise M.	Dem	N.Y.	1	1

Minority

Rank Name	Party	State	Terms in: House	Terms in: Comm.
RM Rinaldo, Matthew J.	Rep	N.J.	8	6
2nd Hammerschmidt, John Paul	Rep	Ark.	11	7
3rd Regula, Ralph S.	Rep	Ohio	8	6
4th Shumway, Norman D.	Rep	Cal.	5	5
5th Snowe, Olympia J. B.	Rep	Me.	5	5
6th Jeffords, James M.	Rep	Vt.	7	4
7th Tauke, Thomas J.	Rep	Iowa	5	4
8th Wortley, George	Rep	N.Y.	4	4
9th Courter, James A.	Rep	N.J.	5	3
10th Schneider, Claudine	Rep	R.I.	4	3
11th Ridge, Thomas J.	Rep	Penn.	3	3
12th Smith, Christopher H.	Rep	N.J.	4	3
13th Boehlert, Sherwood L.	Rep	N.Y.	3	2
14th Saxton, H. James	Rep	N.J.	2	2
15th Bentley, Helen Delich	Rep	Md.	2	2
16th Lightfoot, Jim Ross	Rep	Iowa	2	2
17th Fawell, Harris W.	Rep	Ill.	2	2
18th Meyers, Jan	Rep	Kans.	2	2
19th Blaz, Ben Garrido	Rep	Guam	2	2
20th Swindall, Patrick Lynn	Rep	Ga.	2	2
21st Henry, Paul B.	Rep	Mich.	2	2
22nd Schuette, Bill	Rep	Mich.	2	2
23rd Spence, Floyd	Rep	S.C.	9	1
24th Clinger, William F. Jr.	Rep	Penn.	5	1
25th Morella, Constance A.	Rep	Md.	1	1
26th Saiki, Patricia	Rep	Hai.	1	1

Changes:

Majority:

Boner, William H.	Dem	Tenn.	Oct. 5,1987	Resigned; elected Mayor of Nashville.
Bilbray, James	Dem	Nev.	Oct. 20,1987	Replaced Boner.
Biaggi, Mario	Dem	N.Y.	Aug. 5,1988	Resigned and retired.
Jontz, Jim	Dem	Ind.	Aug. 10,1988	Replaced Biaggi.
Mica, Daniel A.	Dem	Fla.	Oct. 3,1988	Left committee; no new assignment.
Costello, Jerry F.	Dem	Ill.	Oct. 3,1988	Replaced Mica.

Departures from the House:	Majority			Minority		
Elected to U.S. Senate	None			Jeffords, James M.	Vt.	Rep
Defeated for Reelection	None			Swindall, Patrick Lynn	Ga.	Rep
Lost Election to U.S. Senate	MacKay, Kenneth H.	Fla.	Dem	None		
Lost Nomination to U.S. Senate	Bonker, Don L.	Wash.	Dem	None		
Retired	None			Wortley, George	N.Y.	Rep
Departures from Committee:						
No new assignment	Boucher, Frederick C.	Va.	Dem	None		

HOUSE SELECT COMMITTEE: AGING (Permanent) / 101st Congress

Service Dates of Committee Chair: Mar. 8,1989-Jan. 3,1991
Service Dates of Majority Members: Mar. 8,1989-Jan. 3,1991
Service Dates of Minority Members: Apr. 10,1989-Jan. 3,1991

Majority

Rank	Name	Party	State	Terms in: House	Terms in: Comm.
Chr	Roybal, Edward R.	Dem	Cal.	14	8
2nd	Pepper, Claude D.	Dem	Fla.	14	8
3rd	Downey, Thomas J.	Dem	N.Y.	8	8
4th	Florio, James J.	Dem	N.J.	8	8
5th	Ford, Harold E.	Dem	Tenn.	8	8
6th	Hughes, William J.	Dem	N.J.	8	8
7th	Lloyd, Marilyn	Dem	Tenn.	8	8
8th	Oakar, Mary Rose	Dem	Ohio	7	7
9th	Luken, Thomas A.	Dem	Ohio	8	6
10th	Byron, Beverly B.	Dem	Md.	6	6
11th	Waxman, Henry A.	Dem	Cal.	8	6
12th	Synar, Michael L.	Dem	Okla.	6	6
13th	Derrick, Butler C. Jr.	Dem	S.C.	8	5
14th	Vento, Bruce F.	Dem	Minn.	7	5
15th	Frank, Barney	Dem	Mass.	5	5
16th	Lantos, Tom	Dem	Cal.	5	5
17th	Wyden, Ron	Dem	Ore.	5	5
18th	Crockett, George W. Jr.	Dem	Mich.	6	5
19th	Skelton, Ike	Dem	Mo.	7	4
20th	Hertel, Dennis M.	Dem	Mich.	5	4
21st	Borski, Robert A.	Dem	Penn.	4	4
22nd	Erdreich, Ben	Dem	Ala.	4	4
23rd	Sisisky, Norman	Dem	Va.	4	4
24th	Wise, Robert E. Jr.	Dem	W.Va.	4	4
25th	Richardson, Bill	Dem	N.M.	4	4
26th	Volkmer, Harold L.	Dem	Mo.	7	3
27th	Gordon, Bart	Dem	Tenn.	3	3
28th	Manton, Thomas J.	Dem	N.Y.	3	3
29th	Robinson, Tommy F.	Dem	Ark.	3	3
30th	Stallings, Richard H.	Dem	Ida.	3	3
31st	Clarke, James McClure	Dem	N.C.	3	2
32nd	Kennedy, Joseph P. II	Dem	Mass.	2	2
33rd	Slaughter, Louise M.	Dem	N.Y.	2	2
34th	Bilbray, James	Dem	Nev.	2	2
35th	Jontz, Jim	Dem	Ind.	2	2
36th	Costello, Jerry F.	Dem	Ill.	2	2
37th	Staggers, Harley O. Jr.	Dem	W.Va.	4	1
38th	Pallone, Frank Jr.	Dem	N.J.	2	1

Minority

Rank	Name	Party	State	Terms in: House	Terms in: Comm.
RM	Rinaldo, Matthew J.	Rep	N.J.	9	7
2nd	Hammerschmidt, John Paul	Rep	Ark.	12	8
3rd	Regula, Ralph S.	Rep	Ohio	9	7
4th	Shumway, Norman D.	Rep	Cal.	6	6
5th	Snowe, Olympia J. B.	Rep	Me.	6	6
6th	Tauke, Thomas J.	Rep	Iowa	6	5
7th	Courter, James A.	Rep	N.J.	6	4
8th	Schneider, Claudine	Rep	R.I.	5	4
9th	Ridge, Thomas J.	Rep	Penn.	4	4
10th	Smith, Christopher H.	Rep	N.J.	5	4
11th	Boehlert, Sherwood L.	Rep	N.Y.	4	3
12th	Saxton, H. James	Rep	N.J.	3	3
13th	Bentley, Helen Delich	Rep	Md.	3	3
14th	Lightfoot, Jim Ross	Rep	Iowa	3	3
15th	Fawell, Harris W.	Rep	Ill.	3	3
16th	Meyers, Jan	Rep	Kans.	3	3
17th	Blaz, Ben	Rep	Guam	3	3
18th	Henry, Paul B.	Rep	Mich.	3	3
19th	Schuette, Bill	Rep	Mich.	3	3
20th	Spence, Floyd	Rep	S.C.	10	2
21st	Clinger, William F. Jr.	Rep	Penn.	6	2
22nd	Morella, Constance A.	Rep	Md.	2	2
23rd	Saiki, Patricia	Rep	Hai.	2	2
24th	Porter, John Edward	Rep	Ill.	6	1
25th	Duncan, John J. Jr.	Rep	Tenn.	2	1
26th	Stearns, Cliff	Rep	Fla.	1	1
27th	James, Craig T.	Rep	Fla.	1	1

39th Unsoeld, Jolene	Dem	Wash.	1	1
40th DeFazio, Peter A.	Dem	Ore.	2	1

Vacancy Filled:
Majority: 40th seat by DeFazio on Aug. 4,1989.
Minority: 27th seat by James on Apr. 25,1989.

Changes:
Majority:

Pepper, Claude D.	Dem	Cal.	May 30,1989	Died in office.
Lewis, John R.	Dem	Ga.	Aug. 4,1989	Replaced Pepper.
Florio, James J.	Dem	N.J.	Jan. 16,1990	Resigned; elected Governor.
Owens, D. Wayne	Dem	Utah	Apr. 4,1990	Replaced Pepper.

Departures from the House:	Majority		Minority	
Defeated for Reelection	Clarke, James McClure	N.C. Dem	None	
Lost Election to U.S. Senate	None		Saiki, Patricia	Hai. Rep
			Schneider, Claudine	R.I. Rep
			Schuette, Bill	Mich. Rep
			Tauke, Thomas J.	Iowa Rep
Lost Election for Governor	Robinson, Tommy F.	Ark. Dem	Courter, James A.	N.J. Rep
Retired	Crockett, George W. Jr.	Mich. Dem	Shumway, Norman D.	Cal. Rep
	Luken, Thomas A.	Ohio Dem		
Departures from Committee:				
Moved to Select Hunger	Synar, Michael L.	Okla. Dem	None	
Moved to Select Narcotics Abuse & Control	None		Clinger, William F. Jr.	Penn. Rep
No new assignment	None		Ridge, Thomas J.	Penn. Rep

HOUSE SELECT COMMITTEE: AGING (Permanent) / 102nd Congress

Service Dates of Committee Chair: Feb. 21,1991-Jan. 3,1993
Service Dates of Majority Members: Feb. 21,1991-Jan. 3,1993
Service Dates of Minority Members: Feb. 21,1991-Jan. 3,1993

Majority

Rank Name	Party	State	Terms in: House	Terms in: Comm.
Chr Roybal, Edward R.	Dem	Cal.	15	9
2nd Downey, Thomas J.	Dem	N.Y.	9	9
3rd Ford, Harold E.	Dem	Tenn.	9	9
4th Hughes, William J.	Dem	N.J.	9	9
5th Lloyd, Marilyn	Dem	Tenn.	9	9
6th Oakar, Mary Rose	Dem	Ohio	8	8
7th Byron, Beverly B.	Dem	Md.	7	7
8th Waxman, Henry A.	Dem	Cal.	9	7
9th Derrick, Butler C. Jr.	Dem	S.C.	9	6
10th Vento, Bruce F.	Dem	Minn.	8	6
11th Frank, Barney	Dem	Mass.	6	6
12th Lantos, Tom	Dem	Cal.	6	6
13th Wyden, Ron	Dem	Ore.	6	6
14th Skelton, Ike	Dem	Mo.	8	5
15th Hertel, Dennis M.	Dem	Mich.	6	5
16th Borski, Robert A.	Dem	Penn.	5	5
17th Erdreich, Ben	Dem	Ala.	5	5
18th Sisisky, Norman	Dem	Va.	5	5
19th Wise, Robert E. Jr.	Dem	W.Va.	5	5
20th Richardson, Bill	Dem	N.M.	5	5
21st Volkmer, Harold L.	Dem	Mo.	8	4
22nd Gordon, Bart	Dem	Tenn.	4	4
23rd Manton, Thomas J.	Dem	N.Y.	4	4
24th Stallings, Richard H.	Dem	Ida.	4	4
25th Kennedy, Joseph P. II	Dem	Mass.	3	3
26th Slaughter, Louise M.	Dem	N.Y.	3	3
27th Bilbray, James	Dem	Nev.	3	3
28th Jontz, Jim	Dem	Ind.	3	3

Minority

Rank Name	Party	State	Terms in: House	Terms in: Comm.
RM Rinaldo, Matthew J.	Rep	N.J.	10	8
2nd Hammerschmidt, John Paul	Rep	Ark.	13	9
3rd Regula, Ralph S.	Rep	Ohio	10	8
4th Snowe, Olympia J. B.	Rep	Me.	7	7
5th Smith, Christopher H.	Rep	N.J.	6	5
6th Boehlert, Sherwood L.	Rep	N.Y.	5	4
7th Saxton, H. James	Rep	N.J.	4	4
8th Bentley, Helen Delich	Rep	Md.	4	4
9th Lightfoot, Jim Ross	Rep	Iowa	4	4
10th Fawell, Harris W.	Rep	Ill.	4	4
11th Meyers, Jan	Rep	Kans.	4	4
12th Blaz, Ben	Rep	Guam	4	4
13th Henry, Paul B.	Rep	Mich.	4	4
14th Spence, Floyd	Rep	S.C.	11	3
15th Morella, Constance A.	Rep	Md.	3	3
16th Porter, John Edward	Rep	Ill.	7	2
17th Duncan, John J. Jr.	Rep	Tenn.	3	2
18th Stearns, Cliff	Rep	Fla.	2	2
19th James, Craig T.	Rep	Fla.	2	2
20th Houghton, Amory	Rep	N.Y.	3	1
21st Franks, Gary	Rep	Conn.	1	1
22nd Hobson, David L.	Rep	Ohio	1	1
23rd Taylor, Charles H.	Rep	N.C.	1	1
24th Gilchrest, Wayne T.	Rep	Md.	1	1
25th Zimmer, Dick	Rep	N.J.	1	1
26th Nichols, Dick	Rep	Kans.	1	1
27th Nussle, Jim	Rep	Iowa	1	1

29th Costello, Jerry F.	Dem	Ill.	3	3
30th Staggers, Harley O. Jr.	Dem	W.Va.	5	2
31st Pallone, Frank Jr.	Dem	N.J.	3	2
32nd Unsoeld, Jolene	Dem	Wash.	2	2
33rd DeFazio, Peter A.	Dem	Ore.	3	2
34th Lewis, John R.	Dem	Ga.	3	2
35th Owens, D. Wayne	Dem	Utah	4	2
36th Roe, Robert A.	Dem	N.J.	12	1
37th Studds, Gerry E.	Dem	Mass.	10	1
38th Abercrombie, Neil	Dem	Hai.	1	1
39th Swett, Dick	Dem	N.H.	1	1
40th DeLauro, Rosa	Dem	Conn.	1	1
41st Pastor, Ed	Dem	Ariz.	1	1

Vacancy Filled:

Majority: 41st by Pastor on Mar. 4,1992.

Changes:

Minority:

Lightfoot, Jim Ross	Rep	Iowa	Mar. 11,1991	Moved to Appropriations.

HOUSE SELECT COMMITTEE: INTELLIGENCE

Jurisdiction, 1975

From House Resolution 138, 94th Congress, First Session, February 19, 1975:

[Section 2]

The select committee is authorized and directed to conduct an inquiry into--
(1) the collection, analysis, use, and cost of intelligence information and allegations of improper activities of intelligence agencies in the United States and abroad;
(2) the procedures and effectiveness of coordination among and between the various intelligence components of the United States Government;
(3) the nature and extent of executive branch oversight and control of United States intelligence activities;
(4) the need for improved or reorganized oversight by the Congress of the United States intelligence activities;
(5) the necessity, nature, and extent of overt and covert intelligence activities by United States intelligence instrumentalities in the United States and abroad;
(6) the procedures for and means of the protection of sensitive intelligence information; and
(7) such other related matters as the select committee shall deem necessary to carry out the purposes of this resolution.

[Section 3]

In carrying out the purposes of this resolution, the select committee is authorized to inquire into the activities of the following:
(1) the National Security Council;
(2) the United States Intelligence Board;
(3) the President's Foreign Intelligence Advisory Board;
(4) the Central Intelligence Agency;
(5) the Defense Intelligence Agency;
(6) the intelligence components of the Departments of the Army, Navy, and Air Force;
(7) the National Security Agency;
(8) the Intelligence and Research Bureau of the Department of State;
(9) the Federal Bureau of Investigation;
(10) the Department of the Treasury;
(11) the Energy Research and Development Administration; and
(12) any other instrumentalities of the United States Government engaged in or otherwise responsible for intelligence operations in the United States and abroad.

Jurisdiction, 1975

From House Resolution 351, 94th Congress, First Session, July 17, 1975:

[Section 2]

The select committee is authorized and directed to conduct an inquiry into--
(1) the collection, analysis, use, and cost of intelligence information and allegations of illegal or improper activities of intelligence agencies in the United States and abroad;
(2) the procedures and effectiveness of coordination among and between the various intelligence components of the United States Government;
(3) the nature and extent of executive branch oversight and control of United States intelligence activities;
(4) the need for improved or reorganized oversight by the Congress of United States intelligence activities;
(5) the necessity, nature, and extent of overt and covert intelligence activities by United States intelligence instrumentalities in the United States and abroad;
(6) the procedures for and means of the protection of sensitive intelligence information;

(7) procedures for and means of the protection of rights and privileges of citizens of the United States from illegal or improper intelligence activities; and
(8) such other related matters as the select committee shall deem necessary to carry out the purposes of this resolution.

[Section 3]

In carrying out the purposes of this resolution, the select committee is authorized to inquire into the activities of the following:
(1) the National Security Council;
(2) the United States Intelligence Board;
(3) the President's Foreign Intelligence Advisory Board;
(4) the Central Intelligence Agency;
(5) the Defense Intelligence Agency;
(6) the intelligence components of the Departments of the Army, Navy, and Air Force;
(7) the National Security Agency;
(8) the Intelligence and Research Bureau of the Department of State;
(9) the Federal Bureau of Investigation;
(10) the Department of the Treasury and the Department of Justice;
(11) the Energy Research and Development Administration; and
(12) any other instrumentalities of the United States Government engaged in or otherwise responsible for intelligence operations in the United States and abroad.

Termination, 1975

The first Select Committee was terminated by authority of House Resolution 591 (94-1), on July 17, 1975. A second Select Committee took its place and was later extended by House Resolution 982 (94-2). The second Select Committee was terminated upon the filing of its final report, House Report 833 (94-2), on February 11, 1976.

HOUSE SELECT COMMITTEE: INTELLIGENCE (Nedzi) / 94th Congress

Service Dates of Committee Chair: Feb. 19,1975-July 17,1975
Service Dates of Majority Members: Feb. 19,1975-July 17,1975
Service Dates of Minority Members: Feb. 19,1975-July 17,1975

Majority

Rank	Name	Party	State	Terms in: House	Terms in: Comm.
Chr	Nedzi, Lucien N.	Dem	Mich.	8	1
2nd	Giaimo, Robert N.	Dem	Conn.	9	1
3rd	Edwards, Don	Dem	Cal.	7	1
4th	Stanton, James V.	Dem	Ohio	3	1
5th	Harrington, Michael J.	Dem	Mass.	4	1
6th	Dellums, Ronald V.	Dem	Cal.	3	1
7th	Murphy, Morgan F.	Dem	Ill.	3	1

Minority

Rank	Name	Party	State	Terms in: House	Terms in: Comm.
RM	McClory, Robert	Rep	Ill.	7	1
2nd	Treen, David C.	Rep	La.	2	1
3rd	Kasten, Robert W. Jr.	Rep	Wisc.	1	1

Members not assigned to Reorganized Committee:
No new assignment

Majority

Harrington, Michael J. Mass. Dem
Nedzi, Lucien N. Mich. Dem

Minority

None

HOUSE SELECT COMMITTEE: INTELLIGENCE (Pike) / 94th Congress

Service Dates of Committee Chair: July 17,1975-Feb. 11,1976
Service Dates of Majority Members: July 17,1975-Feb. 11,1976
Service Dates of Minority Members: July 17,1975-Feb. 11,1976

Majority

Rank	Name	Party	State	Terms in: House	Terms in: Comm.
Chr	Pike, Otis G.	Dem	N.Y.	8	1
2nd	Giaimo, Robert N.	Dem	Conn.	9	1
3rd	Edwards, Don	Dem	Cal.	7	1
4th	Stanton, James V.	Dem	Ohio	3	1
5th	Dellums, Ronald V.	Dem	Cal.	3	1
6th	Murphy, Morgan F.	Dem	Ill.	3	1
7th	Aspin, Les	Dem	Wisc.	3	1
8th	Milford, Dale	Dem	Tex.	2	1
9th	Hayes, Philip H.	Dem	Ind.	1	1

Minority

Rank	Name	Party	State	Terms in: House	Terms in: Comm.
RM	McClory, Robert	Rep	Ill.	7	1
2nd	Treen, David C.	Rep	La.	2	1
3rd	Johnson, James P.	Rep	Colo.	2	1
4th	Kasten, Robert W. Jr.	Rep	Wisc.	1	1

Changes:

Majority:

Name	Party	State	Date	Change
Edwards, Don	Dem	Cal.	July 22,1975	Left committee; no new assignment.
Lehman, William	Dem	Fla.	July 22,1975	Replaced Edwards.

HOUSE SELECT COMMITTEE: INTELLIGENCE (Permanent)

Jurisdiction, 1977

From House Resolution 658, as amended, 95th Congress, First Session, July 14, 1977:

[Section 1]

There is hereby established a permanent select committee to be known as the Permanent Select Committee on Intelligence...

[Section 2 a]

There shall be referred to the select committee all proposed legislation, messages, petitions, memorials, and other matters relating to the following:

(1) The Central Intelligence Agency and the Director of Central Intelligence.
(2) Intelligence and intelligence-related activities of all other departments and agencies of the Government, including, but not limited to, the intelligence and intelligence-related activities of the Defense Intelligence Agency, the National Security Agency, and other agencies of the Department of Defense; the Department of State; the Department of Justice; and the Department of the Treasury.
(3) The organization or reorganization of any department or agency of the Government to the extent that the organization or reorganization relates to a function or activity involving intelligence or intelligence-related activities.
(4) Authorizations for appropriations, both direct and indirect, for the following:
    (A) The Central Intelligence Agency and Director of Central Intelligence.
    (B) The Defense Intelligence Agency.
    (C) The National Security Agency.
    (D) The intelligence and intelligence-related activities of other agencies and subdivisions of the Department of Defense.
    (E) The intelligence and intelligence related activities of the Department of State.
    (F) The intelligence and intelligence related activities of the Federal Bureau of Investigation, including all activities of the Intelligence Division.
    (G) Any department, agency, or subdivision which is the successor to any agency named in subdivision (A), (B), or (C); and the activities of any department, agency, bureau, or subdivision named in subdivision (D), (E), or (F) to the extent that the activities of such successor department, agency, or subdivision are activities described in subdivision (D), (E), or (F).

[Section 3]

(a) The select committee, for the purposes of accountability to the House, shall make regular and periodic reports to the House on the nature and extent of the intelligence and intelligence-related activities of the various departments and agencies of the United States. Such committee shall promptly call to the attention of the House or to any other appropriate committee or committees of the House any matters requiring the attention of the House or such other committee or committees. . .

(b) The select committee shall obtain an annual report from the Director of the Central Intelligence Agency, the Secretary of Defense, the Secretary of State, and the Director of the Federal Bureau of Investigation. Such reports shall review the intelligence and intelligence-related activities of the agency or department concerned and the intelligence and intelligence-related activities of foreign countries directed at the United States or its interest. An unclassified version of each report may be made available to the public at the discretion of the select committee.

Jurisdiction, 1992

The jurisdiction of the permanent select committee has not changed since its inception in 1977.

HOUSE SELECT COMMITTEE: INTELLIGENCE (Permanent) / 95th Congress

Service Dates of Committee Chair: July 27,1977-Jan. 3,1979
Service Dates of Majority Members: July 27,1977-Jan. 3,1979
Service Dates of Minority Members: July 27,1977-Jan. 3,1979

Majority

Rank	Name	Party	State	Terms in: House	Terms in: Comm.
Chr	Boland, Edward P.	Dem	Mass.	13	1
2nd	Zablocki, Clement J.	Dem	Wisc.	15	1
3rd	Burlison, Bill D.	Dem	Mo.	5	1
4th	Murphy, Morgan F.	Dem	Ill.	4	1
5th	Aspin, Les	Dem	Wisc.	4	1
6th	Rose, Charles G. III	Dem	N.C.	3	1
7th	Mazzoli, Romano L.	Dem	Ky.	4	1
8th	Mineta, Norman Y.	Dem	Cal.	2	1
9th	Fowler, Wyche Jr.	Dem	Ga.	1	1

Minority

Rank	Name	Party	State	Terms in: House	Terms in: Comm.
RM	Wilson, Robert C.	Rep	Cal.	13	1
2nd	Ashbrook, John M.	Rep	Ohio	9	1
3rd	McClory, Robert	Rep	Ill.	8	1
4th	Robinson, J. Kenneth	Rep	Va.	4	1

Note: The Majority and Minority Leaders of the House are *ex officio* members of the committee, but do no vote and are not counted for purposes of determining a quorum.

Departures from Committee:	**Majority**	**Minority**	
No new assignment	None	Wilson, Robert C.	Cal. Rep

HOUSE SELECT COMMITTEE: INTELLIGENCE (Permanent) / 96th Congress

Service Dates of Committee Chair: Jan. 25,1979-Jan. 3,1981
Service Dates of Majority Members: Jan. 25,1979-Jan. 3,1981
Service Dates of Minority Members: Jan. 25,1979-Jan. 3,1981

Majority

Rank	Name	Party	State	Terms in: House	Terms in: Comm.
Chr	Boland, Edward P.	Dem	Mass.	14	2
2nd	Zablocki, Clement J.	Dem	Wisc.	16	2
3rd	Burlison, Bill D.	Dem	Mo.	6	2
4th	Murphy, Morgan F.	Dem	Ill.	5	2
5th	Aspin, Les	Dem	Wisc.	5	2
6th	Rose, Charles G. III	Dem	N.C.	4	2
7th	Mazzoli, Romano L.	Dem	Ky.	5	2
8th	Mineta, Norman Y.	Dem	Cal.	3	2
9th	Fowler, Wyche Jr.	Dem	Ga.	2	2

Minority

Rank	Name	Party	State	Terms in: House	Terms in: Comm.
RM	Robinson, J. Kenneth	Rep	Va.	5	2
2nd	Ashbrook, John M.	Rep	Ohio	10	2
3rd	McClory, Robert	Rep	Ill.	9	2
4th	Whitehurst, G. William	Rep	Va.	6	1
5th	Young, C. W. Bill	Rep	Fla.	5	1

Note: The Majority and Minority Leaders of the House are *ex officio* members of the committee, but do no vote and are not counted for purposes of determining a quorum.

Vacancy Filled:
Minority: 5th seat by Young on Feb. 5,1979.

Departures from the House:	**Majority**		**Minority**
Defeated for Reelection	Burlison, Bill D.	Mo. Dem	None
Retired	Murphy, Morgan F.	Ill. Dem	None
Departures from Committee:			
Moved to Budget	Aspin, Les	Wisc. Dem	None

HOUSE SELECT COMMITTEE: INTELLIGENCE (Permanent) / 97th Congress

Service Dates of Committee Chair: Feb. 3,1981-Jan. 3,1983
Service Dates of Majority Members: Feb. 3,1981-Jan. 3,1983
Service Dates of Minority Members: Feb. 6,1981-Jan. 3,1983

Majority

Rank	Name	Party	State	Terms in: House	Terms in: Comm.
Chr	Boland, Edward P.	Dem	Mass.	15	3
2nd	Zablocki, Clement J.	Dem	Wisc.	17	3
3rd	Rose, Charles G. III	Dem	N.C.	5	3
4th	Mazzoli, Romano L.	Dem	Ky.	6	3
5th	Mineta, Norman Y.	Dem	Cal.	4	3
6th	Fowler, Wyche Jr.	Dem	Ga.	3	3
7th	Hamilton, Lee H.	Dem	Ind.	9	1
8th	Gore, Albert A. Jr.	Dem	Tenn.	3	1
9th	Stump, Robert	Dem	Ariz.	3	1

Minority

Rank	Name	Party	State	Terms in: House	Terms in: Comm.
RM	Robinson, J. Kenneth	Rep	Va.	6	3
2nd	Ashbrook, John M.	Rep	Ohio	11	3
3rd	McClory, Robert	Rep	Ill.	10	3
4th	Whitehurst, G. William	Rep	Va.	7	2
5th	Young, C. W. Bill	Rep	Fla.	6	2

Note: The Majority and Minority Leaders of the House are *ex officio* members of the committee, but do no vote and are not counted for purposes of determining a quorum.

Vacancy Filled:
Majority: 7th seat by Hamilton on Feb. 18,1981.

Changes:
Minority:
Ashbrook, John M. Rep Ohio Apr. 24,1982 Died in office.

	Majority			Minority		
Departures from the House:						
Retired	None			McClory, Robert	Ill.	Rep
Departures from Committee:						
No new assignment	Rose, Charles G. III	N.C.	Dem	None		

HOUSE SELECT COMMITTEE: INTELLIGENCE (Permanent) / 98th Congress

Service Dates of Committee Chair: Feb. 2,1983-Jan. 3,1985
Service Dates of Majority Members: Feb. 2,1983-Jan. 3,1985
Service Dates of Minority Members: Feb. 2,1983-Jan. 3,1985

Majority

Rank	Name	Party	State	Terms in: House		Terms in: Comm.
Chr	Boland, Edward P.	Dem	Mass.	16		4
2nd	Zablocki, Clement J.	Dem	Wisc.	18		4
3rd	Mazzoli, Romano L.	Dem	Ky.	7		4
4th	Mineta, Norman Y.	Dem	Cal.	5		4
5th	Fowler, Wyche Jr.	Dem	Ga.	4		4
6th	Hamilton, Lee H.	Dem	Ind.	10		2
7th	Gore, Albert A. Jr.	Dem	Tenn.	4		2
8th	Stokes, Louis	Dem	Ohio	8		1
9th	McCurdy, Dave	Dem	Okla.	2	*1	1

Minority

Rank	Name	Party	State	Terms in: House	Terms in: Comm.
RM	Robinson, J. Kenneth	Rep	Va.	7	4
2nd	Whitehurst, G. William	Rep	Va.	8	3
3rd	Young, C. W. Bill	Rep	Fla.	7	3
4th	Stump, Robert	Rep	Ariz.	4	2
5th	Goodling, William F.	Rep	Penn.	5	1

*1: Member's 1st period of service on the committee.

Notes: The Majority and Minority Leaders of the House are *ex officio* members of the committee, but do no vote and are not counted for purposes of determining a quorum. Robert Stump of Arizona resigned from the Democratic Party and jointed the Republican Party on Jan. 3,1983. Recognizing Stump's previous service on this committee, the Republican Conference assigned him the 4th minority rank.

Changes:
Majority:
Zablocki, Clement J. Dem Wisc. Dec. 3,1983 Died in office.

Departures from the House:	Majority		Minority	
Elected to U.S. Senate	Gore, Albert A. Jr.	Tenn. Dem	None	
Retired	None		Robinson, J. Kenneth	Va. Rep
Departures from Committee:				
Moved to Budget	None		Goodling, William F.	Penn. Rep
Moved to Standards of Official Conduct	None		Whitehurst, G. William	Va. Rep
No new assignment	Boland, Edward P.	Mass. Dem	Young, C. W. Bill	Fla. Rep
	Fowler, Wyche Jr.	Ga. Dem		
	Mazzoli, Romano L.	Ky. Dem		
	Mineta, Norman Y.	Cal. Dem		

HOUSE SELECT COMMITTEE: INTELLIGENCE (Permanent) / 99th Congress

Service Dates of Committee Chair: Jan. 30,1985-Jan. 3,1987
Service Dates of Majority Members: Jan. 30,1985-Jan. 3,1987
Service Dates of Minority Members: Feb. 7,1985-Jan. 3,1987

Majority

Rank Name	Party	State	Terms in: House		Terms in: Comm.
Chr Hamilton, Lee H.	Dem	Ind.	11		3
2nd Stokes, Louis	Dem	Ohio	9		2
3rd McCurdy, Dave	Dem	Okla.	3	*1	2
4th Beilenson, Anthony C.	Dem	Cal.	5		1
5th Kastenmeier, Robert W.	Dem	Wisc.	14		1
6th Daniel, W. C. (Dan)	Dem	Va.	9		1
7th Roe, Robert A.	Dem	N.J.	9		1
8th Brown, George E. Jr.	Dem	Cal.	11		1
9th McHugh, Matthew F.	Dem	N.Y.	6		1
10th Dwyer, Bernard J.	Dem	N.J.	3		1

Minority

Rank Name	Party	State	Terms in: House	Terms in: Comm.
RM Stump, Robert	Rep	Ariz.	5	3
2nd Ireland, Andrew P.	Rep	Fla.	5	1
3rd Hyde, Henry J.	Rep	Ill.	6	1
4th Cheney, Richard B.	Rep	Wyo.	4	1
5th Livingston, Robert L.	Rep	La.	5	1
6th McEwen, Bob	Rep	Ohio	3	1

*1: Member's 1st period of service on the committee.

Note: The Majority and Minority Leaders of the House are *ex officio* members of the committee, but do no vote and are not counted for purposes of determining a quorum.

Departures from Committee:	Majority		Minority	
Moved to Science, Space & Technology; became Chair of Select Committee on Iran-Contra	Hamilton, Lee H.	Ind. Dem	None	
Moved to Armed Services	None		Ireland, Andrew P.	Fla. Rep
Moved to Veterans' Affairs	None		Stump, Robert	Ariz. Rep

HOUSE SELECT COMMITTEE: INTELLIGENCE (Permanent) / 100th Congress

Service Dates of Committee Chair: Jan. 21,1987-Jan. 3,1989
Service Dates of Majority Members: Jan. 21,1987-Jan. 3,1989
Service Dates of Minority Members: Jan. 28,1987-Jan. 3,1989

Majority

Rank Name	Party	State	Terms in: House		Terms in: Comm.
Chr Stokes, Louis	Dem	Ohio	10		3
2nd McCurdy, Dave	Dem	Okla.	4	*1	3
3rd Beilenson, Anthony C.	Dem	Cal.	6		2
4th Kastenmeier, Robert W.	Dem	Wisc.	15		2
5th Daniel, W. C. (Dan)	Dem	Va.	10		2
6th Roe, Robert A.	Dem	N.J.	10		2
7th Brown, George E. Jr.	Dem	Cal.	12		2
8th McHugh, Matthew F.	Dem	N.Y.	7		2
9th Dwyer, Bernard J.	Dem	N.J.	4		2
10th Wilson, Charles H.	Dem	Tex.	8		1
11th Kennelly, Barbara B.	Dem	Conn.	4		1

Minority

Rank Name	Party	State	Terms in: House	Terms in: Comm.
RM Hyde, Henry J.	Rep	Ill.	7	2
2nd Cheney, Richard B.	Rep	Wyo.	5	2
3rd Livingston, Robert L.	Rep	La.	6	2
4th McEwen, Bob	Rep	Ohio	4	2
5th Lungren, Daniel E.	Rep	Cal.	5	1
6th Shuster, E. G. (Bud)	Rep	Penn.	8	1

*1: Member's 1st period of service on the committee.

Note: The Majority and Minority Leaders of the House are *ex officio* members of the committee, but do no vote and are not counted for purposes of determining a quorum.

Changes:

Majority:

Brown, George E. Jr.	Dem	Cal.	Nov. 18,1987	Left committee; no new assignment.
Glickman, Daniel R.	Dem	Kans.	Nov. 18,1987	Replaced Brown.
McCurdy, Dave	Dem	Okla.	Dec. 21,1987	Left committee; no new assignment (letter dated Dec. 18,1987).
Daniel, W.C. (Dan)	Dem	Va.	Jan. 23,1988	Died in office.
Mavroules, Nicholas	Dem	Mass.	Feb. 1,1988	Replaced McCurdy.
Richardson, Bill	Dem	N.M.	Feb. 1,1988	Replaced Daniel.

	Majority			Minority		
Departures from the House:						
Retired	None			Lungren, Daniel E.	Cal.	Rep
Departures from Committee:						
No new assignment	Stokes, Louis	Ohio	Dem	McEwen, Bob	Ohio	Rep

HOUSE SELECT COMMITTEE: INTELLIGENCE (Permanent) / 101st Congress

Service Dates of Committee Chair: Jan. 19,1989-Jan. 3,1991
Service Dates of Majority Members: Jan. 19,1989-Jan. 3,1991
Service Dates of Minority Members: Jan. 24,1989-Jan. 3,1991

Majority

Rank Name	Party	State	Terms in: House	Terms in: Comm.
Chr Beilenson, Anthony C.	Dem	Cal.	7	3
2nd McCurdy, Dave	Dem	Okla.	5	*2 1
3rd Kastenmeier, Robert W.	Dem	Wisc.	16	3
4th Roe, Robert A.	Dem	N.J.	11	3
5th McHugh, Matthew F.	Dem	N.Y.	8	3
6th Dwyer, Bernard J.	Dem	N.J.	5	3
7th Wilson, Charles H.	Dem	Tex.	9	2
8th Kennelly, Barbara B.	Dem	Conn.	5	2
9th Glickman, Daniel R.	Dem	Kans.	7	2
10th Mavroules, Nicholas	Dem	Mass.	6	2
11th Richardson, Bill	Dem	N.M.	4	2
12th Solarz, Stephen J.	Dem	N.Y.	8	1

Minority

Rank Name	Party	State	Terms in: House	Terms in: Comm.
RM Hyde, Henry J.	Rep	Ill.	8	3
2nd Cheney, Richard B.	Rep	Wyo.	6	3
3rd Livingston, Robert L.	Rep	La.	7	3
4th Shuster, E.G. (Bud)	Rep	Penn.	9	2
5th Combest, Larry	Rep	Tex.	3	1
6th Bereuter, Douglas K.	Rep	Neb.	6	1
7th Rowland, John G.	Rep	Conn.	3	1

*2: Member's 2nd period of service on the committee.

Notes: House Resolution 213 (101-1), agreed to on July 27,1989, stipulated that Anthony C. Beilenson (Dem-Cal.) was allowed to continue serving as Chair of the Select Committee "notwithstanding the provisions of clause 1(c) of rule XLVIII" for the remainder of the 101st Congress. The Majority and Minority Leaders of the House are *ex officio* members of the committee, but do no vote and are not counted for purposes of determining a quorum. Dave McCurdy (Dem-Okla.) returned to the committee in this Congress and was credited for his previous service and ranked 2nd.

Changes:

Minority:

Cheney, Richard B.	Rep	Wyo.	Mar. 17,1989	Resigned; appointed Secretary of Defense.
Dornan, Robert K.	Rep	Cal.	Apr. 10,1989	Replaced Cheney.

	Majority			Minority		
Departures from the House:						
Defeated for Reelection	Kastenmeier, Robert W.	Wisc.	Dem	None		
Lost Election for Governor	None			Rowland, John G.	Conn.	Rep
Departures from Committee:						
Moved to Standards of Official Conduct	McHugh, Matthew F.	N.Y.	Dem	None		
Moved to Select Aging	Roe, Robert A.	N.J.	Dem	None		
Moved to House Administration	None			Livingston, Robert L.	La.	Rep
No new assignment	Beilenson, Anthony C.	Cal.	Dem	Hyde, Henry J.	Ill.	Rep
	Dwyer, Bernard J.	N.J.	Dem			

HOUSE SELECT COMMITTEE: INTELLIGENCE (Permanent) / 102nd Congress

Service Dates of Committee Chair: Feb. 5,1991-Jan. 3,1993
Service Dates of Majority Members: Feb. 5,1991-Jan. 3,1993
Service Dates of Minority Members: Feb. 5,1981-Jan. 3,1993

Majority

Rank Name	Party	State	Terms in: House	Terms in: Comm.
Chr McCurdy, Dave	Dem	Okla.	6 *2	2
2nd Wilson, Charles H.	Dem	Tex.	10	3
3rd Kennelly, Barbara B.	Dem	Conn.	6	3
4th Glickman, Daniel R.	Dem	Kans.	8	3
5th Mavroules, Nicholas	Dem	Mass.	7	3
6th Richardson, Bill	Dem	N.M.	5	3
7th Solarz, Stephen J.	Dem	N.Y.	9	2
8th Dicks, Norman D.	Dem	Wash.	8	1
9th Dellums, Ronald V.	Dem	Cal.	11	1
10th Bonior, David E.	Dem	Mich.	8	1
11th Sabo, Martin Olav	DFL	Minn.	7	1
12th Owens, D. Wayne	Dem	Utah	4	1

Minority

Rank Name	Party	State	Terms in: House	Terms in: Comm.
RM Shuster, E.G. (Bud)	Rep	Penn.	10	3
2nd Combest, Larry	Rep	Tex.	4	2
3rd Bereuter, Douglas K.	Rep	Neb.	7	2
4th Dornan, Robert K.	Rep	Cal.	4	2
5th Young, C.W. Bill	Rep	Fla.	11	1
6th Martin, David O'B.	Rep	N.Y.	6	1
7th Gekas, George W.	Rep	Penn.	5	1

*2: Member's 2nd period of service on the committee.

Note: The Majority and Minority Leaders of the House are *ex officio* members of the committee, but do no vote and are not counted for purposes of determining a quorum.

HOUSE SELECT COMMITTEE: THE OUTER CONTINENTAL SHELF (Ad Hoc)

Jurisdiction, 1975

From House Resolution 412, 94th Congress, First Session, April 22, 1975:

[Section 1]

Resolved (a) That pursuant to rule X, clause 5, the Speaker is authorized to establish an ad hoc Select Committee on the Outer Continental Shelf, to consider and report to the House on the bill H.R. 6218, a bill to establish a policy for the management of oil and natural gas in the Outer Continental Shelf; to protect the marine and coastal environment; to amend the Outer Continental Shelf Lands Act; and for other purposes, and on any related matter on this subject within the jurisdiction of the three committees named in part (b) of this section which may hereafter be referred to it by the Speaker.

Termination, 1980

The Select Committee was terminated upon the filing of its final report, House Report 1214 (96-2), on July 31, 1980.

HOUSE SELECT COMMITTEE: THE OUTER CONTINENTAL SHELF (Ad Hoc) / 94th Congress

Service Dates of Committee Chair: Apr. 22,1975-Jan. 3,1977
Service Dates of Majority Members: Apr. 22,1975-Jan. 3,1977
Service Dates of Minority Members: Apr. 22,1975-Jan. 3,1977

Majority

Rank	Name	Party	State	Terms in: House	Terms in: Comm.
Chr	Murphy, John M.	Dem	N.Y.	7	1
2nd	Udall, Morris K.	Dem	Ariz.	8	1
3rd	Mink, Patsy T.	Dem	Hai.	6	1
4th	Eilberg, Joshua	Dem	Penn.	5	1
5th	Kazen, Abraham Jr.	Dem	Tex.	5	1
6th	Breaux, John B.	Dem	La.	3	1
7th	Studds, Gerry E.	Dem	Mass.	2	1
8th	AuCoin, Les	Dem	Ore.	1	1
9th	Dodd, Christopher J.	Dem	Conn.	1	1
10th	Hughes, William J.	Dem	N.J.	1	1
11th	Russo, Martin A.	Dem	Ill.	1	1

Minority

Rank	Name	Party	State	Terms in: House	Terms in: Comm.
RM	Fish, Hamilton Jr.	Rep	N.Y.	4	1
2nd	Forsythe, Edwin B.	Rep	N.J.	4	1
3rd	du Pont, Pierre S. IV	Rep	Del.	3	1
4th	Young, Donald E.	Rep	Alas.	2	1
5th	Bauman, Robert E.	Rep	Md.	2	1

Additions:

	Rank	Name	Party	State	Date
Majority:	12th	Miller, George	Dem	Cal.	May 6,1975
	13th	de la Garza, E. (Kika)	Dem	Tex.	May 6,1975
Minority:	6th	Wiggins, Charles E.	Rep	Cal.	May 6,1975

	Majority			Minority		
Departures from the House:						
Elected Governor	None			du Pont, Pierre S. IV	Del.	Rep
Lost Nomination to U.S. Senate	Mink, Patsy T.	Hai.	Dem	None		
Departures from Committee:						
Moved to International Relations	de la Garza, E. (Kika)	Tex.	Dem	None		
No new assignment	AuCoin, Les	Ore.	Dem	None		

HOUSE SELECT COMMITTEE: THE OUTER CONTINENTAL SHELF (Ad Hoc) / 95th Congress

Service Dates of Committee Chair: Jan. 26,1977-Jan. 3,1979
Service Dates of Majority Members: Jan. 26,1977-Jan. 3,1979
Service Dates of Minority Members: Jan. 26,1977-Jan. 3,1979

Majority

Rank Name	Party	State	Terms in: House	Terms in: Comm.
Chr Murphy, John M.	Dem	N.Y.	8	2
2nd Udall, Morris K.	Dem	Ariz.	9	2
3rd Eilberg, Joshua	Dem	Penn.	6	2
4th Kazen, Abraham Jr.	Dem	Tex.	6	2
5th Breaux, John B.	Dem	La.	4	2
6th Studds, Gerry E.	Dem	Mass.	3	2
7th Dodd, Christopher J.	Dem	Conn.	2	2
8th Hughes, William J.	Dem	N.J.	2	2
9th Russo, Martin A.	Dem	Ill.	2	2
10th Miller, George	Dem	Cal.	2	1
11th Seiberling, John F.	Dem	Ohio	4	1
12th Ginn, Ronald B. (Bo)	Dem	Ga.	3	1
13th Zeferetti, Leo C.	Dem	N.Y.	2	1

Minority

Rank Name	Party	State	Terms in: House	Terms in: Comm.
RM Fish, Hamilton Jr.	Rep	N.Y.	5	2
2nd Forsythe, Edwin B.	Rep	N.J.	5	2
3rd Young, Donald E.	Rep	Alas.	3	2
4th Bauman, Robert E.	Rep	Md.	3	2
5th Wiggins, Charles E.	Rep	Cal.	6	2
6th Treen, David C.	Rep	La.	3	1

	Majority		Minority	
Departures from the House:				
Defeated for Reelection	Eilberg, Joshua	Penn. Dem	None	
Retired	None		Wiggins, Charles E.	Cal. Rep
Departures from Committee:				
No new assignment	Dodd, Christopher J.	Conn. Dem	Bauman, Robert E.	Md. Rep
			Fish, Hamilton Jr.	N.Y. Rep
			Treen, David C.	La. Rep

HOUSE SELECT COMMITTEE: THE OUTER CONTINENTAL SHELF (Ad Hoc) / 96th Congress

Service Dates of Committee Chair: Apr. 9,1979-July 31,1980
Service Dates of Majority Members: Apr. 9,1979-July 31,1980
Service Dates of Minority Members: Apr. 9,1979-July 31,1980

Majority

Rank Name	Party	State	Terms in: House	Terms in: Comm.
Chr Murphy, John M.	Dem	N.Y.	9	3
2nd Udall, Morris K.	Dem	Ariz.	10	3
3rd Kazen, Abraham Jr.	Dem	Tex.	7	3
4th Breaux, John B.	Dem	La.	5	3
5th Studds, Gerry E.	Dem	Mass.	4	3
6th Hughes, William J.	Dem	N.J.	3	3
7th Russo, Martin A.	Dem	Ill.	3	3
8th Miller, George	Dem	Cal.	3	2
9th Seiberling, John F.	Dem	Ohio	5	2
10th Ginn, Ronald B. (Bo)	Dem	Ga.	4	2
11th Zeferetti, Leo C.	Dem	N.Y.	3	2
12th Bonior, David E.	Dem	Mich.	2	1

Minority

Rank Name	Party	State	Terms in: House	Terms in: Comm.
RM Forsythe, Edwin B.	Rep	N.J.	6	3
2nd Young, Donald E.	Rep	Alas.	4	3
3rd Lott, Trent	Rep	Miss.	4	1
4th Emery, David F.	Rep	Me.	3	1
5th Livingston, Robert L.	Rep	La.	2	1
6th Lewis, Jerry	Rep	Cal.	1	1

Vacancy Filled:
Minority: 6th seat by Lewis on Sep. 12,1979.

Changes:
Majority:

Russo, Martin A.	Dem	Ill.	Oct. 23,1979	Left committee; no new assignment.
Albosta, Donald J.	Dem	Mich.	Dec. 20,1979	Replaced Russo.

HOUSE SELECT COMMITTEE: MISSING PERSONS IN SOUTHEAST ASIA

Jurisdiction, 1975

From House Resolution 335, 94th Congress, First Session, September 11, 1975:

[Section 2]

The select committee is authorized and directed to conduct a full and complete investigation and study of--
(1) the problem of United States servicemen still identified as missing in action, as well as those known dead whose bodies have not been recovered, as a result of military operations in North Vietnam, South Vietnam, Laos, and Cambodia;
(2) the need for additional international inspection teams to determine whether there are servicemen still held as prisoners of war.

Termination, 1977

The Select Committee was extended by House Resolution 1454 on August 2, 1976 until January 3, 1977, or 30 days after filing its final report, whichever was earlier. Its final report, House Report 1764 (94-2), was filed December 13, 1976; thus, the committee was terminated on January 3, 1977.

HOUSE SELECT COMMITTEE: MISSING PERSONS IN SOUTHEAST ASIA / 94th Congress

Service Dates of Committee Chair: Sep. 15,1975-Jan. 3,1977
Service Dates of Majority Members: Sep. 15,1975-Jan. 3,1977
Service Dates of Minority Members: Sep. 15,1975-Jan. 3,1977

Majority

Rank Name	Party	State	Terms in: House	Terms in: Comm.
Chr Montgomery, G.V. (Sonny)	Dem	Miss.	5	1
2nd Gonzalez, Henry B.	Dem	Tex.	8	1
3rd Moakley, John Joseph	Dem	Mass.	2	1
4th Schroeder, Patricia S.	Dem	Colo.	2	1
5th Ottinger, Richard L.	Dem	N.Y.	4	1
6th Harkin, Thomas R.	Dem	Iowa	1	1
7th Lloyd, James F.	Dem	Cal.	1	1

Minority

Rank Name	Party	State	Terms in: House	Terms in: Comm.
RM McCloskey, Paul N. Jr.	Rep	Cal.	5	1
2nd Gilman, Benjamin A.	Rep	N.Y.	2	1
3rd Guyer, Tennyson	Rep	Ohio	2	1

HOUSE SELECT COMMITTEE: PROFESSIONAL SPORTS

Jurisdiction, 1976

From House Resolution 1186, 94th Congress, Second Session, May 18, 1976:

[Section 1.(a)]

Resolved, That (a) there is hereby created a select committee on professional sports to conduct an inquiry into the need for legislation with respect to professional sports.

Termination, 1977

The Select Committee was terminated upon the filing of its final report, House Report 1786 (94-2), on January 3, 1977.

HOUSE SELECT COMMITTEE: PROFESSIONAL SPORTS / 94th Congress

Service Dates of Committee Chair: June 11,1976-Jan. 3,1977
Service Dates of Majority Members: June 11,1976-Jan. 3,1977
Service Dates of Minority Members: June 11,1976-Jan. 3,1977

Majority

Rank Name	Party	State	Terms in: House	Terms in: Comm.
Chr Sisk, B. F.	Dem	Cal.	11	1
2nd Price, C. Melvin	Dem	Ill.	16	1
3rd Rooney, Fred B.	Dem	Penn.	7	1
4th Long, Gillis W.	Dem	La.	3	1
5th Fisher, Joseph L.	Dem	Va.	1	1
6th Mottl, Ronald M.	Dem	Ohio	1	1
7th Zeferetti, Leo C.	Dem	N.Y.	1	1

Minority

Rank Name	Party	State	Terms in: House	Terms in: Comm.
RM Horton, Frank J.	Rep	N.Y.	7	1
2nd Conte, Silvio O.	Rep	Mass.	9	1
3rd Derwinski, Edward J.	Rep	Ill.	9	1
4th Clausen, Don H.	Rep	Cal.	7	1
5th Wydler, John W.	Rep	N.Y.	7	1
6th Gude, Gilbert	Rep	Md.	5	1

HOUSE SELECT COMMITTEE: NARCOTICS ABUSE AND CONTROL

Jurisdiction, 1976

From House Resolution 1350, 94th Congress, Second Session, July 29, 1976:

[Section 2]

The select committee shall not have legislative jurisdiction. The select committee shall have authority--

(1) to conduct a continuing comprehensive study and review of the problems of narcotics abuse and control, including, but not limited to, international trafficking, enforcement, prevention, narcotics-related violations of the Internal Revenue Code of 1954, international treaties, organized crime, drug abuse in the Armed Forces of the United States, treatment and rehabilitation, and the approach of the criminal justice system with respect to narcotics law violations and crimes related to drug abuse; and

(2) to review any recommendations made by the President, or by any department or agency of the executive branch of the Federal Government, relating to programs or policies affecting narcotics abuse or control.

The Select Committee has been recreated each Congress by separate Resolutions: House Resolution 77 (95-1); House Resolution 13 (96-1); House Resolution 13 (97-1); House Resolution 49 (98-1); House Resolution 22 (99-1); House Resolution 26 (100-1); House Resolution 84 (101-1);

Jurisdiction, 1992

From House Resolution 51, 102nd Congress, First Session, February 6, 1991:

[Section 2]

The select committee shall not have legislative jurisdiction. The select committee shall have authority--

(1) to conduct continuing oversight and review of the problems of narcotics, drug, and polydrug abuse and control, including (but not limited to) the study and review of

(A) the abuse and control of opium and its derivatives, other narcotic drugs, psychotropics, and other controlled substances, as defined in the Comprehensive Drug Abuse Prevention and Control Act of 1970, and any such drug or substance when used in combination with any other substance;
(B) domestic and international trafficking, manufacturing, and distribution;
(C) treatment, prevention, and rehabilitation;
(D) narcotics-related violations of the Internal Revenue Code of 1954;
(E) international treaties and agreements relating to the control of narcotics and drug abuse;
(G) problems of narcotics and drug abuse and control in the Armed Forces of the United States;
(H) problems of narcotics and drug abuse and control in industry; and
(I) the approach of the criminal justice system with respect to narcotic and drug law violations and crimes related to drug abuse;

(2) to review any recommendations made by the President, or by any department or agency of the executive branch of the Federal Government, relating to programs or policies affecting narcotics or drug abuse or control; and

(3) to recommend to the appropriate committees of the House legislation or other action the select committee considers necessary with respect to programs or policies affecting narcotics or drug abuse or control.

HOUSE SELECT COMMITTEE: NARCOTICS ABUSE AND CONTROL / 94th Congress

Service Dates of Committee Chair: Aug. 3,1976-Jan. 3,1977
Service Dates of Majority Members: Aug. 3,1976-Jan. 3,1977
Service Dates of Minority Members: Aug. 3,1976-Jan. 3,1977

Majority

Rank	Name	Party	State	Terms in: House	Terms in: Comm.
Chr	Wolff, Lester L.	Dem	N.Y.	6	1
2nd	Rodino, Peter W. Jr.	Dem	N.J.	14	1
3rd	Rogers, Paul G.	Dem	Fla.	11	1
4th	de la Garza, E. (Kika)	Dem	Tex.	6	1
5th	Mann, James R.	Dem	S.C.	4	1
6th	Badillo, Herman	Dem	N.Y.	3	1
7th	Murphy, Morgan F.	Dem	Ill.	3	1
8th	Rangel, Charles B.	Dem	N.Y.	3	1
9th	Stark, Fortney H. (Pete)	Dem	Cal.	2	1
10th	Scheuer, James H.	Dem	N.Y.	5 *1	1
11th	English, Glenn L. Jr.	Dem	Okla.	1	1
12th	Waxman, Henry A.	Dem	Cal.	1	1

Minority

Rank	Name	Party	State	Terms in: House	Terms in: Comm.
RM	Burke, J. Herbert	Rep	Fla.	5	1
2nd	Railsback, Thomas F.	Rep	Ill.	5	1
3rd	Frey, Louis Jr.	Rep	Fla.	4	1
4th	Beard, Robin L. Jr.	Rep	Tenn.	2	1
5th	Gilman, Benjamin A.	Rep	N.Y.	2	1
6th	Guyer, Tennyson	Rep	Ohio	2	1

*1: Member's first period of service on the committee.

HOUSE SELECT COMMITTEE: NARCOTICS ABUSE AND CONTROL / 95th Congress

Service Dates of Committee Chair: Jan. 19,1977-Jan. 3,1979
Service Dates of Majority Members: Jan. 19,1977-Jan. 3,1979
Service Dates of Minority Members: Jan. 19,1977-Jan. 3,1979

Majority

Rank	Name	Party	State	Terms in: House	Terms in: Comm.
Chr	Wolff, Lester L.	Dem	N.Y.	7	2
2nd	Rodino, Peter W. Jr.	Dem	N.J.	15	2
3rd	Rogers, Paul G.	Dem	Fla.	12	2
4th	de la Garza, E. (Kika)	Dem	Tex.	7	2
5th	Mann, James R.	Dem	S.C.	5	2
6th	Badillo, Herman	Dem	N.Y.	4	2
7th	Murphy, Morgan F.	Dem	Ill.	4	2
8th	Rangel, Charles B.	Dem	N.Y.	4	2
9th	Stark, Fortney H. (Pete)	Dem	Cal.	3	2
10th	Scheuer, James H.	Dem	N.Y.	6 *1	2
11th	English, Glenn L. Jr.	Dem	Okla.	2	2
12th	Waxman, Henry A.	Dem	Cal.	2	2

Minority

Rank	Name	Party	State	Terms in: House	Terms in: Comm.
RM	Burke, J. Herbert	Rep	Fla.	6	2
2nd	Railsback, Thomas F.	Rep	Ill.	6	2
3rd	Frey, Louis Jr.	Rep	Fla.	5	2
4th	Beard, Robin L. Jr.	Rep	Tenn.	3	2
5th	Gilman, Benjamin A.	Rep	N.Y.	3	2
6th	Guyer, Tennyson	Rep	Ohio	3	2

*1: Member's first period of service on the committee.

Changes:

Majority:

Name	Party	State	Date	Change
Waxman, Henry A.	Dem	Cal.	Apr. 4,1977	Left committee; no new assignment.
Evans, Billy Lee	Dem	Ga.	Apr. 4,1977	Replaced Waxman.
Scheuer, James H.	Dem	N.Y.	Nov. 4,1977	Moved to Select Population as Chair.
Zeferetti, Leo C.	Dem	N.Y.	Nov. 4,1977	Replaced Scheuer.
Badillo, Herman	Dem	N.Y.	Dec. 31,1977	Resigned; appointed Deputy Mayor New York City.
Akaka, Daniel K.	Dem	Hai.	Mar. 16,1978	Replaced Badillo.

	Majority			Minority		
Departures from the House:						
Defeated for Reelection	None			Burke, J. Herbert	Fla.	Rep
Lost Nomination for Governor	None			Frey, Louis Jr.	Fla.	Rep
Retired	Mann, James R.	S.C.	Dem	None		
	Rogers, Paul G.	Fla.	Dem			
Departures from Committee:						
No new assignment	Akaka, Daniel K.	Hai.	Dem	None		

HOUSE SELECT COMMITTEE: NARCOTICS ABUSE AND CONTROL / 96th Congress

Service Dates of Committee Chair: Apr. 5,1979-Jan. 3,1981
Service Dates of Majority Members: Apr. 5,1979-Jan. 3,1981
Service Dates of Minority Members: Apr. 5,1979-Jan. 3,1981

Majority

Rank	Name	Party	State	Terms in: House	Terms in: Comm.
Chr	Wolff, Lester L.	Dem	N.Y.	8	3
2nd	Rodino, Peter W. Jr.	Dem	N.J.	16	3
3rd	de la Garza, E. (Kika)	Dem	Tex.	8	3
4th	Murphy, Morgan F.	Dem	Ill.	5	3
5th	Rangel, Charles B.	Dem	N.Y.	5	3
6th	Stark, Fortney H. (Pete)	Dem	Cal.	4	3
7th	English, Glenn L. Jr.	Dem	Okla.	3	3
8th	Evans, Billy Lee	Dem	Ga.	2	2
9th	Zeferetti, Leo C.	Dem	N.Y.	3	2
10th	Neal, Stephen L.	Dem	N.C.	3	1
11th	Scheuer, James H.	Dem	N.Y.	7 *2	1

Minority

Rank	Name	Party	State	Terms in: House	Terms in: Comm.
RM	Railsback, Thomas F.	Rep	Ill.	7	3
2nd	Beard, Robin L. Jr.	Rep	Tenn.	4	3
3rd	Gilman, Benjamin A.	Rep	N.Y.	4	3
4th	Guyer, Tennyson	Rep	Ohio	4	3
5th	Coughlin, R. Lawrence	Rep	Penn.	6	1
6th	Dornan, Robert K.	Rep	Cal.	2 *1	1

*1: Member's 1st period of service on the committee; *2: Member's 2nd period of service on the committee.

Changes:
Majority:

Name	Party	State	Date	Change
Murphy, Morgan F.	Dem	Ill.	Dec. 20,1979	Left committee; no new assignment.
Collins, Cardiss	Dem	Ill.	Feb. 20,1980	Replaced Murphy.

	Majority			Minority
Departures from the House:				
Defeated for Reelection	Wolff, Lester L.	N.Y.	Dem	None
Departures from Committee:				
Became Chair of Agriculture	de la Garza, E. (Kika)	Tex.	Dem	None

HOUSE SELECT COMMITTEE: NARCOTICS ABUSE AND CONTROL / 97th Congress

Service Dates of Committee Chair: Feb. 25,1981-Jan. 3,1983
Service Dates of Majority Members: Feb. 25,1981-Jan. 3,1983
Service Dates of Minority Members: Feb. 25,1981-Jan. 3,1983

Majority

Rank	Name	Party	State	Terms in: House	Terms in: Comm.
Chr	Zeferetti, Leo C.	Dem	N.Y.	4	3
2nd	Rodino, Peter W. Jr.	Dem	N.J.	17	4
3rd	Rangel, Charles B.	Dem	N.Y.	6	4
4th	Stark, Fortney H. (Pete)	Dem	Cal.	5	4
5th	English, Glenn L. Jr.	Dem	Okla.	4	4
6th	Evans, Billy Lee	Dem	Ga.	3	3
7th	Neal, Stephen L.	Dem	N.C.	4	2
8th	Scheuer, James H.	Dem	N.Y.	8 *2	2
9th	Collins, Cardiss	Dem	Ill.	5	2
10th	Akaka, Daniel K.	Dem	Hai.	3 *2	1
11th	Guarini, Frank J.	Dem	N.J.	2	1

Minority

Rank	Name	Party	State	Terms in: House	Terms in: Comm.
RM	Railsback, Thomas F.	Rep	Ill.	8	4
2nd	Beard, Robin L. Jr.	Rep	Tenn.	5	4
3rd	Gilman, Benjamin A.	Rep	N.Y.	5	4
4th	Guyer, Tennyson	Rep	Ohio	5	4
5th	Coughlin, R. Lawrence	Rep	Penn.	7	2
6th	Dornan, Robert K.	Rep	Cal.	3 *1	2
7th	DeNardis, Lawrence J.	Rep	Conn.	1	1
8th	Shaw, E. Clay Jr.	Rep	Fla.	1	1

*1: Member's first period of service on the committee;
*2: Member's 2nd period of service on the committee.

Changes:
Majority:

Name	Party	State	Date	Change
Neal, Stephen L.	Dem	N.C.	Mar. 18,1981	Left committee (letter dated Feb. 27,1981); no new assignment.
Matsui, Robert T.	Dem	Cal.	Mar. 18,1981	Replaced Neal.

Minority:

Name	Party	State	Date	Change
Guyer, Tennyson	Rep	Ohio	Apr. 12,1981	Died in office.
Oxley, Michael G.	Rep	Ohio	Sep. 16,1981	Replaced Guyer.

Departures from the House:	Majority		Minority	
Defeated for Reelection	Zeferetti, Leo C.	N.Y. Dem	DeNardis, Lawrence J.	Conn. Rep
Defeated for Renomination	Evans, Billy Lee	Ga. Dem	Railsback, Thomas F.	Ill. Rep
Lost Election to U.S. Senate	None		Beard, Robin L. Jr.	Tenn. Rep
Lost Nomination to U.S. Senate	None		Dornan, Robert K.	Cal. Rep
Departures from Committee:				
No new assignment	English, Glenn L. Jr.	Okla. Dem	None	

HOUSE SELECT COMMITTEE: NARCOTICS ABUSE AND CONTROL / 98th Congress

Service Dates of Committee Chair: Feb. 22,1983-Jan. 3,1985
Service Dates of Majority Members: Feb. 22,1983-Jan. 3,1985
Service Dates of Minority Members: Feb. 22,1983-Jan. 3,1985

Majority

Rank	Name	Party	State	Terms in: House	Terms in: Comm.
Chr	Rangel, Charles B.	Dem	N.Y.	7	5
2nd	Rodino, Peter W. Jr.	Dem	N.J.	18	5
3rd	Stark, Fortney H. (Pete)	Dem	Cal.	6	5
4th	Scheuer, James H.	Dem	N.Y.	9	*2 3
5th	Collins, Cardiss	Dem	Ill.	6	3
6th	Akaka, Daniel K.	Dem	Hai.	4	*2 2
7th	Guarini, Frank J.	Dem	N.J.	3	2
8th	Matsui, Robert T.	Dem	Cal.	3	2
9th	Fascell, Dante B.	Dem	Fla.	15	1
10th	Fauntroy, Walter E.	Dem	D.C.	7	1
11th	Hughes, William J.	Dem	N.J.	5	1
12th	Hall, Sam B. Jr.	Dem	Tex.	5	1
13th	Levine, Mel	Dem	Cal.	1	1
14th	Ortiz, Solomon P.	Dem	Tex.	1	1
15th	Smith, Lawrence J.	Dem	Fla.	1	1
16th	Towns, Edolphus	Dem	N.Y.	1	1

Minority

Rank	Name	Party	State	Terms in: House	Terms in: Comm.
RM	Gilman, Benjamin A.	Rep	N.Y.	6	5
2nd	Coughlin, R. Lawrence	Rep	Penn.	8	3
3rd	Shaw, E. Clay Jr.	Rep	Fla.	2	2
4th	Oxley, Michael G.	Rep	Ohio	2	2
5th	Pritchard, Joel M.	Rep	Wash.	6	1
6th	Parris, Stanford E.	Rep	Va.	3	1
7th	Chappie, Eugene A.	Rep	Cal.	2	1
8th	Hunter, Duncan L.	Rep	Cal.	2	1
9th	Lewis, Tom	Rep	Fla.	1	1

*2: Member's 2nd period of service on the committee.

Departures from the House:	Majority		Minority	
Retired	None		Pritchard, Joel M.	Wash. Rep
Departures from Committee:				
Moved to Agriculture	None		Lewis, Tom	Fla. Rep
No new assignment	Hall, Sam B. Jr.	Tex. Dem		

HOUSE SELECT COMMITTEE: NARCOTICS ABUSE AND CONTROL / 99th Congress

Service Dates of Committee Chair: Mar. 25,1985-Jan. 3,1987
Service Dates of Majority Members: Mar. 25,1985-Jan. 3,1987
Service Dates of Minority Members: Mar. 25,1985-Jan. 3,1987

Majority

Rank	Name	Party	State	Terms in: House	Terms in: Comm.
Chr	Rangel, Charles B.	Dem	N.Y.	8	6
2nd	Rodino, Peter W. Jr.	Dem	N.J.	19	6
3rd	Stark, Fortney H. (Pete)	Dem	Cal.	7	6
4th	Scheuer, James H.	Dem	N.Y.	10	*2 4
5th	Collins, Cardiss	Dem	Ill.	7	4
6th	Akaka, Daniel K.	Dem	Hai.	5	*2 3
7th	Guarini, Frank J.	Dem	N.J.	4	3
8th	Matsui, Robert T.	Dem	Cal.	4	3
9th	Fascell, Dante B.	Dem	Fla.	16	2
10th	Fauntroy, Walter E.	Dem	D.C.	8	2
11th	Hughes, William J.	Dem	N.J.	6	2
12th	Levine, Mel	Dem	Cal.	2	2
13th	Ortiz, Solomon P.	Dem	Tex.	2	2
14th	Smith, Lawrence J.	Dem	Fla.	2	2
15th	Towns, Edolphus	Dem	N.Y.	2	2

Minority

Rank	Name	Party	State	Terms in: House	Terms in: Comm.
RM	Gilman, Benjamin A.	Rep	N.Y.	7	6
2nd	Coughlin, R. Lawrence	Rep	Penn.	9	4
3rd	Shaw, E. Clay Jr.	Rep	Fla.	3	3
4th	Oxley, Michael G.	Rep	Ohio	3	3
5th	Parris, Stanford E.	Rep	Va.	4	2
6th	Chappie, Eugene A.	Rep	Cal.	3	2
7th	Hunter, Duncan L.	Rep	Cal.	3	2
8th	DioGuardi, Joseph J.	Rep	N.Y.	1	1
9th	Strang, Michael L.	Rep	Colo.	1	1
10th	Rowland, John G.	Rep	Conn.	1	1

*2: Member's 2nd period of service on the committee.

Departures from the House:	**Majority**		**Minority**	
Defeated for Reelection	None		Strang, Michael L.	Colo. Rep
Retired	None		Chappie, Eugene A.	Cal. Rep
Departures from Committee:				
Moved to Armed Services	None		Rowland, John G.	Conn. Rep

HOUSE SELECT COMMITTEE: NARCOTICS ABUSE AND CONTROL / 100th Congress

Service Dates of Committee Chair: Jan. 21,1987-Jan. 3,1989
Service Dates of Majority Members: Jan. 21,1987-Jan. 3,1989
Service Dates of Minority Members: Jan. 28,1987-Jan. 3,1989

Majority

Rank	Name	Party	State	Terms in: House	Terms in: Comm.
Chr	Rangel, Charles B.	Dem	N.Y.	9	7
2nd	Rodino, Peter W. Jr.	Dem	N.J.	20	7
3rd	Stark, Fortney H. (Pete)	Dem	Cal.	8	7
4th	Scheuer, James H.	Dem	N.Y.	11 *2	5
5th	Collins, Cardiss	Dem	Ill.	8	5
6th	Akaka, Daniel K.	Dem	Hai.	6 *2	4
7th	Guarini, Frank J.	Dem	N.J.	5	4
8th	Matsui, Robert T.	Dem	Cal.	5	4
9th	Fascell, Dante B.	Dem	Fla.	17	3
10th	Fauntroy, Walter E.	Dem	D.C.	9	3
11th	Hughes, William J.	Dem	N.J.	7	3
12th	Levine, Mel	Dem	Cal.	3	3
13th	Ortiz, Solomon P.	Dem	Tex.	3	3
14th	Smith, Lawrence J.	Dem	Fla.	3	3
15th	Towns, Edolphus	Dem	N.Y.	3	3

Minority

Rank	Name	Party	State	Terms in: House	Terms in: Comm.
RM	Gilman, Benjamin A.	Rep	N.Y.	8	7
2nd	Coughlin, R. Lawrence	Rep	Penn.	10	5
3rd	Shaw, E. Clay Jr.	Rep	Fla.	4	4
4th	Oxley, Michael G.	Rep	Ohio	4	4
5th	Parris, Stanford E.	Rep	Va.	5	3
6th	Hunter, Duncan L.	Rep	Cal.	4	3
7th	DioGuardi, Joseph J.	Rep	N.Y.	2	2
8th	McKinney, Stewart B.	Rep	Conn	9	1
9th	Sensenbrenner, F. James Jr.	Rep	Wisc.	5	1
10th	Dornan, Robert K.	Rep	Cal.	5 *2	1

*2: Member's 2nd period of service on the committee.

Changes:

Majority:

Name	Party	State	Date	Change
Matsui, Robert T.	Dem	Cal.	June 17,1987	Left committee; no new assignment.
Traficant, James A. Jr.	Dem	Ohio	June 17,1987	Replaced Matsui.

Minority:

Name	Party	State	Date	Change
McKinney, Stewart B.	Rep	Conn.	May 7,1987	Died in office.
Lewis, Tom	Rep	Fla.	June 25,1987	Replaced McKinney.
Shaw, E. Clay Jr.	Rep	Fla.	July 7,1988	Moved to Ways and Means.
Hunter, Duncan L.	Rep	Cal.	Oct. 6,1988	Left committee; no new assignment.
Inhofe, James M.	Rep	Okla.	Oct. 6,1988	Replaced Shaw.

Departures from the House:	**Majority**		**Minority**	
Defeated for Reelection	None		DioGuardi, Joseph J.	N.Y. Rep
Retired	Rodino, Peter W. Jr.	N.J. Dem	None	

HOUSE SELECT COMMITTEE: NARCOTICS ABUSE AND CONTROL / 101st Congress

Service Dates of Committee Chair: Mar. 8,1989-Jan. 3,1991
Service Dates of Majority Members: Mar. 8,1989-Jan. 3,1991
Service Dates of Minority Members: Apr. 10,1989-Jan. 3,1991

Majority

Rank Name	Party	State	Terms in: House	Terms in: Comm.
Chr Rangel, Charles B.	Dem	N.Y.	10	8
2nd Brooks, Jack	Dem	Tex.	19	1
3rd Stark, Fortney H. (Pete)	Dem	Cal.	9	8
4th Scheuer, James H.	Dem	N.Y.	12	*2 6
5th Collins, Cardiss	Dem	Ill.	9	6
6th Akaka, Daniel K.	Dem	Hai.	7	*2 5
7th Guarini, Frank J.	Dem	N.J.	6	5
8th Fascell, Dante B.	Dem	Fla.	18	4
9th Fauntroy, Walter E.	Dem	D.C.	10	4
10th Hughes, William J.	Dem	N.J.	8	4
11th Levine, Mel	Dem	Cal.	4	4
12th Ortiz, Solomon P.	Dem	Tex.	4	4
13th Smith, Lawrence J.	Dem	Fla.	4	4
14th Towns, Edolphus	Dem	N.Y.	4	4
15th Traficant, James A. Jr.	Dem	Ohio	3	2
16th Mfume, Kweisi	Dem	Md.	2	1
17th Brennan, Joseph E.	Dem	Me.	2	1
18th Lowey, Nita M.	Dem	N.Y.	1	1

Minority

Rank Name	Party	State	Terms in: House	Terms in: Comm.
RM Coughlin, R. Lawrence	Rep	Penn.	11	6
2nd Gilman, Benjamin A.	Rep	N.Y.	9	8
3rd Oxley, Michael G.	Rep	Ohio	6	6
4th Parris, Stanford E.	Rep	Va.	6	4
5th Sensenbrenner, F. James Jr.	Rep	Wisc.	6	2
6th Dornan, Robert K.	Rep	Cal.	6	*2 2
7th Lewis, Tom	Rep	Fla.	4	2
8th Inhofe, James M.	Rep	Okla.	2	2
9th Herger, Wally	Rep	Cal.	2	1
10th Shays, Christopher	Rep	Conn.	2	1
11th Paxon, L. William	Rep	N.Y.	1	1
12th Grant, Bill	Rep	Fla.	2	1

*2: Member's 2nd period of service on the committee.

Note: As Chair of the Judiciary Committee, Jack Brooks (Dem-Tex.) was ranked second on the committee.

Vacancy Filled:
Minority: 12th by Grant on May 4,1989.

Changes:
Majority:

Akaka, Daniel K.	Dem	Hai.	May 19,1990	Resigned; appointed to the Senate.
Payne, Donald M.	Dem	N.J.	July 19,1990	Replaced Akaka.

Departures from the House:

	Majority		Minority	
Defeated for Reelection	None		Parris, Stanford E.	Va. Rep
			Grant, Bill	Fla. Rep
Lost Election for Governor	Brennan, Joseph E.	Me. Dem	None	
Lost Election for Mayor	Fauntroy, Walter E.	D.C. Dem		

HOUSE SELECT COMMITTEE: NARCOTICS ABUSE AND CONTROL / 102nd Congress

Service Dates of Committee Chair: Feb. 21,1991-Jan. 3,1993
Service Dates of Majority Members: Feb. 21,1991-Jan. 3,1993
Service Dates of Minority Members: Feb. 21,1991-Jan. 3,1993

Majority

Rank Name	Party	State	Terms in: House	Terms in: Comm.
Chr Rangel, Charles B.	Dem	N.Y.	11	9
2nd Brooks, Jack	Dem	Tex.	20	2
3rd Stark, Fortney H. (Pete)	Dem	Cal.	10	9
4th Scheuer, James H.	Dem	N.Y.	13	*2 7
5th Collins, Cardiss	Dem	Ill.	10	7
6th Guarini, Frank J.	Dem	N.J.	7	6
7th Fascell, Dante B.	Dem	Fla.	19	5
8th Hughes, William J.	Dem	N.J.	9	5
9th Levine, Mel	Dem	Cal.	5	5
10th Ortiz, Solomon P.	Dem	Tex.	5	5
11th Smith, Lawrence J.	Dem	Fla.	5	5
12th Towns, Edolphus	Dem	N.Y.	5	5
13th Traficant, James A. Jr.	Dem	Ohio	4	3
14th Mfume, Kweisi	Dem	Md.	3	2
15th Lowey, Nita M.	Dem	N.Y.	2	2
16th Payne, Donald M.	Dem	N.J.	2	2
17th Mazzoli, Romano L.	Dem	Ky.	11	1
18th de Lugo, Ron	Dem	V.I.	9	1
19th Hochbrueckner, George J.	Dem	N.Y.	3	1
20th Washington, Craig	Dem	Tex.	2	1
21st Andrews, Robert E.	Dem	N.J.	2	1

Minority

Rank Name	Party	State	Terms in: House	Terms in: Comm.
RM Coughlin, R. Lawrence	Rep	Penn.	12	7
2nd Gilman, Benjamin A.	Rep	N.Y.	10	9
3rd Oxley, Michael G.	Rep	Ohio	6	6
4th Sensenbrenner, F. James Jr.	Rep	Wisc.	7	3
5th Dornan, Robert K.	Rep	Cal.	7	*2 3
6th Lewis, Tom	Rep	Fla.	5	3
7th Inhofe, James M.	Rep	Okla.	3	3
8th Herger, Wally	Rep	Cal.	3	2
10th Shays, Christopher	Rep	Conn.	3	2
11th Paxon, L. William	Rep	N.Y.	2	2
12th Clinger, William F.	Rep	Penn.	7	1
13th Coble, Howard	Rep	N.C.	4	1
14th Gillmor, Paul E.	Rep	Ohio	2	1
15th Ramstad, Jim	Rep	Minn.	1	1

*2: Member's 2nd period of service on the committee.

Note: As Chair of the Judiciary Committee, Jack Brooks (Dem-Tex.) was ranked second on the committee.

HOUSE SELECT COMMITTEE: ASSASSINATIONS

Jurisdiction, 1976

From House Resolution 1540, 94th Congress, Second Session, September 17, 1976:

[Paragraph 2]

The select committee is authorized and directed to conduct a full and complete investigation and study of the circumstances surrounding the death of John F. Kennedy and the death of Martin Luther King, Junior, and of any others the select committee shall determine.

From House Resolution 222, 95th Congress, First Session, February 2, 1977:

[Paragraph 2]

The select committee or a subcommittee thereof is authorized and directed to conduct a full and complete investigation and study of the circumstances surrounding the assassination and death of President John F. Kennedy and the assassination and death of Martin Luther King, Junior, and of any other persons the select committee shall determine might be related to either death in order to ascertain

(1) whether the existing laws of the United States, including but not limited to laws relating to the safety and protection of the President of the United States, assassinations of the President of the United States, deprivation of civil rights, and conspiracies related thereto, as well as the investigatory jurisdiction and capability of agencies and departments of the United States Government, are adequate, either in their provisions or in the manner of their enforcement; and

(2) whether there was full disclosure and sharing of information and evidence among agencies and departments of the United States Government during the course of all prior investigations into those deaths; and whether any evidence or information which was not in the possession of any agency or department of the United States Government investigating either death would have been of assistance to that agency or department, and why such information was not provided to or collected by the appropriate agency or department; and shall make recommendations to the House, if the select committee deems it appropriate for the amendment of existing legislation or the enactment of new legislation.

Termination, 1979

The Select Committee was extended by House Resolution 433 (95-1) and terminated upon the filing of its final report, House Report 1828 (95-2) on January 2, 1979 with supplemental reports filed March 29, 1979.

HOUSE SELECT COMMITTEE: ASSASSINATIONS / 94th Congress

Service Dates of Committee Chair: Sep. 21,1976-Jan. 3,1977
Service Dates of Majority Members: Sep. 21,1976-Jan. 3,1977
Service Dates of Minority Members: Sep. 21,1976-Jan. 3,1977

Majority

Rank	Name	Party	State	Terms in: House	Terms in: Comm.
Chr	Downing, Thomas N.	Dem	Va.	9	1
2nd	Gonzalez, Henry B.	Dem	Tex.	8	1
3rd	Preyer, L. Richardson	Dem	N.C.	4	1
4th	Stokes, Louis	Dem	Ohio	4	1
5th	Fauntroy, Walter E.	Dem	D.C.	3	1
6th	Burke, Yvonne Brathwaite	Dem	Cal.	2	1
7th	Dodd, Christopher J.	Dem	Conn.	1	1
8th	Ford, Harold E.	Dem	Tenn.	1	1

Minority

Rank	Name	Party	State	Terms in: House	Terms in: Comm.
RM	Devine, Samuel L.	Rep	Ohio	9	1
2nd	Talcott, Burt L.	Rep	Cal.	7	1
3rd	McKinney, Stewart B.	Rep	Conn.	3	1
4th	Thone, Charles	Rep	Neb.	3	1

Departures from the House:	Majority			Minority		
Defeated for Reelection	None			Talcott, Burt L.	Cal.	Rep
Retired	Downing, Thomas N.	Va.	Dem	None		

HOUSE SELECT COMMITTEE: ASSASSINATIONS / 95th Congress

Service Dates of Committee Chair: Ch1 Feb. 2,1977-Mar. 8,1977
Ch2 Mar. 8,1977-Jan. 2,1979
Service Dates of Majority Members: Feb. 2,1977-Jan. 2,1979
Service Dates of Minority Members: Feb. 2,1977-Jan. 2,1979

Majority

Rank Name	Party	State	Terms in: House	Terms in: Comm.
Ch1 Gonzalez, Henry B.	Dem	Tex.	9	2
2nd Preyer, L. Richardson	Dem	N.C.	5	2
Ch2 3rd Stokes, Louis	Dem	Ohio	5	2
4th Fauntroy, Walter E.	Dem	D.C.	4	2
5th Burke, Yvonne Brathwaite	Dem	Cal.	3	2
6th Dodd, Christopher J.	Dem	Conn.	2	2
7th Ford, Harold E.	Dem	Tenn.	2	2
8th Fithian, Floyd J.	Dem	Ind.	2	1

Minority

Rank Name	Party	State	Terms in: House	Terms in: Comm.
RM Devine, Samuel L.	Rep	Ohio	10	2
2nd Anderson, John B.	Rep	Ill.	9	1
3rd McKinney, Stewart B.	Rep	Conn.	4	2
4th Thone, Charles	Rep	Neb.	4	2

Changes:

Chair:				
Ch1 Gonzalez, Henry B.	Dem	Tex.	Mar. 8,1977	Left committee; no new assignment.
Ch2 Stokes, Louis	Dem	Ohio	Mar. 8,1977	Succeeded Gonzalez as Chair.
Majority:				
Gonzalez, Henry B.	Dem	Tex.	Mar. 8,1977	Left committee; no new assignment.
Edgar, Robert W.	Dem	Penn.	Mar. 10,1977	Replaced Gonzalez.
Minority:				
Anderson, John B.	Rep	Ill.	Apr. 21,1977	Moved to Ad Hoc Select Committee on Energy.
Sawyer, Harold S.	Rep	Mich.	Apr. 21,1977	Replaced Anderson.

HOUSE SELECT COMMITTEE: ETHICS

Jurisdiction, 1977

From House Resolution 383, 95th Congress, First Session, March 9, 1977:

[Sections 2.(a) and 2.(b)]

(a) The select committee shall consider and may report to the House on any bills or resolutions which may include provisions incorporating and integrating into permanent law applicable provisions and appropriate modifications of rule XLIII, rule XLIV, rule XLV, rule XLVI, and rule LXVII of the Rules of the House of Representatives, and which may hereafter be referred to the select committee by the Speaker. The select committee shall have exclusive jurisdiction over the bills and resolutions referred to it.
(b) The select committee shall have jurisdiction to adopt regulations, and may issue advisory opinions, respecting the application of rule XLIII, rule XLIV, rule XLV, rule XLVI, and rule XLVII of the Rules of the House of Representatives.

Termination, 1979

The Select Committee was terminated upon filing its final report, House Report 1837 (95-2), on January 3, 1979.

HOUSE SELECT COMMITTEE: ETHICS / 95th Congress

Service Dates of Committee Chair: Mar. 10,1977-Jan. 3,1979
Service Dates of Majority Members: Mar. 10,1977-Jan. 3,1979
Service Dates of Minority Members: Mar. 10,1977-Jan. 3,1979

Majority

Rank	Name	Party	State	Terms in: House	Terms in: Comm.
Chr	Preyer, L. Richardson	Dem	N.C.	5	1
2nd	Bolling, Richard W.	Dem	Mo.	15	1
3rd	Flynt, John James Jr.	Dem	Ga.	13	1
4th	Thompson, Frank Jr.	Dem	N.J.	12	1
5th	Kastenmeier, Robert W.	Dem	Wisc.	10	1
6th	Stratton, Samuel S.	Dem	N.Y.	10	1
7th	Udall, Morris K.	Dem	Ariz.	9	1
8th	Hamilton, Lee H.	Dem	Ind.	7	1
9th	Meeds, Lloyd	Dem	Wash.	7	1
10th	Flowers, Walter	Dem	Ala.	5	1
11th	Obey, David R.	Dem	Wisc.	5	1
12th	Danielson, George E.	Dem	Cal.	4	1
13th	Mazzoli, Romano L.	Dem	Ky.	4	1

Minority

Rank	Name	Party	State	Terms in: House	Terms in: Comm.
RM	Wiggins, Charles E.	Rep	Cal.	6	1
2nd	Cederberg, Elford A.	Rep	Mich.	13	1
3rd	Heckler, Margaret M.	Rep	Mass.	6	1
4th	Frenzel, William E.	Rep	Minn.	4	1
5th	Cochran, Thad	Rep	Miss.	3	1
6th	Sawyer, Harold S.	Rep	Mich.	1	1

Changes:
Minority:

Cochran, Thad	Rep	Miss.	Dec. 26,1978	Resigned; elected to U.S. Senate.
Cederberg, Elford A.	Rep	Mich.	Dec. 31,1978	Defeated for reelection.

HOUSE SELECT COMMITTEE: CONGRESSIONAL OPERATIONS

Jurisdiction, 1977

From House Resolution 420, 95th Congress, First Session, March 28, 1977:

[Section 3]

(a) The committee shall continue the functions of the Joint Committee on Congressional Operations for the House, as follows:
   (1) Making a continuing study of the organization and operation of the Congress of the United States and recommending improvements in such organization and operation with a view toward strengthening the Congress, simplifying its operations, developing cooperation between the Houses of Congress, improving its relationship with other branches of the United States Government, and enabling it to meet its responsibilities under the Constitution of the United States.
   (2) Identifying any court proceeding or action which, in the opinion of the committee, is of vital interest to the Congress, or to the House of Representatives as a constitutionally established institution of the Federal Government, and calling such proceeding or action to the attention of the House.
   (3) Conducting a continuing study of the jurisdiction of the various standing committees of the House of Representatives and their relative workloads, and of ways of rationalizing committee jurisdictions between the two Houses of Congress, and reporting to the Committee on Rules any recommendations on the more equitable distribution of workload or the more rational combination of jurisdictional responsibilities.
   (4) Exercising the functions vested in it by section 6 of this resolution.

(b) In carrying out the functions referred to in subsection (a) of this section, the committee shall at all times avoid conflict or duplication with the activities of other committees, commissions, or other entities established by the House.
(c) The committee shall not have legislative jurisdiction. Nothing in this resolution, except as specifically provided in subsection (a) (3) of this section, shall be construed to authorize the committee to make any recommendations with respect to the rules, parliamentary procedure, practices, or precedents of the House, or the consideration of any matter on the floor of the House.

[Section 6 (a)]

The committee shall supervise and control the functions, as they relate to the House, of the Office of Placement and Office Management established by section 406 of the Legislative Reorganization Act of 1970.

Termination, 1979

The Select Committee filed House Report 1843 on January 2, 1979 on its activities during the 95th Congress.

HOUSE SELECT COMMITTEE: CONGRESSIONAL OPERATIONS / 95th Congress

Service Dates of Committee Chair: Apr. 6,1977-Jan. 2,1979
Service Dates of Majority Members: Apr. 6,1977-Jan. 2,1979
Service Dates of Minority Members: Apr. 6,1977-Jan. 2,1979

Majority

Rank Name	Party	State	Terms in: House	Terms in: Comm.
Chr Brooks, Jack B.	Dem	Tex.	13	1
2nd Giaimo, Robert N.	Dem	Conn.	10	1
3rd Oberstar, James L.	DFL	Minn.	2	1
4th Burton, John L.	Dem	Cal.	3	1
5th Benjamin, Adam Jr.	Dem	Ind.	1	1

Minority

Rank Name	Party	State	Terms in: House	Terms in: Comm.
RM Cleveland, James C.	Rep	N.H.	8	1
2nd Ashbrook, John M.	Rep	Ohio	9	1

HOUSE SELECT COMMITTEE: ENERGY (Ad Hoc)

Jurisdiction, 1977

From House Resolution 508, 95th Congress, First Session, April 21, 1977:

[Section 1]

Resolved, (a) That pursuant to Rule X, clause 5, the Speaker is authorized to establish an ad hoc Committee on Energy to consider and report to the House on the Message of the President dated April 20, 1977 (H. Doc. 95-128), on other messages or communications related thereto, and on any bill or resolution which the Speaker may sequentially refer thereto which the Speaker determines relates to the substance of the President's Message: Provided, however, That this paragraph shall not preclude initial reference to the ad hoc Committee of a bill or resolution incorporating the recommendations of the committees with subject-matter jurisdiction over the substances of the President's Message.

Termination, 1978

The Select Committee filed House Report 1820 (95-2) on December 29, 1978 on its activities during the 95th Congress.

HOUSE SELECT COMMITTEE: ENERGY (Ad Hoc) / 95th Congress

Service Dates of Committee Chair: Apr. 21,1977-Jan. 3,1979
Service Dates of Majority Members: Apr. 21,1977-Jan. 3,1979
Service Dates of Minority Members: Apr. 21,1977-Jan. 3,1979

Majority

Rank	Name	Party	State	Terms in: House	Terms in: Comm.
Chr	Ashley, Thomas L.	Dem	Ohio	12	1
2nd	Bolling, Richard W.	Dem	Mo.	15	1
3rd	Staggers, Harley O.	Dem	W.Va.	15	1
4th	Moss, John E. Jr.	Dem	Cal.	13	1
5th	Reuss, Henry S.	Dem	Wisc.	12	1
6th	Vanik, Charles A.	Dem	Ohio	12	1
7th	Rogers, Paul G.	Dem	Fla.	12	1
8th	Dingell, John D. Jr.	Dem	Mich.	12	1
9th	Ullman, Albert C.	Dem	Ore.	11	1
10th	Young, John A.	Dem	Tex.	11	1
11th	Rostenkowski, Daniel D.	Dem	Ill.	10	1
12th	Corman, James C.	Dem	Cal.	9	1
13th	Udall, Morris K.	Dem	Ariz.	9	1
14th	Waggonner, Joe D. Jr.	Dem	La.	9	1
15th	Bingham, Jonathan B.	Dem	N.Y.	7	1
16th	Foley, Thomas S.	Dem	Wash.	7	1
17th	Eckhardt, Robert C.	Dem	Tex.	6	1
18th	McCormack, Mike	Dem	Wash.	4	1
19th	Rangel, Charles B.	Dem	N.Y.	4	1
20th	Wilson, Charles	Dem	Tex.	3	1
21st	Fisher, Joseph L.	Dem	Va.	2	1
22nd	Moffett, Anthony J.(Toby)	Dem	Conn.	2	1
23rd	Sharp, Philip R.	Dem	Ind.	2	1
24th	Tsongas, Paul E.	Dem	Mass.	2	1
25th	Mikulski, Barbara A.	Dem	Md.	1	1

Minority

Rank	Name	Party	State	Terms in: House	Terms in: Comm.
RM	Anderson, John B.	Rep	Ill.	9	1
2nd	Brown, Clarence J. Jr.	Rep	Ohio	7	1
3rd	Horton, Frank J.	Rep	N.Y.	8	1
4th	Wydler, John W.	Rep	N.Y.	8	1
5th	Brown, Garry E.	Rep	Mich.	6	1
6th	Steiger, William A.	Rep	Wisc.	6	1
7th	Collins, James M.	Rep	Tex.	6	1
8th	Archer, William R.	Rep	Tex.	4	1
9th	Martin, James G.	Rep	N.C.	3	1
10th	Moorhead, Carlos J.	Rep	Cal.	3	1
11th	Edwards, M.H. (Mickey)	Rep	Okla.	1	1
12th	Steers, Newton I. Jr.	Rep	Md.	1	1

Note: House Resolution 509, agreed to on Apr. 21,1977, changed the size and party ratio on this committee to 27 Democrats and 13 Republicans.

Additions:

Majority:	18th	Flowers, Walter	Dem	Ala.	Apr. 22,1977
	27th	Murphy, Austin J.	Dem	Penn.	Apr. 22,1977
Minority:	8th	Goldwater, Barry M. Jr.	Rep	Cal.	Apr. 22,1977

Changes:

Majority:

Moss, John E. Jr.	Dem	Cal.	Dec. 31,1978	Resigned and retired.

Minority:

Steiger, William A.	Rep	Wisc.	Dec. 4,1978	Died in office.

HOUSE SELECT COMMITTEE: POPULATION

Jurisdiction, 1977

From House Resolution 70, 95th Congress, First Session, September 28, 1977:

[Paragraph 2]

The committee is authorized and directed to conduct a full and complete investigation and study of--

(1) the causes of changing population conditions and their consequences for the United States and the world;

(2) national, regional, and global population characteristics relative to the demands on limited resources and the ability of nations to feed, clothe, house, employ, and govern their citizens and otherwise afford them an improved standard of living;

(3) various approaches to population planning (including the study of family planning technology, with emphasis on measures to reduce the frequency of conception rather than the termination of pregnancy, and the relationship of improved economic and social opportunities to family size) in order to ascertain those policies and programs, within the United States as well as other nations, which would be most effective in coping with unplanned population change;

(4) the means by which the United States Government can most effectively cooperate with and assist nations and international agencies in addressing successfully, in a noncoercive manner, various national, regional, and global population-related issues.

Termination, 1979

The Select Committee was terminated upon the filing of its final report, House Report 1842 (95-2), on January 5, 1979.

HOUSE SELECT COMMITTEE: POPULATION / 95th Congress

Service Dates of Committee Chair: Oct. 14,1977-Jan. 5,1979
Service Dates of Majority Members: Oct. 14,1977-Jan. 5,1979
Service Dates of Minority Members: Oct. 14,1977-Jan. 5,1979

Majority

Rank	Name	Party	State	Terms in: House	Terms in: Comm.
Chr	Scheuer, James H.	Dem	N.Y.	6	1
2nd	Harrington, Michael J.	Dem	Mass.	5	1
3rd	Collins, Cardiss	Dem	Ill.	3	1
4th	Neal, Stephen L.	Dem	N.C.	2	1
5th	Richmond, Frederick W.	Dem	N.Y.	2	1
6th	Simon, Paul M.	Dem	Ill.	2	1
7th	Akaka, Daniel K.	Dem	Hai.	1	1
8th	Beilenson, Anthony C.	Dem	Cal.	1	1
9th	Gephardt, Richard A.	Dem	Mo.	1	1
10th	Kildee, Dale E.	Dem	Mich.	1	1
11th	Corrada, Baltasar	Dem	P.R.	1	1

Minority

Rank	Name	Party	State	Terms in: House	Terms in: Comm.
RM	Erlenborn, John N.	Rep	Ill.	7	1
2nd	McCloskey, Paul N. Jr.	Rep	Cal.	6	1
3rd	Kindness, Thomas N.	Rep	Ohio	2	1
4th	Hollenbeck, Harold C.	Rep	N.J.	1	1
5th	Stockman, David A.	Rep	Mich.	1	1

HOUSE SELECT COMMITTEE: COMMITTEES II (Patterson)

Jurisdiction, 1979

From House Resolution 118, 96th Congress, First Session, March 19, 1979:

[Section 2]

(a) The select committee is authorized and directed to conduct a thorough and complete study with respect to the operation and implementation of rules X, XI, and XLVIII of the Rules of the House of Representatives including committee structure of the House, the number of committees and their jurisdiction, committee rules and procedures, media coverage of meetings, staffing, space, equipment, and other committee facilities.
(b) The select committee is authorized and directed to report to the House by bill, resolution, or otherwise, with respect to any matters covered in subparagraph (a): Provided, however, That the select committee shall not report to the House by bill or resolution recommendations relating to the optimum size of committees, the appropriate committee and subcommittee assignments, per Member, or the number of subcommittees or their jurisdictions, but such recommendations may be made to the respective party caucuses.

The Select Committee was extended by House Resolution 533 (96-2) on February 5, 1980 and expired under its authority 30 days after the filing of its final report, House Report 866 (96-2), on April 1, 1980.

HOUSE SELECT COMMITTEE: COMMITTEES II (Patterson) / 96th Congress

Service Dates of Committee Chair: Mar. 28,1979-May 1,1980
Service Dates of Majority Members: Mar. 28,1979-May 1,1980
Service Dates of Minority Members: Mar. 28,1979-May 1,1980

Majority

Rank	Name	Party	State	Terms in: House	Terms in: Comm.
Chr	Patterson, Jerry M.	Dem	Cal.	3	1
2nd	Clay, William L.	Dem	Mo.	6	1
3rd	McCormack, Mike	Dem	Wash.	5	1
4th	Breaux, John B.	Dem	La.	5	1
5th	Schroeder, Patricia S.	Dem	Colo.	4	1
6th	Traxler, J. Bob	Dem	Mich.	4	1
7th	Derrick, Butler C. Jr.	Dem	S.C.	3	1
8th	Fisher, Joseph L.	Dem	Va.	3	1
9th	Kostmayer, Peter H.	Dem	Penn.	2	1
10th	Whitley, Charles O. Sr.	Dem	N.C.	2	1

Minority

Rank	Name	Party	State	Terms in: House	Terms in: Comm.
RM	Cleveland, James C.	Rep	N.H.	9	1
2nd	Horton, Frank J.	Rep	N.Y.	9	1
3rd	Frenzel, William E.	Rep	Minn.	5	1
4th	Leach, James A. S.	Rep	Iowa	2	1
5th	Loeffler, Thomas G.	Rep	Tex.	1	1

Changes:

Minority:

Name	Party	State	Date	Change
Loeffler, Thomas G.	Rep	Tex.	July 10,1979	Left committee; no new assignment.
Solomon, Gerald B.H.	Rep	N.Y.	July 10,1979	Replaced Loeffler.

HOUSE SELECT COMMITTEE: CHILDREN, YOUTH AND FAMILIES

Jurisdiction, 1983

From House Resolution 16, 98th Congress, First Session, February 2, 1983:

[Section 2]

(a) The select committee shall not have legislative jurisdiction. The select committee shall have authority--
- (1) to conduct a continuing comprehensive study and review of the problems of children, youth, and families, including but not limited to income maintenance, health (including medical and child development research), nutrition, education, welfare, employment, and recreation;
- (2) to study the use of all practicable means and methods of encouraging the development of public and private programs and policies which will assist American children and youth in taking a full part in national life and becoming productive citizens; and
- (3) to develop policies that would encourage the coordination of both governmental and private programs designed to address the problems of childhood and adolescence.

The Select Committee has been recreated each Congress by separate Resolutions: House Resolution 25 (99-1); House Resolution 26 (100-1); House Resolution 84 (101-1); and House Resolution 51 (102-1).

Jurisdiction, 1992

The jurisdiction of the Select Committee has not changed since its inception in 1983.

HOUSE SELECT COMMITTEE: CHILDREN, YOUTH AND FAMILIES / 98th Congress

Service Dates of Committee Chair: Feb. 2,1983-Jan. 3,1985
Service Dates of Majority Members: Feb. 2,1983-Jan. 3,1985
Service Dates of Minority Members: Feb. 2,1983-Jan. 3,1985

Majority

Rank Name	Party	State	Terms in: House	Terms in: Comm.
Chr Miller, George	Dem	Cal.	5	1
2nd Lehman, William	Dem	Fla.	6	1
3rd Schroeder, Patricia S.	Dem	Colo.	6	1
4th Boggs, Corinne C. (Lindy)	Dem	La.	6	1
5th McHugh, Matthew F.	Dem	N.Y.	5	1
6th Patterson, Jerry M.	Dem	Cal.	5	1
7th Mikulski, Barbara A.	Dem	Md.	4	1
8th Weiss, Theodore S.	Dem	N.Y.	4	1
9th Anthony, Beryl F. Jr.	Dem	Ark.	3	1
10th Boxer, Barbara	Dem	Cal.	1	1
11th Levin, Sander M.	Dem	Mich.	1	1
12th Morrison, Bruce A.	Dem	Conn.	1	1
13th Richardson, Bill	Dem	N.M.	1	1
14th Rowland, J. Roy	Dem	Ga.	1	1
15th Sikorski, Gerry	Dem	Minn.	1	1
16th Wheat, Alan	Dem	Mo.	1	1

Minority

Rank Name	Party	State	Terms in: House	Terms in: Comm.
RM Marriott, D. Daniel	Rep	Utah	4	1
2nd Fish, Hamilton Jr.	Rep	N.Y.	8	1
3rd Coats, Daniel R.	Rep	Ind.	2	1
4th Bliley, Thomas J. Jr.	Rep	Va.	2	1
5th Wolf, Frank R.	Rep	Va.	2	1
6th Burton, Dan	Rep	Ind.	1	1
7th Johnson, Nancy L.	Rep	Conn.	1	1
8th McKernan, John R. Jr.	Rep	Me.	1	1
9th Vucanovich, Barbara F.	Rep	Nev.	1	1

	Majority			Minority		
Departures from the House:						
Defeated for Reelection	Patterson, Jerry M.	Cal.	Dem	None		
Lost Nomination for Governor	None			Marriott, D. Daniel	Utah	Rep
Departures from Committee:						
No new assignment	Richardson, Bill	N.M.	Dem	None		
	Mikulski, Barbara A.	Md.	Dem	None		

HOUSE SELECT COMMITTEE: CHILDREN, YOUTH AND FAMILIES / 99th Congress

Service Dates of Committee Chair: Mar. 20,1985-Jan. 3,1987
Service Dates of Majority Members: Mar. 20,1985-Jan. 3,1987
Service Dates of Minority Members: Mar. 25,1985-Jan. 3,1987

Majority

Rank	Name	Party	State	Terms in: House	Terms in: Comm.
Chr	Miller, George	Dem	Cal.	6	2
2nd	Lehman, William	Dem	Fla.	7	2
3rd	Schroeder, Patricia S.	Dem	Colo.	7	2
4th	Boggs, Corinne C. (Lindy)	Dem	La.	7	2
5th	McHugh, Matthew F.	Dem	N.Y.	6	2
6th	Weiss, Theodore S.	Dem	N.Y.	5	2
7th	Anthony, Beryl F. Jr.	Dem	Ark.	4	2
8th	Boxer, Barbara	Dem	Cal.	2	2
9th	Levin, Sander M.	Dem	Mich.	2	2
10th	Morrison, Bruce A.	Dem	Conn.	2	2
11th	Rowland, J. Roy	Dem	Ga.	2	2
12th	Sikorski, Gerry	Dem	Minn.	2	2
13th	Wheat, Alan	Dem	Mo.	2	2
14th	Martinez, Matthew G.	Dem	Cal.	3	1
15th	Evans, Lane	Dem	Ill.	2	1

Minority

Rank	Name	Party	State	Terms in: House	Terms in: Comm.
RM	Coats, Daniel R.	Rep	Ind.	3	2
2nd	Fish, Hamilton Jr.	Rep	N.Y.	9	2
3rd	Bliley, Thomas J. Jr.	Rep	Va.	3	2
4th	Wolf, Frank R.	Rep	Va.	3	2
5th	Burton, Dan	Rep	Ind.	2	2
6th	Johnson, Nancy L.	Rep	Conn.	2	2
7th	McKernan, John R. Jr.	Rep	Me.	2	2
8th	Vucanovich, Barbara F.	Rep	Nev.	2	2
9th	Monson, David S.	Rep	Utah	1	1
10th	Smith, Robert C.	Rep	N.H.	1	1

Changes:

Minority:

Name	Party	State	Date	Change
Burton, Dan	Rep	Ind.	Apr. 22,1986	Left committee; no new assignment.
Cobey, William W. Jr.	Rep	N.C.	Apr. 22,1986	Replaced Burton.

	Majority	Minority		
Departures from the House:				
Elected Governor	None	McKernan, John R. Jr.	Me.	Rep
Defeated for Reelection	None	Cobey, William W. Jr.	N.C.	Rep
Retired	None	Monson, David S.	Utah	Rep
Departures from Committee:				
No new assignment	None	Fish, Hamilton Jr.	N.Y.	Rep
		Smith, Robert C.	N.H.	Rep

HOUSE SELECT COMMITTEE: CHILDREN, YOUTH AND FAMILIES / 100th Congress

Service Dates of Committee Chair: Jan. 21,1987-Jan. 3,1989
Service Dates of Majority Members: Jan. 21,1987-Jan. 3,1989
Service Dates of Minority Members: Feb. 2,1987-Jan. 3,1989

Majority

Rank	Name	Party	State	Terms in: House	Terms in: Comm.
Chr	Miller, George	Dem	Cal.	7	3
2nd	Lehman, William	Dem	Fla.	8	3
3rd	Schroeder, Patricia S.	Dem	Colo.	8	3
4th	Boggs, Corinne C. (Lindy)	Dem	La.	8	3
5th	McHugh, Matthew F.	Dem	N.Y.	7	3
6th	Weiss, Theodore S.	Dem	N.Y.	6	3
7th	Anthony, Beryl F. Jr.	Dem	Ark.	5	3
8th	Boxer, Barbara	Dem	Cal.	3	3
9th	Levin, Sander M.	Dem	Mich.	3	3
10th	Morrison, Bruce A.	Dem	Conn.	3	3
11th	Rowland, J. Roy	Dem	Ga.	3	3
12th	Sikorski, Gerry	Dem	Minn.	3	3
13th	Wheat, Alan	Dem	Mo.	3	3
14th	Martinez, Matthew G.	Dem	Cal.	4	2
15th	Evans, Lane	Dem	Ill.	3	2
16th	Durbin, Richard J.	Dem	Ill.	3	1

Minority

Rank	Name	Party	State	Terms in: House	Terms in: Comm.
RM	Coats, Daniel R.	Rep	Ind.	4	3
2nd	Bliley, Thomas J. Jr.	Rep	Va.	4	3
3rd	Wolf, Frank R.	Rep	Va.	4	3
4th	Johnson, Nancy L.	Rep	Conn.	3	3
5th	Vucanovich, Barbara F.	Rep	Nev.	3	3
6th	Kemp, Jack F.	Rep	N.Y.	9	1
7th	Wortley, George C.	Rep	N.Y.	4	1
8th	Packard, Ron	Rep	Cal.	3	1
9th	Boulter, Beau	Rep	Tex.	2	1
10th	Hastert, Dennis	Rep	Ill.	1	1
11th	Holloway, Clyde C.	Rep	La.	1	1
12th	Grandy, Fred	Rep	Iowa	1	1

17th Sawyer, Thomas C.	Dem	Ohio	1	1
18th Skaggs, David E.	Dem	Colo.	1	1

Note: Floyd Flake (Dem-N.Y.) was assigned to the 19th majority rank on Jan. 21,1987, but his assignment was vacated later that day to allow him to serve on the Select Committee on Hunger.

Changes:

Minority:

Coats, Daniel R.	Rep	Ind.	Dec. 12,1988	Resigned; appointed to U.S. Senate.

Departures from the House:	**Majority**			**Minority**		
Lost Nomination for President	None			Kemp, Jack	N.Y.	Rep
Lost Election to U.S. Senate	None			Boulter, Beau	Tex.	Rep
Retired	None			Wortley, George C.	N.Y.	Rep
Departures from Committee:						
Moved to Post Office & Civil Service	Sawyer, Thomas C.	Ohio	Dem	None		
Moved to Ways and Means	None			Johnson, Nancy L.	Conn.	Rep

HOUSE SELECT COMMITTEE: CHILDREN, YOUTH AND FAMILIES / 101st Congress

Service Dates of Committee Chair: Mar. 8,1989-Jan. 3,1991
Service Dates of Majority Members: Mar. 8,1989-Jan. 3,1991
Service Dates of Minority Members: Apr. 4,1989-Jan. 3,1991

Majority

Rank Name	Party	State	Terms in: House	Terms in: Comm.
Chr Miller, George	Dem	Cal.	8	4
2nd Lehman, William	Dem	Fla.	9	4
3rd Schroeder, Patricia S.	Dem	Colo.	9	4
4th Boggs, Corinne C. (Lindy)	Dem	La.	9	4
5th McHugh, Matthew F.	Dem	N.Y.	8	4
6th Weiss, Theodore S.	Dem	N.Y.	7	4
7th Anthony, Beryl F. Jr.	Dem	Ark.	6	4
8th Boxer, Barbara	Dem	Cal.	4	4
9th Levin, Sander M.	Dem	Mich.	4	4
10th Morrison, Bruce A.	Dem	Conn.	4	4
11th Rowland, J. Roy	Dem	Ga.	4	4
12th Sikorski, Gerry	Dem	Minn.	4	4
13th Wheat, Alan	Dem	Mo.	4	4
14th Martinez, Matthew G.	Dem	Cal.	5	3
15th Evans, Lane	Dem	Ill.	4	3
16th Durbin, Richard J.	Dem	Ill.	4	2
17th Skaggs, David E.	Dem	Colo.	2	2
18th Sarpalius, Bill	Dem	Tex.	1	1

Minority

Rank Name	Party	State	Terms in: House	Terms in: Comm.
RM Bliley, Thomas J. Jr.	Rep	Va.	5	4
2nd Wolf, Frank R.	Rep	Va.	5	4
3rd Vucanovich, Barbara F.	Rep	Nev.	4	4
4th Packard, Ron	Rep	Cal.	4	2
5th Hastert, Dennis	Rep	Ill.	2	2
6th Holloway, Clyde C.	Rep	La.	2	2
7th Grandy, Fred	Rep	Iowa	2	2
8th Weldon, Curt	Rep	Penn.	2	1
9th Smith, Lamar S.	Rep	Tex.	2	1
10th Smith, Peter P.	Rep	Vt.	1	1
11th Walsh, James T.	Rep	N.Y.	1	1
12th Machtley, Ronald K.	Rep	R.I.	1	1

Changes:

Minority:

Grandy, Fred	Rep	Iowa	Aug. 4,1989	Moved to Standards of Official Conduct.
Robinson, Tommy F.	Rep	Ark.	Aug. 4,1989	Replaced Grandy.

Departures from the House:	**Majority**			**Minority**		
Defeated for Reelection	None			Smith, Peter	Vt.	Rep
Lost Election for Governor	Morrison, Bruce A.	Conn.	Dem	Robinson, Tommy F.	Ark.	Rep
Retired	Boggs, Corinne C. (Lindy)	La.	Dem	None		
Departures from Committee:						
Became Ranking Minority Member of District of Columbia	None			Bliley, Thomas J. Jr.	Va.	Rep
Moved to Appropriations	None			Vucanovich, Barbara F.	Nev.	Rep
No new assignment	None			Packard, Ron	Cal.	Rep

HOUSE SELECT COMMITTEE: CHILDREN, YOUTH AND FAMILIES / 102nd Congress

Service Dates of Committee Chair: Feb, 21,1991-Jan. 3,1993
Service Dates of Majority Members: Feb. 21,1991-Jan. 3,1993
Service Dates of Minority Members: Feb. 21,1991-Jan. 3,1993

Majority

Rank Name	Party	State	Terms in: House	Terms in: Comm.
Chr Schroeder, Patricia S.	Dem	Colo.	10	5
2nd Miller, George	Dem	Cal.	9	5
3rd Lehman, William	Dem	Fla.	10	5
4th McHugh, Matthew F.	Dem	N.Y.	9	5
5th Weiss, Theodore S.	Dem	N.Y.	8	5
6th Anthony, Beryl F. Jr.	Dem	Ark.	7	5
7th Boxer, Barbara	Dem	Cal.	5	5
8th Levin, Sander M.	Dem	Mich.	5	5
9th Rowland, J. Roy	Dem	Ga.	5	5
10th Sikorski, Gerry	Dem	Minn.	5	5
11th Wheat, Alan	Dem	Mo.	5	5
12th Martinez, Matthew G.	Dem	Cal.	6	4
13th Evans, Lane	Dem	Ill.	5	4
14th Durbin, Richard J.	Dem	Ill.	5	3
15th Skaggs, David E.	Dem	Colo.	3	3
16th Sarpalius, Bill	Dem	Tex.	2	2
17th Johnson, Tim	Dem	S.D.	3	1
18th Collins, Barbara-Rose	Dem	Mich.	1	1
19th Horn, Joan Kelly	Dem	Mo.	1	1
20th Bacchus, Jim	Dem	Fla.	1	1
21st Peterson, Pete	Dem	Fla.	1	1
22nd Cramer, Bud	Dem	Ala.	1	1

Minority

Rank Name	Party	State	Terms in: House	Terms in: Comm.
RM Wolf, Frank R.	Rep	Va.	6	5
2nd Hastert, Dennis	Rep	Ill.	3	3
3rd Holloway, Clyde C.	Rep	La.	3	3
4th Weldon, Curt	Rep	Penn.	3	2
5th Smith, Lamar	Rep	Tex.	3	2
6th Walsh, James T.	Rep	N.Y.	2	2
7th Machtley, Ronald K.	Rep	R.I.	2	2
8th McEwen, Bob	Rep	Ohio	6	1
9th Bilirakis, Michael	Rep	Fla.	5	1
10th Klug, Scott L.	Rep	Wisc.	1	1
11th Santorum, Rick	Rep	Penn.	1	1
12th Camp, David	Rep	Mich.	1	1
13th Riggs, Frank	Rep	Cal.	1	1
14th Barrett, Bill	Rep	Neb.	1	1

Changes:

Majority:

Name	Party	State	Date	Change
Weiss, Theodore S.	Dem	N.Y.	Sep. 14,1992	Died in office.

Minority:

Name	Party	State	Date	Change
Hastert, Dennis	Rep	Ill.	Oct. 8,1991	Left committee; no new assignment.
Fawell, Harris W.	Rep	Ill.	June 16,1992	Replaced Hastert.

HOUSE SELECT COMMITTEE: HUNGER

Jurisdiction, 1985

From House Resolution 20, 99th Congress, First Session, March 7, 1985:

[Section 2 (a)]

The select committee shall not have legislative jurisdiction. The select committee shall have authority--

(1) to conduct a continuing comprehensive study and review of the problems of hunger and malnutrition, including but not limited to, those issues addressed in the reports of the Presidential Commission of World Hunger and the Independent Commission on International Development Issues, which issues include--
 (A) the United States development and economic assistance program and the executive branch structuring responsible for administering the program
 (B) world food security;
 (C) trade relations between the United Sates and less developed countries;
 (D) food production and distribution;
 (E) corporate and agribusiness efforts to further international development;
 (F) policies of multilateral development banks and international development institutions; and
 (G) food assistance programs in the United States;

(2) to review any recommendations made by the President, or by any department or agency of the executive branch of the Federal Government, relating to programs or policies affecting hunger or malnutrition; and

(3) to recommend to the appropriate committees of the House legislation or other action the select committee considers necessary with respect to programs or policies affecting hunger or malnutrition.

The Select Committee has been recreated each Congress by separate Resolutions: House Resolution 26 (100-1); House Resolution 84 (101-1); and House Resolution 51 (102-1).

Jurisdiction, 1992

The jurisdiction of the Select Committee has not changed since its inception in 1983.

HOUSE SELECT COMMITTEE: HUNGER / 99th Congress

Service Dates of Committee Chair: Mar. 20,1985-Jan. 3,1987
Service Dates of Majority Members: Mar. 20,1985-Jan. 3,1987
Service Dates of Minority Members: Mar. 20,1985-Jan. 3,1987

Majority

Rank Name	Party	State	Terms in: House	Terms in: Comm.
Chr Leland, G. T. (Mickey)	Dem	Tex.	4	1
2nd Hall, Tony P.	Dem	Ohio	4	1
3rd Traxler, J. Bob	Dem	Mich.	7	1
4th Panetta, Leon E.	Dem	Cal.	5	1
5th Daschle, Thomas A.	Dem	S.D.	4	1
6th Fazio, Victor H.	Dem	Cal.	4	1
7th Gejdenson, Samuel	Dem	Conn.	3	1
8th Kostmayer, Peter H.	Dem	Penn.	4	1
9th Burton, Sala	Dem	Cal.	2	1
10th Dorgan, Byron L.	Dem	N.D.	3	1

Minority

Rank Name	Party	State	Terms in: House	Terms in: Comm.
VCh Roukema, Margaret	Rep	N.J.	3	1
2nd Emerson, Bill	Rep	Mo.	3	1
3rd Morrison, Sid	Rep	Wash.	3	1
4th Gilman, Benjamin A.	Rep	N.Y.	7	1
5th Evans, T. Cooper	Rep	Iowa	3	1
6th Smith, Robert F.	Rep	Ore.	2	1
7th Bereuter, Douglas K.	Rep	Neb.	4	1

Departures from the House:	**Majority**		**Minority**	
Elected to U.S. Senate	Daschle, Thomas A.	S.D. Dem	None	
Retired	None		Evans, T. Cooper	Iowa Rep
Departures from Committee:				
No new assignment	Fazio, Victor H.	Cal. Dem	None	

HOUSE SELECT COMMITTEE: HUNGER / 100th Congress

Service Dates of Committee Chair: Jan. 21,1987-Jan. 3,1989
Service Dates of Majority Members: Jan. 21,1987-Jan. 3,1989
Service Dates of Minority Members: Feb. 2,1987-Jan. 3,1989

Majority

Rank Name	Party	State	Terms in: House	Terms in: Comm.
Chr Leland, G. T. (Mickey)	Dem	Tex.	5	2
2nd Hall, Tony P.	Dem	Ohio	5	2
3rd Traxler, J. Bob	Dem	Mich.	8	2
4th Panetta, Leon E.	Dem	Cal.	6	2
5th Gejdenson, Samuel	Dem	Conn.	4	2
6th Kostmayer, Peter H.	Dem	Penn.	5	2
7th Burton, Sala	Dem	Cal.	3	2
8th Dorgan, Byron L.	Dem	N.D.	4	2
9th Carr, M. Robert	Dem	Mich.	6	1
10th Penny, Timothy J.	DFL	Minn.	3	1
11th Ackerman, Gary L.	Dem	N.Y.	3	1
12th Espy, Mike	Dem	Miss.	1	1
13th Flake, Floyd H.	Dem	N.Y.	1	1

Minority

Rank Name	Party	State	Terms in: House	Terms in: Comm.
VCh1 Roukema, Margaret	Rep	N.J.	4	2
VCh2 2nd Emerson, Bill	Rep	Mo.	4	2
3rd Morrison, Sid	Rep	Wash.	4	2
4th Gilman, Benjamin A.	Rep	N.Y.	8	2
5th Smith, Robert F.	Rep	Ore.	3	2
6th Bereuter, Douglas K.	Rep	Neb.	5	2
7th Upton, Frederick S.	Rep	Mich.	1	1

Notes: House Resolution 26 (100-1), agreed to Jan. 22,1987, changed the size and party ratio on this committee to 16 Democrats and 10 Republicans. Victor Fazio (Dem-Cal.) was reappointed to the committee on that date and credited with his previous service. On July 13,1987, the Speaker announced a change in the order of minority rankings, with Margaret Roukema (Rep-N.J.) and Bill Emerson (Rep-Mo.) switching ranks.

Additions:

Majority:	14th Fazio, Victor H.	Dem	Cal.	Jan. 22,1987	(ranked 5th)
	15th Bilbray, James H.	Dem	Nev.	Jan. 22,1987	
	16th Mfume, Kweisi	Dem	Md.	Jan. 22,1987	
Minority:	8th Brown, Hank	Rep	Colo.	Apr. 9,1987	
	9th Molinari, Guy V.	Rep	N.Y.	Apr. 22,1987	
	10th Herger, Wally	Rep	Cal.	Mar. 9,1988	

Changes:

Vice Chair:				
Roukema, Margaret	Rep	N.J.	July 13,1987	Moved to second minority rank.
Emerson, Bill	Rep	Mo.	July 13,1987	Became Ranking Minority Member of committee.
Majority:				
Burton, Sala	Dem	Cal.	Feb. 1,1987	Died in office.
Patterson, Elizabeth J.	Dem	S.C.	Feb. 19,1987	Replaced Burton.
Gejdenson, Samuel	Dem	Conn.	Oct. 20,1987	Left committee; no new assignment.
Brennan, Joseph E.	Dem	Me.	Oct. 27,1987	Replaced Gejdenson.
Bilbray, James	Dem	Nev.	Nov. 16,1987	Moved earlier to Select Aging.
Staggers, Harley O. Jr.	Dem	W.Va.	Mar. 22,1988	Replaced Bilbray.
Minority:				
Molinari, Guy V.	Rep	N.Y.	Sep. 7,1988	Left committee; no new assignment.

Departures from Committee:	**Majority**		**Minority**	
Moved to Education & Labor; Select Narcotics, Abuse & Control	Mfume, Kweisi	Md. Dem	None	
Moved to Select Aging	Staggers, Harley O. Jr.	W.Va. Dem	None	
No new assignment	Traxler, J. Bob	Mich. Dem	Brown, Hank	Colo. Rep
	Brennan, Joseph E.	Me. Dem		

HOUSE SELECT COMMITTEE: HUNGER / 101st Congress

Service Dates of Committee Chair: Mar. 8,1989-Aug. 7,1989
Sept. 28,1989-Jan. 3,1991
Service Dates of Majority Members: Mar. 8,1989-Jan. 3,1991
Service Dates of Minority Members: Apr. 4,1989-Jan. 3,1991

Majority

Rank	Name	Party	State	Terms in: House	Terms in: Comm.
Ch1	Leland, G. T. (Mickey)	Dem	Tex.	6	3
Ch2 2nd	Hall, Tony P.	Dem	Ohio	6	3
3rd	Panetta, Leon E.	Dem	Cal.	7	3
4th	Fazio, Victor	Dem	Cal.	6	3
5th	Kostmayer, Peter H.	Dem	Penn.	6	3
6th	Dorgan, Byron L.	Dem	N.D.	5	3
7th	Carr, M. Robert	Dem	Mich.	7	2
8th	Penny, Timothy J.	DFL	Minn.	4	2
9th	Ackerman, Gary L.	Dem	N.Y.	4	2
10th	Espy, Mike	Dem	Miss.	2	2
11th	Flake, Floyd H.	Dem	N.Y.	2	2
12th	Patterson, Elizabeth J.	Dem	S.C.	2	2
13th	Foglietta, Thomas M.	Dem	Penn.	5	1
14th	Bustamante, Albert G.	Dem	Tex.	3	1
15th	McNulty, Michael R.	Dem	N.Y.	1	1
16th	Faleomavaega, Eni F.H.	Dem	AmS	1	1
17th	Engel, Eliot L.	Dem	N.Y.	1	1
18th	AuCoin, Les	Dem	Ore.	8	1

Minority

Rank	Name	Party	State	Terms in: House	Terms in: Comm.
VCh	Emerson, Bill	Rep	Mo.	5	3
2nd	Roukema, Margaret	Rep	N.J.	5	3
3rd	Morrison, Sid	Rep	Wash.	5	3
4th	Gilman, Benjamin A.	Rep	N.Y.	9	3
5th	Smith, Robert F.	Rep	Ore.	4	3
6th	Bereuter, Douglas K.	Rep	Neb.	6	3
7th	Upton, Frederick S.	Rep	Mich.	2	2
8th	Herger, Wally	Rep	Cal.	2	2
9th	Hunter, Duncan L.	Rep	Cal.	5	1
10th	Wolf, Frank R.	Rep	Va.	5	1
11th	Smith, Christopher H.	Rep	N.J.	5	1

Note: The assignment of Jill Long (Dem-Ind.) and Alan Wheat (Dem-Mo.) to this committee was not reported in either the House Journal or The Congressional Record. These Representatives were not listed in the roster of a committee print dated Jan. 24,1990, but were listed in a committee print dated Feb. 8,1990.

Vacancies Filled:
Majority: 16th seat by Faleomavaega on Apr. 4,1989; 17th seat by Engel on Apr. 27,1989; and 18th seat by AuCoin on May 4,1989.
Minority: 11th seat by Smith on Apr. 25,1989.

Addition:
Majority: 19th Wheat, Alan — Dem — Mo. — Feb. 8,1990 (see Note)

Changes:
Chair:

Leland, G.T. (Mickey)	Dem	Tex.	Aug. 7,1989	Died in office.
Hall, Tony P.	Dem	Ohio	Sep. 28,1989	Succeeded Leland as Chair.

Majority:

Leland, G.T. (Mickey)	Dem	Tex.	Aug. 7,1989	Died in office.
Long, Jill	Dem	Ind.	Feb. 8,1990	Replaced Leland (see Note).

Departures from Committee:	Majority	Minority	
No new assignment	None	Herger, Wally	Cal. Rep

HOUSE SELECT COMMITTEE: HUNGER / 102nd Congress

Service Dates of Committee Chair: Feb. 21,1991-Jan. 3,1993
Service Dates of Majority Members: Feb. 21,1991-Jan. 3,1993
Service Dates of Minority Members: Feb. 21,1991-Jan. 3,1993

Majority

Rank Name	Party	State	Terms in: House	Terms in: Comm.
Chr Hall, Tony P.	Dem	Ohio	7	4
2nd Panetta, Leon E.	Dem	Cal.	8	4
3rd Fazio, Victor	Dem	Cal.	7	4
4th Kostmayer, Peter H.	Dem	Penn.	7	4
5th Dorgan, Byron L.	Dem	N.D.	6	4
6th Carr, M. Robert	Dem	Mich.	8	3
7th Penny, Timothy J.	DFL	Minn.	5	3
8th Ackerman, Gary L.	Dem	N.Y.	5	3
9th Espy, Mike	Dem	Miss.	3	3
10th Flake, Floyd H.	Dem	N.Y.	3	3
11th Patterson, Elizabeth J.	Dem	S.C.	3	3
12th Foglietta, Thomas M.	Dem	Penn.	6	2
13th Bustamante, Albert G.	Dem	Tex.	4	2
14th McNulty, Michael R.	Dem	N.Y.	2	2
15th Faleomavaega, Eni F.H.	Dem	AmS	2	2
16th Engel, Eliot L.	Dem	N.Y.	2	2
17th AuCoin, Les	Dem	Ore.	9	2
18th Wheat, Alan	Dem	Mo.	5	2
19th Long, Jill	Dem	Ind.	2	2
20th Synar, Michael L.	Dem	Okla.	7	1

Minority

Rank Name	Party	State	Terms in: House	Terms in: Comm.
RM Emerson, Bill	Rep	Mo.	6	4
2nd Roukema, Margaret	Rep	N.J.	6	4
3rd Morrison, Sid	Rep	Wash.	6	4
4th Gilman, Benjamin A.	Rep	N.Y.	10	4
5th Smith, Robert F.	Rep	Ore.	5	4
6th Bereuter, Douglas K.	Rep	Neb.	7	4
7th Upton, Frederick S.	Rep	Mich.	3	3
8th Hunter, Duncan L.	Rep	Cal.	6	2
9th Wolf, Frank R.	Rep	Va.	6	2
10th Smith, Christopher H.	Rep	N.J.	6	2
11th Gilchrest, Wayne T.	Rep	Md.	1	1
12th Riggs, Frank	Rep	Cal.	1	1

Changes:

Majority:

Name	Party	State	Date	Change
Foglietta, Thomas M.	Dem	Penn.	Mar. 19,1991	Left committee; no new assignment (letter dated Mar. 12,1991).
Moran, James P. Jr.	Dem	Va.	May 14,1992	Replaced Foglietta

Minority:

Name	Party	State	Date	Change
Riggs, Frank	Rep	Cal.	May 15,1991	Left committee; no new assignment (letter dated May 10,1991).
Hastert, Dennis	Rep	Ill.	Aug. 15,1991	Replaced Riggs.

HOUSE SELECT COMMITTEE: INVESTIGATE COVERT ARMS TRANSACTIONS WITH IRAN

Jurisdiction, 1987

From House Resolution 12, 100th Congress, First Session, January 7, 1987:

[Section 1]

...The select committee is authorized and directed to conduct a full and complete investigation and study and to make such findings and recommendations to the House as the select committee deems appropriate...regarding the following matters:

(a) Direct or indirect sale or transfer of arms, technology or intelligence information to Iran or Iraq involving United States Government officers...
(b) Diversion or intended diversion of the funds realized in connection with the sale or transfer in paragraph (a), for financing assistance to anti-Government forces in Nicaragua or any other disposition apart from deposit in the Treasury...

Termination, 1987

The Select Committee was terminated upon the filing of the final report, House Report 433 (100-1), which was filed jointly with the Senate Select Committee on Secret Military Assistance to Iran and the Nicaraguan Opposition on November 17, 1987

HOUSE SELECT COMMITTEE: INVESTIGATE COVERT ARMS TRANSACTIONS WITH IRAN / 100th Congress

Service Dates of Committee Chair: Jan. 7,1987-Jan. 3,1989
Service Dates of Majority Members: Jan. 7,1987-Jan. 3,1989
Service Dates of Minority Members: Jan. 7,1987-Jan. 3,1989

Majority

Rank	Name	Party	State	Terms in: House	Terms in: Comm.
Chr	Hamilton, Lee H.	Dem	Ind.	12	1
VCh	Fascell, Dante B.	Dem	Fla.	17	1
3rd	Foley, Thomas S.	Dem	Wash.	12	1
4th	Rodino, Peter W. Jr.	Dem	N.J.	20	1
5th	Brooks, Jack B.	Dem	Tex.	18	1
6th	Stokes, Louis	Dem	Ohio	10	1
7th	Aspin, Les	Dem	Wisc.	9	1
8th	Boland, Edward P.	Dem	Mass.	18	1
9th	Jenkins, Edgar L.	Dem	Ga.	6	1

Minority

Rank	Name	Party	State	Terms in: House	Terms in: Comm.
RM	Cheney, Richard B.	Rep	Wyo.	5	1
2nd	Broomfield, Williams S.	Rep	Mich.	16	1
3rd	Hyde, Henry J.	Rep	Ill.	7	1
4th	Courter, James A.	Rep	N.J.	5	1
5th	McCollum, Bill	Rep	Fla.	4	1
6th	DeWine, Michael	Rep	Ohio	3	1

HOUSE SELECT COMMITTEE: INVESTIGATE FIRE SAFETY IN THE CAPITOL AND HOUSE OFFICE BUILDINGS

Jurisdiction, 1988

From House Resolution 440, 100th Congress, Second Session:

Resolved, That a Select Committee of the House be appointed, comprised of two members from the majority party and two members from the minority party of the House of Representatives to inquire into the origin of the fire which occurred in the Office of the Speaker, and to meet with Federal and local fire officials to report and list any Federal or local fire code violations or any other potential fire or life safety hazards, and report back to the House any recommendations or measures which they deem necessary to assure the safety of the Members, officers, staff, and visitors in the Capitol, Cannon, Longworth, and Rayburn House Office Buildings.

Termination, 1989

The Select Committee was terminated at the end of the 100th Congress, on January 3, 1989 (per conversation with Chair Douglas Walgren (Dem-Penn.) in October, 1992).

HOUSE SELECT COMMITTEE: INVESTIGATE FIRE SAFETY IN THE CAPITOL AND HOUSE OFFICE BUILDINGS / 100th Congress

Service Dates of Committee Chair: June 16,1988-Jan. 3,1989
Service Dates of Majority Members: June 16,1988-Jan. 3,1989
Service Dates of Minority Members: June 16,1988-Jan. 3,1989

Majority

Rank Name	Party	State	Terms in: House	Terms in: Comm.
Chr Walgren, Douglas	Dem	Penn.	6	1
2nd Manton, Thomas J.	Dem	N.Y.	2	1

Minority

Rank Name	Party	State	Terms in: House	Terms in: Comm.
RM Weldon, Curt	Rep	Penn.	1	1
2nd Boehlert, Sherwood L.	Rep	N.Y.	3	1

PART V
Joint Committees
U.S. Congress, 1947-1992

JOINT COMMITTEE: LIBRARY

Jurisdiction, 1947

From House Concurrent Resolution 47, 72nd Congress, Third Session, February 24, 1933:

[Section 2]

That the Architect of the Capitol, upon the approval of the joint committee on the Library, with the advice of the Commission of Fine Arts, is hereby authorized and directed to relocate within the Capitol any of the statues already received and placed in Statuary Hall, and to provide for the reception and location of the statues received hereafter from the States.

Jurisdiction, 1979

From the Senate Manual for the 96th Congress (1979):

[Title 40, Section 188]

The joint committee on the Library, whenever, in their judgment, it is expedient, are authorized to accept any work of the fine arts, on behalf of Congress, which may be offered, and to assign the same such place in the Capitol as they may deem suitable, and shall have the supervision of all works of art that may be placed in the Capitol.

Jurisdiction, 1979

From Jefferson's Manual and the Rules of the House of Representatives of the United States for the 96th Congress (1979):

[Section 983f]

The Committee considers proposals concerning the management and expansion of the Library of Congress, the development and maintenance of the Botanic Gardens, the receipt of gifts for the benefit of the Library, and certain matters relating to placing of statues and other works of art in the Capitol.

Jurisdiction, 1991

From Paul S. Rundquist, Congressional Research Service, The Library of Congress, August 23, 1984:

"In addition to its basic mandate which dates from 1802 and continues in force, the Joint Committee on the Library is charged by statute with a number of duties involving both the Library of Congress and other components of the legislative branch..."

JOINT COMMITTEE: LIBRARY / 80th Congress

Service Dates of Committee Chair: Jan. 22,1947-Jan. 3,1949
Service Dates of House Members: Jan. 20,1947-Jan. 3,1949
Service Dates of Senate Members: Jan. 10,1947-Jan. 13,1949

HOUSE

Majority Rank Name	Party	State	Terms in: House	Terms in: Comm.	Minority Rank Name	Party	State	Terms in: House	Terms in: Comm.
1st LeCompte, Karl M.	Rep	Iowa	5	1	1st Norton, Mary T.	Dem	N.J.	12	1
2nd Bishop, Cecil W. (Runt)	Rep	Ill.	4	4	2nd Meade, Hugh A.	Dem	Md.	1	1
3rd Landis, Gerald W.	Rep	Ind.	5	1					

SENATE

Majority Rank Name	Party	State	Years in: Senate	Years in: Comm.	Minority Rank Name	Party	State	Years in: Senate	Years in: Comm.
Chr Brooks, C. Wayland	Rep	Ill.	7	1	1st Green, Theodore F.	Dem	R.I.	11	3
2nd Jenner, William E.	Rep	Ind.	1	*1 1	2nd Holland, Spessard L.	Dem	Fla.	1	1
3rd Ives, Irving M.	Rep	N.Y.	1	1					

*1: Member's 1st period of service on the committee.

Changes:
House Minority:

Meade, Hugh A.	Dem	Md.	Jan. 14,1948	Left committee; no new assignment.
Regan, Kenneth M.	Dem	Tex.	Jan. 27,1948	Replaced Meade.

	Majority			Minority		
Departures from the House:						
Defeated for Reelection	Landis, Gerald W.	Ind.	Rep	None		
Departures from the Senate:						
Defeated for Reelection	Brooks, C. Wayland	Ill.	Rep	None		
Departures from Committee:						
Senate:						
Moved to Judiciary	Jenner, William E.	Ind.	Rep	None		
Moved to Agriculture & Forestry	None			Holland, Spessard L.	Fla.	Dem

JOINT COMMITTEE: LIBRARY / 81st Congress

Service Dates of Committee Chair: Jan. 13,1949-Continued
Service Dates of House Members: Jan. 27,1949-Jan. 3,1951
Service Dates of Senate Members: Jan. 13,1949-Jan. 17,1951

HOUSE

Majority Rank Name	Party	State	Terms in: House	Terms in: Comm.	Minority Rank Name	Party	State	Terms in: House	Terms in: Comm.
1st Norton, Mary T.	Dem	N.J.	13	2	1st LeCompte, Karl M.	Rep	Iowa	6	2
2nd Regan, Kenneth M.	Dem	Tex.	2	2	2nd Bishop, Cecil W. (Runt)	Rep	Ill.	5	5
3rd Albert, Carl	Dem	Okla.	2	1					

SENATE

Majority Rank Name	Party	State	Years in: Senate	Years in: Comm.	Minority Rank Name	Party	State	Years in: Senate	Years in: Comm.
Chr Green, Theodore F.	Dem	R.I.	13	5	1st Ives, Irving M.	Rep	N.Y.	3	2
2nd Hayden, Carl	Dem	Ariz.	22	1	2nd Lodge, Henry Cabot Jr.	Rep	Mass.	10	1
3rd Long, Russell B.	Dem	La.	1	1					

Changes:
Senate Majority:

Long, Russell B.	Dem	La.	July 29,1949	Left committee; no new assignment.
Stennis, John C.	Dem	Miss.	July 29,1949	Replaced Long.

Senate Minority:

Ives, Irving M.	Rep	N.Y.	Jan. 25,1950	Left committee; no new assignment.
Hendrickson, Robert C.	Rep	N.J.	Jan. 25,1950	Replaced Ives.

Departures from the House:	Majority		Minority	
Retired	Norton, Mary T.	N.J. Dem	None	
Departures from Committee:				
Senate:				
Moved to Armed Services	Stennis, John C.	Miss. Dem	None	

JOINT COMMITTEE: LIBRARY / 82nd Congress

Service Dates of Committee Chair: Jan. 17,1951-Jan. 3,1953
Service Dates of House Members: Jan. 23,1951-Jan. 3,1953
Service Dates of Senate Members: Jan. 17,1951-Jan. 29,1953

HOUSE

Majority Rank Name	Party	State	Terms in: House	Terms in: Comm.	Minority Rank Name	Party	State	Terms in: House	Terms in: Comm.
1st Stanley, Thomas B.	Dem	Va.	4	1	1st LeCompte, Karl M.	Rep	Iowa	7	3
2nd Regan, Kenneth M.	Dem	Tex.	3	3	2nd Bishop, Cecil W. (Runt)	Rep	Ill.	6	6
3rd Albert, Carl	Dem	Okla.	3	2					

SENATE

Majority Rank Name	Party	State	Years in: Senate	Years in: Comm.	Minority Rank Name	Party	State	Years in: Senate	Years in: Comm.
Chr Green, Theodore F.	Dem	R.I.	15	7	1st Lodge, Henry Cabot Jr.	Rep	Mass.	12	2
2nd Hayden, Carl	Dem	Ariz.	24	3	2nd Hendrickson, Robert C.	Rep	N.J.	3	2
3rd Benton, William	Dem	Conn.	2	1					

Departures from the Senate:	Majority		Minority	
Defeated for Reelection	Benton, William	Conn. Dem	Lodge, Henry Cabot Jr.	Mass. Rep
Departures from Committee:				
House:				
No new assignment	Albert, Carl	Okla. Dem	Bishop, Cecil W. (Runt)	Ill. Rep
	Stanley, Thomas B.	Va. Dem		
Senate:				
Moved to Armed Services	None		Hendrickson, Robert C.	N.J. Rep
No new assignment	Hayden, Carl	Ariz. Dem		

JOINT COMMITTEE: LIBRARY / 83rd Congress

Service Dates of House Members: Feb. 6,1953-Jan. 3,1955
Service Dates of Senate Members: Jan. 29,1953-Feb. 26,1955

HOUSE

Majority Rank Name	Party	State	Terms in: House	Terms in: Comm.	Minority Rank Name	Party	State	Terms in: House	Terms in: Comm.
1st LeCompte, Karl M.	Rep	Iowa	8	4	1st Regan, Kenneth M.	Dem	Tex.	4	4
2nd Harrison, Robert D.	Rep	Neb.	2	1	2nd Burleson, Omar T.	Dem	Tex.	4	1
3rd Corbett, Robert J.	Rep	Penn.	6 *1	1					

SENATE

Majority Rank Name	Party	State	Years in: Senate	Years in: Comm.	Minority Rank Name	Party	State	Years in: Senate	Years in: Comm.
1st Purtell, William A.	Rep	Conn.	1	1	1st Green, Theodore F.	Dem	R.I.	17	9
2nd Jenner, William E.	Rep	Ind.	7 *2	1	2nd Gillette, Guy M.	Dem	Iowa	13	1
3rd Barrett, Frank A.	Rep	Wyo.	1	1					

*1: Member's 1st period of service on the committee; *2: Member's 2nd period of service on the committee.

Note: No committee Chair is listed in Congressional Directory for either session of the 83rd Congress.

Changes:
Senate Majority:

Purtell, William A.	Rep	Conn.	Jan. 25,1954	Left committee; no new assignment.
McCarthy, Joseph R.	Rep	Wisc.	Jan. 25,1954	Replaced Purtell.

	Majority			Minority		
Departures from the House:						
Defeated for Renomination	None			Regan, Kenneth M.	Tex.	Dem
Departures from the Senate:						
Defeated for Reelection	None			Gillette, Guy M.	Iowa	Dem
Departures from Committee:						
House:						
Moved to Joint Disposition of Executive Papers	Corbett, Robert J.	Penn.	Rep	None		
Senate:						
Moved to Joint Immigration & Naturalization	Jenner, William E.	Ind.	Rep	None		

JOINT COMMITTEE: LIBRARY / 84th Congress

Service Dates of Committee Chair: Feb. 18,1955-Jan. 3,1957
Service Dates of House Members: Feb. 2,1955-Jan. 3,1957
Service Dates of Senate Members: Feb. 26,1955-Jan. 30,1957

HOUSE

Majority			Terms in:		Minority			Terms in:	
Rank Name	**Party**	**State**	**House**	**Comm.**	**Rank Name**	**Party**	**State**	**House**	**Comm.**
CVc Burleson, Omar T.	Dem	Tex.	5	2	1st LeCompte, Karl M.	Rep	Iowa	9	5
2nd Jones, Paul C.	Dem	Mo.	5	1	2nd Harrison, Robert D.	Rep	Neb.	3	2
3rd Smith, Frank E.	Dem	Miss.	3	1					

SENATE

Majority			Years in:		Minority			Years in:	
Rank Name	**Party**	**State**	**Senate**	**Comm.**	**Rank Name**	**Party**	**State**	**Senate**	**Comm.**
VcC Green, Theodore F.	Dem	R.I.	19	11	1st Barrett, Frank A.	Rep	Wyo.	3	2
2nd Mansfield, Michael J.	Dem	Mont.	3 *1	1	2nd McCarthy, Joseph R.	Rep	Wisc.	9	2
3rd Gore, Albert A.	Dem	Tenn.	3	1					

*1: Member's 1st period of service on the committee.

	Majority			Minority		
Departures from Committee:						
Senate:						
Moved to Finance	Gore, Albert A.	Tenn.	Dem	None		
Became Senate Majority Whip	Mansfield, Michael J.	Mont.	Dem	None		
Moved to Select Labor & Management	None			McCarthy, Joseph R.	Wisc.	Rep
No new assignment	None			Barrett, Frank A.	Wyo.	Rep

JOINT COMMITTEE: LIBRARY / 85th Congress

Service Dates of Committee Chair: Jan. 28,1957-Jan. 3,1959
Service Dates of House Members: Jan. 28,1957-Jan. 3,1959
Service Dates of Senate Members: Jan. 30,1957-Feb. 2,1959

HOUSE

Majority			Terms in:		Minority			Terms in:	
Rank Name	**Party**	**State**	**House**	**Comm.**	**Rank Name**	**Party**	**State**	**House**	**Comm.**
CVc Burleson, Omar T.	Dem	Tex.	6	3	1st LeCompte, Karl M.	Rep	Iowa	10	6
2nd Jones, Paul C.	Dem	Mo.	6	2	2nd Harrison, Robert D.	Rep	Neb.	4	3
3rd Smith, Frank E.	Dem	Miss.	4	2					

SENATE Majority					Minority				
			Years in:					Years in:	
Rank Name	Party	State	Senate	Comm.	Rank Name	Party	State	Senate	Comm.
VcC Green, Theodore F.	Dem	R.I.	21	13	1st Curtis, Carl T.	Rep	Neb.	3	1
2nd Hennings, Thomas C. Jr.	Dem	Mo.	7	1	2nd Cooper, John Sherman	Rep	Ky.	5 *1	1
3rd Talmadge, Herman E.	Dem	Ga.	1	1					

*1: Member's 1st period of service on the committee.

Departures from the House:	Majority			Minority		
Defeated for Reelection	None			Harrison, Robert D.	Neb.	Rep
Retired	None			LeCompte, Karl M.	Iowa	Rep
Departures from Committee:						
Senate:						
Moved to Finance	Talmadge, Herman E.	Ga.	Dem	Curtis, Carl T.	Neb.	Rep
Moved to Public Works	None			Cooper, John Sherman	Ky.	Rep

JOINT COMMITTEE: LIBRARY / 86th Congress

Service Dates of Committee Chair: Feb. 2,1959-Jan. 3,1961
Service Dates of House Members: Feb. 11,1959-Jan. 3,1961
Service Dates of Senate Members: Feb. 2,1959-Jan. 31,1961

HOUSE Majority					Minority				
			Terms in:					Terms in:	
Rank Name	Party	State	House	Comm.	Rank Name	Party	State	House	Comm.
VcC Burleson, Omar T.	Dem	Tex.	7	4	1st Schenck, Paul F.	Rep	Ohio	5	1
2nd Jones, Paul C.	Dem	Mo.	7	3	2nd Corbett, Robert J.	Rep	Penn.	9 *2	1
3rd Smith, Frank E.	Dem	Miss.	5	3					

SENATE Majority					Minority				
			Years in:					Years in:	
Rank Name	Party	State	Senate	Comm.	Rank Name	Party	State	Senate	Comm.
CVc Green, Theodore F.	Dem	R.I.	23	15	1st Morton, Thruston B.	Rep	Ky.	3	1
2nd Hennings, Thomas C. Jr.	Dem	Mo.	9	3	2nd Keating, Kenneth B.	Rep	N.Y.	1	1
3rd Jordan, B. Everett	Dem	N.C.	1	1					

*2: Member's 2nd period of service on the committee.

Changes:				
Senate Majority:				
Hennings, Thomas C. Jr.	Dem	Mo.	Sep. 13,1960	Died in office.
Senate Minority:				
Morton, Thruston B.	Rep	Ky.	Mar. 24,1960	Left committee; no new assignment.
Brunsdale, C. Norman	Rep	N.D.	Mar. 24,1960	Replaced Morton.
Brunsdale, C. Norman	Rep	N.D.	Aug. 7,1960	Resigned and retired.
Martin, Thomas E.	Rep	Iowa	Aug. 31,1960	Replaced Brunsdale.

Departures from the Senate:	Majority			Minority		
Retired	Green, Theodore F.	R.I.	Dem	Martin, Thomas E.	Iowa	Rep

JOINT COMMITTEE: LIBRARY / 87th Congress

Service Dates of Committee Chair: Feb. 28,1961-Jan. 3,1963
Service Dates of House Members: Feb. 28,1961-Jan. 3,1963
Service Dates of Senate Members: Jan. 31,1961-Mar. 14,1963

HOUSE Majority					Minority				
			Terms in:					Terms in:	
Rank Name	Party	State	House	Comm.	Rank Name	Party	State	House	Comm.
Chr Burleson, Omar T.	Dem	Tex.	8	5	1st Schenck, Paul F.	Rep	Ohio	6	2
2nd Jones, Paul C.	Dem	Mo.	8	4	2nd Corbett, Robert J.	Rep	Penn.	10 *2	2
3rd Smith, Frank E.	Dem	Miss.	6	4					

SENATE **Majority** / **Minority**

Rank	Name	Party	State	Years in: Senate	Years in: Comm.	Rank	Name	Party	State	Years in: Senate	Years in: Comm.
VCh	Mansfield, Michael J.	Dem	Mont.	9	*2 1	1st	Keating, Kenneth B.	Rep	N.Y.	3	2
2nd	Jordan, B. Everett	Dem	N.C.	3	2	2nd	Miller, Jack R.	Rep	Iowa	1	1
3rd	Pell, Claiborne D.	Dem	R.I.	1	*1 1						

*1: Member's 1st period of service on the committee; *2: Member's 2nd period of service on the committee.

Changes:

House Majority:

Smith, Frank E.	Dem	Miss.	Nov. 14,1962	Resigned; defeated for renomination.

Senate Minority:

Keating, Kenneth B.	Rep	N.Y.	Feb. 22,1962	Left committee; no new assignment.
Dirksen, Everett M.	Rep	Ill.	Feb. 22,1962	Replaced Keating.
Miller, Jack R.	Rep	Iowa	Feb. 22,1962	Left committee; no new assignment.
Pearson, James B.	Rep	Kans.	Feb. 22,1962	Replaced Miller.
Pearson, James B.	Rep	Kans.	Aug. 9,1962	Left committee; no new assignment.
Bottum, Joseph H.	Rep	S.D.	Aug. 9,1962	Replaced Pearson.

	Majority			Minority		
Departures from the Senate:						
Defeated for Reelection	None			Bottum, Joseph H.	S.D.	Rep
Departures from Committee:						
Senate:						
Moved to Appropriations	Mansfield, Michael J.	Mont.	Dem	None		
Moved to Finance	None			Dirksen, Everett McK.	Ill.	Rep

JOINT COMMITTEE: LIBRARY / 88th Congress

Service Dates of Committee Chair: Jan. 29,1963-Jan. 3,1965
Service Dates of House Members: Jan. 29,1963-Jan. 3,1965
Service Dates of Senate Members: Mar. 14,1963-Feb. 2,1965

HOUSE **Majority** / **Minority**

Rank	Name	Party	State	Terms in: House	Terms in: Comm.	Rank	Name	Party	State	Terms in: House	Terms in: Comm.
CVc	Burleson, Omar T.	Dem	Tex.	9	6	1st	Schenck, Paul F.	Rep	Ohio	7	3
2nd	Jones, Paul C.	Dem	Mo.	9	5	2nd	Corbett, Robert J.	Rep	Penn.	11	*2 3
3rd	Thompson, Frank Jr.	Dem	N.J.	5	*1 1						

SENATE **Majority** / **Minority**

Rank	Name	Party	State	Years in: Senate	Years in: Comm.	Rank	Name	Party	State	Years in: Senate	Years in: Comm.
VcC	Jordan, B. Everett	Dem	N.C.	5	5	1st	Cooper, John Sherman	Rep	Ky.	11	*2 1
2nd	Pell, Claiborne D.	Dem	R.I.	3	*1 3	2nd	Scott, Hugh D. Jr.	Rep	Penn.	5	*1 1
3rd	Clark, Joseph S.	Dem	Penn.	7	1						

*1: Member's 1st period of service on the committee; *2: Member's 2nd period of service on the committee;

	Majority	Minority		
Departures from the House:				
Defeated for Reelection	None	Schenck, Paul F.	Ohio	Rep

JOINT COMMITTEE: LIBRARY / 89th Congress

Service Dates of Committee Chair: Jan. 28,1965-Jan. 3,1967
Service Dates of House Members: Jan. 28,1965-Jan. 3,1967
Service Dates of Senate Members: Feb. 2,1965-Jan. 26,1967

HOUSE — **Majority** / **Minority**

Rank	Name	Party	State	Terms in: House	Terms in: Comm.	Rank	Name	Party	State	Terms in: House	Terms in: Comm.
CVc	Burleson, Omar T.	Dem	Tex.	10	7	1st	Lipscomb, Glenard P.	Rep	Cal.	7	1
2nd	Jones, Paul C.	Dem	Mo.	10	6	2nd	Corbett, Robert J.	Rep	Penn.	12	*2 4
3rd	Thompson, Frank Jr.	Dem	N.J.	6	*1 2						

SENATE — **Majority** / **Minority**

Rank	Name	Party	State	Years in: Senate	Years in: Comm.	Rank	Name	Party	State	Years in: Senate	Years in: Comm.
VcC	Jordan, B. Everett	Dem	N.C.	7	7	1st	Cooper, John Sherman	Rep	Ky.	13	*2 2
2nd	Pell, Claiborne D.	Dem	R.I.	5	*1 5	2nd	Scott, Hugh D. Jr.	Rep	Penn.	7	*1 2
3rd	Clark, Joseph S.	Dem	Penn.	9	2						

*1: Member's 1st period of service on the committee; *2: Member's 2nd period of service on the committee.

JOINT COMMITTEE: LIBRARY / 90th Congress

Service Dates of Committee Chair: Feb. 15,1967-Jan. 3,1969
Service Dates of House Members: Feb. 15,1967-Jan. 3,1969
Service Dates of Senate Members: Jan. 26,1967-Jan. 31,1969

HOUSE — **Majority** / **Minority**

Rank	Name	Party	State	Terms in: House	Terms in: Comm.	Rank	Name	Party	State	Terms in: House	Terms in: Comm.
CVc	Burleson, Omar T.	Dem	Tex.	11	8	1st	Lipscomb, Glenard P.	Rep	Cal.	8	2
2nd	Jones, Paul C.	Dem	Mo.	11	7	2nd	Corbett, Robert J.	Rep	Penn.	13	*2 5
3rd	Thompson, Frank Jr.	Dem	N.J.	7	*1 3						

SENATE — **Majority** / **Minority**

Rank	Name	Party	State	Years in: Senate	Years in: Comm.	Rank	Name	Party	State	Years in: Senate	Years in: Comm.
VcC	Jordan, B. Everett	Dem	N.C.	9	8	1st	Cooper, John Sherman	Rep	Ky.	15	*2 4
2nd	Pell, Claiborne D.	Dem	R.I.	7	*1 6	2nd	Scott, Hugh D. Jr.	Rep	Penn.	9	*1 4
3rd	Clark, Joseph S.	Dem	Penn.	11	4						

*1: Member's 1st period of service on the committee; *2: Member's 2nd period of service on the committee;

Changes:

House Majority:

Name	Party	State	Date	Change
Burleson, Omar T.	Dem	Tex.	July 30,1968	Left committee; no new assignment.
Friedel, Samuel N.	Dem	Md.	July 31,1968	Replaced Burleson.

	Majority		Minority	
Departures from the House:				
Retired	Jones, Paul C.	Mo. Dem	None	
Departures from the Senate:				
Defeated for Reelection	Clark, Joseph S.	Penn. Dem	None	
Departures from Committee:				
House:				
No new assignment	None		Lipscomb, Glenard P.	Cal. Rep
Senate:				
No new assignment	None		Scott, Hugh D. Jr.	Penn. Rep

JOINT COMMITTEE: LIBRARY / 91st Congress

Service Dates of Committee Chair: Feb. 20,1969-Jan. 3,1971
Service Dates of House Members: Feb. 20,1969-Jan. 3,1971
Service Dates of Senate Members: Jan. 31,1969-Feb. 24,1971

HOUSE

Majority Rank Name	Party	State	Terms in: House	Comm.	Minority Rank Name	Party	State	Terms in: House	Comm.
CVc Friedel, Samuel N.	Dem	Md.	9	1	1st Corbett, Robert J.	Rep	Penn.	14	*2 6
2nd Thompson, Frank Jr.	Dem	N.J.	8	*1 4	2nd Harvey, James	Rep	Mich.	5	1
3rd Podell, Bertram L.	Dem	N.Y.	2	1					

SENATE

Majority Rank Name	Party	State	Years in: Senate	Comm.	Minority Rank Name	Party	State	Years in: Senate	Comm.
VcC Jordan, B. Everett	Dem	N.C.	11	10	1st Cooper, John Sherman	Rep	Ky.	17	*2 6
2nd Pell, Claiborne D.	Dem	R.I.	9	*1 9	2nd Thurmond, J. Strom	Rep	S.C.	14	1
3rd Cannon, Howard W.	Dem	Nev.	11	1					

*1: Member's 1st period of service on the committee; *2: Member's 2nd period of service on the committee;

Changes:

House Majority:

Podell, Bertram L.	Dem	N.Y.	Mar. 11,1969	Left committee; no new assignment.
Brademas, John	Dem	Ind.	Mar. 12,1969	Replaced Podell.

House Minority:

Corbett, Robert J.	Rep	Penn.	Mar. 25,1969	Left committee; no new assignment.
Schwengel, Frederick D.	Rep	Iowa	Apr. 3,1969	Replaced Corbett.

	Majority	Minority
Departures from the House:		
Defeated for Renomination	Friedel, Samuel N. Md. Dem	None
Departures from Committee:		
House:		
No new assignment	Thompson, Frank Jr. N.J. Dem	None
Senate:		
Moved to Veterans' Affairs as Chair	None	Thurmond, J. Strom S.C. Rep

JOINT COMMITTEE: LIBRARY / 92nd Congress

Service Dates of Committee Chair: Feb. 25,1971-Jan. 3,1973
Service Dates of House Members: Feb. 25,1971-Jan. 3,1973
Service Dates of Senate Members: Feb. 24,1971-Jan. 26,1973

HOUSE

Majority Rank Name	Party	State	Terms in: House	Comm.	Minority Rank Name	Party	State	Terms in: House	Comm.
CVc Hays, Wayne L.	Dem	Ohio	12	1	1st Schwengel, Frederick D.	Rep	Iowa	8	2
2nd Nedzi, Lucien N.	Dem	Mich.	6	1	2nd Harvey, James	Rep	Mich.	6	2
3rd Brademas, John	Dem	Ind.	7	2					

SENATE

Majority Rank Name	Party	State	Years in: Senate	Comm.	Minority Rank Name	Party	State	Years in: Senate	Comm.
VcC Jordan, B. Everett	Dem	N.C.	13	13	1st Cooper, John Sherman	Rep	Ky.	19	*2 8
2nd Pell, Claiborne D.	Dem	R.I.	11	*1 11	2nd Scott, Hugh D. Jr.	Rep	Penn.	13	*2 1
3rd Cannon, Howard W.	Dem	Nev.	13	3					

*1: Member's 1st period of service on the committee; *2: Member's 2nd period of service on the committee.

	Majority	Minority
Departures from the House:		
Defeated for Reelection	None	Schwengel, Frederick D. Iowa Rep

Departures from the Senate:

	Majority			Minority		
Defeated for Renomination	Jordan, B. Everett	N.C.	Dem	None		
Retired	None			Cooper, John Sherman	Ky.	Rep

Departures from Committee:

Senate:

	Majority	Minority		
Moved to Joint Printing	None	Scott, Hugh D. Jr.	Penn.	Rep

JOINT COMMITTEE: LIBRARY / 93rd Congress

Service Dates of Committee Chair: Jan. 31,1973-Jan. 3,1975
Service Dates of House Members: Jan. 31,1973-Jan. 3,1975
Service Dates of Senate Members: Jan. 26,1973-Jan. 28,1975

HOUSE

Majority

Rank	Name	Party	State	Terms in: House	Terms in: Comm.
CVc	Nedzi, Lucien N.	Dem	Mich.	7	2
2nd	Hays, Wayne L.	Dem	Ohio	13	2
3rd	Brademas, John	Dem	Ind.	8	3

Minority

Rank	Name	Party	State	Terms in: House	Terms in: Comm.
1st	Harvey, James	Rep	Mich.	7	3
2nd	Hansen, Orval H.	Rep	Ida.	3	1

SENATE

Majority

Rank	Name	Party	State	Years in: Senate	Years in: Comm.
VcC	Cannon, Howard W.	Dem	Nev.	15	4
2nd	Pell, Claiborne D.	Dem	R.I.	13 *1	12
3rd	Williams, Harrison A. Jr.	Dem	N.J.	15	1

Minority

Rank	Name	Party	State	Years in: Senate	Years in: Comm.
1st	Cook, Marlow W.	Rep	Ky.	5	1
2nd	Hatfield, Mark O.	Rep	Ore.	7 *1	1

*1: Member's 1st period of service on the committee.

Changes:

House Minority:

Name	Party	State	Date	Change
Harvey, James	Rep	Mich.	Feb. 7,1973	Left committee; no new assignment.
Devine, Samuel L.	Rep	Ohio	Feb. 7,1973	Replaced Harvey.

Senate Minority:

Name	Party	State	Date	Change
Cook, Marlow W.	Rep	Ky.	Dec. 27,1974	Resigned; defeated for reelection.

Departures from the House:

	Majority	Minority		
Defeated for Renomination	None	Hansen, Orval H.	Ida.	Rep

JOINT COMMITTEE: LIBRARY / 94th Congress

Service Dates of Committee Chair: Mar. 14,1975-Jan. 3,1977
Service Dates of House Members: Mar. 14,1975-Jan. 3,1977
Service Dates of Senate Members: Jan. 28,1975-Mar. 3,1977

HOUSE

Majority

Rank	Name	Party	State	Terms in: House	Terms in: Comm.
CVc	Nedzi, Lucien N.	Dem	Mich.	8	3
2nd	Hays, Wayne L.	Dem	Ohio	14	3
3rd	Brademas, John	Dem	Ind.	9	4

Minority

Rank	Name	Party	State	Terms in: House	Terms in: Comm.
1st	Devine, Samuel L.	Rep	Ohio	9	2
2nd	Moore, W. Henson	Rep	La.	1	1

SENATE

Majority

Rank	Name	Party	State	Years in: Senate	Years in: Comm.
VcC	Cannon, Howard W.	Dem	Nev.	17	6
2nd	Pell, Claiborne D.	Dem	R.I.	15 *1	14
3rd	Williams, Harrison A. Jr.	Dem	N.J.	17	3

Minority

Rank	Name	Party	State	Years in: Senate	Years in: Comm.
1st	Hatfield, Mark O.	Rep	Ore.	9 *1	3
2nd	Griffin, Robert P.	Rep	Mich.	9	1

*1: Member's 1st period of service on the committee.

Changes:
House Majority:

Hays, Wayne L.	Dem	Ohio	Sep. 1,1976	Resigned and retired.
Thompson, Frank Jr.	Dem	N.J.	Sep. 2,1976	Replaced Hays.

Departures from Committee:	Majority	Minority		
House:				
No new assignment	None	Moore, W. Henson	La.	Rep
Senate:				
Moved to Joint Printing	None	Hatfield, Mark O.	Ore.	Rep

JOINT COMMITTEE: LIBRARY / 95th Congress

Service Dates of Committee Chair: Mar. 9,1977-Jan. 3,1979
Service Dates of House Members: Mar. 9,1977-Jan. 3,1979
Service Dates of Senate Members: Mar. 3,1977-Jan. 31,1979

HOUSE — Majority / Minority

Rank	Name	Party	State	Terms in: House	Comm.	Rank	Name	Party	State	Terms in: House	Comm.
Chr	Nedzi, Lucien N.	Dem	Mich.	9	4	1st	Devine, Samuel L.	Rep	Ohio	10	3
2nd	Thompson, Frank Jr.	Dem	N.J.	12	*2 2	2nd	Stockman, David A.	Rep	Mich.	1	1
3rd	Brademas, John	Dem	Ind.	10	5						

SENATE — Majority / Minority

Rank	Name	Party	State	Years in: Senate	Comm.	Rank	Name	Party	State	Years in: Senate	Comm.
VCh	Cannon, Howard W.	Dem	Nev.	19	9	1st	Griffin, Robert P.	Rep	Mich.	11	3
2nd	Pell, Claiborne D.	Dem	R.I.	17	*1 17	2nd	Baker, Howard H. Jr.	Rep	Tenn.	11	1
3rd	Williams, Harrison A. Jr.	Dem	N.J.	19	5						

*1: Member's 1st period of service on the committee; *2: Member's 2nd period of service on the committee.

Departures from the Senate:	Majority	Minority	
Defeated for Reelection	None	Griffin, Robert P.	Mich. Rep

JOINT COMMITTEE: LIBRARY / 96th Congress

Service Dates of Committee Chair: Jan. 31,1979-Jan. 3,1981
Service Dates of House Members: Feb. 8,1979-Jan. 3,1981
Service Dates of Senate Members: Jan. 31,1979-Feb. 5,1981

HOUSE — Majority / Minority

Rank	Name	Party	State	Terms in: House	Comm.	Rank	Name	Party	State	Terms in: House	Comm.
VCh	Nedzi, Lucien N.	Dem	Mich.	10	5	1st	Devine, Samuel L.	Rep	Ohio	11	4
2nd	Thompson, Frank Jr.	Dem	N.J.	13	*2 3	2nd	Stockman, David A.	Rep	Mich.	2	2
3rd	Brademas, John	Dem	Ind.	11	6						

SENATE — Majority / Minority

Rank	Name	Party	State	Years in: Senate	Comm.	Rank	Name	Party	State	Years in: Senate	Comm.
Chr	Pell, Claiborne D.	Dem	R.I.	19	*1 19	1st	Baker, Howard H. Jr.	Rep	Tenn.	13	2
2nd	Cannon, Howard W.	Dem	Nev.	21	11	2nd	Schweiker, Richard S.	Rep	Penn.	11	1
3rd	Williams, Harrison A. Jr.	Dem	N.J.	21	7						

*1: Member's 1st period of service on the committee; *2: Member's 2nd period of service on the committee.

Changes:
House Minority:

Devine, Samuel L.	Rep	Ohio	June 26,1979	Left committee; elected Chair of Republican Conference (reported July 17).
Frenzel, William E.	Rep	Minn.	July 17,1979	Replaced Devine.
Frenzel, William E.	Rep	Minn.	Feb. 28,1980	Left committee; no new assignment.
Gingrich, Newton L.	Rep	Ga.	Feb. 28,1980	Replaced Frenzel.

Departures from the House:	Majority		Minority	
Unassigned in 97th; appointed Director of the Office of Management & Budget, Jan. 27,1987	None		Stockman, David A.	Mich. Rep
Defeated for Reelection	Brademas, John	Ind. Dem	None	
	Thompson, Frank Jr.	N.J. Dem		
Retired	Nedzi, Lucien N.	Mich. Dem	None	
Departures from the Senate:				
Appointed Secretary of Health & Human Services	None		Schweiker, Richard S.	Penn. Rep
Departures from Committee:				
Senate:				
No new assignment	Cannon, Howard W.	Nev. Dem	None	

JOINT COMMITTEE: LIBRARY / 97th Congress

Service Dates of Committee Chair: Feb. 5,1981-Jan. 3,1983
Service Dates of House Members: Feb. 5,1981-Jan. 3,1983
Service Dates of Senate Members: Feb. 3,1981-Feb. 16,1983

HOUSE

Majority Rank Name	Party	State	Terms in: House	Terms in: Comm.	Minority Rank Name	Party	State	Terms in: House	Terms in: Comm.
Chr Hawkins, Augustus F.	Dem	Cal.	10	1	1st Gingrich, Newton L.	Rep	Ga.	2	2
2nd Swift, Allan B.	Dem	Wash.	2	1	2nd Coyne, James K.	Rep	Penn.	1	1
3rd Coyne, William J.	Dem	Penn.	1	1					

SENATE

Majority Rank Name	Party	State	Years in: Senate	Years in: Comm.	Minority Rank Name	Party	State	Years in: Senate	Years in: Comm.
VCh Mathias, Charles McC. Jr.	Rep	Md.	13	1	1st Pell, Claiborne D.	Dem	R.I.	21	*1 21
2nd Hatfield, Mark O.	Rep	Ore.	15	*2 1	2nd Williams, Harrison A. Jr.	Dem	N.J.	23	9
3rd Baker, Howard H. Jr.	Rep	Tenn.	15	4					

*1: Member's 1st period of service on the committee; *2: Member's 2nd period of service on the committee.

Changes:
Senate Minority:

Williams, Harrison A. Jr.	Dem	N.J.	Mar. 11,1982	Resigned and retired.
Inouye, Daniel K.	Dem	Hai.	July 27,1982	Replaced Williams.

Departures from the House:	Majority		Minority	
Defeated for Reelection	None		Coyne, James K.	Penn. Rep
Departures from Committee:				
Senate:				
Moved to Joint Printing	Baker, Howard H. Jr.	Tenn. Rep	Pell, Claiborne D.	R.I. Dem

JOINT COMMITTEE: LIBRARY / 98th Congress

Service Dates of Committee Chair: Feb. 16,1983-Jan. 3,1985
Service Dates of House Members: Feb. 8,1983-Jan. 3,1985
Service Dates of Senate Members: Feb. 16,1983-Apr. 17,1985

HOUSE

Majority Rank Name	Party	State	Terms in: House	Terms in: Comm.	Minority Rank Name	Party	State	Terms in: House	Terms in: Comm.
VCh1 Hawkins, Augustus F.	Dem	Cal.	11	2	1st Gingrich, Newton L.	Rep	Ga.	3	3
VCh2 2nd Swift, Allan B.	Dem	Wash.	3	2	2nd Chandler, Rodney	Rep	Wash.	1	1
3rd Coyne, William J.	Dem	Penn.	2	2					

SENATE	Majority					Minority				
			Years in:						Years in:	
Rank	Name	Party	State	Senate	Comm.	Rank Name	Party	State	Senate	Comm.
Chr	Mathias, Charles McC. Jr.	Rep	Md.	15	3	1st Inouye, Daniel K.	Dem	Hai.	21	1
2nd	Hatfield, Mark O.	Rep	Ore.	17 *2	3	2nd DeConcini, Dennis	Dem	Ariz.	7	1
3rd	Warner, John W.	Rep	Va.	5	1					

*2: Member's 2nd period of service on the committee;

Changes:

Vice Chair:

VCh1 Hawkins, Augustus F.	Dem	Cal.	Sep. 6,1984	Left committee; no new assignment.
VCh2 Swift, Allan B.	Dem	Wash.	Sep. 6,1984	Succeeded Hawkins as Vice Chair.
House Majority:				
Hawkins, Augustus F.	Dem	Cal.	Sep. 6,1984	Left committee; no new assignment.
Annunzio, Frank	Dem	Ill.	Sep. 6,1984	Replaced Hawkins.
House Minority:				
Chandler, Rodney	Rep	Wash.	July 20,1983	Left committee; no new assignment.
Roberts, Pat	Rep	Kans.	July 20,1983	Replaced Chandler.

Departures from Committee:	Majority		Minority	
House:				
Moved to Ways and Means	Coyne, William J.	Penn. Dem	None	
Senate:				
Moved to Joint Printing	None		DeConcini, Dennis	Ariz. Dem

JOINT COMMITTEE: LIBRARY / 99th Congress

Service Dates of Committee Chair: Mar. 28,1985-Jan. 3,1987
Service Dates of House Members: Mar. 28,1985-Jan. 3,1987
Service Dates of Senate Members: Apr. 17,1985-Jan. 29,1987

HOUSE	Majority					Minority				
			Terms in:						Terms in:	
Rank	Name	Party	State	House	Comm.	Rank Name	Party	State	House	Comm.
Chr	Annunzio, Frank	Dem	Ill.	11	2	1st Gingrich, Newton L.	Rep	Ga.	4	4
2nd	Swift, Allan B.	Dem	Wash.	4	3	2nd Roberts, Pat	Rep	Kans.	3	2
3rd	Oakar, Mary Rose	Dem	Ohio	5	1					

SENATE	Majority					Minority				
			Years in:						Years in:	
Rank	Name	Party	State	Senate	Comm.	Rank Name	Party	State	Senate	Comm.
VCh	Mathias, Charles McC. Jr.	Rep	Md.	17	5	1st Inouye, Daniel K.	Dem	Hai.	23	3
2nd	Hatfield, Mark O.	Rep	Ore.	19 *2	5	2nd Pell, Claiborne D.	Dem	R.I.	25 *2	1
3rd	Warner, John W.	Rep	Va.	7	3					

*2: Member's 2nd period of service on the committee.

Departures from the Senate:	Majority		Minority	
Retired	Mathias, Charles McC. Jr.	Md. Rep	None	
Departures from Committee:				
House:				
No new assignment	Swift, Allan B.	Wash. Dem	None	
Senate:				
Moved to Environment & Public Works; Select Intelligence	Warner, John W.	Va. Rep		
Moved to Select Iran-Contra as Chair	None		Inouye, Daniel K.	Hai. Dem

JOINT COMMITTEE: LIBRARY / 100th Congress

Service Dates of Committee Chair: Jan. 29,1987-Jan. 3,1989
Service Dates of House Members: Feb. 10,1987-Jan. 3,1989
Service Dates of Senate Members: Jan. 29,1987-Feb. 2,1989

HOUSE

Majority Rank Name	Party	State	Terms in: House	Terms in: Comm.	Minority Rank Name	Party	State	Terms in: House	Terms in: Comm.
VCh Annunzio, Frank	Dem	Ill.	12	3	1st Gingrich, Newton L.	Rep	Ga.	5	5
2nd Oakar, Mary Rose	Dem	Ohio	6	2	2nd Roberts, Pat	Rep	Kans.	4	*1 3
3rd Jones, Ed	Dem	Tenn.	10	1					

SENATE

Majority Rank Name	Party	State	Years in: Senate	Years in: Comm.	Minority Rank Name	Party	State	Years in: Senate	Years in: Comm.
Chr Pell, Claiborne D.	Dem	R.I.	27	*2 2	1st Hatfield, Mark O.	Rep	Ore.	21	*2 6
2nd DeConcini, Dennis	Dem	Ariz.	11	1	2nd Stevens, Theodore F.	Rep	Alas.	19	1
3rd Moynihan, Daniel Patrick	Dem	N.Y.	11	1					

*1: Member's 1st period of service on the committee; *2: Member's 2nd period of service on the committee.

	Majority		Minority	
Departures from the House:				
Retired	Jones, Ed	Tenn. Dem	None	
Departures from Committee:				
House:				
Moved to Joint Printing	None		Gingrich, Newton L.	Ga. Rep
No new assignment	None		Roberts, Pat	Kans. Rep

JOINT COMMITTEE: LIBRARY / 101st Congress

Service Dates of Committee Chair: Mar. 15,1989-Jan. 3,1991
Service Dates of House Members: Mar. 15,1989-Jan. 3,1991
Service Dates of Senate Members: Feb. 2,1989-Feb. 6,1991

HOUSE

Majority Rank Name	Party	State	Terms in: House	Terms in: Comm.	Minority Rank Name	Party	State	Terms in: House	Terms in: Comm.
Chr Annunzio, Frank	Dem	Ill.	13	4	1st Gillmor, Paul E.	Rep	Ohio	1	1
2nd Oakar, Mary Rose	Dem	Ohio	7	3	2nd Walsh, James T.	Rep	N.Y.	1	1
3rd Clay, William L.	Dem	Mo.	11	1					

SENATE

Majority Rank Name	Party	State	Years in: Senate	Years in: Comm.	Minority Rank Name	Party	State	Years in: Senate	Years in: Comm.
VCh Pell, Claiborne D.	Dem	R.I.	29	*2 4	1st Hatfield, Mark O.	Rep	Ore.	23	*2 8
2nd DeConcini, Dennis	Dem	Ariz.	13	3	2nd Stevens, Theodore F.	Rep	Alas.	21	3
3rd Moynihan, Daniel Patrick	Dem	N.Y.	13	3					

*2: Member's 2nd period of service on the committee.

	Majority		Minority	
Departures from Committee:				
House:				
Moved to Select Narcotics Abuse & Control	None		Gillmor, Paul E.	Ohio Rep
Became Chair of Post Office & Civil Service	Clay, William L.	Mo. Dem	None	
No new assignment	Annunzio, Frank	Ill. Dem	Walsh, James T.	N.Y. Rep
	Oakar, Mary Rose	Tenn. Dem		

JOINT COMMITTEE: LIBRARY / 102nd Congress

Service Dates of Committee Chair: Feb. 6,1991-Jan. 3,1993
Service Dates of House Members: Feb. 21,1991-Jan. 3,1993
Service Dates of Senate Members: Feb. 6,1991-Jan. 3,1993

HOUSE

Majority

Rank	Name	Party	State	Terms in: House	Terms in: Comm.
VCh	Rose, Charles G. III	Dem	N.C.	9	1
2nd	Kolter, Joseph P.	Dem	Penn.	5	1
3rd	Manton, Thomas J.	Dem	N.Y.	4	1

Minority

Rank	Name	Party	State	Terms in: House	Terms in: Comm.
1st	Barrett, William A.	Rep	Neb.	1	1
2nd	Roberts, Pat	Rep	Kans.	6	*2 1

SENATE

Majority

Rank	Name	Party	State	Years in: Senate	Years in: Comm.
Chr	Pell, Claiborne D.	Dem	R.I.	31	*2 6
2nd	DeConcini, Dennis	Dem	Ariz.	15	5
3rd	Moynihan, Daniel Patrick	Dem	N.Y.	15	5

Minority

Rank	Name	Party	State	Years in: Senate	Years in: Comm.
1st	Hatfield, Mark O.	Rep	Ore.	25	*2 11
2nd	Stevens, Theodore F.	Rep	Alas.	23	5

*2: Member's 2nd period of service on the committee.

Note: Senate Concurrent Resolution 10, agreed to on Feb. 6,1991, stipulated that "effective for the One Hundred Second Congress, the Chairman of the Committee on Rules and Administration of the Senate may designate another member of the Committee to serve on the Joint Committee of the Congress on the Library in place of the Chairman."

JOINT COMMITTEE: PRINTING

Jurisdiction, 1947

From the Act entitled "An Act Providing for the public printing and binding and the distribution of public documents," 53rd Congress, Third Session, January 12, 1895 (28 Statutes 601-602):

[Section 2]

The joint committee on printing shall have power to adopt such measures as may be deemed necessary to remedy any neglect or delay in the execution of the public printing; and the committee shall have power to order reprinted not exceeding three hundred copies of a public bill pending before either House of Congress, when the supply shall have become exhausted, and the interests of the public service demand immediate action.

[Section 3]

The joint committee on Printing shall fix upon standards of paper for the different descriptions of public printing and binding . . .

[Section 6]

No contract for furnishing paper shall be valid until it has been approved by the joint committee on printing, if made under their direction . . .

Jurisdiction, 1979

From Jefferson's Manual and Rules of the House of Representatives of the United States for the Ninety-Sixth Congress (1979):

[Section 983h]

The Committee adopts and employs measures necessary to remedy inefficiencies or waste in the public printing, binding, and distribution of Government publications. It has control of the arrangement and style of the Congressional Record (44 U.S.C. 901-910). The joint committee on Printing is authorized and directed to provide for printing in the Daily Record the legislative program for the day, together with a list of congressional committee meetings and hearings and the place of meeting and subject matter; and to cause a brief resume of congressional activities for the previous day to be incorporated in Record, together with an index of its contents. Such data shall be prepared under the supervision of the Secretary of the Senate and the Clerk of the House of Representatives, respectively.

Jurisdiction, 1992

From Authority and Rules of Senate Committees, Senate Document 102-6, printed under the authority of Senate Resolution 58 (102-1), agreed to March 13, 1991:

The Joint Committee on Printing may use any measures it considers necessary to remedy neglect, delay, duplication, or waste in the public printing and binding and the distribution of Government publications.

JOINT COMMITTEE: PRINTING / 80th Congress

Service Dates of Committee Chair: Jan. 22,1947-Jan. 13,1949
Service Dates of House Members: Jan. 20,1947-Jan. 3,1949
Service Dates of Senate Members: Jan. 10,1947-Jan. 13,1949

HOUSE

Majority Rank	Name	Party	State	Terms in: House	Terms in: Comm.	Minority Rank	Name	Party	State	Terms in: House	Terms in: Comm.
VCh	LeCompte, Karl M.	Rep	Iowa	5	1	1st	Pickett, Tom	Dem	Tex.	2	1
2nd	Gamble, Ralph A.	Rep	N.Y.	6	1						

SENATE

Majority Rank	Name	Party	State	Years in: Senate	Years in: Comm.	Minority Rank	Name	Party	State	Years in: Senate	Years in: Comm.
1st	Brooks, C. Wayland	Rep	Ill.	7	1	1st	Hayden, Carl	Dem	Ariz.	20	16
2nd	Knowland, William F.	Rep	Cal.	2	1						

Changes:

House Minority:				
Pickett, Tom	Dem	Tex.	July 24,1947	Left committee; no new assignment.
Burleson, Omar T.	Dem	Tex.	July 24,1947	Replaced Pickett.
Senate Majority:				
Knowland, William F.	Rep	Cal.	Jan. 22,1947	Left committee; no new assignment.
Jenner, William E.	Rep	Ind.	Jan. 22,1947	Replaced Knowland; elected Chair.

	Majority		Minority	
Departures from the Senate:				
Defeated for Reelection	Brooks, C. Wayland	Ill. Rep	None	
Departures from Committee:				
House:				
Moved to Foreign Affairs (Mar. 16,1949)	None		Burleson, Omar T.	Tex. Dem
No new assignment	Gamble, Ralph A.	N.Y. Rep	None	

JOINT COMMITTEE: PRINTING / 81st Congress

Service Dates of Committee Chair: Jan. 13,1949-Continued
Service Dates of House Members: Jan. 27,1949-Jan. 3,1951
Service Dates of Senate Members: Jan. 13,1949-Continued

HOUSE

Majority Rank	Name	Party	State	Terms in: House	Terms in: Comm.	Minority Rank	Name	Party	State	Terms in: House	Terms in: Comm.
VCh	Norton, Mary T.	Dem	N.J.	13	1	1st	LeCompte, Karl M.	Rep	Iowa	6	2
2nd	Deane, Charles B.	Dem	N.C.	2	1						

SENATE

Majority Rank	Name	Party	State	Years in: Senate	Years in: Comm.	Minority Rank	Name	Party	State	Years in: Senate	Years in: Comm.
Chr	Hayden, Carl	Dem	Ariz.	22	18	1st	Jenner, William E.	Rep	Ind.	3	2
2nd	Hunt, Lester C.	Dem	Wyo.	1	1						

Changes:

Senate Majority:				
Hunt, Lester C.	Dem	Wyo.	Sep. 9,1949	Left committee; no new assignment.
Withers, Garrett L.	Dem	Ky.	Sep. 9,1949	Replaced Hunt.
Withers, Garrett L.	Dem	Ky.	Nov. 26,1950	Left committee; no new assignment.
Clements, Earle C.	Dem	Ky.	Dec. 21,1950	Replaced Withers.

	Majority		Minority
Departures from the House:			
Retired	Norton, Mary T.	N.J. Dem	None
Departures from Committee:			
House:			
No new assignment	Deane, Charles B.	N.C. Dem	None

JOINT COMMITTEE: PRINTING / 82nd Congress

Service Dates of Committee Chair: Jan. 23,1951-Jan. 30,1953
Service Dates of House Members: Jan. 23,1951-Jan. 3,1953
Service Dates of Senate Members: Jan. 3,1951-Jan. 30,1953

HOUSE

Majority			Terms in:		**Minority**			Terms in:	
Rank Name	**Party**	**State**	**House**	**Comm.**	**Rank Name**	**Party**	**State**	**House**	**Comm.**
VCh Stanley, Thomas B.	Dem	Va.	4	1	1st LeCompte, Karl M.	Rep	Iowa	7	3
2nd Trimble, James W.	Dem	Ark.	4	1					

SENATE

Majority			Years in:		**Minority**			Years in:	
Rank Name	**Party**	**State**	**Senate**	**Comm.**	**Rank Name**	**Party**	**State**	**Senate**	**Comm.**
Chr Hayden, Carl	Dem	Ariz.	24	20	1st Jenner, William E.	Rep	Ind.	5	4
2nd Clements, Earle C.	Dem	Ky.	1	1					

Departures from Committee:

	Majority			**Minority**		
House:						
No new assignment	Stanley, Thomas B.	Va.	Dem	None		
Senate:						
Moved to Agriculture & Forestry; Became Minority Whip	Clements, Earle C.	Ky.	Dem	None		

JOINT COMMITTEE: PRINTING / 83rd Congress

Service Dates of Committee Chair: Jan. 30,1953-Jan. 26,1955
Service Dates of House Members: Feb. 6,1953-Jan. 3,1955
Service Dates of Senate Members: Jan. 30,1953-Jan. 26,1955

HOUSE

Majority			Terms in:		**Minority**			Terms in:	
Rank Name	**Party**	**State**	**House**	**Comm.**	**Rank Name**	**Party**	**State**	**House**	**Comm.**
VCh LeCompte, Karl M.	Rep	Iowa	8	4	1st Trimble, James W.	Dem	Ark.	5	2
2nd Schenck, Paul F.	Rep	Ohio	2	*1 1					

SENATE

Majority			Years in:		**Minority**			Years in:	
Rank Name	**Party**	**State**	**Senate**	**Comm.**	**Rank Name**	**Party**	**State**	**Senate**	**Comm.**
Chr Jenner, William E.	Rep	Ind.	7	7	1st Hayden, Carl	Dem	Ariz.	26	22
2nd Carlson, Frank	Rep	Kans.	3	1					

*1: Member's 1st period of service on the committee.

Departures from Committee:

	Majority			**Minority**		
House:						
Moved to Rules	None			Trimble, James W.	Ark.	Dem
No new assignment	Schenck, Paul F.	Ohio	Rep	None		
Senate:						
No new assignment	Carlson, Frank	Kans.	Rep	None		

JOINT COMMITTEE: PRINTING / 84th Congress

Service Dates of Committee Chair: Jan. 26,1955-Jan. 30,1957
Service Dates of House Members: Feb. 2,1955-Jan. 3,1957
Service Dates of Senate Members: Jan. 26,1955-Jan. 30,1957

HOUSE

Majority			Terms in:		Minority			Terms in:	
Rank Name	**Party**	**State**	**House**	**Comm.**	**Rank Name**	**Party**	**State**	**House**	**Comm.**
VCh Burleson, Omar T.	Dem	Tex.	5	*2 1	1st LeCompte, Karl M.	Rep	Iowa	9	5
2nd Hays, Wayne L.	Dem	Ohio	4	*1 1					

SENATE

Majority			Years in:		Minority			Years in:	
Rank Name	**Party**	**State**	**Senate**	**Comm.**	**Rank Name**	**Party**	**State**	**Senate**	**Comm.**
Chr Hayden, Carl	Dem	Ariz.	28	24	1st Jenner, William E.	Rep	Ind.	9	9
2nd Green, Theodore F.	Dem	R.I.	19	1					

*1: Member's 1st period of service on the committee; *2: Member's 2nd period of service on the committee.

Departures from Committee:	Majority			Minority		
Senate:						
Moved to Finance	None			Jenner, William E.	Ind.	Rep
No new assignment	Green, Theodore F.	R.I.	Dem	None		

JOINT COMMITTEE: PRINTING / 85th Congress

Service Dates of Committee Chair: Jan. 30,1957-Feb. 2,1959
Service Dates of House Members: Jan. 28,1957-Jan. 3,1959
Service Dates of Senate Members: Jan. 30,1957-Feb. 2,1959

HOUSE

Majority			Terms in:		Minority			Terms in:	
Rank Name	**Party**	**State**	**House**	**Comm.**	**Rank Name**	**Party**	**State**	**House**	**Comm.**
VCh Burleson, Omar T.	Dem	Tex.	6	*2 2	1st LeCompte, Karl M.	Rep	Iowa	10	6
2nd Hays, Wayne L.	Dem	Ohio	5	*1 2					

SENATE

Majority			Years in:		Minority			Years in:	
Rank Name	**Party**	**State**	**Senate**	**Comm.**	**Rank Name**	**Party**	**State**	**Senate**	**Comm.**
Chr Hayden, Carl	Dem	Ariz.	30	26	1st Javits, Jacob K.	Rep	N.Y.	1	1
2nd Hennings, Thomas C. Jr.	Dem	Mo.	7	1					

*1: Member's 1st period of service on the committee; *2: Member's 2nd period of service on the committee.

Departures from the House:	Majority	Minority		
Retired	None	LeCompte, Karl M.	Iowa	Rep
Departures from Committee:				
Senate:				
Moved to Labor & Public Welfare	None	Javits, Jacob K.	N.Y.	Rep

JOINT COMMITTEE: PRINTING / 86th Congress

Service Dates of Committee Chair: Feb. 2,1959-Jan. 31,1961
Service Dates of House Members: Feb. 11,1959-Jan. 3,1961
Service Dates of Senate Members: Feb. 2,1959-Jan. 31,1961

HOUSE

Majority			Terms in:		Minority			Terms in:	
Rank Name	**Party**	**State**	**House**	**Comm.**	**Rank Name**	**Party**	**State**	**House**	**Comm.**
VCh Burleson, Omar T.	Dem	Tex.	7	*2 3	1st Schenck, Paul F.	Rep	Ohio	5	*2 1
2nd Hays, Wayne L.	Dem	Ohio	6	*1 3					

SENATE — **Majority** / **Minority**

Rank	Name	Party	State	Years in: Senate	Years in: Comm.	Rank	Name	Party	State	Years in: Senate	Years in: Comm.
Chr	Hayden, Carl	Dem	Ariz.	32	28	1st	Morton, Thruston B.	Rep	Ky.	3	1
2nd	Hennings, Thomas C. Jr.	Dem	Mo.	9	3						

*1: Member's 1st period of service on the committee; *2: Member's 2nd period of service on the committee.

Changes:

Senate Majority:

Hennings, Thomas C. Jr.	Dem	Mo.	Sep. 13,1960	Died in office.

Senate Minority:

Morton, Thruston B.	Rep	Ky.	Mar. 24,1960	Left committee; no new assignment.
Brunsdale, C. Norman	Rep	N.D.	Mar. 24,1960	Replaced Morton.
Brunsdale, C. Norman	Rep	N.D.	Aug. 7,1960	Resigned and retired.
Martin, Thomas E.	Rep	Iowa	Aug. 31,1960	Replaced Brunsdale.

Departures from the Senate:	Majority	Minority	
Retired	None	Martin, Thomas E.	Iowa Rep

JOINT COMMITTEE: PRINTING / 87th Congress

Service Dates of Committee Chair: Jan. 31,1961-Mar. 14,1963
Service Dates of House Members: Feb. 28,1961-Jan. 3,1963
Service Dates of Senate Members: Jan. 31,1961-Mar. 14,1963

HOUSE — **Majority** / **Minority**

Rank	Name	Party	State	Terms in: House	Terms in: Comm.	Rank	Name	Party	State	Terms in: House	Terms in: Comm.
VCh	Burleson, Omar T.	Dem	Tex.	8 *2	4	1st	Schenck, Paul F.	Rep	Ohio	6 *2	2
2nd	Hays, Wayne L.	Dem	Ohio	7 *1	4						

SENATE — **Majority** / **Minority**

Rank	Name	Party	State	Years in: Senate	Years in: Comm.	Rank	Name	Party	State	Years in: Senate	Years in: Comm.
Chr	Hayden, Carl	Dem	Ariz.	34	30	1st	Miller, Jack R.	Rep	Iowa	1	1
2nd	Mansfield, Michael J.	Dem	Mont.	9	1						

*1: Member's 1st period of service on the committee; *2: Member's 2nd period of service on the committee.

Changes:

Senate Minority:

Miller, Jack R.	Rep	Iowa	Feb. 22,1962	Left committee; no new assignment.
Curtis, Carl T.	Rep	Neb.	Feb. 22,1962	Replaced Miller.

Departures from Committee:	Majority		Minority	
Senate:				
Moved to Appropriations	Mansfield, Michael J.	Mont. Dem	None	
Moved to Aeronautical & Space Sciences	None		Curtis, Carl T.	Neb. Rep

JOINT COMMITTEE: PRINTING / 88th Congress

Service Dates of Committee Chair: Mar. 14,1963-Feb. 2,1965
Service Dates of House Members: Jan. 29,1963-Jan. 3,1965
Service Dates of Senate Members: Mar. 14,1963-Feb. 2,1965

HOUSE — **Majority** / **Minority**

Rank	Name	Party	State	Terms in: House	Terms in: Comm.	Rank	Name	Party	State	Terms in: House	Terms in: Comm.
VCh	Burleson, Omar T.	Dem	Tex.	9 *2	5	1st	Schenck, Paul F.	Rep	Ohio	7 *2	3
2nd	Hays, Wayne L.	Dem	Ohio	8 *1	5						

SENATE

Majority			Years in: Senate	Years in: Comm.	Minority			Years in: Senate	Years in: Comm.
Rank Name	**Party**	**State**	**Senate**	**Comm.**	**Rank Name**	**Party**	**State**	**Senate**	**Comm.**
Chr Hayden, Carl	Dem	Ariz.	36	32	1st Scott, Hugh D. Jr.	Rep	Penn.	5	*1 1
2nd Jordan, B. Everett	Dem	N.C.	5	1					

*1: Member's 1st period of service on the committee; *2: Member's 2nd period of service on the committee.

Departures from the House:

	Majority	Minority		
Defeated for Reelection	None	Schenck, Paul F.	Ohio	Rep

JOINT COMMITTEE: PRINTING / 89th Congress

Service Dates of Committee Chair: Feb. 2,1965-Jan. 26,1967
Service Dates of House Members: Jan. 28,1965-Jan. 3,1967
Service Dates of Senate Members: Feb. 2,1965-Jan. 26,1967

HOUSE

Majority			Terms in: House	Terms in: Comm.	Minority			Terms in: House	Terms in: Comm.
Rank Name	**Party**	**State**	**House**	**Comm.**	**Rank Name**	**Party**	**State**	**House**	**Comm.**
VCh Burleson, Omar T.	Dem	Tex.	10	*2 6	1st Lipscomb, Glenard P.	Rep	Cal.	7	1
2nd Hays, Wayne L.	Dem	Ohio	9	*1 6					

SENATE

Majority			Years in: Senate	Years in: Comm.	Minority			Years in: Senate	Years in: Comm.
Rank Name	**Party**	**State**	**Senate**	**Comm.**	**Rank Name**	**Party**	**State**	**Senate**	**Comm.**
Chr Hayden, Carl	Dem	Ariz.	38	34	1st Scott, Hugh D. Jr.	Rep	Penn.	7	*1 2
2nd Jordan, B. Everett	Dem	N.C.	7	2					

*1: Member's 1st period of service on the committee; *2: Member's 2nd period of service on the committee.

JOINT COMMITTEE: PRINTING / 90th Congress

Service Dates of Committee Chair: Jan. 26,1967-Jan. 31,1969
Service Dates of House Members: Feb. 15,1967-Jan. 3,1969
Service Dates of Senate Members: Jan. 26,1967-Jan. 31,1969

HOUSE

Majority			Terms in: House	Terms in: Comm.	Minority			Terms in: House	Terms in: Comm.
Rank Name	**Party**	**State**	**House**	**Comm.**	**Rank Name**	**Party**	**State**	**House**	**Comm.**
VCh Burleson, Omar T.	Dem	Tex.	11	*2 7	1st Lipscomb, Glenard P.	Rep	Cal.	8	2
2nd Hays, Wayne L.	Dem	Ohio	10	*1 7					

SENATE

Majority			Years in: Senate	Years in: Comm.	Minority			Years in: Senate	Years in: Comm.
Rank Name	**Party**	**State**	**Senate**	**Comm.**	**Rank Name**	**Party**	**State**	**Senate**	**Comm.**
Chr Hayden, Carl	Dem	Ariz.	40	36	1st Scott, Hugh D. Jr.	Rep	Penn.	9	*1 4
2nd Jordan, B. Everett	Dem	N.C.	9	4					

*1: Member's 1st period of service on the committee; *2: Member's 2nd period of service on the committee.

Changes:

House Majority:

Burleson, Omar T.	Dem	Tex.	July 30,1968	Left committee; no new assignment.
Friedel, Samuel N.	Dem	Md.	July 31,1968	Replaced Burleson.

Departures from the Senate:

	Majority			Minority
Retired	Hayden, Carl	Ariz.	Dem	None

Departures from Committee:

House:

No new assignment	Hays, Wayne L.	Ohio	Dem	None

JOINT COMMITTEE: PRINTING / 91st Congress

Service Dates of Committee Chair: Jan. 31,1969-Feb. 24,1971
Service Dates of House Members: Feb. 20,1969-Jan. 3,1971
Service Dates of Senate Members: Jan. 31,1969-Feb. 24,1971

HOUSE

Majority						**Minority**				
			Terms in:						**Terms in:**	
Rank	**Name**	**Party**	**State**	**House**	**Comm.**	**Rank Name**	**Party**	**State**	**House**	**Comm.**
VcC	Friedel, Samuel N.	Dem	Md.	9	2	1st Lipscomb, Glenard P.	Rep	Cal.	9	3
2nd	Dent, John H.	Dem	Penn.	7	1					

SENATE

Majority						**Minority**				
			Years in:						**Years in:**	
Rank	**Name**	**Party**	**State**	**Senate**	**Comm.**	**Rank Name**	**Party**	**State**	**Senate**	**Comm.**
CVc	Jordan, B. Everett	Dem	N.C.	11	6	1st Scott, Hugh D. Jr.	Rep	Penn.	11 *1	6
2nd	Allen, James B.	Dem	Ala.	1	1					

*1: Member's 1st period of service on the committee.

Changes:
House Minority:

Lipscomb, Glenard P.	Rep	Cal.	Feb. 1,1970	Died in office.
Devine, Samuel L.	Rep	Ohio	Feb. 10,1970	Replaced Lipscomb.

	Majority		**Minority**	
Departures from the House:				
Defeated for Renomination	Friedel, Samuel N.	Md. Dem	None	
Departures from Committee:				
House:				
No new assignment	Dent, John H.	Penn. Dem	None	
Senate:				
Moved to Select Secret Documents	None		Scott, Hugh D. Jr.	Penn. Rep

JOINT COMMITTEE: PRINTING / 92nd Congress

Service Dates of Committee Chair: Feb. 24,1971-Jan. 3,1973
Service Dates of House Members: Feb. 25,1971-Jan. 3,1973
Service Dates of Senate Members: Feb. 24,1971-Jan. 26,1973

HOUSE

Majority						**Minority**				
			Terms in:						**Terms in:**	
Rank	**Name**	**Party**	**State**	**House**	**Comm.**	**Rank Name**	**Party**	**State**	**House**	**Comm.**
VcC	Hays, Wayne L.	Dem	Ohio	12 *2	1	1st Devine, Samuel L.	Rep	Ohio	7	2
2nd	Brademas, John	Dem	Ind.	7	1					

SENATE

Majority						**Minority**				
			Years in:						**Years in:**	
Rank	**Name**	**Party**	**State**	**Senate**	**Comm.**	**Rank Name**	**Party**	**State**	**Senate**	**Comm.**
CVc	Jordan, B. Everett	Dem	N.C.	13	8	1st Griffin, Robert P.	Rep	Mich.	5	1
2nd	Allen, James B.	Dem	Ala.	3	3					

*2: Member's 2nd period of service on the committee.

	Majority		**Minority**	
Departures from the Senate:				
Defeated for Renomination	Jordan, B. Everett	N.C. Dem	None	
Departures from Committee:				
House:				
Moved to Joint Library	None		Devine, Samuel L.	Ohio Rep
Senate:				
Moved to Foreign Relations	None		Griffin, Robert P.	Mich. Rep

JOINT COMMITTEE: PRINTING / 93rd Congress

Service Dates of Committee Chair: Jan. 26,1973-Jan. 3,1975
Service Dates of House Members: Jan. 31,1973-Jan. 3,1975
Service Dates of Senate Members: Jan. 26,1973-Jan. 28,1975

HOUSE

Majority						Minority				
			Terms in:						Terms in:	
Rank Name	Party	State	House	Comm.		Rank Name	Party	State	House	Comm.
VcC Hays, Wayne L.	Dem	Ohio	13	*2 2		1st Dickinson, William L.	Rep	Ala.	5	1
2nd Brademas, John	Dem	Ind.	8	2						

SENATE

Majority						Minority				
			Years in:						Years in:	
Rank Name	Party	State	House	Comm.		Rank Name	Party	State	Senate	Comm.
CVc Cannon, Howard W.	Dem	Nev.	15	*1 1		1st Scott, Hugh D. Jr.	Rep	Penn.	15	*2 1
2nd Allen, James B.	Dem	Ala.	5	4						

*1: Member's 1st period of service on the committee; *2: Member's 2nd period of service on the committee.

JOINT COMMITTEE: PRINTING / 94th Congress

Service Dates of Committee Chair: Jan. 28,1975-Jan. 3,1976
Service Dates of House Members: Mar. 14,1975-Jan. 3,1977
Service Dates of Senate Members: Jan. 28,1975-Mar. 3,1977

HOUSE

Majority						Minority				
			Terms in:						Terms in:	
Rank Name	Party	State	House	Comm.		Rank Name	Party	State	House	Comm.
VcC Hays, Wayne L.	Dem	Ohio	14	*2 3		1st Dickinson, William L.	Rep	Ala.	6	2
2nd Brademas, John	Dem	Ind.	9	3						

SENATE

Majority						Minority				
			Years in:						Years in:	
Rank Name	Party	State	Senate	Comm.		Rank Name	Party	State	Senate	Comm.
CVc Cannon, Howard W.	Dem	Nev.	17	*1 3		1st Scott, Hugh D. Jr.	Rep	Penn.	17	*2 3
2nd Allen, James B.	Dem	Ala.	7	6						

*1: Member's 1st period of service on the committee; *2: Member's 2nd period of service on the committee.

Changes:

House Majority:

Hays, Wayne L.	Dem	Ohio	Sep. 1,1976	Resigned and retired.
Thompson, Frank Jr.	Dem	N.J.	Sep. 2,1976	Replaced Hays; became Chair.

Departures from the Senate:	Majority	Minority	
Retired	None	Scott, Hugh D. Jr.	Penn. Rep

Departures from Committee:

House:

No new assignment	Brademas, John	Ind. Dem	None

JOINT COMMITTEE: PRINTING / 95th Congress

Service Dates of Committee Chair: Ch1 Mar. 3,1977-Jan. 27,1978
Ch2 Jan. 27,1978-Jan. 3,1979
Service Dates of House Members: Mar. 9,1977-Jan. 3,1979
Service Dates of Senate Members: Mar. 3,1977-Jan. 31,1979

HOUSE

Majority Rank	Name	Party	State	Terms in: House	Comm.	Minority Rank	Name	Party	State	Terms in: House	Comm.
VCh	Thompson, Frank Jr.	Dem	N.J.	12	2	1st	Dickinson, William L.	Rep	Ala.	7	3
2nd	Hawkins, Augustus F.	Dem	Cal.	8	1						

SENATE

Majority Rank	Name	Party	State	Years in: Senate	Comm.	Minority Rank	Name	Party	State	Years in: Senate	Comm.
Chr	Cannon, Howard W.	Dem	Nev.	19	*1 5	1st	Hatfield, Mark O.	Rep	Ore.	11	*1 1
2nd	Allen, James B.	Dem	Ala.	9	9						

*1: Member's 1st period of service on the committee.

Changes:

Chair:

Ch1	Cannon, Howard W.	Dem	Nev.	Jan. 27,1978	Left committee; no new assignment.
Ch2	Pell, Claiborne D.	Dem	R.I.	Jan. 27,1978	Succeeded Cannon as Chair.

Senate Majority:

Cannon, Howard W.	Dem	Nev.	Jan. 27,1978	Left committee; no new assignment.
Pell, Claiborne D.	Dem	R.I.	Jan. 27,1978	Replaced Cannon.
Allen, James B.	Dem	Ala.	June 1,1978	Died in office.
Cannon, Howard W.	Dem	Nev.	June 28,1978	Replaced Allen.

JOINT COMMITTEE: PRINTING / 96th Congress

Service Dates of Committee Chair: Feb. 8,1979-Jan. 3,1981
Service Dates of House Members: Feb. 8,1979-Jan. 3,1981
Service Dates of Senate Members: Jan. 31,1979-Feb. 5,1981

HOUSE

Majority Rank	Name	Party	State	Terms in: House	Comm.	Minority Rank	Name	Party	State	Terms in: House	Comm.
Ch1	Thompson, Frank Jr.	Dem	N.J.	13	3	1st	Dickinson, William L.	Rep	Ala.	8	4
ChA 2nd	Hawkins, Augustus F.	Dem	Cal.	9	2						

SENATE

Majority Rank	Name	Party	State	Years in: Senate	Comm.	Minority Rank	Name	Party	State	Years in: Senate	Comm.
VCh	Pell, Claiborne D.	Dem	R.I.	19	*1 2	1st	Hatfield, Mark O.	Rep	Ore.	13	*1 2
2nd	Cannon, Howard W.	Dem	Nev.	21	*2 1						

*1: Member's 1st period of service on the committee; *2: Member's 2nd period of service on the committee.

Changes:

Chair:

Ch1	Thompson, Frank Jr.	Dem	N.J.	June 18,1980	Due to Democratic Caucus rules, interrupts service as Chair.
ChA	Hawkins, Augustus F.	Dem	Cal.	June 18,1980	Acting Chair during interruption of service by Thompson.

	Majority		Minority	
Departures from the House:				
Defeated for Reelection	Thompson, Frank Jr.	N.J. Dem	None	
Departures from Committee:				
House:				
No new assignment	None		Dickinson, William L.	Ala. Rep
Senate:				
No new assignment	Pell, Claiborne D.	R.I. Dem	Hatfield, Mark O.	Ore. Rep

JOINT COMMITTEE: PRINTING / 97th Congress

Service Dates of Committee Chair: Feb. 3,1981-Jan. 3,1983
Service Dates of House Members: Feb. 5,1981-Jan. 3,1983
Service Dates of Senate Members: Feb. 5,1981-Feb. 16,1983

HOUSE

Majority Rank	Name	Party	State	Terms in: House	Comm.	Minority Rank	Name	Party	State	Terms in: House	Comm.
VCh	Hawkins, Augustus F.	Dem	Cal.	10	2	1st	Gingrich, Newton L.	Rep	Ga.	2	*1 1
2nd	Gaydos, Joseph M.	Dem	Penn.	8	1	2nd	Martin, Lynn M.	Rep	Ill.	1	1
3rd	Jones, Ed	Dem	Tenn.	7	1						

SENATE

Majority Rank	Name	Party	State	Years in: Senate	Comm.	Minority Rank	Name	Party	State	Years in: Senate	Comm.
Chr	Mathias, Charles McC. Jr.	Rep	Md.	13	1	1st	Cannon, Howard W.	Dem	Nev.	23	*2 3
2nd	Warner, John W.	Rep	Va.	3	1						

*1: Member's 1st period of service on the committee; *2: Member's 2nd period of service on the committee.

Note: Senate Bill 272, agreed to Feb. 3,1981, increased the committee size to 5 House members and 5 Senators.

Additions:

Senate Majority: 3rd Hatfield, Mark O. Rep Ore. Feb. 24,1981
Senate Minority: 2nd Ford, Wendell H. Dem Ky. Feb. 24,1981

	Majority			Minority		
Departures from the Senate:						
Defeated for Reelection	None			Cannon, Howard W.	Nev.	Dem
Departures from Committee:						
House:						
No new assignment	None			Gingrich, Newton L.	Ga.	Rep
Senate:						
Moved to Joint Library	Warner, John W.	Va.	Rep	None		

JOINT COMMITTEE: PRINTING / 98th Congress

Service Dates of Committee Chair: Ch1 Feb. 8,1983-Sep. 6,1984
Ch2 Sep. 6,1984-Jan. 3,1985
Service Dates of House Members: Feb. 8,1983-Jan. 3,1985
Service Dates of Senate Members: Feb. 16,1983-Apr. 17,1985

HOUSE

Majority Rank	Name	Party	State	Terms in: House	Comm.	Minority Rank	Name	Party	State	Terms in: House	Comm.
Ch1	Hawkins, Augustus F.	Dem	Cal.	11	3	1st	Martin, Lynn M.	Rep	Ill.	2	2
2nd	Gaydos, Joseph M.	Dem	Penn.	9	2	2nd	Chandler, Rodney	Rep	Wash.	1	1
3rd	Jones, Ed	Dem	Tenn.	8	2						

SENATE

Majority Rank	Name	Party	State	Years in: Senate	Comm.	Minority Rank	Name	Party	State	Years in: Senate	Comm.
VCh	Mathias, Charles McC. Jr.	Rep	Md.	15	3	1st	Ford, Wendell H.	Dem	Ky.	9	2
2nd	Hatfield, Mark O.	Rep	Ore.	17	*2 2	2nd	Pell, Claiborne D.	Dem	R.I.	23	*2 1
3rd	Baker, Howard H. Jr.	Rep	Tenn.	17	1						

*2: Member's 2nd period of service on the committee.

Changes:

Chair:

Ch1	Hawkins, Augustus F.	Dem	Cal.	Sep. 6,1984	Left committee; no new assignment.
Ch2	Annunzio, Frank	Dem	Ill.	Sep. 6,1984	Succeeded Hawkins as Chair.

House Majority:

Hawkins, Augustus F.	Dem	Cal.	Sep. 6,1984	Left committee; no new assignment.
Annunzio, Frank	Dem	Ill.	Sep. 6,1984	Replaced Hawkins.

House Minority:

Martin, Lynn M.	Rep	Ill.	June 8,1983	Left committee; no new assignment.
Chandler, Rodney	Rep	Wash.	July 20,1983	Left committee; no new assignment.
Vucanovich, Barbara F	Rep	Nev.	July 20,1983	Replaced Martin.
Roberts, Pat	Rep	Kans.	July 20,1983	Replaced Chandler.

Departures from the Senate:	Majority		Minority	
Retired	Baker, Howard H. Jr.	Tenn. Rep	None	
Departures from Committee:				
House:				
No new assignment	None		Vucanovich, Barbara F.	Nev. Rep
Senate:				
Moved to Joint Library	None		Pell, Claiborne D.	R.I. Dem

JOINT COMMITTEE: PRINTING / 99th Congress

Service Dates of Committee Chair: Apr. 17,1985-Jan. 3,1987
Service Dates of House Members: Mar. 28,1985-Jan. 3,1987
Service Dates of Senate Members: Apr. 17,1985-Jan. 29,1987

HOUSE **Majority** / **Minority**

Rank Name	Party	State	Terms in: House	Terms in: Comm.	Rank Name	Party	State	Terms in: House	Terms in: Comm.
VCh Annunzio, Frank	Dem	Ill.	11	2	1st Badham, Robert E.	Rep	Cal.	5	1
2nd Gaydos, Joseph M.	Dem	Penn.	10	3	2nd Roberts, Pat	Rep	Kans.	3	2
3rd Jones, Ed	Dem	Tenn.	9	3					

SENATE **Majority** / **Minority**

Rank Name	Party	State	Years in: Senate	Years in: Comm.	Rank Name	Party	State	Years in: Senate	Years in: Comm.
Chr Mathias, Charles McC. Jr.	Rep	Md.	17	5	1st Ford, Wendell H.	Dem	Ky.	11	5
2nd Hatfield, Mark O.	Rep	Ore.	19	*2 4	2nd DeConcini, Dennis	Dem	Ariz.	9	1
3rd Stevens, Theodore F.	Rep	Alas.	17	1					

*2: Member's 2nd period of service on the committee.

Departures from the Senate:	Majority		Minority
Retired	Mathias, Charles McC. Jr.	Md. Rep	None
Departures from Committee:			
House:			
No new assignment	Jones, Ed	Tenn. Dem	None

JOINT COMMITTEE: PRINTING / 100th Congress

Service Dates of Committee Chair: Feb. 10,1987-Jan. 3,1989
Service Dates of House Members: Feb. 10,1987-Jan. 3,1989
Service Dates of Senate Members: Jan. 29,1987-Feb. 2,1989

HOUSE **Majority** / **Minority**

Rank Name	Party	State	Terms in: House	Terms in: Comm.	Rank Name	Party	State	Terms in: House	Terms in: Comm.
Chr Annunzio, Frank	Dem	Ill.	12	3	1st Badham, Robert E.	Rep	Cal.	6	2
2nd Gaydos, Joseph M.	Dem	Penn.	11	4	2nd Roberts, Pat	Rep	Kans.	4	3
3rd Panetta, Leon E.	Dem	Cal.	6	1					

SENATE **Majority** / **Minority**

Rank Name	Party	State	Years in: Senate	Years in: Comm.	Rank Name	Party	State	Years in: Senate	Years in: Comm.
VCh Ford, Wendell H.	Dem	Ky.	13	6	1st Stevens, Theodore F.	Rep	Alas.	19	2
2nd DeConcini, Dennis	Dem	Ariz.	11	2	2nd Hatfield, Mark O.	Rep	Ore.	21	*2 6
3rd Gore, Albert A. Jr.	Dem	Tenn.	3	1					

*2: Member's 2nd period of service on the committee.

	Majority		Minority	
Departures from the House:				
Retired	None		Badham, Robert E.	Cal. Rep
Departures from Committee:				
House:				
Moved to Budget as Chair	Panetta, Leon E.	Cal. Dem	None	

JOINT COMMITTEE: PRINTING / 101st Congress

Service Dates of Committee Chair: Feb. 2,1989-Jan. 3,1991
Service Dates of House Members: Mar. 15,1989-Jan. 3,1991
Service Dates of Senate Members: Feb. 2,1989-Feb. 6,1991

HOUSE

Majority

Rank	Name	Party	State	Terms in: House	Terms in: Comm.
VCh	Annunzio, Frank	Dem	Ill.	13	4
2nd	Gaydos, Joseph M.	Dem	Penn.	12	5
3rd	Bates, Jim	Dem	Cal.	4	1

Minority

Rank	Name	Party	State	Terms in: House	Terms in: Comm.
1st	Roberts, Pat	Rep	Kans.	5	4
2nd	Walsh, James T.	Rep	N.Y.	1	1

SENATE

Majority

Rank	Name	Party	State	Years in: Senate	Years in: Comm.
Chr	Ford, Wendell H.	Dem	Ky.	15	8
2nd	DeConcini, Dennis	Dem	Ariz.	13	4
3rd	Gore, Albert A. Jr.	Dem	Tenn.	5	3

Minority

Rank	Name	Party	State	Years in: Senate	Years in: Comm.
1st	Stevens, Theodore F.	Rep	Alas.	21	4
2nd	Hatfield, Mark O.	Rep	Ore.	23	*2 8

*2: Member's 2nd period of service on the committee.

Changes:
House Minority:

Walsh, James T.	Rep	N.Y.	Apr. 18,1989	Left committee; no new assignment.
Gingrich, Newton L.	Rep	Ga.	Apr. 18,1989	Replaced Walsh.

	Majority		Minority
Departures from the House:			
Defeated for Reelection	Bates, Jim	Cal. Dem	None
Departures from Committee:			
House:			
No new assignment	Annunzio, Frank	Ill. Dem	None
	Gaydos, Joseph M.	Penn. Dem	

JOINT COMMITTEE: PRINTING / 102nd Congress

Service Dates of Committee Chair: Feb. 21,1991-Jan. 3,1993
Service Dates of House Members: Feb. 21,1991-Jan. 3,1993
Service Dates of Senate Members: Feb. 6,1991-Jan. 3,1993

HOUSE

Majority

Rank	Name	Party	State	Terms in: House	Terms in: Comm.
Chr	Rose, Charles G. III	Dem	N.C.	9	1
2nd	Gejdenson, Samuel	Dem	Conn.	6	1
3rd	Kleczka, Gerald D.	Dem	Wisc.	6	1

Minority

Rank	Name	Party	State	Terms in: House	Terms in: Comm.
1st	Roberts, Pat	Rep	Kans.	6	5
2nd	Gingrich, Newton L.	Rep	Ga.	7	*2 2

SENATE

Majority

Rank	Name	Party	State	Years in: Senate	Years in: Comm.
VCh	Ford, Wendell H.	Dem	Ky.	17	10
2nd	DeConcini, Dennis	Dem	Ariz.	15	6
3rd	Gore, Albert A. Jr.	Dem	Tenn.	7	5

Minority

Rank	Name	Party	State	Years in: Senate	Years in: Comm.
1st	Stevens, Theodore F.	Rep	Alas.	23	6
2nd	Hatfield, Mark O.	Rep	Ore.	25	*2 10

*2: Member's 2nd period of service on the committee.

JOINT COMMITTEE: TAXATION

INTERNAL REVENUE TAXATION

Jurisdiction, 1947

From Public Law 69-20, the Revenue Act of 1926, 69th Congress, First Session, February 26, 1926 (44 Statutes 9, 127-128) describing the joint committee on Internal Revenue Taxation:

[Section 1203. (c)]

(c) It shall be the duty of the joint committee--

(1) To investigate the operation and effects of the Federal system of internal-revenue taxes;
(2) To investigate the administration of such taxes by the Bureau of Internal Revenue or any executive department, establishment, or agency, charged with their administration;
(3) To make such other investigations in respect of such system of taxes as the joint committee may deem necessary;
(4) To investigate measures and methods for the simplification of such taxes, particularly the income tax;
(5) To publish, from time to time, for public examination and analysis, proposed measures and methods for the simplification of such taxes, and to make to the Senate and the House of Representatives, not later than December 31, 1927, a definite report thereon, together with such recommendations as it may deem advisable; and
(6) To report, from time to time, to the Committee on Finance and the Committee on Ways and Means and, in its discretion, to the Senate or the House of Representatives, or both, the results of its investigations, together with such recommendations as it may deem advisable.

TAXATION

The joint committee was renamed the joint committee on Taxation by Public Law 94-455 on October 4, 1976.

Jurisdiction, 1992

From Authority and Rules of Senate Committees for the 102nd Congress, printed under authority of Senate Resolution 58, agreed to March 13, 1991:

[Section 477.5-477.9]

It shall be the duty of the joint committee--

(1) Investigation--
- (A) Operation and effects of law.--To investigate the operation and effects of the Federal system of internal revenue taxes;
- (B) Administration.--To investigate the administration of such taxes by the Internal Revenue Service or any executive department, establishment, or agency charged with their administration; and
- (C) Other investigations.--To make such other investigations in respect of such system of taxes as the joint committee may deem necessary.

(2) Simplification of law.--
- (A) Investigation of methods.--To investigate measures and methods for the simplification of such taxes, particularly the income tax; and
- (B) Publication of proposals.--To publish, from time to time, for public examination and analysis, proposed measures and methods for the simplification of such taxes.

(3) Reports.--
To report, from time to time, to the Committee on Finance and the Committee on Ways and Means, and, in its discretion, to the Senate or the House of Representatives, or both, the results of its investigations, together with such recommendations as it may deem advisable.

JOINT COMMITTEE: INTERNAL REVENUE TAXATION / 80th Congress

Service Dates of Committee Chair: Jan. 17,1947-Jan. 3,1949 (appointments reported Jan. 27,1947)
Service Dates of House Members: Jan. 17,1947-Jan. 3,1949 (appointments reported Jan. 27,1947)
Service Dates of Senate Members: Jan. 24,1947-Continued

HOUSE

Majority Rank	Name	Party	State	Terms in: House	Comm.	Minority Rank	Name	Party	State	Terms in: House	Comm.
CVc	Knutson, Harold	Rep	Minn.	16	3	1st	Doughton, Robert L.	Dem	N.C.	19	5
2nd	Reed, Daniel A.	Rep	N.Y.	15	2	2nd	Cooper, Jere	Dem	Tenn.	10	4
3rd	Woodruff, Roy O.	Rep	Mich.	15	1						

SENATE

Majority Rank	Name	Party	State	Years in: Senate	Comm.	Minority Rank	Name	Party	State	Years in: Senate	Comm.
VcC	Millikin, Eugene D.	Rep	Colo.	6	1	1st	George, Walter F.	Dem	Ga.	25	10
2nd	Taft, Robert A.	Rep	Ohio	9	1	2nd	Barkley, Alben W.	Dem	Ky.	20	6
3rd	Butler, Hugh A.	Rep	Neb.	7 *1	1						

*1: Member's 1st period of service on the committee.

	Majority		Minority	
Departures from the House:				
Lost for Reelection	Knutson, Harold	Minn. Rep	None	
Departures from the Senate:				
Elected Vice President	None		Barkley, Alben W.	Ky. Dem
Departures from Committee:				
Senate:				
No new assignment	Butler, Hugh A.	Neb. Rep	None	

JOINT COMMITTEE: INTERNAL REVENUE TAXATION / 81st Congress

Service Dates of Committee Chair: Jan. 5,1949-Jan. 3,1951
Service Dates of House Members: Jan. 14,1949-Jan. 3,1951 (reported Feb. 2,1949)
Service Dates of Senate Members: Jan. 10,1949-Continued

HOUSE

Majority Rank	Name	Party	State	Terms in: House	Comm.	Minority Rank	Name	Party	State	Terms in: House	Comm.
CVc	Doughton, Robert L.	Dem	N.C.	20	6	1st	Reed, Daniel A.	Rep	N.Y.	16	3
2nd	Cooper, Jere	Dem	Tenn.	11	5	2nd	Woodruff, Roy O.	Rep	Mich.	16	2
3rd	Dingell, John D.	Dem	Mich.	9 *2	1						

SENATE

Majority Rank	Name	Party	State	Years in: Senate	Comm.	Minority Rank	Name	Party	State	Years in: Senate	Comm.
VcC	George, Walter F.	Dem	Ga.	27	12	1st	Millikin, Eugene D.	Rep	Colo.	8	2
2nd	Connally, Thomas T.	Dem	Tex.	20	1	2nd	Taft, Robert A.	Rep	Ohio	11	2
3rd	Byrd, Harry Flood	Dem	Va.	16	1						

*2: Member's 2nd period of service on the committee.

Note: Senate membership on this committee was composed of the three ranking majority members and two ranking minority members of the Senate Finance Committee. Because official reassignment of Senate members was not recorded in the Congressional Record, "Service Dates of Senate Members" reflects members' service on that Standing Committee.

JOINT COMMITTEE: INTERNAL REVENUE TAXATION / 82nd Congress

Service Dates of Committee Chair: Jan. 3,1951-Jan. 3,1953
Service Dates of House Members: Jan. 3,1951-Jan. 3,1953
Service Dates of Senate Members: Jan. 3,1951-Continued

HOUSE

Majority Rank Name	Party	State	Terms in: House	Terms in: Comm.	Minority Rank Name	Party	State	Terms in: House	Terms in: Comm.
CVc Doughton, Robert L.	Dem	N.C.	21	7	1st Reed, Daniel A.	Rep	N.Y.	17	4
2nd Cooper, Jere	Dem	Tenn.	12	6	2nd Woodruff, Roy O.	Rep	Mich.	17	3
3rd Dingell, John D.	Dem	Mich.	10	*2 2					

SENATE

Majority Rank Name	Party	State	Years in: Senate	Years in: Comm.	Minority Rank Name	Party	State	Years in: Senate	Years in: Comm.
VcC George, Walter F.	Dem	Ga.	29	14	1st Millikin, Eugene D.	Rep	Colo.	10	4
2nd Connally, Thomas T.	Dem	Tex.	22	2	2nd Taft, Robert A.	Rep	Ohio	13	4
3rd Byrd, Harry Flood	Dem	Va.	18	2					

*2: Member's 2nd period of service on the committee.

Note: There was no listing for the assignment of House or Senate members to this committee in the 82nd Congress in either the Congressional Record or the House Journal or Senate Journal. All members continued their service from the previous Congress as indicated by the Congressional Directory.

	Majority			Minority		
Departures from the House:						
Retired	Doughton, Robert L.	N.C.	Dem	Woodruff, Roy O.	Mich.	Rep
Departures from the Senate:						
Retired	Connally, Thomas T.	Tex.	Dem	None		
Departures from Committee:						
Senate:						
Became Senate Majority Leader; Moved to Foreign Relations	None			Taft, Robert A.	Ohio	Rep

JOINT COMMITTEE: INTERNAL REVENUE TAXATION / 83rd Congress

Service Dates of Committee Chair: Jan. 16,1953-Jan. 3,1955
Service Dates of House Members: Jan. 16,1953-Jan. 3,1955 (appointments reported Apr. 1,1953)
Service Dates of Senate Members: Jan. 13,1953-Continued

HOUSE

Majority Rank Name	Party	State	Terms in: House	Terms in: Comm.	Minority Rank Name	Party	State	Terms in: House	Terms in: Comm.
CVc Reed, Daniel A.	Rep	N.Y.	18	5	1st Cooper, Jere	Dem	Tenn.	13	7
2nd Jenkins, Thomas A.	Rep	Ohio	15	1	2nd Dingell, John D.	Dem	Mich.	11 *2	3
3rd Simpson, Richard M.	Rep	Penn.	9 *1	1					

SENATE

Majority Rank Name	Party	State	Years in: Senate	Years in: Comm.	Minority Rank Name	Party	State	Years in: Senate	Years in: Comm.
VcC Millikin, Eugene D.	Rep	Colo.	12	6	1st George, Walter F.	Dem	Ga.	31	16
2nd Butler, Hugh A.	Rep	Neb.	13 *2	1	2nd Byrd, Harry Flood	Dem	Va.	20	4
3rd Martin, Edward	Rep	Penn.	7	1					

*1: Member's 1st period of service on the committee; *2: Member's 2nd period of service on the committee.

Note: Senate membership on this committee was composed of the three ranking majority members and two ranking minority members of the Senate Finance Committee. Because official reassignment of Senate members was not recorded in the Congressional Record, "Service Dates of Senate Members" reflects members' service on this Standing Committee.

Changes:
Senate Majority:

Butler, Hugh A.	Rep	Neb.	July 1,1954	Died in office.

Departures from Committee:

	Majority		Minority
House:			
No new assignment	Simpson, Richard M.	Penn. Rep	None

JOINT COMMITTEE: INTERNAL REVENUE TAXATION / 84th Congress

Service Dates of Committee Chair: Jan. 14,1955-Jan. 3,1957
Service Dates of House Members: Jan. 14,1955-Jan. 3,1957 (reported Jan. 17,1955)
Service Dates of Senate Members: Jan. 11,1955-Continued

HOUSE

Majority Rank Name	Party	State	Terms in: House	Comm.	Minority Rank Name	Party	State	Terms in: House	Comm.
CVc Cooper, Jere	Dem	Tenn.	14	8	1st Reed, Daniel A.	Rep	N.Y.	19	6
2nd Dingell, John D.	Dem	Mich.	12	*2 4	2nd Jenkins, Thomas A.	Rep	Ohio	16	2
3rd Mills, Wilbur D.	Dem	Ark.	9	1					

SENATE

Majority Rank Name	Party	State	Years in: Senate	Comm.	Minority Rank Name	Party	State	Years in: Senate	Comm.
VcC Byrd, Harry Flood	Dem	Va.	22	6	1st Millikin, Eugene D.	Rep	Colo.	14	8
2nd George, Walter F.	Dem	Ga.	33	18	2nd Martin, Edward	Rep	Penn.	9	2
3rd Kerr, Robert S.	Dem	Okla.	7	1					

*2: Member's 2nd period of service on the committee.

Note: Senate membership on this committee was composed of the three ranking majority members and two ranking minority members of the Senate Finance Committee. Because official reassignment of Senate members was not recorded in the Congressional Record, "Service Dates of Senate Members" reflects members' service on this Standing Committee.

Changes:

House Majority:

Dingell, John D.	Dem	Mich.	Sep. 19,1955	Died in office.
Gregory, Noble J.	Dem	Ky.	Jan. 16,1956	Replaced Dingell (reported Jan. 26,1956).

Departures from the Senate:

	Majority			Minority	
Retired	George, Walter F.	Ga.	Dem	Millikin, Eugene D.	Colo. Rep

JOINT COMMITTEE: INTERNAL REVENUE TAXATION / 85th Congress

Service Dates of Committee Chair: May 16,1957-Jan. 3,1959
Service Dates of House Members: May 16,1957-Jan. 3,1959 (reported May 22,1957)
Service Dates of Senate Members: Jan. 9,1957-Continued

HOUSE

Majority Rank Name	Party	State	Terms in: House	Comm.	Minority Rank Name	Party	State	Terms in: House	Comm.
CVc Cooper, Jere	Dem	Tenn.	15	9	1st Reed, Daniel A.	Rep	N.Y.	20	7
2nd Mills, Wilbur D.	Dem	Ark.	10	2	2nd Jenkins, Thomas A.	Rep	Ohio	17	3
3rd Gregory, Noble J.	Dem	Ky.	11	2					

SENATE

Majority Rank Name	Party	State	Years in: Senate	Comm.	Minority Rank Name	Party	State	Years in: Senate	Comm.
VcC Byrd, Harry Flood	Dem	Va.	24	8	1st Martin, Edward	Rep	Penn.	11	4
2nd Kerr, Robert S.	Dem	Okla.	9	2	2nd Williams, John J.	Rep	Del.	11	1
3rd Frear, J. Allen Jr.	Dem	Del.	9	1					

Note: Senate membership on this committee was composed of the three ranking majority members and two ranking minority members of the Senate Finance Committee. Because official reassignment of Senate members was not recorded in the Congressional Record, "Service Dates of Senate Members" reflects members' service on this Standing Committee.

Changes:

House Majority:

Cooper, Jere	Dem	Tenn.	Dec. 18,1957	Died in office.
Forand, Aime J.	Dem	R.I.	Jan. 21,1958	Replaced Cooper (reported Jan. 27,1958).

	Majority			Minority		
Departures from the House:						
Defeated for Renomination	Gregory, Noble J.	Ky.	Dem	None		
Retired	None			Jenkins, Thomas A.	Ohio	Rep
Departures from the Senate:						
Retired	None			Martin, Edward	Penn.	Rep

JOINT COMMITTEE: INTERNAL REVENUE TAXATION / 86th Congress

Service Dates of Committee Chair: Jan. 20,1959-Jan. 3,1961
Service Dates of House Members: Jan. 20,1959-Jan. 3,1961
Service Dates of Senate Members: Jan. 20,1959-Feb. 24,1961

HOUSE

Majority			Terms in:		Minority			Terms in:	
Rank Name	Party	State	House	Comm.	Rank Name	Party	State	House	Comm.
CVc Mills, Wilbur D.	Dem	Ark.	11	3	1st Reed, Daniel A.	Rep	N.Y.	21	8
2nd Forand, Aime J.	Dem	R.I.	11	2	2nd Simpson, Richard M.	Rep	Penn.	12 *2	1
3rd King, Cecil R.	Dem	Cal.	10	1					

SENATE

Majority			Years in:		Minority			Years in:	
Rank Name	Party	State	Senate	Comm.	Rank Name	Party	State	Senate	Comm.
VcC Byrd, Harry Flood	Dem	Va.	26	10	1st Williams, John J.	Rep	Del.	13	2
2nd Kerr, Robert S.	Dem	Okla.	11	4	2nd Carlson, Frank	Rep	Kans.	9	1
3rd Frear, J. Allen Jr.	Dem	Del.	11	2					

*2: Member's 2nd period of service on the committee.

Note: Senate membership on this committee was composed of the three ranking majority members and two ranking minority members of the Senate Finance Committee. Because official reassignment of Senate members was not recorded in the Congressional Record, "Service Dates of Senate Members" reflects members' service on this Standing Committee.

Changes:

House Minority:

Reed, Daniel A.	Rep	N.Y.	Feb. 19,1959	Died in office.
Mason, Noah M.	Rep	Ill.	Mar. 3,1959	Replaced Reed.
Simpson, Richard M.	Rep	Penn.	Jan. 7,1960	Died in office.
Byrnes, John W.	Rep	Wisc.	Jan. 27,1960	Replaced Simpson (reported Feb. 1,1960).

	Majority			Minority
Departures from the House:				
Retired	Forand, Aime J.	R.I.	Dem	None
Departures from the Senate:				
Defeated for Reelection	Frear, J. Allen Jr.	Del.	Dem	None

JOINT COMMITTEE: INTERNAL REVENUE TAXATION / 87th Congress

Service Dates of Committee Chair: Feb. 20,1961-Jan. 3,1963
Service Dates of House Members: Feb. 20,1961-Jan. 3,1963 (reported Feb. 21,1961)
Service Dates of Senate Members: Feb. 24,1961-Continued

HOUSE

Majority			Terms in:		Minority			Terms in:	
Rank Name	Party	State	House	Comm.	Rank Name	Party	State	House	Comm.
CVc Mills, Wilbur D.	Dem	Ark.	12	4	1st Mason, Noah M.	Rep	Ill.	13	2
2nd King, Cecil R.	Dem	Cal.	11	2	2nd Byrnes, John W.	Rep	Wisc.	9	2
3rd O'Brien, Thomas J.	Dem	Ill.	13	1					

SENATE **Majority**

Rank	Name	Party	State	Years in: Senate	Comm.
VcC	Byrd, Harry Flood	Dem	Va.	28	13
2nd	Kerr, Robert S.	Dem	Okla.	13	7
3rd	Long, Russell B.	Dem	La.	13	1

Minority

Rank	Name	Party	State	Years in: Senate	Comm.
1st	Williams, John J.	Rep	Del.	15	5
2nd	Carlson, Frank	Rep	Kans.	11	3

Changes:

Senate Majority:

Kerr, Robert S.	Dem	Okla.	Jan. 1,1963	Died in office.

Departures from the House:

	Majority	Minority		
Retired	None	Mason, Noah M.	Ill.	Rep

JOINT COMMITTEE: INTERNAL REVENUE TAXATION / 88th Congress

Service Dates of Committee Chair: Jan. 31,1963-Jan. 3,1965
Service Dates of House Members: Jan. 31,1963-Jan. 3,1965
Service Dates of Senate Members: Feb. 25,1963-Continued

HOUSE **Majority**

Rank	Name	Party	State	Terms in: House	Comm.
CVc	Mills, Wilbur D.	Dem	Ark.	13	5
2nd	King, Cecil R.	Dem	Cal.	12	3
3rd	O'Brien, Thomas J.	Dem	Ill.	14	2

Minority

Rank	Name	Party	State	Terms in: House	Comm.
1st	Byrnes, John W.	Rep	Wisc.	10	3
2nd	Baker, Howard H.	Rep	Tenn.	7	1

SENATE **Majority**

Rank	Name	Party	State	Years in: Senate	Comm.
VcC	Byrd, Harry Flood	Dem	Va.	30	14
2nd	Long, Russell B.	Dem	La.	15	2
3rd	Smathers, George A.	Dem	Fla.	13	1

Minority

Rank	Name	Party	State	Years in: Senate	Comm.
1st	Williams, John J.	Rep	Del.	17	6
2nd	Carlson, Frank	Rep	Kans.	13	4

Note: Senate membership on this committee was composed of the three ranking majority members and two ranking minority members of the Senate Finance Committee. Because official reassignment of Senate members was not recorded in the Congressional Record, "Service Dates of Senate Members" reflects members' service on this Standing Committee.

Changes:

House Majority:

O'Brien, Thomas J.	Dem	Ill.	Apr. 14,1964	Died in office.
Boggs, T. Hale	Dem	La.	May 11,1964	Replaced O'Brien.

House Minority:

Baker, Howard H.	Rep	Tenn.	Jan. 7,1964	Died in office.
Curtis, Thomas B.	Rep	Mo.	Jan. 20,1964	Replaced Baker (reported Jan. 23,1964).

JOINT COMMITTEE: INTERNAL REVENUE TAXATION / 89th Congress

Service Dates of Committee Chair: Mar. 16,1965-Jan. 3,1967
Service Dates of House Members: Mar. 16,1965-Jan. 3,1967 (reported Mar. 22,1965)
Service Dates of Senate Members: Jan. 3,1965-Continued

HOUSE **Majority**

Rank	Name	Party	State	Terms in: House	Comm.
CVc	Mills, Wilbur D.	Dem	Ark.	14	6
2nd	King, Cecil R.	Dem	Cal.	13	4
3rd	Boggs, T. Hale	Dem	La.	11	2

Minority

Rank	Name	Party	State	Terms in: House	Comm.
1st	Byrnes, John W.	Rep	Wisc.	11	4
2nd	Curtis, Thomas B.	Rep	Mo.	8	2

SENATE — Majority / Minority

Rank	Name	Party	State	Years in: Senate	Years in: Comm.	Rank	Name	Party	State	Years in: Senate	Years in: Comm.
VcC	Byrd, Harry Flood	Dem	Va.	32	16	1st	Williams, John J.	Rep	Del.	19	8
VC3 2nd	Long, Russell B.	Dem	La.	17	4	2nd	Carlson, Frank	Rep	Kans.	15	6
3rd	Smathers, George A.	Dem	Fla.	15	2						

Changes:

Vice Chair:

VCh1 Byrd, Harry Flood	Dem	Va.	Nov. 10,1965	Resigned and retired.
VCh2 Long, Russell B.	Dem	La.	Nov. 10,1965	Succeeds Byrd as Vice Chair.

Senate Majority:

Byrd, Harry Flood	Dem	Va.	Nov. 10,1965	Resigned and retired.
Anderson, Clinton P.	Dem	N.M.	Nov. 10,1965	Replaced Byrd.

JOINT COMMITTEE: INTERNAL REVENUE TAXATION / 90th Congress

Service Dates of Committee Chair: Feb. 23,1967-Jan. 3,1969
Service Dates of House Members: Feb. 23,1967-Jan. 3,1969
Service Dates of Senate Members: Jan. 3,1967-Continued

HOUSE — Majority / Minority

Rank	Name	Party	State	Terms in: House	Terms in: Comm.	Rank	Name	Party	State	Terms in: House	Terms in: Comm.
CVc	Mills, Wilbur D.	Dem	Ark.	15	7	1st	Byrnes, John W.	Rep	Wisc.	12	5
2nd	King, Cecil R.	Dem	Cal.	14	5	2nd	Curtis, Thomas B.	Rep	Mo.	9	3
3rd	Boggs, T. Hale	Dem	La.	12	3						

SENATE — Majority / Minority

Rank	Name	Party	State	Years in: Senate	Years in: Comm.	Rank	Name	Party	State	Years in: Senate	Years in: Comm.
VcC	Long, Russell B.	Dem	La.	19	6	1st	Williams, John J.	Rep	Del.	21	10
2nd	Smathers, George A.	Dem	Fla.	17	4	2nd	Carlson, Frank	Rep	Kans.	17	8
3rd	Anderson, Clinton P.	Dem	N.M.	19	2						

	Majority			Minority		
Departures from the House:						
Lost Election for U.S. Senate	None			Curtis, Thomas B.	Mo.	Rep
Retired	King, Cecil R.	Cal.	Dem	None		
Departures from the Senate:						
Retired	Smathers, George A.	Fla.	Dem	Carlson, Frank	Kans.	Rep

JOINT COMMITTEE: INTERNAL REVENUE TAXATION / 91st Congress

Service Dates of Committee Chair: Jan. 29,1969-Jan. 3,1971
Service Dates of House Members: Jan. 29,1969-Jan. 3,1971 (reported Feb. 5,1969)
Service Dates of Senate Members: Jan. 14,1969-Continued

HOUSE — Majority / Minority

Rank	Name	Party	State	Terms in: House	Terms in: Comm.	Rank	Name	Party	State	Terms in: House	Terms in: Comm.
CVc	Mills, Wilbur D.	Dem	Ark.	16	8	1st	Byrnes, John W.	Rep	Wisc.	13	6
2nd	Boggs, T. Hale	Dem	La.	13	4	2nd	Utt, James B.	Rep	Cal.	9	1
3rd	Watts, John C.	Dem	Ky.	10	1						

SENATE — Majority / Minority

Rank	Name	Party	State	Years in: Senate	Years in: Comm.	Rank	Name	Party	State	Years in: Senate	Years in: Comm.
VcC	Long, Russell B.	Dem	La.	21	8	1st	Williams, John J.	Rep	Del.	23	12
2nd	Anderson, Clinton P.	Dem	N.M.	21	4	2nd	Bennett, Wallace F.	Rep	Utah	19	1
3rd	Gore, Albert A.	Dem	Tenn.	17	1						

Note: Senate membership on this committee was composed of the three ranking majority members and two ranking minority members of the Senate Finance Committee. Because official reassignment of Senate members was not recorded in the Congressional Record, "Service Dates of Senate Members" reflects members' service on this Standing Committee.

Changes:

House Minority:

Utt, James B.	Rep	Cal.	Mar. 1,1970	Died in office.
Betts, Jackson E.	Rep	Ohio	Mar. 5,1970	Replaced Utt.

Senate Minority:

Williams, John J.	Rep	Del.	Dec. 31,1970	Resigned and retired.

	Majority			Minority
Departures from the Senate:				
Lost for Reelection	Gore, Albert A.	Tenn.	Dem	None
Departures from Committee:				
House:				
No new assignment	Boggs, T. Hale	La.	Dem	None

JOINT COMMITTEE: INTERNAL REVENUE TAXATION / 92nd Congress

Service Dates of Committee Chair: Feb. 8,1971-Jan. 3,1973
Service Dates of House Members: Feb. 8,1971-Jan. 3,1971
Service Dates of Senate Members: Mar. 30,1971-Continued

HOUSE

Majority			Terms in:		Minority			Terms in:	
Rank Name	**Party**	**State**	**House**	**Comm.**	**Rank Name**	**Party**	**State**	**House**	**Comm.**
CVc Mills, Wilbur D.	Dem	Ark.	17	9	1st Byrnes, John W.	Rep	Wisc.	14	7
2nd Watts, John C.	Dem	Ky.	11	2	2nd Betts, Jackson E.	Rep	Ohio	11	2
3rd Ullman, Albert C.	Dem	Ore.	8	1					

SENATE

Majority			Years in:		Minority			Years in:	
Rank Name	**Party**	**State**	**Senate**	**Comm.**	**Rank Name**	**Party**	**State**	**Senate**	**Comm.**
VcC Long, Russell B.	Dem	La.	23	10	1st Bennett, Wallace F.	Rep	Utah	21	2
2nd Anderson, Clinton P.	Dem	N.M.	23	6	2nd Curtis, Carl T.	Rep	Neb.	17	1
3rd Talmadge, Herman E.	Dem	Ga.	15	1					

Note: "Service Dates of Senate Members" reflect the dates of service of Talmadge and Curtis; all other Senators continued service from the previous Congress without official reassignment recorded in the Congressional Record.

Changes:

House Majority:

Watts, John C.	Dem	Ky.	Sep. 24,1971	Died in office.
Burke, James A.	Dem	Mass.	Sep. 29,1971	Replaced Watts.

	Majority			Minority		
Departures from the House:						
Retired	None			Betts, Jackson E.	Ohio	Rep
				Byrnes, John W.	Wisc.	Rep
Departures from the Senate:						
Retired	Anderson, Clinton P.	N.M.	Dem	None		

JOINT COMMITTEE: INTERNAL REVENUE TAXATION / 93rd Congress

Service Dates of Committee Chair: Jan. 29,1973-Jan. 3,1975
Service Dates of House Members: Jan. 29,1973-Jan. 3,1975
Service Dates of Senate Members: Jan. 4,1973-Continued

HOUSE

Majority			Terms in:		Minority			Terms in:	
Rank Name	**Party**	**State**	**House**	**Comm.**	**Rank Name**	**Party**	**State**	**House**	**Comm.**
CVc Mills, Wilbur D.	Dem	Ark.	18	10	1st Schneebeli, Herman T.	Rep	Penn.	8	1
2nd Ullman, Albert C.	Dem	Ore.	9	2	2nd Collier, Harold R.	Rep	Ill.	9	1
3rd Burke, James A.	Dem	Mass.	8	2					

SENATE	Majority					Minority				
			Years in:						Years in:	
Rank Name	Party	State	Senate	Comm.		Rank Name	Party	State	Senate	Comm.
VcC Long, Russell B.	Dem	La.	25	12		1st Bennett, Wallace F.	Rep	Utah	23	4
2nd Talmadge, Herman E.	Dem	Ga.	17	2		2nd Curtis, Carl T.	Rep	Neb.	19	2
3rd Hartke, R. Vance	Dem	Ind.	15	1						

Note: Senate membership on this committee was composed of the three ranking majority members and two ranking minority members of the Senate Finance Committee. Because official reassignment of Senate members was not recorded in the Congressional Record, "Service Dates of Senate Members" reflects members' service on this Standing Committee.

Changes:

Senate Minority:

Bennett, Wallace F.	Rep	Utah	Dec. 20,1974	Resigned and retired.

	Majority			Minority		
Departures from the House:						
Retired	None			Collier, Harold R.	Ill.	Rep
Departures from Committee:						
House:						
No new assignment	Mills, Wilbur D.	Ark.	Dem	None		

JOINT COMMITTEE: INTERNAL REVENUE TAXATION / 94th Congress

* Name changed to Joint Committee on TAXATION on Oct. 4,1976.

Service Dates of Committee Chair: Jan. 28,1975-Jan. 3,1977
Service Dates of House Members: Jan. 28,1975-Jan. 3,1977
Service Dates of Senate Members: Feb. 5,1975-Continued

HOUSE	Majority					Minority				
			Terms in:						Terms in:	
Rank Name	Party	State	House	Comm.		Rank Name	Party	State	House	Comm.
CVc Ullman, Albert C.	Dem	Ore.	10	3		1st Schneebeli, Herman T.	Rep	Penn.	9	2
2nd Burke, James A.	Dem	Mass.	9	3		2nd Conable, Barber B. Jr.	Rep	N.Y.	6	1
3rd Rostenkowski, Daniel D.	Dem	Ill.	9	1						

SENATE	Majority					Minority				
			Years in:						Years in:	
Rank Name	Party	State	Senate	Comm.		Rank Name	Party	State	Senate	Comm.
VcC Long, Russell B.	Dem	La.	27	14		1st Curtis, Carl T.	Rep	Neb.	21	4
2nd Talmadge, Herman E.	Dem	Ga.	19	4		2nd Fannin, Paul J.	Rep	Ariz.	11	1
3rd Hartke, R. Vance	Dem	Ind.	17	2						

Note: Senate membership on this committee was composed of the three ranking majority members and two ranking minority members of the Senate Finance Committee. Because official reassignment of Senate members was not recorded in the Congressional Record, "Service Dates of Senate Members" reflects members' service on this Standing Committee.

	Majority			Minority		
Departures from the House:						
Retired	None			Schneebeli, Herman T.	Penn.	Rep
Departures from the Senate:						
Defeated for Reelection	Hartke, R. Vance	Ind.	Dem	None		
Retired	None			Fannin, Paul J.	Ariz.	Rep

JOINT COMMITTEE: TAXATION / 95th Congress

Service Dates of Committee Chair: Jan. 24,1977-Jan. 3,1979 (appointments reported Jan. 26,1977)
Service Dates of House Members: Jan. 24,1977-Jan. 3,1979 (appointments reported Jan. 26,1977)
Service Dates of Senate Members: Jan. 10,1977-Feb. 8,1979

HOUSE

Majority			Terms in:		Minority			Terms in:	
Rank Name	**Party**	**State**	**House**	**Comm.**	**Rank Name**	**Party**	**State**	**House**	**Comm.**
CVc Ullman, Albert C.	Dem	Ore.	11	4	1st Conable, Barber B. Jr.	Rep	N.Y.	7	2
2nd Burke, James A.	Dem	Mass.	10	4	2nd Duncan, John J.	Rep	Tenn.	7	1
3rd Rostenkowski, Daniel D.	Dem	Ill.	10	2					

SENATE

Majority			Years in:		Minority			Years in:	
Rank Name	**Party**	**State**	**Senate**	**Comm.**	**Rank Name**	**Party**	**State**	**Senate**	**Comm.**
VcC Long, Russell B.	Dem	La.	29	16	1st Curtis, Carl T.	Rep	Neb.	23	6
2nd Talmadge, Herman E.	Dem	Ga.	21	6	2nd Hansen, Clifford P.	Rep	Wyo.	11	1
3rd Ribicoff, Abraham A.	Dem	Conn.	15	1					

Note: Senate membership on this committee was composed of the three ranking majority members and two ranking minority members of the Senate Finance Committee. Because official reassignment of Senate members was not recorded in the Congressional Record, "Service Dates of Senate Members" reflects members' service on this Standing Committee.

Changes:
Senate Minority:

Hansen, Clifford P.	Rep	Wyo.	Dec. 31,1978	Resigned and retired.

	Majority		Minority	
Departures from the House:				
Retired	Burke, James A.	Mass. Dem	None	
Departures from the Senate:				
Retired	None		Curtis, Carl T.	Neb. Rep

JOINT COMMITTEE: TAXATION / 96th Congress

Service Dates of Committee Chair: Jan. 31,1979-Jan. 3,1981
Service Dates of House Members: Jan. 31,1979-Jan. 3,1981 (appointments reported Feb. 1,1979)
Service Dates of Senate Members: Feb. 8,1979-Continued

HOUSE

Majority			Terms in:		Minority			Terms in:	
Rank Name	**Party**	**State**	**House**	**Comm.**	**Rank Name**	**Party**	**State**	**House**	**Comm.**
CVc Ullman, Albert C.	Dem	Ore.	12	5	1st Conable, Barber B. Jr.	Rep	N.Y.	8	3
2nd Rostenkowski, Daniel D.	Dem	Ill.	11	3	2nd Duncan, John J.	Rep	Tenn.	8	2
3rd Vanik, Charles A.	Dem	Ohio	13	1					

SENATE

Majority			Years in:		Minority			Years in:	
Rank Name	**Party**	**State**	**Senate**	**Comm.**	**Rank Name**	**Party**	**State**	**Senate**	**Comm.**
VcC Long, Russell B.	Dem	La.	31	18	1st Dole, Robert J.	Rep	Kans.	11	1
2nd Talmadge, Herman E.	Dem	Ga.	23	8	2nd Packwood, Robert W.	Rep	Ore.	11	1
3rd Ribicoff, Abraham A.	Dem	Conn.	17	2					

	Majority		Minority
Departures from the House:			
Defeated for Reelection	Ullman, Albert C.	Ore. Dem	None
Retired	Vanik, Charles A.	Ohio Dem	None
Departures from the Senate:			
Defeated for Reelection	Talmadge, Herman E.	Ga. Dem	None
Retired	Ribicoff, Abraham A.	Conn. Dem	None

JOINT COMMITTEE: TAXATION / 97th Congress

Service Dates of Committee Chair: May 11,1981-Jan. 3,1983 (assignments reported May 18,1981)
Service Dates of House Members: May 11,1981-Jan. 3,1983 (assignments reported May 18,1981)
Service Dates of Senate Members: Jan. 5,1981-Continued

HOUSE

Majority			Terms in:		Minority			Terms in:	
Rank Name	**Party**	**State**	**House**	**Comm.**	**Rank Name**	**Party**	**State**	**House**	**Comm.**
CVc Rostenkowski, Daniel D.	Dem	Ill.	12	4	1st Conable, Barber B. Jr.	Rep	N.Y.	9	4
2nd Gibbons, Sam M.	Dem	Fla.	10	1	2nd Duncan, John J.	Rep	Tenn.	9	3
3rd Pickle, J. J. (Jake)	Dem	Tex.	10	1					

SENATE

Majority			Years in:		Minority			Years in:	
Rank Name	**Party**	**State**	**Senate**	**Comm.**	**Rank Name**	**Party**	**State**	**Senate**	**Comm.**
VcC Dole, Robert J.	Rep	Kans.	13	2	1st Long, Russell B.	Dem	La.	33	20
2nd Packwood, Robert W.	Rep	Ore.	13	2	2nd Byrd, Harry Flood Jr.	Ind	Va.	16	1
3rd Roth, William V. Jr.	Rep	Del.	11	1					

Notes: Senate membership on this committee was composed of the three ranking majority members and two ranking minority members of the Senate Finance Committee. Because official reassignment of Senators was not recorded in the Congressional Record, "Service Dates of Senate Members" reflects members' service on this Standing Committee. Harry Flood Byrd Jr. of Virginia was elected as an Independent but assigned to the committee by the Democratic Caucus with his seniority intact.

Departures from the Senate:	**Majority**	**Minority**		
Retired	None	Byrd, Harry Flood Jr.	Va.	Ind

JOINT COMMITTEE: TAXATION / 98th Congress

Service Dates of Committee Chair: Jan. 25,1983-Jan. 3,1985
Service Dates of House Members: Jan. 25,1983-Jan. 3,1985
Service Dates of Senate Members: Jan. 3,1983-Continued

HOUSE

Majority			Terms in:		Minority			Terms in:	
Rank Name	**Party**	**State**	**House**	**Comm.**	**Rank Name**	**Party**	**State**	**House**	**Comm.**
CVc Rostenkowski, Daniel D.	Dem	Ill.	13	5	1st Conable, Barber B. Jr.	Rep	N.Y.	10	5
2nd Gibbons, Sam M.	Dem	Fla.	11	2	2nd Duncan, John J.	Rep	Tenn.	10	4
3rd Pickle, J. J. (Jake)	Dem	Tex.	11	2					

SENATE

Majority			Years in:		Minority			Years in:	
Rank Name	**Party**	**State**	**Senate**	**Comm.**	**Rank Name**	**Party**	**State**	**Senate**	**Comm.**
VcC Packwood, Robert W.	Rep	Ore.	15	4	1st Long, Russell B.	Dem	La.	35	22
2nd Dole, Robert J.	Rep	Kans.	15	4	2nd Bentsen, Lloyd M. Jr.	Dem	Tex.	13	1
3rd Roth, William V. Jr.	Rep	Del.	13	2					

Note: Senate membership on this committee was composed of the three ranking majority members and two ranking minority members of the Senate Finance Committee. Because official reassignment of Senate members was not recorded in the Congressional Record, "Service Dates of Senate Members" reflects members' service on this Standing Committee.

Departures from the House:	**Majority**	**Minority**		
Retired	None	Conable, Barber B. Jr.	N.Y.	Rep

JOINT COMMITTEE: TAXATION / 99th Congress

Service Dates of Committee Chair: Feb. 19,1985-Jan. 3,1987
Service Dates of House Members: Feb. 19,1985-Jan. 3,1987
Service Dates of Senate Members: Jan. 3,1985-Continued

HOUSE

Majority			Terms in:		Minority			Terms in:	
Rank Name	**Party**	**State**	**House**	**Comm.**	**Rank Name**	**Party**	**State**	**House**	**Comm.**
CVc Rostenkowski, Daniel D.	Dem	Ill.	14	6	1st Duncan, John J.	Rep	Tenn.	11	5
2nd Gibbons, Sam M.	Dem	Fla.	12	3	2nd Archer, William R.	Rep	Tex.	8	1
3rd Pickle, J. J. (Jake)	Dem	Tex.	12	3					

SENATE

Majority			Years in:		Minority			Years in:	
Rank Name	**Party**	**State**	**Senate**	**Comm.**	**Rank Name**	**Party**	**State**	**Senate**	**Comm.**
VcC Roth, William V. Jr.	Rep	Del.	15	5	1st Long, Russell B.	Dem	La.	37	24
2nd Packwood, Robert W.	Rep	Ore.	17	6	2nd Bentsen, Lloyd M. Jr.	Dem	Tex.	15	3
3rd Dole, Robert J.	Rep	Kans.	17	6					

Departures from the Senate:

	Majority			Minority		
Retired	None			Long, Russell B.	La.	Dem

Departures from Committee:

Senate:

	Majority			Minority
No new assignment	Roth, William V. Jr.	Del.	Rep	None

JOINT COMMITTEE: TAXATION / 100th Congress

Service Dates of Committee Chair: Feb. 19,1987-Jan. 3,1989
Service Dates of House Members: Feb. 19,1987-Jan. 3,1989
Service Dates of Senate Members: Jan. 12,1987-Feb. 2,1989

HOUSE

Majority			Terms in:		Minority			Terms in:	
Rank Name	**Party**	**State**	**House**	**Comm.**	**Rank Name**	**Party**	**State**	**House**	**Comm.**
CVc Rostenkowski, Daniel D.	Dem	Ill.	15	7	1st Duncan, John J.	Rep	Tenn.	12	6
2nd Gibbons, Sam M.	Dem	Fla.	13	4	2nd Archer, William R.	Rep	Tex.	9	2
3rd Pickle, J. J. (Jake)	Dem	Tex.	13	4					

SENATE

Majority			Years in:		Minority			Years in:	
Rank Name	**Party**	**State**	**Senate**	**Comm.**	**Rank Name**	**Party**	**State**	**Senate**	**Comm.**
VcC Bentsen, Lloyd M. Jr.	Dem	Tex.	17	5	1st Packwood, Robert W.	Rep	Ore.	19	8
2nd Matsunaga, Spark M.	Dem	Hai.	11	1	2nd Dole, Robert J.	Rep	Kans.	19	8
3rd Moynihan, Daniel Patrick	Dem	N.Y.	11	1					

Note: "Service Dates of Senate Members" reflect the dates of service of Matsunaga and Moynihan; all other Senators continued service from the previous Congress without official reassignment recorded in the Congressional Record.

Changes:

House Minority:

Duncan, John J.	Rep	Tenn.	June 21,1988	Died in office.
Vander Jagt, Guy	Rep	Mich.	July 15,1988	Replaced Duncan (reported Aug. 10,1988).

JOINT COMMITTEE: TAXATION / 101st Congress

Service Dates of Committee Chair: Jan. 24,1989-Jan. 3,1991
Service Dates of House Members: Jan. 24,1989-Jan. 3,1991
Service Dates of Senate Members: Feb. 2,1989-Feb. 28,1991

HOUSE **Majority** / **Minority**

Rank Name	Party	State	Terms in: House	Terms in: Comm.	Rank Name	Party	State	Terms in: House	Terms in: Comm.
CVc Rostenkowski, Daniel D.	Dem	Ill.	16	8	1st Archer, William R.	Rep	Tex.	10	3
2nd Gibbons, Sam M.	Dem	Fla.	14	5	2nd Vander Jagt, Guy	Rep	Mich.	13	1
3rd Pickle, J. J. (Jake)	Dem	Tex.	14	5					

SENATE **Majority** / **Minority**

Rank Name	Party	State	Years in: Senate	Years in: Comm.	Rank Name	Party	State	Years in: Senate	Years in: Comm.
VcC Bentsen, Lloyd M. Jr.	Dem	Tex.	19	7	1st Packwood, Robert W.	Rep	Ore.	21	10
2nd Matsunaga, Spark M.	Dem	Hai.	13	3	2nd Dole, Robert J.	Rep	Kans.	21	10
3rd Moynihan, Daniel Patrick	Dem	N.Y.	13	3					

Changes:
Senate Majority:
Matsunaga, Spark M. Dem Hai. Apr. 15,1990 Died in office.

JOINT COMMITTEE: TAXATION / 102nd Congress

Service Dates of Committee Chair: Mar. 7,1991-Jan. 3,1993
Service Dates of House Members: Mar. 7,1991-Jan. 3,1993
Service Dates of Senate Members: Feb. 28,1991-Jan. 3,1993

HOUSE **Majority** / **Minority**

Rank Name	Party	State	Terms in: House	Terms in: Comm.	Rank Name	Party	State	Terms in: House	Terms in: Comm.
CVc Rostenkowski, Daniel D.	Dem	Ill.	17	9	1st Archer, William R.	Rep	Tex.	11	4
2nd Gibbons, Sam M.	Dem	Fla.	15	6	2nd Vander Jagt, Guy	Rep	Mich.	14	2
3rd Pickle, J. J. (Jake)	Dem	Tex.	15	6					

SENATE **Majority** / **Minority**

Rank Name	Party	State	Years in: Senate	Years in: Comm.	Rank Name	Party	State	Years in: Senate	Years in: Comm.
VcC Bentsen, Lloyd M. Jr.	Dem	Tex.	21	9	1st Packwood, Robert W.	Rep	Ore.	23	13
2nd Moynihan, Daniel Patrick	Dem	N.Y.	15	5	2nd Dole, Robert J.	Rep	Kans.	23	13
3rd Baucus, Max	Dem	Mont.	13	1					

JOINT COMMITTEE: REDUCTION OF FEDERAL EXPENDITURES

REDUCTION OF NON-ESSENTIAL FEDERAL EXPENDITURES

Jurisdiction, 1941

From Public Law 77-250, the Revenue Act of 1941, 77th Congress, First Session, September 20, 1941 (55 Statutes 687, 726):

[Section 601.(b)]

(b) It shall be the duty of the committee to make a full and complete study and investigation of all expenditures of the Federal Government with a view to recommending the elimination or reduction of all such expenditures deemed by the committee to be nonessential. The committee shall report to the President and to the Congress the results of its study, together with its recommendation, at the earliest practicable date.

REDUCTION OF FEDERAL EXPENDITURES

The Committee was informally renamed the Joint Committee on Reduction of Federal Expenditures during the 91st Congress.

Termination, 1974

The Joint Committee was terminated by authority of Public Law 93-344, on July 12, 1974.

JOINT COMMITTEE: REDUCTION OF NON-ESSENTIAL FEDERAL EXPENDITURES / 80th Congress

Service Dates of House Members: Jan. 20,1947-Jan. 3,1949
Service Dates of Senate Members: Jan. 3,1947-Continued

HOUSE

Majority Rank Name	Party	State	Terms in: Senate	Terms in: Comm.	Minority Rank Name	Party	State	Terms in: Senate	Terms in: Comm.
1st Knutson, Harold	Rep	Minn.	16	2	1st Doughton, Robert L.	Dem	N.C.	19	4
2nd Reed, Daniel A.	Rep	N.Y.	15	1	2nd Cannon, Clarence	Dem	Mo.	13	4
3rd Taber, John	Rep	N.Y.	13	4					
4th Wigglesworth, Richard B.	Rep	Mass.	11	*1 1					

SENATE

Majority Rank Name	Party	State	Years in: Senate	Years in: Comm.	Minority Rank Name	Party	State	Years in: Senate	Years in: Comm.
1st Butler, Hugh A.	Rep	Neb.	7	2	1st Byrd, Harry Flood	Dem	Va.	14	6
2nd Bridges, H. Styles	Rep	N.H.	11	*1 2	2nd George, Walter F.	Dem	Ga.	25	6
					3rd McKellar, Kenneth D.	Dem	Tenn.	30	6

*1: Member's 1st period of service on the committee.

Note: No committee Chair is listed in Congressional Directory for either session of the 80th Congress.

	Majority		Minority
Departures from the House:			
Defeated for Reelection	Knutson, Harold	Minn. Rep	None
Departures from Committee:			
House:			
No new assignment	Wigglesworth, Richard B.	Mass. Rep	None

JOINT COMMITTEE: REDUCTION OF NON-ESSENTIAL FEDERAL EXPENDITURES / 81st Congress

Service Dates of House Members: Feb. 2,1949-Jan. 3,1951
Service Dates of Senate Members: Jan. 3,1949-Continued

HOUSE

Majority			Terms in:		Minority			Terms in:	
Rank Name	**Party**	**State**	**House**	**Comm.**	**Rank Name**	**Party**	**State**	**House**	**Comm.**
1st Doughton, Robert L.	Dem	N.C.	20	5	1st Reed, Daniel A.	Rep	N.Y.	16	2
2nd Cooper, Jere	Dem	Tenn.	11 *2	1	2nd Taber, John	Rep	N.Y.	14	5
3rd Cannon, Clarence	Dem	Mo.	14	5					
4th Kerr, John H.	Dem	N.C.	14	1					

SENATE

Majority			Years in:		Minority			Years in:	
Rank Name	**Party**	**State**	**Senate**	**Comm.**	**Rank Name**	**Party**	**State**	**Senate**	**Comm.**
1st Byrd, Harry Flood	Dem	Va.	16	8	1st Butler, Hugh A.	Rep	Neb.	9	4
2nd George, Walter F.	Dem	Ga.	27	8	2nd Bridges, H. Styles	Rep	N.H.	13 *1	4
3rd McKellar, Kenneth D.	Dem	Tenn.	32	8					

*1: Member's 1st period of service on the committee; *2: Member's 2nd period of service on the committee.

Note: No committee Chair is listed in Congressional Directory for either session of the 81st Congress.

JOINT COMMITTEE: REDUCTION OF NON-ESSENTIAL FEDERAL EXPENDITURES / 82nd Congress

Service Dates of Committee Chair: Jan. 3,1951-Continued
Service Dates of House Members: Jan. 29,1951-Jan. 3,1953
Service Dates of Senate Members: Jan. 3,1951-Continued

HOUSE

Majority			Terms in:		Minority			Terms in:	
Rank Name	**Party**	**State**	**House**	**Comm.**	**Rank Name**	**Party**	**State**	**House**	**Comm.**
VCh Doughton, Robert L.	Dem	N.C.	21	6	1st Taber, John	Rep	N.Y.	15	6
3rd Cannon, Clarence	Dem	Mo.	15	6	2nd Reed, Daniel A.	Rep	N.Y.	17	3
4th Kerr, John H.	Dem	N.C.	15	2					
5th Cooper, Jere	Dem	Tenn.	12 *2	2					

SENATE

Majority			Years in:		Minority			Years in:	
Rank Name	**Party**	**State**	**Senate**	**Comm.**	**Rank Name**	**Party**	**State**	**Senate**	**Comm.**
Chr Byrd, Harry Flood	Dem	Va.	18	10	1st Bridges, H. Styles	Rep	N.H.	15 *1	6
2nd McKellar, Kenneth D.	Dem	Tenn.	34	10	2nd Butler, Hugh A.	Rep	Neb.	11	6
3rd George, Walter F.	Dem	Ga.	29	10					

*1: Member's 1st period of service on the committee; *2: Member's 2nd period of service on the committee.

Changes:

Senate Minority:

Bridges, H. Styles	Rep	N.H.	Jan. 18,1952	Left committee; no new assignment (reported Jan. 21,1952).
Ferguson, Homer	Rep	Mich.	Jan. 21,1952	Replaced Bridges.

	Majority			**Minority**
Departures from the House:				
Defeated for Renomination	Kerr, John H.	N.C.	Dem	None
Retired	Doughton, Robert L.	N.C.	Dem	None
Departures from the Senate:				
Defeated for Renomination	McKellar, Kenneth D.	Tenn.	Dem	None

JOINT COMMITTEE: REDUCTION OF NON-ESSENTIAL FEDERAL EXPENDITURES / 83rd Congress

Service Dates of Committee Chair: Jan. 3,1953-Continued
Service Dates of House Members: Jan. 26,1953-Jan. 3,1955
Service Dates of Senate Members: Jan. 3,1953-Mar. 30,1955

HOUSE

Majority Rank Name	Party	State	Terms in: House	Comm.	**Minority** Rank Name	Party	State	Terms in: House	Comm.
VCh Reed, Daniel A.	Rep	N.Y.	18	4	1st Cannon, Clarence	Dem	Mo.	16	7
2nd Taber, John	Rep	N.Y.	16	7	2nd Cooper, Jere	Dem	Tenn.	13 *2	3
3rd Wigglesworth, Richard B.	Rep	Mass.	14 *2	1					
4th Kean, Robert W.	Rep	N.J.	8	1					

SENATE

Majority Rank Name	Party	State	Years in: Senate	Comm.	**Minority** Rank Name	Party	State	Years in: Senate	Comm.
1st Butler, Hugh A.	Rep	Neb.	13	8	Chr Byrd, Harry Flood	Dem	Va.	20	12
2nd Ferguson, Homer	Rep	Mich.	11	1	2nd George, Walter F.	Dem	Ga.	31	12
3rd Bridges, H. Styles	Rep	N.H.	17 *2	1	3rd McCarran, Patrick A.	Dem	Nev.	21	1

*2: Member's 2nd period of service on the committee.

Vacancies Filled:
Majority: 3rd seat by Bridges on Feb. 9,1954.
Minority: 3rd seat by McCarran on Feb. 9,1954.

Changes:
Senate Majority:

Butler, Hugh A.	Rep	Neb.	July 1,1954	Died in office.

Senate Minority:

McCarran, Patrick A.	Dem	Nev.	Sep. 28,1954	Died in office.

Departures from the Senate:	**Majority**		**Minority**
Defeated for Reelection	Ferguson, Homer	Mich. Rep	None
Departures from Committee:			
House:			
No new assignment	Kean, Robert W.	N.J. Rep	None
	Wigglesworth, Richard B.	Mass. Rep	
Senate:			
No new assignment	Bridges, H. Styles	N.H. Rep	None

JOINT COMMITTEE: REDUCTION OF NON-ESSENTIAL FEDERAL EXPENDITURES / 84th Congress

Service Dates of Committee Chair: Jan. 3,1955-Continued
Service Dates of House Members: Feb. 3,1955-Jan. 3,1957
Service Dates of Senate Members: Mar. 30,1955-Continued

HOUSE

Majority Rank Name	Party	State	Terms in: House	Comm.	**Minority** Rank Name	Party	State	Terms in: House	Comm.
VCh Cannon, Clarence	Dem	Mo.	17	8	1st Reed, Daniel A.	Rep	N.Y.	19	5
2nd Cooper, Jere	Dem	Tenn.	14 *2	4	2nd Taber, John	Rep	N.Y.	17	8
3rd Dingell, John D.	Dem	Mich.	12	1					
4th Mahon, George H.	Dem	Tex.	11	1					

SENATE

Majority Rank Name	Party	State	Years in: Senate	Comm.	**Minority** Rank Name	Party	State	Years in: Senate	Comm.
Chr Byrd, Harry Flood	Dem	Va.	22	15	1st Martin, Edward	Rep	Penn.	9	1
2nd George, Walter F.	Dem	Ga.	33	15	2nd Dirksen, Everett M.	Rep	Ill.	5	1
3rd Ellender, Allen J.	Dem	La.	19	1					
4th Holland, Spessard L.	Dem	Fla.	9	1					

*2: Member's 2nd period of service on the committee.

Changes:
House Majority:

Dingell, John D.	Dem	Mich.	Sep. 19,1955	Died in office.
Mills, Wilbur D.	Dem	Ark.	Jan. 12,1956	Replaced Dingell.

Departures from the Senate:	Majority			Minority
Retired	George, Walter F.	Ga.	Dem	None

JOINT COMMITTEE: REDUCTION OF NON-ESSENTIAL FEDERAL EXPENDITURES / 85th Congress

Service Dates of Committee Chair: Jan. 3,1957-Continued
Service Dates of House Members: Jan. 22,1957-Jan. 3,1959
Service Dates of Senate Members: Feb. 26,1957-Continued

HOUSE Majority

Rank	Name	Party	State	Terms in: House	Comm.
VCh	Cannon, Clarence	Dem	Mo.	18	9
2nd	Cooper, Jere	Dem	Tenn.	15	*2 5
3rd	Mahon, George H.	Dem	Tex.	12	2
4th	Mills, Wilbur D.	Dem	Ark.	10	2

HOUSE Minority

Rank	Name	Party	State	Terms in: House	Comm.
1st	Reed, Daniel A.	Rep	N.Y.	20	6
2nd	Taber, John	Rep	N.Y.	18	9

SENATE Majority

Rank	Name	Party	State	Years in: Senate	Comm.
Chr	Byrd, Harry Flood	Dem	Va.	24	16
2nd	Ellender, Allen J.	Dem	La.	21	2
3rd	Holland, Spessard L.	Dem	Fla.	11	2
4th	Kerr, Robert S.	Dem	Okla.	9	1

SENATE Minority

Rank	Name	Party	State	Years in: Senate	Comm.
1st	Martin, Edward	Rep	Penn.	11	2
2nd	Dirksen, Everett M.	Rep	Ill.	7	2

*2: Member's 2nd period of service on the committee.

Note: "Service Dates of Senate Members" reflect the dates of service of Kerr; all other Senators continued service from the previous Congress without official reassignment recorded in the Congressional Record.

Changes:
House Majority:

Cooper, Jere	Dem	Tenn.	Dec. 18,1957	Died in office.
Gregory, Noble J.	Dem	Ky.	Jan. 27,1958	Replaced Cooper.

Departures from the House:	Majority			Minority		
Defeated for Renomination	Gregory, Noble J.	Ky.	Dem	None		
Departures from the Senate:						
Retired	None			Martin, Edward	Penn.	Rep

JOINT COMMITTEE: REDUCTION OF NON-ESSENTIAL FEDERAL EXPENDITURES / 86th Congress

Service Dates of Committee Chair: Jan. 3,1959-Continued
Service Dates of House Members: Jan. 19,1959-Jan. 3,1961
Service Dates of Senate Members: Feb. 5,1959-Continued

HOUSE Majority

Rank	Name	Party	State	Terms in: House	Comm.
VCh	Cannon, Clarence	Dem	Mo.	19	10
2nd	Mahon, George H.	Dem	Tex.	13	3
3rd	Mills, Wilbur D.	Dem	Ark.	11	3
4th	Forand, Aime J.	Dem	R.I.	11	1

HOUSE Minority

Rank	Name	Party	State	Terms in: House	Comm.
1st	Reed, Daniel A.	Rep	N.Y.	21	7
2nd	Taber, John	Rep	N.Y.	19	10

SENATE **Majority**

Rank	Name	Party	State	Years in: Senate	Comm.
Chr	Byrd, Harry Flood	Dem	Va.	26	18
2nd	Ellender, Allen J.	Dem	La.	23	4
3rd	Holland, Spessard L.	Dem	Fla.	13	4
4th	Kerr, Robert S.	Dem	Okla.	11	2

Minority

Rank	Name	Party	State	Years in: Senate	Comm.
1st	Dirksen, Everett M.	Rep	Ill.	9	4
2nd	Williams, John J.	Rep	Del.	13	1

Note: "Service Dates of Senate Members" reflect the dates of service of Williams; all other Senators continued service from the previous Congress without official reassignment recorded in the Congressional Record.

Changes:

House Minority:

Reed, Daniel A.	Rep	N.Y.	Feb. 19,1959	Died in office.
Simpson, Richard M.	Rep	Penn.	Feb. 25,1959	Replaced Reed.
Simpson, Richard M.	Rep	Penn.	Jan. 7,1960	Died in office.
Mason, Noah M.	Rep	Ill.	Feb. 9,1960	Replaced Simpson.

Departures from the House:

	Majority			Minority
Retired	Forand, Aime J.	R.I.	Dem	None

JOINT COMMITTEE: REDUCTION OF NON-ESSENTIAL FEDERAL EXPENDITURES / 87th Congress

Service Dates of Committee Chair: Jan. 3,1961- Continued
Service Dates of House Members: Mar. 7,1961-Jan. 3,1963
Service Dates of Senate Members: Jan. 3,1961-Continued

HOUSE **Majority**

Rank	Name	Party	State	Terms in: House	Comm.
VCh	Cannon, Clarence	Dem	Mo.	20	11
2nd	Mahon, George H.	Dem	Tex.	14	4
3rd	Mills, Wilbur D.	Dem	Ark.	12	4
4th	King, Cecil R.	Dem	Cal.	11	1

Minority

Rank	Name	Party	State	Terms in: House	Comm.
1st	Taber, John	Rep	N.Y.	19	11
2nd	Mason, Noah M.	Rep	Ill.	13	1

SENATE **Majority**

Rank	Name	Party	State	Years in: Senate	Comm.
Chr	Byrd, Harry Flood	Dem	Va.	28	20
2nd	Ellender, Allen J.	Dem	La.	25	6
3rd	Holland, Spessard L.	Dem	Fla.	15	6
4th	Kerr, Robert S.	Dem	Okla.	13	4

Minority

Rank	Name	Party	State	Years in: Senate	Comm.
1st	Williams, John J.	Rep	Del.	15	2
2nd	Dirksen, Everett M.	Rep	Ill.	11	6

Changes:

Senate Majority:

Kerr, Robert S.	Dem	Okla.	Jan. 1,1963	Died in office.

Departures from the House:

	Majority	Minority		
Retired	None	Mason, Noah M.	Ill.	Rep
		Taber, John	N.Y.	Rep

Departures from Committee:

Senate:

	Majority	Minority		
Moved to Finance	None	Dirksen, Everett McK.	Ill.	Rep

JOINT COMMITTEE: REDUCTION OF NON-ESSENTIAL FEDERAL EXPENDITURES / 88th Congress

Service Dates of Committee Chair: Jan. 3,1963-Continued
Service Dates of House Members: Jan. 31,1963-Jan. 3,1965
Service Dates of Senate Members: Mar. 8,1963-Continued

HOUSE

Majority			Terms in:		Minority			Terms in:	
Rank Name	**Party**	**State**	**House**	**Comm.**	**Rank Name**	**Party**	**State**	**House**	**Comm.**
VCh Cannon, Clarence	Dem	Mo.	21	12	1st Jensen, Ben F.	Rep	Iowa	13	1
2nd Mahon, George H.	Dem	Tex.	15	5	2nd Byrnes, John W.	Rep	Wisc.	10	1
3rd Mills, Wilbur D.	Dem	Ark.	13	5					
4th King, Cecil R.	Dem	Cal.	12	2					

SENATE

Majority			Years in:		Minority			Years in:	
Rank Name	**Party**	**State**	**Senate**	**Comm.**	**Rank Name**	**Party**	**State**	**Senate**	**Comm.**
Chr Byrd, Harry Flood	Dem	Va.	30	22	1st Williams, John J.	Rep	Del.	17	4
2nd Ellender, Allen J.	Dem	La.	27	8	2nd Saltonstall, Leverett	Rep	Mass.	19	1
3rd Holland, Spessard L.	Dem	Fla.	17	8					
4th Long, Russell B.	Dem	La.	15	1					

Note: "Service Dates of Senate Members" reflect the dates of service of Long and Saltonstall; all other Senators continued service from the previous Congress without official reassignment recorded in the Congressional Record.

Changes:

House Majority:

Cannon, Clarence	Dem	Mo.	May 12,1964	Died in office.

Departures from the House:

	Majority	Minority		
Defeated for Reelection	None	Jensen, Ben F.	Iowa	Rep

JOINT COMMITTEE: REDUCTION OF NON-ESSENTIAL FEDERAL EXPENDITURES / 89th Congress

Service Dates of Committee Chair: Ch1 Jan. 3,1965-Nov. 10,1965
Ch2 Nov. 10,1965-Jan. 3,1967
Service Dates of House Members: Feb. 1,1965-Jan. 3,1967
Service Dates of Senate Members: Jan. 3,1965-Continued

HOUSE

Majority			Terms in:		Minority			Terms in:	
Rank Name	**Party**	**State**	**House**	**Comm.**	**Rank Name**	**Party**	**State**	**House**	**Comm.**
Ch2 Mahon, George H.	Dem	Tex.	16	6	1st Byrnes, John W.	Rep	Wisc.	11	2
2nd Thomas, Albert	Dem	Tex.	15	1	2nd Bow, Frank T.	Rep	Ohio	8	1
3rd Mills, Wilbur D.	Dem	Ark.	14	6					
4th King, Cecil R.	Dem	Cal.	13	3					

SENATE

Majority			Years in		Minority			Years in:	
Rank Name	**Party**	**State**	**Senate**	**Comm.**	**Rank Name**	**Party**	**State**	**Senate**	**Comm.**
Ch1 Byrd, Harry Flood	Dem	Va.	32	24	1st Williams, John J.	Rep	Del.	19	6
2nd Ellender, Allen J.	Dem	La.	29	10	2nd Saltonstall, Leverett	Rep	Mass.	20	2
3rd Holland, Spessard L.	Dem	Fla.	19	10					
4th Long, Russell B.	Dem	La.	17	2					

Changes:

Chair:

Ch1 Byrd, Harry Flood	Dem	Va.	Nov. 10,1965	Resigned and retired.
Ch2 Mahon, George H.	Dem	Tex.	Nov. 10,1965	Succeeded Byrd as Chair.

House Majority:

Thomas, Albert	Dem	Tex.	Feb. 15,1966	Died in office.
Kirwan, Michael J.	Dem	Ohio	June 23,1966	Replaced Thomas.

Senate Majority:

Byrd, Harry Flood	Dem	Va.	Nov. 10,1965	Resigned and retired.
Anderson, Clinton P.	Dem	N.M.	Mar. 1,1966	Replaced Byrd.

Departures from the Senate:	Majority	Minority	
Retired	None	Saltonstall, Leverett	Mass. Rep

JOINT COMMITTEE: REDUCTION OF NON-ESSENTIAL FEDERAL EXPENDITURES / 90th Congress

Service Dates of Committee Chair: Jan. 31,1967-Jan. 3,1969
Service Dates of House Members: Jan. 31,1967-Jan. 3,1969
Service Dates of Senate Members: Jan. 25,1967-Continued

HOUSE

Majority

Rank	Name	Party	State	Terms in: House	Terms in: Comm.
Chr	Mahon, George H.	Dem	Tex.	17	7
2nd	Kirwan, Michael J.	Dem	Ohio	16	2
3rd	Mills, Wilbur D.	Dem	Ark.	15	7
4th	King, Cecil R.	Dem	Cal.	14	4

Minority

Rank	Name	Party	State	Terms in: House	Terms in: Comm.
1st	Byrnes, John W.	Rep	Wisc.	12	3
2nd	Bow, Frank T.	Rep	Ohio	9	2

SENATE

Majority

Rank	Name	Party	State	Years in: Senate	Years in: Comm.
1st	Ellender, Allen J.	Dem	La.	31	12
2nd	Holland, Spessard L.	Dem	Fla.	21	12
3rd	Long, Russell B.	Dem	La.	19	4
4th	Anderson, Clinton P.	Dem	N.M.	19	1

Minority

Rank	Name	Party	State	Years in: Senate	Years in: Comm.
1st	Williams, John J.	Rep	Del.	21	8
2nd	Allott, Gordon L.	Rep	Colo.	13	1

Note: "Service Dates of Senate Members" reflect the dates of service of Allott; all other Senators continued service from the previous Congress without official reassignment recorded in the Congressional Record.

Departures from the House:	Majority		Minority	
Retired	King, Cecil R.	Cal. Dem	None	
Departures from Committee:				
Senate:				
No new assignment	None		Allott, Gordon L.	Colo. Rep

JOINT COMMITTEE: REDUCTION OF NON-ESSENTIAL FEDERAL EXPENDITURES / 91st Congress

* The Committee was informally renamed the Joint Committee on Reduction of Federal Expenditures during this Congress.

Service Dates of Committee Chair: Feb. 3,1969-Jan. 3,1971
Service Dates of House Members: Feb. 3,1969-Jan. 3,1971
Service Dates of Senate Members: Mar. 27,1969-Continued

HOUSE

Majority

Rank	Name	Party	State	Terms in: House	Terms in: Comm.
Chr	Mahon, George H.	Dem	Tex.	18	8
2nd	Kirwan, Michael J.	Dem	Ohio	17	3
3rd	Mills, Wilbur D.	Dem	Ark.	16	8
4th	Boggs, T. Hale	Dem	La.	13	1

Minority

Rank	Name	Party	State	Terms in: House	Terms in: Comm.
1st	Byrnes, John W.	Rep	Wisc.	13	4
2nd	Bow, Frank T.	Rep	Ohio	10	3

SENATE

Majority

Rank	Name	Party	State	Years in: Senate	Years in: Comm.
1st	Ellender, Allen J.	Dem	La.	33	14
2nd	Holland, Spessard L.	Dem	Fla.	23	14
3rd	Long, Russell B.	Dem	La.	21	6
4th	Anderson, Clinton P.	Dem	N.M.	21	3

Minority

Rank	Name	Party	State	Years in: Senate	Years in: Comm.
1st	Williams, John J.	Rep	Del.	23	10
2nd	Hruska, Roman L.	Rep	Neb.	15	1

Note: "Service Dates of Senate Members" reflect the dates of service of Hruska; all other Senators continued service from the previous Congress without official reassignment recorded in the Congressional Record.

Changes:

House Majority:

Kirwan, Michael J.	Dem	Ohio	July 27,1970	Died in office.
Whitten, Jamie L.	Dem	Miss.	Sep. 9,1970	Replaced Kirwan.

Senate Minority:

Williams, John J.	Rep	Del.	Dec. 31,1970	Resigned and retired.

Departures from the Senate:	**Majority**			**Minority**
Retired	Holland, Spessard L.	Fla.	Dem	None
Departures from Committee:				
House:				
Became Majority Leader	Boggs, T. Hale	La.	Dem	None

JOINT COMMITTEE: REDUCTION OF FEDERAL EXPENDITURES / 92nd Congress

Service Dates of Committee Chair: Feb. 10,1971-Jan. 3,1973
Service Dates of House Members: Feb. 10,1971-Jan. 3,1973
Service Dates of Senate Members: Feb. 11,1971-Continued

HOUSE

Majority Rank Name	Party	State	Terms in: House	Comm.	Minority Rank Name	Party	State	Terms in: House	Comm.
Chr Mahon, George H.	Dem	Tex.	19	9	1st Byrnes, John W.	Rep	Wisc.	14	5
2rd Mills, Wilbur D.	Dem	Ark.	17	9	2nd Bow, Frank T.	Rep	Ohio	11	4
3rd Whitten, Jamie L.	Dem	Miss.	16	2					
4th Watts, John C.	Dem	Ky.	11	1					

SENATE

Majority Rank Name	Party	State	Years in: Senate	Comm.	Minority Rank Name	Party	State	Years in: Senate	Comm.
1st Ellender, Allen J.	Dem	La.	35	16	1st Hruska, Roman L.	Rep	Neb.	17	2
2nd Long, Russell B.	Dem	La.	23	8	2nd Bennett, Wallace F.	Rep	Utah	21	1
3rd Anderson, Clinton P.	Dem	N.M.	23	5					
4th McClellan, John L.	Dem	Ark.	29	1					

Note: "Service Dates of Senate Members" reflect the dates of service of McClellan; all other Senators continued service from the previous Congress without official reassignment recorded in the Congressional Record.

Vacancy Filled:
Senate Minority: 2nd by Bennett on Mar. 30,1971.

Changes:

House Majority:

Watts, John C.	Dem	Ky.	Sep. 24,1971	Died in office.
Ullman, Albert C.	Dem	Ore.	Sep. 30,1971	Replaced Watts.

House Minority:

Bow, Frank T.	Rep	Ohio	Nov. 13,1972	Died in office.

Senate Majority:

Ellender, Allen J.	Dem	La.	July 27,1972	Died in office.
Stennis, John C.	Dem	Miss.	Aug. 11,1972	Replaced Ellender.

JOINT COMMITTEE: REDUCTION OF FEDERAL EXPENDITURES / 93rd Congress

Service Dates of Committee Chair: Feb. 7,1973-Jan. 3,1975
Service Dates of House Members: Feb. 7,1973-Jan. 3,1975
Service Dates of Senate Members: Jan. 4,1973-Feb. 5,1975

HOUSE **Majority**

Rank	Name	Party	State	Terms in: House	Terms in: Comm.
Chr	Mahon, George H.	Dem	Tex.	20	10
2rd	Mills, Wilbur D.	Dem	Ark.	18	10
3rd	Whitten, Jamie L.	Dem	Miss.	17	3
4th	Ullman, Albert C.	Dem	Ore.	9	2

Minority

Rank	Name	Party	State	Terms in: House	Terms in: Comm.
1st	Cederberg, Elford A.	Rep	Mich.	11	1
2nd	Collier, Harold R.	Rep	Ill.	9	1

SENATE **Majority**

Rank	Name	Party	State	Years in: Senate	Years in: Comm.
1st	Long, Russell B.	Dem	La.	25	10
2nd	McClellan, John L.	Dem	Ark.	31	2
3rd	Stennis, John C.	Dem	Miss.	26	1
4th	Hartke, R. Vance	Dem	Ind.	15	1

Minority

Rank	Name	Party	State	Years in: Senate	Years in: Comm.
1st	Hruska, Roman L.	Rep	Neb.	19	4
2nd	Bennett, Wallace F.	Rep	Utah	23	2

Note: "Service Dates of Senate Members" reflect the dates of service of Hartke; all other Senators continued service from the previous Congress without official reassignment recorded in the Congressional Record.

JOINT COMMITTEE: REDUCTION OF FEDERAL EXPENDITURES / 94th Congress

Service Dates of Senate Members: Feb. 5,1975-Feb. 24,1975

SENATE **Majority**

Rank	Name	Party	State	Years in: Senate	Years in: Comm.
1st	Long, Russell B.	Dem	La.	27	12
2nd	McClellan, John L.	Dem	Ark.	33	4
3rd	Stennis, John C.	Dem	Miss.	26	3
4th	Hartke, R. Vance	Dem	Ind.	17	2

Minority

Rank	Name	Party	State	Years in: Senate	Years in: Comm.
1st	Hruska, Roman L.	Rep	Neb.	21	6
2nd	Curtis, Carl T.	Rep	Neb.	21	1

Note: "Service Dates of Senate Members" reflect the dates of service of Curtis; all other Senators continued service from the previous Congress without official reassignment recorded in the Congressional Record.

JOINT COMMITTEE: DISPOSITION OF EXECUTIVE PAPERS

Jurisdiction, 1947

From Public Law 78-115, 78th Congress, First Session, July 7, 1943 (57 Statutes 380, 381):

[Section 2]

The National Archives Council shall promulgate regulations, not inconsistent with this Act, establishing
(1) procedures for the compiling and submitting to the Archivist of the United States of lists and schedules of records proposed for disposal,
(2) procedures for the disposal of records authorized for disposal, and
(3) standards for the reproduction of records by photographic or microphotographic processes with a view to the disposal of the original records. Such regulations, when approved by the President, shall be binding on all agencies of the United States Government.

[Section 5]

Whenever the Archivist shall submit lists or schedules to Congress, it shall be the duty of the presiding officer of the Senate to appoint two Senators who, with the members of the Committee on the Disposition of Executive Papers of the House of Representatives, shall constitute a joint committee to which all such lists or schedules shall be referred, and the joint committee shall examine such lists or schedules and submit to the Senate and House of Representatives, respectively, a report of such examination and its recommendations.

[Section 6]

If the joint committee reports that any of the records listed in a list or schedule referred to it do not, or will not after the lapse of the period specified, have sufficient administrative, legal, research, or other value to warrant their continued preservation by the Government, the Archivist shall notify the head of the agency by which the list or schedule was submitted of the action of the joint committee and the head of such agency shall cause such records to be disposed of in accordance with regulations promulgated as provided in section 2 of this Act.

Jurisdiction, 1969

From the Senate Manual for the 91st Congress (1969):

[Section 681]

S3305. Examination of lists and schedules by joint congressional committee and report to Congress.

When the Administrator of General Services submits lists or schedules to Congress, the presiding officer of the Senate shall appoint two Senators who, with the members of the subcommittee on the Disposition of Executive Papers of the House of Representatives Committee on House Administration, shall constitute a joint committee to which lists or schedules shall be referred, and the joint committee shall examine them and submit to the Senate and House of Representatives, respectively, a report of its examination and its recommendations.

[Section 682]

S3306. Disposal of records by head of Government agency upon notification by Administrator of General Services of action by joint congressional committee.

If the joint congressional committee reports that any of the records listed in a list or schedule referred to it do not, or will not after the lapse of the period specified, have sufficient administrative, legal, research, or other value to warrant their continued preservation by the Government, the Administrator of General Services shall notify the agency having the records in its custody of the action of the joint committee, and the agency shall cause the records to be disposed of in accordance with regulations promulgated under section 3302 of this title . . .

Termination, 1970

The Joint Committee was terminated by authority of Public Law 91-287 (84 Statutes 321), agreed to June 23, 1970.

JOINT COMMITTEE: DISPOSITION OF EXECUTIVE PAPERS / 80th Congress

Service Dates of House Members: Feb. 17,1947-Jan. 3,1949
Service Dates of Senate Members: Jan. 27,1947-Jan. 17,1949

HOUSE

Majority Rank	Name	Party	State	Terms in: House	Comm.	Minority Rank	Name	Party	State	Terms in: House	Comm.
1st	Bishop, Cecil W. (Runt)	Rep	Ill.	4	1	1st	Norton, Mary T.	Dem	N.J.	12	1

SENATE

Majority Rank	Name	Party	State	Years in: Senate	Comm.	Minority Rank	Name	Party	State	Years in: Senate	Comm.
1st	Langer, William	Rep	N.D.	7	1	1st	Chavez, Dennis	Dem	N.M.	12	1

Changes:
Senate Minority:

Chavez, Dennis	Dem	N.M.	June 2,1948	Left committee; no new assignment.
McKellar, Kenneth D.	Dem	Tenn.	June 2,1948	Replaced Chavez.

Departures from Committee:

	Majority	Minority		
House:				
Moved to Joint Printing	None	Norton, Mary T.	N.J.	Dem
Senate:				
Moved to Joint Legislative Budget	None	McKellar, Kenneth D.	Tenn.	Dem

JOINT COMMITTEE: DISPOSITION OF EXECUTIVE PAPERS / 81st Congress

Service Dates of House Members: Jan. 27,1949-Jan. 3,1951
Service Dates of Senate Members: Jan. 17,1949-Jan. 8,1951

HOUSE

Majority Rank	Name	Party	State	Terms in: House	Comm.	Minority Rank	Name	Party	State	Terms in: House	Comm.
1st	Garmatz, Edward A.	Dem	Md.	2	1	1st	Bishop, Cecil W. (Runt)	Rep	Ill.	5	2

SENATE

Majority Rank	Name	Party	State	Years in: Senate	Comm.	Minority Rank	Name	Party	State	Years in: Senate	Comm.
1st	Johnston, Olin D.	Dem	S.C.	5	1	1st	Langer, William	Rep	N.D.	9	2

JOINT COMMITTEE: DISPOSITION OF EXECUTIVE PAPERS / 82nd Congress

Service Dates of House Members: Feb. 12,1951-Jan. 3,1953
Service Dates of Senate Members: Jan. 8,1951-Jan. 29,1953

HOUSE

Majority Rank	Name	Party	State	Terms in: House	Comm.	Minority Rank	Name	Party	State	Terms in: House	Comm.
1st	Garmatz, Edward A.	Dem	Md.	3	2	1st	Bishop, Cecil W. (Runt)	Rep	Ill.	6	3

SENATE

Majority Rank	Name	Party	State	Years in: Senate	Comm.	Minority Rank	Name	Party	State	Years in: Senate	Comm.
1st	Johnston, Olin D.	Dem	S.C.	7	2	1st	Langer, William	Rep	N.D.	11	4

Departures from Committee:	Majority		Minority	
Senate:				
Moved to Foreign Relations; Joint Immigration & Naturalization	None		Langer, William	N.D. Rep

JOINT COMMITTEE: DISPOSITION OF EXECUTIVE PAPERS / 83rd Congress

Service Dates of House Members: Jan. 26,1953-Jan. 3,1955
Service Dates of Senate Members: Jan. 29,1953-Feb. 1,1955

HOUSE

Majority Rank	Name	Party	State	Terms in: House	Terms in: Comm.	Minority Rank	Name	Party	State	Terms in: House	Terms in: Comm.
1st	Bishop, Cecil W. (Runt)	Rep	Ill.	7	4	1st	Garmatz, Edward A.	Dem	Md.	4	3

SENATE

Majority Rank	Name	Party	State	Years in: Senate	Years in: Comm.	Minority Rank	Name	Party	State	Years in: Senate	Years in: Comm.
1st	Carlson, Frank	Rep	Kans.	3	1	1st	Johnston, Olin D.	Dem	S.C.	9	5

Departures from the House:	Majority		Minority	
Defeated for Reelection	Bishop, Cecil W. (Runt)	Ill. Rep	None	
Departures from Committee:				
House:				
Moved to Government Operations	None		Garmatz, Edward A.	Md. Dem

JOINT COMMITTEE: DISPOSITION OF EXECUTIVE PAPERS / 84th Congress

Service Dates of House Members: Feb. 3,1955-Jan. 3,1957
Service Dates of Senate Members: Feb. 1,1955-Jan. 25,1957

HOUSE

Majority Rank	Name	Party	State	Terms in: House	Terms in: Comm.	Minority Rank	Name	Party	State	Terms in: House	Terms in: Comm.
1st	Long, George S.	Dem	La.	2	1	1st	Corbett, Robert J.	Rep	Penn.	7	1

SENATE

Majority Rank	Name	Party	State	Years in: Senate	Years in: Comm.	Minority Rank	Name	Party	State	Years in: Senate	Years in: Comm.
1st	Johnston, Olin D.	Dem	S.C.	11	7	1st	Carlson, Frank	Rep	Kans.	5	3

Departures from Committee:	Majority		Minority	
House:				
No new assignment	Long, George S.	La. Dem	None	

JOINT COMMITTEE: DISPOSITION OF EXECUTIVE PAPERS / 85th Congress

Service Dates of House Members: Jan. 28,1957-Jan. 3,1959
Service Dates of Senate Members: Jan. 25,1957-Feb. 2,1959

HOUSE

Majority Rank	Name	Party	State	Terms in: House	Terms in: Comm.	Minority Rank	Name	Party	State	Terms in: House	Terms in: Comm.
1st	Green, Edith S.	Dem	Ore.	2	1	1st	Corbett, Robert J.	Rep	Penn.	8	2

SENATE

Majority Rank	Name	Party	State	Years in: Senate	Years in: Comm.	Minority Rank	Name	Party	State	Years in: Senate	Years in: Comm.
1st	Johnston, Olin D.	Dem	S.C.	13	9	1st	Carlson, Frank	Rep	Kans.	7	4

Departures from Committee:	Majority		Minority	
House:				
No new assignment	Green, Edith S.	Ore. Dem	Corbett, Robert J.	Penn. Rep

JOINT COMMITTEE: DISPOSITION OF EXECUTIVE PAPERS / 86th Congress

Service Dates of House Members: Feb. 11,1959-Jan. 3,1961
Service Dates of Senate Members: Feb. 2,1959-Feb. 20,1961

HOUSE

Majority Rank	Name	Party	State	Terms in: House	Terms in: Comm.	Minority Rank	Name	Party	State	Terms in: House	Terms in: Comm.
1st	Thompson, Frank Jr.	Dem	N.J.	3	1	1st	Curtin, Willard S.	Rep	Penn.	2	1

SENATE

Majority Rank	Name	Party	State	Years in: Senate	Years in: Comm.	Minority Rank	Name	Party	State	Years in: Senate	Years in: Comm.
1st	Johnston, Olin D.	Dem	S.C.	15	11	1st	Carlson, Frank	Rep	Kans.	9	7

Changes:

House Minority:

Name	Party	State	Date	Change
Curtin, Willard S.	Rep	Penn.	Feb. 2,1960	Left committee; no new assignment.
Kyl, John H.	Rep	Iowa	Feb. 2,1960	Replaced Curtin.

JOINT COMMITTEE: DISPOSITION OF EXECUTIVE PAPERS / 87th Congress

Service Dates of House Members: Feb. 28,1961-Jan. 3,1963
Service Dates of Senate Members: Feb. 20,1961-Jan. 17,1963

HOUSE

Majority Rank	Name	Party	State	Terms in: House	Terms in: Comm.	Minority Rank	Name	Party	State	Terms in: House	Terms in: Comm.
1st	Thompson, Frank Jr.	Dem	N.J.	4	2	1st	Kyl, John H.	Rep	Iowa	2	2

SENATE

Majority Rank	Name	Party	State	Years in: Senate	Years in: Comm.	Minority Rank	Name	Party	State	Years in: Senate	Years in: Comm.
1st	Johnston, Olin D.	Dem	S.C.	17	13	1st	Carlson, Frank	Rep	Kans.	11	9

JOINT COMMITTEE: DISPOSITION OF EXECUTIVE PAPERS / 88th Congress

Service Dates of House Members: Jan. 29,1963-Jan. 3,1965
Service Dates of Senate Members: Jan. 17,1963-Feb. 29,1965

HOUSE

Majority Rank	Name	Party	State	Terms in: House	Terms in: Comm.	Minority Rank	Name	Party	State	Terms in: House	Terms in: Comm.
1st	Thompson, Frank Jr.	Dem	N.J.	5	3	1st	Kyl, John H.	Rep	Iowa	3	3

SENATE

Majority Rank	Name	Party	State	Years in: Senate	Years in: Comm.	Minority Rank	Name	Party	State	Years in: Senate	Years in: Comm.
1st	Johnston, Olin D.	Dem	S.C.	19	15	1st	Carlson, Frank	Rep	Kans.	13	10

Departure from the House:

	Majority	Minority	
Defeated for Reelection	None	Kyl, John H.	Iowa Rep

JOINT COMMITTEE: DISPOSITION OF EXECUTIVE PAPERS / 89th Congress

Service Dates of House Members: Feb. 8,1965-Jan. 3,1967
Service Dates of Senate Members: Feb. 29,1965-Feb. 28,1967

HOUSE

Majority			Terms in:		Minority			Terms in:	
Rank Name	**Party**	**State**	**House**	**Comm.**	**Rank Name**	**Party**	**State**	**House**	**Comm.**
1st Thompson, Frank Jr.	Dem	N.J.	6	4	1st Chamberlain, Charles E.	Rep	Mich.	5	1

SENATE

Majority			Years in:		Minority			Years in:	
Rank Name	**Party**	**State**	**Senate**	**Comm.**	**Rank Name**	**Party**	**State**	**Senate**	**Comm.**
1st Johnston, Olin D.	Dem	S.C.	21	17	1st Carlson, Frank	Rep	Kans.	15	13

Changes:
Senate Majority:

Johnston, Olin D.	Dem	S.C.	Apr. 18,1965	Died in office.
Monroney, A. S. Mike	Dem	Okla.	May 3,1965	Replaced Johnston.

Departures from Committee:
House:

	Majority		Minority	
No new assignment	None		Chamberlain, Charles E.	Mich. Rep

JOINT COMMITTEE: DISPOSITION OF EXECUTIVE PAPERS / 90th Congress

Service Dates of House Members: Feb. 1,1967-Jan. 3,1969
Service Dates of Senate Members: Feb. 28,1967-Mar. 17,1969

HOUSE

Majority			Terms in:		Minority			Terms in:	
Rank Name	**Party**	**State**	**House**	**Comm.**	**Rank Name**	**Party**	**State**	**House**	**Comm.**
1st Thompson, Frank Jr.	Dem	N.J.	7	5	1st Cleveland, James C.	Rep	N.H.	3	1

SENATE

Majority			Years in:		Minority			Years in:	
Rank Name	**Party**	**State**	**Senate**	**Comm.**	**Rank Name**	**Party**	**State**	**Senate**	**Comm.**
1st Monroney, A. S. Mike	Dem	Okla.	17	2	1st Carlson, Frank	Rep	Kans.	17	15

Departures from the Senate:	**Majority**		**Minority**	
Defeated for Reelection	Monroney, A. S. Mike	Okla. Dem	None	
Retired	None		Carlson, Frank	Kans. Rep
Departures from Committee:				
House:				
No new assignment	Thompson, Frank Jr.	N.J. Dem	Cleveland, James C.	N.H. Rep

JOINT COMMITTEE: DISPOSITION OF EXECUTIVE PAPERS / 91st Congress

Service Dates of House Members: Feb. 20,1969-July 9,1970
Service Dates of Senate Members: Mar. 17,1969-July 9,1970

HOUSE

Majority			Terms in:		Minority			Terms in:	
Rank Name	**Party**	**State**	**House**	**Comm.**	**Rank Name**	**Party**	**State**	**House**	**Comm.**
1st Nedzi, Lucien N.	Dem	Mich.	5	1	1st Pettis, Jerry L.	Rep	Cal.	2	1

SENATE

Majority			Years in:		Minority			Years in:	
Rank Name	**Party**	**State**	**Senate**	**Comm.**	**Rank Name**	**Party**	**State**	**Senate**	**Comm.**
1st McGee, Gale W.	Dem	Wyo.	11	1	1st Fong, Hiram L.	Rep	Hai.	10	1

JOINT COMMITTEE: ECONOMIC

ECONOMIC REPORT

Jurisdiction, 1947

From Public Law 79-304, the Employment Act of 1946, 79th Congress, Second Session, February 20, 1946 (60 Statutes 23, 25) for the joint committee on the Economic Report:

[Section 5.(b)]

(b) It shall be the function of the joint committee--

(1) to make a continuing study of matters relating to the Economic Report;
(2) to study means of coordinating programs in order to further the policy of this Act; and
(3) as a guide to the several committees of the Congress dealing with legislation relating to the Economic Report, not later than May 1 of each year (beginning with the year 1947) to file a report with the Senate and the House of Representatives containing its findings and recommendations with respect to each of the main recommendations made by the President in the Economic Report, and from time to time to make such other reports and recommendations to the Senate and House of Representatives as it deems advisable.

ECONOMIC

The Committee was renamed the Joint Economic Committee on June 18, 1956 by authority of Public Law 591 (84-2).

Jurisdiction, 1978

From Public Law 95-523, the Full Employment and Balanced Growth Act of 1978, 95th Congress, Second Session (92 Statutes 1887, 1904-1905):

[Section 302]

(a) In conjunction with its review of the Economic Report, and the holding of hearings on the Economic Report under the Employment Act of 1946, the Joint Economic Committee shall review and analyze the short-term and medium-term goals set forth in the Economic Report pursuant to sections 3(a)(2) and 4(b) of the Employment Act of 1946 (as amended by sections 103 and 104 of this Act).

Jurisdiction, 1992

From Authority and Rules of Senate Committees, Senate Document 102-6, printed under the authority of Senate Resolution 58 (102-1), agreed to March 13, 1991:

[Section 1024]

(b) It shall be the function of the joint committee--

(1) to make a continuing study of matters relating to the Economic Report;
(2) to study means of coordinating programs in order to further the policy of this chapter; and
(3) as a guide to the several committees of the Congress dealing with legislation relating to the Economic Report, not later than March 1 of each year (beginning with the year 1947) to file a report with the Senate and the House of Representatives containing its findings and recommendations with respect to each of the main recommendations made by the President in the Economic Report, and from time to time to make such other reports and recommendations to the Senate and House of Representatives as it deems advisable.

JOINT COMMITTEE: ECONOMIC REPORT / 80th Congress

Service Dates of Committee Chair: Jan. 17,1947 Jan. 3,1949
Service Dates of House Members: Jan. 20,1947-Jan. 3,1949
Service Dates of Senate Members: Jan. 17,1947-Jan. 24,1949

HOUSE

Majority Rank Name	Party	State	Terms in: House	Comm.	Minority Rank Name	Party	State	Terms in: House	Comm.
VCh Wolcott, Jesse P.	Rep	Mich.	9	1	1st Hart, Edward J.	Dem	N.J.	7	2
2nd Bender, George H.	Rep	Ohio	5	2	2nd Patman, J.W. Wright	Dem	Tex.	10	2
3rd Judd, Walter H.	Rep	Minn.	3	2	3rd Huber, Walter B.	Dem	Ohio	2	2
4th Rich, Robert F.	Rep	Penn.	9	2					

SENATE

Majority Rank Name	Party	State	Years in: Senate	Comm.	Minority Rank Name	Party	State	Years in: Senate	Comm.
Chr Taft, Robert A.	Rep	Ohio	9	1	1st O'Mahoney, Joseph C.	Dem	Wyo.	14 *1	1
2nd Ball, Joseph H.	Rep	Minn.	7	1	2nd Myers, Francis J.	Dem	Penn.	3	1
3rd Flanders, Ralph E.	Rep	Vt.	1	1	3rd Sparkman, John J.	Dem	Ala.	1	1
4th Watkins, Arthur V.	Rep	Utah	1	1					

*1: Member's 1st period of service on the committee.

Note: "Service Dates of Senate Members" reflect the dates of service of all Senators with Taft, O'Mahoney and Myers continuing their service on the committee from the previous Congress.

Changes:

House Majority:

Judd, Walter H.	Rep	Minn.	Apr. 17,1947	Left committee; no new assignment.
Herter, Christian A.	Rep	Mass.	Apr. 17,1947	Replaced Judd.

	Majority		Minority
Departures from the House:			
Defeated for Reelection	Bender, George H.	Ohio Rep	None
Departures from the Senate:			
Defeated for Reelection	Ball, Joseph H.	Minn. Rep	None

JOINT COMMITTEE: ECONOMIC REPORT / 81st Congress

Service Dates of Committee Chair: Jan. 24,1949-Continued
Service Dates of House Members: Jan. 24,1949-Jan. 3,1951
Service Dates of Senate Members: Jan. 24,1949-Continued

HOUSE

Majority Rank Name	Party	State	Terms in: House	Comm.	Minority Rank Name	Party	State	Terms in: House	Comm.
VCh Hart, Edward J.	Dem	N.J.	8	3	1st Wolcott, Jesse P.	Rep	Mich.	10	2
2nd Patman, J.W. Wright	Dem	Tex.	11	3	2nd Rich, Robert F.	Rep	Penn.	10	3
3rd Huber, Walter B.	Dem	Ohio	3	3	3rd Herter, Christian A.	Rep	Mass.	4	2
4th Buchanan, Frank	Dem	Penn.	3	1					

SENATE

Majority Rank Name	Party	State	Years in: Senate	Comm.	Minority Rank Name	Party	State	Years in: Senate	Comm.
Chr O'Mahoney, Joseph C.	Dem	Wyo.	16 *1	3	1st Taft, Robert A.	Rep	Ohio	11	3
2nd Myers, Francis J.	Dem	Penn.	5	3	2nd Flanders, Ralph E.	Rep	Vt.	3	2
3rd Sparkman, John J.	Dem	Ala.	3	2	3rd Watkins, Arthur V.	Rep	Utah	3	2
4th Douglas, Paul H.	Dem	Ill.	1	1					

*1: Member's 1st period of service on the committee.

	Majority		Minority	
Departures from the House:				
Defeated for Reelection	Huber, Walter B.	Ohio Dem	None	
Retired	None		Rich, Robert F.	Penn. Rep
Departures from the Senate:				
Defeated for Reelection	Myers, Francis J.	Penn. Dem	None	

JOINT COMMITTEE: ECONOMIC REPORT / 82nd Congress

Service Dates of Committee Chair: Jan. 18,1951 Jan. 3,1953
Service Dates of House Members: Feb. 7,1951-Jan. 3,1953
Service Dates of Senate Members: Jan. 18,1951-Jan. 30,1953

HOUSE

Majority

Rank Name	Party	State	Terms in: House	Comm.
VCh Hart, Edward J.	Dem	N.J.	9	4
2nd Patman, J.W. Wright	Dem	Tex.	12	4
3rd Buchanan, Frank	Dem	Penn.	4	2
4th Bolling, Richard W.	Dem	Mo.	2	1

Minority

Rank Name	Party	State	Terms in: House	Comm.
1st Wolcott, Jesse P.	Rep	Mich.	11	3
2nd Herter, Christian A.	Rep	Mass.	5	3
3rd Boggs, J. Caleb	Rep	Del.	3	1

SENATE

Majority

Rank Name	Party	State	Years in: Senate	Comm.
Chr O'Mahoney, Joseph C.	Dem	Wyo.	18	*1 5
2nd Sparkman, John J.	Dem	Ala.	5	4
3rd Douglas, Paul H.	Dem	Ill.	3	2
4th Benton, William	Dem	Conn.	2	1

Minority

Rank Name	Party	State	Years in: Senate	Comm.
1st Taft, Robert A.	Rep	Ohio	13	5
2nd Flanders, Ralph E.	Rep	Vt.	5	4
3rd Watkins, Arthur V.	Rep	Utah	5	4

*1: Member's 1st period of service on the committee.

Note: "Service Dates of Senate Members" reflect the dates of service of Benton; all other Senators continued service from the previous Congress without official reassignment recorded in the Congressional Record.

Changes:

House Majority:

Buchanan, Frank	Dem	Penn.	Apr. 27,1951	Died in office.
McKinnon, Clinton D.	Dem	Cal.	June 13,1951	Replaced Buchanan.

	Majority		Minority	
Departures from the House:				
Elected Governor	None		Boggs, J. Caleb	Del. Rep
			Herter, Christian A.	Mass. Rep
Lost Nomination to U.S. Senate	McKinnon, Clinton D.	Cal. Dem	None	
Departures from the Senate:				
Defeated for Reelection	Benton, William	Conn. Dem	None	
	O'Mahoney, Joseph C.	Wyo. Dem		

JOINT COMMITTEE: ECONOMIC REPORT / 83rd Congress

Service Dates of Committee Chair: Jan. 29,1953-Jan. 3,1955
Service Dates of House Members: Jan. 29,1953-Jan. 3,1955
Service Dates of Senate Members: Jan. 30,1953-Jan. 14,1955

HOUSE

Majority

Rank Name	Party	State	Terms in: House	Comm.
Chr Wolcott, Jesse P.	Rep	Mich.	12	4
2nd Simpson, Richard M.	Rep	Penn.	9	1
3rd Talle, Henry O.	Rep	Iowa	8	1
4th Bender, George H.	Rep	Ohio	7 *2	1

Minority

Rank Name	Party	State	Terms in: House	Comm.
1st Hart, Edward J.	Dem	N.J.	10	5
2nd Patman, J.W. Wright	Dem	Tex.	13	5
3rd Bolling, Richard W.	Dem	Mo.	3	2

SENATE **Majority**

Rank	Name	Party	State	Years in: Senate	Comm.
VCh	Flanders, Ralph E.	Rep	Vt.	7	7
2nd	Taft, Robert A.	Rep	Ohio	15	7
3rd	Watkins, Arthur V.	Rep	Utah	7	7
4th	Goldwater, Barry M.	Rep	Ariz.	1	1

Minority

Rank	Name	Party	State	Years in: Senate	Comm.
1st	Sparkman, John J.	Dem	Ala.	7	7
2nd	Douglas, Paul H.	Dem	Ill.	5	5
3rd	Fulbright, J. William	Dem	Ark.	9	1

*2: Member's 2nd period of service on the committee.

Changes:

House Majority:

Bender, George H.	Rep	Ohio	Dec. 15,1954	Resigned; elected to U.S. Senate.

Senate Majority:

Taft, Robert A.	Rep	Ohio	July 31,1953	Died in office.
Carlson, Frank	Rep	Kans.	Aug. 3,1953	Replaced Taft.

Departures from the House:

	Majority	Minority		
Retired	None	Hart, Edward J.	N.J.	Dem

Departures from Committee:

House:

	Majority			Minority
No new assignment	Simpson, Richard M.	Penn.	Rep	None

Senate:

	Majority			Minority
No new assignment	Carlson, Frank	Kans.	Rep	None

JOINT COMMITTEE: ECONOMIC REPORT / 84th Congress

* Renamed the Joint ECONOMIC Committee on June 18,1956.

Service Dates of Committee Chair: Jan. 14,1955-Jan. 3,1957
Service Dates of House Members: Jan. 20,1955-Jan. 3,1957
Service Dates of Senate Members: Jan. 14,1955-Continued

HOUSE **Majority**

Rank	Name	Party	State	Terms in: House	Comm.
VCh	Patman, J.W. Wright	Dem	Tex.	14	6
2nd	Bolling, Richard W.	Dem	Mo.	4	3
3rd	Mills, Wilbur D.	Dem	Ark.	9	1
4th	Kelley, Augustine B.	Dem	Penn.	8	1

Minority

Rank	Name	Party	State	Terms in: House	Comm.
1st	Wolcott, Jesse P.	Rep	Mich.	13	5
2nd	Talle, Henry O.	Rep	Iowa	9	2
3rd	Curtis, Thomas B.	Rep	Mo.	3	1

SENATE **Majority**

Rank	Name	Party	State	Years in: Senate	Comm.
Chr	Douglas, Paul H.	Dem	Ill.	7	6
2nd	Sparkman, John J.	Dem	Ala.	9	8
3rd	Fulbright, J. William	Dem	Ark.	11	2
4th	O'Mahoney, Joseph C.	Dem	Wyo.	20 *2	1

Minority

Rank	Name	Party	State	Years in: Senate	Comm.
1st	Flanders, Ralph E.	Rep	Vt.	9	8
2nd	Watkins, Arthur V.	Rep	Utah	9	8
3rd	Goldwater, Barry M.	Rep	Ariz.	3	2

*2: Member's 2nd period of service on the committee.

Departures from the House:

	Majority	Minority		
Retired	None	Wolcott, Jesse P.	Mich.	Rep

JOINT COMMITTEE: ECONOMIC / 85th Congress

Service Dates of Committee Chair: Jan. 22,1957-Jan. 3,1959
Service Dates of House Members: Jan. 22,1957-Jan. 3,1959
Service Dates of Senate Members: Jan. 3,1957-Continued

HOUSE

Majority Rank Name	Party	State	Terms in: House	Terms in: Comm.	Minority Rank Name	Party	State	Terms in: House	Terms in: Comm.
Chr Patman, J.W. Wright	Dem	Tex.	15	7	1st Talle, Henry O.	Rep	Iowa	10	3
2nd Bolling, Richard W.	Dem	Mo.	5	4	2nd Curtis, Thomas B.	Rep	Mo.	4	2
3rd Mills, Wilbur D.	Dem	Ark.	10	2	3rd Kilburn, Clarence E.	Rep	N.Y.	10	1
4th Kelley, Augustine B.	Dem	Penn.	9	2					

SENATE

Majority Rank Name	Party	State	Years in: Senate	Years in: Comm.	Minority Rank Name	Party	State	Years in: Senate	Years in: Comm.
VCh Sparkman, John J.	Dem	Ala.	11	10	1st Flanders, Ralph E.	Rep	Vt.	11	10
2nd Douglas, Paul H.	Dem	Ill.	9	8	2nd Watkins, Arthur V.	Rep	Utah	11	10
3rd Fulbright, J. William	Dem	Ark.	13	4	3rd Goldwater, Barry M.	Rep	Ariz.	5	4
4th O'Mahoney, Joseph C.	Dem	Wyo.	22	*2 2					

*2: Member's 2nd period of service on the committee.

Changes:

House Majority:

Mills, Wilbur D.	Dem	Ark.	Jan. 27,1958	Left committee; no new assignment.
Boggs, T. Hale	Dem	La.	Jan. 27,1958	Replaced Mills.
Kelley, Augustine B.	Dem	Penn.	Nov. 20,1957	Died in office.
Reuss, Henry S.	Dem	Wisc.	Feb. 17,1958	Replaced Kelley.

Senate Minority:

Goldwater, Barry M.	Rep	Ariz.	Mar. 20,1958	Left committee; no new assignment.
Hoblitzell, John D. Jr.	Rep	W.Va.	Mar. 20,1958	Replaced Goldwater.
Hoblitzell, John D. Jr.	Rep	W.Va.	Nov. 4,1958	Defeated for election.

	Majority	Minority		
Departures from the House:				
Defeated for Reelection	None	Talle, Henry O.	Iowa	Rep
Departures from the Senate:				
Defeated for Reelection	None	Watkins, Arthur V.	Utah	Rep
Retired	None	Flanders, Ralph E.	Vt.	Rep

JOINT COMMITTEE: ECONOMIC / 86th Congress

Service Dates of Committee Chair: Feb. 4,1959-Jan. 3,1961
Service Dates of House Members: Jan. 27,1959-Jan. 3,1961
Service Dates of Senate Members: Feb. 4,1959-Continued

HOUSE

Majority Rank Name	Party	State	Terms in: House	Terms in: Comm.	Minority Rank Name	Party	State	Terms in: House	Terms in: Comm.
VCh Patman, J.W. Wright	Dem	Tex.	16	8	1st Curtis, Thomas B.	Rep	Mo.	5	3
2nd Bolling, Richard W.	Dem	Mo.	6	5	2nd Kilburn, Clarence E.	Rep	N.Y.	11	2
3rd Boggs, T. Hale	Dem	La.	8	2	3rd Widnall, William B.	Rep	N.J.	6	1
4th Reuss, Henry S.	Dem	Wisc.	3	2					

SENATE

Majority Rank Name	Party	State	Years in: Senate	Years in: Comm.	Minority Rank Name	Party	State	Years in: Senate	Years in: Comm.
Chr Douglas, Paul H.	Dem	Ill.	11	10	1st Bush, Prescott S.	Rep	Conn.	7	1
2nd Sparkman, John J.	Dem	Ala.	13	12	2nd Butler, John Marshall	Rep	Md.	9	1
3rd Fulbright, J. William	Dem	Ark.	15	6	3rd Javits, Jacob K.	Rep	N.Y.	3	1
4th O'Mahoney, Joseph C.	Dem	Wyo.	24	*2 4					

*2: Member's 2nd period of service on the committee.

Notes: "Service Dates of Senate Members" reflect the dates of service of Bush, Butler and Javits; all other Senators continued service from the previous Congress without official reassignment recorded in the Congressional Record. The committee was expanded and party ratio changed to 8 Representatives (5 Democrats and 3 Republicans) and 8 Senators (5 Democrats and 3 Republicans) on Feb. 17,1959.

Additions:

House:	5th	Coffin, Frank M.	Dem	Me.	Feb. 18,1959
Senate:	5th	Kennedy, John F.	Dem	Mass.	Mar. 19,1959

Changes:

Senate Majority:

Kennedy, John F.	Dem	Mass.	Dec. 22,1960	Resigned; elected President.

Departures from the House:	Majority			Minority
Lost Election for Governor	Coffin, Frank M.	Me.	Dem	None
Departures from the Senate:				
Retired	O'Mahoney, Joseph C.	Wyo.	Dem	None

JOINT COMMITTEE: ECONOMIC / 87th Congress

Service Dates of Committee Chair: Feb. 7,1961-Jan. 3,1963
Service Dates of House Members: Feb. 7,1961-Jan. 3,1963
Service Dates of Senate Members: Jan. 26,1961-Continued

HOUSE

Majority			Terms in:		Minority			Terms in:	
Rank Name	Party	State	House	Comm.	Rank Name	Party	State	House	Comm.
Chr Patman, J.W. Wright	Dem	Tex.	17	9	1st Curtis, Thomas B.	Rep	Mo.	6	4
2nd Bolling, Richard W.	Dem	Mo.	7	6	2nd Kilburn, Clarence E.	Rep	N.Y.	12	3
3rd Boggs, T. Hale	Dem	La.	9	3	3rd Widnall, William B.	Rep	N.J.	7	2
4th Reuss, Henry S.	Dem	Wisc.	4	3					
5th Griffiths, Martha W.	Dem	Mich.	4	1					

SENATE

Majority			Years in:		Minority			Years in:	
Rank Name	Party	State	Senate	Comm.	Rank Name	Party	State	Senate	Comm.
VCh Douglas, Paul H.	Dem	Ill.	13	12	1st Bush, Prescott S.	Rep	Conn.	9	2
2nd Sparkman, John J.	Dem	Ala.	15	14	2nd Butler, John Marshall	Rep	Md.	11	2
3rd Fulbright, J. William	Dem	Ark.	17	8	3rd Javits, Jacob K.	Rep	N.Y.	5	2
4th Proxmire, William	Dem	Wisc.	4	1					
5th Pell, Claiborne D.	Dem	R.I.	1	1					

Note: "Service Dates of Senate Members" reflect the dates of service of Proxmire and Pell; all other Senators continued service from the previous Congress without official reassignment recorded in the Congressional Record.

Departures from the Senate:	Majority	Minority		
Retired	None	Bush, Prescott S.	Conn.	Rep
		Butler, John Marshall	Md.	Rep

JOINT COMMITTEE: ECONOMIC / 88th Congress

Service Dates of Committee Chair: Feb, 11,1963-Jan. 3,1965
Service Dates of House Members: Jan. 17,1963-Jan. 3,1965
Service Dates of Senate Members: Feb. 11,1963-Continued

HOUSE

Majority

Rank	Name	Party	State	Terms in: House	Terms in: Comm.
VCh	Bolling, Richard W.	Dem	Mo.	8	7
2nd	Patman, J.W. Wright	Dem	Tex.	18	10
3rd	Boggs, T. Hale	Dem	La.	10	4
4th	Reuss, Henry S.	Dem	Wisc.	5	4
5th	Griffiths, Martha W.	Dem	Mich.	5	2

Minority

Rank	Name	Party	State	Terms in: House	Terms in: Comm.
1st	Curtis, Thomas B.	Rep	Mo.	7	5
2nd	Kilburn, Clarence E.	Rep	N.Y.	13	4
3rd	Widnall, William B.	Rep	N.J.	8	3

SENATE

Majority

Rank	Name	Party	State	Years in: Senate	Years in: Comm.
Chr	Douglas, Paul H.	Dem	Ill.	15	14
2nd	Sparkman, John J.	Dem	Ala.	17	16
3rd	Fulbright, J. William	Dem	Ark.	19	10
4th	Proxmire, William	Dem	Wisc.	6	2
5th	Pell, Claiborne D.	Dem	R.I.	3	2

Minority

Rank	Name	Party	State	Years in: Senate	Years in: Comm.
1st	Javits, Jacob K.	Rep	N.Y.	7	4
2nd	Miller, Jack R.	Rep	Iowa	3	1
3rd	Jordan, Len B.	Rep	Ida.	1	1

Note: "Service Dates of Senate Members" reflect the dates of service of Miller and Jordan; all other Senators continued service from the previous Congress without official reassignment recorded in the Congressional Record.

	Majority		Minority	
Departures from the House:				
Retired	None		Kilburn, Clarence E.	N.Y. Rep
Departures from Committee:				
Senate:				
No new assignment	Pell, Claiborne D.	R.I. Dem	None	

JOINT COMMITTEE: ECONOMIC / 89th Congress

Service Dates of Committee Chair: Feb. 8,1965-Jan. 3,1967
Service Dates of House Members: Feb. 8,1965-Jan. 3,1967
Service Dates of Senate Members: Jan. 12,1965-Continued

HOUSE

Majority

Rank	Name	Party	State	Terms in: House	Terms in: Comm.
Chr	Patman, J.W. Wright	Dem	Tex.	19	11
2nd	Bolling, Richard W.	Dem	Mo.	9	8
3rd	Boggs, T. Hale	Dem	La.	11	5
4th	Reuss, Henry S.	Dem	Wisc.	6	5
5th	Griffiths, Martha W.	Dem	Mich.	6	3

Minority

Rank	Name	Party	State	Terms in: House	Terms in: Comm.
1st	Curtis, Thomas B.	Rep	Mo.	8	6
2nd	Widnall, William B.	Rep	N.J.	9	4
3rd	Ellsworth, Robert F.	Rep	Kans.	3	1

SENATE

Majority

Rank	Name	Party	State	Years in: Senate	Years in: Comm.
VCh	Douglas, Paul H.	Dem	Ill.	17	16
2nd	Sparkman, John J.	Dem	Ala.	19	18
3rd	Fulbright, J. William	Dem	Ark.	21	12
4th	Proxmire, William	Dem	Wisc.	8	4
5th	Talmadge, Herman E.	Dem	Ga.	9	1

Minority

Rank	Name	Party	State	Years in: Senate	Years in: Comm.
1st	Javits, Jacob K.	Rep	N.Y.	9	6
2nd	Miller, Jack R.	Rep	Iowa	5	2
3rd	Jordan, Len B.	Rep	Ida.	3	2

Note: "Service Dates of Senate Members" reflect the dates of service of Talmadge; all other Senators continued service from the previous Congress without official reassignment recorded in the Congressional Record.

	Majority		Minority	
Departures from the House:				
Lost Nomination for U.S. Senate	None		Ellsworth, Robert F.	Kans. Rep
Departures from the Senate:				
Defeated for Reelection	Douglas, Paul H.	Ill. Dem	None	

JOINT COMMITTEE: ECONOMIC / 90th Congress

Service Dates of Committee Chair: Jan. 17,1967-Jan. 3,1969
Service Dates of House Members: Jan. 26,1967-Jan. 3,1969
Service Dates of Senate Members: Jan. 17,1967-Continued

HOUSE **Majority**

Rank Name	Party	State	Terms in: House	Comm.
VCh Patman, J.W. Wright	Dem	Tex.	20	12
2nd Bolling, Richard W.	Dem	Mo.	10	9
3rd Boggs, T. Hale	Dem	La.	12	6
4th Reuss, Henry S.	Dem	Wisc.	7	6
5th Griffiths, Martha W.	Dem	Mich.	7	4
6th Moorhead, William S.	Dem	Penn.	5	1

Minority

Rank Name	Party	State	Terms in: House	Comm.
1st Curtis, Thomas B.	Rep	Mo.	9	7
2nd Widnall, William B.	Rep	N.J.	10	5
3rd Rumsfeld, Donald	Rep	Ill.	3	1
4th Brock, William E. III	Rep	Tenn.	3	1

SENATE **Majority**

Rank Name	Party	State	Years in: Senate	Comm.
Chr Proxmire, William	Dem	Wisc.	10	6
2nd Sparkman, John J.	Dem	Ala.	21	20
3rd Fulbright, J. William	Dem	Ark.	23	14
4th Talmadge, Herman E.	Dem	Ga.	11	2
5th Symington, W. Stuart	Dem	Mo.	15	1
6th Ribicoff, Abraham A.	Dem	Conn.	5	1

Minority

Rank Name	Party	State	Years in: Senate	Comm.
1st Javits, Jacob K.	Rep	N.Y.	11	8
2nd Miller, Jack R.	Rep	Iowa	7	4
3rd Jordan, Len B.	Rep	Ida.	5	4
4th Percy, Charles H.	Rep	Ill.	1	1

Note: "Service Dates of Senate Members" reflect the dates of service of Symington and Percy; all other Senators continued service from the previous Congress without official reassignment recorded in the Congressional Record.

Vacancy Filled:
Senate Majority: 6th seat by Ribicoff on Jan. 25,1967.

Departures from the House:	Majority	Minority		
Lost Senate Election	None	Curtis, Thomas B.	Mo.	Rep

JOINT COMMITTEE: ECONOMIC / 91st Congress

Service Dates of Committee Chair: Jan. 30,1969-Jan. 3,1971
Service Dates of House Members: Jan. 30,1969-Jan. 3,1971
Service Dates of Senate Members: Jan. 3,1969-Continued

HOUSE **Majority**

Rank Name	Party	State	Terms in: House	Comm.
Chr Patman, J.W. Wright	Dem	Tex.	21	13
2nd Bolling, Richard W.	Dem	Mo.	11	10
3rd Boggs, T. Hale	Dem	La.	13	7
4th Reuss, Henry S.	Dem	Wisc.	8	7
5th Griffiths, Martha W.	Dem	Mich.	8	5
6th Moorhead, William S.	Dem	Penn.	6	2

Minority

Rank Name	Party	State	Terms in: House	Comm.
1st Widnall, William B.	Rep	N.J.	11	6
2nd Rumsfeld, Donald	Rep	Ill.	4	2
3rd Brock, William E. III	Rep	Tenn.	4	2
4th Conable, Barber B. Jr.	Rep	N.Y.	3	1

SENATE **Majority**

Rank Name	Party	State	Years in: Senate	Comm.
VCh Proxmire, William	Dem	Wisc.	12	8
2nd Sparkman, John J.	Dem	Ala.	23	22
3rd Fulbright, J. William	Dem	Ark.	25	16
4th Talmadge, Herman E.	Dem	Ga.	13	4
5th Symington, W. Stuart	Dem	Mo.	17	2
6th Ribicoff, Abraham A.	Dem	Conn.	7	2

Minority

Rank Name	Party	State	Years in: Senate	Comm.
1st Javits, Jacob K.	Rep	N.Y.	13	10
2nd Miller, Jack R.	Rep	Iowa	9	6
3rd Jordan, Len B.	Rep	Ida.	7	6
4th Percy, Charles H.	Rep	Ill.	3	2

Changes:
House Minority:

Rumsfeld, Donald	Rep	Ill.	May 25,1969	Resigned; appointed Assistant Director of Office of Economic Opportunity.
Brown, Clarence J. Jr.	Rep	Ohio	June 16,1969	Replaced Rumsfeld.

Departures from the House:	Majority			Minority		
Elected to U.S. Senate	None			Brock, William E. III	Tenn.	Rep
Departures from Committee:						
Senate:						
Moved to Joint Atomic Energy	Symington, W. Stuart	Mo.	Dem	None		
Moved to Veterans' Affairs	Talmadge, Herman E.	Ga.	Dem	None		
No new assignment	None			Jordan, Len B.	Ida.	Rep

JOINT COMMITTEE: ECONOMIC / 92nd Congress

Service Dates of Committee Chair: Jan. 28,1971-Jan. 3,1973
Service Dates of House Members: Feb. 23,1971-Jan. 3,1973
Service Dates of Senate Members: Jan. 28,1971-Continued

HOUSE **Majority**

Rank	Name	Party	State	Terms in: House	Terms in: Comm.
VCh	Patman, J.W. Wright	Dem	Tex.	22	14
2nd	Bolling, Richard W.	Dem	Mo.	12	11
3rd	Boggs, T. Hale	Dem	La.	14	8
4th	Reuss, Henry S.	Dem	Wisc.	9	8
5th	Griffiths, Martha W.	Dem	Mich.	9	6
6th	Moorhead, William S.	Dem	Penn.	7	3

Minority

Rank	Name	Party	State	Terms in: House	Terms in: Comm.
1st	Widnall, William B.	Rep	N.J.	12	7
2nd	Conable, Barber B. Jr.	Rep	N.Y.	4	2
3rd	Brown, Clarence J. Jr.	Rep	Ohio	4	2
4th	Blackburn, Benjamin B.	Rep	Ga.	3	1

SENATE **Majority**

Rank	Name	Party	State	Years in: Senate	Years in: Comm.
Chr	Proxmire, William	Dem	Wisc.	14	10
2nd	Sparkman, John J.	Dem	Ala.	25	24
3rd	Fulbright, J. William	Dem	Ark.	27	18
4th	Ribicoff, Abraham A.	Dem	Conn.	9	4
5th	Humphrey, Hubert H. Jr.	DFL	Minn.	17	1
6th	Bentsen, Lloyd M. Jr.	Dem	Tex.	1	1

Minority

Rank	Name	Party	State	Years in: Senate	Years in: Comm.
1st	Javits, Jacob K.	Rep	N.Y.	15	12
2nd	Miller, Jack R.	Rep	Iowa	11	8
3rd	Percy, Charles H.	Rep	Ill.	5	4
4th	Pearson, James B.	Rep	Kans.	10	1

Note: "Service Dates of Senate Members" reflect the dates of service of Humphrey and Bentsen; all other Senators continued service from the previous Congress without official reassignment recorded in the Congressional Record.

Vacancy Filled:
Senate Minority: 4th seat by Pearson on Feb. 10,1971.

Changes:
House Majority:

Boggs, T. Hale	Dem	La.	Jan. 3,1973	Died in office.

Departures from the Senate:	Majority	Minority		
Defeated for Reelection	None	Miller, Jack R.	Iowa	Rep

JOINT COMMITTEE: ECONOMIC / 93rd Congress

Service Dates of Committee Chair: Feb. 1,1973-Jan. 3,1975
Service Dates of House Members: Feb. 1,1973-Jan. 3,1975
Service Dates of Senate Members: Jan. 11,1973-Continued

HOUSE

Majority Rank	Name	Party	State	Terms in: House	Comm.	Minority Rank	Name	Party	State	Terms in: House	Comm.
Chr	Patman, J.W. Wright	Dem	Tex.	23	15	1st	Widnall, William B.	Rep	N.J.	13	8
2nd	Bolling, Richard W.	Dem	Mo.	13	12	2nd	Conable, Barber B. Jr.	Rep	N.Y.	5	3
3rd	Reuss, Henry S.	Dem	Wisc.	10	9	3rd	Brown, Clarence J. Jr.	Rep	Ohio	5	3
4th	Griffiths, Martha W.	Dem	Mich.	10	7	4th	Blackburn, Benjamin B.	Rep	Ga.	4	2
5th	Moorhead, William S.	Dem	Penn.	8	4						
6th	Carey, Hugh L.	Dem	N.Y.	7	1						

SENATE

Majority Rank	Name	Party	State	Years in: Senate	Comm.	Minority Rank	Name	Party	State	Years in: Senate	Comm.
VCh	Proxmire, William	Dem	Wisc.	16	12	1st	Javits, Jacob K.	Rep	N.Y.	17	14
2nd	Sparkman, John J.	Dem	Ala.	27	26	2nd	Percy, Charles H.	Rep	Ill.	7	6
3rd	Fulbright, J. William	Dem	Ark.	29	20	3rd	Pearson, James B.	Rep	Kans.	11	2
4th	Ribicoff, Abraham A.	Dem	Conn.	11	6	4th	Schweiker, Richard S.	Rep	Penn.	5	1
5th	Humphrey, Hubert H. Jr.	DFL	Minn.	18	2						
6th	Bentsen, Lloyd M. Jr.	Dem	Tex.	3	2						

Note: "Service Dates of Senate Members" reflect the dates of service of Schweiker; all other Senators continued service from the previous Congress without official reassignment recorded in the Congressional Record.

Changes:

House Majority:

Griffiths, Martha W.	Dem	Mich.	Dec. 31,1974	Resigned and retired.
Carey, Hugh L.	Dem	N.Y.	Dec. 31,1974	Resigned; elected Governor.

House Minority:

Widnall, William B.	Rep	N.J.	Dec. 31,1974	Resigned; defeated for reelection.

Senate Majority:

Fulbright, J. William	Dem	Ark.	Dec. 31,1974	Resigned; defeated for renomination.

	Majority	Minority	State	Party
Departures from the House:				
Defeated for Reelection	None	Blackburn, Benjamin B.	Ga.	Rep
Departures from the Senate:				
House:				
Moved to Budget; Joint Internal Revenue Taxation	None	Conable, Barber B. Jr.	N.Y.	Rep
Senate:				
Moved to Joint Atomic Energy	None	Pearson, James B.	Kans.	Rep
No new assignment	None	Schweiker, Richard S.	Penn.	Rep

JOINT COMMITTEE: ECONOMIC / 94th Congress

Service Dates of Committee Chair: Jan. 17,1975-Jan. 3,1977
Service Dates of House Members: Jan. 27,1975-Jan. 3,1977
Service Dates of Senate Members: Jan. 17,1975-Continued

HOUSE

Majority Rank	Name	Party	State	Terms in: House	Comm.	Minority Rank	Name	Party	State	Terms in: House	Comm.
VCh1	Patman, J.W. Wright	Dem	Tex.	24	16	1st	Brown, Clarence J. Jr.	Rep	Ohio	6	4
VCh2	Bolling, Richard W.	Dem	Mo.	14	13	2nd	Brown, Garry E.	Rep	Mich.	5	1
3rd	Reuss, Henry S.	Dem	Wisc.	11	10	3rd	Heckler, Margaret M.	Rep	Mass.	5	1
4th	Moorhead, William S.	Dem	Penn.	9	5	4th	Rousselot, John H.	Rep	Cal.	5	1
5th	Hamilton, Lee H.	Dem	Ind.	6	1						
6th	Long, Gillis W.	Dem	La.	3	1						

SENATE **Majority**

Rank	Name	Party	State	Years in: Senate	Years in: Comm.
Chr	Humphrey, Hubert H. Jr.	DFL	Minn.	20	4
2nd	Sparkman, John J.	Dem	Ala.	29	28
3rd	Proxmire, William	Dem	Wisc.	18	14
4th	Ribicoff, Abraham A.	Dem	Conn.	13	8
5th	Bentsen, Lloyd M. Jr.	Dem	Tex.	5	4
6th	Kennedy, Edward M.	Dem	Mass.	13	1

Minority

Rank	Name	Party	State	Years in: Senate	Years in: Comm.
1st	Javits, Jacob K.	Rep	N.Y.	19	16
2nd	Percy, Charles H.	Rep	Ill.	9	8
3rd	Taft, Robert Jr.	Rep	Ohio	5	1
4th	Fannin, Paul J.	Rep	Ariz.	11	1

Note: "Service Dates of Senate Members" reflect the dates of service of Kennedy and Taft; all other Senators continued service from the previous Congress without official reassignment recorded in the Congressional Record.

Vacancy Filled:
Senate Minority: 4th seat by Fannin on Jan. 28,1975.

Changes:
Vice Chair:

VCh1 Patman, J.W. Wright	Dem	Tex.	Mar. 7,1976	Died in office.
VCh2 Bolling, Richard W.	Dem	Mo.	Mar. 7,1976	Succeeded Patman as Vice Chair.

House Majority:

Patman, J.W. Wright	Dem	Tex.	Mar. 7,1976	Died in office.
Pike, Otis G.	Dem	N.Y.	Mar. 18,1976	Replaced Patman.

Senate Minority:

Fannin, Paul J.	Rep	Ariz.	Sep. 22,1976	Left committee; no new assignment.
Roth, William V. Jr.	Rep	Del.	Sep. 22,1976	Replaced Fannin.
Taft, Robert Jr.	Rep	Ohio	Dec. 28,1976	Resigned; defeated for reelection.

Departures from Committee:
Senate:

	Majority	Minority	
No new assignment	None	Percy, Charles H.	Ill. Rep

JOINT COMMITTEE: ECONOMIC / 95th Congress

Service Dates of Committee Chair: Jan. 13,1977-Jan. 3,1979
Service Dates of House Members: Jan. 13,1977-Jan. 3,1979
Service Dates of Senate Members: Feb. 24,1977-Continued

HOUSE **Majority**

Rank	Name	Party	State	Terms in: House	Terms in: Comm.
Chr	Bolling, Richard W.	Dem	Mo.	15	14
2nd	Reuss, Henry S.	Dem	Wisc.	12	11
3rd	Moorhead, William S.	Dem	Penn.	10	6
4th	Hamilton, Lee H.	Dem	Ind.	7	2
5th	Long, Gillis W.	Dem	La.	4	2
6th	Pike, Otis G.	Dem	N.Y.	9	2

Minority

Rank	Name	Party	State	Terms in: House	Terms in: Comm.
1st	Brown, Clarence J. Jr.	Rep	Ohio	7	5
2nd	Brown, Garry E.	Rep	Mich.	6	2
3rd	Heckler, Margaret M.	Rep	Mass.	6	2
4th	Rousselot, John H.	Rep	Cal.	6	2

SENATE **Majority**

Rank	Name	Party	State	Years in: Senate	Years in: Comm.
VCh1	Humphrey, Hubert H. Jr.	DFL	Minn.	22	6
2nd	Sparkman, John J.	Dem	Ala.	31	30
3rd	Proxmire, William	Dem	Wisc.	20	16
4th	Ribicoff, Abraham A.	Dem	Conn.	15	10
VCh2 5th	Bentsen, Lloyd M. Jr.	Dem	Tex.	7	6
6th	Kennedy, Edward M.	Dem	Mass.	15	2

Minority

Rank	Name	Party	State	Years in: Senate	Years in: Comm.
1st	Javits, Jacob K.	Rep	N.Y.	21	18
2nd	Roth, William V. Jr.	Rep	Del.	7	1
3rd	McClure, James A.	Rep	Ida.	5	1
4th	Hatch, Orrin G.	Rep	Utah	1	1

Note: "Service Dates of Senate Members" reflect the dates of service of minority members only; majority members continued service from the previous Congress without official reassignment recorded in the Congressional Record.

Changes:
Vice Chair:

VCh1 Humphrey, Hubert H. Jr.	DFL	Minn.	Jan. 13,1978	Died in office.
VCh2 Bentsen, Lloyd M. Jr.	Dem	Tex.	Feb. 2,1978	Succeeded Humphrey as Vice Chair.

House Majority:

Pike, Otis G.	Dem	N.Y.	Feb. 23,1978	Left committee; no new assignment (letter dated Feb. 2,1978).
Mitchell, Parren J.	Dem	Md.	Feb. 23,1978	Replaced Pike.

Senate Majority:

Humphrey, Hubert H. Jr.	DFL	Minn.	Jan. 13,1978	Died in office.
McGovern, George S.	Dem	S.D.	Jan. 26,1978	Replaced Humphrey.

	Majority		Minority	
Departures from the House:				
Defeated for Reelection	None		Brown, Garry E.	Mich. Rep
Departures from the Senate:				
Retired	Sparkman, John J.	Ala. Dem	None	
Departures from Committee:				
Senate:				
Moved to Budget	None		Hatch, Orrin G.	Utah Rep

JOINT COMMITTEE: ECONOMIC / 96th Congress

Service Dates of Committee Chair: Jan. 23,1979-Jan. 3,1981
Service Dates of House Members: Feb. 13,1979-Jan. 3,1981
Service Dates of Senate Members: Jan. 23,1979-Continued

HOUSE

Majority			Terms in:		Minority			Terms in:	
Rank Name	**Party**	**State**	**House**	**Comm.**	**Rank Name**	**Party**	**State**	**House**	**Comm.**
VCh Bolling, Richard W.	Dem	Mo.	16	15	1st Brown, Clarence J. Jr.	Rep	Ohio	8	6
2nd Reuss, Henry S.	Dem	Wisc.	13	12	2nd Heckler, Margaret M.	Rep	Mass.	7	3
3rd Moorhead, William S.	Dem	Penn.	11	7	3rd Rousselot, John H.	Rep	Cal.	7	3
4th Hamilton, Lee H.	Dem	Ind.	8	3	4th Wylie, Chalmers P.	Rep	Ohio	7	1
5th Long, Gillis W.	Dem	La.	5	3					
6th Mitchell, Parren J.	Dem	Md.	5	2					

SENATE

Majority			Years in:		Minority			Years in:	
Rank Name	**Party**	**State**	**Senate**	**Comm.**	**Rank Name**	**Party**	**State**	**Senate**	**Comm.**
Chr Bentsen, Lloyd M. Jr.	Dem	Tex.	9	8	1st Javits, Jacob K.	Rep	N.Y.	23	20
2nd Proxmire, William	Dem	Wisc.	22	18	2nd Roth, William V. Jr.	Rep	Del.	9	3
3rd Ribicoff, Abraham A.	Dem	Conn.	17	12	3rd McClure, James A.	Rep	Ida.	7	2
4th Kennedy, Edward M.	Dem	Mass.	17	4	4th Jepsen, Roger W.	Rep	Iowa	1	1
5th McGovern, George S.	Dem	S.D.	17	1					
6th Sarbanes, Paul S.	Dem	Md.	3	1					

Note: "Service Dates of Senate Members" reflect the dates of service of minority members only; majority members continued service from the previous Congress without official reassignment recorded in the Congressional Record.

Vacancy Filled:
Senate Majority: 6th seat by Sarbanes on Mar. 7,1979.

	Majority		Minority	
Departures from the House:				
Retired	Moorhead, William S.	Penn. Dem	None	
Departures from the Senate:				
Defeated for Reelection	McGovern, George S.	S.D. Dem	Javits, Jacob K.	N.Y. Rep
Retired	Ribicoff, Abraham A.	Conn. Dem	None	
Departures from Committee:				
Senate:				
Moved to Rules & Administration	None		McClure, James A.	Ida. Rep

JOINT COMMITTEE: ECONOMIC / 97th Congress

Service Dates of Committee Chair: Jan. 28,1981-Jan. 3,1983
Service Dates of House Members: Jan. 28,1981-Jan. 3,1983
Service Dates of Senate Members: Jan. 6,1981-Continued

HOUSE **Majority**

Rank Name	Party	State	Terms in: House	Terms in: Comm.
Chr Reuss, Henry S.	Dem	Wisc.	14	13
2nd Bolling, Richard W.	Dem	Mo.	17	16
3rd Hamilton, Lee H.	Dem	Ind.	9	4
4th Long, Gillis W.	Dem	La.	6	4
5th Mitchell, Parren J.	Dem	Md.	6	3
6th Richmond, Frederick W.	Dem	N.Y.	4	1

Minority

Rank Name	Party	State	Terms in: House	Terms in: Comm.
1st Brown, Clarence J. Jr.	Rep	Ohio	9	7
2nd Heckler, Margaret M.	Rep	Mass.	8	4
3rd Rousselot, John H.	Rep	Cal.	8	4
4th Wylie, Chalmers P.	Rep	Ohio	8	2

SENATE **Majority**

Rank Name	Party	State	Years in: Senate	Years in: Comm.
VCh Jepsen, Roger W.	Rep	Iowa	3	2
2nd Roth, William V. Jr.	Rep	Del.	11	5
3rd Abdnor, James	Rep	S.D.	1	1
4th Symms, Steven D.	Rep	Ida.	1	1
5th Hawkins, Paula	Rep	Fla.	1	1
6th Mattingly, Mack	Rep	Ga.	1	1

Minority

Rank Name	Party	State	Years in: Senate	Years in: Comm.
1st Bentsen, Lloyd M. Jr.	Dem	Tex.	11	10
2nd Proxmire, William	Dem	Wisc.	24	20
3rd Kennedy, Edward M.	Dem	Mass.	19	6
4th Sarbanes, Paul S.	Dem	Md.	5	2

Note: "Service Dates of Senate Members" reflect the dates of service of majority members; minority members continued service from the previous Congress without official reassignment recorded in the Congressional Record.

Changes:
House Majority:

Richmond, Frederick W.	Dem	N.Y.	Aug. 25,1982	Resigned and retired.
Hawkins, Augustus F.	Dem	Cal.	Sep. 23,1982	Replaced Richmond.

Departures from the House:

	Majority		Minority	
Defeated for Reelection	None		Heckler, Margaret M.	Mass. Rep
			Rousselot, John H.	Cal. Rep
Lost Election for Governor	None		Brown, Clarence J. Jr.	Ohio Rep
Retired	Bolling, Richard W.	Mo. Dem	None	
	Reuss, Henry S.	Wisc. Dem		

Departures from Committee:
Senate:

	Majority		Minority
No new assignment	Hawkins, Paula	Fla. Rep	None

JOINT COMMITTEE: ECONOMIC / 98th Congress

Service Dates of Committee Chair: Jan. 6,1983-Jan. 3,1985
Service Dates of House Majority Members: Jan. 6,1983-Jan. 3,1985
Service Dates of House Minority Members: Jan. 25,1983-Jan. 3,1985
Service Dates of Senate Members: Jan. 3,1983-Mar. 5,1985

HOUSE **Majority**

Rank Name	Party	State	Terms in: House	Terms in: Comm.
VCh Hamilton, Lee H.	Dem	Ind.	10	5
2nd Long, Gillis W.	Dem	La.	7	5
3rd Mitchell, Parren J.	Dem	Md.	7	4
4th Hawkins, Augustus F.	Dem	Cal.	11	2
5th Obey, David R.	Dem	Wisc.	8	1
6th Scheuer, James H.	Dem	N.Y.	9	1

Minority

Rank Name	Party	State	Terms in: House	Terms in: Comm.
1st Wylie, Chalmers P.	Rep	Ohio	9	3
2nd Holt, Marjorie S.	Rep	Md.	6	1
3rd Lungren, Daniel E.	Rep	Cal.	3	1
4th Snowe, Olympia J. B.	Rep	Me.	3	1

SENATE Majority			Years in:		Minority			Years in:	
Rank Name	Party	State	Senate	Comm.	Rank Name	Party	State	Senate	Comm.
Chr Jepsen, Roger W.	Rep	Iowa	5	4	1st Bentsen, Lloyd M. Jr.	Dem	Tex.	13	12
2nd Roth, William V. Jr.	Rep	Del.	13	7	2nd Proxmire, William	Dem	Wisc.	26	22
3rd Abdnor, James	Rep	S.D.	3	2	3rd Kennedy, Edward M.	Dem	Mass.	21	8
4th Symms, Steven D.	Rep	Ida.	3	2	4th Sarbanes, Paul S.	Dem	Md.	7	4
5th Mattingly, Mack	Rep	Ga.	3	2					
6th D'Amato, Alfonse M.	Rep	N.Y.	3	1					

Note: "Service Dates of Senate Members" reflect the dates of service of minority members; majority members continued service from the previous Congress without official reassignment recorded in the Congressional Record.

Vacancy Filled:
Senate Majority: 6th seat by D'Amato on Feb. 3,1983.

	Majority		Minority
Departures from the Senate:			
Defeated for Reelection	Jepsen, Roger W.	Iowa Rep	None
Departures from Committee:			
House:			
No new assignment	Long, Gillis W.	La. Dem	None

JOINT COMMITTEE: ECONOMIC / 99th Congress

Service Dates of Committee Chair: Jan. 31,1985-Jan. 3,1987
Service Dates of House Members: Jan. 31,1985-Jan. 3,1987
Service Dates of Senate Members: Mar. 5,1985-Continued

HOUSE Majority			Terms in:		Minority			Terms in:	
Rank Name	Party	State	House	Comm.	Rank Name	Party	State	House	Comm.
Chr Obey, David R.	Dem	Wisc.	9	2	1st Wylie, Chalmers P.	Rep	Ohio	10	4
2nd Hamilton, Lee H.	Dem	Ind.	11	6	2nd Holt, Marjorie S.	Rep	Md.	7	2
3rd Mitchell, Parren J.	Dem	Md.	8	5	3rd Lungren, Daniel E.	Rep	Cal.	4	2
4th Hawkins, Augustus F.	Dem	Cal.	12	3	4th Snowe, Olympia J. B.	Rep	Me.	4	2
5th Scheuer, James H.	Dem	N.Y.	10	2					
6th Stark, Fortney H. (Pete)	Dem	Cal.	7	1					

SENATE Majority			Years in:		Minority			Years in:	
Rank Name	Party	State	Senate	Comm.	Rank Name	Party	State	Senate	Comm.
VCh Abdnor, James	Rep	S.D.	5	5	1st Bentsen, Lloyd M. Jr.	Dem	Tex.	15	15
2nd Roth, William V. Jr.	Rep	Del.	15	9	2nd Proxmire, William	Dem	Wisc.	28	25
3rd Symms, Steven D.	Rep	Ida.	5	5	3rd Kennedy, Edward M.	Dem	Mass.	23	11
4th Mattingly, Mack	Rep	Ga.	5	5	4th Sarbanes, Paul S.	Dem	Md.	9	7
5th D'Amato, Alfonse M.	Rep	N.Y.	5	3					
6th Wilson, Pete	Rep	Cal.	3	1					

Changes:
House Minority:

Holt, Marjorie S.	Rep	Md.	Mar. 4,1985	Left committee; no new assignment.
Fiedler, Bobbi	Rep	Cal.	Mar. 4,1985	Replaced Holt.

	Majority		Minority	
Departures from the House:				
Lost Nomination to U.S. Senate	None		Fiedler, Bobbi	Cal. Rep
Lost Nomination for Lt. Governor	Mitchell, Parren J.	Md. Dem	None	
Departures from the Senate:				
Defeated for Reelection	Abdnor, James	S.D. Rep	None	
	Mattingly, Mack	Ga. Rep		
Departures from Committee:				
House:				
Moved to Select Intelligence	None		Lungren, Daniel E.	Cal. Rep

JOINT COMMITTEE: ECONOMIC / 100th Congress

Service Dates of Committee Chair: Jan. 12,1987-Continued
Service Dates of House Members: Jan. 21,1987-Jan. 3,1989
Service Dates of Senate Members: Jan. 12,1987-Feb. 2,1989

HOUSE — Majority

Rank	Name	Party	State	Terms in: House	Terms in: Comm.
VCh	Hamilton, Lee H.	Dem	Ind.	12	7
2nd	Obey, David R.	Dem	Wisc.	10	3
3rd	Hawkins, Augustus F.	Dem	Cal.	13	4
4th	Scheuer, James H.	Dem	N.Y.	11	3
5th	Stark, Fortney H. (Pete)	Dem	Cal.	8	2
6th	Solarz, Stephen J.	Dem	N.Y.	7	1

HOUSE — Minority

Rank	Name	Party	State	Terms in: House	Terms in: Comm.
1st	Wylie, Chalmers P.	Rep	Ohio	11	5
2nd	Snowe, Olympia J. B.	Rep	Me.	5	3
3rd	Fish, Hamilton Jr.	Rep	N.Y.	10	1
4th	McMillan, J. Alex	Rep	N.C.	2	1

SENATE — Majority

Rank	Name	Party	State	Years in: Senate	Years in: Comm.
Chr	Sarbanes, Paul S.	Dem	Md.	11	8
2nd	Bentsen, Lloyd M. Jr.	Dem	Tex.	17	16
3rd	Proxmire, William	Dem	Wisc.	30	26
4th	Kennedy, Edward M.	Dem	Mass.	25	12
5th	Melcher, John	Dem	Mont.	11	1
6th	Bingaman, Jeff	Dem	N.M.	5	1

SENATE — Minority

Rank	Name	Party	State	Years in: Senate	Years in: Comm.
1st	Roth, William V. Jr.	Rep	Del.	17	11
2nd	Symms, Steven D.	Rep	Ida.	7	7
3rd	D'Amato, Alfonse M.	Rep	N.Y.	7	5
4th	Wilson, Pete	Rep	Cal.	5	2

Note: "Service Dates of Senate Members" reflect the dates of service of Melcher and Bingaman; all other Senators continued service from the previous Congress without official reassignment recorded in the Congressional Record.

	Majority		Minority	
Departures from the Senate:				
Defeated for Reelection	Melcher, John	Mont. Dem	None	
Retired	Proxmire, William	Wisc. Dem	None	
Departures from Committee:				
House:				
No new assignment	None		McMillan, J. Alex	N.C. Rep
Senate:				
Moved to Select Intelligence	None		D'Amato, Alfonse M.	N.Y. Rep

JOINT COMMITTEE: ECONOMIC / 101st Congress

Service Dates of Committee Chair: Feb. 2,1989-Jan. 3,1991
Service Dates of House Members: Feb. 7,1989-Jan. 3,1991
Service Dates of Senate Members: Feb. 2,1989-Apr. 16,1991

HOUSE — Majority

Rank	Name	Party	State	Terms in: House	Terms in: Comm.
VCh	Hamilton, Lee H.	Dem	Ind.	13	8
2nd	Hawkins, Augustus F.	Dem	Cal.	14	5
3rd	Obey, David R.	Dem	Wisc.	11	4
4th	Scheuer, James H.	Dem	N.Y.	12	4
5th	Stark, Fortney H. (Pete)	Dem	Cal.	9	3
6th	Solarz, Stephen J.	Dem	N.Y.	8	2

HOUSE — Minority

Rank	Name	Party	State	Terms in: House	Terms in: Comm.
1st	Wylie, Chalmers P.	Rep	Ohio	12	6
2nd	Snowe, Olympia J. B.	Rep	Me.	6	4
3rd	Fish, Hamilton Jr.	Rep	N.Y.	11	2
4th	Upton, Frederick S.	Rep	Mich.	2	1

SENATE — Majority

Rank	Name	Party	State	Years in: Senate	Years in: Comm.
Chr	Sarbanes, Paul S.	Dem	Md.	13	11
2nd	Bentsen, Lloyd M. Jr.	Dem	Tex.	19	19
3rd	Kennedy, Edward M.	Dem	Mass.	27	15
4th	Bingaman, Jeff	Dem	N.M.	7	3
5th	Gore, Albert A. Jr.	Dem	Tenn.	5	1
6th	Bryan, Richard H.	Dem	Nev.	1	1

SENATE — Minority

Rank	Name	Party	State	Years in: Senate	Years in: Comm.
1st	Roth, William V. Jr.	Rep	Del.	19	13
2nd	Symms, Steven D.	Rep	Ida.	9	9
3rd	Wilson, Pete	Rep	Cal.	7	4
4th	Mack, Connie III	Rep	Fla.	1	1

	Majority		Minority	
Departures from the House:				
Retired	Hawkins, Augustus	Cal. Dem	None	
Departures from the Senate:				
Elected Governor	None		Wilson, Pete	Cal. Rep
Departures from Committee:				
No new assignment	None		Upton, Frederick S.	Mich. Rep

JOINT COMMITTEE: ECONOMIC / 102nd Congress

Service Dates of Committee Chair: Mar. 7,1989-Jan. 3,1993
Service Dates of House Members: Mar. 7,1991-Jan. 3,1993
Service Dates of Senate Members: Apr. 16,1991-Jan. 3,1993

HOUSE

Majority Rank Name	Party	State	Terms in: House	Comm.	Minority Rank Name	Party	State	Terms in: House	Comm.
Chr Hamilton, Lee H.	Dem	Ind.	14	9	1st Armey, Dick	Rep	Tex.	3	1
2nd Obey, David R.	Dem	Wisc.	12	5	2nd Wylie, Chalmers P.	Rep	Ohio	13	7
3rd Scheuer, James H.	Dem	N.Y.	13	5	3rd Snowe, Olympia J. B.	Rep	Me.	7	5
4th Stark, Fortney H. (Pete)	Dem	Cal.	10	4	4th Fish, Hamilton Jr.	Rep	N.Y.	12	3
5th Solarz, Stephen J.	Dem	N.Y.	9	3					
6th Mfume, Kweisi	Dem	Md.	2	1					

SENATE

Majority Rank Name	Party	State	Years in: Senate	Comm.	Minority Rank Name	Party	State	Years in: Senate	Comm.
VCh Sarbanes, Paul S.	Dem	Md.	15	13	1st Roth, William V. Jr.	Rep	Del.	21	15
2nd Bentsen, Lloyd M. Jr.	Dem	Tex.	21	21	2nd Symms, Steven D.	Rep	Ida.	11	11
3rd Kennedy, Edward M.	Dem	Mass.	29	17	3rd Mack, Connie III	Rep	Fla.	3	3
4th Bingaman, Jeff	Dem	N.M.	9	5	4th Smith, Robert C.	Rep	N.H.	1	1
5th Gore, Albert A. Jr.	Dem	Tenn.	7	3					
6th Bryan, Richard H.	Dem	Nev.	3	3					

JOINT COMMITTEE: ATOMIC ENERGY

Jurisdiction, 1946

From Public Law 79-585, the Atomic Energy Act of 1946, 79th Congress, Second Session, August 1, 1946 (60 Statutes 775, 772-773):

[Section 15]

(b) The joint committee shall make continuing studies of the activities of the Atomic Energy Commission and of problems relating to the development, use, and control of atomic energy. The Commission shall keep the joint committee fully and currently informed with respect to the Commission's activities. All bills, resolutions, and other matters in the Senate or the House of Representatives relating primarily to the Commission or to the development, use, or control of atomic energy shall be referred to the joint committee. The members of the joint committee who are Members of the Senate shall from time to time report to the Senate, and the members of the joint committee who are Members of the House of Representatives shall from time to time report to the House, by bill or otherwise, their recommendations with respect to matters within the jurisdiction of their respective Houses which are (1) referred to the joint committee or (2) otherwise within the jurisdiction of the joint committee.

Jurisdiction, 1954

From Public Law 83-703, the Atomic Energy Act of 1954, 83rd Congress, Second Session, August 30, 1954 (68 Statutes 919, 956):

[Section 202]

. . . During the first sixty days of each session of the Congress, the joint committee shall conduct hearings in either open or executive session for the purpose of receiving information concerning the development, growth, and state of the atomic energy industry. The Commission shall keep the joint committee fully and currently informed with respect to all of the Commission's activities. The Department of Defense shall keep the joint committee fully and currently informed with respect to all matters within the Department of Defense relating to the development, utilization, or application of atomic energy. Any Government agency shall furnish any information requested by the joint committee with respect to the activities or responsibilities of that agency in the field of atomic energy . . . .

Jurisdiction, 1975

From the Senate Manual for the 94th Congress (1975):

[Section 566]

(a) The joint committee shall make continuing studies of the activities of the Atomic Energy Commission and of problems relating to the development, use, and control of atomic energy. During the first ninety days of each session of the Congress, the joint committee may conduct hearings in either open or executive session for the purpose of receiving information concerning the development, growth, and state of the atomic energy industry. The Commission shall keep the joint committee fully and currently informed with respect to all of the Commission's activities. The Department of Defense shall keep the joint committee fully and currently informed with respect to all matters within the Department of Defense relating to the development, utilization, or application of atomic energy. Any Government agency shall furnish any information requested by the joint committee with respect to the activities or responsibilities of that agency in the field of atomic energy. All bills, resolutions, and other matters in the Senate or the House of Representatives relating primarily to the Commission or to the development, use, or control of atomic energy shall be referred to the joint committee. The members of the joint committee who are Members of the Senate shall from time to time report to the Senate, and the members of the joint committee who are Members of the House of Representatives shall from time to time report to the House, by bill or otherwise, their recommendations with respect to matters within the jurisdiction of their respective Houses which are referred to the joint committee or otherwise within the jurisdiction of the joint committee.

(b) The members of the joint committee who are Members of the Senate and the members of the joint committee who are Members of the House of Representatives shall, on or before June 30, of each year, report to their respective Houses on the development, use, and control of nuclear energy for the common defense and security and for peaceful purposes. Each report shall provide facts and information available to the joint committee concerning nuclear energy which will assist the appropriate committees of the Congress and individual members in the exercise of informed judgment on matters of weaponry; foreign policy; defense; international trade; and in respect to the expenditure and appropriation of Government revenues. Each report shall be presented formally under circumstances which provide for clarification and discussion by the Senate and the House of Representatives. In recognition of the need for public understanding, presentations of the reports shall be made to the maximum extent possible in open sessions and by means of unclassified written materials.

Termination, 1977

The Joint Committee was terminated by authority of Public Law 110, signed September 20, 1977.

JOINT COMMITTEE: ATOMIC ENERGY / 80th Congress

Service Dates of Committee Chair: Jan. 20,1947-Jan. 27,1949
Service Dates of House Members: Jan. 20,1947-Jan. 3,1949
Service Dates of Senate Members: Jan. 20,1947-Continued

HOUSE

Majority: Rank Name	Party	State	Terms in: House	Comm.	Minority: Rank Name	Party	State	Terms in: House	Comm.
VCh Cole, W. Sterling	Rep	N.Y.	7	1	1st Thomason, R. Ewing	Dem	Tex.	9	2
2nd Elston, Charles H.	Rep	Ohio	5	2	2nd Durham, Carl T.	Dem	N.C.	5	2
3rd Hinshaw, Carl	Rep	Cal.	5	2	3rd Holifield, Chet	Dem	Cal.	3	2
4th Van Zandt, James E.	Rep	Penn.	4	1	4th Price, C. Melvin	Dem	Ill.	2	2
5th Patterson, James T.	Rep	Conn.	1 *1	1					

SENATE

Majority: Rank Name	Party	State	Years in: Senate	Comm.	Minority: Rank Name	Party	State	Years in: Senate	Comm.
Chr Hickenlooper, Bourke B.	Rep	Iowa	3	1	1st McMahon, Brien	Dem	Conn.	3	1
2nd Vandenberg, Arthur H.	Rep	Mich.	19	1	2nd Russell, Richard B.	Dem	Ga.	14	1
3rd Millikin, Eugene D.	Rep	Colo.	6	1	3rd Johnson, Edwin C.	Dem	Colo.	11	1
4th Knowland, William F.	Rep	Cal.	2	1	4th Connally, Thomas T.	Dem	Tex.	18	1
5th Bricker, John W.	Rep	Ohio	1 *1	1					

*1: Member's 1st period of service on the committee.

Note: John W. Bricker (Rep-Ohio) was the only new Senate member of the committee appointed in the 80th Congress; all others were "hold-over reappointments" whose names were listed Jan. 20,1947 in the Congressional Record.

Changes:
House Minority:

Name	Party	State	Date	Action
Thomason, R. Ewing	Dem	Tex.	July 26,1947	Left committee; no new assignment.
Johnson, Lyndon B.	Dem	Tex.	July 31,1947	Replaced Thomason.

	Majority		Minority	
Departures from the House:				
Elected to U.S. Senate	None		Johnson, Lyndon B.	Tex. Dem
Departures from Committee:				
House:				
Moved to Armed Services	Patterson, James T.	Conn. Rep	None	
Senate:				
Moved to Interstate & Foreign Commerce	Bricker, John W.	Ohio Rep	None	

JOINT COMMITTEE: ATOMIC ENERGY / 81st Congress

Service Dates of Committee Chair: Jan. 24,1949-Jan. 3,1951
Service Dates of House Members: Jan. 27,1949-Jan. 3,1951
Service Dates of Senate Members: Jan. 24,1949-Continued

HOUSE

Majority

Rank Name	Party	State	Terms in: House	Terms in: Comm.
VCh Durham, Carl T.	Dem	N.C.	6	3
2nd Holifield, Chet	Dem	Cal.	4	3
3rd Price, C. Melvin	Dem	Ill.	3	3
4th Kilday, Paul J.	Dem	Tex.	6	1
5th Jackson, Henry M.	Dem	Wash.	5	*1 1

Minority

Rank Name	Party	State	Terms in: House	Terms in: Comm.
1st Cole, W. Sterling	Rep	N.Y.	8	2
2nd Elston, Charles H.	Rep	Ohio	6	3
3rd Hinshaw, Carl	Rep	Cal.	6	3
4th Van Zandt, James E.	Rep	Penn.	5	2

SENATE

Majority

Rank Name	Party	State	Years in: Senate	Years in: Comm.
Chr McMahon, Brien	Dem	Conn.	5	3
2nd Russell, Richard B.	Dem	Ga.	16	3
3rd Johnson, Edwin C.	Dem	Colo.	13	3
4th Connally, Thomas T.	Dem	Tex.	20	3
5th Tydings, Millard E.	Dem	Md.	22	1

Minority

Rank Name	Party	State	Years in: Senate	Years in: Comm.
1st Vandenberg, Arthur H.	Rep	Mich.	21	3
2nd Millikin, Eugene D.	Rep	Colo.	8	3
3rd Knowland, William F.	Rep	Cal.	4	3
4th Hickenlooper, Bourke B.	Rep	Iowa	5	3

*1: Member's first period of service on the committee.

Note: "Service Dates of Senate Members" reflect the dates of service of Tydings; all other Senators continued service from the previous Congress without official reappointment recorded in the Congressional Record.

Changes:

Senate Minority:

Name	Party	State	Date	Change
Vandenberg, Arthur H.	Rep	Mich.	Jan. 30,1950	Left committee; no new assignment.
Bricker, John W.	Rep	Ohio	Jan. 30,1950	Replaced Vandenberg.

Departures from the Senate:

	Majority			Minority
Defeated for Reelection	Tydings, Millard E.	Md.	Dem	None

JOINT COMMITTEE: ATOMIC ENERGY / 82nd Congress

Service Dates of Committee Chair: Ch1 Jan. 18,1951-July 28,1952
ChA July 28,1952-Jan. 3,1953
Service Dates of House Members: Jan. 29,1951-Jan. 3,1953
Service Dates of Senate Members: Jan. 18,1951-Continued

HOUSE

Majority

Rank Name	Party	State	Terms in: House	Terms in: Comm.
VCh Durham, Carl T.	Dem	N.C.	7	4
2nd Holifield, Chet	Dem	Cal.	5	4
3rd Price, C. Melvin	Dem	Ill.	4	4
4th Kilday, Paul J.	Dem	Tex.	7	2
5th Jackson, Henry M.	Dem	Wash.	6	*1 2

Minority

Rank Name	Party	State	Terms in: House	Terms in: Comm.
1st Cole, W. Sterling	Rep	N.Y.	9	3
2nd Elston, Charles H.	Rep	Ohio	7	4
3rd Hinshaw, Carl	Rep	Cal.	7	4
4th Van Zandt, James E.	Rep	Penn.	6	3

SENATE

Majority

Rank Name	Party	State	Years in: Senate	Years in: Comm.
Chr McMahon, Brien	Dem	Conn.	7	5
2nd Russell, Richard B.	Dem	Ga.	18	5
3rd Johnson, Edwin C.	Dem	Colo.	15	5
4th Connally, Thomas T.	Dem	Tex.	22	5
5th Anderson, Clinton P.	Dem	N.M.	3	1

Minority

Rank Name	Party	State	Years in: Senate	Years in: Comm.
1st Hickenlooper, Bourke B.	Rep	Iowa	7	5
2nd Millikin, Eugene D.	Rep	Colo.	10	5
3rd Knowland, William F.	Rep	Cal.	6	5
4th Bricker, John W.	Rep	Ohio	5	*2 2

*1: Member's 1st period of service on the committee; *2: Member's 2nd period of service on the committee.

Note: "Service Dates of Senate Members" reflect the dates of service of Anderson; all other Senators continued service from the previous Congress without official reappointment recorded in the Congressional Record.

Changes:
Chair:

Ch1 McMahon, Brien	Dem	Conn.	July 28,1952	Died in office.
ChA Durham, Carl T.	Dem	N.C.	July 28,1952	Succeeded McMahon as Acting Chair.

Senate Majority:

Connally, Thomas T.	Dem	Tex.	July 5,1952	Left committee; no new assignment.
Johnson, Lyndon B.	Dem	Tex.	July 5,1952	Replaced Connally.
McMahon, Brien	Dem	Conn.	July 28,1952	Died in office.
Pastore, John O.	Dem	R.I.	Aug. 8,1952	Replaced McMahon.

Departures from the House:	**Majority**		**Minority**	
Elected to U.S. Senate	Jackson, Henry M.	Wash. Dem	None	
Retired	None		Elston, Charles H.	Ohio Rep
Departures from Committee:				
House:				
Moved to Interstate & Foreign Commerce	Pastore, John O.	R.I. Dem	None	

JOINT COMMITTEE: ATOMIC ENERGY / 83rd Congress

Service Dates of Committee Chair: Jan. 29,1953-Jan. 3,1955
Service Dates of House Members: Jan. 29,1953-Jan. 3,1955
Service Dates of Senate Members: Jan. 26,1953-Continued

HOUSE

Majority Rank Name	Party	State	Terms in: House	Comm.	Minority Rank Name	Party	State	Terms in: House	Comm.
Chr Cole, W. Sterling	Rep	N.Y.	10	4	1st Durham, Carl T.	Dem	N.C.	8	5
2nd Hinshaw, Carl	Rep	Cal.	8	5	2nd Holifield, Chet	Dem	Cal.	6	5
3rd Van Zandt, James E.	Rep	Penn.	7	4	3rd Price, C. Melvin	Dem	Ill.	5	5
4th Patterson, James T.	Rep	Conn.	4	*2 1	4th Kilday, Paul J.	Dem	Tex.	8	3
5th Jenkins, Thomas A.	Rep	Ohio	15	*1 1					

SENATE

Majority Rank Name	Party	State	Years in: Senate	Comm.	Minority Rank Name	Party	State	Years in: Senate	Comm.
VCh Hickenlooper, Bourke B.	Rep	Iowa	9	7	1st Russell, Richard B.	Dem	Ga.	20	7
2nd Millikin, Eugene D.	Rep	Colo.	12	7	2nd Johnson, Edwin C.	Dem	Colo.	17	7
3rd Knowland, William F.	Rep	Cal.	8	7	3rd Anderson, Clinton P.	Dem	N.M.	5	3
4th Bricker, John W.	Rep	Ohio	7	*2 3	4th Johnson, Lyndon B.	Dem	Tex.	5	*2 1
5th Cordon, Guy	Rep	Ore.	9	1					

*1: Member's 1st period of service on the committee; *2: Member's 2nd period of service on the committee.

Note: "Service Dates of Senate Members" reflect the dates of service of Cordon; all other Senators continued service from the previous Congress without official reappointment recorded in the Congressional Record.

Changes:
Senate Minority:

Johnson, Lyndon B.	Dem	Tex.	June 3,1953	Left committee; no new assignment.
Pastore, John O.	Dem	R.I.	June 3,1953	Replaced Johnson (Lyndon B.).
Johnson, Edwin C.	Dem	Colo.	Nov. 8,1954	Left committee; no new assignment.
Gore, Albert A.	Dem	Tenn.	Nov. 8,1954	Replaced Johnson (Edwin C.).

Departures from the Senate:	**Majority**		**Minority**
Defeated for Reelection	Cordon, Guy	Ore. Rep	None
Departures from Committee:			
House:			
No new assignment	Jenkins, Thomas A.	Ohio Rep	None

JOINT COMMITTEE: ATOMIC ENERGY / 84th Congress

Service Dates of Committee Chair: Jan. 19,1955-Jan. 7,1957 (election reported Jan. 21,1955)
Service Dates of House Members: Jan. 10,1955-Jan. 3,1957
Service Dates of Senate Members: Jan. 14,1955-Continued

HOUSE

Majority Rank	Name	Party	State	Terms in: House	Terms in: Comm.	Minority Rank	Name	Party	State	Terms in: House	Terms in: Comm.
VCh	Durham, Carl T.	Dem	N.C.	9	6	1st	Cole, W. Sterling	Rep	N.Y.	11	5
2nd	Holifield, Chet	Dem	Cal.	7	6	2nd	Hinshaw, Carl	Rep	Cal.	9	6
3rd	Price, C. Melvin	Dem	Ill.	6	6	3rd	Van Zandt, James E.	Rep	Penn.	8	5
4th	Kilday, Paul J.	Dem	Tex.	9	4	4th	Patterson, James T.	Rep	Conn.	5	*2 2
5th	Dempsey, John J.	Dem	N.M.	6	1						

SENATE

Majority Rank	Name	Party	State	Years in: Senate	Years in: Comm.	Minority Rank	Name	Party	State	Years in: Senate	Years in: Comm.
Chr	Anderson, Clinton P.	Dem	N.M.	7	4	1st	Hickenlooper, Bourke B.	Rep	Iowa	11	9
2nd	Russell, Richard B.	Dem	Ga.	22	9	2nd	Millikin, Eugene D.	Rep	Colo.	14	9
3rd	Pastore, John O.	Dem	R.I.	5	*2 2	3rd	Knowland, William F.	Rep	Cal.	10	9
4th	Gore, Albert A.	Dem	Tenn.	3	1	4th	Bricker, John W.	Rep	Ohio	9	*2 5
5th	Jackson, Henry M.	Dem	Wash.	3	*2 1						

*2: Member's 2nd period of service on the committee.

Note: "Service Dates of Senate Members" reflect the dates of service of Jackson; all other Senators continued service from the previous Congress without official reappointment recorded in the Congressional Record.

Changes:
House Minority:
Hinshaw, Carl Rep Cal. Aug. 5,1956 Died in office.

Departures from the Senate:	Majority	Minority	
Retired	None	Millikin, Eugene D.	Colo. Rep

JOINT COMMITTEE: ATOMIC ENERGY / 85th Congress

Service Dates of Committee Chair: Jan. 7,1957-Jan. 3,1959
Service Dates of House Members: Jan. 7,1957-Jan. 3,1959
Service Dates of Senate Members: Jan. 30,1957-Continued

HOUSE

Majority Rank	Name	Party	State	Terms in: House	Terms in: Comm.	Minority Rank	Name	Party	State	Terms in: House	Terms in: Comm.
Chr	Durham, Carl T.	Dem	N.C.	10	7	1st	Cole, W. Sterling	Rep	N.Y.	12	6
2nd	Holifield, Chet	Dem	Cal.	8	7	2nd	Van Zandt, James E.	Rep	Penn.	9	6
3rd	Price, C. Melvin	Dem	Ill.	7	7	3rd	Patterson, James T.	Rep	Conn.	6	*2 3
4th	Kilday, Paul J.	Dem	Tex.	10	5	4th	Jenkins, Thomas A.	Rep	Ohio	17	*2 1
5th	Dempsey, John J.	Dem	N.M.	7	2						

SENATE

Majority Rank	Name	Party	State	Years in: Senate	Years in: Comm.	Minority Rank	Name	Party	State	Years in: Senate	Years in: Comm.
VCh	Anderson, Clinton P.	Dem	N.M.	9	6	1st	Hickenlooper, Bourke B.	Rep	Iowa	13	11
2nd	Russell, Richard B.	Dem	Ga.	24	11	2nd	Knowland, William F.	Rep	Cal.	12	11
3rd	Pastore, John O.	Dem	R.I.	7	*2 4	3rd	Bricker, John W.	Rep	Ohio	11	*2 7
4th	Gore, Albert A.	Dem	Tenn.	5	3	4th	Dworshak, Henry C.	Rep	Ida.	10	1
5th	Jackson, Henry M.	Dem	Wash.	5	*2 2						

*2: Member's 2nd period of service on the committee.

Note: "Service Dates of Senate Members" reflect the dates of service of Dworshak; all other Senators continued service from the previous Congress without official reappointment recorded in the Congressional Record.

Vacancy Filled:
House Minority: 4th seat by Jenkins on Jan. 28,1957.

Changes:
House Majority:

Dempsey, John J.	Dem	N.M.	Mar. 11,1958	Died in office.
Aspinall, Wayne N.	Dem	Colo.	Mar. 17,1958	Replaced Dempsey.

House Minority:

Cole, W. Sterling	Rep	N.Y.	Dec. 1,1957	Resigned; appointed Director General of the International Atomic Energy Agency.

	Majority	Minority		
Departures from the House:				
Defeated for Reelection	None	Patterson, James T.	Conn.	Rep
Retired	None	Jenkins, Thomas A.	Ohio	Rep
Departures from the Senate:				
Defeated for Reelection	None	Bricker, John W.	Ohio	Rep
Lost Election for Governor	None	Knowland, William F.	Cal.	Rep

JOINT COMMITTEE: ATOMIC ENERGY / 86th Congress

Service Dates of Committee Chair: Jan. 29,1959-Feb. 9,1961
Service Dates of House Members: Jan. 19,1959-Jan. 3,1961
Service Dates of Senate Members: Jan. 29,1959-Continued

HOUSE **Majority**

Rank Name	Party	State	Terms in: House	Comm.
VCh Durham, Carl T.	Dem	N.C.	11	8
2nd Holifield, Chet	Dem	Cal.	9	8
3rd Price, C. Melvin	Dem	Ill.	8	8
4th Kilday, Paul J.	Dem	Tex.	11	6
5th Aspinall, Wayne N.	Dem	Colo.	6	2

Minority

Rank Name	Party	State	House	Comm.
1st Van Zandt, James E.	Rep	Penn.	10	7
2nd Hosmer, Craig	Rep	Cal.	4	1
3rd Bates, William H.	Rep	Mass.	6	1
4th Westland, Alfred John	Rep	Wash.	4	1

SENATE **Majority**

Rank Name	Party	State	Years in: Senate	Comm.
Chr Anderson, Clinton P.	Dem	N.M.	11	8
2nd Russell, Richard B.	Dem	Ga.	27	13
3rd Pastore, John O.	Dem	R.I.	9	*2 6
4th Gore, Albert A.	Dem	Tenn.	7	5
5th Jackson, Henry M.	Dem	Wash.	7	*2 4

Minority

Rank Name	Party	State	Years in: Senate	Comm.
1st Hickenlooper, Bourke B.	Rep	Iowa	15	13
2nd Dworshak, Henry C.	Rep	Ida.	12	2
3rd Aiken, George D.	Rep	Vt.	19	1
4th Bennett, Wallace F.	Rep	Utah	9	1

*2: Member's 2nd period of service on the committee.

Notes: On Jan. 29,1959, Senate minority rankings listed Bennett before Aiken. The order was rearranged as listed here on Feb. 5,1959. "Service Dates of Senate Members" reflect the dates of service of Aiken and Bennett; all other Senators continued service from the previous Congress without official reappointment recorded in the Congressional Record.

Changes:
House Majority:

Kilday, Paul J.	Dem	Tex.	Feb. 16,1959	Left committee to become Ranking Minority Member of Armed Services; letter dated Jan. 21,1959.
Thomas, Albert	Dem	Tex.	Feb. 16,1959	Replaced Kilday.

	Majority			Minority
Departures from the House:				
Retired	Durham, Carl T.	N.C.	Dem	None

JOINT COMMITTEE: ATOMIC ENERGY / 87th Congress

Service Dates of Committee Chair: Feb. 9,1961-Jan. 2,1963
Service Dates of House Members: Feb. 9,1961-Jan. 3,1963
Service Dates of Senate Members: Jan. 3,1961-Continued

HOUSE **Majority** / **Minority**

Rank Name	Party	State	Terms in: House	Terms in: Comm.	Rank Name	Party	State	Terms in: House	Terms in: Comm.
Chr Holifield, Chet	Dem	Cal.	10	9	1st Van Zandt, James E.	Rep	Penn.	11	8
2nd Price, C. Melvin	Dem	Ill.	9	9	2nd Hosmer, Craig	Rep	Cal.	5	2
3rd Aspinall, Wayne N.	Dem	Colo.	7	3	3rd Bates, William H.	Rep	Mass.	7	2
4th Thomas, Albert	Dem	Tex.	13	2	4th Westland, Alfred John	Rep	Wash.	5	2
5th Morris, Thomas G.	Dem	N.M.	2	1					

SENATE **Majority** / **Minority**

Rank Name	Party	State	Years in: Senate	Years in: Comm.	Rank Name	Party	State	Years in: Senate	Years in: Comm.
VCh Pastore, John O.	Dem	R.I.	11	*2 8	1st Hickenlooper, Bourke B.	Rep	Iowa	17	15
2nd Russell, Richard B.	Dem	Ga.	28	15	2nd Dworshak, Henry C.	Rep	Ida.	14	4
3rd Anderson, Clinton P.	Dem	N.M.	13	10	3rd Aiken, George D.	Rep	Vt.	21	2
4th Gore, Albert A.	Dem	Tenn.	9	7	4th Bennett, Wallace F.	Rep	Utah	11	2
5th Jackson, Henry M.	Dem	Wash.	9	*2 6					

*2: Member's 2nd period of service on the committee.

Changes:
Senate Minority:

Dworshak, Henry C.	Rep	Ida.	July 23,1962	Died in office.
Dirksen, Everett M.	Rep	Ill.	July 31,1962	Replaced Dworshak.

	Majority	Minority	
Departures from the House:			
Lost Nomination to U.S. Senate	None	Van Zandt, James E.	Penn. Rep
Departures from Committee:			
Senate:			
Moved to Finance	None	Dirksen, Everett McK.	Ill. Rep

JOINT COMMITTEE: ATOMIC ENERGY / 88th Congress

Service Dates of Committee Chair: Feb. 11,1963-Jan. 18,1965
Service Dates of House Members: Jan. 14,1963-Jan. 3,1965
Service Dates of Senate Members: Jan. 11,1963-Continued

HOUSE **Majority** / **Minority**

Rank Name	Party	State	Terms in: House	Terms in: Comm.	Rank Name	Party	State	Terms in: House	Terms in: Comm.
VCh Holifield, Chet	Dem	Cal.	11	10	1st Hosmer, Craig	Rep	Cal.	6	3
2nd Price, C. Melvin	Dem	Ill.	10	10	2nd Bates, William H.	Rep	Mass.	8	3
3rd Aspinall, Wayne N.	Dem	Colo.	8	4	3rd Westland, Alfred John	Rep	Wash.	6	3
4th Thomas, Albert	Dem	Tex.	14	3	4th Anderson, John B.	Rep	Ill.	2	1
5th Morris, Thomas G.	Dem	N.M.	3	2					

SENATE **Majority** / **Minority**

Rank Name	Party	State	Years in: Senate	Years in: Comm.	Rank Name	Party	State	Years in: Senate	Years in: Comm.
Chr Pastore, John O.	Dem	R.I.	13	*2 10	1st Hickenlooper, Bourke B.	Rep	Iowa	19	17
2nd Russell, Richard B.	Dem	Ga.	30	17	2nd Aiken, George D.	Rep	Vt.	23	4
3rd Anderson, Clinton P.	Dem	N.M.	15	12	3rd Bennett, Wallace F.	Rep	Utah	13	4
4th Gore, Albert A.	Dem	Tenn.	11	9	4th Curtis, Carl T.	Rep	Neb.	9	1
5th Jackson, Henry M.	Dem	Wash.	11	*2 8					

*2: Member's 2nd period of service on the committee.

Note: "Service Dates of Senate Members" reflect the dates of service of Curtis; all other Senators continued service from the previous Congress without official reappointment recorded in the Congressional Record.

Vacancy Filled:
House Minority: 4th seat by Anderson on Jan. 31,1963.

Departures from the House:	**Majority**	**Minority**	
Defeated for Reelection	None	Westland, Alfred John	Wash. Rep

JOINT COMMITTEE: ATOMIC ENERGY / 89th Congress

Service Dates of Committee Chair: Jan. 18,1965-Jan. 3,1967
Service Dates of House Members: Jan. 18,1965-Jan. 3,1967
Service Dates of Senate Members: Jan. 3,1965-Continued

HOUSE

Majority Rank Name	Party	State	Terms in: House	Comm.	Minority Rank Name	Party	State	Terms in: House	Comm.
Chr Holifield, Chet	Dem	Cal.	12	11	1st Hosmer, Craig	Rep	Cal.	7	4
2nd Price, C. Melvin	Dem	Ill.	11	11	2nd Bates, William H.	Rep	Mass.	9	4
3rd Aspinall, Wayne N.	Dem	Colo.	9	5	3rd Anderson, John B.	Rep	Ill.	3	2
4th Thomas, Albert	Dem	Tex.	15	4	4th McCulloch, William M.	Rep	Ohio	10	1
5th Morris, Thomas G.	Dem	N.M.	4	3					

SENATE

Majority Rank Name	Party	State	Years in: Senate	Comm.	Minority Rank Name	Party	State	Years in: Senate	Comm.
VCh Pastore, John O.	Dem	R.I.	15 *2	12	1st Hickenlooper, Bourke B.	Rep	Iowa	21	19
2nd Russell, Richard B.	Dem	Ga.	32	19	2nd Aiken, George D.	Rep	Vt.	25	6
3rd Anderson, Clinton P.	Dem	N.M.	17	14	3rd Bennett, Wallace F.	Rep	Utah	15	6
4th Gore, Albert A.	Dem	Tenn.	13	11	4th Curtis, Carl T.	Rep	Neb.	11	2
5th Jackson, Henry M.	Dem	Wash.	13*2	10					

*2: Member's 2nd period of service on the committee.

Vacancy Filled:
House Minority: 4th seat by McCulloch on Feb. 4,1965.

Changes:
House Majority:

Thomas, Albert	Dem	Tex.	Feb. 15,1966	Died in office.
Young, John A.	Dem	Tex.	Mar. 1,1966	Replaced Thomas.

JOINT COMMITTEE: ATOMIC ENERGY / 90th Congress

Service Dates of Committee Chair: Jan. 17,1967-Feb. 3,1969
Service Dates of House Members: Jan. 17,1967-Jan. 3,1969
Service Dates of Senate Members: Jan. 3,1967-Continued

HOUSE

Majority Rank Name	Party	State	Terms in: House	Comm.	Minority Rank Name	Party	State	Terms in: House	Comm.
VCh Holifield, Chet	Dem	Cal.	13	12	1st Hosmer, Craig	Rep	Cal.	8	5
2nd Price, C. Melvin	Dem	Ill.	12	12	2nd Bates, William H.	Rep	Mass.	10	5
3rd Aspinall, Wayne N.	Dem	Colo.	10	6	3rd Anderson, John B.	Rep	Ill.	4	3
4th Morris, Thomas G.	Dem	N.M.	5	4	4th McCulloch, William M.	Rep	Ohio	11	2
5th Young, John A.	Dem	Tex.	6	2					

SENATE **Majority**

Rank	Name	Party	State	Years in: Senate	Comm.
Chr	Pastore, John O.	Dem	R.I.	17	*2 14
2nd	Russell, Richard B.	Dem	Ga.	34	21
3rd	Anderson, Clinton P.	Dem	N.M.	19	16
4th	Gore, Albert A.	Dem	Tenn.	15	13
5th	Jackson, Henry M.	Dem	Wash.	15*2	12

Minority

Rank	Name	Party	State	Years in: Senate	Comm.
1st	Hickenlooper, Bourke B.	Rep	Iowa	23	21
2nd	Aiken, George D.	Rep	Vt.	27	8
3rd	Bennett, Wallace F.	Rep	Utah	17	8
4th	Curtis, Carl T.	Rep	Neb.	13	4

*2: Member's 2nd period of service on the committee.

	Majority		Minority	
Departures from the House:				
Defeated for Reelection	Morris, Thomas G.	N.M. Dem	None	
Departures from the Senate:				
Retired	None		Hickenlooper, Bourke B.	Iowa Rep

JOINT COMMITTEE: ATOMIC ENERGY / 91st Congress

Service Dates of Committee Chair: Feb. 3,1969-Jan. 3,1971
Service Dates of House Members: Feb. 3,1969-Jan. 3,1971
Service Dates of Senate Members: Jan. 23,1969-Continued

HOUSE **Majority**

Rank	Name	Party	State	Terms in: House	Comm.
Chr	Holifield, Chet	Dem	Cal.	14	13
2nd	Price, C. Melvin	Dem	Ill.	13	13
3rd	Aspinall, Wayne N.	Dem	Colo.	11	7
4th	Young, John A.	Dem	Tex.	7	3
5th	Edmondson, Edmond A.	Dem	Okla.	9	1

Minority

Rank	Name	Party	State	Terms in: House	Comm.
1st	Hosmer, Craig	Rep	Cal.	9	6
2nd	Bates, William H.	Rep	Mass.	11	6
3rd	Anderson, John B.	Rep	Ill.	5	4
4th	McCulloch, William M.	Rep	Ohio	12	3

SENATE **Majority**

Rank	Name	Party	State	Years in: Senate	Comm.
VCh	Pastore, John O.	Dem	R.I.	19	*2 16
2nd	Russell, Richard B.	Dem	Ga.	36	23
3rd	Anderson, Clinton P.	Dem	N.M.	21	18
4th	Gore, Albert A.	Dem	Tenn.	17	15
5th	Jackson, Henry M.	Dem	Wash.	17	*2 14

Minority

Rank	Name	Party	State	Years in: Senate	Comm.
1st	Aiken, George D.	Rep	Vt.	29	10
2nd	Bennett, Wallace F.	Rep	Utah	19	10
3rd	Curtis, Carl T.	Rep	Neb.	15	6
4th	Cotton, Norris	Rep	N.H.	15	1

*2: Member's 2nd period of service on the committee.

Note: "Service Dates of Senate Members" reflect the dates of service of Cotton; all other Senators continued service from the previous Congress without official reappointment recorded in the Congressional Record.

Changes:

House Minority:

Bates, William H.	Rep	Mass.	June 22,1969	Died in office.
May, Catherine D.	Rep	Wash.	July 24,1969	Replaced Bates.

Senate Majority:

Russell, Richard B.	Dem	Ga.	Jan. 21,1971	Died in office.

	Majority		Minority	
Departures from the House:				
Defeated for Reelection	None		May, Catherine D.	Wash. Rep
Departures from the Senate:				
Defeated for Reelection	Gore, Albert A.	Tenn. Dem	None	
Departures from Committee:				
Senate:				
No new assignment	None		Cotton, Norris	N.H. Rep
			Curtis, Carl T.	Neb. Rep

JOINT COMMITTEE: ATOMIC ENERGY / 92nd Congress

Service Dates of Committee Chair: Jan. 28,1971-Jan. 26,1973
Service Dates of House Members: Jan. 29,1971-Jan. 3,1973
Service Dates of Senate Members: Jan. 28,1971-Continued

HOUSE

Majority

Rank Name	Party	State	Terms in: House	Terms in: Comm.
VCh Price, C. Melvin	Dem	Ill.	14	14
2nd Holifield, Chet	Dem	Cal.	15	14
3rd Aspinall, Wayne N.	Dem	Colo.	12	8
4th Young, John A.	Dem	Tex.	8	4
5th Edmondson, Edmond A.	Dem	Okla.	10	2

Minority

Rank Name	Party	State	Terms in: House	Terms in: Comm.
1st Hosmer, Craig	Rep	Cal.	10	7
2nd Anderson, John B.	Rep	Ill.	6	5
3rd McCulloch, William M.	Rep	Ohio	13	4
4th Hansen, Orval H.	Rep	Ida.	2	1

SENATE

Majority

Rank Name	Party	State	Years in: Senate	Years in: Comm.
Chr Pastore, John O.	Dem	R.I.	21	*2 18
2nd Anderson, Clinton P.	Dem	N.M.	23	20
3rd Jackson, Henry M.	Dem	Wash.	19	*2 16
4th Symington, W. Stuart	Dem	Mo.	19	1
5th Bible, Alan H.	Dem	Nev.	17	1

Minority

Rank Name	Party	State	Years in: Senate	Years in: Comm.
1st Aiken, George D.	Rep	Vt.	31	12
2nd Bennett, Wallace F.	Rep	Utah	21	12
3rd Dominick, Peter H.	Rep	Colo.	9	1
4th Baker, Howard H. Jr.	Rep	Tenn.	5	1

*2: Member's 2nd period of service on the committee.

Note: "Service Dates of Senate Members" reflect the dates of service of Symington and Bible; all other Senators continued service from the previous Congress without official reappointment recorded in the Congressional Record.

Vacancies Filled:
House Minority: 4th by Hansen on Feb. 10,1971.
Senate Minority: 3rd and 4th by Dominick and Baker respectively on Feb. 10,1971.

	Majority		Minority	
Departures from the House:				
Defeated for Renomination	Aspinall, Wayne N.	Colo. Dem	None	
Lost Election for Senate	Edmondson, Edmond A.	Okla. Dem	None	
Retired	None		McCulloch, William M.	Ohio Rep
Departures from the Senate:				
Retired	Anderson, Clinton P.	N.M. Dem	None	

JOINT COMMITTEE: ATOMIC ENERGY / 93rd Congress

Service Dates of Committee Chair: Jan. 26,1973-Jan. 17,1975
Service Dates of House Members: Jan. 26,1973-Jan. 3,1975
Service Dates of Senate Members: Jan. 4,1973-Continued

HOUSE

Majority

Rank Name	Party	State	Terms in: House	Terms in: Comm.
Chr Price, C. Melvin	Dem	Ill.	15	15
2nd Holifield, Chet	Dem	Cal.	16	15
3rd Young, John A.	Dem	Tex.	9	5
4th Roncalio, Teno	Dem	Wyo.	3	1
5th McCormack, Mike	Dem	Wash.	2	1

Minority

Rank Name	Party	State	Terms in: House	Terms in: Comm.
1st Hosmer, Craig	Rep	Cal.	11	8
2nd Anderson, John B.	Rep	Ill.	7	6
3rd Hansen, Orval H.	Rep	Ida.	3	2
4th Lujan, Manuel Jr.	Rep	N.M.	3	1

SENATE

Majority

Rank Name	Party	State	Years in: Senate	Years in: Comm.
VCh Pastore, John O.	Dem	R.I.	23	*2 20
2nd Jackson, Henry M.	Dem	Wash.	21	*2 18
3rd Symington, W. Stuart	Dem	Mo.	21	2
4th Bible, Alan H.	Dem	Nev.	19	2
5th Montoya, Joseph M.	Dem	N.M.	9	1

Minority

Rank Name	Party	State	Years in: Senate	Years in: Comm.
1st Aiken, George D.	Rep	Vt.	33	14
2nd Bennett, Wallace F.	Rep	Utah	23	14
3rd Dominick, Peter H.	Rep	Colo.	11	2
4th Baker, Howard H. Jr.	Rep	Tenn.	7	2

*2: Member's 2nd period of service on the committee.

Note: "Service Dates of Senate Members" reflect the dates of service of Montoya; all other Senators continued service from the previous Congress without official reappointment recorded in the Congressional Record.

Changes:

House Majority:				
Holifield, Chet	Dem	Cal.	Dec. 13,1974	Left committee; resigned House Dec. 31,1974.
Moss, John E. Jr.	Dem	Cal.	Dec. 13,1974	Replaced Holifield.
House Minority:				
Hosmer, Craig	Rep	Cal.	Dec. 31,1974	Resigned and retired.
Senate Majority:				
Bible, Alan H.	Dem	Nev.	Dec. 17,1974	Resigned and retired.
Senate Minority:				
Bennett, Wallace F.	Rep	Utah	Dec. 20,1974	Resigned and retired.

	Majority	Minority		
Departures from the House:				
Defeated for Renomination	None	Hansen, Orval H.	Ida.	Rep
Departures from the Senate:				
Defeated for Reelection	None	Dominick, Peter H.	Colo.	Rep
Retired	None	Aiken, George D.	Vt.	Rep

JOINT COMMITTEE: ATOMIC ENERGY / 94th Congress

Service Dates of Committee Chair: Jan. 17,1975-Dec. 28,1976
Service Dates of House Members: Jan. 29,1975-Jan. 3,1977
Service Dates of Senate Members: Jan. 17,1975-Continued

HOUSE

Majority			Terms in:		Minority			Terms in:	
Rank Name	Party	State	House	Comm.	Rank Name	Party	State	House	Comm.
VCh Price, C. Melvin	Dem	Ill.	16	16	1st Anderson, John B.	Rep	Ill.	8	7
2nd Young, John A.	Dem	Tex.	10	6	2nd Lujan, Manuel Jr.	Rep	N.M.	4	2
3rd Roncalio, Teno	Dem	Wyo.	4	2	3rd Horton, Frank J.	Rep	N.Y.	7	1
4th McCormack, Mike	Dem	Wash.	3	2	4th Hinshaw, Andrew J.	Rep	Cal.	2	1
5th Moss, John E. Jr.	Dem	Cal.	12	2					

SENATE

Majority			Years in:		Minority			Years in:	
Rank Name	Party	State	Senate	Comm.	Rank Name	Party	State	Senate	Comm.
Chr Pastore, John O.	Dem	R.I.	25	*2 22	1st Baker, Howard H. Jr.	Rep	Tenn.	9	4
2nd Jackson, Henry M.	Dem	Wash.	23	*2 20	2nd Case, Clifford P.	Rep	N.J.	21	1
3rd Symington, W. Stuart	Dem	Mo.	23	4	3rd Pearson, James B.	Rep	Kans.	13	1
4th Montoya, Joseph M.	Dem	N.M.	11	2	4th Buckley, James L.	Con	N.Y.	5	1
5th Tunney, John V.	Dem	Cal.	5	1					

*2: Member's 2nd period of service on the committee.

Notes: James L. Buckley of New York was elected as a Conservative, but was assigned to the committee by the Republican Conference. "Service Dates of Senate Members" reflect the dates of service of Tunney, Case, Pearson and Buckley; all other Senators continued service from the previous Congress without official reappointment recorded in the Congressional Record.

Changes:

House Majority:				
Moss, John E. Jr.	Dem	Cal.	May 3,1976	Left committee; no new assignment.
Brown, George E. Jr.	Dem	Cal.	May 3,1976	Replaced Moss.
Senate Majority:				
Pastore, John O.	Dem	R.I.	Dec. 28,1976	Resigned and retired.
Symington, W. Stuart	Dem	Mo.	Dec. 27,1976	Resigned and retired.
Tunney, John V.	Dem	Cal.	Jan. 1,1977	Resigned; defeated for reelection.
Senate Minority:				
Buckley, James L.	Con	N.Y.	Nov. 30,1976	Left committee; no new assignment (reported Jan. 10,1977).
Domenici, Pete V.	Rep	N.M.	Nov. 30,1976	Replaced Buckley (reported Jan. 10,1977).

JOINT COMMITTEE: ATOMIC ENERGY / 95th Congress

Service Dates of Committee Chair: Feb. 11, 1977-Sep. 20,1977
Service Dates of House Members: Jan. 3,1977-Sep. 20,1977
Service Dates of Senate Members: Jan. 3,1977-Sep. 20,1977

HOUSE

Majority

Rank	Name	Party	State	Terms in: House	Terms in: Comm.
VCh	Price, C. Melvin	Dem	Ill.	17	17
2nd	Young, John A.	Dem	Tex.	11	7
3rd	Roncalio, Teno	Dem	Wyo.	5	3
4th	McCormack, Mike	Dem	Wash.	4	3
5th	Brown, George E. Jr.	Dem	Cal.	7	2

Minority

Rank	Name	Party	State	Terms in: House	Terms in: Comm.
1st	Anderson, John B.	Rep	Ill.	9	8
2nd	Lujan, Manuel Jr.	Rep	N.M.	5	3
3rd	Horton, Frank J.	Rep	N.Y.	8	2
4th	Hinshaw, Andrew J.	Rep	Cal.	3	2

SENATE

Majority

Rank	Name	Party	State	Years in: Senate	Years in: Comm.
Chr	Jackson, Henry M.	Dem	Wash.	25	*2 22
2nd	Montoya, Joseph M.	Dem	N.M.	13	4

Minority

Rank	Name	Party	State	Years in: Senate	Years in: Comm.
1st	Baker, Howard H. Jr.	Rep	Tenn.	11	6
2nd	Case, Clifford P.	Rep	N.J.	23	3
3rd	Pearson, James B.	Rep	Kans.	15	3
4th	Domenici, Pete V.	Rep	N.M.	5	1

*2: Member's 2nd period of service on the committee.

Note: Due to the imminent abolition of the Joint Committee, the membership was not officially reappointed, nor was a full complement of Senate members assigned.

Changes:

Chair:

Jackson, Henry M.	Dem	Wash.	Feb. 11,1977	Confirmed as Committee Chair.

JOINT COMMITTEE: LEGISLATIVE BUDGET

Jurisdiction, 1947

From Public Law 79-601, the Legislative Reorganization Act of 1946, 79th Congress, Second Session, August 2, 1946 (60 Statutes 812, 832-833):

[Section 138]

(a) The Committee on Ways and Means and the Committee on Appropriations of the House of Representatives, and the Committee on Finance and the Committee on Appropriations of the Senate, or duly authorized subcommittees thereof, are authorized and directed to meet jointly at the beginning of each regular session of Congress and after study and consultation, giving due consideration to the budget recommendations of the President, report to their respective Houses a legislative budget for the ensuing fiscal year, including the estimated over-all Federal receipts and expenditures for such year. Such report shall contain a recommendation for the maximum amount to be appropriated for expenditure in such year which shall include such an amount to be reserved for deficiencies as may be deemed necessary by such committees. If the estimated receipts exceed the estimated expenditures, such report shall contain a recommendation for a reduction in the public debt. Such report shall be made by February 15.

(b) The report shall be accompanied by a concurrent resolution adopting such budget, and fixing the maximum amount to be appropriated for expenditure in such year. If the estimated expenditures exceed the estimated receipts, the concurrent resolution shall include a section substantially as follows: "That it is the sense of the Congress that the public debt shall be increased in an amount equal to the amount by which the estimated expenditures for the ensuing fiscal year exceed the estimated receipts, such amount being $."

Termination, 1971

The Joint Committee was officially terminated by authority of Public Law 91-510, the Legislative Reorganization Act, signed into law January 3, 1971. However, no members from the House were ever appointed to the Joint Committee, and a full complement of Senate members was never appointed.

JOINT COMMITTEE: LEGISLATIVE BUDGET / 81st Congress

Service Dates of Senate Members: Feb. 7,1949-Jan. 3,1951

SENATE

Majority Rank Name	Party	State	Years in: Senate	Years in: Comm.	Minority Rank Name	Party	State	Years in: Senate	Years in: Comm.
1st McKellar, Kenneth D.	Dem	Tenn.	32	1	1st Bridges, H. Styles	Rep	N.H.	13	1
2nd Hayden, Carl	Dem	Ariz.	22	1	2nd Gurney, J. Chandler	Rep	S.D.	11	1
3rd Thomas, Elmer	Dem	Okla.	22	1					

Departures from the Senate:	Majority	Minority		
Defeated for Renomination	None	Gurney, J. Chandler	S.D.	Rep

JOINT COMMITTEE: LABOR-MANAGEMENT RELATIONS

Jurisdiction, 1947

From Public Law 80-101, the Labor-Management Relations Act of 1947, 80th Congress, First Session, June 23, 1947 (61 Statutes 136, 160):

[Section 402]

The committee, acting as a whole or by subcommittee, shall conduct a thorough study and investigation of the entire field of labor-management relations, including but not limited to--
(1) the means by which permanent friendly cooperation between employers and employees and stability of labor relations may be secured throughout the United States;
(2) the means by which the individual employee may achieve a greater productivity and higher wages, including plans for guaranteed annual wages, incentive profit-sharing and bonus systems;
(3) the internal organization and administration of labor unions, with special attention to the impact on individuals of collective agreements requiring membership in unions as a condition of employment;
(4) the labor relations policies and practices of employers and associations of employment;
(5) the desirability of welfare funds for the benefit of employees and their relation to the social-security system;
(6) the methods and procedures for best carrying out the collective-bargaining processes, with special attention to the effects of industry-wide or regional bargaining upon the national economy;
(7) the administration and operation of existing Federal laws relating to labor relations; and
(8) such other problems and subjects in the field of labor-management relations as the committee deems appropriate.

Termination, 1949

The joint committee filed its so-called final report, Senate Report #986 (80-2), on December 31, 1948. The joint committee was extended by Senate Concurrent Resolution 10 (81-1), agreed to by both chambers on April 14, 1949, until May 14, 1949. Senate Reports #372 and #374 were filed on May 12 and May 13 respectively by the committee.

JOINT COMMITTEE: LABOR-MANAGEMENT RELATIONS / 80th Congress

Service Dates of Committee Chair: July 3,1947-Jan. 3,1949
Service Dates of House Members: July 17,1947-Jan. 3,1949
Service Dates of Senate Members: July 3,1947-Feb. 3,1949

HOUSE

Majority Rank Name	Party	State	Terms in: House	Comm.	Minority Rank Name	Party	State	Terms in: House	Comm.
VCh Hartley, Fred A. Jr.	Rep	N.J.	10	1	1st Lesinski, John	Dem	Mich.	8	1
2nd Landis, Gerald W.	Rep	Ind.	5	1	2nd Barden, Graham A.	Dem	N.C.	7	1
3rd Hoffman, Clare E.	Rep	Mich.	7	1	3rd Kelley, Augustine B.	Dem	Penn.	4	1
4th McCowen, Edward O.	Rep	Ohio	3	1					

SENATE

Majority Rank Name	Party	State	Years in: Senate	Comm.	Minority Rank Name	Party	State	Years in: Senate	Comm.
Chr Ball, Joseph H.	Rep	Minn.	7	1	1st Murray, James E.	Dem	Mont.	13	1
1st Taft, Robert A.	Rep	Ohio	9	1	2nd Pepper, Claude D.	Dem	Fla.	11	1
3rd Smith, H. Alexander	Rep	N.J.	3	1	3rd Ellender, Allen J.	Dem	La.	11	1
4th Ives, Irving M.	Rep	N.Y.	1	1					

Departures from the House:	Majority			Minority
Defeated for Reelection	Landis, Gerald W.	Ind.	Rep	None
	McCowen, Edward O.	Ohio	Rep	
Retired	Hartley, Fred A. Jr.	N.J.	Rep	None

Departures from the Senate:					
Defeated for Reelection	Ball, Joseph H.	Minn. Rep	None		
Departures from Committee:					
House:					
No new assignment	Hoffman, Clare E.	Mich. Rep	None		
Senate:					
Moved to Appropriations	None		Ellender, Allen J.	La.	Dem

JOINT COMMITTEE: LABOR-MANAGEMENT RELATIONS / 81st Congress

Service Dates of Committee Chair: Feb. 3,1949-May 13,1949
Service Dates of House Members: Jan. 31,1949-May 13,1949
Service Dates of Senate Members: Feb. 3,1949-May 13,1949

HOUSE

Majority Rank Name	Party	State	Terms in: House	Comm.	**Minority** Rank Name	Party	State	Terms in: House	Comm.
VCh Lesinski, John	Dem	Mich.	9	2	1st McConnell, Samuel K. Jr.	Rep	Penn.	4	1
3rd Kelley, Augustine B.	Dem	Penn.	5	2	2nd Gwinn, Ralph W.	Rep	N.Y.	3	1
2nd Barden, Graham A.	Dem	N.C.	8	2	3rd Smith, Wint	Rep	Kans.	2	1
4th Kennedy, John F.	Dem	Mass.	2	1					

SENATE

Majority Rank Name	Party	State	Years in: Senate	Comm.	**Minority** Rank Name	Party	State	Years in: Senate	Comm.
Chr Murray, James E.	Dem	Mont.	15	2	1st Taft, Robert A.	Rep	Ohio	11	2
2nd Pepper, Claude D.	Dem	Fla.	13	2	2nd Smith, H. Alexander	Rep	N.J.	5	2
3rd Neely, Matthew M.	Dem	W.Va.	17	1	3rd Ives, Irving M.	Rep	N.Y.	3	2
4th Humphrey, Hubert H. Jr.	DFL	Minn.	1	1					

JOINT COMMITTEE: HOUSING

Jurisdiction, 1947

From House Concurrent Resolution 104, 80th Congress, First Session, July 26, 1947:

[Section 2]

The committee, acting as a whole or by subcommittee, shall conduct a thorough study and investigation of the entire field of housing, including but not limited to--

(1) the extent of the need for housing in the United States as a whole and in all areas thereof;
(2) the extent, if any, to which shortages in building materials are contributing to the shortage of housing;
(3) the reasons for the existing high cost of building materials and housing and the action which may be taken to reduce such costs;
(4) all factors of whatever kind or nature which contribute to the existing high costs of housing and which prevent the speedy construction of adequate housing to satisfy the needs of the Nation and the action which may be taken to eliminate such factors;
(5) the extent to which archaic building codes and zoning laws contribute to the existing shortage and excessive cost of housing;
(6) the administration and operation of existing Federal laws relating to slum clearance, insurance of mortgages on housing, home loans, guarantees of veterans' housing loans, construction permits, veterans' preference in the renting and purchase of housing, rent control, and all other matters relating to housing;
(7) the availability of private capital and of Government loans to finance the construction of housing;
(8) the organization and operations of Federal, State, and municipal government agencies concerned with housing; and
(9) such other problems and subjects in the field of housing as the committee deems appropriate.

Termination, 1948

The joint committee was extended by House Concurrent Resolution 197 (80-2), agreed to on May 11, 1948, and terminated by its authority on June 15,1948. Its final report, Senate Report #1564 was filed on March 15, 1948, with a minority report, Senate Report #1019, filed March 22, 1948.

JOINT COMMITTEE: HOUSING / 80th Congress

Service Dates of Committee Chair: July 26,1947-Mar. 15,1948
Service Dates of House Members: July 30,1947-Mar. 15,1948
Service Dates of Senate Members: July 26,1947-Mar. 15,1948

HOUSE Majority

Rank Name	Party	State	Terms in: House	Comm.
Chr Gamble, Ralph A.	Rep	N.Y.	6	1
2nd Sundstrom, Frank L.	Rep	N.J.	3	1
3rd McMillen, Rolla C.	Rep	Ill.	3	1
4th Fletcher, Charles K.	Rep	Cal.	1	1

HOUSE Minority

Rank Name	Party	State	Terms in: House	Comm.
1st Patman, J.W. Wright	Dem	Tex.	10	1
2nd Rains, Albert	Dem	Ala.	2	1
3rd Boggs, T. Hale	Dem	La.	2	1

SENATE Majority

Rank Name	Party	State	Years in: Senate	Comm.
VCh McCarthy, Joseph R.	Rep	Wisc.	1	1
2nd Tobey, Charles W.	Rep	N.H.	9	1
3rd Flanders, Ralph E.	Rep	Vt.	1	1
4th Cain, Harry P.	Rep	Wash.	1	1

SENATE Minority

Rank Name	Party	State	Years in: Senate	Comm.
1st Wagner, Robert F.	Dem	N.Y.	21	1
2nd Taylor, Glen H.	Dem	Ida.	3	1
3rd Sparkman, John J.	Dem	Ala.	1	1

JOINT COMMITTEE: FOREIGN ECONOMIC COOPERATION

Jurisdiction, 1948

From Public Law 80-472, the Economic Cooperation Act of 1948, 80th Congress, Second Session, April 3, 1948 (62 Statutes 137, 156):

[Section 124]

(b) It shall be the function of the committee to make a continuous study of the programs of United States economic assistance to foreign countries, and to review the progress achieved in the execution and administration of such programs. Upon request, the committee shall aid the several standing committees of the Congress having legislative jurisdiction over any part of the programs of United States economic assistance to foreign countries; and it shall make a report to the Senate and the House of Representatives, from time to time, concerning the results of its studies, together with such recommendations as it may deem desirable. The Administrator, at the request of the committee, shall consult with the committee from time to time with respect to his activities under this Act.

Termination, 1950

The Joint Committee was terminated upon the filing of its final reports, Senate Documents #142 (81-2), on March 3, 1950, and Senate Document #144 on March 8,1950. Patrick McCarran, Chair of the Joint Committee, read the prepared study entitled "An Analysis of the ECA Program" into the Senate Record on June 16, 1950.

JOINT COMMITTEE: FOREIGN ECONOMIC COOPERATION / 80th Congress

Service Dates of Committee Chair: Apr. 7,1948-Jan. 31,1949
Service Dates of House Members: Apr. 22,1948-Jan. 3,1949
Service Dates of Senate Members: Apr. 7,1948-Jan. 31,1949

HOUSE

Majority			Terms in:		Minority			Terms in:	
Rank Name	Party	State	House	Comm.	Rank Name	Party	State	House	Comm.
1st Taber, John	Rep	N.Y.	13	1	1st Bloom, Sol	Dem	N.Y.	13	1
2nd Vorys, John M.	Rep	Ohio	5	1	2nd Cannon, Clarence	Dem	Mo.	13	1
3rd Fulton, James G.	Rep	Penn.	2	1					

SENATE

Majority			Years in:		Minority			Years in:	
Rank Name	Party	State	Senate	Comm.	Rank Name	Party	State	Senate	Comm.
Chr Bridges, H. Styles	Rep	N.H.	12	1	1st Connally, Thomas T.	Dem	Tex.	20	1
2nd Smith, H. Alexander	Rep	N.J.	4	1	2nd McCarran, Patrick A.	Dem	Nev.	16	1
3rd Lodge, Henry Cabot Jr.	Rep	Mass.	9	1					

Departures from Committee:	Majority		Minority
House:			
No new assignment	Fulton, James G.	Penn. Rep	None
Senate:			
Moved to Joint Library	Lodge, Henry Cabot Jr.	Mass. Rep	None

JOINT COMMITTEE: FOREIGN ECONOMIC COOPERATION / 81st Congress

Service Dates of Committee Chair: Jan. 31,1949-Mar. 8,1950
Service Dates of House Members: Jan. 28,1949-Mar. 8,1950
Service Dates of Senate Members: Jan. 31,1949-Mar. 8,1950

HOUSE

Majority			Terms in:		Minority			Terms in:	
Rank Name	**Party**	**State**	**House**	**Comm.**	**Rank Name**	**Party**	**State**	**House**	**Comm.**
1st Bloom, Sol	Dem	N.Y.	14	2	1st Taber, John	Rep	N.Y.	14	2
2nd Cannon, Clarence	Dem	Mo.	14	2	2nd Vorys, John M.	Rep	Ohio	6	2
3rd Kee, John	Dem	W.Va.	9	1					

SENATE

Majority			Years in:		Minority			Years in:	
Rank Name	**Party**	**State**	**Senate**	**Comm.**	**Rank Name**	**Party**	**State**	**Senate**	**Comm.**
Chr McCarran, Patrick A.	Dem	Nev.	16	1	1st Bridges, H. Styles	Rep	N.H.	13	1
2nd Connally, Thomas T.	Dem	Tex.	20	1	2nd Smith, H. Alexander	Rep	N.J.	5	1
3rd George, Walter F.	Dem	Ga.	27	1					

Note: "Service Dates of Senate Members" reflect the dates of service of member of the Foreign Relations committee: Connally, George and Smith; all other Senators continued service from the previous Congress without official reassignment recorded in the Congressional Record.

Changes:

House Majority:

Bloom, Sol	Dem	N.Y.	Mar. 7,1949	Died in office.
Richards, James P.	Dem	S.C.	Mar. 14,1949	Replaced Bloom.

JOINT COMMITTEE: INAUGURAL CEREMONIES

Jurisdiction, 1948

From Senate Concurrent Resolution 48, 80th Congress, Second Session, April 7, 1948. Passed by the Senate on April 28, 1948; passed by the House of Representatives on May 5, 1948:

Resolved by the Senate (the House of Representatives concurring), That a joint committee consisting of three Senators and three Representatives, to be appointed by the President pro tempore of the Senate and the Speaker of the House of Representatives, respectively, is authorized to make the necessary arrangements for the inauguration of the President-elect of the United States on the 20th day of January 1949.

From Senate Concurrent Resolution 84, 96th Congress, Second Session, March 27, 1980. Passed by the Senate on March 27, 1980; passed by the House of Representatives on April 1, 1980:

Resolved by the Senate (the House of Representatives concurring), That a Joint Congressional Committee on Inaugural Ceremonies consisting of three Senators and three Representatives, to be appointed by the President of the Senate and the Speaker of the House of Representatives, respectively, is authorized to make the necessary arrangements for the inauguration of the President-elect and Vice President-elect of the United States on the 20th day of January 1981.

Note: The committee changed little in its jurisdiction during the nine Congresses in which it was created. Originally, only the President-elect's inauguration was mentioned but beginning in 1956, the Vice-President-elect's inauguration was added to the resolution (Senate Concurrent Resolution 64).

The resolutions and their dates of passage for each of the inaugurations between 1949 and 1993 are listed below:

Harry S. Truman's inauguration in 1949: Senate Concurrent Resolution 48, 80th Congress, Second Session, April 7, 1948. Passed by the Senate on April 28, 1948; passed by the House of Representatives on May 5, 1948.

Dwight D. Eisenhower's first inauguration in 1953: Senate Concurrent Resolution 69, 82nd Congress, Second Session, March 24, 1952. Passed by the Senate on March 25, 1952; passed by the House of Representatives on March 31, 1952.

Eisenhower's second inauguration in 1957: Senate Concurrent Resolution 64, 84th Congress, Second Session, February 3, 1956. Amended by the House to change the date from January 20 to January 21, 1957 on February 7, 1956. Passed the Senate on February 3, 1956; passed by the House of Representatives on February 7, 1956; and passed again as amended by the Senate on February 16, 1956.

John F. Kennedy's inauguration in 1961: Senate Concurrent Resolution 92, 86th Congress, Second Session, February 24, 1960. Passed by the Senate on April 27, 1960; passed by the House of Representatives on April 28, 1960.

Lyndon B. Johnson's inauguration in 1965: Senate Concurrent Resolution 71, 88th Congress, Second Session, February 7, 1964. Passed by the Senate on April 16, 1964; passed by the House of Representatives on April 20, 1964.

Richard M. Nixon's first inauguration in 1969: Senate Concurrent Resolution 73, 90th Congress, Second Session, May 29, 1968. Passed by the Senate on May 29, 1968; passed by the House of Representatives on June 4, 1968.

Nixon's second inauguration in 1973: Senate Concurrent Resolution 63, 92nd Congress, Second Session, February 24, 1972. Passed by the Senate on March 24, 1972; passed by the House of Representatives on March 27, 1972.

Jimmy Carter's inauguration in 1977: Senate Concurrent Resolution 90, 94th Congress, Second Session, January 29, 1976. Passed by the Senate on January 29, 1976; passed by the House of Representatives on February 18, 1976.

Ronald Reagan's inauguration in 1981: Senate Concurrent Resolution 84, 96th Congress, Second Session, March 27, 1980. Passed by the Senate on March 27, 1980; passed by the House of Representatives on April 1, 1980.

Ronald Reagan's inauguration in 1985: Senate Concurrent Resolution 122, 98th Congress, Second Session, June 28, 1984. Passed by the Senate on June 28, 1984; passed by the House of Representatives on June 29, 1984.

George Bush's inauguration in 1989: Senate Concurrent Resolution 105, 100th Congress, Second Session, March 18, 1988. Passed by the Senate on March 18, 1988; passed by the House of Representatives on June 28, 1988.

Bill Clinton's inauguration in 1993: Senate Concurrent Resolution 102, 102nd Congress, Second Session, March 25, 1992. Passed by the Senate on March 25, 1992; passed by the House of Representatives on June 29, 1992.

Note: Much of the work done by this Joint Committee is undertaken during the adjournment of Congress. For this reason, many personnel changes are not reported exactly in official records of Congress.

JOINT COMMITTEE: INAUGURAL CEREMONIES (for Truman) / 80th Congress

Service Dates of Committee Chairs: Ch1 May 5,1948-Nov. 13,1948
Ch2 Nov. 13,1948-Jan. 20,1949
Service Dates of House Members: May 13,1948-Jan. 3,1949
Service Dates of Senate Members: May 5,1948-Jan. 20,1949

HOUSE **Majority**

Rank	Name	Party	State	Terms in: House	Terms in: Comm.
1st	Halleck, Charles A.	Rep	Ind.	7	*1 1
2nd	Arends, Leslie C.	Rep	Ill.	7	*1 1

Minority

Rank	Name	Party	State	Terms in: House	Terms in: Comm.
1st	McCormack, John W.	Dem	Mass.	11	*1 1

SENATE **Majority**

Rank	Name	Party	State	Years in: Senate	Terms in: Comm.
Ch1	Brooks, C. Wayland	Rep	Ill.	8	1
2nd	Wherry, Kenneth S.	Rep	Neb.	6	1

Minority

Rank	Name	Party	State	Years in: Senate	Terms in: Comm.
1st	Barkley, Alben W.	Dem	Ky.	22	1

*1: Member's 1st period of service on the committee.

Note: Republicans Leslie Arends and Wayland Brooks were replaced by Democrats Carl Hayden and Harry Sheppard due to the victory of Democrat Harry S Truman for the Presidency.

Changes:

Chair:					
Ch1	Brooks, C. Wayland	Rep	Ill.	Nov. 13,1948	Left committee due to Democratic victory.
Ch2	Hayden, Carl	Dem	Ariz.	Nov. 13,1948	Succeeded Brooks as Chair.
House Majority:					
	Arends, Leslie C.	Rep	Ill.	Nov. 29,1948	Left committee due to Democratic victory.
	Sheppard, Harry R.	Dem	Cal.	Nov. 29,1948	Replaced Arends.
Senate Majority:					
	Brooks, C. Wayland	Rep	Ill.	Nov. 13,1948	Left committee due to Democratic victory.
	Hayden, Carl	Dem	Ariz.	Nov. 13,1948	Replaced Brooks.
Senate Minority:					
	Barkley, Alben W.	Dem	Ky.	Nov. 13,1948	Left committee; elected Vice President.
	McGrath, J. Howard	Dem	R.I.	Nov. 13,1948	Replaced Barkley.

81st Congress

Service Dates of House Members: Jan. 3,1949-Jan. 20,1949

HOUSE **Majority**

Rank	Name	Party	State	Terms in: House	Terms in: Comm.
1st	McCormack, John W.	Dem	Mass.	12	*1 2
2nd	Sheppard, Harry R.	Dem	Cal.	7	2

Minority

Rank	Name	Party	State	Terms in: House	Terms in: Comm.
1st	Halleck, Charles A.	Rep	Ind.	8	*1 2

*1: Member's 1st period of service on the committee.

JOINT COMMITTEE: INAUGURAL CEREMONIES (for Eisenhower) / 82nd Congress

Service Dates of Committee Chairs: Ch1 Apr. 8,1952-Nov. 1952
Ch2 Nov. 1952-Jan. 20,1953
Service Dates of House Members: May 21,1952-Jan. 3,1953
Service Dates of Senate Members: Apr. 8,1952-Jan. 20,1953

HOUSE

Majority Rank Name	Party	State	Terms in: House	Terms in: Comm.	Minority Rank Name	Party	State	Terms in: House	Terms in: Comm.
1st Rayburn, Sam	Dem	Tex.	20	1	1st Martin, Joseph W. Jr.	Rep	Mass.	14	1
2nd McCormack, John W.	Dem	Mass.	13	*1 3					

SENATE

Majority Rank Name	Party	State	Years in: Senate	Terms in: Comm.	Minority Rank Name	Party	State	Years in: Senate	Terms in: Comm.
Ch1 Hayden, Carl	Dem	Ariz.	26	2	Ch2 1st Bridges, H. Styles	Rep	N.H.	16	1
2nd McFarland, Ernest W.	Dem	Ariz.	12	1					

*1: Member's 1st period of service on the committee.

Changes:

Chair:

Ch1 Hayden, Carl	Dem	Ariz.	Jan. 6,1953	Relinquished Chair due to Republican victory.
Ch2 Bridges, H. Styles	Rep	N.H.	Jan. 6,1953	Succeeded Hayden as Chair.

Senate:

McFarland, Ernest W.	Dem	Ariz.	Nov. 1952	Left committee; defeated for reelection (reported Jan. 3,1953).
Smith, Margaret Chase	Rep	Me.	Nov. 1952	Appointed to replace McFarland, unable to serve (reported Jan. 3,1953).
Welker, Herman	Rep	Ida.	Nov. 1952	Replaced McFarland (reported Jan. 3,1953).

83rd Congress

Service Dates of House Members: Jan. 3,1953-Jan. 20,1953

HOUSE

Majority Rank Name	Party	State	Terms in: Senate	Terms in: Comm.	Minority Rank Name	Party	State	Terms in: Senate	Terms in: Comm.
1st Martin, Joseph W. Jr.	Rep	Mass.	15	2	1st Rayburn, Sam	Dem	Tex.	21	2
2nd Arends, Leslie C.	Rep	Ill.	10	*2 1					

*2: Member's 2nd period of service on the committee.

JOINT COMMITTEE: INAUGURAL CEREMONIES (for Eisenhower) / 84th Congress

Service Dates of House Members: Apr. 18,1956-Jan. 3,1957
Service Dates of Senate Members: Apr. 16,1956-Jan. 20,1957

HOUSE

Majority Rank Name	Party	State	Terms in: House	Terms in: Comm.	Minority Rank Name	Party	State	Terms in: House	Terms in: Comm.
1st Rayburn, Sam	Dem	Tex.	22	3	1st Martin, Joseph W. Jr.	Rep	Mass.	16	3
2nd McCormack, John W.	Dem	Mass.	15	*2 1					

SENATE

Majority Rank Name	Party	State	Years in: Senate	Terms in: Comm.	Minority Rank Name	Party	State	Years in: Senate	Terms in: Comm.
1st Green, Theodore F.	Dem	R.I.	20	1	Chr Bridges, H. Styles	Rep	N.H.	20	2
2nd Sparkman, John J.	Dem	Ala.	10	1					

*2: Member's 2nd period of service on the committee.

85th Congress

Service Dates of House Members: Jan. 3,1957-Jan. 20,1957

HOUSE — Majority / Minority

Rank	Name	Party	State	Terms in: House	Comm.	Rank	Name	Party	State	Terms in: House	Comm.
1st	Rayburn, Sam	Dem	Tex.	23	4	1st	Martin, Joseph W. Jr.	Rep	Mass.	17	4
2nd	McCormack, John W.	Dem	Mass.	16	*2 2						

*2: Member's 2nd period of service on the committee.

JOINT COMMITTEE: INAUGURAL CEREMONIES (for Kennedy) / 86th Congress

Service Dates of Committee Chair: June 20,1960-Jan. 20,1961
Service Dates of House Members: May 25,1960-Jan. 3,1961
Service Dates of Senate Members: June 20,1960-Jan. 20,1961

HOUSE — Majority / Minority

Rank	Name	Party	State	Terms in: Senate	Comm.	Rank	Name	Party	State	Terms in: Senate	Comm.
1st	Rayburn, Sam	Dem	Tex.	24	5	1st	Halleck, Charles A.	Rep	Ind.	13	*2 1
2nd	McCormack, John W.	Dem	Mass.	17	*2 3						

SENATE — Majority / Minority

Rank	Name	Party	State	Years in: House	Terms in: Comm.	Rank	Name	Party	State	Years in: Senate	Terms in: Comm.
Chr	Sparkman, John J.	Dem	Ala.	14	2	1st	Bridges, H. Styles	Rep	N.H.	24	3
2nd	Hennings, Thomas C. Jr.	Dem	Mo.	10	1						

*2: Member's 2nd period of service on the committee.

Changes:

Senate Majority:

Hennings, Thomas C. Jr.	Dem	Mo.	Sep. 13,1960	Died in office.
Hayden, Carl	Dem	Ariz.	Sep. 14,1960	Replaced Hennings (reported after adjournment).

87th Congress

Service Dates of House Members: Jan. 3,1961-Jan. 20,1961

HOUSE — Majority / Minority

Rank	Name	Party	State	Terms in: House	Comm.	Rank	Name	Party	State	Terms in: House	Comm.
1st	Rayburn, Sam	Dem	Tex.	25	6	1st	Halleck, Charles A.	Rep	Ind.	14	*2 2
2nd	McCormack, John W.	Dem	Mass.	18	*2 4						

*2: Member's 2nd period of service on the committee.

JOINT COMMITTEE: INAUGURAL CEREMONIES (for Johnson) / 88th Congress

Service Dates of Committee Chair: May 15,1964-Jan. 20,1965
Service Dates of House Members: Apr. 20,1964-Jan. 3,1965
Service Dates of Senate Members: May 15,1964-Jan. 20,1965

HOUSE — Majority / Minority

Rank	Name	Party	State	Terms in: Senate	Comm.	Rank	Name	Party	State	Terms in: Senate	Comm.
1st	McCormack, John W.	Dem	Mass.	19	*2 5	1st	Halleck, Charles A.	Rep	Ind.	15	*2 3
2nd	Albert, Carl	Dem	Okla.	9	1						

SENATE — **Majority**

Rank	Name	Party	State	Years in: Senate	Terms in: Comm.
Chr	Jordan, B. Everett	Dem	N.C.	7	1
2nd	Sparkman, John J.	Dem	Ala.	18	3

Minority

Rank	Name	Party	State	Years in: Senate	Terms in: Comm.
1st	Saltonstall, Leverett	Rep	Mass.	20	1

*2: Member's 2nd period of service on the committee.

89th Congress

Service Dates of House Members: Jan. 3,1965-Jan. 20,1965

HOUSE — **Majority**

Rank	Name	Party	State	Terms in: House	Terms in: Comm.
1st	McCormack, John W.	Dem	Mass.	20	*2 6
2nd	Albert, Carl	Dem	Okla.	10	2

Minority

Rank	Name	Party	State	Terms in: House	Terms in: Comm.
1st	Ford, Gerald R. Jr.	Rep	Mich.	9	1

*2: Member's 2nd period of service on the committee.

JOINT COMMITTEE: INAUGURAL CEREMONIES (for Nixon) / 90th Congress

Service Dates of Committee Chairs: Ch1 June 6,1968-Nov. 1968
Ch2 Nov. ,1968-Jan. 20,1969
Service Dates of House Members: June 4,1968-Jan. 3,1969
Service Dates of Senate Members: June 6,1968-Jan. 20,1969

HOUSE — **Majority**

Rank	Name	Party	State	Terms in: House	Terms in: Comm.
1st	McCormack, John W.	Dem	Mass.	21	*2 7
2nd	Albert, Carl	Dem	Okla.	11	3

Minority

Rank	Name	Party	State	Terms in: House	Terms in: Comm.
1st	Ford, Gerald R. Jr.	Rep	Mich.	10	2

SENATE — **Majority**

Rank	Name	Party	State	Years in: Senate	Terms in: Comm.
Ch1	Jordan, B. Everett	Dem	N.C.	11	2
2nd	Mansfield, Michael J.	Dem	Mont.	16	1

Minority

Rank	Name	Party	State	Years in: Senate	Terms in: Comm.
Ch2 1st	Dirksen, Everett M.	Rep	Ill.	18	1

*2: Member's 2nd period of service on the committee.

Changes:
Chair:

Ch1	Jordan, B. Everett	Dem	N.C.	Jan. 3,1968	Relinquished Chair due to Republican victory.
Ch2	Dirksen, Everett M.	Rep	Ill.	Jan. 3,1968	Succeeded Jordan as Chair.

91st Congress

Service Dates of House Members: Jan. 3,1969-Jan. 20,1969

HOUSE — **Majority**

Rank	Name	Party	State	Terms in: House	Terms in: Comm.
1st	McCormack, John W.	Dem	Mass.	22	*2 8
2nd	Albert, Carl	Dem	Okla.	12	4

Minority

Rank	Name	Party	State	Terms in: House	Terms in: Comm.
1st	Ford, Gerald R. Jr.	Rep	Mich.	11	3

*2: Member's 2nd period of service on the committee.

JOINT COMMITTEE: INAUGURAL CEREMONIES (for Nixon) / 92nd Congress

Service Dates of Committee Chair: Ch1 Mar. 30,1972-Aug. 2,1972
Ch2 Aug. 2,1972-Jan. 20,1973
Service Dates of House Members: Mar. 27,1972-Jan. 3,1973
Service Dates of Senate Members: Mar. 30,1972-Jan. 20,1973

HOUSE Majority

Rank	Name	Party	State	Terms in: House	Terms in: Comm.
1st	Albert, Carl	Dem	Okla.	13	5
2nd	Boggs, T. Hale	Dem	La.	14	1

Minority

Rank	Name	Party	State	Terms in: House	Terms in: Comm.
1st	Ford, Gerald R. Jr.	Rep	Mich.	12	4

SENATE Majority

Rank	Name	Party	State	Years in: Senate	Terms in: Comm.
Ch1	Jordan, B. Everett	Dem	N.C.	14	3
2nd	Mansfield, Michael J.	Dem	Mont.	20	2

Minority

Rank	Name	Party	State	Years in: Senate	Terms in: Comm.
1st	Cook, Marlow W.	Rep	Ky.	4	1

Changes:

	Name	Party	State	Date	Change
Chair:					
	Ch1 Jordan, B. Everett	Dem	N.C.	Aug. 2,1972	Left committee; defeated for renomination.
	Ch2 Cannon, Howard W.	Dem	Nev.	Aug. 2,1972	Succeeded Jordan as Chair.
House Majority:					
	Boggs, T. Hale	Dem	La.	Jan. 3,1973	Died in office.
Senate Majority:					
	Jordan, B. Everett	Dem	N.C.	Aug. 2,1972	Left committee; defeated for renomination.
	Cannon, Howard W.	Dem	Nev.	Aug. 2,1972	Replaced Jordan.

93rd Congress

Service Dates of House Members: Jan. 3,1973-Jan. 20,1973

HOUSE Majority

Rank	Name	Party	State	Terms in: House	Terms in: Comm.
1st	Albert, Carl	Dem	Okla.	14	6
2nd	O'Neill, Thomas P. Jr.	Dem	Mass.	11	1

Minority

Rank	Name	Party	State	Terms in: House	Terms in: Comm.
1st	Ford, Gerald R. Jr.	Rep	Mich.	13	5

JOINT COMMITTEE: INAUGURAL CEREMONIES (for Carter) / 94th Congress

Service Dates of Committee Chair: Mar. 16,1976-Jan. 20,1977
Service Dates of House Members: Feb. 18,1976-Jan. 3,1977
Service Dates of Senate Members: Mar. 16,1976-Jan. 20,1977

HOUSE Majority

Rank	Name	Party	State	Terms in: House	Terms in: Comm.
1st	Albert, Carl	Dem	Okla.	15	7
2nd	O'Neill, Thomas P. Jr.	Dem	Mass.	12	2

Minority

Rank	Name	Party	State	Terms in: House	Terms in: Comm.
1st	Rhodes, John J.	Rep	Ariz.	12	1

SENATE Majority

Rank	Name	Party	State	Years in: Senate	Terms in: Comm.
Chr	Cannon, Howard W.	Dem	Nev.	18	2
2nd	Byrd, Robert C.	Dem	W.Va.	18	*1 1

Minority

Rank	Name	Party	State	Years in: Senate	Terms in: Comm.
1st	Hatfield, Mark O.	Rep	Ore.	10	1

*1: Member's 1st period of service on the committee.

Departures from the House:	Majority	State	Party	Minority
Retired	Albert, Carl	Okla.	Dem	None

95th Congress

Service Dates of House Members: Jan. 3,1977-Jan. 20,1977

HOUSE

Majority Rank	Name	Party	State	Terms in: House	Terms in: Comm.	Minority Rank	Name	Party	State	Terms in: House	Terms in: Comm.
1st	O'Neill, Thomas P. Jr.	Dem	Mass.	13	3	1st	Rhodes, John J.	Rep	Ariz.	13	2
2nd	Wright, James C. Jr.	Dem	Tex.	12	1						

Departures from the House:

	Majority		Minority
Retired	Albert, Carl	Okla. Dem	None

JOINT COMMITTEE: INAUGURAL CEREMONIES (for Reagan) / 96th Congress

Service Dates of Committee Chairs: Ch1 Apr. 22,1980-Nov. 8,1980
Ch2 Nov. 8,1980-Jan. 20,1981
Service Dates of House Members: Apr. 1,1980-Jan. 3,1981
Service Dates of Senate Members: Apr. 22,1980-Jan. 20,1981

HOUSE

Majority Rank	Name	Party	State	Terms in: House	Terms in: Comm.	Minority Rank	Name	Party	State	Terms in: House	Terms in: Comm.
1st	O'Neill, Thomas P. Jr.	Dem	Mass.	14	4	1st	Rhodes, John J.	Rep	Ariz.	14	3
2nd	Wright, James C. Jr.	Dem	Tex.	13	2						

SENATE

Majority Rank	Name	Party	State	Years in: Senate	Terms in: Comm.	Minority Rank	Name	Party	State	Years in: Senate	Terms in: Comm.
Ch1	Pell, Claiborne D.	Dem	R.I.	20	1	1st	Baker, Howard H. Jr.	Rep	Tenn.	14	1
2nd	Byrd, Robert C.	Dem	W.Va.	22	*1 2						

*1: Member's 1st period of service on the committee.

Changes:

Chair:

Ch1 Pell, Claiborne D.	Dem	R.I.	Nov. 8,1980	Left committee due to Republican victory.
Ch2 Hatfield, Mark O.	Rep	Ore.	Nov. 8,1980	Succeeded Pell as Chair.

Senate Majority:

Pell, Claiborne D.	Dem	R.I.	Nov. 8,1980	Left committee due to Republican victory.
Hatfield, Mark O.	Rep	Ore.	Nov. 8,1980	Replaced Pell.

97th Congress

Service Dates of House Members: Jan. 3,1981-Jan. 20,1981

HOUSE

Majority Rank	Name	Party	State	Terms in: House	Terms in: Comm.	Minority Rank	Name	Party	State	Terms in: House	Terms in: Comm.
1st	O'Neill, Thomas P. Jr.	Dem	Mass.	15	5	1st	Michel, Robert H.	Rep	Ill.	13	1
2nd	Wright, James C. Jr.	Dem	Tex.	14	3						

JOINT COMMITTEE: INAUGURAL CEREMONIES (for Reagan) / 98th Congress

Service Dates of Committee Chair: July 3,1984-Jan. 20,1985
Service Dates of House Members: July 3,1984-Jan. 3,1985
Service Dates of Senate Members: July 3,1984-Jan. 20,1985

HOUSE

Majority Rank Name	Party	State	Terms in: House	Terms in: Comm.	Minority Rank Name	Party	State	Terms in: House	Terms in: Comm.
1st O'Neill, Thomas P. Jr.	Dem	Mass.	16	6	1st Michel, Robert H.	Rep	Ill.	14	2
2nd Wright, James C. Jr.	Dem	Tex.	15	4					

SENATE

Majority Rank Name	Party	State	Years in: Senate	Terms in: Comm.	Minority Rank Name	Party	State	Years in: Senate	Terms in: Comm.
Chr Mathias, Charles McC. Jr.	Rep	Md.	16	*1 1	1st Ford, Wendell H.	Dem	Ky.	10	1
2nd Baker, Howard H. Jr.	Rep	Tenn.	18	2					

*1: Member's 1st period of service on the committee.

Departures from the Senate:	Majority:		Minority
Retired	Baker, Howard H. Jr.	Tenn. Rep	None

99th Congress

Service Dates of House Members: Jan. 3,1985-Jan. 21,1985

HOUSE

Majority Rank Name	Party	State	Terms in: House	Terms in: Comm.	Minority Rank Name	Party	State	Terms in: House	Terms in: Comm.
1st O'Neill, Thomas P. Jr.	Dem	Mass.	17	7	1st Michel, Robert H.	Rep	Ill.	15	3
2nd Wright, James C. Jr.	Dem	Tex.	16	5					

Departures from the House:	Majority		Minority
Retired	O'Neill, Thomas P. Jr.	Mass. Dem	None

JOINT COMMITTEE: INAUGURAL CEREMONIES (for Bush) / 100th Congress

Service Dates of Committee Chair: Aug. 2,1988-Jan. 20,1989
Service Dates of House Members: June 29,1988-Jan. 3,1989
Service Dates of Senate Members: Aug. 2,1988-Jan. 20,1989

HOUSE

Majority Rank Name	Party	State	Terms in: House	Terms in: Comm.	Minority Rank Name	Party	State	Terms in: House	Terms in: Comm.
1st Wright, James C. Jr.	Dem	Tex.	17	6	1st Michel, Robert H.	Rep	Ill.	16	4
2nd Foley, Thomas	Dem	Wash.	12	1					

SENATE

Majority Rank Name	Party	State	Years in: Senate	Terms in: Comm.	Minority Rank Name	Party	State	Years in: Senate	Terms in: Comm.
Chr Ford, Wendell H.	Dem	Ky.	14	2	1st Stevens, Theodore F.	Rep	Alas.	20	1
2nd Byrd, Robert C.	Dem	W.Va.	30	*2 1					

*2: Member's 2nd period of service on the committee.

101st Congress

Service Dates of House Members: Jan. 3,1989-Jan. 20,1989

HOUSE **Majority**

Rank	Name	Party	State	Terms in: House	Terms in: Comm.
1st	Wright, James C. Jr.	Dem	Tex.	18	7
2nd	Foley, Thomas	Dem	Wash.	13	2

Minority

Rank	Name	Party	State	Terms in: House	Terms in: Comm.
1st	Michel, Robert H.	Rep	Ill.	17	5

JOINT COMMITTEE: INAUGURAL CEREMONIES / 102nd Congress

Service Dates of Committee Chair: Aug. 4,1992-Jan. 20,1993
Service Dates of House Members: June 30,1992-Jan. 2,1993
Service Dates of Senate Members: July 2,1992-Jan. 20,1993

HOUSE **Majority**

Rank	Name	Party	State	Terms in: House	Terms in: Comm.
1st	Foley, Thomas	Dem	Wash.	14	3
2nd	Gephardt, Richard A.	Dem	Mo.	8	1

Minority

Rank	Name	Party	State	Terms in: House	Terms in: Comm.
1st	Michel, Robert H.	Rep	Ill.	18	6

SENATE **Majority**

Rank	Name	Party	State	Years in: Senate	Terms in: Comm.
Chr	Ford, Wendell H.	Dem	Ky.	18	3
2nd	Mitchell, George J.	Dem	Me.	12	1

Minority

Rank	Name	Party	State	Years in: Senate	Terms in: Comm.
2nd	Mathias, Charles McC. Jr.	Rep	Md.	24	*2 1

*2: Member's 2nd period of service on the committee.

JOINT COMMITTEE: TRUST TERRITORIES OF THE PACIFIC

Jurisdiction, 1948

From House Concurrent Resolution 129, 80th Congress, Second Session, May 21, 1948:

[Section 2]

The committee shall make a thorough study and investigation of the islands, groups of islands, and other areas included within the trust territory of the Pacific and all other islands, groups of islands, and other areas in the Pacific which are possessions of, or subject to the authority of, the United States, including study and investigation of--

(a) the peoples, customs, laws, economies, resources, and governments of such areas;
(b) the interrelation, and the natural or appropriate integration, of such areas;
(c) the interrelation of the security of such areas and the security of the United States;
(d) measures designed to advance the security and well-being of the peoples and economies of such areas; and
(e) such other matters relating to such areas as the committee may deem appropriate.

Termination, 1948

The Joint Committee was terminated at the end of the Second Session of the 80th Congress on December 31, 1948.

JOINT COMMITTEE: TRUST TERRITORIES OF THE PACIFIC / 80th Congress

Service Dates of House Members: June 19,1948-Jan. 3,1949
Service Dates of Senate Members: June 18,1948-Jan. 3,1949

HOUSE

Majority Rank Name	Party	State	Terms in: House	Comm.	Minority Rank Name	Party	State	Terms in: House	Comm.
1st Crawford, Fred L.	Rep	Mich.	7	1	1st Fernandez, Antonio M.	Dem	N.M.	3	1
2nd Lemke, William	Rep	N.D.	7	1	2nd Pfeifer, Joseph L.	Dem	N.Y.	7	1
3rd Fulton, James G.	Rep	Penn.	2	1					
4th Jackson, Donald L.	Rep	Cal.	1	1					

SENATE

Majority Rank Name	Party	State	Years in: Senate	Comm.	Minority Rank Name	Party	State	Years in: Senate	Comm.
1st Wiley, Alexander	Rep	Wisc.	10	1	1st Barkley, Alben W.	Dem	Ky.	22	1
2nd Smith, H. Alexander	Rep	N.J.	4	1	2nd O'Mahoney, Joseph C.	Dem	Wyo.	15	1
3rd Cordon, Guy	Rep	Ore.	5	1					
4th Malone, George W.	Rep	Nev.	2	1					

JOINT COMMITTEE: NAVAHO-HOPI INDIAN ADMINISTRATION

Jurisdiction, 1950

From Public Law 81-474, 81st Congress, Second Session, April 19, 1950 (64 Statutes 44, 47): and reprinted in the Senate Manual for the 93rd Congress (1973) 640.(b):

[Section 10(b)]

(b) It shall be the function of the committee to make a continuous study of the programs for the administration and rehabilitation of the Navajo and Hopi Indians, and to review the progress achieved in the execution of such programs. Upon request, the committee shall aid the several standing committees of the Congress having legislative jurisdiction over any part of such programs, and shall make a report to the Senate and the House of Representatives, from time to time, concerning the results of its studies, together with such recommendations as it may deem desirable. The Commissioner of Indian Affairs at the request of the committee, shall consult with the committee from time to time with respect to his activities under this Act.

Termination, 1973

The Joint Committee was terminated by authority of Senate Bill 267, which passed the Senate on Feb. 2, 1973, and was sent to the House Committee on Interior and Insular Affairs on February 6, 1973.

JOINT COMMITTEE: NAVAHO-HOPI INDIAN ADMINISTRATION / 81st Congress

Service Dates of House Members: May 18,1950-Jan. 3,1951
Service Dates of Senate Members: May 22,1950-Continued

HOUSE

Majority Rank	Name	Party	State	Terms in: House	Comm.	Minority Rank	Name	Party	State	Terms in: House	Comm.
1st	Murdock, John R.	Dem	Ariz.	7	1	1st	D'Ewart, Wesley A.	Rep	Mont.	3	1
2nd	Morris, Toby	Dem	Okla.	2	1						

SENATE

Majority Rank	Name	Party	State	Years in: Senate	Comm.	Minority Rank	Name	Party	State	Years in: Senate	Comm.
1st	McFarland, Ernest W.	Dem	Ariz.	10	1	1st	Watkins, Arthur V.	Rep	Utah	4	1
2nd	Anderson, Clinton P.	Dem	N.M.	2	1						

Note: No committee Chair is listed in Congressional Directory for either session of this Congress..

JOINT COMMITTEE: NAVAHO-HOPI INDIAN ADMINISTRATION / 82nd Congress

Service Dates of House Members: Jan. 29,1951-Jan. 3,1953
Service Dates of Senate Members: Jan. 3,1951-Continued

HOUSE

Majority Rank	Name	Party	State	Terms in: House	Comm.	Minority Rank	Name	Party	State	Terms in: House	Comm.
1st	Murdock, John R.	Dem	Ariz.	8	2	1st	D'Ewart, Wesley A.	Rep	Mont.	4	2
2nd	Morris, Toby	Dem	Okla.	3	2						

SENATE

Majority Rank	Name	Party	State	Years in: Senate	Comm.	Minority Rank	Name	Party	State	Years in: Senate	Comm.
1st	McFarland, Ernest W.	Dem	Ariz.	11	1	1st	Watkins, Arthur V.	Rep	Utah	5	1
2nd	Anderson, Clinton P.	Dem	N.M.	3	1						

Note: No committee Chair is listed in Congressional Directory for either session of this Congress.

Departures from the House:	Majority		Minority
Defeated for Reelection	Murdock, John R.	Ariz. Dem	None
Defeated for Renomination	Morris, Toby	Okla. Dem	None
Departures from the Senate:			
Defeated for Reelection	McFarland, Ernest W.	Ariz. Dem	None

JOINT COMMITTEE: NAVAHO-HOPI INDIAN ADMINISTRATION / 83rd Congress

Service Dates of House Members: Jan. 26,1953-Jan. 3,1955
Service Dates of Senate Members: Jan. 3,1953-Mar. 30,1955

HOUSE

Majority Rank Name	Party	State	Terms in: House	Terms in: Comm.	Minority Rank Name	Party	State	Terms in: House	Terms in: Comm.
1st D'Ewart, Wesley A.	Rep	Mont.	5	3	1st McCarthy, Eugene J.	DFL	Minn.	3	1
2nd Rhodes, John J.	Rep	Ariz.	1	1					

SENATE

Majority Rank Name	Party	State	Years in: Senate	Years in: Comm.	Minority Rank Name	Party	State	Years in: Senate	Years in: Comm.
1st Watkins, Arthur V.	Rep	Utah	7	3	1st Anderson, Clinton P.	Dem	N.M.	5	3
2nd Barrett, Frank A.	Rep	Wyo.	1	1					

Note: No committee Chair is listed in Congressional Directory for either session of this Congress.

Vacancy Filled:
Senate Majority: 2nd seat by Barrett on Aug. 3,1953.

Departures from the House:	Majority		Minority	
Lost Election to U.S. Senate	D'Ewart, Wesley A.	Mont. Rep	None	
Departures from Committee:				
House:				
Moved to Ways and Means	None		McCarthy, Eugene J.	Minn. DFL
Senate:				
No new assignment	Barrett, Frank A.	Wyo. Rep	None	
	Watkins, Arthur V.	Utah Rep		

JOINT COMMITTEE: NAVAHO-HOPI INDIAN ADMINISTRATION / 84th Congress

Service Dates of House Members: Feb. 3,1955-Jan. 3,1957
Service Dates of Senate Members: Mar. 30,1955-Continued

HOUSE

Majority Rank Name	Party	State	Terms in: House	Terms in: Comm.	Minority Rank Name	Party	State	Terms in: House	Terms in: Comm.
1st Engle, Clair	Dem	Cal.	7	1	1st Rhodes, John J.	Rep	Ariz.	2	2
2nd Udall, Stewart L.	Dem	Ariz.	1	1					

SENATE

Majority Rank Name	Party	State	Years in: Senate	Years in: Comm.	Minority Rank Name	Party	State	Years in: Senate	Years in: Comm.
1st Anderson, Clinton P.	Dem	N.M.	7	5	1st Goldwater, Barry M.	Rep	Ariz.	3	1
2nd Bible, Alan H.	Dem	Nev.	1	1					

Note: No committee Chair is listed in Congressional Directory for either session of this Congress.

JOINT COMMITTEE: NAVAHO-HOPI INDIAN ADMINISTRATION / 85th Congress

Service Dates of House Members: Jan. 28,1957-Jan. 3,1959
Service Dates of Senate Members: Jan. 3,1957-Continued

HOUSE

Majority Rank	Name	Party	State	Terms in: House	Comm.	Minority Rank	Name	Party	State	Terms in: House	Comm.
1st	Engle, Clair	Dem	Cal.	8	2	1st	Rhodes, John J.	Rep	Ariz.	3	3
2nd	Udall, Stewart L.	Dem	Ariz.	2	2						

SENATE

Majority Rank	Name	Party	State	Years in: Senate	Comm.	Minority Rank	Name	Party	State	Years in: Senate	Comm.
1st	Anderson, Clinton P.	Dem	N.M.	9	7	1st	Goldwater, Barry M.	Rep	Ariz.	5	2
2nd	Bible, Alan H.	Dem	Nev.	3	2						

Note: No committee Chair is listed in Congressional Directory for either session of this Congress.

	Majority		Minority	
Departures from the House:				
Elected to U.S. Senate	Engle, Clair	Cal. Dem	None	
Departures from Committee:				
House:				
Moved to Appropriations	None		Rhodes, John J.	Ariz. Rep

JOINT COMMITTEE: NAVAHO-HOPI INDIAN ADMINISTRATION / 86th Congress

Service Dates of House Members: Jan. 29,1959-Jan. 3,1961
Service Dates of Senate Members: Jan. 3,1959-Continued

HOUSE

Majority Rank	Name	Party	State	Terms in: House	Comm.	Minority Rank	Name	Party	State	Terms in: House	Comm.
1st	Udall, Stewart L.	Dem	Ariz.	3	3	1st	Berry, Ellis Y.	Rep	S.D.	5	1
2nd	Anderson, LeRoy H.	Dem	Mont.	2	1						

SENATE

Majority Rank	Name	Party	State	Years in: Senate	Comm.	Minority Rank	Name	Party	State	Years in: Senate	Comm.
1st	Anderson, Clinton P.	Dem	N.M.	11	9	1st	Goldwater, Barry M.	Rep	Ariz.	7	4
2nd	Bible, Alan H.	Dem	Nev.	5	4						

Note: No committee Chair is listed in Congressional Directory for either session of this Congress.

	Majority		Minority
Departures from the House:			
Lost Nomination for U.S. Senate	Anderson, LeRoy H.	Mont. Dem	None
Departures from Committee:			
House:			
Unassigned in 87th; appointed Secretary of the Interior Jan. 18,1961	Udall, Stewart L.	Ariz. Dem	None

JOINT COMMITTEE: NAVAHO-HOPI INDIAN ADMINISTRATION / 87th Congress

Service Dates of House Members: Mar. 7,1961-Jan. 3,1963
Service Dates of Senate Members: Jan. 3,1961-Continued

HOUSE

Majority Rank	Name	Party	State	Terms in: House	Comm.	Minority Rank	Name	Party	State	Terms in: House	Comm.
1st	Haley, James A.	Dem	Fla.	5	1	1st	Berry, Ellis Y.	Rep	S.D.	6	2
2nd	Morris, Thomas G.	Dem	N.M.	2	1						

SENATE

Majority					Minority				
			Years in:					Years in:	
Rank Name	Party	State	Senate	Comm.	Rank Name	Party	State	Senate	Comm.
1st Anderson, Clinton P.	Dem	N.M.	13	11	1st Goldwater, Barry M.	Rep	Ariz.	9	6
2nd Bible, Alan H.	Dem	Nev.	7	6					

Note: No committee Chair is listed in Congressional Directory for either session of this Congress.

JOINT COMMITTEE: NAVAHO-HOPI INDIAN ADMINISTRATION / 88th Congress

Service Dates of House Members: Jan. 31,1963-Jan. 3,1965
Service Dates of Senate Members: Jan. 3,1963-Continued

HOUSE

Majority					Minority				
			Terms in:					Terms in:	
Rank Name	Party	State	House	Comm.	Rank Name	Party	State	House	Comm.
1st Haley, James A.	Dem	Fla.	6	2	1st Berry, Ellis Y.	Rep	S.D.	7	3
2nd Morris, Thomas G.	Dem	N.M.	3	2					

SENATE

Majority					Minority				
			Years in:					Years in:	
Rank Name	Party	State	Senate	Comm.	Rank Name	Party	State	Senate	Comm.
1st Anderson, Clinton P.	Dem	N.M.	15	13	1st Goldwater, Barry M.	Rep	Ariz.	11	8
2nd Bible, Alan H.	Dem	Nev.	9	8					

Note: No committee Chair is listed in Congressional Directory for either session of this Congress.

Changes:
Senate Minority:

Goldwater, Barry M.	Rep	Ariz.	Sep. 19,1963	Left committee; no new assignment.
Mechem, Edwin L.	Rep	N.M.	Sep. 19,1963	Replaced Goldwater.
Mechem, Edwin L.	Rep	N.M.	Nov. 3,1964	Resigned; defeated for election.

JOINT COMMITTEE: NAVAHO-HOPI INDIAN ADMINISTRATION / 89th Congress

Service Dates of House Members: Feb. 3,1965-Jan. 3,1967
Service Dates of Senate Members: Feb. 10,1965-Continued

HOUSE

Majority					Minority				
			Terms in:					Terms in:	
Rank Name	Party	State	House	Comm.	Rank Name	Party	State	House	Comm.
1st Haley, James A.	Dem	Fla.	7	3	1st Berry, Ellis Y.	Rep	S.D.	8	4
2nd Morris, Thomas G.	Dem	N.M.	4	3					

SENATE

Majority					Minority				
			Years in:					Years in:	
Rank Name	Party	State	Senate	Comm.	Rank Name	Party	State	Senate	Comm.
1st Anderson, Clinton P.	Dem	N.M.	17	15	1st Fannin, Paul J.	Rep	Ariz.	1	1
2nd Bible, Alan H.	Dem	Nev.	11	10					

Notes: No committee Chair is listed in Congressional Directory for either session of this Congress. "Service Dates of Senate Members" reflect the dates of service of Fannin; all other Senators continued service from the previous Congress without official reassignment recorded in the Congressional Record.

Changes:
House Majority:

Morris, Thomas G.	Dem	N.M.	Feb. 10,1965	Moved to Appropriations.
Udall, Morris K.	Dem	Ariz.	Feb. 10,1965	Replaced Morris.

JOINT COMMITTEE: NAVAHO-HOPI INDIAN ADMINISTRATION / 90th Congress

Service Dates of House Members: Jan. 30,1967-Jan. 3,1969
Service Dates of Senate Members: Jan. 3,1967-Continued

HOUSE

Majority Rank	Name	Party	State	Terms in: House	Terms in: Comm.	Minority Rank	Name	Party	State	Terms in: House	Terms in: Comm.
1st	Haley, James A.	Dem	Fla.	8	4	1st	Berry, Ellis Y.	Rep	S.D.	9	5
2nd	Udall, Morris K.	Dem	Ariz.	4	2						

SENATE

Majority Rank	Name	Party	State	Years in: Senate	Years in: Comm.	Minority Rank	Name	Party	State	Years in: Senate	Years in: Comm.
1st	Anderson, Clinton P.	Dem	N.M.	19	17	1st	Fannin, Paul J.	Rep	Ariz.	3	2
2nd	Bible, Alan H.	Dem	Nev.	13	12						

Note: No committee Chair is listed in Congressional Directory for either session of this Congress.

Departures from Committee:

House:

	Majority	Minority		
No new assignment	None	Berry, Ellis Y.	S.D.	Rep

JOINT COMMITTEE: NAVAHO-HOPI INDIAN ADMINISTRATION / 91st Congress

Service Dates of House Members: Feb. 17,1969-Jan. 3,1971
Service Dates of Senate Members: Jan. 3,1969-Continued

HOUSE

Majority Rank	Name	Party	State	Terms in: House	Terms in: Comm.	Minority Rank	Name	Party	State	Terms in: House	Terms in: Comm.
1st	Haley, James A.	Dem	Fla.	9	5	1st	Steiger, Sam	Rep	Ariz.	2	1
2nd	Udall, Morris K.	Dem	Ariz.	5	3						

SENATE

Majority Rank	Name	Party	State	Years in: Senate	Years in: Comm.	Minority Rank	Name	Party	State	Years in: Senate	Years in: Comm.
1st	Anderson, Clinton P.	Dem	N.M.	21	19	1st	Fannin, Paul J.	Rep	Ariz.	5	4
2nd	Bible, Alan H.	Dem	Nev.	15	14						

Note: No committee Chair is listed in Congressional Directory for either session of this Congress.

JOINT COMMITTEE: NAVAHO-HOPI INDIAN ADMINISTRATION / 92nd Congress

Service Dates of House Members: Feb. 23,1971-Jan. 3,1973
Service Dates of Senate Members: Jan. 3,1971-Feb. 5,1973

HOUSE

Majority Rank	Name	Party	State	Terms in: House	Terms in: Comm.	Minority Rank	Name	Party	State	Terms in: House	Terms in: Comm.
1st	Haley, James A.	Dem	Fla.	10	6	1st	Steiger, Sam	Rep	Ariz.	3	2
2nd	Udall, Morris K.	Dem	Ariz.	6	4						

SENATE

Majority Rank	Name	Party	State	Years in: Senate	Years in: Comm.	Minority Rank	Name	Party	State	Years in: Senate	Years in: Comm.
1st	Anderson, Clinton P.	Dem	N.M.	23	21	1st	Fannin, Paul J.	Rep	Ariz.	7	6
2nd	Bible, Alan H.	Dem	Nev.	17	16						

Note: No committee Chair is listed in Congressional Directory for either session of the 92nd Congress.

JOINT COMMITTEE: NAVAHO-HOPI INDIAN ADMINISTRATION / 93rd Congress

Service Dates of House Members: Feb. 5,1973-Feb. 6,1973

HOUSE **Majority**

Rank Name	Party	State	Terms in: House	Terms in: Comm.
1st Haley, James A.	Dem	Fla.	11	7
2nd Udall, Morris K.	Dem	Ariz.	7	5

Minority

Rank Name	Party	State	Terms in: House	Terms in: Comm.
1st Steiger, Sam	Rep	Ariz.	4	3

JOINT COMMITTEE: DEFENSE PRODUCTION

Jurisdiction, 1950

From Public Law 81-774, the Defense Production Act of 1950, 81st Congress, Second Session, September 8, 1950 (64 Statutes 798, 820-821):

[Section 712]

(b) It shall be the function of the committee to make a continuous study of the programs authorized by this Act, and to review the progress achieved in the execution and administration of such programs. Upon request, the committee shall aid the standing committees of the Congress having legislative jurisdiction over any part of the programs authorized by this Act; and it shall make a report to the Senate and the House of Representatives, from time to time, concerning the results of its studies, together with such recommendations as it may deem desirable. Any department, official, or agency administering any of such programs shall, at the request of the committee, consult with the committee, from time to time, with respect to their activities under this Act.

Termination, 1977

The joint committee was extended by Public Law 95-37, (S 853 May 19, 1977; HR 4962 May 2, 1977) and officially terminated at the end of the 95th Congress; however, no funds were appropriated after September 30, 1977, at which time the joint committee ceased to function.

JOINT COMMITTEE: DEFENSE PRODUCTION / 81st Congress

Service Dates of Committee Chair: Sep. 1 1950-Continued
Service Dates of House Members: Sep. 20,1950-Jan. 3,1951
Service Dates of Senate Members: Sep. 1,1950-Continued

HOUSE

Majority

Rank	Name	Party	State	Terms in: House	Terms in: Comm.
VCh	Brown, Paul	Dem	Ga.	9	1
2nd	Patman, J.W. Wright	Dem	Tex.	11 *1	1
3rd	Hays, L. Brooks	Dem	Ark.	4	1

Minority

Rank	Name	Party	State	Terms in: House	Terms in: Comm.
1st	Gamble, Ralph A.	Rep	N.Y.	7	1
2nd	Talle, Henry O.	Rep	Iowa	6	1

SENATE

Majority

Rank	Name	Party	State	Years in: Senate	Years in: Comm.
Chr	Maybank, Burnet R.	Dem	S.C.	9	1
2nd	Fulbright, J. William	Dem	Ark.	6	1
3rd	Robertson, A. Willis	Dem	Va.	4 *1	1

Minority

Rank	Name	Party	State	Years in: Senate	Years in: Comm.
1st	Tobey, Charles W.	Rep	N.H.	12	1
2nd	Capehart, Homer E.	Rep	Ind.	6	1

*1: Member's 1st period of service on the committee.

Note: Senate membership on this committee was originally appointed by Burnet R. Maybank (Dem-S.C.) on Sep. 1,1950 as mandated by the conference report on Defense Production, before such legislation had been signed into law.

Departures from Committee:

	Majority		Minority	
House:				
No new assignment	Hays, L. Brooks	Ark. Dem	None	
Senate:				
No new assignment	None		Tobey, Charles W.	N.H. Rep

JOINT COMMITTEE: DEFENSE PRODUCTION / 82nd Congress

Service Dates of Committee Chair: Jan. 3,1951-Jan. 3,1953
Service Dates of House Members: Jan. 19,1951-Jan. 3,1953
Service Dates of Senate Members: Jan. 15,1951-Continued

HOUSE

Majority			Terms in:		Minority			Terms in:	
Rank Name	**Party**	**State**	**House**	**Comm.**	**Rank Name**	**Party**	**State**	**House**	**Comm.**
VCh Brown, Paul	Dem	Ga.	10	2	1st Gamble, Ralph A.	Rep	N.Y.	8	2
2nd Patman, J.W. Wright	Dem	Tex.	12 *1	2	2nd Talle, Henry O.	Rep	Iowa	7	2
3rd Rains, Albert	Dem	Ala.	4 *1	1					

SENATE

Majority			Years in:		Minority			Years in:	
Rank Name	**Party**	**State**	**Senate**	**Comm.**	**Rank Name**	**Party**	**State**	**Senate**	**Comm.**
Chr Maybank, Burnet R.	Dem	S.C.	10	1	1st Capehart, Homer E.	Rep	Ind.	7	1
2nd Fulbright, J. William	Dem	Ark.	7	1	2nd Bricker, John W.	Rep	Ohio	5	1
3rd Robertson, A. Willis	Dem	Va.	5 *1	1					

*1: Member's 1st period of service on the committee.

Note: Senate membership on this committee was composed of the three ranking majority members and two ranking minority members of the Senate Banking and Currency Committee. "Service Dates of Senate Members" reflects members' service on the Standing Committee.

Departures from Committee:

	Majority			Minority
House:				
No new assignment	Rains, Albert	Ala.	Dem	None
Senate:				
No new assignment	Robertson, A. Willis	Va.	Dem	None

JOINT COMMITTEE: DEFENSE PRODUCTION / 83rd Congress

Service Dates of Committee Chair: Jan. 3,1953-Jan. 3,1955
Service Dates of House Members: Jan. 23,1953-Jan. 3,1955 (reported Jan. 26,1953)
Service Dates of Senate Members: Jan. 13,1953-Continued

HOUSE

Majority			Terms in:		Minority			Terms in:	
Rank Name	**Party**	**State**	**House**	**Comm.**	**Rank Name**	**Party**	**State**	**House**	**Comm.**
VCh Gamble, Ralph A.	Rep	N.Y.	9	3	1st Brown, Paul	Dem	Ga.	11	3
2nd Wolcott, Jesse P.	Rep	Mich.	12	1	2nd Patman, J.W. Wright	Dem	Tex.	13 *1	3
3rd Talle, Henry O.	Rep	Iowa	8	3					

SENATE

Majority			Years in:		Minority			Years in:	
Rank Name	**Party**	**State**	**Senate**	**Comm.**	**Rank Name**	**Party**	**State**	**Senate**	**Comm.**
Chr Capehart, Homer E.	Rep	Ind.	9	3	1st Maybank, Burnet R.	Dem	S.C.	12	3
2nd Bricker, John W.	Rep	Ohio	7	2	2nd Fulbright, J. William	Dem	Ark.	9	3
3rd Ives, Irving M.	Rep	N.Y.	7	1					

*1: Member's 1st period of service on the committee.

Note: Senate membership on this committee was composed of the three ranking majority members and two ranking minority members of the Senate Banking and Currency Committee. "Service Dates of Senate Members" reflects members' service on the Standing Committee.

Changes:

House Majority:

Patman, J.W. Wright	Dem	Tex.	Sep. 24,1953	Left committee; no new assignment.
Spence, Brent	Dem	Ky.	Sep. 24,1953	Replaced Patman.

Senate Majority:

Maybank, Burnet R.	Dem	S.C.	Sep. 1,1954	Died in office.
Robertson, A. Willis	Dem	Va.	Sep. 1,1954	Replaced Maybank.

Departures from Committee:	Majority			Minority		
House:						
No new assignment	Wolcott, Jesse P.	Mich.	Rep	Spence, Brent	Ky.	Dem
Senate:						
No new assignment	Ives, Irving M.	N.Y.	Rep	Fulbright, J. William	Ark.	Dem

JOINT COMMITTEE: DEFENSE PRODUCTION / 84th Congress

Service Dates of Committee Chair: Feb. 2,1955-Jan. 3,1957
Service Dates of House Members: Feb. 2,1955-Jan. 3,1957
Service Dates of Senate Members: Jan. 11,1955-Continued

HOUSE — **Majority**

Rank	Name	Party	State	Terms in: House	Terms in: Comm.
Chr	Brown, Paul	Dem	Ga.	12	4
2nd	Patman, J.W. Wright	Dem	Tex.	14	*2 1
3rd	Rains, Albert	Dem	Ala.	6	*2 1

Minority

Rank	Name	Party	State	Terms in: House	Terms in: Comm.
1st	Gamble, Ralph A.	Rep	N.Y.	10	4
2nd	Talle, Henry O.	Rep	Iowa	9	4

SENATE — **Majority**

Rank	Name	Party	State	Years in: Senate	Years in: Comm.
VCh	Robertson, A. Willis	Dem	Va.	9	*2 1
2nd	Sparkman, John J.	Dem	Ala.	9	1
3rd	Frear, J. Allen Jr.	Dem	Del.	7	1

Minority

Rank	Name	Party	State	Years in: Senate	Years in: Comm.
1st	Capehart, Homer E.	Rep	Ind.	11	5
2nd	Bricker, John W.	Rep	Ohio	9	4

*2: Member's 2nd period of service on the committee.

Note: Senate membership on this committee was composed of the three ranking majority members and two ranking minority members of the Senate Banking and Currency Committee. "Service Dates of Senate Members" reflects members' service on the Standing Committee.

Departures from the House:	Majority	Minority		
Retired	None	Gamble, Ralph A.	N.Y.	Rep

JOINT COMMITTEE: DEFENSE PRODUCTION / 85th Congress

Service Dates of Committee Chair: Jan. 3,1957-Jan. 3,1959
Service Dates of House Members: Feb. 5,1957-Jan. 3,1959 (assignments reported Feb. 6, 1957)
Service Dates of Senate Members: Jan. 3,1957-Feb. 17,1959

HOUSE — **Majority**

Rank	Name	Party	State	Terms in: House	Terms in: Comm.
VCh	Brown, Paul	Dem	Ga.	13	5
2nd	Patman, J.W. Wright	Dem	Tex.	15	*2 2
3rd	Rains, Albert	Dem	Ala.	7	*2 2

Minority

Rank	Name	Party	State	Terms in: House	Terms in: Comm.
1st	Talle, Henry O.	Rep	Iowa	10	5
2nd	McDonough, Gordon L.	Rep	Cal.	7	1

SENATE — **Majority**

Rank	Name	Party	State	Years in: Senate	Years in: Comm.
Chr	Robertson, A. Willis	Dem	Va.	11	*2 3
2nd	Sparkman, John J.	Dem	Ala.	11	2
3rd	Frear, J. Allen Jr.	Dem	Del.	9	2

Minority

Rank	Name	Party	State	Years in: Senate	Years in: Comm.
1st	Capehart, Homer E.	Rep	Ind.	13	7
2nd	Bricker, John W.	Rep	Ohio	11	6

*2: Member's 2nd period of service on the committee.

Departures from the House:	Majority	Minority		
Defeated for Reelection	None	Talle, Henry O.	Iowa	Rep
Departures from the Senate:				
Defeated for Reelection	None	Bricker, John W.	Ohio	Rep

JOINT COMMITTEE: DEFENSE PRODUCTION / 86th Congress

Service Dates of Committee Chair: Feb. 13,1959-Jan. 3,1961
Service Dates of House Members: Feb. 13,1959-Jan. 3,1961 (reported Feb. 16,1959)
Service Dates of Senate Members: Feb. 17,1959-Continued

HOUSE **Majority** / **Minority**

Rank Name	Party	State	Terms in: House	Terms in: Comm.	Rank Name	Party	State	Terms in: House	Terms in: Comm.
Chr Brown, Paul	Dem	Ga.	14	6	1st McDonough, Gordon L.	Rep	Cal.	8	2
2nd Patman, J.W. Wright	Dem	Tex.	16	*2 3	2nd Hiestand, Edgar W.	Rep	Cal.	4	1
3rd Rains, Albert	Dem	Ala.	8	*2 3					

SENATE **Majority** / **Minority**

Rank Name	Party	State	Years in: Senate	Years in: Comm.	Rank Name	Party	State	Years in: Senate	Years in: Comm.
1st Robertson, A. Willis	Dem	Va.	13	*2 5	VCh Capehart, Homer E.	Rep	Ind.	15	9
2nd Sparkman, John J.	Dem	Ala.	13	5	2nd Bennett, Wallace F.	Rep	Utah	9	1
3rd Frear, J. Allen Jr.	Dem	Del.	11	5					

*2: Member's 2nd period of service on the committee.

	Majority			Minority		
Departures from the House:						
Retired	Brown, Paul	Ga.	Dem	None		
Departures from the Senate:						
Defeated for Reelection	Frear, J. Allen Jr.	Del.	Dem	None		
Departures from Committee:						
House:						
Moved to House Administration	None			Hiestand, Edgar W.	Cal.	Rep

JOINT COMMITTEE: DEFENSE PRODUCTION / 87th Congress

Service Dates of Committee Chair: Feb. 23,1961-Jan. 3,1963
Service Dates of House Members: Feb. 23,1961-Jan. 3,1963 (reported Feb. 27,1963)
Service Dates of Senate Members: Feb. 28,1961-Continued

HOUSE **Majority** / **Minority**

Rank Name	Party	State	Terms in: House	Terms in: Comm.	Rank Name	Party	State	Terms in: House	Terms in: Comm.
VCh Patman, J.W. Wright	Dem	Tex.	17	*2 4	1st McDonough, Gordon L.	Rep	Cal.	9	3
2nd Rains, Albert	Dem	Ala.	9	*2 4	2nd Widnall, William B.	Rep	N.J.	7	1
3rd Multer, Abraham J.	Dem	N.Y.	8	1					

SENATE **Majority** / **Minority**

Rank Name	Party	State	Years in: Senate	Years in: Comm.	Rank Name	Party	State	Years in: Senate	Years in: Comm.
Chr Robertson, A. Willis	Dem	Va.	15	*2 7	1st Capehart, Homer E.	Rep	Ind.	17	11
2nd Sparkman, John J.	Dem	Ala.	15	6	2nd Bennett, Wallace F.	Rep	Utah	11	2
3rd Douglas, Paul H.	Dem	Ill.	13	1					

*2: Member's 2nd period of service on the committee.

Note: "Service Dates of Senate Members" reflect the dates of service of Douglas; all other Senators continued service from the previous Congress without official reassignment recorded in the Congressional Record.

	Majority	Minority		
Departures from the House:				
Defeated for Reelection	None	McDonough, Gordon L.	Cal.	Rep
Departures from the Senate:				
Defeated for Reelection	None	Capehart, Homer E.	Ind.	Rep

JOINT COMMITTEE: DEFENSE PRODUCTION / 88th Congress

Service Dates of Committee Chair: Jan. 24,1963-Jan. 3,1965
Service Dates of House Members: Jan. 24,1963-Jan. 3,1965
Service Dates of Senate Members: Mar. 4,1963-Feb. 9,1965

HOUSE

Majority Rank Name	Party	State	Terms in: House	Terms in: Comm.	Minority Rank Name	Party	State	Terms in: House	Terms in: Comm.
Chr Patman, J.W. Wright	Dem	Tex.	18	*2 5	1st Widnall, William B.	Rep	N.J.	8	2
2nd Rains, Albert	Dem	Ala.	10	*2 5	2nd Fino, Paul A.	Rep	N.Y.	6	1
3rd Multer, Abraham J.	Dem	N.Y.	9	2					

SENATE

Majority Rank Name	Party	State	Years in: Senate	Years in: Comm.	Minority Rank Name	Party	State	Years in: Senate	Years in: Comm.
VCh Robertson, A. Willis	Dem	Va.	17	*2 9	1st Bennett, Wallace F.	Rep	Utah	13	4
2nd Sparkman, John J.	Dem	Ala.	17	9	2nd Tower, John G.	Rep	Tex.	2	1
3rd Douglas, Paul H.	Dem	Ill.	15	2					

*2: Member's 2nd period of service on the committee.

Note: "Service Dates of Senate Members" reflect the dates of service of Tower; all other Senators continued service from the previous Congress without official reassignment recorded in the Congressional Record.

Departures from the House:	Majority			Minority
Retired	Rains, Albert	Ala.	Dem	None

JOINT COMMITTEE: DEFENSE PRODUCTION / 89th Congress

Service Dates of Committee Chair: Feb. 9,1965-Dec. 30,1966
Service Dates of House Members: Feb. 9,1965-Jan. 3,1967
Service Dates of Senate Members: Feb. 9,1965-Continued

HOUSE

Majority Rank Name	Party	State	Terms in: House	Terms in: Comm.	Minority Rank Name	Party	State	Terms in: House	Terms in: Comm.
VCh Patman, J.W. Wright	Dem	Tex.	19	*2 6	1st Widnall, William B.	Rep	N.J.	9	3
2nd Multer, Abraham J.	Dem	N.Y.	10	3	2nd Fino, Paul A.	Rep	N.Y.	7	2
3rd Barrett, William A.	Dem	Penn.	10	1					

SENATE

Majority Rank Name	Party	State	Years in: Senate	Years in: Comm.	Minority Rank Name	Party	State	Years in: Senate	Years in: Comm.
Chr Robertson, A. Willis	Dem	Va.	19	*2 11	1st Bennett, Wallace F.	Rep	Utah	15	6
2nd Sparkman, John J.	Dem	Ala.	19	11	2nd Tower, John G.	Rep	Tex.	4	2
3rd Douglas, Paul H.	Dem	Ill.	17	4					

*2: Member's 2nd period of service on the committee.

Changes:

Senate Majority:

Robertson, A. Willis — Dem — Va. — Dec. 30,1966 — Resigned; defeated for renomination.

Departures from the Senate:	Majority			Minority
Defeated for Reelection	Douglas, Paul H.	Ill.	Dem	None

JOINT COMMITTEE: DEFENSE PRODUCTION / 90th Congress

Service Dates of Committee Chair: Jan. 20,1967-Jan. 3,1969
Service Dates of House Members: Jan. 20,1967-Jan. 3,1969 (assignments reported Jan. 23,1967)
Service Dates of Senate Members: Jan. 11,1967-Continued

HOUSE

Majority					Minority				
			Terms in:					Terms in:	
Rank Name	**Party**	**State**	**House**	**Comm.**	**Rank Name**	**Party**	**State**	**House**	**Comm.**
Chr Patman, J.W. Wright	Dem	Tex.	20	*2 7	1st Widnall, William B.	Rep	N.J.	10	4
2nd Multer, Abraham J.	Dem	N.Y.	11	4	2nd Fino, Paul A.	Rep	N.Y.	8	3
3rd Barrett, William A.	Dem	Penn.	11	2					

SENATE

Majority					Minority				
			Years in:					Years in:	
Rank Name	**Party**	**State**	**Senate**	**Comm.**	**Rank Name**	**Party**	**State**	**Senate**	**Comm.**
VCh Sparkman, John J.	Dem	Ala.	21	13	1st Bennett, Wallace F.	Rep	Utah	17	8
2nd Proxmire, William	Dem	Wisc.	10	1	2nd Tower, John G.	Rep	Tex.	6	4
3rd Williams, Harrison A. Jr.	Dem	N.J.	9	1					

*2: Member's 2nd period of service on the committee.

Note: Senate membership on this committee was composed of the three ranking majority members and two ranking minority members of the Senate Banking and Currency Committee. "Service Dates of Senate Members" reflects members' service on the Standing Committee.

Changes:

House Majority:

Multer, Abraham J.	Dem	N.Y.	Dec. 31,1967	Resigned; elected to State Supreme Court.
Sullivan, Leonor Kretzer	Dem	Mo.	Feb. 5,1968	Replaced Multer.

House Minority:

Fino, Paul A.	Rep	N.Y.	Dec. 31,1968	Resigned; elected to State Supreme Court.

JOINT COMMITTEE: DEFENSE PRODUCTION / 91st Congress

Service Dates of Committee Chair: Jan. 17,1955-Jan. 3,1971
Service Dates of House Members: Feb. 5,1969-Jan. 3,1971
Service Dates of Senate Members: Jan. 3,1969-Feb. 26,1971

HOUSE

Majority					Minority				
			Terms in:					Terms in:	
Rank Name	**Party**	**State**	**House**	**Comm.**	**Rank Name**	**Party**	**State**	**House**	**Comm.**
VCh Patman, J.W. Wright	Dem	Tex.	21	*2 8	1st Widnall, William B.	Rep	N.J.	11	5
2nd Barrett, William A.	Dem	Penn.	12	3	2nd Brock, William E. III	Rep	Tenn.	4	1
3rd Sullivan, Leonor Kretzer	Dem	Mo.	9	2					

SENATE

Majority					Minority				
			Years in:					Years in:	
Rank Name	**Party**	**State**	**Senate**	**Comm.**	**Rank Name**	**Party**	**State**	**Senate**	**Comm.**
Chr Sparkman, John J.	Dem	Ala.	23	15	1st Bennett, Wallace F.	Rep	Utah	19	10
2nd Proxmire, William	Dem	Wisc.	12	2	2nd Tower, John G.	Rep	Tex.	8	6
3rd Williams, Harrison A. Jr.	Dem	N.J.	11	2					

*2: Member's 2nd period of service on the committee.

Departures from the House:	**Majority**	**Minority**	
Elected to U.S. Senate	None	Brock, William E. III	Tenn. Rep

JOINT COMMITTEE: DEFENSE PRODUCTION / 92nd Congress

Service Dates of Committee Chair: Mar. 2,1971-Jan. 3,1973
Service Dates of House Members: Mar. 2,1971-Jan. 3,1973
Service Dates of Senate Members: Feb. 26,1971-Jan. 31,1973

HOUSE

Majority			Terms in:		Minority			Terms in:	
Rank Name	**Party**	**State**	**House**	**Comm.**	**Rank Name**	**Party**	**State**	**House**	**Comm.**
Chr Patman, J.W. Wright	Dem	Tex.	22	*2 9	1st Widnall, William B.	Rep	N.J.	12	6
2nd Barrett, William A.	Dem	Penn.	13	4	2nd Brown, Garry E.	Rep	Mich.	3	1
3rd Sullivan, Leonor Kretzer	Dem	Mo.	10	3					

SENATE

Majority			Years in:		Minority			Years in:	
Rank Name	**Party**	**State**	**Senate**	**Comm.**	**Rank Name**	**Party**	**State**	**Senate**	**Comm.**
VCh Sparkman, John J.	Dem	Ala.	25	17	1st Bennett, Wallace F.	Rep	Utah	21	12
2nd Proxmire, William	Dem	Wisc.	14	4	2nd Tower, John G.	Rep	Tex.	10	8
3rd Williams, Harrison A. Jr.	Dem	N.J.	13	4					

*2: Member's 2nd period of service on the committee.

JOINT COMMITTEE: DEFENSE PRODUCTION / 93rd Congress

Service Dates of Committee Chair: Jan. 31,1973-Jan. 3,1975
Service Dates of House Members: Feb. 5,1973-Jan. 3,1975 (reported Feb. 6,1973)
Service Dates of Senate Members: Jan. 31,1973-Continued

HOUSE

Majority			Terms in:		Minority			Terms in:	
Rank Name	**Party**	**State**	**House**	**Comm.**	**Rank Name**	**Party**	**State**	**House**	**Comm.**
VCh Patman, J.W. Wright	Dem	Tex.	23	*2 10	1st Widnall, William B.	Rep	N.J.	13	7
2nd Barrett, William A.	Dem	Penn.	14	5	2nd Brown, Garry E.	Rep	Mich.	4	2
3rd Sullivan, Leonor Kretzer	Dem	Mo.	11	4					

SENATE

Majority			Years in:		Minority			Years in:	
Rank Name	**Party**	**State**	**Senate**	**Comm.**	**Rank Name**	**Party**	**State**	**Senate**	**Comm.**
Chr Sparkman, John J.	Dem	Ala.	27	19	1st Tower, John G.	Rep	Tex.	12	10
2nd Proxmire, William	Dem	Wisc.	16	6	2nd Bennett, Wallace F.	Rep	Utah	23	14
3rd Williams, Harrison A. Jr.	Dem	N.J.	15	6					

*2: Member's 2nd period of service on the committee.

Changes:

House Minority:

Widnall, William B.	Rep	N.J.	Dec. 31,1974	Resigned; defeated for reelection.

Senate Minority:

Bennett, Wallace F.	Rep	Utah	Dec. 20,1974	Resigned and retired.

Departures from Committee:

	Majority		Minority
House:			
No new assignment	Barrett, William A.	Penn. Dem	None

JOINT COMMITTEE: DEFENSE PRODUCTION / 94th Congress

Service Dates of Committee Chairs: Ch1 Jan. 28,1975-Mar. 7,1976
Ch2 Mar. 7,1976-Jan. 3,1977
Service Dates of House Members: Jan. 28,1975-Jan. 3,1977
Service Dates of Senate Members: Feb. 5,1975-Mar. 3,1977

HOUSE

Majority			Terms in:		Minority			Terms in:	
Rank Name	**Party**	**State**	**House**	**Comm.**	**Rank Name**	**Party**	**State**	**House**	**Comm.**
Ch1 Patman, J.W. Wright	Dem	Tex.	24	*2 11	1st Brown, Garry E.	Rep	Mich.	5	3
Ch2 Sullivan, Leonor Kretzer	Dem	Mo.	12	5	2nd Johnson, Albert W.	Rep	Penn.	7	1
3rd Reuss, Henry S.	Dem	Wisc.	11	1					

SENATE

Majority			Years in:		Minority			Years in:	
Rank Name	**Party**	**State**	**Senate**	**Comm.**	**Rank Name**	**Party**	**State**	**Senate**	**Comm.**
VCh Proxmire, William	Dem	Wisc.	18	8	1st Tower, John G.	Rep	Tex.	14	12
2nd Sparkman, John J.	Dem	Ala.	29	21	2nd Brooke, Edward W.	Rep	Mass.	9	1
3rd Williams, Harrison A. Jr.	Dem	N.J.	17	8					

*2: Member's 2nd period of service on the committee.

Note: "Service Dates of Senate Members" reflect the dates of service of Brooke; all other Senators continued service from the previous Congress without official reassignment recorded in the Congressional Record.

Changes:

Chair:

Patman, J.W. Wright	Dem	Tex.	Mar. 7,1976	Died in office.
Sullivan, Leonor Kretzer	Dem	Mo.	Mar. 7,1976	Succeeded Patman as Chair.

House Majority:

Reuss, Henry S.	Dem	Wisc.	Jan. 29,1976	Left committee; no new assignment.
Patman, J.W. Wright	Dem	Tex.	Mar. 7,1976	Died in office.
Mitchell, Parren J.	Dem	Md.	May 3,1976	Replaced Reuss (reported May 5,1976).
Evans, David W.	Dem	Ind.	May 3,1976	Replaced Patman (reported May 5,1976).

Departures from the House:	**Majority**			**Minority**	
Defeated for Reelection	None			Johnson, Albert W.	Penn. Rep
Retired	Sullivan, Leonor Kretzer	Mo.	Dem	None	
Departures from Committee:					
Senate:					
No new assignment	Williams, Harrison A.Jr.	N.J.	Dem	None	

JOINT COMMITTEE: DEFENSE PRODUCTION / 95th Congress

Service Dates of Committee Chair: Mar. 3,1977-Sep. 30,1977
Service Dates of House Members: Feb. 2,1977-Sep. 30,1977
Service Dates of Senate Members: Mar. 3,1977-Sep 30,1977

HOUSE

Majority			Terms in:		Minority			Terms in:	
Rank Name	**Party**	**State**	**House**	**Comm.**	**Rank Name**	**Party**	**State**	**House**	**Comm.**
VCh Mitchell, Parren J.	Dem	Md.	4	2	1st Brown, Garry E.	Rep	Mich.	6	4
2nd Evans, David W.	Dem	Ind.	2	2	2nd Wylie, Chalmers P.	Rep	Ohio	6	1
3rd Tsongas, Paul E.	Dem	Mass.	2	1					

SENATE

Majority			Years in:		Minority			Years in:	
Rank Name	**Party**	**State**	**Senate**	**Comm.**	**Rank Name**	**Party**	**State**	**Senate**	**Comm.**
Chr Proxmire, William	Dem	Wisc.	20	10	1st Brooke, Edward W.	Rep	Mass.	11	2
2nd Sparkman, John J.	Dem	Ala.	31	23	2nd Tower, John G.	Rep	Tex.	16	14
3rd McIntyre, Thomas J.	Dem	N.H.	15	1					

JOINT COMMITTEE: RAILROAD RETIREMENT LEGISLATION

Jurisdiction, 1951

From Senate Concurrent Resolution 51, 82nd Congress, First Session, October 18, 1951:

[Section 2.]

It shall be the duty of the joint committee, and it is hereby authorized and directed, to make a full and complete fact-finding study and investigation of the Railroad Retirement Act, and of such related problems as it may deem proper, with a view toward ascertaining what changes should be made in such act. The joint committee shall determine the scope of such study and investigation, without limitation thereon, and the following shall be given consideration:

1. The character and amount of present benefits and the estimated cost of providing such benefits.
2. The existing relationships between the system established by the Railroad Retirement Act and the old-age and survivors insurance system.
3. The changes that should be made in the character and amount of benefits to be provided workers subject to the Railroad Retirement Act and the estimated cost of providing such benefits.
4. Any changes that should be made in the existing relationships between the system established by the Railroad Retirement Act and the old-age and survivors insurance system with a view to simplifying administration, eliminating inequities and anomalies as regards benefits to workers whose earnings are included in whole or in part under either system, and strengthening the financial base for benefits to be provided under one system without impairing the financial base underlying benefits provided under the other system.

Termination, 1953

The Joint Committee was terminated upon the filing of Senate Report #6 (83-1), on January 9, 1953.

JOINT COMMITTEE: RAILROAD RETIREMENT LEGISLATION / 82nd Congress

Service Dates of Committee Chair: During Adjournment-Jan. 9,1953
Service Dates of House Members: Oct. 22,1951-Jan. 9,1953
Service Dates of Senate Members: During Adjournment-Jan. 9,1953

HOUSE

Majority Rank Name	Party	State	Terms in: House	Comm.	Minority Rank Name	Party	State	Terms in: House	Comm.
VCh Beckworth, Lindley G.	Dem	Tex.	7	1	1st Wolverton, Charles A.	Rep	N.J.	13	1
2nd Harris, Oren	Dem	Ark.	6	1					

SENATE

Majority Rank Name	Party	State	Years in: Senate	Comm.	Minority Rank Name	Party	State	Years in: Senate	Comm.
Chr Douglas, Paul H.	Dem	Ill.	4	1	Morse, Wayne	Rep	Ore.	7	1
2nd Hill, Lister	Dem	Ala.	15	1					

Note: The Senate adjourned for the 82nd Congress on Oct. 20,1951, two days after the establishment of this committee. No formal appointment of Senators could be found in the Congressional Record or in the Senate Journal before or after adjournment; however, committee members had been appointed by Mar. 26,1952 when Senate Concurrent Resolution 56 was passed providing a budget for the Joint Committee.

JOINT COMMITTEE: POSTAL SERVICE

Jurisdiction, 1951

From Public Law 82-233, 82nd Congress, First Session, October 30, 1951 (65 Statutes 672, 677-678):

[Section 13 b]

The joint committee, acting as a whole or by subcommittee, shall conduct a thorough study and investigation in respect of the following matters:

(1) Postal rates and charges in relation to the reasonable cost of handling the several classes of mail matter and special services, with due allowances in each class for the care required, the degree of preferment, priority in handling, and economic value of the services rendered and the public interest served thereby.
(2) The extent to which expenditures now charged to the Post Office Department for the following items should be excluded in considering costs for the several classes of mail matter and special services:
  (A) Expenditures for free postal services;
  (B) Expenditures in excess of revenues for international postal services;
  (C) Expenditures for subsidies for postal services pursuant to law or legislative policy of Congress;
  (D) Expenditures in excess of revenues, pursuant to the Act of June 5, 1930 (39 U.S.C. 793), not enumerated in the preceding subparagraphs (A), (B), or (C);
  (E) Expenditures for services of any character not otherwise enumerated herein which may be performed for other departments and agencies of the Government; and
  (F) Expenditures which may be justified only on a national welfare basis and not primarily as a business function.
(3) Expenditures for the Post Office Department by other Government agencies which should be considered in connection with the cost for the handling of the several classes of mail matter and special services, such as employees' retirement, use of Government buildings, and maintenance services.
(4) The extent, if any, to which Post Office Department expenditures in excess of revenue, for its various services and for the handling of various classes of mail, are justified as being in the public interest.

Termination, 1953

The Joint Committee was terminated upon filing Senate Report #7 (83-1) on January 13, 1953.

JOINT COMMITTEE: POSTAL SERVICE / 82nd Congress

Service Dates of Committee Chair: Jan. 10,1952-Jan. 13,1953
Service Dates of House Members: Jan. 31,1952-Jan. 13,1953
Service Dates of Senate Members: Jan. 31,1952-Jan. 13,1953

HOUSE

Majority			Terms in:		Minority			Terms in:	
Rank Name	**Party**	**State**	**House**	**Comm.**	**Rank Name**	**Party**	**State**	**House**	**Comm.**
1st Murray, Thomas J.	Dem	Tenn.	5	1	VCh Rees, Edward H.	Rep	Kans.	8	1
2nd Morrison, James H.	Dem	La.	5	1					

SENATE

Majority			Years in:		Minority			Years in:	
Rank Name	**Party**	**State**	**Senate**	**Comm.**	**Rank Name**	**Party**	**State**	**Senate**	**Comm.**
Chr Johnston, Olin D.	Dem	S.C.	8	1	1st Carlson, Frank	Rep	Kans.	2	1
2nd Underwood, Thomas R.	Dem	Ky.	1	1					

Changes:
Senate Majority:

Underwood, Thomas R.	Dem	Ky.	Nov. 4,1952	Resigned; defeated for election.

JOINT COMMITTEE: IMMIGRATION AND NATIONALITY POLICY

Jurisdiction, 1952

From Public Law 82-414, the Immigration and Nationality Act, 82nd Congress, Second Session, June 27, 1952 (66 Statutes 163, 274)

[Section 401]

(d) It shall be the function of the Committee to make a continuous study of
  (1) the administration of this Act, and its effect on the national security, the economy, and the social welfare of the United States, and
  (2) such conditions within or without the United States which in the opinion of the Committee might have any bearing on the immigration and nationality policy of the United States.

(e) The Committee shall make from time to time a report to the Senate and the House of Representatives concerning the results of its studies together with such recommendations as it may deem desirable.

Termination, 1970

The Joint Committee was terminated by authority of Public Law 91-510 [Part 2, Section 421], the Legislative Reorganization Act, passed October 26, 1970.

JOINT COMMITTEE: IMMIGRATION AND NATIONALITY POLICY / 82nd Congress

Service Dates of House Members: June 30,1952-Jan. 3,1953

HOUSE

Majority Rank	Name	Party	State	Terms in: House	Terms in: Comm.	Minority Rank	Name	Party	State	Terms in: House	Terms in: Comm.
1st	Walter, Francis E.	Dem	Penn.	10	1	1st	Graham, Louis E.	Rep	Penn.	7	1
2nd	Chelf, Frank L.	Dem	Ky.	4	*1 1	2nd	Thompson, Ruth	Rep	Mich.	1	1
3rd	Wilson, J. Frank	Dem	Tex.	3	1						

*1: Member's 1st period of service on the committee.

Note: Senate membership on this committee was appointed by the President of the Senate from among members of the Judiciary Committee. No Senate appointments were made in the 82nd Congress.

Departures from Committee:
House:

	Majority			Minority
No new assignment	Chelf, Frank L.	Ky.	Dem	None

JOINT COMMITTEE: IMMIGRATION AND NATIONALITY POLICY / 83rd Congress

Service Dates of Committee Chair: Feb. 4,1953-Continued
Service Dates of House Members: Jan. 26,1953-Jan. 3,1955
Service Dates of Senate Members: Feb. 4,1953-Mar. 30,1955

HOUSE

Majority Rank	Name	Party	State	Terms in: Senate	Terms in: Comm.	Minority Rank	Name	Party	State	Terms in: Senate	Terms in: Comm.
VCh	Graham, Louis E.	Rep	Penn.	8	2	1st	Walter, Francis E.	Dem	Penn.	11	2
2nd	Thompson, Ruth	Rep	Mich.	2	2	2nd	Wilson, J. Frank	Dem	Tex.	4	2
3rd	Hillings, Patrick J.	Rep	Cal.	2	*1 1						

SENATE — **Majority**

Rank	Name	Party	State	Years in: House	Years in: Comm.
Chr	Watkins, Arthur V.	Rep	Utah	7	1
2nd	Langer, William	Rep	N.D.	13	1
3rd	Dirksen, Everett M.	Rep	Ill.	3	*1 1

Minority

Rank	Name	Party	State	Years in: Senate	Years in: Comm.
1st	McCarran, Patrick A.	Dem	Nev.	20	1
2nd	Eastland, James O.	Dem	Miss.	11	1

*1: Member's 1st period of service on the committee.

Changes:

House Majority:

Hillings, Patrick J.	Rep	Cal.	Mar. 10,1954	Left committee; no new assignment.
Hyde, DeWitt S.	Rep	Md.	Mar. 10,1954	Replaced Hillings.

Senate Minority:

McCarran, Patrick A.	Dem	Nev.	Sep. 28,1954	Died in office.

Departures from the House:	**Majority**		**Minority**	
Defeated for Reelection	Graham, Louis E.	Penn. Rep	None	
Appointed State Judge	None		Wilson, J. Frank	Tex. Dem
Departures from Committee:				
House:				
No new assignment	Hyde, DeWitt S.	Md. Rep	None	
Senate:				
Moved to Joint Federal Expenditures	Dirksen, Everett McK.	Ill. Rep	None	
No new assignment	Langer, William	N.D. Rep	None	

JOINT COMMITTEE: IMMIGRATION AND NATIONALITY POLICY / 84th Congress

Service Dates of Committee Chair: Mar. 30,1955-Jan. 3,1956
Service Dates of House Members: Feb. 25,1955-Jan. 3,1957
Service Dates of Senate Members: Mar. 30,1955-Continued

HOUSE — **Majority**

Rank	Name	Party	State	Terms in: House	Terms in: Comm.
1st	Celler, Emanuel	Dem	N.Y.	17	1
2nd	Walter, Francis E.	Dem	Penn.	12	3
3rd	Feighan, Michael A.	Dem	Ohio	7	1

Minority

Rank	Name	Party	State	Terms in: House	Terms in: Comm.
1st	Thompson, Ruth	Rep	Mich.	3	3
2nd	Reed, Chauncey W.	Rep	Ill.	11	1

SENATE — **Majority**

Rank	Name	Party	State	Years in: Senate	Years in: Comm.
1st	Eastland, James O.	Dem	Miss.	13	3
2nd	Kilgore, Harley M.	Dem	W.Va.	15	1
3rd	Hennings, Thomas C. Jr.	Dem	Mo.	5	1

Minority

Rank	Name	Party	State	Years in: Senate	Years in: Comm.
Chr	Watkins, Arthur V.	Rep	Utah	9	3
2nd	Jenner, William E.	Rep	Ind.	9	1

Note: Arthur V. Watkins (Rep-Utah) was Chair of the committee in the previous Congress, and remained nominal Chair until sometime during the first session of the 84th Congress. No Chair or Vice Chair was listed in the Congressional Directory for the second session of the 84th Congress.

Changes:

House Minority:

Reed, Chauncey W.	Rep	Ill.	Feb. 9,1956	Died in office.
Keating, Kenneth B.	Rep	N.Y.	Apr. 23,1956	Replaced Reed.

Senate Majority:

Kilgore, Harley M.	Dem	W.Va.	Feb. 28,1956	Died in office.
McClellan, John L.	Dem	Ark.	June 7,1956	Replaced Kilgore.

Departures from the House:	**Majority**	**Minority**	
Lost for Renomination	None	Thompson, Ruth	Mich. Rep

JOINT COMMITTEE: IMMIGRATION AND NATIONALITY POLICY / 85th Congress

Service Dates of House Members: Jan. 30,1957-Jan. 3,1959
Service Dates of Senate Members: Jan. 3,1957-Continued

HOUSE

Majority			Terms in:		Minority			Terms in:	
Rank Name	**Party**	**State**	**House**	**Comm.**	**Rank Name**	**Party**	**State**	**House**	**Comm.**
1st Celler, Emanuel	Dem	N.Y.	18	2	1st Keating, Kenneth B.	Rep	N.Y.	6	2
2nd Walter, Francis E.	Dem	Penn.	13	4	2nd Hillings, Patrick J.	Rep	Cal.	4	*2 1
3rd Feighan, Michael A.	Dem	Ohio	8	2					

SENATE

Majority			Years in:		Minority			Years in:	
Rank Name	**Party**	**State**	**Senate**	**Comm.**	**Rank Name**	**Party**	**State**	**Senate**	**Comm.**
1st Eastland, James O.	Dem	Miss.	15	4	1st Watkins, Arthur V.	Rep	Utah	11	4
2nd Hennings, Thomas C. Jr.	Dem	Mo.	7	2	2nd Jenner, William E.	Rep	Ind.	11	2
3rd McClellan, John L.	Dem	Ark.	15	1					

*2: Member's 2nd period of service on the committee.

Note: No committee Chair is listed in Congressional Directory for either session of the 85th Congress.

	Majority	Minority		
Departures from the House:				
Elected to U.S. Senate	None	Keating, Kenneth B.	N.Y.	Rep
Lost Election for Attorney General	None	Hillings, Patrick J.	Cal.	Rep
Departures from the Senate:				
Lost for Reelection	None	Watkins, Arthur V.	Utah	Rep
Retired	None	Jenner, William E.	Ind.	Rep

JOINT COMMITTEE: IMMIGRATION AND NATIONALITY POLICY / 86th Congress

Service Dates of House Members: Jan. 22,1959-Jan. 3,1961
Service Dates of Senate Members: Feb. 5,1959-Continued

HOUSE

Majority			Terms in:		Minority			Terms in:	
Rank Name	**Party**	**State**	**House**	**Comm.**	**Rank Name**	**Party**	**State**	**House**	**Comm.**
1st Celler, Emanuel	Dem	N.Y.	19	3	1st McCulloch, William M.	Rep	Ohio	7	*1 1
2nd Walter, Francis E.	Dem	Penn.	14	5	2nd Moore, Arch A. Jr.	Rep	W.Va.	2	1
3rd Feighan, Michael A.	Dem	Ohio	9	3					

SENATE

Majority			Years in:		Minority			Years in:	
Rank Name	**Party**	**State**	**Senate**	**Comm.**	**Rank Name**	**Party**	**State**	**Senate**	**Comm.**
1st Eastland, James O.	Dem	Miss.	17	6	1st Dirksen, Everett M.	Rep	Ill.	9	*2 1
2nd Hennings, Thomas C. Jr.	Dem	Mo.	9	4	2nd Keating, Kenneth B.	Rep	N.Y.	1	1
3rd McClellan, John L.	Dem	Ark.	17	3					

*1: Member's 1st period of service on the committee; *2: Member's 2nd period of service on the committee.

Notes: No committee Chair is listed in Congressional Directory for either session of the 86th Congress. "Service Dates of Senate Members" reflect the dates of service of Dirksen and Keating; all other Senators continued service from the previous Congress without official reassignment recorded in the Congressional Record.

Changes:
Senate Majority:
Hennings, Thomas C. Jr. Dem Mo. Sep. 13,1960 Died in office.

	Majority	Minority		
Departures from Committee:				
House:				
No new assignment	None	McCulloch, William M.	Ohio	Rep

JOINT COMMITTEE: IMMIGRATION AND NATIONALITY POLICY / 87th Congress

Service Dates of House Members: Mar. 10,1961-Jan. 3,1963
Service Dates of Senate Members: Jan. 10,1961-Continued

HOUSE

Majority Rank Name	Party	State	Terms in: House	Terms in: Comm.	Minority Rank Name	Party	State	Terms in: House	Terms in: Comm.
1st Celler, Emanuel	Dem	N.Y.	20	4	1st Poff, Richard H.	Rep	Va.	5	1
2nd Walter, Francis E.	Dem	Penn.	15	6	2nd Moore, Arch A. Jr.	Rep	W.Va.	3	2
3rd Feighan, Michael A.	Dem	Ohio	10	4					

SENATE

Majority Rank Name	Party	State	Years in: Senate	Years in: Comm.	Minority Rank Name	Party	State	Years in: Senate	Years in: Comm.
1st Eastland, James O.	Dem	Miss.	19	8	1st Dirksen, Everett M.	Rep	Ill.	11 *2	2
2nd Johnston, Olin D.	Dem	S.C.	17	1	2nd Keating, Kenneth B.	Rep	N.Y.	3	2
3rd McClellan, John L.	Dem	Ark.	19	5					

*2: Member's 2nd period of service on the committee.

Note: As a member of the Judiciary Committee, Olin D. Johnston (Dem-S.C.) filled the vacancy created by the death of Thomas Hennings (Dem-Mo.) in the 86th Congress. "Service Dates of Senate Members" reflects members' service on the Judiciary Committee. No committee Chair is listed in Congressional Directory for either session of the 87th Congress.

JOINT COMMITTEE: IMMIGRATION AND NATIONALITY POLICY / 88th Congress

Service Dates of House Members: Jan. 31,1963-Jan. 3,1965
Service Dates of Senate Members: Jan. 3,1963-Continued

HOUSE

Majority Rank Name	Party	State	Terms in: House	Terms in: Comm.	Minority Rank Name	Party	State	Terms in: House	Terms in: Comm.
1st Celler, Emanuel	Dem	N.Y.	21	5	1st Poff, Richard H.	Rep	Va.	6	2
2nd Walter, Francis E.	Dem	Penn.	16	7	2nd Moore, Arch A. Jr.	Rep	W.Va.	4	3
3rd Feighan, Michael A.	Dem	Ohio	11	5					

SENATE

Majority Rank Name	Party	State	Years in: Senate	Years in: Comm.	Minority Rank Name	Party	State	Years in: Senate	Years in: Comm.
1st Eastland, James O.	Dem	Miss.	21	10	1st Dirksen, Everett M.	Rep	Ill.	13 *2	4
2nd Johnston, Olin D.	Dem	S.C.	19	2	2nd Keating, Kenneth B.	Rep	N.Y.	5	4
3rd McClellan, John L.	Dem	Ark.	21	7					

*2: Member's 2nd period of service on the committee.

Note: No committee Chair is listed in Congressional Directory for either session of the 88th Congress.

Changes:

House Majority:

Walter, Francis E.	Dem	Penn.	May 31,1963	Died in office.
Chelf, Frank L.	Dem	Ky.	Aug. 21,1963	Replaced Walter.

Departures from the Senate:	Majority	Minority		
Defeated for Reelection	None	Keating, Kenneth B.	N.Y.	Rep

JOINT COMMITTEE: IMMIGRATION AND NATIONALITY POLICY / 89th Congress

Service Dates of Committee Chair: Feb. 1,1965-Jan. 3,1967
Service Dates of House Members: Feb. 1,1965-Jan. 3,1967
Service Dates of Senate Members: Jan. 3,1965-Continued

HOUSE

Majority Rank	Name	Party	State	Terms in: House	Comm.	Minority Rank	Name	Party	State	Terms in: House	Comm.
Chr	Feighan, Michael A.	Dem	Ohio	12	6	1st	Poff, Richard H.	Rep	Va.	7	3
2nd	Celler, Emanuel	Dem	N.Y.	22	6	2nd	Moore, Arch A. Jr.	Rep	W.Va.	5	4
3rd	Chelf, Frank L.	Dem	Ky.	11	*2 2						

SENATE

Majority Rank	Name	Party	State	Years in: Senate	Comm.	Minority Rank	Name	Party	State	Years in: Senate	Comm.
1st	Eastland, James O.	Dem	Miss.	23	12	1st	Dirksen, Everett M.	Rep	Ill.	15	*2 6
2nd	Johnston, Olin D.	Dem	S.C.	21	4						
3rd	McClellan, John L.	Dem	Ark.	23	9						

*2: Member's 2nd period of service on the committee.

Changes:

House Minority:

Poff, Richard H.	Rep	Va.	Feb. 3,1965	Left committee due to conflicting subcommittee assignment.
McCulloch, William M.	Rep	Ohio	Feb. 3,1965	Replaced Poff (ranked ahead of Moore).

Senate Majority:

Johnston, Olin D.	Dem	S.C.	Apr. 18,1965	Died in office.

Departures from the House:

	Majority			Minority
Defeated for Reelection	Chelf, Frank L.	Ky.	Dem	None

JOINT COMMITTEE: IMMIGRATION AND NATIONALITY POLICY / 90th Congress

Service Dates of Committee Chair: Feb. 2,1967-Jan. 3,1969
Service Dates of House Members: Feb. 2,1967-Jan. 3,1969
Service Dates of Senate Members: Jan. 3,1967-Continued

HOUSE

Majority Rank	Name	Party	State	Terms in: House	Comm.	Minority Rank	Name	Party	State	Terms in: House	Comm.
Chr	Feighan, Michael A.	Dem	Ohio	13	7	1st	McCulloch, William M.	Rep	Ohio	11	*2 2
2nd	Celler, Emanuel	Dem	N.Y.	23	7	2nd	Moore, Arch A. Jr.	Rep	W.Va.	6	5
3rd	Rodino, Peter W. Jr.	Dem	N.J.	10	1						

SENATE

Majority Rank	Name	Party	State	Years in: Senate	Comm.	Minority Rank	Name	Party	State	Years in: Senate	Comm.
1st	Eastland, James O.	Dem	Miss.	25	14	1st	Dirksen, Everett M.	Rep	Ill.	17	*2 8
2nd	McClellan, John L.	Dem	Ark.	25	11						

*2: Member's 2nd period of service on the committee.

Departures from the House:

	Majority	Minority		
Elected Governor	None	Moore, Arch A. Jr.	W.Va.	Rep

JOINT COMMITTEE: IMMIGRATION AND NATIONALITY POLICY / 91st Congress

Service Dates of House Members: Feb. 6,1969-Oct. 26,1970
Service Dates of Senate Members: Jan. 3,1969-Oct. 26,1970

HOUSE

Majority			Terms in:		Minority			Terms in:	
Rank Name	**Party**	**State**	**House**	**Comm.**	**Rank Name**	**Party**	**State**	**House**	**Comm.**
1st Celler, Emanuel	Dem	N.Y.	24	8	1st McCulloch, William M.	Rep	Ohio	12	*2 3
2nd Feighan, Michael A.	Dem	Ohio	14	8	2nd Cahill, William T.	Rep	N.J.	6	1
3rd Rodino, Peter W. Jr.	Dem	N.J.	11	2					

SENATE

Majority			Years in:		Minority			Years in:	
Rank Name	**Party**	**State**	**Senate**	**Comm.**	**Rank Name**	**Party**	**State**	**Senate**	**Comm.**
1st Eastland, James O.	Dem	Miss.	27	16	1st Dirksen, Everett M.	Rep	Ill.	19	*2 10
2nd McClellan, John L.	Dem	Ark.	27	13	2nd Fong, Hiram L.	Rep	Hai.	10	1

*2: Member's 2nd period of service on the committee.

Note: No committee Chair is listed in Congressional Directory for either session of the 91st Congress.

Vacancy Filled:
Senate Minority: 2nd seat by Fong on Mar. 6,1970.

Changes:

House Minority:				
Cahill, William T.	Rep	N.J.	Jan. 19,1970	Resigned; elected Governor.
Meskill, Thomas J.	Rep	Conn.	June 11,1970	Replaced Cahill.
Senate Majority:				
Eastland, James O.	Dem	Miss.	Mar. 6,1970	Left committee; no new assignment.
McClellan, John L.	Dem	Ark.	Mar. 6,1970	Left committee; no new assignment.
Ervin, Samuel J.	Dem	N.C.	Mar. 6,1970	Replaced Eastland.
Senate Minority:				
Dirksen, Everett M.	Rep	Ill.	Mar. 6,1970	Left committee; no new assignment.
Thurmond, J. Strom	Rep	S.C.	Mar. 6,1970	Replaced Dirksen.

JOINT COMMITTEE: CONSTRUCTION OF A BUILDING FOR A MUSEUM OF HISTORY AND TECHNOLOGY FOR THE SMITHSONIAN INSTITUTION

Jurisdiction, 1955

From Public Law 84-106, 84th Congress, First Session, June 28, 1955 (69 Statutes 189):

[Section 1]

Be it enacted by the Senate and House of Representatives of the United States of America in Congress assembled, That the Regents of the Smithsonian Institution are hereby authorized and directed to have prepared drawings and specifications for, and to construct, a suitable building for a Museum of History and Technology (with requisite equipment, approaches, architectural landscape treatment of the grounds, and connections with public utilities and the Federal heating system) for the use of the Smithsonian Institution, . . .

[Section 4]

That there is hereby established a Joint Congressional Committee on Construction of a Building for a Museum of History and Technology for the Smithsonian Institution. it shall be the duty of the joint committee to advise with the Board of Regents of the Smithsonian Institution during the planning and construction of such building.

Termination, 1965

The Joint Committee was terminated upon the filing of its final report, Senate Document #58 (89-1), on September 15, 1965; however, the membership was not reappointed in the 89th Congress.

JOINT COMMITTEE: CONSTRUCTION OF A BUILDING FOR A MUSEUM OF HISTORY AND TECHNOLOGY FOR THE SMITHSONIAN INSTITUTION / 84th Congress

Service Dates of Committee Chair: Aug. 2,1955-Continued
Service Dates of House Members: Sep. 1,1955-Jan. 3,1957
Service Dates of Senate Members: Aug. 2,1955-Continued

HOUSE

Majority

Rank	Name	Party	State	Terms in: House	Terms in: Comm.
1st	Cannon, Clarence	Dem	Mo.	17	1
2nd	Brooks, Overton	Dem	La.	10	1
3rd	Jones, Robert E. Jr.	Dem	Ala.	5	1

Minority

Rank	Name	Party	State	Terms in: House	Terms in: Comm.
1st	Vorys, John M.	Rep	Ohio	9	1
2nd	Curtis, Laurence	Rep	Mass.	2	1

SENATE

Majority

Rank	Name	Party	State	Years in: Senate	Years in: Comm.
Chr	Anderson, Clinton P.	Dem	N.M.	7	1
2nd	Symington, W. Stuart	Dem	Mo.	4	1

Minority

Rank	Name	Party	State	Years in: Senate	Years in: Comm.
1st	Saltonstall, Leverett	Rep	Mass.	11	1
2nd	Smith, H. Alexander	Rep	N.J.	11	1
3rd	Martin, Edward	Rep	Penn.	9	1

Note: Stuart Symington (Dem-Mo.) was appointed after the adjournment of the first session of the 84th Congress; his appointment was reported on Jan. 5,1956.

Vacancy Filled:
Senate Majority: 2nd seat by Symington on Jan. 5,1956.

JOINT COMMITTEE: SMITHSONIAN CONSTRUCTION / 85th Congress

Service Dates of Committee Chair: Jan. 3,1957-Continued
Service Dates of House Members: Jan. 28,1957-Jan. 3,1959
Service Dates of Senate Members: Jan. 3,1957-Continued

HOUSE **Majority**

Rank	Name	Party	State	Terms in: House	Terms in: Comm.
1st	Cannon, Clarence	Dem	Mo.	18	2
2nd	Brooks, Overton	Dem	La.	11	2
3rd	Jones, Robert E. Jr.	Dem	Ala.	6	2

Minority

Rank	Name	Party	State	Terms in: House	Terms in: Comm.
1st	Vorys, John M.	Rep	Ohio	10	2
2nd	Curtis, Laurence	Rep	Mass.	3	2

SENATE **Majority**

Rank	Name	Party	State	Years in: Senate	Years in: Comm.
Chr	Anderson, Clinton P.	Dem	N.M.	9	2
2nd	Symington, W. Stuart	Dem	Mo.	5	2

Minority

Rank	Name	Party	State	Years in: Senate	Years in: Comm.
1st	Saltonstall, Leverett	Rep	Mass.	12	2
2nd	Smith, H. Alexander	Rep	N.J.	13	2
3rd	Martin, Edward	Rep	Penn.	11	2

	Majority	Minority	State	Party
Departures from the House:				
Retired	None	Vorys, John M.	Ohio	Rep
Departures from the Senate:				
Retired	None	Martin, Edward	Penn.	Rep
	None	Smith, H. Alexander	N.J.	Rep

JOINT COMMITTEE: SMITHSONIAN CONSTRUCTION / 86th Congress

Service Dates of Committee Chair: Feb. 9,1959-Continued
Service Dates of House Members: Jan. 29,1959-Jan. 3,1961
Service Dates of Senate Members: Feb. 9,1959-Continued

HOUSE **Majority**

Rank	Name	Party	State	Terms in: House	Terms in: Comm.
1st	Cannon, Clarence	Dem	Mo.	19	3
2nd	Brooks, Overton	Dem	La.	12	3
3rd	Jones, Robert E. Jr.	Dem	Ala.	7	3

Minority

Rank	Name	Party	State	Terms in: House	Terms in: Comm.
1st	Curtis, Laurence	Rep	Mass.	4	3
2nd	Bow, Frank T.	Rep	Ohio	5	1

SENATE **Majority**

Rank	Name	Party	State	Years in: Senate	Years in: Comm.
Chr	Anderson, Clinton P.	Dem	N.M.	11	4
2nd	Symington, W. Stuart	Dem	Mo.	7	4

Minority

Rank	Name	Party	State	Years in: Senate	Years in: Comm.
1st	Saltonstall, Leverett	Rep	Mass.	14	4
2nd	Carlson, Frank	Rep	Kans.	9	1
3rd	Bennett, Wallace F.	Rep	Utah	9	1

Note: "Service Dates of Senate Members" reflect the dates of service of Carlson and Bennett; all other Senators continued service from the previous Congress without official reassignment recorded in the Congressional Record.

Additions:
Senate: 3rd Fulbright, J. William Dem Ark. Mar. 9,1959

Changes:
Senate Minority:
Bennett, Wallace F. Rep Utah Mar. 9,1959 Left committee; no new assignment.

JOINT COMMITTEE: SMITHSONIAN CONSTRUCTION / 87th Congress

Service Dates of Committee Chair: Jan. 3,1961-Continued
Service Dates of House Members: Mar. 7,1961-Sep. 16,1961
Service Dates of Senate Members: Jan. 3,1957-Continued

HOUSE Majority

Rank	Name	Party	State	Terms in: House	Comm.
1st	Cannon, Clarence	Dem	Mo.	20	4
2nd	Brooks, Overton	Dem	La.	13	4
3rd	Jones, Robert E. Jr.	Dem	Ala.	8	4

Minority

Rank	Name	Party	State	Terms in: House	Comm.
1st	Curtis, Laurence	Rep	Mass.	5	4
2nd	Bow, Frank T.	Rep	Ohio	6	2

SENATE Majority

Rank	Name	Party	State	Years in: Senate	Comm.
Chr	Anderson, Clinton P.	Dem	N.M.	13	6
2nd	Fulbright, J. William	Dem	Ark.	17	2
3rd	Symington, W. Stuart	Dem	Mo.	9	6

Minority

Rank	Name	Party	State	Years in: Senate	Comm.
1st	Saltonstall, Leverett	Rep	Mass.	16	6
2nd	Carlson, Frank	Rep	Kans.	11	2

Changes:

House Majority:

Brooks, Overton	Dem	La.	Sep. 16,1961	Died in office.
Kirwan, Michael J.	Dem	Ohio	Jan. 15,1962	Replaced Brooks.

Departures from the House:

	Majority	Minority	
Lost Nomination for U.S. Senate	None	Curtis, Laurence	Mass. Rep

JOINT COMMITTEE: SMITHSONIAN CONSTRUCTION / 88th Congress

Service Dates of Committee Chair: Jan. 3,1963-Jan. 6,1965
Service Dates of House Members: Jan. 31,1963-Jan. 3,1965
Service Dates of Senate Members: Jan. 3,2963-Jan. 6,1965

HOUSE Majority

Rank	Name	Party	State	Terms in: House	Comm.
1st	Cannon, Clarence	Dem	Mo.	21	5
2nd	Jones, Robert E. Jr.	Dem	Ala.	9	5
3rd	Kirwan, Michael J.	Dem	Ohio	14	2

Minority

Rank	Name	Party	State	Terms in: House	Comm.
1st	Bow, Frank T.	Rep	Ohio	7	3
2nd	Fulton, James G.	Rep	Penn.	10	1

SENATE Majority

Rank	Name	Party	State	Years in: Senate	Comm.
Chr	Anderson, Clinton P.	Dem	N.M.	15	8
2nd	Fulbright, J. William	Dem	Ark.	19	4
3rd	Symington, W. Stuart	Dem	Mo.	11	8

Minority

Rank	Name	Party	State	Years in: Senate	Comm.
1st	Saltonstall, Leverett	Rep	Mass.	18	8
2nd	Carlson, Frank	Rep	Kans.	13	4

Changes:

House Majority:

Cannon, Clarence	Dem	Mo.	May 12,1964	Died in office.
Mahon, George H.	Dem	Tex.	May 20,1964	Replaced Cannon.

JOINT COMMITTEE: WASHINGTON METROPOLITAN PROBLEMS

Jurisdiction, 1957

From House Concurrent Resolution 172, as amended, 85th Congress, First Session, August, 29, 1957:

[Section 2]

The joint committee, or any duly authorized subcommittee thereof, shall examine, investigate, and make a complete study of any and all matters pertaining to --

(a) the problems created by the growth and expansion of the District of Columbia and its metropolitan area,
(b) how and with what degree of success such problems are handled and resolved by the various agencies and instrumentalities of the Government which are charged with the duty of resolving such problems, and
(c) how the resolution of such problems is affecting the affairs of the District of Columbia. The joint committee shall report its findings, together with its recommendations for such legislation as it deems advisable, to the Senate and the House of Representatives at the earliest practicable date, . . .

Termination, 1960

The Joint Committee was terminated upon the filing of Senate Report 1903 (86-2), on August 23, 1960.

JOINT COMMITTEE: WASHINGTON METROPOLITAN PROBLEMS / 85th Congress

Service Dates of Committee Chair: Aug. 30,1957-Continued
Service Dates of House Members: Aug. 30,1957-Jan. 3,1959
Service Dates of Senate Members: Aug. 30,1957-Continued

HOUSE — Majority / Minority

Rank	Name	Party	State	Terms in: House	Terms in: Comm.	Rank	Name	Party	State	Terms in: House	Terms in: Comm.
1st	McMillan, John L.	Dem	S.C.	10	1	VCh	Hyde, DeWitt S.	Rep	Md.	3	1
2nd	Smith, Howard W.	Dem	Va.	14	1						

SENATE — Majority / Minority

Rank	Name	Party	State	Years in: Senate	Years in: Comm.	Rank	Name	Party	State	Years in: Senate	Years in: Comm.
Chr	Bible, Alan H.	Dem	Nev.	3	1	1st	Beall, J. Glenn	Rep	Md.	5	1
2nd	Morse, Wayne L.	Dem	Ore.	13	1						

Departures from the House:	Majority	Minority		
Defeated for Reelection	None	Hyde, DeWitt S.	Md.	Rep

JOINT COMMITTEE: WASHINGTON METROPOLITAN PROBLEMS / 86th Congress

Service Dates of Committee Chair: Jan. 3,1959-Aug. 23,1960
Service Dates of House Members: Jan. 21,1959-Aug. 23,1960
Service Dates of Senate Members: Jan. 3,1959-Aug. 23,1960

HOUSE — Majority / Minority

Rank	Name	Party	State	Terms in: House	Terms in: Comm.	Rank	Name	Party	State	Terms in: House	Terms in: Comm.
VCh	McMillan, John L.	Dem	S.C.	11	2	1st	Broyhill, Joel T.	Rep	Va.	4	1
2nd	Smith, Howard W.	Dem	Va.	15	2						

SENATE — Majority / Minority

Rank	Name	Party	State	Years in: Senate	Years in: Comm.	Rank	Name	Party	State	Years in: Senate	Years in: Comm.
Chr	Bible, Alan H.	Dem	Nev.	5	2	1st	Beall, J. Glenn	Rep	Md.	7	2
2nd	Morse, Wayne L.	Dem	Ore.	15	2						

JOINT COMMITTEE: ORGANIZATION OF CONGRESS

Jurisdiction, 1965

From Senate Concurrent Resolution 2, 89th Congress, First Session, March 11, 1965:

[Section 2]

The committee shall make a full and complete study of the organization and operation of the Congress of the United States and shall recommend improvements in such organization and operation with a view toward strengthening the Congress, simplifying its operations, improving its relationships with other branches of the United States Government, and enabling it better to meet its responsibilities under the Constitution. This study shall include, but shall not be limited to, the organization and operation of each House of the Congress; the relationship between the two Houses; the relationships between the Congress and other branches of the Government; the employment and remuneration of officers and employees of the respective Houses and officers and employees of the committees and Members of Congress; and the structure of, and the relationships between, the various standing, special, and select committees of the Congress: *Provided,* That nothing in this Concurrent Resolution shall be construed to authorize the committee to make any recommendations with respect to the rules, parliamentary procedure, practices, and/or precedents of either House, or the consideration of any matter on the floor of either House: *Provided further,* That the language employed herein shall not prohibit the committee from studying and recommending the consolidation and reorganization of committees.

Termination, 1967

The Joint Committee filed its final report, Senate Report #1414 (89-2) (House Report #1781), on July 28, 1966. The Joint Committee was extended by Senate Concurrent Resolution 2 (90-1), agreed to January 31, 1967. It was further extended by Senate Concurrent Resolution 32, agreed to June 12, 1967, and terminated by its authority on December 31, 1967.

JOINT COMMITTEE: ORGANIZATION OF CONGRESS / 89th Congress

Service Dates of House Members: Mar. 11,1965-Jan. 3,1967
Service Dates of Senate Members: Mar. 15,1965-Continued

HOUSE

Majority Rank Name	Party	State	Terms in: House	Comm.	Minority Rank Name	Party	State	Terms in: House	Comm.
CoCh Madden, Ray J.	Dem	Ind.	12	1	1st Curtis, Thomas B.	Rep	Mo.	8	1
2nd Brooks, Jack B.	Dem	Tex.	7	1	2nd Griffin, Robert P.	Rep	Mich.	5	1
3rd Hechler, Kenneth	Dem	W.Va.	4	1	3rd Hall, Durward G.	Rep	Mo.	3	1

SENATE

Majority Rank Name	Party	State	Years in: Senate	Comm.	Minority Rank Name	Party	State	Years in: Senate	Comm.
CoCh Monroney, A. S. Mike	Dem	Okla.	15	1	1st Mundt, Karl E.	Rep	S.D.	17	1
2nd Sparkman, John J.	Dem	Ala.	19	1	2nd Case, Clifford P.	Rep	N.J.	11	1
3rd Metcalf, Lee	Dem	Mont.	5	1	3rd Boggs, J. Caleb	Rep	Del.	5	1

Changes:

House Minority:

Griffin, Robert P.	Rep	Mich.	May 10,1966	Resigned; appointed to U.S. Senate.
Cleveland, James C.	Rep	N.H.	May 18,1966	Replaced Griffin.

JOINT COMMITTEE: ORGANIZATION OF CONGRESS / 90th Congress

Service Dates of House Members: Jan. 31,1967-Dec. 31,1967
Service Dates of Senate Members: Jan. 3,1967-Dec. 31,1967

HOUSE

Majority			Terms in:		Minority			Terms in:	
Rank Name	**Party**	**State**	**House**	**Comm.**	**Rank Name**	**Party**	**State**	**House**	**Comm.**
CoCh Madden, Ray J.	Dem	Ind.	13	2	1st Curtis, Thomas B.	Rep	Mo.	9	2
2nd Brooks, Jack B.	Dem	Tex.	8	2	2nd Hall, Durward G.	Rep	Mo.	4	2
3rd Hechler, Kenneth	Dem	W.Va.	5	2	3rd Cleveland, James C.	Rep	N.H.	3	2

SENATE

Majority			Years in:		Minority			Years in:	
Rank Name	**Party**	**State**	**Senate**	**Comm.**	**Rank Name**	**Party**	**State**	**Senate**	**Comm.**
CoCh Monroney, A. S. Mike	Dem	Okla.	17	2	1st Mundt, Karl E.	Rep	S.D.	19	2
2nd Sparkman, John J.	Dem	Ala.	21	2	2nd Case, Clifford P.	Rep	N.J.	13	2
3rd Metcalf, Lee	Dem	Mont.	7	2	3rd Boggs, J. Caleb	Rep	Del.	7	2

Note: The House voted to continue the Joint Committee on Jan. 31,1967, without renaming the membership of the committee.

JOINT COMMITTEE: CONGRESSIONAL OPERATIONS

Jurisdiction, 1970

From Public Law 91-510, the Legislative Reorganization Act of 1970, 91st Congress, Second Session, October 26, 1970

[Section 402]

(a) The joint committee shall--
   (1) make a continuing study of the organization and operation of the Congress of the United States and shall recommend improvements in such organization and operation with a view toward strengthening Congress, simplifying its operations, improving its relationships with other branches of the United States Government, and enabling it better to meet its responsibilities under the Constitution of the United States; and
   (2) identify any court proceeding or action which, in the opinion of the joint committee, is of vital interest to the Congress, or to either House of the Congress, as a constitutionally established institution of the Federal Government and call such proceeding or action to the attention of that House of the Congress which is specifically concerned or to both Houses of the Congress if both Houses are concerned.

(b) The joint committee shall exercise all functions vested in it by section 406 of this Part,
(c) The joint committee shall report, from time to time, to the Senate and the House of Representatives their recommendations with respect to matters within the jurisdiction of the joint committee.
(d) Nothing in this Part shall be construed to authorize the joint committee to make any recommendations with respect to the rules, parliamentary procedure, practices, or precedents of either House or the consideration of any matter on the floor of either House.

[Section 406 (a)]

There is hereby established for the Congress an Office of Placement and Office Management which shall be subject to the supervision and control of the joint committee. The joint committee is authorized, by record vote of a majority of the members of the joint committee--

(1) to appoint, on a permanent basis, without regard to political affiliation, and solely on the basis of fitness to perform his duties, a Director of the Office of Placement and Office Management to serve as the head of the staff of the Office and such personnel as the joint committee deems necessary;
(2) to prescribe their duties and responsibilities;
(3) to fix their pay at respective per annum gross rates not in excess of the highest rate of basic pay, as in effect from time to time, of the General Schedule of section 5332(a) of title 5, United States Code; and
(4) to terminate their employment, as the joint committee may deem appropriate.

Jurisdiction, 1974

From House Resolution 1395, 93rd Congress, Second Session, October 8, 1974:

[Section 206]

The House members of the joint committee on Congressional Operations shall undertake and conduct a continuing study of the jurisdiction of the various standing committees of the House under Rule X of the Rules of the House and the relative workloads sustained by such committees as a result thereof, and periodically shall prepare for submission to and consideration by the Committee on Rules (and for possible submission by that committee to the full House) a report including any recommended changes in the Rules of the House which may be necessary or appropriate to effect a more equitable distribution of workload or a more rational combination of jurisdictional responsibilities. it is the sense of the House of Representatives that the House members of the joint committee on Congressional Operations should work with the Senate members of such joint committee in an effort to rationalize the committee jurisdiction between the Houses.

Termination, 1977

The Joint Committee was terminated by Senate Resolution 4 (95-1), February 4, 1977, which discontinued Senate participation in the committee. The House Select Committee on Congressional Operations was established on March 28, 1977 to carry on the functions of the joint committee.

JOINT COMMITTEE: CONGRESSIONAL OPERATIONS / 92nd Congress

Service Dates of Committee Chair: Feb. 25,1971-Jan. 3,1973
Service Dates of House Members: Feb. 25,1971-Jan. 3,1973
Service Dates of Senate Majority Members: Jan. 28,1971-Continued
Service Dates of Senate Minority Members: Feb. 18,1971-Jan. 12,1973

HOUSE **Majority**

Rank	Name	Party	State	Terms in: House	Terms in: Comm.
Chr	Brooks, Jack B.	Dem	Tex.	10	1
2nd	Giaimo, Robert N.	Dem	Conn.	7	1
3rd	O'Hara, James G.	Dem	Mich.	7	1

Minority

Rank	Name	Party	State	Terms in: House	Terms in: Comm.
1st	Hall, Durward G.	Rep	Mo.	6	1
2nd	Cleveland, James C.	Rep	N.H.	5	1

SENATE **Majority**

Rank	Name	Party	State	Years in: Senate	Years in: Comm.
VCh	Metcalf, Lee	Dem	Mont.	11	1
2nd	Gravel, Mike	Dem	Alas.	3	1
3rd	Chiles, Lawton M. Jr.	Dem	Fla.	1	1

Minority

Rank	Name	Party	State	Years in: Senate	Years in: Comm.
1st	Case, Clifford P.	Rep	N.J.	17	1
2nd	Schweiker, Richard S.	Rep	Penn.	3	1

	Majority	Minority		
Departures from the House:				
Retired	None	Hall, Durward G.	Mo.	Rep
Departures from Committee:				
Senate:				
Moved to Appropriations	None	Schweiker, Richard S.	Penn.	Rep
No new assignment	None	Case, Clifford P.	N.J.	Rep

JOINT COMMITTEE: CONGRESSIONAL OPERATIONS / 93rd Congress

Service Dates of Committee Chair: Jan. 12,1973-Continued
Service Dates of House Members: Feb. 5,1973-Jan. 3,1975
Service Dates of Senate Members: Jan. 12,1973-Continued

HOUSE **Majority**

Rank	Name	Party	State	Terms in: House	Terms in: Comm.
VCh	Brooks, Jack B.	Dem	Tex.	11	2
2nd	Giaimo, Robert N.	Dem	Conn.	8	2
3rd	O'Hara, James G.	Dem	Mich.	8	2

Minority

Rank	Name	Party	State	Terms in: House	Terms in: Comm.
1st	Cleveland, James C.	Rep	N.H.	6	2
2nd	Dellenback, John R.	Rep	Ore.	4	1

SENATE **Majority**

Rank	Name	Party	State	Years in: Senate	Years in: Comm.
Chr	Metcalf, Lee	Dem	Mont.	13	2
2nd	Gravel, Mike	Dem	Alas.	5	2
3rd	Chiles, Lawton M. Jr.	Dem	Fla.	3	2

Minority

Rank	Name	Party	State	Years in: Senate	Years in: Comm.
1st	Taft, Robert Jr.	Rep	Ohio	3	1
2nd	Weicker, Lowell P. Jr.	Rep	Conn.	3	1

Note: "Service Dates of Senate Members" reflect the dates of service of Taft and Weicker; all other Senators continued service from the previous Congress without official reappointment recorded in the Congressional Record.

Changes:

Senate Minority:

Weicker, Lowell P. Jr.	Rep	Conn.	Mar. 26,1973	Left committee; no new assignment.
Helms, Jesse A.	Rep	N.C.	Mar. 26,1973	Replaced Weicker.

	Majority	Minority	
Departures from the House:			
Defeated for Reelection	None	Dellenback, John R.	Ore. Rep
Departures from the Senate:			
Defeated for Reelection	None	Taft, Robert Jr.	Ohio Rep

JOINT COMMITTEE: CONGRESSIONAL OPERATIONS / 94th Congress

Service Dates of Committee Chair: Jan. 31,1975-Jan. 3,1977
Service Dates of House Members: Jan. 31,1975-Jan. 3,1977
Service Dates of Senate Members: Jan. 29,1975-Continued

HOUSE

Majority

Rank	Name	Party	State	Terms in: House	Terms in: Comm.
Chr	Brooks, Jack B.	Dem	Tex.	12	3
2nd	Giaimo, Robert N.	Dem	Conn.	9	3
3rd	O'Hara, James G.	Dem	Mich.	9	3

Minority

Rank	Name	Party	State	Terms in: House	Terms in: Comm.
1st	Cleveland, James C.	Rep	N.H.	7	3
2nd	Ashbrook, John M.	Rep	Ohio	8	1

SENATE

Majority

Rank	Name	Party	State	Years in: Senate	Years in: Comm.
VCh	Metcalf, Lee	Dem	Mont.	15	4
2nd	Gravel, Mike	Dem	Alas.	7	4
3rd	Chiles, Lawton M. Jr.	Dem	Fla.	5	4

Minority

Rank	Name	Party	State	Years in: Senate	Years in: Comm.
1st	Helms, Jesse A.	Rep	N.C.	3	2
2nd	Domenici, Pete V.	Rep	N.M.	3	1

Note: "Service Dates of Senate Members" reflect the dates of service of Domenici; all other Senators continued service from the previous Congress without official reappointment recorded in the Congressional Record.

	Majority		Minority
Departures from the House:			
Lost Nomination to U.S. Senate	O'Hara, James G.	Mich. Dem	None

JOINT COMMITTEE: CONGRESSIONAL OPERATIONS / 95th Congress

Service Dates of Committee Chair: Jan. 17,1977-Feb. 4,1977
Service Dates of House Members: Jan. 17,1977-Feb. 4,1977
Service Dates of Senate Members: Jan. 3,1977-Feb. 4,1977

HOUSE

Majority

Rank	Name	Party	State	Terms in: House	Terms in: Comm.
VCh	Brooks, Jack B.	Dem	Tex.	13	4
2nd	Giaimo, Robert N.	Dem	Conn.	10	4
3rd	Oberstar, James L.	DFL	Minn.	2	1

Minority

Rank	Name	Party	State	Terms in: House	Terms in: Comm.
1st	Cleveland, James C.	Rep	N.H.	8	4
2nd	Ashbrook, John M.	Rep	Ohio	9	2

SENATE

Majority

Rank	Name	Party	State	Years in: Senate	Years in: Comm.
Chr	Metcalf, Lee	Dem	Mont.	17	6
2nd	Gravel, Mike	Dem	Alas.	9	6
3rd	Chiles, Lawton M. Jr.	Dem	Fla.	7	6

Minority

Rank	Name	Party	State	Years in: Senate	Years in: Comm.
1st	Helms, Jesse A.	Rep	N.C.	5	4
2nd	Domenici, Pete V.	Rep	N.M.	5	2

JOINT COMMITTEE: STUDY BUDGET CONTROL

Jurisdiction, 1972

From Public Law 92-599, 92nd Congress, Second Session, October 27, 1972 (86 Statutes 1324-1325):

[Section 301]

(b) The joint committee created by subsection (a) shall make a full study and review of--

(1) the procedures which should be adopted by the Congress for the purpose of improving congressional control of budgetary outlay and receipt totals, including procedures for establishing and maintaining an overall view of each year's budgetary outlays which is fully coordinated with and overall view of the anticipated revenues for that year, and

(2) the operation of the limitation on expenditures and net lending imposed by section 201 of this Act for the fiscal year ending June 30, 1973.

The joint committee shall report the results of such study and review to the Speaker of the House of Representatives and to the President pro tempore of the Senate, not later than February 15, 1973.

Termination, 1973

The Joint Committee was terminated upon the filing of House Report #147 (93-1), on April 18, 1973 along with House Resolution 7130.

JOINT COMMITTEE: STUDY BUDGET CONTROL / 92nd Congress

Service Dates of House Members: Nov. 27,1972-Jan. 3,1973 (assignments reported Jan. 3,1973)

HOUSE **Majority**

Rank	Name	Party	State	Terms in: House	Terms in: Comm.
CoCh	Whitten, Jamie L.	Dem	Miss.	16	1
CoCh	Ullman, Albert C.	Dem	Ore.	8	1
3rd	Mahon, George H.	Dem	Tex.	19	1
4th	Rooney, John J.	Dem	N.Y.	15	1
5th	Sikes, Robert L. F.	Dem	Fla.	16	1
6th	Griffiths, Martha W.	Dem	Mich.	9	1
7th	Reuss, Henry S.	Dem	Wisc.	9	1
8th	Burke, James A.	Dem	Mass.	7	1
9th	Rostenkowski, Daniel D.	Dem	Ill.	7	1

Minority

Rank	Name	Party	State	Terms in: House	Terms in: Comm.
CoVc	Schneebeli, Herman T.	Rep	Penn.	7	1
2nd	Cederberg, Elford A.	Rep	Mich.	10	1
3rd	Broyhill, Joel T.	Rep	Va.	10	1
4th	Rhodes, John J.	Rep	Ariz.	10	1
5th	Davis, Glenn R.	Rep	Wisc.	9	1
6th	Collier, Harold R.	Rep	Ill.	8	1
7th	Broyhill, James T.	Rep	N.C.	5	1

JOINT COMMITTEE: STUDY BUDGET CONTROL / 93rd Congress

Service Dates of Committee Chair: Jan. 3,1973-Apr. 18,1973
Service Dates of House Members: Jan. 3,1973-Apr. 18,1973
Service Dates of Senate Members: Jan. 3,1973-Apr. 18,1973

HOUSE **Majority**

Rank	Name	Party	State	Terms in: House	Terms in: Comm.
CoCh	Whitten, Jamie L.	Dem	Miss.	17	2
CoCh	Ullman, Albert C.	Dem	Ore.	9	2
3rd	Mahon, George H.	Dem	Tex.	20	2
4th	Rooney, John J.	Dem	N.Y.	16	2
5th	Sikes, Robert L. F.	Dem	Fla.	17	2
6th	Griffiths, Martha W.	Dem	Mich.	10	2
7th	Reuss, Henry S.	Dem	Wisc.	10	2
8th	Burke, James A.	Dem	Mass.	8	2
9th	Rostenkowski, Daniel D.	Dem	Ill.	8	2

Minority

Rank	Name	Party	State	Terms in: House	Terms in: Comm.
CoVc	Schneebeli, Herman T.	Rep	Penn.	8	2
2nd	Cederberg, Elford A.	Rep	Mich.	11	2
3rd	Broyhill, Joel T.	Rep	Va.	11	2
4th	Rhodes, John J.	Rep	Ariz.	11	2
5th	Davis, Glenn R.	Rep	Wisc.	10	2
6th	Collier, Harold R.	Rep	Ill.	9	2
7th	Broyhill, James T.	Rep	N.C.	6	2

SENATE **Majority**

Rank	Name	Party	State	Years in: Senate	Years in: Comm.
CoVc	McClellan, John L.	Dem	Ark.	31	1
2nd	Fulbright, J. William	Dem	Ark.	29	1
3rd	Stennis, John C.	Dem	Miss.	26	1
CoVc	Long, Russell B.	Dem	La.	25	1
5th	Pastore, John O.	Dem	R.I.	23	1
6th	Bible, Alan H.	Dem	Nev.	19	1
7th	Talmadge, Herman E.	Dem	Ga.	17	1
8th	Proxmire, William	Dem	Wisc.	16	1
9th	Hartke, R. Vance	Dem	Ind.	15	1

Minority

Rank	Name	Party	State	Years in: Senate	Years in: Comm.
1st	Young, Milton R.	Rep	N.D.	28	1
2nd	Bennett, Wallace F.	Rep	Utah	23	1
3rd	Cotton, Norris	Rep	N.H.	19	1
CoVc	Hruska, Roman :	Rep	Nev.	19	1
5th	Curtis, Carl T.	Rep	Neb.	19	1
6th	Fannin, Paul J.	Rep	Ariz.	9	1
7th	Roth, William V. Jr.	Rep	Del.	3	1

JOINT COMMITTEE: BICENTENNIAL ARRANGEMENTS

Jurisdiction, 1975

From Senate Concurrent Resolution 44, 94th Congress, First Session, May 22, 1975:

[Section 3]

The joint committee shall--

(1) coordinate the planning and implementation of Bicentennial activities and events of the Congress with the activities and events of other Governmental and non-governmental groups;
(2) consult with the Speaker of the House of Representatives and the President of the Senate to provide for representation of the Congress at appropriate Bicentennial ceremonies and events; and
(3) develop and implement programs to inform and emphasize to the Nation the role of the Congress, as the representative of the people, from its historic beginnings in pre-revolution days through 200 years of growth, challenge and change.

Termination, 1976

The Joint Committee was terminated at the end of the Second Session of the 94th Congress.

JOINT COMMITTEE: BICENTENNIAL ARRANGEMENTS / 94th Congress

Service Dates of Committee Chair: Sep. 5,1975-Dec. 31,1976
Service Dates of House Members: Sep. 5,1975-Dec. 31,1976
Service Dates of Senate Members: Sep. 5,1975-Dec. 31,1976

HOUSE

Majority					Minority				
			Terms in:					Terms in:	
Rank Name	**Party**	**State**	**House**	**Comm.**	**Rank Name**	**Party**	**State**	**House**	**Comm.**
Chr Boggs, Corinne C. (Lindy)	Dem	La.	2	1	1st Butler, M. Caldwell	Rep	Va.	3	1
2nd O'Neill, Thomas P. Jr.	Dem	Mass.	12	1	2nd Rhodes, John J.	Rep	Ariz.	12	1
3rd Pickle, J. J. (Jake)	Dem	Tex.	7	1	3rd Esch, Marvin L.	Rep	Mich.	5	1

SENATE

Majority					Minority				
			Years in:					Years in:	
Rank Name	**Party**	**State**	**Senate**	**Comm.**	**Rank Name**	**Party**	**State**	**Senate**	**Comm.**
1st Montoya, Joseph M.	Dem	N.M.	11	1	VCh Brooke, Edward W.	Rep	Mass.	9	1
2nd Mansfield, Michael J.	Dem	Mont.	23	1	2nd Scott, Hugh D. Jr.	Rep	Penn.	17	1
3rd Humphrey, Hubert H. Jr.	DFL	Minn.	21	1	3rd Hruska, Roman L.	Rep	Neb.	21	1

Note: The joint committee was comprised of the majority and minority leaders of each chamber and two additional members.

Vacancies Filled:
Senate Majority: 3rd seat by Humphrey on Sep. 10,1975.
Senate Minority: 3rd seat by Hruska on Sep. 10,1975.

Changes:
House Minority:

Esch, Marvin L.	Rep	Mich.	June 23,1976	Left committee; no new assignment.
McDade, Joseph M.	Rep	Penn.	June 23,1976	Replaced Esch.

TEMPORARY JOINT COMMITTEE: DEFICIT REDUCTION

Jurisdiction, 1987

From Public Law 99-177, 99th Congress, First Session, December 12, 1985 (99 Statutes 1100):

[Section 274 (f)]

Alternative Procedures for the Joint Reports of the Directors.--

(1) In the event that any of the reporting procedures described in section 251 are invalidated, then any report of the Directors referred to in section 251(a) or (c)(1) shall be transmitted to the joint committee established under this subsection.
(2) Upon the invalidation of any such procedure there is established a Temporary Joint Committee on Deficit Reduction, composed of the entire membership of the Budget Committees of the House of Representatives and the Senate. The Chairmen of these two committees shall act as Co-Chairmen of the Joint Committee. Actions taken by the Joint Committee shall be determined by the majority vote of the members representing each House. The purposes of the Joint Committee are to receive the reports of the Directors as described in paragraph (1), and to report (with respect to each such report of the Directors) a joint resolution as described in paragraph (3).
(3) No later than 5 days after the receipt of a report of the Directors in accordance with paragraph (1), the Joint Committee shall report to the House of Representatives and the Senate a joint resolution setting forth the contents of the report of the Directors.

Termination, 1989

The Joint Committee was terminated upon the adjustment to the Gramm-Rudman-Hollings Act by Public Law 100-119, signed September 29,1987.

TEMPORARY JOINT COMMITTEE: DEFICIT REDUCTION / 100th Congress

Service Dates of Committee Chair: Feb. 23,1987- Sep. 29,1987
Service Dates of House Members: Feb. 23,1987-Sep. 29,1987
Service Dates of Senate Members: Jan. 6,1987-Sep. 29,1987

HOUSE **Majority**

Rank	Name	Party	State	Terms in: House	Terms in: Comm.
CoCh	Gray, William H. III	Dem	Penn.	5 *2	1
2nd	Foley, Thomas S.	Dem	Wash.	12	1
3rd	Lowry, Michael E.	Dem	Wash.	5	1
4th	Derrick, Butler C. Jr.	Dem	S.C.	7 *2	1
5th	Miller, George	Dem	Cal.	7	1
6th	Williams, Pat	Dem	Mont.	5	1
7th	Wolpe, Howard E.	Dem	Mich.	5	1
8th	Frost, J. Martin III	Dem	Tex.	5	1
9th	Fazio, Victor H.	Dem	Cal.	5	1
10th	Russo, Martin A.	Dem	Ill.	7	1
11th	Jenkins, Edgar L.	Dem	Ga.	6	1
12th	Leath, J. Marvin	Dem	Tex.	5	1
13th	Schumer, Charles E.	Dem	N.Y.	4	1
14th	Boxer, Barbara	Dem	Cal.	3	1
15th	MacKay, Kenneth H.	Dem	Fla.	3	1
16th	Slattery, Jim	Dem	Kans.	3	1
17th	Atkins, Chester G.	Dem	Mass.	2	1
18th	Oberstar, James L.	Dem	Minn.	7	1
19th	Guarini, Frank J.	Dem	N.J.	5	1
20th	Durbin, Richard J.	Dem	Ill.	3	1
21st	Espy, Mike	Dem	Miss.	1	1

Minority

Rank	Name	Party	State	Terms in: House	Terms in: Comm.
1st	Latta, Delbert L.	Rep	Ohio	15	1
2nd	Gradison, Willis D. Jr.	Rep	Ohio	7	1
3rd	Mack, Connie III	Rep	Fla.	3	1
4th	Goodling, William F.	Rep	Penn.	7	1
5th	Smith, Denny	Rep	Ore.	4	1
6th	Boulter, Beau	Rep	Tex.	2	1
7th	Edwards, M.H. (Mickey)	Rep	Okla.	6	1
8th	Thomas, William M.	Rep	Cal.	5	1
9th	Rogers, Harold	Rep	Ky.	4	1
10th	Sundquist, Don	Rep	Tenn.	3	1
11th	Johnson, Nancy L.	Rep	Conn.	3	1
12th	Armey, Richard	Rep	Tex.	2	1
13th	Buechner, Jack	Rep	Mo.	1	1
14th	Houghton, Amory Jr.	Rep	N.Y.	1	1

SENATE **Majority**

Rank Name	Party	State	Years in: Senate	Comm.
CoCh Chiles, Lawton M. Jr.	Dem	Fla.	17	1
2nd Hollings, Ernest F.	Dem	S.C.	21	1
3rd Johnston, J. Bennett Jr.	Dem	La.	15	1
4th Sasser, James R.	Dem	Tenn.	11	1
5th Riegle, Donald W. Jr.	Dem	Mich.	11	1
6th Exon, J. James	Dem	Neb.	9	1
7th Lautenberg, Frank R.	Dem	N.J.	5	1
8th Simon, Paul M.	Dem	Ill.	3	1
9th Sanford, Terry	Dem	N.C.	1	1
10th Wirth, Timothy E.	Dem	Colo.	1	1
11th Fowler, Wyche Jr.	Dem	Ga.	1	1
12th Conrad, Kent	Dem	N.D.	1	1
13th Dodd, Christopher J.	Dem	Conn.	7	1

Minority

Rank Name	Party	State	Years in: Senate	Comm.
1st Domenici, Pete V.	Rep	N.M.	15	1
2nd Armstrong, William L.	Rep	Colo.	9	1
3rd Kassebaum, Nancy Landon	Rep	Kans.	9	1
4th Boschwitz, Rudolf E.	Rep	Minn.	9	1
5th Symms, Steven D.	Rep	Ida.	7	1
6th Grassley, Charles E.	Rep	Iowa	7	1
7th Kasten, Robert W. Jr.	Rep	Wisc.	7	1
8th Quayle, J. Danforth	Rep	Ind.	7	1
9th Danforth, John C.	Rep	Mo.	11	1
10th Nickles, Don	Rep	Okla.	7	1
11th Rudman, Warren B.	Rep	N.H.	7	1

*2: Member's 2nd period of service on the committee.

Note: Membership on this Committee was identical to that of the House and Senate Budget Committees. "Service Dates of Senate Members" reflect members' service on the Senate Budget Committee, as no formal assignments to the Joint Committee were listed in either the Congressional Record or The Journal of the Senate.

Addition:

House Minority: 15th McCrery, Jim Rep La. May 18,1988

JOINT COMMITTEE: ORGANIZATION OF CONGRESS (Ad Hoc)

Jurisdiction, 1992

From House Concurrent Resolution 192, 102nd Congress, Second Session, August 6, 1992:

[Section 2(a)]

In General. --The Committee shall--
(1) make a full and complete study of the organization and operation of the Congress of the United States; and
(2) recommend improvements in such organization and operation with a view toward strengthening the effectiveness of the Congress, simplifying its operations, improving its relationships with other branches of the United States Government, and improving the orderly consideration of legislation.

[Section 2(b)]

Focus of Study.--The study shall include and examination of --
(1) the organization and operation of each House of the Congress, including the employment of personnel by the Members and the committees of the Congress and the structure of,a nd the relationships between, the various standing, special, and select committees of the Congress;
(2) the relationship between the 2 Houses; and
(3) the relationship between the Congress and the Executive branch of the Government.

JOINT COMMITTEE: ORGANIZATION OF CONGRESS (Ad Hoc) / 102nd Congress

Service Dates of House Majority Members: Oct. 9,1992-Jan. 3,1993
Service Dates of House Minority Members: Sep. 14,1992-Jan. 3,1993 (appointments made Aug. 10,1992)
Service Dates of Senate Majority Members: Oct. 8,1992-Jan. 3,1993
Service Dates of Senate Minority Members: Sep. 25,1992-Jan. 3,1993

HOUSE Majority

Rank	Name	Party	State	Terms in: House	Terms in: Comm.
CoCh	Hamilton, Lee H.	Dem	Ind.	14	1
2nd	Obey, David R.	Dem	Wisc.	13	1
3rd	Swift, Allan B.	Dem	Wash.	8	1
4th	Gejdenson, Samuel	Dem	Conn.	6	1
5th	Spratt, John M. Jr.	Dem	S.C.	5	1
6th	Norton, Eleanor Holmes	Dem	D.C.	1	1

HOUSE Minority

Rank	Name	Party	State	Terms in: House	Terms in: Comm.
VCh	Gradison, Willis D. Jr.	Rep	Ohio	9	1
2nd	Walker, Robert S.	Rep	Penn.	8	1
3rd	Solomon, Gerald B.	Rep	N.Y.	7	1
4th	Dreier, David	Rep	Cal.	6	1
5th	Emerson, Bill	Rep	Mo.	6	1
6th	Allard, Wayne R.	Rep	Co.	1	1

SENATE Majority

Rank	Name	Party	State	Years in: House	Years in: Comm.
CoCh	Boren, David L.	Dem	Okla.	14	1
2nd	Ford, Wendell H.	Dem	Ky.	18	1
3rd	Pryor, David	Dem	Ark.	14	1
4th	Reid, Harry M.	Dem	Nev.	6	1
5th	Sarbanes, Paul S.	Dem	Md.	16	1
6th	Sasser, James R.	Dem	Tenn.	16	1

SENATE Minority

Rank	Name	Party	State	Years in: House	Years in: Comm.
1st	Domenici, Pete V.	Rep	N.M.	20	1
2nd	Kassebaum, Nancy Landon	Rep	Kans.	14	1
3rd	Lott, Trent	Rep	Miss.	4	1
4th	Stevens, Theodore F.	Rep	Alas.	24	1
5th	Lugar, Richard G.	Rep	Ind.	16	1
6th	Cohen, William S.	Rep	Me.	14	1

Index

A

B

D

E

F

G

H

I

J

K

L

M

N

O

P

W

Y

Z